UPGRADING AND REPAIRING PCs,

18th Edition

Scott Mueller

800 East 96th Street
Indianapolis, Indiana 46240

Contents at a Glance

Upgrading and Repairing PCs, 18th Edition

Copyright © 2008 by Que Publishing

ISBN-13: 978-0-7897-3697-0
ISBN-10: 0-7897-3697-7

Library of Congress Cataloging-in-Publication Data

Mueller, Scott.
  Upgrading and repairing PCs / Scott Mueller.—18th ed.
    p. cm.
  ISBN 0-7897-3697-7
  1. Microcomputers—Maintenance and repair. 2. Microcomputers—Equipment and supplies. 3. Microcomputers—Upgrading. I. Title.
  TK7887.M84 2008
  004.16—dc22

                                                                    2007034956

Printed in the United States of America

First Printing: September 2007

Trademarks

All terms mentioned in this book that are known to be trademarks or service marks have been appropriately capitalized. Que Publishing cannot attest to the accuracy of this information. Use of a term in this book should not be regarded as affecting the validity of any trademark or service mark.

Warning and Disclaimer

Every effort has been made to make this book as complete and as accurate as possible, but no warranty or fitness is implied. The information provided is on an "as is" basis. The author and the publisher shall have neither liability nor responsibility to any person or entity with respect to any loss or damages arising from the information contained in this book or from the use of the DVD accompanying it.

Bulk Sales

Que Publishing offers excellent discounts on this book when ordered in quantity for bulk purchases or special sales. For more information, please contact

U.S. Corporate and Government Sales
1-800-382-3419
corpsales@pearsontechgroup.com

For sales outside the U.S., please contact

International Sales
international@pearsoned.com

This Book Is Safari Enabled

Safari
BOOKS ONLINE
ENABLED

The Safari® Enabled icon on the cover of your favorite technology book means the book is available through Safari Bookshelf. When you buy this book, you get free access to the online edition for 45 days.

Safari Bookshelf is an electronic reference library that lets you easily search thousands of technical books, find code samples, download chapters, and access technical information whenever and wherever you need it.

To gain 45-day Safari Enabled access to this book:

- Go to http://www.quepublishing.com/safarienabled
- Complete the brief registration form
- Enter the coupon code L7LX-5AHN-QRK2-P1NF-IMDP

If you have difficulty registering on Safari Bookshelf or accessing the online edition, please email customer-service@safaribooksonline.com.

Associate Publisher
Greg Wiegand

Executive Editor
Rick Kughen

Development Editors
Todd Brakke
Rick Kughen

Managing Editor
Gina Kanouse

Project Editor
Betsy Harris

Copy Editor
Bart Reed

Indexer
Erika Millen

Proofreader
Editorial Advantage

Technical Editor
Mark Reddin

Publishing Coordinator
Cindy Teeters

Multimedia Developer
Dan Scherf

Book Designer
Anne Jones

Compositor
Nonie Ratcliff

DVD Production
Lynn Mueller

Contents

About the Author

Scott Mueller is president of Mueller Technical Research (MTR), an international research and corporate training firm. Since 1982, MTR has produced the industry's most in-depth, accurate, and effective seminars, books, articles, videos, and FAQs covering PC hardware and data recovery. MTR maintains a client list that includes Fortune 500 companies, the U.S. and foreign governments, major software and hardware corporations, as well as PC enthusiasts and entrepreneurs. His seminars have been presented to several thousands of PC support professionals throughout the world.

Scott personally teaches seminars nationwide covering all aspects of PC hardware (including troubleshooting, maintenance, repair, and upgrade), A+ Certification, and data recovery/forensics. He has a knack for making technical topics not only understandable, but entertaining as well; his classes are never boring! If you have 10 or more people to train, Scott can design and present a custom seminar for your organization.

Although he has taught classes virtually nonstop since 1982, Scott is best known as the author of the longest running, most popular, and most comprehensive PC hardware book in the world, *Upgrading and Repairing PCs*, which has not only been produced in more than 18 editions, but has also become the core of an entire series of books.

Scott has authored many books over the last 20+ years, including *Upgrading and Repairing PCs* (1st through 18th and Academic editions); *Upgrading and Repairing Laptops* (1st and 2nd editions); *Upgrading and Repairing Windows*; *Upgrading and Repairing PCs: A+ Certification Study Guide* (1st and 2nd editions); *Upgrading and Repairing PCs Technician's Portable Reference* (1st and 2nd editions); *Upgrading and Repairing PCs Field Guide*; *Upgrading and Repairing PCs Quick Reference*; *Upgrading and Repairing PCs, Linux Edition*; *Killer PC Utilities*; *The IBM PS/2 Handbook*; and *Que's Guide to Data Recovery*.

Scott has produced several video training packages covering PC hardware, including a 6-hour, CD-based seminar titled *Upgrading and Repairing PCs Training Course: A Digital Seminar from Scott Mueller*. Scott has also produced other videos over the years, including *Upgrading and Repairing PCs Video, 12th Edition*; *Your PC: The Inside Story*; and 2+ hours of free video training included in the 10th and 12th through 18th editions of *Upgrading and Repairing PCs* as well as several editions of *Upgrading and Repairing Laptops* and *Upgrading and Repairing Windows*.

Contact MTR directly if you have a unique book, article, or video project in mind, or if you want Scott to conduct a custom PC troubleshooting, repair, maintenance, upgrade, or data-recovery seminar tailored for your organization:

Mueller Technical Research
3700 Grayhawk Drive
Algonquin, IL 60102-6325
(847) 854-6794
(847) 854-6795 Fax
Internet: scottmueller@compuserve.com
Web: http://www.upgradingandrepairingpcs.com
             http://www.scottmueller.com

Scott has a private forum exclusively for those who have purchased one of his recent books or DVDs. Visit http://forum.scottmueller.com to view the forum. Note that posting is only available to registered members.

Scott's premiere work, *Upgrading and Repairing PCs*, has sold well over 2 million copies, making it by far the most popular and longest-running PC hardware book on the market today. Scott has been featured in *Forbes* magazine and has written several articles for *PC World* magazine, *Maximum PC* magazine, the Scott Mueller Forum, various computer and automotive newsletters, and the *Upgrading and Repairing PCs* website.

If you have suggestions for the next version of this book, any comments about the book in general, or new book or article topics you would like to see covered, send them to Scott via email at scottmueller@compuserve.com.

When he is not working on PC-related books or on the road teaching seminars, Scott can usually be found in the garage working on anything with wheels and an engine.

Dedication

To Emerson: from a boy to a man, you make your father proud!

Acknowledgements

The new 18th edition continues the long tradition of making this the most accurate, in-depth, and up-to-date book of its kind on the market. This new edition is the product of a great deal of additional research and development over the previous editions. Several people have helped me with both the research and production of this book. I would like to thank the following people:

First, a very special thanks to my wife and partner, Lynn. She used her creative and technical skills to shoot and produce the video that is included with this book. I'm extremely proud of her for all I've seen her accomplish. The dedication she has shown to her work has been inspiring.

I must give a *very* special thanks to Rick Kughen at Que. Through the years Rick is the number one person responsible for championing this book and the *Upgrading and Repairing* series. His office is like a shrine to *Upgrading and Repairing PCs*, sporting a complete (and very rare) collection of every single edition of this book. I cannot say enough about Rick and what he means to all the *Upgrading and Repairing* books.

I'd also like to thank Todd Brakke for once again doing the development editing for this edition. His excellent tips and suggestions really help to keep the material concise and up-to-date. Special thanks also go to Bart Reed who helped tremendously with the copy editing, and the job that Gina Kanouse and Betsy Harris did in shepherding my manuscripts through a very tight publishing schedule cannot be overlooked. I'd also like to thank all of the other editors, illustrators, designers, and technicians at Que who work so hard to complete the finished product and get this book out the door! They are a wonderful team that produces clearly the best computer books on the market. I am happy and proud to be closely associated with all the people at Que.

I would also like to say thanks to my publisher Greg Wiegand, who has stood behind all the *Upgrading and Repairing* book and video projects. Greg is a fellow motorcycle enthusiast; someday hopefully we can go riding together.

All the people at Que make me feel as if we are on the same team, and they are just as dedicated as I am to producing the best books possible.

I would also like to say thanks to Mark Soper, who has added considerable expertise in areas that I might tend to neglect. And a very special thanks to Mark Reddin, who has become the primary technical editor for this book since the 13th edition and who not only is extremely diligent in verifying details, but also makes numerous suggestions about additional coverage. His input has been extremely important in helping me to ensure the highest level of technical accuracy and depth of coverage.

Many readers write me with suggestions and even corrections for the book, for which I am especially grateful. However some readers go the extra mile, and their contributions deserve a special mention. Of note are Micah Haber and Chris Beahan, both of whom did thorough readings of the entire book, literally commenting on every chapter, offering numerous comments and suggestions. Please keep those comments coming; I welcome any and all of your comments, and even your criticisms. I take them seriously and apply them to the continuous improvement of this book. Interaction with my readers is the primary force that helps maintain this book as the most up-to-date and relevant work available *anywhere* on the subject of PC hardware.

Finally, I would like to thank the thousands of people who have attended my seminars; you might not realize how much I learn from each of you and all your questions!

We Want to Hear from You!

As the reader of this book, *you* are our most important critic and commentator. We value your opinion and want to know what we're doing right, what we could do better, what areas you'd like to see us publish in, and any other words of wisdom you're willing to pass our way.

As an associate publisher for Que Publishing, I welcome your comments. You can email or write me directly to let me know what you did or didn't like about this book—as well as what we can do to make our books better.

Please note that I cannot help you with technical problems related to the topic of this book. We do have a User Services group, however, where I will forward specific technical questions related to the book.

When you write, please be sure to include this book's title and author as well as your name, email address, and phone number. I will carefully review your comments and share them with the author and editors who worked on the book.

Email: feedback@quepublishing.com

Mail: Greg Wiegand
            Associate Publisher
            Que Publishing
            800 East 96th Street
            Indianapolis, IN 46240 USA

Reader Services

Visit our website and register this book at www.informit.com/title/9780789736970 for convenient access to any updates, downloads, or errata that might be available for this book.

Introduction

Welcome to *Upgrading and Repairing PCs, 18th Edition.* Since debuting as the first book of its kind on the market in 1988, no other book on PC hardware has matched the depth and quality of the information found in this tome. The 18th edition continues *Upgrading and Repairing PCs'* role as not only the best-selling book of its type, but also the most comprehensive and complete PC hardware reference available. This book examines PCs in depth, outlines the differences among them, and presents options for configuring each system.

More than just a minor revision, the 18th edition of *Upgrading and Repairing PCs* contains hundreds of pages of new, revised, and reworked content. The PC industry is moving faster than ever, and this book is the most accurate, complete, in-depth, and up-to-date book of its kind on the market today.

I wrote this book for people who want to know everything about their PCs. How they got started; how they've evolved; how to upgrade, troubleshoot, and repair them; and everything in between. This book is for all those professionals and PC enthusiasts who want to know everything about PC hardware. This book covers the full gamut of PC-compatible systems from the oldest 8-bit machines to the latest in high-end 64-bit quad-core processor systems. If you need to know about everything from the original PC to the latest in PC technology on the market today, this book and the accompanying information-packed disc is definitely for you.

This book covers state-of-the-art hardware and accessories that make the most modern personal computers easier, faster, and more productive to use. Inside these pages you will find in-depth coverage of every PC processor from the original 8088 to the latest quad-core processors from Intel and AMD.

Upgrading and Repairing PCs also doesn't ignore the less glamorous PC components. Every part of your PC plays a critical role in its stability and performance. Over the course of this book's 1,600+ pages, you'll find out exactly why your motherboard's chipset might just be the most important part of your PC and what can go wrong when you settle for a run-of-the-mill power supply that can't get enough juice to that monster processor you just bought. You'll also find in-depth coverage of technologies such as new processors, chipsets, graphics, audio cards, PCI Express 2.x, HD DVD and Blu-ray drives, Serial ATA, USB, and FireWire, and more—it's all in here, right down to the guts-level analysis of your mouse and keyboard.

New in the 18th Edition

Many of you who are reading this have purchased one or more of the previous editions. Based on your letters, emails, and other correspondence, I know that, as much as you value each new edition, you want to know what new information I'm bringing you. So, here is a short list of the major improvements to this edition:

- A completely updated look at the newest processor families from Intel and AMD as well as the chipsets and motherboards that support them. Dual- and quad-core processors are the latest rage, and their impact on our collective computing experiences is not to be underestimated.

- A detailed look at how chipsets and motherboards are evolving, especially with regard to PCI Express. We also examine how the type of bus interconnect technologies implemented for a chipset and CPU affect your entire system's performance.

- The landscape of the graphics card market continues to evolve as quickly as any in the PC industry. In this edition, the latest GPU and graphics chipsets are profiled, with an especially watchful eye on the latest developments in using two graphics cards to double your system's video performance using technologies such as NVIDIA's SLI and ATI's Crossfire.

- With all the power today's PC hardware craves, the venerable PC power supply of yesterday is no longer up to the task of keeping every power-hungry component well fed. Given that, the power supply chapter has been extensively revised to include new information on power use calculations, and how to save power (and money) using ACPI suspend modes.

- As always, we have new, high-quality technical illustrations. Every year we add, modify, and generally improve on the hundreds of figures in this book. These new and revised illustrations provide more technical detail, helping you understand difficult topics or showing you exactly how to complete a task.

- Just like last year, you'll find a DVD-ROM plastered to the inside back cover of this book. On it you'll find all the usual standbys, such as the Technical Reference and complete electronic versions of prior editions. Rather than recycle the same video clips from edition to edition as many of my competitors do, I've once again included new video clips for this edition. For this edition, there are two hours of video on home networking components and technologies.

As with every edition, I've done as much research and homework as humanly possible to ensure that this volume is the most consistent and up-do-date text on PC hardware you're going to find in a book.

Book Objectives

Upgrading and Repairing PCs focuses on several objectives. The primary objective is to help you learn how to maintain, upgrade, and repair your PC system. To that end, *Upgrading and Repairing PCs* helps you fully understand the family of computers that has grown from the original IBM PC, including all PC-compatible systems. This book discusses all areas of system improvement, such as motherboards, processors, memory, and even case and power-supply improvements. The book discusses proper system and component care, specifies the most failure-prone items in various PC systems, and tells you how to locate and identify a failing component. You'll learn about powerful diagnostics hardware and software that enable a system to help you determine the cause of a problem and how to repair it.

PCs are moving forward rapidly in power and capabilities. Processor performance increases with every new chip design. *Upgrading and Repairing PCs* helps you gain an understanding of all the processors used in PC-compatible computer systems.

This book covers the important differences between major system architectures from the original Industry Standard Architecture (ISA) to the latest PCI Express interface standards. *Upgrading and Repairing PCs* covers each of these system architectures and their adapter boards to help you make decisions about which type of system you want to buy in the future and to help you upgrade and troubleshoot such systems.

The amount of storage space available to modern PCs is increasing geometrically. *Upgrading and Repairing PCs* covers storage options ranging from larger, faster hard drives to state-of-the-art storage devices.

When you finish reading this book, you should have the knowledge to upgrade, troubleshoot, and repair almost any system and component.

Is This Book for You?

If you want to know more about PCs, then this book is most definitely for you! *Upgrading and Repairing PCs* is designed for people who want a thorough understanding of PC hardware and how their PC systems work. Each section fully explains common and not-so-common problems, what causes problems, and how to handle problems when they arise. You will gain, for example, an understanding of disk configuration and interfacing that can improve your diagnostics and troubleshooting skills. You'll develop a feel for what goes on in a system so you can rely on your own judgment and observations and not some table of canned troubleshooting steps.

Upgrading and Repairing PCs is written for people who will select, install, configure, maintain, and repair systems they or their companies use. To accomplish these tasks, you need a level of knowledge much higher than that of an average system user. You must know exactly which tool to use for a task and how to use the tool correctly. This book can help you achieve this level of knowledge.

Over the years I have taught millions of people to upgrade and build PCs. Some of my students are computer experts, and some are computer novices. But they all have one thing in common: They believe this book has changed their lives.

Chapter-by-Chapter Breakdown

This book is organized into chapters that cover the components of a PC system. A few chapters serve to introduce or expand in an area not specifically component related, but most parts in the PC have a dedicated chapter or section, which will aid you in finding the information you want. Also note that the index has been improved greatly over previous editions, which will further aid in finding information in a book of this size.

Chapters 1 and 2 of this book serve primarily as an introduction. Chapter 1, "Development of the PC," begins with an introduction to the development of the original IBM PC and PC-compatibles. This chapter incorporates some of the historical events that led to the development of the microprocessor and the PC. Chapter 2, "PC Components, Features, and System Design," provides information about the various types of systems you encounter and what separates one type of system from another, including the types of system buses that differentiate systems. Chapter 2 also provides an overview of the types of PC systems that help build a foundation of knowledge essential for the remainder of the book, and it offers some insight as to how the PC market is driven and where components and technologies are sourced.

Chapter 3, "Microprocessor Types and Specifications," includes detailed coverage of processors from Intel and AMD. Because the processor is one of the most important parts of a PC, this book features more extensive and updated processor coverage than ever before. I dig deeply into the latest processors and the latest socket types designed to interface with them.

Chapter 4, "Motherboards and Buses," covers the motherboard, chipsets, motherboard components, and system buses in detail. This chapter contains discussions of motherboard form factors, including specifications on everything from Baby-AT to the various ATX, BTX and related standards. A chipset can either make a good PC better or choke the life out of an otherwise high-speed CPU. I cover the latest chipsets for current processor families, including chipsets from Intel, AMD, VIA, NVIDIA, SiS, ALi, and more. This chapter also covers special bus architectures and devices, such as high-speed Peripheral Component Interconnect (PCI), including PCI Express. Everything from the specifications of the latest chipsets to the proper spacing of holes on industry standard form factor motherboards can be found here.

Chapter 5, "BIOS," contains a detailed discussion of the system BIOS, including types, features, and upgrades. Also included is updated coverage of the BIOS setup and flash-upgradeable BIOSs. There is also an exhaustive list of BIOS codes and error messages.

Chapter 6, "Memory," provides a detailed discussion of PC memory, including the latest in cache and main memory specifications. Next to the processor and motherboard, system memory is one of the most important parts of a PC. It's also one of the most difficult things to understand because it is somewhat intangible and how it works is not always obvious. If you're confused about the difference between system memory and cache memory; L1 cache and L2 cache; external and integrated on-die L2 cache; SIMMs, DIMMs, and RIMMs; DDR SDRAM versus DDR2 and the new DDR3, this is the chapter that can answer your questions.

Chapter 7, "The ATA/IDE Interface," provides a detailed discussion of ATA/IDE, including types and specifications. This covers the faster parallel and serial ATA modes that allow 133MBps to 300MBps operation and why they might not increase your PC's performance much. There's also more new content on Serial ATA AHCI (Advanced Host Controller Interface) mode, which allows for additional SATA capabilities and performance.

Chapter 8, "Magnetic Storage Principles," details the inner workings of magnetic storage devices such as disk and tape drives. Regardless of whether you understood electromagnetism in high school science, this chapter breaks down these difficult concepts and presents them in a way that will change the way you think about data and drives.

Chapter 9, "Hard Disk Storage," breaks down how data is stored to your drives and how it is retrieved when you double-click a file.

Chapter 10, "Removable Storage," covers every type of removable storage drive you're likely to see used on a system, both young and old. From floppies to Zip disks to flash memory drives and magnetic tape drives, it's all here.

Chapter 11, "Optical Storage," covers optical drives and storage using CD and DVD technology, including rewritable CD and DVD discs as well as the latest HD DVD and Blu-ray technology.

Chapter 12, "Physical Drive Installation and Configuration," covers how to install drives of all types in a PC system. You learn how to format and partition hard drives after they are installed.

Chapter 13, "Video Hardware," covers everything there is to know about video cards and displays. Learn about how both CRT and flat-panel monitors work and which is best suited for you. If you're a gamer or multimedia buff, you'll want to read about choosing the right video card with the right chipset and amount of video memory to fill your needs.

Chapter 14, "Audio Hardware," covers sound and sound-related devices, including sound boards and speaker systems. Quality audio has become an increasingly important part of any good PC, and in this chapter I help you learn which features to look for in an audio card and which types of audio cards and chips are suited to your needs.

Chapter 15, "I/O Interfaces from Serial and Parallel to IEEE 1394 and USB," covers the standard serial and parallel ports still found in most systems, as well as newer technology such as USB and FireWire (IEEE 1394/i.LINK). I also cover the latest developments in USB 2.0, USB On-The-Go, wireless USB, and FireWire 800.

Chapter 16, "Input Devices," covers keyboards, pointing devices, and game ports used to communicate with a PC, including wireless peripherals that finally let you cut the cord without sacrificing responsiveness.

Chapter 17, "Internet Connectivity," compares your options for getting on the information super-highway using either low-speed dialup connections or the multiple high-speed connectivity methods that have come to the home desktop, including DSL, cable modems, and satellite.

Chapter 18, "Local Area Networking," covers setting up a wired or wireless Ethernet network in your home or small office. I show you how to install NICs, make your own Ethernet cables, and set up Windows networking services.

Chapter 19, "Power Supplies," is a detailed investigation of the power supply, which still remains the primary cause of PC system problems and failures. When you buy a new PC, this undervalued compo-nent is the one most likely to be skimped on, which helps explain why it's the source of so many problems often attributed to Windows, memory, and several other components. You'll also find detailed specifications on the power connectors found in systems from AT to ATX and BTX, including some nonstandard connectors that can cause problems. New information added covering power man-agement can be used to save several times the cost of this book in just one year, by properly configur-ing your systems to use less power.

Chapter 20, "Building or Upgrading Systems," is where I show you how to select the parts you'll need for your upgrade or to build a PC from scratch. Then, I walk you step by step through the process. This chapter is loaded with professional photos that help you follow along.

Chapter 21, "PC Mods: Overclocking and Cooling," covers the technology that controls the speed of your system and how to safely run the system faster than the basic specifications call for (called *over-clocking*). A detailed examination of system cooling is also found here, from air cooling, to liquid cool-ing, and even refrigeration. The latest chassis upgrades to improve cooling are also discussed, and a simple modification is detailed that can dramatically improve the cooling in existing systems for less than $10.

Chapter 22, "PC Diagnostics, Testing, and Maintenance," covers diagnostic and testing tools and pro-cedures. This chapter also adds more information on general PC troubleshooting and problem deter-mination. Here, I show you what the prepared PC technician has in his toolkit. I also show you a few tools you might have never seen or used before.

The 18th Edition DVD-ROM

The 18th edition of *Upgrading and Repairing PCs* includes a DVD-ROM that contains nearly as much valuable content as you'll find in the pages of this book.

First, there's the all-new professional-grade video (the DVD will play in your standalone DVD player, too) with all-new segments covering the components and technology that will enable you to create a robust and secure home network including all of your systems.

There's also my venerable Technical Reference material, a PDF repository of material that has appeared in previous editions of *Upgrading and Repairing PCs* but has been moved to the disc to make room for coverage of newer technologies. The disc, combined with the printed content of the book, makes *Upgrading and Repairing PCs* far more than 2,000 pages long! Its contents include a detailed listing of BIOS codes and legacy coverage from earlier editions of the book. It's included on the disc in printable PDF format.

Two appendixes—Appendix A, "Glossary," and Appendix B, "List of Acronyms and Abbreviations"—are also included on the DVD.

Finally, there is also a full PDF version of a previous edition of *Upgrading and Repairing PCs*. All told, there's more PC hardware content and knowledge here than you're likely to find from any other sin-gle source.

My Website: upgradingandrepairingpcs.com

Don't forget about the www.upgradingandrepairingpcs.com website! Here, you'll find a cache of helpful material to go along with the book you're holding. I've loaded this site with tons of material, from video clips to book content and technology updates. These articles are archived so you can refer to them anytime.

If you find that the video on this book's disc isn't enough, you'll find even more of my previously recorded videos on the website. Not to mention that it is the best place to look for information on all of Que's *Upgrading and Repairing* titles. In the last year, we've released *Upgrading and Repairing Servers,* and *Upgrading and Repairing Windows*, and *Upgrading and Repairing Networks 5th edition.* Check the www.upgradingandrepairingpcs.com website to see when new editions of my other books are coming out.

I also have a private forum (www.forum.scottmueller.com) designed exclusively to support those who have purchased my recent books and DVDs. I use the forum to answer questions and otherwise help my loyal readers. If you own one of my current books or DVDs, feel free to join in and post questions. I endeavor to answer each and every question personally, but I also encourage knowledgeable members to respond as well. Anybody can view the forum without registering, but to post a question of your own you will need to join. Even if you don't join in, the forum is a tremendous resource because you can still benefit from all of the reader questions I have answered over the years.

Be sure to check the upgradingandrepairingpcs.com website for more information on all my latest books, videos, articles, FAQs, and more!

A Personal Note

When asked which was his favorite Corvette, Dave McLellan, former manager of the Corvette platform at General Motors, always said, "Next year's model." Now with the new 18th edition, next year's model has just become this year's model, until *next* year that is....

I believe this book is absolutely the best book of its kind on the market, and that is due in large part to the extensive feedback I have received from both my seminar attendees and book readers. I am so grateful to everyone who has helped me with this book through each of its 18 editions, as well as all the loyal readers who have been using this book, many of you since the first edition was published. I have had personal contact with many thousands of you in the seminars I have been teaching since 1982, and I enjoy your comments and even your criticisms tremendously. Using this book in a teaching environment has been a major factor in its development. Some of you might be interested to know that I originally began writing this book in early 1985; back then it was self-published and used exclusively in my PC hardware seminars before being professionally published by Que in 1988.

In one way or another, I have been writing and rewriting this book for more than 20 years! In that time, *Upgrading and Repairing PCs* has proven to be not only the first but also the most comprehensive and yet approachable and easy-to-understand book of its kind. With the new 18th edition, it is even better than ever. Your comments, suggestions, and support have helped this book to become the best PC hardware book on the market. I look forward to hearing your comments after you see this exciting new edition.

Scott

Development of the PC

Computer History: Before Personal Computers

Many discoveries and inventions have directly and indirectly contributed to the development of the PC and other personal computers as we know them today. Examining a few important developmental landmarks can help bring the entire picture into focus.

The first computers of any kind were simple calculators. Even these evolved from mechanical devices to electronic digital devices.

Timeline

The following is a timeline of some significant events in computer history. It is not meant to be complete, just a representation of some of the major landmarks in computer development:

1617   John Napier creates "Napier's Bones," wooden or ivory rods used for calculating.

1642   Blaise Pascal introduces the Pascaline digital adding machine.

1822   Charles Babbage introduces the Difference Engine and later the Analytical Engine, a true general-purpose computing machine.

1906   Lee De Forest patents the vacuum tube triode, used as an electronic switch in the first electronic computers.

1936   Alan Turing publishes "On Computable Numbers," a paper in which he conceives an imaginary computer called the Turing Machine, considered one of the foundations of modern computing. Turing later worked on breaking the German Enigma code.

1936   Konrad Zuse begins work on a series of computers that will culminate in 1941 when he finishes work on the Z3. These are considered the first working electric binary computers, using electromechanical switches and relays.

1937   John V. Atanasoff begins work on the Atanasoff-Berry Computer (ABC), which would later be officially credited as the first electronic computer. Note that an electronic computer uses tubes, transistors, or other solid-state switching devices, whereas an electric computer uses electric motors, solenoids, and/or relays (electromechanical switches).

1943   Thomas (Tommy) Flowers develops the Colossus, a secret British code-breaking computer designed to decode secret messages encrypted by the German Enigma cipher machines.

1945   John von Neumann writes "First Draft of a Report on the EDVAC," in which he outlines the architecture of the modern stored-program computer.

1946   ENIAC is introduced, an electronic computing machine built by John Mauchly and J. Presper Eckert.

1947   On December 23, William Shockley, Walter Brattain, and John Bardeen successfully test the point-contact transistor, setting off the semiconductor revolution.

1949   Maurice Wilkes assembles the EDSAC, the first practical stored-program computer, at Cambridge University.

1950   Engineering Research Associates of Minneapolis builds the ERA 1101, one of the first commercially produced computers.

1952   The UNIVAC I delivered to the U.S. Census Bureau is the first commercial computer to attract widespread public attention.

1953   IBM ships its first electronic computer, the 701.

1954   A silicon-based junction transistor, perfected by Gordon Teal of Texas Instruments, Inc., brings a tremendous reduction in costs.

1954   The IBM 650 magnetic drum calculator establishes itself as the first mass-produced computer, with the company selling 450 in one year.

1955   Bell Laboratories announces the first fully transistorized computer, TRADIC.

1956   MIT researchers build the TX-0, the first general-purpose, programmable computer built with transistors.

1956   The era of magnetic disk storage dawns with IBM's shipment of a 305 RAMAC to Zellerbach Paper in San Francisco.

1958   Jack Kilby creates the first integrated circuit at Texas Instruments to prove that resistors and capacitors can exist on the same piece of semiconductor material.

1959   IBM's 7000 series mainframes are the company's first transistorized computers.

1959   Robert Noyce's practical integrated circuit, invented at Fairchild Camera and Instrument Corp., allows printing of conducting channels directly on the silicon surface.

1960   Bell Labs designs its Dataphone, the first commercial modem, specifically for converting digital computer data to analog signals for transmission across its long-distance network.

1960   The precursor to the minicomputer, DEC's PDP-1, sells for $120,000.

1961   According to *Datamation* magazine, IBM has an 81.2% share of the computer market in 1961, the year in which it introduces the 1400 series.

1964   CDC's 6600 supercomputer, designed by Seymour Cray, performs up to three million instructions per second—a processing speed three times faster than that of its closest competitor, the IBM Stretch.

1964 IBM announces System/360, a family of six mutually compatible computers and 40 peripherals that can work together.

1964 Online transaction processing makes its debut in IBM's SABRE reservation system, set up for American Airlines.

1965 Digital Equipment Corp. introduces the PDP-8, the first commercially successful minicomputer.

1966 Hewlett-Packard enters the general-purpose computer business with its HP-2115 for computation, offering computational power formerly found only in much larger computers.

1969 The root of what is to become the Internet begins when the Department of Defense establishes four nodes on the ARPAnet: two at University of California campuses (one at Santa Barbara and one at Los Angeles) and one each at SRI International and the University of Utah.

1971 A team at IBM's San Jose Laboratories invents the 8" floppy disk.

1971 The first advertisement for a microprocessor, the Intel 4004, appears in *Electronic News*.

1971 The Kenbak-1, one of the first personal computers, is advertised for $750 in *Scientific American*.

1972 Hewlett-Packard announces the HP-35 as "a fast, extremely accurate electronic slide rule" with a solid-state memory similar to that of a computer.

1972 Intel's 8008 microprocessor makes its debut.

1972 Steve Wozniak builds his "blue box," a tone generator to make free phone calls.

1973 Robert Metcalfe devises the Ethernet method of network connection at the Xerox Palo Alto Research Center.

1973 The Micral is the earliest commercial, non-kit personal computer based on a microprocessor, the Intel 8008.

1973 The TV Typewriter, designed by Don Lancaster, provides the first display of alphanumeric information on an ordinary television set.

1974 Researchers at the Xerox Palo Alto Research Center design the Alto, the first workstation with a built-in mouse for input.

1974 Scelbi advertises its 8H computer, the first commercially advertised U.S. computer based on a microprocessor, Intel's 8008.

1975 Telenet, the first commercial packet-switching network and civilian equivalent of ARPAnet, is born.

1975 The January edition of *Popular Electronics* features the Altair 8800, which is based on Intel's 8080 microprocessor, on its cover.

1975 The visual display module (VDM) prototype, designed by Lee Felsenstein, marks the first implementation of a memory-mapped alphanumeric video display for personal computers.

1976 Steve Wozniak designs the Apple I, a single-board computer.

1976 The 5 1/4" flexible disk drive and disk are introduced by Shugart Associates.

1976 The Cray I makes its name as the first commercially successful vector processor.

1977 Tandy RadioShack introduces the TRS-80.

1977 Apple Computer introduces the Apple II.

1977 Commodore introduces the PET (Personal Electronic Transactor).

1978 The VAX 11/780 from Digital Equipment Corp. features the capability to address up to 4.3GB of virtual memory, providing hundreds of times the capacity of most minicomputers.

1979 Motorola introduces the 68000 microprocessor.

1980   John Shoch, at the Xerox Palo Alto Research Center, invents the computer "worm," a short program that searches a network for idle processors.

1980   Seagate Technology creates the first hard disk drive for microcomputers, the ST-506.

1980   The first optical data storage disk has 60 times the capacity of a 5 1/4" floppy disk.

1981   Xerox introduces the Star, the first personal computer with a graphical user interface (GUI).

1981   Adam Osborne completes the first portable computer, the Osborne I, which weighs 24 lbs. and costs $1,795.

1981   IBM introduces its PC, igniting a fast growth of the personal computer market. The IBM PC is the grandfather of all modern PCs.

1981   Sony introduces and ships the first 3 1/2" floppy drives and disks.

1981   Philips and Sony introduce the CD-DA (compact disc digital audio) format.

1982   Sony is the first with a CD player on the market.

1983   Apple introduces its Lisa, which incorporates a GUI that's very similar to the one first introduced on the Xerox Star.

1983   Compaq Computer Corp. introduces its first PC clone that uses the same software as the IBM PC.

1984   Apple Computer launches the Macintosh, the first successful mouse-driven computer with a GUI, with a single $1.5 million commercial during the 1984 Super Bowl.

1984   IBM releases the PC-AT (PC Advanced Technology), three times faster than original PCs and based on the Intel 286 chip. The AT introduces the 16-bit ISA bus and is the computer on which all modern PCs are based.

1985   Philips introduces the first CD-ROM drive.

1986   Compaq announces the Deskpro 386, the first computer on the market to use what was then Intel's new 386 chip.

1987   IBM introduces its PS/2 machines, which make the 3 1/2" floppy disk drive and VGA video standard for PCs. The PS/2 also introduces the MicroChannel Architecture (MCA) bus, the first plug-and-play bus for PCs.

1988   Apple cofounder Steve Jobs, who left Apple to form his own company, unveils the NeXT.

1988   Compaq and other PC-clone makers develop Enhanced Industry Standard Architecture (EISA), which unlike MicroChannel retains backward compatibility with the existing ISA bus.

1988   Robert Morris's worm floods the ARPAnet. The 23-year-old Morris, the son of a computer security expert for the National Security Agency, sends a nondestructive worm through the Internet, causing problems for about 6,000 of the 60,000 hosts linked to the network.

1989   Intel releases the 486 (P4) microprocessor, which contains more than one million transistors. Intel also introduces 486 motherboard chipsets.

1990   The World Wide Web (WWW) is born when Tim Berners-Lee, a researcher at CERN—the high-energy physics laboratory in Geneva—develops Hypertext Markup Language (HTML).

1993   Intel releases the Pentium (P5) processor. Intel shifts from numbers to names for its chips after it learns it's impossible to trademark a number. Intel also releases motherboard chipsets and, for the first time, complete motherboards as well.

1995   Intel releases the Pentium Pro processor, the first in the P6 processor family.

1995 Microsoft releases Windows 95, the first mainstream 32-bit operating system, in a huge rollout.

1997 Intel releases the Pentium II processor, essentially a Pentium Pro with MMX instructions added.

1997 AMD introduces the K6, which is compatible with the Intel P5 (Pentium).

1998 Microsoft releases Windows 98.

1998 Intel releases the Celeron, a low-cost version of the Pentium II processor. Initial versions have no cache, but within a few months Intel introduces versions with a smaller but faster L2 cache.

1999 Intel releases the Pentium III, essentially a Pentium II with SSE (Streaming SIMD Extensions) added.

1999 AMD introduces the Athlon.

1999 The IEEE officially approves the 5GHz band 802.11a 54Mbps and 2.4GHz band 802.11b 11Mbps wireless networking standards. The Wi-Fi Alliance is formed to certify 802.11b products, ensuring interoperability.

2000 The first 802.11b Wi-Fi–certified products are introduced, and wireless networking rapidly builds momentum.

2000 Microsoft releases Windows Me (Millennium Edition) and Windows 2000.

2000 Both Intel and AMD introduce processors running at 1GHz.

2000 AMD introduces the Duron, a low-cost Athlon with reduced L2 cache.

2000 Intel introduces the Pentium 4, the latest processor in the Intel Architecture 32-bit (IA-32) family.

2001 Intel releases the Itanium processor, its first 64-bit (IA-64) processor for PCs.

2001 The industry celebrates the 20th anniversary of the release of the original IBM PC.

2001 Intel introduces the first 2GHz processor, a version of the Pentium 4. It takes the industry 28 1/2 years to go from 108KHz to 1GHz, but only 18 months to go from 1GHz to 2GHz.

2001 Microsoft releases Windows XP Home and Professional, for the first time merging the consumer and business operating system lines under the same code base (NT 5.1).

2001 Atheros introduces the first 802.11a 54Mbps high-speed wireless chips, allowing 802.11a products to finally reach the market.

2002 Intel releases the first 3GHz-class processor, a 3.06GHz version of the Pentium 4. This processor also introduces Intel's Hyper-Threading (HT) technology (which enables a single processor to work with two application threads at the same time) to desktop computing.

2003 Intel releases the Pentium M, a processor designed specifically for mobile systems, offering extremely low power consumption that results in dramatically increased battery life while still offering relatively high performance. The Pentium M becomes the cornerstone of Intel's Centrino brand.

2003 AMD releases the Athlon 64, the first x86-64 (AMD64) 64-bit processor targeted at the mainstream consumer and business markets.

2003 The IEEE officially approves the 802.11g 54Mbps high-speed wireless networking standard, which uses the same 2.4GHz band as (and is backward-compatible with) 802.11b. 802.11g products reach the market quickly, some even before the official standard is approved.

2004 Intel introduces a version of the Pentium 4 codenamed Prescott, the first PC processor built on 90-nanometer technology.

2004	Intel introduces EM64T (Extended Memory 64 Technology), which is a 64-bit extension to Intel's IA-32 architecture based on (and virtually identical to) the x86-64 (AMD64) technology first released by AMD.
2005	Microsoft releases Windows XP x64 Edition, which supports processors with 64-bit AMD64 and EM64T extensions.
2005	The era of multicore PC processors begins as Intel introduces the Pentium D 8xx and Pentium Extreme Edition 8xx dual-core processors. AMD soon follows with the dual-core Athlon 64 X2.
2006	Apple introduces the first Macintosh systems based on PC architecture and technology, indicating they are four times faster than previous non-PC-based Macs.
2006	Intel introduces the Core 2 Extreme, the first quad-core processor for PCs.
2006	Microsoft releases the long-awaited Windows Vista to business users. The PC OEM and consumer market releases would follow in early 2007.
2007	Intel releases the 3x series chipsets with support for DDR3 memory and PCI Express 2.0, which doubles the available bandwidth.

Mechanical Calculators

One of the earliest calculating devices on record is the abacus, which has been known and widely used for more than 2,000 years. The abacus is a simple wooden rack holding parallel rods on which beads are strung. When these beads are manipulated back and forth according to certain rules, several types of arithmetic operations can be performed.

Math with standard Arabic numbers found its way to Europe in the eighth and ninth centuries. In the early 1600s, a man named Charles Napier (the inventor of logarithms) developed a series of rods (later called Napier's Bones) that could be used to assist with numeric multiplication.

Blaise Pascal is usually credited with building the first digital calculating machine in 1642. It could perform the addition of numbers entered on dials and was intended to help his father, who was a tax collector. Then in 1671, Gottfried Wilhelm von Leibniz invented a calculator that was finally built in 1694. His calculating machine not only could add, but by successive adding and shifting, it could also multiply.

In 1820, Charles Xavier Thomas developed the first commercially successful mechanical calculator that not only could add but also subtract, multiply, and divide. After that, a succession of ever-improving mechanical calculators created by various other inventors followed.

The First Mechanical Computer

Charles Babbage, a mathematics professor in Cambridge, England, is considered by many to be the father of computers because of his two great inventions—each a different type of mechanical computing engine.

The Difference Engine, as he called it, was conceived in 1812 and solved polynomial equations by the method of differences. By 1822, he had built a small working model of his Difference Engine for demonstration purposes. With financial help from the British government, Babbage started construction of a full-scale model in 1823. It was intended to be steam-powered and fully automatic, and it would even print the resulting tables.

Babbage continued work on it for 10 years, but by 1833 he had lost interest because he now had an idea for an even better machine, something he described as a general-purpose, fully program-controlled, automatic mechanical digital computer. Babbage called his new machine an Analytical

Engine. The plans for the Analytical Engine specified a parallel decimal computer operating on numbers (words) of 50 decimal digits and with a storage capacity (memory) of 1,000 such numbers. Built-in operations were to include everything that a modern general-purpose computer would need, even the all-important conditional function, which would allow instructions to be executed in an order depending on certain conditions, not just in numerical sequence. In modern computer languages, this conditional capability is manifested in the IF statement. The Analytical Engine was also intended to use punched cards, which would control or program the machine. The machine was to operate automatically by steam power and would require only one attendant.

The Analytical Engine is regarded as the first real predecessor to a modern computer because it had all the elements of what, today, is considered a computer. These included the following:

- **An input device**—Using an idea similar to the looms used in textile mills at the time, a form of punched cards supplied the input.

- **A control unit**—A barrel-shaped section with many slats and studs was used to control or program the processor.

- **A processor (or calculator)**—A computing engine, about 10 feet tall, containing hundreds of axles and thousands of gears.

- **Storage**—A unit containing more axles and gears that could hold 1,000 50-digit numbers.

- **An output device**—Plates designed to fit in a printing press that were used to print the final results.

Alas, this potential first computer was never actually completed because of the problems in machining all the precision gears and mechanisms required. The tooling of the day was simply not good enough.

An interesting side note is that the punched card idea first proposed by Babbage finally came to fruition in 1890. That year a competition was held for a better method to tabulate the U.S. Census information, and Herman Hollerith, a Census Department employee, came up with the idea for punched cards. Without these cards, department employees had estimated the census data would take years to tabulate; with these cards they were able to finish in about six weeks. Hollerith went on to found the Tabulating Machine Company, which later became known as IBM.

IBM and other companies at the time developed a series of improved punch-card systems. These systems were constructed of electromechanical devices, such as relays and motors. Such systems included features to automatically feed in a specified number of cards from a "read-in" station; perform operations, such as addition, multiplication, and sorting; and feed out cards punched with results. These punched-card computing machines could process 50–250 cards per minute, with each card holding up to 80-digit numbers. The punched cards not only provided a means of input and output, but they also served as a form of memory storage. Punched-card machines did the bulk of the world's computing for more than 50 years and gave many of the early computer companies their starts.

The development of mechanical computers culminated with the electromechanical systems developed by Konrad Zuse between 1936 and 1941, ending with what he called the Z3. These are considered the first working electric binary computers, using electromechanical switches and relays.

Electronic Computers

A physicist named John V. Atanasoff (with associate Clifford Berry) is officially credited with creating the first true digital electronic computer during 1937 to 1942, while working at Iowa State University. The Atanasoff-Berry Computer (called the ABC) was the first to use modern digital switching techniques and vacuum tubes as switches, and it introduced the concepts of binary arithmetic and logic circuits. This was made legally official on October 19, 1973, when following a lengthy court trial, U.S. Federal Judge Earl R. Larson voided the ENIAC patent of Eckert and Mauchly and named Atanasoff as the inventor of the first electronic digital computer.

Military needs during World War II caused a great thrust forward in the evolution of computers. In 1943, Tommy Flowers completed a secret British code-breaking computer called Colossus, which was used to decode German secret messages. Unfortunately, that work went largely uncredited because Colossus was kept secret until many years after the war.

Besides code-breaking, systems were needed to calculate weapons trajectory and other military functions. In 1946, John P. Eckert, John W. Mauchly, and their associates at the Moore School of Electrical Engineering at the University of Pennsylvania built the first large-scale electronic computer for the military. This machine became known as ENIAC, the Electrical Numerical Integrator and Calculator. It operated on 10-digit numbers and could multiply two such numbers at the rate of 300 products per second by finding the value of each product from a multiplication table stored in its memory. ENIAC was about 1,000 times faster than the previous generation of electromechanical relay computers.

ENIAC used approximately 18,000 vacuum tubes, occupied 1,800 square feet (167 square meters) of floor space, and consumed around 180,000 watts of electrical power. Punched cards served as the input and output; registers served as adders and also as quick-access read/write storage.

The executable instructions composing a given program were created via specified wiring and switches that controlled the flow of computations through the machine. As such, ENIAC had to be rewired and switched for each program to be run.

Although Eckert and Mauchly were originally given a patent for the electronic computer, it was later voided and the patent awarded to John Atanasoff for creating the Atanasoff-Berry Computer.

Earlier in 1945, the mathematician John von Neumann demonstrated that a computer could have a very simple, fixed physical structure and yet be capable of executing any kind of computation effectively by means of proper programmed control without the need for any changes in hardware. In other words, you could change the program without rewiring the system. The *stored-program technique*, as von Neumann's ideas are known, became fundamental for future generations of high-speed digital computers and has become universally adopted.

The first generation of modern programmed electronic computers to take advantage of these improvements appeared in 1947. This group of machines included EDVAC and UNIVAC, the first commercially available computers. These computers included, for the first time, the use of true random access memory (RAM) for storing parts of the program and the data that is needed quickly. Typically, they were programmed directly in machine language, although by the mid-1950s progress had been made in several aspects of advanced programming. The standout of the era is the UNIVAC (Universal Automatic Computer), which was the first true general-purpose computer designed for both alphabetical and numerical uses. This made the UNIVAC a standard for business, not just science and the military.

Modern Computers

From UNIVAC to the latest desktop PCs, computer evolution has moved very rapidly. The first-generation computers were known for using vacuum tubes in their construction. The generation to follow would use the much smaller and more efficient transistor.

From Tubes to Transistors

Any modern digital computer is largely a collection of electronic switches. These switches are used to represent and control the routing of data elements called *binary digits* (or *bits*). Because of the on or off nature of the binary information and signal routing the computer uses, an efficient electronic switch was required. The first electronic computers used vacuum tubes as switches, and although the tubes worked, they had many problems.

The type of tube used in early computers was called a *triode* and was invented by Lee De Forest in 1906 (see Figure 1.1). It consists of a cathode and a plate, separated by a control grid, suspended in a glass vacuum tube. The cathode is heated by a red-hot electric filament, which causes it to emit electrons that are attracted to the plate. The control grid in the middle can control this flow of electrons. By making it negative, you cause the electrons to be repelled back to the cathode; by making it positive, you cause them to be attracted toward the plate. Thus, by controlling the grid current, you can control the on/off output of the plate.

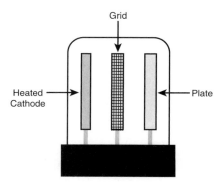

Figure 1.1   The three main components of a basic triode vacuum tube.

Unfortunately, the tube was inefficient as a switch. It consumed a great deal of electrical power and gave off enormous heat—a significant problem in the earlier systems. Primarily because of the heat they generated, tubes were notoriously unreliable—in larger systems, one failed every couple of hours or so.

The invention of the transistor was one of the most important developments leading to the personal computer revolution. The transistor was first invented in 1947 and announced in 1948 by Bell Laboratory engineers John Bardeen and Walter Brattain. Bell associate William Shockley invented the junction transistor a few months later, and all three jointly shared the Nobel Prize in Physics in 1956 for inventing the transistor. The transistor, which essentially functions as a solid-state electronic switch, replaced the less-suitable vacuum tube. Because the transistor was so much smaller and consumed significantly less power, a computer system built with transistors was also much smaller, faster, and more efficient than a computer system built with vacuum tubes.

The conversion from tubes to transistors began the trend toward miniaturization that continues to this day. Today's small laptop (or palmtop) PC and even Tablet PC systems, which run on batteries, have more computing power than many earlier systems that filled rooms and consumed huge amounts of electrical power.

Although there have been many different designs for transistors over the years, the transistors used in modern computers are normally Metal Oxide Semiconductor Field Effect Transistors (MOSFETs). MOSFETs are made from layers of materials deposited on a silicon substrate. Some of the layers contain silicon with certain impurities added by a process called *doping* or *ion bombardment,* whereas other layers include silicon dioxide (which acts as an insulator), polysilicon (which acts as an electrode), and metal to act as the wires to connect the transistor to other components. The composition and arrangement of the different types of doped silicon allows it to act both as a conductor or an insulator, which is why silicon is called a *semiconductor.*

MOSFETs can be constructed as either NMOS or PMOS types, based on the arrangement of doped silicon used. Silicon doped with boron is called P-type (positive) because it lacks electrons, whereas silicon doped with phosphorus is called N-type (negative) because it has an excess of free electrons.

MOSFETs have three connections, called the source, gate, and drain. An NMOS transistor is made by using N-type silicon for the source and drain, with P-type silicon placed in between (see Figure 1.2). The gate is positioned above the P-type silicon, separating the source and drain, and is separated from the P-type silicon by an insulating layer of silicon dioxide. Normally there is no current flow between N-type and P-type silicon, thus preventing electron flow between the source and drain. When a positive voltage is placed on the gate, the gate electrode creates a field that attracts electrons to the P-type silicon between the source and drain, thus changing that area to behave as if it were N-type silicon, creating a path for current to flow and turning the transistor "on."

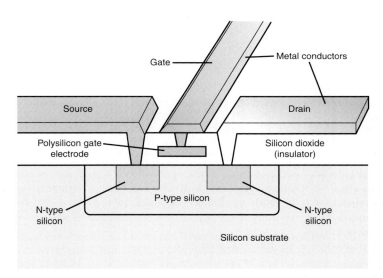

Figure 1.2   Cutaway view of an NMOS transistor.

A PMOS transistor works in a similar but opposite fashion. P-type silicon is used for the source and drain, with N-type silicon positioned in between them. When a negative voltage is placed on the gate, the gate electrode creates a field that repels electrons from the N-type silicon between the source and drain, thus changing that area to behave as if it were P-type silicon, creating a path for current to flow and turning the transistor "on."

When both NMOS and PMOS field-effect transistors are combined in a complementary arrangement, power is used only when the transistors are switching, making very dense, low-power circuit designs possible. Because of this, virtually all modern processors are designed using CMOS (Complementary Metal Oxide Semiconductor) technology.

Compared to a tube, a transistor is much more efficient as a switch and can be miniaturized to microscopic scale. In 2003, IBM researchers unveiled the world's smallest working silicon transistor, only 6 nanometers (billionths of a meter) in size. Other technology, such as carbon nanotubes, is being explored to produce even smaller transistors down to the molecular or even atomic scale.

Although transistors and integrated circuits have replaced vacuum tubes in virtually all consumer applications, vacuum tubes remain popular for high-end audio applications because, in analog circuits, they produce a warmer and richer sound than transistors do. To capitalize on this effect, Acer's Aopen division once released a series of motherboards (the AX4B-533 Tube, for example) designed for audiophiles that used a dual-triode tube along with a special noise-reduction design to produce excellent music playback.

Integrated Circuits

The third generation of modern computers is known for using integrated circuits instead of individual transistors. In 1959, engineers at Texas Instruments invented the *integrated circuit (IC)*, a semiconductor circuit that contains more than one transistor on the same base (or substrate material) and connects the transistors without wires. The first IC contained only six transistors. By comparison, the Intel Core 2 Extreme quad-core processor incorporates two dual-core die internally with 291 million transistors each, for a total of 582 million transistors in the processor package!

The First Microprocessor

Intel was founded on July 18, 1968 (as N M Electronics) by Robert Noyce and Gordon Moore. Almost immediately they changed the company name to Intel and were joined by cofounder Andrew Grove. They had a specific goal: to make semiconductor memory practical and affordable. This was not a given at the time, considering that silicon chip-based memory was at least 100 times more expensive than the magnetic core memory commonly used in those days. At the time, semiconductor memory was going for about a dollar a bit, whereas core memory was about a penny a bit. Noyce said, "All we had to do was reduce the cost by a factor of a hundred; then we'd have the market; and that's basically what we did."

By 1970, Intel was known as a successful memory chip company, having introduced a 1Kb memory chip, much larger than anything else available at the time. (1Kb equals 1,024 bits, and a byte equals 8 bits. This chip, therefore, stored only 128 bytes—not much by today's standards.) Known as the 1103 dynamic random access memory (DRAM), it became the world's largest-selling semiconductor device by the end of the following year. By this time, Intel had also grown from the core founders and a handful of others to more than 100 employees.

Because of Intel's success in memory chip manufacturing and design, Japanese manufacturer Busicom asked Intel to design a set of chips for a family of high-performance programmable calculators. At the time, all logic chips were custom designed for each application or product. Because most chips had to be custom designed specific to a particular application, no one chip could have any widespread usage.

Busicom's original design for its calculator called for at least 12 custom chips. Intel engineer Ted Hoff rejected the unwieldy proposal and instead designed a single-chip, general-purpose logic device that retrieved its application instructions from semiconductor memory. As the core of a four-chip set, a program could control this central processing unit and essentially tailor its function to the task at hand. The chip was generic in nature, meaning it could function in designs other than calculators. Previous designs were hard-wired for one purpose, with built-in instructions; this chip would read a variable set of instructions from memory, which would control the function of the chip. The idea was to design, on a single chip, almost an entire computing device that could perform various functions, depending on which instructions it was given.

There was one problem with the new chip: Busicom owned the rights to it. Hoff and others knew that the product had almost limitless application, bringing intelligence to a host of "dumb" machines. They urged Intel to repurchase the rights to the product. While Intel founders Gordon Moore and Robert Noyce championed the new chip, others within the company were concerned that the product would distract Intel from its main focus—making memory. They were finally convinced by the fact that every four-chip microcomputer set included two memory chips. As the director of marketing at the time recalled, "Originally, I think we saw it as a way to sell more memories, and we were willing to make the investment on that basis."

Intel offered to return Busicom's $60,000 investment in exchange for the rights to the product. Struggling with financial troubles, the Japanese company agreed. Nobody else in the industry at the time, even at Intel, realized the significance of this deal. Of course, it paved the way for Intel's future in processors. The result was the 1971 introduction of the 4-bit Intel 4004 microcomputer set (the term *microprocessor* was not coined until later). Smaller than a thumbnail and packing 2,300 transistors with 10-micron (millionth of a meter) spacing, the $200 chip delivered as much computing power as one of the first electronic computers, ENIAC. By comparison, ENIAC relied on 18,000 vacuum tubes packed into 3,000 cubic feet (85 cubic meters) when it was built in 1946. The 4004 ran at 108KHz (just over one tenth of 1MHz) and executed 60,000 operations in 1 second—primitive by today's standards, but a major breakthrough at the time.

Intel introduced the 8008 microcomputer in 1972, which processed 8 bits of information at a time, twice as much as the original chip. By 1981, Intel's microprocessor family had grown to include the 16-bit 8086 and the 8/16-bit 8088 processors. These two chips garnered an unprecedented 2,500 design wins in a single year. Among those designs was a product from IBM that was to become the first PC.

Note

The term *PC* defines a type of personal computer using Intel architecture processors and loosely based on the original IBM PC, XT, and AT designs. Other types of personal computers have existed both before and after the PC, but what we call PCs today have dominated the personal computer market since they were first introduced in 1981.

In 1982, Intel introduced the 286 chip. With 134,000 transistors, it provided about three times the performance of other 16-bit processors of the time. Featuring on-chip memory management, the 286 also offered software compatibility with its predecessors. This revolutionary chip was first used in IBM's benchmark PC-AT, the system upon which all modern PCs are based.

In 1985 came the Intel 386 processor. With a new 32-bit architecture and 275,000 transistors, the chip could perform more than five million instructions every second (MIPS). Compaq's Deskpro 386 was the first PC based on the new microprocessor.

Next out of the gate was the Intel 486 processor in 1989. The 486 had 1.2 million transistors and the first built-in math coprocessor. It was some 50 times faster than the original 4004, equaling the performance of some mainframe computers.

Then, in 1993, Intel introduced the first P5 family (586) processor, called the Pentium, setting new performance standards with several times the performance of the previous 486 processor. The Pentium processor used 3.1 million transistors to perform up to 90 MIPS—now up to about 1,500 times the speed of the original 4004.

Note

Intel's change from using numbers (386/486) to names (Pentium/Pentium Pro) for its processors was based on the fact that it could not secure a registered trademark on a number and therefore could not prevent its competitors from using those same numbers on clone chip designs.

The first processor in the P6 (686) family, called the Pentium Pro processor, was introduced in 1995. With 5.5 million transistors, it was the first to be packaged with a second die containing high-speed L2 memory cache to accelerate performance.

Intel revised the original P6 (686/Pentium Pro) and introduced the Pentium II processor in May 1997. Pentium II processors had 7.5 million transistors packed into a cartridge rather than a conventional chip, allowing the L2 cache chips to be attached directly on the module. The Pentium II family was augmented in April 1998, with both the low-cost Celeron processor for basic PCs and the high-end Pentium II Xeon processor for servers and workstations. Intel followed with the Pentium III in 1999, essentially a Pentium II with Streaming SIMD Extensions (SSE) added.

Around the time the Pentium was establishing its dominance, AMD acquired NexGen, who had been working on its Nx686 processor. AMD incorporated that design along with a Pentium interface into what would be called the AMD K6. The K6 was both hardware- and software-compatible with the Pentium, meaning it plugged into the same Socket 7 and could run the same programs. As Intel dropped its Pentium in favor of the Pentium II and III, AMD continued making faster versions of the K6 and made huge inroads in the low-end PC market.

During 1998, Intel became the first to integrate L2 cache directly on the processor die (running at the full speed of the processor core), dramatically increasing performance. This was first done on the second-generation Celeron processor (based on the Pentium II core), as well as the Pentium IIPE (performance-enhanced) chip used only in laptop systems. The first high-end desktop PC chip with on-die full-core speed L2 cache was the second-generation (Coppermine core) Pentium III introduced in late 1999. After this, all the major processor manufacturers also integrated the L2 cache on the processor die, a trend that continues today.

AMD introduced the Athlon in 1999 to compete with Intel head to head in the high-end desktop PC market. The Athlon became very successful, and it seemed for the first time that Intel had some real competition in the higher-end systems. In hindsight the success of the Athlon might be easy to see, but at the time it was introduced, its success was anything but assured. Unlike the previous K6 chips, which were both hardware- and software-compatible with Intel processors, the Athlon was only software-compatible and required a motherboard with an Athlon supporting chipset and processor socket.

The year 2000 saw both companies introduce more new chips to the market. AMD premiered Athlons based on a new Thunderbird core, and new Duron processors as well. The Duron was essentially an Athlon with a smaller L2 cache designed for lower-cost systems, whereas the Athlon with the Thunderbird core used integrated on-die L2 cache to ratchet up performance. The Duron was a lower-cost chip primarily targeted as competition for Intel's lower-cost Celeron processors.

Intel introduced the Pentium 4 in late 2000 as a new processor in the Intel Architecture 32-bit (IA-32) family.

2000 also saw another significant milestone written into the history books when both Intel and AMD crossed the 1GHz barrier, a speed that many thought could never be accomplished.

In 2001, Intel introduced a Pentium 4 version running at 2GHz, the first PC processor to achieve that speed. AMD also introduced the Athlon XP, based on its newer Palomino core, as well as the Athlon MP, designed for multiprocessor server systems. During 2001, both AMD and Intel continued to increase the speed of their chips and enhance the existing Pentium III/Celeron, Pentium 4, and Athlon/Duron processors.

In 2002, Intel released a Pentium 4 version running at 3.06GHz, the first PC processor to break the 3GHz barrier, and the first to feature Intel's Hyper-Threading (HT) technology, which turns the processor into a virtual dual-processor configuration. By running two application threads at the same time, HT-enabled processors can perform tasks at speeds 25%–40% faster than non-HT-enabled processors can. This encouraged programmers to write multithreaded applications, which would prepare them for when true multicore processors would be released a few years later.

In 2003, AMD released its first 64-bit processor: the Athlon 64 (previously code named ClawHammer, or K8), which incorporated AMD64 64-bit extensions. Unlike the IA-64 architecture used by the server-oriented Itanium and Itanium 2, AMD64 defined 64-bit extensions to the IA-32 architecture typified by the Athlon, Pentium 4, and earlier processors. That year Intel also released the Pentium 4 Extreme Edition, the first consumer-level processor that incorporated L3 cache. The whopping 2MB of cache added greatly to the transistor count as well as performance.

In 2004 Intel followed AMD by releasing EM64T, basically the same set of 64-bit extensions as previously defined by AMD as AMD64.

In 2005 both Intel and AMD released their first dual-core processors, basically integrating two processors into a single chip. Although boards supporting two or more processors had been commonly used in network servers for many years prior, this brought dual-CPU capabilities in an affordable package to standard PCs. Rather than attempting to increase clock rates, as has been done in the past, adding processing power by integrating two or more processors into a single chip will enable future processors to perform more work with fewer bottlenecks and with a reduction in both power consumption and heat production.

In 2006 Intel released a new processor called the Core 2, based on an architecture that came mostly from its mobile Pentium M/Core duo processors. The Core 2 was released in a dual-core version first, followed by a quad-core version (combining two dual-core die in a single package) later in the year.

History of the PC

The fourth generation of the modern computer includes those that incorporate microprocessors in their designs. Of course, part of this fourth generation of computers is the personal computer, which itself was made possible by the advent of low-cost microprocessors and memory.

Birth of the Personal Computer

In 1973, some of the first microcomputer kits based on the 8008 chip were developed. These kits were little more than demonstration tools and didn't do much except blink lights. In April 1974, Intel introduced the 8080 microprocessor, which was 10 times faster than the earlier 8008 chip and addressed 64KB of memory. This was the breakthrough the personal computer industry had been waiting for.

A company called MITS introduced the Altair kit in a cover story in the January 1975 issue of *Popular Electronics*. The Altair kit, considered the first personal computer, included an 8080 processor, a power supply, a front panel with a large number of lights, and 256 bytes (not kilobytes) of memory. The kit sold for $395 and had to be assembled. Assembly back then meant you got out your soldering iron to actually finish the circuit boards—not like today, where you can assemble a system of premade components with nothing more than a screwdriver.

Note

Micro Instrumentation and Telemetry Systems was the original name of the company founded in 1969 by Ed Roberts and several associates to manufacture and sell instruments and transmitters for model rockets. Ed Roberts became the sole owner in the early 1970s, after which he designed the Altair. By January 1975, when the Altair was introduced, the company was called MITS, Inc., which then stood for nothing more than the name of the company. In 1977, Roberts sold MITS to Pertec, moved to Georgia, went to medical school, and became a practicing physician!

The Altair included an open architecture system bus called the *S-100 bus* because it had 100 pins per slot. The open architecture meant that anybody could develop boards to fit in these slots and interface to the system. This prompted various add-ons and peripherals from numerous aftermarket companies. The new processor inspired software companies to write programs, including the CP/M (control program for microprocessors) operating system and the first version of the Microsoft BASIC (Beginners All-purpose Symbolic Instruction Code) programming language.

IBM introduced what can be called its first personal computer in 1975. The Model 5100 had 16KB of memory, a built-in 16-line–by–64-character display, a built-in BASIC language interpreter, and a built-in DC-300 cartridge tape drive for storage. The system's $8,975 price placed it out of the mainstream personal computer marketplace, which was dominated by experimenters (affectionately referred to as *hackers*) who built low-cost kits ($500 or so) as a hobby. Obviously, the IBM system was not in competition for this low-cost market and did not sell as well by comparison.

The Model 5100 was succeeded by the 5110 and 5120 before IBM introduced what we know as the IBM Personal Computer (Model 5150). Although the 5100 series preceded the IBM PC, the older systems and the 5150 IBM PC had nothing in common. The PC that IBM turned out was more closely related to the IBM System/23 DataMaster, an office computer system introduced in 1980. In fact, many of the engineers who developed the IBM PC had originally worked on the DataMaster.

In 1976, a new company called Apple Computer introduced the Apple I, which originally sold for $666.66. The selling price was an arbitrary number selected by one of Apple's cofounders, Steve Jobs. This system consisted of a main circuit board screwed to a piece of plywood; a case and power supply were not included. Only a few of these computers were made, and they reportedly have sold to collectors for more than $20,000. The Apple II, introduced in 1977, helped set the standard for nearly all the important microcomputers to follow, including the IBM PC.

The microcomputer world was dominated in 1980 by two types of computer systems. One type, the Apple II, claimed a large following of loyal users and a gigantic software base that was growing at a fantastic rate. The other type, CP/M systems, consisted not of a single system but of all the many systems that evolved from the original MITS Altair. These systems were compatible with one another and were distinguished by their use of the CP/M operating system and expansion slots, which followed the S-100 standard. All these systems were built by a variety of companies and sold under various names. For the most part, however, these systems used the same software and plug-in hardware. It is interesting to note that none of these systems was PC compatible or Macintosh compatible, the two primary standards in place today.

A new competitor looming on the horizon was able to see that to be successful, a personal computer needed to have an open architecture, slots for expansion, a modular design, and healthy support from both hardware and software companies other than the original manufacturer of the system. This competitor turned out to be IBM, which was quite surprising at the time because IBM was not known for systems with these open-architecture attributes. IBM, in essence, became more like the early Apple, while Apple became like everybody expected IBM to be. The open architecture of the forthcoming IBM PC and the closed architecture of the forthcoming Macintosh caused a complete turnaround in the industry.

The IBM Personal Computer

At the end of 1980, IBM decided to truly compete in the rapidly growing low-cost personal computer market. The company established the Entry Systems Division, located in Boca Raton, Florida, to develop the new system. The division was intentionally located far away from IBM's main headquarters in New York, or any other IBM facilities, so that it would be able to operate independently as a separate unit. This small group consisted of 12 engineers and designers under the direction of Don Estridge and was charged with developing IBM's first real PC. (IBM considered the previous 5100 system, developed in 1975, to be an intelligent programmable terminal rather than a genuine computer, even though it truly was a computer.) Nearly all these engineers had come to the new division from the System/23 DataMaster project, which was a small office computer system introduced in 1980 and was the direct predecessor of the IBM PC.

Much of the PC's design was influenced by the DataMaster design. In the DataMaster's single-piece design, the display and keyboard were integrated into the unit. Because these features were limiting, they became external units on the PC, although the PC keyboard layout and electrical designs were copied from the DataMaster.

Several other parts of the IBM PC system also were copied from the DataMaster, including the expansion bus (or input/output slots), which included not only the same physical 62-pin connector, but also almost identical pin specifications. This copying of the bus design was possible because the PC used the same interrupt controller as the DataMaster and a similar direct memory access (DMA) controller. Also, expansion cards already designed for the DataMaster could easily be redesigned to function in the PC.

The DataMaster used an Intel 8085 CPU, which had a 64KB address limit and an 8-bit internal and external data bus. This arrangement prompted the PC design team to use the Intel 8088 CPU, which offered a much larger (1MB) memory address limit and an internal 16-bit data bus, but only an 8-bit external data bus. The 8-bit external data bus and similar instruction set enabled the 8088 to be easily interfaced into the earlier DataMaster designs.

IBM brought its system from idea to delivery of functioning systems in one year by using existing designs and purchasing as many components as possible from outside vendors. The Entry Systems Division was granted autonomy from IBM's other divisions and could tap resources outside the company, rather than go through the bureaucratic procedures that required exclusive use of IBM resources. IBM contracted out the PC's languages and operating system to a small company named Microsoft. That decision was the major factor in establishing Microsoft as the dominant force in PC software today.

Note

It is interesting to note that IBM had originally contacted Digital Research (the company that created CP/M, then the most popular personal computer operating system) to have it develop an operating system for the new IBM PC. However, Digital was leery of working with IBM and especially balked at the nondisclosure agreement IBM wanted Digital to sign. Microsoft jumped on the opportunity left open by Digital Research and, consequently became the largest software company in the world. IBM's use of outside vendors in developing the PC was an open invitation for the after-market to jump in and support the system—and it did.

On August 12, 1981, a new standard was established in the microcomputer industry with the debut of the IBM PC. Since then, hundreds of millions of PC-compatible systems have been sold, as the original PC has grown into an enormous family of computers and peripherals. More software has been written for this computer family than for any other system on the market.

The PC Industry More Than 25 Years Later

In the more than 25 years since the original IBM PC was introduced, many changes have occurred. The IBM-compatible computer, for example, advanced from a 4.77MHz 8088-based system to 3GHz or faster Core 2 –based systems—about 50,000 times faster than the original IBM PC (in actual processing speed, not just clock speed). The original PC had only one or two single-sided floppy drives that stored 160KB each using DOS 1.0, whereas modern systems easily can have 1TB (1 trillion bytes) or more of hard disk storage.

A rule of thumb in the computer industry (called Moore's Law, originally set forth by Intel cofounder Gordon Moore) is that available processor performance and disk-storage capacity doubles every one and a half to two years, give or take.

Since the beginning of the PC industry, this pattern has held steady and, if anything, seems to be accelerating.

Moore's Law

In 1965, Gordon Moore was preparing a speech about the growth trends in computer memory and made an interesting observation. When he began to graph the data, he realized a striking trend existed. Each new chip contained roughly twice as much capacity as its predecessor, and each chip was released within 18–24 months of the previous chip. If this trend continued, he reasoned, computing power would rise exponentially over relatively brief periods of time.

Moore's observation, now known as Moore's Law, described a trend that has continued to this day and is still remarkably accurate. It was found to not only describe memory chips, but also accurately describe the growth of processor power and disk drive storage capacity. It has become the basis for many industry performance forecasts. As an example, in 30 years the number of transistors on a processor chip increased more than 18,000 times, from 2,300 transistors on the 4004 processor in 1971 to more than 582 million transistors on the Core 2 Extreme (Quad-Core) processor in November 2006. By 2008, Intel expects to release processors with over one billion transistors.

In addition to performance and storage capacity, another major change since the original IBM PC was introduced is that IBM is not the only manufacturer of PC-compatible systems. IBM originated the PC-compatible standard, of course, but today it no longer sets the standards for the system it originated. More often than not, new standards in the PC industry are developed by companies and organizations other than IBM.

Today, it is Intel, Microsoft, and AMD who are primarily responsible for developing and extending the PC hardware and software standards. Some have even taken to calling PCs "Wintel" systems, owing to the dominance of the first two companies. Although AMD originally produced Intel processors under license and later produced low-cost, pin-compatible counterparts to Intel's 486 and Pentium processors (AMD 486, K5/K6), starting with the Athlon, AMD has created completely unique processors that have been worthy rivals to Intel's current models.

In more recent years the introduction of hardware standards such as the Peripheral Component Interconnect (PCI) bus, Accelerated Graphics Port (AGP) bus, PCI Express bus, ATX and BTX motherboard form factors, as well as processor socket and slot interfaces show that Intel is really pushing PC hardware design these days. Intel's ability to design and produce motherboard chipsets as well as complete motherboards has enabled Intel processor–based systems to first adopt newer memory and bus architectures as well as system form factors. Although in the past AMD has on occasion made chipsets for its own processors, the company's acquisition of ATI will allow it to become more aggressive in the chipset marketplace in the future.

In a similar fashion, Microsoft is pushing the software side of things with the continual evolution of the Windows operating system as well as applications such as the Office suite. All these companies have capitalized on the widespread popularity of the Internet, multimedia, and other types of rich media. Such uses as gaming, video editing, broadband Internet access, and photo-quality printing are giving more and more people important reasons to use a PC. Even though recent sales have leveled off from the explosive growth of the mid-to-late 1990s, the reality is that literally hundreds of system manufacturers follow the collective PC standard and produce computers that are fully PC compatible. In addition, thousands of peripheral manufacturers produce components that expand and enhance PC-compatible systems.

PC-compatible systems have thrived not only because compatible hardware can be assembled easily, but also because the most popular operating system was available not from IBM but from a third party (Microsoft). The core of the system software is the basic input/output system (BIOS), and this was also available from third-party companies, such as AMI, Phoenix, and others. This situation enabled other manufacturers to license the operating system and BIOS software and sell their own compatible systems. The fact that DOS borrowed the functionality and user interface from both CP/M and Unix probably had a lot to do with the amount of software that became available. Later, with the success of Windows, even more reasons would exist for software developers to write programs for PC-compatible systems.

One reason Apple's Macintosh systems have never enjoyed the market success of PC systems is that Apple has often used proprietary hardware and software designs that it was unwilling to license to other companies. This proprietary nature has unfortunately relegated Apple to a meager 3%–5% market share in personal computers.

One fortunate development for Mac enthusiasts is Apple's shift to Intel x86 processors and PC architecture, resulting in far better performance and much greater standardization as compared to the previous non-PC compatible Mac systems. Although Apple still refuses to adopt all of the industry-standard form factors used in PCs, the PC based Macs truly are PCs from a hardware standpoint, using all of the same processors, memory, buses, and other system architectures that PCs have been using for years, finally allowing Macs to perform on par with PCs as well. I've even had people ask me, "Is there a book like *Upgrading and Repairing PCs* that covers Mac systems instead?" Well, since Macs have essentially *become* PCs, they are now covered in this book by default! Time will tell, but I believe that the move to a PC based architecture is without a doubt the smartest move Apple has made in years.

Apple could even become a real contender in the OS arena (taking market share from Microsoft) if the company would only sell its OS in an unlocked version that would run on non-Apple PCs. Unfortunately for now, even though Apple's OS X operating system is designed to run on PC hardware, it is coded to check for a security chip found only on Apple motherboards. There are ways to work around the check (see OSx86project.org), but they are not supported by Apple.

Apple's shift to a PC based architecture is just one more indication of just how popular the PC has become. After 25 years the PC continues to thrive and prosper. With far-reaching industry support and an architecture that is continuously evolving, I would say it is a safe bet that PC-compatible systems will continue to dominate the personal computer marketplace for the next 25 years as well.

Chapter 2

PC Components,
Features, and
System Design

What Is a PC?

When I begin one of my PC hardware seminars, I like to ask the question, "What exactly is a PC?" Most people immediately answer that PC stands for *personal computer*, which in fact it does. Many continue by defining a personal computer as any small computer system purchased and used by an individual. Although all of this is true, that definition is not precise enough when you consider that all PCs are personal computers, but not all personal computers are PCs. For example, all of Apple's Motorola/IBM processor–based Macintosh systems, 8080/Z-80 processor–based CP/M machines, and even my old Apple][+ system are all personal computers, but most people wouldn't call them PCs, least of all the Mac users! For the true definition of what a PC is, we must look deeper.

Calling something a PC implies that it is something much more specific than just any personal computer. One thing it implies is a family relation to the original IBM PC from 1981. In fact, I'll go so far as to say that IBM literally *invented* the type of computer we call a PC today; that is, IBM designed and created the very first one, and IBM originally defined and set all the standards that made the PC distinctive from other personal computers. Note that it is very clear in my mind—as well as in the historical record—that IBM did *not* invent the personal computer. (Many recognize the historical origins of the personal computer in the MITS Altair, introduced in 1975, even though there were many small computers available prior.) So, IBM did not invent the personal computer, but it did invent what today we call the PC. Some people might take this definition a step further and define a PC as any personal computer that is "IBM compatible." In fact, many years back, PCs were called either *IBM compatibles* or *IBM clones*, in essence paying homage to the origins of the PC at IBM.

Some Personal Computer Trivia

Although the 1975 MITS Altair is often credited as the first personal computer, according to the Blinkenlights Archaeological Institute (www.blinkenlights.com), the first personal computer was the Simon created by Edmund C. Berkeley and described in his 1949 book, *Giant Brains, or Machines That Think*. The plans for Simon were available for purchase by Berkeley Enterprises as well as published in a series of 13 articles in *Radio Electronics* magazine during 1950–1951.

The term *personal computer* may have first appeared in a November 3, 1962 *New York Times* article quoting John W. Mauchly (co-creator of ENIAC). The article was reporting on Mauchly's vision of future computing and was quoted as saying, "There is no reason to suppose the average boy or girl cannot be master of a personal computer."

The first machine advertised as a "personal computer" was the Hewlett-Packard 9100A, a 40-lb. programmable desktop electronic calculator released in 1968. Advertisements for the $4900 system called it "The new Hewlett-Packard 9100A personal computer." The end of the ad stated, "If you are still skeptical, or of faint heart, ask for a demonstration. It will affirm, assure (and only slightly delay) your entry into the solid-state of personal computing power." (See www. vintagecalculators.com.)

The reality today is that although IBM clearly designed and created the PC in 1981 and controlled the development and evolution of the PC standard for several years thereafter, IBM is no longer in control of the PC standard; that is, it does not dictate what makes up a PC today. IBM lost control of the PC standard in 1987 when it introduced its PS/2 line of systems. Up until then, other companies that were producing PCs literally copied IBM's systems right down to the chips, connectors, and even the shapes (form factors) of the boards, cases, and power supplies. After 1987, IBM abandoned many of the standards it created in the first place. That's why for many years now I have refrained from using the designation "IBM compatible" when referring to PCs.

If a PC is no longer an IBM-compatible system, then what is it? The real question seems to be, "Who is in control of the PC standard today?" That question is best broken down into two parts. First, who is in control of PC software? Second, who is in control of PC hardware?

Who Controls PC Software?

Most of the people in my seminars don't even hesitate for a split second when I ask this question; they immediately respond, "Microsoft!" I don't think there is any argument with that answer. Microsoft clearly controls the dominant operating systems used on PCs, which has evolved from the original MS-DOS to DOS/Windows 3.x, then to Windows 9x/Me, then to Windows NT/2000/XP, and now to Windows Vista.

Microsoft has effectively used its control of the PC operating systems as leverage to also control other types of PC software, such as utilities and applications. For example, many utility programs originally offered by independent companies, such as disk caching, disk compression, file defragmentation, file structure repair, firewalls and even simple applications such as calculator and notepad programs, are now bundled in Windows. Microsoft has even bundled more comprehensive applications such as Web browsers, word processors, and media players, ensuring an automatic installed base for these applications—much to the dismay of companies who produce competing versions. Microsoft has also leveraged its control of the operating system to integrate its own networking software and applications suites more seamlessly into the operating system than others. That's why it now dominates most of the PC software universe—from operating systems to networking software to utilities, from word processors to database programs to spreadsheets.

In the early days of the PC, IBM hired Microsoft to provide most of the core software for the PC. IBM developed the hardware, wrote the basic input/output system (BIOS), and hired Microsoft to develop the disk operating system (DOS), as well as several other programs and utilities for the PC. In what was later viewed as perhaps the most costly business mistake in history, IBM failed to secure exclusive rights to the DOS it had contracted from Microsoft, either by purchasing it outright or by an exclusive license agreement. Instead, IBM licensed it nonexclusively, which subsequently allowed Microsoft to sell the same MS-DOS code it developed for IBM to any other company that was interested. Early PC cloners such as Compaq eagerly licensed this operating system code, and suddenly consumers could purchase the same basic MS-DOS operating system with several different company names on the box. In retrospect, that single contractual error made Microsoft into the dominant software company it is today and subsequently caused IBM to lose control of the very PC standard it had created.

As a writer (of words, not software), I can appreciate what an incredible oversight this was. Imagine that a book publisher comes up with a great idea for a very popular book and then contracts with an author to write it. Then, by virtue of a poorly written contract, the author discovers that he can legally sell the very same book (perhaps with a different title) to all the competitors of the original publisher. Of course, no publisher I know would allow this to happen; yet that is exactly what IBM allowed Microsoft to do back in 1981. By virtue of its deal with Microsoft, IBM lost control of the software it commissioned for its new PC.

It is interesting to note that in the PC business, software enjoys copyright protection, whereas hardware can be protected only by patents, which are much more difficult, time-consuming, and expensive to obtain. And in the case of U.S. patents, they also expire 20 years after filing. According to the U.S. patent office, "any new and useful process, machine, manufacture, or composition of matter, or any new and useful improvement thereof" can be patented. This definition made it difficult to patent most aspects of the IBM PC because it was designed using previously existing parts that anybody could purchase off the shelf. In fact, most of the important parts for the original PC came from Intel, such as the 8088 processor, 8284 clock generator, 8253/54 timer, 8259 interrupt controller, 8237 DMA (direct memory access) controller, 8255 peripheral interface, and 8288 bus controller. These chips made up the heart and soul of the original PC motherboard.

Because the design of the original PC was not wholly patented and virtually all of the parts were readily available, almost anybody could duplicate the hardware of the IBM PC. All they had to do was purchase the same chips from the same manufacturers and suppliers IBM used and design a new motherboard with a similar circuit. IBM even made it easier by publishing complete schematic diagrams of its motherboards and adapter cards in very detailed and easily available technical reference manuals. These manuals even included fully commented source code listings for the ROM BIOS code as well. I have several of these early IBM manuals and still refer to them for specific component-level PC design information. In fact, I highly recommend these original manuals to anybody who wants to delve deeply into PC hardware design. Although they are long out of print, they do turn up in the used book market and online auction sites such as eBay.

The difficult part of copying the IBM PC was the software, which is protected by copyright law. Both Compaq and Phoenix Software (today known as Phoenix Technologies) were among the first to develop a legal way around this problem, which enabled them to functionally duplicate (but not exactly copy) software such as the BIOS. The *BIOS* is defined as the core set of control software that drives the hardware devices in the system directly. These types of programs are normally called *device drivers*, so in essence, the BIOS is a collection of all the core device drivers used to operate and control the system hardware. The *operating system* (such as DOS or Windows) uses the drivers in the BIOS to control and communicate with the various hardware and peripherals in the system.

▶▶ See Chapter 5, "BIOS," p. 441.

The method they used to legally duplicate the IBM PC BIOS was an ingenious form of reverse-engineering. They used two groups of software engineers, the second of which were specially screened to consist only of people who had never before seen or studied the IBM BIOS code. The first group studied the IBM BIOS and wrote a detailed description of what it did. The second group read the description written by the first group and set out to write from scratch a new BIOS that did everything the first group had described. The end result was a new BIOS written from scratch, and while the resulting code was not identical to IBM's, it had exactly the same functionality.

This is called a "clean room" approach to reverse-engineering software, and if carefully conducted, it can escape any legal attack. Because IBM's original PC BIOS had a limited and yet well-defined set of functions, and was only 8,096 bytes long, duplicating it through the clean-room approach was not very difficult. As the IBM BIOS evolved, keeping up with any changes IBM made was relatively easy. Discounting the power-on self test (POST) and BIOS Setup (used for configuring the system) portion of the BIOS, most motherboard BIOSs, even today, have only about 32KB–128KB of active code, and modern OSs ignore most of it anyway by loading code and drivers from disk. In essence, the modern motherboard BIOS serves only to initialize the system and load the OS. Today, although some PC manufacturers still write some of their own BIOS code, most source their BIOS from one of the independent BIOS developers. Phoenix and American Megatrends (AMI) are the leading developers of BIOS software for PC system and motherboard manufacturers. A third major producer of BIOS software, Award Software, is owned by Phoenix Technologies, which continues to sell Award BIOS–based products.

After the motherboard hardware and BIOS of the IBM PC were duplicated, all that was necessary to produce a fully IBM-compatible system was MS-DOS. Reverse-engineering DOS, even with the clean-room approach, seemed to be a daunting task at the time, because DOS is much larger than the BIOS and consists of many more programs and functions. Also, the operating system has evolved and changed more often than the BIOS, which by comparison has remained relatively constant. This means that the only way to get DOS on an IBM compatible back in the early 1980s was to license it. This is where Microsoft came in. Because IBM (who hired Microsoft to write DOS in the first place) did not ensure that its license agreement with Microsoft was exclusive, Microsoft was free to sell the same DOS it designed for IBM to anybody else who wanted it. With a licensed copy of MS-DOS, the last piece was in place and the floodgates were open for IBM-compatible systems to be produced whether IBM liked it or not.

Note

MS-DOS was eventually cloned, the first of which was DR-DOS, released by Digital Research (developers of CP/M) in 1988. By all rights, DR-DOS was more than just a clone; it had many features not found in MS-DOS at the time, inspiring Microsoft to add similar features in future MS-DOS versions as well. In 1991, Novell acquired DR-DOS, followed by Caldera in 1996 (who released a version of the source code under an open-source license), followed by Lineo in 1998, and finally by DRDOS (www.drdos.com) in 2002.

Free and open-source DOS versions have been independently produced, upgraded, and maintained by the DR-DOS/OpenDOS Enhancement Project (www.drdosprojects.de) as well as the FreeDOS Project (www.freedos.org).

In retrospect, this is exactly why there were no clones or compatibles of the Apple Macintosh systems. It is not that Mac systems couldn't be duplicated; in fact, the older Mac hardware was fairly simple and easy to produce using off-the-shelf parts, and current Macs now use the same hardware as PCs. The real problem is that Apple owns the Mac OS, and so far has refused to license or allow its OS to run on non-Apple hardware. The earlier non-PC-compatible Macs also incorporated a rather large and complex BIOS that was very tightly integrated with the older Mac OS. The greater complexity and integration combined with very low market share allowed the early non-PC-compatible Mac BIOS and OS to escape any clean-room duplication efforts.

Note

During 1996–1997, an effort was made by the more liberated thinkers at Apple to license its BIOS/OS combination, and several Mac-compatible machines were developed, produced, and sold. Companies such as Sony, Power Computing, Radius, and even Motorola invested millions of dollars in developing these systems, but shortly after these first Mac clones were sold, Apple canceled the licensing! By canceling these licenses, Apple virtually guaranteed that its systems would not be competitive with Windows-based PCs. Along with its smaller market share come much higher system costs, fewer available software applications, and fewer options for hardware repair, replacement, or upgrades as compared to PCs. The proprietary form factors also ensure that major components such as motherboards, power supplies, and cases are available only from Apple at very high prices, making out-of-warranty repair, replacement, or upgrades of these components not cost effective.

Now that Apple has converted its Mac systems over to PC architecture, the only difference between a Mac and a PC is the OS they run, so a PC running OS X essentially becomes a Mac, while a Mac running Windows becomes a PC. This means that the only thing keeping Mac systems unique is the ability to run OS X. To this end, Apple includes code in OS X that checks for an Apple specific security chip, thus preventing OS X from running on non-Apple PCs. While this does create an incentive to buy Apple brand PCs, it also overlooks the huge market for selling OS X to non-Apple PC users. For example, if Apple had sold OS X to PC users while Microsoft was delaying the release of Vista, OS X would have taken a large amount of market share from Windows. However, despite Apple's attempts to prevent OS X from running, the OSx86 Project (www.osx86project.org) has information showing how to get OS X installed and running on standard PCs.

Who Controls PC Hardware?

Although it is clear that Microsoft has always had the majority control over PC software by virtue of its control over the dominant PC operating systems, what about the hardware? It is easy to see that IBM controlled the PC hardware standard up through 1987. After all, IBM invented the core PC motherboard design; the original expansion bus slot architecture (8/16-bit ISA bus); ROM BIOS interface, serial and parallel port implementations; video card design through VGA and XGA standards; floppy and hard disk interface and controller implementations; power supply designs; keyboard interfaces and designs; mouse interface; and even the physical shapes (form factors) of everything from the motherboard to the expansion cards, power supplies, and system chassis. All these pre-1987 IBM PC, XT, and AT system design features are still influencing modern systems today.

But to me the real question is which company has been responsible for creating and inventing newer and more recent PC hardware designs, interfaces, and standards? When I ask people that question, I normally see some hesitation in their responses—some people say Microsoft (but it controls the software, not the hardware), and some say HP/Compaq or Dell, or they name a few other big-name system manufacturers. Some, however, surmise the correct answer—Intel.

I can see why many people don't immediately realize this; I mean, how many people actually own an Intel-brand PC? No, not just one that says "Intel inside" on it (which refers only to the system having an Intel processor), but a system that was designed and built by, or even purchased through, Intel. Believe it or not, many people today do have Intel PCs!

Certainly this does not mean that consumers have purchased their systems from Intel because Intel does not sell complete PCs to end users. You can't currently order a system from Intel, nor can you purchase an Intel-brand system from somebody else. What I am talking about is the motherboard. In my opinion, the single most important part in a PC system is the motherboard, and I'd say that whoever made your motherboard would be considered the primary manufacturer of your system.

Even back when IBM was the major supplier of PCs, it primarily made the motherboard and contracted out the other components of the system (power supply, disk drives, and so on) to others.

▶▶ See Chapter 4, "Motherboards and Buses," p. 235.

Many of the top-selling system manufacturers do design and make their own motherboards, especially for their higher-end systems. According to *Computer Reseller News* magazine, the top desktop systems manufacturers for the last several years have consistently been names such as HP, Dell, and Lenovo (formerly IBM). These companies both design and manufacture their own motherboards as well as purchase existing boards from motherboard manufacturers. In rare cases, they even design their own chips and chipset components for their own boards. Although sales are high for these individual companies, a large segment of the market is what those in the industry call the *white-box systems*.

White-box is the term used by the industry to refer to what would otherwise be called *generic* PCs— that is, PCs assembled from a collection of industry-standard, commercially available components. The white-box designation comes from the fact that historically most of the chassis used by this type of system have been white (or ivory or beige).

The great thing about white-box systems is that they use industry-standard components that are interchangeable. This interchangeability is the key to future upgrades and repairs because it ensures that a plethora of replacement parts will be available to choose from and will be interchangeable. For many years, I have recommended avoiding proprietary systems and recommended more industry-standard white-box systems instead.

Companies selling white-box systems do not really manufacture the systems; they assemble them. That is, they purchase commercially available motherboards, cases, power supplies, disk drives, peripherals, and so on, and assemble and market everything together as complete systems. Some companies such as HP and Dell manufacture some of their own systems as well as assemble some from industry-standard parts. In particular, the HP Pavilion and Dell Dimension lines are composed largely of mainstream systems made with mostly industry-standard parts. PC makers using mostly industry-standard parts also include high-end game system builders such as VoodooPC (owned by HP) and Alienware (owned by Dell). Other examples include Gateway and eMachines (owned by Gateway), whose PCs are also constructed using primarily industry-standard components. Note that there can be exceptions for all of these systems; for example, I know that some of the Dell Dimension XPS systems use proprietary parts such as power supplies. I recommend avoiding such systems, due to future upgrade and repair hassles.

Others using industry-standard components include Acer, CyberPower, Micro Express, and Systemax, but hundreds more could be listed. In overall total volume, this ends up being the largest segment of the PC marketplace today. What is interesting about white-box systems is that, with very few exceptions, you and I can purchase the same motherboards and other components any of the white-box manufacturers can (although we would probably pay more than they do because of the volume discounts they receive). We can assemble a virtually identical white-box system from scratch ourselves, but that is a story for Chapter 20, "Building or Upgrading Systems."

Who makes the majority of motherboards for white-box systems? You guessed it—Intel. The only place Intel doesn't have a presence is in the roughly 20% PC marketshare of AMD-based systems designed to support AMD processors.

Although Intel still dominates motherboard sales, that dominance has faltered somewhat from a few years back. Because of Intel's focus on Rambus memory during the early Pentium 4 days, many of the lower-cost system builders switched to alternative products. Also, Intel's boards don't have as many configuration options for overclocking, so "hotrod" system builders often choose non-Intel boards instead.

AMD, on the other hand, manufactures processors and chipsets but not complete motherboards. For that, AMD relies on a number of other motherboard manufacturers to make boards designed to accept AMD processors. These boards use either the AMD/ATI chipsets or other chipsets made by third-party companies specifically to support AMD processors. The same motherboard companies making boards for AMD processor–based systems also make motherboards for Intel processor–based systems, in essence competing directly with Intel's own motherboards.

▶▶ See "Chipsets," p. 273.

How did Intel come to dominate the interior of our PCs? Intel has been the dominant PC processor supplier since IBM chose the Intel 8088 CPU in the original IBM PC in 1981. By controlling the processor, Intel naturally controlled the chips necessary to integrate its processors into system designs. This naturally led Intel into the chipset business. It started its chipset business in 1989 with the 82350 Extended Industry Standard Architecture (EISA) chipset, and by 1993 it had become—along with the debut of the Pentium processor—the largest-volume major motherboard chipset supplier. Now I imagine Intel sitting there, thinking that it makes the processor and all the other chips necessary to produce a motherboard, so why not just eliminate the middleman and make the entire motherboard, too? The answer to this, and a real turning point in the industry, came about in 1994 when Intel became the largest-volume motherboard manufacturer in the world. And Intel has remained solidly on top ever since. It doesn't just lead in this category by any small margin; in fact, during 1997, Intel made more motherboards than the next eight largest motherboard manufacturers combined, with sales of more than 30 million boards, worth more than $3.6 billion! Note that this figure does not include processors or chipsets—only the boards themselves. These boards end up in the various system assembler–brand PCs you and I buy, meaning that most of us are now essentially purchasing Intel-manufactured systems, no matter who actually wielded the screwdriver.

Intel controls the PC hardware standard because it controls the PC motherboard. It not only makes the vast majority of motherboards being used in systems today, but it also supplies the vast majority of processors and motherboard chipsets to other motherboard manufacturers.

Intel also has had a hand in setting several recent PC hardware standards, such as the following:

- Peripheral Component Interconnect (PCI) local bus interface.
- Accelerated Graphics Port (AGP) interface for high-performance video cards.
- PCI Express (originally known as 3GIO), the interface elected by the PCI Special Interest Group (PCI SIG) to replace both PCI and AGP as the high-performance bus for newer PCs.
- Industry-standard motherboard form factors such as ATX (including variations such as microATX and FlexATX) and BTX (including variations such as microBTX, nanoBTX, and picoBTX). ATX is still the most popular, and beginning in 1996–1997 it replaced the somewhat long-in-the-tooth IBM-designed Baby-AT form factor, which had been used since the early 1980s.
- Desktop Management Interface (DMI) for monitoring system hardware functions.
- Dynamic Power Management Architecture (DPMA) and Advanced Power Management (APM) standards for managing power use in the PC.

Intel dominates not only the PC, but the entire worldwide semiconductor industry. According to the sales figures compiled by iSuppli, Intel has about one and a half times the sales of the next closest semiconductor company (Samsung) and more than four times the sales of competitor AMD (see Table 2.1).

Table 2.1   Top 25 Semiconductor Companies Ranked by 2006 Semiconductor Sales

2006 Rank	Country of Company	2006 Origin	Percent Revenue[1]	2005 of Total	2005 Rank	Percent Revenue	Change
1	Intel	USA	31,542	12.1%	1	35,466	−11.1%
2	Samsung	South Korea	19,842	7.6%	2	17,710	+12.0%
3	Texas Instruments	USA	12,600	4.8%	3	10,745	+17.3%
4	Toshiba	Japan	10,141	3.9%	4	9,077	+11.7%
5	STMicroelectronics	Italy/France	9,854	3.8%	5	8,881	+11.0%
6	Renesas	Japan	7,900	3.0%	7	8,107	−2.6%
7	Hynix	South Korea	7,865	3.0%	11	5,560	+41.5%
8	AMD[2]	USA	7,506	2.9%	15	3,917	+91.6%
9	Freescale	USA	5,988	2.3%	10	5,598	+7.0%
10	NXP	Netherlands	5,874	2.3%	9	5,646	+4.0%
11	NEC	Japan	5,679	2.2%	8	5,708	−0.5%
12	Qimonda[3]	Germany	5,413	2.1%	—	—	—
13	Micron	USA	5,210	2.0%	12	4,775	+9.1%
14	Infineon[3]	Germany	5,119	2.0%	6	8,297	−38.3%
15	Sony	Japan	4,852	1.9%	13	4,574	+6.1%
16	Qualcomm	USA	4,529	1.7%	16	3,457	+31.0%
17	Matsushita	Japan	4,022	1.5%	14	4,131	−2.6%
18	Broadcom	USA	3,668	1.4%	20	2,671	+37.3
19	Elpida	Japan	3,527	1.4%	28	1,776	+98.6%
20	Sharp	Japan	3,341	1.3%	17	3,266	+2.3%
21	IBM	USA	3,172	1.2%	19	2,792	+13.6%
22	Rohm	Japan	2,882	1.1%	18	2,909	−0.9%
23	Analog Devices	USA	2,603	1.0%	22	2,428	+7.2%
24	Spansion	Japan/USA	2,579	1.0%	24	2,054	+25.6%
25	NVIDIA	USA	2,574	1.0%	23	2,069	+24.4%
	Others:		81,912	31.5%		76,362	+7.3%
	TOTAL:		260,194	100.0%		237,976	+9.3%

1. *Ranking by Revenue in Millions of U.S. Dollars.*
2. *MD acquired ATI Technologies in 2006, AMD's 2006 revenue includes ATI Technology revenue for all of 2006.*
3. *Qimonda was formed as a spin-off of Infineon's memory division. Revenue for both companies is separated for 2006.*

As you can see by these figures, it is no wonder that a popular industry news website called *The Register* (www.theregister.com) uses the term *Chipzilla* when referring to the industry giant.

Whoever controls the operating system controls the software for the PC, and whoever controls the motherboard—controls the hardware. Because Microsoft and Intel together seem to control software and hardware in the PC today, it is no surprise the modern PC is often called a "Wintel" system.

PC Design Guides

For several years Intel and Microsoft released a series of documents called the "PC *XX* Design Guides" (where *XX* designates the year) as a set of standard specifications to guide both hardware and software developers creating products that work with Windows. The requirements in these guides were part of Microsoft's "Designed for Windows" logo requirement. In other words, if you produced either a hardware or software product and you want the official "Designed for Windows" logo to be on your box, your product had to meet the PC *XX* minimum requirements.

Following are the documents that have been produced in this series:

- "Hardware Design Guide for Microsoft Windows 95"
- "Hardware Design Guide Supplement for PC 95"
- "PC 97 Hardware Design Guide"
- "PC 98 System Design Guide"
- "PC 99 System Design Guide"
- "PC 2000 System Design Guide"
- "PC 2001 System Design Guide"

These documents are available for download from the Microsoft website (http://www.microsoft.com/whdc/system/platform/pcdesign/desguide/pcguides.mspx).

Note

These guides do not mean anything directly for the end user; instead, they were meant to be guides for PC manufacturers to design and build their systems. In some ways, they were a market-control tool for Intel and Microsoft to further wield their influence over PC hardware and software.

The "PC 2001 System Design Guide" is the most recent design guide produced by Microsoft and Intel together. Since then these companies have produced individual whitepapers and other resources for this purpose. For updated system-design information, see the following websites:

- The Microsoft Windows Platform Design–Overview site at http://www.microsoft.com/whdc/system/platform/default.mspx
- The Intel developer website at http://developer.intel.com

System Types

PCs can be broken down into many categories. I like to break them down in two ways—by the type of software they can run and by the motherboard host bus or processor bus design and width. Because this book concentrates mainly on hardware, let's look at that first.

When a processor reads data, the data moves into the processor via the processor's external data bus connection. The processor's data bus is directly connected to the processor host bus on the motherboard. The processor data bus or host bus is also sometimes referred to as the *local bus* because it is local to the processor connected directly to it. Any other devices connected to the host bus essentially appear as if they are directly connected to the processor as well. If the processor has a 32-bit data bus, the motherboard must be wired to have a 32-bit processor host bus. This means the system can move 32 bits of data into or out of the processor in a single cycle.

▶▶ See "Data I/O Bus," p. 48.

Different processors have different data bus widths, and the motherboards designed to accept them require a processor host bus with a matching width. Table 2.2 lists all the Intel and major Intel-compatible processors, their data bus widths, and their internal register sizes.

Table 2.2   Intel and Intel-Compatible Processors and Their Data Bus/Register Widths

Processor	Data Bus Width	Register Size
8088	8-bit	16-bit
8086	16-bit	16-bit
286	16-bit	16-bit
386SX	16-bit	32-bit
386DX	32-bit	32-bit
486/AMD-5x86	32-bit	32-bit
Pentium/AMD-K6	64-bit	32-bit
Pentium Pro/Celeron/II/III/4	64-bit	32-bit
AMD Duron/Athlon/Athlon XP	64-bit	32-bit
AMD64/EM64T	64-bit	64-bit

A common misconception arises in discussions of processor widths. Although most Pentium processors all have 64-bit data bus widths, most include internal registers that are only 32 bits wide, and they process 32-bit commands and instructions. The AMD processors with AMD64 and Intel processors with EM64T have 64-bit internal registers and can run in both 32-bit and 64-bit modes. Thus, from a software point of view, all chips from the 386 to the Athlon/Duron and Celeron/Pentium 4 have 32-bit registers and execute 32-bit instructions. From the electronic or physical perspective, these 32-bit, software-capable processors have been available in physical forms with 16-bit (386SX), 32-bit (386DX and 486), and 64-bit (Pentium and beyond) data bus widths. The data bus width is the major factor in motherboard and memory system design because it dictates how many bits move in and out of the chip in one cycle.

▶▶   See "Internal Registers (Internal Data Bus)," p. 49.

Processors including AMD64 and EM64T technology have an x86-compatible 64-bit architecture but are also designed to use 32-bit instructions written for normal x86 processors.

▶▶   See "Processor Specifications," p. 43.

Referring to Table 2.2, you can see that all Pentium and newer systems have a 64-bit processor bus. Pentium processors, whether they are the original Pentium, Pentium MMX, Pentium Pro, or even the Pentium II/III or 4, all have 64-bit data buses, as do comparable processors from AMD (K6 family, Athlon, Duron, Athlon XP, and Athlon 64).

As you can see from Table 2.2, systems can be broken down into the following hardware categories:

- 8-bit
- 16-bit
- 32-bit
- 64-bit

What is interesting is that besides the bus width, the 16- through 64-bit systems are remarkably similar in basic design and architecture. The older 8-bit systems are very different, however. This gives us two basic system types, or classes, of hardware:

- 8-bit (PC/XT-class) systems
- 16/32/64-bit (AT-class) systems

Here, PC stands for personal computer, XT stands for an extended PC, and AT stands for an advanced-technology PC. The terms *PC*, *XT*, and *AT*, as they are used here, are taken from the original IBM systems of those names. The XT was a PC system that included a hard disk for storage in addition to the floppy drives found in the basic PC system. These systems had an 8-bit 8088 processor and an 8-bit Industry Standard Architecture (ISA) bus for system expansion. The *bus* is the name given to expansion slots in which additional plug-in circuit boards can be installed. The 8-bit designation comes from the fact that the ISA bus found in the PC/XT class systems can send and receive only 8 bits of data in a single cycle. The data in an 8-bit bus is sent along eight wires simultaneously, in parallel.

▶▶ See "The ISA Bus," p. 391.

Systems that are 16-bit and greater are said to be *AT-class*, which indicates that they follow certain standards and that they follow the basic design first set forth in the original IBM AT system. AT is the designation IBM applied to systems that first included more advanced 16-bit (and later, 32- and 64-bit) processors and expansion slots. AT-class systems must have a processor that is compatible with Intel 286 or higher processors, and they must have a 16-bit or greater system bus. The system bus architecture is central to the AT system design, along with the basic memory architecture, interrupt request (IRQ), direct memory access (DMA), and I/O port address design. All AT-class systems are similar in the way these resources are allocated and how they function.

The first AT-class systems had a 16-bit version of the ISA bus, which is an extension of the original 8-bit ISA bus found in the PC/XT-class systems. Eventually, several expansion slot or bus designs were developed for AT-class systems, including the following:

- 16-bit ISA/AT bus
- 16-bit PC Card (PCMCIA) bus
- 16/32-bit Extended ISA (EISA) bus
- 16/32-bit PS/2 Micro Channel Architecture (MCA) bus
- 32-bit VESA Local (VL) bus
- 32/64-bit Peripheral Component Interconnect (PCI) bus
- 32-bit CardBus (PCMCIA) bus
- 32-bit Accelerated Graphics Port (AGP) bus
- PCI Express bus (serial)
- ExpressCard bus (serial)

A system with any of these types of expansion slots is by definition an AT-class system, regardless of the actual Intel or Intel-compatible processor that is used. AT-type systems with 386 or higher processors have special capabilities not found in the first generation of 286-based ATs. These distinct capabilities are in the areas of memory addressing, memory management, and possible 32- or 64-bit wide access to data. Most systems with 386DX or higher chips also have 32-bit bus architectures to take full advantage of the 32-bit data transfer capabilities of the processor.

For a time, PC systems continued to incorporate a 16-bit ISA slot for backward-compatibility and lower-function adapters. However, virtually all motherboards eventually eliminated ISA slots in favor of PCI slots along with an AGP slot for high-performance graphics. However, just as ISA support in motherboards has faded from the landscape, so too will PCI and AGP in favor of the PCI Express standard.

Chapter 4, "Motherboards and Buses," contains in-depth information on these and other PC system buses, including technical information such as pinouts, performance specifications, and bus operation and theory.

Table 2.3 summarizes the primary differences between the older 8-bit (PC/XT) systems and modern AT systems. This information distinguishes between these systems and includes all IBM and compatible models.

Table 2.3   Differences Between PC/XT and AT Systems

System Attributes	(8-Bit) PC/XT Type	(16/32/64-Bit) AT Type
Supported processors	All x86 or x88	286 or higher
Processor modes	Real	Real/Protected/Virtual Real
Software supported	16-bit only	16- or 32-bit
Bus slot width	8-bit	16/32/64-bit
Slot type	ISA only	ISA, EISA, MCA, PC Card, CardBus, ExpressCard, VL-Bus, PCI, PCI Express, and AGP
Hardware interrupts	8 (6 usable)	16 (11 usable)
DMA channels	4 (3 usable)	8 (7 usable)
Maximum RAM	1MB	16MB/4GB or more
Floppy controller speed	250Kbps	250Kbps/300Kbps/500Kbps/1,000Kbps
Standard boot drive	360KB or 720KB	1.2MB/1.44MB/2.88MB
Keyboard interface	Unidirectional	Bidirectional
CMOS memory/clock	None standard	MC146818 compatible
Serial-port UART	8250B	16450/16550A or greater

No PC/XT type (8-bit) systems have been manufactured for many years. Unless you are in a computer museum, virtually every system you encounter today is based on the AT-type design.

System Components

A modern PC is both simple and complicated. It is simple in the sense that over the years, many of the components used to construct a system have become integrated with other components into fewer and fewer actual parts. It is complicated in the sense that each part in a modern system performs many more functions than did the same types of parts in older systems.

This section briefly examines all the components and peripherals in a modern PC system. Each item is discussed further in later chapters.

The components and peripherals necessary to assemble a basic modern PC system are listed in Table 2.4.

Table 2.4   Basic PC Components

Component	Description
Motherboard	The motherboard is the core of the system. It really is the PC; everything else is connected to it, and it controls everything in the system. Motherboards are covered in detail in Chapter 4.
Processor	The processor is often thought of as the "engine" of the computer. It's also called the CPU (central processing unit). Processors are covered in detail in Chapter 3, "Microprocessor Types and Specifications."
Memory (RAM)	The system memory is often called RAM (for random access memory). This is the primary working memory, which holds all the programs and data the processor is using at a given time. Memory is discussed in Chapter 6, "Memory."
Case/chassis	The case is the frame or chassis that houses the motherboard, power supply, disk drives, adapter cards, and any other physical components in the system. The case is covered in detail in Chapter 19, "Power Supplies."
Power supply	The power supply feeds electrical power to the internal components in the PC. The power supply is covered in detail in Chapter 19.
Floppy drive	The floppy drive is a low-capacity, removable-media, magnetic-storage device. Many recent systems use other types of removable magnetic or USB-based flash memory devices instead of floppy drives for removable storage. Removable-media drives are covered in Chapter 10, "Removable Storage," and floppy drives are covered in detail in Chapter 11, "Optical Storage."
Hard drive	The hard disk is the primary high-capacity storagemedia for the system. Hard disk drives are also discussed in Chapter 9, "Hard Disk Storage."
CD or DVD drive	CD (compact disc) and DVD (digital versatile disc) drives are relatively high-capacity, removable-media, optical drives; most newer systems include drives featuring write/rewrite capability. These drives are covered in detail in Chapter 11.
Keyboard	The keyboard is the primary device on a PC that is used by a human to communicate with and control a system. Keyboards are covered in Chapter 16, "Input Devices."
Mouse	Although many types of pointing devices are on the market today, the first and most popular device for this purpose is the mouse. The mouse and other pointing devices are discussed in Chapter 16.
Video card*	The video card controls the information you see on the monitor. Video cards are covered in detail in Chapter 13, "Video Hardware."
Monitor	Monitors are covered in Chapter 13.
Sound card*	A sound card enables the PC to generate complex sounds. Sound cards and speakers are discussed in detail in Chapter 14, "Audio Hardware."
Network/modem*	Most prebuilt PCs ship with a network interface and possibly a modem. Network cards are covered in Chapter 18, "Local Area Networking." Modems are covered in Chapter 17, "Internet Connectivity."

Components marked with an asterisk (*) may be integrated into the motherboard on many recent systems, particularly entry-level systems.

Microprocessor Types and Specifications

Pre-PC Microprocessor History

The brain or engine of the PC is the *processor* (sometimes called *microprocessor*), or *central processing unit (CPU)*. The CPU performs the system's calculating and processing. The processor is often the most expensive single component in the system (although graphics card pricing now surpasses it in some cases); in higher-end systems it can cost up to four or more times more than the motherboard it plugs into. Intel is generally credited with creating the first microprocessor in 1971 with the introduction of a chip called the 4004. Today Intel still has control over the processor market, at least for PC systems, although over the years AMD has garnered a respectable market share. This means that all PC-compatible systems use either Intel processors or Intel-compatible processors from a handful of competitors (such as AMD or VIA/Cyrix).

Intel's dominance in the processor market hadn't always been assured. Although Intel is generally credited with inventing the processor and introducing the first one on the market, by the late 1970s the two most popular processors for personal computers were *not* from Intel (although one was a clone of an Intel processor). Personal computers of that time primarily used the Z-80 by Zilog and the 6502 by MOS Technologies. The Z-80 was noted for being an improved and less expensive clone of the Intel 8080 processor, similar to the way companies such as AMD, VIA/Cyrix, IDT, and Rise Technologies have cloned Intel's Pentium processors. In the Z-80 case, though, the clone had become far more popular than the original. Some might argue that AMD has achieved that type of status over the past year or so, but even though it has made significant gains, Intel still controls the PC processor market.

Back then I had a system containing both of those processors, consisting of a 1MHz (yes, that's *1*, as in one megahertz!) 6502-based Apple II system with a Microsoft Softcard (Z-80 card) plugged into one of the slots. The Softcard contained a 2MHz Z-80 processor. This enabled me to run software for both processors on the one system. The Z-80 was used in systems of the late 1970s and early 1980s that ran the CP/M operating system, whereas the 6502 was best known for its use in the early Apple I and II computers (before the Mac).

The fate of both Intel and Microsoft was dramatically changed in 1981 when IBM introduced the IBM PC, which was based on a 4.77MHz Intel 8088 processor running the Microsoft Disk Operating System (MS-DOS) 1.0. Since that fateful decision was made to use an Intel processor in the first PC, subsequent PC-compatible systems have used a series of Intel or Intel-compatible processors, with each new one capable of running the software of the processor before it—from the 8088 to the current Core 2 and Athlon 64 X2. The following sections cover the various types of processor chips that have been used in personal computers since the first PC was introduced more than two decades ago. These sections provide a great deal of technical detail about these chips and explain why one type of CPU chip can do more work than another in a given period of time.

Microprocessors from 1971 to the Present

It is interesting to note that the microprocessor had existed for only 10 years prior to the creation of the PC! Intel invented the microprocessor in 1971; the PC was created by IBM in 1981. Now more than 20 years later, we are still using systems based more or less on the design of that first PC. The processors powering our PCs today are still backward compatible in many ways with the 8088 that IBM selected for the first PC in 1981.

November 15, 2001 marked the 30th anniversary of the microprocessor, and in those 30 years processor speed had increased more than 18,500 times (from 0.108MHz to 2GHz). The story of the development of the first microprocessor, the Intel 4004, can be read in Chapter 1, "Development of the PC." The 4004 was introduced on November 15, 1971 and originally ran at a clock speed of 108KHz (108,000 cycles per second, or just over one-tenth a megahertz). The 4004 contained 2,300 transistors and was built on a 10-micron process. This means that each line, trace, or transistor could be spaced about 10 microns (millionths of a meter) apart. Data was transferred 4 bits at a time, and the maximum addressable memory was only 640 bytes. The 4004 was designed for use in a calculator but proved to be useful for many other functions because of its inherent programmability. For example, the 4004 was used in traffic light controllers, blood analyzers, and even in the NASA Pioneer 10 deep space probe!

In April 1972, Intel released the 8008 processor, which originally ran at a clock speed of 200KHz (0.2MHz). The 8008 processor contained 3,500 transistors and was built on the same 10-micron process as the previous processor. The big change in the 8008 was that it had an 8-bit data bus, which meant it could move data 8 bits at a time—twice as much as the previous chip. It could also address more memory, up to 16KB. This chip was primarily used in dumb terminals and general-purpose calculators.

The next chip in the lineup was the 8080, introduced in April 1974, running at a clock rate of 2MHz. Due mostly to the faster clock rate, the 8080 processor had 10 times the performance of the 8008. The 8080 chip contained 6,000 transistors and was built on a 6-micron process. Similar to the previous chip, the 8080 had an 8-bit data bus, so it could transfer 8 bits of data at a time. The 8080 could address up to 64KB of memory, significantly more than the previous chip.

It was the 8080 that helped start the PC revolution because this was the processor chip used in what is generally regarded as the first personal computer, the Altair 8800. The CP/M operating system was written for the 8080 chip, and Microsoft was founded and delivered its first product: Microsoft BASIC for the Altair. These initial tools provided the foundation for a revolution in software because thousands of programs were written to run on this platform.

In fact, the 8080 became so popular that it was cloned. A company called Zilog formed in late 1975, joined by several ex-Intel 8080 engineers. In July 1976, it released the Z-80 processor, which was a vastly improved version of the 8080. It was not pin compatible but instead combined functions such as the memory interface and RAM refresh circuitry, which enabled cheaper and simpler systems to be designed. The Z-80 also incorporated a superset of 8080 instructions, meaning it could run all 8080 programs. It also included new instructions and new internal registers, so software designed for the Z-80 would not necessarily run on the older 8080. The Z-80 ran initially at 2.5MHz (later versions ran up to 10MHz) and contained 8,500 transistors. The Z-80 could access 64KB of memory.

RadioShack selected the Z-80 for the TRS-80 Model 1, its first PC. The chip also was the first to be used by many pioneering systems, including the Osborne and Kaypro machines. Other companies followed, and soon the Z-80 was the standard processor for systems running the CP/M operating system and the popular software of the day.

Intel released the 8085, its follow-up to the 8080, in March 1976. Even though it predated the Z-80 by several months, it never achieved the popularity of the Z-80 in personal computer systems. It was popular as an embedded controller, finding use in scales and other computerized equipment. The 8085 ran at 5MHz and contained 6,500 transistors. It was built on a 3-micron process and incorporated an 8-bit data bus.

Along different architectural lines, MOS Technologies introduced the 6502 in 1976. This chip was designed by several ex-Motorola engineers who had worked on Motorola's first processor, the 6800. The 6502 was an 8-bit processor like the 8080, but it sold for around $25, whereas the 8080 cost about $300 when it was introduced. The price appealed to Steve Wozniak, who placed the chip in his Apple I and Apple II designs. The chip was also used in systems by Commodore and other system manufacturers. The 6502 and its successors were also used in game consoles, including the original Nintendo Entertainment System (NES) among others. Motorola went on to create the 68000 series, which became the basis for the original line of Apple Macintosh computers. The second-generation Macs used the PowerPC chip, also by Motorola and a successor to the 68000 series. Of course, the current Macs have adopted PC architecture, using the same processors, chipsets and other components as PCs.

All these previous chips set the stage for the first PC processors. Intel introduced the 8086 in June 1978. The 8086 chip brought with it the original x86 instruction set that is still present in current x86-compatible chips such as the Core 2 and AMD Athlon 64 X2. A dramatic improvement over the previous chips, the 8086 was a full 16-bit design with 16-bit internal registers and a 16-bit data bus. This meant that it could work on 16-bit numbers and data internally and also transfer 16 bits at a time in and out of the chip. The 8086 contained 29,000 transistors and initially ran at up to 5MHz. The chip also used 20-bit addressing, so it could directly address up to 1MB of memory. Although not directly backward compatible with the 8080, the 8086 instructions and language were very similar and enabled older programs to quickly be ported over to run. This later proved important to help jumpstart the PC software revolution with recycled CP/M (8080) software.

Although the 8086 was a great chip, it was expensive at the time and more importantly required expensive 16-bit board designs and infrastructure to support it. To help bring costs down, in 1979 Intel released what some called a *crippled* version of the 8086 called the 8088. The 8088 processor used the same internal core as the 8086, had the same 16-bit registers, and could address the same 1MB of memory, but the external data bus was reduced to 8 bits. This enabled support chips from the older 8-bit 8085 to be used, and far less expensive boards and systems could be made. These reasons are why IBM chose the 8088 instead of the 8086 for the first PC.

This decision would affect history in several ways. The 8088 was fully software compatible with the 8086, so it could run 16-bit software. Also, because the instruction set was very similar to the previous 8085 and 8080, programs written for those older chips could be quickly and easily modified to run. This enabled a large library of programs to be quickly released for the IBM PC, thus helping it become a success. The overwhelming blockbuster success of the IBM PC left in its wake the legacy of requiring backward compatibility with it. To maintain the momentum, Intel has pretty much been forced to maintain backward compatibility with the 8088/8086 in most of the processors it has released since then.

To date, backward compatibility has been maintained, but innovating and adding new features has still been possible. One major change in processors was the move from the 16-bit internal architecture of the 286 and earlier processors to the 32-bit internal architecture of the 386 and later chips, which Intel calls IA-32 (Intel Architecture, 32-bit). Intel's 32-bit architecture dates to 1985, and it took a full 10 years for both a partial 32-bit mainstream OS (Windows 95) as well as a full 32-bit OS requiring 32-bit drivers (Windows NT) to surface, and another 6 years for the mainstream to shift to a fully 32-bit environment for the OS and drivers (Windows XP). That's a total of 16 years from the release of 32-bit computing hardware to the full adoption of 32-bit computing in the mainstream with supporting software. I'm sure you can appreciate that 16 years is a lifetime in technology.

Now we are in the beginning of another major architectural jump, as Intel and AMD are in the process of moving from 32-bit to 64-bit computing for servers, desktop PCs, and even portable PCs. Intel had introduced the IA-64 (Intel Architecture, 64-bit) in the form of the Itanium and Itanium 2 processors several years earlier, but this standard was something completely new and not an extension of the existing 32-bit technology. IA-64 was first announced in 1994 as a CPU development project with Intel and HP (codenamed Merced), and the first technical details were made available in October 1997. The result was the IA-64 architecture and Itanium chip, which was officially released in 2001.

The fact that the IA-64 architecture is not an extension of IA-32 but is instead a whole new and completely different architecture is fine for non-PC environments such as servers (for which IA-64 was designed), but the PC market has always hinged on backward compatibility. Even though emulating IA-32 within IA-64 is possible, such emulation and support is slow.

With the door now open, AMD seized this opportunity to develop 64-bit extensions to IA-32, which it calls AMD64 (originally known as x86-64). Intel eventually released its own set of 64-bit extensions, which it calls EM64T or IA-32e mode. As it turns out, the Intel extensions are almost identical to the AMD extensions, meaning they are software compatible. It seems for the first time that Intel has unarguably followed AMD's lead in the development of PC architecture.

To make 64-bit computing a reality, 64-bit operating systems and 64-bit drivers are also needed. Microsoft began providing trial versions of Windows XP Professional x64 Edition (which supports AMD64 and EM64T) in April 2005, and major computer vendors now offer systems with either Windows XP Professional x64 or Windows Vista 64-bit already installed. Major hardware vendors have also developed 64-bit drivers for current and recent hardware. Linux is also available in 64-bit-compatible versions, making the move to 64-bit computing possible.

The latest development is the introduction of dual- and quad-core processors from both Intel and AMD. Current multi-core processors have two or four full CPU cores operating off of one CPU package—in essence enabling a single processor to perform the work of two or four processors. Although multi-core processors don't make games that use single execution threads play faster, multi-core processors, like multiple single-core processors, split up the workload caused by running multiple applications at the same time. If you've ever tried to scan for viruses while checking email or running another application, you've probably seen how running multiple applications can bring even the fastest processor to its knees. With multi-core processors available from both Intel and AMD, your ability to get more work done in less time by multitasking is greatly enhanced. Current multi-core processors also support AMD64 or EM64T 64-bit extensions, enabling you to enjoy both multicore and 64-bit computing's advantages.

PCs have certainly come a long way. The original 8088 processor used in the first PC contained 29,000 transistors and ran at 4.77MHz. The AMD Athlon 64FX has more than 105 million transistors, whereas the Pentium 4 670 (Prescott core) runs at 3.8GHz and has 169 million transistors thanks to its 2MB L2 cache. Dual-core processors, which include two processor cores and cache memory in a single physical chip, have even higher transistor counts: The Intel Pentium D processor has 230 million transistors, and the AMD Athlon 64 X2 includes over 233 million transistors. The latest Intel Core 2 Duo and Core 2 Quad processors have 291 million and 582 million transistors, respectively, the latter with a whopping 8MB of integrated L2 cache. As multicore processors and large L2 caches continue to be used in more and more designs, look for transistor counts and real-world performance to continue to increase beyond a billion transistors. And the progress won't stop there because, according to Moore's Law, processing speed and transistor counts are doubling every 1.5–2 years.

Processor Specifications

Many confusing specifications often are quoted in discussions of processors. The following sections discuss some of these specifications, including the data bus, address bus, and speed. The next section includes a table that lists the specifications of virtually all PC processors.

Processors can be identified by two main parameters: how wide they are and how fast they are. The speed of a processor is a fairly simple concept. Speed is counted in megahertz (MHz) and gigahertz (GHz), which means millions and billions, respectively, of cycles per second—and faster is better! The width of a processor is a little more complicated to discuss because three main specifications in a processor are expressed in width:

- Data (I/O) bus
- Address bus
- Internal registers

Note that the processor data bus is also called the *front-side bus (FSB), processor side bus (PSB)*, or just *CPU bus*. All these terms refer to the bus that is between the CPU and the main chipset component (North Bridge or Memory Controller Hub). Intel uses the FSB or PSB terminology, whereas AMD uses only FSB. Personally I usually just like to say "CPU bus" in conversation or when speaking during my training seminars because that is the least confusing of the terms while also being completely accurate.

The number of bits a processor is designated can be confusing. All modern processors have 64-bit data buses; however, that does not mean they are classified as 64-bit processors. Processors such as the Pentium 4 and Athlon XP are 32-bit processors because their internal registers are 32 bits wide, although their data I/O buses are 64 bits wide and their address buses are 36 bits wide (both wider than their predecessors, the Pentium and K6 processors). The Core 2 series and the AMD Opteron and Athlon 64 are 64-bit processors because their internal registers are 64 bits wide.

First, I'll present some tables describing the differences in specifications between all the PC processors; then the following sections will explain the width and other specifications in more detail. Refer to these tables as you read about the various processor specifications, and the information in the tables will become clearer.

Tables 3.1 through 3.3 list the Intel processors, AMD processors, and alternative processors from other manufacturers.

Table 3.1   Intel Processor Specifications

Processor	Process (Micron)	Clock	Voltage	Registers	Data Bus	Max. Memory
8088	3.0	1x	5V	16-bit	8-bit	1MB
8086	3.0	1x	5V	16-bit	16-bit	1MB
286	1.5	1x	5V	16-bit	16-bit	16MB
386SX	1.5, 1.0	1x	5V	32-bit	16-bit	16MB
386SL	1.0	1x	3.3V	32-bit	16-bit	16MB
386DX	1.5, 1.0	1x	5V	32-bit	32-bit	4GB
486SX	1.0, 0.8	1x	5V	32-bit	32-bit	4GB
486SX2	0.8	2x	5V	32-bit	32-bit	4GB
487SX	1.0	1x	5V	32-bit	32-bit	4GB
486DX	1.0, 0.8	1x	5V	32-bit	32-bit	4GB
486SL[2]	0.8	1x	3.3V	32-bit	32-bit	4GB
486DX2	0.8	2x	5V	32-bit	32-bit	4GB
486DX4	0.6	2x+	3.3V	32-bit	32-bit	4GB
486 Pentium OD	0.6	2.5x	5V	32-bit	32-bit	4GB
Pentium 60/66	0.8	1x	5V	32-bit	64-bit	4GB
Pentium 75-200	0.6, 0.35	1.5x+	3.3V-3.5V	32-bit	64-bit	4GB
Pentium MMX	0.35, 0.25	1.5x+	1.8V-2.8V	32-bit	64-bit	4GB
Pentium Pro	0.35	2x+	3.3V	32-bit	64-bit	64GB
Pentium II (Klamath)	0.35	3.5x+	2.8V	32-bit	64-bit	64GB
Pentium II (Deschutes)	0.35	3.5x+	2.0V	32-bit	64-bit	64GB
Pentium II PE (Dixon)	0.25	3.5x+	1.6V	32-bit	64-bit	64GB
Celeron (Covington)	0.25	3.5x+	1.8V-2.8V	32-bit	64-bit	64GB
Celeron A (Mendocino)	0.25	3.5x+	1.5V-2V	32-bit	64-bit	64GB
Celeron III (Coppermine)	0.18	4.5x+	1.5-1.75V	32-bit	64-bit	64GB
Celeron III (Tualatin)	0.13	9x+	1.5V	32-bit	64-bit	64GB
Pentium III (Katmai)	0.25	4x+	2.0-2.05V	32-bit	64-bit	64GB
Pentium III (Coppermine)	0.18	4x+	1.6-1.75V	32-bit	64-bit	64GB
Pentium III (Tualatin)	0.13	8.5x+	1.45V	32-bit	64-bit	64GB
Celeron 4 (Willamette)	0.18	4.25x+	1.6V	32-bit	64-bit	64GB
Pentium 4 (Willamette)	0.18	3x+	1.7V	32-bit	64-bit	64GB
Pentium 4A (Northwood)	0.13	4x+	1.3V	32-bit	64-bit	64GB
Pentium 4EE (Prestonia)	0.13	8x+	1.5V	32-bit	64-bit	64GB
Pentium 4E (Prescott)	0.09	8x+	1.3V	32-bit	64-bit	64GB
Celeron D	0.09	4x+	1.25V-1.4V	64-bit	64-bit	1TB
Pentium D (Smithfield)	0.09	3.5x+	1.25V-1.4V	64-bit	64-bit	1TB
Pentium D (Presler)	0.065	3.5x+	1.25V-1.4V	64-bit	64-bit	1TB
Pentium M (Banias)	0.13	2.25x+	0.8-1.5V	32-bit	64-bit	64GB
Pentium M (Dothan)	0.09	4.25x+	1-1.3V	32-bit	64-bit	64GB
Core Duo (Yonah)	0.09	2.25+	0.7-1.3V	32-bit	64-bit	64GB
Core 2 Duo (Conroe)	0.065	1.75x+	0.9-1.3V	64-bit	64-bit	1TB
Core 2 Quad (Kentsfield)	0.065	2.25x+	1.1-1.3V	64-bit	64-bit	1TB

L1 Cache	L2 Cache	L3 Cache	L2/L3 Cache Speed	Multimedia Instructions	Transistors	Introduced
—	—	—	—	—	29,000	June '79
—	—	—	—	—	29,000	June '78
—	—	—	—	—	134,000	Feb. '82
—	—	—	Bus	—	275,000	June '88
0KB[1]	—	—	Bus	—	855,000	Oct. '90
—	—	—	Bus	—	275,000	Oct. '85
8KB	—	—	Bus	—	1.185M	Apr. '91
8KB	—	—	Bus	—	1.185M	Apr. '94
8KB	—	—	Bus	—	1.2M	Apr. '91
8KB	—	—	Bus	—	1.2M	Apr. '89
8KB	—	—	Bus	—	1.4M	Nov. '92
8KB	—	—	Bus	—	1.2M	Mar. '92
16KB	—	—	Bus	—	1.6M	Feb. '94
2x16KB	—	—	Bus	—	3.1M	Jan. '95
2x8KB	—	—	Bus	—	3.1M	Mar. '93
2x8KB	—	—	Bus	—	3.3M	Mar. '94
2x16KB	—	—	Bus	MMX	4.5M	Jan. '97
2x8KB	256KB, 512KB, 1MB	—	Core[3]	—	5.5M	Nov. '95
2x16KB	512KB	—	1/2 core	MMX	7.5M	May '97
2x16KB	512KB	—	1/2 core	MMX	7.5M	May '97
2x16KB	256KB	—	Core	MMX	27.4M	Jan. '99
2x16KB	0KB	—	—	MMX	7.5M	Apr. '98
2x16KB	128KB	—	Core	MMX	19M	Aug. '98
2x16KB	128KB	—	Core	SSE	28.1M[4]	Feb. '00
2x16KB	256KB	—	Core	SSE	44M[5]	Oct. '01
2x16KB	512KB	—	? core	SSE	9.5M	Feb. '99
2x16KB	256KB	—	Core	SSE	28.1M	Oct. '99
2x16KB	512KB	—	Core	SSE	44M	June '01
2x16KB	128KB	—	Core	SSE2	42M[6]	May '02
12+8KB	256KB	—	Core	SSE2	42M	Nov. '00
12+8KB	512KB	—	Core	SSE2	55M	Jan. '02
12+8KB	512KB	2MB	Core	SSE2	178M	Nov. '03
12+16KB	1MB	—	Core	SSE3	125M	Feb. '04
12+16KB	256KB	—	Core	SSE3	125M	June '04
12+16KB (x2)	1MB (x2)	—	Core	SSE3	230M	Apr. '05
12+16KB (x2)	2MB (x2)	—	Core	SSE3	376M	Dec. '05
2x32KB	1MB	—	Core	SSE2	77M	Mar. '03
2x32KB	2MB	—	Core	SSE2	144M	May '04
2x32KB (x2)	1MB (x2)	—	Core	SSE3	151M	Jan. '06
2x32KB (x2)	1/2MB (x2)	—	Core	SSSE3	291M	July '06
2x64KB (x2)	4MB (x2)	—	Core	SSSE3	582M	Dec. '06

Table 3.2   AMD Processor Specifications

Processor	Process (Micron)	Clock	Voltage	Registers	Data Bus	Max. Memory
AMD K5	0.35	1.5x+	3.5V	32-bit	64-bit	4GB
AMD K6	0.35	2.5x+	2.2-3.2V	32-bit	64-bit	4GB
AMD K6-2	0.25	2.5x+	1.9-2.4V	32-bit	64-bit	4GB
AMD K6-3	0.25	3.5x+	1.8-2.4V	32-bit	64-bit	4GB
AMD Athlon	0.25	5x+	1.6-1.8V	32-bit	64-bit	4GB
AMD Duron	0.18	5x+	1.5-1.8V	32-bit	64-bit	4GB
AMD Athlon (Thunderbird)	0.18	5x+	1.5-1.8V	32-bit	64-bit	4GB
AMD Athlon XP (Palomino)	0.18	5x+	1.5-1.8V	32-bit	64-bit	4GB
AMD Athlon XP (Thoroughbred)	0.13	5x+	1.5-1.8V	32-bit	64-bit	4GB
AMD Athlon XP (Barton)	0.13	5.5x+	1.65V	32-bit	64-bit	4GB
Athlon 64 (ClawHammer/ Winchester)	0.13, 0.09	5.5x+	1.5V	64-bit	64-bit	1TB
Athlon 64 FX (SledgeHammer)	0.13	5.5x+	1.5V	64-bit	128-bit	1TB
Athlon 64 X2 (Manchester)	0.09	5x+	1.35V-1.4V	64-bit	128-bit	1TB
Athlon 64 X2 (Toledo)	0.09	5x+	1.35V-1.4V	64-bit	128-bit	1TB
Athlon 64 X2 (Windsor)	0.09	5x+	1.35V-1.4V	64-bit	128-bit	1TB
Athlon X2, 64 X2 (Brisbane)	0.065	5x+	1.25V-1.35V	64-bit	128-bit	1TB

1. The 386SL contains an integral-cache controller, but the cache memory must be provided outside the chip.

2. Intel later marketed SL Enhanced versions of the SX, DX, and DX2 processors. These processors were available in both 5V and 3.3V versions and included power management capabilities.

Table 3.3   Cyrix, NexGen, IDT, Rise, and VIA Processor Specifications

Processor	CPU Clock	Voltage	Internal Register Size	Data Bus Width	Max. Memory
Cyrix 6x86	2x+	2.5–3.5V	32-bit	64-bit	4GB
Cyrix 6x86MX/MII	2x+	2.2–2.9V	32-bit	64-bit	4GB
Cyrix III	2.5x+	2.2V	32-bit	64-bit	4GB
NexGen Nx586	2x	4V	32-bit	64-bit	4GB
IDT Winchip	3x+	3.3–3.5V	32-bit	64-bit	4GB
IDT Winchip2/2A	2.33x+	3.3–3.5V	32-bit	64-bit	4GB
Rise mP6	2x+	2.8V	32-bit	64-bit	4GB
VIA C3[2]	6x+	1.6V	32-bit	64-bit	4GB
VIA C3[3]	6x+	1.35V	32-bit	64-bit	4GB
VIA C3[4]	5.5x+	1.35V	32-bit	64-bit	4GB
VIA C3[5]	7.5x+	1.4V	32-bit	64-bit	4GB

1. L2 cache runs at full-core speed but is contained in a separate chip die.

2. Samuel 2 core (improved version of Cyrix III core).

L1 Cache	L2 Cache	L3 Cache	L2/L3 Cache Speed	Multimedia Instructions	Transistors	Introduced
16+8KB	—	—	Bus	—	4.3M	March '96
2x32KB	—	—	Bus	MMX	8.8M	April '97
2x32KB	—	—	Bus	3DNow!	9.3M	May '98
2x32KB	256KB	—	Core	3DNow!	21.3M	Feb. '99
2x64KB	512KB	—	1/2-1/3 core	Enh. 3DNow!	22M	June '99
2x64KB	64KB	—	Core[3]	Enh. 3DNow!	25M	June '00
2x64KB	256KB	—	Core	Enh. 3DNow!	37M	June '00
2x64KB	256KB	—	Core	3DNow! Pro	37.5M	Oct. '01
2x64KB	256KB	—	Core	3DNow! Pro	37.2M	June '02
2x64KB	512KB	—	Core	3DNow! Pro	54.3M	Feb. '03
2x64KB	1MB	—	Core	3DNow! Pro (SSE3 for 0.09 process)	105.9M	Sept. '03
2x64KB	1MB	—	Core	3DNow! Pro	105.9M	Sept. '03
2x64KB (x2)	256KB/512KB (x2)	—	Core	SSE3	154M	June '05
2x64KB (x2)	512KB/1MB (x2)	—	Core	SSE3	233M	June '05
2x64KB (x2)	512KB/1MB (x2)	—	Core	SSE3	233.2M	May '05
2x64KB (x2)	512KB (x2)	—	Core	SSE3	154M	Dec. '06

3. L2 cache runs at full-core speed but is contained in a separate chip die.

4. 128KB functional L2 cache (256KB total, 128KB disabled) uses the same die as the Pentium IIIE.

5. 256KB functional L2 cache (512KB total, 256KB disabled) uses the same die as the Pentium IIIB.

6. 128KB functional L2 cache (256KB total, 128KB disabled) uses the same die as the Pentium 4.

L1 Cache	L2 Cache	L3 Cache	L2/L3 Cache Speed	Multimedia Instructions	No. of Transistors	Date Introduced
16KB	—	—	Bus	—	3M	Feb. '96
64KB	—	—	Bus	MMX	6.5M	May '97
64KB	256KB	—	Core[1]	3DNow!	22M	Feb. '00
2x16KB	—	—	Bus	—	3.5M	Mar. '94
2x32KB	—	—	Bus	MMX	5.4M	Oct. '97
2x32KB	—	—	Bus	3DNow!	5.9M	Sep. '98
2x8KB	—	—	Bus	MMX	3.6M	Oct. '98
64KB	128KB	—	Bus	MMX, 3DNow!	15.2M	Mar. '01
64KB	128KB	—	Bus	MMX, 3DNow!	15.4M	Mar. '01
64KB	128KB	—	Bus	MMX, 3DNow!	15.5M	Sep. '01
64KB	128KB	—	Bus	MMX, 3DNow!	20.5M	Jan. '02

3. Ezra core.

4. Ezra-T core.

5. Nehemiah core.

Data I/O Bus

Perhaps the most important features of a processor are the speed and width of its external data bus. This defines the rate at which data can be moved into or out of the processor.

The processor bus discussed most often is the external data bus—the bundle of wires (or pins) used to send and receive data. The more signals that can be sent at the same time, the more data can be transmitted in a specified interval and, therefore, the faster (and wider) the bus. A wider data bus is like having a highway with more lanes, which enables greater throughput.

Data in a computer is sent as digital information in which certain voltages or voltage transitions occurring within specific time intervals are used to represent data as 1s and 0s. The more wires you have, the more individual bits you can send in the same time interval. All modern processors from the original Pentium and Athlon through the latest Core 2, Athlon 64 X2, and even the Itanium and Itanium 2 have a 64-bit (8-byte) wide data bus. Therefore, they can transfer 64 bits of data at a time to and from the motherboard chipset or system memory.

A good way to understand this flow of information is to consider a highway and the traffic it carries. If a highway has only one lane for each direction of travel, only one car at a time can move in a certain direction. If you want to increase traffic flow, you can add another lane so that twice as many cars pass in a specified time. You can think of an 8-bit chip as being a single-lane highway because 1 byte flows through at a time. (1 byte equals 8 individual bits.) The 16-bit chip, with 2 bytes flowing at a time, resembles a two-lane highway. You might have four lanes in each direction to move a large number of automobiles; this structure corresponds to a 32-bit data bus, which has the capability to move 4 bytes of information at a time. Taking this further, a 64-bit data bus is like having an 8-lane highway moving data in and out of the chip.

Another ramification of the data bus in a chip is that the width of the data bus also defines the size of a bank of memory. So, a processor with a 32-bit data bus (such as the 486) reads and writes memory 32 bits at a time, whereas processors with a 64-bit data bus (most current processors) read and write memory 64 bits at a time.

In 486 class systems, because standard 72-pin single inline memory modules (SIMMs) are only 32 bits wide, they must be installed one at a time in most 486 class systems. When used in 64-bit Pentium class systems, they must be installed two at a time. The current module standard, dual inline memory modules (DIMMs), are 64 bits wide. So, they are normally installed one at a time, unless the system is designed or configured for dual-channel memory. Dual-channel memory reads and writes two banks simultaneously, as a way to improve system performance, which means two DIMMs must be installed at a time. To improve memory performance, most future chipsets will support and eventually require that DIMM memory modules be installed in identical pairs.

The Rambus inline memory modules (RIMMs) used in some older Pentium III and 4 systems are somewhat of an anomaly because they play by a different set of rules. They are typically only 16 or 32 bits wide. Depending on the module type and chipset, they are either used individually or in pairs.

▶▶   See "Memory Banks," p. 555.

Address Bus

The address bus is the set of wires that carries the addressing information used to describe the memory location to which the data is being sent or from which the data is being retrieved. As with the data bus, each wire in an address bus carries a single bit of information. This single bit is a single digit in the address. The more wires (digits) used in calculating these addresses, the greater the total number of address locations. The size (or width) of the address bus indicates the maximum amount of RAM a chip can address.

The highway analogy in the "Data I/O Bus" section can be used to show how the address bus fits in. If the data bus is the highway and the size of the data bus is equivalent to the number of lanes, the address bus relates to the house number or street address. The size of the address bus is equivalent to the number of digits in the house address number. For example, if you live on a street in which the address is limited to a two-digit (base 10) number, no more than 100 distinct addresses (00–99) can exist for that street (10^2). Add another digit, and the number of available addresses increases to 1,000 (000–999), or 10^3.

Computers use the binary (base 2) numbering system, so a two-digit number provides only four unique addresses (00, 01, 10, and 11), calculated as 2^2. A three-digit number provides only eight addresses (000—111), which is 2^3. For example, the 8086 and 8088 processors use a 20-bit address bus that calculates a maximum of 2^{20}, or 1,048,576 bytes (1MB), of address locations. Table 3.4 describes the memory-addressing capabilities of processors.

Table 3.4   Processor Physical Memory-Addressing Capabilities

Processor Family	Address Bus	Bytes	KiB	MiB	GiB	TiB
8088, 8086	20-bit	1,048,576	1,024	1	—	—
286, 386SX	24-bit	16,777,216	16,384	16	—	—
386DX, 486, Pentium, K6, Athlon	32-bit	4,294,967,296	4,194,304	4,096	4	—
Pentium w/PAE	36-bit	68,719,476,736	67,108,864	65,536	64	—
64-bit Pentium, Athlon, Core	40-bit	1,099,511,627,776	1,073,741,824	1,048,576	1024	1

PAE = Physical Address Extension (supported by Server OS only)

KiB = Kibibytes

MiB = Mebibytes

TiB = Tebibytes

See http://www.iec.ch/zone/si/si_bytes.htm for more information on prefixes for binary multiples.

The data bus and address bus are independent, and chip designers can use whatever size they want for each. Usually, however, chips with larger data buses have larger address buses. The sizes of the buses can provide important information about a chip's relative power, measured in two important ways. The size of the data bus is an indication of the chip's information-moving capability, and the size of the address bus tells you how much memory the chip can handle.

Internal Registers (Internal Data Bus)

The size of the internal registers indicates how much information the processor can operate on at one time and how it moves data around internally within the chip. This is sometimes also referred to as the *internal data bus*. A *register* is a holding cell within the processor; for example, the processor can add numbers in two different registers, storing the result in a third register. The register size determines the size of data on which the processor can operate. The register size also describes the type of software or commands and instructions a chip can run. That is, processors with 32-bit internal registers can run 32-bit instructions that are processing 32-bit chunks of data, but processors with 16-bit registers can't. Processors from the 386 to the Pentium 4 use 32-bit internal registers and can therefore all run essentially the same 32-bit operating systems and software. The Core 2 and Athlon 64 processors have both 32-bit and 64-bit internal registers, which can run existing 32-bit OS and applications as well as newer 64-bit versions.

Some very old processors have an internal data bus (made up of data paths and storage units called registers) that is larger than the external data bus. The 8088 and 386SX are examples of this structure. Each chip has an internal data bus twice the width of the external bus. These designs, which sometimes are called *hybrid designs*, usually are low-cost versions of a "pure" chip. The 386SX, for example, can pass data around internally with a full 32-bit register size; for communications with the outside world, however, the chip is restricted to a 16-bit-wide data path. This design enabled a systems designer to build a lower-cost motherboard with a 16-bit bus design and still maintain software and instruction set compatibility with the full 32-bit 386. However, both the 8088 and the 386SX had lower performance than the 8086 and 386DX processors at the same speeds.

Internal registers often are larger than the data bus, which means the chip requires two cycles to fill a register before the register can be operated on. For example, both the 386SX and 386DX have internal 32-bit registers, but the 386SX must "inhale" twice (figuratively) to fill them, whereas the 386DX can do the job in one "breath." The same thing would happen when the data is passed from the registers back out to the system bus.

The Pentium is an example of this type of design. All Pentiums have a 64-bit data bus and 32-bit registers—a structure that might seem to be a problem until you understand that the Pentium has two internal 32-bit pipelines for processing information. In many ways, the Pentium is like two 32-bit chips in one. The 64-bit data bus provides for very efficient filling of these multiple registers. Multiple pipelines are called *superscalar* architecture, which was introduced with the Pentium processor.

▶▶ See "Pentium Processors," p. 138.

More advanced sixth- and seventh-generation processors from Intel and AMD have as many as six internal pipelines for executing instructions. Although some of these internal pipes are dedicated to special functions, these processors can execute multiple operations in one clock cycle.

Processor Modes

All Intel and Intel-compatible processors from the 386 on up can run in several modes. Processor modes refer to the various operating environments and affect the instructions and capabilities of the chip. The processor mode controls how the processor sees and manages the system memory and the tasks that use it.

The three main modes of operation with several submodes are as follows:

- Real mode (16-bit software)
- IA-32 mode:
  - Protected mode (32-bit software)
  - Virtual real mode (16-bit programs within a 32-bit environment)
- IA-32e 64-bit extension mode (also called AMD64, x86-64, or EM64T):
  - 64-bit mode (64-bit software)
  - Compatibility mode (32-bit software)

Table 3.5 summarizes the processor modes.

Table 3.5   Processor Modes

Mode	Submode	OS Required	Software	Memory Address Size	Default Operand Size	Register Width
Real	—	16-bit	16-bit	24-bit	16-bit	16-bit
IA-32	Protected	32-bit	32-bit	32-bit	32-bit	32/16-bit
	Virtual real	32-bit	16-bit	24-bit	16-bit	16-bit
IA-32e	64-bit	64-bit	64-bit	64-bit	32-bit	64-bit
	Compatibility	64-bit	32-bit	32-bit	32-bit	32/16-bit

Real Mode

Real mode is sometimes called 8086 mode because it is based on the 8086 and 8088 processors. The original IBM PC included an 8088 processor that could execute 16-bit instructions using 16-bit internal registers and could address only 1MB of memory using 20 address lines. All original PC software was created to work with this chip and was designed around the 16-bit instruction set and 1MB memory model. For example, DOS and all DOS software, Windows 1.x through 3.x, and all Windows 1.x through 3.x applications are written using 16-bit instructions. These 16-bit operating systems and applications are designed to run on an original 8088 processor.

◄◄   See "Internal Registers (Internal Data Bus)," p. 49.

◄◄   See "Address Bus," p. 48.

Later processors such as the 286 could also run the same 16-bit instructions as the original 8088, but much faster. In other words, the 286 was fully compatible with the original 8088 and could run all 16-bit software just the same as an 8088, but, of course, that software would run faster. The 16-bit instruction mode of the 8088 and 286 processors has become known as *real mode*. All software running in real mode must use only 16-bit instructions and live within the 20-bit (1MB) memory architecture it supports. Software of this type is usually single-tasking—that is, only one program can run at a time. No built-in protection exists to keep one program from overwriting another program or even the operating system in memory, so if more than one program is running, one of them could bring the entire system to a crashing halt.

IA-32 Mode (32-Bit)

Then came the 386, which was the PC industry's first 32-bit processor. This chip could run an entirely new 32-bit instruction set. To take full advantage of the 32-bit instruction set, a 32-bit operating system and a 32-bit application were required. This new 32-bit mode was referred to as *protected mode*, which alludes to the fact that software programs running in that mode are protected from overwriting one another in memory. Such protection helps make the system much more crash-proof because an errant program can't very easily damage other programs or the operating system. In addition, a crashed program can be terminated while the rest of the system continues to run unaffected.

Knowing that new operating systems and applications—which take advantage of the 32-bit protected mode—would take some time to develop, Intel wisely built a backward compatible real mode into the 386. That enabled it to run unmodified 16-bit operating systems and applications. It ran them quite well—much more quickly than any previous chip. For most people, that was enough. They did not necessarily want any new 32-bit software; they just wanted their existing 16-bit software to run more quickly. Unfortunately, that meant the chip was never running in the 32-bit protected mode, and all the features of that capability were being ignored.

When a processor such as a Pentium 4 is running DOS (real mode), it acts like a "Turbo 8088." Turbo 8088 means the processor has the advantage of speed in running any 16-bit programs; it otherwise can use only the 16-bit instructions and access memory within the same 1MB memory map of the original 8088. Therefore, if you have a 256MB Pentium 4 or Athlon system running Windows 3.x or DOS, you are effectively using only the first megabyte of memory, leaving the other 255MB largely unused!

New operating systems and applications that ran in the 32-bit protected mode of the modern processors were needed. Being stubborn, we resisted all the initial attempts at getting switched over to a 32-bit environment. It seems that as a user community, we are very resistant to change and would be content with our older software running faster rather than adopting new software with new features. I'll be the first one to admit that I was one of those stubborn users myself!

Because of this resistance, true 32-bit operating systems such as Unix or variants (such as Linux), OS/2, and even Windows NT/2000 or XP/Vista have taken a long time in getting a mainstream share in the PC marketplace. Windows XP was the first full 32-bit OS that has become a true mainstream product, and that is primarily because Microsoft has coerced us in that direction with Windows 95, 98, and Me (which are mixed 16-/32-bit systems). Windows 3.x was the last full 16-bit operating system. In fact, it was not really considered a complete operating system because it ran on top of DOS.

The Itanium processor family, the AMD Opteron, and the Intel EM64T-compatible Xeon processors add 64-bit native capability to the table for servers, whereas the AMD Athlon 64 family, the Intel EM64T-compatible Pentium 4, and all Intel Pentium D and Core 2 processors provide this capability for desktop computers. Both processors run all the existing 32-bit software, but to fully take advantage of the processor, a 64-bit OS, drivers, and applications are required. Microsoft has released 64-bit versions of Windows XP and Vista, and several companies have released 64-bit applications for networking and workstation use.

IA-32 Virtual Real Mode

The key to the backward compatibility of the Windows 32-bit environment is the third mode in the processor: virtual real mode. *Virtual real* is essentially a virtual real mode 16-bit environment that runs inside 32-bit protected mode. When you run a DOS prompt window inside Windows, you have created a virtual real mode session. Because protected mode enables true multitasking, you can actually have several real mode sessions running, each with its own software running on a virtual PC. These can all run simultaneously, even while other 32-bit applications are running.

Note that any program running in a virtual real mode window can access up to only 1MB of memory, which that program will believe is the first and only megabyte of memory in the system. In other words, if you run a DOS application in a virtual real window, it will have a 640KB limitation on memory usage. That is because there is only 1MB of total RAM in a 16-bit environment and the upper 384KB is reserved for system use. The virtual real window fully emulates an 8088 environment, so that aside from speed, the software runs as if it were on an original real mode-only PC. Each virtual machine gets its own 1MB address space, an image of the real hardware BIOS routines, and emulation of all other registers and features found in real mode.

Virtual real mode is used when you use a DOS window to run a DOS or Windows 3.x 16-bit program. When you start a DOS application, Windows creates a virtual DOS machine under which it can run.

One interesting thing to note is that all Intel and Intel-compatible (such as AMD and Cyrix) processors power up in real mode. If you load a 32-bit operating system, it automatically switches the processor into 32-bit mode and takes control from there.

It's also important to note that some 16-bit (DOS and Windows 3.x) applications misbehave in a 32-bit environment, which means they do things that even virtual real mode does not support.

Diagnostics software is a perfect example of this. Such software does not run properly in a real-mode (virtual real) window under Windows. In that case, you can still run your Pentium 4 in the original no-frills real mode by either booting to a DOS floppy or, in the case of Windows 9x (excluding Me), interrupting the boot process and commanding the system to boot plain DOS. This is accomplished on Windows 9x systems by pressing the F8 key when you see the prompt Starting Windows... on the screen or immediately after the beep when the power-on self test (POST) is completed. In the latter case, it helps to press the F8 key multiple times because getting the timing just right is difficult and Windows 9x looks for the key only during a short 2-second time window.

If successful, you will then see the Startup menu. You can select one of the command-prompt choices that tell the system to boot plain 16-bit real mode DOS. The choice of Safe Mode Command Prompt is best if you are going to run true hardware diagnostics, which do not normally run in protected mode and should be run with a minimum of drivers and other software loaded.

Even though Windows Me is based on Windows 98, Microsoft removed the DOS Startup menu option in an attempt to further wean us from any 16-bit operation. Windows NT, 2000, XP and Vista also lack the capability to start up DOS in this manner. For these operating systems, you need a startup disk (CD or floppy), which you can use to boot the system in real mode. Generally, you would do this to perform certain maintenance procedures, such as running hardware diagnostics or doing direct disk sector editing.

Although real mode is used by 16-bit DOS and "standard" DOS applications, special programs are available that "extend" DOS and allow access to extended memory (over 1MB). These are sometimes called *DOS extenders* and usually are included as part of any DOS or Windows 3.x software that uses them. The protocol that describes how to make DOS work in protected mode is called *DOS protected mode interface (DPMI)*.

DPMI was used by Windows 3.x to access extended memory for use with Windows 3.x applications. It allowed these programs to use more memory even though they were still 16-bit programs. DOS extenders are especially popular in DOS games because they enable them to access much more of the system memory than the standard 1MB most real mode programs can address. These DOS extenders work by switching the processor in and out of real mode. In the case of those that run under Windows, they use the DPMI interface built into Windows, enabling them to share a portion of the system's extended memory.

Another exception in real mode is that the first 64KB of extended memory is actually accessible to the PC in real mode, despite the fact that it's not supposed to be possible. This is the result of a bug in the original IBM AT with respect to the 21st memory address line, known as A20 (A0 is the first address line). By manipulating the A20 line, real-mode software can gain access to the first 64KB of extended memory—the first 64KB of memory past the first megabyte. This area of memory is called the *high memory area (HMA)*.

IA-32e 64-Bit Extension Mode (AMD64, x86-64, EM64T)

64-bit extension mode is an enhancement to the IA-32 architecture originally designed by AMD and later adopted by Intel. Processors with 64-bit extension technology can run in real (8086) mode, IA-32 mode, or IA-32e mode. IA-32 mode enables the processor to run in protected mode and virtual real mode. IA-32e mode allows the processor to run in 64-bit mode and compatibility mode, which means you can run both 64-bit and 32-bit applications simultaneously. IA-32e mode includes two submodes:

- **64-bit mode**—Enables a 64-bit operating system to run 64-bit applications
- **Compatibility mode**—Enables a 64-bit operating system to run most existing 32-bit software

IA-32e 64-bit mode is enabled by loading a 64-bit operating system and is used by 64-bit applications. In the 64-bit submode, the following new features are available:

- 64-bit linear memory addressing
- Physical memory support beyond 4GB (limited by the specific processor)
- Eight new general-purpose registers (GPRs)
- Eight new registers for streaming SIMD extensions (MMX, SSE, SSE2, and SSE3)
- 64-bit-wide GPRs and instruction pointers

IE-32e compatibility mode enables 32-bit and 16-bit applications to run under a 64-bit operating system. Unfortunately, legacy 16-bit programs that run in virtual real mode (that is, DOS programs) are not supported and will not run, which is likely to be the biggest problem for many users. Similar to 64-bit mode, compatibility mode is enabled by the operating system on an individual code basis, which means 64-bit applications running in 64-bit mode can operate simultaneously with 32-bit applications running in compatibility mode.

What we need to make all this work is a 64-bit operating system and, more importantly, 64-bit drivers for all our hardware to work under that OS. A 64-bit Windows OS already exists in three versions:

- Windows XP 64-bit Edition for Itanium
- Windows XP Professional x64 Edition
- Windows Vista 64-bit (in multiple variants)

Of those, the first is for IA-64 processors, such as Itanium and Itanium 2, and has been available in a released production version since 2001. The latter two are for IA-32 processors with 64-bit extensions, such as the Athlon 64, Opteron, some Semprons, the Core 2, the Pentium D, the Pentium Extreme Edition, and some Xeon and Pentium 4 processors supporting 64-bit extensions, and are now available on shipping systems. Note that Microsoft uses the term *x64* to refer to processors that support either AMD64 or EM64T because AMD and Intel's extensions to the standard IA32 architecture are practically identical and can be supported with a single version of Windows.

Note

Early versions of EM64T-equipped processors from Intel lacked support for the LAHF and SAHF instructions used in the AMD64 instruction set. However, Pentium 4 and Xeon DP processors using core steppings G1 and higher completely support these instructions; a BIOS update is also needed. Newer multicore processors with 64-bit support include these instructions as well.

The physical memory limits for Windows XP and Vista 32-bit and 64-bit editions are shown in Table 3.6.

Table 3.6   Windows Physical Memory Limits

Windows Version	Memory Limit (32-bit)	Memory Limit (64-bit)
Vista Ultimate	4GB	128GB
Vista Business	4GB	128GB
Vista Home Premium	4GB	16GB
Vista Home Basic	4GB	8GB
XP Professional	4GB	128GB
XP Home	4GB	N/A

The major difference between 32-bit and 64-bit Windows is memory support, specifically breaking the 4GB barrier found in 32-bit Windows systems. 32-bit versions of Windows support up to 4GB of physical memory, with up to 2GB of dedicated memory per process. 64-bit versions of Windows support up to 128GB of physical memory, with up to 4GB for each 32-bit process, and up to 8TB for each 64-bit process. Support for more memory means applications can preload more data into memory, which the processor can access much more quickly.

64-bit Windows runs 32-bit Windows applications with no problems, but it does not run 16-bit Windows or DOS applications, or any other programs that run in virtual real mode. Also, drivers are another big problem. 32-bit processes cannot load 64-bit dynamic link libraries (DLLs), and 64-bit processes cannot load 32-bit DLLs. This essentially means that, for all the devices you have connected to your system, you need both 32-bit and 64-bit drivers for them to work. Acquiring 64-bit drivers for older devices or devices that are no longer supported can be difficult or impossible. Even for new devices, it can be a couple of years before manufacturers provide 64-bit drivers as a standard feature. Before installing a 64-bit version of Windows, be sure to check with the vendors of your internal and add-on hardware for 64-bit drivers. Keep in mind that drivers made for Itanium do not work with x64-compatible processors.

You should keep all the memory size, software, and driver issues in mind when considering the transition from 32-bit to 64-bit technology. The transition from 32-bit hardware to mainstream 32-bit computing took 16 years. As I've already stated, it might not take 16 years for 64-bit computing to become mainstream. It's starting to happen now. But it will most likely take at least several years for adoption of 64-bit computing to become the norm.

Processor Speed Ratings

A common misunderstanding about processors is their different speed ratings. This section covers processor speed in general and then provides more specific information about Intel, AMD, and VIA/Cyrix processors.

A computer system's clock speed is measured as a frequency, usually expressed as a number of cycles per second. A crystal oscillator controls clock speeds using a sliver of quartz sometimes housed in what looks like a small tin container. Newer systems include the oscillator circuitry in the motherboard chipset, so it might not be a visible separate component on newer boards. As voltage is applied to the quartz, it begins to vibrate (oscillate) at a harmonic rate dictated by the shape and size of the crystal (sliver). The oscillations emanate from the crystal in the form of a current that alternates at the harmonic rate of the crystal. This alternating current is the clock signal that forms the time base on which the computer operates. A typical computer system runs millions or billions of these cycles per second, so speed is measured in megahertz or gigahertz. (One hertz is equal to one cycle per second.) An alternating current signal is like a sine wave, with the time between the peaks of each wave defining the frequency (see Figure 3.1).

Note

The hertz was named for the German physicist Heinrich Rudolf Hertz. In 1885, Hertz confirmed the electromagnetic theory, which states that light is a form of electromagnetic radiation and is propagated as waves.

A single cycle is the smallest element of time for the processor. Every action requires at least one cycle and usually multiple cycles. To transfer data to and from memory, for example, a modern processor such as the Pentium 4 needs a minimum of three cycles to set up the first memory transfer and then only a single cycle per transfer for the next three to six consecutive transfers. The extra cycles on the first transfer typically are called *wait states*. A wait state is a clock tick in which nothing happens. This ensures that the processor isn't getting ahead of the rest of the computer.

 See "SIMMs, DIMMs, and RIMMs," p. 533.

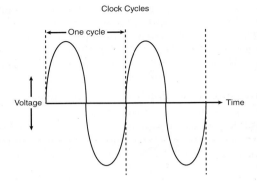

Figure 3.1   Alternating current signal showing clock cycle timing.

The time required to execute instructions also varies:

- **8086 and 8088**—The original 8086 and 8088 processors take an average of 12 cycles to execute a single instruction.

- **286 and 386**—The 286 and 386 processors improve this rate to about 4.5 cycles per instruction.

- **486**—The 486 and most other fourth-generation Intel-compatible processors, such as the AMD 5x86, drop the rate further, to about 2 cycles per instruction.

- **Pentium, K6 series**—The Pentium architecture and other fifth-generation Intel-compatible processors, such as those from AMD and Cyrix, include twin instruction pipelines and other improvements that provide for operation at one or two instructions per cycle.

- **Pentium Pro through Core 2, Athlon through Athlon X2**—These P6 and P7 (sixth- and seventh-generation) processors can execute as many as three or more instructions per cycle, with multiples of that possible on multicore processors.

Different instruction execution times (in cycles) make comparing systems based purely on clock speed or number of cycles per second difficult. How can two processors that run at the same clock rate perform differently with one running "faster" than the other? The answer is simple: efficiency.

The main reason the 486 was considered fast relative to a 386 is that it executes twice as many instructions in the same number of cycles. The same thing is true for a Pentium; it executes about twice as many instructions in a given number of cycles as a 486. Therefore, given the same clock speed, a Pentium is twice as fast as a 486, and consequently a 133MHz 486 class processor (such as the AMD 5x86-133) is not even as fast as a 75MHz Pentium! That is because Pentium megahertz are "worth" about double what 486 megahertz are worth in terms of instructions completed per cycle. The Pentium II and III are about 50% faster than an equivalent Pentium at a given clock speed because they can execute about that many more instructions in the same number of cycles.

Unfortunately, after the Pentium III, it becomes much more difficult to compare processors on clock speed alone. This is because the different internal architectures make some processors more efficient than others, but these same efficiency differences result in circuitry that is capable of running at different maximum speeds. The less efficient the circuit, the higher the clock speed it can attain, and vice versa.

Evaluating CPU performance can be tricky. CPUs with different internal architectures do things differently and can be relatively faster at certain things and slower at others. To fairly compare various CPUs at different clock speeds, Intel has devised a specific series of benchmarks called the *iCOMP (Intel Comparative Microprocessor Performance) index* that can be run against processors to produce a relative gauge of performance. The iCOMP index benchmark has been updated twice and released in original iCOMP, iCOMP 2.0, and now iCOMP 3.0 versions.

Table 3.7 shows the relative power, or iCOMP 2.0 index, for several processors.

Table 3.7   Intel iCOMP 2.0 Index Ratings

Processor	iCOMP 2.0 Index
Pentium 75	67
Pentium 100	90
Pentium 120	100
Pentium 133	111
Pentium 150	114
Pentium 166	127
Pentium 200	142
Pentium-MMX 166	160
Pentium Pro 150	168
Pentium-MMX 200	182
Pentium Pro 180	197
Pentium-MMX 233	203
Celeron 266	213
Pentium Pro 200	220
Celeron 300	226
Pentium II 233	267
Celeron 300A	296
Pentium II 266	303
Celeron 333	318
Pentium II 300	332
Pentium II OverDrive 300	351
Pentium II 333	366
Pentium II 350	386
Pentium II OverDrive 333	387
Pentium II 400	440
Pentium II 450	483

The iCOMP 2.0 index is derived from several independent benchmarks and is a stable indication of relative processor performance. The benchmarks balance integer with floating-point and multimedia performance.

When Intel developed the Pentium III, it discontinued the iCOMP 2.0 index and released the iCOMP 3.0 index. iCOMP 3.0 is an updated benchmark that incorporates an increasing use of 3D, multimedia, and Internet technology and software, as well as the increasing use of rich data streams and computer-intensive applications, including 3D, multimedia, and Internet technology. iCOMP 3.0 combines six benchmarks: WinTune 98 Advanced CPU Integer test, CPUmark 99, 3D WinBench 99-3D Lighting and Transformation Test, MultimediaMark 99, Jmark 2.0 Processor Test, and WinBench 99-FPU WinMark. These newer benchmarks take advantage of the SSE (Streaming SIMD Extensions), additional graphics and sound instructions built into the PIII. Without taking advantage of these new instructions, the PIII would benchmark at about the same speed as a PII at the same clock rate.

Note

Note that this reflects the most recent iCOMP index. Intel uses other benchmarks for the Pentium 4 and subsequent processors.

Table 3.8 shows the iCOMP Index 3.0 ratings for Pentium II and III processors.

Table 3.8   Intel iCOMP 3.0 Ratings

Processor	iCOMP 3.0 Index	Processor	iCOMP 3.0 Index
Pentium II 350	1000	Pentium III 650	2270
Pentium II 450	1240	Pentium III 700	2420
Pentium III 450	1500	Pentium III 750	2540
Pentium III 500	1650	Pentium III 800	2690
Pentium III 550	1780	Pentium III 866	2890
Pentium III 600	1930	Pentium III 1000	3280
Pentium III 600E	2110		

Intel and AMD usually rate their latest processors using the commercially available BAPCo SYSmark benchmark suites. The ratings for the various processors under the 2002 and 2004 benchmark suites are shown in Tables 3.9 and 3.10. Table 3.11 shows benchmarks for the SYSmark 2004 SE suite.

Table 3.9   SYSmark 2002 Scores for Various Processors

CPU	Clock	SYSmark 2002 Rating	CPU	Clock	SYSmark 2002 Rating
Pentium 4 Extreme Edition	3.2GHz	362	AMD Athlon XP	1.72GHz	195
Pentium 4	3.2GHz	344	Pentium 4	1.9GHz	192
Pentium 4	3.0GHz	328	Pentium 4	1.8GHz	187
Pentium 4	3.06GHz	324	Pentium 4	1.7GHz	178
Pentium 4	2.8GHz	312	Pentium 4	1.6GHz	171
Pentium 4	2.6GHz	295	AMD Athlon XP	1.67GHz	171
Pentium 4	2.67GHz	285	Pentium 4	1.5GHz	162
Pentium 4	2.53GHz	273	AMD Athlon XP	1.53GHz	149
Pentium 4	2.4GHz	264	Pentium III	1.2GHz	108
Pentium 4	2.26GHz	252	Pentium III	1.3GHz	104
Pentium 4	2.2GHz	238	Pentium III	1.13GHz	100
Pentium 4	2.0GHz	222	Pentium III	1.0GHz	92

Table 3.10   SYSmark 2004 Scores for Various Processors

CPU	Clock/Cache/FSB	SYSmark 2004 Rating
Intel Core 2 Quad Extreme QX6700	2.66GHz/8MB/1066	413
Intel Core 2 Duo 6600	2.4 GH /4MB/1066	335
Intel Pentium EE 965	3.73GHz/2x2MB/1066	305
AMD Athlon 64 FX-60	2.6GHz/2x1MB/1000	302
Intel Pentium EE 965	3.73GHz/2x2MB/1066	292
AMD Athlon 64 X2 4800+	2.4GHz/1MB/1000	284
AMD Athlon 64 X2 4600+	2.4GHz/512KB/1000	281
Intel Pentium EE 955	3.46GHz/2x2MB/1066	279
Intel Pentium EE 965	3.73GHz/2x2MB/1066	275
AMD Athlon 64 X2 4400+	2.2GHz/1MB/1000	266
Intel Pentium EE 955	3.46GHz/2x2MB/1066	264
Intel Pentium D 950	3.40GHz/2x2MB/800	263
AMD Athlon 64 X2 4200+	2.2GHz/512KB/1000	263
Intel Pentium EE 955	3.46GHz/2x2MB/1066	261
Pentium 4 570J	3.8GHz/1MB/800	245
AMD Athlon 64 X2 3800+	2.0GHz/512KB/1000	242
Intel Pentium 4 570J	3.8GHz/1MB/800	239
Intel Pentium 4 EE 3.73GHz	3.73GHz/2MB/1066	239
Intel Pentium EE 840	3.20GHz/2x1MB/800	238
AMD Athlon 64 FX-55	2.6GHz/1MB/1000	238
Intel Pentium 4 EE 3.73GHz	3.73GHz/2MB/1066	236
Intel Pentium D 840	3.20GHz/2x1MB/800	232
Intel Pentium D 840	3.2GHz/2x1MB/800	232
Intel Pentium EE 840	3.2GHz/2x1MB/800	232
Intel Core Duo T2600	2.16GHz/2MB/667	231
Intel Pentium 4 EE 3.73GHz	3.73GHz/2MB/1066	231
Pentium 4 EE 3.73GHz	3.73GHz/2MB/1066	230
Intel Pentium 4 560	3.6GHz/1MB/800	229
Intel Pentium 4 560	3.6GHz/1MB/800	226
Intel Pentium 4EE	3.4GHz/2MB/800	225
Intel Pentium 4 EE	3.4GHz/512KB+2MB L3/800	225
Intel Pentium 4 570J	3.8GHz/1MB/800	224
AMD Athlon 64 FX-55	2.6GHz/1MB/1000	224
Athlon 64 X2 3800+	2.00GHz/2x512KB/1000	223
AMD Athlon 64 4000+	2.4GHz/1MB/1000	222
Intel Pentium 4 EE	3.4GHz/2MB/800	222
Pentium 4 660	3.6GHz/2MB/800	220
AMD Athlon 64 FX-53	2.4GHz/1MB/1000	219

Table 3.10   Continued

CPU	Clock/Cache/FSB	SYSmark 2004 Rating
Intel Pentium 4E	3.4GHz/1MB/800	218
Intel Pentium 4 550	3.4GHz/1MB/800	216
AMD Athlon 64 FX-53	2.4GHz/1MB/1000	216
Intel Pentium 4 EE	3.2GHz/512KB/2MB L3/800	215
Intel Pentium D 925	3.00GHz/2x2MB/800	214
AMD Athlon 64 3800+	2.4GHz/512KB/1000	214
AMD Athlon FX-53	2.4GHz/1MB/1000	213
AMD Athlon 64 4000+	2.4GHz/1MB/1000	213
AMD Athlon 64 3700+	2.4GHz/1MB/1000	212
Intel Pentium 4C	3.4GHz/512KB/800	212
Intel Pentium 4	3.4GHz/512KB/800	212
Intel Pentium D 820	2.80GHz/2x1MB/800	211
Intel Pentium 4 EE	3.4GHz/512KB+2MB L3/800	207
Intel Pentium 4 540	3.2GHz/1MB/800	207
AMD Athlon 64 3400+	2.4GHz/512KB/1000	207
Athlon 64 4000+	2.40GHz/1MB/1000	205
AMD Athlon 64 3500+	2.2GHz/512KB/1000	205
Intel Pentium 4	3.4GHz/512KB/800	204
AMD Athlon 64	2.4GHz/1MB/1000	204
Intel Pentium 4 640	3.2GHz/2MB/800	204
Intel Pentium 4E	3.2GHz/512KB/800	204
Intel Pentium 4	3.2GHz/512KB/800	203
Intel Pentium 4 560	3.6GHz/1MB/800	203
Intel Pentium 4E	3.4GHz/1MB/800	203
AMD Athlon 64 FX-51	2.2GHz/1MB/1000	200
Intel Pentium 4C	3.4GHz/512KB/800	198
Intel Pentium D 805	2.66GHz/2x1MB/533	196
Athlon 64 3700+	2.20GHz/1MB/1000	196
Intel Pentium D 805	2.66GHz/2x1MB/533	196
AMD Athlon 64 3400+	2.2GHz/1MB/1000	195
AMD Athlon 64 3200+	2.2GHz/512KB/1000	194
Intel Pentium 4E	3.20GHz/1MB/800	194
Intel Core Duo T2300	1.66GHz/2MB/667	193
Intel Pentium 4	3.0GHz/512KB/800	193
Intel Pentium 4	3.4GHz/512KB/800	193
Intel Pentium 4	3.2GHz/512KB/800	192
Intel Pentium 4 540	3.20GHz/1MB/800	192
Intel Pentium 4E	3.0GHz/512KB/800	192

Table 3.10   Continued

CPU	Clock/Cache/FSB	SYSmark 2004 Rating
Intel Pentium 4 630	3.00GHz/2MB/800	190
Intel Pentium 4	3.20GHz/512KB/800	189
Athlon 64 3500+	2.20GHz/512KB/1000	188
AMD Athlon 64 3500+	2.20GHz/512KB/1000	188
Intel Pentium 4 530	3.0GHz/1MB/800	188
Intel Pentium 4	3.0GHz/512KB/800	187
Intel Pentium 4	3.2GHz/512KB/800	186
AMD Athlon 64	2.2GHz/512KB/1000	185
AMD Athlon 64 3400+	2.2GHz/1MB/1000	185
Intel Pentium 4 530	3.00GHz/1MB/800	184
Intel Pentium 4E	2.8GHz/512KB/800	182
Intel Pentium 4 540	3.2GHz/1MB/800	182
Intel Pentium 4	2.8GHz/512KB/800	181
Intel Pentium 4 517	2.93GHz/1MB/533	180
AMD Athlon 64 3200+	2.0GHz/1MB/1000	180
AMD Athlon 64 3000+	2.0GHz/512KB/1000	178
Intel Pentium 4	3.0GHz/512KB/800	177
Athlon 64 3200+	2.00GHz/512KB/1000	176
Intel Pentium 4 520	2.80GHz/1MB/800	175
Intel Pentium 4C	2.80GHz/512KB/800	174
Intel Pentium 4E	2.8GHz/1MB/800	173
AMD Athlon 64 3200+	2.0GHz/1MB/1000	173
Intel Pentium 4	2.8GHz/512KB/800	168
AMD Athlon 64 3000+	2.0GHz/512KB/1000	168
Intel Pentium 4 520	2.8GHz/1MB/800	167
AMD Athlon 64 2800+	1.8GHz/512KB/1000	164
AMD Athlon XP 3200+	2.2GHz/512KB/400	163
Sempron 3400+	2.00GHz/256KB/800	161
Sempron 3300+	2.00GHz/128KB/800	157
AMD Sempron 3100+	1.8GHz/256KB/1000	154
Intel Pentium 4C	2.4GHz/512KB/800	153
Intel Pentium 4 515	2.93GHz/1MB/800	152
AMD Sempron 3100+	1.8GHz/256KB/1000	152
AMD Athlon XP 2800+	2.25GHz/256KB/166	151
Intel Celeron D 346	3.06GHz/256KB/533	151
Sempron 3100+	1.80GHz/256KB/800	149
Intel Pentium 4 520	2.8GHz/1MB/800	149
AMD Athlon XP 2700+	2.18GHz/256KB/166	148

Table 3.10   Continued

CPU	Clock/Cache/FSB	SYSmark 2004 Rating
Intel Pentium 4	2.4GHz/512KB/800	148
Intel Celeron D 341	2.93GHz/256KB/533	146
Sempron 3000+	1.80GHz/128KB/800	145
Intel Pentium 4B	2.80GHz/512KB/533	144
AMD Athlon XP 2600+	2.08GHz/256KB/166	144
Intel Celeron D 336	2.80GHz/256KB/533	143
Intel Pentium M 730	1.60GHz/2MB/533	139
Intel Celeron D 335	2.8GHz/256KB/533	139
Sempron 2800+	1.60GHz/256KB/800	137
AMD Sempron 3100+	1.8GHz/256KB/1000	137
AMD Sempron 3000+	2.0GHz/512KB/333	137
AMD Sempron 2800+	2.0GHz/256KB/333	136
Intel Celeron D 331	2.66GHz/256KB/533	135
AMD Athlon 64	2.2GHz/512KB/1000	135
Intel Celeron D 335	2.8GHz/256KB/533	135
AMD Athlon XP 2400+	2.00GHz/256KB/133	133
Intel Celeron D 326	2.53GHz/256KB/533	133
Sempron 2600+	1.60GHz/128KB/800	133
Intel Celeron D 340	2.93GHz/256KB/533	133
AMD Sempron 2800+	2.0GHz/256KB/333	132
Intel Celeron D 330	2.66GHz/256KB/533	131
Intel Pentium 4B	2.4GHz/512KB/533	130
Intel Celeron D 330	2.67GHz/256KB/533	127
Intel Celeron D 340	2.93GHz/256KB/533	126
Intel Pentium 4	2.8GHz/512KB/800	125
AMD Sempron 2600+	1.833GHz/256KB/333	124
Sempron 2500+	1.40GHz/256KB/800	123
Intel Celeron D 320	2.4GHz/256KB/533	119
Intel Celeron	2.8GHz/128KB/400	117
AMD Sempron 2400+	1.667GHz/256KB/333	117
Intel Celeron	2.7GHz/128KB/400	115
AMD Athlon XP 3200+	2.2GHz/512KB/400	115
AMD Sempron 2300+	1.583GHz/256KB/333	113
AMD Athlon XP 3000+	2.1GHz/512KB/400	112
AMD Athlon XP 2900+	2.0GHz/512KB/400	111
AMD Athlon XP 1800+	1.53GHz/256KB/133	111
Intel Celeron	2.5GHz/128KB/400	110
Pentium-M	1.6GHz/1MB/400	109

Table 3.10   Continued

CPU	Clock/Cache/FSB	SYSmark 2004 Rating
Intel Celeron	2.4GHz/128KB/400	104
Intel Pentium 4	2GHz/512KB/400	104
Intel Pentium 4	2.0GHz/512KB/400	103
Intel Pentium 4 2.0GHz	2.0GHz/512KB/400	98
Intel Pentium 4	2.4GHz/512KB/800	97
Intel Celeron M	1.3GHz/512KB/400	93
Intel Celeron C	2GHz/128KB/400	84
Intel Pentium III	1GHz/256KB/133	64
Intel Pentium III	1GHz/256KB/133	61

Table 3.11   SYSmark 2004 SE Scores for Various Processors

CPU	Clock/Cache/FSB	SYSmark 2004 SE Rating
Intel Core 2 Quad Extreme QX6700	2.66GHz/8MB/1066	440
Intel Core 2 Extreme QX6700	2.66GHz/8MB/1066	421
Intel Core 2 Extreme X6800	2.93GHz/4MB/1066	418
Intel Core 2 Extreme X6800	2.93GHz/4MB/1066	408
Intel Core 2 Extreme E6800	2.93GHz/4MB/1066	404
Intel Core 2 Extreme X6800	2.93GHz/4MB/1066	398
Intel Core 2 Extreme QX6700	2.66GHz/8MB/1066	389
Intel Core 2 Duo E6700	2.66GHz/4MB/1066	378
Intel Core 2 Duo E6700	2.66GHz/4MB/1066	333
AMD Athlon 64 FX-62	2.80GHz/2x1MB/1000	324
AMD Athlon 64 FX-62	2.8GHz/2x1MB/1000	312
AMD Athlon 64 FX-62	2.80GHz/2x1MB/1000	309
Intel Pentium EE 965	3.73GHz/2x2MB/1066	305
AMD Athlon FX-60	2.6GHz/2x1MB/1000	297
Intel Pentium EE 965	3.73GHz/2x2MB/1066	292
AMD Athlon 64 X2 5000+	2.6GHz/2x512KB/1000	290
AMD Athlon 64 X2 5000+	2.60GHz/2x512KB/1000	281
Intel Core 2 Duo E6300	1.86GHz/2MB/1066	280
AMD Athlon 64 X2 4800+	2.4GHz/2x1MB/1000	280
Intel Pentium EE 955	3.46GHz/2x2MB/1066	279
Intel Pentium EE 965	3.73GHz/2x2MB/1066	279
Intel Core 2 Duo T7600	2.33GHz/4MB/667	275
Intel Pentium EE 965	3.73GHz/2x2MB/1066	275
AMD Athlon 64 X2 4600+	2.4GHz/2x512KB/1000	275
AMD Athlon 64 X2 4600+	2.4GHz/2x512KB/1000	273

Table 3.11   **Continued**

CPU	Clock/Cache/FSB	SYSmark 2004 SE Rating
Intel Core 2 Duo E6300	1.86GHz/2MB/1066	259
AMD Athlon 64 X2 4200+	2.2GHz/2x512KB/1000	256
Intel Pentium D 960	3.60GHz/2x2MB/800	254
AMD Athlon 64 X2 4200+	2.20GHz/2x512KB/1000	250
Intel Pentium D 945	3.4GHz/2x2MB/800	246
AMD Athlon 64 X2 3800+	2.0GHz/2x512KB/1000	245
AMD Athlon 64 X2 3800+	2.0GHz/2x512KB/1000	239
Intel Pentium D 960	3.60GHz/2x2MB/800	234
Intel Pentium 4 670	3.80GHz/2MB/800	234
Intel Pentium D 930	3.00GHz/2x2MB/800	223
Intel Pentium 4 661	3.6GHz/2MB/800	220
AMD Athlon 64 3800+	2.4GHz/512KB/1000	217
Intel Core 2 Duo T5500	1.66GHz/4MB/667	204
AMD Athlon 64 3500+	2.2GHz/512KB/1000	201
Athlon 64 3700+	2.20GHz/1MB/1000	196
Intel Pentium D 805	2.66GHz/2x1MB/533	196
Intel Core Duo T2300	1.66GHz/2MB/667	193
Intel Pentium 4 540	3.20GHz/1MB/800	192
Intel Pentium 4 630	3.00GHz/2MB/800	190
Intel Pentium 4 631	3.00GHz/2MB/800	189
Athlon 64 3500+	2.20GHz/512KB/1000	188
AMD Athlon 64 3500+	2.20GHz/512KB	188
Intel Pentium 4 530	3.0GHz/1MB/800	188
Intel Core Duo T2300	1.66GHz/4MB/667	187
Intel Pentium 4 530	3.00GHz/1MB/800	184
Intel Pentium 4 631	3.0GHz/2MB/800	182
Intel Pentium 4 517	2.93GHz/1MB/533	180
Athlon 64 3200+	2.00GHz/512KB/1000	176
Intel Pentium 4 520	2.80GHz/1MB/800	175
AMD Turion X2 TL-52	1.60GHz/2x512KB/1000	171
AMD Turion X2 TL-50	1.60GHz/2x256KB/1000	169
AMD Sempron 3600+	2.0GHz/256KB/1000	163
AMD Sempron 3500+	2.0GHz/128KB/1000	162
Sempron 3400+	2.00GHz/256KB/800	161
Sempron 3300+	2.00GHz/128KB/800	157
Intel Celeron D 346	3.06GHz/256KB/533	151
Sempron 3100+	1.80GHz/256KB/800	149
AMD Sempron 3400+	1.8GHz/256KB/1000	148

Table 3.11   Continued

CPU	Clock/Cache/FSB	SYSmark 2004 SE Rating
AMD Sempron 3200+	1.8GHz/128KB/1000	147
Intel Celeron D 341	2.93GHz/256KB/533	146
Sempron 3000+	1.80GHz/128KB/800	145
Intel Celeron D 336	2.80GHz/256KB/533	143
AMD Sempron 3000+	1.6GHz/256KB/1000	141
Intel Pentium M 730	1.60GHz/2MB/533	139
Sempron 2800+	1.60GHz/256KB/800	137
Intel Celeron D 331	2.66GHz/256KB/533	135
Intel Celeron D 326	2.53GHz/256KB/533	133
Sempron 2600+	1.60GHz/128KB/800	133
Intel Celeron D 340	2.93GHz/256KB/533	133
Sempron 2500+	1.40GHz/256KB/800	123

SYSmark 2002, 2004 and 2004 SE are commercially available application-based benchmarks that reflect the normal usage of business users employing modern Internet content creation and Microsoft Office applications. However, it is important to note that the scores listed here are produced by complete systems and are affected by things such as the specific version of the processor, the motherboard and chipset used, the amount and type of memory installed, the speed of the hard disk, and other factors. For complete disclosure of the other factors resulting in the given scores, see the BAPCo website.

SYSmark 2002 incorporates the following applications, which it uses for testing:

- **Internet Content Creation**—Includes Adobe Photoshop 6.01, Premiere 6.0, Microsoft Windows Media Encoder 7.1, Macromedia Dreamweaver 4, and Flash 5
- **Office Productivity**—Includes Microsoft Word 2002, Excel 2002, PowerPoint 2002, Outlook 2002, Access 2002, Netscape Communicator 6.0, Dragon NaturallySpeaking Preferred v.5, WinZip 8.0, and McAfee VirusScan 5.13

SYSmark 2004 incorporates the following applications, which it uses for testing:

- **Internet Content Creation**—Includes Adobe After Effects 5.5, Adobe Photoshop 7.01, Adobe Premiere 6.5, Discreet 3ds max 5.1, Macromedia Dreamweaver MX, Macromedia Flash MX, Microsoft Windows Media Encoder 9 Series, Network Associates McAfee VirusScan 7.0, and WinZip Computing WinZip 8.1
- **Office Productivity**—Includes Adobe Acrobat 5.0.5, Microsoft Access 2002, Microsoft Excel 2002, Microsoft Internet Explorer 6, Microsoft Outlook 2002, Microsoft PowerPoint 2002, Microsoft Word 2002, Network Associates McAfee VirusScan 7.0, ScanSoft Dragon Naturally Speaking 6 Preferred, and WinZip Computing WinZip 8.1

SYSmark 2004 SE—was introduced in June 2005 and now supports the Windows XP Professional x64 Edition. SYSmark 2004 SE uses the same applications used by SYSmark 2004, but it incorporates changes to its operation that are designed to more closely mirror how a typical user works with the application mix featured in each module.

The latest version of the SYSmark is SYSmark 2007, which is designed to support Windows Vista in addition to XP. A preview version of SYSmark 2007 was released in April 2007.

SYSmark runs various scripts to do actual work using these applications and is used by many companies for testing and comparing PC systems and components. It is a much more modern and real-world benchmark than the iCOMP benchmark Intel previously used, and because it is available to anybody, the results can be independently verified. The SYSmark benchmark software can be purchased from BAPCo at www.bapco.com or from FutureMark at www.futuremark.com.

Processor Speeds and Markings Versus Motherboard Speed

Another confusing factor when comparing processor performance is that virtually all modern processors since the 486DX2 run at some multiple of the motherboard speed. For example, a Pentium 4 2.53GHz chip runs at a multiple of 19/4 (4.75x) times the motherboard speed of 533MHz, whereas an AMD Athlon XP 2800+ using the Barton core (2.083GHz) runs at 75/12 (6.25x) times the motherboard speed of 333MHz.

Up until early 1998, most motherboards ran at 66MHz or less. Starting in April 1998, Intel released both processors and motherboard chipsets designed to run at 100MHz. By late 1999, chipsets and motherboards running at 133MHz became available to support the newer Pentium III processors. At that time, AMD Athlon motherboards and chipsets were introduced running a 100MHz clock but using a double transfer technique for an effective 200MHz data rate between the Athlon processor and the main chipset North Bridge chip.

In 2000 and 2001, processor bus speeds advanced further to 266MHz for the AMD Athlon and Intel Itanium and 400MHz to 533MHz for the Pentium 4. In 2002, the AMD Athlon XP processors began to support a processor bus speed of 333MHz. In 2003, Intel introduced the first Pentium 4 processors that supported a processor bus speed of 800MHz; later that year, Intel introduced the Pentium 4 Extreme Edition, which supports a processor bus speed of 1,066MHz. Today we have AMD processors using the HyperTransport bus running at 1,000MHz, and Intel processors with bus speeds of 1,333MHz.

Note

See Chapter 4, "Motherboards and Buses," for more information on chipsets and bus speeds.

Intel Processor Model Numbers

Most people associate clock speed with the processor, and Intel has always used the raw clock speed of its processors to market them. This has led many people to believe that faster-speed processors always result in faster or better systems, but that is not always the case. Processor architectures have a major effect on the performance of a processor, and it is entirely possible that a slower clock speed processor can handily outperform a faster one when running actual programs or doing real work. Unfortunately, this message is hard to convey when the main attribute used to market a chip is its raw clock speed.

AMD has long been marketing its chips with model numbers, which in this case do relate to speed—but not directly. Starting in 2004, Intel also began to use model numbers, but its model numbering scheme is distinctly different from AMD's. Intel has decided to use a BMW-esque numbering scheme across its various processor families. Currently, it uses 9xx and 8xx designations for its top-of-the-line desktop processors (Pentium Extreme Edition and Pentium D), 7xx for its Pentium M mobile processors, 6xx for advanced Pentium 4 processors, 5xx for mainstream Pentium 4 and mobile Pentium 4 processors, and 4xx and 3xx for economy Celeron D desktop and Celeron M mobile processors. Dual-core Intel Xeon processors are numbered in the 7xxx series.

When creating the specific model number for a chip, Intel takes into account not only the raw clock speed of the chip, but also the internal architecture, cache sizes, bus speeds, and other features. In general, the higher the number, the more feature-rich the processor. In addition, within each series, the higher numbers are generally faster chips.

The model numbers are not strictly comparisons of speed and certainly don't pertain to speed comparisons outside the model line. For example, using the BMW automobile analogy from which these numbers seem to be derived, some 3-series cars are faster than some 5-series cars, and some 5-series cars are faster than some 7-series cars. However, as you go up in the series numbers, the higher-numbered series generally have more features or are premium models. Within a particular series, the model numbers do give somewhat of an indication of speed, in that a Pentium 4 660 is faster than a Pentium 4 650, and so on.

Note that these model numbers are somewhat ambiguous. No matter what the model number is, I wouldn't purchase either an Intel or an AMD chip for an upgrade or as part of a new computer without knowing the true clock speeds and other specifications and features in the chip. The model numbers don't strictly tell that information and are useful only for a rough comparison.

Cyrix Processor Speeds

Older Cyrix/IBM/VIA 6x86 processors—which were designed to compete with the Intel Pentium, early Pentium II, and AMD K5 and K6 series of processors—used a PR (performance rating) scale that was not equal to the true clock speed in megahertz. For example, the Cyrix 6x86MX/MII-PR366 actually runs at only 250MHz (2.5×100MHz). This is a little misleading—you must set up the motherboard as if a 250MHz processor were being installed, instead of the 366MHz you might suspect. Unfortunately, this led people to believe these systems were faster than they really were.

Note that a given P-Rating can mean several different actual CPU speeds—for example, a Cyrix 6x86MX-PR200 might actually be running at 150MHz, 165MHz, 166MHz, or 180MHz, but *not* at 200MHz.

This P-Rating was supposed to indicate speed in relation to an Intel Pentium processor, but the processor being compared to in this case is the original non-MMX, small L1 cache version running on an older motherboard platform with an older chipset and slower technology memory. The P-Rating did not compare well against the Celeron, Pentium II, or Pentium III processors. In other words, the MII-PR366 really ran at only 250MHz and compared well against Intel processors running at closer to that speed, making the ratings somewhat misleading.

AMD Processor Speeds

AMD's Athlon XP processors were excellent performers and included several notable features, but they also brought with them a resurrection of the infamous Cyrix/AMD performance rating. This is a simulated MHz number that does not indicate the actual speed of the chip but instead indicates an estimate of the relative MHz of a first-generation Intel Pentium 4 that would be approximately equal in performance. If this sounds confusing, that's because it is!

As time marched on and CPU architecture evolved, this method of rating chips had to be revised and eventually abandoned. Although AMD uses model numbers to identify the newer Sempron and Athlon 64 product families, the model numbers for these chips are not specifically intended to compare the processors to Intel processors. As is increasingly the case with both Intel and AMD processors, to gauge processor performance, there's no substitute for knowing the particular features (CPU speed, motherboard speed, L2 cache size, and so on) of a given processor.

The marketing problem that led to the need for performance ratings and model numbers for processors is real: How do you market a chip that performs faster than its predecessors or its rivals when both are running at the same clock speed or lower? For example, an AMD Athlon XP with an actual clock speed of 2GHz is significantly faster than a 2GHz Pentium 4 (Northwood) and in fact performs about equal to a 2.4GHz Pentium 4 (hence, AMD called its model the Athlon XP 2400+). This apparent disparity in performance is because the P4 uses a different architecture that utilizes a deeper instruction pipeline with more stages. The original version of the Pentium 4 had a 20-stage pipeline, which compared to a 10-stage pipeline in the original Athlon and Pentium III (see Table 3.12).

Table 3.12   Number of Pipelines per CPU

Processor	Pipeline Depth	Processor	Pipeline Depth
Pentium III	10-stage	Core 2	14-stage
Pentium M/Core	10-stage	Pentium 4	20-stage
Athlon/XP	10-stage	Pentium 4 Prescott	31-stage
Athlon 64	12-stage	Pentium D	31-stage

A deeper pipeline effectively breaks instructions down into smaller microsteps, which allows overall higher clock rates to be achieved using the same silicon technology. However, it also means that overall fewer instructions can be executed in a single cycle as compared to processors with shorter pipelines. This is because, if a branch prediction or speculative execution step fails (which happens fairly frequently inside the processor as it attempts to line up instructions in advance), the entire pipeline has to be flushed and refilled. Thus, if you compared an Athlon to a Pentium III to a Pentium 4 all running at the same clock speed, the Athlon and Pentium III would both beat the Pentium 4 running typical benchmarks because they would execute more instructions in the same number of cycles.Although it might sound like a disadvantage to have a deeper pipeline in terms of instruction efficiency, processors with deeper pipelines can run at higher clock rates on a given manufacturing technology. Even though the deeper pipeline might be 30% less efficient overall, it more than makes up for this by allowing at least 50% greater clock speeds than the Athlon XP or Pentium III could muster. The deeper 20- or 31-stage pipeline in the P4 architecture enabled significantly higher clock speeds to be achieved using the same silicon die process as other chips. As an example, the Athlon XP and Pentium 4 were originally made using the same 0.18-micron process (which describes the line width of components etched on the chips). The P4's 20-stage pipeline enabled the 0.18-micron die process to result in chips running up to 2.0GHz, whereas the same process achieves only 1.73GHz in the 10-stage Athlon XP and only 1.13GHz in the 10-stage Pentium III. Using the newer 0.13-micron process, the Pentium 4 ran up to 3.4GHz and the Athlon XP tops out at 2.2GHz (3200+ model) in the same introduction timeframe. The latest Pentium 4 models (and the dual-core Pentium D and Pentium Extreme Edition) use the 0.09-micron process to reach clock speeds up to 3.8GHz. Even though the Pentium 4 executes fewer instructions in each cycle, the overall higher cycling speeds make up for the loss of efficiency. So, in the end, for the initial crop of Athlon XP and Pentium 4 processors, higher clock speed versus more efficient processing effectively cancelled each other out.

Unfortunately the deep pipeline combined with high clock rates did come with a penalty in power consumption, and therefore heat generation as well. Eventually it was determined that the power penalty was too great, causing Intel to drop back to a more efficient design in its newer Core microarchitecture processors. Rather than solely increasing clock rates, another way performance was increased was by combining multiple processors into a single chip, thus improving the effective instruction efficiency even further.

Note

If you want to determine the designed clock speed for any type of AMD processor (the actual clock speed could vary according to motherboard overclocking, underclocking, or power management clock speed adjustments), go to AMD's website and download the Data Sheet for the processor model you are interested in. You will find a table in each data sheet that lists the actual MHz (divide by 1,000 for the GHz) for each model.

One thing is clear in all of this confusion: Raw clock speed is not always a good way to compare chips, and generating pseudo-MHz or GHz numbers can only make things more confusing for the uninitiated. Even Intel moved away from using clock speed as its primary marketing designation. It still notes the speeds of its chips, but the processors are labeled and marketed primarily by model numbers. This was deemed necessary because the relative difference between each model number is based not just on the CPU's speed, but also on architectural and other differences that affect overall performance.

◄◄ See "Intel Processor Model Numbers," p. 66.

Overclocking

As is discussed in detail in Chapter 21, "PC Mods: Overclocking and Cooling," in some systems, the processor speed can be set higher than the rating on the chip; this is called *overclocking* the chip. In many cases, you can get away with a certain amount of overclocking because Intel, AMD, and others often build safety margins into their ratings. So, a chip rated for, say, 3GHz might in fact run at 3.5GHz or more but instead be down-rated to allow for a greater margin of reliability. By overclocking, you are using this margin and running the chip closer to its true maximum speed. I don't normally recommend overclocking for a novice, but if you are comfortable playing with your system settings, and you can afford and are capable of dealing with any potential consequences, overclocking might enable you to get 10%–20% or more performance from your system.

Overclocking Pitfalls

If you are intent on overclocking, there are several issues to consider. One is that most processors sold since 1998 are multiplier-locked before they are shipped out. Processors that are locked ignore any changes to the multiplier setting on the motherboard. Actually, both Intel and AMD sell some processors that have unlocked multipliers, and in some cases it is possible to modify locked processors to change or un-do the locks. For example, some AMD processors use solder bridges on top of the chip that can be manipulated if you are careful and somewhat mechanically inclined. Although originally done to prevent re-markers from fraudulently relabeling processors (creating "counterfeit" chips), multiplier locking has impacted the computing performance enthusiast, leaving tweaking the motherboard bus speed as the only easy way (or in some cases, the only way possible) to achieve a clock speed higher than standard.

You can run into problems increasing motherboard bus speed, as well. Most older Intel motherboards, for example, simply don't support clock speeds other than the standard settings. Some newer enthusiast-oriented Intel boards have "burn-in" or "override" features that allows you to increase the default processor bus speed (and also the speed of the processor core), voltages, and multiplier (for unlocked CPUs). Most other brands of motherboards also allow changing the bus speeds. Note that small incremental changes in clock multiplier speeds, rather than large jumps, are the best way to coax a bit more performance out of a particular processor. This is because a given chip is generally overclockable by a certain percentage. The smaller the steps you can take when increasing speed, the more likely that you'll be able to come close to the actual maximum speed of the chip without going over that amount and causing system instability.

For example, say you have a Socket 775 motherboard running a 2.4GHz Core 2 Quad processor at a CPU front-side bus speed of 1,066MHz. The motherboard permits 1MHz adjustments of the CPU bus clock speed (which is multiplied by 4 to obtain the front-side bus) to enable you to fine-tune your processor speed. The base clock frequency is 266MHz and is multiplied by 4 to obtain the motherboard bus (FSB) speed, which is then further increased by the CPU multiplier: 800MHz × 3.5 = 2,800MHz, or 2.8GHz.

Using a 2.40GHz Core 2 Quad processor as an example, let's see how the clock speeds work out. The 2.40GHz Core 2 Quad Processor Q6600 runs on a CPU front-side bus speed of 1,066MHz. Both the processor core and bus speeds are derived from the CPU bus clock generated by the motherboard, which defaults to 266MHz in this case. The FSB always runs at a 4X multiple of the CPU clock, while the core of the processor in this example runs at 9X the CPU clock. By adjusting the CPU clock frequency, you can change the FSB and CPU core clock speeds as shown in Table 3.13.

Table 3.13 lists the resulting FSB and CPU core speeds you could achieve by adjusting the CPU frequency from 266MHz (the standard setting for Intel CPUs with a 1,066MHz FSB) to 300MHz:

Table 3.13   Core Clock, FSB, and CPU Speed Relationships

Base Clock Frequency	Bus Multiplier (fixed)	Resulting FSB Speed	CPU Core Multiplier (locked)	Resulting Processor Speed
266 MHz	4X	1,066 MHz	9X	2.400 GHz
268 MHz	4X	1,072 MHz	9X	2.412 GHz
270 MHz	4X	1,080 MHz	9X	2.430 GHz
272 MHz	4X	1,088 MHz	9X	2.448 GHz
274 MHz	4X	1,096 MHz	9X	2.466 GHz
276 MHz	4X	1,104 MHz	9X	2.484 GHz
278 MHz	4X	1,112 MHz	9X	2.502 GHz
280 MHz	4X	1,120 MHz	9X	2.520 GHz
282 MHz	4X	1,128 MHz	9X	2.538 GHz
284 MHz	4X	1,136 MHz	9X	2.556 GHz
286 MHz	4X	1,144 MHz	9X	2.574 GHz
288 MHz	4X	1,152 MHz	9X	2.592 GHz
290 MHz	4X	1,160 MHz	9X	2.610 GHz
292 MHz	4X	1,168 MHz	9X	2.628 GHz
294 MHz	4X	1,176 MHz	9X	2.646 GHz
296 MHz	4X	1,184 MHz	9X	2.664 GHz
298 MHz	4X	1,192 MHz	9X	2.682 GHz
300 MHz	4X	1,200 MHz	9X	2.700 GHz

As you can see in this example, by increasing the base clock from 266MHz to 300MHz, you would increase the FSB from 1,066MHz to 1,200MHz, and the CPU core speed from 2.4GHz to 2.7GHz, nearly a 13% increase. Typically, increases on the order of 10%–20% are successful, possibly more if your system offers excellent cooling and you can also adjust CPU multiplier, voltage, and other settings.

An issue when it comes to increasing CPU bus speeds is that the other buses in the system may be similarly affected. Thus, if you increase the CPU bus speed by 10%, you might also be increasing the memory, PCI, PCI Express or AGP buses by the same amount, and your RAM, video, network, or other components might not be able to keep up. This is something that varies from board to board, so you have to consider each example as a potentially unique case. If possible, change the CPU multiplier to a higher setting (if it is unlocked), and/or configure the other buses to run at their normal speeds through the appropriate BIOS settings. Check with your processor and motherboard documentation to see what settings are possible.

Overclocking Socket A Processors

The AMD Athlon and Duron processors in the FC-PGA (flip-chip pin grid array) format, which plugs into Socket A, have special solder bridges on the top face of the chip that can be modified to change or remove the lock from the internal multiplier on the chip. This can increase the speed of the chip without changing the motherboard bus speed, thus affecting other buses or cards.

The selected multiplier is set or locked by very small solder connections between solder dots (contacts) on the surface of the chip. You can completely unlock the chip by bridging or disconnecting the appropriate dots. Unfortunately, it is somewhat difficult to add or remove these bridges; you usually have to mask off the particular bridge you want to create and, rather than dripping solder onto it, literally paint the bridge with silver or copper paint. For example, you can use the special copper paint sold in small vials at any auto parts store for repairing the window defogger grids. The real problem is that the contacts are very small, and if you bridge to adjacent rather than opposite contacts, you can render the chip nonfunctional. An Xacto knife or razor blade can be used to remove the bridges if desired. If you are not careful, you can easily damage a processor worth several hundred dollars. If you are leery of making such changes, you should try bus overclocking instead because this is done in the BIOS Setup and can easily be changed or undone without any mechanical changes to the chip.

CPU Voltage Settings

Another trick used by overclockers is playing with the voltage settings for the CPU. All modern CPU sockets and slots have automatic voltage detection. With this detection, the system determines and sets the correct voltage by reading certain pins on the processor. Some motherboards do not allow any manual changes to these settings. Other motherboards allow you to tweak the voltage settings from the automatic setting up or down by fractions of a volt. Some experimenters have found that by either increasing or decreasing voltage slightly from the standard, a higher speed of overclock can be achieved with the system remaining stable. Some motherboards allow adjusting the voltage settings for the FSB, chipset, and memory components, allowing for even more control in overclocking situations.

My recommendation is to be careful when playing with voltages because you can damage the processor or other components in this manner. Even without changing voltage, overclocking with an adjustable bus speed motherboard is very easy and fairly rewarding. I do recommend you make sure you are using a high-quality board, good memory, and especially a good system chassis with additional cooling fans and a heavy-duty power supply. See Chapter 19, "Power Supplies," for more information on upgrading power supplies and chassis. Especially when overclocking, it is essential that the system components and the CPU remain properly cooled. Going a little bit overboard on the processor heatsink and adding extra cooling fans to the case never hurts and in many cases helps a great deal when hotrodding a system in this manner.

Cache Memory

As processor core speeds increased, memory speeds could not keep up. How could you run a processor faster than the memory from which you feed it without having performance suffer terribly? The answer was cache. In its simplest terms, *cache memory* is a high-speed memory buffer that temporarily stores data the processor needs, allowing the processor to retrieve that data faster than if it came from main memory. But there is one additional feature of a cache over a simple buffer, and that is intelligence. A cache is a buffer with a brain.

A buffer holds random data, usually on a first in, first out, or first in, last out basis. A cache, on the other hand, holds the data the processor is most likely to need in advance of it actually being needed. This enables the processor to continue working at either full speed or close to it without having to wait for the data to be retrieved from slower main memory. Cache memory is usually made up of static RAM (SRAM) memory integrated into the processor die, although older systems with cache also used chips installed on the motherboard.

▶▶   See "Cache Memory: SRAM," p. 514.

For the vast majority of desktop systems, there are two levels of processor/memory cache used in a modern PC: Level 1 (L1) and Level 2 (L2). Some processors also have Level 3 cache; however, this is rare. These caches and how they function are described in the following sections.

Internal Level 1 Cache

All modern processors starting with the 486 family include an integrated L1 cache and controller. The integrated L1 cache size varies from processor to processor, starting at 8KB for the original 486DX and now up to 32KB, 64KB, or more in the latest processors.

To understand the importance of cache, you need to know the relative speeds of processors and memory. The problem with this is that processor speed usually is expressed in MHz or GHz (millions or billions of cycles per second), whereas memory speeds are often expressed in nanoseconds (billionths of a second per cycle). Most newer types of memory express the speed in either MHz or in megabyte per second (MBps) bandwidth (throughput).

Both are really time- or frequency-based measurements, and a chart comparing them can be found in Table 6.3 in Chapter 6, "Memory." In this table, you will note that a 233MHz processor equates to 4.3-nanosecond cycling, which means you would need 4ns memory to keep pace with a 200MHz CPU. Also note that the motherboard of a 233MHz system typically runs at 66MHz, which corresponds to a speed of 15ns per cycle and requires 15ns memory to keep pace. Finally, note that 60ns main memory (common on many Pentium-class systems) equates to a clock speed of approximately 16MHz. So, a typical Pentium 233 system has a processor running at 233MHz (4.3ns per cycle), a motherboard running at 66MHz (15ns per cycle), and main memory running at 16MHz (60ns per cycle). This might seem like a rather dated example, but in a moment, you will see that the figures listed here make it easy for me to explain how cache memory works.

Because L1 cache is always built into the processor die, it runs at the full-core speed of the processor internally. By full-core speed, I mean this cache runs at the higher clock multiplied internal processor speed rather than the external motherboard speed. This cache basically is an area of very fast memory built into the processor and is used to hold some of the current working set of code and data. Cache memory can be accessed with no wait states because it is running at the same speed as the processor core.

Using cache memory reduces a traditional system bottleneck because system RAM is almost always much slower than the CPU; the performance difference between memory and CPU speed has become especially large in recent systems. Using cache memory prevents the processor from having to wait for code and data from much slower main memory, thus improving performance. Without the L1 cache, a processor would frequently be forced to wait until system memory caught up.

Cache is even more important in modern processors because it is often the only memory in the entire system that can truly keep up with the chip. Most modern processors are clock multiplied, which means they are running at a speed that is really a multiple of the motherboard into which they are plugged. The Core 2 Quad 2.4GHz, for example, runs at a multiple of 9 times the core motherboard clock speed of 266MHz. The main memory in such a system would normally run at either 667MHz or 800MHz. The only memory matching the 2.4GHz speed of the processor in such a system are the L1 and L2 caches built into the processor core. In this example, the Core 2 Quad 2.4GHz processor has 128KiB of integrated L1 cache (32KiB per core) and 8MiB of L2 (2MiB per core), all running at the full speed of the processor.

▶▶ See "Memory Module Speed," p. 557.

If the data the processor wants is already in the internal cache, the CPU does not have to wait. If the data is not in the cache, the CPU must fetch it from the Level 2 cache or (in less sophisticated system designs) from the system bus, meaning main memory directly.

How Cache Works

To learn how the L1 cache works, consider the following analogy.

This story involves a person (in this case you) eating food to act as the processor requesting and operating on data from memory. The kitchen where the food is prepared is the main system memory (typically DDR, DDR2, or DDR3 DIMMs). The cache controller is the waiter, and the L1 cache is the table at which you are seated.

Okay, here's the story. Say you start to eat at a particular restaurant every day at the same time. You come in, sit down, and order a hot dog. To keep this story proportionately accurate, let's say you normally eat at the rate of one bite (byte? <g>) every four seconds (233MHz = about 4ns cycling). It also takes 60 seconds for the kitchen to produce any given item that you order (60ns main memory).

So, when you first arrive, you sit down, order a hot dog, and you have to wait for 60 seconds for the food to be produced before you can begin eating. After the waiter brings the food, you start eating at your normal rate. Pretty quickly you finish the hot dog, so you call the waiter over and order a hamburger. Again you wait 60 seconds while the hamburger is being produced. When it arrives, you again begin eating at full speed. After you finish the hamburger, you order a plate of fries. Again you wait, and after it is delivered 60 seconds later, you eat it at full speed. Finally, you decide to finish the meal and order cheesecake for dessert. After another 60-second wait, you can eat cheesecake at full speed. Your overall eating experience consists of mostly a lot of waiting, followed by short bursts of actual eating at full speed.

After coming into the restaurant for two consecutive nights at exactly 6 p.m. and ordering the same items in the same order each time, on the third night the waiter begins to think, "I know this guy is going to be here at 6 p.m., order a hot dog, a hamburger, fries, and then cheesecake. Why don't I have these items prepared in advance and surprise him? Maybe I'll get a big tip." So you enter the restaurant and order a hot dog, and the waiter immediately puts it on your plate, with no waiting! You then proceed to finish the hot dog and right as you are about to request the hamburger, the waiter deposits one on your plate. The rest of the meal continues in the same fashion, and you eat the entire meal, taking a bite every four seconds, and never have to wait for the kitchen to prepare the food. Your overall eating experience this time consists of all eating, with no waiting for the food to be prepared, due primarily to the intelligence and thoughtfulness of your waiter.

This analogy exactly describes the function of the L1 cache in the processor. The L1 cache itself is the table that can contain one or more plates of food. Without a waiter, the space on the table is a simple food buffer. When stocked, you can eat until the buffer is empty, but nobody seems to be intelligently refilling it. The waiter is the cache controller who takes action and adds the intelligence to decide which dishes are to be placed on the table in advance of your needing them. Like the real cache controller, he uses his skills to literally guess which food you will require next, and if and when he guesses right, you never have to wait.

Let's now say on the fourth night you arrive exactly on time and start off with the usual hot dog. The waiter, by now really feeling confident, has the hot dog already prepared when you arrive, so there is no waiting.

Just as you finish the hot dog, and right as he is placing a hamburger on your plate, you say "Gee, I'd really like a bratwurst now; I didn't actually order this hamburger." The waiter guessed wrong, and the consequence is that this time you have to wait the full 60 seconds as the kitchen prepares your brat. This is known as a *cache miss*, in which the cache controller did not correctly fill the cache with the data the processor actually needed next. The result is waiting, or in the case of a sample 233MHz Pentium system, the system essentially throttles back to 16MHz (RAM speed) whenever a cache miss occurs.

According to Intel, the L1 cache in most of its processors has approximately a 90% hit ratio (some processors, such as the Pentium 4, are slightly higher). This means that the cache has the correct data 90% of the time, and consequently the processor runs at full speed (233MHz in this example) 90% of the time. However, 10% of the time the cache controller guesses wrong and the data has to be retrieved out of the significantly slower main memory, meaning the processor has to wait. This essentially throttles the system back to RAM speed, which in this example was 60ns or 16MHz.

In this analogy, the processor was 14 times faster than the main memory. Memory speeds have increased from 16MHz (60ns) to 333MHz (3.0ns) or faster in the latest systems, but processor speeds have also risen to 3GHz and beyond, so even in the latest systems, memory is still 7.5 or more times *slower* than the processor. Cache is what makes up the difference.

The main feature of L1 cache is that it has always been integrated into the processor core, where it runs at the same speed as the core. This, combined with the hit ratio of 90% or greater, makes L1 cache very important for system performance.

Level 2 Cache

To mitigate the dramatic slowdown every time an L1 cache miss occurs, a secondary (L2) cache is employed.

Using the restaurant analogy I used to explain L1 cache in the previous section, I'll equate the L2 cache to a cart of additional food items placed strategically in the restaurant such that the waiter can retrieve food from the cart in only 15 seconds (versus 60 seconds from the kitchen). In an actual Pentium class (Socket 7) system, the L2 cache is mounted on the motherboard, which means it runs at motherboard speed (66MHz, or 15ns in this example). Now, if you ask for an item the waiter did not bring in advance to your table, instead of making the long trek back to the kitchen to retrieve the food and bring it back to you 60 seconds later, he can first check the cart where he has placed additional items. If the requested item is there, he will return with it in only 15 seconds. The net effect in the real system is that instead of slowing down from 233MHz to 16MHz waiting for the data to come from the 60ns main memory, the system can instead retrieve the data from the 15ns (66MHz) L2 cache. The effect is that the system slows down from 233MHz to 66MHz.

All modern processors have integrated L2 cache that runs at the same speed as the processor core, which is also the same speed as the L1 cache. For the analogy to describe these newer chips, the waiter would simply place the cart right next to the table you were seated at in the restaurant. Then, if the food you desired wasn't on the table (L1 cache miss), it would merely take a longer reach over to the adjacent L2 cache (the cart, in this analogy) rather than a 15-second walk to the cart as with the older designs.

Level 3 Cache

A few processors, primarily those designed for very high-performance desktop operation or enterprise-level servers, contain a third level of cache known as *L3 cache*. Relatively few processors have L3 cache, but those that do access it at the same speed as L1 and L2 cache.

Extending the restaurant analogy I used to explain L1 and L2 caches, I'll equate L3 cache to another cart of additional food items placed in the restaurant next to the cart used to symbolize L2 cache. If the food item needed was not on the table (L1 cache miss) or on the first food cart (L2 cache miss), the waiter could then reach over to the second food cart to retrieve a necessary item.

Although Intel has used L3 caches with the first version of the Pentium 4 Extreme Edition processor and with the Itanium 2 and Xeon MP server processors, more recent desktop processors—including the dual-core Core 2 and Core 2 Extreme processors—use large L2 caches instead of a separate L3 cache. Future processors may eventually include L3 cache as a more standard feature.

Cache Performance and Design

Just as with the L1 cache, most L2 caches have a hit ratio also in the 90% range; therefore, if you look at the system as a whole, 90% of the time it will be running at full speed (233MHz in this example) by retrieving data out of the L1 cache. Ten percent of the time it will slow down to retrieve the data from the L2 cache. Ninety percent of the time the processor goes to the L2 cache, the data will be in the L2, and 10% of that time it will have to go to the slow main memory to get the data because of an L2 cache miss. So, by combining both caches, our sample system runs at full processor speed 90% of the time (233MHz in this case), at motherboard speed 9% (90% of 10%) of the time (66MHz in this case), and at RAM speed about 1% (10% of 10%) of the time (16MHz in this case). You can clearly see the importance of both the L1 and L2 caches; without them the system uses main memory more often, which is significantly slower than the processor.

This brings up other interesting points. If you could spend money doubling the performance of either the main memory (RAM) or the L2 cache, which would you improve? Considering that main memory is used directly only about 1% of the time, if you doubled performance there, you would double the speed of your system only 1% of the time! That doesn't sound like enough of an improvement to justify much expense. On the other hand, if you doubled L2 cache performance, you would be doubling system performance 9% of the time, a much greater improvement overall. I'd much rather improve L2 than RAM performance.

The processor and system designers at Intel and AMD know this and have devised methods of improving the performance of L2 cache. In Pentium (P5) class systems, the L2 cache usually was found on the motherboard and had to therefore run at motherboard speed. Intel made the first dramatic improvement by migrating the L2 cache from the motherboard directly into the processor and initially running it at the same speed as the main processor. The cache chips were made by Intel and mounted next to the main processor die in a single chip housing. This proved too expensive, so with the Pentium II, Intel began using cache chips from third-party suppliers such as Sony, Toshiba, NEC, Samsung, and others. Because these were supplied as complete packaged chips and not raw die, Intel mounted them on a circuit board alongside the processor. This is why the Pentium II was designed as a cartridge rather than what looked like a chip.

One problem was the speed of the available third-party cache chips. The fastest ones on the market were 3ns or higher, meaning 333MHz or less in speed. Because the processor was being driven in speed above that, in the Pentium II and initial Pentium III processors Intel had to run the L2 cache at half the processor speed because that is all the commercially available cache memory could handle. AMD followed suit with the Athlon processor, which had to drop L2 cache speed even further in some models to two-fifths or one-third the main CPU speed to keep the cache memory speed less than the 333MHz commercially available chips.

Then a breakthrough occurred, which first appeared in Celeron processors 300A and above. These had 128KB of L2 cache, but no external chips were used. Instead, the L2 cache had been integrated directly into the processor core just like the L1. Consequently, both the L1 and L2 caches now would run at full processor speed, and more importantly scale up in speed as the processor speeds increased in the future. In the newer Pentium III, as well as all the Xeon and Celeron processors, the L2 cache runs at full processor core speed, which means there is no waiting or slowing down after an L1 cache miss. AMD also achieved full-core speed on-die cache in its later Athlon and Duron chips. Using on-die cache improves performance dramatically because 9% of the time the system would be using the L2, it would now remain at full speed instead of slowing down to one-half or less the processor speed or, even worse, slow down to motherboard speed as in Socket 7 designs. Another benefit of on-die L2 cache is cost, which is less because now fewer parts are involved.

Let's revisit the restaurant analogy using a 3.6GHz processor. You would now be taking a bite every half second (3.6GHz = 0.28ns cycling). The L1 cache would also be running at that speed, so you could eat anything on your table at that same rate (the table = L1 cache). The real jump in speed comes when you want something that isn't already on the table (L1 cache miss), in which case the waiter reaches over to the cart (which is now directly adjacent to the table) and nine out of ten times is able to find the food you want in just over one-quarter second (L2 speed = 3.6GHz or 0.28ns cycling). In this system, you would run at 3.6GHz 99% of the time (L1 and L2 hit ratios combined) and slow down to RAM speed (wait for the kitchen) only 1% of the time, as before. With faster memory running at 800MHz (1.25ns), you would have to wait only 1.25 seconds for the food to come from the kitchen. If only restaurant performance would increase at the same rate processor performance has!

Cache Organization

You know that cache stores copies of data from various main memory addresses. Because the cache cannot hold copies of the data from all the addresses in main memory simultaneously, there has to be a way to know which addresses are currently copied into the cache so that, if we need data from those addresses, it can be read from the cache rather than from the main memory. This function is performed by Tag RAM, which is additional memory in the cache that holds an index of the addresses that are copied into the cache. Each line of cache memory has a corresponding address tag that stores the main memory address of the data currently copied into that particular cache line. If data from a particular main memory address is needed, the cache controller can quickly search the address tags to see whether the requested address is currently being stored in the cache (a hit) or not (a miss). If the data is there, it can be read from the faster cache; if it isn't, it has to be read from the much slower main memory.

Various ways of organizing or mapping the tags affect how cache works. A cache can be mapped as fully associative, direct-mapped, or set associative.

In a fully associative mapped cache, when a request is made for data from a specific main memory address, the address is compared against all the address tag entries in the cache tag RAM. If the requested main memory address is found in the tag (a *hit*), the corresponding location in the cache is returned. If the requested address is not found in the address tag entries, a *miss* occurs and the data must be retrieved from the main memory address instead of the cache.

In a direct-mapped cache, specific main memory addresses are preassigned to specific line locations in the cache where they will be stored. Therefore, the tag RAM can use fewer bits because when you know which main memory address you want, only one address tag needs to be checked and each tag needs to store only the possible addresses a given line can contain. This also results in faster operation because only one tag address needs to be checked for a given memory address.

A set associative cache is a modified direct-mapped cache. A direct-mapped cache has only one set of memory associations, meaning a given memory address can be mapped into (or associated with) only a specific given cache line location. A two-way set associative cache has two sets, so that a given memory location can be in one of two locations. A four-way set associative cache can store a given memory address into four different cache line locations (or sets). By increasing the set associativity, the chance of finding a value increases; however, it takes a little longer because more tag addresses must be checked when searching for a specific location in the cache. In essence, each set in an *n*-way set associative cache is a subcache that has associations with each main memory address. As the number of subcaches or sets increases, eventually the cache becomes fully associative—a situation in which any memory address can be stored in any cache line location. In that case, an *n*-way set associative cache is a compromise between a fully associative cache and a direct-mapped cache.

In general, a direct-mapped cache is the fastest at locating and retrieving data from the cache because it has to look at only one specific tag address for a given memory address. However, it also results in more misses overall than the other designs. A fully associative cache offers the highest hit ratio but is the slowest at locating and retrieving the data because it has many more address tags to check through. An *n*-way set associative cache is a compromise between optimizing cache speed and hit ratio, but the more associativity there is, the more hardware (tag bits, comparator circuits, and so on) is required, making the cache more expensive. Obviously, cache design is a series of tradeoffs, and what works best in one instance might not work best in another. Multitasking environments such as Windows are good examples of environments in which the processor needs to operate on different areas of memory simultaneously and in which an *n*-way cache can improve performance.

The contents of the cache must always be in sync with the contents of main memory to ensure that the processor is working with current data. For this reason, the internal cache in the 486 family was a *write-through* cache. Write-through means that when the processor writes information out to the cache, that information is automatically written through to main memory as well.

By comparison, Pentium and later chips have an internal write-back cache, which means that both reads and writes are cached, further improving performance.

Another feature of improved cache designs is that they are *nonblocking*. This is a technique for reducing or hiding memory delays by exploiting the overlap of processor operations with data accesses. A nonblocking cache enables program execution to proceed concurrently with cache misses as long as certain dependency constraints are observed. In other words, the cache can handle a cache miss much better and enable the processor to continue doing something nondependent on the missing data.

The cache controller built into the processor also is responsible for watching the memory bus when alternative processors, known as *bus masters*, are in control of the system. This process of watching the bus is referred to as *bus snooping*. If a bus master device writes to an area of memory that also is stored in the processor cache currently, the cache contents and memory no longer agree. The cache controller then marks this data as invalid and reloads the cache during the next memory access, preserving the integrity of the system.

All PC processor designs that support cache memory include a feature known as a *translation lookaside buffer (TLB)* to improve recovery from cache misses. The TLB is a table inside the processor that stores information about the location of recently accessed memory addresses. The TLB speeds up the translation of virtual addresses to physical memory addresses. To improve TLB performance, several recent processors have increased the number of entries in the TLB, as AMD did when it moved from the Athlon Thunderbird core to the Palomino core. Pentium 4 processors that support HT Technology have a separate instruction TLB (iTLB) for each virtual processor thread.

▶▶   See "Hyper-Threading Technology," p. 84.

As clock speeds increase, cycle time decreases. Newer systems don't use cache on the motherboard any longer because the faster system memory used in modern systems can keep up with the motherboard speed. Modern processors all integrate the L2 cache into the processor die just like the L1 cache. This enables the L2 to run at full-core speed because it is now a part of the core. Cache speed is always more important than size. The rule is that a smaller but faster cache is always better than a slower but bigger cache. Table 3.14 illustrates the need for and function of L1 (internal) and L2 (external) caches in modern systems.

Table 3.14   CPU Speeds Relative to Cache, RAM, and Motherboard

CPU Type	Pentium	Pentium Pro	Pentium II	AMD K6-2	AMD K6-3
CPU speed	233MHz	200MHz	450MHz	550MHz	450MHz
L1 cache Speed	4.3ns (233MHz)	5.0ns (200MHz)	2.2ns (450MHz)	1.8ns (550MHz)	2.2ns (450MHz)
L1 cache size	16K	32K	32K	64K	64K
L2 cache type	external	on-chip	on-chip	External	on-die
CPU/L2 speed ratio	—	1/1	1/2	—	1/1
L2 cache speed	15ns (66MHz)	5ns (200MHz)	4.4ns (225MHz)	10ns (100MHz)	2.2ns (450MHz)
L2 cache size	—	256K	512K	—	256K
CPU bus bandwidth	533MBps	533MBps	800MBps	800MBps	800MBps
Memory bus speed	60ns (16MHz)	60ns (16MHz)	10ns (100MHz)	10ns (100MHz)	10ns (100MHz)

As you can see, having two levels of cache between the very fast CPU and the much slower main memory helps minimize any wait states the processor might have to endure, especially those with the on-die L2. This enables the processor to keep working closer to its true speed.

Processor Features

As new processors are introduced, new features are continually added to their architectures to help improve everything from performance in specific types of applications to the reliability of the CPU as a whole. The next few sections take a look at some of these technologies, including System Management Mode (SMM), Superscalar Execution, MMX, SSE, 3DNow!, HT Technology, and multi-core processing.

System Management Mode (SMM)

Spurred on initially by the need for more robust power management capabilities in mobile computers, Intel and AMD began adding *System Management Mode* (SMM) to its processors during the early '90s. SMM is a special-purpose operating mode provided for handling low-level system power management and hardware control functions. SMM offers an isolated software environment that is transparent to the operating system or applications software, and is intended for use by system BIOS or low-level driver code.

SMM was first introduced as part of the Intel 386SL mobile processor in Oct. 1990. SMM later appeared as part of the 486SL processor in Nov. 1992, and in the entire 486 line starting in June 1993. SMM was notably absent from the first Pentium processors when they were released in March 1993; however, SMM was included in all 75MHz and faster Pentium processors released on or after October 1994. AMD added SMM to their enhanced Am486 and K5 processors around that time as well. All other Intel and AMD x86-based processors introduced since that time have incorporated SMM as well.

SMM is invoked by signaling a special interrupt pin on the processor, which generates a System Management Interrupt (SMI), the highest priority nonmaskable interrupt available. When SMM starts, the context or state of the processor and currently running programs are saved. Then the processor switches to a separate dedicated address space and executes the SMM code, which runs transparently to the interrupted program as well as any other software on the system. Once the SMM task is

Pentium III	Athlon	Athlon XP	Pentium 4	Athlon 64 X2	Core 2 Duo/Quad
1.4GHz	1.4GHz	2.2GHz	3.8GHz	3GHz	2.93GHz
0.71ns (1.4GHz)	0.71ns (1.4GHz)	0.45ns (2.2GHz)	0.26ns (3.8GHz)	0.33ns (3GHz)	0.34ns (2.93GHz)
32K	128K	128K	20K	256K	64K/128K
on-die	on-die	on-die	on-die	on-die	on-die
1/1	1/1	1/1	1/1	1/1	1/1
0.71ns (1.4GHz)	0.71ns (1.4GHz)	0.45ns (2.2GHz)	0.26ns (3.8GHz)	0.33ns (3GHz)	0.34ns (2.93GHz)
512K	256K	512K	2M	2M	4M/8M
1,066MBps	2,133MBps	3,200MBps	6,400MBps	4,000MBps	8,533MBps
7.5ns (133MHz)	3.8ns (266MHz)	2.5ns (400MHz)	1.25ns (800MHz)	2.5ns (400MHz)	0.94ns (1066MHz)

complete, a resume instruction restores the previously saved context or state of the processor and programs, and the processor resumes running exactly where it left off.

While initially used mainly for power management, SMM was designed to be used by any low-level system functions that need to function independent of the OS and other software on the system. In modern systems, this includes the following:

- ACPI and APM power management functions
- USB legacy (keyboard and mouse) support
- USB boot (drive emulation)
- Password and security functions
- Thermal monitoring
- Fan speed monitoring
- Reading/writing CMOS RAM
- BIOS updating
- Logging memory ECC errors
- Logging hardware errors besides memory
- Wake and Alert functions such as Wake On Lan (WOL)

One example of SMM in operation can be seen when the system tries to access a peripheral device that had been previously powered down to save energy. For example, say that a program makes a request to read a file on a hard drive, but the drive had previously spun down to save energy. Upon access, the host adapter generates a System Management Interrupt (SMI) to invoke System Management Mode (SMM). The SMM software then issues commands to spin up the drive and make it ready. Then SMM returns control to the OS, and the file load continues as if the drive had been spinning all along.

Superscalar Execution

The fifth-generation Pentium and newer processors feature multiple internal instruction execution pipelines, which enable them to execute multiple instructions at the same time. The 486 and all preceding chips can perform only a single instruction at a time. Intel calls the capability to execute more than one instruction at a time *superscalar* technology. This technology provides additional performance compared with the 486.

▶▶   See "Pentium Processors," p. 138.

Superscalar architecture usually is associated with high-output Reduced Instruction Set Computer (RISC) chips. A RISC chip has a less complicated instruction set with fewer and simpler instructions. Although each instruction accomplishes less, overall the clock speed can be higher, which can usually increase performance. The Pentium is one of the first Complex Instruction Set Computer (CISC) chips to be considered superscalar. A CISC chip uses a richer, fuller-featured instruction set, which has more complicated instructions. As an example, say you wanted to instruct a robot to screw in a light bulb. Using CISC instructions, you would say

1. Pick up the bulb.
2. Insert it into the socket.
3. Rotate clockwise until tight.

Using RISC instructions, you would say something more along the lines of

1. Lower hand.
2. Grasp bulb.
3. Raise hand.
4. Insert bulb into socket.
5. Rotate clockwise one turn.
6. Is bulb tight? If not, repeat step 5.
7. End.

Overall, many more RISC instructions are required to do the job because each instruction is simpler (reduced) and does less. The advantage is that there are fewer overall commands the robot (or processor) has to deal with and it can execute the individual commands more quickly, and thus in many cases execute the complete task (or program) more quickly as well. The debate goes on whether RISC or CISC is really better, but in reality there is no such thing as a pure RISC or CISC chip—it is all just a matter of definition, and the lines are somewhat arbitrary.

Intel and compatible processors have generally been regarded as CISC chips, although the fifth- and sixth-generation versions have many RISC attributes and internally break CISC instructions down into RISC versions.

MMX Technology

MMX technology was originally named for *multimedia extensions*, or *matrix math extensions*, depending on whom you ask. Intel officially states that it is actually not an abbreviation and stands for nothing other than the letters MMX (not being an abbreviation was apparently required so that the letters could be trademarked); however, the internal origins are probably one of the preceding. MMX technology was introduced in the later fifth-generation Pentium processors as a kind of add-on that improves video compression/decompression, image manipulation, encryption, and I/O processing—all of which are used in a variety of today's software.

MMX consists of two main processor architectural improvements. The first is very basic; all MMX chips have a larger internal L1 cache than their non-MMX counterparts. This improves the performance of any and all software running on the chip, regardless of whether it actually uses the MMX-specific instructions.

The other part of MMX is that it extends the processor instruction set with 57 new commands or instructions, as well as a new instruction capability called single instruction, multiple data (SIMD).

Modern multimedia and communication applications often use repetitive loops that, while occupying 10% or less of the overall application code, can account for up to 90% of the execution time. SIMD enables one instruction to perform the same function on multiple pieces of data, similar to a teacher telling an entire class to "sit down," rather than addressing each student one at a time. SIMD enables the chip to reduce processor-intensive loops common with video, audio, graphics, and animation.

Intel also added 57 new instructions specifically designed to manipulate and process video, audio, and graphical data more efficiently. These instructions are oriented to the *highly parallel* and often repetitive sequences frequently found in multimedia operations. *Highly parallel* refers to the fact that the same processing is done on many data points, such as when modifying a graphic image. The main drawbacks to MMX were that it worked only on integer values and used the floating-point unit for processing, so time was lost when a shift to floating-point operations was necessary. These drawbacks were corrected in the additions to MMX from Intel and AMD.

Intel licensed the MMX capabilities to competitors such as AMD and Cyrix, who were then able to upgrade their own Intel-compatible processors with MMX technology.

SSE, SSE2, SSE3 and SSSE3

In February 1999, Intel introduced the Pentium III processor and included in that processor an update to MMX called Streaming SIMD Extensions (SSE). These were also called *Katmai New Instructions (KNI)* up until their debut because they were originally included on the Katmai processor, which was the codename for the Pentium III. The Celeron 533A and faster Celeron processors based on the Pentium III core also support SSE instructions. The earlier Pentium II and Celeron 533 and lower (based on the Pentium II core) do not support SSE.

SSE includes 70 new instructions for graphics and sound processing over what MMX provided. SSE is similar to MMX; in fact, besides being called KNI, SSE was also called MMX-2 by some before it was released. In addition to adding more MMX-style instructions, the SSE instructions allow for floating-point calculations and now use a separate unit within the processor instead of sharing the standard floating-point unit as MMX did.

SSE2 was introduced in November 2000, along with the Pentium 4 processor, and adds 144 additional SIMD instructions. SSE2 also includes all the previous MMX and SSE instructions.

SSE3 was introduced in February 2004, along with the Pentium 4 Prescott processor, and adds 13 new SIMD instructions to improve complex math, graphics, video encoding, and thread synchronization. SSE3 also includes all the previous MMX, SSE, and SSE2 instructions.

SSSE3 (Supplemental SSE3) was introduced in June 2006 in the Xeon 5100 series server processors, and in July 2006 in the Core 2 processors. SSSE3 adds 32 new SIMD instructions to SSE3. In addition, Intel has pre-announced SSE4, which will contain another 50 new SIMD instructions.

The Streaming SIMD Extensions consist of new instructions, including SIMD floating-point, additional SIMD integer, and cacheability control instructions. Some of the technologies that benefit from the Streaming SIMD Extensions include advanced imaging, 3D video, streaming audio and video (DVD playback), and speech-recognition applications. The benefits of SSE include the following:

- Higher resolution and higher quality image viewing and manipulation for graphics software
- High-quality audio, MPEG2 video, and simultaneous MPEG2 encoding and decoding for multimedia applications
- Reduced CPU utilization for speech recognition, as well as higher accuracy and faster response times when running speech-recognition software

The SSE*x* instructions are particularly useful with MPEG2 decoding, which is the standard scheme used on DVD video discs. SSE-equipped processors should therefore be more capable of performing MPEG2 decoding in software at full speed without requiring an additional hardware MPEG2 decoder card. SSE-equipped processors are much better and faster than previous processors when it comes to speech recognition, as well.

One of the main benefits of SSE over plain MMX is that it supports single-precision floating-point SIMD operations, which have posed a bottleneck in the 3D graphics processing. Just as with plain MMX, SIMD enables multiple operations to be performed per processor instruction. Specifically, SSE supports up to four floating-point operations per cycle; that is, a single instruction can operate on four pieces of data simultaneously. SSE floating-point instructions can be mixed with MMX instructions with no performance penalties. SSE also supports data *prefetching*, which is a mechanism for reading data into the cache before it is actually called for.

Note that for any of the SSE instructions to be beneficial, they must be encoded in the software you are using, so SSE-aware applications must be used to see the benefits. Most software companies writing graphics- and sound-related software today have updated those applications to be SSE aware and use the features of SSE. For example, high-powered graphics applications such as Adobe Photoshop support SSE instructions for higher performance on processors equipped with SSE. Microsoft included support for SSE in its DirectX 6.1 and later video and sound drivers, which are included with Windows 98 and newer.

Each of the successive sets of SIMD instructions builds on the previous set; for example, processors that support SSE4 also support all the previous SSE instructions all the way back to MMX.

3DNow!, Enhanced 3DNow!, and Professional 3DNow!

3DNow! technology was originally introduced as AMD's alternative to the SSE instructions in the Intel processors. Actually, 3DNow! was first introduced in the K6 series before Intel released SSE in the Pentium III, and then AMD added Enhanced 3DNow! to the Athlon and Duron processors. The latest version, Professional 3DNow!, was introduced in the first Athlon XP processors. AMD licensed MMX from Intel, and all its K6 series, Athlon, Duron, and later processors include full MMX instruction support. Not wanting to additionally license the SSE instructions being developed by Intel, AMD first came up with a different set of extensions beyond MMX called 3DNow!. Introduced in May 1998 in the K6-2 processor and enhanced when the Athlon was introduced in June 1999, 3DNow! and Enhanced 3DNow! are sets of instructions that extend the multimedia capabilities of the AMD chips beyond MMX. This enables greater performance for 3D graphics, multimedia, and other floating-point-intensive PC applications.

3DNow! technology is a set of 21 instructions that uses SIMD techniques to operate on arrays of data rather than single elements. Enhanced 3DNow! adds 24 more instructions (19 SSE and five DSP/communications instructions) to the original 21, for a total of 45 new instructions. Positioned as an extension to MMX technology, 3DNow! is similar to the SSE found in the Pentium III and Celeron processors from Intel. According to AMD, 3DNow! provides approximately the same level of improvement to MMX as did SSE, but in fewer instructions with less complexity. Although similar in capability, they are not compatible at the instruction level, so software specifically written to support SSE does not support 3DNow!, and vice versa.

Just as with SSE, 3DNow! also supports single-precision floating-point SIMD operations and enables up to four floating-point operations per cycle. 3DNow! floating-point instructions can be mixed with MMX instructions with no performance penalties. 3DNow! also supports data prefetching.

Also like SSE, 3DNow! is well supported by software, including Windows 9x and all newer Microsoft operating systems; however, 3DNow!-specific support is no longer an issue if you are using an Athlon XP or newer processors because they support SSE through their support of 3DNow! Professional.

The latest version of 3DNow!, 3DNow! Professional, added 51 SSE commands to 3DNow! Enhanced, meaning that 3DNow! Professional supports all SSE commands. This in turn means that current AMD chips have SSE capability at a minimum. AMD added SSE2 support in the Athlon 64, Athlon 64FX, and Opteron 64-bit processors, and included SSE3 in the 0.09-micron versions of the Athlon 64 and all versions of the dual-core Athlon 64 X2. Future AMD processors are likely to add SSE4 as well.

Dynamic Execution

First used in the P6 (or sixth-generation) processors, dynamic execution enables the processor to execute more instructions on parallel, so tasks are completed more quickly. This technology innovation is composed of three main elements:

- **Multiple branch prediction**—Predicts the flow of the program through several branches
- **Dataflow analysis**—Schedules instructions to be executed when ready, independent of their order in the original program
- **Speculative execution**—Increases the rate of execution by looking ahead of the program counter and executing instructions that are likely to be necessary

Branch Prediction

Branch prediction is a feature formerly found only in high-end mainframe processors. It enables the processor to keep the instruction pipeline full while running at a high rate of speed. A special fetch/decode unit in the processor uses a highly optimized branch-prediction algorithm to predict the direction and outcome of the instructions being executed through multiple levels of branches, calls, and returns. It is similar to a chess player working out multiple strategies in advance of game play by predicting the opponent's strategy several moves into the future. By predicting the instruction outcome in advance, the instructions can be executed with no waiting.

Dataflow Analysis

Dataflow analysis studies the flow of data through the processor to detect any opportunities for out-of-order instruction execution. A special dispatch/execute unit in the processor monitors many instructions and can execute these instructions in an order that optimizes the use of the multiple superscalar execution units. The resulting out-of-order execution of instructions can keep the execution units busy even when cache misses and other data-dependent instructions might otherwise hold things up.

Speculative Execution

Speculative execution is the processor's capability to execute instructions in advance of the actual program counter. The processor's dispatch/execute unit uses dataflow analysis to execute all available instructions in the instruction pool and store the results in temporary registers. A retirement unit then searches the instruction pool for completed instructions that are no longer data dependent on other instructions to run or which have unresolved branch predictions. If any such completed instructions are found, the results are committed to memory by the retirement unit or the appropriate standard Intel architecture in the order they were originally issued. They are then retired from the pool.

Dynamic execution essentially removes the constraint and dependency on linear instruction sequencing. By promoting out-of-order instruction execution, it can keep the instruction units working rather than waiting for data from memory. Even though instructions can be predicted and executed out of order, the results are committed in the original order so as not to disrupt or change program flow. This enables the P6 to run existing Intel architecture software exactly as the P5 (Pentium) and previous processors did—just a whole lot more quickly!

Dual Independent Bus Architecture

The Dual Independent Bus (DIB) architecture was first implemented in the sixth-generation processors from Intel and AMD. DIB was created to improve processor bus bandwidth and performance. Having two (dual) independent data I/O buses enables the processor to access data from either of its buses simultaneously and in parallel, rather than in a singular sequential manner (as in a single-bus system). The main (often called *front-side*) processor bus is the interface between the processor and the motherboard or chipset. The second (back-side) bus in a processor with DIB is used for the L2 cache, enabling it to run at much greater speeds than if it were to share the main processor bus.

Two buses make up the DIB architecture: the L2 cache bus and the main CPU bus, often called *FSB (front-side bus)*. The P6 class processors from the Pentium Pro to the Core 2, and Athlon 64 processors can use both buses simultaneously, eliminating a bottleneck there. The dual bus architecture enables the L2 cache of the newer processors to run at full speed inside the processor core on an independent bus, leaving the main CPU bus (FSB) to handle normal data flowing in and out of the chip. The two buses run at different speeds. The front-side bus or main CPU bus is coupled to the speed of the motherboard, whereas the back-side or L2 cache bus is coupled to the speed of the processor core. As the frequency of processors increases, so does the speed of the L2 cache.

The key to implementing DIB was to move the L2 cache memory off the motherboard and into the processor package. L1 cache always has been a direct part of the processor die, but L2 was larger and originally had to be external. By moving the L2 cache into the processor, the L2 cache could run at speeds more like the L1 cache, much faster than the motherboard or processor bus.

DIB also enables the system bus to perform multiple simultaneous transactions (instead of singular sequential transactions), accelerating the flow of information within the system and boosting performance. Overall, DIB architecture offers up to three times the bandwidth performance over a single-bus architecture processor.

Hyper-Threading Technology

Computers with two or more physical processors have long had a performance advantage over single-processor computers when the operating system supported multiple processors, as is the case with Windows NT 4.0, 2000, XP Professional, Vista (Business, Enterprise, and Ultimate editions), and Linux. However, dual-processor motherboards and systems have always been more expensive than otherwise-comparable single processor systems, and upgrading a dual-processor-capable system to dual-processor status can be difficult because of the need to match processor speeds and specifications. Intel's Hyper-Threading (HT) Technology allows a single processor to handle two independent sets of instructions at the same time. In essence, HT Technology converts a single physical processor into two virtual processors.

Intel originally introduced HT Technology in its line of Xeon processors for servers in March 2002. HT Technology enables multiprocessor servers to act as if they had twice as many processors installed. HT Technology was introduced on Xeon workstation-class processors with a 533MHz system bus and later found its way into standard desktop PC processors starting with the Pentium 4 3.06GHz processor in November 2002. HT Technology is also present in all Pentium 4 processors with 800MHz CPU bus speed (2.4GHz up through 3.8GHz) as well as the Pentium 4 Extreme Edition and the dual-core Pentium Extreme Edition. HT Technology predates true dual-core processors, and neither the dual-core Pentium D nor the Core 2 includes HT Technology because those processors have multiple physical cores instead.

How Hyper-Threading Works

Internally, an HT-enabled processor has two sets of general-purpose registers, control registers, and other architecture components, but both logical processors share the same cache, execution units, and buses. During operations, each logical processor handles a single thread (see Figure 3.2).

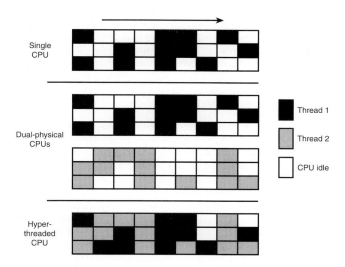

Figure 3.2   A processor with HT Technology enabled can fill otherwise-idle time with a second process, improving multitasking and performance of multithreading single applications.

Although the sharing of some processor components means that the overall speed of an HT-enabled system isn't as high as a true dual-processor system would be, speed increases of 25% or more are possible when multiple applications or a single multithreaded application is being run.

Hyper-Threading Requirements

The first HT-enabled processor was the Intel Pentium 4 3.06GHz. All 3.06GHz and faster Pentium 4 models support HT Technology. However, an HT-enabled P4 processor by itself can't bring the benefits of HT Technology to your system. You also need the following:

- **A compatible motherboard (chipset)**—It might need a BIOS upgrade.
- **BIOS support to enable/disable HT Technology**—If your operating system doesn't support HT Technology, you should disable this feature. Application performance varies (some faster, some slower) when HT Technology is enabled. If this is a matter of concern, you should

perform application-based benchmarks with HT Technology enabled and disabled to determine whether your application mix will benefit from using HT Technology.

■ **A compatible operating system such as Windows XP or Vista**—When hyper-threading is enabled, the Device Manager shows two processors, even though only one physical processor is present.

Although Windows NT 4.0 and Windows 2000 were designed to use multiple physical processors, HT Technology requires specific operating system optimizations to work correctly. Linux distributions based on kernel 2.4.18 and higher also support HT Technology.

Multicore Technology

HT Technology *simulates* two processors in a single physical unit. If two simulated processors are good, having two or more *real* processors would be better. A multicore processor, as the name implies, actually contains two or more processor cores in a single processor package. From outward appearances it still looks like a single processor and is considered as such for Windows licensing purposes, but inside there can be two, four, or even more processor cores. A multicore processor provides virtually all the advantages of having multiple separate physical processors, all at a much lower cost. In addition, a multicore processor can avoid problems with OS licensing. For example, even though Windows Vista Home Basic and Home Premium as well as XP Home only support a single processor, if that is a quad-core unit, all 4 cores will be fully supported and operational. Likewise, Vista Business and Ultimate as well as XP Pro support up to two processors; if both are quad-core units, then all 8 cores will be fully supported and operational.

Both AMD and Intel introduced dual-core x86-compatible desktop processors in 2005. AMD's initial entry—the Athlon 64 X2—can be installed in most Socket 939 motherboards designed for the original single-core Athlon 64 or Athlon 64 FX processors. A BIOS upgrade might be necessary in some situations. AMD also introduced dual-core versions of the Opteron workstation and server processor in 2005. Intel's first dual-core processors—the Pentium Extreme Edition and the Pentium D—use the same Socket 775 as the previous Pentium 4 models. However, they require motherboards using chipsets that support dual-core operation. Newer dual-core processors from Intel include the Core 2 Duo, which still uses Socket 775, albeit with updated chipsets and motherboards. AMD has introduced Socket AM2 versions of the Athlon 64 FX dual-core, Athlon 64 X2 and Athlon X2, with support for DDR2 memory, and Phenom X2 processors designed for Socket AM3, with both DDR2 and DDR3 memory support. Intel introduced the first quad-core processor in November 2006, called the Core 2 Extreme QX and Core 2 Quad. AMD subsequently introduced its first quad-core processor, called the Phenom X4.

▶▶ For more information, see "Multicore Processors," p. 219.

Multicore CPU Benefits

No matter how fast a conventional single-core processor operates or how much RAM is installed in a system, it must ensure that each program and process that is running is properly serviced. As more and more programs are opened, the amount of time the processor can devote to each program is reduced. The result is that system performance declines. Workstations and servers have long enjoyed the benefits of multiple processors, including better responsiveness when multitasking, faster performance in single multithreaded applications, and better overall throughput for both business and creativity applications (in terms of instructions processed per clock cycle).

However, the high cost of multiprocessor motherboards and multiple processors has kept most desktop computer users from enjoying the same benefits.

Note

A multithreaded application can run different parts of the program, known as *threads*, at the same time in the same address space. They can share code and data. A multithreaded program runs faster on a multicore processor or an Intel processor with HT Technology enabled than on a single-core or non-HT processor.

If you use multiple applications at the same time, such as email, web browsers, office suite components (such as word processors and spreadsheets), graphics editors, and so forth, you should consider the latest development in processor technology: a multicore processor. The multicore processors introduced by Intel and AMD are designed to bring the benefits of multiprocessor operation to desktop systems by placing two or more processor cores in a single physical processor.

Multicore processors include two processor cores in the same physical package, providing virtually all the advantages of a multiple-processor computer at a cost lower than that of two matched processors. Unlike Intel's HT Technology—which simulates two processors in a single physical unit—dual-core processors do not need specific application support to improve performance. Multiple processor cores provide more time to service each running application or application thread, providing faster performance in a multitasking environment.

Multicore processors are designed for users who frequently multitask (run multiple programs at the same time) or who use multithreaded applications. That pretty much describes all PC users these days. Figure 3.3 illustrates how a dual-core processor handles multiple applications for faster performance.

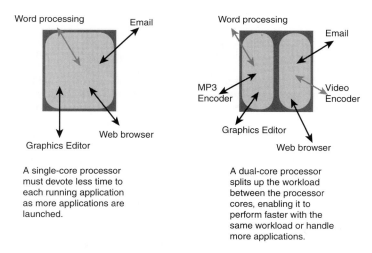

A single-core processor must devote less time to each running application as more applications are launched.

A dual-core processor splits up the workload between the processor cores, enabling it to perform faster with the same workload or handle more applications.

Figure 3.3   How a single-core processor (left) and a dual-core processor (right) handle multitasking.

It's important to realize that a multicore processor does not improve single-task performance. If you play non-multithreaded 3D games on your PC, for example, it's very likely that's all you're doing at the time, so no multitasking is taking place that would take advantage of a dual-core CPU. Fortunately more and more software (including games) is designed to be multithreaded, which will automatically take advantage of multicore processors by breaking the program up into multiple threads, which can be divided among the available CPU cores.

Processor Manufacturing

Processors are manufactured primarily from silicon, the second most common element on the planet (only the element oxygen is more common). Silicon is the primary ingredient in beach sand; however, in that form it isn't pure enough to be used in chips.

The manner in which silicon is formed into chips is a lengthy process that starts by growing pure silicon crystals via what is called the Czochralski method (named after the inventor of the process). In this method, electric arc furnaces transform the raw materials (primarily quartz rock that is mined) into metallurgical-grade silicon. Then to further weed out impurities, the silicon is converted to a liquid, distilled, and then redeposited in the form of semiconductor-grade rods, which are 99.999999% pure. These rods are then mechanically broken up into chunks and packed into quartz crucibles, which are loaded into electric crystal pulling ovens. There the silicon chunks are melted at more than 2,500° Fahrenheit. To prevent impurities, the ovens usually are mounted on very thick concrete cubes—often on a suspension to prevent any vibration, which would damage the crystal as it forms.

After the silicon is melted, a small seed crystal is inserted into the molten silicon and slowly rotated (see Figure 3.4). As the seed is pulled out of the molten silicon, some of the silicon sticks to the seed and hardens in the same crystal structure as the seed. By carefully controlling the pulling speed (10–40 millimeters per hour) and temperature (approximately 2,500°F), the crystal grows with a narrow neck that then widens into the full desired diameter. Depending on the chips being made, each ingot is 200mm (approximately 8") or 300mm (12") in diameter and more than 5 feet long, weighing hundreds of pounds.

The ingot is then ground into a perfect 200mm- (8") or 300mm-diameter (12") cylinder, with a small, flat cut on one side for positioning accuracy and handling. Each ingot is then cut with a high-precision diamond saw into more than a thousand circular wafers, each less than a millimeter thick (see Figure 3.5). Each wafer is then polished to a mirror-smooth surface.

Chips are manufactured from the wafers using a process called *photolithography*. Through this photographic process, transistors and circuit and signal pathways are created in semiconductors by depositing different layers of various materials on the chip, one after the other. Where two specific circuits intersect, a transistor or switch can be formed.

The photolithographic process starts when an insulating layer of silicon dioxide is grown on the wafer through a vapor deposition process. Then a coating of photoresist material is applied, and an image of that layer of the chip is projected through a mask onto the now light-sensitive surface.

Doping is the term used to describe chemical impurities added to silicon (which is naturally a nonconductor), creating a material with semiconductor properties. The projector uses a specially created mask, which is essentially a negative of that layer of the chip etched in chrome on a quartz plate. Modern processors have 20 or more layers of material deposited and partially etched away (each requiring a mask) and up to six or more layers of metal interconnects.

As the light passes through a mask, the light is focused on the wafer surface, exposing the photoresist with the image of that layer of the chip. Each individual chip image is called a *die*. A device called a *stepper* then moves the wafer over a little bit, and the same mask is used to imprint another chip die immediately next to the previous one. After the entire wafer is imprinted with a layer of material and photoresist, a caustic solution washes away the areas where the light struck the photoresist, leaving the mask imprints of the individual chip circuit elements and pathways. Then, another layer of semiconductor material is deposited on the wafer with more photoresist on top, and the next mask is used to expose and then etch the next layer of circuitry. Using this method, the layers and components of each chip are built one on top of the other until the chips are completed.

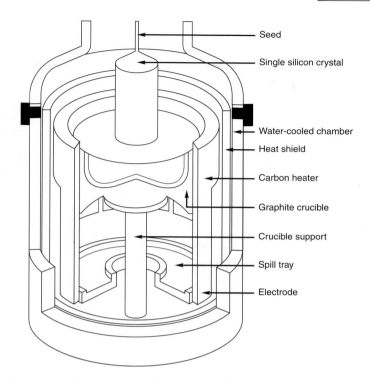

Figure 3.4   Growing a pure silicon ingot in a high-pressure, high-temperature oven.

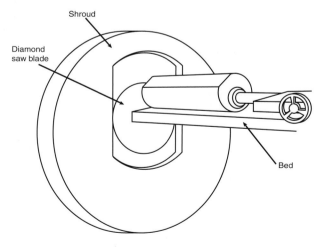

Figure 3.5   Slicing a silicon ingot into wafers with a diamond saw.

Some of the masks are used to add the *metallization* layers, which are the metal interconnects used to tie all the individual transistors and other components together. Most older chips use aluminum interconnects, although during 2002 many moved to copper. The first commercial PC processor chip to use copper was the 0.18-micron Athlon made in AMD's Dresden fab, and Intel shifted the Pentium 4 to copper with the 0.13-micron Northwood version (see Figure 3.6). Copper is a better conductor than aluminum and allows smaller interconnects with less resistance, meaning smaller and faster chips can be made. The reason copper hadn't been used until recently is that there were difficult corrosion problems to overcome during the manufacturing process that were not as much of a problem with aluminum. Now that these problems have been solved, more and more chips are fabricated with copper interconnects.

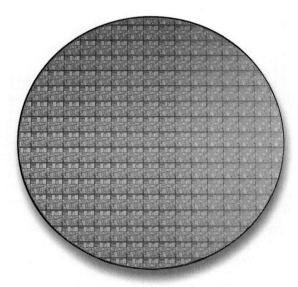

Figure 3.6 200mm wafer of the 0.13-micron Pentium 4 processors.

Note

The Pentium III and Celeron chips with the "coppermine" (codename for the 0.18-micron die used in those chips) die used aluminum and not copper metal interconnects as many people assume. In fact, the chip name had nothing to do with metal; the codename instead came from the Coppermine River in the Northwest Territory of Canada. Intel has long had a fondness for using codenames based on rivers (and sometimes, other geological features), especially those in the northwest region of the North American continent. For example, an older version of the Pentium III (0.25-micron die) was codenamed Katmai, after an Alaskan river. Intel codenames read like the travel itinerary of a whitewater rafting enthusiast: Deerfield, Foster, Northwood, Tualatin, Gallatin, McKinley, and Madison are all rivers in Oregon, California, Alaska, Montana, and—in the case of Deerfield—Massachusetts and Vermont.

Another technology that is becoming common is the use of silicon on insulator (SOI) instead of CMOS technology. AMD uses SOI for its 90-nanometer (0.09-micron) processors, and it's expected that SOI, which provides better insulation than CMOS for transistors, will continue to grow in popularity.

A completed circular wafer has as many chips imprinted on it as can possibly fit. Because each chip usually is square or rectangular, there are some unused portions at the edges of the wafer, but every attempt is made to use every square millimeter of surface.

The industry is going through several transitions in chip manufacturing. The trend in the industry is to use both larger wafers and a smaller chip die process. *Process* refers to the size and spacing of the individual circuits and transistors on the chip. In late 2001 and into 2002, chip manufacturing processes began moving from the 0.18-micron to the 0.13-micron process, the metal interconnects on the die began moving from aluminum to copper, and wafers began moving from 200mm (8") to 300mm (12") in diameter. The larger 300mm wafers alone enable more than double the number of chips to be made, compared to the 200mm used previously. The smaller 0.13-micron and 0.09-micron (90-nanometer) processes enable more transistors to be incorporated into the die while maintaining a reasonable die size and allowing for a sufficient yield. This means the trend for incorporating more and more cache within the die will continue, and transistor counts will rise to 1 billion per chip or more by 2010.

As an example of how this can affect a particular chip, let's look at the original Pentium 4. The standard wafer size used in the industry for many years was 200mm in diameter, or just under 8". This results in a wafer of about 31,416 square millimeters in area. The first version of the Pentium 4 with the Willamette core used a 0.18-micron process with aluminum interconnects on a die that was 217 square millimeters in area, had 42 million transistors, and was made on 200mm wafers. Therefore, up to 145 of these chips could fit on a 200mm (8") wafer.

The Pentium 4 processors with the Northwood core that followed it use a smaller 0.13-micron process with copper interconnects on a die that is 131 square millimeters in area with 55 million transistors. Northwood has double the on-die L2 cache (512KB) as compared to Willamette, which is why the transistor count is significantly higher. Even with the higher transistor count, the smaller 0.13-micron process results in a die that is more than 60% smaller, allowing up to 240 chips to fit on the same 200mm (8") wafer that could hold only 145 Willamette die.

Starting in early 2002, Intel began producing Northwood on the larger 300mm wafers, which have a surface area of 70,686 square millimeters. These wafers have 2.25 times the surface area of the smaller 200mm wafers, enabling more than double the number of chips to be produced per wafer. In the case of the Pentium 4 Northwood, up to 540 chip dies fit on a 300mm wafer. By combining the smaller die with the larger wafer, Pentium 4 production has increased by more than 3.7 times since the chip was first introduced. This is one reason newer chips are often more plentiful and less expensive than older ones.

In 2004, the industry began moving to the 90-nanometer (0.09-micron) process, allowing even smaller and faster chips to be made. Most new chips in 2005 were based on the 0.09-micron process, a trend that continued throughout most of 2006.

In July 2006 Intel introduced the first mainstream processors based on a 65-nanometer process, and AMD followed with its first 65nm chips in December 2006. Both Intel and AMD are now working on 45-nanometer process chips, which are expected in 2008. These advancements in process will allow more than 1 billion transistors per chip! These will still be made on 300mm wafers because the next wafer transition isn't expected until 2012, when a transition to 450mm wafers is being considered. Table 3.15 lists the CPU process transitions.

Table 3.15   Past, Current, and Future CPU Process Transitions

Date:	1989	1991	1993	1995	1997	1999	2001	2004	2006	2008	2010	2012
Process (micron):	1.0	0.8	0.5	0.35	0.25	0.18	0.13	0.09	0.065	0.045	0.032	0.022
Process (nm):	1000	800	500	350	250	180	130	90	65	45	32	22

Note that not all the chips on each wafer will be good, especially as a new production line starts. As the manufacturing process for a given chip or production line is perfected, more and more of the chips will be good. The ratio of good to bad chips on a wafer is called the *yield*. Yields well under 50% are common when a new chip starts production; however, by the end of a given chip's life, the yields are normally in the 90% range. Most chip manufacturers guard their yield figures and are very secretive about them because knowledge of yield problems can give their competitors an edge. A low yield causes problems both in the cost per chip and in delivery delays to their customers. If a company has specific knowledge of competitors' improving yields, it can set prices or schedule production to get higher market share at a critical point.

After a wafer is complete, a special fixture tests each of the chips on the wafer and marks the bad ones to be separated out later. The chips are then cut from the wafer using either a high-powered laser or diamond saw.

After being cut from the wafers, the individual dies are then retested, packaged, and retested again. The packaging process is also referred to as *bonding* because the die is placed into a chip housing in which a special machine bonds fine gold wires between the die and the pins on the chip. The package is the container for the chip die, and it essentially seals it from the environment.

After the chips are bonded and packaged, final testing is done to determine both proper function and rated speed. Different chips in the same batch often run at different speeds. Special test fixtures run each chip at different pressures, temperatures, and speeds, looking for the point at which the chip stops working. At this point, the maximum successful speed is noted and the final chips are sorted into bins with those that tested at a similar speed. For example, the Pentium 4 2.0A, 2.2, 2.26, 2.4, and 2.53GHz are all exactly the same chip made using the same die. They were sorted at the end of the manufacturing cycle by speed.

One interesting thing about this is that as a manufacturer gains more experience and perfects a particular chip assembly line, the yield of the higher-speed versions goes way up. So, of all the chips produced from a single wafer, perhaps more than 75% of them, check out at the highest speed, and only 25% or less run at the lower speeds. The paradox is that Intel often sells a lot more of the lower-priced, lower-speed chips, so it just dips into the bin of faster ones, labels them as slower chips, and sells them that way. People began discovering that many of the lower-rated chips actually ran at speeds much higher than they were rated, and the business of overclocking was born.

Processor Re-marking

As people learned more about how processors are manufactured and graded, an interesting problem arose: Unscrupulous vendors began re-marking slower chips and reselling them as if they were faster. Often the price between the same chip at different speed grades can be substantial—in the hundreds of dollars—so by changing a few numbers on the chip, the potential profits can be huge. Because most of the Intel and AMD processors are produced with a generous safety margin—that is, they typically run well past their rated speeds—the re-marked chips would seem to work fine in most cases. Of course, in many cases they wouldn't work fine, and the system would end up crashing or locking up periodically.

At first, the re-marked chips were just a case of rubbing off the original numbers and restamping with new official-looking numbers. These were easy to detect, though. Re-markers then resorted to manufacturing completely new processor housings, especially for the plastic-encased Slot 1 and Slot A processors from Intel and AMD that were popular in the late '90s and still quite common just a few years ago. Although it might seem to be a huge bother to make a custom plastic case and swap it with the existing case, because the profits can be huge, criminals find it very lucrative. This type of re-marking is a form of organized crime and isn't just some kid in his basement with sandpaper and a rubber stamp.

Intel and AMD have seen fit to put a stop to some of the re-marking by building overclock protection in the form of a multiplier lock into most of their chips dating back nearly 10 years. This is usually done in the bonding or cartridge manufacturing process, where the chips are intentionally altered so they won't run at any speeds higher than they are rated. Usually this involves changing the bus frequency (BF) pins or traces on the chip, which control the internal multipliers the chip uses. At one point, many feared that fixing the clock multiplier would put an end to hobbyist overclocking, but that proved not to be the case. Enterprising individuals found ways to run their motherboards at bus speeds higher than normal, so even though the CPU generally won't allow a higher multiplier, you can still run it at a speed higher than it was designed for by ramping up the speed of the processor bus.

The real problem with the overclock protection as implemented by Intel and AMD is that the professional counterfeiter has often been able to figure out a way around it by modifying the chip physically. Today's socketed processors are much more immune to these re-marking attempts, but it is still possible, particularly because the evidence can be hidden under a heatsink. To protect yourself from purchasing a fraudulent chip, verify the specification numbers and serial numbers with Intel and AMD before you purchase. Also beware where you buy your hardware. Purchasing over online auction sites can be extremely dangerous because defrauding the purchaser is so easy. Also, traveling computer show/flea market arenas can be a hotbed of this type of activity. Finally, I recommend purchasing only "boxed" or retail-packaged versions of the Intel and AMD processors, rather than the raw OEM versions. The boxed versions are shrink-wrapped and contain a high-quality heatsink, documentation, and a 3-year warranty with the manufacturer.

Fraudulent computer components are not limited to processors. I have seen fake memory, fake mice, fake video cards, fake cache memory, counterfeit operating systems and applications, and even fake motherboards. The hardware that is faked usually works but is of inferior quality to the type it is purporting to be. For example, one of the most highly counterfeited pieces of hardware at one time was the Microsoft mouse. They originally sold for $35 wholesale, yet I could purchase cheap mice from overseas manufacturers for as little as $2 each. It didn't take somebody long to realize that if they made the $2 mouse look like a $35 Microsoft mouse, they could sell it for $20 and people would think they were getting a genuine article for a bargain, while the thieves ran off with a substantial profit.

PGA Chip Packaging

Variations on the pin grid array (PGA) chip packaging have been the most commonly used chip packages over the years. They were used starting with the 286 processor in the 1980s and are still used today, although not in all CPU designs. PGA takes its name from the fact that the chip has a grid-like array of pins on the bottom of the package. PGA chips are inserted into sockets, which are often of a zero insertion force (ZIF) design. A ZIF socket has a lever to allow for easy installation and removal of the chip.

Most Pentium processors use a variation on the regular PGA called staggered pin grid array (SPGA), in which the pins are staggered on the underside of the chip rather than in standard rows and columns. This was done to move the pins closer together and decrease the overall size of the chip when a large number of pins is required. Figure 3.7 shows a Pentium Pro that uses the dual-pattern SPGA (on the right) next to an older Pentium 66 that uses the regular PGA. Note that the right half of the Pentium Pro shown here has additional pins staggered among the other rows and columns.

Figure 3.7   PGA on Pentium 66 (left) and dual-pattern SPGA on Pentium Pro (right).

Older PGA variations had the processor die mounted in a cavity underneath the substrate, with the top surface facing up if you turned the chip upside down. The die was then wire-bonded to the chip package with hundreds of tiny gold wires connecting the connections at the edge of the chip with the internal connections in the package. After the wire bonding, the cavity was sealed with a metal cover. This was an expensive and time-consuming method of producing chips, so cheaper and more efficient packaging methods were designed.

Most modern processors are built on a form of flip-chip pin grid array (FC-PGA) packaging. This type still plugs into a PGA socket, but the package itself is dramatically simplified. With FC-PGA, the raw silicon die is mounted face down on the top of the chip substrate, and instead of wire bonding, the connections are made with tiny solder bumps around the perimeter of the die. The edge is then sealed with a fillet of epoxy. With the original versions of FC-PGA, you could see the backside of the raw die sitting on the chip.

Unfortunately, there were some problems with attaching the heatsink to an FC-PGA chip. The heatsink sat on the top of the die, which acted as a pedestal. If you pressed down on one side of the heatsink excessively during the installation process (such as when you were attaching the clip), you risked cracking the silicon die and destroying the chip. This was especially a problem as heatsinks became larger and heavier and the force applied by the clip became greater.

AMD decreased the risk of damage by adding rubber spacers to each corner of the chip substrate for the Athlon XP, thus preventing the heatsink from tilting excessively during installation. Still, these bumpers could compress, and it was all too easy to crack the die.

Intel revised its packaging with a newer FC-PGA2 version used in later Pentium III and all Pentium 4 processors. This incorporates a protective metal cap, dubbed a *heat spreader*, to protect the CPU from damage when the heatsink is attached. Ironically, the first processor for PCs to use a heat spreader was actually made by AMD for its K6 family of processors.

The Athlon 64 processor family uses a heatsink design different from the Athlon XP. On the Athlon 64 family, the heatsink is attached to a clip. The clip is then screwed to the motherboard, which helps prevent damage to the processor. The Athlon 64, Opteron, and Socket 754 versions of the Sempron also use a heat spreader on top of the processor die, enabling larger and heavier heatsinks to be installed without any potential damage to the processor core.

Future packaging directions may include what is called *bumpless build-up layer (BBUL)* packaging. This will embed the die completely in the package; in fact, the package layers will be built up around and on top of the die, fully encapsulating it within the package. This will embed the chip die and allow for a full flat surface for attaching the heatsink, as well as shorter internal interconnections within the package. BBUL is designed to handle extremely high clock speeds of 20GHz or faster.

Single Edge Contact and Single Edge Processor Packaging

Intel and AMD used cartridge- or board-based packaging for some of their processors from 1997 through 2000. This packaging was called *single edge contact cartridge (SECC)* or *single edge processor package (SEPP)* and consisted of the CPU and optional separate L2 cache chips mounted on a circuit board that looked similar to an oversized memory module and that plugged into a slot. In some cases, the boards were covered with a plastic cartridge cover.

The SEC cartridge is an innovative—if a bit unwieldy—package design that incorporates the back-side bus and L2 cache internally. It was used as a cost-effective method for integrating L2 cache into the processor before it was feasible to include the cache directly inside the processor die.

A less expensive version of the SEC is called the *single edge processor (SEP)* package. The SEP package is basically the same circuit board containing processor and (optional) cache, but without the fancy plastic cover. This was used mainly by the lower-cost early Celeron processors. The SEP package plugs directly into the same Slot 1 connector used by the standard Pentium II or III. Four holes on the board enable the heatsink to be installed.

Slot 1, as shown in Figure 3.8, is the connection to the motherboard and has 242 pins. AMD used the same physical slot but rotated it 180° and called it Slot A. The SEC cartridge or SEP processor is plugged into the slot and secured with a processor-retention mechanism, which is a bracket that holds it in place. There also might be a retention mechanism or support for the processor heatsink. Figure 3.9 shows the parts of the cover that make up the SEC package. Note the large thermal plate used to aid in dissipating the heat from this processor. The SEP package is shown in Figure 3.10.

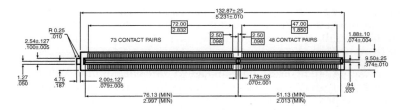

Figure 3.8   Pentium II Processor Slot 1 dimensions (metric/English).

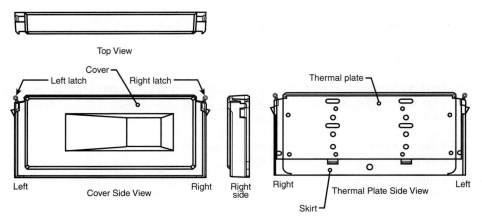

Figure 3.9   Pentium II Processor SEC package parts.

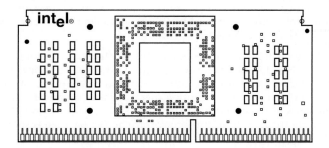

Figure 3.10   Celeron Processor SEP package front-side view.

With the Pentium III, Intel introduced a variation on the SEC packaging called *single edge contact cartridge version 2 (SECC2)*. This new package covered only one side of the processor board with plastic and enables the heatsink to directly attach to the chip on the other side. This more direct thermal interface allowed for better cooling, and the overall lighter package was cheaper to manufacture. A newer Universal Retention System, consisting of a plastic upright stand, was required to hold the SECC2 package chip in place on the board. The Universal Retention System also worked with the older SEC package as used on most Pentium II processors, as well as the SEP package used on the slot-based Celeron processors. This made it the ideal retention mechanism for all Slot 1-based processors. AMD Athlon Slot A processors used the same retention mechanisms as Intel. Figure 3.11 shows the SECC2 package.

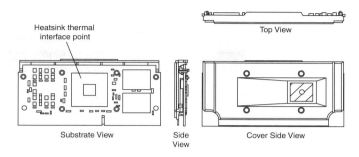

Figure 3.11   SECC2 packaging used in Pentium II and III processors.

The main reason for switching to the SEC and SEP packages in the first place was to be able to move the L2 cache memory off the motherboard and onto the processor in an economical and scalable way. This was necessary because, at the time, it was not feasible to incorporate the cache directly into the CPU core die. After building the L2 directly into the CPU die became possible, the cartridge and slot packaging were unnecessary. Because virtually all modern processors incorporate the L2 cache on-die, the processor packaging has gone back to the PGA socket form.

Processor Socket and Slot Types

Intel and AMD have created a set of socket and slot designs for their processors. Each socket or slot is designed to support a different range of original and upgrade processors. Table 3.16 shows the designations for the various 486 and newer processor sockets/slots and lists the chips designed to plug into them.

Table 3.16   CPU Socket and Slot Types and Specifications

Chip Class	Socket	Pins	Layout	Voltage	Supported Processors	Introduced
Intel/AMD 486 class	Socket 1	169	17×17 PGA	5V	486 SX/SX2, DX/DX2, DX4 OD	Apr. '89
	Socket 2	238	19×19 PGA	5V	486 SX/SX2, DX/DX2, DX4 OD, 486 Pentium OD	Mar. '92
	Socket 3	237	19×19 PGA	5V/3.3V	486 SX/SX2, DX/DX2, DX4, 486 Pentium OD, AMD 5x86	Feb. '94
	Socket 6[1]	235	19×19 PGA	3.3V	486 DX4, 486 Pentium OD	Feb. '94
Intel/AMD 586 (Pentium) class	Socket 4	273	21×21 PGA	5V	Pentium 60/66, OD	Mar. '93
	Socket 5	320	37×37 SPGA	3.3V/3.5V	Pentium 75-133, OD	Mar. '94
	Socket 7	321	37×37 SPGA	VRM	Pentium 75-233+, MMX, OD, AMD K5/K6, Cyrix M1/II	June '95

Table 3.16   Continued

Chip Class	Socket	Pins	Layout	Voltage	Supported Processors	Introduced
Intel 686(Pentium II/III) class	Socket 8	387	Dual-pattern SPGA	Auto VRM	Pentium Pro, OD	Nov. '95
	Slot 1(SC242)	242	Slot	Auto VRM	Pentium II/III, Celeron SECC	May '97
	Socket 370	370	37×37 SPGA	Auto VRM	Celeron/Pentium III PPGA/ FC-PGA	Nov. '98
Intel Pentium4 class	Socket 423	423	39×39 SPGA	Auto VRM	Pentium 4 FC-PGA	Nov. '00
	Socket 478	478	26×26 mPGA	Auto VRM	Pentium 4/Celeron FC-PGA2	Oct. '01
	Socket T (LGA775)	775	30×33 LGA	Auto VRM	Pentium 4/Celeron/ Pentium D/ Pentium Extreme Edition/ LGA775	June '04
AMD K7 class	Slot A	242	Slot	Auto VRM	AMD Athlon SECC	June '99
	Socket A (462)	462	37×37 SPGA	Auto VRM	AMD Athlon/ Athlon XP/ Duron PGA/FC-PGA	June '00
AMD K8 class	Socket 754	754	29×29 mPGA	Auto VRM	AMD Athlon 64	Sep. '03
	Socket 939	939	31×31 mPGA	Auto VRM	AMD Athlon 64 v.2	June '04
	Socket 940	940	31×31 mPGA	Auto VRM	AMD Athlon 64FX, Opteron	Apr. '03
	Socket AM2	940	31×31 mPGA	Auto VRM	AMD Athlon 64FX, X2	May '06
	Socket F (1207FX)	1207	35×35 LGA	Auto VRM	AMD Athlon QuadFX, Opteron	Aug. '06
Intel/AMD server and workstation class	Slot 2(SC330)	330	Slot	Auto VRM	Pentium II/III Xeon	Apr. '98
	Socket 603	603	31×25 mPGA	Auto VRM	Xeon (P4)	May '01
	Socket 604	604	31×25 mPGA	Auto VRM	Xeon (P4)	Oct. '03
	Socket PAC418	418	38×22	Auto VRM split SPGA	Itanium	May '01
	Socket PAC611	611	25×28	Auto VRM mPGA	Itanium 2	July '02
	Socket 940	940	31×31 mPGA	Auto VRM	AMD Athlon 64FX, Opteron	Apr. '03

1. Socket 6 was never actually implemented in any systems.

FC-PGA = Flip-chip pin grid array

FC-PGA2 = FC-PGA with an Integrated Heat Spreader (IHS)

OD = OverDrive (retail upgrade processors)

PAC = Pin array cartridge

PGA = Pin grid array

PPGA = Plastic pin grid array

SC242 = Slot connector, 242 pins

SC330 = Slot connector, 330 pins

SECC = Single edge contact cartridge

SPGA = Staggered pin grid array

mPGA = Micro pin grid array

VRM = Voltage regulator module with variable voltage output determined by module type or manual jumpers

Auto VRM = Voltage regulator module with automatic voltage selection determined by processor Voltage ID (VID) pins

Sockets 1, 2, 3, and 6 are 486 processor sockets and are shown together in Figure 3.12 so you can see the overall size comparisons and pin arrangements between these sockets. Sockets 4, 5, 7, and 8 are Pentium and Pentium Pro processor sockets and are shown together in Figure 3.13 so you can see the overall size comparisons and pin arrangements between these sockets. More detailed drawings of each socket are included throughout the remainder of this section with thorough descriptions of the sockets.

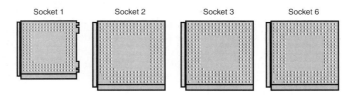

Figure 3.12   486 processor sockets.

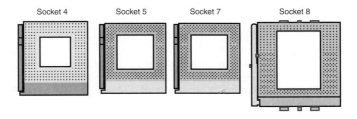

Figure 3.13   Pentium and Pentium Pro processor sockets.

Zero Insertion Force (ZIF)

When the Socket 1 specification was created, manufacturers realized that if users were going to upgrade processors, they had to make the process easier. The socket manufacturers found that 100 lbs. of insertion force is required to install a chip in a standard 169-pin screw Socket 1 motherboard. With this much force involved, you easily could damage either the chip or the socket during removal or reinstallation. Because of this, some motherboard manufacturers began using low insertion force (LIF) sockets, which required only 60 lbs. of insertion force for a 169-pin chip. With the LIF or standard socket, I usually advise removing the motherboard—that way you can support the board from behind when you insert the chip. Pressing down on the motherboard with 60–100 lbs. of force can crack the board if it is not supported properly. A special tool is also required to remove a chip from one of these sockets. As you can imagine, even the low insertion force was relative, and a better solution was needed if the average person was ever going to replace his CPU.

Manufacturers began using ZIF sockets in Socket 1 designs, and all processor sockets from Socket 2 and higher have been of the ZIF design. ZIF is required for all the higher-density sockets because the insertion force would simply be too great otherwise. ZIF sockets almost eliminate the risk involved in installing or removing a processor because no insertion force is necessary to install the chip and no tool is needed to extract one. Most ZIF sockets are handle-actuated: You lift the handle, drop the chip into the socket, and then close the handle. This design makes installing or removing a processor an easy task.

Socket 1

The original OverDrive socket, now officially called Socket 1, is a 169-pin PGA socket. Motherboards that have this socket can support any of the 486SX, DX, and DX2 processors and the DX2/OverDrive versions. This type of socket is found on most 486 systems that originally were designed for OverDrive upgrades. Figure 3.14 shows the pinout of Socket 1.

The original DX processor draws a maximum 0.9 amps of 5V power in 33MHz form (4.5 watts) and a maximum 1 amp in 50MHz form (5 watts). The DX2 processor, or OverDrive processor, draws a maximum 1.2 amps at 66MHz (6 watts). This minor increase in power requires only a passive heatsink consisting of aluminum fins that are glued to the processor with thermal transfer epoxy. Passive heatsinks don't have any mechanical components like fans. Heatsinks with fans or other devices that use power are called *active* heatsinks. OverDrive processors rated at 40MHz or less do not have heatsinks.

Socket 2

When the DX2 processor was released, Intel was already working on the new Pentium processor. The company wanted to offer a 32-bit, scaled-down version of the Pentium as an upgrade for systems that originally came with a DX2 processor. Rather than just increasing the clock rate, Intel created an all-new chip with enhanced capabilities derived from the Pentium.

The chip, called the *Pentium OverDrive processor*, plugs into a processor socket with the Socket 2 or Socket 3 design. These sockets hold any 486 SX, DX, or DX2 processor, as well as the Pentium OverDrive. Because this chip is essentially a 32-bit version of the (normally 64-bit) Pentium chip, many have taken to calling it a Pentium-SX. It was available in 25/63MHz and 33/83MHz versions. The first number indicates the base motherboard speed; the second number indicates the actual operating speed of the Pentium OverDrive chip. As you can see, it is a clock-multiplied chip that runs at 2.5 times the motherboard speed. Figure 3.15 shows the pinout configuration of the official Socket 2 design.

Notice that although the chip for Socket 2 is called Pentium OverDrive, it is not a full-scale (64-bit) Pentium. Intel released the design of Socket 2 a little prematurely and found that the chip ran too hot for many systems. The company solved this problem by adding a special active heatsink to the Pentium OverDrive processor. This active heatsink is a combination of a standard heatsink and a built-in electric fan. Unlike the aftermarket glue-on or clip-on fans for processors that you might have seen, this one actually draws 5V power directly from the socket to drive the fan. No external connection to disk drive cables or the power supply is required. The fan/heatsink assembly clips and plugs directly into the processor and provides for easy replacement if the fan fails.

Another requirement of the active heatsink is additional clearance—no obstructions for an area about 1.4" off the base of the existing socket to allow for heatsink clearance. The Pentium OverDrive upgrade is difficult or impossible in systems that were not designed with this feature.

Another problem with this particular upgrade is power consumption. The 5V Pentium OverDrive processor draws up to 2.5 amps at 5V (including the fan) or 12.5 watts, which is more than double the 1.2 amps (6 watts) drawn by the DX2 66 processor.

Note

Intel no longer markets OverDrive processors, but it maintains technical information about them at www.intel.com/support/processors/overdrive/index.htm.

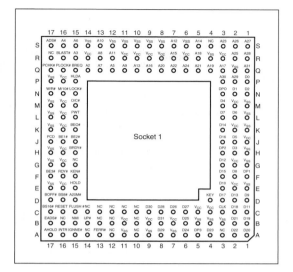

Figure 3.14   Intel Socket 1 pinout.

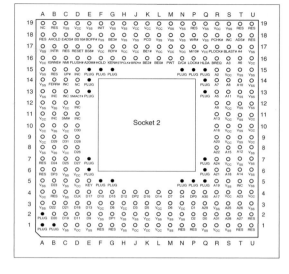

Figure 3.15   238-pin Intel Socket 2 configuration.

Socket 3

Because of problems with the original Socket 2 specification and the enormous heat the 5V version of the Pentium OverDrive processor generates, Intel came up with an improved design. This processor is the same as the previous Pentium OverDrive processor, except that it runs on 3.3V and draws a maximum 3.0 amps of 3.3V (9.9 watts) and 0.2 amp of 5V (1 watt) to run the fan—a total of 10.9 watts. This configuration provides a slight margin over the 5V version of this processor. The fan is easy to remove from the OverDrive processor for replacement, should it ever fail.

Intel had to create a new socket to support both the DX4 processor, which runs on 3.3V, and the 3.3V Pentium OverDrive processor. In addition to the 3.3V chips, this new socket supports the older 5V SX, DX, DX2, and even the 5V Pentium OverDrive chip. The design, called Socket 3, is the most flexible upgradeable 486 design. Figure 3.16 shows the pinout specification of Socket 3.

Notice that Socket 3 has one additional pin and several others plugged in compared with Socket 2. Socket 3 provides for better keying, which prevents an end user from accidentally installing the processor in an improper orientation. However, one serious problem exists: This socket can't automatically determine the type of voltage that is provided to it. You will likely find a jumper on the motherboard near the socket to enable selecting 5V or 3.3V operation.

Caution

Because this jumper must be manually set, a user could install a 3.3V processor in this socket when it is configured for 5V operation. This installation instantly destroys the chip when the system is powered on. So, it is up to the end user to ensure that this socket is properly configured for voltage, depending on which type of processor is installed. If the jumper is set in 3.3V configuration and a 5V processor is installed, no harm will occur, but the system will not operate properly unless the jumper is reset for 5V.

Socket 4

Socket 4 is a 273-pin socket designed for the original Pentium processors. The original Pentium 60MHz and 66MHz version processors had 273 pins and plugged into Socket 4. It is a 5V-only socket because all the original Pentium processors run on 5V. This socket accepts the original Pentium 60MHz or 66MHz processor and the OverDrive processor. Figure 3.17 shows the pinout specification of Socket 4.

Somewhat amazingly, the original Pentium 66MHz processor consumes up to 3.2 amps of 5V power (16 watts), not including power for a standard active heatsink (fan). The 66MHz OverDrive processor that replaced it consumes a maximum 2.7 amps (13.5 watts), including about 1 watt to drive the fan. Even the original 60MHz Pentium processor consumes up to 2.91 amps at 5V (14.55 watts). It might seem strange that the replacement processor, which is twice as fast, consumes less power than the original, but this has to do with the manufacturing processes used for the original and OverDrive processors.

Although both processors run on 5V, the original Pentium processor was created with a circuit size of 0.8 micron, making that processor much more power-hungry than the 0.6-micron circuits used in the OverDrive and the other Pentium processors. Shrinking the circuit size is one of the best ways to decrease power consumption. Although the OverDrive processor for Pentium-based systems draws less power than the original processor, additional clearance might have to be allowed for the active heatsink assembly that is mounted on top. As in other OverDrive processors with built-in fans, the power to run the fan is drawn directly from the chip socket, so no separate power-supply connection is required. Also, the fan is easy to replace should it ever fail.

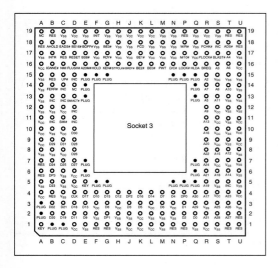

Figure 3.16   237-pin Intel Socket 3 configuration.

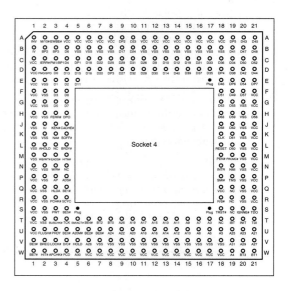

Figure 3.17   273-pin Intel Socket 4 configuration.

Socket 5

When Intel redesigned the Pentium processor to run at 75MHz, 90MHz, and 100MHz, the company went to a 0.6-micron manufacturing process and 3.3V operation. This change resulted in lower power consumption: only 3.25 amps at 3.3V (10.725 watts). Therefore, the 100MHz Pentium processor used far less power than even the original 60MHz version. This resulted in lower power consumption and enabled the extremely high clock rates without overheating.

The Pentium 75 and higher processors actually have 296 pins, although they plug into the official Intel Socket 5 design, which calls for a total of 320 pins. The additional pins are used by the Pentium OverDrive for Pentium processors. This socket has the 320 pins configured in a staggered PGA, in which the individual pins are staggered for tighter clearance.

Several OverDrive processors for existing Pentiums were available. These usually were later design chips with integral voltage regulators to enable operating on the higher voltages the older chips originally required. Intel no longer sells these; however, companies such as PowerLeap do still sell upgrade chips for older systems. Figure 3.18 shows the standard pinout for Socket 5.

The Pentium OverDrive for Pentium processors has an active heatsink (fan) assembly that draws power directly from the chip socket. The chip requires a maximum 4.33 amps of 3.3V to run the chip (14.289 watts) and 0.2 amp of 5V power to run the fan (one watt), which results in a total power consumption of 15.289 watts. This is less power than the original 66MHz Pentium processor requires, yet it runs a chip that is as much as four times faster!

Socket 6

The last 486 socket was designed for the 486 DX4 and the 486 Pentium OverDrive processor. Socket 6 was intended as a slightly redesigned version of Socket 3 and had an additional 2 pins plugged for proper chip keying. Socket 6 has 235 pins and accepts only 3.3V 486 or OverDrive processors. Although Intel went to the trouble of designing this socket, it never was built or implemented in any systems. Motherboard manufacturers instead stuck with Socket 3.

Socket 7 (and Super7)

Socket 7 is essentially the same as Socket 5 with one additional key pin in the opposite inside corner of the existing key pin. Socket 7, therefore, has 321 pins total in a 37×37 SPGA arrangement. The real difference with Socket 7 is not with the socket itself, but with the companion voltage regulator module (VRM) circuitry on the motherboard that must accompany it.

The VRM is either a small circuit board or a group of circuitry embedded in the motherboard that supplies the proper voltage level and regulation of power to the processor.

The main reason for the VRM is that Intel and AMD wanted to drop the voltages the processors would use from the 3.3V or 5V supplied to the motherboard by the power supply. Rather than require custom power supplies for different processors, the VRM converts the 3.3V or 5V to the proper voltage for the particular CPU you are using. Intel released different versions of the Pentium and Pentium-MMX processors that ran on 3.3V (called VR), 3.465V (called VRE), or 2.8V. Equivalent processors from AMD, Cyrix, and others used voltages from 3.3V to 1.8V. Because of the variety of voltages that might be required to support different processors, most motherboard manufacturers started including VRM sockets or building adaptable VRMs into their Pentium motherboards.

Figure 3.19 shows the Socket 7 pinout.

AMD, along with Cyrix and several chipset manufacturers, pioneered an improvement or extension to the Intel Socket 7 design called Super Socket 7 (or Super7), taking it from 66MHz to 95MHz and 100MHz. This enabled faster Socket 7–type systems to be made, supporting processors up to 500MHz, which are nearly as fast as some of the newer Slot 1– and Socket 370–type systems using Intel processors. Super7 systems also have support for the AGP video bus, as well as Ultra DMA hard disk controllers and advanced power management.

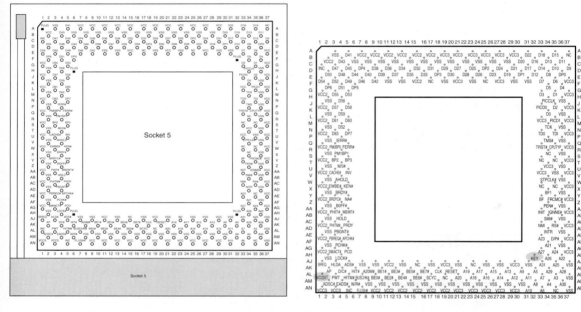

Figure 3.18 320-pin Intel Socket 5 configuration. **Figure 3.19** Socket 7 (Pentium) pinout (top view).

Major third-party chipset suppliers—including Acer Laboratories, Inc. (ALi), VIA Technologies, and Silicon Integrated Systems (SiS)—all released chipsets for Super7 boards. Most of the major motherboard manufacturers made Super7 boards in both Baby-AT and ATX form factors.

Socket 8

Socket 8 is a special SPGA socket featuring a whopping 387 pins! This was specifically designed for the Pentium Pro processor with the integrated L2 cache. The additional pins are required by the P6 processor bus. Figure 3.20 shows the Socket 8 pinout.

Socket 370 (PGA-370)

In November 1998, Intel introduced a new socket for P6 class processors. The socket was called *Socket 370* or *PGA-370* because it has 370 pins and originally was designed for lower-cost PGA versions of the Celeron and Pentium III processors. Socket 370 was originally designed to directly compete in the lower-end system market along with the Super7 platform supported by AMD and Cyrix. However, Intel later used it for the Pentium III processor. Initially all the Celeron and Pentium III processors were made in SECC or SEPP format. These are essentially circuit boards containing the processor and separate L2 cache chips on a small board that plugs into the motherboard via Slot 1. This type of design was necessary when the L2 cache chips were made a part of the processor but were not directly integrated into the processor die. Intel did make a multiple-die chip package for the Pentium Pro, but this proved to be a very expensive way to package the chip, and a board with separate chips was cheaper, which is why the Pentium II looks different from the Pentium Pro.

Starting with the Celeron 300A processor introduced in August 1998, Intel began combining the L2 cache directly on the processor die; it was no longer in separate chips. With the cache fully integrated into the die, there was no longer a need for a board-mounted processor. Because it costs more to make a Slot 1 board or cartridge-type processor instead of a socketed type, Intel moved back to the socket design to reduce the manufacturing cost—especially with the Celeron, which at that time was competing on the low end with Socket 7 chips from AMD and Cyrix.

The Socket 370 (PGA-370) pinout is shown in Figure 3.21.

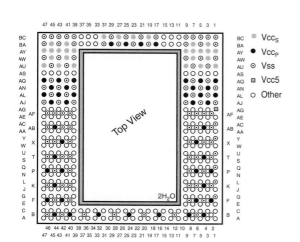

Figure 3.20 Socket 8 (Pentium Pro) pinout showing power pin locations.

Figure 3.21 Socket 370 (PGA-370) Pentium III/Celeron pinout (top view).

The Celeron was gradually shifted over to PGA-370, although for a time both were available. All Celeron processors at 333MHz and lower were available only in the Slot 1 version. Celeron processors from 366MHz to 433MHz were available in both Slot 1 and Socket 370 versions; all Celeron processors from 466MHz and up through 1.4GHz are available only in the Socket 370 version.

Starting in October 1999, Intel also introduced Pentium III processors with integrated cache that plug into Socket 370. These use a packaging called *flip chip pin grid array (FC-PGA)*, in which the raw die is mounted on the substrate upside down. The slot version of the Pentium III was more expensive and no longer necessary because of the on-die L2 cache.

Note that because of some voltage changes and one pin change, many original Socket 370 mother-boards do not accept the later FC-PGA Socket 370 versions of the Pentium III and Celeron. Pentium III processors in the FC-PGA form have two RESET pins and require VRM 8.4 specifications. Prior motherboards designed only for the older versions of the Celeron are referred to as *legacy motherboards*, and the newer motherboards supporting the second RESET pin and VRM 8.4 specification are referred to as *flexible motherboards*. Contact your motherboard or system manufacturer for information to see whether your socket is the flexible version. Some motherboards, such as the Intel CA810, do support the VRM 8.4 specifications and supply proper voltage, but without Vtt support the Pentium III processor in the FC-PGA package will be held in RESET#. The last versions of the Pentium III and Celeron III use the Tualatin core design, which also requires a revised socket to operate. Motherboards that can handle Tualatin-core processors are known as *Tualatin-ready* and use different chipsets from those not designed to work with the Tualatin-core processor. Companies that sell upgrade processors offer products that enable you to install a Tualatin-core Pentium III or Celeron III processor into a motherboard that lacks built-in Tualatin support.

Installing a Pentium III processor in the FC-PGA package into an older motherboard is unlikely to damage the motherboard. However, the processor itself could be damaged. Pentium III processors in the 0.18-micron process operate at either 1.60V or 1.65V, whereas the Intel Celeron processors operate at 2.00V. The motherboard could be damaged if the motherboard BIOS fails to recognize the voltage identification of the processor. Contact your PC or motherboard manufacturer before installation to ensure compatibility.

A motherboard with a Slot 1 can be designed to accept almost any Celeron, Pentium II, or Pentium III processor. To use the socketed Celerons and Pentium III processors, several manufacturers have made available a low-cost slot-to-socket adapter sometimes called a *slot-ket*. This is essentially a Slot 1 board containing only a Socket 370, which enables you to use a PGA processor in any Slot 1 board. A typical slot-ket adapter is shown in the "Celeron" section later in this chapter.

▶▶ See "Celeron," p. 166.

Socket 423

Socket 423 is a ZIF-type socket introduced in November 2000 for the original Pentium 4. Figure 3.22 shows Socket 423.

Socket 423 supports a 400MHz processor bus, which connects the processor to the Memory Controller Hub (MCH), which is the main part of the motherboard chipset and similar to the North Bridge in earlier chipsets. Pentium 4 processors up to 2GHz were available for Socket 423; all faster versions require Socket 478 instead.

Socket 423 uses a unique heatsink mounting method that requires standoffs attached either to the chassis or to a special plate that mounts underneath the motherboard. This was designed to support the weight of the larger heatsinks required for the Pentium 4. Because of this, many Socket 423 motherboards require a special chassis that has the necessary additional standoffs installed. Fortunately, the need for these standoffs was eliminated with the newer Socket 478 for Pentium 4 processors.

The processor uses five voltage ID (VID) pins to signal the VRM built into the motherboard to deliver the correct voltage for the particular CPU you install. This makes the voltage selection completely automatic and foolproof. Most Pentium 4 processors for Socket 423 require 1.7V. A small triangular mark indicates the pin-1 corner for proper orientation of the chip.

Socket 478

Socket 478 is a ZIF-type socket for the Pentium 4 and Celeron 4 (Celerons based on the Pentium 4 core) introduced in October 2001. It was specially designed to support additional pins for future Pentium 4 processors and speeds over 2GHz. The heatsink mounting is different from the previous Socket 423, allowing larger heatsinks to be attached to the CPU. Figure 3.23 shows Socket 478.

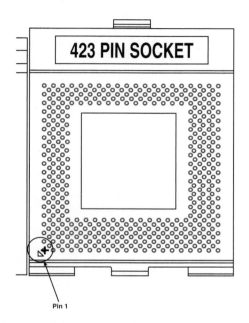

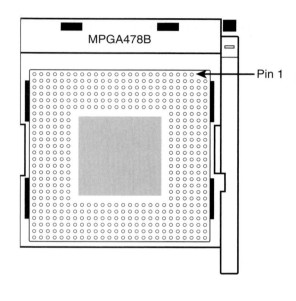

Figure 3.22 Socket 423 (Pentium 4) showing pin 1 location.

Figure 3.23 Socket 478 (Pentium 4) showing pin 1 location.

Socket 478 supports a 400MHz, 533MHz, or 800MHz processor bus that connects the processor to the memory controller hub (MCH), which is the main part of the motherboard chipset.

Socket 478 uses a heatsink attachment method that clips the heatsink directly to the motherboard, and not the CPU socket or chassis (as with Socket 423). Therefore, any standard chassis can be used, and the special standoffs used by Socket 423 boards are not required. This heatsink attachment allows for a much greater clamping load between the heatsink and processor, which aids cooling.

Socket 478 processors use five VID pins to signal the VRM built into the motherboard to deliver the correct voltage for the particular CPU you install. This makes the voltage selection completely automatic and foolproof. A small triangular mark indicates the pin-1 corner for proper orientation of the chip.

Socket A (Socket 462)

AMD introduced Socket A, also called Socket 462, in June 2000 to support the PGA versions of the Athlon and Duron processors. It is designed as a replacement for Slot A used by the original Athlon processor. Because the Athlon has now moved to incorporate L2 cache on-die, and the low-cost Duron was manufactured only in an on-die cache version, there was no longer a need for the expensive cartridge packaging the original Athlon processors used.

Socket A has 462 pins and 11 plugs oriented in an SPGA form (see Figure 3.24). Socket A has the same physical dimensions and layout as Socket 370; however, the location and placement of the plugs prevent Socket 370 processors from being inserted. Socket A supports 31 voltage levels from 1.100V to 1.850V in 0.025V increments, controlled by the VID0–VID4 pins on the processor. The automatic voltage regulator module circuitry typically is embedded on the motherboard.

There are 11 total plugged holes, including two of the outside pin holes at A1 and AN1. These are used to allow for keying to force the proper orientation of the processor in the socket. The pinout of Socket A is shown in Figure 3.25.

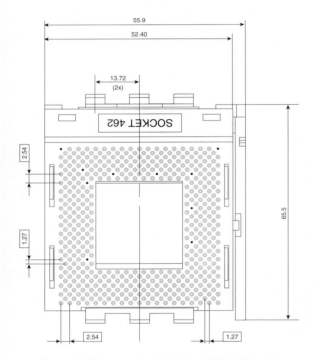

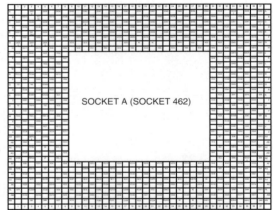

Figure 3.24   Socket A (Socket 462) Athlon/Duron layout.

Figure 3.25   Socket A (Socket 462) Athlon/Duron pinout (top view).

After the introduction of Socket A, AMD moved all Athlon (including all Athlon XP) processors to this form factor, phasing out Slot A. In addition, for a time AMD also sold a reduced L2 cache version of the Athlon, called the *Duron*, in this form factor. In 2005, AMD discontinued the Athlon XP and introduced the AMD Sempron in both Socket A and Socket 754 form factors. The first Athlon 64 processors also used Socket 754, but later switched to Socket 939 and AM2.

Caution

Just because a chip can plug into a socket doesn't mean it will work. The Athlon XP and Socket A Sempron processors require different voltages, BIOS, and chipset support than earlier Socket A Athlon and Duron processors. As always, make sure your motherboard supports the processor you intend to install.

Socket 603

Socket 603 is used with the Intel Xeon processor in DP (dual processor) and MP (multiple processor) configurations. These are typically used in motherboards designed for use in network file servers. Figure 3.26 shows Socket 603.

Socket 754

Socket 754 is used with the initial releases of the AMD Athlon 64 processors. Socket 754 is also used by some versions of the AMD Sempron, AMD's economy processor line. This socket supports single-channel unbuffered DDR SDRAM. Figure 3.27 shows an overhead view of this socket.

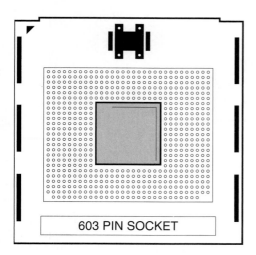

Figure 3.26 Socket 603 is used by the Intel Xeon processor.

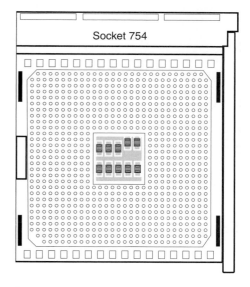

Figure 3.27 Socket 754. The large cutout corner at the lower left indicates pin 1.

Socket 939 and 940

Socket 939 is used with the Socket 939 versions of the AMD Athlon 64, 64 FX, and 64 X2 (see Figure 3.28). It's also used by some recent versions of the AMD Opteron processor for workstations and servers. Motherboards using this socket support conventional unbuffered DDR SDRAM modules in either single- or dual-channel mode, rather than the server-oriented (more expensive) registered modules required by Socket 940 motherboards. Sockets 939 and 940 have different pin arrangements and processors for each and are not interchangeable.

Socket 940 is used with the Socket 940 version of the AMD Athlon 64 FX, as well as most AMD Opteron processors (see Figure 3.29). Motherboards using this socket support only registered DDR SDRAM modules in dual-channel mode. Because the pin arrangement is different, Socket 939 processors do not work in Socket 940, and vice versa.

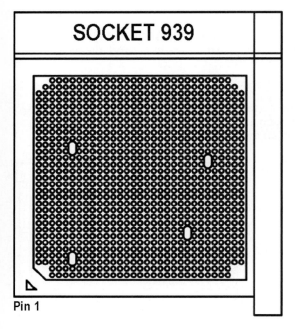

Figure 3.28   Socket 939. The cutout corner and triangle at the lower left indicate pin 1.

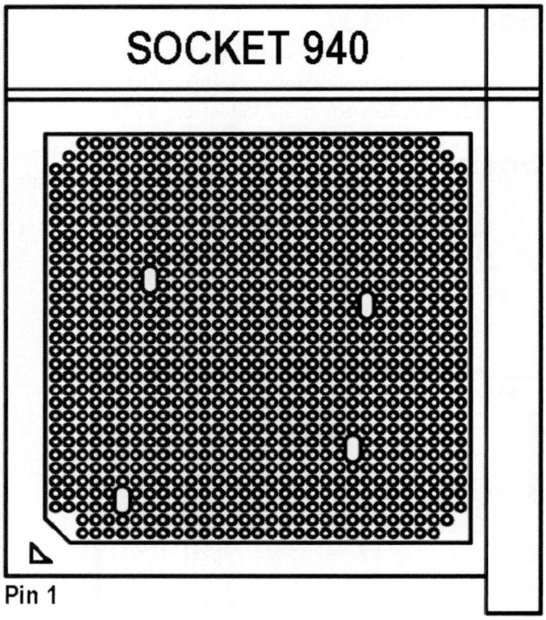

Figure 3.29   Socket 940. The cutout corner and triangle at the lower left indicate pin 1.

Socket LGA775

Socket LGA775 (also called Socket T or 775)) is used by the Core 2 Duo/Quad processors, the latest versions of the Intel Pentium 4 Prescott processor and the Pentium D and Pentium Extreme Edition processors, as well as some versions of the Celeron and Celeron D. Socket LGA775 is unique in that it uses a land grid array format, so the pins are on the socket, rather than the processor. The first LGA processors were the Pentium II and Celeron processors in 1997; in those processors LGA packaging was used for the chip mounted on the Slot-1 cartridge.

LGA uses gold pads (called *lands*) on the bottom of the substrate to replace the pins used in PGA packages. In socketed form, it allows for much greater clamping forces and therefore greater stability and improved thermal transfer (better cooling). LGA is really just a recycled version of what was previously called *leadless chip carrier (LCC)* packaging. This was used way back on the 286 processor in '84, which had gold lands around the edge only (there were far fewer pins back then). In other ways LGA is simply a modified version of ball grid array (BGA), with gold lands replacing the solder balls, making it more suitable for socketed (rather than soldered) applications. The early LCC packages were ceramic, whereas the first Pentium II LGA packages were plastic, with the package soldered to a cartridge substrate. These days (and for the future) the LGA package is organic and directly socketed instead. On a technical level, LGA chips combine several packaging technologies that have all been used in the past, including organic land grid array (OLGA) for the substrate and controlled collapse chip connection (C4) flip-chip for the actual processor die (see Figure 3.30).

Socket AM2

In May 2006, AMD introduced processors that use a new socket, called Socket AM2 (see Figure 3.31). AM2 is the eventual replacement for the confusing array of Socket 754, Socket 939, and Socket 940 form factors for the Athlon 64, Athlon 64 FX, and Athlon 64 X2 processors.

Although Socket AM2 contains 940 pins—the same number as used by Socket 940—Socket AM2 is designed to support the integrated dual-channel DDR2 memory controllers that were added to the Athlon 64 and Opteron processor families in 2006. Processors designed for Sockets 754, 939, and 940 include DDR memory controllers and are not pin compatible with Socket AM2.

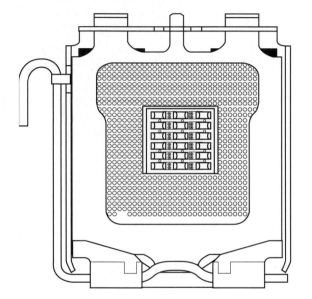

SOCKET M2

Figure 3.30   Socket T. The release lever on the left is used to raise the clamp out of the way to permit the processor to be placed over the contacts.

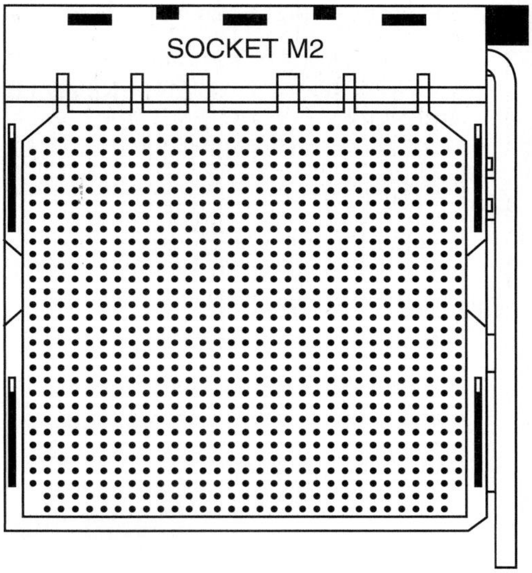

Figure 3.31   Socket AM2. The cutout corner at the lower left indicates pin 1.

Socket F (1207FX)

Socket F (also called 1207FX) was initially introduced by AMD in August 2006 for its Opteron line of server processors. Socket F is AMDs first LGA (Land Grid Array) socket (similar to Intels Socket LGA775), featuring 1207 pins in a 35 by 35 grid, with the pins in the socket instead of on the processor. Socket F normally appears on motherboards in pairs, as it is designed to run dual physical processors on a single motherboard. Socket F was utilized by AMD for its Quad FX processors, which are dual-core processors sold in matched pairs, operating as a dual socket dual-core system. Future versions may support quad-core processors, for a total of 8 cores in the system. Due to the high expense of running dual physical processors, only a very limited number of non-server motherboards are available with Socket F.

Processor Slots

After introducing the Pentium Pro with its integrated L2 cache, Intel discovered that the physical package it chose was very costly to produce. Intel was looking for a way to easily integrate cache and possibly other components into a processor package, and it came up with a cartridge or board design as the best way to do this. To accept its new cartridges, Intel designed two types of slots that could be used on motherboards.

Slot 1 is a 242-pin slot designed to accept Pentium II, Pentium III, and most Celeron processors. Slot 2, on the other hand, is a more sophisticated 330-pin slot designed for the Pentium II Xeon and Pentium III Xeon processors, which are primarily for workstations and servers. Besides the extra pins, the biggest difference between Slot 1 and Slot 2 is the fact that Slot 2 was designed to host up to four-way or more processing in a single board. Slot 1 allows only single or dual processing functionality.

Note that Slot 2 is also called SC330, which stands for slot connector with 330 pins. Intel later discovered less-expensive ways to integrate L2 cache into the processor core and no longer produces Slot 1 and Slot 2 processors. Both Slot 1 and Slot 2 processors are now obsolete, and many systems using these processors have been retired or upgraded with socket-based motherboards.

Slot 1 (SC242)

Slot 1, also called SC242 (slot connector 242 pins), is used by the SEC design that is used with the cartridge-type Pentium II/III and Celeron processors (see Figure 3.32).

◄◄ See "Single Edge Contact and Single Edge Processor Packaging," p. 95.

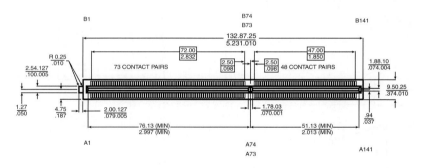

Figure 3.32   Slot 1 connector dimensions and pin layout.

Slot 2 (SC330)

Slot 2, otherwise called SC330 (slot connector 330 pins), is used on high-end motherboards that support the Pentium II Xeon and Pentium III Xeon processors. Figure 3.33 shows the Slot 2 connector.

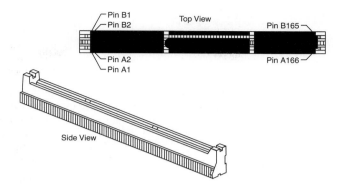

Figure 3.33   Slot 2 (SC330) connector dimensions and pin layout.

The Pentium II Xeon and Pentium III Xeon processors are designed in a cartridge similar to, but larger than, that used for the standard Pentium II/III. Figure 3.34 shows the Xeon cartridge.

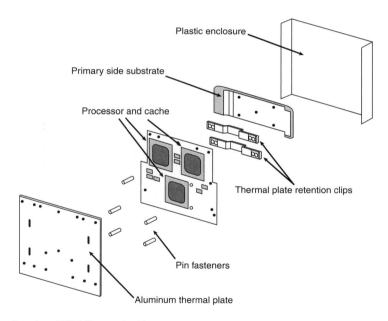

Figure 3.34   Pentium II/III Xeon cartridge.

Slot 2 motherboards were used in higher-end systems such as workstations or servers based on the Pentium II Xeon or Pentium III Xeon. These versions of the Xeon differ from the standard Pentium II and slot-based Pentium III mainly by virtue of having full-core speed L2 cache, and in some versions more of it. The additional pins allow for additional signals needed by multiple processors.

CPU Operating Voltages

One trend that is clear to anybody who has been following processor design is that the operating voltages have gotten lower and lower. The benefits of lower voltage are threefold. The most obvious is that with lower voltage comes lower overall power consumption. By consuming less power, the system is less expensive to run, but more importantly for portable or mobile systems, it runs much longer on existing battery technology. The emphasis on battery operation has driven many of the advances in lowering processor voltage because this has a great effect on battery life.

The second major benefit is that with less voltage and therefore less power consumption, less heat is produced. Processors that run cooler can be packed into systems more tightly and last longer.

The third major benefit is that a processor running cooler on less power can be made to run faster. Lowering the voltage has been one of the key factors in enabling the clock rates of processors to go higher and higher. This is because the lower the voltage, the shorter the time needed to change a signal from low to high.

Until the release of the mobile Pentium and both desktop and mobile Pentium MMX, most processors used a single voltage level to power both the core as well as run the input/output circuits. Originally, most processors ran both the core and I/O circuits at 5V, which was later reduced to 3.5V or 3.3V to lower power consumption. When a single voltage is used for both the internal processor core power as well as the external processor bus and I/O signals, the processor is said to have a single or unified power plane design.

When originally designing a version of the Pentium processor for mobile or portable computers, Intel came up with a scheme to dramatically reduce the power consumption while still remaining compatible with the existing 3.3V chipsets, bus logic, memory, and other components. The result was a dual-plane or split-plane power design in which the processor core ran off a lower voltage while the I/O circuits remained at 3.3V. This originally was called *voltage reduction technology (VRT)* and first debuted in the Mobile Pentium processors released in 1996. Later, this dual-plane power design also appeared in desktop processors such as the Pentium MMX, which used 2.8V to power the core and 3.3V for the I/O circuits. Now most recent processors, whether for mobile or desktop use, feature a dual-plane power design. Some of the more recent Mobile Pentium II processors run on as little as 1.6V for the core while still maintaining compatibility with 3.3V components for I/O.

Knowing the processor voltage requirements is not a big issue with Socket 8, Socket 370, Socket 478, Socket A, Socket 604, Socket 754, Socket 940, Pentium Pro (Socket 8), and Pentium II (Slot 1 or Slot 2) processors because these sockets and slots have special VID pins the processor uses to signal to the motherboard the exact voltage requirements. This enables the voltage regulators built into the motherboard to be automatically set to the correct voltage levels by merely installing the processor.

Unfortunately, this automatic voltage setting feature was not available on Super7, Socket 7, and earlier motherboard and processor designs. Therefore, you usually must set jumpers or otherwise configure the motherboard according to the voltage requirements of the processor you are installing. Pentium (Socket 4, 5, or 7) processors have run on a number of voltages, but the most recent MMX versions all use 2.8V—except for mobile Pentium processors, which are as low as 1.8V. Table 3.17 lists the voltage settings used by Intel Pentium (non-MMX) Socket 7 processors that use a single power plane and a dual power plane. A single power plane means that both the CPU core and the I/O pins run at the same voltage, whereas a dual power plane means that the core and I/O voltage values are different.

Table 3.17   Socket 7 Single- and Dual-Plane Processor Voltages

Voltage Setting	Processor	Core Voltage	I/O Voltage	Voltage Planes
VRE (3.5V)	Intel Pentium	3.5V	3.5V	Single
STD (3.3V)	Intel Pentium	3.3V	3.3V	Single
MMX (2.8V)	Intel MMX Pentium	2.8V	3.3V	Dual
VRE (3.5V)	AMD K5	3.5V	3.5V	Single
3.2V	AMD-K6	3.2V	3.3V	Dual
2.9V	AMD-K6	2.9V	3.3V	Dual
2.4V	AMD-K6-2/K6-3	2.4V	3.3V	Dual
2.2V	AMD-K6/K6-2	2.2V	3.3V	Dual
VRE (3.5V)	Cyrix 6x86	3.5V	3.5V	Single
2.9V	Cyrix 6x86MX/M-II	2.9V	3.3V	Dual
MMX (2.8V)	Cyrix 6x86L	2.8V	3.3V	Dual
2.45V	Cyrix 6x86LV	2.45V	3.3V	Dual

Generally, the acceptable range is plus or minus 5% from the nominal intended setting.

Most Socket 7 and later Pentium motherboards supply several voltages (such as 2.5V, 2.7V, 2.8V, and 2.9V) for compatibility with future devices. A voltage regulator built into the motherboard converts the power supply voltage into the various levels the processor core requires. Check the documentation for your motherboard and processor to find the appropriate settings.

The Pentium Pro and Pentium II processors were the first to automatically determine their voltage settings by controlling the motherboard-based voltage regulator through built-in VID pins. Those are explained in more detail later in this chapter.

▶▶   See "Pentium Pro Processors," p. 150.

▶▶   See "Pentium II Processors," p. 154.

Note that on the STD or VRE settings, the core and I/O voltages are the same; these are single-plane voltage settings. Any time a voltage other than STD or VRE is set, the motherboard defaults to a dual-plane voltage setting where the core voltage can be specifically set, while the I/O voltage remains constant at 3.3V no matter what.

Socket 5 was designed to supply only STD or VRE settings, so any processor that can work at those settings can work in Socket 5 as well as Socket 7. Older Socket 4 designs can supply only 5V, and they have a completely different pinout (fewer pins overall), so using a processor designed for Socket 7 or Socket 5 in Socket 4 is not possible.

Most Socket 7 and later Pentium motherboards supply several voltages (such as 2.2V, 2.4V, 2.5V, 2.7V, 2.8V, and 2.9V as well as the older STD or VRE settings) for compatibility with many processors. A voltage regulator built into the motherboard converts the power supply voltage into the various levels required by the processor core. Check the documentation for your motherboard and processor to find the appropriate settings.

Starting with the Pentium Pro, all newer processors automatically determine their voltage settings by controlling the motherboard-based voltage regulator. That's done through built-in VID pins.

For hotrodding purposes, many newer motherboards for these processors have override settings that allow for manual voltage adjustment if desired. Many people have found that when attempting to overclock a processor, increasing the voltage by a tenth of a volt or so often helps. Of course, this increases the heat output of the processor and must be accounted for with adequate heatsinking and case cooling.

Note

Although modern processors use VID pins to enable the processor to select the correct voltage, newer processor that use the same processor socket as older processors might use a voltage setting not supported by the motherboard. Before upgrading an existing motherboard with a new processor, make sure the motherboard will support the processor's voltage and other features. You might need to install a BIOS upgrade before upgrading the processor to ensure that the processor is properly recognized by the motherboard.

Heat and Cooling Problems

Heat can be a problem in any high-performance system. The higher-speed processors consume more power and therefore generate more heat. The processor is usually the single most power-hungry chip in a system, and in most situations, the fan inside your computer case is incapable of handling the load without some help.

To ensure a constant flow of air and more consistent performance, most processors include some form of heatsink, which is designed to draw heat away from the processor. Additionally, most heatsinks incorporate fans so they don't have to rely on the airflow within the system. Heatsinks with fans are referred to as *active* heatsinks (see Figure 3.35). Active heatsinks have a power connection. Older ones often used a spare disk drive power connector, but most recent heatsinks plug into dedicated heatsink power connections found on the newer motherboards. Heatsink power connections also provide a connection used to monitor fan performance through the BIOS Hardware Monitor or PC Health screen. Fan performance can also be displayed within the operating system by using a monitoring program.

Processor cooling, including heatsinks, is covered in detail in Chapter 21.

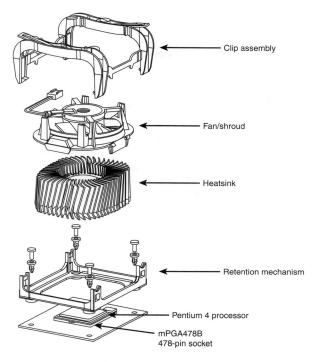

Clip assembly

Fan/shroud

Heatsink

Retention mechanism

Pentium 4 processor

mPGA478B
478-pin socket

Figure 3.35   Active heatsink suitable for a Pentium 4 processor using Socket 478.

Math Coprocessors (Floating-point Units)

This section covers the floating-point unit (FPU) contained in the processor, which was formerly a separate external math coprocessor in the 386 and older chips. Older central processing units designed by Intel (and cloned by other companies) used an external math coprocessor chip. However, when Intel introduced the 486DX, it included a built-in math coprocessor, and every processor built by Intel (and AMD and Cyrix, for that matter) since then includes a math coprocessor. Coprocessors provide hardware for floating-point math, which otherwise would create an excessive drain on the main CPU. Math chips speed your computer's operation only when you are running software designed to take advantage of the coprocessor. All the subsequent fifth- and sixth-generation Intel and compatible processors (such as those from AMD and Cyrix) have featured an integrated floating-point unit.

Math chips (as coprocessors sometimes are called) can perform high-level mathematical operations— long division, trigonometric functions, roots, and logarithms, for example—at 10–100 times the speed of the corresponding main processor. The operations performed by the math chip are all operations that make use of noninteger numbers (numbers that contain digits after the decimal point). The need to process numbers in which the decimal is not always the last character leads to the term *floating point* because the decimal (point) can move (float), depending on the operation. The integer units in the primary CPU work with integer numbers, so they perform addition, subtraction, and multiplication operations. The primary CPU is designed to handle such computations; these operations are not offloaded to the math chip.

The instruction set of the math chip is different from that of the primary CPU. A program must detect the existence of the coprocessor and then execute instructions written explicitly for that coprocessor; otherwise, the math coprocessor draws power and does nothing else. Fortunately, most modern programs that can benefit from the use of the coprocessor correctly detect and use the coprocessor. These programs usually are math intensive: spreadsheet programs, database applications, statistical programs, and graphics programs, such as computer-aided design (CAD) software. Word processing programs do not benefit from a math chip and therefore are not designed to use one. Table 3.18 summarizes the coprocessors available for the Intel family of processors.

Table 3.18   Math Coprocessor Summary

Processor	Coprocessor	Processor	Coprocessor
8086/8088	8087	486DX/DX2/DX4	Built-in FPU
286	287	Cyrix/VIA 6x86 and newer	Built-in FPU
386SX	387SX	Intel Pentium and newer	Built-in FPU
386DX	387DX	AMD Athlon and newer	Built-in FPU
486SX/SX2	487SX, 486DX2		

FPU = Floating-point unit

The 487SX chip is a modified pinout 486DX chip with the math coprocessor enabled. When you plug in a 487SX chip, it disables the 486SX main processor and takes over all processing.

The DX2/OverDrive is equivalent to the SX2 with the addition of a functional FPU.

Virtually all modern processors include a built-in FPU

Although virtually all processors since the 486 series have built-in floating-point units, they may vary in performance. Historically, the Intel processor FPUs have dramatically outperformed those from AMD and Cyrix, although AMD and Cyrix are achieving performance parity in their newer offerings.

Within each of the original 8087 group, the maximum speed of the math chips varies. A suffix digit after the main number, as shown in Table 3.19, indicates the maximum speed at which a system can run a math chip.

Table 3.19   Maximum Math Chip Speeds

Part	Speed	Part	Speed
8087	5MHz	287	6MHz
8087-3	5MHz	287-6	6MHz
8087-2	8MHz	287-8	8MHz
8087-1	10MHz	287-10	10MHz

The 387 math coprocessors and the 486 or 487 and Pentium processors always indicate their maximum speed ratings in MHz in the part number suffix. A 486DX2-66, for example, is rated to run at 66MHz. Some processors incorporate clock multiplication, which means they can run at different speeds compared with the rest of the system.

Most systems that use the 386 or earlier processors are socketed for a math coprocessor as an option, but they do not include a coprocessor as standard equipment. A few systems on the market at that time didn't even have a socket for the coprocessor because of cost and size considerations. These systems were usually low-cost or portable systems, such as older laptops, the IBM PS/1, and the PCjr. For more specific information about math coprocessors, see the discussions of the specific chips—8087, 287, 387, and 487SX—in the later sections. Table 3.20 shows the specifications of the various math coprocessors.

Table 3.20   Older Intel Math Coprocessor Specifications

Name	Power Consumption	Case Minimum Temperature	Case Maximum Temperature	No. of Transistors	Date Introduced
8087	3 watts	0°C, 32°F	85°C, 185°F	45,000	1980
287	3 watts	0°C, 32°F	85°C, 185°F	45,000	1982
287XL	1.5 watts	0°C, 32°F	85°C, 185°F	40,000	1990
387SX	1.5 watts	0°C, 32°F	85°C, 185°F	120,000	1988
387DX	1.5 watts	0°C, 32°F	85°C, 185°F	120,000	1987

Most often, you can learn which CPU and math coprocessor are installed in a particular system by checking the markings on the chip.

Note

Most applications that formerly used floating-point math now use SSE through SSE4 instructions instead. These instructions are faster and more accurate than x87 floating-point math.

Processor Bugs

Processor manufacturers use specialized equipment to test their own processors, but you have to settle for a little less. The best processor-testing device to which you have access is a system that you know is functional; you then can use the diagnostics available from various utility software companies or your system manufacturer to test the motherboard and processor functions.

Perhaps the most infamous of these bugs is the floating-point division math bug in the early Pentium processors. This and a few other bugs are discussed in detail later in this chapter.

Because the processor is the brain of a system, most systems don't function with a defective processor. If a system seems to have a dead motherboard, try replacing the processor with one from a functioning motherboard that uses the same CPU chip. You might find that the processor in the original board is the culprit. If the system continues to play dead, however, the problem is elsewhere, most likely in the motherboard, memory, or power supply. See the chapters that cover those parts of the system for more information on troubleshooting those components. I must say that in all my years of troubleshooting and repairing PCs, I have rarely encountered defective processors.

A few system problems are built in at the factory, although these bugs or design defects are rare. By learning to recognize these problems, you can avoid unnecessary repairs or replacements. Each processor section describes several known defects in that generation of processors, such as the infamous floating-point error in the Pentium. For more information on these bugs and defects, see the following sections, and check with the processor manufacturer for updates.

Microcode and the Processor Update Feature

All processors can contain design defects or errors. Many times, the effects of any given bug can be avoided by implementing hardware or software workarounds. Intel documents these bugs and workarounds well for its processors in its processor Specification Update manual; this manual is available from Intel's website. Most of the other processor manufacturers also have bulletins or tips on their websites listing any problems or special fixes or patches for their chips.

Previously, the only way to fix a processor bug was to work around it or replace the chip with one that had the bug fixed. Starting with the Intel P6 and P7 family processors, including the Pentium Pro through Pentium D and Core 2, many bugs in a processor's design can be fixed by altering the *microcode* in the processor. Microcode is essentially a set of instructions and tables in the processor that control how the processor operates. These processors incorporate a new feature called *reprogrammable microcode*, which enables certain types of bugs to be worked around via microcode updates. The microcode updates reside in either the motherboard ROM BIOS or Windows XP/Vista updates, and are loaded into the processor by the motherboard BIOS during the POST or by Windows during the boot process. Each time the system is rebooted, the updated microcode is reloaded, ensuring that it will have the bug fix installed anytime the system is operating.

The updated microcode for a given processor is provided by Intel to either the motherboard manufacturers or to Microsoft so the code can be incorporated into the flash ROM BIOS for the board, or directly into Windows via WindowsUpdate. This is one reason it is important to keep Windows up to date, as well as to install the most recent motherboard BIOS for your systems. Because it is easier for most people to keep Windows updates as compared to updating the motherboard BIOS, it seems that more recent microcode updates are being distributed via Microsoft instead of the motherboard manufacturers.

Processor Codenames

Intel, AMD, and Cyrix have always used codenames when talking about future processors. The codenames usually are not supposed to become public, but they typically do. They can often be found in online and print news and magazine articles talking about future-generation processors. Sometimes, they even appear in motherboard manuals because the manuals are written before the processors are officially introduced. Table 3.21 lists processor codenames for reference purposes.

Table 3.21   Processor Codenames

AMD Codename	Description
X5	5x86-133 [Socket 3]
SSA5	K5 (original PR75-PR100) [Socket 5, 7]
5k86	K5 (newer PR120-PR200) [Socket 7]
K6	Original AMD K6 core; canceled
NX686	NexGen K6 core; became the K6 [Socket 7]
Little Foot	0.25μm K6 [Socket 7]
Chompers	K6-2 [Socket 7, Super7]
Sharptooth	K6-3 [Super7]
Argon	Formerly K7
K7	Athlon [Slot A]
K75	0.18μm Athlon [Slot A]
K76	0.18μm Athlon (copper interconnects) [Slot A]

Table 3.21   Continued

AMD Codename	Description
K8	Athlon 64
Thunderbird	Athlon [Slot A, Socket A]
Mustang	Athlon w/large L2; canceled
Corvette	Former mobile Athlon (now Palomino)
Palomino	0.18µm Athlon XP/MP, Mobile Athlon 4 [Socket A]
Thoroughbred-A	0.13µm Athlon XP/MP 1700-2100+ [Socket A]
Thoroughbred-B	-0.13µm Athlon XP 1700-2400+, 2600-2800+ [Socket A]; Sempron 2200-2800+ [Socket A]
Barton	0.13µm Athlon XP/MP w/512K L2 [Socket A]
Thorton	Athlon XP (256KB L2 cache) [Socket A]
Spitfire	Duron [Socket A]
Camaro	Former Morgan
Morgan	Mobile Duron and Model 7 Duron 900MHz-1.3GHz [Socket A]
Applebred	Duron 1.4GHz-1.8GHz
Appaloosa	0.13µm Morgan [Socket A]
ClawHammer	Athlon 64 (64-bit CPU) [Socket 754 and Socket 939]
ClawHammer DP	Early name for Opteron DP [Socket 940]
Newcastle	Athlon 64 [Socket 754 and Socket 939]
Winchester	0.09µm Athlon 64 [Socket 939]
San Diego	0.09µm Athlon 64 and Athlon 64 FX w/SSE3 extensions [Socket 939]
Venice	0.09µm Athlon 64 w/SSE3 extensions [Socket 939]
Odessa	0.09µm mobile Athlon 64
Manchester	Athlon 64 X2 w/512KB L2 cache and SSE3 extensions [Socket 939]
Toledo	Athlon 64 X2 w/1024KB L2 cache and SSE3 extensions [Socket 939]
SledgeHammer	Opteron w/large L2 [Socket 940]
Palermo	0.09µm Sempron [Socket 754]
Paris	Sempron [Socket 754]
Oakville	Mobile Athlon 64 and Sempron [Socket 754]
Windsor	Athlon 64 X2 and Athlon 64 FX-62 [Socket AM2]
Orleans	Athlon 64 [Socket AM2]
Manila	Sempron [Socket AM2]
Intel Codename	**Description**
P23	486SX [Socket 1, 2, 3]
P23S	486SX SL-enhanced [Socket 1, 2, 3]
P23N	487SX (coprocessor) [Socket 1]
P4	486DX [Socket 1, 2, 3]
P4S	486DX SL-enhanced [Socket 1, 2, 3]
P24	486DX2 [Socket 1, 2, 3]

Table 3.21   Continued

Intel Codename	Description
P24S	486DX2 SL-enhanced [Socket 1, 2, 3]
P24D	486DX2 (write-back cache) [Socket 3]
P24C	486DX4 [Socket 3]
P23T	486DXODP (486 OverDrive) [Socket 3]
P4T	486DXODPR (486 OverDrive) [Socket 1, 2, 3]
P24T	PODP5V (Pentium OverDrive) [Socket 2, 3]
P24CT	Pentium OverDrive 3.3V [Socket 2, 3]
P5	Pentium 60/66MHz [Socket 4]
P5T	Pentium OverDrive 120/133MHz [Socket 4]
P54C	Pentium 75MHz–120MHz [Socket 5, 7]
P54CQS	Pentium 120MHz–133MHz [Socket 5, 7]
P54CS	Pentium 120MHz–200MHz [Socket 7]
P54CT(A)	Pentium OverDrive [Socket 5, 7]
P55C	Pentium MMX [Socket 7]
P54CTB	Pentium OverDrive MMX [Socket 5, 7]
Tillamook	Mobile Pentium MMX [Mobile Module]
P6	Pentium Pro [Socket 8]
P6T	Pentium II OverDrive [Socket 8]
Klamath	0.35µm Pentium II [Slot 1]
Deschutes	0.25µm Pentium II [Slot 1]
Drake	0.25µm Pentium II Xeon [Slot 2]
Tonga	Mobile Pentium II
Covington	Celeron (cacheless Pentium II) [Slot 1]
Mendocino	0.25µm Celeron w/128KB on-die L2 [Slot 1, Socket 370]
Dixon	Mobile Pentium II w/256KB on-die L2
Katmai	0.25µm Pentium III w/SSE [Slot 1]
Tanner	0.25µm Pentium III Xeon w/SSE [Slot 2]
Coppermine	0.18µm Pentium III w/on-die L2 [Slot 1, Socket 370]
Tualatin	0.13µm Pentium III [Socket 370]
Coppermine-T	0.18µm Pentium III w/Tualatin voltage [Socket 370]
Cascades	0.18µm Pentium III Xeon [Slot 2]
Coppermine-128	0.18µm Celeron w/128KB L2 [Socket 370]
Timna	Mobile Celeron w/DRAM controller; canceled
P68	Willamette
Willamette	0.18µm Pentium 4 [Socket 423, 478]
Northwood	0.13µm Pentium 4 [Socket 478]
Prescott	0.09µm Pentium 4 w/HT; Celeron D [Socket 478]; Celeron D [Socket 775]
Smithfield	Pentium D, Pentium Extreme Edition [Socket 775]

Table 3.21   Continued

Intel Codename	Description
Presler	0.065µm Pentium D
Conroe	0.065µm desktop Core 2
Banias	130nm Pentium M w/1MB L2
Yonah	Core Solo/Duo
Merom	Mobile Core 2
WoodCrest	Server Core 2
Foster	Xeon DP [Socket 603]
Foster MP	Xeon MP [Socket 603]
Prestonia	0.13µm Xeon DP [Socket 603]
Gallatin	0.13µm Xeon MP [Socket 603]
Nocona	0.09µm Xeon [Socket 603]; Pentium 4 Extreme Edition [Socket 478 and Socket 775]
Dothan	90nm Pentium M w/2MB L2
P7	Former Merced (Itanium)
Merced	Itanium [PAC 418]
McKinley	Itanium 2 w/3MB on-die L3 [PAC 418]
Madison	0.13µm Itanium 2
Deerfield	Low-cost Madison
Montecito	0.09µm Madison
Shavano	Future Itanium family chip
Kentsfield	Core 2 Quad
Penryn	Successor to Mobile Core 2
Wolfdale	Successor to Desktop Core 2
Yorkfield	Successor to Core 2 Quad

Note that the codenames and information listed in these tables are used before the processors are officially introduced. After a chip is introduced, the codename is dropped and the chip is thereafter referred to by the marketing name used at the time of the introduction. Because many of these names refer to chips that are not yet officially released, the names or specifications might change. For chipset codenames, see Chapter 4, "Motherboards and Buses."

P1 (086) First-generation Processors

The first generation of processors represents the series of chips from Intel that were found in the first PCs. IBM, as the architect of the PC at the time, chose Intel processors and support chips to build the PC motherboard, setting a standard that would hold for many subsequent processor generations to come.

8088 and 8086 Processors

Intel introduced the 8086 back in June 1978. The 8086 was one of the first 16-bit processor chips on the market; at the time, virtually all other processors were 8-bit designs. The 8086 had 16-bit internal registers and could run a new class of software using 16-bit instructions. It also had a 16-bit external data path, so it could transfer data to memory 16 bits at a time.

The address bus was 20 bits wide, which enabled the 8086 to address a full 1MB (2^{20}) of memory. This was in stark contrast to most other chips of that time that had 8-bit internal registers, an 8-bit external data bus, and a 16-bit address bus allowing a maximum of only 64KB of RAM (2^{16}).

Unfortunately, most of the personal computer world at the time was using 8-bit processors, which ran 8-bit CP/M (Control Program for Microprocessors) operating systems and software. The board and circuit designs at the time were largely 8-bit, as well. Building a full 16-bit motherboard and memory system was costly, pricing such a computer out of the market.

The cost was high because the 8086 needed a 16-bit data bus rather than a less expensive 8-bit bus. Systems available at that time were 8-bit, and slow sales of the 8086 indicated to Intel that people weren't willing to pay for the extra performance of the full 16-bit design. In response, Intel introduced a kind of crippled version of the 8086, called the 8088. The 8088 essentially deleted 8 of the 16 bits on the data bus, making the 8088 an 8-bit chip as far as data input and output were concerned. However, because it retained the full 16-bit internal registers and the 20-bit address bus, the 8088 ran 16-bit software and was capable of addressing a full 1MB of RAM.

For these reasons, IBM selected the 8-bit 8088 chip for the original IBM PC. Years later, IBM was criticized for using the 8-bit 8088 instead of the 16-bit 8086. In retrospect, it was a very wise decision. IBM even covered up the physical design in its ads, which at the time indicated its new PC had a "high-speed 16-bit microprocessor." IBM could say that because the 8088 still ran the same powerful 16-bit software the 8086 ran, just a little more slowly. In fact, programmers universally thought of the 8088 as a 16-bit chip because there was virtually no way a program could distinguish an 8088 from an 8086. This enabled IBM to deliver a PC capable of running a new generation of 16-bit software, while retaining a much less expensive 8-bit design for the hardware. Because of this, the IBM PC was actually priced less at its introduction than the most popular PC of the time, the Apple II. For the trivia buffs out there, the IBM PC listed for $1,265 and included only 16KB of RAM, whereas a similarly configured Apple II cost $1,355.

Even though the 8088 was introduced in June 1979, the original IBM PC that used the processor did not appear until August 1981. Back then, a significant lag time often occurred between the introduction of a new processor and systems that incorporated it. That is unlike today, when new processors and systems using them often are released on the same day.

The 8088 in the IBM PC ran at 4.77MHz; the average instruction on the 8088 took 12 cycles to complete.

Computer users sometimes wonder why a 640KB conventional-memory barrier exists if the 8088 chip can address 1MB of memory. The conventional-memory barrier exists because IBM reserved 384KB of the upper portion of the 1,024KB (1MB) address space of the 8088 for use by adapter cards and system BIOS. The lower 640KB is the conventional memory in which DOS and software applications execute.

80186 and 80188 Processors

After Intel produced the 8086 and 8088 chips, it created versions of these chips with some of the required support components integrated within the processor.

The relationship between the 80186 and 80188 is the same as that of the 8086 and 8088; the 80188 is essentially an 8-bit interface version of the 80186. The advantage of the 80186 and 80188 is that they combine on a single chip 15–20 of the 8086–8088 series system components—a fact that can greatly reduce the number of components in a computer design. The 80186 and 80188 chips were used for highly intelligent peripheral adapter cards of that age, such as network adapters.

8087 Coprocessor

The math coprocessor or floating-point unit that was paired with the 8086 chip was called the 8087 numeric data processor (NDP), the math coprocessor, or simply the math chip. The 8087 is designed to perform high-level math operations at many times the speed of the main processor. The primary advantage of using this chip is the increased execution speed in number-crunching programs, such as spreadsheet applications.

P2 (286) Second-generation Processors

The second generation of PC processors allowed for a great leap in system speed and processing efficiency. With these chips we went from moving 8 bits of data around to moving 16 bits at a time. The following section details the second-generation PC processor, the 286.

286 Processors

The Intel 80286 (normally abbreviated as 286) processor did not suffer from the compatibility problems that damned the 80186 and 80188. The 286 chip, first introduced in 1982, is the CPU behind the original IBM PC AT (Advanced Technology). Other computer makers manufactured what came to be known as IBM clones, with many of these manufacturers calling their systems AT-compatible or AT-class computers.

When IBM developed the AT, it selected the 286 as the basis for the new system because the chip provided compatibility with the 8088 used in the PC and the XT. Therefore, software written for those chips should run on the 286. The 286 chip is many times faster than the 8088 used in the XT, and at the time it offered a major performance boost to PCs used in businesses. The processing speed, or throughput, of the original AT (which ran at 6MHz) is five times greater than that of the PC running at 4.77MHz. The die for the 286 is shown in Figure 3.36.

286 systems are faster than their predecessors for several reasons. The main reason is that 286 processors are much more efficient in executing instructions. An average instruction takes 12 clock cycles on the 8086 or 8088, but takes an average of only 4.5 cycles on the 286 processor. Additionally, the 286 chip can handle up to 16 bits of data at a time through an external data bus twice the size of the 8088.

The 286 chip has two modes of operation: real mode and protected mode. The two modes are distinct enough to make the 286 resemble two chips in one. In real mode, a 286 acts essentially the same as an 8086 chip and is fully *object-code compatible* with the 8086 and 8088. (A processor with object-code compatibility can run programs written for another processor without modification and execute every system instruction in the same manner.)

In the protected mode of operation, the 286 was truly something new. In this mode, a program designed to take advantage of the chip's capabilities believes that it has access to 1GB of memory (including virtual memory). The 286 chip, however, can address only 16MB of hardware memory. A significant failing of the 286 chip is that it cannot switch from protected mode to real mode without a hardware reset (a warm reboot) of the system. (It can, however, switch from real mode to protected mode without a reset.) A major improvement of the 386 over the 286 is that software can switch the 386 from real mode to protected mode, and vice versa. See the section "Processor Modes," earlier in this chapter for more information.

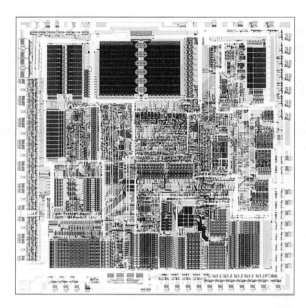

Figure 3.36 286 Processor die. *Photograph used by permission of Intel Corporation.*

Only a small amount of software that took advantage of the 286 chip was sold until Windows 3.0 offered standard mode for 286 compatibility; by that time, the hottest-selling chip was the 386. Still, the 286 was Intel's first attempt to produce a CPU chip that supported multitasking, in which multiple programs run at the same time.

80287 Coprocessor

The 80287, internally, is the same math chip as the 8087, although the pins used to plug them into the motherboard are different. Both the 80287 and the 8087 operate as though they are identical.

In most systems, the 80286 internally divides the system clock by 2 to derive the processor clock. The 80287 internally divides the system-clock frequency by 3. For this reason, most AT-type computers run the 80287 at one-third the system clock rate, which also is two-thirds the clock speed of the 80286. Because the 286 and 287 chips are asynchronous, the interface between the 286 and 287 chips is not as efficient as with the 8088 and 8087.

P3 (386) Third-generation Processors

The third generation represents perhaps the most significant change in processors since the first PC. The big deal was the migration from processors that handled 16-bit operations to true 32-bit chips. The third-generation processors were so far ahead of their time, it took fully 10 years before 32-bit operating systems and software became mainstream, and by that time the third-generation chips had become a memory. The following section details the third-generation processors.

386 Processors

The Intel 80386 (usually abbreviated as 386) caused quite a stir in the PC industry because of the vastly improved performance it brought to the personal computer. Compared with 8088 and 286 systems, the 386 chip offered greater performance in almost all areas of operation.

The 386 is a full 32-bit processor optimized for high-speed operation and multitasking operating systems. Intel introduced the chip in 1985, but the 386 appeared in the first systems in late 1986 and early 1987. The Compaq Deskpro 386 and systems made by several other manufacturers introduced the chip; somewhat later, IBM used the chip in its PS/2 Model 80.

The 386 can execute the real-mode instructions of an 8086 or 8088, but in fewer clock cycles. The 386 was as efficient as the 286 in executing instructions—the average instruction took about 4.5 clock cycles. In raw performance, therefore, the 286 and 386 actually seemed to be at almost equal clock rates. The 386 offered greater performance in other ways, mainly because of additional software capability (modes) and a greatly enhanced memory management unit (MMU). The die for the 386 is shown in Figure 3.37.

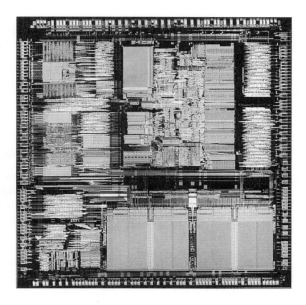

Figure 3.37 *386 processor die. Photograph used by permission of Intel Corporation.*

The 386 can switch to and from protected mode under software control without a system reset—a capability that makes using protected mode more practical. In addition, the 386 includes a new mode, called virtual real mode, which enables several real-mode sessions to run simultaneously under protected mode.

The protected mode of the 386 is fully compatible with the protected mode of the 286. Intel extended the memory-addressing capabilities of 386 protected mode with a new MMU that provided advanced memory paging and program switching. These features were extensions of the 286 type of MMU, so the 386 remained fully compatible with the 286 at the system-code level.

The 386 chip's virtual real mode was also new. In virtual real mode, the processor could run with hardware memory protection while simulating an 8086's real-mode operation. Multiple copies of DOS and other operating systems, therefore, could run simultaneously on this processor, each in a protected area of memory. If the programs in one segment crashed, the rest of the system was protected.

Numerous variations of the 386 chip were manufactured, some of which are less powerful and some of which are less power hungry. The following sections cover the members of the 386-chip family and their differences.

386DX Processors

The 386DX chip was the first of the 386 family members that Intel introduced. The 386 is a full 32-bit processor with 32-bit internal registers, a 32-bit internal data bus, and a 32-bit external data bus. The 386 contains 275,000 transistors in a very large scale integration (VLSI) circuit. The chip comes in a 132-pin package and draws approximately 400 milliamperes (ma), which is less power than even the 8086 requires. The 386 has a smaller power requirement because it is made of Complementary Metal-Oxide Semiconductor (CMOS) materials. The CMOS design enables devices to consume extremely low levels of power.

The Intel 386 chip was available in clock speeds ranging from 16MHz–33MHz; other manufacturers, primarily AMD and Cyrix, offered comparable versions with speeds up to 40MHz.

The 386DX can address 4GB of physical memory. Its built-in virtual memory manager enables software designed to take advantage of enormous amounts of memory to act as though a system has 64TB of memory. (A terabyte, or TB, is 1,099,511,627,776 bytes of memory, or about 1,000GB.)

386SX Processors

The 386SX was designed for systems designers looking for 386 capabilities at 286 system prices. Similar to the 286, the 386SX is restricted to only 16 bits when communicating with other system components, such as memory. Internally, however, the 386SX is identical to the DX chip; the 386SX has 32-bit internal registers and can therefore run 32-bit software. The 386SX uses a 24-bit memory-addressing scheme like that of the 286, rather than the full 32-bit memory address bus of the standard 386. The 386SX, therefore, can address a maximum 16MB of physical memory rather than the 4GB of physical memory the 386DX can address. Before it was discontinued, the 386SX was available in clock speeds ranging from 16MHz to 33MHz.

The 386SX signaled the end of the 286 because of the 386SX chip's superior MMU and the addition of the virtual real mode. Under a software manager such as Windows or OS/2, the 386SX can run numerous DOS programs at the same time. The capability to run 386-specific software is another important advantage of the 386SX over any 286 or older design. For example, Windows 3.1 runs nearly as well on a 386SX as it does on a 386DX.

386SL Processors

The 386SL is another variation on the 386 chip. This low-power CPU had the same capabilities as the 386SX, but it was designed for laptop systems in which low power consumption was necessary. The SL chips offered special power-management features that were important to systems that ran on batteries. The SL chip also offered several sleep modes to conserve power.

The chip included an extended architecture that contained a System Management Interrupt (SMI), which provided access to the power-management features. Also included in the SL chip was special support for LIM (Lotus Intel Microsoft) expanded memory functions and a cache controller. The cache controller was designed to control a 16KB–64KB external processor cache.

These extra functions account for the higher transistor count in the SL chips (855,000) compared with even the 386DX processor (275,000). The 386SL was available in 25MHz clock speed.

Intel offered a companion to the 386SL chip for laptops called the 82360SL I/O subsystem. The 82360SL provided many common peripheral functions, such as serial and parallel ports, a direct memory access (DMA) controller, an interrupt controller, and power-management logic for the 386SL processor. This chip subsystem worked with the processor to provide an ideal solution for the small size and low power-consumption requirements of portable and laptop systems.

80387 Coprocessor

Although the 80387 chips ran asynchronously, 386 systems were designed so that the math chip ran at the same clock speed as the main CPU. Unlike the 80287 coprocessor, which was merely an 8087 with different pins to plug into the AT motherboard, the 80387 coprocessor was a high-performance math chip specifically designed to work with the 386.

All 387 chips used a low power-consumption CMOS design. The 387 coprocessor had two basic designs: the 387DX coprocessor, which was designed to work with the 386DX processor, and the 387SX coprocessor, which was designed to work with the 386SX, SL, or SLC processor.

Intel originally offered several speeds for the 387DX coprocessor. But when the company designed the 33MHz version, a smaller mask was required to reduce the lengths of the signal pathways in the chip. This increased the performance of the chip by roughly 20%.

Note

Because Intel lagged in developing the 387 coprocessor, some early 386 systems were designed with a socket for a 287 coprocessor. Performance levels associated with that combination, however, left much to be desired.

Installing a 387DX is easy, but you must be careful to orient the chip in its socket properly; otherwise, the chip will be destroyed. The most common cause of burned pins on the 387DX is incorrect installation. In many systems, the 387DX was oriented differently from other large chips. Follow the manufacturer's installation instructions carefully to avoid damaging the 387DX; Intel's warranty does not cover chips that are installed incorrectly.

Several manufacturers developed their own versions of the Intel 387 coprocessors, some of which were touted as being faster than the original Intel chips. The general compatibility record of these chips was very good.

P4 (486) Fourth-generation Processors

The third generation had been a large change from the previous generations of processors. With the fourth generation, more refinement than complete redesign was accomplished. Even so, Intel, AMD, and others managed to literally double processor performance with their fourth-generation processors. The following section defines the fourth-generation processors from Intel, AMD, and others.

486 Processors

In the race for more speed, the Intel 80486 (normally abbreviated as 486) was another major leap forward. The additional power available in the 486 fueled tremendous growth in the software industry. Tens of millions of copies of Windows, and millions of copies of OS/2, have been sold largely because the 486 finally made the GUI of Windows and OS/2 a realistic option for people who work on their computers every day.

Four main features make a given 486 processor roughly twice as fast as an equivalent MHz 386 chip:

- **Reduced instruction-execution time**—A single instruction in the 486 takes an average of only two clock cycles to complete, compared with an average of more than four cycles on the 386. Clock-multiplied versions, such as the DX2 and DX4, further reduced this to about two cycles per instruction.

- **Internal (Level 1) cache**—The built-in cache has a hit ratio of 90%–95%, which describes how often zero-wait-state read operations occur. External caches can improve this ratio further.

- **Burst-mode memory cycles**—A standard 32-bit (4-byte) memory transfer takes two clock cycles. After a standard 32-bit transfer, more data up to the next 12 bytes (or three transfers) can be transferred with only one cycle used for each 32-bit (4-byte) transfer. Thus, up to 16 bytes of contiguous, sequential memory data can be transferred in as little as five cycles instead of eight cycles or more. This effect can be even greater when the transfers are only 8 bits or 16 bits each.

- **Built-in (synchronous) enhanced math coprocessor (some versions)**—The math coprocessor runs synchronously with the main processor and executes math instructions in fewer cycles than previous designs did. On average, the math coprocessor built into the DX-series chips provides two to three times greater math performance than an external 387 chip.

The 486 chip is about twice as fast as the 386, so a 386DX-40 is about as fast as a 486SX-20. This made the 486 a much more desirable option, primarily because it could more easily be upgraded to a DX2 or DX4 processor at a later time. You can see why the arrival of the 486 rapidly killed off the 386 in the marketplace.

Most of the 486 chips were offered in a variety of maximum speed ratings, varying from 16MHz up to 133MHz. Additionally, 486 processors have slight differences in overall pin configurations. The DX, DX2, and SX processors have a virtually identical 168-pin configuration, whereas the OverDrive chips have either the standard 168-pin configuration or a specially modified 169-pin OverDrive (sometimes also called 487SX) configuration. If your motherboard has two sockets, the primary one likely supports the standard 168-pin configuration, and the secondary (OverDrive) socket supports the 169-pin OverDrive configuration. Most of the later 486-based motherboards with a single ZIF socket support any of the 486 processors except the DX4. The DX4 is different because it requires 3.3V to operate instead of 5V, like most other chips up to that time.

A processor rated for a given speed always functions at any of the lower speeds. A 100MHz-rated 486DX4 chip, for example, runs at 75MHz if it is plugged into a 25MHz motherboard. Note that the DX2/OverDrive processors operate internally at two times the motherboard clock rate, whereas the DX4 processors operate at two, two-and-one-half, or three times the motherboard clock rate. Table 3.22 shows the various speed combinations that can result from using the DX2 or DX4 processors with different motherboard clock speeds.

Table 3.22   Intel DX2 and DX4 Operating Speeds Versus CPU Bus (Motherboard) Clock Speeds

CPU Bus Speed	DX2/DX4 Speed (2× Mode)	DX4 Speed (2.5× Mode)	DX4 Speed (3× Mode)
16MHz	32MHz	40MHz	48MHz
20MHz	40MHz	50MHz	60MHz
25MHz	50MHz	63MHz	75MHz
33MHz	66MHz	83MHz	100MHz
40MHz	80MHz	100MHz	120MHz
50MHz	100MHz	n/a	n/a

The internal multiplier of the DX4 processor is controlled by the CLKMUL (clock multiplier) signal at pin R-17 (Socket 1) or S-18 (Socket 2, 3, or 6). In most cases, one or two jumpers will be on the board near the processor socket to control the settings for these pins. The motherboard documentation should cover these settings if they can be changed.

One interesting capability here is to run the DX4-100 chip in a doubled mode with a 50MHz motherboard speed. This gives you a very fast memory bus, along with the same 100MHz processor speed, as if you were running the chip in a 33/100MHz tripled mode.

Many VL-Bus motherboards can run the VL-Bus slots in a buffered mode, add wait states, or even selectively change the clock only for the VL-Bus slots to keep them compatible. In most cases, they don't run properly at 50MHz. Consult your motherboard documentation—or even better, your chipset documentation—to see how your board is set up.

Caution

When upgrading an existing system, you should be sure that your socket supports the chip you are installing. This was especially true when putting a DX4 processor in an older system. In that scenario, you needed some type of adapter to regulate the voltage down to 3.3V. Putting the DX4 in a 5V socket destroys the chip! See the earlier section on processor sockets for more information.

486DX Processors

The original Intel 486DX processor was introduced on April 10, 1989, and systems using this chip first appeared during 1990. The first chips had a maximum speed rating of 25MHz; later versions of the 486DX were available in 33MHz- and 50MHz-rated versions. The 486DX originally was available only in a 5V, 168-pin PGA version, but later became available in 5V, 196-pin plastic quad flat pack (PQFP) and 3.3V, 208-pin small quad flat pack (SQFP). These latter form factors were available in SL enhanced versions, which were intended primarily for portable or laptop applications in which saving power is important.

Two main features separate the 486 processor from its predecessors:

■ The 486DX integrates functions such as the math coprocessor, cache controller, and cache memory into the chip.

■ The 486 also was designed with easy installation and upgradeability in mind; double-speed OverDrive upgrades were available for most systems.

The 486DX processor was fabricated with low-power CMOS technology. The chip has a 32-bit internal register size, a 32-bit external data bus, and a 32-bit address bus. These dimensions are equal to those of the 386DX processor. The internal register size is where the "32-bit" designation used in advertisements comes from. The 486DX chip contains 1.2 million transistors on a piece of silicon no larger than your thumbnail. This figure is more than four times the number of components on 386 processors and should give you a good indication of the 486 chip's relative power. The die for the 486 is shown in Figure 3.38.

The standard 486DX contains a processing unit, floating-point unit (math coprocessor), memory-management unit, and cache controller with 8KB of internal-cache RAM. Due to the internal cache and a more efficient internal processing unit, the 486 family of processors can execute individual instructions in an average of only two processor cycles. Compare this figure with the 286 and 386 families, both of which execute an average 4.5 cycles per instruction. Compare it also with the original 8086 and 8088 processors, which execute an average 12 cycles per instruction. At a given clock rate (MHz), therefore, a 486 processor is roughly twice as efficient as a 386 processor; a 16MHz 486SX is roughly equal to a 33MHz 386DX system; and a 20MHz 486SX is equal to a 40MHz 386DX system. Any of the faster 486s are way beyond the 386 in performance.

Figure 3.38   486 processor die. *Photograph used by permission of Intel Corporation.*

The 486 is fully instruction-set-compatible with previous Intel processors, such as the 386, but offers several additional instructions (most of which have to do with controlling the internal cache).

Similar to the 386DX, the 486 can address 4GB of physical memory and manage as much as 64TB of virtual memory. The 486 fully supports the three operating modes introduced in the 386:

- **Real mode**—In this mode, the 486 (similar to the 386) runs unmodified 8086-type software.

- **Protected mode**—In this mode, the 486 (similar to the 386) offers sophisticated memory paging and program switching.

- **Virtual real mode**—In this mode, the 486 (similar to the 386) can run multiple copies of DOS or other operating systems while simulating an 8086's real-mode operation. Under an operating system such as Windows or OS/2, therefore, both 16-bit and 32-bit programs can run simultaneously on this processor with hardware memory protection. If one program crashes, the rest of the system is protected, and you can reboot the blown portion through various means, depending on the operating software.

The 486DX series has a built-in math coprocessor that sometimes is called an MCP (math coprocessor) or FPU. This series is unlike previous Intel CPU chips, which required you to add a math coprocessor if you needed faster calculations for complex mathematics. The FPU in the 486DX series is 100% software-compatible with the external 387 math coprocessor used with the 386, but it delivers more than twice the performance. It runs in synchronization with the main processor and executes most instructions in half as many cycles as the 386.

486SL

The 486SL was a short-lived, standalone chip. The SL enhancements and features became available in virtually all the 486 processors (SX, DX, and DX2) in what are called *SL enhanced versions*. SL enhancement refers to a special design that incorporates special power-saving features.

The SL-enhanced chips originally were designed to be installed in laptop or notebook systems that run on batteries, but they found their way into desktop systems, as well. The SL-enhanced chips featured special power-management techniques, such as sleep mode and clock throttling, to reduce power consumption when necessary. These chips were available in 3.3V versions, as well.

Intel designed a power-management architecture called *System Management Mode (SMM)*. This mode of operation is totally isolated and independent from other CPU hardware and software. SMM provides hardware resources such as timers, registers, and other I/O logic that can control and power down mobile-computer components without interfering with any of the other system resources. SMM executes in a dedicated memory space called *System Management Memory*, which is not visible and does not interfere with operating system and application software. SMM has an interrupt called *System Management Interrupt (SMI)*, which services power-management events and is independent from—and a higher priority than—any of the other interrupts.

SMM provides power management with flexibility and security that were not available previously. For example, an SMI occurs when an application program tries to access a peripheral device that is powered down for battery savings, which powers up the peripheral device and re-executes the I/O instruction automatically.

Intel also designed a feature called Suspend/Resume in the SL processor. The system manufacturer can use this feature to provide the portable computer user with instant on-and-off capability. An SL system typically can resume (instant on) in 1 second from the suspend state (instant off) to exactly where it left off. You do not need to reboot, load the operating system, or load the applications and their data. Instead, simply push the Suspend/Resume button and the system is ready to go.

The SL CPU was designed to consume almost no power in the suspend state. This feature means that the system can stay in the suspend state possibly for weeks and yet start up instantly right where it left off. An SL system can keep working data in normal RAM memory safe for a long time while it is in the suspend state, but saving to a disk still is prudent.

486SX

The 486SX, introduced in April 1991, was designed to be sold as a lower-cost version of the 486. The 486SX is virtually identical to the full DX processor, but the chip does not incorporate the FPU or math coprocessor portion.

As you read earlier in this chapter, the 386SX was a scaled-down (some people would say crippled) 16-bit version of the full-blown 32-bit 386DX. The 386SX even had a completely different pinout and was not interchangeable with the more powerful DX version. The 486SX, however, is a different story. The 486SX is, in fact, a full-blown 32-bit 486 processor that is basically pin compatible with the DX. A few pin functions are different or rearranged, but each pin fits into the same socket.

The 486SX chip was more a marketing quirk than new technology. Early versions of the 486SX chip actually were DX chips that showed defects in the math-coprocessor section. Instead of being scrapped, the chips were packaged with the FPU section disabled and sold as SX chips. This arrangement lasted for only a short time; thereafter, SX chips got their own mask, which is different from the DX mask. (A *mask* is the photographic blueprint of the processor and is used to etch the intricate signal pathways into a silicon chip.) The transistor count dropped to 1.185 million (from 1.2 million) to reflect this new mask.

The 486SX was available in 16MHz-, 20MHz-, 25MHz-, and 33MHz-rated speeds, and a 486 SX/2 was also available that ran at up to 50MHz or 66MHz. The 486SX typically was made in a 168-pin version, although other surface-mount versions were manufactured in SL-enhanced models.

Despite what Intel's marketing and sales information implies, no technical provision exists for adding a separate math coprocessor to a 486SX system; neither was a separate math coprocessor chip ever available to plug in. Instead, Intel wanted you to add a new 486 processor with a built-in math unit and disable the SX CPU that already was on the motherboard.

487SX

The 487SX math coprocessor, as Intel called it, really is a complete 25MHz 486DX CPU with an extra pin added and some other pins rearranged. When the 487SX is installed in the extra socket provided in a 486SX CPU–based system, the 487SX turns off the existing 486SX via a new signal on one of the pins. The extra key pin actually carries no signal itself and exists only to prevent improper orientation when the chip is installed in a socket.

The 487SX takes over all CPU functions from the 486SX and also provides math coprocessor functionality in the system. At first glance, this setup seems rather strange and wasteful, so perhaps further explanation is in order. Fortunately, the 487SX turned out to be a stopgap measure while Intel prepared its real surprise: the OverDrive processor. The DX2/OverDrive speed-doubling chips, which are designed for the 487SX 169-pin socket, have the same pinout as the 487SX. These upgrade chips are installed in exactly the same way as the 487SX; therefore, any system that supports the 487SX also supports the DX2/OverDrive chips.

Originally, Intel discouraged users from removing the existing chip from the socket and replacing it with a 487SX (or even a DX or DX2/OverDrive). Instead, Intel recommended that PC manufacturers include a dedicated upgrade (OverDrive) socket in their systems because several risks were involved in removing the original CPU from a standard socket. (The following section elaborates on those risks.) Later Intel recommended—or even insisted on—the use of a single processor socket of a ZIF design, which makes upgrading an easy task physically.

◄◄   See "Zero Insertion Force (ZIF)," p. 99.

DX2/OverDrive and DX4 Processors

On March 3, 1992, Intel introduced the DX2 speed-doubling processors. On May 26, 1992, Intel announced that the DX2 processors also would be available in a retail version called OverDrive. Originally, the OverDrive versions of the DX2 were available only in 169-pin versions, which meant that they could be used only with 486SX systems that had sockets configured to support the rearranged pin configuration.

On September 14, 1992, Intel introduced 168-pin OverDrive versions for upgrading 486DX systems. These processors could be added to existing 486 (SX or DX) systems as an upgrade, even if those systems did not support the 169-pin configuration. When you use this processor as an upgrade, you install the new chip in your system, which subsequently runs twice as fast.

The DX2/OverDrive processors run internally at twice the clock rate of the host system. If the motherboard clock is 25MHz, for example, the DX2/OverDrive chip runs internally at 50MHz; likewise, if the motherboard is a 33MHz design, the DX2/OverDrive runs at 66MHz. The DX2/OverDrive speed doubling has no effect on the rest of the system; all components on the motherboard run the same as they do with a standard 486 processor. Therefore, you do not have to change other components (such as memory) to accommodate the double-speed chip. The DX2/OverDrive chips have been available in several speeds. Three speed-rated versions have been offered:

- 40MHz DX2/OverDrive for 16MHz or 20MHz systems
- 50MHz DX2/OverDrive for 25MHz systems
- 66MHz DX2/OverDrive for 33MHz systems

Notice that these ratings indicate the maximum speed at which the chip is capable of running. You could use a 66MHz-rated chip in place of the 50MHz- or 40MHz-rated parts with no problem, although the chip will run only at the slower speeds. The actual speed of the chip is double the motherboard clock frequency. When the 40MHz DX2/OverDrive chip is installed in a 16MHz 486SX system, for example, the chip functions only at 32MHz—exactly double the motherboard speed. Intel originally stated that no 100MHz DX2/OverDrive chip would be available for 50MHz systems—which technically has not been true because the DX4 could be set to run in a clock-doubled mode and used in a 50MHz motherboard (see the discussion of the DX4 processor in this section).

The only part of the DX2 chip that doesn't run at double speed is the bus interface unit, a region of the chip that handles I/O between the CPU and the outside world. By translating between the differing internal and external clock speeds, the bus interface unit makes speed doubling transparent to the rest of the system. The DX2 appears to the rest of the system to be a regular 486DX chip, but one that seems to execute instructions twice as fast.

DX2/OverDrive chips are based on the 0.8-micron circuit technology that was first used in the 50MHz 486DX. The DX2 contains 1.2 million transistors in a three-layer form. The internal 8KB cache, integer, and floating-point units all run at double speed. External communication with the PC runs at normal speed to maintain compatibility.

Besides upgrading existing systems, one of the best parts of the DX2 concept was the fact that system designers could introduce very fast systems by using cheaper motherboard designs, rather than the more costly designs that would support a straight high-speed clock. Therefore, a 50MHz 486DX2 system was much less expensive than a straight 50MHz 486DX system. The system board in a 486DX-50 system operates at a true 50MHz. The 486DX2 CPU in a 486DX2-50 system operates internally at 50MHz, but the motherboard operates at only 25MHz.

You might be thinking that a true 50MHz DX processor–based system still would be faster than a speed-doubled 25MHz system, and this generally is true. But, the differences in speed actually are very slight—a real testament to the integration of the 486 processor and especially to the cache design.

When the processor has to go to system memory for data or instructions, for example, it must do so at the slower motherboard operating frequency (for example, 25MHz). Because the 8KB internal cache of the 486DX2 has a hit rate of 90%–95%, however, the CPU must access system memory only 5%–10% of the time for memory reads. Therefore, the performance of the DX2 system can come very close to that of a true 50MHz DX system and cost much less. Even though the motherboard runs at only 33.33MHz, a system with a DX2 66MHz processor ends up being faster than a true 50MHz DX system, especially if the DX2 system has a good L2 cache.

Many 486 motherboard designs also include a secondary cache that is external to the cache integrated into the 486 chip. This external cache allows for much faster access when the 486 chip calls for external-memory access. The size of this external cache can vary anywhere from 16KB to 512KB or more. When you add a DX2 processor, an external cache is even more important for achieving the greatest performance gain. This cache greatly reduces the wait states the processor must add when writing to system memory or when a read causes an internal cache miss. For this reason, some systems perform better with the DX2/OverDrive processors than others, usually depending on the size and efficiency of the external-memory cache system on the motherboard. Systems that have no external cache still enjoy a near-doubling of CPU performance, but operations that involve a great deal of memory access are slower.

Although the standard DX4 technically was not sold as a retail part, it could be purchased from several vendors, along with the 3.3V voltage adapter needed to install the chip in a 5V socket. These adapters have jumpers that enable you to select the DX4 clock multiplier and set it to 2x, 2.5x, or 3x mode. In a 50MHz DX system, you could install a DX4/voltage-regulator combination set in 2x mode for a motherboard speed of 50MHz and a processor speed of 100MHz! Although you might not be able to take advantage of certain VL-Bus adapter cards, you will have one of the fastest 486-class PCs available.

Intel also sold a special DX4 OverDrive processor that included a built-in voltage regulator and heatsink that are specifically designed for the retail market. The DX4 OverDrive chip is essentially the same as the standard 3.3V DX4 with the main exception that it runs on 5V because it includes an on-chip regulator. Also, the DX4 OverDrive chip runs only in the tripled speed mode, and not the 2x or 2.5x modes of the standard DX4 processor. Intel OverDrive products were discontinued several years ago, as were third-party equivalents.

Pentium OverDrive for 486SX2 and DX2 Systems

The Pentium OverDrive Processor became available in 1995. An OverDrive chip for 486DX4 systems had been planned, but poor marketplace performance of the SX2/DX2 chip resulted in it never seeing the light of day. One thing to keep in mind about the 486 Pentium OverDrive chip is that although it was intended primarily for SX2 and DX2 systems, it should work in any upgradeable 486SX or DX system that has a Socket 2 or Socket 3. If you want to install one in an older system, you can check Intel's online upgrade guide for compatibility, located at http://support.intel.com/support/processors/overdrive/.

The Pentium OverDrive processor is designed for systems that have a processor socket that follows the Intel Socket 2 specification. This processor also works in systems that have a Socket 3 design, although you should ensure that the voltage is set for 5V rather than 3.3V. The Pentium OverDrive chip includes a 32KB internal L1 cache and the same superscalar (multiple instruction path) architecture of the real Pentium chip. Besides a 32-bit Pentium core, these processors feature increased clock-speed operation due to internal clock multiplication and incorporate an internal write-back cache (standard with the Pentium). If the motherboard supports the write-back cache function, increased performance is realized. Unfortunately, most motherboards, especially older ones with the Socket 2 design, support only write-through cache.

Most tests of these OverDrive chips show them to be only slightly ahead of the DX4-100 and behind the DX4-120 and true Pentium 60, 66, or 75. Based on the relative affordability of low-end "real" Pentiums (in their day), it was hard not to justify making the step up to a Pentium system.

AMD 486 (5x86)

AMD made a line of 486-compatible chips that installed into standard 486 motherboards. In fact, AMD made the fastest 486 processor available, which it called the Am5x86-P75. The name was a little misleading because the 5x86 part made some people think that this was a fifth-generation Pentium-type processor. In reality, it was a fast clock-multiplied (4x clock) 486 that ran at four times the speed of the 33MHz 486 motherboard you plugged it into.

The 5x86 offered high-performance features such as a unified 16KB write-back cache and 133MHz core clock speed; it was approximately comparable to a Pentium 75, which is why it was denoted with a P-75 in the part number. It was the ideal choice for cost-effective 486 upgrades, where changing the motherboard is difficult or impossible.

Not all 486 motherboards support the 5x86. The best way to verify that your motherboard supports the chip is by checking with the documentation that came with the board. Look for keywords such as "Am5X86," "AMD-X5," "clock-quadrupled," "133MHz," or other similar wording. Another good way to determine whether your motherboard supports the AMD 5x86 is to look for it in the listed models on AMD's website.

There are a few things to note when installing a 5x86 processor into a 486 motherboard:

- The operating voltage for the 5x86 is 3.45V +/- 0.15V. Not all motherboards have this setting, but most that incorporate a Socket 3 design should. If your 486 motherboard is a Socket 1 or 2 design, you cannot use the 5x86 processor directly. The 3.45V processor does not operate in a 5V socket and can be damaged. To convert a 5V motherboard to 3.45V, processors with adapters could be purchased from several vendors, such as Kingston, PowerLeap, and Evergreen. These companies and others sold the 5x86 complete with a voltage regulator adapter attached in an easy-to-install package. These versions are ideal for older 486 motherboards that don't have a Socket 3 design and might still be available in the surplus or closeout market. If not, you can create your own upgrade kit with a processor, voltage adapter, and heatsink/fan.

- It is generally better to purchase a new motherboard, processor, and RAM than to buy one of these adapters. Buying a new motherboard is also better than using an adapter because the older BIOS might not understand the requirements of the processor as far as speed is concerned. BIOS updates often are required with older boards.

- Most Socket 3 motherboards have jumpers, enabling you to set the voltage manually. Some boards don't have jumpers, but have voltage autodetect instead. These systems check the VOLDET pin (pin S4) on the microprocessor when the system is powered on.

- The VOLDET pin is tied to ground (Vss) internally to the microprocessor. If you cannot find any jumpers for setting voltage, you can check the motherboard as follows: Switch the PC off, remove the microprocessor, connect pin S4 to a Vss pin on the ZIF socket, power on, and check any Vcc pin with a voltmeter. This should read 3.45 (± 0.15) volts. See the previous section on CPU sockets for the pinout.

- The 5x86 requires a 33MHz motherboard speed, so be sure the board is set to that frequency. The 5x86 operates at an internal speed of 133MHz. Therefore, the jumpers must be set for "clock-quadrupled" or "4x clock" mode. When you set the jumpers correctly on the motherboard, the CLKMUL pin (pin R17) on the processor will be connected to ground (Vss). If there is no 4x clock setting, the standard DX2 2x clock setting should work.

- Some motherboards have jumpers that configure the internal cache in either write-back (WB) or write-through (WT) mode. They do this by pulling the WB/WT pin (pin B13) on the microprocessor to logic High (Vcc) for WB or to ground (Vss) for WT. For best performance, configure your system in WB mode; however, reset the cache to WT mode if problems running applications occur or the floppy drive doesn't work right (DMA conflicts).

- The 5x86 runs hot, so a heatsink is required. It normally must have a fan, and most upgrade kits included a fan.

In addition to the 5x86, the AMD-enhanced 486 product line included 80MHz, 100MHz, and 120MHz CPUs. These are the A80486DX2-80SV8B (40MHz×2), A80486DX4-100SV8B (33MHz×3), and A80486DX4-120SV8B (40MHz×3).

Cyrix/TI 486

The Cyrix 486DX2/DX4 processors were available in 100MHz, 80MHz, 75MHz, 66MHz, and 50MHz versions. Similar to the AMD 486 chips, the Cyrix versions are fully compatible with Intel's 486 processors and work in most 486 motherboards.

The Cx486DX2/DX4 incorporates an 8KB write-back cache, an integrated floating-point unit, advanced power management, and SMM, and it was available in 3.3V versions.

Note

TI originally made all the Cyrix-designed 486 processors, and under the agreement it also sold them under the TI name. They are essentially the same as the Cyrix chips.

P5 (586) Fifth-generation Processors

After the fourth-generation chips such as the 486, Intel and other chip manufacturers went back to the drawing board to come up with new architectures and features that they would later incorporate into what they called fifth-generation chips. This section defines the fifth-generation processors from Intel, AMD, and others.

Pentium Processors

On October 19, 1992, Intel announced that the fifth generation of its compatible microprocessor line (codenamed P5) would be named the Pentium processor rather than the 586, as everybody had assumed. Calling the new chip the 586 would have been natural, but Intel discovered that it could not trademark a number designation, and the company wanted to prevent other manufacturers from using the same name for any clone chips it might develop. The actual Pentium chip shipped on March 22, 1993. Systems that used these chips were only a few months behind.

The Pentium is fully compatible with previous Intel processors, but it differs from them in many ways. At least one of these differences is revolutionary: The Pentium features twin data pipelines, which enable it to execute two instructions at the same time. The 486 and all preceding chips can perform only a single instruction at a time. Intel calls the capability to execute two instructions at the same time superscalar technology. This technology provides additional performance compared with the 486.

With superscalar technology, the Pentium can execute many instructions at a rate of two instructions per cycle. Superscalar architecture usually is associated with high-output RISC chips. The Pentium is one of the first CISC chips to be considered superscalar. The Pentium is almost like having two 486 chips under the hood. Table 3.23 shows the Pentium processor specifications.

Table 3.23   Pentium Processor Specifications

Introduced	March 22, 1993 (first generation); March 7, 1994 (second generation)
Maximum rated speeds	60/66MHz (first generation); 75/90/100/120/133/150/166/200MHz (second generation)
CPU clock multiplier	1x (first generation); 1.5x–3x (second generation)
Register size	32-bit
External data bus	64-bit
Memory address bus	32-bit
Maximum memory	4GB
Integral-cache size	8KB code; 8KB data
Integral-cache type	Two-way set associative; write-back data
Burst-mode transfers	Yes
Number of transistors	3.1 million (first generation); 3.3 million (second generation)
Circuit size	0.8 micron (60/66MHz); 0.6 micron (75MHz-100MHz); 0.35 micron (120MHz and up)
External package	273-pin PGA; 296-pin SPGA; tape carrier

Table 3.23   Continued

Math coprocessor	Built-in FPU
Power management	SMM; enhanced in second generation
Operating voltage	5V (first generation); 3.465V, 3.3V, 3.1V, 2.9V (second generation)

PGA = Pin grid array
SPGA = Staggered pin grid array

The two instruction pipelines within the chip are called the u- and v-pipes. The *u-pipe*, which is the primary pipe, can execute all integer and floating-point instructions. The *v-pipe* is a secondary pipe that can execute only simple integer instructions and certain floating-point instructions. The process of operating on two instructions simultaneously in the different pipes is called *pairing*. Not all sequentially executing instructions can be paired, and when pairing is not possible, only the u-pipe is used. To optimize the Pentium's efficiency, you can recompile software to enable more instructions to be paired.

The Pentium processor has a branch target buffer (BTB), which employs a technique called *branch prediction*. It minimizes stalls in one or more of the pipes caused by delays in fetching instructions that branch to nonlinear memory locations. The BTB attempts to predict whether a program branch will be taken and then fetches the appropriate instructions. The use of branch prediction enables the Pentium to keep both pipelines operating at full speed. Figure 3.39 shows the internal architecture of the Pentium processor.

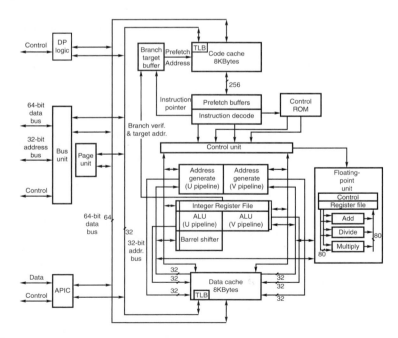

Figure 3.39   Pentium processor internal architecture.

The Pentium has a 32-bit address bus width, giving it the same 4GB memory-addressing capabilities as the 386DX and 486 processors. But the Pentium expands the data bus to 64 bits, which means it can move twice as much data into or out of the CPU, compared with a 486 of the same clock speed. The 64-bit data bus requires that system memory be accessed 64 bits wide, so each bank of memory is 64 bits.

On most Pentium-based motherboards, memory is installed via SIMMs or DIMMs. SIMMs are available in 8-bit-wide and 32-bit-wide versions, whereas DIMMs are 64 bits wide. In addition, versions are available with additional bits for parity or error-correcting code (ECC) data. Most Pentium systems use the 32-bit-wide SIMMs—two of these SIMMs per bank of memory. Most Pentium motherboards have at least four of these 32-bit SIMM sockets, providing for a total of two banks of memory. Later Pentium systems and most Pentium II systems use DIMMs, which are 64 bits wide—just like the processor's external data bus, so only one DIMM is used per bank. This makes installing or upgrading memory much easier because DIMMs can go in one at a time and don't have to be matched up in pairs.

▶▶   See "SIMMs, DIMMs, and RIMMs," p. 533, and "Memory Banks," p. 555.

Even though the Pentium has a 64-bit data bus that transfers information 64 bits at a time into and out of the processor, the Pentium has only 32-bit internal registers. As instructions are being processed internally, they are broken down into 32-bit instructions and data elements and processed in much the same way as in the 486. Some people thought that Intel was misleading them by calling the Pentium a 64-bit processor, but 64-bit transfers do indeed take place. Internally, however, the Pentium has 32-bit registers that are fully compatible with the 486.

The Pentium has two separate internal 8KB caches, compared with a single 8KB or 16KB cache in the 486. The cache-controller circuitry and the cache memory are embedded in the CPU chip. The cache mirrors the information in normal RAM by keeping a copy of the data and code from different memory locations. The Pentium cache also can hold information to be written to memory when the load on the CPU and other system components is less. (The 486 makes all memory writes immediately.)

The separate code and data caches are organized in a two-way set associative fashion, with each set split into lines of 32 bytes each. Each cache has a dedicated translation lookaside buffer (TLB) that translates linear addresses to physical addresses. You can configure the data cache as write-back or write-through on a line-by-line basis. When you use the write-back capability, the cache can store write operations and reads, further improving performance over read-only write-through mode. Using write-back mode results in less activity between the CPU and system memory—an important improvement because CPU access to system memory is a bottleneck on fast systems. The code cache is an inherently write-protected cache because it contains only execution instructions and not data, which is updated. Because burst cycles are used, the cache data can be read or written very quickly.

Systems based on the Pentium can benefit greatly from secondary processor caches (L2), which usually consist of up to 512KB or more of extremely fast (15ns or less) SRAM chips. When the CPU fetches data that is not already available in its internal processor (L1) cache, wait states slow the CPU. If the data already is in the secondary processor cache, however, the CPU can go ahead with its work without pausing for wait states.

The Pentium uses a Bipolar Complementary Metal-Oxide Semiconductor (BiCMOS) process and superscalar architecture to achieve the high level of performance expected from the chip. BiCMOS adds about 10% to the complexity of the chip design, but adds about 30%–35% better performance without a size or power penalty.

All 75MHz and faster Pentium processors are SL enhanced—they incorporate the SMM to provide full control of power-management features, which helps reduce power consumption. The second-generation Pentium processors (75MHz and faster) incorporate a more advanced form of SMM that includes processor clock control. This enables you to throttle the processor up or down to control power use. You can even stop the clock with these more advanced Pentium processors, putting the processor in a state of suspension that requires very little power. The second-generation Pentium processors run on 3.3V power (instead of 5V), reducing power requirements and heat generation even further.

Many Pentium motherboards supply either 3.465V or 3.3V. The 3.465V setting is called VRE (voltage reduced extended) by Intel and is required by some versions of the Pentium, particularly some of the 100MHz versions. The standard 3.3V setting is called STD (standard), which most of the second-generation Pentiums use. STD voltage means anything in a range from 3.135V to 3.465V, with 3.3V nominal. Additionally, a special 3.3V setting called *voltage reduced (VR)* reduces the range from 3.300V to 3.465V, with 3.38V nominal. Some of the processors require this narrower specification, which most motherboards provide. Table 3.24 includes a summary.

Table 3.24   Summary of Voltage Specifications for the Pentium Processor

Voltage Specification	Nominal	Tolerance	Minimum	Maximum
STD (standard)	3.30V	±0.165	3.135V	3.465V
VR (voltage reduced)	3.38V	±0.083	3.300V	3.465V
VRE (VR extended)	3.50V	±0.100	3.400V	3.600V

For even lower power consumption, Intel introduced special Pentium processors with voltage reduction technology in the 75 to 266MHz family; the processors were intended for mobile computer applications. They did not use a conventional chip package and were instead mounted using a new format called tape carrier packaging (TCP). The tape carrier packaging does not encase the chip in ceramic or plastic as with a conventional chip package, but instead covers the actual processor die directly with a thin, protective plastic coating. The entire processor is less than 1mm thick, or about half the thickness of a dime, and weighs less than 1 gram. They were sold to system manufacturers in a roll that looks very much like a filmstrip.

The TCP processor is directly affixed (soldered) to the motherboard by a special machine, resulting in a smaller package, lower height, better thermal transfer, and lower power consumption. Special solder plugs on the circuit board located directly under the processor draw heat away and provide better cooling in the tight confines of a typical notebook or laptop system—no cooling fans are required. For more information on mobile processors and systems, see my book *Upgrading and Repairing Laptops, 2nd Edition.*

The Pentium, like the 486, contains an internal math coprocessor or FPU. The FPU in the Pentium was rewritten to perform significantly better than the FPU in the 486 yet still be fully compatible with the 486 and 387 math coprocessors. The Pentium FPU is estimated to be two to as much as ten times faster than the FPU in the 486. In addition, the two standard instruction pipelines in the Pentium provide two units to handle standard integer math. (The math coprocessor handles only more complex calculations.) Other processors, such as the 486, have only a single-standard execution pipe and one integer math unit. Interestingly, the Pentium FPU contains a flaw that received widespread publicity. See the discussion in the section "Pentium Defects," later in this chapter.

First-generation Pentium Processors

The Pentium was offered in three basic designs, each with several versions. The first-generation design came in 60MHz and 66MHz processor speeds. This design used a 273-pin PGA form factor and ran on 5V power. In this design, the processor ran at the same speed as the motherboard—in other words, a 1x clock was used.

The first-generation Pentium was created through a 0.8-micron BiCMOS process. Unfortunately, this process, combined with the 3.1 million transistor count, resulted in a die that was overly large and complicated to manufacture. As a result, reduced yields kept the chip in short supply; Intel could not make them fast enough. The 0.8-micron process was criticized by other manufacturers, including Motorola and IBM, which had been using 0.6-micron technology for their most advanced chips. The huge die and 5V operating voltage caused the 66MHz versions to consume up to an incredible 3.2 amps or 16 watts of power, resulting in a tremendous amount of heat and problems in some systems that did not employ conservative design techniques. Fortunately, adding a fan to the processor solved most cooling problems, as long as the fan kept running.

Much of the criticism leveled at Intel for the first-generation Pentium was justified. Some people realized that the first-generation design was just that; they knew that new Pentium versions, made in a more advanced manufacturing process, were coming. Many of those people advised against purchasing any Pentium system until the second-generation version became available.

Tip

A cardinal rule of computing is never buy the first generation of any radically new technology. Although you can wait forever because something better always will be on the horizon, a little waiting can be worthwhile in many cases.

Those who purchased first-generation Pentiums still had a way out, however. As with previous 486 systems, Intel released OverDrive upgrade chips that effectively doubled the processor speed of the Pentium 60 or 66. These are a single-chip upgrade, meaning they replace the existing CPU. Because subsequent Pentiums are incompatible with the Pentium 60/66 Socket 4 arrangement, these OverDrive chips and comparable upgrades available from some third-party sources were the only way to upgrade an existing first-generation Pentium without replacing the motherboard.

Generally, it was better to consider a complete motherboard replacement, which would accept a newer design processor that would potentially be many times faster, than to upgrade using just an OverDrive processor, that might only be twice as fast.

Second-generation Pentium Processors

Intel announced the second-generation Pentium on March 7, 1994. This processor was introduced in 90MHz and 100MHz versions, with a 75MHz version not far behind. Eventually, 120MHz, 133MHz, 150MHz, 166MHz, and 200MHz versions were also introduced. The second-generation Pentium uses 0.6-micron (75/90/100MHz) BiCMOS technology to shrink the die and reduce power consumption. The newer, faster 120MHz (and higher) second-generation versions incorporate an even smaller die built on a 0.35-micron BiCMOS process. These smaller dies are not changed from the 0.6-micron versions; they are basically a photographic reduction of the P54C die. The die for the Pentium is shown in Figure 3.40. Additionally, these new processors run on 3.3V power. The 100MHz version consumes a maximum of 3.25 amps of 3.3V power, which equals only 10.725 watts. Further up the scale, the 150MHz chip uses 3.5 amps of 3.3V power (11.6 watts), the 166MHz unit draws 4.4 amps (14.5 watts), and the 200MHz processor uses 4.7 amps (15.5 watts).

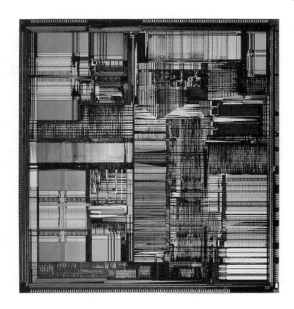

Figure 3.40   Pentium processor die. *Photograph used by permission of Intel Corporation.*

The second-generation Pentium processors use a 296-pin SPGA form factor that is physically incompatible with the first-generation versions. The only way to upgrade from the first generation to the second was to replace the motherboard. The second-generation Pentium processors also have 3.3 million transistors—more than the earlier chips. The extra transistors exist because additional clock-control SL enhancements were added, along with an on-chip advanced programmable interrupt controller (APIC) and dual-processor interface.

The APIC and dual-processor interfaces are responsible for orchestrating dual-processor configurations in which two second-generation Pentium chips can process on the same motherboard simultaneously. Many of the Pentium motherboards designed for file servers come with dual Socket 7 specification sockets, which fully support the multiprocessing capability of the new chips. Software support for what usually is called symmetric multiprocessing (SMP) was integrated into operating systems such as Windows NT and OS/2.

The second-generation Pentium processors use clock-multiplier circuitry to run the processor at speeds faster than the bus. The 150MHz Pentium processor, for example, can run at 2.5 times the bus frequency, which normally is 60MHz. The 200MHz Pentium processor can run at a 3x clock in a system using a 66MHz bus speed.

Virtually all Pentium motherboards had three speed settings: 50MHz, 60MHz, and 66MHz. Pentium chips were available with a variety of internal clock multipliers that caused the processor to operate at various multiples of these motherboard speeds. Refer to Table 3.25 for a list of the speeds of Pentium processors and motherboard bus speeds.

The core-to-bus frequency ratio or clock multiplier is controlled in a Pentium processor by two pins on the chip labeled BF1 and BF2. Table 3.25 shows how the state of the BFx pins affects the clock multiplication in the Pentium processor.

Table 3.25   Pentium BFx Pins and Clock Multipliers

BF1	BF2	Clock Multiplier	Bus Speed (MHz)	Core Speed (MHz)
0	1	3x	66	200
0	1	3x	60	180
0	1	3x	50	150
0	0	2.5x	66	166
0	0	2.5x	60	150
0	0	2.5x	50	125
1	0	2x/4x	66	133/266[1]
1	0	2x	60	120
1	0	2x	50	100
1	1	1.5x/3.5x	66	100/233[1]
1	1	1.5x	60	90
1	1	1.5x	50	75

1. The 233MHz and 266MHz processors have modified the 1.5x and 2x multipliers to 3.5x and 4x, respectively.

Not all chips support all the bus frequency (BF) pins or combinations of settings. In other words, some of the Pentium processors operate only at specific combinations of these settings or might even be fixed at one particular setting. Many of the later Pentium motherboards included jumpers or switches that enabled you to control the BF pins and, therefore, alter the clock-multiplier ratio within the chip. In theory, you could run a 75MHz-rated Pentium chip at 133MHz by changing jumpers on the motherboard. This is called *overclocking* and is discussed in the section "Overclocking," earlier in this chapter. What Intel has done to discourage overclockers in its most recent Pentiums is discussed near the end of the "Processor Manufacturing" section of this chapter.

Intel also offered a single-chip OverDrive upgrade for second-generation Pentiums. These OverDrive chips are fixed at a 3x multiplier; they replace the existing Socket 5 or 7 CPU, increase processor speed up to 200MHz (with a 66MHz motherboard speed), and add MMX capability. Simply stated, a Pentium 100, 133, or 166 system equipped with the OverDrive chip has a processor speed of 200MHz. Perhaps the best feature of these Pentium OverDrive chips is that they incorporate MMX technology to improve multimedia application performance.

Pentium-MMX Processors

A third generation of Pentium processors (codenamed P55C) was released in January 1997, and incorporates what Intel calls MMX technology into the second-generation Pentium design (see Figure 3.41). These Pentium-MMX processors were manufactured in clock rates of 66/166MHz, 66/200MHz, and 66/233MHz and in a mobile-only version, which is 66/266MHz. The MMX processors have a lot in common with other second-generation Pentiums, including superscalar architecture, multiprocessor support, on-chip local APIC controller, and power-management features. New features include a pipelined MMX unit, 16KB code, write-back cache (versus 8KB in earlier Pentiums), and 4.5 million transistors. Pentium-MMX chips are produced on an enhanced 0.35-micron CMOS silicon process that allows for a lower 2.8V voltage level. The newer mobile 233MHz and 266MHz processors are built on a 0.25-micron process and run on only 1.8V. With this newer technology, the 266 processor actually uses less power than the non-MMX 133.

Figure 3.41   Pentium MMX. The left side shows the underside of the chip with the cover plate removed exposing the processor die. *Photograph used by permission of Intel Corporation.*

To use the Pentium-MMX, the motherboard must be capable of supplying the lower (2.8V or less) voltage these processors use. To enable a more universal motherboard solution with respect to these changing voltages, Intel developed the Socket 7 with VRM. The VRM is a socketed module that plugs in next to the processor and supplies the correct voltage. Because the module is easily replaced, reconfiguring a motherboard to support any of the voltages required by the newer Pentium processors is easy.

Of course, lower voltage is nice, but MMX is what this chip is really all about. MMX incorporates a process Intel calls *single instruction multiple data (SIMD)*, which enables one instruction to perform the same function on many pieces of data. Fifty-seven new instructions designed specifically to handle video, audio, and graphics data have been added to the chip.

Pentium Defects

Probably the most famous processor bug in history is the now legendary flaw in the Pentium FPU. It has often been called the FDIV bug because it affects primarily the FDIV (floating-point divide) instruction, although several other instructions that use division are also affected. Intel officially refers to this problem as Errata No. 23, titled "Slight precision loss for floating-point divides on specific operand pairs." The bug has been fixed in the D1 or later steppings of the 60/66MHz Pentium processors, as well as the B5 and later steppings of the 75/90/100MHz processors. The 120MHz and higher processors are manufactured from later steppings, which do not include this problem. Tables listing all the variations of Pentium processors and steppings and how to identify them appear later in this chapter.

This bug caused a tremendous fervor when it first was reported on the Internet by mathematician Thomas R. Nicely of Lynchburg College in Virginia in October 1994. Within a few days, news of the defect had spread nationwide, and even people who did not have computers had heard about it. The Pentium incorrectly performed floating-point division calculations with certain number combinations, with errors anywhere from the third digit on up.

By the time the bug was publicly discovered outside of Intel, the company had already incorporated the fix into the next stepping of both the 60/66MHz and the 75/90/100MHz Pentium processor, along with the other corrections Intel had made.

After the bug was made public and Intel admitted to already knowing about it, a fury erupted. As people began checking their spreadsheets and other math calculations, many discovered they had also encountered this problem and did not know it. Others who had not encountered the problem had their faith in the core of their PCs very shaken. People had come to put so much trust in the PC that they had a hard time coming to terms with the fact that it might not even be capable of doing math correctly!

One interesting result of the fervor surrounding this defect is that people are less likely to implicitly trust their PCs and are therefore doing more testing and evaluating of important results. The bottom line is that if your information and calculations are important enough, you should implement some results tests. Several math programs were found to have problems. For example, a bug was discovered in the yield function of Excel 5.0 that some were attributing to the Pentium processor. In this case, the problem turned out to be the software (which has been corrected in versions 5.0c and later).

Intel finally decided that in the best interest of the consumer and its public image, it would begin a lifetime replacement warranty on the affected processors. Therefore, if you ever encounter one of the Pentium processors with the Errata 23 floating-point bug, Intel will replace the processor with an equivalent one without this problem.

If you are still using a Pentium-based system and wonder whether you might have a system affected by this bug, visit the Intel "FDIV Replacement Program" page at http://support.intel.com/support/processors/pentium/fdiv/. Here you can find information on how to determine whether your processor is affected and how to obtain a free replacement for an affected processor. As long as Intel receives the original CPU back within a specified amount of time, there will be no charges to you. Intel has indicated that these defective processors are destroyed and will not be remarketed or resold in another form.

Testing for the FPU Bug

Testing a Pentium for this bug is relatively easy. All you have to do is execute one of the test division cases cited here and see whether your answer compares to the correct result.

The division calculation can be done in a spreadsheet (such as Lotus 1-2-3, Microsoft Excel, or any other), the Microsoft Windows built-in calculator, or any other calculating program that uses the FPU. Make sure that for the purposes of this test the FPU has not been disabled. That typically requires some special command or setting specific to the application and, of course, ensures that the test comes out correct, regardless of whether the chip is flawed.

The most severe Pentium floating-point errors occur as early as the third significant digit of the result. Here is an example of one of the more severe instances of the problem:

> 962,306,957,033 / 11,010,046 = 87,402.6282027341 (correct answer)
>
> 962,306,957,033 / 11,010,046 = 87,399.5805831329 (flawed Pentium)

Note

Note that your particular calculator program might not show the answer to the number of digits shown here. Most spreadsheet programs limit displayed results to 13 or 15 significant digits.

As you can see in the previous case, the error turns up in the third most significant digit of the result. In an examination of more than 5,000 integer pairs in the 5- to 15-digit range found to produce Pentium floating-point division errors, errors beginning in the sixth significant digit were the most likely to occur.

Several workarounds are available for this bug, but they extract a performance penalty. Because Intel has agreed to replace any Pentium processor with this flaw under a lifetime warranty replacement program, the best workaround is a free replacement or an upgrade to a more modern system.

Power Management Bugs

Starting with the second-generation Pentium processors, Intel added functions that enable these CPUs to be installed in energy-efficient systems. These are usually called *Energy Star systems* because they meet the specifications imposed by the EPA Energy Star program, but they are also unofficially called *green PCs* by many users.

Unfortunately, there have been several bugs with respect to these functions, causing them to either fail or be disabled. These bugs are in some of the functions in the power-management capabilities accessed through SMM. These problems are applicable only to the second-generation 75/90/100MHz processors because the first-generation 60/66MHz processors do not have SMM or power-management capabilities, and all higher-speed (120MHz and up) processors have the bugs fixed.

Most of the problems are related to the STPCLK# pin and the HALT instruction. If this condition is invoked by the chipset, the system will hang. For most systems, the only workaround for this problem is to disable the power-saving modes, such as suspend or sleep. Unfortunately, this means that your green PC won't be so green anymore! The best way to repair the problem is to replace the processor with a later stepping version that does not have the bug. These bugs affect the B1 stepping version of the 75/90/100MHz Pentiums, and they were fixed in the B3 and later stepping versions.

Pentium Processor Models and Steppings

We know that like software, no processor is truly ever perfect. From time to time, the manufacturers gather up what problems they have found and put into production a new stepping, which consists of a new set of masks that incorporate the corrections. Each subsequent stepping is better and more refined than the previous ones. Although no microprocessor is ever perfect, they come closer to perfection with each stepping. In the life of a typical microprocessor, a manufacturer might go through half a dozen or more such steppings.

See *Upgrading and Repairing PCs, Tenth Anniversary Edition*, which is included on the disc, for tables showing the Pentium processor steppings and revisions. This information is also available online from Intel via its website.

To determine the specifications of a given processor, you must look up the S-spec number in the table of processor specifications. To find your S-spec number, you have to read it off the chip directly. It can be found printed on both the top and bottom of the chip. If your heatsink is glued on, remove the chip and heatsink from the socket as a unit and read the numbers from the bottom of the chip. Then, you can look up the S-spec number in the Specification Guide Intel publishes (via its website); it tells you the specifications of that particular processor. Intel is introducing new chips all the time, so visit its website and search for the Pentium processor "Quick Reference Guide" in the developer portion of its site. There you will find a complete listing of all current processor specifications by S-spec number.

One interesting item to note is that several subtly different voltages are required by different Pentium processors. Table 3.26 summarizes the various processors and their required voltages.

Table 3.26   Pentium Processor Voltages

Model	Stepping	Voltage Spec.	Voltage Range
1	—	Std.	4.75V–5.25V
1	—	5V1	4.90V–5.25V
1	—	5V2	4.90V–5.40V
1	—	5V3	5.15V–5.40V

Table 3.26   Continued

Model	Stepping	Voltage Spec.	Voltage Range
2+	B1–B5	Std.	3.135V–3.465V
2+	C2+	Std.	3.135V–3.600V
2+	—	VR	3.300V–3.465V
2+	B1–B5	VRE	3.45V–3.60V
2+	C2+	VRE	3.40V–3.60V
4+	—	MMX	2.70V–2.90V
4	3	Mobile	2.285V–2.665V
4	3	Mobile	2.10V–2.34V
8	1	Mobile	1.850V–2.150V
8	1	Mobile	1.665V–1.935V

Many of the newer Pentium motherboards have jumpers that allow for adjustments to the different voltage ranges. If you are having problems with a particular processor, it might not be matched correctly to your motherboard voltage outputs.

If you are refurbishing an older, used Pentium system today, I recommend using only Model 2 (second-generation) or later version processors that are available in 75MHz or faster speeds. You should definitely get stepping C2 or later. Virtually all the important bugs and problems were fixed in the C2 and later releases. The newer Pentium processors have no serious bugs to worry about.

AMD-K5

The AMD-K5 is a Pentium-compatible processor developed by AMD and available as the PR75, PR90, PR100, PR120, PR133, PR166, and PR200. Because it is designed to be physically and functionally compatible, any motherboard that properly supports the Intel Pentium should support the AMD-K5. However, a BIOS upgrade might be required to properly recognize the AMD-K5. The K5 has the following features:

- 16KB instruction cache, 8KB write-back data cache
- Dynamic execution-branch prediction with speculative execution
- Five-stage, RISC-like pipeline with six parallel functional units
- High-performance floating-point unit
- Pin-selectable clock multiples of 1.5x, 1.75x, and 2x

The K5 is sold under the P-Rating system, which means that the number on the chip does not indicate true clock speed, only apparent speed when running certain applications.

Note that the actual clock speeds of several of these processors are not the same as their apparent rated speeds. For example, the PR-166 version actually runs at only 117 true MHz. Sometimes this can confuse the system BIOS, which might report the true speed rather than the P-Rating, which compares the chip against an Intel Pentium of that speed. AMD's assertion is that because of architecture enhancements over the Pentium, they do not need to run the same clock frequency to achieve that same performance. Even with such improvements, AMD marketed the K5 as a fifth-generation processor, just like the Pentium.

The AMD-K5 operates at 3.52V (VRE setting). Some older motherboards default to 3.3V, which is below specification for the K5 and could cause erratic operation. Because of the relatively low clock speeds and compatibility issues some users experienced with the K5, AMD replaced it with the K6 family of processors.

Intel P6 (686) Sixth-generation Processors

The P6 (686) processors represent a new generation with features not found in the previous generation units. The P6 processor family began when the Pentium Pro was released in November 1995. Since then, Intel has released many other P6 chips, all using the same basic P6 core processor as the Pentium Pro. Table 3.27 shows the variations in the P6 family of processors.

Table 3.27   Intel P6 Processor Variations

Pentium Pro	Original P6 processor, includes 256KB, 512KB, or 1MB of full-core speed L2 cache
Pentium II	P6 with 512KB of half-core speed L2 cache
Pentium II Xeon	P6 with 512KB, 1MB, or 2MB of full-core speed L2 cache
Celeron	P6 with no L2 cache
Celeron-A	P6 with 128KB of on-die full-core speed L2 cache
Pentium III	P6 with SSE (MMX2), 512KB of half-core speed L2 cache
Pentium IIPE	P6 with 256KB of full-core speed L2 cache
Pentium IIIE	P6 with SSE (MMX2) plus 256KB or 512KB of full-core speed L2 cache
Pentium III Xeon	P6 with SSE (MMX2), 512KB, 1MB, or 2MB of full-core speed L2 cache

The main new feature in the fifth-generation Pentium processors was the superscalar architecture, in which two instruction execution units could execute instructions simultaneously in parallel. Later fifth-generation chips also added MMX technology to the mix. So then what did Intel add in the sixth generation to justify calling it a whole new generation of chip? Besides many minor improvements, the real key features of all sixth-generation processors are Dynamic Execution and the Dual Independent Bus (DIB) architecture, plus a greatly improved superscalar design.

Dynamic Execution

Dynamic execution enables the processor to execute more instructions on parallel, so tasks are completed more quickly. This technology innovation is composed of three main elements:

- **Multiple branch prediction**—Predict the flow of the program through several branches
- **Dataflow analysis**—Schedules instructions to be executed when ready, independent of their order in the original program
- **Speculative execution**—Increases the rate of execution by looking ahead of the program counter and executing instructions that are likely to be necessary

Dual Independent Bus

The other main P6 architecture feature is known as the Dual Independent Bus. This refers to the fact that the processor has two data buses: one for the system (motherboard) and the other just for cache. This enables the cache memory to run at speeds previously not possible.

Other Sixth-generation Improvements

Finally, the P6 architecture upgrades the superscalar architecture of the P5 processors by adding more instruction execution units and by breaking down the instructions into special micro-ops. This is where the CISC instructions are broken down into more RISC commands. The RISC-level commands are smaller and easier for the parallel instruction units to execute more efficiently. With this design, Intel has brought the benefits of a RISC processor—high-speed dedicated instruction execution—to the CISC world. Note that the P5 had only two instruction units, whereas the P6 has at least six separate dedicated instruction units. It is said to be three-way superscalar because the multiple instruction units can execute up to three instructions in one cycle.

Other improvements in efficiency also are included in the P6 architecture: built-in multiprocessor support, enhanced error detection and correction circuitry, and optimization for 32-bit software.

Rather than just being a faster Pentium, the Pentium Pro, Pentium II/III, and other sixth-generation processors have many feature and architectural improvements. The core of the chip is very RISC-like, whereas the external instruction interface is classic Intel CISC. By breaking down the CISC instructions into several RISC instructions and running them down parallel execution pipelines, the overall performance is increased.

Compared to a Pentium at the same clock speed, the P6 processors are faster—as long as you're running 32-bit software. The P6 Dynamic Execution is optimized for performance primarily when running 32-bit software. If you are using 16-bit software, the P6 does not provide as marked a performance improvement over similarly speed-rated Pentium and Pentium-MMX processors. That's because the Dynamic Execution capability is not fully exploited.

Note that it is really not so much the operating system but which applications you use. Software developers can take steps to gain the full advantages of the sixth-generation processors. This includes using modern compilers that can improve performance for all current Intel processors, writing 32-bit code where possible, and making code as predictable as possible to take advantage of the processor's Dynamic Execution multiple-branch-prediction capabilities.

Pentium Pro Processors

Intel's successor to the Pentium is called the Pentium Pro. The Pentium Pro was the first chip in the P6 or sixth-generation processor family. It was introduced in November 1995 and became widely available in 1996. The chip is a 387-pin unit that resides in Socket 8, so it is not pin compatible with earlier Pentiums. The chip is unique among processors because it is constructed in a multichip module (MCM) physical format, which Intel calls a *dual-cavity PGA package*. Inside the 387-pin chip carrier are two dies. One contains the actual Pentium Pro processor (shown in Figure 3.42), and the other contains a 256KB, 512KB, or 1MB L2 cache (the Pentium Pro with 256KB cache is shown in Figure 3.43). The processor die contains 5.5 million transistors, the 256KB cache die contains 15.5 million transistors, and the 512KB cache die(s) have 31 million transistors each—for a potential total of nearly 68 million transistors in a Pentium Pro with 1MB of internal cache! A Pentium Pro with 1MB cache has two 512KB cache die and a standard P6 processor die (see Figure 3.44).

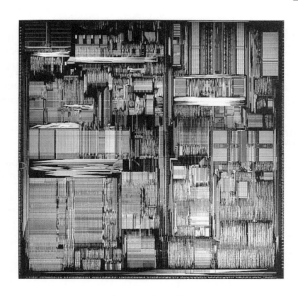

Figure 3.42   Pentium Pro processor die. *Photograph used by permission of Intel Corporation.*

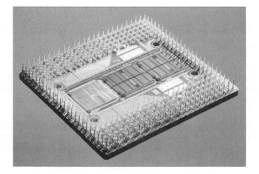

Figure 3.43   Pentium Pro processor with 256KB L2 cache (the cache is on the left side of the processor die). *Photograph used by permission of Intel Corporation.*

Figure 3.44   Pentium Pro processor with 1MB L2 cache (the cache is in the center and right portions of the die). *Photograph used by permission of Intel Corporation.*

The main processor die includes a 16KB split L1 cache with an 8KB two-way set associative cache for primary instructions and an 8KB four-way set associative cache for data.

Another sixth-generation processor feature found in the Pentium Pro is the DIB architecture, which addresses the memory bandwidth limitations of previous-generation processor architectures. Two buses make up the DIB architecture: the L2 cache bus (contained entirely within the processor package) and the processor-to-main memory system bus. The speed of the dedicated L2 cache bus on the

Pentium Pro is equal to the full-core speed of the processor. This was accomplished by embedding the cache chips directly into the Pentium Pro package. The DIB processor bus architecture addresses processor-to-memory bus bandwidth limitations. It offers up to three times the performance bandwidth of the single-bus, "Socket 7" generation processors, such as the Pentium.

Table 3.28 shows Pentium Pro processor specifications, and Table 3.29 shows the specifications for each model within the Pentium Pro family because many variations exist from model to model.

Table 3.28   Pentium Pro Family Processor Specifications

Introduced	November 1995
Maximum rated speeds	150MHz, 166MHz, 180MHz, 200MHz
CPU clock	2x, 2.5x, 3x, 3.5x, 4x
Internal registers	32-bit
External data bus	64-bit
Memory address bus	36-bit
Addressable memory	64GB
Virtual memory	64TB
Integral L1 cache size	8KB code, 8KB data (16KB total)
Integrated L2 cache bus	64-bit, full-core speed
Socket/Slot	Socket 8
Physical package	387-pin dual cavity PGA
Package dimensions	2.46 (6.25cm)×2.66 (6.76cm)
Math coprocessor	Built-in FPU
Power management	SMM
Operating voltage	3.1V or 3.3V

Table 3.29   Pentium Pro Processor Specifications by Processor Model

Pentium Pro Processor (200MHz) with 1MB Integrated Level 2 Cache	
Introduction date	August 18, 1997
Clock speeds	200MHz (66MHz×3)
Number of transistors	5.5 million (0.35-micron process), plus 62 million in 1MB L2 cache (0.35-micron)
Cache memory	8K×2 (16KB) L1, 1MB core-speed L2
Die size	0.552" per side (14.0mm)
Pentium Pro Processor (166/180/200MHz)	
Introduction date	November 1, 1995
Clock speeds	200MHz (66MHz×3), 180MHz (60MHz×3), 166MHz (66MHz×2.5)
Number of transistors	5.5 million (0.35-micron process), plus 15.5 million in 256KB L2 cache (0.6-micron), or 31 million in 512KB L2 cache (0.35-micron)
Cache memory	8K×2 (16KB) L1, 256KB or 512KB core-speed L2
Die size	0.552" per side (14.0mm)

Table 3.29   Continued

Pentium Pro Processor (150MHz)	
Introduction date	November 1, 1995
Clock speeds	150MHz (60MHz×2.5)
Number of transistors	5.5 million (0.6-micron process), plus 15.5 million in 256KB L2 cache (0.6-micron)
Cache memory	8Kx2 (16KB) L1, 256KB core-speed L2
Die size	0.691" per side (17.6mm)

Performance comparisons on the iCOMP 2.0 Index rate a classic Pentium 200MHz at 142, whereas a Pentium Pro 200MHz scores 220. Just for comparison, note that a Pentium MMX 200MHz falls right about in the middle in regards to performance at 182. Keep in mind that using a Pentium Pro with any 16-bit software applications nullifies much of the performance gain shown by the iCOMP 2.0 rating.

Similar to the Pentium before it, the Pentium Pro runs clock multiplied on a 66MHz motherboard. Table 3.30 lists speeds for Pentium Pro processors and motherboards.

Table 3.30   Speeds for Pentium Pro Processors and Motherboards

CPU Type/Speed	CPU Clock	Motherboard Speed
Pentium Pro 150	2.5x	60
Pentium Pro 166	2.5x	66
Pentium Pro 180	3x	60
Pentium Pro 200	3x	66

The integrated L2 cache is one of the really outstanding features of the Pentium Pro. Because the L2 cache is built into the CPU and is off the motherboard, the Pentium Pro can now run the cache at full processor speed rather than the slower 60MHz or 66MHz motherboard bus speed. In fact, the L2 cache features its own internal 64-bit back-side bus, which does not share time with the external 64-bit front-side bus used by the CPU. The internal registers and data paths are still 32-bit, as with the Pentium. Because the L2 cache is built into the system, motherboards can be cheaper because they no longer require separate cache memory. Some boards might still try to include cache memory in their designs, but the general consensus is that L3 cache (as it would be called) would offer less improvement with the Pentium Pro than with the Pentium. The incorporation of L2 cache is one of the most enduring legacies of the Pentium Pro because this feature has been incorporated into virtually every Intel and AMD processor built since, with the notable exception of the original Celeron.

One of the features of the built-in L2 cache is that multiprocessing is greatly improved. Rather than just SMP, as with the Pentium, the Pentium Pro supports a type of multiprocessor configuration called the *Multiprocessor Specification (MPS 1.1)*. The Pentium Pro with MPS enables configurations of up to four processors running together. Unlike other multiprocessor configurations, the Pentium Pro avoids cache coherency problems because each chip maintains a separate L1 and L2 cache internally.

Pentium Pro-based motherboards were pretty much exclusively PCI and ISA bus-based, and Intel has produced its own chipsets for these motherboards. Because of the greater cooling and space requirements, Intel designed the new ATX motherboard form factor to better support the Pentium Pro and other future processors, such as the Pentium II/III/4. However, systems using the Pentium Pro use various types of motherboard form factors, including ATX, Baby-AT, and proprietary models.

▶▶   See "Motherboard Form Factors," p. 235, and "Sixth-generation (P6 Pentium Pro/II/III Class) Chipsets," p. 286.

Four special VID pins are on the Pentium Pro processor. These pins can be used to support automatic selection of power supply voltage. Therefore, a Pentium Pro motherboard does not have voltage regulator jumper settings like most Pentium boards, which greatly eases the setup and integration of a Pentium Pro system. These pins are not actually signals, but are either an open circuit in the package or a short circuit to voltage. The sequence of opens and shorts defines the voltage the processor requires. In addition to allowing for automatic voltage settings, this feature was designed to support voltage specification variations on future Pentium Pro processors. The VID pins are named VID0 through VID3, and the definition of these pins is shown in Table 3.31. A 1 in this table refers to an open pin, and a 0 refers to a short to ground. The voltage regulators on the motherboard should supply the requested voltage or disable themselves.

Table 3.31   Pentium Pro Voltage Identification Definition

VID [3:0]	Voltage Setting	VID [3:0]	Voltage Setting
0000	3.5	1000	2.7
0001	3.4	1001	2.6
0010	3.3	1010	2.5
0011	3.2	1011	2.4
0100	3.1	1100	2.3
0101	3.0	1101	2.2
0110	2.9	1110	2.1
0111	2.8	1111	No CPU present

Most Pentium Pro processors run at 3.3V, but a few run at 3.1V. Note that the 1111 (or all opens) ID can be used to detect the absence of a processor in a given socket.

The Pentium Pro never did become very popular on the desktop, but it did find a niche in file-server applications primarily because of the full-core speed high-capacity internal L2 cache. For a time, Intel offered an OverDrive upgrade processor for the Pentium Pro, but it no longer offers any OverDrive processors. At one time, PowerLeap offered several upgrades for Pentium Pro that used 533MHz–700MHz-class Celeron PPGA processors in an adapter, but these products are no longer available.

Pentium II Processors

Intel revealed the Pentium II in May 1997. Prior to its official unveiling, the Pentium II processor was popularly referred to by its codename, Klamath, and was surrounded by much speculation throughout the industry. The Pentium II is essentially the same sixth-generation processor as the Pentium Pro, with MMX technology added (which included double the L1 cache and 57 new MMX instructions); however, there are a few twists to the design. The Pentium II processor die is shown in Figure 3.45.

From a physical standpoint, it was a big departure from previous processors. Abandoning the chip in a socket approach used by virtually all processors up until this point, the Pentium II chip is characterized by its SEC cartridge design. The processor, along with several L2 cache chips, is mounted on a small circuit board (much like an oversized-memory SIMM), as shown in Figure 3.46, and the circuit board is then sealed in a metal and plastic cartridge. The cartridge is then plugged into the motherboard through an edge connector called Slot 1, which looks very much like an adapter card slot.

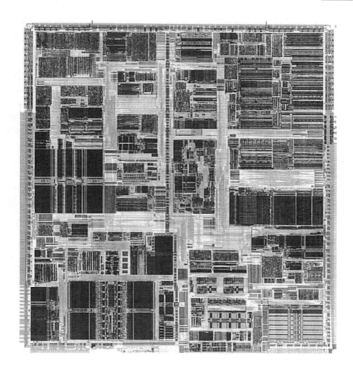

Figure 3.45 Pentium II Processor die. *Photograph used by permission of Intel Corporation.*

Figure 3.46 Pentium II processor board (normally found inside the SEC cartridge). *Photograph used by permission of Intel Corporation.*

The two variations on these cartridges are called SECC (single edge contact cartridge) and SECC2. Figure 3.47 shows a diagram of the SECC package; Figure 3.48 shows the SECC2 package.

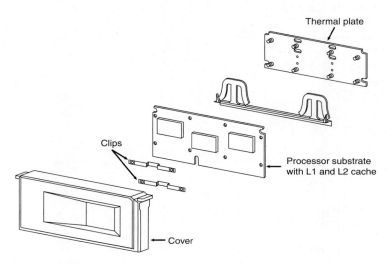

Figure 3.47   SECC components showing an enclosed processor board.

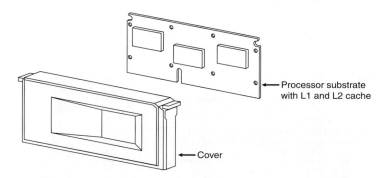

Figure 3.48   SECC, rev. 2 components showing a half-enclosed processor board.

As you can see from these figures, the SECC2 version was cheaper to make because it uses fewer overall parts. It also allowed for a more direct heatsink attachment to the processor for better cooling. Intel transitioned from SECC to SECC2 in the beginning of 1999; all later PII chips, and the Slot 1 PIII chips that followed, use the improved SECC2 design.

By using separate chips mounted on a circuit board, Intel could build the Pentium II much less expensively than the multiple die within a package used in the Pentium Pro. Intel could also use cache chips from other manufacturers and more easily vary the amount of cache in future processors compared to the Pentium Pro design.

Intel offered Pentium II processors with the speeds listed in Table 3.32.

Table 3.32   Speeds for Pentium II Processors and Motherboards

CPU Type/Speed	CPU Clock	Motherboard Speed
Pentium II 233MHz	3.5x	66MHz
Pentium II 266MHz	4x	66MHz
Pentium II 300MHz	4.5x	66MHz
Pentium II 333MHz	5x	66MHz
Pentium II 350MHz	3.5x	100MHz
Pentium II 400MHz	4x	100MHz
Pentium II 450MHz	4.5x	100MHz

The Pentium II processor core has 7.5 million transistors and is based on Intel's advanced P6 architecture. The Pentium II started out using a 0.35-micron process technology, although the 333MHz and faster Pentium IIs are based on 0.25-micron technology. This enables a smaller die, allowing increased core frequencies and reduced power consumption. At 333MHz, the Pentium II processor delivers a 75%–150% performance boost, compared to the 233MHz Pentium processor with MMX technology, and approximately 50% more performance on multimedia benchmarks. As shown earlier in Table 3.8, the iCOMP 2.0 Index rating for the Pentium II 266MHz chip is more than twice as fast as a classic Pentium 200MHz.

Aside from speed, the best way to think of the Pentium II is as a Pentium Pro with MMX technology instructions and a slightly modified cache design. It has the same multiprocessor scalability as the Pentium Pro, as well as the integrated L2 cache. The 57 new multimedia-related instructions carried over from the MMX processors and the capability to process repetitive loop commands more efficiently are included as well. Also included as a part of the MMX upgrade is double the internal L1 cache from the Pentium Pro (from 16KB total to 32KB total in the Pentium II).

Maximum power usage for the Pentium II is shown in Table 3.33.

Table 3.33   Maximum Power Usage for the Pentium II Processor

Core Speed	Power Draw	Process	Voltage
450MHz	27.1w	0.25-micron	2.0V
400MHz	24.3w	0.25-micron	2.0V
350MHz	21.5w	0.25-micron	2.0V
333MHz	23.7w	0.25-micron	2.0V
300MHz	43.0w	0.35-micron	2.8V
266MHz	38.2w	0.35-micron	2.8V
233MHz	34.8w	0.35-micron	2.8V

You can see that the highest speed 450MHz version of the Pentium II actually uses less power than the slowest original 233MHz version! This was accomplished by using the smaller 0.25-micron process and running the processor on a lower voltage of only 2.0V. Pentium III and subsequent processors used even smaller processes and lower voltages to continue this trend.

The Pentium II includes Dynamic Execution, which describes unique performance-enhancing developments by Intel and was first introduced in the Pentium Pro processor. Major features of Dynamic Execution include multiple branch prediction, which speeds execution by predicting the flow of the program through several branches; dataflow analysis, which analyzes and modifies the program order to execute instructions when ready; and speculative execution, which looks ahead of the program counter and executes instruction that are likely to be needed. The Pentium II processor expands on these capabilities in sophisticated and powerful new ways to deliver even greater performance gains.

Similar to the Pentium Pro, the Pentium II also includes DIB architecture. The term *Dual Independent Bus* comes from the existence of two independent buses on the Pentium II processor—the L2 cache bus and the processor-to-main-memory system bus. The Pentium II processor can use both buses simultaneously, thus getting as much as twice as much data in and out of the Pentium II processor as a single-bus architecture processor. The DIB architecture enables the L2 cache of the 333MHz Pentium II processor to run 2 1/2 times as fast as the L2 cache of Pentium processors. As the frequency of future Pentium II processors increases, so will the speed of the L2 cache. Also, the pipelined system bus enables simultaneous parallel transactions instead of singular sequential transactions. Together, these DIB architecture improvements offer up to three times the bandwidth performance over a single-bus architecture as with the regular Pentium.

Table 3.34 shows the general Pentium II processor specifications. Table 3.35 shows the specifications that vary by model.

Table 3.34   Pentium II General Processor Specifications

Bus speeds	66MHz, 100MHz
CPU clock multiplier	3.5x, 4x, 4.5x, 5x
CPU speeds	233MHz, 266MHz, 300MHz, 333MHz, 350MHz, 400MHz, 450MHz
Cache memory	16K×2 (32KB) L1, 512KB 1/2-speed L2
Internal registers	32-bit
External data bus	64-bit system bus w/ ECC; 64-bit cache bus w/ optional ECC
Memory address bus	36-bit
Addressable memory	64GB
Virtual memory	64TB
Physical package	Single edge contact cartridge (S.E), 242 pins
Package dimensions	5.505" (13.98cm) ×2.473" (6.28cm) ×0.647" (1.64cm)
Math coprocessor	Built-in FPU
Power management	SMM

Table 3.35   Pentium II Specifications by Model

Pentium II MMX Processor (350MHz, 400MHz, and 450MHz)	
Introduction date	April 15, 1998
Clock speeds	350MHz (100MHz×3.5), 400MHz (100MHz×4), and 450MHz (100MHz×4.5)
iCOMP Index 2.0 rating	386 (350MHz), 440 (400MHz), and 483 (450MHz)
Number of transistors	7.5 million (0.25-micron process), plus 31 million in 512KB L2 cache
Cacheable RAM	4GB
Operating voltage	2.0V

Table 3.35   Continued

Slot	Slot 1
Die size	0.400" per side (10.2mm)

Mobile Pentium II Processor (266MHz, 300MHz, 333MHz, and 366MHz)

Introduction date	January 25, 1999
Clock speeds	266MHz, 300MHz, 333MHz, and 366MHz
Number of transistors	27.4 million (0.25-micron process), 256KB on-die L2 cache
Ball grid array (BGA)	Number of balls = 615
Dimensions	Width = 31mm; length = 35mm
Core voltage	1.6 volts
Thermal design power ranges by frequency	366MHz = 9.5 watts; 333MHz = 8.6 watts; 300MHz = 7.7 watts; 266MHz = 7.0 watts

Pentium II MMX Processor (333MHz)

Introduction date	January 26, 1998
Clock speed	333MHz (66MHz×5)
iCOMP Index 2.0 rating	366
Number of transistors	7.5 million (0.25-micron process), plus 31 million in 512KB L2 cache
Cacheable RAM	512MB
Operating voltage	2.0V
Slot	Slot 1
Die size	0.400" per side (10.2mm)

Pentium II MMX Processor (300MHz)

Introduction date	May 7, 1997
Clock speed	300MHz (66MHz×4.5)
iCOMP Index 2.0 rating	332
Number of transistors	7.5 million (0.35-micron process), plus 31 million in 512KB L2 cache
Cacheable RAM	512MB
Die size	0.560" per side (14.2mm)

Pentium II MMX Processor (266MHz)

Introduction date	May 7, 1997
Clock speed	266MHz (66MHz×4)
iCOMP Index 2.0 rating	303
Number of transistors	7.5 million (0.35-micron process), plus 31 million in 512KB L2 cache
Cacheable RAM	512MB
Slot	Slot 1
Die size	0.560" per side (14.2mm)

Pentium II MMX Processor (233MHz)

Introduction date	May 7, 1997
Clock speed	233MHz (66MHz×3.5)
iCOMP Index 2.0 rating	267

Table 3.35   Continued

Number of transistors	7.5 million (0.35-micron process), plus 31 million in 512KB L2 cache
Cacheable RAM	512MB
Slot	Slot 1
Die size	0.560" per side (14.2mm)

The L1 cache always runs at full-core speeds because it is mounted directly on the processor die. The L2 cache in the Pentium II normally runs at half-core speed, which saves money and allows for less expensive cache chips to be used. For example, in a 333MHz Pentium II, the L1 cache runs at a full 333MHz, whereas the L2 cache runs at 167MHz. Even though the L2 cache is not at full-core speed as it was with the Pentium Pro, this is still far superior to having cache memory on the motherboard running at the 66MHz motherboard speed of most Socket 7 Pentium designs. Intel claims that the DIB architecture in the Pentium II enables up to three times the bandwidth of normal single-bus processors, such as the original Pentium.

By removing the cache from the processor's internal package and using external chips mounted on a substrate and encased in the cartridge design, Intel could use more cost-effective cache chips and more easily scale the processor up to higher speeds. The Pentium Pro was limited in speed to 200MHz, largely due to the inability to find affordable cache memory that ran any faster. By running the cache memory at half-core speed, the Pentium II can run up to 400MHz while still using 200MHz-rated cache chips. To offset the half-core speed cache used in the Pentium II, Intel doubled the basic amount of integrated L2 cache from 256KB standard in the Pro to 512KB standard in the Pentium II.

Note that the tag RAM included in the L2 cache enables up to 512MB of main memory to be cacheable in PII processors from 233MHz to 333MHz. The 350MHz, 400MHz, and faster versions include an enhanced tag RAM that allows up to 4GB of main memory to be cacheable. If you support systems based on the Pentium II, be aware of the caching limitations in the slower processors before upgrading memory above 512MB. Uncached memory will slow down any system.

The system bus of the Pentium II provides "glueless" support for up to two processors. This enables low-cost, two-way multiprocessing on the L2 cache bus. These system buses are designed especially for servers or other mission-critical system use where reliability and data integrity are important. All Pentium IIs also include parity-protected address/request and response system bus signals with a retry mechanism for high data integrity and reliability. As a result, the Pentium II was used in many servers and workstations.

To install the Pentium II in a system, a special processor-retention mechanism is required. This consists of a mechanical support that attaches to the motherboard and secures the Pentium II processor in Slot 1 to prevent shock and vibration damage. Retention mechanisms should be provided by the motherboard manufacturer. (For example, the Intel Boxed AL440FX and DK440LX motherboards included a retention mechanism, plus other important system integration components.) The retention mechanism sometimes folds out of the way for easier storage of the motherboard component, or it might use a rigid design.

The Pentium II can generate a significant amount of heat that must be dissipated. This is accomplished by installing a heatsink on the processor. Many of the Pentium II processors use an active heatsink that incorporates a fan. Unlike heatsink fans for previous Intel boxed processors, the Pentium II fans draw power from a three-pin power header on the motherboard. Most motherboards provide several fan connectors to supply this power.

Special heatsink supports are necessary to furnish mechanical support between the fan heatsink and support holes on the motherboard. Normally, a plastic support is inserted into the heatsink holes in the motherboard next to the CPU, before installing the CPU/heatsink package. Most fan heatsinks have two components: a fan in a plastic shroud and a metal heatsink. The heatsink is attached to the processor's thermal plate and should not be removed. The fan can be removed and replaced if necessary—for example, if it has failed. Figure 3.49 shows the SEC assembly with fan, power connectors, mechanical supports, and the slot and support holes on the motherboard.

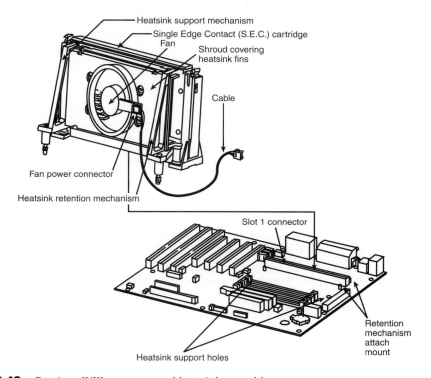

Figure 3.49 Pentium II/III processor and heatsink assembly.

The following tables show the specifications unique to certain versions of the Pentium II processor.

To identify exactly which Pentium II processor you have and what its capabilities are, look at the specification number printed on the SEC cartridge. You will find the specification number in the dynamic mark area on the top of the processor module. See Figure 3.50 to locate these markings.

After you have located the specification number (actually, it is an alphanumeric code), you can look it up in Table 3.36 to see exactly which processor you have.

For example, a specification number of SL2KA identifies the processor as a Pentium II 333MHz running on a 66MHz system bus, with an ECC L2 cache, and indicates that this processor runs on only 2.0V. The stepping is also identified, and by looking in the "Pentium II Specification Update Manual" published by Intel, you could figure out exactly which bugs were fixed in that revision.

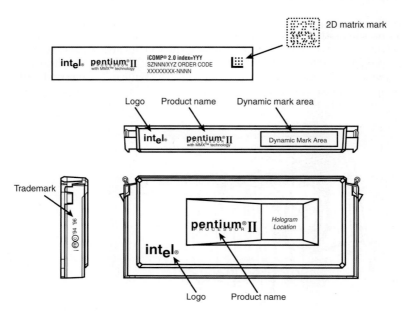

Figure 3.50 Pentium II/III SECC.

Table 3.36 Basic Pentium II Processor Identification Information

S-spec	Core Stepping	CPUID	Core/Bus Speed (MHz)	L2 Cache Size (KB)	L2 Cache Type	CPU Package	Notes (see footnotes)
SL264	C0	0633h	233/66	512	Non-ECC	SECC 3.00	5
SL265	C0	0633h	266/66	512	Non-ECC	SECC 3.00	5
SL268	C0	0633h	233/66	512	ECC	SECC 3.00	5
SL269	C0	0633h	266/66	512	ECC	SECC 3.00	5
SL28K	C0	0633h	233/66	512	Non-ECC	SECC 3.00	1, 3, 5
SL28L	C0	0633h	266/66	512	Non-ECC	SECC 3.00	1, 3, 5
SL28R	C0	0633h	300/66	512	ECC	SECC 3.00	5
SL2MZ	C0	0633h	300/66	512	ECC	SECC 3.00	1, 5
SL2HA	C1	0634h	300/66	512	ECC	SECC 3.00	5
SL2HC	C1	0634h	266/66	512	Non-ECC	SECC 3.00	5
SL2HD	C1	0634h	233/66	512	Non-ECC	SECC 3.00	5
SL2HE	C1	0634h	266/66	512	ECC	SECC 3.00	5
SL2HF	C1	0634h	233/66	512	ECC	SECC 3.00	5
SL2QA	C1	0634h	233/66	512	Non-ECC	SECC 3.00	1, 3, 5
SL2QB	C1	0634h	266/66	512	Non-ECC	SECC 3.00	1, 3, 5
SL2QC	C1	0634h	300/66	512	ECC	SECC 3.00	1, 5

Table 3.36   Continued

S-spec	Core Stepping	CPUID	Core/Bus Speed (MHz)	L2 Cache Size (KB)	L2 Cache Type	CPU Package	Notes (see footnotes)
SL2KA	dA0	0650h	333/66	512	ECC	SECC 3.00	5
SL2QF	dA0	0650h	333/66	512	ECC	SECC 3.00	1
SL2K9	dA0	0650h	266/66	512	ECC	SECC 3.00	
SL35V	dA1	0651h	300/66	512	ECC	SECC 3.00	1, 2
SL2QH	dA1	0651h	333/66	512	ECC	SECC 3.00	1, 2
SL2S5	dA1	0651h	333/66	512	ECC	SECC 3.00	2, 5
SL2ZP	dA1	0651h	333/66	512	ECC	SECC 3.00	2, 5
SL2ZQ	dA1	0651h	350/100	512	ECC	SECC 3.00	2, 5
SL2S6	dA1	0651h	350/100	512	ECC	SECC 3.00	2, 5
SL2S7	dA1	0651h	400/100	512	ECC	SECC 3.00	2, 5
SL2SF	dA1	0651h	350/100	512	ECC	SECC 3.00	1, 2
SL2SH	dA1	0651h	400/100	512	ECC	SECC 3.00	1, 2
SL2VY	dA1	0651h	300/66	512	ECC	SECC 3.00	1, 2
SL33D	dB0	0652h	266/66	512	ECC	SECC 3.00	1, 2, 5
SL2YK	dB0	0652h	300/66	512	ECC	SECC 3.00	1, 2, 5
SL2WZ	dB0	0652h	350/100	512	ECC	SECC 3.00	1, 2, 5
SL2YM	dB0	0652h	400/100	512	ECC	SECC 3.00	1, 2, 5
SL37G	dB0	0652h	400/100	512	ECC	SECC2 OLGA	1, 2, 4
SL2WB	dB0	0652h	450/100	512	ECC	SECC 3.00	1, 2, 5
SL37H	dB0	0652h	450/100	512	ECC	SECC2 OLGA	1, 2
SL2W7	dB0	0652h	266/66	512	ECC	SECC 2.00	2, 5
SL2W8	dB0	0652h	300/66	512	ECC	SECC 3.00	2, 5
SL2TV	dB0	0652h	333/66	512	ECC	SECC 3.00	2, 5
SL2U3	dB0	0652h	350/100	512	ECC	SECC 3.00	2, 5
SL2U4	dB0	0652h	350/100	512	ECC	SECC 3.00	2, 5
SL2U5	dB0	0652h	400/100	512	ECC	SECC 3.00	2, 5
SL2U6	dB0	0652h	400/100	512	ECC	SECC 3.00	2, 5
SL2U7	dB0	0652h	450/100	512	ECC	SECC 3.00	2, 5
SL356	dB0	0652h	350/100	512	ECC	SECC2 PLGA	2, 5
SL357	dB0	0652h	400/100	512	ECC	SECC2 OLGA	2, 5
SL358	dB0	0652h	450/100	512	ECC	SECC2 OLGA	2, 5
SL37F	dB0	0652h	350/100	512	ECC	SECC2 PLGA	1, 2, 5
SL3FN	dB0	0652h	350/100	512	ECC	SECC2 OLGA	2, 5
SL3EE	dB0	0652h	400/100	512	ECC	SECC2 PLGA	2, 5
SL3F9	dB0	0652h	400/100	512	ECC	SECC2 PLGA	1, 2
SL38M	dB1	0653h	350/100	512	ECC	SECC 3.00	1, 2, 5
SL38N	dB1	0653h	400/100	512	ECC	SECC 3.00	1, 2, 5
SL36U	dB1	0653h	350/100	512	ECC	SECC 3.00	2, 5

Table 3.36   Continued

S-spec	Core Stepping	CPUID	Core/Bus Speed (MHz)	L2 Cache Size (KB)	L2 Cache Type	CPU Package	Notes (see footnotes)
SL38Z	dB1	0653h	400/100	512	ECC	SECC 3.00	2, 5
SL3D5	dB1	0653h	400/100	512	ECC	SECC2 OLGA	1, 2

CPUID = The internal ID returned by the CPUID instruction

ECC = Error-correcting code

OLGA = Organic land grid array

PLGA = Plastic land grid array

SECC = Single edge contact cartridge

SECC2 = Single edge contact cartridge revision 2

1. This is a boxed Pentium II processor with an attached fan heatsink.

2. These processors have an enhanced L2 cache, which can cache up to 4GB of main memory. Other standard PII processors can cache only up to 512MB of main memory.

3. These boxed processors might have packaging that incorrectly indicates ECC support in the L2 cache.

4. This is a boxed Pentium II OverDrive processor with an attached fan heatsink, designed for upgrading Pentium Pro (Socket 8) systems.

5. These parts operate only at the specified clock multiplier frequency ratio at which they were manufactured. They can be overclocked only by increasing the bus speed.

The two variations of the SECC2 cartridge vary by the type of processor core package on the board. The plastic land grid array (PLGA) is the older type of packaging used in previous SECC cartridges and was eventually phased out. A newer organic land grid array (OLGA), which is a processor core package that is smaller and easier to manufacture, took its place. It also enabled better thermal transfer between the processor die and the heatsink, which was attached directly to the top of the OLGA chip package. Figure 3.51 shows the open back side (where the heatsink would be attached) of SECC2 processors with PLGA and OLGA cores.

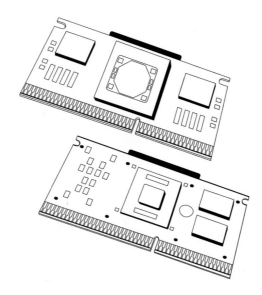

Figure 3.51   SECC2 processors with PLGA (top) and OLGA (bottom) cores.

Pentium II motherboards have an onboard voltage regulator circuit designed to power the CPU. Some Pentium II processors run at several different voltages, so the regulator must be set to supply the correct voltage for the specific processor you are installing. As with the Pentium Pro and unlike the older Pentium, no jumpers or switches must be set; the voltage setting is handled completely automatically through the VID pins on the processor cartridge. Table 3.37 shows the relationship between the pins and the selected voltage.

To ensure the system is ready for all Pentium II processor variations, the values in **bold** must be supported. Most Pentium II processors run at 2.8V, with some newer ones at 2.0V.

The Pentium II Mobile Module is a Pentium II for notebooks that includes the North Bridge of the high-performance 440BX chipset. This was the first chipset on the market that allowed 100MHz processor bus operation, although that feature was not supported in the mobile versions. The 440BX chipset was released at the same time as the 350MHz and 400MHz versions of the Pentium II.

Newer variations on the Pentium II include the Pentium IIPE, which is a mobile version that includes 256KB of L2 cache directly integrated into the die. Therefore, it runs at full-core speed, making it faster than the desktop Pentium II because the desktop chips use half-speed L2 cache.

Table 3.37   Pentium II/III/Celeron Voltage ID Pin Definitions

VID4	VID3	VID2	VID1	VID0	Voltage
0	1	1	1	1	1.30
0	1	1	1	0	1.35
0	1	1	0	1	1.40
0	1	1	0	0	1.45
0	1	0	1	1	1.50
0	1	0	1	0	1.55
0	1	0	0	1	1.60
0	1	0	0	0	1.65
0	0	1	1	1	1.70
0	0	1	1	0	1.75
0	0	1	0	1	**1.80**
0	0	1	0	0	**1.85**
0	0	0	1	1	**1.90**
0	0	0	1	0	**1.95**
0	0	0	0	1	**2.00**
0	0	0	0	0	**2.05**
1	1	1	1	1	**No Core**
1	1	1	1	0	**2.1**
1	1	1	0	1	**2.2**
1	1	1	0	0	**2.3**
1	1	0	1	1	**2.4**
1	1	0	1	0	**2.5**
1	1	0	0	1	**2.6**
1	1	0	0	0	**2.7**

Table 3.37   Continued

VID4	VID3	VID2	VID1	VID0	Voltage
1	0	1	1	1	**2.8**
1	0	1	1	0	2.9
1	0	1	0	1	3.0
1	0	1	0	0	3.1
1	0	0	1	1	3.2
1	0	0	1	0	3.3
1	0	0	0	1	3.4
1	0	0	0	0	3.5

0 = Processor pin connected to Vss.

1 = Open on processor.

VID0–VID3 used on Socket 370.

Socket 370 supports 1.30-2.05V settings only.

VID0–VID4 used on Slot 1.

Slot 1 supports 1.30-3.5V settings.

Celeron

The Celeron processor is a chameleon. It was originally a P6 with the same processor core as the Pentium II in the original two versions; later it came with the same core as the PIII; and more recently it has been based on the various the Pentium 4 cores, including Prescott. It is designed mainly for lower-cost PCs.

Most of the features for the Celeron are the same as the Pentium II, III, or 4 because it uses the same internal processor cores. The main differences are in packaging, L2 cache amount, and CPU bus speed.

The first version of the Celeron was available in a package called the single edge processor package (SEPP or SEP package). The SEP package is basically the same Slot 1 design as the SECC used in the Pentium II/III, with the exception of the fancy plastic cartridge cover. This cover was deleted in the Celeron, making it cheaper to produce and sell. Essentially, the original Celeron used the same circuit board as is inside the Pentium II package.

◀◀ See "Single Edge Contact and Single Edge Processor Packaging," p. 95.

Even without the plastic covers, the Slot 1 packaging was more expensive than it should have been. This was largely due to the processor retention mechanisms (stands) required to secure the processor into Slot 1 on the motherboard, as well as the larger and more complicated heatsinks required. This, plus competition from the lower-end Socket 7 systems using primarily AMD processors, led Intel to introduce the Celeron in a socketed form. The socket is called PGA-370 or Socket 370 because it has 370 pins. The processor package designed for this socket is called the plastic pin grid array (PPGA) package (see Figure 3.52) or flip chip PGA (FC-PGA). Both the PPGA and FC-PGA packages plug into the 370 pin socket and allow for lower-cost, lower-profile, and smaller systems because of the less expensive processor retention and cooling requirements of the socketed processor.

◀◀ See "Socket 370 (PGA-370)," p. 105.

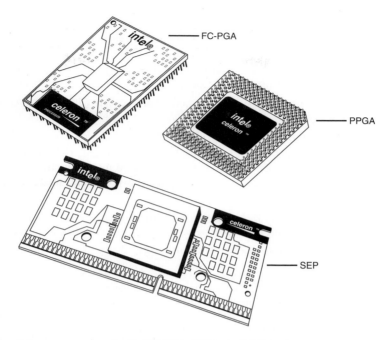

Figure 3.52   Celeron processors in the FC-PGA, PPGA, and SEP packages.

All Celeron processors at 433MHz and lower were available in the SEPP that plugs into the 242-contact slot connector (Slot 1). The 300MHz and higher versions were also made in the PPGA package. This means that the 300MHz to 433MHz have been available in both packages, whereas the 466MHz and higher-speed versions are available only in the PPGA. The fastest Celeron processor for Socket 370 runs at 1.4GHz; faster Celerons use Socket 478 and are based on the Pentium 4 design.

Motherboards that include Socket 370 can accept the PGA versions of both the Celeron and Pentium III in most cases. If you want to use a Socket 370 version of the Celeron in a Slot 1 motherboard, slot-to-socket adapters are available that plug into Slot 1 and incorporate a Socket 370 on the card. Figure 3.53 shows a typical slot-to-socket adapter.

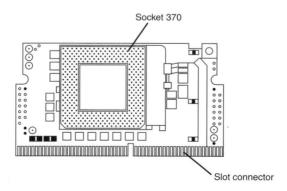

Figure 3.53   Slot-to-socket adapter for installing PPGA processors in Slot 1 motherboards.

Highlights of the Celeron include the following:

- Available at 300MHz (300A) and higher core frequencies with 128KB or more on-die L2 cache; 300MHz and 266MHz core frequencies without L2 cache.

- Uses same processor core as the Pentium II (266MHz through 533MHz), the Pentium III (533A MHz and higher), and the Pentium 4 or Core microarchitecture processors (1.6GHz and higher).

- Operates on a 66MHz, 100MHz, 400MHz, 533MHz or 800MHz CPU bus, depending on the version.

- Specifically designed for lower-cost value PC systems.

- Includes MMX technology; Celeron 533A and higher include SSE; Celeron 1.7GHz and higher include SSE2; Celeron D and Core microarchitecture based models include SSE3.

- More cost-effective packaging technology, including SEP, PPGA, and FC-PGA or FC-PGA2 packages.

- Integrated L1 and L2 cache on most models, with amount and type depending on the version; typically, the Celeron has half the L2 cache of the processor core it is patterned after.

- Integrated thermal diode for temperature monitoring.

The Intel Celeron processors from the 300A and higher include integrated 128KB L2 cache. The core for the 300A through 533MHz versions that are based on the Pentium II core include 19 million transistors because of the addition of the integrated 128KB L2 cache. The 533A and faster versions are based on the Pentium III core and incorporate 28.1 million transistors. The 1.6GHz and faster versions are based on the Pentium 4 or Core microarchitecture processors. The Pentium III and Pentium 4–based versions actually have 256KB of L2 cache on the die; however, 128KB is disabled, leaving 128KB of functional L2 cache. This was done because it was cheaper for Intel to simply make the Celeron using the same die as the Pentium III or 4 and just disable part of the cache on the Celeron versions, rather than coming up with a unique die for the newer Celerons. The Pentium III–based Celeron processors also support the SSE in addition to MMX instructions, whereas the Pentium 4-based versions support SSE2 instructions. The older Celerons based on the Pentium II core support only MMX.

All the Celerons in SEPP and PPGA form are manufactured using the 0.25-micron process, whereas those in FC-PGA and FC-PGA2 form are made using the better 0.18-micron and 0.13-micron processes. The smaller process reduces processor heat and enables higher speeds.

The latest Celeron processors for desktop computers use the Celeron D and Celeron 400 series brand names, whereas the Celeron M brand name identifies Celeron-class processors designed for use in low-cost portable computers. Celeron D processors are manufactured using the 90nm (0.09-micron) process, but Celeron 400 series processors use a 65nm (0.065-micron) process.

A Brief Celeron History

The original Celerons were economy versions of the Intel Pentium II processor. Intel figured that by taking a Pentium II and deleting the separate L2 cache chips mounted inside the processor cartridge (and also deleting the cosmetic cover), it could create a "new" processor that was basically just a slower version of the Pentium II. As such, the first 266MHz and 300MHz Celeron models didn't include any L2 cache. Unfortunately, this proved to have far too great a crippling effect on performance, so starting with the 300A versions, the Celeron received 128KB of on-die full-speed L2 cache, which was actually faster and more advanced than the 512KB of half-speed cache used in the Pentium II it was based on! In fact, the Celeron was the first PC processor to receive on-die L2 cache. It wasn't until the Coppermine version of the Pentium III appeared that on-die L2 cache migrated to Intel's main processors.

Needless to say, this caused a lot of confusion in the marketplace about the Celeron. Considering that the Celeron started out as a "crippled" Pentium II and then was revised so as to actually be superior in some ways to the Pentium II on which it was based (all the while selling for less), many didn't know just where the Celeron stood in terms of performance. Fortunately, the crippling lack of L2 cache existed only in the earliest Celeron versions; all of those at speeds greater than 300MHz have on-die full-speed L2 cache.

The earliest Celerons from 266MHz up through 400MHz were produced in a SEPP design that physically looked like a circuit board and that was designed to fit into Slot 1. This is the same slot the Pentium II used, meaning the Celeron SEPP plugged into any Pentium II Slot-1 motherboard. As the Celeron continued to develop, the form factor was changed to correspond with changes in the Pentium II-, III-, and 4-class processors from which it was adapted. Starting with the 300A processor (300MHz Celeron with 128KB of on-die Level 2 cache), Celerons were produced in a PPGA package using the Socket 370 interface. This socket, with differences in voltage, was later used for most versions of the Pentium III. Celerons using Socket 370 range in speed from 300MHz all the way up to 1.4GHz. Along the way, the packaging changed from PPGA to FC-PGA and FC-PGA2. The latter added a metal heat spreader on top of the die offering better protection for the fragile die.

Celeron processors based on the Pentium 4 are produced in one of two package designs. Some use the FC-PGA2 package that fits into the same Socket 478 used by most Pentium 4 processors. However, the Celeron D is available in both the Socket 478 package and Socket T (LGA775) package used by the Prescott core version of the Pentium 4, but the Celeron 400 series are for LGA775 only. The Celeron was never produced in the short-lived Socket 423 form factor the original Pentium 4 processors used.

As this very brief history shows, the name *Celeron* has never meant anything more specific than a reduced-performance version of Intel's current mainstream processor. Before you can decide whether a particular Celeron processor is a suitable choice, you need to know what its features are and especially on which processor it is based. At least eight discrete variations of the Celeron processor exist, which are detailed in Table 3.38.

Table 3.38 Celeron CPU Variations

Celeron Version	Base On	Codename	Process (Micron)	L2 Cache (KB)
Celeron	Pentium II Deschutes	Covington	0.25	0
Celeron A	Pentium II Deschutes	Mendocino	0.25	128
Celeron A-PGA	Pentium II Deschutes	Mendocino	0.25	128
Celeron III	Pentium III Coppermine	Coppermine-128	0.18	128
Celeron IIIA	Pentium III Tualatin	Tualatin-256	0.13	256
Celeron 4	Pentium 4 Willamette	Willamette-128	0.18	128
Celeron 4A	Pentium 4 Northwood	Northwood-128	0.13	128
Celeron D	Pentium 4 Prescott	Prescott-256	0.09	256
Celeron D	Pentium 4 Cedar Mill	Cedar Mill-512	0.065	512
Celeron 4xx	Core microarchitecture	Conroe-512	0.065	512

1. *All Celeron III below 800MHz use the 66MHz CPU bus; all Celeron III from 800MHz through 1.1GHz use the 100MHz bus.*

SEPP = Single edge processor package.

FC-PGA = Flip chip pin grid array.

FC-PGA2 = FC-PGA with added heat spreader.

MMX = Multimedia extensions; 57 additional instructions for graphics and sound processing.

Figure 3.54 shows most of the various Celeron package types.

Celeron/Celeron A SEPP (Slot-1)

Celeron 4 FC-PGA2 (Socket 478)

Celeron A-PGA PPGA (Socket 370)

Celeron IIIA FC-PGA2 (Socket 370)

Celeron III FC-PGA (Socket 370)

Figure 3.54 Processors released under the Celeron brand. *Photos courtesy of Intel.*

Multimedia Support	Physical Interface	Package	CPU Bus Speed	Min. Speed	Max. Speed
MMX	Slot-1	SEPP	66MHz	266MHz	300MHz
MMX	Slot-1	SEPP	66MHz	300MHz	433MHz
MMX	Socket 370	PPGA	66MHz	300MHz	533MHz
SSE	Socket 370	FC-PGA	66/100MHz[1]	533MHz	1.1GHz
SSE	Socket 370	FC-PGA2	100MHz	900MHz	1.4GHz
SSE2	Socket 478	FC-PGA2	400MHz	1.7GHz	1.8GHz
SSE2	Socket 478	FC-PGA2	400MHz	2.0GHz	2.8GHz
SSE3	Socket 478/LGA775	FC-PGA2	533MHz	2.13GHz	3.33GHz
SSE3	Socket LGA775	FC-PGA2	533MHz	3.06GHz	3.6GHz
SSE3	Socket LGA775	FC-PGA2	800MHz	1.6GHz	2.0GHz

SSE = Streaming SIMD (single instruction multiple data) extensions; MMX plus 70 additional instructions for graphics and sound processing.

SSE2 = Streaming SIMD extensions 2; SSE plus 144 additional instructions for graphics and sound processing.

The "Celeron Version" names listed here are not official; I made them up as a way to clearly identify the different Celeron processors.

Minimum and maximum speeds indicate the slowest and fastest rated speeds of each variation offered.

As you can see, there is a wide range of what is called a Celeron, and you could consider the Celeron as a family of different core processor models in several package variations.

The following sections discuss the differences between these Celeron processors.

Socket 370 Celerons

Socket 370 Celerons are based on various versions of the Pentium II and Pentium III architecture.

Intel offered Celeron IIIA versions for Socket 370 motherboards in speeds from 900MHz to 1.4GHz. These processors have a CPU bus speed of 100MHz. Celeron IIIA versions based on the Pentium III Tualatin core have 256KB of L2 cache, whereas those based on the earlier Pentium III Coppermine core or Pentium II Deschutes core have 128KB of L2 cache. Compared to Celerons based on the previous Pentium III Coppermine core, Tualatin-based Celerons have the following differences:

- Larger L2 memory cache (256KB versus 128KB)
- Improved L2 cache design for better performance
- FC-PGA2 packaging, which includes a metal heat spreader over the fragile CPU core to protect it when attaching a heatsink

Like the Tualatin-core versions of the Pentium III, Celerons based on the Tualatin core don't work in motherboards designed for older Pentium III or Celeron chips. Socket 370 is physically the same, but the Tualatin core redefines 10 pins in the socket, which requires corresponding changes in the chipset and motherboard. So, if you're looking for a way to speed up an older Celeron by installing a Tualatin-core Celeron IIIA, make sure the motherboard is Tualatin-ready. Also note that Tualatin-core Celerons use the FC-PGA2 packaging, which includes a heat spreader on top of the CPU die. This requires a compatible heatsink.

Socket 478 Celeron and Celeron D Processors

Celeron processors in Socket 478 fall into three distinct camps, as Table 3.38 previously demonstrated:

- Celerons running at 1.7GHz and 1.8GHz are based on the original Pentium 4 Willamette core and have a 400MHz CPU bus, 128KB of L2 cache, and SSE2 support.

- Celerons running at 2GHz–2.8GHz with a 400MHz CPU bus are based on the Pentium 4 Northwood core, have 128KB of L2 cache, and have SSE2 support.

- Celeron D processors are based on the Prescott core used by the latest Pentium 4 processors; range in speed from 2.13GHz to 3.2GHz; and feature a 533MHz CPU bus, 256KB of L2 cache, and SSE3 support.

Socket T (LGA 775) Celeron D Processors

Celeron D processors in Socket T (LGA 775) range in speed from 2.4GHz to 3.6GHz and feature a 533MHz CPU bus, 256KB or 512KB of L2 cache, and SSE3 support. They also may have two unique features compared to Celeron D processors in Socket 478:

- Most feature support for the Execute Disable (NX) Bit feature, which helps block buffer overrun virus attacks, when used with a compatible operating system such as Windows XP or Vista.

- Some also feature support for EM64T, Intel's implementation of 64-bit extensions to the IA32 processor architecture. Thus, Celeron D processors with EM64T provide a low-cost way to use 64-bit operating systems such as Windows XP and Vista x64 Editions or 64-bit Linux distributions.

Celeron D processors use the Intel processor numbering scheme introduced in 2004. Use Table 3.39 to determine the specific features supported by a particular Celeron D processor model number.

Table 3.39   Celeron D Model Numbers and Features

Processor Number	CPU Speed	Bus Speed	L2 Cache	Mfg. Process	S-Spec	Stepping	64-bit	NX	Socket
310	2.13GHz	533MHz	256KB	90nm	SL8RZ	E0	—	—	478
310	2.13GHz	533MHz	256KB	90nm	SL8S4	G0	—	—	478
310	2.13GHz	533MHz	256KB	90nm	SL93R	G1	—	—	478
310	2.13GHz	533MHz	256KB	90nm	SL8S2	G1	—	—	478
315	2.26GHz	533MHz	256KB	90nm	SL7XG	C0	—	—	478
315	2.26GHz	533MHz	256KB	90nm	SL7XY	D0	—	—	478
315	2.26GHz	533MHz	256KB	90nm	SL7WS	D0	—	—	478
315	2.26GHz	533MHz	256KB	90nm	SL87K	E0	—	—	478
315	2.26GHz	533MHz	256KB	90nm	SL8AW	E0	—	—	478
315	2.26GHz	533MHz	256KB	90nm	SL8HH	G1	—	—	478
315	2.26GHz	533MHz	256KB	90nm	SL93Q	G1	—	—	478
320	2.40GHz	533MHz	256KB	90nm	SL7C4	C0	—	—	478
320	2.40GHz	533MHz	256KB	90nm	SL7KX	D0	—	—	478
320	2.40GHz	533MHz	256KB	90nm	SL7JV	D0	—	—	478
320	2.40GHz	533MHz	256KB	90nm	SL7VW	E0	—	—	478

Table 3.39   Continued

Processor Number	CPU Speed	Bus Speed	L2 Cache	Mfg. Process	S-Spec	Stepping	64-bit	NX	Socket
320	2.40GHz	533MHz	256KB	90nm	SL7VQ	E0	—	yes	LGA775
320	2.40GHz	533MHz	256KB	90nm	SL8HJ	G1	—	—	478
325	2.53GHz	533MHz	256KB	90nm	SL7C5	C0	—	—	478
325	2.53GHz	533MHz	256KB	90nm	SL7TG	C0	—	—	478
325	2.53GHz	533MHz	256KB	90nm	SL7SS	D0	—	—	LGA775
325	2.53GHz	533MHz	256KB	90nm	SL7ND	D0	—	—	478
325	2.53GHz	533MHz	256KB	90nm	SL7KY	D0	—	—	478
325	2.53GHz	533MHz	256KB	90nm	SL7NU	E0	—	—	478
325J	2.53GHz	533MHz	256KB	90nm	SL7VR	E0	—	yes	LGA775
325	2.53GHz	533MHz	256KB	90nm	SL7VX	E0	—	—	478
325J	2.53GHz	533MHz	256KB	90nm	SL7TL	E0	—	yes	LGA775
325	2.53GHz	533MHz	256KB	90nm	SL8HK	G1	—	—	478
326	2.53GHz	533MHz	256KB	90nm	SL7TU	E0	yes	yes	LGA775
326	2.53GHz	533MHz	256KB	90nm	SL98U	G1	yes	—	LGA775
326	2.53GHz	533MHz	256KB	90nm	SL8H5	G1	yes	yes	LGA775
330	2.66GHz	533MHz	256KB	90nm	SL7VY	—	—	—	478
330	2.66GHz	533MHz	256KB	90nm	SL7TH	C0	—	—	478
330	2.66GHz	533MHz	256KB	90nm	SL7C6	C0	—	—	478
330	2.66GHz	533MHz	256KB	90nm	SL7ST	D0	—	—	LGA775
330	2.66GHz	533MHz	256KB	90nm	SL7DL	D0	—	—	478
330	2.66GHz	533MHz	256KB	90nm	SL7NV	E0	—	—	478
330J	2.66GHz	533MHz	256KB	90nm	SL7TM	E0	—	yes	LGA775
330J	2.66GHz	533MHz	256KB	90nm	SL7VS	E0	—	yes	LGA775
330	2.66GHz	533MHz	256KB	90nm	SL7KZ	E0	—	—-	478
330	2.66GHz	533MHz	256KB	90nm	SL8HL	G1	—	—	478
331	2.66GHz	533MHz	256KB	90nm	SL7TV	E0	yes	yes	LGA775
331	2.66GHz	533MHz	256KB	90nm	SL8H7	G1	yes	—	LGA775
331	2.66GHz	533MHz	256KB	90nm	SL98V	G1	—	—	LGA775
335	2.80GHz	533MHz	256KB	90nm	SL7SU	-	—	—	LGA775
335	2.80GHz	533MHz	256KB	90nm	SL7C7	C0	—	—	478
335	2.80GHz	533MHz	256KB	90nm	SL7L2	C0	—	—	478
335	2.80GHz	533MHz	256KB	90nm	SL7TJ	C0	—	—	478
335	2.80GHz	533MHz	256KB	90nm	SL7DM	D0	—	—	478
335J	2.80GHz	533MHz	256KB	90nm	SL7VT	E0	—	yes	LGA775
335J	2.80GHz	533MHz	256KB	90nm	SL7TN	E0	—	yes	LGA775
335	2.80GHz	533MHz	256KB	90nm	SL7NW	E0	—	—	478
335	2.80GHz	533MHz	256KB	90nm	SL7VZ	E0	—	—	478
335	2.80GHz	533MHz	256KB	90nm	SL8HM	G1	—	—	478

Table 3.39   Continued

Processor Number	CPU Speed	Bus Speed	L2 Cache	Mfg. Process	S-Spec	Stepping	64-bit	NX	Socket
336	2.80GHz	533MHz	256KB	90nm	SL7TW	E0	yes	yes	LGA775
336	2.80GHz	533MHz	256KB	90nm	SL98W	G1	—	—	LGA775
336	2.80GHz	533MHz	256KB	90nm	SL8H9	G1	yes	yes	LGA775
340	2.93GHz	533MHz	256KB	90nm	SL7RN	C0	—	—	478
340	2.93GHz	533MHz	256KB	90nm	SL7SV	D0	—	—	LGA775
340	2.93GHz	533MHz	256KB	90nm	SL7Q9	D0	—	—	478
340J	2.93GHz	533MHz	256KB	90nm	SL7TP	E0	—	yes	LGA775
340	2.93GHz	533MHz	256KB	90nm	SL7W2	E0	—	—	478
340	2.93GHz	533MHz	256KB	90nm	SL7TS	E0	—	—	478
340	2.93GHz	533MHz	256KB	90nm	SL8HN	G1	—	—	478
341	2.93GHz	533MHz	256KB	90nm	SL7TX	E0	yes	yes	LGA775
341	2.93GHz	533MHz	256KB	90nm	SL8HB	G1	yes	yes	LGA775
345	3.06GHz	533MHz	256KB	90nm	SL7DN	D0	—	—	478
345	3.06GHz	533MHz	256KB	90nm	SL7W3	E0	—	—	478
345J	3.06GHz	533MHz	256KB	90nm	SL7VV	E0	—	yes	LGA775
345J	3.06GHz	533MHz	256KB	90nm	SL7TQ	E0	—	yes	LGA775
345	3.06GHz	533MHz	256KB	90nm	SL7NX	E0	—	—	478
345	3.06GHz	533MHz	256KB	90nm	SL8HP	G1	—	—	478
346	3.06GHz	533MHz	256KB	90nm	SL7TY	E0	yes	yes	LGA775
346	3.06GHz	533MHz	256KB	90nm	SL8HD	G1	yes	yes	LGA775
346	3.06GHz	533MHz	256KB	90nm	SL9BR	G1	yes	—	LGA775
347	3.06GHz	533MHz	512KB	65nm	SL9XU	C1	yes	yes	LGA775
350-	3.20GHz	533MHz	256KB	90nm	SL7NY	E0	—	—	478
350	3.20GHz	533MHz	256KB	90nm	SL8HQ	G1	—	—	478
351	3.20GHz	533MHz	256KB	90nm	SL7TZ	E0	yes	yes	LGA775
351	3.20GHz	533MHz	256KB	90nm	SL8HF	G1	yes	yes	LGA775
351	3.20GHz	533MHz	256KB	90nm	SL9BS	G1	yes	yes	LGA775
352	3.20GHz	533MHz	512KB	65nm	SL96P	C1	yes	yes	LGA775
355	3.33GHz	533MHz	256KB	90nm	SL8HS	G1	yes	yes	LGA775
356	3.33GHz	533MHz	512KB	65nm	SL96N	C1	yes	yes	LGA775
360	3.46GHz	533MHz	512KB	65nm	SL9KK	D0	yes	yes	LGA775
365	3.60GHz	533MHz	512KB	65nm	SL9KJ	D0	yes	yes	LGA775

Celeron 400 processors also use the Intel processor numbering scheme introduced in 2004. Use Table 3.40 to determine the specific features supported by a particular Celeron 400 processor model number.

Table 3.40   Celeron 400 Model Numbers and Features

Processor Number	CPU Speed	Bus Speed	L2 Cache	Mfg. Process	S-Spec	Stepping	64-bit	NX	Socket
420	1.60GHz	800MHz	512KB	65nm	SL9XP	A1	yes	yes	LGA775
430	1.80GHz	800MHz	512KB	65nm	SL9XN	A1	yes	yes	LGA775
440	2.00GHz	800MHz	512KB	65nm	SL9XL	A1	yes	yes	LGA775

Because Intel has offered Celeron and Celeron D processors in many distinctive variations, it's easy to get confused as to which is which, or which is available at a specific speed. By reading the spec number off a particular chip and looking up the number on the Intel developer website (http://developer.intel.com) or by using the reference charts in this book, you can find out the exact specification, including socket type, voltage, stepping, cache size, and other information about the chip.

Pentium III

The Pentium III processor, shown in Figure 3.55, was first released in February 1999 and introduced several new features to the P6 family. It is essentially the same core as a Pentium II with the addition of SSE instructions and integrated on-die L2 cache in the later versions. SSE consists of 70 new instructions that dramatically enhance the performance and possibilities of advanced imaging, 3D, streaming audio, video, and speech-recognition applications.

Figure 3.55   Pentium III processor in SECC2 (Slot 1) and FC-PGA (Socket 370) packages.

Originally based on Intel's advanced 0.25-micron CMOS process technology, the PIII core started out with more than 9.5 million transistors. In late 1999, Intel shifted to a 0.18-micron process die (code-named Coppermine) and added 256KB of on-die L2 cache, which brought the transistor count to 28.1 million. The latest version of the Pentium III (codenamed Tualatin) uses a 0.13-micron process and has 44 million transistors; motherboards made before the Tualatin-core versions of the Pentium III generally do not support this processor because of logical pinout changes. The Pentium III was manu-factured in speeds from 450MHz through 1.4GHz, as well as in server versions with larger or faster cache known as the Pentium Xeon. The Pentium III also incorporates advanced features such as a 32KB L1 cache and either half-core speed 512KB L2 cache or full-core speed on-die 256KB or 512KB L2 with cacheability for up to 4GB of addressable memory space. The PIII also can be used in dual-processing systems with up to 64GB of physical memory. A self-reportable processor serial number gives security, authentication, and system management applications a powerful new tool for identify-ing individual systems. Because of privacy concerns when the processor was released, you can disable this feature in the system BIOS on most systems that use the Pentium III or Celeron III processors.

Pentium III processors were first made available in Intel's SECC2 form factor, which replaced the more expensive older SEC packaging. The SECC2 package covers only one side of the chip and allows for better heatsink attachment and less overall weight. Architectural features of the Pentium III processor include the following:

- **Streaming SIMD extensions (SSE)**—Seventy new instructions for dramatically faster processing and improved imaging, 3D streaming audio and video, web access, speech recognition, new user interfaces, and other graphics and sound-rich applications.

- **Intel processor serial number**—The processor serial number serves as an electronic serial number for the processor and, by extension, its system or user. This feature can be enabled or disabled as desired in the BIOS Setup. The serial number enables the system/user to be identified by company internal networks and applications. The processor serial number can be used in applications that benefit from stronger forms of system and user identification, such as the following:

  - **Applications using security capabilities**—Managed access to new Internet content and services; electronic document exchange.

  - **Manageability applications**—Asset management; remote system load and configuration.

Although the initial release of Pentium III processors was made in the improved SECC2 packaging, Intel later switched to the FC-PGA package, which is even less expensive to produce and enables a more direct attachment of the heatsink to the processor core for better cooling. The FC-PGA version plugs into Socket 370 but can be used in Slot 1 with a slot-ket adapter.

All Pentium III processors have either 512KB or 256KB of L2 cache, which runs at either half-core or full-core speed. Pentium III Xeon versions have 512KB, 1MB, or 2MB of L2 cache that runs at full-core speed. The Pentium III Xeon is a more expensive version of the Pentium III designed for servers and

Table 3.41   Intel Pentium III Processor Variations

Speed (MHz)	Bus Speed (MHz)	Multiplier	Boxed CPU S-spec	OEM CPU S-spec	Stepping	CPUID
450	100	4.5x	SL3CC	SL364	kB0	0672
450	100	4.5x	SL37C	SL35D	kC0	0673
500	100	5x	SL3CD	SL365	kB0	0672
500	100	5x	SL365	SL365	kB0	0672
500	100	5x	SL37D	SL35E	kC0	0673
500E	100	5x	SL3R2	SL3Q9	cA2	0681
500E	100	5x	SL45R	SL444	cB0	0683
533B	133	4x	SL3E9	SL3BN	kC0	0673
533EB	133	4x	SL3SX	SL3N6	cA2	0681
533EB	133	4x	SL3VA	SL3VF	cA2	0681
533EB	133	4x	SL44W	SL3XG	cB0	0683
533EB	133	4x	SL45S	SL3XS	cB0	0683
550	100	5.5x	SL3FJ	SL3F7	kC0	0673
550E	100	5.5x	SL3R3	SL3QA	cA2	0681

workstations. All PIII processor L2 caches can cache up to 4GB of addressable memory space and include ECC capability.

Pentium III processors can be identified by their markings, which are found on the top edge of the processor cartridge. Figure 3.56 shows the format and meaning of the markings.

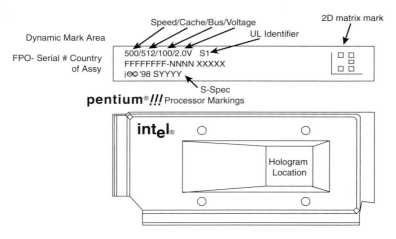

Figure 3.56   Pentium III processor markings.

Table 3.41 shows variations of the Pentium III, indicated by the S-specification number.

L2 Cache	L2 Speed	Max. Temp. (C)	Voltage	Max. Power (W)	Process (Microns)	Transistors	Package
512K	225	90	2.00	25.3	0.25	9.5M	SECC2
512K	225	90	2.00	25.3	0.25	9.5M	SECC2
512K	250	90	2.00	28.0	0.25	9.5M	SECC2
512K	250	90	2.00	28.0	0.25	9.5M	SECC2
512K	250	90	2.00	28.0	0.25	9.5M	SECC2
256K	500	85	1.60	13.2	0.18	28.1M	FC-PGA
256K	500	85	1.60	13.2	0.18	28.1M	FC-PGA
512K	267	90	2.05	29.7	0.25	9.5M	SECC2
256K	533	85	1.65	14.0	0.18	28.1M	SECC2
256K	533	85	1.65	14.0	0.18	28.1M	FC-PGA
256K	533	85	1.65	14.0	0.18	28.1M	SECC2
256K	533	85	1.65	14.0	0.18	28.1M	FC-PGA
512K	275	80	2.00	30.8	0.25	9.5M	SECC2
256K	550	85	1.60	14.5	0.18	28.1M	FC-PGA

Table 3.41   Continued

Speed (MHz)	Bus Speed (MHz)	Multiplier	Boxed CPU S-spec	OEM CPU S-spec	Stepping	CPUID
550E	100	5.5x	SL3V5	SL3N7	cA2	0681
550E	100	5.5x	SL44X	SL3XH	cB0	0683
550E	100	5.5x	SL45T	N/A	cB0	0683
600	100	6x	SL3JT	SL3JM	kC0	0673
600E	100	6x	SL3NA	SL3H6	cA2	0681
600E	100	6x	SL3NL	SL3VH	cA2	0681
600E	100	6x	SL44Y	SL43E	cB0	0683
600E	100	6x	SL45U	SL3XU	cB0	0683
600E	100	6x	n/a	SL4CM	cC0	0686
600E	100	6x	n/a	SL4C7	cC0	0686
600B	133	4.5x	SL3JU	SL3JP	kC0	0673
600EB	133	4.5x	SL3NB	SL3H7	cA2	0681
600EB	133	4.5x	SL3VB	SL3VG	cA2	0681
600EB	133	4.5x	SL44Z	SL3XJ	cB0	0683
600EB	133	4.5x	SL45V	SL3XT	cB0	0683
600EB	133	4.5x	SL4CL	SL4CL	cC0	0686
600EB	133	4.5x	n/a	SL46C	cC0	0686
650	100	6.5x	SL3NR	SL3KV	cA2	0681
650	100	6.5x	SL3NM	SL3VJ	cA20	681
650	100	6.5x	SL452	SL3XK	cB0	0683
650	100	6.5x	SL45W	SL3XV	cB0	0683
650	100	6.5x	n/a	SL4CK	cC0	0686
650	100	6.5x	n/a	SL4C5	cC0	0686
667	133	5x	SL3ND	SL3KW	cA2	0681
667	133	5x	SL3T2	SL3VK	cA2	0681
667	133	5x	SL453	SL3XL	cB0	0683
667	133	5x	SL45X	SL3XW	cB0	0683
667	133	5x	n/a	SL4CJ	cC0	0686
667	133	5x	n/a	SL4C4	cC0	0686
700	100	7x	SL3SY	SL3S9	cA2	0681
700	100	7x	SL3T3	SL3VL	cA2	0681
700	100	7x	SL454	SL453	cB0	0683
700	100	7x	SL45Y	SL3XX	cB0	0683
700	100	7x	SL4M7	SL4CH	cC0	0686
700	100	7x	n/a	SL4C3	cC0	0686
733	133	5.5x	SL3SZ	SL3SB	cA2	0681
733	133	5.5x	SL3T4	SL3VM	cA2	0681
733	133	5.5x	SL455	SL3XN	cB0	0683

L2 Cache	L2 Speed	Max. Temp. (C)	Voltage	Max. Power (W)	Process (Microns)	Transistors	Package
256K	550	85	1.60	14.5	0.18	28.1M	SECC2
256K	550	85	1.60	14.5	0.18	28.1M	SECC2
256K	550	85	1.60	14.5	0.18	28.1M	FC-PGA
512K	300	85	2.00	34.5	0.25	9.5M	SECC2
256K	600	82	1.65	15.8	0.18	28.1M	SECC2
256K	600	82	1.65	15.8	0.18	28.1M	FC-PGA
256K	600	82	1.65	15.8	0.18	28.1M	SECC2
256K	600	82	1.65	15.8	0.18	28.1M	FC-PGA
256K	600	82	1.7	15.8	0.18	28.1M	FC-PGA
256K	600	82	1.7	15.8	0.18	28.1M	SECC2
512K	300	85	2.05	34.5	0.25	9.5M	SECC2
256K	600	82	1.65	15.8	0.18	28.1M	SECC2
256K	600	82	1.65	15.8	0.18	28.1M	FC-PGA
256K	600	82	1.65	15.8	0.18	28.1M	SECC2
256K	600	82	1.65	15.8	0.18	28.1M	FC-PGA
256K	600	82	1.7	15.8	0.18	28.1M	FC-PGA
256K	600	82	1.7	15.8	0.18	28.1M	SECC2
256K	650	82	1.65	17.0	0.18	28.1M	SECC2
256K	650	82	1.65	17.0	0.18	28.1M	FC-PGA
256K	650	82	1.65	17.0	0.18	28.1M	SECC2
256K	650	82	1.65	17.0	0.18	28.1M	FC-PGA
256K	650	82	1.7	17.0	0.18	28.1M	FC-PGA
256K	650	82	1.7	17.0	0.18	28.1M	SECC2
256K	667	82	1.65	17.5	0.18	28.1M	SECC2
256K	667	82	1.65	17.5	0.18	28.1M	FC-PGA
256K	667	82	1.65	17.5	0.18	28.1M	SECC2
256K	667	82	1.65	17.5	0.18	28.1M	FC-PGA
256K	667	82	1.7	17.5	0.18	28.1M	FC-PGA
256K	667	82	1.7	17.5	0.18	28.1M	SECC2
256K	700	80	1.65	18.3	0.18	28.1M	SECC2
256K	700	80	1.65	18.3	0.18	28.1M	FC-PGA
256K	700	80	1.65	18.3	0.18	28.1M	SECC2
256K	700	80	1.65	18.3	0.18	28.1M	FC-PGA
256K	700	80	1.7	18.3	0.18	28.1M	FC-PGA
256K	700	80	1.7	18.3	0.18	28.1M	SECC2
256K	733	80	1.65	19.1	0.18	28.1M	SECC2
256K	733	80	1.65	19.1	0.18	28.1M	FC-PGA
256K	733	80	1.65	19.1	0.18	28.1M	SECC2

Table 3.41   Continued

Speed (MHz)	Bus Speed (MHz)	Multiplier	Boxed CPU S-spec	OEM CPU S-spec	Stepping	CPUID
733	133	5.5x	SL45Z	SL3XY	cB0	0683
733	133	5.5x	SL4M8	SL4CG	cC0	0686
733	133	5.5x	SL4KD	SL4C2	cC0	0686
733	133	5.5x	SL4FQ	SL4CX	cC0	0686
750	100	7.5x	SL3V6	SL3WC	cA2	0681
750	100	7.5x	SL3VC	SL3VN	cA2	0681
750	100	7.5x	SL456	SL3XP	cB0	0683
750	100	7.5x	SL462	SL3XZ	cB0	0683
750	100	7.5x	SL4M9	SL4CF	cC0	0686
750	100	7.5x	SL4KE	SL4BZ	cC0	0686
800	100	8x	SL457	SL3XR	cB0	0683
800	100	8x	SL463	SL3Y3	cB0	0683
800	100	8x	SL4MA	SL4CE	cC0	0686
800	100	8x	SL4KF	SL4BY	cC0	0686
800EB	133	6x	SL458	SL3XQ	cB0	0683
800EB	133	6x	SL464	SL3Y2	cB0	0683
800EB	133	6x	SL4MB	SL4CD	cC0	0686
800EB	133	6x	SL4G7	SL4XQ	cC0	0686
800EB	133	6x	SL4KG	SL4BX	cC0	0686
850	100	8.5x	SL47M	SL43F	cB0	0683
850	100	8.5x	SL49G	SL43H	cB0	0683
850	100	8.5x	SL4MC	SL4CC	cC0	0686
850	100	8.5x	SL4KH	SL4BW	cC0	0686
866	133	6.5x	SL47N	SL43G	cB0	0683
866	133	6.5x	SL49H	SL43J	cB0	0683
866	133	6.5x	SL4MD	SL4CB	cC0	0686
866	133	6.5x	SL4KJ	SL4BV	cC0	0686
866	133	6.5x	SL5B5	SL5QE	cD0	068A
900	100	9x	n/a	SL4SD	cC0	0686
933	133	7x	SL47Q	SL448	cB0	0683
933	133	7x	SL49J	SL44J	cB0	0683
933	133	7x	SL4ME	SL4C9	cC0	0686
933	133	7x	SL4KK	SL4BT	cC0	0686
933	133	7x	n/a	SL5QF	cD0	068A
1000B	133	7.5x	SL4FP	SL48S	cB0	0683
1000B	133	7.5x	SL4C8	SL4C8	cC0	0686
1000B	133	7.5x	SL4MF	n/a	cC0	0686
1000	100	10x	SL4BR	SL4BR	cC0	0686

L2 Cache	L2 Speed	Max. Temp. (C)	Voltage	Max. Power (W)	Process (Microns)	Transistors	Package
256K	733	80	1.65	19.1	0.18	28.1M	FC-PGA
256K	733	80	1.7	19.1	0.18	28.1M	FC-PGA
256K	733	80	1.7	19.1	0.18	28.1M	SECC2
256K	733	80	1.7	19.1	0.18	28.1M	SECC2
256K	750	80	1.65	19.5	0.18	28.1M	SECC2
256K	750	80	1.65	19.5	0.18	28.1M	FC-PGA
256K	750	80	1.65	19.5	0.18	28.1M	SECC2
256K	750	80	1.65	19.5	0.18	28.1M	FC-PGA
256K	750	80	1.7	19.5	0.18	28.1M	FC-PGA
256K	750	80	1.7	19.5	0.18	28.1M	SECC2
256K	800	80	1.65	20.8	0.18	28.1M	SECC2
256K	800	80	1.65	20.8	0.18	28.1M	FC-PGA
256K	800	80	1.7	20.8	0.18	28.1M	FC-PGA
256K	800	80	1.7	20.8	0.18	28.1M	SECC2
256K	800	80	1.65	20.8	0.18	28.1M	SECC2
256K	800	80	1.65	20.8	0.18	28.1M	FC-PGA
256K	800	80	1.7	20.8	0.18	28.1M	FC-PGA
256K	800	80	1.7	20.8	0.18	28.1M	SECC2
256K	800	80	1.7	20.8	0.18	28.1M	SECC2
256K	850	80	1.65	22.5	0.18	28.1M	SECC2
256K	850	80	1.65	22.5	0.18	28.1M	FC-PGA
256K	850	80	1.7	22.5	0.18	28.1M	FC-PGA
256K	850	80	1.7	22.5	0.18	28.1M	SECC2
256K	866	80	1.65	22.9	0.18	28.1M	SECC2
256K	866	80	1.65	22.9	0.18	28.1M	FC-PGA
256K	866	80	1.7	22.5	0.18	28.1M	FC-PGA
256K	866	80	1.7	22.5	0.18	28.1M	SECC2
256K	866	80	1.75	26.1	0.18	28.1M	FC-PGA
256K	900	75	1.7	23.2	0.18	28.1M	FC-PGA
256K	933	75	1.7	25.5	0.18	28.1M	SECC2
256K	933	75	1.7	24.5	0.18	28.1M	FC-PGA
256K	933	75	1.7	24.5	0.18	28.1M	FC-PGA
256K	933	75	1.7	25.5	0.18	28.1M	SECC2
256K	933	77	1.75	27.3	0.18	28.1M	FC-PGA
256K	1000	70	1.7	26.1	0.18	28.1M	SECC2
256K	1000	70	1.7	26.1	0.18	28.1M	FC-PGA
256K	1000	70	1.7	26.1	0.18	28.1M	FC-PGA
256K	1000	70	1.7	26.1	0.18	28.1M	SECC2

Table 3.41   Continued

Speed (MHz)	Bus Speed (MHz)	Multiplier	Boxed CPU S-spec	OEM CPU S-spec	Stepping	CPUID
1000	100	10x	SL4KL	n/a	cC0	0686
1000B	133	7.5x	SL4BS	SL4BS	cC0	0686
1000B	100	10x	n/a	SL5QV	cD0	068A
1000B	133	7.5x	SL5DV	n/a	cD0	068A
1000B	133	7.5x	SL5B3	SL5B3	cD0	068A
1000B	133	7.5x	SL52R	SL52R	cD0	068A
1000B	133	7.5x	SL5FQ	n/a	cD0	068A
1100	100	11x	n/a	SL5QW	cD0	068A
1133	133	8.5x	SL5LT	n/a	tA1	06B1
1133	133	8.5x	SL5GQ	SL5GQ	tA1	06B1
1133-S	133	8.5x	SL5LV	n/a	tA1	06B1
1133-S	133	8.5x	SL5PU	SL5PU	tA1	06B1
1200	133	9x	SL5GN	SL5GN	tA1	06B1
1200	133	9x	SL5PM	n/a	tA1	06B1
1266-S	133	9.5x	SL5LW	SL5QL	tA1	06B1
1333	133	10x	n/a	SL5VX	tA1	06B1
1400-S	133	10.5x	SL657	SL5XL	tA1	06B1

CPUID = The internal ID returned by the CPUID instruction

ECC = Error correcting code

FC-PGA = Flip-chip pin grid array

FC-PGA2 = Flip-chip pin grid array revision 2

SECC = Single edge contact cartridge

SECC2 = Single edge contact cartridge revision 2

Pentium III processors are all clock multiplier locked. This is a means to prevent processor fraud and overclocking by making the processor work only at a given clock multiplier. Unfortunately, this feature can be bypassed by making modifications to the processor under the cartridge cover, and unscrupulous individuals have been selling lower-speed processors re-marked as higher speeds. It pays to purchase your systems or processors from direct Intel distributors or high-end dealers who do not engage in these practices.

Pentium II/III Xeon

The Pentium II and III processors were the basis for special high-end versions called Pentium II Xeon (introduced in June 1998) and Pentium III Xeon (introduced in March 1999). Intel now uses the term *Xeon* by itself to refer to Xeon processors based on the Pentium 4. These differ from the standard Pentium II and III in three ways: packaging, cache size, and cache speed.

Pentium II/III Xeon processors use a larger SEC cartridge than the standard PII/III processors, mainly to house a larger internal board with more cache memory.

L2 Cache	L2 Speed	Max. Temp. (C)	Voltage	Max. Power (W)	Process (Microns)	Transistors	Package
256K	1000	70	1.7	26.1	0.18	28.1M	SECC2
256K	1000	70	1.7	26.1	0.18	28.1M	SECC2
256K	1000	75	1.75	29.0	0.18	28.1M	FC-PGA
256K	1000	75	1.75	29.0	0.18	28.1M	FC-PGA
256K	1000	75	1.75	29.0	0.18	28.1M	FC-PGA
256K	1000	75	1.75	29.0	0.18	28.1M	FC-PGA
256K	1000	75	1.75	29.0	0.18	28.1M	FC-PGA
256K	1100	77	1.75	33.0	0.18	28.1M	FC-PGA
256K	1133	69	1.475	29.1	0.13	44M	FC-PGA2
256K	1133	69	1.475	29.1	0.13	44M	FC-PGA2
512K	1133	69	1.45	27.9	0.13	44M	FC-PGA2
512K	1133	69	1.45	27.9	0.13	44M	FC-PGA2
256K	1200	69	1.475	29.9	0.13	44M	FC-PGA2
256K	1200	69	1.475	29.9	0.13	44M	FC-PGA2
512K	1266	69	1.45	29.5	0.13	44M	FC-PGA2
256K	1333	69	1.475	29.9	0.13	44M	FC-PGA2
512K	1400	69	1.45	29.9	0.13	44M	FC-PGA2

Besides the larger package, the Xeon processors also include more L2 cache. They were produced in three variations, with 512KB, 1MB, or 2MB of L2 cache.

Even more significant than the size of the cache is its speed. All the cache in the Xeon processors run at the full-core speed. This is difficult to do considering that the cache chips were separate chips on the board in most versions. The original Pentium II Xeon processors had 7.5 million transistors in the main processor die, whereas the later Pentium III Xeon came with 9.5 million. When the Pentium III versions with on-die cache were released, the transistor count went up to 28.1 million transistors in the 256KB cache version, 84 million transistors in the 1MB cache version, and 140 million transistors in the 2MB cache version, which set an industry record at the time. The high transistor counts are due to the on-die L2 cache, which is very transistor intensive. The L2 cache in all Pentium II and III Xeon processors has a full 64GB RAM address range and supports ECC.

Table 3.42 provides an overview of the Pentium II and Pentium III Xeon processors.

Table 3.42   Intel Pentium II Xeon/Pentium III Xeon Processor Features

CPU	Processor Speed	FSB Speed	L2 Cache Sizes	Package
PII Xeon	400MHz	100MHz	512KB; 1024KB; 2048KB	SC330
	450MHz	100MHz	512KB; 1024KB; 2048KB	SC330
PIII Xeon	500MHz	100MHz	512KB; 1024KB; 2048KB	SC330
	550MHz	100MHz	512KB; 1024KB; 2048KB	SC330
	600MHz	133MHz	256KB	SC330.1
	667MHz	133MHz	256KB	SC330.1
	700MHz	100MHz	1024KB; 2048KB	SC330.1
	733MHz	133MHz	256KB	SC330.1 or 495-pin SECC
	800MHz	133MHz	256KB	SC330.1 or 495-pin SECC
	866MHz	133MHz	256KB	SC330.1 or 495-pin SECC
	900MHz	100MHz	2048KB	SC330.1
	933MHz	133MHz	256KB	SC330.1 or 495-pin SECC
	1,000MHz	133MHz	256KB	495-pin SECC
Xeon	700MHz*	100MHz	1024KB	SC330.1

Although this processor is listed as a Xeon by Intel, it's obvious from its specifications that it is really a Pentium III Xeon.

PII Xeon = Pentium II Xeon

PIII Xeon = Pentium III Xeon

For more details about Pentium II Xeon and Pentium III Xeon processors, see my book *Upgrading and Repairing Servers*.

Other Sixth-generation Processors

Besides Intel, many other manufacturers have produced P6-type processors, but often with a difference. Most of them were designed to interface with P5 class motherboards for the lower-end markets. AMD later offered up the Athlon and Duron processors, which were true sixth-generation designs using their own proprietary connections to the system.

This section examines the various sixth-generation processors from manufacturers other than Intel.

NexGen Nx586

NexGen was founded by Thampy Thomas, who hired some of the people formerly involved with the 486 and Pentium processors at Intel. At NexGen, developers created the Nx586, a processor that was functionally the same as the Pentium but not pin compatible. As such, it was always supplied with a motherboard; in fact, it was usually soldered in. NexGen did not manufacture the chips or the motherboards they came in; for that it hired IBM Microelectronics. Later NexGen was bought by AMD, right before it was ready to introduce the Nx686—a greatly improved design by Greg Favor and a true competitor for the Pentium. AMD took the Nx686 design and combined it with a Pentium electrical interface to create a drop-in Pentium-compatible chip called the K6, which actually outperformed the original from Intel.

The Nx586 had all the standard fifth-generation processor features, such as superscalar execution with two internal pipelines and a high-performance integral L1 cache with separate code and data caches. One advantage is that the Nx586 includes separate 16KB instruction and 16KB data caches, compared to 8KB each for the Pentium. These caches keep key instruction and data close to the processing engines to increase overall system performance.

The Nx586 also includes branch prediction capabilities, which are one of the hallmarks of a sixth-generation processor. *Branch prediction* means the processor has internal functions to predict program flow to optimize the instruction execution.

The Nx586 processor also featured a RISC core. A translation unit dynamically translates x86 instructions into RISC86 instructions. These RISC86 instructions were designed specifically with direct support for the x86 architecture while obeying RISC performance principles. They are thus simpler and easier to execute than the complex x86 instructions. This type of capability is another feature normally found only in P6 class processors.

The Nx586 was discontinued after the merger with AMD, which then took the design for the successor Nx686 and released it as the AMD-K6.

AMD-K6 Series

The AMD-K6 processor is a high-performance sixth-generation processor that is physically installable in a P5 (Pentium) motherboard. It essentially was designed for AMD by NexGen and was first known as the Nx686. The NexGen version never appeared because it was purchased by AMD before the chip was due to be released. The AMD-K6 delivers performance levels somewhere between the Pentium and Pentium II processor as a result of its unique hybrid design.

The K6 processor contains an industry-standard, high-performance implementation of the new multimedia instruction set, enabling a high level of multimedia performance for the time period. The K6-2 introduced an upgrade to MMX that AMD calls 3DNow!, which adds even more graphics and sound instructions. AMD designed the K6 processor to fit the low-cost, high-volume Socket 7 infrastructure. Initially, it used AMD's 0.35-micron, five-metal layer process technology; later the 0.25-micron process was used to increase production quantities because of reduced die size, as well as to decrease power consumption.

AMD-K6 processor technical features include

- Sixth-generation internal design, fifth-generation external interface
- Internal RISC core, translates x86 to RISC instructions
- Superscalar parallel execution units (seven)
- Dynamic execution
- Branch prediction
- Speculative execution
- Large 64KB L1 cache (32KB instruction cache plus 32KB write-back dual-ported data cache)
- Built-in floating-point unit
- Industry-standard MMX instruction support
- System Management Mode
- Ceramic pin grid array (CPGA) Socket 7 design
- Manufactured using 0.35-micron and 0.25-micron, five-layer designs

The K6-2 adds the following:

- Higher clock speeds
- Higher bus speeds of up to 100MHz (Super7 motherboards)
- 3DNow!; 21 new graphics and sound processing instructions

The K6-3 adds the following:

- 256KB of on-die full-core speed L2 cache

The addition of the full-speed L2 cache in the K6-3 was significant. It enabled the K6 series to fully compete with the Intel Pentium II processors and the Celeron processors based on the Pentium II. The 3DNow! capability added in the K6-2/3 was also exploited by newer graphics programs.

The AMD-K6 processor architecture is fully x86 binary code compatible, which means it runs all Intel software, including MMX instructions. To make up for the lower L2 cache performance of the Socket 7 design, AMD beefed up the internal L1 cache to 64KB total, twice the size of the Pentium II or III. This, plus the dynamic execution capability, enabled the K6 to outperform the Pentium and come close to the Pentium II and III in performance for a given clock rate. The K6-3 was even better with the addition of full-core speed L2 cache; however, this processor ran very hot and was discontinued after a relatively brief period.

Both the AMD-K5 and AMD-K6 processors are Socket 7 bus compatible. However, certain modifications might be necessary for proper voltage setting and BIOS revisions. To ensure reliable operation of the AMD-K6 processor, the motherboard must meet specific voltage requirements.

The AMD processors have specific voltage requirements. Most older split-voltage motherboards default to 2.8V Core/3.3V I/O, which is below specification for the AMD-K6 and could cause erratic operation. To work properly, the motherboard must have Socket 7 with a dual-plane voltage regulator supplying 2.9V or 3.2V (233MHz) to the CPU core voltage (Vcc2) and 3.3V for the I/O (Vcc3). The voltage regulator must be capable of supplying up to 7.5A (9.5A for the 233MHz) to the processor. When used with a 200MHz or slower processor, the voltage regulator must maintain the core voltage within 145mV of nominal (2.9V+/-145mV). When used with a 233MHz processor, the voltage regulator must maintain the core voltage within 100mV of nominal (3.2V+/-100mV).

If the motherboard has a poorly designed voltage regulator that cannot maintain this performance, unreliable operation can result. If the CPU voltage exceeds the absolute maximum voltage range, the processor can be permanently damaged. Also note that the K6 can run hot. Make sure your heatsink is securely fitted to the processor and that the thermally conductive grease or pad is properly applied.

The motherboard must have an AMD-K6 processor-ready BIOS with support for the K6 built in. Award has that support in its March 1, 1997 or later BIOS; AMI had K6 support in any of its BIOSs with CPU Module 3.31 or later; and Phoenix supports the K6 in version 4.0, release 6.0, or release 5.1 with build dates of 4/7/97 or later.

Because these specifications can be fairly complicated, AMD keeps a list of motherboards that have been verified to work with the AMD-K6 processor on its website.

The multiplier, bus speed, and voltage settings for the K6 are shown in Table 3.43. You can identify which AMD-K6 you have by looking at the markings on this chip, as shown in Figure 3.57.

Table 3.43   AMD-K6 Processor Speeds and Voltages

Processor	Core Speed	Clock Multiplier	Bus Speed	Core Voltage	I/O Voltage
K6-3	450MHz	4.5x	100MHz	2.4V	3.3V
K6-3	400MHz	4x	100MHz	2.4V	3.3V
K6-2	475MHz	5x	95MHz	2.4V	3.3V
K6-2	450MHz	4.5x	100MHz	2.4V	3.3V
K6-2	400MHz	4x	100MHz	2.2V	3.3V
K6-2	380MHz	4x	95MHz	2.2V	3.3V
K6-2	366MHz	5.5x	66MHz	2.2V	3.3V
K6-2	350MHz	3.5x	100MHz	2.2V	3.3V
K6-2	333MHz	3.5x	95MHz	2.2V	3.3V
K6-2	333MHz	5.0x	66MHz	2.2V	3.3V
K6-2	300MHz	3x	100MHz	2.2V	3.3V
K6-2	300MHz	4.5x	66MHz	2.2V	3.3V
K6-2	266MHz	4x	66MHz	2.2V	3.3V
K6	300MHz	4.5x	66MHz	2.2V	3.45V
K6	266MHz	4x	66MHz	2.2V	3.3V
K6	233MHz	3.5x	66MHz	3.2V	3.3V
K6	200MHz	3x	66MHz	2.9V	3.3V
K6	166MHz	2.5x	66MHz	2.9V	3.3V

Figure 3.57   AMD Athlon processor for Slot A (cartridge form factor).

Older motherboards achieve the 3.5x setting by setting jumpers for 1.5x. The 1.5x setting for older motherboards equates to a 3.5x setting for the AMD-K6 and newer Intel parts. Getting the 4x and higher setting requires a motherboard that controls three BF pins, including BF2. Older motherboards can control only two BF pins. The settings for the multipliers are shown in Table 3.44.

Table 3.44   AMD-K6 Multiplier Settings

Multiplier Setting	BF0	BF1	BF2	Multiplier Setting	BF0	BF1	BF2
2.5x	Low	Low	High	4.5x	Low	Low	Low
3x	High	Low	High	5x	High	Low	Low
3.5x	High	High	High	5.5x	High	High	Low
4x	Low	High	Low				

These settings usually are controlled by jumpers on the motherboard. Consult your motherboard documentation to see where they are and how to set them for the proper multiplier and bus speed settings.

Unlike Cyrix and some of the other Intel competitors, AMD is a manufacturer and a designer. Therefore, it designs and builds its chips in its own fabs. Similar to Intel, AMD has migrated to 0.25-micron process technology and beyond (the AMD Athlon XP is built on a 0.13-micron process). The original K6 has 8.8 million transistors and is built on a 0.35-micron, five-layer process. The die is 12.7mm on each side, or about 162 square mm. The K6-3 uses a 0.25-micron process and incorporates 21.3 million transistors on a die only 10.9mm on each side, or about 118 square mm.

Because of its performance and compatibility with the Socket 7 interface, the K6 series is often looked at as an excellent processor upgrade for motherboards using older Pentium or Pentium MMX processors. Although they do work in Socket 7, the AMD-K6 processors have different voltage and bus speed requirements from the Intel processors. Before attempting any upgrades, you should check the board documentation or contact the manufacturer to see whether your board meets the necessary requirements. In some cases, a BIOS upgrade also is necessary.

AMD Athlon, Duron, and Athlon XP

The Athlon is AMD's successor to the K6 series (see Figure 3.57). The Athlon was designed as a new chip from the ground up and does not interface via the Socket 7 or Super7 sockets like its previous chips. In the initial Athlon versions, AMD used a cartridge design, called Slot A, almost exactly like that of the Intel Pentium II and III. This was due to the fact that the original Athlons used 512KB of external L2 cache, which was mounted on the processor cartridge board. The external cache ran at one-half core, two-fifths core, or one-third core, depending on which speed processor you had. In June 2000, AMD introduced a revised version of the Athlon (codenamed Thunderbird) that incorporates 256KB of L2 cache directly on the processor die. This on-die cache runs at full-core speed and eliminates a bottleneck in the original Athlon systems. Along with the change to on-die L2 cache, the Athlon was also introduced in a version for AMD's own Socket A (Socket 462), which replaced the Slot A cartridge version. The Athlon XP added several enhancements such as 3DNow! Professional instructions, which also include the Intel SSE instructions. The latest Athlon XP models have 512KB L2 cache, but this time at full processor speed.

Although the Slot A cartridge looks a lot like the Intel Slot 1, and the Socket A looks like Intel's Socket 370, the pinouts are completely different and the AMD chips do not work in the same motherboards as the Intel chips. This was by design because AMD was looking for ways to improve its chip architecture and distance itself from Intel. Special blocked pins in either socket or slot design prevent accidentally installing the chip in the wrong orientation or wrong slot. Figure 3.58 shows the Athlon in the Slot A cartridge. Socket A versions of the Athlon closely resemble the Duron.

Figure 3.58   AMD Athlon XP 0.13-micron processor for Socket A (PGA form factor).

The Athlon was manufactured in speeds from 500MHz up to 1.4GHz and uses a 200MHz or 266MHz processor (front-side) bus called the EV6 to connect to the motherboard North Bridge chip as well as other processors. Licensed from Digital Equipment, the EV6 bus is the same as that used for the Alpha 21264 processor, later owned by Compaq. The EV6 bus uses a clock speed of 100MHz or 133MHz but double-clocks the data, transferring data twice per cycle, for a cycling speed of 200MHz or 266MHz. Because the bus is 8 bytes (64 bits) wide, this results in a throughput of 8 bytes times 200MHz/266MHz, which amounts to 1.6GBps or 2.1GBps. This bus is ideal for supporting PC1600 or PC2100 DDR memory, which also runs at those speeds. The AMD bus design eliminates a potential bottleneck between the chipset and processor and enables more efficient transfers compared to other processors. The use of the EV6 bus is one of the primary reasons the Athlon and Duron chips perform so well.

The Athlon has a very large 128KB of L1 cache on the processor die and one-half, two-fifths, or one-third core speed 512KB L2 cache in the cartridge in the older versions; 256KB of full-core speed cache in Socket A Athlon and most Athlon XP models; and 512KB of full-core speed cache in the latest Athlon XP models. All PGA socket A versions have the full-speed cache. The Athlon also has support for MMX and the Enhanced 3DNow! instructions, which are 45 new instructions designed to support graphics and sound processing. 3DNow! is very similar to Intel's SSE in design and intent, but the specific instructions are different and require software support. The Athlon XP adds the Intel SSE instructions, which it calls 3DNow! Professional. Fortunately, most companies producing graphics software have decided to support the 3DNow! instructions along with the Intel SSE instructions, with only a few exceptions.

The initial production of the Athlon used 0.25-micron technology, with newer and faster versions being made on 0.18-micron and 0.13-micron processes. The latest versions are even built using copper metal technology, a first in the PC processor business.

Table 3.45 shows detailed information on the Slot A version of the Athlon processor.

Table 3.45   AMD Athlon Slot A Cartridge Processor Information

Part Number	Model	Speed (MHz)	Bus Speed (MHz)	Multiplier	L2Cache
AMD-K7500MTR51B	Model 1	500	100x2	5x	512KB
AMD-K7550MTR51B	Model 1	550	100x2	5.5x	512KB
AMD-K7600MTR51B	Model 1	600	100x2	6x	512KB
AMD-K7650MTR51B	Model 1	650	100x2	6.5x	512KB
AMD-K7700MTR51B	Model 1	700	100x2	7x	512KB
AMD-K7550MTR51B	Model 2	550	100x2	5.5x	512KB
AMD-K7600MTR51B	Model 2	600	100x2	6x	512KB
AMD-K7650MTR51B	Model 2	650	100x2	6.5x	512KB
AMD-K7700MTR51B	Model 2	700	100x2	7x	512KB
AMD-K7750MTR52B	Model 2	750	100x2	7.5x	512KB
AMD-K7800MPR52B	Model 2	800	100x2	8x	512KB
AMD-K7850MPR52B	Model 2	850	100x2	8.5x	512KB
AMD-K7900MNR53B	Model 2	900	100x2	9x	512KB
AMD-K7950MNR53B	Model 2	950	100x2	9.5x	512KB
AMD-K7100MNR53B	Model 2	1000	100x2	10x	512KB
AMD-A0650MPR24B	Model 4	650	100x2	6.5x	256KB
AMD-A0700MPR24B	Model 4	700	100x2	7x	256KB
AMD-A0750MPR24B	Model 4	750	100x2	7.5x	256KB
AMD-A0800MPR24B	Model 4	800	100x2	8x	256KB
AMD-A0850MPR24B	Model 4	850	100x2	8.5x	256KB
AMD-A0900MMR24B	Model 4	900	100x2	9x	256KB
AMD-A0950MMR24B	Model 4	950	100x2	9.5x	256KB
AMD-A1000MMR24B	Model 4	1000	100x2	10x	256KB

In most benchmarks the AMD Athlon compares as equal, if not superior, to the Intel Pentium III. AMD beat Intel to the 1GHz mark by introducing its 1GHz Athlon two days before Intel introduced the 1GHz Pentium III.

Table 3.46 shows information on the PGA or Socket A version of the AMD Athlon processor. All Socket A processors are Athlon Model 4.

Note

In Tables 3.46–49, the CPU frequency and CPU frequency multiplier are listed for each processor. These values are used in the system BIOS to configure your AMD processor if the BIOS is unable to manually configure the processor. The multiplier value listed in earlier editions of this book and in other sources is based on multiplying the bus speed to obtain the processor clock speed. However, the processor setup in the BIOS needs the actual values now shown in these tables.

L2 Speed (MHz)	Voltage	Max. Power (W)	Process (Microns)	Transistors	Introduced
250	1.60V	42W	0.25	22M	Jun. 1999
275	1.60V	46W	0.25	22M	Jun. 1999
300	1.60V	50W	0.25	22M	Jun. 1999
325	1.60V	54W	0.25	22M	Aug. 1999
350	1.60V	50W	0.25	22M	Oct. 1999
275	1.60V	31W	0.18	22M	Nov. 1999
300	1.60V	34W	0.18	22M	Nov. 1999
325	1.60V	36W	0.18	22M	Nov. 1999
350	1.60V	39W	0.18	22M	Nov. 1999
300	1.60V	40W	0.18	22M	Nov. 1999
320	1.70V	48W	0.18	22M	Jan. 2000
340	1.70V	50W	0.18	22M	Feb. 2000
300	1.80V	60W	0.18	22M	Mar. 2000
317	1.80V	62W	0.18	22M	Mar. 2000
333	1.80V	65W	0.18	22M	Mar. 2000
650	1.70V	36.1W	0.18	37M	Jun. 2000
700	1.70V	38.3W	0.18	37M	Jun. 2000
750	1.70V	40.4W	0.18	37M	Jun. 2000
800	1.70V	42.6W	0.18	37M	Jun. 2000
850	1.70V	44.8W	0.18	37M	Jun. 2000
900	1.75V	49.7W	0.18	37M	Jun. 2000
950	1.75V	52.0W	0.18	37M	Jun. 2000
1000	1.75V	54.3W	0.18	37M	Jun. 2000

Table 3.46   AMD Athlon PGA (Socket A) Processor Information

Speed (MHz)[1]	CPU Frequency Multiplier	Bus Speed (MHz)[2]	CPU Frequency (MHz)	L2 Cache	L2 Speed (MHz)	Voltage	Max. Power (W)	Process (Microns)	Transistors
650	6.5x	200	100	256KB	650	1.75V	38.5W	0.18	37M
700	7x	200	100	256KB	700	1.75V	40.3W	0.18	37M
750	6.5x	200	100	256KB	750	1.75V	43.8W	0.18	37M
800	8x	200	100	256KB	800	1.75V	45.5W	0.18	37M
850	8.5x	200	100	256KB	850	1.75V	47.3W	0.18	37M
900	9x	200	100	256KB	900	1.75V	50.8W	0.18	37M
950	9.5x	200	100	256KB	950	1.75V	52.5W	0.18	37M
1000	10x	200	100	256KB	1000	1.75V	54.3W	0.18	37M
1000	7.5x	266	133	256KB	1000	1.75V	54.3W	0.18	37M

Table 3.46   Continued

Speed (MHz)[1]	CPU Frequency Multiplier	Bus Speed (MHz)[2]	CPU Frequency (MHz)	L2 Cache	L2 Speed (MHz)	Voltage	Max. Power (W)	Process (Microns)	Transistors
1100	11x	200	100	256KB	1100	1.75V	59.5W	0.18	37M
1133	8.5xx	266	133	256KB	1133	1.75V	63.0W	0.18	37M
1200	12x	200	100	256KB	1200	1.75V	66.5W	0.18	37M
1200	9x	266	133	256KB	1200	1.75V	66.5W	0.18	37M
1300	13x	200	100	256KB	1300	1.75V	68.3W	0.18	37M
1333	10x	266	133	256KB	1333	1.75V	70.0W	0.18	37M
1400	11x	266	133	256KB	1400	1.75V	72.0W	0.18	37M

1. Multiply the CPU frequency by the CPU frequency multiplier to obtain processor clock speed.

2. The CPU frequency is multiplied by 2 to obtain the bus speed. For best performance, use memory with a clock speed as fast as or faster than the bus speed.

Note

To configure an Athlon processor in the system BIOS, select the appropriate CPU frequency and CPU frequency multiplier from Table 3.44. The bus speed shown in Table 3.46 is twice that of the CPU frequency.

AMD Duron

The AMD Duron processor (originally code named Spitfire) was announced in June 2000 and is a derivative of the AMD Athlon processor in the same fashion as the Celeron is a derivative of the Pentium II and III. Basically, the Duron is an Athlon with less L2 cache; all other capabilities are essentially the same. It is designed to be a lower-cost version with less cache but only slightly less performance. In keeping with the low-cost theme, Duron contains 64KB on-die L2 cache and is designed for Socket A, a socket version of the Athlon Slot A (see Figure 3.59). Except for the Duron markings, the Duron is almost identical externally to the Socket A versions of the original Athlon.

Figure 3.59   AMD Duron processor.

Essentially, the Duron was designed to compete against the Intel Celeron in the low-cost PC market, just as the Athlon was designed to compete in the higher-end Pentium III market. The Duron has since been discontinued, but most systems that use the Duron processor can use AMD Athlon or, in some cases Athlon XP or AMD Sempron processors using Socket A, as an upgrade.

Because the Duron processor is derived from the Athlon core, it includes the Athlon 200MHz front-side system bus (interface to the chipset) as well as enhanced 3DNow! instructions in Model 3. Model 7 processors include 3DNow! Professional instructions (which include a full implementation of SSE instructions).

Table 3.47 shows information on the PGA or Socket A version of the AMD Duron processor. Durons that require 1.6V are Model 3 processors, whereas those that require 1.75V are Model 7 processors. The Model 7 version was originally code named Morgan.

Table 3.47   AMD Duron Processor Information

Speed (MHz)[1]	CPU Frequency Multiplier	Bus Speed (MHz)[2]	CPU Frequency (MHz)	L2 Cache	Voltage	Max. Power (W)	Process (Microns)	Transistors
550	5.5x	200	100	64KB	1.6V	25.3W	0.18	25M
600	6x	200	100	64KB	1.6V	27.4W	0.18	25M
650	6.5x	200	100	64KB	1.6V	29.4W	0.18	25M
700	7x	200	100	64KB	1.6V	31.4W	0.18	25M
750	7.5x	200	100	64KB	1.6V	33.4W	0.18	25M
800	8x	200	100	64KB	1.6V	35.4W	0.18	25M
850	8.5x	200	100	64KB	1.6V	37.4W	0.18	25M
900	9x	200	100	64KB	1.6V	39.5W	0.18	25M
900	9x	200	100	64KB	1.75V	42.7W	0.18	25.2M
950	9.5x	200	100	64KB	1.6V	41.5W	0.18	25M
950	9.5x	200	100	64KB	1.75V	44.4W	0.18	25.2M
1000	10x	200	100	64KB	1.75V	46.1W	0.18	25.2M
1100	11x	200	100	64KB	1.75V	50.3W	0.18	25.2M
1200	12x	200	100	64KB	1.75V	54.7W	0.18	25.2M
1300	13x	200	100	64KB	1.75V	60.0W	0.18	25.2M
1400	11x	266	133	64KB	1.5V	45.5W	0.13	37.2M
1600	12x	266	133	64KB	1.5V	48.0W	0.13	37.2M
1800	13.5x	266	133	64KB	1.5V	53.0W	0.13	37.2M

1. *Multiply the CPU frequency by the CPU frequency multiplier to obtain the processor clock speed.*

2. *The CPU frequency is multiplied by 2 to obtain the bus speed. For best performance, use memory with a clock speed as fast as or faster than the bus speed.*

Note

To configure a Duron processor in the system BIOS, select the appropriate CPU frequency and CPU frequency multiplier from Table 3.45. The bus speed shown in Table 3.47 is twice that of the CPU frequency.

AMD Athlon XP

As mentioned earlier, the most recent version of the Athlon is called the Athlon XP. This is basically an improved version of the previous Athlon, with improvements in the instruction set so it can execute Intel SSE instructions and a new marketing scheme that directly competes with the Pentium 4. Athlon XP also adopted a larger (512KB) full-speed on-die cache.

AMD uses the term *QuantiSpeed* (a marketing term, not a technical term) to refer to the architecture of the Athlon XP. AMD defines this as including the following:

- **A nine-issue superscalar, fully pipelined microarchitecture**—This provides more pathways for instructions to be sent into the execution sections of the CPU and includes three floating-point execution units, three integer units, and three address calculation units.

- **A superscalar, fully pipelined floating-point calculation unit**—This provides faster operations per clock cycle and cures a long-time deficiency of AMD processors versus Intel processors.

- **A hardware data prefetch**—This gathers the data needed from system memory and places it in the processor's Level 1 cache to save time.

- **Improved translation look-aside buffers (TLBs)**—These enable the storage of data where the processor can access it more quickly without duplication or stalling for lack of fresh information.

These design improvements wring more work out of each clock cycle, enabling a "slower" Athlon XP to beat a "faster" Pentium 4 processor in doing actual work (and play).

The first models of the Athlon XP used the Palomino core, which is also shared by the Athlon 4 mobile (laptop) processor. Later models have used the Thoroughbred core, which was later revised to improve thermal characteristics. The different Thoroughbred cores are sometimes referred to as Thoroughbred-A and Thoroughbred-B. Athlon XP processors use a core with 512KB on-die full-speed L2 cache known as Barton. Additional features include the following:

- 3DNow! Professional multimedia instructions (adding compatibility with the 70 additional SSE instructions in the Pentium III but not the 144 additional SSE2 instructions in the Pentium 4)

Table 3.48 AMD Athlon XP Processor Information

P-Rating	Actual Speed (MHz)[1]	CPU Frequency Multiplier	CPU Frequency (MHz)	Bus Speed (MHz)[2]
1500+[3]	1333	10x	133	266
1600+[3]	1400	10.5x	133	266
1700+[3]	1467	11x	133	266
1800+[3]	1533	11.5x	133	266
1900+[3]	1600	12x	133	266
2000+[3]	1667	12.5x	133	266
2100+[3]	1733	13x	133	266
1700+[4]	1467	11x	133	266
1700+[5]	1467	11x	133	266
1800+[4]	1533	11.5x	133	266
1800+[5]	1533	11.5x	133	266
1900+[4]	1600	12x	133	266

- 266MHz or 333MHz FSB
- 128KB Level 1 and 256KB or 512KB on-die Level 2 memory caches running at full CPU speed
- Copper interconnects (instead of aluminum) for more electrical efficiency and less heat

Also new to the Athlon XP is the use of a thinner, lighter organic chip packaging compound similar to that used by recent Intel processors. Figure 3.60 shows the latest Athlon XP processors that use the Barton core.

This packaging allows for a more efficient layout of electrical components. The latest versions of the Athlon XP are made using a new 0.13-micron die process that results in a chip with a smaller die that uses less power, generates less heat, and is capable of running faster as compared to the previous models. The newest 0.13-micron versions of the Athlon XP run at actual clock speeds exceeding 2GHz. Table 3.48 provides detailed information about the Athlon XP.

Figure 3.60   AMD Athlon XP 0.13-micron processor with 512KB of L2 cache for Socket A (PGA form factor). *Photo courtesy of Advanced Micro Devices, Inc.*

Multiplier	L2 Cache	Voltage	Max. Power (W)	Process (Microns)	Transistors
5x	256KB	1.75V	60.0W	0.18	37.5
5.25x	256KB	1.75V	62.8W	0.18	37.5
5.5x	256KB	1.75V	64.0W	0.18	37.5
5.75x	256KB	1.75V	66.0W	0.18	37.5
6x	256KB	1.75V	68.0W	0.18	37.5
6.25x	256KB	1.75V	70.0W	0.18	37.5
6.5x	256KB	1.75V	72.0W	0.18	37.5
5.5x	256KB	1.5V	49.4W	0.13	37.2
5.5x	256KB	1.6V	59.8W	0.13	37.2
5.75x	256KB	1.5V	51.0W	0.13	37.2
5.75x	256KB	1.6V	59.8W	0.13	37.2
6x	256KB	1.5V	52.5W	0.13	37.2

Table 3.48   Continued

P-Rating	Actual Speed (MHz)[1]	CPU Frequency Multiplier	CPU Frequency (MHz)	Bus Speed (MHz)[2]
2000+[4]	1667	12.5x	133	266
2000+[5]	1667	12.5x	133	266
2100+[4]	1733	13x	133	266
2100+[5]	1733	13x	133	266
2200+[4]	1800	13.5x	133	266
2200+[5]	1800	13.5x	133	266
2400+[5]	2000	15x	133	266
2500+[5]	1833	11x	166	333
2600+[5]	2133	16x	133	266
2600+[6]	2083	12.5x	166	333
2700+[6]	2167	13x	166	333
2800+[7]	2083	12.5x	166	333
3000+[7]	2167	13x	166	333
3000+[7]	2100	10.5x	200	400
3200+[7]	2200	11x	200	400

1. *Multiply the CPU frequency by the CPU frequency multiplier to obtain the processor clock speed.*
2. *The CPU frequency is multiplied by 2 to obtain the bus speed. For best performance, use memory with a clock speed as fast as or faster than the bus speed.*
3. *Model 6 Athlon XP (Palomino).*

Note

To configure an Athlon XP processor in the system BIOS, select the appropriate CPU frequency and CPU frequency multiplier from Table 3.46. The bus speed shown in Table 3.48 is twice that of the CPU frequency.

The Athlon XP has been replaced by Socket A versions of the Sempron.

Athlon MP

The Athlon MP is AMD's first processor designed for multiprocessor support. Thus, it can be used in servers and workstations that demand multiprocessor support. The Athlon MP comes in the following three versions, which are similar to various Athlon and Athlon XP models:

- **Model 6 (1GHz, 1.2GHz)**—This model is similar to the Athlon Model 4.
- **Model 6 OPGA (1500+ through 2100+)**—This model is similar to the Athlon XP Model 6.
- **Model 8 (2000+, 2200+, 2400+, 2600+)**—This model is similar to the Athlon XP Model 8.
- **Model 10 (2500+, 2800+, 3000+)**—This model is similar to the Athlon XP Model 8, but with 512KB of L2 cache.

Multiplier	L2 Cache	Voltage	Max. Power (W)	Process (Microns)	Transistors
6.25x	256KB	1.6V	60.3W	0.13	37.2
6.25x	256KB	1.6V	61.3W	0.13	37.2
6.5x	256KB	1.6V	62.1W	0.13	37.2
6.5x	256KB	1.6V	62.1W	0.13	37.2
6.75x	256KB	1.65V	67.9W	0.13	37.2
6.75x	256KB	1.6V	62.8W	0.13	37.2
7.5x	256KB	1.65V	68.3W	0.13	37.2
5.5x	512KB	1.65V	68.3W	0.13	54.3
8x	256KB	1.65V	68.3W	0.13	37.2
6.25x	256KB	1.65V	68.3W	0.13	37.2
6.5x	2167	1.65V	68.3W	0.13	37.2
6.25x	2083	1.65V	68.3W	0.13	54.3
6.5x	2167	1.65V	74.3W	0.13	54.3
5.25x	512KB	1.65V	68.3W	0.13	54.3
5.5x	512KB	1.65V	76.8W	0.13	54.3

4. *Model 8 Athlon XP CPUID 680 (Thoroughbred).*
5. *Model 8 Athlon XP CPUID 681 (Thoroughbred).*
6. *Model 8 Athlon XP with 333MHz FSB (Thoroughbred).*
7. *Model 10 Athlon XP (Barton).*

All Athlon MP processors use the same Socket A interface used by later models of the Athlon and all Duron and Athlon XP processors.

The Athlon MP has been replaced by the AMD Opteron. For more details about the Athlon MP, see the AMD website.

Sempron (Socket A)

AMD introduced the Sempron line of processors in 2004 to provide an economy line of processors designed to compete with the Intel Celeron D. As with the Celeron, the Sempron is a chameleon because the Sempron brand is used for both Socket A processors (based on and replacing the Athlon XP series) and Socket 754 processors (based on the Athlon 64). This section discusses Socket A versions of the Sempron. Socket 754 versions of the Sempron are discussed later in this chapter.

▶▶ See "AMD Sempron (Socket 754)," p. 217.

The Socket A version of the AMD Sempron is a replacement for, and is closely based on, the Athlon XP processor's Thoroughbred (Model 8) and Barton (Model 10) versions. The major features of the Sempron are the same as the Athlon XP. Although the Sempron uses processor numbers that appear similar to those used by the Athlon XP, a Sempron with features similar to an Athlon XP does not use the same processor number. As with other AMD processors—and with Intel processors that use one of Intel's new numbering schemes—you need to look up the specifics for a particular processor to determine its exact features.

Table 3.49 provides detailed information about Socket A versions of the Sempron.

Table 3.49   AMD Sempron (Socket A) Processor Information

Model Number	CPU Speed	Bus Speed	L2 Cache	CPU Core	Mfg. Process	Max. Power	SSE	Socket
Sempron 2200+	1.50GHz	333MHz	256KB	Thoroughbred	130nm	62W	SSE	A (462)
Sempron 2200+	1.50GHz	333MHz	256KB	Thorton	130nm	62W	SSE	A (462)
Sempron 2300+	1.58GHz	333MHz	256KB	Thoroughbred	130nm	62W	SSE	A (462)
Sempron 2400+	1.66GHz	333MHz	256KB	Thoroughbred	130nm	62W	SSE	A (462)
Sempron 2400+	1.66GHz	333MHz	256KB	Thorton	130nm	62W	SSE	A (462)
Sempron 2500+	1.75GHz	333MHz	256KB	Thoroughbred	130nm	62W	SSE	A (462)
Sempron 2600+	1.83GHz	333MHz	256KB	Thoroughbred	130nm	62W	SSE	A (462)
Sempron 2800+	2.00GHz	333MHz	256KB	Thoroughbred	130nm	62W	SSE	A (462)
Sempron 2800+	2.00GHz	333MHz	256KB	Thorton	130nm	62W	SSE	A (462)
Sempron 3000+	2.00GHz	333MHz	512KB	Barton	130nm	62W	SSE	A (462)
Sempron 3300+	2.20GHz	400MHz	512KB	Barton	130nm	64W	SSE	A (462)

SSE = Streaming SIMD Instructions (MMX)

Cyrix/IBM 6x86 (M1) and 6x86MX (MII)

The Cyrix 6x86 processor family consists of the now-discontinued 6x86 and 6x86MX processors. They are similar to the AMD-K5 and K6 in that they offer sixth-generation internal designs in a fifth-generation P5 Pentium-compatible Socket 7 exterior.

The Cyrix 6x86 and 6x86MX (later renamed MII) processors incorporate two optimized super-pipelined integer units and an on-chip floating-point unit. These processors include the dynamic execution capability that is the hallmark of a sixth-generation CPU design. This includes branch prediction and speculative execution.

The 6x86MX/MII processor is compatible with MMX technology to run MMX games and multimedia software. With its enhanced memory-management unit, a 64KB internal cache, and other advanced architectural features, the 6x86MX processor achieves higher performance than the standard 6x86.

Note that because of the use of the P-Rating system, the actual speed of the chip is not the same number at which it is advertised. For example, the 6x86MX-PR300 is not a 300MHz chip; it actually runs at only 263MHz or 266MHz, depending on exactly how the motherboard bus speed and CPU clock multipliers are set. Cyrix says it runs as fast as a 300MHz Pentium, hence the P-Rating. Personally, I wish it would label the chip at the correct speed and then say that it runs faster than a Pentium at the same speed.

To install the 6x86 processors in a motherboard, you also must set the correct voltage. Normally, the markings on top of the chip indicate which voltage setting is appropriate. Various versions of the 6x86 run at 3.52V (use VRE setting), 3.3V (VR setting), or 2.8V (MMX) settings. The MMX versions use the standard split-plane 2.8V core 3.3V I/O settings.

Cyrix was acquired by VIA Technologies in 1999.

VIA C3

The VIA C3 was originally known as the VIA Cyrix III and was designed to fit into the same Socket 370 used by the Pentium III and Celeron III. The initial versions of the C3, code named Joshua and

Samuel, had 128KB L1 cache but didn't contain any L2 cache. As a consequence, they had much lower performance than similar 500MHz-class processors. The original Cyrix III/C3, code named Joshua, was developed by former Cyrix engineers after VIA bought Cyrix in late 1998, but the Samuel and subsequent versions are based on the Centaur Winchip (VIA purchased Centaur in 1999). The Samuel was built with a .18-micron process, whereas the Samuel 2 is a development of the Samuel with 64KB of L2 cache on board and is built on a .15-micron process. The Ezra core was the first .13-micron process C3 processor, but it, like previous C3 processors, was not compatible with Tualatin (late Pentium III-compatible) motherboards. The Ezra-T core was the first C3 to reach 1GHz and the first to support Tualatin motherboards. The latest C3 uses the Nehemiah core and features clock speeds over 1GHz and built-in encryption. C3 models feature 100MHz FSB (750MHz and 900MHz models) or 133MHz FSB (733MHz, 800MHz, 866MHz, 933MHz, and higher).

The C3 is fully software compatible with other x86 processors, including Pentium III and Celeron, but its microarchitecture is designed to enhance the performance of most frequently used instructions while reducing the performance of seldom-used instructions. This design feature significantly reduces the die size needed for C3 processors, but it also reduces performance in multimedia and graphics operations. Due to a reduced die size, the C3 in its Nehemiah version offers typical power consumption of only 11.25 watts, making it the coolest running processor available for Socket 370 applications.

Because of its low power consumption, cool operation, and relatively low performance compared to the Intel Celeron, the C3 processor should be considered primarily for computing appliances, set-top boxes, and portable computers in which small size and low power/cooling requirements (rather than performance) are paramount.

The C3 is also available in an enhanced ball grid array (EBGA) package called the E-series. E-series C3 processors are used for permanent installation on motherboards such as the Mini-ITX ultra-compact form factor designs also produced by VIA.

For more details about various versions of the C3, refer to Table 3.3 or the VIA Technologies website.

Intel Pentium 4 (Seventh-generation) Processors

The Pentium 4 was introduced in November 2000 and represented a new generation in processors (see Figure 3.61). If this one had a number instead of a name, it might be called the 786 because it represents a generation beyond the previous 686 class processors. Several variations on the Pentium 4 have been released, based on the processor die and architecture. Several of the processor dies are shown in Figure 3.62.

Figure 3.61   Pentium 4 FC-PGA2 processor.

The main technical details for the Pentium 4 include

- Speeds range from 1.3GHz to 3.8GHz.
- 42 million transistors, 180nm process, 217 sq. mm die (Willamette).
- 55 million transistors, 130nm process, 131 sq. mm die (Northwood).
- 178 million transistors, 130nm process, 237 sq. mm die (Gallatin).
- 125 million transistors, 90nm process, 112 sq. mm die (Prescott).
- 169 million transistors, 90nm process, 135 sq. mm die (Prescott 2M).
- 188 million transistors, 65nm process, 81 sq. mm die (Cedar Mill).
- Software compatible with previous Intel 32-bit processors.
- Some versions support EM64T (64-bit extensions) and Execute Disable Bit (buffer overflow protection).
- Processor (front-side) bus runs at 400MHz, 533MHz, 800MHz, or 1,066MHz.
- Arithmetic logic units (ALUs) run at twice the processor core frequency.
- Hyper-pipelined (20-stage or 31-stage) technology.
- Hyper-Threading Technology support in all 2.4GHz and faster processors running an 800MHz bus and all 3.06GHz and faster processors running a 533MHz bus.
- Very deep out-of-order instruction execution.
- Enhanced branch prediction.
- 8KB or 16KB L1 cache plus 12K micro-op execution trace cache.
- 256KB, 512KB, 1MB, or 2MB of on-die, full-core speed 256-bit-wide L2 cache with eight-way associativity.
- L2 cache can handle all physical memory and supports ECC.
- 2MB of on-die, full-speed L3 cache (Extreme Edition).
- SSE2-SSE plus 144 new instructions for graphics and sound processing (Willamette and Northwood).
- SSE3-SSE2 plus 13 new instructions for graphics and sound processing (Prescott).
- Enhanced floating-point unit.
- Multiple low-power states.

◄◄ See "IA-32e 64-Bit Extension Mode (AMD64, x86-64, EM64T)," p. 53.

Intel abandoned Roman numerals for a standard Arabic numeral 4 designation to identify the Pentium 4. Internally, the Pentium 4 introduces a new architecture Intel calls NetBurst microarchitecture, which is a marketing term and not a technical term. Intel uses NetBurst to describe hyper-pipelined technology, a rapid execution engine, a high-speed (400MHz, 533MHz, 800MHz, or 1,066MHz) system bus, and an execution trace cache. The hyper-pipelined technology doubles or triples the instruction pipeline depth as compared to the Pentium III (or Athlon/Athlon 64), meaning more and smaller steps are required to execute instructions. Even though this might seem less efficient, it enables much higher clock speeds to be more easily attained. The rapid execution engine enables the two integer arithmetic logic units (ALUs) to run at twice the processor core frequency, which means instructions can execute in half a clock cycle. The 400MHz/533MHz/800MHz/1,066MHz system bus is a quad-pumped bus running off a 100MHz/133MHz/200MHz/266MHz system clock transferring data four times per clock cycle. The execution trace cache is a high-performance Level 1 cache that stores approximately 12K decoded micro-operations. This removes the instruction decoder from the main execution pipeline, increasing performance.

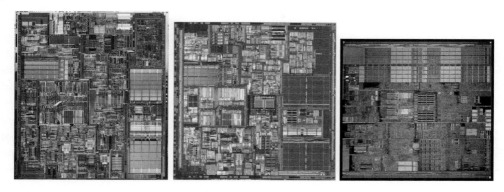

Figure 3.62   The CPU dies for the Pentium 4 CPU based on the Willamette, Northwood, and Prescott cores.

Of these, the high-speed processor bus is most notable. Technically speaking, the processor bus is a 100MHz, 133MHz, 200MHz, or 266MHz quad-pumped bus that transfers four times per cycle (4x), for a 400MHz, 533MHz, 800MHz, or 1,066MHz effective rate. Because the bus is 64 bits (8 bytes) wide, this results in a throughput rate of 3,200MBps, 4,266MBps, 6,400MBps, or 8,533MBps.

In the Pentium 4's 20-stage or 31-stage pipelined internal architecture, individual instructions are broken down into many more substages than with previous processors such as the Pentium III, making this almost like a RISC processor. Unfortunately, this can add to the number of cycles taken to execute instructions if they are not optimized for this processor.Another important architectural advantage is Hyper-Threading Technology, which can be found in all Pentium 4 2.4GHz and faster processors running an 800MHz bus and all 3.06GHz and faster processors running a 533MHz bus. Hyper-threading enables a single processor to run two threads simultaneously, thereby acting as if it were two processors instead of one. For more information on Hyper-Threading Technology, see the section "Hyper-Threading Technology," earlier in this chapter.

The Pentium 4 initially used Socket 423, which has 423 pins in a 39x39 SPGA arrangement. Later versions used Socket 478; recent versions use Socket T (LGA775), which has additional pins to support new features such as EM64T (64-bit extensions), Execute Disable Bit (protection against buffer overflow attacks), Intel Virtualization Technology, and other advanced features. The Celeron was never designed to work in Socket 423, but Celeron and Celeron D versions are available for Socket 478 and Socket T (LGA775), allowing for lower-cost systems compatible with the Pentium 4. Voltage selection is made via an automatic voltage regulator module installed on the motherboard and wired to the socket.

Table 3.50 as a comprehensive guide to Pentium 4 processor features.

Table 3.50   Pentium 4 Processor Information

Processor Model Number	CPU Speed	Bus Speed	L2-Cache	L3 Cache	CPU Core
Pentium 4 1.3	1.30GHz	400MHz	256KB	—	Willamette
Pentium 4 1.4	1.40GHz	400MHz	256KB	—	Willamette
Pentium 4 1.4	1.40GHz	400MHz	256KB	—	Willamette
Pentium 4 1.5	1.50GHz	400MHz	256KB	—	Willamette
Pentium 4 1.5	1.50GHz	400MHz	256KB	—	Willamette
Pentium 4 1.6	1.60GHz	400MHz	256KB	—	Willamette
Pentium 4 1.6	1.60GHz	400MHz	256KB	—	Willamette
Pentium 4 1.6A	1.60GHz	400MHz	512KB	—	Northwood
Pentium 4 1.7	1.70GHz	400MHz	256KB	—	Willamette
Pentium 4 1.7	1.70GHz	400MHz	256KB	—	Willamette
Pentium 4 1.8	1.80GHz	400MHz	256KB	—	Willamette
Pentium 4 1.8	1.80GHz	400MHz	256KB	—	Willamette
Pentium 4 1.8A	1.80GHz	400MHz	512KB	—	Northwood
Pentium 4 1.9	1.90GHz	400MHz	256KB	—	Willamette
Pentium 4 1.9	1.90GHz	400MHz	256KB	—	Willamette
Pentium 4 2.0	2.00GHz	400MHz	256KB	—	Willamette
Pentium 4 2.0	2.00GHz	400MHz	256KB	—	Willamette
Pentium 4 2.0A	2.00GHz	400MHz	512KB	—	Northwood
Pentium 4 2.2	2.20GHz	400MHz	512KB	—	Northwood
Pentium 4 2.26	2.26GHz	533MHz	512KB	—	Northwood
Pentium 4 2.26A	2.26GHz	533MHz	1MB	—	Prescott
Pentium 4 2.4	2.40GHz	400MHz	512KB	—	Northwood
Pentium 4 2.4A	2.40GHz	533MHz	1MB	—	Prescott
Pentium 4 2.4B	2.40GHz	533MHz	512KB	—	Northwood
Pentium 4 2.4C	2.40GHz	800MHz	512KB	—	Northwood
Pentium 4 2.5	2.50GHz	400MHz	512KB	—	Northwood
Pentium 4 2.53	2.53GHz	533MHz	512KB	—	Northwood
Pentium 4 2.6	2.60GHz	400MHz	512KB	—	Northwood
Pentium 4 2.6C	2.60GHz	800MHz	512KB	—	Northwood
Pentium 4 2.66	2.66GHz	533MHz	512KB	—	Northwood
Pentium 4 2.66A	2.66GHz	533MHz	1MB	—	Prescott
Pentium 4 505	2.66GHz	533MHz	1MB	—	Prescott
Pentium 4 505J	2.66GHz	533MHz	1MB	—	Prescott
Pentium 4 506	2.66GHz	533MHz	1MB	—	Prescott
Pentium 4 2.8	2.80GHz	533MHz	512KB	—	Northwood
Pentium 4 2.8	2.80GHz	400MHz	512KB	—	Northwood
Pentium 4 2.8	2.80GHz	400MHz	512KB	—	Northwood
Pentium 4 2.8A	2.80GHz	533MHz	1MB	—	Prescott

Mfg. Process	Max. Power	SSE	HT	64-bit	NX	EIST	VT	Socket
180nm	51.6W	SSE2	—	—	—	—	—	423
180nm	54.7W	SSE2	—	—	—	—	—	423
180nm	55.3W	SSE2	—	—	—	—	—	478
180nm	57.8W	SSE2	—	—	—	—	—	423
180nm	57.9W	SSE2	—	—	—	—	—	478
180nm	61W	SSE2	—	—	—	—	—	423
180nm	60.8W	SSE2	—	—	—	—	—	478
130nm	46.8W	SSE2	—	—	—	—	—	478
180nm	64W	SSE2	—	—	—	—	—	423
180nm	63.5W	SSE2	—	—	—	—	—	478
180nm	66.7W	SSE2	—	—	—	—	—	423
180nm	66.1W	SSE2	—	—	—	—	—	478
130nm	49.6W	SSE2	—	—	—	—	—	478
180nm	69.2W	SSE2	—	—	—	—	—	423
180nm	72.8W	SSE2	—	—	—	—	—	478
180nm	71.8W	SSE2	—	—	—	—	—	423
180nm	75.3W	SSE2	—	—	—	—	—	478
130nm	54.3W	SSE2	—	—	—	—	—	478
130nm	57.1W	SSE2	—	—	—	—	—	478
130nm	58W	SSE2	—	—	—	—	—	478
90nm	89W	SSE3	—	—	—	—	—	478
130nm	59.8W	SSE2	—	—	—	—	—	478
90nm	89W	SSE3	—	—	—	—	—	478
130nm	59.8W	SSE2	—	—	—	—	—	478
130nm	66.2W	SSE2	yes	—	—	—	—	478
130nm	61W	SSE2	—	—	—	—	—	478
130nm	61.5W	SSE2	—	—	—	—	—	478
130nm	62.6W	SSE2	—	—	—	—	—	478
130nm	69W	SSE2	yes	—	—	—	—	478
130nm	66.1W	SSE2	—	—	—	—	—	478
90nm	89W	SSE3	—	—	—	—	—	478
90nm	84W	SSE3	—	—	—	—	—	LGA775
90nm	84W	SSE3	—	—	yes	—	—	LGA775
90nm	84W	SSE3	—	yes	yes	—	—	LGA775
130nm	68.4W	SSE2	—	—	—	—	—	478
130nm	81.8W	SSE2	—	—	—	—	—	478
130nm	81.8W	SSE2	—	—	—	—	—	478
90nm	89W	SSE3	—	—	—	—	—	478

Table 3.50   Continued

Processor Model Number	CPU Speed	Bus Speed	L2-Cache	L3 Cache	CPU Core
Pentium 4 2.8C	2.80GHz	800MHz	512KB	—	Northwood
Pentium 4 2.8E	2.80GHz	800MHz	1MB	—	Prescott
Pentium 4 511	2.80GHz	533MHz	1MB	—	Prescott
Pentium 4 520	2.80GHz	800MHz	1MB	—	Prescott
Pentium 4 520J	2.80GHz	800MHz	1MB	—	Prescott
Pentium 4 521	2.80GHz	800MHz	1MB	—	Prescott
Pentium 4 620	2.80GHz	800MHz	2MB	—	Prescott 2M
Pentium 4 515	2.93GHz	533MHz	1MB	—	Prescott
Pentium 4 515J	2.93GHz	533MHz	1MB	—	Prescott
Pentium 4 516	2.93GHz	533MHz	1MB	—	Prescott
Pentium 4 517	2.93GHz	533MHz	1MB	—	Prescott
Pentium 4 3.0	3.00GHz	800MHz	512KB	—	Northwood
Pentium 4 3.0E	3.00GHz	800MHz	1MB	—	Prescott
Pentium 4 530	3.00GHz	800MHz	1MB	—	Prescott
Pentium 4 530J	3.00GHz	800MHz	1MB	—	Prescott
Pentium 4 531	3.00GHz	800MHz	1MB	—	Prescott
Pentium 4 630	3.00GHz	800MHz	2MB	—	Prescott 2M
Pentium 4 631	3.00GHz	800MHz	2MB	—	Cedar Mill
Pentium 4 631	3.00GHz	800MHz	2MB	—	Cedar Mill
Pentium 4 3.06	3.06GHz	533MHz	512KB	—	Northwood
Pentium 4 3.06	3.06GHz	533MHz	512KB	—	Northwood
Pentium 4 519J	3.06GHz	533MHz	1MB	—	Prescott
Pentium 4 519K	3.06GHz	533MHz	1MB	—	Prescott
Pentium 4 524	3.06GHz	533MHz	1MB	—	Prescott
Pentium 4 3.2	3.20GHz	800MHz	512KB	—	Northwood
Pentium 4 3.2E	3.20GHz	800MHz	1MB	—	Prescott
Pentium 4 3.2E	3.20GHz	800MHz	1MB	—	Prescott
Pentium 4 3.2F	3.20GHz	800MHz	1MB	—	Prescott
Pentium 4 540	3.20GHz	800MHz	1MB	—	Prescott
Pentium 4 540J	3.20GHz	800MHz	1MB	—	Prescott
Pentium 4 541	3.20GHz	800MHz	1MB	—	Prescott
Pentium 4 640	3.20GHz	800MHz	2MB	—	Prescott 2M
Pentium 4 641	3.20GHz	800MHz	2MB	—	Cedar Mill
Pentium 4 641	3.20GHz	800MHz	2MB	—	Cedar Mill
Pentium 4 3.4	3.40GHz	800MHz	512KB	—	Northwood
Pentium 4 3.4E	3.40GHz	800MHz	1MB	—	Prescott
Pentium 4 3.4E	3.40GHz	800MHz	1MB	—	Prescott
Pentium 4 3.4F	3.40GHz	800MHz	1MB	—	Prescott

Mfg. Process	Max. Power	SSE	HT	64-bit	NX	EIST	VT	Socket
130nm	69.7W	SSE2	yes	—	—	—	—	478
90nm	89W	SSE3	yes	—	—	—	—	478
90nm	84W	SSE3	—	yes	yes	—	—	LGA775
90nm	84W	SSE3	yes	—	—	—	—	LGA775
90nm	84W	SSE3	yes	—	yes	—	—	LGA775
90nm	84W	SSE3	yes	yes	yes	—	—	LGA775
90nm	84W	SSE3	yes	yes	yes	—	—	LGA775
90nm	84W	SSE3	—			—	—	LGA775
90nm	84W	SSE3	—		yes	—	—	LGA775
90nm	84W	SSE3	—	yes	yes	—	—	LGA775
90nm	84W	SSE3	yes	yes	yes	—	—	LGA775
130nm	81.9W	SSE2	yes	—	—	—	—	478
90nm	89W	SSE3	yes	—	—	—	—	478
90nm	84W	SSE3	yes	—	—	—	—	LGA775
90nm	84W	SSE3	yes	—	yes	—	—	LGA775
90nm	84W	SSE3	yes	yes	yes	—	—	LGA775
90nm	84W	SSE3	yes	yes	yes	yes	—	LGA775
65nm	86W	SSE3	yes	yes	yes	—	—	LGA775
65nm	65W	SSE3	yes	yes	yes	yes	—	LGA775
130nm	81.8W	SSE2	Yes	—	—	—	—	478
130nm	81.8W	SSE2	yes	—	—	—	—	478
90nm	84W	SSE3	—		yes	—	—	LGA775
90nm	84W	SSE3	—	yes	yes	—	—	LGA775
90nm	84W	SSE3	yes	yes	yes	—	—	LGA775
130nm	82W	SSE2	yes	—	—	—	—	478
90nm	89W	SSE3	yes	—	—	—	—	478
90nm	103W	SSE3	yes	—	—	—	—	478
90nm	103W	SSE3	yes	yes	—	—	—	LGA775
90nm	84W	SSE3	yes	—	—	—	—	LGA775
90nm	84W	SSE3	yes	—	yes	—	—	LGA775
90nm	84W	SSE3	yes	yes	yes	—	—	LGA775
90nm	84W	SSE3	yes	yes	yes	yes	—	LGA775
65nm	86W	SSE3	yes	yes	yes	—	—	LGA775
65nm	65W	SSE3	yes	yes	yes	yes	—	LGA775
130nm	89W	SSE2	yes	—	—	—	—	478
90nm	89W	SSE3	yes	—	—	—	—	478
90nm	103W	SSE3	yes	—	—	—	—	478
90nm	115W	SSE3	yes	yes	—	—	—	LGA775

Table 3.50   Continued

Processor Model Number	CPU Speed	Bus Speed	L2-Cache	L3 Cache	CPU Core
Pentium 4 550	3.40GHz	800MHz	1MB	—	Prescott
Pentium 4 550J	3.40GHz	800MHz	1MB	—	Prescott
Pentium 4 551	3.40GHz	800MHz	1MB	—	Prescott
Pentium 4 650	3.40GHz	800MHz	2MB	—	Prescott 2M
Pentium 4 651	3.40GHz	800MHz	2MB	—	Cedar Mill
Pentium 4 651	3.40GHz	800MHz	2MB	—	Cedar Mill
Pentium 4 3.6F	3.60GHz	800MHz	1MB	—	Prescott
Pentium 4 560	3.60GHz	800MHz	1MB	—	Prescott
Pentium 4 560J	3.60GHz	800MHz	1MB	—	Prescott
Pentium 4 561	3.60GHz	800MHz	1MB	—	Prescott
Pentium 4 660	3.60GHz	800MHz	2MB	—	Prescott 2M
Pentium 4 661	3.60GHz	800MHz	2MB	—	Cedar Mill
Pentium 4 661	3.60GHz	800MHz	2MB	—	Cedar Mill
Pentium 4 662	3.60GHz	800MHz	2MB	—	Prescott 2M
Pentium 4 3.8F	3.80GHz	800MHz	1MB	—	Prescott
Pentium 4 570J	3.80GHz	800MHz	1MB	—	Prescott
Pentium 4 571	3.80GHz	800MHz	1MB	—	Prescott
Pentium 4 670	3.80GHz	800MHz	2MB	—	Prescott 2M
Pentium 4 672	3.80GHz	800MHz	2MB	—	Prescott 2M

SSE = Streaming SIMD Instructions (MMX)

HT = Hyper-Threading Technology

NX = Execute Disable Bit

EIST = Enhanced Intel SpeedStep Technology

VT = Virtualization Technology

For some time now, it has been obvious that "Pentium 4" has been far more of a brand than a single processor family, leading to endless confusion when users have considered processor upgrades or new system purchases. Because of the three form factors (Socket 423, Socket 478, and Socket 775) and the wide range of features available in the Pentium 4 family, it's essential that you determine exactly what the features are of a particular processor before you purchase it as an upgrade to an existing processor or as part of a complete system.

Pentium 4 Extreme Edition

In November 2003, Intel introduced the Extreme Edition of the Pentium 4, which is notable for being the first desktop PC processor to incorporate L3 cache. The Extreme Edition (or Pentium 4EE) is basically a revamped version of the Prestonia core Xeon workstation/server processor, which has used L3 cache since November 2002. The Pentium 4EE has 512KB of L2 cache and 2MB of L3 cache, which increases the transistor count to 178 million transistors and makes the die significantly larger than the standard Pentium 4. Because of the large die based on the 130-nanometer process, this chip is

Mfg. Process	Max. Power	SSE	HT	64-bit	NX	EIST	VT	Socket
90nm	84W	SSE3	yes	—	—	—	—	LGA775
90nm	84W	SSE3	yes	—	yes	—	—	LGA775
90nm	84W	SSE3	yes	yes	yes	—	—	LGA775
90nm	84W	SSE3	yes	yes	yes	yes	—	LGA775
65nm	86W	SSE3	yes	yes	yes	—	—	LGA775
65nm	65W	SSE3	yes	yes	yes	yes	—	LGA775
90nm	115W	SSE3	yes	yes	—	—	—	LGA775
90nm	115W	SSE3	yes	—	—	—	—	LGA775
90nm	115W	SSE3	yes	—	yes	—	—	LGA775
90nm	115W	SSE3	yes	yes	yes	—	—	LGA775
90nm	115W	SSE3	yes	yes	yes	yes	—	LGA775
65nm	86W	SSE3	yes	yes	yes	—	—	LGA775
65nm	65W	SSE3	yes	yes	yes	yes	—	LGA775
90nm	115W	SSE3	yes	yes	yes	yes	—	LGA775
90nm	115W	SSE3	yes	yes	—	—	—	LGA775
90nm	115W	SSE3	yes	—	yes	—	—	LGA775
90nm	115W	SSE3	yes	yes	yes	—	—	LGA775
90nm	115W	SSE3	yes	yes	yes	yes	—	LGA775
90nm	115W	SSE3	yes	yes	yes	yes	yes	LGA775

expensive to produce and the extremely high selling price reflects that. The Extreme Edition is targeted toward the gaming market, where people are willing to spend extra money for additional performance. The additional cache doesn't help standard business applications as well as it helps power-hungry 3D games.

In 2004, revised versions of the Pentium 4 Extreme Edition were introduced. These processors are based on the 90-nanometer (0.09-micron) Pentium 4 Prescott core but with a larger 2MB L2 cache in place of the 512KB L2 cache design used by the standard Prescott-core Pentium 4. Pentium 4 Extreme Edition processors based on the Prescott core do not have L3 cache.

The Pentium 4 Extreme Edition is available in both Socket 478 and Socket T form factors, with clock speeds ranging from 3.2GHz to 3.4GHz (Socket 478) and from 3.4GHz to 3.73GHz (Socket T). For specific features of a particular Pentium 4 Extreme Edition processor, see Table 3.51.

The various Pentium 4 and Pentium 4 Extreme Edition versions are shown in Table 3.49.

Table 3.50   Pentium 4 Extreme Edition Processor Information

Processor Model Number	CPU Core	CPU Speed	Bus Speed	L2-Cache	L3 Cache
Pentium 4 EE	Gallatin	3.20GHz	800MHz	512KB	2MB
Pentium 4 EE	Gallatin	3.40GHz	800MHz	512KB	2MB
Pentium 4 EE	Gallatin	3.40GHz	800MHz	512KB	2MB
Pentium 4 EE	Gallatin	3.46GHz	1066MHz	512KB	2MB
Pentium 4 EE	Prescott 2M	3.73GHz	1066MHz	2MB	—

EE = Extreme Edition   *NX = Execute Disable Bit*
SSE = Streaming SIMD Instructions (MMX)   *EIST = Enhanced Intel SpeedStep Technology*
HT = Hyper-Threading Technology   *VT = Virtualization Technology*

Pentium 4 Power Supply and Cooling Issues

Compared to older processors, the Pentium 4 requires a lot of electrical power, and because of this, starting in February 2000 Intel changed the ATX motherboard and power supply specifications to support a CPU voltage regulator module powered from 12V instead of 3.3V or 5V, as with previous designs. By using the 12V power, more 3.3V and 5V power is available to run the rest of the system and the overall current draw is greatly reduced with the higher voltage as a source. PC power supplies normally generate more than enough 12V power, but the previous ATX motherboard and power supply designs originally allotted only one pin for 12V power (each pin is rated for only 6 amps), so additional 12V lines were necessary to carry this power to the motherboard.

The fix appears in the form of a third power connector, called the ATX12V connector. This new connector is used in addition to any existing connectors. Any motherboard having the ATX12V connector requires that you supply power to it, if you are using an older ATX power supply that lacks the proper ATX12V connector, several companies sell adapters that convert a standard Molex-type peripheral power connector to the ATX12V connector. Typically, a 300-watt (the minimum recommended) or larger power supply has more than adequate levels of 12V power for both the drives and the ATX12V connector.

If your power supply is less than the 300-watt minimum recommended, you may need to purchase a replacement supply.

▶▶ See "Motherboard Power Connectors," p. 1233.

Cooling a high-wattage processor such as the Pentium 4 requires a large active heatsink. These heavy (sometimes more than 1 lb.) heatsinks can damage a CPU or destroy a motherboard when subjected to vibration or shock, especially during shipping. To solve this problem with Pentium 4 motherboards, various methods have been used to secure the heatsink in the system. Intel's specifications for Socket 423 added four standoffs to the ATX chassis design flanking the Socket 423 to support the heatsink retention brackets. These standoffs enabled the chassis to support the weight of the heatsink instead of depending on the motherboard, as with older designs. Vendors also used other means to reinforce the CPU location without requiring a direct chassis attachment. For example, Asus's P4T motherboard was supplied with a metal reinforcing plate to enable off-the-shelf ATX cases to work with the motherboard.

Mfg. Process	Max. Power	SSE	HT	64-bit	NX	EIST	VT	Socket
130nm	92.1W	SSE2	yes	—	—	—	—	478
130nm	102.9W	SSE2	yes	—	—	—	—	478
130nm	109.6W	SSE2	yes	—	—	—	—	LGA775
130nm	110.7W	SSE2	yes	—	—	—	—	LGA775
90nm	115W	SSE3	yes	yes	yes	yes	—	LGA775

Socket 478 systems do not require any special standoffs or reinforcement plates; instead they use a unique scheme in which the CPU heatsink attaches directly to the motherboard rather than to the CPU socket or chassis. Motherboards with Socket 478 can be installed into any ATX chassis-no special standoffs are required.

Socket T (LGA775) systems use a unique locking mechanism that holds the processor in place. The heatsink is positioned over the processor and locking pins attache it to the motherboard.

Because the Pentium 4 processor family has been manufactured in three socket types with a wide variation in clock speed and power dissipation, it's essential that you choose a heatsink made specifically for the processor form factor and speed you have purchased (or intend to purchase). This is just one more reason I think it's worth getting a boxed processor instead of an OEM version when building or upgrading a system. If you purchase the shrink-wrapped or "boxed" processor, you get an Intel-specified high-quality heatsink in the box with the process. In addition, you get a 3-year warranty with Intel, making the boxed version ideal for upgraders and system builders.

Xeon Processors

Xeon processors are based on the Pentium 4 and are designed for Socket 603 and Socket 604. Xeon DP processors (often referred to simply as *Xeon*) are designed for single- and dual-processor workstations:

- Xeon DP processors with a 400MHz CPU bus feature clock speeds from 1.4GHz to 3GHz.
- Xeon DP processors with a 533MHz CPU bus feature clock speeds from 2GHz to 3.2GHz.
- Xeon DP processors with a 667MHz CPU bus (a speed never used by the Pentium 4, by the way) feature clock speeds from 3.33GHz to 3.66GHz.
- Xeon DP processors with an 800MHz CPU bus feature clock speeds from 2.8GHz to 3.8GHz.

Xeon MP processors are designed for four-way and larger servers. They are available in speeds ranging from 1.4GHz to 3GHz, and all support the 400MHz CPU bus.

For more information about Xeon DP and Xeon MP processors, see my book *Upgrading and Repairing Servers*.

Eighth-generation (64-Bit Register) Processors

In 2003, AMD introduced the first 64-bit processor for x86-compatible desktop computers—the Athlon 64—followed by its first 64-bit server processor, the Opteron. In 2004, Intel introduced a series of 64-bit-enabled versions of its Pentium 4 desktop processor. The years that followed saw both companies introducing more and more processors with 64-bit capabilities.

The following sections discuss the major features of these processors and the different approaches taken by Intel and AMD to bring 64-bit computing to the PC server and desktop.

AMD Athlon 64 and 64 FX

The AMD Athlon 64 and 64 FX, introduced in September 2003, are the first 64-bit processors for desktop (and not server) computers. Originally code named ClawHammer, the Athlon 64 and 64 FX are the desktop element of AMD's 64-bit processor family, which also includes the Opteron (code named SledgeHammer) server processor. The Athlon 64 and 64 FX (shown in Figure 3.63) are essentially Opteron chips designed for single-processor systems, and in some cases have decreased cache or memory bandwidth capabilities.

Figure 3.63   AMD Athlon 64 FX (Socket 939 version). *Photo courtesy of AMD.*

Besides support for 64-bit instructions, the biggest difference between the Athlon 64 and 64 FX and other processors is the fact that their memory controller is built in. The memory controller is normally part of the motherboard chipset North Bridge or memory controller hub (MCH) chip, but with the Athlon 64 and 64 FX, the memory controller is now built into the processor. This means that the typical CPU bus architecture is different with these chips. In a conventional design, the processor talks to the chipset North Bridge, which then talks to the memory and all other components in the system. Because the Athlon 64 and 64 FX have integrated memory controllers, they talk to memory directly, and also talk to the North Bridge for other system communications. Separating the memory traffic from the CPU bus allows for improved performance not only in memory transfers, but also in CPU bus transfers. The main difference in the Athlon 64 and 64 FX is in the different configurations of cache sizes and memory bus widths.

The major features of the Athlon 64 design include

- Speeds ranging from 1.0GHz to 3.0GHz.
- Between 68.5 million transistors (512KB L2 cache versions) and 129 million transistors (1MB L2 cache versions).
- 12-stage pipeline.
- DDR memory controller with ECC support integrated into the processor (instead of the North Bridge or MCP, as in other recent chipsets).
- Socket 754 features single-channel memory controller; Socket 940, 939 and AM2 features dual-channel memory controller.
- 128KB L1 cache.
- 512KB or 1MB of on-die full-speed L2 cache.
- Support for AMD64 (also called IA-32e or x86-64) 64-bit extension technology (extends 32-bit x86 architecture).
- Up to 3.2GBps (Socket 754) or 4GBps (Socket 940, 939 and AM2) Hypertransport link to chipset North Bridge.
- Addressable memory size up to 1TB, greatly exceeding the 4GB or 64GB limit imposed by 32-bit processors.
- SSE2 (SSE plus 144 new instructions for graphics and sound processing).
- Multiple low-power states.
- 130-nanometer, 90nm, or 65nm cores.

The Athlon 64 FX differs from the standard Athlon 64 in the following ways:

- Supports only Socket 940, 939, or AM2.
- Has dual-channel DDR or DDR2 memory controller with ECC support.
- Socket 940 versions require registered memory.
- Features speeds from 2.2GHz to 2.8GHz.
- 1MB L2 cache (standard).

Although Socket 939 and AM2 versions of the Athlon 64 have closed the performance gap, the Athlon 64 FX is still the fastest single-core Athlon 64 processor.

Although AMD has been criticized by many, including me, for its confusing performance-rating processor names in the Athlon XP series, AMD also uses this naming scheme with the Athlon 64. As I suggest with the Athlon XP, you should look at the actual performance of the processor with the applications you use most to determine whether the Athlon 64 is right for you and which model is best suited to your needs. The integrated memory bus in the Athlon 64 means that the Athlon 64 connects to memory more directly than any 32-bit chip and makes North Bridge design simpler. AMD offers its own chipsets for the Athlon 64, and since acquiring ATI in 2006, offers ATI chipsets as well. See Chapter 4 for details.

The various models and features of the Athlon 64 and 64 FX are summed up in Tables 3.52 and 3.53.

Table 3.52   Athlon 64 Processor Information

Processor Model Number	CPU Speed	Bus Speed	L2 Cache	CPU Core
Athlon 64 1500+	1.00GHz	1000MHz	512KB	Venice
Athlon 64 2800+	1.80GHz	800MHz	512KB	ClawHammer
Athlon 64 2800+	1.80GHz	800MHz	512KiB	Newcastle
Athlon 64 3000+	1.80GHz	1000MHz	512KB	Newcastle
Athlon 64 3000+	1.80GHz	1000MHz	512KB	Winchester
Athlon 64 3000+	1.80GHz	1000MHz	512KB	Venice
Athlon 64 3000+	1.80GHz	1000MHz	512KB	Orleans
Athlon 64 3000+	2.00GHz	800MHz	512KB	ClawHammer
Athlon 64 3000+	2.00GHz	800MHz	512KB	Newcastle
Athlon 64 3000+	2.00GHz	800MHz	512KB	Venice
Athlon 64 3200+	2.00GHz	800MHz	1MB	ClawHammer
Athlon 64 3200+	2.00GHz	1000MHz	512KB	Newcastle
Athlon 64 3200+	2.00GHz	1000MHz	512KB	Winchester
Athlon 64 3200+	2.00GHz	1000MHz	512KB	Venice
Athlon 64 3200+	2.00GHz	1000MHz	512KB	Manchester
Athlon 64 3200+	2.00GHz	1000MHz	512KB	Orleans
Athlon 64 3200+	2.20GHz	800MHz	512KB	Newcastle
Athlon 64 3200+	2.20GHz	800MHz	512KB	Venice
Athlon 64 3300+	2.40GHz	800MHz	256KB	Newcastle
Athlon 64 3400+	2.20GHz	800MHz	1MB	ClawHammer
Athlon 64 3400+	2.20GHz	800MHz	512KB	Newcastle
Athlon 64 3400+	2.20GHz	800MHz	512KB	Venice
Athlon 64 3400+	2.40GHz	800MHz	512KB	Newcastle
Athlon 64 3400+	2.40GHz	800MHz	512KB	Venice
Athlon 64 3500+	2.20GHz	1000MHz	512KB	ClawHammer
Athlon 64 3500+	2.20GHz	1000MHz	512KB	Newcastle
Athlon 64 3500+	2.20GHz	1000MHz	512KB	Winchester
Athlon 64 3500+	2.20GHz	1000MHz	512KB	Venice
Athlon 64 3500+	2.20GHz	1000MHz	512KB	Manchester
Athlon 64 3500+	2.20GHz	1000MHz	512KB	San Diego
Athlon 64 3500+	2.20GHz	1000MHz	512KB	Orleans
Athlon 64 3500+	2.20GHz	1000MHz	512KB	Orleans
Athlon 64 3500+	2.20GHz	1000MHz	512KB	Orleans
Athlon 64 3500+	2.20GHz	1000MHz	512KB	Lima
Athlon 64 3700+	2.20GHz	1000MHz	1MB	San Diego
Athlon 64 3700+	2.40GHz	800MHz	1MB	ClawHammer
Athlon 64 3800+	2.40GHz	1000MHz	512KB	Newcastle
Athlon 64 3800+	2.40GHz	1000MHz	512KB	Venice

Mfg. Process	Max. Power	SSE	64-bit	NX	Cool'n'Quiet	VT	Socket
90nm	—	SSE3	X	X	X	—	939
130nm	89W	SSE2	X	X	X	—	754
130nm	89W	SSE2	X	X	X	—	754
130nm	89W	SSE2	X	X	X	—	939
90nm	67W	SSE2	X	X	X	—	939
90nm	67W	SSE3	X	X	X	—	939
90nm	62W	SSE3	X	X	X	X	AM2
130nm	89W	SSE2	X	X	X	—	754
130nm	89W	SSE2	X	X	X	—	754
90nm	51W	SSE3	X	X	X	—	754
130nm	89W	SSE2	X	X	X	—	754
130nm	89W	SSE2	X	X	X	—	939
90nm	67W	SSE2	X	X	X	—	939
90nm	67W	SSE3	X	X	X	—	939
90nm	67W	SSE3	X	X	X	—	939
90nm	62W	SSE3	X	X	X	X	AM2
130nm	89W	SSE2	X	X	X	—	754
90nm	59W	SSE3	X	X	X	—	754
130nm	89W	SSE2	X	X	X	—	754
130nm	89W	SSE2	X	X	X	—	754
130nm	89W	SSE2	X	X	X	—	939
90nm	67W	SSE3	X	X	X	—	939
130nm	89W	SSE2	X	X	X	—	754
90nm	67W	SSE3	X	X	X	—	754
130nm	89W	SSE2	X	X	X	—	939
130nm	89W	SSE2	X	X	X	—	939
90nm	67W	SSE2	X	X	X	—	939
90nm	67W	SSE3	X	X	X	—	939
90nm	67W	SSE3	X	X	X	—	939
90nm	67W	SSE3	X	X	X	—	939
90nm	62W	SSE3	X	X	X	X	AM2
90nm	62W	SSE3	X	X	X	X	AM2
90nm	35W	SSE3	X	X	X	X	AM2
65nm	45W	SSE3	X	X	X	X	AM2
90nm	89W	SSE3	X	X	X	—	939
130nm	89W	SSE2	X	X	X	—	754
130nm	89W	SSE2	X	X	X	—	939
90nm	89W	SSE3	X	X	X	—	939

Table 3.52   Continued

Processor Model Number	CPU Speed	Bus Speed	L2 Cache	CPU Core
Athlon 64 3800+	2.40GHz	1000MHz	512KB	Orleans
Athlon 64 3800+	2.40GHz	1000MHz	512KB	Orleans
Athlon 64 3800+	2.40GHz	1000MHz	512KB	Lima
Athlon 64 4000+	2.40GHz	1000MHz	1MB	ClawHammer
Athlon 64 4000+	2.40GHz	1000MHz	1MB	San Diego
Athlon 64 4000+	2.40GHz	1000MHz	1MB	San Diego
Athlon 64 4000+	2.60GHz	1000MHz	512KB	Orleans

SSE = Streaming SIMD Instructions (MMX)   *Cool'n'Quiet = Power Saving Technology*
NX = Execute Disable Bit   *VT = Virtualization Technology*

Table 3.53   Athlon 64 FX Processor Information

Processor Model Number	CPU Speed	Bus Speed	L2 Cache	CPU Core
Athlon 64 FX-51	2.20GHz	800MHz	1MB	SledgeHammer
Athlon 64 FX-51	2.20GHz	800MHz	1MB	SledgeHammer
Athlon 64 FX-53	2.40GHz	800MHz	1MB	SledgeHammer
Athlon 64 FX-53	2.40GHz	1000MHz	1MB	ClawHammer
Athlon 64 FX-55	2.60GHz	1000MHz	1MB	ClawHammer
Athlon 64 FX-55	2.60GHz	1000MHz	1MB	San Diego
Athlon 64 FX-57	2.80GHz	1000MHz	1MB	San Diego

SSE = Streaming SIMD Instructions (MMX)   *Cool'n'Quiet = Power Saving Technology*
NX = Execute Disable Bit   *VT = Virtualization Technology*

The Athlon 64 and 64 FX are available in four socket versions (see Table 3.54). The Athlon 64 is available in Socket 754, 939 and AM2 versions, whereas the 64 FX is available in Socket 940, 939 and AM2 versions. Socket 754 supports only a single-channel memory bus, whereas Sockets 940, 939 and AM2 support dual-channel memory for double the memory bandwidth. Socket 754 and 939 support cheaper unbuffered DDR SDRAM DIMMs, and Socket AM2 supports even faster DDR2; Socket 940 only supports slower and more expensive registered DIMMs. Because of this, you should avoid any Socket 940 processors or motherboards because they require registered modules that are both slower and more expensive than unbuffered DDR/DDR2 types.

Table 3.54   AMD Athlon 64 and 64 FX Socket and Memory Types

Socket	Processor	Channels	Type
754	Athlon 64	Single-channel	DDR
940	Athlon 64 FX	Dual-channel	Registered SDRAM
939	Athlon 64/64 FX	Dual-channel	DDR
AM2	Athlon 64/64 FX	Dual-channel	DDR2

Mfg. Process	Max. Power	SSE	64-bit	NX	Cool'n'Quiet	VT	Socket
90nm	62W	SSE3	X	X	X	X	AM2
90nm	62W	SSE3	X	X	X	X	AM2
65nm	45W	SSE3	X	X	X	X	AM2
130nm	89W	SSE2	X	X	X	—	939
90nm	89W	SSE3	X	X	X	—	939
90nm	89W	SSE3	X	X	X	—	939
90nm	62W	SSE3	X	X	X	X	AM2

Mfg. Process	Max. Power	SSE	64-bit	NX	Cool'n'Quiet	VT	Socket
130nm	89W	SSE2	X	X	—	—	940
130nm	89W	SSE2	X	X	—	—	940
130nm	89W	SSE2	X	X	—	—	940
130nm	89W	SSE2	X	X	X	—	939
130nm	104W	SSE2	X	X	X	—	939
90nm	104W	SSE3	X	X	X	—	939
90nm	104W	SSE3	X	X	X	—	939

The Athlon 64 essentially comes in three versions: a Socket 754 version that has only a single-channel memory bus, and an improved Socket 939 version that has a dual-channel memory bus, and an even better Socket AM2 version that has a dual-channel DDR2 bus. The Athlon 64 FX is also available in three versions: a Socket 940 version that uses expensive (and slower) registered memory, an improved Socket 939 version that uses unbuffered memory, and an updated version that uses dual-channel DDR2. The Socket 939 versions of the Athlon 64 and 64 FX are essentially the same chip, differing only in the amount of L2 cache included. For example, the Athlon 64 3800+ and Athlon 64 FX-53 both run at 2.4GHz and run dual-channel memory. The only difference is that the 3800+ has only 512KB of L2 cache, whereas the FX-53 has 1MB of L2. Because the 64 and 64 FX chips are essentially the same, you need to read the fine print to determine the minor differences in configuration.

The Athlon 64 FX can draw up to 104W or more of power, which is high but still somewhat less than the more power-hungry Pentium 4 processors. As with the Pentium 4, motherboards for the Athlon 64 and 64 FX generally require the ATX12V connector to provide adequate 12V power to run the processor voltage regulator module.

The initial version of the Athlon 64 is built on a 0.13-micron (130-nanometer) process (see Figure 3.64). Subsequent versions use either a 0.09-micron (90nm) or a .065-micron (65nm) process.

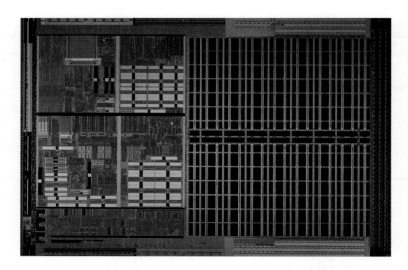

Figure 3.64 AMD Athlon 64 die (130-nanometer process, 106 million transistors, 193 sq. mm).
Photo courtesy of AMD.

Table 3.55 Sempron (Socket 754) Processors

Model Number	CPU Speed	Bus Speed	L2 Cache	CPU Core
Sempron 2500+	1.40GHz	800MHz	256KB	Palermo
Sempron 2600+	1.60GHz	800MHz	128KB	Palermo
Sempron 2800+	1.60GHz	800MHz	256KB	Palermo
Sempron 2800+	1.60GHz	800MHz	128KB	Manila
Sempron 3000+	1.80GHz	800MHz	128KB	Paris
Sempron 3000+	1.80GHz	800MHz	128KB	Palermo
Sempron 3000+	1.80GHz	1000MHz	128KB	Palermo
Sempron 3000+	1.60GHz	800MHz	256KB	Manila
Sempron 3000+	1.60GHz	800MHz	256KB	Manila
Sempron 3100+	1.80GHz	800MHz	256KB	Paris
Sempron 3100+	1.80GHz	800MHz	256KB	Palermo
Sempron 3200+	1.80GHz	1000MHz	256KB	Palermo
Sempron 3200+	1.80GHz	800MHz	128KB	Manila
Sempron 3200+	1.80GHz	800MHz	128KB	Manila
Sempron 3300+	2.00GHz	800MHz	128KB	Palermo
Sempron 3400+	2.00GHz	800MHz	256KB	Palermo
Sempron 3400+	2.00GHz	1000MHz	128KB	Palermo

AMD Sempron (Socket 754)

Just as the Intel Celeron name long ago ceased to identify a particular processor and instead is a brand used by Intel to identify various types of low-cost, reduced-performance processors, AMD's Sempron brand follows a similar course. Sempron is used to identify both Socket A processors that have replaced the Athlon XP and Socket 754 processors that provide a low-cost alternative to the Athlon 64.

◀◀ See "Sempron (Socket A)," p. 197, for more information on the Socket A version of the Sempron.

The Socket 754 Sempron is based on the Socket 754 version of the Athlon 64 processor. However, some versions of the Sempron operate only in a 32-bit mode. The major features of the Socket 754 Sempron include

- 90-nanometer manufacturing process (except as noted in Table 3.52)
- 128KB or 256KB of L2 cache
- 3.2GBps (800MHz) HyperTransport connection to chipset
- 32-bit only or 32/64-bit operation supporting AMD64 (IA-32e or x86-64) applications
- 63.5-68.5 million transistors
- SSE2 or SSE3 instruction support

A system using a Socket 754 Sempron processor can be easily upgraded to a Socket 754 Athlon 64 processor. Table 3.55 provides detailed information about Socket 754 Sempron processors.

Mfg. Process	Max. Power	SSE	64-bit	NX	Cool'n'Quiet	VT	Socket
90nm	62W	SSE3	yes	yes	—	—	754
90nm	62W	SSE2[1]	yes[2]	yes	—	—	754
90nm	62W	SSE2[1]	yes[2]	yes	—	—	754
90nm	62W	SSE3	yes	yes	—	—	AM2
130nm	62W	SSE2	—	yes	—	—	754
90nm	62W	SSE2[1]	yes[2]	yes	yes	—	754
90nm	62W	SSE3	yes[3]	yes	—	—	939
90nm	62W	SSE3	yes	yes	—	—	AM2
90nm	35W	SSE3	yes	yes	—	—	AM2
130nm	62W	SSE2	—	yes	—	—	754
90nm	62W	SSE2[1]	yes[2]	yes	yes	—	754
90nm	62W	SSE3	yes[3]	yes	—	—	939
90nm	62W	SSE3	yes	yes	yes	—	AM2
90nm	35W	SSE3	yes	yes	yes	—	AM2
90nm	62W	SSE2[1]	yes[2]	yes	yes	—	754
90nm	62W	SSE3	yes	yes	yes	—	754
90nm	62W	SSE3	yes	yes	—	—	939

Table 3.55   Sempron (Socket 754) Processors

Model Number	CPU Speed	Bus Speed	L2 Cache	CPU Core
Sempron 3400+	1.80GHz	800MHz	256KB	Manila
Sempron 3400+	1.80GHz	800MHz	256KB	Manila
Sempron 3500+	2.00GHz	1000MHz	256KB	Palermo
Sempron 3500+	2.00GHz	800MHz	128KB	Manila
Sempron 3500+	2.00GHz	800MHz	128KB	Manila
Sempron 3600+	2.00GHz	800MHz	256KB	Manila
Sempron 3800+	2.20GHz	800MHz	256KB	Manila

1. *SSE3 is supported in processors with a part number ending in BO or BX.*
2. *64-bit extensions are supported in processors with a part number ending in BX.*
3. *64-bit extensions are supported in processors with a part number ending in BW.*

As Table 3.55 indicates, most Socket 754 Sempron models include 64-bit support. With both Intel and AMD offering entry-level 64-bit processors, it's easier than ever to move into 64-bit computing.

AMD Opteron

The AMD Opteron is the workstation and server counterpart to the AMD Athlon 64, supporting the same AMD64 (x86-64) architecture as the Athlon 64. The Opteron was introduced in the spring of 2003.

The following are the major features of the Opteron:

- 128KB L1 cache
- 1MB L2 cache
- Clock speeds of 1.8GHz–2.8GHz
- Three 3.2MBps Hypertransport links to chipset
- Socket 939 or 940
- Integrated dual-channel memory controller with ECC
- Maximum addressable memory of 1 terabyte (40-bit physical) and 256 terabytes (48-bit virtual)
- AMD64 (x86-64) architecture
- 130-nanometer or 90-nanometer production process
- Single-core or dual-core design

The Opteron is available in three series: 100 (single-processor workstations), 200 (dual-processor workstations and servers), and 800 (up to eight-way servers). Dual-core versions of Opteron processors are available in all three of these series.

Unlike the Itanium series, which has been supported primarily by Intel chipsets, the Opteron has broad third-party chipset support from companies such as VIA, SiS, ULi, NVIDIA, and ATI (just like the Athlon 64 does).

For more information on Opteron configurations and features, see the book *Upgrading and Repairing Servers*.

Mfg. Process	Max. Power	SSE	64-bit	NX	Cool'n'Quiet	VT	Socket
90nm	62W	SSE3	yes	yes	yes	—	AM2
90nm	35W	SSE3	yes	yes	yes	—	AM2
90nm	62W	SSE3	yes	yes	—	—	939
90nm	62W	SSE3	yes	yes	yes	—	AM2
90nm	35W	SSE3	yes	yes	yes	—	AM2
90nm	62W	SSE3	yes	yes	yes	—	AM2
90nm	62W	SSE3	yes	yes	yes	—	AM2

SSE = Streaming SIMD Instructions (MMX)
NX = Execute Disable Bit
Cool'n'Quiet = Power Saving Technology
VT = Virtualization Technology

Multicore Processors
Intel Pentium D and Pentium Extreme Edition

Intel introduced its first dual-core processors, the Pentium Extreme Edition and Pentium D, in April 2005. Although these processors used the code name Smithfield before their introductions, they are based on the Pentium 4 Prescott core. In fact, to bring dual-core processors to market as quickly as possible, Intel used two Prescott cores in each Pentium D or Pentium Extreme Edition processor. Each core communicates with the other via the MCH (North Bridge) chip on the motherboard (see Figure 3.65).

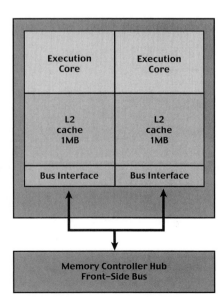

Figure 3.65 The Pentium D and Pentium Extreme Edition's processor cores communicate with each other via the chipset's MCH (North Bridge) chip.

For this reason, Intel 915 and 925 chipsets and some third-party chipsets made for the Pentium 4 cannot be used with the Pentium D or Pentium Extreme Edition. Intel's 945 series, 955X and 975X desktop chipsets, and the E7230 workstation chipset are the first Intel chipsets to support these processors. The nForce 4 series from NVIDIA also works with these processors.

▶▶ See "Intel 945 Express Family," p. 314, and "Intel 955X and 975X Family," p. 314, for more information on these chipsets.

The major features of the Pentium D include

- Clock speeds of 2.66GHz-3.6GHz
- 533MHz or 800MHz processor bus
- EM64T 64-bit extensions
- Execute Disable Bit support
- 65- or 90-nanometer manufacturing process

Table 3.56   Pentium D and Pentium Extreme Edition Processors

Processor Model Number	CPU Speed	Bus Speed	L2 Cache	CPU Core	Mfg. Process
Pentium D 805	2.66GHz	533MHz	2MB	Smithfield	90nm
Pentium D 820	2.80GHz	800MHz	2MB	Smithfield	90nm
Pentium D 915	2.80GHz	800MHz	4MB	Presler	65nm
Pentium D 920	2.80GHz	800MHz	4MB	Presler	65nm
Pentium D 830	3.00GHz	800MHz	2MB	Smithfield	90nm
Pentium D 925	3.00GHz	800MHz	4MB	Presler	65nm
Pentium D 930	3.00GHz	800MHz	4MB	Presler	65nm
Pentium D 840	3.20GHz	800MHz	2MB	Smithfield	90nm
Pentium D 935	3.20GHz	800MHz	4MB	Presler	65nm
Pentium D 940	3.20GHz	800MHz	4MB	Presler	65nm
Pentium EE 840	3.20GHz	800MHz	2MB	Smithfield	90nm
Pentium D 945	3.40GHz	800MHz	4MB	Presler	65nm
Pentium D 950	3.40GHz	800MHz	4MB	Presler	65nm
Pentium EE 955	3.46GHz	1066MHz	4MB	Presler	65nm
Pentium D 960	3.60GHz	800MHz	4MB	Presler	65nm
Pentium EE 965	3.73GHz	1066MHz	4MB	Presler	65nm

Note: Max. power depends on the stepping (internal revision)

EE = Extreme Edition

SSE = Streaming SIMD Instructions (MMX)

HT = Hyper-Threading Technology

NX = Execute Disable Bit

EIST = Enhanced Intel SpeedStep Technology

VT = Virtualization Technology

- 2MB/4MB L2 cache (1MB/2MB per core)
- Socket T (LGA775)

The 830, 840, and 9xx models also include Enhanced Intel Speed Step Technology, which results in cooler and quieter PC operation by providing a wide range of processor speeds in response to workload and thermal issues.

The Pentium Extreme Edition is a high-end version of the Pentium D, but with the following differences:

- HT Technology is supported, enabling each core to simulate two processor cores for even better performance with multithreaded applications.
- Enhanced Intel Speed Step Technology is not supported.
- It includes unlocked clock multipliers, enabling easy overclocking.

Table 3.56 compares the features of the various Pentium D and Pentium Extreme Edition processors.

Max. Power	SSE	HT	64-bit	NX	EIST	VT	Socket
95W	SSE3	—	yes	yes	—	—	LGA775
95W	SSE3	—	yes	—	—	—	LGA775
95W	SSE3	—	yes	yes	yes	—	LGA775
95W	SSE3	—	yes	yes	yes	yes	LGA775
130W	SSE3	—	yes	—	yes	—	LGA775
95W	SSE3	—	yes	yes	yes	—	LGA775
95W	SSE3	—	yes	yes	yes	yes	LGA775
130W	SSE3	—	yes	—	yes	—	LGA775
95W	SSE3	—	yes	yes	yes	—	LGA775
95/130W*	SSE3	—	yes	yes	yes	yes	LGA775
130W	SSE3	yes	yes	yes	—	—	LGA775
95W	SSE3	—	yes	yes	yes	—	LGA775
95/130W*	SSE3	—	yes	yes	yes	yes	LGA775
130W	SSE3	yes	yes	yes	—	yes	LGA775
95/130W*	SSE3	—	yes	yes	yes	yes	LGA775
130W	SSE3	yes	yes	yes	—	yes	LGA775

Intel Core 2

During production of the Pentium 4, Intel realized that the high power consumption of the NetBurst architecture was becoming a serious problem. As the clock speeds increased, so did the power consumption. At the heart of the problem was the 31-stage deep internal pipeline, which made the processor fast but much less efficient. To continue evolving processors with faster versions featuring multiple cores, a solution was needed to increase efficency and reduce power consumption dramatically. Fortunately Intel had the perfect solution in its mobile processors, already regarded as the most efficient PC processors in the world. Starting with the Pentium M, Intel's mobile processors used a completely different internal architecture from its desktop processors such as the Pentium 4. In fact the Pentium M mobile processor was originally based on the Pentium III! To create a powerful new desktop processor, Intel started with the highly efficient mobile processors and then added several new features and technologies to increase performance. These new processors were designed from the outset to be multicore chips, with two or more cores per physical chip. The end result of this development was the Core 2 processor family, which was released on July 27, 2006.

The internal architecture for the Core 2 processors is called Core microarchitecture. The highly efficient Core microarchitecture design featured in the Core 2 processor family provides 40 percent better performance and is 40 percent more energy efficient than the previous generation Pentium D processor. It is also interesting to note that the Core 2 Duo processor is Intel's third-generation dual-core processor; the first generation was the Pentium D processor for desktop PCs, and the second generation was the Core Duo processor for mobile PCs.

The naming of both the Core 2 processor and the Core microarchitecture is somewhat confusing because the Core name was also used on the Core Solo and Core Duo processors, which were the successors to the Pentium M in Intel's mobile processor family. What is strange is that the Core Solo/Duo do *not* incorporate Intel's Core microarchitecture, and although they served as a developmental starting point for the Core 2, the Core Solo/Duo are internally different and not in the same family as the Core 2 processors. Because the Core Solo and Core Duo processors are considered mobile processors only, they are not covered here.

The Core 2 was initially released as a dual-core processor, but since then quad-core versions have also been released. The dual-core versions of the Core 2 processors have 291 million transistors, whereas the quad-core versions have double that, or 582 million. They include 1 or 2MB of L2 cache per core, with up to 8MB total L2 in the quad-core versions. Initially all were built on 300mm wafers using a 65nm process, but since then 45nm versions have been released as well.

The highlights of the Core microarchitecture include

- **Wide Dynamic Execution**—Each internal execution core is 33 percent wider than in previous generations, allowing each core to execute up to four full instructions simultaneously. Further efficiencies are achieved through more accurate branch prediction, deeper instruction buffers for greater execution flexibility, and additional features to reduce execution time.

- **Intelligent Power Capability**—An advanced power gating capability that turns on individual processor subsystems only if and when they are needed.

- **Advanced Smart Cache**—A multicore optimized cache that increases the probability that each execution core can access data from a shared L2 cache.

- **Smart Memory Access**—Includes a capability called "memory disambiguation," which increases the efficiency of out-of-order processing by providing the execution cores with the intelligence to speculatively load data for instructions that are about to execute.

- **Advanced Digital Media Boost**—Improves performance when executing Streaming SIMD Extension (SSE) instructions by enabling 128-bit instructions to be executed at a throughput rate of one per clock cycle. This effectively doubles the speed of execution for these instructions as compared to previous generations.

The Core 2 family now includes both dual-core and quad-core processors under three different names:

- **Core 2 Duo**—Standard dual-core processors
- **Core 2 Quad**—Standard quad-core processors
- **Core 2 Extreme**—High end versions of either dual-core or quad-core processors

Figure 3.66 shows a cutaway view of a Core 2 Duo chip, showing the single dual-core die underneath the heat spreader.

Figure 3.66   Core 2 Duo cutaway view.

All Core 2 family processors support 64-bit extensions, as well as SSSE3 (Supplemental SSE3), which adds 32 new SIMD (Single Instruction Multiple Data) instructions to SSE3. They also support Enhanced Intel Speedstep Technology (EIST) and most provide support for hardware Virtualization Technology as well.

The following tables detail the various processors in the Core 2 family.

Table 3.57   Core 2 Family Dual-Core Processors

Processor Model Number	CPU Speed	Bus Speed	L2 Cache	CPU Core	Mfg. Process
Core 2 Duo E4300	1.80GHz	800MHz	2MB	Allendale	65nm
Core 2 Duo E4400	2.00GHz	800MHz	2MB	Allendale	65nm
Core 2 Duo E4500	2.20GHz	800MHz	2MB	Allendale	65nm
Core 2 Duo E6300	1.86GHz	1066MHz	2MB	Conroe	65nm
Core 2 Duo E6300	1.86GHz	1066MHz	2MB	Allendale	65nm
Core 2 Duo E6320	1.86GHz	1066MHz	4MB	Conroe	65nm
Core 2 Duo E6400	2.13GHz	1066MHz	2MB	Conroe	65nm
Core 2 Duo E6400	2.13GHz	1066MHz	2MB	Allendale	65nm
Core 2 Duo E6420	2.13GHz	1066MHz	4MB	Conroe	65nm
Core 2 Duo E6540	2.33GHz	1333MHz	4MB	Conroe	65nm
Core 2 Duo E6550	2.33GHz	1333MHz	4MB	Conroe	65nm
Core 2 Duo E6600	2.40GHz	1066MHz	4MB	Conroe	65nm
Core 2 Duo E6700	2.66GHz	1066MHz	4MB	Conroe	65nm
Core 2 Duo E6750	2.66GHz	1333MHz	4MB	Conroe	65nm
Core 2 Duo E6850	3.00GHz	1333MHz	4MB	Conroe	65nm
Core 2 Extreme X6800	2.93GHz	1066MHz	4MB	Conroe XE	65nm

Table 3.58   Core 2 Family Quad-Core Processors

Processor Model Number	CPU Speed	Bus Speed	L2 Cache	CPU Core	Mfg. Process
Core 2 Quad Q6600	2.40GHz	1066MHz	8MB	Kentsfield	65nm
Core 2 Quad Q6700	2.66GHz	1066MHz	8MB	Kentsfield	65nm
Core 2 Extreme QX6700	2.66GHz	1066MHz	8MB	Kentsfield XE	65nm
Core 2 Extreme QX6800	2.93GHz	1066MHz	8MB	Kentsfield XE	65nm
Core 2 Extreme QX6850	3.00GHz	1333MHz	8MB	Kentsfield XE	65nm

*Note: Max. power depends on the stepping (internal revision)

EE = Extreme Edition

SSE = Streaming SIMD Instructions (MMX)

HT = Hyper-Threading Technology

NX = Execute Disable Bit

EIST = Enhanced Intel SpeedStep Technology

VT = Virtualization Technology

Max. Power	SSE	64-bit	NX	EIST	VT	Socket
65W	SSSE3	yes	yes	yes	—	LGA775
65W	SSSE3	yes	yes	yes	—	LGA775
65W	SSSE3	yes	yes	yes	—	LGA775
65W	SSSE3	yes	yes	yes	yes	LGA775
65W	SSSE3	yes	yes	yes	yes	LGA775
65W	SSSE3	yes	yes	yes	yes	LGA775
65W	SSSE3	yes	yes	yes	yes	LGA775
65W	SSSE3	yes	yes	yes	yes	LGA775
65W	SSSE3	yes	yes	yes	yes	LGA775
65W	SSSE3	yes	yes	yes	yes	LGA775
65W	SSSE3	yes	yes	yes	yes	LGA775
65W	SSSE3	yes	yes	yes	yes	LGA775
65W	SSSE3	yes	yes	yes	yes	LGA775
65W	SSSE3	yes	yes	yes	yes	LGA775
65W	SSSE3	yes	yes	yes	yes	LGA775
75W	SSSE3	yes	yes	yes	yes	LGA775

Max. Power	SSE	64-bit	NX	EIST	VT	Socket
95/105W*	SSSE3	yes	yes	yes	yes	LGA775
95W	SSSE3	yes	yes	yes	yes	LGA775
130W	SSSE3	yes	yes	yes	yes	LGA775
130W	SSSE3	yes	yes	yes	yes	LGA775
130W	SSSE3	yes	yes	yes	yes	LGA775

AMD Athlon 64 X2 and 64 FX

The 64-bit Athlon 64 processors were designed with multi-core updates in mind from the very beginning. The desktop Athlon 64 X2 was introduced in May 2005. The Athlon 64 X2 uses several core designs, with different options and features.

Major features of the Athlon 64 X2 include

- 65nm or 90nm manufacturing process
- Actual clock speeds of 1.9GHz-3.0GHz
- Socket 939, AM2 or 1207FX form factors
- 1GHz HyperTransport interconnect (4GBps bandwidth)

The design of these processors has always included room for the second processor core along with a crossbar memory controller to enable the processor cores to directly communicate with each other without using the North Bridge, as with Intel's initial dual-core processors. Figure 3.67 illustrates the internal design of the Athlon 64 X2.

The result is that most existing systems based on Socket 939 Athlon 64 can be upgraded to a dual-core processor without a motherboard swap. As long as the motherboard supports the processor and a dual-core BIOS upgrade is available from the motherboard or system vendor, the upgrade is possible.

Another benefit of AMD's approach is the lack of a performance or thermal penalty in moving to a dual-core design. Because the Athlon 64 design included provisions for a dual-core upgrade from the beginning, the thermal impact of the second core is minimal, even though the dual-core processors run at the same speeds as their single-core predecessors.

Table 3.59   Athlon 64 X2 Processor Information

Processor Model Number	CPU Speed	Bus Speed	L2 Cache	CPU Core	Mfg. Process
Athlon 64 X2 3600+	1.90GHz	1GHz	1MB	Windsor	90nm
Athlon 64 X2 3600+	2.00GHz	1GHz	512KB	Manchester	90nm
Athlon 64 X2 3600+	2.00GHz	1GHz	512KB	Windsor	90nm
Athlon 64 X2 3800+	2.00GHz	1GHz	1MB	Manchester	90nm
Athlon 64 X2 3800+	2.00GHz	1GHz	1MB	Toledo	90nm
Athlon 64 X2 3800+	2.00GHz	1GHz	1MB	Windsor	90nm
Athlon 64 X2 3800+	2.00GHz	1GHz	1MB	Windsor	90nm
Athlon 64 X2 3800+	2.00GHz	1GHz	1MB	Windsor	90nm
Athlon 64 X2 3800+	2.00GHz	1GHz	1MB	Windsor	90nm
Athlon 64 X2 4000+	2.00GHz	1GHz	2MB	Windsor	90nm
Athlon 64 X2 4000+	2.00GHz	1GHz	2MB	Windsor	90nm
Athlon 64 X2 4000+	2.10GHz	1GHz	1MB	Windsor	90nm
Athlon 64 X2 4200+	2.20GHz	1GHz	1MB	Manchester	90nm
Athlon 64 X2 4200+	2.20GHz	1GHz	1MB	Toledo	90nm
Athlon 64 X2 4200+	2.20GHz	1GHz	1MB	Windsor	90nm
Athlon 64 X2 4200+	2.20GHz	1GHz	1MB	Windsor	90nm
Athlon 64 X2 4400+	2.20GHz	1GHz	2MB	Toledo	90nm

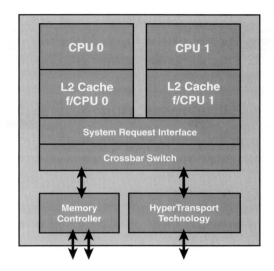

Figure 3.67 The Athlon 64 X2 uses the integrated crossbar memory controller present from the beginning of the Athlon 64 processor design to enable the processor cores to communicate with each other.

Tables 3.59 through 3.61 provide a detailed comparison of the various dual-core Athlon 64 X2, Athlon X2, and Athlon 64 FX processors.

Max. Power	SSE	64-bit	NX	Cool'n'Quiet	VT	Socket
65W	SSE3	X	X	X	X	AM2
110W	SSE3	X	X	X	—	939
65W	SSE3	X	X	X	X	AM2
89W	SSE3	X	X	X	—	939
89W	SSE3	X	X	X	—	939
89W	SSE3	X	X	X	X	AM2
65W	SSE3	X	X	X	X	AM2
65W	SSE3	X	X	X	X	AM2
35W	SSE3	X	X	X	X	AM2
89W	SSE3	X	X	X	X	AM2
65W	SSE3	X	X	X	X	AM2
65W	SSE3	X	X	X	X	AM2
89W	SSE3	X	X	X	—	939
89W	SSE3	X	X	X	—	939
89W	SSE3	X	X	X	X	AM2
65W	SSE3	X	X	X	X	AM2
110W	SSE3	X	X	X	—	939

Table 3.59   Continued

Processor Model Number	CPU Speed	Bus Speed	L2 Cache	CPU Core	Mfg. Process
Athlon 64 X2 4400+	2.20GHz	1GHz	2MB	Toledo	90nm
Athlon 64 X2 4400+	2.20GHz	1GHz	2MB	Windsor	90nm
Athlon 64 X2 4400+	2.20GHz	1GHz	2MB	Windsor	90nm
Athlon 64 X2 4400+	2.30GHz	1GHz	1MB	Windsor	90nm
Athlon 64 X2 4600+	2.40GHz	1GHz	1MB	Manchester	90nm
Athlon 64 X2 4600+	2.40GHz	1GHz	1MB	Toledo	90nm
Athlon 64 X2 4600+	2.40GHz	1GHz	1MB	Windsor	90nm
Athlon 64 X2 4600+	2.40GHz	1GHz	1MB	Windsor	90nm
Athlon 64 X2 4600+	2.40GHz	1GHz	1MB	Windsor	90nm
Athlon 64 X2 4800+	2.40GHz	1GHz	2MB	Toledo	90nm
Athlon 64 X2 4800+	2.40GHz	1GHz	2MB	Windsor	90nm
Athlon 64 X2 4800+	2.40GHz	1GHz	2MB	Windsor	90nm
Athlon 64 X2 4800+	2.50GHz	1GHz	1MB	Windsor	90nm
Athlon 64 X2 5000+	2.60GHz	1GHz	1MB	Windsor	90nm
Athlon 64 X2 5000+	2.60GHz	1GHz	1MB	Windsor	90nm
Athlon 64 X2 5000+	2.60GHz	1GHz	1MB	Windsor	90nm
Athlon 64 X2 5200+	2.60GHz	1GHz	2MB	Windsor	90nm
Athlon 64 X2 5200+	2.60GHz	1GHz	2MB	Windsor	90nm
Athlon 64 X2 5200+	2.70GHz	1GHz	1MB	Windsor	90nm
Athlon 64 X2 5400+	2.80GHz	1GHz	1MB	Windsor	90nm
Athlon 64 X2 5600+	2.80GHz	1GHz	2MB	Windsor	90nm
Athlon 64 X2 6000+	3.00GHz	1GHz	2MB	Windsor	90nm

Table 3.60   Athlon X2 Processor Information

Processor Model Number	CPU Speed	Bus Speed	L2 Cache	CPU Core	Mfg. Process
Athlon X2 BE-2300	1.90GHz	1GHz	1MB	Brisbane	65nm
Athlon X2 BE-2350	2.10GHz	1GHz	1MB	Brisbane	65nm

Table 3.61   Athlon 64 FX Dual-Core Processor Information

Processor Model Number	CPU Speed	Bus Speed	L2 Cache	CPU Core	Mfg. Process
Athlon 64 FX-60	2.60GHz	1GHz	2MB	Toledo	90nm
Athlon 64 FX-62	2.80GHz	1GHz	2MB	Windsor	90nm
Athlon 64 FX-70	2.60GHz	1GHz	2MB	Windsor	90nm
Athlon 64 FX-72	2.80GHz	1GHz	2MB	Windsor	90nm
Athlon 64 FX-74	3.00GHz	1GHz	2MB	Windsor	90nm

SSE = Streaming SIMD Instructions (MMX)   *Cool'n'Quiet = Power Saving Technology*
NX = Execute Disable Bit   *VT = Virtualization Technology*

Max. Power	SSE	64-bit	NX	Cool'n'Quiet	VT	Socket
89W	SSE3	X	X	X	—	939
89W	SSE3	X	X	X	X	AM2
65W	SSE3	X	X	X	X	AM2
65W	SSE3	X	X	X	X	AM2
110W	SSE3	X	X	X	—	939
110W	SSE3	X	X	X	—	939
89W	SSE3	X	X	X	X	AM2
65W	SSE3	X	X	X	X	AM2
65W	SSE3	X	X	X	X	AM2
110W	SSE3	X	X	X	—	939
89W	SSE3	X	X	X	X	AM2
65W	SSE3	X	X	X	X	AM2
65W	SSE3	X	X	X	X	AM2
89W	SSE3	X	X	X	X	AM2
65W	SSE3	X	X	X	X	AM2
65W	SSE3	X	X	X	X	AM2
89W	SSE3	X	X	X	X	AM2
65W	SSE3	X	X	X	X	AM2
65W	SSE3	X	X	X	X	AM2
89W	SSE3	X	X	X	X	AM2
89W	SSE3	X	X	X	X	AM2
125W	SSE3	X	X	X	X	AM2

Max. Power	SSE	64-bit	NX	Cool'n'Quiet	VT	Socket
45W	SSE3	X	X	X	X	AM2
45W	SSE3	X	X	X	X	AM2

Max. Power	SSE	64-bit	NX	Cool'n'Quiet	VT	Socket
110W	SSE3	X	X	X	—	939
125W	SSE3	X	X	X	X	AM2
125W	SSE3	X	X	X	X	1207FX
125W	SSE3	X	X	X	X	1207FX
125W	SSE3	X	X	X	X	1207FX

The ability to upgrade most existing Socket 939 Athlon 64 systems with a dual-core processor opens the way for many users to move into dual-core computing with minimal difficulty.

Processor Upgrades

Since the 486, processor upgrades have been relatively easy for most systems. With the 486 and later processors, Intel designed in the capability to upgrade by designing standard sockets that would take a variety of processors. This trend has continued to the present, with most motherboards being designed to handle a range of processors in the same family.

To maximize your motherboard, you can almost always upgrade to the fastest processor your particular board will support. Because of the varieties of processor sockets and slots—not to mention voltages, speeds, and other potential areas of incompatibility—you should consult with your motherboard manufacturer to see whether a higher-speed processor will work in your board. Usually, that can be determined by the type of socket or slot on the motherboard, but other things such as the voltage regulator and BIOS can be deciding factors as well.

For example, if your motherboard supports Socket LGA775, you might be able to upgrade from a single core Pentium 4 family processor to a dual- or quad-core processor in the Core 2 family, because they all use the same socket. Before purchasing a new CPU, you should verify that the motherboard has proper bus speed, voltage settings, and ROM BIOS support for the new chip. Visit the motherboard or system manufacturer's website to obtain the most up-to-date processor compatibility information and to download BIOS updates that might be necessary.

Tip

If you are trying to upgrade the processor in a pre-assembled or store-bought system, you might have very few processor upgrade options using the BIOS provided by the system vendor. If you can figure out who made the motherboard (and it is not a proprietary unit) then you might be able to contact the motherboard manufacturer for a more updated BIOS that supports more processors.

If you are unable to install a faster processor directly into your system, a variety of third-party solutions are available, including adapters that can help first-generation Socket 423 Pentium 4 motherboards use Socket 478 processors, faster Socket 370 processors for older Slot 1 motherboards, and so on. Rather than purchasing processors and adapters separately, I usually recommend you purchase them together in a module from companies such as PowerLeap.

Upgrading the processor can, in some cases, double the performance of a system. However, if you already have the fastest processor that will fit a particular socket, you need to consider other alternatives. In that case, you really should look into a complete motherboard change, which would let you upgrade to one of the latest processors at the same time. If your chassis design is not proprietary and your system uses an industry-standard ATX motherboard design, I normally recommend changing the motherboard and processor together rather than trying to find an upgrade processor that will work with your existing board.

OverDrive Processors

Intel at one time offered special OverDrive processors for upgrading systems. Often these were repackaged versions of the standard processors, sometimes including necessary voltage regulators and fans. Unfortunately, they frequently were overpriced, even when compared against purchasing a complete new motherboard and processor. They have all been withdrawn, and Intel has not announced any new versions. I don't recommend the OverDrive processors or third-party upgrades unless the deal is too good to pass up and you need to keep a very old system operating.

Processor Benchmarks

People love to know how fast (or slow) their computers are. We have always been interested in speed; it is human nature. To help us with this quest, various benchmark test programs can be used to measure different aspects of processor and system performance. Although no single numerical measurement can completely describe the performance of a complex device such as a processor or a complete PC, benchmarks can be useful tools for comparing different components and systems.

However, the only truly accurate way to measure your system's performance is to test the system using the actual software applications you use. Although you think you might be testing one component of a system, often other parts of the system can have an effect. It is inaccurate to compare systems with different processors, for example, if they also have different amounts or types of memory, different hard disks, video cards, and so on. All these things and more will skew the test results.

Benchmarks can typically be divided into two types: component or system tests. *Component* benchmarks measure the performance of specific parts of a computer system, such as a processor, hard disk, video card, or optical drive, whereas *system* benchmarks typically measure the performance of the entire computer system running a given application or test suite.

Benchmarks are, at most, only one kind of information you can use during the upgrading or purchasing process. You are best served by testing the system using your own set of software operating systems and applications and in the configuration you will be running.

Several companies specialize in benchmark tests and software. Table 3.62 lists the companies and the benchmarks they are known for.

Table 3.62   Companies That Specialize in Benchmark Tests and Software

Company	Benchmarks Published	Benchmark Type
Futuremark (formerly MadOnion.com)	SysMark PCMark Pro 3DMark	System System 3D graphics
Business Applications Performance Corporation (BAPCo)	MobileMark	Notebook battery life
Standard Performance	SPECint	Processor Integer
Evaluation Corporation	SPECfp	Processor floating-point
SiSoftware	Sandra	System, memory, processor, multimedia

Processor Troubleshooting Techniques

Processors are normally very reliable. Most PC problems are with other devices, but if you suspect the processor, there are some steps you can take to troubleshoot it. The easiest thing to do is to replace the microprocessor with a known-good spare. If the problem goes away, the original processor is defective. If the problem persists, the problem is likely elsewhere.

Table 3.63 provides a general troubleshooting checklist for processor-related PC problems.

Table 3.63   Troubleshooting Processor-Related Problems

Problem Identification	Possible Cause	Resolution
System is dead, no cursor, no beeps, no fan.	Power cord failure.	Plug in or replace power cord. Power cords can fail even though they look fine.
	Power supply failure.	Replace the power supply. Use a known-good spare for testing.
	Motherboard failure.	Replace motherboard. Use a known-good spare for testing.
	Memory failure.	Remove all memory except 1 bank and retest. If the system still won't boot, replace bank 1.
System is dead, no beeps, or locks up before POST begins.	All components either not installed or incorrectly installed.	Check all peripherals, especially memory and graphics adapter. Reseat all boards and socketed components.
System beeps on startup, fan is running, no cursor on screen.	Improperly seated or failing graphics adapter.	Reseat or replace graphics adapter. Use known-good spare for testing.
System powers up, fan is running, no beep or cursor.	Processor not properly installed.	Reseat or remove/reinstall processor and heatsink.
Locks up during or shortly after POST.	Poor heat dissipation.	Check CPU heatsink/fan; replace if necessary, use one with higher capacity.
	Improper voltage settings.	Set motherboard for proper core processor voltage.
	Wrong motherboard bus speed.	Set motherboard for proper speed.
	Wrong CPU clock multiplier.	Jumper motherboard for proper clock multiplier.
Improper CPU identification during POST.	Old BIOS.	Update BIOS from manufacturer.
	Board not configured properly.	Check manual and jumper board accordingly to proper bus and multiplier settings.
System won't start after new processor is installed.	Processor not properly installed.	Reseat or remove/reinstall processor and heatsink.
	BIOS doesn't support new processor.	Update BIOS from system or motherboard manufacturer.
	Motherboard can't use new processor.	Verify motherboard support.
Operating system will not boot.	Poor heat dissipation.	Check CPU fan (replace if necessary); it might need a higher-capacity heatsink or heatsink/fan on the North Bridge chip.
	Improper voltage settings.	Jumper motherboard for proper core voltage.
	Wrong motherboard bus speed.	Jumper motherboard for proper speed.
	Wrong CPU clock multiplier.	Jumper motherboard for proper clock multiplier.
	Applications will not install or run.	Improper drivers or incompatible hardware; update drivers and check for compatibility issues.
System appears to work, but no video is displayed.	Monitor turned off or failed.	Check monitor and power to monitor. Replace with known-good spare for testing.

If during the POST the processor is not identified correctly, your motherboard settings might be incorrect or your BIOS might need to be updated. Check that the motherboard is jumpered or configured correctly for your processor, and make sure you have the latest BIOS for your motherboard.

If the system seems to run erratically after it warms up, try setting the processor to a lower speed setting. If the problem goes away, the processor might be defective or overclocked.

Many hardware problems are really software problems in disguise. Be sure you have the latest BIOS for your motherboard, as well as the latest drivers for all your peripherals. Also, it helps to use the latest version of your given operating system because there usually will be fewer problems.

Motherboards and Buses

Motherboard Form Factors

Without a doubt, the most important component in a PC system is the main board or mother-board. Virtually every internal component in a PC connects to the motherboard, and its features largely determine what your computer is capable of, not to mention its overall performance. Although I prefer the term *motherboard*, other terms such as *main board*, *system board*, and *planar* are interchangeable. This chapter examines the various types of motherboards available and those components typically contained on the motherboard and motherboard interface connectors.

Several common form factors are used for PC motherboards. The *form factor* refers to the physical dimensions (size and shape) as well as certain connector, screw hole, and other positions that dictate into which type of case the board will fit. Some are true standards (meaning that all boards with that form factor are interchangeable), whereas others are not standardized enough to allow for interchangeability. Unfortunately, these nonstandard form factors preclude any easy upgrade or inexpensive replacement, which generally means they should be avoided. The more commonly known PC motherboard form factors include the following:

Obsolete Form Factors

- Baby-AT
- Full-size AT
- LPX (semiproprietary)
- WTX (no longer in production)
- ITX (FlexATX variation, never produced)

Modern Form Factors

- BTX
- microBTX
- picoBTX

- ATX
- microATX
- flexATX
- DTX
- Mini-ITX (FlexATX variation)
- NLX

All Others

- Semi or fully proprietary designs (certain Compaq, Dell, Hewlett-Packard, notebook/portable systems, and so on)

Motherboards have evolved over the years from the original Baby-AT form factor boards used in the original IBM PC and XT to the current ATX and BTX boards used in most full-size desktop and tower systems. ATX has a number of variants, including microATX (which is a smaller version of the ATX form factor used in the smaller systems) and FlexATX (an even smaller version for the lowest-cost home PCs and some small-form-factor corporate PCs). The BTX form factor relocates major components to improve system cooling and incorporates a thermal module. BTX also has smaller microBTX and picoBTX variations. Other small form factors are available including DTX and Mini-ITX. NLX is designed for corporate desktop-type systems but has largely been replaced by FlexAXT; WTX was designed for workstations and medium-duty servers, but never became popular. Table 4.1 shows the modern industry-standard form factors and their recommended uses.

Table 4.1   Common Industry-Standard Motherboard Form Factors

Form Factor	Use	Max. Slots
BTX	Tower and desktop systems; popular in high-end major OEM systems starting in 2007.	7
microBTX	Smaller version of BTX; popular in mid-range major OEM systems; fits microBTX or BTX chassis.	4
picoBTX	Smallest version of BTX; used in low-end small form factor, entertainment, or appliance systems from major OEMs; fits the picoBTX, microBTX, or BTX chassis.	1
ATX	Standard tower and desktop systems; most common form factor from mid-1996 through the present; supports high-end systems.	7
Mini-ATX	Slightly smaller version of ATX that fits the ATX chassis; many ATX motherboards are sold as Mini-ATX motherboards.	6
microATX	Smaller version of ATX; used in mid-range systems; fits microATX or ATX chassis.	4
DTX	Smaller version of microATX; used in small form factor, entertainment, or appliance systems; fits DTX, microATX or ATX chassis.	2
FlexATX	Smaller version of microATX; used in low-end small form factor, entertainment, or appliance systems; fits FlexATX, microATX, or ATX chassis.	3
Mini-DTX	Smaller version of FlexATX; used in low-end small form factor, entertainment, or appliance systems; fits DTX, FlexATX, microATX, or ATX chassis.	2
Mini-ITX	Minimum-size FlexATX version; used in set-top boxes and compact/small form factor systems; highly integrated with one PCI expansion slot; fits in the Mini-ITX, FlexATX, microATX, or ATX chassis.	1
NLX	Corporate slim desktop or mini-tower systems; fast and easy serviceability; slots on riser card; largely replaced in recent systems by microATX, FlexATX, and Mini-ITX designs.	Varies

Although the Baby-AT, Full-size AT, and LPX boards were once popular, they have been replaced by more modern and interchangeable form factors. The modern form factors are true standards that provide improved interchangeability within each type. This means one brand of ATX boards can interchange with other brand ATX boards, BTX with other BTX, and so on. The additional features found on these boards as compared to the obsolete form factors, combined with true interchangeability, has made the migration to these newer form factors quick and easy. Today I recommend purchasing only systems with one of the modern industry-standard form factors. Each of these form factors, however, is discussed in more detail in the following sections.

Anything that does not fit into one of the industry-standard form factors should be considered proprietary. Unless there are special circumstances, I do not recommend purchasing systems with proprietary board designs. They will be virtually impossible to upgrade and very expensive to repair later because the motherboard, case, and often power supply will not be interchangeable with other models. I call proprietary form factor systems "disposable" PCs because that's what you must normally do with them when they are too slow or need repair out of warranty.

Caution

"Disposable" PCs might be more common than ever. Some estimate that as much as 60% of all PCs sold today are disposable models, not so much because of the motherboards used, but because of the tiny power supplies and cramped micro-tower cases that are favored on most retail-market PCs today. Although low-cost PCs using small chassis and power supplies are theoretically more upgradeable than past disposable type systems, you'll still hit the wall over time if you need more than three expansion slots or want to use more than two or three internal drives. Because mini-tower systems are so cramped and limited, I consider them to be almost as disposable as the LPX systems they have largely replaced.

You also need to watch out for systems that only appear to meet industry standards, such as certain Dell computer models built from 1996 to the present—especially the XPS line of systems. These computers often use rewired versions of the ATX power supply (or even some that are completely nonstandard in size and shape) and modified motherboard power connectors, which makes both components completely incompatible with standard motherboards and power supplies. In some of the systems, the power supply has a completely proprietary shape as well and the motherboards are not fully standard ATX either. If you want to upgrade the power supply, you must use a special Dell-compatible power supply. And if you want to upgrade the motherboard (assuming you can find one that fits), you must buy a standard power supply to match. The best alternative is to replace the motherboard, power supply, and possibly the case with industry-standard components simultaneously. For more details about how to determine whether your Dell computer uses nonstandard power connectors, see Chapter 19, "Power Supplies."

If you want to have a truly upgradeable system, insist on systems that use ATX or BTX motherboards in a mid-tower or larger case with at least five drive bays.

PC and XT

The first popular PC motherboard was, of course, the original IBM PC released in August 1981. Figure 4.1 shows how this board looked. IBM followed the PC with the XT motherboard in March 1983, which had the same size and shape as the PC board but had eight slots instead of five. Both the IBM PC and XT motherboards were 9"×13" in size. Also, the slots were spaced 0.8" apart in the XT instead of 1" apart as in the PC (see Figure 4.2). The XT also eliminated the little-used cassette port in the back, which was supposed to be used to save BASIC programs on cassette tape instead of the much more expensive (at the time) floppy drive.

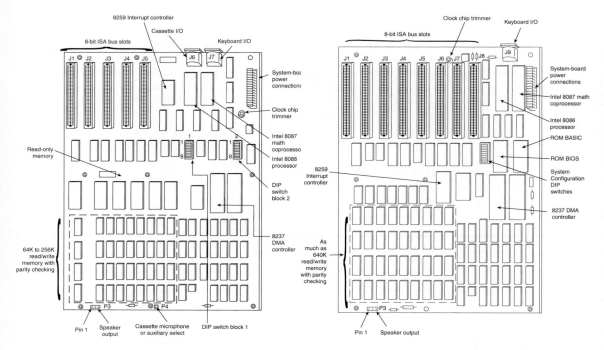

Figure 4.1   IBM PC motherboard (circa 1981).   **Figure 4.2**   IBM PC-XT motherboard (circa 1983).

The minor differences in the slot positions and the deleted cassette connector on the back required a minor redesign of the case. In essence, the XT was a mildly enhanced PC, with a motherboard that was the same overall size and shape, used the same processor, and came in a case that was identical except for slot bracketry and the lack of a hole for the cassette port. Eventually, the XT motherboard design became very popular, and many other PC motherboard manufacturers of the day copied IBM's XT design and produced similar boards.

Full-Size AT

The full-size AT motherboard form factor matches the original IBM AT motherboard design. This allows for a very large board of up to 12" wide by 13.8" deep. The full-size AT board first debuted in August 1984, when IBM introduced the Personal Computer AT (advanced technology). To accommodate the 16-bit 286 processor and all the necessary support components at the time, IBM needed more room than the original PC/XT-sized boards could provide. So for the AT, IBM increased the size of the motherboard but retained the same screw hole and connector positions of the XT design. To accomplish this, IBM essentially started with a PC/XT-sized board and extended it in two directions (see Figure 4.3).

A little more than a year after being introduced, the appearance of chipsets and other circuit consolidation allowed the same motherboard functionality to be built using fewer chips, so the board was redesigned to make it slightly smaller. Then, it was redesigned again as IBM shrank the board down to XT-size in a system it called the XT-286 (introduced in September 1986). The XT-286 board was virtually identical in size and shape to the original XT, a form factor which would later be known as *Baby-AT*.

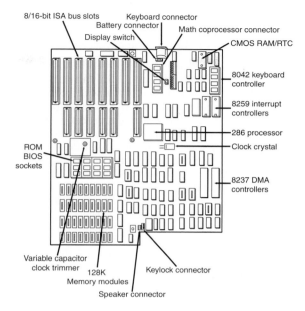

Figure 4.3   IBM AT motherboard (circa 1984).

The keyboard connector and slot connectors in the full-size AT boards still conformed to the same specific placement requirements to fit the holes in the XT cases already in use, but a larger case was still required to fit the larger board. Because of the larger size of the board, a full-size AT motherboard only fits into full-size AT desktop or tower cases. Because these motherboards do not fit into the smaller Baby-AT or mini-tower cases, and because of advances in component miniaturization, they are no longer being produced by most motherboard manufacturers—except in some cases for dual processor server applications.

The important thing to note about the full-size AT systems is that you can always replace a full-size AT motherboard with a Baby-AT (or XT-size) board, but the opposite is not true unless the case is large enough to accommodate the full-size AT design.

Baby-AT

After IBM released the AT in August 1984, component consolidation allowed subsequent systems to be designed using far fewer chips and requiring much less in the way of motherboard real estate. Therefore, all the additional circuits on the 16-bit AT motherboard could fit into boards using the smaller XT form factor.

IBM was one of the first to use the smaller boards when it introduced a system called the XT-286 in September 1986. Unfortunately the "XT" designation in the name of that system caused a lot of confusion, and many people did not want to buy a system they thought used older and slower technology. Sales of the XT-286 were dismal. By this time, other companies had also developed XT-size AT class systems. However, they decided that rather than calling these boards XT-size, which seemed to make people think they were 8-bit designs, they would refer to them as "Baby-AT" designs. The intention was to make people understand that these new boards had AT technology in a smaller form factor and were not souped-up versions of older technology as was seemingly implied by IBM's XT-286 moniker.

Thus, the Baby-AT form factor is essentially the same form factor as the original IBM XT motherboard. The only difference is a slight modification in one of the screw hole positions to fit into an AT-style case. These motherboards also have specific placement of the keyboard and slot connectors to match the holes in the case. Note that virtually all full-size AT and Baby-AT motherboards use the standard 5-pin DIN type connector for the keyboard. Baby-AT motherboards can be used to replace full-size AT motherboards and will fit into several case designs. Because of its flexibility, from 1983 into early 1996, the Baby-AT form factor was the most popular motherboard type. Starting in mid-1996, Baby-AT was replaced by the superior ATX motherboard design, which is not directly interchangeable. Most systems sold since 1996 have used the improved ATX, microATX, or NLX design. Baby-AT motherboards, power supplies, and cases are almost impossible to come by, even at surplus computer hardware outlets—and in any event, they support outdated processors, memory, and other components that are equally difficult to find. Figure 4.5 shows the onboard features and layout of a late-model Baby-AT motherboard. Older Baby-AT motherboards have the same general layout but lack advanced features, such as USB connectors, DIMM memory sockets, and the AGP slot.

Any case that accepts a full-size AT motherboard will also accept a Baby-AT design. PC motherboards using the Baby-AT design have been manufactured to use virtually any processor from the original 8088 to the Pentium III or Athlon, although the pickings are slim where the newer processors are concerned. As such, systems with Baby-AT motherboards were the original upgradeable systems. Because any Baby-AT motherboard can be replaced with any other Baby-AT motherboard, this is an interchangeable design. Even though the Baby-AT design (shown in Figure 4.4) is now obsolete, ATX carries on its philosophy of interchangeability. Figure 4.5 shows a more modern Baby-AT motherboard, which includes USB compatibility, SIMM and DIMM sockets, and even a supplemental ATX power supply connection.

The easiest way to identify a Baby-AT form factor system without opening it is to look at the rear of the case. In a Baby-AT motherboard, the cards plug directly into the board at a 90° angle; in other words, the slots in the case for the cards are perpendicular to the motherboard. Also, the Baby-AT motherboard has only one visible connector directly attached to the board, which is the keyboard connector. Typically, this connector is the full-size 5-pin DIN type connector, although some Baby-AT systems use the smaller 6-pin mini-DIN connector (sometimes called a *PS/2-type connector*) and might even have a mouse connector. All other connectors are mounted on the case or on card edge brackets and are attached to the motherboard via cables. The keyboard connector is visible through an appropriately placed hole in the case.

▶▶   See "Keyboard/Mouse Interface Connectors," p. 1073.

Baby-AT boards all conform to specific widths and screw hole, slot, and keyboard connector locations, but one thing that can vary is the length of the board. Versions have been built that are smaller than the full 9"×13" size; these are often called mini-AT, micro-AT, or even things such as 2/3-Baby or 1/2-Baby. Even though they might not be the full size, they still bolt directly into the same case as a standard Baby-AT board and can be used as a direct replacement for one.

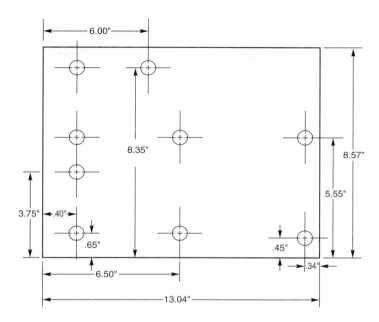

Figure 4.4   Baby-AT motherboard form factor dimensions.

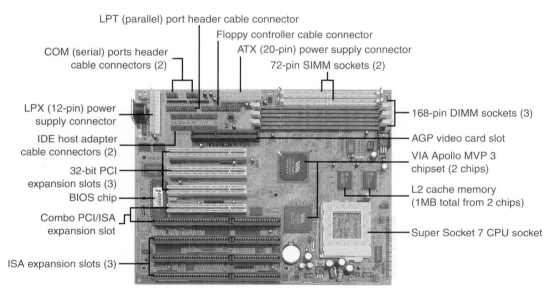

Figure 4.5   A late-model Baby-AT motherboard, the Tyan Trinity 100AT (S1590). *Photo courtesy of Tyan Computer Corporation.*

LPX

The LPX and mini-LPX form factor boards were a semiproprietary design that Western Digital originally developed in 1987 for some of its motherboards. The *LP* in LPX stands for Low Profile, which is so named because these boards incorporate slots that are parallel to the main board, enabling the expansion cards to install sideways. This allows for a slim or low-profile case design and overall a smaller system than the Baby-AT.

Although Western Digital no longer produces PC motherboards, the form factor lives on, and many other motherboard manufacturers have duplicated the general design. Unfortunately, because the specifications were never laid out in exact detail—especially with regard to the bus riser card portion of the design—these boards are termed *semiproprietary* and are not interchangeable between manufacturers. Some vendors, such as IBM and HP, for example, have built LPX systems that use a T-shaped riser card that allows expansion cards to be mounted at the normal 90° angle to the motherboard but still above the motherboard. This lack of standardization means that if you have a system with an LPX board, in most cases you can't replace the motherboard with a different LPX board later. You essentially have a system you can't upgrade or repair by replacing the motherboard with something better. In other words, you have what I call a "disposable PC," something I would not normally recommend that anybody purchase.

Most people were not aware of the semiproprietary nature of the design of these boards, and they were extremely popular in what I call "retail store" PCs from the late 1980s through the late 1990s. This would include primarily Compaq and Packard Bell systems, as well as many others who used this form factor in their lower-cost systems. These boards were most often used in low-profile or Slimline case systems, but were found in tower cases too. These were often lower-cost systems such as those sold at retail electronics superstores. LPX is considered obsolete today.

LPX boards are characterized by several distinctive features (see Figure 4.6). The most noticeable is that the expansion slots are mounted on a bus riser card that plugs into the motherboard. In most designs, expansion cards plug sideways into the riser card. This sideways placement allows for the low-profile case design. Slots are located on one or both sides of the riser card depending on the system and case design. Vendors who use LPX-type motherboards in tower cases sometimes use a T-shaped riser card instead, which puts the expansion slots at the normal right angle to the motherboard but on a raised shelf above the motherboard itself.

Another distinguishing feature of the LPX design is the standard placement of connectors on the back of the board. An LPX board has a row of connectors for video (VGA 15-pin), parallel (25-pin), two serial ports (9-pin each), and mini-DIN PS/2 style mouse and keyboard connectors. All these connectors are mounted across the rear of the motherboard and protrude through a slot in the case. Some LPX motherboards might have additional connectors for other internal ports, such as network or SCSI adapters. Because LPX systems use a high degree of motherboard port integration, many vendors of LPX motherboards, cases, and systems often refer to LPX products as having an "all-in-one" design.

The standard form factor used for LPX and mini-LPX motherboards in many typical low-cost systems is shown in Figure 4.7.

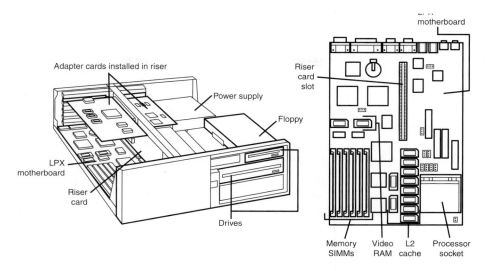

Figure 4.6   Typical LPX system chassis and motherboard.

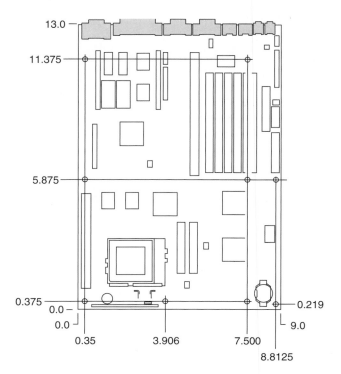

Figure 4.7   LPX motherboard dimensions.

I am often asked, "How can I tell whether a system has an LPX board without opening the cover?" Because of the many variations in riser card design, and because newer motherboards such as NLX also use riser cards, the most reliable way to distinguish an LPX motherboard from other systems is to look at the connector signature (the layout and pattern of connectors on the back of the board). As you can see in Figure 4.8, all LPX motherboards—regardless of variations in riser card shape, size, or location—place all external ports along the rear of the motherboard. By contrast, Baby-AT mother-boards use case-mounted or expansion slot-mounted connectors for serial, parallel, PS/2 mouse, and USB ports, whereas ATX-family and BTX-family motherboards group all external ports together to the left side of the expansion slots.

On an LPX board, the riser is placed in the middle of the motherboard, whereas NLX boards have the riser to the side (the motherboard actually plugs into the riser in NLX).

Figure 4.8 shows two typical examples of the connectors on the back of LPX boards. Note that not all LPX boards have the built-in audio, so those connectors might be missing. Other ports (such as USB) might be missing from what is shown in these diagrams, depending on exactly which options are included on a specific board; however, the general layout will be the same.

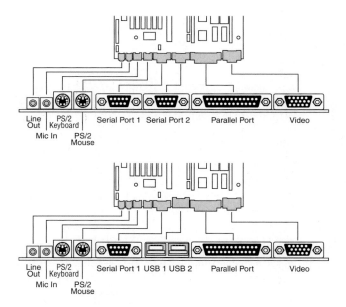

Figure 4.8   LPX motherboard back panel connectors.

The connectors along the rear of the board would interfere with locating bus slots directly on the motherboard, which accounts for why riser cards are used for adding expansion boards.

Although the built-in connectors on the LPX boards were a good idea, unfortunately the LPX design was semiproprietary (not a fully interchangeable standard) and, therefore, not a good choice. Newer motherboard form factors such as ATX, microATX, and NLX have both built-in connectors and use a standard board design. The riser card design of LPX allowed system designers to create a low-profile desktop system, a feature now carried by the much more standardized NLX form factor. In fact, NLX was developed as the modern replacement for LPX.

NLX

NLX is a low-profile form factor designed to replace the nonstandard LPX design used in previous low-profile systems. First introduced in November 1996 by Intel, NLX was a popular form factor in the late 1990s for Slimline corporate desktop systems from vendors such as Compaq, HP, Toshiba, and others. Since 2000, many Slimline systems have used variations on the FlexATX motherboard instead.

NLX is similar in initial appearance to LPX, but with numerous improvements designed to enable full integration of the latest technologies. NLX is basically an improved version of the proprietary LPX design, but, unlike LPX, NLX is fully standardized, which means you should be able to replace one NLX board with another from a different manufacturer—something that was not possible with LPX.

Another limitation of LPX boards is the difficulty in handling the larger physical size of the newer processors and their larger heatsinks, as well as newer bus structures such as AGP for video. The NLX form factor has been designed specifically to address these problems (see Figure 4.9). In fact, NLX provides enough room for some vendors to support dual Slot 1 Pentium III processors in this form factor.

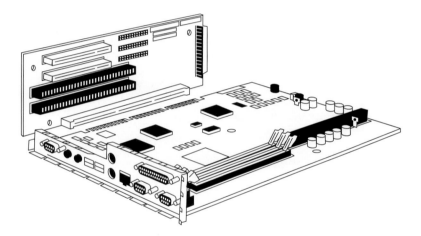

Figure 4.9   NLX motherboard and riser combination.

The main characteristic of an NLX system is that the motherboard plugs into the riser, unlike LPX where the riser plugs into the motherboard. Therefore, the motherboard can be removed from the system without disturbing the riser or any of the expansion cards plugged into it. In addition, the motherboard in a typical NLX system literally has no internal cables or connectors attached to it! All devices that normally plug into the motherboard—such as drive cables, the power supply, the front panel light, switch connectors, and so on—plug into the riser instead (see Figure 4.9). By using the riser card as a connector concentration point, you can remove the lid on an NLX system and literally slide the motherboard out the left side of the system without unplugging a single cable or connector on the inside. This allows for unbelievably quick motherboard changes; in fact, I have swapped motherboards in less than 30 seconds on NLX systems!

As Figure 4.10 shows, by using different sizes and types of riser cards, a system designer can customize the features of a given NLX system.

Such a design was a boon for the corporate market, where ease and swiftness of servicing is a major feature.

Specific advantages of the NLX form factor include

■ **Support for all desktop system processor technologies**—This is especially important because, since the NLX form factor was developed, both AMD and Intel adopted and then abandoned bulkier slot-based processors and returned to more compact socketed processors. NLX can handle both types of processors.

■ **Flexibility in the face of rapidly changing processor technologies**—Backplane-like flexibility has been built into the form by allowing a new motherboard to be easily and quickly installed without tearing your entire system to pieces. But unlike traditional backplane systems, many industry leaders, such as Compaq, Toshiba, and HP, have sold NLX-based systems.

■ **Support for newer technologies than LPX**—This includes Accelerated Graphics Port (AGP) high-performance graphic solutions, Universal Serial Bus (USB), and memory modules in DIMM or RIMM form.

■ **Ease and speed of servicing and repair**—Compared to other industry-standard interchangeable form factors, NLX systems are by far the easiest to work on and allow component swaps or other servicing in the shortest amount of time.

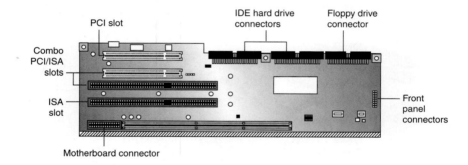

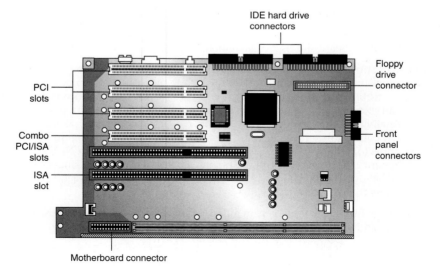

Figure 4.10   Typical NLX riser cards. Although most NLX systems use a low-profile riser card similar to the top riser card, others use a taller riser card to provide more slots for add-on cards.

Figure 4.11 shows the basic NLX system layout. Notice that, similar to ATX, the motherboard is clear of the drive bays and other chassis-mounted components. Also, the motherboard and I/O cards (which, like the LPX form factor, are mounted parallel to the motherboard) can easily be slid into and out of the side of the chassis, leaving the riser card and other cards in place. The processor can be easily accessed and enjoys greater cooling than in a more closed-in layout.

Note the position of the optional AGP slot shown in Figure 4.11. It is mounted on the motherboard itself, not on the riser card as with PCI or ISA slots. This location was necessary because AGP was developed well after the NLX form factor was introduced. Most NLX motherboards use chipset-integrated or motherboard-based video instead of a separate AGP card, but you must remove an AGP card installed in an NLX system before you can remove the motherboard for servicing. Also, the AGP card used in an NLX system must have a different form factor to enable it to clear the rear connector shield at the back of the NLX motherboard (see Figure 4.12).

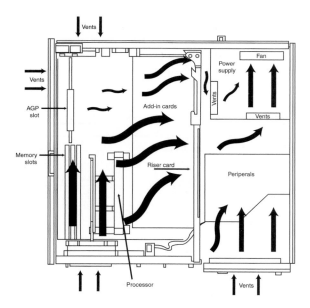

Figure 4.11   NLX system chassis layout and cooling airflow.

The NLX motherboard is specified in three lengths, front to back: 13.6", 11.2", or 10" total (see Figure 4.13). With proper bracketry, the shorter boards can go into a case designed for a longer board.

As with most of the form factors, you can identify NLX via the unique I/O shield or connector area at the back of the board (see Figure 4.14). You only need a quick look at the rear of any given system to determine which type of board is contained within. Figure 4.14 shows the unique stepped design of the NLX I/O connector area. This allows for a row of connectors all along the bottom and has room for double-stacked connectors on one side.

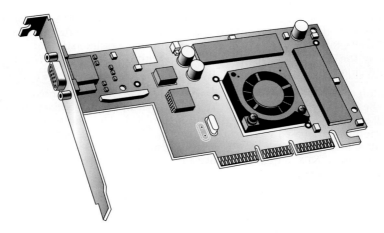

Figure 4.12   An AGP card that can be installed in either a standard ATX/Baby-AT system or an NLX system. This is because of the shape, which leaves room for the NLX motherboard's rear connector shield. *Photo courtesy Elsa AG.*

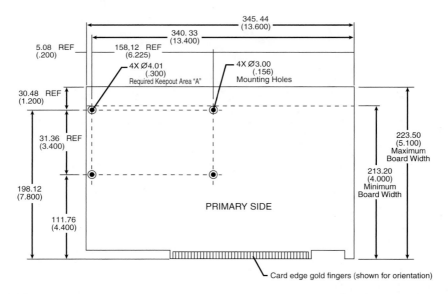

Figure 4.13   NLX form factor. This shows a 13.6"-long NLX board. The NLX specification also allows shorter 11.2" and 10" versions.

As you can see, the NLX form factor has been designed for maximum flexibility and space efficiency. Even extremely long I/O cards will fit easily without getting in the way of other system components—a problem with Baby-AT form factor systems.

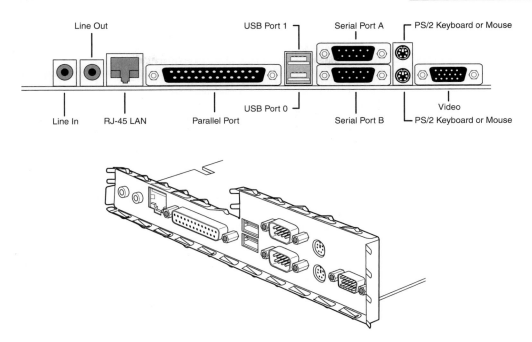

Figure 4.14 Typical NLX motherboard rear connector layout.

Although NLX is a standard form factor—just as the ATX family is—most NLX products have been sold as part of complete systems aimed at the corporate market. Very few aftermarket motherboards have been developed in this form factor. The microATX and FlexATX form factors have largely super-seded NLX in the markets formerly dominated by LPX.

ATX

The ATX form factor was the first of a dramatic evolution in motherboard form factors. ATX is a com-bination of the best features of the Baby-AT and LPX motherboard designs, with many new enhance-ments and features thrown in. The ATX form factor is essentially a Baby-AT motherboard turned sideways in the chassis, along with a modified power supply location and connector. The most impor-tant thing to know initially about the ATX form factor is that it is physically incompatible with either the previous Baby-AT or LPX design. In other words, a different case and power supply are required to match the ATX motherboard. These case and power supply designs have become common and are found in most new systems.

Intel initially released the official ATX specification in July 1995. It was written as an open specifica-tion for the industry. ATX boards didn't hit the market in force until mid-1996, when they rapidly began replacing Baby-AT boards in new systems. The ATX specification was updated to version 2.01 in February 1997, 2.03 in May 2000, 2.1 in June 2002, and 2.2 in February 2004. Intel publishes these detailed specifications so other manufacturers can use the interchangeable ATX design in their sys-tems. The current specifications for ATX and other current motherboard types are available online from the Desktop Form Factors site: www.formfactors.org. ATX is the most popular motherboard form factor for new systems through 2007 and will continue to be popular in the future. An ATX system will be upgradeable for many years to come, exactly like Baby-AT was in the past.

ATX improved on the Baby-AT and LPX motherboard designs in several major areas:

- **Built-in double high external I/O connector panel**—The rear portion of the motherboard includes a stacked I/O connector area that is 6 1/4" wide by 1 3/4" tall. This enables external connectors to be located directly on the board and minimizes the need for cables running from internal connectors to the back of the case as with Baby-AT designs.

- **Single main keyed internal power supply connector**—This is a boon for the average end user who always had to worry about interchanging the Baby-AT power supply connectors and subsequently blowing the motherboard. The ATX specification includes a keyed and shrouded main power connector that is easy to plug in and can't be installed incorrectly. This connector also features pins for supplying 3.3V to the motherboard, so ATX motherboards do not require built-in voltage regulators that are susceptible to failure. The ATX specification was extended to include two additional optional keyed power connectors called the Auxiliary Power connector (3.3V and 5V) and the ATX12V connector for systems that require more power than the original specification would allow. The latest version of the ATX power connector specification uses a 24-pin connector rather than the original 20-pin connector.

▶▶ See "Motherboard Power Connectors," p. 1233.

- **Relocated CPU and memory**—The CPU and memory modules are relocated so they can't interfere with any bus expansion cards and can easily be accessed for upgrade without removing any of the installed bus adapters. The CPU and memory are relocated next to the power supply, which is where the primary system fan is located. Although the improved airflow over the processor helped to eliminate the need for extra-cost CPU fans in older and lower-powered systems, most current ATX systems today require active heatsinks on the processor because of how hot today's CPUs run. There is room for a CPU and a heatsink and fan combination of up to 2.8" in height, as well as more than adequate side clearance provided in that area.

Heatsinks and Boxed Processors

Most systems require cooling in addition to the fan in the power supply—from a secondary case—mounted fan or an active heatsink on the processor with an integral fan. Intel and AMD supply processors with attached high-quality (ball bearing) fans for CPUs sold to smaller vendors. These are so-called "boxed" processors because they are sold in single-unit box quantities instead of cases of 100 or more like the raw CPUs sold to the larger vendors. The included fan heatsink is an excellent form of thermal insurance because most smaller vendors and system self-assemblers lack the engineering knowledge necessary to perform thermal analysis, temperature measurements, and the testing required to select the properly sized passive heatsinks. The only thermal requirement spelled out for the boxed processors is that the temperature of the air entering the active heatsink (usually the same as the system interior ambient temperature) is kept to a specified minimum, usually 38°C (100.4°F) or less (some older processors allow higher inlet temps). By putting a high-quality fan on these "boxed" processors, Intel and AMD can put a warranty on the boxed processors that is independent of the system warranty. Larger vendors have the engineering talent to select the proper passive heatsink, thus reducing the cost of the system as well as increasing reliability. With an OEM non-boxed processor, the warranty is with the system vendor and not the processor manufacturer directly. Heatsink mounting instructions usually are included with a motherboard if non-boxed processors are used.

- **Relocated internal I/O connectors**—The internal I/O connectors for the floppy and hard disk drives are relocated to be near the drive bays and out from under the expansion board slot and drive bay areas. Therefore, internal cables to the drives can be much shorter, and accessing the connectors does not require card or drive removal.

- **Improved cooling**—The CPU and main memory are designed and positioned to improve overall system cooling. This can decrease—but not necessarily eliminate—the need for separate case or CPU cooling fans. Most higher-speed systems still need additional cooling fans for the CPU and chassis. Note that the ATX specification originally specified that the ATX power supply fan blows into the system chassis instead of outward. This reverse flow, or positive pressure design, pressurizes the case and minimizes dust and dirt intrusion. More recently, the ATX specification was revised to allow the more normal standard flow, which negatively pressurizes the case by having the fan blow outward. Because the specification technically allows either type of airflow, and because some overall cooling efficiency is lost with the reverse flow design, most power supply manufacturers provide ATX power supplies with fans that exhaust air from the system, otherwise called a negative pressure design. See Chapter 19 for more detailed information.

- **Lower cost to manufacture**—The ATX specification eliminates the need for the rat's nest of cables to external port connectors found on Baby-AT motherboards, additional CPU or chassis cooling fans, or onboard 3.3V voltage regulators. Instead, ATX allows for shorter internal drive cables and no cables for standard external serial or parallel ports. These all conspire to greatly reduce the cost of the motherboard and the cost of a complete system-including the case and power supply.

Figure 4.15 shows the typical ATX system layout and chassis features, as you would see them looking in with the lid off on a desktop, or sideways in a tower with the side panel removed. Notice how virtually the entire motherboard is clear of the drive bays and how the devices such as CPU, memory, and internal drive connectors are easy to access and do not interfere with the bus slots. Also notice how the processor is positioned near the power supply.

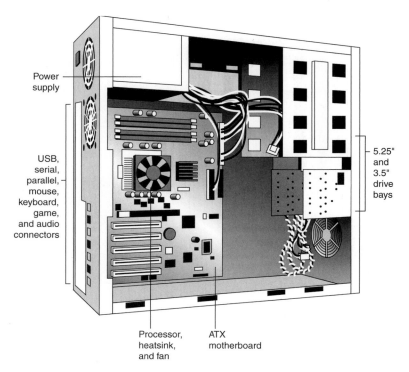

Figure 4.15 Typical ATX system layout.

Note

While most ATX systems mount the power supply near the processor (on top in most tower arrangements), this is not a requirement of the standard. Some systems mount the power supply in other locations (such as on the bottom).

The ATX motherboard shape is basically a Baby-AT design rotated sideways 90°. The expansion slots are now parallel to the shorter side dimension and do not interfere with the CPU, memory, or I/O connector sockets (see Figure 4.16). There are actually two basic sizes of standard ATX boards. In addition to a full-size ATX layout, Intel also specified a MiniATX design, which is a fully compatible subset of ATX that fits into the same case:

- A full-size ATX board is 12" wide × 9.6" deep (305mm×244mm).
- The Mini-ATX board is 11.2"×8.2" (284mm×208mm).

Mini-ATX is not an official standard; instead it is simply referenced as a slightly smaller version of ATX. In fact, all references to Mini-ATX were removed from the ATX 2.1 and later specifications. Two smaller official versions of ATX exist, called microATX and FlexATX. They are discussed in the following sections.

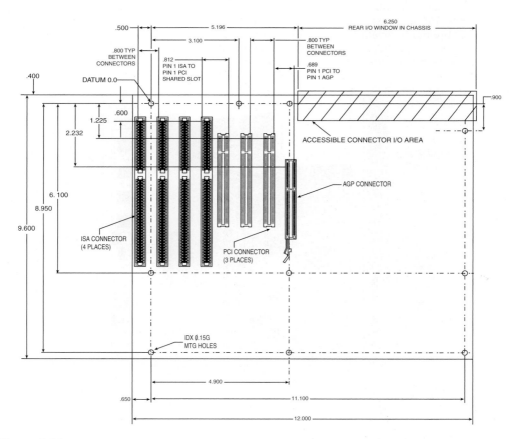

Figure 4.16 ATX specification 2.2 motherboard dimensions. Most recent ATX motherboards no longer use ISA expansion slots.

Although the case holes are similar to the Baby-AT case, cases for Baby-AT and ATX are generally incompatible. The ATX power supply design is identical in physical size to the standard Slimline power supply used with Baby-AT systems; however, they also use different connectors and supply different voltages.

The ATX form factor's design advantages have swept Baby-AT and LPX motherboards off the market. Although other form factors are now available, I have been recommending only ATX (or compatible variations such as microATX or FlexATX) systems for new system purchases since late 1996 and will probably continue to do so for the next several years.

The best way to tell whether your system has an ATX-family motherboard design without removing the lid is to look at the back of the system. Two distinguishing features identify ATX. One is that the expansion boards plug directly into the motherboard. There is usually no riser card as with LPX or NLX (except for certain Slimline systems, such as rack-mounted servers), so the slots are usually perpendicular to the plane of the motherboard. Also, ATX boards have a unique double-high connector area for all the built-in connectors on the motherboard (see Figure 4.17 and Table 4.2). This is found just to the side of the bus slot area and can be used to easily identify an ATX board.

Table 4.2   Built-in Ports Usually Found on ATX Motherboards

Port Description	Connector Type	Connector Color
PS/2 mouse port	6-pin Mini-DIN	Green
PS/2 keyboard port	6-pin Mini-DIN	Purple
USB ports	Dual Stack USB	Black
Parallel port	25-pin D-Submini	Burgundy
Serial port	9-pin D-Submini	Teal
VGA analog video port	15-pin HD D-Submini	Dark blue
MIDI/Game port	15-pin D-Submini	Gold
Audio ports: L/R in, front L/R out, rear L/R out, center/LFE out, Microphone L/R in	1/8" (3.5mm) Mini-Phone	Light blue, lime green, black, black, pink
S-Video TV out	4-pin Mini-DIN	Black
IEEE 1394/FireWire port	6-pin IEEE 1394	Gray
10/100/1000 Ethernet LAN	8-pin RJ-45	Black
Optical S/PDIF audio out	TOSLINK	Black
DVI digital video out (not shown)	DDWG-DVI	White
Digital S/PDIF audio out (not shown)	RCA Jack	Orange
SCSI (not shown)	50/68-pin HD SCSI	Black
Modem (not shown)	4-pin RJ-11	Black
Composite Video out (not shown)	RCA Jack	Yellow

DIN = Deutsches Institut für Normung e.V.
USB = Universal serial bus
VGA = Video graphics array
HD = High density
MIDI = Musical Instrument Digital Interface
L/R = Left and right channel
LFE = Low frequency effects (subwoofer)
S-Video = Super Video
IEEE = Institute of Electrical and Electronics Engineers

LAN = Local area network
RJ = Registered jack
S/PDIF = Sony/Philips Digital Interface
TOSLINK = Toshiba optical link
DVI = Digital visual interface
DDWG = Digital Display Working Group
RCA = Radio Corporation of America
SCSI = Small computer system interface

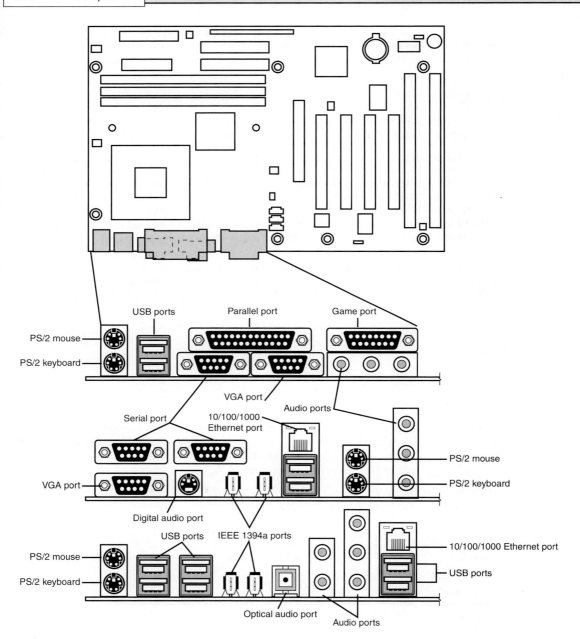

Figure 4.17 ATX motherboard and rear panel connections from systems with onboard sound and video (top and middle), networking and IEEE 1394/FireWire (middle and bottom), and a "legacy-free" system (bottom).

Note

Most ATX motherboards feature connectors with industry-standardized color codes (shown in the previous table). This makes plugging in devices much easier and more foolproof: You merely match up the colors. For example, most keyboards have a cable with a purple plug, whereas most mice have a cable with a green plug. Even though the keyboard and mouse connectors on the motherboard appear the same (both are 6-pin Mini-DIN types), their color-coding matches the plugs on the respective devices. Therefore, to plug them in properly, you merely insert the purple plug into the purple connector and the green plug into the green connector. This saves you from having to bend down to try to decipher small labels on the connectors to ensure you get them right.

The specification and related information about the ATX, Mini-ATX, microATX, FlexATX, or NLX form factor specifications are available from the Form Factors website at www.formfactors.org. The Form Factors site provides form factor specifications and design guides, as well as design considerations for new technologies, information on initiative supporters, vendor products, and a form factor discussion forum.

Note

Some motherboards, especially those used in server systems, come in nonstandard ATX variations collectively called *extended ATX*. This is a term applied to boards that are compatible with ATX but that are deeper. Standard ATX is 12"×9.6" (305mm×244mm), whereas extended ATX boards are up to 12"×13" (305mm×330mm). Because technically no official "extended ATX" standard exists, compatibility problems can exist with boards and chassis claiming to support extended ATX. When purchasing an extended ATX board, be sure it will fit in the chassis you intend to use. Dual Xeon processors fit in a standard ATX-size board, so choose a standard ATX-size board for maximum compatibility with the existing ATX chassis.

ATX Riser

In December 1999, Intel introduced a riser card design modification for ATX motherboards. The design includes the addition of a 22-pin (2×11) connector to one of the PCI slots on the motherboard, along with a two- or three-slot riser card that plugs in. The riser enables two or three PCI cards to be installed, but it does not support AGP.

ATX motherboards typically are found in vertically oriented tower-type cases, but often a horizontal desktop system is desired for a particular application. When ATX boards are installed in desktop cases, PCI cards can be as tall as 4.2", thus requiring a case that is at least 6"–7" tall. For Slimline desktop systems, some manufacturers have used the NLX format, but the more complex design and lower popularity of NLX makes that a more expensive alternative. A low-cost way to use an industry-standard ATX form factor board in a Slimline desktop case is therefore needed. The best long-term solution to this problem is the eventual adoption of a lower-profile PCI card design that is shorter than the current 4.2". The PCI Low-Profile specification was released for engineering review by the Peripheral Component Interconnect Special Interest Group (PCI SIG) on February 14, 2000, and some PCI card products have been produced in this shorter (2.5") form factor. Until Low-Profile PCI becomes widespread, Intel has suggested a riser card approach to enable standard-height PCI cards to be used in Slimline and rack-mount (1U, 2U) systems.

By adding a small 22-pin extension connector to one of the PCI slots on a motherboard, the necessary additional signals for riser card support could be implemented. The current design enables the use of a two- or three-slot riser that is either 2" or 2.8" tall, respectively. To this riser, you can attach full-length cards sideways in the system, and the motherboard can be used with or without the riser. The only caveat is that, if a riser card is installed, the remaining PCI slots on the motherboard can't be used. You can have expansion cards plugged in to only the riser or the motherboard, but not both. Also, the riser card supports only PCI cards—not AGP or ISA cards. A sample ATX board with a riser installed is shown in Figure 4.18.

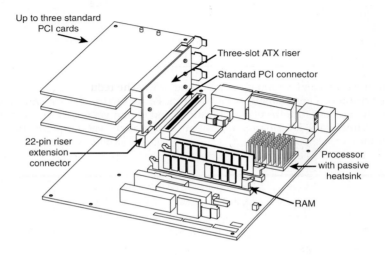

Figure 4.18 A three-slot ATX riser implementation on a microATX motherboard.

The 22-pin extension connector usually is installed in line with PCI slot 6, which is the second one from the right; the slots are usually numbered from right to left (facing the board) starting with 7 as the one closest to the processor. Some boards number the slots from right to left starting with 1; in that case, the extension connector is on PCI slot 2. The pinout of the ATX 22-pin riser extension connector is shown in Figure 4.19.

Signal	Pin	Pin	Signal
Ground	B1	A1	PCI_GNT1#
PCI_ CLK1	B2	A2	Ground
Ground	B3	A3	PCI_GNT2#
PCI_REQ1#	A4	B4	Ground
Ground	A5	B5	PCI_CLK3
PCI_CLK2	A6	B6	RISER_ID1
Ground	A7	B7	Reserved
PCI_REQ2#	A8	B8	RISER_ID2
Ground	A9	B9	NOGO
PC/PCI_DREQ#	A10	B10	+12V
PC/PCI_DGNT#	A11	B11	SER_IRQ

Figure 4.19 An ATX 22-pin riser extension connector pinout.

The PCI connector that is in line with the riser extension connector is just a standard PCI slot; none of the signals are changed.

Systems that use the riser generally are low-profile designs. Therefore, they don't fit normal PCI or AGP cards in the remaining (nonriser-bound) slots. Although the ATX riser standard originally was developed for use with low-end boards—which have integrated video, sound, and network support—some rack-mounted servers are also using the ATX riser because these boards also have most of their required components already integrated.

microATX

microATX is a motherboard form factor Intel originally introduced in December 1997, as an evolution of the ATX form factor for smaller and lower-cost systems. The reduced size as compared to standard ATX allows for a smaller chassis, motherboard, and power supply, thereby reducing the cost of the entire system. The microATX form factor is also backward-compatible with the ATX form factor and can be used in full-size ATX cases. Of course, a microATX case doesn't take a full-size ATX board. This form factor has become popular in the low-cost PC market. Currently, mini-tower chassis systems dominate the low-cost PC market, although their small sizes and cramped interiors severely limit future upgradeability.

The main differences between microATX and standard or Mini-ATX are as follows:

- Reduced width motherboard (9.6" [244mm] instead of 12" [305mm] or 11.2" [284mm])
- Fewer I/O bus expansion slots (four maximum, although most boards feature only three)
- Smaller power supply optional (SFX/TFX form factors)

The microATX motherboard maximum size is only 9.6"×9.6" (244mm×244mm) as compared to the full-size ATX size of 12"×9.6" (305mm×244mm) or the Mini-ATX size of 11.2"×8.2" (284mm×208mm). Even smaller boards can be designed as long as they conform to the location of the mounting holes, connector positions, and so on, as defined by the standard. Fewer slots aren't a problem for typical home or small-business PC users because more components such as sound and video are usually integrated on the motherboard and therefore don't require separate slots. This higher integration reduces motherboard and system costs. External buses, such as USB, 10/100/1000 Ethernet, and optionally 1394 (FireWire), can provide additional expansion out of the box. The specifications for microATX motherboard dimensions are shown in Figure 4.20.

Smaller form factor (called SFX or TFX) power supplies have been defined for optional use with microATX systems, although the standard ATX supply also works fine because the connectors are the same. The smaller size SFX/TFX power supplies encourage flexibility in choosing mounting locations within the chassis and allows for smaller systems that consume less power overall. Although the smaller supplies can be used, they may lack sufficient power output for faster or more fully configured systems. Because of the high power demands of most modern systems, most third-party microATX chassis are designed to accept standard ATX power supplies, although microATX systems sold by vendors such as Compaq, HP, and eMachines typically use some type of SFX or TFX power supply to reduce costs.

▶▶ See "Power Supply Form Factors" p. 1212.

The microATX form factor is similar to ATX for compatibility. The similarities include the following:

- Standard ATX power connectors
- Standard ATX I/O panel
- Mounting holes and dimensions are a subset of ATX

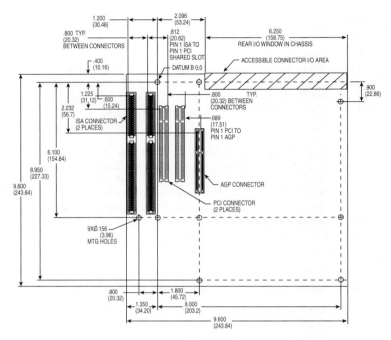

Figure 4.20   microATX specification 1.2 motherboard dimensions.

These similarities ensure that a microATX motherboard can easily work in a standard ATX chassis with a standard ATX power supply, as well as the smaller microATX chassis and SFX/TFX power supply.

The overall system size for a microATX is very small. A typical case is only 12"–14" tall, about 7" wide, and 12" deep. This results in a kind of micro-tower or desktop size. A typical microATX motherboard is shown in Figure 4.21.

As with ATX, Intel released microATX to the public domain to facilitate adoption as a de facto standard. The specification and related information on microATX are available through the Desktop Form Factors site (www.formfactors.org).

FlexATX

In March 1999, Intel released the FlexATX addendum to the microATX specification. This added a new and even smaller variation of the ATX form factor to the motherboard scene. FlexATX's smaller design is intended to allow a variety of new PC designs, especially extremely inexpensive, smaller, consumer-oriented, appliance-type systems. Some of these designs might not even have expansion slots, allowing expansion only through USB or IEEE 1394/FireWire ports.

FlexATX defines a board that is up to 9"×7.5" (229mm×191mm) in size, which is the smallest of the ATX family boards. In all other ways, FlexATX is the same as ATX and microATX, making FlexATX fully backward compatible with ATX or microATX by using a subset of the mounting holes and the same I/O and power supply connector specifications (see Figure 4.22).

Most FlexATX systems likely use SFX/TFX (small or thin form factor) type power supplies (introduced in the microATX specification), although if the chassis allows it, a standard ATX power supply can also be used.

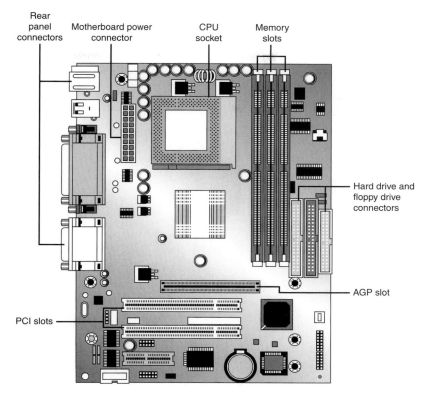

Labels (clockwise from top left):
Rear panel connectors — Motherboard power connector — CPU socket — Memory slots — Hard drive and floppy drive connectors — AGP slot — PCI slots

Figure 4.21 A typical microATX motherboard's dimensions are 9.6"×9.6".

The addition of FlexATX gave the family of ATX boards four definitions of size (three are the official standards), as shown in Table 4.3.

Table 4.3   ATX Motherboard Form Factors

Form Factor	Max. Width	Max. Depth	Max. Area	Size Comparison
ATX	12.0" (305mm)	9.6" (244mm)	115 sq. in. (743 sq. cm)	—
Mini-ATX	11.2" (284mm)	8.2" (208mm)	92 sq. in. (593 sq. cm)	20% smaller
microATX	9.6" (244mm)	9.6" (244mm)	92 sq. in. (595 sq. cm)	20% smaller
Flex ATX	9.0" (229mm)	7.5" (191mm)	68 sq. in. (435 sq. cm)	41% smaller

Note that these dimensions are the maximums allowed. Making a board smaller in any given dimension is always possible as long as it conforms to the mounting hole and connector placement requirements detailed in the respective specifications. Each board has the same basic screw hole and connector placement requirements, so if you have a case that fits a full-size ATX board, you could also mount a microATX, or FlexATX board in that same case. Obviously, if you have a smaller case designed for microATX or FlexATX, you won't be able to put the larger Mini-ATX or full-size ATX boards in that case.

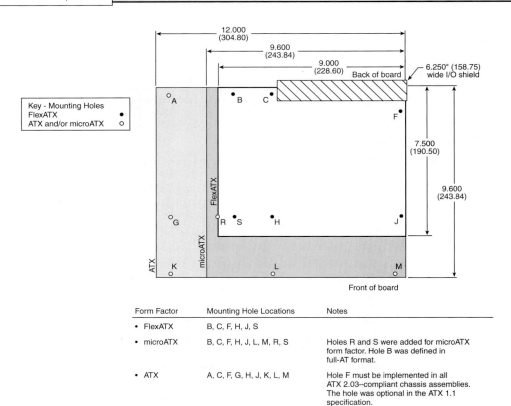

Figure 4.22 Size and mounting hole comparison between ATX, microATX, and FlexATX motherboards.

DTX and Mini-DTX

The DTX (and Mini-DTX) specification was released in Feb. 2007 by AMD, and is available for download from www.dtxpc.org. DTX and Mini-DTX are smaller variations of the microATX and FlexATX specifications respectively. DTX boards are up to 8"×9.6" in size, whereas Mini-DTX boards are a shorter version at only 8"×6.7" in size. Mini-DTX boards incorporate only four mounting holes (C, F, H, and J), whereas DTX boards add two more for a total of six (C, F, H, J, L, and M). Refer to Figure 4.16 for the respective hole locations. The size of the DTX and Mini-DTX boards as they relate to FlexATX are shown in Table 4.4. The narrow 8" width for both DTX and Mini-DTX boards allows for only two expansion slots.

ITX and Mini-ITX

FlexATX defines a board that is *up to* 9"×7.5" in size. Note the *up to* part of the dimensions, which means that, even though those dimensions are the maximums, less is also allowed. Therefore, a FlexATX board can be smaller than that, but how much smaller? By analyzing the FlexATX specification—and, in particular, studying the required mounting screw locations—you can see that a FlexATX board could be made small enough to use only four mounting holes (C, F, H, and J). Refer to Figure 4.16 for the respective hole locations.

According to the FlexATX standard, the distance between holes H and J is 6.2", and the distance between hole J and the right edge of the board is 0.25". By leaving the same margin from hole H to the left edge, you could make a board with a minimum width of 6.7" (0.25" + 6.2" + 0.25") that would conform to the FlexATX specification. Similarly, the distance between holes C and H is 6.1", and the distance between hole C and the back edge of the board is 0.4". By leaving a minimum 0.2" margin from hole H to the front edge, you could make a board with a minimum depth of 6.7" (0.4" + 6.1" + 0.2") that would conform to the FlexATX specification. By combining the minimum width and depth, you can see that the minimum board size that would conform to the FlexATX specification is 6.7"×6.7" (170mm×170mm).

VIA Technologies Platform Solutions Division wanted to create a motherboard as small as possible, yet not define a completely new and incompatible form factor. To accomplish this, in March 2001 VIA created a board that was slightly narrower in width (8.5" instead of 9") but still the same depth as FlexATX, resulting in a board that was 6% smaller and yet still conformed to the FlexATX specification. VIA called this ITX but then realized that the size savings were simply too small to justify developing it further, so it was discontinued before any products were released.

In April 2002, VIA created an even smaller board that featured the absolute minimum width and depth dimensions allowed by FlexATX. The company called it Mini-ITX. In essence, all Mini-ITX boards are simply FlexATX boards that are limited to the minimum allowable dimensions. All other aspects, including the I/O aperture size and location, screw hole locations, and power supply connections, are pure FlexATX. A Mini-ITX board fits in any chassis that accepts a FlexATX board; however, larger boards will not fit into a Mini-ITX chassis.

The Mini-ITX form factor was designed by VIA especially to support VIA's low-power embedded Eden ESP and C3 E-Series processors. Only a very small number of motherboards is available in this form factor, and only from VIA and one or two other manufacturers. Because the processors used on these boards are substantially less powerful than even the old Intel Celeron 4 or AMD Duron entry-level processors, the Mini-ITX form factor is intended for use mainly in nontraditional settings such as set-top boxes and computing appliances. The size of the ITX and Mini-ITX boards as they relate to FlexATX as shown in Table 4.4.

Table 4.4   Comparing the FlexATX, ITX, and Mini-ITX Form Factors

Form Factor	Max. Width	Max. Depth	Max. Area	Size Comparison to FlexATX
DTX	8.0" (203mm)	9.6" (244mm)	77 sq. in. (495 sq. cm)	14% larger
FlexATX	9.0" (229mm)	7.5" (191mm)	68 sq. in. (435 sq. cm)	—
ITX	8.5" (215mm)	7.5" (191mm)	64 sq. in. (411 sq. cm)	6% smaller
Mini-DTX	8.0" (203mm)	6.7" (170mm)	54 sq. in. (346 sq. cm)	21% smaller
Mini-ITX	6.7" (170mm)	6.7" (170mm)	45 sq. in. (290 sq. cm)	34% smaller
Nano-ITX	4.7" (120mm)	4.7" (120mm)	22 sq. in. (144 sq. cm)	67% smaller
Pico-ITX	3.9" (100mm)	2.8" (72mm)	11 sq. in. (72 sq. cm)	83% smaller

Although the still-born ITX format was virtually the same as FlexATX in size (which is probably why it was discontinued before any were sold), Mini-ITX motherboards are 170mm×170mm (6.7"×6.7"), which is 34% smaller than the maximum allowed by FlexATX.

To take advantage of the smaller Mini-ITX format, several chassis makers have produced very small chassis to fit these boards. Most are the shape of a small cube, with one floppy and one optical drive bay visible from the front. The layout of a typical Mini-ITX motherboard, the VIA EPIA-V, is shown in Figure 4.23.

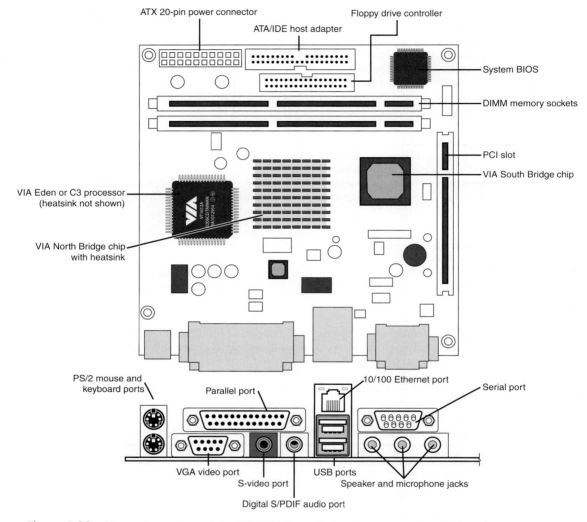

Figure 4.23   Top and rear views of the VIA EPIA-V motherboard, a typical Mini-ITX motherboard. *Photo courtesy VIA Technologies, Inc.*

As Figure 4.23 makes clear, Mini-ITX motherboards can offer a full range of input-output ports. However, several differences exist between the Mini-ITX motherboards and other ATX designs:

- The processor on a Mini-ITX motherboard is usually permanently soldered to the board, making future processor upgrades or replacements impossible.

- Most Mini-ITX chassis use TFX power supplies, for which there are currently only a few suppliers. Consequently, replacements for them are more expensive and more difficult to find.

- The available TFX power supplies are rated for less output than larger supplies, typically up to 240 watts maximum.

- There is no provision for replacing onboard video with an AGP video card.

Because Mini-ITX boards and chassis are made by only a small number of suppliers, future upgrades or parts replacements are limited. However, Mini-ITX boards are actually considered FlexATX boards as well, so they can be installed in any standard FlexATX, microATX, or full-size ATX chassis and use the corresponding power supplies. The only caveats are that the smaller Mini-ITX chassis will not accept larger FlexATX, microATX, or full-size ATX boards and most Mini-ITX chassis accept only TFX power supplies. When you select a Mini-ITX system, you must be sure to select the appropriate processor type and speed necessary for the task you need it to perform because processor replacements or upgrades almost always require changing the entire motherboard.

Note

The official site for ITX information is www.viaembedded.com. The site www.mini-itx.com is often mistaken for an official site, but it is actually a vendor that specializes in ITX systems and component sales.

The latest development in the ITX family are the Nano-ITX and Pico-ITX form factors, ultra-compact (120mm×120mm and 100mm×72mm) platforms that are designed for extreme low-power embedded applications.

BTX

Balanced Technology Extended (BTX) is a motherboard form factor specification Intel originally released in September 2003, with 1.0a and 1.0b updates released in Feb. 2004 and Jul. 2005 respectively. BTX was designed to address the ever-increasing component power and cooling requirements, as well as enabling improved circuit routing and more flexible chassis designs. However, the recent trend toward more power efficient dual-core processor designs has slowed the need for the benefits inherent in the BTX standard, which has in turn slowed the adoption of BTX. BTX became popular in many 2005 and newer mass-produced retail branded PCs such as those by Dell, Gateway, and others.

BTX is not backward-compatible with ATX or other designs. A full-size BTX board is 17% larger than ATX, allowing room for more integrated components onboard. The I/O connectors, slots, and mounting holes are in different locations than with ATX, requiring new chassis designs. However, the power supply interface connectors are the same as in the latest ATX12V specifications, and newer ATX, TFX, SFX, CFX, and LFX power supplies can be used. The latter two power supply form factors were specifically created to support compact and low-profile BTX systems.

The primary advantages to BTX include

- **Optimized inline component layout and routing**—Signals are aligned front to back, allowing connections between components and I/O connectors to run unobstructed.

- **Optimized airflow path**—Allows for a condensed system design and an optimized, unobstructed airflow path for efficient system cooling with fewer fans and lower acoustics.

- **Support and retention module (SRM)**—Offers mechanical support for heavy heatsinks. It also helps to prevent board flexing or damaging board components and traces during shipping and handling.

- **Scalable board dimensions**—Flexible board sizes enable developers to use the same components for a variety of system sizes and configurations.

- **Low-profile options**—Component keep-out specifications enable lower profiles, making it easier to design Slimline or small form factor systems.

- **Flexible, compatible power supply designs**—Connectors are shared with recent ATX designs; smaller, more efficient power supply form factors can be used for small form factor systems, whereas standard ATX12V power supplies can be used for larger tower configurations.

BTX includes three definitions of motherboard size, as shown in Table 4.5.

Table 4.5   BTX Motherboard Form Factors

Form Factor	Max. Width	Depth	Max. Area	Size Versus BTX
BTX	12.8" (325mm)	10.5" (267mm)	134 sq. in. (867 sq. cm)	—
microBTX	10.4" (264mm)	10.5" (267mm)	109 sq. in. (705 sq. cm)	19% smaller
PicoATX	8.0" (203mm)	10.5" (267mm)	84 sq. in. (542 sq. cm)	37% smaller

Each board has the same basic screw hole and connector placement requirements. So, if you have a case that fits a full-size BTX board, you can also mount a microBTX or picoBTX board in that same case (see Figure 4.24). Obviously, if you have a smaller case designed for MicroBTX or picoBTX, you won't be able to put the larger microBTX or BTX boards in that case.

BTX requires up to 10 mounting holes and supports up to seven slots, depending on the size, as shown in Table 4.6.

Table 4.6   BTX Motherboard Mounting Holes

Board Size	Mounting Holes	Max. Slots
BTX	A,B,C,D,E,F,G,H,J,K	7
microBTX	A,B,C,D,E,F,G	4
picoBTX	A,B,C,D	1

BTX also clearly specifies volumetric zones around the motherboard to prevent any interference from the chassis or internal components such as drives, which allows for maximum interchangeability without physical interference or fit problems.

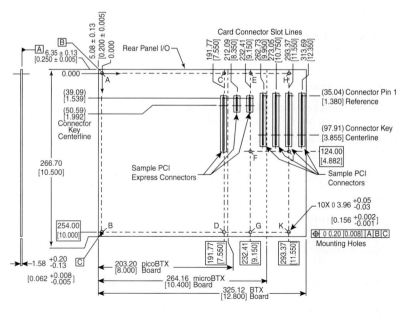

Figure 4.24   BTX specification 1.0a motherboard dimensions.

With processors exceeding 100W in thermal output, as well as voltage regulators, motherboard chipsets, and video cards adding to the thermal load in a system, BTX was designed to allow all the high-heat-producing core components to be mounted inline from front to back, so that a single high-efficiency thermal module (heatsink) can cool the system. This eliminates the need for an excessive number of fans. The thermal module includes a heatsink for the processor, a high-efficiency fan, and a duct to direct airflow through the system. Extra support for the thermal module is provided under the board via a support and retention module (SRM), which provides structural support for heatsinks that are much heavier than allowed in ATX designs (see Figure 4.25).

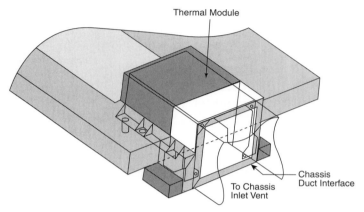

Figure 4.25   BTX thermal module containing a processor heatsink and fan.

BTX uses the same power connectors as in the latest power supply form factor specifications, including a 24-pin main connector for the board and a 4-pin ATX12V connector for the CPU voltage regulator module. The particular power supply form factor used depends mostly on the chassis selected.

A typical tower system has components arranged as shown in Figure 4.26.

From Figure 4.26, you can see that the main heat-producing core components are centrally located inline from front to rear, allowing the most efficient thermal design. Air flows from front to rear through the center, cooling the processor, motherboard chipset, memory, and video card.

To support the heavy processor heatsink and thermal module assembly, an SRM is mounted under the board. The SRM is essentially a metal plate affixed to the chassis under the board, and the thermal module is bolted directly to the SRM instead of to the motherboard. This helps carry the weight of the module and prevents excessive loads from being applied to the processor and motherboard, especially during the shipping and handling of the system.

The BTX I/O connector area is similar to ATX, except that it is at the opposite side of the rear of the board. The size of the area is slightly shorter but wider than ATX, allowing a large number of interfaces and connectors to be built into the motherboard.

While BTX became popular in many 2005 and newer mass-produced retail branded PCs such as those by Dell, Gateway, and others, BTX has definitely not replaced ATX as an overall solution in the marketplace. Other large manufacturers such as HP continue to use ATX, and ATX is by far the more popular choice for all of the smaller manufacturers and system builders as well. BTX motherboards, chassis, and boxed processors are extremely limited in both numbers and availability, and there have been problems with heatsink to chassis standardization as well. Because of the lack of BTX component popularity and other problems, I recommend avoiding BTX systems and components as they will be difficult to upgrade or replace in the future. ATX remains by far the most popular and recommended form factor for system builders and upgraders.

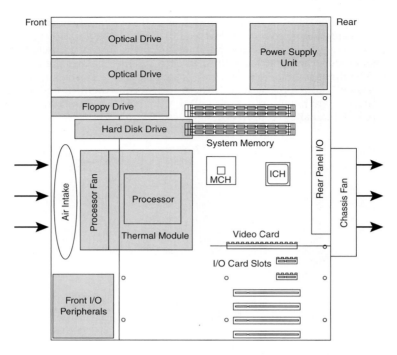

Figure 4.26   BTX tower chassis layout.

WTX

WTX was a board and system form factor developed for the mid-range workstation market; however, most vendors making workstations and servers have used the ATX form factor. WTX went beyond ATX and defined the size and shape of the board and the interface between the board and chassis, as well as required chassis features.

WTX was first released in September 1998 (1.0) and updated in February 1999 (1.1). Since then however, WTX has been officially discontinued and there will be no further updates.

Figure 4.27 shows a typical WTX system with the cover removed. Note that easy access is provided to internal components via pull-out drawers and swinging side panels.

WTX motherboards have a maximum width of 14" (356mm) and a maximum length of 16.75" (425 mm), which is significantly larger than ATX. There are no minimum dimensions, so board designers are free to design smaller boards as long as they meet the mounting criteria. The additional space provided by the WTX form factor provides room for two or more processors and other onboard equipment needed in a workstation or server design.

The WTX specification offers flexibility by leaving motherboard mounting features and locations undefined. Instead of defining exact screw hole positions, WTX motherboards must mount to a standard mounting adapter plate, which must be supplied with the board. The WTX chassis is designed to accept the mounting plate with attached motherboard and not just a bare board alone.

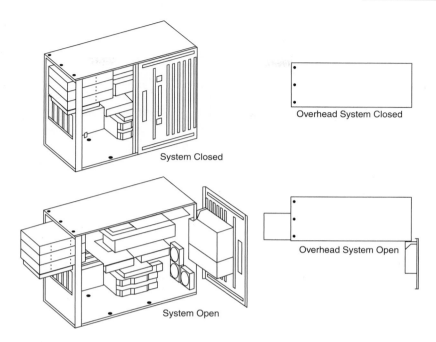

Figure 4.27   Typical WTX system chassis showing internal layout and ease of access.

WTX motherboards use different power connectors than ATX motherboards. Originally, WTX motherboards used a 24-pin power connector that supplied only 5V and 3.3V power to the motherboard and a separate 22-pin power connector that supplied 12V power. Some WTX motherboards use a 24-pin primary power connector, but the connector might use the EPS12V (also known as the Superset ATX or SSI) standard or the older ATX-GES standard. Both ATX-GES and EPS12V provide 3.3V, 5V, and 12V power to the motherboard, but the pinouts are completely different. EPS12V motherboards also use an 8-pin power connector to provide additional 12V power to the processor(s). Table 4.7 compares the pinouts of the ATX-GES and EPS12V 24-pin primary power connectors.

Caution

Keep in mind that motherboards using the WTX, ATX-GES, and EPS12V power supply standards all use the same connector (the 24-pin Molex 39-01-2240 connector, a longer version of the 20-pin Molex connector used by ATX power supplies). However, they use different voltages on almost every wire. If you mismatch the motherboard and power supply, you will destroy one or both of them!

Table 4.7   ATX-GES and EPS12V 24-Pin Primary Power Connector Pinouts

Pin #	ATX-GES	EPS12V	Pin #	ATX-GES	EPS12V
1	+5V red	+3.3V orange	13	+5V red	+3.3V orange and brown
2	+5V red	+3.3V orange	14	+5V red	-12V blue
3	GND black	GND black	15	GND black	GND black
4	GND black	+5V red	16	+5V SB purple	PS-On green

Table 4.7   Continued

Pin #	ATX-GES	EPS12V	Pin #	ATX-GES	EPS12V
5	PS-On green	GND black	17	-12V blue	GND black
6	GND black	+5V red	18	GND black	GND black
7	+3.3V orange + orange	GND black	19	+3.3V orange	GND black
8	+3.3V orange	Pwr-OK gray	20	+3.3V orange	-5V white
9	GND black	+5V SB purple	21	+3.3V orange	+5V red
10	GND black	+12V yellow	22	GND black	+5V red
11	+12V yellow	+12V yellow	23	GND black	+5V red
12	+12V yellow	+3.3V orange	24	+12V yellow	GND black

Proprietary Designs

Motherboards that are *not* one of the industry standard form factors, such as any of the ATX formats, are deemed *proprietary* or *semiproprietary*. LPX, Mini-ITX, and Nano-ITX systems fall into the semiproprietary category for example, while other companies have fully proprietary systems that only they manufacture. Most people purchasing PCs should avoid proprietary designs because they do not allow for a future motherboard, power supply, or case upgrade, which limits future use and serviceability of the system. To me, proprietary systems are disposable PCs because you can neither upgrade them nor easily repair them. The problem is that the proprietary parts can come only from the original system manufacturer, and they usually cost much more than nonproprietary parts. Therefore, after your proprietary system goes out of warranty, not only is it not upgradeable, but it is also essentially no longer worth repairing. If the motherboard or any component on it goes bad, you will be better off purchasing a completely new standard system than paying five times the normal price for a new proprietary motherboard. In addition, a new motherboard in a standard form factor system would be one or more generations newer and faster than the one you would be replacing. In a proprietary system, the replacement board would not only cost way too much, but it would be the same as the one that failed.

Note that you might be able to perform limited upgrades to older systems with proprietary motherboards, in the form of custom (non-OEM) processor replacements with attached voltage regulators, usually called "overdrive" or "turbo" chips. Unfortunately, these often don't perform up to the standards of a less expensive new processor and motherboard combination. Of course, I usually recommend upgrading the motherboard and processor together—but that is something that can't be done with a proprietary system.

If the motherboard in your current ATX form factor system dies, you can find any number of replacement boards that will bolt directly in—with your choice of processors and clock speeds—at great prices. However, if the motherboard dies in a proprietary form factor system, you'll pay for a replacement available only from the original manufacturer, and you have little or no opportunity to select a board with a faster or better processor than the one that failed. In other words, upgrading or repairing one of these systems via a motherboard replacement is difficult and usually not cost-effective.

Systems sold by many of the leading retail and mail-order suppliers are available in industry-standard ATX form factors such as ATX, microATX, and FlexATX. This allows for easy upgrading and system expansion in the future. These standard form factors allow you to replace your own motherboards, power supplies, and other components easily and select components from any number of suppliers other than where you originally bought the system.

Note

Both Dell and Gateway shifted over to BTX form factor systems in 2005. While BTX is considered an industry standard form factor, the lack of available BTX components such as motherboards, chassis, and boxed processors makes BTX systems difficult to repair and/or upgrade in the future, and also makes BTX generally a poor choice for those building systems from scratch as well.

Not all systems from a given manufacturer use the same form factors. For example, while Dell use industry-standard form factors for some of its desktop systems, many of its systems are based on proprietary components, including power supplies with nonstandard pinouts. For this reason, some Dell computers can be difficult to upgrade with aftermarket motherboard and power supply components. Learn more in Chapter 19, "Power Supplies."

Backplane/Blade Systems

One type of design that has been used in some systems over the years is the *backplane* or *blade* system. These systems do not have a motherboard in the true sense of the word. In a backplane system, the components typically found on a motherboard are located instead on an expansion adapter card plugged into a slot.

In these systems, the board with the slots is called a *backplane*, and the boards with the processors and other components are often called *blades*.

The motherboard system design and the backplane system design have advantages and disadvantages. Most original PCs were designed as backplanes in the late 1970s. Apple and IBM shifted the market to the now traditional motherboard with a slot-type design because this kind of system generally is cheaper to mass-produce than one with the backplane design.

Backplane systems come in two main types—passive and active. A *passive* backplane means the main backplane board does not contain any circuitry at all except for the bus connectors and maybe some buffer and driver circuits. All the circuitry found on a conventional motherboard is contained on one or more expansion cards installed in slots on the backplane. Most backplane systems use a passive design that incorporates the entire system circuitry into card-baded motherboards called *blades*. A blade is essentially a complete motherboard designed to plug into a slot in the passive backplane. The passive backplane/blade concept enables the entire system to be easily upgraded by adding or changing one or more cards. The passive backplane/blade design is popular in industrial systems and servers, which are usually rack-mounted. Figure 4.28 shows a typical Pentium 4 blade. Figure 4.29 shows a rack-mount chassis with a passive backplane.

Passive backplane systems with blades (also called *single-board computers* or *SBCs*) are by far the most popular backplane design. They are used in industrial or laboratory-type systems and are rack-mountable. They usually have a large number of slots and extremely heavy-duty power supplies; they also feature high-capacity, reverse flow cooling designed to pressurize the chassis with cool, filtered air.

Note

Many passive backplane systems adhere to the PCI/ISA passive backplane and CompactPCI form factor standards set forth by the PCI Industrial Computer Manufacturers Group (PICMG). You can get more information about these standards from PICMG's website at www.picmg.org. Another standard for SBCs is the PISA standard developed by JUMPtec and Kontron. The PISA standard uses a half-length SBC that plugs in to a backplane slot similar to the old EISA slot. PISA backplanes also support PCI and ISA cards. Learn more at http://www.kontron.com.

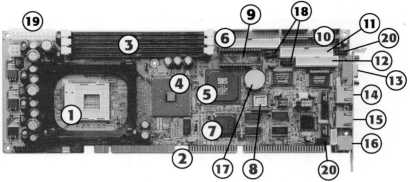

1. Pentium 4 processor socket
2. PICMG interface to backplane
3. DIMM memory sockets (3)
4. North Bridge/MCH
5. SIS 315 graphics chip
6. ATA/IDE host adapters
7. South Bridge/ICH
8. System BIOS
9. JEDEC Disk on Chip socket
10. ATA RAID host adapters
11. Floppy controller
12. Parallel port header cable connector
    PS/2 mouse port
13. VGA port
14. 10/100 Ethernet port
15. 10/100 Ethernet port
16. PS/2 keyboard/mouse port
17. CR-2032 battery
18. USB header cable connectors (2)
19. Power connector
20. Serial port header cable connectors (2)

Figure 4.28 A typical Pentium 4 blade. This single card provides PCI and ISA interfacing; integrated AGP video; two 10/100 Ethernet network interfaces; ATA RAID; and normal parallel, serial, ATA/IDE, USB, and floppy interfaces.

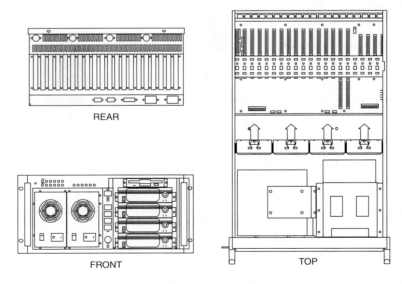

Figure 4.29 A rack-mount chassis with passive backplane.

An *active* backplane means the main backplane board contains bus control and usually other circuitry as well. Most active backplane systems contain all the circuitry found on a typical motherboard except for what is then called the *processor complex*. The processor complex is the name of the circuit board that contains the main system processor and any other circuitry directly related to it, such as clock control, cache, and so forth. The processor's complex design enables the user to easily upgrade the system later to a new processor type by changing one card. In effect, it amounts to a modular motherboard with a replaceable processor section.

Many large PC manufacturers once built systems with an active backplane/processor complex. Unfortunately, because no standards exist for the processor complex interface to the system, these boards are proprietary and can be purchased only from the system manufacturer. This limited market and availability causes the prices of these boards to be higher than most complete motherboards from other manufacturers.

Processor Sockets/Slots

The CPU is installed in either a socket or a slot, depending on the type of chip.

Starting with the 486 processors, Intel designed the processor to be a user-installable and replaceable part and developed standards for CPU sockets and slots that would allow different models of the same basic processor to plug in. One key was to use a zero insertion force (ZIF) socket design, which meant that the processor could be easily installed or removed with no tools. ZIF sockets use a lever to engage or release the grip on the chip, and with the lever released, the chip can be easily inserted or removed. The ZIF sockets were given a designation that was usually imprinted or embossed on the socket indicating what type it was. Different socket types accepted different families of processors. If you know the type of socket or slot on your motherboard, you essentially know which types of processors are designed to plug in.

◄◄ See "Processor Socket and Slot Types," p. 97.

Sockets for processors prior to the 486 were not ZIF designs and, as such, were not designed for easy processor installation or removal. In addition, interchangeability was limited. Table 4.8 shows the designations for the various 486 and newer processor sockets/slots and lists the chips designed to plug into them.

Table 4.8   CPU Socket Specifications

	Socket	Pins	Layout	Voltage	Supported Processors
Intel/AMD 486 class	Socket 1	169	17×17 PGA	5V	486 SX/SX2, DX/DX2, DX4 OD
	Socket 2	238	19×19 PGA	5V	486 SX/SX2, DX/DX2, DX4 OD, 486 Pentium OD
	Socket 3	237	19×19 PGA	5V/3.3V	486 SX/SX2, DX/DX2, DX4, 486 Pentium OD,
	Socket 6[1]	235	19×19 PGA	3.3V	486 DX4, 486 Pentium OD AMD 5x86
Intel/AMD 586 (Pentium) lass	Socket 4	273	21×21 PGA	5V	Pentium 60/66, OD
	Socket 5	320	37×37 SPGA	3.3V/3.5V	Pentium 75-133, OD
	Socket 7	321	37×37 SPGA	VRM	Pentium 75-233+, MMX, OD, AMD K5/K6, Cyrix M1/II

Table 4.8   Continued

	Socket	Pins	Layout	Voltage	Supported Processors
Intel 686 (Pentium II/III) class	Socket 8	387	Dual-pattern SPGA	Auto VRM	Pentium Pro, OD
	Slot 1 (SC242)	242	Slot	Auto VRM	Pentium II/III, Celeron SECC
	Socket 370	370	37×37 SPGA	Auto VRM	Celeron/Pentium III PPGA/FC-PGA
Pentium 4 class	Socket 423	423	39×39 SPGA	Auto VRM	Pentium 4 FC-PGA
	Socket 478	478	26×26 mPGA	Auto VRM	Pentium 4/Celeron FC-PGA2
	Socket T (LGA775)	775	30×33 LGA	Auto VRM	Pentium 4/Celeron LGA775
AMD K7 class	Slot A	242	Slot	Auto VRM	AMD Athlon SECC
	Socket A (462)	462	37×37 SPGA	Auto VRM	AMD Athlon/Athlon XP/ Duron PGA/FC-PGA
AMD K8 class[2]	Socket 754	754	29×29 mPGA	Auto VRM	AMD Athlon 64,
	Socket 939	939	31×31 mPGA	Auto VRM	AMD Athlon 64, 64 FX,
	Socket 940	940	31×31 mPGA	Auto VRM	AMD Athlon 64FX, Opteron
	Socket AM2	940	31×31 mPGA	Auto VRM	AMD Athlon 64, X2, 64 FX, 64 X2, Opteron
Intel/AMD Server and Workstation class	Slot 2 (SC330)	330	Slot	Auto VRM	Pentium II/III Xeon
	Socket 603	603	31×25 mPGA	Auto VRM	Xeon (P4)
	Socket PAC418	418	38×22 split SPGA	Auto VRM	Itanium
	Socket PAC611	611	25×28 mPGA	Auto VRM	Itanium 2
	Socket 940	940	31×31 mPGA	Auto VRM	AMD Athlon 64FX, Opteron

1. Socket 6 was never actually implemented in any systems.

2. AMD transitioned its Athlon 64 family of processors to Socket AM2 in 2006.

FC-PGA = Flip-chip pin grid array

FC-PGA2 = FC-PGA with an integrated heat spreader (IHS)

OD = OverDrive (retail upgrade processors)

PAC = Pin array cartridge

PGA = Pin grid array

PPGA = Plastic pin grid array

SC242 = Slot connector, 242 pins

SC330 = Slot connector, 330 pins

SECC = Single edge contact cartridge

SPGA = Staggered pin grid array

mPGA = Micro pin grid array

VRM = Voltage regulator module with variable voltage output determined by module type or manual jumpers

Auto VRM = Voltage regulator module with automatic voltage selection determined by processor voltage ID (VID) pins

Originally, all processors were mounted in sockets (or soldered directly to the motherboard). With the advent of the Pentium II and original Athlon processors, both Intel and AMD temporarily shifted to a slot-based approach for their processors because the processors now incorporated built-in L2 cache, purchased as separate chips from third-party Static RAM (SRAM) memory chip manufacturers. Therefore, the processor then consisted not of one but of several chips, all mounted on a daughterboard that was then plugged into a slot in the motherboard. This worked well, but there were additional expenses in the extra cache chips, the daughterboard itself, the slot, optional casings or packaging, and the support mechanisms and physical stands and latches for the processor and heatsink. All in all, slot-based processors were expensive to produce compared to the previous socketed versions.

With the advent of the second-generation Celeron, Intel integrated the L2 cache directly into the processor die, meaning within the main CPU chip circuits with no extra chips required. The second-generation (code named Coppermine) Pentium III also received on-die L2 cache, as did the K6-3, Duron (code named Spitfire), and second-generation Athlon (code named Thunderbird) processors from AMD (some early Thunderbird Athlon CPUs were also made in the Slot A configuration). With on-die L2, the processor was back to being a single chip again, which also meant that mounting it on a separate board plugged into a slot was expensive and unnecessary. Because of on-die integrated L2 cache, processor packaging shifted back to sockets and will continue that way for the foreseeable future. All modern processors now have integrated L2 cache (some also have integrated L3 cache) and use the socket form. Besides allowing a return to socketed packaging, the on-die L2 cache runs at full processor speed, instead of the one-half or one-third speed of the previous integrated (but not on-die) L2 cache.

Chipsets

We can't talk about modern motherboards without discussing chipsets. The chipset *is* the motherboard; therefore, any two boards with the same chipsets are functionally identical unless the vendor has added features to those provided by the chipset or removed support for certain chipset features.

The chipset usually contains the processor bus interface (called *front-side bus*, or *FSB*), memory controllers, bus controllers, I/O controllers, and more. All the circuits of the motherboard are contained within the chipset. If the processor in your PC is like the engine in your car, the chipset represents the chassis. It is the framework in which the engine rests and is its connection to the outside world. The chipset is the frame, suspension, steering, wheels and tires, transmission, drive shaft, differential, and brakes. The chassis in your car is what gets the power to the ground, allowing the vehicle to start, stop, and corner. In the PC, the chipset represents the connection between the processor and everything else. The processor can't talk to the memory, adapter boards, devices, and so on without going through the chipset. The chipset is the main hub and central nervous system of the PC. If you think of the processor as the brain, the chipset is the spine and central nervous system.

Because the chipset controls the interface or connections between the processor and everything else, the chipset ends up dictating which type of processor you have; how fast it will run; how fast the buses will run; the speed, type, and amount of memory you can use; and more. In fact, the chipset might be the single most important component in your system, possibly even more important than the processor. I've seen systems with faster processors be outperformed by systems with slower processor but a better chipset, much like how a car with less power might win a race through better cornering and braking. When deciding on a system, I start by choosing the chipset because the chipset decision then dictates the processor, memory, I/O, and expansion capabilities.

Chipset Evolution

When IBM created the first PC motherboards, it used several discrete (separate) chips to complete the design. Besides the processor and optional math coprocessor, many other components were required to complete the system. These other components included items such as the clock generator, bus controller, system timer, interrupt and DMA controllers, CMOS RAM and clock, and keyboard controller. Additionally, many other simple logic chips were used to complete the entire motherboard circuit, plus, of course, things such as the actual processor, math coprocessor (floating-point unit), memory, and other parts. Table 4.9 lists all the primary chip components used on the original PC/XT and AT motherboards.

Table 4.9   Primary Chip Components on PC/XT and AT Motherboards

Chip Function	PC/XT Version	AT Version
Processor	8088	80286
Math Coprocessor (Floating-Point Unit)	8087	80287
Clock Generator	8284	82284
Bus Controller	8288	82288
System Timer	8253	8254
Low-order Interrupt Controller	8259	8259
High-order Interrupt Controller	—	8259
Low-order DMA Controller	8237	8237
High-order DMA Controller	—	8237
CMOS RAM/Real-Time Clock	—	MC146818
Keyboard Controller	8255	8042

In addition to the processor/coprocessor, a six-chip set was used to implement the primary motherboard circuit in the original PC and XT systems. IBM later upgraded this to a nine-chip design in the AT and later systems, mainly by adding more interrupt and DMA controller chips and the nonvolatile CMOS RAM/Real-Time Clock chip. All these motherboard chip components came from Intel or an Intel-licensed manufacturer, except the CMOS/Clock chip, which came from Motorola. To build a clone or copy of one of these IBM systems required all these chips plus many smaller discrete logic chips to glue the design together, totaling 100 or more individual chips. This kept the price of a motherboard high and left little room on the board to integrate other functions.

In 1986, a company called Chips and Technologies introduced a revolutionary component called the 82C206—the main part of the first PC motherboard chipset. This was a single chip that integrated into it all the functions of the main motherboard chips in an AT-compatible system. This chip included the functions of the 82284 Clock Generator, 82288 Bus Controller, 8254 System Timer, dual 8259 Interrupt Controllers, dual 8237 DMA Controllers, and even the MC146818 CMOS/Clock chip. Besides the processor, virtually all the major chip components on a PC motherboard could now be replaced by a single chip. Four other chips augmented the 82C206 acting as buffers and memory controllers, thus completing virtually the entire motherboard circuit with five total chips. This first chipset was called the CS8220 chipset by Chips and Technologies. Needless to say, this was a revolutionary concept in PC motherboard manufacturing. Not only did it greatly reduce the cost of building a PC motherboard, but it also made designing a motherboard much easier. The reduced component count meant the boards had more room for integrating other items formerly found on expansion cards. Later, the four chips augmenting the 82C206 were replaced by a new set of only three chips, and the entire set was called the New Enhanced AT (NEAT) CS8221 chipset. This was later followed by the 82C836 Single Chip AT (SCAT) chipset, which finally condensed all the chips in the set down to a single chip.

The chipset idea was rapidly copied by other chip manufacturers. Companies such as Acer, Erso, Opti, Suntac, Symphony, UMC, and VLSI each gained an important share of this market. Unfortunately for many of them, the chipset market has been a volatile one, and many of them have long since gone out of business. In 1993, VLSI had become the dominant force in the chipset market and had the vast majority of the market share; by the next year, VLSI (which later was merged into Philips Semiconductors), along with virtually everybody else in the chipset market, was fighting to stay alive. This is because a new chipset manufacturer had come on the scene, and within a year or so of getting serious, it was totally dominating the chipset market. That company was Intel, and after 1994, it had a virtual lock on the chipset market. If you have a motherboard built since 1994 that uses or accepts an Intel processor, chances are good that it has an Intel chipset on it as well.

Intel struggled somewhat with chipsets from 1999 through 2001 because of its reliance on RDRAM memory. Intel originally signed a contract with Rambus back in 1996 declaring it would support this memory as its primary focus for desktop PC chipsets through 2001. I suspect this has turned out to be something Intel regrets (the contract has since expired). RDRAM memory had a significantly higher price than DDR SDRAM memory. Consequently, Intel introduced the 845 chipset (code named Brookdale), which supported DDR SDRAM with the Pentium 4. Since that time, all of Intel's Pentium chipsets have supported variations of DDR memory.

Intel is not alone in the chipset business: ATI (now part of AMD), NVIDIA, VIA Technologies, Silicon Integrated Systems (SiS), ATI, and ULi Electronics (formerly ALi Corporation) all make or have made chipsets for Intel-based systems as well.

Although AMD (and ATI which is now a part of AMD) has developed its own chipsets, it also emphasizes encouraging third-party chipset developers to support its products. Today, VIA Technologies is one of the leading developers of chipsets for AMD processors. The popularity of AMD processors has encouraged NVIDIA, SiS, ATI, and ULi Electronics to develop chipsets for AMD-based systems as well.

It is interesting to note that the original PC chipset maker, Chips and Technologies, survived by changing course to design and manufacture video chips and found a niche in that market specifically for laptop and notebook video chipsets. Chips and Technologies was subsequently purchased by Intel in 1998 as a part of Intel's video strategy.

Intel Chipsets

You can't talk about chipsets today without discussing Intel because it currently owns the vast majority of the chipset market. It is interesting to note that we probably have Compaq to thank for forcing Intel into the chipset business in the first place!

The thing that really started it all was the introduction of the EISA bus designed by Compaq in 1989. At that time, it had shared the bus with other manufacturers in an attempt to make it a market standard. However, Compaq refused to share its EISA bus chipset—a set of custom chips necessary to implement this bus on a motherboard.

Enter Intel, who decided to fill the chipset void for the rest of the PC manufacturers wanting to build EISA bus motherboards. As is well known today, the EISA bus failed to become a market success, except for a short-term niche server business, but Intel now had a taste of the chipset business—and this it apparently wouldn't forget. With the introduction of the 286 and 386 processors, Intel became impatient with how long it took the other chipset companies to create chipsets around its new processor designs; this delayed the introduction of motherboards that supported the new processors. For example, it took more than 2 years after the 286 processor was introduced for the first 286 motherboards to appear and just over a year for the first 386 motherboards to appear after the 386 had been introduced. Intel couldn't sell its processors in volume until other manufacturers made motherboards that would support them, so it thought that by developing motherboard chipsets for a new processor in parallel with the new processor, it could jumpstart the motherboard business by providing ready-made chipsets for the motherboard manufacturers to use.

Intel tested this by introducing the 420 series chipsets along with its 486 processor in April 1989. This enabled the motherboard companies to get busy right away, and in only a few months the first 486 motherboards appeared. Of course, the other chipset manufacturers weren't happy; now they had Intel as a competitor, and Intel would always have chipsets for new processors on the market first!

Intel then realized that it made both processors *and* chipsets, which were 90% of the components on a typical motherboard. What better way to ensure that motherboards were available for its Pentium processor when it was introduced than by making its own motherboards as well and having these boards ready on the new processor's introduction date. When the first Pentium processor debuted in 1993, Intel also debuted the 430LX chipset as well as a fully finished motherboard. Now, besides the chipset companies being upset, the motherboard companies weren't too happy, either. Intel was not only the major supplier of parts needed to build finished boards (processors and chipsets), but was now building and selling the finished boards as well. By 1994, Intel dominated the processor and chipset markets and had cornered the motherboard market as well.

Now as Intel develops new processors, it develops chipsets and motherboards simultaneously, which means they can be announced and shipped in unison. This eliminates the delay between introducing new processors and waiting for motherboards and systems capable of using them, which was common in the industry's early days. For the consumer, this means no waiting for new systems. Since the original Pentium processor in 1993, we have been able to purchase ready-made systems on the same day a new processor is released.

In my seminars, I ask how many people in the class have Intel-brand PCs. Of course, Intel does not sell or market a PC under its own name, so nobody thinks they have an "Intel-brand" PC. But, if your motherboard was made by Intel, for all intents and purposes you sure seem to have an Intel-brand PC, at least as far as the components are concerned. Does it really matter whether the Dells or Gateways of the world put that same Intel motherboard into a slightly different-looking case with their name on it? If you look under the covers, you'll find that many, if not most, of the systems from the major manufacturers are really the same because they basically use the same parts. Although more and more major manufacturers are offering AMD-based systems as alternatives to Intel's, no single manufacturer dominates AMD motherboard sales the way Intel has dominated OEM sales to major system manufacturers.

To hold down pricing, many low-cost retail systems based on microATX motherboards use non-Intel motherboards (albeit with Intel chipsets in most cases). But, even though many companies make PC-compatible motherboards for aftermarket upgrades or local computer assemblers, Intel still dominates the major vendor OEM market for midrange and high-end systems.

Intel Chipset Model Numbers

Starting with the 486 in 1989, Intel began a pattern of numbering its chipsets as shown in Table 4.10.

Table 4.10   Intel Chipset Model Numbers

Chipset Series	Supported Processors and Other Features
420xx	P4 (486)
430xx	P5 (Pentium), EDO memory
440xx	P6 (Pentium Pro/PII/PIII), AGP, SDRAM memory
450xx	P6 workstation (Pentium Pro/PII/PIII Xeon), SDRAM memory
8xx	P6/P7 (PII/PIII/P4), AGP, DDR memory
9xx	P7/P8 (Pentium 4/D Core 2), PCI Express, DDR2 memory
3x	P8 (Core 2), PCI Express, DDR2/DDR3 memory
E72xx	P7 (Pentium 4/D), AGP/PCI Express, DDR/DDR2 w/ECC memory
E75xx	P7/P8 workstation (Xeon), dual processor, PCI Express, DDR2 w/ECC memory
5000x	P8 workstation (Xeon dual-core), dual processor, PCI Express, FB-DIMM memory

The chipset numbers listed here are abbreviations of the actual chipset numbers stamped on the individual chips. For example, one of the popular Pentium II/III chipsets was the Intel 440BX chipset, which consisted of two components: the 82443BX North Bridge and the 82371EB South Bridge. Likewise, the 865G chipset supports the Pentium 4 and consists of two main parts: the 82865G graphics memory controller hub (GMCH; replaces the North Bridge and includes integrated video) and an 82801EB or 82801EBR I/O controller hub (ICH5 or ICH5R; replaces the South Bridge). By reading the logo (Intel or others) as well as the part number and letter combinations on the larger chips on your motherboard, you can quickly identify the chipset your motherboard uses.

Intel has used two distinct chipset architectures: a North/South Bridge architecture and a newer hub architecture. All chipsets introduced from the 800 series on use the hub architecture.

Tip

In many cases, the North Bridge/GMCH/MCH chip on recent motherboards is covered up with a passive or active heatsink, and some motherboards also use a heatsink on the South Bridge or ICH chip. To determine the chipset used in these systems, I recommend software such as the Intel Chipset Identification Utility (http://developer.intel.com/support/chipsets/inf/sb/CS-009266.htm) or CPU-Z (http://cpuid.com).

Intel Integrated Graphics Architecture

Intel began producing motherboard chipsets with integrated video starting with the 810 chipset in April 1999. By building the graphics directly into the motherboard chipset, no other graphics chip or video memory was required, meaning that video could be essentially included in a PC for "free." Many of the chipsets including integrated graphics also support either AGP or PCI Express video slots for upgrades, meaning that the integrated graphics could easily be upgraded by adding a discrete graphics card.

Table 4.11 shows the various integrated graphics technologies integrated into Intel chipsets from the 810 to the G35.

Table 4.11   Intel Integrated Graphics and Supporting Chipsets

Intel Integrated Graphics	Supporting Chipsets
Intel Graphics Technology	810/E/E2, 815G/EG
Intel Extreme Graphics	845G, 852/855GM, 865G
GMA 900	910G/GM, 915G/GM
GMA 950	945G/GM
GMA 3000	946GZ, Q963, Q965
GMA 3100	G31, G33, Q33, Q35
GMA X3000	G965
GMA X3100	GM965, GL960
GMA X3500	G35

GMA = Graphics Media Accelerator

With the release of the 845-series chipsets with integrated video (845G-series models, covered later in this chapter), Intel implemented what it called Extreme Graphics Architecture. This architecture supported 3D graphics, featuring the following four technologies aimed at improving 3D rendering speed and quality:

- **Rapid Pixel and Texel Rendering Engine**—Uses pipelines to overlap 2D and 3D operations, provides 8x data compression to improve the use of memory bandwidth, and features a multitier cache for 3D operations

- **Zone Rendering**—Reduces memory bandwidth requirements by dividing the frame buffer into rectangular zones, sorting the triangles into memory by zone, and processing each zone to memory

- **Dynamic Video Memory Technology**—Manages memory sharing between the display, applications, and operating system depending on the memory requirements of the programs running

- **Intelligent Memory Management**—Improves memory addressing, display buffer implementation, and memory efficiency

Extreme Graphics Architecture improved 3D rendering compared to Intel's earlier integrated video chipsets (the 810- and 815-series chipsets, which have limited 3D functions), but its performance and features still lagged behind even the mid-range dedicated graphics cards of the time (such as NVIDIA's GeForce 2 MX 200).

It wasn't until the third time around—when Intel renamed it the Graphics Media Accelerator (GMA) 900—that it added support for most of the core 3D features made standard in DirectX 9. GMA 900 lacks hardware support for vertex shaders, an important feature for systems used in gaming. GMA 900 was included in the 915 family of Intel chipsets.

Next came the Intel Graphics Media Accelerator 950, which is a faster version of GMA 900 and is found in Intel's 945 chipset family. GMA 950 offers a 400MHz clock speed, compared to 333MHz for GMA 900, and features support for 16:9 wide-screen flat panels, motion compensation for DVD playback, HDTV playback (720p and 1080i), digital TV support, and vertex shader 2.0 support. GMA 950 and higher versions are eligible for the Vista Premium logo, as they support running the Vista Aero interface.

The GMA versions from GMA 3000 up to GMA X3500 each add capabilities over the previous versions, such as improved hardware video decoding, enhanced high-definition video playback (Intel calls this Clear Video Technology), and features such as DirectX 10 and OpenGL 1.5 and 2.0 support.

While not designed to challenge discrete graphics chips on dedicated graphics cards, integrated video can offer reasonable graphics performance for virtually no cost. I often recommend using motherboards that feature integrated graphics as well as a slot for adding a video card later, that way you can start off by saving money using the integrated graphics, and later upgrade to a higher performance video solution by merely adding a card.

▶▶ See "Integrated Video/Motherboard Chipsets," p. 928.

AMD Chipsets

AMD took a gamble with its Athlon family of processors. With these processors, AMD decided for the first time to create a chip that was Intel compatible with regard to software but not directly hardware or pin compatible. Whereas the K6 series would plug into the same Socket 7 that Intel designed for the Pentium processor line, the AMD Athlon and Duron would not be pin compatible with the Pentium II/III and Celeron chips. This also meant that AMD could not take advantage of the previously existing chipsets and motherboards when the Athlon and Duron were introduced; instead, AMD would have to either create its own chipsets and motherboards or find other companies who would.

The gamble has paid off. AMD bootstrapped the market by introducing its own chipset, referred to as the AMD-750 chipset (code named Irongate). The AMD 750 chipset consists of the 751 System

Controller (North Bridge) and the 756 Peripheral Bus Controller (South Bridge). AMD followed with the AMD-760 chipset for the Athlon/Duron processors, which was the first major chipset on the market supporting DDR SDRAM for memory. It consists of two chips—the AMD-761 System Bus Controller (North Bridge) and the AMD-766 Peripheral Bus Controller (South Bridge). Similarly, AMD established a new standard chipset architecture for its line of 64-bit processors—the Athlon 64 and Opteron—by developing the AMD-8000 chipset. AMD's pioneering efforts have inspired other companies, such as VIA Technologies, NVIDIA, Ali, SiS, and ATI to develop chipsets specifically designed to interface with AMD processors. Finally in 2007 AMD purchased ATI, essentially bringing both motherboard chipsets and video processors in-house. This puts AMD on a level more equal to Intel, as it gives them the capability to produce most of the chips necessary to build a system around its processors.

Traditional North/South Bridge Architecture

Most of Intel's earlier chipsets (and, until a few years ago, virtually all non-Intel chipsets) are broken into a multitiered architecture incorporating what are referred to as North and South Bridge components, as well as a Super I/O chip:

- **The North Bridge**—So named because it is the connection between the high-speed processor bus (400/266/200/133/100/66MHz) and the slower AGP (533/266/133/66MHz) and PCI (33MHz) buses. The North Bridge is what the chipset is named after, meaning that, for example, what we call the 440BX chipset is derived from the fact that the actual North Bridge chip part number for that set is 82443BX.

- **The South Bridge**—So named because it is the bridge between the PCI bus (66/33MHz) and the even slower ISA bus (8MHz).

- **The Super I/O chip**—It's a separate chip attached to the ISA bus that is not really considered part of the chipset and often comes from a third party, such as National Semiconductor or Standard MicroSystems Corp. (SMSC). The Super I/O chip contains commonly used peripheral items all combined into a single chip. Note that most recent South Bridge chips now include Super I/O functions (such chips are known as Super-South Bridge chips), so that most recent motherboards no longer include a separate Super I/O chip.

▶▶ See "Super I/O Chips," p. 367.

Figure 4.30 shows a typical AMD Socket A motherboard using North/South Bridge architecture with the locations of all chips and components.

The North Bridge is sometimes referred to as the *PAC (PCI/AGP Controller)*. It is essentially the main component of the motherboard and is the only motherboard circuit besides the processor that normally runs at full motherboard (processor bus) speed. Most modern chipsets use a single-chip North Bridge; however, some of the older ones actually consisted of up to three individual chips to make up the complete North Bridge circuit.

The South Bridge is the lower-speed component in the chipset and has always been a single individual chip. The South Bridge is a somewhat interchangeable component in that different chipsets (North Bridge chips) often are designed to use the same South Bridge component. This modular design of the chipset allows for lower cost and greater flexibility for motherboard manufacturers. Similarly, many vendors produce several versions of pin-compatible South Bridge chips with different features to enable more flexible and lower-cost manufacturing and design. The South Bridge connects to the 33MHz PCI bus and contains the interface or bridge to the 8MHz ISA bus (if present). It also typically contains dual ATA/IDE hard disk controller interfaces, one or more USB interfaces, and in later designs even the CMOS RAM and real-time clock functions. In older designs, the South Bridge contained all the components that make up the ISA bus, including the interrupt and DMA controllers.

The third motherboard component, the Super I/O chip, is connected to the 8MHz ISA bus or the low pin count (LPC) bus and contains all the standard peripherals that are built into a motherboard. For example, most Super I/O chips contain the serial ports, parallel port, floppy controller, and keyboard/mouse interface. Optionally, they might contain the CMOS RAM/Clock, IDE controllers, and game port interface as well. Systems that integrate IEEE 1394 and SCSI ports use separate chips for these port types.

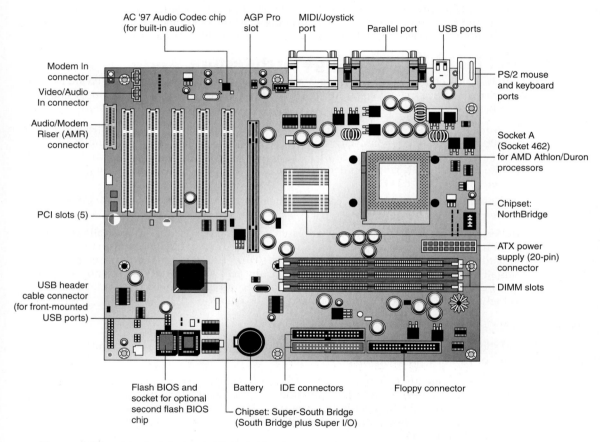

Figure 4.30   A typical Socket A (AMD Athlon/Duron) motherboard showing component locations.

Most recent motherboards that use North/South Bridge chipset designs incorporate a Super-South Bridge, which incorporates the South Bridge and Super I/O functions into a single chip.

Hub Architecture

The newer chipsets from Intel use hub architectures in which the former North Bridge chip is now called a Memory Controller Hub (MCH) and the former South Bridge is called an I/O Controller Hub (ICH). Systems that include integrated graphics use a Graphics Memory Controller Hub (GMCH) in place of the standard MCH. Rather than connect them through the PCI bus as in a standard

North/South Bridge design, they are connected via a dedicated hub interface that is at least twice as fast as PCI. The hub design offers several advantages over the conventional North/South Bridge design:

- **It's faster**—The Accelerated Hub Architecture (AHA) interface used by the 8xx series has twice the throughput of PCI. The 9xx and 3x series chipsets use an even faster version called DMI (Direct Media Interface), which is 7.5x to 14x faster than PCI.

- **Reduced PCI loading**—The hub interface is independent of PCI and doesn't share or steal PCI bus bandwidth for chipset or Super I/O traffic. This improves performance of all other PCI bus-connected devices because the PCI bus is not involved in these transactions.

- **Reduced board wiring**—The accelerated hub architecture (AHA) interface is only 8 bits wide and requires only 15 signals to be routed on the motherboard, while the Direct Media Interface (DMI) is only 4-bits wide requiring only 8 differential pairs of signals. By comparison, PCI requires no less than 64 signals be routed on the board, causing increased electromagnetic interference (EMI) generation, greater susceptibility to signal degradation and noise, and increased board manufacturing costs.

This hub interface design allows for a much greater throughput for PCI devices because there is no South Bridge chip (also carrying traffic from the Super I/O chip) hogging the PCI bus. Due to bypassing PCI, the hub interface also enables greater throughput for devices directly connected to the I/O Controller Hub (formerly the South Bridge), such as the higher-speed ATA-100/133, Serial ATA 3Gbps, and USB 2.0 interfaces.

There are two main variations on the hub interface:

- **AHA (Accelerated Hub Architecture)**—Used by the 8xx series of chipsets. AHA is a 4X (quad-clocked) 66MHz 8-bit (4×66MHz×1 byte = 266MBps) interface, which has twice the throughput of PCI (33MHz×32 bits = 133MBps).

- **DMI (Direct Media Interface)**—Used by the 9xx and 3x series chipsets. DMI is basically a dedicated 4-lane (4 bit wide) PCI Express connection allowing for 250GHz × 4 bits = 1GBps in each direction simultaneously, which is 7.5x to 14x faster than PCI.

These hub interface designs are also very economical, being only 4 or 8 bits wide. Although this seems too narrow to be useful, there is a reason for the design. The lower pin count used by the AHA or DMI hub connections means less circuit routing exists on the board, less signal noise and jitter occur, and the chips themselves have many fewer pins, making them smaller and more economical to produce. So, by virtue of a very narrow—but very fast—design, the hub interface achieves high performance with less cost and more signal integrity than with the previous North/South Bridge design.

The ICH also includes a new low-pin-count (LPC) bus, consisting basically of a stripped 4-bit wide version of PCI designed primarily to support the motherboard ROM BIOS and Super I/O chips. By using the same four signals for data, address, and command functions, only nine other signals are necessary to implement the bus, for a total of only 13 signals. This dramatically reduces the number of traces connecting the ROM BIOS chip and Super I/O chips in a system as compared to the 98 ISA bus signals necessary for older North/South Bridge chipsets that used ISA as the interface to those devices. The LPC bus has a maximum bandwidth of 16.67MBps, which is much faster than ISA and more than enough to support devices such as ROM BIOS and Super I/O chips.

Figure 4.31 shows a typical Intel chipset based motherboard that uses hub architecture.

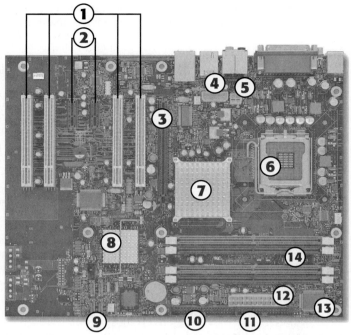

1. PCI expansion slots (4)
2. PCI Express x1 slots (2)
3. PCI Express x16 slot
4. Alternate power connector
5. ATX12V power supply connector
6. Socket LGA775
7. MCH (Memory Controller
   Hub) aka North Bridge
8. ICH (I/O Controller Hub) aka South Bridge
9. SATA/RAID host adapter connectors
10. ATA/IDE host adapter connector
11. Floppy controller connector
12. 24-pin ATX power supply connector
13. Super I/O chip
14. DDR2 DIMM sockets

Figure 4.31   Typical motherboard showing chipset and other component locations. *Illustration courtesy of Intel Corporation.*

High-speed North-South Bridge Connections

Intel is not alone in replacing the slow PCI bus connection between North and South Bridge-type chips with a faster architecture that bypasses the PCI bus. Other companies that have introduced high-speed chipset interconnects include

- **VIA**—VIA created the V-Link architecture to connect its North and South Bridge chips at speeds matching or exceeding Intel hub architecture. V-Link uses a dedicated 8-bit data bus and is currently implemented in three versions: 4x V-Link, 8x V-Link, and Ultra V-Link. 4x V-Link transfers data at 266MBps (4×66MHz), which is twice the speed of PCI and matches the speed of Intel's AHA and HI 1.5 hub architectures. 8x V-Link transfers data at 533MBps (4×133MHz), which is twice the speed of Intel's AHA interface. Ultra V-Link transfers data at 1GBps, which is four times the speed of Intel's AHA interface and equals the speed of Intel's current DMI hub architecture.

- **SiS**—SiS's MuTIOL architecture (also called *HyperStreaming*) provides performance comparable to VIA's 4x V-Link; the second-generation MuTIOL 1G used in SiS's current chipsets provides performance comparable to VIA's Ultra V-Link or Intel's DMI architectures. Chipsets that support MuTIOL use separate address, DMA, input data, and output data buses for each I/O bus master. MuTIOL buffers and manages multiple upstream and downstream data transfers over a bidirectional 16-bit data bus.

- **ATI**—ATI (now owned by AMD) used a high-speed interconnect called A-Link in its 9100-series IGP integrated chipsets. A-Link runs at 266MBps, matching Intel's AHAinterface as well as first-generation V-Link and MuTIOL designs. However, ATI now uses the HyperTransport bus for its current chipsets.

- **NVIDIA**—NVIDIA's nForce chipsets use the HyperTransport bus originally developed by AMD.

Table 4.12 compares the performance features and chipset support of major non-Intel high-speed chipset architectures.

Table 4.12   Non-Intel High-speed Chipset Interconnect Architectures

Chipset Interconnect	Throughput	Chipset Mfr.
HyperTransport 1GHz	3200MBps	AMD/ATI, NVIDIA
HyperTransport 800MHz	4000MBps	AMD/ATI, NVIDIA
A-Link	266MBps	Older ATI
MuTIOL 1G	1066MBps	SiS
MuTIOL	533MBps	SiS
Ultra V-Link	1066MBps	VIA
8x V-Link	533MBps	VIA
4x V-Link	266MBps	VIA

Let's examine the popular chipsets used from the 486 to the present.

Intel's Early 386/486 Chipsets

Intel's first real PC motherboard chipset was the 82350 chipset for the 386DX and 486 processors. This chipset was not very successful, mainly because the EISA bus was not very popular and many other manufacturers were making standard 386 and 486 motherboard chipsets at the time. The market changed very quickly, and Intel dropped the EISA bus support and introduced follow-up 486 chipsets that were much more successful.

Table 4.13 shows the Intel 486 chipsets.

Table 4.13   Intel 486 Motherboard Chipsets

Chipset	420TX	420EX	420ZX
Code name	Saturn	Aries	Saturn II
Date introduced	Nov. 1992	March 1994	March 1994
Processor	5V 486	5V/3.3V 486	5V/3.3V 486
Bus speed	Up to 33MHz	Up to 50MHz	Up to 33MHz
SMP (dual CPUs)	No	No	No

Table 4.13   Continued

Chipset	420TX	420EX	420ZX
Memory types	FPM	FPM	FPM
Parity/ECC	Parity	Parity	Parity
Max. memory	128MB	128MB	160MB
L2 cache type	Async	Async	Async
PCI support	2.0	2.0	2.1
AGP support	No	No	No

AGP = Accelerated graphics port
FPM = Fast page mode
PCI = Peripheral component interconnect
SMP = Symmetric multiprocessing (dual processors)
Note: PCI 2.1 supports concurrent PCI operations.

The 420 series chipsets were the first to introduce the North/South Bridge design that is still used in many chipsets today.

Fifth-generation (P5 Pentium Class) Chipsets

With the advent of the Pentium processor in March 1993, Intel also introduced its first Pentium chipset: the 430LX chipset (code named Mercury). This was the first Pentium chipset on the market and set the stage as Intel took this lead and ran with it. Other manufacturers took months to a year or more to get their Pentium chipsets out the door. Since the debut of its Pentium chipsets, Intel has dominated the chipset market. Table 4.14 shows the Intel Pentium motherboard chipsets. Note that none of these chipsets support AGP; Intel first added support for AGP in its chipsets for the Pentium II/Celeron processors.

Table 4.14   Intel Pentium Motherboard Chipsets (North Bridge)

Chipset	430LX	430NX	430FX	430MX	430HX	430VX	430TX
Code name	Mercury	Neptune	Triton	Mobile Triton	Triton II	Triton III	n/a
Date introduced	March 1993	March 1994	Jan. 1995	Oct. 1995	Feb. 1996	Feb. 1996	Feb. 1997
CPU bus speed	66MHz	66MHz	66MHz	66MHz	66MHz	66MHz	66MHz
CPUs supported	P60/66	P75+	P75+	P75+	P75+	P75+	P75+
SMP (dual CPUs)	No	Yes	No	No	Yes	No	No
Memory types	FPM	FPM	FPM/EDO	FPM/EDO	FPM/EDO	FPM/EDO/ SDRAM	FPM/EDO/ SDRAM
Parity/ECC	Parity	Parity	Neither	Neither	Both	Neither	Neither
Max. memory	192MB	512MB	128MB	128MB	512MB	128MB	256MB
Max. cacheable	192MB	512MB	64MB	64MB	512MB	64MB	64MB
L2 cache type	Async	Async	Async/Pburst	Async/Pburst	Async/Pburst	Async/Pburst	Async/Pburst

Table 4.14   Continued

Chipset	430LX	430NX	430FX	430MX	430HX	430VX	430TX
PCI support	2.0	2.0	2.0	2.0	2.1	2.1	2.1
AGP support	No	No	No	No	No	No	No
South Bridge	SIO	SIO	PIIX	MPIIX	PIIX3	PIIX3	PIIX4

EDO = Extended data out   SDRAM = Synchronous dynamic RAM
FPM = Fast page mode   SIO = System I/O
PIIX = PCI ISA IDE Xcelerator   SMP = Symmetric multiprocessing (dual processors)

Note

PCI 2.1 supports concurrent PCI operations, enabling multiple PCI cards to perform transactions at the same time for greater speed.

Table 4.15 shows the Intel South Bridge chips used with Intel chipsets for Pentium processors. South Bridge chips are the second part of the modern Intel motherboard chipsets.

Table 4.15   Intel South Bridge Chips

Chip Name	SIO	PIIX	PIIX3	PIIX4	PIIX4E	ICH0	ICH
Part number	82378IB/ZB	82371FB	82371SB	82371AB	82371EB	82801AB	82801AA
IDE support	None	BMIDE	BMIDE	UDMA-33	UDMA-33	UDMA-33	UDMA-66
USB support	None	None	Yes	Yes	Yes	Yes	Yes
CMOS/clock	No	No	No	Yes	Yes	Yes	Yes
Power management	SMM	SMM	SMM	SMM	SMM/ACPI	SMM/ACPI	SMM/ACPI

ACPI = Advanced configuration and power interface   SIO = System I/O
BMIDE = Bus master IDE (ATA)   SMM = System management mode
ICH = I/O Controller Hub   UDMA = Ultra-DMA IDE (ATA)
IDE = Integrated Drive Electronics (AT attachment)   USB = Universal serial bus (version 1.1)
PIIX = PCI ISA IDE Xcelerator

The Pentium chipsets listed in Tables 4.14 and 4.15 have been out of production for several years, and most computers that use these chipsets have been retired. For more information about these chipsets, see Chapter 4 in *Upgrading and Repairing PCs, 16th Edition.*

The development of non-Intel Pentium-class chipsets was spurred by AMD's development of its own equivalents to the Pentium processor—the K5 and K6 processor families. Although the K5 was not a successful processor, the K6 family was very successful in the low-cost (under $1,000) market and as an upgrade for Pentium systems. AMD's own chipsets aren't used as often as other third-party chipsets, but AMD's capability to support its own processors with timely chipset deliveries has helped make the K6 and its successors into credible rivals for Intel's processor families and has spurred other vendors, such as VIA, Acer Laboratories, and SiS, to support AMD's processors. Major third-party chipsets for Pentium-class processors include

- AMD 640
- VIA Apollo VP1, VP2, VPX, VP3, MVP3, and MVP4
- ALi Aladdin 4, Aladdin 5, and Aladdin 7
- SiS SiS540, SiS530/5595, SiS5598, SiS5581, SiS5582, SiS5571, SiS5591, and SiS5592

Most computers that use these chipsets have been retired. For more detailed information about these chipsets, see *Upgrading and Repairing PCs, 14th Edition*.

Sixth-generation (P6 Pentium Pro/II/III Class) Chipsets

Just as Intel clearly dominated the Pentium chipset world, it was also the leading vendor for chipsets supporting its P6 processor families.

Note that because the Pentium Pro, Celeron, and Pentium II/III were essentially the same processor with different cache designs and minor internal revisions, the same chipset can be used for Socket 8 (Pentium Pro), Socket 370 (Celeron/Pentium III), and Slot 1 (Celeron/Pentium II/III) designs.

Table 4.16 shows the chipsets used on Pentium Pro motherboards.

Note

PCI 2.1 supports concurrent PCI operations.

Table 4.17   P6 Processor Chipsets Using North/South Bridge Architecture

Chipset	440FX	440LX	440EX
Code name	Natoma	None	None
Date introduced	May 1996	Aug. 1997	April 1998
Part numbers	82441FX, 82442FX	82443LX	82443EX
Bus speed	66MHz	66MHz	66MHz
Supported processors	Pentium II	Pentium II	Celeron
SMP (dual CPUs)	Yes	Yes	No
Memory types	FPM/EDO/BEDO	FPM/EDO/SDRAM	EDO/SDRAM
Parity/ECC	Both	Both	Neither
Maximum memory	1GB	1GB EDO/512MB SDRAM	256MB
Memory banks	4	4	2
PCI support	2.1	2.1	2.1
AGP support	No	AGP 2x	AGP 2x
South Bridge	82371SB (PIIX3)	82371AB (PIIX4)	82371EB (PIIX4E)

Table 4.16   Pentium Pro Motherboard Chipsets (North Bridge)

Chipset	450KX	450GX	440FX
Code name	Orion	Orion Server	Natoma
Workstation date introduced	Nov. 1995	Nov. 1995	May 1996
Bus speed	66MHz	66MHz	66MHz
SMP (dual CPUs)	Yes	Yes (up to 4)	Yes
Memory types	FPM	FPM	FPM/EDO/BEDO
Parity/ECC	Both	Both	Both
Maximum memory	1GB	4GB	1GB
L2 cache type	In CPU	In CPU	In CPU
Maximum cacheable	1GB	4GB	1GB
PCI support	2.0	2.0	2.1
AGP support	No	No	No
AGP speed	n/a	n/a	n/a
South Bridge	Various	Various	PIIX3

AGP = Accelerated graphics port
BEDO = Burst EDO
EDO = Extended data out
FPM = Fast page mode
Pburst = Pipeline burst (synchronous)

PCI = Peripheral component interconnect
PIIX = PCI ISA IDE Xcelerator
SDRAM = Synchronous dynamic RAM
SIO = System I/O
SMP = Symmetric multiprocessing (dual processors)

For the Celeron and Pentium II/III motherboards, Intel offers the chipsets in Table 4.17. 4xx series chipsets incorporate a North/South Bridge architecture, whereas 8xx series chipsets support the newer and faster hub architecture. P6/P7 (Pentium III/Celeron, Pentium 4, and Xeon) processor chipsets using hub architecture are shown in Table 4.18.

440BX	440GX	450NX	440ZX
None	None	None	None
April 1998	June 1998	June 1998	Nov. 1998
82443BX	82443GX	82451NX, 82452NX, 82453NX, 82454NX	82443ZX
66/100MHz	100MHz	100MHz	66/100MHz[1]
Pentium II/III, Celeron	Pentium II/III, Xeon	Pentium II/III, Xeon	Celeron, Pentium II/III
Yes	Yes	Yes, up to four	No
SDRAM	SDRAM	FPM/EDO	SDRAM
Both	Both	Both	Neither
1GB	2GB	8GB	256MB
4	4	4	2
2.1	2.1	2.1	2.1
AGP 2x	AGP 2x	No	AGP 2x
82371EB (PIIX4E)	82371EB (PIIX4E)	82371EB (PIIX4E)	82371EB (PIIX4E)

[1] The 440ZX is available in a cheaper 440ZX-66 version that runs only at 66MHz.

Table 4.18   P6 (Pentium III/Celeron) Processor Chipsets Using Hub Architecture

Chipset	810	810E	815[3]	815E[3]	815EP
Code name	Whitney	Whitney	Solano	Solano	Solano
Date introduced	April 1999	Sept. 1999	June 2000	June 2000	Nov. 2000
Part number	82810	82810E	82815	82815	82815EP
Bus speed	66/100MHz	66/100/ 133MHz	66/100/ 133MHz	66/100/ 133MHz	66/100/ 133MHz
Supported processors	Celeron, Pentium II/III	Celeron, Pentium II/III	Celeron, Pentium II/III	Celeron, Pentium II/III	Celeron, Pentium II/III
SMP(dual CPUs)	No	No	No	No	No
Memory types	EDO SDRAM	SDRAM	SDRAM	SDRAM	SDRAM
Memory speeds	PC100	PC100	PC133	PC133	PC133
Parity/ECC	Neither	Neither	Neither	Neither	Neither
Maximum memory	512MB	512MB	512MB	512MB	512MB
AGP slot	No	No	AGP 4x	AGP 4x	AGP 4x
Integrated video	AGP 2x[1]	AGP 2x[1]	AGP 2x[2]	AGP 2x[2]	No
South Bridge (ICH)	82801AA/AB (ICH/ICH0)	82801AA (ICH)	82801AA (ICH)	82801BA (ICH2)	82801BA (ICH2)

[1] *These 810/815 chipsets have integral AGP 2x 3D video that is NOT upgradeable via an external AGP adapter.*

[2] *The 815/815E chipsets have integral AGP 2x 3D video that IS upgradeable via an APG 4x slot.*

[3] *The only difference between the 815 and 815E is in which I/O controller hub (South Bridge) is used.*

AGP = Accelerated graphics port

BEDO = Burst EDO

EDO = Extended data out

FPM = Fast page mode

Note

Pentium Pro, Celeron, and Pentium II/III CPUs have their secondary caches integrated into the CPU package. Therefore, cache characteristics for these machines are not dependent on the chipset but are quite dependent on the processor instead.

Most Intel chipsets are designed as a two-part system, using a North Bridge (MCH or GMCH in hub-based designs) and a South Bridge (ICH in hub-based designs) component. Often the same South Bridge or ICH component can be used with several different North Bridge (MCH or GMCH) chipsets. Table 4.18 shows a list of all the Intel South Bridge components used with P6-class processors and their capabilities. The ICH2 is also used as part of some of the first seventh-generation (Pentium 4/Celeron 4) Intel chipsets.

820	820E	840	815P	815EG	815G
Camino	Camino	Carmel	Solano	Solano	Solano
Nov. 1999	June 2000	Oct. 1999	March 2001	Sept. 2001	Sept. 2001
82820	82820	82840	82815EP	82815G	82815G
66/100/ 133MHz	66/100/ 133MHz	66/100/ 133MHz	66/100/ 133MHz	66/100/ 133MHz	66/100/ 133MHz
Pentium II/III, Celeron	Pentium II/III, Celeron	Pentium III, Xeon	Celeron, Pentium III	Celeron, Pentium III	Celeron, PentiumIII
Yes	Yes	Yes	No	No	No
RDRAM	RDRAM	RDRAM	SDRAM	SDRAM	SDRAM
PC800	PC800	PC800 dual-channel	PC100, PC133	PC66, PC100, PC133	PC66, PC100, PC133
Both	Both	Both	Neither	Neither	Neither
1GB	1GB	4GB	512MB	512MB	512MB
AGP 4x	AGP 4x	AGP 4x	AGP 4x	No	No
No	No	No	No	AGP 2x[1]	AGP 2x[1]
82801AA (ICH)	82801BA (ICH2)	82801AA (ICH)	82801AA/AB (ICH/ICH0)	82801BA (ICH2)	82801AA/ AB (ICH/ICH0)

ICH = I/O controller hub

Pburst = Pipeline burst (synchronous)

PCI = Peripheral component interconnect

PIIX = PCI ISA IDE Xcelerator

SDRAM = Synchronous dynamic RAM

SIO = System I/O

SMP = Symmetric multiprocessing (dual processors)

The following sections examine the chipsets for P6 processors up through the Celeron and Pentium III, starting with the Intel 800 series chipsets. For a more detailed look at the 400 series, refer to Chapter 4 of *Upgrading and Repairing PCs, 16th Edition*.

Table 4.19   Intel South Bridge-I/O Controller Hub Chips for P6

Chip Name	SIO	PIIX	PIIX3	PIIX4	PIIX4E	ICH0	ICH	ICH2
Part number	82378IB/ZB	82371FB	82371SB	82371AB	82371EB	82801AB	82801AA	82801BA
IDE support	None	BMIDE	BMIDE	UDMA-33	UDMA-33	UDMA-33	UDMA-66	UDMA-100
USB support	None	None	1C/2P	1C/2P	1C/2P	1C/2P	1C/2P	2C/4P
CMOS/clock	No	No	No	Yes	Yes	Yes	Yes	Yes

Table 4.19   Continued

Chip Name	SIO	PIIX	PIIX3	PIIX4	PIIX4E	ICH0	ICH	ICH2
ISA support	Yes	Yes	Yes	Yes	Yes	No	No	No
LPC support	No	No	No	No	No	Yes	Yes	Yes
Power management	SMM	SMM	SMM	SMM	SMM/ACPI	SMM/ACPI	SMM/ACPI	SMM/ACPI

SIO = System I/O
PIIX = PCI ISA IDE (ATA) Xcelerator
ICH = I/O controller hub
USB = Universal serial bus
1C/2P = 1 controller, 2 ports
2C/4P = 2 controllers, 4 ports
IDE = Integrated Drive Electronics (ATA = AT attachment)

BMIDE = Bus master IDE (ATA)
UDMA = Ultra-DMA IDE (ATA)
ISA = Industry standard architecture bus
LPC = Low pin count bus
SMM = System management mode
ACPI = Advanced configuration and power interface

Intel 810, 810E, and 810E2

Introduced in April 1999, the Intel 810 chipset (code named Whitney) represents a major change in chipset design from the standard North and South Bridges that have been used since the 486 days. The 810 chipset allows for improvements in system performance, all for less cost and system complexity. The 810 (which supports 66MHz and 100MHz processor buses) was later revised as the 810E with support for the 133MHz processor bus.

Note

The 810E2 uses the same 82810E GMCH as the 810E but pairs it with the 82801BA I/O Controller Hub (ICH2) used by the Intel 815E. For information about the 82801BA ICH2 chip, see the section "Intel 815 Family," later in this chapter.

The major features of the 810E chipset include

- 66/100/133MHz system bus
- Integrated AGP 2x Intel 3D graphics
- Efficient use of system memory for graphics performance
- Optional 4MB of dedicated display cache video memory
- Digital Video Out port compatible with DVI specification for flat-panel displays
- Software MPEG-2 DVD playback with hardware motion compensation
- 266MBps hub interface
- Support for ATA-66
- Integrated Audio-Codec 97 (AC'97) controller
- Support for low-power sleep modes
- Random number generator (RNG)
- Integrated USB 1.1 controller

- LPC bus for Super I/O and Firmware Hub (ROM BIOS) connection
- Elimination of ISA bus

The 810E chipset consists of three major components:

- **82810E Graphics Memory Controller Hub (GMCH)**—421 BGA package (the original 810 chipset used the 82810 GMCH).
- **82801 Integrated Controller Hub (ICH)**—241 BGA package.
- **82802 Firmware Hub (FWH)**—Come in either 32-pin plastic leaded chip carrier (PLCC) or 40-pin thin small outline package (TSOP) packages. Although a functional part of the chipset, this component is actually sold separately by Intel to motherboard developers.

Compared to the previous North/South Bridge designs, there are some fairly significant changes in the 810 chipset. The previous system designs had the North Bridge acting as the memory controller, talking to the South Bridge chip via the PCI bus. This new design has the GMCH taking the place of the North Bridge, which talks to the ICH via a 66MHz dedicated interface called the *accelerated hub architecture (AHA) bus* instead of the previously used PCI bus. In particular, implementing a direct connection between the North and South Bridges in this manner was key in implementing the new UDMA-66 high-speed IDE interface for hard disks, DVD drives, and other IDE devices.

Figure 4.32 shows a system block diagram for the 810E chipset. With the 810 chipset family, ISA is finally dead.

The 82810E GMCH uses an internal Direct AGP (integrated AGP) interface to create 2D and 3D effects and images. The video capability integrated into the 82810E chip features hardware motion compensation to improve software DVD video quality; it also features both analog and direct digital video out ports, which enable connections to either traditional TVs (via an external converter module) or a direct digital flat-panel display. The GMCH chip also incorporates the System Manageability Bus, which enables networking equipment to monitor the 810 chipset platform. Using ACPI specifications, the system manageability function enables low-power sleep mode and conserves energy when the system is idle.

The 82801 I/O Controller Hub employs AHA for a direct connection from the GMCH chip. This is twice as fast (266MBps) as the previous North/South Bridge connections that used the PCI bus, and it uses far fewer pins for reduced electrical noise. Plus, the AHA bus is dedicated, meaning that no other devices will be on it. The AHA bus also incorporates optimized arbitration rules allowing more functions to run concurrently, enabling better video and audio performance.

The ICH also integrates dual IDE controllers, which run up to either 33MBps (UDMA-33 or Ultra-ATA/33) or 66MBps (UDMA-66 or Ultra-ATA/66). Note that two versions of the ICH chip exist. The 82801AA (ICH) incorporates the 66MBps-capable ATA/IDE and supports up to six PCI slots, whereas the 82801AB (ICH0) supports only 33MBps ATA/IDE maximum and supports up to four PCI slots.

The ICH also integrates an interface to an Audio-Codec 97 (AC'97) controller, dual USB ports, and the PCI bus with up to four or six slots. The Integrated Audio-Codec 97 controller enables software audio and modem by using the processor to run sound and modem software via very simple digital-to-analog conversion circuits. Reusing existing system resources lowers the system cost by eliminating components.

The 82802 Firmware Hub (FWH) incorporates the system BIOS and video BIOS, eliminating a redundant nonvolatile memory component. The BIOS within the FWH is flash-type memory, so it can be field-updated at any time. In addition, the 82802 contains a hardware RNG. The RNG provides truly random numbers to enable fundamental security building blocks supporting stronger encryption, digital signing, and security protocols. Two versions of the FWH are available, called the 82802AB and 82802ACy. The AB version incorporates 512KB (4Mb) of flash BIOS memory, and the AC version incorporates a full 1MB (8Mb) of BIOS ROM.

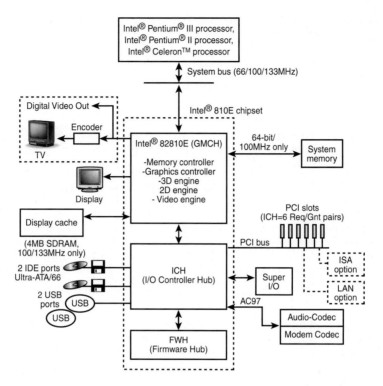

Figure 4.32   Intel 810E chipset system block diagram.

With the Intel 810 and 810E chipsets, Intel did something that many in the industry were afraid of: It integrated the video and graphics controller directly into the motherboard chipset with no means of upgrade. This means systems using the 810 chipset don't have an AGP slot and aren't capable of using conventional AGP video cards. For the low-end market for which this chipset is designed, lacking an AGP slot shouldn't be too much of a drawback. Higher-end systems, on the other hand, use the 815 or other chipsets that do support AGP slots. Intel calls the integrated interface *Direct AGP*, and it describes the direct connection between the memory and processor controllers with the video controller all within the same chip.

This means the video card as we know it will be reserved only for midrange and higher-end systems, as well as gaming-oriented systems. With the 810 as well as subsequent chipsets with integrated video, Intel has let it be known in a big way that it has entered the PC video business.

In fact, the theme with the 810 chipset is one of integration. The integrated video means no video cards are required; the integrated AC'97 interface means that conventional modems and sound cards are not required. Plus, there is an integrated CMOS/Clock chip (in the ICH), and even the BIOS is integrated in the FWH chip.

Intel Random Number Generator

The 8xx chipset series features the Intel Random Number Generator (RNG). The RNG is built into the 82802 FWH, which is the ROM BIOS component used on 8xx-based motherboards. The RNG provides software with true nondeterministic random numbers.

Most security routines, especially those providing authentication or encryption services, require random numbers for purposes such as key code generation. One method of cracking these types of codes is to predict the random numbers being used to generate the keys. Current methods that use system and user input as a seed to a conventional pseudorandom number generator have proven vulnerable to this type of attack. The Intel RNG uses thermal noise across a resistor contained in the FWH (that is, ROM BIOS in 8xx-based boards) to generate true nondeterministic, unpredictable random numbers. Therefore, "random" numbers generated by 8xx-series chipsets really are random.

Intel 815 Family

Introduced in June 2000, the 815 and 815E chipsets are mainstream PC chipsets with integral video that is also upgradeable via an AGP 4x slot. The E versions include the ICH2 I/O controller hub, which features two USB 1.1 controllers (four ports) and ATA-100 support. The 815P and EP versions were introduced later and lacked the integrated video for lower cost. In September 2001, the last members of the family—the 815G and 815EG—were introduced. Note that the G indicates that these chipsets also include integrated video, which was superior to the video included with the original 815 and 815E.

The 815 chipsets are designed for Slot-1 or Socket-370 processors, such as the Celeron or Pentium III. These are the first chipsets from Intel designed to directly support PC133 SDRAM memory, allowing for a more affordable solution than other chipsets using RDRAM memory. Similar to the other 8xx series chipsets from Intel, the 815 uses hub architecture that provides a 266MBps connection between the main chipset components and does not share the PCI bus like the prior North/South Bridge designs.

Although six variations on the 815 chipset are available, only five different parts are used to create the various members of the family: one memory controller hub (82815EP MCH: North Bridge replacement without integrated graphics), two graphics memory controller hubs (82815 or 82815G GMCH: North Bridge replacement with integrated graphics), and two I/O controller hubs (ICH and ICH2).

All 815 chipsets support the following features:

- 66/100/133MHz system bus
- 266MBps hub interface
- ATA-100 (815E/EP/EG) or ATA-66 (815/P/G)
- PC100 or PC133 CL-2 SDRAM (also PC66 with 815G/EG)
- Up to 512MB RAM
- Integrated Audio-Codec 97 (AC'97) controller
- Low-power sleep modes
- RNG for stronger security products
- One (815/P/G) or two (815E/EP/EG) integrated USB 1.1 controllers with either two or four ports, respectively
- LPC bus for Super I/O and Firmware Hub (ROM BIOS) connection
- Elimination of ISA Bus

The 815/E/G/EG also support the following:

- Integrated Intel AGP 2x 3D graphics
- Efficient use of system memory for graphics performance
- Optional 4MB of dedicated display cache video memory
- Digital Video Out port compatible with DVI specification for flat-panel displays
- Software MPEG-2 DVD playback with hardware motion compensation

The 815E/EP/EG uses the ICH2, which is most notable for providing ATA-100 support, allowing 100MBps drive performance. Of course, few drives can really take advantage of this much throughput, but in any case, a bottleneck won't occur there. The other notable feature is having two USB 1.1 controllers and four ports on board. This allows double the USB performance by splitting up devices over the two ports and can allow up to four connections before a hub is required.

Integrated Ethernet

Another important feature of the 815 series is the integration of a fast Ethernet controller directly into the chipset. The integrated LAN controller works with one of three new physical layer components from Intel and enables three distinct solutions for computer manufacturers. These include

- Enhanced 10/100Mbps Ethernet with Alert on LAN technology
- Basic 10/100Mbps Ethernet
- 1Mbps HomePNA (phone-line) home networking

These physical layer components can be placed directly on the PC motherboard (additional chips) or installed via an adapter that plugs into the CNR slot. The CNR slot and cards enable PC assemblers to build network-ready systems for several markets.

AGP Inline Memory Module

Although the 815/815E feature is essentially the same built-in AGP 2x 3D video that comes with the 810 chipset, the difference is upgradeability. The video can easily be upgraded by adding a graphics performance accelerator (GPA) card (see Figure 4.33) or an AGP 4x card for maximum 3D graphics and video performance. The GPA card (also called the AGP Inline Memory Module, or AIMM) is essentially a high-performance video memory card that works in the AGP 4x slot and improves the performance of the integrated video by up to 30%. Unfortunately, these are not commonly sold and are somewhat expensive. For even more performance, you can install a full 4x AGP card in the AGP 4x slot, which disables the integrated video. By having the video integrated, very low-cost systems with reasonable video performance can be assembled. By later installing either the GPA or a full 4x AGP card, you can improve video performance up to 100% or more.

PC133 Memory Support

Another important feature of the 815 chipset is the support of PC133 memory. The 815 family also uses PC100 memory. With PC133 support, Intel has also officially set a standard for PC133 memory that was higher than some of the PC133 memory on the market at the time of introduction. To meet the Intel PC133 specification, the memory must support what is called 2-2-2 timing, sometimes also known as *CAS-2 (column address strobe)* or *CL-2 timing*. The numbers refer to the number of clock cycles for the following functions to complete:

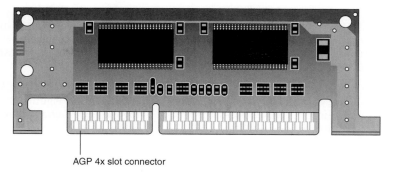

AGP 4x slot connector

Figure 4.33   A typical 4MB GPA/AIMM module, which attaches to the AGP slot of a motherboard using the 815 or 815E chipset.

- **Precharge command to Active command**—Charges the memory's storage capacitors to prepare them for data
- **Active command to Read command**—Selects rows and columns in memory array for reading
- **Read command to Data Out**—Reads data from selected rows and columns for transmission

Some of the PC133 memory on the market takes three cycles for each of these functions and would therefore be termed PC133 3-3-3, CAS-3, or CL-3 memory. Note that the faster PC133 CL-2 can be used in place of the slower CL-3 variety, but not the other way around.

As a result of the tighter cycling timing, PC133 CL-2 offers a lead-off latency of only 30ns, instead of the 45ns required by PC133 CL-3. This results in a 34% improvement in initial access due to the decreased latency.

The 815 chipset was a popular chipset for the mainstream PC market that didn't want to pay the higher prices for RDRAM memory. The 815 was essentially designed to replace the venerable 440BX chipset.

Intel 820 and 820E

The Intel 820 chipsets use the hub-based architecture like all the 800 series chips and are designed to support slot 1 or socket 370 processors, such as the Pentium III and Celeron. The 820 chipset supports RDRAM memory technology, 133MHz system bus, and 4x AGP.

The 82820 MCH provides the processor, memory, and AGP interfaces. Two versions are available: One supports a single processor (82820), whereas the other supports two processors (82820DP). Either is designed to work with the same 82801 ICH is used with the other 800 series chipsets, such as the 810 and 840. The 820 chipset also uses the 82802 FWH for BIOS storage and for the Intel RNG.

The connection between the MCH and ICH uses what is called the *Intel Hub Architecture bus* instead of the PCI bus, as with prior North/South Bridge chipsets. The hub architecture bus provides twice the bandwidth of PCI at 266MB per second, enabling twice as much data to flow between them. The hub architecture bus also has optimized arbitration rules, allowing more functions to run concurrently, as well as far fewer signal pins, reducing the likelihood of encountering or generating noise and signal errors.

The 820 chipset is designed to use RDRAM memory, which has a maximum throughput of up to 1.6GBps. The 820 supports PC600, PC700, and PC800 RDRAM, delivering up to 1.6GBps of theoretical memory bandwidth in the PC800 version. PC800 RDRAM is a 400MHz bus running double-clocked and transferring 16 bits (2 bytes) at a time (2×400MHz×2 bytes = 1.6GBps). Two RIMM sockets are available to support up to 1GB of total system memory.

The AGP interface in the 820 enables graphics controllers to access main memory at AGP 4x speed, which is about 1GB per second—twice that of previous AGP 2x platforms. Figure 4.34 shows the 820 chipset architecture. Because the 820 was designed for midrange to higher-end systems, it does not include integrated graphics, relying instead on the AGP 4x slot to contain a graphics card.

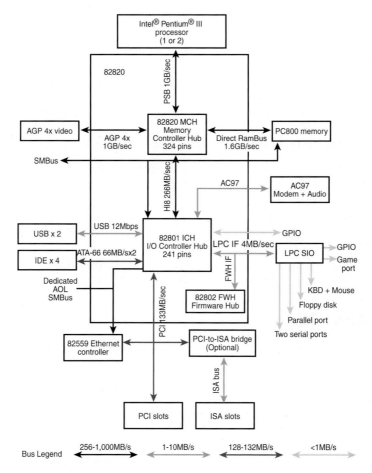

Figure 4.34   Intel 820 chipset architecture.

820 Chipset features include

- 100/133MHz processor bus
- Intel 266MBps hub interface

- PC800 RDRAM RIMM memory support
- AGP 4x support
- ATA-100 (820E) or ATA-66 interface
- Intel RNG
- LPC interface
- AC'97 controller
- One (820) or two (820E) USB 1.1 buses with either two or four ports, respectively

The 820 chipset consists of three main components with a few optional extras. The main component is the 82820 (single-processor) or 82820DP (dual-processor) MCH, which is a 324 BGA chip. That is paired with an 82801 ICH, which is a 241 BGA chip, and finally it has the 82802 FWH, which is really just a fancy Flash ROM BIOS chip. Optionally, there can be an 82380AB PCI-ISA bridge that is used only if the board is equipped with ISA slots.

The newer 820E version uses an updated 82801BA ICH2, which supports ATA-100 and incorporates dual USB 1.1 controllers with two ports each, for a total of four USB 1.1 ports.

820 Chipset MTH Bug

The 820 chipset is designed to support RDRAM memory directly. However, because the market still demanded lower-cost SDRAM, Intel created an RDRAM-to-SDRAM translator chip called the *Memory Translator Hub (MTH)*. This enabled Intel to produce 820 chipset motherboards that supported SDRAM instead of the more expensive RDRAM.

Because the design of the MTH was proven defective, the chip (and any board using it) was simply discontinued. On May 10, 2000, Intel officially announced that it would replace any motherboards using the MTH with a new board lacking the component. The MTH translates signals from SDRAM memory to the Intel 820 chipset and is used only with motherboards utilizing SDRAM and the Intel 820 chipset; boards using RDRAM don't have an MTH and were not affected. Intel found electrical noise issues with the MTH that can cause some systems to intermittently reset, reboot, or hang. In addition, the noise issue can, under extreme conditions, potentially cause data corruption.

The MTH bug forced Intel to recall and replace more than a million motherboards in mid-2000, with new versions lacking the MTH and thus supporting only RDRAM memory. The final bill for this recall was reported at about $253 million, making it perhaps the most costly recall of computer components since the infamous Pentium math bug in 1994. I found it interesting that, due to the fact that Intel did more than $24.4 billion in sales the previous year, at least one article classified the cost of this recall as "chump change" to the chip giant!

At one time, Intel offered an MTH I.D. utility that told you whether you had that component and whether your board was eligible for replacement, including a 128MB RDRAM RIMM. However, Intel is no longer supporting this chipset, and the utility is not available. Again, note that the 820 chipset was really designed to support RDRAM as the native type of memory, and RDRAM-based systems are not affected because they don't use the memory translator hub component.

Intel 840

The Intel 840 is a high-end chipset designed for use in high-performance multiprocessor systems using Slot 1, Slot 2 (Xeon processor), or Socket 370 processors. The 840 chipset uses the same hub architecture and modular design as the rest of the 800 family chipsets, with some additional components enabling more performance.

As with the other 800 series chipsets, the 840 has three main components:

- **82840 Memory Controller Hub**—Provides graphics support for AGP 2x/4x, dual RDRAM memory channels, and multiple PCI bus segments for high-performance I/O.

- **82801 I/O Controller Hub**—Equivalent to the South Bridge in older chipset designs, except it connects directly to the MCH component via the high-speed Intel Hub Architecture bus. The ICH supports 32-bit PCI, IDE controllers, and dual USB ports.

- **82802 Firmware Hub**—Basically an enhanced Flash ROM chip that stores system BIOS and video BIOS, as well as an Intel RNG. The RNG provides truly random numbers to enable stronger encryption, digital signing, and security protocols.

In addition to the core components, parts are available for scaling up to a more powerful design. Three additional components can be added:

- **82806 64-bit PCI Controller Hub (P64H)**—Supports 64-bit PCI slots at speeds of either 33MHz or 66MHz. The P64H connects directly to the MCH using Intel Hub Architecture, providing a dedicated path for high-performance I/O. This is the first implementation of the 66MHz 66-bit PCI on a PC motherboard chipset, allowing for a PCI bus four times faster than the standard 32-bit 33MHz version.

- **82803 RDRAM-based Memory Repeater Hub (MRH-R)**—Converts each memory channel into two memory channels for expanded memory capacity.

- **82804 SDRAM-based Memory Repeater Hub (MRH-S)**—Translates the RDRAM protocol into SDRAM-based signals for system memory flexibility. This would be used only in 840 systems that supported SDRAM.

Figure 4.35 shows the 840 chipset architecture.

840 chipset features include

- 100/133MHz processor bus
- Dual RDRAM memory channels, operating simultaneously and providing up to 3.2GBps memory bandwidth
- 16-bit wide implementation of Intel Hub Architecture (HI16), which enables high-performance concurrent PCI I/O with the optional P64H component
- AGP 4x
- Prefetch cache, unique to the 840 chipset, which enables highly efficient data flow and helps maximize system concurrency
- Intel RNG (see the section "Intel Random Number Generator," earlier in this chapter)
- USB 1.1 support

Optionally, network interface and RAID controller interface chips can be added as well.

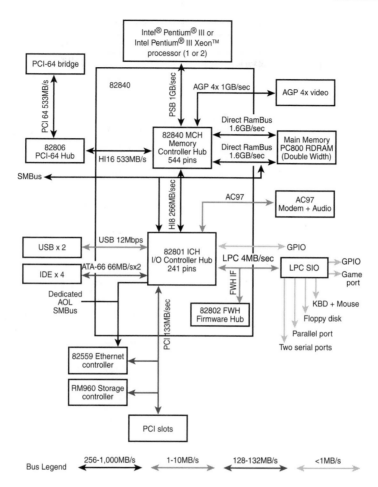

Figure 4.35   Intel 840 chipset architecture.

Third-party (Non-Intel) P6-Class Chipsets

Several companies produce chipsets designed to support P6-class processors, including ALi Corporation (formerly known as Acer Laboratories), VIA Technologies, and SiS. The following sections discuss the offerings from these companies.

ALi/ULi (Acer Labs) Chipsets for P6-Class Processors

ALi (Acer Labs inc) spun off its chipset division in 2003 as ULi Electronics, then ULi was acquired by NVIDIA in 2006. ALi manufactured a variety of chipsets for the P6-class processors. Table 4.20 provides an overview of these chipsets.

Table 4.20   ALi Chipsets for Pentium Pro-II-III-Celeron

Chipset	Aladdin Pro II	Aladdin Pro 4	Aladdin TNT2	Aladdin Pro 5
Date introduced	1999	2000	1999	2000, 2001(T)
Part number	M1621	M1641/M1641B	M1631	M1651, M1651T
Bus speed	60, 66, 100MHz	100, 133, 200, 266MHZ (B)	66, 100, 133MHz	66, 100, 133, 200, 266MHz
Supported processors	Pentium II, Pentium Pro	Pentium II, III, Celeron	Pentium II, III, Celeron	Pentium II, III, Celeron (T version supports Tualatin)
Form factor	Slot 1, Socket 370	Slot 1, Socket 370	Slot 1, Socket 370	Slot 1, Socket 370
SMP (dual CPUs)	Yes	No	No	No
Memory types	FPM, EDO, PC100	PC100, PC133, DDR200, DDR266 (B)	PC66, 100, 133, EDO	PC66, PC100, PC133, DDR200, DDR266
Parity/ECC	ECC	ECC	ECC	Neither
Maximum memory	1GB (SDRAM), 2GB (EDO)	1.5GB	1.5GB	3GB
PCI support	2.2	2.2	2.2	2.2
PCI speed/ width	33MHz/32-bit	33MHz/32-bit	33MHz/32-bit	33MHz/32-bit
AGP slot	1x/2x	1x/2x/4x	No	1x/2x/4x
Integrated video	No	No	Yes—TnT2	No
South Bridge	M1533 or M1543	M1535D	M1543C	M1535D

Table 4.21 provides an overview of the features of the South Bridge chips used in these chipsets.

Table 4.21   ULi (Acer Labs) South Bridge Chips Used with P6-Class Chipsets

South Bridge Chip	Number of USB 1.1 Ports	ATA Support	Integrated Sound	Integrated Super I/O
M1533	2	ATA-33	No	No
M1543	2	ATA-33	No	Yes
M1535D	4	ATA-66	Yes[1]	Yes
M1535D+	6[2]	ATA-100	Yes[3]	Yes
M1543C	3	ATA-66	No	Yes

1. *SoundBlaster 16 compatible with wavetable*
2. *Supports Legacy USB (mouse/keyboard)*
3. *3D PCI audio with Direct3D (DirectX) support, MIDI, SPDIF, SoundBlaster compatibility*

For more information about these chipsets, see *Upgrading and Repairing PCs, 14th Edition.*

VIA Technologies Chipsets for P6-Class Processors

VIA Technologies has a variety of chipsets for the P6 processors. They are discussed in the following sections and Table 4.22.

Silicon Integrated Systems Chipsets for P6-Class Processors

Silicon Integrated Systems has a variety of chipsets for the P6-class processors. They are discussed in the following sections, and Table 4.25 provides a summary of them.

Table 4.22   VIA Technologies Chipsets for Pentium Pro-II-III-Celeron

Chipset	Apollo Pro	Apollo Pro Plus	Apollo PME133 (PM601)	ProSavage PM133	Apollo Pro133	Apollo Pro133A	Apollo Pro PL133T	Apollo Pro266/266T
Part number	VT82C691	VT82C693	VT8601	VT8605	VT82C693A	VT82C694X	VT8605	VT8633
Bus speed	66, 100MHz	66, 100MHz	66, 100, 133MHz	66, 100, 133MHz	66, 100, 133MHz	66, 100, 133MHz	66, 100, 133MHz	66, 100, 133MHz
Supported processors	Pentium Pro, Pentium II, Celeron	Pentium II, Celeron	Pentium II, III, Celeron, VIA C3	Pentium II, III, Celeron, VIA C3	Pentium II, III, Celeron, VIA C3	Pentium II, III, Celeron, VIA C3	Pentium II, III, Celeron (Tualatin), VIA C3	Pentium III, Celeron (Tualatin), VIA C3
Form factor	Socket 8, Slot 1	Slot 1, Socket 370	Slot 1, Socket 370	Slot 1, Socket 370	Slot 1, Socket 370	Slot 1, Socket 370	Slot 1, Socket 370	Socket 370
SMP (dual CPUs)	No	No	No	No	No	Yes	No	No
Memory types	FP, EDO, PC66, 100 SDRAM	FP, EDO, PC66, 100 SDRAM	PC66, 100, 133 SDRAM	PC66, 100, 133 SDRAM	PC66, 100, 133 SDRAM	PC66, 100, 133 SDRAM, EDO	PC100, 133 SDRAM	PC100, 133 SDRAM, DDR200, 266
Parity/ECC	No	No	No	No	No	Yes	No	No
Maximum memory	1GB	1GB	1GB	1.5GB	1.5GB	4GB	1.5GB	4GB
PCI support	2.1	2.1	2.1	2.2	2.1	2.2	2.2	2.2
PCI speed/width	33MHz/32-bit	33MHz/32-bit	33MHz/32-bit	33MHz/32-bit	33MHz/32-bit	33MHz/32-bit	33MHz/32-bit	33MHz/32-bit
AGP slot	1x, 2x	1x, 2x	1x, 2x	2x, 4x	1x, 2x	2x, 4x	2x, 4x	2x, 4x
Integrated video	No	No	Yes[1]	Yes	No	No	Yes[2]	No
South Bridge	VT82C596 or VT82C586B	VT82C596A	VT82C686A	VT8231	VT82C596B or VT82C686A	VT82C596B or VT82C686A	VT8231	VT8233C[3]

1. Trident Blade3D

2. S3 Savage 4 (3D) integrating Savage 2000 (2D)

3. Supports VIA 4x V-Link 266MHz high-speed interconnect between North Bridge and South Bridge

Table 4.23 provides an overview of the features of the South Bridge chips used in these chipsets.

Table 4.23   VIA South Bridge Chips Used with P6-Class Chipsets

South Bridge Chip	Number of USB 1.1 Ports	ATA Support	Integrated Sound	Integrated Super I/O	Integrated 10/100 Ethernet	Supports V-Link
VT82C596	2	ATA-33	No	No	No	No
VT82C596A	2	ATA-33	No	No	No	No
VT82C686A	4	ATA-66	AC'97	Yes	No	No
VT82C586B	2	ATA-33	No	No	No	No
VT8231	4	ATA-100	AC'97	Yes	No	No
VT82C596B	4	ATA-66	AC'97	Yes	No	No
VT82C586A	No	ATA-33	No	No	No	No
VT8233(C)	6	ATA-100	AC'97	Yes	Yes*	Yes

*3Com 10/100 Ethernet on C version only

Seventh/Eighth-generation (Pentium 4/D and Core 2) Chipsets

The Pentium 4 and Celeron processors using Socket 423 and those made for Socket 478 are essentially the same processors with different cache designs and minor internal revisions, so the same chipset can be used for both processors. The Pentium 4 processor in Socket 775 is very different from its predecessors; consequently, most 9xx-series chipsets support only the Socket 775 version of the Pentium 4, as well as the newer Core 2 series of processors.

Tables 4.25 and 4.26 show the 8xx-series chipsets made by Intel for Pentium 4 and Celeron 4 processors. These chipsets use Intel's hub architecture, providing an interconnect speed of 266MBps between the MCH/GMCH and the ICH chips.

Table 4.25   Pentium 4 8xx-Series Chipsets from Intel Introduced 2000–2002

Chipset	850	850E	845	845E
Code name	Tehama	Tehama-E	Brookdale	Brookdale-E
Date introduced	Nov. 2000	May 2002	Sept. 2001 (SDRAM); Jan. 2002 (DDR)	May 2002
Part number	82850	82850E	82845	82845E
Bus speeds	400MHz	400/533MHz	400MHz	400/533MHz
Supported processors	Pentium 4, Celeron[1]	Pentium 4, Celeron[2]	Pentium 4, Celeron[2]	Pentium 4, Celeron[2,4]
SMP (dual CPUs)	No	No	No	No
Memory types	RDRAM (PC800) dual-channel	RDRAM (PC800, 1066 dual-channel)	PC133 SDRAM, SDRAM DDR 200/266 SDRAM	DDR 200/266 SDRAM
Parity/ECC	Both	Both	ECC	ECC
Maximum memory	2GB	2GB (PC800); 1.5GB (PC1066)	2GB(PC2100 DDR); 3GB (PC133 SDRAM)	2GB
Memory banks	2	2	2 (PC2100); 3 (PC133)	2
PCI support	2.2	2.2	2.2	2.2

Table 4.24   SiS 6xx-Series Chipsets for Pentium II/III/Celeron

Chipset	SiS620	SiS630	SiS630E	SiS630ET	SiS630S	SiS630ST
Bus speed	66, 100MHz	66, 100, 133MHz	66, 100, 133MHz	66, 100, 133MHz	66, 100, 133MHz	66, 100, 133MHz
Supported processors	Pentium II	Celeron, Pentium III	Celeron, Pentium III	Celeron, Pentium III, PIII Tualatin	Celeron, Pentium III	Celeron, Pentium III, PIII Tualatin
Form factor	Slot 1	Socket 370	Socket 370	Socket 370	Socket 370	Socket 370
SMP (dual CPUs)	No	No	No	No	No	No
Memory types	SDRAM PC66/100	SDRAM PC100/133	SDRAM PC100/133	SDRAM PC100/133	SDRAM PC100/133	SDRAM PC100/133
Parity/ECC	Neither	Neither	Neither	Neither	Neither	Neither
Maximum memory	1.5GB	3GB	3GB	3GB	3GB	3GB
PCI support	PCI 2.2	PCI 2.2	PCI 2.2	PCI 2.2	PCI 2.2	PCI 2.2
PCI speed/width	33MHz/32-bit	33MHz/32-bit	33MHz/32-bit	33MHz/32-bit	33MHz/32-bit	33MHz/32-bit
AGP slot	None	None	None	None	Yes	Yes
Integrated video	AGP 2.0	AGP 2.0	AGP 2.0	AGP 2.0	AGP 2.0	AGP 2.0
ATA support	ATA-33/66	ATA-33/66	ATA-33/66	ATA-33/66/100	ATA-33/66/100	ATA-33/66/100
USB support/	USB 1.1/2 ports	USB 1.1/5 ports	USB 1.1/5 ports	USB 1.1/5 ports	USB 1.1/6 ports	USB 1.1/6 ports
10/100 Ethernet	No	Yes	Yes	Yes	Yes	Yes
Hardware audio	No	Yes	Yes	Yes	Yes	Yes
South Bridge chip	SiS 5595	No	No	No	No	No
SiS video bridge support	No	Yes	No	No	Yes	Yes

845GL	845G	845GE	845GV	845PE
Brookdale-GL	Brookdale-G	Brookdale-GE	Brookdale-GV	Brookdale-PE
July 2002	July 2002	Oct. 2002	Oct. 2002	Oct. 2002
82845GL	82845G	82845GE	82845GV	82845PE
400MHz	400/533MHz	400/533MHz	400/533MHz	400/533MHz
Pentium 4, Celeron[2]	Pentium 4, Celeron[2,3]	Pentium 4, Celeron[2,3]	Pentium 4, Celeron[2,4]	Pentium 4, Celeron[2,4]
No	No	No	No	No
PC133 SDRAM, DDR 200/266 SDRAM	PC133 SDRAM, DDR 200/266 SDRAM	DDR 333/266 SDRAM	DDR 200/266 SDRAM	DDR333/266 SDRAM
Neither	ECC	Neither	Neither	Neither
2GB	2GB	2GB	2GB	2GB
2	2	2	2	2
2.2	2.2	2.2	2.2	2.2

Table 4.25   Continued

Chipset	850	850E	845	845E
PCI speed/width	33MHz/32-bit	33MHz/32-bit	33MHz/32-bit	33MHz/32-bit
AGP slot	AGP 4x (1.5V)	AGP 4x (1.5V)	AGP 4x (1.5V)	AGP 4x (1.5V)
Integrated video	No	No	No	No
South Bridge (hub)	ICH2	ICH2	ICH2	ICH4

1. *Supports Socket 423 and Socket 478 processors.*
2. *Supports Socket 478 processors only.*
3. *Stepping B-1 supports HT Technology (hyper-threading).*
4. *Supports HT Technology (hyper-threading).*

The Celeron D desktop processor (a successor to the Celeron 4) was introduced after the chipsets listed in Table 4.26. However, it is supported by the 845E, 845G, 845GE, 845PE, and 845GV chipsets. The Celeron D is also supported by all the chipsets listed in Table 4.27.

Table 4.26   Intel 8xx-Series Chipsets Introduced in 2003 for Pentium 4

Chipset	848P	865P	865PE	865G	865GV	875
Codename	Breeds Hill	Springdale-P	Springdale-PE	Springdale-G	Springdale-GV	Canterwood
Date introduced	Feb. '04	May '03	May '03	May '03	May '03	April '03
Part number	82848P	82865P	82865PE	82865G	82865GV	82875
Bus speeds	800/533/ 400MHz	533/ 400MHz	800/533/ 400MHz	800/533/ 400MHz	800/533/ 400MHz	800/ 533MHz
Supported processors	Pentium 4, Celeron, Celeron D	Pentium 4, Celeron, Celeron D	Pentium 4, Celeron, Celeron D	Pentium 4, Celeron, Celeron D	Pentium 4, Celeron, Celeron D	Pentium 4, Celeron, Celeron D
SMP (dual CPUs)	No	No	No	No	No	No
Memory types	DDR266/ 333/400 single-channel	DDR266/ 333 dual-channel	DDR333/ 400 dual-channel	DDR333/ 400 dual-channel	DDR333/ 400 dual-channel	DDR333/ 400 dual-channel
Parity/ECC	Neither	Neither	Neither	Neither	Neither	ECC
Maximum memory	2GB	4GB	4GB	4GB	4GB	4GB
Memory banks	2	2	2	2	2	2
PCI support	2.3	2.3	2.3	2.3	2.3	2.3
PCI speed/width	33MHz/32-bit	33MHz/32-bit	33MHz32-bit /	33MHz/32-bit	33MHz/32-bit	33MHz/32-bit
Video	AGP 8x	AGP 8x	AGP 8x	AGP 8x	—	AGP 8x
Integrated video	No	No	No Graphics 2	Intel Extreme Graphics 2	Intel Extreme	No
Gigabit (GbE) Ethernet support*	No	Yes	Yes	Yes	Yes	Yes
South Bridge (hub)	ICH5/ICH5R	ICH5/ICH5R	ICH5/ICH5R	ICH5/ICH5R	ICH5/ICH5R	ICH5/ICH5R

*GbE connects directly to the MCH/GMCH chip, bypassing the PCI bus. It is implemented by the optional Intel_82547E1 Gigabit Connection chip.

845GL	845G	845GE	845GV	845PE
33MHz/32-bit	33MHz/32-bit	33MHz/32-bit	33MHz/32-bit	33MHz/32-bit
None	AGP 4x (1.5V)	AGP 4x (1.5V)	None	AGP 4x (1.5V)
Intel Extreme Graphics 200MHz	Intel Extreme Graphics 200MHz	Intel Extreme Graphics 266MHz	Intel Extreme Graphics 200MHz	No
ICH4	ICH4	ICH4	ICH4	ICH4

Table 4.27 lists the ICH chips used by 8xx-series Pentium 4/Celeron 4 chipsets made by Intel.

Table 4.27   I/O Controller Hub Chips for Pentium 4 8xx-Series Chipsets

Chip Name	ICH0	ICH	ICH2	ICH4	ICH5	ICH5R
Part number	82801AB	82801AA	82801BA	82801DB	82801EB	82801ER
ATA support	UDMA-33	UDMA-66	UDMA-100	UDMA-100	UDMA-100	UDMA-100
SATA support	No	No	No	No	SATA-150	SATA-150
SATA RAID	No	No	No	No	No	RAID 0, RAID 1
USB support	1C/2P	1C/2P	2C/4P	3C/6P	4C/8P	4C/8P
USB 2.0	No	No	No	Yes	Yes	Yes
CMOS/clock	Yes	Yes	Yes	Yes	Yes	Yes
PCI support	2.2	2.2	2.2	2.2	2.3	2.3
LPC support	Yes	Yes	Yes	Yes	Yes	Yes
Power management	SMM/ACPI 1.0	SMM/ACPI 1.0	SMM/ACPI 1.0	SMM/ACPI 2.0	SMM/ACPI 2.0	SMM/ACPI 2.0
10/100 Ethernet	No	No	No	Yes	Yes	Yes

ICH = I/O controller hub

USB = Universal serial bus

xC/xP = number of controller /number of ports

ATA = AT attachment (IDE)

UDMA = Ultra-DMA ATA

LPC = Low pin count bus

SMM = System management mode

ACPI = Advanced configuration and power interface

Starting in mid-2004, Intel introduced a new 915/925 series of chipsets for the Pentium 4 and Celeron 4. These chipsets, codenamed Grantsdale and Alderwood before their introduction, are optimized for the Pentium 4 Prescott design introduced in early 2004. They are the first Intel chipsets to support several new technologies, including DDR2 memory and PCI-Express for both video and other high-speed I/O uses (such as Gigabit Ethernet). They also include support for the new Socket 775—the first LGA processor socket (also known as Socket-T-instead of Socket 478).

Note

The low-end 910GL Express chipset supports both Socket 478 and Socket 775 processors.

In 2005, Intel introduced its first dual-core chip for desktop processors (the Pentium D) as well as a new processor designed for maximum single-core performance (the Pentium Extreme Edition). To support these new processors as well as Socket 775 Pentium 4 processors with HT Technology, Intel developed the 945, 955, and 975 chipset families.

Table 4.28   Intel 9xx-Series Chipsets for Pentium 4

Chipset	910GL	915P	915PL	915G
Code name	Grantsdale-GL	Grantsdale-P	Grantsdale-PL	Grantsdale-G
Part number	82910GL	828915P	828915GPL	828915G
Bus speeds	533MHz	800/533MHz	800/533MHz	800/533MHz
Supported processors	Pentium 4, Celeron, Celeron D	Pentium 4, Celeron, Celeron D	Pentium 4, Celeron D	Pentium 4, Celeron, Celeron D
SMP (dual CPUs)	No	No	No	No
Memory types	DDR333/400 dual-channel	DDR333/400 dual-channel, DDR2	DDR333/400	DDR333/400 dual-channel DDR2
Parity/ECC	Neither	Neither	Neither	Neither
Maximum memory	2GB	4GB	2GB	4GB
Memory banks	2	2	2	2
PCI support	PCI-Express x1, PCI 2.3	PCI-Express x1, x16, PCI 2.2	PCI-Expres x1, x16, PCI 2.3	PCI-Express x1, x16, PCI 2.2
PCI speed/width	33MHz/32-bit	33MHz/32-bit	33MHz/32-bit	33MHz/32-bit
PCI-Express x16 video	No	Yes	Yes	Yes
AGP slot	No	No	No	No
Integrated video	Intel GMA 900	No	No	Extreme Graphics 3
South Bridge (hub)	ICH6 family	ICH6 family	ICH6 family	ICH6 family

*B-2 stepping and above are required for ECC support.   915GL does not support HT Technology.
GMA 900 = Graphics Media Accelerator 900.

Table 4.29   Intel 9xx-Series Chipsets for Core 2, Pentium D, Pentium Extreme Edition, and Pentium 4

Chipset	975X	955X
Code name	Glenwood	Glenwood
Part number	82975X	82955X
Bus speeds	1066/800MHz	1066/800MHz
Supported processors	Pentium Extreme Edition, Pentium D, Pentium 4 with HT Tech (Socket 775)	Pentium Extreme Edition, Pentium D, Pentium 4 with HT Tech (Socket 775)
SMP (dual CPUs)	No	No
Memory types	DDR2 667/533MHz dual channel	DDR2 667/533MHz dual-channel
Parity/ECC	ECC	ECC

Because of the greater performance needed to support these high-speed technologies, the 9xx-series chipsets use a faster hub architecture than what was used by the 8xx-series chipsets. The new interconnect design, known as *Direct Media Interface (DMI)*, runs at 1GBps in each direction, making it comparable to the latest non-Intel interconnects listed in Table 4.11. Table 4.28 lists the 9xx-series chipsets for the Pentium 4; Table 4.29 lists the 9xx-series chipsets for the Core 2, Pentium D, and Pentium Extreme Edition (they also support the Pentium 4); and Table 4.30 lists the ICH6 and ICH7 families of I/O controller hub chips used with 9xx-series chipsets.

915GV	915GL	925X	925XE
Grantsdale-GV	Grantsdale-GL	Alderwood	Alderwood-E
828915GV	828915GL	82925X	82925XE
800/533MHz	533MHz	800/533MHz	1066/800MHz
Pentium 4, Celeron, Celeron D	Pentium 4, Celeron, Celeron D	Pentium 4, Celeron, Celeron D	Pentium 4 (90nm)
No	No	No	No
DDR333/400 dual-channel DDR2	DDR333/400 dual-channel	DDR2	DDR2 533/400 dual channel
Neither	Neither	ECC*	Neither
4GB	4GB	4GB	4GB
2	2	2	2
PCI-Express x1, PCI 2.2	PCI-Express x1, PCI 2.2	PCI-Express x1, x16, PCI 2.2	PCI-Express x1, x16, PCI 2.3
33MHz/32-bit	33MHz/32-bit	33MHz/32-bit	33MHz/32-bit
No	No	Yes	Yes
No	No	No	No
Extreme Graphics 3	Extreme Graphics 3	No	No
ICH6 family	ICH6 family	ICH6 family	ICH6 family

945G	945P	945PL
Lakeport-G	Lakeport-P	Lakeport-PL
82945G	82945P	82945PL
1066/800/533MHz	1066/800/533MHz	800/533MHz
Pentium D, Pentium 4 with HT Tech (Socket 775)	Pentium D, Pentium 4 with HT Tech (Socket 775)	Pentium D, Pentium 4 with HT Tech (Socket 775)
No	No	No
DDR2 667/533/400MHz, dual-channel	DDR2 667/533/400MHz dual-channel	DDR2 533/400MHz dual-channel
Neither	Neither	Neither

Table 4.29   Continued

Chipset	975X	955X
Maximum memory	8GB	8GB
Memory banks	2	2
PCI support	PCI-Express x1, x16, PCI 2.3	PCI-Express x1, x16, PCI 2.3
PCI speed/width	33MHz, 32-bit	33MHz, 32-bit
PCI-Express x16 video	Yes, dual slots	Yes
AGP slot	No	No
Integrated video	No	No
South Bridge (hub)	ICH7 family	ICH7 family

Table 4.30   I/O Controller Hub Chips for Pentium 4 9xx-Series Chipsets

Chip name	ICH6	ICH6R	ICH7	ICH7R
ATA support*	UDMA-100	UDMA-100	UDMA-100	UDMA-100
SATA-150 support	4 drives	4 drives	4 drives	4 drives
SATA RAID	No	0, 1, 0+1	No	0, 1, 0+1, 5
Matrix storage	No	Yes	No	Yes
USB support	4C/8P	4C/8P	4C/8P	4C/8P
USB 2.0	Yes	Yes	Yes	Yes
CMOS/clock	Yes	Yes	Yes	Yes
PCI support	2.3, PCI-Express	2.3, PCI-Express	2.3, PCI-Express	2.3, PCI-Express
Number of PCI-Express lanes	4	4	4	6
LPC support	Yes	Yes	Yes	Yes
Power management	SMM/ACPI 1.0	SMM/ACPI 1.0	SMM/ACPI 3.0	SMM/ACPI 3.0
10/100 Ethernet	Yes	Yes	Yes	Yes
High-definition audio (Dolby Pro Logic IIx-compatible 7.1-channel)	Yes	Yes	Yes	Yes

ICH = I/O controller hub

USB = Universal serial bus

xC/xP = Number of USB controllers/number of ports

ATA = AT attachment (IDE)

UDMA = Ultra-DMA ATA

ISA = Industry-standard architecture bus

LPC = Low pin count bus

SMM = System management mode

ACPI = Advanced configuration and power interface

Matrix storage = Advanced RAID array technology that supports striped and mirrored arrays with two drives

*One ATA port supporting two ATA/IDE drives

Intel 850 Family

The Intel 850 family contains two members—the original 850 and an enhanced version called the 850E. The 850 is the first chipset for the Intel Pentium 4 processor and therefore is also the first chipset to support the NetBurst microarchitecture. The 850 is designed for high-performance desktop computers and workstations and uses the same hub architecture and modular design as the rest of Intel's 8xx family of chipsets. See Figure 4.36 for a photo of the Intel 850 chipset.

945G	945P	945PL
4GB	4GB	4GB
2	2	2
PCI-Express x1, x16, PCI 2.3	PCI-Express x1, x16, PCI 2.3	PCI-Express x1, x16, PCI 2.3
33MHz, 32-bit	33MHz, 32-bit	33MHz, 32-bit
Yes	Yes	Yes
No	No	No
Intel GMA 900	No	No
ICH7 family	ICH7 family	ICH7 family

Figure 4.36   The Intel 850 chipset. *Photo used by permission of Intel Corporation.*

The 850 has two main components, down from three in earlier 800-series chipsets:

- **82850 Memory Controller Hub**—Provides support for dual 400MHz RDRAM memory channels with a 3.2GBps bandwidth and a 100MHz system bus. The 82850 MCH also supports 1.5V AGP 4x video cards at a bandwidth exceeding 1GBps.

- **82801BA I/O Controller Hub 2**—The ICH2 (an enhanced version of the 82801 used by other 800-series chipsets) supports 32-bit PCI rev. 2.2, dual UDMA 33/66/100 IDE host adapters, four USB ports, an integrated LAN controller, and six-channel AC'97 audio/modem codec, as well as provides FWH interface support, SMBus support, and Alert on LAN and Alert on LAN 2 support.

Optionally, the Intel 82562ET/82562EM Platform LAN communication chips can be added to the 850 chipset to provide support for 10BASE-T and Fast Ethernet networking, building on the LAN features in the 82801BA ICH2 chip.

The 850 chipset, similar to most recent Intel and non-Intel chipsets, also supports the CNR card for integrated audio, modem, and network capabilities. See Figure 4.37 for a diagram of the 850's chipset architecture.

The 850E is an enhanced version of the 850. Its 82850E MCH adds support for dual 533MHz Rambus RDRAM memory channels and support for PC1066 RIMM modules to the 850's standard features. It also uses the same ICH2 hub as the original 850.

Intel 845 Family

Unlike the 850 and 850E chipsets, the 845 family of chipsets is widely used by both Intel and third-party motherboard makers. If you purchased a Pentium 4 system from late 2001 through mid-2003, it probably uses some version of the 845 chipset. The 845, code named Brookdale during its development, was the first Pentium 4 chipset from Intel to support low-cost SDRAM instead of expensive RDRAM. Subsequent variations support DDR SDRAM at speeds up to DDR333, ATA/100, and USB 2.0.

The 845-series chipsets include the following models:

- 845
- 845GL
- 845GV
- 845G
- 845GE
- 845E
- 845PE

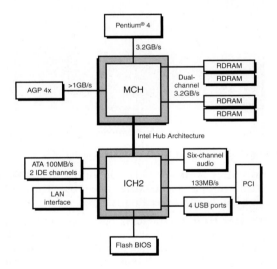

Figure 4.37   Architecture of the Intel 850 chipset.

All members of the 845 family use the same hub-based architecture developed for the 845 family, but they also have onboard audio and support the communications and networking riser (CNR) card for integrated modem and 10/100 Ethernet networking. However, they differ in their support for different types and amounts of memory, integrated graphics, external AGP support, and which ICH chip they use.

Although the original version of the 845 supported only PC133 SDRAM memory, the so-called 845D model (a designation used by review sites but not by Intel) also supports 200/266MHz DDR SDDRAM. The Intel 845's 82845 MCH supports Socket 478-based Celeron or Pentium 4 processors and can support up to two DDR SDRAM modules or three standard SDRAM modules (depending on the motherboard). When DDR SDRAM is used, the 845 supports either 200MHz (PC2100) or 266MHz (PC2700) memory speeds, with an FSB speed of 400MHz. The 845 also supports ECC error correction when parity-checked memory modules are used and offers an AGP 4x video slot, but it has no onboard video.

The 845 uses the same ICH2 I/O controller hub chip (82801-BA) used by the Intel 850 and 850E chipsets in Rambus-based systems and the 815EP in low-cost SDRAM-based systems. The ICH2 supports ATA/100 hard disk interfacing, basic AC'97 sound, and four USB 1.1 ports.

All G-series 845 models feature Intel Extreme Graphics integrated video, which has faster core speeds and adds 3D performance to the bare-bones integrated video used by the 810 and 815 chipset families. Two chipsets—the 845G and 845GE—also offer support for AGP 4x video cards.

The 845E is an updated version of the current 845 model with ECC error correction and support for 533MHz FSB, whereas the 845PE supports the 533MHz FSB, DDR 266, and 333MHz memory, but it doesn't support ECC error correction. All models except the 845 (845D) use the enhanced ICH4 I/O Controller Hub 82801DB, which offers six USB 2.0 ports as well as integrated networking. Additionally, all models except the 845 and 845GL offer enhanced 20-bit audio.

Figure 4.38 compares the system block diagrams of the 845 and 845GE models.

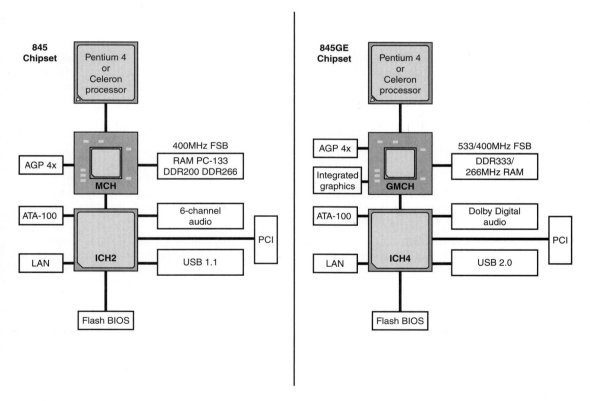

Figure 4.38 The 845GE (right) adds support for faster FSB speeds, memory, integrated graphics, and USB 2.0 to the basic 845 chipset architecture (left).

Intel 865 Family

The Intel 865 chipset family, code named Springdale, was released in May 2003. As the name might suggest, the 865 series is designed to replace the 845 series with chipsets that feature dual-channel memory support, the new communications streaming architecture (CSA) that provides a dedicated connection for the integrated network controller, faster performance, and support for the latest technologies (including optional Gigabit Ethernet and Serial ATA). The features of the 865 and 875 families are summarized in Table 4.27.

The 865 family includes the 865P, 865PE, 865G, and 865GV chipsets. The 865PE, 865G, and 865GV support single-channel or dual-channel DDR266, as well as dual-channel DDR333 and DDR400 SDRAM with FSB speeds up to 800MHz. Dual-channel memory provides a wider memory bandwidth for faster performance. The 865P model supports DDR266/333 and FSB speeds up to 533MHz. All models except the GV support AGP 8x, and the G and GV models include Intel Extreme Graphics 2—a faster version of the integrated graphics technology found in G-series versions of the 845 chipset family. Finally, an optional Gigabit Ethernet (GbE) port is connected to the MCH/GMCH and requires the use of an optional Intel 82547 Gigabit Ethernet controller chip on the motherboard.

All members of the 865 family use the ICH5 or ICH5R I/O controller hub described earlier in this chapter.

Intel 848P

The Intel 848P, code-named Breeds Hill, was introduced in February 2004 as an economy version of the 865 (Springdale) chipset family. Unlike the 865 family, though, it supports only single-channel memory and has a maximum memory size of just 2GB. The 848P also omits Gigabit Ethernet support.

Compared to the 845 family, the 848P offers faster AGP (8x), faster memory (up to DDR400), and the more advanced ICH5 I/O Controller Hub (South Bridge) chip and the Hub Link 1.5 (HL 1.5 or HI 1.5) MCH/ICH interconnect. However, if your intent is to build a new system or upgrade an existing one, your money is better spent on a more modern chipset and motherboard.

ICH5 and ICH5R

ICH5and and ICH5R (RAID) are the latest generation of Intel's I/O controller hub for its AHA and HI 1.5 hub-based architecture, which is the equivalent of the South Bridge in Intel's hub-based architecture introduced with the 800 series of chipsets.

Intel added the ICH5 and ICH5R I/O controller hubs for its AHA and HI 1.5 hub-based architecture chipsets. Both feature four USB 2.0 controllers with eight external ports, two ATA/100 ports, and two Serial ATA/150 ports. ICH5R models add support only for RAID 0 (striping) and RAID 1 (mirroring) on the SATA ports. ICH5/ICH5R also support the PCI 2.3 bus and include an integrated 10/100 Ethernet LAN controller.

Note

RAID 1 (mirroring) support for ICH5R-equipped motherboards requires the installation of the latest version of the Intel Matrix Storage Manager (previously known as the Intel Application Accelerator RAID Edition). In some cases, you might also need to install the latest edition of the Intel RAID Option ROM first. For more information and to download driver and option ROM updates, go to http://support.intel.com/support/chipsets/imsm/. The Intel Matrix Storage Manager also supports motherboards with ICH6R and ICH7R I/O Controller Hub chips.

Intel 875P

The Intel 875P chipset, code named Canterwood during its development, was introduced in April 2003. The 875P chipset supports Intel's HT Technology (hyper-threading), so it fully supports 3.06GHz and faster Pentium 4s, including the newer Prescott (90nm) core versions.

For faster memory access, the 875P supports four standard or ECC memory modules (up to 4GB total) using DDR333 or DDR400 memory in a dual-channel mode, and it offers a new Turbo mode that uses a faster path between DDR400 memory and the MCH to boost enhanced performance. Because multiple memory modules aren't always the same size or type, the 875P also features a new dynamic mode that optimizes system memory when different types or sizes of memory are used at the same time. The 875P also includes both Serial ATA and RAID support and uses the same ICH5/5R I/O controller hub family used by the 865 series.

Intel 915 Family

The Intel 915 chipset family, code named Grantsdale during its development, was introduced in 2004. The Grantsdale family comprises six members (910GL, 915PL, 915P, 915G, 915GV, and 915GL), all of which support the 90nm Pentium 4 Prescott core. These chipsets are the first to support the Socket 775 processor interface outlined in Chapter 3. These chipsets are intended to replace the 865 Springdale family of chipsets.

The 915P, 915G, 915GV, 915GL, and 915PL models are all designed to support the HT Technology feature built into most recent Pentium 4 processors and to support bus speeds up to 800MHz. All five chipsets support dual-channel DDR memory up to 400MHz and PCI-Express x1 and as well as PCI version 2.3 expansion slots. The 915P, 915G, and 915GV chipsets also support the new DDR2 memory standard at speeds up to 533MHz.

The 915P and 915PL use a PCI-Express x16 slot for high-speed graphics, whereas the 915G has a PCI-Express x16 slot as well as integrated Intel Graphics Media Accelerator 900 (originally known as Extreme Graphics 3). The 915GV, 915GL, and 910GL use Intel Graphics Media Accelerator 900 but do not include a PCI-Express x16 slot. Graphics Media Accelerator 900 is a partial implementation of DirectX 9, but it lacks the vertex shaders found on fully compatible DirectX 9 GPUs from ATI and NVIDIA.

The 910GL is the low-end member of the family, lacking support for DDR2 RAM, 800MHz bus speeds, and PCI-Express x16 video. The 910GL is designed to be matched with Intel Celeron or the new Celeron D processors to produce a low-cost system.

All 915-series MCH/GMCH chips use the new ICH6 family of South Bridge replacements detailed in Table 4.31. Note that the wireless versions of ICH6 (ICH6W and ICH6WR) originally announced were discontinued by Intel before being released, and only the standard (ICH6) and RAID (ICH6R) versions are actually available.

Intel 925X Family

The Intel 925 chipset family includes two members: the 925X and the 925XE. The Intel 925X chipset, code named Alderwood, was released in 2004. It was designed to replace the 875P Canterwood chipset. Unlike the 915 series of chipsets, which continue to support older DDR memory, the 925X supports only DDR2 memory. The 925X also supports ECC memory, providing a fast and accurate platform for mission-critical applications. To further improve performance, it uses an optimized memory controller design.

The 925X supports the Pentium 4 Extreme Edition and the Pentium 4 in Socket 775 form factors. It also includes PCI-Express x1, PCI-Express x16 (video), and PCI version 2.3 expansion slots. The I/O Controller Hub uses the ICH6 family of South Bridge replacements detailed in Table 4.30.

The 925XE is an updated version of the 925X, adding support for 1,066MHz FSB speeds; however, it dropped support for the Pentium 4 Extreme Edition processor and for ECC memory.

Intel 945 Express Family

The Intel 945 Express chipset family (code-named Lakeport) was released in 2005 and includes three members: the 945G, 945P, and 945PL. These chipsets, along with the 955X and 975X, are the first to support Intel's new dual-core Pentium D processors, but they also support Pentium 4 HT Technology processors using Socket 775.

The 945G and 945P are aimed at what Intel refers to as the "performance PC" market segment. They offer FSB speeds up to 1,066MHz and up to 4GB of dual-channel DDR2 memory (two pairs) running at up to 667MHz. Both feature PCI Express x16 support, but the 945G also incorporates Intel Graphics Media Accelerator 950 integrated graphics.

The 945PL—aimed at what Intel refers to as the "mainstream PC" segment—supports only two memory modules (one pair of dual-channel modules) running at up to 533MHz and a maximum memory size of 2GB. It also supports PCI-Express x16.

All members of the 945 family support the ICH7 family of I/O controller hub chips listed in Table 4.30. The ICH7 family differs from ICH6 in the following ways:

- It has support for 300MBps Serial ATA.
- It has support for SATA RAID 5 and Matrix RAID (ICH7R only).
- It has support for two additional PCI-Express x1 ports (ICH7R only).

Figure 4.39 compares the features of the 945G and 915G chipsets.

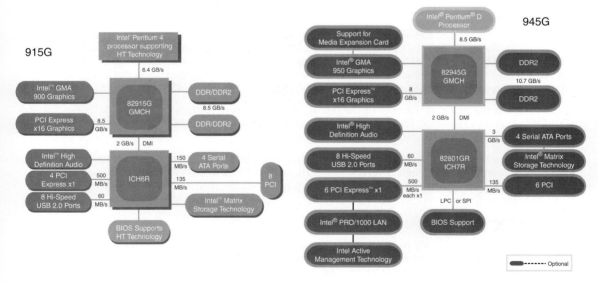

Figure 4.39 The 915G chipset (left) was the first Intel chipset to support both PCI-Express x16 and integrated graphics. The 945G chipset (right) offers similar features but supports faster integrated graphics, faster SATA hard disks, and more PCI-Express x1 slots than the 915G.

Intel 955X and 975X Family

The Intel Glenwood chipset family was released in 2005 and includes two members: the 955X and 975X. These chipsets, along with the 945 family, are the first to support Intel's new dual-core Pentium D processors, but they also support the new high-performance single-core Pentium Extreme Edition processors as well as existing Pentium 4 HT Technology processors using Socket 775. Intel categorizes these chipsets as entry-level workstation and performance PC chipsets.

Although these chipsets are numbered in different series, most of their features are identical. Both support FSB speeds of 800MHz and 1,066MHz and support up to four DDR2 667/533MHz memory modules (two pairs of dual-channel modules) for a maximum 8GB of system memory. Both support ECC memory—a must for workstation operation—and both use the ICH7 family of I/O controller hub chips listed in Table 4.30.

The 955X and 975X differ from each other in their video support. The 955X supports a single PCI-Express x16 video card, whereas the 975X supports two PCI-Express video cards in CrossFire dual-slot operation.

Intel 96x Series

The 96x series (codenamed Broadwater) was introduced in June 2006, and is designed to support the Core 2 processors, including dual and quad-core versions. There are several models in the series, each with slightly different features. The Q963 and Q965 are the most basic versions. Both feature integrated GMA 3000 video, however the Q965 includes support for a PCIe x16 slot (allowing for a video card upgrade), and supports faster 800MHz DDR2 memory as well. The P965 deletes the integrated video for those only wanting to use PCIe x16 cards. Finally, the G965 includes all of the features of the other chipsets, while adding even better integrated GMA X3000 video, along with support for a PCIe x16 upgrade slot as well. Table 4.31 shows the major features of these chipsets.

Table 4.31   Intel 96x Chipsets for Core 2

Feature	Q963	Q965	P965	G965
Introduced	June 2006	June 2006	June 2006	June 2006
Supported Processors	Core 2, Pentium D, Pentium 4	Core 2, Pentium D, Pentium 4	Core 2, Pentium D, Pentium 4	Core 2, Pentium D, Pentium 4
Socket	LGA775	LGA775	LGA775	LGA775
CPU Bus Speed	1066/800/533MHz	1066/800/533MHz	1066/800/533MHz	1066/800/533MHz
Max. Memory	8GB	8GB	8GB	8GB
Memory Type	Dual-Channel DDR2	Dual-Channel DDR2	Dual-Channel DDR2	Dual-Channel DDR2
Memory Speed	667/533MHz	800/667/533MHz	800/667/533MHz	800/667/533MHz
Integrated Graphics	GMA 3000	GMA 3000	—	GMA X3000
Graphics Interface	—	PCI Express x16	PCI Express x16	PCI Express x16
SATA Support	SATA (3 Gbps)/6, External SATA (eSATA)	SATA (3 Gbps)/6, External SATA (eSATA)	SATA (3 Gbps)/6, External SATA (eSATA)	SATA (3 Gbps)/6, External SATA (eSATA)
RAID Support	RAID 0, 1, 5, 10	RAID 0, 1, 5, 10	RAID 0, 1, 5, 10	RAID 0, 1, 5, 10
I/O Controller Hub	ICH8 Family	ICH8 Family	ICH8 Family	ICH8 Family
USB 2.0 Ports	10 ports	10 ports	10 ports	10 ports
Integrated Audio	High Definition Audio, AC'97/20-bit audio	High Definition Audio, AC'97/20-bit audio	High Definition Audio, AC'97/20-bit audio	High Definition Audio, AC'97/20-bit audio

Intel 3x Series Chipsets

First introduced in June 2007, the 3x series chipset family (codenamed Bearlake) is designed to support the Core 2 processors in both dual and quad-core as well as both 65nm Conroe and 45nm Penryn versions. All 3x series chipsets support DDR2 memory up to 800MHz, while some also support DDR3 up to 1333MHz. Some also support Intel Turbo Memory (flash memory used as cache) which can enable faster application loading and boot times in systems running Windows Vista.

Some of the 3x series chipsets also include integrated GMA 3100 graphics, and some of those include Clear Video Technology, which can enhance video playback and support the High Definition Media Interface (HDMI). The Clear Video Technology also supports HD DVD and Blu-ray disc playback using built-in features that might otherwise require a separate graphics card. The GMA 3100 video is Vista Premium ready, as it supports the Vista Aero interface.

The 3x series is available in a number of versions, with the P31 and G31 being the most basic. The only difference between them is that the G31 adds the integrated GMA 3100 video. The P35 has no video, but adds a number of other features, including quad-core support, faster CPU bus speeds, more SATA and USB ports, and support for DDR3 memory. The G33 is the same, except it also adds GMA 3100 video with Clear Video Technology. Table 4.32 shows the different 3x series chipsets.

Table 4.32   Intel 3x Chipsets for Core 2

Feature	P31	G31	P35	G33
Introduced	June 2006	June 2006	June 2006	June 2006
Supported Processors	Core 2 Duo	Core 2 Duo	Core 2 Duo, Core 2 Quad	Core 2 Duo, Core 2 Quad
Socket	LGA775	LGA775	LGA775	LGA775
CPU Bus Speed	1066/800MHz	1066/800MHz	1333/1066/800MHz	1333/1066/800MHz
Max. Memory	8GB	8GB	8GB	8GB
Memory Type	Dual-Channel DDR2	Dual-Channel DDR2	Dual-Channel DDR2/DDR3	Dual-Channel DDR2/DDR3
Memory Speed	DDR2-800MHz	DDR2-800MHz DDR3-1066MHz	DDR2-800MHz DDR2-800MHz	DDR3-1066MHz
Integrated Graphics	—	GMA 3100	—	GMA 3100 w/Clear Video Technology

Table 4.33   SiS North Bridge Chips for Pentium 4 Socket 478 (Up to 533MHz Processor Bus Speed)

Chipset	SiS650	SiS651	SiS645	SiS645DX
Bus speed	400MHz	400/533MHz	400MHz	400/533MHz
Supports Hyper-Threading	No	Yes*	No	Yes*
SMP (dual CPUs)	No	No	No	No
Memory types	PC133, DDR266	PC100/133, DDR200/266/333	PC133, DDR200/266	PC133, DDR266/333
Parity/ECC	Neither	Neither	Neither	Neither
Maximum memory	3GB	3GB	3GB	3GB
PCI support	2.2	2.2	2.2	2.2
PCI speed/width	33MHz/32-bit	33MHz/32-bit	33MHz/32-bit	33MHz/32-bit
AGP slot	4x	4x	4x	4x
Integrated video	Yes	Yes	No	No
South Bridge	SiS961	SiS962	SiS961	SiS961
MuTIOL speed	533MBps	533MBps	533MBps	ß533MBps

*B-stepping only   ^ PCI 2.2 with SiS963 series, PCI 2.3 with SiS964 series

Table 4.32   Continued

Feature	P31	G31	P35	G33
Graphics Interface	PCI Express x16	PCI Express x16	PCI Express x16	PCI Express x16
SATA Support	4 SATA (3 Gbps)	4 SATA (3 Gbps)	6 SATA (3 Gbps), eSATA	6 SATA (3 Gbps), eSATA
RAID Support	RAID 0, 1, 5, 10	RAID 0, 1, 5, 10	RAID 0, 1, 5, 10	RAID 0, 1, 5, 10
I/O Controller Hub	ICH7 Family	ICH7 Family	ICH9 Family	ICH9 Family
USB 2.0 Ports	6 ports	6 ports	12 ports	12 ports
Integrated Audio	High Definition Audio, AC'97/20-bit audio	High Definition Audio, AC'97/20-bit audio	High Definition Audio, AC'97/20-bit audio	High Definition Audio, AC'97/20-bit audio

Third-party Chipsets for Intel Processors

SiS, ULi (now NVIDIA), ATI, and VIA all produce chipsets for the Intel Pentium 4/D and Core 2 processors.

Although Intel's chipsets have dominated the market up to this point, many of these chipsets offer unique features that are worth considering. The following sections discuss these chipsets by vendor.

SiS Chipsets

SiS offers several chipsets for Intel processors, including integrated chipsets, chipsets for use with discrete video accelerator cards, and some that support Rambus RDRAM. Details of SiS's chipsets for the Pentium 4 are available in Tables 4.33–36; chipsets for the Pentium D are listed in Tables 4.35 and 4.37. Unlike most of the chipsets SiS has created for the Pentium II/III/Celeron, the SiS chipsets for the Pentium 4 and Pentium D use one of several high-speed South Bridge equivalents (SiS 96x series Media I/O chips) instead of integrating North and South Bridge functions into a single chip. SiS North and South Bridge chips for the Pentium 4 and Pentium D use a high-speed 16-bit connection known as MuTIOL (Multi-Threaded I/O Link) instead of the slow PCI bus as with older chipsets.

SiS648	SiS655	SiS R658	SiS 661GX
400/533MHz	400/533MHz	400/533MHz	400/533MHz
Yes*	Yes*	Yes*	Yes
No	No	No	No
DDR200/266/333	DDR266/333, dual-channel	1066/800MHz RDRAM	DDR400/333/266
Neither	Neither	Neither	Neither
3GB	4GB	4GB	3GB
^	^	^	^
33MHz/32-bit	33MHz/32-bit	33MHz/32-bit	33MHz32-bit /
8x	8x	8x	8x
No	No	No	Mirage DirectX 7.0, 64MB
SiS963, 964 series	SiS963, 964 series	SiS963, 964 series	SiS963, 964 series
1GBps	1GBps	1GBps	1GBps

Table 4.34 lists the SiS North Bridge chips for Pentium 4 processors with 800MHz FSB.

Table 4.34   SiS North Bridge Chips for Pentium 4 (800MHz Processor Bus Speed)

Chipset	SiS648FX	SiS655FX	SiS655TX	SiS656	SiS R659	SiS661FX
Bus speed	800/533/ 400MHz	800/533/ 400MHz	800/533/ 400MHz	800/533/ 400MHz	800/400/ 533MHz	800/400/ 533MHz
Supports Hyper-Threading	Yes	Yes	Yes	Yes	Yes	Yes
SMP (dual CPUs)	No	No	No	No	No	No
Memory types	DDR400/333	Dual-channel DDR400/333	Dual-channel DDR400/333	Dual-channel DDR400/333, DDR-II	Quad-channel RDRAM PC1200	DDR400/ 222/266
Parity/ECC	Neither	Neither	Neither	ECC	ECC	Neither
Maximum memory	3GB	3GB	4GB	4GB	4GB	3GB
PCI support	2.3	2.3	2.3	2.3	2.3	2.3
PCI speed/ width	33MHz/32-bit	33MHz/32-bit	33MHz32-bit /	33MHz/32-bit	33MHz/32-bit	33MHz/32-bit
Video slot	AGP 8x	AGP 8x	AGP 8x	PCI-Express x16	AGP 8x	AGP 8x
Integrated video	No	No	No	No	No	SiS Mirage Graphics 32/64MB
South Bridge	SiS963L	SiS964/964L	SiS964/964L	SiS965/965L	SiS964/964L	SiS964/964L
MuTIOL speed	1GBps	1GBps	1GBps	1GBps	1GBps	1GBps

Table 4.36 lists the SiS Media I/O (South Bridge) chips referenced in Tables 4.34–36.

Table 4.36   SiS Media I/O (South Bridge) Chips for Intel and AMD Processors

South Bridge Chip	USB Support	# of USB Ports	ATA Support	# of SATA Ports	RAID Levels Supported
SiS961	1.1	6	33/66/100	—	—
SiS961B	1.1	6	33/66/100/133	—	—
SiS962	1.1, 2.0	6	33/66/100/133	—	—
SiS962L	1.1, 2.0	6	33/66/100/133	—	—
SiS963	1.1, 2.0	6	33/66/100/133	—	—
SiS963L	1.1, 2.0	6	33/66/100/133	—	—
SiS964	1.1, 2.0	8	33/66/100/133	2	0, 1, JBOD
SiS964L	1.1, 2.0	8	33/66/100/133	—	—
SiS965	1.1, 2.0	8	33/66/100/133	4	0, 1, 0+1, JBOD
SiS965L	1.1, 2.0	8	33/66/100/133	2	0, 1, JBOD
SiS966	1.1, 2.0	8	33/66/100/133	4*	0, 1, 0+1, JBOD
SiS966L	1.1, 2.0	8	33/66/100/133	2	0, 1, JBOD

* Two ports support AHCI
HDA = High-definition audio

JBOD = Just a bunch of disks (spans all drives into a single logical unit)

Table 4.35 lists the SiS North Bridge chips that support the dual-core Pentium D as well as Socket 775 Pentium 4 processors.

Table 4.35   SiS North Bridge Chips for Pentium D and Pentium 4 (Socket 775)

Chipset	SiS649	SiS649FX	SiS656	SiS656FX	SiS661FX
Bus speed	800/533/ 400MHz	1066MHz	800/533/ 400MHz	1066/800/ 533/400MHz	800/400/ 533MHz
Supports Hyper-Threading	Yes	Yes	Yes	Yes	Yes
SMP (dual CPUs)	No	No	No	No	No
Memory types	Single-channel DDR2 533/400, DDR 400/222/266	Single-channel DDR2 667, DDR 400	Dual-channel DDR2 667/ 533/400	Dual-channel DDR2 667/ 533/400	Single-channel DDR400/222 /266
Parity/ECC	Neither	Neither	ECC	ECC	Neither
Maximum memory	2GB	2GB	4GB	4GB	3GB
PCI support	2.3	2.3	2.3	2.3	2.3
PCI speed/width	33MHz/32-bit	33MHz/32-bit	33MHz/32-bit	33MHz/32-bit	33MHz/32-bit
Video slot	PCI Express x16	PCI Express x16	PCI-Express x16	PCI-Express x16	AGP 8x
Integrated video	No	No	No	No	SiS Mirage Graphics 64MB
South Bridge	SiS965, 966 series	SiS965, 966 series	SiS965, 966 series	SiS965, 966 series	SiS964/964L
MuTIOL speed	1GBps	1GBps	1GBps	1GBps	1GBps

Audio	10/100 Ethernet	Gigabit Ethernet	HomePNA 1.0/2.0	IEEE 1394	PCI-Express x1	MuTIOL Throughput
AC'97 2.2, 5.1 channel	Yes	No	Yes	No	No	533MBps
AC'97 2.2, 5.1 channel	Yes	No	Yes	No	No	533MBps
AC'97 2.2, 5.1 channel	Yes	No	Yes	Yes	No	533MBps
AC'97 2.2, 5.1 channel	Yes	No	Yes	No	No	533MBps
AC'97 2.2, 5.1 channel	Yes	No	Yes	Yes	No	533MBps
AC'97 2.2, 5.1 channel	Yes	No	Yes	No	No	533MBps
AC'97 2.3, 5.1 channel	Yes	No	Yes	No	No	1GBps
AC'97 2.3, 5.1 channel	Yes	No	Yes	No	No	1GBps
AC'97, 7.1 channel	Yes	Yes	Yes	No	Yes	1GBps
AC'97, 7.1 channel	Yes	No	Yes	No	Yes	1GBps
AC'97, 7.1 channel HDA	Yes	Yes	Yes	No	Yes	1GBps
AC'97, 7.1 channel HDA	Yes	No	Yes	No	Yes	1GBps

SiS650/651 Chipsets

The SiS650 and 651 chipsets enable Pentium 4 system builders to create low-cost systems with onboard video that can be enhanced with AGP 4x video cards at a later date. The integrated video features support for high-quality DVD playback and the optional SiS301B video bridge for TV-out and DVI LCD panels.

Both chipsets also feature SiS's own MuTIOL technology for connecting the North Bridge and South Bridge chips with a three-layer high-speed (266MHz/533MBps bandwidth) data highway.

The 650 and 651 both support SDRAM and DDR SDRAM, and the 651 adds support for DDR333 memory, the 533MHz system bus of the latest Pentium 4 processors, and hyper-threading in its B-stepping version.

The 650's SiS961 South Bridge provides USB 1.1, ATA-100 (133 in its 961B version), AC'97 six-channel audio, and integrated Ethernet/HomePNA networking. The 651 also uses the newer SiS962 South Bridge, which provides ATA133 and USB 2.0 support.

SiS645/645DX

The 645 family of SiS chipsets does not include the integrated graphics of the 650/651 family, but they are otherwise similar. They support SDRAM and DDR SDRAM, AGP 4x, and the high-speed MuTIOL North Bridge/South Bridge interface. The 645DX supports DDR333 memory, the 533MHz system bus, and the HT technologies found in the most recent Pentium 4 processors.

Both the 645 and 645DX use the SiS961 South Bridge.

SiS648/648FX/655/655FX/655TX

The SiS648 chipset is a development of the 645DX chipset, with the following differences:

- Support for DDR memory only (up to DDR333)
- 8X AGP slot
- SiS963 South Bridge (USB 2.0, IEEE 1394a support)

The SiS655 chipset is essentially a dual-channel version of the 648, supporting up to 4GB of memory with DDR266/333 memory only.

The SiS648FX chipset is a development of the 648 that supports 800MHz bus speeds of the Pentium 4.

The SiS655FX is a development of the original SiS655 chipset with the following differences:

- Supports dual-channel DDR400 memory
- Supports 800MHz bus speeds of the Pentium 4
- Supports SiS's HyperStreaming Technology, SiS's marketing term for its method of reducing data latency through improved pipelining and splitting transactions
- Has SiS964 South Bridge (eight USB 2.0 ports, eight-channel audio, SATA, RAID)

The SiS655TX is based on the SiS655FX but uses second-generation Advanced HyperStreaming Technology.

SiS R658/R659

The SiS R658 is the first SiS chipset ever to support Rambus RDRAM. Other features include

- Support for Pentium 4 processors with 533MHz and HT (B-stepping only) features
- Dual-channel support for PC1066/PC800 RDRAM (requires identical pairs of memory)
- 4GB maximum memory size
- AGP 8x interface
- MuTIOL 1G (533MHz clock speed providing more than 1GBps throughput) interface to the SiS963 South Bridge

Essentially, the R658 is an RDRAM version of the 655 chipset, and, like the 655, it uses the SiS963 South Bridge.

The R659 is based on the R658 with the following differences:

- Support for 800MHz bus speeds of the Pentium 4
- SiS HyperStreaming Technology
- Quad-channel PC1200 RDRAM
- SiS964 South Bridge

SiS661GX/SiS661FX

The SiS661GX is an integrated chipset with the following features:

- Support for Pentium 4 processors up to 533MHz processor bus with HT Technology
- Up to 2GB of DDR400 (two DIMMs) or up to 3GB of DDR333/266 (three DIMMs)
- AGP 8x video
- Integrated SiS Mirage Graphics (software-compatible with DirectX9) with CRT, TV, and LCD support; hardware acceleration for DVD playback; and shared memory of 32MB or 64MB
- SiS964/964L South Bridge

The SiS661FX is an integrated chipset that is similar to the SiS661GX, but it supports Pentium D dual-core processors and Pentium 4 HT Technology processors up to 800MHz processor bus.

SiS656/SiS656 FX

The SiS656 is the first SiS chipset to support PCI-Express and DDR2 memory. Therefore, it is roughly similar to the Intel 915 series of Pentium 4 chipsets (shown earlier). Other features include

- Support for Pentium 4 processors up to 800MHz FSB, including Prescott as well as the dual-core Pentium D
- Dual-channel DDR400/333 or dual-channel DDR2 533/400MHz memory
- Maximum memory size of 4GB

- ECC memory support
- PCI-Express x16
- SiS965/965L or 966/966L South Bridge

The SiS656FX is based on the SiS656 but offers a faster maximum FSB speed of 1066MHz.

SiS649/SiS649FX

The SiS649 is a single-channel version of the SiS656. Its major features include

- Support for Pentium 4 processors up to 800MHz FSB, including Prescott and the dual-core Pentium D
- Dual-channel DDR400/333/266 or dual-channel DDR2 533/400MHz memory
- Maximum memory size of 2GB
- PCI-Express x16
- SiS965/965L or 966/966L South Bridge

The SiS649FX is based on the SiS649 but offers a faster maximum FSB speed of 1,066MHz and supports DDR2 667 or DDR 400 memory.

ULi Electronics Chipsets

ULi Electronics (formerly known as ALi Corporation and Acer Laboratories, and later acquired by NVIDIA) has produced several chipsets for the Pentium 4 and Celeron 4 processors. Tables 4.37 and 4.39 provide an overview of these chipsets, which are discussed in the following sections.

Table 4.38   ULi South Bridge Chips for Pentium 4, Athlon XP, and Athlon 64

South Bridge Chip	USB Support	Number of USB Ports	ATA Support	SATA
M1535D	1.1	4	33/66	—
M1535D+	1.1	6	33/66/100/133	—
M1563*	2.0	6	66/100/133	—
M1567^	2.0	8	66/100/133	150MBps
M1573^	2.0	8	66/100/133	150MBps
M1575^	2.0	8	66/100/133	300MBps

*Also incorporates SD and Memory Stick flash memory interfaces and supports AMD Athlon 64/Opteron/Mobile Athlon 64 processors.

^Supports Pentium 4 and AMD Athlon 64 processors and third-party North Bridge chips such as the ATI Radeon Xpress 200.

Table 4.37   ULi Chipsets for Pentium 4

Chipset	ALADDiN-P4	M1681	M1683	M1685
North Bridge chip	M1671	M1681	M1563	M1563
Bus speed	400MHz	533/400MHz	800/533/400MHz	800/533/400MHz
Supports HT Technology	No	Yes	Yes	Yes
SMP (dual CPUs)	No	No	No	No
Memory types	PC100/133, DDR200/266/333	PC100/133, DDR200/266/333/400	PC133, DDR266/ 333/400	DDR266/333/400, DDR2 400/533/667
Parity/ECC	Neither	Neither	Neither	Neither
Maximum memory	3GB	3GB	4GB	3.5GB
PCI support	2.2	2.3	2.3	2.3
PCI speed/width	33MHz, 32-bit	33MHz, 32-bit	33MHz, 32-bit	33MHz, 32-bit
Video slot	AGP 4x	AGP 8x	AGP 8x	PCI-Express x16
Integrated video	No	No	No	No
South Bridge	M1535 series	M1535 series	M1535 series	M1575 series
HyperTransport NB/SB Link	N/A	400MBps	400MBps	800MBps

Also supports hyper-threaded processors

Table 4.38 provides an overview of the ULi South Bridge chips used in ULi's chipsets for the Pentium 4; some of these South Bridge chips also support the Athlon XP and Athlon 64 processors from AMD.

SATA RAID	Audio	Soft Modem	10/100 Ethernet	Super I/O	PCI-Express
—	Stereo AC'97	Yes	No	Yes	No
—	6-channel AC'97	Yes	No	Yes	No
—	6-channel AC'97; SPDIF	Yes	Yes	Yes	No
—	7.1-channel HDA	Yes	Yes	Yes	Yes
—	7.1-channel HDA	Yes	Yes	Yes	Yes
0, 1, 0+1, 5, JBOD	7.1-channel HDA	Yes	Yes	Yes	Yes

Aladdin P4 (M1671)

The Aladdin P4 was ULi's first Pentium 4–compatible chipset. Because it uses the same M1535-series South Bridge chips used by its earlier Pentium and Pentium II/III chipsets, the P4 is a traditional North Bridge/South Bridge solution. Therefore, it relies on the slow (133MBps) PCI interface to carry data between the bridge chips.

The P4's major features include the following:

- 400MHz system bus
- Support for PC100/133 and DDR200/266/333 memory
- ATA-133 support (when used with the M1535D+ South Bridge)
- AGP 4x interface
- USB 1.1 ports
- ACPI power management

The P4 is also available in a version for notebook computers, the ALADDiN-P4M, which uses the D1535+ South Bridge.

M1681/M1683

ULi's M1681 chipset for the Pentium 4 processor uses the HyperTransport high-speed direct connection between North and South Bridge chips instead of relying on the PCI bus, as with previous designs.

Its major features include

- Support for hyper-threading and 533MHz system bus
- Support for DDR memory up to DDR400 and PC100/133 SDRAM
- ATA-133
- USB 2.0
- AGP 8x interface
- Memory Stick and SD (Secure Digital) flash memory device interfaces
- ACPI power management
- HyperTransport high-speed link between North and South Bridge chips, running at >400MBps bandwidth in each direction (800MBps total throughput)
- M1563 South Bridge chip

The M1683 chipset is based on the M1681 but supports the 800MHz system bus.

M1685

Although the M1685 chipset is numbered in series with ULi's earlier Pentium 4 chipsets, it represents a major departure from the M1681/M1683 generation. The M1685 is ULi's first chipset for the Pentium 4 to adopt PCI-Express and DDR2 memory. Its major features include

- Support for the 800MHz system bus
- Support for HT Technology processors
- DDR266/333/400 or DDR-II memory

- PCI-Express x16 video slot
- 3.5GB maximum memory size
- M1563, M1567, or M1575 South Bridge chip

Although the M1685 North Bridge supports the same DDR2 memory and PCI-Express x16 technologies used by the latest Intel and SiS chipsets, the companion M1653 South Bridge lacks significant I/O support features, such as Serial ATA and ATA RAID. Therefore, a motherboard using the M1685/M1563 chipset combination will not support the latest hard disks unless a discrete SATA host adapter chip is used. Some motherboards using the M1685 might use the newer M1567 (SATA RAID) or M1575 (SATA RAID 300MBps) South Bridge chip, either of which would be more satisfactory than the M1563.

ATI Chipsets

ATI's original line of chipsets for the Pentium 4 integrate Radeon VE-level 3D graphics, DVD playback, and dual-display features with high-performance North Bridge and South Bridge designs. ATI uses its high-speed A-Link bus to connect its North and South Bridge chips.

The Radeon IGP North Bridge chips for Pentium 4 include the ATI A4 family, composed of

- Radeon IGP 330
- Radeon IGP 340

The Radeon 9x00 IGP family is ATI's second generation of chipsets for the Pentium 4. The 9x00 IGP North Bridge chips feature Radeon 9200-level graphics with DirectX 8.1 hardware support and support for multiple monitors. On the other hand, the companion IXP 300 South Bridge supports Serial ATA and USB 2.0 as well as six-channel audio. The Radeon 9x00 IGP family includes

- Radeon 9100 IGP
- Radeon 9100 Pro IGP
- Radeon 9000 Pro IGP

ATI's current line of Pentium 4–compatible chipsets includes the RC410 (integrates Radeon X300 3D graphics) and the RS400 (integrates Radeon X300 3D graphics and includes support for PCI-Express x16 video). Both are sold under the Radeon Xpress 200 brand name. Although ATI has made South Bridge chips in the past, its current Radeon Xpress 200 North Bridge chips can be paired with either ATI's own IXP 450 or ULi's M157x South Bridge chips.

ATI's South Bridge chips include

- IXP 150
- IXP 200
- IXP 250
- IXP 300
- IXP 400
- IXP 450

Table 4.39 summarizes the major features of the North Bridge chips, and Table 4.40 summarizes the major features of the South Bridge chips used in ATI's integrated chipsets for the Pentium 4. The Radeon IGP 330 and 340 chipsets were not widely used in desktop computers and have now been discontinued.

Table 4.39 Radeon IGP (North Bridge) Chips for Pentium 4

North Bridge Chip	Radeon IGP 330	Radeon IGP 340	Radeon 9100/ PRO[2] IGP	Radeon 9000 PRO IGP	Radeon Xpress 200 (RS 400)	Radeon Xpress 200 (RC 410)
Bus speed	400MHz	400/533MHz	400/533/ 800MHz	400/533/ 800MHz	400/533/ 800MHz	400/533/ 800MHz
Hyper-Threading support	No	No	Yes	Yes	Yes	Yes
Memory types	DDR200/266	DDR200/ 266/333	DDR333/400 dual-channel	DDR333/400	DDR333/400; DDR2 400/ 533/667	DDR333/400; DDR2 400/ 533/667
Parity/ECC	Neither	Neither	Neither	Neither	Neither	Neither
Maximum memory	1GB	1GB	4GB	4GB	4GB	4GB
PCI support	2.2	2.2	2.3	2.3	2.3	2.3
PCI speed/width	33MHz/32-bit	33MHz/32-bit	33MHz/32-bit	33MHz/32-bit	33MHz/32-bit	33MHz/32-bit
AGP support	4x	4x	8x	8x	No	No
PCI-Express x16	No	No	No	No	Yes	No
Integrated video	Radeon VE[1]	Radeon VE[1]	Radeon 9200[3,4]	Radeon 9200[3,4]	Radeon X300	RadeonX300
NS/SB interconnect speed	266MBps	266MBps	266MBps	266MBps	800MBps	800MBps
NS/SB interconnect type	A-Link	A-Link	A-Link	A-Link	HyperTransport	HyperTransport

1. Same core as ATI Radeon 7000 with support for dual displays.

2. The PRO version features improved AGP 8x performance, better memory performance, and improved DDR400 memory compatibility.

3. Two graphics pipelines only; discrete Radeon 9200 GPU has four.

4. Supports ATI SurroundView, which allows a three-monitor setup when a dual-display ATI graphics card is connected to the AGP slot. Some motherboards might not support this feature.

Table 4.40 ATI South Bridge Chips for Pentium 4

South Bridge Chip	USB Support	Number of USB Ports	ATA Support	Audio	10/100 Ethernet	High-speed Interconnect
IXP 150	2.0	6	ATA100	AC'97 2.3; 6-channel	3Com	A-Link
IXP 200/250[1]	2.0	6	ATA100	AC'97 2.3; 6-channel	3Com	A-Link
IXP 300	2.0	8	ATA133, 2 SATA	AC'97 2.3; 6-channel	3Com	A-Link
IXP 400 (SB400)	2.0	8	ATA133, 4 SATA	AC'97 2.3; 6-channel	3Com	A-Link
IXP 450	2.0	8	ATA 133, 4 SATA	AC'97 2.3; 8-channel	Realtek 8101L	HyperTransport 800MHz

1. IXP250 identical features to IXP200, plus it supports Wake On LAN (WOL), Desktop Management Interface (DMI), manage boot agent (MBA), and the Alert Standards Forum (ASF) mechanism.

VIA Chipsets

Although VIA Technologies produces a line of chipsets for the Pentium 4, it initially lacked a license from Intel for the Socket 478 interface. This slowed acceptance of VIA's chipsets by motherboard makers until VIA and Intel reached an agreement in April 2003. Before VIA received a license to the Socket 478 interface, it used its VIA Platform Solutions Division (VPSD) to produce Pentium 4–compatible motherboards for sale under a variety of brand names. With the agreement between VIA and Intel, VIA's chipsets for the Pentium 4 are now being used by most of the major third-party motherboard makers.

Tables 4.41 and 4.42 provide an overview of VIA's chipsets for the Pentium 4, including ProSavage chipsets with integrated graphics.

Table 4.41   VIA Chipsets for Pentium 4 (Up to 533MHz System Bus)

Chipset	P4X266	P4X266A	P4X266E	P4M266	P4X400 (P4X333)	P4X400A	P4X533
North Bridge chip	VT8753	VT8753A	VT8753E	VT8751	VT8754	VT8754CE	P4X533
Bus speed	400MHz	400MHz	400/ 533MHz	400MHz	400/ 533MHz	400/ 533MHz	400/ 533MHz
HT Technology support	No	No	No	No	No	Yes	Yes
SMP (dual CPUs)	No	No	No	No	No	No	No
Memory types	PC100/133, DDR200/266	PC100/133, DDR200/266	DDR200/266	PC100/133, DDR200/266	DDR200/ 266/333	DDR266/ 333/400	DDR200/ 266/333
Parity/ECC	Neither	Neither	Neither	Neither	ECC	ECC	ECC
Maximum memory	4GB	4GB	4GB	4GB	16GB	16GB	16GB
PCI support	2.2	2.2	2.2	2.2	2.2	2.2	2.2
PCI speed/ width	33MHz/ 32-bit*	33MHz/ 32-bit*	33MHz/ 32-bit*	33MHz/ 32-bit	33MHz/ 32-bit*	33MHz/ 32-bit*	33MHz/ 32-bit*
AGP slot	4x	4x	4x	4x	8x	8x	8x
Integrated video	No	No	No	S3 Graphics Pro-Savage8 3D	No	No	No
South Bridge	VT8233, VT8233C, VT8233A	VT8233, VT8233C, VT8233A	VT8233, VT8233C, VT8233A, VT8235	VT8233, VT8233C, VT8233A	VT8235	VT8235	VT8237
V-Link speed	266MBps	266MBps	266MBps	266MBps	533MBps	533MBps	533MBps

Supports 66MHz/64-bit PCI when an optional VPX-64 (VT8101) chip is used.

Table 4.42   VIA Chipsets for Pentium 4 (800MHz System Bus)

Chipset	PT800	PM800	P4M800Pro	PT880	PT880Ultra	PT894	PT894Pro
North Bridge chip	PT800	PM800	P4M800 Pro	PT800	PT880 Ultra	PT894	PT894 Pro
Bus speed	400/533/ 800MHz	400/533/ 800MHz	400/533/ 800MHz	400/533/ 800MHz	1066/80033/ 400MHz /	1066/800/ 533/ 400MHz	1066/800/ 533/ 400MHz
HT Technology support	Yes	Yes	Yes	Yes	Yes	Yes	Yes
SMP (dual- CPUs)	No	No	No	No	No	No	No
Memory types	DDR266/ 333/400	DDR266/ 333/400	DDR266/ 333/400; DDR2 533/400	Dual-channel DDR266/ 33/400	Dual-channel DDR266/333/ 400; DDR2 533/400	Dual-channel DDR266/333/ 400; DDR2 533/400	Dual-channel DDR266/ 333/400; DDR2 533/400
Parity/ECC	ECC	ECC	ECC	ECC	ECC	ECC	ECC
Maximum memory	16GB	16GB	16GB	16GB	16GB	16GB	16GB
PCI support	2.2	2.2	2.2	2.2	2.2	2.2	2.2
PCI speed width /	33MHz/ 32-bit*	33MHz/ 32-bit*	33MHz/ 32-bit*	33MHz/ 32-bit*	33MHz/ 32-bit*	33MHz/ 32-bit*	33MHz/ 32-bit*
AGP slot	8x	8x	8x	8x	8x	No	No
PCI-Express video	No	No	No	No	x4	x16	x16, x4
Integrated video	No	S3 UniChrome Pro#	S3 UniChrome Pro#	No	No	—	—
South Bridge	VT8237	VT8237	VT8237R	VT8237	VT8237R	VT8237R	VT8237R
V-Link speed	533MBps	533MBps	1,066MBps	1,066MBps	1,066MBps	1,066MBps	1,066MBps

The UniChrome Pro features dual-monitor support, 350MHz RAMDAC, enhanced DVD playback, and DirectX 7/8/9 3D graphics support.

* Supports 66MHz/64-bit PCI when optional VPX-64 (VT8101) chip is used.

Table 4.43 lists the major features of the VIA South Bridge chips used in VIA's chipsets for the Pentium 4. Note that these same chips are also used by VIA chipsets for the AMD Athlon family of processors. All chipsets that use these South Bridge chips use VIA's high-speed V-Link interface between North and South Bridge chips. These chipsets connect to the VT1211 LPC (low pin count) or equivalent Super I/O chip for support of legacy devices such as serial, IR, and parallel ports and the floppy drive.

VIA Modular Architecture Platforms (V-MAP) for Pentium 4

VIA's North and South Bridge chips for the Pentium 4 support VIA's Modular Architecture Platforms (V-MAP) designs, which enable motherboard designers to convert quickly to more advanced versions of a chipset because of a common pinout. The North Bridge chips used in all VIA Pentium 4–compatible chipsets are all pin-compatible with each other, as are the 8233/8235/8237-series South Bridge chips.

Therefore, motherboards using these chipsets can be built in a variety of configurations. All these chipsets also support VIA's V-Link high-speed connection between the North and South Bridge chips.

Table 4.43   VIA South Bridge Chips for Pentium 4

South Bridge Chip	USB Support	Number of USB Ports	ATA Support	SATA Support	Raid Support	SATA PCI-Express	Audio	10/100 Ethernet	Home-PNA	AV-Link Throughput
VT8233	1.1	6	33/66/100	No	—	No	AC'97, 6-channel[1]	Yes	Yes	266MBps
VT8233A	1.1	6	33/66/100	No	—	No	AC'97, 6-channel[1]	Yes	No	266MBps
VT8233C	1.1	6	33/66/100	No	—	No	AC'97, 6-channel[1]	Yes[2]	No	266MBps
VT8235	2.0	6	33/66/100/133	No	—	No	AC'97, 5.1 channel[1]	Yes	No	533MBps
VT8237R[5,6]	2.0	8	33/66/100/133	SATA-150	0,1[7]		AC'97, 5.1 channel[1,4]	Yes	No	1,066MBps
VT8251	2.0	8	33/66/100/133	SATA-300[8]	0,1, 0+1, 5	X2 or x1×2	AC'97, 7.1 channel	Yes	No	1,066MBs

1. *Integrated audio requires separate audio codec chip on motherboard; it also supports MC'97 soft modem.*
2. *3Com 10/100 Ethernet.*
3. *4 SATA ports with optional SATALite interface.*
4. *8-channel (7.1) audio when optional VIA Envy 24PT PCI audio controller is used.*
5. *Can also be used with North Bridge chips that support 533MBps interconnect speed.*
6. *Originally known as VT8237.*
7. *Supports RAID 0+1 with optional SATALite.*
8. *Supports NCQ (native command queuing).*

VIA Apollo P4X266 Family

The VIA Apollo P4X266 is its first chipset for the Pentium 4 and Celeron 4 processors, supporting AGP 4x, 4GB of RAM, and the 400MHz system bus used by early Pentium 4/Celeron 4 processors. The P4X266A improves the memory interface and queues more instructions (up to 12) in the processor bus interface to reduce latency and improve performance. The P4X266E adds support for the 533MHz bus used in the 2.53GHz (and faster) Pentium 4 processors. It also supports both the VT8233 and newer VT8235 series of South Bridge chips.

ProSavage P4M266

The VIA ProSavage P4M266 integrates the S3 Graphics ProSavage8 2D/3D graphics accelerators with the features of the P4X266 chipset. Unlike some other chipsets with integrated graphics, the P4M266 retains an AGP 4x slot, so users can add an AGP 4x graphics card for better performance.

The ProSavage8 core uses 32MB of system RAM for its frame buffer, supports AGP 8x bandwidth internally with 128-bit data paths, and features DVD DXVA Motion Compensation to improve the quality of DVD playback. In addition, it supports all members of the 8233 family of South Bridge chips.

Apollo P4X400, P4X400A, and P4X533

The VIA Apollo P4X400 chipset is an improved version of the short-lived P4X333. It's suitable for both server and workstation/desktop computer use, thanks to its support for up to 32GB of RAM and ECC memory. It also supports 400MHz and 533MHz system bus speeds and DDR memory up to 400MHz. It uses the VT8235 South Bridge, so it also supports the latest I/O standards (USB 2.0 and ATA-133).

The P4X400A chipset features improved timings and support for DDR400 memory, supports HT Technology processors, and uses the VT8235 South Bridge.

The P4X533 chipset is similar to the P4X400A but uses the VT8237 as its South Bridge chip, providing support for SATA and RAID as well as eight USB 2.0 ports and optional 7.1 audio.

All three processors use the 8x V-Link connection (533MBps) between North and South Bridge chips.

PT800/PM800/PT880/PM880

The PT8xx-series chipsets are the first VIA Technologies chipsets to support the 800MHz processor bus versions of the Pentium 4. They use the VT8237R South Bridge chips (eight USB 2.0 ports, SATA, RAID, and optional 7.1 audio) or the new VT8251 (SATA 300 with NCQ, RAID 5, and integrated 7.1 audio).

The major differences between these chipsets include

- PT800 uses single-channel DDR 400 memory and AGP 8x video, with 8x V-Link (533MBps).
- PM800 adds S3 UniChrome Pro integrated graphics to the PT800 feature set.
- PT880 is a dual-channel version of the PT800 and uses Ultra V-Link (1,066MBps).
- PM880 adds S3 UniChrome Pro integrated graphics to the PT880 feature set.

PT880 Ultra/PT894/PT894 Pro

The VIA PT880 Ultra, PT894, and PT894 Pro are based on the PT880 chipset, with the following differences:

- These chipsets support DDR2 memory up to 533MHz, while continuing to support DDR memory.
- The PT880 Ultra supports AGP 8x as well as PCI-Express x4 graphics.
- The PT894 and PT894 Pro support PCI-Express x16 instead of AGP 8x graphics; PT894 Pro also adds support for PCI-Express x4 graphics.
- The PT894 and PT894 Pro support the 1066MHz front-side bus.

They use the VT8237R South Bridge chips (eight USB 2.0 ports, SATA, RAID, and optional 7.1 audio) or the new VT8251 (SATA 300 with NCQ, RAID 5, and integrated 7.1 audio).

Figure 4.40 illustrates the PT894 Pro's block diagram.

AMD Athlon Chipsets

The original AMD Athlon was a Slot A processor chip, but subsequent versions used Socket A—as do the Athlon XP, Duron, and some versions of the Sempron. Although similar in some ways to the Pentium III and Celeron, the AMD chips use a different interface and require different chipsets. AMD was originally the only supplier for Athlon chipsets, but VIA Technology, ULi Electronics, SiS, and NVIDIA now provide a large number of chipsets with a wide range of features. These chipsets are covered in the following sections.

AMD Chipsets

AMD makes four chipsets for Athlon and Duron processors: the AMD-750 and AMD-760/MP/MPX. The major features of these chipsets are compared in Table 4.44 and described in greater detail in the following sections.

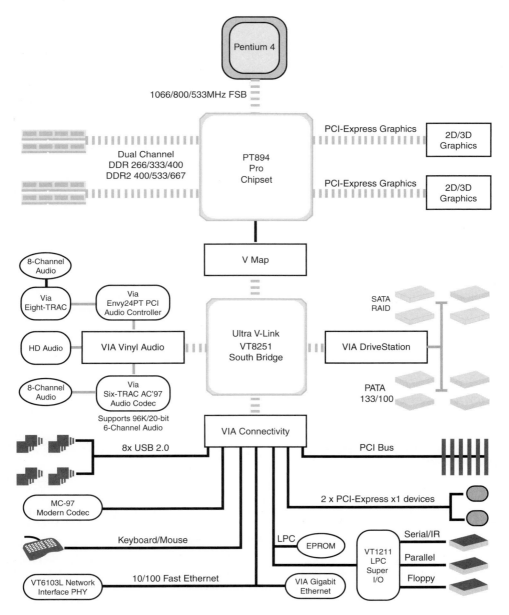

Figure 4.40 VIA's PT894 Pro chipset for the Pentium 4 combines dual-channel DDR/DDR2 memory support with dual PCI-Express video slots and the new VT8251 South Bridge.

Table 4.44   AMD Athlon/Duron Processor Chipsets Using North/South Bridge Architecture

Chipset	AMD-750	AMD-760
Code name	Irongate	None
Date introduced	Aug. 1999	Oct. 2000
Part number	AMD-751	AMD-761
Bus speed	200MHz	200/266MHz
Supported processors	Athlon/Duron	Athlon/Duron
SMP (dual CPUs)	No	Yes
Memory type	SDRAM	DDR SDRAM
Memory speed	PC100	PC1600/PC2100
Parity/ECC	Both	Both
Maximum memory	768MB	2GB buffered, 4GB registered
PCI support	2.2	2.2
AGP support	AGP 2x	AGP 4x
South Bridge	AMD-756	AMD-766
ATA/IDE support	ATA-66	ATA-100
USB support	1C/4P	1C/4P
CMOS/clock	Yes	Yes
ISA support	Yes	No
LPC support	No	Yes
Power management	SMM/ACPI	SMM/ACPI

AGP = Accelerated graphics port
ATA = AT attachment (IDE) interface
DDR-SDRAM = Double data rate SDRAM
ECC = Error-correcting code
ISA = Industry Standard Architecture
LPC = Low pin count bus
PCI = Peripheral component interconnect
SDRAM = Synchronous dynamic RAM
SMP = Symmetric multiprocessing (dual processors)
USB = Universal serial bus

AMD-750

AMD's first chipset for its own Slot A and Socket A processors, called the AMD-750, is a traditional North/South Bridge design specifically for the Athlon and Duron processors. The AMD-750 chipset consists of the AMD-751 North Bridge and the AMD-756 South Bridge.

The AMD-751 system controller connects between the AMD Athlon processor bus to the processor and features the memory controller, AGP 2x controller, and PCI bus controller. The AMD-756 South Bridge includes a PCI-to-ISA bridge, USB controller interface, and ATA 33/66 controller.

The AMD-750 chipset includes the following features:

- AMD Athlon 200MHz processor bus
- PCI 2.2 bus with up to six masters
- AGP 2x
- PC-100 SDRAM with ECC
- Up to 768MB of memory
- ACPI power management
- ATA-33/66 support
- USB controller
- ISA bus support
- Integrated 256-byte CMOS RAM with clock
- Integrated keyboard/mouse controller

AMD-760 Family

The AMD-760 chipset was introduced in October 2000 and is notable as the first chipset supporting DDR SDRAM memory. The AMD-760 chipset consists of the AMD-761 system controller (North Bridge) in a 569-pin plastic ball-grid array (PBGA) package and the AMD-766 peripheral bus controller (South Bridge) in a 272-pin PBGA package. See Figure 4.41 for details of the 760's block diagram.

The AMD-761 North Bridge features the AMD Athlon system bus, DDR-SDRAM system memory controller with support for either PC1600 or PC2100 memory, AGP 4x controller, and PCI bus controller. The 761 allows for 200MHz or 266MHz processor bus operation and supports the newer Athlon chips that use the 266MHz processor (also called front-side) bus.

The AMD-766 South Bridge includes a USB controller, dual UDMA/100 ATA/IDE interfaces, and the LPC bus for interfacing newer Super I/O and ROM BIOS components.

The AMD-760 chipset includes the following features:

- AMD Athlon 200/266MHz processor bus
- Dual processor support
- PCI 2.2 bus with up to six masters
- AGP 2.0 interface that supports 4x mode
- PC1600 or PC2100 DDR SDRAM with ECC
- Support for a maximum of 2GB buffered or 4GB registered DDR SDRAM
- ACPI power management
- ATA-100 support
- USB controller
- LPC bus for Super I/O support

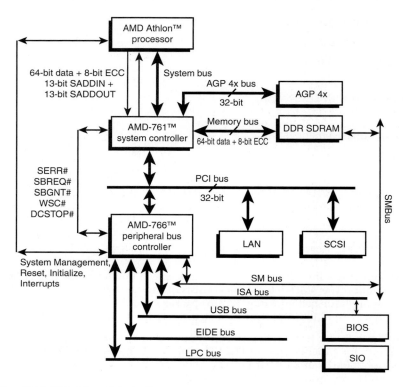

Figure 4.41 AMD-760 chipset block diagram.

The AMD-760MP chipset, which uses the AMD-762 North Bridge chip, is a development of the basic AMD-760 design that supports dual-processor Athlon MP systems. It differs from the standard 760 chipset in the following ways:

- Supports dual AMD Athlon MP processors with 200/266MHz processor bus speeds
- Up to 4GB PC2100 DDR (registered modules)
- Supports 33MHz PCI slots in 32-bit and 64-bit widths

The AMD-760MPX chipset uses the same AMD-762 North Bridge chip as the AMD-760MP to support multiple Athlon MP processors, but it uses the AMD-768 peripheral bus controller (South Bridge) chip. It differs from the 760MP chipset in the following ways:

- The AMD-762 North Bridge chip is used to support two 66MHz 32/64-bit PCI slots.
- The AMD-768 South Bridge chip is used to support 33MHz/32-bit PCI slots.

The 760MPX chipset is a better choice for a server because of its support for 66MHz and 64-bit PCI slots, whereas the 760MP is a suitable choice for a workstation.

None of these chipsets support USB 2.0, ATA-133, or DDR333 or faster memory. If you buy an Athlon, a Duron, or an Athlon XP desktop system, it's far more likely that your system will contain a third-party chipset than an AMD chipset; however, the 760MP and 760MPX chipsets continue to be popular choices for AMD-based workstations and servers. The following sections cover the third-party chipsets made for the Athlon, Duron, and Athlon XP processors.

VIA Chipsets for AMD

VIA Technologies, Inc., is the largest chipset and processor supplier outside of Intel and AMD. Originally founded in 1987, VIA is based in Taipei, Taiwan, and is the largest integrated circuit design firm on the island. VIA is a fabless company, which means it farms out the manufacturing to other companies with chip foundry capability. Although it is best known for its chipsets, in 1999 VIA purchased the Cyrix processor division from National Semiconductor and the Centaur processor division from IDT, respectively, thereby becoming a supplier of processors in addition to chipsets. VIA has also formed a joint venture with SONICblue (formerly S3) as a means of integrating graphics capabilities into various chipset products. This joint venture is known as S3 Graphics Co., Ltd.

VIA makes chipsets for Intel, AMD, and Cyrix (VIA) processors. Table 4.45 provides an overview of VIA's Athlon/Duron chipsets that use the traditional North/South Bridge architecture.

More recently, VIA has converted to an architecture called V-Link, which uses a fast dedicated connection between the North Bridge and South Bridge. V-Link is similar to Intel's hub architecture, as well as HyperTransport (used by ALi, NVIDIA, and ATI), MuTIOL (used by SiS), and A-Link (used by ATI). V-Link is also used by VIA's Pentium 4 chipsets. Tables 4.46–48 provide an overview of V-Link chipsets, which also support the VIA Modular Architecture Platform (V-MAP) design. As with VIA's chipsets for the Pentium 4, V-MAP uses identical pinouts for several ranges of V-Link North and South Bridge chips so vendors can reuse a motherboard design with more advanced chipsets as they are developed.

Both types of chipsets are discussed in the following sections.

Table 4.45   VIA Athlon/Duron/Athlon XP Processor Chipsets Using North/South Bridge Architecture

Chipset	Apollo KX133	Apollo KT133	Apollo KT133A	Apollo KLE133	ProSavage KM133
Introduced	Aug. 1999	June 2000	Dec. 2000	Mar. 2001	Sep. 2000
North Bridge	VT8371	VT8363	VT8363A	VT8361	VT8365
Processor support	Athlon	Athlon/Duron	Athlon/Duron	Athlon/Duron	Athlon/Duron
CPU interface	Slot-A	Socket-A (462)	Socket-A (462)	Socket-A (462)	Socket-A (462)
CPU FSB	200MHz	200MHz	200/266MHz	200/266MHz	200/266MHz
AGP slot	4x	4x	4x	No	AGP 4x
Integrated graphics	No	No	No	Yes	S3 Savage 4
PCI	2.2	2.2	2.2	2.2	2.2
Memory type	SDRAM	SDRAM	SDRAM	SDRAM	SDRAM
Memory speed	PC133	PC133	PC100/133	PC100/133	PC100/133
Maximum memory	1.5GB	1.5GB	1.5GB	1.5GB	1.5GB
South Bridge	VT82C686A	VT82C686A	VT82C686B	VT82C686B	VT8231
ATA/IDE	ATA-66	ATA-66	ATA-100	ATA-100	ATA-100
USB ports	1C4P	1C4P	1C4P	1C4P	1C4P
Power management	SMM/ACPI	SMM/ACPI	SMM/ACPI	SMM/ACPI	SMM/ACPI
Super I/O	Yes	Yes	Yes	Yes	Yes
CMOS/Clock	Yes	Yes	Yes	Yes	Yes
NB pin count	552-pin	552-pin	552-pin	552-pin	552-pin

Table 4.46   VIA Athlon XP/Duron Processor Chipsets Using V-Link Architecture

Chipset	Apollo KT266	Apollo KT266A	Apollo KT333	ProSavage KM266
North Bridge chip	VT8366	VT8633A	VT8753E	VT8375
Bus speed	200/266MHz	200/266MHz	200/266/333MHz	200/266MHz
SMP (dual CPUs)	No	No	No	No
Memory types	PC100/133, DDR200/266	PC100/133, DDR200/266	DDR200/266/333	PC100/133, DDR200/266
Parity/ECC	Neither	Neither	Neither	Neither
Maximum memory	4GB	4GB	4GB	4GB
PCI support	2.2	2.2	2.2	2.2
PCI speed/width	33MHz/32-bit	33MHz/32-bit	33MHz/32-bit	33MHz/32-bit
AGP slot	4x	4x	4x	4x
Integrated video	No	No	No	S3 Graphics ProSavage8 3D
South Bridge	VT8233, VT8233C, VT8233A	VT8233, VT8233C, VT8233A	VT8233, VT8233C, VT8233A	VT8233, VT8233C, VT8233A
V-Link speed	266MBps	266MBps	266MBps	266MBps
NB pin count	552-pin	552-pin	552-pin	552-pin

Table 4.47   VIA South Bridge Chips for Athlon/Duron/Athlon XP

South Bridge Chip	USB Support	Number of USB Ports	ATA Support	Audio	10/100 Ethernet	Home PNA	V-Link Throughput SATA RAID Pin Count)
VT8233	1.1	6	33/66/100	AC'97, 6-channel[1]	Yes	Yes	266MBps (376-pin)
VT8233A	1.1	6	33/66/100/133	AC'97, 6-channel[1]	Yes	No	266MBps (376-pin)
VT8233C	1.1	6	33/66/100	AC'97, 6-channel[1]	Yes[2]	No	266MBps (376-pin)
VT8235CE	2.0	6	33/66/100/133	AC'97, 5.1-channel[1]	Yes	No	533MBps (539-pin)
VT8237R[6]	2.0	8	33/66/100/133	AC'97, 5.1-channel[1,5]	Yes	No	1,066MBps (0, 1, JBOD[4] 539-pin)

1. *Integrated audio requires a separate audio codec chip on the motherboard; it also supports MC'97 soft modem.*

2. *3Com 10/100 Ethernet.*

3. *Four SATA ports with optional SATALite interface.*

4. *RAID 0+1 with optional SATALite. JBOD (just a bunch of disks) means all hard disks are spanned into a single logical drive.*

5. *8-channel (7.1) audio when optional VIA Envy 24PT PCI audio controller is used.*

6. *Can also be used with North Bridge chips that support 1,066MBps Ultra V-Link interconnect speed (originally known as VT8237).*

VIA Technologies Apollo KX133

The VIA Apollo KX133 chipset brings AGP 4x, PC133, a 200MHz FSB, and ATA-66 technologies to the AMD Athlon processor platform, exceeding the performance of AMD's own 750 chipset. It was the first chipset to support AGP 4x.

Apollo KT400	UniChrome KM400	Apollo KT400A	VIA KT600	KT880
VT8377	KM400	VT8377A	KT600	KT800
200/266/333MHz	200/266/333MHz	200/266/333MHz	266/333/400MHz	333/400MHz
No	No	No	No	No
DDR200/266/333	DDR200/266/333	DDR200/266/333/400	DDR200/266/333/400	Dual-channel DDR333/400
Neither	Neither	Neither	Neither	Neither
4GB	4GB	4GB	4GB	8GB
2.2		2.2	2.2	2.2
33MHz/32-bit	33MHz/32-bit	33MHz/32-bit	33MHz/32-bit	33MHz/32-bit
8x	8x	8x	8x	8x
No	S3 Graphics UniChrome	No	No	No
VT8235	VT8235CE or VT8237	VT8235CE or VT8237	VT8237	VT8237
533MBps	533MBps	533MBps	533MBps	533MBps
664-pin	552-pin	664-pin	664-pin	806-pin

Key features include the following:

- 200MHz processor bus
- AGP 4x graphics bus
- PC133 SDRAM memory
- 2GB maximum RAM
- ATA-66 support
- Four USB ports
- AC'97 link for audio and modem
- Hardware monitoring
- Power management

The VIA Apollo KX133 is a two-chip set consisting of the VT8371 North Bridge controller and the VT82C686A South Bridge controller.

VIA Technologies Apollo KT133 and KT133A

The VIA Apollo KT133/A chipsets are designed to support the AMD Athlon and Duron processors in Socket-A (462) form. Based on the prior KX133 chipset, the KT133/A differ mainly in their support for Socket-A (462) over the previous Slot-A processor interface.

The VIA Apollo KT133 and KT133A are both two-chip sets consisting of the VT8363 North Bridge and the VT82C686A South Bridge (KT133) or the VT8363A North Bridge and the VT82C686B South Bridge (KT133A).

Both the KT133 and KT133A support the following standard features:

- Athlon/Duron Socket-A (462) processors
- 200MHz CPU (front-side) bus
- AGP 4x
- 2GB RAM maximum
- PC100/PC133MHz SDRAM
- PCI 2.2
- ATA-66
- USB support
- AC-97 audio
- Integrated Super I/O
- Integrated hardware monitoring
- ACPI power management

The KT133A (VT8363A North Bridge with VT82C686B South Bridge) adds the following features:

- 266MHz CPU (front-side) bus
- ATA-100

ProSavage KM133

The VIA ProSavage KM133 integrates S3 Graphics' S3 Savage 4 and S3 Savage 2000 3D and 2D graphics engines with the Apollo Pro KT133 chipset. The major features of the chipset are the same as for the Apollo Pro KT133, with the following additions:

- 2MB–32MB shared memory architecture integrated with Savage 4 3D and Savage 2000 2D video
- Z-buffering, 32-bit true-color rendering, massive 2K-by-2K textures, single-pass multiple textures, sprite antialiasing, and other 3D features
- Support for DVD playback, DVI LCD displays, and TV-out
- PCI 2.2 compliance

An optional AGP 4x interface enables the integrated AGP 4x video to be upgraded with an add-on card if desired. This two-chip chipset consists of the VT8365 North Bridge and VT8231 South Bridge.

The VT8231 South Bridge integrates the Super I/O and supports the LPC interface.

Apollo KT266 and KT266A

The Apollo KT266 is the first VIA chipset for Athlon-based systems to support VIA's high-speed V-Link system architecture. V-Link connects the 552-pin VT8366 North Bridge to the 376-pin VT8233 series South Bridge with a 266MBps data pathway, which is twice as fast as traditional PCI-based connections.

Major features of the KT266 include system bus speeds of 200/266MHz, AGP 2x/4x interface, and up to 4GB of DDR200/266 DDR SDRAM or PC100/133 SDRAM. Other features vary with the South Bridge (VT8233, VT8233A, or VT8233C) chip used with the VT8366.

The KT266A is a pin-compatible upgrade to the original KT266's North Bridge. The KT266A's VT8366A includes VIA's Performance Driven Design, which is not a technical term but a marketing term for the A-series' chips improved memory timing and deeper command queues to improve chipset performance. Basic features of the KT266A are otherwise similar to the KT266.

ProSavage KM266

The ProSavage KM266 combines the features of the KT266 with the graphics core of the S3 Graphics ProSavage 8 2D/3D accelerator. Unlike some other chipsets with integrated graphics, the KM266 retains an AGP 4x slot, so users can upgrade to faster AGP 4x graphics in the future.

The ProSavage8 core uses 32MB of system RAM for its frame buffer, supports AGP 8x bandwidth internally with 128-bit data paths, and features DVD DXVA Motion Compensation to improve the quality of DVD playback. It supports all members of the VT8233 family of South Bridge chips and has a 266MBps 4x V-Link connection between North and South Bridge chips.

Apollo KT333

The Apollo KT333 is a pin-compatible development of the KT266A, adding support for a 333MHz system bus, 333MHz memory bus, and DDR333 memory. Unlike the KT266A, the KT333 no longer supports PC100/133 memory, but it uses the same KT8233 family of South Bridge chips.

Apollo KT400/KM400

The Apollo KT400 is the first VIA chipset for the Athlon XP processor to offer AGP 8x and a second-generation 533MBps V-Link connection to the South Bridge. It uses the VT8235 South Bridge, which is VIA's first South Bridge chip to support USB 2.0 as well as ATA-133.

The combination of faster video, fast memory and system bus speeds, and faster V-Link connections make the KT400 among the fastest Athlon XP chipsets.

The KM400 has the same basic features as the KT400 but adds integrated UniChrome 2D/3D graphics developed by S3 Graphics. The KM400 can be matched with the VT8235CE South Bridge chip or the top-of-the-line VT8237 South Bridge chip introduced by the KT400A (see the next section).

Apollo KT400A/KT600

In previous A-series chipsets from VIA, the North Bridge component was replaced with an improved chip and the South Bridge component was retained. However, the KT400A features new designs for both its North Bridge (VT8377A) and South Bridge (VT8237) chips. The major features of the VT8377A component include

- System bus support up to 333MHz
- DDR memory support up to DDR400
- Up to 4GB of memory
- An expanded array of prefetch buffers to reduce memory latency and improve throughput (FastStream64)
- AGP 8x interface

Some motherboard vendors use the older VT8235CE South Bridge chip (refer to Table 4.44) with the VT8377A North Bridge component. However, when the VT8237 South Bridge is used, the KT400A chipset has these new features:

- Integrated six-channel Surround Sound AC'97 audio
- Optional eight-channel audio
- Eight USB 2.0 ports
- Integrated MC'97 modem
- Integrated 10/100 Ethernet
- Serial ATA
- ATA RAID 0, 1 (0+1 with optional VIA SATAlite interface for two additional SATA ports)
- ATA 33/66/100/133
- ACPI/OnNow power management
- Optional VIA Velocity Gigabit Ethernet (PCI controller)

KT400A's FastStream64 enables the system to reach 3.2GBps memory transfer speeds without the need for more expensive dual-channel memory support.

Figure 4.42 shows the architecture of the KT400A (with VT8237) chipset.

The VIA KT600 is an improved version of the KT400A/VT3237 combo, adding support for the 400MHz CPU bus versions of the Athlon XP. Although a few motherboards pair the KT600's North Bridge with the older VT8235CE South Bridge, most motherboard vendors use the KT600/VT8237 combo to provide support for Serial ATA, SATA RAID, and other advanced features.

KT880

The VIA KT880 is VIA's first dual-channel chipset for the Athlon XP. Dual-channel memory support enables the system to reach very high memory transfer rates. It has the following features:

- System bus support up to 400MHz
- Dual-channel DDR memory support up to DDR400
- Up to 8GB of memory
- DualStream 64, which is VIA's marketing term for this chipset's combination of improved memory clock timings, larger on-chip branch table, and enhancements to the data prefetch protocol and memory brand predictions feature
- AGP 8x interface
- Integrated six-channel Surround Sound AC'97 audio with optional eight-channel audio
- Eight USB 2.0 ports
- Integrated MC'97 modem
- Integrated 10/100 Ethernet
- Serial ATA and SATA RAID 0, 1 (0+1 with optional VIA SATAlite interface for two additional SATA ports)
- ATA 33/66/100/133
- ACPI/OnNow power management

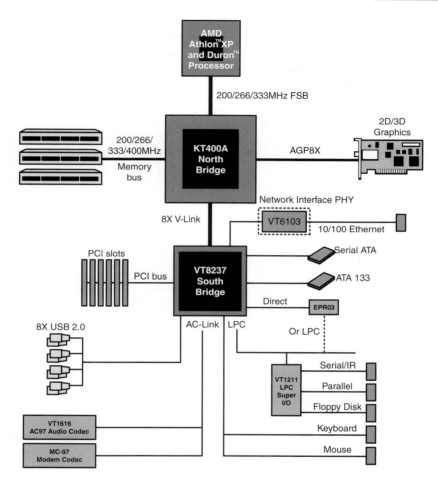

Figure 4.42 VIA KT400A block diagram.

SiS Chipsets for AMD

SiS has a variety of chipsets for the Athlon, Duron, and Athlon XP processors. Tables 4.48 and 4.49 provide an overview of these chipsets, some of which use a single-chip design and others of which use a high-speed two-chip design similar to other vendors' chipsets. These chipsets are discussed in the following sections.

Table 4.48   SiS Chipsets for Athlon/Duron/Athlon XP Processors

Chipset	SiS730S	SiS740	SiS733	SiS735
Bus speed	200/266MHz	266MHz	200/266MHz	200/266MHz
SMP (dual CPUs)	No	No	No	No
Memory type	PC133 SDRAM	DDR266, PC133	PC133	PC133/ DDDR266
Parity/ECC	Neither	Neither	Neither	Neither
Maximum memory	1.5GB	1.5GB	1.5GB	1.5GB
HyperStreaming technology	No	No	No	No
PCI support	2.2	2.2	2.2	2.2
PCI speed/width	33MHz/32-bit	33MHz/32-bit	33MHz32-bit /	33MHz/32-bit
AGP slot	4x	None	4x	4x
Integrated video	Yes[1]	Yes[2]	No	No
South Bridge	N/A[3]	SiS96x series	N/A[3]	N/A[3]
MuTIOL speed	N/A	533MBps	N/A	N/A
ATA support	ATA-100	Varies[4]	ATA-100	ATA-100
USB support	1.1/6 ports	Varies[4]	1.1/6 ports	1.1/6 ports
Audio support	AC'97	Varies[4]	AC'97	AC'97
10/100 Ethernet	Yes	Varies[4]	No	Yes
IEEE 1394a	No	Varies[4]	No	No

1. *2D/3D accelerator with hardware DVD playback and optional SiS301 Video Bridge to TV and secondary monitor.*
2. *DirectX7-compliant 3D features, including two pixel-rendering pipelines and four texture units.*
3. *Single-chip (combined N/S Bridge) design.*

Table 4.49   SiS MuTIOL South Bridge Chips for Athlon XP

South Bridge Chip	USB Support	# of USB Ports	ATA Support	# of SATA Ports	RAID Levels Supported
SiS961	1.1	6	33/66/100	—	—
SiS961B	1.1	6	33/66/100/133	—	—
SiS962	1.1, 2.0	6	33/66/100/133	—	—
SiS962L	1.1, 2.0	6	33/66/100/133	—	—
SiS963	1.1, 2.0	6	33/66/100/133	—	—
SiS963L	1.1, 2.0	6	33/66/100/133	—	—
SiS964	1.1, 2.0	8	33/66/100/133	2	0, 1, JBOD
SiS964L	1.1, 2.0	8	33/66/100/133	—	—
SiS965	1.1, 2.0	8	33/66/100/133	4	0, 1, 0+1, JBOD
SiS965L	1.1, 2.0	8	33/66/100/133	2	0, 1, JBOD

JBOD stands for "just a bunch of disks" (spans all drives into a single logical drive).

SiS745	SiS746	SiS746FX	SiS741GX	SiS748	SiS741
266MHz	266MHz	266/333MHz	266/333MHz	266/333/400MHz	266/333/400MHz
No	No	No	No	No	No
DDR266/333	DDR266/333	DDR266/333/400	DDR266/333	DDR266/333/400	DDR266/333/400
Neither	Neither	Neither	Neither	Neither	Neither
3GB	3GB	3GB	3GB	3GB	3GB
No	No	Yes	Yes	Yes	Yes
2.2	2.2	2.2	2.3	2.2	2.3
33MHz/32-bit	33MHz/32-bit	33MHz/32-bit	33MHz/32-bit	33MHz/32-bit	33MHz/32-bit
4x	8x	8x	8x	8x	8x
No	No	No	SiS Mirage Graphics	No	SiS Mirage Graphics
N/A[3]	SiS963 series	SiS963 series	SiS964 series	SiS963 series	SiS964 series
N/A	1GBps	1GBps[5]	1GBps[5]	1GBps[5]	1GBps[5]
ATA-100	Varies[4]	Varies[4]	Varies[4]	Varies[4]	Varies[4]
1.1/6 ports	Varies[4]	Varies[4]	Varies[4]	Varies[4]	Varies[4]
AC'97	Varies[4]	Varies[4]	Varies[4]	Varies[4]	Varies[4]
No	Varies[4]	Varies[4]	Varies[4]	Varies[4]	Varies[4]
Yes	Varies[4]	Varies[4]	Varies[4]	Varies[4]	Varies[4]

4. Varies with MuTIOL South Bridge chip used.
5. Chipset uses HyperStreaming technology, an improved version of MuTIOL.

Audio	10/100 Ethernet	Gigabit Ethernet	HomePNA 1.0/2.0	IEEE 1394	PCI-Express x1	MuTIOL Throughput
AC'97 2.2, 5.1 channel	Yes	No	Yes	No	No	533MBps
AC'97 2.2, 5.1 channel	Yes	No	Yes	No	No	533MBps
AC'97 2.2, 5.1 channel	Yes	No	Yes	Yes	No	533MBps
AC'97 2.2, 5.1 channel	Yes	No	Yes	No	No	533MBps
AC'97 2.2, 5.1 channel	Yes	No	Yes	Yes	No	533MBps
AC'97 2.2, 5.1 channel	Yes	No	Yes	No	No	533MBps
AC'97 2.3, 5.1 channel	Yes	No	Yes	No	No	1GBps
AC'97 2.3, 5.1 channel	Yes	No	Yes	No	No	1GBps
AC'97, 7.1 channel	Yes	Yes	Yes	No	Yes	1GBps
AC'97, 7.1 channel	Yes	No	Yes	No	Yes	1GBps

SiS MuTIOL High-speed North/South Bridge Connection

The SiS96x-series South Bridge chips use a high-speed bus called MuTIOL to connect with compatible North Bridge chips. The original version of MuTIOL (supported by the SiS961- and 962-series chips) is a 16-bit wide 266MHz connection that provides 533MBps bandwidth, twice the speed of the Intel hub architecture used by Intel's 800-series chipsets.

The SiS963-, 964-, and 965-series and matching North Bridge chips use a second generation of MuTIOL called MuTIOL 1G, which supports a 16-bit wide 533MHz connection to achieve bandwidths exceeding 1GBps.

When connected to the SiS746FX, SiS741GX, SiS748, or SiS741 North Bridge chips and newer models, the SiS963/964-series chips use a further development of MuTIOL called *HyperStreaming*, which integrates the following four technologies to further improve the speed of data transfer:

- **Single Stream with Low Latency Technology**—Improves performance by 5%–43%, depending on the activity.

- **Multiple Stream with Pipelining and Concurrent Execution Technology**—Uses concurrent parallel data pipelines and simultaneous processing of nonsequential data. In file-copy operations, for example, performance increases as data file size increases.

- **Specific Stream with Prioritized Channel Technology**—Improves playback of Internet music, video, and applications such as IP telephony and videoconferencing.

- **Smart Stream Flow Control Technology**—Analyzes characteristics of different interfaces and improves performance.

SiS730S

The SiS730S is a high-performance, low-cost, single-chip chipset with integrated 2D/3D graphics and support for Socket A versions of the AMD Athlon and Duron.

The integrated video is based on a 128-bit graphic display interface with AGP 2x performance. In addition to providing a standard analog interface for CRT monitors, the SiS730S also provides the DFP for a digital flat-panel monitor. An optional SiS301 video bridge supports NTSC/PAL TV output. The SiS730S also supports an AGP 4x slot, enabling users to upgrade to a separate AGP card in the future.

The SiS730S also includes integrated 10/100Mb Fast Ethernet as well as an AC'97-compliant interface that comprises a digital audio engine with 3D-hardware accelerator, on-chip sample rate converter, and professional wavetable along with separate modem DMA controller. SiS730S also incorporates the LPC interface for attaching newer Super I/O chips and a dual USB host controller with six USB ports. The SiS730S can also be used with ISA slots if an optional LPC/ISA bridge chip is used.

Features of the SiS730S include

- Support for AMD Athlon/Duron processors with 200/266MHz system bus
- Support for PC133 SDRAM
- PC99 requirements compliance
- PCI 2.2 compliance
- Four PCI masters
- Support for Ultra DMA100
- Integrated AGP 2x 2D/3D video/graphics accelerator
- Support for digital flat panel
- Hardware DVD decoding

- Built-in secondary CRT controller for independent secondary CRT, LCD, or TV digital output
- LPC interface
- Advanced PCI H/W audio (Sound Blaster 16 and DirectSound 3D compliant) and modem
- ACPI 1.0, APM 1.2 requirements compliance
- PCI Bus Power Management Interface Spec. 1.0
- Integrated keyboard/mouse controller
- Dual USB controller with six USB ports
- Integrated 10/100Mbps Ethernet controller

SiS733 and SiS735

The SiS733 and SiS735 are high-performance single-chip sets that support the AMD Athlon and Duron Socket A processors. Similar to other SiS single-chip sets, the SiS733 and SiS735 incorporate the features of a traditional North Bridge, South Bridge, and Super I/O chip into a single chip.

The SiS733 supports PC133 SDRAM and uses a 682-pin BGA package. The SiS735 supports either PC133 or DDR266 SDRAM and integrates 10/100 Fast Ethernet and HomePNA 1Mbps/10Mbps Home Network interfaces. The SiS735 also uses a 682-pin BGA package.

The SiS733 and SiS735 share the following features:

- Support for 4x AGP
- Up to six PCI masters
- Dual UDMA/100 IDE host adapters
- 1.5GB RAM maximum
- Six USB ports
- AC'97 audio and AMR support
- Integrated RTC
- LPC interface for support of MIDI, joystick, and legacy BIOS devices
- PC2001 compliance

SiS740

The SiS740 is a dual-chip design that provides a high-speed integrated video solution for Athlon-class processors. Its North Bridge and South Bridge chips use the high-speed MuTIOL connection to transfer data. Its major features include

- Integrated Real256 2D/3D graphics core with full DirectX 7 compatibility
- Up to 128MB of shared memory
- Hardware DVD playback
- DDR266 memory support

It is designed to use the SiS961- or 962-series South Bridge chips.

SiS745

The SiS745 is the first single-chip solution to integrate IEEE 1394a (FireWire 400) as part of its I/O. It is designed to provide a high-performance legacy-free solution. Its key features include the following:

- DDR266/333 memory support up to 3GB
- Support for Athlon XP processor as well as earlier models
- Six USB 1.1 ports
- Three IEEE 1394a ports
- Legacy keyboard, mouse, floppy, MIDI, and joystick interfaces
- ATA-100
- AC'97 audio and AMR (audio modem riser) support for a V.90 soft modem

SiS746 and SiS746FX

The SiS746 is the first Athlon/Duron/Athlon XP-compatible chipset on the market to feature an AGP 8x interface. It is a two-piece chipset designed to connect with the SiS963-series South Bridge chipsets. Major features include

- 266MHz processor bus
- DDR266/333 memory (the FX supports DDR400 memory)
- AGP 8x interface
- MuTIOL 1G second-generation connection to South Bridge (1GBps)
- SiS963 or SiS963L South Bridge

The companion SiS963L South Bridge chip adds the following features: ATA-133 support, six USB 2.0 ports, six-channel AC'97 audio, and MII interface for HomePNA or 10/100 Ethernet networking.

The SiS963 South Bridge chip adds IEEE 1394a (FireWire 400) support.

The SiS746FX North Bridge is an enhanced version of the SiS746, adding support for the 333MHz processor bus and approved DDR400 memory. It also uses the SiS963 series of South Bridge chips and uses SiS HyperStreaming technology to reduce latency in the MuTIOL interface.

SiS748

Like the SiS746FX, the SiS748 also uses the SiS963 series of South Bridge chips, as well as the SiS HyperStreaming technology for a lower-latency connection between the chips. Its other major features include

- Up to 400MHz system bus
- DDR266/333/400 memory support
- AGP 8x interface

Figure 4.43 shows the system architecture of the SiS748 chipset when using the SiS963L South Bridge chip. If the SiS963 South Bridge chip is used in place of the SiS963L pictured, three IEEE 1394a ports are also available.

SiS741/741GX

The SiS741 chipset includes integrated SiS Mirage Graphics. Its other features are similar to those of the SiS748 chipset. Major features include

- 400MHz system bus
- DDR400 memory support
- Up to 3GB of memory
- AGP 8x

- Integrated SiS Mirage Graphics with DirectX 8.1 support and 32MB or 64MB of shared memory
- Uses SiS963- or 964-series South Bridge

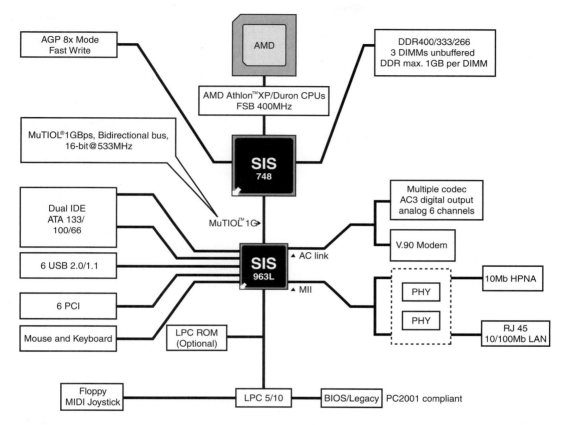

Figure 4.43 Block diagram for SiS748 chipset with SiS963L South Bridge.

The SiS741GX also includes integrated SiS Mirage Graphics. Its other features are similar to those of the SiS746FX, but it is usually paired with the SiS964 South Bridge.

When paired with an SiS964-series South Bridge, the SiS741GX also supports the following:

- Serial ATA (two ports; 964 only)
- Serial ATA RAID (964 only)
- PCI version 2.3
- Up to eight USB 2.0 ports

ULi (ALiMagik1) for AMD

ALi Corporation (now known as ULi Electronics) makes only one chipset for AMD Athlon/Duron processors: the ALiMagik1.

ALiMagik1 is a two-chip chipset that uses the M1647 Super North Bridge and the M1535D+ South Bridge (which is also used by its Pentium III/Celeron chipsets). The M1647 Super North Bridge is a 528-pin BGA chip.

The M1647 Super North Bridge supports SDRAM as well as DDR SDRAM at speeds of 200MHz or 266MHz. It supports up to 3GB of RAM but does not support ECC. Memory timing is x-1-1-1-1-1-1-1 in back-to-back SDRAM reads. Because the M1647 supports both conventional and DDR SDRAM, system manufacturers can use the same chipset for both memory types.

The M1647 supports AGP 4x video, PCI 2.2, up to six PCI masters beyond the North Bridge and PCI bridge, ACPI and Legacy green power management, PCI Mobile CLKRUN#, and AGP Mobile BUSY#/STOP#.

When combined with an M1535+ South Bridge chip, the chipset is called the MobileMagik1 and can be used on Athlon- or Duron-based portable systems.

Because this chipset, unlike others that use DDR memory, still uses the traditional 133MBps PCI bus connection between North and South Bridge chips, its performance is among the lowest of any Athlon chipset. This chipset is now discontinued.

NVIDIA nForce Chipsets for AMD

NVIDIA, although best known for its popular GeForce line of graphics chipsets, has also become a popular vendor of chipsets for the AMD Athlon/Duron/Athlon XP processor family with its nForce and nForce2 product families.

nForce's advanced features include the following:

- 400MBps HyperTransport link between chipset components. nForce is the first PC chipset to use HyperTransport.

- Dual-channel crossbar memory controller to provide high-speed memory access when identical pairs of memory are used. It uses independent 64-bit memory controllers.

Table 4.50   nForce/nForce2 IGP/SPP (North Bridge) Chips

North Bridge Chip	nForce 420	nForce 415	nForce2 IGP	nForce2 SPP
Bus speed	200/266MHz	200/266MHz	200/266/333MHz	200/266MHz
SMP (dual CPUs)	No	No	No	No
Memory type	DDR200/266MHz PC100/133	DDR200/266MHz PC100/133	DDR200/266/ 333/400[1]	DDR200/266/ 333/400[1]
Parity/ECC	Neither	Neither	Neither	Neither
Maximum memory	4GB	4GB	3GB	3GB
Dual-channel mode	Yes[2]	Yes[2]	Yes	Yes
PCI support	2.2	2.2	2.2	2.2
PCI speed/width	33MHz/32-bit	33MHz/32-bit	33MHz/32-bit	33MHz/32-bit
AGP slot	4x	4x	8x	8x
Integrated video	GeForce2 MX	No	GeForce4 MX	No
HyperTransport speed	400MBps	400MBps	800MBps	800MBps
South Bridge chip	nForce MCP, MCP-D	nForce MCP, MCP-D	nForce2 MCP, MCP-T, Gigabit MCP	nForce2 MCP, MCP-T, Gigabit MCP

1. *Requires external AGP card to support DDR400 memory.*   2. *Use only two identical memory modules to enable this mode.*

- nView multidisplay hardware (420 chipset with integrated video) supports dual displays with integrated video.
- AGP 4x interface.
- Dynamic adaptive speculative preprocessor (DASP) to reduce latency and improve prefetching of data.
- StreamThru architecture to improve isochronous (time-dependent) data transfers for network and broadband through the chipset's integrated 10/100 Ethernet port.
- Integrated GeForce2 MX video (420 chipset with integrated video) with support for DVI LCD flat panels.
- True hardware-based audio processing with support for Dolby Digital (AC-3) 5.1 channel audio (SoundStorm chipsets).

nForce2 improvements over nForce include the following:

- 800MHz HyperTransport connection
- DualDDR improved dual-channel memory controller that supports up to DDR400 memory and allows dual-channel operation with two or three DIMMs
- Optional IEEE 1394a support
- Optional GeForce4 MX integrated video
- AGP 8x interface

Table 4.50 provides an overview of the North Bridge chips in the nForce and nForce2 families, and Table 4.52 provides an overview of the nForce/nForce2 South Bridge chips. The nForce is a descendant of the custom chipset NVIDIA created for the Microsoft Xbox console game system.

nForce North Bridge chips with integrated graphics are known as *integrated graphics processors (IGPs)*, whereas those that require separate AGP video are known as *system platform processors (SPPs)*. All South Bridge chips are known as *media and communications processors (MCP)*. IGP/SPP and MCP chips communicate over an 800MBps HyperTransport connection.

nForce2 400	nForce2Ultra 400	nForce 2Ultra 400R	nForce 2Ultra 400 Gb
200/266333/400MHz /	200/266/333/400MHz	200/266333/400MHz /	200/266/333/400MHz
No	No	No	No
DDR200/266/ 333/400[1]	DDR200/266/ 333/400[1]	DDR200/266/ 333/400[1]	DDR200/266/ 333/400[1]
Neither	Neither	Neither	Neither
3GB	3GB	3GB	3GB
No	Yes	Yes	Yes
2.2	2.2	2.2	2.2
33MHz/32-bit	33MHz/32-bit	33MHz/32-bit	33MHz/32-bit
8x	8x	8x	8x
No	No	No	No
800MBps	800MBps	800MBps	800MBps
nForce2 MCP, MCP-T, Gigabit MCP	nForce2 MCP, MCP-T 2 RAID MCP	nForce	nForce2 Gigabit MCP

Table 4.51   nForce/nForce2 MCP (South Bridge) Chips

South Bridge Chip	USB Support	Number of USB Ports	ATA Support	SATA Support	ATA/SATA RAID Support
nForce MCP	1.1	6	33/66/100	No	No
nForce MCP-D[1]	1.1	6	33/66/100	No	No
nForce2 MCP	1.1, 2.0	6	33/66/100/133	No	No
nForce2 MCP-T[1]	1.1, 2.0	6	33/66/100/133	No	No
nForce2 Gigabit MCP	1.1, 2.0	8	33/66/100/133	Yes	Yes
nForce2 RAID MCP	1.1, 2.0	8	33/66/100/133	Yes	Yes

1. Also known as NVIDIA SoundStorm   2. Also supports HomePNA networking

The combination of advanced memory controllers, prefetch design, HyperTransport high-speed connection, and hardware audio processing in MCP-D and MCP-T chips makes the second-generation nForce2 chipsets among the fastest chipsets available for Athlon XP processors. The new Gigabit MCP and RAID MCP chips bring eight-port USB 2.0 and Serial ATA/ATA RAID support to nForce2-based systems. The Gigabit MCP is the first nForce2 MCP chip to offer integrated Gigabit Ethernet.

Figure 4.44 shows the architecture of the nForce2 IGP and MCP-T combination, which provides the greatest versatility. If the SPP North Bridge is used instead of the IGP, integrated video is not present. If the MCP South Bridge is used instead of the MCP-T, then IEEE 1394a, hardware 5.1 Dolby Digital audio, and dual network ports are not available.

ATI Radeon IGP Chipsets

ATI made a series of chipsets for the Athlon series of processors that integrate Radeon VE-level 3D graphics, DVD playback, and dual-display features with high-performance North Bridge and South Bridge designs. These chipsets use ATI's high-speed A-Link bus to connect its North and South Bridge chips, but they also support connections to third-party South Bridge chips via the PCI bus. This has enabled system designers to create an all-ATI or a mix-and-match solution. Many of the first Radeon IGP-based systems on the market used ALi (now ULi) or VIA South Bridge chips. The Radeon IGP 320 North Bridge chip can be matched with either of ATI's South Bridge chips: the IXP 200 or IXP 250. Both of these chips support six USB 2.0 ports and ATA33/66/100. The Radeon 320 IGP is now discontinued. Table 4.52 summarizes the major features of the IGP 320, and Table 4.53 summarizes the major features of the IXP 200 and 250.

Audio	10/100 Ethernet[2]	Gigabit Ethernet	IEEE 1394	Hardware Firewall	Used with
AC'97, 5.1 channel	Yes	No	No	No	nForce IGP, SPP
AC'97, 5.1 channel	Yes	No	No	No	nForce IGP, SPP
AC'97, 6- channel, 20-bit, SPDIF out	Yes	No	No	No	nForce2 IGP, SPP, 400, Ultra 400
All features of MCP, plus AudioProcessing Unit, Dolby Digital 5.1 channel, and DirectX 8 3D audio	Dual NVIDIA and 3Com	No	Yes	No	nForce2 IGP, SPP, 400, Ultra 400
AC'97, 6- channel, 20-bit, SPDIF out	Yes	Yes	No	Yes	nForce2 Ultra 400Gb
AC'97, 6- channel, 20-bit, SPDIF out	Yes	No	No	No	nForce2 Ultra 400R

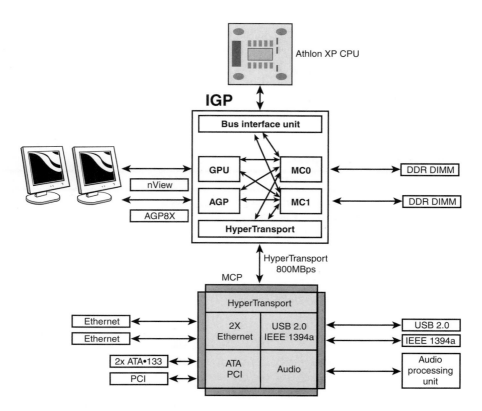

Figure 4.44   NVIDIA nForce2 IGP/MCP2 chipset architecture.

Table 4.52   Radeon IGP (North Bridge) Chip for Athlon

North Bridge Chip	Radeon IGP 320	North Bridge Chip	Radeon IGP 320
Bus speed	200/266MHz	PCI support	2.2
SMP (dual CPUs)	No	PCI speed/width	33MHz/32-bit
Memory type	DDR200/266	AGP slot	4x
Parity/ECC	Neither	Integrated video	Radeon VE*
Maximum memory	1GB	A-Link speed	266MBps

Same core as ATI Radeon 7000, with support for dual displays

Table 4.53   ATI South Bridge Chips for Athlon

South Bridge Chip	IXP 200/250*	South Bridge Chip	IXP 200/250*
USB Support	6 USB 2.0 ports	Ethernet LAN	3Com 10/100
ATA Support	ATA100	Super I/O	Yes
Audio Support	AC'97, S/PDIF	High Speed Interconnect	A-Link

The IXP250 has identical features to IXP200; plus it supports Wake On LAN (WOL), Desktop Management Interface (DMI), manage boot agent (MBA), and the Alert Standards Forum (ASF) mechanism.

Intel Workstation Chipsets

Intel has developed several chipsets for workstations based on the Pentium 4 and Xeon processors. The following sections describe these chipsets in detail; Table 4.54 provides a quick reference to their features.

Table 4.54   Workstation Chipsets

Chipset	860	E7205	E7505	E7525
Code name	Colusa	Granite Bay	Placer	Tumwater
Date introduced	May 2001	Dec. 2002	Dec. 2002	2004
Part number	82860	E7205	E7505	E7525
Bus speeds	400MHz	533/400MHz	533/400MHz	800MHz
Supported processors	Xeon	Pentium 4[5]	Xeon 533MHz FSB and 512KB L2 cache[5]	Xeon 800MHz FSB
SMP (dual CPUs)	Yes (2)	No	Yes (2)	Yes (2)
Memory type	4 RDRAM PC800[1]	DDR200/266 SDRAM (unbuffered)	DDR200/266 dual-channel	DDR333 or DDR2-400 (dual-channel)
Parity/ECC	Both	Both	Both	Both
Maximum memory	4GB (with two MRHR chips)	4GB	16GB	16GB
Memory banks	Up to 43	Up to 4	Up to 6 (registered memory) or 4 (unbuffered memory)	Up to 8

Table 4.54   Continued

Chipset	860	E7205	E7505	E7525
PCI support	2.2	2.2	2.2	2.2
PCI speed/width	32-bit/33MHz[2]	32-bit/33MHz	32-bit/33MHz[4]	32-bit/33MHz[6]
AGP slot	AGP 4x/2x	AGP8x-1x	AGP8x-1x	PCI-Express x16
Integrated video	None	None	None	None
South Bridge (Hub)	ICH2	ICH4	ICH4	ICH5R or 6300ESB[7]

1. *Up to eight on motherboards with MRHR chips.*

2. *64-bit 33/66MHz on motherboards with P64H chips.*

3. *Two banks when MRHR chip is not present.*

4. *64-bit 33/66MHz and PCI-X on motherboards with P64H2 chips.*

5. *Supports HT Technology.*

6. *64-bit 33/66MHz and PCI-X on motherboards with 6700PXH PCI hub chips.*

7. *6300ESB incorporates dual SATA RAID 0,1 host adapters; four USB 2.0 ports; and one PCI-X 64-bit/66MHz (64/66) bus with support for up to 4 PCI-X 64/66 interfaces.*

Intel 860

The Intel 860 is a high-performance chipset designed for the Socket 602 (Pentium 4-based) Xeon processors for DP workstations. The 860 uses the same ICH2 as the Intel 850 but uses a different MCH—the 82860, which supports one or two Socket 602 ("Foster") Xeon processors. The other major features of the 82860 are similar to those of the 82850, including support for dual 400MHz RDRAM memory channels with a 3.2GBps bandwidth and a 400MHz system bus. The 82860 MCH also supports 1.5V AGP 4x video cards at a bandwidth exceeding 1GBps.

The 860 chipset uses a modular design, in which its two core chips can be supplemented by the 82860AA (P64H) 66MHz PCI Controller Hub and the 82803AA MRHR. The 82860AA supports 64-bit PCI slots at either 33MHz or 66MHz, and the 82803AA converts each RDRAM memory channel into two, which doubles memory capacity. Thus, whether a particular 860-based motherboard offers 64-bit or 66MHz PCI slots or dual-channel RDRAM memory depends on whether these supplemental chips are used in its design.

Intel E7205

The Intel E7205 chipset, known as Granite Bay during its development, is designed to support both workstation and high-performance PC applications. It supports DDR200/266 SDRAM modules with a system bus speed up to 533MHz and uses the ICH4 I/O controller hub, just as some versions of the 845 chipset do. However, the E7205 supports ECC and parity-checked memory for better system reliability and supports all standard-voltage speeds of AGP from 1x to 8x with an AGP Pro slot (nonstandard 3.5V versions of AGP once sold by some vendors such as 3dfx will not work). It supports hyper-threading for use with the 3.06GHz and faster Pentium 4 processors.

Intel E7505

The Intel E7505 chipset, known as Placer during its development, is in some ways an updated version of the 860 chipset, adding support for faster processors and more advanced hardware than the 860 offers.

The E7505 supports a system bus of up to 533MHz, matching the single or dual Xeon 533MHz FSB and 512KB L2 cache processors it supports; it also supports the HT Technology included in these processors. The E7505 supports pairs of DDR200/266 memory up to 16GB total, four times as much as the E7205 and the 860. It can use up to six registered or four unbuffered memory modules and supports ECC. Its Intel x4 single-device data correction (SDDC) can correct up to four errors per memory module for better system reliability.

Its AGP Pro slot supports all speeds of AGP from 1x to 8x (except for the nonstandard 3.5V versions of AGP once sold by some vendors), and it uses the ICH4 I/O controller hub. To achieve 66MHz/ 64-bit PCI and 133MHz PCI-X support, the E7505 can be used with up to three optional P64H2 (82870P2) chips, an improved version of the P64H chip that is an optional part of the 860 chipset.

Intel E7525

The Intel E7525 chipset, known as Tumwater during its development, combines features derived from the Intel 9xx series of desktop chipsets with support for the latest 800MHz versions of the Intel Xeon processor and the 64-bit Xeon processor with 2MB L2 cache. The E7525 supports up to 16GB of dual-channel DDR-2 400 (four DIMMs per channel) or DDR333 (three DIMMs per channel) and protects the contents of memory with support for ECC, Intel x4 single-device data correction (SDDC), DIMM sparing, DIMM scrubbing, and memory mirroring. DIMM sparing (also known as *memory mirroring*) sets aside a spare bank of memory that is used automatically if one of the primary banks develops too many single-bit errors. DIMM scrubbing (also known as *memory scrubbing*) tests memory during idle periods. Memory mirroring uses one bank to hold a copy of the other.

The E7525 chipset is Intel's first workstation chipset with support for PCI-Express x16 graphics. It supports either the ICH5R or ESB6300 I/O Controller Hub chip. To achieve 66MHz/64-bit PCI and 133MHz PCI-X support, the E7525 can be used with up to two optional 6700 PXH 64-bit PCI hub chips.

AMD Athlon 64 Chipsets

The Athlon 64 processor requires a new generation of chipsets, both to support its 64-bit processor architecture and to allow for integration of the memory controller into the processor (the memory controller has traditionally been located in the North Bridge chip or equivalent). As a consequence, some vendors do not use the term *North Bridge* to refer to the chipset component that connects the processor to AGP video.

AMD, VIA Technologies, NVIDIA, ATI, SiS, and ULi Electronics (formerly ALi Corporation) have developed chipsets for the Athlon 64.

AMD 8000 (8151) Chipset

The AMD 8000 is AMD's first chipset designed for the Athlon 64 and Opteron families. Its architecture is substantially different from the North Bridge/South Bridge or hub-based architectures we are familiar with from the chipsets designed to support Pentium II/III/4/Celeron and AMD Athlon/Athlon XP/Duron processors.

The AMD-8000 chipset is often referred to as the AMD-8151 because the AMD-8151 provides the connection between the Athlon 64 or Opteron processor and the AGP video slot—the task usually performed by the North Bridge or MCH hub in other chipsets. The name of the North Bridge or MCH hub chip is usually applied to the chipset. However, AMD refers to the AMD-8151 chip as the AGP Graphics Tunnel chip because its only task is to provide a high-speed connection to the AGP slot on the motherboard. The other components of the AMD-8000 chipset include the AMD-8111 HyperTransport I/O hub (South Bridge)and the AMD-8131 PCI-X Tunnel chip.

Due to delays in the development of the AMD-8151 AGP Graphics Tunnel chip, most vendors through late 2003 used the AMD-8111 HyperTransport I/O hub alone or along with the AMD-8131 PCI-X Tunnel chip to provide a mixture of PCI and PCI-X slots on motherboards optimized as servers. Some recent systems have incorporated the AMD-8151 chip to provide AGP video, but the AMD-8000 chipset continues to be used primarily as a workstation/server chipset instead of as a desktop chipset.

The AMD-8151 AGP Graphics tunnel has the following major features:

■ Supports AGP 2.0/3.0 (AGP 1x-8x) graphics cards
■ 16-bit up/down HyperTransport connection to the processor
■ 8-bit up/down HyperTransport connection to downstream chips

The AMD-8111 HyperTransport I/O hub (South Bridge) chip's major features include

■ PCI 2.2-compliant PCI bus (32-bit, 33MHz) for up to eight devices
■ AC'97 2.2 audio (six-channel)
■ Six USB 1.1/2.0 ports (three controllers)
■ Two ATA/IDE host adapters supporting up to ATA-133 speeds
■ RTC
■ Low-pin-count (LPC) bus
■ Integrated 10/100 Ethernet
■ 8-bit up/down HyperTransport connection to upstream chips

The AMD-8131 HyperTransport PCI-X tunnel chip's major features include

■ Two PCI-X bridges (A and B) supporting up to five PCI bus masters each
■ PCI-X transfer rates up to 133MHz
■ PCI 2.2 33MHz and 66MHz transfer rates
■ Independent operational modes and transfer rates for each bridge
■ 8-bit up/down HyperTransport connection to upstream and downstream chips

Figure 4.45 shows the architecture of the AMD-8151 chipset for Athlon 64.

ATI (now AMD)

ATI offers four two-piece chipsets for Athlon 64 processors: the RS480 (which includes Radeon X300 integrated graphics), the RX480, and the RD580. The RS480 and the RX480 typically use the SB400 (also known as the IXP400) or SB450 South Bridge. Aside from the RS480's integrated graphics, both chipsets have the following major features:

■ HyperTransport 16-bit/800MHz processor–to–North Bridge connection
■ PCI-Express x16 graphics card support
■ A-Link II connection between the North and South Bridge chips
■ Four PCI-Express x1 slots

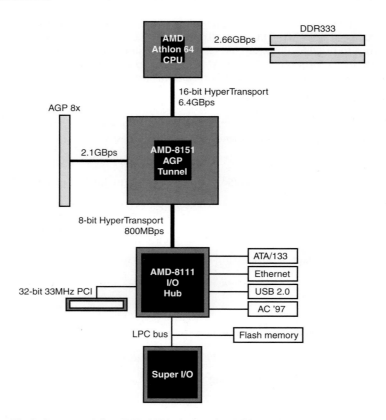

Figure 4.45 Block diagram of the AMD 8000 chipset for Athlon 64.

The RS480's integrated graphics adds these features:

- Radeon X300 integrated graphics with DirectX 9.0 Vertex/Pixel Shader 2.0 support
- Optional dedicated or shared memory design (up to 128MB of RAM)
- Support for up to three monitors with a separate ATI video card
- Support for DVI output

The CrossFire version of the Radeon Express 200—the RD482—supports PCI-Express 2 x8 expansion slots for two PCI-Express video cards; the RD580 supports two x16 PCI-Express expansion slots.

The SB400 South Bridge has these major features:

- Dual ATA-133 host adapters
- Four Serial ATA host adapters with SATA RAID 0, 1
- Eight USB 2.0 ports
- AC'97 2.3 six-channel audio

The SB450 South Bridge used by the RD482 adds support for HDA audio and RAID 0+1 to the SB400's features. The SB600 is designed for use with the RD580. Some motherboard vendors use third-party South Bridge chips from ULi, such as the M1573 or M1575, instead of ATI South Bridge chips.

ULi Chipsets for Athlon 64

Although ULi has largely been absent from chipset development for the Athlon XP, it offers three chipsets for the Athlon 64 and Opteron processors: the M1687, the M1689, and the M1695. The M1687 and M1689 are a traditional two-chip designs, whereas the M1689 is a one-chip design following in the footsteps of SiS and, more recently, NVIDIA.

ULi M1687

The M1687 uses the M1563 as its South Bridge, and the major features of this chipset are similar to the AMD-8151/AMD-8111 design:

- Support for AGP 2.0/3.0 (AGP 1x-8x) graphics cards
- 16-bit up/down HyperTransport connection between processor and M1687
- 8-bit up/down HyperTransport connection between M1687 North Bridge and M1563 South Bridge
- PCI 2.2-compliant PCI bus (32-bit, 33MHz) for up to six devices
- AC'97 2.2 audio (six-channel)
- Six USB 1.1/2.0 ports (three controllers)
- Two ATA/IDE host adapters supporting up to ATA-133 speeds
- RTC
- Low-pin-count (LPC) bus
- Integrated 10/100 Ethernet

Compared to the AMD-8151/AMD-8111, the major advantage of the ALi M1687 is the Secure Digital and Sony Memory Stick interfaces built into the M1563.

ULi M1689

The ULi M1689 is a single-chip chipset for the Athlon 64 and Opteron processors, and it can also be used with the Mobile Athlon 64. It integrates several of the latest technologies, including Serial ATA, support for eight USB 2.0/1.1 ports, and AC'97 2.3 20-bit six-channel audio. Major features include

- AGP 1.5/3.0 (AGP 1x-8x)
- PCI 2.3 with support for up to seven bus masters
- Dual ATA-133 host adapters with support for 48-bit LBA drives
- Four USB host adapters and eight USB 1.1/2.0 ports
- 10/100 Ethernet
- AC'97 2.3 audio with 20-bit sampling
- Two Serial ATA host adapters

ULi M1695

The ULi M1695 is a true second-generation Athlon 64 chipset that offers no-compromise support for both PCI-Express x16 and AGP 8x video at full speed (when used with the M1567 South Bridge). Its

Triple Graphics Interface (TGI) also supports PCI graphics. When PCI-Express, AGP, and PCI graphics cards (all with dual-monitor support) are installed, six screens are supported. The M1695 also supports two PCI-Express x8 slots, enabling configurations similar to NVIDIA's SLI dual-card designs. The M1695 can be used with either ULi's own M1567 South Bridge chip or with other Athlon 64-compatible SB chips. Major features include

- PCI-Express x16 or 2 x8; AGP 8x support is provided by the M1567.
- Two PCI-Express x1.
- PCI 2.3 with support for up to seven bus masters.
- Dual ATA-133 host adapters with support for 48-bit LBA drives.
- Four USB host adapters and eight USB 1.1/2.0 ports.
- 10/100 Ethernet.
- AC'97 2.3 audio with 20-bit sampling.
- Two Serial ATA host adapters with SATA RAID 0, 1 and JBOD.

Figure 4.46 displays the ULi M1695/M1567 block diagram. As Figure 4.47 indicates, the ULi M1695/M1567 can also use third-party PCI-X tunnels such as the AMD-8132.

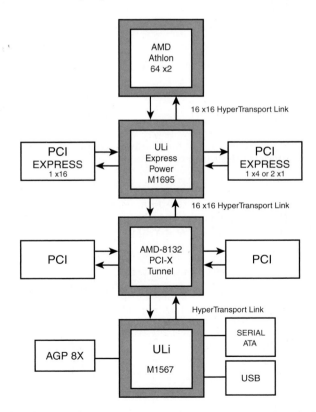

Figure 4.46 The ULi M1695/M1567 combination enables a system to provide full-speed PCI-Express x16 video and AGP 8x video. The AMD-8132 PCI-X tunnel is optional.

VIA Chipsets for Athlon 64

VIA has long been one of the leading developers of chipsets for AMD processors, and this pattern continues with the Athlon 64 and Opteron. VIA offers five chipsets for these processors:

- K8T800 Pro
- K8T800
- K8M800
- K8T890
- K8M890

The following sections cover these chipsets in more detail.

K8T800, K8T800 Pro, and K8M800

The K8T800 (originally known as the K8T400) was VIA's first chipset for the Athlon 64 and Opteron processors. It departs somewhat from the pattern established by AMD's and ALi's chipsets by using VIA's own 8x V-Link (533MBps) interconnect between the North and South Bridge chips instead of HyperTransport (although HyperTransport is used, of course, to connect to the processor). The K8T800 uses the VT8237 South Bridge chip. Major features include

- HyperTransport 16-bit/800MHz link between the processor and North Bridge
- Support for AGP 4x/8x video cards
- PCI 2.23 with support for up to six bus masters
- Dual ATA-133 host adapters
- Eight USB 1.1/2.0 ports
- 10/100 Ethernet
- AC'97 5.1 audio
- Two Serial ATA/SATA RAID host adapters (RAID 0, 1, JBOD)

The K8T800 chipset family also includes the following optional chips, which can be used to add more features:

- SATAlite SATA (two additional ports, adding RAID 0+1)
- VPX2 expansion bridge (adds two PCI-X buses)
- VIA Vinyl Gold (7.1 surround sound via PCI bus)
- Gigabit Ethernet controller (via PCI bus)

The K8T800 Pro is based on the K8T800, but with the following improvements:

- HyperTransport 1GHz link between the processor and North Bridge
- Asynchronous operation of PCI and AGP slots
- Ultra V-Link (1GBps) connection between the North and South Bridges

The most significant of these features is the asynchronous operation of PCI and AGP slots. This feature enables the user to lock the frequency of these slots regardless of the processor bus and clock multiplier used by the processor, enabling more reliable overclocking. Many Athlon 64 chipsets lack this capability.

The K8M800 is based on the K8T800 but adds S3 UniChrome Pro integrated graphics. UniChrome Pro offers a 128-bit 2D/3D engine, dual pixel pipelines, hardware acceleration for MPEG-2 and MPEG-4 video, and support for HDTV up to 1080p and standard TV as well as LCD and CRT displays.

K8T890, K8M890, and K8T900

The VIA K8T890 and K8M890 are VIA's first PCI-Express chipsets for the Athlon 64 and Opteron. These chipsets use the 1GHz HyperTransport processor/NB connection and Ultra V-Link NB/SB connections. These North Bridge chips actually have a 20-lane-wide PCI-Express interface, leaving four lanes available for PCI-Express x1 cards.

These chipsets are also designed to use the new VT8251 South Bridge, which includes several features that once required add-on chips:

■ Four Serial ATA host adapters are included to support SATA RAID 0, 1, and 0+1.

■ Support for Intel's new High-Definition Audio (HDA, formerly code named Azalia) standard. HDA provides Dolby Digital IIfx–compatible (7.1) surround sound and 24-bit/192KHz sampling rates for CE-quality sound.

■ Two PCI-Express x1 slots, for a total of six possible (four connected to North Bridge and two to South Bridge).

Because of delays in production, some systems using the K8T890 and K8M890 used the earlier VT8237R South Bridge instead of the VT8251. Be sure to check specifications for a particular motherboard to determine which South Bridge chip was used.

The K8M890 adds integrated S3 Graphics DeltaChrome 2D/3D graphics with DirectX 9 graphics support to the features of the K8T890.

The K8T900 is based on the K8T890 but adds support for PCI-Express 2 x8 video to support two PCI-Express graphics cards.

NVIDIA Chipsets for Athlon 64

NVIDIA offers more than 14 chipset variations that support the current range of Athlon 64, Sempron, and Opteron processors. Seven of these are single-chip chipsets for use with the Athlon 64:

■ nForce3 150

■ nForce3 250

■ nForce3 250Gb

■ nForce3 250 Ultra

■ nForce4

■ nForce4 Ultra

■ nForce 4 SLI

There are also three two-chip chipsets with integrated video for the Sempron:

■ nForce 410 with GeForce 6100

■ nForce 430 with GeForce 6100

■ nForce 430 with GeForce 6150

NVIDIA also offers four single-chip chipsets for the Opteron:

■ nForce3 Pro 150

■ nForce3 Pro 250

- nForce Professional 2050
- nForce Professional 2200

NVIDIA refers to these chips as *media and communications processors (MCPs)* because a single chip combines the functions of typical North and South Bridge chips. The following sections cover these chips in more detail.

nForce3 150 and nForce3 Pro 150

The NVIDIA nForce3 150 MCP was one of the first chipsets available for the Athlon 64 processor. Although it departs from the two-chip chipset standard used by most Athlon 64 chipsets by combining North Bridge and South Bridge functions, the nForce3 150 has a limited feature set. The short list of features reflects both this chipset's early development and its positioning as an entry-level chipset. The nForce3 150's major features include the following:

- HyperTransport chipset-to-processor connection. However, it offers the standard 16-bit/800MHz speed only in the downstream (processor-to-chipset) direction. Data flowing from the chipset to the processor (upstream) runs in an 8-bit data path at only 600MHz.
- AGP 1x-8x video card support.
- Dual ATA-133 ATA/IDE hard disk host adapters.
- RAID 0, 1, and 0+1.
- AC'97 2.1 audio (six-channel) with 20-bit output and SPDIF support.
- Six USB 1.1/2.0 ports.
- 10/100 Ethernet.

The nForce3 Pro 150 has a similar feature set but is designed for use with the Opteron processor and NVIDIA's Quadro workstation graphics processor.

Note

Although some nForce3 150 and Pro 150 motherboards offer SATA and SATA RAID, this is *not* a function of the chipset; however, it can be performed with the use of an add-on SATA RAID chip.

nForce3 250, 250Gb, and 250 Ultra and nForce3 Professional 250

The nForce3 250 family of MCPs includes four members, all of which include several enhanced features over the original nForce3 150 and 150 Pro. The base model, nForce3 250, has the following major features:

- HyperTransport 16-bit/800MHz upstream/downstream connections between the processor and the MCP
- AGP 8x graphics card support
- Dual independent ATA-133 ATA/IDE host adapters with RAID 0, 1, and 0+1
- SATA and SATA RAID 0, 1, and 0+1
- Eight USB 1.1/2.0 ports
- 10/100 Ethernet with integrated hardware firewall
- AC'97 2.1 audio (six-channel) with 20-bit output and SPDIF support

The 250Gb model has the 250's features and adds support for 10/100/1000 Ethernet with integrated hardware firewall. The 250 Pro has the feature set of the 250 Gb but supports the Opteron workstation processor, and the Athlon 64FX and is optimized to work with NVIDIA's Quadro workstation graphics processor.

The 250 Ultra model has the 250's features and adds support for both 10/100/1000 Ethernet with integrated hardware firewall and an Advanced 16-bit/1GHz HyperTransport upstream/downstream processor/MCP connection.

Note

The integrated firewall included in all nForce3 250-series chipsets and all nForce 4 chipsets is highly configurable and protects the computer as soon as it is turned on. Software firewalls, by contrast, cannot protect the computer until they are loaded, which is often late in the boot process.

nForce4 Series and nForce Professional Series

NVIDIA's nForce4 series combines PCI-Express support with the successful single-chip design used by the nForce3. The nForce4 series includes four models: the nForce4, nForce Ultra, nForce4 SLI, and nForce4 SI x16.

The base model, nForce4, has the following major features:

- HyperTransport 16-bit/800MHz upstream/downstream connections between the processor and the MCP
- PCI-Express x16 graphics support
- Dual independent ATA-133 ATA/IDE host adapters with RAID 0, 1, and 0+1
- SATA and SATA RAID 0, 1, and 0+1
- 10 USB 1.1/2.0 ports
- 10/100/1000 Ethernet with integrated hardware firewall
- AC'97 2.1 audio (six-channel) with 20-bit output and SPDIF support

nForce4 Ultra adds support for 3Gbps SATA drives and the ActiveArmor secure networking edition.

nForce4 SLI supports a flexible PCI-Express design that can use either a single x16 or two x8 NVIDIA PCI-Express graphics cards. It also adds support for bootable RAID 5 to the features of nForce4 Ultra.

nForce4 SLI x16 supports one or two NVIDIA PCI-Express x16 cards running at full speed and supports up to 38 total PCI-Express lanes. Its other features are the same as the nForce4 SLI.

nForce4 Professional chipsets for the Opteron processors are based on the nForce4 series, but with the following differences:

- nForce Professional 2050 has x16 and four x1 PCI-Express lanes; Gigabit Ethernet; and four SATA 3GBps ports with RAID 0,1 and 0+1 support. However, it offers no support for PATA drives, 32-bit PCI, audio, or the low-pin-count (LPC) bus used for legacy devices.
- nForce Professional 2200 has a flexible 20-lane PCI-Express implementation; Gigabit Ethernet; and SATA 3GBps with RAID 0,1, and 0+1. However, it also supports 32-bit PCI, 10 USB 2.0 ports, the LPC bus, AC'97 2.3 audio, and four PATA drives. The 2200 is designed as a workstation processor. Both chipsets support multiple Opteron processors.

nForce 410 and 430 Series

The nForce 410 and 430 are the first NVIDIA chipsets with integrated video for the AMD Sempron, a 32-bit version of the Athlon 64. The nForce 410 and 430 use the GeForce 6100 GPU for integrated video, whereas the 430 can also use the GeForce 6150 GPU.

Table 4.55 lists the major features of each nForce 4xx-series integrated chipset.

SiS Chipsets for Athlon 64

SiS offers eight chipsets for 64-bit AMD processors. The following three chipsets require discrete graphics:

- 755
- 755FX
- 756

SiS also offers four chipsets with integrated graphics for AMD's 64-bit processors:

- 760
- 760GX
- 761
- 761GX
- 761GL

The following sections cover these chipsets in greater detail.

SiS755 and SiS755FX

The SiS 755 is the first SiS chipset to support the AMD Athlon 64, Opteron, and Athlon 64FX chipsets. It is a two-piece chipset that uses the SiS964 as its South Bridge component. Its major features include

- HyperTransport 16-bit/800MHz connection between the processor and North Bridge with HyperStreaming
- Support for AGP 8x graphics
- MuTIOL 1G connection between the North and South Bridge chips with HyperStreaming
- Dual ATA-133 host adapters
- Two Serial ATA ports with SATA RAID 0 and 1
- Eight USB 1.1/2.0 ports
- 10/100 Ethernet
- AC'97 version 2.3 eight-channel audio

The 755FX North Bridge chip is pin-compatible with the 755; however, the preferred South Bridge chip for the 755FX—the SiS965—uses a larger 588-pin socket over the 505-pin socket used by the 964 family. The 755FX/965 chipset has the following major improvements over the 755/964 chipset:

- HyperTransport 16-bit/1GHz connection between the processor and North Bridge with HyperStreaming
- Support for two PCI-Express x1 slots
- Four Serial ATA ports with SATA RAID 0, 1, and 0+1 and JBOD (disk spanning)
- 10/100/1000 Ethernet

Table 4.55 nForce 4xx Integrated Chipsets for AMD Sempron

MCP Model	GPU Model	Video Support	PCI-Express x1 Slots	ATA/Serial ATA Support	RAID	USB Support (# of Ports)	Audio
410	GeForce 6100	PCI-Express x16	1	ATA-133 (4), SATA 3Gbps (2)	0,1	1.1/2.0 (8)	1.1/2.0 (8) HDA, AC'97
430	GeForce 6100	PCI-Express x16	1	ATA-133 (4), SATA 3Gbps (4)	0,1, 0+1, 5	1.1/2.0 (8)	HDA, AC'97
430	GeForce 6150	PCI-Express x16 SATA	1 3Gbps (4)	ATA-133 (4),	0,1, 0+1, 5	1.1/2.0 (8)	HDA, AC'97

HDA = High-Definition Audio (previously code-named Azalia); supports CE-quality (192KHz, 32-bit multichannel) audio, with support for Dolby Pro Logic IIx (7.1 surround) and multiple codecs operating independently.

*Also includes ActiveArmor secure networking engine.

SiS756

The SiS756 chipset is designed specifically for use with the high-performance Athlon 64FX desktop processor. It is the first SiS chipset to support the PCI-Express x16 graphics interface. The SiS756 is usually paired with the SiS965 South Bridge. This chipset's major features include

- HyperTransport 16-bit/1GHz connection between the processor and North Bridge with HyperStreaming
- PCI-Express x16 graphics support
- Two PCI-Express x1 slots
- Eight USB 1.1/2.0 ports
- Four SATA ports with SATA RAID 0, 1, and 0+1 and JBOD
- 10/100/1000 Ethernet
- AC'97 2.3 eight-channel audio

Note

If the SiS965L is used in place of the SiS965, only two SATA ports with SATA RAID 0 and 1 are available. The other features are the same.

PCI-Express x16 replaces the AGP 8x video support found in earlier SiS chipsets.

Figure 4.47 shows the architecture of the SiS756 chipset with the SiS965 South Bridge.

SiS760 and Sis760GX

The SiS760 is the first SiS chipset with integrated graphics for the Athlon 64 and Opteron processors. Otherwise, its major features are similar to those of the SiS755. Both use the SiS964 South Bridge chip. Its features include

- HyperTransport 16-bit/800MHz connection between the processor and North Bridge with HyperStreaming
- Support for AGP 8x graphics
- MuTIOL 1G connection between the North and South Bridge chips with HyperStreaming

LAN	DirectX 9.0 Shader Model 3	TV Encoder	TDM S/ DVI Output	GPU Clock Speed	Video Scaling	1080i/p MPEG-2, WMA Playback
10/100 Ethernet	Yes	No	No	425MHz	2x2 (basic)	No
10/100/ 1000 Ethernet*	Yes	No	No	425MHz	2x2 (basic)	No
10/100/1000 Ethernet	Yes	Yes	Yes	475MHz	5x4 (high-quality)	Yes

- Dual ATA-133 host adapters
- Two Serial ATA ports with SATA RAID 0 and 1
- Eight USB 1.1/2.0 ports
- 10/100 Ethernet
- AC'97 version 2.3 eight-channel audio

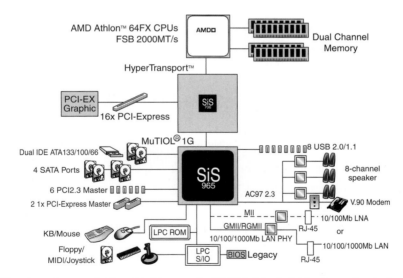

Figure 4.47   As with most Athlon 64 chipsets, the SiS756's North Bridge is used only for connection to discrete graphics (PCI-Express in this case), while a vast majority of the work is performed by the South Bridge.

The integrated SiS Mirage 2 (Ultra256) graphics features of the SiS760 include

- DirectX 8.1–compatible 3D graphics
- Dual-channel 256-bit 3D interface

- 128-bit 2D graphics
- Optional support for TV-out and a secondary CRT or LCD display
- Shared memory up to 128MB

The SiS760GX instead uses Mirage 1 single-channel (128-bit) graphics.

The SiS966 South Bridge is the preferred South Bridge for the SiS760GX, adding the following features:

- Four PCI-Express x1 slots
- SATA, SATA RAID 0, 1, and 0+1
- Ten USB 1.1/2.0 ports
- AC'97 2.3 audio with support for Intel's new High Definition Audio 7.1-channel audio
- 10/100/1000 Ethernet

SiS761GL and SiS761GX

The SiS761GL and SiS761GX integrated graphics chipsets are based on the SiS760 and support all Athlon 64 processors, the Opteron, and the Sempron 32-bit version of the Athlon 64. Both chipsets use the SiS966 as their preferred South Bridge.

Note

The SiS966, SiS965, and SiS965L are pin-compatible. Therefore, some vendors might use the SiS965 or SiS965L in place of the SiS966.

The SiS761GX North Bridge chip has the following major features:

- HyperTransport 16-bit/1GHz connection between the processor and North Bridge with HyperStreaming
- Support for PCI-Express x16 graphics
- MuTIOL 1G connection between the North and South Bridge chips with HyperStreaming
- Integrated Mirage DirectX 7.0 graphics using up to 128MB of video memory

The SiS761GL differs from its sibling in these ways:

- HyperTransport 16-bit/800MHz
- No PCI-Express x16 slot
- Integrated Mirage 1 DirectX 7.0 graphics using up to 128MB of video memory

When the SiS966 South Bridge chip is used, both chipsets also feature the following:

- Four PCI-Express x1 slots
- SATA, SATA RAID 0, 1, and 0+1
- Ten USB 1.1/2.0 ports
- AC'97 2.3 six-channel audio with support for Intel's High Definition Audio standard
- 10/100/1000 Ethernet

Super I/O Chips

The third major chip seen on many PC motherboards is called the Super I/O chip. This is a chip that integrates devices formerly found on separate expansion cards in older systems.

Most Super I/O chips contain, at a minimum, the following components:

- Floppy controller
- One or two serial port controllers
- Parallel port controller

The floppy controllers on some Super I/O chips handle two drives, but some newer models can handle only one. Older systems often required a separate floppy controller card.

The serial port is another item that was formerly on one or more cards. Most of the better Super I/O chips implement a buffered serial port design known as a universal asynchronous receiver transmitter (UART), one for each port. Most mimic the standalone NS16550A high-speed UART, which was created by National Semiconductor. Because the functions of these chips are put into the Super I/O chip, serial ports are essentially built into the motherboard.

Virtually all Super I/O chips also include a high-speed multimode parallel port. Most recent models allow three modes: standard (bidirectional), Enhanced Parallel Port (EPP), and the Enhanced Capabilities Port (ECP) modes. The ECP mode is the fastest and most powerful, but selecting it also causes your port to use an ISA bus 8-bit DMA channel—usually DMA channel 3. As long as you account for this and don't set anything else to that channel (such as a sound card and so on), the ECP mode parallel port should work fine. Some of the newer printers and scanners that connect to the system via the parallel port use ECP mode, which was invented by Hewlett-Packard.

The Super I/O chip can contain other components as well. For example, the Intel VC820 ATX motherboard uses an SMC (Standard Microsystems Corp.) LPC47M102 Super I/O chip. This chip incorporates the following functions:

- Floppy drive interface
- Two high-speed serial ports
- One ECP/EPP multimode parallel port
- 8042-style keyboard and mouse controller

This chip is typical of recent Super I/O chips in that it has an integrated keyboard and mouse controller. Older Super I/O chips lacked this feature.

One thing I've noticed over the years is that the role of the Super I/O chip has decreased more and more in the newer motherboards. This is primarily due to Intel and other chipset manufacturers moving Super I/O functions, such as IDE, directly into the chipset South Bridge or ICH component, where these devices can attach to the PCI bus (North/South Bridge architecture) or to the high-speed hub interface (hub architecture) rather than the ISA bus. One of the shortcomings of the Super I/O chip is that originally it was interfaced to the system via the ISA bus and shared all the speed and performance limitations of that 8MHz bus. Moving the IDE over to the PCI bus allowed higher-speed IDE drives to be developed that could transfer at the faster 33MHz PCI bus speed.

Newer Super I/O chips interface to the system via the LPC bus, an interface designed by Intel to offer a connection running at half the speed of PCI (up to about 16.67MBps) using only 13 signals. LPC is much more efficient than ISA.

Because high-speed devices such as IDE/ATA drives are now interfaced through the South Bridge chip, PCI bus, or hub architectures, nothing interfaced through the current Super I/O chips needs any greater bandwidth anyway.

As the chipset manufacturers combine more and more functions into the main chipset, and as USB- and IEEE 1394–based peripherals replace standard serial, parallel, and floppy controller-based devices, we will probably see the Super I/O chip continue to fade away in motherboard designs. More and more chipsets are combining the South Bridge and Super I/O chips into a single component (often referred to as a *Super South Bridge chip*) to save space and reduce parts count on the motherboard. Several of the SiS and NVIDIA chipsets even integrate all three chips (North Bridge, South Bridge, and Super I/O) into a single chip.

Motherboard CMOS RAM Addresses

In the original AT system, a Motorola 146818 chip was used as the RTC and Complementary Metal-Oxide Semiconductor (CMOS) RAM chip. This was a special chip that had a digital clock and stored 64 bytes of data. The clock used 14 bytes of RAM and an additional 50 more bytes of leftover RAM in which you could store anything you wanted. The designers of the IBM AT used these extra 50 bytes to store the system configuration.

Modern PC systems don't use the Motorola chip; instead, they incorporate the functions of this chip into the motherboard chipset (South Bridge) or Super I/O chip, or they use a special battery and NVRAM module from companies such as Dallas or Benchmarq.

▶▶ For more details on the CMOS RAM addresses, see "Motherboard CMOS RAM Addresses," p. 471.

Motherboard Connectors

A modern motherboard contains a variety of connectors. Figure 4.48 shows the connector locations on a typical motherboard. Several of these connectors, such as power supply connectors, serial and parallel ports, and keyboard/mouse connectors, are covered in other chapters.

This section has figures and tables showing the configurations and pinouts of most of the other interface and I/O connectors you will find.

▶▶ See "AT/LPX Power Supply Connectors," p. 1233.

▶▶ See "Serial Ports," p. 1046, and "Parallel Ports," p. 1053.

▶▶ See "Keyboard/Mouse Interface Connectors," p. 1073.

▶▶ See "Universal Serial Bus," p. 1031.

▶▶ See "An Overview of the IDE Interface," p. 581.

One of the biggest problems many people overlook when building and upgrading systems is the front panel connections. Connectors that don't match between the motherboard and chassis are one of the small but frustrating things that can be problematic in an otherwise smooth upgrade or system build. Having dependable standards for these connections would help, but unfortunately no official standard for the front panel connectors existed until October 2000, when Intel published the "Front Panel I/O Connectivity Design Guide." The latest version of this guide can be found, along with the motherboard form factor specifications, at www.formfactors.org.

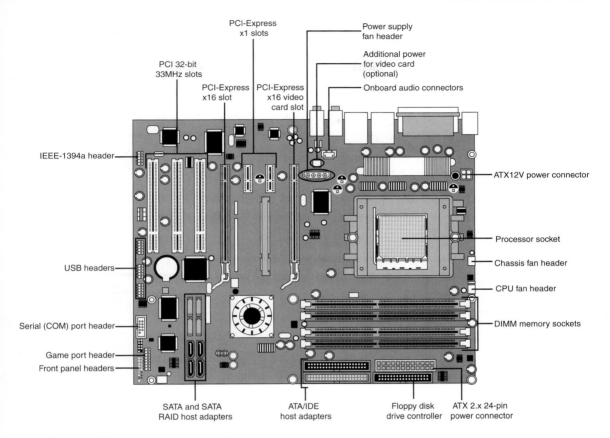

Figure 4.48 Typical motherboard connectors.

Before this standard was published, no official standard existed (and anarchy ruled). In addition, even though most chassis gave you individual tiny connectors for each function, some of the bigger system builders (for example, Dell, Gateway, MicronPC [now MPC], and so on) began using specialized inline or dual-row header connectors so they could build systems more quickly and efficiently. Coincidentally, most of those vendors used Intel boards, hence Intel's development of a standard.

The front panel guide details a 10-pin keyed header connector for the main front panel switch/LED functions, as well as a 10-pin keyed USB header, a 10-pin keyed IEEE 1394 (FireWire/i.LINK) header, a 10-pin keyed audio header, and a 6-pin keyed IR header. The pinouts and configurations of these and other motherboard-based connectors are shown in the following figures and tables. Figure 4.49 details the front panel switch/LED header connector.

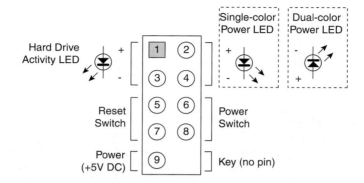

Figure 4.49   Front panel switch/LED header connector.

The pinout of the standard front panel switch/LED connector is shown in Table 4.56.

Table 4.56   Front Panel Switch/LED Connector Pinout

Signal	Description	Pin	Pin	Signal	Description
Hard Disk Activity LED			**Power/Sleep/Message LED**		
HD_LED+	Hard disk LED+	1	2	PWR_LED GRN+	Single-color LED+
HD_LED-	Hard disk LED-	3	4	PWR_LED_YEL+	Dual-color LED+
Reset Button			**Power On/Off Button**		
GND	Ground	5	6	FP_PWR	Power switch
FP_RESET	Reset switch	7	8	GND	Ground
Power			**Not Connected**		
+5V	Power	9	10	N/C	Not connected

Some chassis provide a single 10-pin header connector for the front panel switch/LED connections, but most provide individual 2-pin connectors for the various functions. If 2-pin connectors are used, they are connected as shown in Figure 4.50. Note that you can easily replace the multiple 2-pin connectors with a single 10-pin connector, some chassis even include an adapter for this purpose.

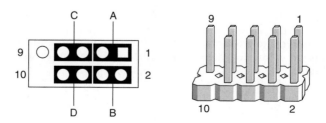

Figure 4.50   Standard front panel switch/LED connections using 2-pin connectors.

The 2-pin connections to a standard 10-pin front panel switch/LED connector are shown in Table 4.57.

Table 4.57   Front Panel Switch/LED Connections Using Multiple Connectors

Connector	Pins	Description
A	1 and 3	Hard disk activity LED
B	2 and 4	Power LED
C	5 and 7	Reset switch
D	6 and 8	Power switch

A chassis can use either a single-color or dual-color LED for the Power LED function. A dual-color LED can provide more information about the various power and message states the system might be in, including power on/off, sleep, and message-waiting indications. Table 4.58 shows the possible states and meanings for both single- and dual-color power LEDs.

Table 4.58   Power LED Indications

LED Type	LED State	Description	ACPI State
Single-color	Off	Power off or sleeping	S1, S3, S5
	Steady green	Running	S0
	Blinking green	Running, message waiting	S0
Dual-color	Off	Power off	S5
	Steady green	Running	S0
	Blinking green	Running, message waiting	S0
	Steady yellow	Sleeping	S1, S3
	Blinking yellow	Sleeping, message waiting	S1, S3

Many motherboards do not follow the industry-standard guidelines for front panel switch/LED connections, and many use alternative designs instead, one of which is shown in Figure 4.51.

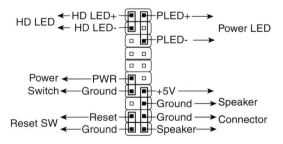

Figure 4.51   Alternative front panel switch/LED connector configuration.

Some of Intel's older motherboards, as well as those made by other motherboard manufacturers, used a single-row pin header connector for the front panel connections, as shown in Figure 4.52.

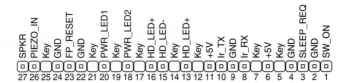

Figure 4.52   Alternative single-row front panel connector configuration.

Table 4.59 shows the designations for the front panel motherboard connectors used on some motherboards.

Table 4.59   Alternative Single-Row Front Panel Connector Pinout

Connector	Pin	Signal Name
Speaker	27	SPKR
	26	PIEZO_IN
	25	Key (no pin)
	24	GND
Reset	23	FP_RESET
	22	GND
None	21	Key (no pin)
Sleep/Power LED	20	PWR_LED1 (green)
	19	Key (no pin)
	18	PWR_LED2 (yellow)
None	17	Key (no pin)
Hard Drive LED	16	HD_LED+
	15	HD_LED-
	14	Key (no pin)
	13	HD_LED+
None	12	Key (no pin)
IrDA	11	+5V
	10	Ir_TX
	9	GND
	8	Ir_RX
	7	Key (no pin)
	6	+5V
None	5	Key (no pin)
Sleep/Resume	4	GND
	3	SLEEP_REQ
Power On	2	GND
	1	SW_ON

To adapt the connectors in your chassis to those on your motherboard, in some cases you might need to change the connector ends by removing the terminals and reinserting them into different positions. For example, I had a chassis that used a 3-pin power LED connection, whereas the motherboard only had a 2-pin connection. I had to remove one of the terminals, reinsert it into the middle position on the 3-pin connector, and then plug the connector into the motherboard so that two pins were mated and the third empty position was hanging off the end of the connector. Fortunately, the terminals are easy to remove by merely lifting a latch on the side of the connector and then sliding the terminal and wire back out. When the terminal is inserted, the latch automatically grabs the terminal and locks it into position.

Most motherboards include USB connectors, which are designed to be connected to front-mounted or rear bracket USB connectors in the chassis. The standard uses a single 10-pin keyed connector to provide two USB connections. The pinout of a standard dual USB motherboard header connector is shown in Figure 4.53 and Table 4.60.

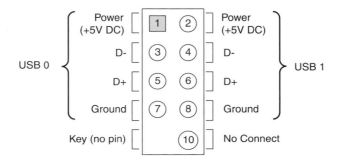

Figure 4.53 Dual-USB header connector configuration.

Table 4.60   USB Header Connector Pinout

Description	Signal Names	Pin	Pin	Signal Names	Description
Port 0 +5V	USB0_PWR	1	2	USB1_PWR	Port 1 +5V
Port 0 Data-	USB_D0-	3	4	USB_D1-	Port 1 Data-
Port 0 Data+	USB_D0+	5	6	USB_D1+	Port 1 Data+
Port 0 Ground	GND	7	8	GND	Port 1 Ground
No pin	Key	9	10	NC/Shield	No Connect/Shield

Many chassis includes multiple inline connectors for the dual USB–to–front panel or rear bracket connection, instead of a single keyed connector. An example of this is shown in Figure 4.54.

Using the multiple individual connectors shown in the previous figure, you would have to plug each individual connector into the proper pin. Some internal chassis USB cables use two 5-pin inline connectors, in which case you just need to ensure that you don't put them on backward. Consult your motherboard and chassis manual for more information if you are unsure about your particular connections.

Caution

If your chassis uses multiple individual non-keyed connections, you must be sure to connect them properly to the connector on the motherboard. If you connect them improperly, you can cause a short circuit to occur that can damage the motherboard or any USB peripherals you plug into the front panel connectors. Higher-quality motherboards usually have self-healing fuses on the power signals, which can prevent damage if such a situation occurs.

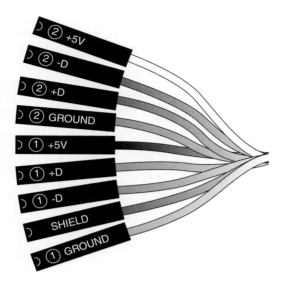

Figure 4.54   Front panel USB cable using multiple individual non-keyed connectors.

Although IEEE 1394 (FireWire/i.LINK) is not found on most motherboards, some boards do incorporate this feature or offer it as an option. FireWire can also be added via an expansion card, and many of the cards have header connectors for front panel or rear bracket connections similar to that found on a motherboard. Figure 4.55 and Table 4.61 show the pinout of the industry-standard FireWire header connector.

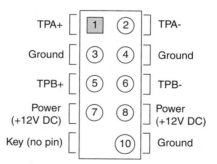

Figure 4.55   IEEE 1394 (FireWire/i.LINK) header connector configuration.

Table 4.61   IEEE 1394 (FireWire/i.LINK) Connector Pinout

Pin	Signal Name	Pin	Signal Name
TPA+	1	2	TPA-
Ground	3	4	Ground
TPB+	5	6	TPB-
+12V (Fused)	7	8	+12V (Fused)
Key (no pin)	9	10	Ground

Note that the FireWire header connector has the same physical configuration and keying as a USB connector. This is unfortunate because it enables a USB front panel cable to be plugged into a FireWire connector, and vice versa. Either situation could cause a short circuit.

Caution

You must not plug a USB cable into a FireWire header connector, or a FireWire cable into a USB header connector. Doing so causes a short circuit that can damage the motherboard, as well as any peripherals you plug into the front panel connectors. Higher-quality motherboards usually have self-healing fuses on the power signals, which can prevent damage if such a situation occurs.

Motherboards that have integrated audio hardware usually feature a front panel audio header connector. The pinout of the industry-standard front panel audio header connector is shown in Figure 4.56 and Table 4.62.

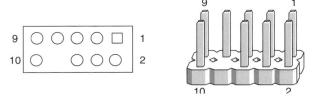

Figure 4.56   Front panel audio header connector configuration.

Table 4.62   Front Panel Audio Connector Pinout

Description	Signal Name	Pin	Pin	Signal Name	Description
Microphone input	AUD_MIC	1	2	AUD_GND	Analog audio ground
Microphone power audio	AUD_MIC_BIAS	3	4	AUD_VCC	Filtered +5V for analog
Right channel audio	AUD_FPOUT_R	5	6	AUD_RET_R	Right channel return
Ground or headphone amplifier control	GND/HP_ON	7	8	KEY	No pin
Left channel audio	AUD_FPOUT_L	9	10	AUD_RET_L	Left channel return

Some motherboards include an infrared data connector that connects to an infrared optical transceiver on the chassis front panel. This enables communication via infrared with cell phones, PDAs, laptops, printers, or other IrDA devices. The industry-standard pinout for IrDA connections on a motherboard is shown in Figure 4.57 and Table 4.63.

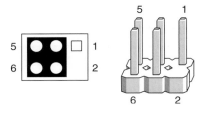

Figure 4.57   Infrared data front panel header connector configuration.

Other miscellaneous connectors might appear on motherboards as well; several are shown in Tables 4.64–4.72.

Table 4.63   Infrared Data Front Panel Connector Pinout

Description	Signal	Pin	Pin	Signal	Description
No connect	NC	1	2	Key	No pin
IR_power	+5V	3	4	GND	Ground
IrDA serial output	IR_TX	5	6	IR_RX	IrDA serial input

Table 4.64   Battery Connector

Pin	Signal	Pin	Signal
1	Gnd	3	KEY
2	Unused	4	+4 to 6V

Table 4.65   LED and Keylock Connector

Pin	Signal	Pin	Signal
1	LED Power (+5V)	4	Keyboard Inhibit
2	KEY	5	Gnd
3	Gnd		

Table 4.66   Speaker Connector

Pin	Signal	Pin	Signal
1	Ground	3	Board-Mounted Speaker
2	KEY	4	Speaker Output

Table 4.67   Chassis Intrusion (Security) Pin-Header

Pin	Signal Name
1	Ground
2	CHS_SEC

Table 4.68   Wake on LAN Pin-Header

Pin	Signal Name
1	+5 VSB
2	Ground
3	WOL

Table 4.69   Wake on Ring Pin-Header

Pin	Signal Name
1	Ground
2	RINGA

Table 4.70   CD Audio Connector

Pin	Signal Name	Pin	Signal Name
1	CD_IN-Left	3	Ground
2	Ground	4	CD_IN-Right

Table 4.71   Telephony Connector

Pin	Signal Name	Pin	Signal Name
1	Audio Out (monaural)	3	Ground
2	Ground	4	Audio In (monaural)

Table 4.72   ATAPI-Style Line In Connector

Pin	Signal Name	Pin	Signal Name
1	Left Line In	3	Ground
2	Ground	4	Right Line In (monaural)

Note

Some boards have a board-mounted piezo speaker. It is enabled by placing a jumper over pins 3 and 4, which routes the speaker output to the board-mounted speaker. Removing the jumper enables a conventional speaker to be plugged in.

Most modern motherboards have three or four fan connectors for use with the processor fan, rear chassis fan, front chassis fan, and voltage regulator (power) fan (see Table 4.73). They all generally use the same 3-pin connector, with the third pin providing a tachometer signal for optional speed monitoring. If the motherboard is capable of monitoring the fan speed, it can sound an alarm when the fans begin to slow down due to bearing failure or wear. The alarm sound can vary, but it normally comes from the internal speaker and might be an ambulance siren-type sound.

Table 4.73   Fan Power Connectors

Pin	Signal Name
1	Ground
2	+12V
3	Sense tachometer

Caution

Do not place a jumper on this connector; serious board damage will result if the 12V is shorted to ground.

System Bus Types, Functions, and Features

The heart of any motherboard is the various buses that carry signals between the components. A *bus* is a common pathway across which data can travel within a computer. This pathway is used for communication and can be established between two or more computer elements.

The PC has a hierarchy of different buses. Most modern PCs have at least three buses; some have four or more. They are hierarchical because each slower bus is connected to the faster one above it. Each device in the system is connected to one of the buses, and some devices (primarily the chipset) act as bridges between the various buses.

The main buses in a modern system are as follows:

- **Processor bus**—Also called the front-side bus (FSB), this is the highest-speed bus in the system and is at the core of the chipset and motherboard. This bus is used primarily by the processor to pass information to and from cache or main memory and the North Bridge of the chipset. The processor bus in a modern system runs at 66MHz, 100MHz, 133MHz, 200MHz, 266MHz, 400MHz, 533MHz, 800MHz, or 1,066MHz and is normally 64 bits (8 bytes) wide.

- **AGP bus**—This is a 32-bit bus designed specifically for a video card. It runs at 66MHz (AGP 1x), 133MHz (AGP 2x), 266MHz (AGP 4x), or 533MHz (AGP 8x), which allows for a bandwidth of up to 2,133MBps. It is connected to the North Bridge or Memory Controller Hub of the chipset and is manifested as a single AGP slot in systems that support it. Newer systems are phasing out AGP slots in favor of PCI-Express.

- **PCI-Express**—The PCI-Express bus is a third-generation development of the PCI bus. PCI-Express is a differential signaling bus that can be generated by either the North Bridge or South Bridge. The speed of PCI-Express is described in terms of lanes. Each bidirectional dual-simplex lane provides a 2.5Gbps or 5Gbps transfer rate in each direction (250MBps or 500MBps effective speed). PCI-Express video cards generally use the x16 slot, which provides 4,000MBps or 8,000MBps in each direction.

- **PCI-X**—PCI-X is a second-generation development of the PCI bus that provides faster speeds than PCI but is backward-compatible with PCI. It is used primarily in workstation and server installations. PCI-X supports 64-bit slots that are backward-compatible with 64-bit and 32-bit PCI cards. PCI-X version 1 runs at 133MHz, whereas PCI-X 2.0 supports operation at up to 533MHz. Typically, PCI-X 2.0's bandwidth is subdivided among multiple PCI-X and PCI slots. Although a few South Bridge chips can generate the PCI-X bus, most chipsets that support PCI-X use a separate PCI-X bus chip.

- **PCI bus**—This is usually a 33MHz 32-bit bus found in virtually all systems since the days of the Intel 486 CPU. Some newer systems include an optional 66MHz 64-bit version-mostly workstations or server-class systems. This bus is generated by either the chipset North Bridge in North/South Bridge chipsets or the I/O Controller Hub in chipsets using hub architecture. This bus is manifested in the system as a collection of 32-bit slots, normally white in color and numbering from four to six on most motherboards. High-speed peripherals, such as SCSI adapters, network cards, video cards, and more, can be plugged into PCI bus slots. PCI-X and PCI-Express are faster developments of the PCI bus. PCI-Express motherboards and systems began to appear in mid-2004.

■ **ISA bus**—This is an 8MHz 16-bit bus that has disappeared from recent systems after first appearing in the original PC in 8-bit, 5MHz form and in the 1984 IBM AT in full 16-bit 8MHz form. It is a very slow-speed bus, but it was ideal for certain slow-speed or older peripherals. It has been used in the past for plug-in modems, sound cards, and various other low-speed peripherals. The ISA bus is created by the South Bridge part of the motherboard chipset, which acts as the ISA bus controller and the interface between the ISA bus and the faster PCI bus above it. The Super I/O chip usually was connected to the ISA bus on systems that included ISA slots.

Some motherboards feature a special connector called an *Audio Modem Riser (AMR)* or a *Communications and Networking Riser (CNR)*. These are dedicated connectors for cards that are specific to the motherboard design to offer communications and networking options. They are *not* designed to be general-purpose bus interfaces, and few cards for these connectors are offered on the open market. Usually, they're offered only as an option with a given motherboard. They are designed such that a motherboard manufacturer can easily offer its boards in versions with and without communications options, without having to reserve space on the board for optional chips. Normal network and modem options offered publicly, for the most part, will still be PCI based because the AMR/CNR connection is somewhat motherboard specific. Figure 4.58 compares these connectors, and Figure 4.59 compares typical AMR and CNR riser cards. Note that the newest motherboards have largely abandoned AMR and CNR slots.

Several hidden buses exist on modern motherboards—buses that don't manifest themselves in visible slots or connectors. I'm talking about buses designed to interface chipset components, such as the Hub Interface and the LPC bus. The Hub Interface is a quad-clocked (4x) 66MHz 8-bit bus that carries data between the MCH and ICH in hub architecture chipsets made by Intel. It operates at a bandwidth of 266MBps and was designed as a chipset component connection that is faster than PCI and yet uses fewer signals for a lower-cost design. Some recent workstation/server chipsets and the latest 9xx-series desktop computer chipsets from Intel use faster versions of the hub interface. The most recent chipsets from major third-party vendors also bypass the PCI bus with direct high-speed connections between chipset components.

◀◀ See "High-speed North-South Bridge Connections," p. 282.

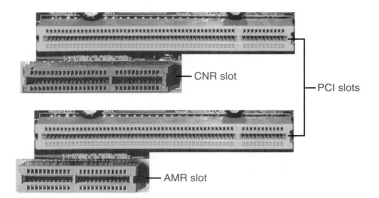

Figure 4.58 The AMR slot (top left) and CNR slot (top center) compared to PCI slots. When the AMR slot is used, the PCI slot paired with it cannot be used.

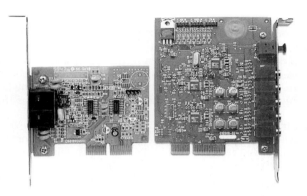

Figure 4.59 A typical AMR riser card (right) with connections for soft modem and 10/100 Ethernet ports. A typical CNR riser card (right) with analog and SPDIF digital audio ports.

In a similar fashion, the LPC bus is a 4-bit bus that has a maximum bandwidth of 16.67MBps; it was designed as an economical onboard replacement for the ISA bus. In systems that use LPC, it typically is used to connect Super I/O chip or motherboard ROM BIOS components to the main chipset. LPC is faster than ISA and yet uses far fewer pins and enables ISA to be eliminated from the board entirely.

The system chipset is the conductor that controls the orchestra of system components, enabling each to have its turn on its respective buses. Table 4.74 shows the widths, speeds, data cycles, and overall bandwidth of virtually all PC buses.

Table 4.74   Bandwidth (in MBps) and Detailed Comparison of Most PC Buses and Interfaces

Bus Type	Bus Width (Bits)	Bus Speed (MHz)	Data Cycles per Clock	Bandwidth (MBps)
8-bit ISA (PC/XT)	8	4.77	1/2	2.39
8-bit ISA (AT)	8	8.33	1/2	4.17
LPC bus	4	33	1	16.67
16-bit ISA (AT-Bus)	16	8.33	1/2	8.33
DD Floppy Interface	1	0.25	1	0.03125
HD Floppy Interface	1	0.5	1	0.0625
ED Floppy Interface	1	1	1	0.125
EISA Bus	32	8.33	1	33
VL-Bus	32	33	1	133
MCA-16	16	5	1	10
MCA-32	32	5	1	20
MCA-16 Streaming	16	10	1	20
MCA-32 Streaming	32	10	1	40
MCA-64 Streaming	64	10	1	80

Table 4.74   Continued

Bus Type	Bus Width (Bits)	Bus Speed (MHz)	Data Cycles per Clock	Bandwidth (MBps)
MCA-64 Streaming	64	20	1	160
PC-Card (PCMCIA)	16	10	1	20
CardBus	32	33	1	133
PCI	32	33	1	133
PCI 66MHz	32	66	1	266
PCI 64-bit	64	33	1	266
PCI 66MHz/64-bit	64	66	1	533
PCI-X 66	64	66	1	533
PCI-X 133	64	133	1	1066
PCI-X 266	64	266	1	2133
PCI-X 533	64	533	1	4266
PCI-Express 1.x	1	2500	0.8	250
PCI-Express 1.x	16	2500	0.8	4000
PCI-Express 1.x	32	2500	0.8	8000
PCI-Express 2.x	1	5000	0.8	500
PCI-Express 2.x	16	5000	0.8	8000
PCI-Express 2.x	32	5000	0.8	16000
Intel Hub Interface 8-bit	8	66	4	266
Intel Hub Interface 16-bit	16	66	4	533
AMD HyperTransport 2x2	2	200	2	100
AMD HyperTransport 4x2	4	200	2	200
AMD HyperTransport 8x2	8	200	2	400
AMD HyperTransport 16x2	16	200	2	800
AMD HyperTransport 32x2	32	200	2	1600
AMD HyperTransport 2x4	2	400	2	200
AMD HyperTransport 4x4	4	400	2	400
AMD HyperTransport 8x4	8	400	2	800
AMD HyperTransport 16x4	16	400	2	1600
AMD HyperTransport 32x4	32	400	2	3200
AMD HyperTransport 2x8	2	800	2	400
AMD HyperTransport 4x8	4	800	2	800
AMD HyperTransport 8x8	8	800	2	1600
AMD HyperTransport 16x8	16	800	2	3200
AMD HyperTransport 32x8	32	800	2	6400

Table 4.74 Continued

Bus Type	Bus Width (Bits)	Bus Speed (MHz)	Data Cycles per Clock	Bandwidth (MBps)
ATI A-Link	16	66	2	266
SiS MuTIOL	16	133	2	533
SiS MuTIOL 1G	16	266	2	1066
VIA V-Link 4x	8	66	4	266
VIA V-Link 8x	8	66	8	533
AGP	32	66	1	266
AGP 2X	32	66	2	533
AGP 4X	32	66	4	1066
AGP 8X	32	66	8	2133
RS-232 Serial	1	0.1152	1/10	0.01152
RS-232 Serial HS	1	0.2304	1/10	0.02304
IEEE 1284 Parallel	8	8.33	1/6	1.38
IEEE 1284 EPP/ECP	8	8.33	1/3	2.77
USB 1.1/2.0 low-speed	1	1.5	1	0.1875
USB 1.1/2.0 full-speed	1	12	1	1.5
USB 2.0 high-speed	1	480	1	60
IEEE 1394a S100	1	100	1	12.5
IEEE 1394a S200	1	200	1	25
IEEE 1394a S400	1	400	1	50
IEEE 1394b S800	1	800	1	100
IEEE 1394b S1600	1	1600	1	200
ATA PIO-4	16	8.33	1	16.67
ATA-UDMA/33	16	8.33	2	33
ATA-UDMA/66	16	16.67	2	66
ATA-UDMA/100	16	25	2	100
ATA-UDMA/133	16	33	2	133
SATA-150	1	750	2	150
SATA-300	1	1500	2	300
SATA-600	1	3000	2	600
SCSI	8	5	1	5
SCSI Wide	16	5	1	10
SCSI Fast	8	10	1	10
SCSI Fast/Wide	16	10	1	20
SCSI Ultra	8	20	1	20
SCSI Ultra/Wide	16	20	1	40
SCSI Ultra2	8	40	1	40

Table 4.74   Continued

Bus Type	Bus Width (Bits)	Bus Speed (MHz)	Data Cycles per Clock	Bandwidth (MBps)
SCSI Ultra2/Wide	16	40	1	80
SCSI Ultra3 (Ultra160)	16	40	2	160
SCSI Ultra4 (Ultra320)	16	80	2	320
FPM DRAM	64	22	1	177
EDO DRAM	64	33	1	266
PC66 SDRAM DIMM	64	66	1	533
PC100 SDRAM DIMM	64	100	1	800
PC133 SDRAM DIMM	64	133	1	1066
PC1600 DDR DIMM (DDR200)	64	100	2	1600
PC2100 DDR DIMM (DDR266)	64	133	2	2133
PC2700 DDR DIMM (DDR333)	64	167	2	2666
PC3200 DDR DIMM (DDR400)	64	200	2	3200
PC3500 DDR (DDR433)	64	216	2	3466
PC3700 DDR (DDR466)	64	233	2	3733
PC2-3200 DDR2 (DDR2-400)	64	200	2	3200
PC2-4300 DDR2 (DDR2-533)	64	267	2	4266
PC2-5400 DDR2 (DDR2-667)	64	333	2	5333
PC2-6400 DDR2 (DDR2-800)	64	400	2	6400
RIMM1200 RDRAM (PC600)	16	300	2	1200
RIMM1400 RDRAM (PC700)	16	350	2	1400
RIMM1600 RDRAM (PC800)	16	400	2	1600
RIMM2100 RDRAM (PC1066)	16	533	2	2133
RIMM2400 RDRAM (PC1200)	16	600	2	2400
RIMM3200 RDRAM (PC800)	32	400	2	3200
RIMM4200 RDRAM (PC1066)	32	533	2	4266
RIMM4800 RDRAM (PC1200)	32	600	2	4800
33MHz 486 FSB	32	33	1	133
66MHz Pentium I/II/III FSB	64	66	1	533
100MHz Pentium I/II/III FSB	64	100	1	800
133MHz Pentium I/II/III FSB	64	133	1	1066
200MHz Athlon FSB	64	100	2	1600
266MHz Athlon FSB	64	133	2	2133
333MHz Athlon FSB	64	167	2	2666
400MHz Athlon FSB	64	200	2	3200
533MHz Athlon FSB	64	267	2	4266
400MHz Pentium 4 FSB	64	100	4	3200

Table 4.74   Continued

Bus Type	Bus Width (Bits)	Bus Speed (MHz)	Data Cycles per Clock	Bandwidth (MBps)
533MHz Pentium 4 FSB	64	133	4	4266
800MHz Pentium 4 FSB	64	200	4	6400
1066MHz Pentium 4 FSB	64	267	4	8533
266MHz Itanium FSB	64	133	2	2133
400MHz Itanium 2 FSB	128	100	4	6400

Note: ISA, EISA, VL-Bus, and MCA are no longer used in current motherboard designs.

MBps = Megabytes per second

ISA = Industry Standard Architecture, also known as the PC/XT (8-bit) or AT-Bus (16-bit)

LPC = Low Pin Count bus

DD Floppy = Double Density (360/720KB) Floppy

HD Floppy = High Density (1.2/1.44MB) Floppy

ED Floppy = Extra-high Density (2.88MB) Floppy

EISA = Extended Industry Standard Architecture (32-bit ISA)

VL-Bus = VESA (Video Electronics Standards Association) Local Bus (ISA extension)

MCA = MicroChannel Architecture (IBM PS/2 systems)

PC-Card = 16-bit PCMCIA (Personal Computer Memory Card International Association) interface

CardBus = 32-bit PC-Card

Hub Interface = Intel 8xx chipset bus

HyperTransport = AMD chipset bus

V-Link = VIA Technologies chipset bus

MuTIOL = Silicon Integrated System chipset bus

PCI = Peripheral Component Interconnect

AGP = Accelerated Graphics Port

RS-232 = Standard Serial port, 115.2Kbps

RS-232 HS = High Speed Serial port, 230.4Kbps

IEEE 1284 Parallel = Standard Bidirectional Parallel Port

IEEE 1284 EPP/ECP = Enhanced Parallel Port/Extended Capabilities Port

USB = Universal serial bus

IEEE 1394 = FireWire, also called i.LINK

ATA PIO = AT Attachment (also known as IDE) Programmed I/O

ATA-UDMA = AT Attachment Ultra DMA

SCSI = Small computer system interface

FPM = Fast Page Mode, based on X-3-3-3 (1/3 max) burst mode timing on a 66MHz bus

EDO = Extended Data Out, based on X-2-2-2 (1/2 max) burst mode timing on a 66MHz bus

SDRAM = Synchronous dynamic RAM

RDRAM = Rambus dynamic RAM

DDR = Double data rate SDRAM

DDR2 = Next-generation DDR

CPU FSB = Processor front-side bus

Note that many of the buses use multiple data cycles (transfers) per clock cycle to achieve greater performance. Therefore, the data transfer rate is higher than it would seem for a given clock rate, which allows for an easy way to take an existing bus and make it go faster in a backward-compatible way.

The following sections discuss the processor and other subset buses in the system and the main I/O buses mentioned in the previous table.

The Processor Bus (Front-side Bus)

The processor bus (also called the *front-side bus* or *FSB*) is the communication pathway between the CPU and motherboard chipset—more specifically the North Bridge or Memory Controller Hub. This bus runs at the full motherboard speed—typically between 66MHz and 800MHz in modern systems, depending on the particular board and chipset design. This same bus also transfers data between the CPU and an external (L2) memory cache on Socket 7 (Pentium class) systems. Figure 4.60 shows how this bus fits into a typical Socket 7 PC system.

Figure 4.60 also shows where and how the other main buses, such as the PCI and ISA buses, fit into the system. As you can see, there is clearly a three-tier architecture with the fastest CPU bus on top, the PCI bus next, and the ISA bus at the bottom. Various components in the system are connected to one of these three main buses.

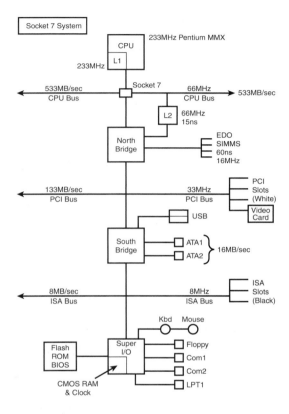

Figure 4.60 Typical Socket 7 (Pentium class) system architecture.

Socket 7 systems have an external (L2) cache for the CPU; the L2 cache is mounted on the motherboard and connected to the main processor bus that runs at the motherboard speed (usually between 66MHz and 100MHz). Thus, as the Socket 7 processors became available in faster and faster versions (through increasing the clock multiplier in the chip), the L2 cache unfortunately remained stuck on the motherboard running at the relatively slow (by comparison) motherboard speed. For example, the fastest Intel Socket 7 systems ran the CPU at 233MHz, which was 3.5x the CPU bus speed of 66MHz. Therefore, the L2 cache ran at only 66MHz. The fastest Socket 7 systems used the AMD K6-2 550 processor, which ran at 550MHz—5.5x a CPU bus speed of 100MHz. In those systems, the L2 cache ran at only 100MHz.

The problem of the slow L2 cache was first solved in the P6 class processors, such as the Pentium Pro, Pentium II, Celeron, Pentium III, and AMD Athlon and Duron. These processors used either Socket 8, Slot 1, Slot 2, Slot A, Socket A, or Socket 370. They moved the L2 cache off the motherboard and directly onto the CPU and connected it to the CPU via an on-chip back-side bus. Because the L2 cache bus was called the back-side bus, some in the industry began calling the main CPU bus the front-side bus. I still usually refer to it simply as the CPU bus.

With the L2 cache incorporated into the CPU, it can run at speeds up to the same as the processor itself. Most processors now incorporate the L2 cache directly on the CPU die, so the L2 cache runs at the same speed as the rest of the CPU. Others (mostly older versions) used separate dies for the cache integrated into the CPU package, which ran the L2 cache at some lower multiple (one-half, two-fifth, or one-third) of the main CPU. Even if the L2 ran at half or one-third of the processor speed, it still was significantly faster than the motherboard-bound cache on the Socket 7 systems.

In a Slot-1 type system the L2 cache is built into the CPU, but running at only half the processor speed. Slot A systems run the cache at one-half or one-third speed. The CPU bus speed increased from 66MHz (used primarily in Socket 7 systems) to 100MHz, enabling a bandwidth of 800MBps. Note that most of these systems included AGP support. Basic AGP was 66MHz (twice the speed of PCI), but most of these systems incorporated AGP 2x, which operated at twice the speed of standard AGP and enabled a bandwidth of 533MBps. These systems also typically used PC-100 SDRAM DIMMs, which have a bandwidth of 800MBps, matching the processor bus bandwidth for the best performance.

Slot 1 was dropped in favor of Socket 370 for the Pentium III and Celeron systems. This was mainly because these newer processors incorporated the L2 cache directly into the CPU die (running at the full-core speed of the processor) and an expensive cartridge with multiple chips was no longer necessary. At the same time, processor bus speeds increased to 133MHz, which enabled a throughput of 1,066MBps. Figure 4.61 shows a typical Socket 370 system design. AGP speed was also increased to AGP 4x, with a bandwidth of 1,066MBps.

Note the use of what Intel calls *hub architecture* instead of the older North/South Bridge design. This moves the main connection between the chipset components to a separate 266MBps hub interface (which has twice the throughput of PCI) and enables PCI devices to use the full bandwidth of PCI without fighting for bandwidth with a South Bridge. Also note that the flash ROM BIOS chip is now referred to as a *Firmware Hub* and is connected to the system via the LPC bus instead of via the Super I/O chip as in older North/South Bridge designs. The ISA bus is no longer used in most of these systems, and the Super I/O is connected via the LPC bus instead of ISA. The Super I/O chip also can easily be eliminated in these designs. This is commonly referred to as a *legacy-free* system because the ports supplied by the Super I/O chip are now known as *legacy* ports. Devices that would have used legacy ports must then be connected to the system via USB instead, and such systems would feature two USB controllers, with up to four total ports (more can be added by attaching USB hubs).

AMD processor systems adopted a Socket A design, which is similar to Socket 370 except it uses faster processor and memory buses. Although early versions retained the older North/South Bridge design, more recent versions use a design similar to Intel's hub architecture. Note the high-speed CPU bus running up to 333MHz (2,667MBps throughput) and the use of DDR SDRAM DIMM modules that support a matching bandwidth of 2667MBps. It is always best for performance when the bandwidth of memory matches that of the processor. Finally, note how most of the South Bridge components include functions otherwise found in Super I/O chips; when these functions are included the chip is called a *Super South Bridge*.

The Pentium 4 uses a Socket 423 or Socket 478 design with hub architecture (see Figure 4.62). This design is most notable for including a 400MHz, 533MHz, or 800MHz CPU bus with a bandwidth of 3,200MBps, 4,266MBps, or 6,400MBps. The 533MHz and 800MHz models are currently faster than anything else on the market. In this example, note the use of dual-channel PC3200 (DDR400) SDRAM. A single PC-3200 DIMM has a bandwidth of 3,200MBps, but when running dual-channel (identical pairs of memory) mode, it has a bandwidth of 6,400MBps—which matches the bandwidth of the 800MHz CPU bus models of the Pentium 4 for best performance. Processors with the 533MHz CPU bus can use pairs of PC2100 (DDR266) or PC2700 (DDR333) memory modules in dual-channel mode to match the 4,266MBps throughput of this memory bus. It is always best when the throughput of the memory bus matches that of the processor bus.

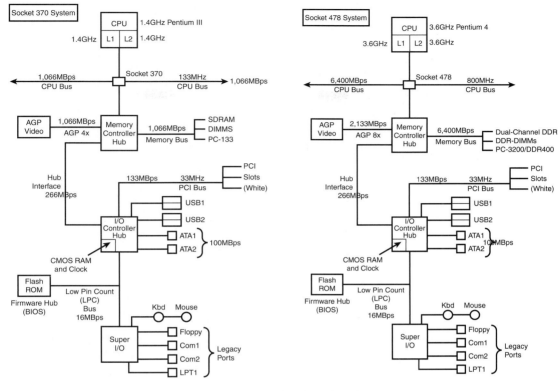

Figure 4.61   Typical Socket 370 (Pentium III/ Celeron class) system architecture

Figure 4.62   Typical Socket 478 (Pentium 4) system architecture.

The Athlon 64 uses the high-speed HyperTransport architecture to connect the North Bridge or AGP Graphics Tunnel chip to the processor (Socket 754, 939, or 940). Most Athlon 64 chipsets use the 16-bit/800MHz version, but the latest chipsets designed for the new Socket 939 Athlon 64 FX-53 use the faster 16-bit/1GHz version to support faster DDR-2 memory.

However, the Athlon 64's most significant departure from conventional computer architecture is the location of the memory controller. Rather than the memory controller being located in the North Bridge/MCH/GMCH chip, the Athlon 64/FX/Opteron architecture places it in the processor itself. This eliminates slow-downs caused by the use of an external memory controller and helps boost performance.

One drawback to the design, however, is that new memory technologies, such as DDR-2, require that the processor itself be redesigned.

Figure 4.63 illustrates an Athlon 64 FX-53–based system that uses the new PCI-Express x1 and PCI-Express x16 expansion slot designs.

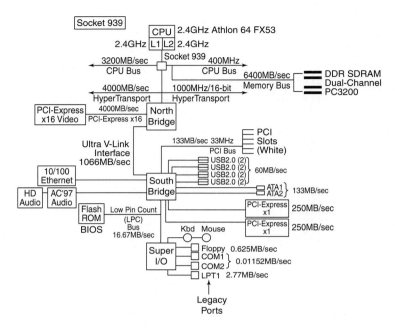

Figure 4.63   Typical Socket 939 (Athlon 64 FX-53) system architecture using PCI-Express slots.

Because the purpose of the processor bus is to get information to and from the CPU at the fastest possible speed, this bus typically operates at a rate faster than any other bus in the system. The bus consists of electrical circuits for data, addresses (the address bus, which is discussed in the following section), and control purposes. Most processors since the original Pentium have a 64-bit data bus, so they transfer 64 bits (8 bytes) at a time over the CPU bus.

The processor bus operates at the same base clock rate as the CPU does externally. This can be misleading because most CPUs these days run at a higher clock rate internally than they do externally. For example, an AMD Athlon 64 3800+ system has a processor running at 2.4GHz internally but only 400MHz externally, whereas a Pentium 4 3.4GHz runs at 3.4GHz internally but only 800MHz externally. In newer systems, the actual processor speed is some multiple (2x, 2.5x, 3x, and higher) of the processor bus.

◄◄   See "Processor Speed Ratings," p. 55.

The processor bus is tied to the external processor pin connections and can transfer 1 bit of data per data line every cycle. Most modern processors transfer 64 bits (8 bytes) of data at a time.

To determine the transfer rate for the processor bus, you multiply the data width (64 bits or 8 bytes for a Celeron/Pentium III/4 or Athlon/Duron/Athlon XP/Athlon 64) by the clock speed of the bus (the same as the base or unmultiplied clock speed of the CPU).

For example, if you are using a Pentium 4 3.6GHz processor that runs on an 800MHz processor bus, you have a maximum instantaneous transfer rate of roughly 6,400MBps. You get this result by using the following formula:

800MHz × 8 bytes (64 bits) = 6,400MBps

With slower versions of the Pentium 4, you get either

533.33MHz × 8 bytes (64 bits) = 4,266MBps

or

400MHz × 8 bytes (64 bits) = 3,200MBps

With Socket A (Athlon XP), you get

333.33MHz × 8 bytes (64 bits) = 2,667MBps

or

266.66MHz × 8 bytes (64 bits) = 2,133MBps

or

200MHz × 8 bytes (64 bits) = 1,600MBps

With Socket 370 (Pentium III), you get

133.33MHz × 8 bytes (64 bits) = 1,066MBps

or

100MHz × 8 bytes (64 bits) = 800MBps

This transfer rate, often called the *bandwidth* of the processor bus, represents the maximum speed at which data can move. Refer to Table 4.71 for a more complete list of various processor bus bandwidths.

The Memory Bus

The memory bus is used to transfer information between the CPU and main memory—the RAM in your system. This bus is usually connected to the motherboard chipset North Bridge or Memory Controller Hub chip. Depending on the type of memory your chipset (and therefore motherboard) is designed to handle, the North Bridge runs the memory bus at various speeds. The best solution is if the memory bus runs at the same speed as the processor bus. Systems that use PC133 SDRAM have a memory bandwidth of 1,066MBps, which is the same as the 133MHz CPU bus. In another example, Athlon systems running a 266MHz processor bus also run PC2100 DDR-SDRAM, which has a bandwidth of 2,133MBps—exactly the same as the processor bus in those systems. Systems running a Pentium 4 with its 400MHz processor bus also use dual-channel RDRAM memory, which runs 1,600MBps for each channel, or a combined bandwidth (both memory channels run simultaneously) of 3,200MBps, which is exactly the same as the Pentium 4 CPU bus. Pentium 4 systems with the 533MHz bus run dual-channel DDR PC2100 or PC2700 modules, which match or exceed the throughput of the 4,266MBps processor bus.

Running memory at the same speed as the processor bus negates the need for having cache memory on the motherboard. That is why when the L2 cache moved into the processor, nobody added an L3 cache to the motherboard. Some very high-end processors, such as the Intel Pentium 4 Extreme Edition, have integrated 2MB–4MB of full-core speed L3 cache into the CPU. However, the most recent high-performance chips, such as the new Core 2 Duo and Quad processors, use only L1 and L2 cache. Therefore, it appears that L2 cache will continue to be the most common type of secondary cache for the foreseeable future.

Note

Notice that the main memory bus must transfer data in the same width as the processor bus. This defines the size of what is called a *bank of memory*, at least when dealing with anything but RDRAM. Memory banks and their widths relative to processor buses are discussed in the section "Memory Banks" in Chapter 6.

The Need for Expansion Slots

The I/O bus or expansion slots enable your CPU to communicate with peripheral devices. The bus and its associated expansion slots are needed because basic systems can't possibly satisfy all the needs of all the people who buy them. The I/O bus enables you to add devices to your computer to expand its capabilities. The most basic computer components, such as sound cards and video cards, can be plugged into expansion slots; you also can plug in more specialized devices, such as network interface cards, audio cards, and others.

Note

In most modern PC systems, a variety of basic peripheral devices are built into the motherboard. Most systems today have at least dual (primary and secondary) IDE interfaces, four USB ports, a floppy controller, two serial ports, a parallel port, keyboard, and mouse controller built directly into the motherboard. These devices are usually distributed between the motherboard chipset South Bridge and the Super I/O chip. (Super I/O chips are discussed earlier in this chapter.)

Many add even more items, such as a sound card, video adapter, SCSI host adapter, network interface, or IEEE 1394a port, that also are built into the motherboard. Those items, however, might not be built into the motherboard chipset or Super I/O chip; they are sometimes configured as additional chips installed on the board. Nevertheless, these built-in controllers and ports still use the I/O bus to communicate with the CPU. In essence, even though they are built in, they act as if they were cards plugged into the system's bus slots, including using system resources in the same manner.

Types of I/O Buses

Since the introduction of the first PC, many I/O buses have been introduced. The reason is simple: Faster I/O speeds are necessary for better system performance. This need for higher performance involves three main areas:

- Faster CPUs
- Increasing software demands
- Greater multimedia requirements

Each of these areas requires the I/O bus to be as fast as possible.

One of the primary reasons new I/O bus structures have been slow in coming is compatibility—that old catch-22 that anchors much of the PC industry to the past. One of the hallmarks of the PC's success is its standardization. This standardization spawned thousands of third-party I/O cards, each originally built for the early bus specifications of the PC. If a new high-performance bus system was introduced, it often had to be compatible with the older bus systems so the older I/O cards would not be obsolete. Therefore, bus technologies seem to evolve rather than make quantum leaps forward.

You can identify different types of I/O buses by their architectures. The main types of I/O buses are detailed earlier in this chapter.

The main differences among buses consist primarily of the amounts of data they can transfer at one time and the speeds at which they can do it. The following sections describe the various types of PC buses.

The ISA Bus

Industry Standard Architecture (ISA) is the bus architecture that was introduced as an 8-bit bus with the original IBM PC in 1981; it was later expanded to 16 bits with the IBM PC/AT in 1984. ISA is the basis of the modern personal computer and was the primary architecture used in the vast majority of PC systems until the late 1990s. It might seem amazing that such a presumably antiquated architecture was used for so long, but it provided reliability, affordability, and compatibility, plus this old bus is still faster than many of the peripherals we connect to it!

Note

The ISA bus has vanished from all recent desktop systems, and few companies make or sell ISA cards anymore. The ISA bus continues to be popular with industrial computer (PICMG) designs, but it is expected to eventually fade away from these as well.

Two versions of the ISA bus exist, based on the number of data bits that can be transferred on the bus at a time. The older version is an 8-bit bus; the newer version is a 16-bit bus. The original 8-bit version ran at 4.77MHz in the PC and XT, and the 16-bit version used in the AT ran at 6MHz and then 8MHz. Later, the industry as a whole agreed on an 8.33MHz maximum standard speed for 8/16-bit versions of the ISA bus for backward-compatibility. Some systems have the capability to run the ISA bus faster than this, but some adapter cards will not function properly at higher speeds. ISA data transfers require anywhere from two to eight cycles. Therefore, the theoretical maximum data rate of the ISA bus is about 8MBps, as the following formula shows:

$$8.33\text{MHz} \times 2 \text{ bytes (16 bits)} \div 2 \text{ cycles per transfer} = 8.33\text{MBps}$$

The bandwidth of the 8-bit bus would be half this figure (4.17MBps). Remember, however, that these figures are theoretical maximums. Because of I/O bus protocols, the effective bandwidth is much lower—typically by almost half. Even so, at about 8MBps, the ISA bus is still faster than many of the peripherals connected to it, such as serial ports, parallel ports, floppy controllers, keyboard controllers, and so on.

The 8-Bit ISA Bus

This bus architecture is used in the original IBM PC computers and was retained for several years in later systems. Although virtually nonexistent in new systems today, this architecture still exists in hundreds of thousands of PC systems in the field, including systems with 286 and 386 processors.

Physically, the 8-bit ISA expansion slot resembles the tongue-and-groove system furniture makers once used to hold two pieces of wood together. It is specifically called a *card/edge connector*. An adapter card with 62 contacts on its bottom edge plugs into a slot on the motherboard that has 62 matching contacts. Electronically, this slot provides eight data lines and 20 addressing lines, enabling the slot to handle 1MB of memory.

Figure 4.64 describes the pinouts for the 8-bit ISA bus; Figure 4.65 shows how these pins are oriented in the expansion slot.

Signal	Pin	Pin	Signal
Ground	B1	A1	-I/O CH CHK
RESET DRV	B2	A2	Data Bit 7
+5 Vdc	B3	A3	Data Bit 6
IRQ 2	B4	A4	Data Bit 5
-5 Vdc	B5	A5	Data Bit 4
DRQ 2	B6	A6	Data Bit 3
-12 Vdc	B7	A7	Data Bit 2
-CARD SLCTD	B8	A8	Data Bit 1
+12 Vdc	B9	A9	Data Bit 0
Ground	B10	A10	-I/O CH RDY
-SMEMW	B11	A11	AEN
-SMEMR	B12	A12	Address 19
-IOW	B13	A13	Address 18
-IOR	B14	A14	Address 17
-DACK 3	B15	A15	Address 16
DRQ 3	B16	A16	Address 15
-DACK 1	B17	A17	Address 14
DRQ 1	B18	A18	Address 13
-Refresh	B19	A19	Address 12
CLK(4.77MHz)	B20	A20	Address 11
IRQ 7	B21	A21	Address 10
IRQ 6	B22	A22	Address 9
IRQ 5	B23	A23	Address 8
IRQ 4	B24	A24	Address 7
IRQ 3	B25	A25	Address 6
-DACK 2	B26	A26	Address 5
T/C	B27	A27	Address 4
BALE	B28	A28	Address 3
+5 Vdc	B29	A29	Address 2
OSC(14.3MHz)	B30	A30	Address 1
Ground	B31	A31	Address 0

Figure 4.64   Pinouts for the 8-bit ISA bus.

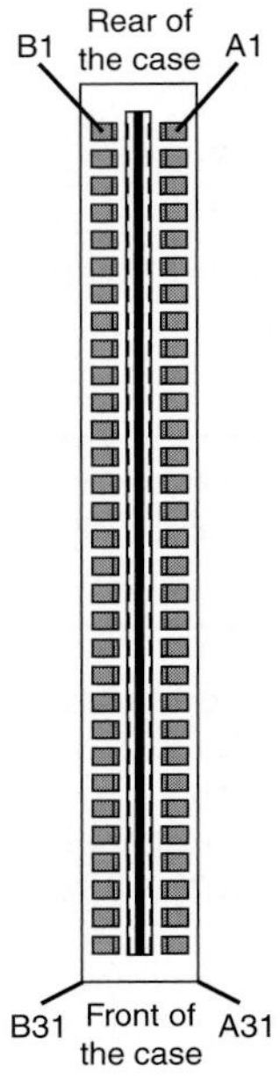

Figure 4.65   The 8-bit ISA bus connector.

Although the design of the bus is simple, IBM waited until 1987 to publish full specifications for the timings of the data and address lines, so in the early days of PC compatibles, manufacturers had to do their best to figure out how to make adapter boards. This problem was solved, however, as PC-compatible personal computers became more widely accepted as the industry standard and manufacturers had more time and incentive to build adapter boards that worked correctly with the bus.

The dimensions of 8-bit ISA adapter cards are as follows:

4.2" (106.68mm) high

13.13" (333.5mm) long

0.5" (12.7mm) wide

The 16-Bit ISA Bus

IBM threw a bombshell on the PC world when it introduced the AT with the 286 processor in 1984. This processor had a 16-bit data bus, which meant communications between the processor and motherboard as well as memory would now be 16 bits wide instead of only 8. Although this processor could have been installed on a motherboard with only an 8-bit I/O bus, that would have meant a huge sacrifice in the performance of any adapter cards or other devices installed on the bus.

Rather than create a new I/O bus, at that time IBM instead came up with a system that could support both 8- and 16-bit cards by retaining the same basic 8-bit connector layout but adding an optional 16-bit extension connector. This first debuted on the PC/AT in August 1984, which is why we also refer to the ISA bus as the *AT-bus*.

The extension connector in each 16-bit expansion slot adds 36 connector pins (for a total of 98 signals) to carry the extra signals necessary to implement the wider data path. In addition, two of the pins in the 8-bit portion of the connector were changed. These two minor changes did not alter the function of 8-bit cards.

Figure 4.66 describes the pinouts for the full 16-bit ISA expansion slot, and Figure 4.67 shows how the additional pins are oriented in the expansion slot.

Because of physical interference with some ancient 8-bit card designs, IBM left 16-bit extension connectors off two of the slots in the AT. This was not a problem in newer systems, so any system with ISA slots would have all of them as full 16-bit versions.

The dimensions of a typical AT expansion board are as follows:

4.8" (121.92mm) high

13.13" (333.5mm) long

0.5" (12.7mm) wide

Two heights actually are available for cards commonly used in AT systems: 4.8" and 4.2" (the height of older PC-XT cards). The shorter cards became an issue when IBM introduced the XT Model 286. Because this model has an AT motherboard in an XT case, it needs AT-type boards with the 4.2" maximum height. Most board makers trimmed the height of their boards; most manufacturers who still make ISA cards now make only 4.2"-tall (or less) boards so they will work in systems with either profile.

32-Bit Buses

After 32-bit CPUs became available, it was some time before 32-bit bus standards became available. Before MCA and EISA specs were released, some vendors began creating their own proprietary 32-bit buses, which were extensions of the ISA bus. Fortunately, these proprietary buses were few and far between.

The expanded portions of the bus typically are used for proprietary memory expansion or video cards. Because the systems are proprietary (meaning that they are nonstandard), pinouts and specifications are not available.

The Micro Channel Bus

The introduction of 32-bit chips meant that the ISA bus could not handle the power of another new generation of CPUs. The 386DX chips could transfer 32 bits of data at a time, but the ISA bus can handle a maximum of only 16 bits. Rather than extend the ISA bus again, IBM decided to build a new bus; the result was the MCA bus. *MCA* (an abbreviation for microchannel architecture) is completely different from the ISA bus and is technically superior in every way.

IBM wanted not only to replace the old ISA standard, but also to require vendors to license certain parts of the technology. Many owed for licenses on the ISA bus technology that IBM also created, but because IBM had not been aggressive in its licensing of ISA, many got away without any license. Problems with licensing and control led to the development of the competing EISA bus (see the next section on the EISA bus) and hindered acceptance of the MCA bus.

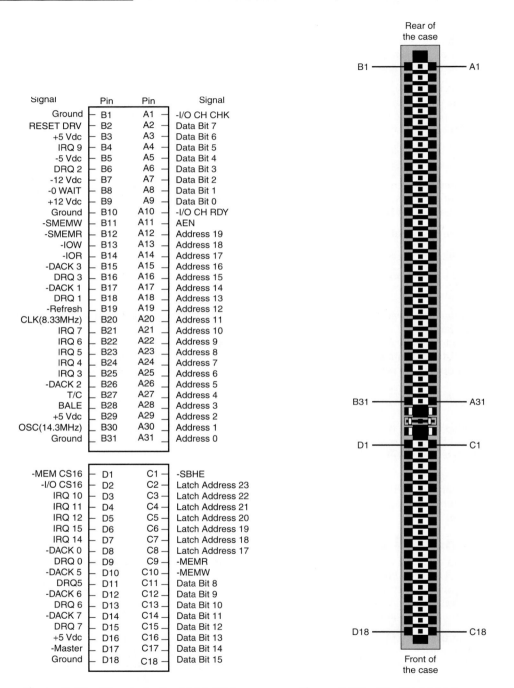

Signal	Pin	Pin	Signal
Ground	B1	A1	-I/O CH CHK
RESET DRV	B2	A2	Data Bit 7
+5 Vdc	B3	A3	Data Bit 6
IRQ 9	B4	A4	Data Bit 5
-5 Vdc	B5	A5	Data Bit 4
DRQ 2	B6	A6	Data Bit 3
-12 Vdc	B7	A7	Data Bit 2
-0 WAIT	B8	A8	Data Bit 1
+12 Vdc	B9	A9	Data Bit 0
Ground	B10	A10	-I/O CH RDY
-SMEMW	B11	A11	AEN
-SMEMR	B12	A12	Address 19
-IOW	B13	A13	Address 18
-IOR	B14	A14	Address 17
-DACK 3	B15	A15	Address 16
DRQ 3	B16	A16	Address 15
-DACK 1	B17	A17	Address 14
DRQ 1	B18	A18	Address 13
-Refresh	B19	A19	Address 12
CLK(8.33MHz)	B20	A20	Address 11
IRQ 7	B21	A21	Address 10
IRQ 6	B22	A22	Address 9
IRQ 5	B23	A23	Address 8
IRQ 4	B24	A24	Address 7
IRQ 3	B25	A25	Address 6
-DACK 2	B26	A26	Address 5
T/C	B27	A27	Address 4
BALE	B28	A28	Address 3
+5 Vdc	B29	A29	Address 2
OSC(14.3MHz)	B30	A30	Address 1
Ground	B31	A31	Address 0

Signal	Pin	Pin	Signal
-MEM CS16	D1	C1	-SBHE
-I/O CS16	D2	C2	Latch Address 23
IRQ 10	D3	C3	Latch Address 22
IRQ 11	D4	C4	Latch Address 21
IRQ 12	D5	C5	Latch Address 20
IRQ 15	D6	C6	Latch Address 19
IRQ 14	D7	C7	Latch Address 18
-DACK 0	D8	C8	Latch Address 17
DRQ 0	D9	C9	-MEMR
-DACK 5	D10	C10	-MEMW
DRQ5	D11	C11	Data Bit 8
-DACK 6	D12	C12	Data Bit 9
DRQ 6	D13	C13	Data Bit 10
-DACK 7	D14	C14	Data Bit 11
DRQ 7	D15	C15	Data Bit 12
+5 Vdc	D16	C16	Data Bit 13
-Master	D17	C17	Data Bit 14
Ground	D18	C18	Data Bit 15

Figure 4.66   Pinouts for the 16-bit ISA bus.

Figure 4.67   The ISA 16-bit bus connector.

MCA systems produced a new level of ease of use; they were plug-and-play before the official Plug and Play specification even existed. An MCA system had no jumpers and switches—neither on the motherboard nor on any expansion adapter. Instead you used a special Reference disk, which went with the particular system, and Option disks, which went with each of the cards installed in the system. After a card was installed, you loaded the Option disk files onto the Reference disk; after that, you didn't need the Option disks anymore. The Reference disk contained the special BIOS and system setup program necessary for an MCA system, and the system couldn't be configured without it.

For more information on the MCA bus, see the previous editions of this book on the included disc.

The EISA Bus

The Extended Industry Standard Architecture (EISA) standard was announced in September 1988 as a response to IBM's introduction of the MCA bus—more specifically, to the way IBM wanted to handle licensing of the MCA bus. Vendors did not feel obligated to pay retroactive royalties on the ISA bus, so they turned their backs on IBM and created their own buses.

The EISA standard was developed primarily by Compaq and was intended to be its way of taking over future development of the PC bus from IBM. Compaq knew that nobody would clone its bus if it was the only company that had it, so it essentially gave the design to other leading manufacturers. Compaq formed the EISA committee, a nonprofit organization designed specifically to control development of the EISA bus. Very few EISA adapters were ever developed. Those that were developed centered mainly around disk array controllers and server-type network cards.

The EISA bus was essentially a 32-bit version of ISA. Unlike the MCA bus from IBM, you could still use older 8-bit or 16-bit ISA cards in 32-bit EISA slots, providing for full backward-compatibility. As with MCA, EISA also allowed for automatic configuration of EISA cards via software.

The EISA bus added 90 new connections (55 new signals plus grounds) without increasing the physical connector size of the 16-bit ISA bus. At first glance, the 32-bit EISA slot looks a lot like the 16-bit ISA slot. The EISA adapter, however, has two rows of stacked contacts. The first row is the same type used in 16-bit ISA cards; the other, thinner row extends from the 16-bit connectors. Therefore, ISA cards can still be used in EISA bus slots. Although this compatibility was not enough to ensure the popularity of EISA buses, it is a feature that was carried over into the VL-Bus standard that followed. The physical specifications of an EISA card are as follows:

- 5" (127mm) high
- 13.13" (333.5mm) long
- 0.5" (12.7mm) wide

The EISA bus can handle up to 32 bits of data at an 8.33MHz cycle rate. Most data transfers require a minimum of two cycles, although faster cycle rates are possible if an adapter card provides tight timing specifications. The maximum bandwidth on the bus is 33MBps, as the following formula shows:

$$8.33\text{MHz} \times 4 \text{ bytes (32 bits)} = 33\text{MBps}$$

Figure 4.68 describes the pinouts for the EISA bus. Figure 4.69 shows the locations of the pins; note how some pins are offset to allow the EISA slot to accept ISA cards. Figure 4.70 shows the card connector for the EISA expansion slot.

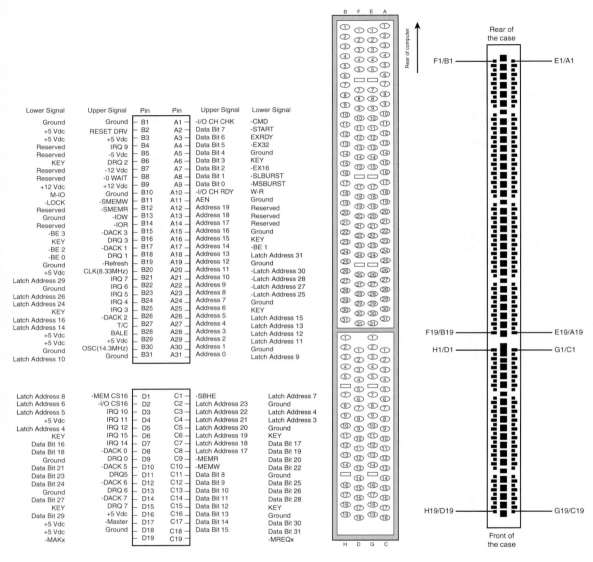

Figure 4.68 Pinouts for the EISA bus.

Figure 4.69
Pin locations inside the EISA bus connector.

Figure 4.70
The EISA bus connector.

Local Buses

The I/O buses discussed so far (ISA, MCA, and EISA) have one thing in common: relatively slow speed. The next three bus types that are discussed in the following few sections all use the *local bus* concept explained in this section to address the speed issue. The main local buses found in PC systems are

- VL-Bus (VESA local bus)
- PCI
- AGP
- PCI Express

The speed limitation of ISA, MCA, and EISA is a carryover from the days of the original PC when the I/O bus operated at the same speed as the processor bus. As the speed of the processor bus increased, the I/O bus realized only nominal speed improvements, primarily from an increase in the bandwidth of the bus. The I/O bus had to remain at a slower speed because the huge installed base of adapter cards could operate only at slower speeds.

Figure 4.71 shows a conceptual block diagram of the buses in a computer system.

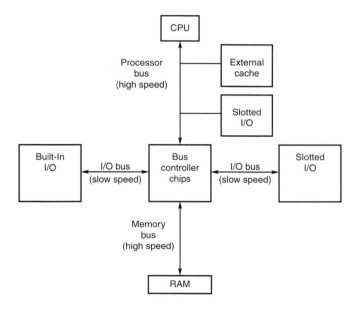

Figure 4.71   Bus layout in a traditional PC.

The thought of a computer system running more slowly than it could is very bothersome to some computer users. Even so, the slow speed of the I/O bus is nothing more than a nuisance in most cases. You don't need blazing speed to communicate with a keyboard or mouse—you gain nothing in performance. The real problem occurs in subsystems in which you need the speed, such as video and disk controllers.

The speed problem became acute when graphical user interfaces (such as Windows) became prevalent. These systems require the processing of so much video data that the I/O bus became a literal bottle-neck for the entire computer system. In other words, it did little good to have a processor that was capable of 66MHz–450MHz or faster if you could put data through the I/O bus at a rate of only 8MHz.

An obvious solution to this problem is to move some of the slotted I/O to an area where it could access the faster speeds of the processor bus—much the same way as the external cache. Figure 4.72 shows this arrangement.

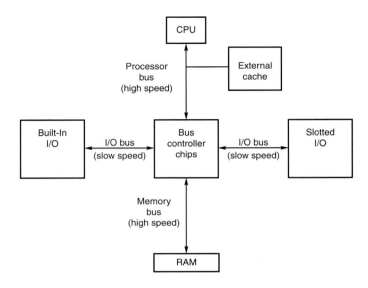

Figure 4.72 How a local bus works.

This arrangement became known as *local bus* because external devices (adapter cards) now could access the part of the bus that was local to the CPU—the processor bus. Physically, the slots provided to tap this new configuration would need to be different from existing bus slots to prevent adapter cards designed for slower buses from being plugged into the higher bus speeds, which this design made accessible.

It is interesting to note that the very first 8-bit and 16-bit ISA buses were a form of local bus architecture. These systems had the processor bus as the main bus, and everything ran at full processor speeds. When ISA systems ran faster than 8MHz, the main ISA bus had to be decoupled from the processor bus because expansion cards, memory, and so on could not keep up. In 1992, an extension to the ISA bus called the *VESA local bus (VL-Bus)* started showing up on PC systems, indicating a return to local bus architecture. Since then, the peripheral component interconnect (PCI) local bus has supplanted VL-Bus, and the AGP bus has been introduced to complement PCI.

Note

A system does not have to have a local bus expansion slot to incorporate local bus technology; instead, the local bus device can be built directly into the motherboard. (In such a case, the local bus-slotted I/O shown in Figure 4.72 would in fact be built-in I/O.) This built-in approach to local bus is the way the first local bus systems were designed.

Local bus solutions do not necessarily replace earlier standards, such as ISA; they are designed into the system as a bus that is closer to the processor in the system architecture. Older buses such as ISA were kept around for backward compatibility with slower types of adapters that didn't need any faster connection to the system (such as modems). Therefore, until recently a typical system might have AGP, PCI, and ISA slots. Older cards still are compatible with such a system, but high-speed adapter cards can take advantage of the AGP and PCI local bus slots as well. With the demise of ISA slots and the movement of traditionally ISA-based motherboard devices to the LPC interface, today's motherboards essentially use other buses or dedicated interfaces for most of the connections that would have previously used ISA.

The performance of graphical user interfaces such as Windows and graphical Linux interfaces such as KDE and GNOME have been tremendously improved by moving the video cards off the slow ISA bus and onto faster PCI and now AGP local buses.

VESA Local Bus

The Video Electronics Standards Association (VESA) local bus was the most popular local bus design from its debut in August 1992 through 1994. It was created by the VESA committee, a nonprofit organization originally founded by NEC to further develop video display and bus standards. In a similar fashion to how EISA evolved, NEC had done most of the work on the VL-Bus (as it would be called) and, after founding the nonprofit VESA committee, NEC turned over future development to VESA. At first, the local bus slot seemed designed to be used primarily for video cards. Improving video performance was a top priority at NEC to help sell its high-end displays as well as its own PC systems. By 1991, video performance had become a real bottleneck in most PC systems.

The VL-Bus can move data 32 bits at a time, enabling data to flow between the CPU and a compatible video subsystem or hard drive at the full 32-bit data width of the 486 chip. The maximum rated throughput of the VL-Bus is 133MBps. In other words, local bus went a long way toward removing the major bottlenecks that existed in earlier bus configurations.

Unfortunately, the VL-Bus did not seem to be a long-lived concept. The design was simple indeed—just take the pins from the 486 processor and run them out to a card connector socket. So, the VL-Bus is essentially the raw 486 processor bus. This allowed for a very inexpensive design because no additional chipsets or interface chips were required. A motherboard designer could add VL-Bus slots to its 486 motherboards very easily and at a very low cost. This is why these slots appeared on virtually all 486 system designs overnight.

Problems arose with timing glitches caused by the capacitance introduced into the circuit by different cards. Because the VL-Bus ran at the same speed as the processor bus, different processor speeds meant different bus speeds, and full compatibility was difficult to achieve. Although the VL-Bus could be adapted to other processors—including the 386 or even the Pentium—it was designed for the 486 and worked best as a 486 solution only. Despite the low cost, after a new bus called PCI appeared, VL-Bus fell into disfavor very quickly. It never did catch on with Pentium systems, and there was little or no further development of the VL-Bus in the PC industry.

Physically, the VL-Bus slot was an extension of the slots used for whatever type of base system you have. If you have an ISA system, the VL-Bus is positioned as an extension of your existing 16-bit ISA slots. The VESA extension has 112 contacts and uses the same physical connector as the MCA bus.

The PCI Bus

In early 1992, Intel spearheaded the creation of another industry group. It was formed with the same goals as the VESA group in relation to the PC bus. Recognizing the need to overcome weaknesses in the ISA and EISA buses, the PCI Special Interest Group was formed.

The PCI bus specification was released in June 1992 as version 1.0 and since then has undergone several upgrades. Table 4.75 shows the various releases of PCI.

Table 4.75   PCI Specifications

PCI Specification	Released	Major Change
PCI 1.0	June 1992	Original 32/64-bit specification
PCI 2.0	April 1993	Defined connectors and expansion boards
PCI 2.1	June 1995	66MHz operation, transaction ordering, latency changes

Table 4.75   Continued

PCI Specification	Released	Major Change
PCI 2.2	Jan. 1999	Power management, mechanical clarifications
PCI-X 1.0	Sept. 1999	133MHz operation, addendum to 2.2
Mini-PCI	Nov. 1999	Small form-factor boards, addendum to 2.2
PCI 2.3	March 2002	3.3V signaling, low-profile add-in cards
PCI-X 2.0	July 2002	266MHz and 533MHz operation, supports subdivision of 64-bit data bus into 32-bit or 16-bit segments for use by multiple devices, 3.3V/1.5V signaling
PCI-Express 1.0	July 2002	2.5GBps per lane per direction, using 0.8V signaling, resulting in 250MBps per lane
PCI-Express 2.0	Jan. 2007	5GBps per lane per direction, using 0.8V signaling, resulting in 500MBps per lane

PCI redesigned the traditional PC bus by inserting another bus between the CPU and the native I/O bus by means of bridges. Rather than tap directly into the processor bus, with its delicate electrical timing (as was done in the VL-Bus), a new set of controller chips was developed to extend the bus, as shown in Figure 4.73.

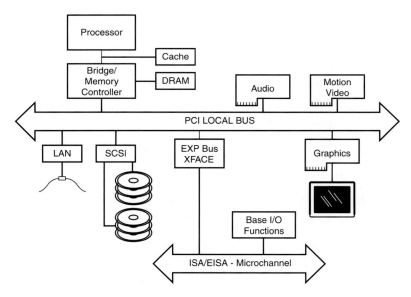

Figure 4.73   Conceptual diagram of the PCI bus.

The PCI bus often is called a *mezzanine bus* because it adds another layer to the traditional bus configuration. PCI bypasses the standard I/O bus; it uses the system bus to increase the bus clock speed and take full advantage of the CPU's data path. Systems that integrate the PCI bus became available in mid-1993 and have since become a mainstay in the PC.

Information typically is transferred across the PCI bus at 33MHz and 32 bits at a time. The bandwidth is 133MBps, as the following formula shows:

33.33MHz × 4 bytes (32 bits) = 133MBps

Although 32-bit 33MHz PCI is the standard found in most PCs, there are now several variations on PCI, as shown in Table 4.76. Many recent PCs now also feature PCI-Express x1 and PCI-Express x16 slots.

Table 4.76   PCI Bus Types

PCI Bus Type	Bus Width (Bits)	Bus Speed (MHz)	Data Cycles per Clock	Bandwidth (MBps)
PCI	32	33	1	133
PCI 66MHz	32	66	1	266
PCI 64-bit	64	33	1	266
PCI 66MHz/64-bit	64	66	1	533
PCI-X 64	64*	66	1	533
PCI-X 133	64*	133	1	1,066
PCI-X 266	64*	133	2	2,132
PCI-X 533	64*	133	4	4,266
PCI-Express 1.x**	1	2,500	0.8	250
PCI-Express 1.x**	16	2,500	0.8	4,000
PCI-Express 1.x**	32	2,500	0.8	8,000
PCI-Express 2.x**	1	5,000	0.8	500
PCI-Express 2.x**	16	5,000	0.8	8,000
PCI-Express 2.x**	32	5,000	0.8	16,000

Bus width on PCI-X devices can be shared by multiple 32-bit or 16-bit devices.

**PCI-Express uses 8b/10b encoding, which transfers 8 bits for every 10 bits sent and can transfer 1–32 bits at a time, depending on how many lanes are in the implementation.*

Currently, the 64-bit or 66MHz and 133MHz variations are used only on server- or workstation-type boards and systems. Aiding performance is the fact that the PCI bus can operate concurrently with the processor bus; it does not supplant it. The CPU can be processing data in an external cache while the PCI bus is busy transferring information between other parts of the system—a major design benefit of the PCI bus.

A PCI adapter card uses its own unique connector. This connector can be identified within a computer system because it typically is offset from the normal ISA, MCA, or EISA connectors found in older motherboards. See Figure 4.74 for an example. The size of a PCI card can be the same as that of the cards used in the system's normal I/O bus.

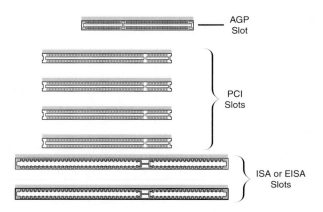

Figure 4.74   Typical configuration of 32-bit 33MHz PCI slots in relation to ISA or EISA and AGP slots.

The PCI specification identifies three board configurations, each designed for a specific type of system with specific power requirements; each specification has a 32-bit version and a longer 64-bit version. The 5V specification is for stationary computer systems (using PCI 2.2 or earlier versions), the 3.3V specification is for portable systems (also supported by PCI 2.3), and the universal specification is for motherboards and cards that work in either type of system. 64-bit versions of the 5V and universal PCI slots are found primarily on server motherboards. The PCI-X 2.0 specifications for 266 and 533 versions support 3.3V and 1.5V signaling; this corresponds to PCI version 2.3, which supports 3.3V signaling.

Note

The pinouts for the 5V, 3.3V, and universal PCI slots can be found on the disc in the Technical Reference section.

Figure 4.75 compares the 32-bit and 64-bit versions of the standard 5V PCI slot to a 64-bit universal PCI slot. Figure 4.76 shows how the connector on a 64-bit universal PCI card compares to the 64-bit universal PCI slot.

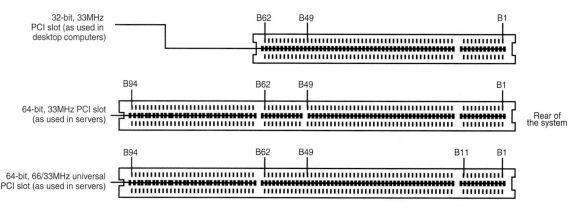

Figure 4.75   A 32-bit 33MHz PCI slot (top) compared to a 64-bit 33MHz PCI slot (center) and a 64-bit universal PCI slot that runs at 66MHz (bottom).

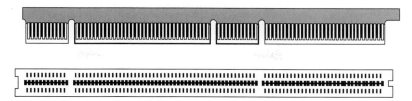

Figure 4.76   A 64-bit universal PCI card (top) compared to the 64-bit universal PCI slot (bottom).

Notice that the universal PCI board specifications effectively combine the 5V and 3.3V specifications. For pins for which the voltage is different, the universal specification labels the pin V I/O. This type of pin represents a special power pin for defining and driving the PCI signaling rail.

Another important feature of PCI is the fact that it was the model for the Intel PnP specification. Therefore, PCI cards do not have jumpers and switches and are instead configured through software. True PnP systems are capable of automatically configuring the adapters, whereas non-PnP systems with ISA slots must configure the adapters through a program that is usually a part of the system CMOS configuration. Starting in late 1995, most PC-compatible systems have included a PnP BIOS that allows the automatic PnP configuration.

PCI-Express

During 2001, a group of companies called the Arapahoe Work Group (led primarily by Intel) developed a draft of a new high-speed bus specification code named 3GIO (third-generation I/O). In August 2001, the PCI Special Interest Group (PCI-SIG) agreed to take over, manage, and promote the 3GIO architecture specification as the future generation of PCI. In April 2002, the 3GIO draft version 1.0 was completed, transferred to the PCI-SIG, and renamed PCI-Express. Finally in July 2002, the PCI-Express 1.0 specification was approved. The specification was updated to 1.1 in April 2005, and 2.0 in January 2007.

The original 3GIO code name was derived from the fact that this new bus specification was designed to initially augment and eventually replace the previously existing ISA/AT-Bus (first-generation) and PCI (second-generation) bus architectures in PCs. Each of the first two generations of PC bus architectures was designed to have a 10- to 15-year useful life in PCs. In being adopted and approved by the PCI-SIG, PCI-Express is now destined to be the dominant PC bus architecture designed to support the increasing bandwidth needs in PCs over the next 10–15 years.

The key features of PCI-Express are as follows:

- Compatibility with existing PCI enumeration and software device drivers.
- Physical connection over copper, optical, or other physical media to allow for future encoding schemes.
- Maximum bandwidth per pin allows for small form factors, reduced cost, simpler board designs and routing, and reduced signal integrity issues.
- Embedded clocking scheme enables easy frequency (speed) changes as compared to synchronous clocking.
- Bandwidth (throughput) increases easily with frequency and width (lane) increases.
- Low latency suitable for applications requiring isochronous (time-sensitive) data delivery, such as streaming video.
- Hot-plugging and hot-swapping capabilities.
- Power management capabilities.

PCI-Express is another example of how the PC is moving from parallel to serial interfaces. Earlier generation bus architectures in the PC have been of a parallel design, in which multiple bits are sent simultaneously over several pins in parallel. The more bits sent at a time, the faster the bus throughput is. The timing of all the parallel signals must be the same, which becomes more and more difficult to do over faster and longer connections. Even though 32 bits can be transmitted simultaneously over a bus such as PCI or AGP, propagation delays and other problems cause them to arrive slightly skewed at the other end, resulting in a time difference between when the first and last of all the bits arrive.

A serial bus design is much simpler, sending 1 bit at a time over a single wire, at much higher rates of speed than a parallel bus would allow. By sending the bits serially, the timing of individual bits or the length of the bus becomes much less of a factor. By combining multiple serial data paths, even faster throughputs can be realized that dramatically exceed the capabilities of traditional parallel buses.

PCI-Express is a very fast serial bus design that is backward-compatible with current PCI parallel bus software drivers and controls. In PCI-Express, data is sent full duplex (simultaneously operating one-way paths) over two pairs of differentially signaled wires called a *lane*. Each lane allows for about 250MBps throughput in each direction initially, and the design allows for scaling from 1 to 2, 4, 8, 16, or 32 lanes. For example, a high-bandwidth configuration with 16 lanes allowing 16 bits to be sent in each direction simultaneously would allow up to 4,000MBps bandwidth each way. PCIe 2.0 increases the transfer rate to 500MBps per lane, or 8,000MBps for an x16 connector. This compares to PCI, which has only 133MBps bandwidth (one way at a time). Figure 4.77 compares the PCI-Express x1–x16 connectors, and Figure 4.78 shows how PCI-Express x1 and x16 slots compare to PCI slots on a typical motherboard implementation. Note that the PCI-Express x4 and x8 connectors shown in Figure 4.77 are intended primarily for use in servers.

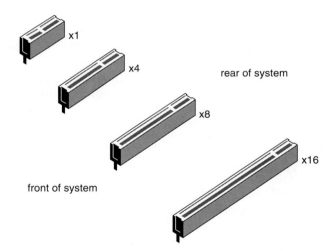

Figure 4.77   PCI-Express x1, x4, x8, and x16 slots.

PCI-Express uses an IBM-designed 8-bit-to-10-bit encoding scheme, which allows for self-clocked signals that will easily allow future increases in frequency. The starting frequency is 2.5GHz, and the specification will allow increasing up to 10GHz in the future, which is about the limit of copper connections. By combining frequency increases with the capability to use up to 32 lanes, PCI-Express will be capable of supporting future bandwidths up to 32GBps.

PCI-Express is designed to augment and eventually replace many of the buses currently used in PCs. It will not only be a supplement to (and the eventual replacement for) PCI slots, but can also be used to replace the existing Intel hub architecture, HyperTransport, and similar high-speed interfaces between motherboard chipset components. Additionally, it will replace video interfaces such as AGP and act as a mezzanine bus to attach other interfaces, such as Serial ATA, USB 2.0, 1394b (FireWire or i.LINK), Gigabit Ethernet, and more.

Because PCI-Express can be implemented over cables as well as onboard, it can be used to create systems constructed with remote "bricks" containing the bulk of the computing power. Imagine the motherboard, processor, and RAM in one small box hidden under a table, with the video, disk drives, and I/O ports in another box sitting out on a table within easy reach. This will enable a variety of flexible PC form factors to be developed in the future without compromising performance.

PCI-Express has not and will not replace PCI or other interfaces overnight. System developers will continue to integrate PCI, AGP, and other bus architectures into system designs for several more years. Just as with PCI and the ISA/AT-Bus before, there will likely be a long period of time during which both buses will be found on motherboards. Gradually, though, fewer PCI and more PCI-Express connections will appear. Over time, PCI-Express will eventually become the preferred general-purpose I/O interconnect over PCI. I expect the move to PCI-Express will be similar to the transition from ISA/AT-Bus to PCI during the 1990s. Current full-size ATX motherboards have about half their slots as PCI and half as PCI-Express.

Although it will take some time for PCI-Express to completely replace PCI, PCI-Express x16 has already replaced AGP 8x.

Most recent desktop motherboard designs feature a mix of PCI, PCI-Express x1, and x16 slots; workstation and server motherboards are also adding PCI-Express slots to their typical PCI-X and PCI slots.

For more information on PCI-Express, I recommend consulting the PCI-SIG website (www.pcisig.org).

Accelerated Graphics Port

In the mid 1990s Intel created AGP as a new bus specifically designed for high-performance graphics and video support. AGP is based on PCI, but it contains several additions and enhancements and is physically, electrically, and logically independent of PCI. For example, the AGP connector is similar to PCI, although it has additional signals and is positioned differently in the system. Unlike PCI, which is a true bus with multiple connectors (slots), AGP is more of a point-to-point high-performance connection designed specifically for a video card in a system because only one AGP slot is allowed for a single video card. Intel originally released the AGP specification 1.0 in July 1996 and defined a 66MHz clock rate with 1x or 2x signaling using 3.3V. AGP version 2.0 was released in May 1998 and added 4x signaling as well as a lower 1.5V operating capability.

The final revision for the AGP specification for PCs is AGP 8x, also called AGP 3.0. AGP 8x defines a transfer speed of 2,133MBps, which is twice that of AGP 4x. The AGP 8x specification was first publicly announced in November 2000. AGP 8x support is now widely available in motherboard chipsets and graphics chipsets from major vendors. Although AGP 8x has a maximum speed twice that of AGP 4x, the real-world differences between AGP 4x- and 8x-compatible devices with otherwise identical specifications are minimal. However, many 3D chipsets that support AGP 8x have also upgraded memory and 3D graphics core speeds and designs to better support the faster interface.

Most of the last generation of AGP video cards are designed to conform to the AGP 4X or AGP 8X specification, each of which runs on only 1.5 volts. Most older motherboards with AGP 2X slots are designed to accept only 3.3V cards. If you plug a 1.5V card into a 3.3V slot, both the card and motherboard could be damaged, so special keys have been incorporated into the AGP specification to prevent such disasters. Normally, the slots and cards are keyed such that 1.5V cards fit only in 1.5V sockets and 3.3V cards fit only in 3.3V sockets. However, universal sockets do exist that accept either 1.5V or 3.3V cards. The keying for the AGP cards and connectors is dictated by the AGP standard, as shown in Figure 4.79.

As you can see from Figure 4.78, AGP 4X or 8X (1.5V) cards fit only in 1.5V or universal (3.3V or 1.5V) slots. Due to the design of the connector and card keys, a 1.5V card cannot be inserted into a 3.3V slot. So, if your new AGP card won't fit in the AGP slot in your existing motherboard, consider that a good thing because if you were able to plug it in, you would fry the card and possibly the board as well! In that case, you'd either have to return the 4X/8X card or get a new motherboard that supports the 4X/8X (1.5V) cards.

Caution

Some AGP 4x/8x-compatible motherboards require you to use 1.5V AGP 4x/8x cards only; be sure to check compatibility between the motherboard and the AGP card you want to buy to avoid problems. Some AGP 4x/8x-compatible slots use the card retention mechanism shown in Figure 4.79. Note that AGP 1x/2x slots have a visible divider not present on the newer AGP 4x slot. AGP 4x slots can also accept AGP 8x cards, and vice versa.

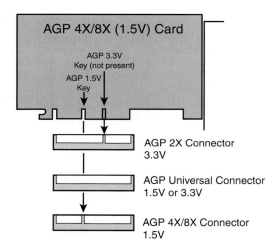

Figure 4.78   AGP 4X/8X (1.5V) card and AGP 3.3V, universal, and 1.5V slots.

Additionally, a newer specification was introduced as AGP Pro 1.0 in August 1998 and was revised in April 1999 as AGP Pro 1.1a. It defines a slightly longer slot with additional power pins at each end to drive bigger and faster AGP cards that consume more than 25 watts of power, up to a maximum of 110 watts. AGP Pro cards are likely to be used for high-end graphics workstations and are not likely to be found in any normal PCs. However, AGP Pro slots are backward-compatible, meaning a standard AGP card will plug in, and a number of motherboard vendors began using AGP Pro slots rather than AGP 4x slots in their products. Because AGP Pro slots are longer, an AGP 1x/2x card can be incorrectly inserted into the slot, which could damage it, so some vendors supply a cover or an insert for the AGP Pro extension at the rear of the slot. This protective cover or insert should be removed only if you want to install an AGP Pro card.

The standard AGP 1x/2x, AGP 4x, and AGP Pro slots are compared to each other in Figure 4.79.

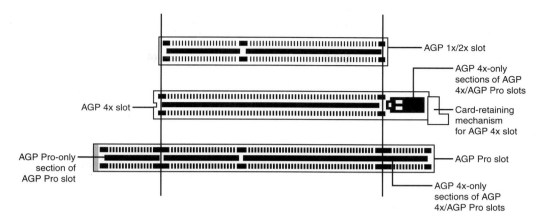

Figure 4.79 AGP standard (1x/2x), AGP 4x, and AGP Pro slots compared to each other. AGP 4x and AGP Pro can accept AGP 1x, 2x, and 4x cards. AGP 4x and AGP Pro slots can also accept AGP 8x cards.

AGP runs at a base frequency of 66MHz (actually 66.66MHz), which is double that of standard PCI. In the basic AGP mode, called 1x, a single transfer is done every cycle. Because the AGP bus is 32 bits (4 bytes) wide, at 66 million times per second it would be capable of transferring data at a rate of about 266MBps! The original AGP specification also defines a 2x mode, in which two transfers are performed every cycle, resulting in 533MBps. Using an analogy in which every cycle is equivalent to the back-and-forth swing of a pendulum, the 1x mode is thought of as transferring information at the start of each swing. In 2x mode, an additional transfer would occur every time the pendulum completed half a swing, thereby doubling performance while technically maintaining the same clock rate, or in this case, the same number of swings per second. Although the earliest AGP cards supported only the AGP 1x mode, most vendors quickly shifted to the AGP 2x mode. The newer AGP 2.0 specification adds the capability for 4x transfers, in which data is transferred four times per cycle and equals a data transfer rate of 1,066MBps. Most current AGP cards have support for the 4x standard as a minimum, and many graphics chipsets from NVIDIA and ATI support AGP 8x. Table 4.77 shows the differences in clock rates and data transfer speeds (bandwidth) for the various AGP modes.

Table 4.77   AGP Modes Showing Clock Speeds and Bandwidth

AGP Bus Type	Bus Width (Bits)	Bus Speed (MHz)	Data Cycles per Clock	Bandwidth (MBps)
AGP	32	66	1	266
AGP 2x	32	66	2	533
AGP 4x	32	66	4	1,066
AGP 8x	32	66	8	2,133

Because AGP is independent of PCI, using an AGP video card frees up the PCI bus for more traditional input and output, such as for IDE/ATA or SCSI controllers, USB controllers, sound cards, and so on.

Besides faster video performance, one of the main reasons Intel designed AGP was to allow the video card to have a high-speed connection directly to the system RAM, which would enable a reasonably fast and powerful video solution to be integrated at a lower cost. AGP allows a video card to have direct access to the system RAM, either enabling lower-cost video solutions to be directly built into a motherboard without having to include additional video RAM or enabling an AGP card to share the main system memory. However, few AGP cards in recent years share main memory. Instead, they have their own high-speed memory (as much as 256MB in some recent models). Using dedicated memory directly on the video card is especially important when running high-performance 3D video applications. AGP enables the speed of the video card to pace the requirements for high-speed 3D graphics rendering as well as full-motion video on the PC.

Although AGP 8x (2,133MBps) is 16 times faster than 32-bit 33MHz PCI (133MBps), AGP 8x is only about half as fast as PCI-Express x16 (4,000MBps). Starting in mid-2004, motherboard and system vendors began to replace AGP 8x with PCI-Express x16 expansion slots in high-performance systems using Pentium 4 and Athlon 64 processors. As of early 2006, most motherboards in all price ranges feature PCI-Express x16 slots in place of AGP. This trend will eventually spell the end of AGP.

Note

If you want to purchase a motherboard that uses PCI-Express x16 but don't want to replace your AGP video card at the same time, look for motherboards that offer both AGP 8x and PCI-Express x16 slots.

System Resources

System resources are the communications channels, addresses, and other signals hardware devices use to communicate on the bus. At their lowest level, these resources typically include the following:

- Memory addresses
- IRQ (interrupt request) channels
- DMA (direct memory access) channels
- I/O port addresses

I have listed these roughly in the order you would experience problems with them. Memory conflicts are perhaps the most troublesome of these and certainly the most difficult to fully explain and overcome. These are discussed in Chapter 6, "Memory." This chapter focuses on the others listed here in the order you will likely have problems with them.

Historically, IRQs have caused more problems than DMAs because they are in much higher demand; virtually all cards use IRQ channels. Fewer problems exist with DMA channels because fewer cards use them, DMA channels are used only by the obsolete ISA standard, and there are usually more than enough channels to go around. I/O ports are used by all hardware devices on the bus, but there are technically 64KB of them, which means there are plenty to go around. For any individual resource that is used, you must ensure that only a single card or hardware function uses the given resource; in most cases they cannot or should not be shared.

These resources are required and used by many components of your system. Adapter cards need these resources to communicate with your system and accomplish their purposes. Not all adapter cards have the same resource requirements. A serial communications port, for example, needs an IRQ channel and I/O port address, whereas a sound card needs these resources and at least one DMA channel. Most network cards use an IRQ channel and an I/O port address, and some also use a 16KB block of memory addresses.

As your system increases in complexity, the chance for resource conflicts increases. Modern systems with several additional devices can really push the envelope and become a configuration nightmare for the uninitiated. Sometimes under these situations the automatic configuration capability of Plug and Play can get confused or fail to optimally configure resources so that everything will work. Most adapter cards enable you to modify resource assignments by using the Plug and Play software that comes with the card or the Device Manager in Windows 9x and later, thus you can sometimes improve on a default configuration by making some changes. Even if the automatic configuration gets confused (which happens more often than it should), fortunately, in almost all cases a logical way to configure the system exists—once you know the rules.

Fortunately, modern systems with ACPI and modern buses like PCI and PCI Express rarely have problems configuring these resources. In virtually all cases the configuration will be automatic and trouble-free.

Interrupts

Interrupt request channels, or hardware interrupts, are used by various hardware devices to signal the motherboard that a request must be fulfilled. This procedure is the same as a student raising his hand to indicate that he needs attention.

These interrupt channels are represented by wires on the motherboard and in the slot connectors. When a particular interrupt is invoked, a special routine takes over the system, which first saves all the CPU register contents in a stack and then directs the system to the interrupt vector table. This vector table contains a list of memory addresses that correspond to the interrupt channels. Depending on which interrupt was invoked, the program corresponding to that channel is run.

The pointers in the vector table point to the address of whatever software driver is used to service the card that generated the interrupt. For a network card, for example, the vector might point to the address of the network drivers that have been loaded to operate the card; for a hard disk controller, the vector might point to the BIOS code that operates the controller.

After the particular software routine finishes performing whatever function the card needed, the interrupt-control software returns the stack contents to the CPU registers, and the system then resumes whatever it was doing before the interrupt occurred.

Through the use of interrupts, your system can respond to external events in a timely fashion. Each time a serial port presents a byte to your system, an interrupt is generated to ensure that the system reads that byte before another comes in. Keep in mind that in some cases a port device—in particular, a modem with a 16550 or higher UART chip—might incorporate a byte buffer that allows multiple characters to be stored before an interrupt is generated.

Hardware interrupts are generally prioritized by their numbers; with some exceptions, the highest-priority interrupts have the lowest numbers. Higher-priority interrupts take precedence over lower-priority interrupts by interrupting them. As a result, several interrupts can occur in your system concurrently, with each interrupt nesting within another.

If you overload the system—in this case, by running out of stack resources (too many interrupts were generated too quickly)—an internal stack overflow error occurs and your system halts. The message usually appears as `Internal stack overflow - system halted` at a DOS prompt. If you experience this type of system error and run DOS, you can compensate for it by using the `STACKS` parameter in your `CONFIG.SYS` file to increase the available stack resources. Most people will not see this error in Windows 9x or later.

The ISA bus uses *edge-triggered* interrupt sensing, in which an interrupt is sensed by a changing signal sent on a particular wire located in the slot connector. A different wire corresponds to each possible hardware interrupt. Because the motherboard can't recognize which slot contains the card that used an interrupt line and therefore generated the interrupt, confusion results if more than one card is set to use a particular interrupt. Each interrupt, therefore, is usually designated for a single hardware device. Most of the time, interrupts can't be shared.

Originally, IBM developed ways to share interrupts on the ISA bus, but few devices followed the necessary rules to make this a reality. The PCI bus inherently allows interrupt sharing; in fact, virtually all PCI cards are set to PCI interrupt A and share that interrupt on the PCI bus. The real problem is that there are technically two sets of hardware interrupts in the system: PCI interrupts and ISA interrupts. For PCI cards to work in a PC, the PCI interrupts are first mapped to ISA interrupts, which are then configured as non-shareable. Therefore, in many cases you must assign a nonconflicting interrupt for each card, even PCI cards. The conflict between assigning ISA IRQs for PCI interrupts caused many configuration problems for early users of PCI motherboards and continued to cause problems even after the development of Windows 95 and its Plug and Play technology.

The solution to the interrupt sharing problem for PCI cards was something called *PCI IRQ Steering*, which has been supported in operating systems (starting with Windows 95 OSR 2.x) and BIOS for more than a decade. PCI IRQ Steering allows a plug-and-play operating system such as Windows to dynamically map or "steer" PCI cards (which almost all use PCI INTA#) to standard PC interrupts and allows several PCI cards to be mapped to the same interrupt. More information on PCI IRQ Steering is found in the section "PCI Interrupts," later in this chapter.

Hardware interrupts are sometimes referred to as *maskable interrupts*, which means the interrupts can be masked or turned off for a short time while the CPU is used for other critical operations. It is up to the system BIOS and programs to manage interrupts properly and efficiently for the best system performance.

Because interrupts usually can't be shared in an ISA bus system, you often run into conflicts and can even run out of interrupts when you are adding boards to a system. If two boards or onboard devices use the same IRQ to signal the system, the resulting conflict prevents either board from operating properly. The following sections discuss the IRQs that any standard devices use, as well as what might be free in your system.

8-Bit ISA Bus Interrupts

The PC and XT (the systems based on the 8-bit 8086 CPU) provide for eight different external hardware interrupts. Table 4.78 shows the typical uses for these interrupts, which are numbered 0–7.

Table 4.78   8-Bit ISA Bus Default Interrupt Assignments

IRQ	Function	Bus Slot
0	System Timer	No
1	Keyboard Controller	No
2	Available	Yes (8-bit)
3	Serial Port 2 (COM2:)	Yes (8-bit)
4	Serial Port 1 (COM1:)	Yes (8-bit)
5	Hard Disk Controller	Yes (8-bit)
6	Floppy Disk Controller	Yes (8-bit)
7	Parallel Port 1 (LPT1:)	Yes (8-bit)

If you have a system that has one of the original 8-bit ISA buses, you will find that the IRQ resources provided by the system present a severe limitation. Installing several devices that need the services of system IRQs in a PC/XT-type system can be a study in frustration because the only way to resolve the interrupt-shortage problem is to remove the adapter board that you need the least.

16-Bit ISA, EISA, and MCA Bus Interrupts

The introduction of the AT, based on the 286 processor, was accompanied by an increase in the number of external hardware interrupts the bus would support. The number of interrupts was doubled to 16 by using two Intel 8259 interrupt controllers, piping the interrupts generated by the second one through the unused IRQ2 in the first controller. This arrangement effectively makes only 15 IRQ assignments available, and IRQ2 effectively became inaccessible.

By routing all the interrupts from the second IRQ controller through IRQ2 on the first, all these new interrupts are assigned a nested priority level between IRQ1 and IRQ3. Thus, IRQ15 ends up having a higher priority than IRQ3. Figure 4.80 shows how the two 8259 chips were wired to create the cascade through IRQ2 on the first chip.

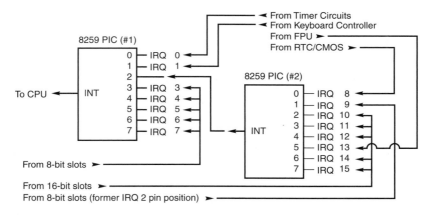

Figure 4.80   Interrupt controller cascade wiring.

To prevent problems with boards set to use IRQ2, the AT system designers routed one of the new interrupts (IRQ9) to fill the slot position left open after removing IRQ2. This means that any card you install in a modern system that claims to use IRQ2 is really using IRQ9 instead.

Table 4.79 shows the typical uses for interrupts in the 16-bit ISA and 32-bit PCI/AGP buses and lists them in priority order from highest to lowest. The obsolete EISA and MCA buses used a similar IRQ map.

Table 4.79   16/32-Bit ISA/PCI/AGP Default Interrupt Assignments

IRQ	Standard Function	Bus Slot	Card Type	Recommended Use
0	System Timer	No	—	—
1	Keyboard Controller	No	—	—
2	2nd IRQ Controller Cascade	No	—	—
8	Real-Time Clock	No	—	—
9	Avail. (as IRQ2 or IRQ9)	Yes	8/16-bit	Network Card
10	Available	Yes	16-bit	USB
11	Available	Yes	16-bit	SCSI Host Adapter
12	Mouse Port/Available	Yes	16-bit	Mouse Port

Table 4.79   Continued

IRQ	Standard Function	Bus Slot	Card Type	Recommended Use
13	Math Coprocessor	No	—	—
14	Primary IDE	Yes	16-bit	Primary IDE (hard disks)
15	Secondary IDE	Yes	16-bit	2nd IDE (CD-ROM/Tape)
3	Serial 2 (COM2:)	Yes	8/16-bit	COM2:/Internal Modem
4	Serial 1 (COM1:)	Yes	8/16-bit	COM1:
5	Sound/Parallel 2 (LPT2:)	Yes	8/16-bit	Sound Card
6	Floppy Controller	Yes	8/16-bit	Floppy Controller
7	Parallel 1 (LPT1:)	Yes	8/16-bit	LPT1:

Notice that interrupts 0, 1, 2, 8, and 13 are not on the bus connectors and are not accessible to adapter cards. Interrupts 8, 10, 11, 12, 13, 14, and 15 are from the second interrupt controller and are accessible only by boards that use the 16-bit extension connector because this is where these wires are located. IRQ9 is rewired to the 8-bit slot connector in place of IRQ2, so IRQ9 replaces IRQ2 and, therefore, is available to 8-bit cards, which treat it as though it were IRQ2.

Note

Although the 16-bit ISA bus has twice as many interrupts as systems that have the 8-bit ISA bus, you still might run out of available interrupts because only 16-bit adapters can use most of the newly available interrupts. Any 32-bit PCI adapter can be mapped to any ISA IRQs.

The extra IRQ lines in a 16-bit ISA system are of little help unless the adapter boards you plan to use enable you to configure them for one of the unused IRQs. Some devices are hard-wired so they can use only a particular IRQ, and some of the early 16-bit ISA adapters weren't designed to use 16-bit IRQs (9–15). If you have a device that already uses that IRQ, you must resolve the conflict before installing the second adapter. If neither adapter enables you to reconfigure its IRQ use, chances are that you can't use the two devices in the same system.

PCI Interrupts

The PCI bus supports hardware interrupts (IRQs) that can be used by PCI devices to signal to the bus that they need attention. The four PCI interrupts are called INTA#, INTB#, INTC#, and INTD#. These INTx# interrupts are *level-sensitive*, which means that the electrical signaling enables them to be shared among PCI cards. In fact, all single device or single function PCI chips or cards that use only one interrupt must use INTA#. This is one of the rules in the PCI specification. If additional devices are within a chip or onboard a card, the additional devices can use INTB# through INTD#. Because there are very few multifunction PCI chips or boards, practically all the devices on a given PCI bus share INTA#.

For the PCI bus to function in a PC, the PCI interrupts must be mapped to ISA interrupts. Because ISA interrupts can't be shared, in most cases each PCI card using INTA# on the PCI bus must be mapped to a different non-shareable ISA interrupt. For example, you could have a system with four PCI slots and four PCI cards installed, each using PCI interrupt INTA#. These cards would each be mapped to a different available ISA interrupt request, such as IRQ9, IRQ10, IRQ11, or IRQ5 in most cases.

Finding unique IRQs for each device on both the ISA and PCI buses has always been a problem; there simply aren't enough free ones to go around. Setting two ISA devices to the same IRQ has never been possible (the so-called *IRQ sharing* of IRQ4 by COM1/3 and IRQ3 by COM2/4 didn't allow both COM ports to work at the same time), but on most newer systems sharing IRQs between multiple PCI devices might be possible. Newer system BIOSs as well as plug-and-play operating systems, such as Windows 95B (OSR 2) or later, Windows 98, and Windows 2000/XP, all support a function known as PCI IRQ Steering. For this to work, both your system BIOS and operating system must support IRQ Steering. Older system BIOSs and Windows 95 or 95A do not have support for PCI IRQ Steering.

Generally, the BIOS assigns unique IRQs to PCI devices. If your system supports PCI IRQ Steering and it is enabled, Windows assigns IRQs to PCI devices. Even when IRQ Steering is enabled, the BIOS still initially assigns IRQs to PCI devices. Although Windows has the capability to change these settings, it typically does not do so automatically, except where necessary to eliminate conflicts. If there are insufficient free IRQs to go around, IRQ Steering allows Windows to assign multiple PCI devices to a single IRQ, thus enabling all the devices in the system to function properly. Without IRQ Steering, Windows begins to disable devices after it runs out of free IRQs to assign.

To determine whether your Windows 9x/Me system is using IRQ Steering, you can follow these steps:

1. Open the Device Manager.
2. Double-click the System Devices branch.
3. Double-click the PCI Bus, and then click the IRQ Steering tab. There will be a check that displays IRQ Steering as either Enabled or Disabled. If enabled, it also specifies where the IRQ table has been read from.

Note that with Windows 2000, XP, and Vista, you can't disable IRQ Steering and no IRQ Steering tab appears in the Device Manager.

IRQ Steering is controlled by one of four routing tables Windows attempts to read. Windows searches for the tables in order and uses the first one it finds. You can't control the order in which Windows searches for these tables, but by selecting or deselecting the Get IRQ Table Using check boxes, you can control which table Windows finds first by disabling the search for specific tables. Windows searches for the following tables:

- ACPI BIOS table
- MS Specification table
- Protected Mode PCIBIOS 2.1 table
- Real Mode PCIBIOS 2.1 table

Windows first tries to use the ACPI BIOS table to program IRQ Steering, followed by the MS Specification table, the Protected Mode PCIBIOS 2.1 table, and the Real Mode PCIBIOS 2.1 table. Windows 95 OSR2 and later versions offer only a choice for selecting the PCIBIOS 2.1 tables via a single check box, which is disabled by default. Under Windows 98, all IRQ table choices are selected by default, except the third one, which is the Protected Mode PCIBIOS 2.1 table.

If you are having a problem with a PCI device related to IRQ settings under Windows 95, try selecting the PCIBIOS 2.1 table and restarting. Under Windows 98, try clearing the ACPI BIOS table selection and restarting. If the problem persists, try selecting the Protected Mode PCIBIOS 2.1 table and restarting. You should select Get IRQ Table from Protected Mode PCIBIOS 2.1 Call only if a PCI device is not working properly. To access these settings in the Windows 98 Device Manager, do the following:

1. Open the Device Manager.
2. Scroll down to the System Devices category, and double-click to open it.

3. Select PCI Bus and click Properties.

4. Click the IRQ Steering tab to see or change the current settings.

If IRQ Steering is shown as disabled in Device Manager, be sure the Use IRQ Steering check box is selected. After you select this and restart, if IRQ Steering is still showing as disabled, the IRQ routing table that must be provided by the BIOS to the operating system might be missing or contain errors. Check your BIOS Setup to ensure PCI IRQ Steering is enabled. If there is still no success, you might have to select the Get IRQ Table from Protected Mode PCIBIOS 2.1 Call check box, or your BIOS might not support PCI bus IRQ Steering. Contact the manufacturer of your motherboard or BIOS to see whether your board or BIOS supports IRQ Steering.

On systems that have support for IRQ Steering, an IRQ Holder for PCI Steering might be displayed when you view the System Devices branch of Device Manager. This indicates that an IRQ has been mapped to PCI and is unavailable for ISA devices, even if no PCI devices are currently using the IRQ. To view IRQs programmed for PCI-mode, follow these steps:

1. Select Start, Settings, Control Panel, and then double-click System.

2. Click the Device Manager tab.

3. Double-click the System Devices branch.

4. Double-click the IRQ Holder for PCI Steering you want to view, and then click the Resources tab.

I have found this interrupt steering or mapping to be the source of a great deal of confusion. Even though PCI interrupts (INTx#) can be (and are by default) shared, each card or device that might be sharing a PCI interrupt must be mapped or steered to a unique ISA IRQ, which in turn can't normally be shared. You can have several PCI devices mapped to the same ISA IRQ only if

- No ISA devices are using the IRQ.
- The BIOS and operating system support PCI IRQ Steering.
- PCI IRQ Steering is enabled.

Without PCI IRQ Steering support, the sharing capabilities of the PCI interrupts are of little benefit because all PCI-to-ISA IRQ assignments must then be unique. Without PCI IRQ Steering, you can easily run out of available ISA interrupts. If IRQ Steering is supported and enabled, multiple PCI devices will be capable of sharing a single IRQ, allowing for more system expansion without running out of available IRQs. Better support for IRQ Steering is one of the best reasons for upgrading to Windows 98 or newer versions, especially if you are using the original OSR1 release of 95.

Another source of confusion is that the interrupt listing shown in the Windows 9x Device Manager might show the PCI-to-ISA interrupt mapping as multiple entries for a given ISA interrupt. One entry would be for the device actually mapped to the interrupt—for example, a built-in USB controller—whereas the other entry for the same IRQ would say IRQ Holder for PCI Steering. This latter entry, despite claiming to use the same IRQ, does not indicate a resource conflict; instead it represents the chipset circuitry putting a reservation on that interrupt for mapping purposes. This is part of the plug-and-play capabilities of PCI and the modern motherboard chipsets. Windows 2000 and later can also map multiple devices to the same IRQ, but they don't use the term *IRQ Holder* to avoid confusion.

Note that you can have internal devices on the PCI bus even though all the PCI slots are free. For example, most systems today have two IDE controllers and at least one USB controller as devices on the PCI bus. Normally, the PCI IDE controllers are mapped to ISA interrupts 14 (primary IDE) and 15 (secondary IDE), whereas the USB controller can be mapped to the available ISA interrupts 9, 10, 11, and 5. Many recent systems have two or more USB controllers (typically one per every two USB ports), so each USB controller needs to be mapped to an ISA interrupt.

▶▶ See "Universal Serial Bus," p. 1031.

The PCI bus enables two types of devices to exist, called *bus masters* (initiators) and *slaves* (targets). A bus master is a device that can take control of the bus and initiate a transfer. The target device is the intended destination of the transfer. Most PCI devices can act as both masters and targets, and to be compliant with the PC'97 and newer system design guides, all PCI slots must support bus master cards.

The PCI bus is an arbitrated bus: A central arbiter (part of the PCI bus controller in the motherboard chipset) governs all bus transfers, giving fair and controlled access to all the devices on the bus. Before a master can use the bus, it must first request control from the central arbiter, and then it is granted control for only a specified maximum number of cycles. This arbitration allows equal and fair access to all the bus master devices, prevents a single device from hogging the bus, and also prevents dead-locks because of simultaneous multiple device access. In this manner, the PCI bus acts much like a local area network (LAN), albeit one that is contained entirely within the system and runs at a much higher speed than conventional external networks between PCs.

Advanced Programmable Interrupt Controller

As a replacement for the traditional pair of 8259 interrupt controllers, Intel developed the Advanced Programmable Interrupt Controller (APIC) in the mid-1990s. Although all processors since the original Pentium contain an APIC, an APIC must also be present in the motherboard's chipset, and the BIOS and operating system must also support APIC. APIC support is present on most recent motherboards and has been supported in all Windows releases since Windows 2000. You can enable or disable APIC support in the system BIOS.

APIC provides support for multiple processors, but it is also used on single-processor computers. The major benefit of APIC for a single processor is support for virtual PCI IRQs above 15. Most APIC implementations support virtual IRQs up to 24. Although Windows 2000 tends to place PCI IRQs into the traditional ISA range of 0–15, even when APIC is enabled, Windows XP and Vista make full use of APIC services when installed on a system with APIC enabled. With Windows XP and Vista, APIC limits IRQ sharing to enable devices to perform better with fewer conflicts. For example, on one typical system with APIC enabled, PCI IRQs are assigned as follows:

- **PCI IRQ 16**—Onboard audio/AGP graphics (shared)
- **PCI IRQ 17**—Add-on card USB 1.1 controller (nonshared)
- **PCI IRQ 18**—Add-on card USB 1.1 controller (nonshared)
- **PCI IRQ 19**—10/100 Ethernet adapter/add-on card USB 2.0 controller (shared)
- **PCI IRQ 21**—Onboard USB 1.1 controllers (3)/onboard USB 2.0 controller (shared)

The traditional ISA IRQs 0–15 on the sample system are used only for ISA devices, thus preventing ISA-PCI IRQ conflicts.

APIC must be enabled in the system BIOS when Windows 2000, XP or Vista is installed to make APIC services available.

Note

APIC must be enabled in the system BIOS before x64 editions of Windows XP, 2003, or Vista can be installed.

IRQ Conflicts

One of the more common IRQ conflicts in older systems is the potential one between the integrated COM2: port found in most modern motherboards and an internal (card-based) ISA modem. The problem stems from the fact that true PC card-based modems (not the so-called WinModems, which are software based) incorporate a serial port as part of the card's circuitry. This serial port is set as COM2: by default. Your PC sees this as having two COM2: ports, each using the same IRQ and I/O port address resources.

The solution to this problem is easy: Enter the system BIOS Setup and disable the built-in COM2: port in the system. While you are there, you might think about disabling the COM1: port too, because you are unlikely to use it. Disabling unused COMx: ports is one of the best ways to free up a couple of IRQs for other devices to use.

Another common IRQ conflict also involves serial (COM) ports. You might have noticed in the preceding two sections that two IRQs are set aside for two COM ports. IRQ3 is used for COM2:, and IRQ4 is used for COM1:. The problem occurs when you have more than two serial ports in a system. When people add COM3: and COM4: ports, they often don't set them to nonconflicting interrupts, which results in a conflict and the ports not working.

Contributing to the problem are poorly designed COM port boards that do not allow IRQ settings other than 3 or 4. What happens is that they end up setting COM3: to IRQ4 (sharing it with COM1:), and COM4: to IRQ3 (sharing it with COM2:). This is not acceptable because it prevents you from using the two COM ports on any one of the interrupt channels simultaneously. This was somewhat acceptable under plain DOS because single-tasking (running only one program at a time) was the order of the day, but it is totally unacceptable under Windows. If you must share IRQs, you can usually get away with sharing devices on the same IRQ as long as they use different COM ports. For instance, a scanner and an internal modem could share an IRQ, but if the two devices are used simultaneously, a conflict results. Fortunately, most devices that formerly used serial ports (such as mice and other pointing devices, label printers, external modems, and PDA cradles) have been redesigned to use USB ports. Therefore, many users no longer have any devices that must be plugged into a serial port.

If you need to use serial ports, the best solution is to purchase a multiport serial I/O card that allows nonconflicting interrupt settings or an intelligent card with its own processor that can handle the multiple ports onboard and use only one interrupt in the system. Some older multiport serial cards used the ISA slot, but PCI-slot cards have replaced these in recent systems and have the additional advantages of faster speed and a sharable interrupt.

▶▶ See "Serial Ports," p. 1046.

If a device listed in the table is not present, such as the motherboard mouse port (IRQ12) or parallel port 2 (IRQ5), you can consider those interrupts as available. For example, a second parallel port is a rarity, and most systems have a sound card installed and set for IRQ5 (if it is used to emulate a SoundBlaster Pro or 16). Also, on most systems IRQ15 is assigned to a secondary IDE controller. If you do not have an IDE hard or optical drive connected to the secondary controller, you could disable the secondary IDE controller to free up that IRQ for another device.

Note that an easy way to check your interrupt settings is to use the Device Manager in Windows. By double-clicking the Computer Properties icon in the Device Manager, you can get concise lists of all used system resources. Microsoft has also included a program called HWDIAG on Windows 95B; Windows 98 and above feature the System Information program. HWDIAG and System Information do an excellent job of reporting system resource usage, as well as details about device drivers and Windows Registry entries for each hardware component. If you are running Windows XP or Vista, a program called MSinfo32 will also give you a report of detailed system information.

To provide the maximum number of shareable interrupts in a recent system without ISA slots, I recommend performing the following steps in the system BIOS:

1. Disable any unused legacy ports in the system BIOS. For example, if you use USB ports instead of serial and parallel ports, disable the serial and parallel ports. This can free up as many as three IRQs.

2. Select the IRQs freed up in step 1 as available for PCI/PnP use. Depending on the BIOS, the screen to use might be known as the PnP/PCI Resource Exclusion screen or the PnP/PCI Configuration screen.

3. Enable the Reset Configuration Data option so the IRQ routing tables in the CMOS are cleared.

4. Save your changes and exit the BIOS setup program.

DMA Channels

Direct memory access (DMA) channels are used by communications devices that must send and receive information at high speeds. A serial or parallel port does not use a DMA channel, but an ISA-based sound card or SCSI adapter often does. DMA channels sometimes can be shared if the devices are not the type that would need them simultaneously. For example, you can have a network adapter and a tape backup adapter sharing DMA channel 1, but you can't back up while the network is running. To back up during network operation, you must ensure that each adapter uses a unique DMA channel.

Note

There are several types of DMA in a modern PC. The DMA channels referred to in this section involve the ISA bus. Other buses, such as the ATA/IDE bus used by hard drives, have different DMA uses. The DMA channels explained here don't involve your ATA/IDE drives, even if they are set to use DMA or Ultra DMA transfers.

8-Bit ISA Bus DMA Channels

In the 8-bit ISA bus, four DMA channels support high-speed data transfers between I/O devices and memory. Three of the channels are available to the expansion slots. Table 4.80 shows the typical uses of these DMA channels.

Table 4.80   8-Bit ISA Default DMA-Channel Assignments

DMA	Standard Function	Bus Slot
0	Dynamic RAM Refresh	No
1	Available	Yes (8-bit)
2	Floppy disk controller	Yes (8-bit)
3	Hard disk controller	Yes (8-bit)

Because most systems typically have both a floppy and hard disk drive, only one DMA channel is available in 8-bit ISA systems.

16-Bit ISA DMA Channels

Since the introduction of the 286 CPU, the ISA bus has supported eight DMA channels, with seven channels available to the expansion slots. Similar to the expanded IRQ lines described earlier in this chapter, the added DMA channels were created by cascading a second DMA controller to the first one.

DMA channel 4 is used to cascade channels 0–3 to the microprocessor. Channels 0–3 are available for 8-bit transfers, and channels 5–7 are for 16-bit transfers only. Table 4.81 shows the typical uses for the DMA channels.

Table 4.81   16-Bit ISA Default DMA-Channel Assignments

DMA	Standard Function	Bus Slot	Card Type	Transfer	Recommended Use
0	Available	Yes	16-bit	8-bit	Sound
1	Available	Yes	8/16-bit	8-bit	Sound
2	Floppy Disk Controller	Yes	8/16-bit	8-bit	Floppy Controller
3	Available	Yes	8/16-bit	8-bit	LPT1: in ECP Mode
4	1st DMA Controller Cascade	No	—	16-bit	—
5	Available	Yes	16-bit	16-bit	Sound
6	Available	Yes	16-bit	16-bit	Available
7	Available	Yes	16-bit	16-bit	Available

Note that PCI adapters don't use these ISA DMA channels; these are only for ISA cards. However, some PCI cards emulate the use of these DMA channels (such as sound cards) to work with older software.

The only standard DMA channel used in all systems is DMA 2, which is universally used by the floppy controller. DMA 4 is not usable and does not appear in the bus slots. DMA channels 1 and 5 are most commonly used by ISA sound cards, such as the Sound Blaster 16, or by newer PCI sound cards that emulate an older one for backward compatibility. These cards use both an 8-bit and a 16-bit DMA channel for high-speed transfers. DMA 3 is used when a parallel port is configured to work in ECP mode or EPP/ECP mode. Some nonstandard systems, such as older Packard Bell computers, use DMA 1 instead of DMA 3 for the parallel port by default. However, a jumper block on the motherboard on many of these systems can be set to use DMA 3 for the parallel port and avoid conflicts with sound cards that use DMA 1.

Note

Although DMA channel 0 appears in a 16-bit slot connector extension and therefore can be used only by a 16-bit card, it performs only 8-bit transfers! Because of this, you generally don't see DMA 0 as a choice on 16-bit cards. Most 16-bit cards (such as SCSI host adapters) that use DMA channels have their choices limited to DMA 5–7.

I/O Port Addresses

Your computer's I/O ports enable communications between devices and software in your system. They are equivalent to two-way radio channels. If you want to talk to your serial port, you need to know on which I/O port (radio channel) it is listening. Similarly, if you want to receive data from the serial port, you need to listen on the same channel on which it is transmitting.

Unlike IRQs and DMA channels, our systems have an abundance of I/O ports. There are exactly 65,536 ports—numbered from 0000h to FFFFh—which is a feature of the Intel x86 processor design. Even though most devices use up to eight ports for themselves, with that many to spare, you won't run out anytime soon. The biggest problem you have to worry about is setting two devices to use the same port.

Most modern plug-and-play systems resolve any port conflicts and select alternative ports for one of the conflicting devices.

One confusing issue is that I/O ports are designated by hexadecimal addresses similar to memory addresses. They are not memory; they are ports. The difference is that when you send data to memory address 1000h, it gets stored in your SIMM or DIMM memory. If you send data to I/O port address 1000h, it gets sent out on the bus on that "channel," and anybody listening in could then "hear" it. If nobody is listening to that port address, the data reaches the end of the bus and is absorbed by the bus terminating resistors.

Driver programs are primarily what interact with devices at the various port addresses. The driver must know which ports the device is using to work with it, and vice versa. That is not usually a problem because the driver and device come from the same company.

Motherboard and chipset devices usually are set to use I/O port addresses 0h–FFh, and all other devices use 100h–FFFFh. Table 4.82 shows the commonly used motherboard and chipset-based I/O port usage.

Table 4.82   Motherboard and Chipset-Based Device Port Addresses

Address (hex)	Size	Description
0000–000F	16 bytes	Chipset – 8237 DMA 1
0020–0021	2 bytes	Chipset – 8259 interrupt controller 1
002E–002F	2 bytes	Super I/O controller configuration registers
0040–0043	4 bytes	Chipset – Counter/Timer 1
0048–004B	4 bytes	Chipset – Counter/Timer 2
0060	1 byte	Keyboard/Mouse controller byte – reset IRQ
0061	1 byte	Chipset – NMI, speaker control
0064	1 byte	Keyboard/Mouse controller, CMD/STAT byte
0070, bit 7	1 bit	Chipset – Enable NMI
0070, bits 6:0	7 bits	MC146818 – Real-time clock, address
0071	1 byte	MC146818 – Real-time clock, data
0078	1 byte	Reserved – Board configuration
0079	1 byte	Reserved – Board configuration
0080–008F	16 bytes	Chipset – DMA page registers
00A0–00A1	2 bytes	Chipset – 8259 interrupt controller 2
00B2	1 byte	APM control port
00B3	1 byte	APM status port
00C0–00DE	31 bytes	Chipset – 8237 DMA 2
00F0	1 byte	Math Coprocessor Reset Numeric Error

To find out exactly which port addresses are being used on your motherboard, consult the board documentation or look up these settings in the Windows Device Manager.

Bus-based devices typically use the addresses from 100h on up. Table 4.83 lists the commonly used bus-based device addresses and some common adapter cards and their settings.

Table 4.83 Bus-Based Device Port Addresses

Address (hex)	Size	Description
0130–0133	4 bytes	Adaptec SCSI adapter (alternate)
0134–0137	4 bytes	Adaptec SCSI adapter (alternate)
0168–016F	8 bytes	Fourth IDE interface
0170–0177	8 bytes	Secondary IDE interface
01E8–01EF	8 bytes	Third IDE interface
01F0–01F7	8 bytes	Primary IDE/AT (16-bit) hard disk controller
0200–0207	8 bytes	Gameport or joystick adapter
0210–0217	8 bytes	IBM XT expansion chassis
0220–0233	20 bytes	Creative Labs Sound Blaster 16 audio (default)
0230–0233	4 bytes	Adaptec SCSI adapter (alternate)
0234–0237	4 bytes	Adaptec SCSI adapter (alternate)
0238–023B	4 bytes	MS bus mouse (alternate)
023C–023F	4 bytes	MS bus mouse (default)
0240–024F	16 bytes	SMC Ethernet adapter (default)
0240–0253	20 bytes	Creative Labs Sound Blaster 16 audio (alternate)
0258–025F	8 bytes	Intel above board
0260–026F	16 bytes	SMC Ethernet adapter (alternate)
0260–0273	20 bytes	Creative Labs Sound Blaster 16 audio (alternate)
0270–0273	4 bytes	Plug and Play I/O read ports
0278–027F	8 bytes	Parallel port 2 (LPT2)
0280–028F	16 bytes	SMC Ethernet adapter (alternate)
0280–0293	20 bytes	Creative Labs Sound Blaster 16 audio (alternate)
02A0–02AF	16 bytes	SMC Ethernet adapter (alternate)
02C0–02CF	16 bytes	SMC Ethernet adapter (alternate)
02E0–02EF	16 bytes	SMC Ethernet adapter (alternate)
02E8–02EF	8 bytes	Serial port 4 (COM4)
02EC–02EF	4 bytes	Video, 8514, or ATI standard ports
02F8–02FF	8 bytes	Serial port 2 (COM2)
0300–0301	2 bytes	MPU-401 MIDI port (secondary)
0300–030F	16 bytes	SMC Ethernet adapter (alternate)
0320–0323	4 bytes	XT (8-bit) hard disk controller
0320–032F	16 bytes	SMC Ethernet adapter (alternate)
0330–0331	2 bytes	MPU-401 MIDI port (default)
0330–0333	4 bytes	Adaptec SCSI adapter (default)
0334–0337	4 bytes	Adaptec SCSI adapter (alternate)
0340–034F	16 bytes	SMC Ethernet adapter (alternate)
0360–036F	16 bytes	SMC Ethernet adapter (alternate)
0366	1 byte	Fourth IDE command port

Table 4.83   Continued

Address (hex)	Size	Description
0367, bits 6:0	7 bits	Fourth IDE status port
0370–0375	6 bytes	Secondary floppy controller
0376	1 byte	Secondary IDE command port
0377, bit 7	1 bit	Secondary floppy controller disk change
0377, bits 6:0	7 bits	Secondary IDE status port
0378–037F	8 bytes	Parallel Port 1 (LPT1)
0380–038F	16 bytes	SMC Ethernet adapter (alternate)
0388–038B	4 bytes	Audio – FM synthesizer
03B0–03BB	12 bytes	Video, Mono/EGA/VGA standard ports
03BC–03BF	4 bytes	Parallel port 1 (LPT1) in some systems
03BC–03BF	4 bytes	Parallel port 3 (LPT3)
03C0–03CF	16 bytes	Video, EGA/VGA standard ports
03D0–03DF	16 bytes	Video, CGA/EGA/VGA standard ports
03E6	1 byte	Third IDE command port
03E7, bits 6:0	7 bits	Third IDE status port
03E8–03EF	8 bytes	Serial port 3 (COM3)
03F0–03F5	6 bytes	Primary floppy controller
03F6	1 byte	Primary IDE command port
03F7, bit 7	1 bit	Primary floppy controller disk change
03F7, bits 6:0	7 bits	Primary IDE status port
03F8–03FF	8 bytes	Serial port 1 (COM1)
04D0–04D1	2 bytes	Edge/level triggered PCI interrupt controller
0530–0537	8 bytes	Windows sound system (default)
0604–060B	8 bytes	Windows sound system (alternate)
0678–067F	8 bytes	LPT2 in ECP mode
0778–077F	8 bytes	LPT1 in ECP mode
0A20–0A23	4 bytes	IBM Token-Ring adapter (default)
0A24–0A27	4 bytes	IBM Token-Ring adapter (alternate)
0CF8–0CFB	4 bytes	PCI configuration address registers
0CF9	1 byte	Turbo and reset control register
0CFC–0CFF	4 bytes	PCI configuration data registers
FF00–FF07	8 bytes	IDE bus master registers
FF80–FF9F	32 bytes	Universal serial bus
FFA0–FFA7	8 bytes	Primary bus master IDE registers
FFA8–FFAF	8 bytes	Secondary bus master IDE registers

To find out exactly what your devices are using, again I recommend consulting the documentation for the device or looking up the device in the Windows Device Manager. Note that the documentation for some devices might list only the starting address instead of the full range of I/O port addresses used.

Virtually all devices on the system buses use I/O port addresses. Most of these are fairly standardized, meaning conflicts or problems won't often occur with these settings. In the next section, you learn more about working with I/O addresses.

Resolving Resource Conflicts

The resources in a system are limited. Unfortunately, the demands on those resources seem to be unlimited. As you add more and more adapter cards to your system, you will find that the potential for resource conflicts increases. If your system is fully PnP-compatible, potential conflicts should be resolved automatically, but often are not.

How do you know whether you have a resource conflict? Typically, one of the devices in your system stops working. Resource conflicts can exhibit themselves in other ways, though. Any of the following events could be diagnosed as a resource conflict:

- A device transfers data inaccurately.
- Your system frequently locks up.
- Your sound card doesn't sound quite right.
- Your mouse doesn't work.
- Garbage appears on your video screen for no apparent reason.
- Your printer prints gibberish.
- You can't format a floppy disk.
- The PC starts in Safe mode (Windows 9x/Me) or can start only in Last Known Good Configuration (Windows 2000/XP).

Windows also show conflicts by highlighting a device in yellow or red in the Device Manager representation. By using the Windows Device Manager, you can usually spot the conflicts quickly.

In the following sections, you learn some of the steps you can take to head off resource conflicts or track them down when they occur.

Caution

Be careful when diagnosing resource conflicts; a problem might not be a resource conflict at all, but a computer virus. Many computer viruses are designed to exhibit themselves as glitches or periodic problems. If you suspect a resource conflict, it might be worthwhile to run a virus check first to ensure that the system is clean. This procedure could save you hours of work and frustration.

One way to resolve conflicts is to help prevent them in the first place. Especially if you are building up a new system, you can take several steps to avoid problems. One is to avoid using older ISA devices. By definition, they cannot share IRQs, and that is the resource most in demand. PCI (and AGP) cards can share IRQs with IRQ Steering and as such are a much better choice.

Tip

The serial, PS/2 mouse, and parallel ports still found in most recent systems are all ISA devices that cannot share IRQs. If you no longer use these ports, you can use these devices' IRQs for other devices if you do the following:

- Disable the unused port in the system BIOS.
- Configure the system BIOS to use the IRQ formerly used by the device(s) for PnP configuration (this might be automatic in some systems).

Another way you can help is to install cards in a particular sequence, and not all at once. Modifying the installation sequence often helps because many cards can use only one or two out of a predefined selection of IRQs that is specific to each brand or model of card. When the cards are installed in a controlled sequence, the plug-and-play software can more easily work around IRQ conflicts caused by the default configurations of different cards.

The first time you start up a new system you have assembled or done major upgrades on, the first thing you should check is the BIOS Setup. If you have a setting for PnP Operating System in your BIOS, be sure it is enabled if you are running an operating system with plug-and-play support, such as Windows. Otherwise, make sure it's disabled if you are running an OS that is not plug-and-play, such as Windows NT or Windows 3.x.

On initial startup I recommend a minimum configuration with only the graphics card, memory, and storage drives (floppy, hard disk, CD-ROM, and DVD). This allows for the least possibility of system conflicts in the initial configuration. If your motherboard came with a CD including drivers specific to the chipset or other built-in features of the board, now is the time to load or install them. Complete the configuration of all built-in devices before installing any other cards or external devices.

After the basic system has been configured (and after you have successfully loaded your operating system and any updates or patches), you can then begin adding one device at a time in a specific order. So, you will power down, install the new device, power up, and proceed to install any necessary drivers and configure the device. You'll probably have to restart your system after you are done to fully complete the configuration.

Tip

I sometimes recommend that between installing devices you enter the Device Manager in Windows and print out the resource settings as they are configured at the time. This way you have a record of how the configuration changes during the entire device installation and configuration process.

Here's the loading sequence for additional cards:

1. Sound card
2. Internal or external modem
3. Network card
4. Auxiliary video devices, such as MPEG decoders, 3D accelerators, and so on
5. SCSI adapter
6. Anything else

Normally, using this controlled sequence of configuring or building up your system results in easier integration with fewer conflicts and configuration hassles.

Resolving Conflicts Manually

In the past, the only way to resolve conflicts manually was to take the cover off your system and start changing switches or jumper settings on the adapter cards. Fortunately, this is a bit easier with plug-and-play because all the configuration is done via the Device Manager software included in the operating system. Although some early plug-and-play cards also had jumper switches or setup options to enable them to be configured manually, this feature was found primarily on ISA PnP-compatible cards.

Be sure you write down or print out your current system settings before you start making changes. That way, you will know where you began and can go back to the original configuration (if necessary).

Finally, dig out the manuals for all your adapter boards; you might need them, particularly if they can be configured manually or be switched to PnP mode. Additionally, you could look for more current information online at the manufacturers' websites.

Now you are ready to begin your detective work. As you try various resource settings, keep the following questions in mind; the answers will help you narrow down the conflict areas:

- **When did the conflict first become apparent?** If the conflict occurred after you installed a new adapter card, that new card probably is causing the conflict. If the conflict occurred after you started using new software, the software probably uses a device that is taxing your system's resources in a new way.

- **Are there two similar devices in your system that do not work?** For example, if your modem, integrated serial ports, or mouse—devices that use a COM port—do not work, chances are good that these devices are conflicting with each other.

- **Have other people had the same problem, and if so, how did they resolve it?** Public forums, such as those on CompuServe, Internet newsgroups, and America Online, are great places to find other users who might be able to help you solve the conflict.

Whenever you make changes in your system, reboot and see whether the problem persists. When you believe that you have solved the problem, be sure to test all your software. Fixing one problem often seems to cause another to crop up. The only way to ensure that all problems are resolved is to test everything in your system.

One of the best pieces of advice I can give you is to try changing one thing at a time, and then retest. That is the most methodical and simplest way to isolate a problem quickly and efficiently.

As you attempt to resolve your resource conflicts, you should work with and update a system-configuration template, as discussed in the following section.

Using a System-configuration Template

A *system-configuration template* is helpful because remembering something that is written down is easier than keeping it in your head. To create a configuration template, you need to start writing down which resources are used by which parts of your system. Then, when you need to make a change or add an adapter, you can quickly determine where conflicts might arise. You can also use the Windows Device Manager to list and print this information.

I like to use a worksheet split into three main areas—one for interrupts, another for DMA channels, and a middle area for devices that do not use interrupts. Each section lists the IRQ or DMA channel on the left and the I/O port device range on the right. This way, I get the clearest picture of which resources are used and which ones are available in a given system.

The next page shows the system-configuration template I have developed over the years and still use almost daily.

This type of configuration sheet is resource-based instead of component-based. Each row in the template represents a different resource and lists the component using the resource as well as the resources used. The chart has pre-entered all the fixed items in a modern PC for which the configuration cannot be changed.

To fill out this type of chart, you would perform the following steps:

1. Enter the default resources used by standard components, such as serial and parallel ports, disk controllers, and video. You can use the filled-out example I have provided to see how most standard devices are configured.

2. Enter the default resources used by additional add-on components, such as sound cards, SCSI cards, network cards, proprietary cards, and so on. In the case of PnP hardware, there are no real defaults. Instead, use Windows Device Manager or comparable diagnostic programs to determine the settings used for the device.

3. Change any configuration items that are in conflict. Try to leave built-in devices at their default settings, as well as sound cards. Other installed adapters might have their settings changed, but be sure to document the changes.

Of course, a template such as this is best used when first installing components, not after. After you have it completely filled out to match your system, you can label it and keep it with the system. Whenever you add more devices, the template will be your guide as to how any new devices should be configured if you need to configure devices manually.

Note

Thanks to plug-and-play configuration, the days of fixed IRQ and other hardware resources are over. Don't be surprised if your system has assigned different IRQ, I/O port address, or DMA settings after you install a new card. That's why I recommend recording information both before and after you add a new device to your system.

You also might want to track which PCI slot is used by a particular card because some systems convert PCI IRQs to different ISA IRQs depending on which slot is used for a card. Also, some systems pair PCI slots or might pair the AGP slot and a PCI slot, assigning cards installed in both paired slots to the same ISA IRQ. Check the system or motherboard documentation to determine which slots and onboard devices share a particular IRQ.

Page 427 shows the same template filled out for a typical PC system with a mixture of PCI and ISA devices.

System Resource Map

PC Make and Model: _____

Serial Number: _____

Date: _____

Interrupts (IRQs):

  0 - Timer Circuits _____

  1 - Keyboard/Mouse Controller _____

  2 - 2nd 8259 IRQ Controller _____

  8 - Real-time Clock/CMOS RAM _____

  9 - _____

10 - _____

11 - _____

12 - _____

13 - Math Coprocessor _____

14 - _____

15 - _____

  3 - _____

  4 - _____

  5 - _____

  6 - _____

  7 - _____

I/O Port Addresses:

040-04B _____

060 & 064 _____

0A0-0A1 _____

070-071 _____

0F0 _____

Virtual IRQs (used by PCI devices only):

16 - _____

17 - _____

18 - _____

19 - _____

20 - _____

21 - _____

22 - _____

23 - _____

24 - _____

DMA Channels:

0 - _____

1 - _____

2 - _____

3 - _____

4 - DMA Channel 0-3 Cascade_____

5 - _____

6 - _____

7 - _____

Devices Not Using Interrupts:_____

      Mono/EGA/VGA Standard Ports _____

      EGA/VGA Standard Ports _____

      CGA/EGA/VGA Standard Ports _____

      _____

      _____

      _____

      _____

I/O Port Addresses:

3B0-3BB _____

3C0-3CF _____

3D0-3DF _____

_____

_____

_____

_____

System Resource Map

PC Make and Model: Intel SE440BX-2 _____

Serial Number: 100000 _____

Date: 06/09/99 _____

Interrupts (IRQs):

		I/O Port Addresses:
0	- Timer Circuits _____	040-04B _____
0	- Timer Circuits _____	040-04B _____
1	- Keyboard/Mouse Controller _____	060 & 064 _____
2	- 2nd 8259 IRQ Controller _____	0A0-0A1 _____
8	- Real-time Clock/CMOS RAM _____	070-071 _____
9	- SMC EtherEZ Ethernet Card _____	340-35F _____
10	- _____	_____
11	- Adaptec 1542CF SCSI Adapter (scanner)334-337[1]	
12	- Motherboard Mouse Port_____	060 and 064 _____
13	- Math Coprocessor _____	0F0 _____
14	- Primary IDE (hard disk 1 and 2) _____	1F0-1F7, 3F6 _____
15	- Secondary IDE (CD-ROM/tape) _____	170-177, 376 _____
3	- Serial Port 2 (Modem) _____	3F8-3FF _____
4	- Serial Port 1 (COM1) _____	2F8-2FF _____
5	- Sound Blaster 16 Audio _____	220-233 _____
6	- Floppy Controller _____	3F0-3F5 _____
7	- Parallel Port 1 (Printer)_____	378-37F _____

Devices Not Using Interrupts:

	I/O Port Addresses:
Mono/EGA/VGA Standard Ports _____	3B0-3BB _____
Mono/EGA/VGA Standard Ports _____	3B0-3BB _____
EGA/VGA Standard Ports _____	3C0-3CF _____
CGA/EGA/VGA Standard Ports _____	3D0-3DF _____
ATI Mach 64 Video Card Additional Ports ____	102,1CE-1CF, 2EC-2EF _____
Sound Blaster 16 MIDI Port_____	330-331 _____
Sound Blaster 16 Game Port (joystick) _____	200-207 _____
Sound Blaster 16 FM Synthesizer (music) _____	388-38B _____
_____	_____

DMA Channels:

0	- _____
1	- Sound Blaster 16 (8-bit DMA) _____
2	- Floppy Controller _____
3	- Parallel Port 1 (in ECP mode) _____
4	- DMA Channel 0-3 Cascade _____
5	- Sound Blaster 16 (16-bit DMA) _____
6	- Adaptec 1542CF SCSI Adapter[1] _____
7	- _____

1. Represents a resource setting that had to be changed to resolve a conflict.

As you can see from this template, only one IRQ and two DMA channels remain available, and that would be *no* IRQs if I enabled the USB on the motherboard! As you can see, interrupt shortages are a big problem in modern systems, particularly when ISA and PCI devices are in use. In that case, I would probably find a way to recover one of the other interrupts; for example, I am not really using COM1:, so I could disable that port and gain back IRQ4. In this sample configuration, the primary and secondary IDE connectors were built into the motherboard:

- Floppy controller
- Two serial ports
- One parallel port

Whether these devices are built into the motherboard or on a separate card makes no difference because the resource allocations are the same in either case. All default settings are typically used for these devices and are indicated in the completed configuration. Next, the accessory cards were configured. In this example, the following cards were installed:

- SVGA video card (ATI Mach 64)
- Sound card (Creative Labs Sound Blaster 16)
- SCSI host adapter (Adaptec AHA-1542CF)
- Network interface card (SMC EtherEZ)

It helps to install the cards in this order. Start with the video card; next, add the sound card. Because of problems with software that must be configured to the sound card, it is best to install it early and ensure that only default settings are used. It is better to change settings on cards other than the sound card.

After the sound card, the SCSI adapter was installed; however, the default I/O port addresses (330–331) and DMA channel (DMA 5) used were in conflict with other cards (mainly the sound card). These settings were changed to their next logical settings that did not cause a conflict.

Finally, the network card was installed, which also had default settings that conflicted with other cards. In this case, the Ethernet card came preconfigured to IRQ3, which was already in use by COM2:. The solution was to change the setting, and IRQ9 was the next logical choice in the card's configuration settings.

Even though this is a fully loaded configuration, only three individual items among all the cards had to be changed to achieve an optimum system configuration. As you can see, using a configuration template such as the one shown can make what would otherwise be a jumble of settings lay out in an easy-to-follow manner. The only real problems you will run into after you work with these templates are cards that do not allow for enough adjustment in their settings or cards that are lacking in documentation. As you can imagine, you will need the documentation for each adapter card, as well as the motherboard, to accurately complete a configuration table such as the one shown.

Tip

Do not rely too much on third-party DOS-based software diagnostics, such as MSD.EXE, which claim to be capable of showing hardware settings such as IRQ and I/O port settings. Even though they can be helpful in certain situations, they are often wrong with respect to at least some of the information they display about your system. One or two items shown incorrectly can be very troublesome if you believe the incorrect information and configure your system based on it!

Some third-party products such as AMIDiag and CheckIt do a better job, but a much better utility to view these settings is the Device Manager built into Windows. With plug-and-play hardware, it not only reports settings, but it allows you to change them in some cases (sometimes this requires moving the card to another PCI slot). On older legacy hardware, you can view the settings but not change them. To change the settings of legacy (non-plug-and-play) hardware, you must manually move jumpers or switches and run the special configuration software that came with the card. Consult the card manufacturer or documentation for more information.

Heading Off Problems: Special Boards

A number of devices that you might want to install in a computer system require IRQ lines or DMA channels, which means that a world of conflict could be waiting in the box the device comes in. As mentioned in the preceding section, you can save yourself problems if you use a system-configuration template to keep track of the way your system is configured.

You also can save yourself trouble by carefully reading the documentation for a new adapter board before you attempt to install it, particularly if you are still using ISA boards. The documentation details the IRQ lines the board can use as well as its DMA channel requirements. In addition, the documentation details the adapter's upper-memory needs for ROM and adapter.

Note

Although PCI cards also use all the resources discussed earlier except DMA channels, most are designed to use any available resource. Thus, the resources used by a particular PCI card are controlled less by the card's design than by the configuration of the particular system in use. For example, if IRQ3 or IRQ4 (normally set aside for use by COM2: and COM1:) are not used by COM ports and are made available for PCI/PnP use on a given system, a PCI card might use one of these IRQs. However, on a system that has only IRQ9, IRQ10, and IRQ11 available for PCI/PnP configuration, the identical card might use one of these IRQs instead. In addition, some systems assign different IRQs to different PCI expansion slots.

The following sections describe some of the conflicts you might encounter when you install some popular adapter boards. Although the list of adapter boards covered in these sections is far from comprehensive, the sections serve as a guide to installing complex hardware with minimum hassle. Included are tips on soundboards, SCSI host adapters, and network adapters.

Sound Cards

Sound cards are probably the biggest single resource hog in your system. They typically use at least one IRQ, two DMA channels (in DOS emulation mode), and multiple I/O port address ranges. This is because a sound card is actually several different pieces of hardware all on one board. Most sound cards, including PCI-based models, emulate the Sound Blaster 16 from Creative Labs.

Table 4.84 shows the default resources used by a typical PCI sound card, the Creative Labs SB512. Because sound cards are multifunction devices, each function is listed separately as it appears in the Windows Device Manager.

Table 4.84   Default Resources Used by Creative Labs SB512

Device	IRQ	I/O Port Address	16-Bit DMA Channel	8-Bit DMA Channel
Sound Blaster 16 emulation	5	0220-022F 0330-0331[1] 0388-038B[2]	5	1
Creative Multimedia Interface	N/A	D400-D407	n/a	n/a
Creative Gameport Joystick	N/A	0200-0207	n/a	n/a
Creative SB512	9[3]	C860-C87F	n/a	n/a

1. *Used for MIDI interface*
2. *Used for FM Synthesis*
3. *Varies with system and PCI expansion slot used*

Although other brands of sound cards might use a slightly different configuration, the pattern is the same; Sound Blaster emulation requires a large number of resources. Even if SB emulation isn't used (you might be able to disable it if you no longer play DOS games), the card still uses a single IRQ and several I/O port address ranges. If you read your soundboard's documentation and determine its communications-channel needs, compare those needs to the IRQ lines and DMA channels that already are in use in your system, and then change the settings of the other adapters to avoid conflicts with the sound card, your installation will go quickly and smoothly. Unfortunately, many vendors no longer provide detailed information on their plug-and-play-compatible cards. That's why you need to install the sound card first and use the system resource map to record which settings the card uses before you install other cards.

Tip

The best advice I can give you for installing a sound card is to put the sound card in before all other cards—except for video. In other words, let the sound card retain all its default settings if you can. Try to change the settings of other adapters when a conflict with the sound card arises. The problem here is that many older programs that use sound are very poorly written with respect to supporting alternative resource settings on sound cards. Save yourself some grief, and let the sound card have its way!

Even the latest sound cards can have problems if they're installed after other cards. I know a user who had to remove all his plug-and-play cards before his system would recognize his plug-and-play sound card.

If your system has integrated sound but you prefer to use a sound card, don't forget to use the BIOS configuration program to disable onboard sound before you install the sound card.

One example of a potential soundboard conflict is the combination of a Sound Blaster 16 and an Adaptec SCSI adapter, as I noted earlier in this chapter. The Sound and SCSI adapters conflict on DMA 5 as well as on I/O ports 330–331. Rather than changing the settings of the sound card, it is best to alter the SCSI adapter to the next available settings that will not conflict with the sound card or anything else. The reason to use the defaults for the sound card is that some older (mostly DOS-based) software often assumes default settings for sound hardware and won't work when alternative settings are used. However, devices that use SCSI ports can use any available setting. The final settings are shown in the previous configuration template.

The cards in question (Sound Blaster 16 and AHA-1542CF) are not singled out here because there is something wrong with them, but instead because they happen to be very popular cards of their respective types and, as such, often are paired together in older systems.

Most people would be using PCI versions of these cards today, but they still require the same types of resource settings with the only exception being DMA channels. Unfortunately, it wasn't DMA channels that we were really running out of! The interrupt shortage often continues even with PCI cards because for older real-mode applications or Windows 95 and earlier, they must be mapped to discrete ISA IRQs. The real solutions to the ISA IRQ problem are to use only PCI cards, use Windows 98 or newer (which support IRQ Steering), and have that support in your ROM BIOS. Then, full sharing is possible. Every desktop system sold today is equipped with a motherboard that lacks ISA slots and breaks ties with that bus forever. These motherboards free us of the interrupt restrictions we have been under for so many years.

Tip

The newer PCI sound cards are largely incompatible with older DOS-based software because they don't use DMA channels like their ISA counterparts. If you don't update your software to 32-bit Windows versions, you won't be able to use these newer PCI bus sound cards. Most of the newer PCI cards do include an emulation program that allows the card to work with older DMA-dependent software, but the results are often problematic. If you use integrated sound, the drivers for your motherboard might include a Sound Blaster emulation driver.

For the best results, use the PC/PCI connector found on some motherboards to connect a patch cable to a PC/PCI-compatible sound card. The PC/PCI connector enables the sound card to use ISA-style DMA channels without clumsy emulation software.

SCSI Adapter Boards

SCSI adapter boards use more resources than just about any other type of add-in device except perhaps a sound card. They often use resources that are in conflict with sound cards or network cards, especially if the card has an onboard BIOS for handling bootable drives. A typical ISA SCSI host adapter with onboard BIOS requires an IRQ line, a DMA channel, a range of I/O port addresses, plus a 16KB range of unused upper memory for its ROM and possible scratch-pad RAM use. Even a simple SCSI host adapter designed for use with scanners still requires an IRQ and a range of I/O port addresses. Fortunately, the typical SCSI adapter is also easy to reconfigure, and changing any of these settings should not affect performance or software operation. PCI-based SCSI host adapters require all of the preceding, except for the DMA channel.

Before installing a SCSI adapter, be sure to read the documentation for the card, and ensure that any IRQ lines, DMA channels, I/O ports, and upper memory the card needs are available. If the system resources the card needs are already in use, use your system-configuration template to determine how you can alter the settings on the SCSI card or other cards to prevent any resource conflicts before you attempt to plug in the adapter card.

Note

Some ISA-based SCSI and network cards can be configured to work in PnP mode or use manual configuration settings. With these cards, you can use the configuration method you prefer. If PnP doesn't work, set the card manually (through jumpers, DIP switches, or software).

Network Interface Cards

Networks are becoming more and more popular all the time, thanks to the rise of easy-to-configure small office/home office networks and the use of network cards to connect to broadband Internet devices such as cable and DSL modems. A typical network adapter does not require as many resources as some of the other cards discussed here, but it requires at least a range of I/O port addresses and an interrupt. Some network interface cards (NICs) also require a 16KB range of free upper memory to be used for the RAM transfer buffer on the network card. As with any other cards, be sure that all these resources are unique to the card and are not shared with any other devices. If your network adapter is built into the motherboard, it still uses IRQ and I/O port address resources.

Multiple-COM-Port Adapters

A serial port adapter usually has two or more ports onboard. These COM ports require an interrupt and a range of I/O ports each. There aren't too many problems with the I/O port addresses because the ranges used by up to four COM ports in a system are fairly well defined. The real problem is with the interrupts. Most older installations of more than two serial ports have any additional ones sharing the same interrupts as the first two. This is incorrect and causes nothing but problems with software that runs under Windows. With these older boards, ensure that each serial port in your system has a unique I/O port address range and, more importantly, a unique interrupt setting.

Many newer multiport adapter cards—such as those offered by Byte Runner Technologies—allow "intelligent" interrupt sharing among ports. In some cases, you can have up to 12 COM port settings without conflict problems. Check with your adapter card's manufacturer to determine whether it allows for automatic or "intelligent" interrupt sharing.

Although most people have problems incorrectly trying to share interrupts when installing more than two serial ports in a system, a fairly common problem exists with the I/O port addressing that should be mentioned. Some video chipsets use additional I/O port addresses that conflict with the standard I/O port addresses used by COM4:.

In the sample system configuration just covered, you can see that the ATI video card uses some additional I/O port addresses, specifically 2EC–2EF. This is a problem because COM4: usually is configured as 2E8–2EF, which overlaps with the video card. The video cards that use these addresses are not normally adjustable for this setting, so you either must change the address of COM4: to a nonstandard setting or disable COM4: and restrict yourself to using only three serial ports in the system. If you do have a serial adapter that supports nonstandard I/O address settings for the serial ports, you must ensure that those settings are not used by other cards, and you must inform any software or drivers, such as those in Windows, of your nonstandard settings.

In many cases, USB or 10/100 Ethernet connections can be used to perform the tasks formerly handled by serial ports. If you no longer need serial ports for any devices in your system, I recommend that you disable the onboard serial ports, remove multiport serial cards, and assign the IRQs used by the serial ports in the BIOS to be available for PCI/AGP Plug and Play assignment. This helps eliminate any IRQ conflicts that could occur.

Universal Serial Bus

USB ports corresponding to USB 1.1 or USB 2.0 are found on most motherboards since 1996. One potential problem is that USB takes another interrupt from your system (in some cases, more than one), and many computers either don't have any free or are down to their last one. If your system supports PCI IRQ Steering, this shouldn't be much of a problem because the IRQ used by your USB controller should be sharable with other PCI devices. If you are out of interrupts, you should look at what other devices you can disable (such as COM or LPT ports) to gain back a necessary interrupt for other devices.

The big advantage of either type of USB from an IRQ or a resource perspective is that the USB bus uses only one IRQ no matter how many devices (up to 127) are attached or how many USB ports are installed on systems with a single USB controller. Some systems with multiple USB controllers use additional IRQs, but USB controllers can share IRQs with each other or with other PCI devices. Therefore, you can freely add or remove devices from the USB without worrying about running out of resources or having resource conflicts.

If you aren't using any USB devices, you should turn off the port using your motherboard CMOS Setup so that the IRQ it was using will be freed. As we continue to move to USB-based keyboards, mice, modems, printers, and so on, the IRQ shortage will be less of a problem. As we have already seen, the elimination of the ISA bus in our systems will also go a long way toward solving this problem.

For the best performance—especially with high-capacity removable media, CD/DVD rewriteable drives, scanners, and printers—look for motherboards that have USB 2.0 (High-speed USB) ports. These ports are also completely backward compatible with USB 1.1 devices and provide better performance when several USB devices are in use simultaneously. You can also add a USB 2.0 card to an existing motherboard to provide the same benefits to an existing system.

Miscellaneous Boards

Some video cards ship with advanced software that allows special video features, such as oversized desktops, custom monitors, switch modes on-the-fly, and so on. Unfortunately, this software requires that the card be configured to use an IRQ. If your video card doesn't require an IRQ, I suggest you dispense with this unnecessary software and configure the card to free up the interrupt for other devices. However, keep in mind that many of the latest 3D accelerators must use an IRQ to enable their bus-mastering feature to work correctly. See your video card's manual for details.

Also related to video is the use of an MPEG decoder add-on card that works in addition to your normal graphics adapter. These are used more in specialized video production and editing and in playing DVD movies; however, they do use additional system resources that must be available. If your CPU runs at speeds above 300MHz and you have an AGP video card, you can probably use your video card for DVD playback and remove the MPEG decoder card. You will need a DVD player program, which might be supplied with your video card. See your video card's manual for details.

Plug-and-Play Systems

Plug and Play (PnP) represents a major revolution in interface technology. PnP first came on the market in 1995, and most motherboards and adapter cards since 1996 take advantage of it. Prior to that, PC users were forced to muddle through a nightmare of DIP switches and jumpers every time they wanted to add new devices to their systems. The results, all too often, were system resource conflicts and nonfunctioning cards.

PnP was not an entirely new concept. It was a key design feature of MCA and EISA interfaces that preceded it by almost 10 years, but the limited appeal of MCA and EISA meant that they never became true de facto industry standards. Therefore, mainstream PC users still had to worry about I/O addresses, DMA channels, and IRQ settings. Early PCI-based systems also used a form of PnP configuration, but because there was no provision for managing conflicts between PCI and ISA cards, many users still had configuration problems. But now that PnP has become prevalent, worry-free hardware setup is available to all computer buyers.

For PnP to work, the following components are desired:

- PnP hardware
- PnP BIOS
- PnP operating system

Each of these components needs to be PnP-compatible, meaning that it complies with the PnP specifications. Of course, support for these features is found in all modern systems.

The Hardware Component

The *hardware component* refers to both computer systems and adapter cards. The term does not mean, however, that you can't use your older ISA adapter cards (referred to as *legacy cards*) in a PnP system. You can use these cards; in fact, your PnP BIOS automatically reassigns PnP-compatible cards around existing legacy components. Also, many late-model ISA cards can be switched into PnP-compatible mode.

PnP adapter cards communicate with the system BIOS and the operating system to convey information about which system resources are necessary. The BIOS and operating system, in turn, resolve conflicts (wherever possible) and inform the adapter card which specific resources it should use. The adapter card then can modify its configuration to use the specified resources.

The BIOS Component

The BIOS component means that most users of pre-1996 PCs need to update their BIOSs or purchase new machines that have PnP BIOSs. For a BIOS to be compatible, it must support 13 additional system function calls, which can be used by the OS component of a PnP system. The PnP BIOS specification was developed jointly by Compaq, Intel, and Phoenix Technologies.

The PnP features of the BIOS are implemented through an expanded POST. The BIOS is responsible for identification, isolation, and possible configuration of PnP adapter cards. The BIOS accomplishes these tasks by performing the following steps:

1. Disables any configurable devices on the motherboard or on adapter cards.
2. Identifies any PnP PCI or ISA devices.
3. Compiles an initial resource-allocation map for ports, IRQs, DMAs, and memory.
4. Enables I/O devices.
5. Scans the ROMs of ISA devices.
6. Configures initial program-load (IPL) devices, which are used later to boot the system.
7. Enables configurable devices by informing them which resources have been assigned to them.
8. Starts the bootstrap loader.
9. Transfers control to the operating system.

The Operating System Component

The operating system component is found in most modern operating systems since Windows 95. In some cases system manufacturers have provided extensions to the operating system for their specific hardware. Such is especially true for notebook systems, for example. Be sure you load these extensions if they are required by your system.

It is the responsibility of the operating system to inform users of conflicts that can't be resolved by the BIOS. Depending on the sophistication of the operating system, the user then could configure the offending cards manually (onscreen) or turn off the system and set switches on the physical cards. When the system is restarted, it is checked for remaining (or new) conflicts, any of which are brought to the user's attention. Through this repetitive process, all system conflicts are resolved.

Note

Because of revisions in some of the Plug and Play specifications, especially the ACPI specification, it can help to ensure you are running the latest BIOS and drivers for your system. With the flash ROM used in most PnP systems, you can download the new BIOS image from the system vendor or manufacturer and run the supplied BIOS update program.

Motherboard Selection Criteria (Knowing What to Look For)

I am often asked to make a recommendation for purchases. Without guidance, many individuals don't have any rhyme or reason to their selections and instead base their choices solely on magazine reviews or, even worse, on some personal bias. To help eliminate this haphazard selection process, I have developed a simple checklist that will help you select a system. This list takes into consideration several important system aspects overlooked by most checklists. The goal is to ensure that the selected system truly is compatible and has a long life of service and upgrades ahead.

It helps to think like an engineer when you make your selection. Consider every aspect and detail of the motherboards in question. For instance, you should consider any future uses and upgrades. Technical support at a professional (as opposed to a user) level is extremely important. What support will be provided? Is there documentation, and does it cover everything else?

In short, a checklist is a good idea. Here is one for you to use in evaluating any PC-compatible system. A system might not have to meet every one of these criteria for you to consider purchasing it, but if it misses more than a few, consider staying away from that system. The items at the top of the list are the most important, and the items at the bottom are perhaps of lesser importance (although I think each item is important). The rest of this chapter discusses in detail the criteria in this checklist:

- **Motherboard chipset**—Motherboards should use a high-performance chipset that supports DDR2 or DDR3 SDRAM DIMMs. Also look for PCI-Express x16 video support and multiple Serial ATA connectors. The motherboard chipset is the backbone of a system and is perhaps the single most important part you'll consider. I spend the most time deciding on my next chipset because it affects and influences virtually every other component in the system.

- **Processor**—A modern system should use a socket-based processor with on-die L2 cache. Evaluate the processor choices you have, and try to get the one with the highest-speed CPU bus (front-side bus). Don't get too hung up on L2 cache size; a little cache goes a long way. It is more important that the cache run at full core speed (which it will if it is on-die). Current processors all meet this criteria. I usually recommend only "boxed" processors as sold by Intel and AMD, which include a high-quality active heatsink as well as installation instructions and a 3-year warranty direct with the manufacturer.

- **Processor sockets**—For maximum upgradeability and performance, you should stick with a system that uses a socket for the CPU. The main sockets in use today on new systems include Socket AM2 for the Athlon 64 models and Socket LGA775 for the Intel Core 2 series. As long as your motherboard has one of these sockets, you should be in good shape.

- **Motherboard speed**—The motherboard typically offers a choice of CPU bus speeds, check to ensure the board you are buying runs at the speeds necessary to support the processors you want to install.

- **Cache memory**—All modern systems use processors with integral cache, most of them now having the cache directly on the processor die for maximum speed. As such, there won't be any cache memory on the motherboard in a modern system. The tip is to make sure you are using a processor with full-core-speed on-die L2 cache because this offers the maximum in performance. All the modern processors now incorporate full-speed on-die L2 cache.

- **DIMM memory**—Current systems use either DDR, DDR2, or DDR3 DIMMs. Older memory types, such as the now-ancient SIMMs and more recent SDRAM DIMM and RIMM memory, are obsolete and should be avoided. What you use depends mainly on your motherboard chipset, so choose the chipset and board that accepts the memory type you want to use.

  Mission-critical systems might consider ECC memory (ensure that the motherboard fully supports ECC operation first). Note that many of the standard chipsets from Intel and others do not support ECC, so this is something you should know before purchasing the system.

  Finally, note that most full-size motherboards support four DIMM sockets. Be sure that you populate them wisely so you don't have to resort to removing memory later to add more, which is not very cost-effective. Most systems support one or two pairs of dual-channel memory. On these systems, install memory in matched pairs for best performance.

- **Bus type**—Current systems offer one to five or more PCI and PCI Express slots. Take a look at the layout of the slots to ensure that cards inserted in them will not block access to memory sockets or be blocked by other components in the case. Systems without onboard video should also feature one PCI-Express x16 slot instead of (or sometimes along with) the older AGP 4x/8x slot.

- **BIOS**—The motherboard should use an industry-standard BIOS, such as those from AMI, Phoenix, or Award. The BIOS should be of a flash ROM or EEPROM design for easy updating. Look for a BIOS Recover jumper or mode setting, as well as possibly a flash ROM write-protect jumper on some systems.

- **Form factor**—For maximum flexibility, performance, reliability, and ease of use, the ATX form factor (including microATX and FlexATX) cannot be beat. The newest form factor, BTX, offers superior cooling in some designs, but is more expensive than ATX, with far fewer motherboards, chassis and boxed processors to choose from.

- **Built-in interfaces**—Ideally, a motherboard should contain as many built-in standard controllers and interfaces as possible. If choosing a board with integrated video, I recommend insuring that there is also a PCIe x16 slot available for a future video card upgrade.

  Built-in gigabit Ethernet network adapters are also handy, especially if you are using a cable modem or DSL connection to the Internet. A built-in sound card is a great feature, usually offering full Sound Blaster compatibility and functions, and possibly offering additional features such as 5.1 (six-channel) or 7.1 (eight-channel) surround sound and SPDIF connections to a home theater system. If your sound needs are more demanding, you might find the built-in solutions less desirable, and you might want to have a separate sound card in your system.

- **Onboard ATA interfaces**—All motherboards on the market have included onboard ATA and SATA interfaces for some time now, but not all are equal. Look for boards that include 4 to 6 SATA connectors, with support for 3Gbps operation as well as RAID functionality.

Tip

With a never-ending stream of motherboards coming onto the market, finding motherboards with the features you want can be difficult. Motherboard Homeworld's Mobot search engine helps you find motherboards based on your choice of form factor, platform, chipset, CPU type, processor, manufacturer, memory type, slot types, built-on ports, and more. Check it out at http://www.motherboards.org/mobot/.

- **Power management**—The motherboard should fully support the latest standard for power management, which is ACPI. An Energy Star–compliant system is also a bonus because it uses less than 30 watts of electrical energy when in sleep mode, saving energy as well as your electric bill.

- **Documentation**—Good technical documentation is a requirement. Documents should include information on any and all jumpers and switches found on the board, connector pinouts for all connectors, specifications for other plug-in components, and any other applicable technical information. Most vendors provide this information in electronic form (using the Adobe Reader PDF format) on their websites, so you can preview the information available for a given motherboard before you buy.

- **Technical support**—Good online technical support goes beyond documentation. It includes driver and BIOS updates, FAQs, updated tables of processor and memory compatibility, and utility programs to help you monitor the condition of your system. In addition to these online support features, make sure the vendor can be contacted through email and by phone.

You might notice that these selection criteria seem fairly strict and might disqualify many motherboards on the market, including what you already have in your system! These criteria will, however, guarantee you the highest-quality motherboard offering the latest in PC technology that will be upgradeable, be expandable, and provide good service for many years.

Most of the time I recommend purchasing boards from better-known motherboard manufacturers such as Intel, Acer, ABIT, AsusTek, SuperMicro, Tyan, FIC, and others. These boards might cost a little more, but there is some safety in the more well-known brands. That is, the more boards they sell, the more likely that any problems will have been discovered by others and solved long before you get yours. Also, if service or support is necessary, the larger vendors are more likely to be around in the long run.

Documentation

As mentioned, documentation is an important factor to consider when you're planning to purchase a motherboard. Most motherboard manufacturers design their boards around a particular chipset, which actually counts as the bulk of the motherboard circuitry. Many manufacturers, such as Intel, VIA, ALi, SiS, and others, offer chipsets. I recommend obtaining the data book or other technical documentation on the chipset directly from the chipset manufacturer.

For example, one of the more common questions I hear about a system relates to the BIOS Setup program. People want to know what the "Advanced Chipset Setup" features mean and what the effects of changing them will be. Often they go to the BIOS manufacturer thinking that the BIOS documentation will offer help. Usually, however, people find that there is no real coverage of what the chipset setup features are in the BIOS documentation. You will find this information in the data book provided by the chipset manufacturer. Although these books are meant to be read by the engineers who design the boards, they contain all the detailed information about the chipset's features, especially those that might be adjustable. With the chipset data book, you will have an explanation of all the controls in the Advanced Chipset Setup section of the BIOS Setup program.

Besides the main chipset data books, I also recommend collecting any data books on the other major chips in the system. This includes any floppy or IDE controller chips, Super I/O chips, and of course the main processor. You will find an incredible amount of information on these components in the data books.

Caution

Most chipset manufacturers make a particular chip for only a short time, rapidly superseding it with an improved or changed version. The data books are available only during the time the chip is being manufactured, so if you wait too long, you will find that such documents might no longer be available. The time to collect documentation on your motherboard is *now*!

Using Correct Speed-rated Parts

Some vendors use substandard parts in their systems to save money. Because the CPU is one of the most expensive components on the motherboard, and motherboards are sold to system assemblers without the CPU installed, it is tempting for the assembler to install a CPU rated for less than the actual operating speed. A system could be sold as a 2.4GHz system, for example, but when you look under the hood, you might find it's rated for only 2GHz. This is called *overclocking*, and many vendors have engaged in this practice. Some even go so far as to re-mark the CPUs, so that even if you look, the part appears to have the correct rating. The best way to stop this is to purchase systems from known, reliable vendors and purchase processors from distributors that are closely connected with the manufacturer. Overclocking is fine if you want to do it yourself and understand the risks, but when I purchase a new system, I expect that all the parts included will be rated to run at the speed to which they are set.

◄◄   See "Processor Speed Ratings," p. 55.

When a chip is run at a speed higher than it is rated for, it runs hotter than it would normally. This can cause the chip to occasionally overheat, which would appear as random lockups, glitches, and frustration. I highly recommend that you check to ensure you are getting the right speed-rated parts you are paying for.

Also be sure to use the recommended heatsink thermal interface material (TIM). This can improve the efficiency of your heatsink by up to 30%.

This practice is easy to fall into because the faster-rated chips cost more money. Intel and other chip manufacturers usually rate their chips very conservatively. Over the years, I have overclocked many processors, running them sometimes well beyond their rated speeds. Although I might purchase a Pentium 4 2.4GHz and run it at 2.6GHz, if I were to experience lockups or glitches in operation, I would immediately return it to the original speed and retest. If I purchase a 2.6GHz system from a vendor, I fully expect it to have a 2.6GHz part, not slower parts running past their rated speeds!

Overclocking has been made more difficult by Intel and AMD, who have both started locking the bus multipliers in their chips to prevent easy overclocking by changing the multiplier setting on the motherboard. This is done mainly to combat re-marking CPUs and deceiving customers, although it unfortunately can also prevent those who want to from hotrodding their chips. Still, you can overclock most chips by increasing the CPU bus (front-side bus) speed within certain tolerances. Many of the motherboards on the market have tweakable CPU bus speeds specifically designed to allow overclocking. Check with your motherboard manual, or download the documentation from the manufacturer's website. You might find that your board is capable of things you didn't realize.

If you purchase a processor or system, verify that the markings are the original Intel or AMD markings and that the speed rating on the chip is what you really paid for.

The bottom line: If the price is too good to be true, ask before you buy. Are the parts really manufacturer-rated for the system speed?

To determine the rated speed of a CPU chip, look at the writing on the chip. Refer to Chapter 3 for details on how to interpret the marks to see what the rating on the chip actually is.

Caution

Be careful when running software to detect processor speed. Most programs can only estimate at what speed the chip is currently running, not what the true original rating is. The current speed of the processor might not be its actual rated speed, either because of overclocking or because some recent systems reduce processor speed when the system is not heavily tasked. One exception to this is the Intel Processor Frequency ID Utility, which can determine whether an Intel processor is operating at the correct and rated frequency intended. Although it gives only basic information about any Intel processor, it can uniquely identify the original speed ratings of the Pentium III, third-generation Celeron (Coppermine-based), and any newer processors, accurately determining whether they have been overclocked. For Pentium 4 and later processors, use the Intel Processor Identification Utility. Both are available from http://support.intel.com/support/processors/tools/piu/.

For AMD processors, use the AMD CPUInfo and AMDClock utilities to identify your processor type and speed. Download these and other utilities from:

http://www.amd.com/us-en/assets/content_type/utilities/CPUsetup.exe

http://www.amd.com/us-en/assets/content_type/utilities/amdclock.zip

Another excellent utility is the CPU-Z program available from http://www.cpuid.com.

Most of these programs read the processor ID and stepping information, as well as show current operating (but not rated) speed. You can consult the processor manufacturer or Chapter 3 for tables listing the various processor steppings to see exactly how yours stacks up.

BIOS

BIOS Basics

It is often difficult for people to understand the difference between hardware and software in a PC system. The differences can be difficult to understand because both are very much intertwined in the system design, construction, and operation. Understanding these differences is essential to understanding the role of the BIOS in the system.

BIOS stands for *basic input/output system*, which consists of low-level software that controls the system hardware and acts as an interface between the operating system and the hardware. Most people know the term *BIOS* by another name—*device drivers*, or just *drivers*. In other words, the BIOS is drivers, meaning all of them. The BIOS is essentially the link between hardware and software in a system.

When the PC was first introduced, the BIOS software containing all the device drivers for the entire system was collectively burned into one or more nonvolatile read-only memory (ROM) chips (*nonvolatile* means they retain their data even when the power is turned off) and placed on the motherboard. In essence, the drivers were self-contained, preloaded into memory, and accessible any time the PC was powered on.

This ROM chip also contained a power-on self test (POST) program and a bootstrap loader. The bootstrap program was designed to initiate the loading of an OS by checking for and loading the boot sector from a floppy disk or, if one was not present, a hard disk. After the OS was loaded, it could call on the low-level routines (device drivers) in the BIOS to interact with the system hardware. In the early days, all the necessary device drivers were in the BIOS stored in the motherboard ROM. This included drivers for the keyboard, MDA/CGA video adapters, serial/parallel ports, floppy controller, hard disk controller, joystick, and clock.

When the OS loaded, you didn't have to load a driver to interact with those pieces of hardware because the drivers were already preloaded in the ROM. That worked great as long as you didn't add any new hardware for which there wasn't a driver in ROM. If you did, you then had two choices. If the hardware you were adding was an adapter card, that card could include a ROM onboard containing the necessary device drivers. The motherboard ROM was programmed to scan a predetermined area of memory looking for any adapter card ROMs, and if any were found, their code was executed, essentially adding their functionality to the existing BIOS. In essence, the motherboard ROM "assimilated" any adapter card ROMs, adding to the "collective" functionality.

This method of adding drivers was required for items such as video cards, which needed to be functional immediately when the PC was powered on. The BIOS code in the motherboard ROM had drivers only for the IBM monochrome display adapter (MDA) and color graphics adapter (CGA) video cards. If you added any video card other than those, the drivers in the motherboard ROM would not support it. That wouldn't be a problem if the new video card had its own drivers in an onboard ROM that would be linked into the BIOS immediately upon throwing the power switch.

If the device did not use an adapter card, there had to be another way to add the necessary driver to the BIOS collective. A scheme was devised whereby during the early stages of loading, the MS-DOS startup file (IO.SYS) checked for a configuration file (called CONFIG.SYS) that specified any additional drivers to load to support new hardware. The CONFIG.SYS file, along with any drivers named within, would be placed on the boot drive. When booting, the IO.SYS program would load the specified drivers into memory and link them into the rest of the BIOS, again adding their functionality to the collective whole. In essence, these drivers were loaded from disk into RAM and linked into the BIOS so they could be called on when necessary.

At this point, the BIOS had grown from being entirely contained in the motherboard ROM, to having additional drivers linked in from adapter card ROMs, to having even more drivers linked in after being loaded into RAM during the early stages of the boot process. The BIOS was now constructed of programs located in three different physical locations in the system, and yet it functioned as a single entity because all the programs were linked together via the BIOS subroutine calling system-of-software interrupts. The OS or an application program needing to talk to a specific piece of hardware (for example, to read from the CD-ROM drive) would make a call to a specific software interrupt, and the interrupt vector table would then route the call to the specific part of the BIOS (meaning the specific driver) for the device being called. It did not matter whether that driver was in the motherboard ROM, adapter ROM, or RAM. As far as the system was concerned, memory is memory, and as long as the routine existed at a known memory address, it could be called.

The combination of the motherboard ROM, adapter card ROM, and device drivers loaded from disk into RAM contributed to the BIOS as a whole. The portion of the BIOS contained in ROM chips, both on the motherboard and in some adapter cards, is sometimes called *firmware*, which is a name given to software stored in ROM chips rather than on disk. Of course, after you turned off the system, the drivers in nonvolatile ROM would remain intact, but those in volatile RAM would instantly vanish. That was not a problem, however, because the next time the system was turned back on, it went through the boot process and again loaded the necessary drivers from disk all over again.

As the PC has evolved, more and more accessories and new hardware have been devised to add to the system. This means that more and more drivers have to be loaded to support this hardware. Adding new drivers to the motherboard ROM is difficult because ROM chips are relatively fixed (difficult to change) and limited space is available. The PC architecture allows only 128KB for the motherboard ROM, and most of it was already used by the existing drivers, POST, BIOS Setup program, and of course the bootstrap loader. Putting drivers on adapter card ROMs is also expensive, and only 128KB is allocated for all adapter card ROMs, not to mention the fact that the video card takes 32KB of that. So, most companies developing new hardware for the PC simply wrote drivers designed to be loaded into RAM during the boot process.

As time went on, more and more drivers were being loaded from disk—in some cases, even drivers that were replacing those in the motherboard. For example, Windows 95 introduced a new hard disk driver that used 32-bit code, which superseded the existing 16-bit driver that existed in the motherboard ROM. In other words, the 16-bit hard disk driver in the motherboard ROM was used to begin loading the OS and other drivers, and after the 32-bit driver was loaded into RAM during the boot process, the vector table was changed to point to the 32-bit driver in RAM instead of the 16-bit driver in ROM. Windows 95, 98, and Me allowed the use of both 16-bit and 32-bit drivers, easing the transition to full 32-bit operation.

This has progressed to today, when 32-bit and 64-bit drivers have been designed to be loaded from disk to replace *all* the drivers in the motherboard ROM. This is the case for any system today running Windows NT, 2000, XP, or Vista. Those operating systems cannot use any of the 16-bit drivers found in either the motherboard ROMs or any adapter card ROMs and must use only 32-bit or 64-bit drivers, depending on the version. The 16-bit code in the motherboard ROM is used only to get the system functioning long enough to get the drivers and OS loaded, at which point they take over. In other words, once Windows is loaded, the BIOS (meaning all of the drivers) essentially resides entirely in RAM. The motherboard ROM exists only to get the system started, to initialize specific hardware, to offer security in the way of power-on passwords and such, and to perform some basic initial configuration. Once the OS is loaded, a whole new set of drivers takes over.

A PC system can be described as a series of layers—some hardware and some software—that interface with each other. In the most basic sense, you can break a PC down into four primary layers, each of which can be broken down further into subsets. Figure 5.1 shows the four layers in a typical PC.

The purpose of the layered design is to enable a given operating system and applications to run on different hardware. Figure 5.1 shows how two different machines with different hardware can each use different sets of drivers (BIOS) to interface the unique hardware to a common operating system and applications. Thus, two machines with different processors, storage media, video display units, and so on, can run the same OS and applications.

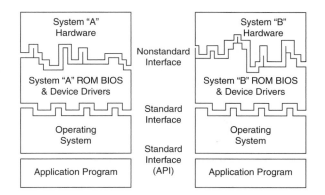

Figure 5.1   PC system layers.

In this layered architecture, the application software programs talk to the operating system via what is called an *application programming interface (API)*. The API varies according to the operating system you are using and consists of the various commands and functions the operating system can perform for an application. For example, an application can call on the operating system to load or save a file. This prevents the application itself from having to know how to read the disk, send data to a printer, or perform any other of the many functions the operating system can provide. Because the application is completely insulated from the hardware, you can essentially run the same applications on different machines; the application is designed to talk to the operating system rather than the hardware.

The operating system then interfaces with or talks to the BIOS or driver layer. The BIOS consists of all the individual driver programs that operate between the operating system and the actual hardware.

As such, the operating system never talks to the hardware directly; instead, it must always go through the appropriate drivers. This provides a consistent way to talk to the hardware. It is usually the responsibility of the hardware manufacturer to provide drivers for its hardware. Because the drivers must act between both the hardware and the operating system, the drivers typically are operating system specific. Thus, the hardware manufacturer must offer different drivers so that its hardware works under DOS, Windows, OS/2, Linux, and so on. Because many operating systems use the same internal interfaces, some drivers can work under multiple operating systems. For example, a driver that works under Windows Me will usually also work under Windows 98 and 95, and a driver that works under Windows XP will also often work under Windows 2000 and NT (and vice versa). This is because Windows 95, 98, and Me are essentially variations on the same core OS, as are Windows NT, 2000, and XP. Although Vista is based on NT, the driver model for Vista has changed enough that Vista generally can't use drivers for NT through XP.

Because the BIOS layer looks the same to the operating system no matter what hardware is above it (or underneath, depending on your point of view), the same operating system can run on a variety of systems. For example, you can run Windows Vista on two systems with different processors, hard disks, video adapters, and so on, yet Windows Vista will look and feel pretty much the same to the users on both of them. This is because the drivers provide the same basic functions no matter which specific hardware is used.

As you can see from Figure 5.1, the application and operating system's layers can be identical from system to system, but the hardware can differ radically. Because the BIOS consists of drivers that act to interface the hardware to the software, the BIOS layer adapts to the unique hardware on one end but looks consistently the same to the operating system at the other end.

The hardware layer is where most differences lie between the various systems. It is up to the BIOS to mask the differences between unique hardware so that the given operating system (and subsequently the application) can be run. This chapter focuses on the BIOS layer of the PC.

BIOS Hardware/Software

The BIOS itself is software running in memory that consists of all the various drivers that interface the hardware to the operating system. The BIOS is unique compared to normal software in that some of it is preloaded into read-only memory (or ROM), and some is loaded into RAM from disk.

The BIOS in a PC comes from three possible sources:

- Motherboard ROM
- Adapter card ROMs (such as that found on a video card)
- Loaded into RAM from disk (device drivers)

The motherboard ROM BIOS is most often associated with hardware rather than software. This is because the BIOS on the motherboard is contained in a ROM chip on the board, which contains the initial software drivers needed to get the system running. Years ago, when only DOS was running on basic PCs, this was enough, so no other drivers were needed—the motherboard BIOS had everything that was necessary. The motherboard BIOS usually includes drivers for all the basic system components, including the keyboard, floppy drive, hard drive, serial and parallel ports, and more. As systems became more complex, new hardware was added for which no motherboard BIOS drivers existed. These included devices such as newer video adapters, optical drives, SCSI hard disks, USB ports, drive arrays, and so on.

Rather than requiring a new motherboard BIOS that would specifically support the new devices, it was far simpler and more practical to copy any new drivers that were necessary onto the system hard disk and configure the operating system to load them at boot time. This is how most optical drives, sound cards, scanners, printers, PC Card (PCMCIA) devices, and so on are supported. Because these devices don't need to be active during boot time, the system can boot up from the hard disk and wait to load the drivers during the initial operating system load.

Some drivers, however, must be active during boot time. For example, how can you boot from a hard disk if the drivers necessary to make the disk interface work must be loaded from that disk? Obviously, the hard disk drivers must be preloaded into ROM either on the motherboard or on an adapter card.

How will you be able to see anything onscreen if your video card doesn't have a set of drivers in a ROM? The solution to this could be to provide a motherboard ROM with the appropriate video drivers built in; however, this is impractical because of the variety of video cards, each needing its own drivers. You would end up with hundreds of different motherboard ROMs, depending on which video card you had. Instead, when IBM designed the original PC, it created a better solution. It designed the PC's motherboard ROM to scan the slots, looking for adapter cards with ROMs on them. If a card was found with a ROM on it, the ROM was executed during the initial system startup phase, before the system began loading the operating system from the hard disk.

By putting the ROM-based drivers right on the card, you didn't have to change your motherboard ROM to have built-in support for new devices, especially those that needed to be active during boot time. A few cards (adapter boards) almost always have a ROM onboard, including the following:

- **Video cards**—All have an onboard BIOS.

- **SCSI adapters**—Those that support booting from SCSI hard drives or optical drives have an onboard BIOS. Note that, in most cases, the SCSI BIOS does not support any SCSI devices other than a hard disk; if you use a SCSI optical drive, scanner, Zip drive, and so on, you still need to load the appropriate drivers for those devices from your hard disk. Most newer SCSI adapters support booting from a SCSI optical drive, but drivers are still necessary to access the drive when booting from another drive or device.

- **Network cards**—Those that support booting directly from a file server have what is usually called a *boot ROM* or *IPL (initial program load) ROM* onboard. This enables PCs to be configured on a LAN as diskless workstations—also called Net PCs, NCs (network computers), thin clients, or even smart terminals.

- **ATA or floppy upgrade boards**—Boards that enable you to attach more or different types of drives than what is typically supported by the motherboard alone. These cards require an onboard BIOS to enable these drives to be bootable.

- **RAID (Redundant Array of Inexpensive Disks) cards**—Adapters that enable you to attach multiple drives and array them in different ways to improve reliability, redundancy, and/or performance. These cards require an onboard BIOS to enable the array to be bootable.

- **Y2K boards**—Boards that incorporate BIOS fixes to update the century byte in the CMOS RAM. These boards have a small driver contained in the BIOS that monitors the year byte for a change from 99 to 00. When this is detected, the driver updates the century byte from 19 to 20, correcting a flaw in some older motherboard ROM BIOS.

BIOS and CMOS RAM

Some people confuse BIOS with the CMOS RAM in a system. This confusion is aided by the fact that the Setup program in the BIOS is used to set and store the configuration settings in the CMOS RAM. They are, in fact, two totally separate components.

The BIOS on the motherboard is stored in a fixed ROM chip. Also on the motherboard is a chip called the *RTC/NVRAM chip*, which stands for real-time clock/nonvolatile memory. This is where the settings in the BIOS Setup are stored, and it is actually a clock chip with a few extra bytes of memory thrown in. It is usually called the CMOS chip because it happens to be made using CMOS (complementary metal-oxide semiconductor) technology.

The first example of this ever used in a PC was the Motorola MC146818 chip, which had 64 bytes of storage, of which 14 bytes were dedicated to the clock function, leaving 50 bytes to store BIOS Setup settings. Although it is called nonvolatile, the chip is actually volatile, meaning that without power, the time/date settings and the data in the RAM portion will in fact be erased. This chip is considered nonvolatile by many because it is designed using CMOS technology, which results in a chip that still requires very little power compared to other chips. A small battery can provide that power when the system is unplugged. This battery-powered clock/memory chip is commonly referred to as "the" CMOS RAM chip; although that is somewhat misleading (almost all modern chips use a form of CMOS technology), the term has stuck. Most RTC/NVRAM chips run on as little as 1 micro amp (millionth of an amp), so they use very little battery power to run. Most lithium coin cell batteries can last up to 5 years or more before they die and the information stored (including the date and time) is lost.

When you enter your BIOS Setup, configure your hard disk parameters or other BIOS Setup settings, and save them, these settings are written to the storage area in the RTC/NVRAM chip (otherwise called the CMOS RAM chip). Every time your system boots up, it reads the parameters stored in the CMOS RAM chip to determine how the system should be configured. A relationship exists between the BIOS and CMOS RAM, but they are two distinctly different parts of the system.

Some systems used special versions of these chips made by Dallas Semiconductor, Benchmarq, or Odin (such as the DS12885 and DS12887) that include both the RTC/NVRAM chip and the battery in a single component. However, those are uncommon in modern systems today. Although the so-called CMOS RAM chip started out as a discrete chip on the motherboard, in modern systems it is no longer a separate chip, but instead included as one of the functions in the South Bridge or I/O Controller Hub component of the motherboard chipset.

Motherboard ROM BIOS

All motherboards have a special chip containing software called the *ROM BIOS*. This ROM chip contains the startup programs and drivers used to get the system running and act as the interface to the basic hardware in the system. When you turn on a system, the power-on self test (POST) in the BIOS also tests the major components in the system. Additionally, you can run a setup program to store system configuration data in the CMOS memory, which is powered by a battery on the motherboard. This CMOS RAM is often called *NVRAM (nonvolatile RAM)* because it runs on about 1 millionth of an amp of electrical current and can store data for years when powered by a tiny lithium battery.

The motherboard ROM contains a collection of programs embedded in one or more chips, depending on the design of your computer. That collection of programs is the first thing loaded when you start your computer, even before the operating system. Simply put, the BIOS in most PCs has four main functions:

- **POST (power-on self test)**—The POST tests your computer's processor, memory, chipset, video adapter, disk controllers, disk drives, keyboard, and other crucial components.

- **Setup**—The system configuration and setup program is usually a menu-driven program activated by pressing a special key during the POST, and it enables you to configure the motherboard and chipset settings along with the date and time, passwords, disk drives, and other basic system settings. You also can control the power-management settings and boot-drive sequence from the BIOS Setup, and on some systems, you can also configure CPU timing and clock-multiplier settings. Some older 286 and 386 systems did not have the Setup program in ROM and required that you boot from a special setup disk, and some newer systems use a Windows-based application to access BIOS Setup settings.

- **Bootstrap loader**—A routine that reads the first physical sector of various disk drives looking for a valid master boot record (MBR). If one meeting certain minimum criteria (ending in the signature bytes 55AAh) is found, the code within is executed. The MBR program code then continues the boot process by reading the first physical sector of the bootable volume, which is the start of the volume boot record (VBR). The VBR then loads the first operating system startup file, which is usually IO.SYS (DOS/Windows 9x/Me), ntldr (Windows NT/2000/XP), or bootmgr (Vista), upon which the operating system is then in control and continues the boot process.

- **BIOS (basic input/output system)**—This refers to the collection of actual drivers used to act as a basic interface between the operating system and your hardware when the system is booted and running. When running DOS or Windows in Safe mode, you are running almost solely on ROM-based BIOS drivers because none are loaded from disk.

ROM Hardware

Read-only memory (ROM) is a type of memory that can permanently or semi-permanently hold data. It is called *read-only* because it is either impossible or difficult to write to. ROM is also often called *nonvolatile memory* because any data stored in ROM remains even if the power is turned off. As such, ROM is an ideal place to put the PC's startup instructions—that is, the software that boots the system (the BIOS).

Note that ROM and RAM are not opposites, as some people seem to believe. In fact, ROM is technically a subset of the system's RAM. In other words, a portion of the system's random access memory address space is mapped into one or more ROM chips. This is necessary to contain the software that enables the PC to boot up; otherwise, the processor would have no program in memory to execute when it is powered on.

For example, when a PC is turned on, the processor automatically jumps to address FFFF0h, expecting to find instructions to tell the processor what to do. This location is exactly 16 bytes from the end of the first megabyte of RAM space, as well as the end of the ROM itself. If this location were mapped into regular RAM chips, any data stored there would have disappeared when the power was previously turned off, and the processor would subsequently find no instructions to run the next time the power was turned on. By placing a ROM chip at this address, a system startup program can be permanently loaded into the ROM and will be available every time the system is turned on.

▶▶ For more information about Dynamic RAM, see "DRAM," p. 512.

Normally, the system ROM starts at address E0000h or F0000h, which is 128KB or 64KB prior to the end of the first megabyte. Because the ROM chip usually is up to 128KB in size, the ROM programs are allowed to occupy the entire last 128KB of the first megabyte, including the critical FFFF0h startup instruction address, which is located 16 bytes from the end of the BIOS space. Some motherboard ROM chips are larger, up to 256KB or 512KB in size. The additional code in these is configured to act as a video card ROM (addresses C0000h–C7FFFh) on motherboards with built-in video and might even contain additional ROM drivers configured anywhere from C8000h to DFFFFh to support additional onboard devices, such as SCSI or network adapters.

Figure 5.2 shows a map of the first megabyte of memory in a PC; notice the upper memory areas reserved for adapter card and motherboard ROM BIOS at the end of the first megabyte.

```
        . = RAM
        G = Graphics Mode Video RAM
        M = Monochrome Text Mode Video RAM
        C = Color Text Mode Video RAM
        V = Video adapter ROM BIOS
        a = Reserved for other adapter board ROM
        r = Additional Motherboard ROM BIOS in some systems
        R = Motherboard ROM BIOS

        Conventional (Base) Memory

             : 0---1---2---3---4---5---6---7---8---9---A---B---C---D---E---F---
        000000: ................................................................
        010000: ................................................................
        020000: ................................................................
        030000: ................................................................
        040000: ................................................................
        050000: ................................................................
        060000: ................................................................
        070000: ................................................................
        080000: ................................................................
        090000: ................................................................

        Upper Memory Area (UMA)

             : 0---1---2---3---4---5---6---7---8---9---A---B---C---D---E---F---
        0A0000: GGGGGGGGGGGGGGGGGGGGGGGGGGGGGGGGGGGGGGGGGGGGGGGGGGGGGGGGGGGGGGGG
        0B0000: MMMMMMMMMMMMMMMMMMMMMMMMMMMMMMMMMMCCCCCCCCCCCCCCCCCCCCCCCCCCCCCCCC
             : 0---1---2---3---4---5---6---7---8---9---A---B---C---D---E---F---
        0C0000: VVVVVVVVVVVVVVVVVVVVVVVVVVVVVVVVVaaaaaaaaaaaaaaaaaaaaaaaaaaaaaaaa
        0D0000: aaaaaaaaaaaaaaaaaaaaaaaaaaaaaaaaaaaaaaaaaaaaaaaaaaaaaaaaaaaaaaaa
             : 0---1---2---3---4---5---6---7---8---9---A---B---C---D---E---F---
        0E0000: rrrrrrrrrrrrrrrrrrrrrrrrrrrrrrrrrrrrrrrrrrrrrrrrrrrrrrrrrrrrrrrr
        0F0000: RRRRRRRRRRRRRRRRRRRRRRRRRRRRRRRRRRRRRRRRRRRRRRRRRRRRRRRRRRRRRRRR
```

Figure 5.2   PC memory map showing ROM BIOS.

Some think it is strange that the PC would start executing BIOS instructions 16 bytes from the end of the ROM, but this design is intentionally built into Intel's x86 processors. All the ROM programmer has to do is place a JMP (jump) instruction at that address that instructs the processor to jump to the actual beginning of the ROM—in most cases, close to F0000h—which is about 64KB earlier in the memory map. It's like deciding to read every book starting 16 pages from the end and then having all book publishers agree to place an instruction there to jump back the necessary number of pages to get to page 1. By setting the processor startup location in this way, Intel enabled the ROM to grow to be any size, all the while keeping it at the upper end of addresses in the first megabyte of the memory address space.

Adapter card ROMs are automatically scanned and read by the motherboard ROM during the early part of the boot process—during the POST. The motherboard ROM scans a special area of RAM reserved for adapter ROMs (addresses C0000–DFFFFh) looking for 55AAh signature bytes. This area indicates the start of a ROM.

All adapter ROMs must start with 55AAh; otherwise, the motherboard won't recognize them. The third byte indicates the size of the ROM in 512-byte units called *paragraphs*, and the fourth byte is the actual start of the driver programs. The size byte is used by the motherboard ROM for testing purposes. The motherboard ROM adds all the bytes in the ROM and divides the sum by the number of bytes. The result should produce a remainder of 100h. Thus, when creating a ROM for an adapter, the programmer typically uses a "fill" byte at the end to get the checksum to come out right. Using this checksum, the motherboard tests each adapter ROM during the POST and flags any that appear to have been corrupted.

The motherboard ROM automatically runs the programs in any adapter ROMs it finds during the scan. You see this in most systems when you turn them on, and during the POST you see the video card BIOS initialize and announce its presence.

ROM Shadowing

ROM chips by their natures are very slow, with access times of 150ns (nanoseconds, or billionths of a second), compared to DRAM access times of well under 10ns on most systems. Because of this, in virtually all systems the ROMs are *shadowed*, which means they are copied into RAM at startup to allow faster access during normal operation. The shadowing procedure copies the ROM into RAM and then assigns that RAM the same address as the ROM originally used, disabling the actual ROM in the process. This makes the system seem as though it has ROM running at the same speed as RAM.

The performance gain from shadowing adapter card ROMs is often very slight, and it can cause problems if not set up properly. Therefore, in most cases, it is wise to shadow only the motherboard (and maybe the video card BIOS) and leave the others alone.

Typically, shadowing is useful only if you are running a 16-bit operating system, such as DOS or Windows 3.x. If you are running a 32-bit or 64-bit operating system, shadowing is virtually useless because those operating systems do not use the 16-bit ROM code while running. Instead, those operating systems load drivers into RAM, which replace the 16-bit ROM code used only during system startup.

If present, shadowing options are found in the CMOS Setup program in the motherboard ROM, which is covered in more detail later in this chapter.

ROM Chip Types

The four main types of ROM chips that have been used in PCs are as follows:

- **ROM**—Read-only memory
- **PROM**—Programmable ROM
- **EPROM**—Erasable PROM
- **EEPROM**—Electrically erasable PROM, also sometimes called a *flash ROM*

No matter which type of ROM your system uses, the data stored in a ROM chip is nonvolatile and remains indefinitely unless intentionally erased or overwritten (in those cases where that is possible).

Table 5.1 lists the identifying part numbers typically used for each type of ROM chip, along with any other identifying information.

Table 5.1   ROM Chip Part Numbers

ROM Type	Part Number
ROM	No longer in use
PROM	27xxxx
EPROM*	27xxxx

xxxx = numbers normally indicating capacity in kilobits or megabits

*Has a clear quartz window over the internal chip die allowing UV (ultraviolet) exposure to erase the chip.

ROM (True or Mask ROM)

Originally, most ROMs were manufactured with the binary data (0s and 1s) already "cast in" or integrated into the die. The die represents the actual silicon chip itself. These are called *Mask ROMs* because the data is formed into the mask from which the ROM die is photolithographically produced. This type of manufacturing method is economical if you are making hundreds of thousands of ROMs with the same information. If you must change a single bit, however, you must remake the mask, which is an expensive proposition. Because of costs and inflexibility, nobody uses Mask ROMs anymore.

Mask ROMs are exactly analogous to prerecorded CD-ROMs. Some people think a CD-ROM is first manufactured as a blank and then the data is written to it by a laser, but that is not true. A CD-ROM is literally a piece of plastic that is stamped in a press, and the data is directly molded in, not written. The only actual recording is done with the master disc from which the molds or stamps are made.

PROM

PROMs are a type of ROM that is blank when new and must be programmed with whatever data you want. The PROM was invented in the late 1970s by Texas Instruments and has been available in sizes from 1KB (8Kb) to 2MB (16Mb) or more. They can be identified by their part numbers, which usually are 27xxxx—where the 27 indicates the TI type PROM and the nnnn indicates the size of the chip in kilobits (not bytes). For example, most PCs that used PROMs came with 27512 or 271000 chips, which indicate 512Kb (64KB) or 1Mb (128KB), respectively.

Note

Since 1981, all cars sold in the United States have used onboard computers with some form of ROM containing the control software. For example, my 1989 Pontiac Turbo Trans Am came with an onboard computer containing a 2732 PROM, which was a 32Kb (4KB) chip in the ECM (electronic control module or vehicle computer) under the dash. This chip contained the vehicle operating software as well as all the data tables describing spark advance, fuel delivery, and other engine and vehicle operating parameters. Many devices with integrated computers use PROMs to store their operating programs.

Although we say these chips are blank when new, they are technically preloaded with binary 1s. In other words, a 1Mb ROM chip used in a PC would come with 1 million (actually 1,048,576) bit locations, each containing a binary 1. A blank PROM can then be programmed, which is the act of writing to it. This usually requires a special machine called a device programmer, ROM programmer, or ROM burner (see Figure 5.3).

Programming the ROM is sometimes referred to as *burning* it because that is technically an apt description of the process. Each binary 1 bit can be thought of as a fuse, which is intact. Most chips run on 5 volts, but when a PROM is programmed, a higher voltage (normally 12 volts) is placed at the various addresses within the chip. This higher voltage actually blows or burns the fuses at the desired locations, thus turning any given 1 into a 0. Although you can turn a 1 into a 0, you should note that the process is irreversible; that is, you can't turn a 0 back into a 1.

The device programmer examines the program you want to write into the chip and then selectively changes only the 1s to 0s where necessary in the chip.

PROM chips are often referred to as *one-time programmable (OTP)* chips for this reason. They can be programmed once and never erased. Most PROMs are very inexpensive (about $3 for a typical PC motherboard PROM), so if you want to change the program in a PROM, you discard it and program a fresh one with the new data.

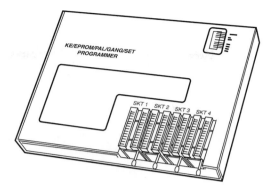

Figure 5.3   Typical gang (multisocket) device programmer (PROM burner).

The act of programming a PROM takes anywhere from a few seconds to a few minutes, depending on the size of the chip and the algorithm used by the programming device. Figure 5.3 shows an illustration of a typical PROM programmer that has multiple sockets. This is called a *gang programmer* and can program several chips at once, saving time if you have several chips to write with the same data. Less expensive programmers are available with only one socket, which is fine for most individual use.

I use and recommend a very inexpensive programmer from a company called Andromeda Research Labs (www.arlabs.com). Besides being economical, its unit has the advantage of connecting to a PC via the parallel port for fast and easy data transfer of files between the PC and programming unit. The unit is also portable and comes built into a convenient carrying case. It is operated by a menu-driven program you install on the connected PC. The program contains several features, including a function that enables you to read the data from a chip and save it in a file on your system, as well as write a chip from a data file, verify that a chip matches a file, and verify that a chip is blank before programming begins. A low-cost BIOS backup option makes backing up the flash BIOS chip in your system easy (if it is removable) as a safeguard against disaster.

Custom Programming of PROM Chips

I even used my PROM programmer to reprogram the chip in my 1989 Turbo Trans Am, changing the factory preset speed and rpm limiters, turbocharger boost, torque converter lockup points, spark advance, fuel delivery, idle speed, and much more! I also incorporated a switch box under the dash that enables me to switch from among four different chips, even while the vehicle is running. One chip I created I call the "valet chip," which, when engaged, cuts off the fuel injectors at 36 miles per hour and restarts them when the vehicle coasts down to 35 mph. By rewriting the chip, I could set the cutoff/restore speeds anywhere from 0 mph to 255 mph. I imagine this type of modification would be useful for those with teenage drivers because you could set the mph or engine rpm limit to whatever you want! Another chip I created cuts off fuel to the engine altogether, which I engage for security purposes when the vehicle is parked. No matter how clever, a thief will not be able to steal this car unless he tows it away. If you are interested in such a chip-switching device or custom chips for your Turbo Trans Am or Buick Grand National, I recommend you contact Casper's Electronics (www.casperselectronics.com). For other vehicles with replaceable PROMs, companies such as Fastchip (www.fastchip.com), Superchips (www.superchips.com), Hypertech (www.hypertech.com), and Mopar Performance (www.mopar.com) offer custom PROMs or vehicle powertrain control modules (PCMs) for improved performance. For example, I installed a Mopar Performance PCM in my 5.9L Jeep Grand Cherokee, and it made a noticeable improvement in engine/transmission operation and overall vehicle performance.

EPROM

One variation of the PROM that has been very popular is the EPROM. An *EPROM* is a PROM that is erasable. An EPROM chip can be easily recognized by the clear quartz crystal window set in the chip package directly over the die (see Figure 5.4). You can actually see the die through the window! EPROMs have the same 27xxxx part-numbering scheme as the standard PROM, and they are functionally and physically identical except for the clear quartz window above the die.

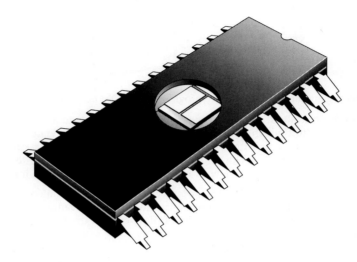

Figure 5.4   An EPROM showing the quartz window for ultraviolet erasing.

The purpose of the window is to allow ultraviolet light to reach the chip die because the EPROM is erased by exposure to intense UV light. The window is quartz crystal because regular glass blocks UV light. You can't get a suntan through a glass window!

Note

The quartz window makes the EPROMs more expensive than the OTP PROMs. This extra expense is needless if erasability is not important.

The UV light erases the chip by causing a chemical reaction, which essentially melts the fuses back together. Thus, any binary 0s in the chip become 1s, and the chip is restored to a new condition with binary 1s in all locations. To work, the UV exposure must be at a specific wavelength (2,537 angstroms), at a fairly high intensity (12,000 uw/cm²), in close proximity (2cm–3cm, or about 1"), and last for between 5 and 15 minutes. An EPROM eraser is a device that contains a UV light source (usually a sunlamp-type bulb) above a sealed compartment drawer in which you place the chip or chips (see Figure 5.5).

Figure 5.5 shows a professional-type EPROM eraser that can handle up to 50 chips at a time. I use a much smaller and less expensive one called the DataRase by the Walling Company. This device erases up to four chips at a time and is both economical and portable. The current version is called DataRase II; the DataRase II and similar products are sold by DigiKey (www.digikey.com) and other sources of EPROM programming equipment.

The quartz crystal window on an EPROM typically is covered by tape, which prevents accidental exposure to UV light. UV light is present in sunlight, of course, and even in standard room lighting, so that over time a chip exposed to the light can begin to degrade. For this reason, after a chip is programmed, you should put a sticker over the window to protect it.

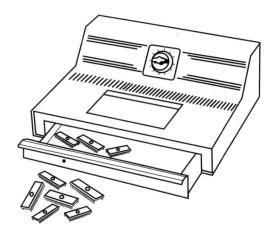

Figure 5.5   A professional EPROM eraser.

EEPROM/Flash ROM

A newer type of ROM is the EEPROM, which stands for *electrically erasable PROM*. These chips are also called *flash ROMs* and are characterized by their capability to be erased and reprogrammed directly in the circuit board they are installed in, with no special equipment required. By using an EEPROM, or flash ROM, you can erase and reprogram the motherboard ROM in a PC without removing the chip from the system or even opening up the system chassis.

With a flash ROM or EEPROM, you don't need a UV eraser or device programmer to program or erase chips. Not only do virtually all PC motherboards built since 1994 use flash ROMs or EEPROMs, but most automobiles built since then use them as well.

The EEPROM or flash ROM can be identified by a 28xxxx or 29xxxx part number, as well as by the absence of a window on the chip. Having an EEPROM or a flash ROM in your PC motherboard means you now can easily upgrade the motherboard ROM without having to swap chips. In most cases, you download the updated ROM from the motherboard manufacturer's website and then run a special program it provides to update the ROM. This procedure is described in more detail later in this chapter.

I recommend that you periodically check with your motherboard manufacturer to see whether an updated BIOS is available for your system. An updated BIOS might contain bug fixes or enable new features or device support not originally found in your system.

▶▶   For more information on updating your PC motherboard flash ROMs, see "Upgrading the BIOS," p. 459.

Non-PC ROM Upgrades

For the auto enthusiasts out there, you might want to do the same for your car; that is, check to see whether ROM upgrades are available for your vehicle's computer. Now that updates are so easy and inexpensive, vehicle manufacturers are releasing bug-fix ROM upgrades that correct operational problems or improve vehicle performance. In most cases, you must check with your dealer to see whether any new vehicle ROMs are available. If you have a GM car, GM has a website where you can get information about the BIOS revisions available for your car, which it calls Vehicle Calibrations. The GM Vehicle Calibration Information site address is http://calid.gm.com.

When you enter your VIN (vehicle identification number), this page displays the calibration history for the vehicle, which is a list of all the different flash ROM upgrades (calibrations) developed since the vehicle was new. For example, when I entered the VIN from the 1994 Impala SS I owned, I discovered that the PCM (powertrain control module or computer) had been programmed with the second of five flash ROM calibrations that had been released over the years, meaning there had been three newer ROM versions than the one I had! The fixes included in the available updates are also listed. Armed with this information I made a visit to the dealer to have them reprogram the PCM with the latest calibration. In this specific case the upgraded software fixed several problems, including the engine surging under specific conditions, transmission clunks when shifting, erroneous "check engine" light warnings, and several other minor problems.

Knowing the flash ROM capability, I began experimenting with running calibrations originally intended for other vehicles. In my case, I ran a '94 Camaro Z28 calibration in the '94 Impala SS, which made a noticeable improvement in performance. The spark-advance curve and fuel-delivery parameters were much more aggressive in the Camaro calibration, as were the transmission shift points and other features. Today there are even better options—a number of companies produce ROM upgrades for many different vehicles. If you are interested in having a custom program installed in your flash ROM–equipped vehicle, I recommend Fastchip (www.fastchip.com), Hypertech (www.hypertech.com), and Superchips (www.superchips.com). If you want to develop your own vehicle calibrations, see www.diy-efi.org for more information.

Flash ROM updates can also be used to add new capabilities to existing peripherals—for example, updating a modem to support newer communications standards or updating CD or DVD rewritable drives to support new media.

These days, many objects with embedded computers controlling them are using flash ROMs; for example, I have updated the flash ROM code (often called *firmware*) in my network routers, wireless access points, network attached storage drives, and even some digital cameras. Installing flash ROM or firmware upgrades is as easy as downloading a file from the device manufacturer website and running the update program included in the file. Who knows, one day you might find yourself downloading flash ROM upgrades for your toaster!

ROM BIOS Manufacturers

Several popular BIOS manufacturers in the market today supply the majority of motherboard and system manufacturers with the code for their ROMs. This section discusses the various available versions.

Several companies have specialized in the development of a compatible ROM BIOS product. The three major companies that come to mind in discussing ROM BIOS software are American Megatrends, Inc. (AMI), Phoenix Technologies, and Award Software (now owned by Phoenix Technologies). Each company licenses its ROM BIOS to motherboard manufacturers so those manufacturers can worry about the hardware rather than the software. To obtain one of these ROMs for a motherboard, the original equipment manufacturer (OEM) must answer many questions about the design of the system so that the proper BIOS can be either developed or selected from those already designed. Combining a ROM BIOS and a motherboard is not a haphazard task. No single, generic, compatible ROM exists, either. AMI, Award, and Phoenix ship many variations of their BIOS code to different board manufacturers, each one custom-tailored to that specific motherboard.

Over the years, some major changes have occurred in the BIOS industry. Intel, perhaps the largest BIOS customer, has switched between Phoenix and AMI for most of its motherboards. Intel originally used a Phoenix BIOS core in its motherboards up through 1995, when it changed to an AMI core. It then used AMI until 1997, when it switched back to Phoenix. In 1999 Intel switched again, this time back to AMI. In each case note that while Intel gets the core BIOS from Phoenix or AMI, they are highly customized for the individual motherboards they are installed in.

Another major development occurred in late 1998, when Phoenix bought Award. Since then Phoenix has sold both the Phoenix and Award BIOS as different products. The Award BIOS is sold as its standard product, while the Phoenix BIOS is sold as a more feature-rich BIOS for high-end systems. Currently, the BIOS market is mostly divided between AMI and Phoenix; however, Phoenix not only develops the BIOS for many systems, but is also the primary BIOS developer responsible for new BIOS development and new BIOS standards.

Another development in recent years has been the creation of separate BIOS products for 32-bit and 64-bit desktop systems, mobile systems, 32-bit and 64-bit servers, and embedded devices. Although all BIOS chips must perform some of the same tasks, a BIOS product optimized for a mobile computer often needs additional support for features such as docking modules, advanced battery power management, as well as bootable USB and removable flash memory devices, whereas a BIOS optimized for a server needs support for features such as advanced hardware monitoring and 64-bit PCI slots. By creating customized BIOS versions for different platforms, BIOS vendors provide support for the features needed by a particular computing platform and provide better performance and stability.

OEMs

Most OEMs contract with AMI or Phoenix for motherboard BIOS core, and then perform their own customizations for specific chipsets and motherboards. Although most use either the AMI or Phoenix core offerings, some OEMs have developed their own compatible BIOS ROMs independently. Companies such as Dell, HP/Compaq, AT&T, and Acer have developed several of their own BIOS products. In some cases they may have started with an AMI or Phoenix core that they licensed years ago, and continued development in-house after that.

Even though AMI or Phoenix might have done the initial development, you still must get upgrades or fixes from the system or motherboard manufacturer. This is really true for all systems because the system or motherboard manufacturers customize the BIOS for their boards.

AMI

The AMI BIOS is currently the most popular BIOS in PC systems. Some versions of the AMI BIOS are called *Hi-Flex* because of the high flexibility found in the BIOS configuration program. The AMI Hi-Flex BIOS products are used in Intel, AMI, and many other manufacturers' motherboards. One special AMI feature is that it is the only third-party BIOS manufacturer to make its own motherboards and other hardware devices.

During power up, the AMI BIOS ID string is displayed on the lower-left part of the screen. This string tells you valuable information about which BIOS version you have and about certain settings that are determined by the built-in setup program.

Tip

A good trick to help you view the BIOS ID string is to shut down and either unplug your keyboard or hold down a key as you power it back on. This causes a keyboard error, and the string remains displayed.

You also can download the AMI Motherboard ID Utility program (AMIMBID) from AMI's website (http://www.ami.com/support/mbid.cfm) and run it to determine the contents of ID String 1.

The primary BIOS identification string (ID String 1) is displayed by any AMI BIOS during the POST in the bottom-left corner of the screen, below the copyright message. Two additional BIOS ID strings (ID Strings 2 and 3) can be displayed by the AMI Hi-Flex BIOS by pressing the Insert key during the POST. These additional ID strings display the options installed in the BIOS.

The general BIOS ID String 1 format for older AMI BIOS versions is shown in Table 5.2. In addition, the BIOS ID String 1 format for AMI Hi-Flex BIOS versions is shown in Table 5.3, the AMI Hi-Flex BIOS ID String 2 in Table 5.4, and the AMI Hi-Flex BIOS ID String 3 in Table 5.5.

Table 5.2   The ABBB-NNNN-mmddyy-KK String 1 Format for Older AMI BIOS Versions

Position	Description
A	BIOS options: D = Diagnostics built in S = Setup built in E = Extended Setup built in
BBB	Chipset or motherboard identifier: C&T = Chips & Technologies chipset NET = C&T NEAT 286 chipset 286 = Standard 286 motherboard SUN = Suntac chipset PAQ = Compaq motherboard INT = Intel motherboard AMI = AMI motherboard G23 = G2 chipset 386 motherboard
NNNN	The manufacturer license code reference number
mmddyy	The BIOS release date, mm/dd/yy

Table 5.3   The AB-CCcc-DDDDDD-EFGHIJKL-mmddyy-MMMMMMMM-N String 1 Format for the AMI Hi-Flex BIOS

Position	Description
A	Processor type: 0 = 8086 or 8088 2 = 286 3 = 386 4 = 486 5 = Pentium 6 = Pentium Pro/II/III/Celeron/Athlon/Duron
B	Size of BIOS: 0 = 64KB BIOS 1 = 128KB BIOS 2 = 256KB BIOS
CCcc	Major and minor BIOS version number
DDDDDD	Manufacturer license code reference number 0036xx = AMI 386 motherboard, xx = Series # 0046xx = AMI 486 motherboard, xx = Series # 0056xx = AMI Pentium motherboard, xx = Series # 0066xx = AMI Pentium Pro motherboard, xx = Series #

Table 5.3   Continued

Position	Description
E	1 = Halt on POST error
F	1 = Initialize CMOS every boot
G	1 = Block pins 22 and 23 of the keyboard controller
H	1 = Mouse support in BIOS/keyboard controller
I	1 = Wait for <F1> key on POST errors
J	1 = Display floppy error during POST
K	1 = Display video error during POST
L	1 = Display keyboard error during POST
mmddyy	BIOS date, mm/dd/yy
MMMMMMMMM	Chipset identifier or BIOS name

Table 5.4   The AAB-C-DDDD-EE-FF-GGGG-HH-II-JJJ Format for the AMI Hi-Flex BIOS String 2

Position	Description
AA	Keyboard controller pin number for clock switching
B	Keyboard controller clock switching pin function: H = High signal switches clock to high speed L = High signal switches clock to low speed
C	Clock switching through chipset registers: 0 = Disable 1 = Enable
DDDD	Port address to switch clock high
EE	Data value to switch clock high
FF	Mask value to switch clock high
GGGG	Port address to switch clock low
HH	Data value to switch clock low
II	Mask value to switch clock low

Table 5.5   The AAB-C-DDD-EE-FF-GGGG-HH-II-JJ-K-L Format for the AMI Hi-Flex BIOS ID String 3

Position	Description
AA	Keyboard controller pin number for cache control.
B	Keyboard controller cache control pin function: H = High signal enables the cache L = High signal disables the cache
C	1 = High signal is used on the keyboard controller pin
DDD	Cache control through chipset registers: 0 = Cache control off 1 = Cache control on

Table 5.5   Continued

Position	Description
EE	Port address to enable cache
FF	Data value to enable cache
GGGG	Mask value to enable cache
HH	Port address to disable cache
II	Data value to disable cache
JJ	Mask value to disable cache
K	Pin number for resetting the 82335 memory controller
L	BIOS modification flag: 0 = The BIOS has not been modified

The AMI BIOS has many features, including a built-in setup program normally activated by pressing the Delete or Esc key within the first few seconds of powering on the system. In most cases the BIOS prompts you briefly on the screen as to which key to press and when to press it.

A unique feature of some of the AMI BIOS versions was that in addition to the setup, they had a built-in, menu-driven diagnostics package—essentially a very limited version of the standalone AMIDIAG product. The internal diagnostics are not a replacement for more comprehensive disk-based programs, but they can help in a pinch. The menu-driven diagnostics do not do extensive memory testing, for example, and the hard disk low-level formatter works only at the BIOS level rather than at the controller register level. These limitations often have prevented it from being capable of formatting severely damaged disks. Most newer AMI BIOS versions no longer include the full diagnostics.

AMI has provided detailed documentation for its BIOS called the *Programmer's Guide to the AMIBIOS: Includes Descriptions of PCI, APM, and Socket Services BIOS Functions*, published by Windcrest/McGraw-Hill (ISBN 0-07-001561-9). This book, written by AMI engineers, describes the AMI BIOS functions, features, error codes, and more. Unfortunately this book is out of print; however, you can often find used copies at Amazon.com.

AMI produces upgrades only for its own motherboards. If you have a non-AMI motherboard with a customized AMI BIOS, you must contact the motherboard or system manufacturer for an upgrade or use a third-party BIOS upgrade vendor such as eSupport.com.

Phoenix Award BIOS

Phoenix now refers to the family of products built on its Award BIOS as *Phoenix Award BIOS*. For several years it was also called the Phoenix FirstBIOS. The Award BIOS has all the features you expect, including a built-in setup program activated by pressing a particular key on startup (usually prompted on the screen). The POST is good, although the few beep codes supported means that a POST card may be helpful if you want to diagnose power-on fatal error problems. Phoenix provides technical support for the Award BIOS on its website at www.phoenix.com. eSupport.com also provides limited Award BIOS upgrades for some systems.

Phoenix

The Phoenix BIOS is currently licensed by Phoenix under the *SecureCore* and *TrustedCore* brands. For many years it has been a standard of compatibility by which others are judged. Phoenix was one of the first third-party companies to legally reverse-engineer the IBM BIOS using a *clean-room* approach. In this approach, a group of engineers studied the IBM BIOS and wrote a specification for how that

BIOS should work and what features should be incorporated. This information then was passed to a second group of engineers who had never seen the IBM BIOS. They could then legally write a new BIOS to the specifications set forth by the first group. This work was then unique and not a copy of IBM's BIOS; however, it functioned the same way.

The Phoenix BIOS has a built-in setup program that is normally activated by pressing F1 or F2 during the POST. The Phoenix BIOS includes a built-in setup program normally activated by pressing the F1 or F2 keys within the first few seconds of powering on the system. In most cases the BIOS will prompt you briefly on the screen as to which key to press and when to press it.

Phoenix has produced a wealth of BIOS-related documentation, including a detailed set of BIOS technical reference manuals. The original set consists of three books, titled *System BIOS for IBM PC/XT/AT Computers and Compatibles, CBIOS for IBM PS/2 Computers and Compatibles,* and *ABIOS for IBM PS/2 Computers and Compatibles;* an updated version is titled *System BIOS for IBM PCs, Compatibles, and EISA Computers: The Complete Guide to ROM-Based System Software.* In addition to being excellent references for the Phoenix BIOS, these books serve as an outstanding overall reference to the BIOS in general. These are out of print but are often available used through bookfinder services such as Amazon.com.

Phoenix has extensive technical support and documentation on its website at www.phoenix.com, and you can also find additional documentation on the eSupport site (www.esupport.com).

Microid Research BIOS

Microid Research (MR) primarily marketed upgrade BIOS for older Pentium and 486 motherboards that were abandoned by their original manufacturers. Microid Research was later acquired by Unicore, which was then acquired by Phoenix.

Tip

If you support several BIOS types, consider adding Phil Croucher's *The BIOS Companion* to your bookshelf or PDF file collection. This book provides detailed BIOS options and configuration information for today's leading BIOSs. You can purchase various editions from Amazon.com and other bookstores, but for the most up-to-date (and least expensive) edition, I suggest ordering the PDF (Adobe Acrobat) version of *The BIOS Companion* from Electrocution.com.

Upgrading the BIOS

Motherboard manufacturers tailor the BIOS code to the specific hardware on each board. This is what makes upgrading a BIOS somewhat problematic; the BIOS usually resides in one or more ROM chips on the motherboard and contains code specific to that motherboard model or revision. In other words, you must get your BIOS upgrades from your motherboard manufacturer or from a BIOS upgrade company that supports the motherboard you have, rather than directly from the original core BIOS developer.

Often you must upgrade the BIOS to take advantage of some other upgrade. For example, a BIOS upgrade will often add support for newer processors to a motherboard. To install larger hard drives in older machines, you might need a BIOS upgrade as well. For example, some of the machines you have might be equipped with an older BIOS that does not support hard drives larger than 137GB, and an upgrade may provide this support.

The following list shows some of the primary functions of a ROM BIOS upgrade; the exact features and benefits of a particular BIOS upgrade depend on your system:

- Support for newer and faster processors
- Support for bootable optical drives (called the *El Torito specification*)

- Support for bootable USB drives (including flash drives)
- Fast POST for quicker booting
- Support for Ultra-DMA/100 or Ultra-DMA/133 ATA modes
- Support for Serial ATA (SATA) drives in native Advanced Host Controller Interface (AHCI) mode
- Support for ATA/SATA hard drives greater than 8.4GB or 137GB (48-bit LBA)
- Plug and Play (PnP) device support and compatibility
- Correction of calendar-related and leap-year bugs
- Correction of bugs or compatibility problems with certain hardware and application or operating system software
- Support for ACPI (Advanced Configuration and Power Interface) power management
- Support for temperature and fan speed monitoring and control
- Support for legacy USB devices (keyboards and mice)
- Support for Wake On Lan (WOL) and network boot
- Support for chassis intrusion detection

Part of the PC 2001 standard published by Intel and Microsoft requires something called *Fast POST* to be supported. Fast POST means that the time it takes from turning on the power until the system starts booting from disk must be 12 seconds or less (for systems not using SCSI as the primary storage connection). This time limit includes the initialization of the keyboard, video card, and ATA bus. For systems containing adapters with onboard ROMs, an additional 4 seconds are allowed per ROM. Intel calls the Fast POST feature *Rapid BIOS Boot (RBB)* and is supported in all its motherboards from 2001 and beyond—some of which can begin booting from power-on in 6 seconds or less.

If you install newer hardware or software and follow all the instructions properly, but you can't get it to work, specific problems might exist with the BIOS that an upgrade can fix. This is especially true for newer operating systems. Many older systems need to have a BIOS update to properly work with the Plug and Play and ACPI power management features of Windows XP and Vista. Because these problems vary from board to board, it pays to periodically check the board manufacturer's website to see whether any updates are posted and what problems they fix. Because new hardware and software that are not compatible with your system could cause it to fail, I recommend you check the BIOS upgrades available for your system before you install new hardware or software—particularly processors and operating systems.

You can use the BIOS Wizard utility available from eSupport.com to test your BIOS for compatibility with popular BIOS features.

Where to Get Your BIOS Update

Most BIOS upgrades must be downloaded from the system or motherboard manufacturer's website. The BIOS manufacturers do not offer BIOS upgrades because the BIOS in your motherboard did not come directly from them. In other words, although you think you have a Phoenix, AMI, or Award BIOS, you really don't! Instead, you have a *custom* version of one of these BIOSs, which was licensed by your motherboard manufacturer and uniquely customized for your particular motherboard. As such, you must get any BIOS upgrades from the motherboard or system manufacturer because they must be customized for your board or system as well. You may be able to get updates from eSupport.com if you can't find your motherboard manufacturer or if it is out of business.

Determining Your BIOS Version

When seeking a BIOS upgrade for a particular motherboard (or system), you need to know the following information:

- The make and model of the motherboard (or system)
- The version of the existing BIOS

You usually can identify the BIOS you have by watching the screen when the system is first powered up. It helps to turn on the monitor first because some take a few seconds to warm up and the BIOS information is often displayed for only a few seconds. You usually can press the Pause key on the keyboard when the BIOS ID information is being displayed, which freezes it so you can record the information. Pressing any other key allows the system startup to resume.

Note

Many PCs do not display the typical POST screen. Instead, they show a logo for the motherboard or PC manufacturer, which is usually referred to as a *splash screen*. To enter BIOS Setup, you must press a key or keys (specific to the BIOS manufacturer). See the section "Running or Accessing the CMOS Setup Program," later in this chapter, for more information. You might hear some in the industry refer to displaying a manufacturer's logo instead of the default POST screen as a *quiet boot*. Often you can change these BIOS splash screens to your own liking, even including your own company logo or graphic of choice. Intel has free software at developer.intel.com/design/motherbd/gen_indx.htm that enables you to change or restore the splash screen on Intel motherboards.

Tip

Look for any copyright notices or part number information. Sometimes you can press the Pause key on the keyboard to freeze the POST, which allows you to take your time to write down the information. Pressing any other key then causes the POST to resume.

In addition, you often can find the BIOS ID information in the BIOS Setup screens. eSupport also offers a downloadable BIOS Agent program that can be used to determine this information, as well as the motherboard chipset and Super I/O chip used by your motherboard. After you have this information, you should be able to contact the motherboard manufacturer to see whether a new BIOS is available for your system. If you go to the website, check to see whether a version exists that is newer than the one you have. If so, you can download it and install it in your system.

Checking the BIOS Date

One method of determining the relative age and capabilities of your motherboard ROM is to check the date. The BIOS date is stored in virtually all PCs as an 8-byte text string at memory address FFFF5h. The date generally indicates when the BIOS code was last updated or compiled by the motherboard manufacturer. Knowing the date of a particular BIOS might give you some clue as to which features might or might not be present. You can use the DEBUG command-line utility supplied with Windows and DOS to view these addresses. DEBUG is a command-line program that presents a - prompt of its own, to which you can enter various commands. For example, the ? command displays help information. To find the BIOS date, open a command-prompt window (or boot to a DOS floppy) and execute the DEBUG command. Then at the DEBUG - prompt, enter D FFFF:5 L 8, which instructs DEBUG to display memory at FFFF5 for a length of 8 bytes. DEBUG then displays both the hexadecimal and ASCII codes found at those addresses. When the - prompt returns, you can enter Q to quit DEBUG and return to the command prompt. Figure 5.6 shows how this looked when I ran it on one of my systems.

Figure 5.6   Using DEBUG to display the motherboard ROM BIOS date.

In this example, the system shows a motherboard ROM BIOS date of 03/22/05.

Backing Up Your BIOS

Before updating a BIOS, it is generally a good idea to see if it is possible to save a backup copy of the existing BIOS. That is because some motherboard manufacturers only offer the latest BIOS for a given motherboard, and sometimes a newer BIOS may cause problems or have consequences you are not ready to live with. By having a backup you will be able to go back to the previous version. To make the backup, run the BIOS upgrade program for your board, and check to see if there is an option to save the existing BIOS to a file. If that option is not available, check to see if your motherboard manufacturer offers older versions (including the one you have) for download. If there is no option to back up and no older versions can be downloaded, there may be other ways to make a copy of the BIOS.

One benefit of an EPROM programmer is that you can use it to back up socketed ROMs in case they are later damaged. This works extremely well for socketed ROMs, but most motherboards today have Flash ROMs that are soldered. In that case you can use the Windows DEBUG program to read the ROM contents from memory and save it to a disk file.

Besides being useful as a backup, a file-based copy of your ROMs can also prove interesting for snooping around because you can look for copyright notices and other strings, disassemble the code to see how it works, and otherwise check it out.

The ROM code in a PC normally consumes 128KB of RAM in two 64KB segments, E0000–EFFFF and F0000–FFFFF. Video and other auxiliary BIOS routines normally reside in C0000–CFFFF and D0000–DFFFF. Because of the nature of DEBUG, each 64KB segment must be saved separately.

To use DEBUG to save segments E000 and F000 in this manner, open up a command prompt and follow these instructions:

```
C:\>DEBUG                 ;Run DEBUG
-R BX                     ;Change BX register (high-order file size)
BX 0000                   ;   from 0
:1                        ;   to 1 (indicates 64K file)
-N SEG-E.ROM              ;Name the file
-M E000:0 FFFF CS:0       ;Move 64K of BIOS data to current code segment
-W 0                      ;Write file from offset 0 in code segment
Writing 10000 bytes       ;   10000h = 64K
-N SEG-F.ROM              ;Name the file
-M F000:0 FFFF CS:0       ;Move 64K of BIOS data to current code segment
-W 0                      ;Write file from offset 0 in code segment
Writing 10000 bytes       ;   10000h = 64K
-Q                        ;Quit DEBUG
```

Figure 5.7 shows how this will look when entered at a Windows command prompt.

These instructions effectively save the 64K segment ranges E0000–EFFFF and F0000–FFFFF as files by first setting up the size of the file to be saved, then setting up the name of the file, and then moving (essentially, copying) the ROM BIOS code to the current code segment when DEBUG was loaded. The data then can be written to the disk.

Figure 5.7   Using DEBUG to save E0000–EFFFF and F0000–FFFFF as files.

If you want to save the segments including the video BIOS and other possible adapter card ROMs in your system, repeat the previous procedure but use C000:0 and D000:0 as the starting addresses in the DEBUG commands. Be sure to use different filenames as well. Note that the video BIOS might not use all of the C0000 segment; also, you might not have any other adapters using ROM in the remainder of the C0000 and D0000 segments, in which case Windows can sometimes use this area for other code.

One important quirk of this procedure is that the commands should be entered in the relative order indicated here. In particular, the Name command must precede the Move command; otherwise, some of the data at the beginning of the current code-segment area will be trashed.

Backing Up Your BIOS Setup (CMOS RAM) Settings

A motherboard BIOS upgrade often wipes out the BIOS Setup settings in the CMOS RAM. Therefore, you should record these settings, especially important ones such as hard-disk related settings and parameters. Some BIOS Setup programs offer the ability to save and restore CMOS settings, but unfortunately this capability is not universal. Also in some cases the new BIOS offers new settings or changes the positions of the stored data in the CMOS RAM, which means a backup and restore won't work.

In many cases you are better off manually recording your BIOS Setup parameters. You can do so by pressing the appropriate key during boot to start the BIOS setup program (usually F1, F2, or Del) and writing down any changes you've made from default settings. If you have a parallel printer connected, you also might be able to print the screens using the PrtScr key on the keyboard. Turn on the printer, start your computer normally, and restart it without turning off the system to initialize the printer. Note that this won't work for printers connected via USB, as only parallel printers are directly supported via the BIOS. When recording any changes you made from default settings, pay special attention to any hard-drive settings, especially SATA modes (IDE/AHCI/RAID), drive geometry (Cylinder/Head/Sectors per track), or translation (LBA, Large, CHS). These are important because if you fail to reset them as they were, you might not be able to boot from or access the drives.

Tip

If you are unable to print your screens, use a digital camera to take a picture of each BIOS setup screen. Be sure to set the camera to its close-up mode, and unless the camera is an SLR (Single Lens Reflex) type, use the LCD display rather than the optical viewfinder to ensure you get the entire screen in the photo.

Keyboard Controller Chips

In addition to the main system ROM, AT-class computers also have a keyboard controller or keyboard ROM, which is a keyboard-controller microprocessor with its own built-in ROM. The original keyboard controller was an Intel 8042 micro-controller, which incorporates a microprocessor, RAM, ROM, and I/O ports. This was a 40-pin chip that often had a copyright notice identifying the BIOS code programmed into the chip. Modern motherboards have this function integrated into the chipset, specifically the Super I/O or South Bridge chips.

The keyboard controller controls the reset and A20 lines and also deciphers the keyboard scan codes. The A20 line is used in extended memory and other protected-mode operations. In many systems, one of the unused ports is used to select the CPU clock speed as well.

Because of the tie-in with the keyboard controller and protected-mode operation, some problems with keyboard controllers became evident on certain mid-1990s and older systems when moving from DOS to Windows. Fortunately this is not an issue for most systems built after that time.

Upgrading a Flash BIOS

Virtually all PCs built since 1996 use a flash ROM to store the BIOS. A flash ROM is a type of EEPROM chip you can erase and reprogram directly in the system without special equipment. Older EPROMs required a special ultraviolet light source and an EPROM programmer device to erase and reprogram them, whereas flash ROMs can be erased and rewritten without you even removing them from the system. On some systems, the flash ROM is not a separate chip but may instead be incorporated into the South Bridge chip.

Using flash ROM enables you to load the upgrade into the flash ROM chip on the motherboard with-out removing and replacing the chip. Normally, these upgrades are downloaded from the manufac-turer's website. Depending on the design, some update programs require that you place the software on a bootable floppy or optical disc, while others will configure the program to run on the next startup (before Windows loads), while others will actually run in Windows as a Windows application.

Some systems allow the flash ROM in a system to be locked (write-protected). In that case you must disable the protection before performing an update—usually by means of a jumper or switch. Without the lock, any program that knows the correct instructions can rewrite the ROM in your system—not a comforting thought. Without the write-protection, virus programs could be written that overwrite or damage the ROM BIOS code in your system. The CIH virus (also called the Chernobyl virus) was one example that could overwrite the BIOS code on certain motherboards. Instead of a physical write-protect lock, some flash ROM BIOSs have a security algorithm that prevents unauthorized updates. This is the technique Intel uses on its motherboards, eliminating the need for a lock jumper or switch.

Note that motherboard manufacturers will not normally notify you when they upgrade the BIOS for a particular board. You must periodically log on to their websites to check for updates, which can then be downloaded and installed for no charge.

Before proceeding with a BIOS upgrade, you first must locate and download the updated BIOS from your motherboard manufacturer. Log on to its website, and follow the menus to the BIOS updates page; then select and download the new BIOS for your motherboard.

Note

If a flash BIOS upgrade is identified as being for only certain board revisions of a particular model, be sure you deter-mine that it will work with your motherboard before you install it. You might need to open your system and look for a revi-sion number on the motherboard or for a particular component. Check the vendor's website for details.

Some motherboard manufacturers may offer several different ways to update the BIOS on a given motherboard, some may run directly from within Windows, others may need to be run from bootable removable media such as optical, USB, or floppy. You only need to use one of them, so if you have choices, in most cases you should choose the one that is the easiest to perform. Which one you choose may depend on the current state of the system. For example, if the BIOS is corrupt, you may have no other choice but to use the emergency recovery procedures shown in the next section. If the system you are updating is one you are building for the first time and does not yet have working copy of Windows 2000 or later installed on the hard drive, then you may want to use a method that works with other bootable media such as an optical drive, USB flash drive, or floppy drive. If the update files and programs are too large to fit on a floppy, then you should run the update from either an optical drive or a USB flash drive.

Most downloadable flash ROM upgrades fit into four main types:

- Windows executable upgrades
- Automated images of bootable media
- User-created bootable media
- Emergency recovery media

The following sections examine each of these in more detail.

Windows Executable Upgrade

The Windows executable is generally the easiest and most popular method. It might not be available for older motherboards, but most new boards offer this type of procedure. Performing the actual upgrade couldn't be much easier, as basically all you have to do is download the executable upgrade program and run it. The program either runs directly in Windows, or it runs an install routine that temporarily installs the flash upgrade software so it will automatically run on the next startup and then automatically reboot the system and begin the upgrade. In either case, once the upgrade is finished, the system reboots again, and the upgrade is complete. The only drawback to this procedure is that it requires that Windows 2000 or later be installed on the system, so it might not be appropriate for new system builds where the OS isn't installed yet or if you are running an alternative OS, such as Linux.

Automated Bootable Media Images

Using automated bootable images is the next easiest method and works with any (or no) OS installed on the system. This is ideal for non-Windows systems or new systems where the OS hasn't yet been installed. Being able to use this procedure depends on your motherboard manufacturer supplying bootable floppy or CD images containing the necessary upgrade files, which you would then use to create the actual upgrade media.

In the case of a floppy, you download the floppy image creation program from the motherboard manufacturer. When you run it, the program prompts you to insert a blank floppy disk into the drive, after which it overwrites the disk with a bootable image containing the bootable OS (most likely DOS or a DOS variant) plus all of the files necessary to perform the upgrade. Then to perform the upgrade, you would first ensure that the floppy drive is set first in the boot sequence and then restart the system with the upgrade floppy disk in the drive. The system should then boot from the floppy, and the upgrade procedure should start and run automatically. Follow any on-screen prompts to complete the upgrade and then when the upgrade is complete, remove the floppy and reboot the system.

Because floppy drives are no longer installed in most newer systems and the BIOS images for newer motherboards are often too large to fit on a floppy anyway, many motherboard manufacturers now offer downloadable images of bootable CDs for BIOS upgrades. These are normally in the form of an *.ISO file, which is a CD-ROM image file containing a sector by sector copy of a CD. In order to perform the upgrade, you need to write the ISO bootable image file to a blank CD-R or RW disc. Unfortunately, neither Windows Vista, XP, nor any earlier versions include CD/DVD burning software that can read or write ISO images, which means that you need a third-party CD/DVD burning program to accomplish this. Commercial CD/DVD burning programs like those from Roxio, Nero, or Sonic are sometimes included with new systems or optical drives, so you might already have the necessary software on your system. If you don't already have one of these programs, then I recommend ImgBurn (www.imgburn.com), which is an excellent free CD/DVD burning application.

Use your CD/DVD burning program to generate the disc image by copying the ISO file to a blank CD-R or RW disc. Then, to perform the upgrade, first ensure that the optical drive is set first in the boot sequence and then restart the system with the upgrade disc in the drive. The system should boot from the CD and the upgrade procedure should start and run automatically. Merely follow the prompts to complete the upgrade and then, once the upgrade is complete, remove the CD and reboot the system.

User-created Bootable Media

Many motherboard manufacturers also offer BIOS upgrades in the form of a raw DOS-based flash utility combined with an image file, which you can run manually from any DOS bootable media. Using this technique, the upgrade can be performed from a bootable floppy, CD, or even a USB flash drive, regardless of whether the system hard drive is running Windows, Linux, or even if it has no OS at all. The necessary files are normally contained in an archive that can be downloaded from the motherboard manufacturer. Unfortunately, this type of procedure is much more labor-intensive than the others because several steps are involved. One particularly difficult part is the manual creation of the bootable media to which you will copy the files. While it is fairly straightforward and simple to create a bootable floppy, the procedure for creating bootable CDs or USB flash drives is more involved.

Fortunately, some free utilities are very helpful. For creating a bootable CD for BIOS upgrades, I recommend the Clean Boot CD package, which can be downloaded for free from www.nu2.nu/bootcd/#clean. Download the self-extracting executable package into a new folder and run it, which extracts the additional files and folders within. Then follow the directions to copy the flash utility and image files for your motherboard into the proper folder. After the files are in place, you can run the "build-clean" command, which automatically builds and creates an ISO image of a bootable CD, complete with an OS and your files included. You then use a third-party CD/DVD burning program such as ImgBurn (www.imgburn.com) to copy the ISO image to an actual CD-R or RW disc.

After you have burned the CD, you can boot from it, navigate to the folder where your flash utility and image files are located, and enter the appropriate command to execute the upgrade. For Intel motherboards that use the IFLASH.EXE utility and image files with an *.BIO extension, the proper command would be `IFLASH /PF XXX.BIO`, where you would replace `XXX.BIO` with the actual name of the BIO file you have.

The same procedure can be accomplished with a bootable USB flash drive, but just as with the creation of a bootable CD, creating a bootable USB flash drive can be somewhat involved. Fortunately, a Windows-based USB format utility is available for free from HP at tinyurl.com/ydao7p. To make the flash drive bootable, this program requires a set of DOS system files (`command.com`, `io.sys`, and `msdos.sys`) to write to the flash drive during the format. You can use several different versions of DOS, but in most cases I recommend using the system files from DOS 6.22. If you don't have a copy, you can download the DOS 6.22 system files in the form of a bootable floppy image from www.bootdisk.com.

Note

BIOS and motherboard manufacturers began adding USB boot support during 2001, so if your system dates from around that time or earlier it might not be able to boot from a USB drive.

When setting up a system to boot from a USB flash drive, the flash drive must be plugged in prior to restarting the system and entering the BIOS setup. In the BIOS setup startup sequence (boot order) the USB flash drive might appear as either a "generic" storage device hard disk or as a type of removable drive, which you should set as the first device in the boot order. In most systems, when the USB flash drive is unplugged it is automatically be removed from the boot order on the next restart.

After the USB flash drive is formatted as a bootable drive, you can add the BIOS flash utility and image files for the motherboard. Plug the bootable USB flash drive into the system you wish to upgrade and then restart the system, run the BIOS setup, and set the USB flash drive to be first in the boot sequence. After saving and exiting, the system should boot to DOS from the USB flash drive. At the DOS command prompt you can then run the proper command to reflash your BIOS.

Tip

Before you start the flash BIOS upgrade process, you should disconnect all USB and IEEE 1394 (FireWire) devices except for your keyboard and mouse. If you are booting from a USB flash drive to perform the upgrade, make sure all other USB drives are disconnected. On some systems, leaving additional external drives connected prevents a BIOS upgrade from working properly.

If you have Byte Merge enabled in the BIOS Setup on an Award BIOS-based system, disable this feature as a precaution before you perform the BIOS upgrade. This is recommended because on some older systems, leaving Byte Merge enabled during a BIOS upgrade can cause the upgrade to fail, corrupting the BIOS in the process. You can reenable this feature after you complete the upgrade. Some BIOS upgrades contain fixes for this problem so it can't happen in the future.

Emergency Flash BIOS Recovery

When you perform a flash BIOS upgrade, you should normally see a warning message onscreen similar to the following:

```
The BIOS is currently being updated. DO NOT REBOOT OR POWER DOWN until the update
is completed (typically within three minutes)...
```

If you fail to heed this warning or something interrupts the update procedure, you can be left with a system that has a corrupted BIOS. This means you will not be able to restart the system and redo the procedure, at least not easily. Depending on the motherboard, you might have to replace the flash ROM chip with one that was preprogrammed by the motherboard manufacturer. This is an unfortunate necessity because a motherboard is nonfunctional until a valid ROM is present. This is one reason I still keep my trusty ROM burner around; it is very useful for motherboards with socketed flash ROM chips. In minutes, I can use the ROM burner to reprogram the chip and reinstall it in the board. If you need a ROM programmer, I recommend the EPROM+ from Andromeda Research Labs (www.arlabs.com).

In most systems however, the flash ROM is soldered into the motherboard so it can't be easily replaced, rendering the external reprogramming idea moot. However, this doesn't mean the only way out is a complete motherboard replacement. Most motherboards with soldered-in flash ROMs have a special BIOS Recovery procedure that can be performed, which restores the contents of the chip. This hinges on a special protected part of the flash ROM that is reserved for this purpose, called the boot block. The boot block holds a recovery routine that can be used to restore the main BIOS code.

Note

Because of the small amount of code in the boot block area, on-screen prompts are not usually available to direct the procedure. This means that during the procedure the screen remains dark—as if nothing is happening. The procedure can instead be monitored by listening to the internal speaker and/or looking at the access LED on the drive containing the upgrade media. Normally the procedure causes the system to beep once when it begins, and several more times when it ends. During the procedure, you should be able to observe drive activity, indicating that the BIOS image is being read from the drive and written into the flash device.

Different motherboards and BIOS versions may have different recovery techniques. Most motherboards (including those from Intel) that support BIOS recover incorporate a BIOS configuration jumper, which can set several modes, including a built-in recovery mode. Figure 5.8 shows this jumper on a typical motherboard.

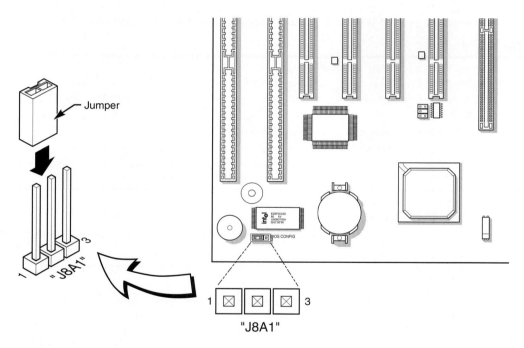

Figure 5.8   BIOS configuration jumper.

In addition to moving the jumper, the recovery requires that either a floppy or optical drive containing media with the BIOS image file is attached to the system and properly configured. Some motherboards may be able to use either type of drive to perform the recovery process, but in most cases you can only use one or the other. That is because most older motherboards only support recovery from a floppy drive, and many newer motherboards either lack floppy support entirely (no built-in floppy controller) or have BIOS images that are too large to fit on a floppy. The general rule is that you should use the floppy drive method if the recovery file (*.BIO) is small enough to fit on a floppy (1.44MB or less in size) and the motherboard includes a built-in floppy controller. If a floppy drive is not installed, you can temporarily install one. As a technician I always carry a spare floppy drive and cable in my toolkit just for this purpose. Note that the floppy drive doesn't have to be permanently mounted; I usually just open the case, attach the drive power and data cables, and leave the drive loose on the table next to the system. The floppy disk inserted into the drive should only contain the *.BIO file. No other files are necessary (that is, the disk should *not* be bootable) and if present may even prevent the *.BIO file from fitting on the disk.

Before beginning either the floppy disk or optical disc recovery procedure, you need to download the proper recovery image (*.BIO) file for the motherboard you are recovering. Obviously this needs to be done using another system if the system to be recovered is non-functional. The *.BIO image file can be downloadable separately, or it can be part of an archive with other files, such as flash programming tools, documentation, and so on. In this case you only need the actual *.BIO image file; none of the other programs or files will be used. You will also need to ensure that either a working floppy or optical drive is properly installed in the system.

To recover the BIOS using the floppy recovery method, perform the following steps:

1. Copy only the proper recovery image file (*.BIO) to a blank formatted floppy disk.

2. Place the disk in the primary floppy drive attached to the system to be recovered.

3. Power off the system and remove the BIOS configuration jumper to enable BIOS Recovery mode. (See Figure 5.8.)

4. Power on the system; the recovery should begin automatically. You should hear a beep at the start and see activity on the floppy drive during the procedure.

5. The recovery should complete in 2 to 5 minutes, after which the system will remain running, power off automatically, or prompt you to turn it off manually.

6. With the system powered off, remove the floppy disk and restore the BIOS configuration jumper to enable normal operation.

You can use the optical drive method on newer motherboards that do not have a built-in floppy controller or for which the recovery file (*.BIO) won't fit on a 1.44MB floppy. Although the drive can be virtually any type of CD or DVD optical drive, the actual disc you use should be a CD-R or RW that is burned with the *.BIO file and finalized (closed). You can burn the disc using the built-in CD burning software found in Windows XP and Vista, or you can use third-party software like the free ImgBurn application (www.imgburn.com), which is more powerful, easier to use, and works with older versions of Windows also.

To recover the BIOS using the optical drive method, perform the following steps:

1. Burn and finalize a CD with a copy of the recovery image file (*.BIO).

2. Place the CD in the primary optical drive of the system to be recovered.

3. Power off the system and remove the BIOS configuration jumper to enable BIOS Recovery mode.

4. Power on the system; the recovery should begin automatically.

5. The recovery should complete in 2 to 5 minutes, after which the system will remain running, turn off automatically, or prompt you to turn it off manually.

6. With the system powered off, restore the BIOS configuration jumper to enable normal operation.

Note

A BIOS recovery may corrupt the BIOS Setup information stored in the CMOS RAM. If the error message "CMOS/GPNV Checksum Bad...Press F1 to Run SETUP" appears during the first boot after the update, to correct the problem press F1 to go into the BIOS Setup Utility, press F9 to load setup defaults, and then press F10 to save and exit.

If your motherboard does not include a BIOS configuration jumper, there might still be a recovery procedure that could work. For example, some AMI BIOS have boot block code with a recovery procedure that works even without a recovery jumper. If the main BIOS is damaged, the boot block code is designed to look for a file called AMIBOOT.ROM on a floppy disk and flash it into the ROM if found. To perform a recovery, first download the latest BIOS image file for the motherboard, copy the file to a blank formatted floppy, and then rename the image file to AMIBOOT.ROM. Power off the system to be recovered, insert the floppy, and then power on—the recovery process should start automatically.

Some Award BIOS also have a boot block with recovery capabilities. These are designed to automatically boot from a floppy disk if the main BIOS is damaged. To perform a recovery, first download the latest BIOS upgrade files for the motherboard. Extract the files and copy the Award flash program (awdflash.exe) and the correct BIOS image (*.bin) file to a bootable formatted floppy, and then create an AUTOEXEC.BAT file on the floppy with the command awdflash.exe *.bin, replacing the *.bin with the actual name of the BIOS image file for the specific motherboard being recovered. Power off the system to be recovered, insert the floppy, and then power on. The system should boot from the floppy and the recovery process should start automatically.

With any of these procedures, wait at least several minutes after all disk and beeping activity stops before removing the floppy or CD and restarting the system. When you power the system back on, the new BIOS should be installed and functional. If nothing at all happens, then the recovery may have failed, or the board may not feature a separate boot-block section (which contains the recovery code).

Note

Note that the BIOS recovery procedure is often the fastest way to update a large number of machines, especially if you are performing other upgrades at the same time, and/or the machines are new and do not have a bootable OS installed. For example, this is how updates are sometimes done in a system assembly or production environment.

IML System Partition BIOS

Some older IBM and Compaq used a scheme similar to a flash ROM, called Initial Microcode Load (IML), in some of their older Pentium and 486 systems. IML is a technique in which the BIOS code is installed on the hard disk in a special hidden-system partition and is loaded every time the system is powered up. Of course, the system still has a core BIOS on the motherboard, but all that BIOS does is locate and load updated BIOS code from the system partition. This technique enabled Compaq and IBM to distribute ROM updates on disk for installation in the system partition. The IML BIOS is loaded every time the system is reset or powered on.

Along with the system BIOS code, the system partition contains a complete copy of the Setup and Diagnostics or Reference Disk, which provides the option of running the setup and system-configuration software at any time during a reboot operation. This option eliminates the need to boot from this disk to reconfigure the system and gives the impression that the entire Setup and Diagnostics or Reference Disk is contained in ROM.

One drawback to this technique is that the BIOS code is installed on the hard disk; the system can't function properly without the correctly set-up hard disk connected. You can always boot from the

Reference Disk floppy should the hard disk fail or become disconnected, but you can't boot from a standard floppy disk.

Although this might seem similar to newer systems using the host protected area (reserved space past the "end" of the hard disk), it is not quite the same thing. Systems using the HPA use it only for recovery, diagnostic, and backup applications. The BIOS itself, as well as the BIOS Setup, is still contained in the actual ROM (flash ROM) chip.

Motherboard CMOS RAM Addresses

In the original IBM AT system, a Motorola 146818 chip was used as the real-time clock (RTC) and CMOS RAM chip. This special chip had a simple digital clock that used 14 bytes of RAM and an additional 50 more bytes of leftover RAM in which you could store anything you wanted. The designers of the IBM AT used these extra 50 bytes to store the system configuration.

Modern PC systems don't use the Motorola chip; instead, they incorporate the functions of this chip into the motherboard chipset (South Bridge) or Super I/O chip, or they use a special battery and NVRAM module from companies such as Dallas Semiconductor or Benchmarq.

Table 5.6 shows the standard format of the information stored in the 64-byte standard CMOS RAM module. This information controls the configuration of the system and is read and written by the system setup program.

Table 5.6   CMOS RAM Addresses

Offset (hex)	Offset (dec)	Field Size	Function
00h	0	1 byte	Current second in BCD (00–59)
01h	1	1 byte	Alarm second in BCD
02h	2	1 byte	Current minute in BCD (00–59)
03h	3	1 byte	Alarm minute in BCD
04h	4	1 byte	Current hour in BCD (00–23)
05h	5	1 byte	Alarm hour in BCD
06h	6	1 byte	Current day of week in BCD (00–06)
07h	7	1 byte	Current day of month in BCD (00–31)
08h	8	1 byte	Current month in BCD (00–12)
09h	9	1 byte	Current year in BCD (00–99)
0Ah	10	1 byte	Status register A
0Bh	11	1 byte	Status register B
0Ch	12	1 byte	Status register C
0Dh	13	1 byte	Status register D
0Eh	14	1 byte	Diagnostic status
0Fh	15	1 byte	Shutdown code
10h	16	1 byte	Floppy drive types
11h	17	1 byte	Advanced BIOS Setup options
12h	18	1 byte	Hard disk 0/1 types (0–15)
13h	19	1 byte	Keyboard typematic rate and delay
14h	20	1 byte	Installed equipment

Table 5.6   Continued

Offset (hex)	Offset (dec)	Field Size	Function
15h	21	1 byte	Base memory in 1K multiples, LSB
16h	22	1 byte	Base memory in 1K multiples, MSB
17h	23	1 byte	Extended memory in 1K multiples, LSB
18h	24	1 byte	Extended memory in 1K multiples, MSB
19h	25	1 byte	Hard Disk 0 Extended Type (0–255)
1Ah	26	1 byte	Hard Disk 1 Extended Type (0–255)
1Bh	27	9 bytes	Hard Disk 0 user-defined type information
24h	36	9 bytes	Hard Disk 1 user-defined type information
2Dh	45	1 byte	Advanced BIOS Setup options
2Eh	46	1 byte	CMOS checksum MSB
2Fh	47	1 byte	CMOS checksum LSB
30h	48	1 byte	POST reported extended memory LSB
31h	49	1 byte	POST reported extended memory MSB
32h	50	1 byte	Date century in BCD (00–99)
33h	51	1 byte	POST information flag
34h	52	2 bytes	Advanced BIOS Setup options
36h	54	1 byte	Chipset-specific BIOS Setup options
37h	55	7 bytes	Power-On Password (usually encrypted)
3Eh	62	1 byte	Extended CMOS checksum MSB

BCD = Binary-coded decimal
LSB = Least significant byte
MSB = Most significant byte
POST = Power-on self test

Note that many newer systems have extended CMOS RAM with 2KB, 4KB, or more. The extra room is used to store the Plug and Play information detailing the configuration of adapter cards and other options in the system. As such, no 100%-compatible standard exists for how CMOS information is stored in all systems. You should consult the BIOS manufacturer for more information if you want the full details of how CMOS is stored because the CMOS configuration and setup programs typically are part of the BIOS. This is another example of how close the relationship is between the BIOS and the motherboard hardware.

Backup programs and utilities are available in the public domain for CMOS RAM information, which can be useful for saving and later restoring a configuration. Unfortunately, these programs are BIOS specific and function only on a BIOS for which they are designed. As such, I don't usually rely on these programs because they are too motherboard and BIOS specific and will not work on all my systems seamlessly.

Table 5.7 shows the values that might be stored by your system BIOS in a special CMOS byte called the *diagnostic status byte*. By examining this location with a diagnostics program, you can determine whether your system has set trouble codes, which indicate that a problem previously has occurred.

Table 5.7   CMOS RAM Diagnostic Status Byte Codes

Bit Number									
7	6	5	4	3	2	1	0	Hex	Function
1	■	■	■	■	■	■	■	80	Real-time clock (RTC) chip lost power.
■	1	■	■	■	■	■	■	40	CMOS RAM checksum is bad.
■	■	1	■	■	■	■	■	20	Invalid configuration information found at POST.
■	■	■	1	■	■	■	■	10	Memory size compare error at POST.
■	■	■	■	1	■	■	■	08	Fixed disk or adapter failed initialization.
■	■	■	■	■	1	■	■	04	Real-time clock (RTC) time found invalid.
■	■	■	■	■	■	1	■	02	Adapters do not match configuration.
■	■	■	■	■	■	■	1	01	Timeout reading an adapter ID.

If the diagnostic status byte is any value other than 0, you typically get a CMOS configuration error on bootup. These types of errors can be cleared by rerunning the setup program.

Replacing a Socketed ROM

Systems dating from 1995 or earlier usually don't have a flash ROM and instead use an EPROM. To upgrade the BIOS in one of these systems, you replace the EPROM chip with a new one preloaded with the new BIOS. As with a flash ROM upgrade, you usually would get this from your motherboard manufacturer.

The procedure for replacing the BIOS chip is also useful if you have made a backup copy of your socketed system BIOS chip and need to replace a damaged original with the backup copy. This can also be useful if you have a socketed flash ROM, which was common on motherboards without a BIOS recovery jumper.

To replace the BIOS chip, follow these steps:

1. Back up the CMOS RAM settings.
2. Power down the system and unplug the power cord.
3. Remove the cover and any other components in the way of the BIOS EPROM chip. Remember to use caution with respect to static discharges; you should wear an antistatic wrist strap for this procedure or ground yourself to the chassis before touching any internal components.
4. Using a chip puller or a thin flat-blade screwdriver, gently pry the chip out of its socket.
5. Remove the new EPROM from the antistatic packing material in which it came.
6. Install the new EPROM chip into the socket. A standard rectangular BIOS chip has a dimple at one end that corresponds to a cutout on the socket. You can install the chip in the socket backward, but if you do, you will destroy the chip.
7. Reinstall anything you removed to gain access to the chip.
8. Put the cover back on, plug in the system, and power on.
9. Enter the BIOS setup information you saved earlier.
10. Save the BIOS setup settings and restart the system.

As you can see, things are much easier with a flash ROM because you usually don't even have to remove the lid.

Year 2000 BIOS Issues

All systems now in use should be compliant with twenty-first century dates, either through BIOS updates or through software or hardware patches. However, if you are returning stored systems built before 1999 to service, you might want to test them for year-2000 compliance. For details, see *Upgrading and Repairing PCs, 12th Edition.*

Preboot Environment

The Phoenix BIOS preboot environment has a graphical user interface that allows a user to access the BIOS Setup, extended diagnostics, a backup/restore application, or a full recovery of the original system contents (product restoration to factory-delivered contents). All these applications (except the BIOS Setup) are stored in the HPA (Host Protected Area), a hidden area of the hard drive literally situated past the reported end of the drive. The number and type of applications accessible via the preboot environment depend on which options the OEM selected when designing the system. Figure 5.9 shows the IBM/Lenovo implementation of the Phoenix BIOS preboot environment. This environment is activated by pressing the Enter key on the keyboard during the POST.

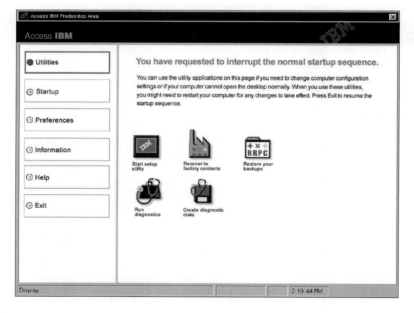

Figure 5.9   IBM/Lenovo implementation of the Phoenix BIOS preboot environment.

A graphical preboot environment is especially useful for product recovery. For example, most of the larger system OEMs do a lot more than just install Windows on a system before they deliver it. After installing Windows, they install all the service packs and updates available at the time, as well as all the updated drivers unique to their systems. Then they add customizations, such as special wallpapers or interface customizations, support contact information, online system documentation, and custom utilities designed to make their systems easier to use. Finally, they install applications such as DVD players, Office applications or other productivity software, and more.

This OEM customization represents a lot of work if a user were to have to duplicate this from scratch, so most manufacturers like to include the ability to easily recover the system to the factory-delivered contents, including the OS, drivers, application, and custom configuration. This was originally provided via several CDs or DVDs, which could be lost or damaged by the user, are sometimes problematic to use, and cost money to produce and deliver with the system. By using a BIOS with a preboot environment, an OEM can instead deliver the contents of the recovery CDs directly on the hard disk and make it accessible via the preboot menu in the BIOS.

Originally, this was done using a hidden partition, which unfortunately could easily be damaged or overwritten by partitioning software or other utilities. In many newer systems, the contents of the recovery disks are instead preinstalled in the HPA, which is accessible via Protected Area Run Time Interface Extension Services (PARTIES), a standard supported on all ATA-4 or newer drives. HPA/ PARTIES works by using the ATA SET MAX ADDRESS command to essentially make the drive appear to the system as a slightly smaller drive. Most manufacturers use the last 3GB of the drive for the HPA. Anything from the new max address (the newly reported end of the drive) to the true end of the drive is considered the HPA and is accessible only using PARTIES commands. Figure 5.10 shows the contents of the HPA and the relationship between the HPA and the rest of the drive.

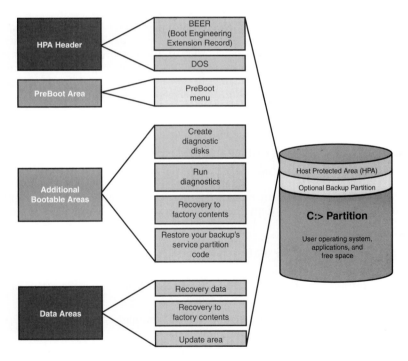

Figure 5.10   The Host Protected Area (HPA).

The HPA is more secure than a hidden partition because any data past the end of the drive simply cannot be seen by any normal application, or even a partitioning utility such as Partition Magic or Partition Commander. This makes it far more secure and immune to damage. Still, if you wanted to remove the HPA, there is a way to reset the max address, thus exposing the HPA. Then you could run something like Partition Magic or Partition Commander to resize the main partition to include the extra space that was formerly hidden and unavailable. The only consequence is that you would lose access to the product recovery, diagnostics, and backup applications preloaded by the OEM. For some people, this might be desirable because future product recoveries could still be done via the recovery discs (not usually shipped with the system anymore, but still available separately either for free or for a minimal charge), and true hardware diagnostics can still be run via bootable floppies or optical discs. Also, if you are replacing the hard disk, you can temporarily unhide the HPA on the original drive, allowing it to be copied to a new drive. Alternatively, you can use the OEM-supplied recovery discs to install the HPA on the new drive.

Most new systems using Phoenix BIOS come with their recovery software and diagnostics in the HPA because this is part of the newer Phoenix BIOS cores used by a large number of OEMs on desktop and laptop systems built in 2003 or later.

CMOS Setup Specifications

The CMOS RAM must be configured with information about your system's drives and user-selected options before you can use your computer. The Setup program provided with your system is used to select the options you want to use to start your computer.

Running or Accessing the CMOS Setup Program

If you want to run the BIOS Setup program, you usually have to reboot and press a particular key or key combination during the POST. Normally, the correct key to press is displayed onscreen momentarily during the POST. If it flashes past too quickly to read, try pressing the Pause key on the keyboard when it appears. This freezes the system, allowing you to read the display. Pressing any other key (such as the spacebar) unpauses the system and allows the POST to continue. The major vendors have standardized the following keystrokes to enter the BIOS Setup in recent systems:

- **AMI BIOS**—Press F1 or Del (Delete) during POST.
- **Phoenix BIOS**—Press F1 or F2 during POST.
- **Award BIOS**—Press Delete or Ctrl+Alt+Esc during POST.
- **Microid Research (MR) BIOS**—Press Esc during POST.

If your system does not respond to one of these common keystroke settings, you might have to contact the manufacturer or read the system documentation to find the correct keystrokes.

Some unique ones are as follows:

- **IBM Aptiva/Valuepoint or ThinkPad**—Press F1 during POST or while powering on the system.
- **Toshiba notebook/laptop**—Press Esc while powering on the system; then press F1 when prompted.
- **Older Phoenix BIOS**—Boot to a safe-mode DOS command prompt and then press Ctrl+Alt+Esc or Ctrl+Alt+S.
- **Compaq**—Press F10 during POST.

After you are at the BIOS Setup main screen, you'll usually find a main menu allowing access to other menus and menus of different sections or screens. In the following sections I go through the menus and submenus found on most Intel motherboards. While not all motherboards will have all of these settings, and other brands may use slightly different settings and terminology, most will be similar in content.

BIOS Setup Menus

Most modern BIOSs offer a menu bar at the top of the screen when you're in the BIOS Setup that controls navigation through the various primary menus. A typical menu bar offers the choices shown in Table 5.8.

Note

Because most common BIOSs use similar settings, I've chosen the Setup used by modern Intel motherboards as an example in the following tables. Because the BIOS is customized by the motherboard manufacturer, even the same BIOS can offer different options for different boards. The settings covered here will help you get a general idea of the type of settings to expect and how the BIOS Setup settings affect your computer.

Table 5.8   BIOS Setup Menus

Setup Menu	Description
Maintenance	Clears passwords and displays processor information. The maintenance menu is displayed only when the BIOS Configuration jumper is set to configure mode.
Main	Processor and time/date configuration.
Advanced	Configures advanced chipset and hardware features.
Security	Sets passwords and security features.
Power	Configures power management features and power supply controls.
Boot	Selects boot options.
Exit	Saves or discards changes to Setup program options.

Choosing each of these selections takes you to another menu with more choices.

Maintenance Menu

The Maintenance menu is a special menu for setting the processor speed and clearing the setup passwords. Older motherboards used jumpers to configure the processor bus speed (motherboard speed) and processor multiplier. Most newer boards from Intel and others now offer this control via the BIOS Setup rather than moving jumpers. In the case of Intel, one jumper still remains on the board called the *configuration jumper*, and it must be set to Configure mode for the Maintenance menu to be available.

Setup displays this menu only if the system is set in Configure mode. To set Configure mode, power off the system and move the configuration jumper on the motherboard from *Normal* to *Configure* (see Figure 5.8, earlier in this chapter). Because this is the only jumper on a modern Intel board, it is pretty easy to find. When the system is powered back on, the BIOS Setup automatically runs, and you will be able to select the Maintenance menu shown in Table 5.9. After making changes and saving, power off the system and reset the jumper to Normal mode for normal operation.

Table 5.9   Maintenance Menu Settings

Setting	Options	Description
Board ID	—	Value that uniquely identifies the board.
C1E	Enabled Disabled	Allows the system to reduce processor voltage when no work is being done.
Clear All Passwords	OK Cancel	Clears both user and supervisor passwords.
Clear Trusted Platform Module	OK Cancel	Used to clear the Trusted Platform Module (TPM) if you are transferring ownership of the system to a new user.
CPU Frequency Multiplier	User Defined	Sets the ratio between CPU Core Clock and the Front Side Bus (FSB). This setting is present only when Default Frequency Ratio is disabled.
CPU Microcode Update Revision	—	Displays processor's Microcode Update Revision.
CPU Stepping Signature	—	Displays processor's Stepping Signature.
Default Frequency Ratio	Enabled Disabled	Enabled: uses processor default frequency ratio. Disabled: allows programming of frequency ratio.
Fixed Disk Boot Sector	Enable Disable	Master Boot Record (MBR) virus protection, Enable: master boot record is write protected.
Microcode Revision	—	Displays the processor microcode revision.
Processor Stepping	—	Displays the processor stepping.
Ratio Actual Value	—	Displays the processor core/bus ratio.
Reset Intel AMT to default factory settings	—	Resets Intel Active Management Technology (AMT) to the default factory settings.
Use Maximum Multiplier	Automatic Disabled	Works only on multiplier-unlocked processors: sets CPU speed to default or maximum rated multiplier.

Note that most newer Intel processors are designed to allow operation only at or below their rated speeds (a feature called *speed locking*), whereas others allow higher-than-rated speeds to be selected.

If a user forgets his password, all he has to do is set the configuration jumper, enter the Maintenance menu in BIOS Setup, and use the option provided to clear the password. This function doesn't tell the user what the password was; it simply clears it, allowing a new one to be set if desired. This means the security is only as good as the lock on the system case because anybody who can get to the configuration jumper can clear the password and access the system. This is why most better cases come equipped with locks.

Main Menu

The standard CMOS Setup menu dates back to the 286 days, when the complete BIOS Setup consisted of only one menu. In the standard menu, you can set the system clock and record hard-disk and floppy-drive parameters and the basic video type. Newer BIOSs have more complicated setups with more menus and submenus, so the main menu often is fairly sparse compared to older systems.

The main menu in a modern system reports system information such as the BIOS version, the processor type and speed, the amount of memory, and whether the memory or cache is configured for ECC functionality. The main menu also can be used to set the system date and time.

Table 5.10 shows a typical main menu.

Table 5.10   Main Menu Settings

Setting	Options	Description
Additional System Information	—	Displays System Information, Motherboard Information, Chassis Information, etc.
BIOS Version	—	Displays the version of the BIOS currently installed.
Core Multiplexing Technology	Enabled Disabled	When disabled, turns off all but one processor core. You may need to set this for legacy operating systems that do not support multiple cores. Depending on the particular processor, the remaining core may have access to more cache, resulting in better performance under certain applications.
Front Side Bus (FSB) Frequency	—	Displays the Front Side Bus (FSB) Frequency
Hyper-Threading Technology	Enabled Disabled	Enables or disables Hyper-Threading Technology (HTT).
L2 Cache RAM	—	Displays the size of L2 cache.
Language	English French	Selects the language used by the BIOS.
Processor Speed	—	Displays processor speed.
Processor Type	—	Displays processor type.
System Bus Speed	—	Displays the system bus speed.
System Date	Month/day/year	Sets the current date.
System Memory Speed	—	Displays the system memory speed.
System Time	Hour:minute:second	Sets the current time.
Total Memory	—	Displays the total amount of RAM

ECC stands for *error-correcting code*, which is the use of extra bits on the memory modules to detect and even correct memory errors on-the-fly. For ECC to be enabled, more expensive ECC DIMMs would have to be installed in the system. Note that all DIMMs would need to be ECC versions for this to work; if even one is non-ECC, ECC can't be enabled. For mission-critical systems (such as servers), I recommend purchasing ECC memory and enabling this function because it makes the system more fault tolerant and prevents corrupted data due to soft errors in memory. Random memory errors can occur at the rate of up to 1 bit error per month for every 64–256 megabytes installed. ECC ensures that these errors don't creep into your data files, corrupt the system, or cause it to crash.

▶▶ See "Error-correcting Code (ECC)," p. 564.

Be sure to check whether your motherboard supports ECC before purchasing ECC memory. You can install ECC memory in a non-ECC-capable board, but the ECC functionality will not be available. Also, make sure you are aware of the memory requirements for your board. Don't try to install more memory than the board supports, and be sure the modules you use meet the specifications required by the board. See the documentation for the motherboard for more information on the type and amount of memory that can be installed.

Most older BIOSs report memory as base and extended memory instead of as a single value. Base memory is typically 640KB and sometimes is called *conventional memory*. Extended memory is that which is beyond the first megabyte in the system.

You can't change any values in the memory fields; they are only for your information because they are automatically counted up by the system. If the memory count doesn't match what you have installed, a problem has likely occurred with some of the memory: It is defective, is not fully seated or properly installed, or is a type that is incompatible with your system.

Advanced Menus

The Advanced menus are used for setting advanced features that are typically controlled by the motherboard chipset. This part of your BIOS setup is somewhat specific to the particular chipset the motherboard uses. Many chipsets are available on the market today, and each has unique features. The chipset setup is designed to enable the user to customize these features and control some of the chipset settings. Table 5.11 shows the typical Advanced menus available.

Table 5.11   Advanced BIOS Menus

Advanced Menu	Description
PCI Configuration	Configures the IRQ priority of individual PCI slots
PCI Express Configuration	Configures PCI express slots
Memory Configuration	Configures memory controller and modules
Boot Configuration	Configures Plug and Play and configures the NumLock key
Chipset Configuration	Configures advanced chipset features
Peripheral Configuration	Configures peripheral ports and devices
Drive Configuration	Configures ATA devices
Floppy Configuration	Configures the floppy drive
Event Log Configuration	Configures event logging
Video Configuration	Configures video features
USB Configuration	Configures USB support
Fan Control Configuration	Configures fan operation
Hardware Monitoring	Displays voltage, temperature, and fan speeds

Advanced PCI Configuration

The PCI Configuration menu is used to select the IRQ priority of add-on cards plugged into the PCI slots. Auto (the default) should be used to allow the BIOS and operating system to assign IRQs to each slot unless specific PCI cards require unique IRQs. See Table 5.12 for a typical example.

Table 5.12   Advanced PCI Configuration Menu Settings

Feature	Options	Description
PCI Slot 1 IRQ Priority	Auto (default), 3, 5, 9, 10, 11	Allows selection of the IRQ priority for PCI bus connector 1
PCI Slot 2 IRQ Priority	Auto (default), 3, 5, 9, 10, 11	Allows selection of the IRQ priority for PCI bus connector 2
PCI Slot 3 IRQ Priority	Auto (default), 3, 5, 9, 10, 11	Allows selection of the IRQ priority for PCI bus connector 3
PCI Slot 4 IRQ Priority	Auto (default), 3, 5, 9, 10, 11	Allows selection of the IRQ priority for PCI bus connector 4

Additional IRQs might be available if onboard devices such as the serial and parallel ports are disabled.

Advanced PCI Express Configuration

The PCI Express Configuration menu is used to configure settings related to the PCI Express bus and slots. See Table 5.13 for a typical example.

Table 5.13   Advanced PCI Express Configuration Menu Settings

Setting	Options	Description
Compliance Test Pattern	Enabled Disabled	Used to verify a PCI Express slot remains functional and enabled per PCI Express specification for compliance test card testing.
Link Stability Algorithm	Enabled Disabled	Used for verifying x16 PCIe Link is up and running for x16 graphics cards.
PCIE x16 Link Retrain	GFX Card Disabled Enabled	Used to adjust the configuration for devices which may need accommodations to function properly when link training. Some PCI Express cards may not be detected properly. Link retraining allows the system to keep trying to train or detect and configure the card. This setting increases boot time.
PEG Negotiated Width	—	Displays the link train width (x1, x4, x8, x16) of the PCIe device connected in the x16 PCIe slot. This information is provided for determining performance issues with x4, x8, and x16 PCIe cards in an x16 PCIe slot while the Intel Integrated video (PCIe graphics) is enabled and the "PEG Allow > 1" option is disabled on the Advanced Chipset menu.

Advanced Memory Configuration

The options in Table 5.14 set the system's memory configuration. You can possibly change some of these settings in order to overclock the memory; however, if you run into any system instability or other problems, it is recommended to reset all settings back to default values.

Table 5.14   Advanced Memory Configuration Menu Settings

Setting	Options	Description
CPC Override	Auto Enabled Disabled	Controls Command Per Clock/1n rule mode. When enabled, allows DRAM controller to attempt Chip Select assertions in two consecutive common clocks.
Memory Frequency	Options vary	Allows you to manually set the memory speed.
Memory Correction	Non-ECC ECC	Allows you to turn error reporting on or off if the system and all the memory installed supports ECC (Error Correction Code).
Memory Mode	—	Displays single or dual channel operation.
SDRAM CAS# Latency	2.0 2.5 3.0	Selects the number of clock cycles required to address a column in memory. Corresponds to CL.
SDRAM Frequency	Auto 266 MHz 333 MHz 400 MHz	Allows override of detected memory frequency value.

Table 5.14 Continued

Setting	Options	Description
SDRAM RAS Act. To Pre.	8 7 6 5	Selects length of time from read to pre-change. Corresponds to tRAS, min.
SDRAM RAS# Precharge	4 3 2	Selects the length of time required before accessing a new row.
SDRAM RAS# to CAS# delay	4 3 2	Selects the number of clock cycles between addressing a row and addressing a column. Corresponds to tRCD.
SDRAM Timing Control	Auto Manual—Aggressive Manual—User Defined	Auto sets memory timings according to the memory detected. Manual—Aggressive selects the most aggressive user defined timings. Manual—User Defined allows manual override of detected settings.
Total Memory	—	Displays the total amount of RAM.

Advanced Boot Configuration

The options in Table 5.15 sets the system's boot time options including PnP and keyboard configuration.

Table 5.15 Advanced Boot Configuration Menu Settings

Setting	Options	Description
ASF Support	Enabled Disabled	Disables or enables Alert Standard Format (ASF) support.
Display Setup Prompt	On Off	Displays the "F2 to enter BIOS setup" message during boot.
Limit CPUID MaxVal	Enabled Disabled	Enable: allows some legacy operating systems to boot on processors with extended CPUID functions.
Numlock	Off On	Specifies the power-on state of the Numlock feature on the numeric keypad of the keyboard.
Plug & Play O/S	No Yes	Specifies if manual configuration is desired. No lets the BIOS configure all devices in the system. Yes lets the operating system configure Plug & Play (PnP) devices.

Advanced Chipset Configuration Menu

Chipset configuration allows access to settings that control the very core of the system. Because of the wide variations in different chipset, motherboard and BIOS designs, the options you see here may vary greatly from board to board.

Many motherboards include features designed to overclock the system, which enables you to set the system to run the CPU bus (and therefore the CPU itself) and possibly other buses at higher-than-normal rated speeds. These settings are especially useful for stress-testing a system after initial assembly, which is often called a *burn-in test*.

These settings can be used to speed up the processor and interconnected buses such as PCI and AGP. For specifically testing AGP video or PCI adapter cards, some motherboards allow the AGP/PCI bus speed to be set independently of the CPU bus. If you intend to use these settings to speed up a system, be aware that—depending on the specific hardware and software you have—running faster than the default clock speed can reduce system stability and shorten the useful life of the processor, and it might not be covered under warranty. You also might need to invest in better system cooling to offset the extra heat generated by overclocking your system. In general, if you don't know what a particular setting is designed for, it is best to leave it at the default or automatic setting. If any problems occur, start by returning all frequency and timing settings to their default values.

Table 5.16 lists settings used by a typical motherboard's Advanced Chipset Configuration menu.

Table 5.16   Advanced Chipset Configuration Menu

Setting	Options	Description
AGP/PCI Burn-in Mode	Default 63.88/31.94 MHz 68.05/34.02 MHz 69.44/34.72 MHz 70.83/35.41 MHz 72.22/36.11 MHz 73.60/36.80 MHz	Enables under- or overclocking the AGP/PCI bus at specific frequencies. The host clock (system bus speed) is not changed. If this option is set to anything other than Default (66.66/33.33 MHz), the Host and I/O Burn-In Mode is automatically set to Default.
CSA Device	Auto Disable	Enables or disables Communication Streaming Architecture (CSA) interface. CSA bypasses the PCI bus to provide a fast dedicated connection for on-board gigabit ethernet adapters. Auto leaves the CSA device enabled if a device is found on the bus, else the device is disabled.
DDR2 Voltage	Automatic 1.8 1.9	Automatic: memory voltage will be adjusted according to the memory detected. Memory voltage can also be manually set for testing or overclocking purposes.
Extended Burn-in Mode	Enabled Disabled	Enabling this option allows the user to select additional values for system overclocking.
Extended Configuration	Default User Defined	Chooses the default or user defined settings for the extended configuration options.
Host Burn-in Mode	<percentage>	Alters host and I/O clock frequencies in order to under or overclock the system. Percentage options are dependent on board and processor models; may be set up to 30%.
Host Burn-in Mode Type	Positive Negative	Reads the percentage set in Host Burn-in Mode Percentage as either a positive number (increases speed) or a negative number (decreases speed).
Host Spread Spectrum	Down Center	Adjust the mean frequencies for core system clocks to help prevent electromagnetic interference. Requires additional POST time.
HPET	Enabled Disabled	Enables or disables HPET (High Precision Event Timer) support.
IOAPIC Enable	Enabled Disabled	Enables or disables the I/O Programmable Interrupt Controller.

Table 5.16 Continued

Setting	Options	Description
ISA Enable Bit	Enabled Disabled	When enabled a PCI-to-PCI bridge recognizes only 16-bit I/O addresses that are not aliases of 10-bit ISA addresses (within the bridge's assigned I/O range). This helps prevent resource conflicts with ISA devices that might be present in the system (such as serial or parallel ports) and allows VGA-compatible address range mapping for ISA devices. Some older expansion devices require this to be enabled.
MCH Voltage Override	Default 1.525V 1.600V 1.625V 1.725V	Allows you to set the Memory Controller Hub (MCH or Northbridge) voltage for testing or overclocking purposes.
PCI Burn-in Mode	Default 36.36 MHz 40.00 MHz	Enables the selection of specific PCI clock frequencies for testing or overclocking purposes. Default is 33.33 MHz.
PCI Express Burn-in Mode	Default 101.32 MHz 102.64 MHz 103.96 MHz 105.28 MHz 106.6 MHz 107.92 MHz 109.24 MHz	Enables the selection of specific PCI Express clock frequencies for testing or overclocking purposes. Default is 100.00 MHz.
PCI Latency Timer	32 64 96 128 160 192 224 248	Allows you to control the time (in PCI bus clock cycles) that an agent on the PC bus can hold the bus when another agent has requested the bus.
PEG Allow > x1	Enabled Disabled	Enabled: allows the system to link train PCI express devices of width x4, x8, and x16 in the GMCH x16 slot while leaving the Intel Integrated Graphics (PCIe graphics) enabled as well. Disabled: all devices plugged into the GMCH x16 slot will link train as x1 PCIe devices if the Intel Integrated Graphics (PCIe graphics) controller is enabled.
Watchdog Timer	Enabled Disabled	Enabled: monitors the system for timeouts and takes corrective action if they occur.

Advanced Peripheral Configuration

The Peripheral Configuration menu is used to configure the devices built into the motherboard, such as serial ports, parallel ports, and built-in audio and USB ports.

Table 5.19 shows a typical Peripheral Configuration menu and its choices.

Table 5.19   Peripheral Configuration Menu Settings

Setting	Options	Description
Auxiliary Power	Enabled Disabled	Enables or disables on the onboard auxiliary power connector.
Base I/O Address (for the Parallel Port)	378 278	Specifies the base I/O address for the parallel port, if enabled.
Base I/O Address (for the Serial Port)	3F8 2F8 3E8 2E8	Specifies the base I/O address for serial port A if enabled.
ECP Mode Use DMA	—	DMA Channel 3 is used by default.
Front Panel 1394 Port 1	1394A 1394B	Sets the IEEE 1394 (FireWire) mode for the front panel 1394 Port.
Front Panel 1394 Port 2	1394A 1394B	Sets the IEEE 1394 (FireWire) mode for the 2nd front panel 1394 Port.
Interrupt (for the Parallel Port)	IRQ 5 IRQ 7	Specifies the interrupt for the parallel port, if enabled.
Interrupt (for the Serial Port)	IRQ 3 IRQ 4	Specifies the interrupt for the serial port, if enabled.
Legacy Front Panel Audio	Enabled Disabled	When enabled, the system assumes that a High Definition audio connector is not present in the system (Legacy audio is present) When disabled, the system assumes that a High Definition audio connector is present in the system.
Parallel Port Mode	Output only Bi-directional EPP ECP	Output Only operates in AT-compatible mode. Bidirectional operates in PS/2-compatible mode. EPP is Enhanced Parallel Port mode, a high-speed bidirectional mode for nonprinter peripherals. ECP is Enhanced Capability Port mode, a high-speed bidirectional mode for printers and scanners.
Onboard 1394	Enabled Disabled	Enables or disables the onboard IEEE 1394.
Onboard Audio	Enabled Disabled	Enables or disables the onboard audio.
Onboard LAN Boot ROM	Enabled Disabled	Disables or enables booting from the network.
Onboard LAN	Enabled Disabled	Enables or disables the onboard LAN.
Parallel Port	Disabled Enabled Auto	Auto assigns LPT1 the address 378h and the interrupt IRQ7. An * (asterisk) displayed next to an address indicates a conflict with another device.
Secondary SATA Controller	Enabled Disabled	Enables or disables the secondary SATA controller.
Serial Port	Disabled Enabled Auto	Auto assigns COM1 the address 3F8h, and the interrupt IRQ4. An * (asterisk) displayed next to an address indicates a conflict with another device.
Trusted Platform Module	Enabled Disabled	Disables or enables the Trusted Platform Module (TPM) security chip.

I usually recommend disabling the serial and parallel ports if they are not being used because this frees up those resources for other devices, and potentially speeds up boot time.

Advanced Drive Configuration

Of all the BIOS Setup menus, the hard-disk settings are some of the most important.

As with many BIOS Setup settings, the default or automatic values are generally recommended. With Auto settings, the BIOS sends a special Identify Drive command to the drive, which responds with information about the correct settings. From this, the BIOS can automatically detect the specifications and optimal operating mode of almost all ATA and SATA hard drives. When you select Auto for a hard drive, the BIOS redetects the drive specifications during POST, every time the system boots. You could swap drives with the power off, and the system would automatically detect the new drive the next time it was turned on.

In addition to the Auto setting, most older BIOSs offered a standard table of up to 47 drive types with specifically prerecorded parameters. Each defined drive type had a specified number of cylinders, number of heads, write precompensation factor, landing zone, and number of sectors. This often was used many years ago, but it is not used today because no current drives conform to the older type parameters.

Note that systems dating from 1997 and earlier usually are limited to a maximum drive size of 8.4GB unless they have a BIOS upgrade. Systems from 1998 and later usually support drives up to 137GB; systems dating from 2002 and beyond usually support drives beyond 137GB (48-bit LBA support), although a BIOS upgrade might be necessary for some systems.

Table 5.20 shows the Drive Configuration menu and options for a typical modern motherboard.

Table 5.20   Advanced Drive Configuration Menu Settings

Setting	Options	Description
Access Mode	CHS LBA Large Auto	Allows you to select the sector translation and addressing mode for drives under 137GB. CHS (cylinder, head, sector) mode supports up to 528MB hard disks. LBA (logical block addressing) mode supports hard disks up to 137GB in size. Large mode supports hard disks above 528MB in size, but does not support LBA mode.
ATA/IDE Configuration	Disabled Legacy Enhanced	Specifies the integrated ATA controller. Disabled disables the integrated ATA controller. Legacy enables up to two PATA channels for OS requiring legacy IDE operation. Enhanced (or Native) enables all SATA and PATA resources.
Cable Detected	—	Displays the type of cable connected to the IDE interface: 40-conductor, 80-conductor, or Serial ATA.
Configure SATA as...	IDE AHCI RAID	IDE allows for backward compatibility with non-SATA aware OS or drivers. AHCI: enables the Advanced Host Controller Interface, which supports features such as Native Command Queuing (NCQ), Hot plugging, etc. RAID: enables both AHCI and RAID capability. RAID must be configured using the RAID Configuration Utility.

Table 5.20 Continued

Setting	Options	Description
DMA Mode	Auto SWDMA 0 SWDMA 1 SWDMA 2 MWDMA 0 MWDMA 1 MWDMA 2 UDMA 0 UDMA 1 UDMA 2 UDMA 3 UDMA 4 UDMA 5	Specifies the DMA mode for the drive.
Drive Installed	—	Displays the type of drive installed.
Hard Disk Pre-Delay	Disabled 3 Seconds 6 Seconds 9 Seconds 12 Seconds 15 Seconds 21 Seconds 30 Seconds	Causes the BIOS to insert a delay before attempting to detect IDE drives in the system. Designed to give time for slower drives to spin-up.
Intel RAID Technology	Enabled Disabled	Enables or disables Intel Matrix Storage RAID technology.
Legacy IDE Channels	PATA Pri only PATA Sec only PATA PRI and Sec SATA P0/P1 only SATA P0/P1, PATA Sec SATA P0/P1, PATA Pri	Configures PATA and SATA resources for OS requiring legacy IDE operation. P0 = SATA connector 0, P1 = SATA connector 1.
Maximum Capacity	—	Displays the capacity of the drive.
Onboard Chip SATA	IDE Controller SATA Disabled	IDE Controller—both IDE and SATA channels will be detected. SATA Disabled—SATA channels will not be detected.
PCI IDE Bus Master	Disabled Enabled	Allows a PCI ATA device to initiate a transaction as a master.
PIO Mode	Auto 0 1 2 3 4	Specifies the ATA PIO mode.
Primary IDE Master	[drive]	Displays the drive installed on this IDE channel. Shows [None] if no drive is installed.
Primary IDE Slave	[drive]	Displays the drive installed on this IDE channel. Shows [None] if no drive is installed.

Table 5.20   Continued

Setting	Options	Description
Secondary IDE Master	[drive]	Displays the drive installed on this IDE channel. Shows [None] if no drive is installed.
Secondary IDE Slave	[drive]	Displays the drive installed on this IDE channel. Shows [None] if no drive is installed.
S.M.A.R.T.	Auto Disable Enable	Enable or Disable support for the hard disk's S.M.A.R.T. (Self Monitoring Analysis and Reporting Technology) capability. S.M.A.R.T. allows the early prediction and warning of impending hard disk failures.
First SATA Master	[drive]	Displays the drive installed on this SATA channel. Shows [None] if no drive is installed.
Second SATA Master	[drive]	Displays the drive installed on this SATA channel. Shows [None] if no drive is installed.
Third SATA Master	[drive]	Displays the drive installed on this SATA channel. Shows [None] if no drive is installed.
Fourth SATA Master	[drive]	Displays the drive installed on this SATA channel. Shows [None] if no drive is installed.
Fifth SATA Master	[drive]	Displays the drive installed on this SATA channel. Shows [None] if no drive is installed.
Sixth SATA Master	[drive]	Displays the drive installed on this SATA channel. Shows [None] if no drive is installed.
Type	Auto User	Specifies the IDE configuration mode for IDE devices. Auto fills-in capabilities from ATA/ATAPI device. User allows capabilities to be changed.
Use Automatic Mode	Enabled Disabled	Allows you to manually set the bootable devices configuration for legacy operating systems (OS). Legacy OS may only allow 4 devices, which means you must choose to use the IDE controller as one of your 4 devices.

The SATA controller mode setting is of particular importance. This setting controls how SATA hard drives function and appear to the system and can have a major effect on OS installation and driver issues.

One of the requirements of SATA is that it be capable of fully emulating ATA. This means that a SATA drive should be able to be supported by the same drivers and software as Parallel ATA drives. While this is true, adherence to this would mean that additional capabilities such as native command queuing could never be supported. To support features beyond standard ATA, SATA has a more powerful "native" mode interface called AHCI (advanced host controller interface).

The SATA controller on most motherboards has three modes of operation:

- IDE mode—Provides legacy ATA emulation with no AHCI or RAID support
- AHCI mode—Provides support for native SATA functionality without RAID
- RAID mode—Provides both RAID and AHCI support

Any OS or software that supports standard ATA drives also supports SATA drives if the host adapter is set to IDE mode. This means that, for example, you could install Windows XP on a SATA drive without having to press the F6 key to specify and load any additional drivers. However, if you choose AHCI or RAID/AHCI modes, the standard ATA drivers will not work, and you will need AHCI/RAID drivers instead. This means that if you are installing Windows XP on a system with SATA drives set to AHCI mode, you need to press the F6 key and install the AHCI/RAID drivers from a floppy disk. Note that Windows Vista has AHCI/RAID drivers for most SATA host adapters on the installation DVD, and it is also possible to integrate these drivers into a Windows XP install disc as well.

Switching SATA modes in the BIOS setup *after* the OS is installed can cause problems if a SATA drive is the boot drive, and you have not loaded the proper drivers in advance. For example, switch modes on a system running Windows XP, on the next boot you will most likely have an immediate blue screen error as follows:

```
STOP: 0x0000007B (parameter1, parameter2, parameter3, parameter4)
INACCESSIBLE_BOOT_DEVICE
```

In this case, changing the host adapter back to IDE mode should allow the system to boot again. Then you can install the AHCI/RAID drivers and turn AHCI/RAID mode back on. You do not usually see this problem in Windows Vista because Vista has most AHCI/RAID drivers on the installation disc.

The hard disk pre-delay function is to delay accessing drives that are slow to spin up. Some drives aren't ready when the system begins to look for them during boot time, causing the system to display Fixed Disk Failure messages and fail to boot. Setting this delay allows time for the drive to become ready before continuing the boot process. Of course, this slows down the boot process, so if your drives don't need this delay, it should be disabled.

Advanced Floppy Configuration

The Floppy Configuration menu is for configuring the floppy drive and interface. Table 5.22 shows the options in a typical BIOS Setup.

Table 5.22   Advanced Floppy Configuration Menu

Setting	Options	Description
Diskette Controller	Enabled Disabled	Configures the integrated floppy controller.
Diskette Write Protect	Enabled Disabled	Disables or enables diskette drive write protection.
Floppy A	Disabled 360 KB 5 1/4" 1.2 MB 5 1/4" 720 KB 3 1/2" 1.44 MB 3 1/2" 2.88 MB 3 1/2"	Selects the floppy drive type.

By enabling the write-protect feature, you can disallow writing to floppy disks. This can help prevent the theft of data as well as help to prevent infecting disks with viruses should they be on the system.

Advanced Event Log Configuration

The Event Logging menu is for configuring the System Management (SMBIOS) and AMT (Active Management Technology) event-logging features. SMBIOS is a DMI-compliant method for managing computers on a managed network. DMI stands for *Desktop Management Interface*, a special protocol that software can use to communicate with the motherboard. AMT allows for powerful remote access and troubleshooting capabilities, including hardware and software inventory, proactive alterting, and remote troubleshooting and recovery.

Using SMBIOS and AMT, a system administrator can remotely obtain information about a system. Applications such as the LANDesk Management Suite can use SMBIOS and AMT to report the following DMI information:

- BIOS data, such as the BIOS revision level
- System data, such as installed peripherals, serial numbers, and asset tags
- Resource data, such as memory size, cache size, and processor speed
- Dynamic data such as event detection, including event detection and error logging

Table 5.23 shows a typical Event Logging menu in BIOS Setup.

Table 5.23   Advanced Event Log Configuration Menu

Setting	Options	Description
Clear All DMI Event Log	Yes No	Yes—the DMI Event Log will be cleared at next POST and then this option automatically resets to No.
DMI Event Log	Enabled Disabled	Enable or disable the storing of POST error messages to the DMI Event Log.
ECC Event Logging	Enabled Disabled	Enables or disables event logging of ECC events.
Event Log Capacity	—	Indicates if there is space available in the event log.
Event Log Validity	—	Indicates if the event log information is valid.
Mark DMI Events As Read	[Enter]	Marks all DMI events in the event log as read.
View Event Log	[Enter]	Press Enter to show all DMI Event logs.

Some motherboards with ECC memory also support logging ECC events. I find event logging particularly useful for tracking errors such as ECC errors. Using the View Log feature, you can see whether any errors have been detected (and corrected) by the system.

Advanced Video Configuration

The Video Configuration menu is for configuring video features. Table 5.24 shows the functions of this menu in a typical modern motherboard BIOS.

Table 5.24   Advanced Video Configuration Menu

Setting	Options	Description
Aperture Size	4MB 8MB 16MB 32MB 128MB 256MB	Establishes the maximum amount of system memory that the operating system can use for video memory. This is primarily used for buffering textures for the AGP video device.

Table 5.24   Continued

Setting	Options	Description
DVMT Mode	DVMT Fixed Both	Dynamic Video Memory Technology (DVMT)—Dynamically allocates video memory based on memory requests made by applications; memory is released once the requesting application has been terminated. Fixed—Video memory is allocated during driver initialization to provide a static amount of memory. Both—Allows the combination of both Fixed and DVMT type driver allocation methods; used to guarantee a minimum amount of video memory but give the flexibility of DVMT for enhanced performance.
Frame Buffer Size	1 MB 8 MB 16 MB	Sets the frame buffer size. Frame buffer size is the total amount of system memory locked by the BIOS for video. A larger frame buffer size should result in higher video performance.
Onboard Video Memory Size	32MB 64MB 128MB 256MB	Amount of system memory available for direct access by the graphics device.
PCI/VGA Palette Snoop	Enabled Disabled	Some special VGA cards and high-end hardware MPEG decoders need to be able to look at the video card's VGA palette to determine what colors are currently in use. Enabling this feature turns on this palette "snoop." This option is only very rarely needed and should be left Disabled unless a video device specifically requires the setting enabled upon installation.
Primary Video Adapter	AGP PCI PCIe Onboard Auto	Allows selecting a specific video controller as the display device that will be active when the system boots.
Secondary Video Adapter	AGP PCI PCIe Onboard Auto	Allows selecting a specific video controller as the secondary display device.

The most common use of this menu is to change the primary video device. This is useful for dual-monitor configurations. Using this feature, you can set the PCI Express, AGP, or PCI video card to be the primary boot device.

Advanced USB Configuration Menu

The USB Configuration menu is used for configuring the USB ports on the system. Table 5.25 shows the functions of this menu in a typical modern motherboard BIOS.

Table 5.25   Advanced USB Configuration Menu

Setting	Options	Description
USB 2.0	Enabled Disabled	Disabled will turn off all USB functionality. This feature can be used for security purposes.
USB 2.0 Legacy Support	Full-Speed Hi-Speed	Configures the USB 2.0 legacy support to Full-Speed (12 Mbps) or Hi-Speed (480 Mbps).
USB EHCI Controller	Enabled Disabled	Enables or disables high-speed USB transfers (USB 2.0).
USB Function	Enabled Disabled	Disables or enables USB functionality. If Disabled, the Advanced USB Configuration menu will *not* include any changeable options. The menu will appear blank. This setting is present only when the BIOS configuration jumper is set to Maintenance mode.
USB Legacy	Enabled Disabled	USB Legacy support allows the BIOS to interact with a USB keyboard, and in limited cases, a USB mouse.
USB Ports	Enabled Disabled	Enables or disables all USB ports.
USB ZIP Emulation Type	Floppy Hard Disk	Allows you to set the emulation type for USB zip drives.

Legacy USB support means support for USB keyboards and mice independent of the OS or drivers. If you are using USB keyboards and mice with this option disabled, you will find that the keyboard and mouse are not functional until a USB-aware operating system is loaded. This can be a problem when running diagnostics software, older operating systems, or other applications that run outside of USB-aware operating systems or environments.

Note that even with legacy support disabled, the system still recognizes a USB keyboard and enables it to work during the POST and BIOS Setup. If USB legacy support is disabled (the default on some systems), the system operates as follows:

1. When you power up the computer, USB legacy support is disabled.
2. POST begins.
3. USB legacy support is temporarily enabled by the BIOS. This enables you to use a USB keyboard to enter the setup program or Maintenance mode.
4. POST completes and disables USB legacy support (unless it was set to *Enabled* while in Setup).
5. The operating system loads. While the operating system is loading, USB keyboards and mice are not recognized. After the operating system loads the USB drivers, the USB devices are recognized.

To install an operating system that supports USB when using a USB keyboard and/or mouse, enable USB legacy support in BIOS Setup and follow the operating system's installation instructions. After the operating system is installed and the USB drivers are configured, USB legacy support is no longer used and the operating system USB drivers take over. However, I recommend that you leave legacy support enabled so the USB keyboard and mouse will function while running self-booting or DOS-based diagnostics or when running other non-USB-aware operating systems.

USB legacy support is for keyboards and mice only; it won't work for USB hubs or other USB devices. For devices other than keyboards or mice to work, you need a USB-aware operating system with the appropriate USB drivers.

Advanced Fan Control Configuration Menu

Most systems have one or more chassis fans to help cool the system. Table 5.26 shows the function of the Fan Control Configuration menu on a typical high-performance PC.

Table 5.26   Advanced Fan Control Configuration Menu

Setting	Options	Description
Automatic Fan Detection	Next Boot Disable Always	Next Boot: Will detect fans added to the motherboard upon next boot only. Disabled: Will not detect fans added to the motherboard, new fans may perform erratically. Always: Will detect fans added to the motherboard, may cause a slight delay and increased noise during startup.
Lowest System Fan Speed	Slow Off	This option defines the system fan speed at the lowest system temperature. Slow—Allows the fans to continue to run at a reduced speed at low system temperatures. Off—Turns off the system fans at low system temperatures.
Processor Zone Response	Aggressive Normal Slow	To adjust acoustics for fan heatsink solutions. For less efficient fan heatsink solutions, set CPU Zone Response to Aggressive. For more efficient fan heatsink solutions, set the CPU Zone Response to Slow.
Unlock Intel(R) QST	No Yes	Unlocking Quiet System Technology (QST) allows the fan control settings to be changed using software.
CPU Fan Control	Enabled Disabled	Allows the CPU fan to be controlled in order to optimize acoustics. If disabled, the CPU fan will run at 100%.
System Fan Control	Enabled Disabled	Allows the system fans to be controlled in order to optimize acoustics. If disabled, system fans will run at 100%.

Many newer boards have built-in monitor chips that can read temperature, voltage, and fan speeds. Those that do often include a screen in the BIOS Setup that allows you to view the readings from the monitor chip. Usually such boards also include a hardware monitor program that runs under Windows for more convenient monitoring while the system is in use (see Table 5.27).

Table 5.27   Advanced Hardware Monitoring Display

Feature	Description
+1.5V in	Displays the +1.5V input level.
+12V in	Displays the +12V input level.
+3.3V in	Displays the +3.3V input level.
+5V in	Displays the +5V input level.
Ambient Air Temperature	Displays the remote thermal diode temperature.
Aux Fan	Displays the aux fan speed.
Chassis Inlet Fan	Displays the front chassis fan speed.
Chassis Outlet Fan	Displays the rear chassis fan speed.
CPU Cooling Fan	Displays the fan speed of the CPU fan.

Table 5.27   Continued

Feature	Description
CPU Temperature	Displays the processor temperature.
ICH Temperature	Displays the I/O Controller Hub (ICH) Southbridge temperature.
MCH Temperature	Displays the Memory Controller Hub (MCH) Northbridge temperature.
VCORE Voltage	Displays the CPU core operating voltage.

Security Menu

Most BIOSs include two passwords for security, called the *supervisor and user passwords.* These passwords help control who is allowed to access the BIOS Setup program and who is allowed to boot the computer. The supervisor password is also called a *setup password* because it controls access to the setup program. The user password is also called a *system password* because it controls access to the entire system.

If a supervisor password is set, a password prompt is displayed when an attempt is made to enter the BIOS Setup menus. When entered correctly, the supervisor password gives unrestricted access to view and change all the Setup options in the Setup program. If the supervisor password is not entered or is entered incorrectly, access to view and change Setup options in the Setup program is restricted.

If the user password is set, the password prompt is displayed before the computer boots up. The password must be entered correctly before the system is allowed to boot. Note that if only the supervisor password is set, the computer boots without asking for a password because the supervisor password controls access only to the BIOS Setup menus. If both passwords are set, the password prompt is displayed at boot time, and either the user or the supervisor password can be entered to boot the computer. In most systems, the password can be up to seven or eight characters long.

If you forget the password, most systems have a jumper on the board that allows all passwords to be cleared. This means that for most systems, the password security also requires that the system case be locked to prevent users from opening the cover and accessing the password-clear jumper. This jumper is often not labeled on the board for security reasons, but it can be found in the motherboard or system documentation.

Provided you know the password and can get into the BIOS Setup, a password can also be cleared by entering the BIOS Setup and selecting the Clear Password function. If no Clear function is available, you can still clear the password by selecting the Set Password function and pressing Enter (for no password) at the prompts.

Table 5.28 shows the security functions in a typical BIOS Setup.

Table 5.28   Security Settings Menu

Setting	Options	Description
Chassis Intrusion	Enabled Disabled	Enables or disables the chassis intrusion feature.
Clear User Password	Yes No	Clears the user password.
Security Option	Setup System	If you set a Supervisor or User password, selects whether the password is required every time the system boots or only when you enter Setup.

Table 5.28   Continued

Setting	Options	Description
Set Supervisor Password	—	Specifies the supervisor password, which can be up to seven alphanumeric characters.
Set User Password	—	Specifies the user password, which can be up to seven alphanumeric characters.
Supervisor Password	—	Reports if there is a supervisor password set.
User access Level	Limited No Access View Only Full	Sets BIOS Setup Utility access rights for user level. This BIOS setting is present only if both a user password and a supervisor password have been set.
User Password	—	Reports if there is a user password set.
VT Technology	Enabled Disabled	Enables or disables Virtualization Technology.
XD Technology	Enabled Disabled	Enables or disables Execute Disable memory protection, which can prevent buffer overflow attacks.

To clear passwords if the password is forgotten, most motherboards have a password-clear jumper or switch. Intel motherboards require that you set the configuration jumper, enter the Maintenance menu in BIOS Setup, and select the Clear Password feature. If you can't find the documentation for your board and aren't sure how to clear the passwords, you can try removing the battery for 15 minutes or so—it clears the CMOS RAM. It can take that long for the CMOS RAM to clear on some systems because they have capacitors in the circuit that retain a charge. Note that this also erases all other BIOS settings, including the hard disk settings, so they should be recorded beforehand.

Power Menu

Power management is defined as the capability of the system to automatically enter power-conserving modes during periods of inactivity. Two main classes of power management exist; the original standard was called Advanced Power Management (APM) and was supported by most systems since the 386 and 486 processors. More recently, a new type of power management called Advanced Configuration and Power Interface (ACPI) has been developed and began appearing in systems during 1998. Most systems sold in 1998 or later support the more advanced ACPI type of power management. In APM, the BIOS does the actual power management, and the operating system or other software had little control. With ACPI, the power management is done by the operating system and BIOS together. This makes the control more centralized, easier to access, and enables applications to work with the power management. Instead of using the BIOS Setup options, you merely ensure that ACPI is enabled in the BIOS Setup and then manage all the power settings through the Power configuration settings in Windows 98 and later.

Table 5.29 shows the typical power settings found in a managed system.

Table 5.29   Power Settings Menu

Setting	Options	Description
ACPI Suspend Mode (or ACPI Suspend State)	S1 State S3 State	Specifies the ACPI sleep state.
After Power Failure	Stay Off Last State Power On	Determines the mode of operation once power is restored after a power loss occurs. Stay Off keeps the power off until the power button is pressed. Last State restores the previous power state before power loss occurs. Power On restores power to the computer.
APM	Enabled Disabled	Disables or enables APM (advanced power management).
EIST	Enabled Disabled	Enables or disables Enhanced Intel Speedstep Technology (EIST), advanced CPU power management that includes adjustable frequency and voltage.
Energy Lake	Enabled Disabled	Disables or enables Energy Lake power management technology. Energy Lake technology introduces two main end-user features: Consumer Electronics (CE) style power behavior and the ability to maintain system state and data integrity during power loss events.
Hard Drive	Enabled Disabled	Enables power management for hard disks during APM standby mode.
Inactivity Timer	Off 1 Minute 5 Minutes 10 Minutes 20 Minutes 30 Minutes 60 Minutes 120 Minutes	Specifies the amount of time before the computer enters APM standby mode.
Intel Quick Resume Technology	Enabled Disabled	Enables or disables Intel Quick Resume Technology (QRT), a component of Intel Viiv Technology.
Keyboard Select	Disable Keyboard	Select Keyboard to allow a PS/2 keyboard to wake the system from the S5 state.
Video Repost	Enabled Disabled	Allows the video BIOS to be initialized coming out of the S3 state. Some video controllers require this option to be enabled. This BIOS setting is present only when ACPI Suspend State is set to S3.
Wake on LAN from S5	Stay Off Power-On	In ACPI soft-off mode only, determines how the system responds to a LAN wake up event when the system is in the ACPI soft-off mode. This BIOS setting is present only on Intel Desktop Boards that include onboard LAN.
Wake on Modem Ring	Stay Off Power-On	Specifies how the computer responds to an incoming call on an installed modem when the power is off.
Wake on PCI PME	Stay Off Power-On	Determines how the system responds to a PCI PME wake up event.
Wake on PS/2 Mouse from S3	Stay Off Power-On	Determines how the system responds to a PS/2 mouse wake up event.

When in Standby mode, the BIOS reduces power consumption by spinning down hard drives and reducing power to or turning off monitors that comply with Video Electronics Standards Organization

(VESA) and Display Power Management Signaling (DPMS). While in Standby mode, the system can still respond to external interrupts, such as those from keyboards, mice, fax/modems, or network adapters. For example, any keyboard or mouse activity brings the system out of Standby mode and immediately restores power to the monitor.

In most systems, the operating system takes over most of the power management settings, and in some cases, it can even override the BIOS settings. This is definitely true if the operating system and motherboard both support ACPI.

Some systems feature additional power management settings in their BIOS. These options are listed in "Additional Power Management Settings" in the Technical Reference section of the DVD packaged with this book.

Boot Menu (Boot Sequence, Order)

The Boot menu is used for setting the boot features and the boot sequence (through menus). If your operating system includes a bootable CD—Windows XP, for example—use this menu to change the boot drive order to check your CD before your hard drive. Table 5.30 shows the functions and settings available on a typical motherboard.

Table 5.30   Boot Menu Settings

Setting	Options	Description
1st ATAPI CD-ROM Drive	Dependent on installed drives	Specifies the boot sequence from the available optical drives. This list will display up to four ATAPI drives.
1st Hard Disk Drive	Dependent on installed drives	Specifies the boot sequence from the available hard disk drives. This list will display up to 12 hard disk drives.
1st Removable Device	Dependent on installed devices	Specifies the boot sequence from the available removable devices. This list will display up to four removable devices.
1st Boot Device	Removable Device Hard Drive ATAPI CD-ROM Network Disabled	Specifies the boot sequence from the available devices.
2nd Boot Device	Removable Device Hard Drive ATAPI CD-ROM Network Disabled	Specifies the boot sequence from the available devices.
3rd Boot Device	Removable Device Hard Drive ATAPI CD-ROM Network Disabled	Specifies the boot sequence from the available devices.
4th Boot Device	Removable Device Hard Drive ATAPI CD-ROM Network Disabled	Specifies the boot sequence from the available devices.

Table 5.30   Continued

Setting	Options	Description
AddOn ROM Display Mode	Enabled Disabled	Enabled—Adapter card ROM messages are visible. Disabled—Adapter card ROM messages are hidden.
Boot to Network	Enabled Disabled	Disables or enables booting from the network.
Boot to Optical Devices	Enabled Disabled	Disables or enables booting from optical devices (CD/DVD).
Boot to Removable Devices	Enabled Disabled	Disables or enables booting from removable devices (floppy/USB).
Halt On	All Errors No Errors All, But Keyboard	Used to configure what types of POST errors will halt the system boot.
Intel Rapid BIOS Boot	Enabled Disabled	Allows BIOS to skip certain tests while booting.
PXE Boot to LAN	Enabled Disabled	Disables or enables Preboot eXecution Environment boot to LAN.
Scan User Flash Area	Disabled Enabled	Enables the BIOS to scan the flash ROM for user binary files that are executed at boot time.
Silent Boot	Enabled Disabled	Disabled—Displays normal POST messages. Enabled—Displays OEM logo instead of POST messages.
USB Boot	Enabled Disabled	Disables or enables booting from USB boot devices.
USB Mass Storage Emulation Type	Auto All Removable All Fixed Disc Size	Allows you to set the emulation type for USB drives. Auto—Relies on USB device design and media format to set emulation type. All Removable—Sets USB mass devices to emulate removable drives. Master Boot Record format required for USB storage devices. All Fixed Disc—Sets USB mass devices to emulate fixed discs. Size—Sets emulation type based on media size.
ZIP Emulation Type	Floppy Hard Disk	Allows you to set the emulation type for USB zip drives

Using this menu, you can configure which devices your system boots from and in which order the devices are sequenced. From this menu, you also can access Hard Drive and Removable Devices menus, which enable you to configure the ordering of these devices in the boot sequence. For example, you can set hard drives to be the first boot choice, and then in the hard drive menu, decide to boot from the secondary drive first and the primary drive second. Normally, the default with two drives would be the other way around.

The Boot Menu lists up to 12 hard disks and 4 removable devices, enabling you to choose the preferred boot device; older systems usually list only primary and secondary master and slave (four) drives. This BIOS option enables you to install more than one bootable hard disk in your computer and select which one you want to boot from at a BIOS level, rather than by using a boot manager program. If you need to work with multiple operating systems, this menu can be very useful.

Most recent systems also enable you to boot from external USB drives, including Flash or thumb drives.

Exit Menu

The Exit menu is for exiting the Setup program, saving changes, and loading and saving defaults. Table 5.31 shows the typical selections found in most motherboard BIOSs.

Table 5.31   Exit Menu Settings

Feature	Description
Exit Saving Changes	Exits and saves the changes in CMOS RAM.
Exit Discarding Changes	Exits without saving any changes made in the BIOS Setup.
Load Optimal Defaults	Loads the factory (optimal) default values for all the Setup options.
Load Custom Defaults	Loads the custom defaults for Setup options.
Save Custom Defaults	Saves the current values as custom defaults in CMOS RAM. Normally, the BIOS reads the saved Setup values from CMOS RAM. If this memory is corrupted, the BIOS reads the custom defaults. If no custom defaults are set, the BIOS reads the factory defaults from the flash ROM.
Discard Changes	Discards changes without exiting Setup. The option values present when the computer was turned on are used.

After you have selected an optimum set of BIOS Setup settings, you can save them using the Save Custom Defaults option. This enables you to quickly restore your settings if they are corrupted or lost. All BIOS settings are stored in the CMOS RAM memory, which is powered by a battery attached to the motherboard.

Additional BIOS Setup Features

Some systems have additional features in their BIOS Setup screens, which might not be found in all BIOSs. Some of the more common features you might see are listed in Table 5.32.

Table 5.32   Additional BIOS Setup Features

Feature	Description
Virus Warning	When this feature is enabled, you receive a warning message if a program attempts to write to the boot sector or the partition table of the hard disk drive. If you get this warning during normal operation, you should run an antivirus program to see whether an infection has occurred. This feature protects only the master boot sector, not the entire hard drive. Note that programs that usually write to the master boot sector, such as FDISK, can trigger the virus warning message.
CPU Internal Cache/External Cache	This allows you to disable the L1 (internal) and L2 (external) CPU caches. This is often used when testing memory, in which case you don't want the cache functioning. For normal operation, both caches should be enabled.

Table 5.32   Continued

Feature	Description
Quick Power On Self Test	When enabled, this feature reduces the amount of time required to run the POST. A quick POST skips certain steps, such as the memory test. If you trust your system, you can enable the quick POST, but in most cases I recommend leaving it disabled so you get the full-length POST version.
Swap Floppy Drive	This field is functional only in systems with two floppy drives. Selecting Enabled assigns physical drive B: to logical drive A: and physical drive A: to logical drive B:.
Boot Up Floppy Seek	When this feature is enabled, the BIOS tests (seeks) floppy drives to determine whether they have 40 or 80 tracks. Only 360KB floppy drives have 40 tracks; drives with 720KB, 1.2MB, and 1.44MB capacity all have 80 tracks. Because very few modern PCs have 40-track floppy drives, you can disable this function to save time.
Boot Up System Speed	Select High to boot at the default CPU speed; select Low to boot at a simulated 8MHz speed. The 8MHz option often was used in the past with certain copy-protected programs, which would fail the protection scheme if booted at full speed. This option is not used today.
Gate A20 Option	Gate A20 refers to the way the system addresses memory above 1MB (extended memory). When set to Fast, the system chipset controls Gate A20. When set to Normal, a pin in the keyboard controller controls Gate A20. Setting Gate A20 to Fast improves system speed, particularly with protected-mode operating systems such as Windows 9x and Windows 2000/XP.
Typematic Rate Setting	When this feature is disabled, the following two items (Typematic Rate and Typematic Delay) are irrelevant. Keystrokes repeat at a rate determined by the keyboard controller in your system. When this feature is enabled, you can select a typematic rate and typematic delay.
Typematic Rate	When the Typematic Rate setting is enabled, you can select a typematic rate—the rate (Chars/Sec) at which characters repeat when you hold down a key—of 6, 8, 10, 12, 15, 20, 24, or 30 characters per second.
Typematic Delay (Msec)	When the Typematic Rate setting is enabled, you can select a typematic delay (the delay before key strokes begin to repeat) of 250, 500, 750, or 1,000 milliseconds.
Report No FDD for	Select Yes to release IRQ6 when the system contains no floppy drive, for compatibility Windows 95 with Windows 95 logo certification. In the Integrated Peripherals screen, select Disabled or the Onboard FDC Controller field.
ROM Shadowing	ROM chips typically are very slow, around 150ns (nanoseconds), and operate only 8 bits at a time, whereas RAM runs 60ns or even 10ns or less and is either 32 bits or 64 bits wide in most systems. Shadowing is the copying of BIOS code from ROM into RAM, where the CPU can read the BIOS drivers at the higher speed of RAM.

Plug and Play BIOS

Originally, installing and configuring devices in PCs was a difficult process. During installation, the user was faced with the task of configuring the new card by selecting the IRQ, I/O ports, and DMA channel. In the past, users were required to move jumpers or set switches on the add-in cards to control these settings. They needed to know exactly which resources were already in use so they could find a set of resources that did not conflict with the devices already in the system. If a conflict existed, the system might not boot and the device might fail or cause the conflicting hardware to fail.

Plug and Play (PnP) is technology designed to prevent configuration problems and provide users with the capability to easily expand a PC. With PnP, the user simply plugs in the new card and the system configures it automatically for proper operation.

PnP is composed of three principal components:

- Plug and Play BIOS
- Extended System Configuration Data (ESCD)
- Plug and Play operating system

The PnP BIOS initiates the configuration of the PnP cards during the bootup process. If the cards previously were installed, the BIOS reads the information from ESCD, initializes the cards, and boots the system. During the installation of new PnP cards, the BIOS consults the ESCD to determine which system resources are available and needed for the add-in cards. If the BIOS is capable of finding sufficient available resources, it configures the cards. However, if the BIOS is incapable of locating sufficient available resources, the Plug and Play routines in the operating system complete the configuration process. During the configuration process, the configuration registers (in flash BIOS) on the cards and the ESCD are updated with the new configuration data.

PnP Device IDs

All Plug and Play devices must contain a Plug and Play device ID to enable the operating system to uniquely recognize the device so it can load the appropriate driver software. Each device manufacturer is responsible for assigning the Plug and Play ID for each product and storing it in the hardware.

Each manufacturer of Plug and Play devices must be assigned an industry-unique, three-character vendor ID. Then, the device manufacturer is responsible for assigning a unique product ID to each individual product model. After an ID is assigned to a product model, it must not be assigned to any other product model manufactured by the same company (that is, one that uses the same vendor ID).

Note

For a comprehensive list of PnP device IDs, see the file PCDEVS.TXT, which is part of the PCI32 diagnostic program available from http://members.datafast.net.au/dft0802

ACPI

ACPI stands for *Advanced Configuration and Power Interface*, which defines a standard method for integrating power management as well as system-configuration features throughout a PC, including the hardware, operating system, and application software. ACPI goes far beyond the previous standard, called *Advanced Power Management (APM)*, which consists mainly of processor, hard disk, and display control. ACPI controls not only power, but also all the Plug and Play hardware configuration throughout the system. With ACPI, system configuration (Plug and Play) as well as power management configuration are no longer controlled via the BIOS Setup; they are controlled entirely within the operating system instead.

The ACPI specification was created by Intel, Microsoft, and Toshiba; version 1.0 was first released in 1996. ACPI became one of the major requirements for Microsoft's "PC'97" logo certification program, causing motherboard and BIOS manufacturers to work on integrating ACPI into systems during that time. Intel integrated ACPI support in chipsets starting in April 1998 with the PIIX4E southbridge, and Microsoft added ACPI support in Windows starting with the release of Windows 98 (June 25, 1998) as part of what Microsoft called "OnNow" design. By the time Windows 2000 was released (February 17, 2000), ACPI had universally replaced APM as the primary power management and control interface on new systems.

ACPI enables the system to automatically turn peripherals on and off (such as CD-ROMs, network cards, hard disk drives, and printers), as well as external devices connected to the PC (such as VCRs, televisions, telephones, and stereos). ACPI technology also enables peripherals to turn on or activate the PC. For example, inserting a tape into a VCR can turn on the PC, which could then activate a large-screen television and high-fidelity sound system.

ACPI enables system designers to implement a range of power management features with various hardware designs while using the same operating system driver. ACPI also uses the Plug and Play BIOS data structures and takes control over the Plug and Play interface, providing an operating system–independent interface for configuration and control. Microsoft has included support for ACPI since Windows 98.

During the system setup and boot process, Windows versions supporting ACPI perform a series of checks and tests to see whether the system hardware and BIOS support ACPI. If support for ACPI is either not detected or found to be faulty, the system typically reverts to standard Advanced Power Management control, but problems can also cause a lockup with either a red or blue screen with an ACPI error code.

Red screens indicate that the problem is probably related to hardware or the BIOS. Blue screens, on the other hand, indicate that the problem is probably related to software or is an obscure problem. The ACPI error codes are described in Table 5.33.

Table 5.33   ACPI Error Codes

Error Code	Description
1xxx -	Indicates an error during the initialization phase of the ACPI driver and usually means the driver can't read one or more of the ACPI tables
2xxx -	Indicates an ACPI machine language (AML) interpreter error
3xxx -	Indicates an error within the ACPI driver event handler
4xxx -	Indicates thermal management errors

Virtually all these errors are the result of partial or incomplete ACPI implementations or incompatibilities in either the BIOS or device drivers. If you encounter any of these errors, contact your motherboard manufacturer for an updated BIOS or the device manufacturers for updated drivers.

Initializing a PnP Device

One responsibility of a Plug and Play BIOS during POST is to isolate and initialize all Plug and Play cards and assign them a valid Card Select Number (CSN). After a CSN is assigned, the system BIOS can then designate resources to the cards. The BIOS is responsible only for the configuration of boot devices; all the remaining Plug and Play devices can be configured dynamically by the operating system software.

The following steps outline a typical flow of a Plug and Play BIOS during the POST:

1. Disable all configurable devices.
2. Identify all Plug and Play devices.

3. Construct a resource map of resources that are statically allocated to devices in the system.

4. Enable input and output devices.

5. Perform ISA ROM scan.

6. Configure the boot device.

7. Enable Plug and Play ISA and other configurable devices.

8. Start the bootstrap loader.

If the loaded operating system is Plug and Play compliant, it takes over management of the system resources. Any unconfigured Plug and Play devices are configured by the appropriate system software or the Plug and Play operating system.

At this point, the operating system is loaded and takes control over Plug and Play system resources. Using the Device Manager in the operating system (such as Windows), the user can now control any Plug and Play devices.

BIOS/MBR Error Messages

When a PC system is first powered on, the system runs a POST. If errors are encountered during the POST, you usually see a text error message displayed onscreen. Errors that occur very early in the POST might happen before the video card is initialized. These types of errors can't be displayed, so the system uses two other alternatives for communicating the error message. One is beeping—the system beeps the speaker in a specific pattern that indicates which error has occurred.

▶▶ For detailed lists of the BIOS POST beep codes, see Chapter 22, "PC Diagnostics, Testing, and Maintenance," p. 1367.

The alternative is to send a hexadecimal error code to I/O port address 80h, which can be read by a special card in one of the bus slots. When the ROM BIOS is performing the POST, in most systems the results of these tests are continuously sent to I/O Port 80h so they can be monitored by special diagnostics cards called *POST cards* (see Figure 5.11). These tests sometimes are called *manufacturing tests* because they were designed into the system for testing it on the assembly line without a video display attached.

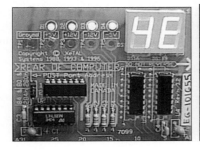

Figure 5.11   A two-digit hexadecimal code display (left) and a POST card in operation (right).

The POST cards have a two-digit hexadecimal display used to report the number of the currently executing test routine. Before each test is executed, a hexadecimal numeric code is sent to the port and then the test is run. If the test fails and locks up the machine, the hexadecimal code of the last test being executed remains on the card's display.

Many tests are executed in a system before the video display card is enabled, especially if the display is EGA or VGA. Therefore, many errors can occur that would lock up the system before the system could possibly display an error code through the video system. Because not all these errors generate beep codes, to most normal troubleshooting procedures, a system with this type of problem (such as a memory failure in Bank 0) would appear completely "dead." By using one of the commercially available POST cards, however, you can often diagnose the problem.

These codes are completely BIOS dependent because the card does nothing but display the codes sent to it. Some BIOSs have more detailed POST procedures and therefore send more informative codes. POST cards can be purchased from JDR Microdevices or other sources and are available in both ISA and PCI bus versions.

For simple but otherwise fatal errors that can't be displayed onscreen, most of the BIOS versions also send audio codes that can be used to help diagnose such problems. The audio codes are similar to POST codes, but they are "read" by listening to the speaker beep rather than by using a special card.

▶▶   The following section details the text error codes for all the popular BIOS versions. For detailed lists of the BIOS POST beep codes, see Chapter 22, "PC Diagnostics, Testing, and Maintenance," p. 1367.

Note

The DVD accompanying this book contains an exhaustive listing of additional error codes, error messages, and BIOS POST codes for BIOSs from Phoenix, AMI, Award, Microid Research, and IBM.

BIOS Boot Error Messages

During the boot process, the bootstrap loader routine in the motherboard ROM BIOS reads the first physical sector of each of the bootable drives or devices, which is cylinder 0, head 0, sector 1 in CHS mode or logical block address 0 in LBA mode. The code from the first sector is loaded into RAM, and the last two bytes are checked to see whether they match a signature value of 55AAh. If the signature bytes match, that tells the ROM that the first sector contains a valid MBR and that the ROM can continue by transferring control to the MBR code.

If the last two bytes of the first physical sector do not match 55AAh, the ROM continues by checking the first physical sector of the next bootable device in the boot sequence until it either finds one with a valid MBR or runs out of devices to check. If after checking all the drives or devices in the boot sequence, none are found to have the proper signature bytes indicating a valid MBR, the ROM invokes an interrupt (18h) that calls a subroutine that displays an error message. The specific text or wording of the message varies according to the ROM manufacturer and version. The messages are detailed in the following sections.

IBM BIOS Messages

With no valid MBR or bootable device found, systems with a very old IBM BIOS display the infamous ROM BASIC interpreter, which looks like this:

```
The IBM Personal Computer Basic
Version C1.10 Copyright IBM Corp 1981
62940 Bytes free
Ok
```

IBM ROM BASIC

The ROMs of most PCs are similar to the original IBM systems with which they are compatible—with the exception of the ROM BASIC interpreter (also called *Cassette BASIC*). It might come as a surprise to some PC users, but the original IBM PC actually had a jack on the rear of the system for connecting a cassette tape recorder. This was to be used for loading programs and data to or from a cassette tape. IBM included the cassette port because cassette tapes were used by several early personal computers (including the Apple) because floppy drives were very expensive and hard disks were not even an option yet. However, floppy drives came down in price quickly right at the time the PC was first released, and the cassette port never appeared on any subsequent IBM systems. The cassette port also never appeared on any PC-compatible systems because floppy drives were cheap by the time they came out.

The reason for having BASIC in ROM was so the original PC could come standard with only 16KB of memory and no floppy drives in the base configuration. Many computer users at the time either wrote their own programs in the BASIC language or ran BASIC programs written by others. The BASIC language interpreter built into the ROM BIOS of these early IBM systems was designed to access the cassette port on the back of the system, and by having the interpreter in ROM, all the 16KB of RAM could be used to store a program.

Even after the cassette port was eliminated, IBM left the BASIC code in the motherboard ROM until the early 1990s! I liken this to humans having an appendix. The ROM BASIC in those IBM systems is sort of like a vestigial organ—a leftover that had some use in prehistoric evolutionary ancestors but has no function today.

You can catch a glimpse of this ROM BASIC on older IBM systems that have it by disabling all the disk drives in the system. In that case, with nothing to boot from, those systems unceremoniously dump you into the strange (vintage 1981) ROM BASIC screen.

People used to dread seeing this because it usually meant that the floppy disk or hard disk they were trying to boot from had become corrupted or had failed. Because no compatible systems ever had the BASIC interpreter in ROM, they came up with different messages to display for the same situations in which an IBM system would invoke this BASIC. The most confusing of these was the message from AMI BIOS, which simply said **NO ROM BASIC - SYSTEM HALTED**, which really meant that the system was incapable of booting.

With no valid MBR or bootable device found, some IBM systems display a screen using text graphic characters that look similar to Figure 5.12.

The meaning here is, "Insert a bootable floppy disk into the A: drive and press the F1 key."

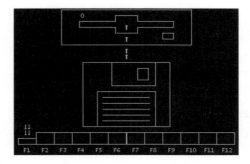

Figure 5.12   IBM ROM BIOS display indicating an invalid master boot record.

AMI BIOS Messages

With no valid MBR or bootable device found, systems with an AMI BIOS display the following message:

```
NO ROM BASIC - SYSTEM HALTED
```

This message is confusing to some because it seems to point to a problem with ROM BASIC, which of course is not what it really means! The AMI ROM does not include a BASIC interpreter in the ROM (neither does any other ROMs except those found in very old IBM machines), so instead of jumping into BASIC or displaying a useful message indicating there are no bootable devices, it displays this confusing message. The real meaning is the same as for all these messages, which is to say that none of the bootable devices in the boot sequence were found to contain signature bytes indicating a valid MBR in their first physical sectors.

Compaq BIOS Messages

With no valid MBR or bootable device found, systems with a Compaq BIOS display the following message:

```
Non-System disk or disk error
replace and strike any key when ready
```

This is another confusing message because this very same (or similar) error message is contained in the DOS/Windows 9X/Me VBR and normally is displayed if the system files are missing or corrupted. So, if you see this message on a Compaq system, you can't be sure whether the problem is in the MBR, VBR, or the system files, which makes tracking down and solving the problem more difficult.

Award BIOS Messages

With no valid MBR or bootable device found, systems with an Award BIOS display the following message:

```
DISK BOOT FAILURE, INSERT SYSTEM DISK AND PRESS ENTER
```

So far, this appears to be the least confusing of these messages. You don't need a secret decoder ring to figure out what it is really trying to say.

Phoenix BIOS Messages

With no valid MBR or bootable device found, systems with a Phoenix BIOS display either the message

```
No boot device available -
strike F1 to retry boot, F2 for setup utility
```

or this one:

```
No boot sector on fixed disk -
strike F1 to retry boot, F2 for setup utility
```

Which of these two messages you see depends on whether no boot devices were found or readable, or a boot sector could be read but was found not to have the proper signature bytes.

MBR Boot Error Messages

If the BIOS has successfully loaded the MBR and checked the signature, and if the signature bytes are correct, the BIOS then passes control to the MBR by running the MBR code. The program code in the MBR performs a test of the partition table (also contained in the MBR) by checking the Boot Indicator bytes in each of the four partition table entries. These bytes are at offsets 446 (1BEh), 462 (1CEh), 478 (1DEh), and 494 (1EEh) in the MBR. These bytes are used to indicate which of the four possible primary partition table entries contains an active (bootable) partition. A value of 80h at any of these byte locations indicates that particular table entry contains the active partition. Only one of the four Boot Indicator bytes at a time is allowed to indicate an active partition (containing a value of 80h), meaning that if one of them is 80h, the other three must all contain 00h. Going by the rules initially set forth by IBM and Microsoft, only two possible conditions are allowed with respect to all four Boot Indicator bytes:

- All four Boot Indicator bytes are 00h, indicating no Active (bootable) partitions.
- One Boot Indicator byte is 80h and the other three are 00h, indicating one Active (bootable) partition.

If all four Boot Indicator bytes are 00h—which indicates that no active (bootable) partitions exist—then the MBR returns control back to the motherboard ROM, which will then normally display one of the error messages listed earlier. This would be an expected result if you were to remove the existing partitions from a drive but had not created new partitions on the drive, or if you had failed to make one of the partitions Active (bootable) when partitioning or repartitioning the drive. For example, when creating multiple partitions on a drive, it is possible to forget to set one of them as Active. If you do this by accident and render your hard drive nonbootable, you can easily correct the problem by booting from a floppy or CD with partitioning software such as FDISK or DISKPART and setting the partition where your OS is installed as Active.

If only one of the Boot Indicator bytes is 80h and the rest are 00h (required for a properly booting system), the system will then continue the standard boot process by loading the volume boot record (VBR) from the active partition.

Invalid Partition Table

Any other Boot Indicator byte conditions are not allowed and, if present, indicate that the partition table is corrupt, causing the MBR code to generate an error message and stop. For example, if two or more of the Boot Indicator bytes are 80h (indicating multiple Active partitions, which is not allowed) or if any one of the Boot Indicator bytes is any value *other* than 00h or 80h, the partition table is considered corrupt and the MBR code will display the following error message and halt the system:

```
Invalid partition table
```

If you see this message, you can try rebooting from alternate media or a different drive and then see if you can access the data on the problem drive. Depending on how much of the partition table, MBR, or other sectors on the drive are corrupted, it may be easiest to simply start over by removing and re-creating all of the partitions (which will lose any and all data they contain), or investigate data recovery options if you don't have any backups and need the data back.

Error Loading Operating System

Once the MBR code makes it past the Boot Indicator byte check, and one of the partitions was marked active (bootable), the MBR code continues by looking at the rest of the information in the active partition table entry to determine the starting sector location for the active partition. The starting sector location is a sector address indicated by both CHS (cylinder/head/sector) and LBA (logical block address) values. The CHS value is used for drives 8.4GB or smaller in capacity, whereas the LBA value is used for drives larger than 8.4GB (pretty much all drives today). The first sector of a partition contains the volume boot record (VBR), which is also known as the *operating system boot record* because it is installed on the drive during the OS partition format process. Once the VBR address of the active partition has been determined, the MBR code then reads that sector from the drive.

If the VBR of the active partition can't be read successfully due to a read error (physical problem with the disk), a series of five retries will occur. If after all of the retries the VBR still cannot be read, the following message is displayed and the system stops:

```
Error loading operating system
```

This is a bad message to see because it generally indicates physical problems with the drive. However, this message can also appear if the drive parameters are incorrectly entered in the BIOS Setup, or if the VBR sector location as listed in the MBR partition table is invalid. For example, if the MBR contains an invalid VBR address that points to a sector beyond the physical end of the drive, this message will result.

If you see this message unexpectedly, first check the BIOS Setup settings for the drive to be sure they are correct, then check the partition table entries, and finally run a diagnostic test of the drive itself. If the drive is bad or going bad and you need the data back, you may require the services of a professional data-recovery outfit.

Missing Operating System

If the MBR code has successfully loaded the VBR with no read errors, then the MBR code will check the last two bytes of the VBR for the 55AAh signature. If the signature is not present, the MBR will display the following error message and halt the system:

```
Missing operating system
```

This would be an expected occurrence if, for example, you had just created the partition and had not yet done a high-level format, meaning that the partition has not yet been formatted by the OS, or no OS is yet installed.

Geometry Translation Problems

Some of the aforementioned errors can also occur with older, smaller hard disks that are between 528MB (504MiB) and 8.4GB (7.9GiB) in size. The problem is caused by tampering with the translation mode set in the BIOS Setup. Geometry translation is used by drives between 528MB (504MiB) and 8.4GB (7.9GiB), which alters the reported CHS geometry of the drive into a format that enables the entire disk to be used by operating systems such as DOS and Windows. Typically, three settings exist for translation: It can be disabled (often indicated by a setting of "normal"), or it can be enabled using either CHS or LBA values. Translation using CHS values is often indicated by a setting of "large," and translation using LBA values is indicated by a setting of "LBA." If a drive is partitioned and formatted with LBA translation and the setting is later changed to CHS (often indicated in the BIOS Setup as "large"), the bootstrap loader in the BIOS translates drive sector locations differently and might not properly load the VBR of the bootable volume, causing either the `Missing operating system` or `Error loading operating system` message to be displayed.

Thus, if you see such errors on a system with a hard drive between 528MB (504MiB) and 8.4GB (7.9GiB), be sure to check the translation settings for the drive. On some of the older AMI BIOS Hi-Flex and WinBIOS (graphical) versions, the translation mode setting is not on the same screen as the hard disk setup but is buried in the Advanced or Built-in Peripherals setup screen, where it can be turned off by autoconfiguring BIOS setup options.

Caution

Although most versions of Windows will not boot if the translation is disabled on the bootable drive, a dangerous situation can take place if a hard disk between 528MB (504MiB) and 8.4GB (7.9GiB) is partitioned with MS-DOS and translation mode is turned off afterward. In such cases, if a write occurs beyond the first 1,024 cylinders, the hard disk loops back to the beginning and overwrites the master boot record! All the data on the drive will remain inaccessible until the MBR and partition tables are restored. To learn more about the MBR and partition tables, including techniques for MBR and partition table recovery, refer to the latest edition of my book *Upgrading and Repairing Microsoft Windows*.

6

Memory

Memory Basics

This chapter discusses memory from both a physical and logical point of view. First, we'll examine what memory is, where it fits into the PC architecture, and how it works. Then we'll look at the various types of memory, speeds, and packaging of the chips and memory modules you can buy and install.

This chapter also covers the logical layout of memory, defining the various areas of memory and their uses from the system's point of view. Because the logical layout and uses are within the "mind" of the processor, memory mapping and logical layout remain perhaps the most difficult subjects to grasp in the PC universe. This chapter contains useful information that removes the mysteries associated with memory and enables you to get the most out of your system.

Memory is the workspace for the processor. It is a temporary storage area where the programs and data being operated on by the processor must reside. Memory storage is considered temporary because the data and programs remain there only as long as the computer has electrical power or is not reset. Before the computer is shut down or reset, any data that has been changed should be saved to a more permanent storage device (usually a hard disk) so it can be reloaded into memory in the future.

Memory often is called *RAM*, for *random access memory*. Main memory is called RAM because you can randomly (as opposed to sequentially) access any location in memory. This designation is somewhat misleading and often misinterpreted. Read-only memory (ROM), for example, is also randomly accessible, yet is usually differentiated from the system RAM because it maintains data without power and can't normally be written to. Although a hard disk can be used as virtual random access memory, we don't consider that RAM either.

Over the years, the definition of RAM has changed from a simple acronym to become something that means the primary memory workspace the processor uses to run programs, which usually is constructed of a type of chip called dynamic RAM (DRAM). One of the characteristics of DRAM chips (and therefore most types of RAM in general) is that they store data dynamically, which really has two meanings. One meaning is that the information can be written to RAM repeatedly at any time. The other has to do with the fact that DRAM requires the data to be refreshed (essentially rewritten) every few milliseconds or so; faster RAM requires refreshing more often than slower RAM. A type of RAM called static RAM (SRAM) does not require the periodic refreshing. An important characteristic of RAM in general is that data is stored only as long as the memory has electrical power.

Note

Both DRAM and SRAM memory maintain their contents only as long as power is present. However, a different type of memory known as Flash memory does not. Flash memory can retain its contents without power, and it is most commonly used today in digital camera and player media and USB Flash drives. As far as the PC is concerned, a Flash memory device emulates a disk drive (not RAM) and is accessed by a drive letter, just as with any other disk or optical drive.

When we talk about a computer's memory, we usually mean the RAM or physical memory in the system, which is mainly the memory chips or modules the processor uses to store primary active programs and data. This often is confused with the term *storage*, which should be used when referring to things such as disk and tape drives (although they can be used as a form of RAM called virtual memory).

RAM can refer to both the physical chips that make up the memory in the system and the logical mapping and layout of that memory. *Logical mapping* and *layout* refer to how the memory addresses are mapped to actual chips and what address locations contain which types of system information.

People new to computers often confuse main memory (RAM) with disk storage because both have capacities that are expressed in similar megabyte or gigabyte terms. The best analogy to explain the relationship between memory and disk storage I've found is to think of an office with a desk and a file cabinet.

In this popular analogy, the file cabinet represents the system's hard disk, where both programs and data are stored for long-term safekeeping. The desk represents the system's main memory, which allows the person working at the desk (acting as the processor) direct access to any files placed on it. Files represent the programs and documents you can "load" into the memory. For you to work on a particular file, it must first be retrieved from the cabinet and placed on the desk. If the desk is large enough, you might be able to have several files open on it at one time; likewise, if your system has more memory, you can run more or larger programs and work on more or larger documents.

Adding hard disk space to a system is similar to putting a bigger file cabinet in the office—more files can be permanently stored. And adding more memory to a system is like getting a bigger desk—you can work on more programs and data at the same time.

One difference between this analogy and the way things really work in a computer is that when a file is loaded into memory, it is a copy of the file that is actually loaded; the original still resides on the hard disk. Because of the temporary nature of memory, any files that have been changed after being loaded into memory must then be saved back to the hard disk before the system is powered off (which erases the memory). If the changed file in memory is not saved, the original copy of the file on the hard disk remains unaltered. This is like saying that any changes made to files left on the desktop are discarded when the office is closed, although the original files are still preserved in the cabinet.

Memory temporarily stores programs when they are running, along with the data being used by those programs. RAM chips are sometimes termed *volatile storage* because when you turn off your computer or an electrical outage occurs, whatever is stored in RAM is lost unless you saved it to your hard drive.

Because of the volatile nature of RAM, many computer users make it a habit to save their work frequently—a habit I recommend. Many software applications perform periodic saves automatically in order to minimize the potential for data loss.

Physically, the *main memory* in a system is a collection of chips or modules containing chips that are usually plugged into the motherboard. These chips or modules vary in their electrical and physical designs and must be compatible with the system into which they are being installed to function properly. This chapter discusses the various types of chips and modules that can be installed in different systems.

How much you spend on memory for your PC depends mostly on the amount and type of modules you purchase. It is typical to spend the same amount on memory as you do for the motherboard in a system, which is usually anywhere from $50 to $150.

Before the big memory price crash in mid-1996, memory had maintained a fairly consistent price for many years of about $40 per megabyte. A typical configuration back then of 16MB cost more than $600. In fact, memory was so expensive at that time that it was worth more than its weight in gold. These high prices caught the attention of criminals and memory module manufacturers were robbed at gunpoint in several large heists. These robberies were partially induced by the fact that memory was so valuable, the demand was high, and stolen chips or modules were virtually impossible to trace. After the rash of armed robberies and other thefts, memory module manufacturers began posting armed guards and implementing beefed-up security procedures.

By the end of 1996, memory prices had cooled considerably to about $4 per megabyte—a tenfold price drop in less than a year. Prices continued to fall after the major crash until they were at or below 50 cents per megabyte in 1997. All seemed well, until events in 1998 conspired to create a spike in memory prices, increasing them by four times their previous levels. The main culprit was Intel, who had driven the industry to support Rambus DRAM (RDRAM) and then failed to deliver the supporting chipsets on time. The industry was caught in a bind by shifting production to a type of memory for which there were no chipsets or motherboards to plug into, which then created a shortage of the existing (and popular) SDRAM memory. An earthquake in Taiwan (where much of the world's RAM is manufactured) during that year served as the icing on the cake, disrupting production and furthering the spike in prices.

Since then, things have cooled considerably, and memory prices have dropped to all-time lows, with actual prices of under 6 cents per megabyte. In particular, 2001 was a disastrous year in the semiconductor industry, prompted by the dot-com crash as well as worldwide events, and sales dropped well below that of previous years. This conspired to bring memory prices down further than they had ever been and even forced some companies to merge or go out of business.

Memory is less expensive now than ever, but its useful life has also become shorter. New types and speeds of memory are being adopted more quickly than before, and any new systems you purchase now most likely will not accept the same memory as your existing ones. In an upgrade or a repair situation, that means you often have to change the memory if you change the motherboard. The chance that you can reuse the memory in an existing motherboard when upgrading to a new one is slim.

Because of this, you should understand all the various types of memory on the market today, so you can best determine which types are required by which systems, and thus more easily plan for future upgrades and repairs.

To better understand physical memory in a system, you should understand what types of memory are found in a typical PC and what the role of each type is. Three main types of physical memory are used in modern PCs. (Remember, I'm talking about the type of memory chip, not the type of module that memory is stored on.)

- **ROM**—Read-only memory
- **DRAM**—Dynamic random access memory
- **SRAM**—Static RAM

The only type of memory you normally need to purchase and install in a system is DRAM. The other types are built in to the motherboard (ROM), processor (SRAM), and other components such as the video card, hard drives, and so on.

ROM

Read-only memory, or ROM, is a type of memory that can permanently or semipermanently store data. It is called read-only because it is either impossible or difficult to write to. ROM also is often referred to as *nonvolatile memory* because any data stored in ROM remains there, even if the power is turned off. As such, ROM is an ideal place to put the PC's startup instructions—that is, the software that boots the system.

Note that ROM and RAM are not opposites, as some people seem to believe. Both are simply types of memory. In fact, ROM could be classified as technically a subset of the system's RAM. In other words, a portion of the system's random access memory address space is mapped into one or more ROM chips. This is necessary to contain the software that enables the PC to boot up; otherwise, the processor would have no program in memory to execute when it was powered on.

◀◀ For more information on ROM, see "Motherboard ROM BIOS," p. 446.

The main ROM BIOS is contained in a ROM chip on the motherboard, but there are also adapter cards with ROMs on them as well. ROMs on adapter cards contain auxiliary BIOS routines and drivers needed by the particular card, especially for those cards that must be active early in the boot process, such as video cards. Cards that don't need drivers active at boot time typically don't have a ROM because those drivers can be loaded from the hard disk later in the boot process.

Most systems today use a type of ROM called *electrically erasable programmable ROM (EEPROM)*, which is a form of flash memory. Flash is a truly nonvolatile memory that is rewritable, enabling users to easily update the ROM or firmware in their motherboards or any other components (video cards, SCSI cards, peripherals, and so on).

◀◀ For more information on BIOS upgrades, see "Upgrading the BIOS," p. 459.

DRAM

Dynamic RAM (DRAM) is the type of memory chip used for most of the main memory in a modern PC. The main advantages of DRAM are that it is very dense, meaning you can pack a lot of bits into a very small chip, and it is inexpensive, which makes purchasing large amounts of memory affordable.

The memory cells in a DRAM chip are tiny capacitors that retain a charge to indicate a bit. The problem with DRAM is that it is dynamic—that is, its contents can be changed. With every keystroke or every mouse swipe, the contents of RAM change. And the entire contents of RAM can be wiped out by a system crash. Also, because of the design, it must be constantly refreshed; otherwise, the electrical charges in the individual memory capacitors will drain and the data will be lost. Refresh occurs when the system memory controller takes a tiny break and accesses all the rows of data in the memory chips. Most systems have a memory controller (normally built into the North Bridge portion of the motherboard chipset or located within the CPU in the case of the AMD Athlon 64 and Opteron processors), which is set for an industry-standard refresh time of 15ms (milliseconds). This means that every 15ms, all the rows in the memory are automatically read to refresh the data.

◄◄   See "Chipsets," p. 273.

Refreshing the memory unfortunately takes processor time away from other tasks because each refresh cycle takes several CPU cycles to complete. In older systems, the refresh cycling could take up to 10% or more of the total CPU time, but with modern systems running in the multi-gigahertz range, refresh overhead is now on the order of a fraction of a percent or less of the total CPU time. Some systems allow you to alter the refresh timing parameters via the CMOS Setup. The time between refresh cycles is known as *tREF* and is expressed not in milliseconds, but in clock cycles (see Figure 6.1).

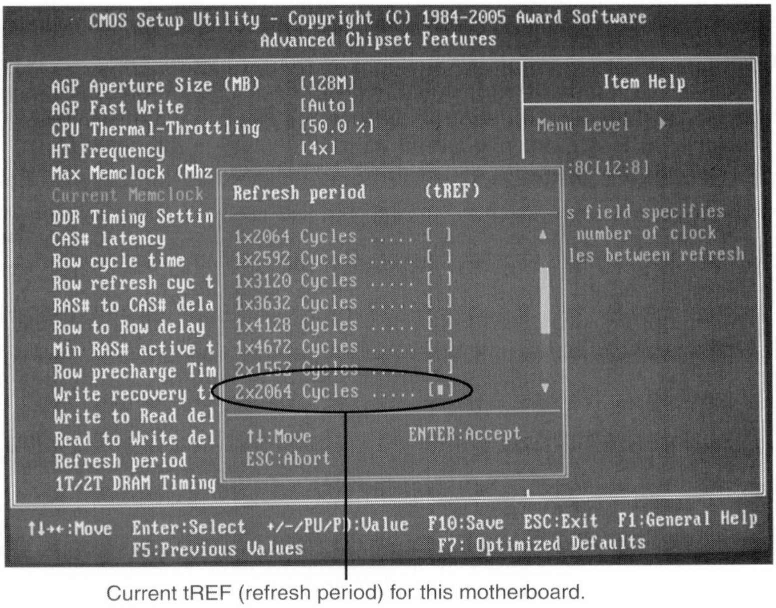

Current tREF (refresh period) for this motherboard.

Figure 6.1   The refresh period dialog box and other advanced memory timings can be adjusted manually through the system CMOS setup program.

It's important to be aware that increasing the time between refresh cycles (tREF) to speed up your system can allow some of the memory cells to begin draining prematurely, which can cause random soft memory errors to appear.

A *soft error* is a data error that is not caused by a defective chip. To avoid soft errors, it is usually safer to stick with the recommended or default refresh timing. Because refresh consumes less than 1% of modern system overall bandwidth, altering the refresh rate has little effect on performance. It is almost always best to use default or automatic settings for any memory timings in the BIOS Setup. Many modern systems don't allow changes to memory timings and are permanently set to automatic settings. On an automatic setting, the motherboard reads the timing parameters out of the serial presence detect (SPD) ROM found on the memory module and sets the cycling speeds to match.

DRAMs use only one transistor and capacitor pair per bit, which makes them very dense, offering more memory capacity per chip than other types of memory. DRAM chips are currently being prepared for production with densities up to 2Gb. This means that DRAM chips are available with over one billion transistors! Compare this to a Core 2 Duo, which has 291 million transistors, and it makes the processor look wimpy by comparison. The difference is that in a memory chip, the transistors and capacitors are all consistently arranged in a (normally square) grid of simple repetitive structures, unlike the processor, which is a much more complex circuit of different structures and elements interconnected in a highly irregular fashion.

The transistor for each DRAM bit cell reads the charge state of the adjacent capacitor. If the capacitor is charged, the cell is read to contain a 1; no charge indicates a 0. The charge in the tiny capacitors is constantly draining, which is why the memory must be refreshed constantly. Even a momentary power interruption, or anything that interferes with the refresh cycles, can cause a DRAM memory cell to lose the charge and thus the data. If this happens in a running system, it can lead to blue screens, global protection faults, corrupted files, and any number of system crashes.

DRAM is used in PC systems because it is inexpensive and the chips can be densely packed, so a lot of memory capacity can fit in a small space. Unfortunately, DRAM is also relatively slow, typically much slower than the processor. For this reason, many types of DRAM architectures have been developed to improve performance. These architectures are covered later in the chapter.

Cache Memory: SRAM

Another distinctly different type of memory exists that is significantly faster than most types of DRAM. SRAM stands for *static RAM*, which is so named because it does not need the periodic refresh rates like DRAM. Because of how SRAMs are designed, not only are refresh rates unnecessary, but SRAM is much faster than DRAM and much more capable of keeping pace with modern processors.

SRAM memory is available in access times of 2ns or less, so it can keep pace with processors running 500MHz or faster. This is because of the SRAM design, which calls for a cluster of six transistors for each bit of storage. The use of transistors but no capacitors means that refresh rates are not necessary because there are no capacitors to lose their charges over time. As long as there is power, SRAM remembers what is stored. With these attributes, why don't we use SRAM for all system memory? The answers are simple.

Compared to DRAM, SRAM is much faster but also much lower in density and much more expensive (see Table 6.1). The lower density means that SRAM chips are physically larger and store fewer bits overall. The high number of transistors and the clustered design mean that SRAM chips are both physically larger and much more expensive to produce than DRAM chips. For example, a DRAM module might contain 64MB of RAM or more, whereas SRAM modules of the same approximate physical size would have room for only 2MB or so of data and would cost the same as the 64MB DRAM module. Basically, SRAM is up to 30 times larger physically and up to 30 times more expensive than DRAM. The high cost and physical constraints have prevented SRAM from being used as the main memory for PC systems.

Table 6.1   Comparing DRAM and SRAM

Type	Speed	Density	Cost
DRAM	Slow	High	Low
SRAM	Fast	Low	High

Even though SRAM is too expensive for PC use as main memory, PC designers have found a way to use SRAM to dramatically improve PC performance. Rather than spend the money for all RAM to be SRAM memory, which can run fast enough to match the CPU, designing in a small amount of high-speed SRAM memory, called *cache memory*, is much more cost-effective. The cache runs at speeds close to or even equal to the processor and is the memory from which the processor usually directly reads from and writes to. During read operations, the data in the high-speed cache memory is resupplied from the lower-speed main memory or DRAM in advance. To convert access time in nanoseconds to MHz, use the following formula:

1 / nanoseconds × 1000 = MHz

Likewise, to convert from MHz to nanoseconds, use the following inverse formula:

1 / MHz × 1000 = nanoseconds

Today we have memory that runs faster than 1GHz (1 nanosecond), but up until the late 1990s, DRAM was limited to about 60ns (16MHz) in speed. Up until processors were running at speeds of 16MHz, the available DRAM could fully keep pace with the processor and motherboard, meaning that there was no need for cache. However, as soon as processors crossed the 16MHz barrier, the available DRAM could no longer keep pace, and SRAM cache began to enter PC system designs. This occurred way back in 1986 and 1987 with the debut of systems with the 386 processor running at speeds of 16MHz to 20MHz or faster. These were among the first PC systems to employ what's called *cache memory*, a high-speed buffer made up of SRAM that directly feeds the processor. Because the cache can run at the speed of the processor, it acts as a buffer between the processor and the slower DRAM in the system. The cache controller anticipates the processor's memory needs and preloads the high-speed cache memory with data. Then, as the processor calls for a memory address, the data can be retrieved from the high-speed cache rather than the much lower-speed main memory.

Cache effectiveness can be expressed by a hit ratio. This is the ratio of cache hits to total memory accesses. A *hit* occurs when the data the processor needs has been preloaded into the cache from the main memory, meaning the processor can read it from the cache. A cache *miss* is when the cache controller did not anticipate the need for a specific address and the desired data was not preloaded into the cache. In that case the processor must retrieve the data from the slower main memory, instead of the faster cache. Anytime the processor reads data from main memory, the processor must wait longer because the main memory cycles at a much slower rate than the processor. As an example, if the processor with integral on-die cache is running at 3.6GHz (3,600MHz) on an 800MHz bus, both the processor and the integral cache would be cycling at 0.28ns, while the main memory would most likely be cycling almost five times more slowly at 800MHz (1.25ns) DDR2. So, every time the 3.6GHz processor reads from main memory, it would effectively slow down to only 800MHz! The slowdown is accomplished by having the processor execute what are called *wait states*, which are cycles in which nothing is done; the processor essentially cools its heels while waiting for the slower main memory to return the desired data. Obviously, you don't want your processors slowing down, so cache function and design become more important as system speeds increase.

To minimize the processor being forced to read data from the slow main memory, two or three stages of cache usually exist in a modern system, called Level 1 (L1), Level 2 (L2), and Level 3 (L3). The L1 cache is also called *integral* or *internal cache* because it has always been built directly into the processor as part of the processor die (the raw chip). Because of this, L1 cache always runs at the full speed of the processor core and is the fastest cache in any system. All 486 and higher processors incorporate integral L1 cache, making them significantly faster than their predecessors. L2 cache was originally called *external cache* because it was external to the processor chip when it first appeared. Originally, this meant it was installed on the motherboard, as was the case with all 386, 486, and first generation Pentium systems. In those systems, the L2 cache runs at motherboard and CPU bus speed because it is installed on the motherboard and is connected to the CPU bus. You typically find the L2 cache physically adjacent to the processor socket in Pentium and earlier systems.

◀◀   See "How Cache Works," p. 73.

In the interest of improved performance, later processor designs from Intel and AMD included the L2 cache as a part of the processor. In all processors since late 1999 (and some earlier models), the L2 cache is directly incorporated as a part of the processor die just like the L1 cache. In chips with on-die L2, the cache runs at the full core speed of the processor and is much more efficient. By contrast, most processors from 1999 and earlier with integrated L2 had the L2 cache in separate chips that were external to the main processor core. The L2 cache in many of these older processors ran at only half or one-third the processor core speed. Cache speed is very important, so systems having L2 cache on the motherboard were the slowest. Including L2 inside the processor made it faster, and including it directly on the processor die (rather than as chips external to the die) is the fastest yet. Any chip that has on-die full core speed L2 cache has a distinct performance advantage over any chip that doesn't.

A third-level or L3 cache has been present in some high-end workstation and server processors since 2001. The first desktop PC processor with L3 cache was the Pentium 4 Extreme Edition, a high-end chip introduced in late 2003 with 2MB of on-die L3 cache. Although it seemed at the time that this would be a forerunner of widespread L3 cache in desktop processors, later versions of the Pentium 4 Extreme Edition (as well as its successor, the Pentium Extreme Edition) dropped the L3 cache. Instead, larger L2 cache sizes are used to improve performance. Although L3 cache may eventually become a standard feature in processors, the current trend is to use the extra die space for multiple cores with larger L2 caches instead.

The key to understanding both cache and main memory is to see where they fit in the overall system architecture.

See Chapter 4, "Motherboards and Buses," for diagrams showing recent systems with different types of cache memory. Table 6.2 illustrates the need for and function of cache memory in modern systems.

Cache designs originally were *asynchronous*, meaning they ran at a clock speed that was not identical or in sync with the processor bus. Starting with the 430FX chipset released in early 1995, a new type of synchronous cache design was supported. It required that the chips now run in sync or at the same identical clock timing as the processor bus, further improving speed and performance. Also added at that time was a feature called *pipeline burst mode*, which reduces overall cache latency (wait states) by allowing single-cycle accesses for multiple transfers after the first one. Because both synchronous and pipeline burst capability came at the same time in new modules, specifying one usually implies the other. Synchronous pipeline burst cache allowed for about a 20% improvement in overall system performance, which was a significant jump.

The cache controller for a modern system is contained in either the North Bridge of the chipset, as with Pentium and lesser systems, or within the processor, as with the Pentium II, Athlon, and newer systems. The capabilities of the cache controller dictate the cache's performance and capabilities. One important thing to note for older systems is that most external cache controllers have a limitation on the amount of memory that can be cached. Often, this limit can be quite low, as with the 430TX chipset–based Pentium systems from the late '90s. Most original Pentium-class chipsets from that time, such as the 430FX/VX/TX, can cache data only within the first 64MB of system RAM. If you add more memory than that to those systems, you will see a noticeable slowdown in system performance because all data outside the first 64MB is never cached and is always accessed with all the wait states required by the slower DRAM. Depending on what software you use and where data is stored in memory, this can be significant. For example, 32-bit operating systems such as Windows load from the top down, so if you had 96MB of RAM, the operating system and applications would load directly into the upper 32MB, which is beyond the 64MB cacheability limit and therefore not cached. This results in a dramatic slowdown in overall system use. Removing memory to bring the system total down to the cacheable limit of 64MB would actually speed up the system in this case. In short, it is unwise to install more main RAM memory than your system (CPU or chipset) can cache. Fortunately, this limitation does not affect modern systems with Pentium III and newer processors because they can cache all addressable memory.

Chipsets made for the Pentium Pro and later processors do not control the L2 cache because the cache was moved into the processor instead. So, with the Pentium Pro and beyond, the processor sets the cacheability limits. The Pentium Pro and some of the earlier Pentium IIs can only cache memory within the first 512MB of address space. The later Pentium IIs can cache up to 4GB, whereas the Pentium III and later can cache any and all addressable memory up to 64GB, well beyond the maximum RAM support of any chipsets.

Table 6.2 shows the evolutionary changes in cache and main memory in processors since the first-generation Pentium. Note especially how the L2 cache moved from being external to on-chip and then on-die, while also getting larger and larger. In addition, there have been significant increases in CPU speed as well as cache, memory, and bus speeds.

RAM Types and Performance

The speed and performance issue with memory is confusing to some because memory speed is sometimes expressed in nanoseconds (ns) and processor speed has always been expressed in megahertz (MHz) or gigahertz (GHz). Newer and faster types of memory usually have speeds expressed in MHz, thus adding to the confusion. Fortunately, you can easily translate MHz/GHz to ns, and vice versa.

A *nanosecond* is defined as one billionth of a second—a very short time indeed. To put some perspective on that, the speed of light is 186,282 miles (299,792 kilometers) per second in a vacuum. In one billionth of a second, a beam of light travels a mere 11.80 inches or 29.98 centimeters—less than the length of a typical ruler!

Chip and system speeds have often been expressed in megahertz (MHz), which is millions of cycles per second, or gigahertz (GHz), which is billions of cycles per second. Today's processors run in the 2GHz–4GHz range with most performance improvements coming from changes in CPU design (such as multiple cores) rather than pure clock speed increases.

Because it is confusing to speak in these different terms for speeds, I thought it would be interesting to see how they compare. Earlier in this chapter I listed formulas you could use to mathematically convert these values. Table 6.3 shows the relationship between common nanosecond (ns) and megahertz (MHz) speeds associated with PCs from yesterday to today and tomorrow.

Table 6.2   Evolutionary Changes in L1 (Internal) Cache, L2 (External) Cache, and Main Memory in Modern Processors

CPU Type Extreme	Pentium	Pentium Pro	Pentium II	AMD K6-2	AMD K6-3
CPU speed	233MHz	200MHz	450MHz	550MHz	450MHz
L1 cache speed	4.3ns (233MHz)	5.0ns (200MHz)	2.2ns (450MHz)	1.8ns (550MHz)	2.2ns (450MHz)
L1 cache size	16K	32K	32K	64K	64K
L2 cache type	external	on-chip	on-chip	external	on-die
CPU/L2 speed ratio	—	1/1	1/2	—	1/1
L2 cache speed	15ns (66MHz)	5ns (200MHz)	4.4ns (225MHz)	10ns (100MHz)	2.2ns (450MHz)
L2 cache size	—	256K	512K	—	256K
CPU bus bandwidth	533MBps	533MBps	800MBps	800MBps	800MBps
Memory bus speed	60ns (16MHz)	60ns (16MHz)	10ns (100MHz)	10ns (100MHz)	10ns (100MHz)

1. 4M total L2 cache / 2M per core
2. 8M total L2 cache / 4M per core

Table 6.3   The Relationship Between Megahertz (MHz) and Cycle Times in Nanoseconds (ns)

Clock Speed	Cycle Time	Clock Speed	Cycle Time	Clock Speed	Cycle Time	Clock Speed	Cycle Time
4.77MHz	210ns	150MHz	6.7ns	550MHz	1.82ns	1,000MHz	1.00ns
6MHz	167ns	166MHz	6.0ns	566MHz	1.77ns	1,100MHz	0.91ns
8MHz	125ns	180MHz	5.6ns	600MHz	1.67ns	1,133MHz	0.88ns
10MHz	100ns	200MHz	5.0ns	633MHz	1.58ns	1,200MHz	0.83ns
12MHz	83ns	225MHz	4.4ns	650MHz	1.54ns	1,300MHz	0.77ns
16MHz	63ns	233MHz	4.3ns	666MHz	1.50ns	1,400MHz	0.71ns
20MHz	50ns	250MHz	4.0ns	700MHz	1.43ns	1,500MHz	0.67ns
25MHz	40ns	266MHz	3.8ns	733MHz	1.36ns	1,600MHz	0.63ns
33MHz	30ns	300MHz	3.3ns	750MHz	1.33ns	1,700MHz	0.59ns
40MHz	25ns	333MHz	3.0ns	766MHz	1.31ns	1,800MHz	0.56ns
50MHz	20ns	350MHz	2.9ns	800MHz	1.25ns	1,900MHz	0.53ns
60MHz	17ns	366MHz	2.7ns	833MHz	1.20ns	2,000MHz	0.50ns
66MHz	15ns	400MHz	2.5ns	850MHz	1.18ns	2,100MHz	0.48ns
75MHz	13ns	433MHz	2.3ns	866MHz	1.15ns	2,200MHz	0.45ns
80MHz	13ns	450MHz	2.2ns	900MHz	1.11ns	2,300MHz	0.43ns
100MHz	10ns	466MHz	2.1ns	933MHz	1.07ns	2,400MHz	0.42ns
120MHz	8.3ns	500MHz	2.0ns	950MHz	1.05ns	2,500MHz	0.40ns
133MHz	7.5ns	533MHz	1.88ns	966MHz	1.04ns	2,600MHz	0.38ns

Pentium III	Athlon	Athlon XP	Pentium 4	Athlon 64 X2	Core 2 Duo	Core 2
1.4GHz	1.4GHz	2.2GHz	3.8GHz	3GHz	2.66GHz	2.93GHz
0.71ns (1.4GHz)	0.71ns (1.4GHz)	0.45ns (2.2GHz)	0.26ns (3.8GHz)	0.33ns (3GHz)	0.37ns (2.66GHz)	0.34ns (2.93GHz)
32K	128K	128K	20K	256K	64K	64K
on-die	on-die	on-die	on-die	on-die	On-die	on-die
1/1	1/1	1/1	1/1	1/1	1/1	1/1
0.71ns (1.4GHz)	0.71ns (1.4GHz)	0.45ns (2.2GHz)	0.26ns (3.8GHz)	0.33ns (3GHz)	0.37ns (2.66GHz)	0.34ns (2.93GHz)
512K	256K	512K	2M	2M	4M[1]	8M[2]
1,066MBps	2,133MBps	3,200MBps	6,400MBps	4,000MBps	8,533MBps	8,533MBps
7.5ns (133MHz)	3.8ns (266MHz)	2.5ns (400MHz)	1.25ns (800MHz)	2.5ns (400MHz)	0.94ns (1066MHz)	0.94ns (1066MHz)

Table 6.3   Continued

Clock Speed	Cycle Time	Clock Speed	Cycle Time	Clock Speed	Cycle Time	Clock Speed	Cycle Time
2,700MHz	0.37ns	3,300MHz	0.303ns	3,900MHz	0.256ns	4,500MHz	0.222ns
2,800MHz	0.36ns	3,400MHz	0.294ns	4,000MHz	0.250ns	4,600MHz	0.217ns
2,900MHz	0.34ns	3,500MHz	0.286ns	4,100MHz	0.244ns	4,700MHz	0.213ns
3,000MHz	0.333ns	3,600MHz	0.278ns	4,200MHz	0.238ns	4,800MHz	0.208ns
3,100MHz	0.323ns	3,700MHz	0.270ns	4,300MHz	0.233ns	4,900MHz	0.204ns
3,200MHz	0.313ns	3,800MHz	0.263ns	4,400MHz	0.227ns	5,000MHz	0.200ns

As you can see from Table 6.3, as clock speeds increase, cycle time decreases proportionately.

Over the development life of the PC, memory has had a difficult time keeping up with the processor, requiring several levels of high-speed cache memory to intercept processor requests for the slower main memory. More recently, however, systems using DDR, DDR2, and DDR3 SDRAM have memory bus performance equaling that of the processor bus. When the speed of the memory bus equals the speed of the processor bus, main memory performance is optimum for that system.

For example, using the information in Table 6.3, you can see that the 60ns DRAM memory used in the original Pentium and Pentium II PCs up until 1998 works out to be an extremely slow 16.7MHz! This slow 16.7MHz memory was installed in systems running processors up to 300MHz or faster on a processor bus speed of 66MHz, resulting in a large mismatch between processor bus and main memory performance. However, starting in 1998 the industry shifted to faster SDRAM memory, which was able to match the 66MHz speed of the processor bus at the time. From that point forward, memory has largely evolved in step with the processor bus, with newer and faster types coming out to match any increases in processor bus speeds.

By the year 2000 the dominant processor bus and memory speeds had increased to 100MHz and even 133MHz (called PC100 and PC133 SDRAM, respectively). Starting in early 2001, double data rate (DDR) SDRAM memory of 200MHz and 266MHz become popular. In 2002 DDR memory increased to 333MHz, and in 2003 the speeds increased further to 400MHz. During 2004 we saw the introduction of DDR2, first at 400MHz and then at 533MHz. DDR2 memory continued to match processor bus speed increases in PCs during 2005 and 2006, rising to 667MHz and 800MHz during that time. By 2007 DDR2 memory was available at speeds of up to 1,066MHz, and DDR3 came on the market at 1,066MHz and faster. Table 6.4 lists the primary types and performance levels of PC memory.

Table 6.4   Types and Performance Levels of Memory Used in PCs

Memory Type	Years Popular	Module Type	Voltage	Max. Clock Speed	Max. Throughput Single-Channel	Max. Throughput Dual-Channel
Fast Page Mode (FPM) DRAM	1987–1995	30/72-pin SIMM	5V	22MHz	177MBps	N/A
Extended Data Out (EDO) DRAM	1995–1998	72-pin SIMM	5V	33MHz	266MBps	N/A
Single Data Rate (SDR) SDRAM	1998–2002	168-pin DIMM	3.3V	133MHz	1,066MBps	N/A
Rambus DRAM (RDRAM)	2000–2002	184-pin RIMM	2.5V	1,066MTps	2,133MBps	4,266MBps
Double Data Rate (DDR) SDRAM	2002–2005	184-pin DIMM	2.5V	400MTps	3,200MBps	6,400MBps
DDR2 SDRAM	2005–2008	240-pin DDR2 DIMM	1.8V	1,066MTps	8,533MBps	17,066MBps
DDR3 SDRAM	2008+	240-pin DDR3 DIMM	1.5V	1,600MTps	12,800MBps	25,600MBps

MHz = Megacycles per second

MTps = Megatransfers per second

MBps = Megabytes per second

SIMM = Single inline memory module

DIMM = Dual inline memory module

The following sections look at these memory types in more detail.

Fast Page Mode DRAM

Standard DRAM is accessed through a technique called *paging*. Normal memory access requires that a row and column address be selected, which takes time. Paging enables faster access to all the data within a given row of memory by keeping the row address the same and changing only the column. Memory that uses this technique is called *Page Mode* or *Fast Page Mode* memory. Other variations on Page Mode were called *Static Column* or *Nibble Mode* memory.

Paged memory is a simple scheme for improving memory performance that divides memory into pages ranging from 512 bytes to a few kilobytes long. The paging circuitry then enables memory locations in a page to be accessed with fewer wait states. If the desired memory location is outside the current page, one or more wait states are added while the system selects the new page.

To improve further on memory access speeds, systems have evolved to enable faster access to DRAM. One important change was the implementation of burst mode access in the 486 and later processors. Burst mode cycling takes advantage of the consecutive nature of most memory accesses. After setting up the row and column addresses for a given access, using burst mode, you can then access the next three adjacent addresses with no additional latency or wait states. A burst access usually is limited to four total accesses. To describe this, we often refer to the timing in the number of cycles for each access. A typical burst mode access of standard DRAM is expressed as x-y-y-y; x is the time for the first access (latency plus cycle time), and y represents the number of cycles required for each consecutive access.

Standard 60ns-rated DRAM normally runs 5-3-3-3 burst mode timing. This means the first access takes a total of five cycles (on a 66MHz system bus, this is about 75ns total, or 5×15ns cycles), and the consecutive cycles take three cycles each (3×15ns = 45ns). As you can see, the actual system timing is somewhat less than the memory is technically rated for. Without the bursting technique, memory access would be 5-5-5-5 because the full latency is necessary for each memory transfer. The 45ns cycle time during burst transfers equals about a 22.2MHz effective clock rate; on a system with a 64-bit (8-byte) wide memory bus, this would result in a maximum throughput of 177MBps (22.2MHz × 8 bytes = 177MBps).

DRAM memory that supports paging and this bursting technique is called *Fast Page Mode (FPM)* memory. The term comes from the capability of memory accesses to data on the same page to be done with less latency. Most 386, 486, and Pentium systems from 1987 through 1995 used FPM memory, which came in either 30-pin or 72-pin SIMM form.

Another technique for speeding up FPM memory is called *interleaving*. In this design, two separate banks of memory are used together, alternating access from one to the other as even and odd bytes. While one is being accessed, the other is being precharged, when the row and column addresses are being selected. Then, by the time the first bank in the pair is finished returning data, the second bank in the pair is finished with the latency part of the cycle and is now ready to return data. While the second bank is returning data, the first bank is being precharged, selecting the row and column address of the next access. This overlapping of accesses in two banks reduces the effect of the latency or precharge cycles and allows for faster overall data retrieval. The only problem is that to use interleaving, you must install identical pairs of banks together, doubling the number of modules required. This was popular on 32-bit wide memory systems for 486 processors but fell out of favor on Pentium systems because of their 64-bit wide memory widths. To perform interleaving on a Pentium machine using FPM memory, you would need to install memory 128 bits at a time, meaning four 72-pin SIMMs at a time.

Extended Data Out RAM (EDO)

In 1995, a newer type of DRAM called *extended data out (EDO)* RAM became available for Pentium systems. EDO, a modified form of FPM memory, is sometimes referred to as *Hyper Page mode*. EDO was invented and patented by Micron Technology, although Micron licensed production to many other memory manufacturers.

EDO memory consists of specially manufactured chips that allow a timing overlap between successive accesses. The name *extended data out* refers specifically to the fact that unlike FPM, the data output drivers on the chip are not turned off when the memory controller removes the column address to begin the next cycle. This enables the next cycle to overlap the previous one, saving approximately 10ns per cycle.

The effect of EDO is that cycle times are improved by enabling the memory controller to begin a new column address instruction while it is reading data at the current address. This is almost identical to what was achieved in older systems by interleaving banks of memory, but unlike interleaving, with EDO you didn't need to install two identical banks of memory in the system at a time.

EDO RAM allows for burst mode cycling of 5-2-2-2, compared to the 5-3-3-3 of standard fast page mode memory. To do four memory transfers, then, EDO would require 11 total system cycles, compared to 14 total cycles for FPM. This is a 22% improvement in overall cycling time. The resulting two-cycle (30ns) cycle time during burst transfers equals a 33.3MHz effective clock rate, compared to 45ns/22MHz for FPM. On a system with a 64-bit (8-byte) wide memory bus, this would result in a maximum throughput of 266MBps (33.3MHz × 8 bytes = 266MBps). Due to the processor cache, EDO typically increased overall system benchmark speed by only 5% or less. Even though the overall system improvement was small, the important thing about EDO was that it used the same basic DRAM chip design as FPM, meaning that there was practically no additional cost over FPM. In fact, in its heyday EDO cost less than FPM and yet offered higher performance.

EDO RAM generally came in 72-pin SIMM form. Figure 6.4 (later in this chapter) shows the physical characteristics of these SIMMs.

To actually use EDO memory, your motherboard chipset had to support it. Most motherboard chipsets introduced on the market from 1995 (Intel 430FX) through 1997 (Intel 430TX) offered support for EDO, making EDO the most popular form of memory in PCs from 1995 through 1998. Because EDO memory chips cost the same to manufacture as standard chips, combined with Intel's support of EDO in motherboard chipsets, the PC market jumped on the EDO bandwagon full force.

◀◀   See "Fifth-generation (P5 Pentium Class) Chipsets," p. 284, and "Sixth-generation (P6 Pentium Pro/II/III Class) Chipsets," p. 286.

EDO RAM was used in systems with CPU bus speeds of up to 66MHz, which fit perfectly with the PC market up through 1998. However, starting in 1998, with the advent of 100MHz and faster system bus speeds, the market for EDO rapidly declined, and faster SDRAM architecture became the standard.

One variation of EDO that never caught on was called burst EDO (BEDO). BEDO added burst capabilities for even speedier data transfers than standard EDO. Unfortunately, the technology was owned by Micron and not a free industry standard, so only one chipset (Intel 440FX Natoma) ever supported it. BEDO was quickly overshadowed by industry-standard SDRAM, which came into favor among PC system chipset and system designers over proprietary designs. As such, BEDO never really saw the light of production, and to my knowledge no systems ever used it.

SDRAM

SDRAM is short for *synchronous DRAM*, a type of DRAM that runs in synchronization with the memory bus. SDRAM delivers information in very high-speed bursts using a high-speed clocked interface. SDRAM removes most of the latency involved in asynchronous DRAM because the signals are already in synchronization with the motherboard clock.

As with any type of memory on the market, motherboard chipset support is required before it can be usable in systems. Starting in 1996 with the 430VX and 430TX, most of Intel's chipsets began to support industry-standard SDRAM, and in 1998 the introduction of the 440BX chipset caused SDRAM to eclipse EDO as the most popular type on the market.

SDRAM performance is dramatically improved over that of FPM or EDO RAM. However, because SDRAM is still a type of DRAM, the initial latency is the same, but burst mode cycle times are much faster than with FPM or EDO. SDRAM timing for a burst access would be 5-1-1-1, meaning that four memory reads would complete in only eight system bus cycles, compared to 11 cycles for EDO and 14 cycles for FPM. This makes SDRAM almost 20% faster than EDO.

Besides being capable of working in fewer cycles, SDRAM is also capable of supporting up to 133MHz (7.5ns) system bus cycling. Most PC systems sold from 1998 through 2002 included SDRAM memory.

SDRAM is sold in DIMM form and is normally rated by clock speed (MHz) rather than cycling time (ns), which was confusing during the initial change from FPM and EDO DRAM. Figure 6.5 (later in this chapter) shows the physical characteristics of DIMMs.

To meet the stringent timing demands of its chipsets, Intel created specifications for SDRAM called PC66, PC100, and PC133. For example, you would think 10ns would be considered the proper rating for 100MHz operation, but the PC100 specification promoted by Intel calls for faster 8ns memory to ensure all timing parameters could be met with sufficient margin for error.

In May 1999, the Joint Electron Device Engineering Council (JEDEC) created a specification called PC133. It achieved this 33MHz speed increase by taking the PC100 specification and tightening up the timing and capacitance parameters. The faster PC133 quickly caught on for any systems running a 133MHz processor bus. The original chips used in PC133 modules were rated for exactly 7.5ns or 133MHz; later ones were rated at 7.0ns, which is technically 143MHz. These faster chips were still used on PC133 modules, but they allowed for improvements in column address strobe latency (abbreviated as CAS or CL), which somewhat improves overall memory cycling time.

Note

JEDEC is the semiconductor engineering standardization body of the Electronic Industries Alliance (EIA), a trade association that represents all areas of the electronics industry. JEDEC was originally created in 1960 and governs the standardization of all types of semiconductor devices, integrated circuits, and modules. JEDEC has about 300 member companies, including memory, chipset, and processor manufacturers as well as practically any company involved in manufacturing computer equipment using industry-standard components.

The idea behind JEDEC is simple: to create open standards that can be freely adopted throughout the industry. For example, if one company were to create a proprietary memory technology, other companies who wanted to manufacture components compliant with that memory would have to pay license fees, assuming the company that owned the technology was interested in licensing at all! Parts would be more proprietary in nature, causing problems with interchangeability or sourcing reasonably priced replacements. In addition, those companies licensing the technology would have no control over the evolution of the technology or any future changes made by the owner company.

JEDEC prevents this type of scenario for things such as memory by getting all the memory manufacturers to work together to create shared industry standards covering memory chips and modules. JEDEC-approved standards for memory can then be freely shared by all the member companies, and no one single company has control over a given standard, or any of the companies producing compliant components. FPM, SDRAM, DDR, DDR2, and DDR3 are all examples of JEDEC memory standards used in PCs, whereas memory such as EDO and RDRAM are proprietary examples. You can find out more about JEDEC standards for memory and other semiconductor technology at www.jedec.org.

Table 6.5 shows the timing, rated chip speeds, and standard module speeds for various SDRAM DIMMs.

Table 6.5   SDRAM Timing, Actual Speed, and Rated Speed

Timing	Rated Chip Speed	Standard Module Speed
15ns	66MHz	PC66
10ns	100MHz	PC66
8ns	125MHz	PC100
7.5ns	133MHz	PC133
7.0ns	143MHz	PC133

SDRAM normally came in 168-pin DIMMs, running at several different speeds. Table 6.6 shows the standard single data rate SDRAM module speeds and resulting throughputs.

Table 6.6   JEDEC Standard SDRAM Module (168-pin DIMM) Speeds and Transfer Rates

Module Standard	Chip Type	Clock Speed (MHz)	Cycles per Clock	Bus Speed (MTps)	Bus Width (Bytes)	Transfer Rate (MBps)
PC66	10ns	66	1	66	8	533
PC100	8ns	100	1	100	8	800
PC133	7ns	133	1	133	8	1,066

MTps = Megatransfers per second
MBps = Megabytes per second
ns = Nanoseconds (billionths of a second)
DIMM = Dual inline memory module

▶▶   See "SIMMs, DIMMs, and RIMMS," p. 533.

Some module manufacturers sold modules they claimed were "PC150" or "PC166," even though those speeds did not exist as official JEDEC or Intel standards, and no chipsets or processors officially supported those speeds. These modules actually used hand-picked 133MHz rated chips that could run overclocked at 150MHz or 166MHz speeds. In essence, PC150 or PC166 memory was PC133 memory that was tested to run at overclocked speeds not supported by the original chip manufacturer. This overclockable memory was sold at a premium to enthusiasts who wanted to overclock their motherboard chipsets, thereby increasing the speed of the processor and memory bus.

Caution

In general, PC133 memory is considered to be backward compatible with PC100 memory. However, some chipsets or motherboards had more specific requirements for specific types of 100MHz or 133MHz chips and module designs. If you need to upgrade an older system that requires PC100 memory, you should not purchase PC133 memory unless the memory is specifically identified by the memory vendor as being compatible with the system. You can use the online memory-configuration tools provided by most major memory vendors to ensure that you get the right memory for your system.

DDR SDRAM

Double data rate (DDR) SDRAM memory is a JEDEC standard that is an evolutionary upgrade in which data is transferred twice as quickly as standard SDRAM. Instead of doubling the actual clock rate, DDR memory achieves the doubling in performance by transferring twice per transfer cycle: once at the leading (falling) edge and once at the trailing (rising) edge of the cycle (see Figure 6.2). This effectively doubles the transfer rate, even though the same overall clock and timing signals are used.

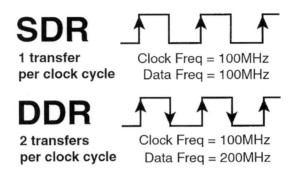

Figure 6.2 SDR (single data rate) versus DDR (double data rate) cycling.

DDR SDRAM first came to market in the year 2000 and was initially used on high-end graphics cards since there weren't any motherboard chipsets to support it at the time. DDR finally became popular in 2002 with the advent of mainstream supporting motherboards and chipsets. From 2002 through 2005, DDR was the most popular type of memory in mainstream PCs. DDR SDRAM uses a DIMM module design with 184 pins. Figure 6.6 (later in this chapter) shows the 184-pin DDR DIMM.

DDR DIMMs come in a variety of speed or throughput ratings and normally run on 2.5 volts. They are basically an extension of the standard SDRAM DIMMs redesigned to support double clocking, where data is sent on each clock transition (twice per cycle) rather than once per cycle as with standard SDRAM. To eliminate confusion with DDR, regular SDRAM is often called *single data rate (SDR)*. Table 6.7 compares the various types of industry-standard DDR SDRAM modules. As you can see, the raw chips are designated by their speed in megatransfers per second, whereas the modules are designated by their approximate throughput in megabytes per second.

Table 6.7 JEDEC Standard DDR Module (184-pin DIMM) Speeds and Transfer Rates

Module Standard	Chip Type	Clock Speed (MHz)	Cycles per Clock	Bus Speed (MTps)	Bus Width (Bytes)	Transfer Rate (MBps)	Dual-Channel Transfer Rate (MBps)
PC1600	DDR200	100	2	200	8	1,600	3,200
PC2100	DDR266	133	2	266	8	2,133	4,266
PC2700	DDR333	166	2	333	8	2,667	5,333
PC3200	DDR400	200	2	400	8	3,200	6,400

MTps = Megatransfers per second   *DIMM = Dual inline memory module*
MBps = Megabytes per second   *DDR = Double data rate*

The major memory chip and module manufacturers normally produce parts that conform to the official JEDEC standard speed ratings. However, to support overclocking, several memory module manufacturers purchase unmarked and untested chips from the memory chip manufacturers, then independently test and sort them by how fast they run. These are then packaged into modules with unofficial designations and performance figures that exceed the standard ratings. Table 6.8 shows the popular unofficial speed ratings I've seen on the market. Note that since the speeds of these modules are beyond the standard default motherboard and chipset speeds, you won't see any advantage to using these unless you are overclocking your system to match.

Table 6.8   Overclocked (non-JEDEC) DDR Module (184-pin DIMM) Speeds and Transfer Rates

Module Standard	Chip Type	Clock Speed (MHz)	Cycles per Clock	Bus Speed (MTps)	Bus Width (Bytes)	Transfer Rate (MBps)	Dual-Channel Transfer Rate (MBps)
PC3500	DDR433	216	2	433	8	3,466	6,933
PC3700	DDR466	216	2	466	8	3,733	7,466
PC4000	DDR500	250	2	500	8	4,000	8,000
PC4200	DDR533	266	2	533	8	4,266	8,533
PC4400	DDR550	275	2	550	8	4,400	8,800
PC4800	DDR600	300	2	600	8	4,800	9,600

MTps = Megatransfers per second
MBps = Megabytes per second
DIMM = Dual inline memory module
DDR = Double data rate

The bandwidths listed in these tables are per module. Most chipsets that support DDR also support dual-channel operation—a technique in which two matching DIMMs are installed to function as a single bank, with double the bandwidth of a single module. For example, if a chipset supports standard PC3200 modules, the bandwidth for a single module would be 3,200MBps. However, in dual-channel mode, the total bandwidth would double to 6,400MBps. Dual-channel operation optimizes PC design by ensuring that the CPU bus and memory bus both run at exactly the same speeds (meaning throughput, not MHz) so that data can move synchronously between the buses without delays.

DDR2 SDRAM

DDR2 is simply a faster version of DDR memory: It achieves higher throughput by using differential pairs of signal wires to allow faster signaling without noise and interference problems. DDR2 is still double data rate, just as with DDR, but the modified signaling method enables higher clock speeds to be achieved with more immunity to noise and cross-talk between the signals. The additional signals required for differential pairs add to the pin count—DDR2 DIMMs have 240 pins, which is more than the 184 pins of DDR. The original DDR specification officially topped out at 400MHz (although faster unofficial overclocked modules were produced), whereas DDR2 starts at 400MHz and goes up to an official maximum of 1,066MHz. Table 6.9 shows the various official JEDEC-approved DDR2 module types and bandwidth specifications.

Table 6.9   JEDEC Standard DDR2 Module (240-pin DIMM) Speeds and Transfer Rates

Module Standard	Chip Type	Clock Speed (MHz)	Cycles per Clock	Bus Speed (MTps)	Bus Width (Bytes)	Transfer Rate (MBps)	Dual-Channel Transfer Rate (MBps)
PC2-3200	DDR2-400	200	2	400	8	3,200	6,400
PC2-4200	DDR2-533	266	2	533	8	4,266	8,533
PC2-5300	DDR2-667	333	2	667	8	5,333	10,667
PC2-6400	DDR2-800	400	2	800	8	6,400	12,800
PC2-8500	DDR2-1066	533	2	1066	8	8,533	17,066

MTps = Megatransfers per second
MBps = Megabytes per second
DIMM = Dual inline memory module
DDR = Double data rate

The fastest official JEDEC-approved standard is DDR2-1066, which are chips that run at an effective speed of 1,066MHz (really megatransfers per second), resulting in modules designated PC2-8500 having a bandwidth of 8,533MBps. However, just as with DDR, many of the module manufacturers produce even faster modules designed for overclocked systems. These are sold as modules with unofficial designations and performance figures that exceed the standard ratings. Table 6.10 shows the popular unofficial speed ratings I've seen on the market. Note that since the speeds of these modules are beyond the standard default motherboard and chipset speeds, you won't see any advantage to using these unless you are overclocking your system to match.

Table 6.10   Overclocked (non-JEDEC) DDR2 Module (240-pin DIMM) Speeds and Transfer Rates

Module Standard	Chip Type	Clock Speed (MHz)	Cycles per Clock	Bus Speed (MTps)	Bus Width (Bytes)	Transfer Rate (MBps)	Dual-Channel Transfer Rate (MBps)
PC2-6000	DDR2-750	375	2	750	8	6,000	12,000
PC2-7200	DDR2-900	450	2	900	8	7,200	14,400
PC2-8000	DDR2-1000	500	2	1000	8	8,000	16,000
PC2-8800	DDR2-1100	550	2	1100	8	8,800	17,600
PC2-8888	DDR2-1111	556	2	1111	8	8,888	17,777
PC2-9136	DDR2-1142	571	2	1142	8	9,136	18,272
PC2-9200	DDR2-1150	575	2	1150	8	9,200	18,400
PC2-9600	DDR2-1200	600	2	1200	8	9,600	19,200
PC2-10000	DDR2-1250	625	2	1250	8	10,000	20,000

MTps = Megatransfers per second
MBps = Megabytes per second
DIMM = Dual inline memory module
DDR = Double data rate

In addition to providing greater speeds and bandwidth, DDR2 has other advantages. It uses lower voltage than conventional DDR (1.8V versus 2.5V), so power consumption and heat generation are reduced. Because of the greater number of pins required on DDR2 chips, the chips typically use fine-pitch ball grid array (FBGA) packaging rather than the thin small outline package (TSOP) chip packaging used by most DDR and conventional SDRAM chips. FPGA chips are connected to the substrate (meaning the memory module in most cases) via tightly spaced solder balls on the base of the chip.

DDR2 DIMMs resemble conventional DDR DIMMs but have more pins and slightly different notches to prevent confusion or improper application. For example, the different physical notches prevent you from plugging a DDR2 module into a conventional DDR (or SDR) socket. DDR2 memory module designs incorporate 240 pins, significantly more than conventional DDR or standard SDRAM DIMMs.

JEDEC began working on the DDR2 specification in April 1998, and published the standard in September 2003. DDR2 chip and module production actually began in mid-2003 (mainly samples and prototypes), and the first chipsets, motherboards, and systems supporting DDR2 appeared for Intel processor–based systems in mid-2004. At that time variations of DDR2 such as G-DDR2 (Graphics DDR2) began appearing in graphics cards as well. Mainstream motherboard chipset support for DDR2 on Intel processor–based systems appeared in 2005. Notable for its lack of DDR2 support through 2005 was AMD, whose Athlon 64 and Opteron processor families included integrated DDR memory controllers. AMD processor–based systems first supported DDR2 in mid-2006, with the release of socket AM2 motherboards and processors to match. (AMD's Socket F, also known as 1207 FX, also supports DDR2 memory.)

It is interesting to note that AMD was almost two years behind Intel in the transition from DDR to DDR2. This is because AMD included the memory controller in its Athlon 64 and newer processors, rather than incorporating the memory controller in the chipset North Bridge, as with more traditional Intel designs. Although there are advantages to integrating the memory controller in the CPU, a major disadvantage is the inability to quickly adopt new memory architectures, because doing so requires that both the processor and processor socket be redesigned. With the memory controller in the chipset, Intel can more quickly adopt newer and faster memory architectures without having to redesign existing processors. These transitional differences will likely become apparent again in the expected transition from DDR2 to DDR3 in 2008.

DDR3

DDR3 isis the latest JEDEC memory standard, which will enable higher levels of performance along with lower power consumption and higher reliability than DDR2. JEDEC began working on the DDR3 specification in June of 2002, and the first DDR3 memory modules and supporting chipsets (Intel 3xx series) were released for Intel-based systems in mid-2007. AMD is expected to introduce new processors and sockets supporting DDR3 memory sometime during 2008. Initially DDR3 will be more expensive than DDR2, and will be used in systems requiring extremely high-performance memory. DDR3 is expected to achieve mainstream status in the 2008 to 2009 timeframe.

DDR3 modules use advanced signal designs, including self-driver calibration and data synchronization, along with an optional onboard thermal sensor. DDR3 memory runs on only 1.5V, which is nearly 20% less than the 1.8V used by DDR2 memory. The lower voltage combined with higher efficiency is expected to reduce overall power consumption by up to 30% compared to DDR2.

DDR3 modules are expected to initially become popular for systems where the processor and/or memory bus runs at 1,333MHz, which is faster than the 1,066MHz maximum supported by DDR2. For higher-speed memory in standard (non-overclocked) systems, DDR3 modules rated PC3-10600 and PC3-12800 will allow for throughputs of 10,667MBps and 12,800MBps, respectively. When combined in dual-channel operation, a pair of PC3-12800 modules will result in a total throughput of an incredible 25,600MBps. Table 6.11 shows the various official JEDEC-approved DDR3 module types and bandwidth specifications.

Table 6.11   JEDEC Standard DDR3 Module (240-pin DIMM) Speeds and Transfer Rates

Module Standard	Chip Type	Clock Speed (MHz)	Cycles per Clock	Bus Speed (MTps)	Bus Width (Bytes)	Transfer Rate (MBps)	Dual-Channel Transfer Rate (MBps)
PC3-6400	DDR3-800	400	2	800	8	6,400	12,800
PC3-8500	DDR3-1066	533	2	1066	8	8,533	17,066
PC3-10600	DDR3-1333	667	2	1333	8	10,667	21,333
PC3-12800	DDR3-1600	800	2	1600	8	12,800	25,600

MTps = Megatransfers per second
MBps = Megabytes per second
DIMM = Dual inline memory module
DDR = Double data rate

240-pin DDR3 modules are similar in pin count, size, and shape to DDR2 modules; however, DDR3 modules are incompatible with DDR2 circuits, and are designed with different keying to make them physically noninterchangeable.

RDRAM

Rambus DRAM (RDRAM) was a proprietary (non-JEDEC) memory technology found mainly in certain Intel-based Pentium III and 4 systems from 2000 through 2002. Intel had signed a contract with Rambus in 1996 ensuring it would both adopt and support RDRAM memory into 2001. Believing that any memory it endorsed would automatically become the most popular in the industry, Intel also invested heavily in Rambus at the time. Since RDRAM was a proprietary standard owned by Rambus, using or producing it would require licensing from Rambus, something that was not very popular with other memory and chipset manufacturers. Still, the technology was licensed and Intel originally promised that supporting chipsets and motherboards would be available in 1998.

Unfortunately there were problems in getting the supporting chipsets to market, with delays of many months resulting in memory manufacturers stockpiling RDRAM chips with no systems to support them, while conventional SDRAM and DDR meanwhile came into short supply. The delays resulted in an industry-wide debacle that caused Intel to rethink and eventually abandon its investment in the technology. After 2001, Intel continued to support RDRAM in existing systems; however, new chipsets and motherboards rapidly shifted to DDR SDRAM. AMD wisely never invested in the RDRAM technology, and as a result no AMD-based systems were ever designed to use RDRAM.

Although RDRAM standards had been proposed that would support faster processors through 2006, without Intel's commitment to future chipset development and support, very few RDRAM-based systems were sold after 2002. Due to the lack of industry support from chipset and motherboard manufacturers, RDRAM was only used in PCs for a short time, and will most likely not play a big part in any future PCs.

With RDRAM, Rambus developed what is essentially a chip-to-chip memory bus, with specialized devices that communicate at very high rates of speed. What might be interesting to some is that this technology was first developed for game systems and first made popular by the Nintendo 64 game system, and it subsequently was used in the Sony Playstation 2.

Conventional memory systems that use SDRAM are known as *wide-channel systems*. They have memory channels as wide as the processor's data bus, which for the Pentium and up is 64 bits, or even wider in dual-channel modes. The dual inline memory module (DIMM) is a 64-bit wide device, meaning data can be transferred to it 64 bits (or 8 bytes) at a time.

RDRAM modules, on the other hand, are narrow-channel devices. They transfer data only 16 bits (2 bytes) at a time (plus 2 optional parity bits), but at faster speeds. This was a shift away from a more parallel to a more serial design for memory and is similar to what has been happening with other evolving buses in the PC.

Each individual chip is serially connected to the next on a package called a *Rambus inline memory module (RIMM)*, which looks similar to a DIMM module but which is not interchangeable. All memory transfers are done between the memory controller and a single device, not between devices. A single Rambus channel typically has three RIMM sockets and can support up up to 32 individual RDRAM devices (the RDRAM chips) and more if buffers are used. However, most motherboards implement only two modules per channel (four sockets in a dual-channel design) to avoid problems with signal noise.

The RDRAM memory bus is a continuous path through each device and module on the bus, with each module having input and output pins on opposite ends. Therefore, any RIMM sockets not containing a RIMM must then be filled with a continuity module to ensure that the path is completed. The signals that reach the end of the bus are terminated on the motherboard.

16-bit single channel RIMMs originally ran at 800MHz, so the overall throughput is 800×2, or 1.6GB per second for a single channel—the same as PC1600 DDR SDRAM. Pentium 4 systems typically used two banks simultaneously, creating a dual-channel design capable of 3.2GBps, which matched the bus speed of the original Pentium 4 processors. The RDRAM design features less latency between transfers because they all run synchronously in a looped system and in only one direction.

Newer RIMM versions ran at 1,066MHz in addition to the original 800MHz rate, but very few chipsets or motherboards were released to support the higher speed.

Each RDRAM chip on a RIMM1600 essentially operates as a standalone device sitting on the 16-bit data channel. Internally, each RDRAM chip has a core that operates on a 128-bit wide bus split into eight 16-bit banks running at 100MHz. In other words, every 10ns (100MHz), each RDRAM chip can transfer 16 bytes to and from the core. This internally wide yet externally narrow high-speed interface is the key to RDRAM.

Other improvements to the design include separating control and data signals on the bus. Independent control and address buses are split into two groups of pins for row and column commands, while data is transferred across the 2-byte wide data bus. The actual memory bus clock runs at 400MHz; however, data is transferred on both the falling and rising edges of the clock signal, or twice per clock pulse. The falling edge is called an *even cycle*, and the rising edge is called an *odd cycle*. Complete memory bus synchronization is achieved by sending packets of data beginning on an even cycle interval. The overall wait before a memory transfer can begin (latency) is only one cycle, or 2.5ns maximum.

Figure 6.2 (shown earlier) depicts the relationship between clock and data cycles; you can see the DDR clock and data cycles used by RDRAM and DDR SDRAM. An RDRAM data packet always begins on an even (falling) transition for synchronization purposes.

The architecture also supports multiple, simultaneous interleaved transactions in multiple separate time domains. Therefore, before a transfer has even completed, another can begin.

Another important feature of RDRAM is that it is designed for low power consumption. The RIMMs themselves as well as the RDRAM devices run on only 2.5 volts and use low-voltage signal swings from 1.0V to 1.8V, a swing of only 0.8V total. RDRAMs also have four power-down modes and can automatically transition into standby mode at the end of a transaction, which offers further power savings.

A RIMM is similar in size and physical form to a DIMM, but they are not interchangeable. RIMMs are available in module sizes up to 1GB or more and can be added to a system one at a time because each individual RIMM technically represents multiple banks to a system. Note, however, that they have to be added in pairs if your motherboard implements dual-channel RDRAM and you are using 16-bit wide RIMMs.

RIMMs are available in four primary speed grades and usually run in a dual-channel environment, so they have to be installed in pairs, with each one of the pairs in a different set of sockets. Each set of RIMM sockets on such boards is a channel. The 32-bit version incorporates multiple channels within a single device and, as such, is designed to be installed individually, eliminating the requirement for matched pairs. Table 6.12 compares the various types of RDRAM modules. Note that the once-common names for RIMM modules, such as PC800, have been replaced by names that reflect the actual bandwidth of the modules to avoid confusion with DDR memory.

Table 6.12 RDRAM Module Types and Bandwidth

Module Standard	Chip Type	Clock Speed (MHz)	Cycles per Clock	Bus Speed (MTps)	Bus Width (Bytes)	Transfer Rate (MBps)
RIMM1200	PC600	300	2	600	2	1,200
RIMM1400	PC700	350	2	700	2	1,400
RIMM1600	PC800	400	2	800	2	1,600
RIMM2100	PC1066	533	2	1,066	2	2,133

MTps = Megatransfers per second

MBps = Megabytes per second

RIMM = Rambus inline memory module

When Intel initially threw its weight behind the Rambus memory, it seemed destined to be a sure thing for success. Unfortunately, technical delays in the chipsets caused the supporting motherboards to be significantly delayed, and with few systems to support the RIMMs, most memory manufacturers went back to making SDRAM or shifted to DDR SDRAM instead. This caused the remaining available RIMMs being manufactured to be originally priced three or more times that of a comparatively sized DIMM. More recently, the cost for RDRAM RIMMs has come down to approximately that of DDR SDRAM, but by the time that happened, Intel had shifted all future chipset development to support only DDR and DDR2 memory.

As I've stated many times, one of the main considerations for memory is that the throughput of the memory bus should match the throughput of the processor bus, and in that area RDRAM RIMMs were originally more suited to the initial Pentium 4 processor systems. However, with the increases in speed of the Pentium 4 processor bus along with the advent of chipsets supporting dual-channel DDR memory, DDR, DDR2, and DDR3 became the best choices for the CPU bus speeds of both Intel and AMD processors. In short, the advent of newer chipsets has rendered DDR memory types as the best choices for modern systems, offering the maximum memory performance possible.

Note

Unfortunately for the memory chip manufacturers, Rambus has claimed patents that cover both standard and DDR SDRAM designs. So, regardless of whether these companies manufacture SDRAM, DDR, or RDRAM, it is the contention of Rambus that these memory manufacturers must pay the company royalties. Several court cases are ongoing with companies challenging these patents, and a lot is riding on the outcome. Most of the cases that have gone to trial have so far ruled against Rambus, essentially invalidating its patents and claims on DDR and SDRAM. Many appeals are pending, and it will likely be a long time before the patent issues are resolved.

With support for RDRAM memory essentially gone in 2003, RDRAM quickly disappeared from the PC marketplace. Because RDRAM is in such limited supply, if you have existing systems with RDRAM memory, it is generally not cost effective to upgrade them by adding more memory.

Memory Modules

The CPU and motherboard architecture (chipset) dictates a particular computer's physical memory capacity and the types and forms of memory that can be installed. Over the years, two main changes have occurred in computer memory—it has gradually become faster and wider. The CPU and the memory controller circuitry indicate the speed and width requirements. The memory controller in a modern PC resides in the motherboard chipset. Even though a system might physically support a given amount of memory, the type of software you run could dictate whether all the memory can be used.

The 8088 and 8086 CPUs, with 20 address lines, can use as much as 1MB (1,024KB) of RAM. The 286 and 386SX CPUs have 24 address lines and can keep track of as much as 16MB of memory. The 386DX, 486, Pentium, and Pentium-MMX CPUs have a full set of 32 address lines, so they can keep track of 4GB of memory; the Pentium Pro, Pentium II/III, and 4, as well as the AMD Athlon and Duron, have 36 address lines and can manage an impressive 64GB. The Itanium processor, on the other hand, has 44-bit addressing, which allows for up to 16TB (terabytes) of physical RAM!

◄◄   See "Processor Specifications," p. 43.

When the 286 and higher chips emulate the 8088 chip (as they do when running 16-bit software, such as DOS or Windows 3.x), they implement a hardware operating mode called *real mode*. Real mode is the only mode available on the 8086 and 8088 chips used in PC and XT systems. In real mode, all Intel processors—even the mighty Pentium family—are restricted to using only 1MB of memory, just as their 8086 and 8088 ancestors were, and the system design reserves 384KB of that amount. Only in protected mode can the 286 or better chips use their maximum potentials for memory addressing.

◄◄   See "Processor Modes," p. 50.

P5 class systems can address as much as 4GB of memory, and P6/P7 class systems can address up to 64GB. To put these memory-addressing capabilities into perspective, 64GB (65,536MB) of memory would cost more than $10,000! Even if you could afford all this memory, some of the largest memory modules available for desktop PCs today are 1GB DIMMs. Installing 64GB of RAM would require 64 1GB DIMMs, and most systems today support up to only four DIMM sockets.

Although memory sizes are increasing and some current desktop motherboards support 2GB modules, the real limitations on memory sizing in any system are the chipset and the number of sockets on the motherboard. Most desktop motherboards incorporate from two to four memory sockets, which allows a maximum of 4GB–8GB if all the sockets are filled. These limitations are from the chipset, not the processor or RAM modules. Some processors can address 64GB, but no chipset on the market will allow that!

Note

See the "Chipsets" section in Chapter 4 for the maximum cacheable limits on all the Intel and other motherboard chipsets.

SIMMs, DIMMs, and RIMMs

Originally, systems had memory installed via individual chips. They are often referred to as dual inline package (DIP) chips because of their designs. The original IBM XT and AT had 36 sockets on the motherboard for these individual chips; then more of them were installed on the memory cards plugged into the bus slots. I remember spending hours populating boards with these chips, which was a tedious job.

Besides being a time-consuming and labor-intensive way to deal with memory, DIP chips had one notorious problem—they crept out of their sockets over time as the system went through thermal cycles. Every day, when you powered the system on and off, the system heated and cooled, and the chips gradually walked their way out of the sockets—a phenomenon called *chip creep*. Eventually, good contact was lost and memory errors resulted. Fortunately, reseating all the chips back in their sockets usually rectified the problem, but that method was labor intensive if you had a lot of systems to support.

The alternative to this at the time was to have the memory soldered into either the motherboard or an expansion card. This prevented the chips from creeping and made the connections more permanent, but it caused another problem. If a chip did go bad, you had to attempt desoldering the old one and resoldering a new one or resort to scrapping the motherboard or memory card on which the chip was installed. This was expensive and made memory troubleshooting difficult.

A chip was needed that was both soldered and removable, and that is exactly what was found in the module called a SIMM. For memory storage, most modern systems have adopted the single inline memory module (SIMM) or the more recent DIMM and RIMM module designs as an alternative to individual memory chips. These small boards plug into special connectors on a motherboard or memory card. The individual memory chips are soldered to the module, so removing and replacing them is impossible. Instead, you must replace the entire module if any part of it fails. The module is treated as though it were one large memory chip.

Two main types of SIMMs, three main types of DIMMs, and one type of RIMM have been commonly used in desktop systems. The various types are often described by their pin count, memory row width, or memory type.

SIMMs, for example, are available in two main physical types—30-pin (8 bits plus an option for 1 additional parity bit) and 72-pin (32 bits plus an option for 4 additional parity bits)—with various capacities and other specifications. The 30-pin SIMMs are physically smaller than the 72-pin versions, and either version can have chips on one or both sides. SIMMs were widely used from the late 1980s to the late 1990s but have become obsolete.

DIMMs are also available in three main types. DIMMs usually hold standard SDRAM or DDR SDRAM chips and are distinguished by different physical characteristics. Standard DIMMs have 168 pins, one notch on either side, and two notches along the contact area. DDR DIMMs, on the other hand, have 184 pins, two notches on each side, and only one offset notch along the contact area. DDR2 DIMMs have 240 pins, two notches on each side, and one in the center of the contact area. All DIMMs are either 64-bits (non-ECC/parity) or 72-bits (parity or error-correcting code [ECC]) wide (data paths). The main physical difference between SIMMs and DIMMs is that DIMMs have different signal pins on each side of the module. That is why they are called dual inline memory modules, and why with only 1" of additional length, they have many more pins than a SIMM.

Note

There is confusion among users and even in the industry regarding the terms *single-sided* and *double-sided* with respect to memory modules. In truth, the single- or double-sided designation actually has nothing to do with whether chips are physically located on one or both sides of the module, and it has nothing to do with whether the module is a SIMM or DIMM (meaning whether the connection pins are single- or double-inline). Instead the terms single-sided and double-sided are used to indicate whether the module has one or two banks of memory chips installed. A double-banked DIMM module has two complete 64-bit wide banks of chips logically stacked so that the module is twice as deep (has twice as many 64-bit rows). In most (but not all) cases, this requires chips to be on both sides of the module; therefore, the term double-sided has often been used to indicate that a module has two banks, even though the term is technically incorrect. Single-banked modules (incorrectly referred to as single-sided) can have chips physically mounted on both sides of the module, and double-banked modules (incorrectly referred to as double-sided) can have chips physically mounted on only one side. I recommend using the terms *single-banked* and *double-banked* instead because they are much more accurate and easily understood.

RIMMs also have different signal pins on each side. Three different physical types of RIMMs are available: a 16/18-bit version with 184 pins, a 32/36-bit version with 232 pins, and a 64/72-bit version with 326 pins. Each of these plugs into the same sized connector, but the notches in the connectors and RIMMs are different to prevent a mismatch. A given board will accept only one type. By far the most common type is the 16/18-bit version. The 32-bit version was introduced in late 2002, and the 64-bit version was introduced in 2004.

The standard 16/18-bit RIMM has 184 pins, one notch on either side, and two notches centrally located in the contact area. The 16-bit versions are used for non-ECC applications, whereas the 18-bit versions incorporate the additional bits necessary for ECC.

Figures 6.3 through 6.9 show a typical 30-pin (8-bit) SIMM, 72-pin (32-bit) SIMM, 168-pin SDRAM DIMM, 184-pin DDR SDRAM (64-bit) DIMM, 240-pin DDR2 DIMM, 240-pin DDR3 DIMM, and 184-pin RIMM, respectively. The pins are numbered from left to right and are connected through to both sides of the module on the SIMMs. The pins on the DIMM are different on each side, but on a SIMM, each side is the same as the other and the connections carry through. Note that all dimensions are in both inches and millimeters (in parentheses), and modules are generally available in error-correcting code (ECC) versions with 1 extra ECC (or parity) bit for every 8 data bits (multiples of 9 in data width) or versions that do not include ECC support (multiples of 8 in data width).

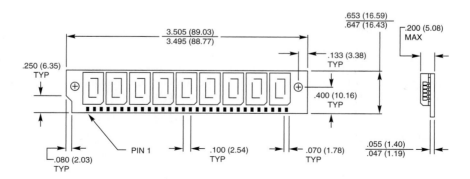

Figure 6.3 A typical 30-pin SIMM.

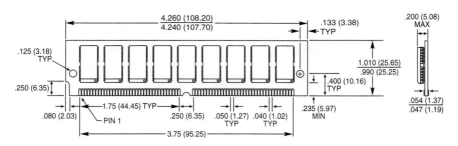

Figure 6.4   A typical 72-pin SIMM.

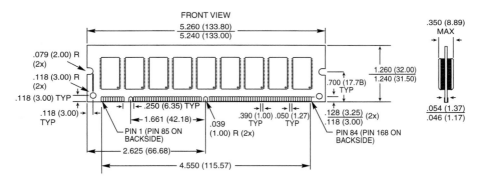

Figure 6.5   A typical 168-pin SDRAM DIMM.

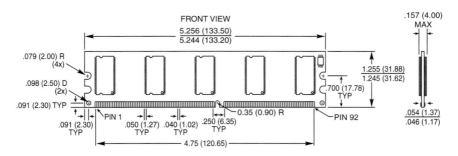

Figure 6.6   A typical 184-pin DDR DIMM.

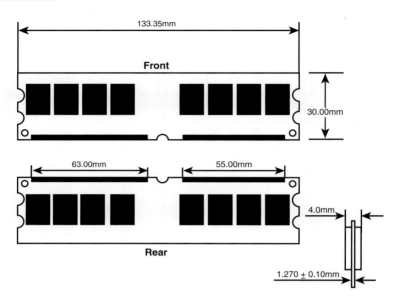

Figure 6.7 A typical 240-pin DDR2 DIMM.

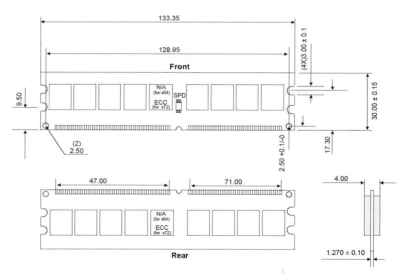

Figure 6.8 A typical 240-pin DDR3 DIMM.

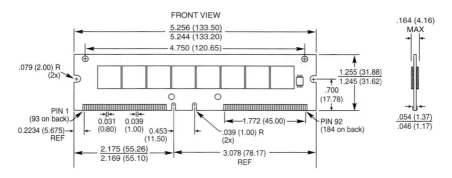

FRONT VIEW

Figure 6.9   A typical 184-pin RIMM.

All these memory modules are fairly compact considering the amount of memory they hold and are available in several capacities and speeds. Table 6.13 lists the various capacities available for SIMMs, DIMMs, and RIMMs.

Table 6.13   SIMM, DIMM, and RIMM Capacities

Capacity	Standard	Parity/ECC
30-Pin SIMM		
256KB	256KB×8	256KB×9
1MB	1MB×8	1MB×9
4MB	4MB×8	4MB×9
16MB	16MB×8	16MB×9
72-Pin SIMM		
1MB	256KB×32	256KB×36
2MB	512KB×32	512KB×36
4MB	1MB×32	1MB×36
8MB	2MB×32	2MB×36
16MB	4MB×32	4MB×36
32MB	8MB×32	8MB×36
64MB	16MB×32	16MB×36
128MB	32MB×32	32MB×36
168/184-Pin DIMM/DDR DIMM		
8MB	1MB×64	1MB×72
16MB	2MB×64	2MB×72
32MB	4MB×64	4MB×72
64MB	8MB×64	8MB×72
128MB	16MB×64	16MB×72
256MB	32MB×64	32MB×72
512MB	64MB×64	64MB×72
1,024MB	128MB×64	128MB×72

Table 6.13   Continued

Capacity	Standard	Parity/ECC
2,048MB	256MB×64	256MB×72
240-Pin DDR2 DIMM		
256MB	32MB×64	32MB×72
512MB	64MB×64	64MB×72
1,024MB	128MB×64	128MB×72
2,048MB	256MB×64	256MB×72
240-Pin DDR3 DIMM		
256MB	32MB×64	32MB×72
512MB	64MB×64	64MB×72
1,024MB	128MB×64	128MB×72
2,048MB	256MB×64	256MB×72
184-Pin RIMM		
64MB	32MB×16	32MB×18
128MB	64MB×16	64MB×18
256MB	128MB×16	128MB×18
512MB	256MB×16	256MB×18
1,024MB	512MB×16	512MB×18

Memory modules of each type and capacity are available in various speed ratings. Consult your motherboard documentation for the correct memory speed and type for your system. It is usually best for the memory speed (also called throughput or bandwidth) to match the speed of the processor data bus (also called the front side bus, or FSB).

If a system requires a specific speed memory module, you can almost always substitute faster speeds if the one specified is not available. Generally, no problems occur in mixing module speeds, as long as you use modules equal to or faster than what the system requires. Because there's little price difference between the various speed versions, I often buy faster modules than are necessary for a particular application. This might make them more usable in a future system that could require the faster speed.

Because SDRAM and newer modules have an onboard serial presence detect (SPD) ROM that reports their speed and timing parameters to the system, most systems run the memory controller and memory bus at the speed matching the slowest module installed.

Note

A bank is the smallest amount of memory needed to form a single row of memory addressable by the processor. It is the minimum amount of physical memory that is read or written by the processor at one time and usually corresponds to the data bus width of the processor. If a processor has a 64-bit data bus, a bank of memory also is 64 bits wide. If the memory is interleaved or runs dual-channel, a virtual bank is formed that is twice the absolute data bus width of the processor.

You can't always replace a module with a higher-capacity unit and expect it to work. Systems might have specific design limitations for the maximum capacity of module they can take. A larger-capacity module works only if the motherboard is designed to accept it in the first place. Consult your system documentation to determine the correct capacity and speed to use.

Registered Modules

SDRAM through DDR3 modules are available in unbuffered and registered versions. Most PC motherboards are designed to use unbuffered modules, which allow the memory controller signals to pass directly to the memory chips on the module with no interference. This is not only the cheapest design, but also the fastest and most efficient. The only drawback is that the motherboard designer must place limits on how many modules (meaning module sockets) can be installed on the board, and possibly also limit how many chips can be on a module. So-called double-sided modules that really have multiple banks of chips onboard might be restricted on some systems in certain combinations.

Systems designed to accept extremely large amounts of RAM (such as servers) often require registered modules. A registered module uses an architecture that has register chips on the module that act as an interface between the actual RAM chips and the chipset. The registers temporarily hold data passing to and from the memory chips and enable many more RAM chips to be driven or otherwise placed on the module than the chipset could normally support. This allows for motherboard designs that can support many modules and enables each module to have a larger number of chips. In general, registered modules are required by server or workstation motherboards designed to support more than four sockets. One anomaly is the initial version of the AMD Athlon 64 FX processor, which also uses registered memory because its Socket 940 design was based on the AMD Opteron workstation and server processor. Subsequent Socket 939, AM2, and Socket F versions of the Athlon FX no longer require registered memory.

To provide the space needed for the buffer chips, a registered DIMM is often taller than a standard DIMM. Figure 6.10 compares a typical registered DIMM to a typical unbuffered DIMM.

Tip

If you are installing registered DIMMs in a slimline case, clearance between the top of the DIMM and the case might be a problem. Some vendors sell low-profile registered DIMMs that are about the same height as an unbuffered DIMM. Use this type of DIMM if your system does not have enough head room for standard registered DIMMs. Some vendors sell only this type of DIMM for particular systems.

Registered DIMM

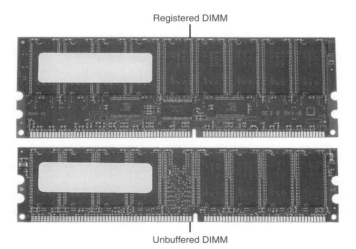

Unbuffered DIMM

Figure 6.10   A typical registered DIMM is taller than a typical unbuffered DIMM to provide room for buffer chips.

The important thing to note is that you can use only the type of module your motherboard (or chipset) is designed to support. For most, that is standard unbuffered modules or, in some cases, registered modules.

SIMM Pinouts

Table 6.14 shows the interface connector pinouts for standard 72-pin SIMMs. They also include a special presence detect table that shows the configuration of the presence detect pins on various 72-pin SIMMs. The motherboard uses the presence detect pins to determine exactly what size and speed SIMM is installed. Industry-standard 30-pin SIMMs do not have a presence detect feature, but IBM did add this capability to its modified 30-pin configuration. Note that all SIMMs have the same pins on both sides of the module.

Table 6.14   Standard 72-Pin SIMM Pinout

Pin	SIMM Signal Name	Pin	SIMM Signal Name	Pin	SIMM Signal Name	Pin	SIMM Signal Name
1	Ground						
2	Data Bit 0	21	Data Bit 20	40	Column Address Strobe 0	56	Data Bit 27
3	Data Bit 16	22	Data Bit 5			57	Data Bit 12
4	Data Bit 1	23	Data Bit 21	41	Column Address Strobe 2	58	Data Bit 28
5	Data Bit 17	24	Data Bit 6	42	Column Address Strobe 3	59	+5 Vdc
6	Data Bit 2	25	Data Bit 22			60	Data Bit 29
7	Data Bit 18	26	Data Bit 7	43	Column Address Strobe 1	61	Data Bit 13
8	Data Bit 3	27	Data Bit 23			62	Data Bit 30
9	Data Bit 19	28	Address Bit 7	44	Row Address Strobe 0	63	Data Bit 14
10	+5 Vdc	29	Address Bit 11	45	Row Address Strobe 1	64	Data Bit 31
11	Presence Detect 5	30	+5 Vdc	46	Reserved	65	Data Bit 15
12	Address Bit 0	31	Address Bit 8	47	Write Enable	66	EDO
13	Address Bit 1	32	Address Bit 9	48	ECC Optimized	67	Presence Detect 1
14	Address Bit 2	33	Address Bit 12	49	Data Bit 8	68	Presence Detect 2
15	Address Bit 3	34	Address Bit 13	50	Data Bit 24	69	Presence Detect 3
16	Address Bit 4	35	Parity Data Bit 2	51	Data Bit 9	70	Presence Detect 4
17	Address Bit 5	36	Parity Data Bit 0	52	Data Bit 25	71	Reserved
18	Address Bit 6	37	Parity Data Bit 1	53	Data Bit 10	72	Ground
19	Address Bit 10	38	Parity Data Bit 3	54	Data Bit 26		
20	Data Bit 4	39	Ground	55	Data Bit 11		

Notice that the 72-pin SIMMs use a set of four or five pins to indicate the type of SIMM to the motherboard. These presence detect pins are either grounded or not connected to indicate the type of SIMM to the motherboard. Presence detect outputs must be tied to the ground through a 0-ohm resistor or jumper on the SIMM—to generate a high logic level when the pin is open or a low logic level when the motherboard grounds the pin. This produces signals the memory interface logic can decode. If the motherboard uses presence detect signals, a power-on self test (POST) procedure can determine the size and speed of the installed SIMMs and adjust control and addressing signals automatically. This enables autodetection of the memory size and speed.

Note

In many ways, the presence detect pin function is similar to the industry-standard DX coding used on modern 35mm film rolls to indicate the ASA (speed) rating of the film to the camera. When you drop the film into the camera, electrical contacts can read the film's speed rating via an industry-standard configuration.

Presence detect performs the same function for 72-pin SIMMs that the serial presence detect (SPD) chip does for DIMMs.

Table 6.15 shows the Joint Electronic Devices Engineering Council (JEDEC) industry-standard presence detect configuration listing for the 72-pin SIMM family. JEDEC is an organization of U.S. semiconductor manufacturers and users that sets semiconductor standards.

Table 6.15   Presence Detect Pin Configurations for 72-Pin SIMMs

Size	Speed	Pin 67	Pin 68	Pin 69	Pin 70	Pin 11
1MB	100ns	Gnd	—	Gnd	Gnd	—
1MB	80ns	Gnd	—	—	Gnd	—
1MB	70ns	Gnd	—	Gnd	—	—
1MB	60ns	Gnd	—	—	—	—
2MB	100ns	—	Gnd	Gnd	Gnd	—
2MB	80ns	—	Gnd	—	Gnd	—
2MB	70ns	—	Gnd	Gnd	—	—
2MB	60ns	—	Gnd	—	—	—
4MB	100ns	Gnd	Gnd	Gnd	Gnd	—
4MB	80ns	Gnd	Gnd	—	Gnd	—
4MB	70ns	Gnd	Gnd	Gnd	—	—
4MB	60ns	Gnd	Gnd	—	—	—
8MB	100ns	—	—	Gnd	Gnd	—
8MB	80ns	—	—	—	Gnd	—
8MB	70ns	—	—	Gnd	—	—
8MB	60ns	—	—	—	—	—
16MB	80ns	Gnd	—	—	Gnd	Gnd
16MB	70ns	Gnd	—	Gnd	—	Gnd
16MB	60ns	Gnd	—	—	—	Gnd
16MB	50ns	Gnd	—	Gnd	Gnd	Gnd
32MB	80ns	—	Gnd	—	Gnd	Gnd
32MB	70ns	—	Gnd	Gnd	—	Gnd
32MB	60ns	—	Gnd	—	—	Gnd
32MB	50ns	—	Gnd	Gnd	Gnd	Gnd

— = No connection (open)
Gnd = Ground
Pin 67 = Presence detect 1
Pin 68 = Presence detect 2
Pin 69 = Presence detect 3
Pin 70 = Presence detect 4
Pin 11 = Presence detect 5

Unfortunately, unlike the film industry, not everybody in the computer industry follows established standards. As such, presence detect signaling is not a standard throughout the PC industry. Different system manufacturers sometimes use different configurations for what is expected on these four pins. Compaq, IBM (mainly PS/2 systems), and Hewlett-Packard are notorious for this type of behavior. Many of the systems from these vendors require special SIMMs that are basically the same as standard 72-pin SIMMs, except for special presence detect requirements. Table 6.16 shows how IBM defines these pins.

Table 6.16 Presence Detect Pins for IBM 72-Pin SIMMs

67	68	69	70	SIMM Type	IBM Part Number
—	—	—	—	Not a valid SIMM	n/a
Gnd	—	—	—	1MB 120ns	n/a
—	Gnd	—	—	2MB 120ns	n/a
Gnd	Gnd	—	—	2MB 70ns	92F0102
—	—	Gnd	—	8MB 70ns	64F3606
Gnd	—	Gnd	—	Reserved	n/a
—	Gnd	Gnd	—	2MB 80ns	92F0103
Gnd	Gnd	Gnd	—	8MB 80ns	64F3607
—	—	—	Gnd	Reserved	n/a
Gnd	—	—	Gnd	1MB 85ns	90X8624
—	Gnd	—	Gnd	2MB 85ns	92F0104
Gnd	Gnd	—	Gnd	4MB 70ns	92F0105
—	—	Gnd	Gnd	4MB 85ns	79F1003 (square notch) L40-SX
Gnd	—	Gnd	Gnd	1MB 100ns	n/a
Gnd	—	Gnd	Gnd	8MB 80ns	79F1004 (square notch) L40-SX
—	Gnd	Gnd	Gnd	2MB 100ns	n/a
Gnd	Gnd	Gnd	Gnd	4MB 80ns	87F9980
Gnd	Gnd	Gnd	Gnd	2MB 85ns	79F1003 (square notch) L40SX

— = No connection (open)

Gnd = Ground

Pin 67 = Presence detect 1

Pin 68 = Presence detect 2

Pin 69 = Presence detect 3

Pin 70 = Presence detect 4

Because these pins can have custom variations, you often must specify IBM, Compaq, HP, or generic SIMMs when you order memory for systems using 72-pin SIMMs. Although very few (if any) of these systems are still in service, keep this information in mind if you are moving 72-pin modules from one system to another or are installing salvaged memory into a system. Also, be sure you match the metal used on the module connectors and sockets. SIMM pins can be tin or gold plated, and the plating on the module pins must match that on the socket pins; otherwise, corrosion will result.

Caution

To have the most reliable system when using SIMM modules, you must install modules with gold-plated contacts into gold-plated sockets and modules with tin-plated contacts into tin-plated sockets only. If you mix gold contacts with tin sockets, or vice versa, you are likely to experience memory failures from 6 months to 1 year after initial installation because a type of corrosion known as *fretting* will take place. This has been a major problem with 72-pin SIMM-based systems because some memory and motherboard vendors opted for tin sockets and connectors while others opted for gold. According to connector manufacturer AMP's "Golden Rules: Guidelines for the Use of Gold on Connector Contacts" (available at http://www.tycoelectronics.com/documentation/whitepapers/pdf/aurulrep.pdf) and "The Tin Commandments: Guidelines for the Use of Tin on Connector Contacts" (available at http://www.tycoelectronics.com/documentation/whitepapers/pdf/sncomrep.pdf), you should match connector metals.

If you are maintaining systems with mixed tin/gold contacts in which fretting has already occurred, use a wet contact cleaner. After cleaning, to improve electrical contacts and help prevent corrosion, you should use a liquid contact enhancer and lubricant called Stabilant 22 from D.W. Electrochemicals when installing SIMMs or DIMMs. The company's website (http://www.stabilant.com) has detailed application notes on this subject that provide more technical details.

DIMM Pinouts

Table 6.17 shows the pinout configuration of a 168-pin standard unbuffered SDRAM DIMM. Note again that the pins on each side of the DIMM are different. All pins should be gold plated.

Table 6.17   168-Pin SDRAM DIMM Pinouts

Pin	Signal	Pin	Signal	Pin	Signal	Pin	Signal
1	GND	43	GND	85	GND	127	GND
2	Data Bit 0	44	Do Not Use	86	Data Bit 32	128	Clock Enable 0
3	Data Bit 1	45	Chip Select 2#	87	Data Bit 33	129	Chip Select 3#
4	Data Bit 2	46	I/O Mask 2	88	Data Bit 34	130	I/O Mask 6
5	Data Bit 3	47	I/O Mask 3	89	Data Bit 35	131	I/O Mask 7
6	+3.3V	48	Do Not Use	90	+3.3V	132	Reserved
7	Data Bit 4	49	+3.3V	91	Data Bit 36	133	+3.3V
8	Data Bit 5	50	NC	92	Data Bit 37	134	NC
9	Data Bit 6	51	NC	93	Data Bit 38	135	NC
10	Data Bit 7	52	Parity Bit 2	94	Data Bit 39	136	Parity Bit 6
11	Data Bit 8	53	Parity Bit 3	95	Data Bit 40	137	Parity Bit 7
12	GND	54	GND	96	GND	138	GND
13	Data Bit 9	55	Data Bit 16	97	Data Bit 41	139	Data Bit 48
14	Data Bit 10	56	Data Bit 17	98	Data Bit 42	140	Data Bit 49
15	Data Bit 11	57	Data Bit 18	99	Data Bit 43	141	Data Bit 50
16	Data Bit 12	58	Data Bit 19	100	Data Bit 44	142	Data Bit 51
17	Data Bit 13	59	+3.3V	101	Data Bit 45	143	+3.3V
18	+3.3V	60	Data Bit 20	102	+3.3V	144	Data Bit 52
19	Data Bit 14	61	NC	103	Data Bit 46	145	NC
20	Data Bit 15	62	NC	104	Data Bit 47	146	NC

Table 6.17   Continued

=Pin	Signal	Pin	Signal	Pin	Signal	Pin	Signal
21	Parity Bit 0	63	Clock Enable 1	105	Parity Bit 4	147	NC
22	Parity Bit 1	64	GND	106	Parity Bit 5	148	GND
23	GND	65	Data Bit 21	107	GND	149	Data Bit 53
24	NC	66	Data Bit 22	108	NC	150	Data Bit 54
25	NC	67	Data Bit 23	109	NC	151	Data Bit 55
26	+3.3V	68	GND	110	+3.3V	152	GND
27	WE#	69	Data Bit 24	111	CAS#	153	Data Bit 56
28	I/O Mask 0	70	Data Bit 25	112	I/O Mask 4	154	Data Bit 57
29	I/O Mask 1	71	Data Bit 26	113	I/O Mask 5	155	Data Bit 58
30	Chip Select 0#	72	Data Bit 27	114	Chip Select 1#	156	Data Bit 59
31	Do Not Use	73	+3.3V	115	RAS#	157	+3.3V
32	GND	74	Data Bit 28	116	GND	158	Data Bit 60
33	Address Bit 0	75	Data Bit 29	117	Address Bit 1	159	Data Bit 61
34	Address Bit 2	76	Data Bit 30	118	Address Bit 3	160	Data Bit 62
35	Address Bit 4	77	Data Bit 31	119	Address Bit 5	161	Data Bit 63
36	Address Bit 6	78	GND	120	Address Bit 7	162	GND
37	Address Bit 8	79	Clock 2	121	Address Bit 9	163	Clock 3
38	Address Bit 10	80	NC	122	Bank Address 0	164	NC
39	Bank Address 1	81	SPD Write Protect	123	Address Bit 11	165	SPD Address 0
40	+3.3V	82	SPD Data	124	+3.3V	166	SPD Address 1
41	+3.3V	83	SPD Clock	125	Clock 1	167	SPD Address 2
42	Clock 0	84	+3.3V	126	Reserved	168	+3.3V

Gnd = Ground
SPD = Serial presence detect
NC = No connection

The DIMM uses a completely different type of presence detect than a SIMM, called *serial presence detect (SPD)*. It consists of a small EEPROM or flash memory chip on the DIMM that contains specially formatted data indicating the DIMM's features. This serial data can be read via the serial data pins on the DIMM, and it enables the motherboard to autoconfigure to the exact type of DIMM installed.

DIMMs can come in several varieties, including unbuffered and buffered as well as 3.3V and 5V. Buffered DIMMs have additional buffer chips on them to interface to the motherboard. Unfortunately, these buffer chips slow down the DIMM and are not effective at higher speeds. For this reason, most PC systems (those that do not use registered DIMMs) use unbuffered DIMMs. The voltage is simple—DIMM designs for PCs are almost universally 3.3V. If you install a 5V DIMM in a 3.3V socket, it would be damaged, but fortunately keying in the socket and on the DIMM prevents that.

Modern PC systems use only unbuffered 3.3V DIMMs. Apple and other non-PC systems can use the buffered 5V versions. Fortunately, the key notches along the connector edge of a DIMM are spaced differently for buffered/unbuffered and 3.3V/5V DIMMs, as shown in Figure 6.11. This prevents inserting a DIMM of the wrong type into a given socket.

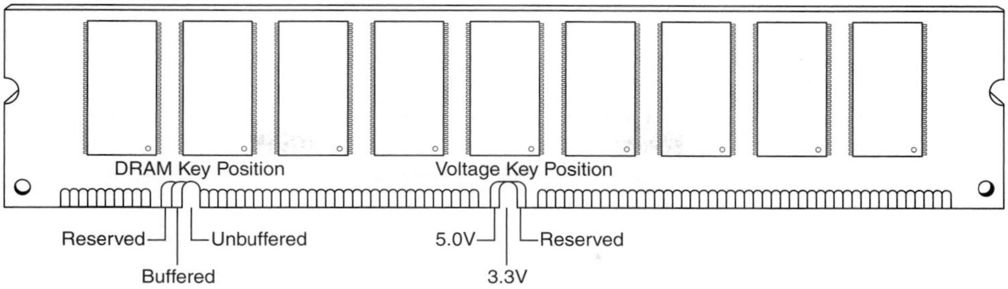

Figure 6.11   168-pin DRAM DIMM notch key definitions.

DDR DIMM Pinouts

Table 6.18 shows the pinout configuration of a 184-pin DDR SDRAM DIMM. Note again that the pins on each side of the DIMM are different. All pins should be gold plated.

Table 6.18   184-Pin DDR DIMM Pinouts

Pin	Signal	Pin	Signal	Pin	Signal	Pin	Signal
1	Reference +1.25V	47	Data Strobe 8	93	GND	139	GND
2	Data Bit 0	48	Address Bit 0	94	Data Bit 4	140	Data Strobe 17
3	GND	49	Parity Bit 2	95	Data Bit 5	141	Address Bit 10
4	Data Bit 1	50	GND	96	I/O +2.5V	142	Parity Bit 6
5	Data Strobe 0	51	Parity Bit 3	97	Data Strobe 9	143	I/O +2.5V
6	Data Bit 2	52	Bank Address 1	98	Data Bit 6	144	Parity Bit 7
7	+2.5 V	53	Data Bit 32	99	Data Bit 7	145	GND
8	Data Bit 3	54	I/O +2.5 V	100	GND	146	Data Bit 36
9	NC	55	Data Bit 33	101	NC	147	Data Bit 37
10	NC	56	Data Strobe 4	102	NC	148	+2.5V
11	GND	57	Data Bit 34	103	Address Bit 13	149	Data Strobe 13
12	Data Bit 8	58	GND	104	I/O +2.5V	150	Data Bit 38
13	Data Bit 9	59	Bank Address 0	105	Data Bit 12	151	Data Bit 39
14	Data Strobe 1	60	Data Bit 35	106	Data Bit 13	152	GND
15	I/O +2.5V	61	Data Bit 40	107	Data Strobe 10	153	Data Bit 44
16	Clock 1	62	I/O +2.5V	108	+2.5V	154	RAS#
17	Clock 1#	63	WE#	109	Data Bit 14	155	Data Bit 45
18	GND	64	Data Bit 41	110	Data Bit 15	156	I/O +2.5V
19	Data Bit 10	65	CAS#	111	Clock Enable 1	157	S0#
20	Data Bit 11	66	GND	112	I/O +2.5V	158	S1#
21	Clock Enable 0	67	Data Strobe 5	113	Bank Address 2	159	Data Strobe 14
22	I/O +2.5V	68	Data Bit 42	114	Data Bit 20	160	GND
23	Data Bit 16	69	Data Bit 43	115	Address Bit 12	161	Data Bit 46
24	Data Bit 17	70	+2.5V	116	GND	162	Data Bit 47
25	Data Strobe 2	71	S2#	117	Data Bit 21	163	S3#
26	GND	72	Data Bit 48	118	Address Bit 11	164	I/O +2.5V

Table 6.18   Continued

Pin	Signal	Pin	Signal	Pin	Signal	Pin	Signal
27	Address Bit 9	73	Data Bit 49	119	Data Strobe 11	165	Data Bit 52
28	Data Bit 18	74	GND	120	+2.5V	166	Data Bit 53
29	Address Bit 7	75	Clock 2#	121	Data Bit 22	167	FETEN
30	I/O +2.5V	76	Clock 2	122	Address Bit 8	168	+2.5V
31	Data Bit 19	77	I/O +2.5V	123	Data Bit 23	169	Data Strobe 15
32	Address Bit 5	78	Data Strobe 6	124	GND	170	Data Bit 54
33	Data Bit 24	79	Data Bit 50	125	Address Bit 6	171	Data Bit 55
34	GND	80	Data Bit 51	126	Data Bit 28	172	I/O +2.5V
35	Data Bit 25	81	GND	127	Data Bit 29	173	NC
36	Data Strobe 3	82	+2.5VID	128	I/O +2.5V	174	Data Bit 60
37	Address Bit 4	83	Data Bit 56	129	Data Strobe 12	175	Data Bit 61
38	+2.5V	84	Data Bit 57	130	Address Bit 3	176	GND
39	Data Bit 26	85	+2.5V	131	Data Bit 30	177	Data Strobe 16
40	Data Bit 27	86	Data Strobe 7	132	GND	178	Data Bit 62
41	Address Bit 2	87	Data Bit 58	133	Data Bit 31	179	Data Bit 63
42	GND	88	Data Bit 59	134	Parity Bit 4	180	I/O +2.5V
43	Address Bit 1	89	GND	135	Parity Bit 5	181	SPD Address 0
44	Parity Bit 0	90	SPD Write Protect	136	I/O +2.5V	182	SPD Address 1
45	Parity Bit 1	91	SPD Data	137	Clock 0	183	SPD Address 2
46	+2.5V	92	SPD Clock	138	Clock 0#	184	SPD +2.5V

Gnd = Ground

SPD = Serial presence detect

NC = No connection

DDR DIMMs use a single key notch to indicate voltage, as shown in Figure 6.12.

The 184-pin DDR DIMMs use two notches on each side to enable compatibility with both low- and high-profile latched sockets. Note that the key position is offset with respect to the center of the DIMM to prevent inserting it backward in the socket. The key notch is positioned to the left, centered, or to the right of the area between pins 52 and 53. This is used to indicate the I/O voltage for the DDR DIMM and to prevent installing the wrong type into a socket that might damage the DIMM.

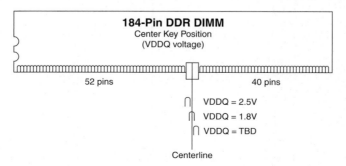

Figure 6.12   184-pin DDR SDRAM DIMM keying.

DDR2 DIMM Pinouts

Table 6.19 shows the pinout configuration of a 240-pin DDR2 SDRAM DIMM. Pins 1–120 are on the front side, and pins 121–240 are on the back. All pins should be gold plated.

Table 6.19   240-Pin DDR2 DIMM Pinouts

Pin	Signal	Pin	Signal	Pin	Signal	Pin	Signal
1	VREF	61	A4	121	VSS	181	VDDQ
2	VSS	62	VDDQ	122	DQ4	182	A3
3	DQ0	63	A2	123	DQ5	183	A1
4	DQ1	64	VDD	124	VSS	184	VDD
5	VSS	65	VSS	125	DM0	185	CK0
6	-DQS0	66	VSS	126	NC	186	-CK0
7	DQS0	67	VDD	127	VSS	187	VDD
8	VSS	68	NC	128	DQ6	188	A0
9	DQ2	69	VDD	129	DQ7	189	VDD
10	DQ3	70	A10/-AP	130	VSS	190	BA1
11	VSS	71	BA0	131	DQ12	191	VDDQ
12	DQ8	72	VDDQ	132	DQ13	192	-RAS
13	DQ9	73	-WE	133	VSS	193	-CS0
14	VSS	74	-CAS	134	DM1	194	VDDQ
15	-DQS1	75	VDDQ	135	NC	195	ODT0
16	DQS1	76	-CS1	136	VSS	196	A13
17	VSS	77	ODT1	137	CK1	197	VDD
18	NC	78	VDDQ	138	-CK1	198	VSS
19	NC	79	SS	139	VSS	199	DQ36
20	VSS	80	DQ32	140	DQ14	200	DQ37
21	DQ10	81	DQ33	141	DQ15	201	VSS
22	DQ11	82	VSS	142	VSS	202	DM4
23	VSS	83	-DQS4	143	DQ20	203	NC
24	DQ16	84	DQS4	144	DQ21	204	VSS
25	DQ17	85	VSS	145	VSS	205	DQ38
26	VSS	86	DQ34	146	DM2	206	DQ39
27	-DQS2	87	DQ35	147	NC	207	VSS
28	DQS2	88	VSS	148	VSS	208	DQ44
29	VSS	89	DQ40	149	DQ22	209	DQ45
30	DQ18	90	DQ41	150	DQ23	210	VSS
31	DQ19	91	VSS	151	VSS	211	DM5
32	VSS	92	-DQS5	152	DQ28	212	NC
33	DQ24	93	DQS5	153	DQ29	213	VSS
34	DQ25	94	VSS	154	VSS	214	DQ46

Table 6.19   Continued

Pin	Signal	Pin	Signal	Pin	Signal	Pin	Signal
35	VSS	95	DQ42	155	DM3	215	DQ47
36	-DQS3	96	DQ43	156	NC	216	VSS
37	DQS3	97	VSS	157	VSS	217	DQ52
38	VSS	98	DQ48	158	DQ30	218	DQ53
39	DQ26	99	DQ49	159	DQ31	219	VSS
40	DQ27	100	VSS	160	VSS	220	CK2
41	VSS	101	SA2	161	NC	221	-CK2
42	NC	102	NC	162	NC	222	VSS
43	NC	103	VSS	163	VSS	223	DM6
44	VSS	104	-DQS6	164	NC	224	NC
45	NC	105	DQS6	165	NC	225	VSS
46	NC	106	VSS	166	VSS	226	DQ54
47	VSS	107	DQ50	167	NC	227	DQ55
48	NC	108	DQ51	168	NC	228	VSS
49	NC	109	VSS	169	VSS	229	DQ60
50	VSS	110	DQ56	170	VDDQ	230	DQ61
51	VDDQ	111	DQ57	171	CKE1	231	VSS
52	CKE0	112	VSS	172	VDD	232	DM7
53	VDD	113	-DQS7	173	NC	233	NC
54	NC	114	DQS7	174	NC	234	VSS
55	NC	115	VSS	175	VDDQ	235	DQ62
56	VDDQ	116	DQ58	176	A12	236	DQ63
57	A11	117	DQ59	177	A9	237	VSS
58	A7	118	VSS	178	VDD	238	VDDSPD
59	VDD	119	SDA	179	A8	239	SA0
60	A5	120	SCL	180	A6	240	SA1

The 240-pin DDR2 DIMMs use two notches on each side to enable compatibility with both low- and high-profile latched sockets. The connector key is offset with respect to the center of the DIMM to prevent inserting it backward in the socket. The key notch is positioned in the center of the area between pins 64 and 65 on the front (184/185 on the back), and there is no voltage keying because all DDR2 DIMMs run on 1.8V.

DDR3 DIMM Pinouts

Table 6.20 shows the pinout configuration of a 240-pin DDR3 SDRAM DIMM. Pins 1–120 are on the front side, and pins 121–240 are on the back. All pins should be gold plated.

Table 6.20   240-Pin DDR3 DIMM Pinouts

Pin	Signal Front	Pin	Signal Back	Pin	Signal Front	Pin	Signal Back	Pin	Signal Front	Pin	Signal Back
1	VREFDQ	121	VSS	42	DQS8	162	DQS17	82	DQ33	202	VSS
2	VSS	122	DQ4	43	DQS8	163	VSS	83	VSS	203	DM4, DQS13
3	DQ0	123	DQ5	44	VSS	164	CB6	84	DQS4	204	DQS13
4	DQ1	124	VSS	45	CB2	165	CB7	85	DQS4	205	VSS
5	VSS	125	DM0,DQS9	46	CB3	166	VSS	86	VSS	206	DQ38
6	DQS0	126	NC,DQS9	47	VSS	167	TEST	87	DQ34	207	DQ39
7	DQS0	127	VSS	48	NC	168	Reset	88	DQ35	208	VSS
8	VSS	128	DQ6	Key	Key	Key	Key	89	VSS	209	DQ44
9	DQ2	129	DQ7	49	NC	169	CKE1	90	DQ40	210	DQ45
10	DQ3	130	VSS	50	CKE0	170	VDD	91	DQ41	211	VSS
11	VSS	131	DQ12	51	VDD	171	A15	92	VSS	212	DM5, DQS14
12	DQ8	132	DQ13	52	BA2	172	A14	93	DQS5	213	DQS14
13	DQ9	133	VSS	53	ERR-OUT(NC)	173	VDD	94	DQS5	214	VSS
14	VSS	134	DM1, DQS10	54	VDD	174	A12	95	VSS	215	DQ46
15	DQS1	135	NC,DQS10	55	A11	175	A9	96	DQ42	216	DQ47
16	DQS1	136	VSS	56	A7	176	VDD	97	DQ43	217	VSS
17	VSS	137	DQ14	57	VDD	177	A8	98	VSS	218	DQ52
18	DQ10	138	DQ15	58	A5	178	A6	99	DQ48	219	DQ53
19	DQ11	139	VSS	59	A4	179	VDD	100	DQ49	220	VSS
20	VSS	140	DQ20	60	VDD	180	A3	101	VSS	221	DM6, DQS15
21	DQ16	141	DQ21	61	A2	181	A1	102	DQS6	222	DQS15
22	DQ17	142	VSS	62	VDD	182	VDD	103	DQS6	223	VSS
23	VSS	143	DQS11	63	CK1/NC	183	VDD	104	VSS	224	DQ54
24	DQS2	144	DQS11	64	CK1/NC	184	CK0	105	DQ50	225	DQ55
25	DQS2	145	VSS	65	VDD	185	CK0	106	DQ51	226	VSS
26	VSS	146	DQ22	66	VDD	186	VDD	107	VSS	227	DQ60
27	DQ18	147	DQ23	67	VREFCA	187	NF	108	DQ56	228	DQ61
28	DQ19	148	VSS	68	Par_In(NC)	188	A0	109	DQ57	229	VSS
29	VSS	149	DQ28	69	VDD	189	VDD	110	VSS	230	DM7, DQS16
30	DQ24	150	DQ29	70	A10	190	BA1/BA0	111	DQS7	231	DQS16
31	DQ25	151	VSS	71	BA0/BA1	191	VDD	112	DQS7	232	VSS
32	VSS	152	DM3, DQS12	72	VDD	192	RAS	113	VSS	233	DQ62

Table 6.20   Continued

Pin	Signal Front	Pin	Signal Back	Pin	Signal Front	Pin	Signal Back	Pin	Signal Front	Pin	Signal Back
33	DQS3	153	DQS12	73	WE	193	S0	114	DQ58	234	DQ63
34	DQS3	154	VSS	74	CAS	194	VDD	115	DQ59	235	VSS
35	VSS	155	DQ30	75	VDD	195	ODT0	116	VSS	236	VDDSPD
36	DQ26	156	DQ31	76	S1	196	A13	117	SA0	237	SA1
37	DQ27	157	VSS	77	ODT1	197	VDD	118	SCL	238	SDA
38	VSS	158	CB4	78	VDD	198	NF	119	VSS	239	VSS
39	CB0	159	CB5	79	RFUSPD	199	VSS	120	VTT	240	VTT
40	CB1	160	VSS	80	VSS	200	DQ36				
41	VSS	161	DM8,DQS17	81	DQ32	201	DQ37				

NC = No Connect
NF = No Function
NU = Not Usable
RFU = Reserved Future Use

The 240-pin DDR3 DIMMs use two notches on each side to enable compatibility with both low- and high-profile latched sockets. The connector key is offset with respect to the center of the DIMM to prevent inserting it backward in the socket. The key notch is positioned in the center of the area between pins 48 and 49 on the front (168/169 on the back), and there is no voltage keying because all DDR3 DIMMs run on 1.5V.

RIMM Pinouts

RIMM modules and sockets are gold plated and designed for 25 insertion/removal cycles. Each RIMM has 184 pins, split into two groups of 92 pins on opposite ends and sides of the module. The pinout of the RIMM is shown in Table 6.21.

Table 6.21   RIMM Pinout

Pin	Signal	Pin	Signal	Pin	Signal	Pin	Signal
A1	GND	B1	GND	A47	NC	B47	NC
A2	LData Bit A8	B2	LData Bit A7	A48	NC	B48	NC
A3	GND	B3	GND	A49	NC	B49	NC
A4	LData Bit A6	B4	LData Bit A5	A50	NC	B50	NC
A5	GND	B5	GND	A51	VREF	B51	VREF
A6	LData Bit A4	B6	LData Bit A3	A52	GND	B52	GND
A7	GND	B7	GND	A53	SPD Clock	B53	SPD Address 0
A8	LData Bit A2	B8	LData Bit A1	A54	+2.5V	B54	+2.5V
A9	GND	B9	GND	A55	SDA	B55	SPD Address 1
A10	LData Bit A0	B10	Interface Clock+	A56	SVDD	B56	SVDD
A11	GND	B11	GND	A57	SPD Write Protect	B57	SPD Address 2
A12	LCTMN	B12	Interface Clock-	A58	+2.5V	B58	+2.5V
A13	GND	B13	GND	A59	RSCK	B59	RCMD

Table 6.21   Continued

Pin	Signal	Pin	Signal	Pin	Signal	Pin	Signal
A14	LCTM	B14	NC	A60	GND	B60	GND
A15	GND	B15	GND	A61	Rdata Bit B7	B61	RData Bit B8
A16	NC	B16	LROW2	A62	GND	B62	GND
A17	GND	B17	GND	A63	Rdata Bit B5	B63	RData Bit B6
A18	LROW1	B18	LROW0	A64	GND	B64	GND
A19	GND	B19	GND	A65	Rdata Bit B3	B65	RData Bit B4
A20	LCOL4	B20	LCOL3	A66	GND	B66	GND
A21	GND	B21	GND	A67	Rdata Bit B1	B67	RData Bit B2
A22	LCOL2	B22	LCOL1	A68	GND	B68	GND
A23	GND	B23	GND	A69	RCOL0	B69	RData Bit B0
A24	LCOL0	B24	LData Bit B0	A70	GND	B70	GND
A25	GND	B25	GND	A71	RCOL2	B71	RCOL1
A26	LData Bit B1	B26	LData Bit B2	A72	GND	B72	GND
A27	GND	B27	GND	A73	RCOL4	B73	RCOL3
A28	LData Bit B3	B28	LData Bit B4	A74	GND	B74	GND
A29	GND	B29	GND	A75	RROW1	B75	RROW0
A30	LData Bit B5	B30	LData Bit B6	A76	GND	B76	GND
A31	GND	B31	GND	A77	NC	B77	RROW2
A32	LData Bit B7	B32	LData Bit B8	A78	GND	B78	GND
A33	GND	B33	GND	A79	RCTM	B79	NC
A34	LSCK	B34	LCMD	A80	GND	B80	GND
A35	VCMOS	B35	VCMOS	A81	RCTMN	B81	RCFMN
A36	SOUT	B36	SIN	A82	GND	B82	GND
A37	VCMOS	B37	VCMOS	A83	Rdata Bit A0	B83	RCFM
A38	NC	B38	NC	A84	GND	B84	GND
A39	GND	B39	GND	A85	Rdata Bit A2	B85	RData Bit A1
A40	NC	B40	NC	A86	GND	B86	GND
A41	+2.5V	B41	+2.5V	A87	Rdata Bit A4	B87	RData Bit A3
A42	+2.5V	B42	+2.5V	A88	GND	B88	GND
A43	NC	B43	NC	A89	Rdata Bit A6	B89	RData Bit A5
A44	NC	B44	NC	A90	GND	B90	GND
A45	NC	B45	NC	A91	Rdata Bit A8	B91	RData Bit A7
A46	NC	B46	NC	A92	GND	B92	GND

The 16/18-bit RIMMs are keyed with two notches in the center. This prevents a backward insertion and prevents the wrong type (voltage) RIMM from being used in a system. Currently, all RIMMs run on 2.5V, but proposed 64-bit versions will run on only 1.8V. To allow for changes in the RIMMs, three keying options are possible in the design (see Figure 6.13). The left key (indicated as "DATUM A" in Figure 6.13) is fixed in position, but the center key can be in three different positions spaced 1mm or

2mm to the right, indicating different types of RIMMs. The current default is option A, as shown in Figure 6.13 and Table 6.22, which corresponds to 2.5V operation.

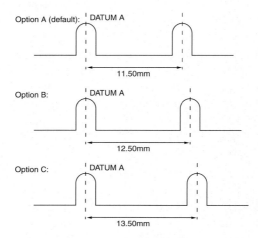

Figure 6.13   RIMM keying options.

Table 6.22   Possible Keying Options for RIMMs

Option	Notch Separation	Description
A	11.5mm	2.5V RIMM
B	12.5mm	Reserved
C	13.5mm	Reserved

RIMMs incorporate an SPD device, which is essentially a flash ROM onboard. This ROM contains information about the RIMM's size and type, including detailed timing information for the memory controller. The memory controller automatically reads the data from the SPD ROM to configure the system to match the RIMMs installed.

Figure 6.14 shows a typical PC RIMM installation. The RDRAM controller and clock generator are typically in the motherboard chipset North Bridge component. As you can see, the Rambus memory channel flows from the memory controller through each of up to three RIMM modules in series. Each module contains 4, 8, 16, or more RDRAM devices (chips), also wired in series, with an onboard SPD ROM for system configuration. Any RIMM sockets without a RIMM installed must have a continuity module, shown in the last socket in Figure 6.13. This enables the memory bus to remain continuous from the controller through each module (and, therefore, each RDRAM device on the module) until the bus finally terminates on the motherboard. Note how the bus loops from one module to another. For timing purposes, the first RIMM socket must be 6" or less from the memory controller, and the entire length of the bus must not be more than it would take for a signal to go from one end to another in four data clocks, or about 5ns.

Interestingly, Rambus does not manufacture the RDRAM devices (the chips) or the RIMMs; that is left to other companies. Rambus is merely a design company, and it has no chip fabs or manufacturing facilities of its own. It licenses its technology to other companies who then manufacture the devices and modules.

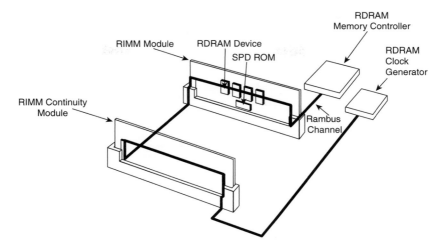

Figure 6.14   Typical RDRAM bus layout showing a RIMM and one continuity module.

Determining a Memory Module's Size and Features

Most memory modules are labeled with a sticker indicating the module's type, speed rating, and manufacturer. If you are attempting to determine whether existing memory can be used in a new computer, or if you need to replace memory in an existing computer, this information can be essential. Figure 6.15 illustrates the markings on typical 512MB and 1GB DDR memory modules from Crucial Technologies.

However, if you have memory modules that are not labeled, you can still determine the module type, speed, and capacity if the memory chips on the module are clearly labeled. For example, assume you have a memory module with chips labeled as follows:

MT46V64M8TG-75

By using an Internet search engine such as Google and entering the number from one of the memory chips, you can usually find the data sheet for the memory chips. Consider the following example: Say you have a registered memory module and want to look up the part number for the memory chips (usually eight or more chips) rather than the buffer chips on the module (usually from one to three, depending on the module design). In this example, the part number turns out to be a Micron memory chip that decodes like this:

MT = Micron Technologies (the memory chip maker)

46 = DDR SDRAM

V = 2.5V DC

64M8 = 8 million rows × 8 (equals 64) × 8 banks (often written as 64 Meg × 8)

TG = 66-pin TSOP chip package

−75 = 7.5ns @ CL2 latency (DDR 266)

1. Module size
2. Module type and speed
3. CAS Latency
4. Crucial Technology part number

Figure 6.15   Markings on 512MB (top) and 1GB (bottom) DDR memory modules from Crucial Technology.

The full datasheet for this example is located at http://download.micron.com/pdf/datasheets/dram/ddr/512MBDDRx4x8x16.pdf.

From this information, you can determine that the module has the following characteristics:

■ The module runs at DDR266 speeds using standard 2.5V DC voltage.

■ The module has a latency of CL2, so it can be used on any system that requires CL2 or slower latency (such as CL2.5 or CL3).

■ Each chip has a capacity of 512Mb (64 × 8 = 512).

■ Each chip contains 8 bits. Because it takes 8 bits to make 1 byte, the capacity of the module can be calculated by grouping the memory chips on the module into groups of eight. If each chip contains 512Mb, a group of eight means that the module has a size of 512MB (512Mb × 8 = 512MB). A dual-bank module has two groups of eight chips for a capacity of 1GB (512Mb × 8 = 1024MB, or 1GB).

If the module has nine instead of eight memory chips (or 18 instead of 16), the additional chips are used for parity checking and support ECC error correction on servers with this feature.

To determine the size of the module in MB or GB and to determine whether the module supports ECC, count the memory chips on the module and compare them to Table 6.23. Note that the size of each memory chip in Mb is the same as the size in MB if the memory chips use an 8-bit design.

Table 6.23   Module Capacity Using 512Mb (64Mbit × 8) Chips

Number of Chips	Number of Bits in Each Bank	Module Size	Supports ECC?	Single or Dual-bank
8	64	512MB	No	Single
9	72	512MB	Yes	Single
16	64	1GB	No	Dual
18	72	1GB	Yes	Dual

The additional chip used by each group of eight chips provides parity checking, which is used by the ECC function on most server motherboards to correct single-bit errors.

A registered module contains 9 or 18 memory chips for ECC plus additional memory buffer chips. These chips are usually smaller in size and located near the center of the module, as shown previously in Figure 6.9.

Note

Some modules use 16-bit wide memory chips. In such cases, only four chips are needed for single-bank memory (five with parity/ECC support) and eight are needed for double-bank memory (10 with parity/ECC support). These memory chips use a design listed as capacity × 16, like this: 256Mb × 16.

You can also see this information if you look up the manufacturer, the memory type, and the organization in a search engine. For example, a web search for Micron "64 Meg x 8" DDR DIMM locates a design list list for Micron's 64MB–512MB modules at http://www.micron.com/support/designsupport/tools/ddrtoolbox/designfiles. The table lists the DIMM organization, SDRAM density, and other information for listed modules.

As you can see, with a little detective work, you can determine the size, speed, and type of a memory module—even if the module isn't marked, as long as the markings on the memory chips themselves are legible.

Tip

If you are unable to decipher a chip part number, you can use a program such as HWiNFO or SiSoftware Sandra to identify your memory module, as well as many other facts about your computer, including chipset, processor, empty memory sockets, and much more. You can download shareware versions of HWiNFO from www.hwinfo.com and SiSoftware Sandra from www.sisoftware.net.

Memory Banks

Memory chips (DIPs, SIMMs, SIPPs, and DIMMs) are organized in banks on motherboards and memory cards. You should know the memory bank layout and position on the motherboard and memory cards.

You need to know the bank layout when adding memory to the system. In addition, memory diagnostics report error locations by byte and bit addresses, and you must use these numbers to locate which bank in your system contains the problem.

The banks usually correspond to the data bus capacity of the system's microprocessor. Table 6.24 shows the widths of individual banks based on the type of PC.

Table 6.24   Memory Bank Widths on Various Systems

Processor	Data Bus	Memory Bank Width	Memory Bank Width (Parity/ECC)	8/9-bit SIMMs per Bank	32/36-bit SIMMs per Bank	64/72-bit DIMMs per Bank
8088	8-bit	8 bits	9 bits	1	—	—
8086	16-bit	16 bits	18 bits	2	—	—
286	16-bit	16 bits	18 bits	2	—	—
386SX, SL, SLC	16-bit	16 bits	18 bits	2	—	—
486SLC, SLC2	16-bit	16 bits	18 bits	2	—	—
386DX	32-bit	32 bits	36 bits	4	1	—
486SX, DX, DX2, DX4, 5x86	32-bit	32 bits	36 bits	4	1	—
Pentium, Athlon and newer running Single-Channel mode	64-bit	64 bits	72 bits	—	—	1
Pentium, Athlon and newer running Dual-Channel mode	64-bit	128 bits	144 bits	—	—	2

Dual-channel mode requires matched pairs of memory inserted into the memory sockets designated for dual-channel mode. If a single module or two different-size modules are used, or the dual-channel sockets are not used, the system runs in single-channel mode.

The number of bits for each bank can be made up of single chips, SIMMs, or DIMMs. Modern systems don't use individual chips; instead, they use only SIMMs or DIMMs. If the system has a 16-bit processor, such as a 386SX, it probably uses 30-pin SIMMs and has two SIMMs per bank. All the SIMMs in a single bank must be the same size and type.

A 486 system requires four 30-pin SIMMs or one 72-pin SIMM to make up a bank. A single 72-pin SIMM is 32 bits wide, or 36 bits wide if it supports parity. You can often tell whether a SIMM supports parity by counting its chips. To make a 32-bit SIMM, you could use 32 individual 1-bit wide chips, or you could use eight individual 4-bit wide chips to make up the data bits. If the system uses parity, 4 extra bits are required (36 bits total), so you would see one more 4-bit wide or four individual 1-bit wide chips added to the bank for the parity bits.

As you might imagine, 30-pin SIMMs are less than ideal for 32-bit or 64-bit systems (that is, 486 or Pentium) because you must use them in increments of four or eight per bank. Consequently, only a few 32-bit systems were ever built using 30-pin SIMMs, and no 64-bit systems have ever used 30-pin SIMMs. If a 32-bit system (such as any PC with a 386DX or 486 processor) uses 72-pin SIMMs, each SIMM represents a separate bank and the SIMMs can be added or removed on an individual basis rather than in groups of four, as would be required with 30-pin SIMMs. This makes memory configuration much easier and more flexible. In 64-bit systems that use SIMMs, two 72-pin SIMMs are required per bank.

DIMMs are ideal for Pentium and higher systems because the 64-bit width of the DIMM exactly matches the 64-bit width of the Pentium processor data bus. Therefore, each DIMM represents an individual bank, and they can be added or removed one at a time. Many recent systems have been designed to use matched pairs of memory modules for faster performance. So-called "dual-channel" designs treat a matched pair of modules as a single 128-bit device (or a 144-bit device if parity or ECC memory is used). In those cases, although a single module can be used, modules must be installed in pairs to achieve best performance.

The physical orientation and numbering of the SIMMs or DIMMs used on a motherboard is arbitrary and determined by the board's designers, so documentation covering your system or card comes in handy. You can determine the layout of a motherboard or an adapter card through testing, but that takes time and might be difficult, particularly after you have a problem with a system.

Caution

If your system supports dual-channel memory, be sure you use the correct memory sockets to enable dual-channel operation. Check the documentation to ensure that you use the correct pair of sockets. Most dual-channel systems will still run if the memory is not installed in a way that permits dual-channel operation, but performance is lower than if the memory were installed properly. Some systems provide dual-channel support if an odd number of modules are installed, as long as the total capacity of two modules installed in one channel equals the size of the single module in the other channel and all modules are the same speed and latency. Again, check your documentation for details.

Memory Module Speed

When you replace a failed memory module or install a new module as an upgrade, you typically must install a module of the same type and speed as the others in the system. You can substitute a module with a different (faster) speed but only if the replacement module's speed is equal to or faster than that of the other modules in the system.

Some people have had problems when "mixing" modules of different speeds. With the wide variety of motherboards, chipsets, and memory types, few ironclad rules exist. When in doubt as to which speed module to install in your system, consult the motherboard documentation for more information.

Substituting faster memory of the same type doesn't result in improved performance if the system still operates the memory at the same speed. Systems that use DIMMs or RIMMs can read the speed and timing features of the module from a special SPD ROM installed on the module and then set chipset (memory controller) timing accordingly. In these systems, you might see an increase in performance by installing faster modules, to the limit of what the chipset will support.

To place more emphasis on timing and reliability, there are Intel and JEDEC standards governing memory types that require certain levels of performance. These standards certify that memory modules perform within Intel's timing and performance guidelines.

The same common symptoms result when the system memory has failed or is simply not fast enough for the system's timing. The usual symptoms are frequent parity check errors or a system that does not operate at all. The POST might report errors, too. If you're unsure of which chips to buy for your system, contact the system manufacturer or a reputable chip supplier.

▶▶ See "Parity Checking," p. 560.

Parity and ECC

Part of the nature of memory is that it inevitably fails. These failures are usually classified as two basic types: hard fails and soft errors.

The best understood are hard fails, in which the chip is working and then, because of some flaw, physical damage, or other event, becomes damaged and experiences a permanent failure. Fixing this type of failure normally requires replacing some part of the memory hardware, such as the chip, SIMM, or DIMM. Hard error rates are known as HERs.

The other, more insidious type of failure is the soft error, which is a nonpermanent failure that might never recur or could occur only at infrequent intervals. (Soft fails are effectively "fixed" by powering the system off and back on.) Soft error rates are known as SERs.

More than 20 years ago, Intel made a discovery about soft errors that shook the memory industry. It found that alpha particles were causing an unacceptably high rate of soft errors or single event upsets (SEUs, as they are sometimes called) in the 16KB DRAMs that were available at the time. Because alpha particles are low-energy particles that can be stopped by something as thin and light as a sheet of paper, it became clear that for alpha particles to cause a DRAM soft error, they would have to be coming from within the semiconductor material. Testing showed trace elements of thorium and uranium in the plastic and ceramic chip packaging materials used at the time. This discovery forced all the memory manufacturers to evaluate their manufacturing processes to produce materials free from contamination.

Today, memory manufacturers have all but totally eliminated the alpha-particle source of soft errors. Many people believed that was justification for the industry trend to drop parity checking. The argument is that, for example, a 16MB memory subsystem built with 4MB technology would experience a soft error caused by alpha particles only about once every 16 years! The real problem with this thinking is that it is seriously flawed, and many system manufacturers and vendors were coddled into removing parity and other memory fault-tolerant techniques from their systems even though soft errors continue to be an ongoing problem. More recent discoveries prove that alpha particles are now only a small fraction of the cause of DRAM soft errors.

As it turns out, the biggest cause of soft errors today are cosmic rays. IBM researchers began investigating the potential of terrestrial cosmic rays in causing soft errors similar to alpha particles. The difference is that cosmic rays are very high-energy particles and can't be stopped by sheets of paper or other more powerful types of shielding. The leader in this line of investigation was Dr. J.F. Ziegler of the IBM Watson Research Center in Yorktown Heights, New York. He has produced landmark research into understanding cosmic rays and their influence on soft errors in memory.

One example of the magnitude of the cosmic ray soft-error phenomenon demonstrated that with a certain sample of non-IBM DRAMs, the SER at sea level was measured at 5950 FIT (failures in time, which is measured at 1 billion hours) per chip. This was measured under real-life conditions with the benefit of millions of device hours of testing. In an average system, this would result in a soft error occurring every 6 months or less. In power-user or server systems with a larger amount of memory, it could mean one or more errors per month! When the exact same test setup and DRAMs were moved to an underground vault shielded by more than 50 feet of rock, thus eliminating all cosmic rays, absolutely no soft errors were recorded. This not only demonstrates how troublesome cosmic rays can be, but it also proves that the packaging contamination and alpha-particle problem has indeed been solved.

Cosmic-ray-induced errors are even more of a problem in SRAMs than DRAMS because the amount of charge required to flip a bit in an SRAM cell is less than is required to flip a DRAM cell capacitor. Cosmic rays are also more of a problem for higher-density memory. As chip density increases, it becomes easier for a stray particle to flip a bit. It has been predicted by some that the soft error rate of a 64MB DRAM will be double that of a 16MB chip, and a 256MB DRAM will have a rate four times higher. As memory sizes continue to increase, it's likely that soft error rates will also increase.

Unfortunately, the PC industry has largely failed to recognize this cause of memory errors. Electrostatic discharge, power surges, or unstable software can much more easily explain away the random and intermittent nature of a soft error, especially right after a new release of an operating system or major application.

Studies have shown that the soft error rate for ECC systems is on the order of 30 times greater than the hard error rate. This is not surprising to those familiar with the full effects of cosmic-ray-generated soft errors. The number of errors experienced varies with the density and amount of memory present. Studies show that soft errors can occur from once a month or less to several times a week or more!

Although cosmic rays and other radiation events are the biggest cause of soft errors, soft errors can also be caused by the following:

- **Power glitches or noise on the line**—This can be caused by a defective power supply in the system or by defective power at the outlet.

- **Incorrect type or speed rating**—The memory must be the correct type for the chipset and match the system access speed.

- **RF (radio frequency) interference**—Caused by radio transmitters in close proximity to the system, which can generate electrical signals in system wiring and circuits. Keep in mind that the increased use of wireless networks, keyboards, and mouse devices can lead to a greater risk of RF interference.

- **Static discharges**—Causes momentary power spikes, which alter data.

- **Timing glitches**—Data doesn't arrive at the proper place at the proper time, causing errors. Often caused by improper settings in the BIOS Setup, by memory that is rated slower than the system requires, or by overclocked processors and other system components.

- **Heat buildup**—High-speed memory modules run hotter than older modules. RDRAM RIMM modules were the first memory to include integrated heat spreaders, and many high-performance DDR and DDR2 memory modules now include heat spreaders to help fight heat buildup.

Most of these problems don't cause chips to permanently fail (although bad power or static can damage chips permanently), but they can cause momentary problems with data.

How can you deal with these errors? Just ignoring them is certainly not the best way to deal with them, but unfortunately that is what many system manufacturers and vendors are doing today. The best way to deal with this problem is to increase the system's fault tolerance. This means implementing ways of detecting and possibly correcting errors in PC systems. Three basic levels and techniques are used for fault tolerance in modern PCs:

- Nonparity
- Parity
- ECC

Nonparity systems have no fault tolerance at all. The only reason they are used is because they have the lowest inherent cost. No additional memory is necessary, as is the case with parity or ECC techniques. Because a parity-type data byte has 9 bits versus 8 for nonparity, memory cost is approximately 12.5% higher. Also, the nonparity memory controller is simplified because it does not need the logic gates to calculate parity or ECC check bits. Portable systems that place a premium on minimizing power might benefit from the reduction in memory power resulting from fewer DRAM chips. Finally, the memory system data bus is narrower, which reduces the amount of data buffers. The statistical probability of memory failures in a modern office desktop computer is now estimated at about one error every few months. Errors will be more or less frequent depending on how much memory you have.

This error rate might be tolerable for low-end systems that are not used for mission-critical applications. In this case, the extreme market sensitivity to price probably can't justify the extra cost of parity or ECC memory, and such errors then must be tolerated.

At any rate, having no fault tolerance in a system is simply gambling that memory errors are unlikely. You further gamble that if they do occur, memory errors will result in an inherent cost less than the additional hardware necessary for error detection. However, the risk is that these memory errors can lead to serious problems. A memory error in a calculation could cause the wrong value to go into a bank check. In a server, a memory error could force a system to hang and bring down all LAN-resident client systems with subsequent loss of productivity. Finally, with a nonparity or non-ECC memory system, tracing the problem is difficult, which is not the case with parity or ECC. These techniques at least isolate a memory source as the culprit, thus reducing both the time and cost of resolving the problem.

Parity Checking

One standard IBM set for the industry is that the memory chips in a bank of nine each handle 1 bit of data: 8 bits per character plus 1 extra bit called the parity bit. The parity bit enables memory-control circuitry to keep tabs on the other 8 bits—a built-in cross-check for the integrity of each byte in the system. If the circuitry detects an error, the computer stops and displays a message informing you of the malfunction. If you are running a GUI operating system, such as Windows or OS/2, a parity error generally manifests itself as a locked system. When you reboot, the BIOS should detect the error and display the appropriate error message.

SIMMs and DIMMs are available both with and without parity bits. Originally, all PC systems used parity-checked memory to ensure accuracy. Starting in 1994, a disturbing trend developed in the PC-compatible marketplace. Most vendors began shipping systems without parity checking or any other means of detecting or correcting errors! These systems can use cheaper nonparity SIMMs, which saves about 10%–15% on memory costs for a system. Parity memory results in increased initial system cost, primarily because of the additional memory bits involved. Parity can't correct system errors, but because parity can detect errors, it can make the user aware of memory errors when they happen. This has two basic benefits:

- Parity guards against the consequences of faulty calculations based on incorrect data.
- Parity pinpoints the source of errors, which helps with problem resolution, thus improving system serviceability.

PC systems can easily be designed to function using either parity or nonparity memory. The cost of implementing parity as an option on a motherboard is virtually nothing; the only cost is in actually purchasing the parity SIMMs or DIMMs. This enables a system manufacturer to offer its system purchasers the choice of parity if the purchasers feel the additional cost is justified for their particular applications.

Unfortunately, several of the big names began selling systems without parity to reduce their prices, and they did not make it well known that the lower cost meant parity memory was no longer included as standard. This began happening mostly in 1994 and 1995, and it has continued until recently, with few people understanding the full implications. After one or two major vendors did this, most of the others were forced to follow to remain price-competitive.

Because nobody wanted to announce this information, it remained sort of a dirty little secret within the industry. Originally, when this happened you could still specify parity memory when you ordered a system, even though the default configurations no longer included it. There was a 10%–15% surcharge on the memory, but those who wanted reliable, trustworthy systems could at least get them, provided they knew to ask, of course. Then a major bomb hit the industry, in the form of the Intel Triton 430FX Pentium chipset, which was the first major chipset on the market that did not support parity checking at all! It also became the most popular chipset of its time and was found in practically all Pentium motherboards sold in the 1995 timeframe. This set a disturbing trend for the next few years. All but one of Intel's Pentium processor chipsets after the 430FX did not support parity-checked memory; the only one that did was the 430HX Triton II.

Since then, Intel and other chipset manufacturers have put support for parity and ECC memory in most of their chipsets (especially so in their higher-end models). The low-end chipsets, however, typically do lack support for either parity or ECC. If more reliability is important to you, make sure the systems you purchase have this support. In Chapter 4, you can learn which recent chipsets support parity and ECC memory and which ones do not.

Let's look at how parity checking works, and then examine in more detail the successor to parity checking, called ECC, which not only can detect but also correct memory errors on-the-fly.

How Parity Checking Works

IBM originally established the odd parity standard for error checking. The following explanation might help you understand what is meant by odd parity. As the 8 individual bits in a byte are stored in memory, a parity generator/checker, which is either part of the CPU or located in a special chip on the motherboard, evaluates the data bits by adding up the number of 1s in the byte. If an even number of 1s is found, the parity generator/checker creates a 1 and stores it as the ninth bit (parity bit) in the parity memory chip. That makes the sum for all 9 bits (including the parity bit) an odd number. If the original sum of the 8 data bits is an odd number, the parity bit created would be a 0, keeping the sum for all 9 bits an odd number. The basic rule is that the value of the parity bit is always chosen so that the sum of all 9 bits (8 data bits plus 1 parity bit) is stored as an odd number. If the system used even parity, the example would be the same except the parity bit would be created to ensure an even sum. It doesn't matter whether even or odd parity is used; the system uses one or the other, and it is completely transparent to the memory chips involved. Remember that the 8 data bits in a byte are numbered 0 1 2 3 4 5 6 7. The following examples might make it easier to understand:

```
Data bit number:     0 1 2 3 4 5 6 7     Parity bit
Data bit value:      1 0 1 1 0 0 1 1     0
```

In this example, because the total number of data bits with a value of 1 is an odd number (5), the parity bit must have a value of 0 to ensure an odd sum for all 9 bits.

Here is another example:

```
Data bit number:     0 1 2 3 4 5 6 7     Parity bit
Data bit value:      1 1 1 1 0 0 1 1     1
```

In this example, because the total number of data bits with a value of 1 is an even number (6), the parity bit must have a value of 1 to create an odd sum for all 9 bits.

When the system reads memory back from storage, it checks the parity information. If a (9-bit) byte has an even number of bits, that byte must have an error. The system can't tell which bit has changed or whether only a single bit has changed. If 3 bits changed, for example, the byte still flags a parity-check error; if 2 bits changed, however, the bad byte could pass unnoticed. Because multiple bit errors (in a single byte) are rare, this scheme gives you a reasonable and inexpensive ongoing indication that memory is good or bad.

The following examples show parity-check messages for three types of older systems:

For the IBM PC: `PARITY CHECK x`

For the IBM XT: `PARITY CHECK x      yyyyy (z)`

For the IBM AT and late model XT: `PARITY CHECK x      yyyyy`

where x is 1 or 2:

> 1 = Error occurred on the motherboard

> 2 = Error occurred in an expansion slot

In this example, yyyyy represents a number from 00000 through FFFFF that indicates, in hexadecimal notation, the byte in which the error has occurred.

Where (z) is (S) or (E):

> (S) = Parity error occurred in the system unit

> (E) = Parity error occurred in an optional expansion chassis

Note

An expansion chassis was an option IBM sold for the original PC and XT systems to add more expansion slots.

When a parity-check error is detected, the motherboard parity-checking circuits generate a nonmaskable interrupt (NMI), which halts processing and diverts the system's attention to the error. The NMI causes a routine in the ROM to be executed. On some older IBM systems, the ROM parity-check routine halts the CPU. In such a case, the system locks up, and you must perform a hardware reset or a power-off/power-on cycle to restart the system. Unfortunately, all unsaved work is lost in the process.

Most systems do not halt the CPU when a parity error is detected; instead, they offer you the choice of rebooting the system or continuing as though nothing happened. Additionally, these systems might display the parity error message in a different format from IBM, although the information presented is basically the same. For example, most systems with a Phoenix BIOS display one of these messages:

```
Memory parity interrupt at xxxx:xxxx
Type (S)hut off NMI, Type (R)eboot, other keys to continue
```

or

```
I/O card parity interrupt at xxxx:xxxx
Type (S)hut off NMI, Type (R)eboot, other keys to continue
```

The first of these two messages indicates a motherboard parity error (Parity Check 1), and the second indicates an expansion-slot parity error (Parity Check 2). Notice that the address given in the form xxxx:xxxx for the memory error is in a segment:offset form rather than a straight linear address, such as with IBM's error messages. The segment:offset address form still gives you the location of the error to a resolution of a single byte.

You have three ways to proceed after viewing this error message:

- You can press S, which shuts off parity checking and resumes system operation at the point where the parity check first occurred.

- You can press R to force the system to reboot, losing any unsaved work.
- You can press any other key to cause the system to resume operation with parity checking still enabled.

If the problem occurs, it is likely to cause another parity-check interruption. It's usually prudent to press S, which disables the parity checking so you can then save your work. In this case, it's best to save your work to a floppy disk or USB flash drive to prevent the possible corruption of the hard disk. You should also avoid overwriting any previous (still good) versions of whatever file you are saving because you could be saving a bad file caused by the memory corruption. Because parity checking is now disabled, your save operations will not be interrupted. Then, you should power the system off, restart it, and run whatever memory diagnostics software you have to try to track down the error. In some cases, the POST finds the error on the next restart, but you usually need to run a more sophisticated diagnostics program—perhaps in a continuous mode—to locate the error.

Systems with an AMI BIOS display the parity error messages in the following forms:

```
ON BOARD PARITY ERROR ADDR (HEX) = (xxxxx)
```

or

```
OFF BOARD PARITY ERROR ADDR (HEX) = (xxxxx)
```

These messages indicate that an error in memory has occurred during the POST, and the failure is located at the address indicated. The first one indicates that the error occurred on the motherboard, and the second message indicates an error in an expansion slot adapter card. The AMI BIOS can also display memory errors in the following manners:

```
Memory Parity Error at xxxxx
```

or

```
I/O Card Parity Error at xxxxx
```

These messages indicate that an error in memory has occurred at the indicated address during normal operation. The first one indicates a motherboard memory error, and the second indicates an expansion slot adapter memory error.

Although many systems enable you to continue processing after a parity error and even allow disabling further parity checking, continuing to use your system after a parity error is detected can be dangerous. The idea behind letting you continue using either method is to give you time to save any unsaved work before you diagnose and service the computer, but be careful how you do this.

Note that these messages can vary depending not only on the ROM BIOS but also on your operating system. Protected mode operating systems, such as most versions of Windows, trap these errors and run their own handler program that displays a message different from what the ROM would have displayed. The message might be associated with a blue screen or might be a trap error, but it usually indicates that it is memory or parity related. For example, Windows 98 displays a message indicating "Memory parity error detected. System halted." when such an error has occurred.

Caution

When you are notified of a memory parity error, remember the parity check is telling you that memory has been corrupted. Do you want to save potentially corrupted data over the good file from the last time you saved? Definitely not! Be sure you save your work with a different filename. In addition, after a parity error, save only to a floppy disk or USB flash drive if possible and avoid writing to the hard disk; there is a slight chance that the hard drive could become corrupt if you save the contents of corrupted memory.

After saving your work, determine the cause of the parity error and repair the system. You might be tempted to use an option to shut off further parity checking and simply continue using the system as though nothing were wrong. Doing so is like unscrewing the oil pressure warning indicator bulb on a car with an oil leak so the oil pressure light won't bother you anymore!

Several years ago, when memory was more expensive, a few companies marketed SIMMs with bogus parity chips. Instead of actually having the extra memory chips needed to store the parity bits, these "logic parity" or parity "emulation" SIMMs used an onboard parity generator chip. This chip ignored any parity the system was trying to store on the SIMM, but when data was retrieved, it always ensured that the correct parity was returned, thus making the system believe all was well even though there might have been a problem.

These bogus parity modules were used because memory was much more expensive and a company could offer a "parity" SIMM for only a few dollars more with the fake chip. Unfortunately, identifying them can be difficult. The bogus parity generator doesn't look like a memory chip and has different markings from the other memory chips on the SIMM. Most of them had a "GSM" logo, which indicated the original manufacturer of the parity logic device, not necessarily the SIMM itself.

One way to positively identify these bogus fake parity SIMMs is by using a hardware SIMM test machine, such as those by Tanisys (www.tanisys.com), CST (www.simmtester.com), or Innoventions (www.memorytest.com). I haven't seen DIMMs or RIMMs with fake parity/ECC bits, and memory prices have come down far enough that it probably isn't worth the trouble anymore.

Error-correcting Code (ECC)

ECC goes a big step beyond simple parity-error detection. Instead of just detecting an error, ECC allows a single bit error to be corrected, which means the system can continue without interruption and without corrupting data. ECC, as implemented in most PCs, can only detect, not correct, double-bit errors. Because studies have indicated that approximately 98% of memory errors are the single-bit variety, the most commonly used type of ECC is one in which the attendant memory controller detects and corrects single-bit errors in an accessed data word (double-bit errors can be detected but not corrected). This type of ECC is known as *single-bit error-correction double-bit error detection (SEC-DED)* and requires an additional 7 check bits over 32 bits in a 4-byte system and an additional 8 check bits over 64 bits in an 8-byte system. ECC in a 4-byte (32-bit, such as a 486) system obviously costs more than nonparity or parity, but in an 8-byte wide bus (64-bit, such as Pentium/Athlon) system, ECC and parity costs are equal because the same number of extra bits (8) is required for either parity or ECC. Because of this, you can purchase parity SIMMs (36-bit), DIMMs (72-bit), or RIMMs (18-bit) for 32-bit systems and use them in an ECC mode if the chipset supports ECC functionality. If the system uses SIMMs, two 36-bit (parity) SIMMs are added for each bank (for a total of 72 bits), and ECC is done at the bank level. If the system uses DIMMs, a single parity/ECC 72-bit DIMM is used as a bank and provides the additional bits. RIMMs are installed in singles or pairs, depending on the chipset and motherboard. They must be 18-bit versions if parity/ECC is desired.

ECC entails the memory controller calculating the check bits on a memory-write operation, performing a compare between the read and calculated check bits on a read operation, and, if necessary, correcting bad bits. The additional ECC logic in the memory controller is not very significant in this age of inexpensive, high-performance VLSI logic, but ECC actually affects memory performance on writes. This is because the operation must be timed to wait for the calculation of check bits and, when the system waits for corrected data, reads. On a partial-word write, the entire word must first be read, the affected byte(s) rewritten, and then new check bits calculated. This turns partial-word write operations into slower read-modify writes. Fortunately, this performance hit is very small, on the order of a few percent at maximum, so the tradeoff for increased reliability is a good one.

Most memory errors are of a single-bit nature, which ECC can correct. Incorporating this fault-tolerant technique provides high system reliability and attendant availability. An ECC-based system is a good choice for servers, workstations, or mission-critical applications in which the cost of a potential memory error outweighs the additional memory and system cost to correct it, along with ensuring that it does not detract from system reliability. If you value your data and use your system for important (to you) tasks, you'll want ECC memory. No self-respecting manager would build or run a network server, even a lower-end one, without ECC memory.

By designing a system that allows for the choice of ECC, parity, or nonparity, you allow the users to choose the level of fault tolerance desired, as well as how much they want to gamble with their data.

Installing RAM Upgrades

Adding memory to a system is one of the most useful upgrades you can perform and also one of the least expensive—especially when you consider the increased performance of Windows and Linux when you give them access to more memory. In some cases, doubling the memory can practically double the speed of a computer.

The following sections discuss adding memory, including selecting memory chips, installing memory chips, and testing the installation.

Upgrade Options and Strategies

Adding memory can be an inexpensive solution; at this writing, the cost of memory has fallen to about 12 cents per megabyte or less. A small dose can give your computer's performance a big boost.

How do you add memory to your PC? You have two options, listed in order of convenience and cost:

- Adding memory in vacant slots on your motherboard
- Replacing your current motherboard's memory with higher-capacity memory

If you decide to upgrade to a more powerful computer system or motherboard, you usually can't salvage the memory from your previous system. Most of the time it is best to plan on equipping a new board with the optimum type of memory that it supports.

Be sure to carefully weigh your future needs for computing speed and a multitasking operating system against the amount of money you spend to upgrade current equipment.

To determine at what point you should add memory, you can use the Performance Monitor (Perfmon.msc) built into Windows 2000 and Windows XP. You can launch it remotely or from the server's own console. To check memory usage, select Memory as the Performance object and enable the following counters:

- **Pages/Sec**—This counter measures the number of times per second that the system uses virtual (swapfile) memory rather than physical memory. A value above 20 indicates a potential problem. Check the virtual memory settings; if the counter remains above 20, install more memory.
- **Committed Bytes and Available Bytes**—Committed Bytes tracks virtual memory in use; Available Bytes tracks physical memory available. Add more memory if you run short of available bytes.
- **Cache Bytes**—Measures the amount of RAM used for file system cache. Add more RAM if this amount exceeds 4MB.

To gather this same information in Windows Vista, open the Reliability and Performance Monitor, select the Performance Monitor, and use the Add tool to select these counters from the Memory category.

Before you add RAM to a system (or replace defective RAM chips), you must determine the memory modules required for your system. Your system documentation has this information.

If you need to replace a defective memory module or add more memory to your system, there are several ways to determine the correct module for your system:

- **Inspect the modules installed in your system**. Each module has markings that indicate its capacity and speed. RAM capacity and speed were discussed in detail earlier in this chapter. You can write down the markings on the memory module and use them to determine the type of memory you need. Check with a local store or an online memory vendor for help.

- **Look up your system using the online memory-configuration utility provided by your preferred memory vendor**. Originally, these configuration utilities were primarily for users of name-brand systems. However, most vendors have now added major motherboard brands and models to their databases. Therefore, if you know your system or motherboard brand and model, you can find the memory that is recommended.

- **Download and run analysis software provided by the memory module maker or from a third party**. SiSoftware Sandra and similar programs use the SPD chip on each module to determine this information.

- **Consult your system documentation**. I list this option last for a reason. If you have installed BIOS upgrades, you might be able to use larger and faster memory than your documentation lists as supported by your system. You should check the latest tech notes and documentation available online for your system and check the BIOS version installed in your system to determine which memory-related features it has. A BIOS upgrade might enable your system to use faster memory.

Adding the wrong modules to a system can make it as unreliable as leaving a defective module installed and trying to use the system in that condition.

Note

Before upgrading an older Pentium (P5 class) system beyond 64MB of RAM, be sure your chipset supports caching more than 64MB. Adding RAM beyond the amount supported by your L2 cache slows performance rather than increases it. See the section "Cache Memory: SRAM," earlier in this chapter, and the discussion of chipsets in Chapter 4 for a more complete explanation of this common system limitation. This limitation was mostly with Pentium (P5) class chipsets. Pentium II and later processors, including the AMD Athlon, Duron, and Sempron famiies have the L2 cache controller integrated in the processor (not the chipset), which supports caching up to 4GB and beyond on most newer models. With the higher price of older SIMM-type memory modules per megabyte compared to SDRAM and DDR-SDRAM, you might find it more cost-effective to replace your motherboard, processor, and memory with new components than to add memory to an older system that uses SIMMs.

Selecting and Installing Memory

Installing extra memory on your motherboard is an easy way to add memory to your computer. Most systems have at least one vacant memory socket where you can install extra memory at a later time and speed up your computer.

If your system requires dual-channel memory, as some high-performance systems do, you must use two identical memory modules (same size, speed, and type).

Purchasing Memory

When purchasing memory, there are some issues you need to consider. Some are related to the manufacturing and distribution of memory, whereas others depend on the type of memory you are purchasing. This section covers some of the issues you should consider when purchasing memory.

Suppliers

Many companies sell memory, but only a few companies actually make memory. Additionally, only a few companies make memory chips, but many more companies make memory modules such as SIMMs, DIMMs, and RIMMs. Most of the companies that make the actual RAM chips also make modules containing their own chips. Other companies, however, strictly make modules; these companies purchase memory chips from several chip makers and then produce modules with these chips. Finally, some companies don't make either the chips or modules. Instead, they purchase modules made by other companies and relabel them.

I refer to memory modules made by the chip manufacturers as *first-party modules*, whereas those made by module (but not chip) manufacturers I call *second-party modules*. Finally, those that are simply relabeled first- or second-party modules under a different name are called *third-party modules*. I always prefer to purchase first- or second-party modules if I can because they are better documented. In essence they have a better pedigree and their quality is generally more assured. Not to mention that purchasing from the first or second party eliminates one or more middlemen in the distribution process as well.

First-party manufacturers (where the same company makes the chips and the modules) include Micron (www.crucial.com), Infineon (formerly Siemens), Samsung, Mitsubishi, Toshiba, NEC, and others. Second-party companies that make the modules (but not the chips) include Kingston, Viking, PNY, Simple Tech, Smart, Mushkin, and OCZ Technologies. At the third-party level you are not purchasing from a manufacturer but from a reseller or remarketer instead.

Most of the large manufacturers don't sell small quantities of memory to individuals, but some have set up factory outlet stores where individuals can purchase as little as a single module. One of the largest memory manufacturers in the world, Micron, sells direct to the consumer at www.crucial.com. Because you are buying direct, the pricing at these outlets is often highly competitive with second- and third-party suppliers.

Considerations in Purchasing or Reusing SIMMs

When purchasing SIMMs, the main things to consider are as follows:

- Do you need FPM (Fast Page Mode) or EDO (extended data out) versions?
- Do you need ECC or non-ECC?
- What speed grade do you need?
- Can you use memory from other systems or from parts stores as an alternative to purchasing (very expensive) new memory?

Most Pentium systems after 1995 used EDO SIMMs that were non-ECC and rated for 60ns access time. If your system is older than that, you might need regular FPM versions. The FPM and EDO types are interchangeable in many systems, but some older systems do not accept the EDO type. If your system is designed for high-reliability using ECC, you might need (or want) ECC versions; otherwise, standard non-ECC types are typically used. You can mix the two, but in that case the system defaults to non-ECC mode.

Unfortunately, FPM and EDO SIMMs are obsolete by today's standards, so they are much more expensive than newer, better, and faster types of memory. This can make adding memory to older systems cost prohibitive.

Tip

Instead of buying new SIMM memory for older systems, check with computer repair shops or other users who might have a collection of old parts.

Considerations in Purchasing DIMMs

When purchasing DIMMs, the main things to consider are as follows:

- Do you need SDR, DDR, DDR2, or DDR3 versions?
- Do you need ECC or non-ECC?
- Do you need registered or standard (unbuffered) versions?
- What speed grade do you need?
- Do you need a specific column address strobe (CAS) latency?

Currently, DIMMs come in SDR (SDRAM), DDR, DDR2, and DDR3 versions. They are not interchangeable because they use completely different signaling and have different notches to prevent a mismatch. High-reliability systems such as servers can use ECC versions, although most desktop systems use the less-expensive non-ECC types. Most systems use standard unbuffered DIMMs, but file server or workstation motherboards designed to support very large amounts of memory might require registered DIMMs (which also include ECC support). Registered DIMMs contain their own memory registers, enabling the module to hold more memory than a standard DIMM. DIMMs come in a variety of speeds, with the rule that you can always substitute a faster one for a slower one, but not vice versa. As an example, if your system requires PC2700 DDR DIMMs, you can install faster PC3200 DDR DIMMs but not slower PC2100 versions.

Another speed-related issue is the column address strobe (CAS) latency. Sometimes this specification is abbreviated CAS or CL and is expressed in a number of cycles, with lower numbers indicating higher speeds (fewer cycles). The lower CAS latency shaves a cycle off a burst mode read, which marginally improves memory performance. Single data rate DIMMs are available in CL3 or CL2 versions.. DDR DIMMs are available in CL2.5 or CL2 versions. DDR2 DIMMs are available in CL 3, 4 or 5. DDR3 DIMMs are available in CL 7, 8, and 9. With all memory types, the lowest CL number is the fastest (and usually the most expensive) memory type. You can mix DIMMs with different CAS latency ratings, but the system usually defaults to cycling at the slower speeds of the lowest common denominator.

Considerations in Purchasing RIMMs

When purchasing RIMMs, the main things to consider are as follows:

- Do you need 184-pin (16/18-bit) or 232-pin (32/36-bit) versions?
- Do you need ECC or non-ECC?
- What speed grade do you need?

RIMMs are available in 184-pin and 232-pin versions, and although they appear to be the same size, they are not interchangeable. Differences exist in the notches that prevent a mismatch. High-reliability systems might want or need ECC versions, which have extra ECC bits. As with other memory types, you can mix ECC and non-ECC types, but systems can't use the ECC capability.

Replacing Modules with Higher-capacity Versions

If all the memory module slots on your motherboard are occupied, your best option is to remove an existing bank of memory and replace it with higher-capacity modules. For example, if you have a motherboard that supports two DIMM modules (each representing one bank on a processor with a 64-bit data bus) and runs in single-channel mode, you could remove one of them and replace it with a higher-capacity version. For example, if you have two 256MB modules, giving you a total of 512MB, you could remove one of the 256MB modules and replace it with a 512MB unit, in which case you'd then have a total of 768MB of RAM.

However, just because higher-capacity modules are available that are the correct pin count to plug into your motherboard, don't automatically assume the higher-capacity memory will work. Your system's chipset and BIOS set limits on the capacity of the memory you can use. Check your system or motherboard documentation to see which size modules work with it before purchasing the new RAM. You should make sure you have the latest BIOS for your motherboard when installing new memory.

If your system supports dual-channel memory, you must use matched pairs of DDR or DDR2 modules (depending on which type your system supports) and install them in the correct location on the motherboard to achieve the superior memory performance that dual-channel access offers. You should consult your motherboard manual for details.

Installing DIMM or RIMM Modules

This section discusses installing memory—specifically, SIMM or DIMM modules. It also covers the problems you are most likely to encounter and how to avoid them. You also get information on configuring your system to use new memory.

When you install or remove memory, you are most likely to encounter the following problems:

■ Electrostatic discharge

■ Improperly seated modules

■ Incorrect memory configuration settings in the BIOS Setup

To prevent electrostatic discharge (ESD) when you install sensitive memory chips or boards, you shouldn't wear synthetic-fiber clothing or leather-soled shoes because these promote the generation of static charges. Remove any static charge you are carrying by touching the system chassis before you begin, or better yet, wear a good commercial grounding strap on your wrist. You can order one from any electronics parts store. A grounding strap consists of a conductive wristband grounded at the other end through a 1-meg ohm resistor by a wire clipped to the system chassis. Be sure the system you are working on is unplugged.

Caution

Be sure to use a properly designed commercial grounding strap; do not make one yourself. Commercial units have a 1-meg ohm resistor that serves as protection if you accidentally touch live power. The resistor ensures that you do not become the path of least resistance to the ground and therefore become electrocuted. An improperly designed strap can cause the power to conduct through you to the ground, possibly killing you.

Follow this procedure to upgrade DIMM or RIMM memory on a typical desktop PC:

1. Shut down the system and unplug it. As an alternative to unplugging it, you can turn off the power supply using the on/off switch on the rear of some power supplies. Wait about 10 seconds for any remaining current to drain from the motherboard.

2. Open the system. See the system or case instructions for details.

3. Connect a static guard wrist strap to your wrist and then to a metal portion of the system chassis, such as the frame. Make sure the metal plate on the inside of the wrist strap is tight against the skin of your wrist.

4. Some motherboards feature an LED that glows as long as the motherboard is receiving power. Wait until the LED dims before removing or installing memory.

5. Move obstructions inside the case, such as cables or wires, out of the way of the memory modules and empty sockets. If you must remove a cable or wire, note its location and orientation so you can replace it later.

6. If you need to remove an existing DIMM or RIMM, flip down the ejector tab at each end of the module and lift the module straight up out of the socket. Note the keying on the module.

7. Note the specific locations needed if you are inserting modules to operate in dual-channel mode. The sockets used for dual-channel memory might use a different-colored plastic to distinguish them from other sockets, but ultimately you should consult the documentation for your motherboard or system to determine the proper orientation.

8. To insert a DIMM or RIMM module into a socket, ensure that the ejector tabs are flipped down on the socket you plan to use. DIMMs and RIMMs are keyed by notches along the bottom connector edges that are offset from the center so they can be inserted in only one direction, as shown in Figure 6.16.

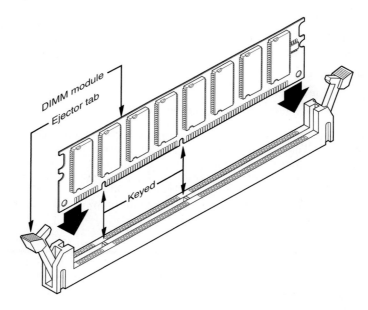

Figure 6.16   DIMM keys match the protrusions in the DIMM sockets. DDR DIMM and RIMM keys are similar but not exactly the same.

9. Push down on the DIMM or RIMM until the ejector tabs lock into place in the notch on the side of the module. It's important that you not force the module into the socket. If the module does not slip easily into the slot and then snap into place, it is probably not oriented or aligned correctly. Forcing the module could break it or the socket. When installing RIMMs, you need to fill any empty RIMM sockets with continuity modules. Refer to Figure 6.14 for details.

10. Replace any cables or wires you disconnected.

11. Close the system, reconnect the power cable, and turn on the PC.

After adding the memory and putting the system back together, you might have to run the BIOS Setup and resave with the new amount of memory being reported. Most newer systems automatically detect the new amount of memory and reconfigure the BIOS Setup settings for you. Most newer systems also don't require setting any jumpers or switches on the motherboard to configure them for your new memory.

After configuring your system to work properly with the additional memory, you might want to run a memory-diagnostics program to ensure that the new memory works properly. Some are run automatically for you. At least two and sometimes three memory-diagnostic programs are available for all systems. In order of accuracy, these programs are as follows:

■ POST (power-on self test)

■ Disk-based advanced diagnostics software

The POST is used every time you power up the system.

Many additional diagnostics programs are available from aftermarket utility software companies.

Installing SIMM Modules

SIMM memory is oriented by a notch on one side of the module that is not present on the other side, as shown in Figure 6.17. The socket has a protrusion that must fit into this notched area on one side of the module. This protrusion makes installing a SIMM backward impossible unless you break the connector or the module. Figure 6.18 details the notch and locking clip.

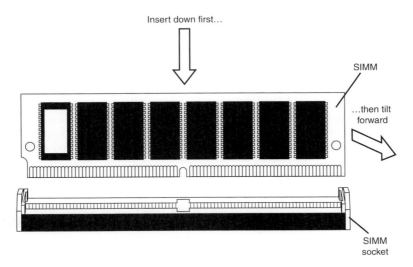

Figure 6.17   The notch on this SIMM is shown on the left side. Insert the SIMM at a 45° angle and then tilt it forward until the locking clips snap into place.

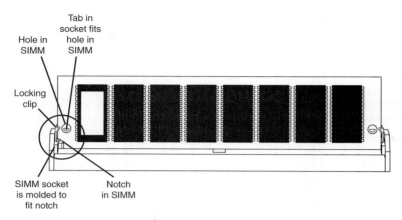

Figure 6.18   This figure shows the SIMM inserted in the socket with the notch aligned, the locking clip locked, and the hole in the SIMM aligned with the tab in the socket.

Troubleshooting Memory

Memory problems can be difficult to troubleshoot. For one thing, computer memory is still mysterious to people because it is a kind of "virtual" thing that can be hard to grasp. The other difficulty is that memory problems can be intermittent and often look like problems with other areas of the system, even software. This section shows simple troubleshooting steps you can perform if you suspect you are having a memory problem.

To troubleshoot memory, you first need some memory-diagnostics testing programs. You already have several and might not know it. Every motherboard BIOS has a memory diagnostic in the POST that runs when you first turn on the system. In most cases, you also receive a memory diagnostic on a utility disk that came with your system. Many commercial diagnostics programs are on the market, and almost all of them include memory tests.

When the POST runs, it not only tests memory, but also counts it. The count is compared to the amount counted the last time BIOS Setup was run; if it is different, an error message is issued. As the POST runs, it writes a pattern of data to all the memory locations in the system and reads that pattern back to verify that the memory works. If any failure is detected, you see or hear a message. Audio messages (beeping) are used for critical or "fatal" errors that occur in areas important for the system's operation. If the system can access enough memory to at least allow video to function, you see error messages instead of hearing beep codes.

See the disc accompanying this book for detailed listings of the BIOS beep and other error codes, which are specific to the type of BIOS you have. These BIOS codes are found in the Technical Reference section of the disc in printable PDF format for your convenience. For example, most Intel motherboards use the Phoenix BIOS. Several beep codes are used in that BIOS to indicate fatal memory errors.

If your system makes it through the POST with no memory error indications, there might not be a hardware memory problem, or the POST might not be able to detect the problem. Intermittent memory errors are often not detected during the POST, and other subtle hardware defects can be hard for the POST to catch. The POST is designed to run quickly, so the testing is not nearly as thorough as it could be. That is why you often have to boot from a standalone diagnostic disk and run a true hardware diagnostic to do more extensive memory testing. These types of tests can be run continuously and be left running for days if necessary to hunt down an elusive intermittent defect.

Fortunately several excellent memory test programs are available for free download. The ones I recommend include

- **Microsoft Windows Memory Diagnostic**—http://oca.microsoft.com/en/windiag.asp
- **DocMemory Diagnostic**—http://www.simmtester.com/page/products/doc/docinfo.asp
- **Memtest86**—http://www.memtest86.com

Not only are all these free, but they are available in a bootable CD format, which means you don't have to install any software on the system you are testing. The bootable format is actually required in a way since Windows and other OSs prevent the direct access to memory and other hardware required for testing. These programs use algorithms that write different types of patterns to all of the memory in the system, testing every bit to ensure it reads and writes properly. They also turn off the processor cache in order to ensure direct testing of the modules and not the cache. Some, such as Windows Memory Diagnostic, will even indicate the module that is failing should an error be encountered.

Still, even these programs do only pass/fail type testing; that is, all they can do is write patterns to memory and read them back. They can't determine how close the memory is to failing—only whether it worked. For the highest level of testing, the best thing to have is a dedicated memory test machine, usually called a *module tester*. These devices enable you to insert a module and test it thoroughly at a variety of speeds, voltages, and timings to let you know for certain whether the memory is good or bad. Versions of these testers are available to handle all types of memory modules. I have defective modules, for example, that work in some systems (slower ones) but not others. What I mean is that the same memory test program fails the module in one machine but passes it in another. In the module tester, it is always identified as bad right down to the individual bit, and it even tells me the actual speed of the device, not just its rating. Companies that offer memory module testers include Tanisys (www.tanisys.com), CST (www.simmtester.com), and Innoventions (www.memorytest.com). They can be expensive, but for a professional in the PC repair business, using one of these module testers can save time and money in the long run.

After your operating system is running, memory errors can still occur, typically identified by error messages you might receive. Here are the most common:

- **Parity errors**—Indicates that the parity-checking circuitry on the motherboard has detected a change in memory since the data was originally stored. (See the "How Parity Checking Works" section earlier in this chapter.)

- **General or global protection faults**—A general-purpose error indicating that a program has been corrupted in memory, usually resulting in immediate termination of the application. This can also be caused by buggy or faulty programs.

- **Fatal exception errors**—Error codes returned by a program when an illegal instruction has been encountered, invalid data or code has been accessed, or the privilege level of an operation is invalid.

- **Divide error**—A general-purpose error indicating that a division by 0 was attempted or the result of an operation does not fit in the destination register.

If you are encountering these errors, they could be caused by defective or improperly configured memory, but they can also be caused by software bugs (especially drivers), bad power supplies, static discharges, close proximity radio transmitters, timing problems, and more.

If you suspect the problems are caused by memory, there are ways to test the memory to determine whether that is the problem. Most of this testing involves running one or more memory test programs.

I am amazed that most people make a critical mistake when they run memory test software. The biggest problem I see is that people run memory tests with the system caches enabled. This effectively invalidates memory testing because most systems have what is called a *write-back cache*. This means that data written to main memory is first written to the cache. Because a memory test program first writes data and then immediately reads it back, the data is read back from the cache, not the main memory. It makes the memory test program run very quickly, but all you tested was the cache. The bottom line is that if you test memory with the cache enabled, you aren't really writing to the SIMM/DIMMs, but only to the cache. Before you run any memory test programs, be sure your cache is disabled. The system will run very slowly when you do this, and the memory test will take much longer to complete, but you will be testing your actual RAM, not the cache.

The following steps enable you to effectively test and troubleshoot your system RAM. Figure 6.19 provides a boiled-down procedure to help you step through the process quickly.

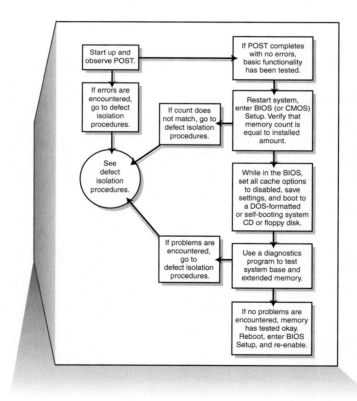

Figure 6.19   Testing and troubleshooting memory.

First, let's cover the memory-testing and troubleshooting procedures.

1. Power up the system and observe the POST. If the POST completes with no errors, basic memory functionality has been tested. If errors are encountered, go to the defect isolation procedures.

2. Restart the system and then enter your BIOS (or CMOS) Setup. In most systems, this is done by pressing the Del or F2 key during the POST but before the boot process begins (see your system or motherboard documentation for details). Once in BIOS Setup, verify that the memory count is equal to the amount that has been installed. If the count does not match what has been installed, go to the defect isolation procedures.

3. Find the BIOS Setup options for cache and then set all cache options to disabled. Figure 6.20 shows a typical Advanced BIOS Features menu with the cache options highlighted. Save the settings and reboot to a DOS-formatted or self-booting CD or floppy disk containing the diagnostics program of your choice. If your system came with a diagnostics disk, you can use that, or you can use one of the many commercial PC diagnostics programs on the market, such as PC-Technician by Windsor Technologies, Norton System Works by Symantec, or Doc Memory from SIMMTester.

Cache options to disable in BIOS

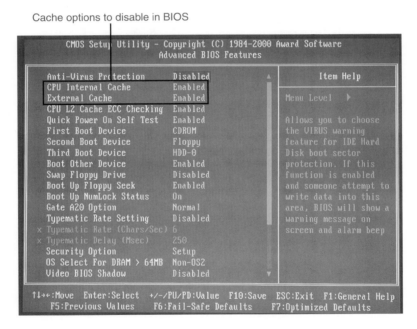

Figure 6.20 The CPU Internal (L1) and External (L2) caches must be disabled in the system BIOS setup before you test system memory; otherwise, your test results will be inaccurate.

4. Follow the instructions that came with your diagnostic program to have it test the system base and extended memory. Most programs have a mode that enables them to loop the test—that is, to run it continuously, which is great for finding intermittent problems. If the program encounters a memory error, proceed to the defect isolation procedures.

5. If no errors are encountered in the POST or in the more comprehensive memory diagnostic, your memory has tested okay in hardware. Be sure at this point to reboot the system, enter the

BIOS Setup, and re-enable the cache. The system will run very slowly until the cache is turned back on.

6. If you are having memory problems yet the memory still tests okay, you might have a problem undetectable by simple pass/fail testing, or your problems could be caused by software or one of many other defects or problems in your system. You might want to bring the memory to a SIMM/DIMM tester for a more accurate analysis. Most PC repair shops have such a tester. I would also check the software (especially drivers, which might need updating), power supply, and system environment for problems such as static, radio transmitters, and so forth.

Memory Defect Isolation Procedures

To use these steps, I am assuming you have identified an actual memory problem that is being reported by the POST or disk-based memory diagnostics. If this is the case, see the following steps and Figure 6.21 for the steps to identify or isolate which SIMM or DIMM in the system is causing the problem.

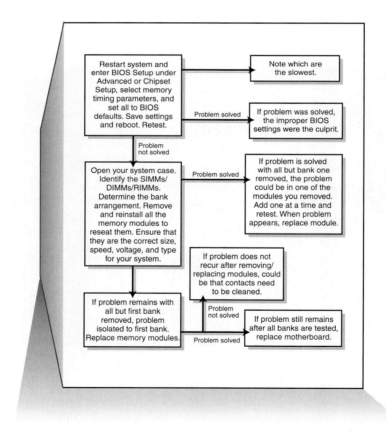

Figure 6.21   Follow these steps if you are still encountering memory errors after completing the steps in Figure 6.19.

1. Restart the system and enter the BIOS Setup. Under a menu usually called Advanced or Chipset Setup might be memory timing parameters. Select BIOS or Setup defaults, which are usually the slowest settings. If the memory timings have been manually set, as shown in Figure 6.20, reset the memory configuration to By SPD.

2. Save the settings, reboot, and retest using the testing and troubleshooting procedures listed earlier. If the problem has been solved, improper BIOS settings were the problem. If the problem remains, you likely do have defective memory, so continue to the next step.

3. Open the system for physical access to the SIMM/DIMM/RIMMs on the motherboard. Identify the bank arrangement in the system. Using the manual or the legend silk-screened on the motherboard, identify which modules correspond to which banks. Remember that if you are testing a dual-channel system, you must be sure you remove both Channel A and Channel B modules in the same logical bank.

4. Remove all the memory except the first bank and then retest using the troubleshooting and testing procedures listed earlier (see Figure 6.22). If the problem remains with all but the first bank removed, the problem has been isolated to the first bank, which must be replaced.

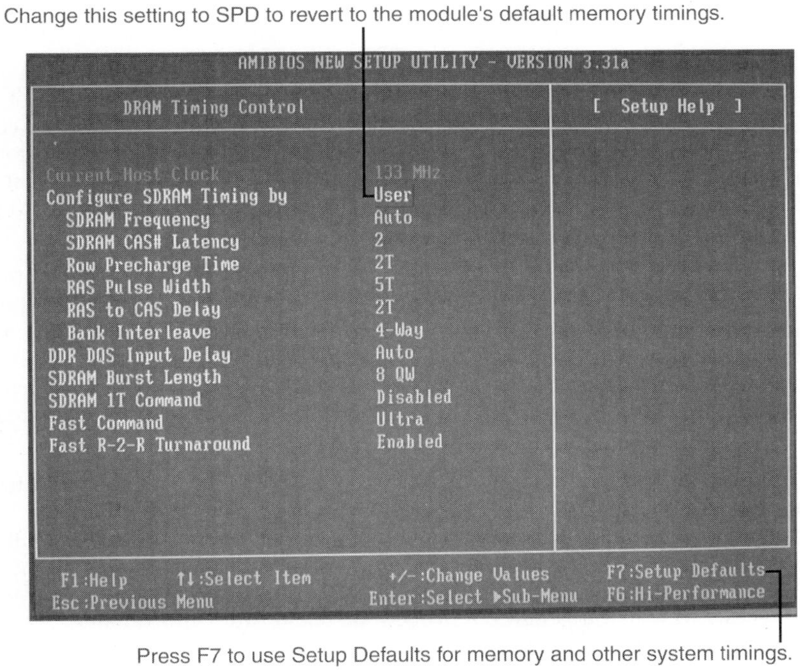

Change this setting to SPD to revert to the module's default memory timings.

```
                  AMIBIOS NEW SETUP UTILITY - VERSION 3.31a

    DRAM Timing Control                              [ Setup Help ]

  Current Host Clock            133 MHz
  Configure SDRAM Timing by     User
    SDRAM Frequency             Auto
    SDRAM CAS# Latency          2
    Row Precharge Time          2T
    RAS Pulse Width             5T
    RAS to CAS Delay            2T
    Bank Interleave             4-Way
  DDR DQS Input Delay           Auto
  SDRAM Burst Length            8 QW
  SDRAM 1T Command              Disabled
  Fast Command                  Ultra
  Fast R-2-R Turnaround         Enabled


  F1:Help        ↑↓:Select Item      +/-:Change Values    F7:Setup Defaults
  Esc:Previous Menu                  Enter:Select ▶Sub-Menu  F6:Hi-Performance
```

Press F7 to use Setup Defaults for memory and other system timings.

Figure 6.22   This system is using user-defined memory timings, which could cause the memory to be unstable.

5. Replace the memory in the first bank (preferably with known good spare modules, but you can also swap in others that you have removed) and then retest. If the problem still remains after testing all the memory banks (and finding them all to be working properly), it is likely the motherboard itself is bad (probably one of the memory sockets). Replace the motherboard and retest.

6. At this point, the first (or previous) bank has tested good, so the problem must be in the remaining modules that have been temporarily removed. Install the next bank of memory and retest. If the problem resurfaces now, the memory in that bank is defective. Continue testing each bank until you find the defective module.

7. Repeat the preceding step until all remaining banks of memory are installed and have been tested. If the problem has not resurfaced after you have removed and reinstalled all the memory, the problem was likely intermittent or caused by poor conduction on the memory contacts. Often simply removing and replacing memory can resolve problems because of the self-cleaning action between the module and the socket during removal and reinstallation.

The System Logical Memory Layout

The original PC had a total of 1MB of addressable memory, and the top 384KB of that was reserved for use by the system. Placing this reserved space at the top (between 640KB and 1,024KB, instead of at the bottom, between 0KB and 640KB) led to what is often called the *conventional memory barrier.* The constant pressures on system and peripheral manufacturers to maintain compatibility by never breaking from the original memory scheme of the first PC has resulted in a system memory structure that is (to put it kindly) a mess. Almost two decades after the first PC was introduced, even the newest Core 2 Extreme or Athlon 64 x2–based systems are limited in many important ways by the memory map of the first PCs.

What we end up with is a PC with a split personality. There are two primary modes of operation that are very different from each other. The original PC used an Intel 8088 processor that could run only 16-bit instructions or code, which ran in what was called the *real mode* of the processor. These early processors had only enough address lines to access up to 1MB of memory, and the last 384KB of that was reserved for use by the video card as video RAM, other adapters (for on-card ROM BIOS or RAM buffers), and finally the motherboard ROM BIOS.

The 286 processor brought more address lines, enough to allow up to 16MB of RAM to be used, and a new mode called protected mode that you had to be in to use it. Unfortunately, all the operating system's software at the time was designed to run only within the first 1MB, so extender programs were added and other tricks performed to eventually allow DOS and Windows 3.x access up to the first 16MB. One area of confusion was that RAM was now noncontiguous; that is, the operating system could use the first 640KB and the last 15MB, but not the 384KB of system reserved area that sat in between.

When Intel released the first 32-bit processor in 1985 (the 386DX), the memory architecture of the system changed dramatically. There were now enough address lines for the processor to use 4GB of memory, but this was accessible only in a new 32-bit protected mode in which only 32-bit instructions or code could run. This mode was designed for newer, more advanced operating systems, such as Windows 9x, NT, 2000, XP, Vista OS/2, Linux, UNIX, and so forth. With the 386 came a whole new memory architecture in which this new 32-bit software could run. Unfortunately, it took 10 years for the mainstream user to upgrade to 32-bit operating systems and applications, which shows how stubborn we are! From a software instruction perspective, all the 32-bit processors since the 386 are really just faster versions of the same. Other than the more recent additions of MMX and SSE (or AMD's 3DNow) instructions to the processor, for all intents and purposes, a Pentium 4 or Athlon is just a "turbo" 386. Even more advanced server-oriented, 64-bit instruction set processors such as the Intel Itanium and AMD Opteron processors fit into this category because they can also run 32-bit software.

The real problem now is that the 32-bit processors have two distinctly different modes, with different memory architectures in each. For backward compatibility, you could still run the 32-bit processors in real mode, but only 16-bit software could run in that mode, and such software could access only the first 1MB or 16MB, depending on how it was written. For example, 16-bit drivers could load into and access only the first 1MB. Also, it is worth noting that the system ROM BIOS, including the POST, BIOS configuration, boot code, and all the internal drivers, is virtually all 16-bit software. This is because all Intel-compatible PC processors begin operation in 16-bit real mode when they are powered on. When a 32-bit operating system loads, it is that operating system code that instructs the processor to switch into 32-bit protected mode.

When an operating system such as Windows is loaded, the processor is switched into 32-bit protected mode early in the loading sequence. Then, 32-bit drivers for all the hardware can be loaded, and then the rest of the operating system can load. In 32-bit protected mode, the operating systems and applications can access all the memory in the system, up to the maximum limit of the processor (64GB for most of the Pentium II and later chips). Similarly, on a 64-bit operating system, the system switches into 64-bit protected mode early in the boot process and loads 64-bit drivers, followed by the remainder of the operating system.

Unfortunately, one problem with protected mode is just that: It is protected. The name comes from the fact that only driver programs are allowed to talk directly to the hardware in this mode; programs loaded by the operating system, such as by clicking an icon in Windows, are not allowed to access memory or other hardware directly. This protection is provided so that a single program can't crash the machine by doing something illegal. You might have seen the error message in Windows indicating this, and that the program will be shut down.

Diagnostics software by nature must talk to the hardware directly. This means that little intensive diagnostics testing can be done while a protected mode operating system such as Windows 9x, NT, 2000, XP, Vista, Linux, and so forth is running. For system testing, you usually have to boot from a DOS or self-booting floppy or CD or interrupt the loading of Windows (press the F8 key when Starting Windows appears during the boot process) and select Command Prompt Only, which boots you into DOS. In Windows 9x (but not Me), you can execute a shutdown and select Restart the Computer in MS-DOS mode. Many of the higher-end hardware diagnostics programs include their own special limited 16-bit operating systems so they can more easily access memory areas even DOS would use. With Windows 2000 and XP, you can format a floppy disk with MS-DOS startup files by selecting that option from the Format menu in My Computer. In Windows Vista, use the Format menu in Computer.

For example, when you boot from a Windows 9x startup disk, you are running 16-bit DOS, and if you want to access your CD-ROM drive to install Windows, you must load a 16-bit CD-ROM driver program from that disk as well. In this mode, you can do things such as partition and format your hard disk, install Windows, and test the system completely. OEM versions of Windows 98 and all versions of Windows Me and newer come on bootable CDs, so if your system supports booting from a CD-ROM drive, be sure to set that option in the BIOS Setup to eliminate the need for a formatted floppy disk.

The point of all this is that although you might not be running DOS very much these days, at least for system configuration and installation, as well as for high-level hardware diagnostics testing, data recovery, and so forth, you might still have to boot to a 16-bit OS occasionally. When you are in that mode, the system's architecture changes, less memory is accessible, and some of the software you are running (16-bit drivers and most application code) must fight over the first 1MB or even 640KB for space.

System memory areas, including the 384KB at the top of the first megabyte, which is used for video, adapter BIOS, and motherboard BIOS, as well as the remaining extended memory, are all part of the PC hardware design. They exist whether you are running 16-bit or 32/64-bit software; however, the limitations on their use in 16-bit (real) mode are much more severe. Because most people run 32-bit operating systems, such as Windows 9x, 2000, XP, Vista, Linux, and so on (or 64-bit operating systems such as Windows XP, Vista, or Linux), these operating systems automatically manage the use of RAM, meaning you don't have to interact with and manage this memory yourself as you often did with the 16-bit operating systems.

If you are using DOS or 16-bit Windows operating systems or are using legacy hardware that uses the ISA, EISA, MCA, or VL-Bus architectures, you need to have a detailed understanding of the logical memory map to avoid conflicts between devices and to optimize the performance of your system.

To learn more about the logical memory map and how to optimize its use, see Chapter 6 of *Upgrading and Repairing PCs, 17th Edition*, available in electronic form on the disc packaged with this book.

The ATA/IDE Interface

An Overview of the IDE Interface

The interface used to connect hard disk and optical drives to a modern PC is typically called IDE (Integrated Drive Electronics); however, I always like to point out that the true name of this interface is ATA (AT Attachment). The ATA designation refers to the fact that this interface was originally designed to connect a combined drive and controller directly to the 16-bit bus found in the 1984 vintage IBM AT (Advanced Technology) and compatible computers. The AT bus is otherwise known as the ISA (Industry Standard Architecture) bus. Although ATA is the official name of the interface, *IDE* is a marketing term originated by some of the drive manufacturers to describe the drive/controller combination used in drives with the ATA interface. *Integrated Drive Electronics* refers to the fact that the interface electronics or controller is built in to the drive and is not a separate board, as with earlier drive interfaces. Although the correct name for the particular IDE interface we most commonly use is technically ATA, many persist in using the IDE designation today. If you are being picky, you could say that *IDE* refers generically to any drive interface in which the controller is built in to the drive, whereas *ATA* refers to the specific implementation of IDE that is used in most PCs.

Over the years, ATA has been used to connect not only hard disks, but also optical (CD and DVD) drives, high-capacity floppy drives such as SuperDisk and Zip, and some tape drives. Even so, ATA is still thought of primarily as a hard disk interface, and it evolved directly from the separate controller and hard drive interfaces that were used prior to ATA. This chapter covers the standard parallel version of ATA as well as the newer Serial ATA interfaces in detail; it also briefly mentions the original interfaces from which ATA evolved. Because the ATA interface is directly integrated into virtually all motherboard chipsets, ATA is the primary storage device interface used by most PCs.

ATA was originally a 16-bit parallel interface, meaning that 16 bits are transmitted simultaneously down the interface cable. A newer interface, called Serial ATA, was officially introduced in late 2000 and was adopted in desktop systems starting in 2003 and in laptops starting in late 2005. Serial ATA (SATA) sends 1 bit down the cable at a time, enabling thinner and smaller cables to be used, as well as providing higher performance due to the higher cycling speeds it enables. Although SATA is a completely different physical interface design, it is also backward compatible on the software level with Parallel ATA. Throughout this book, *ATA* refers to either just the parallel version or both the parallel and serial versions, whereas *Parallel ATA (PATA)* refers specifically to the parallel version and *Serial ATA (SATA)* refers specifically to the serial version.

Precursors to IDE

A variety of hard disk interfaces has been used for PC hard disks over the years. As time has passed, the number of choices has increased; however, many of the older interface standards are obsolete and no longer viable in newer systems.

The primary job of the hard disk controller or interface is to transmit and receive data to and from the drive. The various interface types limit how fast data can be moved from the drive to the system and offer different features as well as levels of performance. If you are putting together a system in which performance is a primary concern, you need to know how these various interfaces affect performance and what you can expect from them. Many statistics that appear in technical literature are not indicative of the real performance figures you will see in practice. I will separate the myths presented by some of these overly optimistic figures from the reality of what you will actually see.

Several types of hard disk interfaces have been used in PCs over the years, as shown in Table 7.1.

Table 7.1   PC Drive Interfaces

Interface	When Used
ST-506/412	1978–1989 (obsolete)
ESDI	1983–1991 (obsolete)
Non-ATA IDE	1987–1993 (obsolete)
SCSI	1986–present
Parallel ATA (IDE)	1986–present
Serial ATA	2003–present

Of these interfaces, only ST-506/412 and ESDI are what you could call true disk-controller-to-drive interfaces, and they are obsolete. Non-ATA versions of IDE were used primarily in the IBM PS/2 systems and are also obsolete. Current SCSI, ATA, and Serial ATA are system-level interfaces that usually internally incorporate a chipset-based controller interface. For example, many SCSI, Parallel ATA, and Serial ATA drives incorporate the same basic controller circuitry inside the actual drive. The SCSI interface then adds another layer that connects between the drive controller and the PCI (or ISA) bus, whereas PATA and Serial ATA have a more direct connection from the controller to the AT bus attachment interface. Despite their differences, we call a SCSI, Parallel ATA (PATA), or Serial ATA (SATA) card a *host interface adapter* instead of a controller card because the actual controllers are inside the drives. Virtually all modern disk drives use Parallel ATA, Serial ATA, or SCSI interfaces to connect to a system.

IDE Origins

Any drive with an integrated controller could be called an IDE drive, although normally when we say *IDE*, we really mean the specific version of IDE called ATA. No matter what you call it, combining the drive and controller greatly simplifies installation because no separate power or signal cables run from the controller to the drive. Also, when the controller and drive are assembled as a unit, the number of total components is reduced, signal paths are shorter, and the electrical connections are more noise-resistant. This results in a more reliable and less expensive design than is possible when a separate controller, connected to the drive by cables, is used.

Placing the controller, including the digital-to-analog encoder/decoder (endec), on the drive offers an inherent reliability advantage over interfaces with separate controllers such as ST506 and ESDI. Reliability is increased because the data encoding, from digital to analog, is performed directly on the drive in a tight noise-free environment. The timing-sensitive analog information does not have to travel along crude ribbon cables that are likely to pick up noise and insert propagation delays into the signals. The integrated configuration enables increases in the clock rate of the encoder and the storage density of the drive.

Integrating the controller and drive also frees the controller and drive engineers from having to adhere to the strict guidelines imposed by the earlier interface standards. Engineers can design what essentially are custom drive and controller implementations because no other controller will ever have to be connected to the drive. The resulting drive and controller combinations can offer higher performance than earlier standalone controller and drive setups. IDE drives sometimes are called drives with embedded controllers.

The earliest IDE drives were called hardcards and were nothing more than hard disks and controllers bolted directly together and plugged into a slot as a single unit. Companies such as the Plus Development Division of Quantum took small 3 1/2" drives (either ST-506/412 or ESDI) and attached them directly to a standard controller. The drive/controller assembly then was plugged into an ISA bus slot as though it were a normal disk controller card. Unfortunately, the mounting of a heavy, vibrating hard disk in an expansion slot with nothing but a single screw to hold it in place left a lot to be desired—not to mention the physical interference with adjacent cards, because many of these units were much thicker than a controller card alone.

Several companies got the idea to redesign the controller to replace the logic board assembly on a standard hard disk and then mount it in a standard drive bay just like any other drive. Because the built-in controller in these drives still needed to plug directly into the expansion bus just like any other controller, a cable was run between the drive and one of the slots. This is the origin of IDE.

IDE Variations

There have been four main types of IDE interfaces based on three bus standards:

- Serial AT Attachment (SATA)
- Parallel AT Attachment (ATA, based on the 16-bit AT-bus, also called ISA and sometimes referred to as PATA)
- XT IDE (based on 8-bit ISA, obsolete)
- MCA IDE (based on 16-bit Micro Channel, obsolete)

Of these, only the Parallel and Serial ATA versions are used today. ATA and Serial ATA have evolved with newer, faster, and more powerful versions. The most recent versions of Parallel ATA are referred to as ATA-2 and higher. They are also sometimes called EIDE (Enhanced IDE), Fast-ATA, Ultra-ATA, or Ultra-DMA. Even though Parallel ATA has hit the end of the evolutionary road with ATA-7, Serial ATA picks up where Parallel ATA leaves off and offers greater performance, higher reliability, easier installation, lower cost, and an established roadmap for future upgrades.

In 1987 IBM developed its own Micro Channel Architecture (MCA) IDE drives for systems such as the PS/2 Model 70, and connected them to the bus through a bus adapter device called an *interposer card*. These bus adapters (sometimes called *paddle boards* or *angle boards*) needed only a few buffer chips and did not require any real circuitry because the drive-based controller was designed to plug directly into the bus. The *paddle board* nickname came from the fact that they resemble game paddle or joystick adapters, which do not have much circuitry on them. MCA IDE uses a nonstandard 72-pin connector and was designed for MCA bus systems only.

An 8-bit variation of IDE appeared in 8-bit ISA systems such as the PS/2 Model 30. The XT IDE interface used a 40-pin connector similar to, but not compatible with, the 16-bit version. Neither MCA nor XT versions of IDE became very popular, and they have been off the market for several years.

Note

It is important to note that only the ATA IDE interface has been standardized by the industry. The XT and MCA IDE interfaces never were adopted as industry-wide standards and never became very popular. These interfaces were only used from 1987 to 1993 and only in IBM PS/2 (and some early ThinkPad) systems.

In most modern systems you will find at least two ATA connectors on the motherboard, and systems that offer ATA RAID have two additional ATA connectors that can be used for an ATA RAID array or for additional ATA drives running as independent devices. If your motherboard does not have one of these connectors and you want to attach an ATA drive to your system, you can purchase an adapter card that adds an ATA interface (or two) to a system via the ISA or PCI bus slots. Some of the cards offer additional features, such as an onboard ROM BIOS and cache memory.

Because only the Parallel and Serial ATA versions of IDE are in use today, they are what this chapter focuses on.

Origins of ATA

Control Data Corporation (CDC; its disk drive division was later called Imprimis), Western Digital, and Compaq actually created what could be called the first ATA IDE interface drive and were the first to establish the 40-pin ATA connector pinout. The first ATA IDE drive was a 5 1/4" half-height CDC Wren II 40MB drive with an integrated WD controller and was initially used in the first Compaq 386 systems in 1986. I remember seeing this drive for the first time in 1986 at the fall Comdex show, and besides the (at the time) unique 40-pin ribbon cable, I remember being surprised by the green activity LED on the front bezel (most drives up until then used red LEDs).

Compaq was the first to incorporate a special bus adapter in its system to adapt the 98-pin AT-bus (also known as ISA) edge connector on the motherboard to a smaller 40-pin, header-style connector into which the drive would plug. The 40-pin connector was all that was necessary because it was known that a disk controller never would need more than 40 of the ISA bus lines. Smaller 2 1/2" ATA drives found in notebook computers use a superset 44-pin or 50-pin connection, which includes additional pins for power and configuration. The pins from the original ISA bus used in ATA are the only signal pins required by a standard-type AT hard disk controller. For example, because a primary AT-style disk controller uses only interrupt request (IRQ) line 14, the primary motherboard ATA connector supplies only that IRQ line; no other IRQ lines are necessary. Even if your ATA interface is integrated within the motherboard chipset South Bridge or I/O Controller Hub chip (as it would be in newer systems) and runs at higher bus speeds, the pinout and functions of the pins are still the same as the original design taken right off the ISA bus.

◄◄   See "Motherboard Connectors," p. 368.

◄◄   See "The ISA Bus," p. 391.

Note

Many people who use systems with ATA connectors on the motherboard believe that a hard disk controller is built in to their motherboards, but in a technical sense the controller is actually in the drive. Although the integrated ATA ports on a motherboard often are referred to as *controllers*, they are more accurately called *host adapters* (although you'll rarely hear this term). A host adapter can be thought of as a device that connects a controller to a bus.

Eventually, the 40-pin ATA connector and drive interface design was placed before one of the ANSI standards committees that, in conjunction with drive manufacturers, ironed out some deficiencies, tied up some loose ends, and then published what was known as the CAM ATA (Common Access Method AT Attachment) interface. The CAM ATA Committee was formed in October 1988, and the first working document of the AT Attachment interface was introduced in March 1989. Before the CAM ATA standard, many companies, such as Conner Peripherals (which later merged with Seagate Technology), made proprietary changes to the original interface as designed by CDC. As a result, many older ATA drives from the late 1980s are very difficult to integrate into a dual-drive setup because minor differences in the interfaces can cause compatibility problems among the drives. By the early 1990s, most drive manufacturers brought their drives into full compliance with the official standard, which eliminated many of these compatibility problems.

Some areas of the ATA standard have been left open for vendor-specific commands and functions. These vendor-specific commands and functions are the main reason it is so difficult to low-level format ATA drives. To work to full capability, the format program you are using typically must know the specific vendor-unique commands for remapping defects. Unfortunately, these and other specific drive commands differ from OEM to OEM, clouding the "standard" somewhat. Most ATA drive manufacturers publish their drive-formatting/initialization software on their websites.

Note

Many people are confused about 16- versus 32-bit bus connections and 16- versus 32-bit hard drive connections. A PCI bus connection allows for a 32-bit (and possibly 64-bit in some versions) connection between the bus and the ATA host interface, which is typically in the motherboard chipset South Bridge or I/O Controller Hub (ICH) chip. However, the actual Parallel ATA interface between the host connector on the motherboard and the drive (or drives) itself is only a 16-bit interface. Thus, in a Parallel ATA drive configuration, you are still getting only 16-bit transfers between the drive and the motherboard-based host interface. Even so, the clock speeds of the ATA interface are high enough that one or two hard drives normally can't supply the controller enough data to saturate even a 16-bit channel. The same is true with Serial ATA—although it transmits only 1 bit at a time, it does so at extremely high speeds.

As I noted at the start of this chapter, Parallel ATA is a 16-bit parallel interface that is slowly being phased out in favor of the serial interface of SATA. Serial ATA's thinner and smaller cables provide higher performance due to the higher cycling speeds allowed and are considerably easier to work with than the wide PATA ribbon cables. Figure 7.1 shows how the power and data cables used by SATA compare in size to those used by Parallel ATA.

The primary advantage of ATA drives over the older, separate controller-based interfaces and newer host bus interface alternatives, such as USB, SCSI, and IEEE 1394 (i.LINK or FireWire), is cost. Because the separate controller or host adapter is eliminated and the cable connections are simplified, ATA drives cost much less than a standard controller and drive combination.

▶▶ See "Introduction to Input/Output Ports," p. 1025.

In terms of performance, ATA drives are often some of the highest performance drives available—but they can also be among the lowest performance drives. This apparent contradiction is a result of the fact that all ATA drives are different. You can't make a blanket statement about the performance of ATA drives because each drive is unique. The high-end models, however, offer performance equal or superior to that of any other type of drive available in a similar form factor.

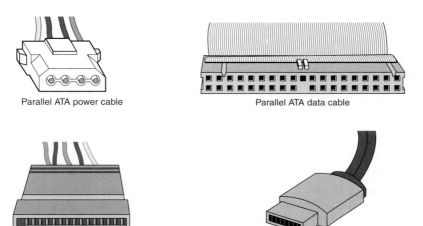

Parallel ATA power cable

Parallel ATA data cable

SATA power cable

SATA data cable

Figure 7.1   Serial ATA data cables (lower right) are much smaller than those used by Parallel ATA (upper right), whereas the power cables (left) are similar in size.

ATA Standards

Today, the ATA interface is controlled by an independent group of representatives from major PC, drive, and component manufacturers. This group is called Technical Committee T13 (http://www.t13.org) and is responsible for all standards relating to the Parallel and Serial AT Attachment storage interfaces. T13 is a part of the International Committee on Information Technology Standards (INCITS), which operates under rules approved by the American National Standards Institute (ANSI), a governing body that sets rules that control nonproprietary standards in the computer industry as well as many other industries. A second group called the Serial ATA International Organization (http://www.serialata.org) was formed to initially create the Serial ATA standards, which are then passed on to the T13 Committee for refinement and official publication under ANSI. The ATA-7 and ATA-8 standards incorporate both parallel and serial interfaces.

The rules these committees operate under are designed to ensure that voluntary industry standards are developed by the consensus of people and organizations in the affected industry. INCITS specifically develops Information Processing System standards, whereas ANSI approves the process under which these standards are developed and then publishes them. Because T13 is essentially a public organization, all the working drafts, discussions, and meetings of T13 are open for all to see.

Copies of any of the published standards can be purchased from ANSI (www.ansi.org) or Global Engineering Documents (http://global.ish.com). Draft versions of the standards can be downloaded from the T13 Committee or Serial ATA International Organization (SATA-IO) website.

The Parallel ATA interface has evolved into several successive standard versions, introduced as follows:

- ATA-1
- ATA-2 (also called Fast-ATA, Fast-ATA-2, or EIDE)
- ATA-3

- ATA-4 (Ultra-ATA/33)
- ATA-5 (Ultra-ATA/66)
- ATA-6 (Ultra-ATA/100)
- ATA-7 (Ultra-ATA/133 or Serial ATA)
- ATA-8 (Ultra-ATA/133 or Serial ATA)

Since ATA-1, newer versions of the ATA interface and complementary BIOS support larger and faster drives, as well as different types of devices other than hard disks. ATA-2 and later have improved the original ATA interface in five main areas:

- Secondary two-device channel
- Increased maximum drive capacity
- Faster data transfer
- ATAPI (ATA Program Interface)
- SATA (Serial ATA)

Each newer version of ATA is backward compatible with the previous versions. In other words, older ATA-1 and ATA-2 devices work fine on ATA-6 and ATA-8 interfaces. ATA-7 and ATA-8 include both Parallel and Serial ATA. Newer versions of ATA are normally built on older versions, and with few exceptions can be thought of as extensions of the previous versions. This means that ATA-8, for example, is generally considered equal to ATA-7 with the addition of some features.

Table 7.2 breaks down the various ATA standards. The following sections describe all the ATA versions in more detail.

ATA-1 (AT Attachment Interface for Disk Drives)

ATA-1 defined the original AT Attachment interface, which was an integrated bus interface between disk drives and host systems based on the ISA (AT) bus. These major features were introduced and documented in the ATA-1 specification:

- 40/44-pin connectors and cabling
- Master/slave or cable select drive configuration options
- Signal timing for basic Programmed I/O (PIO) and direct memory access (DMA) modes
- Cylinder, head, sector (CHS) and logical block address (LBA) drive parameter translations supporting drive capacities up to 2^{28}–2^{20} (267,386,880) sectors, or 136.9GB

Although ATA-1 had been in use since 1986, work on turning it into an official standard began in 1988 under the Common Access Method (CAM) committee. The ATA-1 standard was finished and officially published in 1994 as "ANSI X3.221-1994, AT Attachment Interface for Disk Drives." ATA-1 was officially withdrawn as a standard on August 6, 1999.

Although ATA-1 supported theoretical drive capacities up to 136.9GB (2^{28}–2^{20} = 267,386,880 sectors), it did not address BIOS limitations that stopped at 528MB (1024×16×63 = 1,032,192 sectors). The BIOS limitations would be addressed in subsequent ATA versions because, at the time, no drives larger than 528MB existed.

Table 7.2   ATA Standards

Standard	Proposed	Published	With-drawn	PIO Modes	DMA Modes	UDMA Modes	Parallel Speed (MBps)	Serial Speed (MBps)	Features
ATA-1	1988	1994	1999	0-2	0	—	8.33	—	Drives support up to 136.9GB; BIOS issues not addressed.
ATA-2	1993	1996	2001	0-4	0-2	—	16.67	—	Faster PIO modes; CHS/LBA BIOS translation defined up to 8.4GB; PC-Card.
ATA-3	1995	1997	2002	0-4	0-2	—	16.67	—	S.M.A.R.T.; improved signal integrity; LBA support mandatory; eliminated single-word DMA modes.
ATA-4	1996	1998	—	0-4	0-2	0-2	33.33	—	Ultra-DMA modes; ATAPI Packet Interface; BIOS support up to 136.9GB.
ATA-5	1998	2000	—	0-4	0-2	0-4	66.67	—	Faster UDMA modes; 80-pin cable with autodetection.
ATA-6	2000	2002	—	0-4	0-2	0-5	100	—	100MBps UDMA mode; extended drive and BIOS support up to 144PB.
ATA-7	2001	2004	—	0-4	0-2	0-6	133	150	133MBps UDMA mode; Serial ATA.
ATA-8	2004	2007	—	0-4	0-2	0-6	133	150	Minor revisions.

S.M.A.R.T. = Self-Monitoring, Analysis, and Reporting Technology
ATAPI = AT Attachment Packet Interface
MB = Megabyte; million bytes
GB = Gigabyte; billion bytes
PB = Petabyte; quadrillion bytes
CHS = Cylinder, Head, Sector
LBA = Logical block address
PIO = Programmed I/O
DMA = direct memory access
UDMA = Ultra DMA (direct memory access)

ATA-2 (AT Attachment Interface with Extensions-2)

ATA-2 first appeared in 1993 and was a major upgrade to the original ATA standard. Perhaps the biggest change was almost a philosophical one. ATA-2 was updated to define an interface between host systems and storage devices in general and not only disk drives. The major features added to ATA-2 as compared to the original ATA standard include the following:

- Faster PIO and DMA transfer modes
- Support for power management
- Support for removable devices
- PCMCIA (PC Card) device support
- Identify Drive command that reports more information
- Defined standard CHS/LBA translation methods for drives up to 8.4GB in capacity

The most important additions in ATA-2 were the support for faster PIO and DMA modes, as well as methods to enable BIOS support up to 8.4GB. The BIOS support was necessary because, although ATA-1 was designed to support drives of up to 136.9GB in capacity, the PC BIOS could originally handle drives of up to 528MB. Adding parameter-translation capability now allowed the BIOS to handle drives up to 8.4GB. This is discussed in more detail later in this chapter.

ATA-2 also featured improvements in the Identify Drive command that enabled a drive to tell the software exactly what its characteristics are; this is essential for both Plug and Play (PnP) and compatibility with future revisions of the standard.

ATA-2 was also known by unofficial marketing terms such as fast-ATA or fast-ATA-2 (Seagate/Quantum) and EIDE (Enhanced IDE, Western Digital).

Although work on ATA-2 began in 1993, the standard was not officially published until 1996 as "ANSI X3.279-1996 AT Attachment Interface with Extensions." ATA-2 was officially withdrawn in 2001.

ATA-3 (AT Attachment Interface-3)

First appearing in 1995, ATA-3 was a comparatively minor revision to the ATA-2 standard that preceded it. It consisted of a general cleanup of the specification and had mostly minor clarifications and revisions. The most major changes included the following:

- Eliminated single-word (8-bit) DMA transfer protocols.
- Added S.M.A.R.T. (Self-Monitoring, Analysis, and Reporting Technology) support for prediction of device performance degradation.
- LBA mode support was made mandatory (previously it had been optional).
- Added ATA Security mode, allowing password protection for device access.
- Provided recommendations for source and receiver bus termination to solve noise issues at higher transfer speeds.

ATA-3 built on ATA-2, adding improved reliability, especially of the faster PIO mode 4 transfers; however, ATA-3 did not define any faster modes. ATA-3 did add a simple password-based security scheme, more sophisticated power management, and S.M.A.R.T. This enables a drive to keep track of problems that might result in a failure and thus avoid data loss. S.M.A.R.T. is a reliability prediction technology that IBM initially developed.

Work on ATA-3 began in 1995, and the standard was finished and officially published in 1997 as "ANSI X3.298-1997, AT Attachment 3 Interface." ATA-3 was officially withdrawn in 2002.

ATA/ATAPI-4 (AT Attachment with Packet Interface Extension-4)

First appearing in 1996, ATA-4 included several important additions to the standard. It included the Packet Command feature known as the AT Attachment Packet Interface (ATAPI), which allowed devices such as CD-ROM and CD-RW drives, LS-120 SuperDisk floppy drives, Zip drives, tape drives, and other types of storage devices to be attached through a common interface. Until ATA-4 came out, ATAPI was a separately published standard. ATA-4 also added the 33MB per second (MBps) transfer mode known as Ultra-DMA or Ultra-ATA. ATA-4 is backward compatible with ATA-3 and earlier definitions of the ATAPI.

Work on ATA-4 began in 1996, and the standard was finished and officially published in 1998 as "ANSI NCITS 317-1998, AT Attachment - 4 with Packet Interface Extension."

The major revisions added in ATA-4 were as follows:

- Ultra-DMA (UDMA)or Ultra-ATA/33) transfer modes up to Mode 2, which is 33MBps (called UDMA/33 or Ultra-ATA/33)
- Integral ATAPI support
- Advanced power management support
- An optional 80-conductor, 40-pin cable defined for improved noise resistance
- Host protected area (HPA) support
- Compact Flash Adapter (CFA) support
- Enhanced BIOS support for drives over 9.4ZB (zettabytes or trillion gigabytes) in size (even though ATA was still limited to 136.9GB)

The speed and level of ATA support in your system is mainly dictated by your motherboard chipset. Most motherboard chipsets come with a component called either a South Bridge or an I/O Controller Hub that provides the ATA interface (as well as other functions) in the system. Check the specifications for your motherboard or chipset to see whether yours supports the faster ATA/33, ATA/66, ATA/100, or ATA/133 mode. One indication is to enter the BIOS Setup, put the hard disk on manual parameter settings (user defined), and see which (if any) Ultra-DMA modes are listed. Most boards built during 1998 support ATA/33; in 2000 they began to support ATA/66; and by late 2000 most started supporting ATA/100. ATA/133 support became widespread in mid-2002.

◄◄   See "Chipsets," p. 273.

ATA-4 made ATAPI support a full part of the ATA standard; therefore, ATAPI was no longer an auxiliary interface to ATA but merged completely within it. Thus, ATA-4 promoted ATA for use as an interface for many other types of devices. ATA-4 also added support for new Ultra-DMA modes (also called *Ultra-ATA*) for even faster data transfer. The highest-performance mode, called *UDMA/33*, had 33MBps bandwidth—twice that of the fastest programmed I/O mode or DMA mode previously supported. In addition to the higher transfer rate, because UDMA modes relieve the load on the processor, further performance gains were realized.

An optional 80-conductor cable (with cable select) is defined for UDMA/33 transfers. Although this cable was originally defined as optional, it would later be required for the faster ATA/66, ATA/100, and ATA/133 modes in ATA-5 and later.

Support for a reserved area on the drive called the *host protected area (HPA)* was added via an optional SET MAX ADDRESS command. This enables an area of the drive to be reserved for recovery software.

Also included was support for queuing commands, similar to those provided in SCSI-2. This enabled better multitasking as multiple programs make requests for ATA transfers.

Another standard approved by the T13 committee in 1998 was "ANSI NCITS 316-1998 1394 to AT Attachment - Tailgate," which is a bridge protocol between the IEEE 1394 (i.LINK/FireWire) bus and ATA that enables ATA drives to be adapted to FireWire. A *tailgate* is an adapter device (basically a small circuit board) that converts IEEE 1394 (i.LINK or FireWire) to ATA, essentially allowing ATA drives to be plugged into a FireWire bus. This has enabled vendors to quickly develop IEEE 1394 (FireWire) external drives for backup and high-capacity removable data storage. Inside almost any external FireWire drive enclosure you will find the tailgate device and a standard ATA drive.

 See "IEEE 1394," p. 1042.

ATA/ATAPI-5 (AT Attachment with Packet Interface-5)

ATA-5 first appeared in 1998 and was built on the previous ATA-4 interface. ATA-5 includes Ultra-ATA/66 (also called Ultra-DMA or UDMA/66), which doubles the Ultra-ATA burst transfer rate by reducing setup times and increasing the clock rate. The faster clock rate increases interference, which causes problems with the standard 40-pin cable used by ATA and Ultra-ATA. To eliminate noise and interference, the newer 40-pin, 80-conductor cable was made mandatory for drives running in UDMA/66 or faster modes. This cable adds 40 additional ground lines between each of the original 40 ground and signal lines, which helps shield the signals from interference. Note that this cable works with older, non-Ultra-ATA devices as well because it still has the same 40-pin connectors.

Work on ATA-5 began in 1998, and the standard was finished and officially published in 2000 as "ANSI NCITS 340-2000, AT Attachment - 5 with Packet Interface."

The major additions in the ATA-5 standard include the following:

- Ultra-DMA (UDMA) transfer modes up to Mode 4, which is 66MBps (called UDMA/66 or Ultra-ATA/66).
- 80-conductor cable now mandatory for UDMA/66 operation.
- Automatic detection of 40- or 80-conductor cables.
- UDMA modes faster than UDMA/33 are enabled only if an 80-conductor cable is detected.

The 40-pin, 80-conductor cables support the cable select feature and have color-coded connectors. The blue (end) connector should be connected to the ATA host interface (usually the motherboard). The black (opposite end) connector is known as the *master position*, which is where the primary drive plugs in. The gray (middle) connector is for slave devices.

To use either the UDMA/33 or UDMA/66 mode, your ATA interface, drive, BIOS, and cable must be capable of supporting the mode you want to use. The operating system also must be capable of handling direct memory access. Windows 95 OSR2 and later versions are ready out of the box, but older versions of Windows 95 and NT (prior to Service Pack 3) require additional or updated drivers to fully exploit these faster modes. Contact the motherboard or system vendor for the latest drivers.

For reliability, Ultra-DMA modes incorporate an error-detection mechanism known as *cyclical redundancy checking (CRC)*. CRC is an algorithm that calculates a checksum used to detect errors in a stream of data. Both the host (controller) and the drive calculate a CRC value for each Ultra-DMA transfer. After the data is sent, the drive calculates a CRC value, and this is compared to the original host CRC value. If a difference is reported, the host might be required to select a slower transfer mode and retry the original request for data.

ATA/ATAPI-6 (AT Attachment with Packet Interface-6)

ATA-6 began development during 2000 and includes Ultra-ATA/100 (also called *Ultra-DMA* or *UDMA/100*), which increases the Ultra-ATA burst transfer rate by reducing setup times and increasing the clock rate. As with ATA-5, the faster modes require the improved 80-conductor cable. Using the ATA/100 mode requires both a drive and motherboard interface that supports that mode.

Work on ATA-6 began in 2000, and the standard was finished and officially published in 2002 as "ANSI NCITS 361-2002, AT Attachment - 6 with Packet Interface."

The major changes or additions in the standard include the following:

- Ultra-DMA (UDMA) Mode 5 added, which allows 100MBps (called *UDMA/100*, *Ultra-ATA/100*, or just *ATA/100*) transfers.
- Sector count per command increased from 8 bits (256 sectors, or 131KB) to 16 bits (65,536 sectors, or 33.5MB), allowing larger files to be transferred more efficiently.
- LBA addressing extended from 2^{28} to 2^{48} (281,474,976,710,656) sectors, supporting drives up to 144.12PB (petabytes = quadrillion bytes). This feature is often referred to as *48-bit LBA* or *greater than 137GB* support by vendors; Maxtor referred to this feature as *Big Drive*.
- CHS addressing was made obsolete; drives must use 28-bit or 48-bit LBA addressing only.

Besides adding the 100MBps UDMA Mode 5 transfer rate, ATA-6 also extended drive capacity greatly, and just in time. ATA-5 and earlier standards supported drives of up to only 137GB in capacity, which became a limitation as larger drives were becoming available. Commercially available 3 1/2" drives exceeding 137GB were introduced during 2001, but they were originally available only in SCSI versions because SCSI doesn't have the same limitations as ATA. With ATA-6, the sector addressing limit has been extended from 2^{28} sectors to 2^{48} sectors. What this means is that LBA addressing previously could use only 28-bit numbers, but with ATA-6, LBA addressing can use larger 48-bit numbers if necessary. With 512 bytes per sector, this raises the maximum supported drive capacity to 144.12PB. That is equal to more than 144.12 quadrillion bytes! Note that the 48-bit addressing is optional and necessary only for drives larger than 137GB. Drives 137GB or smaller can use either 28-bit or 48-bit addressing.

ATA/ATAPI-7 (AT Attachment with Packet Interface-7)

Work on ATA-7, which began late in 2001, was completed and officially published in 2004. As with the previous ATA standards, ATA-7 is built on the standard that preceded it (ATA-6), with some additions.

The primary additions to ATA-7 include the following:

- Ultra-DMA (UDMA) Mode 6 was added. This allows for 133MBps transfers (called *UDMA/133*, *Ultra-ATA/133*, or just *ATA/133*). As with UDMA Mode 5 (100MBps) and UDMA Mode 4 (66MBps), the use of an 80-conductor cable is required.
- Added support for long physical sectors. This allows a device to be formatted so that there are multiple logical sectors per physical sector. Each physical sector stores an ECC field, so long physical sectors allow increased format efficiency with fewer ECC bytes used overall.
- Added support for long logical sectors. This enables additional data bytes to be used per sector (520 or 528 bytes instead of 512 bytes) for server applications. Devices using long logical sectors are not backward compatible with devices or applications that use 512-byte sectors, such as standard desktop and laptop systems.
- Serial ATA incorporated as part of the ATA-7 standard.

- The ATA-7 document has been split into three volumes. Volume 1 covers the command set and logical registers, Volume 2 covers the parallel transport protocols and interconnects, and Volume 3 covers the serial transport protocols and interconnects.

Note that although the throughput has been increased from the drive controller (on the drive) to the motherboard via the UDMA modes, most ATA drives—even those capable of UDMA Mode 6 (133MBps) from the drive to the motherboard—still have an average maximum sustained transfer rate while reading data of under 60MBps. This means that although newer ATA drives can transfer at speeds up to 133MBps from the circuit board on the drive to the motherboard, data from the drive media (platters) through the heads to the circuit board on the drive moves at less than half that rate. For that reason, running a drive capable of UDMA Mode 6 (133MBps) on a motherboard capable of only UDMA Mode 5 (100MBps) really doesn't slow things down much, if at all. Likewise, upgrading your ATA host adapter from one that does 100MBps to one that can do 133MBps won't help much if your drive reads data off the disk platters at only half that speed. Always remember that the media transfer rate is far more important than the interface transfer rate when selecting a drive because the media transfer rate is the limiting factor.

The ATA/133 transfer mode was originally proposed by Maxtor, and only a few other drive and chipset manufacturers adopted it. Among the chipset manufacturers, VIA, ALi, and SiS added ATA/133 support to their chipsets, prior to moving on to Serial ATA, but Intel decided from the outset to skip ATA/133 in its chipsets in lieu of adding Serial ATA (150MBps or 300MBps) instead. This means the majority of systems that utilize Parallel ATA do not have support for ATA/133; however, all ATA/133 drives do work in ATA/100 mode.

As a historical note, ATA-7 is the last revision of the venerable Parallel ATA standard. In new systems, ATA has predominantly evolved into Serial ATA, which was incorporated into the ATA-7 specification and is covered in detail later in this chapter.

SATA/ATAPI-8

In 2004 work began on SATA-8, which is a new ATA standard based on ATA-7 that will carry forward the development of Serial ATA while still including Parallel ATA. The main features of ATA-8 include the following:

- The replacement of read long/write long functions
- Improved HPA management

As the development of ATA-8 progresses, it is expected that newer features designed by the SATA-IO committee will be incorporated, including the faster SATA 3Gbps transfer speed. It is expected that ATA-8 will be finalized and officially published sometime in 2007 or 2008.

Parallel ATA

Parallel ATA has unique specifications and requirements regarding the physical interface, cabling, and connectors as compared to Serial ATA. The following sections detail the unique features of Parallel ATA.

Parallel ATA I/O Connector

The Parallel ATA interface connector is normally a 40-pin header-type connector with pins spaced 0.1" (2.54mm) apart, and generally it is keyed to prevent the possibility of installing it upside down (see Figures 7.2 and 7.3). To create a keyed connector, the manufacturer usually removes pin 20 from the male connector and blocks pin 20 on the female cable connector, which prevents the user from installing the cable backward. Some cables also incorporate a protrusion on the top of the female cable connector that fits into a notch in the shroud surrounding the mating male connector on the device. The use of keyed connectors and cables is highly recommended. Plugging an ATA cable in backward normally doesn't cause any permanent damage; however, it can lock up the system and prevent it from running.

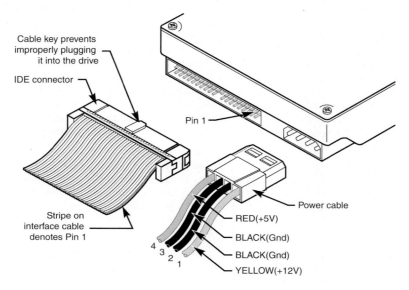

Figure 7.2 Typical Parallel ATA (IDE) hard drive connectors.

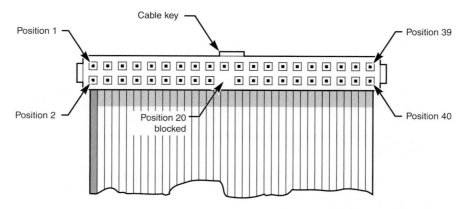

Figure 7.3 Parallel ATA (IDE) 40-pin interface connector detail.

Table 7.3 shows the standard 40-pin Parallel ATA (IDE) interface connector pinout.

Table 7.3   Pinout for the 40-Pin Parallel ATA Connector

Signal Name	Pin	Pin	Signal Name
-RESET	1	2	GROUND
Data Bit 7	3	4	Data Bit 8
Data Bit 6	5	6	Data Bit 9
Data Bit 5	7	8	Data Bit 10
Data Bit 4	9	10	Data Bit 11
Data Bit 3	11	12	Data Bit 12
Data Bit 2	13	14	Data Bit 13
Data Bit 1	15	16	Data Bit 14
Data Bit 0	17	18	Data Bit 15
GROUND	19	20	KEY (pin missing)
DRQ 3	21	22	GROUND
-IOW	23	24	GROUND
-IOR	25	26	GROUND
I/O CH RDY	27	28	CSEL:SPSYNC[1]
-DACK 3	29	30	GROUND
IRQ 14	31	32	Reserved[2]
Address Bit 1	33	34	-PDIAG
Address Bit 0	35	36	Address Bit 2
-CS1FX	37	38	-CS3FX
-DA/SP	39	40	GROUND
+5V (Logic)	41	42	+5V (Motor)
GROUND	43	44	Reserved

1. *Pin 28 is usually cable select, but some older drives could use it for spindle synchronization between multiple drives.*

2. *Pin 32 was defined as -IOCS16 in ATA-2 but is no longer used.*

Note that "-" preceding a signal name (such as -RESET) indicates the signal is "active low."

The 2 1/2" drives found in notebook/laptop-size computers typically use a smaller unitized 50-pin header connector with pins spaced only 2.0mm (0.079") apart. The main 40-pin part of the connector is the same as the standard Parallel ATA connector (except for the physical pin spacing), but there are added pins for power and jumpering. The cable that plugs into this connector typically has 44 pins, carrying power as well as the standard ATA signals. The jumper pins usually have a jumper on them (the jumper position controls cable select, master, or slave settings). Figure 7.4 shows the unitized 50-pin connector used on the 2 1/2" Parallel ATA drives in laptop or notebook computers.

Note the jumper pins at positions A–D and that the pins at positions E and F are removed. A jumper usually is placed between positions B and D to set the drive for cable select operation. On this connector, pin 41 provides +5V power to the drive logic (circuit board), pin 42 provides +5V power to the motor (2 1/2" drives use 5V motors, unlike larger drives that typically use 12V motors), and pin 43 provides a power ground. The last pin (44) is reserved and not used.

Table 7.4 shows the 50-pin unitized Parallel ATA interface connector pinout as used on most 2 1/2" (laptop or notebook computer) drives.

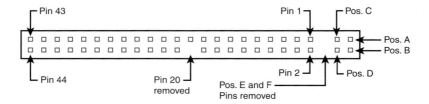

Figure 7.4   The 50-pin unitized Parallel ATA connector detail (used on 2 1/2" notebook/laptop Parallel ATA drives with a 44-pin cable).

Table 7.4   The 50-Pin Unitized Parallel ATA 2 1/2" (Notebook/Laptop Drive) Connector Pinout

Signal Name	Pin	Pin	Signal Name
Jumper pin	A	B	Jumper pin
Jumper pin	C	D	Jumper pin
KEY (pin missing)	E	F	KEY (pin missing)
-RESET	1	2	GROUND
Data Bit 7	3	4	Data Bit 8
Data Bit 6	5	6	Data Bit 9
Data Bit 5	7	8	Data Bit 10
Data Bit 4	9	10	Data Bit 11
Data Bit 3	11	12	Data Bit 12
Data Bit 2	13	14	Data Bit 13
Data Bit 1	15	16	Data Bit 14
Data Bit 0	17	18	Data Bit 15
GROUND	19	20	KEY (pin missing)
DRQ 3	21	22	GROUND
-IOW	23	24	GROUND
-IOR	25	26	GROUND
I/O CH RDY	27	28	CSEL
-DACK 3	29	30	GROUND
IRQ 14	31	32	Reserved
Address Bit 1	33	34	-PDIAG
Address Bit 0	35	36	Address Bit 2
-CS1FX	37	38	-CS3FX
-DA/SP	39	40	GROUND
+5V (Logic)	41	42	+5V (Motor)
GROUND	43	44	Reserved

Note

Many lower-cost board and cable manufacturers leave out the keying. Cheaper motherboards often don't have pin 20 removed on their ATA connectors; consequently, they don't supply a cable with pin 20 blocked. If they don't use a shrouded connector with a notch and a corresponding protrusion on the cable connector, no keying exists and the cables can be inserted backward. Fortunately, the only consequence of this in most cases is that the device won't work until the cable is attached with the correct orientation.

Note that some systems do not display any video until the ATA drives respond to a spin-up command, which they can't receive if the cable is connected backward. So, if you connect an unkeyed ATA drive to your computer, turn on the computer, and it seems as if the system is locked up (you don't see anything on the screen), check the ATA cable. (See Figure 7.6 for examples of unkeyed and keyed ATA cables.)

In rare situations in which you are mixing and matching items, you might encounter a cable with pin 20 blocked (as it should be) and a board with pin 20 still present. In that case, you can break off pin 20 from the board—or for the more squeamish, remove the block from the cable or replace the cable with one without the blocked pin. Some cables have the block permanently installed as a part of the connector housing, in which case you must break off pin 20 on the board or device end or use a different cable.

The simple rule of thumb is that pin 1 should be oriented toward the power connector on the device, which normally corresponds to the stripe on the cable.

Parallel ATA I/O Cable

A 40-conductor ribbon cable is specified to carry signals between the bus adapter circuits and the drive (controller). To maximize signal integrity and eliminate potential timing and noise problems, the cable should not be longer than 18" (0.46 meters), although testing shows that 80-conductor cables can be used reliably up to 27" (0.69 meters) in length.

Note that ATA drives supporting the higher-speed transfer modes, such as PIO Mode 4 or any of the Ultra-DMA (UDMA) modes, are especially susceptible to cable integrity problems. If the cable is too long, you can experience data corruption and other errors that can be maddening. This is manifested in problems reading from or writing to the drive. In addition, any drive using UDMA Mode 5 (66MBps transfer rate), Mode 6 (100MBps transfer rate), or Mode 7 (133MBps transfer rate) must use a special, higher-quality 80-conductor cable. I also recommend this type of cable if your drive is running at UDMA Mode 2 (33MBps) or slower because it can't hurt and can only help. I always keep a high-quality 80-conductor ATA cable in my toolbox for testing drives where I suspect cable integrity or cable length problems. Figure 7.5 shows the typical ATA cable layout and dimensions.

Note

Most 40-conductor cables do not have color-coded connectors, whereas all 80-conductor cables have color-coded connectors.

The two primary variations of Parallel ATA cables in use today—one with 40 conductors and the other with 80 conductors—are shown in Figure 7.6. As you can see, both use 40-pin connectors, and the additional wires in the 80-conductor version are simply wired to ground. The additional conductors are designed to reduce noise and interference and are required when setting the interface to run at 66MBps (ATA/66) or faster. The drive and host adapter are designed to disable the higher-speed ATA/66, ATA/100, and ATA/133 modes if an 80-conductor cable is not detected. In such cases, you might see a warning message when you start your computer if an ATA/66 or faster drive is connected to a 40-conductor cable. The 80-conductor cable can also be used at lower speeds; although this is unnecessary, it improves the signal integrity. Therefore, it is the recommended version no matter which drive you use.

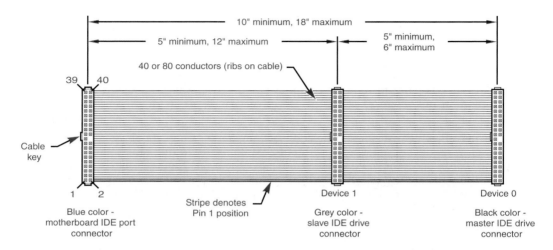

Figure 7.5   Parallel ATA (IDE) cable, with 40-pin connectors and either 40- or 80-conductor cables (additional wires are grounded in 80-conductor versions).

I once had a student ask me how to tell an 80-conductor cable from a 40-conductor cable. The simple answer is to count the ridges (conductors) in the cable. If you count only 40, it must be a 40-conductor cable, and if you count to 80, well... you get the idea! If you observe them side by side, the difference is clear: The 80-conductor cable has an obviously smoother, less ridged appearance than the 40-conductor cable.

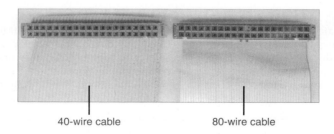

Figure 7.6   40-conductor (left) and 80-conductor (right) Parallel ATA cables.

Note the keying on the 80-conductor cable that is designed to prevent backward installation. Note also that the poorly constructed 40-conductor cable shown in this example lacks keying. Most good 40-conductor cables include the keying; however, because it is optional, many cheaply constructed versions do not include it. Keying was made mandatory for all 80-conductor cables as part of the standard.

Longer and/or Rounded Cables

The official Parallel ATA standard limits cable length to 18" (0.46 meters); however, many of the cables sold are longer, up to even 36" (0.91 meters) or more in length. I've had many readers write me questioning the length, asking, "Why would people sell cables longer than 18" if the standard doesn't allow it?" Well, just because something is for sale doesn't mean it conforms to the standards and will work properly! I see improperly designed, poorly manufactured, and nonconforming items for sale all the time. Still, many people have used the longer cables and yet their systems seem to work fine, but I've also documented numerous cases where using longer cables has caused problems, so I decided to investigate this issue more thoroughly.

What I've discovered is that you can use longer 80-conductor cables reliably up to 27" (0.69 meters) in length, but 40-conductor cables should remain limited to 18", just as the standard indicates.

In fact, an attempt was made to change the Parallel ATA standard to allow 27" cables. If you read http://www.t13.org/Documents/UploadedDocuments/technical/e00151r0.pdf, you'll see data from a proposal that shows "negligible differences in Ultra DMA Mode 5 signal integrity between a 27", 80-conductor cable and an 18", 80-conductor cable." This extended cable design was actually proposed back in October 2000, but it was never incorporated into the standard. Even though it was never officially approved, I take the information presented in this proposal as empirical evidence for allowing the use of 80-conductor cables up to 27" in length without problems.

To that, I would add another recommendation, which is that in general I do not recommend "rounded" ATA cables. A rounded design has not been approved in the ATA standard, and there is some evidence that it can cause problems with crosstalk and noise. The design of 80-conductor cables is such that a ground wire is interspersed between each data wire in the ribbon, and *rounding* the cable causes some of the data lines to run parallel or adjacent to each other at random, thereby causing crosstalk and noise and resulting in signal errors.

In support of this, I read an interview with Rahul Sood in the March 2004 issue of *CPU* (www.computerpoweruser.com). Sood is the chief technology officer of a popular builder of high-end systems, called VoodooPC (www.voodoopc.com), since acquired by HP. In the *CPU* interview, he said, "I don't agree with rounded cables, I never have. SATA cables are great, of course, but rounded [Parallel ATA] cables are a different story because there is potential for noise. Any benchmarks that I've run on any of the rounded cables that we've tested show either errors generating over time or they're slower than good quality flat IDE cables."

Of course, many people are using rounded cables with success, but my knowledge of electrical engineering as well as the ATA standard has always made me somewhat uncomfortable with their use. Although I cannot offer any specific test data to corroborate the findings of Sood, I prefer to stick with 80-conductor ribbon cables of 27" or less in length in my own systems.

Parallel ATA Signals

This section describes some of the most important Parallel ATA signals having to do with drive configuration and installation in more detail. This information can help you understand how the cable select feature works, for example.

Pin 20 is used as a key pin for cable orientation and is not connected to the interface. This pin should be missing from any ATA connectors, and the cable should have the pin-20 hole in the connector plugged off to prevent the cable from being plugged in backward.

Pin 39 carries the drive active/slave present (DASP) signal, which is a dual-purpose, time-multiplexed signal. During power-on initialization, this signal indicates whether a slave drive is present on the interface. After that, each drive asserts the signal to indicate that it is active. Early drives could not multiplex these functions and required special jumper settings to work with other drives. Standardizing this function to allow for compatible dual-drive installations is one of the features of the ATA standard. This is why some drives require a slave present (SP) jumper, whereas others do not.

Pin 28 carries the cable select signal (CSEL). In some older drives, it could also carry a spindle synchronization signal (SPSYNC), but that is not commonly found on newer drives. The CSEL function is the most widely used and is designed to control the designation of a drive as master (drive 0) or slave (drive 1) without requiring jumper settings on the drives. If a drive sees the CSEL as being grounded, the drive is a master; if CSEL is open, the drive is a slave.

You can install special cabling to ground CSEL selectively. This installation usually is accomplished through a cable that has pin 28 missing from the middle connector, put present in the connectors on each end. In that arrangement, with one end plugged into the motherboard, and two drives set to cable select, the drive plugged into the end connector will automatically be configured as master, whereas the drive attached to the middle connector will be configured as slave. Note that while that is the most common arrangement, it is also possible to make cables where the middle connector is master (and the end is slave), or even to use a Y-cable arrangement, with the motherboard ATA bus connector in the middle, and each drive at opposite ends of the cable. In this arrangement, one leg of the Y would have the CSEL line connected through (master), and the other leg has the CSEL line open (conductor interrupted or removed), making the drive at that end the slave.

Parallel ATA Dual-drive Configurations

Dual-drive Parallel ATA installations can be problematic because each drive has its own controller, and both controllers must function while being connected to the same bus. There has to be a way to ensure that only one of the two controllers will respond to a command at a time.

The ATA standard provides the option of operating on the AT bus with two drives in a daisy-chained configuration. The primary drive (drive 0) is called the *master*, and the secondary drive (drive 1) is called the *slave*. You designate a drive as being master or slave by setting a jumper or switch on the drive or by using a special line in the interface called the *cable select (CS) pin* and setting the CS jumper on the drive.

When only one drive is installed, the controller responds to all commands from the system. When two drives (and, therefore, two controllers) are installed, both controllers receive all commands from the system. Each controller then must be set up to respond only to commands for itself. In this situation, one controller must be designated as the master and the other as the slave. When the system sends a command for a specific drive, the controller on the other drive must remain silent while the selected controller and drive are functioning. Setting the jumper to master or slave enables discrimination between the two controllers by setting a special bit (the DRV bit) in the drive/head register of a command block.

Configuring ATA drives can be simple, as is the case with most single-drive installations. Or it can be troublesome, especially when it comes to mixing two older drives from different manufacturers on a single cable.

Most ATA drives can be configured with four possible settings:

- Master (single-drive)
- Master (dual-drive)
- Slave (dual-drive)
- Cable select

Many drives simplify this to three settings: master, slave, and cable select. Because each ATA drive has its own controller, you must specifically tell one drive to be the master and the other to be the slave. No functional difference exists between the two, except that the drive that's specified as the slave will assert a signal called DASP after a system reset informs the master that a slave drive is present in the system. The master drive then pays attention to the drive select line, which it otherwise ignores. Telling a drive that it's the slave also usually causes it to delay its spin-up for several seconds to allow the master to get going and thus to lessen the load on the system's power supply.

Until the ATA specification, no common implementation for drive configuration was in use. Some drive companies even used different master/slave methods for different models of drives. Because of these incompatibilities, some drives work together only in a specific master/slave or slave/master order. This situation mostly affects older IDE drives introduced before the ATA specification.

Most drives that fully follow the ATA specification now need only one jumper (master/slave) for configuration. A few also need a slave present jumper as well. Table 7.5 shows the jumper settings that most ATA drives require.

Table 7.5   Jumper Settings for Most ATA-Compatible Drives on Standard (Non–Cable Select) Cables

Jumper Name	Single-Drive	Dual-Drive Master	Dual-Drive Slave
Master (M/S)	On	On	Off
Slave Present (SP)	Off	On	Off
Cable Select (CS)	Off	Off	Off

Note

If a cable select cable is used, the CS jumper should be set On and all others should be Off. The cable connector then determines which drive will be master or slave.

Figure 7.7 shows the jumpers on a typical ATA drive.

The master jumper indicates that the drive is a master or a slave. Some drives also require a slave present jumper, which is used only in a dual-drive setup and then installed only on the master drive— which is somewhat confusing. This jumper tells the master that a slave drive is attached. With many Parallel ATA drives, the master jumper is optional and can be left off. Installing this jumper doesn't hurt in these cases and can eliminate confusion; I recommend that you install the jumpers listed here.

Note

Note that some drives have these jumpers on the drive circuit board on the bottom of the drive, and as such they might not be visible on the rear.

To eliminate confusion over master/slave settings, most newer systems now use the cable select option. This involves two things. The first is having a special Parallel ATA cable that has all the wires except pin 28 running from the motherboard connector to both drive connectors. Pin 28 is used for cable select and is connected to one of the drive connectors (labeled master) and not to the other (labeled slave). Both drives are then configured in cable select mode via the CS jumper on each drive.

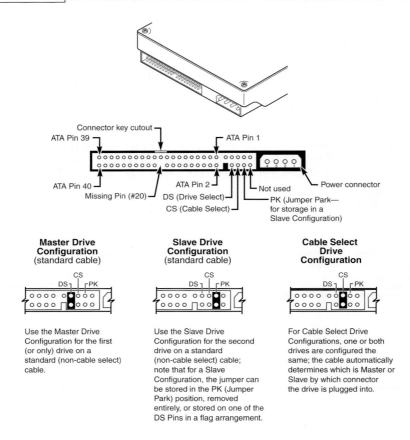

Figure 7.7   Parallel ATA (IDE) drive jumpers for most drives.

With cable select, the drive that receives signals on pin 28 automatically becomes the master, and the other becomes the slave. Most cables implement this by removing the metal insulation displacement bit from the pin-28 hole, which can be difficult to see at a glance. Other cables have a section of pin 28 visibly cut from the cable somewhere along the ribbon. Because this is such a minor modification to the cable and can be difficult to see, cable select cables typically have the connectors labeled master, slave, and system, indicating that the cable controls these options rather than the drive. All 80-conductor Ultra-ATA cables are designed to use cable select.

With cable select, you simply set the CS jumper on all drives and then plug the drive you want to be the master into the connector labeled master on the cable and the drive you want to be the slave into the connector labeled slave.

The only downside I see to using cable select is that it can restrict how the cable is routed or where you mount the drive that is to be master versus slave because they must be plugged in to specific cable connector positions.

Parallel ATA PIO Transfer Modes

ATA-2 and ATA-3 defined the first of several higher-performance modes for transferring data over the Parallel ATA interface, to and from the drive. These faster modes were the main part of the newer specifications and were the main reason they were initially developed. The following section discusses these modes.

The PIO (programmed I/O) mode determines how fast data is transferred to and from the drive using PIO transfers. In the slowest possible mode—PIO Mode 0—the data cycle time can't exceed 600 nanoseconds (ns). In a single cycle, 16 bits are transferred in to or out of the drive, making the theoretical transfer rate of PIO Mode 0 (600ns cycle time) 3.3MBps, whereas PIO Mode 4 (120ns cycle time) achieves a 16.6MBps transfer rate.

Table 7.6 shows the PIO modes, with their respective transfer rates.

Table 7.6   PIO Modes and Transfer Rates

PIO Mode	Bus Width (Bits)	Cycle Speed (ns)	Bus Speed (MHz)	Cycles per Clock	Transfer Rate (MBps)	ATA Specification
0	16	600	1.67	1	3.33	ATA-1
1	16	383	2.61	1	5.22	ATA-1
2	16	240	4.17	1	8.33	ATA-1
3	16	180	5.56	1	11.11	ATA-2
4	16	120	8.33	1	16.67	ATA-2

ATA-2 was also referred to as EIDE (Enhanced IDE) or Fast-ATA.

ns = nanoseconds (billionths of a second)

MB = million bytes

Most motherboards with ATA-2 or greater support have dual ATA connectors on the motherboard. Most of the motherboard chipsets include the ATA interface in their South Bridge components, which in most systems is tied into the PCI bus.

Older 486 and some early Pentium boards have only the primary connector running through the system's PCI local bus. The secondary connector on those boards usually runs through the ISA bus and therefore supports up to Mode 2 operation only.

When interrogated with an Identify Drive command, a hard disk returns, among other things, information about the PIO and DMA modes it is capable of using. Most enhanced BIOSs automatically set the correct mode to match the capabilities of the drive. If you set a mode faster than the drive can handle, data corruption results.

ATA-2 and newer drives also perform Block Mode PIO, which means they use the Read/Write Multiple commands that greatly reduce the number of interrupts sent to the host processor. This lowers the overhead, and the resulting transfers are even faster.

Parallel ATA DMA Transfer Modes

ATA drives also support *direct memory access (DMA)* transfers. DMA means that the data is transferred directly between drive and memory without using the CPU as an intermediary, as opposed to PIO. This has the effect of offloading much of the work of transferring data from the processor, in effect allowing the processor to do other things while the transfer is taking place.

There are two distinct types of direct memory access: singleword (8-bit) and multiword (16-bit) DMA. Singleword DMA modes were removed from the ATA-3 and later specifications and are obsolete. DMA modes are also sometimes called *busmaster* ATA modes because they use a host adapter that supports busmastering. Ordinary DMA relies on the legacy DMA controller on the motherboard to perform the complex task of arbitration, grabbing the system bus and transferring the data. In the case of busmastering DMA, all this is done by a higher-speed logic chip in the host adapter interface (which is also on the motherboard).

Systems using the Intel PIIX (PCI IDE ISA eXcelerator) and later South Bridge chips (or equivalent) have the capability of supporting busmaster ATA. The singleword and multiword busmaster ATA modes and transfer rates are shown in Tables 7.7 and 7.8.

Table 7.7   Singleword (8-bit) DMA Modes and Transfer Rates

8-bit DMA Mode	Bus Width (Bits)	Cycle Speed (ns)	Bus Speed (MHz)	Cycles per Clock	Transfer Rate (MBps)	ATA Specification
0	16	960	1.04	1	2.08	ATA-1*
1	16	480	2.08	1	4.17	ATA-1*
2	16	240	4.17	1	8.33	ATA-1*

Singleword (8-bit) DMA modes were removed from the ATA-3 and later specifications.

Table 7.8   Multiword (16-bit) DMA Modes and Transfer Rates

16-bit DMA Mode	Bus Width (Bits)	Cycle Speed (ns)	Bus Speed (MHz)	Cycles per Clock	Transfer Rate (MBps)	ATA Specification
0	16	480	2.08	1	4.17	ATA-1
1	16	150	6.67	1	13.33	ATA-2*
2	16	120	8.33	1	16.67	ATA-2*

ATA-2 was also referred to as EIDE (Enhanced IDE) or Fast-ATA.

Note that multiword DMA modes are also called busmaster DMA modes by some manufacturers. Unfortunately, even the fastest multiword DMA Mode 2 results in the same 16.67MBps transfer speed as PIO Mode 4. However, even though the transfer speed is the same as PIO, because DMA offloads much of the work from the processor, overall system performance is higher. Even so, multiword DMA modes were never very popular and have been superseded by the newer Ultra-DMA modes supported in devices that are compatible with ATA-4 through ATA-7.

Table 7.9 shows the Ultra-DMA modes now supported in the ATA-4 through ATA-7 specifications. Note that you need to install the correct drivers for your host adapter and version of Windows to use this feature.

Table 7.9   Ultra-DMA Support in ATA-4 Through ATA-7

Ultra DMA Mode	Bus Width (Bits)	Cycle Speed (ns)	Bus Speed (MHz)	Cycles per Clock	Transfer Rate (MBps)	ATA Specification
0	16	240	4.17	2	16.67	ATA-4
1	16	160	6.25	2	25.00	ATA-4
2	16	120	8.33	2	33.33	ATA-4
3	16	90	11.11	2	44.44	ATA-5
4	16	60	16.67	2	66.67	ATA-5
5	16	40	25.00	2	100.00	ATA-6
6	16	30	33.00	2	133.00	ATA-7

ATA-4 UDMA Mode 2 is sometimes called Ultra-ATA/33 or ATA-33.
ATA-5 UDMA Mode 4 is sometimes called Ultra-ATA/66 or ATA-66.
ATA-6 UDMA Mode 5 is sometimes called Ultra-ATA/100 or ATA-100.
ATA-7 UDMA Mode 6 is sometimes called Ultra-ATA/133 or ATA-133.

Serial ATA

With the development of ATA-8, it seems that the Parallel ATA standard that has been in use for more than 10 years has finally reached the end of the line. Sending data at rates faster than 133MBps down a parallel ribbon cable is fraught with all kinds of problems because of signal timing, electromagnetic interference (EMI), and other integrity problems. The solution is called Serial ATA, which is an evolutionary replacement for the venerable Parallel ATA physical storage interface. Serial ATA is software-compatible with Parallel ATA, which means it fully emulates all the commands, registers, and controls so existing software will run on the new architecture without any changes. In other words, the existing BIOSs, operating systems, and utilities that work on Parallel ATA also work on Serial ATA.

Of course, they do differ physically—that is, you can't plug Parallel ATA drives into Serial ATA host adapters, and vice versa, although signal converters make that possible. The physical changes are all for the better because Serial ATA uses much smaller and thinner cables with only seven conductors that are easier to route inside the PC and easier to plug in with smaller, redesigned cable connectors. The interface chip designs also are improved with far fewer pins and lower voltages. These improvements are all designed to eliminate the design problems inherent in Parallel ATA.

Figure 7.8 shows the official Serial ATA International Organization working group logo used to identify most Serial ATA devices.

Figure 7.8   Serial ATA official logo, which is used to identify SATA devices.

Although Serial ATA didn't immediately replace Parallel ATA, most new systems following Serial ATA's standardization included Serial ATA interfaces alongside Parallel ATA interfaces. Over time, SATA has predominantly replaced Parallel ATA as the de facto standard internal storage device interface found in PCs. The transition from ATA to SATA has been a gradual one, and during this transition Parallel ATA capabilities continue to be available.

Development for Serial ATA started when the Serial ATA Working Group effort was announced at the Intel Developer Forum in February 2000. The initial members of the Serial ATA Working Group included APT Technologies, Dell, IBM, Intel, Maxtor, Quantum, and Seagate. The original group later became known as the Serial ATA II Working Group, and finally in July 2004 it became the Serial ATA International Organization. The first Serial ATA 1.0 draft specification was released in November 2000 and was officially published as a final specification in August 2001. The first Serial ATA II Working Group extensions to this specification, which make Serial ATA suitable for network storage, were released in October 2002. The Serial ATA Revision 2.6 specification is the latest release. The released specifications can be downloaded from the Serial ATA International Organization website at http://www.serialata.org. Since forming, the group has grown to include more than 130 Contributor and Adopter companies from all areas of industry. Systems using Serial ATA were first released in late 2002 using discrete PCI interface boards and chips. SATA was finally integrated directly into the motherboard chipset in April 2003 with the introduction of the Intel ICH5 chipset component. Since then, most new motherboard chipsets have included Serial ATA.

The performance of SATA is impressive, although current hard drive designs can't fully take advantage of its bandwidth. This may change somewhat as hybrid drives incorporating larger flash memory caches arrive on the scene. Three variations of the standard have been proposed that all use the same cables and connectors; they differ only in transfer rate performance. Currently, only the first two speeds are available, with higher speeds coming in the future. Table 7.10 shows the specifications for the current and future proposed SATA versions; the second-generation 300MBps (3.0Gbps) version became available in 2005, whereas the third-generation 600MBps (6.0Gbps) versions aren't expected for several more years.

Table 7.10   Serial ATA Transfer Modes

SATA Type	Signal Rate (Gbps)	Bus Width (Bits)	Bus Speed (MHz)	Data Cycles per Clock	Throughput (MBps)
SATA-150	1.5	1	1500	1	150
SATA-300	3.0	1	3000	1	300
SATA-600	6.0	1	6000	1	600

From Table 7.10, you can see that Serial ATA sends data only a single bit at a time. The cable used has only seven wires (four signal and three ground) and is a very thin design, with keyed connectors only 14mm (0.55") wide on each end. This eliminates problems with airflow compared to the wider Parallel ATA ribbon cables. Each cable has connectors only at each end, and each cable connects the device directly to the host adapter (typically on the motherboard). There are no master/slave settings because each cable supports only a single device. The cable ends are interchangeable—the connector on the motherboard is the same as on the device, and both cable ends are identical. Maximum SATA cable length is 1 meter (39.37"), which is considerably longer than the 18" maximum for Parallel ATA. Even with this thinner, longer, and less-expensive cable, you initially get transfer rates of 150MBps (nearly 13% greater than Parallel ATA/133). Second-generation Serial ATA supports 300Mbps, and future variations of SATA will support 600Mbps.

Serial ATA uses a special encoding scheme called 8B/10B to encode and decode data sent along the cable. The 8B/10B transmission code originally was developed (and patented) by IBM in the early 1980s for use in high-speed data communications. Many high-speed data transmission standards, including Gigabit Ethernet, Fibre Channel, FireWire, and others, use this encoding scheme. The main purpose of the 8B/10B encoding scheme is to guarantee that there are never more than four 0s (or 1s) transmitted consecutively. This is a form of Run Length Limited (RLL) encoding called RLL 0,4, in which the 0 represents the minimum and the 4 represents the maximum number of consecutive 0s or 1s in each encoded character.

8B/10B encoding also ensures that there are never more than six or fewer than four 0s (or 1s) in a single encoded 10-bit character. Because 1s and 0s are sent as voltage changes on a wire, this ensures that the spacing between the voltage transitions sent by the transmitter is fairly balanced, with a more regular and steady stream of pulses. This presents a steadier load on the circuits, increasing reliability. The conversion from 8-bit data to 10-bit encoded characters for transmission leaves several 10-bit patterns unused. Many of these additional patterns are used to provide flow control, delimit packets of data, perform error checking, or perform other special functions.

Serial ATA Cables and Connectors

The physical transmission scheme for SATA uses *differential NRZ (Non Return to Zero)*. This uses a balanced pair of wires, each carrying +0.25V (one-quarter volt). The signals are sent differentially: If one wire in the pair carries +0.25V, the other wire carries -0.25V, where the differential voltage between the two wires is always 0.5V (one-half volt). So, for a given voltage waveform, the opposite voltage waveform is sent along the adjacent wire. Differential transmission minimizes electromagnetic radiation and makes the signals easier to read on the receiving end.

A 15-pin power cable and power connector is optional with SATA, providing 3.3V power in addition to the 5V and 12V provided via the industry-standard 4-pin device power connectors. Although it has 15 pins, this new power connector design is only 24mm (0.945"). With 3 pins designated for each of the 3.3V, 5V, and 12V power levels, enough capacity exists for up to 4.5 amps of current at each voltage, which is plenty for even the most power-hungry drives. For compatibility with existing power supplies, SATA drives can be made with the original, standard 4-pin device power connector or the new 15-pin SATA power connector—or both. If the drive doesn't have the type of connector you need, adapters are available to convert from one type to the other.

Figure 7.9 shows what the new SATA signal and power connectors look like.

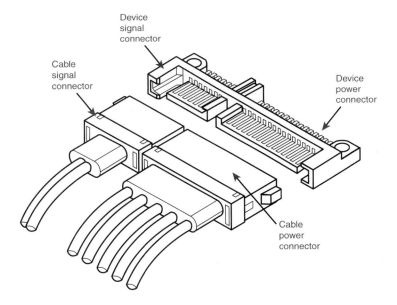

Figure 7.9   SATA (Serial ATA) signal and power connectors on a typical SATA hard drive.

Figure 7.10 shows SATA and Parallel ATA host adapters on a typical motherboard.

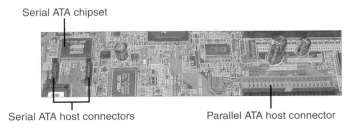

Figure 7.10   A motherboard with Serial and Parallel ATA host adapters.

The pinouts for the Serial ATA data and optional power connectors are shown in Tables 7.11 and 7.12, respectively.

Table 7.11   Serial ATA Data Connector Pinout

Signal Pin	Signal	Description
S1	Gnd	First mate
S2	A+	Host Transmit +
S3	A-	Host Transmit -
S4	Gnd	First mate
S5	B-	Host Receive -
S6	B+	Host Receive +
S7	Gnd	First mate

All pins are in a single row spaced 1.27mm (.050") apart.
All ground pins are longer so they will make contact before the signal/power pins to allow hot plugging.

Table 7.12   Serial ATA Optional Power Connector Pinout

Power Pin	Signal	Description
P1	+3.3V	3.3V power
P2	+3.3V	3.3V power
P3	+3.3V	3.3V power
P4	Gnd	First mate
P5	Gnd	First mate
P6	Gnd	First mate
P7	+5V	5V power
P8	+5V	5V power
P9	+5V	5V power
P10	Gnd	First mate
P11	Gnd	First mate
P12	Gnd	First mate
P13	+12V	12V power
P14	+12V	12V power
P15	+12V	12V power

All pins are in a single row spaced 1.27mm (.050") apart.
All ground pins are longer so they will make contact before the signal/power pins to allow hot-plugging.
Three power pins are used to carry 4.5 amps, a maximum current for each voltage.

Serial ATA Configuration

Configuration of Serial ATA devices is also much simpler because the master/slave or cable select jumper settings used with Parallel ATA are no longer necessary.

BIOS setup for Serial ATA drives is also quite simple. Because Serial ATA is based on ATA, autodetection of drive settings on systems with Serial ATA connectors is performed in the same way as on Parallel ATA systems. Depending on the system, Serial ATA interfaces might be enabled by default or might need to be enabled in the BIOS setup program (see Chapter 5, "BIOS," for details).

If you want to use Serial ATA drives but don't want to install a new motherboard with Serial ATA host adapters already included, you can install a separate Serial ATA host adapter into a PCI expansion slot (see Figure 7.11). Most of these adapters include ATA RAID functions.

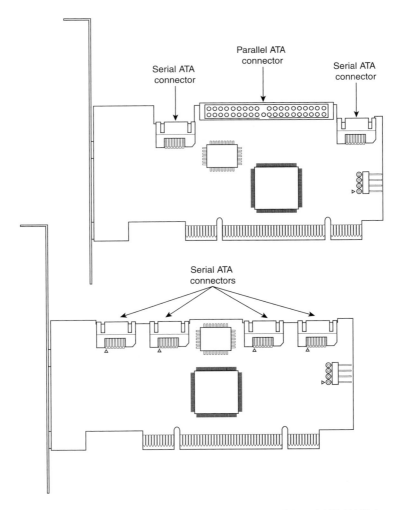

Figure 7.11 Typical two-channel (top) and four-channel (bottom) Serial ATA RAID host adapters. The two-channel adapter also includes a Parallel ATA host adapter.

Some of the first Serial ATA host adapters, such as models from HighPoint and 3Ware, use a Parallel-to-Serial ATA bridge technology that consumes as much as half of the available bandwidth. Other adapters, such as those made by Promise Technology, use native Serial ATA controller chips, which is a better solution in theory because it preserves all the bandwidth for use by the drive. However, current Serial ATA drives, like their Parallel ATA siblings, cannot transfer data at anything close to the 150MBps rate of the host adapter; 40MBps–50MBps is the typical range for average transfer speeds of 7200 rpm Serial ATA drives.

Second-generation Serial ATA

As with Parallel ATA, Serial ATA was designed to be the primary storage interface used inside a PC and was not initially designed to be used as an external interface. However, with Serial ATA Revision 2.x and later, Serial ATA is evolving to include several new features including:

- 3Gbit/sec transfer rate
- Advanced Host Controller Interface (AHCI)
- Native Command Queing (NCQ)
- Hot Plugging
- External SATA (eSATA)
- Port Multipliers
- Staggered Spin-Up

Because of the lower cost and smaller size of the internal cabling, it's no mystery as to why Serial ATA is overtaking Parallel ATA inside both desktop and laptop systems.

Advanced Host Controller Interface (AHCI)

Serial ATA was designed not only as a replacement for Parallel ATA, but also as an interface that would evolve into something with many more capabilities and features than its predecessor. Initially, compatibility with Parallel ATA was one of the most important features of Serial ATA because it enabled a smooth and easy transition from one to the other. This compatibility extends to the driver level, allowing Serial ATA devices to use the same BIOS-level drivers and software as legacy Parallel ATA devices.

Although the intent of Serial ATA was to allow an easy transition from Parallel ATA, it was also designed to allow future growth and expansion of capabilities. To accomplish this, an enhanced software interface called the Advanced Host Controller Interface (AHCI) was initially developed by the AHCI Contributor Group, a group chaired by Intel and originally consisting of AMD, Dell, Marvell, Maxtor, Microsoft, Red Hat, Seagate, and StorageGear. The AHCI Contributor Group released a preliminary version of AHCI v0.95 in May 2003 and released the 1.0 version of the specification in April 2004. The current version is 1.1, and can be downloaded from Intel at www.intel.com/technology/serialata/ahci.htm.

AHCI provides an industry-standard, high-performance interface to system driver/OS software for discovering and implementing such advanced SATA features as command queuing, hot-plugging, and power management. AHCI was integrated into Serial ATA–supporting chipsets in 2004 and is supported by AHCI drivers for Windows. The main idea behind AHCI is to have a single driver-level interface supported by all advanced SATA host adapters. This greatly simplifies the installation of operating systems, eliminating the need for custom SATA drivers for each different manufacturer's SATA host adapter. For example, Windows Vista includes AHCI drivers and will automatically support any advanced SATA host adapters that are AHCI compatible.

Unfortunately the AHCI drivers are not included by default on the Windows XP and earlier installation CDs, because AHCI was developed long after XP was released. This means, for example, that if you are installing Windows XP on a system with an integrated SATA host adapter set to AHCI mode, you will probably need to press the F6 key at the beginning of the installation and provide a floppy disk with the AHCI drivers; otherwise, Windows XP will not be able to recognize the drives. The implication here is that the system must include a floppy drive, and that you must have copied the drivers to a floppy disk in advance. But what if your system doesn't even include a floppy drive? Fortunately there are several solutions.

One option is to keep a spare floppy drive in your toolkit and temporarily connect it during the installation. Just open the case, plug in a floppy cable from the floppy drive connector (FDC) on the motherboard to the drive, and connect power to the drive. There is no need to actually mount the drive in the chassis, because you will only need to read the disk once at the beginning of the installation.

Another option is to set the SATA host adapter to ATA compatibility mode (disable AHCI) in the BIOS Setup, after which you can boot from a standard Windows XP CD and install Windows without requiring any special drivers. You could leave the adapter in compatibility mode, but you might be missing out on the performance offered by the advanced SATA II capabilities supported by your hard drives. Fortunately, you can easily reenable AHCI mode once Windows XP is installed. To do this, first download or copy the AHCI driver (that is, Intel Matrix Storage Manager Driver) to the hard disk and then enable AHCI in the BIOS Setup. During the next boot, Windows will see the "new" AHCI host adapter and automatically run the Found New Hardware Wizard, which you would instruct to install the AHCI drivers you previously downloaded. At this point, you would have Windows installed with the adapter in AHCI mode and the proper AHCI drivers loaded. Unfortunately, many non-Intel motherboards or motherboards using non-Intel chipsets don't support ATA compatibility mode, so this technique may not work for those boards.

Although the first two options can work in most situations, I think the best overall solution is to simply create a custom Windows XP installation disc that already has the SATA AHCI (and even RAID) drivers preinstalled. This can be accomplished via a somewhat tedious manual integration process for each different set of drivers, but to make things really easy you can use the menu-driven BTS DriverPacks from www.driverpacks.net to integrate virtually all of the popular mass storage drivers directly into your Windows XP install disc. The DriverPacks allow you to easily add all kinds of drivers to your Windows XP installation discs. For example, in addition to the mass storage drivers, I also like to integrate the various processor, chipset, and network (both wired and wireless) drivers, because all of these will still fit on a CD. If you are willing to move to a DVD instead of a CD, you can fit all of the available DriverPacks on a single DVD.

Serial ATA Transfer Modes

Serial ATA transfers data in a completely different manner from Parallel ATA. As indicated previously, the transfer rates are 1.5GBps (150MBps), 3.0GBps (300MBps), and 6.0GBps (600MBps), with most drives today supporting either the 1.5GBps or 3.0GBps rate. Note that speeds are backward compatible—for example, all drives supporting the 3.0GBps rate also work at 1.5GBps. Note that because SATA is designed to be backward compatible with Parallel ATA, some confusion can result because SATA drives can report speeds and modes that emulate Parallel ATA settings for backward compatibility. This means the drive is merely lying for backward compatibility with existing software.

For example, many motherboards detect and report a Serial ATA drive as supporting Ultra DMA Mode 5 (ATA/100), which is a Parallel ATA mode operating at 100MBps. This is obviously incorrect because even the slowest Serial ATA mode (1.5GBps) is 150MBps and Ultra DMA modes simply do not apply to Serial ATA drives.

Parallel and Serial ATA are completely different electrical and physical specifications, but Serial ATA does *emulate* Parallel ATA in a way that makes it completely software transparent. In fact, the Parallel ATA emulation in Serial ATA specifically conforms to the ATA-5 specification.

This is especially apparent in the IDENTIFY DEVICE command used by the autodetect routines in the BIOS to read the drive parameters. The Serial ATA specification indicates that many of the items returned by IDENTIFY DEVICE are to be "set as indicated in ATA/ATAPI-5," including available UDMA modes and settings.

The SATA 1 specification also says, "Emulation of parallel ATA device behavior, as perceived by the host BIOS or software driver, is a cooperative effort between the device and the Serial ATA host adapter hardware. The behavior of Command and Control Block registers, PIO and DMA data transfers, resets, and interrupts are all emulated. The host adapter contains a set of registers that shadow the contents of the traditional device registers, referred to as the Shadow Register Block. All Serial ATA devices behave like Device 0 devices. Devices shall ignore the DEV bit in the Device/Head field of received Register FISs, and it is the responsibility of the host adapter to gate transmission of Register FISs to devices, as appropriate, based on the value of the DEV bit."

This means the shadow register blocks are "fake" Parallel ATA registers, allowing all ATA commands, modes, and so on to be emulated. Serial ATA was designed to be fully software compatible with ATA/ATAPI-5, which is why a Serial ATA drive can report in some ways as if it were Parallel ATA or running in Parallel ATA modes, even though it isn't.

ATA Features

The ATA standards have gone a long way toward eliminating incompatibilities and problems with interfacing IDE drives to ISA/PCI bus systems. The ATA specifications define the signals on the 40-pin connector, the functions and timings of these signals, cable specifications, and so on. The following section lists some of the elements and functions defined by the ATA specifications.

ATA Commands

One of the best features of the ATA interface is the enhanced command set. The ATA interface was modeled after the WD1003 controller IBM used in the original AT system. All ATA drives must support the original WD command set (eight commands) with no exceptions, which is why ATA drives are so easy to install in systems today. All IBM-compatible systems have built-in ROM BIOS support for the WD1003, so they essentially support ATA as well.

In addition to supporting all the WD1003 commands, the ATA specification added numerous other commands to enhance performance and capabilities. These commands are an optional part of the ATA interface, but several of them are used in most drives available today and are very important to the performance and use of ATA drives in general.

Perhaps the most important is the IDENTIFY DRIVE command. This command causes the drive to transmit a 512-byte block of data that provides all details about the drive. Through this command, any program (including the system BIOS) can find out exactly which type of drive is connected, including the drive manufacturer, model number, operating parameters, and even the serial number of the drive. Many modern BIOSs use this information to automatically receive and enter the drive's parameters into CMOS memory, eliminating the need for the user to enter these parameters manually during system configuration. This arrangement helps prevent mistakes that can later lead to data loss when the user no longer remembers what parameters he used during setup.

The Identify Drive data can tell you many things about your drive, including the following:

- Number of logical block addresses available using LBA mode
- Number of physical cylinders, heads, and sectors available in P-CHS mode
- Number of logical cylinders, heads, and sectors in the current translation L-CHS mode

- Transfer modes (and speeds) supported
- Manufacturer and model number
- Internal firmware revision
- Serial number
- Buffer type/size, indicating sector buffering or caching capabilities

Several freely available programs can execute this command and report the information onscreen, including ATAINF, which is available as part of a free collection of diagnostic tools called the Ultimate Boot CD. You can download the entire disc or most of the utilities individually from http://ultimatbootcd.com. I find these programs especially useful when I am trying to install ATA drives on a system that has a user-defined drive type but doesn't support autodetection and I need to know the correct parameters for a user-definable BIOS type. These programs get the information directly from the drive.

Two other important commands are the Read Multiple and Write Multiple commands. These commands permit multiple-sector data transfers and, when combined with block-mode PIO capabilities in the system, can result in incredible data-transfer rates many times faster than single-sector PIO transfers. Some older systems require you to select the correct number of sectors supported by the drive, but most recent systems automatically determine this information for you.

Many other enhanced commands are available, including room for a given drive manufacturer to implement what are called *vendor-unique* commands. Certain vendors often use these commands for features unique to that vendor. Often, vendor-unique commands control features such as low-level formatting and defect management. This is why low-level format programs can be so specific to a particular manufacturer's ATA drives and why many manufacturers make their own LLF programs available.

ATA Security Mode

Support for hard disk passwords (called ATA Security Mode) was added to the ATA-3 specification during 1995. The proposal adopted in the ATA specification was originally from IBM, which had developed this capability and had already begun incorporating it into ThinkPad systems and IBM 2.5" drives. Because it was then incorporated into the official ATA-3 standard (finally published in 1997), most other drive and system manufacturers have also adopted this, especially for laptop systems and 2.5" drives. Note that these passwords are *very* secure. Also, if you lose or forget them, they usually cannot be recovered and you will never be able to access the drive. More on that later....

Hard disk security passwords are set via the BIOS Setup, and not all systems support this feature. Most laptops support hard disk security, but most desktops do not. If supported, two types of hard disk passwords can be set, called user and master. The user password locks and unlocks the disk, whereas the master password is used to only unlock. You can set only a user password, or you can set user+master, but you cannot set a master password alone.

When a user password is set (with no master), or when both user+master passwords are set, access to the drive is prevented (even if the drive is moved to a different system), unless the user (or master) password is entered upon system startup.

The master password is designed to be an alternative or backup password for system administrators as a master unlock. With both master and user passwords set, the user is told the user password but not the master password. Subsequently, the user can change the user password as desired; however, a system administrator can still gain access by using the master password.

If a user or user+master password is set, the disk must be unlocked at boot time via a BIOS-generated password prompt. The appearance of the prompt varies from system to system, but in IBM systems the prompt is graphical. An icon consisting of a cylinder with a number above it (indicating the drive number) next to a padlock appears onscreen. If the hard disk password prompt appears, you must enter it; otherwise, you will be denied access to the drive and the system will not boot.

As I said earlier, if you forget the user password (with no master) or both the user and master passwords (if both are set), you will not be able to gain access to the drive, even if you move it to another system and even if the other system does not support ATA Security Mode. The drive will have essentially become a paper weight.

As with many security features, a workaround might be possible if you forget your password. In this case, at least one company can either restore the drive to operation (with all the data lost) or restore the drive and the data. That company is Nortek (see http://www.nortek.on.ca for more information). The password-removal procedure costs $85–$295, and you must provide proof of ownership when you send in the drive. As you can see, the cost is generally more than the cost of a new drive, so it is worthwhile only if you absolutely need the data back.

Hard disk passwords are not preset on a brand-new drive, but they might be preset if you are buying a used drive or if the people or company you purchased the drive or system from entered them. This is a common ploy when selling drives or systems on eBay—for example, the seller might set supervisor or hard disk passwords and hold them until payment is received. Or he might be selling a used product "as is," for which he doesn't have the passwords, which renders them useless to the purchaser. Because of this, I *never* recommend purchasing a laptop or hard drive used unless you are certain that no supervisor or hard disk passwords are set.

Most systems also support other power-on or supervisor passwords in the BIOS Setup. In most systems, when you set a supervisor password, it automatically sets the hard disk password to the same value as well. In most cases, if a supervisor password is set and it matches the hard disk user or master password, when you enter the supervisor password, the BIOS automatically enters the hard disk password at the same time. This means that even though a hard disk password is set, you might not even know it because the hard disk password is entered automatically at the same time as you enter the supervisor password; therefore, you won't see a separate prompt for the hard disk password. However, if the drive is later separated from the system, it will not work on another system until the correct hard disk password is entered. Without the services of a company such as Nortek, you can remove a hard disk password only if you know the password to begin with.

Host Protected Area

Most PCs sold on the market today include some form of automated product recovery or restoration feature that allows a user to easily restore the operating system and other software on the system to the state it was in when the system was new. Originally, this was accomplished via one or more product-recovery CDs containing automated scripts that reinstalled all the software that came preinstalled on the system when it was new.

Unfortunately, the CDs could be lost or damaged, they were often problematic to use, and including them by default cost manufacturers a lot of money. This prompted PC manufacturers to move the recovery software to a hidden partition of the boot hard drive. However, this does waste some space on the drive; the recovery software normally fits on from one to four CDs, which occupies 1GB–3GB of drive space. With 60GB or larger drives, this amounts to 5% or less of the total space. Still, even the hidden partition was less than satisfactory because the partition could easily be damaged or overwritten by partitioning software or other utilities, so there was no way to make it secure.

In 1996, Gateway proposed a change to the ATA-4 standard under development that would allow a space called the *host protected area (HPA)* to be reserved on a drive. This change was ratified, and the HPA feature set was incorporated into the ATA-4 specification that was finally published in 1998. A separate BIOS firmware interface specification called Protected Area Run Time Interface Extension Services (PARTIES) was initiated in 1999 that defined services an operating system could use to access the HPA. The PARTIES standard was completed and published in 2001 as "NCITS 346-2001, Protected Area Run Time Interface Extension Services."

The HPA works by using the optional ATA SET MAX ADDRESS command to make the drive appear to the system as a slightly smaller drive. Anything from the new max address (the newly reported end of the drive) to the true end of the drive is considered the HPA and is accessible only using PARTIES commands. This is more secure than a hidden partition because any data past the end of the drive simply cannot be seen by any normal application, or even a partitioning utility such as PartitionMagic or Partition Commander. Still, if you want to remove the HPA, you can use some options in the BIOS Setup or separate commands to reset the max address, thus exposing the HPA. At that point, you can run something such as PartitionMagic or Partition Commander to resize the adjacent partition to include the extra space that was formerly hidden and unavailable.

Most new systems using Phoenix BIOS come with their recovery software and diagnostics in the HPA because this is part of the new Phoenix BIOS core, which is used by a large number of OEMs (including IBM/Lenovo) on most desktop and laptop systems starting in 2003.

◄◄ For more information on the HPA and what might be stored there, see "Preboot Environment," p. 474.

ATA Packet Interface

ATA Packet Interface (ATAPI) is a standard designed to provide the commands necessary for devices such as optical drives, removable media drives such as SuperDisk and Zip, and tape drives that plug in to an ordinary ATA (IDE) connector. The principal advantage of ATAPI hardware is that it's cheap and works on your current adapter. For optical drives, it has a somewhat lower CPU usage compared to proprietary adapters, but there's no performance gain otherwise. For tape drives, ATAPI has the potential for superior performance and reliability compared to the popular floppy controller attached tape devices. Although ATAPI optical drives use the hard disk interface, this does not mean they look like ordinary hard disks. To the contrary, from a software point of view, they are a completely different kind of animal. They most closely resemble a SCSI device. All modern ATA optical drives support the ATAPI protocols, and generally the terms are synonymous. In other words, an ATAPI optical drive is an ATA optical drive, and vice versa.

Caution

Most systems starting in 1998 began supporting the Phoenix El Torito specification, which enables booting from ATAPI CD or DVD drives. Systems without El Torito support in the BIOS can't boot from an ATAPI CD or DVD drive. Even with ATAPI support in the BIOS, you still must load a driver to use ATAPI under DOS or Windows. Windows 95 and later (including 98 and Me) and Windows NT (including Windows 2000, XP, and Vista) have native ATAPI support. Some versions of the Windows 98 and Me CD-ROMs are bootable, whereas all NT, 2000, XP, and Vista discs are directly bootable on those systems, thus greatly easing installation.

I normally recommend keeping ATA devices you will be accessing simultaneously on separate channels. Because ATA does not typically support overlapping access, when one drive is being accessed on a given channel, the other drive on the same channel can't be accessed. By keeping the CD-ROM and hard disk on separate channels, you can more effectively overlap accessing between them. One other caveat is that a Parallel ATA device such as a hard drive might be incapable of functioning if another Parallel ATAPI device (CD or DVD drive) is master. Therefore, in most cases, you should try to set Parallel ATA hard drives as master (device 0) and Parallel ATAPI drives as slave (device 1) on a given cable.

ATA Drive Capacity Limitations

ATA interface versions up through ATA-5 suffered from a drive capacity limitation of about 137GB (billion bytes). Depending on the BIOS used, this limitation can be further reduced to 8.4GB, or even as low as 528MB (million bytes). This is due to limitations in both the BIOS and the ATA interface, which when combined create even further limitations. To understand these limits, you have to look at the BIOS (software) and ATA (hardware) interfaces together.

Note

In addition to the BIOS/ATA limitations discussed in this section, various operating system limitations also exist. These are described later in this chapter.

The limitations when dealing with ATA drives are those of the ATA interface itself as well as the BIOS interface used to talk to the drive. A summary of the limitations is shown in Table 7.13.

This section details the differences between the various sector-addressing methods and the limitations incurred by using them.

Prefixes for Decimal and Binary Multiples

Many readers are unfamiliar with the MiB (mebibyte), GiB (gibibyte), and so on designations I am using in this section and throughout the book. These are part of a standard designed to eliminate confusion between decimal- and binary-based multiples, especially in computer systems. Standard SI (system international or metric system) units are based on multiples of 10. This worked well for most things, but not for computers, which operate in a binary world where most numbers are based on powers of 2. This has resulted in different meanings being assigned to the same prefix—for example 1KB (kilobyte) could mean either 1,000 (10^3) bytes or 1,024 (2^{10}) bytes. To eliminate confusion, in December 1998 the International Electrotechnical Commission (IEC) approved as an international standard the prefix names and symbols for binary multiples used in data processing and transmission. Some of these prefixes are shown in Table 7.14.

Under this standard terminology, MB (megabyte) would be 1,000,000 bytes, whereas MiB (mebibyte) would be 1,048,576 bytes.

Note

For more information on these industry-standard decimal and binary prefixes, check out the National Institute for Standards and Technology (NIST) website at physics.nist.gov/cuu/Units/prefixes.html.

Table 7.13   ATA/IDE Capacity Limitations for Various Sector Addressing Methods

Sector Addressing Method	Total Sectors Calculation	Maximum Total Sectors	Maximum Capacity (Bytes)	Capacity (Decimal)	Capacity (Binary)
CHS: BIOS w/o TL	1024×16×63	1,032,192	528,482,304	528.48MB	504.00MiB
CHS: BIOS w/bit-shift TL	1024×240×63	15,482,880	7,927,234,560	7.93GB	7.38GiB
CHS: BIOS w/LBA-assist TL	1024×255×63	16,450,560	8,422,686,720	8.42GB	7.84GiB
CHS: BIOS INT13h	1024×256×63	16,515,072	8,455,716,864	8.46GB	7.88GiB
CHS: ATA-1/ATA-5	65536×16×255	267,386,880	136,902,082,560	136.90GB	127.50GiB
LBA: ATA-1/ATA-5	2^{28}	268,435,456	137,438,953,472	137.44GB	128.00GiB
LBA: ATA-6+	2^{48}	281,474,976,710,655	144,115,188,075,855,872	144.12PB	128.00PiB
LBA: EDD BIOS	2^{64}	18,446,744,073,709,551,616	9,444,732,965,739,290,427,392	9.44ZB	8.00ZiB

BIOS = Basic input/output system
ATA = AT Attachment (IDE)
CHS = Cylinder head sector
LBA = Logical block (sector) address
w/ = with
w/o = without
TL = Translation
INT13h = Interrupt 13 hex
EDD = Enhanced Disk Drive specification (Phoenix/ATA)
MB = megabyte (million bytes)
MiB = mebibyte
GB = gigabyte (billion bytes)
GiB = gibibyte
PB = petabyte (quadrillion bytes)
PiB = pebibyte
ZB = zettabyte (sextillion bytes)
ZiB = zebibyte

Table 7.14 Standard Prefix Names and Symbols for Decimal and Binary Multiples

Decimal Prefixes:				Binary Prefixes:				
Factor	Symbol	Name	Value	Factor	Symbol	Name	Derivation	Value
10^3	k	Kilo	1,000	210	Ki	Kibi	Kilobinary	1,024
10^6	M	Mega	1,000,000	220	Mi	Mebi	Megabinary	1,048,576
10^9	G	Giga	1,000,000,000	230	Gi	Gibi	Gigabinary	1,073,741,824
10^{12}	T	Tera	1,000,000,000,000	240	Ti	Tebi	Terabinary	1,099,511,627,776
10^{15}	P	Peta	1,000,000,000,000,000	250	Pi	Pebi	Petabinary	1,125,899,906,842,624
10^{18}	E	Exa	1,000,000,000,000,000,000	260	Ei	Exbi	Exabinary	1,152,921,504,606,846,976
10^{21}	Z	Zetta	1,000,000,000,000,000,000,000	270	Zi	Zebi	Zettabinary	1,180,591,620,717,411,303,424

Note that the symbol for kilo (k) is in lowercase (which is technically correct according to the SI standard), whereas all other decimal prefixes are uppercase.

BIOS Limitations

Motherboard ROM BIOSs have been updated throughout the years to support larger and larger drives. Table 7.15 shows the most important relative dates when drive capacity limits were changed.

Table 7.15   Dates of Changes to Drive Capacity Limitations in the ROM BIOS

BIOS Date	Capacity Limit
August 1994	528MB
January 1998	8.4GB
September 2002	137GB

These are when the limits were broken, such that BIOSs older than August 1994 are generally limited to drives of up to 528MB, whereas BIOSs older than January 1998 are generally limited to 8.4GB. Most BIOSs dated 1998 or newer support drives up to 137GB, and those dated September 2002 or newer should support drives larger than 137GB. These are only general guidelines, though; to accurately determine this for a specific system, you should check with your motherboard manufacturer. You can also use the BIOS Wizard utility from http://www.unicore.com/bioswiz/index2.html, which will tell you the BIOS date from your system and specifically whether your system supports the Enhanced Hard Disk Drive specification (which means drives over 8.4GB).

If your BIOS does not support EDD (drives over 8.4GB), the three possible solutions are as follows:

- Upgrade your motherboard BIOS to a 1998 or newer version that supports >8.4GB.
- Install a BIOS upgrade card, such as the UltraATA cards from www.siig.com.
- Install a software patch to add >8.4GB support.

Of these, the first one is the most desirable because it is usually free. Visit your motherboard manufacturer's website to see whether it has any newer BIOSs available for your motherboard that will support large drives. If it doesn't, the next best thing is to use a card such as one of the UltraATA cards from SIIG (www.siig.com). I almost never recommend the software-only solution because it merely installs a software patch in the boot sector area of the hard drive, which can result in numerous problems when booting from different drives, installing new drives, or recovering data.

CHS Versus LBA

There are two primary methods to address (or number) sectors on an ATA drive. The first method is called *CHS (cylinder head sector)* after the three respective coordinate numbers used to address each sector of the drive. The second method is called *LBA (logical block address)* and uses a single number to address each sector on a drive. CHS was derived from the physical way drives were constructed (and is how they work internally), whereas LBA evolved as a simpler and more logical way to number the sectors regardless of the internal physical construction.

▶▶ For more information on cylinders, heads, and sectors as they are used internally within the drive, see "Hard Disk Drive Operation," p. 668.

The process of reading a drive sequentially in CHS mode starts with cylinder 0, head 0, and sector 1 (which is the first sector on the disk). Next, all the remaining sectors on that first track are read; then the next head is selected; and then all the sectors on that track are read—and so on until all the heads on the first cylinder are read. Then the next cylinder is selected, and the sequence starts again. Think of CHS as an odometer of sorts: The sector numbers must roll over before the head number can change, and the head numbers must roll over before the cylinder can change.

The process of reading a drive sequentially in LBA mode starts with sector 0, then read 1, then 2, and so on. The first sector on the drive in CHS mode would be 0,0,1, and the same sector in LBA mode would be 0.

As an example, imagine a drive with one platter, two heads (both sides of the platter are used), two tracks on each platter (cylinders), and two sectors on each track. We would say the drive has two cylinders (tracks per side), two heads (sides), and two sectors per track. This would result in a total capacity of eight (2×2×2) sectors. Noting that cylinders and heads begin numbering from 0—whereas physical sectors on a track number from 1—using CHS addressing, we would say the first sector on the drive is cylinder 0, head 0, sector 1 (0,0,1); the second sector is 0,0,2; the third sector is 0,1,1; the fourth sector is 0,1,2; and so on until we get to the last sector, which would be 1,1,2.

Now imagine that we could take the eight sectors and—rather than refer directly to the physical cylinder, head, and sector—number the sectors in order from 0 to 7. Thus, if we wanted to address the fourth sector on the drive, we could reference it as sector 0,1,2 in CHS mode or as sector 3 in LBA mode. Table 7.16 shows the correspondence between CHS and LBA sector numbers for this eight-sector imaginary drive.

Table 7.16   CHS and LBA Sector Numbers for an Imaginary Drive with Two Cylinders, Two Heads, and Two Sectors per Track (Eight Sectors Total)

Mode	Equivalent Sector Numbers							
CHS:	0,0,1	0,0,2	0,1,1	0,1,2	1,0,1	1,0,2	1,1,1	1,1,2
LBA:	0	1	2	3	4	5	6	7

As you can see from this example, using LBA numbers is simpler and generally easier to handle; however, when the PC was first developed, all BIOS and ATA drive-level addressing was done using CHS addressing.

CHS/LBA and LBA/CHS Conversions

You can address the same sectors in either CHS or LBA mode. The conversion from CHS to LBA is always consistent in that for a given drive, a particular CHS address always converts to a given LBA address, and vice versa. The ATA-1 document specifies a simple formula that can be used to convert CHS parameters to LBA:

$$LBA = (((C \times HPC) + H) \times SPT) + S - 1$$

By reversing this formula, you can convert the other way—that is, from LBA back to CHS:

$$C = int (LBA / SPT / HPC)$$

$$H = int ((LBA / SPT) \bmod HPC)$$

$$S = (LBA \bmod SPT) + 1$$

For these formulas, the abbreviations are defined as follows:

LBA = Logical block address

C = Cylinder

H = Head

S = Sector

HPC = Heads per cylinder (total number of heads)

SPT = Sectors per track

int X = Integer portion of X

X mod Y = Modulus (remainder) of X/Y

Using these formulas, you can calculate the LBA for any given CHS address, and vice versa. Given a drive of 16,383 cylinders, 16 heads, and 63 sectors per track, Table 7.17 shows the equivalent CHS and LBA addresses.

Table 7.17   Equivalent CHS and LBA Sector Numbers for a Drive with 16,383 Cylinders, 16 Heads, and 63 Sectors per Track (16,514,064 Sectors Total)

Cylinder	Head	Sector	LBA
0	0	1	0
0	0	63	62
0	1	0	63
999	15	63	1,007,999
1,000	0	1	1,008,000
9,999	15	63	10,079,999
10,000	0	1	10,080,000
16,382	15	63	16,514,063

BIOS Commands Versus ATA Commands

In addition to the two methods of sector addressing (CHS or LBA), there are two levels of interface where sector addressing occurs. One interface is where the operating system talks to the BIOS (using driver commands); the other is where the BIOS talks to the drive (using ATA commands). The specific commands at these levels are different, but both support CHS and LBA modes. Figure 7.12 illustrates the two interface levels.

When the operating system talks to the BIOS to read or write sectors, it issues commands via software interrupt (not the same as an IRQ) INT13h, which is how the BIOS subroutines for disk access are called. Various INT13h subfunctions allow sectors to be read or written using either CHS or LBA addressing. The BIOS routines then convert the BIOS commands into ATA hardware-level commands, which are sent over the bus I/O ports to the drive controller. Commands at the ATA hardware level can also use either CHS or LBA addressing, although the limitations are different. Whether your BIOS and drive use CHS or LBA addressing depends on the drive capacity, age of the BIOS and drive, BIOS Setup settings used, and operating system used.

CHS Limitations (the 528MB Barrier)

The original BIOS-based driver for hard disks is accessed via software interrupt 13h (13 hex) and offers functions for reading and writing drives at the sector level. Standard INT13h functions require that a particular sector be addressed by its cylinder, head, and sector location—otherwise known as *CHS addressing*. This interface is used by the operating system and low-level disk utilities to access the drive. IBM originally wrote the INT13h interface for the BIOS on the PC XT hard disk controller in 1983, and in 1984 the company incorporated it into the AT motherboard BIOS. This interface used numbers to define the particular cylinder, head, and sector being addressed. Table 7.18, which shows the standard INT13h BIOS CHS parameter limits, includes the maximum values for these numbers.

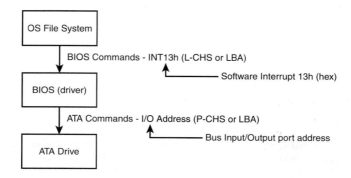

Figure 7.12   The relationship between BIOS and physical sector addressing. (In this figure, L-CHS stands for Logical CHS, and P-CHS stands for Physical CHS.)

Table 7.18   INT13h BIOS CHS Parameter Limits

Field	Field Size	Maximum Value	Range	Total Usable
Cylinder	10 bits	1024	0–1023	1024
Head	8 bits	256	0–255	256
Sector	6 bits	64	1–63	63

The concept of a maximum value given a number of digits is simple: If you had, for example, a hotel with two-digit decimal room numbers, you could have only 100 (10^2) rooms, numbered 0–99. The CHS numbers used by the standard BIOS INT13h interface are binary, and with a 10-bit number being used to count cylinders, you can have only 1,024 (2^{10}) maximum, numbered 0–1023. Because the head is identified by an 8-bit number, the maximum number of heads is 256 (2^8), numbered 0–255. Finally, with sectors per track there is a minor difference. Sectors on a track are identified by a 6-bit number, which would normally allow a maximum of 64 (2^6) sectors; however, because sectors are numbered starting with 1 (instead of 0), the range is limited to 1–63, which means a total of 63 sectors per track is the maximum the BIOS can handle.

These BIOS limitations are true for all BIOS versions or programs that rely on CHS addressing. Using the maximum numbers possible for CHS at the BIOS level, you can address a drive with 1,024 cylinders, 256 heads, and 63 sectors per track. Because each sector is 512 bytes, the math works out as follows:

```
                Max. Values
     --------------------------
      Cylinders         1,024
         Heads            256
  Sectors/Track            63
     =========================
  Total Sectors     16,515,072
     --------------------------
  Total Bytes   8,455,716,864
  Megabytes (MB)        8,456
  Mebibytes (MiB)       8,064
  Gigabytes (GB)          8.4
  Gibibytes (GiB)         7.8
```

From these calculations, you can see that the maximum capacity drive addressable via the standard BIOS INT13h interface is about 8.4GB (where GB equals roughly 1 billion bytes), or 7.8GiB (where GiB means *gigabinarybytes*).

Unfortunately, the BIOS INT13h limits are not the only limitations that apply. Limits also exist in the ATA interface itself. The ATA CHS limits are shown in Table 7.19.

Table 7.19   Standard ATA CHS Parameter Limitations

Field	Field Size	Maximum Value	Range	Total Usable
Cylinder	16 bits	65536	0–65535	65536
Head	4 bits	16	0–15	16
Sector	8 bits	256	1–255	255

As you can see, the ATA interface uses different-sized fields to store CHS values. Note that the ATA limits are higher than the BIOS limits for cylinders and sectors but lower than the BIOS limit for heads. The CHS limits for capacity according to the ATA-1 through ATA-5 specification are as follows:

```
                 Max. Values
- - - - - - - - - - - - - - - - - - - - - - - - - -
     Cylinders         65,536
        Heads              16
Sectors/Track             255
===================================
Total Sectors    267,386,880
- - - - - - - - - - - - - - - - - - - - - - - - - -
Total Bytes   136,902,082,560
Megabytes (MB)       136,902
Mebibytes (MiB)      130,560
Gigabytes (GB)         136.9
Gibibytes (GiB)        127.5
```

When you combine the limitations of the BIOS and ATA CHS parameters, you end up with the situation shown in Table 7.20.

Table 7.20   Combined BIOS and ATA CHS Parameter Limits

	BIOS CHS Parameter Limits	ATA CHS Parameter Limits	Combined CHS Parameter Field Limits
Cylinder	1,024	65,536	1,024
Head	256	16	16
Sector	63	255	63
Total sectors	16,515,072	267,386,880	1,032,192
Maximum capacity	8.4GB	136.9GB	528MB

As you can see, the lowest common denominator of the combined CHS limits results in maximum usable parameters of 1,024 cylinders, 16 heads, and 63 sectors, which results in a maximum drive capacity of 528MB. This became known as the *528MB barrier* (also called the *504MiB barrier*), and it affects virtually all PCs built in 1993 or earlier.

CHS Translation (Breaking the 528MB Barrier)

Having a barrier limiting drive capacity to 528MB or less wasn't a problem when the largest drives available were smaller than that. But by 1994, drive technology had developed such that making drives larger than what the combined BIOS and ATA limitations could address was possible. Clearly a fix for the problem was needed.

Starting in 1993, the BIOS developer Phoenix Technologies began working on BIOS extensions to work around the combined CHS limits. In January 1994 the company released the "BIOS Enhanced Disk Drive (EDD) Specification," which was later republished by the T13 committee (also responsible for ATA) as "BIOS Enhanced Disk Drive Services (EDD)." The EDD documents detail several methods for circumventing the limitations of older BIOSs without causing compatibility problems with existing software. These include the following:

- BIOS INT13h extensions supporting 64-bit LBA
- Bit-shift geometric CHS translation
- LBA-assist geometric CHS translation

The method for dealing with the CHS problem was called *translation* because it enabled additional subroutines in the BIOS to translate CHS parameters from ATA maximums to BIOS maximums (and vice versa). In an effort to make its methods standard among the entire PC industry, Phoenix released the EDD document publicly and allowed the technology to be used free of charge, even among its competitors such as AMI and Award. The T13 committee in charge of ATA subsequently adopted the EDD standard and incorporated it into official ATA documents.

Starting in 1994, most BIOSs began implementing the Phoenix-designed CHS translation methods, which enabled drives up to the BIOS limit of 8.4GB to be supported. The fix involved what is termed *parameter translation* at the BIOS level, which adapted or translated the cylinder, head, and sector numbers to fit within the allowable BIOS parameters. There are two types of translation: One works via a technique called *CHS bit-shift* (usually called "Large" or "Extended CHS" in the BIOS Setup), and the other uses a technique called *LBA-assist* (usually called "LBA" in the BIOS Setup). These refer to the different mathematical methods of doing essentially the same thing: converting one set of CHS numbers to another.

CHS bit-shift translation manipulates the cylinder and head numbers but does not change the sector number. It begins with the physical (drive reported) cylinders and heads and, using some simple division and multiplication, comes up with altered numbers for the cylinders and heads. The sectors-per-track value is not translated and is passed unaltered. The term *bit-shift* is used because the division and multiplication math is actually done in the BIOS software by shifting bits in the CHS address.

With CHS bit-shift translation, the drive reported (physical) parameters are referred to as *P-CHS*, and the BIOS-altered logical parameters are referred to as *L-CHS*. After the settings are made in the BIOS Setup, L-CHS addresses are automatically translated to P-CHS at the BIOS level. This enables the operating system to send commands to the BIOS using L-CHS parameters, which the BIOS automatically converts to P-CHS when it talks to the drive using ATA commands. Table 7.21 shows the rules for calculating CHS bit-shift translation.

CHS bit-shift translation is based on dividing the physical cylinder count by a power of 2 to bring it under the 1,024 cylinder BIOS INT13h limit and then multiplying the heads by the same power of 2, leaving the sector count unchanged. The power of 2 used depends on the cylinder count, as indicated in Table 7.21.

Table 7.21   CHS Bit-Shift Translation Rules

Physical (Drive Reported) Cylinders	Physical Heads	Logical Cylinders	Logical Heads	Max. Capacity
1 < C <= 1,024	1 < H <= 16	C = C	H = H	528MB
1,024 < C <= 2,048	1 < H <= 16	C = C/2	H = H×2	1GB
2,048 < C <= 4,096	1 < H <= 16	C = C/4	H = H×4	2.1GB
4,096 < C <= 8,192	1 < H <= 16	C = C/8	H = H×8	4.2GB
8,192 < C <= 16,384	1 < H <= 16	C = C/16	H = H×16	8.4GB

The drive reported sector count is not translated.

The logical heads value can't exceed 255 with some operating systems, such as DOS/Win9x/Me.

Here is an example of CHS bit-shift translation:

```
                                       Bit-shift
                          P-CHS           L-CHS
                      Parameters      Parameters
        ---------------------------------------------
        Cylinders          8,000           1,000
            Heads             16             128
     Sectors/Track             63              63
        =============================================
     Total Sectors      8,064,000       8,064,000
        ---------------------------------------------
       Total Bytes  4,128,768,000   4,128,768,000
     Megabytes (MB)          4,129           4,129
    Mebibytes (MiB)          3,938           3,938
     Gigabytes (GB)           4.13            4.13
    Gibibytes (GiB)           3.85            3.85
```

This example shows a drive with 8,000 cylinders and 16 heads. The physical cylinder count is way above the BIOS limit of 1,024, so if CHS bit-shift translation is selected in the BIOS Setup, the BIOS then divides the cylinder count by 2, 4, 8, or 16 to bring it below 1,024. In this case, it would divide by 8, which results in a new logical cylinder count of 1,000—which is below the 1,024 maximum. Because the cylinder count is divided by 8, the head count is then multiplied by the same number, resulting in 128 logical heads, which is also below the limit the BIOS can handle.

So, although the drive reports having 8,000 cylinders and 16 heads, the BIOS and all software (including the operating system) instead see the drive as having 1,000 cylinders and 128 heads. Note that the 63 sectors/track figure is simply carried over without change. The result is that by using the logical parameters, the BIOS can see the entire 4.13GB drive and won't be limited to just the first 528MB.

When you install a drive, you don't have to perform the translation math to convert the cylinders and heads; the BIOS does that for you automatically. All you have to do is allow the BIOS to autodetect the P-CHS parameters and then enable the translation in the BIOS Setup. Selecting Large or ECHS translation in the BIOS Setup enables the CHS bit-shift. The BIOS does the rest of the work for you.

CHS bit-shift is a simple and fast (code-wise) scheme that can work with all drives, but unfortunately it can't properly translate all theoretically possible drive geometries for drives under 8.4GB. To solve this, an addendum was added to the ATA-2 specification to specifically require drives to report certain ranges of geometries to allow bit-shift translation to work. Thus, all drives that conform to the ATA-2 specification (or higher) can be translated using this method.

The 2.1GB and 4.2GB Barriers

Some BIOSs incorrectly allocated only 12 bits for the P-CHS cylinder field, thereby allowing a maximum of 4,096 cylinders. Combined with the standard 16-head and 63-sector limits, this resulted in the inability to support any drives over 2.1GB in capacity. Fortunately, this BIOS defect affected only a limited number of systems with BIOS dates prior to about mid-1996.

Even so, some problems still existed with bit-shift translation. Because of the way DOS and Windows 9x/Me were written, they could not properly handle a drive with 256 heads. This was a problem for drives larger than 4.2GB because the CHS bit-shift translation rules typically resulted in 256 heads as a logical value, as seen in the following example:

```
                                      Bit-shift
                         P-CHS          L-CHS
                      Parameters      Parameters
--------------------------------------------------
      Cylinders          12,000             750
          Heads              16             256
   Sectors/Track              63              63
==================================================
   Total Sectors      12,096,000      12,096,000
--------------------------------------------------
     Total Bytes   6,193,152,000   6,193,152,000
   Megabytes (MB)          6,193           6,193
  Mebibytes (MiB)          5,906           5,906
  Gigabytes (GB)            6.19            6.19
  Gibibytes (GiB)           5.77            5.77
```

This scheme failed when you tried to install Windows 9x/Me (or DOS) on a drive larger than 4.2GB because the L-CHS parameters included 256 heads. Any BIOS that implemented this scheme essentially had a 4.2GB barrier, so installing a drive larger than that and selecting CHS bit-shift translation caused the drive to fail. Note that this was not a problem for Windows NT or later.

Note

It is interesting to note that the BIOS is not actually at fault here; the problem instead lies with the DOS/Win9x/Me file system code, which stores the sector per track number as an 8-bit value. The number 256 causes a problem because 256 equals 100000000b, which takes 9 bits to store. The value 255 (which equals 11111111b) is the largest value that can fit in an 8-bit binary register and is therefore the maximum number of heads those operating systems can support.

To solve this problem, CHS bit-shift translation was revised by adding a rule such that if the drive reported 16 heads and more than 8,192 cylinders (which would result in a 256-head translation), the P-CHS head value would be assumed to be 15 (instead of 16) and the P-CHS cylinder value would be multiplied by 16/15 to compensate. These adjusted cylinder and head values would then be translated. The following example shows the results:

```
                                      Bit-shift     Revised Bit-
                         P-CHS          L-CHS       shift L-CHS
                      Parameters      Parameters     Parameters
----------------------------------------------------------------
      Cylinders          12,000             750            800
          Heads              16             256            240
```

Sectors/Track	63	63	63
Total Sectors	12,096,000	12,096,000	12,096,000
Total Bytes	6,193,152,000	6,193,152,000	6,193,152,000
Megabytes (MB)	6,193	6,193	6,193
Mebibytes (MiB)	5,906	5,906	5,906
Gigabytes (GB)	6.19	6.19	6.19
Gibibytes (GiB)	5.77	5.77	5.77

As you can see from this example, a drive with 12,000 cylinders and 16 heads translates to 750 cylinders and 256 heads using the standard CHS bit-shift scheme. The revised CHS bit-shift scheme rule does a double translation in this case, first changing the 16 heads to 15 and then multiplying the 12,000 cylinders by 16/15, resulting in 12,800 cylinders. Then, the new cylinder value is CHS bit-shift-translated by dividing it by 16, resulting in 800 logical cylinders. Likewise, the 15 heads are multiplied by 16, resulting in 240 logical heads. If the logical cylinder count calculates to over 1,024, it is truncated to 1,024. In this case, what started out as 12,000 cylinders and 16 heads P-CHS becomes 800 cylinders and 240 heads (instead of 750 cylinders and 256 heads) L-CHS, which works around the bug in the DOS/Win9x/Me operating systems.

So far, all my examples have been very clean—that is, the L-CHS parameters have calculated to the same capacity as the P-CHS parameters. Unfortunately, it doesn't always work out that way. The following example shows a more typical example in the real world. Several 8.4GB drives from Maxtor, Quantum, Seagate, and others report 16,383 cylinders and 16 heads P-CHS. For those drives, the translations would work out as follows:

	P-CHS Parameters	Bit-shift L-CHS Parameters	Revised Bit-shift L-CHS Parameters
Cylinders	16,383	1,023	1,024
Heads	16	256	240
Sectors/Track	63	63	63
Total Sectors	16,514,064	16,498,944	15,482,880
Total Bytes	8,455,200,768	8,447,459,328	7,927,234,560
Megabytes (MB)	8,455	8,447	7,927
Mebibytes (MiB)	8,064	8,056	7,560
Gigabytes (GB)	8.46	8.45	7.93
Gibibytes (GiB)	7.87	7.87	7.38

Note that the revised CHS bit-shift translation rules result in supporting only 7.93GB of the 8.46GB total on the drive. In fact, the parameters shown (with 240 heads) are the absolute maximum that revised CHS bit-shift supports. Fortunately, another translation mode is available that improves this situation.

LBA-assist Translation

The LBA-assist translation method places no artificial limits on the reported drive geometries, but it works only on drives that support LBA addressing at the ATA interface level. Fortunately, though, virtually all ATA drives larger than 2GB support LBA. LBA-assist translation takes the CHS parameters the drive reports, multiplies them together to get a calculated LBA maximum value (total number of sectors), and then uses this calculated LBA number to derive the translated CHS parameters. Table 7.22 shows the rules for LBA-assist translation.

Table 7.22   LBA-assist Translation Rules

Total Sectors	Logical Cylinders	Logical Heads	Logical Sectors
1 < T <= 1,032,192	T/1,008	16	63
1,032,192 < T <= 2,064,384	T/2,016	32	63
2,064,384 < T <= 4,128,768	T/4,032	64	63
4,128,768 < T <= 8,257,536	T/8,064	128	63
8,257,536 < T <= 16,450,560	T/16,065	255	63

T = Total sectors, calculated by multiplying the drive-reported P-CHS parameters (C×H×S)

LBA-assist translation fixes the sectors at 63 no matter what and divides and multiplies the cylinders and heads by predetermined values depending on the total number of sectors. This results in a set of L-CHS parameters the operating system uses to communicate with the BIOS. The L-CHS numbers are then translated to LBA numbers at the ATA interface level. Because LBA mode is more flexible at translating, it should be used in most cases instead of CHS bit-shift.

Normally, both the CHS bit-shift and LBA-assist translations generate the same L-CHS geometry for a given drive. This should always be true if the drive reports 63 sectors per track and 4, 8, or 16 heads. In the following example, both translation schemes result in identical L-CHS values:

```
                                Revised bit-      LBA-assist
                    P-CHS       shift L-CHS        L-CHS
                    Parameters  Parameters         Parameters
      -----------------------------------------------------------
      Cylinders     8,192       1,024              1,024
      Heads         16          128                128
      Sectors/Track 63          63                 63
      =============================================================
      Total Sectors 8,257,536   8,257,536          8,257,536
      -------------------------------------------------------------
      Total Bytes   4,227,858,432  4,227,858,432  4,227,858,432
      Megabytes (MB) 4,228      4,228              4,228
      Mebibytes (MiB) 4,032     4,032              4,032
      Gigabytes (GB) 4.23       4.23               4.23
      Gibibytes (GiB) 3.94      3.94               3.94
```

However, if the drive reports a value other than 63 sectors per track or has other than 4, 8, or 16 heads, LBA-assist translation does not result in the same parameters as CHS bit-shift translation. In the following example, different translations result:

```
                                Revised bit-      LBA-assist
                    P-CHS       shift L-CHS        L-CHS
                    Parameters  Parameters         Parameters
      -----------------------------------------------------------
      Cylinders     16,383      1,024              1,024
      Heads         16          240                255
      Sectors/Track 63          63                 63
      =============================================================
      Total Sectors 16,514,064  15,482,880         16,450,560
      -------------------------------------------------------------
      Total Bytes   8,455,200,768  7,927,234,560  8,422,686,720
      Megabytes (MB) 8,455      7,927              8,423
```

Mebibytes (MiB)	8,064	7,560	8,033
Gigabytes (GB)	8.46	7.93	8.42
Gibibytes (GiB)	7.87	7.38	7.84

The LBA-assist translation supports 8.42GB, which is nearly 500MB more than the revised CHS bit-shift translation. More importantly, these translations are different, which can result in problems if you change translation modes with data on the drive. If you were to set up and format a drive using CHS bit-shift translation and then change to LBA-assist translation, the interpreted geometry could change and the drive could then become unreadable until it is repartitioned and reformatted (which would destroy all the data). Bottom line: After you select a translation method, don't plan on changing it unless you have your data securely backed up.

Virtually all PC BIOS since 1994 have translation capability in the BIOS Setup, and virtually all offer both translation modes as well as an option to disable translation entirely. If both CHS bit-shift and LBA-assist translation modes are offered, you should probably choose the LBA method of translation because it is the more efficient and flexible of the two. LBA-assist translation also gets around the 4.2GB operating system bug because it is designed to allow a maximum of 255 logical heads no matter what.

You usually can tell whether your BIOS supports translation by the capability to specify more than 1,024 cylinders in the BIOS Setup, although this can be misleading. The best clue is to look for the translation setting parameters in the ATA/IDE drive setup page in the BIOS Setup. See Chapter 5, "BIOS," for more information on how to enter the BIOS Setup on your system. If you see drive-related settings, such as LBA or ECHS (sometimes called Large or Extended), these are telltale signs of a BIOS with translation support. Most BIOSs with a date of 1994 or later include this capability, although some AMI BIOS versions from the mid-1990s locate the LBA setting on a screen different from the hard drive configuration screen. If your system currently does not support parameter translation, you might be able to get an upgrade from your motherboard manufacturer or install a BIOS upgrade card with this capability, such as the LBA Pro card from eSupport.com.

Table 7.23 summarizes the four ways today's BIOSs can handle addressing sectors on the drive: Standard CHS (no translation), Extended CHS translation, LBA translation, and pure LBA addressing.

Table 7.23   Drive Sector Addressing Methods

BIOS Mode	OS to BIOS	BIOS to Drive
Standard (Normal), no translation	P-CHS	P-CHS
CHS Bit-Shift (ECHS) translation	L-CHS	P-CHS
LBA-Assist (LBA) translation	L-CHS	LBA
Pure LBA (EDD BIOS)	LBA	LBA

Standard CHS has only one possible translation step internal to the drive. The drive's actual physical geometry is completely invisible from the outside with all zoned recorded ATA drives today. The cylinders, heads, and sectors printed on the label for use in the BIOS Setup are purely logical geometry and do not represent the actual physical parameters. Standard CHS addressing is limited to 16 heads and 1,024 cylinders, which provides a limit of 504MiB (528MB).

This is often called "Normal" in the BIOS Setup and causes the BIOS to behave like an old-fashioned one without translation. Use this setting if your drive has fewer than 1,024 cylinders or if you want to use the drive with an operating system that doesn't require translation.

ECHS, or "Large" in the BIOS Setup, is CHS bit-shift, and most BIOS from 1997 and later use the revised method (240 logical heads maximum).

LBA, as selected in the BIOS Setup, indicates LBA-assist translation, not pure LBA mode. This enables software to operate using L-CHS parameters while the BIOS talks to the drive in LBA mode.

The only way to select a pure LBA mode, from the OS to the BIOS as well as from the BIOS to the drive, is with a drive that is over 8.4GB. All drives over 137GB must be addressed via LBA at both the BIOS and drive levels, and most PC BIOSs automatically address any drive over 8.4GB in that manner, as well. In that case, no special BIOS Setup settings are necessary, other than setting the type to auto or autodetect.

Caution

A word of warning with these BIOS translation settings: If you have a drive 8.4GB or less in capacity and switch between Standard CHS, ECHS, or LBA, the BIOS can change the (translated) geometry. The same thing can happen if you transfer a disk that has been formatted on an old, non-LBA computer to a new one that uses LBA. This causes the logical CHS geometry seen by the operating system to change and the data to appear in the wrong location from where it actually is! This can cause you to lose access to your data if you are not careful. I always recommend recording the CMOS Setup screens associated with the hard disk configuration so you can properly match the setup of a drive to the settings to which it was originally set. This does not affect drives over 8.4GB because in those cases pure LBA is automatically selected.

The 8.4GB Barrier

Although CHS translation breaks the 528MB barrier, it runs into another barrier at 8.4GB. Supporting drives larger than 8.4GB requires leaving CHS behind and changing from CHS to LBA addressing at the BIOS level. The ATA interface had always supported LBA addressing, even in the original ATA-1 specification. One problem was that LBA support at the ATA level originally was optional, but the main problem was that there was no LBA support at the BIOS interface level. You could set LBA-assist translation in the BIOS Setup, but all that did was convert the drive LBA numbers to CHS numbers at the BIOS interface level.

Phoenix Technologies recognized that the BIOS interface needed to move from CHS to LBA early on and, beginning in 1994, published the "BIOS Enhanced Disk Drive Specification (EDD)," which addressed this problem with new extended INT13h BIOS services that worked with LBA rather than CHS addresses.

To ensure industry-wide support and compatibility for these new BIOS functions, in 1996 Phoenix turned this document over to the International Committee on Information Technology Standards (INCITS) T13 technical committee for further enhancement and certification as a standard called the "BIOS Enhanced Disk Drive Specification (EDD)." Starting in 1998, most of the other BIOS manufacturers began installing EDD support in their BIOS, enabling BIOS-level LBA mode support for ATA drives larger than 8.4GB. Coincidentally (or not), this support arrived just in time because ATA drives of that size and larger became available that same year.

The EDD document describes new extended INT13h BIOS commands that allow LBA addressing up to 2^{64} sectors, which results in a theoretical maximum capacity of more than 9.44ZB (zettabytes, or quadrillion bytes). That is the same as saying 9.44 trillion GB, which is 9.44×10^{21} bytes or, to be more precise, 9,444,732,965,739,290,427,392 bytes! I say theoretical capacity because even though by 1998 the BIOS could handle up to 2^{64} sectors, ATA drives were still using only 28-bit addressing (2^{28} sectors) at the ATA interface level. This limited an ATA drive to 268,435,456 sectors, which was a capacity of

137,438,953,472 bytes, or 137.44GB. Thus, the 8.4GB barrier had been broken, but another barrier remained at 137GB because of the 28-bit LBA addressing used in the ATA interface. The numbers work out as follows:

```
                         Max. Values
--------------------------------------
Total Sectors            268,435,456
--------------------------------------
Total Bytes          137,438,953,472
Megabytes (MB)               137,439
Mebibytes (MiB)              131,072
Gigabytes (GB)                137.44
Gibibytes (GiB)               128.00
```

By using the new extended INT13h 64-bit LBA mode commands at the BIOS level, as well as the existing 28-bit LBA mode commands at the ATA level, no translation would be required and the LBA numbers would be passed unchanged. The combination of LBA at the BIOS as well as the ATA interface levels meant that the clumsy CHS addressing could finally die. This also means that when you install an ATA drive larger than 8.4GB in a PC that has an EDD-capable BIOS (1998 or newer), both the BIOS and the drive are automatically set to use LBA mode.

An interesting quirk is that to allow backward compatibility when you boot an older operating system that doesn't support LBA mode addressing (DOS or the original release of Windows 95, for example), most drives larger than 8.4GB report 16,383 cylinders, 16 heads, and 63 sectors per track, which is 8.4GB. For example, this enables a 120GB drive to be seen as an 8.4GB drive by older BIOSs or operating systems. That sounds strange, but I guess having a 120GB drive being recognized as an 8.4GB is better than not having it work at all. If you did want to install a drive larger than 8.4GB into a system dated before 1998, the recommended solution is either a motherboard BIOS upgrade or an add-on BIOS card with EDD support.

The 137GB Barrier and Beyond

By 2001 the 137GB barrier had become a problem because 3 1/2" hard drives were poised to breach that capacity level. The solution came in the form of ATA-6, which was being developed during that year. To enable the addressing of drives of greater capacity, ATA-6 upgraded the LBA functions from using 28-bit numbers to using larger 48-bit numbers.

The ATA-6 specification extends the LBA interface such that it can use 48-bit sector addressing. This means that the maximum capacity is increased to 2^{48} (281,474,976,710,656) total sectors. Because each sector stores 512 bytes, this results in the maximum drive capacity shown here:

```
                         Max. Values
--------------------------------------------
Total Sectors        281,474,976,710,656
--------------------------------------------
Total Bytes      144,115,188,075,855,872
Megabytes (MB)           144,115,188,076
Mebibytes (MiB)          137,438,953,472
Gigabytes (GB)               144,115,188
Gibibytes (GiB)              134,217,728
Terabytes (TB)                   144,115
Tebibytes (TiB)                  131,072
Petabytes (PB)                    144.12
Pebibytes (PiB)                   128.00
```

As you can see, the 48-bit LBA in ATA-6 allows a capacity of just over 144PB (petabytes = quadrillion bytes)!

Because the EDD BIOS functions use a 64-bit LBA number, they have a much larger limit:

```
                         Max. Values
------------------------------------------------
Total Sectors    18,446,744,073,709,551,616
------------------------------------------------
Total Bytes     9,444,732,965,739,290,427,392
Megabytes (MB)      9,444,732,965,739,290
Mebibytes (MiB)     9,007,199,254,740,992
Gigabytes (GB)          9,444,732,965,739
Gibibytes (GiB)         8,796,093,022,208
Terabytes (TB)              9,444,732,966
Tebibytes (TiB)             8,589,934,592
Petabytes (PB)                  9,444,733
Pebibytes (PiB)                 8,388,608
Exabytes (EB)                       9,445
Exbibytes (EiB)                     8,192
Zettabytes (ZB)                      9.44
Zebibytes (ZiB)                      8.00
```

Although the BIOS services use 64-bit LBA (allowing up to 2^{64} sectors) for even greater capacity, the 144 petabyte ATA-6 limitation is the lowest common denominator that would apply. Still, that should hold us for some time to come.

Because hard disk drives have been doubling in capacity every 1.5 to 2 years (a corollary of Moore's Law), I estimate that it will take us until sometime between the years 2031 and 2041 before we reach the 144PB barrier (assuming hard disk technology hasn't been completely replaced by then). Similarly, I estimate that the 9.44ZB EDD BIOS barrier won't be reached until between the years 2055 and 2073! Phoenix originally claimed that the EDD specification would hold us until 2020, but it seems they were being quite conservative.

The 137GB barrier proved a bit more complicated than previous barriers because, in addition to BIOS issues, operating system issues also had to be considered.

Internal ATA drives larger than 137GB require 48-bit LBA (logical block address) support. This support absolutely needs to be provided in the OS, but it can also be provided in the BIOS. It is best if both the OS and BIOS provide this support, but it can be made to work if only the OS has the support.

To have 48-bit LBA support in the OS requires one of the following:

- Windows XP with Service Pack 1 (SP1) or later.
- Windows 2000 with Service Pack 4 (SP4) or later.
- Windows 98/98SE/Me or NT 4.0 with the Intel Application Accelerator (IAA) loaded. This solution works only if your motherboard has an IAA-supported chipset. See http://www.intel.com/support/chipsets/IAA/ for more information.

To have 48-bit LBA support in the BIOS requires either of the following:

- A motherboard BIOS with 48-bit LBA support (most of those dated September 2002 or later)
- An ATA host adapter card with onboard BIOS that includes 48-bit LBA support

If your motherboard BIOS does not have the support and an update is not available from your motherboard manufacturer, you may be able to use a card. Promise Technology (www.promise.com) makes several different PCI cards with either PATA or SATA interfaces as well as an onboard BIOS that adds 48-bit LBA support.

Note that if you have both BIOS and OS support, you can simply install and use the drive like any other. If you have no BIOS support, but you do have OS support, portions of the drive past 137GB are not recognized or accessible until the OS is loaded. If you are installing the OS to a blank hard drive and booting from an original XP (pre-SP1) CD or earlier, you need to partition and install up to the first 137GB of the drive at installation time. After installing the OS and then the SP1 update, you can either partition the remainder of the drive using standard partitioning software or use a third-party partitioning program such as PartitionMagic or Partition Commander to resize the first partition to use the full drive. If you are booting from an XP SP1 or later CD, you can recognize and access the entire drive during the OS installation and partition the entire drive as a single partition greater than 137GB, if you want.

Finally, keep in mind that the original version of Windows XP, as well as Windows 2000/NT or Windows 95/98/Me, does not provide native support for ATA hard drives that are larger than 137GB. However, as indicated earlier, that can easily be solved by loading the appropriate service packs or the Intel Application Accelerator.

Operating System and Other Software Limitations

Note that if you use older software, including utilities, applications, or even operating systems that rely exclusively on CHS parameters, these items will see all drives over 8.4GB as 8.4GB only. You will need not only a newer BIOS, but also newer software designed to handle the direct LBA addressing to work with drives over 8.4GB.

Operating system limitations with respect to drives over 8.4GB are shown in Table 7.24.

Table 7.24   Operating System Limitations

Operating System	Limitations for Hard Drive Size
DOS/Windows 3x	DOS 6.22 or lower can't support drives greater than 8.4GB. DOS 7.0 or higher (included with Windows 95 or later) is required to recognize a drive over 8.4GB.
Windows 9x/Me	Windows 95a (original version) does support the INT13h extensions, which means it does support drives over 8.4GB; however, due to limitations of the FAT16 file system, the maximum individual partition size is limited to 2GB. Windows 95B/OSR2 and later (including Windows 98/Me) support the INT13h extensions, which allows drives over 8.4GB, and they also support FAT32, which allows partition sizes up to the maximum capacity of the drive. However, Windows 95 doesn't support hard drives larger than 32GB because of limitations in its design. Windows 98 requires an update to FDISK to partition drives larger than 64GB.
Windows NT	Windows NT 3.5x does not support drives greater than 8.4GB. Windows NT 4.0 does support drivers greater than 8.4GB; however, when a drive larger than 8.4GB is being used as the primary bootable device, Windows NT will not recognize more than 8.4GB. Microsoft has released Service Pack 4, which corrects this problem.
Windows 2000/XP/Vista	Windows 2000, XP, and Vista support drives greater than 8.4GB.
OS/2 Warp	Some versions of OS/2 are limited to a boot partition size of 3.1GB or 4.3GB. IBM has a Device Driver Pack upgrade that enables the boot partition to be as large as 8.4GB. The HPFS file system in OS/2 will support drives up to 64GB.
Novell	NetWare 5.0 and later support drives greater than 8.4GB.

In the case of operating systems that support drives over 8.4GB, the maximum drive size limitations are dependent on the BIOS and hard drive interface standard, not the OS. Instead, other limitations come into play for the volumes (partitions) and files that can be created and managed by the various operating systems. These limitations are dependent on not only the operating system involved, but also the file system that is used for the volume. Table 7.25 shows the minimum and maximum volume (partition) size and file size limitations of the various Windows operating systems. As noted in the previous section, the original version of XP, as well as Windows 2000/NT or Windows 95/98/Me, does not currently provide native support for ATA hard drives that are larger than 137GB. You will need to use Vista or XP with Service Pack 1 or later installed to use an ATA drive over 137GB. This does not affect drives interfaced via USB, FireWire, SCSI, or other interfaces.

Table 7.25   Operating System Volume/File Size Limitations by File System

OS Limitations by File System	FAT16	FAT32	NTFS
Min. Volume Size (9x/Me)	2.092MB	33.554MB	—
Max. Volume Size (95)	2.147GB	33.554MB	—
Max. Volume Size (98)	2.147GB	136.902GB	—
Max. Volume Size (Me)	2.147GB	8.796TB	—
Min. Volume Size (NT+)	2.092MB	33.554MB	1.000MB
Max. Volume Size (NT+)	4.294GB	8.796GB	281.475TB
Max. File Size (all)	4.294GB	4.294GB	16.384TB

— = not applicable
NT+ = Windows NT, 2000, XP and Vista
MB = megabyte = 1,000,000 bytes
GB = gigabyte = 1,000,000,000 bytes
TB = terabyte = 1,000,000,000,000 bytes

PATA/SATA RAID

RAID is an acronym for *redundant array of independent (or inexpensive) disks* and was designed to improve the fault tolerance and performance of computer storage systems. RAID was first developed at the University of California at Berkeley in 1987, and was designed so that a group of smaller, less expensive drives could be interconnected with special hardware and software to make them appear as a single larger drive to the system. By using multiple drives to act as one drive, increases in fault tolerance and performance could be realized.

Initially, RAID was conceived to simply enable all the individual drives in the array to work together as a single, larger drive with the combined storage space of all the individual drives added up. However, this actually reduced reliability and didn't do much for performance, either. For example, if you had four drives connected in an array acting as one drive, you would be four times as likely to experience a drive failure than if you used just a single larger drive. To improve the reliability and performance, the Berkeley scientists proposed six levels (corresponding to different methods) of RAID. These levels provide varying emphasis on either fault tolerance (reliability), storage capacity, performance, or a combination of the three.

Although it no longer exists, an organization called the RAID Advisory Board (RAB) was formed in July 1992 to standardize, classify, and educate on the subject of RAID. The RAB developed specifications for RAID, a conformance program for the various RAID levels, and a classification program for RAID hardware.

The RAID Advisory Board defined seven standard RAID levels, called RAID 0–6. RAID typically is implemented by a RAID controller board, although software-only implementations are possible (but not recommended). The levels are as follows:

- **RAID Level 0: Striping**—File data is written simultaneously to multiple drives in the array, which act as a single larger drive. This offers high read/write performance but very low reliability. Requires a minimum of two drives to implement.

- **RAID Level 1: Mirroring**—Data written to one drive is duplicated on another, providing excellent fault tolerance (if one drive fails, the other is used and no is data lost) but no real increase in performance as compared to a single drive. Requires a minimum of two drives to implement (same capacity as one drive).

- **RAID Level 2: Bit-level ECC**—Data is split one bit at a time across multiple drives, and error correction codes (ECCs) are written to other drives. This is intended for storage devices that do not incorporate ECC internally (all SCSI and ATA drives have internal ECC). It's a standard that theoretically provides high data rates with good fault tolerance, but seven or more drives are required for greater than 50% efficiency, and no commercial RAID 2 controllers and/or drives without ECC are available.

- **RAID Level 3: Striped with parity**—Combines RAID Level 0 striping with an additional drive used for parity information. This RAID level is really an adaptation of RAID Level 0 that sacrifices some capacity, for the same number of drives. However, it also achieves a high level of data integrity or fault tolerance because data usually can be rebuilt if one drive fails. Requires a minimum of three drives to implement (two or more for data and one for parity).

- **RAID Level 4: Blocked data with parity**—Similar to RAID 3 except data is written in larger blocks to the independent drives, offering faster read performance with larger files. Requires a minimum of three drives to implement (two or more for data and one for parity).

- **RAID Level 5: Blocked data with distributed parity**—Similar to RAID 4 but offers improved performance by distributing the parity stripes over a series of hard drives. Requires a minimum of three drives to implement (two or more for data and one for parity).

- **RAID Level 6: Blocked data with double distributed parity**—Similar to RAID 5 except parity information is written twice using two different parity schemes to provide even better fault tolerance in case of multiple drive failures. Requires a minimum of four drives to implement (two or more for data and two for parity).

Additional RAID levels exist that were not supported by the RAID Advisory Board, but instead are custom implementations specific companies have used. Note that a higher number doesn't necessarily mean increased performance or fault tolerance; the numbered order of the RAID levels was entirely arbitrary.

At one time virtually all RAID controllers were SCSI based, meaning they used SCSI drives. For a professional setup, SCSI RAID is definitely the best choice because it combines the advantages of RAID with the advantages of SCSI—an interface that already was designed to support multiple drives. Now, however, SATA RAID controllers are available that allow for even less expensive RAID implementations, and most new motherboards have integrated SATA RAID support as well.

Most ATA RAID implementations are much simpler than the professional SCSI RAID adapters used on network file servers. ATA RAID is designed more for the individual who is seeking performance or simple drive mirroring for redundancy. When set up for performance, ATA RAID adapters typically run RAID Level 0, which incorporates data striping. Unfortunately, RAID 0 also sacrifices reliability such that if one drive fails, all data is lost. With RAID 0, performance scales up with the number of drives you add in the array. If you use four drives, you won't necessarily have four times the performance of a single drive, but it can be close to that for sustained transfers. Some overhead is still involved in the controller performing the striping and issues still exist with latency—that is, how long it takes to find the data—but performance will be higher than any single drive can normally achieve.

When set up for reliability, ATA RAID adapters generally run RAID Level 1, which is simple drive mirroring. All data written to one drive is written to the other. If one drive fails, the system can continue to work on the other drive. Unfortunately, this does not increase performance at all, and it also means you get to use only half of the available drive capacity. In other words, you must install two drives, but you get to use only one (the other is the mirror). However, in an era of high capacities and low drive prices, this is not a significant issue.

Combining performance with fault tolerance requires using one of the other RAID levels, such as RAID 5. For example, virtually all professional RAID controllers used in network file servers are designed to use RAID Level 5. Controllers that implement RAID Level 5 used to be very expensive, and RAID 5 requires that at least three drives must be connected. Many RAID controllers enable combinations of the RAID levels—such as 0 and 1 combined. This usually requires four drives, two of which are striped together in a RAID Level 0 arrangement, which is then redundantly written to a second set of two drives in a RAID Level 1 arrangement. This enables you to have approximately double the performance of a single drive, and you have a backup set should one of the primary sets fail.

A typical low-cost SATA RAID controller enables four to six drives to be attached, and you can run them in RAID Level 0, 1, 5, or 0+1 mode. Four-channel Parallel ATA RAID cards are available, but most RAID cards have moved to Serial ATA, which doesn't have the master/slave channel-sharing problems of Parallel ATA. Serial ATA RAID cards use a separate Serial ATA data channel (cable) for each drive, allowing maximum performance. I recommend Serial ATA RAID over Parallel ATA for best performance.

If you are considering an SATA RAID controller (or a motherboard with an integrated SATA RAID controller), things to look for include the following:

- RAID levels supported. (Most better ones support 0, 1, 5 and 0+1 combined, a lack of RAID 5 support indicates a very low-end product)
- Four, six, or eight channels.
- Support for 3Gbits/sec Serial ATA transfer rates.
- PCIe bus interface for best performance and future compatiblity.

If you want to experiment with RAID inexpensively, you can implement software based RAID without a custom controller when using certain operating systems. For example, Windows NT/2000 and later provide a software implementation for RAID using both striping and mirroring. In these operating systems, the Disk Administrator tool is used to set up and control the RAID functions, as well as to reconstruct the volume when a failure has occurred. Normally, though, if you want performance and reliability, you should look for Serial ATA RAID controllers that support RAID Level 5.

Magnetic Storage Principles

Magnetic Storage

Permanent or semipermanent computer data storage works by either optical or magnetic principles—or, in some cases, a combination of the two. In the case of magnetic storage, a stream of binary computer data bits (0s and 1s) is stored by magnetizing tiny pieces of metal embedded on the surface of a disk or tape in a pattern that represents the data. Later, this magnetic pattern can be read and converted back into the exact same stream of bits you started with. This is the principle of magnetic storage and the subject of this chapter.

Magnetic storage is often difficult for people to understand because magnetic fields can't be seen by the human eye. This chapter explains the principles, concepts, and techniques behind modern computer magnetic storage, enabling you to understand what happens behind the scenes. This information is designed for those who have an insatiable curiosity about how these things work; it is not absolutely necessary to know this to use a PC or perform routine troubleshooting, maintenance, or upgrades. Because the data I store on my hard drives, tape drives, floppy drives, and other magnetic storage devices happens to be far more important to me than the devices themselves, knowing how my data is handled makes me feel much more comfortable with the system in general. Having an understanding of the underlying technology does help when it comes to dealing with problems that might arise.

This chapter covers magnetic storage principles and technology and can be considered an introduction to several other chapters in the book, including the following:

- Chapter 9, "Hard Disk Storage"
- Chapter 10, "Removable Storage"

- Chapter 11, "Optical Storage"
- Chapter 12, "Physical Drive Installation and Configuration"

Consult these chapters for more specific information on various types of magnetic and optical storage, as well as drive installation and configuration.

History of Magnetic Storage

Before there was magnetic storage for computers, the primary storage medium was punch cards (paper cards with holes punched in to indicate character or binary data), originally invented by Herman Hollerith for use in the 1890 Census. What amazes me is that I missed contact with punch cards by about a year; the college I went to discontinued using them during my freshman year, before I was able to take any computer-related courses. I have to believe that this was more a reflection on their budget and lack of focus on current technology at the time (in 1979, there really weren't many punch-card readers being used in the field) than it is on my age! Although long obsolete in computer use, punch cards in various forms are still used in older voting equipment.

The history of magnetic storage dates back to June 1949, when a group of IBM engineers and scientists began working on a new storage device. What they were working on was the first magnetic storage device for computers, and it revolutionized the industry. On May 21, 1952, IBM announced the IBM 726 Tape Unit with the IBM701 Defense Calculator, marking the transition from punched-card calculators to electronic computers.

Four years later, on September 13, 1956, a small team of IBM engineers in San Jose, California, introduced the first computer disk storage system as part of the 305 RAMAC (Random Access Method of Accounting and Control) computer.

The 305 RAMAC drive could store 5 million characters (that's right, only 5MB!) of data on 50 disks, each a whopping 24 inches in diameter. Individual bits were stored at a density of only 2Kbits/sq. inch. Unlike tape drives, RAMAC's recording heads could go directly to any location on a disk surface without reading all the information in between. This random accessibility had a profound effect on computer performance at the time, enabling data to be stored and retrieved significantly faster than if it were on tape.

From these beginnings, the magnetic storage industry has progressed in just over 50 years such that today you can store 1TB (1,000GB) or more on tiny 3 1/2" drives that fit into a single computer drive bay.

IBM's contributions to the history and development of magnetic storage are incredible; in fact, most have either come directly from IBM or as a result of IBM research. Not only did IBM invent computer magnetic tape storage as well as the hard disk drive, but it also invented the floppy drive. The same San Jose facility where the hard drive was created introduced the first floppy drive, then using 8" diameter floppy disks, in 1971. The team that developed the drive was led by the late Alan Shugart, a legendary figure in computer storage.

Since then, IBM has pioneered advanced magnetic data encoding schemes, such as Modified Frequency Modulation (MFM) and Run Length Limited (RLL); drive head designs, such as Thin Film, magneto-resistive (MR), and giant magneto-resistive (GMR) heads; and drive technologies, such as Partial Response Maximum Likelihood (PRML), No-ID recording, and Self-Monitoring Analysis and Reporting Technology (S.M.A.R.T.). Today, the combined hard disk drive operations of IBM and Hitachi (called Hitachi Global Storage Technologies) is still one of the leaders in developing and implementing new drive technology and is second in sales only to Seagate Technology in PC hard drives.

How Magnetic Fields Are Used to Store Data

All magnetic storage devices read and write data by using electromagnetism. This basic principle of physics states that as an electric current flows through a conductor (wire), a magnetic field is generated around the conductor (see Figure 8.1). Note that electrons actually flow from negative to positive as shown in the figure, although we normally think of current flowing in the other direction.

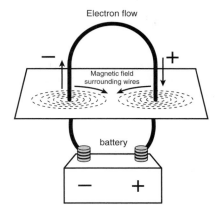

Figure 8.1   A magnetic field is generated around a wire when current is passed through it.

Electromagnetism was discovered in 1819 by Danish physicist Hans Christian Oersted, when he found that a compass needle would deflect away from pointing north when brought near a wire conducting an electric current. When the current was shut off, the compass needle resumed its alignment with the Earth's magnetic field and again pointed north.

The magnetic field generated by a wire conductor can exert an influence on magnetic material in the field. When the direction of the flow of electric current or polarity is reversed, the magnetic field's polarity also is reversed. For example, an electric motor uses electromagnetism to exert pushing and pulling forces on magnets attached to a rotating shaft.

Another effect of electromagnetism was discovered by Michael Faraday in 1831. He found that if a conductor is passed through a moving magnetic field, an electrical current is generated. As the polarity of the magnetic field changes, so does the direction of the electric current's flow (see Figure 8.2).

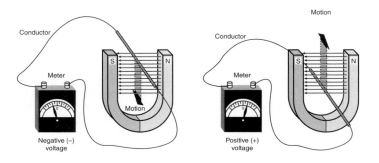

Figure 8.2   Current is induced in a wire when passed through a magnetic field.

For example, an alternator, which is a type of electrical generator used in automobiles, operates by rotating electromagnets on a shaft past coils of stationary wire conductors, which consequently generates large amounts of electrical current in those conductors. Because electromagnetism works two ways, a motor can become a generator and vice versa. When applied to magnetic storage devices, this two-way operation of electromagnetism makes it possible to record data on a disk and read that data back later. When recording, the head changes electrical impulses to magnetic fields, and when reading, the head changes magnetic fields back into electrical impulses.

The read/write heads in a magnetic storage device are U-shaped pieces of conductive material, with the ends of the U situated directly above (or next to) the surface of the actual data storage medium. The U-shaped head is wrapped with coils or windings of conductive wire, through which an electric current can flow (see Figure 8.3). When the drive logic passes a current through these coils, it generates a magnetic field in the drive head. Reversing the polarity of the electric current also causes the polarity of the generated field to change. In essence, the heads are electromagnets whose voltage can be switched in polarity very quickly.

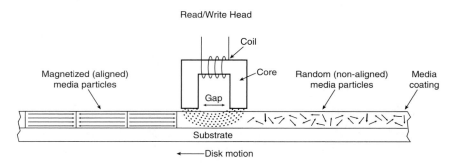

Figure 8.3   A magnetic read/write head.

The disk or tape that constitutes the actual storage medium consists of some form of substrate material (such as Mylar for floppy disks or aluminum or glass for hard disks) on which a layer of magnetizable material has been deposited. This material usually is a form of iron oxide with various other elements added. Each of the individual magnetic particles on the storage medium has its own magnetic field. When the medium is blank, the polarities of those magnetic fields are normally in a state of random disarray. Because the fields of the individual particles point in random directions, each tiny magnetic field is canceled out by one that points in the opposite direction; the cumulative effect of this is a surface with no observable field polarity. With many randomly oriented fields, the net effect is no observable unified field or polarity.

When a drive's read/write head generates a magnetic field (as when writing to a disk), the field jumps the gap between the ends of the U shape. Because a magnetic field passes through a conductor much more easily than through the air, the field bends outward from the gap in the head and actually uses the adjacent storage medium as the path of least resistance to the other side of the gap. As the field passes through the medium directly under the gap, it polarizes the magnetic particles it passes through so they are aligned with the field. The field's polarity or direction—and, therefore, the polarity or direction of the field induced in the magnetic medium—is based on the direction of the flow of electric current through the coils. A change in the direction of the current flow produces a change in the direction of the magnetic field. During the development of magnetic storage, the distance between the read/write head and the media has decreased dramatically. This enables the gap to be smaller and also makes the size of the recorded magnetic domain smaller. The smaller the recorded magnetic domain, the higher the density of data that can be stored on the drive.

When the magnetic field passes through the medium, the particles in the area below the head gap are aligned in the same direction as the field emanating from the gap. When the individual magnetic domains of the particles are in alignment, they no longer cancel one another out, and an observable magnetic field exists in that region of the medium. This local field is generated by the many magnetic particles that now are operating as a team to produce a detectable cumulative field with a unified direction.

The term *flux* describes a magnetic field that has a specific direction or polarity. As the surface of the medium moves under the drive head, the head can generate what is called a *magnetic flux* of a given polarity over a specific region of the medium. When the flow of electric current through the coils in the head is reversed, so is the magnetic field polarity or flux in the head gap. This flux reversal in the head causes the polarity of the magnetized particles on the disk medium to reverse.

The flux reversal (or flux transition) is a change in the polarity of the aligned magnetic particles on the surface of the storage medium. A drive head creates flux reversals on the medium to record data. For each data bit (or bits) that a drive writes, it creates a pattern of positive-to-negative and negative-to-positive flux reversals on the medium in specific areas known as *bit cells* or *transition cells*. A bit cell or transition cell is a specific area of the medium—controlled by the time and speed at which the medium travels—in which the drive head creates flux reversals. The particular pattern of flux reversals within the transition cells used to store a given data bit (or bits) is called the *encoding method*. The drive logic or controller takes the data to be stored and encodes it as a series of flux reversals over a period of time, according to the pattern dictated by the encoding method it uses.

Note

The two most popular encoding methods for magnetic media are Modified Frequency Modulation (MFM) and Run Length Limited (RLL). All floppy disk drives and some older hard disk drives use the MFM scheme. Today's hard disk drives use one of several variations on the RLL encoding method. These encoding methods are described in more detail later in this chapter in the section "Data Encoding Schemes."

During the write process, voltage is applied to the head. As the polarity of this voltage changes, the polarity of the magnetic field being recorded also changes. The flux transitions are written precisely at the points where the recording polarity changes. Strange as it might seem, during the read process, a head does not generate exactly the same signal that was written. Instead, the head generates a voltage pulse or spike only when it crosses a flux transition. When the transition changes from positive to negative, the pulse that the head detects is a negative voltage. When the transition changes from negative to positive, the pulse is a positive voltage spike. This effect occurs because current is generated in a conductor only when passing through lines of magnetic force at an angle. Because the head moves parallel to the magnetic fields it created on the media, the only time the head generates voltage when reading is when passing through a polarity or flux transition (flux reversal).

In essence, while reading from the medium, the head becomes a flux transition detector, emitting voltage pulses whenever it crosses a transition. Areas of no transition generate no pulse. Figure 8.4 shows the relationship between the read and write waveforms and the flux transitions recorded on a storage medium.

You can think of the write pattern as being a square waveform that is at a positive or negative voltage level. When the voltage is positive, a field is generated in the head, which polarizes the magnetic media in one direction. When the voltage changes to negative, the magnetic field induced in the media also changes direction. Where the waveform actually transitions from positive to negative voltage, or vice versa, the magnetic flux on the disk also changes polarity. During a read, the head senses these flux transitions and generates a pulsed positive or negative waveform, rather than the continuously positive or negative waveform used during the original recording. In other words, the signal when reading is 0 volts unless the head detects a magnetic flux transition, in which case it generates a positive or negative pulse accordingly. Pulses appear only when the head is passing over flux transitions on the medium. By knowing the clock timing the drive uses, the controller circuitry can determine whether a pulse (and therefore a flux transition) falls within a given transition cell time period.

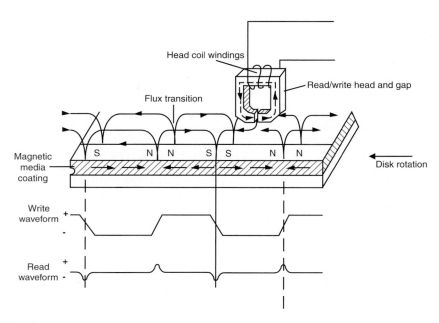

Figure 8.4   Magnetic write and read processes.

The electrical pulse currents generated in the head while it is passing over the storage medium in read mode are very weak and can contain significant noise. Sensitive electronics in the drive and controller assembly amplify the signal above the noise level and decode the train of weak pulse currents back into binary data that is (theoretically) identical to the data originally recorded.

As you can see, hard disk drives and other storage devices read and write data by means of basic electromagnetic principles. A drive writes data by passing electrical currents through an electromagnet (the drive head), generating a magnetic field that is stored on the medium. The drive reads data by passing the head back over the surface of the medium. As the head encounters changes in the stored magnetic field, it generates a weak electrical current that indicates the presence or absence of flux transitions in the signal as it was originally written.

Read/Write Head Designs

As disk drive technology has evolved, so has the design of the read/write head. The earliest heads were simple iron cores with coil windings (electromagnets). By today's standards, the original head designs were enormous in physical size and operated at very low recording densities. Over the years, head designs have evolved from the first simple ferrite core designs into the several types and technologies available today. This section discusses the various types of heads found in PC hard disk drives, including the applications and relative strengths and weaknesses of each.

Six main types of heads have been used in hard disk drives over the years:

- Ferrite
- Metal-In-Gap (MIG)
- Thin-film (TF)
- Magneto-resistive (MR)
- Giant magneto-resistive (GMR)
- Perpendicular magnetic recording (PMR)

Note

By the end of 2005, hard drives based on perpendicular magnetic recording (PMR) were being used in devices such as portable music players and laptop PCs. Desktop PC hard drives based on the technology became available in 2006. PMR is covered in more detail at the end of this chapter.

Ferrite

Ferrite heads, the traditional type of magnetic-head design, evolved from the original IBM 30-30 Winchester drive. These heads have an iron-oxide core wrapped with electromagnetic coils. The drive produces a magnetic field by energizing the coils or passing a magnetic field near them. This gives the heads full read/write capability. Ferrite heads are larger and heavier than thin-film heads and therefore require a larger floating height to prevent contact with the disk while it is spinning.

Manufacturers have made many refinements to the original (monolithic) ferrite head design. One type of ferrite head, called a *composite ferrite head*, has a smaller ferrite core bonded with glass in a ceramic housing. This design permits a smaller head gap, which enables higher track densities. These heads are less susceptible to stray magnetic fields than the older monolithic design heads.

During the 1980s, composite ferrite heads were popular in many low-end drives, such as the Seagate ST-225. As density demands grew, the competing MIG and thin-film head designs came to be used in place of ferrite heads, which are virtually obsolete today. Ferrite heads can't write to the higher coercivity media necessary for high-density disk designs and have poor frequency response with higher noise levels. The main advantage of ferrite heads is that they are the cheapest type available.

Metal-In-Gap

Metal-In-Gap heads are a specially enhanced version of the composite ferrite design. In MIG heads, a metal substance is applied to the head's recording gap. Two versions of MIG heads are available: single-sided and double-sided. Single-sided MIG heads are designed with a layer of magnetic alloy placed along the trailing edge of the gap. Double-sided MIG designs apply the layer to both sides of the gap. The metal alloy is applied through a vacuum-deposition process called *sputtering*.

This magnetic alloy has twice the magnetization capability of raw ferrite and enables the head to write to the higher coercivity thin-film media needed at the higher densities. MIG heads also produce a sharper gradient in the magnetic field for a better-defined magnetic pulse. Double-sided MIG heads offer even higher coercivity capability than the single-sided designs.

Because of these increases in capabilities through improved designs, MIG heads were for a time the most popular head design and were used in many hard disk drives in the late '80s and early '90s, and most recently in LS-120 (SuperDisk) drives as well.

Thin-film

Thin-film heads are manufactured much the same way as a semiconductor chip—through a photo-lithographic process. This process creates many thousands of heads on a single circular wafer and produces a very small, high-quality product.

TF heads have an extremely narrow and controlled head gap that is created by sputtering a hard aluminum material. Because this material completely encloses the gap, the area is very well protected, minimizing the chance of damage from contact with the spinning disk. The core is a combination of iron and nickel alloy that has two to four times more magnetic power than a ferrite head core.

TF heads produce a sharply defined magnetic pulse that enables them to write at extremely high densities. Because they do not have a conventional coil, TF heads are more immune to variations in coil impedance. These small, lightweight heads can float at a much lower height than the ferrite and MIG heads; in some designs, the floating height is 2 micro-inches or less. Because the reduced height enables the heads to pick up and transmit a much stronger signal from the platters, the signal-to-noise ratio increases and improves accuracy. At the high track and linear densities of some drives, a standard ferrite head would not be capable of picking out the data signal from the background noise. Another advantage of TF heads is that their small size enables the platters to be stacked closer together, enabling more platters to fit into the same space.

When first introduced, TF heads were relatively expensive compared with older technologies, such as ferrite and MIG. Better manufacturing techniques and the need for higher densities, however, have driven the market to TF heads. The widespread use of these heads has also made them cost-competitive with, if not cheaper than, MIG heads.

Many of the drives in the 100MB–2GB range used TF heads, especially in the smaller form factors. TF heads displaced MIG heads as the most popular head design, but they have now themselves been displaced by newer magneto-resistive heads.

Magneto-resistive Heads

Magneto-resistive heads, sometimes also referred to as the *anisotropic magneto-resistant (AMR)* heads, are capable of increasing density four times or greater as compared to the previous inductive-only heads. IBM introduced the first commercially available drive with MR heads in 1991, in a 1GB 3 1/2" model, and other manufacturers quickly followed suit.

All heads are detectors; that is, they are designed to detect the flux transitions in the media and convert them back to electrical signals that can be interpreted as data. One problem with magnetic recording is the ever-increasing desire for more and more density, which is putting more information (flux transitions) in a smaller and smaller space. As the magnetic domains on the disk get smaller, the signal from the heads during reading operations becomes weaker; distinguishing the true signal from the random noise or stray fields present becomes difficult. A more efficient read head, which is a more efficient way to detect these transitions on the disk, is therefore necessary.

Another magnetic effect that is well known today is being used in modern drives. When a wire is passed through a magnetic field, not only does the wire generate a small current, but the resistance of the wire also changes. Standard read heads use the head as a tiny generator, relying on the fact that the heads will generate a pulsed current when passed over magnetic flux transitions. A newer type of head design pioneered by IBM instead relies on the fact that the resistance in the head wires will also change.

Rather than use the head to generate tiny currents, which must then be filtered, amplified, and decoded, a magneto-resistive head uses the head as a resistor. A circuit passes a voltage through the head and watches for the voltage to change, which will occur when the resistance of the head changes as it passes through the flux reversals on the media. This mechanism for using the head results in a much stronger and clearer signal of what was on the media and enables the density to be increased.

MR heads rely on the fact that the resistance of a conductor changes slightly when an external magnetic field is present. Rather than put out a voltage by passing through a magnetic-field flux reversal—as a normal head would—the MR head senses the flux reversal and changes resistance. A small current flows through the heads, and this sense current measures the change in resistance. This design provides an output that is three or more times more powerful than a TF head during a read. In effect, MR heads are power-read heads, acting more like sensors than generators.

MR heads were more costly and complex to manufacture than older thin-film heads because of the additional components and manufacturing steps that were required:

- Additional wires must be run to and from the head to carry the sense current.
- Four to six more masking steps are required.
- Because MR heads are so sensitive, they are very susceptible to stray magnetic fields and require additional shielding.

Because the MR principle can only read data and is not used for writing, MR heads are really two heads in one. The assembly includes a standard inductive TF head for writing data and an MR head for reading. Because two separate heads are built into one assembly, each head can be optimized for its task. Ferrite, MIG, and TF heads are known as *single-gap heads* because the same gap is used for both reading and writing, whereas the MR head uses a separate gap for each operation.

The problem with single-gap heads is that the gap length is always a compromise between what is best for reading and what is best for writing. The read function needs a thinner gap for higher resolution; the write function needs a thicker gap for deeper flux penetration to switch the medium. In a dual-gap MR head, the read and write gaps can be optimized for both functions independently. The write (TF) gap writes a wider track than the read (MR) gap reads. Thus, the read head is less likely to pick up stray magnetic information from adjacent tracks.

A typical IBM-designed MR head is shown in Figure 8.5. This figure first shows the complete MR head-and-slider assembly on the end of an actuator arm. This is the part you would see if you opened up a drive. The slider is the block device on the end of the triangular-shaped arm that carries the head. The actual head is the tiny piece shown magnified at the end of the slider, and then the MR read sensor in the head is shown further magnified.

The read element, which is the actual magneto-resistive sensor, consists of a nickel-ferrite (NiFe) film separated by a spacer from a magnetically soft layer. The NiFe film layer changes resistance in the presence of a magnetic field. Layers of shielding protect the MR sensor read element from being corrupted by adjacent or stray magnetic fields. In many designs, the second shield also functions as one pole of the write element, resulting in what is called a *merged* MR head. The write element is not of MR design but is instead a traditional thin-film inductive head.

IBM's MR head design employs a Soft Adjacent Layer (SAL) structure, consisting of the MR NiFe film, as well as a magnetically soft alloy layer separated by a film with high electrical resistance. In this design, a resistance change occurs in the NiFe layer as the MR sensor passes through a magnetic field.

As areal densities have increased, heads have been designed with narrower and thinner MR elements. More recent designs have reduced the film width between the side contacts to as little as half a micron or less.

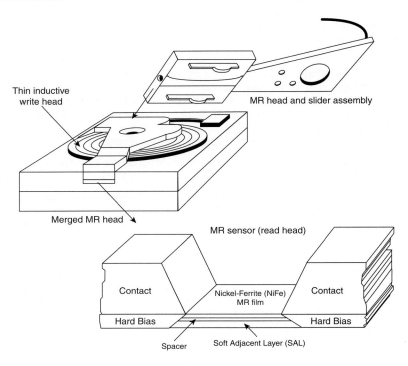

Figure 8.5   Cross-section of a magneto-resistive head.

Giant Magneto-resistive Heads

In the quest for even greater density, IBM introduced a new type of MR head in 1997. Called *giant magneto-resistive heads*, they are physically smaller than standard MR heads but are so named for the GMR effect on which they are based. The design is very similar; however, additional layers replace the single NiFe layer in a conventional MR design. In MR heads, a single NiFe film changes resistance in response to a flux reversal on the disk. In GMR heads, two films (separated by a very thin copper conducting layer) perform this function.

The GMR effect was first discovered in 1988 in crystal samples that were exposed to high-powered magnetic fields (1,000 times the fields used in hard disk drives). Scientists Peter Gruenberg of Julich, Germany, and Albert Fert of Paris discovered that large resistance changes were occurring in materials composed of alternating very thin layers of various metallic elements. The key structure in GMR materials is a spacer layer of a nonmagnetic metal between two layers of magnetic metals. One of the magnetic layers is *pinned*, which means it has a forced magnetic orientation. The other magnetic layer is *free*, which means it is free to change orientation or alignment. Magnetic materials tend to align themselves in the same direction. So if the spacer layer is thin enough, the free layer takes on the same orientation as the pinned layer. What was discovered was that the magnetic alignment of the free magnetic layer would periodically swing back and forth from being aligned in the same magnetic direction as the pinned layer to being aligned in the opposite magnetic direction. The overall resistance is relatively low when the layers are in the same alignment and relatively high when in opposite magnetic alignment.

Figure 8.6 shows a GMR read element.

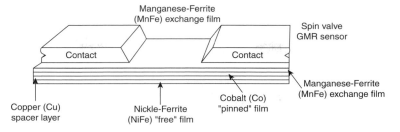

Figure 8.6   Cross-section of a giant magneto-resistive head.

When a weak magnetic field, such as that from a bit on a hard disk, passes beneath a GMR head, the magnetic orientation of the free magnetic layer rotates relative to that of the other and generates a significant change in electrical resistance due to the GMR effect. Because the physical nature of the resistance change was determined to be caused by the relative spin of the electrons in the different layers, GMR heads are often referred to as *spin-valve heads*.

IBM announced the first commercially available drive using GMR heads (a 16.8GB 3 1/2" drive) in December 1997. Since then, GMR heads became the standard in most 3.5" drives from 20GB up to 500GB, and in 2.5" drives of up to 120GB. GMR enables areal densities of up to around 100Gbits/sq. inch, to produce drives with even higher densities required a switch to perpendicular recording technology.

Head Sliders

The term *slider* is used to describe the body of material that supports the actual drive head itself. The slider is what actually floats or slides over the surface of the disk, carrying the head at the correct distance from the medium for reading and writing. Older sliders resemble a trimaran, with two outboard pods that float along the surface of the disk media and a central "hull" portion that actually carries the head and read/write gap. Figure 8.7 shows a typical mini slider. Note that the actual head, with the read/write gap, is on the trailing end of the slider.

The trend toward smaller and smaller form factor drives has forced sliders to become smaller as well. The typical Mini-Winchester slider design was about 4mm×3.2mm×0.86mm in size. Most head manufacturers have since shifted to smaller Micro, Nano, Pico, or Femto sliders. The Femto sliders in use today are extremely small—about the size of the ball in the tip of a ballpoint pen. Pico and Femto sliders are assembled by using flex interconnect cable (FIC) and chip on ceramic (COC) technology that enables the process to be completely automated.

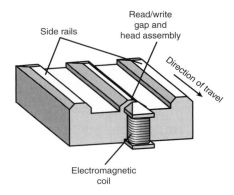

Figure 8.7   The underside of a typical head mini slider.

Table 8.1 shows the characteristics of the various types of sliders used in hard disk drives.

Table 8.1   Hard Disk Drive Slider Types

Slider Type	Year Introduced	Relative Size	Dimensions			
			L (mm)	W (mm)	H (mm)	Mass (mg)
Mini	1980	100%	4.00	3.20	0.86	55.0
Micro	1986	70%	2.80	2.24	0.60	16.2
Nano (+ Pressure)	1991	62%	2.50	1.70	0.43	7.8
Nano (- Pressure)	1994	50%	2.00	1.60	0.43	5.9
Pico	1997	30%	1.25	1.00	0.30	1.6
Femto	2003	20%	0.85	0.70	0.23	0.6

Smaller sliders reduce the mass carried at the end of the head actuator arms, which provides increased acceleration and deceleration, thus leading to faster seek times. The smaller sliders also require less surface area, allowing the head to track closer to the outer and inner diameters, thus increasing the usable area of the disk platters. Further, the smaller slider contact area reduces the slight wear on the platter surface that occurs during normal startup and spindown of the drive platters. Figure 8.8 shows a magnified photo of a Femto slider mounted on the head gimbal assembly, which is on the end of the head actuator arm.

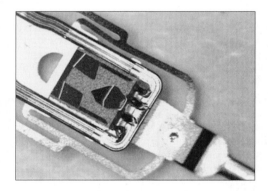

Figure 8.8   Magnified head gimbal assembly featuring a Femto slider. (Photo courtesy Hitachi Global Storage Technologies.)

The newer slider designs also have specially modified surface patterns that are designed to maintain the same floating height above the disk surface, whether the slider is positioned above the inner or outer cylinders. Conventional sliders would increase or decrease their floating heights considerably according to the velocity of the disk surface traveling beneath them. Above the outer cylinders, the velocity and floating height would be higher. This arrangement is undesirable in newer drives that use zoned bit recording, in which the bit density is the same on all the cylinders. When the bit density is uniform throughout the drive, the head floating height should also be relatively constant for maximum performance. Special textured surface patterns and manufacturing techniques enable the sliders to float at a much more consistent height, making them ideal for zoned bit recording drives. For more information on zoned recording, see the section "Disk Formatting" in Chapter 9.

A typical Femto air-bearing slider surface design is shown in Figure 8.9.

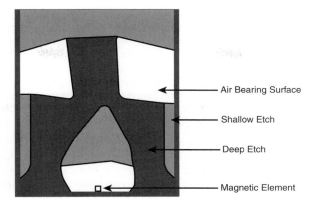

Figure 8.9 Femto air-bearing slider surface design.

A Femto slider has three distinct areas with complex shapes designed to achieve a consistent head-to-disk floating height across the disk as well as minimal height loss under high-altitude (low-pressure) conditions. The shallow etch area creates a stepped air inlet allowing airflow to create a positive pressure under the air-bearing surface that lifts the slider away from the disk. The deep etch area creates an opposite negative pressure pocket that simultaneously pulls the slider closer to the disk surface. The combination of positive and negative pressures is designed to balance the force of the suspension arm pushing the slider toward the disk, while keeping the slider at the desired floating height away from the disk surface. The balance of positive and negative pressures stabilizes and reduces the floating height variations commonly found in older slider designs. The first drive using the Femto slider design was the Hitachi 7K60 2 1/2" drive released in May 2003. Most of the higher-capacity drives on the market today use this design.

Data Encoding Schemes

Magnetic storage is essentially an analog medium. The data a PC stores on it, however, is digital information—that is, 1s and 0s. When the drive sends digital information to a magnetic recording head, the head creates magnetic domains on the storage medium with specific polarities corresponding to the positive and negative voltages the drive applies to the head. The flux reversals form the boundaries between the areas of positive and negative polarity that the drive controller uses to encode the digital data onto the analog medium. During a read operation, each flux reversal the drive detects generates a positive or negative pulse that the device uses to reconstruct the original binary data.

To optimize the placement of flux transitions during magnetic storage, the drive passes the raw digital input data through a device called an encoder/decoder (endec), which converts the raw binary information to a waveform designed to optimally place the flux transitions (pulses) on the media. During a read operation, the endec reverses the process and decodes the pulse train back into the original binary data. Over the years, several schemes for encoding data in this manner have been developed; some are better or more efficient than others, which you see later in this section.

Other descriptions of the data encoding process might be much simpler, but they omit the facts that make some of the issues related to hard drive reliability so critical—namely, timing. Engineers and designers are constantly pushing the envelope to stuff more and more bits of information into the limited quantity of magnetic flux reversals per inch. What they've come up with, essentially, is a design in which the bits of information are decoded not only from the presence or absence of flux reversals, but from the timing between them. The more accurately they can time the reversals, the more information that can be encoded (and subsequently decoded) from that timing information.

In any form of binary signaling, the use of timing is significant. When a read or write waveform is interpreted, the timing of each voltage transition event is critical. Timing is what defines a particular bit or transition cell—that is, the time window within which the drive is either writing or reading a transition. If the timing is off, a given voltage transition might be recognized at the wrong time as being in a different cell, which would throw the conversion or encoding off, resulting in bits being missed, added, or misinterpreted. To ensure that the timing is precise, the transmitting and receiving devices must be in perfect synchronization. For example, if recording a 0 is done by placing no transition on the disk for a given time period or cell, imagine recording ten 0 bits in a row—you would have a long period of time (ten cells) with no activity, no transitions at all.

Imagine now that the clock on the encoder was slightly off time while reading data as compared to when it was originally written. If it were fast, the encoder might think that during this long stretch of 10 cells with no transitions, only nine cells had actually elapsed. Or if it were slow, it might think that 11 cells had elapsed instead. In either case, this would result in a read error, meaning the bits that were originally written would not be read as being the same. To prevent timing errors in drive encoding/decoding, perfect synchronization is necessary between the reading and writing processes. This synchronization often is accomplished by adding a separate timing signal, called a *clock signal*, to the transmission between the two devices. The clock and data signals also can be combined and transmitted as a single signal. Most magnetic data encoding schemes use this type of combination of clock and data signals.

Adding a clock signal to the data ensures that the communicating devices can accurately interpret the individual bit cells. Each bit cell is bounded by two other cells containing the clock transitions. By sending clock information along with the data, the clocks remain in sync, even if the medium contains a long string of identical 0 bits. Unfortunately, the transition cells used solely for timing take up space on the medium that could otherwise be used for data.

Because the number of flux transitions a drive can record in a given space on a particular medium is limited by the physical nature or density of the medium and the head technology, drive engineers have developed various ways of encoding the data by using a minimum number of flux reversals (taking into consideration the fact that some flux reversals used solely for clocking are required). Signal encoding enables the system to make the maximum use of a given drive hardware technology.

Although various encoding schemes have been tried, only a few are popular today. Over the years, these three basic types have been the most popular:

- Frequency Modulation
- Modified Frequency Modulation
- Run Length Limited

The following sections examine these codes, how they work, where they are used, and any advantages or disadvantages that apply to them. It will help to refer to Figure 8.10 (later in the chapter) as you read the descriptions of each of these encoding schemes because this figure depicts how each of these schemes would store an "X" on the same media.

FM Encoding

One of the earliest techniques for encoding data for magnetic storage is called Frequency Modulation encoding. This encoding scheme—sometimes called *Single-Density encoding*—was used in the earliest floppy disk drives installed in PC systems. The original Osborne portable computer, for example, used these Single-Density floppy disk drives, which stored about 80KB of data on a single disk. Although it was popular until the late 1970s, FM encoding is no longer used.

MFM Encoding

Modified Frequency Modulation encoding was devised to reduce the number of flux reversals used in the original FM encoding scheme and, therefore, to pack more data onto the disk. MFM encoding minimizes the use of clock transitions, leaving more room for the data. It records clock transitions only when a stored 0 bit is preceded by another 0 bit; in all other cases, a clock transition is not required. Because MFM minimizes the use of clock transitions, it can double the clock frequency used by FM encoding, enabling it to store twice as many data bits in the same number of flux transitions.

Because MFM encoding writes twice as many data bits by using the same number of flux reversals as FM, the clock speed of the data is doubled and the drive actually sees the same number of total flux reversals as with FM. This means a drive using MFM encoding reads and writes data at twice the speed of FM, even though the drive sees the flux reversals arriving at the same frequency as in FM.

Because it is twice as efficient as FM encoding, MFM encoding also has been called Double-Density recording. MFM is used in virtually all PC floppy disk drives today and was used in nearly all PC hard disks for a number of years. Today, virtually all hard disks use variations of RLL encoding, which provides even greater efficiency than MFM.

Table 8.2 shows the data bit-to-flux reversal translation in MFM encoding.

Table 8.2   MFM Data-to-Flux Transition Encoding

Data Bit Value	Flux Encoding
1	NT
0 preceded by 0	TN
0 preceded by 1	NN

T = Flux transition
N = No flux transition

RLL Encoding

Today's most popular encoding scheme for hard disks, called Run Length Limited, packs up to twice the information on a given disk than MFM does and three times as much information as FM. In RLL encoding, the drive combines groups of bits into a unit to generate specific patterns of flux reversals. By combining the clock and data signals in these patterns, the clock rate can be further increased while maintaining the same basic distance between the flux transitions on the storage medium.

IBM invented RLL encoding and first used the method in many of its mainframe disk drives. During the late 1980s, the PC hard disk industry began using RLL encoding schemes to increase the storage capabilities of PC hard disks. Today, virtually every drive on the market uses some form of RLL encoding.

Instead of encoding a single bit, RLL typically encodes a group of data bits at a time. The term *Run Length Limited* is derived from the two primary specifications of these codes, which are the minimum number (the run length) and maximum number (the run limit) of transition cells allowed between two actual flux transitions. Several variations of the scheme are achieved by changing the length and limit parameters, but only two have achieved any real popularity: RLL 2,7 and RLL 1,7.

You can even express FM and MFM encoding as a form of RLL. FM can be called RLL 0,1 because as few as zero and as many as one transition cells separate two flux transitions. MFM can be called RLL 1,3 because as few as one and as many as three transition cells separate two flux transitions. (Although these codes can be expressed as variations of RLL form, it is not common to do so.)

RLL 2,7 was initially the most popular RLL variation because it offers a high-density ratio with a transition detection window that is the same relative size as that in MFM. This method provides high storage density and fairly good reliability. In very high-capacity drives, however, RLL 2,7 did not prove to be reliable enough. Most of today's highest capacity drives use RLL 1,7 encoding, which offers a density ratio 1.27 times that of MFM and a larger transition detection window relative to MFM. Because of the larger relative timing window or cell size within which a transition can be detected, RLL 1,7 is a more forgiving and more reliable code, which is important when media and head technology are being pushed to their limits.

Another little-used RLL variation called RLL 3,9—sometimes also called Advanced RLL (ARLL)—allows an even higher density ratio than RLL 2,7. Unfortunately, reliability suffered too greatly under the RLL 3,9 scheme; the method was used by only a few now-obsolete controllers and has all but disappeared.

Understanding how RLL codes work is difficult without looking at an example. Within a given RLL variation, such as RLL 2,7 or 1,7, you can construct many flux transition encoding tables to demonstrate how particular groups of bits are encoded into flux transitions.

In the conversion table shown in Table 8.3, specific groups of data that are 2, 3, and 4 bits long are translated into strings of flux transitions 4, 6, and 8 transition cells long, respectively. The selected transitions for a particular bit sequence are designed to ensure that flux transitions do not occur too closely together or too far apart.

Limiting how close two flux transitions can be is necessary because of the fixed resolution capabilities of the head and storage medium. Limiting how far apart two flux transitions can be ensures that the clocks in the devices remain in sync.

Table 8.3   RLL 2,7 Data-to-Flux Transition Encoding

Data Bit Values	Flux Encoding
10	NTNN
11	TNNN
000	NNNTNN
010	TNNTNN
011	NNTNNN
0010	NNTNNTNN
0011	NNNNTNNN

T = Flux transition

N = No flux transition

In studying Table 8.3, you might think that encoding a byte value such as 00000001b would be impossible because no combinations of data bit groups fit this byte. Encoding this type of byte is not a problem, however, because the controller does not transmit individual bytes; instead, the controller sends whole sectors, making encoding such a byte possible by including some of the bits in the following byte. The only real problem occurs in the last byte of a sector if additional bits are necessary to complete the final group sequence. In these cases, the endec in the controller adds excess bits to the end of the last byte. These excess bits are then truncated during any reads so the controller always decodes the last byte correctly.

Encoding Scheme Comparisons

Figure 8.10 shows an example of the waveform written to store the ASCII character X on a hard disk drive by using three different encoding schemes.

In each of these encoding scheme examples, the top line shows the individual data bits (01011000b, for example) in their bit cells separated in time by the clock signal, which is shown as a period (.). Below that line is the actual write waveform, showing the positive and negative voltages as well as head voltage transitions that result in the recording of flux transitions. The bottom line shows the transition cells, with T representing a transition cell that contains a flux transition and N representing a transition cell that is empty.

The FM encoding example shown in Figure 8.10 is easy to explain. Each bit cell has two transition cells: one for the clock information and one for the data itself. All the clock transition cells contain flux transitions, and the data transition cells contain a flux transition only if the data is a 1 bit. No transition is present when the data is a 0 bit. Starting from the left, the first data bit is 0, which decodes as a flux transition pattern of TN. The next bit is a 1, which decodes as TT. The next bit is 0, which decodes as TN, and so on.

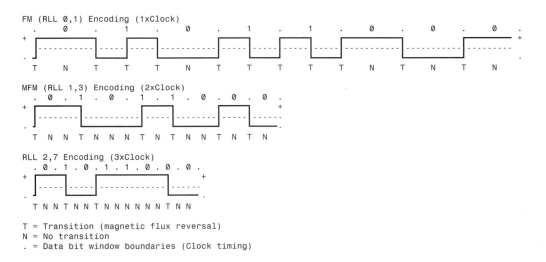

```
FM (RLL 0,1) Encoding (1xClock)
    .    0    .    1    .    0    .    1    .    1    .    0    .    0    .    0    .
  +
  -
    T    N    T    T    T    N    T    T    T    T    T    N    T    N    T    N

MFM (RLL 1,3) Encoding (2xClock)
    .  0  .  1  .  0  .  1  .  1  .  0  .  0  .  0  .
  +
  -
    T  N  N  T  N  N  N  T  N  T  N  N  T  N  T  N

RLL 2,7 Encoding (3xClock)
    .  0  .  1  .  0  .  1  .  1  .  0  .  0  .  0  .
  +
  -
    T N N T N N T N N N N N T N N

T = Transition (magnetic flux reversal)
N = No transition
. = Data bit window boundaries (Clock timing)
```

Figure 8.10   ASCII character X write waveforms using FM; MFM; and RLL 2,7 encoding.

The MFM encoding scheme also has clock and data transition cells for each data bit to be recorded. As you can see, however, the clock transition cells carry a flux transition only when a 0 bit is stored after another 0 bit. Starting from the left, the first bit is a 0, and the preceding bit is unknown (assume 0), so the flux transition pattern is TN for that bit. The next bit is a 1, which always decodes to a transition-cell pattern of NT. The next bit is 0, which was preceded by 1, so the pattern stored is NN. By using Table 8.2 (shown earlier), you easily can trace the MFM encoding pattern to the end of the byte. You can see that the minimum and maximum numbers of transition cells between any two flux transitions are one and three, respectively, which explains why MFM encoding can also be called RLL 1,3.

The RLL 2,7 pattern is more difficult to see because it encodes groups of bits rather than individual bits. Starting from the left, the first group that matches the groups listed in Table 8.3 is the first three bits, 010. These bits are translated into a flux transition pattern of TNNTNN. The next two bits, 11, are translated as a group to TNNN; and the final group, 000 bits, is translated to NNNTNN to complete the byte. As you can see in this example, no additional bits are needed to finish the last group.

Notice that the minimum and maximum numbers of empty transition cells between any two flux transitions in this example are 2 and 6, although a different example could show a maximum of seven empty transition cells. This is where the RLL 2,7 designation comes from. Because even fewer transitions are recorded than in MFM, the clock rate can be increased to three times that of FM or 1.5 times that of MFM, thus storing more data in the same space. Notice, however, that the resulting write waveform itself looks exactly like a typical FM or MFM waveform in terms of the number and separation of the flux transitions for a given physical portion of the disk. In other words, the physical minimum and maximum distances between any two flux transitions remain the same in all three of these encoding scheme examples.

Partial-Response, Maximum-Likelihood Decoders

Another feature often used in modern hard disk drives involves the disk read circuitry. Read channel circuits using Partial-Response, Maximum-Likelihood (PRML) technology enable disk drive manufacturers to increase the amount of data stored on a disk platter by up to 40%. PRML replaces the standard "detect one peak at a time" approach of traditional analog peak-detect, read/write channels with digital signal processing.

As the data density of hard drives increases, the drive must necessarily record the flux reversals closer together on the medium. This makes reading the data on the disk more difficult because the adjacent magnetic peaks can begin to interfere with each other. PRML modifies the way the drive reads the data from the disk. The controller analyzes the analog data stream it receives from the heads by using digital signal sampling, processing, and detection algorithms (this is the partial response element) and predicts the sequence of bits the data stream is most likely to represent (the maximum likelihood element). PRML technology can take an analog waveform, which might be filled with noise and stray signals, and produce an accurate reading from it.

This might not sound like a very precise method of reading data that must be bit-perfect to be usable, but the aggregate effect of the digital signal processing filters out the noise efficiently enough to enable the drive to place the flux change pulses much more closely together on the platter, thus achieving greater densities. Most drives with capacities of 2GB or above use PRML technology in their endec circuits.

Capacity Measurements

In December 1998, the International Electrotechnical Commission (IEC)—the leading international organization for worldwide standardization in electrotechnology—approved as an IEC International Standard the names and symbols for prefixes for binary multiples for use in the fields of data processing and data transmission. Prior to this, a lot of confusion had existed as to whether a megabyte stood for 1 million bytes (10^6) or 1,048,576 bytes (2^{20}). Even so, these new prefixes have yet to be widely adopted and confusion still reigns. The industry-standard abbreviations for the units used to measure the capacity of magnetic (and other) drives are shown in Table 8.4.

Table 8.4   Standard Abbreviations and Meanings

Abbreviation	Description	Power	Value
K	Kilo	10^3	1,000
Ki	Kibi	2^{10}	1,024
M	Mega	10^6	1,000,000
Mi	Mebi	2^{20}	1,048,576
G	Giga	10^9	1,000,000,000
Gi	Gibi	2^{30}	1,073,741,824

Table 8.4 Continued

Abbreviation	Description	Power	Value
T	Tera	10^{12}	1,000,000,000,000
Ti	Tebi	2^{40}	1,099,511,627,776
P	Peta	10^{15}	1,000,000,000,000,000
Pi	Pebi	2^{50}	1,125,899,906,842,624

According to this prefix standard, 1 mebibyte (1 MiB = 2^{20} B = 1,048,576 B) and 1 megabyte (1MB = 10^6 B = 1,000,000 B) are not equal. Because these prefixes are not in widespread use (and they might never be), M in most cases can indicate both decimal *millions of bytes* and binary *megabytes*. Similarly, G is often used to refer to decimal *billions of bytes* and binary *gigabytes*. In general, memory values are expressed by using the binary values, although disk capacities can go either way. This often leads to confusion in reporting disk capacities because many manufacturers tend to use whichever value makes their products look better. For example, drive capacities are often rated in decimal billions (G - Giga), whereas most BIOS chips and operating system utilities, such as the Windows FDISK, rate the same drive in binary gigabytes (Gi - Gibi). Note also that when bits and bytes are used as part of some other measurement, the difference between bits and bytes is often distinguished by the use of a lower- or uppercase *B*. For example, megabits are typically abbreviated with a lowercase *b*, resulting in the abbreviation *Mbps* for *megabits per second*, whereas *MBps* indicates *megabytes per second*.

Areal Density

Areal density is often used as a technology growth-rate indicator for the hard disk drive industry. *Areal density* is defined as the product of the linear bits per inch (BPI), measured along the length of the tracks around the disk, multiplied by the number of tracks per inch (TPI), measured radially on the disk (see Figure 8.11). The results are expressed in units of megabits or gigabits per square inch (Mbit/sq. inch or Gbit/sq. inch) and are used as a measure of efficiency in drive recording technology. Current high-end 2.5" drive drives record at areal densities exceeding 148Gbit/sq. inch (such as the 1TB Hitachi 7K1000, whereas 2 1/2" drives such as the 250GB Hitachi 5K250 record at areal densities of 205Gbit/sq. inch or more. Prototype drives with more than double these densities now exist, which will enable drives with twice the capacity or more in the next couple years.

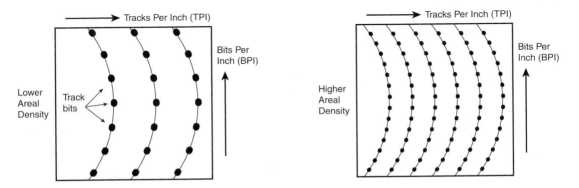

Figure 8.11 Areal density, combining tracks per inch and bits per inch.

Drives record data in tracks, which are circular bands of data on the disk. Each track is divided into sectors. Figure 8.12 shows an actual floppy disk sprayed with magnetic developer (powdered iron)

such that an image of the actual tracks and sectors can be clearly seen. The disk shown is a 5 1/4"
360KB floppy, which has 40 tracks per side, with each track divided into nine sectors. Note that each
sector is delineated by gaps in the recording, which precede and follow the track and sector headers
(where ID and address information resides). You can clearly see the triple gap preceding the first sector, which includes the track and sector headers. Then following in a counterclockwise direction, you
see each subsequent sector, preceded by gaps delineating the header for that sector. The area between
the headers is where the sector data is written.

Notice that sector 9 is longer than the others; this is to enable rotational speed differences between
drives, so that all the data can be written before running into the start of the track. Also notice that a
good portion of the disk surface isn't used because it is simply impractical to have the heads travel in
and out that far, and the difference in length between the sectors on the inner and outer tracks
becomes more of a problem.

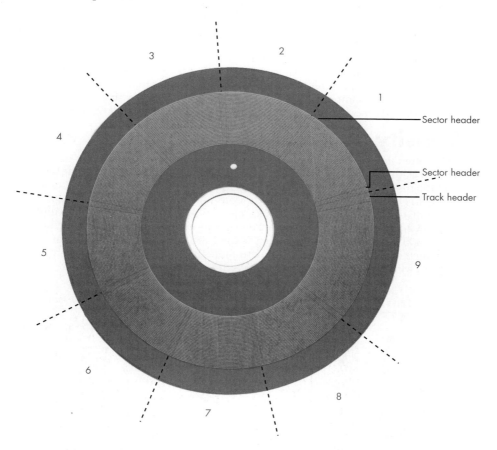

Figure 8.12 360KB floppy disk media sprayed with magnetic developer (powdered iron) showing the
actual track and sector images.

Areal density has been rising steadily since the first magnetic storage drive (the IBM RAMAC featuring
an areal density of 2Kbits/sq. inch) was introduced in 1956. Density initially grew at a rate of about
25% per year (doubling every four years), then in the early 1990s the rate accelerated to a growth rate

of about 60% per year (doubling every year and a half). The development and introduction of magneto-resistive heads in 1991, giant magneto-resistive heads in 1997, and AFC pixie dust media in 2001 (see the next section) subsequently drove a further increase in the areal density growth rate to 100% annually. The end result of all of this growth in density is amazing, in just slightly more than 50 years since the RAMAC drive was introduced, the areal density of magnetic storage has increased more than 100 million fold, from 2Kbits/sq. inch in the 1956 RAMAC (5MB of storage on 50 24-inch platters) to 205Gbits/sq. inch in production drives like the Hitachi 5K250 (250GB of storage on 2 2.5-inch platters) in 2007.

Current drives have used perpendicular recording techniques to go well-past what was previously considered the point at which the superparamagnetic effect takes place. This is an effect in which the magnetic domains become so small that they are intrinsically unstable at room temperature. Techniques such as perpendicular recording combined with extremely high coercivity media are being employed to enable future magnetic storage densities of 500Gbit/sq. inch to 1000Gbit/sq. inch or more, but beyond that, scientists and engineers might have to look toward other technologies. One such technology being considered for the future is patterned media, where a disk is preformatted with magnetic domains that can be more tightly packed without interfering with each other. Another possible future technology is holographic storage, in which a laser writes data three-dimensionally in a crystal plate or cube.

Figure 8.13 shows how areal density has increased by a factor of more than 100 million times from when magnetic storage was first developed (1956 RAMAC) to the present.

To increase areal density while maintaining the same external drive form factors, drive manufacturers have developed media and head technologies to support these higher areal densities, such as ceramic/glass platters, GMR heads, pseudo-contact recording, and PRML electronics, as discussed earlier in this chapter. The primary challenge in achieving higher densities is manufacturing drive heads and disks to operate at closer tolerances. Improvements in tolerances and the use of more platters in a given form factor continue to fuel improvements in drive capacity, but drive makers continue to seek even greater capacity increases, both by improving current technologies and by developing new ones.

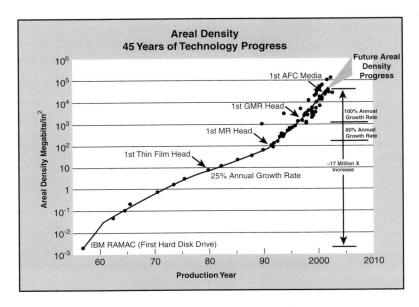

Figure 8.13   Evolution of areal density in magnetic disk storage.

To fit more data on a platter of a given size, the tracks must be placed more closely together and the heads must be capable of achieving greater precision in their placements over the tracks. This also means that as hard disk capacities increase, heads must float ever closer to the disk surface during operation. The gap between the head and disk is as close as 10 nanometers (0.01 microns) in some drives, which is approximately the thickness of a cell membrane. By comparison, a human hair is typically 80 microns in diameter, which is 8,000 times thicker than the gap between the head and disk in some drives. The prospect of actual contact or near contact recording is being considered for future drives to further increase density.

Increasing Areal Density with Pixie Dust

In 1990, IBM scientists discovered that a thin layer of the element ruthenium was the most effective nonmagnetic element that could be used for spacers in devices such as GMR heads. However, more than a decade passed before the first commercially available application of this principle was used to increase disk drive storage densities by improving the storage density of the drives' platters.

In May 2001, IBM began to produce drives using "pixie dust" technology in its Travelstar 2 1/2" hard drive series for notebook computers. In November 2001, Deskstar GXP drives using the same technology were introduced, and these drives had capacities of 80GB and 120GB.

These drives achieved data densities exceeding 25Gb per square inch through the use of a thin (three-atom-thick) layer of ruthenium used to separate two magnetic surfaces on each side of the drive's platters. Traditional drives use platters with a single magnetic surface per side. Media using the ruthenium coating, commonly referred to as *pixie dust*, is technically known as antiferromagnetically coupled (AFC) media. IBM continues to use AFC media in its latest drives for notebook, desktop, and server computers and has licensed AFC media to other drive and media vendors.

AFC media was developed because achieving greater and greater densities of magnetic storage requires individual magnetic areas on the media to become smaller and smaller. However, when magnetic areas become too small, a problem called the superparamagnetic effect (which causes magnetic areas to lose their magnetism over time) can occur.

When a thin layer of ruthenium is placed between two magnetic layers, the layers are forced to orient themselves magnetically in opposite directions to each other. Although the three-layer structure is physically thicker than a conventional magnetic surface, the opposing magnetic orientations make the layers appear to be thinner than a conventional surface. As a result, disk drive read/write heads can record smaller, high-density signals, increasing the storage capacity of a given platter size without the risk of the signal degrading. Figure 8.14 compares a normal single-layer disk platter to a disk platter using pixie dust AFC media technology.

Just as GMR heads use two layers separated by a thin conductive layer to increase data storage density, AFC media uses a similar principle. In essence, AFC media represents an extension of GMR principles from the read/write heads to the media's data recording surfaces. Over time, AFC media more than quadrupled the storage capacity of magnetic media, enabling drives to reach densities of 100Gbits/sq. inch.

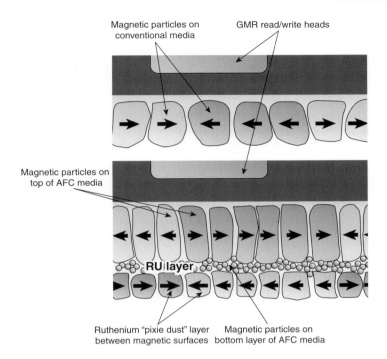

Magnetic particles on conventional media

GMR read/write heads

Magnetic particles on top of AFC media

RU layer

Ruthenium "pixie dust" layer between magnetic surfaces

Magnetic particles on bottom layer of AFC media

Figure 8.14   Conventional media uses a single magnetic surface, whereas AFC media uses two magnetic surfaces separated by a thin layer of ruthenium, a process IBM refers to as *pixie dust*.

Perpendicular Magnetic Recording

Originally all hard drives and other types of magnetic media recorded data using longitudinal recording, which stores magnetic bits horizontally across the surface of the media. Today, however, perpendicular recording, which aligns magnetic signals vertically on the media surface, is being incorporated in modern drives to achieve higher data densities. This process works because vertically oriented magnetic bits use less space than longitudinally stored bits (see Figure 8.15). Virtually all the major drive vendors are working with perpendicular recording as a way to achieve signal density surpassing that achievable even with AFC pixie dust media.

Conventional magnetic recording places magnetic domains longitudinally, meaning the domains lie end to end on the disk. This not only limits the density of the domains, but also helps to enable the superparamagnetic effect. Long ago it was realized that if one could place the domains perpendicular to the media (also called a *vertical recording*), the density could be increased, as well as the resistance of the domains to the superparamagnetic effect. Although the concept was easy to understand, actually implementing it has been difficult.

Unlike GMR heads and AFC media—both of which can be added relatively easily to existing drive technologies—perpendicular recording requires entirely new read/write head designs. Figure 8.15 shows the difference between perpendicular and longitudinal recording. You can get at least twice the number of magnetic domains in the same space with perpendicular recording.

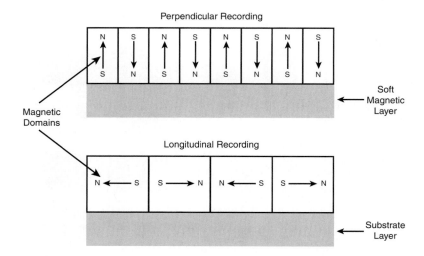

Figure 8.15   Perpendicular versus longitudinal recording.

Using perpendicular recording, the heads are designed to write deep into the media, using a thicker soft magnetic underlayer as a return path for the magnetic field. This enables the domains to be vertically aligned, and therefore placed much more closely together without unwanted interaction problems.

Perpendicular recording was first demonstrated in the late nineteenth century by Danish scientist Valdemar Poulsen, who was also the first person to demonstrate that sound could be recorded magnetically. There weren't many advances in perpendicular recording until 1976 when Dr. Shun-ichi Iwasaki (president of the Tohoku Institute of Technology in Japan) verified the distinct density advantages in perpendicular recording. Then in 1978, Dr. T. Fujiwara began an intensive research and development program at the Toshiba Corporation that eventually resulted in the perfection of floppy disk media optimized for perpendicular recording and the first commercially available magnetic storage devices using the technique.

The first use of perpendicular recording in PCs was with the 3 1/2", 2.88MB ED (extra-high density) floppy format developed by Toshiba and officially announced in 1987, with the ED drives and disks finally reaching production in 1989. IBM officially adopted these drives in its PS/2 systems in 1991, and a number of manufacturers began making them for IBM and other PC manufacturers, including Toshiba, Mitsubishi, Sony, and Panasonic. Because a 2.88MB ED drive can fully read and write 1.44MB HD disks (due to BIOS manufacturers fully integrating 2.88MB floppy support in the BIOS) and because DOS 5.0 and later included support for the 2.88MB format, the change to 2.88MB was an easy one. Unfortunately, due to high media costs and a relatively low increase in data capacity at a time when floppy disks were being replaced by writable CDs, these drives never caught on.

Despite the 2.88MB ED floppy's failure in the marketplace, Toshiba and other companies continued developing perpendicular magnetic recording for other media, especially hard disk drives. Unfortunately they would find that perpendicular recording technology was too far ahead of its time when it came to hard drives, where the existing technology was well entrenched, and where density evolution was already progressing at rates almost too fast for the industry to assimilate. It would take almost 20 more years before the existing longitudinal recording would begin to run out of steam as it reached 100Gbits/sq. inch, and the looming superparamagnetic limit would cause drive engineers to finally find justification for switching to perpendicular recording.

In April 2002, Read-Rite Corporation, a major maker of read/write heads, reached areal densities of 130Gb/sq. inch in a prototype drive using media provided by Maxtor subsidiary MMC Technology. In November 2002, Seagate Technology announced it had achieved areal densities of more than 100Gb/sq. inch in a prototype drive using this technology as well. According to two independent studies published in 2000, perpendicular recording was projected to enable densities of 500Gb to 1000Gb (1 terabit) per square inch in the future, a prediction which is well on its way to becoming true.

Perpendicular recording finally became commercially available in hard disk drives on August 16, 2005, when Toshiba's Storage Device Division announced shipment of the world's first hard disk using PMR technology. These were 1.8" drives used primarily in portable consumer electronics devices—most notably the Apple iPod media players, but also found in some of the smallest laptop PCs, such as the Toshiba Libretto series. The first 1.8" drives using PMR were the 40GB and 80GB models, which store 40GB on a single platter and are available in single-platter 40GB and dual-platter 80GB versions. These drives featured the highest areal density of any drives then on the market at 133Gb/sq. inch (206Mb/sq. mm). Although not normally used in PCs, these drives can be found in some of the extremely small and lightweight laptop systems such as the Toshiba Libretto.

In June 2006 Toshiba introduced a 200GB 2.5" PMR drive only 9.5mm thick and weighing only 98 grams. This became the highest capacity 2.5" drive available at the time, and also featured the world's highest areal density (178.8Gb/sq. inch or 277Mb/sq. mm) in a production drive. In October 2006 Toshiba announced it had produced more than one million drives using PMR technology.

Seagate introduced the world's first 2.5" PMR-based hard disk with the Momentus 5400.3 160, a 160GB 2.5" drive designed primarily for laptops. Although Seagate announced the drive in June 2005, it wasn't actually available for purchase until January 2006. In April 2006 Seagate introduced the Barracuda 7200.10 drive, which was both the first 750GB drive on the market as well as the first 3.5" drive to use perpendicular recording. Seagate also demonstrated recording an areal density of 245Gb/sq. inch with a data rate of 480Mbps using PMR and has indicated it will be able to achieve 500Gb/sq. inch in the future, which will increase the capacity of drives five times compared to those using conventional longitudinal recording. At an areal density of 500Gb/sq. inch, a 3.5" drive could store 2TB, a 2.5" drive in a laptop could hold 500GB, and a 1" Microdrive could store as much as 50GB of data.

Other manufacturers have also developed PMR drives. In April 2005 Hitachi demonstrated a perpendicular recording data density of 230Gb/sq. inch, which it indicated could result in a 20Gb Microdrive being released in 2007. Note that Microdrives are used in portable media players such as the Apple iPod Mini and Creative Zen Micro. In January 2007 Hitachi introduced the Deskstar 7K1000, which used perpendicular recording to achieve the milestone of being the world's first 1TB (terabyte) drive. At the introduction, Hitachi noted that it took the storage industry 35 years to move drive capacity from 5MB to 1GB (1956 to 1991), 14 more years to get to 500GB (1991 to 2005), and only two more years (2005 to 2007) to hit 1TB. This clearly shows Moore's law in effect for magnetic storage. Later in June 2007 Hitachi introduced the 5K250, a 250GB 2.5" drive storing data at an incredible 205Gbits/sq. inch areal density.

In the future, it is expected that all hard drive manufacturers will shift the bulk of their product to PMR-based drives in order to continue the incredible capacity growth trends in magnetic storage.

Chapter

9

Hard Disk Storage

Definition of a Hard Disk

To many users, the hard disk drive is the most important and yet the most mysterious part of a computer system. A *hard disk drive* is a sealed unit that a PC uses for nonvolatile data storage. *Nonvolatile*, or semipermanent, storage means that the storage device retains the data even when no power is supplied to the computer. Because the hard disk drive is expected to retain data until deliberately erased or overwritten, the hard drive is used to store crucial programming and data. As a result, when the hard disk fails, the consequences are usually very serious. To maintain, service, and upgrade a PC system properly, you must understand how the hard disk functions.

A hard disk drive contains rigid, disk-shaped platters, usually constructed of aluminum or glass (see Figure 9.1). Unlike floppy disks, the platters can't bend or flex—hence the term *hard disk*. In most hard disk drives, you can't remove the platters, which is why they are sometimes called *fixed* disk drives. Removable hard disk drives are also available. Usually, this term refers to a device in which the entire drive unit (that is, the disk unit containing the platters as well as the rest of the drive) is removable, but it can also refer to cartridge drives, where the platters are contained in a removable cartridge.

Note

Hard disk drives are sometimes referred to as *Winchester drives*. This term dates back to 1973, when IBM introduced the model 3340 drive, which had 30MB of fixed platter and 30MB of removable platter storage on separate spindles. The drive was codenamed Winchester by project leader Ken Haughton because the original capacity designation (30-30) sounded like the popular .30-30 (caliber-grains of charge) cartridge used by the Winchester 94 rifle introduced in 1895. The original 3340 "Winchester" drive was the first to use a sealed head/disk assembly, and the name has since been applied to all subsequent drives with similar technology.

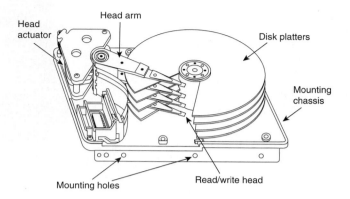

Figure 9.1   Hard disk heads and platters.

Hard Drive Advancements

The first hard drive appeared in 1956. One year later in 1957, Cyril Northcote Parkinson published his famous compilation of essays titled *Parkinson's Law*, which begins with the statement, "Work expands so as to fill the time available for its completion." A corollary of Parkinson's most famous "law" can be applied to hard drives: "Data expands so as to fill the space available for its storage." This, of course, means that no matter how big a drive you get, you *will* find a way to fill it. I know that I have lived by that dictum since purchasing my first hard disk drive nearly 25 years ago.

Note

The book *Parkinson's Law* (ISBN: 1-56849-015-1) is still in print and is in fact considered one of the essential tomes of business and management study even today.

Even though I am well aware of the exponential growth of everything associated with computers, I am still amazed at how large and fast modern drives have become. The first hard drive I purchased in 1983 was a 10MB (that's 10 megabyte, *not* gigabyte) Miniscribe model 2012, which was a 5 1/4" (platter) drive that was 203.2mm×146mm×82.6mm or 8"×5.75"×3.25" in overall size and weighed 2.5kg (5.5 lb., which is heavier than some of today's laptop computers)! By comparison, one of the biggest drives available to date—the Hitachi 7K1000 SATA drive—uses smaller 3 1/2" platters, is about 5 3/4"×4"×1" (146mm×102mm×25mm) in overall size, weighs only 1.54 lb. (0.70kg), and stores a whopping 1TB (which is 100,000 times more storage in a package that is about one-sixth the size and one-fourth the weight of my old Miniscribe).

Obviously, the large storage capacities found on modern drives are useless unless you can also transfer the data to and from the disk quickly. The hard disk as found in the original IBM XT in 1983 had a constant data transfer rate from the media of about 100KBps. Today, most commonly used drives feature the Serial ATA interface, which offers variable media data transfer rates of up to 300MBps (average rates are lower, up to about 50MBps). Much like the increase in drive capacity, the speed of the interface has also come a long way since the MFM and RLL interfaces that were commonplace in the 80s. As always, the interfaces are much faster than the actual drives. The Parallel ATA, Serial ATA, SCSI and Serial Attached SCSI (SAS) interfaces are commonplace now and offer data transfer rates of up to 133MBps for Parallel ATA, 150 and 300MBps for Serial ATA, 320MBps bandwidth for Ultra-320 SCSI, and 300MBps or 600MBps for SAS. All these interfaces are much faster than the drives they support, meaning that the true transfer rate you will see is almost entirely limited by the drive and not the interface you choose. The modern interfaces have bandwidth to spare for future developments and advances in hard disk technology.

In 2006 the hard disk drive celebrated its 50th anniversary, a milestone in computing technology. By the time PCs arrived on the scene in 1981, hard drives of 5MB in capacity were available. To give you an idea of how far hard drives have come in the 25+ years they have been used in PCs, I've outlined some of the more profound changes in PC-based hard disk storage:

- Maximum storage capacities have increased from the 5MB 5 1/4" full-height drives available in 1981 to 1TB in 2007 for 3 1/2" half-height drives (Hitachi 7K1000), 200GB for laptop 2 1/2" drives (Toshiba MK2035GSS), and 100GB for 1.8" drives (Toshiba MK1011GAH). Hard drives smaller than 40GB are rare in new desktop or even laptop systems.

- Data transfer rates to and from the media (sustained transfer rates) have increased from about 100KBps for the original IBM XT in 1983 to an average of 50MBps for some of the fastest drives today (Western Digital Raptor WD74GD), or more than 80MBps for the fastest SCSI drive (Seagate Cheetah 15K.4).

- Average seek times (how long it takes to move the heads to a particular cylinder) have decreased from more than 85ms (milliseconds) for the 10MB drives IBM used in the 1983 vintage PC-XT to 3.3ms for some of the fastest drives today (Seagate Cheetah 15K.4).

- In 1982 a 10MB drive and controller cost more than $2,000 ($200,000 per gigabyte), a figure which would actually be more than double that amount in today's dollars. Currently, the cost of desktop hard drives (with integrated controllers) has dropped to $0.28 per gigabyte or less—or about 500GB for $140! Laptop drives have fallen to $0.67 per gigabyte or less, or about 120GB for $80.

Note

IBM sold its Hard Disk Drive operations division to Hitachi on January 6, 2003. The resulting new company, called Hitachi Global Storage Technologies (www.hitachigst.com), comprises the hard disk drive operations of Hitachi and IBM and is headquartered in San Jose, California. Hitachi Global Storage Technologies now manufactures, sells, and supports the former IBM Travelstar, Microdrive, Ultrastar, and Deskstar product lines. The new company is 70% owned by Hitachi, with the remaining shares held by IBM. Hitachi assumed full ownership at the end of 2005, and IBM has no involvement in the management of the new company. IBM invented the hard drive, so it is sad to see the company exit the business.

Form Factors

The cornerstone of the PC industry has always been standardization. With disk drives, this is evident in the physical and electrical form factors that comprise modern drives. By using industry-standard form factors, you can purchase a system or chassis from one manufacturer and yet physically and electrically install a drive from a different manufacturer. Form factor standards ensure that available drives will fit in the bay, the screw holes will line up, and the standard cables and connections will plug in. Without these industry standards, there would be no compatibility between different chassis, motherboards, cables, and drives.

You might wonder how these form factors are established. In some cases, it is simply that one manufacturer makes a popular product of a particular shape and connection protocol, and others copy or clone those parameters, making other products that are physically and/or electrically compatible. In other cases, various committees or groups have been formed to dictate certain industry standards. Then it is up to the companies that make applicable products to create them to conform to these standards.

Over the years, disk drives have been introduced in several industry-standard form factors, usually identified by the approximate size of the platters contained inside the drive. Table 9.1 lists the various disk drive form factors that have been used in PCs and portables.

Table 9.1   Hard Disk Form Factors

Height	Width	Depth	Volume
	5 1/4" Drives		
3.25" (82.6mm)	5.75" (146.0mm)	8" (203.2mm)	149.5 ci (2449.9 cc)
	5 1/4" Half-Height Drives		
1.63" (41.3mm)	5.75" (146.0mm)	8.00" (203.2mm)	74.8 ci (1224.9 cc)
	3 1/2" Half-Height Drives		
1.63" (41.3mm)	4" (101.6mm)	5.75" (146.0mm)	37.4 ci (612.5 cc)
	3 1/2" 1/3-Height Drives		
1.00" (25.4mm)	4" (101.6mm)	5.75" (146.0mm)	23.0 ci (376.9 cc)
	2 1/2" Drives		
19.0mm (0.75")	70.0mm (2.76")	100.0mm (3.94")	133.0 cc (8.1 ci)
17.0mm (0.67")			119.0 cc (7.3 ci)
12.7mm (0.50")			88.9 cc (5.4 ci)
12.5mm (0.49")			87.5 cc (5.3 ci)
9.5mm (0.37")			66.5 cc (4.1 ci)
8.5mm (0.33")			59.5 cc (3.6 ci)
	1.8" Drives		
9.5mm (0.37")	70.0mm (2.76")	60.0mm (2.36")	39.9 cc (2.4 ci)
7.0mm (0.28")			29.4 cc (1.8 ci)
	1.8" PC Card Drives		
8.0mm (0.31")	54.0mm (2.13")	78.5mm (3.09")	33.9 cc (2.1 ci)
5.0mm (0.20")			21.2 cc (1.3 ci)
	1" Microdrives		
5.0mm (0.20")	42.8mm (1.69")	36.4mm (1.43")	7.8 cc (0.5 ci)

The first figure listed for each dimension is the dimension on which the standard is based; the second one is derived through a conversion. Some standards are based on SAE (English) measurements, whereas others are based on SI (metric) measurements.

Currently, 3 1/2" drives are the most popular for desktops, whereas 2 1/2" and smaller drives are popular in laptops and other portable devices. Parallel ATA 3 1/2" drives are quickly being phased out to be replaced by Serial ATA drives, which are now the most commonplace drive interfaces in new desktop systems. Notebooks, meanwhile, are just beginning to transition toward 2 1/2" drives featuring the Serial ATA interface. Part of the reason most laptop systems continue to support Parallel ATA is that, until recently, the motherboard chipsets supported only Parallel ATA natively and adding an extra chip for SATA support was cost-, space-, and power-prohibitive. Not to mention that there were originally no SATA 2 1/2" drives on the market. But that is changing. The 900 series chipsets from Intel that are found in newer systems include native SATA support, and SATA 2 1/2" drives are now available as well.

5 1/4" Drive

Shugart Associates first introduced the 5 1/4" form factor along with the first 5 1/4" floppy drive in 1976. The story goes that founder Al Shugart then left that company and founded Seagate Technologies, which introduced the first 5 1/4" (Model ST-506, 5MB capacity) hard disk in 1980, pre-dating the IBM PC. IBM later used the Seagate ST-412 (10MB) drive in some of its PC-XT models, which were among the first PCs to be sold with hard drives built in. The physical format of the 5 1/4" hard disk back then was the same as the 5 1/4" full-height floppy drive, so both fit the same size bay in a chassis. For example, the original IBM PC and XT models had two 5 1/4" full-height bays that could accept these drives. The first portable systems (such as the original Compaq Portable) used these drives as well. Later, the 5 1/4" form factor was reduced in height by one-half when the appropriately named 5 1/4" half-height floppy drives and hard drives were introduced. This allowed two drives to fit in a bay originally designed for one. The 5 1/4" half-height form factor is still used as the form factor for modern desktop CD-ROM and DVD drives and is the standard form factor for larger drive bays in all modern desktop PC chassis. Early portable PCs, such as the IBM Portable PC, used this form factor as well.

3 1/2" Drive

Sony introduced the first 3 1/2" floppy drive in 1981, which used a smaller width and depth but the same height as the half-height 5 1/4" form factor. These were called *3 1/2" half-height drives*, even though there was no such thing as a "full-height" 3 1/2" drive. Rodime followed with the first 3 1/2" half-height hard disk in 1983. Later 3 1/2" floppy and hard drives would be reduced in height to only 1", which was just under one-third of the original 5 1/4" full-height form factor (these were sometimes called *1/3-height drives*). Today, the 1" high version has become the modern industry-standard 3 1/2" form factor.

2 1/2" Drive

PrairieTek introduced the 2 1/2" form factor in 1988, which proved to be ideal for laptop and note-book computers. As laptop sales grew, so did sales of the 2 1/2" drives. Although PrairieTek was the first with that form factor, other drive manufacturers quickly capitalized on the market by also intro-ducing 2 1/2" drives. Finally, in 1994 Conner Peripherals, Inc., paid $18 million for PrairieTek's 2 1/2" disk drive technology and PrairieTek went out of business. Since the 2 1/2" drives first appeared, virtu-ally all laptop and notebook systems have used them. Although 2 1/2" drives can also be used in desk-top systems, the 3 1/2" drive continues to dominate the desktop market due to greater capacity and speed and lower cost.

The 2 1/2" drives have been manufactured in various thicknesses (or heights), and many notebook or laptop systems are restricted as to how thick a drive they can support. Here are the common thick-nesses that have been available:

- 8.5mm
- 9.5mm
- 12.5mm
- 12.7mm
- 17.0mm
- 19.0mm

By far, the most popular sizes are 9.5mm and 12.5mm, which are the sizes used by most laptop and notebook systems. Currently, most drive manufacturers are concentrating on the 9.5mm form factor. A thinner drive can almost always be installed in place of a thicker one; however, most systems do not have the room to accept a thicker drive than they were originally designed to use.

1.8" Drive

The 1.8" drive was first introduced by Integral Peripherals in 1991 and has had problems gaining acceptance in the marketplace ever since. This size was initially created because it fit perfectly in the PC Card (PCMCIA) form factor, making it ideal as add-on removable storage for laptop and notebook systems. Unfortunately, the 1.8" drive market has been slow to take shape, and in 1998 an investment group called Mobile Storage bought Integral Peripherals' 1.8" drive technology for $5.5 million; Integral Peripherals then went out of business. Several other companies have introduced 1.8" drives over the years—most notably HP, Calluna, Toshiba, and Hitachi. Of those, only Toshiba and Hitachi continue to manufacture drives in that format. HP exited the disk drive market completely in 1996, and Calluna finally ceased operation in 2001. Toshiba introduced its 1.8" drives (available in the physical format of a Type II PC Card) in 2000, and Hitachi entered the 1.8" drive market in 2003. The 1.8" drives are available in capacities of up to 100GB or more.

1" Drives

During 1998, IBM introduced a 1" drive called the Microdrive, incorporating a single platter about the size of a quarter! Current versions of the Microdrive can store up to 8GB or more. These drives are available with several interfaces including that of a Type II Compact Flash (CF) card, which means they can be used in almost any device that takes CF cards, including digital cameras, personal digital assistants (PDAs), and MP3 players. IBM's disk drive division was sold to Hitachi in 2003 and combined with Hitachi's storage technology business as Hitachi Global Storage Technologies.

Note

HP introduced a 20MB 1.3" disk drive called the KittyHawk in 1992, originally intended for the handheld computer market. In 1994, HP followed with a 40MB model. These small drives were expensive and proved to be too far ahead of their time, as were the handheld computers they were intended for. After two years of low sales, HP discontinued the KittyHawk family.

In 2004, Toshiba introduced the smallest drive to date: the 0.85" drive, which is about the size of a postage stamp and stores up to 4GB. This drive is not really designed for PCs but will be used in cell phones, digital audio players, PDAs, digital still cameras, camcorders, and more.

Hard Disk Drive Operation

The basic physical construction of a hard disk drive consists of spinning disks with heads that move over the disks and store data in tracks and sectors. The heads read and write data in concentric rings called *tracks*, which are divided into segments called *sectors*, which typically store 512 bytes each (see Figure 9.2).

Hard disk drives usually have multiple disks, called *platters*, that are stacked on top of each other and spin in unison, each with two sides on which the drive stores data. Most drives have two or three platters, resulting in four or six sides, but some PC hard disks have up to 12 platters and 24 sides with 24 heads to read them (Seagate Barracuda 180). The identically aligned tracks on each side of every platter together make up a cylinder (see Figure 9.3). A hard disk drive usually has one head per platter side, with all the heads mounted on a common carrier device or rack. The heads move radially across the disk in unison; they can't move independently because they are mounted on the same carrier or rack, called an *actuator*.

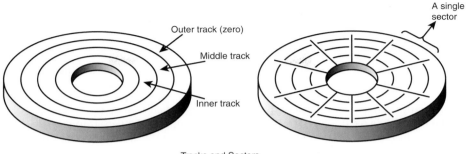

Tracks and Sectors

Figure 9.2 The tracks and sectors on a disk.

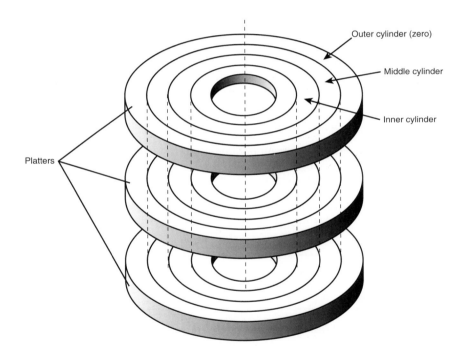

Figure 9.3 Hard disk cylinders.

Originally, most hard disks spun at 3,600 rpm—approximately 10 times faster than a floppy disk drive. For many years, 3,600 rpm was pretty much a constant among hard drives. Now, however, most drives spin much faster. Although speeds can vary, modern drives typically spin the platters at either 4,200 rpm, 5,400 rpm, 7,200 rpm, 10,000 rpm, or 15,000 rpm. Most standard-issue drives found in PCs today spin at 7,200 rpm, with high-performance models spinning at 10,000 rpm, although many less-expensive drives still spin at 5,400 rpm. Some of the small 2 1/2" notebook drives run at only 4,200 rpm to conserve power, and 15,000 rpm drives are usually found only in very high-performance workstations or servers, where their higher prices, heat generation, and noise can be more easily dealt with. High rotational speeds combined with a fast head-positioning mechanism and more sectors per track are what make one hard disk faster overall than another.

The heads in most hard disk drives do not (and should not!) touch the platters during normal operation. However, on most drives, the heads do rest on the platters when the drive is powered off. In most drives, when the drive is powered off, the heads move to the innermost cylinder, where they land on the platter surface. This is referred to as *contact start stop (CSS)* design. When the drive is powered on, the heads slide on the platter surface as they spin up, until a very thin cushion of air builds up between the heads and platter surface, causing the heads to lift off and remain suspended a short distance above or below the platter. If the air cushion is disturbed by a particle of dust or a shock, the head can come into contact with the platter while it is spinning at full speed. When contact with the spinning platters is forceful enough to do damage, the event is called a *head crash*. The result of a head crash can be anything from a few lost bytes of data to a completely ruined drive. Most drives have special lubricants on the platters and hardened surfaces that can withstand the daily "takeoffs and landings" as well as more severe abuse.

Some newer drives do not use CSS design and instead use a load/unload mechanism that does not allow the heads to contact the platters, even when the drive is powered off. First used in the 2 1/2" form factor notebook or laptop drives where resistance to mechanical shock is more important, traditional load/unload mechanisms use a ramp positioned just off the outer part of the platter surface, whereas some newer designs position the ramp near the spindle. When the drive is powered off or in a power-saving mode, the heads ride up on the ramp. When the drive is powered on, the platters are allowed to come up to full speed before the heads are released down the ramp, allowing the airflow (air bearing) to prevent any head/platter contact.

Because the platter assemblies are sealed and nonremovable, the track densities on the disk can be very high. Hard drives today have up to 96,000 or more tracks per inch (TPI) recorded on the media (Hitachi Travelstar 5K80). Head disk assemblies (HDAs), which contain the platters, are assembled and sealed in clean rooms under absolutely sanitary conditions. Because few companies repair HDAs, repair or replacement of the parts inside a sealed HDA can be expensive. Every hard disk ever made eventually fails. The only questions are when the failure will occur and whether your data is backed up.

Caution

It is strongly recommended that you do not even attempt to open a hard disk drive's HDA unless you have the equipment and expertise to make repairs inside. Most manufacturers deliberately make the HDA difficult to open to discourage the intrepid do-it-yourselfer. Opening the HDA voids the drive's warranty.

Many PC users know that hard disks are fragile, and comparatively speaking, they are certainly one of the more fragile components in your PC. That being the case, it comes as somewhat of a surprise to the students in some of my PC Hardware and Troubleshooting or Data Recovery seminars when I run various hard disks with the covers removed—and in some cases I've even removed and installed the covers while the drives were operating! Those drives continue to store data perfectly to this day with their lids either on or off. Of course, I do not recommend that you try this with your own drives.

The Ultimate Hard Disk Drive Analogy

There is an old analogy that compares the interaction of the heads and the medium in a typical hard disk drive as being similar in scale to a 747 Jumbo Jet flying a few feet off the ground at cruising speed (500+ mph). I have heard this analogy used repeatedly for years, and in the past I even used it myself without checking to see whether the analogy is technically accurate with respect to modern hard drives. It isn't.

Perhaps the most inaccurate aspect of the 747 analogy is the use of an airplane of any type to describe the head-and-platter interaction. This analogy implies that the heads fly very low over the surface of the disk, but technically, this is not true. The heads do not fly at all in the traditional aerodynamic sense; instead, they float or ski on a cushion of air that is being dragged around by the platters.

A much better analogy would use a hovercraft instead of an airplane; the action of a hovercraft much more closely emulates the action of the heads in a hard disk drive. Like a hovercraft, the drive heads rely somewhat on the shape of the bottom of the head to capture and control the cushion of air that keeps them floating over the disk. By nature, the cushion of air on which the heads float forms only in very close proximity to the platter and is often called an *air bearing* by those in the disk drive industry.

I thought it was time to come up with a new analogy that more correctly describes the dimensions and speeds at which a hard disk drive operates today. I looked up the specifications on a specific modern hard disk drive and then magnified and rescaled all the dimensions involved by a factor of more than 300,000. For my example, I use an IBM Deskstar 75GXP drive, which is a 75GB (formatted capacity), 3 1/2" ATA (AT Attachment interface) drive. The head sliders (called *pico* sliders) in this drive are about 0.049" long, 0.039" wide, and 0.012" high. They float on a cushion of air about 15 nanometers (nm or billionths of a meter) over the surface of the disk while traveling at an average true speed of 53.55 miles per hour (figuring an average track diameter of about 2 1/2"). These heads read and write individual bits spaced only 2.56 micro-inches (millionths of an inch) apart, along tracks separated by only 35.27 micro-inches. The heads can move from one track to another in 8.5 milliseconds during an average seek.

To create my analogy, I magnified the scale to make the head floating height equal to 5 millimeters (about 0.2"). Because 5 millimeters is about 333,333 times greater than 15 nanometers (nm), I scaled up everything else by the same amount.

Magnified to such a scale, the heads in this typical hard disk would be about 1,361 feet long, 1,083 feet wide, and 333 feet high (the length and height would be about equal to the Sears Tower if it were tipped over sideways). These skyscraper-sized heads would float on a cushion of air that to scale would be only 5mm thick (about 0.2") while traveling at a speed of 17.8 million miles per hour (4,958 miles per second), all while reading data bits spaced a mere 0.85" apart on tracks separated by only 0.98 feet!

The proportionate forward speed of this imaginary head is difficult to comprehend, so I'll elaborate. The diameter of the Earth at the equator is 7,926 miles, which means a circumference of about 24,900 miles. At 4,958 miles per second, this imaginary skyscraper-sized head would circle the earth once every 5 seconds (at only two-tenths of an inch over the surface)! It would also read 231.33MB in one lap around this equatorial track.

There is also sideways velocity to consider. Because the average seek time of 8.5 milliseconds is defined as the time it takes to move the heads over one-third of the total tracks (about 9,241 tracks in this example), the heads could move sideways within a scale distance of 1.71 miles in that short time. This results in a scale-seek velocity of more than 726,321 mph, or 202 miles per second!

This analogy should give you a new appreciation of the technological marvel that the modern hard disk drive actually represents. It makes the old Jumbo Jet analogy look rather pathetic (not to mention grossly inaccurate), doesn't it?

Tracks and Sectors

A *track* is a single ring of data on one side of a disk. A disk track is too large to manage data effectively as a single storage unit. Many disk tracks can store 100,000 or more bytes of data, which would be very inefficient for storing small files. For that reason, tracks are divided into several numbered divisions known as *sectors*. These sectors represent arc-shaped pieces of the track.

Various types of disk drives split their disk tracks into different numbers of sectors, depending on the density of the tracks. For example, floppy disk formats use 8–36 sectors per track, although hard disks usually store data at a higher density and today can have 900 or more sectors per track physically. The sectors created by the standard formatting procedure on a PC system have a capacity of 512 bytes, which has been one constant throughout the history of the PC. One interesting phenomenon of the PC standard is that to be compatible with most older BIOS and drivers, drives usually perform an internal translation so that they pretend to have 63 sectors per track when addressed in CHS (cylinder, head, sector) mode.

The sectors on a track are numbered starting with 1, unlike the heads or cylinders that are numbered starting with 0. For example, a 1.44MB floppy disk contains 80 cylinders numbered 0–79 and two heads numbered 0 and 1, whereas each track on each cylinder has 18 sectors numbered 1–18.

When a disk is formatted, the formatting program creates ID areas before and after each sector's data that the disk controller uses for sector numbering and identifying the start and end of each sector. These areas precede and follow each sector's data area and consume some of the disk's total storage capacity. This accounts for the difference between a disk's unformatted and formatted capacities. Note that most modern hard drives are sold preformatted and advertise only the formatted capacity. The unformatted capacity is usually not mentioned anymore. Another interesting development is that many new drives use what is called *No-ID sector formatting*, which means the sectors are recorded without ID marks before and after each sector. Therefore, more of the disk can be used for actual data.

Each sector on a disk usually has a prefix portion, or header, that identifies the start of the sector and contains the sector number, as well as a suffix portion, or trailer, that contains a checksum (which helps ensure the integrity of the data contents). Many newer drives omit this header and have what is called a *No-ID recording*, thus allowing more space for actual data. With a No-ID recording, the start and end of each sector are located via predetermined clock timing.

Each sector contains 512 bytes of data. The low-level formatting process typically fills the data bytes with some specific value, such as F6h (hex), or some other repeating test pattern used by the drive manufacturer. Some patterns are more difficult for the electronics on the drive to encode/decode, so these patterns are used when the manufacturer is testing the drive during initial formatting. A special test pattern might cause errors to surface that a normal data pattern would not show. This way, the manufacturer can more accurately identify marginal sectors during testing.

Note

The type of disk formatting discussed here is a physical or low-level format, not the high-level format you perform when you use a Windows DOS-based FORMAT program. See the section "Disk Formatting," later in this chapter, to learn about the difference between these two types of formatting.

The sector headers and trailers are independent of the operating system, file system, and files stored on the drive. In addition to the headers and trailers, gaps exist within the sectors, between the sectors on each track, and between tracks, but none of these gaps contain usable data space. The gaps are created during the low-level format process when the recording is turned off momentarily. They serve the same function as having gaps of no sound between the songs recorded on a cassette tape. The prefix, suffix, and gaps account for the lost space between the unformatted capacity of a disk and the formatted capacity. For example, a 4MB (unformatted) floppy disk (3 1/2") has a capacity of 2.88MB when it is formatted, a 2MB (unformatted) floppy has a formatted capacity of 1.44MB, and an older 38MB unformatted capacity (for instance, Seagate ST-4038) hard disk has a capacity of only 32MB when it is formatted. Because the ATA hard drives you purchase today are low-level formatted at the factory, the manufacturers now advertise only the formatted capacity. Even so, nearly all drives use some reserved space for managing the data that will be stored on the drive. Therefore, although I stated earlier that each disk sector is 512 bytes in size, this statement is technically untrue. Each sector does allow for the storage of 512 bytes of data, but the data area is only a portion of the sector. Each sector on a disk typically occupies up to 571 bytes of the disk, of which only 512 bytes are available for the storage of user data. The actual number of additional bytes required for the sector header and trailer can vary from drive to drive. As mentioned earlier, though, many modern drives now use a No-ID recording scheme that virtually eliminates the storage overhead of the sector header information.

You might find it helpful to think of each disk sector as being a page in a book. In a book, each page contains text, but the entire page is not filled with text; rather, each page has top, bottom, left, and right margins. Information such as chapter titles (track and cylinder numbers) and page numbers (sector numbers) is placed in the margins. The "margin" areas of a sector are created during the low-level formatting process. Formatting also fills the data area of each sector with dummy values. After you perform a high-level format on the disk, the PC's file system can write to the data area of each sector, but the sector header and trailer information can't be altered during normal write operations unless the disk is low-level formatted again.

Table 9.2 shows the format for each track and sector on a typical hard disk drive with 17 sectors per track.

Table 9.2   Typical Disk Track/Sector Format Using ID Marks

Bytes	Name	Description
16	POST INDEX GAP	All 4Eh, at the track beginning after the Index mark.

The following sector data (shown between the lines in this table) is repeated as many times as there are sectors on the track.

Bytes	Name	Description
13	ID VFO LOCK	All 00h; synchronizes the VFO for the sector ID.
1	SYNC BYTE	A1h; notifies the controller that data follows.
1	ADDRESS MARK	FEh; defines that ID field data follows.
2	CYLINDER NUMBER	A value that defines the head actuator position.
1	HEAD NUMBER	A value that defines the particular head selected.
1	SECTOR NUMBER	A value that defines the sector.
2	CRC	Cyclic Redundancy Check to verify ID data.
3	WRITE TURN-ON GAP	00h written by format to isolate the ID from DATA.
13	DATA SYNC VFO LOCK	All 00h; synchronizes the VFO for the DATA.
1	SYNC BYTE	A1h; notifies the controller that data follows.
1	ADDRESS MARK	F8h; defines that user DATA field follows.
512	DATA	The area for user DATA.
2	CRC	Cyclic Redundancy Check to verify DATA.
3	WRITE TURN-OFF GAP	00h; written by DATA update to isolate DATA.
15	INTER-RECORD GAP	All 00h; a buffer for spindle speed variation.
693	PRE-INDEX GAP	All 4Eh, at track end before Index mark.

571 = Total bytes per sector; 512 = Data (usable) bytes per sector

Note: "All XXh" indicates that field will be filled with XXh bytes.

As you can see, the usable space for data on each track is about 15% less than its total unformatted capacity. This is true for most disks, although the percentage can vary slightly, depending on how many sectors exist per track. The following paragraphs detail each piece of the sector data listed in Table 9.2.

The POST INDEX GAP provides a head-switching recovery period, so when switching from one track to another, the heads can read sequential sectors without waiting for an additional revolution of the disk. Because the disk is continuously spinning and the heads take some small amount of time to move radially from track to track, reading consecutive sectors on two different tracks, one right after the other, is not possible. By the time the head moves to the new track, the beginning of the second sector has already spun past it. Leaving a gap between sectors provides the heads with time to move to another track.

In some drives, this gap does not provide sufficient time for the heads to move. When this is the case, a drive can gain additional time by skewing the sectors on different tracks so the arrival of the first sector is delayed. In other words, the low-level formatting process offsets the sector numbering, so instead of the same numbered sectors on each track being adjacent to each other, Sector 9 on one track might be next to Sector 8 of the next track, which is next to Sector 7 on the next, and so forth. The optimum skew value is based on the rotational speed of the disk as compared to the lateral speed of the heads.

Note

At one time, the head skew was a parameter you could set yourself while low-level formatting a drive. Today's drives are low-level formatted at the factory with the optimum interleave and skew values, and these values are not changeable.

The Sector ID data consists of the Cylinder, Head, and Sector Number fields, as well as a CRC field used to verify the ID data. Most controllers use bit 7 of the Head Number field to mark a sector as bad during a low-level format or surface analysis. This convention is not absolute, however. Some controllers use other methods to mark a bad sector, but the mark usually involves one of the ID fields.

The WRITE TURN-ON GAP follows the ID field's CRC bytes and provides a pad to ensure a proper recording of the user data area that follows, as well as to enable full recovery of the ID CRC.

The user DATA field consists of all 512 bytes of data stored in the sector. This field is followed by a CRC field to verify the data. Although many controllers use two bytes of CRC here, the controller might implement a longer error correction code (ECC) that requires more than two CRC bytes to store. The ECC data stored here provides the possibility of correcting errors in the DATA field as well as detecting them. The correction/detection capabilities depend on the ECC code the drive uses and its implementation by the controller. The WRITE TURN-OFF GAP is a pad that enables the ECC (CRC) bytes to be fully recovered.

The INTER-RECORD GAP provides a means to accommodate variances in drive spindle speeds. A track might have been formatted while the disk was running slightly more slowly than normal and then written to while the disk was running slightly more quickly than normal. In such cases, this gap prevents the accidental overwriting of any information in the next sector. The actual size of this padding varies, depending on the speed of the DATA disk's rotation when the track was formatted and each time the DATA field is updated.

The PRE-INDEX GAP enables speed tolerance over the entire track. This gap varies in size, depending on the variances in disk rotation speed and write-frequency tolerance at the time of formatting.

This sector prefix information is extremely important because it contains the numbering information that defines the cylinder, head, and sector. So this information, except the DATA field, DATA CRC bytes, and WRITE TURN-OFF GAP, is written only during a low-level format.

Disk Formatting

Two formatting procedures are required before you can write user data to a disk:

- Physical, or low-level formatting
- Logical, or high-level formatting

When you format a blank floppy disk, the Windows Explorer or DOS FORMAT command performs both types of formats simultaneously. If the floppy was already formatted, DOS and Windows will default to doing only a high-level format.

A hard disk, however, requires a third step, between the two formatting procedures, to write the partitioning information to the disk. In addition, the low-level formatting is done at the factory on all modern drives. Partitioning is required because a hard disk is designed to be used with more than one operating system or file system. Using multiple operating and/or file systems on one hard drive is possible by partitioning, which creates multiple volumes on the drive. A *volume* or *logical drive* is any section of the disk to which the operating system assigns a drive letter or name.

Consequently, preparing a hard disk drive for data storage involves three steps:

1. Low-level formatting (LLF – done at the factory)
2. Partitioning
3. High-level formatting (HLF)

Low-Level Formatting

During a low-level format, the tracks are divided into a specific number of sectors, creating the inter-sector and intertrack gaps and recording the sector header and trailer information. The sector's data areas are filled with a dummy byte value or a pattern of test values. For floppy disks, the number of sectors recorded on each track depends on the type of diskette and drive. For hard disks, the number of sectors per track depends on the drive and the controller interface.

Originally, PC hard disk drives used a separate controller that took the form of an expansion card or was integrated into the motherboard. Because the controller could be used with various disk drives and might even have been made by a different manufacturer, some uniformity had to exist in the communications between the controller and the drive. For this reason, the number of sectors written to a track tended to be relatively consistent.

The original ST-506/412 MFM controllers always placed 17 sectors per track on a disk, although ST-506/412 controllers with RLL encoding increased the number of sectors to 25 or 26 per track; ESDI drives had 32 or more sectors per track. The ATA drives found in PCs today can have anywhere from 17 to 2500 or more sectors per track, and the number of sectors can vary among different tracks as well.

Virtually all ATA drives use a technique called *zoned-bit recording (ZBR)*, sometimes shortened to *zoned recording*, which writes a variable number of sectors per track. Without zoned recording, the number of sectors (and therefore bits) on each track is a constant. This means the actual number of bits per inch will vary. More bits per inch will exist on the inner tracks, and fewer will exist on the outer. The data rate and rotational speed will remain constant, as will the number of bits per track. Figure 9.4 shows a drive recorded with the same number of sectors per track.

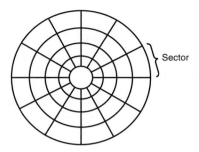

Figure 9.4   Standard recording, where the same number of sectors comprise every track.

A standard recording wastes capacity on the outer tracks because it is longer and yet holds the same amount of data (more loosely spaced) as the inner tracks. One way to increase the capacity of a hard drive during the low-level format is to create more sectors on the disks' outer cylinders than on the inner ones. Because they have a larger circumference, the outer cylinders can hold more data. Drives without zoned recording store the same amount of data on every cylinder, even though the tracks of the outer cylinders might be twice as long as those of the inner cylinders. The result is wasted storage capacity because the disk medium must be capable of storing data reliably at the same density as on the inner cylinders. When the number of sectors per track is fixed, as in older controllers, the drive capacity is limited by the density of the innermost (shortest) track.

Drives that use zoned recording split the cylinders into groups called *zones*, with each successive zone having more sectors per track as you move outward from the center of the disk. All the cylinders in a particular zone have the same number of sectors per track. The number of zones varies with specific drives, but most drives have 10 or more zones.

Figure 9.5 shows a drive with zoned-bit recording.

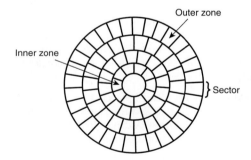

Figure 9.5   Zoned recording, where the number of sectors per track increases within each zone, moving out from the center.

Another effect of zoned recording is that transfer speeds vary depending on which zone the heads are in. A drive with zoned recording still spins at a constant speed. Because more sectors exist per track in the outer zones, however, data transfer is fastest there. Consequently, data transfer is slowest when reading or writing to the inner zones. That is why virtually all drives today report minimum and maximum sustained transfer rates, which depend on where on the drive you are reading from or writing to.

As an example, see Table 9.3, which shows the zones defined for an Hitachi Travelstar 7K60 2 1/2" notebook drive, the sectors per track for each zone, and the resulting data transfer rate.

**Table 9.3   Zoned Recording Information for the Hitachi Travelstar 7K60 2 1/2"
Hard Disk Drive**

	Sectors per Track	Bytes per Track	Transfer Zone Rate (MBps)
0	720	368640	44.24
1	704	360448	43.25
2	696	356352	42.76
3	672	344064	41.29
4	640	327680	39.32
5	614	314368	37.72
6	592	303104	36.37
7	556	284672	34.16
8	528	270336	32.44
9	480	245760	29.49
10	480	245760	29.49
11	456	233472	28.02
12	432	221184	26.54
13	416	212992	25.56
14	384	196608	23.59
15	360	184320	22.12

This drive has a total of 54,288 cylinders, which are divided into 16 zones averaging 3,393 cylinders each. Zone 0 consists of the outermost cylinders, which are the longest and contain the most sectors: 720 for each track. Because each sector is 512 bytes, each track in the outer zone contains 368,640 bytes of data. The inner zone has only 360 sectors per track, which means each track in the inner zone holds 184,320 bytes.

With zoned recording, this drive averages 545.63 sectors per track. Without zoned recording, the number of sectors per track would be limited to 360 for all tracks. The use of zoned recording therefore provides nearly a 52% increase in the storage capacity of this particular drive.

Also notice the difference in the data transfer rates for each of the zones. Because the drive spins at 7,200 rpm, it completes a single revolution every 1/120 of a second, or every 8.33 milliseconds. Therefore, the data transfer speed varies depending on which zone you are reading and writing. In the outer zone, the data transfer rate is 44.24MBps, whereas in the inner zone it is only 22.12MBps. The average transfer rate for this drive is 33.52MBps. This is one reason you might notice huge discrepancies in the results produced by disk drive benchmark programs. A test that reads or writes files on the outer tracks of the disk naturally yields far better results than one conducted on the inner tracks. It might appear as though your drive is running more slowly when the problem is actually that the test results you are comparing stem from disk activity on different zones.

Another thing to note is that this drive conforms to the ATA-6 specification and is capable of running in Ultra-ATA/100 mode (also called UDMA-100), which implies a transfer speed of 100MBps. As you can see, that is entirely theoretical because the true media transfer speed of this drive varies between about 22MBps and 44MBps, averaging about 33MBps overall. The interface transfer rate is just that: what the interface is capable of. It has little bearing on the actual capabilities of the drive.

Drives with separate controllers used in the past could not handle zoned recording because no standard way existed to communicate information about the zones from the drive to the controller.

With ATA disks, however, formatting individual tracks with different numbers of sectors became possible because these drives have the disk controller built in. The built-in controllers on these drives are fully aware of the zoning algorithm and can translate the physical cylinder, head, and sector numbers to logical cylinder, head, and sector numbers so the drive appears to have the same number of sectors on each track. Because the PC BIOS is designed to handle only a single number of sectors per track throughout the entire drive, a zoned drive must run by using a sector-translation scheme.

The use of zoned recording enables drive manufacturers to increase the capacity of their hard drives by 20%–50% or more when compared with a fixed-sector-per-track arrangement. All modern drives use zoned recording.

Partitioning

Creating a partition on a hard disk drive enables it to support separate file systems, each in its own partition.

Each file system can then use its own method to allocate file space in logical units called *clusters* or *allocation units*. Every hard disk drive must have at least one partition on it and can have up to four partitions, each of which can support the same or different type file systems. Three common file systems are used by PC operating systems today:

- **FAT (file allocation table)**—The standard file system supported by DOS and Windows 9x/Me. FAT partitions support filenames of 11 characters maximum (8 characters + a 3-character extension) under DOS, and 255 characters under Windows 9x (or later). The standard FAT file system uses 12- or 16-bit numbers to identify clusters, resulting in a maximum volume size of 2GB.

  Using FDISK, you can create only two physical FAT partitions on a hard disk drive—primary and extended—but you can subdivide the extended partition into as many as 25 logical volumes. Alternative partitioning programs, such as Partition Magic, can create up to four primary partitions or three primary and one extended.

- **FAT32 (file allocation table, 32-bit)**—An optional file system supported by Windows 95 OSR2 (OEM Service Release 2) and later.

  FAT32 uses 32-bit numbers to identify clusters, resulting in a maximum single volume size of 2TB or 2,048GB.

- **NTFS (Windows NT File System)**—The native file system for Windows NT and later, which supports filenames up to 256 characters long and partitions up to (a theoretical) 16 exabytes. NTFS also provides extended attributes and file system security features that do not exist in the FAT file system.

Up until the release of XP, FAT32 was by far the most popular file system. Because NTFS is native to XP and Vista (and required for Vista boot volumes), NTFS is now more popular in newer systems. Still, the FAT file system is accessible by nearly every operating system, which makes it the most compatible format for external drives in a mixed OS environment. FAT32 and NTFS provide additional features but are not universally accessible by other operating systems.

Partitioning normally is accomplished by running the disk partitioning program that comes with your operating system. The name and exact operation of the disk partitioning program varies with the operating system. For example, FDISK is used by DOS and Windows 9x/Me for this task, whereas the FDISK, DISKPART command or the Disk Management snap-in component of the Computer

Management service is used with Windows XP and Vista. FDISK, DISKPART, and other disk-partitioning tools enable you to select the amount of space on the drive to use for a partition, from a single megabyte (or 1%) of the drive up to the entire capacity of the drive or as much as the particular file system will allow. You usually should have as few partitions as possible, and many people (myself included) try to stick with only one or two at the most. This was more difficult before FAT32 because the maximum partition size for a FAT16 partition was only 2GB. With FAT32, though, the maximum partition size can be up to 2048GB.

Caution

FDISK, DISKPART, Disk Management, and other disk-partitioning tools included in operating systems can't be used to change the size of a partition; all they can do is remove or create partitions. The act of removing or creating a partition destroys and loses access to data that was contained in the partition or that was on that part of the disk. To manipulate partitions without destroying data, you can use a third-party utility program such as Partition Magic from Symantec or Partition Commander from V-Communications.

After a drive is partitioned, each partition must then be high-level formatted by the operating system that will use it.

High-Level Formatting

During the high-level format, the operating system writes the structures necessary for managing files and data on the disk. For example, FAT partitions have a Volume Boot Sector (VBS), two copies of a file allocation table (FAT), and a root directory on each formatted logical drive. These data structures enable the operating system to manage the space on the disk, keep track of files, and even manage defective areas so they do not cause problems.

High-level formatting is not really a physical formatting of the drive, but rather the creation of a table of contents for the disk. In low-level formatting, which is the real physical formatting process, tracks and sectors are written on the disk. As mentioned, the DOS and Windows 9x/Me FORMAT command can perform both low-level and high-level format operations on a floppy disk, but it performs only the high-level format for a hard disk. True low-level formats of ATA drives are performed by the manufacturer and technically cannot be performed by the end user. Most manufacturers make initialization programs available, which are the modern substitute for low-level format programs. While the initialization programs do not technically re-create the sector marks, they do rewrite the data portion of all sectors as well as manage defects, including the ability to reassign spare sectors to replace defective sectors. Normally the only time you run an initialization program is when you are attempting to repair a format that has become damaged (parts of the disk become unreadable) or in some cases when you want to wipe away all data on the drive.

Basic Hard Disk Drive Components

Many types of hard disk drives are on the market, but nearly all share the same basic physical components. Some differences might exist in the implementation of these components (and in the quality of the materials used to make them), but the operational characteristics of most drives are similar. The basic components of a typical hard disk drive are as follows (see Figure 9.6):

- Disk platters
- Read/write heads
- Head actuator mechanism
- Spindle motor (inside platter hub)

- Logic board (controller or Printed Circuit Board)
- Cables and connectors
- Configuration items (such as jumpers or switches)

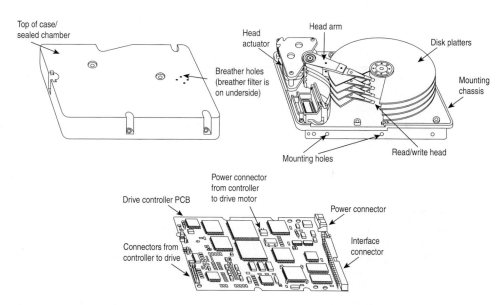

Figure 9.6   Typical hard disk drive components.

The platters, spindle motor, heads, and head actuator mechanisms usually are contained in a sealed chamber called the *head disk assembly (HDA)*. The HDA is usually treated as a single component; it is rarely opened. Other parts external to the drive's HDA, such as the logic boards, bezel, and other configuration or mounting hardware, can be disassembled from the drive.

Hard Disk Platters (Disks)

A hard disk drive has one or more platters, or disks. Hard disks for PC systems have been available in several form factors over the years. Normally, the physical size of a drive is expressed as the size of the platters. Table 9.4 lists the platter sizes that have been associated with PC hard disk drives.

Table 9.4   Hard Disk Form Factors Versus Actual Platter Sizes

Hard Disk Form Factor	Actual Platter Diameter (mm)	Actual Platter Diameter (in.)	Year Introduced
5.25"	130	5.12	1980
3.5"	95	3.74	1983
2.5"	65	2.56	1988
1.8"	48	1.89	1991
1"	34	1.33	1999
0.85"	21.5	0.85	2004

Larger hard disk drives that have 8", 14", or even larger platters are available, but these drives are not used with PC systems. Currently, the 3 1/2" drives are the most popular for desktop and some portable systems, whereas the 2 1/2" and smaller drives are very popular in portable or notebook systems.

Most hard disk drives have two or more platters, although some of the smaller drives used in portable systems and some entry-level drives for desktop computers have only one. The number of platters a drive can have is limited by the drive's vertical physical size. The maximum number of platters I have seen in any 3 1/2" drive is 12; however, most drives have six or fewer.

Platters were originally made from an aluminum/magnesium alloy, which provides both strength and light weight. However, manufacturers' desire for higher and higher densities and smaller drives has led to the use of platters made of glass (or, more technically, a glass-ceramic composite). One such material, produced by the Dow Corning Corporation, is called MemCor. MemCor is composed of glass with ceramic implants, enabling it to resist cracking better than pure glass. Glass platters offer greater rigidity than metal (because metal can be bent and glass can't) and can therefore be machined to one-half the thickness of conventional aluminum disks—sometimes less. Glass platters are also much more thermally stable than aluminum platters, which means they do not expand or contract very much with changes in temperature. Virtually all modern drives use use glass or glass-ceramic platters.

Recording Media

No matter which substrate is used, the platters are covered with a thin layer of a magnetically retentive substance, called the *medium*, on which magnetic information is stored. Three popular types of magnetic media are used on hard disk platters:

- Oxide media
- Thin-film media
- AFC (antiferromagnetically coupled) media

Oxide Media

The oxide medium is made of various compounds, containing iron oxide as the active ingredient. The magnetic layer is created on the disk by coating the aluminum platter with a syrup containing iron-oxide particles. This syrup is spread across the disk by spinning the platters at high speed; centrifugal force causes the material to flow from the center of the platter to the outside, creating an even coating of the material on the platter. The surface is then cured and polished. Finally, a layer of material that protects and lubricates the surface is added and burnished smooth. The oxide coating is usually about 30 millionths of an inch thick. If you could peer into a drive with oxide-coated platters, you would see that the platters are brownish or amber.

As drive density increases, the magnetic medium needs to be thinner and more perfectly formed. The capabilities of oxide coatings have been exceeded by most higher-capacity drives. Because the oxide medium is very soft, disks that use it are subject to head-crash damage if the drive is jolted during operation. Most older drives, especially those sold as low-end models, use oxide media on the drive platters. Oxide media, which have been used since 1955, remained popular because of their relatively low cost and ease of application. Today, however, very few if any drives use oxide media.

Thin-Film Media

The thin-film medium is thinner, harder, and more perfectly formed than oxide medium. Thin film was developed as a high-performance medium that enabled a new generation of drives to have lower head-floating heights, which in turn made increases in drive density possible.

The thin-film medium is aptly named. The coating is much thinner than can be achieved by the oxide-coating method. Thin-film media are also known as *plated* or *sputtered media* because of the various processes used to deposit the thin film on the platters.

Thin-film plated media are manufactured by depositing the magnetic medium on the disk with an electroplating mechanism, in much the same way that chrome plating is deposited on the bumper of a car. The aluminum/magnesium or glass platter is immersed in a series of chemical baths that coat the platter with several layers of metallic film. The magnetic medium layer itself is a cobalt alloy about 1 µ-inch thick.

Thin-film sputtered media are created by first coating the aluminum platters with a layer of nickel phosphorus and then applying the cobalt-alloy magnetic material in a continuous vacuum-deposition process called *sputtering*. This process deposits magnetic layers as thin as 1 µ-inch or less on the disk, in a fashion similar to the way that silicon wafers are coated with metallic films in the semiconductor industry. The same sputtering technique is again used to lay down an extremely hard, 1 µ-inch protective carbon coating. The need for a near-perfect vacuum makes sputtering the most expensive of the processes described here.

The surface of a sputtered platter contains magnetic layers as thin as 1 µ-inch. Because this surface also is very smooth, the head can float more closely to the disk surface than was previously possible. Floating heights as small as 10nm (nanometers, or about 0.4 µ-inch) above the surface are possible. When the head is closer to the platter, the density of the magnetic flux transitions can be increased to provide greater storage capacity. Additionally, the increased intensity of the magnetic field during a closer-proximity read provides the higher signal amplitudes necessary for good signal-to-noise performance.

Both the sputtering and plating processes result in a very thin, hard film of magnetic medium on the platters. Because the thin-film medium is so hard, it has a better chance of surviving contact with the heads at high speed. In fact, modern thin-film media are virtually uncrashable. If you could open a drive to peek at the platters, you would see that platters coated with the thin-film medium look like mirrors.

AFC Media

The latest advancement in drive media is called *antiferromagnetically coupled (AFC)* media and is designed to allow densities to be pushed beyond previous limits. Anytime density is increased, the magnetic layer on the platters must be made thinner and thinner. Areal density (tracks per inch times bits per inch) has increased in hard drives to the point where the grains in the magnetic layer used to store data are becoming so small that they become unstable over time, causing data storage to become unreliable. This is referred to as the *superparamagnetic limit*, and it was originally determined to be between 30Gb/sq. in. and 50Gb/sq. in. However, as technology has advanced, this so-called limit has been pushed further and further back, and commercially produced drives now routinely exceed 100Gb/sq. in. Drives exceeding 200Gb/sq. in. will be possible in the future, with several new technologies in the works.

AFC media consists of two magnetic layers separated by a very thin 3-atom (6 angstrom) film layer of the element ruthenium. IBM has coined the term "pixie dust" to refer to this ultra-thin ruthenium layer. This sandwich produces an antiferromagnetic coupling of the top and bottom magnetic layers, which causes the apparent magnetic thickness of the entire structure to be the difference between the top and bottom magnetic layers. This allows the use of physically thicker magnetic layers with more stable larger grains, so they can function as if they were really a single layer that was much thinner overall.

IBM introduced AFC media starting with the 2 1/2" Travelstar 30GN series of notebook drives introduced in 2001; they were the first drives on the market to use AFC media. IBM then introduced AFC
media in desktop 3 1/2" drives starting with the Deskstar 120 GXP. AFC media is now used by Hitachi
Global Storage Technologies, which owns the former IBM hard drive division, as well as virtually all
other hard drive manufacturers. The use of AFC media allowed areal densities to be extended to
100Gb/sq. in. and beyond, and when combined with perpendicular magnetic recording (PMR), densities can grow to more than twice that. It's also notable that, being a form of thin-film media, if the
protective casing around the drive platters were removed, you would find that AFC media looks like a
mirror.

◄◄　For more information about AFC media and other advanced storage technologies, see Chapter 8, "Magnetic
Storage Principles," p. 637.

Read/Write Heads

A hard disk drive usually has one read/write head for each platter surface (meaning that each platter
has two sets of read/write heads—one for the top side and one for the bottom side). These heads are
connected, or *ganged*, on a single movement mechanism. The heads, therefore, move across the platters in unison.

Mechanically, read/write heads are simple. Each head is on an actuator arm that is spring-loaded to
force the head into contact with a platter. Few people realize that each platter actually is "squeezed"
by the heads above and below it. If you could open a drive safely and lift the top head with your finger, the head would snap back down into the platter when you released it. If you could pull down on
one of the heads below a platter, the spring tension would cause it to snap back up into the platter
when you released it.

Figure 9.7 shows a typical hard disk head-actuator assembly from a voice coil drive.

When the drive is at rest, the heads are forced into direct contact with the platters by spring tension,
but when the drive is spinning at full speed, air pressure develops below the heads and lifts them off
the surface of the platter. On a drive spinning at full speed, the distance between the heads and the
platter can be anywhere from 0.5 µ-inches to 5 µ-inches or more in a modern drive.

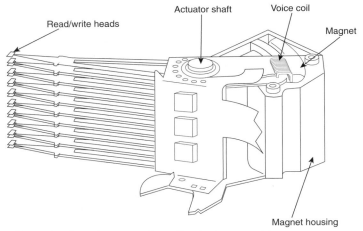

Figure 9.7　Read/write heads and rotary voice coil actuator assembly.

In the early 1960s, hard disk drive recording heads operated at floating heights as large as 200 μ-inches–300 μ-inches; today's drive heads are designed to float as low as 10nm (nanometers) or 0.4 μ-inches above the surface of the disk. To support higher densities in future drives, the physical separation between the head and disk is expected to drop even further, such that on some drives there will even be contact with the platter surface. New media and head designs will be required to make full or partial contact recording possible.

Caution

The small size of the gap between the platters and the heads is why you should never open the disk drive's HDA except in a clean-room environment. Any particle of dust or dirt that gets into this mechanism could cause the heads to read improperly or possibly even to strike the platters while the drive is running at full speed. The latter event could scratch the platter or the head, causing permanent damage.

To ensure the cleanliness of the interior of the drive, the HDA is assembled in a class-100 or better clean room. This specification means that a cubic foot of air can't contain more than 100 particles that measure up to 0.5 microns (19.7 μ-inches). A single person breathing while standing motionless spews out 500 such particles in a single minute! These rooms contain special air-filtration systems that continuously evacuate and refresh the air. A drive's HDA should not be opened unless it is inside such a room.

Although maintaining a clean-room environment might seem to be expensive, many companies manufacture tabletop or bench-size clean rooms that sell for only a few thousand dollars. Some of these devices operate like a glove box; the operator first inserts the drive and any tools required, closes the box, and then turns on the filtration system. Inside the box, a clean-room environment is maintained, and a technician can use the built-in gloves to work on the drive.

In other clean-room variations, the operator stands at a bench where a forced-air curtain maintains a clean environment on the bench top. The technician can walk in and out of the clean-room field by walking through the air curtain. This air curtain is very similar to the curtain of air used in some stores and warehouses to prevent heat from escaping in the winter while leaving a passage wide open.

Because the clean environment is expensive to produce, few companies except those that manufacture the drives are properly equipped to service hard disk drives.

Read/Write Head Designs

As disk drive technology has evolved, so has the design of the read/write head. The earliest heads were simple iron cores with coil windings (electromagnets). By today's standards, the original head designs were enormous in physical size and operated at very low recording densities. Over the years, head designs have evolved from the first simple ferrite core designs into the magneto-resistive and giant magneto-resistive types available today.

For more information on the various head designs, see Chapter 8.

Head Actuator Mechanisms

Possibly more important than the heads themselves is the mechanical system that moves them: the head actuator. This mechanism moves the heads across the disk and positions them accurately above the desired cylinder. Many variations on head actuator mechanisms are in use, but all fall into one of two basic categories:

- Stepper motor actuators
- Voice coil actuators

The use of one or the other type of actuator has profound effects on a drive's performance and reliability. The effects are not limited to speed; they also include accuracy, sensitivity to temperature, position, vibration, and overall reliability. The head actuator is the single most important specification in the drive, and the type of head actuator mechanism in a drive tells you a great deal about the drive's performance and reliability characteristics. Table 9.5 shows the two types of hard disk drive head actuators and the affected performance characteristics.

Table 9.5   Characteristics of Stepper Motor Versus Voice Coil Drives

Characteristic	Stepper Motor	Voice Coil
Relative access speed	Slow	Fast
Temperature sensitive	Yes (very)	No
Positionally sensitive	Yes	No
Automatic head parking	Not usually	Yes
Preventive maintenance	Periodic reformat	None required
Relative reliability	Poor	Excellent

Stepper motor actuators were commonly used on hard drives made during the 1980s and early 1990s with capacities of 100MB or less. All the drives I've seen with greater storage capacity use a voice coil actuator.

Floppy disk drives position their heads by using a stepper motor actuator. The accuracy of the stepper mechanism is suited to a floppy disk drive because the track densities usually are nowhere near those of a hard disk. The track density of a 1.44MB floppy disk is 135 tracks per inch, whereas hard disk drives have densities of more than 5,000 tracks per inch. All hard disk drives being manufactured today use voice coil actuators because stepper motors can't achieve the degree of accuracy necessary.

Stepper Motor Actuators

A stepper motor is an electrical motor that can "step," or move, from position to position, with mechanical detents or click-stop positions. If you were to grip the spindle of one of these motors and spin it manually, you would hear a clicking or buzzing sound as the motor passed each detent position with a soft click.

Stepper motors can't position themselves between step positions; they can stop only at the predetermined detent positions. The motors are small (between 1" and 3") and can be square, cylindrical, or flat. Stepper motors are outside the sealed HDA, although the spindle of the motor penetrates the HDA through a sealed hole.

Stepper motor mechanisms are affected by a variety of problems, but the greatest problem is temperature. As the drive platters heat and cool, they expand and contract, and the tracks on the platters move in relation to a predetermined track position. The stepper mechanism can't move in increments of less than a single track to correct for these temperature-induced errors. The drive positions the heads to a particular cylinder according to a predetermined number of steps from the stepper motor, with no room for nuance.

Figure 9.8 shows a common stepper motor design, in which a split metal band is used to transfer the movement from the rotating motor shaft to the head actuator itself.

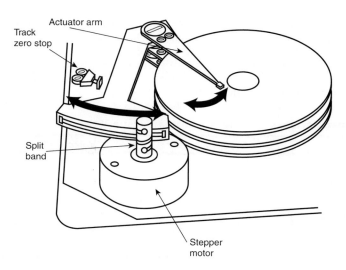

Figure 9.8   A stepper motor actuator.

Voice Coil Actuators

The voice coil actuators used in virtually all hard disk drives made today—unlike stepper motor actuators—use a feedback signal from the drive to accurately determine the head positions and adjust them, if necessary. This arrangement provides significantly greater performance, accuracy, and reliability than traditional stepper motor actuator designs.

A voice coil actuator works by pure electromagnetic force. The construction of the mechanism is similar to that of a typical audio speaker, from which the term *voice coil* is derived. An audio speaker uses a stationary magnet surrounded by a voice coil, which is connected to the speaker's paper cone. Energizing the coil causes it to move relative to the stationary magnet, which produces sound from the cone. In a typical hard disk drive's voice coil system, the electromagnetic coil is attached to the end of the head rack and placed near a stationary magnet. No physical contact occurs between the coil and the magnet; instead, the coil moves by pure magnetic force. As the electromagnetic coils are energized, they attract or repulse the stationary magnet and move the head rack. Systems like these are extremely quick, efficient, and usually much quieter than systems driven by stepper motors.

Unlike a stepper motor, a voice coil actuator has no click-stops or detent positions; rather, a special guidance system stops the head rack above a particular cylinder. Because it has no detents, the voice coil actuator can slide the heads in and out smoothly to any position desired. Voice coil actuators use a guidance mechanism called a *servo* to tell the actuator where the heads are in relation to the cylinders and to place the heads accurately at the desired positions. This positioning system often is called a *closed loop feedback mechanism*. It works by sending the index (or servo) signal to the positioning electronics, which return a feedback signal that is used to position the heads accurately. The system also is called *servo-controlled*, which refers to the index or servo information that is used to dictate or control head-positioning accuracy.

A voice coil actuator with servo control is not affected by temperature changes, as a stepper motor is. When temperature changes cause the disk platters to expand or contract, the voice coil system compensates automatically because it never positions the heads in predetermined track positions. Rather, the voice coil system searches for the specific track, guided by the prewritten servo information, and then positions the head rack precisely above the desired track, wherever it happens to be. Because of the continuous feedback of servo information, the heads adjust to the current position of the track at all times. For example, as a drive warms up and the platters expand, the servo information enables the heads to "follow" the track. As a result, a voice coil actuator is sometimes called a *track-following system.*

The two main types of voice-coil positioner mechanisms are

- Linear voice-coil actuators
- Rotary voice-coil actuators

The two types differ only in the physical arrangement of the magnets and coils.

A linear actuator moves the heads in and out over the platters in a straight line (see Figure 9.9). The coil moves in and out on a track surrounded by the stationary magnets. The primary advantage of the linear design is that it eliminates the head azimuth variations that occur with rotary positioning systems. (*Azimuth* refers to the angular measurement of the head position relative to the tangent of a given cylinder.) A linear actuator does not rotate the head as it moves from one cylinder to another, thus eliminating this problem.

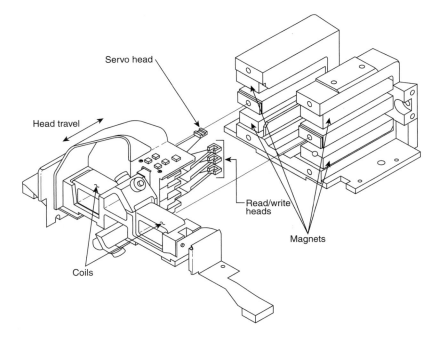

Figure 9.9   A linear voice coil actuator.

Although the linear actuator seems to be a good design, it has one fatal flaw: The devices are much too heavy. As drive performance has increased, the desire for lightweight actuator mechanisms has become very important. The lighter the mechanism, the faster it can accelerate and decelerate from one cylinder to another. Because they are much heavier than rotary actuators, linear actuators were popular only for a short time; they are virtually nonexistent in drives manufactured today.

Rotary actuators also use stationary magnets and a movable coil, but the coil is attached to the end of an actuator arm. As the coil moves relative to the stationary magnet, it swings the head arms in and out over the surface of the disk. The primary advantage of this mechanism is its light weight, which means the heads can accelerate and decelerate very quickly, resulting in very fast average seek times. Because of the lever effect on the head arm, the heads move faster than the actuator, which also helps to improve access times. (Refer to Figure 9.7, which shows a rotary voice coil actuator.)

The disadvantage of a rotary system is that as the heads move from the outer to the inner cylinders, they rotate slightly with respect to the tangent of the cylinders. This rotation results in an azimuth error and is one reason the area of the platter in which the cylinders are located is somewhat limited. By limiting the total motion of the actuator, the azimuth error is contained to within reasonable specifications. Virtually all voice coil drives today use rotary actuator systems.

Servo Mechanisms

Three servo mechanism designs have been used to control voice coil positioners over the years:

- Wedge servo
- Embedded servo
- Dedicated servo

The three designs are slightly different, but they accomplish the same basic task: They enable the head positioner to adjust continuously so it is precisely positioned above a given cylinder on the disk. The main difference between these servo designs is where the gray code information is actually written on the drive.

All servo mechanisms rely on special information that is written to the disk when it is manufactured. This information is usually in the form of a special code called a *gray code*—a special binary notational system in which any two adjacent numbers are represented by a code that differs in only one bit place or column position. This system enables the head to easily read the information and quickly determine its precise position.

At the time of manufacture, a special machine called a *servowriter* writes the servo gray code on the disk. The servowriter is basically a jig that mechanically moves the heads to a given reference position and then writes the servo information at that position. Many servowriters are themselves guided by a laser-beam reference that determines its own position by calculating distances in wavelengths of light. Because the servowriter must be capable of moving the heads mechanically, the process requires either that the lid of the drive be removed or that access be available through special access ports in the HDA. After the servowriting is complete, these ports are usually covered with sealing tape. You often see these tape-covered holes on the HDA, usually accompanied by warnings that you will void the warranty if you remove the tape. Because servowriting exposes the interior of the HDA, it requires a clean-room environment.

A servowriter is an expensive piece of machinery, costing up to $50,000 or more, and often must be custom-made for a particular make or model of drive. Some drive-repair companies have servowriting capability, which means they can rewrite the servo information on a drive if it becomes damaged. If a servowriter is not available, a drive with servo-code damage must be sent back to the drive manufacturer for the servo information to be rewritten.

Fortunately, damaging the servo information through disk read and write processes is impossible. Drives are designed so the heads can't overwrite the servo information, even during a low-level format. One myth that has been circulating (especially with respect to ATA drives) is that you can damage the servo information by improper low-level formatting. This is not true. An improper low-level format can compromise the performance of the drive, but the servo information is totally protected and can't be overwritten. Even so, the servo information on some drives can be damaged by a strong adjacent magnetic field or by jarring the drive while it is writing, which causes the heads to move off track.

The track-following capabilities of a servo-controlled voice coil actuator eliminate the positioning errors that occur over time with stepper motor drives. Voice coil drives are not affected by conditions such as thermal expansion and contraction of the platters. In fact, many voice coil drives today perform a special thermal-recalibration procedure at predetermined intervals while they run. This procedure usually involves seeking the heads from cylinder 0 to some other cylinder one time for every head on the drive. As this sequence occurs, the control circuitry in the drive monitors how much the track positions have moved since the last time the sequence was performed, and a thermal-recalibration adjustment is calculated and stored in the drive's memory. This information is then used every time the drive positions the heads to ensure the most accurate positioning possible.

At one time, most drives had to perform the thermal-recalibration sequence every 5 minutes for the first 30 minutes that the drive was powered on and then once every 25 minutes after that. With some drives, this thermal-recalibration sequence was very noticeable because the drive essentially stopped what it was doing, and you heard rapid ticking for a second or so. This was often misinterpreted as the drive having a problem reading data and having to reread it, but this was not true.

As multimedia applications grew in popularity, thermal recalibration became a problem with some manufacturers' drives. The thermal-recalibration sequence sometimes interrupted the transfer of a large data file, such as an audio or a video file, which resulted in audio or video playback jitter. Consequently, some companies released special A/V (audio visual) drives that hide the thermal-recalibration sequences so they never interrupt a file transfer. Virtually all of today's ATA drives are A/V capable, which means the thermal-recalibration sequences do not interrupt a data transfer. A/V-capable ATA drives are also used in set-top boxes that are utilized for digital recording, such as the popular TiVo and ReplayTV devices.

While we are on the subject of automatic drive functions, most of the drives that perform thermal-recalibration sequences also automatically perform a function called a *disk sweep*. Also called *wear leveling* by some manufacturers, this procedure is an automatic head seek that occurs after the drive has been idle for a period of time. The disk-sweep function moves the heads to a cylinder in the outer portion of the platters, which is where the head float-height is highest (because the head-to-platter velocity is highest). Then, if the drive continues to remain idle for another period, the heads move to another cylinder in this area, and the process continues indefinitely as long as the drive is powered on.

The disk-sweep function is designed to prevent the head from remaining stationary above one cylinder in the drive for too long, where friction between the head and platter eventually would dig a trench in the medium. Although the heads are not in direct contact with the medium, they are so close that the constant air pressure from the head floating above a single cylinder could cause friction and excessive wear. Figure 9.10 shows both a wedge and an embedded servo.

Wedge Servo

Early servo-controlled drives used a technique called a *wedge servo*. In these drives, the gray-code guidance information is contained in a "wedge" slice of the drive in each cylinder immediately preceding the index mark. The index mark indicates the beginning of each track, so the wedge-servo information was written in the PRE-INDEX GAP, which is at the end of each track. This area is provided for speed tolerance and normally is not used by the controller.

Some controllers had to be notified that the drive was using a wedge servo so they could shorten the sector timing to allow for the wedge-servo area. If they were not correctly configured, these controllers would not work properly with the drive.

Another problem was that the servo information appears only one time every revolution, which means that the drive often needed several revolutions before it could accurately determine and adjust the head position. Because of these problems, the wedge servo never was a popular design; it no longer is used in drives.

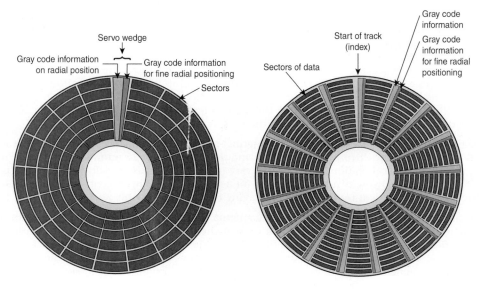

Figure 9.10   A wedge and an embedded servo.

Embedded Servo

An embedded servo is an enhancement of the wedge servo. Instead of placing the servo code before the beginning of each cylinder, an embedded servo design writes the servo information before the start of each sector. This arrangement enables the positioner circuits to receive feedback many times in a single revolution, making the head positioning much faster and more precise. Another advantage is that every track on the drive has its own positioning information, so each head can quickly and efficiently adjust position to compensate for any changes in the platter or head dimensions, especially for changes due to thermal expansion or physical stress.

Most drives today use an embedded servo to control the positioning system. As in the wedge servo design, the embedded servo information is protected by the drive circuits and any write operations are blocked whenever the heads are above the servo information. Thus, it is impossible to overwrite the servo information with a low-level format, as some people incorrectly believe.

Although the embedded servo works much better than the wedge servo because the servo feedback information is made available several times in a single disk revolution, a system that offered continuous servo feedback information would be better.

Dedicated Servo

A dedicated servo is a design in which the servo information is written continuously throughout the entire track, rather than just once per track or at the beginning of each sector. Unfortunately, if this procedure were used on the entire drive, no room would be left for data. For this reason, a *dedicated servo* uses one side of one of the platters exclusively for the servo-positioning information. The term *dedicated* comes from the fact that this platter side is completely dedicated to the servo information and can't contain any data.

When building a dedicated servo drive, the manufacturer deducts one side of one platter from normal read/write usage and records a special set of gray-code data there that indicates the proper track positions. Because the head that rests above this surface can't be used for normal reading and writing, the gray code can never be erased and the servo information is protected—as in the other servo designs. No low-level format or other procedure can possibly overwrite the servo information. Figure 9.11 shows a dedicated servo mechanism. Typically, the head on top or one in the center is dedicated for servo use.

When the drive moves the heads to a specific cylinder, the internal drive electronics use the signals received by the servo head to determine the position of the read/write heads. As the heads move, the track counters are read from the dedicated servo surface. When the servo head detects the requested track, the actuator stops. The servo electronics then fine-tune the position so the heads are precisely above the desired cylinder before any writing is permitted. Although only one head is used for servo tracking, the other heads are attached to the same rack so that if one head is above the desired cylinder, all the others are as well.

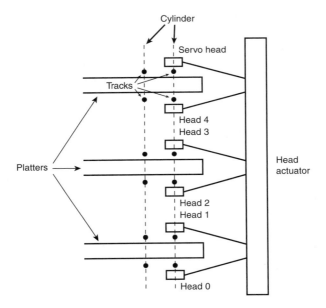

Figure 9.11   A dedicated servo, showing one entire head/side used for servo reading.

One way of telling whether a drive uses a dedicated servo platter is if it has an odd number of heads. For example, the Toshiba MK-538FB 1.2GB drive that I used to have in one of my systems had eight platters, but only 15 read/write heads. That drive uses a dedicated servo positioning system, and the 16th head is the servo head. The advantage of the dedicated servo concept is that the servo information is continuously available to the drive, making the head positioning process faster and more precise.

The drawback to a dedicated servo is that dedicating an entire platter surface for servo information is wasteful. Virtually all drives today use a variation on the embedded servo technique instead. Some drives combined a dedicated servo with an embedded servo, but this type of hybrid design is rare. Regardless of whether the servo mechanism is dedicated or embedded, it is far more accurate than the stepper motor mechanisms of the past.

Of course, as mentioned earlier, today's ATA drives have head, track, and sector-per-track parameters that are translated from the actual physical numbers. Therefore, you usually can't tell from the published numbers exactly how many heads or platters are contained within a drive.

Automatic Head Parking

When you power off a hard disk drive using CSS (contact start stop) design, the spring tension in each head arm pulls the heads into contact with the platters. The drive is designed to sustain thousands of takeoffs and landings, but it is wise to ensure that the landing occurs at a spot on the platter that contains no data. Older drives required manual head parking; you had to run a program that positioned the drive heads to a landing zone—usually the innermost cylinder—before turning off the system. Modern drives automatically park the heads, so park programs are no longer necessary.

Some amount of abrasion occurs during the landing and takeoff process, removing just a "micro puff" from the magnetic medium, but if the drive is jarred during the landing or takeoff process, real damage can occur. Newer drives that use load/unload designs incorporate a ramp positioned outside the outer surface of the platters to prevent any contact between the heads and platters, even if the drive is powered off. Load/unload drives automatically park the heads on the ramp when the drive is powered off.

One benefit of using a voice coil actuator is automatic head parking. In a drive that has a voice coil actuator, the heads are positioned and held by magnetic force. When the power to the drive is removed, the magnetic field that holds the heads stationary over a particular cylinder dissipates, enabling the head rack to skitter across the drive surface and potentially cause damage. In the voice coil design, the head rack is attached to a weak spring at one end and a head stop at the other end. When the system is powered on, the spring is overcome by the magnetic force of the positioner. When the drive is powered off, however, the spring gently drags the head rack to a park-and-lock position before the drive slows down and the heads land. On some drives, you could actually hear the "ting...ting...ting...ting" sound as the heads literally bounce-parked themselves, driven by this spring.

On a drive with a voice coil actuator, you activate the parking mechanism by turning off the computer; you do not need to run a program to park or retract the heads, as was necessary with early hard disk designs. In the event of a power outage, the heads park themselves automatically. (The drives unpark automatically when the system is powered on.)

Air Filters

Nearly all hard disk drives have two air filters. One is called the recirculating filter, and the other is called either a barometric or breather filter. These filters are permanently sealed inside the drive and are designed never to be changed for the life of the drive, unlike many older mainframe hard disks that had changeable filters.

A hard disk on a PC system does not circulate air from inside to outside the HDA or vice versa. The recirculating filter permanently installed inside the HDA is designed to filter only the small particles scraped off the platters during head takeoffs and landings (and possibly any other small particles dislodged inside the drive). Because PC hard disk drives are permanently sealed and do not circulate outside air, they can run in extremely dirty environments (see Figure 9.12).

The HDA in a hard disk drive is sealed but not airtight. The HDA is vented through a barometric or breather filter element that enables pressure equalization (breathing) between the inside and outside of the drive. For this reason, most hard drives are rated by the drive's manufacturer to run in a specific range of altitudes, usually from 1,000 feet below to 10,000 feet above sea level. In fact, some hard drives are not rated to exceed 7,000 feet while operating because the air pressure would be too low inside the drive to float the heads properly. As the environmental air pressure changes, air bleeds into or out of the drive so internal and external pressures are identical. Although air does bleed through a vent, contamination usually is not a concern because the barometric filter on this vent is designed to filter out all particles larger than 0.3 microns (about 12 μ-inches) to meet the specifications for cleanliness inside the drive. You can see the vent holes on most drives, which are covered internally by this breather filter. Some drives use even finer grade filter elements to keep out even smaller particles.

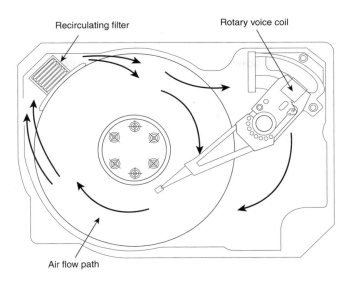

Figure 9.12   Air circulation in a hard disk.

I conducted a seminar in Hawaii several years ago, and several of the students were from one of the astronomical observatories atop Mauna Kea. They indicated that virtually all the hard disk drives they had tried to use at the observatory site had failed very quickly, if they worked at all. This was no surprise because the observatories are at the 13,796-foot peak of the mountain, and at that altitude, even people don't function very well! At the time, they had to resort to solid-state (RAM) disks, tape drives, or even floppy disk drives as their primary storage medium. Some manufacturers produce drives that are hermetically sealed (airtight), although they do still have air inside the HDA. Because they carry their own internal air under pressure, these drives can operate at any altitude and can withstand extremes of shock and temperature. The drives are designed for military and industrial applications, such as systems used aboard aircraft and in extremely harsh environments. They are, of course, more expensive than typical hard drives that operate under ambient pressures.

Hard Disk Temperature Acclimation

Because most hard drives have a filtered port to bleed air into or out of the HDA, moisture can enter the drive, and after some period of time, it must be assumed that the humidity inside any hard disk is similar to that outside the drive. Humidity can become a serious problem if it is allowed to condense—and especially if you power up the drive while this condensation is present. Most hard disk manufacturers have specified procedures for acclimating a hard drive to a new environment with different temperature and humidity ranges, and especially for bringing a drive into a warmer environment in which condensation can form. This situation should be of special concern to users of laptop or portable systems. If you leave a portable system in an automobile trunk during the winter, for example, it could be catastrophic to bring the machine inside and power it up without allowing it to acclimate to the temperature indoors.

The following text and Table 9.6 are taken from the factory packaging that Control Data Corporation (later Imprimis and eventually Seagate) used to ship with its hard drives:

> If you have just received or removed this unit from a climate with temperatures at or below 50°F (10°C) do not open this container until the following conditions are met, otherwise condensation could occur and damage to the device and/or media may result. Place this package in the operating environment for the time duration according to the temperature chart.

Table 9.6   Hard Disk Drive Environmental Acclimation Table

Previous Climate Temperature	Acclimation Time	Previous Climate Temperature	Acclimation Time
+40°F (+4°C)	13 hours	−10°F (−23°C)	20 hours
+30°F (−1°C)	15 hours	−20°F (−29°C)	22 hours
+20°F (−7°C)	16 hours	−30°F (−34°C) or less	27 hours
+10°F (−12°C)	17 hours		
0°F (−18°C)	18 hours		

As you can see from this table, you must place a hard disk drive that has been stored in a colder-than-normal environment into its normal operating environment for a specified amount of time to allow it to acclimate before you power it on.

Spindle Motors

The motor that spins the platters is called the *spindle motor* because it is connected to the spindle around which the platters revolve. Spindle motors in hard disk drives are always connected directly; no belts or gears are involved. The motor must be free of noise and vibration; otherwise, it can transmit a rumble to the platters, which can disrupt reading and writing operations.

The spindle motor also must be precisely controlled for speed. The platters in hard disk drives revolve at speeds ranging from 3,600 rpm to 15,000 rpm (60–250 revolutions per second) or more, and the motor has a control circuit with a feedback loop to monitor and control this speed precisely. Because the speed control must be automatic, hard drives do not have a motor-speed adjustment. Some diagnostics programs claim to measure hard drive rotation speed, but all these programs do is estimate the rotational speed by the timing at which sectors pass under the heads.

There is actually no way for a program to measure the hard disk drive's rotational speed; this measurement can be made only with sophisticated test equipment. Don't be alarmed if some diagnostics program tells you that your drive is spinning at an incorrect speed; most likely, the program is wrong, not the drive. Platter rotation and timing information is not provided through the hard disk controller interface. In the past, software could give approximate rotational speed estimates by performing multiple sector read requests and timing them, but this was valid only when all drives had the same number of sectors per track and spun at the same speed. Zoned-bit recording—combined with the many various rotational speeds used by modern drives, not to mention built-in buffers and caches—means that these calculation estimates can't be performed accurately by software.

On most drives, the spindle motor is on the bottom of the drive, just below the sealed HDA. Many drives today, however, have the spindle motor built directly into the platter hub inside the HDA. By using an internal hub spindle motor, the manufacturer can stack more platters in the drive because the spindle motor takes up no vertical space.

Note

Spindle motors, particularly on the larger form-factor drives, can consume a great deal of 12-volt power. Most drives require two to three times the normal operating power when the motor first spins the platters. This heavy draw lasts only a few seconds or until the drive platters reach operating speed. If you have more than one drive, you should try to sequence the start of the spindle motors so the power supply does not have to provide such a large load to all the drives at the same time. Most SCSI and some ATA drives have a delayed spindle-motor start feature.

Fluid Dynamic Bearings

Traditionally, spindle motors have used ball bearings in their design, but limitations in their performance have now caused drive manufacturers to look for alternatives. The main problem with ball bearings is that they have approximately 0.1 micro-inch (millionths of an inch) of runout, which is lateral side-to-side play in the bearings. Even though that might seem small, with the ever-increasing density of modern drives, it has become a problem. This runout allows the platters to move randomly that distance from side to side, which causes the tracks to wobble under the heads. Additionally, the runout plus the metal-to-metal contact nature of ball bearings allows an excessive amount of mechanical noise and vibration to be generated, and that is becoming a problem for drives that spin at higher speeds.

The solution is a new type of bearing called a fluid dynamic bearing, which uses a highly viscous lubricating fluid between the spindle and sleeve in the motor. This fluid serves to dampen vibrations and movement, allowing runout to be reduced to 0.01 micro-inches or less. Fluid dynamic bearings also allow for better shock resistance, improved speed control, and reduced noise generation. The first drives on the market to use fluid dynamic bearings were advanced drives designed for very high spindle speeds, high areal densities, or low noise. Over the last few years, fluid dynamic bearings have become standard issue in most hard drives.

Logic Boards

All hard disk drives have one or more logic boards mounted on them. The logic boards contain the electronics that control the drive's spindle and head actuator systems and present data to the controller in some agreed-upon form. On ATA drives, the boards include the controller itself, whereas SCSI drives include the controller and the SCSI bus adapter circuit.

Many disk drive failures occur in the logic board, not in the mechanical assembly. (This statement does not seem logical, but it is true.) Therefore, you sometimes can repair a failed drive by replacing the logic board rather than the entire drive. Replacing the logic board, moreover, enables you to regain access to the data on the drive—something that replacing the entire drive does not provide. Unfortunately, none of the drive manufacturers sell logic boards separately. The only way to obtain a replacement logic board for a given drive is to purchase a functioning identical drive and then cannibalize it for parts. Of course, it doesn't make sense to purchase an entire new drive just to repair an existing one except in cases in which data recovery from the old drive is necessary. Cannibalizing new drives to repair old drives is a common practice among companies that offer data recovery services. They stock a large number of popular drives they can use for parts to allow data recovery from defective customer drives they receive.

Most of the time the boards are fairly easy to change with nothing more than a screwdriver. Merely removing and reinstalling a few screws as well as unplugging and reconnecting a cable or two are all that is required to remove and replace a typical logic board.

Cables and Connectors

Hard disk drives typically have several connectors for interfacing to the computer, receiving power, and sometimes grounding to the system chassis. Most drives have at least these three types of connectors:

- Interface connector(s)
- Power connector
- Optional ground connector (tab)

Of these, the interface connectors are the most important because they carry the data and command signals between the system and the drive. In most cases, the drive interface cables can be connected in a daisy-chain or bus-type configuration. Most interfaces support at least two devices. Older interfaces, such as ST-506/412 or ESDI (Enhanced Small Device Interface), used separate cables for data and control signals, but today's SCSI, ATA (AT Attachment), and Serial ATA drives have a single data connector on each drive.

◄◄ See "Parallel ATA I/O Connector," p. 593.

The power is supplied via the larger 4-pin peripheral power connector found on all PC power supplies. Most hard disk drives use both 5- and 12-volt power, although some of the smaller drives designed for portable applications use only 5-volt power. In most cases, the 12-volt power runs the spindle motor and head actuator, and the 5-volt power runs the circuitry. Make sure your power supply can supply adequate power for the hard disk drives installed in your system.

The 12-volt power consumption of a drive usually varies with the physical size of the unit. The larger the drive is, the faster it spins. In addition, the more platters there are to spin, the more power it requires. For example, most of the 3 1/2" drives on the market today use roughly one-half to one-fourth the power (in watts) of the older 5 1/4" drives. Some of the very small (2 1/2" or 1.8") hard disks barely sip electrical power and actually use 1 watt or less!

A grounding tab provides an optional ground connection between the drive and the system's chassis. In most computers, the hard disk drive is mounted directly to the chassis using screws, or the drive is grounded via the ground wires in the power connector, so an extra ground wire is unnecessary.

Configuration Items

To configure a hard disk drive for installation in a system, you usually must set several jumpers (and, possibly, terminating resistors) properly. These items typically vary according to the type of interface the drive supports but can vary somewhat from drive to drive as well.

►► See Chapter 12, "Physical Drive Installation and Configuration," p. 851.

Hard Disk Features

To make the best decision in purchasing a hard disk for your system or to understand what distinguishes one brand of hard disk from another, you must consider many features. This section examines some of the issues you should consider when you evaluate drives:

- Capacity
- Performance
- Reliability
- Cost

Capacity

As stated earlier, a corollary of Parkinson's famous "law" can be applied to hard drives: "Data expands so as to fill the space available for its storage." This, of course, means that no matter how big a drive you get, you *will* find a way to fill it.

If you've exhausted the space on your current hard disk, you might be wondering, How much storage space is enough? Because you are more likely to run out of space than have too much, you should aim high and get the largest drive that will fit within your budget. Modern systems are used to store many space-hungry file types, including digital photos, music, video, newer operating systems, applications, and games. Photo, audio, and especially video files can take up huge amounts of storage, easily running into hundreds of gigabytes or even terabytes of storage. Although most drives today can hold hundreds of gigabytes, many people are storing several times that information.

Running out of space causes numerous problems in a modern system, mainly because Windows, as well as many newer applications, uses a large amount of drive space for temporary files and virtual memory. When Windows runs out of room, system instability, crashes, and data loss are inevitable.

Capacity Limitations

How big a hard drive you can use depends on many factors, including the interface, drivers, operating system, as well as the file system you choose.

When the ATA interface was first created in 1986, it had a maximum capacity limitation of 137GB (65,536×16×255 sectors). BIOS issues further limited capacity to 8.4GB in systems produced earlier than 1998, and as low as 528MB in systems earlier than 1994. Even after the BIOS issues were resolved, however, the initial 137GB limit of ATA remained. Fortunately, this was broken in the ATA-6 specification drafted in 2001. ATA-6 augments the addressing scheme used by ATA to allow drive capacity to grow to 144PB (petabytes, or quadrillion bytes), which is 2^{48} sectors. This has opened the door allowing PATA and SATA drives over 137GB to be released.

BIOS Limitations

If the drive in a system is 8GB or smaller, the system might not be capable of handling a larger drive without a BIOS upgrade because many older (pre-1998) BIOSs can't handle drives above the 8.4GB limit, and other BIOSs (pre-2002) have other limits, such as 137GB. Some drives ship with a setup or installation disc containing a software BIOS substitute such as Ontrack's Disk Manager or Phoenix Technologies' EZ-Drive (Phoenix purchased EZ-Drive creator StorageSoft in January 2002), but I don't recommend using these software BIOS replacements. EZ-Drive, Disk Manager, and their OEM offshoots (Drive Guide, MAXBlast, Data Lifeguard, and others) can cause problems if you need to boot from floppy or CD media or if you need to repair the nonstandard master boot record these products' use.

If your motherboard ROM BIOS dates before 1998 and is limited to 8.4GB or dates before 2002 and is limited to 137GB, and you want to install a larger drive, I recommend you first contact your motherboard (or system) manufacturer to see whether an update is available. Virtually all motherboards incorporate a flash ROM, which allows for easy updates via a utility program.

Internal ATA drives larger than 137GB require 48-bit logical block address (LBA) support. This support *must* be provided in the operating system; it can also be provided in the BIOS, or both. It is best if both the OS and the BIOS support it, but it can be made to work if only the OS has the support.

48-bit LBA support in the OS requires one of the following:

- Windows Vista.
- Windows XP with Service Pack 1 (SP1) or later.
- Windows 2000 with Service Pack 4 (SP4) or later.
- Windows 98/98SE/Me or NT 4.0 with the Intel Application Accelerator (IAA) loaded. This solution works only if your motherboard has an IAA-supported chipset. See www.intel.com/support/chipsets/iaa for more information.

48-bit LBA support in the BIOS requires either of the following:

- A motherboard BIOS with 48-bit LBA support (usually dated September 2002 or later)
- An adapter card with onboard BIOS that includes 48-bit LBA support

If you have both OS and BIOS support for 48-bit LBA, you can simply install and use the drive like any other internal drive. On the other hand, if you do not have 48-bit LBA support in the BIOS, but you do have it in the OS, portions of the drive past 137GB are not recognized or accessible until the OS is loaded. This means that if you are installing the OS to a blank hard drive and booting from an original XP (pre-SP1) CD or earlier, you need to partition up to the first 137GB of the drive at installation time. After the OS is fully installed and the service packs added, the remainder of the drive beyond 137GB is recognized. At that point, you can then either partition the remainder of the drive beyond 137GB using the XP Disk Management tools or use a third-party partitioning program such as PartitionMagic or Partition Commander to resize the first partition to use the full drive.

If you are booting from an XP SP1 or later CD (meaning a CD with Service Pack 1 already applied), you can recognize and access the entire drive during the OS installation and partition the entire drive as a single partition greater than 137GB if you like.

If you need more or faster PATA or SATA interface connections, you can use PCI-based add-on cards from companies such as Promise Technology (www.promise.com). These cards support drives up to and beyond the 137GB limit imposed by the ATA-5 and older standards.

External USB and FireWire drives don't have these capacity issues because they don't rely on the ROM BIOS for support and use OS-managed drivers instead.

SCSI was designed from the beginning with fewer limitations than ATA, which is why SCSI is more commonly used in high-performance file servers, workstations, and other high-performance computer systems. Even though SCSI originated prior to ATA, the architects had the foresight to allow SCSI to address devices up to 2.2TB (terabytes, or trillion bytes) in capacity (2^{32} sectors). In 2001, the SCSI command set was further upgraded to support drives up to 9.44ZB (zettabytes, or sextillion bytes) in capacity (2^{64} sectors). Because SCSI was initially designed with fewer limitations and greater performance in mind, manufacturers have traditionally released their largest capacity drives in SCSI versions first. With the advent of Serial ATA, however, the gap is quickly closing.

Because of the changes in 2001 to both ATA and SCSI, it will be many years before the capacity limitations of either interface become a problem.

Operating System Limitations

More recent operating systems don't have any problems with larger drives. However, older operating systems might have limitations when it comes to using large drives.

DOS generally does not recognize drives larger than 8.4GB because those drives are accessed using LBA and DOS versions 6.x and lower use only CHS addressing.

Windows 95 has a 32GB hard disk capacity limit, and there is no way around it other than upgrading to Windows 98 or newer. Additionally, the retail or upgrade versions of Windows 95 (also called Windows 95 OSR 1 or Windows 95a) are further limited to using only the FAT16 (16-bit file allocation table) file system, which carries a maximum partition size limitation of 2GB. Therefore, if you had a 30GB drive, you would be forced to divide it into 15 2GB partitions, with each appearing as a separate drive letter (drives C:–Q: in this example). Windows 95B and 95C can use the FAT32 file system, which allows partition sizes up to 2TB. Note that because of internal limitations, no version of FDISK can create partitions larger than 512GB.

Windows 98 supports large drives, but a bug in the FDISK program included with Windows 98 reduces the reported drive capacity by 64GB for drives over that capacity. The solution is an updated version of FDISK that can be downloaded from Microsoft. Another bug appears in the FORMAT command with Windows 98: If you run FORMAT from a command prompt on a partition over 64GB, the size isn't reported correctly, although the entire partition is formatted.

Performance

When you select a hard disk drive, one of the important features you should consider is the performance (speed) of the drive. Hard drives can have a wide range of performance capabilities. As is true of many things, one of the best indicators of a drive's relative performance is its price. An old saying from the automobile-racing industry is appropriate here: "Speed costs money. How fast do you want to go?"

The speed of a disk drive is typically measured in two ways:

- Transfer rate
- Average access time

Transfer Rate

The transfer rate is probably more important to overall system performance than any other statistic, but it is also one of the most misunderstood specifications. The problem stems from the fact that several transfer rates can be specified for a given drive; however, the most important of these is usually overlooked.

Don't be fooled by interface transfer rate hype, especially around ATA-133 or SATA-150. A far more important gauge of a drive's performance is the average media transfer rate, which is significantly lower than the interface rate of 133MBps or 150MBps. The media transfer rate represents the average speed at which the drive can actually read or write data. By comparison, the interface transfer rate merely indicates how quickly data can move between the motherboard and the buffer on the drive. The rotational speed of the drive has the biggest effect on the drive's true transfer speed; in general, drives that spin at 10,000 rpm transfer data faster than 7,200 rpm drives, and 7,200 rpm drives transfer data faster than those that spin at 5,400 rpm. If you are looking for performance, be sure to check the true *media* transfer rates of any drives you are comparing.

The confusion results from the fact that drive manufacturers can report up to seven different transfer rates for a given drive. Perhaps the least important (but one that people seem to focus on the most) is the raw interface transfer rate, which for most PATA drives is either 100MBps or 133MBps, and either 150MBps or 300MBps for Serial ATA drives. Unfortunately, few people seem to realize that the drives actually read and write data much more slowly than that. The more important transfer rate specifications are the media transfer rates, which express how fast a drive can actually read or write data. Media transfer rates can be expressed as a raw maximum, a raw minimum, a formatted maximum, formatted minimum, or averages of either. Few report the averages, but they can be easily calculated.

The media transfer rate is far more important than the interface transfer rate because the media transfer rate is the true rate at which data can be read from (or written to) the disk. In other words, it tells how fast data can be moved to and from the drive platters (media). It is the rate that any sustained transfer can hope to achieve. This rate is usually reported as a minimum and maximum figure, although many drive manufacturers report the maximum only.

Media transfer rates have minimum and maximum figures because drives today use zoned recording with fewer sectors per track on the inner cylinders than the outer cylinders. Typically, a drive is divided into 16 or more zones, with the inner zone having about half the sectors per track (and therefore about half the transfer rate) of the outer zone. Because the drive spins at a constant rate, data can be read twice as fast from the outer cylinders than from the inner cylinders.

Another issue is the raw transfer rate versus the formatted transfer rate. The *raw* rate refers to how fast bits can be read off the media. Because not all bits represent data (some are intersector, servo, ECC, or ID bits), and because some time is lost when the heads have to move from track to track (latency), the *formatted* transfer rate represents the true rate at which user data can be read from or written to the drive.

Note that some manufacturers report only raw internal media transfer rates, but you usually can calculate that the formatted transfer rates are about three-fourths of the raw rates. This is because the user data on each track is only about three-fourths of the actual bits stored due to servo, ECC, ID, and other overhead that is stored. Likewise, some manufacturers report only maximum transfer rates (either raw, formatted, or both); in that case, you generally can assume the minimum transfer rate is one-half of the maximum and that the average transfer rate is three-fourths of the maximum.

Let's look at a specific drive as an example. The Hitachi Deskstar T7K500 is considered a fast SATA drive. It spins at 7,200 rpm and supports the SATA 3Gbps interface transfer rate (300MBps from the drive controller to the motherboard host adapter). As with all drives I know of, the actual (media) transfer rate is much less.

Table 9.7 shows the specifications for the 7,200 rpm 3Gbps Hitachi Deskstar T7K500 drive.

Table 9.7   Media Transfer Rate Specifications for the Hitachi Deskstar T7K500 Drive

Media Zone	Sectors/Track	Rotational Speed	Transfer Rate
Outer Zone	1440	7,200 rpm	88.47MBps
Inner Zone	720	7,200 rpm	44.24MBps
Average	1080	7,200 rpm	66.36MBps

As you can see, the *true* transfer rate for this drive is between 88.47MBps and 44.24MBps, or an average of about 66.36MBps—less than one-fourth of the 300MBps SATA interface transfer rate. Of course, if this were your drive, you wouldn't be disappointed because 66.36MBps is excellent performance. In fact, this is one of the fastest SATA drives on the market.

A common question I get is about upgrading the ATA interface in a system. Many people are using older motherboards that support only ATA/100 (Ultra DMA Mode 5) or SATA/150 (1.5Gbps) specifications. After studying the true formatted media transfer rates of most drives, you can see why I generally do not recommend installing a separate ATA/133 or SATA/300 (3GBps) host adapter for those systems, unless you need the additional host adapters to attach more drives. From a pure performance perspective, those who perform such an upgrade will most likely see little, if any, increase in performance. This is because in almost all cases, the drives they are using are on average slower than even ATA/66—and often significantly slower than the ATA/133, SATA 150, or SATA 300 interface speeds.

Two primary factors contribute to transfer rate performance: rotational speed and the linear recording density or sector-per-track figures. When you're comparing two drives with the same number of sectors per track, the drive that spins more quickly transfers data more quickly. Likewise, when you're comparing two drives with identical rotational speeds, the drive with the higher recording density (more sectors per track) is faster. A higher-density drive can be faster than one that spins faster—both factors have to be taken into account.

As you can see from this example, the interface transfer speed is almost meaningless. So, if you were thinking about getting a new motherboard or maybe a separate host adapter card for the sole purpose of increasing drive performance, save your money. To be fair, there will be a slight benefit to higher interface transfer speeds in that data from the buffer on the drive controller can be transferred to the motherboard at interface speed, rather than media speed. These buffers are usually 4MB or less and help only with repetitive transfers of small amounts of data. However, if you perform repetitive transfers frequently, drives with larger 16MB buffers can improve performance with applications that perform repetitive transfers. More recently, drives with large flash memory buffers, called *hybrid* drives, are being manufactured to support the SuperFetch cache in Windows Vista; however since flash memory is relatively slow, this technology is designed more to improve laptop battery life than desktop performance.

All other things being equal, a drive that spins faster transfers data faster, regardless of the interface transfer rate. Unfortunately, it is rare that all other things are exactly equal, so you should consult the drive specifications listed in the data sheet or manual for the drive to be sure.

When evaluating drive performance, don't just compare one specification, such as interface speed or rotational speed, because these can be misleading. The interface speed is relatively meaningless, and although the rotational speed is much more important, some drives have a slower media transfer rate than others even though they spin faster. Be careful with simplistic comparisons. With hard drives, the bottom line is that the media transfer rate is probably the most important specification you can know about a drive—and faster is better.

To find the transfer specifications for a given drive, look in the data sheet or preferably the documentation or manual for the drive. These can usually be downloaded from the drive manufacturer's website. This documentation often reports the maximum and minimum sector per track specifications, which—combined with the rotational speed—can be used to calculate true formatted media performance. You should be looking for the true number of physical sectors per track for the outer and inner zones. Therefore, you should be aware that many drives (especially zoned-bit recording drives) are configured with sector translation, which means the number of sectors per track reported by the BIOS has little to do with the actual physical characteristics of the drive. You must know the drive's true physical parameters, rather than the values the BIOS uses.

When you know the sector per track (SPT) and rotational speed figures, you can use the following formula to determine the true media data transfer rate in millions of bytes per second (MBps):

Media Transfer Rate (MBps) = SPT×512 bytes×rpm/60 seconds/1,000,000 bytes

For example, the Hitachi Deskstar T7K500 drive spins at 7,200 rpm and has an average of 1080 sectors per track. The average media transfer rate for this drive is figured as follows:

$$1080×512×(7,200/60)/1,000,000 = 66.36\text{MBps}$$

Using this formula, you can calculate the media transfer rate of any drive if you know the rotational speed and average sectors per track.

Average Seek Time

Average seek time, usually measured in milliseconds (ms), is the average amount of time it takes to move the heads from one cylinder to another a random distance away. One way to measure this specification is to run many random track-seek operations and then divide the timed results by the number of seeks performed. This method provides an average time for a single seek.

The standard method used by many drive manufacturers when reporting average seek times is to measure the time it takes the heads to move across one-third of the total cylinders. Average seek time depends only on the drive itself; the type of interface or controller has little effect on this specification. The average seek rating is primarily a gauge of the capabilities of the head actuator mechanism.

Note

Be wary of benchmarks that claim to measure drive seek performance. Most ATA drives use a scheme called *sector translation*, so any commands the drive receives to move the heads to a specific cylinder might not actually result in the intended physical movement. This situation renders some benchmarks meaningless for those types of drives. SCSI drives also require an additional step because the commands first must be sent to the drive over the SCSI bus. These drives might seem to have the fastest access times because the command overhead is not factored in by most benchmarks. However, when this overhead is factored in by benchmark programs, these drives receive poor performance figures.

Latency

Latency is the average time (in milliseconds) it takes for a sector to be available after the heads have reached a track. On average, this figure is half the time it takes for the disk to rotate once. A drive that spins twice as fast would have half the latency.

Latency is a factor in disk read and write performance. Decreasing the latency increases the speed of access to data or files and is accomplished only by spinning the drive platters more quickly. Latency figures for most popular drive rotational speeds are shown in Table 9.8.

Table 9.8   Hard Disk Rotation Speeds and Their Latencies

Revs/Minute	Revs/Second	Latency
3,600	60	8.33
4,200	70	7.14
5,400	90	5.56
7,200	120	4.17
10,000	167	3.00
15,000	250	2.00

Many drives today spin at 7,200 rpm, resulting in a latency time of only 4.17ms, whereas others spin at 10,000 rpm or even 15,000 rpm, resulting in incredible 3.00ms or 2.00ms latency figures. In addition to increasing performance where real-world access to data is concerned, spinning the platters more quickly also increases the data-transfer rate after the heads arrive at the desired sectors.

Average Access Time

A measurement of a drive's average access time is the sum of its average seek time plus latency. The average access time is usually expressed in milliseconds.

A measurement of a drive's average access time (average seek time plus latency) provides the average total amount of time required for the drive to access a randomly requested sector.

Cache Programs and Caching Controllers

At the software level, disk cache programs such as SMARTDRV (DOS) and VCACHE (Windows) can have a major effect on disk drive performance. These cache programs hook into the BIOS hard drive interrupt and intercept the read and write calls to the disk BIOS from application programs and device drivers.

When an application program wants to read data from a hard drive, the cache program intercepts the read request, passes the read request to the hard drive controller in the usual way, saves the data read from the disk in its cache memory buffer, and then passes the data back to the application program. Depending on the size of the cache buffer, data from numerous sectors can be read into and saved in the buffer.

When the application wants to read more data, the cache program again intercepts the request and examines its buffers to see whether the requested data is still in the cache. If so, the program passes the data back from the cache to the application immediately, without another hard drive operation. Because the cached data is stored in memory, this method speeds access tremendously and can greatly affect disk drive performance measurements.

Most controllers now have some form of built-in hardware buffer or cache that doesn't intercept or use any BIOS interrupts. Instead, the drive caches data at the hardware level, which is invisible to normal performance-measurement software. Manufacturers originally included track read-ahead buffers in controllers to permit 1:1 interleave performance. Some manufacturers now increase the size of these read-ahead buffers in the controller, whereas others add intelligence by using a cache instead of a simple buffer.

Many ATA and SCSI drives have cache memory built directly into the drive's onboard controller. Most newer ATA drives have 2MB of built-in cache; many high-performance ATA drives have 16MB of cache. I remember the days when 1MB or 2MB of RAM was a lot of memory for an entire system. Nowadays, some 3 1/2" hard disk drives can have up to 16MB of cache memory built right in!

Although software and hardware caches can make a drive faster for routine or repetitive data transfer operations, a cache will not affect the true maximum transfer rate the drive can sustain.

Interleave Selection

In a discussion of disk performance, the issue of interleave often comes up. Although traditionally this was more a controller performance issue than a drive issue, modern ATA hard disk drives with built-in controllers are fully capable of processing the data as fast as the drive can send it. In other words, all modern ATA drives are formatted with no interleave (sometimes expressed as a 1:1 interleave ratio). On older hard drive types, such as MFM and ESDI, you could modify the interleave during a low-level format to optimize the drive's performance. Today, drives are low-level formatted at the factory and interleave adjustments are a moot topic.

Note

For more information on interleaving and cylinder skewing as used on older drives, see the sections "Interleave Selection" and "Head and Cylinder Skewing" in Chapter 10 of *Upgrading and Repairing PCs, 12th Edition*.

Reliability

When you shop for a drive, you might notice a statistic called the *mean time between failures (MTBF)* described in the drive specifications. MTBF figures usually range from 300,000 to 1,000,000 hours or more. I usually ignore these figures because they are derived theoretically.

In understanding the MTBF claims, you must understand how the manufacturers arrive at them and what they mean. Most manufacturers have a long history of building drives, and their drives have seen millions of hours of cumulative use. They can look at the failure rate for previous drive models with the same components and calculate a failure rate for a new drive based on the components used to build the drive assembly. For the electronic circuit board, they also can use industry-standard techniques for predicting the failure of the integrated electronics. This enables them to calculate the predicted failure rate for the entire drive unit.

To understand what these numbers mean, you must know that the MTBF claims apply to a population of drives, not an individual drive. This means that if a drive claims to have an MTBF of 500,000 hours, you can expect a failure in that population of drives in 500,000 hours of total running time. If 1,000,000 drives of this model are in service and all 1,000,000 are running simultaneously, you can expect one failure out of this entire population every half-hour. MTBF statistics are not useful for predicting the failure of any individual drive or a small sample of drives.

You also need to understand the meaning of the word *failure*. In this sense, a failure is a fault that requires the drive to be returned to the manufacturer for repair, not an occasional failure to read or write a file correctly.

Finally, as some drive manufacturers point out, this measure of MTBF should really be called *mean time to first failure*. "Between failures" implies that the drive fails, is returned for repair, and then at some point fails again. The interval between repair and the second failure here would be the MTBF. Because in most cases, a failed hard drive that would need manufacturer repair is replaced rather than repaired, so the whole MTBF concept is misnamed.

The bottom line is that I do not really place much emphasis on MTBF figures. For an individual drive, they are not accurate predictors of reliability. However, if you are an information systems manager considering the purchase of thousands of PCs or drives per year or a system vendor building and supporting thousands of systems, it might be worth your while to examine these numbers and study the methods used to calculate them by each vendor. Most hard drive manufacturers designate their premium drives as Enterprise class drives, meaning they are designed for use in environments requiring full-time usage and high reliability and carry the highest MTBF ratings. If you can understand the vendor's calculations and compare the actual reliability of a large sample of drives, you can purchase more reliable drives and save time and money in service and support.

S.M.A.R.T.

Self-Monitoring, Analysis, and Reporting Technology (S.M.A.R.T.) is an industry standard providing failure prediction for disk drives. When S.M.A.R.T. is enabled for a given drive, the drive monitors predetermined attributes that are susceptible to or indicative of drive degradation. Based on changes in the monitored attributes, a failure prediction can be made. If a failure is deemed likely to occur, S.M.A.R.T. makes a status report available so the system BIOS or driver software can notify the user of the impending problems, perhaps enabling the user to back up the data on the drive before any real problems occur.

Predictable failures are the types of failures S.M.A.R.T. attempts to detect. These failures result from the gradual degradation of the drive's performance. According to Seagate, 60% of drive failures are mechanical, which is exactly the type of failures S.M.A.R.T. is designed to predict.

Of course, not all failures are predictable, and S.M.A.R.T. can't help with unpredictable failures that occur without any advance warning. These can be caused by static electricity, improper handling or sudden shock, or circuit failure (such as thermal-related solder problems or component failure).

S.M.A.R.T. was originally created by IBM in 1992. That year IBM began shipping 3 1/2" hard disk drives equipped with Predictive Failure Analysis (PFA), an IBM-developed technology that periodically measures selected drive attributes and sends a warning message when a predefined threshold is exceeded. IBM turned this technology over to the ANSI organization, and it subsequently became the ANSI-standard S.M.A.R.T. protocol for SCSI drives, as defined in the ANSI-SCSI Informational Exception Control (IEC) document X3T10/94-190.

Interest in extending this technology to ATA drives led to the creation of the S.M.A.R.T. Working Group in 1995. Besides IBM, other companies represented in the original group were Seagate Technology, Conner Peripherals (now a part of Seagate), Fujitsu, Hewlett-Packard, Maxtor, Quantum, and Western Digital. The S.M.A.R.T. specification produced by this group and placed in the public domain covers both ATA and SCSI hard disk drives and can be found in most of the more recently produced drives on the market.

The S.M.A.R.T. design of attributes and thresholds is similar in ATA and SCSI environments, but the reporting of information differs.

In an ATA environment, driver software on the system interprets the alarm signal from the drive generated by the S.M.A.R.T. "report status" command. The driver polls the drive on a regular basis to check the status of this command and, if it signals imminent failure, sends an alarm to the operating system where it is passed on via an error message to the end user. This structure also enables future enhancements, which might allow reporting of information other than drive failure conditions.

The system can read and evaluate the attributes and alarms reported in addition to the basic "report status" command.

SCSI drives with S.M.A.R.T. communicate a reliability condition only as either good or failing. In a SCSI environment, the failure decision occurs at the disk drive and the host notifies the user for action. The SCSI specification provides for a sense bit to be flagged if the drive determines that a reliability issue exists. The system then alerts the end user via a message.

Note that traditional disk diagnostics such as Scandisk work only on the data sectors of the disk surface and do not monitor all the drive functions that are monitored by S.M.A.R.T. Most modern disk drives keep spare sectors available to use as substitutes for sectors that have errors. When one of these spares is reallocated, the drive reports the activity to the S.M.A.R.T. counter but still looks completely defect-free to a surface analysis utility, such as Scandisk.

Drives with S.M.A.R.T. monitor a variety of attributes that vary from one manufacturer to another. Attributes are selected by the device manufacturer based on their capability to contribute to the prediction of degrading or fault conditions for that particular drive. Most drive manufacturers consider the specific set of attributes being used and the identity of those attributes as vendor specific and proprietary.

Some drives monitor the floating height of the head above the magnetic media. If this height changes from a nominal figure, the drive could fail. Other drives can monitor different attributes, such as ECC circuitry that indicates whether soft errors are occurring when reading or writing data. Some of the attributes monitored on various drives include the following:

- Head floating height
- Data throughput performance
- Spin-up time
- Reallocated (spared) sector count
- Seek error rate
- Seek time performance
- Drive spin-up retry count
- Drive calibration retry count

Each attribute has a threshold limit that is used to determine the existence of a degrading or fault condition. These thresholds are set by the drive manufacturer, can vary among manufacturers and models, and can't be changed.

The basic requirements for S.M.A.R.T. to function in a system are simple: You just need a S.M.A.R.T.-capable hard disk drive and a S.M.A.R.T.-aware BIOS or hard disk driver for your particular operating system. If your BIOS does not support S.M.A.R.T., utility programs are available that can support it on a given system. These include Norton Utilities from Symantec, EZ-Drive from StorageSoft, and Data Advisor from Ontrack.

When sufficient changes occur in the monitored attributes to trigger a S.M.A.R.T. alert, the drive sends an alert message via an IDE/ATA or a SCSI command (depending on the type of hard disk drive you have) to the hard disk driver in the system BIOS, which usually reports the problem during the POST the next time the system boots.

If you want more immediate reporting, you can run a utility that queries the S.M.A.R.T. status of the drive, such as S.M.A.R.T. Explorer by Adenix (www.adenix.net) or HDD Health by Panterasoft (www.panterasoft.com).

The first thing to do if you receive a S.M.A.R.T. warning is to back up all the data on the drive. I recommend you back up to new media and do not overwrite any previous backups you might have, just in case the drive fails before the new backup is complete.

After backing up your data, what should you do? S.M.A.R.T. warnings can be caused by an external source and might not actually indicate that the drive itself is going to fail. For example, environmental changes such as high or low ambient temperatures can trigger a S.M.A.R.T. alert, as can excessive vibration in the drive caused by an external source. Additionally, electrical interference from motors or other devices on the same circuit as your PC can induce these alerts.

If the alert was not caused by an external source, a drive replacement might be indicated. If the drive is under warranty, contact the vendor and ask whether they will replace it. If no further alerts occur, the problem might have been an anomaly, and you might not need to replace the drive. If you receive further alerts, replacing the drive is recommended. If you can connect both the new and existing (failing) drive to the same system, you might be able to copy the entire contents of the existing drive to the new one, saving you from having to install or reload all the applications and data from your backup. Because standard copy commands or drag-and-drop methods don't copy system files, hidden files, or files that are open, to copy an entire drive successfully and have the destination copy remain bootable, you need a special application such as Symantec Norton Ghost or Acronis True Image.

Cost

The cost of hard disk storage is continually falling. You can now purchase a 500GB ATA drive for around $140, which is about $0.28 dollars per gigabyte.

A drive I bought in 1983 had a maximum capacity of 10MB and cost $1,800. At current pricing ($0.28 dollars per gigabyte), that drive is worth less than one-third of a penny!

Of course, as the cost of drives continues to fall, we can expect even greater capacities and lower prices in the future.

Chapter

10

Removable Storage

The Role of Removable-media Drives

Since the mid-1980s, the primary storage device used by computers has been the hard disk drive. However, for data backup, data transport between computers, and temporary storage, secondary removable storage devices such as removable media hard drives, floptical drives, magneto-optical drives, flash memory devices, tape drives, and even the ages-old floppy drive have been useful supplements to primary storage. Pure optical storage—such as CD, DVD, HD-DVD, and Blu-ray—can also be used as a supplement to hard disk storage as well as for primary storage. You'll find them covered in Chapter 11, "Optical Storage."

The options for purchasing removable devices vary. Some removable-media drives use media as small as a quarter or your index finger, whereas others use larger media up to 5 1/4".

The capacities of removable-media drives also vary. Whereas the venerable 3 1/2" floppy drive has a capacity of only 1.44MB (big enough for a few driver or data files), others have capacities as large as 100GB or more (enough to store a complete hard disk image).

The next four sections examine the primary roles of these devices.

Extra Storage

As operating systems and applications continue to grow in size and features, more and more storage space is needed for these programs as well as for the data they create.

Operating systems aren't the only program types that are growing. Applications whose MS-DOS versions once fit on a floppy disk have now mutated into "everything but the kitchen sink" do-it-all behemoths like Microsoft Office, which can take hundreds of megabytes of disk space. The multimedia revolution—fueled by millions upon millions of digital music files, low-cost digital cameras, scanners, and video recorders—enables you to capture and store music and images that easily can consume hundreds of gigabytes of space.

High-capacity removable storage devices provide the capability to easily transport huge data files from one computer to another. Or, you can use removable storage to backup or archive important data as well as protect it from prying eyes or environmental disasters (such as fires, floods, and so on). Some types of removable-media storage feature archival durability, whereas others are designed for more short-term storage.

The Importance of Data Backups

Any computer book worth reading warns repeatedly that you should back up your system regularly. Backups are necessary because at any time a major problem, or even some minor ones, can corrupt the important information and programs stored on your computer's hard disk drive and render this information useless. A wide range of problems can damage the data on your hard drive. Here is a list of just some of these data-damaging problems:

- Sudden fluctuations in the electricity that powers your computer (power spikes), resulting in data damage or corruption
- Overwriting a file by mistake
- Performing an unconditional deletion of the wrong file
- Mistakenly formatting a disk containing important data
- Hard drive failure resulting in loss of data that has not been backed up
- Catastrophic damage to your computer (storm, flood, lightning strike, fire, theft, and so on)
- Loss of valuable data due to malware or vandalism

Backups are also the cure for such common headaches as a full hard drive and the need to transfer data between computers. By backing up data you rarely use and deleting the original data from your hard drive, you free up space once occupied by that data. If you later need a particular data file, you can retrieve that file from your backup. You also can more easily share large amounts of data between computers—when you send data from one city to another, for example—by backing up the data to removable media and sending the media.

Regardless of how important regular backups are, many people avoid making them. A major reason for this lapse is that for many people, backing up their systems is tedious work, even more so if the backup medium is low-capacity and cannot hold much data. When you use these media, you might have to insert and remove many disks to back up all the important programs and data.

Optical storage, high-capacity magnetic media, and tape backups are all useful devices for making backups. With the high capacity of today's hard drives, it can be difficult to find an appropriate backup media to hold all of the data.

Additional Boot Devices

Generally, today's systems are started from a hard disk. However, if you need to perform hard disk or system diagnostics, the most thorough tests are those that are performed by booting the system with a specially prepared floppy disk, CD, DVD, or flash drive.

Floppy disks generally must be used to boot older systems that don't support the El Torito (CD/DVD) boot specification or bootable USB drives. In such cases, the floppy drive is the only way to load an operating system from scratch or run bootable diagnostics.

Newer systems support booting from CD/DVD discs as well as bootable USB drives, which can include external USB hard drives in addition to flash drives. Using bootable optical or flash drives is especially useful for running hardware diagnostics or portable operating systems.

Data Transfer Between Systems

Until recently, the only universal method for transferring data between systems was the floppy disk. The 1.44MB 3 1/2" floppy drive type has been standard for well over a decade, and virtually all desktop and laptop computers have included floppy drives. However, more recently the floppy drive has finally been pushed into obsolescence by the USB flash memory drive. Occasionally, a floppy drive might be needed on some systems for diagnostic or other purposes, but in terms of transferring data between systems, it no longer plays any practical role. Even for things like running diagnostics or reflashing motherboard BIOS, the preferred media is bootable CD/DVD discs or USB flash drives.

The USB flash memory drive, even in its smallest capacities can hold many times the capacity of a floppy disk, cannot be damaged by stray magnetic signals, and is both more durable and more compact. With many systems no longer including floppy drives, the USB flash memory drive is even more universal than the floppy drive because virtually all systems built since 1996 have featured USB ports, and most systems built since 2001 support booting from USB devices like flash drives as well.

Floppy-based Driver Installation for Removable-media Devices

Although most devices use CD-ROM media for driver installation, several types of mass storage host adapters have drivers that might be provided on floppy disks:

- ATA/IDE host adapters (add-on card)
- ATA RAID host adapters (motherboard or add-on card)
- SATA host adapters (add-on card)
- SATA RAID host adapters (motherboard or add-on card)
- SCSI host adapters (motherboard or add-on card)
- Serial Attached SCSI (SAS) host adapters

With so many systems today no longer including floppy disk drives, why do vendors provide these drivers on floppy disks?

The design of Windows 2000 and Windows XP is the main reason. When you install these versions of Windows, you are prompted very early in the loading process to press F6 if you need to install a third-party SATA, RAID, or SCSI driver. Windows 2000/XP can only load third-party mass-storage drivers from floppy disks during installation (see Figure 10.1). Note that Windows Vista doesn't have this problem. Vista fully supports loading SATA, RAID, or SCSI drivers from CD or DVD media as well as USB flash drives.

Thus, although floppy disk drives have too little storage to be useful for backup or additional storage, they may still be useful under certain conditions.

Tip

What should you do if you are installing Windows 2000/XP and need to load a mass storage driver, but don't have a floppy drive installed in your system? If the system can be configured to boot from a USB floppy drive, you can temporarily plug in a USB floppy drive and use it as the source for a mass storage driver. To check your system for USB floppy drive support, restart the system and enter the BIOS setup program. Check your BIOS setup program's boot menu to see if you can include USB devices in the boot sequence. See your motherboard or system manual for details.

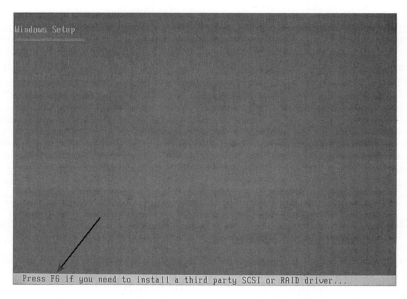

Windows Setup

Press F6 if you need to install a third party SCSI or RAID driver...

Figure 10.1   This prompt appears at the beginning of the Windows 2000 and Windows XP loading process. To load the necessary drivers from this prompt, you need a floppy disk.

Comparing Disk, Tape, and Flash Memory Technologies

Several types of removable-media disk drives are commonly used. Traditionally, the most common varieties have used magnetic media, but some use one of two combinations of magnetic and optical storage: floptical or magneto-optical. Floptical and magneto-optical media drives encode information on disk by using different combinations of laser and magnetic technologies.

Flash memory devices, which have largely replaced the floppy disk for data transfer, emulate disk drives and are discussed in this chapter. Some tape drives are also capable of emulating disk drives by providing drive letter access to a portion of the media, but these drives are used primarily to perform streaming backups of large disk drives and network drive arrays.

Magnetic Disk Media

Whether you are looking at "pure" magnetic media, floptical media, or magneto-optical drives, all types of magnetic disk media share similar characteristics. Disk media is more expensive per megabyte or gigabyte than tape, usually has a lower capacity, and is more easily used on a file-by-file basis as compared to tape. Disk media uses random access, which enables you to find, use, modify, or delete any file or group of files on a disk without disturbing the rest of the disk's contents. When used as a backup medium, most types of disk media are faster for copying a few files but are typically slower for copying large numbers of files or entire drives.

Magnetic Tape Media

Tape media has much less expensive costs overall per megabyte or gigabyte than disk media, has a higher total capacity, and is more easily used on an image or multiple-file basis. Tape drives use sequential access, meaning that the contents of a tape must be read from the beginning and that individual files must be retrieved in the order found on the tape. Also, individual files usually can't be modified on the tape or removed from the tape; the contents of the entire cartridge must be deleted and rewritten. Thus, tape drives are more suited for complete backups of entire hard disks, including all applications and data. Because it is suited for mass backup, tape can be difficult to use for copying single files.

Note

Removable-media disk drives can be used as system backup devices similar to tape. However, the higher price of the medium itself (disks or cartridges) and the generally slower speed at which they perform can make this use somewhat prohibitive on a large scale. For file-by-file backups, disk media is ideal; if, however, you're completely backing up entire drives or systems, external hard drives are much faster and lately have become more economical as well.

Flash Memory Media

Flash memory is a special type of solid-state memory chip that requires no power to maintain its contents. Flash memory cards can easily be moved from digital cameras to laptop or desktop computers and can even be inserted into photo printers or self-contained photo display devices. Flash memory can be used to store any type of computer data, but its original primary application was digital photography. However, more and more digital music players have removable flash memory cards, and so-called *thumb* or *keychain* flash memory devices that plug directly into a USB port are helping to make flash memory a mainstream storage medium and an increasingly popular replacement for some types of magnetic removable-media storage, particularly floppy disks, Zip drives, and SuperDisk drives.

Interfaces for Removable-media Drives

In addition to choosing a type of device, you must choose which type of interface is ideally suited for connecting it to your PC. Several connection options are available for various types of removable-media drives. Table 10.1 provides a cross-reference to current types of removable-media drives and the interfaces they support.

Table 10.1   Removable-Media Drives and Interface Types

Removable-Media Drive Type	Interface Types Supported	Notes
3 1/2" floppy disk	Floppy interface USB	USB-based drives must be supported by the system BIOS if you plan to boot from them or use them to install mass-storage drivers during a Windows 2000/XP installation.
Flash memory	USB	Front-mounted flash memory card readers plug into a USB port on the motherboard or add-on card; USB flash drives plug into a USB port or hub.
Tape drive	ATA SCSI USB	Most tape drives with 2:1 compressed capacities of 100GB or larger use SCSI interfaces.
High-capacity magnetic storage (Zip, REV, Orb)	ATA SCSI USB	Available interfaces vary by drive brand and model.
Magneto-optical	ATA SCSI USB	Available interfaces vary by drive brand and model.

The most common interface (and one of the fastest) for internally mounted drives is the same Parallel AT Attachment (PATA) or Serial ATA (SATA) interface used for most hard drives. SCSI interfacing is as fast or even faster for use with either internal or external drives but requires adding an interface card to most systems. Most high-end tape backups require a SCSI interface.

The most common external interface is now the USB port, which has largely replaced the venerable parallel port for printing as well as for interfacing low-cost external drives and other types of I/O devices. The USB port is available on virtually all PCs since 1996 (and can easily be added via an expansion card if it was not built-in), can be hot-swapped, and is supported by Windows 98 and later. For small-capacity (under 300MB) removable-media devices, the performance of USB 1.1 (12Mbps) is adequate, but larger removable-media devices should be connected to faster USB 2.0 ports (480Mbps) instead. Most flash memory devices must be connected either directly to a USB port or to a flash card reader, which usually plugs into a USB port. Some can be plugged into a CardBus adapter on laptop computers, and some recent laptop computers have integrated slots for some types of flash memory cards.

All current flash memory card readers and USB flash drives now support Hi-Speed USB (USB 2.0), so if your system has slower USB 1.1 ports you should consider installing an expansion card with USB 2.0 ports, which are 40 times faster for greatly improved performance.

Older interfaces such as the parallel port and PC Card (for laptop computers) are still used on some devices but have limited performance. These are recommended only for systems that don't support USB, such as those still running Windows 95 or Windows NT. Some external removable-media drives allow you to interchange interfaces to enable a single drive to work with a variety of systems.

Note

Although late versions of Windows 95 ("Win95C" or OSR2.1 and above) also have USB drivers, many developers of USB devices do not support their use with Windows 95. For reliable results and manufacturer support, use Windows 98 or newer.

Hi-Speed USB ports can be added to desktop systems that have an available PCI slot and to laptop computers that have an available CardBus (32-bit PC Card) slot.

As you will see in the following sections, most removable-media drives are available in two or more of these interface types, allowing you to choose the best interface option for your needs.

Note

Connecting or installing removable-media drives is similar to connecting and installing other internal and external peripherals. The external USB, IEEE 1394, and parallel port drives are the simplest of the available interfaces, requiring only a special cable that comes with the drive and installation of special software drivers. See the instructions that come with each drive for the specifics of its installation.

Refer to Chapter 7, "The ATA/IDE Interface," and Chapter 15, "I/O Interfaces from Serial and Parallel to IEEE 1394 and USB," for details on how these interfaces operate. For information on the SCSI interface, refer to Chapter 8 in *Upgrading and Repairing PCs, 16th Edition*.

The following sections provide details on each of the removable-media drive types discussed in this section, starting with the floppy disk drive.

Floppy Disk Drives, Past and Present

Alan Shugart is generally credited with inventing the floppy disk drive in 1967 while working for IBM. One of Shugart's senior engineers, David Noble, actually proposed the flexible medium (then 8" in diameter) and the protective jacket with the fabric lining. Shugart left IBM in 1969, and in 1976 his company, Shugart Associates, introduced the minifloppy (5 1/4") disk drive. It, of course, became the standard eventually used by personal computers, rapidly replacing the 8" drives. He also helped create the Shugart Associates System Interface (SASI), which was later renamed small computer system interface (SCSI) when approved as an ANSI standard.

Sony introduced the first 3 1/2" microfloppy drives and disks in 1981. The first significant company to adopt the 3 1/2" floppy for general use was Hewlett-Packard in 1984 with its partially PC-compatible HP-150 system. The adoption of the 3 1/2" drive in the PC was solidified when IBM started using the drive in 1986 in some systems and finally switched its entire PC product line to 3 1/2" drives in 1987.

Note that all PC floppy disk drives are still based on (and mostly compatible with) the original Shugart designs, including the electrical and command interfaces. Compared to other parts of the PC, the floppy disk drive has undergone relatively few changes over the years.

The following sections discuss standard 3 1/2" 1.44MB floppy disk drives and media, how they function, and how to properly install and service them. Older types of floppy disk drives, including 3 1/2" 720KB, 3 1/2" 2.88MB, 5 1/4" 1.2MB, and 5 1/4" floppy drives, are no longer in common use. If you need more information about these drives, see the Technical Reference section of the DVD included with this book.

Table 10.2 provides a brief comparison of these drives to each other. As you can see, the different disk capacities are determined by several parameters, some of which seem to remain constant on all drives. Others, however, change from drive to drive. For example, all drives use 512-byte physical sectors, which is true for hard disks as well.

◄◄ For information on magnetic storage in general—that is, how data is actually stored on the disk media—see Chapter 8, "Magnetic Storage Principles," p. 637.

Table 10.2   Floppy Disk Logical Formatted Parameters

	Current Formats					Obsolete Formats		
Disk Size (Inches)	3 1/2	3 1/2	3 1/2	5 1/4	5 1/4	5 1/4	5 1/4	5 1/4
Disk Capacity (KB)	2,880	1,440	720	1,200	360	320	180	160
Media descriptor byte	F0h	F0h	F9h	F9h	FDh	FFh	FCh	FEh
Sides (heads)	2	2	2	2	2	2	1	1
Tracks per side	80	80	80	80	40	40	40	40
Sectors per track	36	18	9	15	9	8	9	8
Bytes per sector	512	512	512	512	512	512	512	512
Sectors per cluster	2	1	2	1	2	2	1	1
FAT length (sectors)	9	9	3	7	2	1	2	1
Number of FATs	2	2	2	2	2	2	2	2
Root dir. length (sectors)	15	14	7	14	7	7	4	4
Maximum root entries	240	224	112	224	112	112	64	64
Total sectors per disk	5,760	2,880	1,440	2,400	720	640	360	320
Total available sectors	5,726	2,847	1,426	2,371	708	630	351	313
Total available clusters	2,863	2,847	713	2,371	354	315	351	313

Alternatives to Floppy Drives

In 2002, many companies started selling systems without floppy drives. This started with laptop computers, where internal floppy drives were first eliminated and replaced with external (normally USB) drives. Most newer laptops no longer include a floppy drive with the system, offering only external USB models as an option. Starting in 2003, many desktop system manufacturers likewise stopped including floppy drives in their standard system configurations. An optional USB floppy drive can be used as a bootable drive if the BIOS permits it, as is the case with many recent systems.

Several alternatives to floppy storage are available, although both Zip and LS-120/LS-240 (SuperDisk) drives have failed in the marketplace as floppy drive replacements in new PCs. The Mount Rainier (EasyWrite) standard, which was introduced in 2002, allows CD-RW and DVD+-RW drives to serve as replacements for the floppy. Prior to Mount Rainier, the CD/DVD drives lacked defect management, as well as native OS support.

▶▶ See "Mount Rainier," p. 795.

Many people are also now using USB flash memory devices, often called *thumb drives* or *keychain drives*, to transport small to medium amounts of data (up to 2GB or more) between systems. However, floppy drives remain useful for data recovery or computer forensics, where data retrieval from older media is often necessary. Even though I don't use floppy drives much for storing new information, I maintain systems with both 5 1/4" and 3 1/2" drives so I can read data from older media in a forensics or data-recovery situation.

1.44MB 3 1/2" Drives

The 3 1/2", 1.44MB, high-density (HD) drives first appeared from IBM in the PS/2 product line introduced in 1987. Most other computer vendors started offering the drives as an option in their systems immediately afterward. For systems that include floppy drives, the 1.44MB type is still by far the most popular.

The drive records 80 cylinders consisting of two tracks each with 18 sectors per track, resulting in a formatted capacity of 1.44MB. Some disk manufacturers label these disks as 2.0MB, and the difference between this unformatted capacity and the formatted usable result is lost during the format. Note that the 1440KB of total formatted capacity does not account for the areas the FAT file system reserves for file management, leaving only 1423.5KB of actual file-storage area.

The drive spins at 300 rpm and in fact must spin at that speed to operate properly with existing high- and low-density controllers. To use the 500KHz data rate (the maximum from most standard high- and low-density floppy controllers), these drives must spin at a maximum of 300 rpm. If the drives were to spin at the faster 360 rpm rate of the 5 1/4" drives, they would have to reduce the total number of sectors per track to 15; otherwise, the controller could not keep up. In short, the 1.44MB 3 1/2" drives store 1.2 times the data of the 5 1/4" 1.2MB drives, and the 1.2MB drives spin exactly 1.2 times faster than the 1.44MB drives. The data rates used by both of these HD drives are identical and compatible with the same controllers. In fact, because these 3 1/2" HD drives can run at the 500KHz data rate, a controller that can support a 1.2MB 5 1/4" drive can also support the 1.44MB drives.

Other types of floppy drives that have been used in the past include the following:

- **2.88MB 3 1/2"**—This size was used on some IBM PS/2 and ThinkPad models in the early 1990s.
- **720KB 3 1/2"**—This size was used by IBM and others starting in 1986 before the 1.44MB 3 1/2" drive was introduced.
- **1.2MB 5 1/4"**—This was introduced by IBM for the IBM AT in 1984 and widely used throughout the rest of the decade.

■ **360KB 5 1/4"**—An improved version of the floppy disk drive originally used by the IBM PC, it was used throughout the 1980s on XT-class machines and some AT-class machines.

Floppy Drive Interfaces

Floppy drives are interfaced to the PC in several ways. Many still include the traditional floppy controller interface (even if a drive is not installed in the system), but some now use the USB interface; this is covered later in this chapter. Because the traditional floppy controller only works internally, all external drives are interfaced via USB or some other alternative interface. USB drives often have a standard floppy drive inside an external box with a USB-to-floppy-controller interface converter inside. Newer, *legacy-free* systems don't include a traditional floppy controller and typically use USB as the floppy interface. In the past, some drives have been available in FireWire (IEEE 1394) or even parallel interfaces as well. For more information on USB or the parallel port, see Chapter 15.

Drive Components

All floppy disk drives, regardless of type, consist of several basic common components. To properly install and service a disk drive, you must be able to identify these components and understand their functions (see Figure 10.2).

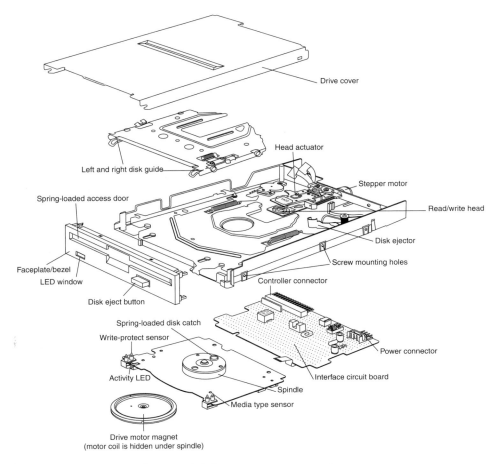

Figure 10.2   A typical 3 1/2" floppy disk drive.

Read/Write Heads

A floppy disk drive usually has two read/write heads—one for each side of the disk, with both heads being used for reading and writing on their respective disk sides (see Figure 10.3). At one time, single-sided drives were available for PC systems (the original PC had such drives), but today single-sided drives are a faded memory.

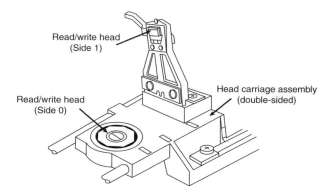

Read/write head
(Side 1)

Head carriage assembly
(double-sided)

Read/write head
(Side 0)

Figure 10.3   A double-sided drive head assembly.

Note

Many people do not realize that Head 0, or the first head on a floppy disk drive, is the bottom one. Single-sided drives, in fact, used only the bottom head; the top head has been replaced by a felt pressure pad. Another bit of disk trivia is that the top head (Head 1) is not positioned directly over the bottom head (Head 0). The top head is instead offset by either four or eight tracks inward from the bottom head, depending on the drive type.

A motor called a *head actuator* moves the head mechanism. The heads can move in and out over the surface of the disk in a straight line to position themselves over various tracks. On a floppy drive, the heads move in and out tangentially to the tracks they record on the disk. This is different from hard disks, where the heads move on a rotating arm similar to the tone-arm of a record player. Because the top and bottom heads are mounted on the same rack, or mechanism, they move in unison and can't move independently of each other. The upper and lower head each defines tracks on its respective side of the disk medium. At any given head position, the tracks under the top and bottom head simultaneously are called a *cylinder*. Most floppy disks are recorded with 80 tracks on each side (160 tracks total), which is 80 cylinders.

The heads themselves are made of soft ferrous (iron) compounds with electromagnetic coils. Each head is a composite design, with a read/write head centered within two tunnel-erase heads in the same physical assembly (see Figure 10.4).

Floppy disk drives use a recording method called *tunnel erasure*. As the drive writes to a track, the trailing tunnel-erase heads erase the outer bands of the track, trimming it cleanly on the disk. The heads force the data into a specified narrow "tunnel" on each track. This process prevents the signal from one track from being confused with the signals from adjacent tracks, which would happen if the signal were allowed to naturally "taper off" to each side. *Alignment* is the placement of the heads with respect to the tracks they must read and write. Head alignment can be checked only against some sort of reference-standard disk recorded by a perfectly aligned machine. These types of disks are available, and you can use one to check your drive's alignment. However, this is usually not practical for the end user because one calibrated analog alignment disk can cost more than a new drive.

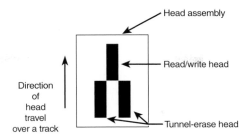

Figure 10.4   Composite construction of a typical floppy disk drive head.

The floppy disk drive's two heads are spring-loaded and physically grip the disk with a small amount of pressure, which means they are in direct contact with the disk surface while reading from and writing to the disk. Because floppy disk drives spin at only 300 rpm or 360 rpm, this pressure does not present an excessive friction problem. Some newer disks are specially coated with Teflon or other compounds to further reduce friction and enable the disk to slide more easily under the heads. Because of the contact between the heads and disk, a buildup of the magnetic material from the disk eventually forms on the heads. The buildup should periodically be cleaned off the heads as part of a preventive maintenance or normal service program. Most manufacturers recommend cleaning the heads after every 40 hours of drive operation, which—considering how often people use these drives today—could be a lifetime.

To read and write to the disk properly, the heads must be in direct contact with the magnetic medium. Very small particles of loose oxide, dust, dirt, smoke, fingerprints, or hair can cause problems with reading and writing the disk. Disk and drive manufacturers' tests have found that a spacing as little as .000032" (32 millionths of an inch) between the heads and medium can cause read/write errors. You now can understand why it is important to handle disks carefully and avoid touching or contaminating the surface of the disk medium in any way. The rigid jacket and protective shutter for the head access aperture on 3 1/2" disks is excellent for preventing problems caused by contamination. Disks that are 5 1/4" do not have the same protective elements, which is perhaps one reason they initially began to fall into disuse. If you still use 5 1/4" floppy disks, you should exercise extra care in their handling. I recommend copying any archival data over to recordable CD or DVD media if your situation doesn't require keeping the data on the original media.

The Head Actuator

The *head actuator* for a floppy disk drive is what moves the heads across the disk and is driven by a special kind of motor, called a *stepper motor* (see Figure 10.5). This type of motor does not spin around continuously; rather, the motor turns a precise specified distance and stops. Stepper motors are not infinitely variable in their positioning; they move in fixed increments—or *detents*—and must stop at a particular detent position. This is ideal for disk drives because the location of each track on the disk can then be defined by moving one or more increments of the motor's motion. The disk controller can instruct the motor to position itself any number of steps within the range of its travel. To position the heads at cylinder 25, for example, the controller instructs the motor to go to the 25th detent position or step from Cylinder 0.

The stepper motor can be linked to the head rack in one of two ways. In the first, the link is a coiled, split-steel band. The band winds and unwinds around the spindle of the stepper motor, translating the rotary motion into linear motion. Most 3 1/2" drives use the more compact worm-gear arrangement rather than a band. In this type of drive, the head assembly rests on a worm gear driven directly off the stepper motor shaft. Most stepper motors used in floppy disk drives can step in specific increments that relate to the track spacing on the disk. The ancient 5 1/4" 360KB drives are the only 48 TPI drives that use the 3.6° increment stepper motor; all other drive types typically use the 1.8° stepper motor. On most drives, the stepper motor is a small, cylindrical object near one corner of the drive.

A stepper motor usually has a full travel time of about one fifth of a second—about 200ms. On average, a one-half stroke is 100ms, and a one-third stroke is 66ms. The timing of a one-half or one-third stroke of the head-actuator mechanism is often used to determine the reported average access time for a disk drive. Average access time is the normal amount of time the heads spend moving at random from one track to another.

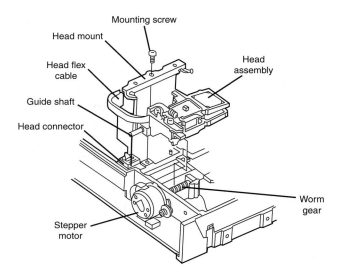

Figure 10.5   An expanded view of a stepper motor and head actuator.

Floppy Drive Spindle Motor

The *spindle motor* is what spins the disk. The normal speed of rotation is either 300 rpm or 360 rpm, depending on the type of drive. The 5 1/4" high-density (HD) drive is the only drive that spins at 360 rpm. All others, including the 5 1/4" double-density (DD), 3 1/2" DD, 3 1/2" HD, and 3 1/2" extra-high density (ED) drives, spin at 300 rpm. This is a slow speed when compared to a hard disk drive, which helps explain why floppy disk drives have much lower data transfer rates. However, this slow speed also enables the drive heads to be in physical contact with the disk while it is spinning, without causing friction damage.

The spindle motor in early drives used a belt-driven mechanism to spin the disk, but all modern drives use a direct-drive system with no belts. The direct-drive systems are more reliable and less expensive to manufacture, as well as smaller in size. The earlier belt-driven systems did have more rotational torque available to turn a sticky disk because of the torque multiplication factor of the belt system. Most newer direct-drive systems, on the other hand, use an automatic torque-compensation capability that sets the disk-rotation speed to a fixed 300 rpm or 360 rpm and compensates with additional torque for high-friction disks or less torque for more slippery ones. Besides compensating for varying amounts of friction, this arrangement eliminates the need to adjust the rotational speed of the drive—something that was frequently required on older drives.

Floppy Drive Circuit Boards

A disk drive always incorporates one or more *logic boards*, which are circuit boards that contain the circuitry used to control the head actuator, read/write heads, spindle motor, disk sensors, and other components on the drive. The logic board implements the drive's interface to the controller board in the system unit.

The standard interface that all PC floppy disk drives use is called the Shugart Associates SA400 interface. It was invented in the 1970s and is based on the NEC 765 controller chip. All modern floppy controllers contain circuits that are compatible with the original NEC 765 chip. This industry-standard interface is why you can purchase drives from almost any manufacturer and they will all be compatible.

The Floppy Controller

At one time, the controller for a computer's floppy disk drives took the form of a dedicated expansion card installed in an Industry Standard Architecture (ISA) bus slot. Later implementations used a multifunction card that provided the IDE/ATA, parallel, and serial port interfaces in addition to the floppy disk drive controller. Today's PCs have the floppy controller integrated into the motherboard. Some systems use a Super I/O chip that also includes the serial and parallel interfaces, among other things; other systems might use a South Bridge chip that contains the Super I/O functions. Regardless of the location of the floppy controller logic, it is still interfaced to the system via the ISA or LPC (low pin count) bus and functions exactly as if it were a card installed in an ISA slot. These built-in controllers are typically configured via the system BIOS Setup routines and can be disabled if an actual floppy controller card is going to be installed.

Whether it is built in or not, each primary floppy controller uses a standard set of system resources:

- IRQ 6 (interrupt request)
- DMA 2 (direct memory address)
- I/O ports 3F0–3F5, 3F7 (input/output)

These system resources are standardized and generally not changeable. This usually does not present a problem because no other devices will try to use these resources (which would result in a conflict). Systems advertised as "legacy-free" don't include a Super I/O chip and therefore don't have a built-in floppy controller. Such systems can still use a floppy drive, but only in the form of an external USB drive.

Unlike the ATA interface used primarily by hard disks and optical drives, the floppy disk controller has not changed much over the years. Virtually the only thing that has changed is the controller's maximum speed. As the data density of floppy disks (and their capacity) has increased over the years, the controller speed has had to increase as well. Nearly all floppy disk controllers in computers today support speeds of up to 1 megabit per second (Mbps), which supports all the standard floppy disk drives. 500 kilobits per second (Kbps) controllers can support all floppy disk drives except the 2.88MB extra high-density models. Very old computers used 250Kbps controllers that could support only 360KB 5 1/4" and 720KB 3 1/2" drives.

Tip

The best way to determine the speed of the floppy disk drive controller in your computer is to examine the floppy disk drive options provided by the system BIOS.

◄◄ See Chapter 5, "BIOS," p. 441.

Although traditional floppy controller cards and multi I/O cards have provisions for two floppy drives—A: and B:—many recent systems that integrate Super I/O features into the South Bridge chip on the motherboard support only a single floppy drive.

The Faceplate

The *faceplate*, or *bezel*, is the plastic piece that comprises the front of the drive. This piece, usually removable, comes in various colors and configurations.

Most floppy drive manufacturers offer drives with matching faceplates in gray, beige, or black and with a choice of red, green, or yellow activity LEDs in their retail-packaged drives. This enables a system builder to better match the drive to the aesthetics of the case for a seamless, integrated, and more professional look.

Tip

OEM "bare" floppy drives might not include faceplate or LED options. Some OEM drives don't even include a faceplate at all because they were manufactured for systems that use a custom-made front panel that incorporates a protective door and pushbutton for ejecting disks from the drive.

Power and Data Connectors

External USB floppy drives use the USB connector for power and data. However, nearly all internal floppy disk drives have two connectors—one for power to run the drive and the other to carry the control and data signals to and from the drive. These connectors are fairly standardized in the computer industry. A 4-pin inline connector (called Mate-N-Lock by AMP) in both large (Molex) and small (Berg) styles is used for power (see Figure 10.6), and a 34-pin connector in both edge and pin header designs is used for the data and control signals. Typically, 5 1/4" drives use the large-style power connector (the same as used by ATA/IDE hard disks and CD/DVD drives) and the 34-pin edge-type connector, whereas most 3 1/2" drives use the smaller version of the power connector and the 34-pin header-type logic connector. The drive controller and logic connectors and pinouts are detailed later in this chapter, as well as on the Vendor List on this book's DVD.

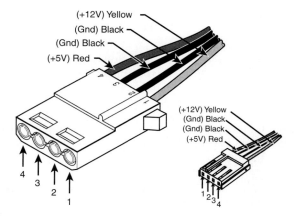

Figure 10.6 Large (Molex) connector for 5 1/4" drives and small (Berg) connector for 3 1/2" drives.

Both the Molex and Berg power connectors from the power supply are female plugs. They plug in to the male portion, which is attached to the drive itself. Note that the pin-to-signal designations on the small connector are the opposite of those on the large connector.

One common problem with installing 3 1/2" drives in some systems is that the power supply might not have an available small-style (Berg) power connector used by the smaller drives. An adapter cable that converts the Molex peripheral power connector to the proper Berg connector used on most 3 1/2" drives is available from Dalco (www.dalco.com) under p/n 47425 and from other sources. You can also use a splitter that converts a Molex connector into one each, Berg and Molex (Dalco p/n 43435), or into two Berg connectors (Dalco p/n 51075). Splitters are also available from other sources.

The Floppy Disk Controller Cable

The 34-pin connector on an internal floppy disk drive takes the form of either an edge connector (on 5 1/4" drives) or a pin connector (on 3 1/2" drives). The pinouts for the floppy controller connector are shown in Table 10.3.

Table 10.3   Floppy Disk Drive Controller Connector Pinout

Pin	Signal	Pin	Signal
1	Ground	2	DD/HD Density Select
3	Key[1]	4	Reserved (unused)
5	Key[1]	6	ED Density Select[2]
7	Ground	8	Index
9	Ground	10	Motor-On 0 (A:)
11	Ground	12	Drive Select 1 (B:)
13	Ground	14	Drive Select 0 (A:)
15	Ground	16	Motor-On 1 (B:)
17	Ground	18	Direction (stepper motor)
19	Ground	20	Step Pulse
21	Ground	22	Write Data
23	Ground	24	Write Enable
25	Ground	26	Track 0
27	Ground	28	Write Protect
29	Ground	30	Read Data
31	Ground	32	Head Select
33	Ground	34	Disk Change

1. Controllers and drives can use one, both, or no key (missing) pins.
2. For controllers supporting ED (Extra-high Density 2.88M) drives only; otherwise unused.

The cable used to connect the floppy disk drive(s) to the controller on the motherboard is sometimes quite strange. To support various drive configurations, the cable might have up to five connectors on it—two edge connectors and two pin connectors to attach to the drives and one pin connector to connect to the controller. The cable has redundant connectors for each of the two drives (A and B) supported by the standard floppy disk drive controller, so you can install any combination of 5 1/4" and 3 1/2" drives (see Figure 10.7).

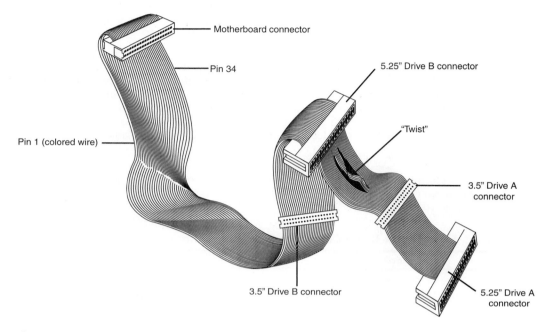

Figure 10.7   Standard five-connector floppy interface cable.

You can also purchase floppy drive cables made for only 3 1/2" drives. These omit the edge connectors shown in Figure 10.7.

In addition to the connectors, the cable has a special twist that inverts the signals of wires 10–16. These are the wires carrying the Drive Select (DS) and Motor Enable signals for each of the two drives. Very old floppy disk drives have DS jumpers designed to enable you to select whether a given drive should be recognized as A or B (really old ones allow a third and fourth setting as well).

You might not even know that these jumpers exist because the twist in the cable prevents you from having to adjust them, and as such they have been eliminated from most newer drives. When two floppy disk drives are installed in one system (admittedly a rarity nowadays), the cable electrically changes the DS configuration of the drive that is plugged in after the twist. Thus, the twist causes a drive physically set to the second DS position (B) to appear to the controller to be set to the first DS position (A). The adoption of this cable has enabled the use of a standard jumper configuration for all floppy disk drives, regardless of whether you install one or two drives in a computer.

If you install only a single floppy disk drive, you use the connector after the twist, which causes the drive to be recognized as drive A. Although it's seldom necessary today, many computer BIOS setup programs have an option enabling you to swap drives A: and B: without adjusting drive cables. If you have a computer with the old 5 1/4" floppy as B: for use with old software and need to use it as A:, you can use this BIOS option, if present, to change the drive setup without opening your system.

Note

The original Shugart SA400 floppy interface made for 5 1/4" floppy drives supported up to four drives on a single cable. However, IBM modified the controller pinout to support only two drives and eliminate the need to change drive select jumpers on the drive. To learn more about these changes, see "Secrets of the Cable Twist" in Chapter 11 of *Upgrading and Repairing PCs, 16th Edition*.

How the Operating System Uses a Floppy Disk

The physical operation of a 3 1/2" disk drive is fairly simple to describe. The disk rotates in the drive at 300 rpm. With the disk spinning, the heads can move in and out approximately 1 inch and write 80 tracks. The tracks are written on both sides of the disk and are therefore sometimes called *cylinders*. A single cylinder comprises the tracks on the top and bottom of the disk. The heads record by using a tunnel-erase procedure that writes a track to a specified width and then erases the edges of the track to prevent interference with any adjacent tracks.

To the operating system, data on your PC disks is organized in tracks and sectors, just as on a hard disk drive. *Tracks* are narrow, concentric circles on a disk; *sectors* are pie-shaped slices of the individual tracks. A 3 1/2" 1.44MB floppy disk drive has the following specifications:

- Bytes per sector: 512
- Sectors per track: 18
- Tracks per side: 80
- Track width (mm): .115
- Sides: 2
- Capacity (KiB): 1,440
- Capacity (MiB): 1.406
- Capacity (MB): 1.475

For the specifications for obsolete disk drive types, see the Technical Reference section of the DVD packaged with this book.

The floppy disk's capacity can actually be expressed in various ways. For example, what we call a 1.44MB disk really stores 1.475MB if you go by the correct decimal prefix definition for a megabyte. The discrepancy comes from the fact that in the past floppies were designated by their kilobinary (1,024-byte) capacities, which were originally (and improperly) abbreviated as KB. To prevent ambiguities in binary versus decimal number interpretations, the International Electrotechnical Commission (IEC) has designated KiB as the correct abbreviation for kilobinary.

Despite the IEC standards, the traditional method when discussing floppy drives or disks is to refer to the capacity of a floppy by the number of kilobinary bytes (1,024 bytes equals 1KiB) but to use the otherwise improper abbreviation KB instead. This has also been improperly extended to the abbreviation MB. Therefore, a floppy disk with an actual capacity of 1,440KiB is instead denoted as a 1.44MB disk, even though it would really be 1.406MiB (megabinary bytes) or 1.475MB (million bytes) if we went by the correct definitions for MiB (mebibyte) and MB (megabyte).

For the remainder of this chapter, I will refer to the capacity of the various floppy disks according to the previously used conventions rather than the more technically accurate IEC-designated binary and decimal prefixes.

Note

As with hard disk drives, using the same prefixes for both decimal and binary multiples has resulted in a great deal of confusion. The IEC prefixes for binary multiples were designed to eliminate this confusion. For more information on prefixes for binary multiples, see http://physics.nist.gov/cuu/Units/binary.html. Also, refer to the section "Capacity Measurements" in Chapter 8, "Magnetic Storage Principles."

Like blank sheets of paper, new, unformatted disks contain no information. Formatting a disk is similar to adding lines to the paper so you can write straight across. Formatting the disk writes the information the operating system needs to maintain a directory and file table of contents. A full format rewrites the file system structures, removing any existing data in the process. This is the equivalent of both a high-level and low-level format on a hard disk. However, unlike a hard disk, a floppy disk does not need to be partitioned.

Note

The Quick Format option available in most versions of Windows, including Windows XP and Vista, erases the contents of the disk and verifies the file system rather than rewriting the file system. If you run FORMAT.EXE from the command line, the /Q option also performs a quick format. Unfortunately, Quick Format is not very good at determining whether you have problems with your floppy disk's file system. If you need to ensure that the floppy disk is properly formatted (such as in the case of a used disk you want to use for another task), you should not use the Quick Format option. Windows NT, 2000, XP, and Vista perform a full (low-level) format that rewrites the file system and clears the disk if Quick Format is not selected. Windows 9x/Me offers Quick (erase), which is the same as selecting Quick Format, Full, Copy System Files Only in Windows XP and Vista. Select Full to rewrite the file system and clear the disk of existing data.

When you format a floppy disk, the operating system reserves the track nearest to the outside edge of a disk (track 0) almost entirely for its purposes. Track 0, Side 0, Sector 1 contains the Volume Boot Record (VBR), or Boot Sector, that the system needs to begin operation. The next few sectors contain the file allocation tables (FATs), which keep records of which clusters or allocation units on the disk contain file information and which are empty. Finally, the next few sectors contain the root directory, in which the operating system stores information about the names and starting locations of the files on the disk.

Note that floppy disks have been sold in preformatted form for a few years now. This saves time because the formatting can take a minute or more per disk. Even if disks come preformatted, they can always be reformatted later. This is useful if you accidentally purchased Mac-formatted disks for your PC; a PC can't use a Mac-formatted disk unless you reformat it.

Cylinders

When the location of data on a floppy disk is discussed, the cylinder number is normally used in place of the track number because all floppy drives today are double-sided. A cylinder on a floppy disk includes two tracks: the one on the bottom of the disk above Head 0 and the one on the top of the disk below Head 1. Because a disk can't have more than two sides and the drive has two heads, there are always two tracks per cylinder for floppy disks. Hard disk drives, on the other hand, can have multiple disk platters—each with two heads—resulting in many tracks per single cylinder. The simple rule is that there are as many tracks per cylinder as there are heads on the drive.

Cylinders were discussed in more detail in Chapter 9, "Hard Disk Storage."

Clusters or Allocation Units

A *cluster* also is called an *allocation unit*. The term is appropriate because a single cluster is the smallest unit of the disk that the operating system can allocate when it writes a file. A cluster or an allocation unit consists of one or more sectors—usually a power of two (1, 2, 4, 8, and so on). Having more than one sector per cluster reduces the FAT size and enables the OS to run more quickly because it has fewer individual clusters to manage. The tradeoff is in some wasted disk space. Because the OS can manage space only in the cluster size unit, every file consumes space on the disk in increments of one cluster. However, 3 1/2" 1.44MB floppy drives store so little information that the default cluster (allocation unit) size is one sector (512 bytes).

Disk Change

The standard PC floppy controller and drive use a special signal on pin 34 called *Disk Change* to determine whether the disk has been changed—or more accurately, to determine whether the same disk loaded during the previous disk access is still in the drive. Disk Change is a pulsed signal that changes a status register in the controller to let the system know that a disk has been either inserted or ejected. This register is set to indicate that a disk has been inserted or removed (changed) by default.

The register is cleared when the controller sends a step pulse to the drive and the drive responds, acknowledging that the heads have moved. At this point, the system knows that a specific disk is in the drive. If the Disk Change signal is not received before the next access, the system can assume that the same disk is still in the drive. Any information read into memory during the previous access can therefore be reused without rereading the disk.

Because of this process, systems can buffer or cache the contents of the FAT or directory structure of a disk in the system's memory. By eliminating unnecessary rereads of these areas of the disk, the apparent speed of the drive is increased. If you move the door lever or eject button on a drive that supports the Disk Change signal, the DC pulse is sent to the controller, thus resetting the register and indicating that the disk has been changed. This procedure causes the system to purge buffered or cached data that had been read from the disk because the system can't be sure that the same disk is still in the drive.

One interesting problem can occur when certain drives are installed in a 16-bit or greater system. Some drives use pin 34 for a "Ready" (RDY) signal. The RDY signal is sent whenever a disk is installed and rotating in the drive. If you install a drive that has pin 34 set to send RDY, the system thinks it is continuously receiving a Disk Change signal, which causes problems. Usually, the drive fails with a Drive Not Ready error and is inoperable. The only reason the RDY signal exists on some drives is that it happens to be a part of the standard Shugart SA400 disk interface; however, it has never been used in PC systems.

The biggest problem occurs if the drive should be sending the DC signal on pin 34 but isn't. If a system is told (through CMOS setup) that the drive is any type other than a 360KB (which can't ever send the DC signal), the system expects the drive to send DC whenever a disk has been ejected. If the drive is not configured properly to send the signal, the system never recognizes that a disk has been changed. Therefore, even if you do change the disk, the system still acts as though the first disk is in the drive and holds the first disk's directory and FAT information in RAM. This can be dangerous because the FAT and directory information from the first disk can be partially written to any subsequent disks written to in the drive.

Caution

If you have ever seen a system with a floppy disk drive that shows "phantom directories" of the previously installed disk, even after you have changed or removed it, you have experienced this problem firsthand. The negative side effect is that all disks after the first one you place in this system are in extreme danger. You likely will overwrite the directories and FATs of many disks with information from the first disk.

If it's even possible at all, data recovery from such a catastrophe can require quite a bit of work with utility programs, such as Norton Utilities (part of the Norton SystemWorks suite). These problems with Disk Change most often are traced to an incorrectly configured drive. A damaged floppy cable can also cause Disk Change to fail.

Windows Explorer doesn't always display the new contents of a drive. Press the F5 key to refresh the display after you change floppy disks to force the computer to read the new disk.

If the drive you are installing is a 5 1/4" 1.2MB or 3 1/2" 720KB, 1.44MB, or 2.88MB drive, be sure to set pin 34 to send the Disk Change (DC) signal. Most drives come permanently preset this way, but some older drives have used a jumper (usually labeled DC) to set this option.

Analyzing 3 1/2" Floppy Disk Media Construction

3 1/2" disks differ from the older 5 1/4" disks in both construction and physical properties. The flexible (or floppy) disk is contained within a plastic jacket. The 3 1/2" disks are covered by a more rigid jacket than are the 5 1/4" disks. The disks within the jackets, however, are virtually identical except, of course, for size.

The 3 1/2" disks use a much more rigid plastic case than 5 1/4" disks, which helps stabilize the magnetic medium inside. Therefore, the disks can store data at track and data densities greater than the 5 1/4" disks (see Figure 10.8). A metal shutter protects the media-access hole. The drive manipulates the shutter, leaving it closed whenever the disk is not in a drive. The medium is then completely insulated from the environment and from your fingers. The shutter also obviates the need for a disk jacket.

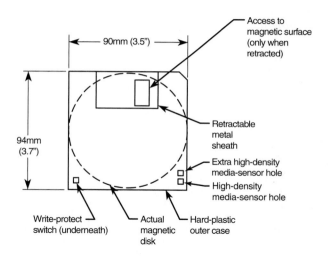

Figure 10.8 Construction of a 3 1/2" floppy disk.

Because the shutter is not necessary for the disk to work, you can remove it from the plastic case if it becomes bent or damaged. Pry it off the disk case; it will pop off with a snap. You also should remove the spring that pushes it closed. Additionally, after removing the damaged shutter, you should copy the data from the damaged disk to a new one.

Rather than an index hole in the disk, the 3 1/2" disks use a metal center hub with an alignment hole. The drive "grasps" the metal hub, and the hole in the hub enables the drive to position the disk properly.

On the lower-left part of the disk is a hole with a plastic slider—the write-protect/enable hole. When the slider is positioned so the hole is visible, the disk is *write-protected*, meaning the drive is prevented from recording on the disk. When the slider is positioned to cover the hole, writing is enabled, and you can save data to the disk. For more permanent write-protection, some commercial software programs are supplied on disks with the slider removed so you can't easily enable recording on the disk. This is exactly opposite of a 5 1/4" floppy, in which covered means write-protected, not write-enabled.

On the other (right) side of the disk from the write-protect hole is usually another hole called the *media-density-selector* hole. If this hole is present, the disk is constructed of a special medium and is therefore an HD or ED disk. If the media-sensor hole is exactly opposite the write-protect hole, it indicates a 1.44MB HD disk. If the media-sensor hole is located more toward the top of the disk (the metal shutter is at the top of the disk), it indicates a 2.88MB ED disk. No hole on the right side means that the disk is a low-density disk. Most 3 1/2" drives have a media sensor that controls recording capability based on the absence or presence of these holes.

The actual magnetic medium in both the 3 1/2" and 5 1/4" disks is constructed of the same basic materials. They use a plastic base (usually Mylar) coated with a magnetic compound. High-density disks use a cobalt-ferric compound; extended-density disks use a barium-ferric media compound. The rigid jacket material on the 3 1/2" disks has occasionally caused people to believe incorrectly that these disks are some sort of "hard disk" and not really a floppy disk. The disk cookie inside the 3 1/2" case is just as floppy as the 5 1/4" variety.

Floppy Disk Media Types and Specifications

This section examines the types of disks that have been available to PC owners over the years. Especially interesting are the technical specifications that can separate one type of disk from another, as Table 10.4 shows. The following sections define all the specifications used to describe a typical disk.

Table 10.4   Floppy Disk Media Specifications

Media Parameters	5 1/4"			3 1/2"		
	Double-Density (DD)	Quad-Density (QD)	High-Density (HD)	Double-Density (DD)	High-Density (HD)	Extra High-Density (ED)
Tracks per inch (TPI)	48	96	96	135	135	135
Bits per inch (BPI)	5,876	5,876	9,646	8,717	17,434	34,868
Media formulation	Ferrite	Ferrite	Cobalt	Cobalt	Cobalt	Barium
Coercivity (oersteds)	300	300	600	600	720	750
Thickness (micro-in.)	100	100	50	70	40	100
Recording polarity	Horiz.	Horiz.	Horiz.	Horiz.	Horiz.	Vert.

5 1/4" quad-density (QD) disks were never used as an official standard for PCs. They were widely used, however, by the Tandy 2000 (a semicompatible MS-DOS computer that used the rare Intel 80186 processor and was introduced shortly before the IBM AT in 1984), the Tandy Color Computer, and other computers running the OS-9 operating system, and some CP/M computers. A QD disk can be reformatted as a double-density disk by a PC that has a 360KB floppy drive.

Density

Density, in simplest terms, is a measure of the amount of information that can be reliably packed into a specific area of a recording surface. The keyword here is *reliably*.

Disks have two types of densities: longitudinal density and linear density. *Longitudinal density* is indicated by how many tracks can be recorded on the disk and is often expressed as a number of tracks per inch (TPI). *Linear density* is the capability of an individual track to store data and is often indicated as a number of bits per inch (BPI). Unfortunately, these types of densities are often confused when different disks and drives are discussed.

Media Coercivity and Thickness

The *coercivity* specification of a disk refers to the magnetic-field strength required to make a proper recording. Coercivity, measured in oersteds, is a value indicating magnetic strength. A disk with a higher coercivity rating requires a stronger magnetic field to make a recording on that disk. With lower ratings, the disk can be recorded with a weaker magnetic field. In other words, the lower the coercivity rating, the more sensitive the disk.

HD media demands higher coercivity ratings so the adjacent magnetic domains don't interfere with each other. For this reason, HD media is actually less sensitive and requires a stronger recording signal strength.

Another factor is the thickness of the disk. The thinner the disk, the less influence a region of the disk has on another adjacent region. The thinner disks, therefore, can accept many more bits per inch without eventually degrading the recording.

Caring for and Handling Floppy Disks and Drives

Most computer users know the basics of disk care. Disks can be damaged or destroyed easily by the following:

- Touching the recording surface with your fingers or anything else
- Writing on a disk label (which has been affixed to a disk) with a ball-point pen or pencil
- Bending the disk
- Spilling coffee or other substances on the disk
- Overheating a disk (leaving it in the hot sun or near a radiator, for example)
- Exposing a disk to stray magnetic fields

Despite all these cautions, disks are rather hardy storage devices; I can't say that I have ever destroyed one by just writing on it with a pen, and I do so all the time. I am careful, however, not to press too hard, so I don't put a crease in the disk. Also, touching a disk's magnetic surface does not necessarily ruin a disk, but rather makes the disk and your drive head dirty with oil and dust. The real danger to your disks comes from magnetic fields that, because they are unseen, can sometimes be found in places you never imagined.

For example, all color monitors (and color TV sets) that use cathode-ray tube (CRT) technology have a degaussing coil around the face of the tube that demagnetizes the shadow mask when you turn on the monitor. If you place any floppy disks closer than about 12 inches (30 cm) from the front of a color monitor, they will be exposed to a strong magnetic field every time you turn on the monitor. Keeping disks in this area is not a good idea because the field is designed to demagnetize objects, and it indeed works well for demagnetizing disks. The effect is cumulative and irreversible. Note that LCD or plasma displays don't have degaussing coils and therefore do not affect magnetic media.

Another source of powerful magnetic fields is an electric motor found in vacuum cleaners, heaters, air conditioners, fans, electric pencil sharpeners, and so on. Do not place these devices near areas where you store disks. Audio speakers also contain magnets, but most of the speakers sold for use with PCs are shielded to minimize disk corruption.

Store 3 1/2" disks between 40° and 127° Fahrenheit (4°–53° Celsius), and store 5 1/4" disks between 40° and 140° Fahrenheit (4°–60° Celsius). In both cases, humidity should not exceed 90%.

Airport X-Ray Machines and Metal Detectors

One of my favorite myths to dispel is that the airport X-ray machine somehow damages disks. I have a great deal of experience in this area from having traveled around the country for the past 20 years or so with disks and portable computers in hand. I fly about 150,000 miles per year, and my portable computer equipment and disks have been through X-ray machines hundreds of times.

X-rays are essentially just a form of light, and disks and computers are not affected by X-rays at anywhere near the levels found in these machines.

What could potentially damage your magnetic media is the metal detector. Metal detectors work by monitoring disruptions in a weak magnetic field. A metal object inserted in the field area causes the field's shape to change, which the detector observes. This principle, which is the reason the detectors are sensitive to metal objects, can be dangerous to your disks; the X-ray machine, however, is the safest area through which to pass either your disk or your computer.

The X-ray machine is not dangerous to magnetic media because it merely exposes the media to electromagnetic radiation at a particular (very high) frequency. Blue light is an example of electromagnetic radiation of a different frequency. The only difference between X-rays and blue light is in the frequency, or wavelength, of the emission.

Some people worry about the effect of X-ray radiation on their system's EPROM (erasable programmable read-only memory) chips. This concern might actually be more valid than worrying about disk damage because EPROMs are erased by certain forms of electromagnetic radiation. In reality, however, you do not need to worry about this effect either. EPROMs are erased by direct exposure to very intense ultraviolet light. Specifically, to be erased, an EPROM must be exposed to a $12,000uw/cm^2$ UV light source with a wavelength of 2,537 angstroms for 15–20 minutes, and at a distance of 1". Increasing the power of the light source or decreasing the distance from the source can shorten the erasure time to a few minutes.

The airport X-ray machine is different by a factor of 10,000 in wavelength. The field strength, duration, and distance from the emitter source are nowhere near what is necessary for EPROM erasure. Many circuit-board manufacturers even use X-ray inspection on circuit boards (with components including EPROMs installed) to test and check quality control during manufacture.

Now, you might not want to take my word for it, but scientific research has been published that corroborates what I have stated. A study was published by two scientists—one of whom actually designs X-ray tubes for a major manufacturer. Their study was titled "Airport X-rays and Floppy Disks: No Cause for Concern" and was published in 1993 in the journal *Computer Methods and Programs in Biomedicine*. The abstract stated the following:

> "A controlled study was done to test the possible effects of X-rays on the integrity of data stored on common sizes of floppy disks. Disks were exposed to doses of X-rays up to seven times that to be expected during airport examination of baggage. The readability of nearly 14 megabytes of data was unaltered by X-irradiation, indicating that floppy disks need not be given special handling during X-ray inspection of baggage."

In fact, the disks were retested after two years of storage, and there was still no measurable degradation following the exposure.

Floppy Drive Installation Procedures

In most cases, installing a floppy disk drive is a matter of physically attaching the drive to the computer chassis or case and then plugging the power and signal cables into the drive. Some types of brackets and screws are usually required to attach the drive to the chassis, and these are normally included with the chassis or case itself. Several companies listed in the Vendor List on the DVD specialize in cases, cables, brackets, screw hardware, and other items useful in assembling systems or installing drives.

Note

Because floppy disk drives are generally installed into the same half-height bays as hard disk drives, the physical mounting of the drive in the computer case is the same for both units. See the section "Hard Disk Installation Procedures" in Chapter 12, "Physical Drive Installation and Configuration," for more information on the process.

Troubleshooting Floppy Drives

For information on troubleshooting floppy drives, see "Troubleshooting Floppy Drives" in the Technical Reference section on the DVD packaged with this book.

High-capacity Magnetic Storage Devices

High-capacity removable media drives are an ever-shrinking category. With competition from USB flash drives (up to 16GB or larger), rewritable DVD (4.7/8.5GB), and external USB and FireWire hard disks (20GB and up), there are only two current product families left, both from Iomega, and as they haven't been updated in a long time, are likely to be discontinued as well:

- **Zip**—Flexible media, with capacities of 100MB, 250MB, and 750MB
- **REV**—Rigid media, with capacities of 35GB and 70GB

Neither of these is recommended, because, compared to other options, these have low storage capacities combined with extremely high prices. Other removable-media drives manufactured in the last few years have been discontinued for similar reasons. These include

- Iomega PocketZip (originally Clik!)
- Imation LS-120 SuperDisk
- Imation LS-240 SuperDisk
- SyQuest (SparQ, SyJet, and all other models)
- Iomega Jaz
- Castlewood Orb
- Iomega Peerless

If you use any of these drives, you should consider moving your data to current storage technologies. A discontinued removable-storage drive is essentially an orphan. There are three reasons for this:

- Repairs can be difficult to come by, especially in the case of a product such as the Castlewood Orb, whose manufacturer (Castlewood Systems) went bankrupt in 2004 and no longer offers online or other forms of support.
- Unlike other storage technologies such as floppy, CD, DVD, and tape, media for removable-media drives is usually proprietary and can only be obtained from the original manufacturer in most cases.
- Most removable-media drives require special drivers to function. As new versions of Windows and other operating systems are delivered, a removable-media drive that works, mechanically speaking, might not be compatible.

Table 10.5 provides an overview of current and recent high-capacity (100MB and larger) magnetic removable-media drives. The following sections provide additional detail about current models.

Table 10.5   Current and Recent High-Capacity Magnetic Removable-Media Drives

Removable Media Drive	Manufacturer	Media Type (Technology)	Capacity	Status	Notes
PocketZip	Iomega	Flexible (magnetic)	40MB	Discontinued	1
Zip 100	Iomega	Flexible (magnetic)	100MB	Current	2
LS-120 SuperDisk	Imation, others	Flexible (floptical)	120MB	Discontinued	3, 4
LS-240 SuperDisk	Imation, others	Flexible (floptical)	240MB	Discontinued	3, 4, 5
Zip 250	Iomega	Flexible (magnetic)	250MB	Current	2, 6
Zip 750	Iomega	Flexible (magnetic)	750MB	Current	2, 7
SparQ	SparQ	Rigid (magnetic)	1GB	Discontinued	8
Jaz	Iomega	Rigid (magnetic)	1GB	Discontinued	9
Jaz	Iomega	Rigid (magnetic)	2GB	Discontinued	9, 10
Orb 2.2GB	Castlewood	Rigid (magnetic)	2.2GB	Discontinued	11
Orb 5.7GB	Castlewood	Rigid (magnetic)	5.7GB	Discontinued	11, 12
Peerless	Iomega	Rigid (magnetic)	10GB	Discontinued	13
Peerless	Iomega	Rigid (magnetic)	20GB	Discontinued	13

1. Originally known as Clik! Media, available from Iomega (www.iomega.com).
2. Media available from Iomega (www.iomega.com) and Fujifilm (www.fujifilm.com).
3. Media available from Maxell (www.maxell.com).
4. Read/write compatible with standard 720KB and 1.44MB 3 1/2" floppy disks.
5. Supports special 32MB format for 1.44MB 3 1/2" floppy disks.
6. Drive read-write compatible with Zip 100 media.
7. Drive read-write compatible with Zip 250 media; read-compatible with Zip 100 media.
8. Limited tech support, drive and media availability from SYQT, Inc. (www.syquest.com); see website for support and media availability for older SyQuest products (SyJet, others).
9. Media available from Iomega (www.iomega.com).
10. Read/write compatible with 1GB Jaz media.
11. No support available from manufacturer; some stores still have media and drives. Check DriverGuide (www.driverguide.com) or other websites for drivers.
12. Read-compatible with 2.2GB Orb media.
13. Drivers available from Iomega (www.iomega.com); some stores still have media and drives.

Iomega Zip

Although Iomega Zip drives are no longer as popular as they were in the late 1990s, their widespread industry adoption and easy media and drive availability make them the leading and—with the demise of SuperDisk—the only bigger-than-floppy magnetic removable-media storage de facto standard. Various models can be purchased as upgrades for existing computers, and media is available from both Iomega and Fujifilm.

Unlike the LS-120 and LS-240 SuperDisk drives, the Iomega Zip drive can't use standard 3 1/2" floppy disks. Zip is a proprietary descendent of a long line of removable-media drives from Iomega that go back to the first Bernoulli cartridge drives released in the early 1980s.

The current form of Bernoulli-technology drive from Iomega is the popular Zip drive. These devices are available in 100MB, 250MB, and 750MB versions with either ATAPI (internal) or USB (external) interfaces.

Zip 100 drives can store up to 100MB of data on a small removable magnetic cartridge that resembles a 3 1/2" floppy disk. Zip 250 drives store up to 250MB of data on the same size cartridge and can read and write to the Zip 100 cartridges. The most recent Zip drive holds 750MB of data. It has read/write compatibility with Zip 250 media, but it has read-only compatibility with Zip 100 media. For best performance, you should use the native media size with Zip 250 and Zip 750 drives; these drives read and write much more slowly when smaller Zip media is used than when their native media size is used.

Zip drives are not recommended for new purchases because, compared to USB flash drives, they offer low capacity, low reliability, and extremely high cost. Today the only reason to purchase a Zip drive is to support legacy Zip hardware or applications. In other words, if you have a stockpile of Zip backups, you might consider purchasing a Zip drive just so you will be able to read them in the future.

Iomega REV

Iomega REV was introduced in 2004, and uses 35GB or 70GB hard-disk-type removable-media cartridges. They are essentially hard drives with removable platters contained in a cartridge. As with Zip they are no longer recommended for new purchases due to low capacity, low performance, and extremely high cost as compared to other options such as external USB hard drives. The only reason to purchase one of these drives today is to support legacy Rev hardware or applications.

Magneto-optical Drives

Magneto-optical (MO) drives were once a popular form of removable media technology. Introduced commercially in 1985 with initial capacities of 230MB through 640MB, magneto-optical drives with capacities of up to 9.1GB were available in 2000. Since then, the popularity of this type of storage has declined and most have been discontinued. The media and some drives are still available to support legacy applications.

Originally, magneto-optical drives were strictly WORM (write once, read many) drives that produced media that could be written to but not erased.

Magneto-optical Technology

At normal temperatures, the magnetic surface of an MO disk is very stable, with archival ratings of up to 30 years, which is one reason this technology was popular for backup and archival storage in larger companies.

One surface of an MO disk faces a variable-power laser, whereas the other surface of the disk faces a magnet. Both the laser beam and the magnet are used to change the data on an MO disk. Figure 10.9 illustrates the magneto-optical writing and reading process.

The "optical" portion of an MO drive is the laser beam, which is used at high power during the erasing process to heat the destination area of the MO drive to a temperature of about 200° Celsius (the Curie point, at which a normally magnetic surface ceases to be magnetic). This enables any existing information in that area to be erased by a uniform magnetic field, which doesn't affect the other portions of the disk that are at normal temperature.

Next, the laser beam and magnetic field are used together to write information to the location by applying high power to the laser and applying a controlled magnetic signal to the media to change it to either a binary 0 or 1.

During the read process, the laser is used at low power to send neutrally polarized light to the surface of the MO disk. The areas of the MO disk that store binary 0s reflect light at a polarization angle different from those that store binary 1s. This difference of 1 degree is called the *Kerr effect*.

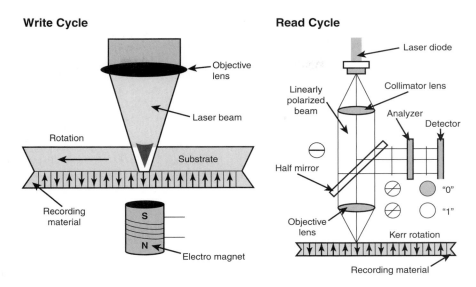

Write Cycle

Read Cycle

Figure 10.9   Magneto-optical drives use the laser at high power to heat the magnetic surface to enable its contents to be magnetically changed during the write cycle (left) and use the laser at low power to determine the angle of polarization (the Kerr effect) during the read cycle (right).

In older MO drives, the erase and write process involved two separate operations, but most MO drives since 1997 use the LIMDOW method (light intensity modulated direct overwrite) for a single-pass operation with some media types. LIMDOW drives use magnets built into the disk itself, rather than separate magnets as in older MO drives. LIMDOW drives are fast enough to store MPEG-2 streaming video and make achieving higher capacities easier.

Flash Memory Devices

Flash memory has been around for several years as a main or an auxiliary storage medium for laptop computers. However, the rise of devices such as digital cameras and music players and the presence of USB ports on practically all recent systems have transformed this technology from a niche product into a mainstream must-have storage technology.

Flash memory is a type of nonvolatile memory that is divided into blocks rather than bytes, as with normal RAM memory modules. Flash memory, which also is used in most recent computers for BIOS chips, is changed by a process known as *Fowler-Nordheim tunneling*. This process removes the charge from the floating gate associated with each memory cell. Flash memory then must be erased before it can be charged with new data.

The speed, low reprogramming current requirements, and compact size of recent flash memory devices have made flash memory a perfect counterpart for portable devices such as laptop computers and digital cameras, which often refer to flash memory devices as so-called "digital film." Unlike real film, digital film can be erased and reshot. Ultra-compact, USB flash memory drives have all but replaced both traditional floppy drives and Zip/SuperDisk drives for transporting data between systems.

Types of Flash Memory Devices

Several types of flash memory devices are in common use today, including the following:

- ATA Flash
- CompactFlash (CF)
- SmartMedia (SM)
- MultiMediaCards (MMC)
- Reduced Size MMC (RS-MMC)
- SecureDigital (SD)
- MiniSD
- Memory Stick
- Memory Stick PRO
- Memory Stick PRO Duo
- xD-Picture Card
- USB flash devices

Some of these are available in different sizes (Type I/Type II). Table 10.7 shows the various types of solid-state storage used in digital cameras and other devices, listed in order of introduction.

Table 10.7   Different Flash Memory Devices and Physical Sizes

Type	L (mm)	W (mm)	H (mm)	Volume (cc)	Date Introduced
ATA Flash Type II	54.00	85.60	5.00	23.11	Nov. 1992
ATA Flash Type I	54.00	85.60	3.30	15.25	Nov. 1992
CompactFlash (CF) Type I	42.80	36.40	3.30	5.14	Oct. 1995
SmartMedia (SM)	37.00	45.00	0.76	1.27	Apr. 1996
CompactFlash (CF) Type II	42.80	36.40	5.00	7.79	Mar. 1998
Memory Stick	21.45	50.00	2.80	3.00	Jul. 1998
Secure Digital (SD)	24.00	32.00	2.10	1.61	Aug. 1999
MultiMediaCard (MMC)	24.00	32.00	1.40	1.08	Nov. 1997
xD-Picture Card (xD)	20.00	25.00	1.70	0.85	Jul. 2002
Memory Stick Duo	20.00	31.00	1.6	0.99	Jul. 2002
Reduced Size MMC (RS-MMC)	24.00	18.00	1.40	0.60	Nov. 2002
MiniSD	20.00	21.5	1.4	0.59	Mar. 2003
MicroSD	15.00	11.00	1.0	0.165	Jul. 2005
Memory Stick Micro	15.00	12.5	1.2	0.225	Sep. 2005

Note: USB flash drives are not listed because they do not have a standardized form factor.

CompactFlash

CompactFlash was developed by SanDisk Corporation in 1994 and uses ATA architecture to emulate a disk drive; a CompactFlash device attached to a computer has a disk drive letter just like your other drives. Later types of flash memory also use ATA architecture, either implemented in the device itself or in its controller.

The original size was Type I (3.3mm thick); a newer Type II size (5mm thick) accommodates higher-capacity devices. Both CompactFlash cards are 1.433" wide by 1.685" long, and adapters allow them to be inserted into laptop computer PC Card slots. The CompactFlash Association (http://www.compactflash.org) oversees development of the standard.

SmartMedia

Ironically, SmartMedia (originally known as SSFDC for *solid state floppy disk card*) is the simplest of any flash memory device; SmartMedia cards contain only flash memory on a card without any control circuits. This simplicity means that compatibility with different generations of SmartMedia cards can require manufacturer upgrades of SmartMedia-using devices. The Solid State Floppy Disk Forum (http://www.ssfdc.or.jp/english) oversees development of the SmartMedia standard.

Tip

If you use a SmartMedia-based Olympus digital camera that has the panorama feature, be sure to use Olympus-brand SmartMedia because other brands lack support for the panorama feature.

MultiMediaCard

The MultiMediaCard (MMC) was codeveloped by SanDisk and Infineon Technologies AG (formerly Siemens AG) in November 1997 for use with smart phones, MP3 players, digital cameras, and camcorders. The MMC uses a simple 7-pin serial interface to devices and contains low-voltage flash memory. The MultiMediaCard Association (www.mmca.org) was founded in 1998 to promote the MMC standard and aid development of new products. In November 2002, MMCA announced the development of the Reduced Size MultiMediaCard (RS-MMC), which reduces the size of the standard MMC by about 40% and can be adapted for use with standard MMC devices. The first flash memory cards in this form factor were introduced in early 2004 to support compact smart phones.

SecureDigital

A SecureDigital (SD) storage device is about the same size as an MMC (many devices can use both types of flash memory), but it's a more sophisticated product. SD, which was codeveloped by Toshiba, Matsushita Electric (Panasonic), and SanDisk in 1999, gets its name from two special features. The first is encrypted storage of data for additional security, meeting current and future Secure Digital Music Initiative (SDMI) standards for portable devices. The second is a mechanical write-protection switch. The SD slot can also be used for adding memory to Palm PDAs. The SDIO standard was created in January 2002 to enable SD slots to be used for small digital cameras and other types of expansion with various brands of PDAs and other devices. The SD Card Association (www.sdcard.org) was established in 2000 to promote the SD standard and aid the development of new products. Note that some new laptop computers have built-in SD slots.

Reduced-size versions of SD include MiniSD (introduced in 2003) and MicroSD (introduced in 2005). MiniSD and MicroSD are very popular choices for smart phones, and can be adapted to a standard SD slot. MicroSD is compatible with the TransFlash standard for mobile phones.

Sony Memory Stick and Memory Stick Pro

Sony, which is heavily involved in both laptop computers and a wide variety of digital cameras and camcorder products, has its own proprietary version of flash memory known as the Sony Memory Stick. This device features an erase-protection switch, which prevents accidental erasure of your photographs. Sony has also licensed Memory Stick technology to other companies, such as Lexar Media and SanDisk.

Lexar introduced the enhanced Memory Stick PRO in 2003. Memory Stick Pro includes MagicGate encryption technology, which enables digital rights management, and Lexar's proprietary high-speed memory controller. Memory Stick Pro is sometimes referred to as MagicGate Memory Stick.

The Memory Stick Pro Duo is a reduced-size, reduced-weight version of the standard Memory Stick Pro. It can be adapted to devices designed for the Memory Stick Pro.

ATA Flash PC Card

Although the PC Card (PCMCIA) form factor is now used for everything from game adapters to modems, from SCSI interfacing to network cards, its original use was computer memory, as the old PCMCIA (Personal Computer Memory Card International Association) acronym indicated.

Unlike normal RAM modules, PC Card memory acts like a disk drive, using the PCMCIA ATA (AT Attachment) standard. PC Cards come in three thicknesses (Type I is 3.3mm, Type II is 5mm, and Type III is 10.5mm), but all are 3.3" long by 2.13" wide. Type I and Type II cards are used for ATA-compliant flash memory and the newest ATA-compliant hard disks. Type III cards are used for older ATA-compliant hard disks; a Type III slot also can be used as two Type II slots.

xD-Picture Card

In July 2002, Olympus and Fujifilm, the major supporters of the SmartMedia flash memory standard for digital cameras, announced the xD-Picture Card as a much smaller, more durable replacement for SmartMedia. In addition to being about one-third the size of SmartMedia—making it the smallest flash memory format yet—xD-Picture Card media has a faster controller to enable faster image capture.

16MB and 32MB cards (commonly packaged with cameras) record data at speeds of 1.3MBps, whereas 64MB and larger cards record data at 3MBps. The read speed for all sizes is 5MBps. The media is manufactured for Olympus and Fujifilm by Toshiba, and because xD-Picture media is optimized for the differences in the cameras (Olympus's media supports the panorama mode found in some Olympus xD-Picture cameras, for example), you should buy media that's the same brand as your digital camera.

USB Flash Drives

As an alternative to floppy and Zip/SuperDisk-class removable-media drives, USB-based flash memory devices are rapidly becoming the preferred way to move data between systems. The first successful drive of this type—Trek's ThumbDrive—was introduced in 2000, and since then hundreds of others have been introduced.

Note

Some USB flash memory drives are even built into watches, pens, or knives, such as the Victorinox SwissMemory Swiss Army Knife, with capacities up to 1GB.

Unlike other types of flash memory, USB flash drives don't require a separate card reader; they can be plugged into any USB port or hub. Although a driver is usually required for Windows 98 and Windows 98SE, most USB flash drives can be read immediately by current versions of Windows, such as Windows XP and Vista. As with other types of flash memory, USB flash drives are assigned a drive letter when connected to the computer. Most have capacities ranging from 16MB to 16GB. Typical read/write performance of USB 1.1–compatible drives is about 1MBps. Hi-Speed USB 2.0 flash drives are much faster, providing read speeds ranging from 5MBps to 15MBps and write speeds ranging from 5MBps to 13MBps. Because Hi-Speed USB flash drives vary in performance, be sure to check the specific read/write speeds for the drives you are considering before you purchase one.

Tip

If you have a card reader or scanner plugged into a USB hub or port on your computer, you might need to disconnect it before you can attach a USB flash drive. This is sometimes necessary because of conflicts between the drivers used by some devices. Use the Windows Safely Remove Hardware icon in the system tray to stop the card reader before you insert the USB flash drive. After the USB flash drive has been recognized by the system, you should be able to reattach the card reader.

For additional protection of your data, some USB flash drives have a mechanical write-protect switch. Others include or support password-protected data encryption as an option, and most are capable of being a bootable device (if supported in the BIOS). Some drives feature biometric security—your fingerprint is the key to using the contents of the drive—whereas others include more traditional security software.

There are even bare USB flash drives that act as readers for MMC, SD, xD-Picture Card, Memory Stick, or Memory Stick Pro flash memory cards. These USB flash readers are essentially USB flash drives without flash memory storage onboard. You can use them as a card reader or as a USB drive with removable storage.

Comparing Flash Memory Devices

As with any storage issue, you must compare each product's features to your needs. You should check the following issues before purchasing flash memory-based devices:

- **Which flash memory products does your camera or other device support?** Although adapters allow some interchange of the various types of flash memory devices, for best results, you should stick with the flash memory type your device was designed to use.

- **Which capacities does your device support?** Flash memory devices are available in ever-increasing capacities, but not every device can handle the higher-capacity devices. Check the device and flash memory card's websites for compatibility information.

- **Are some flash memory devices better than others?** Some manufacturers have added improvements to the basic requirements for the flash memory device, such as faster write speeds and embedded security. Note that these features usually are designed for use with particular digital cameras only. Don't spend the additional money on enhanced features if your camera or other device can't use those features.

Only the ATA Flash cards can be attached directly to a laptop computer's PC Card slots. All other devices need their own socket or some type of adapter to transfer data. Figure 10.10 shows how the most common types of flash memory cards compare in size to each other and to a penny.

Table 10.8 provides an overview of the major types of flash memory devices and their current capacities. Note that smaller-capacity cards might be bundled with some digital cameras.

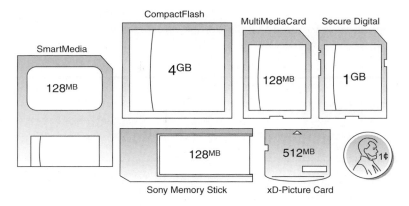

Figure 10.10 SmartMedia, CompactFlash, MultiMediaCard, SecureDigital, xD-Picture Card, and Sony Memory Stick flash memory devices. Shown in relative scale to a U.S. penny (lower right).

Table 10.8   Flash Memory Card Capacities

Device	Minimum Capacity	Maximum Capacity	Notes
CompactFlash+	16MB	16GB	Highest capacity; most flexible format; supported by most digital SLR cameras. Lexar Media and SanDisk also make faster versions of CF+ media; Lexar Media also makes LockTight secured access media.
SmartMedia	16MB	128MB	Popular choice for older Fujifilm and Olympus digital cameras.
MultiMediaCard	16MB	128MB	MMC cards can work in most SD slots. (MMC)
RS-MMC	128MB	2GB	Use adapter to plug into MMC slots.
Secure Digital (SD)	16MB	8GB	SD cards do not work in MMC slots. Used by most brands of consumer-level digital cameras.
MiniSD	128MB	2GB	Use adapter to plug in to SD slots.
MicroSD	128MB	2GB	Use adapter to plug in to SD slots.
Memory Stick	16MB	1GB	This was developed by Sony and licensed to other vendors.
Memory Stick PRO (also known as Memory Stick Magic Gate)	256MB	4GB	This is the enhanced high-speed version of Memory Stick with digital rights management support.
Memory Stick Pro Duo	256MB	4GB	Reduced-size version of Memory Stick PRO.
ATA Flash	16MB	2GB	This plugs directly into a PC Card (PCMCIA) slot without an adapter.
xD-Picture Card	16MB	2GB	Use the same brand as your digital camera for the best results.
USB flash drive	16MB	16GB	Some include password-protection and write-protect features.

I normally recommend only devices (cameras, PDAs, and so on) that use CompactFlash (CF), Secure Digital (SD), or USB flash memory cards. Any of the others I generally do not recommend due to limitations in capacity, performance, proprietary designs, and higher costs.

CompactFlash is the most widely used format in professional and consumer devices and offers the highest capacity, at the lowest prices, in a reasonably small size. CF cards plug directly into PC Card slots on all laptops by using a simple passive adapter that is extremely inexpensive. Therefore, when you're not using one of those cards in your camera, you can use it as a solid-state hard disk in a laptop. For a long time I would not even consider a camera or other device that did not use CF storage. I have relaxed on that stance a little bit, but it is still by far the best overall format and is available in capacities of up to 16GB or higher. It is also significantly faster than the other formats.

Secure Digital has also become quite popular, is reasonably fast, and is available in capacities up to 8GB. SD sockets also take MultiMediaCard (MMC) cards, which are basically thinner versions of SD. Note that the opposite is not true—MMC sockets do not accept SD cards.

USB flash memory is not generally used in cameras and PDAs due to the larger format; however, the USB interface is certainly universal, making this the ideal format for flash memory storage in PCs or anything with any devices sporting USB connectors.

In general I would not consider any device that uses other formats, as they are either proprietary (like Memory Stick or xD-Picture Card), or they are limited in capacity, popularity, availability, or all of the above.

Moving Data in Flash Memory Devices to Your Computer

Several types of devices can be purchased to enable the data on flash memory cards to be moved from digital cameras and other devices to a computer. Although some older digital cameras come with an RS-232 serial cable for data downloading, this is a painfully slow method, even for low-end cameras with less than a megapixel (1,000 pixel horizontal width) resolution.

Card Readers

The major companies who produce flash card products sell card readers that can be used to transfer data from proprietary flash memory cards to PCs. These card readers typically plug into the computer's USB ports (some older versions might use the parallel port) for fast access to the data on the card.

In addition to providing fast data transfer, card readers enable the reuse of expensive digital film after the photos are copied from the camera and save camera battery power because the camera is not needed to transfer information. External card readers can be used with any computer with the correct port type and a supported operating system. USB readers, for example, should be used with Windows 98 or above. Some older readers don't support write functions (such as erasing pictures after they're transferred from the media to your computer); I recommend devices with read/write functionality.

Because many computer and electronics device users might have devices that use two or more types of flash memory, many vendors now offer multiformat flash memory card readers, such as the SanDisk 12-in-1 Card Reader/Writer shown in Figure 10.11.

Before you purchase a card reader, check your PC and your photo printer. You might already have a card reader built into your PC or photo printer. Many PCs, including those that use Windows XP Media Center Edition, include a three- or four-slot card reader built into the front panel. This type of card reader plugs into a USB port header on the motherboard.

Figure 10.12 shows the integrated card reader built into an Epson Stylus Photo R300 printer. A CompactFlash card is inserted into the printer.

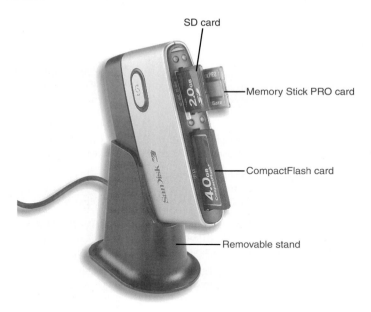

Figure 10.11 The SanDisk 12-in-1 Card Reader/Writer plugs into a Hi-Speed USB (USB 2.0) port and features a removable stand. *Photo courtesy of SanDisk.*

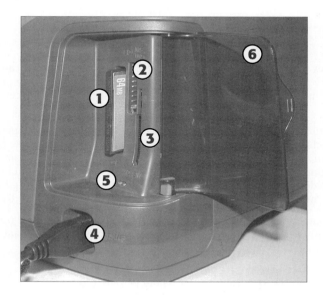

1. CompactFlash card in slot
2. SD/MMC/Memory Stick/Memory Stick PRO slot
3. SmartMedia/XD-Picture Card slot
4. USB cable from external drive
5. Media activity signal lights
6. Protective cover (open)

Figure 10.12 A three-slot card reader built into an Epson Stylus Photo R300 inkjet printer.

Type II PC Card Adapters

For use in the field, you might prefer to adapt flash memory cards to the Type II PC Card or CardBus slot found in most laptop computers. You insert the flash memory into the adapter; then, you slide the adapter into the laptop computer's Type II PC Card slot. Figure 10.13 shows how a CompactFlash card Type II PC Card adapter works. As with card readers, check with the major companies that produce your type of flash memory device for the models available.

Typical Type II PC Card adapter   ATA DataFlash card

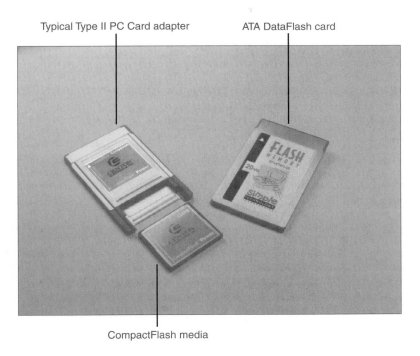

CompactFlash media

Figure 10.13   A typical Type II PC Card adapter for CompactFlash media (left) compared to an ATA DataFlash card (right).

Key Factors in Selecting a Removable-media Drive

When shopping for a removable-media drive, keep the following in mind:

- **Price per megabyte/gigabyte of storage**—Take the cost of the drive's cartridge or disk and divide it by the storage capacity to see how much you are paying per megabyte or gigabyte of storage. This difference in price becomes quite apparent as you buy more cartridges or disks for the drive. (Don't forget to factor in the cost of the drive itself if you are trying to decide which removable-media drive to buy!) If you plan to use removable storage for temporary data storage only, as with flash memory devices, the cost per megabyte or gigabyte is a less important factor than if you plan to leave data on a cartridge or disk for long periods of time.

- **Access time versus need of access**—The access and data transfer speeds are important only if you need to access the data frequently or quickly. If your primary use is archiving data, a slower drive might be fine. However, if you plan to run programs off the drive, choose a faster drive instead.

- **Compatibility and portability**—For maximum portability and compatibility, opt for a USB-based solution. Although some removable-media drives also support FireWire (IEEE 1394), SCSI, or parallel ports, Hi-Speed USB is the lowest-cost and friendliest solution because it's built into recent systems, supports hot-swapping, and can be used on machines with USB 1.1 ports (albeit with much slower data transfer and access speeds). Also verify that drivers are available for each type of machine and operating system you want to use with the drive, and consider whether you need to exchange disks with other users. If you don't want the expense of buying a separate drive for each machine, USB flash storage devices using flash memory or USB-based external hard disks can perform the same tasks and don't need a separate drive for each computer. For some users, this might be the most important factor in choosing a drive.

- **Storage capacity**—For maximum safety and ease of use, the capacity of your storage device should be the largest available that meets your other requirements. Digital camera users, for example, will want the largest possible flash or disk storage supported by their cameras to allow more photos or higher-quality photos to be stored. Desktop and laptop computer users will want the largest drives possible for data backup or program storage.

Note

For many uses, the rewritable DVD drive is the best choice for two reasons: low media cost (under 25 cents each in quantity for writable CD or DVD media; and near-universal compatibility (virtually all systems sold since the mid-1990s can read writable CD media in ordinary CD-ROM drives, and systems with DVD-ROM drives can read writable DVD media).

USB flash drives are now available in capacities up to 16GB for situations demanding high storage density in a very small space.

- **Internal versus external**—Most users find external USB drives the easiest to install; additionally, they give you the option of using the drive on several systems. Internal drives are usually faster because of their ATA, Serial ATA, or SCSI interfaces and are more cleanly integrated into the system from a physical perspective.

- **Bootable or not**—Most systems dating from 1995 or later have a BIOS that supports the Phoenix El Torito standard, which enables them to boot from CD or DVD drives or drives that emulate them, such as the Iomega REV. Most also support the ATAPI/IDE version of the Imation LS-120 or LS-240 SuperDisk as a bootable device; however, those drives are obsolete and difficult to find. Some systems support ATA Zip drives as a bootable drive, but Zip drives are a proprietary format and incompatible with standard 3 1/2" floppy disks. The newest systems support USB floppy drives for booting, enabling you to dispense with a traditional internal floppy disk drive for diagnostics or mass storage device driver installation.

Use the Disk Management snap-in module in Windows 2000 (or later) to change the drive letter assigned by Windows to a removable-media drive. With older versions of Windows, the next available drive letter will be assigned and cannot be changed.

Microdrive Technology

The Hitachi Microdrive was originally developed by IBM and is now manufactured and sold by Hitachi Global Storage Technologies. The Hitachi Microdrive has also been sold by various other companies under OEM agreements. The Microdrive is a true hard disk that spins at 3,600 rpm and features a 128KB cache buffer.

Since its introduction by IBM, the Microdrive in its CompactFlash Type II-compatible form factor has increased in capacity from 170MB up to 8GB. Table 10.9 compares the specifications for current Microdrive models that use CompactFlash (CF) Type II interfaces. These drives are available in travel kits and can be used with many digital cameras and other devices that are compatible with CompactFlash Type II cards.

Tip

Hitachi uses a standard formula for its Microdrive model numbers. Use this information to quickly identify the features of a particular Microdrive model.

For example, a Microdrive with a model number of HMS361008M5CE00 has the following features:

H = Hitachi

M = Microdrive

S = Standard

36 = 3600 rpm

10= Reserved (also 04, 06)

08 = Capacity – 8GB (06 = 6GB, 04 = 4GB, 03 = 3GB)

M = Generation code (D = earlier generation)

5 = 5mm z – height

CE = ZIF connector PATA interface (CA = CE-ATA)

CM = ATA on MMC (CF = CompactFlash Type II)

0 = Reserved

0 = Reserved

Table 10.9   Hitachi Microdrives in CompactFlash Type II Interface

Specifications	3K4-4	3K6-6	3K8
Capacity	4GB	6GB	8GB
Size (mm)	42.8×36.4×5	42.8×36.4×5	40×30×5
Weight	16g	16g	13g
Seek time (ms)	12ms	12ms	12ms
Media transfer rate (max)	97.9Mbps	125Mbps	131Mbps
Interface transfer rate (max)	33MBps	33MBps	33MBps
Sustained data transfer rate (max)	7.2MBps	9.4MBps	10.0MBps
Operating shock	200G	200G	400G
Nonoperating shock	2,000G	2,000G	2,000G

The 3K8 Microdrive series for embedded applications has capacities of up to 8GB. The 3K8 series uses a ZIF connector to interface to Compact Flash, PATA, CE-ATA, or ATA on MMC interfaces in devices such as mobile phones and ultra-small consumer electronics devices. CE-ATA is a standard interface based on the MMC (Multi-Media Card) electrical interface and using a subset of the ATA command set. Despite its higher capacity, the 3K8 actually has a smaller form factor than the 3K6 and previous Microdrive generations: It weighs just 13g, with dimensions of 40×30×5mm. The 3K8 series also features increased shock resistance—it can handle an operational shock of up to 400G (2ms).

Areal density has increased with each Microdrive generation, from as little as 5.04Gb/square inch with the original 170MB model up to 119Gb/square inch in the 3K8 series. In 4GB and larger drives, Hitachi uses a five-layer version of the Pixie Dust AFC media technology originally developed by IBM. To enable the increased areal density to be used as completely as possible, Hitachi also developed smaller hard disk read/write head technology.

Starting in 2003, Hitachi began to use femto sliders for the read/write heads used in several small hard disk series including the Microdrive 3K6 and 3K8. Femto sliders are only 20% of the size of the pioneering Mini hard disk slider introduced in 1980.

See the www.hitachigst.com website for more information about Microdrive products, a compatibility matrix, and other information.

Hard-disk-based Backup

Because the capacities of hard drives have rapidly outstripped the capabilities and costs of tape drives, in most cases I now recommend external hard drive storage for backup purposes. With this in mind, there are several alternatives to consider:

- **External hard drives**—Maxtor, Western Digital, Seagate, SimpleTech, and others have developed external hard drives with capacities up to 1TB (1000GB). These drives attach through USB or FireWire ports and can be used for data backup with backup software or drag-and-drop file copying. Many external drives include backup software, and some offer additional features such as one-button backup.

- **Network Attached Storage (NAS) drives**—A NAS device is basically a simple file server with drives that are visible on a network. The drives can be seen individually, or in higher-end NAS units, they can be combined in a RAID array. NAS units range from the simple and inexpensive (under $100) Linksys NSLU2 to much faster and more powerful devices such as the Intel SS4000-E and the US Robotics USR8700 (about $500). Combining an NAS device with one or more drives is one of the best ways to share and back up data on a home or small office network.

- **RAID arrays**—By connecting identical hard disks to a RAID array using RAID 1 data mirroring, RAID 0+1 (RAID 10) data striping plus mirroring, or RAID 5 data striping with parity, you make your data safer than if you just stored it on a standard drive. However, although RAID offers redundancy, it is not a substitute for backups. The best solution for combining redundancy and backup is to set up drives in a RAID configuration for primary storage, and then use one or more separate drives (or additional RAID arrays) for backups.

▶▶ To learn more about RAID, see "PATA/SATA RAID," p. 634.

Tape Drives

The data backup and archive needs of a personal computer can be overwhelming. People with large hard drives and numerous applications installed and those who generate a large amount of data might need to back up their computers on a weekly or even a daily basis.

In addition, a critical need on today's PCs is data storage space. Sometimes it seems as though the storage requirements of a PC can never be satisfied. On nearly any PC used for business, study, or even fun, the amount of software installed can quickly overwhelm even a large hard drive. To save space on the primary storage devices, you can archive infrequently used data to another storage medium. Depending on the method you use for archiving data to secondary storage, you might be able to read the data directly from the device, or you might need to restore the data to the drive before you can access it. If you copy data to the drive with drag-and-drop, the data can be read from the media directly. However, if you use a backup program to create the backup, you will need to use that same program to access the data and restore it to a drive before it can be reused.

Historically, a popular method for backing up full hard disks or modified files has been a tape backup drive. This section focuses on current tape backup drive technologies to help you determine whether this type of storage technology is right for you.

Tape backup drives are the most simple and efficient devices for creating a full backup of your hard disk if the tape is large enough. With a tape backup drive installed on your computer, you insert a tape into the drive, start your backup software, and select the drive and files you want to back up. The backup software copies your selected files onto the tape while you attend to other business. Later, when you need to retrieve some or all of the files on the backup tape, you insert the tape into the drive, start your backup program, and select the files you want to restore. The tape backup drive takes care of the rest of the job.

Disadvantages of Tape Backup Drives

Many computer users who once used tape backups for data backup purposes have turned to other technologies for the following reasons:

- Creating a tape backup copy of files or of a drive requires the use of a special backup program in almost all cases. A few tape drives allow drive letter access to at least part of the tape capacity, but this feature is far from universal, and a special driver program must be used.

- Retrieving data from most tape backup drives requires that the data files be restored to the hard disk. Other types of backup storage can be treated as a drive letter for direct use from the media.

- Tape backups store and retrieve data sequentially. The last file backed up can't be accessed until the rest of the tape is read; other types of backup storage use random access, which enables any file on the device to be located and used in mere seconds.

- Low-cost tape backups using QIC (Quarter Inch Committee), QIC-Wide, or Travan technology once had little problem keeping up with increases in hard disk capacity and once sold for prices comparable to or less than the hard disks they protected. Today's hard disks have capacities up to 500GB or larger and are far less expensive than most comparably sized tape backups. As a result, more expensive, higher-capacity tape drives are needed to achieve single-cartridge backups. Otherwise, you must load multiple tapes manually or use an autoloader.

- Newer backup and restore techniques, such as drive imaging/ghosting, rival the ease of use of tape backups and permit data restoration with lower-cost optical storage devices such as rewritable DVD drives. These alternatives are particularly useful if only a few GB of data need to be backed up on a continuing basis.

For these reasons, the once-unassailable position of a tape backup drive as being the must-have data-protection accessory is no longer a secure one; plenty of rivals to tape backups are on the market. However, if you can afford a high-quality DDS, DAT 72, or AIT tape drive, you can get a high-performance and high-reliability solution because these same drives are used in the demanding roles of network backup.

Advantages of Tape Backup Drives

Although tape backup drives are no longer the one-size-fits-all panacea for all types of bigger-than-floppy storage problems, they have their place in keeping your data safe. Following are several good reasons for using tape backup drives:

- Tape backups are a true one-cartridge backup process for individual client PCs, standalone computers, or network servers when high-capacity tape drives and cartridges are used. Anytime multiple tapes or disks must be used to make a backup, the chances of backup failure increase.

- If you or your company has made previous backup tapes, you must keep a tape drive to access that data or perform a restore from it. Tape backup drives are necessary if you need to restore from previously made backup tapes.

- If you want an easy media rotation method for preserving multiple full-system backups, tape backup drives are a good choice.

In general, tape drives are used where high capacity and high reliability are paramount. They can be expensive initially but are extremely inexpensive when you factor in the low cost of the media over time.

For more information on tape drives, see the "Tape Drives" section of Chapter 10 of *Upgrading and Repairing PCs, 17th Edition.*

Optical Storage

Optical Technology

There are basically two types of disk storage for computers: magnetic and optical. *Magnetic* storage is represented by the standard floppy and hard disks installed in most PC systems, where the data is recorded magnetically on rotating disks. *Optical* disc storage is similar to magnetic disk storage in basic operation, but it reads and records using light (optically) instead of magnetism. Although most magnetic disk storage is fully read- and write-capable many times over, many optical storage media are either read-only or write-once. Note the convention in which we refer to magnetic as *disk* and optical as *disc*. This is not a law or rule but seems to be followed by most in the industry.

Some media combine magnetic and optical techniques, using either an optical guidance system (called a laser servo) to position a magnetic read/write head or a laser to heat the disk so it can be written magnetically, thus polarizing areas of the track, which can then be read by a lower-powered laser, as in magneto-optical (MO) drives. These technologies were covered in Chapter 10, "Removable Storage."

At one time, it was thought that optical storage would replace magnetic as the primary online storage medium. However, optical storage has proven to be much slower and far less dense than magnetic storage and is much more adaptable to removable-media designs. As such, optical storage is more often used for backup or archival storage purposes and as a mechanism by which programs or data can be loaded onto magnetic drives. Magnetic storage, being significantly faster and capable of holding much more information than optical media in the same amount of space, is more suited for direct online storage and most likely won't be replaced in that role by optical storage anytime soon.

The most promising development in the optical area is that rewritable DVD drives have become so inexpensive that they've largely replaced compact disc-rewritable (CD-RW) drives on all but the least expensive systems, providing a truly high-capacity optical medium on which to distribute or back up data.

Optical technology standards for computers can be divided into three major types:

- CD (CD-ROM, CD-R, CD-RW)
- DVD (DVD-ROM, DVD-RAM, DVD-RW, DVD-R, DVD-R DL, DVD+RW, DVD+R, DVD+R DL,)
- High capacity DVD formats including HD-DVD and Blu-ray Disc (BD)

Both CD and DVD storage devices are descended from popular entertainment standards; CD-based devices can also play music CDs, and DVD-based devices can play the same DVD videos you can purchase or rent. However, computer drives that can use these types of media also offer many additional features.

In the following sections, you will learn how CD and DVD drives and media are similar, how they differ from each other, and how they can be used to enhance your storage and playback options.

CD-based Optical Technology

The first type of optical storage that became a widespread computing standard is the CD-ROM. CD-ROM, or *compact disc read-only memory*, is an optical read-only storage medium based on the original CD-DA (digital audio) format first developed for audio CDs. Other formats, such as CD-R (CD-recordable) and CD-RW (CD-rewritable), expanded the compact disc's capabilities by making it writable. As you will see later in this chapter, technologies such as DVD (digital versatile disc) enable you to store more data than ever on the same size disc.

CD-ROM drives were considered standard equipment on most PCs for many years. The primary exceptions to this rule are *thin clients*—PCs intended for use only on networks and which normally lack drives of any type.

Older CD-ROM discs held 74 minutes of high-fidelity audio in CD audio format or 650MiB (682MB) of data. However, the current CD-ROM standard is an 80-minute disc with a data capacity of 700MiB (737MB). When MP3, WMA, or similar compressed audio files are stored on CD, several hours of audio can be stored on a single disc (depending upon the compression format and bit rate used). Music only, data only, or a combination of music and data (Enhanced CD) can be stored on one side (only the bottom is used) of a 120mm (4.72") diameter, 1.2mm (0.047") thick plastic disc.

CD-ROM has exactly the same form factor (physical shape and layout) of the familiar CD-DA audio compact disc and can, in fact, be inserted in a normal audio player. Sometimes, it isn't playable, though, because the player reads the subcode information for the track, which indicates that it is data and not audio. If it could be played, the result would be noise-unless audio tracks precede the data on the CD-ROM (see the section "Blue Book—CD EXTRA," later in this chapter).

Accessing data from a CD-ROM using a computer is much faster than from a floppy disk but slower than a modern hard drive. The term *CD-ROM* refers to both the discs themselves and the drive that reads them.

Although only a few dozen CD-ROM discs, or titles, were published by 1988, currently hundreds of thousands of individual titles exist that contain data and programs ranging from worldwide agricultural statistics to preschool learning games. Individual businesses, local and federal government offices, and large corporations also publish thousands of their own limited-use titles. As one example, the storage space and expense that so many business offices once dedicated to the maintenance of a telephone book library can now be replaced by two discs containing the telephone listings for the entire United States.

CDs: A Brief History

In 1979, the Philips and Sony corporations joined forces to coproduce the CD-DA (Compact Disc-Digital Audio) standard. Philips had already developed commercial laserdisc players, and Sony had a decade of digital recording research under its belt. The two companies were poised for a battle—the introduction of potentially incompatible audio laser disc formats—when instead they came to terms on an agreement to formulate a single industry-standard digital audio technology.

Philips contributed most of the physical design, which was similar to the laserdisc format it had previously created with regards to using pits and lands on the disk that are read by a laser. Sony contributed the digital-to-analog circuitry, and especially the digital encoding and error-correction code designs.

In 1980, the companies announced the CD-DA standard, which has since been referred to as the *Red Book format* (so named because the cover of the published document was red). The Red Book included the specifications for recording, sampling, and—above all—the 120mm (4.72") diameter physical format you live with today. This size was chosen, legend has it, because it could contain all of Beethoven's approximately 70-minute Ninth Symphony without interruption, compared to 23 minutes per side of the then-mainstream 33rpm LP record.

After the specification was set, both manufacturers were in a race to introduce the first commercially available CD audio drive. Because of its greater experience with digital electronics, Sony won that race and beat Philips to market by one month, when on October 1, 1982 Sony introduced the CDP-101 player and the world's first commercial CD recording—Billy Joel's *52nd Street* album. The player was first introduced in Japan and then Europe; it wasn't available in the United States until early 1983. In 1984, Sony also introduced the first automobile and portable CD players.

Sony and Philips continued to collaborate on CD standards throughout the decade, and in 1983 they jointly released the Yellow Book CD-ROM standard. It turned the CD from a digital audio storage medium to one that could now store read-only data for use with a computer. The Yellow Book used the same physical format as audio CDs but modified the decoding electronics to allow data to be stored reliably. In fact, all subsequent CD standards (usually referred to by their colored book binders) have referred back to the original Red Book standard for the physical parameters of the disc. With the advent of the Yellow Book standard (CD-ROM), what originally was designed to hold a symphony could now be used to hold practically any type of information or software.

For more information on the other CD book formats, see the section "Compact Disc and Drive Formats," later in this chapter.

CD-ROM Construction and Technology

Although identical in appearance to CD-DAs, CD-ROMs store data instead of (or in addition to) audio. The CD-ROM drives in PCs that read the data discs are almost identical to audio CD players, with the main changes in the circuitry to provide additional error detection and correction. This is to ensure data is read without errors because what would be a minor—if not unnoticeable—glitch in a song would be unacceptable as missing data in a file.

A CD is made of a polycarbonate wafer, 120mm in diameter and 1.2mm thick, with a 15mm hole in the center. This wafer base is stamped or molded with a single physical track in a spiral configuration starting from the inside of the disc and spiraling outward. The track has a pitch, or spiral separation, of 1.6 microns (millionths of a meter, or thousandths of a millimeter). By comparison, an LP record has a physical track pitch of about 125 microns. When viewed from the reading side (the bottom), the disc rotates counterclockwise. If you examined the spiral track under a microscope, you would see that along the track are raised bumps, called *pits*, and flat areas between the pits, called *lands*. It seems strange to call a raised bump a *pit*, but that is because when the discs are pressed, the stamper works from the top side. So, from that perspective, the pits are actually depressions made in the plastic.

The laser used to read the disc would pass right through the clear plastic, so the stamped surface is coated with a reflective layer of metal (usually aluminum) to make it reflective. Then, the aluminum is coated with a thin protective layer of acrylic lacquer, and finally a label or printing is added.

Caution

CD-ROM media should be handled with the same care as a photographic negative. The CD-ROM is an optical device and degrades as its optical surface becomes dirty or scratched. Also it is important to note that, although discs are read from the bottom, the layer containing the track is actually much closer to the top of the disc because the protective lacquer overcoat is only 6–7 microns thick. Writing on the top surface of a disc with a ballpoint pen, for example, will easily damage the recording underneath. You need to be careful even when using a marker to write on the disc. The inks and solvents used in some markers can damage the print and lacquer overcoat on the top of the disc, and subsequently the information layer right below. Use only markers designed for, or tested as being compatible with, CD-ROM and CD-R media. The important thing is to treat both sides of the disc carefully, especially the top (label) side.

Mass-producing CD-ROMs

Commercial mass-produced CDs are stamped or pressed and not burned by a laser as many people believe (see Figure 11.1). Although a laser is used to etch data onto a glass master disc that has been coated with a photosensitive material, using a laser to directly burn discs would be impractical for the reproduction of hundreds or thousands of copies.

The steps in manufacturing CDs are as follows (use Figure 11.1 as a visual):

1. **Photoresist coating**—A circular 240mm diameter piece of polished glass 6mm thick is spin-coated with a photoresist layer about 150 microns thick and then hardened by baking at 80°C (176°F) for 30 minutes.

2. **Laser recording**—A Laser Beam Recorder (LBR) fires pulses of blue/violet laser light to expose and soften portions of the photoresist layer on the glass master.

3. **Master development**—A sodium hydroxide solution is spun over the exposed glass master, which then dissolves the areas exposed to the laser, thus etching pits in the photoresist.

4. **Electroforming**—The developed master is then coated with a layer of nickel alloy through a process called *electroforming*. This creates a metal master called a *father*.

5. **Master separation**—The metal master father is then separated from the glass master. The father is a metal master that can be used to stamp discs, and for short runs, it may in fact be used that way. However, because the glass master is damaged when the father is separated, and because a stamper can produce only a limited number of discs before it wears out, the father often is electroformed to create several reverse image *mothers*. These mothers are then subsequently electroformed to create the actual stampers. This enables many more discs to be stamped without ever having to go through the glass mastering process again.

6. **Disc stamping operation**—A metal stamper is used in an injection molding machine to press the data image (pits and lands) into approximately 18 grams of molten (350°C or 662°F) polycarbonate plastic with a force of about 20,000psi. Normally, one disc can be pressed every 2–3 seconds in a modern stamping machine.

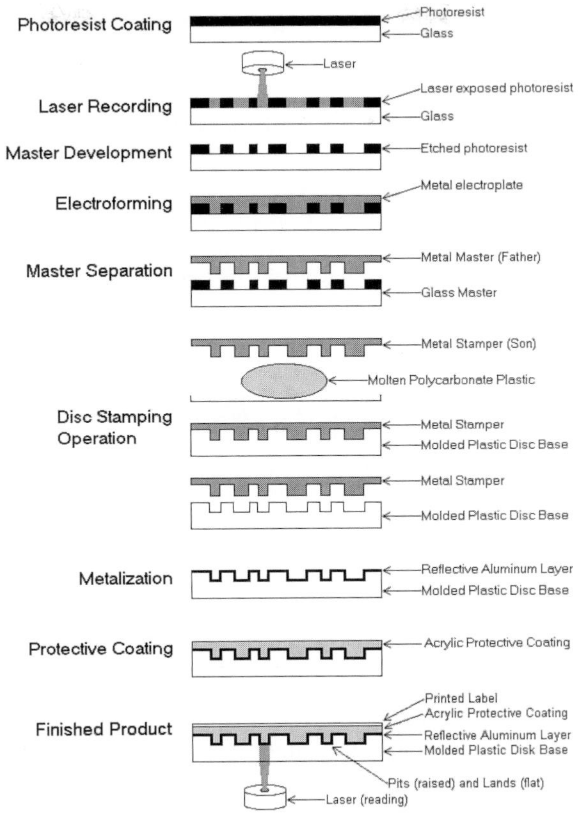

Figure 11.1 CD manufacturing process.

7. **Metalization**—The clear stamped disc base is then sputter-coated with a thin (0.05–0.1 micron) layer of aluminum to make the surface reflective.

8. **Protective coating**—The metalized disc is then spin-coated with a thin (6–7 micron) layer of acrylic lacquer, which is then cured with UV (ultraviolet) light. This protects the aluminum from oxidation.

9. **Finished product**—Finally, a label is affixed or printing is screen-printed on the disc and cured with UV light.

This manufacturing process is identical for both data CD-ROMs and audio CDs.

Pits and Lands

Reading the information back from a disc is a matter of bouncing a low-powered laser beam off the reflective layer in the disc. The laser shines a focused beam on the underside of the disc, and a photo-sensitive receptor detects when the light is reflected back. When the light hits a land (flat spot) on the track, the light is reflected back; however, when the light hits a pit (raised bump), no light is reflected back.

As the disc rotates over the laser and receptor, the laser shines continuously while the receptor sees what is essentially a pattern of flashing light as the laser passes over pits and lands. Each time the laser passes over the edge of a pit, the light seen by the receptor changes in state from being reflected to not reflected, or vice versa. Each change in state of reflection caused by crossing the edge of a pit is translated into a 1 bit digitally. Microprocessors in the drive translate the light/dark and dark/light (pit edge) transitions into 1 bits, translate areas with no transitions into 0 bits, and then translate the bit patterns into actual data or sound.

The individual pits on a CD are 0.125 microns deep and 0.6 microns wide. Both the pits and lands vary in length from about 0.9 microns at their shortest to about 3.3 microns at their longest. The track is a spiral with 1.6 microns between adjacent turns (see Figure 11.2).

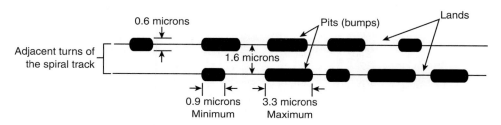

Figure 11.2   Pit, land, and track geometry on a CD.

The height of the pits above the land is especially critical because it relates to the wavelength of the laser light used when reading the disc. The pit (bump) height is exactly 1/4 of the wavelength of the laser light used to read the disc. Therefore, the light striking a land travels 1/2 of a wavelength of light farther than light striking the top of a pit (1/4 + 1/4 = 1/2). This means the light reflected from a pit is 1/2 wavelength out of phase with the rest of the light being reflected from the disc. The out-of-phase waves cancel each other out, dramatically reducing the light that is reflected back and making the pit appear dark even though it is coated with the same reflective aluminum as the lands.

The read laser in a CD drive is a 780nm (nanometer) wavelength laser of about 1 milliwatt in power. The polycarbonate plastic used in the disc has a refractive index of 1.55, so light travels through the plastic 1.55 times more slowly than through the air around it. Because the frequency of the light passing through the plastic remains the same, this has the effect of shortening the wavelength inside the plastic by the same factor. Therefore, the 780nm light waves are now compressed to 500nm (780/1.55). One quarter of 500nm is 125nm, which is 0.125 microns—the specified height of the pit.

Note

Drives compatible with CD and DVD media use two different lasers, a 780nm laser for CD media and a 650nm laser for DVD media. Consequently, a drive designed for CD or DVD media could suffer a failure of one laser, causing it to no longer read (or write) one type of media while continuing to read (or write) the other type of media.

Drive Mechanical Operation

A CD-ROM drive operates by using a laser to reflect light off the bottom of the disc. The reflected light is then read by a photo detector. The overall operation of a CD-ROM drive is as follows (see Figure 11.3):

1. The laser diode emits a low-energy infrared beam toward a reflecting mirror.

2. The servo motor, on command from the microprocessor, positions the beam onto the correct track on the CD-ROM by moving the reflecting mirror.

3. When the beam hits the disc, its refracted light is gathered and focused through the first lens beneath the platter, bounced off the mirror, and sent toward the beam splitter.

4. The beam splitter directs the returning laser light toward another focusing lens.

5. The last lens directs the light beam to a photo detector that converts the light into electric impulses.

6. These incoming impulses are decoded by the microprocessor and sent along to the host computer as data.

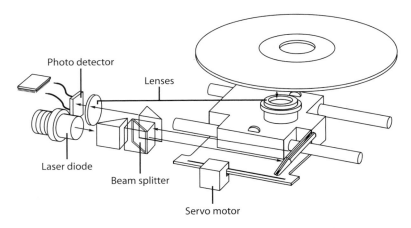

Figure 11.3 Typical components inside a CD-ROM drive.

When first introduced, CD-ROM drives were too expensive for widespread adoption. In addition, drive manufacturers were slow in adopting standards, causing a lag time for the production of CD-ROM titles. Without a wide base of software to drive the industry, acceptance was slow.

After the production costs of both drives and discs began to drop, however, CD-ROMs were rapidly assimilated into the PC world. This was particularly due to the ever-expanding size of PC applications. Virtually all software is now supplied on CD-ROM (although operating systems and games are now being distributed on DVD-ROMs due to their larger storage capacity), even if the disc doesn't contain data representing a tenth of its potential capacity.

Note

Microsoft Windows Vista is distributed at retail only on DVD media. However, you can purchase CD media direct from Microsoft for a nominal fee. For more information, see http://www.microsoft.com/windowsvista/1033/ordermedia/default.mspx.

Tracks and Sectors

On the traditional 74-minute CD, the pits are stamped into a single spiral track with a spacing of 1.6 microns between turns, corresponding to a track density of 625 turns per millimeter, or 15,875 turns per inch. This equates to a total of 22,188 turns for a typical 74-minute (650MiB) disc. Current 80-minute CDs gain their extra capacity by decreasing the spacing between turns. See Table 11.1 for more information about the differences between 74-minute and 80-minute CDs.

The disc is divided into six main areas (discussed here and shown in Figure 11.4):

- **Hub clamping area**—The hub clamp area is just that: a part of the disc where the hub mechanism in the drive can grip the disc. No data or information is stored in that area.

- **Power calibration area (PCA)**—This is found only on writable (CD-R/RW) discs and is used only by recordable drives to determine the laser power necessary to perform an optimum burn. A single CD-R or CD-RW disc can be tested this way up to 99 times.

- **Program memory area (PMA)**—This is found only on writable (CD-R/RW) discs and is the area where the TOC (table of contents) is temporarily written until a recording session is closed. After the session is closed, the TOC information is written to the lead-in area.

- **Lead-in**—The lead-in area contains the disc (or session) TOC in the Q subcode channel. The TOC contains the start addresses and lengths of all tracks (songs or data), the total length of the program (data) area, and information about the individual recorded sessions. A single lead-in area exists on a disc recorded all at once (Disc At Once or DAO mode), or a lead-in area starts each session on a multisession disc. The lead-in takes up 4,500 sectors on the disc (1 minute if measured in time, or about 9.2MB worth of data). The lead-in also indicates whether the disc is multisession and what the next writable address on the disc is (if the disc isn't closed).

- **Program (data) area**—This area of the disc starts at a radius of 25mm from the center.

- **Lead-out**—The lead-out marks the end of the program (data) area or the end of the recording session on a multisession disc. No actual data is written in the lead-out; it is simply a marker. The first lead-out on a disc (or the only one if it is a single session or Disk At Once recording) is 6,750 sectors long (1.5 minutes if measured in time, or about 13.8MB worth of data). If the disc is a multisession disc, any subsequent lead-outs are 2,250 sectors long (0.5 minutes in time, or about 4.6MB worth of data).

The hub clamp, lead-in, program, and lead-out areas are found on all CDs, whereas only recordable CDs (such as CD-Rs and CD-RWs) have the additional power calibration area and program memory area at the start of the disc.

Figure 11.4 shows these areas in actual relative scale as they appear on a disc.

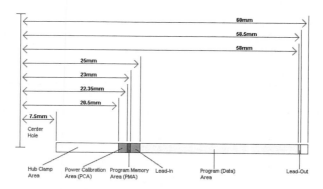

Figure 11.4   Areas on a CD (side view).

Officially, the spiral track of a standard CD-DA or CD-ROM disc starts with the lead-in area and ends at the finish of the lead-out area, which is 58.5mm from the center of the disc, or 1.5mm from the outer edge. This single spiral track is about 5.77 kilometers, or 3.59 miles, long. An interesting fact is that in a 56x CAV (constant angular velocity) drive, when reading the outer part of the track, the data moves at an actual speed of 162.8 miles per hour (262km/h) past the laser. What is more amazing is that even when the data is traveling at that speed, the laser pickup can accurately read bits (pit/land transitions) spaced as little as only 0.9 microns (or 35.4 millionths of an inch) apart!

Table 11.1 shows some of the basic information about the two main CD capacities, which are 74 and 80 minutes. The CD standard originally was created around the 74-minute disc; the 80-minute versions were added later and basically stretch the standard by tightening up the track spacing within the limitations of the original specification. A poorly performing or worn out drive can have trouble reading the 80-minute discs.

Table 11.1   CD-ROM Technical Parameters

	74	80
Advertised CD length (minutes)	74	80
Advertised CD capacity (MiB)	650	700
1x read speed (m/sec)	1.3	1.3
Laser wavelength (nm)	780	780
Numerical aperture (lens)	0.45	0.45
Media refractive index	1.55	1.55
Track (turn) spacing (um)	1.6	1.48
Turns per mm	625	676
Turns per inch	15,875	17,162
Total track length (m)	5,772	6,240
Total track length (feet)	18,937	20,472
Total track length (miles)	3.59	3.88
Pit width (um)	0.6	0.6
Pit depth (um)	0.125	0.125
Min. nominal pit length (um)	0.90	0.90
Max. nominal pit length (um)	3.31	3.31
Lead-in inner radius (mm)	23	23
Data zone inner radius (mm)	25	25
Data zone outer radius (mm)	58	58
Lead-out outer radius (mm)	58.5	58.5
Data zone width (mm)	33	33
Total track area width (mm)	35.5	35.5
Max. rotating speed 1x CLV (rpm)	540	540
Min. rotating speed 1x CLV (rpm)	212	212
Track revolutions (data zone)	20,625	22,297
Track revolutions (total)	22,188	23,986

B = Byte (8 bits)
KB = Kilobyte (1,000 bytes)
KiB = Kibibyte (1,024 bytes)
MB = Megabyte (1,000,000 bytes)
MiB = Mebibyte (1,048,576 bytes)

m = Meters
mm = Millimeters (thousandths of a meter)
um = Micrometers = microns (millionths of a meter)
CLV = Constant linear velocity
rpm = Revolutions per minute

The spiral track is divided into sectors that are stored at the rate of 75 sectors per second. On a disc that can hold a total of 74 minutes of information, that results in a maximum of 333,000 sectors. Each sector is then divided into 98 individual frames of information. Each frame contains 33 bytes: 24 bytes are audio data, 1 byte contains subcode information, and 8 bytes are used for parity/ECC (error correction code) information. Table 11.2 shows the sector, frame, and audio data calculations.

Table 11.2   CD-ROM Sector, Frame, and Audio Data Information

Advertised CD length (minutes)	74	80
Sectors/second	75	75
Frames/sector	98	98
Number of sectors	333,000	360,000
Sector length (mm)	17.33	17.33
Byte length (um)	5.36	5.36
Bit length (um)	0.67	0.67
Each Frame:		
Subcode bytes	1	1
Data bytes	24	24
Q+P parity bytes	8	8
Total bytes/frame	33	33
Audio Data:		
Audio sampling rate (Hz)	44,100	44,100
Samples per Hz (stereo)	2	2
Sample size (bytes)	2	2
Audio bytes per second	176,400	176,400
Sectors per second	75	75
Audio bytes per sector	2,352	2,352
Each Audio Sector (98 Frames):		
Q+P parity bytes	784	784
Subcode bytes	98	98
Audio data bytes	2,352	2,352
Bytes/sector RAW (unencoded)	3,234	3,234

Hz = Hertz (cycles per second)
mm = Millimeters (thousandths of a meter)
um = Micrometers = microns (millionths of a meter)

Sampling

When music is recorded on a CD, it is sampled at a rate of 44,100 times per second (Hz). Each music sample has a separate left and right channel (stereo) component, and each channel component is digitally converted into a 16-bit number. This allows for a resolution of 65,536 possible values, which represents the amplitude of the sound wave for that channel at that moment.

The sampling rate determines the range of audio frequencies that can be represented in the digital recording. The more samples of a wave that are taken per second, the closer the sampled result will be to the original. The Nyquist theorem (originally published by American physicist Harry Nyquist in 1928) states that the sampling rate must be at least twice the highest frequency present in the sample to reconstruct the original signal accurately. That explains why Philips and Sony intentionally chose the 44,100Hz sampling rate when developing the CD—that rate could be used to accurately reproduce sounds of up to 20,000Hz, which is the upper limit of human hearing.

So, you can see that audio sectors combine 98 frames of 33 bytes each, which results in a total of 3,234 bytes per sector, of which only 2,352 bytes are actual audio data. Besides the 98 subcode bytes per frame, the other 784 bytes are used for parity and error correction.

▶▶ Parity and error correction for CDs is discussed in "Handling Read Errors," p. 758.

◀◀ To learn more about the concepts behind parity and error correction, which were originally used to guard against errors in memory and modem communications, see Chapter 6, "Memory," and Chapter 17, "Internet Connections."

Subcodes

Subcode bytes enable the drive to find songs (which are confusingly also called *tracks*) along the spiral track and also contain or convey additional information about the disc in general. The subcode bytes are stored as 1 byte per frame, which results in 98 subcode bytes for each sector. Two of these bytes are used as start block and end block markers, leaving 96 bytes of subcode information. These are then divided into eight 12-byte subcode blocks, each of which is assigned a letter designation P-W. Each subcode channel can hold about 31.97MB of data across the disc, which is about 4% of the capacity of an audio disc. The interesting thing about the subcodes is that the data is woven continuously throughout the disc; in other words, subcode data is contained piecemeal in every sector on the disc.

The P and Q subcode blocks are used on all discs, and the R-W subcodes are used only on CD+G (graphics) or CD TEXT-type discs.

The P subcode is used to identify the start of the tracks on the CD. The Q subcode contains a multitude of information, including

- Whether the sector data is audio (CD-DA) or data (CD-ROM). This prevents most players from trying to "play" CD-ROM data discs, which might damage speakers due to the resulting noise that would occur.
- Whether the audio data is two or four channel. Four channel is rarely if ever used.
- Whether digital copying is permitted. PC-based CD-R and RW drives ignore this; it was instituted to prevent copying to DAT (digital audio tape) or home audio CD-R/RW drives.
- Whether the music is recorded with pre-emphasis. This is a hiss or noise reduction technique.
- The track (song) layout on the disc.
- The track (song) number.
- The minutes, seconds, and frame number from the start of the track (song).
- A countdown during an intertrack (intersong) pause.
- The minutes, seconds, and frames from the start of the first track (song).

- The barcode of the CD.
- The ISRC (International Standard Recording Code). This is unique to each track (song) on the disc.

The R-W subcodes are used on CD+G (graphics) discs to contain graphics and text. This enables a limited amount of graphics and text to be displayed while the music is being played. The most common use for CD+G media is karaoke "singalong" media. These same subcodes are used on CD TEXT discs to store disc- and track-related information that is added to standard audio CDs for playback on compatible CD audio players. The CD TEXT information is stored as ASCII characters in the R-W channels in the lead-in and program areas of a CD. On a CD TEXT disc, the lead-in area subcodes contain text information about the entire disc, such as the album, track (song) titles, and artist names. The program area subcodes, on the other hand, contain text information for the current track (song), including track title, composer, performers, and so on. The CD TEXT data is repeated throughout each track to reduce the delay in retrieving the data.

CD TEXT–compatible players typically have a text display to show this information, ranging from a simple one- or two-line, 20-character display, such as on many newer RBDS (radio broadcast data system) automobile radio/CD players, to up to 21 lines of 40-color, alphanumeric or graphics characters on home- or computer-based players. The specification also allows for future additional data, such as Joint Photographic Experts Group (JPEG) images. Interactive menus also can be used for the selection of text for display.

Note

Current versions of Windows Media Player do not support CD TEXT for either playback or during the creation of music CDs. However, other media players, such as VuPlayer (www.vuplayer.com), RealPlayer (www.realplayer.com), and Winamp (www.winamp.com), support CD TEXT. Popular CD mastering programs with support for CD TEXT include Nero 6, Nero 7, and Nero Express 7 (www.nero.com); Roxio Easy Media Creator 7.5, 8.0, and 9.0 (www.roxio.com).

Handling Read Errors

Handling errors when reading a disc was a big part of the original Red Book CD standard. CDs use parity and interleaving techniques called *cross-interleave Reed-Solomon code (CIRC)* to minimize the effects of errors on the disk. This works at the frame level. When being stored, the 24 data bytes in each frame are first run through a Reed-Solomon encoder to produce a 4-byte parity code called "Q" parity, which then is added to the 24 data bytes. The resulting 28 bytes are then run though another encoder that uses a different scheme to produce an additional 4-byte parity value called "P" parity. These are added to the 28 bytes from the previous encoding, resulting in 32 bytes (24 of the original data plus the Q and P parity bytes). An additional byte of subcode (tracking) information is then added, resulting in 33 bytes total for each frame. Note that the P and Q parity bytes are not related to the P and Q subcodes mentioned earlier.

To minimize the effects of a scratch or physical defect that would damage adjacent frames, several interleaves are added before the frames are actually written. Parts of 109 frames are cross-interleaved (stored in different frames and sectors) using delay lines. This scrambling decreases the likelihood of a scratch or defect affecting adjacent data because the data is actually written out of sequence.

With audio CDs and CD-ROMs, the CIRC scheme can correct errors up to 3,874 bits long (which would be 2.6mm in track length). In addition, for audio CDs, only the CIRC can also conceal (through interpolation) errors up to 13,282 bits long (8.9mm in track length). *Interpolation* is the process in which the data is estimated or averaged to restore what is missing. That would of course be unacceptable on a CD-ROM data disc, so this applies only to audio discs. The Red Book CD standard defines the *block error rate (BLER)* as the number of frames (98 per sector) per second that have any bad bits (averaged over 10 seconds) and requires that this be less than 220. This allows a maximum of up to about 3% of the frames to have errors, and yet the disc will still be functional.

An additional layer of error detection and correction circuitry is the key difference between audio CD players and CD-ROM drives. Audio CDs convert the digital information stored on the disc into analog signals for a stereo amplifier to process. In this scheme, some imprecision is acceptable because it would be virtually impossible to hear in the music. CD-ROMs, however, can't tolerate any imprecision. Each bit of data must be read accurately. For this reason, CD-ROM discs have a great deal of additional ECC information written to the disc along with the actual stored information. The ECC can detect and correct most minor errors, improving the reliability and precision to levels that are acceptable for data storage.

In the case of an audio CD, missing data can be interpolated—that is, the information follows a predictable pattern that enables the drive to guess the missing values. For example, if three values are stored on an audio disc, say 10, 13, and 20 appearing in a series, and the middle value is missing—because of damage or dirt on the CD's surface—you could interpolate a middle value of 15, which is midway between 10 and 20. Although this might not be exactly correct, in the case of audio recording, it probably won't be noticeable to the listener. If those same three values appear on a CD-ROM in an executable program, there is no way to guess at the correct value for the middle sample. Interpolation can't work because executable program instructions or data must be exact; otherwise, the program will crash or improperly read data needed for a calculation. Using the previous example with a CD-ROM running an executable program, guessing 15 is not merely slightly off—it is completely wrong.

In a CD-ROM on which data is stored instead of audio information, additional information is added to each sector to detect and correct errors as well as to identify the location of data sectors more accurately. To accomplish this, 304 bytes are taken from the 2,352 that originally were used for audio data and are instead used for sync (synchronizing bits), ID (identification bits), ECC, and EDC information. This leaves 2,048 bytes for actual user data in each sector. Just as when reading an audio CD, on a 1x (standard speed) CD-ROM, sectors are read at a constant speed of 75 per second. This results in a standard CD-ROM transfer rate of 153,600 bytes per second (2,048×75), which is expressed as either 153.6KBps or 150KiBps.

Note

Some of the copy-protection schemes used on audio CDs intentionally interfere with the audio data and CIRC information in such a way as to make the disc appear to play correctly, but copies of the audio files or of the entire disc will be filled with noise. Copy protection for both audio and data CDs is discussed in more detail later in this chapter.

CD Capacity

Each second of a CD contains 75 blocks of data containing 2,048 bytes per block. From this information, you can calculate the absolute maximum storage capacity of an 80-minute or 74-minute CD-ROM, as shown in Table 11.3. Table 11.3 also shows the structure and layout of each sector on a CD-ROM on which data is stored.

Table 11.3   CD-ROM Sector Information and Capacity

Each Data Sector (Mode 1):	74-Minute	80-Minute
Q+P parity bytes	784	784
Subcode bytes	98	98
Sync bytes	12	12
Header bytes	8	8
ECC/EDC bytes	284	284
Data bytes	2,048	2,048
Bytes/sector RAW (unencoded)	3,234	3,234
Actual CD-ROM Data Capacity:		
B	681,984,000	737,280,000
KiB	666,000	720,000
KB	681,984	737,280
MiB	650.39	703.13
MB	681.98	737.28

B = Byte (8 bits)
KB = Kilobyte (1,000 bytes)
KiB = Kibibyte (1,024 bytes)
MB = Megabyte (1,000,000 bytes)

MiB = Mebibyte (1,048,576 bytes)
ECC = Error correction code
EDC = Error detection code

This information assumes the data is stored in Mode 1 format, which is used on virtually all data discs. You can learn more about the Mode 1/Mode 2 formats in the section on the Yellow Book and XA standards later in this chapter.

With data sectors, you can see that out of 3,234 actual bytes per sector, only 2,048 are actual CD-ROM user data. Most of the 1,186 other bytes are used for the intensive error-detection and -correction schemes to ensure error-free performance.

Data Encoding on the Disc

The final part of how data is actually written to the CD is very interesting. After all 98 frames are composed for a sector (whether audio or data), the information is then run through a final encoding process called *EFM (eight to fourteen modulation)*. This scheme takes each byte (8 bits) and converts it into a 14-bit value for storage. The 14-bit conversion codes are designed so that there are never fewer than two or more than ten adjacent 0 bits. This is a form of Run Length Limited (RLL) encoding called RLL 2,10 (RLL x,y, where x equals the minimum and y equals the maximum run of 0s). This is designed to prevent long strings of 0s, which could more easily be misread, as well as to limit the minimum and maximum frequency of transitions actually placed on the recording media. With as few as two or as many as ten 0 bits separating 1 bits in the recording, the minimum distance between 1s is 3 bit time intervals (usually referred to as 3T) and the maximum spacing between 1s is 11 time intervals (11T).

Because some of the EFM codes start and end with a 1 or more than five 0s, three additional bits called *merge bits* are added between each 14-bit EFM value written to the disc. The merge bits usually are 0s but might contain a 1 if necessary to break a long string of adjacent 0s formed by the adjacent

14-bit EFM values. In addition to the now 17 bits created for each byte (EFM plus merge bits), a 24-bit sync word (plus three more merge bits) is added to the beginning of each frame. This results in a total of 588 bits (73.5 bytes) actually being stored on the disc for each frame. Multiply this for 98 frames per sector and you have 7,203 bytes actually being stored on the disc to represent each sector. An 80-minute disc, therefore, really has something like 2.6GB of actual data being written, which, after being fully decoded and stripped of error-correcting codes and other information, results in about 737MB (703MiB) of actual user data.

The calculations for EFM-encoded frames and sectors are shown in Table 11.4.

Table 11.4   EFM-Encoded Data Calculations

EFM-Encoded Frames:	74-Minute	80-Minute
Sync word bits	24	24
Subcode bits	14	14
Data bits	336	336
Q+P parity bits	112	112
Merge bits	102	102
EFM bits per frame	588	588
EFM-Encoded Sectors:		
EFM bits per sector	57,624	57,624
EFM bytes per sector	7,203	7,203
Total EFM data on disc (MB)	2,399	2,593

B = Byte (8 bits)
KB = Kilobyte (1,000 bytes)
KiB = Kibibyte (1,024 bytes)

MB = Megabyte (1,000,000 bytes)
MiB = Mebibyte (1,048,576 bytes)
EFM = Eight to fourteen modulation

To put this into perspective, see Table 11.5 for an example of how familiar data would actually be encoded when written to a CD. As an example, I'll use the letters *N* and *O* as they would be written on the disk.

Table 11.5   EFM Data Encoding on a CD

Character	N	O
ASCII decimal code	78	79
ASCII hexadecimal code	4E	4F
ASCII binary code	01001110	01001111
EFM code	00010001000100	00100001000100

ASCII = American Standard Code for Information Interchange
EFM = Eight to fourteen modulation

Figure 11.5 shows how the encoded data would actually appear as pits and lands stamped into a CD.

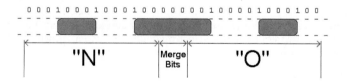

Figure 11.5   EFM data physically represented as pits and lands on a CD.

The edges of the pits are translated into the binary 1 bits. As you can see, each 14-bit grouping is used to represent a byte of actual EFM-encoded data on the disc, and each 14-bit EFM code is separated by three merge bits (all 0s in this example). The three pits produced by this example are 4T (4 transitions), 8T, and 4T long. The string of 1s and 0s on the top of the figure represent how the actual data would be read; note that a 1 is read wherever a pit-to-land transition occurs. It is interesting to note that this drawing is actually to scale, meaning the pits (raised bumps) would be about that long and wide relative to each other. If you could use a microscope to view the disc, this is what the word "NO" would look like as actually recorded.

Caring for Optical Media

Some people believe that optical discs and drives are indestructible when compared to their magnetic counterparts. While optical discs and drives are more reliable than the now-obsolete floppy disks and floppy disk drives, modern optical drives are far less reliable than modern hard disk drives. Reliability is the bane of any removable media, and CD-ROMs and DVD-ROMs are no exceptions.

By far the most common causes of problems with optical discs and drives are scratches, dirt, and other contamination. Small scratches or fingerprints on the bottom of the disc should not affect performance because the laser focuses on a point inside the actual disc, but dirt or deep scratches can interfere with reading a disc.

To remedy this type of problem, you can clean the bottom surface of the CD with a soft cloth, but be careful not to scratch the surface in the process. The best technique is to wipe the disc in a radial fashion, using strokes that start from the center of the disc and emanate toward the outer edge. This way, any scratches will be perpendicular to the tracks rather than parallel to them, minimizing the interference they might cause. You can use any type of solution on the cloth to clean the disc, so long as it will not damage plastic. Most window cleaners are excellent at removing fingerprints and other dirt from the disc and don't damage the plastic surface.

If your disc has deep scratches, they can often be buffed or polished out. A commercial plastic cleaner such as that sold in auto parts stores for cleaning plastic instrument cluster and tail-lamp lenses is very good for removing these types of scratches. This type of plastic polish or cleaner has a very mild abrasive that polishes scratches out of a plastic surface. Products labeled as cleaners usually are designed for more serious scratches, whereas those labeled as polishes are usually milder and work well as a final buff after using the cleaner. Polishes can be used alone if the surface is not scratched very deeply. The SkipDR device made by Digital Innovations can be used to make the polishing job easier.

Most people are careful about the bottom of the disc because that is where the laser reads, but the top is actually more fragile! This is because the lacquer coating on top of the disc is very thin, normally only 6–7 microns (0.24–0.28 thousandths of an inch). If you write on a disc with a ball point pen, for example, you will press through the lacquer layer and damage the reflective layer underneath, ruining the disc. Also, certain types of markers have solvents that can eat through the lacquer and damage the disc as well. You should write on discs only with felt tip pens that have compatible inks, such as the Sharpie or Staedtler Lumocolor brands, or other markers specifically sold for writing on CDs, such as Maxell's DiscWriter pens. In any case, remember that scratches or dents on the top of the disc are more fatal than those on the bottom. It's also important to keep in mind that many household chemicals (and even certain beverages), if spilled on an optical disc, can damage the coating and cause the material to crack or flake off. This, of course, renders the media useless.

Read errors can also occur when dust accumulates on the read lens of your CD-ROM drive. You can try to clean out the drive and lens with a blast of "canned air" or by using a drive cleaner (which can be purchased at most stores that sell audio CDs).

If your discs and your drive are clean, but you still can't read a particular disc, your trouble might be due to disc capacity. Many older CD-ROM drives are unreliable when they try to read the outermost tracks of newer discs where the last bits of data are stored. You're more likely to run into this problem with a CD that has a lot of data—including some multimedia titles. If you have this problem, you might be able to solve it with a firmware or driver upgrade for your CD-ROM drive, but the only solution might be to replace the drive.

Sometimes too little data on the disc can be problematic as well. Some older CD-ROM drives use an arbitrary point on the disc's surface to calibrate their read mechanism, and if there happens to be no data at that point on the disc, the drive will have problems calibrating successfully. Fortunately, this problem usually can be corrected by a firmware or driver upgrade for your drive.

If you are having problems reading media with an older drive and firmware upgrades are not available or did not solve the problem, consider replacing the drive. With new high-speed drives with read/write CD and DVD support available for well under $100, it does not make sense to spend any time messing with an older drive that is having problems. In almost every case, it is more cost-effective to upgrade to a new drive (which won't have these problems and will likely be much faster) instead.

If you have problems reading a particular brand or type of disk in some drives but not others, you might have a poor drive/media match. Use the media types and brands recommended by the drive vendor.

If you are having problems with only one particular disc and not the drive in general, you might find that your difficulties are in fact caused by a defective disc. See whether you can exchange the disc for another to determine whether that is indeed the cause.

DVD

DVD stands for *digital versatile disc* and in simplest terms is a high-capacity CD. In fact, every DVD-ROM drive *is* a CD-ROM drive; that is, it can read CDs as well as DVDs (many standalone DVD players can't read CD-R or CD-RW discs, however). DVD uses the same optical technology as CD, with the main difference being higher density. The DVD standard dramatically increases the storage capacity of, and therefore the useful applications for, CD-ROM-sized discs. A CD-ROM can hold a maximum of about 737MB (80-minute disc) of data, which might sound like a lot but is simply not enough for many applications, especially where the use of video is concerned. DVDs, on the other hand, can hold up to 4.7GB (single layer) or 8.5GB (dual layer) on a single side of the disc, which is more than 11 1/2 times greater than a CD. Double-sided DVDs can hold up to twice that amount, although you currently must manually flip the disc over to read the other side.

Up to two layers of information can be recorded to DVDs, with an initial storage capacity of 4.7GB of digital information on a single-sided, single-layer disc—a disc that is the same overall diameter and thickness of a current CD-ROM. With Moving Picture Experts Group standard 2 (MPEG-2) compression, that's enough to contain approximately 133 minutes of video, which is enough for a full-length, full-screen, full-motion feature film—including three channels of CD-quality audio and four channels of subtitles. Using both layers, a single-sided disc could easily hold 240 minutes of video or more. This initial capacity is no coincidence; the creation of DVD was driven by the film industry, which has long sought a storage medium cheaper and more durable than videotape.

Note

It is important to know the difference between the DVD-Video and DVD-ROM standards. DVD-Video discs contain only video programs and are intended to be played in a DVD player connected to a television and possibly an audio system. DVD-ROM is a data-storage medium intended for use by PCs and other types of computers. The distinction is similar to that between an audio CD and a CD-ROM. Computers might be capable of playing audio CDs as well as CD-ROMs, but dedicated audio CD players can't use a CD-ROM's data tracks. Likewise, computer DVD drives can play DVD-Video discs (with MPEG-2 decoding in either hardware or software), but DVD-Video players can't access data on a DVD-ROM. This is the reason you must select the type of DVD you are trying to create when you make a writable or rewritable DVD.

The initial application for DVDs was as an upgrade for CDs as well as a replacement for prerecorded videotapes. DVDs can be rented or purchased like prerecorded VCR tapes, but they offer much higher resolution and quality with greater content. As with CDs, which initially were designed only for music, DVDs have since developed into a wider range of uses, including computer data storage and high-quality audio.

DVD History

DVD had a somewhat rocky start. During 1995, two competing standards for high-capacity CD-ROM drives were being developed to compete with each other for future market share. One standard, called Multimedia CD, was introduced and backed by Philips and Sony, whereas a competing standard, called the Super Density (SD) disc, was introduced and backed by Toshiba, Time Warner, and several other companies. If both standards had hit the market as is, consumers as well as entertainment and software producers would have been in a quandary over which one to choose.

Fearing a repeat of the Beta/VHS situation that occurred in the videotape market, several organizations, including the Hollywood Video Disc Advisory Group and the Computer Industry Technical Working Group, banded together to form a consortium to develop and control the DVD standard. The consortium insisted on a single format for the industry and refused to endorse either competing proposal. With this incentive, both groups worked out an agreement on a single, new, high-capacity CD-type disc in September 1995. The new standard combined elements of both previously proposed standards and was called DVD, which originally stood for *digital video disc*, but has since been changed to *digital versatile disc*. The single DVD standard has avoided a confusing replay of the VHS versus Beta tape fiasco for movie fans and has given the software, hardware, and movie industries a single, unified standard to support.

After agreeing on copy protection and other items, the DVD-ROM and DVD-Video standards were officially announced in late 1996. Players, drives, and discs were announced in January 1997 at the Consumer Electronics Show (CES) in Las Vegas, and the players and discs became available in March 1997. The initial players were about $1,000 each. Only 36 movies were released in the first wave, and they were available only in seven cities nationwide (Chicago, Dallas, Los Angeles, New York, San Francisco, Seattle, and Washington, D.C.) until August 1997 when the full release began. After a somewhat rocky start (much had to do with agreements on copy protection to get the movie companies to go along, and there was a lack of titles available in the beginning), DVD has become an incredible success. It will continue to grow as DVD moves from a read-only to a fully rewritable consumer as well as computer device.

The organization that controls the DVD video standard is called the DVD Forum and was founded by 10 companies, including Hitachi, Matsushita, Mitsubishi, Victor, Pioneer, Sony, Toshiba, Philips, Thomson, and Time Warner. Since its founding in April 1997, more than 230 companies have joined the forum. Because it is a public forum, anybody can join and attend the meetings; the site for the DVD Forum is www.dvdforum.org. Because the DVD Forum was unable to agree on a universal recordable format, its members who are primarily responsible for CD and DVD technology (Philips, Sony, and others) split off to form the DVD+RW Alliance in June 2000; their site is www.dvdrw.com. They have since introduced the DVD+RW format, which is the fastest, most flexible and backward-compatible recordable DVD format. DVD-R/RW and DVD+R/RW are not just for computer uses either: You can purchase DVD set-top recorders from many vendors (some of which also contain VCRs to enable you to dub non-copy-protected VCR tapes to DVD).

Note

Although DVD set-top recorders can record information at higher qualities than VCRs, they are not nearly as popular for time-shifting as digital video recorders (DVRs) such as TiVo, RePlay TV, and units provided by cable and satellite TV providers. DVRs use hard disks to achieve storage capacities far beyond that possible with DVD technologies.

DVD Construction and Technology

DVD technology is similar to CD technology. Both use the same size discs (120mm diameter, 1.2mm thick, with a 15mm hole in the center) with pits and lands stamped in a polycarbonate base. Unlike a CD, though, DVDs can have two layers of recordings on a side and be double-sided as well. Each layer is separately stamped, and they are all bonded together to make the final 1.2mm-thick disc. The manufacturing process is largely the same, with the exception that each layer on each side is stamped from a separate piece of polycarbonate plastic and are then bonded together to form the completed disc. The main difference between CD and DVD is that DVD is a higher-density recording read by a laser with a shorter wavelength, focused more closely to the disc, which enables more information to be stored. Also, whereas CDs are single-sided and have only one layer of stamped pits and lands, DVDs can have up to two layers per side and can have information on both sides.

As with CDs, each layer is stamped or molded with a single physical track in a spiral configuration starting from the inside of the disc and spiraling outward. The disc rotates counterclockwise (as viewed from the bottom), and each spiral track contains pits (bumps) and lands (flat portions), just as on a CD. Each recorded layer is coated with a thin film of metal to reflect the laser light. The outer layer has a thinner coating to allow the light to pass through to read the inner layer. If the disc is single-sided, a label can be placed on top; if it's double-sided, only a small ring near the center provides room for labeling.

Just as with a CD, reading the information back on a DVD is a matter of bouncing a low-powered laser beam off one of the reflective layers in the disc. The laser shines a focused beam on the underside of the disc, and a photosensitive receptor detects when the light is reflected back. When the light hits a land (flat spot) on the track, the light is reflected back; when the light hits a pit (raised bump), the phase differential between the projected and reflected light causes the waves to cancel and no light is reflected back.

The individual pits on a DVD are 0.105 microns deep and 0.4 microns wide. Both the pits and lands vary in length from about 0.4 microns at their shortest to about 1.9 microns at their longest (on single-layer discs).

Refer to the section "CD-ROM Construction and Technology," earlier in this chapter, for more information on how the pits and lands are read and converted into actual data, as well as how the drives physically and mechanically work.

DVD uses the same optical laser read pit and land storage that CDs do. The greater capacity is made possible by several factors, including the following:

■ A 2.25 times smaller pit length (0.9-0.4 microns)

■ A 2.16 times reduced track pitch (1.6–0.74 microns)

■ A slightly larger data area on the disc (8,605–8,759 square millimeters)

■ About 1.06 times more efficient channel bit modulation

■ About 1.32 times more efficient error-correction code

■ About 1.06 times less sector overhead (2,048/2,352–2,048/2,064 bytes)

The DVD disc's pits and lands are much smaller and closer together than those on a CD, allowing the same physical-sized platter to hold much more information. Figure 11.6 shows how the grooved tracks with pits and lands are just over four times as dense on a DVD as compared to a CD.

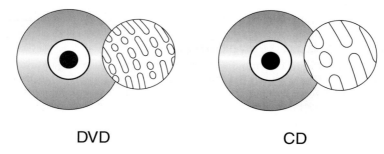

DVD   CD

Figure 11.6 DVD data markings (pits and lands) versus those of a standard CD.

DVD drives use a shorter wavelength laser (650nm) to read these smaller pits and lands. A DVD can have nearly double the initial capacity by using two separate layers on one side of a disc and double it again by using both sides of the disc. The second data layer is written to a separate substrate below the first layer, which is then made semireflective to enable the laser to penetrate to the substrate beneath it. By focusing the laser on one of the two layers, the drive can read roughly twice the amount of data from the same surface area.

DVD Tracks and Sectors

The pits are stamped into a single spiral track (per layer) with a spacing of 0.74 microns between turns, corresponding to a track density of 1,351 turns per millimeter or 34,324 turns per inch. This equates to a total of 49,324 turns and a total track length of 11.8km or 7.35 miles in length. The track is composed of sectors, with each sector containing 2,048 bytes of data. The disc is divided into four main areas:

■ **Hub clamping area**—The hub clamp area is just that, a part of the disc where the hub mechanism in the drive can grip the disc. No data or information is stored in that area.

■ **Lead-in zone**—The lead-in zone contains buffer zones, reference code, and mainly a control data zone with information about the disc. The control data zone consists of 16 sectors of information repeated 192 times, for a total of 3,072 sectors. Contained in the 16 (repeated) sectors is information about the disc, including disc category and version number, disc size and maximum transfer rate, disc structure, recording density, and data zone allocation. The entire lead-in zone takes up to 196,607 (2FFFFh) sectors on the disc. Unlike CDs, the basic structure of all sectors on a DVD are the same. The buffer zone sectors in the lead-in zone have all 00h (zero hex) recorded for data.

- **Data zone**—The data zone contains the video, audio, or other data on the disc and starts at sector number 196,608 (30000h). The total number of sectors in the data zone can be up to 2,292,897 per layer for single-layer discs.

- **Lead-out (or middle) zone**—The lead-out zone marks the end of the data zone. The sectors in the lead-out zone all contain zero (00h) for data. This is called the middle zone if the disc is dual-layer and is recorded in opposite track path (OPT) mode, in which the second layer starts from the outside of the disc and is read in the opposite direction from the first layer.

The center hole in a DVD is 15mm in diameter, so it has a radius of 7.5mm from the center of the disc. From the edge of the center hole to a point at a radius of 16.5mm is the hub clamp area. The lead-in zone starts at a radius of 22mm from the center of the disc. The data zone starts at a radius of 24mm from the center and is followed by the lead-out (or middle) zone at 58mm. The disc track officially ends at 58.5mm, which is followed by a 1.5mm blank area to the edge of the disc. Figure 11.7 shows these zones in actual relative scale as they appear on a DVD.

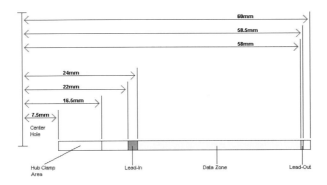

Figure 11.7 Areas on a DVD (side view).

Officially, the spiral track of a standard DVD starts with the lead-in zone and ends at the finish of the lead-out zone. This single spiral track is about 11.84 kilometers or 7.35 miles long. An interesting fact is that in a 20x CAV drive, when the outer part of the track is being read, the data moves at an actual speed of 156 miles per hour (251km/h) past the laser. What is more amazing is that even when the data is traveling at that speed, the laser pickup can accurately read bits (pit/land transitions) spaced as little as only 0.4 microns or 15.75 millionths of an inch apart!

DVDs come in both single- and dual-layer as well as single- and double-sided versions. The double-sided discs are essentially the same as two single-sided discs glued together back to back, but subtle differences do exist between the single- and dual-layer discs. Table 11.6 shows some of the basic information about DVD technology, including single- and dual-layer DVDs. The dual-layer versions are recorded with slightly longer pits, resulting in slightly less information being stored in each layer.

Table 11.6   DVD Technical Parameters

DVD Type:	Single-Layer	Dual-Layer
1x read speed (m/sec)	3.49	3.84
Laser wavelength (nm)	650	650
Numerical aperture (lens)	0.60	0.60
Media refractive index	1.55	1.55
Track (turn) spacing (um)	0.74	0.74
Turns per mm	1,351	1,351
Turns per inch	34,324	34,324
Total track length (m)	11,836	11,836
Total track length (feet)	38,832	38,832
Total track length (miles)	7.35	7.35
Media bit cell length (nm)	133.3	146.7
Media byte length (um)	1.07	1.17
Media sector length (mm)	5.16	5.68
Pit width (um)	0.40	0.40
Pit depth (um)	0.105	0.105
Min. nominal pit length (um)	0.40	0.44
Max. nominal pit length (um)	1.87	2.05
Lead-in inner radius (mm)	22	22
Data zone inner radius (mm)	24	24
Data zone outer radius (mm)	58	58
Lead-out outer radius (mm)	58.5	58.5
Data zone width (mm)	34	34
Data zone area (mm2)	8,759	8,759
Total track area width (mm)	36.5	36.5
Max. rotating speed 1x CLV (rpm)	1,515	1,667
Min. rotating speed 1x CLV (rpm)	570	627
Track revolutions (data zone)	45,946	45,946
Track revolutions (total)	49,324	49,324
Data zone sectors per layer per side	2,292,897	2,083,909
Sectors per second	676	676
Media data rate (mbits/sec)	26.15625	26.15625
Media bits per sector	38,688	38,688
Media bytes per sector	4,836	4,836
Interface data rate (mbits/sec)	11.08	11.08
Interface data bits per sector	16,384	16,384
Interface data bytes per sector	2,048	2,048

DVD Type:	Single-Layer	Dual-Layer
Track time per layer (minutes)	56.52	51.37
Track time per side (minutes)	56.52	102.74
MPEG-2 video per layer (minutes)	133	121
MPEG-2 video per side (minutes)	133	242

B = Byte (8 bits)
KB = Kilobyte (1,000 bytes)
KiB = Kibibyte (1,024 bytes)
MB = Megabyte (1,000,000 bytes)
MiB = Mebibyte (1,048,576 bytes)
GB = Gigabyte (1,000,000,000 bytes)
GiB = Gibibyte (1,073,741,824 bytes)

m = Meters
mm = Millimeters (thousandths of a meter)
mm2 = Square millimeters
um = Micrometers = microns
  (millionths of a meter)
nm = Nanometers (billionths of a meter)

rpm = Revolutions per minute
ECC = Error correction code
EDC = Error detection code
CLV = Constant linear velocity
CAV = Constant angular velocity

As you can see from the information in Table 11.6, the spiral track is divided into sectors that are stored at the rate of 676 sectors per second. Each sector contains 2,048 bytes of data.

When being written, the sectors are first formatted into data frames of 2,064 bytes: 2,048 are data, 4 bytes contain ID information, 2 bytes contain ID error-detection (IED) codes, 6 bytes contain copyright information, and 4 bytes contain EDC for the frame.

The data frames then have ECC information added to convert them into ECC frames. Each ECC frame contains the 2,064-byte data frame plus 182 parity outer (PO) bytes and 120 parity inner (PI) bytes, for a total of 2,366 bytes for each ECC frame.

Finally, the ECC frames are converted into physical sectors on the disc. This is done by taking 91 bytes at a time from the ECC frame and converting them into recorded bits via 8–to–16 modulation. This is where each byte (8 bits) is converted into a special 16-bit value, which is selected from a table. These values are designed using an RLL 2,10 scheme, which is designed so that the encoded information never has a run of fewer than two or more than ten 0 bits in a row. After each group of 91 bytes is converted via the 8–to–16 modulation, 32 bits (4 bytes) of synchronization information is added. After the entire ECC frame is converted into a physical sector, 4,836 total bytes are stored.

Table 11.7 shows the sector, frame, and audio data calculations.

Table 11.7   DVD Data Frame, ECC Frame, and Physical Sector Layout and Information

DVD Data Frame:	
Identification data (ID) bytes	4
ID error detection code (IED) bytes	2
Copyright info (CI) bytes	6
Data bytes	2,048
Error detection code (EDC)	4
Data frame total bytes	2,064

Table 11.7   Continued

DVD ECC Frame:	
Data frame total bytes	2,064
Parity outer (PO) bytes	182
Parity inner (PI) bytes	120
ECC frame total bytes	2,366
DVD Media Physical Sectors:	
ECC frame bytes	2,366
8–to–16 modulation bits	37,856
Synchronization bits	832
Total encoded media bits/sector	38,688
Total encoded media bytes/sector	4,836
Original data bits/sector	16,384
Original data bytes/sector	2,048
Ratio of original to media data	2.36

Unlike CDs, DVDs do not use subcodes and instead use the ID bytes in each data frame to store the sector number and information about the sectors.

Handling DVD Errors

DVDs use more powerful error-correcting codes than were first devised for CDs. Unlike CDs, which have different levels of error correction depending on whether audio/video or data is being stored, DVDs treat all information equally and apply the full error correction to all sectors.

The main error correcting in DVDs takes place in the ECC frame. Parity Outer (column) and Parity Inner (row) bits are added to detect and correct errors. The scheme is simple and yet very effective. The information from the data frames is first broken up into 192 rows of 172 bytes each. Then, a polynomial equation is used to calculate and add 10 PI bytes to each row, making the rows now 182 bytes each. Finally, another polynomial equation is used to calculate 16 PO (Parity Outer) bytes for each column, resulting in 16 bytes (rows) being added to each column. What started out as 192 rows of 172 bytes becomes 208 rows of 182 bytes with the PI and PO information added.

The function of the PI and PO bytes can be explained with a simple example using simple parity. In this example, 2 bytes are stored (01001110 = N, 01001111 = O). To add the error-correcting information, they are organized in rows, as shown here:

```
              Data bits
              1 2 3 4 5 6 7 8
- - - - - - - - - - - - - - - - - - - - - - - - - - -
Byte 1        0 1 0 0 1 1 1 0
Byte 2        0 1 0 0 1 1 1 1
```

Then, one PI bit is added for each row, using odd parity. This means you count up the 1 bits: In the first row there are four, so the parity bit is created as a 1, making the sum an odd number.

In the second row, the parity bit is a 0 because the sum of the 1s was already an odd number. The result is as follows:

```
              Data bits      |
              1 2 3 4 5 6 7 8 |  PI
- - - - - - - - - - - - - - - - - - - -|- - - - - -
Byte 1        0 1 0 0 1 1 1 0 |  1
Byte 2        0 1 0 0 1 1 1 1 |  0
- - - - - - - - - - - - - - - - - - - -|- - - - - -
```

Next, the parity bits for each column are added and calculated the same as before. In other words, the parity bit will be such that the sum of the 1s in each column is an odd number. The result is as follows:

```
              Data bits      |
              1 2 3 4 5 6 7 8 |  PI
- - - - - - - - - - - - - - - - - - - -|- - - - - -
Byte 1        0 1 0 0 1 1 1 0 |  1
Byte 2        0 1 0 0 1 1 1 1 |  0
- - - - - - - - - - - - - - - - - - - -|- - - - - -
PO            1 1 1 1 1 1 1 0 |  1
```

Now the code is complete, and the extra bits are stored along with the data. So, instead of just the 2 bytes being stored, 11 additional bits are stored for error correction. When the data is read back, the error-correction-bit calculations are repeated and they're checked to see whether they are the same as before. To see how it works, let's change one of the data bits (due to a read error) and recalculate the error-correcting bits as follows:

```
              Data bits      |
              1 2 3 4 5 6 7 8 |  PI
- - - - - - - - - - - - - - - - - - - -|- - - - - -
Byte 1        0 1 0 0 1 0 1 0 |  0
Byte 2        0 1 0 0 1 1 1 1 |  0
- - - - - - - - - - - - - - - - - - - -|- - - - - -
PO            1 1 1 1 1 0 1 0 |  1
```

Now, when you compare the PI and PO bits you calculated after reading the data to what was originally stored, you see a change in the PI bit for byte (row) 1 and in the PO bit for bit (column) 6. This identifies the precise row and column where the error was, which is at byte 1 (row 1), bit 6 (column 6). That bit was read as a 0, and you now know it is wrong, so it must have been a 1. The error-correction circuitry then simply changes it back to a 1 before passing it back to the system. As you can see, with some extra information added to each row and column, error-correction codes can indeed detect and correct errors on-the-fly.

Besides the ECC frames, DVDs also scramble the data in the frames using a bit-shift technique and also interleave parts of the ECC frames when they are actually recorded on the disc. These schemes serve to store the data somewhat out of sequence, preventing a scratch from corrupting consecutive pieces of data.

DVD Capacity (Sides and Layers)

Four main types of DVDs are available, categorized by whether they are single- or double-sided, and single- or dual-layered. They are designated as follows:

- **DVD-5 - 4.7GB single-side, single-layer**—A DVD-5 is constructed from two substrates bonded together with adhesive. One is stamped with a recorded layer (called Layer 0), and the other is blank. An aluminum coating typically is applied to the single recorded layer.

- **DVD-9 - 8.5GB single-side, dual-layer**—A DVD-9 is constructed of two stamped substrates bonded together to form two recorded layers for one side of the disc, along with a blank substrate for the other side. The outer stamped layer (0) is coated with a semitransparent gold coating to both reflect light if the laser is focused on it and pass light if the laser is focused on the layer below. A single laser is used to read both layers; only the focus of the laser is changed.

- **DVD-10 - 9.4GB double-side, single-layer**—A DVD-10 is constructed of two stamped substrates bonded together back to back. The recorded layer (Layer 0 on each side) usually is coated with aluminum. Note that these discs are double-sided; however, drives have a read laser only on the bottom, which means the disc must be removed and flipped to read the other side.

- **DVD-18 - 17.1GB double-side, dual-layer**—A DVD-18 combines both double layers and double sides. Two stamped layers form each side, and the substrate pairs are bonded back to back. The outer layers (Layer 0 on each side) are coated with semitransparent gold, whereas the inner layers (Layer 1 on each side) are coated with aluminum. The reflectivity of a single-layer disc is 45%–85%, and for a dual-layer disc the reflectivity is 18%–30%. The automatic gain control (AGC) circuitry in the drive compensates for the different reflective properties.

Figure 11.8 shows the construction of each of the DVD disc types.

Note that although Figure 11.8 shows two lasers reading the bottom of the dual-layer discs, in actual practice only one laser is used. Only the focus is changed to read the different layers.

Dual-layer discs can have the layers recorded in two ways: either OTP or parallel track path (PTP). OTP minimizes the time needed to switch from one layer to the other when reading the disc. When reaching the inside of the disc (end of Layer 0), the laser pickup remains in the same location—it merely moves toward the disc slightly to focus on Layer 1. When written in OTP mode, the lead-out zone toward the outer part of the disc is called a middle zone instead.

Discs written in PTP have both spiral layers written (and read) from the inside out. When changing from Layer 0 to Layer 1, PTP discs require the laser pickup to move from the outside (end of the first layer) back to the inside (start of the second layer), as well as for the focus of the laser to change. Virtually all discs are written in OTP mode to make the layer change quicker. OTP recording is also used by dual-layer (DL) DVD rewritable drives.

To allow the layers to be read more easily even though they are on top of one another, discs written in PTP mode have the spiral direction changed from one layer to the other. Layer 0 has a spiral winding clockwise (which is read counterclockwise), whereas Layer 1 has a spiral winding counterclockwise. This typically requires that the drive spin the disc in the opposite direction to read that layer, but with OTP the spiral is read from the outside in on the second layer. So Layer 0 spirals from the inside out, and Layer 1 spirals from the outside in.

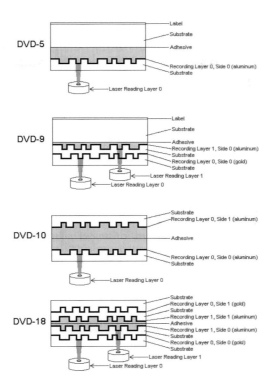

Figure 11.8   DVD disk types and construction.

Figure 11.9 shows the differences between PTP and OTP on a DVD.

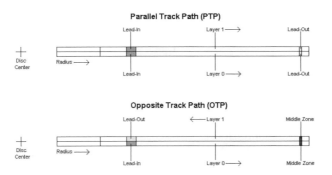

Figure 11.9   PTP versus OTP.

DVDs store up to 4.7GB–17.1GB, depending on the type. Table 11.8 shows the precise capacities of the various types of DVDs.

Table 11.8   DVD Capacity

	Single-Layer	Dual-Layer
DVD Designation	DVD-5	DVD-9
B	4,695,853,056	8,535,691,264
KiB	4,585,794	8,335,636
KB	4,695,853	8,535,691
MiB	4,478	8,140
MB	4,696	8,536
GiB	4.4	7.9
GB	4.7	8.5
MPEG-2 video (approx. minutes)	133	242
MPEG-2 video (hours:minutes)	2:13	4:02
	Single-Layer Double-Sided	Dual-Layer Double-Sided
DVD Designation	DVD-10	DVD-18
B	9,391,706,112	17,071,382,528
KiB	9,171,588	16,671,272
KB	9,391,706	17,071,383
MiB	8,957	16,281
MB	9,392	17,071
GiB	8.7	15.9
GB	9.4	17.1
MPEG-2 video (approx. minutes)	266	484
MPEG-2 video (hours:minutes)	4:26	8:04

B = Byte (8 bits)   *MiB = Mebibyte (1,048,576 bytes)*
KB = Kilobyte (1,000 bytes)   *GB = Gigabyte (1,000,000,000 bytes)*
KiB = Kibibyte (1,024 bytes)   *GiB = Gibibyte (1,073,741,824 bytes)*
MB = Megabyte (1,000,000 bytes)

As you might notice, the capacity of dual-layer discs is slightly less than twice of single-layer discs, even though the layers take up the same space on the discs (the spiral tracks are the same length). This was done intentionally to improve the readability of both layers in a dual-layer configuration. To do this, the bit cell spacing was slightly increased, which increases the length of each pit and land. When reading a dual-layer disc, the drive spins slightly faster to compensate, resulting in the same data rate. However, because the distance on the track is covered more quickly, less overall data can be stored.

Besides the standard four capacities listed here, a double-sided disc with one layer on one side and two layers on the other can also be produced. This would be called a DVD-14 and have a capacity of 13.2GB, or about 6 hours and 15 minutes of MPEG-2 video. Additionally, 80mm discs, which store less data in each configuration than the standard 120mm discs, can be produced.

Because of the manufacturing difficulties and the extra expense of double-sided discs—and the fact that they must be ejected and flipped to play both sides—most DVDs are configured as either a DVD-5 (single-sided, single-layer) or a DVD-9 (single-sided, dual-layer), which allows up to 8.5GB of data or 242 minutes of uninterrupted MPEG-2 video to be played. The 133-minute capacity of DVD-5 video discs accommodates 95% or more of the movies ever made.

Note

When you view a dual-layer DVD movie, you will see a momentary pause onscreen when the player starts to play the second layer. This is normal, and it takes so little time that if you blink, you might miss it.

Data Encoding on the Disc

As with CDs, the pits and lands themselves do not determine the bits; instead, the transitions (changes in reflectivity) from pit to land and land to pit determine the actual bits on the disc. The disc track is divided into bit cells or time intervals (T), and a pit or land used to represent data is required to be a minimum of 3T or a maximum of 11T intervals (cells) long. A 3T long pit or land represents a 1001, and a 11T long pit or land represents a 100000000001.

Data is stored using 8 to 16 modulation, which is a modified version of the 8 to 14 modulation (EFM) used on CDs. Because of this, 8 to 16 modulation is sometimes called EFM+. This modulation takes each byte (8 bits) and converts it into a 16-bit value for storage. The 16-bit conversion codes are designed so that there are never fewer than two or more than ten adjacent 0 bits (resulting in no fewer than three or no more than 11 time intervals between 1s). EFM+ is a form of RLL encoding called RLL 2,10 (RLL x,y, where x equals the minimum and y equals the maximum run of 0s). This is designed to prevent long strings of 0s, which could more easily be misread due to clocks becoming out of sync, as well as to limit the minimum and maximum frequency of transitions actually placed on the recording media. Unlike CDs, no merge bits exist between codes. The 16-bit modulation codes are designed so that they will not violate the RLL 2,10 form without needing merge bits. Because the EFM used on CDs really requires more than 17 bits for each byte (because of the added merge and sync bits), EFM+ is slightly more efficient since only slightly more than 16 bits are generated for each byte encoded.

Note that although no more than ten 0s are allowed in the modulation generated by EFM+, the sync bits added when physical sectors are written can have up to thirteen 0s, meaning a time period of up to 14T between 1s written on the disc and pits or lands up to 14T intervals or bit cells in length.

Blu-ray Disc (BD)

In February 2002, the leading optical storage companies formed the Blu-ray Disc Founders (BDF) and announced the initial specifications for Blu-ray Disc, a high-capacity CD/DVD-type optical disc format. By May 2002, the Blu-ray Disc (BD) specification 1.0 was released, and in April 2003, Sony released the BDZ-S77 for the Japanese market, the first commercially available BD recorder. In January 2006, the Blu-ray Disc Association also released a 2.0 specification for BD-RE discs. Blu-ray is a fully rewritable format that enables recording up to 25GB of data or up to 11.5 hours of standard-definition video on a single-sided, single-layer 12cm diameter disc (which is the same as existing CDs and DVDs) using a 405nm blue-violet laser. Dual-layer BD recorders are also being developed and will record up to 50GB or 23 hours of standard-definition video. Although backward compatibility with DVD and CD is not a requirement of the Blu-ray specification, it is a feature drive manufacturers can easily include. In fact, all the Blu-ray drives announced so far have full backward compatibility with DVD and CD formats. One of the main applications for higher-capacity optical storage is recording high-definition TV, which takes an incredible amount of storage. Current DVD recorders can't store enough data to handle high-definition video. Blu-ray, on the other hand, is designed to store up to 4.5 hours of high-definition video (or more than 13 hours of standard broadcast-quality TV) on a single-layer disc, and 9 hours on dual-layer versions. As with DVD, Blu-ray uses the industry-standard MPEG-2 compression technology.

Note

When a mixture of HD video and standard video is stored on a Blu-ray disc, you can store up to 2.25 hours of HD video and 2 hours of standard video (used for bonus features) on a single-layer disc. A dual-layer Blu-ray disc can store up to 3 hours of HD video and 9 hours of standard video. Capacities can also vary with bit rates used for movie storage, as Blu-ray can support a wide range of bit rates.

The Blu-ray Disc 1.0 specification includes the following formats:

- **BD-ROM**—Read-only for prerecorded content
- **BD-R**—Recordable for PC data storage
- **BD-RW**—Rewritable for PC data storage

The BD-RE format for rewritable HDTV recording is now available in version 2.0.

Standard CDs use a 780nm (infrared) laser combined with a 0.45 numerical aperture lens, whereas DVDs use a 650nm (red) laser combined with a 0.60 numerical aperture lens. Blu-ray uses a much shorter 405nm (blue-violet) laser with a 0.85 numerical aperture lens. *Numerical aperture* is a measurement of the light-gathering capability of a lens, as well as the focal length and relative magnification. The numerical aperture of a lens is derived by taking the sine of the maximum angle of light entering the lens. For example, the lens in a CD-ROM drive gathers light at up to a 26.7° angle, which results in a numerical aperture of SIN(26.7) = 0.45. By comparison, the lens in a DVD drive gathers light at up to a 36.9° angle, resulting in a numerical aperture of SIN(36.9) = 0.60. Blu-ray drives gather light at up to a 58.2° angle, resulting in a numerical aperture of SIN(58.2) = 0.85. Higher numerical apertures allow increasingly oblique (angled) rays of light to enter the lens and therefore produce a more highly resolved image.

The higher the aperture, the shorter the focal length and the greater the magnification. The lens in a CD-ROM drive magnifies roughly 20 times, whereas the lens in a DVD drive magnifies about 40 times. The Blu-ray lens magnifies about 60 times. This greater magnification is necessary because the distance between tracks on a Blu-ray disc is reduced to 0.32um, which is almost half that of a regular DVD. Because of the very high densities involved, a simple cartridge is normally used to hold the disc, which prevents it from being impaired by dust, fingerprints, or scratches.

HD-DVD

HD-DVD, also known as *Advanced Optical Disc (AOD),* is another next-generation blue laser optical disc format developed by Toshiba and NEC. HD-DVD is similar to Blu-ray (but not compatible) and also uses blue-laser technology to achieve a higher storage capacity. HD-DVD-R (recordable) versions store 15GB on a single-layer disc and 30GB on a dual-layer disc. HD-DVD-RW (rewritable) versions store 20GB on a single-layer disc and 32GB on a dual-layer disc. The DVD Forum has approved the HD-DVD format for further study as the successor to the current DVD technology.

A comparison of Blu-ray Disc, HD-DVD, and standard DVD is shown in Table 11.9.

Table 11.9   Comparison of Blu-ray Disc, HD-DVD, and DVD Specifications

Disc Type	Blu-ray Disc (BD)	HD-DVD ROM	DVD ROM
Laser	405nm	405nm	650nm
Numerical aperture	0.85	0.65	0.60
Storage capacity (single layer)	25GB	15GB	4.7GB
Storage capacity (dual layer)	50GB	30GB	8.5GB
SD Video (single layer)	11.5 hours	6.9 hours	2 hours
SD Video (dual layer)	23 hours	13.8 hours	4 hours
HD Video (single layer)	4.5 hours	2.7 hours	—
HD Video (dual layer)	9 hours	5.4 hours	—
Video codecs	MPEG-4 AVC (H.264), VC-1, MPEG-2	MPEG-4 AVC (H.264), VC-1, MPEG-2	MPEG-2
Lossless audio codecs optional: MLP(True HD) [2-ch, 8-ch]*	Linear PCM Linear PCM/MLP (True HD)[2-ch, 8-ch]*	Linear PCM[2ch]	
Lossy audio codecs	Dolby Digital Plus/DTS/ Dolby Digital/MPEG Audio	Dolby Digital Plus/DTS/ Dolby Digital/MPEG Audio	Dolby Digital/ MPEG Audio
Max. transfer rate	54.0Mbps	36.55Mbps	11.08Mbps
Content protection	AACS-128bit	AACS-128bit	CSS 40-bit
Max. video resolution	1920×1080p (HDTV)	1920×1080p (HDTV)	720×480p (SDTV)

Requires HDMI 1.1 or greater for 8-channel support; most home theater systems downmix to 2-channel or use a lossy codec for 5.1 or 7.1 surround audio.

Unfortunately, the development of HD-DVD and the endorsement by the DVD Forum means that there will be another format war over the next-generation blue laser DVD drives. HD-DVD and Blu-ray products first appeared in 2006.

Although a few combo Blu-ray writable/HD-DVD readable drives (which also feature backwards-compatibility with standard DVD and CD media) have been introduced (the first combo drives feature LG's Super Multi Blue drive technology), it will be a few years before one (or both) of these technologies become replacements for today's DVD drives.

Note

For more information about Blu-ray Disc, see www.blu-raydisc.com, and for more information on HD-DVD, see www.dvdforum.org.

Optical Disc Formats

CD and DVD drives can use many types of disc formats and standards. The following sections discuss the formats and file systems used by CD and DVD drives, so you can make sure you can use media recorded in a particular format with your drive.

Compact Disc and Drive Formats

After Philips and Sony created the Red Book CD-DA format discussed earlier in the chapter, they began work on other format standards that would allow CDs to store computer files, data, and even video and photos. These standards control how the data is formatted so that the drive can read it, and additional file format standards can then control how the software and drivers on your PC can be designed to understand and interpret the data properly. Note that the physical format and storage of data on the disc as defined in the Red Book was adopted by all subsequent CD standards. This refers to the encoding and basic levels of error correction provided by CD-DA discs. The other "books" specify primarily how the 2,352 bytes in each sector are to be handled, what type of data can be stored, how it should be formatted, and more.

All the official CD standard books and related documents can be purchased from Philips for $100—$150 each. See the Philips licensing site at www.licensing.philips.com for more information.

Table 11.10 describes the various standard CD formats, which are discussed in more detail in the following sections.

Table 11.10   Compact Disc Formats

Format	Name	Introduced	Notes
Red Book	CD-DA (compact disc digital audio)	1980 – by Philips and Sony	• The original CD audio standard on which all subsequent CD standards are based.
Yellow Book	CD-ROM (compact disc read-only memory)	1983 – by Philips and Sony	• Specifies additional ECC and EDC for data in several sector formats, including Mode 1 and Mode 2.
Green Book	CD-i (compact disc-interactive)	1986 – by Philips and Sony	• Specifies an interactive audio/video standard for non-PC-dedicated player hardware (now mostly obsolete) and discs used for interactive presentations. • Defines Mode 2, Form 1 and Mode 2, Form 2 sector formats along with interleaved MPEG-1 video and ADPCM audio.
CD-ROM XA	CD-ROM XA (extended architecture)	1989 – by Philips, Sony, and Microsoft	• Combines Yellow Book and CD-i to bring CD-i audio and video capabilities to PCs.
Orange Book	CD-R (recordable) and CD-RW (rewritable)	1989 – by Philips and Sony (Part I/II); 1996 – by Philips and Sony (Part III)	• Defines single session, multisession, and packet writing on recordable discs. • Part I—CD-MO (magneto-optical, withdrawn). • Part II—CD-R (recordable). • Part III—CD-RW (rewritable).
Photo-CD	CD-P	1990 – by Philips and Kodak	• Combines CD-ROM XA with CD-R multisession capability in a standard for photo storage on CD-R discs.
White Book	Video CD	1993 – by Philips, JVC, Matsushita, and Sony	• Based on CD-i and CD-ROM XA. It stores up to 74 minutes of MPEG-1 video and ADPCM digital audio data.
Blue Book	CD EXTRA (formerly CD-Plus or enhanced music)	1995 –by Philips and Sony	• Multisession format for stamped discs; used by musical artists to incorporate videos, liner notes, and other information on audio CDs.
Purple Book	CD Double-Density	2000 – by Philips and Sony	• Double-density (1.3GB) versions of CD-ROM, CD-R, and CD-RW (DD-ROM, DD-R, DD-RW).

Format	Name	Introduced	Notes
Scarlet Book	Super Audio CD	1999 – by Philips and Sony	• High-capacity (4.7GiB) music disc; hybrid SA-CD discs also features a CD-DA layer for compatibility with standard players
DualDisc	DualDisc	2004 – by Sony BMG, EMI, Universal Music Group, and Warner Music Group	• Double-sided disc; modified CD-DA format for music on one side; flip side is DVD-Video for videos and other content; slightly thicker than normal CD or DVD media.

Red Book—CD-DA

The Red Book introduced by Philips and Sony in 1980 is the father of all compact-disc specifications because all other "books" or formats are based on the original CD-DA Red Book format. The Red Book specification includes the main parameters, audio specification, disc specification, optical stylus, modulation system, error correction system, and control and display system. The latest revision of the Red Book is dated May 1999.

For more information on the original Red Book format, see the section "CDs: A Brief History," earlier in this chapter.

Yellow Book—CD-ROM

The Yellow Book was first published by Philips, Sony, and Microsoft in 1983 and has been revised and amended several times since. The Yellow Book standard took the physical format of the original CD-DA, or Red Book, standard and added another layer of error detection and correction to enable data to be stored reliably. It also added additional synchronization and header information to enable sectors to be more accurately located. Yellow Book specifies two types of sectoring—called Mode 1 (with error correction) and Mode 2—which offer different levels of error-detection and -correction schemes. Some data (computer files, for example) can't tolerate errors. However, other data, such as a video image or sound, can tolerate minor errors. By using a mode with less error-correction information, more data can be stored, but with the possibility of uncorrected errors.

In 1989, the Yellow Book was issued as an international standard by the ISO as *ISO/IEC 10149, Data Interchange on Read-Only 120mm Optical Discs (CD-ROM)*. The latest version of the Yellow Book is dated May 1999.

Green Book—CD-i

The Green Book was published by Philips and Sony in 1986. CD-i is much more than just a disc format; instead it is a complete specification for an entire interactive system consisting of custom hardware (players) designed to be connected to a television, software designed to deliver video and audio together with user interactivity in real time, and the media and format. A CD-i player is actually a dedicated computer usually running a variant on the Motorola 68000 processor line, as well as a customized version of the Microware OS/9 Real Time Operating System.

CD-i enables both audio and video to share a disc and enables the information to be interleaved so as to maintain synchronization between the pictures and sounds. To fit both audio and video in the same space originally designed for just audio, compression was performed. The video was compressed using the Moving Picture Experts Group-1 (MPEG-1) compression standard, whereas the audio was compressed with adaptive differential pulse code modulation (ADPCM). ADPCM is an audio encoding algorithm that takes about half the space for the same quality of standard PCM, and even less if quality is reduced by lowering the sampling rate or bits per sample. Using ADPCM, up to 8 hours of stereo or 16 hours of mono sound can fit on one CD. The "differential" part of ADPCM refers to the fact that it records the differences between one signal and the next (using only 4-bit numbers), which reduces the total amount of data involved. ADPCM audio can be interleaved with video in CD-i (and CD-ROM XA) applications.

The Yellow Book defines two CD-ROM sector structures, called Mode 1 and Mode 2. The Green Book (CD-i) refines the Mode 2 sector definition by adding two forms, called *Mode 2, Form 1* and *Mode 2, Form 2*. The Mode 2, Form 1 sector definition uses ECC and allows for 2,048 bytes of data storage like the Yellow Book Mode 1 sectors, but it rearranged things slightly to use the 8 bytes formerly unused (blank or 0) as a subheader containing additional information about the sector. The Mode 2, Form 2 definition drops the ECC and allows 2,324 bytes for data. Without the ECC, only video or audio information should be stored in Form 2 sectors because that type of information can tolerate minor errors.

All types of media were produced for CD-i, but because the files use the OS/9 file format, they can't be viewed by a PC without special drivers. One of the best resources for CD-i technical information, utility software, drivers, and emulators is The New International CD-I Association website at www.icdia.org.

Today, the CD-i format is largely obsolete. The last revision of the standard was produced in May 1994. Philips sold off its entire consumer CD-i catalog to Infogrames Multimedia in 1998, which now owns the rights for virtually all consumer CD-i titles ever produced. Philips made a final run of CD-i players in 1999, and it is doubtful any new ones will ever be produced. The legacy of CD-i lives on in the other formats that use specifications originally devised for CD-i, such as the Mode 2, Form 1 and Form 2 sector structures found in CD-XA and the MPEG-1 video format later used in the White Book (CD-Video).

CD-ROM XA

CD-ROM XA originally was defined in 1989 by Philips, Sony, and Microsoft as a supplement to the Yellow Book. CD-ROM XA brings some of the features originally defined in the Green Book (CD-i) to the Yellow Book (CD-ROM) standard, especially for multimedia use. CD-ROM XA adds three main features to the Yellow Book standard. The first consists of the CD-i-enhanced sector definitions (called forms) for the Mode 2 sectors; the second is a capability called interleaving (mixing audio and video information); and the third is ADPCM for compressed audio. The latest version of the CD-ROM XA standard was released in May 1991.

Interleaving

CD-ROM XA drives can employ a technique known as *interleaving*. The specification calls for the capability to encode on disc whether the data directly following an identification mark is graphics, sound, or text. Graphics can include standard graphics pictures, animation, or full-motion video. In addition, these blocks can be interleaved, or interspersed, with each other. For example, a frame of video can start a track followed by a segment of audio, which would accompany the video, followed by yet another frame of video. The drive picks up the audio and video sequentially, buffering the information in memory and then sending it along to the PC for synchronization.

In short, the data is read off the disc in alternating pieces and then synchronized at playback so that the result is a simultaneous presentation of the data. Without interleaving, the drive would have to read and buffer the entire video track before it could read the audio track and synchronize the two for playback.

Sector Modes and Forms

Mode 1 is the standard Yellow Book CD sector format with ECC and EDC to enable error-free operation. Each Mode 1 sector is broken down as shown in Tables 11.11 and 11.12.

Table 11.11   Yellow Book Mode 1 Sector Format Breakdown

Yellow Book (CD-ROM) Sectors (Mode 1):	
Q+P parity bytes	784
Subcode bytes	98
Sync bytes	12
Header bytes	4
Data bytes	2,048
EDC bytes	4
Blank (0) bytes	8
ECC bytes	276
Bytes/sector RAW (unencoded)	3,234

Table 11.12   Yellow Book (CD-ROM) Mode 1 Sector Format

Sync	Header	User Data	EDC	Blank	ECC
12	4	2,048	4	8	276

In the original Yellow Book, Mode 2 was defined as a sector without any ECC or EDC. Unfortunately, Mode 1 (which had ECC and EDC) couldn't be mixed with Mode 2 sectors on the same track (program or song). To enable data with and without error detection and correction in a single track, new sector format subsets for Mode 2 sectors were added in the Green Book (CD-i) and subsequently adopted in the CD-ROM XA extensions. This enabled information that would not tolerate errors (such as programs or computer data) to be interleaved or mixed within the same track with information that would tolerate errors (such as audio or video data). These variations on Mode 2 include Form 1 and Form 2 sectors. Each Mode 2, Form 1 sector is broken down as shown in Tables 11.13, 11.14, 11.15, and 11.16.

Table 11.13   Green Book Mode 2 Sector Format Breakdown

Green Book/CD-ROM XA Sectors (Mode 2, Form 1):	
Q+P parity bytes	784
Subcode bytes	98
Sync bytes	12
Header bytes	4
Subheader bytes	8
Data bytes	2,048
EDC bytes	4
ECC bytes	276
Bytes/sector RAW (unencoded)	3,234

Table 11.14   Green Book/CD-ROM XA (Yellow Book Extensions) Mode 2, Form 1 Sector Format

Sync	Header	Subheader	User Data	EDC	ECC
12	4	8	2,048 bytes	4	276

Table 11.15   Green Book Mode 2 Sector Format Breakdown

Green Book/CD-ROM XA Sectors (Mode 2, Form 2):	
Q+P parity bytes	784
Subcode bytes	98
Sync bytes	12
Header bytes	4
Subheader bytes	8
Data bytes	2,324
EDC bytes	4
Bytes/sector RAW (unencoded)	3,234

Table 11.16   Green Book/CD-ROM XA (Yellow Book Extensions) Mode 2, Form 2 Sector Format

Sync	Header	Subheader	User Data	EDC
12	4	8	2,324 bytes	4

Both Mode 2 sector formats add a subheader field that identifies the type of information (such as audio or video) carried in the user data field. The Form 2 sector lacks the ECC of the Form 1 sector and increases the size of the user data field instead. This type of sector is for storing audio or video data that can tolerate errors.

Because they don't use any third-level error correction, CD-ROMs that use the Mode 2, Form 2 sector format (such as MPEG video CDs) can hold more user information than other CD-ROM types in the same number of sectors and as a result also have a higher data transfer rate of 174.3KBps instead of the standard 153.6KBps. Note that Form 2 sectors are never used to store data or program files because errors can't be tolerated in that type of information. In that case, the Mode 2, Form 1 sector format would be used.

For a drive to be truly XA compatible, the audio data written in Form 2 sectors on the disc as audio must be ADPCM audio—specially compressed and encoded audio. This requires that the drive or the SCSI controller have a signal processor chip that can decompress the audio during the synchronization process.

Some earlier drives were called XA-ready, which meant they were capable of Mode 2, Form 1 and Form 2 reading but did not incorporate the ADPCM chip. This is not a significant shortcoming, however, because only certain multimedia titles use the ADPM encoding (with interleaved audio and video). The main benefit XA brought to the table was the additional sector modes and forms taken from the Green Book.

Orange Book

The Orange Book defines the standards for recordable CDs and originally was announced in 1989 by Philips and Sony. The Orange Book comes in three parts: Part I describes a format called CD-MO (magneto-optical), which was to be a rewritable format but was withdrawn before any products really came to market; Part II (1989) describes CD-R; and Part III (1996) describes CD-RW. Note that originally CD-R was referred to as CD-WO (write-once), and CD-RW originally was called CD-E (erasable).

The Orange Book Part II CD-R design is known as a WORM (write once read mostly) format. After a portion of a CD-R disc is recorded, it can't be overwritten or reused. Recorded CD-R discs are Red Book and Yellow Book compatible, which means they are readable on conventional CD-DA or CD-ROM drives. The CD-R definition in the Orange Book Part II is divided into two volumes. Volume 1 defines recording speeds of 1x, 2x, and 4x the standard CD speed; the last revision, dated December 1998, is 3.1. Volume 2 defines recording speeds up to 48x the standard CD speed. The latest version released, 1.2, is dated April 2002.

The Orange Book Part III describes CD-RW. As the name implies, CD-RW enables you to erase and overwrite information in addition to reading and writing. The Orange Book Part III CD-RW definition is broken into three volumes. Volume 1 defines recording speeds of 1x, 2x, and 4x times the standard CD speed; the latest version, 2.0, is dated August 1998. Volume 2 (high-speed) defines recording speeds from 4x to 10x standard CD speed; the latest version, 1.1, is dated June 2001. Volume 3 (ultra-speed) defines recording speeds from 8x to 32x; the latest version, 1.0, is dated September 2002.

Besides the capability to record on CDs, the most important feature instituted in the Orange Book specification is the capability to perform multisession recording.

Multisession Recording Overview

Before the Orange Book specification, CDs had to be written as a single session. A *session* is defined as a lead-in, followed by one or more tracks of data (or audio), followed by a lead-out. The lead-in takes up 4,500 sectors on the disc (1 minute if measured in time or about 9.2MB worth of data). The lead-in also indicates whether the disc is multisession and what the next writable address on the disc is (if the disc isn't closed). The first lead-out on a disc (or the only one if it is a single session or Disk At Once recording) is 6,750 sectors long (1.5 minutes if measured in time or about 13.8MB worth of data). If the disc is a multisession disc, any subsequent lead-outs are 2,250 sectors long (0.5 minutes in time or about 4.6MB worth of data).

A multisession CD has multiple sessions, with each individual session complete from lead-in to lead-out. The mandatory lead-in and lead-out for each session do waste space on the disc. In fact, 48 sessions would literally use up all of a 74-minute disc even with no data recorded in each session! Therefore, the practical limit for the number of sessions you can record on a disc would be much less than that.

CD-DA and older CD-ROM drives couldn't read more than one session on a disc, so that is the way most pressed CDs are recorded. The Orange Book allows multiple sessions on a single disc. To allow this, the Orange Book defines three main methods or modes of recording:

- Disk-at-Once (DAO)
- Track-at-Once (TAO)
- Packet Writing

Disc-at-Once

Disc-at-Once means pretty much what it says: It is a single-session method of writing CDs in which the lead-in, data tracks, and lead-out are written in a single operation without ever turning off the writing laser; then the disc is closed. A disc is considered closed when the last (or only) lead-in is fully written and the next usable address on the disc is not recorded in that lead-in. In that case, the CD recorder is incapable of writing any further data on the disc. Note that it is not necessary to close a disc to read it in a normal CD-ROM drive, although if you were submitting a disc to a CD-duplicating company for replication, most require that it be closed.

Track-at-Once

Multisession discs can be recorded in either Track-at-Once (TAO) or Packet Writing mode. In Track-at-Once recording, each track can be individually written (laser turned on and off) within a session, until the session is closed. Closing a session is the act of writing the lead-out for that session, which means no more tracks can be added to that session. If the disc is closed at the same time, no further sessions can be added either.

The tracks recorded in TAO mode are typically divided by gaps of 2 seconds. Each track written has 150 sectors of overhead for run-in, run-out, pre-gap, and linking. A CD-R/RW drive can read the tracks even if the session is not closed, but to read them in a CD-DA or CD-ROM drive, the session must be closed. If you intend to write more sessions to the disc, you can close the session and not close the disc. At that point, you could start another session of recording to add more tracks to the disc. The main thing to remember is that each session must be closed (lead-out written) before another session can be written or before a normal CD-DA or CD-ROM drive can read the tracks in the session.

Packet Writing

Packet writing is a method whereby multiple writes are allowed within a track, thus reducing the overhead and wasted space on a disc. Each packet uses four sectors for run-in, two for run-out, and one for linking. Packets can be of fixed or variable length, but most drives and packet-writing software use a fixed length because dealing with file systems that way is much easier and more efficient.

With packet writing, you use the Universal Disk Format (UDF) version 1.5 or later file system, which enables the CD to be treated essentially like a big floppy drive. That is, you can literally drag and drop files to it, use the copy command to copy files onto the disc, and so on. The packet-writing software and UDF file system manage everything. If the disc you are using for packet writing is a CD-R, every time a file is overwritten or deleted, the file seems to disappear, but you don't get the space back on the disc. Instead, the file system simply forgets about the file. If the disc is a CD-RW, the space is indeed reclaimed and the disc won't be full until you literally have more than the limit of active files stored there.

Unfortunately, Windows versions up through Windows XP don't support packet writing or the UDF file system directly, so drivers must be loaded to read packet-written discs and a packet-writing application must be used to write them. Fortunately, though, these typically are included with CD-RW drives. One of the most popular packet-writing programs is DirectCD from Roxio. You can even download a universal UDF reader application from Roxio for free that enables you to read UDF 1.5 (packet-written) discs on any CD-ROM or CD-RW drive.

Windows Vista supports UDF much more thoroughly than previous Windows versions. It is able to format both CD and DVD media using the Live File System (LFS—Microsoft's term for UDF 2.01), older UDF versions (1.02, 1.5), and the new UDF version 2.5, as well as mastered. UDF 2.01 discs can be read by Windows XP, Windows Server 2003, or Windows Vista systems, and support drag and drop file copying on Windows Vista. UDF version 1.02 is designed for use with DVD-RAM media and is supported by Windows 98 and many Apple computers. UDF version 1.5 works with Windows 2000/XP and Windows Server 2003 as well as Linux systems using kernel version 2.6 or greater. UDF version 2.5 is supported by Windows Vista. For Linux kernel 2.6.20 and later support of UDF version 2.5, install the UDF-2.50 patch available from http://sourceforge.net.

Note

By default, Windows Vista uses Live File System (UDF 2.01) to format CDs and DVDs. To choose between Live File System or Mastered (copies all files at once; does not support drag and drop file copying), select Show Formatting Options in the Burn a Disc dialog. To choose a different UDF version, select Show Formatting Options, and then Change Version in the Burn a Disc dialog.

Note

Windows XP also has limited CD-RW support in the form of something called IMAPI (image mastering application program interface), which enables data to be temporarily stored on the hard drive (staged) before being written to the CD in one session. Additional sessions can be written to the same disc, but a 50MB overhead exists for each session. This gives some of the appearance of packet writing, but it is not really the same thing. To read packet-written discs in the UDF 1.5 or later format, you must install a UDF reader just as with previous versions of Windows. Instead of using IMAPI, I recommend installing a third-party CD-mastering program that also includes packet-writing UDF support, such as Roxio's Easy Media Creator or Nero AG's Nero Premium.

When you remove a packet-written disc from the drive, the packet-writing software first asks whether you want the files to be visible to normal CD-ROM drives. If you do then the session must be closed. Even if the session is closed, you can still write more to the disc later, but there is an overhead of wasted space every time you close a session. If you are going to read the disc in a CD-RW drive, you don't have to close the session because it will be capable of reading the files even if the session isn't closed.

Caution

If you are not sure what type of drive will be used to read the media, I recommend closing the media. This enables users of varying types of drives to read the media, although a compatible UDF reader program must be installed in some cases.

A newer standard called Mount Rainier (Mt. Rainier) adds even more capability to packet writing. With Mount Rainier, packet writing can become an official part of the operating system and the drives can support the defect management necessary to make them usable as removable storage in the real world. For more information, see the section "Mount Rainier" later in this chapter.

Note

As part of Service Pack 1, Microsoft released updates for Windows XP that add native support for the Mount Rainier standard, which supports full drag-and-drop packet writing through CD-MRW drives as well as DVD+MRW drives. Microsoft Windows Vista includes native support of Mount Rainier.

Photo CD

First announced back in 1990 but not available until 1992, Photo CD was a standard that used CD-R discs and drives to store photos. Although Kodak originally sold Photo CD "players" that were connected to TVs, most Photo CD users used CD-ROM drives along with software to decode and display the photos.

Perhaps the main benefit Photo CD brought to the table is that it was the first CD format to use the Orange Book Part II (CD-R) specification with multisession recordings. Additionally, the data is recorded in CD-ROM XA Mode 2, Form 2 sectors so more photo information could be stored on the disc.

Kodak's own PhotoYCC encoding format was used to store up to six resolutions for each image, as shown in Table 11.17. The x64 resolution was supported only by the Pro Photo CD master version of the service.

Table 11.17   Photo CD Resolutions

Base	Resolution (Pixels)	Description
/16	128×192	Thumbnail
/4	256×384	Thumbnail
x1	512×768	TV resolution
x4	1,024×1,536	HDTV resolution
x16	2,048×3,072	Print size
x64	4,096×6,144	Pro Photo CD master only

At a time when photo-editing software was in its infancy, the ability to select different sizes optimized for different purposes was quite useful. However, with the rise of high-speed PCs running Adobe Photoshop, Adobe Photoshop Elements, and other photo editing programs, along with high-speed, low-cost recordable, and rewritable CD and DVD drives, the Photo CD format became obsolete. Kodak discontinued development in the early twenty-first century, and third-party labs that offered the service discontinued it in 2004. Kodak still offers drivers, software, and firmware for Pro Photo CD at http://www.kodak.com/global/en/service/professional/products/ekn017045.jhtml.

Picture CD

As a replacement for Photo CD, Kodak now offers the simpler Picture CD service. Unlike Photo CD, Picture CD uses the industry-standard JPEG file format. It uses a CD-R, with up to 40 images stored at a single medium-resolution scan of 1,024×1,536 pixels. This resolution is adequate for 4"×6" and 5"×7" prints. The images can also be made available via Kodak PhotoNet, where the same images are posted online and can be downloaded. In addition, Kodak has a service called Picture Disk that stores up to 28 images on a 1.44MB floppy disk at a resolution of 400×600, suitable for screensavers and slide shows.

The software provided with Picture CD enables the user to manipulate images with various automatic or semiautomatic operations, but unlike Photo CD, the standard JPEG (JPG) file format used for storage enables any popular image-editing program to work with the images without conversion. Although the image quality of Picture CD isn't as high as with Photo CD, the much lower price of the service makes it far more popular with amateur photographers. Services similar to Picture CD are also offered by Fujifilm and Agfa, and some stores allow you to order Kodak Picture CD with your choice of store-brand or Kodak film processing.

Note

By scanning your own 35mm negatives with a high-performance flatbed or dedicated film scanner, you can achieve much higher resolutions (up to 4800 dpi optical) that support larger images sizes than what Picture CD offers. For example, a 3200 dpi scan of a full-frame 35mm film negative has a resolution of about 2570×4450 pixels. By scanning negatives yourself, you can also select the quality of JPEG images and save images in other formats, such as TIFF. Some photo labs offer high-resolution film developing and scanning services if you prefer not to scan your own film.

White Book—Video CD (VCD)

The White Book standard was introduced in 1993 by Philips, JVC, Matsushita, and Sony. It is based on the Green Book (CD-i) and CD-ROM XA standards and allows for storing up to 74 minutes of MPEG-1 video and ADPCM digital audio data on a single disc. The latest version (2.0) was released in April 1995. Video CD (VCD) 2.0 supports MPEG-1 compression with a 1.15Mbps bit rate. The screen resolution is 352×240 for NTSC format and 352×288 for European PAL format. In addition, it supports Dolby Pro Logic–compatible stereo sound.

You can think of Video CDs as a sort of poor man's DVD format, although the picture and sound quality can actually be quite good—certainly better than VHS or most other videotape formats. You can play video CDs on virtually any PC with a CD-ROM drive using the free Windows Media Player (other media player applications can be used as well). They also can be played on most DVD players and even some game consoles, such as the Playstation (with the correct options). Although you can create VCDs with popular DVD production programs such as Roxio Easy Media Creator, prerecorded VCD media is difficult to find today, thanks to the popularity of the higher-quality (and easier to copy-protect) DVD format and its higher-resolution siblings (Blu-ray and HD DVD).

Super Video CD

The Super Video CD specification 1.0, published in May 1999, is an enhanced version of the White Book Video CD specification. It uses MPEG-2 compression, an NTSC screen resolution of 480×480, and a PAL screen resolution of 480×576; it also supports MPEG-2 5.1 surround sound and multiple languages.

Most home DVD-creation programs can create Video CDs or Super Video CDs.

Blue Book—CD EXTRA

Manufacturers of CD-DA media were looking for a standard method to combine both music and data on a single CD. The intention was for a user to be able to play only the audio tracks in a standard audio CD player while remaining unaware of the data track. However, a user with a PC or dedicated combination audio/data player could access both the audio and data tracks on the same disc.

The fundamental problem with nonstandard mixed-mode CDs is that if or when an audio player tries to play the data track, the result is static that could conceivably damage speakers and possibly hearing if the volume level has been turned up. Various manufacturers originally addressed this problem in different ways, resulting in a number of confusing methods for creating these types of discs, some of which still allowed the data tracks to be accidentally "played" on an audio player. In 1995, Philips and Sony developed the CD EXTRA specification, as defined in the Blue Book standard. CDs conforming to this specification usually are referred to as CD EXTRA (formerly called CD Plus or CD Enhanced Music) discs and use the multisession technology defined in the CD-ROM XA standard to separate the audio and data tracks. These are a form of stamped multisession disc. The audio portion of the disc can consist of up to 98 standard Red Book audio tracks, whereas the data track typically is composed of XA Mode 2 sectors and can contain video, song lyrics, still images, or other multimedia content. Such discs can be identified by the CD EXTRA logo, which is the standard CD-DA logo with a plus sign to the right. Often the logo or markings on the disc package are overlooked or somewhat obscure, and you might not know that an audio CD contains this extra data until you play it in a CD-ROM drive.

A CD EXTRA disc normally contains two sessions. Because audio CD players are only single-session capable, they play only the audio session and ignore the additional session containing the data. A CD-ROM drive in a PC, however, can see both sessions on the disc and access both the audio and data tracks.

Note

Many artists have released audio CDs in the CD EXTRA format that include things such as lyrics, video, artist bio, photos, and so on in data files on the disc. *Tidal* by Fiona Apple (released in 1996) was one of the first CD EXTRA discs from Sony Music. There have been many CD EXTRA releases since then. For examples of other CD EXTRA (Enhanced CD) discs, including current releases, see www.musicfan.com.

Purple Book

The Purple Book defines the standards for double-density CD-ROM (DDCD), CD-R (DDCD-R), and CD-RW (DDCD-RW) media and drives. It was announced by Sony and Philips in July 2000, and the current standard (1.0) was released in July 2001.

Purple Book–compliant rewritable drives can read and write standard CD, CD-R, and CD-RW media and achieve their higher 1.3GiB capacity (versus 650MiB/703MiBfor standard drives) by modifying the following features of existing CD-ROM, CD-R, and CD-RW standards:

- The track pitch has been reduced from 1.6 micrometers to 1.1 micrometers, and the minimum pit length has been reduced from 0.833 micrometers to 0.623 micrometers to enable double-density recording.
- CIRC7 (instead of regular CIRC) error correction is used.
- An expanded ATIP address format is used.

DD drives support digital rights management (DRM). They are designed to prevent the creation of DD music CDs. Tables 11.18 and 11.19 provide the details of the sector format used by DD drives.

Table 11.18   Purple Book Mode 2 Sector Format Breakdown

Purple Book/DD CD-ROM Sectors (Mode 2, Form 2):	
Q+P parity bytes	276
Subcode bytes	98
Sync bytes	12
Header bytes	4
Subheader bytes	8
Data bytes	2,048
EDC bytes	4
Bytes/sector RAW (unencoded)	2,352

Table 11.19   Purple Book/DD CD-ROM Mode 2, Form 2 Sector Format

Sync	Header	Subheader	User Data	EDC
12	4	8	2,048 bytes	4

Although DDCD drives have twice the capacity of traditional drives, very few of them were sold. Sony several models in 2001 but has since discontinued them, although DDCD media is still available.

▶▶   For more information about digital rights management, see "CD Digital Rights Management (DRM)," p.830.

Scarlet Book (SA-CD)

The Scarlet Book defines the official standard for Super Audio CD (SA-CD, also referred to as SACD) media and drives. It was co-developed by Philips Electronics and Sony in 1999. Unlike the original Red Book CD-Audio standard, which samples music at 44.1KHz, Scarlet Book uses Direct Stream Digital encoding with a sampling rate of 2.822MHz—64 times the sampling frequency of Red Book.

Because of the higher sampling rate and the larger disc capacity necessary to store the audio (as well as SA-CD's support for video and text contents), you cannot play standard or dual-layer SA-CD media in a standard CD player or computer's CD or DVD drive. Although standard SA-CD media has a capacity of 4.7GiB (the same as that of single-layer DVD), the formats are not interchangeable. SA-CD contents are copy-protected by a physical watermark known as Pit Signal Processing, which cannot be detected by standard computer DVD drives.

To ease the transition from CD-Audio to SA-CD, almost all SA-CD albums use a hybrid dual-layer design, in which the top layer stores standard CD audio playable on standard CD players and computer CD/DVD drives, and the lower layer contains the higher-density SA-CD content. Hybrid SA-CD albums can be played in standard CD players and computer CD/DVD drives Essentially, a hybrid SA-CD disc is like a CD-audio disc and a standard SA-CD disc in a single-sided disc (see Figure 11.10).

Note

Although hybrid SA-CD media can be played in standalone CD or computer CD/DVD drives, these devices are only playing the CD layer. To enjoy the enhanced audio of SA-CD, you must use a standalone SA-CD player.

A SA-CD disc (or the SA-CD layer of a hybrid disc) includes the stereo version of the album in its inner portion, a six-channel surround audio mix in the middle portion, and extra data such as lyrics, graphics, and video in the outer portion.

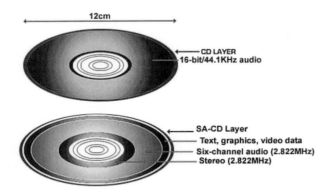

Figure 11.10 The structure of a hybrid SA-CD disc.

For listings of SA-CD albums and players and additional SA-CD information, see www.sa-cd.net.

DualDisc

DualDisc, introduced by a consortium of major record labels in the summer of 2004 (see http://sonybmg.com/dualdisc/ for details), is a combination of two different formats, music CD and DVD, on a single two-sided disc. DualDisc, as the name suggests, is two discs in one: One side is a music CD, typically featuring support for surround audio or other advanced audio formats, and the other side is a DVD (using the single-layer DVD-5 format) that can include music videos, concert footage, web links and other features.

Although DualDisc is designed to work in standard CD drives and players, it is not completely compatible with Red Book standards because the CD layer is only 0.9mm, compared to the RedBook standard of 1.1mm. To compensate for spherical aberration caused by a thinner CD layer, one method used is to increase the size of the pits on the CD side of a DualDisc, reducing playing time to 60 minutes. (Some later DualDisc media uses different methods to increase playtime.)

The total thickness of a DualDisc is 1.5mm, compared to 1.2mm for standard CD or DVD media, causing DualDiscs to be incompatible with slot-loading drives in car stereo, PCs, or mega-disc changers. Because DualDisc media is thicker than normal CD media and because the internal structure of the CD side is not compatible with Red Book standards, Philips and Sony (the co-creators of the CD format) do not use the CD logo on DualDisc media, and most DualDisc albums include warning labels that the disc will not work in slot-loaded drives or mega-disc changers, and might not play in other types of players. Essentially, then, a DualDisc is best considered as a combo disc with full DVD and partial CD compatibility.

DualDisc albums are typically packaged in CD-style jewel cases, and are usually marked with the DualDisc logo.

Caution

Some music vendors use the term DualDisc to refer to SA-CD as well as actual DualDisc albums. Be sure to check details of the media carefully to assure that you can play the disc in your equipment.

Although DualDisc media, unlike SA-CD media, supports two standard formats, it is not nearly as popular as SA-CD media. Thousands of albums are available in SA-CD format, but only a few hundred (at most) are available in DualDisc format. SA-CD provides far better audio quality than DualDisc (which provides only CD quality music), making it a better format for the serious audiophile. However, DualDisc provides DVD-quality video and other extras as well as standard CD-quality music on devices that can play the CD side.

CD-ROM File Systems

Manufacturers of early CD-ROM discs required their own custom software to read the discs. This is because the Yellow Book specification for CD-ROM details only how data sectors—rather than audio sectors—can be stored on a disc and did not cover the file systems or deal with how data should be stored in files and how these should be formatted for use by PCs with different operating systems. Obviously, noninterchangeable file formats presented an obstacle to the industry-wide compatibility for CD-ROM applications.

In 1985–1986, several companies got together and published the High Sierra file format specification, which finally enabled CD-ROMs for PCs to be universally readable. That was the first industry-standard CD-ROM file system that made CD-ROMs universally usable in PCs. Today several file systems are used on CDs, including

- High Sierra
- ISO 9660 (based on High Sierra)
- Joliet
- UDF (Universal Disk Format)
- Mac HFS (Hierarchical File Format)
- Rock Ridge
- Mount Rainier (also known as Mt. Rainier)

Not all CD file system formats can be read by all operating systems. Table 11.20 shows the primary file systems used and which operating systems support them.

Table 11.20   CD File System Formats

CD File System	DOS/ Win 3.x	Win 9x/ Me	Win NT/ 2000/XP	Win Vista	Mac OS
High Sierra	Yes	Yes	Yes	Yes	Yes
ISO 9660	Yes	Yes	Yes	Yes	Yes
Joliet	Yes[1]	Yes	Yes	Yes	Yes[1]
UDF	No	Yes[2]	Yes[2]	Yes	Yes[2]
Mac HFS	No	No	No	No	Yes
Rock Ridge (RockRidge)	Yes[1]	Yes[1]	Yes[1]	Yes[1]	Yes[1]
Mount Rainier	No	Yes[3]	Yes[3]	Yes	Yes[3]

1. *A short name, such as (SHORTN~1.TXT), will be shown in place of long filenames.*
2. *Only if a third-party UDF reader is installed.*
3. *Requires Mount Rainier (also called EasyWrite) hardware and driver software (Win98 or above) or a third-party reader program.*

Note

The Mac HFS and Unix Rock Ridge file systems are not supported by PC operating systems such as DOS or Windows and therefore are not covered in depth here.

High Sierra

To make CD-ROM discs readable on all systems without having to develop custom file systems and drivers, it was in the best interests of all PC hardware and software manufacturers to resolve the CD-ROM file format standardization issue. In 1985, representatives from TMS, DEC, Microsoft, Hitachi, LaserData, Sony, Apple, Philips, 3M, Video Tools, Reference Technology, and Xebec met at what was then called the High Sierra Hotel and Casino in Lake Tahoe, Nevada, to create a common logical format and file structure for CD-ROMs. In 1986, they jointly published this standard as the "Working Paper for Information Processing: Volume and File Structure of CD-ROM Optical Discs for Information Exchange (1986)." This standard was subsequently referred to as the High Sierra format.

This agreement enabled all drives using the appropriate driver (such as MSCDEX.EXE supplied by Microsoft with DOS) to read all High Sierra format discs, opening the way for the mass production and acceptance of CD-ROM software publishing. Adoption of this standard also enabled disc publishers to provide cross-platform support for their software and easily manufacture discs for DOS, Unix, and other operating system formats. Without this agreement, the maturation of the CD-ROM marketplace would have taken years longer and the production of CD-ROM-based information would have been stifled.

The High Sierra format was submitted to the International Organization for Standardization (ISO). Two years later (in 1988), with several enhancements and changes, it was republished as the ISO 9660 standard. ISO 9660 was not exactly the same as High Sierra, but all drivers that would read High Sierra–formatted discs were quickly updated to handle both ISO 9660 and the original High Sierra format on which it was based.

For example, Microsoft wrote the MSCDEX.EXE (Microsoft CD-ROM extensions) driver in 1988 and licensed it to CD-ROM hardware and software vendors to include with their products. It wasn't until 1993 when MS-DOS 6.0 was released that MSCDEX was included with DOS as a standard feature. MSCDEX enables DOS to read ISO 9660–formatted (and High Sierra–formatted) discs. This driver works with the AT Attachment Packet Interface (ATAPI) or Advanced SCSI Programming Interface (ASPI) hardware-level device driver that comes with the drive. Microsoft built ISO 9660 and Joliet file system support directly into Windows 95 and later, with no additional drivers necessary.

ISO 9660

The ISO 9660 standard enabled full cross-compatibility among different computer and operating systems. ISO 9660 was released in 1988 and was based on the work done by the High Sierra group. Although based on High Sierra, ISO 9660 does have some differences and refinements. It has three levels of interchange that dictate the features that can be used to ensure compatibility with different systems.

ISO 9660 Level 1 is the lowest common denominator of all CD file systems and is capable of being read by almost every computer platform, including Unix and Macintosh. The downside of this file system is that it is very limited with respect to filenames and directories. Level 1 interchange restrictions include

- Only uppercase characters A–Z, numbers 0–9, and the underscore (_) are allowed in filenames.
- Only 8.3 characters maximum for the name.extension (based on DOS limits).
- Directory names are eight characters maximum (no extension allowed).
- Directories are limited to eight levels deep.
- Files must be contiguous.

Level 2 interchange rules have the same limitations as Level 1, except that the filename and extension can be up to 30 characters long (both added together, not including the . separator). Finally, Level 3 interchange rules are the same as Level 2 except that files don't have to be contiguous.

Note that Windows 95 and later versions enable you to use file and folder names up to 255 characters long, which can include spaces as well as lowercase and many other characters not allowed in ISO 9660. To maintain backward compatibility with DOS, Windows 95 and later associate a short 8.3 format filename as an alias for each file that has a longer name. These alias short names are created automatically by Windows and can be viewed in the Properties for each file or by using the DIR command at a command prompt. To create these alias names, Windows truncates the name to six (or fewer) characters followed by a tilde (~) and a number starting with 1 and truncates the extension to three characters. Other numbers are used in the first part if other files that would have the same alias when truncated already exist. For example, the filename This is a.test gets THISIS~1.TES as an alias.

This filename alias creation is independent of your CD drive, but it is important to know that if you create or write to a CD using the ISO 9660 format using Level 1 restrictions, the alias short names are used when recording files to the disc, meaning any long filenames will be lost in the process. In fact, even the alias short name will be modified because ISO 9660 Level 1 restrictions don't allow a tilde— that character is converted to an underscore in the names written to the CD.

The ISO 9660 data starts at 2 seconds and 16 sectors into the disc, which is also known as *logical sector 16 of track one*. For a multisession disc, the ISO 9660 data is present in the first data track of each session containing CD-ROM tracks. This data identifies the location of the volume area—where the actual d ta is stored. The system area also lists the directories in this volume as the volume table of content (VTOC), with pointers or addresses to various named areas, as illustrated in Figure 11.11.

A significant difference between the CD directory structure and that of a normal hard disk is that the CD's system area also contains direct addresses of the files within the subdirectories, allowing the CD to seek specific sector locations on the spiral data track. Because the CD data is all on one long spiral track, when speaking of tracks in the context of a CD, we're actually talking about sectors or segments of data along that spiral.

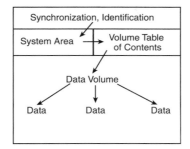

Figure 11.11 A diagram of basic ISO 9660 file organizational format.

To put the ISO 9660 format in perspective, the disc layout is roughly analogous to that of a floppy disk. A floppy disk has a system track that not only identifies itself as a floppy disk and reveals its density and operating system, but also tells the computer how it's organized (into directories, which are made up of files).

Joliet

Joliet is an extension of the ISO 9660 standard that Microsoft developed for use with Windows 95 and later. Joliet enables CDs to be recorded using filenames up to 64 characters long, including spaces and other characters from the Unicode international character set. Joliet also preserves an 8.3 alias for those programs that can't use the longer filenames.

In general, Joliet features the following specifications:

- File or directory names can be up to 64 Unicode characters (128 bytes) in length.
- Directory names can have extensions.
- Directories can be deeper than eight levels.
- Multisession recording is inherently supported.

Tip

Because Joliet supports a shorter path than Windows 9x and newer versions, you might have difficulties mastering a Joliet-format CD that contains extremely long pathnames. I recommend you shorten folder names in the file structure you create with the CD mastering software to avoid problems. Unfortunately, some CD mastering programs don't warn you about a pathname that is too long until after the burning process starts. If your CD mastering program offers an option to validate your disc structure, use this option to determine if you need to shorten folder names. Some CD mastering programs will provide a suggested short name and shorten too-long folder names for you.

Due to backward-compatibility provisions, systems that don't support the Joliet extensions (such as older DOS systems) should still be capable of reading the disc. However, it will be interpreted as an ISO 9660 format using the short names instead.

Note

A bit of trivia: "Chicago" was the code name used by Microsoft for Windows 95. Joliet is the town outside of Chicago where Jake was locked up in the movie *The Blues Brothers*.

Universal Disk Format

UDF is a file system created by the Optical Storage Technology Association (OSTA) as an industry-standard format for use on optical media such as CD-ROM and DVD, but it can also be used by other types of removable-media drives, such as the Iomega REV drives. UDF has several advantages over the ISO 9660 file system used by standard CD-ROMs but is most noted because it is designed to work with packet writing, a technique for writing small amounts of data to a CD-R/RW disc, treating it much like a standard magnetic drive. The UDF file system allows long filenames up to 255 characters per name. There have been several versions of UDF, with most packet-writing software using UDF 1.5 or later. Packet-writing software such as Roxio's DirectCD and Drag-to-Disc's, Nero AG's InCD, and Veritas and Sonic Solutions' DLA use the UDF file system. However, standard CD-ROM drives, drivers, or operating systems such as DOS can't read UDF-formatted discs. Recordable drives can read them, but regular CD-ROM drives must conform to the MultiRead specification (see the section "MultiRead Specifications," later in this chapter) to be capable of reading UDF discs.

After you are sure that your drive can read UDF, you must check the OS. Most operating systems can't read UDF natively—the support has to be added via a driver. DOS can't read UDF at all; however, with Windows 95 and later, UDF-formatted discs can be read by installing a UDF driver. Typically, such a driver is included with the software that comes with most CD-RW and rewritable DVD drives drives.

If you don't have a UDF reader, you can download one from the following websites:

- Get Roxio's UDF Volume Reader from the support section of www.roxio.com
- Get Nero AG's InCD Reader from the support section of www.nero.com

After the UDF driver is installed, you do not need to take any special steps to read a UDF-formatted disc. The driver will be in the background waiting for you to insert a UDF-formatted disc.

If you are unable to read a disc written with UDF on another system, return it to the original system and close the media. This option is usually displayed as part of the Eject Settings dialog. Closing the disc converts the filenames to Joliet format and causes them to be truncated to 64 characters.

You can download the latest (revision 2.60) version of the Universal Disk Format from the OSTA website at www.osta.org/specs/index.htm.

Tip

UDF discs can become unreadable for a variety of reasons, including incompatible UDF reader installed, disc not closed before removal of drive, table of contents not written due to system lockup, and so on. To recover data from UDF discs, try CD Roller (available from www.cdroller.com). It supports the most commonly-used UDF versions (v1.02 through 2.01, and UDF Bridge) and also works with CD and DVD discs created by digital cameras, DVD recorders, and DVD camcorders. Another CD/DVD recovery program to consider is IsoBuster (www.smart-projects.net). IsoBuster also works with Blu-ray and HD DVD formats.

Macintosh HFS

HFS is the file system used by the Macintosh OS. HFS can also be used on CD-ROMs; however, if that is done, they will not be readable on a PC. A hybrid disc can be produced with both Joliet and HFS or ISO 9660 and HFS file systems, and the disc would then be readable on both PCs and Macs. In that case, the system will see only the disc that is compatible, which is ISO 9660 or Joliet in the case of PCs.

Rock Ridge

The Rock Ridge Interchange Protocol (RRIP) was developed by an industry consortium called the Rock Ridge group. It was officially released in 1994 by the IEEE CD-ROM File System Format Working Group and specifies an extension to the ISO 9660 standard for CD-ROM that enables the recording of additional information to support Unix/POSIX file system features. Neither DOS nor Windows include support for the Rock Ridge extensions. However, because it is based on ISO 9660, the files are still readable on a PC and the RRIP extensions are simply ignored.

Note

An interesting bit of trivia is that the Rock Ridge name was taken from the fictional Western town in the movie *Blazing Saddles*.

Mount Rainier

Mount Rainier was a rewritable CD and DVD standard developed byPhilips, Sony, Microsoft, and HP (Compaq). Also called EasyWrite (see Figure 11.12), Mount Rainier was designed to enable native operating system support for data storage on CD-RW and DVD+RW.

Figure 11.12   The EasyWrite logo was used on some CD-RW and DVD+R/RW drives manufactured in 2003 and beyond that support the Mount Rainier standard.

Mount Rainier's main features included:

- **Integral defect management**—Standard drives rely on driver software to manage defects.
- **Direct addressing at the 2KB sector level to minimize wasted space**—Standard CD-RW media uses a block size of 64KB.
- **Background formatting so that new media can be used in seconds after first insertion**—Standard CD-RW formatting can take up to 45 minutes depending on drive speed.
- **Standardized command set**—Standard software cannot work with new drives until revised command files are available.
- **Standardized physical layout**—Differences in standard UDF software can make reading media written by another program difficult.

Mount Rainier compatibility is also known as CD-MRW or DVD+MRW compatibility. Drives with the Mount Rainier or EasyWrite logo have this compatibility built-in, but some existing CD-RW drives can be updated to MRW status by reflashing the firmware in the drive.

You must also have operating system or application support to use Mount Rainier. The first version of Windows to include Mount Rainier support is Windows Vista; Linux kernel version 2.6.2 and above also include Mount Rainier support. For Windows XP or older editions, you must use recent versions of Nero AG's InCD or Roxio's DirectCD or Drag-to-Disc or other Mount Rainier-compatible programs to support Mount Rainier media.

Note

Software Architects (www.softarch.com) produces WriteCD-RW Pro! Software, which enables interchange between Mount Rainier and conventional UDF media, as well as between UDF media written with different programs and to different standards.

Although Mount Rainier was a promising technology, it has become outdated. Many users who formerly relied upon the not-always-reliable UDF format for treating CD-RW and rewritable DVD discs as floppy drives are now using USB flash memory drives for file transport. DVD-RAM (which has native drag-and-drop and file-erasure capabilities) is now making a comeback for both file transport and backup thanks to widespread support in recent DVD rewritable drives. Consequently, most recent rewritable DVD drives no longer include hardware support for Mount Rainier.

DVD Formats and Standards

As with the CD standards, the DVD standards are published in reference books produced mainly by the DVD Forum, but also by other companies, such as the DVD+RW Alliance. The DVD Forum's DVD-Video and DVD-ROM standards are well established and are supported by virtually every DVD drive, regardless of age. However, rival recordable and rewritable DVD standards have been developed by both organizations. The DVD Forum developed

- DVD-RAM (drag and drop file storage and erasure without using add-on software)
- DVD-R (recordable DVD)
- DVD-RW (rewritable DVD)

After the development of DVD-RAM and DVD-R, the rival DVD+RW Alliance developed:

- DVD+RW (rewritable DVD with support for lossless linking to prevent buffer underrun)
- DVD+R (recordable DVD)

Early rewritable DVD drives supported either DVD-RW or DVD+RW, but recent DVD rewritable drives support DVD+/-R/RW media, and so-called "Super Multi" drives using an LG-designed drive mechanism add support for DVD-RAM media as well. As a result, you can now choose the best DVD media for the task.

The current standard and high-capacity DVD formats are shown in Table 11.21.

Table 11.21   Standard and High-Capacity DVD Formats and Capacities

Format	Data Size	Sides	Layers	Data Capacity	MPEG-2 Video Capacity
DVD-ROM Formats and Capacities					
DVD-5	120mm	Single	Single	4.7GB	2.2 hours
DVD-9	120mm	Single	Double	8.5GB	4.0 hours
DVD-10	120mm	Double	Single	9.4GB	4.4 hours
DVD-14	120mm	Double	Both	13.2GB	6.3 hours
DVD-18	120mm	Double	Double	17.1GB	8.1 hours
DVD-1	80mm	Single	Single	1.5GB	0.7 hours
DVD-2	80mm	Single	Double	2.7GB	1.3 hours
DVD-3	80mm	Double	Single	2.9GB	1.4 hours
DVD-4	80mm	Double	Double	5.3GB	2.5 hours
Recordable DVD Formats and Capacities					
DVD-R 1.0	120mm	Single	Single	3.95GB	1.9 hours
DVD-R 2.0	120mm	Single	Single	4.7GB	2.2 hours
DVD-R DL	120mm	Single	Double	8.5GB	4.0 hours
DVD-RAM 1.0	120mm	Single	Single	2.58GB	N/A
DVD-RAM 1.0	120mm	Double	Single	5.16GB	N/A
DVD-RAM 2.0	120mm	Single	Single	4.7GB	N/A
DVD-RAM 2.0	120mm	Double	Single	9.4GB	N/A
DVD-RAM 2.0	80mm	Single	Single	1.46GB	N/A
DVD-RAM 2.0	80mm	Double	Single	2.65GB	N/A
DVD-RW 2.0	120mm	Single	Single	4.7GB	N/A
DVD+RW 2.0	120mm	Single	Single	4.7GB	2.2hours
DVD+RW 2.0	120mm	Double	Single	9.4GB	4.4 hours
DVD+R 1.0	120mm	Single	Single	4.7GB	2.2 hours
DVD+R DL	120mm	Single	Double	8.5GB	4.0 hours
High Capacity DVD Formats and Capacities					
HD DVD-ROM	120mm	Single	Single	15GB	4.0 hours HD
HD DVD-ROM	120mm	Single	Double	30GB	8.0 hours HD
HD DVD-R	120mm	Single	Single	15GB	4.0 hours HD
HD DVD-RW	120mm	Single	Single	20GB, 32GB	5.5/8.4 hours HD
Blu-Ray	120mm	Single	Single	25GB	4.5 hours HD
Blu-Ray	120mm	Single	Double	50GB	9 hours HD
CD-ROM Formats and Capacities (for Comparison)					
CD-ROM/R/RW	120mm	Single	Single	0.737GB	N/A
CD-ROM/R/RW	80mm	Single	Single	0.194GB	N/A

HD – HD TV (720p, 1080i, or 1080p resolutions)

DVD drives are fully backward-compatible and as such are capable of playing today's CD-ROMs as well as audio CDs. When playing existing CDs, the performance of current models is equivalent to a 40x or faster CD-ROM drive. DVD-rewritable drives, which also fully support CD formats, have replaced CD-RW drives at virtually every price point in both new systems and as upgrades at retail (a few very low-cost systems still include combo DVD-ROM/CD-RW drives, but expect to see these disappear by 2008). The main reason to use CD media instead of DVD media at this point is for near-universal compatibility (especially when CD-R discs are used) with both older and recent systems.

With the development of Blu-ray and HD DVD, rewritable Blu-ray drives with backward-compatibility with DVD and CD media are now available (some also have read compatibility with HD DVD). These drives are much more expensive than rewritable DVD drives, however, and until the availability of low-cost media and more movies in Blu-ray and HD DVD formats increase, these drives will continue to represent a very small percentage of the rewritable optical drive market.

DIVX (Discontinued Standard)

DIVX (Digital Video Express) was a short-lived proprietary DVD format developed by Digital Video Express (a Hollywood law firm) and Circuit City. It was discontinued on June 16, 1999, less than a year after it was released.

The name now lives on as an open encoding standard for DVD video. However, this encoding standard actually has no relation to the original DIVX format other than the name.

Note

More detailed coverage of DIVX is included in Chapter 13 of the 11th and 12th editions of this book.

DVD Drive Compatibility

When DVD drives first appeared on the market, they were touted to be fully backward-compatible with CD-ROM drives. Although that might be the case when reading commercially pressed CD-ROM discs, that was not necessarily true when reading CD-R or CD-RW media. Fortunately, the industry has responded with standards that let you know in advance how compatible your DVD drive will be. These standards are called *MultiRead* for computer-based drives and *MultiPlay* for consumer standalone devices, such as DVD-Video or CD-DA players. See the section "MultiRead Specifications," later in this chapter.

DVD Movie Playback on a PC

Almost all DVD-ROM and rewritable DVD drives (except for some DVD-RAM drives) include a DVD playback program such as MyDVD or SoftDVD. These programs enable you to interact with a DVD movie the same way you would if it were being played through a DVD player. All recent ATI and NVIDIA chipsets support MPEG-2 decoding in hardware for high-quality DVD movie playback. If your computer has a 1GHz or faster processor, you do not need a separate MPEG-2 hardware decoder card.

DVD Copy Protection

DVD-Video discs employ several levels of protection that are mainly controlled by the DVD Copy Control Association (DVD CCA) and a third-party company called Macrovision. This protection typically applies only to DVD-Video discs, not DVD-ROM software. So, for example, copy protection might affect your ability to make backup copies of *The Matrix*, but it won't affect a DVD encyclopedia or other software application distributed on DVD-ROM discs.

Note that every one of these protection systems has been broken, so with a little extra expense or the correct software, you can defeat the protection and make copies of your DVDs either to other digital media (hard drive, DVD+RW, CD-R/RW, and so on) or analog media (such as a VHS or other tape format).

A lot of time and money are wasted on these protection schemes, which can't really foil the professional bootleggers willing to spend the time and money to work around them. But they can make it difficult for the average person to legitimately back up his expensive media.

The four main protection systems used with DVD-Video discs are as follows:

- Regional Playback Control (RPC)
- Content Scrambling System (CSS)
- Analog Protection System (APS)
- ProtectDisc

Caution

The Digital Millennium Copyright Act (DMCA) signed into law in 1998 prohibits the breaking of copy-protection schemes or the distribution of information (such as tools, website links, and so forth) on how to break these schemes.

Regional Playback Control

Regional playback was designed to allow discs sold in specific geographical regions of the world to play only on players sold in those same regions. The idea was to allow a movie to be released at different times in different parts of the world and to prevent people from ordering discs from regions in which the movie had not been released yet.

Eight regions are defined in the RPC standard. Discs (and players) usually are identified by a small logo or label showing the region number superimposed on a world globe. Multiregion discs are possible, as are discs that are not region locked. If a disc plays in more than one region, it has more than one number on the globe. The regions are

- **Region Code 1**—United States, Canada, U.S. Territories
- **Region Code 2**—Japan, Europe, South Africa, and the Middle East
- **Region Code 3**—Southeast Asia and East Asia
- **Region Code 4**—Australia, New Zealand, Pacific Islands, Central America, Mexico, South America, and the Caribbean
- **Region Code 5**—Eastern Europe (east of Poland and the Balkans), Indian subcontinent, Africa, North Korea, and Mongolia
- **Region Code 6**—China and Tibet
- **Region Code All**—Special international or mobile venues, such as airplanes, cruise ships, and so on

The region code is embedded in the hardware of DVD video players. Most players are preset for a specific region and can't be changed. Some companies who sell the players modify them to play discs from all regions; these are called *region-free* or *code-free* players. Some newer discs have an added region code enhancement (RCE) function that checks to see whether the player is configured for multiple or all regions and then, if it is, refuses to play. Most newer region-free modified players know how to query the disc first to circumvent this check as well.

DVD-ROM drives used in PCs originally did not have RPC in the hardware, placing that responsibility instead on the software used to play DVD video discs on the PC. The player software would usually lock the region code to the first disc that was played and then from that point on, play only discs from that region. Reinstalling the software enabled the region code to be reset, and numerous patches were posted on websites to enable resetting the region code even without reinstalling the software. Because of the relative ease of defeating the region-coding restrictions with DVD-ROM drives, starting on January 1, 2000, all DVD-ROM and rewritable DVD drives were required to have RPC-II, which embeds the region coding directly into the drive.

RPC-II (or RPC-2) places the region lock in the drive, and not in the playing or MPEG-2 decoding software. You can set the region code in RPC-II drives up to five times total, which basically means you can change it up to four times after the initial setting. Usually, the change can be made using the player software you are using, or you can download region change software from the drive manufacturer. Upon making the fourth change (which is the fifth setting), the drive is locked on the last region set.

Region Codes Used by Blu-ray Disc

A different region code that divides the world into three regions is used by Blu-ray Disc:

- Region A includes North America, Central America, South America, Korea, Japan, and South East Asia
- Region B includes Europe, the Middle East, Africa, Australia, and New Zealand
- Region C includes Russia, India, China, and the rest of the world

A Blu-ray disc without a region code can be played by players with any region code.

Content Scramble System

The Content Scramble System (CSS) provides the main protection for DVD-Video discs. It wasn't until this protection was implemented that the Motion Picture Association of America (MPAA) agreed to release movies in the DVD format, which is the main reason the rollout of DVD had been significantly delayed.

CSS originally was developed by Matsushita (Panasonic) and is used to digitally scramble and encrypt the audio and video data on a DVD-Video disc. Descrambling requires a pair of 40-bit (5-byte) keys (numeric codes). One of the keys is unique to the disc, whereas the other is unique to the video title set (VTS file) being descrambled. The disc and title keys are stored in the lead-in area of the disc in an encrypted form. The CSS scrambling and key writing are carried out during the glass mastering procedure, which is part of the disc manufacturing process.

You can see this encryption in action if you put a DVD disc into a DVD-ROM drive on a PC, copy the files to your hard drive, and then try to view the files. The files are usually called VTS_xx_yy.VOB (video object), where xx represents the title number and yy represents the section number. Typically, all the files for a given movie have the same title number and the movie is spread out among several 1GB or smaller files with different section numbers. These .VOB files contain both the encrypted video and audio streams for the movie interleaved together. Other files with an .IFO extension contain information used by the DVD player to decode the video and audio streams in the .VOB files. If you copy the .VOB and .IFO files onto your hard drive and try to click or play the .VOB files directly, you either see and hear scrambled video and audio or receive an error message about playing copy-protected files.

This encryption is not a problem if you use a CSS-licensed player (either hardware or software) and play the files directly from the DVD disc. All DVD players, whether they are consumer standalone units or software players on your PC, have their own unique CSS unlock key assigned to them. Every DVD video disc has 400 of these 5-byte keys stamped onto the disc in the lead-in area (which is not usually accessible by programs) on the DVD in encrypted form. The decryption routine in the player uses its unique code to retrieve and unencrypt the disc key, which is then used to retrieve and unencrypt the title keys. CSS is essentially a three-level encryption that originally was thought to be very secure but has proven otherwise.

In October 1999, a 16-year-old Norwegian programmer was able to extract the first key from one of the commercial PC-based players, which allowed him to very easily decrypt disc and title keys. A now famous program called DeCSS was then written that can break the CSS protection on any DVD video title and save unencrypted .VOB files to a hard disk that can be played by any MPEG-2 decoder program. Needless to say, this utility (and others based on it) has been the cause of much concern in the movie industry and has caused many legal battles over the distribution and even links to this code on the Web. Do a search on DeCSS for some interesting legal reading.

As if that weren't enough, in March 2001, two MIT students published an incredibly short (only seven lines long!) and simple program that can unscramble CSS so quickly that a movie can essentially be unscrambled in real time while it is playing. They wrote and demonstrated the code as part of a two-day seminar they conducted on the controversial Digital Millennium Copyright Act, illustrating how trivial the CSS protection really is.

Because of the failure of CSS, the DVD Forum is now actively looking into other means of protection, especially including digital watermarks, which consists essentially of digital noise buried into the data stream, which is supposed to be invisible to normal viewing. Unfortunately, when similar technology was applied to DIVX (the discontinued proprietary DVD standard), these watermarks caused a slight impairment of the image—a raindrop or bullet-hole effect could be seen by some in the picture. Watermarks also might require new equipment to play the discs.

Analog Protection System

APS (also called CopyGuard by Macrovision) is an analog protection system developed by Macrovision and is designed to prevent making VCR tapes of DVD-Video discs. APS requires codes to be added to the disc, as well as special modifications in the player. APS starts with the creation or mastering of a DVD, where APS is enabled by setting predefined control codes in the recording. During playback in an APS-enabled (Macrovision-enabled) player, the digital-to-analog converter (DAC) chip inside the player adds the APS signals to the analog output signal being sent to the screen. These additions to the signal are designed so that they are invisible when viewed on a television or monitor but cause copies made on most VCRs to appear distorted. Unfortunately, some TVs or other displays can react to the distortions added to create a less-than-optimum picture.

APS uses two signal modifications called automatic gain control and colorstripe. The automatic gain control process consists of pulses placed in the vertical scan interval of the video signal, which TVs can't detect but which cause dim and noisy pictures, loss of color, loss of video, tearing, and so forth on a VCR. This process has been used since 1985 on many prerecorded video tapes to prevent copying. The colorstripe process modifies colorburst information that is also transparent on television displays but produces lines across the picture when recorded on a VCR.

Note that many older players don't have the licensed Macrovision circuits and simply ignore the code to turn on the APS signal modifications. Also, various image stabilizer, enhancer, or copyguard decoder units are available that can plug in between the player and VCR to remove the APS copyguard signal and allow a perfect recording to be made.

ProtectDisc

The newest copy protection system is called ProtectDisc. Its DVD-Video version changes the standard structure of the disc to prevent copying. Unfortunately, a DVD movie created using ProtectDisc cannot be viewed with PC-based player programs such as Windows Media Player or WinDVD.

Despite the claims of "unbreakable" copy protection, ProtectDisc's method, like the others discussed here, was quickly overcome. As with other copy protection schemes, legitimate users who don't try to "beat the system" are winding up victimized—in the case of ProtectDisk, by being unable to use a PC to watch the movie.

CD/DVD Read-only Drives and Specifications

Although rewritable DVD drives have largely replaced CD-ROM or DVD-ROM drives, you may still want to install a DVD-ROM drive alongside your rewritable DVD drive to permit disc-to-disc backup. Whether you are evaluating a CD-ROM, DVD-ROM or a rewritable CD or DVD drive for your system, you should consider three distinct sets of criteria, as follows:

- The drive's performance specifications
- The interface the drive requires for connection to your PC
- The physical disc-handling system the drive uses

These criteria will affect how fast the drive operates, how it is connected to your system, and how convenient (or inconvenient) it is to use. These same criteria, plus media and speed issues, are also important considerations when selecting a rewritable drive.

Performance Specifications

Many factors in a drive can affect performance, and several specifications are involved. Typical performance figures published by manufacturers are the data transfer rate, the access time, the internal cache or buffers (if any), and the interface the drive uses. The following sections examine these specifications.

CD Data Transfer Rate

The data transfer rate for a CD-ROM or CD-RW drive tells you how quickly the drive can read from the disc and transfer to the host computer. Normally, transfer rates indicate the drive's capability for reading large, sequential streams of data.

Transfer speed is measured two ways. The one most commonly quoted with CD/DVD drives is the "x" speed, which is defined as a multiple of the particular standard base rate. For example, CD-ROM drives transfer at 153.6KBps according to the original standard. Drives that transfer twice that are 2x, 40 times that are 40x, and so on. DVD drives transfer at 1,385KBps at the base rate, whereas drives that are 20 times faster than that are listed as 20x. Note that because almost all faster drives feature CAV, the "x" speed usually indicated is a maximum that is seen only when reading data near the outside (end) of a disc. The speed near the beginning of the disc might be as little as half that, and of course, average speeds are somewhere in the middle.

With today's optical drives supporting multiple disc formats, multiple read and write specifications are given for each form of media a drive supports. Drives that read from and write to CD-R and CD-RW media typically can read and write at speeds between 4x and 48x (CAV).

CD Drive Speed

When a drive seeks out a specific data sector or musical track on the disc, it looks up the address of the data from a table of contents contained in the lead-in area and positions itself near the beginning of this data across the spiral, waiting for the right string of bits to flow past the laser beam.

Because CDs originally were designed to record audio, the speed at which the drive reads the data had to be constant. To maintain this constant flow, CD-ROM data is recorded using a technique called *constant linear velocity (CLV)*. This means that the track (and thus the data) is always moving past the read laser at the same speed, which originally was defined as 1.3 meters per second. Because the track is a spiral that is wound more tightly near the center of the disc, the disc must spin at various rates to maintain the same track linear speed. In other words, to maintain a CLV, the disk must spin more quickly when reading the inner track area than when reading the outer track area. The speed of rotation in a 1x drive (1.3 meters per second is considered 1x speed) varies from 540 rpm when reading the start (inner part) of the track down to 212 rpm when reading the end (outer part) of the track.

In the quest for greater performance, drive manufacturers began increasing the speeds of their drives by making them spin more quickly. A drive that spins twice as fast was called a 2x drive, one that spins four times faster was called 4x, and so on. This was fine until about the 12x point, where drives were spinning discs at rates from 2,568 rpm to 5,959 rpm to maintain a constant data rate. At higher speeds than this, it became difficult to build motors that could change speeds (spin up or down) as quickly as necessary when data was read from different parts of the disc. Because of this, most drives rated faster than 12x spin the disc at a fixed rotational, rather than linear speed. This is termed *constant angular velocity (CAV)* because the angular velocity (or rotational speed) remains a constant.

CAV drives are also generally quieter than CLV drives because the motors don't have to try to accelerate or decelerate as quickly. A drive (such as most rewritables) that combines CLV and CAV technologies is referred to as *Partial-CAV* or *P-CAV*. Most writable drives, for example, function in CLV mode when burning the disc and in CAV mode when reading. Table 11.22 compares CLV and CAV.

Table 11.22   CLV Versus CAV Technology Quick Reference

	CLV (Constant Linear Velocity)	CAV (Constant Angular Velocity)
Speed of CD rotation	Varies with data position on CD—faster on inner tracks than on outer tracks	Constant
Data transfer rate	Constant	Varies with data position on CD—faster on outer tracks than on inner tracks
Average noise level	Higher	Lower

CD-ROM drives have been available in speeds from 1x up to 52x and beyond. Most nonrewritable drives up to 12x were CLV; most drives from 16x and up are CAV. With CAV drives, the disc spins at a constant speed, so track data moves past the read laser at various speeds, depending on where the data is physically located on the CD (near the inner or outer part of the track). This also means that CAV drives read the data at the outer edge (end) of the disk more quickly than data near the center (beginning). This allows for some misleading advertising. For example, a 12x CLV drive reads data at 1.84MBps no matter where that data is on the disc. On the other hand, a 16x CAV drive reads data at speeds up to 16x (2.46MBps) on the outer part of the disc, but it also reads at a much lower speed of only 6.9x (1.06MBps) when reading the inner part of the disc (that is the part they don't tell you). On average, this would be only 11.5x, or about 1.76MBps. In fact, the average is actually overly optimistic because discs are read from the inside (slower part) out, and an average would relate only to reading completely full discs. The real-world average could be much less than that.

What this all means is that on average the 12x CLV drive would be noticeably faster than the 16x drive, and faster than even a 20x drive! Remember that all advertised speeds on CAV drives are only the maximum transfer speed the drive can achieve, and it can achieve that only when reading the very outer (end) part of the disc.

Table 11.23 contains data showing CD-ROM drive speeds along with transfer rates and other interesting data. This information also applies to DVD-ROM and rewritable DVD drives when CDs are used.

Vibration problems can cause high-speed drives to drop to lower speeds to enable reliable reading of CD-ROMs. Your CD-ROM can become unbalanced, for example, if you apply a small paper label to its surface to identify the CD or affix its serial number or code for easy reinstallation. For this reason, many of the faster CD and DVD drives come with autobalancing or vibration-control mechanisms to overcome these problems. The only drawback is that if they detect a vibration, they slow down the disc, thereby reducing the transfer rate performance.

Most recent CD and DVD drives use Z-CLV (zoned CLV) or P-CAV (partial CAV) designs, which help increase average performance while keeping rotational speeds under control.

Table 11.23   CD-ROM Drive Speeds and Transfer Rates

Advertised CD-ROM Speed (Max. if CAV)	Time to Read 74-Minute CD if CLV	Time to Read 80-Minute CD if CLV	Transfer Rate (Bps) (Max. if CAV)	Actual CD-ROM Speed Minimum in CAV	Minimum Transfer Rate if CAV (Bps)
1x	74.0	80.0	153,600	0.4x	61,440
2x	37.0	40.0	307,200	0.9x	138,240
4x	18.5	20.0	614,400	1.7x	261,120
6x	12.3	13.3	921,600	2.6x	399,360
8x	9.3	10.0	1,228,800	3.4x	522,240
10x	7.4	8.0	1,536,000	4.3x	660,480
12x	6.2	6.7	1,843,200	5.2x	798,720
16x	4.6	5.0	2,457,600	6.9x	1,059,840
20x	3.7	4.0	3,072,000	8.6x	1,320,960
24x	3.1	3.3	3,686,400	10.3x	1,582,080
32x	2.3	2.5	4,915,200	13.8x	2,119,680
40x	1.9	2.0	6,144,000	17.2x	2,641,920
48x	1.5	1.7	7,372,800	20.7x	3,179,520
50x	1.5	1.6	7,680,000	21.6x	3,317,760
52x	1.4	1.5	7,987,200	22.4x	3,440,640
56x	1.3	1.4	8,601,600	24.1x	3,701,760

Each of the columns in Table 11.23 is explained here:

Column 1 indicates the advertised drive speed. This is a constant speed if the drive is CLV (most 12x and lower) or a maximum speed only if CAV.

Columns 2 and 3 indicate how long it would take to read a full disc if the drive was CLV. For CAV drives, those figures would be longer because the average read speed is less than the advertised speed. The fourth column indicates the data transfer rate, which for CAV drives would be a maximum figure only when reading the end of a disc.

Columns 3–6 indicate the actual minimum "x" speed for CAV drives, along with the minimum transfer speed (when reading the start of any disc) and an optimistic average speed (true only when reading a full disc; otherwise, it would be even lower) in both "x" and byte-per-second formats.

Note

A company called Zen Research developed a technology called TrueX in the late 1990s, which used multiple laser beams to achieve constant high transfer rates with lower spin rates. Unfortunately, TrueX drives made by vendors such as Kenwood didn't live up to the promised performance of TrueX technology and suffered from many reliability problems. Zen Research closed in mid-2002, and TrueX drives are no longer sold.

DVD Drive Speed

As with CDs, DVDs rotate counterclockwise (as viewed from the reading laser) and typically are recorded at a constant data rate called CLV. Therefore, the track (and thus the data) is always moving past the read laser at the same speed, which originally was defined as 3.49 meters per second (or 3.84mps on dual-layer discs). Because the track is a spiral that is wound more tightly near the center

Average CD-ROM Speed if CAV	Average Transfer Rate if CAV (Bps)	Maximum Linear Speed (mps)	Maximum Linear Speed (mph)	Rotational Speed Min. if CLV Max. if CAV (rpm)	Rotational Speed Max. if CLV (rpm)
0.7x	107,520	1.3	2.9	214	497
1.5x	222,720	2.6	5.8	428	993
2.9x	437,760	5.2	11.6	856	1,986
4.3x	660,480	7.8	17.4	1,284	2,979
5.7x	875,520	10.4	23.3	1,712	3,973
7.2x	1,098,240	13.0	29.1	2,140	4,966
8.6x	1,320,960	15.6	34.9	2,568	5,959
11.5x	1,758,720	20.8	46.5	3,425	7,945
14.3x	2,196,480	26.0	58.2	4,281	9,931
17.2x	2,634,240	31.2	69.8	5,137	11,918
22.9x	3,517,440	41.6	93.1	6,849	15,890
28.6x	4,392,960	52.0	116.3	8,561	19,863
34.4x	5,276,160	62.4	139.6	10,274	23,835
35.8x	5,498,880	65.0	145.4	10,702	24,828
37.2x	5,713,920	67.6	151.2	11,130	25,821
40.1x	6,151,680	72.8	162.8	11,986	27,808

Columns 7–8 indicate the maximum linear speeds the drive will attain, in both meters per second and miles per hour. CLV drives maintain those speeds everywhere on the disc, whereas CAV drives reach those speeds only on the outer part of a disc.

Columns 9–12 indicate the rotational speeds of a drive. The first of these shows how fast the disc spins when being reading from the start; this applies to either CAV or CLV drives. For CAV drives, the figure is constant no matter where on the disc it is being read. The last column shows the maximum rotational speed if the drive were a CLV type. Because most drives over 12x are CAV, these figures are mostly theoretical for the 16x and faster drives.

of the disc, the disc must spin at varying rates to maintain the same track linear speed. In other words, to maintain a CLV, the disk must spin more quickly when reading the inner track area and more slowly when reading the outer track area. The speed of rotation in a 1x drive (3.49 meters per second is considered 1x speed) varies from 1,515 rpm when reading the start (inner part) of the track down to 570 rpm when reading the end (outer part) of the track.

Single-speed (1x) DVD-ROM drives provide a data transfer rate of 1.385MBps, which means the data transfer rate from a DVD-ROM at 1x speed is roughly equivalent to a 9x CD-ROM (1x CD-ROM data transfer rate is 153.6KBps, or 0.1536MBps). This does not mean, however, that a 1x DVD drive can read CDs at 9x rates: DVD drives actually spin at a rate that is just under three times faster than a CD-ROM drive of the same speed. So, a 1x DVD drive spins at about the same rotational speed as a 2.7x CD drive. Many DVD drives list two speeds, one for reading DVDs and another for reading CDs. For example, a DVD-ROM drive listed as a 16x/40x would indicate the performance when reading DVDs/CDs, respectively.

Table 11.24   DVD Speeds and Transfer Rates

Advertised CD-ROM Speed (Max. if CAV)	Time to Read 74-Minute CD if CLV	Time to Read 80-Minute CD if CLV	Transfer Rate (Bps) (Max. if CAV)	Actual CD-ROM Speed Minimum in CAV	Minimum Transfer Rate if CAV (Bps)	
1x	56.5	51.4	1,384,615	0.4x	553,846	0.7x
2x	28.3	25.7	2,769,231	0.8x	1,107,692	1.4x
4x	14.1	12.8	5,538,462	1.7x	2,353,846	2.9x
6x	9.4	8.6	8,307,692	2.5x	3,461,538	4.3x
8x	7.1	6.4	11,076,923	3.3x	4,569,231	5.7x
10x	5.7	5.1	13,846,154	4.1x	5,676,923	7.1x
12x	4.7	4.3	16,615,385	5.0x	6,923,077	8.5x
16x	3.5	3.2	22,153,846	6.6x	9,138,462	11.3
20x	2.8	2.6	27,692,308	8.3x	11,492,308	14.2
24x	2.4	2.1	33,230,769	9.9x	13,707,692	17.0
32x	1.8	1.6	44,307,692	13.2x	18,276,923	22.6
40x	1.4	1.3	55,384,615	16.6x	22,984,615	28.3
48x	1.2	1.1	66,461,538	19.9x	27,553,846	34.0
50x	1.1	1.0	69,230,769	20.7x	28,661,538	35.4

Column 1 indicates the advertised drive speed. This is a constant speed if the drive is CLV or a maximum speed only if CAV (most DVD-ROM drives are CAV).

Columns 2 and 3 indicate how long it would take to read a full disc (single- or dual-layer) if the drive were CLV. For CAV drives, those figures are longer because the average read speed is less than the advertised speed. The fourth column indicates the data transfer rate, which for CAV drives is a maximum figure seen only when reading the end of a disc.

Columns 4--8 indicate the actual minimum "x" speed for CAV drives, along with the minimum transfer speed (when reading the start of any disc) and an optimistic average speed (true only when reading a full disc; otherwise, it's even lower) in both "x" and byte-per-second formats.

Columns 9 and 10 indicate the maximum linear speeds the drive attains, in both meters per second and miles per hour. CLV drives maintain those speeds everywhere on the disc, whereas CAV drives reach those speeds only on the outer part of a disc.

As with CDs, drive manufacturers began increasing the speeds of their drives by making them spin more quickly. A drive that spins twice as fast was called a 2x drive, a drive that spins four times as fast was 4x, and so on. At higher speeds, it became difficult to build motors that could change speeds (spin up or down) as quickly as needed when data was read from different parts of the disc. Because of this, faster DVD drives spin the disc at a fixed rotational, rather than linear speed. This is termed *constant angular velocity (CAV)* because the angular velocity (or rotational speed) remains a constant.

The faster drives are useful primarily for data, not video. Having a faster drive can reduce or eliminate the pause during layer changes when playing a DVD video disc, but having a faster drive has no effect on video quality.

DVD-ROM drives have been available in speeds up to 20x or more, but because virtually all are CAV, they actually achieve the rated transfer speed only when reading the outer part of a disc. Table 11.24 shows the data rates for DVD drives reading DVDs and how that rate compares to a CD-ROM drive.

Average CD-ROM Speed if CAV	Average Transfer Rate if CAV (Bps)	Maximum Linear Speed (mps)	Maximum Linear Speed (mph)	Rotational Speed Min. if CLV Max. if CAV (rpm)	Rotational Speed Max. if CLV (rpm)
969,231	3.5	7.8	570	1,515	2.7x
1,938,462	7.0	15.6	1,139	3,030	5.4x
3,946,154	14.0	31.2	2,279	6,059	11x
5,884,615	20.9	46.8	3,418	9,089	16x
7,823,077	27.9	62.5	4,558	12,119	21x
9,761,538	34.9	78.1	5,697	15,149	27x
11,769,231	41.9	93.7	6,836	18,178	32x
15,646,154	55.8	124.9	9,115	24,238	43x
19,592,308	69.8	156.1	11,394	30,297	54x
23,469,231	83.8	187.4	13,673	36,357	64x
31,292,308	111.7	249.8	18,230	48,476	86x
39,184,615	139.6	312.3	22,788	60,595	107x
47,007,692	167.5	374.7	27,345	72,714	129x
48,946,154	174.5	390.3	28,485	75,743	134x

Columns 11 and 12 indicate the rotational speeds of a drive. The first of these shows how quickly the disc spins when being read from the start. This applies to either CAV or CLV drives. For CAV drives, the figure is constant no matter where on the disc it is being read. The second of these two columns shows the maximum rotational speed if the drive were a CLV type. Because most faster drives are CAV, these figures are mostly theoretical for the faster drives.

Column 13 shows the speed the drive would be rated if it were a CD-ROM drive. This is based on the rotational speed, not the transfer rate. In other words, a 12x DVD drive would perform as a 32x CD-ROM drive when reading CDs. Most DVD drives list their speeds when reading CDs in the specifications. Due to the use of PCAV (Partial CAV) designs, some might have higher CD performances than the table indicates.

Access Time

The access time for a CD or DVD drive is measured the same way as for PC hard disk drives. In other words, the access time is the delay between the drive receiving the command to read and its actual first reading of a bit of data. The time is recorded in milliseconds; a typical manufacturer's rating would be listed as 95ms. This is an average access rate; the true access rate depends entirely on where the data is located on the disc. When the read mechanism is positioned to a portion of the disc nearer to the narrower center, the access rate is faster than when it is positioned at the wider outer perimeter. Access rates quoted by many manufacturers are an average taken by calculating a series of random reads from a disc.

Obviously, a faster (that is, a lower) average access rate is desirable, especially when you rely on the drive to locate and pull up data quickly. Access times for CD and DVD drives have been steadily improving, and the advancements are discussed later in this chapter. Note that these average times are significantly slower than PC hard drives, running around 130-160ms for both CD and DVD media in current drive models, compared to the 8ms access time of a typical hard disk drive. Most of the speed difference lies in the construction of the drive itself. Hard drives have multiple-read heads that range over a smaller surface area of the medium; CD/DVD drives have only one laser pickup, and it must be capable of accessing the entire range of the disc. In addition, the data on a CD is organized in a single long spiral. When the drive positions its head to read a track, it must estimate the distance into the disc and skip forward or backward to the appropriate point in the spiral. Reading off the outer edge requires a longer access time than the inner segments, unless you have a CAV drive, which spins at a constant rate so the access time to the outer tracks is equal to that of the inner tracks.

Buffer/Cache

Most CD/DVD drives include internal buffers or caches of memory installed onboard. These buffers are actual memory chips installed on the drive's circuit board that enable it to stage or store data in larger segments before sending it to the PC. A typical buffer for a CD-ROM drive is 128KB, although drives are available that have either more or less (more is usually better). DVD-ROM drives usually have 256KB buffers. Recordable CD or DVD drives typically have much larger buffers of 2MB–8MB or more to prevent buffer underrun problems and to smooth writing operations. Generally, faster drives come with more buffer memory to handle the higher transfer rates. Combo DVD-ROM/CD-RW drives usually have buffers of 1.5–2MB. Including buffer or cache memory in CD/DVD drives offers a number of advantages. Buffers can ensure that the PC receives data at a constant rate; when an application requests data from the drive, the data can be found in files scattered across different segments of the disc. Because the drive has a relatively slow access time, the pauses between data reads can cause a drive to send data to the PC sporadically. You might not notice this in typical text applications, but on a drive with a slower access rate coupled with no data buffering, it is very noticeable—and even irritating—during the display of video or some audio segments. In addition, a drive's buffer, when under the control of sophisticated software, can read and have ready the disc's table of contents, speeding up the first request for data.

CPU Utilization

A once-neglected but very real issue in calculating computer performance is the impact that any piece of hardware or software has on the central processing unit (CPU). This "CPU utilization" factor refers to how much attention the CPU (such as Core Duo, Athlon 64 x2, and so on) must provide to the hardware or software to help it work. A low CPU utilization percentage score is desirable because the less time a CPU spends on any given hardware or software process, the more time it has for other tasks and thus the greater the performance for your system. On CD-ROM drives, three factors influence CPU utilization: drive speed, drive buffer size, and interface type.

Drive buffer size can influence CPU utilization. For CD-ROM drives with similar performance ratings, the drive with a larger buffer is likely to require less CPU time (lower CPU utilization percentage) than the one with a smaller buffer.

Because drive speed and buffer size are more of a given, the most important factor influencing CPU utilization is the interface type. Before the use of busmastering ATA/IDE host adapters, SCSI CD-ROM drives featured far lower CPU utilization rates than ATAPI drives of similar ratings. One review of 12x drives done several years ago rated CPU utilization for ATAPI CD-ROM drives at 65%—80%, whereas SCSI CD-ROM drives checked in at less than 11%. By using DMA or Ultra-DMA modes with an ATA interface drive, near-SCSI levels of low CPU utilization can be realized.

Direct Memory Access and Ultra-DMA

Busmastering ATA controllers use Direct Memory Access (DMA) or Ultra-DMA transfers to improve performance and reduce CPU utilization. Virtually all modern ATA drives support Ultra-DMA. With busmastering, CPU utilization for ATA/ATAPI and SCSI CD-ROM drives is about equal at around 11%. Therefore, it's to your benefit to enable DMA access for your CD-ROM drives (and your ATA hard drives, too) if your system permits it.

Most recent ATA/ATAPI CD-ROM drives support DMA or Ultra-DMA transfers, as does Windows 95B and above and most recent Pentium-class or newer motherboards. To determine whether your Win9x, Me, XP, or Vista system has this feature enabled, open the Device Manager and click the + mark next to Hard Disk Controllers (known as IDE ATA/ATAPI Controllers in newer Windows versions). Some older drive interfaces capable of handling DMA transfers may list "Bus Master" in the name. However, with most recent systems, you will need to open the properties sheet for the controller to view its capabilities.

Next, check the hard drive and optical drive (CD/DVD) information for your system. You can use the properties sheet for your system's CD-ROM drives under Windows 9x/Me and Windows 2000/XP/ Vista to find this information; you might need to open the system to determine your hard drive brand and model on older Windows versions. Hard disk drives and CD or DVD drives that support MultiWord DMA Mode 2 (16.6MBps), UltraDMA Mode 2 (33MBps), UltraDMA Mode 4 (66MBps), or faster can use DMA transfers. Check your product literature or the manufacturer's website for information.

To enable DMA transfers if your motherboard and drives support it, open the Device Manager and then open the properties sheet for the controller or drive. Click the Settings or Advanced Settings tab, and make sure DMA is enabled if available. Depending on which version of Windows you are using, some have the DMA setting in the controller properties and others have it with the individual drives.

Repeat the same steps to enable DMA transfers for any additional hard drives and ATAPI CD-ROM drives in your computer. Restart your computer after making these changes.

Note

If your system hangs after you enable this feature, you must restart the system in Safe mode and uncheck the DMA box. Because DMA transfers bypass the CPU to achieve greater speed, DMA problems could result in data loss. Make backups first, instead of wishing you had later.

Also, if your drive is a parallel ATA model that supports any of the Ultra-DMA (also called Ultra-ATA) modes, you should be sure to use the 80-conductor-style ATA cables. Also be wary of using cables longer than the 18" limit according to the ATA standard. Using these cables prevents noise and signal distortion that will occur if you try to use a standard 40-conductor cable with the Ultra-DMA modes.

Most drives and motherboards refuse to enable Ultra-DMA modes faster than 33MBps if an 80-conductor cable is not detected. Note that these cabling issues affect only parallel ATA drives. If your drives are Serial ATA (SATA) models, these cabling issues do not apply.

Drive interfaces that don't mention busmastering either can't perform this speedup or need to have the correct driver installed. In some cases, depending on your Windows version and when your motherboard chipset was made, you must install chipset drivers to enable Windows to properly recognize the chipset and enable DMA modes. Virtually all motherboard chipsets produced since 1995 provide busmaster ATA support. Most of those produced since 1997 also provide UltraDMA support for up to 133MHz (Ultra ATA/133) speed operation. Still, you should make sure that DMA is enabled to ensure you are benefiting from the performance it offers. Enabling DMA can dramatically improve DVD performance, for example.

Interface

The drive's interface is the physical connection of the drive to the PC's expansion bus. The interface is the data pipeline from the drive to the computer, and its importance shouldn't be minimized. Six types of interfaces have been used for attaching a CD or DVD drive to your system:

- SATA (Serial ATA)
- ATA/ATAPI (AT Attachment/AT Attachment Packet Interface)
- USB port
- FireWire (IEEE 1394)
- SCSI/ASPI (Small Computer System Interface/Advanced SCSI Programming Interface)
- Parallel port

The following sections examine the SATA, ATA, USB, and FireWire interface choices. For more information on SCSI or Parallel, refer to Chapter 13 of *Upgrading and Repairing PCs, 16th Edition.*

SATA

The SATA interface is the same interface used by most recent computers for connecting their hard disk drives. With many recent systems featuring support for as little as one ATA/ATAPI drive, but support for eight or more SATA drives, many rewritable DVD drive vendors are now producing SATA versions of their ATA/ATAPI drives. Expect to see SATA rewritable DVD drives largely replace ATA/ATAPI drives over the next couple of years.

Compared to similar ATA/ATAPI rewritable DVD drives, SATA rewritable DVD drives feature equal performance, but are easier to install because it is not necessary to jumper the drive for master/slave or cable select. An SATA host adapter connects directly to an SATA drive.

SATA rewritable DVD drives typically work only with Windows XP and Windows Vista, so if you need to use a drive with older versions of Windows or with other operating systems, use an ATA/ATAPI optical drive if your system supports it.

SATA emulates ATA and ATAPI devices, enabling an SATA DVD drive to be used as a bootable device.

◀◀ See "An Overview of the IDE Interface," p. 581.

▶▶ See "Bootable CDs and DVDs—El Torito," p. 842.

ATA/ATAPI

The ATA/ATAPI (AT Attachment/AT Attachment Packet Interface) is an extension of the same ATA (AT Attachment) interface most older computers use to connect to their hard disk drives. ATA is sometimes also referred to as *IDE (Integrated Drive Electronics)*. ATAPI is an industry-standard ATA interface used for CD/DVD and other drives. ATAPI is a software interface that adapts the SCSI/ASPI commands to the ATA interfaceThis enables the ATA drives to remain compatible with the extensions that provide the CD/DVD drive with a software interface with DOS. With Windows 9x and later, the CD-ROM extensions are contained in the CD file system (CDFS) VxD (virtual device) driver.

ATA/ATAPI drives are sometimes also called enhanced IDE (EIDE) drives because this is an extension of the original IDE (technically the ATA) interface. On systems with two (or more) ATA/IDE host adapters, an ATA CD or DVD drive connects to the system via a second ATA interface connector and channel, leaving the primary one for hard disk drives only. This is preferable because ATA does not share the single channel well and would cause a hard disk drive to wait for CD/DVD commands to complete and vice versa. SCSI does not have this problem because a SCSI host adapter can send commands to different devices without having to wait for each previous command to complete.

If your system does not support SATA, the ATA interface represents the most cost-effective and high-performance interface for CD-ROM and DVD drives.

Virtually all systems on the market today can use the ATA/ATAPI CD/DVD drive as a bootable device, which allows the vendor to supply a recovery CD that can restore the computer's software to its factory-shipped condition. Later, you'll see how bootable CDs differ from ordinary CDs and how you can use low-cost CD-R/CD-RW drives, along with mastering and imaging software to make your own bootable CDs with your own preferred configuration.

◀◀   See "An Overview of the IDE Interface," p. 581.

▶▶   See "Bootable CDs and DVDs—El Torito," p. 842.

USB Interface

Universal Serial Bus (USB) has proven to be extremely flexible and has been used for everything from keyboards and joysticks to CD/DVD drives from several vendors.

USB 1.1 and earlier drives provide read and write transfer rates that match the fastest rates possible with IEEE 1284 parallel ports, with read rates on typical 6x models ranging from 1,145KBps to 1,200KBps. USB 2.0 and later provide a transfer rate up to 60MBps, which is 40 times faster than USB 1.1 and yet is fully backward-compatible.

USB also provides benefits that no parallel port drive can match: for example, hot-swappability, which is the capability to be plugged in or unplugged without removing the power or rebooting the system. Additionally, USB devices are fully Plug and Play, allowing the device to be automatically recognized by the system and the drivers automatically installed.

For Windows 98/Me or Windows 2000/XP/Vista systems with USB ports, USB-based DVD rewritable drives are an excellent solution for backup and archiving of data onto low-cost, durable optical media.

FireWire

In addition, external CD/DVD drives are now available on the market with a FireWire (also called IEEE 1394 or i.LINK) interface. FireWire is a high-performance external interface designed mainly for video use. It evolved as an Apple standard and is used primarily on Macintosh systems. Because few PCs include FireWire ports as a standard item—whereas all PCs include USB—I usually recommend the more universally supported USB for external CD/DVD drives. Make sure any external drives you purchase use the faster USB 2.0 (also known as Hi-Speed USB), which is faster and far more readily available than FireWire versions. FireWire drives can be useful if you work in a two-platform environment (both PCs and Macs). However, because most Macs also support USB (and you can easily add a USB interface to those that don't), if your primary platform is the PC, I'd still recommend USB over FireWire.

If you do want to use a FireWire drive and your system does not include FireWire integrated into the motherboard, you can easily add a FireWire interface card to your PC. Additionally, some video and sound cards are available with FireWire ports as an option.

▶▶ See "Universal Serial Bus," p. 1031, and "IEEE 1394," p. 1042.

Loading Mechanism

Three distinctly different mechanisms exist for loading a disc into a CD/DVD drive: the tray, caddy, and slot. Each one offers some benefits and features. Which type you select has a major impact on your use of the drive because you interact with this mechanism every time you load a disc.

Tray

Most current SATA, ATA/ATAPI, and SCSI CD/DVD drives use a tray-loading mechanism. This is similar to the mechanism used with a stereo system. Because you don't need to put each disc into a separate caddy, this mechanism is much less expensive overall. However, it also means that you must handle each disc every time you insert or remove it.

Tray loading is less expensive than a caddy system (see the next section, "Caddy") because you don't need a caddy. It is also more convenient, unless you have caddies for all your discs. However, this can make it much more difficult for young children or those who work in harsh environments to use the discs without smudging or damaging them due to excess handling.

The tray loader itself is also subject to damage. The trays can easily break if bumped or if something is dropped on them while they are extended. Also, any contamination you place on the tray or disc is brought right into the drive when the tray is retracted. Tray-loaded drives should not be used in a harsh environment, such as a commercial or an industrial application. Make sure both the tray and the data surface of the disc are clean whenever you use a tray-loading drive.

The tray mechanism also does not hold the disc as securely as the caddy. If you don't have the disc placed in the tray properly when it retracts, the disc or tray can be damaged. Even a slight misalignment can prevent the drive from reading the disc properly, forcing you to open the tray and reset the disc.

Some tray drives can't operate in a vertical (sideways) position because gravity prevents proper loading and operation. Check to see whether the drive tray has retaining clips that grab the hub of the disc or tabs that fold in or flip over from the outside of the tray to retain the disc. If so, you can run the drive in either a horizontal or vertical position.

The main advantage of the tray mechanism over the others is in cost, and that is a big factor. Most drives today use the tray mechanism for handling discs.

Caddy

At one time, the caddy system was used on most high-end CD-ROM drives as well as the early CD-R and DVD-RAM drives. The caddy system requires that you place the disc itself into a special caddy, which is a sealed container with a metal shutter. The caddy has a hinged lid you open to insert the disc, but after that the lid remains shut. When you insert the caddy containing the disc into the drive, the drive opens a metal shutter on the bottom of the caddy, allowing access to the disc by the laser.

When caddy-loaded drives were popular, they were extremely convenient to use if you had a caddy for each drive and extremely inconvenient if you shared a single caddy among all your media. The caddy was inserted into the drive, much the way you would insert a 3 1/2" floppy disk. The caddy protected the CD from scratches, contamination, and careless handling.

The drawbacks to the caddy system included the expense and the inconvenience of having to put the discs into the caddies.

When DVD-RAM was first introduced, the disc had to remain in a caddy because the recordable surface is delicate. Since then, DVD-RAM drives have been made caddy-less, but especially with double-sided discs the information is at risk every time you handle the disc. The caddy-loading system is no longer used in CD and DVD drive designs because of the convenience of the tray. Although the original design of Blu-ray used a caddy, improved protective coating over the data area enabled the designers of Blu-ray drives and media to eliminate the caddy,

Slot

Some drives now use a slot-loading mechanism, identical to that used in most automotive CD players. This is very convenient because you just slip the disc into the slot, where the mechanism grabs it and draws it inside. Some drives can load several CDs at a time this way, holding them internally inside the drive and switching discs as access is required.

The primary drawback to this type of mechanism is that if a jam occurs, it can be much more difficult to repair because you might have to remove the drive to free the disc. Another drawback is that slot-loading drives usually can't handle the smaller 80mm discs, card-shaped discs, or other modified disc physical formats or shapes, such as DualDisc.

DVD and CD Jukeboxes

Several years ago, some CD drive vendors produced internal multi-CD changers. These have become obsolete, but the basic idea of having multiple CDs and DVDs available has migrated from inside the PC (where size limitations prevented support for more than six discs per drive) to external devices that can hold hundreds of discs.

Many of these devices, such as the Niveus Ice Vault, Sony VGP-XL 1B series Media Changer, and others, are designed to hold DVD movies and CD audio for playback under Windows XP Media Center Edition or Windows Vista Ultimate's Media Center. These devices connect to the PC via the IEEE-1394a (FireWire, i.Link) interface.

For network use where CD and DVD data discs rather than movies or music need to be shared across a network, you will get faster performance with DVD-ROM or CD-ROM servers. These devices include several DVD-ROM or CD-ROM drives and a Fast Ethernet network adapter, enabling access from any other station on the network. If you need access to more CDs or DVDs than a tower can hold (and the media is not copy-protected), a disc-caching server copies CDs or DVDs to its hard disk, and provides access to the CD or DVD image to other stations on the network. DVD-ROM and CD-ROM towers are available from CD Dimensions (www.cddimensions.com), Kintronics (www.kintronics.com), JES Hardware Solutions (www.jescdrom.com), and others. DVD and CD servers are available in either tower or rack-mount versions.

Other Drive Features

Although drive specifications are of the utmost importance, you should also consider other factors and features when evaluating CD-ROM drives. Besides quality of construction, the following criteria bear scrutiny when making a purchasing decision:

- Drive sealing
- Self-cleaning lenses
- Internal versus external drive

Drive Sealing

Dirt is your CD/DVD drive's biggest enemy. Dust or dirt, when it collects on the lens portion of the mechanism, can cause read errors or severe performance loss. Many manufacturers seal off the lens and internal components from the drive bay in airtight enclosures. Other drives, although not sealed, have double dust doors—one external and one internal—to keep dust from the inside of the drive. All these features help prolong the life of your drive.

Some drives are sealed, which means no air flows through the chamber in which the laser and lens reside. Always look for sealed drives in harsh industrial or commercial environments. In a standard office or home environment, it is probably not worth the extra expense.

To determine if a particular drive is sealed, you may need to view FAQ or support questions considering drive cleaning; this information may not always be listed on the drives' spec sheet.

Self-cleaning Lenses

If the laser lens gets dirty, so does your data. The drive will spend a great deal of time seeking and reseeking or will finally give up. Lens-cleaning discs are available, but built-in cleaning mechanisms are now included on virtually all good-quality drives. This might be a feature you'll want to consider, particularly if you work in a less-than-pristine work environment or have trouble keeping your desk clean, let alone your drive laser lens. You can clean the lens manually, but it is generally a delicate operation requiring that you partially disassemble the drive. Also, damaging the lens mechanism by using too much force is pretty easy to do. Because of the risks involved, in most cases I do not recommend the average person disassemble and try to manually clean the laser lens.

Note

Before using a cleaning disc, check the drive vendor's recommendations to determine if this method of maintenance is recommended. Some vendors do not recommend the use of cleaning discs because the felt pads or brushes used can scratch the laser lens.

Internal Versus External Drives

When deciding whether you want an internal or external drive, think about where and how you're going to use your drive. What about the future expansion of your system? Both types of drives have advantages and disadvantages, such as the following:

- **External enclosure**—These tend to be rugged, portable, and large-in comparison to their internal versions. External drives are ideal for sharing a drive with multiple systems or especially with laptops or notebook portable systems. USB 2.0 (Hi-Speed USB) drives can be used on virtually any recent system. If you have an IEEE 1394 (FireWire, i.LINK) port and don't have a USB 2.0 port, this port type provides speed comparable to SCSI and USB 2.0 and the hot-swappability of USB. Some optical drives are now equipped with both USB 2.0 and IEEE 1394 ports.

- **Internal enclosure**—Internal drives won't take up any space on your desk. Buy an internal drive if you have a free drive bay and a sufficient power supply and you plan to keep the drive exclusively on one machine. The internal drives are also nice because you can connect the audio connector to your sound card and leave the external audio connectors free for other inputs. Internal drives are typically ATA/ATAPI, although many vendors are now producing SATA versions as the industry continues to move away from the ATA/ATAPI interface.

Writable CDs

Virtually all recent systems include rewritable CD or DVD drives (which can also write CDs). Although DVD rewritable media is now less expensive on a cost per megabyte basis, using CD-R and CD-RW media is still useful for transferring data to older systems. In fact, a CD-R recorded in a single session is the most compatible way to send data to another use.

CD recording has come a long way since 1988, when the first CD-R recording system was introduced at the cost of $50,000 (back then, they used a $35,000 Yamaha audio recording drive along with thousands of dollars of additional error correction and other circuitry for CD-ROM use), operated at 1x speed only, and was part of a subsystem that was the size of a washing machine! The blank discs also cost about $100 each—compared to less than 5 cents each in bulk cakebox form. (You provide your own jewel or slimline cases.) Originally, the main purpose for CD recording was to produce prototype CDs that could then be replicated via the standard stamping process.

In 1991, Philips introduced the first 2x recorder (the CDD 521), which was about the size of a stereo receiver and cost about $12,000. Sony in 1992 and then JVC in 1993 followed with their 2x recorders, and the JVC was the first drive that had the half-height 5 1/4" form factor that most desktop system drives still use today. In 1995, Yamaha released the first 4x recorder (the CDR100), which sold for $5,000. A breakthrough in pricing came in late 1995 when Hewlett-Packard released a 2x recorder (the 4020i, which was actually made for them by Philips) for under $1,000. This proved to be exactly what the market was waiting for. With a surge in popularity after that, prices rapidly fell to below $500, and then down to $200 or less. In 1996, Ricoh introduced the first CD-RW drive.

Today, most vendors have largely switched their production from CD-RW to rewritable DVD drives. However, these drives function exactly like a CD-RW drive, writing both CD-RW and CD-R media. If you need to create data backups that can be used on both recent and older systems, you can use CD media. However, if you want to store more on a disc, you can use DVD media.

Two main types of recordable CD discs are available, called CD-R (recordable) and CD-RW (rewritable). However, because the CD-RW discs are 1.5–2 times more expensive than CD-R discs, only half as fast (or less) as CD-R discs, and won't work in all CD audio or CD-ROM drives, people usually write to CD-R media in their CD-RW drives.

Note

Because of differences in reflectivity of the media, older CD and DVD drives can't read CD-RW media. Most newer CD or DVD-ROM drives conform to the MultiRead specification and as such can read CD-RWs. But many older drives are still out there that do not conform. As such, if you are recording something that many people or systems will need to read, CD-R is your best choice for overall compatibility.

CD-R media is a WORM (write once, read many) media, meaning that after you fill a CD-R with data, it is permanently stored and can't be erased. The write-once limitation makes this type of disc less than ideal for system backups or other purposes in which it would be preferable to reuse the same media over and over. However, because of the low cost of CD-R media, you might find that making permanent backups to essentially disposable CD-R discs is as economically feasible as tape or other media.

CD-RW discs can be reused up to 1,000 times, making them suitable for almost any type of data storage task. The following sections examine these two standards and how you can use them for your own data storage needs.

CD-R

Once recorded, CD-R discs can be played back or read in any standard CD-ROM drive. CD-R discs are useful for archival storage and creating master CDs, which can be duplicated for distribution within a company.

CD-Rs function using the same principle as standard CD-ROMs, by bouncing laser light off the disc and tracking the changes in reflectivity when pit/land and land/pit boundaries are encountered. The main difference is that instead of being stamped or embossed into plastic as on regular CDs, CD-Rs have images of pits burned onto a raised groove instead. Therefore, the pits are not really raised bumps like on a standard CD, but instead are rendered as dark (burned) areas on the groove that reflect less light. Because the overall reflectivity of pit and land areas remains the same as on a stamped disc, normal CD-ROM or CD audio drives can read CD-Rs exactly as if they were stamped discs.

Part of the recording process with CD-Rs starts before you even insert the disc into the drive. CD-R media is manufactured much like a standard CD—a stamper is used to mold a base of polycarbonate plastic. However, instead of stamping pits and lands, the stamper imprints a spiral groove (called a *pre-groove*), into the disc. From the perspective of the reading (and writing) laser underneath the disc, this groove is seen as a raised spiral ridge and not a depression.

The pre-groove (or ridge) is not perfectly straight; instead it has a slight wobble. The amplitude of the wobble is generally very small compared to the track pitch (spacing). The groove separation is 1.6 microns, but it wobbles only 0.030 microns from side to side. The wobble of a CD-R groove is modulated to carry supplemental information read by the drive. The signal contained in the wobble is called absolute time in pre-groove (ATIP) because it is modulated with time code and other data. The time code is the same minutes:seconds:frame format that will eventually be found in the Q-subcode of the frames after they are written to the disc. The ATIP enables the drive to locate positions on the disc before the frames are actually written. Technically, the wobble signal is frequency shift keyed with a carrier frequency of 22.05KHz and a deviation of 1KHz. The wobble uses changes in frequency to carry information.

To complete the CD-R disc, an organic dye is evenly applied across the disc by a spin-coating process. Next, a gold or silver reflective layer is applied (some early low-cost media used aluminum), followed by a protective coat of UV-cured lacquer to protect the reflective and dye layers. Gold or silver is used in recent and current CD-R discs to get the reflectivity as high as possible (gold is used in archival CD-Rs designed for very long-term storage), and it was found that the organic dye tends to oxidize aluminum. Then, silk-screen printing is applied on top of the lacquer for identification and further protection. When seen from the underside, the laser used to read (or write) the disc first passes through the clear polycarbonate and the dye layer, hits the gold layer where it is reflected back through the dye layer and the plastic, and finally is picked up by the optical pickup sensor in the drive.

The dye and reflective layer together have the same reflective properties as a *virgin* CD. In other words, a CD reader would read the groove of an unrecorded CD-R disc as one long land. To record on a CD-R disc, a laser beam of the same wavelength (780nm) as is normally used to read the disc, but with 10 times the power, is used to heat up the dye. The laser is fired in a pulsed fashion at the top of the ridge (groove), heating the layer of organic dye to between 482°F and 572°F (250°–300°C). This temperature literally burns the organic dye, causing it to become opaque. When read, this prevents the light from passing through the dye layer to the gold and reflecting back, having the same effect of canceling the laser reflection that an actual raised pit would on a normal stamped CD.

Figure 11.13 shows the CD-R media layers, along with the pre-groove (raised ridge from the laser perspective) with burned pits.

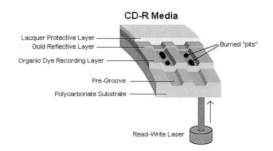

Figure 11.13 CD-R media layers.

The drive reading the disc is fooled into thinking a pit exists, but no actual pit exists—there's simply a spot of less-reflective material on the ridge. This use of heat to create the pits in the disc is why the recording process is often referred to as *burning* a CD. When burned, portions of the track change from a reflective to a nonreflective state. This change of state is permanent and can't be undone, which is why CD-R is considered a write-once medium.

CD-R Capacity

All CD-R drives can work with the standard 650MiB (682MB) CD-R media (equal to 74 minutes of recorded music), as well as the higher-capacity 700MiB (737MB) CD-R blanks (equal to 80 minutes of recorded music). The 80-minute discs cost only about 2 cents more than the 74-minute discs, so most would figure why not purchase only the higher-capacity media? Although the extra 55MB of storage can be useful and the cost difference is negligible, the 80-minute discs can actually be harder to read on older CD-ROM and CD-DA drives, especially car audio units. This is because to get the extra 55MB/6 minutes of capacity, the spiral track is wound a little more tightly, making them a bit more difficult to read. If you'll be using the discs for audio or interchange purposes and might be dealing with older equipment, you might want to stick with the 74-minute discs instead. If not, the 80-minute media will be just fine.

Some drives and burning software are capable of overburning, whereby they write data partially into the lead-out area and essentially extend the data track. This is definitely risky as far as compatibility is concerned. Many drives, especially older ones, fail when reading near the end of an overburned disc. It's best to consider this form of overclocking CDs somewhat experimental. It might be useful for your own purposes if it works with your drives and software, but interchangeability will be problematic.

Some vendors sell 90-minute (790MiB) and 99-minute (870MiB) media to make overburning easier. Although experiments performed by the Tom's Hardware website (www.tomshardware.com) indicate that most standard CD-RW drives can reliably burn up to 89:59 of music onto the 90-minute media and the CD-R can be played on a wide variety of auto and home electronics players, very few drives can burn a full 90 minutes or more of music (or the equivalent amount of computer data) to this media.

Tip

Wondering whether your drive can handle 90-minute or 99-minute media? Your drive vendor will probably say it can't, but the media compatibility list put together by DVD-Supply.com can provide a field-tested answer: http://www.dvd-supply.com/90—min-compatibility-chart.html

Check drive compatibility before you buy the longer media.

Note that Roxio (makers of Easy Media Creator and other CD mastering/writing programs) states that trying to write 90-minute or longer media could result in damage to the drive that is writing or reading the media.

CD-R Media Color

There has been some controversy over the years about which colors of CD-R media provide the best performance. Table 11.25 shows the most common color combinations, along with which brands use them and some technical information.

Some brands are listed with more than one color combination, due to production changes or different product lines. You should check color combinations whenever you purchase a new batch of CD-R media if you've found that particular color combinations work better for you in your applications.

Table 11.25   CD-R Media Color and Its Effect on Recording

Media Color (first color is reflective layer; second is die layer)	Brands	Technical Notes
Gold-gold	Mitsui, Kodak, Maxell, Ricoh	Phthalocyanine dye. Less tolerance for power variations. Has a rate life span of up to 100 years. Might be less likely to work in a wide variety of drives. Invented by Mitsui Toatsu Chemicals. Works best in drives that use a Long Write Strategy (longer laser pulse) to mark media.
Gold-green	Imation (nee 3M), Memorex, Kodak, BASF, TDK, Verbatim	Cyanine dye. More forgiving of disc-write and disc-read variations. Has a rated lifespan of 10 years (older media). Recent media has a rated lifespan of 20–50 years (silver/green). Color combination developed by Taiyo Yuden. Used in the development of the original CD-R standards. De facto standard for CD-R industry and was the original color-combination used during the development of CD-R technology. Works best in drives that use a Short Write Strategy (shorter laser pulse) to mark media.
Silver-blue	Verbatim,DataLifePlus, HiVal, Maxell, TDK	Process developed by Verbatim. Azo dye. Similar performance to green media, plus rated to last up to 100 years. A good choice for long-term archiving.

Note

Original Playstation games came on discs that were tinted black for appearance. Soon blank CD-R recordable discs were also available with this same black tint in the polycarbonate. The black tint is purely cosmetic—it is invisible to the infrared laser that reads/writes the disc. In other words, "black" CD-R discs are functionally identical to clear discs and can be made using any of the industry-standard dyes in the recording layer. The black tint hides the recording layer visually, so although the laser passes right through it, the black tint prevents you from observing the color of the dye in the recording layer directly.

Ultimately, although the various color combinations have their advantages, the best way to choose a media type is to try a major brand of media in your CD or DVD drive with both full-disc and small-disc recording jobs and then try the completed CD-R in as wide a range of CD-ROM drive brands and speeds as you can.

Note

If you are planning to record music mixes for use in auto CD players or portable CD players, be sure to test compatibility in these devices as well.

The perfect media for you will be the ones that offer you the following:

- High reliability in writing (check your drive model's list of recommended media)
- No dye or reflective surface dropouts (areas where the media won't record properly)
- Durability through normal handling (scratch-resistant coating on media surface)
- Compatibility across the widest range of CD-ROM drives
- Lowest unit cost

If you have problems recording reliably with certain types of media, or if you find that some brands with the same speed rating are much slower than others, contact your drive vendor for a firmware upgrade. Firmware upgrades can also help your drive recognize new types of faster media from different vendors.

▶▶ See "Updating the Firmware in a CD-RW or Rewritable DVD Drive," p. 847.

Choosing the Best Media

After you determine which media works best for you and your target drives, you might still be faced with a wide variety of choices, including conventional surface, printable surface, unbranded, jewel case, and bulk on spindle. The following list discusses these options:

- **Conventional surface**—Choose this type of media if you want to use a marker to label the CD rather than adding a paper label. This type of CD often has elaborate labeling, including areas to indicate CD title, date created, and other information as well as prominent brand identification. Because of the surface marking, it's not suitable for relabeling unless you use very opaque labels. It's a good choice for internal backups and data storage, though, where labeling is less important.

- **Printable surface**—Choose this type of media if you have a CD/DVD printer (a special type of inkjet printer that can print directly onto the face of the CD or DVD). The Epson R-series inkjet printers offer this capability, as well as some CD and DVD duplicators. Because the brand markings are usually low-contrast or even nonexistent (to allow overprinting), this type also works well with labeling kits such as NEATO and others. These are available in white or silver.

- **Unbranded**—Usually sold in bulk on spindle, these are good choices for economy or use with labeling kits.

- **Jewel case**—Any of the preceding versions can be sold with jewel cases (the same type of case used for CD-ROM software and music CDs). This is a good choice if you plan to distribute the media in a jewel case, but it raises your costs if you plan to distribute or store the media in paper, Tyvek, or plastic sleeves. Hint: Use extra jewel cases to replace your broken jewel cases in your CD software or music collection!

- **Slimline case**—This variation on the classic jewel case holds the CD and an information page in a thinner case. In fact, two slimline cases are as thick as a jewel case. Slimline cases are often harder to crack than jewel cases, but are not thick enough for a booklet.

- **Bulk on spindle**—This media generally comes with no sleeves and no cases. It is usually the lowest-priced packaging within any brand of media. This is an excellent choice for mass duplication, or for those who don't use jewel cases or slimline cases for distribution.

CD-R Media Recording Speed Ratings

With CD-R mastering speeds ranging from 1x (now-discontinued first-generation units) up through the latest state-of-the-art 48x–52x rates, it's important to check the speed rating (x-rating) of your CD-R media.

Most branded media on the market today is rated to work successfully at up to 52x recording speeds. Some brands indicate this specifically on their packaging, whereas you must check the websites for others to get this information. If necessary, install the latest firmware updates to reach maximum recording speed.

▶▶ See "Updating the Firmware in a CD-RW or Rewritable DVD Drive," p. 847.

Note

The current 52x CD-R recording speed is the fastest speed that will be achieved by CD-RW or rewritable DVD drives. Many vendors believe that the risk of damage to media and drives at faster spin rates and the technical difficulties in reliably recording data at higher speeds, plus the rising popularity of rewritable DVD, makes the 52x generation the last generation of CD-RW drives.

If speed ratings are unavailable for your media, you might want to restrict your burning to 32x or lower for data. If you are burning audio CDs, you might find that some devices work better with media burned at 8x or lower speeds than with media burned at higher speeds.

Tip

Some drives and mastering software support a setting that automatically determines the best speed to use for burning a CD-R. Software that supports this type of feature analyzes the media and adjusts writing methods and write speed during the write process to ensure the best results. Using this feature with media with an unknown speed rating helps you get a reliable burn no matter what the speed rating of the media is.

CD-RW

Beginning in early 1996, an industry consortium that included Ricoh, Philips, Sony, Yamaha, Hewlett-Packard, and Mitsubishi Chemical Corporation announced the CD-RW format. The design was largely led by Ricoh, and it was the first manufacturer to introduce a CD-RW drive in May 1996. This drive was the MP6200S, which was a 2/2/6 (2x record, 2x rewrite, 6x read) rated unit. At the same time, the Orange Book Part III was published, which officially defined the CD-RW standard.

CD-RW drives rapidly replaced CD-R-only drives, and although rewritable DVD drives have largely replaced CD-RW drives, any rewritable DVD drive can function as a CD-R/CD-RW drive.

CD-RW discs can be burned or written to just like CD-Rs; the main difference is that they can be erased and reburned again and again. They are very useful for prototyping a disc that will then be duplicated in less expensive CD-R or even stamped CDs for distribution. They can be rewritten at least 1,000 times or more. Additionally, with packet-writing software, they can even be treated like giant floppy disks, where you can simply drag and drop or copy and delete files at will. Although CD-RW discs are about 1.5×2 times more expensive than CD-R media, CD-RWs are still far cheaper than optical cartridges and other removable formats. This makes CD-RW a viable technology for system backups, file archiving, and virtually any other data storage task where rewritable DVD is not suitable.

Note

The CD-RW format originally was referred to as CD-Erasable, or CD-E.

Four main differences exist between CD-RW and CD-R media. In a nutshell, CD-RW discs are

- Rewritable
- More expensive
- Slower when writing
- Less reflective

Besides the CD-RW media being rewritable and costing a bit more, it is also writable at about half (or less) the speed of CD-R discs. This is because the laser needs more time to operate on a particular spot on the disk when writing. This media also has a lower reflectivity, which limits readability in older drives. Many older standard CD-ROM and CD-R drives can't read CD-RWs. However, MultiRead capability is now found in virtually all CD-ROM drives of 24x speed or above, enabling them to read CD-RWs without problems. In general, CD-DA drives—especially the car audio players-—seem to have the most difficulty reading CD-RWs. So, for music recording or compatibility with older drives, you should probably stick to CD-R media. Look for the MultiRead logo on a CD-ROM drive, which indicates the capability to read CD-RW. When you shop for a new standalone CD player, look for those that specify the capability to read CD-R/CD-RW media.

CD-RW drives and media use a phase-change process to create the illusion of pits on the disc. As with CD-R media, the disc starts out with the same polycarbonate base with a wobbled pre-groove molded in, which contains ATIP information. Then, on top of the base a special dielectric (insulating) layer is spin-coated, followed by the phase-change recording layer, another dielectric layer, an aluminum reflective layer, and finally a UV-cured lacquer protective layer (and optional screen printing). The dielectric layers above and below the recording layer are designed to insulate the polycarbonate and reflective layers from the intense heat used during the phase-change process.

Figure 11.14 shows the CD-RW media layers, along with the pre-groove (raised ridge from the laser perspective) with burned pits in the phase change layer.

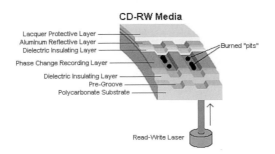

Figure 11.14 CD-RW media layers.

Instead of burning an organic dye as with CD-R, the recording layer in a CD-RW disc is made up of a phase-change alloy consisting of silver, indium, antimony, and tellurium (AgInSbTe). The reflective part of the recording layer is an aluminum alloy, the same as used in normal stamped discs. As a result, the recording side of CD-RW media looks like a mirror with a slight blue tint. The read/write laser works from the underside of the disk, where the groove again appears like a ridge, and the recording is made in the phase-change layer on top of this ridge. The recording layer of Ag-In-Sb-Te alloy normally has a polycrystalline structure that is about 20% reflective. When data is written to a CD-RW disc, the laser in the drive alternates between two power settings, called P-write and P-erase. The higher power setting (P-write) is used to heat the material in the recording layer to a temperature between 500°C and 700°C (932°–1,292°F), causing it to melt. In a liquid state the molecules of the material flow freely, losing their polycrystalline structure and taking what is called an *amorphous* (random) state. When the material then solidifies in this amorphous state, it is only about 5% reflective. When being read, these areas lower in reflectivity simulate the pits on a stamped CD-ROM disc.

That would be all to the story if CD-RW discs were read-only, but because they can be rewritten, there must be a way to bring the material back to a polycrystalline state. This is done by setting the laser to the lower-power P-erase mode. This heats the active material to approximately 200°C (392°F), which is well below the liquid melting point but high enough to soften the material. When the material is softened and allowed to cool more slowly, the molecules realign from a 5% reflective amorphous state back to a 20% reflective polycrystalline state. These higher reflective areas simulate the lands on a stamped CD-ROM disc.

Note that despite the name of the P-erase laser power setting, the disc is not ever explicitly "erased." Instead, CD-RW uses a recording technique called *direct overwrite*, in which a spot doesn't have to be erased to be rewritten; it is simply rewritten. In other words, when data is recorded the laser remains on and pulses between the P-write and P-erase power levels to create amorphous and polycrystalline areas of low and high reflectivity, regardless of which state the areas were in prior. It is similar in many ways to writing data on a magnetic disk that also uses direct overwrite. Every sector already has data patterns, so when you write data, all you are really doing is writing new patterns. Sectors are never really erased; they are merely overwritten. The media in CD-RW discs is designed to be written and rewritten up to 1,000 times.

CD-RW Speeds

The original Orange Book Part III Volume 1 (CD-RW specification) allowed for CD-RW writing at up to 4x speeds. New developments in the media and drives were required to support speeds higher than that. So in May 2000, Part III Volume 2 was published, defining CD-RW recording at speeds from 4x to 10x. This revision of the CD-RW standard is called High-Speed Rewritable, and both the discs and drives capable of CD-RW speeds higher than 4x will indicate this via the logos printed on them. Part III Volume 3 was published in September 2002 and defines Ultra-Speed drives, which are CD-RW drives capable of recording speeds 8x–24x.

Because of the differences in High-Speed and Ultra-Speed media, High-Speed media can be used only in High-Speed and Ultra-Speed drives; Ultra-Speed Media can be used only in Ultra-Speed drives. Both High-Speed and Ultra-Speed drives can use standard 2x–4x media, enabling them to interchange data with computers that have standard-speed CD-RW drives. Thus, choosing the wrong media to interchange with another system can prevent the other system from reading the media. If you don't know which speed of CD-RW media the target computer supports, I recommend you either use standard 2x–4x media or create a CD-R.

Because of differences in the UDF standards used by the packet-writing software that drags and drops files to CD-RW drives, the need to install a UDF reader on systems with CD-ROM drives, and the incapability of older CD-ROM and first-generation DVD-ROM drives to read CD-RW media, I recommend using CD-RW media for personal backups and data transfer between your own computers. However, when you send CD data to another user, CD-R is universally readable, making it a better choice.

MultiRead Specifications

The original Red and Yellow Book CD standards specified that on a CD the lands should have a minimum reflectance value of about 70% and the pits should have a maximum reflectance of about 28%. Therefore, the area of a disc that represents a land should reflect back no less than 70% of the laser light directed at it, whereas the pits should reflect no more than 28%. In the early 1980s when these standards were developed, the photodetector diodes used in the drives were relatively insensitive, and these minimum and maximum reflectance requirements were deliberately designed to create enough brightness and contrast between pits and lands to accommodate them.

On a CD-RW disc, the reflectance of a land is approximately 20% (plus or minus 5%) and the reflectivity of a pit is only 5%—obviously well below the original requirements. Fortunately, it was found that by the addition of a relatively simple AGC circuit, the ratio of amplification in the detector circuitry can be changed dynamically to allow for reading the lower-reflective CD-RW discs. Therefore, although CD-ROM drives were not initially capable of reading CD-RW discs, modifying the existing designs to enable them to do so wasn't difficult. Where you might encounter problems reading CD-RW discs is with CD audio drives, especially older ones. Because CD-RW first came out in 1996 (and took a year or more to become popular), most CD-ROM drives manufactured in 1997 or earlier have problems reading CD-RW discs. Reflectivity is also a problem on DVD-Video and DVD-ROM drives—because they use a different frequency laser, they actually have more trouble reading CD-R discs than CD-RWs.

DVDs also have some compatibility problems. With DVD, the problem isn't just simple reflectivity as it is an inherent incompatibility with the laser wavelength used for DVD versus CD-R and RW. The problem in this case stems from the dyes used in the recording layer of CD-R and RW discs, which are very sensitive to the wavelength of light used to read them. At the proper CD laser wavelength of 780nm, they are very reflective, but at other wavelengths, the reflectivity falls off markedly. Normally, CD-ROM drives use a 780nm (infrared) laser to read the data, whereas DVD drives use a shorter wavelength 650nm (red) laser. Although the shorter wavelength laser works well for reading commercial CD-ROM discs because the aluminum reflective layer they use is equally reflective at the shorter DVD laser wavelength, it doesn't work well at all for reading CD-R or RW discs.

Fortunately, a solution was first introduced by Sony and then similarly by all the other DVD drive manufacturers. This solution consists of a dual-laser pickup that incorporates both a 650nm (DVD) and 780nm (CD) laser. Some of these used two discrete pickup units with separate optics mounted to the same assembly, but they eventually changed to dual-laser units that use the same optics for both, making the pickup smaller and less expensive. Because most manufacturers wanted to make a variety of drives—including cheaper ones without the dual-laser pickup—a standard needed to be created so that someone purchasing a drive would know the drive's capabilities.

So, how can you tell whether your CD-ROM or DVD-ROM drive is compatible with CD-R and RW discs? In the late 1990's, the OSTA OSTA created the MultiRead specifications to guarantee specific levels of compatibility:

- **MultiRead**—For CD-ROM drives
- **MultiRead2**—For DVD-ROM drives

In addition, a similar MultiPlay standard exists that is for consumer DVD-Video and CD-DA devices.

Table 11.26 shows the two levels of MultiRead capability that can be assigned to drives and the types of media guaranteed to be readable in such drives.

Table 11.26   MultiRead and MultiRead2 Compatibility Standards for CD/DVD Drives

Media	MultiRead	MultiRead2	Media	MultiRead	MultiRead2
CD-DA	X	X	DVD-ROM	—	X
CD-ROM	X	X	DVD-Video	—	X
CD-R	X	X	DVD-Audio	—	X
CD-RW	X	X	DVD-RAM	—	X

X = Compatible; drive will read this media

— = Incompatible; drive won't read

Note that MultiRead also indicates that the drive is capable of reading discs written in Packet Writing mode because this mode is now being used more commonly with both CD-R and DVD rewritable media.

If you use only rewritable CD or DVD drives, you don't need to worry about compatibility. However, if you still use CD-ROM, DVD-ROM or DVD-ROM/CD-RW combo drives, you should check compatibility with other types of media. Although the MultiRead or MultiRead2 logos shown in Figure 11.15 are not widely used today, you can determine a particular drive's compatibility with a give media type by viewing its specification sheet.

Figure 11.15   MultiRead and MultiRead2 logos. These logos can be found on some older drives meeting these specifications.

You can obtain the MultiRead specification (revision 1.11, October 23, 1997) and MultiRead 2 specification (revision 1.0, December 6, 1999) from the OSTA website.

How to Reliably Record CDs

Five major factors influence your ability to create a working CD-R: interface type, drive buffer size, the location and condition of the data you want to record to CD-R, the recording speed, and whether the computer is performing other tasks while trying to create the CD-R.

Recent and current CD-RW and rewritable DVD drives can normally burn CD-R discs without difficulty, but if you are having problems, check the following:

- **Make sure the drive has some form of buffer underrun protection**—The data buffer in the drive holds information read from the original data source, so that if a pause in data reading occurs, there's less of a possibility of a buffer underrun until the on-drive buffer runs empty. Newer drives with buffer underrun protection virtually eliminate this problem, no matter what size buffer is in the drive. Some CD and DVD mastering programs might offer an option to disable buffer underrun protection. However, you should leave it enabled at all times unless you are using an old drive that does not support this feature.

■ **Support for UDMA operating modes**—As you've already seen, UDMA modes transfer data more quickly and with less CPU intervention than earlier versions of ATA. To use this feature, you'll also need a motherboard with a busmastering UDMA interface with the appropriate drivers installed.

Tip

Also, if you have problems with reliable CD-R creation at the drive's maximum speed, try using a lower speed (24x instead of 52x, for example). Your mastering job will take twice as long, but it's better to create a working CD-R slowly than ruin a blank quickly.

An alternative approach is to use packet-writing software to create your CD-R. All recent CD-RW and rewritable DVD drives support packet writing, which allows drag-and-drop copying of individual files to the CD-R/RW rather than transferring all the files at once as with normal mastering software. This "a little at a time" approach means that less data must be handled in each write and can make the difference between success and failure. If your drive supports this feature, it probably includes packet-writing software in the package. Note that although packet-written CDs can be read with Windows 9x/Me and NT/2000/XP/Vista, they can't be read with Windows 3.1 and MS-DOS because these operating systems don't have drivers available that support packet-written CDs. Note that some CD-mastering software supports packet-writing to CD-Rs, but others don't. For example, the DirectCD and Drag to Disc programs included with Roxio Easy CD Creator can packet-write to both CD-R and CD-RW media and close CD-R media for reading on any drive, but Nero's InCD packet-writing software doesn't support CD-R.

Note

Imaging software such as Norton Ghost or Acronis True Image works from a DOS prompt but uses packet-writing to copy data to CD-R media. Because a backup created with these programs must be restored from a DOS prompt in some versions of the program, they include a special DOS-compatible packet-writing driver that is loaded during its startup process.

Buffer Underruns

Whenever a drive writes data to a CD-R/RW disc in either Disk-at-Once or Track-at-Once mode, it writes to the spiral track on the CD, alternating on and off to etch the pattern into the raw media. Originally, it was not possible for a drive to realign where it starts and stops writing like a hard drive can, after it starts writing it was necessary to continue until it's finished with the track or disc. Otherwise, the recording (and disc if it is a CD-R) would be ruined, creating a useless disc often referred to as a 'coaster.' To avoid this problem, the CD recording software, in combination with your system hardware, must be capable of delivering a consistent stream of data to the drive while it's writing.

Although vendors added larger buffers (up to 8MB) to CD-RW drives and users were often reminded to perform no other tasks while burning a CD, buffer underruns and spoiled media still took place all too often.

Buffer Underrun Protection

Sanyo was the first to develop a technology that eliminates buffer underruns once and for all. It calls the technology BURN-Proof (BURN stands for "buffer underrun"), which sounds a little confusing (some people thought it prevented any writing on discs), but in practice it has proven to be excellent. Other technologies were developed by various vendors, including Ricoh's JustLink, Waste-Proof and Safeburn from Yamaha, SMART-Burn from Lite-On, and Superlink from Mediatek among others. For several years, all CD-RW, combo DVD-ROM/CD-RW and rewritable DVD drives have included some type of buffer underrun protection.Buffer underrun protection technology involves having a special chipset in the drive that monitors the drive buffer. When it anticipates that a buffer underrun might occur (the buffer is running low on data), it temporarily suspends the recording until more data fills the buffer. When the buffer is sufficiently restocked, the drive then locates exactly where the recording left off earlier and restarts recording again immediately after that position.

According to the Orange Book specification, gaps between data in a CD recording must not be more than 100 milliseconds in length. The buffer underrun technology can restart the recording with a gap of 40–45 milliseconds or less from where it left off, which is well within the specification. These small gaps are easily compensated for by the error correction built into the recording, so no data is lost.

Note that it is important that the drive incorporate buffer underrun technology, but the recording software must support it as well for everything to work properly. Fortunately, all the popular CD and DVD recording programs on the market now support this technology.

If your drive incorporates buffer underrun protection, you can multitask—do other things while burning CDs—without fear of producing a bad recording.

Note

Another method used to produce high-quality recording is intelligent disk burning. Virtually all recent rewritable CD and DVD drives include this feature, which determines the type of media in use and the best burn strategy. If the media type unknown, drives might use a utility program to test a representative sample of the media to determine the best strategy.

CD (and DVD) burning problems can also be caused by inadequate power supplies and by failures of the CD or DVD laser. If you are using a late-model CD or DVD drive and have buffer underrun or unreadable media problems, determine whether the problem happens only with CD media, only with DVD media, or with both types of media. If the problem happens only with CD or DVD media, replace the drive (one of the lasers has failed). However, if the drive can't burn either type of media, the power supply may be to blame. I've seen cases in which the system seemed to be normal in most respects, but there were tremendous problems recording CDs, from buffer underruns to power calibration errors. After upgrading the power supply with a high-quality, high-output unit, the problems all but disappeared. I've said it many times, but the power supply is the foundation of a PC, and in general it is the most failure-prone or problematic piece of hardware in the system. See Chapter 19, "Power Supplies," for more information on power supplies, including recommended suppliers for upgraded units.

If you have a drive that does not feature buffer underrun protection, see Chapter 13 of *Upgrading and Repairing PCs, 14th Edition*, for suggestions on producing error-free recordings.

Recording Software

Another difficulty with CD-R/RW devices is that they usually require special software to write them. Although most cartridge drives and other removable media mount as standard devices in the system and can be accessed exactly like a hard drive, the CD-R/RW drives and most types of rewritable DVD drives use special CD-ROM/DVD burning software to write to the disc (DVD-RAM drives don't require special software to write to DVD-RAM media). This software handles the differences between how data is stored on a CD and how it is stored on a hard drive. As you learned earlier, there are several CD-ROM standards for storing information. The CD-ROM-burning software arranges the data into one of these formats so a CD-ROM reader can read the CD later.

Windows XP is the first version of Windows to include native support for writing CD-R and CD-RW media (Windows Vista also supports writing to DVD+R/RW and DVD-R/RW media). Previous versions of Windows must use CD-mastering or drag and drop software (usually supplied as a bundle) to write to this media.

Although Windows XP and Vista write to CD media, the method used is slow and clumsy. You may prefer to use a special CD/DVD mastering program to create your disks. Some of the most popular choices include Nero Premium and Roxio Easy Media Creator. These and other programs are far more powerful and easier to use than what Windows includes or what is packaged with some drives.

Note

Most rewritable CD and DVD drive vendors include some type of CD/DVD mastering and packet-writing software with their drives. However, these programs do not always support backup, DVD creation or other advanced features. If you are not satisfied with the bundled applications, look for a third-party application with the features you want.

At one time, CD recording technology required that you have what amounted to a replica of the CD on a local hard drive. In fact, some software packages even required a separate, dedicated disk partition for this purpose. You would copy all the files to the appropriate place on the hard drive, creating the directory structure for the CD, and then the software would create an exact replica of every sector for the proposed CD-ROM—including every file, all the directory information, and the volume information—and copy it to the CD-R drive. The result was that you had to have about 1.5GiB of storage to burn a single CD (650MiB/CD × 2 = 1.3GiB + overhead = 1.5GiB). This is no longer a requirement because most software supports virtual images. You select the files and directories you want to write to the CD from your hard drive and create a virtual directory structure for the CD-ROM in the software. This means you can select files from different directories on different hard drives, or even files from network or other CD-ROM drives, and combine them any way you want on the CD-R. This works well provided the drives have adequate speed and your drive has buffer underrun protection. The software assembles the directory information, burns it onto the CD, opens each file on the CD, and copies the data directly from the original source. This generally works well, but you must be aware of the access times for the media you select as data sources. If, for example, you select directories from a slow hard drive or from a busy network, the software might not be capable of reading the data quickly enough to maintain a consistent stream to the recorder. In drives lacking buffer underrun protection, this causes the write to fail, resulting in a wasted disc.

Don't Forget the Software!

If you have persistent problems with making CDs, your recording software or drive might be to blame. Check the vendor's website for tips and software updates. Some drives offer software-upgradeable firmware similar to the motherboard's flash BIOS; if so, be sure your drive has the latest firmware available. Also make sure that your recording software is up-to-date and compatible with your drive and your drive's firmware revision.

Each of the major CD-R/CD-RW drive vendors provides extensive technical notes to help you achieve reliable recordings. You can also find helpful information on SCSI adapter vendors' websites and the websites of the media vendors.

▶▶ See "Updating the Firmware in a CD-RW or Rewritable DVD Drive," p. 847.

Digital Audio Extraction (DAE)

All CD-ROM drives can *play* Red Book–formatted CD-DA discs, but not all CD-ROM drives can *read* CD-DA discs. The difference sounds subtle, but it is actually quite dramatic. If you enjoy music and want to use your PC to manage your music collection, the ability to read the audio data digitally is an important function for your CD (and DVD) drives because it enables you to much more easily and accurately store, manipulate, and eventually write back out audio tracks.

CD-ROM drives installed in PCs can play audio discs. The playing function is simple: Using a CD or Media player application (such as the one included with Windows), you can insert a CD-DA disc into a CD-ROM drive and play it just as you could with a standard audio CD player. While playing, the analog sound waveform is sent over a thin stereo cable (usually referred to as the CD audio cable) connected between your CD-ROM drive and the sound card in your PC. The same analog waveform usually is also sent to the headphone jack on the front of the drive (or sound card). Your sound card then amplifies the analog signal so you can hear it through the speakers plugged into your sound card or via headphones plugged into the front of the drive (or the sound card).

To record a song from CD to your hard disk, it was once necessary to play the disc at normal speed and capture the audio output as analog, hence the need for the four-wire analog audio cable connection from the rear of CD and DVD drives to your sound card. Fortunately, for several years drives have supported *digital audio extraction (DAE)*. In this process they read the digital audio sectors directly and, rather than decode them into analog signals, pass each 2,352-byte sector of raw (error-corrected) digital audio data directly to the PC's processor via the drive interface cable (ATA, SATA, SCSI, USB, or FireWire). Therefore, no digital-to-analog conversion (and back) occurs, and you essentially get the audio data exactly as it was originally recorded on the CD (within the limits of the CD-DA error-correction standards). You would have essentially extracted the exact digital audio data from the disc onto your PC.

Another term for digital audio extraction is *ripping*, so named because you can "rip" the raw audio data from the drive at full drive read speed, rather than the normal 1x speed at which you listen to audio discs. Actually, most drives can't perform DAE at their full rated speeds. Although some are faster (or slower) than others, most perform DAE at speeds from about one-half to two-thirds of their rated CD read speed. So, you might be able to extract audio data at speeds only up to 28x on a 40x rated drive. However, that is still quite a bit better than at 1x as it would be on drives that can't do DAE (not to mention skipping the conversion to analog and back to digital with the resultant loss of information).

Virtually all newer CD/DVD drives can perform digital audio extraction on music discs. How fast or accurately they do this varies from model to model. One might think any extraction (digital copy) of a given track (song) should be the same because it is a digital copy of the original; however, that is not always the case. The CD-DA format was designed to play music, not to transfer data with 100% accuracy. Errors beyond the capability of the CIRC in the CD-DA format cause the firmware in the drive to interpolate or approximate the data. In addition, time-based problems due to clock inaccuracies can occur in the drive, causing it to get slightly out of step when reading the frames in the sector (this is referred to as *jitter*). Differences in the internal software (firmware) in the drive and differences in the drivers used are other problems that can occur.

Positioning can also be a problem because the CD-DA format was designed to stream (play continuously) and not to read individual sectors. CD-ROM sectors are 2,352 bytes long, and these bytes are further divided into 2,048 bytes of data plus 304 bytes of synchronization, header, and additional ECC information to control positioning and allow for error-free reads. No such synchronization, header, or extra ECC information exists for audio sectors; instead, all 2,352 bytes are used for pure audio data. To address an audio sector, the Q subcode information is used instead (see the section "Subcodes," earlier in this chapter). Most audio players position to within only 75 sectors (1 second) using the Q subcode information. CD-ROM drives that can perform digital audio extraction are usually much more accurate than that, but because of how the subcode works (as well as the cross-interleaved way audio data is stored), designing a drive that can position every time to the precise audio sector that starts the track can be difficult.

All of this conspires to cause inaccuracies or slight differences in multiple extractions of the same track (song). Perfect extractions are possible, but making perfect extractions is difficult to achieve for many reasons. For example, even a slight amount of dirt or scratches on the disc has a great effect on the quality of your extractions, so be sure the discs are clean. As a test of your drive's capability to perform DAE, try extracting the same track (song) multiple times from a new, clean, scratch-free disc, using a different filename for each extraction. Then, bring up a command prompt and use the FC (file compare) command to compare the different files to each other. If they compare exactly, you have a combination of hardware and software that can do perfect or near-perfect extractions.

If you intend to do a lot of extracting, you should ask around to see what hardware and software others are using for this purpose. Websites such as Tom's Hardware (www.tomshardware.com) and Anandtech (www.anandtech.com) typically include DAE or similar benchmark tests for DVD (and CD) drives. The bottom line is that DAE enables you to extract audio data tracks directly to your PC as WAV files. Once the WAV files are on the PC, you can play them as is or convert them to other (usually more compressed) formats, such as MP3 (MPEG-1/2 Layer III) for use with the MP3 audio players on the market.

Note

Because the WAV files extracted match the high 44.1KHz sampling rate used on the CD, you have 176,400 bytes per second of sound information, which means 1 minute of music consumes nearly 10.6MB worth of space on your hard drive! MP3 compression can reduce that by a factor of 6 or more, with little to no perceptible loss in quality.

You can also use a CD-R/RW drive that can perform DAE to make copies of audio CDs (for backup purposes only) or to compile several songs into your own greatest hits collections that you can use to burn your own custom audio CDs.

"For Music Use Only" CD-R/RW Discs

According to the Audio Home Recording Act of 1992, consumer CD recordable drives *and media* sold specifically for recording music are required to have specific safeguards against copying discs, mainly SCMS. That means these recorders can make digital copies only from original prerecorded discs. You can copy a copy, but in that case, the data being recorded goes from digital to analog and back to digital on the second copy, resulting in a generational loss of quality.

The media for these recorders must be special as well. They work only with special discs labeled "For Music Use," "For Audio," or "For Consumer." These carry the standard Compact Disk Digital Audio Recordable logo that most are familiar with, but below that, as part of the logo, is an added line that says "For Consumer." These discs feature a special track prerecorded onto the disc, which the consumer music recorders look for. Built into the price of the AHRA-compliant media is a royalty for the music industry that this track protects. The media costs about 20%–30% more than what regular CD-R/RW media costs. If you try to use standard non-AHRA-compliant CD-R/RW discs in these drives, the drive refuses to recognize the disc. These music devices also refuse to copy CD-ROM or data discs.

Note that this does not apply to the CD-R/RW drive you have installed or attached to your PC. It does not have to be AHRA compliant, nor does it need to use AHRA-compliant "For Music Use" media, even if you are copying or recording music discs. Additionally, you can make digital copies of copies—the SCMS does not apply, either. The bottom line is that you do not have to purchase AHRA-compliant discs for the CD-R/RW drives in your PC. If you do purchase such discs, despite the "For Music Use Only" designation, AHRA-compliant discs can be used in your CD-R/RW drives just as regular CD-R/RW discs can be used for storing data. The extra information indicating AHRA compliance is simply ignored.

CD Copy Protection

Worries about the public copying of software and music CDs has prompted the development of copy protection techniques that attempt to make these discs uncopyable. There are different methods of protecting software CDs versus music CDs, but the end result is the same: You are prevented from making normal copies, or the copies don't work properly. In the case of music CDs, the copy protection can be quite obtrusive, adding noise to the recording, and in extreme cases preventing the disc from even playing in a PC drive.

Several copy protection schemes are available for CD-DA (digital audio) discs, ranging from the simple to sophisticated. The most popular protection scheme for digital audio discs is called SafeAudio by Macrovision. Macrovision won't explain exactly how SafeAudio works, but it purchased the technology from a company called TTR Technologies and patents filed by TTR describe the scheme in detail. According to the patents, the disc is deliberately recorded with grossly erroneous values (bursts of noise) in both the audio data and the codes, which would typically be used to correct these errors. When reading the disc, the normal error-correction scheme fails, leaving small gaps in the music.

When this happens on a standard audio CD player, the gaps are automatically bridged by circuitry or code in the player, which looks at the audio data on either side of the gap and interpolates (guesses) the missing values. The CD drive in a PC can do the same thing, so the interpolation occurs only when playing CDs in an audio player mode. However, the drive in a PC does not perform this same interpolation when "ripping" the data—that is, copying it directly to a hard drive, another CD, or some other medium. In that case the unbridged gaps are heard as extremely loud clicks, pops, and noise. Both TTR and Macrovision claim that the interpolation that occurs when playing a SafeAudio disc is not discernable to the human ear, but many audio experts disagree. To an audiophile, the addition of any distortion or noise to the audio signal is unconscionable.

Even more rigorous protection can be added that can render the audio disc unplayable on a PC and even cause problems on audio players. Of course, the final problem is that you can't make legal backups of your music—something that is allowed by law.

For software (rather than audio), several protection schemes are used, although most are similar to one another. Again the most popular is by Macrovision, but for CD-ROMs it is called SafeDisc. As with SafeAudio, Macrovision purchased the technology from another company; in this case it was a company called C-Dilla.

SafeDisc works by first encrypting all the software code on the disc and then adding a routine to the code that looks for a unique authentication signature (called a *watermark*), which would have been added to the disc during the mastering process. When executed, the authentication code attempts to read the watermark on the disc. If the watermark is present, the main program code is unencrypted and executed. But if the watermark is not present, the program does not run. Because the watermark does not conform to the normal structures written to a CD, most CD burners can't duplicate it.

The authentication process basically requires that the original CD be present in the drive whenever the program is run. This, however, can be set up so that the original disc is required only during program installation, or it can be checked anytime the program is run, even if run from a hard disk. The latter is quite inconvenient because it requires you to have the original CD with you at all times to run the program.

To circumvent this type of protection, people have developed software that can fool the authentication code into believing the watermark is present. Some software even strips the authentication code from the software completely. Others have found ways to copy the watermark such that it would appear on any copies of the original CD. As with other forms of copy protection, it has been easily defeated and represents more of a nuisance to the legitimate user rather than to the thief.

CD Digital Rights Management (DRM)

Digital rights management (DRM) goes a step beyond standard copy protection by specifying what you can and cannot do with a recorded CD or other type of commercial media. When applied to downloaded music, for example, DRM features in audio tracks can prevent you from burning a song to CD an unlimited amount of times, playing a song past a particular date, or limit the number of times you can copy a song from one PC to another.

Although the use of DRM on CD media (as opposed to downloadable audio tracks) has been rare, the Sony rootkit scandal of 2005 is a useful case to keep in mind.

Sony Rootkit Scandal

Sony BMG, one of the biggest music CD distributors, introduced a controversial method of copy-protection and DRM in the fall of 2005 by adding copy protection and DRM to some of its music CDs. Affected CDs used either XCP (Extended Copy Protection, developed by First 4 Internet, now known as Fortium Technologies, Inc.) or MediaMax CD-3 (developed by SunnComm).

These programs limited the user's ability to work freely with the songs (as they can with normal music CDs), and, worse yet, were installed on PCs without notifying the user. The type of installer Sony used is called a 'rootkit,' which is a program that hides its presence from the operating system and makes it easier for worms and other malware to attack the system.

After security and privacy advocates attacked Sony's use of DRM and rootkits without adequate notice to music purchasers, Sony introduced a rootkit removal tool and eventually recalled all albums in 2006, settling a lawsuit with the Federal Trade Commission. Although Sony's attempt to use DRM was botched by its failure to inform customers that CDs contained DRM software and the software did not provide a way for users to block installation, it's possible that DRM features that avoid Sony's mistakes may be used on CD and other types of media in the future.

Recordable DVD Standards

The history of recordable DVD drives has been a troubled one. It dates back to April 1997, when the DVD Forum announced specifications for rewritable and recordable DVD: DVD-RAM, and DVD-R. Later, it added DVD-RW to the mix. Dissatisfied with these standards, the industry leaders in optical recording and drives formed their own group called the DVD+RW Alliance and created another stan-dard—DVD+R and DVD+RW. For several years, drives based on one family of standards could not freely interchange media with drives using the other family of standards.

Fortunately, all recent drives support both DVD-R/RW and DVD+R/RW media, including dual-layer (DL) DVD+R media, and most also support DVD-RAM. The move to support multiple standards in a single drive means that the recordable/rewritable DVD industry is no longer forcing you to decide what drive is the best. Instead, you can choose the right media for a particular task.

Table 11.27 compares the competing recordable DVD standards, and Table 11.28 breaks down the compatibilities between the drives and media.

Table 11.27 Recordable DVD Standards

Format	Introduced	Capacity	Compatibility
DVD-RAM	July 1997	Up to 4.7GB per side	Incompatible with existing DVD drives unless they support the MultiRead2 standard
DVD-R/RW	July 1997; Nov. 1999	4.7GB per side	Readable by many existing DVD recorders/drives
DVD+R/RW	Mar. 2001; May 2001	4.7GB per side	Readable by most existing DVD recorders/drives, with enhancements for video and data recording
DVD+R DL	Oct. 2003	8.5GB	Older DVD drives may require firmware updates to read DL media.

Table 11.27   Continued

Format	Introduced	Capacity	Compatibility
DVD-R DL	Feb. 2005	8.5GB	For compatibility with older DVD drives, use the Layer Jump Recording method. Older DVD drives may also require firmware updates to read DL media.

Table 11.28   DVD Drive and Media Compatibility

						Media (Discs)				
Drives	CD-ROM	CD-R	CD-RW	DVD Drive	DVD-ROM	DVD-R	DVD-RAM	DVD-RW	DVD+RW	DVD+R
DVD-Video Player	R	?	?	R	—	R	?	R	R	R
DVD-ROM Drive	R	R	R	R	R	R	?	R	R¹	R
DVD-R Drive	R	R/W	R/W	R	R	R/W	—	R	R	R
DVD-RAM Drive	R	R	R	R	R	R⁶	R/W	R	R¹	R
DVD-RW Drive	R	R/W	R/W	R	R	R/W	—	R/W	R	R
DVD+R/RW Drive	R	R/W	R/W	R	R	R	R³	R	R/W	R/W²
DVD-Multi Drive⁴	R	R/W	R/W	R	R	R	R/W	R/W	R¹	R
DVD±R/RW Drive	R	R/W	R/W	R	R	R/W	R⁵	R/W	R/W	R/W
DVD Super Multi Drive⁷	R	R/W	R/W	R	R	R/W⁸	R/W	R/W	R/W	R/W⁹

R = Read.

W = Write.

— = Will not read or write.

? = MultiRead/MultiPlay drives will read.

1 = Might require media's compatibility bit be changed to alternate (Type 2).

2 = Some first-generation DVD+RW drives will not write DVD+R discs; see your drive manufacturer for an update or trade-in.

3 = Read compatibility with DVD-RAM varies by drive; check documentation for details.

4 = DVD Forum specification for drives that are compatible with all DVD Forum standards (DVD+R/RW is not a DVD Forum standard).

5 = Some of these drives can also write to DVD-RAM media.

6 = Some of these drives can also write to DVD-R media.

7 = Identifies drives that work with DVD+R/RW, DVD-R/RW, DVD+R DL and DVD-RAM media.

8 = Some of these drives also work with dual-layer (DL) media

9 = Also supports dual-layer (DL) media

DVD+R/RW offers low drive and media prices, provides the highest compatibility with existing formats, and has features that make it the most ideal for both video recording and data storage in PCs. However, with most recent drives, you can now select the best media for the job.

DVD-RAM

DVD-RAM is the rewritable DVD standard endorsed by Panasonic, Hitachi, and Toshiba; it is part of the DVD Forum's list of supported standards. DVD-RAM uses a phase-change technology similar to that of CD-RW. Unfortunately, DVD-RAM discs can't be read by most standard DVD-ROM drives because of differences in both reflectivity of the media and the data format. (DVD-R, by comparison, is backward-compatible with DVD-ROM.)

DVD-ROM drives that can read DVD-RAM discs began to come on the market in early 1999 and follow the MultiRead2 specification. DVD-ROM drives and DVD-Video players labeled as MultiRead2 compliant are capable of reading DVD-RAM discs. See the section "MultiRead Specifications," earlier in this chapter, for more information. Although the MultiRead2 logo is not used on current products, some recent and current DVD-ROM drives can read DVD-RAM media; check the specification sheet for a particular drive to verify compatibility.

The first DVD-RAM drives were introduced in spring 1998 and had a capacity of 2.6GB (single-sided) or 5.2GB (double-sided). DVD-RAM Version 2 discs with 4.7GB arrived in late 1999, and double-sided 9.4GB discs arrived in 2000. DVD-RAM drives typically read DVD-Video, DVD-ROM, and CD media. Although DVD-ROM drives, older DVD+R/RW and DVD-R/RW drives and DVD-Video players can't read DVD-RAM media, DVD Multi and DVD Super Multi drives can read/write DVD-RAM.

DVD-RAM uses what is called the wobbled land and groove recording method, which records signals on both the lands (the areas between grooves) and inside the grooves that are preformed on the disc. The tracks wobble, which provides clock data for the drive. Special sector header pits are prepressed into the disc during the manufacturing process as well. See Figure 11.16, which shows the wobbled tracks (lands and grooves) with data recorded both on the lands and in the grooves. This is unlike CD-R or CD-RW, in which data is recorded on the groove only.

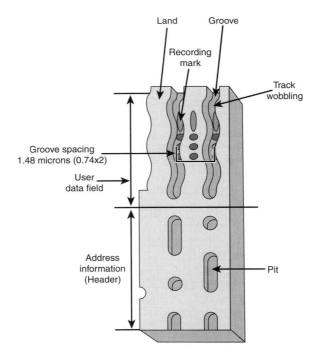

Figure 11.16 DVD-RAM wobbled land and groove recording.

The disc is recorded using phase-change recording, in which data is written by selectively heating spots in the grooves or on the lands with a high-powered laser. The DVD-RAM drive write laser transforms the film from a crystalline to an amorphous state by heating a spot, which is then rendered less reflective than the remaining crystalline portions. The signal is read as the difference of the laser reflection rate between the crystalline and amorphous states. The modulation and error-correction codes are the same as for DVD-Video and DVD-ROM, ensuring compatibility with other DVD formats. For rewriting, a lower-powered laser reheats the spot to a lower temperature, where it recrystallizes.

Disc cartridges or caddies originally were required for both single- and double-sided discs but have now been made optional for single-sided discs. Double-sided discs must remain inside the caddy at all times for protection; however, single-sided discs can be taken out of the cartridge if necessary.

Specifications for DVD-RAM Version 2 are shown in Table 11.29.

Table 11.29   DVD-RAM Version 2 Specifications

Storage capacity	4.7GB single-sided; 9.4GB double-sided
Disc diameter	80mm–120mm
Disc thickness	1.2mm (0.6mm×2: bonded structure)
Recording method	Phase change
Laser wavelength	650nm
Data bit length	0.28 microns
Recording track pitch	0.615 microns
Track format	Wobbled land and groove

In the past, I have been opposed to DVD-RAM because of a lack of compatibility with other drive types. However, if you use drives supporting the DVD Super Multi standard, you can read and write DVD-RAM as well as other rewritable DVD formats. With the ability to read, write, and erase data without the need to use UDF packet-writing software, DVD-RAM can be a useful alternative to other types of rewritable DVD—assuming all of your drives can use it.

DVD-R

DVD-R is a write-once medium very similar to CD-R, which was originally created by Pioneer and released by the DVD Forum in July 1997. DVD-R discs can be played on standard DVD-ROM drives. Some DVD-RAM drives can also write to DVD-R media.

DVD-R has a single-sided storage capacity of 4.7GB—about seven times that of a CD-R-and double that for a double-sided disc. These discs use an organic dye recording layer that allows for a low material cost, similar to CD-R.

To enable positioning accuracy, DVD-R uses a wobbled groove recording, in which special grooved tracks are pre-engraved on the disc during the manufacturing process. Data is recorded within the grooves only. The grooved tracks wobble slightly right and left, and the frequency of the wobble contains clock data for the drive to read, as well as clock data for the drive. The grooves are spaced more closely together than with DVD-RAM, but data is recorded only in the grooves and not on the lands (see Figure 11.17).

Table 11.30 has the basic specifications for DVD-R drives.

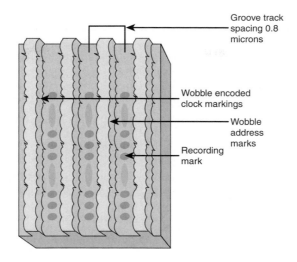

Figure 11.17 DVD-R wobbled groove recording.

Table 11.30 DVD-R Specifications

Storage capacity	4.7GB single-sided; 9.4GB double-sided
Disc diameter	80mm–120mm
Disc thickness	1.2mm (0.6mm×2: bonded structure)
Recording method	Organic dye layer recording method
Laser wavelength	635nm (recording); 635/650nm (playback)
Data bit length	0.293 microns
Recording track pitch	0.80 microns
Track format	Wobbled groove

DVD-R media is currently available in speeds up to 16x, although some drives feature faster burn speeds. Some vendors are now producing double-sided single-layer DVD-R media with capacities of 9.4GB. This media is designed primarily for DVD jukeboxes, although it can be used by standard DVD rewritable drives.

DVD-R DL

DVD-R DL was introduced in February 2005, and is sometimes known as DVD-R for Dual Layer or DVD-R9. DVD-R DL is essentially a dual-layer version of the DVD-R disc, using the same recording method, laser wavelength and other specifications. However, DVD-R DL discs have two recording layers, with the reflective surface of the top layer being semi-transparent to permit recording on the second layer. Because of the lower reflectivity of the top layer, some DVD-ROM drives cannot read DVD-R DL media.

Note

If you are unable to read DVD-R DL media with a DVD-ROM drive, try using the Layer Jump Recording (LJR) recording method in your DVD mastering software if your drive and software support it. LJR alternates between recording layers during the writing process, rather than filling one layer before writing to the other layer. This permits a disc to support multi-session recording and is intended to make it easier for DVD-ROM drives to read dual-layer media.

DVD-R DL media is currently available in 4x speed, although some rewritable DVD drives support faster write speeds.

DVD-RW

The DVD Forum introduced DVD-RW in November 1999. Created and endorsed originally by Pioneer, DVD-RW is basically an extension to DVD-R, just as CD-RW is an extension to CD-R. DVD-RW uses a phase-change technology and is somewhat more compatible with standard DVD-ROM drives than DVD-RAM. Drives based on this technology began shipping in late 1999, but early models achieved only moderate popularity because Pioneer was the only source for the drives and because of limitations in their performance.DVD-RW media is currently available in speeds up to 6x, although 1x, 2x, and 4x media is also available. Drives supporting 2x/4x and faster media have several advantages over original 1x/2x DVD-RW drives, including these:

- **Quick formatting**—1x/2x drives require that the entire DVD-RW disc be formatted before the media can be used, a process that can take about an hour. 2x/4x and faster drives can use DVD-RW media in a few seconds after inserting, formatting the media in the background as necessary. This is similar to the way in which DVD+RW drives work.

- **Quick grow**—Instead of erasing the media to add files, as with 1x/2x DVD-RW drives, 2x/4x and faster DVD-RW drives can unfinalize the media and add more files without deleting existing files.

- **Quick finalizing**—2x/4x DVD-RW drives close media containing small amounts of data (under 1GB) more quickly than 1x/2x drives.

However, most DVD-RW drives still don't support lossless linking, Mount Rainier, or selective deletion of files—all of which are major features of DVD+RW.

Note

Plextor's Zero Link technology does support selective file erasure on DVD-RW media. Essentially, Zero Link provides an equivalent to DVD+RW's lossless link feature, enabling DVD-Video players that support DVD-RW media to play edited disks.

DVD+RW and DVD+R

DVD+RW, also called DVD Phase Change Rewritable, has become the premier DVD recordable standard because it is the least expensive, easiest to use, fastest and most compatible with existing formats. It was developed and is supported by Philips, Sony, Hewlett-Packard, Mitsubishi Chemical (MCC/Verbatim), Ricoh, Yamaha, and Thomson, who are all part of an industry standard group called the DVD+RW Alliance (www.dvdrw.com). Microsoft joined the alliance in February 2003. DVD+RW is also supported by major DVD/CD creation software vendors and many drive vendors, including HP, Philips, Ricoh, and many remarketers of OEM drive mechanisms. Although DVD-RW has increased in popularity with the advent of faster and easier burning times, DVD+RW is the most popular rewritable DVD format.

Table 11.31 lists the basic specifications for DVD+RW drives.

Table 11.31   DVD+RW Specifications

Storage capacity	4.7GB single-sided; 9.4GB double-sided (future product)
Disc diameter	120mm
Disc thickness	1.2mm (0.6mm×2: bonded structure)
Recording method	Phase change
Laser wavelength	650nm (recording/playback)
Data bit length	0.4 microns
Recording track pitch	0.74 microns
Track format	Wobbled groove

Note that DVD+R, the recordable version of DVD+RW, was actually introduced *after* DVD+RW. This is the opposite of DVD-RW, which grew out of DVD-R. One of the major reasons for the development of DVD+R was to provide a lower-cost method for permanent data archiving with DVD+RW drives, and another was because of compatibility issues with DVD-ROM and DVD video players being incapable of reading media created with DVD+RW drives. However, most standard DVD-ROM drives or DVD players can read both DVD+R and DVD+RW media without problems. See the section "DVD+RW Compatibility Mode," later in this chapter, for details.

The basic structure of a DVD+RW or DVD+R disc resembles that of a DVD-R disc with data written in the grooves only (refer to Figure 11.18), but the groove is wobbled at a frequency different from that used by DVD-R/RW or DVD-RAM. The DVD+R/RW groove also contains positioning information. These differences mean that DVD+R/RW media offers more accurate positioning for lossless linking, but drives made only for DVD+R/RW media can't write to other types of DVD rewritable or recordable media.

Although some first-generation DVD+RW drives worked only with rewritable media, all current and future DVD+RW drives are designed to work with both DVD+R (writable) and DVD+RW (rewritable) media. The +R discs can be written only once and are less expensive than the +RW discs.

Some of the features of DVD+RW includes are as follows:

- Single-sided discs (4.7GB).
- Double-sided discs (9.4GB).
- Up to 4 hours video recording (single-sided discs).
- Up to 8 hours video recording (double-sided discs).
- Bare discs—no caddy required.
- 650nm laser (same as DVD-Video).
- Constant linear data density.
- CLV and CAV recording.
- Write speeds 1x–4x and higher (depending on the drive).
- DVD-Video data rates.
- UDF (Universal Disc Format) file system.
- Defect management integral to the drive.

- Quick formatting.
- Uses same 8 to 16 modulation and error-correcting codes as DVD-ROM.
- Sequential and random recording.
- Lossless linking (multiple recording sessions don't waste space).
- Spiral groove with radial wobble.
- After recording, all physical parameters comply with the DVD-ROM specification.

DVD+RW technology is very similar to CD-RW, and DVD+RW drives can read DVD-ROMs and all CD formats, including CD-R and CD-RW.

With DVD+RW, the writing process can be suspended and continued without a loss of space linking the recording sessions together. This increases efficiency in random writing and video applications. This "lossless linking" also enables the selective replacement of any individual 32KB block of data (the minimum recording unit) with a new block, accurately positioning with a space of 1 micron. To enable this high accuracy for placement of data on the track, the pre-groove is wobbled at a higher frequency. The timing and addressing information read from the groove is very accurate.

The quick formatting feature means you can pop a DVD+R or DVD+RW blank into the drive and almost instantly begin writing to it. The actual formatting is carried out in the background ahead of where any writing will occur.

Note

Current DVD set-top players are designed to work with a variety of DVD types. However, if you are not sure of a particular device's compatibility and your drive uses only DVD+R/RW media, you might prefer to create a DVD+R disc to improve the likelihood of the disc's working in many different devices.

DVD+RW is the format I prefer and recommend, and I expect that in the long run it will be the one preferred by most users. However, today's multiformat drives support both DVD+R/RW and DVD-R/RW (and Super Multi Drives also support DVD-RAM), so you can choose the right media for a particular task.

DVD+RW Compatibility Mode

When DVD+RW drives were introduced in 2001, some users of DVD-ROM and standalone DVD players were unable to read DVD+RW media, even though others were able to do so. The first drives to support DVD+R (writable) media (which works with a wider range of older drives) was not introduced until mid-2002, so this was a significant problem.

The most common reason for this problem turned out to be the contents of the Book Type Field located in the lead-in section of every DVD disc. Some drives require that this field indicate that the media is a DVD-ROM before they can read it. However, by default, DVD+RW drives write DVD+RW as the type into this field when DVD+RW media is used.

The following are three possible solutions:

- Upgrade the firmware in the DVD+RW recorder so it writes compatible information into the Book Type Field automatically.
- Change the Book Type Field during the creation of a disc with a DVD mastering program.
- Use a compatibility utility to change the contents of the Book Type Field for a particular DVD+RW disc as necessary. These utilities may be provided by the drive manufacturer (sometimes a firmware upgrade is also necessary), or by a third-party utility.

Changing the Book Type Field is known as bitsetting.

▶▶ See "Updating the Firmware in a CD-RW or Rewritable DVD Drive," p. 847.

DVD+R DL

DVD+R DL, also known as DVD-R9, is a dual-layer version of the DVD+R standard, and was introduced in October 2003. DVD+R DL is essentially a dual-layer version of the DVD+R disc, using the same recording method, laser wavelength and other specifications. However, DVD+R DL discs have two recording layers, with the reflective surface of the top layer being semi-transparent to permit recording on the second layer. Because of the lower reflectivity of the top layer, some DVD-ROM drives cannot read DVD+R DL media.

Current DVD+R DL media is available in speeds up to 8x, although drives support up to 10x burn speeds.

Multiformat Rewritable DVD Drives

The DVD Multi specification from the DVD Forum was developed for drives and players that are compatible with all DVD Forum standards, including DVD-R/RW, DVD-RAM, DVD-ROM, DVD-Video, and eventually DVD Audio (DVD+R/RW are not DVD Forum specifications and are not supported). The original version of DVD Multi was published in February 2001; the current version, version 1.01, was approved by the DVD Forum and published in December 2001. The first DVD Multi products for computers reached the market in early 2003.

To provide support for different types of DVD media in a single drive, all rewritable DVD drive vendors now sell drives compatible with both DVD+R/RW and DVD-R/RW discs. These drives are commonly known as DVD±R/RW. LG's Super Multi Drive series was the first to also add compatibility with DVD-RAM, and most current DVD±R/RW drives from other makers are also compatible with DVD-RAM. Many (but not all) current drives also support DVD-R DL, so you can now buy a single drive that supports all common formats supported by both the DVD Forum and the DVD+RW Alliance.

CD/DVD Drive and Software Installation and Support

CD and DVD drives are installed and configured in the same way as any other drive with the same interface. For details, see the appropriate section:

■ For ATA/IDE drives, see Chapter 7, "The ATA/IDE Interface," and Chapter 12, "Physical Drive Installation and Configuration."

■ For IEEE 1394a and USB drives, see Chapter 15, "I/O Interfaces from Serial and Parallel to IEEE 1394 and USB."

After you've physically installed the drive, you're ready for the last step—installing the drivers and other CD-ROM/DVD-ROM software. As usual, this process can be simple with a PnP operating system such as Windows 9x or later. In that case the drivers for Windows will automatically be installed. Things are different, however, if you need to access the drive after booting from a floppy, such as when installing an operating system, running diagnostics, or running DOS.

Booting from a Floppy Disk with CD/DVD Drive Support

Although modern operating systems (Windows XP and Vista among others) are distributed on bootable CDs or DVDs, you might need to boot from a floppy disc to start a restore process from a disk imaging utility or to install an older operating system, such as Windows 9x or Me. Even if you are installing Windows 9x or Me in a virtualized environment such as those created with Microsoft

Virtual PC or VMware, you will need to boot the virtual machine with a floppy disc containing CD-ROM support before you can install the operating system into the VM.

For a CD or DVD drive to function in a floppy (or CD) boot environment, several drivers might be necessary:

- **An ATAPI host adapter driver (not needed for SCSI drives)**—This driver is included with your motherboard, or you can use the generic ATAPI drivers found on Windows 98 and later startup disks.

- **SCSI adapter drivers (not needed for ATAPI drives)**—Most SCSI cards include these drivers, or you can use the generic versions included on Windows 98 and later startup disks.

- **MSCDEX**—Microsoft CD Extensions, which is included with DOS 6.0 and later. It is also built into Windows 95 and later as the CDFS VxD.

If you need to start a PC from a bootable floppy, the floppy must contain not only a bootable OS, but also the previously mentioned drivers; otherwise, the CD-ROM will be inaccessible.

Generic ATAPI and SCSI drivers can be found on the Windows 98 and newer startup disks. Rather than create custom CONFIG.SYS and AUTOEXEC.BAT files, the best advice I can give is to merely boot from a Windows 98 or Me startup floppy because each time you boot from these, the proper drivers load and autodetect the CD/DVD drives, after which the drives are accessible. You can generate a Windows 98/Me startup disk on any system running Windows 98 or Me. If you don't have access to a Windows 98 or Me system, you can download an equivalent bootable floppy from www.bootdisk.com.

After you boot from a Win98/Me floppy, you see a menu that asks whether you want to boot with or without CD-ROM (and DVD) support. If you select yes, after the floppy finishes loading, you should be able to read any disc in the CD or DVD drive.

One possible, and useful, task with this capability is to install any version of Windows in a situation where the installation CD is not bootable (such as with most versions of Windows 9x/Me) or where the system is older than 1998 and cannot boot from a CD. In such a case, all you need to install any version of Windows is the Windows CD and your bootable Windows 98/Me startup floppy. In addition, the fact that the startup floppy is from Windows 98 or Me does not matter—you can install *any* Windows OS using that floppy.

For example, to install Windows 9x/Me onto a system, you could do the following:

1. Boot from the Windows 98/Me startup floppy, and then select Start Computer with CD-ROM support from the menu. Wait for the A: prompt to appear.

2. Insert the operating system CD you want to install (Windows 95, 98, or Me) into the CD/DVD drive.

3. Type D:SETUP at the A: prompt and press Enter. Make sure you substitute the drive letter of your CD/DVD drive for the D:.

4. The SETUP program will run from the CD and begin the operating system installation. Merely follow the prompts as necessary to complete the install.

To install Windows NT, 2000, or XP onto a system, do the following:

1. Boot from the Windows 98/Me startup floppy and select Start Computer with CD-ROM Support from the menu. Wait for the A: prompt to appear.

2. Insert the operating system CD you want to install (Windows NT, 2000, or XP) into the CD/DVD drive.

3. Type D:\i386\WINNT at the A: prompt and press Enter. Make sure you substitute the drive letter of your CD/DVD drive for the D:.

4. The WINNT program will run from the CD and begin the operating system installation. Merely follow the prompts as necessary to complete the install.

Note

You can also create boot disks for Windows 2000 using files in the \bootdisk folder. See Microsoft Knowledge Base article 197063 at http://support.microsoft.com for details.

Another useful function you can perform with a Windows 98/Me startup floppy is to format a hard drive larger than 32GiB with FAT32 for use with Windows 2000 or XP. The Format program in Windows 2000 and XP is intentionally restricted by Microsoft from formatting volumes larger than 32GiB even though Windows 2000 and XP support FAT32 volumes up to 2TiB in size. In most cases it is recommended to use NTFS on Windows 2000 or XP systems, but if you are creating a dual-boot environment in which you want to run other operating systems that do not support NTFS, FAT32 is the best choice. The restriction on the Windows 2000/XP format command is a nuisance in such a situation, but the only way around it is to use the format from 98/Me.

Windows Vista can be installed only to an NTFS drive, so if you want to have a dual-boot environment that uses a FAT32 drive, you should prepare a portion of the hard disk as FAT32, leave the remainder unformatted, and use the Windows Vista installer to prepare the unformatted section as NTFS.

Although I've often used a Windows 98/Me startup floppy to install Windows XP, Microsoft does have official XP startup floppies available for downloading from its website. To locate the appropriate files for your Windows XP release, visit the Microsoft Knowledge Base at http://support.microsoft.com/ and search for article number 310994.

Using a CD-ROM or DVD-ROM drive that conforms to the ATAPI specification under Windows does not require you to do anything. All the driver support for these drives is built into Windows 9x and later versions, including the ATAPI driver and the CDFS VxD driver.

If you are running a SCSI CD-ROM drive under Windows, you may still need the ASPI driver that goes with your drive. The ASPI driver for your drive usually comes from the drive manufacturer and is included with the drive in most cases. However, by arrangement with hardware manufacturers, Windows typically includes the ASPI driver for most SCSI host adapters and also automatically runs the CDFS VxD virtual device driver. In some rare cases, you might have to install an updated driver that you have obtained from the manufacturer.

When you install a PnP SCSI host adapter in a Windows system, simply booting the computer should cause the operating system to detect, identify, and install drivers for the new device. When the driver for the host adapter is active, the system should detect the SCSI devices connected to the adapter and again load the appropriate drivers automatically.

For DOS users, merely use the Windows 98 or Me startup disk, which includes the necessary DOS SCSI and CD-ROM drivers that support most SCSI cards and CD/DVD drives on the market.

To learn more about the process of preparing to use a CD/DVD drive from a DOS prompt, see "DOS ATAPI CD-ROM Device Driver" in the Technical Reference portion of the disc packaged with this book.

Bootable CDs and DVDs—El Torito

If your system BIOS is a version dated from 1998 or later, most likely it has "El Torito" support, which means it supports booting from a bootable CD or DVD. The El Torito name comes from the Phoenix/ IBM Bootable CD-ROM Format Specification, which was actually named after the El Torito restaurant located near the Phoenix Software offices where the two engineers who developed the standard ate lunch. What El Torito means for the PC is the capability to boot from CDs or DVDs, which opens up several new possibilities, including creating bootable CD/DVD rescue discs, booting from newer OS discs when installing to new systems, creating bootable diagnostics and test CDs, and more.

To create a bootable CD, ideally you need a CD/DVD-burning application that allows the creation of bootable discs. Additionally, in some cases you need a bootable floppy that contains the drivers to support your CD drive in DOS mode (sometimes called real-mode drivers). The best source for these drivers (if needed) is a Windows 98 or Me startup floppy, which can be generated by any Windows 98 or Me system. Windows 98/Me startup disks can be used because these have the DOS-level CD-ROM support already configured and installed. If you don't have access to such a system to generate the disk, you can download one from www.bootdisk.com.

Before creating the bootable CD/DVD, test your boot floppy (with CD-ROM drivers) by first booting to the floppy. Then, with a CD or DVD containing files in the CD/DVD drive, see whether you can change to the CD/DVD drive and read a directory of the files (try the DIR command). The CD/DVD usually is the next drive letter after your last hard drive letter. For example, if your last hard drive letter is C:, the CD/DVD will be D:.

If you can display a directory listing of the CD/DVD after booting from the floppy, your drivers are properly loaded.

To create a bootable CD or DVD, simply follow the directions included with your CD/DVD-burning application. Programs such as Easy Media Creator by Roxio and Nero AG's Nero make the creation of bootable discs a relatively easy procedure.

Creating a Rescue CD

Several programs on the market today allow you to make a compressed image file of the contents of any drive. These programs, such as the Ghost program sold by Symantec or Acronis' True Image, enable you to lock in the condition of any drive as of a particular time.

This enables you to create an image file of your system when it's working and use the image-restore feature to reset your system when it fails.

The perfect place to store a compressed image file is on a CD-R (for older operating systems) or a DVD+R (for Windows XP or Vista). At a minimum, your rescue disk should contain the compressed image file (a 737MB, 80-minute CD-R/RW could contain the equivalent of a nearly 1.5GB drive's normal contents if the maximum compression option is used). It's also desirable to place a copy of the image-restore program on the CD. Mastering this type of rescue CD is done exactly the same as a conventional CD-mastering process. To use the rescue CD, you must boot your system with drivers that allow the CD or DVD drive to work, run the restore program to read the data from the media, and overwrite the drive's existing contents.

If you're looking for a single-CD solution to rescuing your system, one that won't require you to lug around a bootable floppy disk, you can burn a rescue CD that is bootable all by itself.

Making a Bootable CD/DVD for Emergencies

A little-known capability to PC users is that they can create their own versions of what is standard with more and more new computers: a bootable CD/DVD that can be used to start up a system and restore it to a previously saved state.

The minimum requirements for a bootable CD/DVD include the following:

■ A system supporting the El Torito standard in which the CD/DVD can be designated as a boot drive. Check your BIOS under Advanced Setup or similar options. Recent and current BIOS code supplied by AMI, Award Software, and Phoenix Technologies typically support El Torito, meaning the CD/DVD can be assigned as a bootable device.

■ A CD/DVD burner and media.

■ Recording software that allows creation of a bootable CD. Most modern CD recording software, such as NERO and Roxio Easy Media Creator, support creating bootable CD/DVDs. If your current CD/DVD-recording software lacks this option, you must upgrade to something that does.

■ A floppy disk containing your operating system boot files.

ATAPI Drives Are Bootable

Most ATAPI drives connected to a motherboard ATA interface can be used as bootable devices if the BIOS is configured to use the drive as a bootable device. Similarly, you can boot from SATA rewritable DVD drives connected to the motherboard. If your CD/DVD is connected to a SCSI interface, you'll need a SCSI interface with a BIOS chip that permits booting as well as a bootable disc.

Check your BIOS Setup for a page on which boot devices are listed to see whether yours supports a CD/DVD drive as a bootable device.

Because the procedures can vary for different burning software, you should follow the directions that come with your software for the exact procedure for creating a bootable CD or DVD.

Using LightScribe and Other Direct Disc Labeling Systems

The LightScribe direct disc labeling system was developed by Hewlett-Packard (HP) in 2005 as a method for labeling CD (and later, DVD) discs without the need to print labels or use an inkjet printer equipped to print on CD or DVD media.

The top surface of a LightScribe disc is coated with a reactive dye that changes color when exposed to laser light. LightScribe uses the recording laser to etch text and graphics on the top surface of special LightScribe media. After the disc is recorded, the user flips the disc over and runs a LightScribe program to transfer the desired design to the top of the disc. To prevent fading and surface damage, LightScribe discs should be stored in cases away from light when not in use.

Although HP was the original developer of LightScribe, it has licensed the LightScribe technology to most major rewritable DVD drive manufacturers and to Verbatim, Imation, TDK, and other disc makers. LightScribe media is currently available in CD-R, DVD+R, and DVD-R formats. Many DVD mastering and label programs support LightScribe, and LightScribe software and utilities are available for Windows, Linux, and MacOS. For an updated list of products supporting LightScribe and for drivers and utilities, visit the LightScribe website at www.lightscribe.com.

LightScribe discs and media are identified by the LightScribe logo.

A rival technology, Labelflash, was announced in October 2005 by Yamaha and Fujifilm. Labelflash is based on the DiscT@2 ("disk tatoo") technology originally developed by Yamaha for writing text and graphics into the unused portion of the data side of a CD-R disc. However, Labelflash can also write to the top side of media by flipping the disc, just as with LightScribe. The top side of Labelflash media is designed to be more resistant to damage and to produce better image quality than LightScribe, because the Labelflash recording surface is 0.6mm beneath the surface, the same distance as the data recording layer is from the back side surface.

Labelflash is not as widely supported as LightScribe. Media is available only from Fujifilm (DVD-R) as of mid-2007, and Labelflash-compatible products were not available in the US until Toshiba introduced two lines of laptops, the P205 and A205 series, with Labelflash-enabled drives in April 2007. Labeling software supporting Labelflash does not always support the DiscT@2 data-surface labeling feature; check before buying or downloading.

Labelflash discs and media are identified by the Labelflash logo. For more information about Labelflash, visit the official Labelflash website at http://labelflash.jp.

Troubleshooting Optical Drives

Failure Reading a CD/DVD

If your drive fails to read a CD or DVD, try the following solutions:

- Check for scratches on the disc data surface.
- Check the drive for dust and dirt; use a cleaning disc.
- Make sure the drive shows up as a working device in System Properties.
- Try a disc that you know works.
- Restart the computer (the magic cure-all).
- Remove the drive from Device Manager in Windows 9x or later versions, allow the system to redetect the drive, and then reinstall the drivers (if PnP-based system).

Failure to Read CD-R, CD-RW Discs in CD-ROM or DVD Drive

If your CD-ROM or DVD drive fails to read CD-R and CD-RW discs, try the following solutions:

- Check compatibility; some very old 1x CD-ROM drives can't read CD-R media. Replace the drive with a newer, faster, cheaper model.
- Many early-model DVD drives can't read CD-R, CD-RW media; check compatibility.
- The CD-ROM drive must be MultiRead compatible to read CD-RW because of the lower reflectivity of the media; replace the drive.
- If some CD-Rs but not others can be read, check the media color combination to see whether some color combinations work better than others; change the brand of media.
- Packet-written CD-Rs (from Adaptec DirectCD or Drag to Disc and backup programs) can't be read on MS-DOS/Windows 3.1 CD-ROM drives because of the limitations of the operating system.
- Record the media at a slower speed. The pits/lands created at faster speeds sometimes can't be read by older drives.
- If you are trying to read a packet-written CD-R created with DirectCD or Drag to Disc on a CD-ROM drive, reinsert the media into the original drive, eject the media, and select the option Close to Read on Any Drive.

- Download and install a UDF reader compatible with the packet-writing software used to create the CD-RW on the target computer. If you are not sure how the media was created, Software Architects offers a universal UDF reader/media repair program called FixUDF! (also included as part of WriteCD-RW! Pro). WriteDVD! Pro includes the similar FixDVD! UDF reader/media repair program for DVD drives.

Failure to Read a Rewritable DVD in DVD-ROM Drive or Player

If your DVD-ROM or DVD player fails to read a rewritable DVD, try the following solutions:

- Reinsert DVD-RW media into the original drive and finalize the media. Make sure you don't need to add any more data to the media if you use a first-generation (DVD-R 2x/DVD-RW 1x) drive because you must erase the entire disc to do so. You can unfinalize media written by second-generation DVD-R 4x/DVD-RW 2x drives. See your DVD-RW disc-writing software instructions or help file for details.

- Reinsert DVD+RW media into the original drive and change the compatibility setting to emulate DVD-ROM. See the section "DVD+RW Compatibility Mode," earlier in this chapter, for details.

- If the media is dual-layer, write a single-layer disc and retry. Most DVD-ROM drives can't read DL media.

- Make sure the media contains more than 521MB of data. Some drives can't read media that contains a small amount of data.

Failure to Create a Writable DVD

If you can't create a writable DVD but the drive can be used with CD-R, CD-RW, or rewritable DVD media, try the following solutions:

- Make sure you are using the correct media. +R and -R media can't be interchanged unless the drive is a DVD±R/RW dual-mode drive.

- Be sure you select the option to create a DVD project in your mastering software. Some CD/DVD-mastering software defaults to the CD-R setting.

- Select the correct drive as the target. If you have both rewritable DVD and rewritable CD drives on the same system, be sure to specify the rewritable DVD drive.

- Try a different disc.

- Contact the mastering software vendor for a software update.

Failure Writing to CD-RW or DVD-RW 1x Media

If you can't write to CD-RW or DVD-RW 1x media, try the following solutions:

- Make sure the media is formatted. Use the format tool provided with the UDF software to prepare the media for use.

- If the media was formatted, verify it was formatted with the same or compatible UDF program. Different packet-writing programs support different versions of the UDF standard. I recommend you use the same UDF packet-writing software on the computers you use or use drives that support the Mount Rainier standard.

- Make sure the system has identified the media as CD-RW or DVD-RW. Eject and reinsert the media to force the drive to redetect it.

- Contact the packet-writing software vendor for a software update.

- The disc might have been formatted with Windows XP's own limited CD-writing software (which uses the CDFS instead of UDF) instead of a UDF packet-writing program. Erase the disc with Windows XP after transferring any needed files from the media; then format it with your preferred UDF program.

- Contact the drive vendor for a firmware update. See "Updating the Firmware in a CD-RW or Rewritable DVD Drive," later in this chapter.

ATAPI CD-ROM or DVD Drive Runs Slowly

If your ATAPI CD-ROM or DVD drive performs poorly, check the following items:

- Check the cache size in the Performance tab of the System Properties control panel. Select the quad-speed setting (largest cache size).

- Check to see whether the drive is set as the slave to your hard disk; move the drive to the secondary controller if possible.

- Your PIO (Programmed I/O) or UDMA mode might not be set correctly for your drive in the BIOS; check the drive specs and use autodetect in BIOS for the best results (refer to Chapter 5, "BIOS").

- Check that you are using busmastering drivers on compatible systems; install the appropriate drivers for the motherboard's chipset and the operating system in use. See the section "Direct Memory Access and Ultra-DMA," earlier in this chapter.

- Check to see whether you are using the CD-ROM interface on your sound card instead of the ATA connection on the motherboard. Move the drive connection to the ATA interface on the motherboard and disable the sound card ATA if possible to free up IRQ and I/O port address ranges.

- Open the System Properties control panel and select the Performance tab to see whether the system is using MS-DOS Compatibility Mode for CD-ROM drive. If all ATA drives are running in this mode, see www.microsoft.com and query on "MS-DOS Compatibility Mode" for a troubleshooter. If only the CD-ROM drive is in this mode, see whether you're using CD-ROM drivers in CONFIG.SYS and AUTOEXEC.BAT. Remove the lines containing references to the CD-ROM drivers (don't actually delete the lines but instead REM them), reboot the system, and verify that your CD-ROM drive still works and that it's running in 32-bit mode. Some older drives require at least the CONFIG.SYS driver to operate.

Can't Use CD or DVD Drive or Write to Media in Windows XP or Vista

Windows XP's built-in CD-writing feature works only on drives that are listed in the Windows Hardware Compatibility List of supported drives and devices (http://www.microsoft.com/whdc/hcl/default.mspx). To install the latest updates for Windows XP, including updates to the CD writing feature, use Windows Update. Microsoft Knowledge Base article 320174 discusses an update to the CD-writing feature. Search the Microsoft website for other solutions.

If you are using third-party CD or DVD writing applications, you may prefer to disable Windows XP or Vista's built-in writing feature. This feature is enabled or disabled with Windows Explorer. Open the drive's properties sheet's Recording tab and clear the Enable CD Recording checkbox to disable recording, or click the empty box to enable recording.

If you have problems writing media or using your CD or DVD drive in either Windows XP or Windows Vista, see Microsoft Knowledge Base article 314060 for solutions.

Tip

If you are unable to create DVDs or CDs with Windows Vista and you have a USB flash memory drive connected to your computer, eject the drive, and try the burn again.

Poor Results or Slow Performance When Writing to CD-R Media

If you are having problems successfully writing data to a CD, see "How to Reliably Record CDs," earlier in this chapter. Also see the section "Updating the Firmware in a CD-RW or Rewritable DVD Drive."

Trouble Reading CD-RW Discs on CD-ROM

If you can't read CD-RW discs in your CD-ROM, try the following solutions:

- Check the vendor specifications to see whether your drive is MultiRead compliant. Some are not.

- If your drive is MultiRead compliant, try the CD-RW disc on a known-compliant CD-ROM drive (a drive with the MultiRead feature).

- Insert CD-RW media back into the original drive and check it for problems with the packet-writing software program's utilities.

- Insert CD-RW media back into the original drive and eject the media. Use the right-click Eject command in My Computer or Windows Explorer to properly close the media.

- Create a writable CD or DVD to transfer data to a computer that continues to have problems reading rewritable media.

Trouble Reading CD-R Discs on DVD Drive

If your DVD drive can't read a CD-R disc, check to see that the drive is MultiRead2 compliant because noncompliant DVDs can't read CD-R media. Newer DVD drives generally support reading CD-R media.

Trouble Making Bootable CDs

If you are having problems creating a bootable CD, try these possible solutions:

- Check the contents of the bootable floppy disk from which you copied the boot image. To access the entire contents of a CD, a bootable disk must contain CD-ROM drivers, AUTOEXEC.BAT, and CONFIG.SYS.

- Use the ISO 9660 format. Don't use the Joliet format because it is for long-filename CDs and can't boot.

- Check your system's BIOS for boot compliance and boot order; the CD-ROM should be listed first.

- SCSI CD-ROMs need a SCSI card with BIOS and bootable capability as well as special motherboard BIOS settings.

Updating the Firmware in a CD-RW or Rewritable DVD Drive

Just as updating the motherboard BIOS can solve compatibility problems with CPU and memory, support, USB ports, and system stability, upgrading the firmware in a rewritable CD or DVD drive can also solve problems with media compatibility, writing speed, and digital audio extraction from scratched discs and can even prevent potentially fatal mismatches between media and drives.

For example, I noticed that a Plextor CD-RW drive with a maximum CD-R writing speed of 40x was working near its maximum speed when writing to green-gold media brands such as Philips and Imation. However, when azo blue/silver Verbatim media was used, performance sank to an average of 10x or less. A check of the Plextor website (www.plextor.com) revealed that the latest firmware upgrade improved results when Verbatim media was used. After I installed the update, the drive wrote at top speed to azo blue/silver, green-gold, and other types of CD-R media.

To determine exactly which problems a firmware update can solve for you, be sure to check your drive vendor's website.

Determining Whether You Might Need a Firmware Update

If you encounter any of the following issues, a firmware update might be necessary:

- Your drive can't use a particular type of media, or it performs much more slowly with one type of media than other types/brands of media.
- Your writing software stops recognizing the drive as a rewritable drive.
- You want to use faster media than what the drive was originally designed to use.

Because any firmware update runs a risk of failure and a failed firmware update can render your drive useless (I've seen it happen), you shouldn't install firmware updates casually. However, as the preceding examples make clear, sooner or later you'll probably need one.

Note that firmware updates don't fix the following problems:

- Drive not recognized by a newly installed CD or DVD mastering program
- Drive not recognized by Windows XP's built-in CD writing program or Vista's CD/DVD writing program

Because each rewritable CD or DVD drive has special characteristics at present, CD- or DVD-writing programs you buy at retail must have model-specific updates to work. Get the update from the software vendor, or use the software provided with the drive. If you are trying to use an OEM version of a program with a different drive model from the original, you will also need an update from the software vendor (in some cases, an OEM version works only with the original drive with which it was packaged).

Determining Which Drive Model and Firmware Are Installed

Before you can determine whether you need a firmware update for your rewritable drive, you need to know your drive model and which firmware version it's using. This is especially important if you use a drive that is an OEM product produced by a vendor other than the one that packaged the drive for resale. You can use the following methods to determine this information:

- Windows Device Manager
- CD/DVD mastering software drive information

With the Windows Device Manager, follow this procedure:

1. Right-click My Computer and select Properties.
2. Click the Device Manager tab.
3. Click the plus (+) sign next to DVD/CD-ROM in the list of device types.
4. Double-click the rewritable drive icon to display its properties sheet.

5. With older Windows versions, click the Settings tab; the firmware version and drive name will be displayed.

6. On Windows XP SP2 and Windows Vista, click the Details tab and select Hardware Ids. The firmware revision is usually displayed with several underscores on either side of it as part of the hardware ids listed. For example, my Lite-On SHW-160P6S DVD drive is using firmware version PS08, displayed as _____PS08_____

With Roxio Easy Media Creator 7 and newer, follow this procedure:

1. Start Creator Classic

2. Click Tools.

3. Click Disc and Device Utility.

4. Expand the CD/DVD drive listing.

5. Expand Device Properties. The Drive firmware revision is listed along with other information.

With Nero Burning ROM 5.5 and later, follow this procedure:

1. Click Recorder from the top-level menu.

2. Click the drive desired.

3. The drive model and firmware version are displayed along with other information.

After you have this information, you can go to your rewritable drive vendor's website and see whether a firmware update is available and what the benefits of installing the latest version would be.

Installing New Drive Firmware

Generally speaking, the firmware update procedure works like this, but you should be sure to follow the particular instructions given for your drive:

1. If the firmware update is stored as a Zip file, you need to use an unzipping program or the integrated unzipping utility found in some versions of Windows to uncompress the update to a folder. Some vendors ship firmware updates as .rar files (.rar is a Linux compressed archive; it can be opened by many uncompression utilities for Windows).

2. If the drive maker provides a readme file, be sure to read it for help and troubleshooting. If the update file is an EXE file, it might display a readme file as part of step 3.

3. Double-click the EXE file to start the update process. Be sure to leave the system powered on during the process (which can take 2–3 minutes).

4. Follow the vendor's instructions for restarting your system.

5. After you restart your system, the computer might redetect the drive and assign it the next available drive letter. If you previously assigned the drive a customized drive letter (for example, on one computer in my organization, Q: is used for a CD-RW drive, and R: for a DVD+RW drive), use the Device Manager in Windows 9x/Me or the Computer Management service in Windows 2000/XP/Vista to reassign the correct drive letter to the drive.

Troubleshooting Firmware Updates

If you have problems performing a rewritable drive firmware update, check the vendor's readme file or website for help. In addition, here are some tips I've found useful.

If the firmware update fails to complete, there might be interference from programs that control the drive, such as packet-writing programs (InCD, DirectCD) or the built-in Windows XP CD writing feature. To disable resident software, restart the computer in Safe Mode (Windows 2000/XP) and retry the update. Restart the system normally after the update is complete.

With Windows 9x/Me, you can use MSConfig (System Configuration Utility), select the Selective Startup option, and uncheck Load Startup Group Items and Process Win.INI File Before Restarting. After completing the firmware update, be sure to rerun MSConfig and select Normal Startup before restarting the computer.

To disable Windows XP's own CD-writing feature for a particular drive, right-click the drive icon in My Computer, select Properties, click the Recording tab, and clear the check mark in the box next to Enable CD Recording on This Drive. The same method is used to disable CD/DVD recording with Windows Vista.

If the firmware update doesn't improve drive performance on a system running Windows 9x/Me, DMA might not be enabled on the rewritable drive. Refer to the section "Direct Memory Access and Ultra-DMA," earlier in this chapter, for details.

Physical Drive Installation and Configuration

Installing All Types of Drives

This chapter covers the actual installation of hard drives, optical drives (CD/DVD) and floppy drives. This includes everything from preparing the components to setting jumpers to installing the actual cabling and performing the physical installation. I also dig into some initial system software configuration issues, right up to the point of installing the operating system. From that point on, the steps you take depend on which operating system you are installing.

For more information on drive interfaces, magnetic storage, drive operation, and operating system issues, see the following chapters:

- Chapter 7, "The ATA/IDE Interface"
- Chapter 8, "Magnetic Storage Principles"
- Chapter 9, "Hard Disk Storage"
- Chapter 10, "Removable Storage"
- Chapter 11, "Optical Storage"
- Chapter 15, "I/O Interfaces from Serial and Parallel to IEEE 1394 and USB"

Although most of the drives you would install in a PC are covered here, the primary emphasis is on internal hard disks and other devices using Serial ATA (SATA) or Parallel ATA (also called PATA, ATA, or IDE). Other interfaces such as SCSI (Small Computer System Interface) or SAS (Serial Attached SCSI) are often used in servers, and are covered in more detail in my book *Upgrading and Repairing Servers* instead. For external USB or FireWire (IEEE 1394) devices, see Chapter 15.

Hard Disk Installation Procedures

This section describes the hard disk drive installation process, particularly the configuration, physical installation, and formatting of a hard disk drive.

To install a hard drive in a PC, you must perform some or all of the following procedures:

- Configure the drive.
- Configure the host adapter.
- Physically install the drive.
- Configure the system to recognize the drive.
- Initialize and partition the drive.
- High-level format the partitions or volumes.

As you perform these procedures, you might need to know a few details about the drive, host adapter, and system ROM BIOS. This information usually appears in the various manuals or reference sheets that come with these devices.

If you are like me, however, and want all the detailed technical documentation on the device you can get, you should contact the original manufacturer and see if you can download any more in-depth datasheets or technical manuals for the device. For example, if you purchase a system that includes a particular SATA drive, the system builder may give you some limited information on the drive, but not nearly the amount that the datasheet and technical manual for the drive provides. To get this documentation, you normally download it from the drive manufacturer's website. The same rule applies for any of the other components in most of the systems sold today. I find the OEM technical manuals essential in providing the highest level of technical support possible.

Drive Configuration

Before you physically install a hard disk drive in the computer, you must ensure that it is properly configured. For Parallel ATA drives, this generally means designating a drive as either master/slave or cable select (CS) and using an 80-conductor cable to determine the relationship.

◀◀ To learn more about configuring PATA drives, see "ATA Standards," p. 586.

Because Serial ATA drives connect to the SATA host adapter in a point-to-point configuration using a dedicated cable, there is no master, slave, or cable select setting as there is with Parallel ATA drives. Note, however, that some SATA drives might have jumpers to help solve compatibility issues, such as to lock a newer 300/150MBps interface speed drive into the slower 150MBps mode to work around problems with certain older host adapters. For driver and other software compatibility reasons, most SATA host adapters can operate in a compatibility mode in which they emulate master and slave configurations, even though no such settings are made physically.

Host Adapter Configuration

Older hard disk drive interfaces used separate disk controller cards you had to install in a bus slot. The PATA and SATA hard disk drives used in today's PCs, however, have the disk controller integrated directly into the drive assembly. For ATA drives, the host adapter interface is nearly always integrated into the system's motherboard, and you configure the interface through the BIOS Setup. In these cases, no separate host adapter exists. Some systems might use adapter card–based host adapters in lieu of the built-in interfaces. This is because some of the motherboard-integrated PATA and SATA interfaces might not support the faster modes (300MBps for SATA or 133MBps for PATA) that most newer drives can use. In most cases, I would recommend upgrading the motherboard rather than installing a separate host adapter because a new motherboard has other benefits and the cost may not be that much higher. Still, in some cases adding a card-based host adapter makes sense—for example, you can add SATA drives to an older system that doesn't have a SATA host adapter built in to the motherboard by installing an SATA adapter card (see Figure 12.1).

Card-based host adapters require some combination of the following system resources:

- Boot ROM address (optional)
- Interrupt request (IRQ)
- Direct memory access (DMA) channel
- I/O port address

Not all adapters use every one of these resources, but some might use them all. In most cases with modern Plug and Play adapters and systems, the BIOS and your operating system automatically configure these resources. The computer sets the required hardware resources using values that do not conflict with other devices in the computer.

◀◀   See "Plug and Play BIOS," p. 500.

If your hardware or operating system does not support Plug and Play, you must manually configure the adapter to use the appropriate resources. Some adapters provide software that enables you to reconfigure or change the hardware resources, whereas others might use jumpers or DIP switches on the adapter card.

◀◀   See "System Resources," p. 408.

The ATA interface driver is part of the standard PC BIOS, which enables booting from either PATA or SATA drives. Systems that include SATA interfaces on the motherboard also incorporate support for SATA into the BIOS. The BIOS provides the device driver functionality the system needs to access the drive before any files can be loaded from disk.

Note

Although standard ATA drivers are provided with Windows, this interface is typically built in to the motherboard chipset South Bridge or I/O Controller Hub (ICH) component, and often requires that specific chipset drivers be loaded. If you are using a motherboard that is newer than your operating system version (for example, a board purchased new after 2002 that is used with Windows XP), be sure you install the chipset drivers that came with your motherboard immediately after installing Windows. If the board supports SATA in AHCI (Advanced Host Controller Interface) mode or features such as SATA RAID (Redundant Array of Independent Disks) and you are running Windows XP or earlier, in most cases you will either need to supply the drivers via a floppy disk at the start of the installation, or have them preloaded on your Windows install disc. Note that these drivers are built in to the Windows Vista install DVD. If the board is older than the OS, the chipset drivers will most likely be present on the OS installation CD; however, it is still a good idea to update to the latest chipset drivers immediately after the OS installation.

Some SATA host adapters include a host adapter BIOS to add support for AHCI, RAID, large drives, or other features. If your standard motherboard BIOS already includes this support, or if you will not be using these features, then use of the accessory BIOS is optional. Most card-based host adapters have switches, jumpers, or configuration software you can use to enable or disable BIOS support.

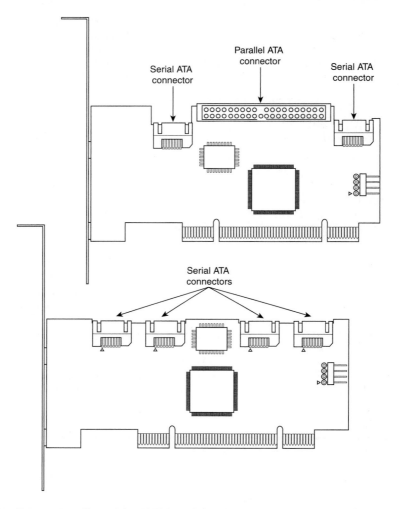

Figure 12.1   You can install a combo SATA/ATA host adapter (top) or a pure SATA host adapter (bottom). This enables you to install SATA drives into a computer that has standard ATA host adapters.

In addition to providing boot functionality, the host adapter BIOS can provide many other functions, including any or all of the following:

- RAID configuration
- Host adapter configuration
- Diagnostics

If the adapter's BIOS is enabled, it uses specific memory address space in the upper memory area (UMA). The UMA is the top 384KB in the first megabyte of system memory. It is divided into three areas of two 64KB segments each, with the first and last areas being used by the video adapter circuits and the motherboard BIOS, respectively. Segments C000h and D000h are reserved for use by adapter ROMs, such as those found on video cards and host adapters.

Note

You must ensure that any adapters using space in these segments of the UMA (upper memory area) do not overlap with another adapter that uses this space. No two adapters can share this memory space. Most adapters have software, jumpers, or switches that can adjust the configuration of the board and change the addresses it uses to prevent conflict.

Physical Installation

The procedure for the physical installation of a hard disk drive is much the same as that for installing any other type of drive. You must have the correct screws, brackets, and faceplates for the specific drive and system before you can install the drive.

Some computer cases require plastic or metal rails that are secured to the sides of a hard disk drive so it can slide into the proper place in the system (see Figure 12.2). Other case designs have drive bays that directly accept the drive via screws through the side supports and no other hardware is necessary, whereas others use a cage arrangement where you first install the drives into a cage and then slide the cage into the case (see Figure 12.3). If your case uses rails or a cage, these are usually included with the case. With the proper mounting mechanism supplied via the case, all you need is the bare drive to install.

Because PATA and SATA drives use different cables, be sure you have the proper cable for both your drive and controller/host adapter. For example, to run PATA 66MBps and faster modes (through 133MBps), you need an 80-conductor cable. This cable is also recommended even if you are running 33MBps and slower modes as well. To determine whether your cable has 40 or 80 conductors, simply count the ridges on the ribbon cable—each ridge contains a conductor (wire). Another indication is that the 80-conductor cable typically has the motherboard connector end color-coded blue, and the master and slave drive connectors color-coded black and gray, respectively.

If you need additional drive-mounting hardware not included with either your case or the drive, several companies specialize in drive-mounting brackets, cables, and other hardware accessories, including Ci Design (www.cidesign.com), Micro Accessories (www.micro-a.com), Jameco (www.jameco.com), NewEgg (www.newegg.com), and more. If you intend to install a 3 1/2" hard drive in a 5 1/4" drive bay, you need yet another type of mounting bracket (as shown in Figure 12.4). Many 3 1/2" hard drives come with these brackets, or one might be supplied with your case or chassis.

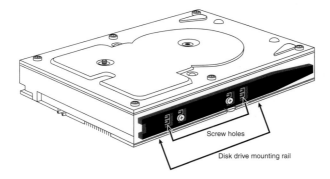

Figure 12.2   A typical 3 1/2" hard disk with mounting rails for a 3 1/2" drive bay.

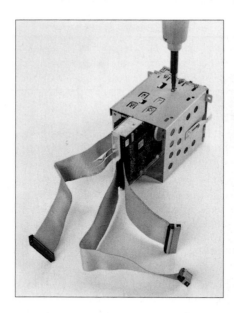

Figure 12.3   A typical hard disk mounted in a removable drive cage.

Note

You should also note the length of the drive cable itself when you plan to add a hard disk drive. It can be very annoying to assemble everything you think you'll need to install a drive and then find that the drive cable is not long enough to reach the new drive location. You can either try to reposition the drive to a location closer to the interface connector on the host adapter or motherboard or just get a longer cable. PATA ribbon cables are technically limited to 18" in overall length according to the standard; however, in most cases you can get away with cables of up to 27" in length as long as they are an 80-conductor ribbon type. Cable lengths longer than that, as well as "rounded" types, are generally not recommended. This is most important if your drive is going to use the fastest 133MBps mode. Using a cable that is too long causes timing errors and signal degradation, possibly corrupting the data on your drive. I see many 36" cable assemblies being sold or used in systems; you are asking for trouble if you violate the 18" maximum-length specification by that amount.

Different faceplate, or bezel, options are also available. Make sure you have the correct bezel for your application. Some systems, for example, do not need a bezel; if a bezel exists on the drive, you must remove it.

Caution

Be sure you use only the screws that come with your new drive. Many drives come with special short-length screws that may have the same size thread as other screws you might use in your system, but these screws should not be interchanged. If you use screws that are too long, they might protrude too far into the drive casing and cause problems.

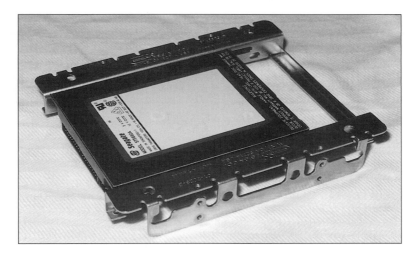

Figure 12.4   A typical bracket used to mount a 3 1/2" drive in a 5 1/4" drive bay. The bracket is screwed to the drive and then mounted in the bay by using screws or rails, as determined by the case.

After unpacking a new internal drive, you should have the following pieces:

- The drive
- The internal CD-audio cable (optional)
- Software (optional)
- Drive rails and mounting screws

Drives sold as OEM or bare drives may include only the drive, and you will need to supply any screws, cables, and/or software.

Parallel ATA (PATA) Hard Disk Drive Installation

The step-by-step procedures for installing an ATA hard drive are as follows:

1. Check your computer for an unused 40-pin PATA/IDE connector. Typical PCs have one or two of these connectors, allowing for up to four PATA devices.

   You might need an additional cable if both master and slave connectors are used on the primary cable and you are adding a third device.

Tip

For best performance, keep devices that will be simultaneously active, such as hard drives and optical drives, on separate cables.

2. Double-check the pin configuration and cable type. The colored stripe on one edge of the ribbon cable goes to pin 1 of the drive's data connector. Most cable and drive connectors are keyed to prevent improper (backward) installation, but many are not. Keying can be done via missing and/or plugged pins, a ridge on one side of the connector, or both. One tip to note is that pin 1 on the drive connector is almost always oriented nearest to the 4-pin power connector.

Tip

Newer ATA drives that operate in the faster Ultra-DMA modes (66MBps through 133MBps) require 80-conductor cables, whereas 33MBps and slower drives can use 40-conductor cables. However, because the superior 80-conductor cables will also work for slower drives, I recommend using only 80-conductor cables where possible. Another benefit is that with 80-conductor cables, you can set all of the drives to CS (cable select) instead of independent master/slave settings.

3. **Configure the drive jumpers.** If the drive is PATA/IDE and you are using an 80-conductor cable (that supports CS), you should set jumpers to the CS position on any drives connected to that cable. Otherwise, you must set the drives on the cable separately as either master or slave. Note that some older drives also required a slave-present jumper be set if the drive was configured as a master with a slave drive on the same cable.

4. **Slide the drive into an available 3 1/2" drive bay,** and secure it using the screws, rails, or brackets provided with either the drive or chassis. If you have no 3 1/2" drive bays left for your hard disk, attach a drive-adapter kit to the sides of the drive to make it wide enough to fit into a 5 1/4"-wide drive bay (refer to Figure 12.4). Some case designs require you to attach rails to the side of the hard drive. If so, attach them to the drive using the screws supplied with either the case or the drive. Be sure the screws aren't too long; if the screws are longer than the hole is deep, or if they bottom out against the sealed HDA (Head Disk Assembly), you can damage the drive. Slide the drive into the bay in the case until the rails latch into place.

Note

You can find more visual step-by-step instructions for installing a hard drive in Chapter 20, "Building or Upgrading Systems."

5. **Connect the ribbon cable between the drive and the host adapter** (usually the motherboard). If you're using an 80-conductor cable, the blue connector attaches to the host adapter, the black connector goes to the drive you want to be master, and the gray connector (usually in the middle) goes to the drive you want to be slave.

6. **Attach the power connector to the drive.** If necessary, you can use a Y-splitter cable (see Figure 12.5) to create two power connectors from one (some computers have fewer power connectors than drive bays).

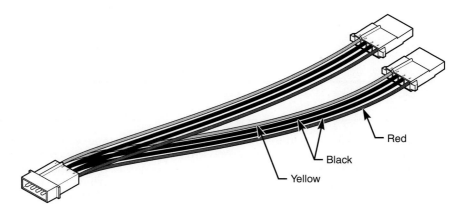

Figure 12.5 Power cord splitter and connector.

Serial ATA (SATA) Hard Disk Drive Installation

The step-by-step procedure for installing a SATA hard drive is as follows:

1. Check your computer for an unused SATA host adapter connector (usually on the mother-board). Most motherboards have from two to six SATA connectors on-board, but for older boards without a built-in SATA host adapter, you might need to install a separate SATA host adapter card instead. If you install a SATA host adapter card, consult the documentation included with the card for installation instructions.

2. Slide the drive into an available 3 1/2" drive bay, and secure it using the screws, rails, or brackets provided with either the drive or chassis.

3. Connect a SATA cable between the drive and the SATA host adapter. In some cases, SATA data cables can be combined with the SATA power cable. If the SATA data cable is separate from the SATA power cable, either end of the cable can be used for the drive or host adapter (see Figure 12.6).

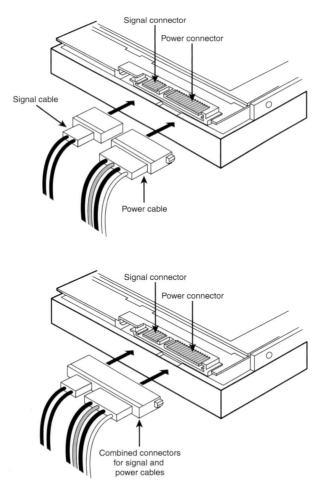

Figure 12.6   SATA data and power cables can be separate (top) or combined into a single molded assembly (bottom).

4. Attach a power connector to the drive. Some SATA drives have both conventional 4-pin peripheral power connectors as well as SATA 15-pin power connectors, in which case you can use one or the other, but *not* both simultaneously. If your drive has only a SATA power connector and your power supply doesn't have SATA power connectors available, you might need to purchase a peripheral-to-SATA power cable adapter if one was not provided with your drive. This type of adapter changes a standard 4-pin peripheral power connector into a 15-pin SATA power connector.

Caution

If a drive has both conventional (also called *peripheral* or *legacy*) and SATA-type power connectors, you must *not* plug in both power connectors at the same time, or the drive may be damaged!

System Configuration

After your drive is physically installed, you must provide the computer with basic information about the drive so the system can access and boot from it.

With your operating system boot CD or floppy in the appropriate drive, restart the computer. If you intend to install the operating system, Windows 98 or later will automatically guide you through the partitioning and formatting process during the operating system installation. If you want, you can partition and format the drive before installing the OS, by using the operating system's disk-partitioning software.

If you use Windows 9x or Me, FDISK can be found on the operating system startup floppy. Simply boot from the startup floppy and type the FDISK command at the A: prompt. Windows 2000, XP, and Vista use the DISKPART command or the Disk Management utility, which can be found on the bootable OS optical disc. If you are installing an operating system on the new drive, you would normally perform the partitioning and formatting during the early part of the OS installation process.

◀◀ See "ATA Standards," p. 586.

Automatic Drive Detection

For PATA and SATA drives, virtually all new BIOS versions in today's PCs have automatic parameter detection (autodetect). The BIOS sends a special Identify Drive command to all the devices connected during the system startup sequence; the drives are intelligent enough to respond with the correct parameters. The BIOS then automatically enters the parameter information returned by the drive. This procedure eliminates errors or confusion in parameter selection:

Start the computer and press the appropriate key to access the BIOS Setup screens to configure the drive. If your BIOS has an autodetect or auto type setting, I recommend you use it because it will configure the parameters automatically using optimal settings. With SATA drives you may also have options to configure AHCI (Advanced Host Controller Interface) support or set multiple drives in a RAID (Redundant Array of Independent Disks) configuration. Once the settings are made, save the BIOS Setup settings and exit the BIOS Setup to continue.

◀◀ See "Advanced Host Controller Interface (AHCI)," p. 610.

2. Restart the system. If the drive you are installing was not the boot drive and you are running Windows 9x or later, the OS should automatically detect the new drive upon loading, and install the necessary drivers. Note that the drive will not be visible to the OS as a volume (that is, a drive letter) until it is partitioned and formatted. If the drive is the boot drive, you can continue by booting from an OS installation disc in order to partition, format, and install the OS to

the boot drive. If the motherboard supports SATA in AHCI mode or features such as SATA RAID, and you are running Windows XP or earlier, in most cases you will either need to supply host adapter drivers via a floppy disk at the start of the installation or have them preloaded on your Windows install disc. Note that these drivers are built in to the Windows Vista install DVD.

Manual Drive Parameters

If you are dealing with an ancient motherboard that does not support autodetect, you must enter the appropriate drive information in the system BIOS manually. The BIOS has a selection of preconfigured drive types, but these are woefully outdated in most cases, providing support only for drives holding a few hundred megabytes or less. In nearly every case, you must select the user-defined drive type and provide values for the following settings:

- Cylinders
- Heads
- Sectors per track

The values you use for these settings should be provided in the documentation for the hard disk drive, but they also might be printed on the drive itself. It's a good idea to check for these settings and write them down because they might not be visible after you've installed the drive. You also should maintain a copy of these settings in case your system BIOS loses its data due to a battery failure. One of the best places to store this information is inside the computer itself. Taping a note with vital settings such as these to the inside of the case can be a lifesaver.

In the event that you are unable to determine the correct settings for your hard drive from either the drive case or the Technical Reference, utility programs are available on the Internet that can query the drive for this information.

Depending on the maker and version of your system BIOS, you might have to configure other settings as well, such as which transfer mode to use and whether the BIOS should use logical block addressing.

◀◀ See "ATA Drive Capacity Limitations," p. 616.

Formatting

Proper setup and formatting are critical to a drive's performance and reliability. This section describes the procedures used to partition and format a hard disk drive correctly. Use these procedures when you install a new drive in a system or immediately after you recover data from a hard disk that has been exhibiting problems.

The three major steps in the formatting process for a hard disk drive subsystem are as follows:

1. Low-level formatting
2. Partitioning
3. High-level formatting

The low-level format (LLF) option is not considered a normal part of a new drive installation, but can often bring back a failing drive from the dead. For more information on low-level formatting drives, see the section "Low-level Formatting (Initializing)" later in this chapter. During normal drive installation and configuration procedures, you will only need to partition the drive into volumes and then high-level format each volume. These procedures are covered in the following sections.

Partitioning

Partitioning a hard disk is the act of defining areas of the disk for an operating system to use as a volume.

When you partition a disk, the partitioning software writes a master partition boot sector at Cylinder 0, Head 0, Sector 1 (also known as Logical Block Address 0)—the first sector on the hard disk. This sector contains data that describes the partitions by their starting and ending sector locations. The partition table also indicates which of the partitions is bootable and, therefore, where to look for an operating system to load.

The FDISK program is the accepted standard for partitioning hard disk drives for use with all operating systems up through Windows Me. Windows 2000, XP, and Vista use a similar command-line program called DISKPART, or you can partition and format hard disks with the Disk Management tool. All versions of Windows starting with Windows 95 can also partition and format a drive using the SETUP program when the OS is installed. These programs are included with the operating systems, and although they might have the same name and basic functions with different OSs, you should typically use the tools that specifically came with or were designed for your specific OS. Partitioning prepares the boot sector of the disk in such a way that it can be recognized as one or more volumes for storing files. Partitioning also enables multiple operating systems to coexist on a single hard disk. No matter which operating system you use, it should come with an FDISK, DISKPART, Disk Management, or SETUP utility that can be used to partition the drive.

Note

Because FDISK, DISKPART, Disk Management, and SETUP depend on BIOS information about the hard disk to determine the size and drive geometry of the hard disk, having correct BIOS settings saved in the BIOS Setup is vital to the correct operation of these programs. If a 100GB hard drive is defined in the BIOS as a 100MB hard drive, for example, all these programs will see is 100MB. To prevent confusion and improper geometry definition, it is best to set the BIOS Setup drive types to Auto or Autodetect, that way the geometry will be read directly from the drives and should always be correct.

The two main types of partitions for DOS or Windows systems are primary and extended. A primary partition can be bootable, but an extended partition can't. If you have only a single hard disk in your system, at least part of the drive must be prepared as a primary partition if you want to start your computer from the hard disk (and who doesn't?). A primary partition is seen as a single volume or drive letter (C: on one-drive systems), whereas an extended partition acts as a sort of logical container for additional volumes (drive letters D: and beyond). A single extended partition can contain a single volume (also referred to by FDISK as a *logical DOS drive*) or several volumes (logical DOS drives) of various sizes.

Don't get hung up on the fact that FDISK calls partitions "DOS" partitions or "DOS" drives. This is true even though the operating system you are installing is Windows 95, 98, Me, NT, 2000, XP, Vista, Linux, and so on.

Depending on the version of Windows in use (and with any version of MS-DOS), you might need to subdivide a hard drive through the use of FDISK. The original release of Windows 95 and all MS-DOS versions support a file system known as FAT16, which allows no more than 65,536 files per drive and a single drive letter or volume size of no more than 2.1GB. Thus, a 10GB hard disk prepared with MS-DOS or the original Windows 95 (or 95A) must be divided into a minimum of five volumes, and could have more (see Figure 12.7).

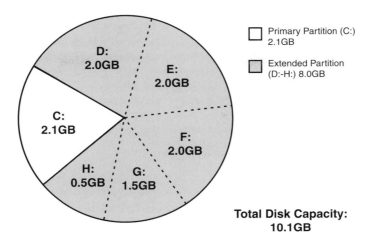

Total Disk Capacity:
10.1GB

Figure 12.7   Adding a hard drive above 2.1GB in size to an MS-DOS or original Windows 95A computer forces the user to create multiple drive letters to use the entire drive capacity. The logical DOS drives are referenced like any other drive, although they are portions of a single physical hard disk.

Another reason for subdividing a single drive into multiple volumes is increased data security. For example, a common scheme is to use a two-volume partitioning scheme that looks like this:

- C: for the operating system and applications
- D: for data

In this example, primary and extended partitions would be assigned as shown here:

- C: for the primary partition
- D: for the logical drive (volume) in an extended partition

FDISK is artificially limited to creating only a single primary partition per drive, but other partitioning programs can create multiple primary partitions, up to a limit of 4 per drive. Normally I prefer creating only primary partitions unless more than 4 volumes are needed on a single drive.

With two partitions, managing backups can be easier because normally you only want to back up your data, and not the OS or applications.

Note

Although external USB and FireWire (IEEE 1394) drives are usually pre-partitioned and formatted to allow immediate use, you can change the partitions and/or file system used on the drive. For example, most external USB/FireWire drives come preformatted using FAT32 because it is the most universally supported file system; however, most people using Windows XP or Vista would want to reformat FAT32 volumes as NTFS for improved integrity and performance.

Large Hard Disk Support

If you use the Windows 95B or above (Win95 OSR 2.x), Windows 98, Windows Me, or Windows 2000 version of FDISK with a hard drive greater than 512MB, the utility offers to enable large disk support.

Choosing to enable large disk support provides the following benefits:

■ You can use a large hard disk (greater than 2.1GB) as a single drive letter. In fact, your drive can be as large as 2TB and still be identified by a single drive letter. This is because the FAT32 file system allows for many more files per drive than FAT16.

■ Because of the more efficient storage methods of FAT32, your files will use less hard disk space overall.

However, keep in mind that all disk operations must be performed through an operating system with FAT32 support (Windows 95B or later, Windows 98, Windows Me, or Windows 2000). If you have old MS-DOS games or applications that are bootable, you won't be able to access a FAT32 volume unless you replace the DOS version on the disk with the DOS included on Windows 95B or Windows 98. This normally can be done by using the SYS A: command from the \Windows\Command folder. Another option is to use the Windows Startup menu in Windows 95B or Windows 98 (press F8 as Windows starts to load) and select Command Prompt to get to a FAT32-capable DOS. On the other hand, you can select Start, Shutdown, Restart the Computer in MS-DOS Mode from the Windows desktop.

A drive prepared with the large hard disk support (FAT32) option enabled can still be partitioned into primary and secondary partitions with FDISK, as with FAT16 for the data-security reasons listed earlier.

Another type of file system is NTFS, which is supported by Windows NT–based operating systems, including NT, 2000, XP, and Vista. This is a high-performance file system with additional security and networking features. Note that Windows 9x can't read NTFS partitions, and Windows NT can't read FAT32 partitions. Windows 2000, XP, and Vista, however, can handle both FAT32 and NTFS.

Assigning Drive Letters with FDISK

FDISK can be used in many ways, depending on the number of hard drives you have in your system and the number of drive letters you want to create.

With a single drive, creating a primary partition (C:) and an extended partition with two logical DOS drives within it results in the following drive letters:

Partition Type	Drive Letter(s)
Primary	C:
Extended	D: and E:

Most people think that a second physical drive added to this system should have drive letters that follow the E: drive.

However, you must understand how the system allocates drive letters to know how to use FDISK correctly in this situation. Table 12.1 shows how FDISK assigns drive letters by drive and partition type.

Table 12.1   Drive Letter Allocations by Drive and Partition Type

Drive	Partition	Order	Drive Letter
1st	Primary	1st	C:
1st	Extended	3rd	E:
2nd	Primary	2nd	D:
2nd	Extended	4th	F:

How does this affect you when you add another hard drive? If you prepare the second hard drive with a primary partition and your first hard drive has an extended partition on it, the second hard drive takes the primary partition's D: drive letter. This moves all the drive letters in the first hard drive's extended partition up one drive letter.

In the first example, a drive is listed with C: (primary partition), D:, and E: (extended partition volumes) as the drive letters (D: and E: were in the extended partition). Table 12.2 indicates what happens if a second drive is added with a primary partition and an extended partition with two volumes (same setup as the first drive).

Table 12.2   Drive Letter Changes Caused by the Addition of a Second Drive with a Primary Partition

Drive	Partition Type	Order	Original Drive Letters (First Drive Only)	New Drive Letters After Adding Second Drive
1st	Primary	1st	C:	C:
1st	Extended	3rd	D:, E:	E:, F:
2nd	Primary	2nd		D:
2nd	Extended	4th		G:, H:

After the second drive is added, the original drive letters D: and E: now become E: and F:. The primary partition on the new drive becomes D:, and the extended partition volumes on the second drive are G: and H:. Confused? Well, you better not be or you'll find yourself deleting or copying data to or from the wrong drive.

This principle extends to third and fourth physical drives as well: The primary partitions on each drive get their drive letters first, followed by logical DOS drives in the extended partitions.

One way to affect this is to partition additional drives with only extended partitions—in other words, do not create primary partitions on them. That enables the new drive's partitions to be seen only as additional letters, and the letters used by the first drive's partitions to remain unchanged.

If you're *adding* a drive to your system, you should now understand why preparing that second, third, or fourth drive with a primary partition is a bad idea. If you're installing an additional hard drive (not a replacement), remember that it can't be a bootable drive. And if it can't be bootable, there's no reason to make it a primary partition. FDISK allows you to create an extended partition using 100% of the space on any drive. Table 12.3 shows the same example used in Table 12.2 with the second drive installed as an extended partition.

Table 12.3   Drive Letter Allocations After the Addition of a Second Drive with an Extended Partition Only

Drive	Partition Type	Order	Original Drive Letters (First Drive Only)	New Drive Letters After Adding Second Drive
1st	Primary	1st	C:	C:
1st	Extended	3rd	D:, E:	D:, E:
2nd	Primary	2nd	—	—
2nd	Extended	4th		F:

When a new drive is added with only extended partition volumes, you can see that the original drive letters remain undisturbed. This arrangement is much easier to understand, and it prevents accidents with data because of drive letters changing. This operating system behavior also explains why some of the first computers with ATA-based (ATAPI) Iomega Zip drives had the Zip drive as D:, with a single hard disk identified as C: and E:. The Zip drive was treated as the second hard drive with a primary partition. Subsequently, Iomega changed the Zip drive format and driver so that the Zip disk is recognized as an extended partition at the end of the drive letter chain.

Running FDISK

When you run newer versions of FDISK, the first thing that happens is you are prompted with the following:

```
Do you wish to enable large disk support (Y/N)...........? [Y]
```

If you answer Yes to this question, FDISK creates FAT32 volumes for all volumes created that are larger than 512MB. Answering No to this question forces FDISK to create only FAT16 volumes, which are limited to a 2GB maximum size and waste more space on the disk due to larger cluster sizes.

Normally, in a modern system you would answer Yes, allowing the use of FAT32. After you answer the question, FDISK shows a menu similar to the following:

```
Current fixed disk drive: 1

    Choose one of the following:

    1. Create DOS partition or Logical DOS Drive
    2. Set active partition
    3. Delete partition or Logical DOS Drive
    4. Display partition information
    5. Change current fixed disk drive

    Enter choice: [1]
```

Option 5 is shown only if FDISK detects more than one drive on your system (if more than one is entered via your BIOS Setup). In that case, FDISK defaults to the first drive, and via option 5 you can cause FDISK to work with any of the other hard disks on the system.

To create partitions, you select option 1. If the drive is already partitioned, however, you can use option 4 to display the current layout of the drive.

After you select option 1, the menu changes to enable you to create primary or extended partitions on a drive, as follows:

```
Create DOS Partition or Logical DOS Drive

    Current fixed disk drive: 1

    Choose one of the following:

    1. Create Primary DOS Partition
    2. Create Extended DOS Partition
    3. Create Logical DOS Drive(s) in the Extended DOS Partition

    Enter choice: [1]
```

The rules require you to create a primary partition first on the boot drive, but on a secondary or non-boot drive, you can create just an extended partition if you choose. So, if you are partitioning the first drive in a system and it will be bootable, you would choose option 1.

At this point, you are prompted to decide whether you want to use the maximum available size for a Primary DOS Partition. If you answer Yes and you're using FAT32, the primary partition uses the entire drive. Conversely, if you answer Yes and you did not enable large drive support (meaning you are using FAT16), the partition uses the entire drive or 2GB, whichever is smaller.

If you decide to create a primary partition that is not the full drive, you should go back through the menus and create an extended partition using the rest of the drive, and then further divide it into logical drives. Normally, I recommend making the primary partition the full size of the drive, keeping all of the drive as one letter. But there are various reasons you might want to split the drive into multiple partitions, such as for different operating systems, file systems, applications, and so on.

After all the partitions are created, the final operation is to make one of them active (bootable), which is option 2 from the main FDISK menu. Typically, the only one that can be active is the primary partition. After that is done, all FDISK operations are complete, and you can exit the program.

When you exit FDISK after making partition changes, the system must be rebooted before these changes will be recognized. After rebooting, you must then high-level format each of the volumes with the operating system FORMAT command, which then allows the operating system to store files on these volumes.

The C: volume usually must be formatted with the system files, although when you install Windows via the Windows Setup command, it detects whether the system files are present and offers to install them for you.

Drive Partitioning and Formatting with Disk Management

Even though Windows 2000, XP, and Vista have a very powerful command-line tool called DISKPART that provides FDISK-like capabilities, along with additional options useful for working with advanced disk structures such as RAID arrays and dynamic disks, most people utilize the GUI-based Disk Management component of the Microsoft Management Console to perform hard disk partitioning and formatting when installing a new hard disk on an existing system.

As with FDISK, you can select the type of file system you want to use, but the following differences exist between FDISK and Disk Management:

■ Disk Management is a true GUI-based utility. Color-coded indicators for partition type and drive condition let you easily see which tasks you've performed with a drive. Wizards enable you to partition and format a drive under the guidance of Windows.

■ Disk Management supports more file systems than FDISK. Whereas FDISK is limited to FAT16 (and FAT32 on Windows 95B and above, Windows 98, and Windows Me), Disk Management also supports NTFS.

■ Disk Management partitions and formats hard disks with a simple process. Unlike FDISK, which requires you to restart the system before a new hard disk can be formatted and uses a separate FORMAT program to finish the job, Disk Management can perform both tasks without the need to restart the computer.

■ Disk Management can create multiple primary partitions on a drive. Unlike FDISK, which can only create a single primary partition, Disk Management can create up to four primary partitions on a drive. Unlike logical volumes in extended partitions, primary partitions can be bootable and are generally easier to manage.

■ Disk Management uses drive letters not already in use for hard disk or optical drives, regardless of the partition type. Unlike FDISK, which can scramble existing drive letter assignments if you prepare a new hard disk with a primary partition, Disk Management assigns a drive letter (or letters) to the new hard drive that follows those already in use. And, if installing a new drive causes conflicts with removable-media drives such as USB keychain or flash memory card readers you use occasionally, you can use Disk Management to select a different drive letter for the new hard disk or for existing hard disks or optical drives.

To use Disk Management to partition a new hard disk in Windows XP or Vista, do the following:

1. Open the Start menu, select Run, type **diskmgmt.msc**, then click **OK**.

2. The current hard disk drive letter is displayed in the upper-right window, and physical hard disks are displayed in the bottom-right window (see Figure 12.8). A newly installed drive is shown as unallocated space.

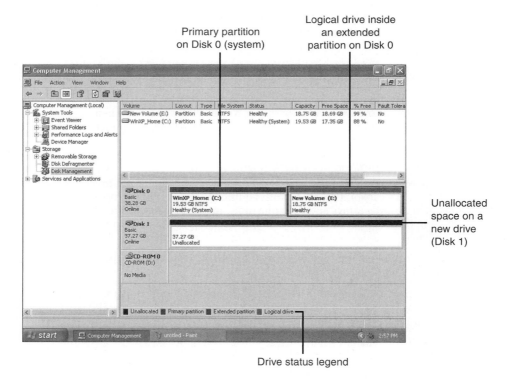

Primary partition
on Disk 0 (system)

Logical drive inside
an extended
partition on Disk 0

Unallocated
space on a
new drive
(Disk 1)

Drive status legend

Figure 12.8 The Disk Management view of a system with a newly installed hard disk (Disk 1). Because New Volume (E:) was prepared after the CD-ROM drive (D:) was installed, it has a higher drive letter.

3. Select the new hard disk, right-click it, and select New Partition from the right-click menu to start the partitioning process.

4. Click Next at the opening screen of the New Partition Wizard.

5. Select Primary or Extended partition. Generally, you should choose an extended partition unless you want to create a primary partition that you can use to start the computer. Click Next to continue.

6. If you want to leave part of the hard disk unallocated, change the partition size. Otherwise, click Next to continue.

7. The New Partition Wizard displays the changes it's about to make to the new drive (see Figure 12.9). Click Finish to complete the partitioning process.

Figure 12.9   The New Partition Wizard prepares to create an extended partition from Disk 1.

8. After the wizard finishes, the Computer Management view displays the newly partitioned hard disk as free space. Right-click the partition, and select New Logical Drive to continue.

9. Click Next to continue with the wizard. Click Next again to select a logical drive.

10. To create more than one logical drive, change the maximum size of the partition size. To create a single logical drive, click Next.

11. Select the drive letter to assign. By default, the next available drive letter is displayed, but you can choose any unused drive letter. If you prefer, you can mount the new logical drive into an empty NTFS folder, or even not assign a drive letter or path. Click Next to continue.

12. Select the format options. By default, the new logical drive is formatted with NTFS, but you can choose FAT32 if the logical drive is 34.36GB (32GiB) or less. If the logical drive is larger than 32GiB, XP and Vista can only format the drive using NTFS. You can also specify the volume label, select a particular allocation unit (cluster) size, enable file/folder compression, and perform a quick format. If you want to format the drive later, select Do Not Format This Partition. Click Next to continue.

13. Again, the New Partition Wizard displays a list of changes to be made. Click Back to return to a particular menu if you need to make any changes, or click Finish to format the logical drive with the options selected (see Figure 12.10).

14. Repeat steps 10–13 if you didn't use all the free space as a logical drive and want to prepare additional logical drives.

No rebooting is necessary, and the color-coded legend at the bottom of the Disk Management display helps you track the status of the disk-preparation process.

Figure 12.10   The New Partition Wizard prepares to format a logical drive on Disk 1 with the options shown.

Drive Partitioning with Third-party Utilities

Alternative partitioning programs enable you to take an existing hard drive and perform the following changes to it without loss of data:

- Create, resize, split, move, and merge partitions on the fly without losing data.
- Convert between file systems without losing data—conversions include FAT to FAT32 and NTFS; FAT32 to FAT; NTFS to FAT and FAT32; primary to logical and vice versa; and FAT32 to NTFS. They also often include support for ext2/ext3 and Linux SWAP file systems as well.
- Move applications between partitions and automatically update the drive-letter references after partitioning.
- Undelete FAT, FAT32, Linux ext2, and NTFS partitions. You can restore partitions that have been deleted on disk as long as the space has not been reallocated or written over.
- Copy or move a partition to another partition or drive.

Several third-party programs are available, including popular commercial utilities such as PartitionMagic by Symantec and Partition Commander by V-Communications. In addition, a number of free or open-source partitioning programs are available, with several that rival the commercial utilities. As an excellent source for free partitioning programs, I recommend the following two projects:

- **Ultimate Boot CD**—www.ultimatebootcd.com
- **Ultimate Boot CD for Windows**—www.ubcd4win.com

Both of these projects offer incredible collections of free or open-source partitioning programs, which you can link to and download individually or on a bootable CD.

Tip

I still recommend FDISK, DISKPART, Disk Management, or SETUP be used for the initial partitioning and setup of any drive (these utilities normally destroy any existing data), but third-party utilities can be very useful for reconfiguring a system that is already partitioned, or for performing more complex operations not possible using the standard programs.

Although the program recommends a full backup before starting, I've used these utilities many times to turn a single "big drive" into two or more drive letters in less than 10 minutes. Performing the same task with backup software and FDISK/FORMAT can take several hours because you must back up your existing drive, remove existing partitions with FDISK, create new partitions with FDISK, restart your computer, format the new drives, and reload your operating system and your backup.

High-level (Operating System) Formatting

The final step in the installation of a hard disk drive is the high-level format. Similar to the partitioning process, the high-level format is specific to the file system you've chosen to use on the drive. On Windows 9x and DOS systems, the primary function of the high-level format is to create a FAT and a directory system on the disk so the operating system can manage files. You must run FDISK before formatting a drive. Each drive letter created by FDISK must be formatted before it can be used for data storage. As you learned in the section "Drive Partitioning and Formatting with Disk Management," earlier in this chapter, Windows 2000, XP, and Vista perform the high-level format with the New Partition Wizard.

Usually, you perform the high-level format with the FORMAT.COM program or the formatting utility in Windows Explorer. FORMAT.COM uses the following syntax:

```
FORMAT C: /S /V
```

This command high-level formats drive C:, writes the hidden operating system files in the first part of the partition, and prompts for the entry of a volume label to be stored on the disk at the completion of the process.

The FAT high-level format program performs the following functions and procedures:

1. Scans the disk (read-only) for tracks and sectors marked as bad during the LLF, and notes these tracks as being unreadable.

2. Returns the drive heads to the first cylinder of the partition, and at that cylinder (Head 1, Sector 1) writes a DOS volume boot sector.

3. Writes a FAT at Head 1, Sector 2. Immediately after this FAT, it writes a second copy of the FAT. These FATs are essentially blank except for bad-cluster marks noting areas of the disk that were found to be unreadable during the marked-defect scan.

4. Writes a blank root directory.

5. If the /S parameter is specified, the program copies the system files, IO.SYS and MSDOS.SYS (or IBMBIO.COM and IBMDOS.COM, depending on which DOS you run), and COMMAND.COM to the disk (in that order).

6. If the /V parameter is specified, the program prompts the user for a volume label, which is written as the fourth file entry in the root directory.

Now, the operating system can use the disk for storing and retrieving files, and the disk is a bootable disk.

During the first phase of the high-level format, the program performs a marked-defect scan. Defects marked by the LLF operation show up during this scan as being unreadable tracks or sectors. When the high-level format encounters one of these areas, it automatically performs up to five retries to read these tracks or sectors. If the unreadable area was marked by the LLF, the read fails on all attempts.

After five retries, the DOS FORMAT program gives up on this track or sector and moves to the next one. If an area remains unreadable after the initial read and five retries, it is marked in the FAT as a bad cluster.

Note

Because the high-level format doesn't overwrite data areas beyond the root directory of the hard disk, using programs such as Norton Utilities to unformat the hard disk that contains data from previous operations is possible, provided no programs or data has been copied to the drive after the high-level formatting. Unformatting can be performed because the data from the drive's previous use is still present.

If you create an extended partition, the logical DOS drive letters found there need a simpler FORMAT command because system files aren't necessary—for example, FORMAT D:/V for drive D:, FORMAT E:/V for drive E:, and so on.

FDISK and FORMAT Limitations

The biggest problem with FDISK is that it is destructive. If you change your mind about disk structure, you must back up your system and start over again. That alone is cause for using FDISK with care, but here are other limitations you should keep in mind:

- FDISK doesn't provide any help with issues of drive letter changes.
- FDISK requires FORMAT before the drive is ready for use.
- FORMAT must check the entire drive before making it ready for use. Its error management is rudimentary and can waste a lot of disk space with older drives that have disk errors.
- FDISK and FORMAT are designed for a single operating system environment, with no provision for multiboot options (Windows 9x and NT or Windows 9x and Linux, for example).
- FDISK and FORMAT offer no procedure for migrating data to a new drive, and the XCOPY command is tricky to use.
- FDISK and FORMAT might cause conflicts with existing CD-ROM drives, which often use the next available drive letter after the existing hard drive.

Although Disk Management in Windows 2000 and later does a better job than FDISK/FORMAT of avoiding drive letter conflicts with existing drives, it's still a mostly destructive process if you need to change your disk partitions, and it has no provision for migrating data. One exception is the new ability in Disk Management under Vista to be able to non-destructively shrink or extend volumes.

For these reasons, many drive vendors offer some type of automatic disk installation software with their hard drives.

Typical features of automatic disk installation programs include the following:

- Replacement for FDISK and FORMAT. A single program performs both functions more quickly than FDISK and FORMAT separately.
- A database of drive jumpers for major brands and models.
- A drive-copy or migration function. Contents of an existing drive or volume are copied to the new drive while retaining long filenames, file attributes, and so on. This is generally the most useful function of these programs.
- A CD-ROM drive letter relocation utility. The CD-ROM is moved to a new drive letter (to make room for new hard drive letters) and Windows Registry and INI file references are reset to the new drive letter so CD-ROM software works without reinstallation.
- A menu-driven or wizard-driven process for installing a new hard drive.
- Optional override of BIOS limitations for installation of large hard drives (not recommended).

Examples of these types of programs include DiskManager (OnTrack), EZ-Drive (StorageSoft), DiscWizard (Seagate), MaxBlast (Maxtor, now owned by Seagate), and Data Lifeguard (Western Digital). In most cases I recommend using these programs for their drive copy/migration functions, but for general purpose drive installation, partitioning, and formatting I recommend using the standard operating system tools instead.

Replacing an Existing Drive

Previous sections discussed installing a single hard drive or adding a new hard drive to a system. Although formatting and partitioning a new hard disk can be challenging, replacing an existing drive and moving your programs and files to it can be a lot more challenging.

Drive Migration for MS-DOS Users

When MS-DOS 6.x was dominant, many users used this straightforward method to transfer the contents of their old hard drive to their new hard drive:

1. The user creates a bootable disk containing FDISK, FORMAT, and XCOPY.

2. The new hard drive is prepared with a primary partition (and possibly an extended partition, depending on the user's desires).

3. The new hard drive is formatted with system files, although the operating system identifies it as D:.

4. The XCOPY command is used to transfer all nonhidden files from C:\ (the old hard drive) to D:\, as in the following example:

   XCOPY C:\ D:\ /S/E

   The XCOPY command also is used as necessary to transfer files from any remaining drive letters on the old hard drive to the corresponding drive letters on the new drive.

Because the only hidden files such a system would have were probably the operating system boot files (already installed) and the Windows 3.1 permanent swap file (which could be re-created after restarting Windows), this "free" data transfer routine worked well for many people.

After the original drive was removed from the system, the new drive would be jumpered as master and assigned C:. The user then would need to run FDISK from a floppy and set the primary partition on the new C: drive as Active. Then, the user would exit FDISK and the drive would boot.

Drive Migration for Windows 9x/Me Users

Windows 9x/Me have complicated the once-simple act of data transfer to a new system by their frequent use of hidden files and folders (such as \Windows\Inf, where Windows 9x hardware drivers are stored). The extensive use of hidden files was a major reason for a greatly enhanced version of XCOPY being included in Windows 9x/Me.

Note

XCOPY32 is automatically used in place of XCOPY when XCOPY is started within a command prompt session under Windows.

Compared to "classic" XCOPY, XCOPY32 can copy hidden files; can preserve file attributes such as system, hidden, read-only, and archive; can automatically create folders; and is compatible with long filenames. Thus, using it to duplicate an existing drive is possible, but with these cautions:

- The XCOPY32 command is much more complex.
- Errors might occur during the copy process because of Windows' use of temporary files during normal operation, but XCOPY32 can be forced to continue.

This command line calls XCOPY32 and transfers all files and folders with their original attributes intact from the original drive (C:) to the new drive (D:). This command, however, must be run from an MS-DOS prompt window (and not MS-DOS Mode) under Windows 9x/Me, as follows:

```
xcopy32 c:\. d:\ /e/c/h/r/k
```

The command switches are explained here:

- /e—Copies folders, even if empty; also copies all folders beneath the starting folder.
- /c—Continues to copy after errors. The Windows swap file can't be copied due to being in use.
- /h—Copies hidden and system files.
- /r—Overwrites read-only files.
- /k—Preserves file attributes.

Repeat the command with appropriate drive-letter changes for any additional drive letters on your old drive.

After the original drive is removed from the system, the new drive must be jumpered as master (or single), and the operating system assigns it C:. You next need to run FDISK from a floppy and set the primary partition on the new C: drive as Active. Then, exit FDISK, and the drive will boot.

Note that although the XCOPY method has worked for me, some people have problems with it. A much more automated and easy approach to cloning drives is to use commercial software designed for that purpose, such as PartitionMagic Drive Copy or Norton Ghost by Symantec. Drive-copying programs included with older versions of hard disk installation programs provided by drive vendors have not always worked well, but the latest versions of these programs can be very useful for drive copying and other preparation tasks. In recent installations, I've found that the MaxBlast disk-copying program worked perfectly in transferring a Windows XP installation to a much larger target drive. So, I recommend you try the drive vendor's copying program first. If you have problems, you can use a third-party product instead.

Drive Migration for Windows 2000/XP/Vista Users

Windows 2000 and later place additional difficulties on the copying or migration of the system (boot) drive, because so many files are open while the OS is running, and open files are generally not copied by most simple file copying programs. To copy the contents of a bootable volume from one drive to another, you can use several tools or procedures.

One technique is to use the Windows backup program to make a complete backup of a volume and then restore the volume to the other drive. This will work in XP and Vista Business, Ultimate, and Enterprise but has unfortunately been intentionally disabled in Vista Home and Home Premium.

You can also use any disk imaging program to make a complete image of a disk or volume and then restore that image to another disk or volume. Commercial tools available for this include Symantec Ghost, Acronis True Image or Migrate Easy, and WinImage. Free tools include:

- EaseUS Disk Copy (www.easeus.com/disk-copy)
- Runtime Software DriveImage XML (www.runtime.org/dixml.htm)
- Gnome Partition Editor LiveCD (http://gparted.sourceforge.net)

Also you may have free tools included with your drive such as Maxtor/Seagate MaxBlast, DiskManager, and so on. These tools may check for specific drive types or manufacturers so they may not work on all systems.

Using these tools you can either directly copy one drive, partition or volume to another, or save an image, which you can then later restore.

Hard Disk Drive Troubleshooting and Repair

If a hard drive has a mechanical problem inside the sealed head disk assembly (HDA), repairing the drive is usually unfeasible. It might be physically doable, but purchasing a new drive will be far less expensive. However, if the goal is data recovery instead of merely repairing the drive, the value of the data may well exceed the cost of a new drive, and justify the expense in any attempts at getting the drive to work. If the failure is in the logic board, that board can be replaced with one from a donor drive. Typically, this is done only for the purposes of reading the information on the failed drive because you must purchase a complete second drive to cannibalize for the logic board. The drive manufacturers usually don't sell spare parts for their drives anymore.

Most hard disk drive problems are not mechanical hardware problems; instead, they are "soft" problems that can be solved by re-initializing the drive, which replaces bad sectors with remapped spare sectors. Soft problems are characterized by a drive that sounds normal but produces various read and write errors.

Hard problems are mechanical, such as when the drive sounds as though it contains loose marbles. Constant scraping and grinding noises from the drive, with no reading or writing capability, also qualify as hard errors. In these cases, re-initializing the drive is unlikely to put the drive back into service. If a hardware problem is indicated, first replace the logic-board assembly. You can make this repair yourself and, if successful, you can recover the data from the drive.

If replacing the logic assembly does not solve the problem, contact the manufacturer or a specialized repair shop that has clean-room facilities for hard disk repair. For example, Seagate Recovery Services (formerly ActionFront) and Kroll OnTrack both offer data recovery services. If you are only interested in drive repair, check to see if the drive is covered by a warranty; if not, it is most likely more cost-effective to replace the drive rather than to repair it.

Testing a Drive

When you're accessing a drive, determining whether the drive has been partitioned and formatted properly is easy. A simple test can tell you whether a stored drive is in its "raw" condition or has been partitioned and formatted properly. These tests work best if you have a boot disk available and if the spare hard drive is the only hard drive attached.

First, attach the drive to your system. If you can attach power and data cables to it, you need not install it into a drive bay unless you are planning to use it immediately. If the drive will be run loose, I recommend placing it on a nonconductive foam pad or other soft surface. This insulates the drive from potential shocks and other hazards. After detecting the drive in the BIOS and saving the changes, start your operating system from the boot disk.

Then, from the A: prompt, enter the following command:

```
DIR C:
```

This produces one of the following responses:

- **Invalid drive specification**—This indicates the drive does not have a valid partition or that the existing Master Boot Sector or partition tables have been damaged. No matter what, the drive must be partitioned and formatted before use. You also get this warning on a FAT32 or NTFS partitioned drive if you use a Windows 95 (original version) or MS-DOS boot disk when checking. Use a Windows 95B, Windows 98/Me, or Windows 2000 boot disk to avoid this false message from FAT32 partitions. Or, use a Windows NT, 2000, XP, or Vista boot disk to detect NTFS partitions.

■ **Invalid media type**—This drive has been partitioned but not formatted, or the format has been corrupted. You should use FDISK or Disk Management to examine the drive's existing partitions and either delete them and create new ones or keep the existing partitions and reformat them.

■ **Directory of C:**—The contents of the C: drive are listed, indicating the volume and file system structures and data are valid.

Tip

If you know to which computer the drive was previously connected, you should connect the drive to that computer to perform the test. If you move the drive to another computer, differences in BIOS and host adapter translation could cause a working drive with data to appear to be empty. This is particularly the case with systems that have drives setup in RAID configurations—or in some cases if you move the drive from a system using an Award or AMI BIOS to a system with a Phoenix BIOS.

If you have a drive that has been exhibiting problems, and you don't need to recover any data from the drive, you can try re-initializing the drive using the drive manufacturer's format or initialization software. These utilities will test the drive for bad sectors, and either replace them with good spare sectors and/or mark them such that data will never be written to them in the future (all data will be destroyed in the process). A complete initialization is generally considered the last thing to try before deciding that a given drive is defective or unusable. The following section discusses low-level formatting (initializing) in more detail.

Low-level Formatting (Initializing)

All new hard disk drives are low-level formatted by the manufacturer when they are made, and you do not have to perform another LLF before you install the drive. In fact, under normal circumstances, you should not ever have to perform a low-level format on ATA drives because technically such drives can only be truly low-level formatted at the factory. What passes for a low-level format today is really more of an initialization and/or surface test of the drive, because it writes to all of the sectors, overwriting the entire drive in the process. Unless you are having problems, a full initialization or surface test isn't necessary.

Using the term *low-level format* in conjunction with ATA drives has been the source of some myths. Many people say, for example, that you can't perform a low-level format on an ATA drive, and that if you do, you will destroy the drive. This statement is half true. The truth is that what we call a low-level format is technically an initialization or surface test on ATA drives, and will not cause any harm! The myth of destruction was borne out of some truth, in that if you low-level formatted some of the earliest ATA drives from the late 1980s, you might lose the optimal head and cylinder skew factors that were set by the manufacturer for the drive, as well as the map of drive defects, and this could have a negative effect on the drive's performance. This problem went away long ago; all drives that internally use a zoned recording (where there is a variable number of sectors per track internally) are immune to any problems due to low-level formatting because the actual sector marks can't be rewritten. This includes pretty much all ATA drives made since the late '80s.

However, sometimes you must perform a low-level format on an ATA or a SCSI drive. The following sections discuss the software you can use to do this.

ATA Low-level Format Software

ATA drive manufacturers have defined and standardized extensions to the original WD1002/1003 hard disk controller card to AT-bus (ISA) interface, which is known as the ATA (AT Attachment) interface. The ATA specification provides for vendor-unique commands, which are manufacturer proprietary extensions to the standard. To prevent improper low-level formatting, many of these ATA drives have special codes that must be sent to the drive to unlock the format routines. These codes vary among manufacturers. If possible, you should obtain LLF and defect management software from the drive manufacturer; this software usually is specific to that manufacturer's products and often is model specific. Check the brand and model number of your hard disk to determine the utility program you need.

Modern ATA drives are protected from any alteration to the skew factors or defect map erasure because they are always in a translated mode internally. Zoned bit recording drives are always under translation and are fully protected. Most ATA drives have a custom command set that must be used in the format process; the standard format commands defined by the ATA specification usually do not work, especially with intelligent or zoned bit recording ATA drives.

Spare sectors can also be allocated automatically by using the drive manufacturer format or initialization software. Without the proper manufacturer-specific commands, you can't perform the defect management by the manufacturer-specified method, in which bad sectors often can be replaced by spare sectors from pools of spares that are intentionally allocated throughout modern drives explicitly for this purpose. Whenever a bad sector is found, it is deallocated and a spare sector from the closest available pool is reassigned to replace it.

Most manufacturers supply low-level format (initialization and test) programs for their drives. Here are a few examples:

- **Seagate/Conner Peripherals**

   ftp://ftp.seagate.com/techsuppt/seagate_utils/sgatfmt4.zip or www.seagate.com/support/seatools

- **Hitachi/IBM**

   www.hitachigst.com/hdd/support/download.htm

- **Maxtor/Quantum**

   http://www.seagate.com/www/en-us/support/downloads/maxtor_desktop

- **Samsung**

   www.samsung.com/Products/HardDiskDrive/utilities/hutil.htm,
   www.samsung.com/Products/HardDiskDrive/utilities/sutil.htm, or
   www.samsung.com/Products/HardDiskDrive/utilities/shdiag.htm

- **Western Digital**

   http://support.wdc.com/download/

You should try the manufacturer-specific programs first. They are free, and can often work at a lower level and handle defects in ways that the more generic ones can't. If initialization/test/formatting software is not available from your drive's manufacturer, I recommend the Hitachi (formerly IBM) Drive Fitness Test (DFT) program. The Drive Fitness Test program works on non-Hitachi and non-IBM drives as well and performs a detailed and thorough test of your hard drive. This is one of the better general-purpose drive test programs because it can do a fairly thorough test in nondestructive mode. Although it can test any drive, one limitation is that it performs destructive read/write tests only on IBM- and Hitachi-brand drives. You can download DFT from the Hitachi site listed previously.

Note

You can find most if not all of these drive initialization/testing/formatting tools as well as many other drive test programs and utilities on the Ultimate Boot CD (UBCD). The UBCD is a fantastic collection of free diagnostic tools collected and integrated into a single bootable CD. You can download a copy of the UBCD from www.ultimatebootcd.com.

Nondestructive Formatters

General-purpose, BIOS-level, nondestructive formatters, such as Calibrate (older Symantec Norton Utilities) and SpinRite (Gibson Research), are not recommended in most situations in which a real LLF or full initialization is required. These programs have several limitations and problems that decrease their effectiveness; in some cases, they can even cause problems with the way defects are handled on a drive. These programs attempt to perform a track-by-track or sector-by-sector reformat, while backing up and restoring the track and sector data as they go.

These programs do not perform defect mapping in the way the manufacturer-supplied programs do, and in some cases with older drives they even can remove the carefully applied sector header defect marks applied during a proper LLF. This situation potentially enables data to be stored in sectors that originally were marked defective and might actually void the manufacturer's warranty on some drives. Another problem is that these programs work only on drives that have already been formatted and they can format only drives that are formattable through BIOS functions.

Note

SpinRite can be useful for recovering data on drives with read errors because of its method of repeatedly rereading the errors and analyzing the results to reconstruct the missing data.

The drive manufacturer programs bypass the system BIOS and send commands directly to the disk controller hardware (on the drive). For this reason, many LLF programs are specific to the disk controller hardware for which they are designed. Having a single format program that will run on all types of controllers is virtually impossible. Many hard drives have been incorrectly diagnosed as being defective because the wrong format program was used and the program did not operate properly.

Installing an Optical Drive

Installation of a CD or DVD drive is pretty much the same as for a hard drive, except these drives don't require partitioning or formatting.

This section walks you through the installation of a typical internal (PATA or SATA) optical drive, with tips that often aren't included in the manufacturers' installation manuals. After you install the hardware, you may need to load additional software, especially in the case of writeable drives (CD or DVD burners).

Note

Optical drives use the same PATA and SATA interfaces and can be installed using the same basic procedures as hard drives. Some older DVD drives came with an MPEG-2 decoder board, whereas virtually all drives today use (and generally include) MPEG decoder software that enables you to view DVD movies and video on your PC. If a board was included, it usually installs in a PCI bus slot like any other expansion card and performs the video-decoding process that would otherwise fall to the system processor. Software decoding does not require a board and instead uses your processor to do the decoding work. Software decoding normally requires a 300MHz or faster processor; otherwise, the video appears jumpy, jerky, or unsynchronized with the sound. Although many DVD drives included hardware decoding for this reason in the past, today's computers typically have 1GHz and faster processors to make software decoding smooth.

Drive Configuration

Configuration of optical drives is the same as for hard disk drives—that is, it depends largely on the interface. Those using the PATA interface will require jumpers be set as either master, slave, or cable select (see Figure 12.11). Those using SATA don't normally require any jumper settings at all. For a PATA drive, here are the typical ways to jumper the drive:

- As the primary (master) drive on the secondary ATA connection
- As the secondary (slave) drive to a current hard disk drive
- Using cable select (CS), where the cable connector determines which drive is master or slave automatically

If the drive is to be the only device on your secondary ATA interface, the default settings (either CS or master) are usually correct.

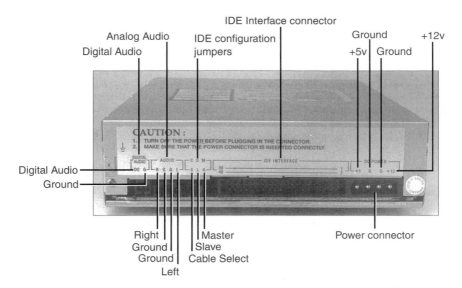

Figure 12.11 The rear connection interfaces of a typical ATA internal CD-ROM drive.

When you install the optical drive as a secondary drive—that is, the second drive on the same ribbon cable with another device—be sure it is either jumpered as CS (cable select) if attached to an 80-conductor cable or set as the slave drive if using a 40-conductor cable (see Figure 12.12).

Caution

Whenever possible, you should try not to connect an optical drive to the same PATA channel as a hard disk drive because devices on the same channel can't simultaneously read or write data. If your computer has the two PATA channels, I recommend you connect the optical drive to the secondary channel, even if you have only one hard disk drive on the primary.

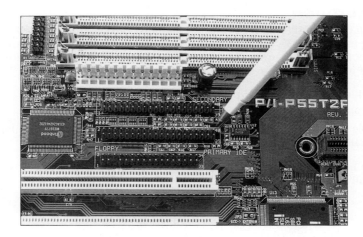

Figure 12.12   An embedded ATA interface with primary and secondary ATA connections (the pen is pointing to the primary ATA connector).

◀◀   These procedures are covered in "Parallel ATA," p. 593.

Internal Drive Installation

After unpacking a new internal drive, you should have the following pieces:

- The drive
- The internal CD-audio cable (optional)
- Software (optional)
- Drive rails and mounting screws

Drives sold as OEM or bare drives may include only the drive; you will need to supply any screws, cables, and/or software.

Parallel ATA Optical Drive Installation

The step-by-step procedure for installing a parallel ATA optical drive is as follows:

1. Check your computer for an unused 40-pin PATA/IDE connector. Typical PCs have one or two of these connectors, allowing for up to four PATA devices.

   You might need an additional cable if both master and slave connectors are used on the primary cable and you are adding a third device.

Tip

For best performance, keep devices that will be simultaneously active, such as hard drives and optical drives, on separate cables.

2. Double-check the pin configuration and cable type. The colored stripe on one edge of the ribbon cable goes to pin 1 of the drive's data connector. Most cable and drive connectors are keyed to prevent improper (backward) installation, but many are not. Keying can be done via missing and/or plugged pins, a ridge on one side of the connector, or both. One tip to note is that pin 1 on the drive connector is almost always oriented nearest to the 4-pin power connector.

Tip

Although there are a few exceptions, most PATA optical drives support interface transfer modes up to UltraDMA mode 2 (33MBps), which is also the fastest speed supported by standard 40-conductor cables. This means you can use 40-conductor cables with nearly all PATA optical drives without any performance penalty. However, because the superior 80-conductor cables required for transfer speeds over 33MBps will also work for slower drives, I recommend using only 80-conductor cables where possible. Another benefit is that with 80-conductor cables you can set all of the drives to CS (cable select) instead of independent master/slave settings.

3. Configure the drive jumpers. If the drive is PATA/IDE and you are using an 80-conductor cable (that supports CS), you should set jumpers to the CS position on any drives connected to that cable. Otherwise, you must set the drives on the cable separately as either master or slave.

4. Slide the drive into an available 5 1/4" drive bay, and secure it using the screws, rails, or brackets provided with either the drive or chassis.

Note

You can find more visual step-by-step instructions for installing optical drives in Chapter 20, "Building or Upgrading Systems."

5. Connect the ribbon cable between the drive and the host adapter (usually the motherboard). If you're using an 80-conductor cable, the blue connector attaches to the host adapter, the black connector goes to drive you want to be master, and the gray connector (usually in the middle) goes to the drive you want to be slave.

6. Attach the power connector to the drive. If necessary, you can use a Y-splitter cable (see Figure 12.5) to create two power connectors from one (some computers have fewer power connectors than drive bays).

Serial ATA Optical Drive Installation

The step-by-step procedure for installing a SATA optical drive is as follows:

1. Check your computer for an unused SATA host adapter connector (usually on the motherboard). Most motherboards have from two to six SATA connectors onboard, but for older boards without a built-in SATA host adapter, you might need to install a separate SATA host adapter card instead. If you install a SATA host adapter card, consult the documentation included with the card for installation instructions.

2. Slide the drive into an available 5 1/4" drive bay, and secure it using the screws, rails, or brackets provided with either the drive or chassis.

3. Connect a SATA cable between the drive and the SATA host adapter. Because both ends are the same, and the connectors are keyed, the orientation doesn't matter.

4. Attach a power connector to the drive. Some SATA drives have both conventional 4-pin peripheral power connectors as well as SATA 15-pin power connectors, in which case you can use one or the other, but *not* both simultaneously. If your drive has only a SATA power connector and your power supply doesn't have SATA power connectors available, you might need to purchase a peripheral-to-SATA power cable adapter if one was not provided with your drive. This type of adapter changes a standard 4-pin peripheral power connector into a 15-pin SATA power connector.

Caution

If a drive has both conventional (also called *peripheral* or *legacy*) and SATA-type power connectors, you must *not* plug in both power connectors at the same time, or the drive may be damaged. Use one or the other, but not both.

System Configuration

From this point, the remainder of the installation is the same for both PATA and SATA optical drives:

1. Start the computer and press the appropriate key to access the BIOS Setup screens to configure the drive. If your BIOS has an autodetect or auto type setting, I recommend you use it because it will configure the parameters automatically using optimal settings. Some BIOSs may require you set the type to CD/DVD, Optical, or ATAPI (ATA Packet Interface).

2. Restart the system. If you are running Windows 9x or later, the OS should automatically detect the drive upon loading and then install the necessary drivers to support reading discs. If the drive is a writable (burner) type, then depending on which version of Windows or other operating system you are using, you will most likely need to install additional software to take full advantage of the burning capabilities. If the drive is capable of reading DVDs, you will also want to install a compatible DVD decoder driver, after which you can play DVD movies and videos using Windows Media Player or other video-playing applications.

Internal Floppy Drive Installation

A floppy drive is one of the simplest types of drives to install. In most cases, installing a floppy disk drive is a matter of attaching the drive to the computer chassis or case and then plugging the power and signal cables into the drive. Some type of brackets and screws are usually required to attach the drive to the chassis; however, some chassis are designed to accept the drive with no brackets at all. Any brackets, if necessary, are normally included with the chassis or case itself.

Note

Because floppy disk drives are generally installed into the same half-height bays as hard disk drives, the physical mounting of the drive in the computer case is the same for both units. See the section "Hard Disk Installation Procedures," earlier in this chapter, for more information on the process.

When you connect the drive, make sure the power cable is installed properly. The cable is usually keyed so you can't plug it in backward, but the keying can be defeated by somebody forcing the connection. If that is done, the drive will be fried the instant the power is turned on.

Next, install the interface cable. A floppy interface cable is a 34-pin cable that typically has a twist in it near one end. What I mean is that pins 10–16 are twisted around before they reach the last (A:)

drive connector. Normally, the A: drive must be plugged in after this twist; any drive plugged into a connector before the twist is seen by the system as drive B:. The twist reverses the drive select and motor enable signals, letting A: and B: drives coexist without rejumpering. This is similar to the way cable select (CS) works for PATA/IDE drives. Because of this, all floppy drives are jumpered the same way, in the second drive select (DS) position. Most drives are preset this way and in fact don't have any visible jumpers to change.

Older drives used to require various jumpers to be set to enable the drive to work properly. The two most common jumpers were the drive select jumper and the disk change (DC) jumper. If you encounter an older drive with these jumpers, you should follow a few simple rules. The DS jumper typically has two positions, labeled 0 and 1—or in some cases, 1 and 2. In all PC installations, the DS jumper should be set on the second position, no matter what it is numbered. This enables the drive on the cable before the twist to function as drive B:, and the drive at the end of the cable after the twist to function as drive A:. The DC jumper setting is normally an on or off setting. For PC use, if the drive has a DC jumper, it must be set on or enabled. This enables the PC to detect when you have changed disks in the drive. For more information on floppy drives and interfacing, see Chapter 10.

The interface cable is usually keyed to prevent backward installation. If no key exists in this cable, use the colored wire in the cable as a guide to the position of pin 1. Normally, pin 1 is oriented closest to the power connector, which is the same as other drives. If the drive LED stays on continuously when you power up the system or when the system is running, that is a sure sign you have the floppy cable on backward either at the drive end or at the controller (motherboard) end.

Chapter

13

Video Hardware

Video Display Technologies

Although a video display is as vital to a PC's user interface as the mouse and keyboard, the video display is actually a latecomer to computing. Before CRT (cathode ray tube) monitors came into general use, the teletypewriter was the standard computer interface—a large, loud device that printed the input and output characters on a roll of paper. Early personal computers often used nothing more than a panel of blinking LEDs for a display.

The first CRT displays used on computers were primitive by today's standards; they displayed only text in a single color (usually green), but to users at the time they were a great improvement, allowing real-time display of input and output data. Over time, color displays were introduced, screen sizes increased, and LCD technologies moved from the portable computer to the desktop. The latest trends reflect the increasing convergence of entertainment and computer technologies.

Today, PC video displays are much more sophisticated, but you must be careful when selecting video hardware for your computer. A poor display can cause eyestrain or otherwise significantly diminish the experience of using your PC.

The video subsystem of a PC consists of two main components:

- **Monitor (or video display)**—The monitor is usually a CRT or an LCD panel, but may also be a wide-screen LCD TV, plasma display, or projector using LCD or DLP technology.

- **Display adapter (also called the video card or graphics adapter or graphics processing unit)**—While usually referring to an adapter card plugged into a bus slot, on many systems, the video adapter circuitry might be built into the motherboard or included as part of the motherboard's chipset. Although it sounds strange, the circuitry is still called an *adapter* or *card*, even if it is fully integrated into the motherboard. You can add a PCI, AGP, or PCI-Express video card to some systems with integrated video.

This chapter explores the range of PC video adapters on the market today and the displays that work with them. The remainder of this section covers the various types of display technologies.

Note

The term *video*, as it is used in this context, does not necessarily imply the existence of a moving image, such as on a television screen. Any circuitry that feeds signals to a monitor or another display is a video or display adapter, regardless of whether it is used with applications that display moving images, such as multimedia or videoconferencing software.

For this reason, video cards are sometimes referred to as *graphics cards* or *display adapters*.

A PC monitor is typically based on one of two display technologies: liquid crystal display (LCD) or cathode-ray tube (CRT). Projectors, on the other hand, are usually based on LCD or digital light processing (DLP) technology. The following sections discuss each type of display technology.

LCD Panels

Because of their light weight, smaller overall size, and clarity, LCD panels have largely supplanted CRT displays in new computer installations. Desktop LCD panels use technology that first appeared in laptop computers. Compared to CRTs, LCDs have completely flat, thin screens and low power requirements (5 watts versus nearly 100 watts for an ordinary CRT monitor). The color quality of a good active-matrix LCD panel can exceed that of many CRT displays, particularly when viewed from head on.

How LCD Displays Work

In an LCD, polarizing filters allow only light waves that are aligned with the filter to pass through. After passing through one polarizing filter, the light waves are all aligned in the same direction. By aligning a second polarizing filter at a right angle to the first, all those waves are blocked. By changing the angle of the second polarizing filter, the amount of light allowed to pass can be changed accordingly. It is the role of the liquid crystal cell to act as a polarizing filter that can change the angle of polarization and control the amount of light that passes. The liquid crystals are tiny rod-shaped molecules that flow like a liquid. They enable light to pass straight through, but an electrical charge alters their orientation, which subsequently alters the orientation of light passing through them.

In a color LCD, there are three cells for each pixel—one each for displaying red, green, and blue—with a corresponding transistor for each cell. The red, green, and blue cells that make up a pixel are sometimes referred to as *subpixels*.

Bad Pixels

A so-called *bad pixel* is one in which the red, green, or blue sub-pixel cell remains permanently on or off. Those that are permanently on are often called *stuck pixels*, while those that are permanently off are called *dead pixels*. Failures in the on state seem to be more common. In particular, pixels stuck on are very noticeable on a dark background as tiny red, green, or blue dots. Although even one of these can be distracting, manufacturers vary in their warranty policies regarding how many bad pixels are required before you can get a replacement display. Some vendors look at both the total number of bad pixels and their locations. Fortunately, improvements in manufacturing quality make it less and less likely that you will see LCD screens with bad pixels.

Although there is no standard way to repair bad pixels, a couple of simple fixes might help. One involves tapping or rubbing on the screen. For example, I have actually repaired stuck pixels on several occasions by tapping with my index finger on the screen directly over the pixel location (with the screen powered on). Because I find a constantly lit pixel to be more irritating than one that is constantly dark, this fix has saved me a lot of aggravation (when it has worked). A similar technique is to use the tip of a PDA stylus or ballpoint pen to apply pressure or to tap directly on the stuck pixel. I recommend you wrap a damp cloth over the tip to prevent scratching the screen. Some have had success by merely rubbing the area where the stuck or dead pixel is located.

Another potential fix involves using software to rapidly cycle the stuck pixel (as well as some adjacent ones), which sometimes causes the stuck pixel to become unstuck and function properly. The two main programs for doing this are Udpixel (http://udpix.free.fr) and Jscreenfix (www.jscreenfix.com).

Unfortunately, none of these fixes work all the time; in fact, in most cases the pixel will likely remain stuck on or dead no matter what you try. If you have stuck or dead pixels that do not respond to any of the fixes I've detailed, you might want to contact the screen or laptop manufacturer to inquire about its bad pixel replacement policy. Although the policies can vary among different manufacturers, Table 13.1 shows the maximum allowable defects in LCD panels from most manufacturers. To find the allowable defect limits for your specific display, consult the manufacturer's documentation.

Table 13.1   Maximum Allowable Defects for LCD Panels (Typical)

LCD Type	Resolution	Stuck Pixels	Dead Pixels	Combined Stuck/ Dead Pixels
SVGA	800×600	5	5	9
XGA	1024×768	8	8	9
WXGA	1280×800	8	8	9
SXGA	1280×1024	5	7	8
WXGA+	1440×900	11	13	16
SXGA+	1400×1050	11	13	16
WSXGA+	1680×1050	11	13	16
UXGA	1600×1200	11	16	16
QXGA	2048×1536	11	16	16

Active-matrix Displays

LCD panels use a type of active-matrix technology known as a *thin-film transistor (TFT)* array. TFT is a method for packaging from one (monochrome) to three (RGB color) transistors per pixel within a flexible material that is the same size and shape as the display. Thus, the transistors for each pixel lie directly behind the liquid crystal cells they control.

Two TFT manufacturing processes account for most of the active-matrix displays on the market today: hydrogenated amorphous silicon (a-Si) and low-temperature polysilicon (p-Si). These processes differ primarily in their costs. At first, most TFT displays were manufactured using the a-Si process because it required lower temperatures (less than 400°C) than the p-Si process of the time. Now, lower-temperature p-Si manufacturing processes are making this method an economically viable alternative to a-Si.

To improve horizontal viewing angles in the latest LCDs, some vendors have modified the classic TFT design. For example, Hitachi's in-plane switching (IPS) design—also known as STFT—aligns the individual cells of the LCD parallel to the glass, running the electric current through the sides of the cells and spinning the pixels to provide more even distribution of the image to the entire panel area. Hitachi's Super-IPS technology also rearranges the liquid crystal molecules into a zigzag pattern, rather than the typical row-column arrangement, to reduce color shift and improve color uniformity. The similar multidomain vertical alignment (MVA) technology developed by Fujitsu divides the screen into different regions and changes the angle of the regions.

Both Super-IPS and MVA provide a wider viewing angle than traditional TFT displays. Other companies have different names for the same technology—for example, Sharp calls it Ultra High Aperture (UHA). Because larger LCDs (17" and wider) are large enough to cause shifts in viewing angle even for an individual user, these advanced technologies are being used primarily on larger and more expensive panels and have been licensed to other display vendors. Note that many low-cost LCD displays use a twisted nematic design and frame rate control to stimulate true 24-bit color.

LCD Display Sizes and Resolutions

Standard 4:3 ratio LCD panels are available in sizes ranging from 15" up to 23" diagonal measure. LCD screens from 15–18.1" in size are usually more limited in resolution than comparably sized CRTs, although LCD displays and CRT displays at larger sizes offer similar resolutions. Table 13.2 compares the typical resolutions of LCD monitors from 15" to 23" to mainstream CRT monitors ranging from 17" to 21" with comparable viewable areas.

Table 13.2   LCD and CRT Resolutions Compared

LCD Size	LCD Resolution	Comparable CRT Size	Comparable CRT Viewable Area	Comparable CRT Maximum Resolution
15"	1024×768	17"	16"	1024×768
				1280×1024
				1600×1200*
17"	1280×1024	—	—	—
18.1"	1280×1024	19"	18"	1600×1200
				1920×1440*
19"	1280×1024	—	—	—
20.1"	1600×1200	21"	20"	1600×1200
				1920×1440*
				2048×1536*
21.3"	1600×1200	—	—	—
23"	1920×1200	—	—	—

Available on high-end monitors only

As you can see from Table 13.2, you must choose a 20.1" or larger LCD panel to achieve resolutions above 1280×1024, although most 18" or larger CRT displays can run 1600×1200.

LCD panels are also available in widescreen (16:9 or 16:10) form factors, which are recommended for viewing widescreen DVDs and for use with Windows Vista (which can use the additional horizontal space for the new Sidebar utility and its gadgets). Figure 13.1 compares a typical 4:3 19-inch LCD panel to a widescreen 19-inch LCD panel.

LCD panels are generally more expensive than comparably sized CRTs; however, prices have been falling. Prices for LCD panels have been falling such that, especially for the lower-end models, they cost about the same as bulky CRTs. This relative price equality has meant that LCDs are outselling CRTs by a wide margin, and CRTs are now being purchased for specialized uses. Of course, extremely large high-end LCDs still command very high prices.

Note

Some specialized LCD products, such as wide-screen LCDs or TV/monitor combinations, are more expensive. Wide-screen LCDs designed for TV/monitor use can be as large as 46" diagonal measure.

However, as Table 13.2 shows, it is important to consider that an LCD screen typically provides a larger viewable image than a CRT monitor of the same size.

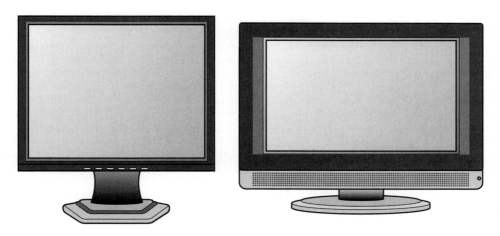

Figure 13.1   A traditional (4:3) LCD panel (left) compared to a widescreen (16:10) LCD panel (right).

Two basic LCD choices are available today on notebook computers: active-matrix analog color and active-matrix digital (the latest development). Monochrome LCDs are obsolete for PCs; however, they are sometimes used for industrial display panels. Passive-matrix displays using dual-scan technology once were popular for low-cost laptop models until a few years ago, but they have been completely replaced by active-matrix displays.

Note

The most common type of passive-matrix display used a supertwist pneumatic design, so these panels were often referred to as *STNs*. Active-matrix panels generally use a thin-film transistor design and are therefore referred to as *TFTs*.

Benefits of LCD Panels

LCD monitors offer a number of benefits when compared to conventional CRT glass tube monitors. LCD panels feature a larger effective viewable area than CRTs; a 17" LCD is essentially equal in usability to a 19" CRT (refer to Table 13.2). Because LCDs use direct addressing of the display (each pixel in the picture corresponds with a transistor), they produce a high-precision image. LCDs can't have the common CRT display problems of pincushion or barrel distortion, nor do they experience convergence errors (halos around the edges of onscreen objects).

LCD panels are less expensive to operate than CRTs because they feature lower power consumption and much less heat buildup than CRTs. Because LCD units lack a CRT, no concerns exist about electromagnetic VLF or ELF emissions. Although LCDs offer a comparable mean time between failures (MTBF) to CRT displays, the major reason for LCD failures is the inverter or backlight, which might be relatively inexpensive to replace in some models. CRT failures usually involve the picture tube, which is the most expensive portion of the display and is often not cost-effective to replace.

LCD panels offer a significantly smaller footprint (front-to-back dimensions), and some offer optional wall or stand mounting. Some LCD panels offer a pivoting feature, enabling the unit to swivel 90° and providing a choice between the traditional landscape horizontal mode for web surfing and the portrait vertical mode for word processing and page-layout programs. LCD panels also weigh substantially less than comparably sized CRTs. For example, a typical 17" LCD weighs less than 10 lbs., compared to the 50 lbs. weight of typical 19" CRTs with a similar viewing area.

LCD Panel Display Connections

Although LCD panels are inherently digital, many computers, particularly low-cost units and those with integrated graphics, lack digital video connections. Therefore, a particular desktop LCD panel might use either a traditional analog VGA connector or a digital DVI connector, or offer both connections. Typically, lower-cost 15"–19" LCD panels use the traditional analog VGA connector and must convert analog signals back into digital, whereas larger and more expensive LCD panels provide both the analog VGA and the DVI digital connector found on most high-end and mid-range video cards. Note that some LCD vendors of VGA/DVI-compatible panels might provide only the cheaper analog VGA cable, leaving it to you to buy your own DVI cable. If you plan to connect your new LCD to your video card's DVI port, be sure that the panel supports DVI and that you have the necessary cable. And, while you're shopping for an LCD panel, be sure to note which models include the DVI cable; the presence of a DVI cable in the box of a nominally more expensive display can more than make up the difference in price between it and an apparently less-expensive panel that doesn't include the cable.

▶▶ For more information about VGA ports, see "The Video Graphics Array (VGA) Standard," p. 924.

DFP and DVI Interfaces for Digital LCD Panels

As I mentioned earlier in this chapter, all LCD panels internally use digital signaling, as do the display adapters in a PC. Unfortunately for many years the primary connection standard between PCs and displays has been analog VGA. When analog VGA is used to connect an LCD panel to a PC, the digital signal in the PC's display adapter is converted to analog VGA, sent over the monitor cable in analog fashion, then converted back to digital inside the LCD panel. This digital-to-analog-to-digital connection unfortunately causes a loss of signal quality from end to end. To avoid this double conversion, it is desirable to have an entirely digital connection from one end to the other. In order to facilitate a digital video connection between PCs and displays, several digital video signal standards and specifications have been developed to permit standardized all-digital connections between display adapters and displays:

■ **Digital Flat Panel (DFP), approved by the Video Electronic Standards Association (VESA) in February 1999**—DFP was previously known as PanelLink; DFP has now been replaced by DVI.

■ **Digital Visual Interface (DVI), proposed by the Digital Display Working Group (DDWG) in April 1999**—DVI has become the de facto standard supported by most recent mid-range and high-end VGA display cards, including models with dual-display capabilities. DVI-D is also known as DVI HDCP. This port is used on many LCD and plasma TVs.

Figure 13.2 shows how DFP and DVI connectors found on some video cards and digital LCDs compare to the standard VGA connector used on conventional video cards, CRTs, and analog-compatible LCDs.

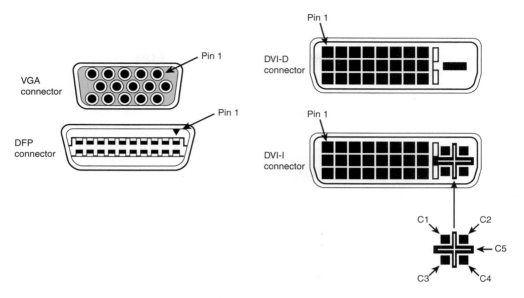

Figure 13.2 Conventional VGA cards, CRTs, and analog-compatible LCDs use the standard VGA connector. Early digital LCDs and their matching video cards often used the DFP connector. Most recent digital LCD panels and LCD TVs use the DVI-D (also known as the DVI-HDCP) connector, whereas video cards used with both analog and digital displays use the DVI-I connector.

The DVI-I connector shown in Figure 13.2 can be converted into a VGA port for use with CRTs or with analog LCD panels via an adapter, as shown in Figure 13.3. Often new graphics cards purchased at retail that support only DVI come with an adapter like this one that allows you to connect a traditional VGA connector from the display to the adapter.

HDMI

The High Definition Multimedia Interface (HDMI) was designed by a group of multimedia companies (Hitachi, Panasonic, Philips, Silicon Image, Sony, Thompson, and Toshiba) as a way to provide a single-cable connection for transporting digital video and audio signals between AV hardware components such as big-screen TVs, video games, DVD players, digital audio ampliers, and home theater systems. The original version 1.0 of HDMI was introduced in December 2002, and the current version 1.3 was introduced in June 2006.

The current version of HDMI, version 1.3, can carry up to eight-channel uncompressed digital audio at 24-bit/192KHz along with Dolby Digital, DTS, Dolby TrueHD, DTS-HD Master Audio compressed audio formats. HDMI 1.3 provides video bandwidth up to 10.2Gbps (equivalent to 340MHz), which enables HDMI to support billions of colors ("Deep Color"), resolutions beyond WQXGA (2560×1600), and improvements in lip sync in HDTV among others. The higher video bandwidth provided by HDMI 1.3 can be used in various ways: for higher-resolution displays, Deep Color support, or higher refresh rates.

Because it uses a single cable for both audio and video signals, HDMI provides an excellent way to reduce the cabling tangle present in home theater systems that use conventional analog audio and video cables. For home theater users who subscribe to HDTV satellite or cable services, HDMI is ideal because it supports high-bandwidth digital content protection (HDCP), which is used by these services to protect content from piracy while assuring high-quality viewing and listening. To avoid reduced-quality playback of protected content, all devices, including the DVD player or set-top box, AV receiver, and display must support HDCP.

VGA cable from monitor   DVI-I / VGA adapter

VGA female port on adapter

DVI-I port on video card

Figure 13.3   Adapting a video card with a DVI-I port to use a VGA cable from a CRT or analog LCD panel.

In addition to transmitting high-quality audio and video between devices, HDMI carries additional signals. HDMI uses the display data channel (DDC) to identify the capabilities of an HDMI display, such as resolutions, color depth, and audio. DDC enables optimal playback quality on different devices. HDMI also supports the optional consumer electronic control (CEC) feature, which enables one-button control of all CEC-enabled devices for one-touch play or record or other features.

Table 13.3 compares the major features of HDMI 1.3 and earlier versions.

Table 13.3   HDMI Versions

Version	Release Date	Maximum Bandwidth	Video Support	Audio Support	Notes
1.0	December 2002	4.9Gbps	1080p 60Hz, UXGA, 24-bit color	8-channel 24-bit audio at 192KHz	
1.1	May 2004	4.9Gbps	1080p 60Hz, UXGA, 24-bit color	8-channel 24-bit audio at 192KHz, DVD audio	

Table 13.3   Continued

Version	Release Date	Maximum Bandwidth	Video Support	Audio Support	Notes
1.2	August 2005	4.9Gbps	1080p 60Hz, UXGA, 24-bit color	8-channel 24-bit audio at 192KHz, DVD audio, Super Audio CD audio	New Type A connector for PCs; native RGB and YCbCr CE color spaces
1.2a	December 2005	4.9Gbps	1080p 60Hz, UXGA, 24-bit color	8-channel 24-bit audio at 192KHz, DVD audio, Super Audio CD audio	Adds specifications for CEC features
1.3	June 2006	10.2Gbps	1080p 60Hz, UXGA,24-bit color; optional support for 30-bit, 36-bit, 48-bit color	8-channel 24-bit audio at 192KHz, DVD audio, Super Audio CD audio; Dolby TrueHD and DT-HD Master Audio Support; auto lip sync	New compact connector option for camcorders and other small devices
1.3a	November 2006	10.2Gbps	1080p 60Hz, UXGA, 24-bit color; optional support for 30-bit, 36-bit, 48-bit color	8-channel 24-bit audio at 192KHz, DVD audio, Super Audio CD audio; Dolby TrueHD and DT-HD Master Audio Support	Various adjustments to CEC and other specifications; new compliance test
1.3b	March 2007	10.2Gbps	1080p 60Hz, UXGA, 24-bit color; optional support for 30-bit, 36-bit, 48-bit color	8-channel 24-bit audio at 192KHz, DVD audio, Super Audio CD audio; Dolby TrueHD and DT-HD Master Audio Support	Revised compliance test

HDMI is backward-compatible with DVI-I and DVI-D video connectors found on most recent mid-range and high-end video cards, enabling a PC to drive an HDTV. This is useful for users of Windows Media Center Edition for Windows XP, Windows Vista Media Center (Home Premium and Ultimate editions), and other PC-based multimedia programs. However, unless the video card supports HDCP, you might not be able to play premium HDTV content through your PC, or, if you can do so, the resolution might be reduced. Although some graphics cards claimed HDCP support as early as early 2006, changes in the HDCP standard may prevent early cards from working properly. You should contact your graphics card or chipset vendor to detemine if a particular video card works with HDCP.

Current HDMI cables correspond to HDMI Type A or Type C. Type A is a 19-pin connector. Type C is a smaller version of Type A, designed for use in DV camcorders or other portable devices. It uses the same pinout, and Type A to Type C adapter are available from various vendors. HDMI version 1.0 also defined a 29-pin Type B cable that is not in general use.

Figure 13.4 illustrates a typical HDMI Type A cable and the location of pin 1 on the cable and connector.

The pinout for HDMI Type and Type C cables is shown in Table 13.4.

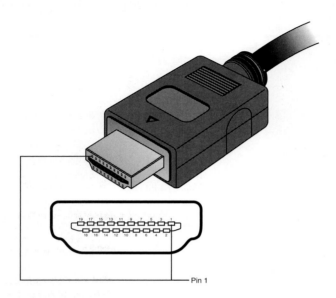

Pin 1

Figure 13.4   HDMI Type A cable and socket use a two-row 19-pin interface.

Table 13.4   HDMI Type A/Type C Pinout

Pin Number	Description	Pin Number	Description
1	TMDS Data2 +	11	TMDS Clock Shield
2	TMDS Data2 Shield	12	TMDS Clock -
3	TMDS Data2 -	13	CEC
4	TMDS Data1+	14	Reserved
5	TMDS Data1 Shield	15	SCL
6	TMDS Data1 -	16	SDA
7	TMDS Data0+	17	DDC/CEC ground
8	TMDS Data0 Shield	18	+5V power
9	TMDS Data0 -	19	Hot Plug Detect
10	TMDS Clock +	—	—

Figure 13.5 illustrates a typical HDMI-DVI adapter cable.

Note

The adapter cable shown in Figure 13.5 is not designed to work with graphics cards and drivers that do not support HDTV resolutions and timings. You may need to upgrade your graphics card driver before using an HDMI-DVI cable. Although some set-top boxes include DVI ports, this type of adapter cable is only intended for PC-HDTV connections.

Figure 13.5 HDMI–DVI adapter cable.

Starting in late 2006, some vendors began to release PCI-Express cards including HDMI ports. Some provide HDMI input and output for use with HDV camcorders, while others using ATI or NVIDIA chipsets are graphics cards that also include HDMI output.

For more information about HDMI, see the HDMI Founders website at www.hdmi.org.

Wide-screen LCD Panels

Although most LCD panels use the 4:3 (also known as 1.33:1) aspect ratio used by CRTs, an increasing number of LCD panels now feature a 16:10 aspect ratio, similar to the 16:9 aspect ratio used by wide-screen TVs. Wide-screen LCD panels offer many benefits:

- You can watch wide-screen TV programs and movies on DVD with the entire screen area, rather than in letterbox mode as with 4:3 ratio displays.

- Most support digital connections to your PC via the DVI port for greatest picture quality and include component and S-video connections to work with mid-range and high-end DVD and VCR set-top boxes, as well as VGA and composite connections for use with low-end PCs or DVD/VCR units.

- Some support portrait mode for easier document editing.

- You can view more documents onscreen at the same time or increase the magnification level used for detail work on documents and photos.

- There's plenty of room for floating menus, a common feature with photo and video-editing programs.

However, you need to ensure that the LCD panel provides sufficient resolution for high-quality computer use. Many wide-screen LCDs in 20" or larger sizes are designed primarily for use as televisions. These units can have resolutions as low as 640×480. A true wide-screen LCD monitor has vertical resolutions similar to a comparably sized 4:3 LCD panel, with proportionally wider horizontal resolutions. For example, a typical 21" wide-screen LCD monitor offers a horizontal resolution of 1680 pixels and a vertical resolution of 1050 pixels. This is comparable to the resolutions provided by a typical 19" 4:3 ratio LCD panel, which features a 1280×1024 resolution. Table 13.5 lists typical resolutions for wide-screen LCD panels and LCD TVs that support PC video inputs (TV/monitors) in sizes from 17" to 32".

Table 13.5   Wide-screen LCD Panel and LCD TV Resolutions

LCD Size	Intended Use	Resolution	Sample Unit
17"	TV/monitor	1280×768	Planar XP17W
19"	TV/monitor	1280×768	Samsung SM940MW
20"	TV/monitor	1366×768	ViewSonic N2060W
20"	Monitor	1680×1050	Apple M9177LL/A
21"	Monitor	1680×1050	Samsung SyncMaster 215TW
23"	TV/monitor	1366×768	Philips 23PF5320
23"	Monitor	1920×1200	HP L2335
26"	TV/monitor	1366×768	Sharp LD=26SH1U
27"	TV/monitor	1366×768	Westinghouse LTV-27w6
32"	TV/monitor	1366×768	Sony BRAVIA KDL32S3000

As you can see from Table 13.5, wide-screen LCD panels designed primarily for TV use offer lower resolutions than those designed as monitors.

▶▶   For more information about display resolution standards, see Table 13.6, p. 905.

The resolutions offered by TV/monitor-type panels are satisfactory for watching TV, DVDs, and video content, for using Windows Media Center, and for console gaming, but they are not high enough for detail work. I recommend using a wide-screen LCD monitor if you want a unit optimized for computer use with a secondary use as a TV monitor. If you buy an LCD panel designed for TV use, I recommend that you use it as an additional monitor, not as your primary monitor.

Note

LCD TVs have built-in TV tuners, and some also feature built-in HDTV tuners. If you want to watch TV on an LCD monitor, you need to use an external tuner, such as a TV tuner card or a set-top TV tuner with suitable connections.

Potential Drawbacks of LCD Panels

Many users are replacing their CRT displays with LCD panels or using a mixture of CRT and LCD displays. As the industry continues to move to LCD panels, there are some potential drawbacks to consider:

■ If you routinely switch display resolutions (as web developers do to preview their work), LCD monitors must take one of two approaches to change resolutions. Some older units might reduce the onscreen image to occupy only the pixels of the new resolution, thus using only a portion of a typical 1024×768 LCD panel to display a 640×480 image, whereas newer units might scale the image to occupy the entire screen. Although scaling is common on recent displays, some displays provide better-quality scaling than others. Typically, though, a CRT can handle a wider range of resolutions than an LCD.

■ If you choose an analog LCD panel, you'll usually save money and be able to use your existing video card or onboard video port. However, image quality for both text and graphics can suffer because of the conversion of the computer's digital signal to analog (at the video card) and back to digital again (inside the LCD panel). The conversion can lead to pixel jitter or pixel swim, in which adjacent LCD cells are turned on and off by the display's incapability to determine which cells should stay on and stay off. Most panels come with adjustment software to reduce this display-quality problem, but you might not be able to eliminate it entirely.

- Digital LCD panels avoid conversion problems when attached to a digital-compatible display card. However, some low-cost, off-the-shelf display cards don't support digital signals yet, and the onboard video circuits built into some motherboards don't support DVI yet.

Note

Although most recent video chipsets made by NVIDIA, ATI, and Matrox include support for digital and analog display panels, low-cost video cards often omit the DVI connector or don't provide a DVI/VGA adapter. Check the specifications for a particular video card to verify support for the display type you want to use.

- High-quality LCD panels of either digital or analog type are great for displaying sharp text and graphics. But they sometimes can't display as wide a range of very light and very dark colors as CRTs can.

- Many LCDs don't react to changes in the images being displayed as quickly as CRTs. This can cause full-motion video, full-screen 3D games, and animation to look smeared onscreen. To avoid this problem, look for LCDs that offer a gray-to-gray response time of 5ms or faster. Some LCDs now have gray-to-gray response times under 2ms (the lower the number, the better). Note that LCD makers use various methods of measuring response time, including black to white. Gray-to-gray response times are shorter than black to white response times on identical hardware.

Shopping Criteria for LCD Panels

Thanks to price decreases, larger panel sizes, improved performance, and widespread support for DVI digital connectors on current video cards, this is the best time ever to consider buying an LCD panel for your desktop PC.

Be sure that you use the following criteria when you consider purchasing an LCD monitor:

- Evaluate the panel both at its native resolution and at any other resolutions you plan to use. This is especially important for web design, games, and video editing.

- If you're considering a digital LCD panel, determine whether your existing video card or onboard video supports the features you need. You might need to upgrade to a PCI-Express (or AGP) video card that features a DVI port because many low-cost systems with integrated video or low-end video cards don't have a DVI port. For maximum flexibility without upgrading existing video while preserving the ability to move to digital display support later, consider a display that features both analog and digital connectors.

- Look for displays that support both analog and DVI inputs if you want to use the same display on different systems. If the graphics card has only DVI connectors, make sure you can use a DVI-VGA adapter to provide analog support. Because LCD panels are much lighter and smaller than normal CRT displays, they're a natural choice for connecting to both desktop and notebook computers. If you use multiple computers in a small work area, you might also want to look for displays that support multiple inputs, which enables you to connect two computers to one screen.

- Make sure your system has a suitable expansion slot for the recommended video card type. Many low-cost systems feature onboard PCI-Express (or AGP) video but no PCI-Express or AGP slot, which can't be upgraded unless the user opts for the obsolescent (for video) PCI slot. As the move to LCD panels continues, more of these systems should feature built-in support for LCDs, but this could be a problem for some time to come.

Note

Although many recent chipsets with integrated video feature DVI support, most motherboards using these chipsets do not provide a built-in DVI port. Instead, an optional add-on card that plugs into the AGP or PCI-Express slot (if present) is used to enable DVI support. Otherwise, the onboard video can be disabled and replaced with a dual-display video card with VGA and DVI ports.

- Evaluate the panel and card combo's performance on video clips and animation if you work with full-motion video, animated presentation programs, or games. Look for gray-to-gray response times of 5ms or faster for best results.

- Although active-matrix (analog) and digital LCD monitors have much wider viewing areas than do passive-matrix and dual-scan LCD panels used in older notebook computers, some displays have viewing angles that are much less than CRTs. This is an important consideration if you're planning to use your LCD monitor for group presentations. To improve the horizontal viewing area, several vendors have developed patented improvements to the basic TFT display, such as Hitachi's in-plane switching (IPS), Fujitsu's multidomain vertical adjustment (MVA), and Mitsubishi's FFD—all of which have been licensed to other leading LCD makers. By using such improvements, as well as increased contrast ratios, horizontal viewing angles exceeding 170° have been achieved in some recent designs.

- A high-contrast ratio (luminance difference between white and black) makes for sharper text and vivid colors. A typical CRT has a contrast ratio of about 245:1. Some recent LCD panels have contrast ratios as high as 700:1 or more. Higher contrast ratios help improve horizontal viewing angles and improve the appearance of movies and TV shows.

- Features such as integrated speakers and Universal Serial Bus (USB) hubs are pleasant additions, but your eyes should make the final decision about which panel is best for you. Because reviews of LCD panels often don't provide detailed analysis of horizontal and vertical viewing angles and contrast ratios, check display units in stores yourself as well as the specification sheets for models you're considering. Be sure to view the displays from several angles. If you're adding the panel as a second display, be sure to check its off-axis image quality.

- Look for pivoting displays that enable you to rotate the display to match an upright page layout if you use your computer for text-editing or page layout. This feature is supported by many LCD panels—particularly those that are 17" or larger—but the display performance in portrait mode is usually lower than in normal landscape mode, especially for rapid motion. If possible, test the display in portrait mode if you plan to use this mode frequently.

How CRT Display Technology Works

Cathode-ray tube (CRT) technology is the same used in older television sets. In the last couple of years, CRTs have become scarce on store shelves, mainly due to the availability of lower cost LCDs.

CRTs consist of a vacuum tube enclosed in glass. One end of the tube contains an electron gun assembly that projects three electron beams, one each for the red, green, and blue phosphors used to create the colors you see onscreen; the other end contains a screen with a phosphorous coating.

When heated, the electron gun emits a stream of high-speed electrons that are attracted to the other end of the tube. Along the way, a focus control and deflection coil steer the beam to a specific point on the phosphorous screen. When struck by the beam, the phosphor glows. This light is what you see when you watch TV or look at your computer screen. Three layers of phosphors are used: red, green, and blue. A metal plate called a *shadow mask* is used to align the electron beams; it has slots or holes that divide the red, green, and blue phosphors into groups of three (one of each color). Various types of shadow masks affect picture quality, and the distance between each group of three (the *dot pitch*) affects picture sharpness.

▶▶   See "Dot Pitch (CRTs)," p. 907.

Figure 13.6 illustrates the interior of a typical CRT.

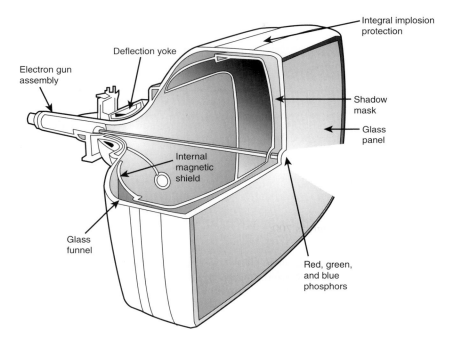

Figure 13.6   A typical CRT monitor is a large vacuum tube. It contains three electron guns (red, green, and blue) that project the picture toward the front glass of the monitor. High voltage is used to produce the magnetism that controls the electron beams that create the picture displayed on the front of the CRT.

The phosphor chemical has a quality called *persistence*, which indicates how long this glow remains onscreen. Persistence is what causes a faint image to remain on your TV screen for a few seconds after you turn off the set. The scanning frequency of the display specifies how often the image is refreshed. You should have a good match between persistence and scanning frequency so the image has less flicker (which occurs when the persistence is too low) and no ghost images (which occurs when the persistence is too high).

The electron beam moves very quickly, sweeping the screen from left to right in lines from top to bottom, in a pattern called a *raster*. The horizontal scan rate refers to the speed at which the electron beam moves laterally across the screen.

During its sweep, the beam strikes the phosphor wherever an image should appear onscreen. The beam also varies in intensity to produce different levels of brightness. Because the glow begins to fade almost immediately, the electron beam must continue to sweep the screen to maintain an image—a practice called *redrawing* or *refreshing* the screen.

Most current CRT displays have an ideal refresh rate (also called the vertical scan frequency) of about 85 hertz (Hz), which means the screen is refreshed 85 times per second. Refresh rates that are too low cause the screen to flicker, contributing to eyestrain. The higher the refresh rate, the better for your eyes. Low-cost monitors often have flicker-free refresh rates (72Hz or higher) available only at 640×480 and 800×600 resolutions; you should insist on high refresh rates at resolutions such as 1024×768 or higher.

Tip

I use the 72Hz refresh rate (the minimum flicker-free refresh rate) as a shortcut for determining the highest usable resolution for a CRT. Many CRTs offer a maximum resolution that supports refresh rates lower than 72Hz. Because low refresh rates cause flicker and eyestrain, I won't use them. For example, a 17" monitor might offer a maximum refresh rate of 1280×1024 at 66Hz and a 1024×768 mode at 87Hz. As far as I'm concerned, that monitor has a usable maximum resolution of 1024×768.

It is important that the refresh rates expected by your monitor match those produced by your video card. If you have mismatched rates, you will not see an image and can actually damage your monitor. Generally speaking, video card refresh rates cover a higher range than most monitors. For this reason, the default refresh rate used by most video cards is relatively low (usually 60Hz) to avoid monitor damage. The refresh rate can be adjusted through the Windows Display properties sheets.

Multiple Frequency Monitors

Although a few very old monitors had fixed refresh rates, virtually all monitors in use support a range of frequencies. This support provides built-in compatibility with a wide range of current and future video standards (described in the "Video Display Adapters" section later in this chapter). A monitor that supports many video standards is called a *multiple-frequency monitor*. Virtually all monitors sold today are multiple frequency, which means they support operation with a variety of popular video signal standards. Different vendors have used a variety of trade names to identify their multiple-frequency monitors, including multisync, multifrequency, multiscan, autosynchronous, and auto-tracking, among others.

Note

Even though a monitor is capable of displaying a wide range of video standards, you usually need to fine-tune the display through its onscreen display (OSD) controls and Windows Display properties sheets to achieve the best possible pictures.

Curved Versus Flat Picture Tubes

Phosphor-based screens come in two styles: curved and flat. Older CRT monitors used a curved picture tub; it bulges outward from the middle of the screen. This design is consistent with the vast majority of CRT designs (the same as the tube in most television sets). Although this type of CRT is inexpensive to produce, the curved surface can cause distortion and glare, especially when used in a brightly lit room. Some vendors use antiglare treatments to reduce the reflectivity of the typical curved CRT surface.

The traditional screen is curved both vertically and horizontally. Some monitor models used the Sony Trinitron CRT, some versions of which are curved only horizontally and flat vertically; these are referred to as *flat square tube (FST)* designs.

Virtually all manufacturers have switched their remaining CRT monitor product lines to CRTs that are flat both horizontally and vertically. Many people prefer this type of flatter screen because these picture tubes show less glare and provide a higher-quality, more accurate image.

Figure 13.7 compares the cross-section of typical curved and flat CRT picture tubes.

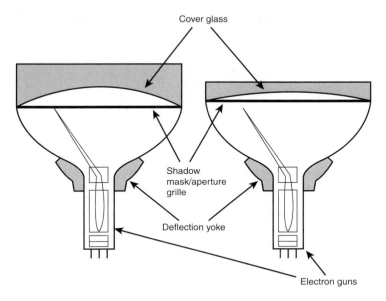

Figure 13.7   A typical curved-tube CRT (left) compared to a Sony FD Trinitron flat tube (right).

CRT Interfaces

Most CRTs are designed to connect to the traditional 15-pin VGA port, although a few high-end models also support BNC connections for use with other types of video sources. A few CRTs in the past have used DVI ports, but DVI never caught on as a video source for CRTs and these monitors have been discontinued.

▶▶   For VGA port pinouts, see "The Video Graphics Array (VGA) Standard," p. 924.

CRT Versus LCD Displays

For many years CRT displays were the leading display type. However, in the last few years LCDs have become the predominant type of display for PCs. There are, however, some benefits to sticking with a CRT monitor, including the following:

■ **Widest viewing angle without color distortion**—If you plan to use a monitor, rather than a projector, to show a presentation to a small group, a monitor provides accurate color rendition and image details to almost anyone who can see the screen, even at a significant angle from a straight-on view. Although recent LCD displays offer wider viewing angles (up to 170° or more horizontal and up to 120° vertical), a CRT is still superior for enabling everyone to see a presentation.

■ **Lower initial cost**—Although LCDs have dropped in price, you can generally purchase CRT displays at a lower cost, especially if you are willing to purchase used equipment. In fact, used CRTs can be found for very little money, or even for free in some cases.

■ **Resolution flexibility**—Although late-model LCD panels offer greater quality when used at non-native resolutions than older designs, high-end CRTs still rule if you need support for a wide range of resolutions. Keep in mind that you will need to fine-tune each resolution and refresh rate combination using your monitor's onscreen display (OSD) controls the first time you use a particular combination. The monitor's nonvolatile RAM will remember your settings and apply them the next time you enter that mode.

■ **Response time**—Even a low-cost CRT offers an instant, ghost-free response time when you're playing back full-motion video or playing games if the recommended refresh rate is selected for the resolution (72Hz–85Hz). However, if you use an LCD panel, you must ensure that the panel supports gray-to-gray response times of 5ms or faster. Many low-cost LCD panels offer slower response times.

Caution

The lower initial cost of a large CRT can be offset by higher shipping costs if you order by mail or over the Internet. CRTs are expensive to ship because of their bulk and weight. If possible, buy your CRT monitor locally to avoid the additional cost of shipping.

Plasma Displays

Plasma, the latest technology for large wide-screen displays, actually has a long history. In the late 1980s, IBM developed a monochrome plasma screen that displayed orange text and graphics on a black background. Toshiba used this display in its T3100 and T3200 laptop computers, which featured double-scan CGA/AT&T 6300–compatible 640×400 graphics.

Unlike the early IBM monochrome plasma screen, today's plasma displays are RGB devices capable of displaying 24-bit or 32-bit color, TV, or DVD signals. Plasma screens produce an image by using electrically charged gas (plasma) to illuminate triads of red, green, and blue phosphors, as shown in Figure 13.8.

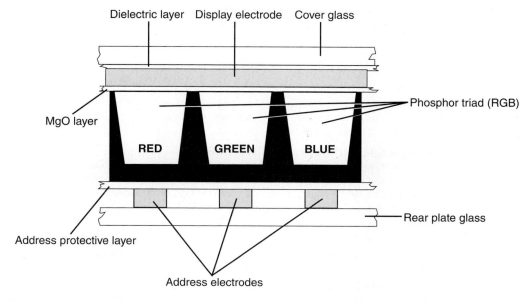

Figure 13.8   A cross-section of a typical plasma display.

The display and address electrodes create a grid that enables each subpixel to be individually addressed. By adjusting the differences in charge between the display and address electrodes for each triad's subpixels, the signal source controls the picture.

Typical plasma screens range in size from 42" to 50" or larger. Because they are primarily designed for use with DVD, TV, or HDTV video sources, they are optimized for video rather than computer use. Typical resolutions include 852×480 or 1366×768 (Wide XGA). Note that some plasma screens can also support 1024×768 or 1280×1024 (4:3 ratio) VGA video. Given the limited resolution of plasma screens, they are best suited for entertainment rather than computer use, although some do include DVI-HDCP (DVI-D) and VGA ports for use with computer-based video.

Monitor Selection Criteria

Stores offer a dizzying variety of monitor choices, from the low-cost units bundled with computers to large-screen tubes that cost more than many systems. Because a monitor can account for a large part of the price of your computer system, you need to know what to look for when you shop for a monitor.

Important factors to consider include

- Viewable image size
- Resolution
- Dot pitch (CRTs)
- Image brightness and contrast (LCDs)
- Power management and safety certifications
- Vertical and horizontal frequencies
- Picture controls
- Environmental issues (lighting, size, weight)

This section helps you understand these issues so you can make a wise choice for your next display, regardless of the display technology you prefer.

The Right Size

CRT-based monitors come in various sizes ranging from 15" to 42" diagonal measurement. The larger the monitor, the higher the price tag—after you get beyond 19" displays, the prices skyrocket. The most common CRT monitor sizes are 17", 19", and 21". These diagonal measurements, unfortunately, often represent not the size of the actual image the screen displays, but the size of the tube.

Although some vendors manufacture LCD panels as small as 14", most vendors are now concentrating on LCD panels with sizes from 17" and larger. If you are comparing CRT and LCD displays, keep in mind that the size of an LCD panel is the same as its active screen area, whereas a CRT's viewable area is typically at least 1" smaller. The *active screen area* refers to the diagonal measurement of the lighted area on the screen. In other words, if you are running Windows, the viewing area is the actual diagonal measure of the desktop. Refer to Table 13.2 to see how typical CRT monitors' viewing areas compare to LCD panels' actual sizes. As a result, LCD displays give you more active screen area for a given screen size than CRTs. Most recent CRT models have an active screen area that is 1" smaller than the CRT's diagonal measurement, but some models might differ slightly. Check the specifications for a particular monitor to determine its actual active screen area. The active screen area is also known as the *viewable image size (VIS)*.

You can adjust many better-quality CRT monitors to display a high-quality image that completely fills the tube from edge to edge. Less-expensive monitors can fill the screen also, but some of them do so only by pushing the monitor beyond its comfortable limits. The result is a distorted image that is worse than the monitor's smaller, properly adjusted picture.

If initial cost is more important than other factors, the 17" CRT monitor is the best bargain in the industry. A 17" monitor is recommended for new systems, especially when running Windows. I recommend a 17" CRT monitor as the minimum you should consider for most normal applications. Displays of 19"–21" or larger are recommended for high-end systems, especially in situations where graphics applications are the major focus.

Larger monitors are particularly handy for applications such as CAD and desktop publishing, in which the smallest details must be clearly visible. With a 17" or larger display, you can see nearly an entire 8 1/2"×11" print page in 100% view; in other words, what you see onscreen virtually matches the page that will be printed. Being able to see the entire page at its actual size can save you the trouble of printing several drafts of a document or project to get it right.

With the popularity of the Internet, monitor size and resolution become even more of an issue. Many web pages are designed for 800×600 or higher resolutions. Whereas a 15" monitor can handle 800×600 fairly well, a 17" monitor set to 1024×768 resolution enables you to comfortably view any website without eyestrain (if the monitor supports 75Hz or higher refresh rates) or excessive scrolling.

Note

Although many monitors smaller than 17" are physically capable of running at 1024×768 and even higher resolutions, most people have trouble reading print at that size. A partial solution is to enable large icons in the Windows Display properties sheet (right-click your desktop and select Properties). In Windows 98/Me/2000/XP, open the Appearance tab, select Effects, Use Large Icons. In Windows Vista, right-clicking the desktop and selecting Properties opens the Personalization menu. Click Adjust Font Size (DPI) in the Tasks pane to change icon size.

Windows 95 doesn't have an option to enlarge only the icons; you can use the Settings tab to select Large Fonts, but some programs will not work properly with font sizes larger than the default Small Fonts setting.

Resolution

Resolution is the amount of detail a monitor can render. This quantity is expressed in the number of horizontal and vertical picture elements, or *pixels*, contained in the screen. The greater the number of pixels, the more detailed the images. The resolution required depends on the application. Character-based applications (such as DOS command-line programs) require little resolution, whereas graphics-intensive applications (such as desktop publishing and Windows software) require a great deal.

It's important to realize that CRTs are designed to handle a range of resolutions natively, but LCD panels (both desktop and notebook) are built to run a single native resolution and must scale to other choices. Older LCD panels handled scaling poorly, but even though current LCD panels perform scaling better, the best results with various resolutions are still found with CRTs.

As PC video technology developed, the screen resolutions video adapters support grew at a steady pace. Table 13.6 shows standard resolutions used in PC graphics adapters and displays and the terms commonly used to describe them.

Table 13.6   Graphics Display Resolution Standards

Display Standard	Linear Pixels (HxV)	Total Pixels	Aspect Ratio
CGA	320×200	64,000	1.60
EGA	640×350	224,000	1.83
VGA	640×480	307,200	1.33
WVGA	854×480	409,920	1.78
SVGA	800×600	480,000	1.33
XGA	1024×768	786,432	1.33
XGA+	1152×864	995,328	1.33
WXGA	1280×800	1,024,000	1.60
WEXGA	1280×854	1,093,120	1.50
QVGA	1280×960	1,228,800	1.33
WXGA+	1440×900	1,296,000	1.60
SXGA	1280×1024	1,310,720	1.25
SXGA+	1400×1050	1,470,000	1.33
WSXGA	1600×1024	1,638,400	1.56
WSXGA+	1680×1050	1,764,000	1.60
UXGA	1600×1200	1,920,000	1.33
HDTV	1920×1080	2,073,600	1.78
WUXGA	1920×1200	2,304,000	1.60
QXGA	2048×1536	3,145,728	1.33
QSXGA	2560×2048	5,242,880	1.25
QUXGA-W	3840×2400	9,216,000	1.60

Aspect ratios:

1.25 = 5:4   *1.60 = 16:10*
1.33 = 4:3   *1.78 = 16:9*
1.56 = 25:16   *1.83 = 11:6*
W = Wide-screen (aspect ratios wider than 1.33)

The Color Graphics Adapter (CGA) and Enhanced Graphics Adapter (EGA) cards and monitors were the first PC graphics standards in the early-to-mid 1980s. The Video Graphics Array (VGA) standard was released by IBM in April 1987, and all the subsequent resolutions and modes introduced since then have been based on it in one way or another. VGA mode is still in common use as a reference to the standard 640×480 16-color display that most versions of the Windows operating systems use as their default; Windows XP and Vista, however, default to SVGA mode, which is 800×600. The 15-pin connector through which you connect the analog display to most video adapters is also often called a *VGA port*. A larger 24-pin connector is used on DVI-D displays, whereas DVI-I displays use a 29-pin version of the DVI-D connector (refer to Figure 13.2).

Nearly all video adapters sold today support UXGA (1600×1200) or higher resolutions. Typically, in addition to the highest setting your card and display will support, any lower settings are automatically supported as well.

Because all CRT and almost all recent and current LCDs can handle various resolutions, you have a choice. As you'll see later in this chapter, the combinations of resolution and color depth (number of colors onscreen) you can choose might be limited by how much RAM your graphics adapter has onboard or, if you have motherboard chipset-based video, how much system memory is allocated to your video function. If you switch to a larger display and you can't set the color depth you want to use, a new video card with more RAM is a desirable upgrade. Video cards once featured upgradeable memory, but this is not usually an option with current models.

Which resolution do you want for your display? Generally, the higher the resolution, the larger the display you will want. Why? Because Windows icons and text normally use a constant number of pixels, higher display resolutions make these screen elements smaller onscreen. By using a larger display (17" or larger), you can use higher resolution settings and still have text and icons that are large enough to be readable. Although it is possible to change icon and text size, this often causes other problems with formatting in various windows and dialog boxes, such that in most cases it is best to stick with the default sizes.

To understand this issue, you might want to try various resolutions on your system. As you change from 1024×768 to 1280×1024 and beyond, you'll notice several changes to the appearance of your screen.

At 1024×768 or lower resolutions, text and onscreen icons are very large. Because the screen elements used for the Windows desktop and software menus are at a fixed pixel width and height, you'll notice that they shrink in size onscreen as you change to the higher resolutions. You'll be able to see more of your document or web page onscreen at the higher resolutions because each object requires less of the screen.

If you are using a 1024×768 resolution, for example, you should find a 17" CRT or 15" LCD monitor to be comfortable. At 1280×1024, you probably will find that the display of a 17" CRT monitor is too small; therefore, you will probably prefer to use a larger one, such as a 19" CRT or 17" LCD monitor. Table 13.7 shows the smallest 4:3 ratio monitors I recommend to properly display the resolutions users typically select.

Table 13.7   Recommended Resolutions for CRT and LCD Displays (4:3 Ratio)

Minimum Recommended Resolution	Minimum Recommended CRT Monitor	Minimum Recommended LCD Panel
800×600	15"	14"
1024×768	17"	15"
1280×1024	19"	17"
1600×1200	21"	18"

Many LCD panels on the market in the 19" and larger sizes use widescreen 16:10 designs. Table 13.8 lists typical sizes and their resolutions.

Table 13.8   Typical Sizes and Resolutions for LCD Widescreen Panels

LCD Panel Size	Typical Native Resolution
19"	1440×900
20.1"	1680×1050
24"	1920×1200
30"	2560×1600

If you compare the recommended resolutions for CRTs in Table 13.7 with those listed in Table 13.2, you'll notice that the recommended resolutions are not necessarily the limits of a given CRT monitor's capabilities. However, I recommend these resolutions to help ensure a comfortable computing experience. On small CRT monitors set to high resolutions, characters, icons, and other information are too small for most users and can cause eyestrain. Low-cost CRT monitors often produce blurry results when set to their maximum resolution and often have low refresh rates at their highest resolution. Low refresh rates cause screen flicker, leading to increased eyestrain.

LCDs have another issue: They work best at their native resolution. This means that if you have a 19" 4:3 LCD with a native resolution of 1280×1024, then you should always run at that resolution to have images and especially text that is crisp and clean. Changing the display adapter resolution to something other than the LCD panel's native resolution results in the image being either compressed or expanded to fill the screen, with often less than perfect results.

Note

If you have a widescreen LCD monitor or laptop display, some of the non-native resolutions you can select are standard 4:3 resolutions. These will result in a "squashed" look on your display. Generally, you should use 4:3 resolutions (such as 1024×768) only if you must configure your display to match the resolution of a cloned display or projector, or to product screen captures at a specified resolution. Although your widescreen display is distorted by running at the wrong ratio, screen captures and output to a 4:3 display will have the correct proportions.

Whereas CRTs can produce poor-quality results at very high resolutions, LCDs, as long as they are run at their native resolution, are crisp and perfectly focused by nature. Also, the dimensions advertised for the LCD screens represent the exact size of the viewable image, unlike most conventional CRT-based monitors. In addition, the LCD is so crisp that screens of a given size can easily handle resolutions that are higher than what would otherwise be acceptable on a CRT.

For example, many of the high-end notebook systems now use 15.4" or 17" widescreen LCD panels that feature 1280×800 or 1440×900 resolutions. Although these resolutions would be unacceptable on a CRT display of the same size, they work well on the LCD panel built into the laptop because of the crystal-clear image and because you generally sit closer to a laptop display. In fact, it is for this reason that such high resolutions might not work on desktop LCD panels unless they are larger 17" or 18" models.

Dot Pitch (CRTs)

Another important specification that denotes the quality of a given CRT monitor is its dot pitch, which is controlled by the design of the shadow mask or aperture grille inside the CRT. A *shadow mask* is a metal plate built into the front area of the CRT, next to the phosphor layers. It has thousands of holes that are used to help focus the beam from each electron gun so that it illuminates only one correctly colored phosphor dot at a time. Because of the immense speed of screen rewriting (60–85 times per second), all dots appear to be illuminated at the same time. The mask prevents the electron gun from illuminating the wrong dots.

In a monochrome monitor, the picture element is a screen phosphor, but in a color monitor, the picture element is a phosphor triad—which is a group of three phosphor dots (red, green, and blue). Dot pitch, which applies only to color monitors, is the distance (in millimeters) between phosphor triads, measured from the center of a phosphor dot in a given triad to the same color phosphor dot in the next triad. Screens with a small dot pitch have a smaller space between the phosphor triads. As a result, the picture elements are closer together, producing a sharper picture onscreen. Conversely, screens with a large dot pitch tend to produce images that are less clear. Figure 13.9 illustrates dot pitch.

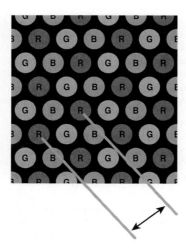

Figure 13.9 Dot pitch is the distance between each group (triad) of red, green, and blue (RGB) phosphors. A smaller dot pitch helps produce sharper, clearer images.

Note

Dot pitch is not an issue with LCD portable or desktop display panels because of their designs, which use transistors rather than phosphor triads.

The original IBM PC color monitor had a dot pitch of .43mm, which is considered to be poor by almost any standard. Smaller pitch values indicate sharper images. Most recent monitors have a dot pitch between .25mm and .27mm, with state-of-the-art monitors down to .24mm or less. To avoid grainy images, look for a dot pitch of .26mm or smaller. Be wary of monitors with anything larger than a .28mm dot pitch; they lack clarity for fine text and graphics. Although you can save money by buying monitors with smaller tubes or a higher dot pitch, the trade-off isn't worth it.

Monitors based on Sony's Trinitron picture tubes and Mitsubishi's DiamondTron picture tubes used an aperture grille, which uses vertical stripes (rather than a shadow mask) to separate red, green, and blue phosphors. This produces a brighter picture, although the stabilizing wires shown in Figure 13.10 are visible on close examination. Monitors using an aperture grille-type picture tube use a stripe pitch measurement instead of dot pitch. An aperture grille monitor stripe pitch of .25mm is comparable to a .27mm dot pitch on a conventional monitor.

Some of NEC's monitors used a variation on the aperture grille called the slotted mask, which is brighter than standard shadow-mask monitors and more mechanically stable than aperture grille-based monitors (see Figure 13.10).

The dot pitch or stripe pitch measurement is one of the most important specifications of any CRT monitor, but it is not the only specification. You might find the image on a CRT monitor with a slightly higher dot pitch superior to that of a CRT monitor with a lower dot pitch. There is no substitute for actually looking at images and text on the monitors you're considering purchasing.

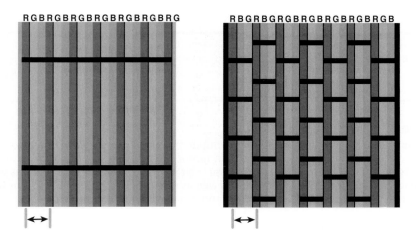

RGBRGBRGBRGBRGBRGBRGBRG   RBGRBGRGBRGBRGBRGBRGBRGB

Figure 13.10 Aperture-grille picture tubes (left) have their phosphors arranged in vertical stripes with one or two reinforcing wires, depending on CRT size. NEC's CromaClear slotted mask picture tube design (right) provides many of the benefits of both the shadow-mask and aperture-grille designs.

Image Brightness and Contrast (LCD Panels)

As previously mentioned, dot pitch is not a factor in deciding which LCD panel to purchase. Although it's a consideration that applies to both LCDs and CRTs, the brightness of a display is especially important in judging the quality of an LCD panel.

Although a dim CRT display is almost certainly a sign of either improper brightness control or a dying monitor, brightness in LCD panels can vary a great deal from one model to another. Brightness for LCD panels is measured in candelas per square meter, which is abbreviated "nt" and pronounced as a *nit*. Typical ratings for good display panels are between 200 and 450 nits, but the brighter the better. A good combination is a rating of 300 nits or higher and a contrast rating of 800:1 or higher.

Note

When you evaluate an LCD TV monitor, be sure to note the brightness settings available in computer mode and TV mode. Many of these displays provide a brighter picture in TV mode than in computer mode.

Interlaced Versus Noninterlaced

CRT monitors and video adapters can support interlaced or noninterlaced resolution. In *noninterlaced* (conventional) mode, the electron beam sweeps the screen in lines from top to bottom, one line after the other, completing the screen in one pass. In *interlaced* mode, the electron beam also sweeps the screen from top to bottom, but it does so in two passes—sweeping the odd lines first and the even lines second. Each pass takes half the time of a full pass in noninterlaced mode. Early high-resolution monitors, such as the IBM 8514/A, used interlacing to reach their maximum resolutions, but all recent and current high-resolution (1,024×768 and higher) CRT monitors are noninterlaced, avoiding the slow screen response and flicker caused by interlacing.

Note

The 1080i HDTV standard is an interlaced standard. However, you will not see a DLP, LCD, or plasma TV flicker when it receives a 1080i signal. The signal is converted into a progressive signal and scaled to the display's native resolution. The only time you might see flicker on a current display is if you run a CRT-based HDTV connected to a computer at a 4:3 non-native resolution such as 1024×768.

Energy and Safety

Monitors, like virtually all power-consuming computer devices, have been designed to save energy for a number of years. Virtually all monitors sold in recent years have earned the Environmental Protection Agency's Energy Star logo by reducing their current draw to 15 watts or less when idle. Power-management features in the monitor, as well as controls provided in the system BIOS and in the latest versions of Windows, help monitors and other types of computing devices use less power.

▶▶ For more information about power management, see Chapter 19, "Power Supplies," p. 1207.

Power Management

One of the first energy-saving standards for monitors was VESA's Display Power-Management Signaling (DPMS) spec, which defined the signals a computer sends to a monitor to indicate idle times. The operating system normally decides when to send these signals.

In Windows 9x/Me/2000/XP, you must enable this feature if you want to use it because it's turned off by default. To enable it in Windows 9x/Me, open the Display properties sheet in the Control Panel, switch to the Screen Saver tab, and make sure the Energy Star Low-Power settings and Monitor Shutdown settings are checked. You can adjust how long the system remains idle before the monitor picture is blanked or the monitor shuts down completely. Use the Power icon in Windows 2000/XP/ Vista to set power management for the monitor and other peripherals. You can also access power management by selecting the Screen Saver tab on the Display properties sheet and clicking the Power button. In Windows Vista, access the Screen Saver control through the Personalization menu.

Intel and Microsoft jointly developed the Advanced Power Management (APM) specification, which defines a BIOS-based interface between hardware that is capable of power-management functions and an operating system that implements power-management policies. In short, this means you can configure an OS such as Windows 9x to switch your monitor into a low-power mode after an interval of nonuse and even to shut it off entirely. For these actions to occur, however, the monitor, system BIOS, and operating system must all support the APM standard.

With Windows 98, Windows Me, Windows 2000, and Windows XP, Microsoft introduced a more comprehensive power-management method called Advanced Configuration and Power Interface (ACPI). ACPI also works with displays, hard drives, and other devices supported by APM and allows the computer to automatically turn peripherals, such as CD-ROMs, network cards, hard disk drives, and printers, on and off. It also enables the computer to turn consumer devices connected to the PC, such as VCRs, televisions, telephones, and stereos, on and off.

Although APM compatibility has been standard in common BIOSs for several years, a number of computers from major manufacturers required BIOS upgrades to add ACPI support when Windows 98 was introduced.

Note

ACPI support is installed with Windows 98 and newer *only* if an ACPI-compliant BIOS is present when Windows is first installed. If an ACPI-compliant BIOS is installed after the initial Windows installation, it is ignored.

Use Table 13.9 to select the most appropriate DPMS power-management setting(s) for your needs. Most recent systems enable you to select separate values for standby (which saves minimal amounts of power) and for monitor power-down (which saves more power but requires the user to wait several seconds for the monitor to power back up).

Table 13.9   Display Power Management Signaling

State	Horizontal	Vertical	Video	Power Savings	Recovery Time
On	Pulses	Pulses	Active	None	n/a
Stand-By	No pulses	Pulses	Blanked	Minimal	Short
Suspend	Pulses	No pulses	Blanked	Substantial	Longer
Off	No pulses	No pulses	Blanked	Maximum	System dependent

Virtually all monitors with power management features meet the requirements of the United States EPA's Energy Star labeling program, which requires that monitor power usage be reduced to 15 watts or less in standby mode. However, some current monitors also comply with the far more stringent Energy 2000 (E2000) standard developed in Switzerland. E2000 requires that monitors use less than 5 watts when in standby mode. Note that LCD displays use far less power than CRTs in either operating or standby modes.

Emissions (CRTs)

Another trend in green CRT monitor design is to minimize the user's exposure to potentially harmful electromagnetic fields. Several medical studies indicate that these electromagnetic emissions can cause health problems, such as miscarriages, birth defects, and cancer. The risk might be low, but if you spend a third of your day (or more) in front of a CRT monitor, that risk is increased.

The concern is that VLF (very low frequency) and ELF (extremely low frequency) emissions might affect the body. These two emissions come in two forms: electric and magnetic. Some research indicates that ELF magnetic emissions are more threatening than VLF emissions because they interact with the natural electric activity of body cells. Monitors are not the only culprits; significant ELF emissions also come from electric blankets and power lines.

Note

ELF and VLF are a form of electromagnetic radiation; they consist of radio frequencies below those used for normal radio broadcasting.

The standards shown in Table 13.10 have been established to regulate emissions and other aspects of monitor operations. Even though these standards originated with Swedish organizations, they are recognized and supported throughout the world.

Table 13.10   Monitor Emissions Standards

Standard Name	Established By	Date Established	Regulates	Notes
MPR I	SWEDAC[1]	1987	Monitor emissions	Replaced by MPR II.
MPR II	SWEDAC[1]	1990	Monitor emissions	Added maximums for ELF and VLF; minimum standard in recent monitors.
TCO[2]	TCO[2]	1992, 1995, 1999, 2003		Tighter monitor emissions limits than MPR- II; power management TCO '95, '99, and '03 add other classes of devices to the TCO standard.

1. The Swedish Board for Accreditation and Conformity Assessment
2. Swedish abbreviation for the Swedish Confederation of Professional Employees

Today, virtually all monitors on the market support TCO standards.

If you are using an older monitor that does not meet TCO standards, you can take other steps to protect yourself. The most important is to stay at arm's length (about 28 inches) from the front of your monitor. When you move a couple of feet away, ELF magnetic emission levels usually drop to those of a typical office with fluorescent lights. Likewise, monitor emissions are weakest at the front of a monitor, so stay at least 3 feet from the sides and backs of nearby monitors and 5 feet from any photocopiers, which are also strong sources of ELF.

Electromagnetic emissions should not be your only concern; you also should be concerned about screen glare. In fact, some of the antiglare panels that fit in front of a monitor screen not only reduce eyestrain, but also cut ELF and VLF emissions.

Note that because plasma and LCD panels don't use electron guns or magnets, they don't produce ELF emissions.

Frequencies

One essential buying decision is to choose a monitor that works with your selected video adapter. Today, virtually all monitors are multiple-frequency (also called multiscanning and multifrequency) units that accommodate a range of standards, including those that are not yet standardized. However, big differences exist in how well various monitors cope with various video adapters.

Tip

High-quality monitors retain their value longer than most other computer components. Although it's common for a newer, faster processor to come out right after you have purchased your computer or to find the same model with a bigger hard disk for the same money, a good quality monitor should outlast your computer. If you purchase a unit with the expectation that your own personal requirements will grow over the years, you might be able to save money on your next system by reusing your old monitor.

Some useful features include the following:

■ Front-mounted digital controls that can memorize screen settings

■ Onscreen programmability to enable you to precisely set desired values for screen size and position

■ Self-test mode, which displays a picture even when your monitor is not receiving a signal from the computer

With multiple-frequency CRT monitors, you must match the range of horizontal and vertical frequencies the monitor accepts with those generated by your video adapter. The wider the range of signals, the more expensive—and more versatile—the monitor. Your video adapter's vertical and horizontal frequencies must fall within the ranges your monitor supports. The vertical frequency (or refresh/frame rate) determines the stability of your image (the higher the vertical frequency, the better). Typical vertical frequencies range from 50Hz to 160Hz, but multiple-frequency monitors support different vertical frequencies at different resolutions. You might find that a bargain CRT monitor has a respectable 120Hz vertical frequency at 640×480 but drops to a less desirable 66Hz at 1280×1024. The horizontal frequency (or line rate) typically ranges from 31.5KHz to 90KHz or more. By default, most video adapters use a 60Hz default vertical scan frequency to avoid monitor damage.

Although LCD monitors use lower vertical frequencies than CRTs, they avoid problems with screen flicker because of their design. Because they use transistors to activate all the pixels in the image at once, as opposed to a scanning electron beam that must work its way from the top to the bottom of the screen to create an image, LCD panels never flicker.

Refresh Rates (Vertical Scan Frequency)

The *refresh rate* (also called the *vertical scan frequency*) is the rate at which the screen display is rewritten. This is measured in hertz. A refresh rate of 72Hz means that the screen is refreshed 72 times per second. A refresh rate that is too low causes CRT screens to flicker, contributing to eyestrain. The higher the refresh rate you use with a CRT display, the better for your eyes and your comfort during long sessions at the computer.

A *flicker-free refresh rate* is a refresh rate high enough to prevent you from seeing any flicker. The flicker-free refresh rate varies with the resolution of your monitor setting (higher resolutions require higher refresh rates) and must be matched by both your monitor and display card. Because a refresh rate that is too high can slow down your video display, use the lowest refresh rate that is comfortable for you.

One important factor to consider when purchasing a CRT monitor is the refresh rate, especially if you are planning to use the monitor at 1024×768 or higher resolutions. Low-cost monitors sometimes have refresh rates that are too low to achieve flicker-free performance for most users and thus can lead to eyestrain.

Table 13.11 compares two typical 19" CRT monitors. Note the differences in the refresh rates supported by two 19" CRT monitors from ViewSonic: the E90fB and G90fB.The E90fB sells for around $200, and the G225fB sells for about $230. The G90fB offers flicker-free refresh rates at higher resolutions than the cheaper E90fB. All recent video cards support higher refresh rates than either monitor, but you can't safely use refresh rates higher than the displays can support. Use of video adapter refresh rates in excess of the monitor's maximum refresh rate can damage the monitor!

Table 13.11   Refresh Rates Comparison

Resolution	ViewSonic E90fB 19" CRT	ViewSonic G90fB 19" CRT
1024×768	106Hz[1]	118Hz[1]
1280×1024	80Hz[2]	90Hz[1]
1600×1200	68Hz	77Hz[2]
1792×1344	61Hz	69Hz
1856×1392	Not supported	66Hz
1920×1440	Not supported	64Hz

1. *Meets or exceeds the VESA standard for flicker-free refresh (85Hz or above).*

2. *Although this refresh rate is lower than the VESA standard for flicker-free refresh (85Hz), it will be flicker-free for many users.*

To determine a monitor's refresh rates for the resolutions you're planning to use, check out the monitor manufacturer's website.

Note

Many manufacturers use the term *optimal resolution* to refer to the highest CRT monitor resolution that supports the VESA standard for flicker-free viewing (85Hz or higher). I recommend that you consider the monitor's optimal resolution as its highest practical resolution because higher resolutions, which don't support flicker-free viewing, are likely to provide poor visual quality.

During installation, Windows 2000, Windows 98, Windows 95B (OSR 2.x), Windows Me, Windows XP and Windows Vista support Plug and Play (PnP) monitor configuration if both the monitor and video adapter support the Data Display Channel (DDC) feature. When DDC communication is available, the monitor can send signals to the operating system that indicate which refresh rates it supports, as well as other display information; this data is reflected by the Display properties sheet for that monitor.

Monitors that don't support PnP configuration via DDC can be configured with an .INF (information) file, just as with other Windows-compatible devices. This might be supplied with a setup disk or CD or can be downloaded from the monitor vendor's website.

Note

Because CRT monitors are redrawing the screen many times per second, the change in a noninterlaced CRT screen display is virtually invisible to the naked eye, but it is very obvious when computer screens are photographed, filmed, or videotaped. Because these cameras aren't synchronized to the monitor's refresh cycle, it's inevitable that the photo, film, or videotape will show the refresh in progress as a line across the picture.

If you need to capture moving images from a monitor to videotape, use a video card with a TV-out option to send your picture to a VCR. If you need to take still photos of a monitor (for example, to record BIOS/CMOS setup information), use an LCD display instead of a CRT monitor.

In my experience, a 72Hz vertical scan frequency (frame rate) is the minimum anybody should use with a CRT, especially at resolutions of 1024×768 and higher. Lower resolutions produce a noticeable flicker, which can cause eyestrain, fatigue, and headaches. 72Hz is the minimum refresh rate I recommend because most people do not notice flicker at this refresh rate or higher. Most modern mid-range or better CRT displays easily handle vertical frequencies up to 85Hz or more at resolutions up to 1024×768. This greatly reduces the flicker a user sees. However, note that, although increasing the frame rate improves the quality of the image, it can also slow down the video hardware because it now needs to display each image more times per second. If you're a gamer, slower frame rates can reduce your score. In general, I recommend that you set the lowest frame rate you find comfortable. To adjust the video card's refresh rate with Windows 9x/Me/2000/XP, use the Display icon in Control Panel. Click Settings and then Advanced to access the tabs for refresh rate. In Windows Vista, open the Personalization menu and select the Display Settings icon.

Tip

If you use multiple monitors, be sure to select the monitor you want to adjust in the Settings dialog box before opening the Advanced dialog box to select a refresh rate.

You can also use the Adapter tab to select the resolution, color quality, and refresh rate with a single click.

Optimal is the default setting, but this really is a "safe" setting for any monitor. Select a refresh rate of at least 72Hz or higher to reduce or eliminate flicker. Click Apply for the new setting to take effect. If you choose a refresh rate other than Optimal, you might see a warning about possible monitor damage. This is a warning you should take seriously, especially if you don't have detailed information about your monitor available. You can literally smoke a monitor if you try to use a refresh rate higher than the monitor is designed to accept. Before you try using a custom refresh rate, do the following:

- Make sure Windows has correctly identified your monitor as either a Plug and Play monitor or by brand and model.

- Check the manual supplied with the monitor (or download the statistics) to determine which refresh rates are supported at a given resolution. As in the example listed earlier in Table 13.11, low-cost monitors often don't support high refresh rates at higher resolutions.

Click OK to try the new setting. The screen changes to show the new refresh rate. If the screen display looks scrambled, wait a few moments and the screen will be restored to the previous value; you'll see a dialog box asking whether you want to keep the new setting. If the display was acceptable, click Yes; otherwise, click No to restore your display. If the screen is scrambled and you can't see your mouse pointer, just press the Enter key on your keyboard because No is the default answer. With some older video drivers, this refresh rate dialog box is not available. Get an updated video driver, or check with the video card vendor for a separate utility program that sets the refresh rate for you.

If you have a scrambled display with a high refresh rate, but you think the monitor should be capable of handling the refresh rate you chose, you might not have the correct monitor selected. To check your Windows 9x/Me/2000/XP monitor selection, check the Display Properties dialog box. In Windows Vista, open the Display Settings dialog. If your monitor is listed as Standard VGA, Super VGA, or Default Monitor, Windows is using a generic driver that will work with a wide variety of monitors. However, this generic driver doesn't support refresh rates above 75Hz because some monitors could be damaged by excessively high refresh rates.

In some cases, you might need to manually select the correct monitor brand and model in the Windows Display Properties dialog box. If you don't find your brand and model of monitor listed, check with your monitor vendor for a driver specific for your model. After you install it, see whether your monitor will safely support a higher refresh rate.

Tip

If you try to use a refresh rate higher than an LCD panel can support, you might see a message that you have selected an out-of-range frequency. Typically, LCD panels do not accept a vertical refresh rate higher than 75Hz. Keep in mind that LCDs do not flicker, so it's acceptable to use refresh rates as low as 60Hz with an LCD display. If you use a dual-head video card, keep in mind that some models don't permit you to assign different refresh rates to each monitor. If you have a CRT and an LCD connected to such a video card, use the highest refresh rate supported by both displays (usually 75Hz) to minimize flicker on the CRT.

Horizontal Frequency

Different video resolutions use different horizontal frequencies. For example, the standard VGA resolution of 640×480 requires a horizontal resolution of 31.5KHz, whereas the 800×600 resolution requires a vertical frequency of at least 72Hz and a horizontal frequency of at least 48KHz. The 1024×768 image requires a vertical frequency of 60Hz and a horizontal frequency of 58KHz, and the 1280×1024 resolution requires a vertical frequency of 60Hz and a horizontal frequency of 64KHz. If the vertical frequency increases to 75Hz at 1280×1024, the horizontal frequency must be 80KHz. For a super-crisp display, look for available vertical frequencies of 75Hz or higher and horizontal frequencies of up to 90KHz or more. My favorite 17" CRT NEC monitor supports vertical resolutions of up to 75Hz at 1600×1200 pixels, 117Hz at 1024×768, and 160Hz at 640×480!

Because literally hundreds of manufacturers have produced thousands of CRT and LCD monitor models, it is impractical to discuss the technical aspects of each monitor model in detail. Suffice it to say that before investing in a monitor, you should check the technical specifications to ensure that the monitor meets your needs. If you are looking for a place to start, check out some of the magazines that periodically feature reviews of monitors. If you can't wait for a magazine review, investigate monitors at the websites run by any of the following vendors: Apple, Sony, NEC Display Solutions, and ViewSonic. Each of these manufacturers creates monitors that set the standards by which other monitors can be judged. Although you typically pay a bit more for these manufacturers' monitors, they offer a known, high level of quality and compatibility, as well as service and support.

Controls

Virtually all recent CRT monitors and LCD panels use digital controls instead of analog controls. This has nothing to do with the signals the monitor receives from the computer, but only the controls (or lack of them) on the front panel that enable you to adjust the display. Monitors with digital controls have a built-in menu system that enables you to set parameters such as brightness (which adjusts the black level of the display), contrast (which adjusts the luminance of the display), screen size, vertical and horizontal shifts, color, phase, and focus. A button brings the menu up onscreen, and you use controls to make menu selections and vary the settings. When you complete your adjustments, the monitor saves the settings in nonvolatile RAM (NVRAM) located inside the monitor. This type of memory provides permanent storage for the settings with no battery or other power source. You can unplug the monitor without losing your settings, and you can alter them at any time in the future. Digital controls provide a much higher level of control over the monitor and are highly recommended.

Tip

Digital video engineer Charles Poynton's notes on adjusting brightness and contrast controls provide an excellent tutorial on the use of these often misunderstood monitor adjustments. Find them online at www.poynton.com/GammaFAQ.html.

Digital controls make adjusting CRT monitors suffering from any of the geometry errors shown in Figure 13.11 easy. Before making these adjustments, be sure the vertical and horizontal size and position are correct.

Tip

Get a monitor with positioning and image controls that are easy to reach, preferably on the front of the case. Look for more than just basic contrast and brightness controls; a good monitor should enable you to adjust the width and height of your screen images and the placement of the image on the screen. The monitor should also be equipped with a tilt-swivel stand so you can adjust the monitor to the best angle for your use.

Figure 13.12 shows a typical onscreen display used to correct the screen geometry errors shown in Figure 13.11. The OSD shown is from a Samsung SyncMaster 955DF, but other brands use somewhat similar displays. Buttons below the screen are used to make and store the adjustments.

Figure 13.11 Typical geometry errors in CRT monitors; these can be corrected on most models that have digital picture controls.

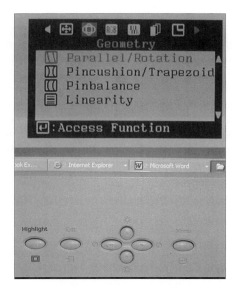

Figure 13.12 Using an OSD to correct CRT screen geometry errors.

Although LCD panels aren't affected by geometry errors as CRT monitors can be, they can have their own set of image-quality problems, especially if they use the typical 15-pin analog VGA video connector. Pixel jitter and pixel swim (in which adjacent pixels turn on and off) are relatively common problems that occur when using an LCD monitor connected to your PC with an analog VGA connector.

The Auto-Tune option available in many LCD panels' OSDs can be used to fix these and other LCD display problems, as shown in Figure 13.13. The OSD shown in Figure 13.13 is from a KDS Rad-5, but other brands offer similar options.

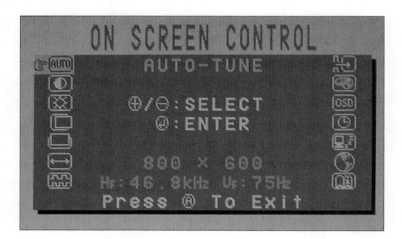

Figure 13.13   Using an OSD to correct LCD image quality problems.

Testing a Display

Unlike most of the other peripherals you can connect to your computer, you can't really tell whether a monitor suits you by examining its technical specifications. Price might not be a reliable indicator either. Testing monitors is a highly subjective process, and it is best to "kick the tires" of a few at a dealer showroom or in the privacy of your home or office (if the dealer has a liberal return policy).

Testing should also not be simply a matter of looking at whatever happens to be displayed on the monitor at the time. Many computer stores display movies, scenic photos, or other flashy graphics that are all but useless for a serious evaluation and comparison. If possible, you should look at the same images on each monitor you try and compare the manner in which they perform a specific series of tasks.

Before running the tests listed here, set your display to the highest resolution and refresh rate allowed by your combination of display and graphics card.

One good series of tasks is as follows:

■ Draw a perfect circle with a graphics program. If the displayed result is an oval, not a circle, this monitor will not serve you well with graphics or design software.

■ Using a word processor, type some words in 8- or 10-point type (1 point equals 1/72"). If the words are fuzzy or the black characters are fringed with color, select another monitor.

■ Display a screen with as much white space as possible and look for areas of color variance. This can indicate a problem with only that individual unit or its location, but if you see it on more than one monitor of the same make, it might indicate a manufacturing problem; it could also indicate problems with the signal coming from the graphics card. Move the monitor to another system equipped with a different graphics card model and retry this test to see for certain whether it's the monitor or the video card.

■ Display the Microsoft Windows desktop to check for uniform focus (with CRT displays) and brightness (with CRT and LCD displays). Are the corner icons as sharp as the rest of the screen? Are the lines in the title bar curved or wavy? Monitors usually are sharply focused at the center, but seriously blurred corners indicate a poor design. Bowed lines on a CRT can be the result of a poor video adapter or incorrect configuration of the monitor's digital picture controls. Before you decide to replace the monitor, you should first adjust the digital picture controls to improve the display. Next, try attaching the monitor to another display adapter. If the display quality does not improve, replace the monitor.

Adjust the brightness up and down to see whether the image blooms or swells, which indicates the monitor is likely to lose focus at high brightness levels. You can also use diagnostics that come with the graphics card or third-party system diagnostics programs to perform these tests.

■ With LCD panels in particular, change to a lower resolution from the panel's native resolution using the Microsoft Windows Display properties settings. Because LCD panels have only one native resolution, the display must use scaling to handle other resolutions full-screen. If you are a web designer, are a gamer, or must capture screens at a particular resolution, this test will show you whether the LCD panel produces acceptable display quality at resolutions other than normal. You can also use this test on a CRT, but CRTs, unlike LCD panels, are designed to handle a wide variety of resolutions.

■ A good CRT monitor is calibrated so that rays of red, green, and blue light hit their targets (individual phosphor dots) precisely. If they don't, you have bad convergence. This is apparent when edges of lines appear to illuminate with a specific color. If you have good convergence, the colors are crisp, clear, and true, provided there isn't a predominant tint in the phosphor.

■ If the monitor has built-in diagnostics (a recommended feature), try them as well to test the display independently of the graphics card and system to which it's attached. A display with built-in diagnostics displays text or a test pattern onscreen if it is receiving power when the host system is turned off or if the monitor is not connected to a host system.

LCD and DLP Projectors

Originally, data projectors were intended for use in boardrooms and training facilities. However, with the rise of home theater systems, the increasing popularity of working from home, and major price reductions and improvements in projector technology, portable projectors are an increasingly popular alternative to large-screen TVs and plasma displays. They can be used with Windows Vista editions supporting Media Center and Windows XP Media Center PCs and video players as well as their traditional partners, conventional laptop and desktop computers running any operating system.

Two technologies are used in the construction of data projectors:

■ Liquid crystal display (LCD)

■ Digital light processing (DLP)

Instead of using triads of subpixels as in a flat-panel or portable LCD, an LCD projector works by separating white light into red, green, and blue wavelengths and directing each wavelength through a corresponding LCD panel. Each LCD panel's pixels are opened or closed according to the signals received from the signal source (computer, DVD, or video player) and are combined into a single RGB image that is projected onto the screen. A relatively hot projection lamp must be used to project LCD images, so LCD projectors require some cool-down time before they can be stored.

The other major technology for presentation and home theater projectors uses Texas Instruments' own digital light processing (DLP) technology. DLP projectors use a combination of a rapidly spinning color wheel and a microprocessor-controlled array of tiny mirrors known as a *digital micromirror device (DMD)*. Each mirror in a DMD corresponds to a pixel, and the mirrors reflect light toward or away from the projector optics. Depending on how frequently the mirrors are switched on, the image varies from white (always on) to black (never on) through as many as 1,024 gray shades. The color wheel provides color data to complete the projected image. Compared to LCD projectors, DLP projectors are more compact, are lighter, and cool down more quickly after use. Although DLP projects were originally more expensive than LCD projectors, they are now about the same price. You can purchase a variety of LCD and DLP projectors providing 800×600 SVGA images for around $700, and LCD and DLP 1024×768 XGA projectors are available for about $900. Most current projectors also support HDTV resolutions of 720p and 1080i and component video inputs, enabling a single projector to work as either a PC or TV display.

Figure 13.14 illustrates how a DLP-based projector produces the image.

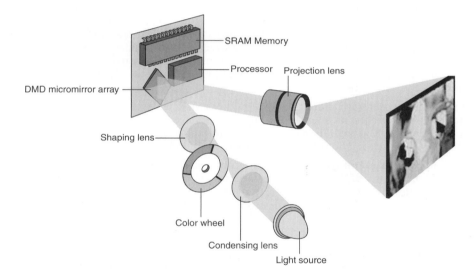

Figure 13.14 How a typical DLP projector works.

The earliest DLP projectors used a simple three-color (RGB) wheel, as shown in Figure 13.14. However, more recent models have used a four-segment (RGB and clear) or a six-segment (RGBRGB) wheel to improve picture quality.

Note

For more information about digital light processing, see the official Texas Instruments website about DLP technology at www.dlp.com.

Projector Selection Criteria

If you're in the market for a projector, the choices are dizzying. A wide variety of models with many different feature combinations awaits you. The following sections will help you find the right model for your needs.

PC Resolutions

If you are purchasing a projector for use with a PC, a model with 1024×768 resolution is the minimum I recommend. This resolution enables you to run any Windows-based or other GUI-based application correctly. Although you can run Windows XP and Windows Vista at 800×600, some menus may be cut off and you might find it necessary to hide the toolbar to be able to use some menus.

HDTV Resolutions

If you are purchasing a projector for HDTV use, make sure the projector supports HDTV 720p resolution or better. Some (but not all) widescreen projectors also support PC display standards, enabling you to use a single projector for movies and for data projection. Projectors that support a native 4:3 aspect ratio display widescreen DVD and HDTV content in a "letterbox" format just as 4:3 TVs do.

Input Types

If you are using your projector strictly with PCs, the minimum requirement is a VGA or DVI port. Because LCD and DLP are digital standards, a projector with a DVI port is a better choice if your computer includes DVI output.

However, if you are using your projector for DVD or HDTV use, or as a PC/HDTV projector, you need additional ports. At a minimum, you need a composite or S-video output to connect your projector to a DVD player or VCR. However, component, DVI, or HDMI support is necessary for true HDTV support.

Figure 13.15 compares composite, S-video, and component cables and ports.

Lumens

Projector brightness is measured in lumens. Generally, the higher the lumens, the better the projector. Most low-cost (under $1,000) projectors have lumen ratings of around 1,500 to 2,000. A 2,000-lumen projector works well in rooms in which the lighting can be reduced—for example, by turning off the lights next to the screen and leaving other room lights on. However, if the projector will be used in an environment in which room lights cannot be dimmed or where exterior windows cannot be covered, the projector needs a rating well in excess of 3,000 lumens.

Zoom Lens

Very low-cost projectors may omit a zoom lens. With these projectors, you must move the projector further away from the screen (reducing its effective brightness) to increase the projected image size. If you will be using the projector in different-sized rooms, consider projectors with zoom lenses.

Size and Weight

Compared to the first "portable" projectors of a decade ago, today's lightweight projectors are amazing. Most offer weights well under 10 pounds. To reduce weight, some models omit features such as integrated speakers or zoom lenses. Be sure to balance weight against features.

Projector Bulb Life and Cost

Most portable projectors have a rated bulb life of 2,000 hours or longer. When comparing projectors, be sure to see if bulb life is rated for maximum or reduced brightness. If you will be using your projector in a bright room, you may need to run it at full brightness (reducing lamp life) to have satisfactory output.

Replacement projector bulbs can cost between $200 and $400 each. Be sure to order one when the projector warns that the bulb is about to fail.

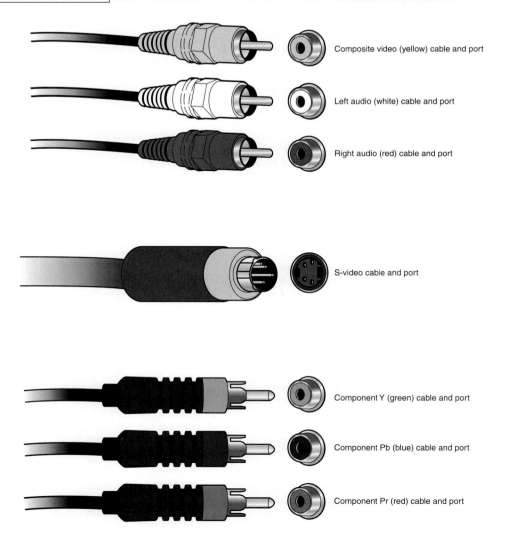

Composite video (yellow) cable and port

Left audio (white) cable and port

Right audio (red) cable and port

S-video cable and port

Component Y (green) cable and port

Component Pb (blue) cable and port

Component Pr (red) cable and port

Figure 13.15 Composite, S-video, and component cables and ports are used on LCD TV/monitors and projectors that support DVD and HDTV connections.

Other Features

Projectors vary widely in their features. If you plan to mount the projector on the ceiling, determine if the projector can automatically rotate the image for proper orientation. Whether the projector will be used on a table, a cart, or a ceiling mount, you might encounter keystoning (the sides of the projected image are not parallel because the projector is not centered on the screen). Be sure to determine how the projector compensates for keystoning. Other features to look for include

- Image quality adjustments for each input type.
- An easy-to-understand remote.

Maintaining Your Monitor

Because a good 17" or larger CRT or 15" or larger LCD monitor can be used for several years on more than one computer, proper care is essential to extend its life to the fullest extent.

Use the following guidelines for proper care of your monitor:

- Although phosphor burn (in which an image left onscreen eventually leaves a permanent shadow onscreen) is next to impossible with VGA-type displays—unlike the old TTL displays—screensavers are still useful for casual security. You can password-protect your system with both the standard Windows screensaver and third-party programs (although a determined snoop can easily thwart screensaver password protection). Windows includes several screensavers that can be enabled via the Display control panel. A bevy of free and inexpensive screensavers is available for download from the Internet. Keep in mind, though, that add-on screensavers can cause crashes and lockups if they're poorly written or out of date and that many "free" versions available online might install spyware (software that reports your web-surfing habits to advertisers). Use screensavers written for your particular operating system version to minimize problems.

Note

Phosphor burn *is* possible with plasma displays, so if you decide to connect a plasma display to your PC, be sure to use a screensaver to protect your display.

- To prevent premature failure of the monitor's power supply, use the power-management feature of the Display Properties or Power (Management) sheet to put the monitor into a low-power standby mode after a reasonable period of inactivity (10–15 minutes) and to turn it off after about 60 minutes. Using the power management feature is far better than using the on/off switch when you are away from the computer for brief periods. Turn off the monitor only at the end of your computing "day."

  How can you tell whether the monitor is really off or in standby mode? Look at the power LCD on the front of the monitor. A monitor that's in standby mode usually has a blinking green or solid amber LCD in place of the solid green LCD displayed when it's running in normal mode. Because monitors in standby mode still consume some power, they should be shut off at the end of the computing day.

  If the monitor will not go into standby when the PC isn't sending signals to it, make sure the monitor is properly defined in the Display properties sheet in Windows. In addition, the Energy Star check box should be selected for any monitor that supports power management, unless the monitor should be left on at all times (such as when used in a retail kiosk or self-standing display).

- Make sure the monitor has adequate ventilation along the sides, rear, and top. Because monitors use passive cooling, a lack of adequate airflow caused by piling keyboards, folders, books, or other office debris on top of the monitor will cause it to overheat and considerably shorten its life. If you're looking at a monitor with a partly melted grille on the top of the case, you're looking at a victim of poor cooling. If you need to use a monitor in an area with poor airflow, use an LCD panel instead of a CRT because LCDs run much cooler than CRTs.

- The monitor screen and case should be kept clean. Turn off the power, spray a cleaner such as Endust for Electronics onto a soft cloth (never directly onto the monitor!), and wipe the screen and the case gently.

- If your CRT monitor has a degaussing button or feature, use it periodically to remove stray magnetic signals. Keep in mind that CRTs have powerful magnets around the picture tube, so keep magnetic media away from them.

Video Display Adapters

A video adapter provides the interface between your computer and your monitor and transmits the signals that appear as images on the display. Throughout the history of the PC, there has been a succession of standards for video display characteristics that represent a steady increase in screen resolution and color depth. The following list of standards can serve as an abbreviated history of PC video-display technology:

> MDA (Monochrome Display Adapter)
>
> HGC (Hercules Graphics Card)
>
> CGA (Color Graphics Adapter)
>
> EGA (Enhanced Graphics Adapter)
>
> VGA (Video Graphics Array)
>
> SVGA (Super VGA)
>
> XGA (Extended Graphics Array)
>
> UGA (Ultra Video Graphics Array)

IBM pioneered most of these standards, but other manufacturers of compatible PCs adopted them as well. Today, IBM no longer sets standards for the PC business (it even sold its PC business to China's Lenovo in 2005), and many of these standards are obsolete. Those that aren't obsolete seldom are referred to by these names anymore. The sole exception to this is *VGA*, which is a term that is still used to refer to a baseline graphics display capability supported by virtually every video adapter on the market today.

When you shop for a video adapter today, you are more likely to see specific references to the screen resolutions and color depths that the device supports than a list of standards such as VGA, SVGA, XGA, and UVGA. However, reading about these standards gives you a good idea of how video-display technology developed over the years and prepares you for any close encounters you might have with legacy equipment from the dark ages.

Today's VGA and later video adapters can also display most older color graphics software written for CGA, EGA, and most other obsolete graphics standards. This enables you to use older graphics software (such as games and educational programs) on your current system. Although not a concern for most users, some older programs wrote directly to hardware registers that are no longer found on current video cards.

The Video Graphics Array (VGA) Standard

When IBM introduced the PS/2 systems on April 2, 1987, it also introduced the VGA display. On that day, in fact, IBM also introduced the lower-resolution MCGA and higher-resolution 8514 adapters. The MCGA and 8514 adapters did not become popular standards like the VGA did, and both were discontinued.

All current display adapters that connect to the 15-pin VGA analog connector or the DVI analog/digital connector are based on the VGA standard. The VGA connector is shown in Figure 13.16; the pinouts are shown in Table 13.12.

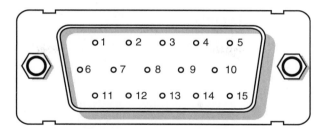

Figure 13.16　VGA connector used for VGA, SVGA, and other VGA-based standards.

Table 13.12　Standard 15-Pin VGA Connector Pinout

Pin #	Function	Direction
1	Red video	Out
2	Green video	Out
3	Blue video	Out
4	Monitor ID 2	In
5	TTL Ground (monitor self-test)	—
6	Red analog ground	—
7	Green analog ground	—
8	Blue analog ground	—
9	Key (plugged hole)	—
10	Synch Ground	—
11	Monitor ID 0	In
12	Monitor ID 1	In
13	Horizontal Synch	Out
14	Vertical Synch	Out
15	Monitor ID 3	In

On the VGA cable connector that plugs into your video adapter, pin 9 is often pinless. Pin 5 is used only for testing purposes, and pin 15 is rarely used (these are often pinless as well). To identify the type of monitor connected to the system, some manufacturers use the presence or absence of the monitor ID pins in various combinations.

Digital Versus Analog Signals

Unlike earlier video standards, which are digital, VGA is an analog system. Why have displays gone from digital to analog when most other electronic systems have gone digital? Compact disc players (digital) have replaced most turntables (analog), mini DV camcorders are replacing 8mm and VHS-based analog camcorders, and TiVo and UltimateTV digital video recorders are performing time-shifting in place of analog VCRs for many users. With a digital television set, you can watch several channels on a single screen by splitting the screen or placing a picture within another picture.

Most personal computer displays introduced before the PS/2 are digital. This type of display generates different colors by firing the RGB electron beams in on-or-off mode, which allows for the display of up to eight colors (2^3). In the IBM displays and adapters, another signal doubles the number of color combinations from 8 to 16 by displaying each color at one of two intensity levels. This digital display is easy to manufacture and offers simplicity with consistent color combinations from system to system. The real drawback of the older digital displays such as CGA and EGA is the limited number of possible colors.

In the PS/2 systems, IBM went to an analog display circuit. Analog displays work like the digital displays that use RGB electron beams to construct various colors, but each color in the analog display system can be displayed at varying levels of intensity-64 levels, in the case of the VGA. This versatility provides 262,144 possible colors (64^3), of which 256 could be simultaneously displayed. For realistic computer graphics, color depth is often more important than high resolution because the human eye perceives a picture that has more colors as being more realistic. IBM moved to analog graphics to enhance the color capabilities of its systems.

VGA Features

PS/2 systems incorporated the primary display adapter circuitry onto the motherboard, and both IBM and third-party companies introduced separate VGA cards to enable other types of systems to enjoy the advantages of VGA.

Although the IBM MicroChannel (MCA) computers, such as the PS/2 Model 50 and above, introduced VGA, it's impossible today to find a brand-new replacement for VGA that fits into the obsolete MCA-bus systems. However, a few surplus and used third-party cards might be available if you look hard enough.

The VGA BIOS is the control software residing in the system ROM for controlling VGA circuits. With the BIOS, software can initiate commands and functions without having to manipulate the VGA directly. Programs become somewhat hardware independent and can call a consistent set of commands and functions built into the system's ROM-control software.

Other implementations of the VGA differ in their hardware but respond to the same BIOS calls and functions. New features are added as a superset of the existing functions, and VGA remains compatible with the graphics and text BIOS functions built into the PC systems from the beginning. The VGA can run almost any software that originally was written for the CGA or EGA, unless it was written to directly access the hardware registers of these cards.

A standard VGA card displays up to 256 colors onscreen, from a palette of 262,144 (256KB) colors; when used in the 640×480 graphics or 720×400 text mode, 16 colors at a time can be displayed. Because the VGA outputs an analog signal, you must have a monitor that accepts an analog input.

VGA displays originally came not only in color, but also in monochrome VGA models, which use color summing. With color summing, 64 gray shades are displayed instead of colors. The summing routine is initiated if the BIOS detects a monochrome display when the system boots. This routine uses an algorithm that takes the desired color and rewrites the formula to involve all three color guns, producing varying intensities of gray. Users who preferred a monochrome display, therefore, could execute color-based applications.

Even the least-expensive video adapters on the market today can work with modes well beyond the VGA standard. VGA, at its 16-color, 640×480 graphics resolution, has come to be the baseline for PC graphical display configurations. VGA is accepted as the least common denominator for all Windows systems and must be supported by the video adapters in all systems running Windows. The installation programs of all Windows versions use these VGA settings as their default video configuration. In addition to VGA, virtually all adapters support a range of higher screen resolutions and color depths, depending on the capabilities of the hardware. If a Windows 9x/Me or Windows XP/2000 system must be started in Safe Mode because of a startup problem, the system defaults to VGA in the 640×480, 16-color mode. Windows 2000, Windows XP, and Windows Vista also offer a VGA Mode startup that also uses this mode (Windows XP and Windows Vista use 800×600 resolution) but doesn't slow down the rest of the computer the way Safe Mode (which replaces 32-bit drivers with BIOS services) does.

IBM introduced higher-resolution versions of VGA called XGA and XGA-2 in the early 1990s, but most of the development of VGA standards has come from the third-party video card industry and its trade group, the Video Electronic Standards Association (VESA).

Super VGA

When IBM's XGA and 8514/A video cards were introduced, competing manufacturers chose not to attempt to clone these incremental improvements on their VGA products. Instead, they began producing lower-cost adapters that offered even higher resolutions. These video cards fall into a category loosely known as Super VGA (SVGA). Unlike the display adapters discussed so far, SVGA refers not to an adapter that meets a particular specification, but to a group of adapters that have different capabilities.

For example, one card might offer several resolutions (such as 800×600 and 1024×768) that are greater than those achieved with a regular VGA, whereas another card might offer the same or even greater resolutions but also provide more color choices at each resolution. These cards have different capabilities; nonetheless, both are classified as SVGA.

The SVGA cards look much like their VGA counterparts. They have the same connectors, but because the technical specifications from different SVGA vendors vary tremendously, it is impossible to provide a definitive technical overview in this book.

VESA SVGA Standards

The Video Electronics Standards Association includes members from various companies associated with PC and computer video products. In October 1989, VESA recognized that programming applications to support the many SVGA cards on the market was virtually impossible and proposed a standard for a uniform programmer's interface for SVGA cards; it is known as the VESA BIOS extension (VBE). VBE support might be provided through a memory-resident driver (used by older cards) or through additional code added to the VGA BIOS chip itself (the more common solution). The benefit of the VESA BIOS extension is that a programmer needs to worry about only one routine or driver to support SVGA. Various cards from various manufacturers are accessible through the common VESA interface. Today, VBE support is a concern primarily for real-mode DOS applications, usually older games, and for non-Microsoft operating systems that need to access higher resolutions and color depths. VBE supports resolutions up to 1280×1024 and color depths up to 24-bit (16.8 million colors), depending on the mode selected and the memory on the video card. VESA compliance is of virtually no consequence to Windows versions 95 and up. These operating systems use custom video drivers for their graphics cards.

Note

For a listing of VESA BIOS modes by resolution, color depth, and scan frequency, see "VESA SVGA Standards" in the Technical Reference portion of the disc accompanying this book.

Video Adapter Types

A monitor requires a source of input. The signals that run to your monitor come from a video adapter inside or plugged in to your computer.

The three ways computer systems connect to either CRT or LCD panels are as follows:

- **Add-on video cards**—This method requires the use of a PCI-Express, AGP, or a PCI expansion slot or slots, but provide the highest possible level of performance, the greatest amount of memory, and the largest choice of features.

- **Video-only chipset on the motherboard**—Performance is generally less than with add-on video cards because older chipset designs are often used. Although many systems with the LPX design used this type of video, it has fallen out of fashion on recent systems. Mid-range and high-end notebook computers typically use a discrete video chip instead of integrated video.

- **Motherboard chipset with integrated video**—This has the lowest cost of any video solution, but performance can also be very low, especially for 3D gaming or other graphics-intensive applications. Resolution and color-depth options are also more limited than those available with add-on video cards. Most low-end and some mid-range notebooks use this type of video instead of a discrete video chip on the motherboard.

Typically, desktop computers that use microATX, FlexATX, microBTX, PicoBTX, or Mini-ITX motherboards feature integrated video using chipsets made by Intel, VIA Technology, SiS, or other vendors. Some microATX or microBTX motherboards might also have a provision for a PCI-Express x16 or AGP video card. For more information, see the next section, "Integrated Video/Motherboard Chipsets."

▶▶   See "3D Chipsets," p. 961.

The term *video adapter* applies to either integrated or separate video circuitry. The term *graphics adapter* is essentially interchangeable with *video adapter* because all video options developed since the original IBM monochrome display adapter (MDA) can display graphics as well as text.

Integrated Video/Motherboard Chipsets

Although built-in video has been a staple of low-cost computing for a number of years, until the late 1990s most motherboard-based video simply moved the standard video components discussed earlier in this chapter to the motherboard. Many low-cost systems—especially those using the semiproprietary LPX motherboard form factor—have incorporated standard VGA-type video circuits on the motherboard. The performance and features of the built-in video differed only slightly from add-on cards using the same or similar chipsets, and in most cases the built-in video could be replaced by adding a video card. Some motherboard-based video also had provisions for memory upgrades.

◀◀   See "LPX," p. 242.

However, in recent years the move toward increasing integration on the motherboard has led to the development of chipsets that include 3D accelerated video and audio support as part of the chipset design. In effect, the motherboard chipset takes the place of most of the video card components listed earlier and uses a portion of main system memory as video memory. The use of main system memory for video memory is often referred to as *unified memory architecture (UMA)*, and although this memory-sharing method was also used by some built-in video that used its own chipset, it has become much more common with the rise of integrated motherboard chipsets.

Cyrix Semiconductor (now owned by VIA Technologies) pioneered chipsets with integrated audio and video with its two-chip MediaGX product. MediaGX incorporated the functions of a CPU, memory controller, sound, and video and made very low-cost (albeit low-performance) computers. National Semiconductor and later AMD developed improved versions of the MediaGX known as the Geode GX series.

Intel became the next major player to develop integrated chipsets, with its 810 chipset for the Pentium III and Celeron processors. The 810 (codenamed Whitney before its official release) heralded the beginning of widespread industry support for this design. Intel later followed the release of the 810 series (810 and 810E) with the 815 series for the Pentium III and Celeron, most of which also feature integrated video. Currently, Intel offers integrated video for Socket 775 processors such as the Pentium 4, Celeron 4, Pentium D, and Core 2 families in the 845, 865, 91x, 94x, 965 chipset families, and for the Core 2 family in the new G3x chipset family. Table 13.13 compares the major video features of Intel's 8xx, 9xx, and G3x series chipsets, which include integrated video. Note that chipsets listed together share the same video features but differ in other ways such as memory support, I/O features, and so forth.

Table 13.13   Integrated Video Features of Intel 8xx/9xx Chipsets

Chipset	Supported Processors	Integrated Graphics Type	External AGP Graphics Support	Video Memory Size
810, 810E, 810E2	Pentium III, Celeron III	Intel 3D with Direct AGP	—	6MB[1], 10MB[2], 12MB[3]
815, 815E	Pentium III, Celeron III	Intel 3D with Direct AGP	AGP 4x	6MB[1], 10MB[2], 12MB[3]
815G, 815EG	Pentium III, Celeron III	Intel 3D with Direct AGP	—	6MB[1], 10MB[2], 12MB[3]
845GL	Pentium 4, Celeron 4	Intel Extreme Graphics	—	32MB[4], 64MB[5]
845G, 845GE	Pentium 4, Celeron 4	Intel Extreme Graphics	AGP 4x	32MB[6], 64MB[7]
845GV	Pentium 4, Celeron 4	Intel Extreme Graphics	—	32MB[6], 64MB[7]
865GV	Pentium 4, Celeron 4, Celeron D	Intel Extreme Graphics 2	—	32MB[4], 64MB[5]
865G	Pentium 4, Celeron 4, Celeron D	Intel Extreme Graphics 2	AGP 8x	32MB[4], 64MB[5]
910GL[8]	Pentium 4, Celeron 4, Celeron D	Intel Graphics Media Accelerator 900	—	32MB[4], up to 128MB[5]
915G[8]	Pentium 4, Celeron 4, Celeron D	Intel Graphics Media Accelerator 900	PCI Express x16	32MB[4], up to 128MB[5]
915GV, 915GL[8]	Pentium 4, Celeron 4, Celeron D	Intel Graphics Media Accelerator 900	—	32MB[4], up to 128MB[5]
945G	Pentium D, Pentium 4, Celeron D, Celeron 4	Intel Graphics Media Accelerator 950	PCI Express x16	Up to 256MB[9]
945GZ	Pentium D, Pentium 4, Celeron D, Celeron 4	Intel Graphics Media Accelerator 950	—	Up to 256MB[9]

Table 13.13   Continued

Chipset	Supported Processors	Integrated Graphics Type	External AGP Graphics Support	Video Memory Size
946GZ	Pentium D, Pentium 4 HT, Celeron D, Celeron 4, Core 2 Duo	Intel Graphics Media Accelerator 3000	PCI Express x16	Up to 256MB[9]
Q963	Pentium D, Pentium 4 HT, Core 2 Duo	Intel Graphics Media Accelerator 3000	PCI Express x16	Up to 256MB[9]
Q965	Pentium D, Pentium 4 HT, Core 2 Duo	Intel Graphics Media Accelerator 3000	PCI Express x16	Up to 256MB[9]
G965	Pentium D, Pentium 4 HT, Core 2 Duo	Intel Graphics Media Accelerator X3000	PCI Express x16	Up to 384MB[9]
G31	Core 2 Duo, Core 2 Quad	Intel Graphics Media Accelerator 3100	PCI Express x16 (v1.1)	Up to 384MB[9]
G33	Core 2 Duo, Core 2 Quad	Intel Graphics Media Accelerator 3100	PCI Express x16 (v1.1)	Up to 384MB[9]

1. *Systems with 32MB of RAM, PV 5.x, or greater graphics drivers.*
2. *Systems with 64MB of RAM, PV 5.x, or greater graphics drivers.*
3. *Systems with 128MB or more of RAM, PV 5.x, or greater graphics drivers.*
4. *Systems with up to 128MB of RAM.*
5. *Systems with more than 128MB of RAM.*
6. *Systems with up to 255MB of RAM.*
7. *Systems with 256MB or more of RAM.*
8. *This family of chipsets was code-named Grantsdale before its release.*
9. *Amount of memory actually used varies by task and onboard system memory. See Intel's website for details.*

Intel 3D with Direct AGP—Basic 2D and 3D acceleration.

Intel Extreme Graphics—Supports alpha blending, fog, anisotropic filtering, hardware motion compensation, and advanced textures.

Intel Extreme Graphics 2—Enhanced version of original Extreme Graphics, adding better memory management, zone rendering, and faster pixel and texturing rendering.

Intel Graphics Media Accelerator 900—Originally known as Extreme Graphics 3, this is an enhanced version of Extreme Graphics 2, adding support for most DirectX 9 features (does not support vertex shaders), optional dual-display support (requires ADD2 card), and support for wide-screen LCD panels.

Intel Graphics Media Accelerator 950—A faster version of Intel Graphics Media Accelerator 900. Supports Shader Model 2.0. Supports Open GL 1.4 + Extensions.

Intel Graphics Media Accelerator 3000—Includes execution units that can perform vertex and pixel shading for 3D graphics (supports DirectX 9.0c Shader Model 3) or video processing for video playback. Supports OpenGL 1.4 + Extensions.

Intel Graphics Media Accelerator X3000—Enhanced version of GMA 3000 with support for high dynamic range (HDR) visuals and Clear Video Technology for better video playback. Hardware T&L. Supports OpenGL 1.5.

Intel Graphics Media Accelerator 3100—Supports DirectX 10 Shader Model 4 for high dynamic range (HDR) visuals and Clear Video Technology for better video playback. Hardware T&L. Supports OpenGL 1.5.

◀◀   To learn more about the integrated graphics included with a given chipset, see the appropriate section following the "Chipsets" heading on p. 273.

Besides Intel, other major vendors of integrated chipsets include AMD, NVIDIA, SiS, and VIA. Table 13.14 compares the video features of current integrated chipsets supporting PCI-Express from these vendors.

Table 13.14   Video Features of Current Non-Intel Integrated Chipsets with PCI-Express Support

Vendor	Chipset	Supported Processors	Integrated Graphics Type	External Graphics Support	Maximum Video Memory Size
AMD	AMD 690 series (RS690)	AMD Athlon 64 X2, other AMD socket AM2 processors	ATI RADEON X1250	PCI Express x16	256MB
AMD	RADEON Xpress 1150 for AMD	AMD Athlon 64 X2, Athlon 64 FX, FX/X2, Athlon 64, Sempron	ATI RADEON X300	PCI Express x16	128MB
ATI	RADEON Xpress 200 for Intel	Intel Pentium 4, Celeron 4	ATI RADEON X300	PCI Express x16	256MB
ATI	RADEON Xpress 200 for AMD	AMD Athlon 64 family (including Socket 754 Sempron)	ATI RADEON X300	PCI Express x16	128MB
NVIDIA	NVIDIA nForce 630a	AMD Athlon 64 X2, Athlon 64 FX, FX/X2, Athlon 64, Sempron	GeForce 7050PV	PCI Express x16	256MB or 512MB
NVIDIA	NVIDIA nForce 630a	AMD Athlon 64 X2, Athlon 64 FX, FX/X2, Athlon 64, Sempron	GeForce 7025	PCI Express x16	256MB
NVIDIA	NVIDIA nForce 430	AMD Athlon 64 X2, Athlon 64 FX, FX/X2, Athlon 64, Sempron	GeForce 6150 SE	PCI Express x16	256MB
NVIDIA	NVIDIA nForce 430	AMD Athlon 64 X2, Athlon 64 FX, FX/X2, Athlon 64, Sempron	GeForce 6100	PCI Express x16	128MB
NVIDIA	NVIDIA nForce 405	AMD Athlon 64 X2, Athlon 64 FX, FX/X2, Athlon 64, Sempron	GeForce 6100	PCI Express x16	128MB
SiS	SiS771	AMD Athlon 64 X2, Athlon 64 FX, FX/X2, Athlon 64, Sempron	SiS Mirage 3	PCI Express x16	256MB
SiS	SiS671	Intel Core 2 Duo, Pentium D, Pentium 4	SiS Mirage 3	PCI Express x16	256MB
SiS	SiS672	Intel Core 2 Duo, Pentium D, Pentium 4	SiS Mirage 3+	PCI Express x16	256MB

Table 13.14 Continued

Vendor	Chipset	Supported Processors	Integrated Graphics Type	External Graphics Support	Maximum Video Memory Size
SiS	SiS672FX	Intel Core 2 Duo, Pentium D, Pentium 4	SiS Mirage 3+	PCI Express x16	256MB
SiS	SiS662	Intel Core 2 Duo, Pentium D, Pentium 4	SiS Mirage 1	PCI Express x16	64MB
SiS	SiS761GX	AMD Athlon 64 FX	SiS Mirage 1	PCI Express x16	128MB
VIA	K8M890	AMD Athlon 64, FX, X2, Sempron	VIA Chrome 9 HC	PCI-Express x16	256MB
VIA	P4M900	Intel Core 2 Duo, Pentium D, Pentium 4, Celeron	VIA Chrome 9 HC	PCI-Express x16	128MB
VIA	KM960	AMD Athlon 64, FX, X2, Sempron	VIA Chrome 9 HC	PCI-Express x16	256MB

RADEON X1250—DirectX 9.0b (Shader Model 2.0x). Supports DVI and HDMI with HDCP. Based on Radeon X700.RADEON X300—DirectX 9 (Shader Model 2.0). Optional DVI support.

GeForce 7050PV—DirectX 9.0c (Shader Model 3.0). DVI and HDMI with HDCP. PureVideo video playback. Based on GeForce 7 series.

GeForce 7025—DirectX 9.0c (Shader Model 3.0), DVI with HDCP. Based on GeForce 7 series.

GeForce 6150 SE— DirectX 9.0c (Shader Model 3.0), DVI. Based on GeForce 6 series.

GeForce 6100— DirectX 9.0c (Shader Model 3.0), DVI on nForce 430 only. Based on GeForce 6 series.

Mirage 3—DirectX 9 (Shader Model 2.0). RealVideo support for Windows Vista.

Mirage 3+—DirectX 9 (Shader Model 2.0). RealVideo. Reduces power requirements when 3D not in use.

Mirage 1—DirectX 7. MPEG2/DVD acceleration. HD Video support.

Chrome9 HC (DeltaChrome)—DirectX 9 (Shader Model 2.0). MPEG video acceleration.

For information about older non-Intel integrated chipsets, see Chapter 15 of *Upgrading and Repairing PCs, 17th Edition.*

◄◄ To learn more about the integrated graphics included with a given chipset, see the appropriate section following the "Chipsets" heading on p. 273.

Some integrated chipsets support DVI output for use with digital LCD panels and HDMI output for use with HDTV and other home theater components. Figure 13.17 shows a typical arrangement of these ports.

Although a serious 3D gamer will not be satisfied with the performance of integrated graphics, business, home/office, and casual gamers will find that integrated chipset-based video on Core 2 Duo or Athlon 64 X2 platforms is satisfactory in performance and provides cost savings compared with a separate video card. If you decide to buy a motherboard with an integrated chipset, I recommend that you select one that also supports a PCI Express x16 video expansion slot. This enables you to add a faster video card in the future if you decide you need it.

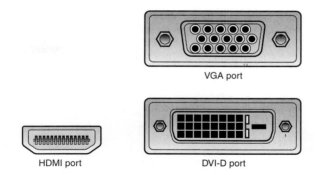

VGA port

HDMI port   DVI-D port

Figure 13.17   A typical port cluster from a system with integrated video outputs for analog, digital, and HDTV support.

Video Adapter Components

All video display adapter cards contain certain basic components, such as the following:

- Video BIOS.
- Video processor/video accelerator.
- Video memory.
- Digital-to-analog converter (DAC). Formerly a separate chip, the DAC is usually incorporated into the video processor/accelerator chip on recent chipsets. The DAC is not necessary on a purely digital subsystem (digital video card and display), but because most display subsystems have an analog VGA video card, an analog display, or both, video cards will continue to have DAC features for some time to come.
- Bus connector.
- Video driver.

On the highest-performing video cards, such as the card shown in Figure 13.18, most of the components are underneath the cooling system. This card uses a combination of a fan and heatpipe to cool its graphics processing unit (GPU).

Virtually all video adapters on the market today use chipsets that include 3D acceleration features. The following sections examine these components and features in greater detail.

The Video BIOS

Video adapters include a BIOS that is similar in construction but completely separate from the main system BIOS. (Other devices in your system, such as SATA host adapters, might also include their own BIOS.) If you turn on your monitor first and look quickly, you might see an identification banner for your adapter's video BIOS at the very beginning of the system startup process.

Similar to the system BIOS, the video adapter's BIOS takes the form of a ROM (read-only memory) chip containing basic instructions that provide an interface between the video adapter hardware and the software running on your system. The software that makes calls to the video BIOS can be a standalone application, an operating system, or the main system BIOS. The programming in the BIOS chip enables your system to display information on the monitor during the system POST and boot sequences, before any other software drivers have been loaded from disk.

◄◄ See "BIOS Basics," p. 441.

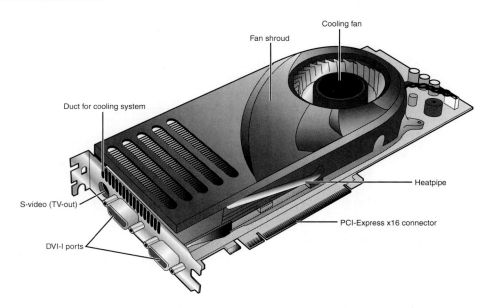

Cooling fan

Fan shroud

Duct for cooling system

Heatpipe

S-video (TV-out)

PCI-Express x16 connector

DVI-I ports

Figure 13.18   A typical example of a high-end video card based on the NVIDIA GeForce 8800, a GPU optimized for gaming and dual-display support.

The video BIOS also can be upgraded, just like a system BIOS, in one of two ways. The BIOS uses a rewritable chip called an EEPROM (electrically erasable programmable read-only memory) that you can upgrade with a utility the adapter manufacturer provides. On very old cards, you might be able to completely replace the chip with a new one—again, if supplied by the manufacturer and if the manufacturer did not hard solder the BIOS to the printed circuit board. Most recent video cards use a surface-mounted BIOS chip rather than a socketed chip. A BIOS you can upgrade using software is referred to as a *flash* BIOS, and most current-model video cards that offer BIOS upgrades use this method. However, most vendors now prefer to update drivers rather than perform BIOS updates to fix card problems.

Video BIOS upgrades (sometimes referred to as *firmware* upgrades) are sometimes necessary in order to use an existing adapter with a new operating system, or when the manufacturer encounters a significant bug in the original programming. Occasionally, a BIOS upgrade is necessary because of a major revision to the video card chipset's video drivers. As a general rule, the video BIOS is a component that falls into the "if it ain't broke, don't fix it" category. Try not to let yourself be tempted to upgrade just because you've discovered that a new BIOS revision is available. Check the documentation for the upgrade, and unless you are experiencing a problem with the upgrade addresses, leave it alone.

The Video Processor

The video processor (also known as the video chipset, video graphics processor, or GPU) is the heart of any video adapter and essentially defines the card's functions and performance levels. Two video adapters built using the same chipset often have many of the same capabilities and deliver comparable performance. Also, the software drivers that operating systems and applications use to address the video adapter hardware are written primarily with the chipset in mind. You often can use a driver intended for an adapter with a particular chipset on any other adapter using the same chipset. Of course, cards built using the same chipset can differ in the amount and type of memory installed, so performance can vary.

Since the first VGA cards were developed, several main types of processors have been used in video adapters; these technologies are compared in Table 13.15.

Table 13.15   Video Processor Technologies

Processor Type	Where Video Processing Takes Place	Relative Speed	Relative Cost	How Used Today
Frame-buffer	Computer's CPU.	Very slow	Very low	Obsolete; mostly ISA video cards.
Graphics coprocessor	Video card's own processor.	Very fast	Very high	CAD and engineering workstations.
Graphics accelerator	Video chip draws lines, circles, shapes; CPU sends commands to draw them.	Fast	Low to moderate	All mainstream video cards; it's combined with 3D GPU on current cards.
3D graphics processor (GPU)	Video card's 3D GPU (in accelerator chipset) renders polygons and adds lighting and shading effects as needed	Fast 2D and 3D display	All price ranges depending on chipset, memory, and RAMDAC speed	All mainstream video cards.

Identifying the Video and System Chipsets

Before you purchase a system or a video card, you should find out which chipset the video card or video circuit uses or, for systems with integrated chipset video, which integrated chipset the system uses. This allows you to have the following:

■ Better comparisons of card or system to others

■ Access to technical specifications

■ Access to reviews and opinions

■ Better buying decisions

■ Choice of card manufacturer or chipset manufacturer support and drivers

Because video card performance and features are critical to enjoyment and productivity, find out as much as you can before you buy the system or video card by using the chipset or video card manufacturer's website and third-party reviews. Poorly written or buggy drivers can cause several types of problems, so be sure to check periodically for video driver updates and install any that become available. With video cards, support after the sale can be important. So, you should check the manufacturer's website to see whether it offers updated drivers and whether the product seems to be well supported.

The Vendor List on the disc has information on most of the popular video chipset manufacturers, including how to contact them. You should note that NVIDIA (the leading video chipset vendor) makes only chipsets, whereas ATI (the #2 video vendor) makes branded video cards and supplies chipsets to vendors. This means a wide variety of video cards use the same chipset; it also means that you are likely to find variations in card performance, software bundles, warranties, and other features between cards using the same chipset.

Video RAM

Most video adapters rely on their own onboard memory that they use to store video images while processing them; although the AGP specification supports the use of system memory for 3D textures, this feature is seldom supported now that video cards routinely ship with as much as 256MB or more onboard memory and with the move away from AGP to PCI Express x16 video cards. Many low-cost systems with onboard video use the universal memory architecture (UMA) feature to share the main system memory. In any case, the memory on the video card or borrowed from the system performs the same tasks.

The amount of memory on the adapter or used by integrated video determines the maximum screen resolution and color depth the device can support. You often can select how much memory you want on a particular video adapter; for example, 128MB, 256MB, and 512MB are common choices today. Although adding more memory is not guaranteed to speed up your video adapter, it can increase the speed if it enables a wider bus (for example, from 128 bits wide to 256 bits wide) or provides nondisplay memory as a cache for commonly displayed objects. It also enables the card to generate more colors and higher resolutions and, for AGP cards, allows 3D textures to be stored and processed on the card, rather than in slower main memory.

Many types of memory have been used with video adapters. These memory types are summarized in Table 13.16.

Table 13.16   Memory Types Used in Video Display Adapters

Memory Type	Definition	Relative Speed	Usage
FPM DRAM	Fast Page-Mode RAM	Slow	Low-end ISA cards; obsolete
VRAM[1]	Video RAM	Fast	Expensive; obsolete
WRAM[1]	Window RAM	Fast	Expensive; obsolete
EDO DRAM	Extended Data Out DRAM	Moderate	Low-end PCI-bus; obsolete
SDRAM	Synchronous DRAM	Fast	Low-end PCI/AGP
MDRAM	Multibank DRAM	Fast	Little used; obsolete
SGRAM	Synchronous Graphics DRAM	Very fast	High-end PCI/AGP; replaced by DDR SDRAM
DDR SDRAM	Double-Data Rate SDRAM	Very fast	High-end AGP; replaced by DDR2 and GDDR2 SDRAM
DDR2 SDRAM	DDR allowing higher clock rates	Extremely fast	High-end AGP, PCI Express
GDDR3 SDRAM	Graphics Double Data Rate version 3 SDRAM	Extremely fast	PCI Express and AGP.
GDDR4 SDRAM	Graphics Double Data Rate version 4 SDRAM	Extremely fast	PCI Express.

1. *VRAM and WRAM are dual-ported memory types that can read from one port and write data through the other port. This improves performance by reducing wait times for accessing the video RAM compared to FPM DRAM and EDO DRAM.*

SGRAM, SDRAM, DDR, DDR2 SDRAM, and GDDR3 SDRAM—which are derived from popular motherboard memory technologies—have replaced VRAM, WRAM, and MDRAM as high-speed video RAM solutions. Their high speeds and low production costs have enabled even inexpensive video cards to have 64MB or more of high-speed RAM onboard.

SDRAM

Synchronous DRAM (SDRAM) is the same type of RAM used on many systems based on processors such as the Pentium III, early Pentium 4, Athlon, and Duron. The SDRAMs found on video cards are usually surface-mounted individual chips; on a few early models, a small module containing SDRAMs might be plugged into a proprietary connector. This memory is designed to work with bus speeds up to 200MHz and provides performance just slightly slower than SGRAM. SDRAM is used primarily in older AGP 2x/4x low-end video cards and chipsets such as NVIDIA's GeForce2 MX and ATI's Radeon VE.

SGRAM

Synchronous Graphics RAM (SGRAM) was designed to be a high-end solution for very fast video adapter designs. SGRAM is similar to SDRAM in its capability to be synchronized to high-speed buses up to 200MHz, but it differs from SDRAM by including circuitry to perform block writes to increase the speed of graphics fill or 3D Z-buffer operations. Although SGRAM is faster than SDRAM, most video card makers have dropped SGRAM in favor of even faster DDR SDRAM in their newest products.

DDR SDRAM

Double Data Rate SDRAM (also called DDR SDRAM) is the most common video RAM technology on recent video cards. It is designed to transfer data at speeds twice that of conventional SDRAM by transferring data on both the rising and falling parts of the processing clock cycle. Video cards based on chipsets such as NVIDIA's GeForce FX and ATI's Radeon 9xxx and X300–700 series use DDR SDRAM for video memory.

DDR2 SDRAM

The second generation of DDR SDRAM uses differential signaling, which allows for much higher clock rates than the first generation DDR.

GDDR3 SDRAM

GDDR3 SDRAM, which is used on NVIDIA GeForce 8 and high-end GeForce 7 series GPUs and ATI's current HD series and X800/850 and X1xx series GPUs, is based on DDR2 memory, but with two major differences:

- GDDR3 separates reads and writes with a single-ended unidirectional strobe, whereas DDR2 uses differential bidirectional strobes. This method enables much higher data transfer rates.

- GDDR3 uses an interface technique known as *pseudo-open drain*, which uses voltage instead of current. This method makes GDDR3 memory compatible with GPUs designed to use DDR or DDR2 memory. As a result, many current GPUs are available in video card designs that feature DDR2 or GDDR3 memory. To determine the type of memory used on a particular video card, check the video card manufacturer's specification sheet.

GDDR4 SDRAM

GDDR4 SDRAM was introduced by ATI's X1950 XTX card, and is also used by the RADEON HD 2600 and 2900 cards. Compared to GDDR3, GDDR4 memory features

- Higher bandwidth; GDDR4 running at half the speed of GDDR3 provides comparable bandwidth to its predecessor.

- Greater memory density, enabling fewer chips to be needed to reach a particular memory size.

◀◀ For more information about DDR, DDR2, and GDDR3, see Chapter 6, "Memory," p. 509.

Video RAM Speed

Video RAM speed is typically measured in MHz, and video card makers often match different memory speeds with different versions of the same basic GPU, as with NVIDIA's GeForce 8800 Ultra (2160MHz GDDR2 memory) and GeForce 8800 GTS (1600MHz memory). Faster memory and faster GPUs produce better gaming performance, but at a higher cost. However, if you are primarily concerned about business or productivity application performance, you can save money by using a video card with a slower GPU and slower memory.

Unless you dig deeply into the technical details of a particular 3D graphics card, determining whether a particular card uses SDRAM, DDR SDRAM, DDR2, SGRAM, or GDDR3 can be difficult. Because none of today's 3D accelerators feature upgradeable memory, I recommend that you look at the performance of a given card and choose the card with the performance, features, and price that's right for you.

RAM Calculations

The amount of memory a video adapter needs to display a particular resolution and color depth is based on a mathematical equation. A location must be present in the adapter's memory array to display every pixel on the screen, and the resolution determines the number of total pixels. For example, a screen resolution of 1024×768 requires a total of 786,432 pixels.

If you were to display that resolution with only two colors, you would need only 1 bit of memory space to represent each pixel. If the bit has a value of 0, the dot is black, and if its value is 1, the dot is white. If you use 24 bits of memory space to control each pixel, you can display more than 16.7 million colors because 16,777,216 combinations are possible with a four-digit binary number ($2^{24}=16,777,216$). If you multiply the number of pixels necessary for the screen resolution by the number of bits required to represent each pixel, you have the amount of memory the adapter needs to display that resolution. Here is how the calculation works:

$$1024 \times 768 = 786432 \text{ pixels} \times 24 \text{ bits per pixel}$$
$$= 18,874,368 \text{ bits}$$
$$= 2,359,296 \text{ bytes}$$
$$= 2.25\text{MB}$$

As you can see, displaying 24-bit color (16,777,216 colors) at 1024×768 resolution requires exactly 2.25MB of RAM on the video adapter. Because most adapters support memory amounts of only 256KB, 512KB, 1MB, 2MB, or 4MB, you would need to use a video adapter with at least 4MB of RAM onboard to run your system using that resolution and color depth.

To use the higher-resolution modes and greater numbers of colors common today, you would need much more memory on your video adapter than the 256KB found on the original IBM VGA. Table 13.17 shows the memory requirements for some of the most common screen resolutions and color depths used for 2D graphics operations, such as photo editing, presentation graphics, desktop publishing, and web page design.

Table 13.17   Video Display Adapter Minimum Memory Requirements for 2D Operations

Resolution	Color Depth	Max. Colors	Memory Required	Memory Used
640×480	16-bit	65,536	1MB	614,400 bytes
640×480	24-bit	16,777,216	1MB	921,600 bytes
640×480	32-bit	4,294,967,296	2MB	1,228,800 bytes
800×600	16-bit	65,536	1MB	960,000 bytes
800×600	24-bit	16,777,216	2MB	1,440,000 bytes
800×600	32-bit	4,294,967,296	2MB	1,920,000 bytes
1024×768	16-bit	65,536	2MB	1,572,864 bytes
1024×768	24-bit	16,777,216	4MB	2,359,296 bytes
1024×768	32-bit	4,294,967,296	4MB	3,145,728 bytes
1280×1024	16-bit	65,536	4MB	2,621,440 bytes
1280×1024	24-bit	16,777,216	4MB	3,932,160 bytes
1280×1024	32-bit	4,294,967,296	8MB	5,242,880 bytes
1400×1050	16-bit	65,536	4MB	2,940,000 bytes
1400×1050	24-bit	16,777,216	8MB	4,410,000 bytes
1400×1050	32-bit	4,294,967,296	8MB	5,880,000 bytes
1600×1200	16-bit	65,536	4MB	3,840,000 bytes
1600×1200	24-bit	16,777,216	8MB	5,760,000 bytes
1600×1200	32-bit	4,294,967,296	8MB	7,680,000 bytes

As you can see from Table 13.17, any current graphics card or integrated graphics solution has more than enough memory to provide true color (24-bit or 32-bit) rendition at any popular resolution. Current video cards and integrated graphics solutions provide much more memory than the amounts listed in Table 13.17 because of the additional memory needs of 3D operation.

3D video cards require more memory for a given resolution and color depth because the video memory must be used for three buffers: the front buffer, back buffer, and Z-buffer. The amount of video memory required for a particular operation varies according to the settings used for the color depth and Z-buffer. Triple buffering allocates more memory for 3D textures than double buffering but can slow down performance of some games. The buffering mode used by a given 3D video card usually can be adjusted through its properties sheet.

Table 13.18 lists the memory requirements for 3D cards in selected modes.

Table 13.18   Video Display Adapter Memory Requirements for 3D Operations

Resolution	Color Depth	Z-Buffer Depth	Buffer Mode	Actual Memory Used	Onboard Video Memory Size Required
640×480	16-bit	16-bit	Double	1.76MB	2MB
			Triple	2.34MB	4MB
	24-bit	24-bit	Double	2.64MB	4MB
			Triple	3.52MB	4MB
	32-bit	32-bit	Double	3.52MB	4MB
			Triple	4.69MB	8MB

Table 13.18 Continued

Resolution	Color Depth	Z-Buffer Depth	Buffer Mode	Actual Memory Used	Onboard Video Memory Size Required
800×600	16-bit	16-bit	Double	2.75MB	4MB
			Triple	3.66MB	4MB
	24-bit	24-bit	Double	4.12MB	8MB
			Triple	5.49MB	8MB
	32-bit	32-bit	Double	5.49MB	8MB
			Triple	7.32MB	8MB
1024×768	16-bit	16-bit	Double	4.50MB	8MB
			Triple	6.00MB	8MB
	24-bit	24-bit	Double	6.75MB	8MB
			Triple	9.00MB	16MB
	32-bit	32-bit	Double	9.00MB	16MB
			Triple	12.00MB	16MB
1280×1024	16-bit	16-bit	Double	7.50MB	8MB
			Triple	10.00MB	16MB
	24-bit	24-bit	Double	11.25MB	16MB
			Triple	15.00MB	16MB
	32-bit	32-bit	Double	15.00MB	16MB
			Triple	20.00MB	32MB
1600×1200	16-bit	16-bit	Double	10.99MB	16MB
			Triple	14.65MB	16MB
	24-bit	24-bit	Double	16.48MB	32MB
			Triple	21.97MB	32MB
	32-bit	32-bit	Double	21.97MB	32MB
			Triple	29.30MB	32MB

Note

Although 3D adapters typically operate in a 32-bit mode (refer to Table 13.18), this does not necessarily mean they can produce more than the 16,277,216 colors of a 24-bit true-color display. Video processors and video memory buses designed for 3D video are optimized to move data in 32-bit words, and they actually display 24-bit color while operating in a 32-bit mode, instead of the 4,294,967,296 colors you would expect from a true 32-bit color depth.

As you can see from comparing Table 13.18 to the specifications of a current video card (even a low-end model) today's PCI-Express and AGP cards feature much more RAM than the minimums needed for even very high-resolution displays. Additional RAM is utilitized to hold larger 3D textures and to improve 3D transfer rates.

Although current integrated graphics solutions feature 3D support, the performance they offer is limited by being based on older, less powerful 3D GPUs and by the narrow data bus they use to access memory. Because integrated graphics solutions share video memory with the processor, they use the same data bus as the processor. In a single-channel-based system, this restricts the data bus to 64 bits. A dual-channel system has a 128-bit data bus, but today's fastest 3D video cards feature a 512-bit or wider data bus. The wider the data bus, the more quickly graphics data can be transferred.

For these reasons, you are likely to be disappointed (and lose a lot of games!) if you play 3D games using integrated graphics. To enjoy 3D games and give yourself a fighting chance of winning, opt for a mid-range to high-end 3D video card based on a current ATI or NVIDIA chipset with 256MB of RAM or more. If your budget permits, you might also consider using a dual-card solution from ATI or NVIDIA that allows you to use two PCI-Express video cards to double your graphics processing performance.

◄◄ See "Dual-GPU Scene Rendering," p. 959.

Note

If your system uses integrated graphics and you have less than 256MB of RAM, you might be able to increase your available graphics memory by upgrading system memory (system memory is used by the integrated chipset). Some Intel chipsets with integrated graphics automatically detect additional system memory and adjust the size of graphics memory automatically. Refer to Table 13.13 for details.

Video Bus Width

Another issue with respect to the memory on the video adapter is the width of the bus connecting the graphics chipset and memory on the adapter. The chipset is usually a single large chip on the card that contains virtually all the adapter's functions. It is wired directly to the memory on the adapter through a local bus on the card. Most of the high-end adapters use an internal memory bus that is 256 or 512 bits wide, but the latest NVIDIA GeForce 8 cards use 384-bit and 320-bit memory buses because of their memory controller design. This jargon can be confusing because video adapters that take the form of separate expansion cards also plug into the main system bus, which has its own speed rating. When you read about a 128-bit or 256-bit video adapter, you must understand that this refers to the local video bus and that the bus connecting the adapter to the system is actually the PCI-Express or AGP bus on the system's motherboard. In two cards with otherwise similar GPU, memory type and memory size specifications, the card with the wider memory bus is preferable because a wider memory bus boosts performance.

◄◄ See "System Bus Types, Functions, and Features," p. 378.

The Digital-to-analog Converter (RAMDAC)

The digital-to-analog converter on a video adapter (commonly called a RAMDAC) does exactly what its name describes. The RAMDAC is responsible for converting the digital images your computer generates into analog signals the monitor can display. The speed of the RAMDAC is measured in MHz; the faster the conversion process, the higher the adapter's vertical refresh rate. The speeds of the RAMDACs used in today's high-performance video adapters range from 300MHz to 500MHz. Most of today's video card chipsets include the RAMDAC function inside the 3D accelerator chip, but some dual-display-capable video cards use a separate RAMDAC chip to allow the second display to work at different refresh rates than the primary display. Systems that use integrated graphics include the RAMDAC function in the North Bridge or GMCH chip portion of the motherboard chipset.

The benefits of increasing the RAMDAC speed include higher vertical refresh rates, which allows higher resolutions with flicker-free refresh rates (72Hz–85Hz or above). Typically, cards with RAMDAC speeds of 300MHz or above display flicker-free (75Hz or above) at all resolutions up to 1920×1200. Of course, as discussed earlier in this chapter, you must ensure that any resolution you want to use is supported by both your monitor and video card.

The Bus

You've learned in this chapter that certain video adapters were designed for use with certain system buses. Earlier bus standards, such as the IBM MCA, ISA, EISA, and VL-Bus, have all been used for VGA and other video standards. Because of their slow performances, all are now obsolete; current video cards use the PCI, AGP, or PCI-Express bus standard.

In current and forthcoming systems, PCI Express x16 is the standard video card slot design, replacing the long-time standard AGP 8x. Some systems can support both types of video cards, enabling you to move to PCI Express x16 at your own pace. PCI video cards are limited in quantity and performance and are sold primarily as upgrades for systems with integrated video that lack AGP or PCI Express slots.

◄◄ See "The PCI Bus," p. 399.

◄◄ See "PCI-Express," p. 403.

◄◄ See "Accelerated Graphics Port," p. 405.

AGP Video Cards

The Accelerated Graphics Port (AGP), an Intel-designed dedicated video bus introduced in 1997, delivers a maximum bandwidth up to 16 times larger than that of a comparable PCI bus. AGP has been the mainstream high-speed video standard for several years but has now been replaced by the more versatile and faster PCI Express x16 standard.

The AGP slot is essentially an enhancement to the existing PCI bus; however, it's intended for use only with video adapters and provides them with high-speed access to the main system memory array. This enables the adapter to process certain 3D video elements, such as texture maps, directly from system memory rather than having to copy the data to the adapter memory before the processing can begin. This saves time and eliminates the need to upgrade the video adapter memory to better support 3D functions. Although AGP version 3.0 provides for two AGP slots, this feature has never been implemented in practice. Systems with AGP have only one AGP slot.

Note

Although the earliest AGP cards had relatively small amounts of onboard RAM, most recent and all current implementations of card-based AGP use large amounts of on-card memory and use a memory aperture (a dedicated memory address space above the area used for physical memory) to transfer data more quickly to and from the video card's own memory. Integrated chipsets featuring built-in AGP do use system memory for all operations, including texture maps.

Although AGP was introduced during the same time period in which Windows NT 4.0 and Windows 95 were the current versions of Windows, those versions of Windows do not support AGP's Direct Memory Execute (DIME) feature. DIME uses main memory instead of the video adapter's memory for certain tasks to lessen the traffic to and from the adapter. Windows 98/Me and Windows 2000/XP support this feature. However, with the large amounts of memory found on current AGP video cards, this feature is seldom implemented.

Four speeds of AGP are available: 1x, 2x, 4x, and 8x (see Table 13.19 for details). Current AGP video cards support AGP 8x and can fall back to AGP 4x or 2x on systems that don't support AGP 8x.

Table 13.19   AGP Speeds and Technical Specifications

AGP Speed	AGP Specification	Clock Speed	Transfer Rate	Slot Voltages
1x	1.0	66MHz	266MBps	3.3V
2x	1.0	133MHz	533MBps	3.3V, 1.5V[1]
4x	2.0	266MHz	1066MBps	1.5V
8x	3.0	533MHz	2133MBps	1.5V[2]

1. Varies with card implementation.

2. Uses 0.8V internal signaling.

Because of the bandwidth AGP 3.0 requires, systems featuring this version of AGP also support DDR333 or faster memory, which is significantly faster than DDR266 (also known as PC2100 memory). AGP 3.0 was announced in 2000, but support for the standard required the development of motherboard chipsets that were not introduced until mid-2002. Almost all current motherboard chipsets with AGP support feature AGP 8x support; however, differences in GPU design, memory bus design, and core and memory clock speed mean (as always) that AGP 8x cards with faster and wider memory and faster GPU speeds provide faster performance than AGP 8x cards with slower and narrower components.

Although some systems with AGP 4x or 8x slots use a universal slot design that can handle 3.3V or 1.5V AGP cards, others do not. If a card designed for 3.3V (2x mode) is plugged into a motherboard that supports only 1.5V (4x mode) signaling, the motherboard will be damaged.

◀◀   See "Accelerated Graphics Port," p. 405.

Caution

Be sure to check AGP compatibility before you insert an older (AGP 1x/2x) card into a recent or current system. Even if you can physically insert the card, a mismatch between the card's required voltage and the AGP slot's voltage output can damage the motherboard. Check the motherboard manual for the card types and voltage levels supported by the AGP slot.

Some AGP cards can use either 3.3V or 1.5V voltage levels by adjusting an onboard jumper. These cards typically use an AGP connector that is notched for use with either AGP 2x or AGP 4x slots, as pictured in Chapter 4, "Motherboards and Buses." Be sure to set these cards to use 1.5V before using them in motherboards that support only 1.5V signaling, such as motherboards based on the Intel 845 or 850 chipsets.

PCI Express Video Cards

PCI Express, which has largely replaced AGP in new systems, began to show up in high-performance systems in mid-2004 and has filtered down to almost all systems that use discrete video cards or have integrated video that can be upgraded. Despite the name, PCI Express uses a high-speed bidirectional serial data transfer method, and PCI Express channels (also known as *lanes*) can be combined to create wider and faster expansion slots (each lane provides 250MBps data rate in each direction). Unlike PCI, PCI Express slots do not compete with each other for bandwidth. PCI Express graphics cards use 16 lanes (x16) to enable speeds of 4GBps in each direction; when PCI Express is used for other types of cards, fewer lanes are used.

PCI, AGP, and x16 PCI Express have some important differences, as Table 13.20 shows.

Table 13.20   High-Speed Video Card Bus Specifications

Feature	PCI	AGP	PCI Express
Theoretical maximum	133MBps[1]	533MBps throughput (2x) 1,066MBps throughput (4x)[2] 2,133MBps throughput (8x)[2]	250MBps/lane[3] 4GBps (x16)[3]
Slots[2]	4/5 (typical)	1	1/more[4]

1. *At 33MHz bus speed and 32 bits.*
2. *Most current systems support AGP 4X/8X only.*
3. *In each direction; multiply by 2 for bidirectional throughput.*
4. *Typical PCI Express implementations include one x16 slot for video and two or more x1 slots for other add-on cards, as well as legacy PCI slots. Systems that support NVIDIA's SLI or ATI's CrossFire dual PCI Express video card technologies have two PCI Express video slots running at x8 or x16 speed.*

The Video Driver

The software driver is an essential, and often problematic, element of a video display subsystem. The driver enables your software to communicate with the video adapter. You can have a video adapter with the fastest processor and the most efficient memory on the market but still have poor video performance because of a badly written driver.

Video drivers generally are designed to support the processor on the video adapter. All video adapters come equipped with drivers the card manufacturer supplies, but often you can use a driver the chipset maker created as well. Sometimes you might find that one of the two provides better performance than the other or resolves a particular problem you are experiencing.

Most manufacturers of video adapters and chipsets maintain websites from which you can obtain the latest drivers; drivers for chipset-integrated video are supplied by the system board or system vendor. A driver from the chipset manufacturer can be a useful alternative, but you should always try the adapter manufacturer's driver first. Before purchasing a video adapter, you should check out the manufacturer's site and see whether you can determine how up to date the available drivers are. At one time, frequent driver revisions were thought to indicate problems with the hardware, but the greater complexity of today's systems means that driver revisions are a necessity. Even if you are installing a brand-new model of a video adapter, be sure to check for updated drivers on the manufacturer's website for best results.

Note

Although most devices work best with the newest drivers, video cards can be a notable exception. Both NVIDIA and ATI now use unified driver designs, creating a single driver installation that can be used across a wide range of graphics chips. However, in some cases, older versions of drivers sometimes work better with older chipsets than the newest drivers do. If you find that system performance or stability, especially in 3D gaming, drops when you upgrade to the newest driver for your 3D graphics card, revert to the older driver.

The video driver also provides the interface you can use to configure the display your adapter produces. On a Windows 9x/Me/2000/XP system, the Display properties sheet's Settings tab identifies the monitor(s) and video adapter installed on your system and enables you to select the color depth and screen resolution you prefer. Windows Vista's Display Settings dialog performs the same task. The driver controls the options that are available for these settings, so you can't choose parameters the hardware doesn't support. For example, you cannot select resolutions not supported by your display, even though your video card might support them.

When you click the Advanced button on the Settings page, you see the Properties dialog box for your particular video display adapter. The contents of this dialog box can vary, depending on the driver and the capabilities of the hardware. Typically, on the General page of this dialog box, you can select the size of the fonts (large or small) to use with the resolution you've chosen. Windows 98/Me/2000 (but not Windows XP or Vista) also add a control to activate a convenient feature. The Show Settings Icon on Task Bar check box activates a tray icon that enables you to quickly and easily change resolutions and color depths without having to open the Control Panel. This feature is often called QuickRes. The Adapter page displays detailed information about your adapter and the drivers installed on the system, and it enables you to set the refresh rate for your display; with Windows XP and Windows Vista, you can use the List All Modes button to view and choose the resolution, color depth, and refresh rate with a single click. The Monitor page lets you display and change the monitor's properties and switch monitor drivers if necessary. In Windows XP and Windows Vista, you can also select the refresh rate on this screen.

If your adapter includes a graphics accelerator, the Performance page contains a Hardware Acceleration slider you can use to control the degree of graphic display assistance provided by your adapter hardware. In Windows XP and Windows Vista, the Performance page is referred to as the Troubleshoot page.

Note

Although Windows Vista includes the Troubleshoot page, most current video drivers for Windows Vista do not permit adjustments to video acceleration. When Windows Vista video drivers permit adjustments to video acceleration, use Table 13.21 to help make adjustments. Note that you must be an administrator or use administrator credentials to change video acceleration.

Setting the Hardware Acceleration slider to the Full position activates all the adapter's hardware acceleration features. The necessary adjustments for various problems can be seen in Table 13.21 for Windows XP and in Table 13.22 for other versions of Windows.

Table 13.21   Using Graphics Acceleration Settings to Troubleshoot Windows XP

Acceleration Setting	When to Use	Effect of Setting	Long-Term Solution
Left*	The display works in Safe or VGA mode but is corrupted in other modes.	There's no acceleration.	Update display, DirectX, and mouse drivers.
One click from left*	2D and 3D graphics driver problems; mouse driver problems.	It disables all but basic acceleration.	Update display, DirectX, and mouse drivers.
Two clicks from left*	3D acceleration problems.	It disables DirectX, DirectDraw, and Direct 3D acceleration (mainly used by 3D games).	Update DirectX drivers.

Table 13.21   Continued

Acceleration Setting	When to Use	Effect of Setting	Long-Term Solution
Two clicks from right*	Display driver problems.	It disables cursor and drawing accelerations.	Update display drivers.
One click from right*	Mouse pointer corruption.	It disables mouse and pointer acceleration.	Update mouse drivers.
Right	Normal operation.	It enables full acceleration.	N/A

Disable write combining, which is a method for speeding up screen display, whenever you select any setting other than full acceleration to improve stability. Reenable write combining after you install updated drivers and retry.

Table 13.22   Using Graphics Acceleration Settings to Troubleshoot Older Windows Versions

Mouse Pointer Location	When to Use	Effects of Setting	Long-Term Solution
Left	Display works in Safe or VGA mode, but it is corrupted in other modes.	It disables all acceleration.	Update display and mouse drivers.
One click from left	2D and 3D graphics driver problems, mouse driver problems.	Basic acceleration only.	Update display and mouse drivers.
One click from right	Mouse pointer corruption.	It disables mouse pointer acceleration.	Update mouse drivers.
Right	Normal operation.	Full acceleration.	N/A

If you're not certain of which setting is the best for your situation, use this procedure: Move the slider one notch to the left to address mouse display problems by disabling the hardware's cursor support in the display driver. This is the equivalent of adding the SWCursor=1 directive to the [Display] section of the System.ini file in Windows 9x/Me.

If you are having problems with 2D graphics in Windows XP only, but 3D applications work correctly, move the slider to the second notch from the right to disable cursor drawing and acceleration.

Moving the slider another notch (to the third notch from the right in Windows XP or the second notch from the right in earlier versions) prevents the adapter from performing certain bit-block transfers; it disables 3D functions of DirectX in Windows XP. With some drivers, this setting also disables memory-mapped I/O. This is the equivalent of adding the Mmio=0 directive to the [Display] section of System.ini and the SafeMode=1 directive to the [Windows] section of Win.ini (and the SWCursor directive mentioned previously) in Windows 9x/Me.

Moving the slider to the None setting (the far left) adds the SafeMode=2 directive to the [Windows] section of the Win.ini file in Windows 9x/Me. This disables all hardware acceleration support on all versions of Windows and forces the operating system to use only the device-independent bitmap (DIB) engine to display images, rather than bit-block transfers. Use this setting when you experience frequent screen lockups or receive invalid page fault error messages.

Note

If you need to disable any of the video hardware features listed earlier, this often indicates a buggy video or mouse driver. If you download and install updated video and mouse drivers, you should be able to revert to full acceleration. You should also download an updated version of DirectX for your version of Windows.

In most cases, another tab called Color Management is also available. You can select a color profile for your monitor to enable more accurate color matching for use with graphics programs and printers.

Video cards with advanced 3D acceleration features often have additional properties; these are discussed later in this chapter.

Multiple Monitors

Macintosh systems pioneered multiple-monitor support long before Windows, but starting with Windows 98, all current Windows versions also offer the ability to use multiple monitors on a single system. Windows 98/Me support up to nine monitors (and video adapters), each of which can provide a different view of the desktop. Windows 2000 and Windows XP support up to 10 monitors and video adapters. Windows Vista supports multiple monitors, but the details of support vary from Windows XP when Vista-specific WDDM display drivers are used. When you configure a Windows system to use multiple monitors, the operating system creates a virtual desktop—that is, a display that exists in video memory that can be larger than the image actually displayed on a single monitor. You use the multiple monitors to display various portions of the virtual desktop, enabling you to place the windows for different applications on separate monitors and move them around at will.

Unless you use multiple-head video cards, each monitor you connect to the system requires its own video adapter. So, unless you have nine bus slots free, the prospects of seeing a nine-screen Windows display are slim, for now. However, even two monitors can be a boon to computing productivity. For example, you can leave an email client or web browser maximized on one monitor and use the other monitor for additional programs.

Multiple Monitor Support on Windows 98 Through XP

On a multimonitor Windows system, one display is always considered to be the primary display. The primary display can use any PCI or AGP VGA video adapter that uses a Windows minidriver with a linear frame buffer and a packed (nonplanar) format, meaning that most of the brand-name adapters sold today are eligible. Additional monitors are called *secondaries* and are much more limited in their hardware support. To install support for multiple monitors, be sure you have only one adapter installed first; then reboot the system, and install each additional adapter one at a time. Table 13.23 lists the most significant multiple-monitor support articles available for Windows 98 through XP on the Microsoft support website (http://support.microsoft.com).

Table 13.23   Selected Multiple-Monitor Support Articles from the Microsoft Knowledge Base for Windows 98–XP

Article Subject	Windows Versions Supported	Article Number
Video card chipsets with multiple-monitor support	Windows 98	182708
Enabling multiple-monitor support	Windows 98	179602
Troubleshooting multiple displays	Windows 98/Me	182930
Setting up and troubleshooting multiple monitors	Windows 2000	238886
Video card chipsets with multiple-monitor support	Windows XP	296538
Supported display adapters for multiple monitors/DualView	Windows XP	307397
DualView	Windows XP	283674
Configuring multiple monitors	Windows XP	307873

It's important that the computer correctly identifies which of the video adapters is the primary one. This is a function of the system BIOS, and if the BIOS on your computer does not let you select which device should be the primary VGA display, it decides based on the order of the PCI slots in the machine. Therefore, you should install the primary adapter in the highest-priority PCI slot. In some cases, an AGP adapter might be considered secondary to a PCI adapter. Depending on the BIOS used by your system, you might need to check in various places for the option to select the primary VGA display. For example, the AMI BIOS used by the MSI KT4 Ultra motherboard for Socket A processors lists this option, which it calls Primary Graphics Adapter, in the PCI/PnP menu. In contrast, the Intel/AMI BIOS used by the Intel D865PERL motherboard lists this option, which it calls Primary Video Adapter, in the Video Configuration menu.

◄◄   See "The PCI Bus," p. 399.

After the hardware is in place, you can configure the display for each monitor from the Display control panel's Settings page. The primary display is always fixed in the upper-left corner of the virtual desktop, but you can move the secondary displays to view any area of the desktop you like. You can also set the screen resolution and color depth for each display individually. Windows XP also supports DualView, an enhancement to Windows 2000's multiple-monitor support. DualView supports the increasing number of dual-head video cards as well as notebook computers connected to external displays. With systems supporting DualView, the first video port is automatically assigned to the primary monitor. On a notebook computer, the primary display is the built-in LCD panel.

Note

To determine whether your notebook computer supports DualView, open its Display properties sheet and click the Settings tab. If two monitor icons are visible, your computer supports DualView. You can activate secondary monitor support after you attach a monitor to the external VGA port.

Even if your BIOS enables you to specify the primary video card and you use video cards that are listed as compatible, determining exactly which display cards will work successfully in a multimonitor configuration can be difficult. Consequently, you should check with your video card or chipset maker for the latest information on Windows 2000 or Windows XP and multiple-monitor support issues.

Because new chipsets, updated drivers, and combinations of display adapters are a continuous issue for multiple-monitor support when separate video cards are used, I recommend the following online resources:

■ http://www.realtimesoft.com/ultramon is the home of the UltraMon multiple-monitor support enhancement program ($39.95). It's an extensive database of user-supplied multiple-monitor configurations for Windows 98/Me, Windows 2000/XP, and Linux, as well as product reviews and tips.

■ http://www.digitalroom.net (click Tech Articles and then Multiple Monitor Guide) provides excellent tips on multiple-monitor setups and links to other resources.

Multiple Monitor Support in Windows Vista

Windows Vista's Aero 3D desktop requires a new Windows display driver model known as WDDM, but you can also run Windows Vista using Vista Basic or other non-3D color schemes if your video card(s) supports Windows XP drivers. These drivers use the Windows XP driver model (XPDM). If you are using Windows XP video drivers, you can mix and match AGP and PCI or PCI-Express and PCI video cards using different GPUs from different manufacturers, just as in Windows XP. To configure the primary display, use the methods discussed in the previous section.

However, if you prefer to use WDDM drivers, which use a new architecture designed to promote improved system stability, you can only use multiple video cards if they use the same WDDM driver. Because ATI and NVIDIA use a unified driver architecture to support their current product lines, you can use two (or more) ATI-based or NVIDIA-based cards to create the desired multiple–monitor configuration. However, you cannot use an ATI and an NVIDIA GPU in the same system (or any other combination of GPUs that use different drivers) when WDDM drivers are used.

You can run either XPDM or WDDM display drivers in your system. If you attempt to run two video cards, one of each with XPDM and WDDM drivers, your system will display an "Incompatible display adapter has been disabled" error message.

For more information about multiple monitor support in Windows Vista, see www.microsoft.com/whdc/device/display/multimonVista.mspx.

Multiple Monitor Hardware

Multiple-monitor support can be enabled through either of the following:

- Installation of a separate PCI Express, AGP, or PCI graphics card for each monitor you want to use
- Installation of a single PCI Express, AGP, or PCI graphics card that can support two or more monitors

A card that supports multiple monitors (also called a multiple-head or dual-head card) saves slots inside your system and eliminates the headaches of driver and BIOS updates or system reconfiguration sometimes necessary when using two or more video cards for multiple-monitor capability. Most recent video cards with multiple-monitor support feature either a 15-pin analog VGA connector for CRTs and a DVI-I digital/analog connector for digital LCD panels (adaptable to VGA) or two DVI-I connectors, and a TV-out connector for S-video or composite output to TVs and VCRs. North American cards normally use S-video (adaptable to composite) for TV-out and cards built for other areas normally use composite. Thus, you can connect any of the following to these cards:

- Two digital LCD panels (on cards with two DVI-I connectors)
- One analog LCD panel or CRT display *and* one digital LCD panel
- Two analog LCD panel or CRT displays (when the DVI-I-to-VGA adapter is used)
- One analog LCD panel or CRT display *and* one TV
- One digital LCD panel *and* one TV
- One digital LCD panel *and* one TV

Virtually all video chipsets that support DirectX 8 support two or more displays, and most support two CRT monitors or LCD panels along with TV–out. However, some low-end video cards, particularly those based on older GPUs, might not always provide all of the outputs supported by the GPU. To determine the exact dual-display support provided by a particular video card, see its specification sheet.

▶▶ For a listing of GPUs from major vendors that support DirectX 8 and above, see Table 13.26, p. 962.

Caution

Some vendors whose cards provide a single VGA or DVI-I port (DVI-I ports can be converted to VGA with an adapter) and a TV-out port refer to such cards as "supporting multiple monitors."

Adding Multiple-monitor Support to Laptops and Desktops with Integrated Graphics

Matrox offers two lines of graphics expansion modules that split the existing single VGA signal coming from compatible laptops or desktops into two or more separate displays that can host their own applications, just as if your system had a multihead-compatible graphics card installed:

- DualHead 2Go Analog Edition—Hosts two analog displays
- DualHead 2Go Digital Edition—Hosts two digital displays
- TripleHead 2Go Analog Edition—Hosts three analog displays
- TripleHead 2Go Digital Edition—Hosts three digital displays The Matrox device and driver software transforms the video signal coming from your computer's integrated video into an ultra wide-screen signal by using Extended Display Identification Data (EDID) and splits it into two or three parts that can be transmitted to different screens. Each display connected to the device can display a separate program, or you can stretch a single program across all displays. See Figure 13.19 for examples.

Figure 13.19 Using the Matrox DualHead2Go device to host separate applications (top) or to stretch a single application across two windows (bottom). *Photos courtesy Matrox Graphics.*

To learn more about DualHead2Go and TripleHead2Go, which support Windows XP, 2000, Vista, and MacOS X 10.4, see www.matrox.com/graphics/en/gxm/.

3D Graphics Accelerators

Since the late 1990s, 3D acceleration—once limited to exotic add-on cards designed for hardcore game players—has become commonplace in the PC world. With the introduction of Windows Vista, 3D imaging is now available in the user interface when the Aero desktop is enabled, joining other full-motion 3D uses such as sports, first-person shooters, team combat, driving, and many other types of PC gaming. Because even low-cost integrated chipsets offer some 3D support and 3D video cards are now in their tenth generation of development, virtually any user of a recent-model computer has the ability to enjoy 3D lighting, perspective, texture, and shading effects in her favorite games. The latest 3D sports games provide lighting and camera angles so realistic that a casual observer could almost mistake the computer-generated game for an actual broadcast, and the latest 3D accelerator chips enable fast PCs to compete with high-performance dedicated game machines, such as Sony's PlayStation 3, Nintendo's Wii, and Microsoft's Xbox 360, for the mind and wallet of the hard-core game player.

Note

At a minimum, Windows Vista requires graphics hardware that supports DirectX 7 3D graphics; however, for maximum functionality of its 3D Aero GUI, graphics hardware that supports DirectX 9 or greater is required. Games are now being released that require DirectX 10, which is available exclusively for Windows Vista.

How 3D Accelerators Work

To construct an animated 3D sequence, a computer can mathematically animate the sequences between keyframes. A keyframe identifies specific points. A bouncing ball, for example, can have three keyframes: up, down, and up. Using these frames as a reference point, the computer can create all the interim images between the top and bottom. This creates the effect of a smoothly bouncing ball.

After it has created the basic sequence, the system can then refine the appearance of the images by filling them in with color. The most primitive and least effective fill method is called *flat shading*, in which a shape is simply filled with a solid color. *Gouraud shading*, a slightly more effective technique, involves the assignment of colors to specific points on a shape. The points are then joined using a smooth gradient between the colors.

A more processor-intensive, and much more effective, type of fill is called *texture mapping*. The 3D application includes patterns—or textures—in the form of small bitmaps that it tiles onto the shapes in the image, just as you can tile a small bitmap to form the wallpaper for your Windows desktop. The primary difference is that the 3D application can modify the appearance of each tile by applying perspective and shading to achieve 3D effects. When lighting effects that simulate fog, glare, directional shadows, and others are added, the 3D animation comes very close indeed to matching reality.

Until the late 1990s, 3D applications had to rely on support from software routines to convert these abstractions into live images. This placed a heavy burden on the system processor in the PC, which has a significant impact on the performance not only of the visual display, but also of any other applications the computer might be running. Starting in the period from 1996 to 1997, chipsets on most video adapters began to take on many of the tasks involved in rendering 3D images, greatly lessening the load on the system processor and boosting overall system performance.

There have been roughly ten generations of 3D graphics hardware on PCs, a process that has lasted over a decade, as detailed in Table 13.24.

Table 13.24 Brief 3D Acceleration History

Generation	Dates	Technologies	Example Product/Chipset
1st	1996–1997	3D PCI card with passthrough to 2D graphics card; OpenGL and GLIDE APIs	3dfx Voodoo
2nd	1997–1998	2D/3D PCI card	ATI Rage, NVIDIA RIVA 128
3rd	1999	2D/3D AGP 1x/2x card	3dfx Voodoo 3, ATI Rage Pro, NVIDIA TnT2
4th	1999–2000	DirectX 7 API, AGP 4x	NVIDIA GeForce 256, ATI Radeon
5th	2001	DirectX 8 API, programmable vertex and pixel shaders	NVIDIA GeForce 3, NVIDIA GeForce 4 Ti
6th	2001–2002	DirectX 8.1 API	ATI Radeon 8500, ATI Radeon 9000
7th	2002–2003	DirectX 9 API, AGP 8x	ATI Radeon 9700, NVIDIA GeForce FX 5900
8th	2004–2005	PCI Express, DirectX 9.0c	ATI X800, NVIDIA GeForce 6800
9th	2004–2006	Dual-GPU rendering with PCI Express x8, x16	ATI X1900, NVIDIA GeForce 7800; ATI CrossFire, NVIDIA nForce SLI motherboard chipsets and compatible cards
10th	2007–present	DirectX 10, Windows Vista	ATI HD 2xxx, NVIDIA GeForce 8 series

With virtually every recent graphics card on the market featuring DirectX 9.0 or greater capabilities, you don't need to spend a fortune to achieve a reasonable level of 3D graphics. Many cards in the $75–$200 range use lower-performance variants of current high-end GPUs, or they might use the previous year's leading GPU. These cards typically provide more-than-adequate performance for 2D business applications. Most current 3D accelerators also support dual-display and TV-out capabilities, enabling you to work and play at the same time.

However, keep in mind that the more you spend on a 3D accelerator card, the greater the onboard memory and faster the accelerator chip you can enjoy. If money is no object, and you are a hardcore gamer, you can buy a 768MB NVIDIA graphics card featuring its fastest GPU for more than $700 (around $900 for a water-cooled version). Fortunately, there are plenty of choices using either NVIDIA or ATI GPUs in the $400–$500 price range that still offer 512MB or more RAM and plenty of 3D gaming performance, including support for dual-GPU operations (NVIDIA SLI or ATI CrossFire), which split rendering chores across the GPUs in both video cards for faster game display than with a single card.

NVIDIA GeForce 8 series and ATI HD 2xxx series GPUs support DirectX 10, and DirectX 10 GPUs are the preferred choice for a serious gamer who wants to play the newest games.

Mid-range cards costing $200–$300 are often based on GPUs that use designs similar to the high-end products but might have slower memory and core clock speeds or a smaller number of rendering pipelines. These cards provide a good middle ground for users who play games fairly often but can't cost-justify high-end cards.

At virtually any price range, from under $100 to the top of the video card heap, you can buy into the latest DirectX 10 3D rendering technology.

Before purchasing a 3D accelerator adapter, you should familiarize yourself with some of the terms and concepts involved in the 3D image generation process.

The basic function of 3D software is to convert image abstractions into the fully realized images that are then displayed on the monitor. The image abstractions typically consist of the following elements:

- **Vertices**—Locations of objects in three-dimensional space, described in terms of their x, y, and z coordinates on three axes representing height, width, and depth.

- **Primitives**—The simple geometric objects the application uses to create more complex constructions, described in terms of the relative locations of their vertices. This serves not only to specify the location of the object in the 2D image, but also to provide perspective because the three axes can define any location in three-dimensional space.

- **Textures**—Two-dimensional bitmap images or surfaces designed to be mapped onto primitives. The software enhances the 3D effect by modifying the appearance of the textures, depending on the location and attitude of the primitive. This process is called *perspective correction*. Some applications use another process, called *MIP mapping*, which uses different versions of the same texture that contain varying amounts of detail, depending on how close the object is to the viewer in the three-dimensional space. Another technique, called *depth cueing*, reduces the color and intensity of an object's fill as the object moves farther away from the viewer.

Using these elements, the abstract image descriptions must then be rendered, meaning they are converted to visible form. Rendering depends on two standardized functions that convert the abstractions into the completed image that is displayed onscreen. The standard functions performed in rendering are

- **Geometry**—The sizing, orienting, and moving of primitives in space and the calculation of the effects produced by the virtual light sources that illuminate the image

- **Rasterization**—The converting of primitives into pixels on the video display by filling the shapes with properly illuminated shading, textures, or a combination of the two

A modern video adapter that includes a chipset capable of 3D video acceleration has special built-in hardware that can perform the rasterization process much more quickly than if it were done by software (using the system processor) alone. Most chipsets with 3D acceleration perform the following rasterization functions right on the adapter:

- **Scan conversion**—The determination of which onscreen pixels fall into the space delineated by each primitive

- **Shading**—The process of filling pixels with smoothly flowing color using the flat or Gouraud shading technique

- **Texture mapping**—The process of filling pixels with images derived from a 2D sample picture or surface image

- **Visible surface determination**—The identification of which pixels in a scene are obscured by other objects closer to the viewer in three-dimensional space

- **Animation**—The process of switching rapidly and cleanly to successive frames of motion sequences

- **Antialiasing**—The process of adjusting color boundaries to smooth edges on rendered objects

Typical 3D Techniques

Typical 3D techniques include the following:

- **Fogging**—Fogging simulates haze or fog in the background of a game screen and helps conceal the sudden appearance of newly rendered objects (buildings, enemies, and so on).

- **Gouraud shading**—Interpolates colors to make circles and spheres look more rounded and smooth.

- **Alpha blending**—One of the first 3D techniques, alpha blending creates translucent objects onscreen, making it a perfect choice for rendering explosions, smoke, water, and glass. Alpha blending also can be used to simulate textures, but it is less realistic than environment-based bump mapping.

- **Stencil buffering**—Stencil buffering is a technique useful for games such as flight simulators in which a static graphic element—such as a cockpit windshield frame, which is known as a heads-up display (HUD) and used by real-life fighter pilots—is placed in front of dynamically changing graphics (such as scenery, other aircraft, sky detail, and so on). In this example, the area of the screen occupied by the cockpit windshield frame is not re-rendered. Only the area seen through the "glass" is re-rendered, saving time and improving frame rates for animation.

- **Z-buffering**—The Z-buffer portion of video memory holds depth information about the pixels in a scene. As the scene is rendered, the Z-values (depth information) for new pixels are compared to the values stored in the Z-buffer to determine which pixels are in "front" of others and should be rendered. Pixels that are "behind" other pixels are not rendered. This method increases speed and can be used along with stencil buffering to create volumetric shadows and other complex 3D objects. Z-buffering was originally developed for computer-aided drafting (CAD) applications.

- **Environment-based bump mapping**—Environment-based bump mapping (standard starting in DirectX 6) introduces special lighting and texturing effects to simulate the rough texture of rippling water, bricks, and other complex surfaces. It combines three separate texture maps (for colors; for height and depth; and for environment, including lighting, fog, and cloud effects). This creates enhanced realism for scenery in games and can also be used to enhance terrain and planetary mapping, architecture, and landscape-design applications. This represents a significant step beyond alpha blending.

- **Displacement mapping**—Special grayscale maps called *displacement maps* have long been used for producing accurate maps of the globe. Microsoft DirectX 9 and 10 support the use of grayscale hardware displacement maps as a source for accurate 3D rendering. GPUs that fully support DirectX 9 and 10 in hardware support displacement mapping.

Advanced 3D Filtering and Rendering

To improve the quality of texture maps, several filtering techniques have been developed, including MIP mapping, bilinear filtering, trilinear filtering, and anisotropic filtering. These techniques and several other advanced techniques found in recent 3D GPUs are explained here:

- **Bilinear filtering**—Improves the image quality of small textures placed on large polygons. The stretching of the texture that takes place can create blockiness, but bilinear filtering applies a blur to conceal this visual defect.

- **MIP mapping**—Improves the image quality of polygons that appear to recede into the distance by mixing low-res and high-res versions of the same texture; a form of antialiasing.

- **Trilinear filtering**—Combines bilinear filtering and MIP mapping, calculating the most realistic colors necessary for the pixels in each polygon by comparing the values in two MIP maps. This method is superior to either MIP mapping or bilinear filtering alone.

Note

Bilinear and trilinear filtering work well for surfaces viewed straight on, but might not work so well for oblique angles (such as a wall receding into the distance).

- **Anisotropic filtering**—Some video card makers use another method, called anisotropic filtering, for more realistically rendering oblique-angle surfaces containing text. This technique is used when a texture is mapped to a surface that changes in two of three spatial domains, such as text found on a wall down a roadway (for example, advertising banners at a raceway). The extra calculations used take time, and for that reason, it can be disabled. To balance display quality and performance, you can also adjust the sampling size: Increase the sampling size to improve display quality, or reduce it to improve performance.

- **T-buffer**—This technology eliminates aliasing (errors in onscreen images due to an undersampled original) in computer graphics, such as the "jaggies" seen in onscreen diagonal lines; motion stuttering; and inaccurate rendition of shadows, reflections, and object blur. The T-buffer replaces the normal frame buffer with a buffer that accumulates multiple renderings before displaying the image. Unlike some other 3D techniques, T-buffer technology doesn't require rewriting or optimization of 3D software to use this enhancement. The goal of T-buffer technology is to provide a movie-like realism to 3D-rendered animations. The downside of enabling antialiasing using a card with T-buffer support is that it can dramatically impact the performance of an application. This technique originally was developed by now-defunct 3dfx. However, it is incorporated into Microsoft DirectX 8.0 and above.

- **Integrated transform and lighting (T&L)**—The 3D display process includes transforming an object from one frame to the next and handling the lighting changes that result from those transformations. T&L is a standard feature of DirectX starting with version 7. The NVIDIA GeForce 256 and original ATI Radeon were the first GPUs to integrate the T&L engines into the accelerator chip, a now-standard feature.

- **Full-screen antialiasing**—This technology reduces the jaggies visible at any resolution by adjusting color boundaries to provide gradual, rather than abrupt, color changes. Whereas early 3D products used antialiasing for certain objects only, recent accelerators from NVIDIA and ATI use various types of highly optimized FSAA methods that allow high visual quality at high frame rates.

- **Vertex skinning**—Also referred to as *vertex blending*, this technique blends the connection between two angles, such as the joints in an animated character's arms or legs.

- **Keyframe interpolation**—Also referred to as *vertex morphing*, this technique animates the transitions between two facial expressions, allowing realistic expressions when skeletal animation can't be used or isn't practical. See the ATI website for details.

- **Programmable vertex and pixel shading**—Programmable vertex and pixel shading became a standard part of DirectX starting with version 8.0. However, NVIDIA introduced this technique with the GeForce3's nfiniteFX technology, enabling software developers to customize effects such as vertex morphing and pixel shading (an enhanced form of bump mapping for irregular surfaces that enables per-pixel lighting effects), rather than applying a narrow range of predefined effects. DirectX 8 and 9-based GPUs use separate vertex and pixel shaders, but DirectX 10 supports a new architecture permitting unified shaders that can perform both vertex and pixel shading on a demand-driven basis.

- **Floating-point calculations**—Microsoft DirectX 9 and above support floating-point data for more vivid and accurate color and polygon rendition. In DirectX 9, vertex shaders used 32-bit precision, while pixel shaders used 24-bit precision. However, Shader Model 3.0 (DirectX 9.0c) increased pixel shader precision to 32-bit, the same precision used by DirectX 10's unified shader design.

Table 13.25 shows when various 3D rendering features were added to DirectX versions from 6.0 to 10.

Table 13.25 3D Rendering Features in DirectX

Feature	DX 6.0	DX 7.0	DX 8.x	DX 9.0	DX 9.0c	DX 10
3D Sky effects	No	Yes	Yes	Yes	Yes	Yes
Smoke and fog effects (volumetric effects)	No	Limited	Yes	Yes	Yes	Yes
Dynamic refraction	No	No	Limited	Yes	Yes	Yes
Transform and Lighting methods	Fixed function in software	Fixed function in hardware	Shader Model 1.0	Shader Model 2.0	Shader Model 3.0	Shader Model 4.0
Bump mapping	No	No	Yes	Yes	Yes	Yes
Texture resolutions	128×128, 256×256	256×256	512×512	512×512	4096×4096	8192×8192
Number of Textures for Pixel Shader	—	—	8	16	4	—
Number of Textures for Vertex Shader	—	—	—	—	16	—
Number of Textures for Unified Shader	—	—	—	—	—	128
Displacement maps resolutions	Low	Medium	Medium to high with bump mapping	High with bump mapping	High with bump mapping	Very high with bump mapping
Appearance of water	Poor	Fair	Good	Excellent	Excellent	Lifelike

Single- Versus Multiple-Pass Rendering

Various video card makers handle application of these advanced rendering techniques differently. The current trend is toward applying the filters and basic rendering in a single pass rather than in multiple passes. Video cards with single-pass rendering and filtering typically provide higher frame-rate performance in 3D-animated applications and avoid the problems of visible artifacts caused by errors in multiple floating-point calculations during the rendering process. Single-pass rendering in standard in DirectX 9 and 10.

Hardware Acceleration Versus Software Acceleration

Compared to software-only rendering, hardware-accelerated rendering provides faster animation. Although most software rendering would create more accurate and better-looking images, software rendering is too slow. Using special drivers, these 3D adapters can take over the intensive calculations needed to render a 3D image that software running on the system processor formerly performed. This is particularly useful if you are creating your own 3D images and animation, but it is also a great enhancement to the many modern games that rely extensively on 3D effects. Note that motherboard-integrated video solutions, such as those listed in Tables 13.13 and 13.14, typically have significantly lower 3D performance than even low-end GPUs because they use the CPU for more of the 3D rendering than 3D video adapter chipsets do.

To achieve greater performance, many of the latest 3D accelerators run their accelerator chips at very high speeds, and many even allow overclocking of the default RAMDAC frequencies. Just as CPUs at high speeds produce a lot of heat, so do high-speed video accelerators. Both the chipset and the memory are heat sources, so most mid-range and high-end 3D accelerator cards feature a fan to cool the chipset. Also, most current high-end 3D accelerators use cooling shrouds and fans to cool the memory chips and make overclocking the video card easier (refer to Figure 13.18).

Software Optimization

It's important to realize that the presence of an advanced 3D-rendering feature on any given video card is meaningless unless game and application software designers optimize their software to take advantage of the feature. Although various 3D standards exist (OpenGL and DirectX), video card makers provide drivers that make their games play with the leading standards. Because some cards do play better with certain games, you should read the reviews in publications such as *Maximum PC* to see how your favorite graphics card performs with them. Typically, it can take several months or longer after a new version of DirectX or OpenGL is introduced before 3D games take full advantage of the 3D rendering features provided by the new API.

Some video cards allow you to perform additional optimization by adjusting settings for OpenGL, Direct 3D, RAMDAC, and bus clock speeds, as well as other options. Note that the bare-bones 3D graphics card drivers provided as part of Microsoft Windows usually don't provide these dialog boxes. Be sure to use the drivers provided with the graphics card or download updated versions from the graphics card vendor's website. Although you can sometimes use generic drivers provided by the GPU vendor, you should use drivers that have been specifically developed for your card to ensure that your card's particular features are fully supported.

Note

If you want to enjoy the features of your newest 3D card immediately, be sure to purchase the individual retail-packaged version of the card from a hardware vendor. These packages typically come with a sampling of games (full and demo versions) designed or compiled to take advantage of the card with which they're sold. The lower-cost OEM or "white box" versions of video cards are sold without bundled software, come only with driver software, and might differ in other ways from the retail advertised product. Some even use modified drivers, use slower memory or RAMDAC components, or lack special TV-out or other features. Some 3D card makers use different names for their OEM versions to minimize confusion, but others don't. Also, some card makers sell their cards in bulk packs, which are intended for upgrading a large organization with its own support staff. These cards might lack individual documentation or driver CDs and also might lack some of the advanced hardware features found on individual retail-pack video cards.

Application Programming Interfaces

Application programming interfaces (APIs) provide hardware and software vendors a means to create drivers and programs that can work quickly and reliably across a wide variety of platforms. When APIs exist, drivers can be written to interface with the API rather than directly with the operating system and its underlying hardware.

Currently, the leading game APIs include SGI's OpenGL and Microsoft's Direct3D (part of DirectX). OpenGL and Direct3D are available for virtually all leading graphics cards. At one time, a third popular game API was Glide, an enhanced version of OpenGL that is restricted to graphics cards that use 3dfx chipsets, which are no longer on the market.

OpenGL

The latest version of OpenGL is version 2.1, released onAugust 2, 2006. OpenGL 2.1 includes the core features of OpenGL 2.0, including the OpenGL shading language (now in revision 1.20), programmable vertex and fragment shaders, multiple render targets, and adds support for non-square matrices, pixel buffer objects, sRGB textures, non-power-of-two textures, point sprites, and separate stencils for the front and back faces of graphics primitives.

Although OpenGL is a popular gaming API, it is also widely used in 3D rendering for specialized business applications, including mapping, life sciences, and other fields. Windows XP and Windows Vista can support OpenGL either through software or through hardware acceleration. For a particular graphics card to support hardware acceleration of OpenGL, the driver developer must include an installable client driver (ICD). The ICD is distributed as part of the driver package provided by the video card or GPU vendor. Thus, driver updates can improve OpenGL performance as well as DirectX (Direct3D) performance.

To learn more about OpenGL, see the OpenGL website at www.opengl.org.

Microsoft DirectX 9.0c and 10

Direct3D is part of Microsoft's comprehensive multimedia API, DirectX. Although the most recent versions of DirectX,, 9.0c and 10 both provide support for higher-order surfaces (converting 3D surfaces into curves), vertex shaders, and pixel shaders, significant differences exist between DirectX versions in how these operations are performed.

DirectX 9.0c, like DirectX 8.0, 8.1, and 9.0, uses separate pixel and vertex shaders to create 3D objects. Although DirectX 9.0c provides greater precision in data handling, support for support for more instructions, more textures, and more registers than its predecessors, its use of separate shaders can still lead to slow 3D rendering when more pixels must be rendered than shaders, or vice versa. Shader Model 3.0 (used by DirectX 9.0c), is simply a development of the split-function design first developed for Shader Model 1 (used by DirectX 8.0) back in 2001, adding support for more instructions and greater numerical accuracy.

DirectX 10, developed for Windows Vista, includes a completely rebuilt Direct3D rendering engine with a brand-new shader design, Shader Model 4.0. Shader Model 4.0 adds a geometry shader to the vertex shader and pixel shader design used in earlier shader models to improve the handling of real-time scene changes such as explosions. However, the biggest single change in Shader Model 4.0 is the use of unified shaders that can be switched between vertex, pixel, and geometry shader operations on-the-fly, eliminating bottlenecks and improving performance, no matter what types of 3D data exist in a scene.

Note

With the replacement of dedicated vertex and pixel shaders in the DirectX 10 3D rendering pipeline, DirectX 10 GPUs are rated in terms of the number of stream processors on board. Each stream processor performs vertex, geometry, and pixel shading as needed.

When comparing two otherwise-equal DirectX 10 GPUs (same GPU, memory size and speed, motherboard and memory bus designs), the GPU with a larger number of stream processors will be faster

Other architectural changes in DirectX 10 include process optimizations to reduce the load on the CPU. In a sample of different types of images rendered, DirectX 10 reduced the command cycles by as much as 90% over DirectX 9.

It's important to realize that DirectX 10 GPUs and Windows Vista retain full compatibility with DirectX 9.0c and earlier DirectX 10 versions, so you can play the latest games as well as old favorites with a DX10-compliant video card. Links to updates for DirectX 9.0c and 10 are provided at www.gamesforwindows.com/en-US/AboutGFW/Pages/DirectX10.aspx.

Note

DirectX 9.0c supports Windows 98 through Windows XP SP1. (It's included in Windows XP SP2.)

Although it's not well known, a version of DirectX 9.0c is integrated into Windows Vista and is used to run the Aero 3D desktop. To keep DirectX updated in both Windows Vista and Windows XP, install the latest DirectX End-User Runtime. Check the system requirements to assure that your version of Windows is supported.

For more information about DirectX 8.0, 8.1 and 9.0, see Chapter 13 of *Upgrading and Repairing PCs, 17th Edition*.

Dual-GPU Scene Rendering

In Table 13.24, I placed the development of dual PCI Express graphics card solutions as the ninth generation of 3D acceleration. The ability to connect two cards together to render a single display more quickly isn't exactly new: The long-defunct 3dfx Voodoo 2 offered an option called *scan-line interfacing (SLI)*, which pairs two Voodoo 2 cards together on the PCI bus with each card writing half the screen in alternating lines. With 3dfx's version of SLI, card number one wrote the odd-numbered screen lines (one, three, five, and so on), while card number two wrote the even-numbered screen lines (two, four, six, and so on). Although effective, use of SLI with Voodoo 2 was an expensive proposition that only a handful of deep-pocketed gamers took advantage of.

A few companies also experimented with using multiple GPUs on a single card to gain a similar performance advantage, but these cards never became popular. However, the idea of doubling graphics performance via multiple video cards has proven too good to abandon entirely, even after 3dfx went out of business.

NVIDIA SLI

When NVIDIA bought what was left of 3dfx, it inherited the SLI trademark and, in mid-2004, reintroduced the concept of using two cards to render a screen under the same acronym. However, NVIDIA's version of SLI has a different meaning and much more intelligence behind it.

NVIDIA uses the term *SLI* to refer to scalable link interface. The *scaling* refers to load-balancing, which adjusts how much of the work each card performs to render a particular scene, depending on how complex the scene is. To enable SLI, the following components are needed:

- **A PCI Express motherboard with an SLI-compatible chipset and two PCI Express video slots designed for SLI operation**—SLI-compatible chipsets include all models in the nForce Professional series, as well as SLI models of the nForce 4 series, nForce 5 series, and nForce 6 series. Versions are available for current Intel and AMD processors.
- **Two NVIDIA-based video cards in the GeForce 8, 7, or 6 series with SLI support**—In most cases, a special bridge device known as a *multipurpose I/O (MIO)* is used to connect the cards to each other. The MIO is supplied with SLI-compatible motherboards, but some SLI-compatible cards don't use it.

Note

Originally, you needed to use two identical cards for NVIDIA SLI. With the introduction of NVIDIA ForceWare v81.85 or higher driver versions, this is no longer necessary. Just as with the ATI CrossFire multi-GPU solution, the cards need to be from the same GPU family (two 8800 Ultras, two 7900 GTs, two 6800LEs, and so on), but they don't need to be from the same manufacturer. You can obtain updated drivers from your video card maker or from the NVIDIA website (www.nvidia.com). To learn more about SLI and for a list of SLI-compatible GPUs and nForce motherboard chipsets, visit NVIDIA's SLI Zone (http://sg.slizone.com).

For best results, SLI should be used with games that have been optimized for SLI. More than 500 games feature SLI support provided by the NVIDIA Control Panel, , and you can also create your own application profiles using the NVIDIA Control Panel.

Figure 13.20 illustrates a typical SLI hardware configuration. Note the MIO device connecting the cards to each other.

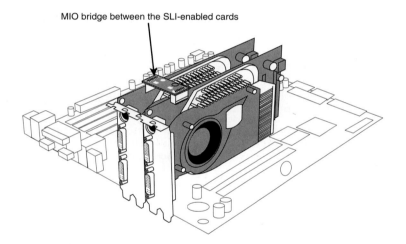

MIO bridge between the SLI-enabled cards

Figure 13.20   How NVIDIA SLI looks in a typical installation.

ATI CrossFire

ATI's CrossFire multi-GPU technology uses three methods to speed up display performance: alternate frame rendering; *supertiling*, which divides the scene into alternating sections and uses each card to render parts of the scene; and load-balancing scissor operation (similar to SLI's load-balancing). The ATI Catalyst driver uses alternate frame rendering for best performance, but automatically switches to one of the other modes for games that don't work with alternate frame rendering.

To achieve better image quality than with a single card, CrossFire offers various SuperAA (antialiasing) modes, which blend the results of antialiasing by each card. CrossFire also improves anisotropic filtering by blending the filtering performed by each card.

To use CrossFire, you need the following components:

■ A PCI Express motherboard with a CrossFire-compatible chipset and two PCI Express video slots designed for CrossFire operation. CrossFire compatible chipsets include AMD 580X and 480X, ATI CrossFire Xpress 3200, and Intel 975X Express and P965 Express.

- A supported combination of ATI CrossFire-supported cards. Cards in the Radeon X850, X1300, X1550, X1600, X1650, X1800, X1900, X1950, HD 2600 XT, and 2900XT support CrossFire.

Note

For specific models of motherboards, video cards, power supplies, memory, and cases designed to support CrossFire, see http://ati.amd.com/technology/crossfire/buildyourown.html

First-generation CrossFire cards required users to buy special CrossFire Edition cards that contained the composting engine (an Xilinx XC3S400 chip) and used a proprietary DMS-59 port for interconnecting the cards. One of these cards was paired with a standard Radeon card from the same series via a clumsy external cable between the CrossFire Edition's DMS port and the DVI port on the standard card. The X1300 and X1600 series use the PCI Express bus to transfer information between the cards.

Current implementations of CrossFire use a CrossFire bridge interconnect (similar in concept to the SLI MIO component) to connect matching cards. The CrossFire Bridge interconnect works with matched pairs of cards in the X1950, X1650, HD 2900 XT, or HD 2600 XT series cards.

CrossFire can be disabled to permit multimonitor operation, and CrossFire cards can also be used to implement physics effects in games that use the HavokFX physics technology (www.havok.com).

For more information about CrossFire, see the AMD website at http://ati.amd.com.

3D Chipsets

Virtually every mainstream video adapter in current production features a 3D acceleration-compatible chipset. With several generations of 3D adapters on the market from the major vendors, keeping track of the latest products can be difficult. Table 13.26 lists the major 3D chipset manufacturers, the various chipsets they make, and the major features of each chipset.

Professional graphics workstation cards and chipsets from vendors such as 3Dlabs (www.3dlabs.com), ATI, and NVIDIA are not listed in Table 13.26 because these cards are not found in standard desktop computers. See the vendors' websites for details about these products.

Note

Table 13.26 is designed to be a reference to recent and current GPUs from AMD (ATI), Matrox, and NVIDIA. Only GPUs that meet fifth -generation (DirectX 8) or newer standards are included. Refer to Table 13.24 for the criteria I use to describe each 3D generation. Because most graphics card vendors now use the GPU name as part of the product name, Table 13.26 does not include product examples. Be sure to use this information in conjunction with application-specific and game-specific tests to help you choose the best card/chipset solution for your needs. Consult the chipset vendors' websites for the latest information about third-party video card sources using a specific chipset.

Most chipsets in Table 13.26 feature some level of dual-display support, typically offering VGA and/or DVI-I, and TV-out. See the specifications for a particular video card to determine which features it implements as well as its memory size and other particulars. See "NVIDIA SLI," (p. 959) and "ATI CrossFire," (p. 960) to determine which chipsets and specific video card models support dual-GPU operation.

Table 13.26   3D Video Chipset Manufacturers and Products

Manufacturer: AMD (ATI)

GPU/ Card (Codename)	DirectX Version	Hard- ware T&L	Number of Pixel Shaders	Number of Vertex Shaders
RADEON 8500 (R200), 8500 LE	8.1	Yes	4	2
RADEON 9000 PRO, 9000 (RV250)	8.1	Yes	4	1
RADEON 9200, SE, std (RV280)	8.1	Yes	4	1
RADEON 9250 (RV280)	8.1	Yes	4	1
RADEON 9500 (R300)	9	Yes	4	4
RADEON 9500 PRO (R300)	9	Yes	8	4
RADEON 9600 PRO, XT, std (RV350)	9	Yes	4	2
RADEON 9600 LE (RV350)	9	Yes	4	2
RADEON 9600XT (RV360)	9	Yes	4	2
RADEON 9700 PRO, 9700 (R300)	9	Yes	8	4
RADEON 9800 PRO, 9800 (R350)	9	Yes	8	4
RADEON 9800 PRO, 9800 std (R350)	9	Yes	8	4
RADEON 9800 SE (R350)	9	Yes	4	4
RADEON 9800XT (R360)	9	Yes	8	4
RADEON X300 SE, X300 (RV370)	9	Yes	4	2
RADEON X550 SE, X550 (RV370)	9	Yes	4	2
RADEON X600 PRO, XT (RV380)	9	Yes	4	2
RADEON X700, PRO, XT (RV410)	9.0b	Yes	8	6
RADEON X800 (R430)	9.0b	Yes	12	6
RADEON X800 SE, GT (R420)	9.0b	Yes	8	6

Number of Rendering Pipelines	Number of Unified Shader (Stream)	Memory Bus	Memory Size and Type	Mfr. Process (microns)	Interface	Notes
4	—	128-bit	64MB, 128MB DDR	.15	AGP 4x	LE is slower
4	—	128-bit	64MB DDR	.15	AGP 8x	Updated 8500 core
4	—	64-bit (SE); 128-bit	128MB, 256MB (AGP)	.15	AGP 8x, PCI	—
4	—	128-bit	128MB, 256MB	.15	AGP 8x	—
4	—	128-bit	128MB DDR	.15	AGP 8x	—
8	—	128-bit	128MB DDR	.15	AGP 8x	
4	—	128-bit	128MB DDR	.13	AGP 8x	
4	—	64-bit	128MB DDR	.13	AGP 8x	
4	—	128-bit	128MB, 256MB DDR	.13	AGP 8x	—
8	—	256-bit	128MB DDR	.15	AGP 8x	AIW
8	—	128-bit	128MB, 256MB DDR	.15	AGP 8x	Pro is faster
8	—	256-bit	128MB DDR (PRO/std), 256MB GDDR2 (PRO)	.15	AGP 8x	Pro is faster
4	—	128-bit, 256-bit	128MB DDR, DDR2 (256-bit)	.15	AGP 8x	
4	—	256-bit	256MB	.15	AGP 8x	—
4	—	64-bit (SE), 128-bit	64MB, 128MB, 256MB DDR or GDDR2	.11	PCIe	
4	—	64-bit (SE), 128-bit	64MB, 128MB, 256MB DDR or GDDR2	.11	PCIe	Faster version of X300 series
4	—	128-bit	128MB,256MB DDR or GDDR2	.13	PCIe	XT is faster version
8	—	128-bit	128MB and 256MB DDR, GDDR2, GDDR3 (PRO, XT)	.11	PCIe	XT fastest, then PRO
12	—	256-bit	128MB and 256MB DDR, GDDR2, GDDR3	.11	PCIe	
8	—	256-bit	256MB DDR, GDDR2, GDDR3	.13	AGP 8x	GT is faster version

Table 13.26   Continued

Manufacturer: AMD (ATI)

GPU/ Card (Codename)	DirectX Version	Hard-ware T&L	Number of Pixel Shaders	Number of Vertex Shaders	Number of Rend-ering Pipelines
RADEON X800 PRO (R423)	9.0b	Yes	12	6	12
X800GTO, GTO2 (R423, R480)	9.0b	Yes	12	6	12
RADEON X800 XT, XT Platinum (R420)	9.0b	Yes	16	6	16
RADEON X800 XT, XT Platinum (R423)	9.0b	Yes	16	6	16
RADEON X800 GT 128, GT 256 (R423, R480)	9.0b	Yes	8	6	8
RADEON X800 XL (R423)	9.0b	Yes	16	6	16
RADEON X800 XL (R430)	9.0b	Yes	12	6	12
RADEON X850 PRO (R480)	9.0b	Yes	12	6	12
RADEON X850 XT, XT PE (R480)	9.0b	Yes	16	6	16
RADEON X850 PRO (R481)	9.0b	Yes	12	6	12
RADEON X850 XT, XT PE (R481)	9.0b	Yes	16	6	12
RADEON X1050 (RV370)	9	Yes	4	2	12
RADEON X1300 (RV515)	9.0c	Yes	4	2	4
RADEON X1300 PRO (RV515)	9.0c	Yes	4	2	4
RADEON X1300 XT (RV535)	9.0c	Yes	12	5	4
RADEON X1550 (RV516)	9.0c	Yes	12	5	4
RADEON X1600 PRO; XT; CrossFire Edition (RV530)	9.0c	Yes	12	5	4
RADEON X1650, PRO, (RV530, RV535) .08 (RV535)	9.0c	Yes	12	5	4
RADEON X1650 XT (RV560) .08 (RV535)	9.0c	Yes	24	8	8
RADEON X1800 GTO (R520)	9.0c	Yes	12	8	12
RADEON X1800 XL, XT,	9.0c	Yes	16	8	16
RADEON X1900 GT (R580)	9.0c	Yes	36	8	12
RADEON X1900 AIW, CF (R580)	9.0c	Yes	48	8	16
RADEON X1900 XTX, XT, CrossFire Edition (R580)	9.0c	Yes	48	8	16

Number of Unified Shader (Stream)	Memory Bus	Memory Size and Type	Mfr. Process (microns)	Interface	Notes
—	256-bit		.13	PCIe	
—	256-bit	128MB, 256MB DDR, GDDR2, GDDR3	.13	PCIe	GTO uses GDDR1 or GDDR2; GTO2 uses GDDR3
—	256-bit	256MB GDDR3	.13	AGP 8x	Platinum runs at faster core, memory clock speeds; AIW
—	256-bit	256MB GDDR3	.13	PCIe	Platinum runs at faster core, memory clock speeds
—	256-bit	128MB, 256MB DDR, GDDR2, GDDR3	.13	PCIe	
—	256-bit	256MB GDDR3	.11	AGP 8x	
—	256-bit	256MB, 512MB GDDR3	.11	PCIe	
—	256-bit	256MB GDDR3	.13	PCIe	
—	256-bit	256MB GDDR3	.13	PCIe	
—	256-bit	256MB GDDR3	.13	AGP 8x	
—	256-bit	256MB GDDR3	.13	AGP 8x	
—	64-bit, 128bit	256MB DDR, DDR2	.11	PCIe, AGP8 8x	
—	64-bit or 128-bit	128MB, 256MB, 512MB	.09	PCIe, AGP 8x, PCI	
—	128-bit	256MB	.09	PCIe PCIe, AGP 8x	
—	128-bit	256MB	.09	PCIe	
—	128-bit	256MB	.09	PCIe, AGP8x, PCI	
—	128-bit	128MB, 256 MB (XT and PRO), 512MB GDDR2, GDDR3 (XT)	.09	PCIe, AGP8x	
—	128-bit	256MB, 512MB GDDR2	.09 (RV530)	PCIe, AGP8x	PRO is faster version
—	128-bit	256MB, 512MB GDDR2	.09 (RV530)	PCIe, AGP8x	PRO is faster version
—	256-bit	256MB GDDR3	.09	PCIe	
—	256-bit	256MB, 512MB (XT only) GDDR3	.09	PCIe	
—	256-bit	256MB GDDR3	.09	PCIe	
—	256-bit	256MB (AIW), 512MB (CF) GDDR3	.09	PCIe	
—	256-bit	512MB	.09	PCIe	XTX has fastest core and memory speed, followed by XT and CrossFire1 Edition

Table 13.26 Continued

Manufacturer: AMD (ATI)

GPU/ Card (Codename)	DirectX Version	Hard-ware T&L	Number of Pixel Shaders	Number of Vertex Shaders	Number of Rend-ering Pipelines
RADEON X1950 GT, PRO (RV570)	9.0c	Yes	36	12	12
RADEON X1950 XT 256, XT 512 (R580)	9.0c	Yes	48	16	48
RADEON X1950 XTX (R580+)	9.0c	Yes	48	16	16
RADEON HD 2400 PRO, XT (RV610)	10	Yes	—	—	4
RADEON HD 2600 PRO, XT (RV630)	10	Yes	—	—	4
RADEON HD 2900 XT (R610)	10	Yes	—	—	16

Manufacturer: Matrox

Millennium P650	8.1	Yes	2	2	2
Millennium P750	8.1	Yes	2	2	2
Parhelia 128MB, 256MB	8.1	Yes	4	4	4
Parhelia APVe	8.1	Yes	4	4	4
Parhelia PCI 256MB	8.1	Yes	4	4	4
Parhelia DL256 PCI	8.1	Yes	4	4	4

Number of Unified Shader (Stream)	Memory Bus	Memory Size and Type	Mfr. Process (microns)	Interface	Notes
—	256-bit	256MB, 512MB GDDR3	.08	PCIe, AGP8x	PRO is faster version
—	256-bit	256MB (XT 256), 512MB (XT 512) GDDR3	.09	PCIe, AGP8x	
—	256-bit	512MB GDDR4	.09	PCIe	
40	64-bit	256MB (DDR2 PRO, GDDR3 XT)	.065	PCIe	
120	128-bit	256MB DDR2 (PRO), GDDR3, GDDR4 (XT)	.065	PCIe	
320	512-bit	512MB, 1024MB GDDR3, GDDR4	.08	PCIe	
—	128-bit	64MB, 128MB DDR	.15	PCIe, AGP 8x, or PCI	TripleHead analog or DualHead digital/analog monitor support
—	128-bit	64MB DDR	.15	AGP 8x or PCIe	TripleHead analog or DualHead digital/analog monitor support
—	256-bit	128MB, 256MB DDR	.15	AGP 8x	Some DirectX 9 features; TripleHead analog or DualHead digital/analog monitor support
—	256-bit	128MB DDR	.15	PCIe	Some DirectX 9 features; TripleHead analog or DualHead digital/analog monitor support
—	256-bit	256MB DDR	.15	PCI 64-bit/66MHz	Some DirectX 9 features; TripleHead analog or DualHead digital/analog monitor support
—	256-bit	256MB DDR	.15	PCI 64-bit/66MHz	Some DirectX 9 features; DualHead analog + digital monitor support

Table 13.26   Continued

Manufacturer: AMD (ATI)

GPU/ Card (Codename)	DirectX Version	Hard- ware T&L	Number of Pixel Shaders	Number of Vertex Shaders	Number of Rend- ering Pipelines
QID	8.1	Yes	4	4	4
QID PRO	8.1	Yes	4	4	4
QID LP PCIe	8.1	Yes	4	4	4
QID LP PCI	8.1	Yes	4	4	4

Manufacturer: NVIDIA

GPU/ Card (Codename)	DirectX Version	Hard- ware T&L	Number of Pixel Shaders	Number of Vertex Shaders	Number of Rend- ering Pipelines
GeForce3, GeForce Ti 200, 500 (NV20)	8	Yes	4	1	4
GeForce4 Ti 4600, 4400, 4200 (NV25)	8	Yes	4	2	4
GeForce4 Ti 4600-8x, 4200-8x (NV28)	8	Yes	4	2	4
GeForce FX 5800 (NV30)	9	Yes	8	1	8
GeForce FX 5600 (NV31)	9	Yes	4	1	4
GeForce FX 5200 (NV34)	9	Yes	4	1	4
GeForce FX 5900 (NV35)	9	Yes	4	1	4
GeForce FX 5700 (NV36)	9	Yes	4	1	4
GeForce FX 5950 Ultra (NV38)	9	Yes	8	1	4
GeForce 6200 (NV43V, NV44)	9.0c	Yes	4	3	2
GeForce 6200 TurboCache (NV44)	9.0c	Yes	4	3	2

Number of Unified Shader (Stream)	Memory Bus	Memory Size and Type	Mfr. Process (microns)	Interface	Notes
—	256-bit	128MB DDR	.15	AGP 4x	Some DirectX 9 features; supports up to four displays
—	256-bit	256MB DDR	.15	PCI 64-bit/ 66MHz	Some DirectX 9 features; supports up to four displays
—	256-bit	128MB DDR	.15	PCIe	Some DirectX 9 features; supports up to four displays
—	256-bit	128MB DDR	.15	PCI	Some DirectX 9 features; supports up to four displays
—	128-bit		.15	AGP 4x	
—	128-bit		.15	AGP 4x	Most 4200 use standard memory; others use faster BGA
—	128-bit		.15	AGP 8x	Based on GeForce 4 Ti 4600 and 4200; dual-display
—	128-bit		.13	AGP 8x	
—	128-bit		.13		
—	128-bit		.13	AGP 8x	
—	256-bit		.13	AGP 8x	Requires two slots for fan
—	128-bit		.13	AGP 8x	Based on FX 5900
—	256-bit		.13	AGP 8x	Requires two slots for fan
—	64-bit or 128-bit	128MB, 256MB, 512MB DDR	.11	PCIe or AGP 8x (64-bit only)	Early PCIe versions based on NV42 core
—	32-bit or 64-bit	16MB, 32MB, 64MB, 128MB DDR	.11	PCIe	16/32MB cards use up to 96MB of system memory for a total of 128MB video RAM; 64/128MB cards use up to 192MB of RAM for a total of 256MB video memory

Table 13.26   Continued

Manufacturer: NVIDIA

GPU/ Card (Codename)	DirectX Version	Hardware T&L	Number of Pixel Shaders	Number of Vertex Shaders	Number of Rendering Pipelines
GeForce 6200 (NV44a)	9.0c	Yes	4	3	2
GeForce 6500 (NV44)	9.0c	Yes	4	4	4
GeForce 6600 LE (NV43)	9.0c	Yes	4	3	4
GeForce 6600, 6610 XL, 6700 XL (NV43)	9.0c	Yes	8	3	8
GeForce 6600, 6600GT (NV43)	9.0c	Yes	8	3	8
GeForce 6800, GS (NV40)	9.0c	Yes	12	5	12
GeForce 6800, GS (NV42)	9.0c	Yes	12	5	12
GeForce 6800 GT, Ultra (NV40)	9.0c	Yes	16	6	16
GeForce 6800 GS, GT, Ultra (NV45)	9.0c	Yes	16	6	16
GeForce 6800 GT (NV42)	9.0c	Yes	16	6	16
GeForce 7100 GS (G70 aka NV47)	9.0c	Yes	4	3	2
GeForce 7200 GS (G72)	9.0c	Yes	2	2	2
GeForce 7300 SE (G72)	9.0c	Yes	2	2	2
GeForce 7300 LE, GS (G72)	9.0c	Yes	4	3	2
GeForce 7500 LE (G72)	9.0c	Yes	2	2	2
GeForce 7300 GT (G73)	9.0c	Yes	8	4	8
GeForce 7600 GS (G73)	9.0c	Yes	12	5	8
GeForce 7600 GT (G73)	9.0c	Yes	12	5	8
GeForce 7800 GT (G70)	9.0c	Yes	20	7	16

Number of Unified Shader (Stream)	Memory Bus	Memory Size and Type	Mfr. Process (microns)	Interface	Notes
—	128-bit	128MB, 256MB DDR or DDR2	.11	AGP 8x or PCI	
—	64-bit	128MB, 256MB DDR	.11	PCIe	Faster version of 6200 series
—	128-bit	128MB, 256MB DDR	.11	AGP 8x or PCIe	
—	128-bit	128MB DDR	.11	PCIe	6700 XL is fastest
—	128-bit	128MB GDDR3	.11	PCIe	
—	256-bit	128MB DDR	.13	AGP 8x	
—	256-bit	128MB DDR	.11	PCIe	
—	256-bit	256MB GDDR3	.13	AGP 8x	Ultra is faster
—	256-bit	256MB GDDR3	.13	PCIe	Uses integrated PCIe bridge; Ultra is faster
—	256-bit	256MB GDDR3	.11	PCIe	Native PCIe
—	64-bit	128MB DDR	.11	PCIe	
—	64-bit	64MB, 128MB, 256MB DDR2	.09	PCIe	
—	64-bit	128MB, 256MB DDR	.09	PCIe	
—	64-bit	128MB, 256MB DDR (LE), DDR2 (GS)	.09	PCIe	
—	64-bit	128MB DDR2	.09	PCIe	OEM product for Hewlett-Packard and Packard Bell; TurboCache uses up to 128MB of system memory below 1GB; up to 384MB of system memory at 1GB or larger
—	128-bit	256MB DDR2, DDR3	.09	PCIe, AGP 8x	
—	128-bit	256MB, 512MB DDR2, DDR3	.09	PCIe, AGP 8x	
—	128-bit	256MB GDDR3	.09, .08	PCIe, AGP 8x (.09 micron only)	.08 micron version is faster
—	256-bit	256MB GDDR3	.11	PCIe	

Table 13.26   Continued

Manufacturer: NVIDIA

GPU/ Card (Codename)	DirectX Version	Hard- ware T&L	Number of Pixel Shaders	Number of Vertex Shaders	Number of Rend- ering Pipelines
GeForce 7800 GTX (G70)	9.0c	Yes	24	8	16
GeForce 7800 GS (G70)	9.0c	Yes	16	6	8
GeForce 7900 GS (G71)	9.0c	Yes	20	7	16
GeForce 7900 GT, GTO (G71)	9.0c	Yes	24	8	16
GeForce 7900 GTX, GTX 512 (G71)	9.0c	Yes	24	8	16
GeForce 7900 GX2 (two G71)	9.0c	Yes	24×2	8×2	16×2
GeForce 7950 GT (G71)	9.0c	Yes	24	8	16
GeForce 7950 GX2 (two G71)	9.0c	Yes	24×2	8×2	16×2
GeForce 8400 GS, GT (G86)	10	Yes	4	—	—
GeForce 8600 GT, GTS (G84)	10	Yes	8	—	—
GeForce 8800 GTS (G80)	10	Yes	20	—	—
GeForce 8800 GTX, Ultra (G80)	10	Yes	24	—	—

CF: Card version that can be paired with a standard Radeon in the same series on a CrossFire-enabled motherboard.

PCIe: PCI Express x16.

TurboCache: Uses portion of system memory to supplement onboard memory

Upgrading or Replacing Your Video Card

If you need more powerful 3D rendering, support for DVI or dual monitors, and faster game performance, replacing your video card is the only way to go. In the current market, you can choose from video cards offering lifelike 3D graphics supporting DirectX 10 and OpenGL 2.1, multiple-monitor support, and massive amounts of display memory (up to 768MB!). However, if you want to use your computer for TV or video capture, you may need to add additional hardware to your PC, such as:

- TV tuners, permitting you to watch cable or broadcast TV on your monitor
- Video capture devices, allowing you to capture still or moving video to a file

In many cases, a single device provides both features.

TV Tuner and Video Capture Upgrades

With a few notable past exceptions, such as ATI's Radeon All-in-Wonder and NVIDIA's Personal Cinema series or cards with VIVO (video-in/video-out ports), most video cards don't have TV tuner or

Number of Unified Shader (Stream)	Memory Bus	Memory Size and Type	Mfr. Process (microns)	Interface	Notes
—	256-bit	256MB GDDR3	.11	PCIe	
—	256-bit	256MB GDDR3	.11	AGP 8x	
—	256-bit	256MB GDDR3	.09	PCIe	
—	256-bit	256MB (GT), 512MB (GTO) GDDR3	.09	PCIe	GTO is faster
—	256-bit	256MB (GTX), 512MB (GTX 512)	.11	PCIe	GTX 512 is faster
—	256-bit ×2	512MB×2 GDDR3	.09	PCI	First GeForce design to use two GPUs; Quad-SLI when used with another 7900 GX2; sold as OEM part only
—	256-bit	256MB, 512MB GDDR3	.09	PCIe, AGP 8x	
—	256-bit×2	512MB×2 GDDR3	.09	PCIe, AGP 8x	
16	64-bit (GS), 128-bit (GT)	256MB DDR2	.08	PCIe	
32	128-bit	256MB GDDR3	.08	PCIe	GTS is faster
96	320-bit	320MB, 640MB	.08	PCIe	
128	384-bit	768MB	.08	PCIe	Ultra is faster

video capture upgrade features built in. This trend is likely to continue. AMD, which owns ATI, for example, has not developed an All-in-Wonder (AIW) card that supports Windows Vista's Media Center features, and apparently has no plans to do so. NVIDIA has not developed any products in its Personal Cinema product line since the GeForce 6 series of GPUs.

If you want to capture analog video from a legacy camcorder or VCR or digital video from a DV camcorder, HD video from broadcast HD video sources, or simply watch TV, you will need a dedicated video capture or TV tuner/video capture card to work alongside your standard 3D video graphics card.

USB 2.0 ports can be used to connect TV tuner and video-capture options compatible with any manufacturer's video card from vendors such as Dazzle, Hauppauge, and others. Because the wide variety of TV and computer hardware on the market can cause compatibility problems with USB TV/capture devices, be sure to check review sites such as http://reviews.cnet.com and www.epinions.com. For HDTV support, look for products compatible with HDTV, such as an HDTV tuner (some plug in to an empty PCI slot, and others plug in to a USB 2.0 port). HDTV tuners enable you to watch HDTV broadcasts on any monitor connected to your PC, including large-screen monitors and projectors.

Warranty and Support

Because a video card can go through several driver changes during its effective lifetime (about 3 years or two operating-system revisions), buying a video card from a major manufacturer usually assures you of better support during the card's lifetime. If you buy a card that uses widely available chipsets (such as NVIDIA's or ATI's), you might be able to try a different vendor's version of drivers or use the chipset vendor's "generic" drivers if you don't get satisfactory support from your card vendor.

Keep in mind that using generic drivers (chipset level) or a different brand of drivers can cause problems if your original card's design was tweaked from the chipset maker's reference design. Look at the vendor's technical support forums or third-party discussions on newsgroups, computer information websites such as ZDNet, or magazine websites to get a feel for the stability, reliability, and usefulness of a vendor's support and driver services. These sources generally also provide alternatives in case of difficulties with a specific brand or chipset. If you use Windows Me, Windows 2000, or Windows XP, make sure you use WHQL-certified drivers for best results. These drivers have been passed by Microsoft's Windows Hardware Quality Labs and might be available through Windows Update or from the vendor's own website. For Windows Vista, make sure you use WDDM drivers that are digitally signed.

Note

With the rise in popularity of Linux, many graphics card and GPU vendors now provide downloadable Linux drivers. Be sure to check compatibility carefully because some vendors customize drivers for different Linux distributions or might provide drivers that work with only certain Linux kernels or XFree86 drivers.

Comparing Video Cards with the Same Chipset

Many manufacturers create a line of video cards with the same chipset to sell at different pricing points. Why not save some dollars and get the cheapest model? Why not say "price is no object" and get the most expensive one? When you're faced with various cards in the "chipset X" family, look for differences such as those shown in Table 13.27.

Table 13.27   Comparing Video Cards with the Same Chipset

Feature	Effect on You
RAMDAC speed	Most current high-end 3D GPUs integrate 400MHz or faster RAMDACs to provide flicker-free resolutions beyond 1280×1024. However, less-expensive cards and older designs often incorporate a slower RAMDAC, which reduces maximum and flicker-free resolutions. If you use a 17" or larger CRT monitor, this could be an eye-straining problem.
Amount of RAM	Although AGP video cards can use AGP memory (a section of main memory borrowed for texturing), performing as much work as possible on the card's own memory is still faster. PCI and PCI Express cards must perform all functions within their own memory. Less expensive cards in a chipset family often have lower amounts of memory onboard, and graphics cards haven't featured expandable memory for several years. Buy a card with enough memory for your games or applications, today and tomorrow; at least 128MB or more for business and 256MB or more for gaming, 3D graphics, and videorelated work. If you plan to upgrade to Windows Vista, consider a video card with 256MB or more and DirectX 10 hardware support to enable you to use the optional Aero GUI and play DirectX 10 games.
Memory type and speed	Virtually all video cards on the market today use GDDR2, GDDR3, or GDDR4 SDRAM. Any of these provide you with high performance in business applications, although GDDR3 or GDDR4 SDRAM is preferable for running high-resolution, high-quality 3D games faster.

Table 13.27   Continued

Feature	Effect on You
Core clock speed	Many suppliers adjust the recommended speed of graphics controllers in an effort to provide users with maximum performance. Sometimes the supplier can choose to exceed the rated specification of the graphics chip. Be cautious: Current controller chips are large and can overheat. An overclocked device in an open system with great airflow might work, or it might fail in a period of months from overstress of the circuitry. If you have questions about the rated speed of a controller, check the chip supplier's website. Many reputable companies do use overclocked parts, but the best vendors supply large heatsinks or powered fans to avoid overheating. Some vendors even provide on-card temperature monitoring.
RAM speed (MHz rating)	Just as faster system RAM improves overall computer performance, faster video card RAM improves video card performance. The higher the MHz rating, the faster the memory. The faster the memory, the faster the card if other components (GPU, shader and pipeline design, and memory bus size) are similar.
TV-out	Once a rare feature, most video cards at all price points now feature TV-out, enabling you to display DVD movies or video games on a big-screen TV. Most use the S-video port, which can be adapted to composite video if your TV or VCR does not have an S-video port. Some of the latest models have hardware-based MPEG-2 compression for higher video quality in less disk space. Some of the latest video cards are now using a VIVO port to support either RCA or S-video inputs on VCRs and TVs.

The speed of the RAMDAC is not the same as the core clock speed of a given graphics card. Even though most current GPUs incorporate the RAMDAC in the GPU, the RAMDAC and the GPU core run at different speeds.

Video Output Devices

When video technology first was introduced, it was based on television. However, a difference exists between the signals used by a television and those used by a computer. In the United States, the National Television System Committee (NTSC) established color TV standards in 1953. Some other countries, such as Japan, followed this standard. Many countries in Europe, though, developed more sophisticated standards, including Phase Alternate Line (PAL) and Sequential Couleur Avec Mémoire (SECAM). Table 13.28 shows the differences among these standards.

Table 13.28   Television Versus Computer Monitors

Standard	Year Est.	Country	Lines	Rate
		Television		
NTSC	1953 (color) 1941 (B&W)	U.S., Japan	525	60 fields/sec
PAL	1941	Europe[1]	625	50 fields/sec
SECAM	1962	France	625	25 fields/sec
HDTV[2]		Various countries	1080p 720p	25 fields/sec 60 frames/sec
NTSC	1953 (color) 1941 (B&W)	U.S., Japan	525	60 fields/sec
PAL	1941	Europe[1]	625	50 fields/sec
SECAM	1962	France	625	25 fields/sec

Table 13.28   Television Versus Computer Monitors

Standard	Year Est.	Country	Lines	Rate
HDTV[2]		Various countries	1080i 1080/720p	25 fields/sec 60 frames/sec
		Computer		
VGA	1987	U.S.	640×480[3]	72Hz

Field = 1/2 (0.5 frame)

1. England, Holland, and West Germany.

2. Various analog and digital HDTV standards have been introduced around the world, starting in France in 1948 (SECAM 755i, a now-discontinued analog version); Japan's analog MUSE 1035i is the oldest system (1979–present) in use. The U.S. standards (both digital) are listed above; other countries use various analog and digital standards.

3. VGA is based on more lines and uses pixels (480) versus lines; genlocking is used to lock pixels into lines and synchronize computers with TV standards.

A video-output (or VGA-to-NTSC) adapter enables you to display computer screens on a TV set or record them onto videotape for easy distribution. These products fall into two categories: those with genlocking (which enables the board to synchronize signals from multiple video sources or video with PC graphics) and those without. Genlocking provides the signal stability necessary to obtain adequate results when recording to tape, but it isn't necessary for using a television as a video display.

VGA-to-NTSC converters are available as internal expansion boards, external boxes that are portable enough to use with a laptop for presentations on the road, and, most commonly today, TV-out ports on the rear of most video cards using chipsets from NVIDIA, ATI, and others. Most VGA-to-TV converters support the standard NTSC television format and might also support the European PAL format. The resolution these devices display on a TV set or record on videotape often is limited to straight VGA at 640×480 pixels, although some TV-out ports on recent video cards can also display 800×600 resolution. The converter also might contain an antiflicker circuit to help stabilize the picture because VGA-to-TV products, as well as TV-to-VGA solutions, often suffer from a case of the jitters.

To connect your PC to an HDTV monitor, use an HDMI cable if your system has an HDMI port. Otherwise, use a DVI-D-to-HDMI adapter or DVI-to-component adapter. If you need HDCP support for watching HD premium content, make sure your display and card support HDCP. Otherwise, you may not be able to watch the program or it may be displayed at reduced resolution.

Video Capture Devices

You can capture individual screen images or full-motion video for reuse in several ways, including

- 3D accelerator cards with TV-in ports
- TV tuner cards
- USB-based devices such as TV tuner/capture devices
- Webcams with video input ports

These units capture still or moving images from NTSC video sources, such as camcorders and VCRs. Although image quality is limited by the input signal, the results are still good enough for presentations and desktop publishing applications. These devices work with VGA cards set for 24-bit or 32-bit color and usually accept video input from VHS, Super VHS, and Hi-8 devices. As you might expect, however, Super VHS and Hi-8 video sources give better results, as do configurations using more than 256 colors. For the best results, use DV camcorders equipped with IEEE 1394 (i.LINK/FireWire) connectors; these can output high-quality digital video direct to your computer without the need to perform an analog-to-digital conversion. If your computer doesn't include an IEEE 1394a or 1394b port, you must install an IEEE 1394 add-in card if you want to capture output from a DV camcorder.

Tip

If you need to convert existing analog video tape to digital format and you also have a DV camcorder (which interfaces via the IEEE 1394 port), check the documentation for your camcorder to see whether it can be used as a passthrough device for analog video. DV camcorders that support passthrough enable you to capture analog video via the 1394 port for better image quality than if you used a USB-based capture device.

HD Video is a new HDTV-compatible video standard that can be captured by HDTV cards with HDMI input ports.

Desktop Video Boards

You can also capture standard or HD television signals to your computer system for display or editing. In other words, you can literally watch TV in a window on your computer. When capturing video, you should think in terms of digital versus analog. In order to edit video, you must capture it, which means it must be converted into digital data stored in a file on your system.

Actually capturing and recording video from external sources and saving the files onto your PC requires special technology. To do this, you need a device called a *video capture board* (also called a TV tuner, video digitizer, or video grabber).

Note

In this context, the technical nomenclature again becomes confusing because the term *video* here has its usual connotation; that is, it refers to the display of full-motion photography on the PC monitor. When evaluating video hardware, be sure to distinguish between devices that capture still images from a video source and those that capture full-motion video streams.

Today, video sources come in two forms:

- Analog
- Digital

Analog video can be captured from traditional sources such as broadcast or cable TV, VCRs, and camcorders using VHS or similar tape standards. This process is much more demanding of storage space and system performance than still images are. Here's why:

The typical computer screen was designed to display mainly static images. The storing and retrieving of these images requires managing huge files. Consider this: A single, full-screen color image in an uncompressed format can require as much as 2MB of disk space; a 1-second video would therefore require 45MB. Likewise, any video transmission you want to capture for use on your PC must be converted from an analog NTSC signal to a digital signal your computer can use. On top of that, the video signal must be moved inside your computer at 10 times the speed of the conventional ISA bus structure. You need not only a superior video card and monitor, but also an excellent expansion bus, such as PCI Express or AGP.

Considering that full-motion video can consume massive quantities of disk space, it becomes apparent that data compression is all but essential. Compression and decompression apply to both video and audio. Not only does a compressed file take up less space, it also performs better simply because less data must be processed. When you are ready to replay the video/audio, the application decompresses the file during playback. In any case, if you are going to work with video, be sure that your hard drive is large enough and fast enough to handle the huge files that can result.

Compression/decompression programs and devices are called *codecs*. Two types of codecs exist: hardware-dependent codecs and software (or hardware-independent) codecs. Hardware codecs typically perform better; however, they require additional hardware—either an add-on card or a high-end video card with hardware codecs built in. Software codes do not require hardware for compression or playback, but they typically do not deliver the same quality or compression ratio. Following are two of the major codec algorithms:

- **JPEG (Joint Photographic Experts Group)**—Originally developed for still images, JPEG can compress and decompress at rates acceptable for nearly full-motion video (30 fps). JPEG still uses a series of still images, which makes editing easier. JPEG is typically lossy (meaning that a small amount of the data is lost during the compression process, slightly diminishing the quality of the image), but it can also be lossless. JPEG compression functions by eliminating redundant data for each individual image (intraframe). Compression efficiency is approximately 30:1 (20:1–40:1).

- **MPEG (Motion Picture Experts Group)**—MPEG by itself compresses video at approximately a 30:1 ratio, but with precompression through oversampling, the ratio can climb to 100:1 and higher, while retaining high quality. Thus, MPEG compression results in better, faster videos that require less storage space. MPEG is an interframe compressor. Because MPEG stores only incremental changes, it is not used during editing phases.

If you will be capturing or compressing video on your computer, you'll need software based on standards such as Microsoft's DirectShow (the successor to Video for Windows and ActiveMovie), Windows Vista and Microsoft Media Foundation, Real Network's Real Producer series, or Apple's QuickTime Pro. Players for files produced with these technologies can be downloaded free from the vendors' websites.

To play or record analog video on your multimedia PC (MPC), you need some extra hardware and software:

- Video system software, such as Apple's QuickTime for Windows or Microsoft's Windows Media Player.

- A compression/digitization video adapter that enables you to digitize and play large video files. When you record an animation file, you can save it in a variety of file formats: AVI (Audio Video Interleave), MOV (Apple QuickTime format), or MPG (MPEG format).

- A TV-out or video-out adapter that connects your system to a VCR or standard TV.

Depending on the video-capture product you use, you have several choices for capturing analog video. The best option is to use component video. Component video uses three RCA-type jacks to carry the luminance (Y) and two chrominance (PR and PB) signals; this type of connector commonly is found on DVD players and high-end conventional and HDTV television sets. However, most home-market video-capture devices usually don't support component video. A typical professional capture and video-editing device designed for component video, such as Pinnacle Systems' Avid Liquid Pro 7, retails for about $1,000.

The next best choice, and one that is supported by many home-market video-capture devices, is the S-video (S-VHS) connector. This cable transmits separate signals for color (chroma) and brightness (luma). Otherwise, you must use composite video, which mixes luma and chroma. This results in a lower-quality signal, and the better your signal, the better your video quality will be.

For capturing TV signals, use a TV tuner with DVR (digital video recorder) capabilities. These devices plug into a USB 2.0 port, PCI, or PCI-Express card slot and contain one or more TV tuners. Some TV tuners include DVR software that enables you to record live TV to your hard disk and pause a broadcast, or you can use the built-in DVR features in Windows XP Media Center Edition or Vista's Media Center. If you want to use the DVR, look for devices that include (or support) a remote control and include access to a TV program guide if you are not using Windows Vista. (Windows Vista Media Center provides access to a TV program guide.)

Until recently, only analog broadcast or cable TV was supported by typical TV tuners, but several vendors are now producing TV tuners that support ATSC (over-the-air HDTV) signals; some support both standard and HDTV signals. Devices that support Clear QAM permit recording of unencrypted cable HDTV signals, and ATI's TV Wonder Digital Cable Tuner supports CableCARD devices used by many cable TV providers for reception of premium HDTV content.

Note

ATI's TV Wonder Digital Cable Tuner is not available as an aftermarket product: It is only available as part of a home media PC because the system BIOS must contain support for digital rights management. For more information, see the AMD website.

TV tuners that provide Windows Vista drivers can be used by Windows Vista's Media Center feature for live TV recording, pausing, and playback on the Vista PC and other PCs and devices throughout the home. Manufacturers of TV tuners include ADS Tech, AMD (ATI), AVerMedia, DVICO, Hauppauge, Macro Image, Pinnacle, Plextor, V-Box, and others.

Note

Some TV tuner devices can also capture S-video and composite video signals, enabling you to use a single device to capture video from TV and from VCRs or analog camcorders.

Table 13.29 provides a breakdown of some common capture devices supporting key features. This table is not inclusive and is meant to serve only as a reference example.

Table 13.29   Video Capture Devices

Device Type	Example
PCI, PCI-Express TV-tuner and PVR	ATI TV Wonder 650
USB TV-tuner and PVR	Hauppauge WinTV-PVR-USB2
USB port video capture	Dazzle Digital Video Creator series
IEEE 1394 (FireWire)	AVerMedia DVD EzMaker

Figure 13.21 shows a typical PCI-Express TV tuner and video capture card: the ATI TV Wonder 650 PCI-Express from AMD. This example featuresa PCI-Express x1 interface, but other TV tuner cards use the PCI interface.

Each type of device has advantages and potential disadvantages. Table 13.30 provides a summary that will help you decide which solution is best for you.

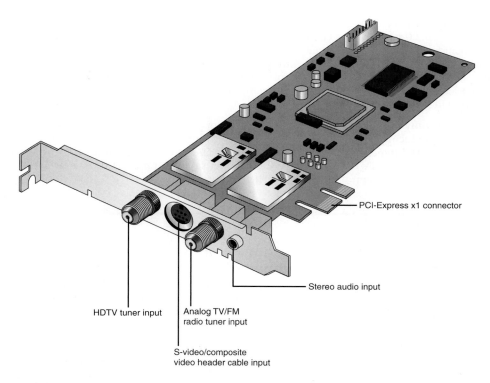

PCI-Express x1 connector

Stereo audio input

HDTV tuner input

Analog TV/FM
radio tuner input

S-video/composite
video header cable input

Figure 13.21 ATI's TV Wonder 650 PCI-Express plugs into a PCI-Express x1 slot and provides analog TV, FM radio, S-video, composite video, stereo audio, and HDTV inputs. A multihead AV input cable and remote control are also included. *Photo courtesy of Advanced Micro Devices.*

Table 13.30 Multimedia Device Comparison

Device Type	Pros	Cons
Graphics card with built-in TV tuner and capture	Convenience; single-slot solution.	Upgrading requires card replacement. Latest GPUs from ATI and NVIDIA not supported.
TV-tuner card	Allows upgrade to existing graphics cards; might be movable to newer models.	PCI-based versions might not support latest HDTV standards; PCI-Express versions not compatible with older systems.
USB port attachment	Easy installation and transfer between different computers; USB 2.0–compatible devices fast enough for high-quality video.	Must use USB 2.0 (Hi-Speed USB) port for adequate performance. Some devices don't support hardware encoding.
IEEE 1394 (FireWire)	No conversion from analog to digital; all-digital image is very high digital video source; high image quality without compressions artifacts; can be used for analog transfer via a DV camcorder with analog video passthrough.	Requires IEEE 1394 port, IEEE 1394 connection to digital video; uses PCI slot (desktop); CardBus or ExpressCard slot (laptop) for installation; not compatible with analog TV source. May require separate software purchase for video capture.

Troubleshooting Video Capture Devices

Table 13.31 provides some advice for troubleshooting problems with video-capture devices. Note that IRQ conflicts can be an issue with both parallel port and add-on card devices and that low-bandwidth devices such as parallel port or USB devices might not be capable of supporting full-motion video capture except in a small window.

Table 13.31   Troubleshooting Video Capture Devices

Device Type	Problem	Solutions
TV tuners	No picture or poor-quality picture.	Check cabling. Set signal source correctly in software. Update software. For Windows XP Media Center Edition or Windows Vista Media Center, check device compatibility and install latest drivers. On devices with multiple coaxial inputs, assure that correct signal source is connected to each input. Use an amplified TV antenna. Aim antenna for better reception of HDTV signals.
All devices	Video capture is jerky.	Frame rate is too low. Increasing it might require capturing video in a smaller window; use faster CPU and increase RAM to improve results. Verify USB ports are configured as Hi-Speed (USB 2.0) ports if you use USB 2.0 devices. Use video-capture devices with hardware rendering.
All devices	Video playback has pauses, dropped frames.	Hard disk might be pausing for thermal recalibration; use AV-rated SCSI hard drives, UDMA EIDE drives or SATA drives; install correct busmastering EIDE drivers for motherboard chipset and make sure UDMA mode is enabled for ATA/IDE ports to improve speed. Reinstall video playback software. Update device drivers. Use video-capture devices with hardware rendering.
USB devices	Device can't be detected or doesn't work properly.	If you use a USB hub, be sure it's self-powered; make sure USB 2.0 port is configured to operate in Hi-Speed mode; use USB 2.0-compatible devices; update drivers; use a USB 2.0 hub for USB 2.0 and USB 1.1 devices
Interface cards (all types)	Card can't be detected or doesn't work.	Check for IRQ conflicts in Windows Device Manager; move card to different slot if possible; make sure additional power is provided for card if card requires it.
IEEE 1394 cards	Card can't be detected or doesn't work.	Make sure power connector is attached to card if card has 4-pin power jack. Make sure correct drivers are installed.
All devices	Capture or installation problems.	Use the newest drivers available for your operating system; check manufacturers' website for updates, FAQs, and so on. Check cables. For external devices, check AC power source.

Adapter and Display Troubleshooting

Solving most graphics adapter and monitor problems is fairly simple, although costly, because replacing the adapter or display is the normal procedure. However, before you take this step, be sure you have exhausted all your other options. One embarrassingly obvious fix to monitor display problems that is often overlooked by many users is to adjust the controls on the monitor, such as contrast and brightness. Although most recent CRT and LCD monitors use front-mounted controls with onscreen display (OSD), other adjustments might be possible as well.

Some NEC CRT monitors, for example, have a focus adjustment screw on the left side of the unit. Because the screw is deep inside the case, the only evidence of its existence is a hole in the plastic grillwork on top of it. To adjust the monitor's focus, you must stick a long-shanked screwdriver about 2" into the hole and feel around for the screw head. This type of adjustment can save you both an expensive repair bill and the humiliation of being ridiculed by the repair technician. Always examine the monitor case, documentation, and manufacturer's website or other online services for the locations of adjustment controls.

A defective or dysfunctional adapter or display usually is replaced as a single unit rather than being repaired. Except for specialized CAD or graphics workstation-oriented adapters, virtually all of today's adapters cost more to service than to replace, and the documentation required to service the hardware properly is not always available. You usually can't get schematic diagrams, parts lists, wiring diagrams, and other documents for most adapters or monitors. Also, virtually all adapters now are constructed with surface-mount technology that requires a substantial investment in a rework station before you can remove and replace these components by hand. You can't use a $25 pencil-type soldering iron on these boards!

Servicing monitors is a slightly different proposition. Although a display often is replaced as a whole unit, some displays—particularly 20" or larger CRTs or most LCD panels—might be cheaper to repair than to replace. If you decide to repair the monitor, your best bet is to either contact the company from which you purchased the display or contact one of the companies that specializes in monitor depot repair. If your CRT monitor has a 15" diagonal measurement or less, consider replacing it with a unit that is 17" or larger because repair costs on small monitors come close to replacement costs and large monitors aren't much more expensive these days.

Depot repair means you send in your display to repair specialists who either fix your particular unit or return an identical unit they have already repaired. This usually is accomplished for a flat-rate fee; in other words, the price is the same no matter what they have done to repair your actual unit.

Because you usually get a different (but identical) unit in return, they can ship out your repaired display immediately upon receiving the one you sent in, or even in advance in some cases. This way, you have the least amount of downtime and can receive the repaired display as quickly as possible. In some cases, if your particular monitor is unique or one they don't have in stock, you must wait while they repair your specific unit.

Troubleshooting a failed monitor is relatively simple. If your display goes out, for example, a swap with another monitor can confirm that the display is the problem. If the problem disappears when you change the display, the problem is almost certainly in the original display or the cable; if the problem remains, it is likely in the video adapter or PC itself.

Many of the better quality, late-model monitors have built-in self-diagnostic circuitry. Check your monitor's manual for details. Using this feature, if available, can help you determine whether the problem is really in the monitor, in a cable, or somewhere else in the system. If self diagnostics produce an image onscreen, look to other parts of the video subsystem for your problem.

The monitor cable can sometimes be the source of display problems. A bent pin in the connector that plugs in to the video adapter can prevent the monitor from displaying images, or it can cause color shifts. Most of the time, you can repair the connector by carefully straightening the bent pin with sharp-nosed pliers. A loose cable or DVI/VGA adapter can also cause color shifts; tighten the cable and adapter securely.

If the pin breaks off or the connector is otherwise damaged, you can sometimes replace the monitor cable. Some monitor manufacturers use cables that disconnect from the monitor and video adapter, whereas others are permanently connected. Depending on the type of connector the device uses at the monitor end, you might have to contact the manufacturer for a replacement.

If you narrow down the problem to the display, consult the documentation that came with the monitor or call the manufacturer for the location of the nearest factory repair depot. Third-party depot repair service companies are also available that can repair most displays (if they are no longer covered by a warranty); their prices often are much lower than factory service. Check the Vendor List on the disc for several companies that do depot repair of computer monitors and displays.

Caution

You should *never* attempt to repair a CRT monitor yourself. Touching the wrong component can be fatal. The display circuits can hold extremely high voltages for hours, days, or even weeks after the power is shut off. A qualified service person should discharge the cathode-ray tube and power capacitors before proceeding.

For most displays, you are limited to making simple adjustments. For color displays, the adjustments can be quite formidable if you lack experience. Use the OSD controls to adjust color, brightness, picture size, and other settings. To quickly adjust an LCD, try the auto-tune feature available on many models. Even factory service technicians often lack proper documentation and service information for newer models; they usually exchange your unit for another and repair the defective one later. Never buy a display for which no local factory repair depot is available.

If you have a problem with a display or an adapter, it pays to call the manufacturer, who might know about the problem and make repairs available. Sometimes, when manufacturers encounter numerous problems with a product, they might offer free repair, replacements, or another generous offer that you would never know about if you did not call.

Remember, also, that many of the problems you might encounter with modern video adapters and displays are related to the drivers that control these devices rather than to the hardware. Be sure you have the latest and proper drivers before you attempt to have the hardware repaired; a solution might already be available.

Troubleshooting Monitors

Problem

No picture.

Solution

If the LED on the front of the monitor is yellow or flashing green, the monitor is in power-saving mode. Move the mouse or press Alt+Tab on the keyboard and wait up to 1 minute to wake up the system if the system is turned on.

If the LED on the front of the monitor is green, the monitor is in normal mode (receiving a signal), but the brightness and contrast are set incorrectly; adjust them.

If no lights are lit on the monitor, check the power and power switch. Check the surge protector or power director to ensure that power is going to the monitor. Replace the power cord with a known-working spare if necessary. Retest. Replace the monitor with a known-working spare to ensure that the monitor is the problem.

Check data cables at the monitor and video card end.

Problem

Jittery picture quality.

Solution

LCD monitors. Use display-adjustment software or onscreen menus to reduce or eliminate pixel jitter and pixel swim caused by running the digital LCD display with an analog (VGA) video source. Use the DVI connector instead of the VGA connector if both the display and the video card support DVI to avoid digital-analog-digital conversion problems like these.

All monitors. Check cables for tightness at the video card and the monitor (if removable):

- Remove the extender cable and retest with the monitor plugged directly into the video card. If the extended cable is bad, replace it.
- Check the cables for damage; replace as needed.
- If problems are intermittent, check for interference. (Microwave ovens near monitors can cause severe picture distortion when turned on.)

CRT monitors. Check refresh-rate settings; reduce them until acceptable picture quality is achieved:

- Use onscreen picture adjustments until an acceptable picture quality is achieved.
- If problems are intermittent and can be "fixed" by waiting or gently tapping the side of the monitor, the monitor power supply is probably bad or has loose connections internally. Service or replace the monitor.

Troubleshooting Video Cards and Drivers

Problem

Display works in DOS (command-prompt mode) but not in Windows.

Solution

If you have an acceptable picture quality in MS-DOS mode (system boot) but no picture in Windows, most likely you have an incorrect or corrupted video driver installed in Windows. Boot Windows 9x/Me in Safe Mode (which uses a VGA driver), boot Windows 2000/XP/Vista in Enable VGA mode, or install the VGA driver and restart Windows. If Safe Mode or VGA Mode works, get the correct driver for the video card and reinstall.

If you have overclocked your card with a manufacturer-supplied or third-party utility, you might have set the speed too high. Restart the system in Safe Mode and reset the card to run at its default speed. If you have adjusted the speed of AGP/PCI/PCI-Express slots in the BIOS setup program, restart the system, start the BIOS setup program, and reset these slots to run at the normal speed.

Problem

Can't replace built-in video card with add-on PCI, AGP, or PCI Express video card.

Solution

Check with the video card and system vendor for a list of acceptable replacement video cards. Try another video card with a different chipset. Check the BIOS or motherboard for jumper or configuration settings to disable built-in video. Place the add-on card in a different PCI slot. Be sure the card is fully inserted into the slot.

Problem

Can't select desired color depth and resolution combination.

Solution

Verify that the card is properly identified in Windows and that the card's memory is working properly. Use diagnostic software provided by the video card or chipset maker to test the card's memory. If the hardware is working properly, check for new drivers. Use the vendor's drivers rather than the ones provided with Windows.

Problem

Can't select desired refresh rate.

Solution

Verify that the card and monitor are properly identified in Windows. Obtain updated drivers for the card and monitor.

Problem

Can't adjust OpenGL or Direct3D (DirectX) settings.

Solution

Install the graphic card or chipset vendor's latest drivers instead of using the drivers included with Microsoft Windows. Standard Microsoft drivers often don't include 3D or other advanced dialog boxes.

Problem

Can't enable secondary monitor.

Solution

If you are using a dual-head graphics card, make sure the secondary monitor has been enabled in the manufacturer's driver. This might require you to open the Advanced settings for your driver. If you are using two video cards in an SLI (NVIDIA) or CrossFire (ATI) configuration, you must disable SLI or CrossFire before you can enable additional monitors. If you are using an AGP and a PCI video card in separate slots, check the BIOS configuration for primary VGA BIOS. Change the current setting and restart the system. Update video card drivers.

Problem

Can't enable SLI operation.

Solution

Make sure the MIO (SLI bridge) device is properly installed between your video cards (refer to Figure 13.20). If you are not using identical video cards, you must use NVIDIA ForceWare v81.85 or new drivers to enable SLI operation. Make sure both cards use the same GPU family as discussed in "NVIDIA SLI," p. 959. Make sure SLI operation is enabled in the ForceWare driver.

Problem

Can't enable CrossFire operation.

Solution

If you use the Radeon X800, X850, or X1800 card, make sure you have paired up a CrossFire Edition and standard Radeon card from the same GPU family. Also, make sure you have properly connected the CrossFire Edition and standard card to each other via the DMS and DVI ports.

If you use later-model cards that use a CrossFire bridge interconnect, make sure the interconnect is properly attached to both cards. Make sure you are using pairs of cards with the same GPU as discussed in "ATI CrossFire," p. 960.

Update ATI CATALYST display drivers to the latest production version. Be sure you have enabled CrossFire in your display driver.

Problem

Can't enable Aero 3D desktop in Windows Vista.

Solution

Make sure your video card or integrated video is running a WDDM (Windows driver display model) driver and supports DirectX 9.0 or later. Update the driver if the hardware can support Aero. Update the card if the card does not have WDDM drivers available.

DisplayMate

DisplayMate is a unique diagnostic and testing program designed to thoroughly test your video adapter and display. It is somewhat unique in that most conventional PC hardware diagnostics programs do not emphasize video testing the way this program does.

I find it useful not only in testing whether a video adapter is functioning properly, but also in examining video displays. You easily can test the image quality of a display, which allows you to make focus, centering, brightness and contrast, color level, and other adjustments much more accurately than before. If you are purchasing a new monitor, you can use the program to evaluate the sharpness and linearity of the display and to provide a consistent way of checking each monitor you are considering. If you use projection systems for presentations—as I do in my PC hardware seminars—you will find it invaluable for setting up and adjusting the projector.

DisplayMate also can test a video adapter thoroughly. It sets the video circuits into each possible video mode so you can test all its capabilities. It even helps you determine the performance level of your card, both with respect to resolution and colors as well as speed. You can then use the program to benchmark the performance of the display, which enables you to compare one type of video adapter system to another. The Video Edition also supports various types of multimedia projectors and TVs used in home theater and presentation environments.

For more information on DisplayMate (formerly Sonera) Technologies, visit www.displaymate.com.

Some video-card vendors supply a special version of DisplayMate for use in diagnostics testing.

Audio Hardware

Since the first edition of this book was published in 1988, a lot has happened to audio hardware. Although rudimentary audio capabilities were part of the original IBM PC of 1981 and its many successors, audio was used on early computers for troubleshooting rather than for creative tasks. Computers used beeps for little other than to signal problems such as a full keyboard buffer or errors during the power-on self test (POST) sequence. The Macintosh, first introduced in 1984, included high-quality audio capabilities in its built-in hardware, but PCs did not gain comparable audio capabilities until the first add-on sound cards from companies such as Ad Lib and Creative Labs were developed in the late 1980s.

Thanks to competition among many companies, we now enjoy widely supported de facto hardware and software standards for audio. Audio hardware has gone from being an expensive, exotic add-on to being an assumed part of virtually any system configuration.

Today's PC audio hardware might take one of the following forms:

- An audio adapter on a PCI expansion card that you install into a bus slot in the computer.

- An AC'97 sound codec chip located on the motherboard, using sound chips from companies such as Crystal, Analog Devices, Sigmatel, ESS, or others.

- Hardware that's integrated into the motherboard's main chipset. Intel, SiS, NVIDIA, AOpen, and VIA have all released products in this category at one point or another.

Regardless of their location, the audio features use jacks for speakers and a microphone. In addition, many of them provide dedicated jacks for MIDI hardware (older cards usually provided an analog game port for joysticks). As you will see later in this chapter, many mid-range and high-end audio adapters also support sophisticated digital audio input and output. On the software side, the audio adapter requires the support of a driver that you install either directly from an application or in your computer's operating system. This chapter focuses on the audio products found in today's PCs, their uses, and how you install and operate them.

Early PC Audio Adapters

When the first audio adapters were introduced in the late 1980s by companies such as AdLib, Roland, and Creative Labs, they were aimed squarely at a gaming audience, were not compatible with each other, and often cost more than $100.

Note

About the same time as the release of the Creative Labs Game Blaster, hardware supporting the Musical Instrument Digital Interface (MIDI) became available for the PC. At this time, however, such hardware was used only in very specialized recording applications. As MIDI support became a more common feature in musical instruments, though, it also became a more affordable PC add-on.

The Game Blaster, which was compatible with only a handful of games, was soon replaced by the Sound Blaster, which was compatible with the AdLib sound card and the Creative Labs Game Blaster card, enabling it to support games that specified one sound card or the other. The Sound Blaster included a built-in microphone jack, stereo output, and a MIDI port for connecting the PC to a synthesizer or other electronic musical instrument. This established a baseline of features that would be supported by virtually all other sound cards and onboard sound features up to the present. Finally, the audio adapter had the potential for uses other than games. The follow-up Sound Blaster Pro featured improved sound when compared to the original Sound Blaster. The Sound Blaster Pro and its successors eventually triumphed over earlier rivals to become de facto standards for PC sound reproduction.

Note

Unlike de jure standards such as the IEEE-1394 port, which is an official standard of the IEEE organization, de facto standards are those that develop informally due to the widespread acceptance of the market leader's products in a particular segment of the marketplace. The Sound Blaster Pro is just one of many examples of a de facto standard: IBM's VGA card became a de facto baseline standard for video, and HP and Apple's different printer languages (HP PCL and Adobe PostScript) became de facto standards for printers.

Limitations of Sound Blaster Pro Compatibility

Through the mid-1990s, while MS-DOS was the standard PC gaming platform, many users of non–Creative Labs sound cards struggled with the limitations of their hardware's imperfect emulation of the Sound Blaster Pro. Unfortunately, some cards required two separate sets of hardware resources, using one set of IRQ, DMA, and I/O port addresses for native mode and a second set for Sound Blaster Pro compatibility. Others worked well within Windows or within an MS-DOS session running with Windows in the background but required the user to install a DOS-based Terminate and Stay Resident (TSR) driver program to work in MS-DOS itself.

However, the rise of 32-bit Windows games has made audio support very simple by comparison. Windows applications use the operating system's drivers to interface with hardware, relieving the software developer from needing to write different code for different sound cards, 3D graphics cards, and so on. For 3D sound and gaming graphics, Microsoft Windows uses a technology called DirectX, which was first introduced in December 1995. Currently, Microsoft supports two distinct families of DirectX: DirectX 9.0c for Windows XP and DirectX 10 for Windows Vista.

DirectX and Audio Adapters

Microsoft's DirectX is a series of application programming interfaces (APIs) that sits between multimedia applications and hardware. Unlike MS-DOS applications, which required developers to develop direct hardware support for numerous models and brands of audio cards, video cards, and game controllers, Windows applications use DirectX to "talk" to hardware in a more direct manner than normal Windows drivers do. This improves program performance and frees the software developer from the need to change the program to work with different devices. Instead, a game developer must work with only the DirectX sound engine, DirectX 3D renderer, and other DirectX interface routines.

Historically, DirectX has meant that sound card and chipset developers are assured that their products will work with recent and current versions of Windows. However, changes in how DirectX audio works in DirectX 10, which is supported only in Windows Vista, are causing special challenges for audio vendors.

▶▶ For more information about DirectX and sound hardware, see "3D Audio," p. 1007.

Legacy Audio Support Through Virtualization

What about legacy software users? If you still enjoy playing MS-DOS-based games, then current audio adapters, chipsets, and integrated audio solutions still might present a compatibility challenge to you because of fundamental hardware differences between the ISA expansion slots used by classic Creative Labs and other sound cards and PCI slots, chipsets, and integrated audio.

At one time, the only way to achieve reliable audio compatibility with legacy games was to use a legacy operating system such as MS-DOS 6.x (with Windows 3.1 if needed) and a Sound Blaster Pro-compatible ISA audio card. This has become impossible because the ISA bus has been removed from recent designs. Some early PCI audio sound cards provided fairly good emulation of the Sound Blaster Pro but required additional audio drivers or proprietary patch cables to provide emulation. Modern audio hardware is geared toward supporting Windows and often is not capable of providing legacy audio support if a legacy application is run directly in a modern operating system such as Windows XP or Windows Vista.

However, you can now run legacy operating systems and applications with full support for legacy audio by creating a virtual PC environment using applications such as Microsoft Virtual PC 2007 (for Windows XP Professional, Tablet, and some editions of Windows Vista), Parallels Desktop (Mac OS running on Intel-based systems), VMWare Workstation (Windows, Linux, FreeBSD, Solaris), and others.

In a virtual PC environment, you create a virtual machine on a host operating system by installing a virtualization application. Next, install a guest operating system into the virtual machine, configure it to provide audio support, and install legacy games. The virtual machine translates audio and other hardware requests made by the legacy game and operating system to the host operating system, which then communicates with the hardware it supports. As a result, a legacy game running in an MS-DOS virtual machine "thinks" that a Sound Blaster Pro or similar sound card is available, even though the audio is actually being played by a modern Sound Blaster Audigy X-Fi, host-based audio, or 'AC 97 audio codec. You hear sound effects and music playback generated by the game just as you would if the game were being run on a system with legacy audio hardware.

PC Multimedia History

Virtually every computer on the market today is equipped with some type of audio adapter and optical drive such as a CD-RW or DVD drive. Computers equipped with an audio adapter and a CD-ROM-compatible drive are often referred to as *multimedia* PCs after the old MPC-1, MPC-2, and MPC-3 standards that were used to rate early multimedia computers. Since 1996, all computers with onboard sound and a CD-ROM or compatible optical drive have exceeded MPC-3 standards by increasingly huge margins.

Note

For more information about the MPC series of multimedia standards, see the section "Multimedia" in Chapter 20 of *Upgrading and Repairing PCs, 11th Edition.*

Because the MPC specifications reflect multimedia's past, users who want to know what comes next need to turn somewhere else for guidance. Microsoft and Intel have jointly produced a series of PC System Design Guides. Although the PC System Design Guide's last version is known as PC 2001 and no further updates are planned, it and its predecessor (PC 99) are still useful references for multimedia hardware and software design and are still widely followed by the industry. For example, most I/O ports on recent systems use the PC 99 color-coding standard.

Note

You can download the PC 2001 and earlier PC System Design Guides from Microsoft's website at http://www. microsoft.com/whdc/system/platform/pcdesign/desguide/pcguides.mspx.

Updated Microsoft-specific system design information is available at http://www.microsoft.com/whdc/system/platform/ pcdesign/desguide/default.mspx.

Although virtually every computer is a "multimedia PC" today, the features of the audio adapter or onboard audio solution in your system will help determine how satisfied you will be with the wide range of specialized uses for multimedia-equipped systems.

Later in this chapter, you learn more about the features you need to specify to ensure your audio adapter—regardless of type—is ready to work for you.

Audio Adapter Features

To make an intelligent purchasing decision, you should be aware of some audio adapter basic components and the features they provide, as well as the advanced features you can get on better audio adapters. The following sections discuss the features you should consider while evaluating audio adapters for your PC.

Basic Connectors

Most audio adapters have the same basic external connectors. These 1/8" minijack connectors provide the means of passing sound signals from the adapter to speakers, headphones, and stereo systems, and of receiving sound from a microphone, CD player, tape player, or stereo. Laptop computers with integrated audio often include only two jacks: stereo line out and line in. However, sound cards and motherboards with integrated audio often include additional jacks for supporting 5.1 or 7.1 surround audio and digital audio.

Figure 14.1 shows a typical arrangement of external and internal audio jacks on a sound card, and Figure 14.2 shows typical external audio jacks on a motherboard with integrated audio.

The jacks shown in Figure 14.1 and 14.2 are usually labeled, but when you're setting up a computer on or under a desk, the labels on the back of the PC can be difficult to see. One of the most common reasons a PC fails to produce any sound is that the speakers are plugged into the wrong socket. To avoid this problem, many consumer-oriented audio cards color-code the jacks according to specifications found in the PC 99 Design Guide available from the Microsoft website. The color-coding can vary on some audio adapters (or not be present at all).

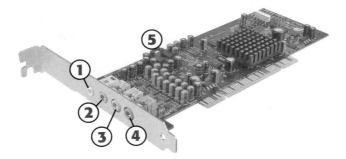

1. FlexiJack (white; provides line-in, microphone-in, or optical digital out; software controlled)
2. Stereo line out (green)
3. Rear audio out (grey; supports 5.1, 6.1 and 7.1 configurations)
4. Subwoofer/center audio out (orange; supports 5.1, 6.1, and 7.1 configurations)
5. Aux audio (black; receives audio from sources such as internal TV tuners).

Figure 14.1 Typical input and output jacks on a typical sound card (the Creative Labs Sound Blaster X-Fi XtremeGamer).

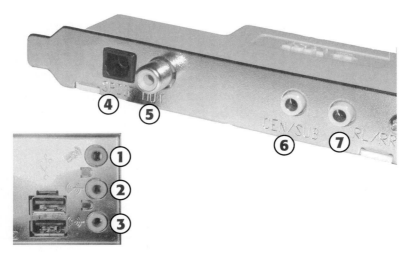

1. Microphone in (pink)
2. Line in (blue)
3. Stereo speaker out (lime green)
4. SPDIF optical out (black)
5. SPDIF coaxial out (yellow)
6. Subwoofer/center audio out (lime green; supports 5.1 surround configuration)
7. Rear audio out (lime green; supports 5.1 surround configuration)

Figure 14.2 Typical input and output jacks on a typical motherboard with 5.1 surround audio support. The SPDIF and surround audio ports on this motherboard are located on a plug-in header cable that uses an expansion slot.

A second method used on many recent systems with motherboard-based audio is universal audio jack sensing, a feature of the AC'97 version 2.3 audio standard. When a device is plugged into an audio jack, the audio driver pops up a dialog asking the type of audio device in use, such as microphone, stereo speakers, stereo headphones, and so on. The audio driver dynamically assigns the jack to support the device plugged in, even if the "wrong" device is being used in a jack according to the color-coding. This feature is sometimes referred to as auto-sensing.

Tip

To avoid confusing the jack sensing feature, plug each device into the audio jacks separately and be sure to confirm the device type in the configuration program before continuing.

Regardless, the basic set of connections included on most audio cards and onboard audio include the following:

- **Stereo line out, or audio out connector (lime green)**—The line-out connector is used to send sound signals from the audio adapter to a stereo device outside the computer. You can hook up the cables from the line-out connector to stereo speakers, a headphone set, or your stereo system. If you hook up the PC to your stereo system, you can have amplified sound. As shown in Figure 14.2, some systems use the same lime-green color for surround audio jacks as for the stereo/headphone jack. Check additional markings on the jacks or your system documentation for help.

- **Stereo line, or audio, in connector (light blue)**—With the line-in connector, you can record or mix sound signals from an external source, such as a stereo system or VCR, to the computer's hard disk. Some sound cards, such as the Creative Labs Sound Blaster X-Fi Xtreme Gamer card shown in Figure 14.1, use a multipurpose jack (Creative calls it a "FlexiJack") to support line-in, optical out, or microphone in or line-in, microphone, and digital optical-in in place of a dedicated line-in jack. See the audio card or motherboard documentation for details.

- **Rear out and subwoofer/center or speaker connectors (no standard color)**—Virtually all modern sound cards and desktop systems with integrated audio include jacks that support rear, center, and subwoofer output for use in 5.1 and greater surround audio systems. Systems that support 5.1 audio use three jacks: one for front (stereo) audio, one for rear audio, and one for center/subwoofer audio. Systems that support 6.1 or 7.1 audio might feature additional jacks or might reassign rear and center/subwoofer jacks with software to provide additional output. Depending upon your software driver, you might need to run a proprietary setup program to enable surround audio, or selecting the surround audio setup you use through your operating system's speaker configuration utility might be sufficient.

Note

If you have only a single speaker/line-out connector, you must carefully adjust your mixer volume control and the volume control on your amplified speakers to find the best quality sound. Don't use powered speakers with an already-amplified sound if you can avoid it.

- **Microphone, or mono, in connector (pink)**—The mono-in connector is used to connect a microphone for recording your voice or other sounds to disk. This microphone jack records in mono—not in stereo—and is therefore not suitable for high-quality music recordings. To record in stereo, use the line-in jack. Many audio adapter cards use Automatic Gain Control (AGC) to improve recordings. This feature adjusts the recording levels on-the-fly. A 600ohm–10,000ohm dynamic or condenser microphone works best with this jack. Some inexpensive audio adapters use the line-in connector instead of a separate microphone jack. Some sound cards use a multipurpose jack in place of a dedicated microphone jack.

In addition to the external connections, some older sound cards featured at least one (and possibly multiple) internal CD-audio connectors. This is a 4-pin connector you can use to plug an internal optical drive directly into the audio adapter, using a small round cable. This connection enables the drive to send analog audio signals from the disc directly to the audio adapter, so you can play the sound through the computer's speakers. Some sound cards use a different connector than the CD-ROM, whereas others use the same type of connector as the CD-ROM.

Note

See Figure 14.7, later in this chapter, for an example of a typical sound card with analog and digital audio cables attached.

To play audio CDs, you have two choices: The playback can be either analog or digital. Analog playback is supported via an analog audio cable connected between the drive and sound card. This cable does not carry data from the CD-ROM to the system bus; it connects the analog audio output of the CD-ROM drive directly to the audio amplifier in the sound card. This cable connection was necessary on many older drives and legacy audio solutions to enable music CD or game audio playback.

Recent drives, audio cards, and integrated audio solutions support digital playback as well as direct analog connection. To determine if you can use digital audio playback, open the properties sheet for your CD or DVD drive in Device Manager and click the Properties tab. Look for a checkbox in the Digital CD Playback portion of the tab. If the box is grayed out (meaning you can't check it), digital audio is not supported for that drive or card.

Using digital audio enables multiple drives to play audio CDs. Typically, a sound card has only a single analog audio connector, so if you have multiple optical drives, only one can have an analog audio connection to the sound card for playing audio CDs. If you want to play audio CDs on multiple drives, you must either enable digital CD audio for those drives or purchase a CD audio Y-cable. By either enabling digital audio or installing an analog audio cable, you should be able to play audio CDs with any given CD/DVD drive.

Note

Most modern audio player programs, such as Windows Media Player, can perform digital audio playback without using the two-wire digital audio cable between the CD-ROM drive and sound card. Instead, these programs read the CD music tracks and convert them on-the-fly into digital form.

Connectors for Advanced Features

Many of the newest sound cards and motherboards with onboard sound are designed for advanced gaming, DVD audio playback, or sound production and have additional connectors to support these uses, such as the following:

- **MIDI in and MIDI out**—Older sound cards with game ports (a 15-pin female connector) also supported MIDI in and MIDI out through adapters that plugged into the game port. With current high-end sound cards, MIDI ports are located on a proprietary I/O port adapter that slides into a 5.25-inch drive bay or sits on the tabletop (see Figure 14.3).

- **SPDIF (also called S/PDIF) in and SPDIF out**—The Sony/Philips Digital Interface receives digital audio signals directly from compatible devices without converting them to analog format first. The SPDIF out interface might be built into the sound card using a dedicated or multipurpose jack. Some motherboards include an SPDIF out jack on the rear port cluster, while others, such as the one shown in Figure 14.2, use a plug-in header cable to provide output. SPDIF ports may also be included on drive bay or external I/O port adapters (see Figure 14.3).

Note

SPDIF interfaces are also referred to by some vendors as "Dolby Digital" interfaces. SPDIF connectors use cables with the standard RCA jack connector but are designed to work specifically at an impedance of 75ohms—the same as composite video cables. Thus, you can use RCA-jack composite video cables with your SPDIF connectors. Although audio cables are also equipped with RCA jacks, their impedance is different, making them a less desirable choice.

- **CD SPDIF**—A two-wire connection that interfaces compatible CD-ROM drives with SPDIF output to the digital input of the sound card. Typical location: side of audio card. See Figure 14.7, later in this chapter, for an example of a typical sound card using a CD SPDIF cable.

- **TAD in**—Connects internal modems with Telephone Answering Device support to the sound card for sound processing of voice messages. Typical location: side of audio card.

- **Optical SPDIF in/out**—This supports home theater and digital speaker systems with optical inputs. Typical locations: rear of card or external device (see Figure 14.3). Motherboard-based audio solutions may include optical SPDIF out on the port cluster or on a header cable that uses an expansion slot, as in Figure 14.2.

- **Aux in**—Provides input for other sound sources, such as a TV tuner card. Typical location: side of audio card (refer to Figure 14.1).

Sometimes these additional connectors are found on the card itself, or sometimes they are attached to an internal or external breakout box, daughtercard, or external rack. Among others, the Platinum family of Audigy and X-Fi sound cards from Creative are two-piece units. Although details vary from card to card, most two-piece models feature a PCI-based sound card with basic I/O ports and a separate internal or external component with additional and more advanced I/O ports. The Creative X-Fi Fatal1ty, for example, routes its additional connections to an internal breakout box that fits into an unused 5 1/4" drive bay (see Figure 14.3). The Creative X-Fi Elite Pro, on the other hand, uses an external breakout box with the same connection options.

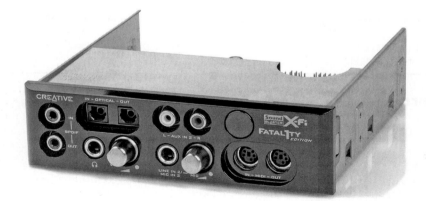

Figure 14.3   The Creative Sound Blaster X-Fi Fatal1ty's internal breakout box provides support for MIDI in/out, coaxial and digital SPDIF in/out, convenient volume control knobs, stereo out, headphone out and line-in jacks, and support for an IR remote control. *Photo courtesy of Creative Technology Ltd.*

Adding Advanced Sound Features Without Replacing Onboard Audio

If you use a laptop computer or an all-in-one desktop computer that lacks expansion slots, or don't want to open your system to perform an audio upgrade, you can now install USB-based audio processors.

When you consider a USB-based solution, keep in mind that, unlike a normal sound card upgrade, you don't need to disable your existing onboard sound or remove a sound card. USB-based audio can coexist with existing sound cards. Typically, as with most hardware, the most recently installed hardware in a category becomes the default, but you can switch back to the original audio hardware through the Windows Control Panel Sound properties sheet.

Beyond the ability to add audio to almost any recent system, USB-based audio is particularly appealing if your current sound card or onboard audio doesn't support 5.1 or 7.1 audio, can't digitize sound at 24-bit/96KHz rates, or lacks digital outputs. Table 14.1 lists the major features of current and recent USB-based audio products.

Table 14.1   USB-Based Audio Processors

Manufacturer	Product	Output Quality	Recording Quality	Speaker Support	Notes
Audiotrak	MAYA EX	16-bit/48KHz	16-bit/48KHz	Up to 5.1	Dolby Digital AC-3
Audiotrak	MAYA EX7	16-bit/48KHz	16-bit/48KHz	Up to 7.1	Dolby Digital AC-3
Creative Labs	Sound Blaster Extigy	24-bit/96KHz	16-bit/48KHz	Up to 5.1	Dolby Digital AC-3
Creative Labs	Sound Blaster MP3+	16-bit/48KHz	16-bit/48KHz	2.1	Optical SPDIF input/output
Creative Labs	Xmod	24-bit/96KHz	N/A	2.1	Upconverts 16-bit CD and compressed audio to 24-bit quality
Creative Labs	Audigy 2 NX	24-bit/96KHz	24-bit/96KHz	Up to 7.1	Dolby Digital AC-3, EX; supports Hi-Speed USB
Creative Labs	Audigy 2 ZS Notebook	24-bit/ 192KHz	24-bit	Up to 7.1	—
Hercules	Gamesurround MUSE Pocket	16-bit/ 48KHz	16-bit/ 48KHz	Up to 5.1	No SPDIF connector
M-Audio	Sonica	24-bit/96KHz	N/A	Up to 5.1	Dolby Digital AC-3 with optical output only
M-Audio	Sonica Theater	24-bit/96KHz	24-bit/96KHz	Up to 7.1	Dolby Digital AC-3
Philips Aurilium	PSC805	24-bit/96KHz	N/A	Up to 5.1	Dolby Digital AC-3; supports Hi- Speed USB
TerraTec	Aureon 5.1 USB	16-bit/48KHz	16-bit/48KHz	Up to 5.1	Dolby Digital AC-3
Turtle Beach	Audio Advantage Micro	16-bit/48KHz	N/A	Up to 5.1 (passthrough)	Dolby Digital AC-3; DTS
Turtle Beach	Audio Advantage Amigo	6-bit/ 148KHz	16-bit/ 48KHz	Up to 5.1 (passthrough)	Dolby Digital AC-3; DTS
Turtle Beach	Audio Advantage SRM	16-bit/ 48KHz	16-bit/ 48KHz	Up to 7.1	Dolby Digital AC-3; DTS

The connectors and controls on the Creative Labs Sound Blaster Audigy 2 NX are shown in Figure 14.4.

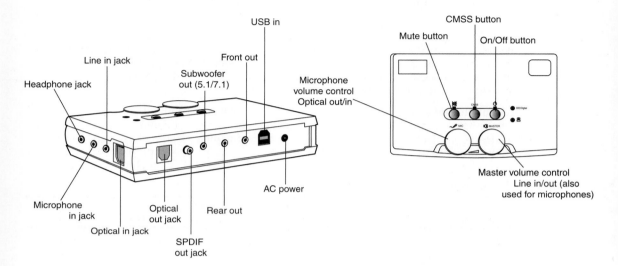

Figure 14.4   The Sound Blaster Audigy 2 NX expands bare-bones onboard audio by adding advanced I/O and sampling features similar to those found on the Sound Blaster Audigy 2 series.

TIP

Before you purchase a new sound card or USB-based audio solution for a desktop computer, you should check your system or motherboard documentation to see whether you already have six-channel audio onboard. If your motherboard features six-channel (5.1) or better audio output but the only ports built into the rear of the motherboard are for a normal stereo (2.0/2.1) configuration, you need to add a header cable to the motherboard similar to the one shown in Figure 14.2. If the motherboard did not ship with the header cable, contact the vendor.

Volume Control

With virtually all recent sound cards, the volume is controlled through a Windows Control Panel speaker icon that can also be found in the system tray (near the onscreen clock). If you're switching from a bare-bones stereo sound card to a more sophisticated one featuring Dolby Digital 5.1, 6.1, or 7.1 output or input, you will need to use the mixing options in the volume control to select the proper sources and appropriate volume levels for incoming and outgoing audio connected to the card or a breakout box. Keep in mind that if you are sending sound to an external audio receiver, you will need to adjust the volume on that device as well. Don't forget to enable digital output if you are using the SPDIF output jack.

If the PC speakers are amplified but you aren't hearing any sound, remember to check that the power is on, the volume control on the speakers is turned up, and the correct speakers are selected and properly connected.

MIDI Support Features

At one time, when evaluating audio adapters, you had to decide whether to buy a monophonic or stereophonic card. Today, all audio adapters are stereophonic and can play music using the MIDI standard, which plays scores using either synthesized instruments or digital samples stored on the audio adapter or in RAM.

Stereophonic cards produce many voices concurrently and from two sources. A voice is a single sound produced by the adapter. A string quartet uses four voices, one for each instrument. On the other hand, a polyphonic instrument, such as a piano, requires one voice for each note of a chord. Thus, fully reproducing the capabilities of a pianist requires 10 voices—one for each finger. The more voices an audio adapter is capable of producing, the better the sound fidelity. The best audio adapters on the market today can produce up to 1,024 simultaneous voices.

Early audio adapters used FM synthesis for MIDI support; the Yamaha OPL2 (YM3812) featured 11 voices, whereas the OPL3 (YMF262) featured 20 voices and stereophonic sound. However, virtually all audio adapters today use recorded samples for MIDI support; audio adapters using this feature are referred to as *wavetable* adapters.

Wavetable audio adapters use digital recordings of real instruments and sound effects instead of imitations generated by an FM chip. When you hear a trumpet in a MIDI score played on a wavetable sound card, you hear the sound of an actual trumpet, not a synthetic imitation of a trumpet. The first cards featuring wavetable support stored 1MB of sound clips embedded in ROM chips on the card or on an optional daughtercard. However, with the ascension of the PCI bus for sound cards and large amounts of RAM in computers, most soundcards adopted a so-called "soft wavetable" approach, loading 2MB–8MB of sampled musical instruments into the computer's RAM.

Whereas early games supported only digitized audio samples (because most early sound cards had very poor MIDI support), late DOS games such as *DOOM* began to exploit the widespread wavetable-based MIDI support found on most mid-1990s and more recent sound cards. With all current sound hardware supporting wavetable MIDI and the improvements in DirectX 8.x and above for MIDI support, MIDI sound has become far more prevalent for game soundtracks. Many websites also offer instructions for patching existing games to allow MIDI support. Whether you play the latest games or like music, good MIDI performance is likely to be important to you.

The most important factor for high-performance MIDI is the number of hardware voices. Even the best sound cards, such as Creative Labs' Sound Blaster X-Fi series, support only 128 voices in hardware; the remainder of the voices required by a MIDI soundtrack must come from software. If your sound card supports only 32 MIDI voices in hardware or uses software synthesis only, consider replacing it with a newer model. Many of the models currently on the market support more than 500 simultaneous voices and 64 hardware voices for under $50.

Data Compression

Virtually all audio adapters on the market today can easily produce CD-quality audio, which is sampled at 44.1KHz. At this rate, recorded files (even of your own voice) can consume more than 10MB for every minute of recording. To counter this demand for disk space, many audio adapters include their own data-compression capability. For example, the Sound Blaster series includes on-the-fly compression of sound files in ratios of 2:1, 3:1, and 4:1.

Most manufacturers of audio adapters use an algorithm called *Adaptive Differential Pulse Code Modulation (ADPCM) compression* (it's also called IMA-ADPCM), which was developed by the Interactive Multimedia Association (IMA) to reduce file size by more than 4:1. IMA-ADPCM compresses 16-bit linear samples down to 4 bits per sample. However, a simple fact of audio technology is that when you use such compression, you lose sound quality. Unfortunately, no standard exists for the use of ADPCM. For example, although both Apple and Microsoft support IMA-ADPCM compression, they implement it in different ways. Apple's standard AIFF and Microsoft's standard WAV file formats are incompatible with each other unless you use a media player that can play both.

When you install an audio adapter, several codecs (programs that perform compression and decompression) are installed. Typically, some form of ADPCM is installed along with many others. To see which codecs are available on your system, open the Windows Control Panel and open the Multimedia icon (Windows 9x), the Sounds and Multimedia icon (Windows 2000), or the Sounds and Audio Devices icon (Windows XP). In Windows 9x, click the Devices tab followed by the plus sign next to Audio Compression to see the installed codecs. In Windows 2000 and Windows XP, click the Hardware tab, followed by Audio Codecs and Properties. The codecs are listed in order of priority, highest to lowest. You can also change the priority if you prefer a different order of priority.

In Windows Vista, finding the codec information is more difficult. To see installed codecs, open Windows Media Player, Show Classic Menus, click Help, About Windows Media Player, and click the Technical Support Information link. Scroll down to see audio codecs.

If you create your own recorded audio for use on another computer, both computers must use the same codec. You can select which codec you want to use for recording sounds with most programs, including the Windows Sound Recorder (up through Windows XP; the Windows Vista Sound Recorder does not offer the option to select the codec).

The most popular compression standard is the Motion Pictures Experts Group (MPEG) standard, which works with both audio and video compression and is gaining support in the non-PC world from products such as DVD players. MPEG by itself provides a potential compression ratio of 30:1, and largely because of this, full-motion-video MPEG DVD and CD-ROM titles are now available. The popular MP3 sound compression scheme is an MPEG format, and it can be played back on most versions of the Windows Media Player, as well as by various other audio player programs and devices.

Multipurpose Digital Signal Processors

Many audio adapters use digital signal processors (DSPs) to add intelligence to the adapter, freeing the system processor from work-intensive tasks such as filtering noise from recordings and compressing audio on-the-fly. The DSP can be upgraded with software downloads to accommodate more simultaneous audio streams. The widespread use of DSPs in better-quality audio adapters enables you to upgrade them through software instead of the time-consuming, expensive process of physical replacement. For a list of DSPs and their developers, see the section "Who's Who in Audio," later in this chapter.

Sound Drivers

As with many PC components, a software driver provides a vital link between an audio adapter and the application or operating system that uses it. Operating systems such as Windows 9x/Me and Windows 2000/XP/Vista include a large library of drivers for most of the audio adapters on the market (Windows NT 4.0 also supports some sound hardware but not as much as other versions of Windows). In most cases, these drivers are written by the manufacturer of the audio adapter and distributed only by Microsoft. You might find that the drivers that ship with the adapter are more recent than those included with the operating system. Although traditionally the best place to find the most recent drivers for a piece of hardware has been the manufacturer's own website or other online service, Windows Me and newer prefer digitally signed drivers that have been certified by the Microsoft Hardware Quality Labs. You might find these drivers available at the vendor's own website, but you can also download and install them automatically through Windows Update.

Older ISA Sound Blaster cards provided hardware support for DOS games, but modern models (including the Sound Blaster Audigy and X-Fi series), as well as most comparable sound cards, require you to run software drivers to obtain Sound Blaster compatibility for DOS games. This software must be run before the game starts. If you use a virtualization environment to run MS-DOS and games, you set up the virtual PC as if you have a Sound Blaster Pro card, and the virtualization environment takes care of the translation necessary to enable the game's audio to play properly.

If your game program locks up when you try to detect the sound card during configuration, set the card type and settings manually. This is often a symptom of inadequate emulation for Sound Blaster by a third-party card. If you have problems, check the game developer's or audio adapter's website for patches or workarounds.

Note

Support for the classic Sound Blaster Pro standard and 15-pin game port were once the primary requirements for a good gaming audio adapter. However, with the rise of great Windows-based games, the development of DirectX, and the replacement of game ports by USB ports, these are no longer issues for many users.

If you need to play MS-DOS games or work with game ports, see Chapter 16 of *Upgrading and Repairing PCs, 15th Anniversary Edition,* to learn about compatibility considerations.

Sound Cards for Sound Producers

Sound producers are people who intend to create their own sound files. These can range from casual business users recording low-fidelity voice annotations to professional musicians and MIDI maniacs. These users need an adapter that can perform as much of the audio processing as possible itself, so they don't place an additional burden on the system processor. Adapters that use digital signal processors (DSPs) to perform compression and other tasks are highly recommended in this case. Musicians will certainly want an adapter with as many voices as possible and a wavetable synthesizer. Adapters with expandable memory arrays and the capability to create and modify custom wavetables are also preferable.

Many of the best sound cards for hard-core gamers can also be made suitable for sound producers by adding the appropriate sound-editing programs, such as Sound Forge, and by equipping the card with the appropriate connectors for SPDIF digital audio and MIDI interfaces. The Sound Blaster X-Fi Platinum includes an internal breakout box with these features. The Creative Labs Audigy 2 NX and other USB devices with 24-bit/96KHz sampling provide similar features but can be added to any system with a USB port. Creative's Sound Blaster X-Fi Elite Pro is the next step and is a great sound card for sound producers. Capable of recording at 96KHz and with playback at up to 192KHz, the card includes three usage modes that allow you to customize your experience:

- **Creation mode**—This mode is ideal for music recording and creation.
- **Gaming mode**—This mode optimizes gaming performance and realism.
- **Entertainment mode**—This mode is configured specifically for listening to music and watching movies.

If you need to edit or output multiple audio sources, you need a sound card designed to handle multiple I/O sources. Some products in this category include M-Audio's Delta and Audiophile series cards, Creative's E-Mu/Creative Professional cards, and others. These products often include an external breakout box.

Note

The Recording Review website at http://www.recordingreview.com is an outstanding resource for researching advanced sound cards and other audio hardware designed specifically for audio production.

Audio Adapter Concepts and Terms

To fully understand audio adapters and their functions, you need to understand various concepts and terms. Terms such as 16-bit, 24-bit CD quality, and MIDI port are just a few. Concepts such as sampling and digital-to-audio conversion (DAC) are often sprinkled throughout stories about new sound products. You've already learned about some of these terms and concepts; the following sections describe many others.

The Nature of Sound

To understand an audio adapter, you must understand the nature of sound. Every sound is produced by vibrations that compress air or other substances. These sound waves travel in all directions, expanding in balloon-like fashion from the source of the sound. When these waves reach your ear, they cause vibrations that you perceive as sound.

Two of the basic properties of any sound are its pitch and intensity.

Pitch is the rate at which vibrations are produced. It is measured in the number of hertz (Hz), or cycles per second. One cycle is a complete vibration back and forth. The number of Hz is the frequency of the tone; the higher the frequency, the higher the pitch.

Humans can't hear all possible frequencies. Very few people can hear sounds with frequencies less than 16Hz or greater than about 20KHz (kilohertz; 1KHz equals 1000Hz). In fact, the lowest note on a piano has a frequency of 27Hz, and the highest note has a frequency a little higher than 4KHz. Frequency-modulation (FM) radio stations can broadcast notes with frequencies as high as 15KHz.

The amazing compression ratios possible with MP3 files, compared to regular CD-quality WAV files, is due in part to the discarding of sound frequencies that are higher or lower than normal hearing range during the ripping process.

The intensity of a sound is called its *amplitude*. This intensity determines the sound's volume and depends on the strength of the vibrations producing the sound. A piano string, for example, vibrates gently when the key is struck softly. The string swings back and forth in a narrow arc, and the tone it sends out is soft. If the key is struck more forcefully, however, the string swings back and forth in a wider arc, producing a greater amplitude and a greater volume. The loudness of sounds is measured in decibels (db). The rustle of leaves is rated at 20db, average street noise at 70db, and nearby thunder at 120db.

Evaluating the Quality of Your Audio Adapter

The quality of an audio adapter is often measured by three criteria: frequency response (or range), total harmonic distortion, and signal-to-noise ratio.

The *frequency response* of an audio adapter is the range in which an audio system can record or play at a constant and audible amplitude level. Many cards support 30Hz–20KHz. The wider the spread, the better the adapter.

The *total harmonic distortion* measures an audio adapter's linearity and the straightness of a frequency response curve. In layman's terms, the harmonic distortion is a measure of accurate sound reproduction. Any nonlinear elements cause distortion in the form of harmonics. The smaller the percentage of distortion, the better. This harmonic distortion factor might make the difference between cards that use the same audio chipset. Cards with cheaper components might have greater distortion, making them produce poorer-quality sound.

The *signal-to-noise ratio (S/N or SNR)* measures the strength of the sound signal relative to background noise (hiss). The higher the number (measured in decibels), the better the sound quality. For example, the top-of-the-line Sound Blaster X-Fi Elite Pro delivers pristine 136dB SNR audio playback quality as compared to the Audigy 2 sound card (106db) or the older Sound Blaster Audigy (100db).

These factors affect all types of audio adapter use, from WAV file playback to speech recognition. Keep in mind that low-quality microphones and speakers can degrade the performance of a high-quality sound card.

Sampling

With an audio adapter, a PC can record waveform audio. Waveform audio (also known as *sampled* or *digitized sound*) uses the PC as a recording device (like a tape recorder). Small computer chips built into the adapter, called *analog-to-digital converters (ADCs)*, convert analog sound waves into digital bits that the computer can understand. Likewise, digital-to-analog converters (DACs) convert the recorded sounds to an audible analog format.

Sampling is the process of turning the original analog sound waves into digital (binary) signals that the computer can save and later replay (see Figure 14.5). The system samples the sound by taking snapshots of its frequency and amplitude at regular intervals. For example, at time X the sound might be measured with an amplitude of Y. The higher (or more frequent) the sample rate, the more accurately the digital sound replicates its real-life source and the larger the amount of disk space needed to store it.

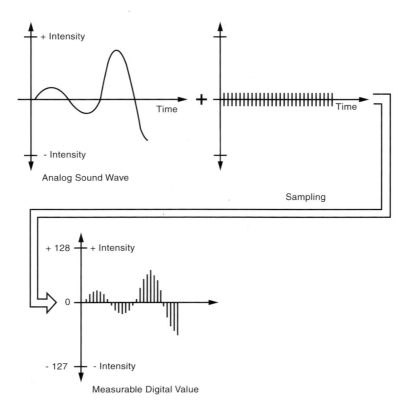

Figure 14.5 Sampling turns a changing sound wave into measurable digital values.

Originally, sound cards used 8-bit digital sampling, which provided for only 256 values (2^8) that could be used to convert a sound. More recently, sound cards have increased the quality of digitized sound by using 16-bit (2^{16}) sampling to produce 65,536 distinct values. Today's highest-quality sound cards feature 24-bit sampling (2^{24}), which translates into more than 14.8 million possible digital values that can be matched to a given sound.

Note

For more information on the differences between 8-bit and 16-bit audio sampling, see "8-Bit Versus 16-Bit," in Chapter 16 of *Upgrading and Repairing PCs, 13th Edition.*

You can experiment with the effects of various sampling rates (and compression technologies) by recording sound with the Windows Sound Recorder (in Windows XP or earlier versions; Windows Vista's Sound Recorder does not permit selection of different sampling rates) or a third-party application set to CD-quality sound. Save the sound and play it back at that highest-quality setting. Then convert the file to a lower-quality setting, and save the sound file again with a different name. Play back the various versions, and determine the lowest quality (and smallest file size) you can use without serious degradation to sound quality.

Who's Who in Audio

Because audio adapters are found in virtually all systems, many vendors have produced audio adapters, audio chips, integrated motherboard chipsets with audio features, and even specialized vacuum tube audio. This section examines some of these companies and their products.

As you've learned in other chapters, I believe it is very important to get all the technical information you can about your computer and its components. By knowing who makes the audio chip your computer depends on, you can find out what the hardware can do and be better able to find upgrades to the software drivers you need to get the most out of your audio hardware.

Chipset Makers Who Make Their Own Audio Adapters

Just as graphics card vendors are divided into two camps, chipset makers are divided into these two categories:

- Card and device makers who produce their own chipsets
- Card and device makers who use chipsets from other vendors

Audio adapter vendors fall into the same categories. One of the pioneers of the audio adapter business, Creative (formerly known as Creative Labs), has also been among the leaders in developing audio chips. Creative develops audio chips primarily for its own Sound Blaster–branded products, but it has sold some of its older Sound Blaster 16 products into OEM markets.

Creative's major audio chips have included the following:

- **Vibra-16**—This was used in the later Sound Blaster 16 cards; it doesn't support wavetable or 3D effects.
- **Ensoniq ES137x series (ES1370/71/73)**—These were used in the Sound Blaster PCI64 and PCI 128 series as well as the Ensoniq Audio PCI and Vibra PCI series. They support soft wavetable features, four speakers on some models, and Microsoft Direct 3D, but don't support 3D acceleration or EAX positional audio.

- **EMU-8000**—This audio chip was used by the AWE32/64 series and features 32-voice wavetable synthesis but no 3D acceleration. The AWE64 used software to generate 32 additional voices for a total of 64 voices.

- **EMU10K1**—This audio chip was at the heart of the Live! and Live 5.1 series sound cards as well as the PCI 512; it features 3D acceleration, EAX positional audio for one audio stream, a reprogrammable DSP, and soft wavetable support.

- **EMU10K2 (also known as Audigy)**—This is the audio chip at the heart of Creative's Sound Blaster Audigy series sound cards; it features 3D acceleration, EAX HD positional audio for up to four audio streams, a reprogrammable DSP, and soft wavetable support. This chip supports professional-level 24-bit sampling at 96KHz and real-time Dolby Digital–quality 24-bit samples at 48KHz.

- **CA0102 (also known as Audigy 2)**—This audio chip is the one used by Creative's Audigy 2 series. It's a development of the EMU10K2 chip, adding support for 24-bit 96KHz output, Dolby Digital EX 6.1 decoding and 6.1 sound in DirectX games, and 64 hardware polyphonic voices.

- **CA0185**—This audio chip is used by the Sound Blaster MP3+. It features 2.1 audio support for analog and digital speakers, 48KHz/16-bit playback and recording, and 3D acceleration.

- **CA0186**—This audio chip is used by the Audigy 2 NX. It features Dolby Digital EX 7.1 decoding, 7.1 sound in DirectX games, 96KHz/24-bit stereo output, and 3D audio acceleration.

- **CA0102-ICT (also known as Audigy 2 ZS)**—This audio chip is used by the Creative Labs Audigy 2 ZS series. It's a development of the CA0102 chip, adding support for Dolby Digital EX 7.1 decoding, Dolby ETS decoding, 7.1 sound in DirectX games, and 192KHz/24-bit stereo output.

- **Extreme Fidelity (X-Fi)**—This is the chip used in Creative's X-Fi line of sound cards. The Creative X-Fi Xtreme Fidelity audio processor has over 51 million transistors capable of handling more than 10,000 millions of instructions per second (MIPS). This is 24 times more powerful than its predecessor, the Sound Blaster Audigy 2 ZS.

Various other companies have produced their own sound chips in the past but no longer do so. The primary makers that fit in this category are

- **Aureal**—Its A3D technology was regarded by many as superior to Creative's original EAX 3D positional audio, but the company was absorbed by Creative in mid-2000. Because Creative's EAX HD is superior to A3D, there will be no further development of this technology.

- **Yamaha**—Its OPL2 and OPL3 chips were among the best FM-synthesis chips used on older sound cards, and its MIDI performance in later models was outstanding. However, its emphasis is now on MIDI daughtercards and professional sound-recording cards such as the SW1000XG. Some of its retail and OEM products might still be available, though.

- **Philips**—Its ThunderBird Q3D (SAA7780) and ThunderBird Avenger (SAA7785) chips, jointly developed with QSound Labs, provided high-quality 3D acceleration for Philips's now-discontinued line of PCI-based sound cards. Some third-party sound cards also used the SAA7780 chip, but the six-channel SAA7785 was used only by Philips. See Table 14.2 for details.

Should you panic if your favorite audio adapter is an "orphan?" Not necessarily. If the audio adapter vendor provides good technical support and up-to-date drivers, you're okay for now. However, with the introduction of Microsoft Windows Vista and the changes in how 3D audio is supported in DirectX 10 (an integral part of Vista), you might find it is necessary to replace your audio adapter to take full advantage of the audio features of Vista.

Table 14.2   Philips ThunderBird Audio Chips

Audio Chip	Sound Cards	3D Audio	Speaker Support	Other Features
ThunderBird Q3D	Philips PSC702, PSC704; Aztech PCI-368DSP; I/O Magic MagicQuad 8; Labway Thunder	64 3D hardware streams; EAX and QSound	4.1	DOS Sound (SAA7780) 3D Blaster emulation; wavetable MIDI
ThunderBird Avenger (SAA7785)	Philips PSC604, PSC605, PSC703, PSC705, PSC706	96 3D hardware streams; EAX and QSound	Dolby Digital 5.1	DOS Sound Blaster emulation; wavetable MIDI

Major Sound Chip Makers

Most companies other than Creative depend on third parties to make their audio chips. Some of the major vendors include Cirrus Logic/Crystal Semiconductor; ESS Technology; C-Media Electronics; ForteMedia, Inc.; and VIA Technologies.

Discontinued and Orphan Sound Chips and Sound Card Producers

Orphan sound chips include Oak Technologies OTI-601 series and Trident 4DWave-NX series. If your sound card or integrated audio is based on one of these chips, you might need to upgrade if you can't get drivers for new and forthcoming operating systems.

Motherboard Chipsets with Integrated Audio

The Intel 810 chipset was the first mainstream chipset for a major CPU to integrate audio; it works with Pentium III-based Celeron CPUs. Its inspiration might have been the Cyrix/National Semiconductor Media GX series, which used a trio of chips to substitute for the CPU, VGA video, onboard audio, memory, and I/O tasks.

Thanks to improvements in chipset design and faster CPU performance, today's best integrated chipsets can provide solid mid-range performance. Almost all recent chipsets from Intel, VIA, ALi, and SiS have integrated audio (see Chapter 4, "Motherboards and Buses," for details). Current systems support at least one of the following audio standards: AC'97 or Intel High Definition Audio (Azalia).

AC'97 Integrated Audio

The phrase *AC'97 integrated audio* can be found in the descriptions of many recent systems. Because AC'97 can replace the need for a separate audio card but might not be a satisfactory replacement, you need to understand what it is and how it works.

AC'97 (often referred to as *AC97*) is an Intel specification that connects an audio codec (compression/decompression) architecture to a section of a South Bridge, an I/O Communications Hub chip called the AC-Link control, or an audio controller such as the VIA Envy24 series. The AC-Link control works with the CPU and an AC'97 digital signal processor (DSP) to create audio.

The AC'97 audio codec could be a physical chip on the motherboard (the most common form in recent systems), a chip on a small daughterboard called a *communications and networking riser (CNR)*, or a software program. Thus, a motherboard with AC'97 integrated sound support doesn't require the use of a separate audio card for sound playback. Sometimes *AC'97* is also used to refer to audio chips on a sound card, but in this discussion we will use it to refer only to integrated audio. Sometimes motherboards also integrate an analog modem through an MC '97 codec chip, or they might have an AMC '97 (audio/modem) codec chip to combine both functions.

Note

Some low-cost sound cards and some USB-based audio products use AC'97 codec chips along with additional components instead of traditional single-chip audio solutions.

It's important to realize that, although most recent chipsets support AC'97 audio, this does not mean that every motherboard built on a particular chipset uses the same AC'97 codec, or even the same method of creating sound. In most cases, AC'97 is implemented through a small AC'97 codec chip on the motherboard (see Figure 14.6). It can be surface-mounted as shown in Figure 14.6, but many vendors use a small socket instead.

Figure 14.6   The Realtek ALC850 is a typical AC'97 2.3–compliant codec chip with surround audio support.

A few motherboards use an AMR or a CNR riser card to implement AC'97 audio along with audio ports.

For various reasons, including audio codec features and price, different motherboard vendors might use different AC'97 codec chips on motherboards that use the same chipset.

Major vendors of AC'97 codecs include Analog Devices (SoundMAX), C-Media, Cirrus Logic (Crystal Audio), National Semiconductor, Realtek (includes former Avance Logic products), SigmaTel (STAC C-Major), VIA Technologies, and Wolfson Microelectronics plc.

Note

The drivers for a particular AC'97 codec chip are supplied by your motherboard vendor because they must be customized to the combination of codec and South Bridge/ICH chip your motherboard uses.

Although the AC'97 specification recommends a standard pinout, differences do exist between AC'97 codec chips. Some vendors of AC'97 chips provide technical information to help motherboard builders design sockets that can be used with different models of the AC'97 codec chip. However, in other cases, AC'97 codecs are surface-mounted to the motherboard, as in Figure 14.6.

The four versions of the AC'97 codec are as follows:

- **AC'97 1.0**—Has fixed 48KHz sampling rate and stereo output.
- **AC'97 2.1**—Has options for variable sampling rate and multichannel output.
- **AC'97 2.2**—Has AC'97 2.1 features plus optional S/PDIF digital audio and enhanced riser card support; released in September 2000.
- **AC'97 2.3**—Has AC'97 2.1/2.2 features plus support for true Plug and Play detection of audio devices; released in July 2002.

Note

Audio solutions that use AC'97 2.3–compliant codecs can detect whether you have connected a speaker to the microphone jack or a microphone to the speaker jack and warn you that the wrong jack is being used for the device. This helps eliminate one of the most common causes of audio failures.

Most recent motherboards with integrated audio support AC'97 2.2 or 2.3. To learn more about the AC'97 specifications, see the Intel – Technology & Research Audio Codec site at http://www.intel.com/technology/computing/audio/

To determine whether a particular motherboard's implementation of AC'97 audio will be satisfactory, follow these steps:

1. Determine which codec chip the motherboard uses. Read the motherboard manual or see which driver the motherboard uses for audio.
2. Look up the chip's features and specifications. If you are not sure of the chip manufacturer, look up the part number with a search engine such as Google.
3. Use a search engine to find reviews of the chip's sound quality and performance (typically found as part of a motherboard review).
4. Look at the motherboard's features to determine whether it uses the full capabilities of the codec chip. Chips that support AC'97 2.1 can offer up to six-channel analog audio; those that support AC'97 2.2 can also offer S/PDIF digital audio. However, motherboard makers don't always provide the proper outputs.
5. Analyze how you use audio. If you play a lot of 3D games, you're not likely to be satisfied with the performance of any integrated audio solution, no matter what its features might be. You can disable onboard audio with a BIOS setting if you prefer to install your own audio card.

◀◀ For details on how to enable and disable onboard audio, see "Advanced Peripheral Configuration," p. 484.

Intel "Azalia" HD Audio

In 2004, Intel released Intel High Definition (HD) Audio in 2004 for delivering high-definition audio capable of playing back more channels at higher quality than AC'97 integrated audio formats. The hardware based on Intel HD Audio specifications is capable of delivering 192KHz/32-bit quality for eight channels, and supports up to 7.1 surround audio. During its development, HD Audio was known by the code-name "Azalia," and some vendors still refer to it by this name.

Although HD Audio was developed by Intel and is included in Intel's current chipset series, HD Audio is also supported by most third-party audio codec vendors. Most recent systems with integrated surround audio now include support for HD Audio as well as the older AC'97 audio standard.

HD Audio is the foundation for the Unified Audio Architecture (UAA) audio design used in Windows Vista.

HD Audio can not only detect when devices are plugged into an audio jack but can also change the default assignment of the audio jack to match the device being inserted. This helps to reduce audio failures caused by mismatched devices and jacks.

Vacuum Tube Audio for the PC

The Taiwan-based motherboard maker AOpen, part of the Acer Group, came up with a very interesting gimmick in June 2002 when it introduced the world's first PC motherboard with a vacuum tube–based audio amplifier—the AOpen AX4B-533 Tube, which was optimized for classical music. Other products with onboard tube audio include the AX4GE Tube and AX4PE Tube for Pentium 4 processors and the AK79G Tube for Athlon XP processors. These motherboards are optimized for rock and pop music, thanks to a slightly revised tube and amplifier design. Tube audio provides PC users the same rich audio that serious audiophiles enjoy through vacuum-tube amplifiers.

Although AOpen is not currently producing tube-based motherboards, the idea of using tube-based audio in a PC isn't dead. The MSI K8N Diamond Plus motherboard for Athlon 64/FX/X2 processors in Socket 939 includes a tube-based amplifier that uses an empty 5.25-inch drive bay. The same component is available separately as the Cooler Master Musketeer III (or Musketeer 3).

Note

To learn more about AOpen's Tube motherboards, go to http://usa.aopen.com/ and click the Innovation Link.

For more information about the MSI K8N Diamond Plus motherboard, go to http://www.msicomputer.com.

For more information about the Cooler Master Musketeer III, go to http://www.coolermaster.com.

3D Audio

One of the biggest issues for serious game players when audio adapters are considered is how well they perform 3D audio tasks. This has been complicated by several factors, including the following:

- Differing standards for positional audio
- Hardware versus software processing of 3D audio
- DirectX support issues
- Windows Vista and DirectX10 support issues

Positional Audio

The underlying issue common to all 3D sound cards is that of positional audio, which refers to adjusting features such as reverberation, balance, and apparent sound "location" to produce the illusion of sound coming from in front of, beside, or even behind the user. One very important element in positional audio is HRTF (Head Related Transfer Function), which refers to how the shape of the ear and the angle of the listener's head changes the perception of sound. Because HRTF factors mean that a "realistic" sound at one listener's head angle might sound artificial when the listener turns to one side or the other, the addition of multiple speakers that "surround" the user, as well as sophisticated sound algorithms that add controlled reverberation to the mix, are making computer-based sound more and more realistic.

Creative's Environmental Audio Extensions (EAX) has become the de facto standard for 3D audio since the demise of Aureal's A3D in mid-2000. There are five versions of EAX:

- EAX 1.0
- EAX 2.0
- EAX Advanced HD (also known as EAX 3.0)
- EAX 4.0 Advanced HD
- EAX 5.0 Advanced HD

EAX 1.0 introduced 26 presets designed to simulate the audio effects caused by typical building and natural environments along with the capability to adjust volume, reverberation, decay time, and damping. EAX 2.0 adds occlusions (how sound originating in one room is heard in another room) and obstructions (how sound is heard when an object blocks direct sound waves and only reflections can be heard).

EAX 1.0 and EAX 2.0 are supported both by Creative's Sound Blaster and Audigy series of sound cards but also by most recent third-party sound cards and integrated audio solutions, thanks to Creative's release of these standards to the industry.

EAX Advanced HD, introduced by the Sound Blaster Audigy, adds support for multienvironment—each sound (up to four) can have its own environmental effects. It also adds environment morphing, environment panning, and environment reflection, three methods used to change environment sounds as the player moves through the game. Environmental filtering fine-tunes how sounds change from environment to environment. Audigy 2's version of EAX Advanced HD adds the capability to convert DirectX 3D audio (Direct3D) into 6.1 audio on systems with 6.1 speaker systems. EAX Advanced HD supports up to 32 channels of Direct 3D hardware voice acceleration.

EAX 4.0 Advanced HD, introduced by the Sound Blaster Audigy 2 ZS and also used with the Audigy 4, adds sound effects such as pitch and frequency shifting, automatic gain control compression, a wah-wah pedal, chorus, distortion, a whooshing effect (flanger), and a ring modulator. EAX 4.0 Advanced HD also adds a comb filter to remove audio artifacts, HRTF filters, cross-talk cancellation algorithms that support speaker types from headphones (2.0) up through 7.1, and 64 channels of Direct 3D hardware voice acceleration.

Sound Blaster introduced EAX 5.0 Advanced HD to exploit the full potential of the Creative X-Fi Xtreme Fidelity Audio Processor. It delivers double the voice count, giving you more detail and speed in your games and letting developers more easily add interactive music to games. EAX Advanced HD 5.0 adds a dedicated bass feed for each of the 128 voices, so gaming audio becomes more cinematic. A feature called Environment FlexiFX gives developers the freedom to use any of four simultaneous effects with any of the 128 voices.

Note

Audigy 2 cards (but not the low-end Audigy LS) can also use EAX 4.0 Advanced HD through a driver update.

The major alternative to EAX is Sensaura's 3D positional audio technology (3DPA). Most third-party sound cards support Sensaura 3DPA along with EAX 1.0/2.0. The full range of Sensaura 3DPA features include

- **Digital Ear**—HRTF filters.
- **Virtual Ear**—Customizes Digital Ear for the listener's ear size and positioning.
- **MacroFX**—Improves realism of close sound sources, such as a buzzing insect.
- **ZoomFX**—Improves realism of sounds from different sizes of objects, such as trains versus motorcycles.
- **EnvironmentFX**—Preset environments with adjustable properties.
- **XTC and MultiDrive**—Crosstalk cancellation for speaker systems up to 7.1.
- **Headphone Theater**—Simulates 5.1 audio for headset users.
- **GameCODA audio middleware**—Developed using Sensaura's core suite of technologies, this feature empowers PC, PlayStation 2, Xbox, and Nintendo Game Cube developers to easily integrate high-quality audio into their game titles.

Note

Some audio cards that use Sensaura 3DPDA technology might not support all the features, or they might require a software upgrade. Contact your audio card or motherboard vendor for details.

3D Audio Processing

A second important issue for game players is how the sound cards produce 3D audio. As with 3D video, there are two major methods:

- Host-based processing (which uses the CPU to process 3D, which can slow down overall system operation). This is the only technique supported by Windows Vista; it is also supported by Windows XP and older Windows versions

- Processing on the audio adapter (referred to as *3D acceleration*); supported by Windows XP and older Windows versions

Some 3D audio cards perform some or all of the processing necessary for 3D using the host's CPU, whereas others use a powerful DSP that performs the processing on the audio adapter itself. Cards that use host-based processing for 3D audio as well as systems that use AC'97 audio codecs for integrated 3D audio can cause major drops in frame rate (frames per second of animation displayed onscreen by a 3D game) when 3D sound is enabled on systems with processors running at speeds under 1GHz. However, cards with their own 3D audio processors onboard have little change in frame rate whether 3D sound is enabled or disabled. Many of the latest chips from major audio adapter and chipset vendors support 3D acceleration, but the number of 3D audio streams supported varies greatly by chip—and can sometimes be limited by problems with software drivers. Windows Vista supports only host-based.

A good rule of thumb for realistic gaming is to have an overall average frame rate of at least 30 fps (frames per second). With CPUs running at 1GHz or above, this is easy to achieve with any recent 3D audio card or recent onboard integrated audio solutions. However, gamers using older CPUs, such as those running slower than 1GHz, will find that cards using the host CPU for some of the 3D processing will have frame rates that fall below the desired average of 30 fps, making for clumsy gameplay. To see the effect of enabling 3D sound on the speed of popular games, you can use the built-in frame-rate-tracking feature found in many games or check online game-oriented hardware review sources, such as www.anandtech.com. Frame rates are closely related to CPU utilization; the more CPU attention your 3D audio card or integrated audio solution requires, the slower the frame rate will be. As with 3D video, the main users of 3D sound are game developers, but business uses for ultra-realistic sound will no doubt follow.

DirectX Support Issues

DirectX 9.0c, which is used by Windows XP, is designed to give all sound cards with 3D support a major boost in performance compared to DirectX 8.x and earlier versions. Previous versions of DirectX supported 3D with DirectSound3D, but the performance of DirectSound3D was limited. Game programmers needed to test the audio adapter to see whether it supported DirectSound3D acceleration and then would either enable or disable 3D sounds based on the host hardware. Starting with DirectX 5.0, DirectSound3D works with third-party 3D acceleration features. Compared to DirectX 8.x, DirectX 9.0c improves 3D audio quality and performance. You can download it from the Microsoft DirectX website at www.microsoft.com/windows/directx.

Windows Vista and DirectX 10 Audio Support Issues

Windows Vista includes a new version of DirectX, DirectX 10, which has created some major problems for gamers running sound cards with hardware-based audio processors, such as Creative's Audigy series. In DirectX 10, DirectSound (the audio component of DirectX) no longer receives hardware acceleration because the hardware abstraction layer (HAL) has been removed. As a result, audio cards with onboard audio processors lose the ability to produce environmental audio (EAX) and surround audio. Host-based audio, which uses the CPU along with audio drivers, supports environmental and surround audio as in previous DirectX versions.

The new Universal Audio Architecture (UAA) used in Windows Vista no longer runs in kernel mode to avoid crashing the system if the audio driver failed. While this design feature promotes better system stability (one of the major goals for Windows Vista), it prevents audio acceleration. As a result, games that are not designed to use UAA will produce only software-rendered stereo sound with no environmental effects. Surround audio is not available, either.

To achieve high-quality audio in Windows Vista, what are your alternatives? Many recent games such as Battlefield 2142, Doom3, Quake 4, Prey and others support a new audio standard known as OpenAL. The new Creative X-Fi cards support OpenAL natively. To learn more about OpenAL, and to get a list of OpenAL-compatible games, visit the OpenAL website at http://www.openal.org.

To support older games that do not support OpenAL, Creative's ALchemy Project enables X-Fi sound cards running under Windows Vista to provide 3D acceleration and environmental audio for many games. To use the ALchemy application, install the latest drivers for your X-Fi card first, then use the application to set up your game. For more information on Creative ALchemy, visit the ALchemy home page at http://connect.creativelabs.com/alchemy/default.aspx.

If you have an older Creative sound card, such as a SoundBlaster Live! or Audigy, Audigy 2, or Audigy 4 card, you should consider switching to the onboard host-based audio in your system (most recent systems now include 5.1 or 7.1 surround audio) instead of a sound card. This is your least expensive alternative and also assures compatibility with Windows Vista and DirectX 10. Upgrading to an X-Fi card that supports Creative ALchemy is an alternative, but ALchemy does not support all games.

Installing the Sound Card

Before you can install a sound card, you must open your computer. In almost all cases today, you will install a PCI audio adapter that supports Plug and Play configuration. Compared to the previous generation of ISA audio adapters, PCI audio adapters use fewer hardware resources, feature a lower CPU utilization rate, and provide better support for advanced 3D gaming APIs.

Note

If you need to install an ISA audio adapter, see "Installing the Sound Card (Detailed Procedure)" in Chapter 20 of *Upgrading and Repairing PCs, 11th Edition*.

If your computer has integrated audio, in most cases you should disable it. You could have audio conflicts with AC'97 or Intel HD Audio codec-based solutions and resource conflicts with solutions that emulate the Creative Sound Blaster. Refer to Chapter 5, "BIOS," for details.

Selecting an Expansion Slot

If you have several empty bus slots from which to choose, install the audio adapter in the slot that is as far away as possible from the other cards in the computer. This reduces any possible electromagnetic interference; that is, it reduces stray radio signals from one card that might affect the sound card. The analog components on audio adapters are highly susceptible to interference, and even though they are shielded, they should be protected as well as is possible. Next, you must remove the screw that holds the metal cover over the empty expansion slot you've chosen. Remove your audio adapter from its protective packaging. When you open the bag, carefully grab the card by its metal bracket and edges. Do not touch any of the components on the card because any static electricity you might transmit can damage the card. Also, do not touch the gold-edge connectors. You might want to invest in a grounding wrist strap, which continually drains you of static build-up as you work on your computer.

Before you make your final decision about which slot to use for your audio adapter, take a careful look at the external cables you must attach to the card. Front and rear speakers, microphone, game controller, line in, S/PDIF, and other cables that attach to your system can interfere with (or be interfered by) existing cables already attached to your system. It's usually best to choose a slot that allows you to route the audio cables away from other cables. If you're installing a sound card that uses an internal 5 1/4" breakout box, be sure the ribbon cable from the drive bay used for the breakout box can comfortably reach the connector on the sound card. You might have to move a CD-ROM, CD-RW, or DVD drive to a different drive bay to free up a drive bay needed by the breakout box.

Figure 14.7 shows a sound card after installation in a computer. The four-wire analog and two-wire digital cables to the CD-ROM drive are connected to the card, as is the ribbon cable to the card's internal breakout box.

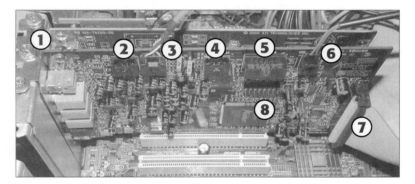

1. Mounting screw
2. TAD (telephone answering device) analog audio connector
3. CD audio analog cable
4. Aux in analog audio connector
5. SB1394 (IEEE-1394a) I/0 connector
6. CD SPDIF digital audio cable
7. Audigy Drive I/O cable
8. Game port (joystick) header pins

Figure 14.7   A sound card installed in a typical PC with analog and digital cables from the optical drive attached.

If your system has an internal CD or DVD drive with an analog audio cable, connect the audio cable to the adapter's CD Audio In connector, as shown in Figure 14.7. This connector is a 4-pin connector and is keyed so that you can't insert it improperly. Note that no true standard exists for this audio cable, so be sure you get the correct one that matches your drive and adapter. If you need to purchase one, you can find cables with multiple connectors designed for various brands of CD-ROM drives. This will allow you to play music CDs through the sound card's speakers and to use analog ripping if you want to create MP3 files from your CDs.

Note

If your PC doesn't include an analog or digital audio cable but you can play and rip music CD's, you don't need to install either cable. However, these cables may be needed on systems running Windows 9x or other legacy operating systems and music player programs.

Many CD-ROM and DVD drives also have a digital audio connector that supports a two-wire connector. Attach one end of the digital audio cable to the rear of the drive and the other end to the CD SPDIF or CD Digital Audio connector on the sound card (refer to Figure 14.7). This enables you to perform digital ripping if you want to create MP3 files from your CDs. Note that most recent ripping programs can also use digital signals received through the drive's data cable.

Next, insert the adapter's edge connector in the bus slot, but first touch a metal object, such as the inside of the computer's cover, to drain yourself of static electricity. When the card is firmly in place, attach the screw (refer to Figure 14.7) to hold the expansion card and then reassemble your computer.

Connecting PC Speakers and Completing the Installation

After the adapter card is installed, you can connect small speakers to the external speaker jack(s). Typically, sound cards provide 4 watts of power per channel to drive unpowered bookshelf speakers. If you are using speakers rated for less than 4 watts, do not turn up the volume on your sound card to the maximum; your speakers might burn out from the overload. You'll get better results if you plug your sound card into powered speakers—that is, speakers with built-in amplifiers. If your sound card supports a four-speaker system, check the documentation to see which jack is used for the front speakers and which for the rear speakers. To use the rear speakers for 3D audio, adjust the properties with the mixer control software supplied with your sound card.

Tip

If you have powered speakers but don't have batteries in them or have them connected to an AC adapter, don't turn on the speakers! Turning on the speakers without power will prevent you from hearing anything at all. Leave the speakers turned off and use the volume control built into your sound card's mixer software instead. Powered speakers sound better, but most small models can run without power in an emergency.

Some computer power supplies feature small jacks to provide power for computer speakers.

When the sound card installation is finished, you should have a speaker icon in the Windows System Tray. If the speaker icon (indicating the Volume Control) isn't visible, you can install it through the Control Panel's Add/Remove Programs icon. With Windows 9x/Me, select the Windows Setup tab and open the Multimedia section. Then, check the box labeled Volume Control. With Windows XP, open the Sounds and Audio Devices icon in Control Panel, click the Volume tab, and click the Place Volume icon in the task bar box. With Windows Vista, open the Taskbar and Start Menu properties dialog, click the Notification Area tab, and check the volume checkbox to add the volume control to the desktop.

In some cases you might be asked to insert the Windows CD-ROM if additional drivers are required to complete the installation.

If you use digital sound sources or output such as Dolby 5.1, CD digital, or S/PDIF, open the properties sheet for your mixer device and enable the display of these volume controls.

Use the Volume Control to ensure your speakers are receiving a sound signal. The mixer sometimes defaults to Mute. You can usually adjust volume separately for wave (WAV) files, MIDI, microphone, and other components.

Using Your Stereo Instead of Speakers

Another alternative is to patch your sound card into your stereo system for greatly amplified sound and for support of advanced Dolby Digital sound for DVD playback. Check the plugs and jacks at both ends of the connection. Most stereos use pin plugs, also called RCA or phono plugs, for input. Although pin plugs are standard on some sound cards and breakout boxes, most use miniature 1/8" phono plugs, which require an adapter for connecting to your stereo system. For example, from RadioShack you can purchase an audio cable that provides a stereo 1/8" miniplug on one end and phono plugs on the other. If you want to attach your sound card to Dolby 5.1 speakers, be sure you use cabling designed for the S/PDIF connectors on your sound card. Some might use RCA-type plugs, whereas others use an optical cable with a square end (also known as a Toslink connector).

Make sure that you get stereo—not mono—plugs, unless your sound card supports only mono. To ensure that you have enough cable to reach from the back of your PC to your stereo system, get a 6-foot-long cable.

Hooking up your stereo to an audio adapter is a matter of connecting the plugs into the proper jacks. If your audio adapter gives you a choice of outputs—speaker/headphone and stereo line-out—choose the stereo line-out jack for the connection. This will give you the best sound quality because the signals from the stereo line-out jack are not amplified. The amplification is best left to your stereo system. In some cases, you'll attach a special DIN plug to your audio adapter that has multiple connections to your stereo system.

Connect this cable output from your audio adapter to the auxiliary input of your stereo receiver, pre-amp, or integrated amplifier. If your stereo doesn't have an auxiliary input, other input options include—in order of preference—tuner, CD, or Tape 2. (Do not use phono inputs, however, because the level of the signals will be uneven.) You can connect the cable's single stereo miniplug to the sound card's stereo line-out jack, for example, and then connect the two RCA phono plugs to the stereo's Tape/VCR 2 Playback jacks.

The first time you use your audio adapter with a stereo system, turn down the volume on your receiver to prevent blown speakers. Barely turn up the volume control and then select the proper input (such as Tape/VCR 2) on your stereo receiver. Finally, start your PC. Never increase the volume to more than three-fourths of the way up. Any higher and the sound might become distorted.

Note

If your stereo speakers are not magnetically shielded, you might hear a lot of crackling if they are placed close to your computer. Try moving them away from the computer, or use magnetically shielded speakers.

Tricks for Using the Tape Monitor Circuit of Your Stereo

Your receiver might be equipped with something called a *tape monitor*. This outputs the sound coming from the tuner, tape, or CD to the tape-out port on the back; it then expects the sound to come back in on the tape-in port. These ports, in conjunction with the line-in and line-out ports on your audio adapter, enable you to play computer sound and the radio through the same set of speakers.

Here's how you do it:

1. Turn off the tape monitor circuit on your receiver.
2. Turn down all the controls on the sound card's mixer application.
3. Connect the receiver's tape-out ports to the audio adapter's line-in port.

4. Connect the audio adapter's line-out port to the receiver's tape-in ports.

5. Turn on the receiver, select some music, and set the volume to a medium level.

6. Turn on the tape monitor circuit.

7. Slowly adjust the line-in and main-out sliders in the audio adapter's mixer application until the sound level is about the same as before.

8. Disengage and re-engage the tape monitor circuit while adjusting the output of the audio adapter so that the sound level is the same regardless of whether the tape monitor circuit is engaged.

9. Start playing a WAV file.

10. Slowly adjust up the volume slider for the WAV file in the audio adapter's mixer application until it plays at a level (slightly above or below the receiver) that is comfortable.

Now you can get sounds from your computer and the radio through the receiver's speakers.

Different connectors might be needed if you have digital surround speakers and newer PCI-based sound cards. Check your speakers and sound card before you start this project.

Troubleshooting Sound Card Problems

To operate, an audio adapter needs hardware resources, such as IRQ numbers, a base I/O address, and DMA channels that don't conflict with other devices. Most adapters come preconfigured to use the standard Sound Blaster resources that have come to be associated with audio adapters. However, problems occasionally arise even with Plug and Play adapters. Troubleshooting might mean that you have to change the settings used by your system BIOS for PnP devices, move the sound card to another slot, or even reconfigure the other devices in your computer. No one said life was fair.

Hardware (Resource) Conflicts

At one time, the most common problem for audio adapters (particularly if you still use ISA cards) is that they might conflict with other devices installed in your PC. Although this isn't as common as it used to be, you might still run into situations where you notice that your audio adapter simply doesn't work (no sound effects or music), repeats the same sounds over and over, or causes your PC to freeze. This situation is called a device conflict (or hardware conflict). What are they fighting over? Mainly the same bus signal lines or channels (called resources) used for talking to your PC. The sources of conflict in audio adapter installations are generally threefold:

- **Interrupt requests (IRQs)**—Hardware devices use IRQs to "interrupt" your PC's CPU and get its attention. PCI cards can share IRQs, but ISA cards and onboard legacy ports such as serial, parallel, and PS/2 mouse ports can't.

- **Direct Memory Access (DMA) channels**—DMA channels move information directly to your PC's memory, bypassing the system processor. DMA channels enable sound to play while your PC is doing other work. ISA sound cards and PCI sound cards emulating the Sound Blaster standard require DMA settings; PCI sound cards running in native mode don't use DMA channels.

- **Input/output (I/O) port addresses**—Your PC uses I/O port addresses to channel information between the hardware devices on your audio adapter and PC. The addresses usually mentioned in a sound card manual are the starting or base addresses. An audio adapter has several devices on it, and each one uses a range of addresses starting with a particular base address.

PCI-based sound cards and PCI-based onboard audio can share IRQs, don't use DMA channels (except when emulating a Sound Blaster card), and can use a wide variety of I/O port addresses.

Consequently, resource conflicts involving PCI-based audio are extremely rare today, in part because systems no longer use ISA slots or ISA cards (ISA devices cannot share IRQs). However, if you still work with ISA sound cards or ISA or PCI cards that use game ports, you might encounter resource conflicts. Resource conflicts can also happen in a virtualized environment.

Note

See Chapter 20 of *Upgrading and Repairing PCs, 12th Edition*, for details on resolving conflicts involving ISA sound cards and game ports.

Other Sound Card and Onboard Audio Problems

Like the common cold, audio adapter problems have common symptoms. Use the following sections to diagnose your problem.

No Sound

If you don't hear anything from your audio adapter, consider these solutions:

- Make sure the audio adapter is set to use all default resources and that all other devices using these resources have been either reconfigured or removed if they cause a conflict. Use the Device Manager to determine this information.

- Are the speakers connected? Check that the speakers are plugged into the sound card's stereo line-out or speaker jack (not the line-in or microphone jack).

- Are the speakers receiving power? Check that the power "brick" or power cord is plugged in securely and that the speakers are turned on.

- Are the speakers stereo? Check that the plug inserted into the jack is a stereo plug, not mono.

- Are the mixer settings correct? Many audio adapters include a sound mixer application. The mixer controls the volume settings for various sound devices, such as the microphone or the CD player. There might be separate controls for both recording and playback. Increase the master volume or speaker volume when you are in the play mode.

  If the Mute option is selected in your sound mixer software, you won't hear anything. Depending on the speaker type and sound source type, you might need to switch from analog to digital sound for some types of sound output. Make sure that the correct digital audio volume controls are enabled in your audio device's mixer control.

- Use your audio adapter's setup or diagnostic software to test and adjust the volume of the adapter. Such software usually includes sample sounds used to test the adapter.

- Turn off your computer for 1 minute and then turn it back on. A hard reset (as opposed to pressing the Reset button or pressing Ctrl+Alt+Delete) might clear the problem.

- If your computer game lacks sound, check that it is designed to work with your audio adapter. For example, some legacy (DOS-based) and early Windows games might require the exact settings of IRQ 7 (or IRQ 5), DMA 1, and I/O address 220 to be Sound Blaster compatible. You also might need to load DOS drivers to enable some recent sound cards to work with DOS games.

- If you're using motherboard-integrated audio, make sure the onboard audio is enabled (check the BIOS setup program) and that the proper drivers and player program have been installed (check the Windows Control Panel). With some motherboards, you might need to run a setup program on the motherboard driver CD to enable onboard sound.

- If you're using motherboard-integrated audio that uses a removable header cable (such as with many SDPIF optical or 4/6-channel analog speaker configurations), make sure the header cable is properly connected to the motherboard.

One-sided Sound

If you hear sound coming from only one speaker, check out these possible causes:

- **Are you using a mono plug in the stereo jack?** A common mistake is to use a mono plug in the sound card's speaker or stereo-out jacks. Seen from the side, a stereo connector has two darker stripes. A mono connector has only one stripe.

- **If you're using amplified speakers, are they powered on?** Check the strength of the batteries or the AC adapter's connection to the electrical outlet. If each speaker is powered separately, be sure that both have working batteries.

- **Are the speakers wired correctly?** When possible, use keyed and color-coded connectors to avoid mistakes.

- **Is the audio adapter driver loaded?** Some sound cards provide only left-channel sound if the driver is not loaded correctly. Rerun your adapter's setup software or reinstall it in the operating system.

- **Are both speakers set to the same volume?** Some speakers use separate volume controls on each speaker. Balance them for best results. Separate speaker volume controls can be an advantage if one speaker must be farther away from the user than the other.

- **Is the speaker jack loose?** If you find that plugging your speaker into the jack properly doesn't produce sound but pulling the plug half-way out or "jimmying" it around in its hole can temporarily correct the problem, you're on the road to a speaker jack failure. There's no easy solution; buy a new adapter or whip out your soldering iron and spend a lot more time on the test bench than most audio adapters are worth. To avoid damage to the speaker jack, be sure you insert the plug straight in, not at an angle.

Volume Is Low

If you can barely hear your sound card, try these solutions:

- **Are the speakers plugged into the proper jack?** Speakers require a higher level of drive signal than headphones. Again, adjust the volume level in your mixer application.

- **Are the mixer settings too low?** Again, adjust the volume level in your mixer application. If your mixer lets you choose between speakers and headphones, be sure to select the correct speaker configuration.

- **Is the initial volume too low?** If your audio adapter has an external thumbwheel volume control located on the card bracket, check to ensure that it is not turned down too low. Check the speakers' own volume controls as well.

- **Are the speakers too weak?** Some speakers might need more power than your audio adapter can produce. Try other speakers or put a stereo amplifier between your sound card and speakers.

Some Speakers Don't Play

If you can hear sound coming from some speakers, but not others, check the following:

- **Incorrect sound mixer settings**—Most systems assume that you are using two-channel (stereophonic) sound, even if you have plugged in four or more speakers. Select the correct speaker type with the Windows Speaker icon or a third-party sound mixer.

- **Additional speakers are connected to the wrong jacks**—Make sure you connect the additional speakers needed for four-channel or six-channel audio to the correct jacks. If you connect them to line-in or microphone jacks, they won't work.

- **Incorrect balance settings**—The volume control also adjusts the balance between the left and right speakers. If you hear audio from the left speakers only or the right speakers only, the balance control needs to be centered with the Windows Speaker icon or a third-party sound mixer.

Note

On some systems with integrated audio, audio jacks have multiple uses. For example, in six-channel mode on some systems, the normal line-in and microphone jacks might be reconfigured to work with rear and center/subwoofer speakers. In such cases, the mixer controls need to be reset.

Some Types of Sounds Play, But Others Don't

If you can hear CDs but not WAV or MP3 digital music, or can play WAV and MP3 but not CD or MIDI files, check the following:

- **Low volume or mute settings for some audio types**—Some audio mixers have separate volume controls for WAV/MP3, MIDI, CD digital, CD audio, and other sound types and sources. Unmute any audio types you play back and adjust the volume as desired.

- **I/O port or DMA conflicts when playing DOS games**—On most ISA-based sound cards or PCI-based sound cards or integrated audio solutions, separate I/O port address ranges and DMA channels are used for MIDI, FM synthesis, and normal audio. A conflict can cause some types of sounds not to play.

- Check the CD audio connection from your optical drive to your sound card.

Note

See Chapter 20 of *Upgrading and Repairing PCs, 12th Edition,* for details on resolving conflicts involving ISA sound cards and game ports.

Scratchy Sound

Scratchy or static-filled sound can be caused by several problems. Improving the sound can be as simple as rearranging your hardware components. The following list suggests possible solutions to the problem of scratchy sound:

- **Is your audio adapter near other expansion cards?** The adapter might be picking up electrical interference from other expansion cards inside the PC. Move the audio card to an expansion slot as far away as possible from other cards.

- **An ISA-based audio adapter requires a lot of CPU attention.** Frequent hard disk access can cause dropouts due to the CPUs switching between managing the sound card and the hard drive.

- **Are your speakers too close to your monitor?** The speakers can pick up electrical noise from your monitor. Move them farther away. Subwoofers should *never* be placed near the monitor because their powerful magnets can interfere with the picture. They should be on the floor to maximize low-frequency transmission.

■ **Are you experiencing compatibility problems between particular games and your sound card?** If you notice sound problems such as stuttering voices and static on some games but not others, check with the game vendor for a software patch or with the sound card vendor for updated drivers. If the game uses DirectX under Windows XP or older versions, run the DXDIAG diagnostics program from the Windows Run dialog. Click Start, Run, type **dxdiag** and click OK. (Windows Vista also includes DXDIAG, but it does not support hardware audio acceleration.) In DXDIAG, click the Sound tab. Adjust the slider for Hardware Sound Acceleration Level down one notch from Full (the default) to Standard, click Save All Information, and exit. Retry the game. If the problem persists, adjust the Hardware Sound Acceleration Level to Basic. If other games have performance problems after you adjust the Hardware Sound Acceleration Level, be sure to reset it to Full before playing those games.

Your Computer Won't Start

If your computer won't start at all, you might not have inserted the audio adapter completely into its slot. Turn off the PC and then press firmly on the card until it is seated correctly.

If you can't start your computer after installing a new sound card and its drivers, you can use the Windows "bootlog" feature to record every event during startup; this file records which hardware drivers are loaded during startup and indicates whether the file loaded successfully, didn't load successfully, or froze the computer. See the documentation for your version of Windows for details on how to create a bootlog when necessary.

Parity Errors or Other Lockups

Your computer might display a memory parity error message or simply crash. This is usually caused by resource conflicts in one of the following areas:

■ IRQ

■ DMA

■ I/O ports

If other devices in your system are using the same resources as your audio adapter, crashes, lockups, or parity errors can result. You must ensure that multiple devices in your system do not share these resources.

Note

See Chapter 20 of *Upgrading and Repairing PCs, 12th Edition,* for details on resolving conflicts involving ISA sound cards and game ports.

Advanced Features

If you are having problems playing DVD audio, playing MP3 files, or using SPDIF connections, make sure of the following:

■ You have enabled the hardware resources on the sound card.

■ You are using the correct playback program.

■ Your mixer has the correct volume control setting for the device.

■ You have enabled digital playback (if you are using coaxial or optical SPDIF output).

■ Your cabling is correct for the device.

Other Problems

Sometimes sound problems can be difficult to solve. Due to quirks and problems with the way DMA is implemented in some motherboard chipsets, problems interacting with certain cards or drivers can occur. Sometimes altering the Chipset Setup options in your CMOS settings can resolve problems. These types of problems can take a lot of trial and error to solve.

The PC standard is based loosely on the cooperation among a handful of companies. Something as simple as one vendor's BIOS or motherboard design can make the standard nonstandard.

A good way to solve problems of all types with Plug and Play cards, a PnP BIOS, and a PnP operating system (Windows 9x/Me/2000/XP/Vista) is to use the Device Manager to remove the sound card, restart the system, and allow the card's components to be redetected. This installs a "fresh" copy of the software and reinserts Registry entries.

If you are using a motherboard with a VIA chipset, be sure to download and install the latest versions of VIA drivers.

Speakers

Successful business presentations, multimedia applications, and MIDI work demand external high-fidelity stereo speakers. Although you can use standard stereo speakers, they are often too big to fit on or near your desk. Smaller bookshelf speakers are better.

Sound cards offer little or none of the amplification needed to drive external speakers. Although some sound cards have small 4-watt amplifiers, they are not powerful enough to drive quality speakers. Also, conventional speakers sitting near your display can create magnetic interference, which can distort colors and objects onscreen or jumble the data recorded on nearby floppy disks or other magnetic media.

To solve these problems, computer speakers need to be small, efficient, and self-powered. Also, they should be provided with magnetic shielding, either in the form of added layers of insulation in the speaker cabinet or electronic cancellation of the magnetic distortion.

Caution

Although most computer speakers are magnetically shielded, do not leave recorded tapes, watches, credit cards, or floppy disks in front of the speakers for long periods of time.

Quality sound depends on quality speakers. A 16-bit audio adapter might provide better sound to computer speakers, but even an 8-bit adapter sounds good from a good speaker. Conversely, an inexpensive speaker makes both 8-bit and 16-bit adapter cards sound tinny.

Now dozens of models of PC speakers are on the market, ranging from inexpensive minispeakers from Sony, Creative, and LabTech to larger self-powered models from prestigious audio companies such as Bose, Cambridge Sound Works, Klipsch, Monsoon, and Altec Lansing. Many of the medium- to higher-end speaker systems even include subwoofers to provide additional bass response. To evaluate speakers, it helps to know the jargon. Speakers are measured by three criteria:

- **Frequency response**—A measurement of the range of high and low sounds a speaker can reproduce. The ideal range is 20Hz–20KHz, the range of human hearing. No speaker system reproduces this range perfectly. In fact, few people hear sounds above 18KHz. An exceptional speaker might cover a range of 30Hz–23000Hz, and lesser models might cover only 100Hz–20000Hz. Frequency response is the most deceptive specification because identically rated speakers can sound completely different.

- **Total Harmonic Distortion (THD)**—An expression of the amount of distortion or noise created by amplifying the signal. Simply put, distortion is the difference between the sound sent to the speaker and the sound you hear. The amount of distortion is measured in percentages. An acceptable level of distortion is less than .1% (one-tenth of 1%). For some CD-quality recording equipment, a common standard is .05%, but some speakers have a distortion of 10% or more. Headphones often have a distortion of about 2% or less.

- **Watts**—Usually stated as watts per channel, this is the amount of amplification available to drive the speakers. Check that the company means "per channel" (or RMS) and not total power. Many audio adapters have built-in amplifiers, providing up to 8 watts per channel (some provide 4 watts). This wattage is not enough to provide rich sound, however, which is why many speakers have built-in amplifiers. With the flick of a switch or the press of a button, these speakers amplify the signals they receive from the audio adapter. If you do not want to amplify the sound, you typically leave the speaker switch set to "direct." In most cases, you'll want to amplify the signal.

Before purchasing a speaker set, be sure to do your research and look at some reviews to see what others think about the speakers you are considering. You can see CNET's speaker review and compare speakers side by side at http://reviews.cnet.com/4566-3179_7-0.html.

Inexpensive PC speakers sometimes use batteries to power the amplifiers. Because these speakers require so much power, you might want to invest in an AC adapter or purchase speakers that use AC power. With an AC adapter, you won't have to buy new batteries every few weeks. If your speakers didn't come with an AC adapter, you can pick one up from your local RadioShack or hardware store. Be sure that the adapter you purchase matches your speakers in voltage and polarity; most third-party adapters are multiple voltage, featuring interchangeable tips and reversible polarity.

You can control the volume and other sound attributes of your speakers in various ways, depending on their complexity and cost. Typically, each speaker has a volume knob, although some share a single volume control. If one speaker is farther away than the other, you might want to adjust the volume accordingly. Many computer speakers include a dynamic bass boost (DBB) switch. This button provides a more powerful bass and clearer treble, regardless of the volume setting. Other speakers have separate bass and treble boost switches or a three-band equalizer to control low, middle, and high frequencies. When you rely on your audio adapter's power rather than your speakers' built-in amplifier, the volume and dynamic bass boost controls have no effect. Your speakers are at the mercy of the adapter's power.

For best audio quality, adjust the master volume on the sound card near the high end and use the volume control on powered speakers to adjust the volume. Otherwise, your speakers will try to amplify any distortions coming from the low-power input from the PC's audio adapter.

A 1/8" stereo minijack connects from the audio adapter's output jack to one of the speakers. The speaker then splits the signal and feeds through a separate cable from the first speaker to the second one (often referred to as the *satellite speaker*).

Before purchasing a set of speakers, check that the cables between the speakers are long enough for your computer setup. For example, a tower case sitting alongside your desk might require longer speaker wires than a desktop computer.

Beware of speakers that have a tardy built-in sleep feature. Such speakers, which save electricity by turning themselves off when they are not in use, might have the annoying habit of clipping the first part of a sound after a period of inactivity.

Speakers that are USB based will not be capable of playing CD music unless the optical drive can perform digital audio extraction. Check your drive's specifications for information.

Headphones are an option when you can't afford a premium set of speakers. Headphones also provide privacy and enable you to play your PC audio as loud as you like.

For best results with newer sound cards that support four speakers or more, check the properties sheet for the audio adapter and set whether you're using headphones, stereo speakers, or a larger number of speakers. Use your audio software to set up 3D or other audio effects.

Make sure that speakers are placed properly. If you use a subwoofer, put it on the floor for better bass sound and to reduce EMI interference with other devices.

How can you tell whether wireless satellite speakers are causing interference? Watch your monitor; frequencies as high as 2KHz can interfere with your video display. Move the speakers away from the monitor and check the display again.

Theater and Surround Sound Considerations

If you're a serious gamer or DVD movie lover, you won't be content with ordinary stereophonic sound. Most audio adapters now support front and rear speakers, and many of the best audio adapters also support Dolby-compatible 4.1 and 5.1 speaker setups. If you are using Windows XP Media Center Edition or a version of Windows Vista that includes Media Center, such as Home Premium or Ultimate, you may prefer to connect your PC's audio subsystem to a home theater system.

To ensure you get the sound you expect from four or more speakers, either directly connected to the system or via a home theater amplifier, check the following:

- **Use the properties sheet for your audio adapter to properly describe your speaker setup.** This includes selecting the number of speakers you are using, setting options for 3D environmental audio and positional sound such as reverb, and setting up your subwoofer if present.

- **Make sure you use the correct cabling between your speakers and audio adapter.** If you are planning to use AC3/Dolby speaker setups, such as 4.1, 5.1, 6.1, or 7.1, be sure you use the correct S/PDIF connection and configuration. This varies from audio adapter to audio adapter; check the vendor's website for details.

- **Make sure you have placed your speakers correctly.** In some cases you can adjust the audio adapter's properties to improve sound quality, but sometimes you might need to move the speakers themselves.

- **Make sure you have connected your speakers to the proper jacks.** Mixing up left and right or front and rear causes poor sound quality.

- **Select the correct setting in your amplifier configuration.** If you are sending your computer's audio signals to a home theater's amplifier, make sure you select the output option corresponding to the input jacks you used. For example, many home theater amps have DVD and Video selections. If you also have a DVD player connected to your home theater, use the DVD connection for the DVD player and the Video connection for your PC. When you turn on your amplifier, select Video if you want to hear PC audio.

Typical Speaker Setups

The simplest audio configuration available today is stereo, which uses two speakers placed to overlap sound. Most audio adapters now support at least four speakers, but depending on the audio adapter, settings, and sound output options in the program, the rear speakers might simply mirror the front speakers' output, or you might have four distinct sound streams.

Four-point surround sound uses four speakers plus a subwoofer to surround you with music and gaming sound effects; the four speakers are placed around the listener, and the subwoofer is usually placed near a wall or in the corner to amplify its low-frequency sound. The subwoofer in stereo or four-point surround sound setups is not on a separate circuit but is controlled by the same signals sent to the other speakers. A stereo speaker system with a subwoofer is often referred to as a *2.1 speaker configuration*, and a four-point surround sound configuration with a subwoofer is often referred to as a *4.1 speaker configuration*.

5.1 Surround sound, also referred to as Dolby Digital or DTS Surround sound, uses five speakers plus a subwoofer. The fifth speaker is placed between the front two speakers to fill in any missing sound caused by incorrect speaker placement. The subwoofer is independently controlled. This is the preferred sound system for use with DVD movies. Most lower-cost audio adapters lack support for 5.1 Surround sound.

Some of the latest sound cards and motherboards with integrated audio support 6.1 and 7.1 Surround sound. The 6.1 configuration resembles the 5.1 Surround setup but adds a middle speaker along with a subwoofer. 7.1 Surround sound uses left-middle and right-middle speakers to flank the listener, along with a subwoofer. Depending on the sound card, some cards play back 5.1 or greater Surround sound configurations with analog speakers only, whereas others can also transmit Dolby Digital (AC-3), DTS Surround, or Dolby EX digital audio through the SPDIF digital audio port to a home theater system.

Microphones

Some audio adapters come complete with a microphone, but most do not. You'll need one to record your voice to a WAV file. Selecting a microphone is quite simple. You need one that has a 1/8" mini-jack to plug into your audio adapter's microphone jack (or audio in jack). Most handheld microphones have an on/off switch. However, you can also use the Mute control in the audio mixer to shut off the microphone.

Like speakers, microphones are measured by their frequency ranges. This is not an important buying factor, however, because the human voice has a limited range. If you are recording only voices, consider an inexpensive microphone that covers a limited range of frequencies. An expensive microphone's recording capabilities extend to frequencies outside the voice's range. Why pay for something you won't be needing?

If you are recording music, invest in an expensive microphone, but be sure that your audio adapter can do justice to the signal produced by the microphone. A high-quality microphone can produce mediocre results when paired with a cheap 8-bit audio adapter.

Your biggest decision is to select a microphone that suits your recording style. If you work in a noisy office, you might want a unidirectional microphone that will prevent extraneous noises from being recorded. An omnidirectional microphone is best for recording a group conversation.

Some audio adapters include a microphone. This can be a small lapel microphone, a handheld microphone, or one with a desktop stand. If you want to keep your hands free, you might want to shun the traditional handheld microphone for a lapel or desktop model. If your audio adapter does not come with a microphone, see your local stereo or electronics parts store. Be sure that any microphone you purchase has the correct impedance to match the audio adapter's input.

If you're using software such as Dragon NaturallySpeaking, Microsoft's integrated voice-recognition, IBM ViaVoice, Philips FreeSpeech, or other voice-recognition software, use the microphone supplied with the software or choose from alternative models the software vendor recommends. Run the microphone setup program again if your software has trouble recognizing your voice. Some models feature a battery pack to boost sound quality; be sure to check the batteries and replace them to keep recognition quality high.

If you're talking but your voice-recognition or recording software isn't responding, check the following:

- **Incorrect jack.** It's easy to plug the microphone into the wrong jack. Try using a magic marker to color-code the microphone wire and jack to make matching up easier if your microphone or audio jack isn't color-coded or uses competing standards. If your sound card or motherboard-based audio supports the auto-recognition feature included in AC'97 v2.3, make sure you plug in one cable at a time and select the device you connected when you are prompted by the audio setup program.

- **Check the recording volume in the mixer control.** This usually defaults to Mute to avoid spurious noise.

- **Make sure the microphone is turned on in the voice-recognition or recording software.** You must click the Record button in recording software, and many voice-recognition programs let you "pick up" the microphone for use or "put it down" when you need to answer the phone. Look for an onscreen microphone icon in the Windows System Tray for fast toggling between modes.

I/O Interfaces from Serial and Parallel to IEEE 1394 and USB

Introduction to Input/Output Ports

This chapter covers the primary external peripheral input/output ports on a modern PC system. This includes a discussion of both the legacy serial and parallel ports that have been standard on PCs since the beginning, as well as a discussion of the universal serial bus (USB, which has largely replaced the older serial and parallel ports) and IEEE 1394 (FireWire/i.LINK) interfaces. (IEEE stands for the Institute of Electrical and Electronic Engineers.) Although eSATA is also considered an external I/O interface, it is a derivative of SATA, which is mainly used as an internal interface. SATA is covered in Chapter 7, "The ATA/IDE Interface." SCSI is another type of internal/external interface; however, desktop PCs today rarely implement SCSI. If you want to learn more about this architecture, refer to *Upgrading and Repairing Servers*.

Currently, the two most popular high-speed serial-bus architecture families for desktop and portable PCs are universal serial bus (USB) and IEEE 1394, which is also called FireWire or i.LINK. Each interface type is available in two versions: USB 1.1 and USB 2.0; IEEE 1394a (FireWire 400) and IEEE 1394b (FireWire 800). The USB and IEEE 1394 port families are high-speed communications ports that far outstrip the capabilities of older standard serial and parallel ports. They can also be used as an alternative to SCSI for high-speed external peripheral connections. In addition to performance, these newer ports offer I/O device consolidation, which means that all types of external peripherals can connect to these ports.

Why Serial?

As mentioned in the previous section, the technology behind both USB and IEEE 1394 is serial in nature. The current trend in high-performance peripheral bus design is to use a serial architecture, in which 1 bit at a time is sent down a wire. Because parallel architecture uses 8, 16, or more wires to send bits simultaneously, the parallel bus is actually much faster at the same clock speed. However, a serial bus still has the advantage in that increasing the clock speed of a serial connection is much easier than increasing that of a parallel connection, so much so that the higher attainable speeds completely offset the difference in the number of bits sent at a time.

Parallel connections in general suffer from several problems, the biggest being signal skew and jitter. Skew and jitter are the reasons high-speed parallel buses such as SCSI (small computer systems interface) are limited to short distances of 3 meters or less. The problem is that, although the 8 or 16 bits of data are fired from the transmitter at the same time, by the time they reach the receiver, propagation delays have conspired to allow some bits to arrive before the others. The longer the cable, the longer the time variation between the arrival of the first and last bits at the other end! This *signal skew*, as it is called, prevents you from running a high-speed transfer rate or a longer cable—or both. *Jitter* is the tendency for the signal to reach its target voltage and float above and below for a short period of time.

With a serial bus, the data is sent 1 bit at a time. Because there is no worry about having multiple bits arrive simultaneously, the clocking rate can be increased dramatically. For example, the top transfer rate possible with EPP/ECP parallel ports is 2.77MBps, whereas IEEE 1394a ports (which use high-speed serial technology) support transfer rates as high as 400Mbps (50MBps)—25 times faster than parallel ports. USB 2.0 supports transfer rates of 480Mbps (60MBps), which is about 30 times faster than parallel ports, and the newer IEEE 1394b (FireWire 800) ports reach transfer rates as high as 800Mbps (100MBps), which is about 50 times faster than parallel ports!

At high clock rates, parallel signals tend to interfere with each other. Serial again has an advantage because, with only one or two signal wires, crosstalk and interference between the wires in the cable are negligible.

In general, parallel cabling is more expensive than serial cabling. Besides the many additional wires needed to carry the multiple bits in parallel, the cable also must be specially constructed to prevent crosstalk and interference between adjacent data lines. This is one reason external SCSI cables are so expensive. Serial cabling, by comparison, is very inexpensive. For one thing, it has significantly fewer wires. Furthermore, the shielding requirements are far simpler, even at very high speeds. Because of this, transmitting serial data reliably over longer distances is also easier, which is why parallel interfaces have shorter recommended cable lengths than do serial interfaces.

For these reasons—in addition to the need for Plug and Play external peripheral interfaces and the elimination of the physical port crowding on portable computers—these high-performance serial buses were developed. USB is a standard feature on virtually all PCs today. It is used for most general-purpose, high-speed external interfacing and is the most compatible, widely available, and fastest general-purpose external interface. In addition, IEEE 1394 (more commonly known as FireWire), although mainly used in certain niche markets, such as connecting DV (digital video) camcorders, has also spread into other high-bandwidth uses, such as high-resolution scanners and external hard drives.

Comparing IEEE 1394 and USB

Although both USB and IEEE 1394 are discussed in detail in the following sections, it's helpful to first compare them. Because of the similarity in both the form and function of USB and 1394 ports, there has been some confusion about the differences between them. Table 15.1 summarizes the differences between these technologies.

Table 15.1   IEEE 1394 and USB Comparison

	IEEE 1394a (also called I.LINK or FireWire 400)	IEEE 1394b (also called FireWire 800)	USB 1.1	USB 2.0
PC-host required	No	No	Yes	Yes/No[1]
Maximum number of devices	63	63	127	127
Hot-swappable	Yes	Yes	Yes	Yes
Maximum cable length between devices	4.5 meters	4.5 meters (9-pin copper); 100 meters (glass optical fiber)[2]	5 meters	5 meters
Transfer rate	400Mbps (50MBps)	800Mbps (100MBps)	12Mbps (1.5MBps)	480Mbps (60MBps)
Proposed future transfer rates	None	1,600Mbps (400MBps); 3,200Mbps (800MBps)	None	None
Typical devices	DV camcorders, high-res digital cameras, HDTV, set-top boxes, high-speed drives, high-res scanners, and electronic musical instruments	All 1394a devices	Keyboards, mice, joysticks, low-res digital cameras, low-speed drives, modems, printers, and low-res scanners	All USB 1.1 devices, DV camcorders, high-res digital cameras, HDTV, set-top boxes, high-speed drives, and high-res scanners

1. *No with USB On-The-Go.*
2. *CAT-5 UTP supported for 100Mbps speeds (100 meters max.); step-index plastic optical fiber supported for 100Mbps and 200Mbps speeds (50 meters max.).*

Currently, USB is by far the most popular external interface for PCs, eclipsing all others by comparison. This is primarily because Intel developed most of the USB specifications and has placed built-in USB support in all its motherboard chipsets and motherboards since 1996, a trend followed by other chipset manufacturers. Few motherboard chipsets integrate 1394a or 1394b; in most cases, it has to be added as an extra-cost chip to the motherboard. The cost of the additional 1394 circuitry (and a $0.25 royalty paid to Apple Computer per system) and the fact that all motherboards already have USB, have limited the popularity of 1394 (FireWire) in the PC marketplace.

1394 has one advantage over USB 1.1 and USB 2.0: it does not need to use a PC as a host. USB 1.1 and USB 2.0 devices can only communicate with each other by means of a PC. On the other hand, 1394 supports the connection of two devices directly because the bus is designed such that any device can control transfers. This can play a big part in performance, as the transfer rate between devices over USB depends greatly on the horsepower of the PC controlling the bus, whereas the transfer rate over FireWire is independent of the PC, and solely dependent on the devices doing the transfers. For example, 1394 can be used to directly connect a DV camcorder to a DV-VCR for dubbing tapes or editing. USB-On-The-Go, a development of USB introduced in 2001, provides a similar "no-host" connection capability for USB. However, USB-On-The-Go is not intended to supplant FireWire. Instead, USB-On-The-Go is designed to support the ever-increasing numbers of portable electronic devices, such as digital cameras, cell phones, and digital media players, enabling them to exchange information with each other or with USB devices such as printers and drives without a PC host.

The latest member of the USB family, Certified Wireless USB, was introduced in 2005, although widespread product support is not expected until late 2007 or beyond.

Because both USB 2.0 and 1394a (FireWire) offer relatively close to the same overall capabilities and performance, you should make your choice based on which devices you intend to connect. If the digital video camera you want to connect has only a 1394 (FireWire/i.LINK) connection, you will need to add a 1394 FireWire card to your system, if such a connection isn't already present on your motherboard. Most general-purpose PC storage, I/O peripherals, and other devices are USB, whereas only video and some storage devices usually have 1394 connections. However, many devices now offer both USB 2.0 and 1394 interfaces to enable use with the widest range of computers.

Performance Myths and Realities

A student once wrote me to enquire about a question that appeared on a test in a computer class he and his classmates had taken. The question was, "Which is faster, USB 2.0 or FireWire 400 (1394a)?" They had answered that USB 2.0 was faster, because USB 2.0 was rated 480Mbps (60MBps), whereas FireWire 400 was rated 400Mbps (50MBps). Well, after the test was graded the students were shocked to find their answer had been marked wrong! Upon discussing the question in class, the teacher confirmed the technical specifications, but then went on to say that due to less internal "overhead," FireWire was faster than USB in the real-world, even though the raw transfer speed might be less on paper. The student was basically asking me what the correct answer to the question really was.

I had to sigh. I *despise* questions like that because from a technical standpoint the question is so poorly and imprecisely written that *both* answers are arguably correct. For example, it obviously wasn't clear whether the question meant "faster" as in the raw bus speed or as in real-world throughput, such as reading or writing files. And if it did mean real-world throughput, then under what circumstances exactly? Well, when confronted with questions like that, where you *have* to make a choice one way or another, in general the best thing you can do is to keep it simple and avoid overthinking the answer. Because real-world testing involves many unknown variables, the simplest and most definitive answer would be based on the raw transfer speeds alone. In that case, choosing the best answer would be simple: Because USB 2.0 transfers at 480Mbps (60MBps), and 1394a transfers at 400Mbps (50MBps), USB is faster.

Now I know some people reading this might disagree, including the teacher who gave the test referenced by the student. Many people believe (and many tests have shown) that whereas USB is faster on paper, FireWire is faster in the real world. Although I hesitate to make blanket statements, I would agree that just as with any interface or bus in a PC, there are many more factors contributing to performance for a specific task under a specific set of conditions than can be assumed from just looking at a raw bus speed specification. Although many people assume that FireWire is faster in the real world, the truth is that the designs of USB and FireWire are very different, and one cannot necessarily predict the results of a specific example without knowing all of the relevant details.

To help make my point, I ran some tests and recorded the results. I had a 7200 rpm Maxtor 250MB drive mounted in an external enclosure that supports *both* FireWire 400 (1394a) and USB 2.0 interfaces. The drive was formatted as a single FAT32 partition, and was about half full. I created a TEMP folder, copied a 300MB video file into the folder, and named it TEMP1.AVI. I specifically selected a large file that would not fit in any of the caches or buffers for either the drive or systems involved.

I used two different systems to conduct the tests, and both included FireWire 400 and USB 2.0 interfaces. The systems were as follows:

- System 1: Desktop, 3.6GHz Pentium 4 processor, 1GB RAM, Windows XP
- System 2: Laptop, 1.7GHz Pentium M processor, 1GB RAM, Windows XP

To test the throughput, I copied the file TEMP1.AVI to TEMP2.AVI in the TEMP folder, and measured the time in seconds for the command to complete. This meant that the file would be read from and written back to the same drive, which amounts to essentially a two-way trip over the interface (from the drive to the PC and back to the drive). I used two different commands (COPY and XCOPY), running each one four times consecutively, discarding the results of the first run and recording the other three. Here are the commands I used to copy the files:

```
COPY /Y TEMP1.AVI TEMP2.AVI

XCOPY /Y TEMP1.AVI TEMP2.AVI
```

NOTE

The /Y switch forces an overwrite of the destination file without prompting, allowing you to repeat the command without having to worry about the destination file left over from the previous execution.

To measure the time it took for each file copy, you can use the **TimeIt** utility, which is a command-line tool that records the time a specified command takes to run. **TimeIt.exe** is included with the Windows Server 2003 Resource Kit Tools, which you can download from Microsoft (http://go.microsoft.com/fwlink/?LinkId=4544).

The times, in seconds, to copy the file for each run using the faster desktop system are shown in Table 15.2.

Table 15.2   Comparing the Time Required to Copy a 300MB File via USB and FireWire on a 3.6GHz Desktop PC

3.6GHz Pentium 4 Desktop		USB 2.0	FireWire 400
COPY 300MB file:	First run	20.65	23.23
	Second run	20.60	23.45
	Third run	20.76	23.28
	Average:	20.67	23.32
USB vs. FireWire		12.82%	−11.36%
XCOPY 300MB file:	First run	12.41	15.66
	Second run	12.47	15.60
	Third run	12.69	15.60
	Average:	12.52	15.62
USB vs. FireWire		24.73%	−19.83%
XCOPY vs. COPY		65.05%	49.30%

As you can see from the results, when using the faster desktop system, copying the file was from 13% (using COPY) to 25% (using XCOPY) *faster* over USB than it was over FireWire. Also note that using the XCOPY command was from 49% to 65% faster than COPY on either interface.

The times, in seconds, to copy the file for each run using the slower laptop system are shown in Table 15.3.

Table 15.3   Comparing the Time Required to Copy a 300MB File via USB and FireWire on a 1.7GHz Laptop PC

1.7GHz Pentium M Laptop		USB 2.0	FireWire 400
COPY 300MB file:	First run	30.59	23.95
	Second run	30.48	24.66
	Third run	30.42	23.79
	Average:	30.50	24.13
USB vs. FireWire		−20.87%	26.37%
XCOPY 300MB file:	First run	19.83	15.71
	Second run	19.16	15.81
	Third run	19.12	15.98
	Average:	19.37	15.83
USB vs. FireWire		−18.26%	22.34%
XCOPY vs. COPY		57.44%	52.42%

As you can see from the results, when using the slower laptop system, copying the file was from 21% (using COPY) to 18% (using XCOPY) *slower* over USB than it was over FireWire. Also note that using the XCOPY command was from 52% to 57% faster than using COPY on either interface.

So which is faster in the "real world"? In this example, when copying the file on the higher performance desktop PC, USB 2.0 was faster; however, on the slower laptop PC, FireWire was faster. But that's not all; I noticed another interesting detail: It seems that the relative speed and performance of the PC had a *large effect* on the throughput of the USB 2.0 transfers, whereas it had virtually *no effect* on the FireWire 400 transfers. Table 15.4 shows a comparison.

Table 15.4   Speed Improvements in the Time to Copy a 300MB File on a 3.6GHz Pentium 4 Desktop vs. a 1.7GHz Pentium M Laptop

Action	USB 2.0	FireWire 400
COPY 300MB file	47.54% faster	3.49% faster
XCOPY 300MB file	54.67% faster	1.37% faster

The desktop system was from 48% to 55% faster than the laptop on USB transfers, and yet only 1% to 3% faster on FireWire transfers. In other words, the FireWire transfer times were virtually *identical* on both the desktop and laptop systems, even though the systems varied greatly in speed. This is understandable because FireWire uses a peer-to-peer connection design, which does not use the PC to manage the interface. On the other hand, USB is a PC-centric design using the PC as the host controller. In other words, because of the internal design differences in USB and FireWire, the PC processor and overall PC system performance has a much greater effect on USB than it does on FireWire.

Another very interesting point: The method used to copy the file (COPY vs. XCOPY in this case) actually made *more* of a difference than the interface or the system speed. This brings up many more questions: Would there have been other differences had the drive been formatted with NTFS instead of FAT32? What if I had copied many small files instead of one large file? Or what if I had used the exact same FireWire and USB interface chipsets on each system (which would probably require using two different desktops in which I could install the same USB/FireWire cards)?

So what is the "correct" answer when all is said and done? If the question merely stated, "Which is faster, USB 2.0 or FireWire 400 (1394a)?", I would have answered *USB*, based solely on the raw bus speeds (480Mbps vs. 400Mbps). However, if the question stated, "When copying a 300MB file on a FAT32 formatted drive under Windows XP, which would be faster, USB 2.0 or FireWire 400 (1394a)?", I would answer, "Either one is faster, depending on the hardware and software used to copy the file." You get the idea. The only thing that went "wrong" with the original test question and answer was failing to understand that in any benchmark or comparison a huge number of variables to must be considered—and there are no simple answers to ambiguous questions!

Universal Serial Bus

Universal serial bus (USB) is an external peripheral bus standard designed to bring Plug and Play capability for attaching peripherals externally to the PC. USB eliminates the need for special-purpose ports, reduces the need to use special-purpose I/O cards (thus reducing the need to reconfigure the system with each new device added), and saves important system resources such as interrupts (IRQs); regardless of the number of devices attached to a system's USB ports, only one IRQ is required. PCs equipped with USB enable peripherals to be automatically recognized and configured as soon as they are physically attached, without the need to reboot or run setup. USB allows up to 127 devices to run simultaneously on a single bus, with peripherals such as monitors and keyboards acting as additional plug-in sites, or hubs. USB cables, connectors, hubs, and peripherals can be identified by icons, as shown in Figure 15.1. Note the "plus" symbol added to the right icon, which indicates that port supports USB 2.0 (Hi-Speed USB) in addition to the standard 1.x support. Keep in mind that on virtually all systems built in the last several years, USB ports support both standards, so the "plus" symbol is no longer widely used.

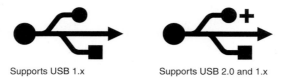

Supports USB 1.x   Supports USB 2.0 and 1.x

Figure 15.1   These icons identify USB cables, connectors, hubs, and peripherals.

Intel has been the primary proponent of USB, and all its PC chipsets starting with the PIIX3 South Bridge chipset component (introduced in February 1996) have included USB support as standard. Other chipset vendors have followed suit, making USB as standard a feature of today's desktop and notebook PCs as serial and parallel ports once were.

Six other companies initially worked with Intel in codeveloping USB, including Compaq, Digital, IBM, Microsoft, NEC, and Northern Telecom. Together, these companies have established the USB Implementers Forum (USB-IF) to develop, support, and promote USB architecture.

◀◀   See "Chipsets," p. 273.

The USB-IF formally released USB 1.0 in January 1996, USB 1.1 in September 1998, and USB 2.0 in April 2000. The 1.1 revision was mostly a clarification of some issues related to hubs and other areas of the specification. Most devices and hubs should be 1.1 compliant, even if they were manufactured before the release of the 1.1 specification. The biggest change was USB 2.0, which is 40 times faster than the original USB and yet fully backward compatible. USB ports can be retrofitted to older computers that lack built-in USB connectors through the use of either an add-on PCI card (for desktop computers) or a PC Card on CardBus-compatible notebook computers. You can also use USB add-on cards to update an older system that has only USB 1.1 on the motherboard. As of mid-2002, virtually all motherboards include four or more USB 2.0 ports as standard. Notebook computers were slower to catch on—it wasn't until early 2003 that most notebook or laptop computers included USB 2.0 ports as standard.

USB Technical Details

USB 1.1 runs at 12Mbps (1.5MBps) over a simple four-wire connection. The bus supports up to 127 devices (including both functions and hubs) connected to a single root hub and uses a tiered-star topology, built on expansion hubs that can reside in the PC, any USB peripheral, or even standalone hub boxes.

Note that although the standard allows up to 127 devices to be attached, they all must share the 12Mbps bandwidth, meaning that for every active device you add, the bus will slow down some. In practical reality, few people will have more than eight devices attached at any one time.

For low-speed peripherals, such as pointing devices and keyboards, the USB also has a slower 1.5Mbps subchannel. The subchannel connection is used for slower interface devices, such as keyboards and mice.

USB employs what is called Non Return to Zero Invert (NRZI) data encoding. NRZI is a method of encoding serial data in which 1s and 0s are represented by opposite and alternating high and low voltages, where there is no return to a zero (or reference) voltage between the encoded bits. In NRZI encoding, a 1 is represented by no change in signal level, and a 0 is represented by a change in level. A string of 0s causes the NRZI data to toggle each bit time; a string of 1s causes long periods with no transitions in the data. This is an efficient transfer encoding scheme because it eliminates the need for additional clock pulses that would otherwise waste time and bandwidth.

USB devices are considered either hubs or functions, or both. *Functions* are the individual devices that attach to the USB, such as a keyboard, mouse, camera, printer, telephone, and so on. *Hubs* provide additional attachment points to the USB, enabling the attachment of more hubs or functions. The initial ports in the PC system unit are called the *root hubs*, and they are the starting point for the USB. Most motherboards have two, three, or four USB ports, any of which can be connected to functions or additional hubs. Generally, there are two USB ports per root hub.

Some systems place one or two of the USB ports in the front of the computer, which is very convenient for devices you use only occasionally, such as digital cameras or flash memory card readers. External hubs (also called *generic hubs*) are essentially wiring concentrators, and through a star-type topology they allow the attachment of multiple devices. Each attachment point is referred to as a *port*. Most hubs have either four or eight ports, but more are possible. For more expandability, you can connect additional hubs to the ports on an existing hub. The hub controls both the connection and distribution of power to each of the connected functions.

Besides providing additional sockets for connecting USB peripherals, a hub provides power to any attached peripherals. A hub recognizes the dynamic attachment of a peripheral and provides at least 0.5W of power per peripheral during initialization. Under control of the host PC driver software, the hub can provide more device power, up to a maximum of 2.5W, for peripheral operation.

Different types of USB devices require different amounts of power, measured in milliamps (mA). Bus-powered USB devices (devices that draw power from the USB port) might require as much as 500mA (the maximum amount of power available through a USB port) or as little as 100mA or less. Self-powered devices also draw power from the USB port, but might draw as little as 2mA.

The PnP aspects of USB enable the system to query the attached peripherals as to their power requirements and issue a warning if available power levels are being exceeded. This is important for USB when it is used in portable systems because the battery power that is allocated to run the external peripherals might be limited, and it is also important because of the differences in hubs.

Root hubs and self-powered hubs (hubs connected to an AC adapter) provide a full 500mA of power to each USB port. However, bus-powered hubs (hubs without an AC adapter) provide only 100mA per port because they use power provided by the upstream USB port and subdivide it among the ports. If you connect a USB device that requires more power than the port provides, the device will not work. In a worst-case scenario, you might damage the device. For example, the contents of some USB flash memory drives (which typically require 200–500mA) can be destroyed by inserting them into a bus-powered hub (which provides only 100mA per port). Some vendors are now including overcurrent protection in their latest designs, but because of the risk factors, I would never plug a USB flash memory drive or a USB card reader into a bus-powered hub.

To determine the power requirements of a particular USB device before you purchase it, check the product's specifications or contact the vendor. To determine the power available per port and the power usage of the devices plugged into the port in Windows, open the Control Panel, open the properties sheet for each root or generic hub, and click the Power tab. The Power tab lists the hub type (self-powered or bus powered) and the amount of power per port in the hub information section of the properties sheet. In the attached devices section, each device connected to the hub is listed by its category and power required (see Figure 15.2).

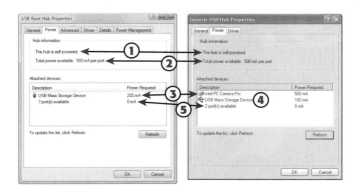

1. Hub type
2. Power per port
3. High-power devices
4. Low-power device
5. Remaining ports

Figure 15.2   Examples of USB hub and device power usage from Windows Vista (left) and Windows XP (right).

Because of the wide variance in the power requirements of different USB devices and the possibility of damage, I recommend that you use only self-powered USB hubs. Keep in mind that some USB hubs on the market do not include an AC adapter, and there are still a number of USB 1.1 hubs on the market. A USB 1.1 hub runs USB 2.0 devices plugged into it to run at USB 1.1 speeds.

Devices that use more than 100mA, such as the webcam and USB mass storage device shown in Figure 15.2, must be connected to a root hub or a self-powered generic hub. Devices that use 100mA or less can be connected to bus-powered hubs, such as those built in to some keyboards and monitors.

Tip

If a device plugged in to a self-powered hub stops working, check the power source for the self-powered hub—it might have failed or been disconnected. In such cases, a self-powered hub becomes a bus-powered hub, providing only 100mA per port instead of the 500mA per port available in self-powered mode.

A newly attached hub is assigned a unique address, and hubs can be cascaded up to five levels deep (see Figure 15.3). A hub operates as a bidirectional repeater and repeats USB signals as required both upstream (toward the PC) and downstream (toward the device). A hub also monitors these signals and handles transactions addressed to itself. All other transactions are repeated to attached devices. In Figure 15.3, host refers to a PC. Hub refers to PCs, standalone hubs, or devices that contain a hub. Function refers to USB devices connected to a root hub or generic hubs.

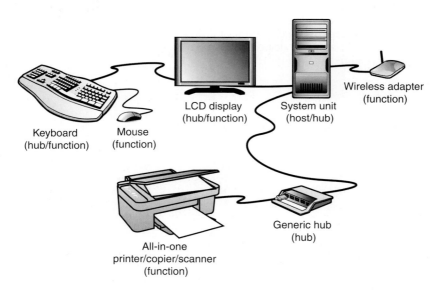

Figure 15.3   A typical PC with USB devices can use multiple USB hubs to support a variety of peripherals, connected to whichever hub is most convenient.

Note

A USB 1.1 hub supports both 12Mbps (full-speed) and 1.5Mbps (low-speed) peripherals. A USB 2.0 hub supports USB 1.1 12Mbps and 1.5Mbps speeds as well as the 480Mbps speed used by native USB 2.0 devices.

Maximum cable length between two high-speed (USB 2.0 480Mbps) or USB 2.0/USB 1.1 full-speed (12Mbps) devices or a device and a hub is 5 meters using twisted-pair shielded cable with 20-gauge wire. Maximum cable length for low-speed (1.5Mbps) devices using non-twisted-pair wire is 3 meters. These distance limits are shorter if smaller-gauge wire is used (see Table 15.5).

Table 15.5   Maximum Cable Lengths Versus Wire Gauge

Gauge	Resistance (in Ohms/Meter Ω/m)	Length (Max.)
28	0.232 Ω/m	0.81m
26	0.145 Ω/m	1.31m
24	0.091 Ω/m	2.08m
22	0.057 Ω/m	3.33m
20	0.036 Ω/m	5.00m

Although USB 1.1 is not as fast at data transfer as FireWire or SCSI, it is still more than adequate for the types of peripherals for which it is designed. USB 2.0 operates a surprising 40 times faster than USB 1.1 and allows transfer speeds of 480Mbps or 60MBps, making it very suitable for external hard disks, USB flash cards, photo printers, and scanners. With very few exceptions, virtually all current motherboards and add-in USB cards support the faster USB 2.0 (Hi-Speed USB) standard. Most generic hubs on the market are also USB 2.0-compliant, although a few vendors continue to sell USB 1.1 hubs. One of the additional benefits of USB 2.0 is the capability to handle concurrent transfers, which enables your USB 1.1 devices to transfer data at the same time without tying up the USB bus.

▶▶ For more information about USB 2.0, see "USB 2.0/Hi-Speed USB," p. 1039.

The USB family of specifications (USB 1.1, USB 2.0, and USB On-the-Go) has included numerous connector styles since it was first introduced. Initially, four main styles of connectors were specified: Series A, Series B, Mini-A, and Mini-B. The A connectors are used for upstream connections between a device and the host or a hub. The USB ports on motherboards and hubs are usually Series A connectors. Series B connectors are designed for the downstream connection to a device that has detachable cables. The mini connector is simply a smaller version of the larger ones, in a physically smaller form factor for smaller devices, such as digital cameras, PDAs, and media players. For USB On-the-Go devices, a Mini-AB connector was developed to permit a device to act as either an upstream or downstream device in relationship to another device.

In April 2006, the Micro-B and Micro-AB connectors were added as approved connectors, and in May 2007, the Mini-A and Mini-AB connectors were removed from the approved list of USB connectors. Thus, as of mid-2007, new and forthcoming USB devices can use only the following connectors: Series A, Series B, Mini-B, Micro-B, and Micro-AB (Micro-AB is used only by OTG products).

The physical USB plugs are small (especially the Mini and Micro plugs) and, unlike a typical serial or parallel cable, the plug is not attached by screws or thumbscrews. There are no pins to bend or break, making USB devices very user friendly to install and remove. The USB plugs shown in Figure 15.4 snap into place on the corresponding USB sockets.

Note that a Mini-AB socket is a dual-purpose socket that can accept either Mini-A or Mini-B plugs. Likewise, a Micro-AB socket is a dual-purpose socket for either Micro-A or Micro-B plugs (there is no Micro-A socket). The newer mini and micro plugs and sockets have plastic portions inside the connectors that are required to be color-coded, as shown in Table 15.6.

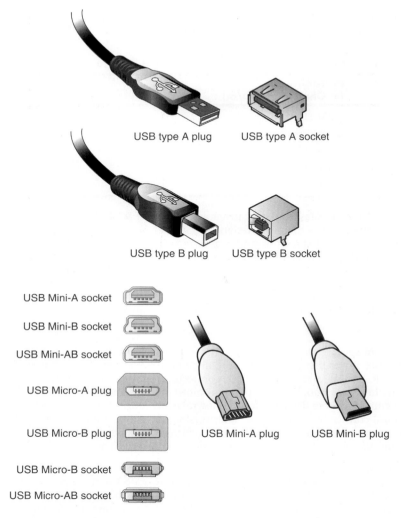

Figure 15.4   USB plugs and sockets.

Table 15.6   Color-Coding for USB Mini-Plugs and Sockets

Connector	Color
Mini-A socket	White
Mini-A or Micro-A plug	White
Mini-B or Micro-B socket	Black
Mini-B or Micro-B plug	Black
Mini-AB or Micro AB socket	Gray

Tables 15.7 and 15.8 show the pinouts for the USB connectors and cables. Most systems with USB connectors feature one or two pairs of Series A plugs on the rear of the system. Some also feature one or two pairs on the front of the system for ease of use with items that are not permanently connected.

Table 15.7   USB Connector Pinouts for Series A/B Connectors

Pin	Signal Name	Wire Color	Comment
1	VBUS	Red	Bus power
2	– Data	White	Data transfer
3	+ Data	Green	Data transfer
4	Ground	Black	Cable ground
Shell	Shield	—	Drain wire

Table 15.8   USB Connector Pinouts for Mini and Micro A/B Connectors

Pin	Signal Name	Wire Color	Comment
1	VBUS	Red	Bus power
2	– Data	White	Data transfer
3	+ Data	Green	Data transfer
4	ID	—	A/B identification*
4	Ground	Black	Cable ground
Shell	Shield	—	Drain wire

Used to identify a Mini-A from a Mini-B or a Micro-A from a Micro-B connector to the device. ID is connected to Ground in a Mini-A or Micro-A plug and not connected (open) in a Mini-B or Micro-B plug.

USB conforms to Intel's Plug and Play (PnP) specification, including hot plugging, which means that devices can be plugged in dynamically without powering down or rebooting the system. Simply plug in the device, and the USB controller in the PC detects the device and automatically determines and allocates the required resources and drivers.

Windows 95B and 95C have very limited support for USB 1.1; the necessary drivers are not present in the original Windows 95 or 95A. With Windows 95B, the USB drivers are not automatically included; they are provided separately, although a late release of Windows 95—Windows 95C—includes USB support. Many USB devices will not work with *any* Windows 95 release, including those that have the USB support files included.

Windows 98 and later have USB 1.1 support built in; however, additional drivers are required for USB 2.0 or later. In most cases, these drivers can be downloaded from Microsoft using the Windows Update feature. Windows Vista, of course, natively supports the USB 2.0 standard.

USB support is also required in the BIOS for devices such as keyboards and mice. This is included in all modern systems with USB ports built in. Aftermarket PCI and PC Card boards also are available for adding USB to systems that don't include it as standard on the motherboard. USB peripherals include printers, external storage drives, modems, scanners, VoIP telephones, game controllers, keyboards, and pointing devices such as mice and trackballs.

Another of the benefits of the USB specification is the self-identifying peripheral, a feature that greatly eases installation because you don't have to set unique IDs or identifiers for each peripheral—the USB handles that automatically. Also, USB devices can be "hot" plugged or unplugged, meaning that you do not have to turn off your computer or reboot every time you want to connect or disconnect a peripheral. However, to prevent data loss with USB drives and storage devices, you need to use the Eject Hardware or Safely Remove Hardware feature in the Windows system tray. Click the device, select Stop, click OK, and wait for the system to indicate that the device has been stopped before you remove it.

Note

Although USB devices support PnP and hot-plugging, you may need to install drivers for particular USB devices. If your USB device is labeled "install software first," be sure to do so, otherwise the system will not be able to recognize the device. However, even if you receive a driver CD with your device, I recommend checking for updated drivers on the vendor's website.

Enabling USB Support

Many systems shipped before Windows 98 was introduced in mid-1998 have onboard USB ports that were disabled at the factory. In some cases, especially with Baby-AT motherboards, there is no way to tell from the outside which systems have USB support built in. This is because many of these same systems were not shipped with the USB header cables necessary to bring the USB root hub connectors from the motherboard to the rear of the system.

If USB support is disabled in the system BIOS, restart your system and locate the BIOS setup screen that refers to the USB ports. Enable the USB feature. If you see a separate entry for USB IRQ, enable this as well. After you restart the computer with a USB-aware operating system, your "new" USB root hub will be detected and the drivers will be installed if you are using Windows 98 or newer; you might need to manually install drivers with late releases of Windows 95. USB 2.0 drivers were not provided with the initial launch of Windows XP but are available through system update downloads or service packs. Use the Windows Update feature to connect to the Microsoft site and download any updates as necessary. Add-on USB 2.0 cards might include their own drivers, which should be installed

If your system has USB connectors present, you also will be able to use the "new" USB ports as soon as the system is rebooted after the USB drivers are installed. However, if your motherboard vendor didn't provide USB connectors, you must buy USB header cables. Before you order them, check the configuration of your motherboard's USB header pins. The standard is two rows of five pins each. Companies such as Belkin, CyberGuys, and Cables To Go sell header cables that are compatible with standard USB header pins if your motherboard supplier doesn't have the header cable in stock. Figure 15.5 shows a typical USB header cable set.

One of the biggest advantages of an interface such as USB is that it requires only a single interrupt (IRQ) from the PC. Therefore, you can connect up to 127 devices and they will not use separate interrupts, as they might if each were connected over a separate interface. This is a major benefit of the USB interface.

The USB interface can also be adapted to older peripherals. See the section "USB Adapters," later in this chapter, for details.

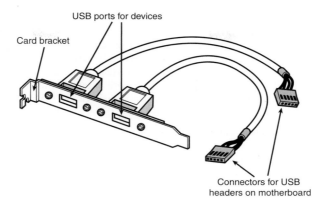

Figure 15.5 A typical USB header cable set; plug it into your motherboard to connect devices to the additional onboard USB ports (if present).

USB 2.0/Hi-Speed USB

USB 2.0 (also called Hi-Speed USB) is a backward-compatible extension of the USB 1.1 specification that uses the same cables, connectors, and software interfaces, but it runs 40 times faster than the original 1.0 and 1.1 versions. The higher speed enables higher-performance peripherals, such as higher-resolution web/videoconferencing cameras, scanners, and faster printers, to be connected externally with the same easy Plug and Play installation of current USB peripherals. From the end user's point of view, USB 2.0 works exactly the same as 1.1—only faster and with more interesting, higher-performance devices available. All existing USB 1.1 devices work in a USB 2.0 bus because USB 2.0 supports all the slower-speed connections. USB data rates are shown in Table 15.9.

Table 15.9   USB Data Rates

Interface	Megabits per Second	Megabytes per Second
USB 1.1 low speed	1.5Mbps	0.1875MBps
USB 1.1 full speed	12Mbps	1.5MBps
USB 2.0 high speed	480Mbps	60MBps

If your motherboard or system features USB 2.0–compatible (Hi-Speed USB) ports, you might need to enable USB 2.0/Hi-Speed USB support in the system BIOS and install an appropriate driver. Otherwise, USB 2.0/Hi-Speed USB ports will be used as USB 1.1 ports.

◄◄ For details, see "Advanced USB Configuration Menu," p. 491.

To support higher-speed USB 2.0 peripherals, use a USB 2.0 hub. You can still use older USB 1.1 hubs on a 2.0 bus, but any peripherals or additional hubs connected downstream from a 1.1 hub will operate at the slower 12Mbps (1.5MBps) USB 1.1 maximum speed. Devices connected to USB 2.0 hubs will operate at the maximum speed of the device, up to the full USB 2.0 speed of 480Mbps (60MBps). The higher transmission speeds through a 2.0 hub are negotiated on a device-by-device basis, and if the higher speed is not supported by a peripheral, the link operates at a lower USB 1.1 speed.

As such, a USB 2.0 hub accepts high-speed transactions at the faster USB 2.0 frame rate and must deliver them to high-speed USB 2.0 peripherals as well as USB 1.1 peripherals. This data rate matching responsibility requires increased complexity and buffering of the incoming high-speed data. When communicating with an attached USB 2.0 peripheral, the 2.0 hub simply repeats the high-speed signals; however, when communicating with USB 1.1 peripherals, a USB 2.0 hub buffers and manages the transition from the high speed of the USB 2.0 host controller (in the PC) to the lower speed of a USB 1.1 device using a component called a transaction translator (TT). This feature of USB 2.0 hubs means that USB 1.1 devices can operate along with USB 2.0 devices and not consume any additional bandwidth. Some manufacturers of add-on USB 2.0 cards are equipping the cards with both external and internal USB 2.0 ports.

Note

If a hub uses only a single TT for all ports, USB 1.1 performance suffers. For best performance, choose hubs that use a separate TT for each USB port. These hubs tend to be more expensive than hubs with a single TT.

How can you tell which devices are designed to support a particular version of USB and have been certified by the USB Implementer's Forum (USB-IF)? Look for logos on the packaging and the devices indicating that devices have passed the USB-IF's certification tests for USB, USB OTG, and Wireless USB..

USB On-The-Go

In December 2001 the USB-IF released a supplement to the USB 2.0 standard called USB On-The-Go (often referred to as USB OTG or simply as OTG). It was designed to address the one major shortcoming of USB: the fact that a PC was required to transfer data between two devices. In other words, you couldn't connect two cameras together and transfer pictures between them without a PC orchestrating the transfer. With USB On-The-Go, however, devices that conform to the specification still work normally when they are connected to a PC, but they also have additional capabilities when connected to other devices supporting the standard.

Although this capability can also work with PC peripherals, it was mainly added to address issues using USB devices in the consumer electronics area, where a PC might not be available. Using this standard, devices such as digital video recorders can connect to other recorders to transfer recorded movies or shows, items such as personal organizers can transfer data to other organizers, and so on. The addition of the On-The-Go supplement to USB 2.0 greatly enhances the use and capabilities of USB both in the PC and consumer electronics markets.

The current version of USB OTG, version 1.3, was released in December 2006, and includes several changes from previous versions, including the mandating of micro ports in place of the mini ports specified in previous versions. By specifying the smaller micro port designs, USB OTG v1.3 enables more compact portable electronic devices containing USB OTG support.

Wireless USB

With the widespread popularity of USB and the increasing popularity of wireless connections, it was only a matter of time until a wireless version of USB was developed. Actually, two competing visions for wireless USB have been introduced, each using a different ultra wide band (UWB) radio technology:

- CableFree USB
- Certified Wireless USB

CableFree USB was developed by FreeScale Semiconductor, using direct sequence UWB signaling (UWB-DS) developed by the UWB Forum. CableFree USB has been largely ignored by vendors, with its main achievement the Belkin CableFree wireless USB hub introduced in 2006.

The Certified Wireless USB specification was announced in 2004 by the USB-IF, and version 1.0 was introduced in May 2005, with several adjustments to its content since. Certified Wireless USB uses the Wi-Media MB-OFDM ultra-wide band radio technology developed by the WiMedia Alliance (www.wimedia.org), which uses radio frequencies running in the 3.1GHz to 10.6GHz range. By using frequencies above the 2.4GHz frequency used by most 802.11-based networks, interference with the most popular wireless network standards is avoided. And, by dividing up this broad range into 528MHz-wide channels, UWB can work in different countries that may have different regulations for allowable frequencies for wireless communications.

Certified Wireless USB offers speeds up to 480Mbps (the same as USB 2.0's Hi-Speed mode) at ranges up to three meters, dropping to 110Mbps for distances up to ten meters. The first Certified Wireless USB products were introduced in 2007. Ironically, Belkin, which introduced one of the first CableFree USB hubs, has introduced the first Certified Wireless USB hub.

Both wireless USB standards require the user to associate connected products with each other through the use of dongles or one-time cable connections. This permits a secure, encrypted connection between devices.

USB Adapters

If you still have a variety of older peripherals and yet you want to take advantage of the USB connector on your motherboard, several signal converters or adapters are available. Companies such as Belkin and others currently have adapters in the following types:

- USB-to-parallel (printer)
- USB-to-serial
- USB-to-SCSI
- USB-to-Ethernet
- USB-to-keyboard/mouse
- USB-to-TV/video

These adapters usually look just like a cable, with a USB connector at one end (which you plug into your USB port) and various other interface connectors at the other end. In some cases, you attach standard USB and device cables to a standalone adapter.

There is more to these devices than just a cable: If the unit is a one-piece device, active electronics are hidden in a module along the cable or are sometimes packed into one of the cable ends. The electronics are powered by the USB bus and convert the signals to the appropriate other interface. If you cannot install a native adapter card for your device, converting it to use the USB port through an adapter is much better than not using the device at all. For example, a USB-to-Ethernet adapter can enable a computer without expansion slots to connect to a broadband Internet device such as a cable or DSL modem.

However, some drawbacks do exist to these adapters. For example, USB-to-parallel converters work only with printers and not other parallel-connected devices, such as scanners, cameras, external drives, and so on. Before purchasing one of these adapters, ensure that it will work with the device or devices you have in mind. If you need to use more than one non-USB device with your system, consider special USB hubs that also contain various combinations of other port types; these are sometimes referred to as *multifunction USB hubs*, *USB port replicators*, or *USB docking stations*. These special hubs are more expensive than USB-only hubs but are less expensive than the combined cost of a comparable USB hub and two or more USB adapters.

Another type of adapter available is a direct-connect cable, which enables you to connect two USB-equipped PCs directly together using USB as a network. These are popular for transferring files because this connection usually works as well or better than the direct parallel connection that otherwise might be used. Also available are USB switchboxes that enable one peripheral to be shared among two or more USB buses. Note that both the direct connect cables and USB switchboxes are technically not allowed as a part of the USB specification, although they do exist.

IEEE 1394

The Institute of Electrical and Electronic Engineers Standards Board introduced IEEE 1394 (or just 1394 for short) in late 1995. The number comes from the fact that this happened to be the 1,394th standard the institute published. It is the result of the large data-moving demands of today's audio and video multimedia devices. The key advantage of 1394 is that it's extremely fast; the popular 1394a standard supports data transfer rates up to an incredible 400Mbps.

1394 Standards

The most common version of the 1394 standard is actually referred to as 1394a, or sometimes as 1394a-2000 for the year it was adopted. The 1394a standard was introduced to solve interoperability and compatibility issues in the original 1394 standard; it uses the same connectors and supports the same speeds as the original 1394 standard.

The 1394 family also includes the 1394b standard, introduced in early 2003. Initially, 1394b supports 800Mbps transfer rates, but future versions of the standard might reach speeds of up to 3,200Mbps. 1394b reaches much higher speeds than the current 1394/1394a standard and will also support network technologies such as glass and plastic fiber-optic cable and Category 5 UTP cable, increased distances when Category 5 cabling is used between devices, and improvements in signaling. 1394b is fully backward-compatible with 1394a devices.

1394 is also known by two other common names: i.LINK and FireWire. *i.LINK* is an IEEE 1394 designation initiated by Sony in an effort to put a more user-friendly name on IEEE 1394 technology. Most companies that produce 1394 products for PCs have endorsed this new name initiative. Originally, the term *FireWire* was an Apple-specific trademark that Apple licensed to vendors on a fee basis. However, in May 2002, Apple and the 1394 Trade Association announced an agreement to allow the trade association to provide no-fee licenses for the FireWire trademark on 1394-compliant products that pass the trade association's tests. Apple continues to use *FireWire* as its marketing term for IEEE 1394 devices. FireWire 400 refers to Apple's IEEE 1394a–compliant products, whereas FireWire 800 refers to Apple's IEEE 1394b–compliant products.

1394a Technical Details

The IEEE 1394a standard currently exists with three signaling rates—100Mbps, 200Mbps, and 400Mbps (12.5MBps, 25MBps, and 50MBps). Most PC adapter cards support the 400Mbps (50MBps) rate, although device speeds can vary. A maximum of 63 devices can be connected to a single IEEE 1394 adapter card by way of daisy-chaining or branching. 1394 devices, unlike USB devices, can be used in a daisy-chain without using a hub, although hubs are recommended for devices that will be hot-swapped. Cables for IEEE 1394/1394a devices use Nintendo Game Boy–derived connectors and consist of six conductors: Four wires transmit data, and two wires conduct power. Connection with the motherboard is made either by a dedicated IEEE 1394 interface or by a PCI adapter card. Figure 15.6 shows the 1394/1394a cable, socket, and connector.

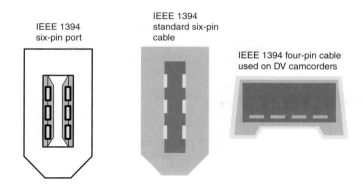

IEEE 1394
six-pin port

IEEE 1394
standard six-pin
cable

IEEE 1394 four-pin cable
used on DV camcorders

Figure 15.6   IEEE 1394 port, 6-pin cable, and 4-pin cable.

The 1394 bus was derived from the FireWire bus originally developed by Apple and Texas Instruments. 1394a uses a simple six-wire cable with two differential pairs of clock and data lines, plus two power lines; the four-wire cable end shown in Figure 15.7 is used with self-powered devices, such as DV camcorders. Just as with USB, 1394 is fully PnP, including the capability for hot-plugging (insertion and removal of components without powering down). Unlike the much more complicated parallel SCSI bus, 1394 does not require complicated termination, and devices connected to the bus can draw up to 1.5 amps of electrical power.

1394 is built on a daisy-chained and branched topology, and it allows up to 63 nodes, with a chain of up to 16 devices on each node. If this is not enough, the standard also calls for up to 1,023 bridged buses, which can interconnect more than 64,000 nodes! Additionally, 1394 can support devices with various data rates on the same bus. Most 1394 adapters have three nodes, each of which can support 16 devices in a daisy-chain arrangement. Some 1394 adapters also support internal 1394 devices.

The types of devices that can be connected to the PC via 1394 mainly include video cameras, editing equipment, and all forms of disk drives, including hard disk, optical, floppy, CD-ROM, and DVD-rewritable drives. Also, digital cameras, tape drives, high-resolution scanners, and many other high-speed peripherals that feature 1394 have interfaces built in. The 1394 bus appears in some desktop and portable computers as a supplement to other external high-speed buses, such as USB.

Chipsets and PCI adapters for the 1394 bus are available from a number of manufacturers, including some models that support both 1394 and other port types in a single slot. Microsoft has developed drivers to support 1394 in Windows 9x and later. The most popular devices that conform to the IEEE 1394 standard are camcorders and VCRs with digital video capability. Sony was among the first to release such devices (under the i.LINK name). In typical Sony fashion, however, many Sony products have a unique four-wire connector that requires an adapter cord to be used with IEEE 1394 PC Cards, and Sony doesn't even call it IEEE 1394 or FireWire—it created its own designation (i.LINK) instead. (Some recent Sony systems use the standard 6-wire 1394 port, while continuing to use the i.Link name.) DV products using 1394 also are available from Panasonic, Sharp, JVC, and others. Noncomputer IEEE 1394 applications include DV conferencing devices, satellite audio and video data streams, audio synthesizers, DVD, and other high-speed storage devices.

Because of the current DV emphasis for IEEE 1394 peripherals, many FireWire cards currently offered are bundled with DV capturing and editing software. With a DV camera or recording equipment, these items provide substantial video-editing and dubbing capabilities on your PC. Of course, you need IEEE 1394 I/O connectivity, which is a growing, but still somewhat rare, feature on current motherboards.

1394b Technical Details

IEEE 1394b is the second generation of the 1394 standard, with the first products (high-performance external hard drives) introduced in January 2003. IEEE 1394b uses one of two 9-pin cables and connectors to support speeds of 800Mbps–3200Mbps with copper or fiber-optic cabling. In addition to supporting faster transfer rates, 1394b has the following features:

- Self-healing loops. If you improperly connect 1394b devices together to create a logical loop, the interface corrects the problem instead of failing, as with 1394a.

- Continuous dual simplex. Of the two wire pairs used, each pair transmits data to the other device, so that speed remains constant.

- Support for fiber-optic and CAT5 network cable as well as standard 1394a and 1394b copper cable.

- Improved arbitration of signals to support faster performance and longer cable distances.

- Support for CAT5 cable, even though it uses pairs on pins 1, 2, 7, and 8 only for greater reliability. It also doesn't require crossover cables.

Note

Microsoft Windows Vista did not include 1394b support when it was introduced. However, 1394b support is forthcoming. In some cases, you may be able to use Windows XP 1394b drivers until native Vista drivers are introduced.

The initial implementations of IEEE 1394b use a nine-wire interface with two pairs of signaling wires. However, to enable a 1394b port to connect to 1394a-compatible devices, two different versions of the 1394b port are available:

- Beta
- Bilingual

Beta connectors support only 1394b devices, whereas bilingual connectors can support both 1394b and 1394a devices. As Figure 15.7 shows, the connectors and cables have the same pinout but are keyed differently.

Note that bilingual sockets and cables have a narrower notch than beta sockets and cables. This prevents cables designed for 1394a devices from being connected to the beta socket. Figure 15.8 compares a beta-to-beta 1394b cable to bilingual-to-1394a cables.

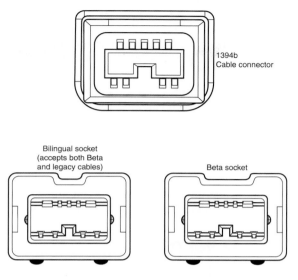

Figure 15.7   Bilingual and beta 1394b connectors and cables. Many 1394b implementations use both types of connectors.

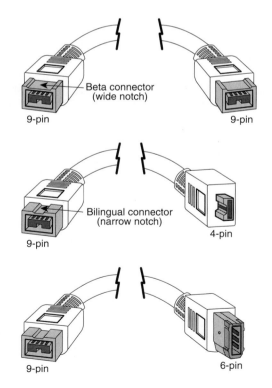

Figure 15.8   A beta-to-beta cable (top) compared to bilingual–to–4-pin (middle) and bilingual–to–6-pin 1394a devices (bottom).

Serial Ports

The asynchronous serial interface was designed as a system-to-system communications port. *Asynchronous* means that no synchronization or clocking signal is present, so characters can be sent with any arbitrary time spacing.

Each character that is sent over a serial connection is framed by a standard start-and-stop signal. A single 0 bit, called the *start bit*, precedes each character to tell the receiving system that the next eight bits constitute a byte of data. One or two stop bits follow the character to signal that the character has been sent. At the receiving end of the communication, characters are recognized by the start-and-stop signals instead of by the timing of their arrival. The asynchronous interface is character oriented and has an approximate 20% overhead for the extra information that is needed to identify each character.

Serial refers to data that is sent over a single wire, with each bit lining up in a series as the bits are sent. This type of communication is used over the phone system because it provides one wire for data in each direction.

Typical Locations for Serial Ports

Typical desktop systems include one or two serial ports, with connectors typically located at the rear of the system, although most recent laptops no longer feature serial ports, and some older consumer-oriented computers also included a front-mounted serial port labeled for use with digital cameras (but operating as a normal serial port). On recent systems, these built-in serial ports are controlled by a highly integrated South Bridge chip.

If you need more serial ports than your system has as standard, you can purchase single-port or multi-port serial port cards or so-called *multi-I/O* cards that feature one or two serial ports and one or two parallel ports.

Note that card-based modems may also incorporate a built-in serial port on the card as part of the modem circuitry (except controller-less software modems). Figure 15.9 shows the standard 9-pin connector used with most modern external serial ports. Figure 15.10 shows the original standard 25-pin version.

Serial ports have been used to connect to a variety of devices, such as modems, plotters, printers, PDA docking devices, other computers, bar code readers, scales, and device control circuits. Although most devices that formerly used serial ports now use USB ports, you might still encounter some serial-based devices.

The official RS-232 specification recommends a maximum cable length of 50 feet. The limiting factor is the total load capacitance of cable and input circuits of the interface. The maximum capacitance is specified as 2500pF (picofarads). Special low-capacitance cables can effectively increase the maximum cable length greatly, to as much as 500 feet or more. Also available are line drivers (amplifier/repeaters) that can extend cable length even further. Tables 15.10, 15.11, and 15.12 show the pinouts of the 9-pin (AT-style), 25-pin, and 9-pin–to–25-pin serial connectors, respectively.

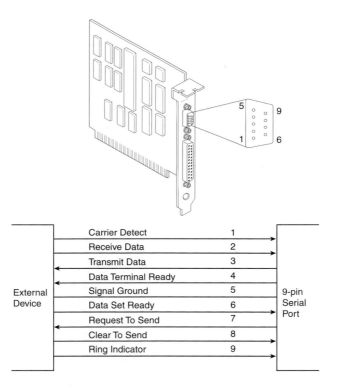

Figure 15.9 AT-style 9-pin serial-port connector specifications.

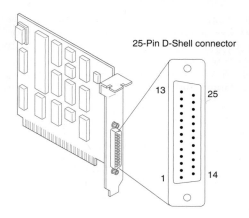

25-Pin D-Shell connector

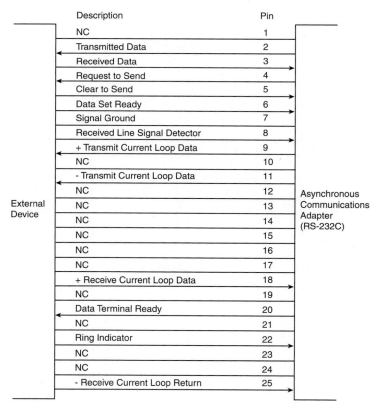

Description	Pin
NC	1
Transmitted Data	2
Received Data	3
Request to Send	4
Clear to Send	5
Data Set Ready	6
Signal Ground	7
Received Line Signal Detector	8
+ Transmit Current Loop Data	9
NC	10
- Transmit Current Loop Data	11
NC	12
NC	13
NC	14
NC	15
NC	16
NC	17
+ Receive Current Loop Data	18
NC	19
Data Terminal Ready	20
NC	21
Ring Indicator	22
NC	23
NC	24
- Receive Current Loop Return	25

External Device

Asynchronous Communications Adapter (RS-232C)

Figure 15.10 Standard 25-pin serial-port connector specifications. NC stands for *no connect,* which indicates a dead pin.

Table 15.10   Pinouts for the 9-Pin (AT) Serial Port Connector

Pin	Signal	Description	I/O
1	CD	Carrier detect	In
2	RD	Receive data	In
3	TD	Transmit data	Out
4	DTR	Data terminal ready	Out
5	SG	Signal ground	—
6	DSR	Data set ready	In
7	RTS	Request to send	Out
8	CTS	Clear to send	In
9	RI	Ring indicator	In

Table 15.11   Pinouts for the 25-Pin (PC, XT, and PS/2) Serial Port Connector

Pin	Signal	Description	I/O
1	—	Chassis ground	—
2	TD	Transmit data	Out
3	RD	Receive data	In
4	RTS	Request to send	Out
5	CTS	Clear to send	In
6	DSR	Data set ready	In
7	SG	Signal ground	—
8	CD	Carrier detect	In
9	—	+Transmit current loop return	Out
11	—	−Transmit current loop data	Out
18	—	+Receive current loop data	In
20	DTR	Data terminal ready	Out
22	RI	Ring indicator	In
25	—	−Receive current loop return	In

Table 15.12   The 9-Pin–to–25-Pin Serial Cable Adapter Connections

9-Pin	25-Pin	Signal	Description
1	8	CD	Carrier detect
2	3	RD	Receive data
3	2	TD	Transmit data
4	20	DTR	Data terminal ready
5	7	SG	Signal ground
6	6	DSR	Data set ready
7	4	RTS	Request to send
8	5	CTS	Clear to send
9	22	RI	Ring indicator

Note

Older Macintosh systems used a similar serial interface, defined as RS-422 (recent PowerPC-based Macs and all Intel-based Macs no longer include RS-422 ports). Most serial-based external modems can interface with RS-232 or RS-422, but it is safest to make sure that the external modem you get for your PC is designed for a PC, not a Macintosh.

The UART Chip

The heart of any serial port is the Universal Asynchronous Receiver/Transmitter (UART) chip. This chip completely controls the process of breaking the native parallel data within the PC into serial format and later converting serial data back into the parallel format.

Several types of UART chips have been available on the market. The original PC and XT used the 8250 UART, which was used for many years in low-priced serial cards. Starting with the first 16-bit systems, the 16450 UART typically was used. The only difference between these chips is their suitability for high-speed communications. The 16450 is better suited for high-speed communications than is the 8250; otherwise, both chips appear identical to most software. The 16550 UART was the first serial chip used in the IBM PS/2 line. Other 386 and higher systems rapidly adopted it. The 16550 functioned as the earlier 16450 and 8250 chips, but it also included a 16-byte buffer that aided in faster communications. This is sometimes referred to as a *FIFO (first in first out)* buffer. Unfortunately, the early 16550 chips had a few bugs, particularly in the buffer area. These bugs were corrected with the release of the 16550A. The most current version of the chip is the 16550D, which was released in 1995 and is produced by National Semiconductor. The 16550D or equivalent can be found in virtually all PCs and serial-port boards produced since the late 1990s. In the case of recent PCs with a Super-I/O or Super South Bridge chip on the motherboard, these chips emulate the functionality of the 16550D.

◀◀   See "Super I/O Chips," p. 367.

For more information about the 8250 and 16450 UART chips, see *Upgrading and Repairing PCs, 15th Edition.*

Several companies have produced versions of the 16550, which has a top speed of 115Kbps, that include larger buffers:

- The 16550 has a 32-byte buffer.
- The 16750 has a 64-byte buffer.
- The 16850 has a 128-byte buffer.
- The 16950 has a 128-byte buffer and the option to run at normal or 4× normal baud rates.

These chips are not from National Semiconductor, and the designations only imply that they are compatible with the 16550, but have a larger buffer. These larger-buffered versions allow speeds of 230Kbps (16650), 460Kbps (16750), and 920Kbps (16850 and 16950) and are recommended when running a high-speed external communications link, such as an ISDN terminal adapter or external 56Kbps modem. Lava Computer Mfg. and SIIG are two of the companies that offer a complete line of high-speed serial and parallel port cards that include serial ports based on these chips.

High-speed Serial Port Cards

If you are using external RS-232 devices designed to run at speeds higher than 115Kbps (the maximum speed of the 16550 series UARTs and equivalents), you can't achieve maximum performance unless you replace your existing serial ports with add-on cards using one of the 16650, 16750, 16850, or 16950 UARTs discussed earlier. Most cards allow raw port speed settings of 230Kbps, 460Kbps, or even higher, which is valuable when connecting a PC to a high-speed external component that is connected to a serial port, such as an ISDN terminal adapter. You can't really get the full-speed benefit of an external ISDN modem (terminal adapter) unless your serial port can go at least 230Kbps.

Serial Port Configuration

Each time a character is received by a serial port, it has to get the attention of the computer by raising an interrupt request line (IRQ). Eight-bit ISA bus systems have eight of these lines, and systems with a 16-bit ISA bus have 16 lines. The 8259 interrupt controller chip or equivalent typically handles these requests for attention. In a standard configuration, COM1 uses IRQ4, and COM2 uses IRQ3. Even on the latest systems, the default COM port assignments remain the same for compatibility with older software and hardware.

When a serial port is installed in a system, it must be configured to use specific I/O addresses (called ports) and interrupts (called IRQs). The best plan is to follow the existing standards for how these devices are to be set up. For configuring serial ports, use the addresses and interrupts indicated in Table 15.13.

Table 15.13   Standard Serial I/O Port Addresses and Interrupts

COMx	I/O Ports	IRQ
COM1	3F8–3FFh	IRQ4
COM2	2F8–2FFh	IRQ3
COM3	3E8–3EFh	IRQ4[1]
COM4	2E8–2EFh[2]	IRQ3[1]

1. Note that although many serial ports can be set up to share IRQ3 and IRQ4 with COM1 and COM2, it is not recommended. The best recommendation is setting COM3 to IRQ10 and COM4 to IRQ11 (if available). If ports above COM3 are required, it is recommended that you purchase a special multiport serial board, preferably a PCI-based board that supports IRQ sharing without conflicts.

2. This I/O address can conflict with registers in some video cards. In such cases, you cannot use COM4 unless COM4 or the video card can be configured to use a different I/O port address range.

Be sure that, if you are adding more than the standard COM1 and COM2 serial ports, they use unique and nonconflicting interrupts. If you purchase a serial port adapter card and intend to use it to supply ports beyond the standard COM1 and COM2, be sure it can use interrupts other than IRQ3 and IRQ4; PCI-based serial port boards take advantage of IRQ sharing features to allow COM3 and above to use a single IRQ without conflicts.

Note that BIOS manufacturers never built support for COM3 and COM4 into the BIOS. Therefore, DOS can't work with serial ports above COM2 because DOS gets its I/O information from the BIOS. The BIOS finds out what is installed in your system, and where it is installed, during the power-on self test (POST). The POST checks only for the first two installed ports. This is not a problem under Windows because Windows 95 and later have built-in support for up to 128 ports.

With support for up to 128 serial ports in Windows, using multiport boards in the system is much easier. Multiport boards give your system the capability to collect or share data with multiple devices while using only one slot and one interrupt.

Caution

Sharing interrupts between COM ports—or any devices—can function properly sometimes and not at others. It is recommended that you never share interrupts between multiple ISA-based serial ports, such as the COM ports built into your motherboard or found on an ISA modem. Trying to track down drivers, patches, and updates to allow this to work successfully—if it's even possible in your system—can cause you hours of frustration.

◄◄   See "Resolving Resource Conflicts," p. 422.

Testing Serial Ports

You can perform several tests on serial and parallel ports. The two most common types of tests are those that involve software only and those that involve both hardware and software. The software-only tests are done with diagnostic programs, such as the Modem diagnostics built into Windows, whereas the hardware and software tests involve using a wrap plug to perform loopback testing.

►►   See "Advanced Diagnostics Using Loopback Testing," p. 1053.

►►   See "Testing Parallel Ports," p. 1057.

Using MSInfo32 to View Serial Port Information

Microsoft includes diagnostics programs with different versions of Windows, which can be useful in testing and configuring serial and parallel ports. Windows NT and later include the System Information tool, otherwise known as WinMSD.exe in Windows NT and Msinfo32.exe in Windows 2000, XP and Vista. A DOS-based tool called Microsoft Diagnostics (MSD) is included with MS-DOS 6.x, Windows 3.x, and Windows 9x/Me. The System Information tool is automatically copied to the hard drive when Windows NT and later are installed. To run it, select Start, Run. Then type **Msinfo32** in the Open box and click OK. If the System Information tool doesn't start, use the Search function to locate either Msinfo32.exe or WinMSD.exe on the hard disk, and double click it when found.

Using System Information, you can view information about which type of serial chip you have in your system as well as information about which ports are available. If any of the ports are in use (with a mouse, for example), that information is provided as well.

These diagnostic tools are helpful in determining whether your serial ports are responding, as well as how they are configured.

Troubleshooting Ports in Windows

Windows 9x/Me can tell you whether your ports are functioning. First, you must verify that the required communications files are present to support the serial ports in your system:

1. Verify the 16-bit serial driver (COMM.DRV) and 32-bit serial driver (SERIAL.VXD) are present in the WINDOWS\SYSTEM folder.

2. Confirm that the following lines are present in SYSTEM.INI:

```
[boot]
comm.drv=comm.drv
[386enh]
device=*vcd
```

Note that the SERIAL.VXD driver is not loaded in SYSTEM.INI; instead, it is loaded through the Registry.

For Windows 2000, XP, and Vista:

Look for the `SERIAL.SYS` and `SERENUM.SYS` drivers in the `WINDOWS\SYSTEM32\DRIVERS` folder for handling RS-232 devices instead.

If both drivers are present and accounted for, you can determine whether a particular serial port's I/O address and IRQ settings are properly defined by following these steps:

1. Right-click the My Computer icon on the desktop and select Properties, or double-click the System icon in the Control Panel. Click the Device Manager tab, click Ports, and then select a specific port (such as COM1).

2. Click the Properties button, and then click the Resources tab to display the current resource settings (IRQ, I/O) for that port.

3. Check the Conflicting Devices List to see whether the port is using resources that conflict with other devices. If the port is in conflict with other devices, click the Change Setting button, and then select a configuration that does not cause resource conflicts. You might need to experiment with these settings until you find the correct one.

4. If the resource settings can't be changed, most likely they must be changed via the BIOS Setup. Shut down and restart the system, enter the BIOS Setup, and change the port configurations there.

◄◄   See "Resolving Resource Conflicts," p. 422.

Advanced Diagnostics Using Loopback Testing

One of the most useful types of diagnostic test is the loopback test, which can be used to ensure the correct function of the serial port and any attached cables. Loopback tests are basically internal (digital) or external (analog). You can run internal tests by simply unplugging any cables from the port and executing the test via a diagnostics program.

The external loopback test is more effective. This test requires that a special loopback connector or wrap plug be attached to the port in question. When the test is run, the port is used to send data out to the loopback plug, which simply routes the data back into the port's receive pins so the port is transmitting and receiving at the same time. A loopback or wrap plug is nothing more than a cable that is doubled back on itself. Most diagnostics programs that run this type of test include the loopback plug, and if not, these types of plugs easily can be purchased or even built.

Most diagnostic programs that can perform loopback tests include serial port loopback plugs. If you need to build your own, see Chapter 17 of *Upgrading and Repairing PCs, 15th Edition*.

If you need to test serial ports further, see Chapter 22, "PC Diagnostics, Testing, and Maintenance," which describes third-party testing software.

Parallel Ports

Parallel ports are normally used for connecting printers to a PC. Even though that was their sole original intention, parallel ports became much more useful over the years as a more general-purpose, relatively high-speed interface between devices (when compared to serial ports). However, on today's systems, USB 2.0 ports have largely replaced parallel ports for either printing or for interfacing to devices such as scanners and external drives. I recommend using USB devices in place of parallel devices, but if you are supporting older operating systems or older printers, you might still need to work with parallel ports and devices.

Parallel ports are so named because they have eight lines for sending all the bits that comprise 1 byte of data simultaneously across eight wires.

Table 15.14 shows the pinout for a standard PC parallel port.

Table 15.14   Pinout for a 25-Pin PC-Compatible Parallel Port Connector

Pin	Description	I/O	Pin	Description	I/O
1	–Strobe	Out	14	–Auto Feed	Out
2	+Data Bit 0	Out	15	–Error	In
3	+Data Bit 1	Out	16	–Initialize Printer	Out
4	+Data Bit 2	Out	17	–Select Input	Out
5	+Data Bit 3	Out	18	–Data Bit 0 Return (GND)	In
6	+Data Bit 4	Out	19	–Data Bit 1 Return (GND)	In
7	+Data Bit 5	Out	20	–Data Bit 2 Return (GND)	In
8	+Data Bit 6	Out	21	–Data Bit 3 Return (GND)	In
9	+Data Bit 7	Out	22	–Data Bit 4 Return (GND)	In
10	–Acknowledge	In	23	–Data Bit 5 Return (GND)	In
11	+Busy	In	24	–Data Bit 6 Return (GND)	In
12	+Paper End	In	25	–Data Bit 7 Return (GND)	In
13	+Select	In			

IEEE 1284 Parallel Port Standard

The IEEE 1284 standard, called *Standard Signaling Method for a Bidirectional Parallel Peripheral Interface for Personal Computers*, was approved for final release in March 1994. This standard defines the physical characteristics of the parallel port, including data-transfer modes and physical and electrical specifications. IEEE 1284 defines the electrical signaling behavior external to the PC for a multimodal parallel port that can support 4-bit modes of operation. Not all modes are required by the 1284 specification, and the standard makes some provision for additional modes.

The IEEE 1284 specification is targeted at standardizing the behavior between a PC and an attached device, specifically attached printers. However, the specification is also of interest to users of parallel port peripherals (removable-media drives, scanners, and so on).

IEEE 1284 enables much higher throughput in a connection between a computer and a printer or two computers. The result is that the printer cable is no longer the standard printer cable. The IEEE 1284 printer cable uses twisted-pair technology, which results in a much more reliable and error-free connection.

The IEEE 1284 standard also defines the parallel port connectors, including the two preexisting types (called Type A and Type B), as well as an additional high-density Type C connector. Type A refers to the standard DB25 connector used on most PC systems for parallel port connections, whereas Type B refers to the standard 36-pin Centronics-style connector found on most printers. Type C is a high-density 36-pin connector that can be found on some parallel printers, such as those from HP. The three connectors are shown in Figure 15.11.

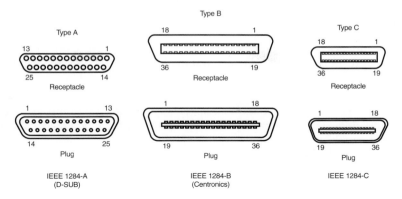

Figure 15.11   The three different types of IEEE 1284 parallel port connectors.

The IEEE 1284 parallel port standard defines five port-operating modes, emphasizing the higher-speed EPP and ECP modes. Some of the modes are input only, whereas others are output only. These five modes combine to create four types of ports, as shown in Table 15.15.

Table 15.15   Types of IEEE 1284 Ports

Parallel Port Type	Input Mode	Output Mode	Comments
SPP (Standard Parallel Port)	Nibble	Compatible	4-bit input, 8-bit output
Bidirectional	Byte	Compatible	8-bit I/O
EPP (Enhanced Parallel Port)	EPP	EPP	8-bit I/O
ECP (Enhanced Capabilities Port)	ECP	ECP	8-bit I/O, uses DMA

The 1284-defined parallel port modes are shown in Table 15.16, which also shows the approximate transfer speeds.

Table 15.16   IEEE 1284 Parallel Port Modes

Parallel Port Mode	Direction	Transfer Rate
Nibble (4-bit)	Input only	50KBps
Byte (8-bit)	Input only	150KBps
Compatible	Output only	150KBps
EPP (Enhanced Parallel Port)	Input/output	500KBps–2.77MBps
ECP (Enhanced Capabilities Port)	Input/output	500KBps–2.77MBps

Modern parallel port devices are designed to use the EPP or ECP modes shown in Table 15.16. If you need more information about the older standard or bidirectional printer port modes, see Chapter 17 of *Upgrading and Repairing PCs, 15th Edition*.

Enhanced Parallel Port

EPP is sometimes referred to as the Fast Mode parallel port. Intel, Xircom, and Zenith Data Systems developed and announced the EPP in October 1991. The first products to offer EPP were Zenith Data Systems laptops, Xircom Pocket LAN adapters, and the Intel 82360 SL I/O chip. On current systems that include parallel ports, EPP is one of the operating modes supported.

EPP operates at almost ISA bus speed and offers a tenfold increase in the raw throughput capability over a conventional parallel port. EPP was especially designed for parallel port peripherals, such as LAN adapters, disk drives, and tape backups. EPP is included in the IEEE 1284 Parallel Port standard. Transfer rates of up to 2.77MBps are possible with EPP. EPP version 1.7 (March 1992) identifies the first popular version of the hardware specification. With minor changes, this was later abandoned and folded into the IEEE 1284 standard. Some technical reference materials have erroneously made reference to "EPP specification version 1.9," causing confusion about the EPP standard. Note that "EPP version 1.9" technically does not exist, and any EPP specification after the original version 1.7 is more accurately referred to as a part of the IEEE 1284 specification.

Unfortunately, this has resulted in two somewhat incompatible standards for EPP parallel ports: the original EPP Standards Committee version 1.7 standard and the IEEE 1284 Committee standard, usually called EPP version 1.9. The two standards are similar enough that new peripherals can be designed to support both, but older EPP 1.7 peripherals might not operate with EPP 1284 (EPP 1.9) ports. For this reason, many multimode ports allow configuration in either EPP 1.7 or 1.9 mode, normally selected via the BIOS Setup.

Enhanced Capabilities Port

In 1992 Microsoft and Hewlett-Packard announced the Enhanced Capabilities Port (ECP), another type of high-speed parallel port. Similar to EPP, ECP offers improved performance for the parallel port and requires special hardware logic.

Since the original announcement, ECP is included in IEEE 1284—just like EPP. Unlike EPP, however, ECP is not tailored to support portable PCs' parallel port peripherals; its purpose is to support an inexpensive attachment to a very high-performance printer or scanner. Furthermore, ECP mode requires the use of a DMA channel, which EPP did not define and which can cause troublesome conflicts with other devices that use DMA, such as ISA sound cards or high-performance ISA SCSI host adapters. Most PCs built since the mid-1990s support both EPP and ECP modes. If you use parallel devices, it's recommended that the port be placed in ECP mode (or a combination mode known as EPP/ECP) for the best throughput.

The DMA channel assignment used for ECP mode on a built-in parallel port is usually performed through the BIOS setup program, but on some very old systems you might need to move a jumper block on the motherboard itself.

Parallel Port Configuration

The configuration of parallel ports is not as complicated as it is for serial ports. Even the original IBM PC had BIOS support for three LPT ports. Table 15.17 shows the standard I/O address and interrupt settings for parallel port use.

Table 15.17   Parallel Interface I/O Port Addresses and Interrupts

Standard LPTx	Alternate LPTx	I/O Ports	IRQ
LPT1	—	3BC–3BFh	IRQ7
LPT1	LPT2	378–37Ah	IRQ5
LPT2	LPT3	278h–27Ah	IRQ5

Because the BIOS and DOS have always provided three definitions for parallel ports, problems with parallel ports are infrequent.

To configure parallel ports, you normally use the BIOS Setup program for ports that are built in to the motherboard, or you might need to set jumpers and switches or use a setup program for adapter card–based ports. Because each board on the market is different, you always should consult the OEM manual for that particular card if you need to know how the card should be configured.

◄◄   See "BIOS Hardware/Software," p. 444.

If you need to connect two systems together via their serial or parallel ports, see Chapter 15 of *Upgrading and Repairing PCs, 17th Edition.*

Testing Parallel Ports

The procedures for testing parallel ports are effectively the same as those used for serial ports, except that when you use the diagnostics software, you (obviously) select choices for parallel ports rather than serial ports.

Even though the software tests are similar, the hardware tests require the proper plugs for the loopback tests on the parallel port. Several loopback plugs are required, depending on what software you are using.

Chapter

16

Input Devices

Keyboards

One of the most basic system components is the keyboard, which is the primary input device. Keyboards are used for entering commands and data into the system. This section looks at keyboards for PCs, examining the various types of keyboards, how they function, the keyboard-to-system interfaces, and keyboard troubleshooting and repair.

In the years following the introduction of the original IBM PC, IBM created three keyboard designs for PC systems, and since then Microsoft has augmented one of them. Together these designs have become de facto standards in the industry and are shared by virtually all PC manufacturers.

The primary keyboard types are as follows:

- 101-key Enhanced keyboard
- 104-key Windows keyboard
- 83-key PC and XT keyboard (obsolete)
- 84-key AT keyboard (obsolete)

This section discusses the 101-key Enhanced and 104-key Windows keyboards, showing the layout and physical appearance of both. Although you may still find old 83-key and 84-key designs, these are rare today.

Note

If you need to learn more about the 83-key PC and XT keyboard or the 84-key AT keyboard, see Chapter 7 of *Upgrading and Repairing PCs, 10th Anniversary Edition.*

Enhanced 101-Key (or 102-Key) Keyboard

In 1986 IBM introduced the Enhanced 101-key keyboard for the XT and AT models. This design first appeared in IBM's RT PC, which was a RISC (reduced instruction set computer) system designed for scientific and engineering applications. Keyboards with this design were soon supplied with virtually every type of system and terminal IBM sold. Other companies quickly copied this design, which became the standard on virtually all PCs until the introduction of the 104-key Windows keyboard in 1995 (discussed later in this chapter).

The layout of the enhanced keyboard was improved over that of the 84-key unit, with the possible exception of the Enter key, which reverted to a smaller size. The 101-key Enhanced keyboard was designed to conform to international regulations and specifications for keyboards. In fact, other companies such as Digital Equipment Corporation (DEC) and Texas Instruments (TI) had already been using designs similar to the IBM 101-key unit. The IBM 101-key units originally came in versions with and without the status-indicator LEDs, depending on whether the unit was sold with an XT or AT system. (XT systems didn't support the LEDs.) Currently there are many variations from which to choose, including some with integrated pointing devices, such as the IBM TrackPoint pointing stick, trackballs, and/or touch pads, as well as programmable keys useful for automating routine tasks.

IBM (with its Lexmark keyboard and printer spin-off) and Unicomp (which now produces these keyboards) have produced a number of keyboard models, including versions with built-in pointing devices and new ergonomic layouts. Several connector variations are possible as well. Whereas PC keyboards started out using a larger 5-pin DIN (an acronym for Deutsches Institut für Normung e.V.) keyboard connector, current designs use either the smaller 6-pin mini-DIN connector (often called a PS/2 connector because it first came on the IBM PS/2 systems) or industry standard USB.

Although the connectors might be physically different between the larger and smaller DIN types, the keyboards are not, and you can either interchange the cables or use a cable adapter to plug one type into the other; some keyboards you can buy at retail include the adapter in the package. See the section "Keyboard/Mouse Interface Connectors" and Figure 16.8, later in this chapter, for the physical and electronic details of these connectors. Many keyboards now include both the standard mini-DIN as well as USB connectors for maximum flexibility when attaching to newer systems. See the section "USB Keyboards," later in this chapter, for details on connecting keyboards via USB.

The 101-key keyboard layout can be divided into the following four sections:

- Typing area
- Numeric keypad
- Cursor and screen controls
- Function keys

The 101-key arrangement is similar to the Selectric keyboard layout, with the exception of the Enter key. The Tab, Caps Lock, Shift, and Backspace keys have a larger striking area and are located in the familiar Selectric locations. The Ctrl and Alt keys are on each side of the spacebar, and the typing area and numeric keypad have home-row identifiers for touch typing.

The cursor- and screen-control keys have been separated from the numeric keypad, which is reserved for numeric input. (As with other PC keyboards, you can use the numeric keypad for cursor and screen control when the keyboard is not in Num Lock mode.) A division-sign key (/) and an additional Enter key have been added to the numeric keypad.

The cursor-control keys are arranged in the inverted T format that is now expected on all computer keyboards. The Insert, Delete, Home, End, Page Up, and Page Down keys, located above the dedicated cursor-control keys, are separate from the numeric keypad. The function keys, spaced in groups of four, are located across the top of the keyboard. The keyboard also has two additional function keys: F11 and F12. The Esc key is isolated in the upper-left corner of the keyboard. In addition, dedicated Print Screen/Sys Req, Scroll Lock, and Pause/Break keys are provided for commonly used functions.

Foreign-language versions of the Enhanced keyboard include 102 keys and a slightly different layout from the 101-key U.S. versions.

One of the many useful features of the IBM/Lexmark enhanced keyboard (now manufactured by Unicomp) is removable keycaps. This permits the replacement of broken keys and provides access for easier cleaning. Also, with clear keycaps and paper inserts, you can customize the keyboard. Keyboard templates are also available to provide specific operator instructions.

104-Key (Windows 9x/Me/2000/XP) Keyboard

When Microsoft released Windows 95, it also introduced the Microsoft Natural Keyboard, which implemented a revised keyboard specification that added three new Windows-specific keys to the keyboard.

The Microsoft Windows keyboard specification, which has since become standard for many desktop and laptop keyboards, outlines a set of additional keys and key combinations. The 104-key layout includes left and right Windows keys and an Application key (see Figure 16.1). These keys are used for operating system and application-level keyboard combinations, similar to the existing Ctrl and Alt combinations. You don't need the new keys to use Windows, but many software vendors have added specific functions to their Windows products that use the new Application key (which provides the same functionality as clicking the right mouse button). The recommended Windows keyboard layout calls for the left and right Windows keys (called WIN keys) to flank the Alt keys on each side of the spacebar, as well as an Application key on the right of the right Windows key. Note that the exact placement of these keys is up to the keyboard designer, so variations exist from keyboard to keyboard.

The WIN keys open the Windows Start menu, which you can then navigate with the cursor keys. The Application key simulates the right mouse button; in most applications, it brings up a context-sensitive pop-up menu. Several WIN key combinations offer preset macro commands as well. For example, you can press WIN+E to launch the Windows Explorer application. Table 16.1 shows a list of all the Windows key combinations used with the 104-key keyboard

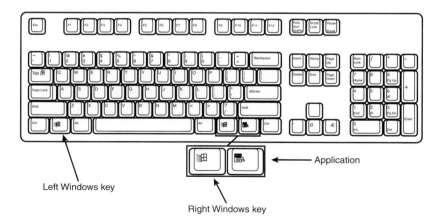

Figure 16.1   The 104-key Windows keyboard layout.

Table 16.1   Windows 9x/Me/2000/XP Key Combinations

Key Combination	Resulting Action
WIN+R	Open the Run dialog box
WIN+M	Minimize All
Shift+WIN+M	Undo Minimize All
WIN+D	Minimize All or Undo Minimize All
WIN+F1	Help
WIN+E	Starts Windows Explorer
WIN+F	Find Files or Folders
Ctrl+WIN+F	Find Computer
WIN+Tab	Cycles through taskbar buttons; opens Flip 3D in Vista (if supported)
WIN+Break	Displays the System Properties dialog box
Application key	Displays a context menu for the selected item

The preceding keystroke combinations work with any manufacturer's 104-key keyboard, but users of certain Microsoft 104-key keyboards can enhance their keyboard use further by installing the IntelliType Pro software supplied by Microsoft with the keyboard.

The Windows and Application keys are not mandatory when running Windows. In fact, preexisting standard key combinations can perform the same functions as these newer keys.

The Windows keyboard specification requires that keyboard makers increase the number of trilograms in their keyboard designs. A *trilogram* is a combination of three rapidly pressed keys that perform a special function, such as Ctrl+Alt+Delete. Designing a keyboard so that the switch matrix correctly registers the additional trilograms plus the additional Windows keys adds somewhat to the cost of these keyboards compared to the previous 101-key standard models.

Many keyboard manufacturers have standardized on 104-key keyboards that include these Windows-specific keys. Some manufacturers have added browser control or other keys that, although not standard, can make them easier to use for navigating web pages and launching various applications.

Num Lock

As a bit of PC trivia, on older IBM systems that support the Enhanced keyboard, when the system detects the keyboard on power-up, it enables the Num Lock feature and the light goes on. If the system detects an older 84-key AT-type keyboard, it does not enable the Num Lock function because these keyboards do not have cursor keys separate from the numeric keypad. When the Enhanced keyboards first appeared in 1986, many users (including me) were irritated to find that the numeric keypad was automatically enabled every time the system booted. Most system manufacturers subsequently began integrating a function into the BIOS setup that enabled one to specify the Num Lock status imposed during the boot process.

Some users thought that the automatic enabling of Num Lock was a function of the Enhanced keyboard because none of the earlier keyboards seemed to operate in this way. But this function was not really a keyboard function at all, but instead a function of the motherboard ROM BIOS, which identified an Enhanced 101-key unit and turned on the Num Lock as a "favor." In systems with a BIOS that can't control the status of the numeric keypad, you can use the DOS 6 or higher version NUMLOCK= parameter in CONFIG.SYS to turn Num Lock on or off, as desired. Some versions of Windows, particularly

Windows NT and Windows 9x, disable Num Lock by default, whereas Windows 2000 and later save the Num Lock status for each user when he or she logs off, and reset Num Lock to the saved state when the user logs back on.

Keyboard Technology

The technology that makes up a typical PC keyboard is very interesting. This section focuses on all the aspects of keyboard technology and design, including the keyswitches, the interface between the keyboard and the system, the scan codes, and the keyboard connectors.

Keyswitch Design

Today's keyboards use any one of several switch types to create the action for each key. Most keyboards use a variation of the mechanical keyswitch. A mechanical keyswitch relies on a mechanical momentary contact-type switch to make the electrical contact that forms a circuit. Some high-end keyboards use a more sophisticated design that relies on capacitive switches. This section discusses these switches and the highlights of each design.

The most common type of keyswitch is the mechanical type, available in the following variations:

- Pure mechanical
- Foam element
- Rubber dome
- Membrane

Pure Mechanical Switches

The pure mechanical type is just that—a simple mechanical switch that features metal contacts in a momentary contact arrangement. The switch often includes a tactile feedback mechanism, consisting of a clip and spring arrangement designed to give a "clicky" feel to the keyboard and offer some resistance to the keypress (see Figure 16.2).

Mechanical switches are very durable, usually have self-cleaning contacts, and are normally rated for 20 million keystrokes (which is second only to the capacitive switch in longevity). They also offer excellent tactile feedback.

Despite the tactile feedback and durability provided by mechanical keyswitch keyboards, they have become much less popular than membrane keyboards (discussed later in this chapter). In addition, many companies that produce keyboards that use mechanical keyswitches either use them for only a few of their high-priced models or have phased out their mechanical keyswitch models entirely. With the price of keyboards nose-diving along with other traditional devices, such as mice and drives, the pressure on keyboard makers to cut costs has led many of them to abandon or deemphasize mechanical-keyswitch designs in favor of the less expensive membrane keyswitch.

The Alps Electric mechanical keyswitch is used by many of the vendors who produce mechanical-switch keyboards, including Alps Electric itself. Other vendors who use mechanical keyswitches for some of their keyboard models include Adesso, Inc. (www.adesso.com), Avant Prime and Stellar (revivals of the classic Northgate keyboards are available from Ergonomic Resources; www.ergonomicsmadeeasy.com), Kinesis (www.kinesis-ergo.com), and SIIG (www.siig.com). Many of these vendors sell through the OEM market, so you must look carefully at the detailed specifications for the keyboard to see whether it is a mechanical keyswitch model.

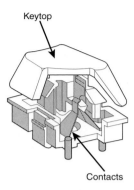

Figure 16.2   A typical mechanical switch used in older NMB Technologies keyboards. As the key is pressed, the switch pushes down on the contacts to make the connection.

Foam Element Switches

Foam element mechanical switches were a very popular design in some older keyboards. Most of the older PC keyboards, including models made by Key Tronic and many others, used this technology. These switches are characterized by a foam element with an electrical contact on the bottom. This foam element is mounted on the bottom of a plunger that is attached to the key (see Figure 16.3).

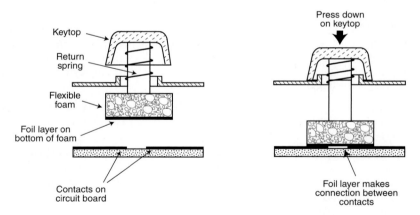

Figure 16.3   Typical foam element mechanical keyswitch.

When the switch is pressed, a foil conductor on the bottom of the foam element closes a circuit on the printed circuit board below. A return spring pushes the key back up when the pressure is released. The foam dampens the contact, helping to prevent bounce, but unfortunately it gives these keyboards a "mushy" feel. The big problem with this type of keyswitch design is that little tactile feedback often exists. These types of keyboards send a clicking sound to the system speaker to signify that contact has been made. Preferences in keyboard feel are somewhat subjective; I personally do not favor the foam element switch design.

Another problem with this type of design is that it is more subject to corrosion on the foil conductor and the circuit board traces below. When this happens, the key strikes can become intermittent, which can be frustrating. Fortunately, these keyboards are among the easiest to clean. By disassembling the keyboard completely, you usually can remove the circuit board portion—without removing each foam pad separately—and expose the bottoms of all the pads. Then, you easily can wipe the corrosion and dirt off the bottoms of the foam pads and the circuit board, thus restoring the keyboard to a "like-new" condition. Unfortunately, over time, the corrosion problem will occur again. I recommend using some Stabilant 22a from D.W. Electrochemicals (www.stabilant.com) to improve the switch contact action and prevent future corrosion. Because of such problems, the foam element design is not used much anymore and has been superseded in popularity by the rubber dome design.

KeyTronicEMS, the most well-known user of this technology, now uses a center-bearing membrane switch technology in its keyboards, so you are likely to encounter foam-switch keyboards only on very old systems.

Rubber Dome Switches

Rubber dome switches are mechanical switches similar to the foam element type but are improved in many ways. Instead of a spring, these switches use a rubber dome that has a carbon button contact on the underside. As you press a key, the key plunger presses on the rubber dome, causing it to resist and then collapse all at once, much like the top of an oil can. As the rubber dome collapses, the user feels the tactile feedback, and the carbon button makes contact between the circuit board traces below. When the key is released, the rubber dome re-forms and pushes the key back up.

The rubber eliminates the need for a spring and provides a reasonable amount of tactile feedback without any special clips or other parts. Rubber dome switches use a carbon button because it resists corrosion and has a self-cleaning action on the metal contacts below. The rubber domes themselves are formed into a sheet that completely protects the contacts below from dirt, dust, and even minor spills. This type of switch design is the simplest, and it uses the fewest parts. This made the rubber dome keyswitch very reliable for several years. However, its relatively poor tactile feedback has led most keyboard manufacturers to switch to the membrane switch design covered in the next section.

Membrane Switches

The membrane keyswitch is a variation on the rubber dome type, using a flat, flexible circuit board to receive input and transmit it to the keyboard microcontroller. Industrial versions of membrane boards use a single sheet for keys that sits on the rubber dome sheet for protection against harsh environments. This arrangement severely limits key travel. For this reason, flat-surface membrane keyboards are not considered usable for normal touch typing. However, they are ideal for use in extremely harsh environments. Because the sheets can be bonded together and sealed from the elements, membrane keyboards can be used in situations in which no other type could survive. Many industrial applications use membrane keyboards for terminals that do not require extensive data entry but are used instead to operate equipment, such as cash registers and point-of-sale terminals in restaurants.

Membrane keyswitches are not just relegated to fast food or industrial uses, though. The membrane keyswitch used with conventional keyboard keytops has become the most popular keyswitch used in low-cost to mid-range keyboards, and even some high-end units. Although low-end membrane keyswitches have a limited life of only 5–10 million keystrokes, some of the better models are rated to handle up to 20 million keystrokes, putting them in the range of pure mechanical switches for durability (see Figure 16.4). A few membrane switches are even more durable: Cherry Corporation's G8x-series keyboards use Cherry's own 50-million-keystroke membrane switch design (www.cherrycorp.com).

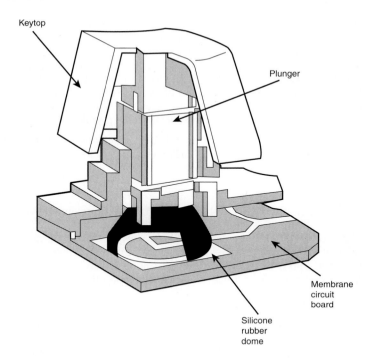

Figure 16.4 A typical membrane keyswitch used in NMB keyboards.

Membrane keyboards typically provide a firmer touch than rubber dome keyboards or the old foam-element keyboards, and those with buckling spring designs can provide the ultimate in tactile feedback. One interesting variation includes the line of keyboards made by KeyTronicEMS using its center-bearing version of membrane keyswitches. Most of its keyboards feature Ergo Technology, which has five levels of force from 35 grams to 80 grams, depending on the relative strength of the fingers used to type various keys. As little as 35 grams of force is required for keys that are used by the little finger, such as Q, Z, and A, and greater levels of force are required for keys used by the other fingers (see Figure 16.5). The spacebar requires the most force: 80 grams. This compares to the standard force level of 55 grams for all keys on normal keyboards. For more information about keyboards with Ergo Technology, visit the KeyTronicEMS website (www.keytronic.com).

Figure 16.5 Force levels used on KeyTronicEMS keyboards with Ergo Technology.

Perhaps the most well-known type of membrane keyboards are the IBM/Lexmark "Model M" keyboards, which combine IBM's legendary buckling spring design with a high-end membrane switch. To find the best membrane keyboards from the vast numbers on the market, look at the lifespan rating of the keyswitches. Longer-lasting keyswitches make the keyboard cost more but will lead to a better experience over the life of the keyboard.

Buckling Spring Capacitive and Membrane Switches

The keyboard included with the original IBM PC, XT and AT systems used capacitive switches combined with a buckling spring mechanism to provide the ultimate in performance and tactile feedback. Capacitive switches are technically the only truly nonmechanical keyswitches in use today (see Figure 16.6). Although the movement of the key and buckling spring is mechanical in nature, in the original designs these components do not close a mechanical contact or switch. Because of the high cost of the capacitive switches, IBM switched its buckling spring keyboards from capacitive to membrane switches in the mid-1980s. However, unlike more common membrane keyboards, all of the buckling spring keyboards feature extremely high-end designs. Regardless of whether capacitive or membrane designs are used, buckling spring keyswitches are considered to be among the best in the world, offering the highest-quality tactile feedback of any type of switch. They are called *buckling spring* keyboards because of the coiled spring and rocker used in each keyswitch to provide tactile and audible feedback.

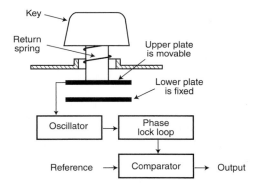

Figure 16.6 A capacitive buckling spring keyswitch.

A capacitive switch does not work by making contact between conductors. Instead, two plates usually made of plastic are connected in a switch matrix designed to detect changes in the capacitance of the circuit. The membrane version of the switch uses upper and lower electrical contact sheets separated by an insulating sheet with small holes.

When a key is pressed, the plunger moves the top plate in relation to the fixed bottom plate, or presses a hammer over the membranes, allowing the top and bottom contacts to touch. The buckling spring mechanism provides for distinct over-center tactile feedback with a resounding "click." As the capacitance between the two plates changes or the two membranes make contact, the comparator circuitry in the keyboard detects this as a keypress.

The tactile feedback is unsurpassed because the buckling spring design provides a relatively loud click and a strong over-center feel. The only drawback to the design is the cost. Buckling spring keyboards are among the most expensive designs, whether they use capacitive or membrane switches. The quality of the feel and their durability make them worth the price, however.

Although some of IBM's older keyboards featured capacitive keyswitches, most current IBM/Lenovo keyboards use either membrane, rubber dome, or other lower-cost keyswitches. In 1991, IBM spun off its keyboard/printer division as Lexmark, which then spun off the keyboard division as Unicomp in 1996. Today, Unicomp still manufactures and sells "IBM" keyboards with buckling spring membrane switch ("clickety" as some would say) technology. As a bonus, it also has models with the IBM TrackPoint built in. You can purchase new Unicomp (IBM) keyboards direct by calling the company's toll-free number (800-777-4886) or by visiting its online store (http://www.pckeyboard.com).

▶▶ See "TrackPoint II/III/IV," p. 1090.

My personal recommendations are for either the EnduraPro/104 (http://www.pckeyboard.com/ep104.html) or the Customizer 101 or 104 (http://www.pckeyboard.com/customizer.html). These are brand-new (not reconditioned or rebuilt) keyboards.

The EnduraPro/104 is notable for including a built-in TrackPoint pointing device and a pass-through mini-DIN mouse port, being programmable and reconfigurable, requiring no special drivers, and of course having the famous buckling spring keyswitches.

Because of the buckling spring keyswitches (and the resulting clickety feel), I've always been a huge fan of the IBM, Lexmark, and now Unicomp keyboards. In my opinion, they are the best keyboards in the world and the only ones I willingly use on desktop systems. I especially like the fact that they include the IBM TrackPoint because I use a laptop system as my main machine and therefore use only laptops that include the TrackPoint device (mainly IBM/Lenovo, Toshiba, and some Dell, HP, and others). The feel and durability of the buckling spring keyswitches is outstanding, and with the integrated TrackPoint, I never have to move my hands off the keyboard, resulting in much greater efficiency when working with my systems.

The Keyboard Interface

A keyboard consists of a set of switches mounted in a grid or an array called the *key matrix*. When a switch is pressed, a processor in the keyboard identifies which key is pressed by determining which grid location in the matrix shows continuity. The keyboard processor, which also interprets how long the key is pressed, can even handle multiple keypresses at the same time. A 16-byte hardware buffer in the keyboard can handle rapid or multiple keypresses, passing each one to the system in succession.

When you press a key, the contact bounces slightly in most cases, meaning that several rapid on/off cycles occur just as the switch makes contact. This is called *bounce*. The processor in the keyboard is designed to filter this, or "debounce" the keystroke. The keyboard processor must distinguish bounce from a double key strike the keyboard operator intends to make. This is fairly easy, though, because the bouncing is much more rapid than a person could simulate by striking a key quickly several times.

The keyboard in a PC is actually a computer itself. It communicates with the main system in one of two ways:

- Through a special serial data link if a standard PS/2 keyboard connector is used
- Through the USB port

The serial data link used by conventional keyboards transmits and receives data in 11-bit packets of information, consisting of 8 data bits, plus framing and control bits. Although it is indeed a serial link (in that the data flows on one wire), the keyboard interface is incompatible with the standard RS-232 serial port commonly used to connect modems.

The processor in the original PC keyboard was an Intel 8048 microcontroller chip. Newer keyboards often use an 8049 version that has built-in ROM or other microcontroller chips compatible with the

8048 or 8049. For example, in its Enhanced keyboards, IBM has always used a custom version of the Motorola 6805 processor, which is compatible with the Intel chips. The keyboard's built-in processor reads the key matrix, debounces the keypress signals, converts the keypress to the appropriate scan code, and transmits the code to the motherboard. The processors built in to the keyboard contain their own RAM, possibly some ROM, and a built-in serial interface.

In the original PC/XT design, the keyboard serial interface is connected to an 8255 Programmable Peripheral Interface (PPI) chip on the motherboard of the PC/XT. This chip is connected to the interrupt controller IRQ1 line, which is used to signal to the system that keyboard data is available. The data is then sent from the 8255 to the processor via I/O port address 60h. The IRQ1 signal causes the main system processor to run a subroutine (INT 9h) that interprets the keyboard scan code data and decides what to do.

In an AT-type keyboard design, the keyboard serial interface is connected to a special keyboard controller on the motherboard. This controller was an Intel 8042 Universal Peripheral Interface (UPI) slave microcontroller chip in the original AT design. This microcontroller is essentially another processor that has its own 2KB of ROM and 128 bytes of RAM. An 8742 version that uses erasable programmable read-only memory (EPROM) can be erased and reprogrammed. In the past, when you purchased a motherboard ROM upgrade for an older system from a motherboard manufacturer, the upgrade included a new keyboard controller chip as well because it had somewhat dependent and updated ROM code in it. Some older systems might use the 8041 or 8741 chips, which differ only in the amount of built-in ROM or RAM. However, recent systems incorporate the keyboard controller into the main system chipset.

In an AT system, the (8048-type) microcontroller in the keyboard sends data to the (8042-type) keyboard controller on the motherboard. The motherboard-based controller also can send data back to the keyboard. When the keyboard controller on the motherboard receives data from the keyboard, it signals the motherboard with an IRQ1 and sends the data to the main motherboard processor via I/O port address 60h, just as in the PC/XT. Acting as an agent between the keyboard and the main system processor, the 8042-type keyboard controller can translate scan codes and perform several other functions as well. The system also can send data to the 8042 keyboard controller via port 60h, which then passes it on to the keyboard. Additionally, when the system needs to send commands to or read the status of the keyboard controller on the motherboard, it reads or writes through I/O port 64h. These commands usually are followed by data sent back and forth via port 60h.

In older systems, the 8042 keyboard controller is also used by the system to control the A20 memory address line, which provides access to system memory greater than 1MB. More modern motherboards typically incorporate this functionality directly into the motherboard chipset. The AT keyboard connector was renamed the "PS/2" port after the IBM PS/2 family of systems debuted in 1987. That was the time when the connector changed in size from the DIN to the mini-DIN, and even though the signals were the same, the mini-DIN version became known from that time forward as the PS/2 port.

Keyboards connected to a USB port work in a surprisingly similar fashion to those connected to conventional DIN or mini-DIN (PS/2) ports after the data reaches the system. Inside the keyboard a variety of custom controller chips is used by various keyboard manufacturers to receive and interpret keyboard data before sending it to the system via the USB port. Some of these chips contain USB hub logic to enable the keyboard to act as a USB hub. After the keyboard data reaches the USB port on the system, the USB port routes the data to the 8042-compatible keyboard controller, where the data is treated as any other keyboard information.

This process works very well after a system has booted into Windows. But what about users who need to use the keyboard at a command prompt or within the BIOS configuration routine? That problem is solved by ensuring that USB Legacy support is present and enabled in the BIOS Setup. A BIOS with USB Legacy support is capable of performing the following tasks:

- Configuring the host controller
- Enabling a USB keyboard and mouse
- Setting up the host controller scheduler
- Routing USB keyboard and mouse input to the 8042 Keyboard Controller

Systems with USB Legacy support enabled use the BIOS to control the USB keyboard until a supported operating system is loaded. At that point, the USB host controller driver in the operating system takes control of the keyboard by sending a command called StopBIOS to the BIOS routine that was managing the keyboard. When Windows 9x/Me shuts down to MS-DOS, the USB host controller sends a command called StartBIOS to restart the BIOS routine that manages the keyboard.

When the BIOS controls the keyboard, after the signals reach the 8042 Keyboard Controller, the USB keyboard is treated just like a conventional keyboard if the BIOS is correctly designed to work with USB keyboards. Note that a BIOS upgrade might be necessary to provide proper support of USB keyboards on some older systems. The system chipset also must support USB Legacy features.

Typematic Functions

If a key on the keyboard is held down, it becomes *typematic*, which means the keyboard repeatedly sends the keypress code to the motherboard. In the AT-style keyboards, the typematic rate is adjusted by sending the appropriate commands to the keyboard processor. This is impossible for the earlier PC/XT keyboard types because the keyboard interface for these types is not bidirectional.

AT-style keyboards have programmable typematic repeat rate and delay parameters. You can adjust the typematic repeat rate and delay parameters with settings in your system BIOS (although not all BIOS chips can control all functions) or in your operating system. In Windows you can use either the MODE command or the Keyboard icon in the Control Panel. Using either method you can set the repeat rate from about 2cps (characters per second) minimum to 30cps maximum, and the delay from 0.25 seconds minimum to 1 second maximum.

For the fastest keyboard operation, I like to set the repeat rate to the maximum (30cps) and the delay to the minimum (0.25 seconds), which can be accomplished with the following command:

```
MODE CON: RATE=31 DELAY=0
```

Likewise, slowing the repeat rate to the minimum (2cps) and increasing the delay to the maximum (1 second), can be accomplished with the following command:

```
MODE CON: RATE=0 DELAY=3
```

Entering MODE CON: with no other parameters will show the current status of the settings. You can also modify these settings using the Keyboard icon in the Control Panel. The Repeat Delay slider, shown in Figure 16.7, controls the duration for which a key must be pressed before the character begins to repeat, and the Repeat Rate slider controls how fast the character repeats after the delay has elapsed.

Note

The increments on the Repeat Delay and Repeat Rate sliders in Keyboard Properties in the Control Panel correspond to the timings given for the **MODE** command's **RATE** and **DELAY** values. Each mark in the Repeat Delay slider adds about 0.25 seconds to the delay, and the marks in the Repeat Rate slider are worth about one character per second (1cps) each.

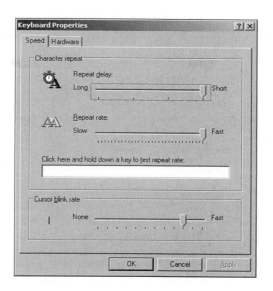

Figure 16.7   Setting the keyboard repeat delay and repeat rate in Windows.

The dialog box also contains a text box you can use to test the settings you have chosen before committing them to your system. When you click in the box and press a key, the keyboard reacts using the settings currently specified by the sliders, even if you have not yet applied the changes to the Windows environment.

Keyboard Key Numbers and Scan Codes

When you press a key on the keyboard, the processor built in to the keyboard (8048 or 6805 type) reads the keyswitch location in the keyboard matrix. The processor then sends to the motherboard a serial packet of data containing the scan code for the key that was pressed.

This is called the *Make code*. When the key is released, a corresponding *Break code* is sent, indicating to the motherboard that the key has been released. The Break code is equivalent to the Make scan code plus 80h. For example, if the Make scan code for the "A" key is 1Eh, the Break code would be 9Eh. By using both Make and Break scan codes, the system can determine whether a particular key has been held down and determine whether multiple keys are being pressed.

In motherboards that use an 8042-type keyboard controller, the 8042 chip translates the actual keyboard scan codes into one of up to three sets of system scan codes, which are sent to the main processor. It can be useful in some cases to know what these scan codes are, especially when you're troubleshooting keyboard problems or when reading the keyboard or system scan codes directly in software.

When a keyswitch on the keyboard sticks or otherwise fails, the Make scan code of the failed keyswitch usually is reported by diagnostics software, including the power-on self test (POST), as well as conventional disk-based diagnostics. This means you must identify the malfunctioning key by its scan code. By looking up the reported scan code, you can determine which keyswitch is defective or needs to be cleaned.

Note

The 101-key Enhanced keyboards are capable of three scan code sets. Set 1 is the default. Some systems, including some of the IBM PS/2 machines, use one of the other scan code sets during the POST. For example, the PS/2 P75 uses Scan Code Set 2 during the POST but switches to Set 1 during normal operation. This is rare, but on one occasion it really threw me off in diagnosing a stuck key problem. It is useful to know whether you are having difficulty interpreting the scan code number, however.

IBM originally assigned each key a unique key number to distinguish it from the others. This is helpful when you are trying to identify keys on foreign keyboards that might use symbols or characters different from what the U.S. models do. In the Enhanced keyboard, most foreign models are missing one of the keys (key 29) found on the U.S. version and have two additional keys (keys 42 and 45). This accounts for the 102-key total instead of the 101 keys found on the U.S. version.

Note

Knowing these key number figures and scan codes can be useful when you are troubleshooting stuck or failed keys on a keyboard. Diagnostics can report the defective keyswitch by the scan code, which varies from keyboard to keyboard as to the character it represents and its location.

Many keyboards feature hotkeys that either have fixed uses—such as opening the default web browser, sending the system into standby mode, and adjusting the speaker volume—or are programmable for user-defined functions. Each of these keys also has scan codes. USB keyboards use a special series of codes called Human Interface Device (HID), which are translated into PS/2 scan codes.

International Keyboard Layouts

After the keyboard controller in the system receives the scan codes generated by the keyboard and passes them to the main processor, the operating system converts the codes into the appropriate alphanumeric characters. In the United States, these characters are the letters, numbers, and symbols found on the standard American keyboard.

However, no matter which characters you see on the keytops, adjusting the scan code conversion process to map different characters to the keys is relatively simple. Windows (post 3.x) takes advantage of this capability by enabling you to install multiple keyboard layouts to support various languages.

In Windows 9x/Me, open the Keyboard icon in the Control Panel and select the Language page. The Language box should display the keyboard layout you selected when you installed the operating system. In Windows XP/Vista, you can select any one of several additional keyboard layouts supporting other languages through the Regional and Language Options applet (in the Windows Control Panel).

These keyboard layouts map various characters to certain keys on the standard keyboard. The standard French layout provides easy access to the accented characters commonly used in that language. For example, pressing the 2 key produces the é character. To type the numeral 2, you press the Shift+2 key combination. Other French-speaking countries have different keyboard conventions for the same characters, so Windows includes support for several keyboard layout variations for some languages, based on nationality.

Note

It is important to understand that this feature is not the same as installing the operating system in a different language. These keyboard layouts do not modify the text already displayed onscreen; they only alter the characters generated when you press certain keys.

The alternative keyboard layouts also do not provide support for non-Roman alphabets, such as Russian and Chinese. The accented characters and other symbols used in languages such as French and German are part of the standard ASCII character set. They are always accessible to English-language users through the Windows Character Map utility or through the use of Alt+keypad combinations. An alternative keyboard layout simply gives you an easier way to access the characters used in certain languages.

If you work on documents using more than one language, you can install as many keyboard layouts as necessary and switch between them at will. Using the settings in the Regional and Language Options applet, you can enable both a selector in the taskbar notification area as well as a key combination that switches between the installed keyboard layouts.

Keyboard/Mouse Interface Connectors

Keyboards typically have a cable with one of three primary types of connectors at the system end. On most aftermarket keyboards, the cable is connected inside the keyboard case on the keyboard end, requiring you to open the keyboard case to disconnect or test it; different vendors use different connections, making cable interchange between brands of keyboards unlikely. When IBM manufactured its own enhanced keyboards, it used a unique cable assembly that plugged into both the keyboard and the system unit to make cable replacement or interchange easy. Current IBM keyboards, unfortunately, no longer use either the shielded data link (SDL) connector inside the keyboard or the telephone cable-style removable plug-in external keyboard connector used on some more recent models.

Although the method of connecting the keyboard cable to the keyboard can vary (some even use wireless connections), all PC keyboards use one of the following three connectors to interface the keyboard (or wireless transceiver) to the computer:

- **5-pin DIN connector**—Used on most obsolete PC systems with Baby-AT form factor motherboards.

- **6-pin mini-DIN connector**—Often called a PS/2 connector because it was first used on IBM PS/2 systems.

- **USB connector**—Most recent systems use USB keyboards and mice.

Figure 16.8 and Table 16.2 show the physical layout and pinouts of the respective keyboard connector plugs and sockets (except USB); although the 6-pin SDL connector is not used in this form by most keyboard vendors, most non-IBM keyboards use a somewhat similar connector to attach the keyboard cable to the inside of the keyboard. You can use the pinouts listed in Table 16.2 to test the continuity of each wire in the keyboard connector.

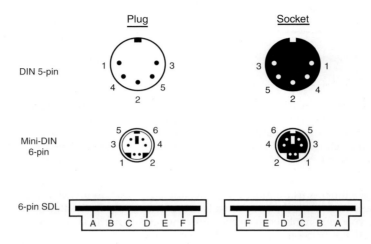

Figure 16.8   Keyboard and mouse connectors.

Table 16.2   Keyboard Connector Signals and Specifications

Signal Name	5-Pin DIN	6-Pin Mini-DIN	6-Pin SDL	Test Voltage
Keyboard Data	2	1	B	+4.8V to +5.5V
Ground	4	3	C	—
+5V Power	5	4	E	+2.0V to +5.5V
Keyboard Clock	1	5	D	+2.0V to +5.5V
Not Connected	—	2	A	—
Not Connected	—	6	F	—
Not Connected	3	—	—	—

DIN = Deutsches Institut für Normung e.V., a committee that sets German dimensional standards.

SDL = Shielded data link, a type of shielded connector created by AMP and used by IBM and others for keyboard cables.

The 6-pin mini-DIN is usually called a PS/2 connector.

PS/2 mouse devices also use the 6-pin mini-DIN connector and have the same pinout and signal descriptions as the keyboard connector; however, the data packets are incompatible. Therefore, you can easily plug a motherboard mouse (PS/2-style) into a mini-DIN keyboard connector or plug the mini-DIN keyboard connector into a motherboard mouse port. Neither one will work properly in this situation, though.

Caution

I have also seen PCs with external power supplies that used the same or similar mini-DIN connectors to attach the power supply. Although cross-connecting the mini-DIN connectors of a mouse and keyboard is a harmless annoyance, connecting a power supply to a keyboard socket would be disastrous.

USB keyboards use the Series A USB connector to attach to the USB port built in to modern computers. For more information on USB, refer to Chapter 15, "I/O Interfaces from Serial and Parallel to IEEE 1394 and USB."

USB Keyboards

Most keyboards now on the market can connect to the PC via a USB port instead of the standard PS/2 keyboard port. Because USB is a universal bus that uses a hub to enable multiple devices to connect to a single port, a single USB port in a system can replace the standard serial and parallel ports as well as the keyboard and mouse ports. Most current systems and motherboards still include the standard ports (now called *legacy* ports) as well as USB, but most so-called *legacy-free* systems and replacement motherboards have only USB ports for interfacing external devices.

Most keyboard manufacturers now market USB keyboards, but if you want to use your keyboard with both legacy (PS/2) and legacy-free (USB) systems, the most economic way to do so is to specify a keyboard that includes both a USB connector and an adapter to permit the keyboard to work with PS/2 ports. Although Microsoft's Natural Keyboard Elite was the first widely available model to offer USB and PS/2 compatibility, most other wired and wireless models from Microsoft, Logitech, Belkin, and others also offer this feature. You can also purchase third-party USB-to-PS/2 adapters, but these can be expensive and might not work with all keyboards.

Although rare in modern systems, not all systems accept USB keyboards, even those with USB ports, because the standard PC BIOS has a keyboard driver that expects a standard keyboard port interface to be present. When a USB keyboard is installed on a system that lacks USB keyboard support, the system can't use it because no driver exists in the BIOS to make it work. In fact, some systems see the lack of a standard keyboard as an error and halt the boot process until one is installed.

To use a keyboard connected via the USB port, you must meet three requirements:

- Have a USB port in the system
- Run Microsoft Windows 98 or newer (previous versions did not include USB keyboard drivers)
- Have a system chipset and BIOS that feature USB Legacy support

USB Legacy support means your motherboard has a chipset and ROM BIOS drivers that enable a USB keyboard to be used outside the Windows GUI environment. Almost all 1998 and newer systems with USB ports include a chipset and BIOS with USB Legacy (meaning USB Keyboard) support, although it might be disabled by default in the system BIOS.

Even though USB Legacy support enables you to use a USB keyboard in almost all situations, don't scrap your standard-port keyboards just yet. Some Windows-related bugs and glitches reported by users include the following:

- **Can't log on to Windows the first time after installing a USB keyboard**. The solution is to leave the USB keyboard unplugged when first booting and then plug it in after the OS desktop is up and running. This allows the keyboard to be detected and drivers loaded. If the system won't boot without a keyboard, then either disable keyboard error detection in the BIOS setup, or temporarily plug in a PS/2 keyboard (or use a USB to PS/2 adapter) instead.

- **Some USB keyboards won't work when the Windows Emergency Boot Disk (EBD) is used to start the system**. The solution is to turn off the system, connect a standard keyboard, and restart the system.

- **Some users of Windows 98 and Windows 98 SE have reported conflicts between Windows and the BIOS when USB Legacy support is enabled on some systems**. This conflict can result in an incapability to detect the USB keyboard if you use the Windows 9x shutdown menu and choose to restart the computer in MS-DOS mode. Check with the system or BIOS vendor for an updated BIOS or a patch to solve this conflict.

If you have problems with Legacy USB support, look at these possible solutions:

- Microsoft's Knowledge Base (http://support.microsoft.com) might address your specific combination of hardware.

- Your keyboard vendor might offer new drivers.

- Your system or motherboard manufacturer might have a BIOS upgrade you can install.

- Connect the keyboard to the PS/2 port with its adapter (or use a PS/2 keyboard) until you resolve the problem.

◀◀ See "Universal Serial Bus," p. 1031.

Keyboards with Special Features

Several keyboards on the market have special features not found in standard designs. These additional features range from simple things, such as built-in calculators, clocks, and volume control, to more complicated features, such as integrated pointing devices, special character layouts, shapes, internal lighting, and even programmable keys.

Note

In 1936 August Dvorak patented a simplified character layout called the Dvorak Simplified Keyboard (DSK). The Dvorak keyboard was designed to replace the common QWERTY layout used on nearly all keyboards available today. The Dvorak keyboard was approved as an ANSI standard in 1982 but has seen limited use.

Ergonomic Keyboards

A trend that began in the late 1990s is to change the shape of the keyboard instead of altering the character layout. This trend has resulted in several so-called *ergonomic* designs. The goal is to shape the keyboard to better fit the human hand. The most common of these designs splits the keyboard in the center, bending the sides outward. Some designs allow the angle between the sides to be adjusted, such as the now-discontinued Lexmark Select-Ease, the Goldtouch keyboard designed by Mark Goldstein (who also designed the Select-Ease), and the Kinesis Maxim split keyboards. Others, such as the Microsoft Natural keyboard series, PC Concepts Wave, and Cirque Smooth Cat, are fixed. These split or bent designs more easily conform to the hands' natural angles while typing than the standard keyboard. They can improve productivity and typing speed and help prevent repetitive strain injuries (RSI), such as carpal tunnel syndrome (tendon inflammation). Even more radical keyboard designs are available from some vendors, including models such as the 3-part Comfort and ErgoMagic keyboards, the Kinesis concave contoured keyboard, and others. A good source for highly ergonomic keyboards, pointing devices, and furniture is Ergonomic Resources (www.eergonomicsmadeeasy.com).

Because of their novelty and trendy appeal, some ergonomic keyboards can be considerably more expensive than traditional designs, but for users with medical problems caused or exacerbated by improper positioning of the wrists at the keyboard, they can be an important remedy to a serious problem. General users, however, are highly resistant to change, and these designs have yet to significantly displace the standard keyboard layout. If you don't want to spend big bucks on the more radical ergonomic keyboards but want to give yourself at least limited protection from RSI, consider keyboards with a built-in wrist rest or add a gel-based wrist rest to your current keyboard. These provide hand support without making you learn a modified or brand-new keyboard layout.

USB Keyboards with Hubs

Some USB keyboards feature a built-in USB hub designed to add two or more USB ports to your system. Even though this sounds like a good idea, keep in mind that a keyboard-based hub won't provide additional power to the USB connectors. Powered hubs work better with a wider variety of devices than unpowered hubs do. I wouldn't choose a particular model based solely on this feature, although if your keyboard has it and your devices work well when plugged into it, that's great. I'd recommend that you use this type of keyboard with your USB mouse or other devices that don't require much power. Bus-powered devices such as scanners and webcams should be connected to a self-powered hub or directly to the USB ports built in to the computer. USB keyboards and mice correspond to the USB 1.1 standard but can also be connected to the faster USB 2.0 ports on the latest systems.

Multimedia and Web-Enabled Keyboards

As I discussed earlier in this chapter, many keyboards sold at retail and bundled with systems today feature fixed-purpose or programmable hotkeys that can launch web browsers, run the Microsoft Media Player, adjust the volume on the speakers, change tracks on the CD player, and so forth. You need Windows 98 or later to use these hotkeys; more recent Windows versions add additional support for these keyboards.

For the best results, you should download the latest drivers for your keyboard and version of Windows from the keyboard vendor's website.

Keyboard Troubleshooting and Repair

Keyboard errors are usually caused by two simple problems. Other more difficult, intermittent problems can arise, but they are much less common. The most frequent problems are as follows:

- Defective cables
- Stuck keys

Many older keyboards, such as the heavy-duty units made by IBM, had replaceable cables. Defective cables are easy to spot if the failure is not intermittent. If the keyboard stops working altogether or every keystroke results in an error or incorrect character, the cable is likely the culprit. Troubleshooting is simple if your keyboard has a detachable cable, especially if you have a spare cable on hand. Simply replace the suspected cable with one from a known, working keyboard to verify whether the problem still exists. If it does, the problem must be elsewhere.

Most modern keyboards have non-replaceable cables, at least from the outside. In some cases you can open up the keyboard case, and you will see that the cable is internally connected via a removable plug. Unfortunately, those cables are not sold separately, meaning that the only source for one would be from another keyboard, making a replacement implausible.

If the cable is removable, you can test it for continuity with a digital multimeter (DMM). DMMs that have an audible continuity tester built in make this procedure much easier to perform. To test each wire of the cable, insert the DMM's red pin into the keyboard connector and touch the DMM's black pin to the corresponding wire that attaches to the keyboard's circuit board. Wiggle the ends of the cable as you check each wire to ensure no intermittent connections exist. If you discover a problem with the continuity in one of the wires, replace the cable or the entire keyboard, whichever is cheaper. Because replacement keyboards are so inexpensive, it's almost always cheaper to replace the entire unit than to get a new cable, unless the keyboard is an expensive unit like an older IBM Model M. You can get replacement cables (and other parts) for older IBM Model M type keyboards from www.clickykeyboards.com.

For more information about using digital multimeters for testing hardware, see Chapter 22, "PC Diagnostics, Testing, and Maintenance."

Many times you first discover a problem with a keyboard because the system has an error during the POST. Many systems use error codes in a 3xx numeric format to distinguish the keyboard. If you encounter any such errors during the POST, write them down. Some BIOS versions do not use cryptic numeric error codes; they simply state something such as the following:

```
Keyboard stuck key failure
```

This message is usually displayed by a system with a Phoenix BIOS if a key is stuck. Unfortunately, the message does not identify which key it is!

If your system displays a 3xx (keyboard) error preceded by a two-digit hexadecimal number, the number is the scan code of a failing or stuck keyswitch. Look up the scan code to determine which keyswitch is the culprit. By removing the keycap of the offending key and cleaning the switch, you often can solve the problem.

For a simple test of the motherboard keyboard connector, you can check voltages on some of the pins. Using Figure 16.8 (shown earlier in the chapter) as a guide, measure the voltages on various pins of the keyboard connector. To prevent possible damage to the system or keyboard, turn off the power before disconnecting the keyboard. Then, unplug the keyboard and turn the power back on. Make measurements between the ground pin and the other pins according to Table 16.2, shown earlier in the chapter. If the voltages are within these specifications, the motherboard keyboard circuitry is probably okay.

If your measurements do not match these voltages, the motherboard might be defective. Otherwise, the keyboard cable or keyboard might be defective. If you suspect that the keyboard and/or cable is the problem, the easiest thing to do is to connect a known-good keyboard as a test. If the system works properly with the known-good keyboard, then you know the original keyboard and/or cable is defective. If the system still does not work normally, you might have to replace the motherboard.

In many newer systems, the motherboard's keyboard and mouse connectors are protected by a fuse that can be replaced. Look for any type of fuse on the motherboard in the vicinity of the keyboard or mouse connectors. Other systems might have a socketed keyboard controller chip (8042-type). In that case, you might be able to repair the motherboard keyboard circuit by replacing this chip. Because these chips have ROM code in them, you should get the replacement from the motherboard or BIOS manufacturer. If the motherboard uses a soldered keyboard controller chip or a chipset that integrates the keyboard controller with other I/O chips, you'll need to replace the motherboard.

Keyboard Disassembly

Although disassembling a keyboard is possible, most likely you won't need or want to do that given how inexpensive new keyboards have become.

Cleaning a Keyboard

One of the best ways to keep a keyboard in top condition is periodic cleaning. As preventive maintenance, you should vacuum the keyboard weekly, or at least monthly. When vacuuming, you should use a soft brush attachment; this will help dislodge the dust. Also note that many keyboards have keycaps that can come off easily. Be careful when vacuuming; otherwise, you'll have to dig them out of the vacuum cleaner. I recommend using a small, handheld vacuum cleaner made for cleaning computers and sewing machines; these have enough suction to get the job done with little risk of removing your keytops.

You also can use canned compressed air to blow the dust and dirt out instead of using a vacuum. Before you dust a keyboard with the compressed air, turn the keyboard upside down so that the particles of dirt and dust collected inside can fall out.

On all keyboards, each keycap is removable, which can be handy if a key sticks or acts erratically. For example, a common problem is a key that does not work every time you press it. This problem usually results from dirt collecting under the key. An excellent tool for removing keycaps on almost any keyboard is the U-shaped chip puller included in many computer tool kits. Simply slip the hooked ends of the tool under the keycap, squeeze the ends together to grip the underside of the keycap, and lift up. IBM sells a tool designed specifically for removing keycaps from its keyboards, but the chip puller works even better. After removing the cap, spray some compressed air into the space under the cap to dislodge the dirt. Then replace the cap and check the action of the key.

Caution

When you remove keycaps, be careful not to remove the spacebar on the original 83-key PC and the 84-key AT-type keyboards. This bar is difficult to reinstall. The newer 101-key units use a different wire support that can be removed and replaced much more easily.

When you remove the keycap on some keyboards, you are actually detaching the entire key from the keyswitch. Be careful during the removal or reassembly of the keyboard; otherwise, you'll break the switch. The classic IBM/Lexmark-type Model M keyboards (now made by Unicomp) use a removable keycap that leaves the actual key in place, enabling you to clean under the keycap without the risk of breaking the switches. If your keyboard doesn't have removable keycaps, consider using cleaning wands with soft foam tips to clean beneath the keytops.

Spills can be a problem, too. If you spill a soft drink or cup of coffee into a keyboard, you do not necessarily have a disaster. Many keyboards that use membrane switches are spill resistant. However, you should immediately (or as soon as possible) disconnect the keyboard and flush it out with distilled water. Partially disassemble the keyboard and use the water to wash the components. If the spilled liquid has dried, soak the keyboard in some of the water for a while. When you are sure the keyboard is clean, pour another gallon or so of distilled water over it and through the keyswitches to wash away any residual dirt. After the unit dries completely, it should be perfectly functional. You might be surprised to know that drenching your keyboard with water does not harm the components. Just make sure you use distilled water, which is free from residue or mineral content (bottled water is *not* distilled; the distinct taste of many bottled waters comes from the trace minerals they contain!). Also, make sure the keyboard is fully dry before you try to use it; otherwise, some of the components might short out. Some have even put keyboards in a dishwasher (top rack, no detergent) in order to clean them, and with good results.

Tip

If you expect spills or excessive dust or dirt because of the environment or conditions in which the PC is used, several companies make thin membrane skins that mold over the top of the keyboard, protecting it from liquids, dust, and other contaminants. These skins are generally thin enough so that they don't interfere too much with the typing or action of the keys.

Keyboard Recommendations

In most cases, replacing a keyboard is cheaper or more cost effective than repairing it. This is especially true if the keyboard has an internal malfunction or if one of the keyswitches is defective. Replacement parts for keyboards are almost impossible to procure, and installing any repair part is usually difficult. In addition, many of the keyboards supplied with lower-cost PCs leave much to be desired. They often have a mushy feel, with little or no tactile feedback. A poor keyboard can make using a system a frustrating experience, especially if you are a touch typist. For all these reasons, it is often a good idea to replace an existing keyboard with something better.

Perhaps the highest-quality keyboards in the entire computer industry are those made by IBM, or, more accurately today, Unicomp. Unicomp maintains an extensive selection of more than 1,400 Lexmark and IBM keyboard models and continues to develop and sell a wide variety of traditional and customized models, including keyboards that match the school colors of several universities. Unicomp sells keyboards directly via its website at www.pckeyboard.com. My personal favorite is the black EnduraPro 104.

Some of the classic-design IBM keyboards are available in the retail market under either the IBM or IBM Options brand name. Items under the IBM Options program can be found through the Lenovo Group (www.lenovo.com) or through normal retail channels, such as CompUSA and Computer Discount Warehouse (CDW). These items are also priced much more cheaply than items purchased as spare parts. They include a full warranty and are sold as complete packages, including cables. Table 16.3 lists some of the IBM Options keyboards and part numbers; even though the IBM website no longer offers these models, they can be purchased from various online retailers. Models marked with an asterisk (*) are also available from Unicomp.

Table 16.3   IBM Options Keyboards (Sold Retail)

Description	Part Number
IBM Enhanced keyboard (cable w/DIN plug)	92G7454*
IBM Enhanced keyboard (cable w/mini-DIN plug)	92G7453*
IBM Enhanced keyboard, built-in Trackball (cable w/DIN plug)	92G7456*
IBM Enhanced keyboard, built-in Trackball (cable w/mini-DIN plug)	92G7455*
IBM Enhanced keyboard, integrated TrackPoint II (cables w/mini-DIN plugs)	92G7461*
IBM TrackPoint IV keyboard, Black	01K1260
IBM TrackPoint IV keyboard, White	01K1259
IBM TrackPoint USB Space Saver keyboard (black)	22P5150
IBM USB Keyboard with two-port hub (black)	10K3849
IBM Rapid Access III (black)	22P5185

Keep in mind, though, that because IBM spun off its keyboard business some years ago, many recent and current IBM-labeled keyboards no longer have the distinct feel, quality, or durability found in the older models. Ironically, one of the best ways to get an "IBM" keyboard is to buy the model with the features you want from Unicomp, most of whose keyboards still use the capacitive buckling spring technology IBM originally made famous.

The extremely positive tactile feedback of the IBM/Lexmark/Unicomp design is also a benchmark for the rest of the industry. Although keyboard feel is an issue of personal preference, I have never used a keyboard that feels better than the IBM/Lexmark/Unicomp designs. I now equip every system I use with a Unicomp keyboard, including the many non-IBM systems I use. You can purchase these keyboards directly from Unicomp at very reasonable prices.

Many models are available, including some with a built-in trackball or even the revolutionary TrackPoint pointing device. (TrackPoint refers to a small stick mounted between the G, H, and B keys.) This device was first featured on the IBM ThinkPad laptop systems, although the keyboards are now sold for use on other manufacturers' PCs. The technology is being licensed to many other manufacturers as well. Other manufacturers of high-quality keyboards that are similar in feel to the IBM/Lexmark/Unicomp units are Alps, Lite-On, NMB Technologies, and the revived Northgate designs sold under the Avant Prime and Avant Stellar names by Creative Vision Technologies. These keyboards have excellent tactile feedback, with a positive click sound. They are my second choice, after a Unicomp unit. Another great source for IBM external keyboards is www.clickykeyboard.com, which offers a number of used and even new-old stock keyboards, including those with integral TrackPoints.

Pointing Devices

The mouse was invented in 1964 by Douglas Engelbart, who at the time was working at the Stanford Research Institute (SRI), a think tank sponsored by Stanford University. The mouse was officially called an X-Y Position Indicator for a Display System. Xerox later applied the mouse to its revolutionary Alto computer system in 1973. At the time, unfortunately, these systems were experimental and used purely for research.

In 1979 several people from Apple—including Steve Jobs—were invited to see the Alto and the software that ran the system. Steve Jobs was blown away by what he saw as the future of computing, which included the use of the mouse as a pointing device and the graphical user interface (GUI) it operated. Apple promptly incorporated these features into what was to become the Lisa computer and lured away 15–20 Xerox scientists to work on the Apple system.

Although Xerox released the Star 8010 computer, which used this technology, in 1981, it was expensive, poorly marketed, and perhaps way ahead of its time. Apple released the Lisa computer, its first system that used the mouse, in 1983. It was not a runaway success, largely because of its $10,000 list price, but by then Jobs already had Apple working on the low-cost successor to the Lisa: the Macintosh. The Apple Macintosh was introduced in 1984. Although it was not an immediate hit, the Macintosh has grown in popularity since that time.

Many credit the Macintosh with inventing the mouse and GUI, but as you can see, this technology was actually borrowed from others, including SRI and Xerox. Certainly Microsoft Windows has popularized this interface and brought it to the legion of Intel-based PC systems.

Although the mouse did not catch on quickly in the PC marketplace, today the GUIs for PC systems, such as Windows, practically demand the use of a mouse. Therefore, virtually every new system sold at retail comes with a mouse. And, because the mice packaged with retail systems are seldom high-quality or up-to-date designs, sooner or later most users are in the market for a better mouse or compatible pointing device.

Mice come in many shapes and sizes from many manufacturers. Some have taken the standard mouse design and turned it upside down, creating the trackball. In the trackball devices, you move the ball with your hand directly rather than moving the unit itself. Trackballs were originally found on arcade video games, such as Missile Command, and are popular with users who have limited desk space. In most cases, the dedicated trackballs have a much larger ball than would be found on a standard mouse. Other than the orientation and perhaps the size of the ball, a trackball is identical to a mouse in design, basic function, and electrical interface. Like many recent mice, trackballs often come in ergonomic designs, and the more recent models even use the same optical tracking mechanisms used by the latest Microsoft and Logitech mice.

The largest manufacturers of mice are Microsoft and Logitech; these two companies provide designs that inspire the rest of the industry and each other and are popular OEM choices as well as retail brands. Even though mice can come in different varieties, their actual use and care differ very little. The standard mouse consists of several components:

■ A housing that you hold in your hand and move around on your desktop.

■ A method of transmitting movement to the system: either ball/roller or optical sensors.

■ Buttons (two or more, and often a wheel or toggle switch) for making selections.

■ Wheel for vertical scrolling. Some wheels tilt for horizontal scrolling and/or can be pressed to act as a button.

■ An interface for connecting the mouse to the system. Conventional mice use a wire and connector, whereas wireless mice use a radio-frequency or infrared transceiver in both the mouse and a separate unit connected to the computer to interface the mouse to the computer.

The housing, which is made of plastic, consists of very few moving parts. On top of the housing, where your fingers normally rest, are buttons. There might be any number of buttons, but mice designed for PCs have always had two buttons, and since 1996 a scroll wheel as well. Although the latest versions of Windows support scrolling mice, other features supported by the vendor, including additional buttons, still require installing the vendor's own mouse driver software.

Ball-type Mice

The bottom of the mouse housing is where the detection mechanisms or electronics are located. On traditional mice, the bottom of the housing contains a small, rubber ball that rolls as you move the mouse across the tabletop. The movements of this rubber ball are translated into electrical signals transmitted to the computer across the cable.

Internally, a ball-driven mouse is very simple, too. The ball usually rests against two rollers: one for translating the x-axis movement and the other for translating the y-axis movement. These rollers are typically connected to small disks with shutters that alternately block and allow the passage of light. Small optical sensors detect movement of the wheels by watching an internal infrared light blink on and off as the shutter wheel rotates and "chops" the light. These blinks are translated into movement along the axes (see Figure 16.9). Figure 16.10 shows a PS/2 mouse connector.

Optical Mice

The other major method of motion detection is optical. Some of the early mice made by Mouse Systems and a few other vendors used a sensor that required a special grid-marked pad. Although these mice were very accurate, the need to use them with a pad caused them to fall out of favor.

Microsoft's IntelliMouse Explorer pioneered the rebirth of optical mice. The IntelliMouse Explorer and the other new-style optical mice from Logitech and other vendors use optical technology to detect movement, and they have no moving parts of their own (except for the scroll wheel and buttons on top). Today's optical mice need no pad; they can work on virtually any surface. This is done by upgrading the optical sensor from the simple type used in older optical mice to a more advanced CCD (charge coupled device). This essentially is a crude version of a video camera sensor that detects movement by seeing the surface move under the mouse. An LED or diode laser is used to provide light for the sensor.

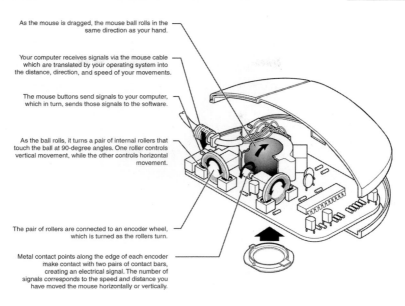

As the mouse is dragged, the mouse ball rolls in the same direction as your hand.

Your computer receives signals via the mouse cable which are translated by your operating system into the distance, direction, and speed of your movements.

The mouse buttons send signals to your computer, which in turn, sends those signals to the software.

As the ball rolls, it turns a pair of internal rollers that touch the ball at 90-degree angles. One roller controls vertical movement, while the other controls horizontal movement.

The pair of rollers are connected to an encoder wheel, which is turned as the rollers turn.

Metal contact points along the edge of each encoder make contact with two pairs of contact bars, creating an electrical signal. The number of signals corresponds to the speed and distance you have moved the mouse horizontally or vertically.

Figure 16.9 Typical opto-mechanical mouse mechanism.

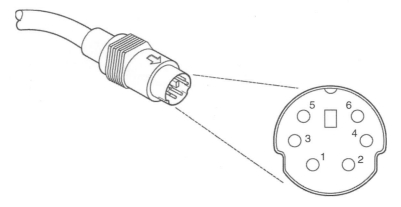

Figure 16.10 Typical PS/2-type mouse connector.

The IntelliMouse Explorer revolutionized the mouse industry; first Logitech, then virtually all other mouse makers, including both retail and OEM suppliers, have moved to optical mice for most of their product lines, offering a wide variety of optical mice in most price ranges. Figure 16.11 shows the essential features of a typical optical mouse.

Their versatility and low maintenance (not to mention that neat red or blue glow out the sides!) make optical mice an attractive choice, and the variety of models available from both vendors means you can have the latest optical technology for about the price of a good ball-type mouse. Figure 16.12 shows the interior of a typical optical mouse.

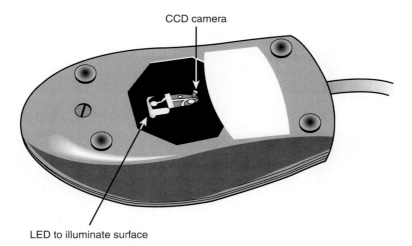

Figure 16.11   The bottom of the Logitech iFeel optical mouse.

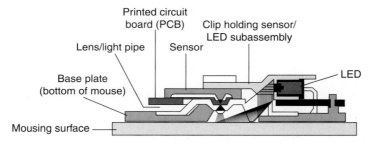

Figure 16.12   The LED inside an optical mouse illuminates the surface by blinking many times per second. The light is reflected from the mousing surface back to the sensor, which converts the information into digital form and sends it to the computer.

All optical mice have a resolution of at least 400 dpi, however, for better performance, some optical mice have adjustable sensors that offer up to 2000dpi resolution. These are often sold as gaming mice because the higher resolution offers faster response for quick game movements. Many mice now incorporate infrared laser technology sensors, which increase the resolution of the sensor, allowing for improved tracking on glossy or transparent surfaces.

Optical mice are available as corded or wireless models, which use either infrared or RF transceivers to replace the cable. A receiver is plugged into the USB or mouse port, while the battery-powered mouse contains a compatible transmitter. Wireless ball-type mice are usually much larger than ordinary mice because of the need to find room for both the bulky ball mechanism and batteries, but wireless optical mice are about the same size as high-end corded mice.

Tip

Corded mice have cables that are typically 4 to 6 feet in length. If you have a choice on the length of cable to buy, get a longer one. This allows easier placement of the mouse in relation to your computer. Extension cables can be used if necessary to extend the distance.

After the mouse is connected to your computer, it communicates with your system through the use of a device driver, which can be loaded explicitly or built in to the operating system software. For example, no separate drivers are necessary to use a mouse with modern operating systems like Windows, but using the mouse with older operating systems like DOS requires a separate driver to be loaded from the CONFIG.SYS or AUTOEXEC.BAT file. Regardless of whether it is built in, the driver translates the electrical signals sent from the mouse into positional information and indicates the status of the buttons.

The standard mouse drivers in Windows are designed for the traditional two-button mouse or scroll mouse (in Windows Me or later), but increasing numbers of mice feature additional buttons, toggles, or wheels to make them more useful. These additional features require special mouse driver software supplied by the manufacturer.

Pointing Device Interface Types

The connector used to attach your mouse to the system depends on the type of interface you are using. Mice are most commonly connected to your computer through the following interfaces:

- Serial interface (obsolete)
- Dedicated motherboard (PS/2) mouse port
- USB port
- Bluetooth/wireless (transceiver connected via USB)

Serial

A popular method of connecting a mouse to older PCs is through the standard serial interface. As with other serial devices, the connector on the end of the mouse cable is typically a 9-pin female connector; some very old mice used a 25-pin female connector. Only a couple of pins in the DB-9 or DB-25 connector are used for communications between the mouse and the device driver, but the mouse connector typically has all 9 or 25 pins present.

Because most older PCs come with two serial ports, a serial mouse can be plugged into either COM1 or COM2. The device driver, when initializing, searches the ports to determine to which one the mouse is connected. Some mouse drivers can't function if the serial port is set to COM3 or COM4, but most can work with any COM port (1–4).

Because a serial mouse does not connect to the system directly, it does not use system resources by itself. Instead, the resources are those used by the serial port to which it is connected. For example, if you have a mouse connected to COM2, and if COM2 is using the default IRQ and I/O port address range, both the serial port and the mouse connected to it use IRQ3 and I/O port addresses 2F8h–2FFh.

◀◀ See "Serial Ports," p. 1046.

Motherboard Mouse Port (PS/2)

Most computers include a dedicated mouse port built in to the motherboard. This practice was introduced by IBM with the PS/2 systems in 1987, so this interface is often referred to as a *PS/2 mouse interface*. This term does not imply that such a mouse can work only with a PS/2; instead, it means the mouse can connect to any system that has a dedicated mouse port on the motherboard.

From a hardware perspective, a motherboard mouse connector is usually exactly the same as the mini-DIN connector used for keyboards. In fact, the motherboard mouse port is connected to the

8042-type keyboard controller found on the motherboard. All the PS/2 computers include mini-DIN keyboard and mouse port connectors on the back. Most computers based on the semiproprietary LPX motherboards and all ATX-series motherboards use these same connectors for space reasons. Most Baby-AT motherboards have a pin-header-type connector for the mouse port because most standard cases do not have a provision for the mini-DIN mouse connector. If that is the case, an adapter cable is usually supplied with the system. This cable adapts the pin-header connector on the motherboard to the standard mini-DIN type connector used for the motherboard mouse.

Caution

As mentioned in the "Keyboard/Mouse Interface Connectors" section earlier in this chapter, the mini-DIN sockets used for both keyboard and mouse connections on many systems are physically and electrically interchangeable, but the data packets they carry are not. Be sure to plug each device into the correct socket; otherwise, neither will function correctly. Don't panic if you mix them up, though. They are electrically identical to each other, so you can't damage the ports or the devices.

Connecting a mouse to the built-in mouse port is the best method of connection on systems that don't have USB ports because you do not sacrifice any of the system's interface slots or any serial ports, and the performance is not limited by the serial port circuitry. The standard resource usage for a motherboard (or PS/2) mouse port is IRQ12, as well as I/O port addresses 60h and 64h. Because the motherboard mouse port uses the 8042-type keyboard controller chip, the port addresses are those of this chip. IRQ12 is an interrupt that is usually free on most systems, but if you use a USB mouse, you can probably disable the mouse port to make IRQ12 available for use by another device.

Hybrid Mice

Hybrid mice are those designed to plug into two types of ports. Although a few low-cost mice sold at retail are designed to plug into either the serial port or the PS/2 port, most mice on the retail market today are designed to plug into either the PS/2 port or the USB port. These combination mice are more flexible than the mice typically bundled with systems, which are designed to work only with the PS/2 or USB port to which they attach.

Circuitry in a hybrid mouse automatically detects the type of port to which it is connected and configures the mouse automatically. Serial-PS/2 hybrid mice usually come with a mini-DIN connector on the end of their cable and an adapter that converts the mini-DIN to a 9- or 25-pin serial port connector, although the reverse is sometimes true on early examples of these mice. PS/2-USB mice usually come with the USB connector on the end of their cable and include a mini-DIN (PS/2) adapter, as shown in Figure 16.13.

Sometimes people use adapters to try to connect a serial mouse to a motherboard mouse port or a motherboard mouse to a serial port. If this does not work, it is not the fault of the adapter. If the mouse does not explicitly state that it is both a serial and a PS/2-type mouse, it works only on the single interface for which it was designed. Most of the time, you find the designation for which type of mouse you have printed on its underside. A safe rule of thumb to follow is if the mouse didn't come with an adapter or come bundled with a system, it probably won't work with an adapter.

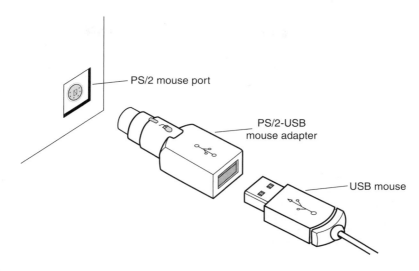

Figure 16.13   A typical USB mouse with a PS/2 adapter.

USB

The extremely flexible USB port has become the most popular port to use for mice as well as keyboards and other I/O devices. Compared to the other interfaces, USB mice (and other USB pointing devices such as trackballs) have the following advantages:

- **USB mice move much more smoothly than the traditional PS/2 type**. This is because the frequency with which the mouse reports its position is much higher. A typical PS/2 mouse has a reporting rate of about 40Hz, whereas an average USB-wired mouse has a reporting rate of 125Hz (most USB wireless mice have a reporting rate of 40Hz–50Hz). Several utilities are available to test and adjust the mouse frequency.

- **USB mice and pointing devices, similar to all other USB devices, are hot-swappable**. If you like to use a trackball and your computing partners prefer mice, you can just lean over and unplug the other users' pointing device and plug in your own, or move it from PC to PC. You can't do that with the other port types.

- **Multiple pointing devices**. With USB, you can easily have multiple pointing devices connected simultaneously, and easily switch between them or use them together in collaboration. Microsoft recently introduced MultiPoint technology, which allows multiple pointing devices to work separately on a single system, with each mouse controlling a separate and distinctly colored pointer.

- **USB mice can be attached to a USB hub, such as the hubs contained in some USB keyboards, as well as standalone hubs**. Using a hub makes attaching and removing your mouse easy without crawling around on the floor to reach the back of the computer. Many computers now have front-mounted USB ports, letting you easily attach and remove a USB mouse without the use of an external hub.

Although the early USB mice were decidedly on the premium end of the price scale, low-cost USB mice are now available for as little as $10. That said, plenty of optical and laser mice are available with premium prices up to $100 and more.

If you want to use a USB mouse at an MS-DOS prompt, in Windows Safe mode, or in some other environment outside of normal Windows 98 or later, make sure that USB Legacy mode is enabled in your PC's BIOS, as discussed earlier in this chapter. Legacy mode enables non-USB-aware systems to recognize a USB keyboard and mouse.

A fourth type of connection, the bus mouse (referred to by Microsoft as the Inport mouse), used a dedicated ISA bus adapter card and is considered long obsolete.

Mouse Troubleshooting

If you are experiencing problems with your mouse, you need to look in only two general places—hardware and software. Because mice are basically simple devices, looking at the hardware takes very little time. Detecting and correcting software problems can take a bit longer, however. To troubleshoot wireless mice, see "Troubleshooting Wireless Input Devices," later in this chapter.

Cleaning Your Mouse

If you notice that the mouse pointer moves across the screen in a jerky fashion, it might be time to clean your mouse. For a mouse with a roller-ball, this jerkiness is caused when dirt and dust become trapped around the mouse's ball-and-roller assembly, thereby restricting its free movement.

From a hardware perspective, the mouse is a simple device, so cleaning it is easy. The first step is to turn the mouse housing over so that you can see the ball on the bottom. Notice that surrounding the ball is an access panel you can open. Sometimes instructions indicate how the panel is to be opened. (Some off-brand mice might require you to remove some screws to get at the roller ball.) Remove the panel to see more of the roller ball and the socket in which it rests.

If you turn the mouse back over, the rubber roller ball should fall into your hand. Take a look at the ball. It might be gray or black, but it should have no visible dirt or other contamination. If it does, wash it in soapy water or a mild solvent, such as contact lens cleaner solution or alcohol, and dry it off.

Now take a look at the socket in which the roller ball normally rests. You will see two or three small wheels or bars against which the ball usually rolls. If you see dust or dirt on or around these wheels or bars, you need to clean them. The best way is to use a compressed air duster, which can blow out any dust or dirt. You also can use some electrical contact cleaner to clean the rollers. Remember, any remaining dirt or dust impedes the movement of the roller ball and results in the mouse not working as it should.

Put the mouse back together by inserting the roller ball into the socket and then securely attaching the cover panel. The mouse should look just as it did before you removed the panel, except that it will be noticeably cleaner.

One of the major advantages of the new breed of optical mice is the lack of moving parts. Just wipe away dust from the optical sensor, and that's all the cleaning an optical mouse needs.

Interrupt Conflicts

Interrupts are internal signals used by your computer to indicate when something needs to happen. With a mouse, an interrupt is used whenever the mouse has information to send to the mouse driver. If a conflict occurs and the same interrupt used by the mouse is used by a different device, the mouse will not work properly—if at all.

Interrupt conflicts caused by mice can occur when a serial or PS/2 mouse is used, but not when a USB mouse is used. Mouse ports built in to modern motherboards are almost always set to IRQ12. If your system has a motherboard mouse port, be sure you don't set any other adapter cards to IRQ12; otherwise, a conflict will result.

If you are using a serial mouse, interrupt conflicts typically occur if you add third and fourth serial ports, using either an expansion card or internal serial device, such as a modem. This happens because in ISA bus systems, the odd-numbered serial ports (1 and 3) usually are configured to use the same interrupts, and the even-numbered ports (2 and 4) are as well; that is, IRQ4 is shared by default between COM1 and COM3, and IRQ 2 is shared by default between COM2 and COM4. Therefore, if your mouse is connected to COM2 and an internal modem uses COM4, they both might use the same interrupt, and you can't use them at the same time.

Because the mouse generates interrupts only when it is moved, you might find that the modem functions properly until you touch the mouse, at which point the modem is disconnected. Another example is when your system will run properly until you try to go online with your modem; then the conflict usually locks up the system. You might be able to use the mouse and modem at the same time by moving one of them to a different serial port. For instance, if your mouse uses COM1 and the modem still uses COM4, you can use them both simultaneously because odd and even ports use different interrupts.

The best way around these interrupt conflicts is to make sure no two devices use the same interrupt. Serial port adapters are available for adding COM3 and COM4 serial ports that do not share the interrupts used by COM1 and COM2. These boards enable the new COM ports to use other normally available interrupts, such as IRQs 10, 11, 12, 15, and 5 (listed in priority order). I never recommend configuring a system with shared ISA interrupts; it is a sure way to run into problems later. However, interrupts used by PCI boards can be shared if you use Windows 95 OSR 2.x, Windows 98, Windows Me, Windows 2000, or Windows XP with recent chipsets that support a feature called IRQ steering.

◄◄ See "Interrupts," p. 409.

If you suspect an interrupt problem with a bus-type mouse, you can use the Device Manager built in to Windows (which is accessible from the System control panel).

►► See "Operating System Diagnostics," p. 1382.

The Device Manager in Windows 9x and later is part of the Plug and Play (PnP) software for the system, and it is usually 100% accurate on PnP hardware. Although some of these interrupt-reporting programs can have problems, most can easily identify the mouse IRQ if the mouse driver has been loaded. After the IRQ is identified, you might need to change the IRQ setting of the bus mouse adapter or one or more other devices in your system so that everything works together properly.

If your driver refuses to recognize the mouse at all, regardless of its type, try using a different mouse that you know works. Replacing a defective mouse with a known good one might be the only way to know whether the problem is indeed caused by a bad mouse.

I have had problems in which a bad PS/2 interface mouse caused the system to lock right as the driver loaded or when third-party diagnostics were being run on the system. Try unplugging the mouse to see if the system will boot, if it does, then the mouse or mouse port (meaning the motherboard) may be the problem. If a motherboard-based mouse port goes bad, you can replace the entire motherboard—which is usually expensive—or you can just disable the motherboard mouse port via jumpers or the system BIOS setup program and install a serial or USB mouse instead.

Driver Software

Most mice and other pointing devices in use today emulate a Microsoft mouse, enabling you to have basic two-button plus scrolling functions with current versions of Windows without loading any special drivers. However, if your mouse has additional buttons or other special features, you will need to install device-specific drivers available from the mouse vendor.

Scroll Wheels

Late in 1996 Microsoft introduced the IntelliMouse, which differed from standard Microsoft mice by adding a small gray wheel between the mouse buttons. While this was not technically the first scrolling mouse on the market (Mouse Systems introduced the ProAgio and Genius EasyScroll in 1995), it was the first to have widespread support. Since then, Logitech, IBM, and virtually all other mouse vendors have made scroll wheels or similar devices compatible with the Microsoft design as standard across almost all models, including OEM mice bundled with computer systems.

The wheel has two main functions. The primary function is to act as a scrolling device, enabling you to scroll through documents or web pages by manipulating the wheel with your index finger. The wheel also functions as a third mouse button when you press it.

Although three-button mice have been available for years from vendors such as Logitech, the scrolling function provided a real breakthrough. No longer do you have to move the mouse pointer to click the scrollbar on the right side of your screen or take your hand off the mouse to use the arrow keys on the keyboard. You just push or pull on the wheel. This is a major convenience, especially when browsing web pages or working with word processing documents or spreadsheets. Also, unlike three-button mice, the IntelliMouse's wheel-button doesn't seem to get in the way and you are less likely to click it by mistake. Although it took a while for software vendors to support the wheel, improvements in application software and Windows support allow today's wheel mice to be fully useful with almost any recent or current Windows program.

Each vendor's mouse driver software offers unique features to enhance the basic operation of the mouse. For example, Logitech's MouseWare drivers enable you to select which function the OS should perform when you click one of the mouse's extra buttons. (The more you spend on a mouse these days, the more buttons it's likely to have.) The drivers also provide various options for how to scroll with each wheel click (three lines, six lines, or one screen). Microsoft's IntelliMouse driver offers a feature called ClickLock, which allows you to drag items without holding down the primary mouse button. In addition, it offers a Universal Scroll feature that adds scrolling mouse support to applications that lack such support. To get the most from whatever scrolling or other advanced-feature mouse you have, be sure you periodically download and install new mouse drivers.

Instead of the wheel used by Microsoft and Logitech, IBM and other mouse vendors frequently use various types of buttons for scrolling. Some inexpensive mice use a rocker switch, but the most elegant of the non-wheel alternatives is IBM's ScrollPoint Pro, which uses a pressure-sensitive scroll stick similar to the TrackPoint pointing device used on IBM's laptop computer and some PC keyboards made by IBM and Unicomp. The scrollpointer in the center of the mouse enables you to smoothly scroll through documents without having to lift your finger to roll the wheel, as you do on the Microsoft version, which makes it much easier and more convenient to use. Because no moving parts exist, the ScrollPoint is also more reliable.

TrackPoint II/III/IV

On October 5, 1992, IBM introduced a revolutionary new pointing device called *TrackPoint* as an integrated feature of its new ThinkPad 700 and 700C computers. Often referred to as a *pointing stick*, the TrackPoint appears as a small rubber cap on the keyboard just above the B key, and between the G and H keys. This was in my opinion the most significant new pointing device since the mouse was invented nearly 30 years earlier!

The TrackPoint device occupies no space on a desk, does not have to be adjusted for left-handed or right-handed use, has no moving parts to fail, and (most importantly) does not require you to move your hands from the home row to use it. This is an absolute boon for touch typists.

I was fortunate enough to meet the actual creator of this device in early 1992 at the spring Comdex/Windows World show in Chicago. While attending the show I had stumbled upon a gentleman wearing suspenders and sporting a pony-tail in a small corner of the IBM booth. His appearance piqued my interest because he was clearly not a "suit," but instead looked to be some sort of scientist or engineer. I was right, and he was there showing off custom-made prototype keyboards with a small stick in the middle. The stick was covered with a soft cream-colored silicone rubber coating that allowed you to press on the stick without your finger slipping off. In fact, he told me that these were hand-built prototypes he had installed in standard desktop keyboards, and that he was there trying to get public reaction and feedback on the invention. I was invited to play with one of the keyboards, which was connected to a demonstration system. I found that by pressing on the stick with my index finger, I could easily move the mouse pointer around on the screen. The stick itself did not move (it was not a joystick). Instead, it was connected to pressure transducers that measured the amount and direction of the force applied by my finger, and moved the mouse pointer accordingly. The harder I pressed, the faster the pointer moved. After playing around for just a few minutes, the pointer movements became automatic—almost as though I could just "think" about where I wanted the pointer to go, and it would go there.

The gentleman at the booth turned out to be Dr. Ted Selker, the primary inventor of the device. He and Joseph Rutledge created this integrated pointing device at the IBM T.J. Watson Research Center. When I asked him when such keyboards would become available, he could not answer—at the time there were apparently no plans for production, and he was only trying to test user reaction to the device. I filled out one of the survey forms, indicating that I was extremely interested in the revolutionary device and would gladly purchase one if they became available in the future.

Well, the feedback must have helped, because just over six months later, IBM had announced the ThinkPad 700, which included this revolutionary device—then known as the TrackPoint II. Since the original version came out, enhanced versions with even greater control and sensitivity have become available.

Note

The reason the device was initially called TrackPoint II is that IBM had previously been selling a convertible mouse/ trackball device called the TrackPoint. No relationship exists between the original TrackPoint mouse/trackball, which has since been discontinued, and the TrackPoint II and later integrated devices. Since the original TrackPoint II came out, improved versions known as TrackPoint III and TrackPoint IV have become available. In the interest of simplicity, I refer to all the TrackPoint II, III, and successive devices as just *TrackPoint*.

Although the prototypes I used were cream-colored, in its final production form, the TrackPoint consists of a small, red, silicone rubber knob nestled between the G, H, and B keys on the keyboard. The primary and secondary mouse buttons are placed below the spacebar where you can easily reach them with your thumbs without taking your hands off the keyboard. Newer versions also include a third button which can be used for scrolling.

Studies conducted by Selker found that the act of removing your hand from the keyboard (to reach for a mouse) and then replacing your hand back on the keyboard takes approximately 1.75 seconds.

If you type at 60 wpm (words per minute), that can equal nearly two lost words every minute, not including the time lost while you regain your train of thought. Almost all of this time can be saved if you use the TrackPoint to move the pointer or make a selection (click or double-click) instead of a mouse. The TrackPoint also enables you to perform drag-and-drop functions easily.

IBM's research also found that people can get up to 20% more work accomplished using the TrackPoint instead of a mouse, especially when the application involves a mix of typing and pointing activities, such as with word processing, spreadsheets, and other typical office applications. In usability tests with the TrackPoint, IBM gave a group of desktop computer users both a TrackPoint and a traditional mouse. After two weeks, 80% of the users had unplugged their mice and switched solely to the TrackPoint device. Selker is convinced (as am I) that the TrackPoint is the best pointing solution for both laptop and desktop systems.

Another feature of the TrackPoint is that a standard mouse can be connected to the system at the same time to enable dual-pointer use. This setup not only enables a single person to use both devices, but also enables two people to use the TrackPoint and the mouse simultaneously to move the pointer on the screen. The first pointing device that moves (thus issuing a system interrupt) takes precedence and retains control over the mouse pointer on the screen until it completes its movement action. The second pointing device is automatically locked out until the primary device is stationary. This enables the use of both devices and yet prevents each one from interfering with the other.

IBM/Lenovo has added various versions of the TrackPoint to its laptop computers, as well as to high-end keyboards sold under the IBM/Lenovo, Lexmark, and Unicomp names. Laptop computer makers, such as HP/Compaq, Dell, and Toshiba, have licensed the TrackPoint device (Toshiba calls it Accupoint) and use it on various models.

I have compared the TrackPoint device to other pointing devices for laptops (especially touch pads), but nothing compares in terms of accuracy and control—and, of course, the fact that you don't have to take your hands off the keyboard to use it!

Unfortunately, most of the TrackPoint devices used by laptops other than IBM/Lenovo don't have the full features of the IBM/Lenovo versions, especially including the multiple tip choices, the third scroll button, and "negative intertia" control. One important feature to look for is the ability to accept different IBM/Lenovo TrackPoint caps. These have a square hole in them and allow choosing from several different types.

Over the years IBM/Lenovo has upgraded the TrackPoint pointing stick to the TrackPoint III and the current TrackPoint IV. Two main differences exist in the III/IV system, but the most obvious one is the rubber cap. The original caps were made from pure silicone rubber, which was grippy and worked well in most situations. However, if the user has greasy fingers, the textured surface of the rubber can become slippery. Cleaning the cap (and the user's hands) solves the problem, but it can be annoying at times. The TrackPoint III and later standard caps are made from a different type of rubber, which Selker calls "plastic sandpaper." This type of cap is much more grippy and does not require cleaning except for cosmetic purposes. More recently IBM/Lenovo introduced other caps that do not feature the sandpaper surface, but have either a wider soft dome or a wider concave surface for additional grip. IBM/Lenovo now has three different types of caps for the TrackPoint to suit different needs and tastes. These different caps are interchangeable with the older styles as well (see Figure 16.14):

- **Classic dome (p/n 84G6537)**—The traditional "pencil eraser" cap with a sandpaper surface.
- **Soft rim (p/n 91P8423)**—A larger concave non-sandpaper design creates a mechanical advantage, requiring less force for pointer motion.
- **Soft dome (p/n 91P8422)**—A larger convex design with a soft texture non-sandpaper surface.

Figure 16.14   Classic, soft rim, and soft dome TrackPoint caps.

Note

If your keyboard uses the same physical caps as the IBM/Lenovo designs, you can change to the newer IBM/Lenovo caps as well. You can get these caps by ordering them from IBM Parts directly or from others who sell IBM/Lenovo parts, such as Compu-Lock (www.compu-lock.com). The cost is less than $15 for a set of four caps. Replacing the cap is easy—grab the existing cap with your fingers and pull straight up; it pops right off. Then, simply push on the new cap.

The other difference between the IBM/Lenovo TrackPoint and some of the others on the market is the control software. IBM/Lenovo added routines that implement a subtle technique Selker calls "negative inertia," which is marketed under the label *QuickStop response*. This software not only takes into account how far you push the pointer in any direction, but also how quickly you push or release it. Selker found that the improved software and caps enable people to make selections up to 8% faster.

The latest incarnation (called TrackPoint IV) includes an extra scroll button, as well as the ability to press the TrackPoint cap to select as if using the left mouse button. These new features make the TrackPoint even better.

The bottom line is that anyone who touch types should strongly consider only laptops that include a TrackPoint device. TrackPoints are far superior to other pointing devices such as touch pads, because the TrackPoint is faster to use (you don't have to take your hands off the keyboard's home row), easier to adapt to (especially for speedy touch typists), and far more precise to control. It takes some getting accustomed to, but the benefits are worth it. I know many people who have converted from using touch pads to TrackPoints, but few who have willingly gone the other way.

Note that the benefits of the TrackPoint are not limited to portable systems; you can have the same features on your desktop keyboard. For desktop systems, I use an IBM/Lenovo keyboard with the TrackPoint built in. This makes for a more consistent interface between desktop and laptop systems because I can use the same pointing device in both environments. You can buy these keyboards directly from IBM/Lenovo, Unicomp (Unicomp keyboards are TrackPoint III compatible), or www.clickykeyboard.com.

Mouse and Pointing Stick Alternatives

Because of Windows, many users spend at least as much time moving pointers around the screen as they do in typing, making pointing device choices very important. In addition to the mouse and the pointing stick choices discussed earlier in this chapter, several other popular pointing devices are available:

- Track pads, such as the Cirque GlidePoint
- Trackballs from many vendors
- Upright mice, such as the 3M Renaissance Mouse

All these devices are treated as mice by the operating system but offer radically different options for the user in terms of comfort. If you're not satisfied with a regular mouse and don't want to use an integrated pointing stick such as the TrackPoint II/III/IV, look into these options.

GlidePoint/Touch Pad

The first touch pad was included on the ill-fated Gavilan portable computer in 1982; however, it didn't catch on until many years later. Cirque originated the modern touch pad (also called a *track pad*) pointing device in 1994. Cirque refers to its technology as the GlidePoint and has licensed the technology to other vendors such as Alps Electric, which also uses the term GlidePoint for its touch pads. The GlidePoint uses a flat, square pad that senses finger position through body capacitance. This is similar to the capacitance-sensitive elevator button controls you sometimes encounter in office buildings or hotels.

When it is used on a portable computer's keyboard, the touch pad is mounted below the spacebar, and it detects pressure applied by your thumbs or fingers. Transducers under the pad convert finger movement into pointer movement. Several laptop manufacturers have licensed this technology from Cirque and have incorporated it into their portable systems. Touch pads are also integrated into a number of mid-range to high-end keyboards from many vendors. When used on a desktop keyboard, touch pads are often offset to the right side of the keyboard's typing area.

Touch pads feature mouse buttons, although the user also can tap or double-tap on the touch pad's surface to activate an onscreen button located under the touch pad's cursor. Dragging and dropping is accomplished without touching the touch pad's buttons; just move the cursor to the object to be dragged, press down on the pad, hold while moving the cursor to the drop point, and raise the finger to drop the object. Some recent models also feature additional hot buttons with functions similar to those on hot-button keyboards, as well a vertical scrollbar on the side and the capability to tap the touch pad to simulate a mouse click.

The primary use for touch pads has been for laptop computer– and desktop keyboard–integrated pointing devices, although Cirque and Alps have both sold standalone versions of the touch pad for use as a mouse alternative on desktop systems. Cirque's touch pads are now available at retail under the Fellowes brand name, as well as direct from the Cirque website. The Internet Touchpad (also sold by Fellowes) has enhanced software to support touch gestures, has programmable hot buttons, and includes other features to make web surfing easier.

Although it has gained wide acceptance, especially on portable computers, touch pad technology can have many drawbacks for some users. Operation of the device can be erratic, depending on skin resistance and moisture content. The biggest drawback is that to operate the touch pad, users must remove their hands from the home row on the keyboard, which dramatically slows their progress. In addition, the operation of the touch pad can be imprecise, depending on how pointy your finger or thumb is! On the other hand, if you're not a touch typist, removing your hands from the keyboard to operate the touch pad might be easier than using a TrackPoint. Even with their drawbacks, touch pad pointing devices are still vastly preferable to using a trackball or a cumbersome external mouse with portable systems.

Unless you want to use a "real" mouse with a portable system, I recommend you sit down with portable computers that have both touch pad and TrackPoint pointing devices. Try them yourself for typing, file management, and simple graphics and see which type of integrated pointing device you prefer. I know what I like, but you might have different tastes.

Trackballs

The first trackball I ever saw outside of an arcade was the Wico trackball, a perfect match for mid-1980s video games and computer games, such as Missile Command and others. It emulated the eight-position Atari 2600 analog joystick but was capable of much more flexibility.

Unlike the mid-80s trackballs, today's trackballs are used primarily for business instead of gaming. Most trackballs use a mouse-style positioning mechanism—the differences being that the trackball is on the top or side of the case and is much larger than a mouse ball. The user moves the trackball rather than the input device case, but rollers or wheels inside most models translate the trackball's motion and move a cursor onscreen the same way that mouse rollers or wheels convert the mouse ball's motion into cursor movement.

Trackballs come in a variety of forms, including ergonomic models shaped to fit the (right) hand, ambidextrous models suitable for both lefties and right-handers, optical models that use the same optical sensors found in the latest mice in place of wheels and rollers, and multibutton monsters that look as if they're the result of an encounter with a remote control.

Because they are larger than mice, trackballs lend themselves well to the extra electronics and battery power needed for wireless use. Logitech offers several wireless trackball models that use radio-frequency transceivers; for details of how this technology works, see the section "Wireless Input Devices," later in this chapter.

Trackballs use the same drivers and connectors as conventional mice. For basic operations, the operating system–supplied drivers will work, but you should use the latest version of the vendor-supplied drivers to achieve maximum performance with recent models.

Trackball troubleshooting is similar to mouse troubleshooting. For issues other than cleaning the trackball, see the section "Mouse Troubleshooting," earlier in this chapter.

Because trackballs are moved by the user's hand rather than by rolling against a tabletop or desktop, they don't need to be cleaned as often as mouse mechanisms do. However, occasional cleaning is recommended, especially with trackballs that use roller movement-detection mechanisms. If the trackball pointer won't move, skips, or drags when you move the trackball, try cleaning the trackball mechanism.

Trackballs can be held into place by a retaining ring, an ejection tab, or simply by gravity. Check the vendor's website for detailed cleaning instructions if your trackball didn't come with such instructions. Swabs and isopropyl alcohol are typically used to clean the trackball and rollers or bearings; see the trackball's instructions for details.

3M's Ergonomic Mouse

Many PC users who grew up using joysticks on the older video games experienced some "interface shock" when they turned in their joysticks for mice. And even long-time mouse users nursing sore arms and elbows have wondered whether the mouse was really as "ergonomic" as it is sometimes claims to be.

3M's solution, developed late in 2000, is to keep the traditional ball-type mouse positioning mechanism but change the user interface away from the hockey puck/soap bar design used for many years to a slanted handle that resembles a joystick. 3M's Ergonomic Mouse (originally called the Renaissance Mouse) is available in two hand sizes and attaches to either the PS/2 port or USB port (serial ports are not supported). The single button on the top of the handle is a rocker switch; push on the left side to left-click and on the right side to right-click. The front handgrip provides scrolling support when the special Ergonomic Mouse driver software is installed.

The Ergonomic Mouse enables the user to hold the pointing device with a "handshake"-style hand and arm position. 3M's website provides detailed ergonomic information to encourage the proper use of the Ergonomic Mouse, which comes with software to support scrolling and other advanced functions. It's available in two sizes, along with various colors and separate models for Windows-based PCs and Macs.

Input Devices for Gaming

Originally, game players on the PC used the arrow keys or letter keys on the keyboard to play all types of games. As you can imagine, this limited the number and type of games that could be played on the PC.

Analog Joysticks and the Game Port

As video standards improved, making games more realistic, input devices made especially for game play also became more and more popular. The first joysticks made for the IBM PC were similar to joysticks made for its early rival, the Apple II series. Both the IBM and Apple II joysticks were analog devices that lacked much of the positive feedback game players were accustomed to from the Atari 2600, Commodore 64, or arcade joysticks. These joysticks also required frequent recalibration to work properly and were far from satisfactory to hardcore game players. Also, these devices required their own connector—the 15-pin game port. The game port found its way onto many sound cards as well as onto multi-I/O cards made for ISA and VL-Bus systems.

Even though joysticks began to add better features, including spring action, video game-style gamepads, and flight control options, the analog nature and slow speed of the gameport began to restrict performance as CPU speeds climbed above 200MHz and improved video cards made ultra-realistic flying, driving, and fighting simulators possible. USB controllers offer the additional speed necessary for more sophisticated gamers.

USB Ports for Gaming

The USB port has become the preferred connector for all types of gaming controllers, including joysticks, gamepads, and steering wheels. Instead of making a single inadequate joystick work for all types of games, users can now interchange controllers using the hot-swap benefits of USB and use the best controller for each type of game.

Although a few low-end game controllers still on the market can connect to either the venerable game port or the serial port, serious gamers want USB because of its higher speed, better support for force feedback (which shakes the game controller realistically to match the action onscreen), and tilting (tilt the gamepad and the onscreen action responds).

As with USB mice, your USB-connected gaming controllers are only as good as their software drivers. Be sure to install the latest software available to keep up with the latest games.

Compatibility Concerns

If you play a lot of older games designed in the heyday of the 15-pin gameport, consider keeping a gameport-type controller. Even though the vendors of USB game controllers strive to make the USB port emulate a game port for use with older games, some older games can't be fooled. If you have problems using a USB game controller with a specific game, check the game's website for patches, as well as your game controller's website for tips and workarounds. Note, however, that analog controllers may not work well when running a game in a DOS window under newer operating systems such as Windows XP and Vista. In that case, your best bet may be to use a virtual machine under VMWare or VirtualPC, or simply create a bootable DOS partition or drive on which to run older games.

Wireless Input Devices

For several years, many manufacturers have offered wireless versions of mice and keyboards. In most cases, these devices have used either infrared or short-range radio transceivers to attach to standard USB or PS/2 ports, with matching transceivers located inside the mouse or keyboard. Wireless input devices are designed to be easier to use in cramped home-office environments and where a large-screen TV/monitor device is used for home entertainment and computing.

Many manufacturers, including Microsoft, Logitech, and second-tier vendors, offer bundled kits that include a wireless keyboard and mouse that share a transceiver. Because many of these keyboards and mice have the latest features, including programmable keys, multimedia and Internet-access keys, and optical sensors, these wireless combos are often the top-of-the-line products from a given vendor and are often less expensive than buying the keyboard and mouse separately.

How Wireless Input Devices Work

The three major technologies used by wireless input devices are as follows:

- Infrared (IR)
- Proprietary radio frequency
- Bluetooth

All three technologies normally use a transceiver connected to the USB or PS/2 ports on the computer. Because many wireless transceivers are designed for use with a mouse and keyboard, PS/2-compatible versions have two cables—one for the mouse port and one for the keyboard port. A USB-compatible transceiver needs only one USB port to handle both devices if the system supports USB Legacy (keyboard) functions. The transceiver attached to the computer draws its power from the port.

The transceiver receives signals from the transceiver built in to the mouse or keyboard. These devices require batteries to function; therefore, a common cause of wireless device failure is battery rundown. Early generations of wireless devices used unusual battery types, but most recent products use off-the-shelf alkaline AA or AAA batteries. Many models now use lithium-ion or NiMH rechargeable batteries in which the transceiver connected to the PC also doubles as a charger.

Although all three technologies rely on battery power, the similarities end there. IR devices have a relatively short range (12 ft. maximum), and a clear line-of-sight must exist between the input device and transceiver. Anything from a Mountain Dew can to a sheet of paper can block the IR signal from reaching the transceiver, assuming you're aiming the transmitter built in to your input device correctly in the first place. Some late-model IR devices have transceivers that can receive signals through a relatively wide 120° range, but this technology is much more temperamental than the others and has been abandoned by most vendors. Figure 16.15 shows how range and line-of-sight issues can prevent IR input devices from working correctly.

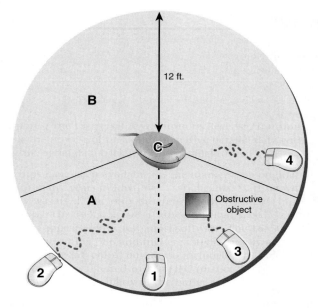

A. Acceptable angle for receiving transmissions
B. Not acceptable
C. IR transceiver

1. Mouse with IR-connection to transceiver
2. Mouse can't connect (out of range)
3. Mouse can't connect (line-of-sight blocked)
4. Mouse can't connect (wrong angle to transceiver)

Figure 16.15   A wireless mouse using IR technology must be within range of the transceiver, at the correct angle to the transceiver, and not blocked by any objects. Otherwise, it cannot work.

Because of the problems with IR devices shown in Figure 16.16, almost all vendors of wireless input devices now use radio waves (RF) for transmission between the device and transceiver. RF-based wireless devices have no line-of-sight problems, but most have a limited range of about 6 ft. from the transmitter (see Figure 16.16).

Although RF overcomes line-of-sight issues that can cripple an IR mouse, early versions of RF products had a high potential for interference from other devices and from other devices in use in the same room because of a limited range of channels. For example, early Logitech wireless MouseMan products required the user to manually select the channel used by the transceiver and mouse. If more than six users in a small room had wireless devices, interference was practically inevitable and user error could lead to a user's mouse movements showing up on the wrong computer screen.

Fortunately, improvements in frequency bands used and automatic tuning have enabled all users of a particular type of device to avoid interference with other electronic devices or with each other. For example, the 27MHz frequency pioneered by Logitech's Palomar line of peripherals has become a de facto standard for most recent wireless input devices (it has also been used by Microsoft and IBM for their wireless products). Logitech allows users to enable a digital security feature that uses one of more than 4,000 unique codes to prevent accidentally activating another computer with a wireless device or signal snooping by another user. Most vendors use similar technology, but some might use a much smaller number of codes. The range of 27MHz RF devices is short—about 6 ft.—but the transmitter can be located behind the computer or under the desk without loss of signal. Many recent wireless products use FastRF technology, which provides 2.5 times the transmission rate of conventional 27MHz devices. The responsiveness of a FastRF connection is all but indistinguishable from a corded mouse or keyboard.

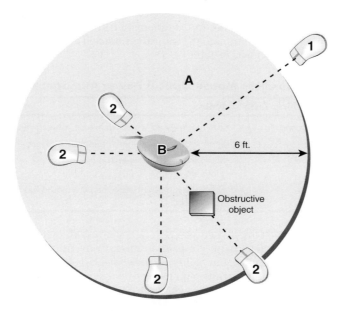

A. Acceptable angle for receiving transmissions (360)
B. RF transceiver

1. Mouse can't connect (out of range)
2. Mouse with connection to RF transceiver

Figure 16.16   A wireless mouse using RF must be within range of the transceiver, but unlike IR-based wireless mice, the angle of the mouse to the transceiver doesn't matter and radio signals can't be blocked by books, paper, or other obstacles.

Finally, there's Bluetooth. Although most wireless products use proprietary radio transceivers, Microsoft, Logitech, and some others have developed wireless mouse and keyboard products using the Bluetooth wireless standard. Bluetooth-enabled devices have an effective range of up to 30 ft. and might be compatible with other brands of devices that are also Bluetooth enabled.

▶▶ For more information about Bluetooth, see Chapter 18, "Local Area Networking," p. 1151.

Having used both IR and RF types of wireless devices, I can tell you that a radio-frequency input device beats an infrared input device hands down for use at home or in a small one- or two-person office. It's little wonder that IR-based mouse devices and keyboards are now all but impossible to find on a retail shelf. Today, there is little reason not to opt for an RF device even if you have the choice of purchasing a less-expensive IR peripheral. Because the cost of RF wireless products, including attractive keyboard and mouse combinations, varies widely, RF input devices are affordable for almost everyone. If you're planning to use a computer to drive a big-screen TV or as a presentation unit, consider Bluetooth-enabled devices available from Microsoft, Logitech, and others because of their longer range (up to 10 meters, or 33 ft.).

Power Management Features of Wireless Input Devices

A wireless mouse is useless if its batteries fail, so several vendors of wireless products have developed sophisticated power-management features to help preserve battery life—especially with optical mice, which use power-eating LEDs to illuminate the mousing surface. For example, Logitech Cordless mice have four operating modes, as shown in Table 16.5.

Table 16.5   Logitech Cordless Mouse Optical Power Management

Mode	Sensor Flashing Rate	Notes
Bright	1,500 per second	Run mode: Used when the mouse is being moved across a surface
Glow	1,000 per second	Walk mode: Used when the mouse stops moving
Strobe	10 per second	Sleep mode: Used when the mouse has not moved for more than 1 minute
Flash	2 per second	Deep sleep mode: Used when the mouse has not moved for more than 10 minutes

Wireless keyboards are activated only when you press a key or use the scroll wheel available on some models, so they tend to have longer battery lives than mice. Conventional ball-type mice also have longer battery lives than optical mice, but ball-type mice have largely been discontinued, as the convenience and accuracy of optical mice outweigh battery-life issues for most users.

Troubleshooting Wireless Input Devices

If your wireless input device does not work, check the following:

- **Battery failure**—The transceivers attached to the computer are powered by the computer, but the input devices themselves are battery-powered. Check the battery life suggestions published by the vendor; if your unit isn't running as long as it should, try using a better brand of battery or turning off the device if possible.

- **Lost synchronization between device and transceiver**—Both the device and the transceiver must be using the same frequency to communicate. Depending on the device, you might be able to resynchronize the device and transceiver by pressing a button, or you might need to remove the battery, reinsert the battery, and wait for several minutes to reestablish contact.

- **Interference between units**—Check the transmission range of the transceivers in your wireless units and visit the manufacturer's website for details on how to reduce interference. Typically, you should use different frequencies for wireless devices on adjacent computers.

- **Blocked line of sight**—If you are using infrared wireless devices, check the line of sight carefully at the computer, the space between your device and the computer, and the device itself. You might be dangling a finger or two over the infrared eye and cutting off the signal—the equivalent of putting your finger over the lens on a camera.

- **Serial port IRQ conflicts**—If the wireless mouse is connected to a serial port and it stops working after you install another add-on card, check for conflicts using the Windows Device Manager.

- **Disconnected transceiver**—If you have moved the computer around, you might have disconnected the transceiver from its keyboard, PS/2 mouse, serial, or USB port. You can plug a USB device in without shutting down the system, but the other types require you to shut down the PC, reattach the cable, and restart the PC to work correctly.

- **USB Legacy support not enabled**—If your wireless keyboard uses a transceiver connected to the USB port and the device works in Windows, but not at a command prompt, make sure you have enabled USB Legacy support in the BIOS or use the PS/2 connector from the transceiver to connect to the PS/2 keyboard port.

Chapter

17

Internet Connectivity

Relating Internet and LAN Connectivity

Communication between computers is a major part of the PC computing industry. Thanks to the World Wide Web (WWW), no computer user is an island. Whether using a dialup modem or broadband technology, virtually all PCs can be connected to other computers, enabling them to share files, send and receive email, and access the Internet. This chapter explores the various technologies you can use to expand the reach of your PC around the block and around the world.

It might surprise you to see discussions of protocols and networking setup in both this chapter and the LAN chapter of this book, but a modem connection is really just another form of networking. In fact, Windows NT and Windows 9x all the way through Windows Vista have all but blended the two services into a single entity.

The reason for this combination is that the typical target for a modem connection has changed over the years. Computer users a decade ago dialed in to *bulletin board systems (BBSs)*, which are proprietary services that provide terminal access to other computers. However, BBSs are practically extinct today. Similarly, proprietary online services such as America Online and CompuServe (now owned by AOL but maintained as a separate service), which have also been around for many years, have almost entirely dropped their proprietary client software and protocols and have been reborn as gateways to the Internet.

With the explosive growth of the Internet, modem and network technologies were joined because both could use the same client software and protocols. Today, the most popular suite of networking protocols—TCP/IP—is used on both LANs and the Internet. When you dial into an Internet service provider (ISP), you are actually connecting to a network using a modem instead of a network interface card, and when you use most broadband services, your path to the Internet typically starts with a network interface card, built-in network port, network-to-USB adapter, or even a wireless connection.

Although some new PCs still include a dialup modem, an increasing number of PC users are abandoning dialup Internet access for the faster world of broadband access. In fact, according to a report by
J.D. Power, 2006 marked the first time that the number of broadband users exceeded the number of
dialup users in the United States, with 56% of residential ISP customers using broadband and 44%
using dialup. According to the Broadband Worldwide report by eMarketer.com, by 2006 the number
of broadband households in the United States reached 54.6 million, or 45.9% of the total households
(see Table 17.1). Not bad when you consider that in 1995 no one had a broadband connection in
their home and in 2000 only 8.9% of home users had access to broadband.

Table 17.1   Worldwide Broadband Penetration in 2006

Country	Broadband Households (millions)	Percent of Total Households
US	54.6	45.9%
China	46.6	12.6%
Japan	23.7	52.3%
South Korea	12.7	78.8%
UK	12.0	47.1%
Germany	11.8	30.8%
France	11.2	42.3%
Italy	7.9	35.4%
Canada	7.4	58.0%
Spain	5.5	41.7%
Brazil	4.9	10.6%
Australia	3.5	45.4%
Mexico	3.0	12.3%
India	2.3	1.2%
Argentina	1.4	13.1%
All Others	42.7	3.0%
Worldwide	251.2	10.5%

Source: www.eMarketer.com

Broadband = 200Kbps in at least one direction

Although broadband has replaced dialup for the majority of users, dialup connections still have their
uses and a large user base. Those without broadband options, those on a budget, or those who travel
still need a dialup connection. They can also serve as a valuable backup Internet access source. Even
though I use broadband when I can, I still configure new PCs with dialup modems for emergency use
when the broadband connection is down. You'll find dialup modem coverage in the second portion
of this chapter.

Comparing Broadband and Dialup Modem Internet Access

Even though many new PCs purchased at retail include some type of dialup modem you can use for
Internet and email access, you are likely to find that Internet and email access with a dialup modem
aren't sufficient for your needs if you use these services for more than a few minutes each day. If you
haven't already, here are some reasons you should consider switching to a broadband service:

- **Speed**—The fastest dialup modems can download data at a maximum rate of 56Kbps (limited
  in the United States to just 53Kbps by the FCC), whereas broadband services start at 128Kbps

for ISDN. Newer forms of broadband, such as DSL and cable modems, start at 384Kbps and typically exceed 500Kbps. Many of the latest services offer 4Mbps–8Mbps download speeds. Similarly, broadband services can upload data at several times the speed of a dialup modem.

■ **Convenience**—Cable modems and some types of DSL and satellite broadband Internet service are always on, providing you with an immediate connection as soon as you open your web browser or email client. Dialup modems require you to dial up the server and wait up to a minute before you can check your email or surf the Web. Similarly, always-on broadband services can provide you with immediate notification of incoming email, whereas dialup systems can check for incoming email only if you stay online and tie up your phone line.

■ **Telephone line usage**—Keeping telephone communications lines open for emergencies—or for convenience—has been a major consideration for many people. Most dialup modems do not support call waiting, making it difficult for callers to reach you with important messages while you're online unless you use call-forwarding or call-notification software. Although some dialup ISPs provide software that can alert you to incoming calls, in most cases you must find and install such software yourself. By contrast, most broadband services keep your telephone line free so you can check email or surf the Web and use the telephone at the same time.

■ **Price**—One disadvantage of broadband communications is apparent when you see your bill: It can cost two to three times as much per month as dialup access with a dialup modem. However, prices of some broadband options like DSL are falling, and millions of U.S. users believe the additional speed and convenience of broadband make the extra cost of the service per month a worthwhile investment. If you use the Internet enough to justify installing a second phone line just for Internet use, the price gap narrows considerably because you can use most broadband services without tying up your single existing phone line. If you have cable TV, most cable TV providers now also offer cable broadband service and provide a discount off the normal price for customers who have both cable TV and cable Internet service.

■ **Ease of reconnection after an operating system upgrade**—Because broadband Internet is usually based on automatically configured TCP/IP network settings, you should be able to keep your broadband connection running during a Windows upgrade with little difficulty. Just verify that you have the correct drivers for your Ethernet adapter (used for most broadband connections) before you perform the upgrade, note your computer and workgroup name, and you should be able to go online as soon as the upgrade is completed. A dialup connection is often much tougher to keep working, especially because of the different methods used by various Windows versions for handling dialup networking.

Broadband Internet Access Types

Thanks to the combination of huge multimegabyte downloads needed to update software and support hardware, dynamic websites with music and full-motion video, and increased demand for online services, even the fastest dialup modem (which can download at just 53Kbps) isn't sufficient for heavy Internet use. More and more users are taking advantage of various types of broadband Internet access solutions, including the following:

■ Cable modem

■ DSL

■ Fixed-base wireless

■ Satellite-based services

■ ISDN

■ Leased lines

At least one of these services might be available to you, and if you live in a large- to medium-size city, you might be able to choose from two or more of these broadband solutions. The first portion of this chapter focuses on these solutions.

High Speed = Less Freedom

Although high-speed services such as cable modems, DSL, and others all represent major improvements in speed over existing dialup 56Kbps connections, one big drawback you should consider is the loss of freedom in choosing an ISP.

With a 56Kbps dialup modem, you can choose from a wide variety of services, including

- Local ISPs (personalized service)
- National ISPs with dialup access across the country (great for travelers)
- Online services with customized content plus web access (AOL and CompuServe)
- Family-friendly filtered Internet access (Mayberry USA and Lightdog)
- Business-oriented web hosting plus Internet access plans from many vendors

At present, if you want faster speed, you must use the ISP provided with your high-speed service. Whether it's your local telephone company, a third-party vendor, or your friendly cable TV operator, their ISP is your ISP. When you evaluate a high-speed service, remember to look at the special features and services provided by the ISP and its track record for reliability and keeping customers happy. After all, the quality of the work your ISP does is reflected in the quality of your broadband connection.

Cable Modems

For many users, cable modem service—which piggybacks on the same cable TV (CATV) service lines that bring your TV many channels—represents both a big boost in speed from that available with ISDN and a major savings in initial costs and monthly charges. Unlike ISDN, cable modem service normally is sold as an "all you can eat" unlimited-access plan with a modest installation charge (often waived) and a small monthly fee for the rental of the cable modem. Because more and more cable networks support a single standard, you can also choose to buy your cable modem from any of several vendors in some cases, saving even more money over the long term.

Connecting to the Internet with a "Cable Modem"

As with ISDN, the device used to connect a PC to a CATV network is somewhat inaccurately called a modem. In fact, the so-called "cable modem" (a name I will continue to use, for the sake of convenience) is actually a great deal more. The device does indeed modulate and demodulate, but it also functions as a tuner, a network bridge, an encryptor, and an SNMP agent. To connect your PC to a CATV network, you do not use a serial port as with dialup modem technologies or ISDN terminal adapters. Instead, the most typical connection today runs the incoming cable connection to an external cable modem, which has an Ethernet connection to a router, which then connects to 1–255 PCs via Ethernet as well. Although you can directly connect most PCs to a cable modem using USB, I do not recommend that option because it precludes using a router. I always recommend running a router between a cable or DSL modem and a PC because a router not only allows more than one PC to be connected, but also provides a robust hardware firewall that helps shield the PCs connected to it from Internet-based attacks. Some cable modems have a built-in router, in which case you don't need to purchase a separate one. If your computer doesn't include an Ethernet adapter built into the motherboard or a separate Ethernet card, you can install an Ethernet card into an available internal expansion slot or use a USB-based Ethernet adapter instead. Some older cable modem services utilize an internal adapter for one-way service and use the conventional modem for uploads; this type of service is called *telco return* and is largely obsolete. Even though you get fast downloading, telco return systems tie up your phone line and are not recommended.

Tip

For maximum security, speed, and ease of sharing among multiple systems, I recommend that you connect your cable modem to a router and then connect the router to an Ethernet card or port in your system. Combination cable modems and routers are available that include both functions in one box.

The Cable Modem and the CATV Network

The cable modem connects to the CATV network using the same coaxial cable connection as your cable TV service (see Figure 17.1). Thus, the cable modem functions as a bridge between the tiny twisted-pair network in your home and the hybrid fiber/coax (HFC) network that connects all the cable customers in your neighborhood.

A few cable modem CATV systems have been built using the older one-way (download-only) coax cable, but this type of cable is much slower for cable modem use and is obsolete for both CATV and data communications. The industry has largely replaced coax with HFC. Before you sign up for CATV Internet service, find out which type of service is being offered. Only the two-way, HFC-based systems allow you to use the Internet independently of the telephone system; one-way cable modem service requires a dialup modem for uploading page requests, files, and email. The modem can be built into your one-way cable modem (these are called *bundled* cable modems) or be a separate external dialup modem. In either case, going online with a one-way cable modem ties up your phone line.

Digital CATV service, which brings your TV many more channels and a clearer picture, requires the cable TV provider to upgrade to an HFC physical plant. Thus, digital CATV service is a precursor to two-way cable modem service; pure-coax CATV systems can't be used to transmit digital service or handle two-way cable modem traffic. CATV systems that have been upgraded to digital service are capable of providing two-way cable modem service, after suitable head-end equipment is installed at the CATV central office. A good rule of thumb, therefore, is that CATV systems that don't offer digital cable TV might offer only one-way cable modem service or no cable modem service at all. A typical two-way cable modem connection is shown in Figure 17.1.

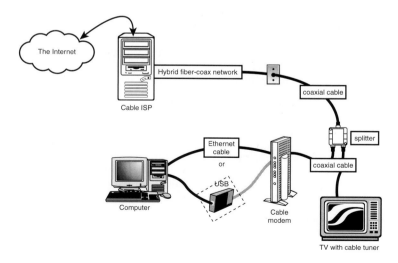

Figure 17.1   A typical hybrid fiber-coax cable TV network that also includes two-way cable modem service.

Originally, cable modems were not sold to users of CATV Internet access but were leased by the CATV companies offering Internet access to their cable modem customers. This is because each cable modem on a particular CATV network had to match the proprietary technology used by the network. In late 1998, DOCSIS-compliant cable modems began to be used by some CATV companies. DOCSIS refers to devices that meet the Data Over Cable Service Interface Specification standards established by Cable Television Laboratories, Inc. (CableLabs). Modems that meet DOCSIS standards are now referred to as *CableLabs Certified cable modems*. Visit the CableLabs website at www.cablelabs.com for a complete list of cable modems that are CableLabs Certified.

Many vendors of traditional modems and other types of communications products, such as 3Com, Motorola, Cisco, D-Link, and many others, now make CableLabs Certified Cable Modem–compliant hardware. The models supported by your CATV Internet provider might vary according to the DOCSIS standard it supports. Table 17.2 provides a brief overview of the differences in these standards.

Table 17.2 DOCSIS Standards Overview

DOCSIS Standard	Benefits	Notes
1.0	Basic broadband CATV (cable modem) service	Original DOCSIS version released March 1997.
1.1	Supports tiered service (different speeds at different costs), faster uploading, home networking, and packet telephony while reducing costs	Backward-compatible with DOCSIS 1.0—released April 1999
2.0	Faster performance for downloading and uploading compared to DOCSIS 1.0 and 1.1; supports high-speed two-way business services	Backward-compatible with DOCSIS 1.1, 1.0—released Dec. 2001
3.0	Faster performance, channel bonding, support for Internet Protocol version 6 (IPv6)	Backward-compatible with DOCSIS 2.0—released Aug. 2006

Many cable providers require modems that are DOCSIS 1.1 or 2.0 certified at a minimum. Check with your cable service provider for the minimum required standard before you purchase or install a cable modem. To check the certification level of a specific modem, you can look it up in the current cable modem certification list (Certified_Products.pdf), which can be downloaded from CableLabs (www.cablemodem.com). In some cases, cable service providers have upgraded their service, causing older modems to work unreliably. If you are suddenly experiencing problems with your cable modem, I recommend you contact your provider to find out if the requirements have changed. If so, an upgraded modem might be required.

Although most cable modems are now available for about $50–$100, compared to $5–$40 for typical dialup modems, you should check with your CATV Internet provider before purchasing one to determine which models are supported by your provider and whether your CATV Internet provider still requires you to lease the cable modem.

If you plan to keep cable modem service for more than a year, I recommend purchasing a CableLabs Certified cable modem, but if you're unsure of your long-term plans, leasing isn't all that expensive. Typical lease costs for the device add only about $5/month to the monthly rate of $30–$60 for cable modem service.

Cable modems normally come in an external box that has a cable connection for connecting to the cable network, along with USB and ethernet ports to connect to your network. While the cable modem can be directly connected to a single PC, this is not recommended for security reasons as well as for sharing the connection. By connecting the cable modem to a router, you can share the connection among several PCs, with the router's built-in firewall providing security and protection. Some cable modems include a built-in router, although I prefer to keep them as separate units. If the router is built-in, you can disable it and use an external router if you choose. A typical cable modem is shown in Figure 17.2.

Figure 17.2   Linksys BEFCMU10 Cable Modem—CableLabs Certified DOCSIS 2.0

CATV Bandwidth

Cable TV uses what is known as a *broadband network*, meaning the bandwidth of the connection is split to simultaneously carry many signals at different frequencies. These signals correspond to the channels you see on your TV. A typical HFC network provides approximately 750MHz of bandwidth, and each channel requires 6MHz. Therefore, because the television channels start at about 50MHz, you would find channel 2 in the 50MHz–56MHz range, channel 3 at 57MHz–63MHz, and so on up the frequency spectrum. At this rate, an HFC network can support about 110 channels.

For data networking purposes, cable systems typically allocate one channel's worth of bandwidth in the 50MHz–750MHz range for downstream traffic—that is, traffic coming into the cable modem from the CATV network. In this way, the cable modem functions as a tuner, just like your cable TV box, ensuring that your PC receives signals from the correct frequency.

Upstream traffic (data sent from your PC to the network) uses a different channel. Cable TV systems commonly reserve the bandwidth from 5MHz to 42MHz for upstream signals of various types (such as those generated by cable TV boxes that enable you to order pay-per-view programming). Depending on the bandwidth available, you might find that your CATV provider does not furnish the same high speed upstream as it does downstream. This is called an *asymmetrical network*.

Note

Because the upstream speed often does not match the downstream speed (and to minimize noise, which tends to accumulate because of the tree-and-branch nature of the network), cable TV connections usually are not practical for hosting web servers and other Internet services. This is largely deliberate because most CATV providers are currently targeting their traditional home user market. As the technology matures, however, this type of Internet connection is likely to spread to the business world as well. There are now specialized domain name services that can be used to "point" web surfers to your cable modem or DSL connection.

Some cable ISPs require you to switch to a more expensive business plan if you want to host a server (including a P2P server such as Gnutella) on your cable modem connection. In fact, hosting a server on a residential cable modem service could be a violation of your contract and could lead to cancellation of your service.

The amount of data throughput that the single 6MHz downstream channel can support depends on the type of modulation used at the head end (that is, the system to which your PC connects over the network). Using a technology called 64 QAM (quadrature amplitude modulation), the channel might be capable of carrying up to 27Mbps of downstream data. A variant called 256 QAM can boost this to 36Mbps. Unfortunately, those speeds are theoretical; most cable providers limit download speeds to 6Mbps or 8Mbps sustained, with bursts of up to 12Mbps. Upload speeds are much lower, normally 384Kbps or 768Kbps, depending on the package you choose.

CATV Performance

The fact that you are sharing the CATV network with other users doesn't mean the performance of a cable modem isn't usually spectacular. Although the CATV network takes a big cut out of the maximum speeds, you'll still realize a throughput that hovers between 6Mbps and 8Mbps, over100 times that of the fastest modem connection. You will find the Web to be an entirely new experience at this speed. Those huge audio and video clips you avoided in the past now download in seconds, and you will soon fill your hard drives with all the free software available.

Add to this the fact that the service is typically quite reasonably priced. Remember that the CATV provider is replacing both the telephone company (if you have two-way service) and your ISP in your Internet access solution. The price can be about $30–$60 per month, which is several times that of a normal dialup ISP account, but it does not require a telephone line, and provides 24-hour access to the Internet. The only drawback is that the service might not be available yet in your area. In my opinion, this technology exceeds all the other Internet access solutions available today in speed, economy, convenience, and widespread availability. Its nearest rival is DSL, which is still not as widely available geographically and is plagued with poor coordination between ISPs and telephone companies. Because cable modem Internet service providers provide the physical plant, provide ISP services, and can provide equipment, you can get service installed in just days and avoid the finger-pointing common with other types of broadband Internet service.

CATV Internet Connection Security

Because your PC is sharing a network with other users in your neighborhood and because the traffic is bidirectional on systems using two-way cable modems, the security of your PC and the network becomes an issue. In most cases, some form of encryption is involved to prevent unauthorized access to the network. CableLabs Certified (DOCSIS) cable modems have built-in encryption, however older one-way modems might not have this feature.

If you use an operating system that has built-in peer networking capabilities and your provider doesn't use CableLabs Certified cable modems or some other form of encryption, and you don't use a router, you might be able to see your neighbors' computers on the network. The operating system has settings that enable you to specify whether other network users can access your drives. If these settings are configured improperly, your neighbors might be able to view, access, and even delete the files on your hard drives. Be sure the technician from the cable company installing the service addresses this problem if your cable modem hardware doesn't provide encryption—although this is rare today. If you want to use a cable modem along with sharing access on your computer (for printing, file storage, and so on), I'd recommend that you use passwords for any shared drives, but you're even safer if you disable file and printer sharing on the system you connect to the cable modem.

▶▶ For more information on securing any type of Internet access, see "Securing Your Internet Connection," p. 1127.

Digital Subscriber Line

The biggest rival to the cable modem in the broadband Internet business is the digital subscriber line (DSL). DSL, like its predecessor ISDN, appeals to the telephone companies who might be able to use the existing POTS wiring to provide high-speed Internet access. Not every type of DSL is suitable for existing wiring; however, all but the fastest, most expensive types can sometimes be used with the existing POTS plant. DSL is also appealing to businesses that don't have access to cable modems but are looking for a high-performance, lower-cost alternative to the expensive ISDN services that top out at 128Kbps.

Note

Some technical discussions of DSL refer to xDSL. The x stands for the various versions of DSL being proposed and offered by local telephone companies and ISPs. DSL generally is used to refer to any type of digital subscriber line service.

One advantage of DSL compared to its most popular rival—cable modems—is that cable modems share common bandwidth, which means that a lot of simultaneous use by your neighbors can slow down your connection. If you use DSL you don't have this concern; whatever bandwidth speed you pay for is yours—period.

How DSL Works

DSL takes advantage of the broadband nature of the telephone system, using the system's capability to carry signals at multiple frequencies to allow both high-speed Internet traffic and phone calls at the same time. Two methods for sending and receiving signals are used by the most common type of DSL, Asymmetric DSL (ADSL):

- Carrierless Amplitude/Phase (CAP)
- Discrete Multitone (DMT)

Most early DSL installations used CAP, which splits the telephone line into three frequency bands. Exact frequency usage varies by system, but most typically, the divisions resemble the following:

- Voice calls use frequencies from 30Hz to 4KHz. This frequency is also used by answering machines, fax machines, and alarm systems.
- Upstream data such as web page requests and sent email uses frequencies between 25Hz and 160Hz.
- Downstream data such as received web pages and email uses frequencies between 240KHz and 1.5MHz.

Some systems use the 300Hz–700Hz range for downstream data and frequencies of 1MHz and above for upstream data.

Because voice, downstream, and upstream data use different frequencies, you can talk, surf, and send email at the same time.

DMT, the system used by most recent ADSL installations, divides the telephone line into 247 channels that are 4KHz wide. If a particular channel has problems, a different channel with better signal quality is used automatically. Unlike CAP, DMT uses some channels starting at around 8KHz to send and receive information.

Both types of signaling can have problems with interference from telephones and similar devices, so devices called *low-pass filters* are used to prevent telephone signals from interfering with signals above the 4KHz range, where DSL signals begin. The location of these filters depends on the type of DSL you use and whether you are installing DSL service yourself.

At the central switch, DSL data is transferred to a device called a *DSL access multiplexer (DSLAM)*, which transfers outgoing signals to the Internet and sends incoming signals to the correct DSL *transceiver* (the correct name for the so-called "DSL modem" that connects to your computer).

Who Can Use DSL—and Who Can't

DSL services have been slowly rolling out across the country for years, first to major cities and then to smaller cities and towns. As with 56Kbps modems, rural and small-town users are often the last to receive this service. If you live in an area without access to cable or Internet, you should consider satellite-based or fixed wireless Internet services where available for a faster-than-56Kbps experience.

Just as distance to a telephone company's central switch (CS) is an important consideration for people purchasing an ISDN connection, distance also affects who can use DSL in the markets offering it. For example, most DSL service types require that you be within about 18,000 feet (about 3 miles) wire distance to a telco offering DSL; some won't offer it if you're beyond 15,000 feet wire distance because the speed drops significantly at longer distances. Repeaters or a local loop that has been extended by the telco with fiber-optic line might provide longer distances. The speed of your DSL connection varies with distance: The closer you are to the telco, the faster your DSL access is. Many telcos that offer some type of DSL service provide websites that help you determine whether, and what type of, DSL is available to you.

If you want to locate DSL service providers in your area, compare rates, and see reviews from users of the hundreds of ISPs now providing DSL service, set your browser to http://www.dslreports.com. The site provides a verdict on many of the ISPs reviewed, summarizing users' experiences and ranking each ISP in five categories.

Note

If you want to connect DSL to your SOHO or office LAN, check first to see what the provider's attitude is. Some users report good cooperation, whereas others indicate they were told "we can't help you" or were told that DSL "couldn't be connected to a LAN." Fortunately, as home LANs continue to proliferate, this is becoming a less frequent problem. Again, check around for the best policies. Low-cost switch/router combinations from companies such as Linksys and D-Link and Microsoft's Internet Connection Sharing provide relatively easy ways to share both DSL and other types of high-speed connections.

Even if your telco's central switch is well within wire distance range of your location, that's no guarantee that you qualify for DSL service. The design and condition of the wiring plant connecting your location with the central switch can prevent you from qualifying for DSL service. Because DSL service depends on successful sending and receiving of high-frequency data, a telephone wiring plant that blocks high-frequency signals can't be used for DSL service. Some of the typical issues with telephone lines that aren't DSL-friendly include

- **Loading coils**—These amplifiers boost voice signals and are sometimes called voice coils. Unfortunately, these block the high-frequency signals needed by DSL service.

- **Bridge taps**—Used to extend service to new customers without running separate lines all the way back to the central switch. Bridge taps can create a circuit that's too long for DSL service.

- **Fiber-optic cables**—Used to carry a lot of signals in a small physical space, fiber-optic cables use analog-to-digital (A/D) and digital-to-analog (D/A) converters where they connect to copper telephone lines. A/D and D/A converters can't pass DSL signals through to their destinations.

Major Types of DSL

Although the term *DSL* is used in advertising and popular discussions to refer to any form of DSL, many, many variations of DSL are used in different markets and for different situations. This section discusses the most common forms of DSL and provides a table that compares the various types of DSL service. Although many types of DSL service exist, you can choose only from the service types offered by your DSL provider:

- **ADSL (Asymmetrical DSL)**—The type of DSL used most often, especially in residential installations. Asymmetrical means that downstream (download) speeds are much faster than upstream (upload) speeds. For most users, this is no problem because downloads of web pages, graphics, and files are the major use of Internet connections. Maximum downstream speeds are up to 9Mbps, with up to 640Kbps upstream. Most vendors who offer ADSL provide varying levels of service at lower speeds and prices, as well. Voice calls are routed over the same wire using a small amount of bandwidth, making a single-line service that carries voice and data possible. ADSL is more expensive to set up than some other forms of DSL because a splitter must be installed at the customer site, meaning that you must pay for a service call (also called a *truck roll*) as part of the initial setup charge.

- **CDSL (Consumer DSL)**—A slower (1Mbps downstream) form of DSL that was developed by modem chipset maker Rockwell. It doesn't require a service call because no splitter is required at the customer site.

- **G.Lite (Universal DSL, and also called DSL Lite or Splitterless DSL)**—Another version that splits the line at the telco end rather than at the consumer end. Downstream speeds range from 1.544Mbps to 6.0Mbps, and upstream speeds can be from 128Kbps to 384Kbps. This is becoming one of the most popular forms of DSL because it enables consumers to use self-install kits. Note that the DSL vendor might cap the service at rates lower than those listed earlier in the chapter; check with the vendor for details.

- **SDSL (Symmetrical DSL)**—This type of DSL service provides the same speed for upstream as for downstream service. Generally, SDSL is offered to business rather than residential customers because it requires new cabling (rather than reusing existing phone lines). A long-term contract frequently is required.

Table 17.3 summarizes the various types of DSL.

Table 17.3   DSL Type Comparison

DSL Type	Description	Data Rate Downstream; Upstream	Distance Limit	Application
IDSL wire	ISDN Digital Subscriber Line	128Kbps	18,000 feet on 24-gauge wire	Similar to the ISDN BRI service but data only (no voice on the same line)
CDSL wire	Consumer DSL from Rockwell	1Mbps downstream; less upstream	18,000 feet on 24-gauge wire	Splitterless home and small business service; similar to DSL Lite
DSL Lite (same as G.Lite)	Splitterless DSL	From 1.544Mbps depending on the subscribed service	18,000 feet on 24-gauge wire	Sacrifices speed for not having to install splitters
HDSL	High bit-rate Digital Subscriber Line	1.544Mbps duplex on two twisted-pair lines; 2.048Mbps duplex three twisted-pair lines	12,000 feet on 24-gauge wire	T-1/E1 service between server and phone company or within a on company

Table 17.3   Continued

DSL Type	Description	Data Rate Downstream; Upstream	Distance Limit	Application
SDSL	Symmetric DSL	1.544Mbps duplex (U.S. and Canada); 2.048Mbps (Europe) on a single-duplex line downstream and upstream	12,000 feet on 24-gauge wire	Same as for HDSL but requiring only one line of twisted pair
ADSL	Asymmetric Digital Subscriber Line	1.544Mbps to 8.448Mbps downstream; 16Kbps to 640Kbps upstream	1.544Mbps at 18,000 feet; 2.048Mbps at 16,000 feet; 6.312Mbps at 12,000 feet; 8.448Mbps at 9,000 feet	The most common DSL used for Internet access
VDSL	Very High Digital Subscriber Line 5	12.9Mbps to 2.8Mbps downstream; 1.6Mbps to 2.3Mbps upstream	4,500 feet at 12.96Mbps; 3,000 feet at 25.82Mbps; 1,000 feet at 51.84Mbps	ATM networks; Fiber to the Neighborhood

With any type of DSL, an external device called a DSL *modem* is attached to the computer through either of the following:

- A crossover cable running to an Ethernet card or port in the computer
- A USB cable running to a USB port in the computer

An RJ-11 (standard telephone) cable is attached between the DSL modem and the RJ-11 port that has been set up for DSL service.

To prevent telephone signals from interfering with DSL frequencies, splitters or microfilters must be installed on a DSL line. If you choose a technician-installed form of DSL, a device called a *splitter* is used at your location to prevent interference. Splitter-based DSL allows faster speeds than splitterless DSL installations, but the wait for a technician to show up and add the splitter can add days or weeks to your installation process.

If you self-install DSL, you will install small devices called *microfilters* to block interference from telephones, answering machines, and similar devices. These devices might fit behind the faceplate of the wall outlet used for DSL service or inline between the phone, answering machine, or fax machine and the wall outlet (see Figure 17.3).

Tip

If you have a security system attached to your telephone line, watch out for problems if you select DSL as your preferred broadband access method. Security systems are often designed to seize the line, interrupting a phone call in progress to send an alarm to the security company. This feature won't work with normal microfilters, so you should purchase a special DSL Alarm filter to allow your alarm system to coexist with your DSL installation. Get more information about the alarm microfilter and alternative DSL installation options from http://www.hometech.com/learn/dsl.html.

DSL Installation with In-line Microfilter

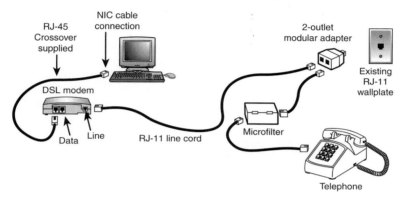

DSL Installation with Wall Outlet Microfilter

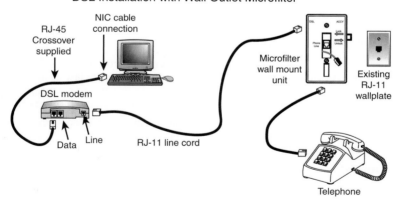

Figure 17.3   Two types of DSL self-installations; if a splitter is used to set up a separate DSL line, the microfilters shown here are not necessary.

DSL Pricing

DSL pricing varies widely, with different telephone companies offering different speeds of DSL and different rates. One thing that's true about the most commonly used flavors of DSL is that they are usually an asymmetrical service—with download speeds faster than upload speeds. ADSL installations can typically be run over existing copper wires, whereas SDSL installations usually require that new high-quality copper wires be installed between the CO and the subscriber's location.

For unlimited use, typical residential DSL pricing ranges anywhere from $15 to $80 a month depending on whether you want a static or dynamic IP address and the download speed, which ranges from 256Kbps to 1.5Mbps. Business DSL pricing ranges from $50 to as high as $500 per month.

The wide variance is partly due to the upload speeds permitted. The lower-cost plans typically use a lower upload speed (some variation on ADSL or G.Lite); in contrast, the more expensive plans often use SDSL. Check carefully with your vendor because your traditional telephone company might not be the only DSL game in town. Some major cities might have as many as half a dozen vendors selling various flavors of DSL.

DSL Security Issues

Unlike other types of broadband access, DSL is a direct one-to-one connection that isn't shared; you have no digital "neighbors" who could casually snoop on your activities. However, as with any broadband "always-on" connection, intrusion from the Internet to your computer is a very real possibility and you should safeguard your system behind a router with firewall capabilities. Using an additional software firewall, such as the one included with Windows XP or Vista, is also a good idea.

▶▶ For more information on securing any type of Internet access, see "Securing Your Internet Connection," p. 1127.

Technical Problems with DSL

Telecommunications has always had its share of difficulties, starting with the incredibly slow and trouble-plagued 300bps modems used on early PCs, but as speed increases, so do problems. DSL connections are often very difficult to get working correctly because DSL, as you've seen, combines the problems of adding high-speed data access to the telephone line with network configuration using TCP/IP (the most powerful and most complex network protocol in widespread use; see Chapter 18, "Local Area Networking," for details).

A review of comments from DSL users in various forums, such as DSLReports.com and others, shows that the most common problems include the following:

- **Poor coordination between the DSL sales department of the telco or third-party provider and the installers**—This can lead to broken or very late appointments for installation; if possible, contact the installer company to verify the appointment. If possible, opt for a self-install version of DSL to avoid problems with late or missing appointments.

- **Installers who install the hardware and software and then leave without verifying it works properly**—Ask whether the installer carries a notebook computer that can test the line; don't let the installer leave until the line is working.

- **Poor technical support before and after installation**—Record the IP address and other information used during the installation; read reviews and tips from sources listed earlier in the chapter to help you find better DSL providers and solutions you can apply yourself or ask your telco or provider to perform.

- **Lower speeds than anticipated**—This can be due to a poor-quality connection to the telco from your home or business or problems at the central switch; ask the installer to test the line for you during initial installation and tell you the top DSL speed the line can reach. On a healthy line, the problem is often traceable to a very low value for the Windows Registry key called RWIN (receive window), which should be adjusted from its default of 8192 (8KB) to a value as high as 32768 (32KB) or even 65535 (64KB). If your system previously was used with a dialup modem, the value for RWIN can be as low as 2144; low values force your DSL connection to receive data at rates hardly faster than those for a dialup modem connection. For interactive tests that will help you find the best value to use for `RWIN` or other Registry options, find line problems, and adjust your configuration, go to http://www.dslreports.com and follow the Tools link from the home page.

Because of the problems with trying to retrofit an aging voice-oriented telephone network with high-speed Internet service, many pure DSL companies are having financial problems. Some once-prominent DSL ISPs went out of business in 2000–2001, leading to service cancellations in some cases. Before you sign a long-term contract for DSL service, you should determine what your options are if your telco, DSL line provider, or ISP drops DSL service.

Fixed-base Wireless Broadband

If cable modem or DSL service isn't available at your location, you still might be able to get broadband Internet service through a fixed wireless broadband Internet provider. These services use various frequencies of microwave signals to connect to the Internet. Most of these are based on the same 2.4GHz frequencies 802.11 Wi-Fi connections use. These services typically require a small directional panel antenna to be mounted at the highest point on your roof and must have a clear line-of-sight view of the transmitter, which is usually mounted on a tower only a few miles away. Such services are therefore local, so you generally need to check your area to see whether they are available. Normally, I recommend fixed-base wireless only if cable modem or DSL service is unavailable, but I'd place it as a better overall choice than satellite service. In general, the initial equipment fees are less than satellite and the signals are more immune to weather problems.

WiMax is a newer standard for fixed-base wireless broadband, offering speeds comparable to dedicated T1 lines (1.5 to 3Mbps duplex) for fees in the $500 per month range, with even higher speeds available for additional cost.

Cellphone providers like AT&T and Verizon also offer high-speed internet access through the cellular network. This is usually in the form of dedicated CardBus or ExpressCard based modems for laptop systems. While it is possible to connect these modems to a desktop using a USB or PCI adapter, the high expense and low performance as compared to conventional Cable or DSL service makes cellular modems a poor choice for a desktop system.

Whereas most cellular broadband connections are made with a dedicated cellular modem, in many cases you can also connect through your existing cellphone by attaching the phone to the system via USB or Bluetooth (called *tethering*), and then using the phone as a high-speed modem connection. Some phones only allow tethering via USB, while others support both USB and Bluetooth. For example, using my laptop, I can link to the cellphone in my pocket via Bluetooth, then instruct the cellphone to connect to the Internet, in essence creating a double-wireless connection.

The connection speeds available depend on the carrier and services offered, but so-called 3G (3rd Generation) technologies offer speeds in the 400 to 700Kbps range. Although this is quite a bit less than the 11MBps provided by the most basic WiFi hotspots, this type of service is available anywhere you can get a cell phone signal. Note that connections via a tethered cell phone are generally much lower in performance (depending on the phone) than via dedicated cards.

In general, you must purchase a modem card along with a service package from your cell phone provider. Because the service packages and networks vary and the technologies are constantly changing, you should contact your local cell phone providers for more information on their current offerings. In most cases, a laptop cellular modem card will run in the $100-$200 range, with ongoing service rates of $60 per month. Although this is expensive when compared to normal cable or DSL connection prices, cellular broadband can be worthwhile for those who travel with a laptop and require access away from hotel rooms or WiFi hotspots.

Internet Connectivity via Satellite with HughesNet or StarBand

If you're in an area where cable modem, DSL, or fixed wireless services don't exist, you might be able to use a satellite connection as a last resort. To see whether this is possible, take a look at the southern sky from your home, condo, or apartment building. If you have a good, clear 45° window view to the sky toward the equator and you want fast downloads of big files, a satellite-based service such as HughesNet or StarBand might be the best (or only viable) high-speed choice for you.

Note

Geosynchronous satellites used for satellite Internet/TV service are visible in the southern sky for users in the Northern Hemisphere (North America, Europe, and Asia); if you're in the Southern Hemisphere (South America, Australia, Africa), these satellites are located in the northern sky.

Depending on the product you choose for satellite Internet, you might be able to use a single dish for both satellite Internet and satellite TV.

Tip

If you want both high-speed Internet access and satellite TV with a single dish, you can add DirecTV to the HughesNet dish at any time. The StarBand dish can work with both Dish Network (TV) and StarBand (Internet) services in the continental United States and Canada. However, if you decide to add HughesNet to an existing DirecTV setup, you will need to replace your existing DirecTV dish unless you installed the larger DirecDUO dish (which works with DirecTV and HughesNet).

HughesNet

HughesNet was originally called DirecPC, but Hughes Network Systems renamed it DirecWay in mid-2001, shortly after rolling out a two-way version of the service, then renamed it again to HughesNet in 2006. The original version of DirecPC was a one-way service that used satellite for downloading and a conventional dialup modem for uploads. Starting in 2002, this was replaced with a two-way satellite connection.

Currently, HughesNet Home is advertised at 700Kbps for downloads, although most people experience much higher speeds of 1,000Kbps–2,000Kbps. Uploads are more limited in speed, to about 60Kbps. This might be slower than cable modems or DSL, but satellite connections are often the only available broadband connection for people living away from urban areas. If you're willing to spend a little more, HughesNet also sells a Professional package that offers download speeds at 1Mbps.

HughesNet Requirements

The HughesNet service requires you to purchase and install a small satellite dish as part of the necessary hardware. It's similar to and slightly larger than the dishes used for satellite TV services, such as DirecTV and DishNetwork. In fact, you can combine DirecTV and HughesNet service on the same dish in many cases, although generally you are better off keeping them separate. HughesNet uses a 35"-wide HughesNet satellite dish to send and receive data. The dish is connected to a DW6000 satellite modem, which provides a shareable Ethernet connection to which you can plug an individual PC or a router to share the access on your network for Windows PC, Mac, and other systems. The

DW6000 is functionally identical to a cable modem as far as setup and operation is concerned. This means that no custom software is required on the PC end. Older modems connected via USB and required a PC for connection, but those have since been phased out.

Purchasing HughesNet Service

HughesNet can be purchased from HughesNet (www.HughesNet.com) as well as from partners such as EarthLink (www.earthlink.com).

You can either purchase the equipment up front (installation is included) and then pay a lower monthly fee or pay a higher monthly fee and avoid the greater upfront costs. Either way, you have to accept a minimum 15-month contract with penalties for early termination.

HughesNet's FAP—Brakes on High-speed Downloading?

A big concern for those wanting to exploit the high-speed download feature continues to be HughesNet's Fair Access Policy (FAP). FAP uses unpublished algorithms to determine who is "abusing" the service with large downloads. This has proven to be a controversial feature. For example, the current guidelines for residential customers state that you might experience the FAP if the cumulative requested downloads in a 1-hour to 4-hour time period exceeds 169MB. The restrictions are lifted within 8–12 hours of the original application of the FAP if the usage in that period stays below the FAP threshold. The limits are higher for those using the Professional service and for business customers. For a more detailed discussion of the real-world impact of FAP on both residential and business users and software you can use to track downloading, see the Fair Access Policy page at at http://www.copperhead.cc/fap.html.

Note

Because different satellites are used by the different HughesNet partners, it pays to research which HughesNet versions perform best. In addition to the HughesNet newsgroup, check out the HughesNet Uncensored! website at www.copperhead.cc as well as the forums on www.dslreports.com for speed tests and tweaks you can make to your system.

StarBand

In April 2000, StarBand—the first consumer-oriented two-way satellite network—was introduced after being tested as Gilat-At-Home. After some initial teething pains, StarBand has achieved success but is not as popular as HughesNet. Even so, the feature set of StarBand in its current two-way form is almost identical to HughesNet.

StarBand provides download speeds ranging from 500Kbps to 1,000Kbps and upload speeds ranging from 50Kbps to 100Kbps, depending on the satellite modem used. StarBand equipment pricing and monthly service fees are generally similar to HughesNet's two-way price structure, although some vendors might offer special promotional packages and bundles.

Tip

You can find excellent tips, tricks, utility software, and user-provided help at the StarBand Users website (www.starbandusers.com) as well as www.dslreports.com.

HughesNet and StarBand services work as shown in Figure 17.4.

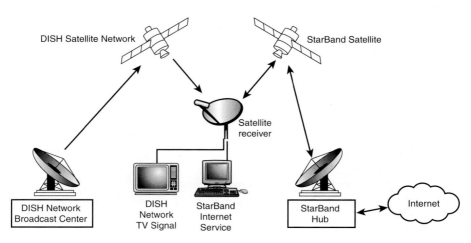

Figure 17.4 The HughesNet and StarBand services can receive both TV programs (left) and Internet traffic (right) with a single 24"×36" satellite dish.

Real-world Satellite Performance

Benchmark addicts will find that satellite Internet access performs poorly on ping tests because the complex pathway your data must travel (ground to space and back again) results in pings taking at least 400ms–600ms. Interactive benchmarks are also disappointing. The delays caused by communicating with a geosynchronous satellite over 22,500 miles in space make satellite a poor choice for these applications, although download speeds are significantly faster than dialup modems. Although they vary widely, speeds of 1,000Kbps are common, and some can reach download speeds of more than 2,000Kbps. To achieve results like this, use the tips available on the various forums and sites covering satellite connections to adjust your system's configuration.

Weather can be a problem for satellite connections, but not in the way you might think. Clouds and storms don't generally affect the signal, unless the storm is so severe you should probably be taking shelter anyway. What can be a problem, however, is snow and ice accumulation on the dish. If you live in an area where it snows, you can have signal problems even though the sky is clear; those problems are invariably caused by snow and ice accumulation on the dish. With that in mind, try to have the dish mounted in a location where you can periodically get to it to brush off any snow and ice accumulation.

Because of the higher latency, slower overall speeds, greater equipment costs, and sensitivity to snow and ice, few would recommend satellite service when alternatives are available. But when the only alternatives are dialup or having an expensive T1 line, satellite is certainly more attractive than the alternatives. Although the costs are higher than cable modem or DSL access, satellite might be the only even remotely cost-effective option for people outside urban areas. Many people have creatively adapted the dishes for use on a recreational vehicle (RV) when stationary or in various tripods and platforms for use while camping.

Integrated Services Digital Network

The connection speed of dialup modems is limited by Shannon's Law (see the section "56Kbps Modems," later in this chapter). To surpass the speed limitations of dialup modems, you need to use digital signals. Integrated Services Digital Network (ISDN) was the first step in the move to digital telecommunications. With ISDN, you can connect to the Internet at speeds of up to 128Kbps. Because

ISDN was developed by the telephone companies, you can purchase a variety of service plans. Depending on the ISDN service you choose, you can use it strictly for Internet service or use it to service multiple telephony applications such as voice, fax, and teleconferencing.

Depending on where you live, you might find that ISDN service is available for Internet uses, or your local telco might offer faster DSL service as an alternative. Because ISDN was not originally designed for Internet use, its speed is much lower than other broadband options. Also, ISDN costs about twice what a typical ADSL or cable modem connection costs per month.

ISDN doesn't require as high a line quality as DSL, so it can be offered in areas where DSL can't work without a major upgrade of the telephone system.

How Standard ISDN Works

Because ISDN carries three channels, it allows integrated services that can include combinations such as voice+data, data+data, voice+fax, fax+data, and so on (see Figure 17.5).

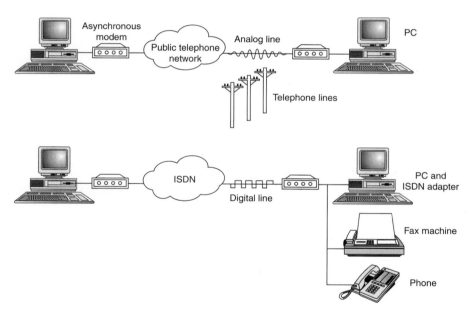

Figure 17.5 A dialup modem connection (top) connects only your PC to the Internet or other online services, whereas ISDN (bottom) can connect your computer, fax, and many other devices via a single ISDN terminal adapter.

On a standard ISDN connection, bandwidth is divided into bearer channels (B channels) that run at 64Kbps and a delta channel (D channel) that runs at either 16Kbps or 64Kbps, depending on the type of service. The B channels carry voice transmissions or user data, and the D channel carries control traffic. In other words, you talk, surf, or fax through the B-channel lines.

Two types of ISDN service exist: basic rate interface (BRI) and primary rate interface (PRI). The BRI service is intended for private and home users and consists of two B channels and one 16Kbps D channel, for a total of 144Kbps. The typical BRI service enables you to use one B channel to talk at 64Kbps and one B channel to run your computer for web surfing at 64Kbps. Hang up the phone, and both

B channels become available. If your ISDN service is configured appropriately, your web browsing becomes supercharged because you're now running at 128Kbps.

The PRI service is oriented more toward business use, such as for PBX connections to the telephone company's central office. In North America and Japan, the PRI service consists of 23 B channels and one 64Kbps D channel for a total of 1,536Kbps, running over a standard T-1 interface. In Europe, the PRI service is 30 B channels and one 64Kbps D channel, totaling 1,984Kbps, which corresponds to the E1 telecommunications standard. For businesses that require more bandwidth than one PRI connection provides, one D channel can be used to support multiple PRI channels using non-facility associated signaling (NFAS).

The BRI limit of two B channels might seem constraining to anyone other than a small office or home office user, but this is misleading. The BRI line can actually accommodate up to eight ISDN devices, each with a unique ISDN number. The D channel provides call routing and "on-hold" services, also called *multiple call signaling*, allowing all the devices to share the two B channels.

Note

When speaking of ISDN connections, 1 kilobyte equals 1,000 bytes, not 1,024 bytes as in standard computer applications.

As you saw earlier, this is also true of speed calculations for modems. Calculations that use 1,000 as a base are often referred to as *decimal* kilobytes, whereas the ones based on 1,024 are now called *kibibytes* or *binary* kilobytes.

If you need a more powerful, more flexible (and more expensive) version of ISDN, use the PRI version along with a switching device, such as a PBX or server. Although PRI allows only one device per B channel, it can dynamically allocate unused channels to support high-bandwidth uses, such as video-conferencing, when a switching device is in use along with PRI.

Acquiring ISDN Service

To have an ISDN connection installed, you must be within 18,000 wire feet (about 3.4 miles or 5.5km) of the CO (telco central office or central switch) for the BRI service; *wire feet* refers to the distance traveled by the telephone wires serving your location, not straight-line distance. For greater distances, expensive repeater devices are needed, and some telephone companies might not offer the service at all.

Prices for ISDN service vary widely depending on your location. In the United States, the initial installation fee can range from $35 to $150, depending on whether you are converting an existing line or installing a new one. The monthly charges typically range from $30 to $50, and sometimes you must pay a connect-time charge as well, ranging from 1 to 6 cents per minute or more, depending on the state. Keep in mind that you also must purchase an ISDN terminal adapter for your PC and possibly other hardware as well, and these charges are only for the telephone company's ISDN service. In addition, you must pay your ISP for access to the Internet at ISDN speeds. Typically, when all charges are included, you can pay up to $100 or more per month for ISDN service in a residential setting, and more for a small business connection. Residential plans are often dialup, requiring you to make a connection to the ISP's server every time you want to go online, whereas business plans are usually always-on, with immediate connection.

Note

Although ISDN Internet access provided by your local telephone company usually has a single price for the ISDN line and ISDN Internet access, most third-party ISDN ISPs provide pricing for only Internet access. These costs might appear to be much less expensive at startup and per month than what the telco's ISDN package costs, but this is misleading because the telco's charges for ISDN service aren't included. Add up the costs from both the ISP and the telephone company for a true picture of third-party ISDN Internet service pricing.

Because ISDN pricing plans offer many options depending on the channels you want and how you want to use them, be sure you carefully plan how you want to use ISDN. Check the telco's website for pricing and package information to get a jump on the decision-making process. Although ISDN is unique among broadband Internet services for its capability to handle both voice and data traffic, its relatively high cost and low speed make it a poor choice for most small-office and home-office users.

ISDN Hardware

To connect a PC to an ISDN connection, you must have a hardware component called a *terminal adapter (TA)*. The terminal adapter takes the form of an expansion board or an external device connected to a serial port, much like a modem. In fact, terminal adapters often are mistakenly referred to as ISDN modems. Actually, they are not modems at all because they do not perform analog/digital conversions.

Because an ISDN connection originally was designed to service telephony devices, most ISDN terminal adapters have connections for telephones, fax machines, and similar devices, as well as for your computer. Some terminal adapters can also be used as routers to enable multiple PCs to be networked to the ISDN connection.

Caution

To achieve the best possible performance, you should either purchase an external ISDN terminal adapter that connects to your computer's USB port or use an internal version. A terminal adapter with compression enabled easily can exceed a serial port's capability to reliably send and receive data. Consider that even a moderate 2:1 compression ratio exceeds the maximum rated speed of 232Kbps, which most high-speed COM ports support. USB 1.1 ports, on the other hand, can handle signals up to 12Mbps, easily supporting even the fastest ISDN connection. USB 2.0 ports available on the latest computers support speeds up to 480Mbps.

Comparing High-speed Internet Access

One way of making sense out of the confusing morass of plans available from cable modem, DSL, fixed wireless Internet, and satellite vendors is to calculate the average cost per Kbps of data downloaded ($/Kbps). You can calculate this figure yourself by dividing the service cost ($SC) per month by the rated or average speed of the service ($SPD):

$$\$SC\ /\ \$SPD = \$/Kbps$$

For example, a typical cable modem service costs $50 per month, including cable modem lease, and has an average (not peak) speed of 1,000Kbps. Divide $50 by 1000Kbps, and the cost per Kbps equals 5 cents.

Use this formula with any broadband or dialup service to find the best values. Don't forget to calculate the cost of required equipment (as in the example). If you must pay for equipment or installation upfront—as you will need to do with satellite, fixed wireless, and ISDN Internet plans—divide the upfront cost by the number of months you plan to keep the service and add the result to the monthly service charge to get an accurate figure.

How does a typical 56Kbps modem compare, assuming 50Kbps download speeds? Using Juno Web ($14.95 per month) and assuming no charge for a dialup modem, the cost per Kbps is 29.9 cents per

Kbps—almost three times as much for service that is at least 10 times slower than a typical cable modem.

Generally, the services stack up as shown in Table 17.4, from slowest to fastest when download speeds are compared.

Table 17.4 Comparing Typical Speeds for Various Types of Internet Connections

Connection Type	Speed (Kbps)	Connection Type	Speed (Kbps)
V.34 dialup	33.6/33.6	Basic DSL	384/128
V.90/92 dialup	53/33.6	Satellite (two-way)	500/60
ISDN (1BRI)	64/64	Premium DSL	3000/128
ISDN (2BRI)	128/128	Premium wireless	3000/256
Basic wireless	256/256	Cable modem	8000/384

The values in this table indicate various vendor maximum ratings; maximum values available in your area will depend on specific vendors and offerings. These figures do not indicate actual average speeds and do not take into account turn-around (ping) speeds or other issues such as network traffic.

Another way to compare Internet connection types is by feature, as in Table 17.5.

Table 17.5 Comparing High-speed Internet Access by Feature

Service	Always On?	Reliability Affected By?
Cable modem	Yes	Cable outages
DSL	Yes	Phone line outages
Fixed wireless	Yes	Transmitter outages; obstructions
Satellite (two-way)	Yes	Weather; satellite outages

Having a Backup Plan in Case of Service Interruptions

Because no high-speed connection is immune to service interruptions, you should consider having some type of backup plan in place in case of a significant service outage.

If your high-speed Internet access uses an ISP that can also accept dialup connections, you can use your regular modem for emergencies. However, this might require an extra charge in some cases. You could also consider using a free trial subscription to an ISP that uses a conventional modem. If you temporarily switch to a different ISP—especially one that uses its own client, such as AOL—be sure to back up your current Internet configuration information before you install the client software. Your best bet is to use an Internet-only ISP whose dialup connection can be added as a new connection without destroying your existing configuration.

If you don't want to spend $15–$25/month for an additional dialup service, or if you travel occasionally and want a low-cost way to work online when you're away from broadband, consider using a broadband vendor who also offers dialup connections such as EarthLink (www.earthlink.com) or SpeakEasy (www.speakeasy.net). Having both broadband and dialup access is essential for those who travel because broadband connections are not always available when on the road. Also, if your broadband connection goes down for some reason, you can usually check the broadband carrier or network status online using a dialup connection to access the company's web pages.

Note

Each type of Internet connection uses a particular combination of TCP/IP settings. TCP/IP is the protocol (software rules) used by all computers on the Internet. TCP/IP is covered in Chapter 18, "Local Area Networking," but for now keep in mind that different TCP/IP settings are required for modem access and access through a NIC or USB port device (cable modem, DSL, and HughesNet or StarBand). Modems usually have an IP address provided dynamically by the ISP when they connect with the ISP. The other types of Internet access devices might have static IP addresses that don't change or have dynamically assigned IP addresses. IP addresses are just one of the network settings that, if changed, prevent you from connecting to the Internet.

Leased Lines

For users with high bandwidth requirements (and deep pockets), dedicated leased lines provide digital service between two locations at speeds that can far exceed ISDN and are as fast or faster than DSL or cable modem. A *leased line* is a permanent 24-hour connection to a particular location that can be changed only by the telephone company. Businesses use leased lines to connect LANs in remote locations or to connect to the Internet through a service provider. Leased lines are available at various speeds, as described in the following sections.

T-1 and T-3 Connections

To connect networks in distant locations, networks that must support a large number of Internet users, or especially organizations that will be hosting their own Internet services, a T-1 connection might be a wise investment. A *T-1* is a digital connection running at about 1.5Mbps. This is more than 10 times faster than an ISDN link and is more than double the speed of most fast DSL connections. A T-1 can be split (or fractioned), depending on how it is to be used. It can be split into 24 individual 64Kbps lines or left as a single high-capacity pipeline. Some ISPs allow you to lease any portion of a T-1 connection that you want (in 64Kbps increments). SBC (formerly Ameritech), for example, offers a flexible T-1 service it calls DS1; it's available at full bandwidth or in various fractional sizes. Figure 17.6 shows how a T-1 line is fractioned.

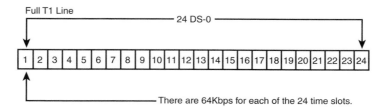

Figure 17.6   Full T-1 service uses all 24 lines (each one is 64Kbps) as a single pipeline; a fractional T-1 service of 256Kbps could use slots 1–4 only, for example.

An individual user of the Internet interacts with a T-1 line only indirectly. No matter how you're accessing the Internet (dialup modem, ISDN, DSL, cable modem, HughesNet, StarBand, or fixed-base wireless), your ISP typically will have a connection to one or more T-1 or T-3 lines, which connect to the backbone of the Internet. This connection to the backbone is sometimes referred to as a *point of presence (PoP)*. When you make your connection to the Internet, your ISP shares a small chunk of that T-1 pipe with you. Depending on how many other users are accessing the Internet at your ISP or elsewhere, you might experience very fast to slow throughput, even if your modem connection speed remains constant. It's a bit like splitting up a pizza into smaller and smaller slices to accommodate more people at a party: The more users of a high-speed connection, the slower each individual part of it will be. To keep user connections fast while growing, ISPs add full or fractional T-1 lines to their points of presence. Or, they might switch from a T-1 connection to the even faster T-3 if available.

Note

Equivalent in throughput to approximately 28 T-1 lines, a T-3 connection runs at 45Mbps and is suitable for use by very large networks and university campuses. Pricing information falls into the "if-you-have-to-ask-you-can't-afford-it" category.

If your Internet connection is on a corporate LAN or your office is located in a downtown building, your relationship to a T-1 line might be much closer. If your building or office is connected directly to a T-1, you're sharing the capacity of that line with just a relatively few other users rather than with the hundreds or thousands of dialup users a normal ISP is hosting at one time. Full or fractional T-1 lines are being added to more and more apartments and office buildings in major cities to allow residents and workers faster Internet access. In these cases, a LAN connection to the T-1 is usually provided, so your Internet access device is a network card, rather than a modem or ISDN terminal adapter.

With the rise of the Internet and the demand for high-speed data access for networks, the price of T-1 links in the United States has fallen drastically since the late 1990s, although you will still pay in the hundreds of dollars for typical service offerings. T-1 service can be acquired from either your local telco or third-party firms. Fractional T-1 or burstable T-1 (which allows you to have differing levels of bandwidth up to the entire T-1 1.5Mbps depending on demand) costs less than full T-1 service. For a large organization that requires a lot of bandwidth, the lower cost of T-1 services today make installing a higher-capacity service and growing into it—rather than constantly upgrading the link—more economical than ever. Although the speed of T-1 links resembles the maximum rates available with DSL or cable modem service, most types of T-1 service provide constant bandwidth (unlike cable modems) and bypass the potentially severe problems of trying to retrofit old phone lines with digital service (unlike DSL).

Comparing Conventional High-speed Services

Some telcos who formerly posted pricing for ISDN, T-1, or other high-end telecommunications services now have a "call us" button on their websites because pricing is complicated by many factors, including

■ Location (state and locality because telephone companies are regulated public utilities)

■ Fixed and variable costs

■ Usage

■ Installation costs

■ Your needs

Be sure to consider hardware and usage costs when you price services, and (for items such as ISDN terminal adapters and network cards) compare the official offerings with products available elsewhere. If you decide to provide some of the equipment yourself, find out whose responsibility repairs become. Some companies provide lower-cost "value" pricing for services in which you agree to configure the hardware yourself and maintain it. If you have knowledgeable staffers who can handle routers and other network configuration, you can save money every month, but if not, go with the full-service option.

Securing Your Internet Connection

Because any Internet connection must use TCP/IP, which uses built-in logical ports numbered 0–65,535 to service different types of activity, any user of the Internet can be vulnerable to various types of Internet attacks, even if precautions such as turning off drive and folder sharing have been followed. Such vulnerabilities increase drastically with always-on broadband services such as DSL and cable modems.

Steve Gibson of Gibson Research Corporation (makers of the classic SpinRite disk maintenance program) has established a free web-based service called Shields Up that you can use on an Internet-connected PC to see how safe or vulnerable it is. The Shields Up portion of the Gibson Research Corporation website (www.grc.com) probes your system's Internet connection security and Internet service ports and reports any potential problems.

Chapter 18 discusses how using a router to share your Internet connection can also help protect your system against intruders.

Note

Proxy servers and firewalls are subjects that go far beyond the scope of this book. If you want to learn more, I suggest you pick up a copy of *Upgrading and Repairing Networks*, also published by Que.

Que's *Absolute Beginner's Guide to Security, Spam, and Spyware*, by Andy Walker, is another excellent resource for users who want to install a personal firewall or otherwise protect their systems from the darker denizens of the Internet.

Asynchronous (Dialup) Modems

If you want to connect to the Internet without spending a lot of money, a dialup modem can serve as your on-ramp to the rest of the computing world. Modems are standard equipment with most recent systems and continue to be popular upgrades for systems that do not have access to broadband solutions, such as two-way cable modem or DSL lines. Even with some types of broadband access (such as one-way HughesNet and one-way cable modem), modems are still needed to send page requests and email.

The word *modem* (from modulator/demodulator) basically describes a device that converts the digital data used by computers into analog signals suitable for transmission over a telephone line and converts the analog signals back to digital data at the destination. To distinguish modems that convert analog and digital signals from other types of access devices, modems are frequently referred to as *analog modems*; because you must dial a telephone number to reach a remote computer, they are also referred to as *dialup modems*. The typical PC modem is an asynchronous device, meaning it transmits data in an intermittent stream of small packets. The receiving system takes the data in the packets and reassembles it into a form the computer can use.

Note

Because it has become such a familiar term, even to inexperienced computer users, the word *modem* is sometimes used to describe devices that are, strictly speaking, not modems at all. For example, earlier in this chapter you read about broadband solutions such as ISDN, cable modems, HughesNet, DSL, and StarBand. Although all these services use devices commonly called "modems" to connect your PC to fast online services, not all of them convert digital information to analog signals. However, because these devices look similar to a standard modem and are used to connect PCs to the Internet or to other networks, they are called modems.

Asynchronous modems transmit each byte of data individually as a separate packet. One byte equals 8 bits, which, using the standard ASCII codes, is enough data to transmit a single alphanumeric character. For a modem to transmit asynchronously, it must identify the beginning and end of each byte to the receiving modem. It does this by adding a start bit before and a stop bit after every byte of data, thus using 10 bits to transmit each byte (see Figure 17.7). For this reason, asynchronous communications have sometimes been referred to as *start-stop* communications. This is in contrast to synchronous communications, in which a continuous stream of data is transmitted at a steady rate.

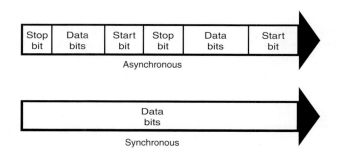

Figure 17.7   Asynchronous modems frame each byte of data with a start bit and a stop bit, whereas synchronous communications use an uninterrupted stream of data.

Synchronous modems generally are used in leased-line environments and in conjunction with multiplexers to communicate between terminals to Unix- or Linux-based servers and mainframe computers. Therefore, this type of modem is outside the scope of this book.

Whenever modems are referred to in this book, I will be discussing the asynchronous, analog variety. (Synchronous modems are not found in typical computer stores and aren't included in normal computer configurations, so you might not ever see one unless you go into the data center of a corporation that uses them.)

Note

During high-speed modem communications, the start and stop bits are usually not transmitted over the telephone line. Instead, the modem's data compression algorithm eliminates them. However, these bits are part of the data packets generated by the communications software in the computer, and they exist until they reach the modem hardware. If both ends of a dialup modem connection don't use the same value for start and stop bits, the connection transmits gibberish instead of usable data.

The use of a single start bit is required in all forms of asynchronous communication, but some protocols use more than one stop bit. To accommodate systems with different protocols, communications software products usually enable you to modify the format of the frame used to transmit each byte. The standard format used to describe an asynchronous communications format is parity/data bits/stop bits. Almost all asynchronous connections today are therefore abbreviated as N-8-1 (No parity/8 data bits/1 stop bit). The meanings for each of these parameters and their possible variations are as follows:

- **Parity**—Before error-correction protocols became standard modem features, a simple parity mechanism was used to provide basic error checking at the software level. Today, this is almost never used, and the value for this parameter is nearly always set to none. Other possible parity values you might see in a communications software package are odd, even, mark, and space.

As with modulation, both modems must adhere to the same standard for error correction to work. Fortunately, most modem manufacturers use the same error-correction protocols.

V.42, MNP10, and MNP10EC Error-correction Protocols

The current error-correction protocols supported by modems include Microcom's proprietary MNP10 (developed to provide a better way to cope with changing line conditions) and MNP10EC (an enhanced version developed to enable modems to use constantly changing cellular telephone connections).

V.90 and V.92 modems (as well as some older models) also support the ITU V.42 error-correction protocol, with fallback to the MNP 4 protocol (which also includes data-compression). Because the V.42 standard includes MNP compatibility through Class 4, all MNP 4–compatible modems can establish error-controlled connections with V.42 modems.

This standard uses a protocol called Link Access Procedure for Modems (LAPM). LAPM, similar to MNP, copes with phone-line impairments by automatically retransmitting data corrupted during transmission, ensuring that only error-free data passes between the modems. V.42 is considered to be better than MNP 4 because it offers approximately a 20% higher transfer rate due to its more intelligent algorithms.

Note

For information about the MNP 1–4 protocols, see Chapter 18 of *Upgrading and Repairing PCs, 11th Edition.*

Data-compression Standards

Data compression refers to a built-in capability in some modems to compress the data they're sending, thus saving time and money for modem users. Depending on the type of files the modem is sending, data can be compressed to nearly one-fourth its original size, effectively quadrupling the speed of the modem—at least in theory. This assumes that the modem has V.42bis data compression built in (true since about 1990) *and* that the data hasn't already been compressed by software. Thus, in reality, the higher throughput caused by data compression applies only to HTML and plain-text files on the Web. Graphics and Zip or EXE archives have already been compressed, as have most PDF (Adobe Acrobat Reader) files. Another factor that influences the throughput of a modem is the type of UART chip used by the serial port included in an internal modem or connected to an external modem, or the use of a USB port instead of a serial port.

Note

To learn more, see "Can Non-56Kbps Modems Achieve Throughput Speeds Above 115,200bps?" in the Technical Reference section of the disc packaged with this book.

As with error correction, data compression can also be performed with software. Data can be compressed only once, so if you are transmitting files that are already in a compressed form, such as Zip archives, GIF or JPEG images, or Adobe Acrobat PDF files, there will be no palpable increase in speed from the modem's hardware compression. The transmission of plain-text files (such as HTML pages) and uncompressed bitmaps, however, is accelerated greatly by modem compression.

MNP5 and V.42bis

Current data-compression standards in modems include Microcom's MNP 5 and the ITU V.42bis protocols. V.42bis is a CCITT data-compression standard similar to MNP Class 5, but it provides about

35% better compression. V.42bis is not actually compatible with MNP Class 5, but nearly all V.42bis modems include the MNP 5 data-compression capability as well.

V.42bis is superior to MNP 5 because it analyzes the data first and then determines whether compression would be useful. V.42bis compresses only data that needs compression. MNP 5, on the other hand, always attempts to compress the data, which slows down throughput on previously compressed files.

To negotiate a standard connection using V.42bis, V.42 also must be present. Therefore, a modem with V.42bis data compression is assumed to include V.42 error correction. When combined, these two protocols result in an error-free connection that has the maximum data compression possible.

V.44

At the same time that the V.92 protocol was introduced by the ITU in mid-2000, a companion data-compression protocol called V.44 was also introduced by the ITU. V.44 uses a lossless LZJH compression protocol designed by Hughes Network Systems (developers of the HughesNet satellite broadband Internet service) to achieve performance more than 25% better than that of V.42. Data throughput with V.44 can reach rates of as much as 300Kbps, compared to 150Kbps–200Kbps with V.42bis. V.42bis was developed in the late 1980s, long before the advent of the World Wide Web, so it is not optimized for web surfing the way V.44 is. V.44 is especially designed to optimize compression of HTML text pages.

Note

V.44 is the latest compression algorithm to be based in part on the work of mathematicians Abraham Lempel and Jakob Ziv in the late 1970s. Lempel and Ziv's work also has been used in the development of LZW (Lempel-Ziv-Welch) compression for TIFF image files, GIF compressed image files, PKZIP-compatible compression, and other data compression methods.

Proprietary Standards

In addition to the industry-standard protocols for modulation, error correction, and data compression that are generally defined and approved by the ITU-T, several protocols in these areas were invented by various companies and included in their products without any official endorsement by any standards body. Some of these protocols have been quite popular at times and became pseudo-standards of their own. The only proprietary standards that continue to enjoy widespread support are the Microcom MNP standards for error correction and data compression. Others, such as 3Com's HST, CompuCom's DIS, and Hayes' V-series, are no longer popular.

56Kbps Modems

At one time, the V.34 annex speed of 33,600bps (33.6Kbps) was regarded as the absolute speed limit for asynchronous modem usage. However, starting in 1996, modem manufacturers began to produce modems that supported speeds of up to 56,000bps. These so-called "56K" or "56Kbps" modems are now universal, although the methods for breaking the 33.6Kbps barrier have changed several times. To understand how this additional speed was achieved, you must consider the basic principle of modem technology—that is, the digital-to-analog conversion.

As you've learned, a traditional modem converts data from digital to analog form so it can travel over the Public Switched Telephone Network (PSTN). At the destination system, another modem converts the analog data back to its digital form. This conversion from digital to analog and back causes some speed loss. Even though the phone line is physically capable of carrying data at 56Kbps or more, the effective maximum speed because of the conversions is about 33.6Kbps. An AT&T engineer named

Claude Shannon came up with a law (Shannon's Law) stating that the maximum possible error-free data communications rate over an all-analog PSTN is approximately 35Kbps, depending on the noise present.

However, because many parts of the United States' urban telephone system is digital—being converted to analog only when signals reach the telephone company's central office (or central switch)—it's possible to "break" Shannon's Law and achieve faster download rates. You can, in some cases, omit the initial digital-to-analog conversion and send a purely digital signal over the PSTN to the recipient's CO (see Figure 17.9). Thus, only one digital-to-analog conversion is necessary, instead of two or more. The result is that you theoretically can increase the speed of the data transmission, in one direction only, beyond the 35Kbps specified by Shannon's Law—to nearly the 56Kbps speed supported by the telephone network. Prior to the new ITU V.92 standard, the transmission in the other direction was still limited to the V.34 annex maximum of 33.6Kbps. However, both the modem and the ISP must have support for the ITU V.92 standard to overcome this limitation for uploading speeds.

▶▶ See "ITU V.92 and V.44—Breaking the Upload Barrier," p. 1137, for more information on how the V.92 standard enables faster uploading.

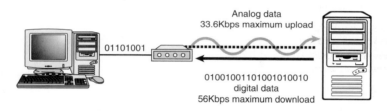

Figure 17.9 V.90-based 56Kbps connections enable you to send data at standard analog modem rates (33.6Kbps maximum) but enable you to receive data nearly twice as fast, depending on line conditions.

56Kbps Limitations

Although 56Kbps modems can increase data transfer speeds beyond the limits of V.34 modems, they are subject to certain limitations. Unlike with standard modem technologies, you can't buy two 56Kbps modems, install them on two computers, and achieve 56Kbps speeds. One side of the connection must use a special digital modem that connects directly to the PSTN without a digital-to-analog conversion.

Therefore, 56Kbps modems can be used at maximum speeds only to connect to ISPs or other hosting services that have invested in the necessary infrastructure to support the connection. Because the ISP has the digital connection to the PSTN, its downstream transmissions to your computer are accelerated. If both sides of the connection support standards predating V.92, your communications back to the ISP are not accelerated.

On a practical level, this means you can surf the Web and download files more quickly, but if you host a web server on your PC, your users will realize no speed gain because the upstream traffic is not accelerated unless you and your ISP both use V.92-compliant modems. If you connect to another regular modem, your connection is made at standard V.34 annex rates (33.6Kbps or less).

Also, only one digital-to-analog conversion can be in the downstream connection from the ISP to your computer. This is dictated by the nature of the physical connection to your local telephone carrier. If additional conversions are involved in your connection, 56Kbps technology will not work for you; 33.6Kbps will be your maximum possible speed.

Note

Although most advertising for 56Kbps modems refers to them as simply "56K" modems, this is inaccurate. "K" is most often used in the computer business to refer to kilobytes. If that were true, a "real" 56K modem would be downloading at 56,000 bytes per second (or 448,000 bits per second)!

With the way the telephone system has had to grow to accommodate new exchanges and devices, even neighbors down the street from each other might have different results when using a 56Kbps modem.

Caution

56Kbps modem communications are highly susceptible to slowdowns caused by line noise. Your telephone line might be perfectly adequate for voice communications and even lower-speed modem communications, but inaudible noise easily can degrade a 56Kbps connection to the point at which there is only a marginal increase over a 33.6Kbps modem, or even no increase at all. If you do have a problem with line noise, getting a surge suppressor with noise filtration might help.

Hotel connections through telephones with data jacks typically provide very slow connections with any type of modem. Even if you have a V.90- or V.92-compliant 56Kbps modem, you will be lucky to achieve even a 24Kbps transmission rate. The analog-to-digital conversions that occur between your room's telephone and the hotel's digital PBX system eliminate the possibility of using any of the 56Kbps standards the modem supports because they depend on a direct digital connection to the central switch (CS).

As an alternative, more and more hotels and motels provide Ethernet-based access to broadband Internet service; a growing number even provide wireless Ethernet access with Wi-Fi/IEEE-802.11b hardware. Depending on the location, you might be able to use your normal Ethernet card or connect to a USB adapter provided by the hotel. If you want high-speed Internet access as part of the package with your next hotel or motel stay, contact the specific lodging location or chain website for details and pricing.

Early 56Kbps Standards

To achieve a high-speed connection, both modems and your ISP (or other hosting service to which you connect) must support the same 56Kbps technology. The first 56Kbps chipsets were introduced in late 1996:

- U.S. Robotics' x2 used Texas Instruments (TI) chipsets.
- Rockwell's K56flex was supported by Zoom and other modem makers.

These rival methods for achieving performance up to 56Kbps were incompatible with each other and were replaced in 1998 by the ITU's V.90 standard.

Note

For more information about K56flex and x2, see *Upgrading and Repairing PCs, 11th Edition*.

Unfortunately, the 56Kbps name is rather misleading, in regards to actual transmission speeds. Although all 56Kbps modems theoretically are capable of this performance on top-quality telephone lines, the power requirements for telephone lines specified in the FCC's Part 68 regulation limit the top speed of these modems to 53Kbps. The FCC has been considering lifting this speed limitation since the fall of 1998, but it remains in place to date.

V.90

V.90 was introduced on February 5, 1998, and was ratified by the ITU-T on September 15, 1998. Its ratification ended the K56flex/x2 standards "war": Shortly thereafter, most modem manufacturers announced upgrade options for users of x2 and K56flex modems to enable these products to become V.90 compliant.

Some modem vendors offer upgrades for K56flex and x2 modems to the V.90 standard. If you purchased your modem before the V.90 standard became official, see your modem vendor's website for information about upgrading to V.90.

ITU V.92 and V.44—Breaking the Upload Barrier

56Kbps protocols, such as the early proprietary x2 and K56flex and the ITU V.90 standard, increased the download speed from its previous maximum of 33.6Kbps to 56Kbps. However, upload speeds, which affect how quickly you can send email, page requests, and file transfers, were not affected by the development of 56Kbps technologies. Upload speeds with any of these 56Kbps technologies are limited to a maximum of 33.6Kbps. This causes severe speed lags for both pure dialup users and those who depend on dialup modems for upstream traffic, such as users of one-way broadband solutions— for example, one-way (Telco Return) cable modems, one-way HughesNet, and one-way (Telco Return) fixed-base wireless Internet services. Other shortcomings of existing 56Kbps technology include the amount of time it takes the user's modem to negotiate its connection with the remote modem and the lack of uniform support for call-waiting features.

In mid-2000, the ITU unveiled a multifaceted solution to the problem of slow connections and uploads: the V.92 and V.44 protocols (V.92 was previously referred to as V.90 Plus).

V.92, as the name implies, is a successor to the V.90 protocol, and any modem that supports V.92 also supports V.90. V.92 doesn't increase the download speed beyond the 56Kbps barrier, but offers these major features:

- **QuickConnect**— QuickConnect cuts the amount of time needed to make a connection by storing telephone line characteristics and using the stored information whenever the same phone line is used again. For users who connect to the Internet more than once from the same location, the amount of time the modem beeps and buzzes to make the connection will drop from as much as 27 seconds to about half that time. Bear in mind, though, that this reduction in connection time does not come about until after the initial connection at that location is made and its characteristics are stored for future use.

- **Modem-on-Hold**—The Modem-on-Hold feature allows the user to pick up incoming calls and talk for a longer amount of time than the few seconds allowed by current proprietary call-waiting modems. Modem-on-Hold enables the ISP to control how long you can take a voice call while online without interrupting the modem connection; the minimum amount of time supported is 10 seconds, but longer amounts of time (up to unlimited!) are also supported by this feature. Modem-on-Hold also allows you to make an outgoing call without hanging up the modem connection. Modem-on-Hold, similar to previous proprietary solutions, requires that you have the call-waiting feature enabled on your telephone line and also requires that your ISP support this feature of V.92.

Note

Although Modem-on-Hold is good for the Internet user with only one phone line (because it allows a single line to handle incoming as well as outgoing calls), it's not as good for ISPs because when you place your Internet connection on hold, the ISP's modem is not capable of taking other calls. ISPs that support Modem-on-Hold might need to add more modems to maintain their quality of service if this feature is enabled. More modems are necessary because the ISP won't be able to count on users dropping their Internet connections to make or receive voice calls when Modem-on-Hold is available.

■ **PCM Upstream**—PCM Upstream breaks the 33.6Kbps upload barrier, boosting upload speed to a maximum of 48Kbps. Unfortunately, because of power issues, enabling PCM Upstream can reduce your downstream (download) speed by 1.3Kbps–2.7Kbps or more. PCM Upstream is an optional feature of V.92, and ISPs who support V.92 connections might not support this feature.

Modems that support V.92 typically also support the V.44 data-compression standard. V.44, which replaces V.42bis, provides for compression of data at rates up to 6:1—that's more than 25% better than V.42bis. This enables V.92/V.44 modems to download pages significantly faster than V.90/V.42bis modems can at the same connection speed.

When will you be able to enjoy the benefits of V.92/V.44? Although most major modem vendors have been offering V.92/V.44-compliant modems since late 2000, ISP interest in this standard has been tepid. Only one national ISP, Navipath (which provided support for many local and regional ISPs), offered V.92 access in 2001, and Navipath went out of business in September 2001. Prodigy began to offer V.92 service early in 2002.

According to the V.92 News & Updates page at Richard Gamberg's Modemsite (http://www.modemsite.com/56k/v92.asp), many vendors of ISP equipment continue to drag their feet on V.92/V.44 support, in part because it often requires expensive upgrades to terminal equipment. Even after upgrading to support V.92/V.44, some existing terminal hardware is incapable of working with the desirable PCM Upstream feature. Additionally, many major modem vendors have produced so-called "V.92" modems that don't support major V.92 features. Check user reviews available at the Modemsite website and others before you buy a particular V.92 modem model.

Tip

Wondering whether it's time to get a V.92/V.44 modem? Before you update your current model or buy a new modem, do the following:

■ Contact your ISP to see whether (or when) it plans to support V.92/V.44 and to determine which features will be supported.

■ Check the V.92 ISPs listing at (www.v92.com) and contact ISPs in your area for more details.

Although the change from x2/K56flex to V.90 was a no-cost one for many modem owners, the upgrade from V.90 to V.92/V.44 isn't as painless. In many cases, only the most recent V.90 modems will be eligible for a free upgrade to V.92/V.44 firmware. Contact your modem vendor for details.

Can your existing V.90-compatible modem be upgraded to V.92/V.44? As with earlier 56Kbps modem standards, the answer will likely be, "It depends." Some Lucent LT Winmodem (Agere Systems) modem drivers for V.90 also might include V.92 commands; see Modemsite's Lucent modem section for the latest information (http://www.modemsite.com/56k/ltwin.asp). For modems based on other chipsets, check with your modem vendor.

As with earlier 56Kbps standards, you shouldn't worry about V.92/V.44 support until your ISP announces that it is supporting these standards. Because the V.92 standard has several components, find out which features of V.92 your ISP is planning to support before you look into a modem firmware update or modem replacement.

Fax Modem Standards

Even though the first experimental facsimile equipment was developed at the end of World War II, it took many years for faxing to become commonplace. Similarly, the first fax boards for computers were not introduced until the late 1980s as separate devices. Later, fax capabilities were incorporated into modems. Today, virtually all modems also meet the ITU-T Class 3 fax standards, enabling them to send data to and receive data from other ITU-T Class 3 fax machines and multifunction devices.

If you have a scanner and a fax-modem, Windows XP and Vista (Business, Ultimate, and Enterprise editions only) provide built-in scanning and faxing capabilities also.Many recent multifunction devices also support the newer ITU-T.30E recommendation for color faxing. Fax modems don't meet this standard as shipped from the manufacturer, but you can download free color fax software developed by HP (Impact ColorFax) that works with most fax modems. Find Impact ColorFax at the BlackICE Software website (www.blackice.com).

For more information about ITU-T fax protocols, see "ITU-T Fax Protocols" in the Technical Reference on the disc packaged with this book.

Dialup Modem Recommendations

A dialup modem for a PC can take the form either of an external device with its own power supply that plugs into a PC's serial port or USB port or of an internal expansion card you insert into a PCI or PC Card bus slot inside the computer. Very few ISA-slot dialup modems are still on the market because the majority of recent systems no longer have ISA slots.

External versions of dialup modems are slightly more expensive because they include a separate case and power supply and sometimes require you to buy a serial modem cable or USB cable. The decision as to which type to use should typically depends on whether you have a free bus slot or serial port, whether you have USB ports and Windows 98 or later, how much room you have on your desk, the capabilities of your system's internal power supply, and how comfortable you are with opening up your computer.

I often prefer external modems because of the visual feedback they provide through their LED indicator lights. These lights let you easily see whether the modem is still connected and transmitting or receiving data. However, Windows and many communication programs today include onscreen indicators that provide some of the same information.

In many situations, however, an internal modem is preferable. If you are using an older computer whose serial ports do not have buffered UART chips, such as the 16550, some more advanced controller-based internal modems include an onboard 16550 UART-equivalent controller chip. This onboard UART with the modem saves you the trouble of upgrading the UART serial port. However, controller-less (or "Windows") modems do not include such chips and rely on the processor for their power and speed, which can degrade the performance of other applications while online. External 56Kbps modems can be hampered from achieving their full speeds by the limitations of the computer's serial port. An external USB model or an internal model using the PCI slot might be preferable instead. Use Table 17.6 to see how internal and external units compare.

Table 17.6   External Versus Internal Modems

Features	External	Internal
Price	Higher	Lower
Extras required	Serial or USB cable	Nothing
Migration between systems	Easy	Difficult (must open case)
Power supply	External AC adapter brick	None—powered by host bus
Status monitoring	External signal LEDs	Tray icon or none
Interface	Serial or USB	PCI or ISA

Although late versions of Windows 95 OSR 2.x have USB support, many USB devices actually require Windows 98 or better. Use Windows 98/Me/2000/XP to achieve more reliable support for USB devices.

◄◄ See "The UART Chip," p. 1050.

Not all modems that function at the same speed have the same functionality. Many modem manufacturers produce modems running at the same speed but with different feature sets at different price points. The more expensive modems usually support advanced features, such as distinctive ring support, caller ID, voice and data, video teleconferencing, and call-waiting support. When purchasing a modem, be sure it supports all the features you need. You also should make sure the software you plan to use, including the operating system, has been certified for use with the modem you select.

If you live in a rural area, or in an older city neighborhood, your telephone line quality might influence your decision. Look at comparison test results carefully and pay particular attention to how well various modems perform with noisy lines. If your phone line sounds crackly during a rainstorm, that poor-quality line makes reliable modem communications difficult, too, and it can limit your ability to connect at speeds above 33.6Kbps.

Another feature to consider is the modem's resistance to electrical damage. Some brands feature built-in power protection to shield against damage from digital telephone lines (higher powered and not compatible with modems) or power surges. However, every modem should be used with a surge protector that allows you to route the RJ-11 telephone cable through the unit for protection against high-voltage surges.

All modems on the market today support V.90 or V.92, and even if your particular location can't support those speeds, your modem might still offer advanced features, such as voicemail or simultaneous voice and data. Keep in mind that V.90/V.92 connections seem to work better for many users if their modems also support x2. If you prefer a modem made by a vendor that also supports K56flex, try to buy a modem that contains both types of standards in its firmware (referred to by some vendors as "Dualmode" modems).

Modems Without a UART (WinModems)

Modems without a UART chip, sometimes referred to as *WinModems* after the pioneering U.S. Robotics version, can save you money at purchase time but can cause problems with speed and operating-system compatibility later.

For users wanting an inexpensive internal modem, a modem that doesn't use a traditional UART instead of a UART-equipped internal or external modem looks like a great deal, often costing less than $40, compared to $80 or more for a UART-equipped "hardware" modem. But, there is no free lunch for modem users. What can you lose with a modem that lacks a UART?

First, you need to realize that there are actually two types of UART-less modems: those that rely on Windows and the CPU for all operations (these modems are also called *controllerless* modems) and those that use a programmable digital signal processor (DSP) chip to replace the UART. Both types of modems use less power than traditional UART-based modems, making them better for use with notebook computers. Although both are "software modems," there's an enormous difference in what you're getting.

A Windows-based modem must run under Windows because Windows provides the brains of the modem, a cost-cutting move similar to that used by some low-cost host-based printers. You should avoid this if you're planning to try Linux, move the modem to a Macintosh, or use an old MS-DOS-based communications program. If you have no drivers for your modem/operating system combination, you'll have no luck using the software modem.

Software modems that lack a DSP have a second major strike against them: They make your CPU do all the work. Although today's computers have much faster CPUs than those required for typical software modems (Pentium 133 minimum), your modem can still slow down your computer if you multitask while downloading or surfing the Web.

Most of the modems bundled with computer systems are software modems, and the major chipsets used include Lucent LT (then Agere Systems, now LSI), Conexant (formerly Rockwell) HCF, U.S. Robotics WinModem, ESS Technology's HSP-compliant chipsets, Intel's Modem Silicon Operation (formerly Ambient), and PCTel.

Except for U.S. Robotics, the other companies produce chipsets that can be found in the modems made by many manufacturers.

For best results, do the following:

- Make sure your modem uses a DSP. Typically, these modems don't require a particular CPU or a particular speed of CPU.

- Consider modems built around the Lucent/Agere LT chipset. These modems have a DSP, and Lucent/Agere's firmware is frequently revised to achieve the best results in a rapidly changing telephony environment.

- Use the modem manufacturer's own drivers first. However, software modems can often use any manufacturer's drivers for the same chipset with excellent results; in particular, Lucent/Agere LT chipset modems typically can use any Lucent/Agere LT driver from any modem manufacturer.

- Don't delete the old software driver when you download and install new modem software. As with UART-equipped modems, the latest firmware isn't always the best.

- Look carefully at the CPU, RAM, and operating system requirements before you buy your modem.

Tip

Many manufacturers sell both traditional and UART-free modems. If you have an older system or want the option to use MS-DOS-based or Linux-based communications programs, the hardware modem with a traditional UART might cost more but be a better choice.

Finding Support for "Brand-X" Modems

Many computer users today didn't install their modems, or even purchase them as a separate unit. Their modems came bundled inside the computer and often have a bare-bones manual that makes no mention of the modem's origin or where to get help. Getting V.90 firmware updates, drivers, or even jumper settings for OEM modems such as this can be difficult.

One of the best websites for getting help when you don't know where to start is the "Who Made My Modem?" page (www.56K.com), which features the following:

- Links to the FCC's equipment authorization database (enter the FCC ID to locate the vendor)
- ATI commands used to query the modem chipset
- Lookup by chipset manufacturer
- Search engine tips
- Links to major modem and chipset manufacturers

Squeezing Performance from Your 56Kbps Modem

Although many users of 56Kbps modems have seen significant improvements in their connect speeds and throughputs over their previous V.34-type modems, many have not or have seen only sporadic improvements. According to the research of Richard Gamberg, available online at his Modemsite website (www.modemsite.com), a combination of five factors comes into play to affect your ability to get reliable connections in the range of 45Kbps–53Kbps (the current FCC maximum):

- The modem
- The modem firmware/driver
- Your line conditions
- The ISP's modems
- The ISP's modem firmware

It's up to you to ensure that you match your modem's 56Kbps type to the 56Kbps standards your ISP supports, and that you use the best (not always the latest!) modem firmware and drivers, as discussed in the previous section.

Other modem adjustments recommended by Modemsite include

- Modifying existing modem `.INF` files used by Windows 9x to accurately reflect connection speed
- Disabling 56Kbps connections (!) when playing games to minimize lag times

Note

This last suggestion might seem odd, but "fast" modems are designed to push a large amount of data through for downloads, and gameplay over modems actually deals with small amounts of data instead. The lag time caused by 56Kbps data handling can make a regular "fast" modem seem slow.

The site also hosts a forum area for discussing modem configuration, reliability, and performance issues.

Telco "Upgrades" and Your Modem

In addition to the well-known analog-to-digital conversion issue that prevents some phone lines from handling 56Kbps modems at anything beyond 33.6Kbps, other local telephone company (telco) practices and services can either prevent 56Kbps from ever working or take it away from you after you've enjoyed it for a while.

If you were getting 45Kbps or faster connections with your 56Kbps modem but can no longer get past 33.6Kbps, what happened? Some local telephone companies have been performing network "upgrades" that improve capacity for voice calls but prevent 56Kbps modems from running faster than 28Kbps. The cause seems to be the telephone companies' change from a signaling type called RBS (Robbed Bit Signaling) to SS7 (Signaling System 7), which changes how data used by the modem for high-speed access is detected. Caller ID devices connected to your phone line use RBS or SS7 signals to obtain information from incoming phone calls. If you use a caller ID box on the same phone circuit as your modem (even if it's connected in another room), you might not be able to get fast connections, or you might experience frequent disconnects. If you notice a drop in connection speed or reliability after you install caller ID, disconnect the caller ID box from the wall jack while you're online and see whether the speed and reliability of your modem connections improve.

What else can you do? You can install the latest firmware available for your modem model or chipset. You can also check with your local telephone company to see whether it can update its firmware to solve the problem. Even if your modem has different firmware, checking on an upgrade might still be useful because this problem is likely to become widespread as telephone numbers, exchanges, and area codes continue to multiply like weeds and telephone network upgrades must keep pace.

Sharing Your Internet Connection

Whether you have a 56Kbps dialup modem or a broadband connection, one connection is often not enough for a home or small-office setting. You can share your connection with other computer users with one of the following methods:

- **Computer-based sharing solutions**—These work by connecting the computer with Internet access to a network with the other computers with which you want to share the connection. The computer with the connection acts as a gateway to the Internet.

- **Router-based sharing solutions**—These work by connecting all the computers on a network with a router or gateway connected to the Internet. Most routers are designed to work with broadband devices that use a USB or 10BASE-T connection, but a few work with dialup modems.

Typical computer-based sharing solutions include

- Microsoft Internet Connection Sharing (ICS), introduced in Windows 98 Second Edition (Win98SE) and also a part of Windows Me, Windows 2000, XP, and Windows Vista

- Third-party gateway or proxy-server programs such as Wingate, Winproxy, and others

Both ICS and third-party programs can also work with non-Windows computers because the TCP/IP network protocol, the standard protocol of the Internet, is used for networking.

▶▶ See "Network Protocols," p. 1191, for details of the TCP/IP protocol.

Router-based solutions are available for popular types of home and small-office networks, including the following:

- Wired Ethernet

- IEEE 802.11b and 802.11g wireless (Wi-Fi) Ethernet

- HomePNA (phone-line) networks

Comparing Gateways, Proxy Servers, and Routers

To the typical user, it doesn't matter whether a gateway, proxy server, or router is used to provide shared Internet access. Traditional gateway programs such as Microsoft Internet Connection Sharing use a method of shared access called Network Address Translation (NAT), which enables sharing by converting network addresses into Internet-compatible addresses during the file request and download process. This process requires little client PC configuration but doesn't permit page caching, content filtration, firewalls, or other useful services that can be provided by a proxy server. Proxy servers traditionally have required tricky configuration—sometimes at an individual application level. However, products such as WinProxy combine the ease of configuration of a gateway with the extra features of a proxy server.

Popular third-party sharing programs include WinProxy (www.winproxy.com) and WinGate (www.wingate.com). Many home-oriented networks and modems are bundled with these or similar products, so if you're in the market for a new modem or are building a small network, ask whether a proxy server or gateway program for Internet sharing is included. If not, you can download free trial versions from the previously listed websites.

If you don't like leaving a computer on at all times to provide Internet access to the network, a router is the only way to go. Routers also provide better firewall protection for all computers on the network, and some, such as certain Linksys models, can be configured to require networked PCs to be running specified firewall or antivirus software before Internet access is granted. The most common routers for broadband Internet access also contain a switch, so you won't need a separate connection device for your home network.

Routers for Internet Sharing

Just as an ICS gateway has two IP addresses—one for the network and one for the Internet—so does a router. Most routers are sold for use with two-way broadband Internet access devices such as two-way cable modems and fixed wireless broadband services or DSL lines. Most of these devices connect to the computer via a 10BASE-T Ethernet port, as seen in Figure 17.10.

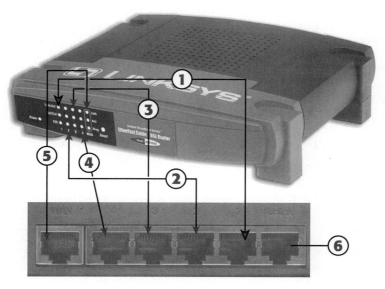

1. LAN port #1
2. LAN port #2
3. LAN port #3
4. LAN port #4
5. WAN port (connects to cable or DSL modem)
6. Uplink port (connects to a hub or switch to allow additional users to connect to the Internet)

Figure 17.10   Front (top) and rear (bottom) views of a typical broadband router with a built-in four-port switch, the Linksys EtherFast Cable/DSL Router, BEFSR41. *Top photo courtesy Linksys.*

When you use a router to share your Internet connection, the WAN port on the router replaces the network card connection originally used to connect your computer with the cable modem or DSL modem. All computers on the network connect to LAN ports and can share files and printers with each other as well as share Internet access.

The router can be configured to provide either dynamically assigned or fixed IP addresses to each computer connected to it through the LAN ports and can be configured to use the same MAC address (a unique hardware address assigned to each network component) originally used by the network card first connected to the cable modem or DSL modem. This prevents the ISP from determining that you're sharing the connection. The WAN port on the router can be configured to obtain an IP address from the cable modem or DSL modem or to have a fixed IP address, depending on the configuration required by the ISP.

As long as the router is running and properly connected to the cable modem or DSL modem, any computer connected to it can go online just by opening its email client or web browser.

Figure 17.11 shows a typical Ethernet home network configuration that uses a router with a built-in switch to share a cable modem.

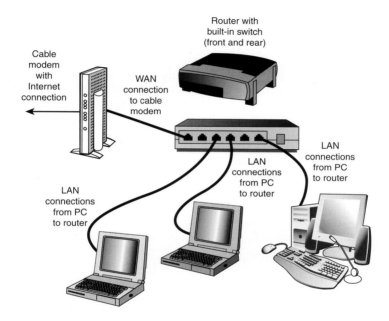

Figure 17.11   When you use a router to share a cable modem or DSL modem, you need only one network card in each computer. This router incorporates a switch that can connect up to four computers to the cable modem.

If you have a wireless network, connect the wireless access point or gateway device designed for your network to the cable modem or other broadband Internet device (some also work with dialup modems). The wireless access point or gateway device will transfer data to and from computers on the wireless network and the Internet.

For more information about choosing and installing wired and wireless networks, see Chapter 18.

Internet Troubleshooting

This section deals with hardware problems that can cause Internet problems. Software problems usually are caused by incorrect configuration of the TCP/IP protocol required by all types of Internet connections. For more information about TCP/IP or other software problems, see Chapter 18.

Diagnosing Problems with a Shared Internet Connection

Although each Internet sharing product has individual configuration issues, the following tips provide general guidelines useful for solving problems with all of them.

Check Your Host Configuration

If your host isn't set up correctly, it can't share its connection with clients. Check the bindings for TCP/IP or other protocols used to create the shared connection. If you are using Microsoft's ICS and two Ethernet cards, you will see entries in the Network configuration on the host computer for each Ethernet card and for the ICS software itself.

Check Your Client Configuration

Make sure your clients have correct TCP/IP, DHCP, and other protocol settings for the host. The ping command can be used at a command prompt to check the Internet connection; try pinging a website by opening a Windows command prompt and typing a command such as ping www.dslreports.com. Note that many sites are designed to reject ping requests, in which case you receive timeout errors. If you have a working Internet connection and are pinging a site not designed to reject ping requests, you should see the IP address for the website you specify and the roundtrip time (or ping rate) for four signals sent to the website. If you are pinging a site that normally responds and yet you still get no response or see an error message, you might have a configuration problem with your TCP/IP configuration.

Note

Because pinging can also be used for denial-of-service (DoS) attacks by hackers on websites, some websites don't respond to pings. Use ping when your system is working properly to find a website that will respond to ping and use that site for troubleshooting as described previously.

Verify that the host has a working Internet connection that's active before you try to share it. Check the sharing program's documentation to see how guests can dial the host's modem to start a connection if necessary.

Speed Will Drop with Multiple Users

It's normal for the speed of an Internet connection to drop with multiple users, but if you're concerned about the degree of decline, check with the sharing software provider for Registry tweaks and other options to improve performance.

Diagnosing Connection Problems with Signal Lights

Signal lights are found on most external broadband devices, such as cable modems, wireless broadband routers, and DSL modems. The signal lights indicate whether the unit is receiving signals from the computer, sending data to the network, or receiving data from the network and whether the unit can "see" the network—even if no data is currently flowing through the unit.

On many units, the power light also is used to indicate problems. If the light is normally green, for example, a red light might indicate the unit has failed. Other lights flash when data is being sent or received. On cable modem or wireless broadband routers, look for a signal lock light; this light flashes if the unit is trying to lock onto a signal from the cable network or wireless transmitter.

Learn the meaning of the lights on your broadband device to help you diagnose problems; the user manual or vendor's website will provide the troubleshooting information you need for the particular broadband device you use.

Modem Fails to Dial

1. Check line and phone jacks on the modem. Use the line jack to attach the modem to the telephone line. The phone jack takes the same RJ-11 silver cord cable, but it's designed to let you

daisy-chain a telephone to your modem, so you need only a single line for modem and telephone use. If you have reversed these cables, you will not get a dial tone.

2. If the cables are attached properly, check the cable for cuts or breaks. The outer jacket used on RJ-11 telephone cables is minimal. If the cable looks bad, replace it.

3. If the modem is external, make sure the RS-232 modem cable is running from the modem to a working serial port on your computer and that it is switched on. Signal lights on the front of the modem can be used to determine whether the modem is on and whether it is responding to dialing commands.

4. If the modem is a PC Card (PCMCIA card), make sure it is fully plugged into the PCMCIA/PC slot. With Windows 9x and later you should see a small PCMCIA/PC Card icon on the toolbar. Double-click it to view the cards that are currently connected. If your modem is properly attached, it should be visible. Otherwise, remove it, reinsert it into the PCMCIA/PC Card slot, and see whether the computer detects it.

Connecting a PC Card Modem via a Dongle

Some PC Card modems do not use a standard RJ-11 cable because the card is too thin. Instead, they use a connection called a *dongle*, which runs from the PC Card to the telephone. If this proprietary cable is damaged, your modem is useless. You should purchase a spare from the modem vendor and carry it with you. And if you find the dongle is too short to reach the data jacks in a hotel room, buy a coupler from your local RadioShack or telephone-parts department and attach a standard RJ-11 cable to your dongle via the coupler. Dongles are also used with some PC Card network cards for the same reason; the RJ-45 twisted-pair cable connector is too wide to attach to a standard PC Card. To avoid using dongles, look for a network or modem card that has a standard RJ-11 or RJ-45 connection built into it.

5. Make sure your modem has been properly configured by your OS. With Windows 9x and later, use the Modems or Phone and Modems tool in the control panel to view and test your modem configuration. Select the Diagnostics tab under Modem Properties, then click on the More Info or Query Modem button to run the test. This sends test commands to the modem and displays the results.

6. If you get a `Couldn't Open Port` error message, your modem isn't connected properly. It might be in use already by a program running in the background, or there might be an IRQ or I/O port address conflict with another card in your computer. If you have a modem installed, every COM port that is working will display its IRQ, I/O port address, and UART chip type when you run Diagnostics. The UART type should be 16550 or above for use with any modern modem.

Note

You can also test your modem response by setting up a HyperTerminal session (discussed earlier) to send the modem commands. If the modem fails to respond, this is another indication of a problem with the modem-PC connection.

Computer Locks Up After Installing or Using Internal Modem, Terminal Adapter, or Network Card

The usual cause of lockups after you install an internal card is an IRQ conflict. Internal dialup modems that use ISA slots typically cause the "curse of the shared IRQ," especially if a serial mouse is also used. PC Card and PCI modems can share IRQs safely, and USB mice use the same IRQ as the USB port itself. For more information about shared IRQs with ISA modems and serial mice, see the Technical Reference section on the disc packaged with this book.

Computer Can't Detect External Modem

1. Make sure the modem has been connected to the computer with the correct type of cable.

For external modems that use an RS-232 serial port, you might need a separate RS-232 modem cable, which has a 9-pin connector on one end (to connect to the computer) and a 25-pin connector on the other end (to connect to the modem). Some external modems have an integrated modem cable. Because RS-232 is a very flexible standard encompassing many pinouts, be sure the cable is constructed according to the following diagram.

If you purchase an RS-232 modem cable prebuilt at a store, you'll have a cable that works with your PC and your modem. However, you can use the following chart to build your own cable or, by using a cable tester, determine whether an existing RS-232 cable in your office is actually made for modems or some other device.

PC (9-pin port—female)	Signal	Modem (25-pin port—male)
3	TX data	2
2	RX data	3
7	RTS	4
8	CTS	5
6	DSR	6
5	SIG GND	7
1	CXR	8
4	DTR	20
9	RI	22

2. Make sure the COM (serial) port or USB port to which the modem is connected to is working.

The Windows diagnostics test listed earlier can be useful in testing the serial port, but third-party testing programs such as AMIDIAG have more thorough methods for testing the system's COM ports. These programs can use loopback plugs to test the serial ports. The loopback plug loops signals that would be sent to the modem or other serial device back to the serial port. These programs normally work best when run from the MS-DOS prompt.

Some diagnostics include a loopback plug to test serial ports. Loopback plugs may vary in design depending on the vendor.

To ensure that the USB port is working, check the Device Manager in Windows; a working USB port is listed as a USB Root hub and a PCI-to-USB Universal Host Controller in the Universal Serial Bus device category. Any external USB hubs also are listed in the same category. If this category is not listed and the ports are physically present on the computer, make sure you are using Windows 98 or later and that the USB ports are enabled in the system BIOS.

3. Check the power cord and power switch.

Using Your Modem Sound to Diagnose Your Modem

If you listen to your modem when it makes a connection, you might have realized that different types of modems make distinctive connection sounds and that different connection speeds also make distinctive sounds.

The various types of 56Kbps modems have distinctly different handshakes of tones, buzzes, and warbles as they negotiate speeds with the ISP's modem. Learning what your modem sounds like when it makes a 56Kbps connection and when it settles for a V.34-speed connection can help you determine when you should hang up and try to connect at a faster speed.

The Modemsite's troubleshooting section has a number of sound samples of various modems during the handshaking process. Use RealPlayer to play the samples, available at http://www.modemsite.com/56k/trouble.asp (click the Handshakes link).

Compare these sound samples to your own modem; be sure you adjust the speaker volume for your modem so you can hear it during the call.

Chapter

18

Local Area Networking

Focus of This Chapter

This chapter concentrates on how to build and use a peer-to-peer network, the lowest-cost network that is still highly useful to small business and home-office users. This type of network can be created utilizing required network hardware along with any recent version of Windows, from Windows 9x and NT through Windows Vista. As you'll see, most peer-to-peer networks can be "grown" into client/server networks at a later point by adding a dedicated server and the appropriate software to the server and client PCs.

Thus, this chapter provides the hands-on and practical information you need to create a small-office, workgroup, or home-office network. If you manage a corporate network using Linux, Unix, Windows Server, or Novell NetWare, you will also be concerned with matters such as security, user profiles, SIDs, and other factors beyond the scope of this book.

Note

Networking is an enormous topic. For more information about client/server networking, wide area networking, the Internet, and corporate networking, I recommend *Upgrading and Repairing Networks* from Que.

Defining a Network

A *network* is a group of two or more computers that *intelligently* share hardware or software devices with each other. A network can be as small and simple as two computers that share the printer and DVD drive attached to one of them or as large as the world's largest network: the Internet.

Intelligently sharing means that each computer that shares resources with another computer or computers maintains control of that resource. Thus, a switchbox for sharing a single printer between two computers doesn't qualify as a network device; because the switchbox—not the computers—handles the print jobs, neither computer knows when the other one needs to print, and print jobs can interfere with each other.

A shared printer, on the other hand, can be controlled remotely and can store print jobs from different computers on the print server's hard disk. Users can change the sequence of print jobs, hold them, or cancel them. And, sharing of the device can be controlled through passwords, further differentiating it from a switchbox.

Virtually any storage or output device can be shared over a network, but the most common devices include the following:

- Printers
- Disk drives
- Optical drives
- Modems
- Fax machines
- Tape backup units
- Scanners

Entire drives or just selected folders can be shared with other users via the network.

In addition to reducing hardware costs by sharing expensive printers and other peripherals among multiple users, networks provide additional benefits to users:

- Multiple users can share access to software and data files.
- Electronic mail (email) can be sent and received.
- Multiple users can contribute to a single document using collaboration features.
- Remote-control programs can be used to troubleshoot problems or show new users how to perform a task.
- A single Internet connection can be shared among multiple computers.

Types of Networks

Several types of networks exist, from small two-station arrangements, to networks that interconnect offices in many cities:

- **Local area networks**—The smallest office network is referred to as a *local area network (LAN)*. A LAN is formed from computers and components in a single office or building. A LAN can also be built at home from the same components used in office networking.

- **Wide area networks**—LANs in different locations can be connected by high-speed fiber-optic, satellite, or leased phone lines to form a wide area network (WAN).

- **The Internet**—The World Wide Web is the most visible part of the world's largest network, the Internet. Although many users of the Internet still use modems over a dialup connection rather than a LAN or WAN connection, any user of the Internet is a network user. The Internet is really a network of networks, all of which are connected to each other through the TCP/IP protocol. It's a glorified WAN in many respects. Programs such as web browsers, File Transfer Protocol (FTP) clients, and email clients are some of the most common ways users work with the Internet.

- **Intranets**—Intranets use the same web browsers and other software and the same TCP/IP protocol as the public Internet, but intranets exist as a portion of a company's private network. Typically, intranets comprise one or more LANs that are connected to other company networks, but, unlike the Internet, the content is restricted to authorized company users only. Essentially, an intranet is a private Internet.

■ **Extranets**—Intranets that share a portion of their content with customers, suppliers, or other businesses, but not with the general public, are called *extranets*. As with intranets, the same web browsers and other software are used to access the content.

Note

Both intranets and extranets rely on firewalls and other security tools and procedures to keep their private contents private.

Requirements for a Network

Unless the computers that are connected know they are connected and agree on a common means of communication and what resources are to be shared, they can't work together. Networking software is just as important as networking hardware because it establishes the logical connections that make the physical connections work.

At a minimum, each network requires the following:

■ Physical (cable) or wireless (usually via radio-frequency) connections between computers.

■ A common set of communications rules, known as a *network protocol*.

■ Software that enables resources to be shared with other PCs and controls access to shared resources. This can be in the form of a *network operating system* or NOS (such as older versions of Novell Netware) that runs on top of a disk operating system; currently, operating systems such as Windows, MacOS, Linux, BSD, and Unix also provide network services, eliminating the need for a specialized NOS.

■ Resources that can be shared, such as printers, disk drives, and CD-ROMs.

■ Software that enables computers to access other computers with shared resources, known as a *network client*; network client software is provided as part of current operating systems, including Windows, MacOS, Linux, BSD, and Unix.

These rules apply both to the simplest and the most powerful networks, and all the ones in between, regardless of their nature. The details of the hardware and software you need are discussed more fully later in this chapter.

About Wireless Networking

Various forms of wireless networks using either radio or IR (infrared) have been developed over the years, but until recently, the benefits of a wireless network (no wires to pull or holes to drill) were outweighed by the lack of standards and relatively slow speed. In conventional Ethernet networks, you can use various brands of NICs, hubs, and switches without any problems, as long as each device corresponds to the same Ethernet standard. That distinction, as you're likely well aware, has changed considerably.

Even though early forms of wireless networking were much slower than wired networks and often were single-vendor proprietary solutions, today's newest wireless networks offer speeds that can outpace Fast Ethernet. Prices have also dropped dramatically, making wireless networking an increasingly appealing alternative to traditional wired network solutions.

Client/Server Versus Peer Networks

Although every computer on a LAN is connected to every other computer, they do not necessarily all communicate with each other. There are two basic types of LANs, based on the communication patterns between the machines—client/server networks and peer-to-peer networks.

Client/Server Networks

On a *client/server* network, every computer has a distinct role, that of either a client or a server. A *server* is designed to share its resources among the client computers on the network. Typically, servers are located in secured areas, such as locked closets or data centers (server rooms), because they hold an organization's most valuable data and do not have to be accessed by operators on a continuous basis. The rest of the computers on the network function as *clients* (see Figure 18.1).

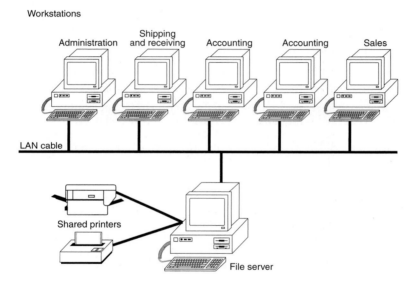

Workstations

Administration Shipping and receiving Accounting Accounting Sales

LAN cable

Shared printers

File server

Figure 18.1 The components of a client/server LAN.

A dedicated server computer typically has faster processors, more memory, and more storage space than a client because it might have to service dozens or even hundreds of users at the same time. High-performance servers typically use from two to eight processors (and that's not counting dual-core CPUs), have several gigabytes of memory installed, use the 64-bit version of the PCI expansion slot or the faster PCI-X expansion slot for server-optimized network interface cards, and have redundant power supplies. The server runs a special network operating system—such as Windows Server, Linux, Unix, or Novell NetWare—that is designed solely to facilitate the sharing of its resources. These resources can reside on a single server or on a group of servers. When more than one server is used, each server can "specialize" in a particular task (file server, print server, fax server, email server, and so on) or provide redundancy (duplicate servers) in case of server failure. For very demanding computing tasks, several servers can act as a single unit through the use of parallel processing.

A client computer typically communicates only with servers, not with other clients. A client system is a standard PC that is running an operating system such as Windows XP or Windows Vista. These versions of Windows contain the client software that enables the client computers to access the resources that servers share. Older operating systems, such as Windows 3.x and DOS, required add-on network client software to join a network.

Peer-to-peer Network

By contrast, on a peer-to-peer network, every computer is equal and can communicate with any other computer on the network to which it has been granted access rights (see Figure 18.2). Essentially, every computer on a peer-to-peer network can function as both a server and a client; any computer on a peer-to-peer network is considered a server if it shares a printer, a folder, a drive, or some other resource with the rest of the network. This is why you might hear about client and server activities, even when the discussion is about a peer-to-peer network. Peer-to-peer networks can be as small as two computers or as large as hundreds of systems. Although there is no theoretical limit to the size of a peer-to-peer network, performance drops significantly and security becomes a major headache on peer-based networks with more than 10 computers. Also, Microsoft imposes a 10-station limit on computers running Windows 2000 Professional or Windows XP Professional that are sharing resources with other systems. Windows Vista Home Basic, Starter, and Home Premium editions have a three-station connection limit, whereas Windows Vista Ultimate, Business, and Enterprise editions have a ten-station connection limit. However, if more stations attempt to connect to the same resource in Windows Vista using the standard IIS 7.0 server software, Vista queues the request instead of displaying a 403.9 Access Forbidden error as in earlier Windows releases. For these reasons, I recommend that you switch to a client/server network when your network climbs above 10 stations.

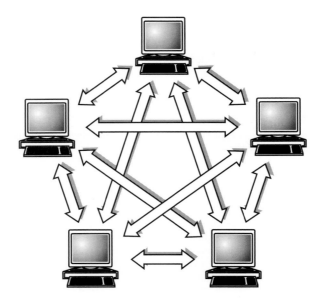

Figure 18.2   The logical architecture of a typical peer-to-peer network.

Peer-to-peer networks are more common in small offices or within a single department of a larger organization. The advantage of a peer-to-peer network is that you don't have to dedicate a computer to function as a file server. Instead, every computer can share its resources with any other. The potential disadvantages to a peer-to-peer network are that typically less security and less control exist because users normally administer their own systems, whereas client/server networks have the advantage of centralized administration.

Comparing Client/Server and Peer-to-peer Networks

Client/server LANs offer enhanced security for shared resources, greater performance, increased backup efficiency for network-based data, and the potential for the use of redundant power supplies and RAID drive arrays. Client/server LANs also have a much greater cost to purchase and maintain. Table 18.1 compares client/server and peer-to-peer server networking.

Table 18.1   Comparing Client/Server and Peer-to-Peer Networking

Item	Client/Server	Peer-to-Peer
Access control	Via user/group lists of permissions stored on a server; user has access to only the resources granted, and different users can be given different levels of access.	Resources are managed by each system with shared resources. Depending upon the operating system, resources may be controlled by separate passwords for each shared resource or by a user list stored on each system with shared resources. Some operating systems do not use passwords or user/group lists, enabling access to shared resources for anyone accessing the network*
Security	High; access is controlled by user or by group identity.	Varies; if password-protected, anyone who knows the password can access a shared resource. If no passwords are used, anyone who can access the workgroup can access shared resources. However, if user/group names are used, security is comparable to a client/server network.
Performance	High; the server is dedicated and doesn't handle other tasks.	Low; servers often act as workstations.
Hardware cost	High; specialized high-performance server hardware with redundancy features.	Low; any workstation can become a server by sharing resources.
Software cost	Higher; license fees per user are part of the cost of the server OS.	Lower; client software is included with OS.
Backup	Centralized on the server; managed by network administrator, backup by device and media only required at server.	Decentralized; managed by users, backup devices and media required at each workstation.
Redundancy	Yes; duplicate power supplies, hot-swappable drive arrays, and even redundant servers are common; network OS normally is capable of using redundant devices automatically.	No true redundancy among peer "servers" or clients; failures require manual intervention to correct, with a high possibility of data loss.

Windows XP Professional with simple file sharing disabled and Windows Vista with password-protected sharing enabled can also set up groups or individual users with varying access rights. Windows 2000 Professional can also set up groups or individual users with varying access rights. Windows 9x/Me use password-protected sharing; Windows XP Home cannot use passwords, groups, or users to control file sharing, nor can Windows XP Professional if simple file sharing is enabled (its default setting).

Network Architecture Overview

The architecture on which you choose to base your network is the single most important decision you make when setting up a local area network. The architecture defines the speed of the network, the medium access control mechanism it uses, the types of cables you can use, the network interface adapters you must buy, and the adapter drivers you install in the network client software.

The Institute of Electrical and Electronic Engineers (IEEE) has defined and documented a set of standards for the physical characteristics of both collision-detection and token-passing networks. These standards are known as IEEE 802.3 (Ethernet) and IEEE 802.5 (Token-Ring), respectively. IEEE 802.11 (Wi-Fi) defines wireless versions of Ethernet.

Note

Be aware, however, that the colloquial names Ethernet and Token-Ring actually refer to earlier versions of these architectures, on which the IEEE standards were based. Minor differences exist between the frame definitions for true Ethernet and true IEEE 802.3. In terms of the standards, IBM's 16Mbps Token-Ring products are an extension of the IEEE 802.5 standard.

New Token-Ring installations are very rare today and are not covered in detail in this book.

The most common choice today for new networks is Ethernet (both wired and wireless), although you might still see some Token-Ring installations in older environments. Other network data-link architectures you might encounter are summarized in Table 18.2. The abbreviations used for the cable types are explained in the following sections.

Table 18.2   LAN Architecture Summary

Network Type	Speed	Maximum Number of Stations	Transmission Types	Notes
Ethernet	10Mbps	Per network: 1,024; per segment: 10BASE-T=2 10BASE-2=30 10BASE-5=100 10BASE-FL=2	Cable: UTP Cat 3 (10BASE-T), Thicknet (coax; 10BASE-5), Thinnet (RG-58 coax; 10BASE-2), fiber-optic (10BASE-F)	Replaced by Fast Ethernet; backward compatible with Fast or Gigabit Ethernet.
Fast Ethernet	100Mbps	Per network: 1,024; per segment: 1	Cable: Cat 5 UTP; can also be run over Cat 5e/6/7 UTP	The most popular wired networking standard.
Gigabit Ethernet	1,000Mbps	Per network: 1,024; per segment: 1	Cable: Cat 5/5e/6 UTP	Uses all four signal pairs in the cable.
802.11a Wireless Ethernet	54Mbps	Per network: 1,024; per segment: n/a	RF 5GHz band (up to 75 ft. outdoors)	Dual-band hardware needed to connect with 802.11b or 802.11g or 802.11n.
802.11b Wireless Ethernet	11Mbps	Per network: 1,024; per segment: n/a	RF 2.4GHz band (up to 150 ft. indoors)	Interoperable with 802.11g and n; dual-band hardware needed to connect with 802.11a.
802.11g Wireless Ethernet	54Mbps	Per network: 1,024; per segment: n/a	RF 2.4GHz band (up to 150 ft. indoors)	Interoperable with 802.11b; dual-band hardware needed to connect with 802.11a.

Table 18.2 Continued

Network Type	Speed	Maximum Number of Stations	Transmission Types	Notes
802.11n Wireless Ethernet	250Mbps	Per network: 1,024; per segment: n/a	RF 2.4GHz band (up to 150 ft. indoors)	Interoperable with 802.11b, g; dual-band hardware needed to connect with 802.11a. Not due for approval until late 2008; pre-n products might not be fully compliant with products meeting the final 802.11n standard.
Token-Ring	4Mpbs; 16Mbps; 100Mbps	72 on UTP; 250–260 on type 1 STP	UTP, Type 1 STP, and fiber optic	Replaced by Fast Ethernet; obsolete for new installations.
ARCnet	2.5Mbps	255	RG-62 coax UTP/ Type 1 STP	Obsolete for new installations; uses same cable as IBM 3270 terminals.

Wired Ethernet

With tens of millions of computers connected by Ethernet cards and cables, Ethernet is the most widely used data-link layer protocol in the world. Ethernet-based LANs enable you to interconnect a wide variety of equipment, including Unix and Linux workstations, Apple computers, printers, and PCs. You can buy Ethernet adapters from dozens of competing manufacturers, and most recent desktop, laptop, and x86 servers incorporate one or more Ethernet ports. Older adapters supported one, two, or all three of the cable types defined in the standard: Thinnet, Thicknet, and unshielded twisted pair (UTP). Current adapters, on the other hand, typically support only UTP. Traditional Ethernet operates at a speed of 10Mbps, but the more recent (and most popular of the Ethernet flavors) Fast Ethernet standards push this speed to 100Mbps. Although many recent desktop computers now incorporate Gigabit Ethernet (1000Mbps), the most recent and fastest version of Ethernet is 10 Gigabit Ethernet (also known as 10G Ethernet). 10G Ethernet runs at 10000Mbps, and is used primarily in enterprise data centers and server blades.

Note

Throughout the remainder of this chapter, be aware that discussion of older Ethernet solutions, such as those using Thicknet or Thinnet, or Token-Ring are only included for reference. You will usually work with these technologies only when installing new workstations or servers into older, existing networks. Most new network installations today use Gigabit, Fast, or Wireless Ethernet.

Fast Ethernet

Fast Ethernet requires adapters, hubs, switches, and UTP or fiber-optic cables designed to support the higher speed. Some early Fast Ethernet products supported only 100Mbps, but almost all current Fast Ethernet products are combination devices that run at both 10Mbps and 100Mbps, enabling you to gradually upgrade an older 10Mbps Ethernet network by installing new NICs and hubs over an extended period of time.

Note

When Fast Ethernet runs in full-duplex mode (sends/receives data simultaneously), it has an effective speed of 200Mbps. Full-duplex operation requires that all hardware in the connection, including adapters and switches, be capable of running in full-duplex and be configured to run in full duplex (or automatically detect full-duplex signals).

Both the most popular form of Fast Ethernet (100BASE-TX) and 10BASE-T standard Ethernet use two of the four wire pairs found in UTP Category 5 cable. (These wire pairs are also found in CAT 5e, CAT 6, and CAT 7 cable.) An alternative Fast Ethernet standard called 100BASE-T4 uses all four wire pairs in UTP Category 5 cable, but this Fast Ethernet standard was never popular and is seldom seen today.

Gigabit Ethernet

Gigabit Ethernet also requires special adapters, hubs, switches, and cables. When Gigabit Ethernet was introduced, most installations used fiber-optic cables, but today it is just as common—if not more common—to run Gigabit Ethernet over the same Category 5 UTP (although better CAT 5e or CAT6 is recommended) cabling that Fast Ethernet and newer installations of standard Ethernet use. Gigabit Ethernet for UTP is also referred to as 1000BASE-T.

Unlike Fast Ethernet and standard Ethernet over UTP, Gigabit Ethernet uses all four wire pairs. Thus, Gigabit Ethernet requires dedicated Ethernet cabling; you can't "borrow" two wire pairs for telephone or other data signaling with Gigabit Ethernet as you can with the slower versions. Most Gigabit Ethernet adapters can also handle 10BASE-T and 100BASE-TX Fast Ethernet traffic, enabling you to interconnect all three UTP-based forms of Ethernet on a single network.

Neither Fast Ethernet nor Gigabit Ethernet support the use of thin or thick coaxial cable originally used with traditional Ethernet, although you can interconnect coaxial cable–based and UTP-based Ethernet networks by using media converters or specially designed hubs and switches.

Note

For more information about Ethernet, Fast Ethernet, Token-Ring, and other network data-link standards, see the "Data Link Layer Protocols" and "High-Speed Networking Technologies" sections found in Chapter 19 of *Upgrading and Repairing PCs, 11th Edition*.

Wireless Ethernet

The most common forms of wireless networking in the United States and Canada are built around various versions of the IEEE 802.11 wireless Ethernet standards, including IEEE 802.11b, IEEE 802.11a, and the newer (and more popular) IEEE 802.11g standard. A fourth member of the family, IEEE 802.11n, is currently in draft form and is scheduled to be officially adopted in late 2008.

Wireless Fidelity (Wi-Fi) is a logo and term given to any IEEE 802.11 wireless network product certified to conform to specific interoperability standards. Wi-Fi Certification comes from the Wi-Fi Alliance, a nonprofit international trade organization that tests 802.11-based wireless equipment to ensure it meets the Wi-Fi standard. To carry the Wi-Fi logo, an 802.11 networking product must pass specific compatibility and performance tests, which ensure that the product will work with all other manufacturers' Wi-Fi equipment on the market. This certification arose from the fact that certain ambiguities in the 802.11 standards allowed for potential problems with interoperability between devices. By purchasing only devices bearing the Wi-Fi logo, you ensure that they will work together and not fall into loopholes in the standards.

Note

The Bluetooth standard for short-range wireless networking, covered later in this chapter, is designed to complement, rather than rival, IEEE 802.11–based wireless networks. In Europe, the HiperLAN family, which has performance and frequency usage similar to that of 802.11a, is the wireless networking standard. HiperLAN/1 runs at up to 20Mbps, while HiperLAN/2 runs at up to 54Mbps.

The widespread popularity of IEEE 802.11–based wireless networks has led to the abandonment of other types of wireless networking, including RadioLAN and HomeRF. RadioLAN now markets long-range antennas that work with 802.11a-based wireless networks.

Note

Although products that are certified and bear the Wi-Fi logo for a particular speed (IEEE standard), such as 802.11g, are designed and tested to work together, most vendors of SOHO wireless networking equipment ship devices that also feature proprietary technologies to raise the speed of the wireless network even further. Linksys calls its solution SpeedBooster, for example, which is advertised as providing "performance increases of up to 30% from old 802.11g standards." Just beware that most, if not all, of these vendor-specific solutions are not interoperable with solutions from other vendors. When different vendor-specific solutions are mixed on a single network, they use the slower standard all have in common to communicate with each other.

Wi-Fi

When the first 802.11b networking products appeared, compatibility problems existed due to certain aspects of the 802.11 standards being ambiguous or leaving loopholes. A group of companies formed an alliance designed to ensure that their products would work together, eliminating any ambiguities or loopholes in the standards. This was originally known as the Wireless Ethernet Compatibility Alliance (WECA) but is now known simply as the Wi-Fi Alliance (www.wi-fi.org). In the past, the term *Wi-Fi* has been used as a synonym for IEEE 802.11b hardware. However, because the Wi-Fi Alliance now certifies other types of 802.11 wireless networks (802.11a and 802.11g, for example), the term *Wi-Fi* should always be accompanied by the frequency band (as in Wi-Fi 2.4GHz band) to make it clear which products will work with the device. Currently, the alliance has certified products that meet the final versions of the 802.11b, 802.11a, and 802.11g standards. The Wi-Fi Alliance also certifies dual-band (a/b/g) products and, as of June 2007, certifies products that meet the specifications of the Draft 2.0 version of the 802.11n standard, which is due for final approval in late 2008.

Caution

Dual-band hardware can access the 802.11a, 802.11b, and 802.11g flavors of Wi-Fi. The newer 802.11g wireless standard has the speed of 802.11a but connects to 802.11b networks without special hardware. 802.11n hardware can also connect to 802.11b and 802.11g networks without special hardware; some implementations of 802.11n can also connect to 802.11a networks.

Be sure you find out which flavor of Wi-Fi is in use in a particular location to determine whether you can connect to it.

The Wi-Fi Alliance currently uses a color-coded certification label to indicate the standard(s) supported by a particular device. Figure 18.3 shows the most common versions of the label, along with the official IEEE standard(s) that the label corresponds to: 802.11a—orange background; 802.11b—dark blue background; 802.11g—lime green background; 802.11n Draft 2—violet background with DRAFT along the right edge.

802.11n Draft 2; also supports
to 802.11a, 802.11b, and 802.11g

802.11n Draft 2; also supports
802.11b and 802.11g

802.11g; also supports 802.11b

802.11a; also supports 802.11b and 802.11g

Figure 18.3   The Wi-Fi Alliance's certification labels for Wi-Fi–compliant 802.11 hardware.

IEEE 802.11b

IEEE 802.11b (Wi-Fi, 2.4GHz band–compliant, also known as Wireless-B) wireless networks run at a maximum speed of 11Mbps, about the same as 10BASE-T Ethernet (the original version of IEEE 802.11 supported data rates up to 2Mbps only). 802.11b networks can connect to conventional Ethernet networks or be used as independent networks, similar to other wireless networks. Wireless networks running 802.11b hardware use the same 2.4GHz spectrum that many portable phones, wireless speakers, security devices, microwave ovens, and the Bluetooth short-range networking products use. Although the increasing use of these products is a potential source of interference, the short range of wireless networks (indoor ranges up to approximately 150 feet and outdoor ranges up to about 300 feet, varying by product) minimizes the practical risks. Many devices use a spread-spectrum method of connecting with other products to minimize potential interference.

Although 802.11b supports a maximum speed of 11Mbps, that top speed is seldom reached in practice, and speed varies by distance. Most 802.11b hardware is designed to run at four speeds, using one of four data-encoding methods, depending on the speed range:

- **11Mbps**—Uses quaternary phase-shift keying/complementary code keying (QPSK/CCK)
- **5.5Mbps**—Also uses quaternary phase-shift keying/complementary code keying (QPSK/CCK)
- **2Mbps**—Uses differential quaternary phase-shift keying (DQPSK)
- **1Mbps**—Uses differential binary phase-shift keying (DBPSK)

As distances change and signal strength increases or decreases, 802.11b hardware switches to the most suitable data-encoding method. The overhead required to track and change signaling methods, along with the additional overhead required when security features are enabled, helps explain why wireless hardware throughput is consistently lower than the rated speed. Figure 18.4 is a simplified diagram showing how speed is reduced with distance. Figures given are for best-case situations—building design and antenna positioning can also reduce speed and signal strength, even at relatively short distances.

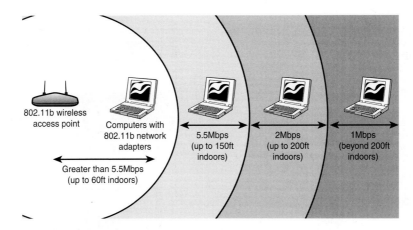

Figure 18.4   At short distances, 802.11b devices can connect at top speed (up to 11Mbps). However, as distance increases, speed decreases because the signal strength is reduced.

IEEE 802.11a

The second flavor of Wi-Fi is the wireless network known officially as IEEE 802.11a. 802.11a (also referred to as Wireless-A) uses the 5GHz frequency band, which allows for much higher speeds (up to 54Mbps) and helps avoid interference from devices that cause interference with lower-frequency 802.11b networks. Although real-world 802.11a hardware seldom, if ever, reaches that speed (almost five times that of 802.11b), 802.11a maintains relatively high speeds at both short and long distances.

For example, in a typical office floor layout, the real-world throughput (always slower than the rated speed due to security and signaling overhead) of a typical 802.11b device at 100 feet might drop to about 5Mbps, whereas a typical 802.11a device at the same distance could have a throughput of around 15Mbps. At a distance of about 50 feet, 802.11a real-world throughput can be four times faster than 802.11b. 802.11a has a shorter maximum distance than 802.11b (approximately 75 feet indoors), but you get your data much more quickly.

Given the difference in throughput (especially at long distances), and if we take the existence of 802.11g out of the equation for a moment, why not skip 802.11b altogether? In a single word: *frequency*. By using the 5GHz frequency instead of the 2.4GHz frequency used by 802.11b/g, standard 802.11a hardware cuts itself off from the already vast 802.11b/g universe, including the growing number of public and semipublic 802.11b/g wireless Internet connections (called *hot spots*) showing up in cafes, airports, hotels, and business campuses.

The current solution for maximum flexibility is to use dual-band hardware. Dual-band hardware can work with either 802.11a or 802.11b/g networks, enabling you to move from an 802.11b/g wireless network at home or at Starbucks to a faster 802.11a office network.

802.11g

IEEE 802.11g, also known to some as *Wireless-G*, is a newer standard that combines compatibility with 802.11b with the speed of 802.11a at longer distances, all at a price only slightly higher than 802.11b hardware. The final 802.11g standard was ratified in mid-2003.

Although 802.11g promises to connect seamlessly with existing 802.11b hardware, early 802.11g hardware was slower and less compatible than the specification promised. In some cases, problems with early-release 802.11g hardware can be solved through firmware upgrades. 802.11g is currently the predominant wireless networking standard, with 802.11b and 802.11a fading into the background.

Note

Although 802.11b wireless hardware uses the same frequencies as 802.11g and can coexist on the same network, most 802.11g-based networks slow down to 802.11b speeds when both types of hardware are on the same network (an option referred to as "mixed mode" in wireless router/access point configuration). To prevent slow-downs, some 802.11g wireless networks are configured to prevent 802.11b devices from joining them (an option known as "G-only mode"). If you need to connect 802.11b devices to an 802.11g-based network and are unable to, configure the wireless router or access point to run in mixed mode.

As happened earlier with 802.11b, the 802.11g market has become fragmented with various faster-than-standard product lines available from major makers. These include:

- SpeedBooster, SRX (Linksys)
- Range Max, Range Max 240 (Netgear)
- 108G Range Booster, Super G with MIMO, Range Booster G (D-Link)

These products use different chipsets, antennas, and other methods to achieve faster rates and, in some cases, longer ranges than standard 802.11g hardware. To achieve the promised performance and distance boosts with any faster-than-standard product, you must upgrade all adapters and routers to the same standard.

802.11n

The latest wireless network standard, 802.11n (also known as Wireless-N) will not be ratified until late 2008 but is already available from leading wireless network vendors. 802.11n hardware uses a technology called multiple input, multiple output (MIMO) to increase throughput and range. MIMO uses multiple radios and antennas to transmit multiple data streams (also known as spatial streams) between stations. Unlike earlier 802.11 implementations, in which reflected radio signals slowed down throughput, reflected radio signals can be used to improve throughput as well as increase useful range.

802.11n is the first wireless Ethernet standard to support two frequency ranges:

- 2.4GHz (same as 802.11b/g)
- 5GHz (same as 802.11a)

Thus, depending on the specific implementation of 802.11n in use, an 802.11n device may be able to connect with 802.11b, 802.11g, and 802.11a devices, or with 802.11b and 802.11g devices only.

How fast is 802.11n? It's significantly faster than 802.11g. But by how much? That depends in part upon whether the device supports only the standard features of 802.11n (two 20MHz channels, 800ns guard interval) or supports one or more of the optional features of 802.11n (two 40MHz channels, 400ns guard interval). 40MHz channels provide up to double the data rate of 20MHz channels, up to 270Mbps in the 5GHz frequency range, compared to 135Mbps when the standard 20MHz channels are used. As with other members of the 802.11 family of standards, 802.11n supports fall-back rates when a connection cannot be made at the maximum data rate.

Note

Another optional feature of the 802.11n standard is support for a faster guard interval (GI) than the one used by 802.11b, 802.11g and 802.11a. The GI is the amount of time (in nanoseconds) the system waits between transmitting OFDM symbols. The standard GI is 800ns; when a 400ns GI is used, the maximum data rate for 802.11n with two 40MHz channels increases to 300Mbps. A 400ns GI is supported by both the 2.4GHz and 5GHz frequency ranges.

Table 18.3 compares the standard and optional speeds supported by 802.11n Draft 2 to those supported by 802.11b, 802.11a, and 802.11g.

Table 18.3 Standard and Optional Wireless Ethernet Speeds

Wireless Ethernet Type	Frequency Band	Radio Speed	GI	Speed Range (one data stream)	Speed Range (two data streams)	Optional 802.11n Feature
802.11a	5GHz	20MHz	800ns	6–54Mbps	—	No
802.11b	2.4GHz	20MHz	800ns	1–11Mbps	—	No
802.11g	2.4GHz	20MHz	800ns	1–54Mbps	—	No
802.11n	2.4GHz	20MHz	800ns	6.5–65Mbps	13–130Mbps	No
802.11n	5GHz	20MHz	800ns	6.5–65Mbps	13–130Mbps	No
802.11n	5GHz	40MHz	800ns	13.5–135Mbps	27–270Mbps	Yes
802.11n	2.4GHz, 5GHz	20MHz	400ns	7.2–72.2Mbps	14.4–144Mbps	Yes
802.11n	2.4GHz, 5GHz	40MHz	400ns	15–150Mbps	30–300Mbps	Yes

300Mbps isn't the end of the road. According to the Wi-Fi Alliance, 600Mbps data rates are possible if four 40MHz streams are used with a 400ns GI setting.

As you can see from Table 18.3, rated speeds above 130Mbps require that 802.11n Draft 2 wireless routers and adapters use optional features. If routers and adapters only support standard 802.11n speeds, the speed advantage of 802.11n over 802.11g drops to about 2.4x faster. However, whether 802.11n Draft 2 equipment supports optional features or not, the range you can expect is about double of older 802.11 standards, thanks to 802.11n's support of MIMO technology.

Although the 802.11n standard is not yet in its final form, the Wi-Fi Alliance began certifying products that support 802.11n in its Draft 2 form in June 2007. As with previous Wi-Fi certifications, the Wi-Fi 802.11n Draft 2 certification requires that 802.11n Draft 2 hardware from different makers interoperate properly with each other. 802.11n Draft 2 hardware uses chips from makers including Atheros, Broadcom, Cisco, Intel, Marvell, and Ralink. Although the 802.11n standard will undergo one more draft revision (Draft 3) before final approval in late 2008, it is expected that 802.11n Draft 2 products will also be compliant with the final 802.11n standard. In some cases, driver or firmware updates might be necessary.

Which Wireless Ethernet Standard Is Best?

Of the fourers to the same standard major flavors of Wireless Ethernet now available, it's time to set the pioneering 802.11b standard and its offshoots aside. 802.11b is much slower than other versions, and, more significantly, most 802.11b hardware supports only the original (and not very secure) WEP wireless network security standard. If you use 802.11b hardware on the same network with 802.11g or 802.11n hardware, you cannot use the much more secure WPA or WPA2 wireless network security standards supported by these newer wireless standards. Even if your 802.11b hardware supports WPA, running a mixture of 802.11b and 802.11g clients with an 802.11g wireless router or access point slows down 802.11g clients, in some cases to 802.11b speeds.

802.11a is also out of date, even though its performance is higher than 802.11b. The main problem with 802.11a is its inability to connect to public and subscription-based hot spots in airports, hotels, libraries, and other public places because it uses a different frequency (5GHz) than 802.11b and g (2.4GHz), the standards commonly supported for hot spots. If you need 802.11a support to connect to an existing corporate network, use a dual-band 802.11a/g network adapter.

Note

Some vendors have offered products that can transmit on the 2.4GHz (802.11g) and 5GHz (802.11a) frequencies at the same time, a feature designed to route multimedia traffic over 802.11a while using 802.11g for web surfing and standard networking. One example is the NetGear Double 108Mbps Wireless Firewall Router WGU624 and the companion WG511U network adapter. However, most vendors have switched to developing 802.11n-based products to provide speed improvements for multimedia file sharing.

802.11g remains an excellent choice for web-surfing or light-duty file sharing and provides full support for the stronger WPA wireless security standard. Although it includes support for quality of service (QoS), which places a higher priority on streaming media and voice over IP (VoIP) traffic than web-surfing or file transfers, 802.11g is not really fast enough to support VoIP or multimedia traffic. Multimedia file sharing (video, audio, photos) is an increasingly important use for home networks, especially with the advent of Microsoft Windows Vista, which includes full-featured media playback, editing, and creation tools such as Windows Media Player 11, Windows Media Center, Windows Movie Maker, and Windows Photo Gallery. While many vendors offer proprietary extensions to 802.11g to improve speed and range, a better long-term solution is to use 802.11n.

Although 802.11n will not be a finalized standard until late 2008, it already represents a standards-based way to achieve both faster performance and longer range. Some vendors are already developing various extensions of the 802.11n standard, so shop carefully to get the performance you want.

Regardless of the wireless network type(s) you support, I recommend you consider only products that have received Wi-Fi Alliance certification to avoid problems in interoperability. This is critical when you have a mixture of different hardware brands on a wireless network, as is always the case when you have notebook or other portable devices with integrated 802.11-based wireless adapters and use wireless routers or access points to connect them to each other and to the Internet.

▶▶ For more information about wireless security standards, see "Wireless Network Security," p. 1188.

Bluetooth

Bluetooth is a low-speed, low-power standard originally designed to interconnect notebook computers, PDAs, cell phones, and pagers for data synchronization and user authentication in public areas, such as airports, hotels, rental car pickups, and sporting events. Bluetooth is also used for a wide variety of wireless devices on PCs, including printer adapters, keyboards and mice (Microsoft's Bluetooth keyboard and mouse are available at many stores selling computer hardware), DV camcorders, data projectors, and many others. A list of Bluetooth products and announcements is available at the official Bluetooth wireless information website: www.bluetooth.com.

Bluetooth devices also use the same 2.4GHz frequency range that Wi-Fi/IEEE 802.11b and 802.11g devices use. However, in an attempt to avoid interference with Wi-Fi, Bluetooth uses a signaling method called *frequency hopping spread spectrum (FHSS)*, which switches the exact frequency used during a Bluetooth session 1,600 times per second over the 79 channels Bluetooth uses. Unlike Wi-Fi, which is designed to allow a device to be part of a network at all times, Bluetooth is designed for ad hoc temporary networks (known as piconets) in which two devices connect only long enough to transfer data and then break the connection. The basic data rate supported by Bluetooth is currently 1Mbps (up from 700Kbps in earlier versions), but devices that support enhanced data rate (EDR) can reach a transfer rate up to 3Mbps.

The current version of Bluetooth, version 2.1+EDR, supports easier connections between devices such as phones and headsets (a process known as pairing), longer battery life, and improved security compared with older versions.

Interference Issues Between Bluetooth and IEEE 802.11b/g

Despite the frequency-hopping nature of Bluetooth, studies have shown that Bluetooth (up through version 1.1) and IEEE 802.11b devices can interfere with each other, particularly at close range (under 2 meters) or when users attempt to use both types of wireless networking at the same time (as with an 802.11b wireless Internet connection on a computer with a Bluetooth wireless keyboard and mouse). Although 802.11g has not been specifically studied, it uses the same frequencies as 802.11b, and interference between 802.11g and Bluetooth can also take place under similar circumstances. Interference reduces throughput and in some circumstances can cause data loss.

An improved version of the Bluetooth specification (version 1.2) adds adaptive frequency hopping to solve interference problems when devices are more than 1 meter (3.3 feet) away from each other. However, close-range (less than 1 meter) interference can still take place. IEEE has developed 802.15.2, a specification for enabling coexistence between 802.11b/g and Bluetooth. It can use various time-sharing or time-division methods to enable coexistence. However, these specifications are not yet part of typical 802.11b/g implementations. The newest version of Bluetooth, version 2.1 (code-named 'Lisbon') is designed to minimize interference by using an improved adaptive hopping method. To avoid interference between 802.11b/g/n (2.4GHz) and Bluetooth, the best bet is to use Bluetooth 2.1 and 802.11-based chipsets from the same vendor. Companies that develop both Bluetooth and 802.11-family chipsets, such as Atheros and Texas Instruments (TI), have developed methods for avoiding interference that work especially well when same-vendor products are teamed together.

Hardware Elements of Your Network

The choice of a data-link protocol affects the network hardware you choose. Because Fast Ethernet, Gigabit Ethernet, Wireless Ethernet, and other data-link protocols use different hardware, you must select the architecture before you can select appropriate hardware, including network interface cards, cables, and switches.

Network Interface Cards for Wired Ethernet Networks

On most recent computers, a wired Ethernet network adapter is integrated into the chipset (desktop computers) or into a mini-PCI internal card (notebook computers). If the integrated component fails or is not fast enough, a replacement network interface card (NIC) can be added through the PCI or PCI-Express slot (desktop computers), CardBus PC Card (PCMCIA) or ExpressCard slot on a notebook computer, or a PCI-X or 64-bit/66MHz PCI slot (servers).

Network adapters (both wired and wireless) have unique hardware addresses coded into their firmware. The hardware address is known as the MAC address. You can see the MAC address on a label on the side of the adapter, or view it after the adapter is installed with operating system utilities such as ipconfig.exe (Windows NT/2000/XP/Vista) or winipcfg.exe (Windows 9x/Me). The data-link layer protocol uses these addresses to identify the other systems on the network. A packet gets to the correct destination because its data-link layer protocol header contains the hardware addresses of both the sending and receiving systems.

Wired Ethernet network adapters range in price from less than $20 for client adapters to over $100 for single-port server-optimized Gigabit Ethernet adapters; four-port Gigabit Ethernet adapters sell for around $500-600 each. 10G Ethernet adapters can sell for over $1000.

Note

Token-Ring adapters have dropped in price recently, reflecting the reduced demand in the corporate networking world. Client adapters typically range in price from less than $40 to around $70, supporting PCI and CardBus as well as older bus designs such as ISA and EISA. Some adapters support 100Mbps speeds as well as the older 4Mbps and 16Mbps speeds. Server-optimized adapters are more expensive, costing around $200–$250.

Although you can connect two computers directly to each other via their Ethernet ports with a crossover RJ-45 cable, larger networks need a switch, which is frequently incorporated into a router or wireless router. The network runs at the speed of the slowest component, so if you use a switch that runs at a slower speed than the network clients, the clients will run at that speed. Some 802.11n or 802.11g wireless routers now include Gigabit Ethernet ports instead of Fast Ethernet ports.

For client workstations on wired Ethernet networks (including peer servers on peer-to-peer networks), the following sections contain my recommendations on the features you need.

Speed

Your NIC should run at the maximum speed you want your network to support. For a Gigabit Ethernet network, for example, you should purchase Ethernet cards that support 1000BASE-T's 1000Mbps speed. Most Gigabit Ethernet and Fast Ethernet cards also support slower speeds, such as Fast Ethernet's 100Mbps speed or standard Ethernet's 10Mbps speed, allowing the same card to be used on both older and newer portions of the network. To verify multispeed operation, look for network cards identified as 10/100 or 10/100/1000 Ethernet. Your NIC should support both half-duplex and full-duplex operation:

- *Half-duplex* means that the network card can only send or only receive data in a single operation.

- *Full-duplex* means that the network card can both receive and send simultaneously. Full-duplex options boost network speed if switches are used in place of hubs. For example, 100Mbps Fast Ethernet cards running in full-duplex mode have a maximum true throughput of 200Mbps, with half going in each direction.

Note

Unlike hubs, which broadcast data packets to all computers connected to them, switches create a direct connection between the sending and receiving computers. Thus, switches provide faster performance than hubs; most switches also support full-duplex operation, doubling the rated speed of the network when full-duplex network cards are used.

▶▶ For more information about switches, see "Switches and Hubs for Ethernet Networks," p. 1182.

Bus Type

If you need to install a network adapter for use with a 10Mbps or Fast Ethernet (10/100Mbps) network, any of the following buses have more than adequate performance:

- PCI (33MHz or faster; 32-bit or 64-bit); the integrated NIC built into most recent desktops or the Mini-PCI card used in notebook computers are also PCI devices.
- USB 2.0 (also known as Hi-Speed USB)
- CardBus (32-bit PC Card slot for notebook computers)

All three of these buses also support Gigabit Ethernet adapters, but USB 2.0 (480Mbps) is not fast enough to fully support Gigabit Ethernet's 1000Mbps bandwidth.

For the best performance with a Gigabit Ethernet network on a desktop computer, use PCI-Express x1 adapters. Servers can use 64-bit/66MHz PCI or PCI-X adapters. For notebook computers, best performance is achieved with an ExpressCard adapter. ExpressCard supports the PCI Express bus but is available only on some late-model notebook computers.

Table 18.4 summarizes the differences between all the types of interfaces network cards use.

Table 18.4   Bus Choices for Client PC NICs

Bus Type	Bus Width (Bits)	Bus Speed (MHz)	Data Cycles per Clock	Bandwidth (MBps)
8-bit ISA (AT)	8	8.33	1/2	4.17
16-bit ISA (AT-Bus)	16	8.33	1/2	8.33
EISA Bus	32	8.33	1	33
MCA-16 Streaming	16	10	1	20
MCA-32 Streaming	32	10	1	40
MCA-64 Streaming	64	10	1	80
PC Card (PCMCIA)	16	10	1	20
CardBus	32	33	1	133
PCI	32	33	1	133
PCI 66MHz	32	66	1	266
PCI 64-bit	64	33	1	266
PCI 66MHz/64-bit	64	66	1	533
PCI Express x1	1	5000*	1	400*
USB 1.1	1	12	1	1.5
USB 2.0	1	480	1	60

Note: ISA, EISA, and MCA are no longer used in current motherboard designs.

MBps = Megabytes per second

ISA = Industry Standard Architecture, also known as the PC/XT (8-bit) or AT-Bus (16-bit)

EISA = Extended Industry Standard Architecture (32-bit ISA)

MCA = Microchannel Architecture (IBM PS/2 systems)

PC Card = 16-bit PCMCIA (Personal Computer Memory Card International Association) interface

CardBus = 32-bit PC Card

PCI = Peripheral Component Interconnect

USB = universal serial bus

*bidirectional throughput; 2500Mbps(2.5Gbps)/200MBps in each direction

Wired Network Adapter Connectors

Wired Ethernet adapters typically have an eight position, eight conductor (8P8C) connector commonly known as an RJ-45 connector, which looks like a large telephone jack. Fast Ethernet and Gigabit Ethernet twisted-pair cables use these connectors, but you might still find a few older adapters that support a single BNC connector (for Thinnet coaxial cables), or a D-shaped 15-pin connector called a DB-15 (for Thicknet coaxial cables). A few older 10Mbps adapters have a combination of two or all three of these connector types; adapters with two or more connectors are referred to as *combo adapters*. Token-Ring adapters can have a 9-pin connector called a DB-9 (for Type 1 STP cable) or sometimes an RJ-45 jack (for Type 3 UTP cable). Figure 18.5 shows all three of the Ethernet connectors.

Note

Although RJ-45 is the common name for the UTP Ethernet connector, this is a misnomer. The actual RJ45S connector is an eight-position connector but is used for telephone rather than computer data. An RJ45S jack has a slightly different shape than the connector used for Ethernet, and includes a cutout on one side to prevent unkeyed connectors from being inserted into the jack.

To see drawings of the true RJ45S jack and other telephone jacks, see http://www.siemon.com/us/standards/13-24_modular_wiring_reference.asp

Virtually all 10/100 Ethernet NICs made for client-PC use on the market today are designed to support unshielded twisted-pair (UTP) cable exclusively; Gigabit Ethernet cards made for wired (not fiber-optic) networks also use only UTP cable. If you are adding a client PC to an existing network that uses some form of coaxial cable, you have four options:

- Purchase a combo NIC that supports coaxial cable as well as RJ-45 twisted-pair cabling.
- Purchase a media converter that can be attached to the coaxial cable to allow the newer UTP-based NICs to connect to the existing network.
- Use a switch or hub that has both coaxial cable and RJ-45 ports. A dual-speed (10/100) device is needed if you are adding one or more Fast Ethernet clients.
- Replace the coaxial installation with an updated Ethernet installation.

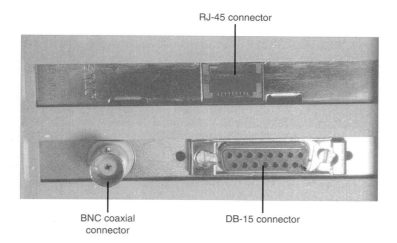

Figure 18.5 Three Ethernet connectors on two NICs: RJ-45 connector (top center), DB-15 connector (bottom right), and BNC connector (bottom left).

For maximum economy, NICs and network cables must match, although media converters can be used to interconnect networks based on the same standard, but using different cable.

Network Cables for Wired Ethernet

Originally, all networks used some type of cable to connect the computers on the network to each other. Although various types of wireless networks are now on the market, many office and home networks still use twisted-pair Ethernet cabling. Occasionally you might still find some based on Thick or Thin Ethernet coaxial cable.

Thick and Thin Ethernet Coaxial Cable

The first versions of Ethernet were based on coaxial cable. The original form of Ethernet, 10BASE-5, used a thick coaxial cable (called Thicknet) that was not directly attached to the NIC. A device called an attachment unit interface (AUI) ran from a DB-15 connector on the rear of the NIC to the cable. The cable had a hole drilled into it to allow the "vampire tap" to be connected to the cable. NICs designed for use with thick Ethernet cable are almost impossible to find as new hardware today.

10BASE-2 Ethernet cards use a BNC (Bayonet-Neill-Concelman) connector on the rear of the NIC. Although the thin coaxial cable (called Thinnet or RG-58) used with 10BASE-2 Ethernet has a bayonet connector that can physically attach to the BNC connector on the card, this configuration is incorrect and won't work. Instead, a BNC T-connector attaches to the rear of the card, allowing a thin Ethernet cable to be connected to either both ends of the T (for a computer in the middle of the network) or to one end only (for a computer at the end of the network). A 50-ohm terminator is connected to the other arm of the T to indicate the end of the network and prevent erroneous signals from being sent to other clients on the network. Some early Ethernet cards were designed to handle thick (AUI/DB-15), thin (RG-58), and UTP (RJ-45) cables. Combo cards with both BNC and RJ-45 connectors are still available on the surplus equipment market but can run at only standard 10Mbps Ethernet speeds.

Figure 18.6 compares Ethernet DB-15 to AUI, BNC coaxial T-connector, and RJ-45 UTP connectors to each other, and Figure 18.7 illustrates the design of coaxial cable.

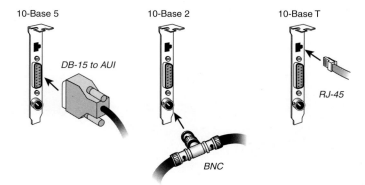

Figure 18.6 An Ethernet network card with thick Ethernet (DB-15), thin Ethernet (RG-58 with T-connector), and UTP (RJ-45) connectors.

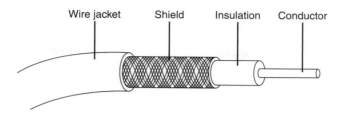

Figure 18.7   Coaxial cable.

Twisted-Pair Cable

Twisted-pair cable is just what its name implies: insulated wires within a protective casing with a specified number of twists per foot. Twisting the wires reduces the effect of electromagnetic interference (that can be generated by nearby cables, electric motors, and fluorescent lighting) on the signals being transmitted. Shielded twisted pair (STP) refers to the amount of insulation around the cluster of wires and therefore its immunity to noise. You are probably familiar with unshielded twisted-pair (UTP) cable; it is often used for telephone wiring. Figure 18.8 shows unshielded twisted-pair cable; Figure 18.9 illustrates shielded twisted-pair cable.

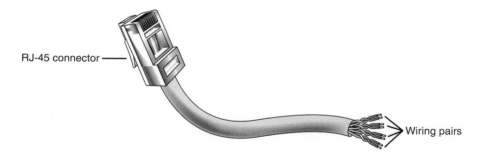

Figure 18.8   An unshielded twisted-pair (UTP) cable.

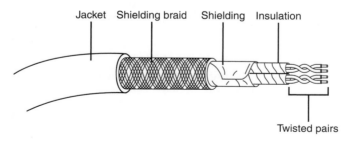

Figure 18.9   A shielded twisted-pair (STP) cable.

Shielded Versus Unshielded Twisted Pair

When cabling was being developed for use with computers, it was first thought that shielding the cable from external interference was the best way to reduce interference and provide for greater transmission speeds. However, it was discovered that twisting the pairs of wires is a more effective way to prevent interference from disrupting transmissions. As a result, earlier cabling scenarios relied on shielded cables rather than the unshielded cables more commonly in use today.

Shielded cables also have some special grounding concerns because one, and only one, end of a shielded cable should be connected to an earth ground; issues arose when people inadvertently caused grounding loops to occur by connecting both ends or caused the shield to act as an antenna because it wasn't grounded.

Grounding loops are situations in which two different grounds are tied together. This is a bad situation because each ground can have a slightly different potential, resulting in a circuit that has very low voltage but infinite amperage. This causes undue stress on electrical components and can be a fire hazard.

Most Ethernet and Fast Ethernet installations that use twisted-pair cabling use UTP because the physical flexibility and small size of the cable and connectors makes routing it very easy. However, its lack of electrical insulation can make interference from fluorescent lighting, elevators, and alarm systems (among other devices) a major problem. If you use UTP in installations where interference can be a problem, you need to route the cable away from the interference, use an external shield, or substitute STP for UTP near interference sources.

Four standard types of unshielded twisted-pair cabling exist and are still used to varying degrees:

- **Category 3 cable**—The original type of UTP cable used for Ethernet networks was also the same as that used for business telephone wiring. This is known as Category 3, or voice-grade UTP cable, and is measured according to a scale that quantifies the cable's data-transmission capabilities. The cable itself is 24 AWG (American Wire Gauge, a standard for measuring the diameter of a wire) and copper-tinned with solid conductors, with 100–105 ohm characteristic impedance and a minimum of two twists per foot. Category 3 cable is largely obsolete because it is only adequate for networks running at up to 16Mbps, so it cannot be used with Fast or Gigabit Ethernet.

- **Category 5 cable**—The faster network types require greater performance levels. Fast Ethernet (100BASE-TX) uses the same two-wire pairs as 10BASE-T, but Fast Ethernet needs a greater resistance to signal crosstalk and attenuation. Therefore, the use of Category 5 UTP cabling is essential with 100BASE-TX Fast Ethernet. Although the 100BASE-T4 version of Fast Ethernet can use all four-wire pairs of Category 3 cable, this flavor of Fast Ethernet is not widely supported and has practically vanished from the marketplace. If you try to run Fast Ethernet 100BASE-TX over Category 3 cable, you will have a slow and unreliable network. Category 5 cable is commonly called CAT 5 and is also referred to as Class D cable.

  Many cable vendors also sell an enhanced form of Category 5 cable called Category 5e (specified by Addendum 5 of the ANSI/TIA/EIA-568-A cabling standard). Category 5e cable can be used in place of Category 5 cable and is especially well suited for use in Fast Ethernet networks that might be upgraded to Gigabit Ethernet in the future. Category 5e cabling must pass several tests not required for Category 5 cabling. Even though you can use both Category 5 and Category 5e cabling on a Gigabit Ethernet (1000BASE-TX) network, Category 5e cabling provides better transmission rates and a greater margin of safety for reliable data transmission.

- **Category 6 cable**—Category 6 cabling (also called CAT 6 or Class E) can be used in place of CAT 5 or 5e cabling and uses the same RJ-45 connectors as CAT 5 and 5e. CAT 6 cable handles a frequency range of 1MHz–250MHz, compared to CAT 5 and 5e's 1MHz–100MHz frequency range.

- **Category 7 cable**—Category 7 (also called CAT 7 or Class F) is the newest cabling standard and handles a frequency range of 1MHz–600MHz, which reduces propagation delay and delay skew. This enables longer network cables and larger numbers of workstations on a network. CAT 7 uses the GG45 connector developed by Nexans. This connector resembles the RJ-45 connector but has four additional contacts (see Figure 18.10). The GG45 connector contains a switch that activates a maximum of eight out of 12 contacts. The upper 8 RJ-45 contacts are used for up to 250MHz (CAT 6) operation, whereas the eight contacts in the outer edges are used for 600MHz (CAT 7) operation. Only eight contacts are used at a given time. In other words, this connector is designed to be backward compatible with cables using RJ-45 connectors while supporting the newer standard.

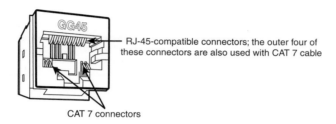

Figure 18.10 The GG45 connector from Nexans can accept CAT 5 and other standard network cabling using the RJ-45 connector or the new CAT 7 cabling.

Caution

If you choose to install Category 5/5e UTP cable, be sure that all the connectors, wall plates, and other hardware components involved are also Category 5–rated.

If you are trying to connect prebuilt Category 5 cabling together on a Fast Ethernet network, use Category 5–grade or better connectors; otherwise, you'll create a substandard section that might fail in your network.

Choosing the correct type of Category 5/5e/6/7 cable is also important. Use solid PVC cable for network cables that represent a permanent installation. However, the slightly more expensive stranded cables are a better choice for a notebook computer or temporary wiring of no more than 10-feet lengths (from a computer to a wall socket, for example) because they are more flexible and therefore capable of withstanding frequent movement.

If you plan to use air ducts or suspended ceilings for cable runs, you should use Plenum cable, which doesn't emit harmful fumes in a fire. It is much more expensive, but the safety issue is a worthwhile reason to use it (some localities require you to use Plenum cabling).

Building Your Own Twisted-Pair Cables

When it's time to wire your network, you have two choices. You can opt to purchase prebuilt cables, or you can build your own cables from bulk wire and connectors.

You should build your own twisted-pair cables if you

- Plan to perform a lot of networking.
- Need cable lengths longer than the lengths you can buy preassembled at typical computer departments.
- Want to create both standard and crossover cables.

- Want to choose your own cable color.
- Want maximum control over cable length.
- Want to save money.
- Have the time necessary to build cables.

Twisted-Pair Wiring Standards

If you want to create twisted-pair (TP) cables yourself, be sure your cable pairs match the color-coding of any existing cable or the color-coding of any prebuilt cabling you want to add to your new network. Because there are eight wires in TP cables, many incorrect combinations are possible. Several standards exist for UTP cabling.

Tip

The keys are to be consistent, use the same scheme for all your cables, and ensure that anyone else working on your network understands the scheme used in it.

One common standard is the AT&T 258A configuration (also called EIA/TIA 568B). Table 18.5 lists the wire pairing and placement within the standard RJ-45 connector.

Table 18.5   RJ-45 Connector Wire Pairing and Placement for AT&T 258A/EIA 568B Standard

Wire Pairing	Wire Connected to Pin #	Pair Used For
White/blue and blue	White/blue - #5–Blue - #4	Not used*
White/orange and orange	White/orange - #1–Orange - #2	Transmit
White/green and green	White/green - #3–Green - #6	Receive
White/brown and brown	White/brown - #7–Brown - #8	Not used*

This pair is not used with 10BASE-T or Fast Ethernet 100BASE-TX, but all four pairs are used with Fast Ethernet 100BASE-T4 and Gigabit Ethernet 1000BASE-TX standards.

In Figure 18.11 an RJ-45 cable connector is wired to the AT&T 258A/EIA 568B standard.

Note

You also might encounter the similar EIA 568A standard. It reverses the position of the orange and green pairs listed previously.

Crossover UTP Cables

Crossover cables, which change the wiring at one end of the cable, are used to connect two (and only two) computers when no hub or switch is available or to connect a hub or switch without an uplink port to another hub or switch. The pinout for a crossover cable is shown in Table 18.6. This pinout is for one end of the cable only; the other end of the cable should correspond to the standard EIA 568B pinout, as shown previously in Figure 18.11.

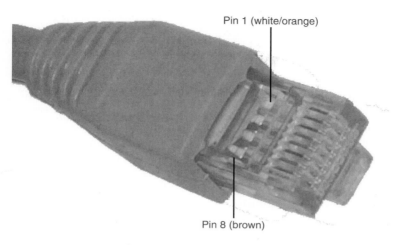

Pin 1 (white/orange)

Pin 8 (brown)

Figure 18.11   An AT&T 258A/EIA 568B standard–compliant RJ-45 connector.

Table 18.6   RJ-45 Connector Wire Pairing and Placement for Crossover Variation on EIA 568B Standard

Wire	Pin #	Wire	Pin #
White/blue	5	White/orange	3
Blue	4	Orange	6
White/green	1	White/brown	7
Green	2	Brown	8

Note

It should be noted that other wiring schemes exist, such as IEEE and USOC. All told, at least eight agreed-on standards exist for connecting UTP cables and RJ-45 connectors. The ones listed in this chapter are the most common.

Constructing the Cable

Making your own UTP cables requires a few tools that aren't commonly found in a typical toolbox. Those items that you might not already have you can typically purchase for a single price from many network-products vendors. You will need the following tools and supplies to build your own Ethernet cables:

- UTP cable (Category 5 or better)
- RJ-45 connectors
- Wire stripper
- RJ-45 crimping tool

Before you make a "real" cable of any length, you should practice on a short length of cable. RJ-45 connectors and bulk cable are cheap; network failures are not. Follow these steps for creating your own twisted-pair cables:

1. Determine how long your UTP cable should be. You should allow adequate slack for moving the computer and for avoiding strong interference sources. Keep the maximum distances for UTP cables of about 100 meters in mind.

2. Roll out the appropriate length of cable.

3. Cut the cable cleanly from the box of wire.

4. Use the wire stripper to strip only the insulation jacket off the cable, exposing the TP wires (see Figure 18.12); you'll need to rotate the wire about 1 1/4 turns to strip away all the jacket. If you turn it too far, you'll damage the wires inside the cable.

5. Check the outer jacket and inner TP wires for nicks; adjust the stripper tool and repeat steps 3 and 4 if you see damage.

6. As shown in Figure 18.13, arrange the wires according to the EIA 568B standard. This arrangement is listed previously, in the section "Twisted-Pair Wiring Standards."

7. Trim the wire edges so the eight wires are even with one another and are slightly less than 1/2" past the end of the jacket. If the wires are too long, crosstalk (wire-to-wire interference) can result; if the wires are too short, they can't make a good connection with the RJ-45 plug.

8. With the clip side of the RJ-45 plug facing away from you, push the cable into place (see Figure 18.14). Verify that the wires are arranged according to the EIA/TIA 568B standard *before* you crimp the plug onto the wires (refer to Table 18.5 and Figure 18.11 earlier in this chapter). Adjust the connection as necessary.

9. Use the crimping tool to squeeze the RJ-45 plug onto the cable (see Figure 18.15). The end of the cable should be tight enough to resist being removed by hand.

10. Repeat steps 4–9 for the other end of the cable. Recut the end of the cable if necessary before stripping it.

11. Label each cable with the following information:
    - Wiring standard
    - Length
    - End with crossover (if any)
    - _____ (a blank) for computer ID

Figure 18.12   Carefully strip the cable jacket away to expose the four wire pairs.

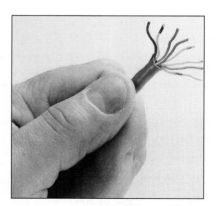

Figure 18.13   Arrange the wire pairs for insertion into the RJ-45 connector according to your chosen scheme (EIA 568B, for instance).

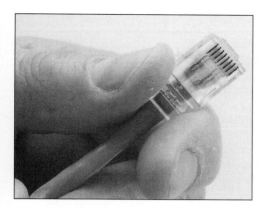

Figure 18.14 Push the RJ-45 connector into place, ensuring the cable pairs are ordered properly.

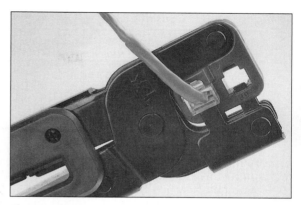

Figure 18.15 Firmly squeeze the crimping tool to attach the connector to the cable.

The cables should be labeled at both ends to make matching the cable with the correct computer easy and to facilitate troubleshooting at the hub. Check with your cable supplier for suitable labeling stock or tags you can attach to each cable.

Cable Distance Limitations

The people who design computer systems love to find ways to circumvent limitations. Manufacturers of Ethernet products have made possible the building of networks in star, branch, and tree designs that overcome the basic limitations already mentioned (for more information, see the "Wired Network Topologies" section later in this chapter). Strictly speaking, you can have thousands of computers on a complex Ethernet network.

LANs are local because the network adapters and other hardware components typically can't send LAN messages more than a few hundred feet. Table 18.7 lists the distance limitations of various types of LAN cable. In addition to the limitations shown in the table, keep the following points in mind:

- You can't connect more than 30 computers on a single Thinnet Ethernet segment.
- You can't connect more than 100 computers on a Thicknet Ethernet segment.
- You can't connect more than 72 computers on a UTP Token-Ring cable.
- You can't connect more than 260 computers on an STP Token-Ring cable.

Table 18.7   Network Distance Limitations

Network Adapter	Cable Type	Maximum	Minimum
Ethernet	10BASE-2	185m (607 ft.)	0.5m (1.6 ft.)
	10BASE-5 (drop)	50m (164 ft.)	2.5m (8.2 ft.)
	10BASE-5 (backbone)	500m (1,640 ft.)	2.5m (8.2 ft.)
	10BASE-T	100m (328 ft.)	2.5m (8.2 ft.)
	100BASE-TX	100m (328 ft.)	2.5m (8.2 ft.)
	1000BASE-TX	100m (328 ft.)	2.5m (8.2 ft.)

Table 18.7   Continued

Network Adapter	Cable Type	Maximum	Minimum
Token-Ring	STP	100m (328 ft.)	2.5m (8.2 ft.)
	UTP	45m (147 ft.)	2.5m (8.2 ft.)
ARCnet	Passive hub drop	30m (98 ft.)	Varies by cable type
	Active hub	600m (1,968 ft.)	Varies by cable type

If you have a station wired with Category 5 cable that is more than 328 feet (100 meters) from a hub, you must use a repeater. If you have two or more stations beyond the 328 feet limit of UTP Ethernet, connect them to a hub or switch that is less than 328 feet away from the primary hub or switch and connect the new hub or switch to the primary hub or switch via its uplink port. Because hubs and switches can act as repeaters, this feature enables you to extend the effective length of your network (see Figure 18.16).

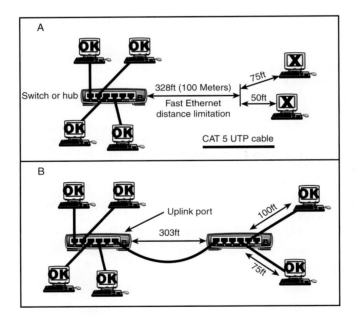

Figure 18.16   In case A (top), the workstations on the right are too far away from the hub to connect to a Fast Ethernet network. In case B (bottom), an additional hub or switch is used to allow the workstations to be added to the network.

Wired Network Topologies

Each computer on the network is connected to the other computers with cable (or some other medium, such as wireless using radio frequency signals). The physical arrangement of the cables connecting computers on a network is called the network *topology*.

Over the last 15 years the three types of basic topologies used in computer networks have been as follows:

- **Bus**—Connects each computer on a network directly to the next computer in a linear fashion. The network connection starts at the server and ends at the last computer in the network. (Obsolete.)
- **Star**—Connects each computer on the network to a central access point.
- **Ring**—Connects each computer to the others in a loop or ring. (Obsolete.)

For a long while, these different topologies were often mixed, forming what is called a *hybrid network*. For example, you can link the hubs of several star networks together with a bus, forming a star-bus network. Rings can be connected in the same way.

Table 18.8 summarizes the relationships between network types and topologies.

Table 18.8   Network Cable Types and Topologies

Network Type	Standard	Cable Type	Topology
Ethernet	10BASE-2	Thin (RG-58) coaxial	Bus
Ethernet	10BASE-5	Thick coaxial	Bus
Ethernet	10BASE-T	Cat 3 or Cat 5 UTP	Star
Fast Ethernet	100BASE-TX	Cat 5 UTP	Star
Gigabit Ethernet	1000BASE-TX	Cat 5, 5e, 6, 7 UTP	Star
Token-Ring	(all)	UTP or STP	Logical ring

The bus, star, and ring topologies are discussed in the following sections. Wireless networking, which technically doesn't have a physical topology as described here, does still employ two logical (virtual) topologies, which I discuss here as well.

Bus Topology

The earliest type of network topology was the *bus topology*, which uses a single cable to connect all the computers in the network to each other, as shown in Figure 18.17. This network topology was adopted initially because running a single cable past all the computers in the network is easier and less wiring is used than with other topologies. Because early bus topology networks used bulky coaxial cables, these factors were important advantages. Both 10BASE-5 (thick) and 10BASE-2 (thin) Ethernet networks are based on the bus topology.

However, the advent of cheaper and more compact unshielded twisted-pair cabling, which also supports faster networks, has made the disadvantages of a bus topology apparent. If one computer or cable connection malfunctions, it can cause all the stations beyond it on the bus to lose their network connections. Thick Ethernet (10BASE-5) networks often fail because the vampire tap connecting the AUI device to the coaxial cable comes loose. In addition, the T-adapters and terminating resistors on a 10BASE-2 Thin Ethernet network can also come loose or be removed by the user, causing all or part of the network to fail. Another drawback of Thin Ethernet (10BASE-2) networks is that adding a new computer to the network between existing computers might require replacement of the existing network cable between the computers with shorter segments to connect to the new computer's network card and T-adapter, thus creating downtime for users on that segment of the network.

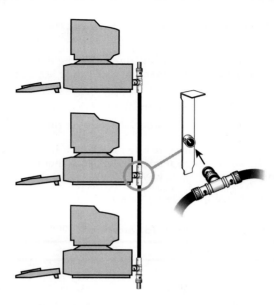

Figure 18.17   A 10BASE-2 network is an example of a linear bus topology, attaching all network devices to a common cable.

Note

Although 10BASE-2 Thin Ethernet networks are no longer common in PC installations, you might encounter them in industrial control environments. Because 10BASE-2 combines a positive-locking bayonet connector with a shielded coaxial cable, it's a better choice for rough environments than UTP or Thick Ethernet networks.

Ring Topology

Another topology often listed in discussions of this type is a *ring*, in which each workstation is connected to the next and the last workstation is connected to the first again (essentially a bus topology with the two ends connected). Two major network types use the ring topology:

- **Fiber Distributed Data Interface (FDDI)**—A network topology used for large, high-speed networks using fiber-optic cables in a physical ring topology
- **Token-Ring**—Uses a logical ring topology

A Token-Ring network resembles a 10BASE-T or 10/100 Ethernet network at first glance because both networks use a central connecting device and a physical star topology. Where is the "ring" in Token-Ring?

The ring exists only within the device that connects the computers, which is called a *multistation access unit (MSAU)* on a Token-Ring network (see Figure 18.18).

Signals generated from one computer travel to the MSAU, are sent out to the next computer, and then go back to the MSAU again. The data is then passed to each system in turn until it arrives back at the computer that originated it, where it is removed from the network. Therefore, although the physical wiring topology is a star, the data path is theoretically a ring. This is called a *logical ring*.

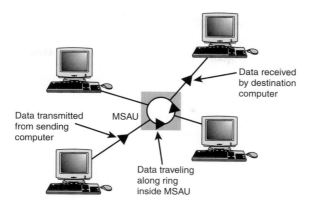

Figure 18.18   A Token-Ring network during the sending of data from one computer to another.

A logical ring that Token-Ring networks use is preferable to a physical ring network topology because it affords a greater degree of fault tolerance. As on a bus network, a cable break anywhere in a physical ring network topology, such as FDDI, affects the entire network. FDDI networks use two physical rings to provide a backup in case one ring fails. By contrast, on a Token-Ring network, the MSAU can effectively remove a malfunctioning computer from the logical ring, enabling the rest of the network to function normally.

Star Topology

By far the most popular type of topology in use today has separate cables to connect each computer to a central wiring nexus, often called a *switch* or *hub*. Figure 18.19 shows this arrangement, which is called a *star topology*.

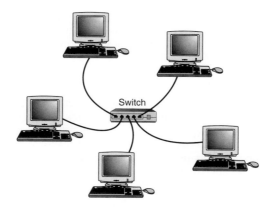

Figure 18.19   The star topology, linking the LAN's computers and devices to one or more central switches, or access units.

Because each computer uses a separate cable, the failure of a network connection affects only the single machine involved. The other computers can continue to function normally. Bus cabling schemes use less cable than the star but are harder to diagnose or bypass when problems occur. At this time, Fast Ethernet and Gigabit Ethernet in a star topology are the most commonly implemented types of wired LAN. 10BASE-T Ethernet also uses the star topology.

Switches and Hubs for Ethernet Networks

As you have seen, modern Ethernet workgroup networks—whether wireless or wired with UTP cable—are usually arranged in a star topology. The center of the star uses a multiport connecting device that can be either a hub or a switch. Although hubs and switches can be used to connect the network—and can have several features in common—the differences between them are also significant and are covered in the following sections.

All Ethernet hubs and switches have the following features:

- Multiple RJ-45 UTP connectors (wireless switches still include wired ports)
- Diagnostic and activity lights
- A power supply

Ethernet hubs and switches are made in two forms: managed and unmanaged. *Managed* hubs and switches can be directly configured, enabled or disabled, or monitored by a network operator. They are commonly used on corporate networks. Workgroup and home-office networks use less expensive *unmanaged* hubs, which simply connect computers on the network using the systems connected to it to provide a management interface for its configurable features.

Signal lights on the front of the hub or switch indicate which connections are in use by computers; switches also indicate whether a full-duplex connection is in use. Multispeed hubs and switches also indicate which connection speed is in use on each port. Your hub or switch must have at least one RJ-45 UTP connector for each computer you want to connect to it.

How Hubs Work

A computer on an Ethernet network broadcasts (sends) a request for network information or programs from a specific computer through the cable to the hub, which broadcasts the request to all computers connected to it. When the destination computer receives the message, it sends the requested information back to the hub, which broadcasts it again to all computers, although only the requesting computer acts on the information. Thus, a hub acts similarly to a radio transmitter and receiver that sends a signal to all radios, but only the radios set for the correct station can send or receive the information. Switches, due to the features explained in the next section, have replaced hubs on retail store shelves.

How Switches Differ from Hubs

Switches, as shown in Figure 18.20, are similar to hubs in both form factor and function. As with hubs, they connect computers on an Ethernet network to each other. However, instead of broadcasting data to all computers on the network as hubs do, switches use a feature called *address storing*, which checks the destination for each data packet and sends it directly to the computer for which it's intended. Thus, a switch can be compared to a telephone exchange, making direct connections between the originator of a call and the receiver.

Because switches establish a direct connection between the originating and receiving PC, they also provide the full bandwidth of the network to each port. Hubs, by contrast, must subdivide the network's bandwidth by the number of active connections on the network, meaning that bandwidth rises and falls depending on network activity.

For example, assume you have a four-station network workgroup using 10/100 NICs and a Fast Ethernet hub. The total bandwidth of the network is 100Mbps. However, if two stations are active, the effective bandwidth available to each station drops to 50Mbps (100Mbps divided by 2). If all four stations are active, the effective bandwidth drops to just 25Mbps (100Mbps divided by 4)! Add more active users, and the effective bandwidth continues to drop.

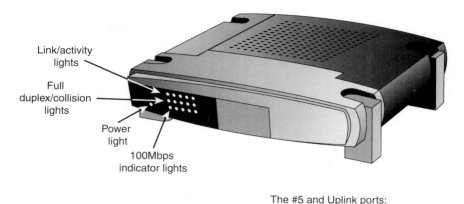

Figure 18.20 Front (top) and rear (bottom) of a typical five-port, 10/100 Ethernet switch.

By replacing the hub with a switch, the effective bandwidth for each station remains 100Mbps because the switch doesn't broadcast data to all stations.

Most 10/100 NICs and Fast Ethernet or 10/100 switches also support full-duplex (simultaneous transmit and receive), enabling actual bandwidth to be double the nominal 100Mbps rating: 200Mbps. Table 18.9 summarizes the differences between the two devices.

Table 18.9   Ethernet Hub and Switch Comparison

Feature	Hub	Switch
Bandwidth	Divided by total number of ports in use	Dedicated to each port in use
Data transmission	Broadcast to all connected computers	Broadcast only to the receiving computer
Duplex support	Half-duplex	Full-duplex when used with full-duplex NICs

As you can see, using a switch instead of a hub greatly increases the effective speed of a network, even if all other components remain the same.

Note

Both wired and wireless routers (a router connects a local area network to a device that provides Internet access, such as a cable or DSL modem) typically incorporate full-duplex 10/100 (Fast Ethernet) or 10/100/1000 (Gigabit Ethernet) switches. Thus, a router can be used in place of a switch.

◄◄   For more information about routers, see "Comparing Gateways, Proxy Servers, and Routers," p. 1143, and "Routers for Internet Sharing," p. 1144.

If you are satisfied with the performance of your network using hubs, you do not need to replace them with switches. However, keep in mind that newer network uses such as VoIP, multimedia content viewing, and others require much more performance than a hub can provide.

Additional Switch Features You Might Need

Although older hubs and switches run at only a single speed and have only a few RJ-45 connectors, it makes sense to upgrade to newer, more flexible equipment. Most recent switches have the following useful features, which are worth asking for:

- **Multispeed switches**—If you are adding Gigabit Ethernet (1000BASE-TX) or Fast Ethernet (100BASE-TX) clients to an existing 10BASE-T network, you need a multispeed switch to connect the various types of Ethernet together.

  Even if you are building a brand-new Gigabit Ethernet or Fast Ethernet network, a multispeed switch is useful for occasionally hosting a "guest" PC that has only a slower-speed NIC onboard. Even though most Gigabit Ethernet and Fast Ethernet switches on the market today are actually 10/100/1000 or 10/100 multispeed models, you might still encounter a single-speed only unit. These single-speed units should be used only on networks that will never have a need to support a slower connection.

- **Wireless access point**—Many switches today also feature a built-in wireless access point or router that supports 802.11b/g, 802.11a, or 802.11n (some access points supports 802.11b/g/n or 802.11b/a/g/n). If you plan to implement a wireless network in the future, getting a switch with a wireless access point built in now is worth the minimal increase in cost.

- **Stackable switch with an uplink port**—A *stackable* hub or switch is one that can be connected to another hub or switch (and often stacked on top of it), enabling you to add computers to your network without replacing the hub or switch every time it runs out of connections. Most switches on the market today are stackable, but some older models might lack this feature. You can use this feature to add 10/100/1000 features to an older 10BASE-T-only network and connect a multispeed switch to the uplink port on your 10BASE-T switch. The uplink port includes a built-in crossover, so you can use a standard cable.

Tip

To determine whether a switch (or hub) is stackable, look for an uplink port. This port looks like an ordinary RJ-45 UTP port, but it is wired differently, enabling you to use a standard-pinout RJ-45 UTP cable to connect it to another switch. Without the uplink port, you'd have to use a specially wired crossover cable.

- **"Extra" ports beyond your current requirements**—If you are connecting four computers together into a small network, you need a four-port switch (the smallest available). But, if you buy a switch with only four ports and want to add another client PC to the network, you must add a second switch or replace the switch with a larger one with more ports.

  Instead, plan for the future by buying a switch that can handle your projected network growth over the next year. If you plan to add two workstations, buy at least an eight-port switch (the cost per connection drops as you buy hubs and switches with more connections). Even though most hubs and switches are stackable to support the growth of your network, the more ports a hub or switch has, the less expensive per port it will be.

Note

The uplink port on your switch (or hub) is also used to connect the device to a router or gateway device that provides an Internet connection for your network. In cases where multiple switches are to be used, they are usually connected directly to the router or gateway instead of chained (or stacked) off each other.

Typically, switches (or hubs) with an uplink port allow you to use the port along with all but one of the normal ports on the switch (or hub). See Figure 18.20 for an example of a switch with an uplink port.

For example, one of my associates uses a five-port switch from Linksys that also contains a router (for Internet access) and an uplink port. If his office network expands beyond five computers, he can use the uplink port to add another switch to expand the network and provide the new stations, as well as the original network, with Internet access.

Switch Placement

Although large networks have a wiring closet near the server, the workgroup-size LANs found in a small office or home office network obviously don't require anything of the sort. However, the location of the switch is important, even if your LAN is currently based solely on a wireless Ethernet architecture.

Ethernet switches (and hubs) require electrical power, whether they are small units that use a power "brick" or larger units that have an internal power supply and a standard three-prong AC cord.

In addition to electrical power, consider placing the hub or switch where its signal lights will be easy to view for diagnostic purposes and where its RJ-45 connectors can be reached easily. This is important both when it's time to add another user or two and when you need to perform initial setup of the switch (requiring a wired connection) or need to troubleshoot a failed wireless connection. In many offices, the hub or switch sits on the corner of the desk, enabling the user to see network problems just by looking at the hub or switch.

If the hub or switch also integrates a router for use with a broadband Internet device, such as a DSL or cable modem, you can place it near the cable or DSL modem or at a distance if the layout of your home or office requires it. Because the cable or DSL modem usually connects to your computer by the same Category 5/5e/6/7 cable used for UTP Ethernet networking, you can run the cable from the cable or DSL modem to the router/switch's WAN port and connect all the computers to the LAN ports on the router/switch.

Except for the 328-ft. (100-meter) limit for all forms of UTP Ethernet (10BASE-T, 100BASE-TX, and 1000BASE-TX), distances between each computer on the network and the switch (or hub) aren't critical, so put the switch (or hub) wherever you can supply power and gain easy access.

Although wireless networks do offer more freedom in terms of placing the switch/access point, you should keep in mind the distances involved (generally up to 150 feet indoor for 802.11b/g) and any walls or devices using the same 2.4GHz spectrum that might interfere with the signal.

Tip

Decide where you plan to put your hub or switch before you buy prebuilt UTP wiring or make your own; if you move the hub or switch, some of your wiring will no longer be the correct length. Although excess lengths of UTP cable can be coiled and secured with cable ties, cables that are too short should be replaced. You can buy RJ-45 connectors to create one long cable from two short cables, but you must ensure the connectors are Category 5 if you are running Fast Ethernet; some vendors still sell Category 3 connectors that support only 10Mbps. You're really better off replacing the too-short cable with one of the correct length.

Wireless Ethernet Hardware

All types of 802.11 wireless networks have two basic components:

- Access points
- NICs equipped with radio transceivers

An *access point* is a bookend-size device that uses one or more RJ-45 ports to attach to a 10BASE-T or 10/100 Ethernet network (if desired) and contains a radio transceiver, encryption, and communications software. It translates conventional Ethernet signals into wireless Ethernet signals that it broadcasts to wireless NICs on the network and then performs the same role in reverse to transfer signals from wireless NICs to the conventional Ethernet network.

Note

In home and small-office networks that provide Internet access, the access point is usually incorporated into a wireless router that also includes an Ethernet switch.

For coverage of a large area, purchase two or more access points and connect them to an Ethernet switch. This enables users to roam inside a building without losing contact with the network. Some access points can communicate directly with each other via radio waves, enabling you to create a wireless backbone that can cover a wide area (such as a warehouse) without the need to run any network cabling. You can also purchase a wireless Ethernet range extender that can receive and boost weak Wi-Fi signals. Some access points are designed to be used as either access points or range extenders. Some range extenders are designed only to work with the same brand of access point or router.

Access points are not necessary for direct peer-to-peer networking (also called *ad hoc mode*), but they are required for a shared Internet connection or a connection with another network. When access points are used, the network is operating in the *infrastructure mode*.

Note

Wireless clients running in ad hoc mode cannot connect to the Internet unless one of the stations on the network is connected to a bridge or uses another network adapter as a bridge.

NICs equipped for wireless Ethernet communications have a fixed or detachable radio antenna. Wireless NICs come in four forms:

- CardBus (32-bit PC Card) cards for use in notebook computers that do not include "integrated" wireless support
- Mini-PCI cards that provide wireless and wired Ethernet and dial-up modem support for notebook computers
- PCI cards for use in desktop computers with PCI slots
- USB adapters for use in both desktop and notebook computers

Most notebook computers with Wi-Fi hardware onboard use the mini-PCI interface for the wireless adapter and place the antenna inside the screen housing. This enables computers with built-in Wi-Fi hardware to have one more open PC Card slot than computers that must use an external PC Card adapter and antenna.

Note

Mini-PCI cards are built into notebook computers. (They can be removed by opening a plate on the bottom of the unit and unsnapping the card.) Because mini-PCI cards are customized to the particular design of a given notebook computer, they are not sold at retail. However, when you customize a notebook computer during the buying process, the manufacturer will use different models of the card depending upon the communication features you specify. You can also buy a replacement card from the vendor's parts department.

Because you can mix and match Wi-Fi-certified products that use the same frequency band, you can incorporate any mix of desktop and notebook computers into your wireless network. Figure 18.21 illustrates typical wireless network hardware.

Figure 18.21   A typical family of Wi-Fi 2.4GHz band (802.11g) wireless products, including a wireless router, USB, CardBus, and PCI wireless network adapters. *Photos courtesy of Linksys.*

Although most recent notebook computers include 802.11g wireless Ethernet or dual-mode 802.11g/a support through an integrated mini-PCI card, you can add support for other 802.11 wireless networks through the CardBus slot or USB 2.0 port.

In cases where a Wi-Fi-enabled system receives multiple Wi-Fi signals, client systems lock onto the strongest signal from access points and automatically roam (switch) to another access point when the signal strength is stronger and the error level is lower than the current connection. Of course, if you want the system to lock onto a specific signal, that can be done via the OS or manufacturer-provided software.

Additional hardware you might need to add to your network includes the following:

- **Wireless bridges**—These devices enable you to connect a wired Ethernet device, including noncomputer items such as video games or set-top boxes, to a wireless network.

- **Wireless repeaters/range extenders**—A repeater can be used to stretch the range of an existing wireless network. Some can also be used as access points or wireless bridges.

- **Wireless router**—Use this in place of a standard access point to enable a wireless network to connect to the Internet through a cable modem or other broadband device (refer to Chapter 17, "Internet Connectivity," for details). For additional flexibility, many wireless routers also include a multiport switch for use with wired Ethernet networks, and some also include a print server.

- **Specialized antennas**—The "rabbit ears" antennas used by most access points and routers are adequate for short distances, but longer distances or problems with line-of-sight reception can be solved by attaching specialized ceiling, wall, omnidirectional, or directional antennas in place of the standard antenna.

- **Signal boosters**—In addition to or as an alternative to replacement antennas, some vendors also sell signal boosters that piggyback onto an existing access point or router. Note that, in most cases, these signal boosters are vendor specific.

Wireless Network Logical Topologies

Wireless networks have different topologies, just as wired networks do. However, wireless networks use only two logical topologies:

- **Star**—The star topology, used by Wi-Fi/IEEE 802.11–based products in the infrastructure mode, resembles the topology used by 10BASE-T and faster versions of Ethernet that use a switch (or hub). The access point takes the place of the switch because stations connect via the access point, rather than directly with each other. This method is much more expensive per unit but permits performance in excess of 10BASE-T Ethernet speeds and has the added bonus of being easier to manage.

- **Point-to-point**—Bluetooth products (as well as Wi-Fi products in the *ad hoc* mode) use the point-to-point topology. These devices connect directly with each other and require no access point or other hub-like device to communicate with each other, although shared Internet access does require that all computers connect to a common wireless gateway. The point-to-point topology is much less expensive per unit than a star topology. It is, however, best suited for temporary data sharing with another device (Bluetooth) and is currently much slower than 100BASE-TX networks.

Figure 18.22 shows a comparison of wireless networks using these two topologies.

Wireless Network Security

When I was writing the original edition of *Upgrading and Repairing PCs* twenty years ago, the hackers' favorite way of trying to get into a network without authorization was discovering the telephone number of a modem on the network, dialing in with a computer, and guessing the password, as in the movie *War Games*. Today, *war driving* has largely replaced this pastime as a popular hacker sport. War driving is the popular name for driving around neighborhoods with a notebook computer equipped with a wireless network card on the lookout for unsecured networks. They're all too easy to find, and after someone gets onto your network, all the secrets in your computer can be theirs for the taking.

Because wireless networks can be accessed by anyone within signal range who has a NIC matching the same IEEE standard of that wireless network, wireless NICs and access points provide for encryption options. Most access points (even cheaper SOHO models) also provide the capability to limit connections to the access point by using a list of authorized MAC numbers (each NIC has a unique MAC). It's designed to limit access to authorized devices only.

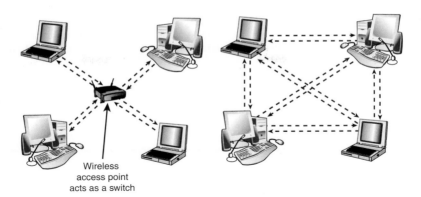

Wireless
access point
acts as a switch

Figure 18.22   A logical star topology (left) as used by IEEE 802.11–based wireless Ethernet in infrastructure
mode compared to a point-to-point topology as used by Bluetooth and 802.11 in ad hoc mode (right).

While MAC address filtering can be helpful in stopping bandwidth borrowing by your neighbors, it
cannot stop determined attacks. Linux-based systems can change the MAC addresses of their network
adapters. Consequently, you also need to look at other security features included in wireless networks,
such as encryption.

Caution

In the past, it was thought that the SSID feature provided by the IEEE 802.11 standards was also a security feature. That's
not the case. A Wi-Fi network's SSID is nothing more than a network name for the wireless network, much the same as
workgroups and domains have network names that identify them. The broadcasting of the SSID can be turned off (when
clients look for networks, they won't immediately see the SSID), which has been thought to provide a minor security benefit. However, Microsoft has determined that a non-broadcast SSID is actually a greater security risk than a broadcast SSID,
especially with Windows XP and Windows Server 2003. For details, see "Non-broadcast Wireless Networks with
Microsoft Windows" at http://www.microsoft.com/technet/network/evaluate/hiddennet.mspx. In fact, many freely available (and quite powerful) tools exist that allow snooping individuals to quickly discover your SSID even if it's not being
broadcast, allowing them to connect to your unsecured wireless network.

The only way that the SSID can provide a small measure of security for your wireless network is if you change the default
SSID provided by the wireless access point or router vendor. The default SSID typically identifies the manufacturer of the
device (and sometimes even its model number). A hacker armed with this information can look up the default password
and user name for the router or access point and the default network address range by downloading the documentation
from the vendor's website. Using this information, the hacker could compromise your network if you do not use other security measures, such as WPA or WEP encryption. By using a non-standard SSID and changing the password used by your
router's web-based configuration program, you make it a little more difficult for hackers to attack your network. Follow up
these changes by enabling the strongest form of encryption supported by your wireless network.

All Wi-Fi products support at least 40-bit encryption through the wired equivalent privacy (WEP)
specification, but the minimum standard on recent products is 64-bit WEP encryption. Many vendors
offer 128-bit or 256-bit encryption on some of their products. However, the 128-bit and stronger
encryption feature is more common among enterprise products than small-office/home-office--
oriented products. Unfortunately, the WEP specification at any encryption strength has been shown

to be notoriously insecure against determined hacking. Enabling WEP will keep a casual snooper at bay, but someone who wants to get into your wireless network won't have much trouble breaking WEP. For that reason, all wireless network products introduced after 2003 incorporate a different security standard known as Wi-Fi Protected Access (WPA). WPA is derived from the developing IEEE 802.11i security standard. WPA-enabled hardware works with existing WEP-compliant devices, and software upgrades are often available for existing devices to make them WPA capable. The latest 802.11g and 802.11n devices also support WPA2, an updated version of WPA that uses a stronger encryption method (WPA uses TKIP, and WPA2 uses AES).

Note

Unfortunately, most 802.11b wireless network hardware supports only WEP encryption. The lack of support for more powerful encryption standards is a good reason to retire your 802.11b hardware in favor of 802.11g or 802.11n Draft 2 hardware, all of which support WPA or WPA2 encryption.

Upgrading to WPA or WPA2 may also require updates to your operating system. For example, Windows XP Service Pack 2 includes support for WPA encryption. However, to use WPA2 with Windows XP Service Pack 2, you must also download the Wireless Client Update for Windows XP with Service Pack 2. At the http://support.microsoft.com website, look up Knowledge Base article 917021.You should match the encryption level and encryption type used on both the access points and the NICs for best security. Remember that if some of your network supports WPA but other parts support only WEP, your network must use the lesser of the two security standards (WEP). If you want to use the more robust WPA security, you must ensure that all the devices on your wireless network support WPA. Because WEP is easily broken and the specific WEP implementations vary among manufacturers, I recommend using only devices that support WPA or WPA2.

Management and DHCP Support

Most wireless access points can be managed via a web browser and provide diagnostic and monitoring tools to help you optimize the positioning of access points. Most products feature support for Dynamic Host Configuration Protocol (DHCP), allowing a user to move from one subnet to another without difficulties.

Figure 18.23 illustrates how a typical IEEE 802.11 wireless network uses multiple access points.

Users per Access Point

The number of users per access point varies with the product; Wi-Fi access points are available in capacities supporting anywhere from 15 to as many as 254 users. You should contact the vendor of your preferred Wi-Fi access point device for details.

Although wired Ethernet networks are still the least expensive network to build if you can do your own wiring, Wi-Fi networking is now cost-competitive with wired Ethernet networks when the cost of a professional wiring job is figured into the overall expense.

Because Wi-Fi is a true standard, you can mix and match access point and wireless NIC hardware to meet your desired price, performance, and feature requirements for your wireless network, just as you can for conventional Ethernet networks, provided you match up frequency bands or use dual-band hardware.

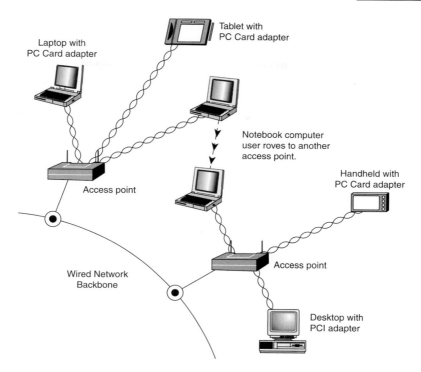

Figure 18.23   A typical wireless network with multiple access points. As users with wireless NICs move from one office to another, the roaming feature of the NIC automatically switches from one access point to another, permitting seamless network connectivity without wires or logging off the network and reconnecting.

Network Protocols

A few years ago, the second-most important choice you had to make when you created a network was which network protocol to use because the network protocol affects which types of computers your network can connect. Today, the choice has largely been made for you: TCP/IP has replaced other network protocols such as IPX/SPX (used in older versions of Novell NetWare) and NetBEUI (used in older Windows and DOS-based peer-to-peer networks and with Direct Cable Connection) because it can be used both for Internet and LAN connectivity. TCP/IP is also a universal protocol that can be used by virtually operating system.

Although data-link protocols such as Ethernet require specific types of hardware, network protocols are software and can be installed to or removed from any computer on the network at any time as necessary. Table 18.10 summarizes the differences between these protocols.

Table 18.10   Overview of Network Protocols and Suites

Protocol	Best Used for	Notes
TCP/IP	Most Windows-based networks, as well as Linux, Unix, MacOS and other networks	Native protocol suite for Windows 2000/XP/Vista; Novell NetWare 5.x and above; Linux; Unix; MacOS; also used for dial-up Internet access
IPX/SPX	Novell 4.x and earlier networks	Used by NetWare 5.x for certain special features only
NetBIOS	Older Windows for Workgroups or DOS-based peer networks	Simplest protocol; can't be routed between networks; also used with Direct Cable Connection "networking" via USB, parallel or serial ports

All the computers on any given network must use the same network protocol or protocol suite to communicate with each other.

IP and TCP/IP

IP stands for Internet Protocol; it is the network layer of the collection of protocols (or protocol suite) developed for use on the Internet and commonly known as TCP/IP (Transmission Control Protocol/Internet Protocol).

Later, the TCP/IP protocols were adopted by the Unix operating systems, and they have now become the most commonly used protocol suite on PC LANs. Virtually every operating system with networking capabilities supports TCP/IP, and it has largely displaced all the other competing protocols. Novell NetWare 6 and above, Linux, Windows XP and Windows Vista use TCP/IP as their native network protocol.

TCP/IP—LAN and Dialup Networks

TCP/IP, unlike the other network protocols listed in the previous section, is also a protocol used by people who have never seen a NIC. People who access the Internet via modems (this is referred to as Dial-Up Networking in some older Windows versions) use TCP/IP just as those whose web access is done with their existing LANs. Although the same protocol is used in both cases, the settings vary a great deal.

Table 18.11 summarizes the differences you're likely to encounter. If you access the Internet with both modems and a LAN, you must ensure that the TCP/IP properties for modems and LANs are set correctly. You also might need to adjust your browser settings to indicate which connection type you are using. Table 18.11 provides general guidelines; your ISP or network administrator can give you the specific details.

Table 18.11   TCP/IP Properties by Connection Type—Overview

TCP/IP Property Tab	Setting	Modem Access (Dialup Adapter)	LAN Access (Network Card)
IP Address	IP Address	Automatically assigned by ISP	Specified (get value from network administrator) or automatically assigned by a DHCP server on the network (DHCP servers are often built into gateways and routers)
WINS Configuration	Enable/Disable WINS Resolution	Disabled	Indicate server or enable DHCP to allow NetBIOS over TCP/IP

Table 18.11   Continued

TCP/IP Property Tab	Setting	Modem Access (Dialup Adapter)	LAN Access (Network Card)
Gateway	Add Gateway/ List of Gateways	Automatically assigned by ISP	IP address of gateway used to connect LAN to Internet
DNS Configuration	Enable/Disable Host Domain	Automatically assigned by ISP	Enabled, with host and domain specified (get value from network administrator)

As you can see from Table 18.11, correct settings for LAN access to the Internet and dialup networking (modem) settings are almost always completely different. In general, the best way to get your dialup networking connection working correctly is to use your ISP's automatic setup software. This is usually supplied as part of your ISP's signup software kit. After the setup is working, view the properties and record them for future troubleshooting use.

Note

In Windows 98 and Me, Microsoft recommends that TCP/IP properties be viewed through the Dial-Up Networking icon for the connection, rather than through the Network icon in the Control Panel. This is because different dialup connections could use different TCP/IP properties, which would override the default properties for the Dial-Up Adapter listing in the Network properties.

In Windows 2000 and XP, all types of networking are viewed and configured through a single interface. Windows Vista also uses a single interface that also controls folder sharing and network discovery (also known as Universal Plug and Play).

IPX

The IPX protocol suite (often referred to as IPX/SPX) is the collective term for the proprietary protocols Novell created for its NetWare operating system. Although based loosely on some of the TCP/IP protocols, Novell privately holds the IPX protocol standards. However, this has not prevented Microsoft from creating its own IPX-compatible protocol for the Windows operating systems.

IPX (Internetwork Packet Exchange) itself is a network layer protocol that is equivalent in function to IP. The suite's equivalent to TCP is the Sequenced Packet Exchange (SPX) protocol, which provides connection-oriented, reliable service at the transport layer.

The IPX protocols typically are used today only on networks with NetWare servers running older versions of NetWare and often are installed along with another protocol suite, such as TCP/IP. Novell has phased out its use of IPX for NetWare support and switched to TCP/IP—along with the rest of the networking industry—starting with NetWare 5. NetWare 5 uses IPX/SPX only for specialized operations. Most of the product uses TCP/IP. NetWare version 6 and above use TCP/IP exclusively.

NetBEUI

NetBIOS Extended User Interface (NetBEUI) is a protocol that was used primarily on small Windows NT networks, as well as on peer networks based on Windows for Workgroups and Windows 9x. It was the default protocol in Windows NT 3.1, the first version of that operating system. Later versions, however, use the TCP/IP protocols as their default.

NetBEUI is a simple protocol that lacks many of the features that enable protocol suites such as TCP/IP to support networks of almost any size. NetBEUI is not routable, so it can't be used on large internetworks. It is suitable for small peer-to-peer networks, but the last Windows versions to include it as a normal component were Windows Me and Windows 2000. Windows XP does not install NetBEUI as part of its standard network components, but it can be installed from the Windows XP CD. Windows Vista does not support (or include) NetBEUI.

Note

For more information on installing and using NetBEUI in Windows XP, see the Microsoft Knowledge Base article "How to install NetBEUI on Windows XP" (article number 301041) available at http://support.microsoft.com

NetBEUI is still useful for creating "instant networks" with the Direct Cable Connection, and it is the minimum protocol required for use in a Windows 9x peer-to-peer network.

Other Home Networking Solutions

If you are working at home or in a small office, you have an alternative to hole-drilling; pulling specialized network cabling; and learning how to configure TCP/IP, IPX, or NetBEUI protocols.

So-called "home" networking is designed to minimize the complexities of cabling and protocol configuration by providing users with a sort of instant network that requires no additional wiring and configures with little technical understanding.

The two major standards in this area are

- HomePNA (uses existing telephone wiring)
- HomePlug (uses existing powerlines and outlets)

HomePNA

Other than using Ethernet (wired or wireless), the most popular form of home networking involves adapting existing telephone wiring to networking by running network signals at frequencies above those used by the telephone system. Because it is the most developed and most broadly supported type of home networking, this discussion focuses on the HomePNA standards the Home Phoneline Networking Alliance (www.homepna.org) has created. This alliance has most of the major computer hardware and telecommunications vendors among its founding and active membership.

Note

The http://www.homepna.com website focuses on products using HomePNA standards, but is very out-of-date. For the most up-to-date product information, see the HomePNA website at http://www.homepna.org.

The Home Phoneline Networking Alliance has developed three versions of its HomePNA standard. HomePNA 1.0, introduced in 1998, ran at only 1Mbps, and was quickly superseded by HomePNA 2.0 in late 1999. HomePNA 2.0 supported up to 32Mbps, although most products ran at 10Mbps, bringing it to parity with 10BASE-T Ethernet. Although some vendors produced HomePNA 1.0 and 2.0 products, these versions of HomePNA never became very popular. Both of these products use a bus topology that runs over existing telephone wiring, and are designed for PC networking only.

With the development of HomePNA 3.1, the emphasis of HomePNA has shifted from strictly PC networking to a true "digital home" solution that incorporates PCs, set-top boxes, TVs and other multimedia hardware on a single network.

HomePNA 3.1 and the Digital Home

HomePNA 3.1 is the latest version of the HomePNA standard. In addition to telephone wiring, HomePNA 3.1 also supports coaxial cable used for services such as TV, set-top boxes and IP phones. HomePNA 3.1 incorporates both types of wiring into a single network (see Figure 18.24) that runs at speeds up to 320Mbps, carries voice, data, and IPTV service, and provides guaranteed quality of service (QoS) to avoid data collisions and avoid disruptions to VoIP and streaming media. HomePNA refers to the ability to carry VoIP, IPTV, and data as a "triple-play." HomePNA 3.1 also supports remote management of the network by the service provider.

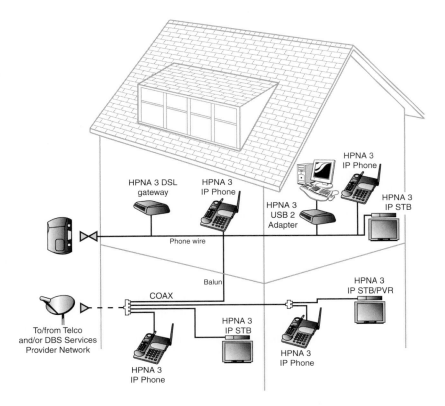

Figure 18.24   A typical HomePNA 3.1 network interconnecting PC, telephone, and TV service via telephone and coaxial cables.

Because HomePNA 3.1 has been designed to handle a mixture of traditional data and Internet telephone (VoIP) and TV (IPTV) service, HomePNA 3.1 hardware is being installed and distributed by telephone and media providers, rather than being sold primarily through retail channels. For example, AT&T uses HomePNA 3.1 for its AT&T U-verse IPTV, broadband, and forthcoming VoIP service.

Note

For more information about AT&T U-verse, see the AT&T U-verse website at https://uverse1.att.com/launchAMSS.do. AT&T U-verse users and others share information at the UverseUsers website (http://www.uverseusers.com).

◄◄ For more information about sharing Internet access and broadband Internet devices, see Chapter 17, "Internet Connectivity," p. 1103.

Powerline Networking

Home networking via power lines has been under development for several years, but electrical interference, inconsistent voltage, and security issues made the creation of a workable standard difficult until mid-2001. In June 2001, the HomePlug Powerline Alliance, a multivendor industry trade group, introduced its HomePlug 1.0 specification for 14Mbps home networking using power lines. The HomePlug Powerline Alliance (www.homeplug.org) conducted field tests in about 500 households early in 2001 to develop the HomePlug 1.0 specification.

HomePlug 1.0 is based on the PowerPacket technology developed by Intellon. PowerPacket uses a signaling method called *orthogonal frequency division multiplexing (OFDM)*, which combines multiple signals at different frequencies to form a single signal for transmission. Because OFDM uses multiple frequencies, it can adjust to the constantly changing characteristics of AC power. To provide security, PowerPacket also supports 56-bit DES encryption and an individual key for each home network. By using PowerPacket technology, HomePlug 1.0 is designed to solve the power quality and security issues of concern to a home or small-office network user. Although HomePlug 1.0 is rated at 14Mbps, typical real-world performance is usually around 4Mbps for LAN applications and around 2Mbps when connected to a broadband Internet device such as a cable modem.

HomePlug 1.0 products include USB and Ethernet adapters, bridges, and routers, enabling most recent PCs with USB or Ethernet ports to use powerline networking for LAN and Internet sharing. Linksys was the first to introduce HomePlug 1.0 products in late 2001; other leading vendors producing HomePlug hardware include Phonex, NetGear, and Asoka. HomePlug Turbo, an updated version of the HomePlug 1.0 standard, supports data rates up to 85Mbps, with typical throughput in the 15-20Mbps range.

An improved HomePlug AV specification with support for faster speeds (up to 200Mbps), multimedia hardware, and guaranteed bandwidth for multimedia applications was announced in the fall of 2002; the final HomePlug AV specification was approved in August 2005.

The HomePlug Powerline Alliance is also developing standards for broadband over power line (BPL) and for command and control of household lighting and appliances (CC). As a consequence, a new certification mark has been developed to indicate which HomePlug certifications are supported by a particular device. Figure 18.25 shows the original and new HomePlug certification marks.

Figure 18.25   The HomePlug Powerline Alliance certification marks. The original mark (left) for HomePlug 14Mbps network devices only is being replaced by the new multi-purpose mark (right).

Putting Your Network Together

You've bought or built your cables, bought your NICs and hub, and located your Windows disc. Now it's time to make your network a reality!

In this section is a detailed checklist of the hardware and software you need to build your network.

First, start with the number of computers you plan to network together. You need the items discussed in the following sections to set up your network.

Network Adapter

You need a network adapter for every computer on the network that doesn't have a network port or wireless network adapter already included; if the computer has a built-in network port or wireless network adapter, be sure it will work with your network.

Traditionally, network adapters are also called *network interface cards (NICs)*, but the widespread use of USB devices and built-in ports makes this term less accurate. To simplify technical support, use the same model of NIC for each computer in your network (if possible). If you are creating a Windows Server or Novell NetWare network with a dedicated server, you should buy server-optimized NICs for the server and less-expensive client NICs for the client PCs. However, you should still purchase the same brand to simplify support issues. Some vendors use the same driver for both their server and client NICs, further simplifying your support issue.

For the best performance, I recommend that you use PCI-Express based NICs for desktop computers or ExpressCard NICs for notebook computers with ExpressCard slots. (ExpressCard includes the PCI-Express bus.) If these slots are not available, use PCI or CardBus.

USB devices are more convenient, but USB 1.1 devices are much slower than 10/100 Ethernet. USB 2.0 devices are a satisfactory substitute for 10/100 Ethernet but require that both the computer and the device be USB 2.0–compliant to achieve the 480Mbps speed of USB 2.0. If either the device or the computer is only USB 1.1–compliant, the connection is limited to 12Mbps.

You should record the brand name and model number of the network adapters you are using, as well as the driver version or source. Use Table 18.12 in the "Recording Information About Your Network" section, later in this chapter, as a template for storing this information.

Installing the Network Adapter

Before you can connect computers to the network, you must install network adapters. If the network adapter is an internal card, follow this procedure:

1. Open the case and locate an open expansion slot that matches the type of NIC you purchased (preferably PCI or PCI-Express).
2. Using a screwdriver, remove the screw securing the slot cover at the rear of the case.
3. Insert the card gently, ensuring that the edge connector is seated solidly in the slot.
4. Fasten down the card with the same screw that held the slot cover.

▶▶ See Figures 20.26 and 20.27 in Chapter 20, "Building or Upgrading Systems," p. 1330, for an example of installing an add-on card.

Tip

If you are a realist like me, you might not want to close the case until you are certain the NIC is working (see the next section, "Testing Your Network Adapters and Connections").

A NIC uses the same hardware configuration settings most other expansion cards use:

- An IRQ
- An I/O port address range

Note

Some older network cards might require an upper memory block range for RAM buffers. Cards used on diskless workstations use a boot ROM, which also requires an upper memory block range. See your network card's documentation to find out whether this issue applies to you.

If you are using Windows 9x or newer with a PnP (Plug and Play) BIOS and a PnP NIC, the computer and Windows configure your card for you in most cases. In a few cases, you might need to adjust PnP settings in the BIOS, and in a rare case you might even need to remove your other PnP cards and put the NIC in first if your system doesn't recognize it after you restart the system.

◀◀ For general BIOS information, see Chapter 5, "BIOS," p. 441, or see your system manual for details about your computer's BIOS.

If you install the card in a non-PnP system or under Windows NT, be sure the card comes with configuration software or manual switch settings for hardware configuration. A pure PnP card can't be installed on a system that lacks PnP support.

USB and PC Card/CardBus network adapters are automatically detected and installed when connected because USB ports and PC Card/CardBus slots are hot-swap connections.

And, if you are using an older network adapter with Windows XP, you might need to download drivers from the adapter vendors' websites. Even if you have drivers for your current version of Windows, getting the latest driver release will help you avoid setup and installation problems.

Windows Vista includes a large library of network adapter drivers, but it doesn't include drivers for some older network adapters. However, you can use Windows XP drivers if Windows Vista drivers are not available.

Testing Your Network Adapters and Connections

The configuration software disc included with the network adapter usually features diagnostic software. Some diagnostics should be performed before the card is connected to the network and should be run from a command prompt.

After the network adapter passes these tests, connect the network adapter to the network. With an Ethernet network using UTP cable, run the cable from the card to the hub or switch, turn on the computer and hub, and watch for signal lights to light up on the NIC's back bracket (if so equipped) and on the hub or switch. Hubs and switches use green LEDs to indicate the presence of a computer on a particular RJ-45 port. Connect a second computer with a NIC installed to the hub or switch. Then, run the diagnostics program on both computers to send and receive data. For other types of networks, see the diagnostics provided with the network hardware for testing details.

Cables and Connections Between Computers

Depending on the network architecture you choose, you might need to run cables. If you are installing a 100BASE-TX or 1000BASE-TX Ethernet network (both of which use UTP cables), you need cables that are long enough to reach comfortably between each computer's network port and the network's hub or switch. Use Table 18.11 in the "Recording Information About Your Network" section, later in this chapter, as a template for storing this information.

Because HomePNA networks are based on your existing telephone line, the patch cord included with the NIC is usually long enough to connect with your existing RJ-11 telephone jack. The HomePNA NIC has two jacks: one for the connection to the telephone line and the other to enable you to connect your telephone to the NIC. Be sure you use the correct jack for each cable; otherwise, your network won't work. HomePNA enables you to use your telephone system for voice and networking at the same time.

Wireless network NICs use an external antenna to make the connection between computers. In some cases, the antenna is built into the NIC, whereas in other cases the antenna is attached to the NIC or needs to be extended from a storage position inside the NIC.

Hub/Switch/Access Point

UTP Ethernet networks require a hub or switch if more than two computers will be networked (you can use a crossover cable between two computers only). Wireless Ethernet networks also require an access point if more than two computers will be networked, or if the network will be used to share an Internet connection.

For a UTP-based Ethernet network, buy a hub or switch (preferred) of the correct speed with at least enough RJ-45 ports for each computer on the network. For a wireless Ethernet network, you will need at least one access point, depending on the range of your wireless network. Most IEEE 802.11b/g network access points have a range of 150 feet indoors (and up to 300 feet outdoors), which should be adequate for most homes and many small businesses. You can add more access points if you need a wider area of coverage or use a larger antenna.

If you are going to use the network to share Internet access, you can save money if you buy a router that contains a switch for a wired Ethernet network or a wireless access point that contains a router for a wireless Ethernet network.

Use Table 18.12 in the "Recording Information About Your Network" section as a template for storing this information. Table 18.12 also provides a space for recording whether you plan to use the network for Internet sharing.

Gateways for Non-Ethernet Networks

If you plan to share Internet access through a non-Ethernet network such as HomePNA or HomePlug and you don't want to use a software-sharing solution such as Microsoft Internet Connection Sharing, you must install a gateway or router between the broadband device (such as a cable or DSL modem) and your network. Some gateway/router devices can also act as print servers; in addition, some, such as those from 2Wire, support HomePNA, Ethernet, or Wi-Fi networks.

Recording Information About Your Network

Networks are terrific when they work, but they're a potential nightmare when they fail. By keeping careful notes about network configuration, you can reinstall network drivers, set up new computers on the network, and handle other network crises without breaking a sweat.

Use the worksheet shown in Table 18.12 as a guide for recording information about your network hardware.

Table 18.12   Network Hardware Worksheet

Network Type:	Number of Stations:	Internet Sharing:	
Computer Location/ID:	Brand Name/Model:	NIC Brand/Model:	Speed:
Driver:	Cable Type/ Wiring Standard:	Cable Length:	
Hub/Switch /Location/ID:	Hub/Switch Brand Model:	Hub/Switch Speed:	
No. Ports:	Hub or Switch:		
Router Location/ID:	Router Brand/Model:	Router Speed:	
No. Ports:	Router IP Address:	Router Password:	

Installing Networking Software

To access network resources with a PC—whether it is connected to a client/server or peer-to-peer network—you must install network client software on the computer. The network client can be part of the operating system or a separate product, but it is this software that enables the system to use the network interface adapter to communicate with other machines.

On a properly configured network workstation, accessing network resources is no different from accessing local ones (except that they might be slightly slower). You can open a file on a network drive just as you would open the same file on your local hard disk. This is because the network client software is completely integrated into every level of the computer's operating system.

In most cases, the network client software is part of the operating system. Windows 9x, NT, 2000, XP and Vista, for example, include all the software you need to participate in a peer-to-peer Windows network or to connect to Windows NT, Windows 2000, Windows Server 2003, Windows Server 2008 ("Longhorn Server") and Novell NetWare servers. To connect to a network using DOS or Windows 3.1, however, you must install a separate client software package.

When you install a NIC under Windows 95 or Windows 98, the following network protocols are installed by default:

- NetBEUI
- TCP/IP
- IPX/SPX

Windows Me, Windows 2000, Windows XP, and Windows Vista use TCP/IP by default. If you need to install particular protocols or other network components, use the Networks icon in the Windows Control Panel or right-click the Network Neighborhood (Windows 9x) or My Network Places (Windows Me/2000) icon on the Windows desktop and select Properties.

Configuring Your Network Software

You might have a few problems installing your NICs. They might pass their diagnostics flawlessly, but until each station on your network can speak the same language, has correct client or server software setups, and uses the same protocols, your network will not function properly.

Table 18.13 shows the minimum network software configuration you must install for Windows 9x/Me, Windows NT, Windows 2000, and Windows XP peer-to-peer networking. Windows Vista uses the Network and Sharing Center to configure peer-to-peer networking.

Table 18.13   Minimum Network Software for Peer-to-Peer Networking

Item	Workstation	Server
Windows Network client	Yes	No
NetBEUI or TCP/IP* protocol	Yes	Yes
File and print sharing for Microsoft Networks	No	Yes
NIC installed and bound to protocols and services above	Yes	Yes
Workgroup identification (same for all PCs in workgroup)	Yes	Yes
Computer name (each PC needs a unique name)	Yes	Yes

If TCP/IP is used as the standard protocol, each workstation must have a different IP address—either manually assigned or received from a DHCP server built into a server, router, or gateway computer or device.

▶▶ For more information about Windows Vista and networks, see "Networking with Windows Vista," p. 1202.

Although the networking settings in Table 18.13 enable a Windows peer-to-peer network to function, you might need to add more networking components. If the computer can access a Novell NetWare client/server network running NetWare 4.x, the IPX/SPX protocol must also be installed. It also might be required for certain operations with NetWare 5. If the computer is used to access the Internet or any other TCP/IP-based network, the TCP/IP protocol must also be installed. In most cases, you can now use TCP/IP as the only network protocol because it can be used for both Internet and LAN access.

Use the Network icon in the Windows Control Panel to select your network settings. To set up your network, you'll need the operating system CDs, disks, or hard-disk image files and the network adapter drivers. (Workgroup hubs and switches require no software.)

To install a network component, follow this procedure:

1. Open the Network icon in the Control Panel.
2. The Configuration tab is displayed; select Add.
3. Select from the following:
   - **Client**—Select if you want to install the Microsoft or other network clients for your network. Every PC on a peer-to-peer network needs the Client for Microsoft Networks.
   - **Adapter**—This should already be installed, but you can use this option to install a new adapter.
   - **Protocol**—For a simple, non-Internet network with versions of Windows before XP, install NetBEUI. If you want to use Internet Connection Sharing along with networking, install both TCP/IP and NetBEUI. With Windows XP, use the Network Setup Wizard to configure TCP/IP easily.

■ **Service**—Install File and Printer Sharing for Microsoft Networks on any computer that will be used as a server.

4. Click the Identification tab. Enter a unique name for each computer on the network; use the same workgroup name for all computers on the network.

5. Click OK. Supply the Windows CD-ROM or other media as necessary to install the network components you requested.

6. You are prompted to insert a CD or disk or browse to the appropriate files during the installation procedure, if they're not available on the Windows CD-ROM or on your hard disk in the default location.

You might need to reboot your PC to complete the process, particularly if you're using Windows 9x or Me. After this is completed, you'll be ready to share resources.

After the network hardware and software installation is complete, your network is ready to use. However, if you are using Windows NT, Windows 2000, or Windows XP Professional, you must set up users and groups for security. Windows 9x, Me, and Windows XP Home Edition use peer-to-peer access control, which can be protected with passwords if you desire.

For more information about these processes, see "Configuring Users, Groups, and Resources" in the Technical Reference section of the disc packaged with this book.

Networking with Windows Vista

Although Windows Vista includes TCP/IP as its default protocol, enabling it to connect to other computers running Windows or other operating systems, its network management and configuration processes are much different than those used by earlier Windows versions.

Network management is performed through the new Network and Sharing Center. The Network and Sharing Center displays the status of the network, signal strength for wireless networks, and the status of network discovery and the sharing of files, the Public folder (Vista's equivalent to the Shared Files folder), printer sharing and media sharing. The Network and Sharing Center can change these settings as desired and also controls whether password-protected sharing is enabled or disabled. When disabled, Vista acts like Windows XP Professional when the default simple file sharing feature is enabled. When enabled, you must set up users and assign them rights as with Windows 2000 Professional or Windows XP Professional with simple file sharing disabled.

The Network and Sharing Center can also provide a map of your network, showing the relationship of devices such as routers and switches and Windows Vista-based computers on the network. To add Windows XP-based systems to the network map, you can install the Link Layer Topology Discoverer (LLTD) responder. To get this feature and learn how it works, look up Knowledge Base article 922120, "Network Map in Windows Vista does not display computers that are running Windows XP," at http://support.microsoft.com.

To add a protocol or component to a particular network connection, open Networks, select Network and Sharing Center, and select Manage Network Connections from the task list. Right-click the network adapter and select Properties.

Other differences include enhancements in the use and management of wireless networks, improvements to the Windows Firewall, and improvements in the network repair and diagnostics procedure. Windows Vista also adds support for network projectors and online meetings, using its new People Near Me and Windows Meeting Space utilities.

To learn more about networking in Windows Vista, I recommend the book *Special Edition Using Windows Vista* by Robert Cowart and Brian Knittel (Que Publishing, ISBN: 0789734729), as well as

Upgrading and Repairing Windows, Second Edition, by Scott Mueller and Brian Knittel (Que, ISBN: 0789736950).

Tips and Tricks

Network configuration can take a long time unless you have a few tricks up your sleeve. Use this section to help you find faster, easier, and better ways to set up and use your network.

Installation

- If you are setting up several systems with identical hardware, NICs, and software, consider making an image file of the first system after you complete its installation with a program such as Drive Image Professional and then connecting the other computers and "cloning" the first computer's hard disk to each additional system. Check with the imaging software vendor for details.

- Don't click OK in the Windows Networks properties sheet until you have made all the changes you want to make (see the previous list) on a Windows 9x or Me system. Whenever you click OK, you are prompted to reboot the system to apply the changes.

- If you're salvaging old 10BASE-T Ethernet cards for a network, use Category 5 UTP and dual-speed hubs to make switching to Fast Ethernet in the future easier. I recommend this only if your systems use ISA cards; new 10/100 Ethernet cards cost less than $20 each.

Sharing Resources

- If you want to have network drives or folders show up as part of My Computer (known as Computer in Windows Vista) so you can search them and see them easily in Windows Explorer, map a drive letter to each one. This step is desirable with any combination of operating systems and is a virtual necessity on networks in which Windows 2000, XP, or Vista computers are accessing shared resources on a Windows 9x computer. Browsing the network is very slow without mapped drives, but access to shares through a mapped drive letter is very fast.

- To more easily keep drive mappings straight, I use the drive letter I plan to use for mapping on other workstations as the name of the shared resource on my peer server. In other words, if I want to map the D: drive on my peer server as "P:", I name it "P" when I set its sharing properties. Then, as I view the folder from another computer, I know from its name that I should map it as "P:". This enables multiple PCs to easily map the same resource as the same drive letter on different systems, which makes it easier if people in your office play musical computers.

Setting Up Security

- If you're building a peer-to-peer network, keep in mind that security varies according to the operating system(s) used. Passwords are implemented on a resource-by-resource basis in Windows 9x/Me, but on a user or group basis in Windows 2000, XP Professional, and Windows Vista. (Windows XP Professional requires you to disable Simple File Sharing before you can set up users and groups.) Windows XP Home Edition does not support passwords, making it the least secure peer server operating system of any recent Windows version.

- Create a group of several users and assign rights on a group basis when you have several users who need the same access rights.

Sharing Internet Connections

- If you are planning to share an Internet connection using Microsoft Internet Connection Sharing or other computer-based sharing programs, *don't* set up File and Printer Sharing on the computer that does the sharing (the proxy server or gateway computer); share drives on other computers instead, or install a self-contained network storage device. You can use Windows Firewall in Windows XP SP2 or Windows Vista to protect your computer from inbound threats. However, you will also want to refer to Chapter 17 for third-party software you can add to your computer to keep it safe on the Internet from both inbound and outbound threats.

■ Routers and gateway devices are an economical way to share broadband access in a home or small office, and they are easier to manage and more reliable than using ICS or other sharing programs. Routers and gateways can also act as firewalls to protect your computer from unauthorized access from the Internet.

Direct Cable Connections

Direct Cable Connection is a technology that enables you to connect two PCs together via their serial, parallel, or IR ports to make an instant network. Windows 9x, Me, 2000, and XP all include Direct Connect client and server software, but special parallel (preferred) or serial cables are required; IR (infrared) ports on notebook computers can also be used for direct connections. See the section "Direct Cable Connections" in Chapter 17, "Local Area Networking," of *Upgrading and Repairing PCs, 12th Edition*, for details.

Direct Cable Connection is not included as part of Windows Vista. However, data files, user settings, and (in some cases) applications can be transferred between Windows XP and Vista systems (or between Windows Vista systems) by using a new Windows Vista feature known as Windows Easy Transfer along with a USB Easy Transfer Cable. Network and disk-based transfer methods are also supported. To transfer applications, download and use the Windows Easy Transfer Companion from the Microsoft Download Center at http://www.microsoft.com/downloads. Windows Easy Transfer for Windows XP can also be downloaded from this site.

Troubleshooting a Network

The following sections list a series of common networking problems along with solutions that can usually set things right again.

Network Software Setup

Problem

Duplicate computer names.

Solution

Make sure that every computer on the network has a unique name. Otherwise, you'll get an error message when you reboot the workstations with networking cables attached. (You can change the computer name from the System applet of the Control Panel, although you must restart the system for it to be effective.)

Problem

Different workgroup names.

Solution

Make sure every computer that's supposed to be working together has the same workgroup name. The Windows 9x/NT Network Neighborhood and Windows Me/2000/XP My Network Places icons display computers by workgroup name. In Windows Vista, use the Network Explorer. Different workgroup names actually create different workgroups, and you'd need to access them by browsing via Entire Network. You can also make this change from the System applet, although it, too, requires rebooting the system to become effective.

Problem

Shared resources are not available.

Solution

Make sure that shared resources have been set for any servers on your network (including peer servers on Windows). If you can't share a resource through Windows Explorer on the peer server, ensure that File and Printer Sharing has been installed. In Windows Vista, enable file and printer sharing through the Network and Sharing Center.

Problem

Network doesn't work after making changes.

Solution

Did you reboot? Any change in the Network icon in Windows 9x/Me Control Panel requires a system reboot!

Did you log in? Any network resources can't be accessed unless you log in when prompted. You can use Start, Shutdown, and Close All Programs and Logon As a New User with Windows 9x/Me to recover quickly from a failure to log on.

Networks in Use

Problem

A user can't access any shared resources (but others can).

Solution

First, have the user log off and log back on. Pressing Cancel or Esc instead of logging in would keep a user off the network.

Next, check cable connections at the server and workstation. Loose terminators or BNC T-connectors can cause trouble for all workstations on a Thinnet cable segment. A loose or disconnected RJ-45 cable affects only the computer (or hub) using it. If a Category 5 UTP cable seems to be connected tightly but the user still can't get on the network, check the cable with a cable tester or replace the cable.

Problem

Wrong access level.

Solution

If you save your passwords in a password cache, entering the read-only password instead of the full-access password limits your access with peer servers. Try unsharing the resource and try to reshare it, or have the user of that peer server set up new full-access and read-only passwords. Alternatively, don't use password caching by unchecking the Save Password box when you log onto a shared resource. With a client/server network with user lists and rights, check with your network administrator because she will need to change the rights for you. On a peer network that uses user lists, check with the administrator of each computer with shared resources to add your user name and appropriate access rights to the computer.

TCP/IP

Problem

Incorrect settings in Network Properties.

Solution

Get the correct TCP/IP settings from the administrator and enter them; restart the PC if you're using Windows 9x. Windows 2000 and newer do not require the PC to be restarted after changing TCP/IP settings.

Problem

Can't keep connection running in Dial-Up Networking.

Solution

You might have the wrong version of PPP running; change the server type in Properties under Dial-Up Networking, not Networks.

Problem

Message about duplicate IP addresses—can't connect to anything.

Solution

Duplicate IP addresses disable both TCP/IP and NetBEUI networking. Internet sharing products such as ICS, third-party sharing programs, and routers are usually configured to assign IP addresses automatically to avoid duplication. If some computers on a network have fixed IP addresses and others have dynamically assigned IP addresses, conflicts could occur. The entire network should use dynamic IP addressing (DHCP) or each computer should be assigned a unique IP address.

Problem

No error message—can't connect to Internet or other computers.

Solution

Check the router, switch, or hub used to connect the computers to each other and the Internet. It needs to be powered, and the data cables must be properly connected between it and each PC (and between the Internet connection and the switch or hub, if applicable).

If your network uses DHCP to dynamically assign IP addresses and the router has lost power or connection, users won't have valid IP addresses. Restart the router, and have all users log off and shut down. When they restart their systems, they should be able to obtain valid IP addresses and connect with each other.

Power Supplies

Considering the Importance of the Power Supply

The power supply is not only one of the most important parts in a PC, but it is unfortunately also one of the most overlooked. The power supply, in the words of the late Rodney Dangerfield, gets no respect! People spend hours discussing their processor speeds, memory capacity, disk storage capacity and speed, video adapter performance, monitor size, and so forth, but rarely even mention or consider their power supply. When a system is put together to meet the lowest possible price point, what component do you think the manufacturer skimps on? Yes, the power supply. To most people, the power supply is a rather unglamorous metal box that sits inside their systems, something to which they pay virtually no attention at all. The few who do pay any mind seem concerned only with how many watts of power it is rated to put out (even though no practical way exists to verify those ratings), without regard to whether the power being produced is clean and stable or whether it is full of noise, spikes, and surges.

I have always placed great emphasis on selecting a power supply for my systems. I consider the power supply the core of the system and am willing to spend more to get a more robust and reliable unit. The power supply is critical because it supplies electrical power to every other component in the system. In my experience, the power supply is also one of the most failure-prone components in any computer system. I have replaced more power supplies in PCs than any other part. This is especially due to the fact that, to keep system prices down, many system builders use the cheapest power supplies they can find. A malfunctioning power supply not only can cause other components in the system to malfunction, but also can damage the other components in your computer by delivering improper or erratic voltages. Because of its importance to proper and reliable system operation, you should understand both the function and limitations of a power supply, as well as its potential problems and their solutions.

This chapter covers the power supply in detail. I focus on the electrical functions of the supply and the mechanical form factors and physical designs that have been used in PC systems in the past, as well as today. Because the physical shape (*form factor*) of the power supply relates to the case, some of this information also relates to the type of chassis or case you have.

The industry-standard ATX power supply used in PCs has been evolving, with new connectors appearing on newer power supplies as well as motherboards and video cards. There are adapters to convert the new power connectors to the old ones (and vice versa). However, in most cases these adapters aren't necessary because, by virtue of their design, several of the old and new connectors are actually compatible. For those who are either building new systems from scratch or upgrading and repairing existing systems, knowledge of the new connectors and how you can almost always build, upgrade, or repair a system without purchasing unnecessary adapters will be invaluable. This chapter examines the evolutionary changes to the ATX power supply connectors and highlights the new connectors designed for the latest systems.

Primary Function and Operation

The basic function of the power supply is to convert the electrical power available at the wall socket to that which the computer circuitry can use. The power supply in a conventional desktop system is designed to convert either 120-volt (nominal) 60Hz AC (alternating current) or 240V (nominal) 50Hz AC power into +3.3V, +5V, and +12V DC (direct current) power. Some power supplies require you to switch between the two input ranges, whereas others auto-switch.

Technically, the power supply in most PCs is described as a *constant voltage switching power supply*, which is defined as follows:

- *Constant voltage* means the power supply puts out the same voltage to the computer's internal components, no matter the voltage of AC current running it or the capacity (wattage) of the power supply.

- *Switching* refers to the design and power regulation technique that most suppliers use. Compared to other types of power supplies, this design provides an efficient and inexpensive power source and generates a minimum amount of heat. It also maintains a small size and low price.

Positive DC Voltages

Usually, the digital electronic components and circuits in the system (motherboard, adapter cards, and disk drive logic boards) use the +3.3V or +5V power, and the motors (disk drive motors and any fans) use the +12V power. Table 19.1 lists these devices and their power consumptions.

Table 19.1 Power Consumption Ratings for PC Devices

Voltage	Devices Powered
+3.3V	Chipsets, DIMMs, PCI/AGP/PCIe cards, miscellaneous chips
+5V	Disk drive logic, low-voltage motors, SIMMs, PCI/AGP cards, ISA cards, voltage regulators, miscellaneous chips
+12V	Motors, high output voltage regulators, AGP/PCIe cards

Voltage Rails

Each of the voltages generated by the power supply is normally delivered to the motherboard over multiple wires connected to the same source circuit (called a *rail* or *tap*) inside the supply. Multiple wires are used because, if all of the current were carried over a single wire, the wire and the terminals, connectors, and even the traces on the circuit boards would all have to be extremely large and thick to handle the load. Instead, it is cheaper and more efficient to spread the load out among multiple smaller and thinner wires instead.

You can think of each rail as a separate power circuit, kind of like a power supply within the power supply. Normally each rail is rated for a specified maximum amount of current in amperes. Because the extreme amount of 12V current required by newer CPU voltage regulators and high-end video cards can exceed the output of common 12V rails, some power supply designs use multiple +12V rails. This means that essentially they have two separate 12V circuits internally, with some wires tapping off of the first circuit and others tapping off of the second. Unfortunately, this can lead to significant power problems, especially if you fail to balance the loads on both rails to ensure you don't exceed the load capacity on one or the other. In other words, it is far better to have a single 12V rail that can supply 40 amps versus two 12V rails supplying 20 amps each, because with the single rail you don't have to worry which connectors derive power from which rail and then try to ensure that you don't overload one or the other.

Whereas the +3.3V, +5V, and +12V rails are technically independent inside the power supply, many cheaper designs have them sharing some circuitry, making them less independent than they should be. This manifests itself in voltage regulation problems in which a significant load on one rail causes a voltage drop on the others. Components such as processors and video cards can vary their power consumption greatly by their activity. Transitioning from sitting at the Windows desktop to loading a 3D game can cause both the processor and video card to more than double the draw on the +12V rail, which on some cheaper power supplies can cause the voltages on the other rails to fall out of spec (drop greater than 5%), causing the system to crash. Better designed power supplies feature truly independent rails with tighter regulation in the 1% to 3% range.

Voltage Regulators

The power supply must deliver a good, steady supply of DC power so the system can operate properly. Devices that run on voltages other than these directly must then be indirectly powered through onboard voltage regulators, which take the 5V or 12V from the power supply and convert that to the lower voltages required by various components. For example, DDR DIMMs (dual inline memory modules) and RIMMs (Rambus inline memory modules) require 2.5V, DDR2 and DDR3 DIMMs require 1.8V and 1.5V, AGP 4x/8x cards require 1.5V, and PCI Express cards use only 0.8V differential signaling—all of which are supplied by simple onboard regulators. Processors also require a wide variety of voltages (as low as 1.3V or less) that are supplied by a sophisticated voltage regulator module (VRM) that is either built into or plugged into the motherboard as well. You'll commonly find three or more different voltage regulator circuits on a modern motherboard.

Note

When Intel began releasing processors that required a +3.3V power source, power supplies that supplied the additional output voltage were not yet available. As a result, motherboard manufacturers began adding voltage regulators to their boards, which converted +5V to +3.3V for the processor. When other chips began using 3.3V as well, Intel created the ATX power supply specification, which supplied 3.3V to the motherboard. You would think that having 3.3V direct from the power supply would have eliminated the need for onboard voltage regulators, but by that time, processors, memory, and other components began running on a wide variety of voltages lower than 3.3V. Motherboard manufacturers then included adaptable regulator circuits called voltage regulator modules to accommodate the widely varying processor voltage requirements. Additional regulators are also used to power any other devices on the motherboard that don't use +3.3V, +5V, or +12V.

◀◀ See "CPU Operating Voltages," p. 114.

Negative DC Voltages

If you look at a specification sheet for a typical PC power supply, you can see that the supply generates not only +3.3V, +5V, and +12V, but also –12V and possibly –5V. Although –12V and possibly –5V are supplied to the motherboard via the power supply connectors, the motherboard normally uses only the +3.3V, +5V, and +12V. If present, the –5V is simply routed to the ISA bus on pin B5 so any ISA cards can use it, even though very few ever have. However, as an example, the analog data separator circuits found in older floppy controllers did use –5V. The motherboard logic typically doesn't use –12V either; however, it might be used in some board designs for serial port or LAN circuits.

The positive voltages seemingly power everything in the system (logic and motors), so what are the negative voltages used for? The answer is, not much! In fact, –5V was removed from the ATX12V 1.3 and later specifications. The only reason it remained in most power supply designs for many years is that –5V was required on the Industry Standard Architecture (ISA) bus for full backward compatibility. Because modern PCs no longer include ISA slots, the –5V signal was deemed as no longer necessary. However, if you are installing a new power supply in a system with an older motherboard that incorporates ISA Bus slots, you will want a supply that does include the –5V signal.

Note

The load placed on the –12V output by an integrated LAN adapter is very small. For example, the integrated 10/100 Ethernet adapter in the Intel D815EEAL motherboard uses only 10mA of +12V and 10mA of –12V (0.01 amps each) to operate.

Although older serial port circuits used +/–12V outputs, today most run only on +3.3V or +5V.

The main function of the +12V power is to run disk drive motors as well as the higher-output processor voltage regulators in some of the newer boards. Usually, a large amount of +12V current is available from the power supply, especially in those designed for systems with a large number of drive bays (such as in a tower configuration). Besides disk drive motors and newer CPU voltage regulators, the +12V supply is used by any cooling fans in the system—which, of course, should always be running. A single cooling fan can draw between 100mA and 250mA (0.1–0.25 amps); however, most newer fans use the lower 100mA figure. Note that although most fans in desktop systems run on +12V, portable systems can use fans that run on +5V or even +3.3V.

Systems with modern form factors based on the ATX or BTX standards include another special signal. This feature, called PS_ON, can be used to turn the power supply (and thus the system) on or off via software. It is sometimes known as the *soft-power feature*. PS_ON is most evident when you use it with an operating system such as Windows that supports the Advanced Power Management (APM) or Advanced Configuration and Power Interface (ACPI) specification. When you shut down a PC from the Start menu, Windows automatically turns off the computer after it completes the OS shutdown sequence. A system without this feature only displays a message that it's safe or ready for you to shut down the computer manually.

The Power Good Signal

In addition to supplying electrical power to run the system, the power supply also ensures that the system does not run unless the voltages supplied are sufficient to operate the system properly. In other words, the power supply actually prevents the computer from starting up or operating until all the power supply voltages are within the proper ranges.

The power supply completes internal checks and tests before allowing the system to start. If the tests are successful, the power supply sends a special signal to the motherboard called Power_Good. This signal must be continuously present for the system to run. Therefore, when the AC voltage dips and the power supply can't maintain outputs within regulation tolerance, the Power_Good signal is withdrawn (goes low) and forces the system to reset. The system will not restart until the Power_Good signal returns.

The Power_Good signal (sometimes called Power_OK or PWR_OK) is a +5V (nominal) active high signal (with a variation from +2.4V through +6.0V generally being considered acceptable) that is supplied to the motherboard when the power supply has passed its internal self tests and the output voltages have stabilized. This typically takes place anywhere from 100ms to 500ms (0.1–0.5 seconds) after you turn on the power supply switch. The power supply then sends the Power_Good signal to the motherboard, where the processor timer chip that controls the reset line to the processor receives it.

In the absence of Power_Good, the timer chip holds the reset line on the processor, which prevents the system from running under bad or unstable power conditions. When the timer chip receives the Power_Good signal, it releases the reset and the processor begins executing whatever code is at address FFFF0h (occupied by the motherboard ROM).

If the power supply can't maintain proper outputs (such as when a brownout occurs), the Power_Good signal is withdrawn and the processor is automatically reset. When the power output returns to its proper levels, the power supply regenerates the Power_Good signal and the system again begins operation (as if you had just powered on). By withdrawing Power_Good before the output voltages fall out of regulation, the system never sees the bad power because it is stopped quickly (reset) rather than being allowed to operate using unstable or improper power levels, which can cause memory parity errors and other problems.

Note

You can use the Power_Good feature as a method of implementing a reset switch for the PC. The Power_Good line is wired to the clock generator circuit, which controls the clock and reset lines to the microprocessor. When you ground the Power_Good line with a switch, the timer chip and related circuitry reset the processor. The result is a full hardware reset of the system.

◄◄ See "Parity and ECC," p. 557.

On pre-ATX systems, the Power_Good connection is made via connector P8-1 (P8 pin 1) from the power supply to the motherboard. ATX, BTX, and later systems use pin 8 of the 20/24-pin main power connector, which is usually a gray wire.

A properly designed power supply delays the arrival of the Power_Good signal until all the voltages stabilize after you turn on the system. Poorly designed power supplies, which are found in many low-cost systems, often do not delay the Power_Good signal properly and enable the processor to start too soon. (The normal Power_Good delay is 0.1–0.5 seconds.) Improper Power_Good timing also causes CMOS memory corruption in some systems.

Note

If you find that a system consistently fails to boot up properly the first time you turn on the switch, but that it subsequently boots up if you press the reset or Ctrl+Alt+Delete warm boot command, you likely have a problem with the Power_Good timing. You should install a new, higher-quality power supply and see whether that solves the problem.

Some cheaper power supplies do not have proper Power_Good circuitry and might just tie any +5V line to that signal. Some motherboards are more sensitive to an improperly designed or improperly functioning Power_Good signal than others. Intermittent startup problems are often the result of improper Power_Good signal timing. A common example is when you replace a motherboard in a system and then find that the system intermittently fails to start properly when you turn on the power. This can be very difficult to diagnose, especially for the inexperienced technician, because the problem appears to be caused by the new motherboard. Although it seems as though the new mother-board is defective, it usually turns out that the power supply is poorly designed. It either can't pro-duce stable enough power to properly operate the new board or has an improperly wired or timed Power_Good signal (which is more likely). In these situations, replacing the supply with a higher-quality unit, in addition to the new motherboard, is the proper solution.

Power Supply Form Factors

The shape and general physical layout of a component is called the *form factor*. Items that share a form factor are generally interchangeable, at least as far as their sizes and fits are concerned. When designing a PC, the engineers can choose to use one of the popular standard power supply unit (PSU) form factors, or they can elect to build their own custom design. Choosing the former means that a virtually inexhaustible supply of inexpensive replacement parts will be available in a variety of quality and power output levels. Going the custom route means additional time and expense for develop-ment. In addition, the power supply is unique to the system and generally available for replacement only from the original manufacturer. This precludes any upgrades as well, such as installing higher-output replacement models.

If you can't tell already, I am a fan of the industry-standard form factors! Having standards and then following them allows us to upgrade and repair our systems by easily replacing physically (and electri-cally) interchangeable components. Having interchangeable parts means that we have a better range of choices for replacement items, and the competition makes for better pricing, too.

In the PC market, IBM originally defined the form factor standards and everybody else copied them—and this included power supplies. All the popular PC power supply form factors up through 1995 were based on one of three IBM models, including the PC/XT, AT, and PS/2 Model 30. The interesting thing is that these three original IBM power supply form factors all had the same motherboard con-nectors and pinouts; where they differed was mainly in shape, maximum power output, the number of peripheral power connectors, and switch mounting. PC systems using knock-offs of one of those three designs were popular up through 1996 and beyond; in fact, even the current industry standard ATX12V models are based on the PS/2 Model 30 physical form factor, but with different connectors.

Intel defined a new power supply form factor in 1995 with the introduction of the ATX form factor. ATX became popular in 1996 and started a shift away from the previous IBM-based standards. ATX and the standards that have followed since use different connectors with additional voltages and sig-nals that allow systems with greater power consumption and additional features that would otherwise not be possible with the AT-style supplies.

Note

Although two power supplies can share the same basic design and form factor, they can differ greatly in quality and effi-ciency. Later in this chapter, you'll learn about some of the features and specifications to look for when evaluating PC power supplies.

More than 10 different power supply form factors have existed that can be called industry standards. Many of these are or were based on designs IBM created in the 1980s, whereas the rest are based on Intel designs from the 1990s to the present. The industry-standard form factors can be broken down into two main categories: those that are currently in use in modern systems and those that are largely obsolete.

Note that although the names of some of the power supply form factors seem to be the same as those of motherboard form factors, the power supply form factor relates more to the system chassis (case) than to the motherboard. That is because all the form factors use one of only two main types of connector designs: either AT or ATX, with subtle variations on each. So, although a particular power supply form factor might be *typically* associated with a particular motherboard form factor, many other power supplies would plug in as well.

For example, all modern ATX form factor motherboards with PCI Express slots have two main power connectors, including a 24-pin ATX main connector along with a 4-pin +12V connector. All the modern power supply form factors, including ATX12V, SFX12V, EPS12V, TFX12V, CFX12V, and LFX12V, include these same connectors and therefore are capable of plugging into the same motherboards. In other words, no matter what the form factor of the motherboard (ATX, BTX, or any of the smaller variants of either), virtually any of the modern industry-standard power supplies will plug in.

Plugging the power supply connectors into the motherboard is one thing, but for the power supply to work in the system, it must physically fit inside the chassis or case—and that is what the different modern power supply form factors are all about. The bottom line is that it is up to you to ensure that the power supply you purchase not only plugs in to your motherboard, but also fits into the chassis or case you plan to use.

Tables 19.2 and 19.3 show the industry-standard power supply form factors, their connector types, and the motherboard form factors with which they are *usually* associated.

Table 19.2   Modern Industry-Standard Power Supply Form Factors

Modern Power Supply Form Factors	Year Introduced	Connector Types	Normally Associated Motherboard Form Factors
ATX/ATX12V	1995	20/24-pin Main, 4-pin +12V	ATX, microATX, BTX, microBTX
SFX/SFX12V/PS3	1997	20/24-pin Main, 4-pin +12V	microATX, FlexATX, microBTX, picoBTX, Mini-ITX, DTX
EPS/EPS12V	1998	24-pin Main, 8-pin +12V	ATX, extended ATX
TFX12V	2002	20/24-pin Main, 4-pin +12V	microATX, FlexATX, microBTX, picoBTX, Mini-ITX, DTX
CFX12V	2003	20/24-pin Main, 4-pin +12V	microBTX, picoBTX, DTX
LFX12V	2004	24-pin Main, 4-pin +12V	picoBTX, nanoBTX, DTX

SFX12V also includes the PS3 form factor, which is a shortened version of ATX12V.
12V versions include a 4-pin or 8-pin +12V connector.

Table 19.3   Obsolete Industry Standard Power Supply Form Factors

Obsolete Power Supply Form Factors	Year Introduced	Connector Type	Normally Associated Motherboard Form Factors
PC/XT	1981	PC/XT	PC/XT, Baby-AT
AT/Desk	1984	AT	Full-size AT, Baby-AT
AT/Tower	1984	AT	Full-size AT, Baby-AT
Baby-AT	1984	AT	Full-size AT, Baby-AT
LPX (PS/2)	1987	AT	Baby-AT, Mini-AT, LPX

PC/XT connectors were the same as AT connectors, except one +5V pin (P8 pin 2) was not used.
LPX is also sometimes called PS/2 or Slimline.

Each of these power supply form factors is, or has been, available in numerous configurations and power output levels. The obsolete LPX form factor supply originated in the IBM PS/2 Model 30 in April 1987 and was the standard used on most systems from the late 1980s to mid-1996, when the ATX form factor started to gain in popularity. Since then, ATX and the many variants based on ATX have become by far the dominant form factors for power supplies. It is interesting to note that IBM's legacy lives on even now because ATX, PS3, and EPS are all based on the LPX (PS/2) physical form factor. Any power supply that does not conform to one of these standards is considered *proprietary*. Systems that use proprietary power supply designs should generally be avoided because replacements are difficult to obtain and upgrades are generally not available. When you consider that the power supply is one of the most failure-prone components, purchasing systems that use proprietary designs can be a significant liability in the future.

◄◄ See "Motherboard Form Factors," p. 235.

Obsolete Form Factors

The following sections explain in detail the form and function of power supply variants that are no longer in use today. Although most users aren't likely to encounter these designs, if you support older PCs, you may.

PC/XT

IBM's PC and XT systems (circa 1981 and 1983, respectively) used the same power supply form factor; the only difference was that the XT supply had more than double the power output capability. Because they were identical in external appearance and the type of connectors they used, you easily could install the higher-output XT supply as an upgrade for a PC system; thus, the idea of upgrading the power supply was born. The tremendous popularity of the original PC and XT systems led several manufacturers to begin building systems that mimicked their shapes and layouts. These *clones* or compatibles, as they have been called, could interchange virtually all components with the IBM systems, including power supplies. Numerous manufacturers then began producing components that followed the form factors used in these systems. The PC/XT power supply and connectors are shown in Figure 19.1. This form factor, however, is considered obsolete.

AT/Desk

The AT desktop system that IBM introduced in August 1984 had a larger power supply and a form factor different from the original PC/XT. Other manufacturers rapidly cloned this system, which represented the basis for many subsequent IBM-compatible designs. The power supply used in these systems was called the *AT/Desktop-style power supply* (see Figure 19.2). Hundreds of manufacturers began making motherboards, power supplies, cases, and other components that were physically interchangeable with the original IBM AT. This form factor is considered obsolete.

AT/Tower

The AT/Tower configuration was basically a full-sized, AT-style desktop system running on its side. The tower configuration was not new; in fact, even IBM's original AT had a specially mounted logo that could be rotated when you ran the system on its side in the tower configuration.

The type of power supply used in most of the AT tower systems was identical to that used in a desktop system, except for the location of the power switch. On the original AT/Desktop systems, the power switch was built into the side of the power supply (usually in the form of a large toggle switch).

AT/Tower systems instead used an external switch attached to the power supply through a four-wire cable. A full-sized AT power supply with a remote switch is called an *AT/Tower form factor power supply* and is identical to the AT/Desktop supply in size and dimensions. The only difference is the use of an external switch (see Figure 19.3). This form factor is considered obsolete.

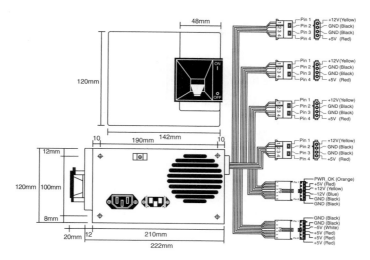

Figure 19.1   PC/XT form factor power supply.

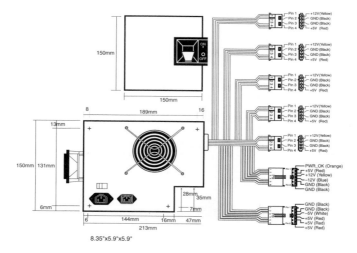

Figure 19.2   AT/Desktop form factor power supply.

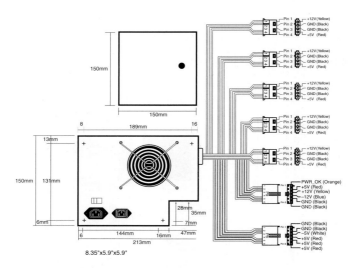

Figure 19.3   AT/Tower form factor power supply.

Baby-AT

Another type of AT-based form factor is the so-called *Baby-AT*, which is a shortened version of the full-size AT form factor. The power supply in these systems is shortened in one dimension but matches the AT design in all other respects. Baby-AT–style power supplies could fit in place of the larger AT/Desktop-style supply; however, the full-size AT/Tower supply would not fit in the Baby-AT chassis (see Figure 19.4). Because the Baby-AT PSU performed the same functions as the AT-style power supply but was in a smaller package, it became a common form factor until it was overtaken by later designs. This form factor is considered obsolete.

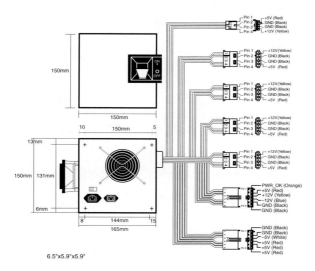

Figure 19.4   Baby-AT form factor power supply.

LPX

The next power supply form factor to gain popularity was the LPX style, also called the *PS/2 type*, *Slimline*, or *slim style* (see Figure 19.5). The PS/2 designation is in reference to the fact that this design originated in the IBM PS/2 Model 30 introduced in April 1987. The LPX-style power supply used the exact same motherboard and disk drive connectors as the previous PC/XT and AT-based standard power supply form factors. LPX power supplies were used primarily in systems with LPX, Baby-AT, or Mini-AT motherboards.

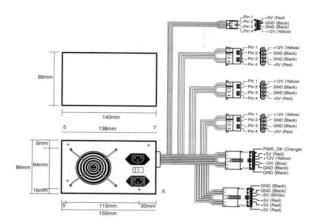

Figure 19.5   LPX form factor power supply.

The LPX power supply quickly found its way into many manufacturers' systems and soon became a de facto standard. This style of power supply became the staple of the industry for many years, coming in everything from low-profile systems using actual LPX motherboards to desktop or mid-tower systems with Baby-AT or Mini-AT motherboards, as well as full-size towers using Baby-AT or even full-size AT motherboards. Although considered obsolete, the LPX (PS/2) design is still sold today; however, you certainly won't find it in any new PCs. The mechanical form factor lives on, though, because it was the basis for the ATX and PS3 designs that are used in modern systems.

Modern Form Factors

The power supply form factors detailed in the following sections are the standards that continue to be implemented in current systems. ATX is far and away the most common of these, but if you work on a variety of PC types, you are likely to encounter the other types listed here.

ATX/ATX12V

In 1995, Intel saw that the existing power supply designs were literally running out of power. The problem was that the existing standards used two connectors with a total of only 12 pins providing power to the motherboard. In addition, the connectors used were difficult to properly key and plugging them in improperly resulted in short-circuiting and damage to both the motherboard and the power supply. To solve these problems, in 1995 Intel took the existing popular LPX (PS/2) design and simply changed the internal circuitry and connectors (while leaving the mechanical shape the same), giving birth to the ATX power supply form factor (see Figure 19.6).

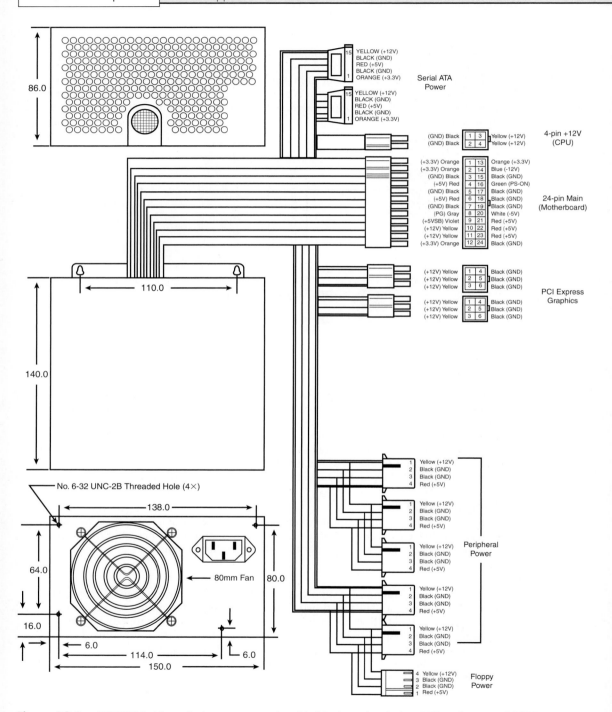

Figure 19.6   ATX12V 2.x form factor power supply with 24-pin main, 4-pin +12V, and optional PCI Express Graphics connectors.

Intel first released the ATX specification in 1995 and in 1996, it started to become increasingly popular in Pentium and Pentium Pro–based PCs, capturing 18% of the market within the first year. Since 1996, ATX variants have become both the dominant motherboard and power supply form factors, replacing the previously popular Baby-AT/LPX designs. ATX12V power supplies are also used with newer motherboard form factors such as BTX, ensuring that ATX and its derivatives will remain the most popular power supply form factors for several years to come.

The ATX12V specification defines the physical or mechanical form as well as the electrical connectors for the power supply. From 1995 through early 2000, the ATX power supply form factor was defined as part of the ATX motherboard specification. However, in February 2000, Intel took the power supply specification out of the then-current ATX 2.03 motherboard/chassis specification and created the ATX/ATX12V power supply specification 1.0, adding an optional 4-pin +12V connector at the same time (those with the +12V connector were called ATX12V supplies). The +12V connector was made a requirement in version 1.3 (April 2002), whereupon the specification became only ATX12V. The ATX12V 2.0 specification (February 2003) dropped the 6-pin auxiliary connector, changed the main power connector to 24 pins, and made Serial ATA power connectors a requirement as well. The current version is ATX12V 2.2, which was released in March 2005 and contains only minor changes from the previous releases, such as the use of high current system (HCS) terminals in the connectors.

As the ATX power supply specification has evolved, there have been some changes in the cooling fan orientation and design. The ATX specification originally called for an 80mm fan to be mounted along the inner side of the supply, where it could draw air in from the rear of the chassis and blow it inside across the motherboard. This kind of airflow runs in the opposite direction than most standard supplies, which exhaust air out the back of the supply through a hole in the case where the fan protrudes. The idea was that the reverse-flow design could cool the system more efficiently with only a single fan, eliminating the need for a fan (active) heatsink on the CPU.

Another benefit of the reverse-flow cooling is that the system would run cleaner, freer from dust and dirt. The case would be pressurized, so air would be continuously forced out of the cracks in the case—the opposite of what happens with a negative pressure design. For this reason, the reverse-flow cooling design is often referred to as a positive-pressure-ventilation design. On an ATX system with reverse-flow cooling, the air is blown out away from the drive because the only air intake is the single fan vent on the power supply at the rear. For systems that operate in extremely harsh environments, you can add a filter to the fan intake vent to further ensure that all the air entering the system is clean and free of dust.

Although this sounds like a good way to ventilate a system, the positive-pressure design needs to use a more powerful fan to pull the required amount of air through a filter and pressurize the case. Also, if a filter is used, it must be serviced on a periodic basis—depending on operating conditions, it could need changing or cleaning as often as every week. In addition, the heat load from the power supply on a fully loaded system heats the air being ingested, blowing warm air over the CPU and reducing the overall cooling capability.

As CPUs evolved to generate more and more heat, the cooling capability of the system became more critical and the positive-pressure design was simply not up to the task. Therefore, subsequent versions of the ATX specification were rewritten to allow both positive- and negative-pressure designs, but they emphasized the standard negative-pressure system with an exhaust fan on the power supply and an additional high-quality cooling fan blowing cool air right on the CPU as the best solution.

Because a standard negative-pressure system offers the greatest cooling capacity for a given fan's air-speed and flow, virtually all recent ATX-style power supplies use a negative-pressure design, in which air flows out the back of the power supply. Most use an 80mm fan mounted on the rear of the unit blowing outward, but some use an 80mm, a 92mm, or a 120mm fan mounted on the inside upper or lower surface, with open vents on the rear of the system. In either example, the flow of air is such that air is always exhausted out of the system through the rear of the supply.

The ATX power supply form factor addressed several problems with the previous PC/XT, AT, and LPX-type supplies. One is that the power supplies used with PC/XT/AT boards had only two connectors that plugged into the motherboard. If you inserted these connectors backward or out of their normal sequence, you would usually fry both the motherboard and the power supply! Most responsible system manufacturers tried to "key" the motherboard and power supply connectors so you couldn't install them backward or out of sequence. However, most vendors of cheaper systems did not feature this keying on the boards or supplies they used. The ATX form factor includes intelligently designed and keyed power plugs to prevent users from incorrectly plugging in their power supplies. The ATX connectors also supply +3.3V, reducing the need for voltage regulators on the motherboard to power +3.3V-based circuits.

Besides the new +3.3V outputs, ATX power supplies furnish another set of outputs that is not typically seen on standard power supplies. The set consists of the Power_On (PS_ON) and 5V_Standby (5VSB) outputs mentioned earlier, known collectively as *Soft Power*. This enables features to be implemented, such as Wake on Ring or Wake on LAN, in which a signal from a modem or network adapter can actually cause a PC to wake up and power on. Many such systems also have the option of setting a wake-up time, at which the PC can automatically turn itself on to perform scheduled tasks. These signals also can enable the optional use of the keyboard to power the system on—an option you can set on some systems. These features are possible because the +5V Standby power is always active, giving the motherboard a limited source of power even when off. Check your BIOS Setup for control over these types of features.

SFX/SFX12V

Intel released the smaller microATX motherboard form factor in December 1997, and at the same time also released the SFX (small form factor) power supply design to go with it. Even so, most microATX chassis continued to use the standard ATX power supply instead. Then in March 1999, Intel released the FlexATX addendum to the microATX specification, which was a very small board designed for low-end PCs or PC-based appliances. Since then, the SFX supply has found use in many new compact system designs. Unlike most of the power supply form factor specifications in which a single mechanical or physical outline is defined, the SFX standard actually defines five different physical shapes, some of which are not directly interchangeable. In addition, there have been changes to the connectors required as the specification has evolved. Therefore, when replacing an SFX/SFX12V-type supply, you need to ensure you are purchasing the correct type—which is to say the type that will physically install in your chassis—as well as have the correct connectors for your motherboard.

The number and types of connectors have changed over the life of the specification. The original SFX power supply specification included a single 20-pin motherboard connector. The 4-pin +12V connector to provide independent CPU power was added as an option in the 2.0 revision (May 2001) and was made a requirement in revision 2.3 (April 2003), causing the spec to be renamed as SFX12V in the process. SFX12V version 3.0 changed the main motherboard power connector from 20 pins to 24 pins and made Serial ATA power connectors a requirement as well. The current SFX12V version 3.1 was released in March 2005 and contains a few additional minor revisions, including a change to HCS terminals in the connectors. SFX12V includes several physical designs, including one called the PS3 form factor.

On a standard SFX/SFX12V power supply, a 60mm diameter cooling fan is located inside the power supply housing, facing the inside of the computer's case (see Figure 19.7). The fan draws the air into the power supply housing from the system cavity and expels it through a port at the rear of the system. Internalizing the fan in this way reduces system noise and results in a standard negative-pressure design. The system can also use additional processor and chassis cooling fans, which are separate from the power supply.

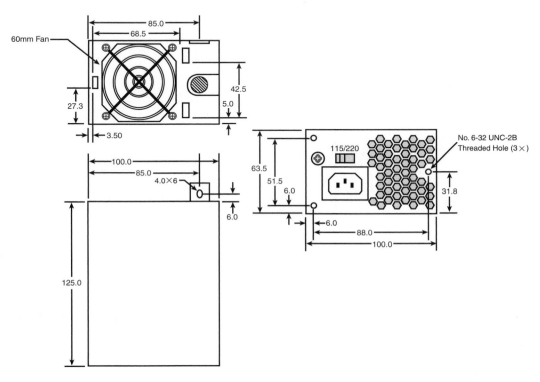

Figure 19.7 SFX/SFX12V standard power supply with internal 60mm fan.

For systems that require more cooling capability, a version that allows for a larger, 80mm top-mounted cooling fan also is available. The larger fan provides more cooling capability and airflow for systems that need it (see Figure 19.8).

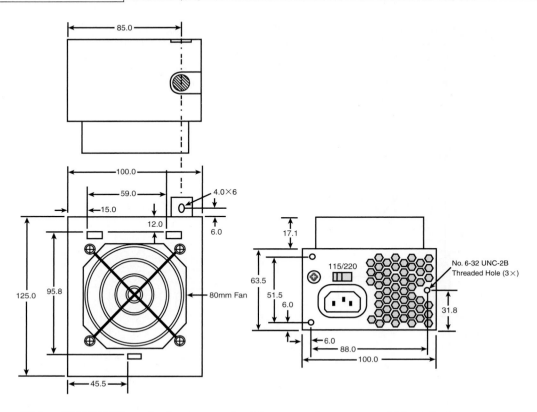

Figure 19.8   SFX/SFX12V standard power supply with a recessed, top-mounted 80mm fan.

Another variation of SFX12V also uses a recessed top-mounted 80mm cooling fan, but it has the body of the power supply rotated for greater width but reduced depth, as shown in Figure 19.9.

A special low-profile version of SFX12V designed for a slim chassis is only 50mm tall with an internal 40mm cooling fan, as shown in Figure 19.10.

Finally, a more recent variation on SFX is called the *PS3 form factor*, defined in Appendix E of the SFX12V specification. Although defined as part of SFX12V, the PS3 form factor is actually a shortened version of ATX12V and is generally used in systems with microATX chassis and motherboards that require higher power output than the smaller SFX variants can supply (see Figure 19.11).

SFX12V power supplies are specifically designed for use in small systems containing a limited amount of hardware and limited upgradeability. Most SFX supplies are designed to provide 80–300 watts of continuous power in four voltages (+5V, +12V, –12V, and +3.3V). This amount of power has proven to be sufficient for a small system with a processor, an AGP or PCI Express x16 interface, up to four expansion slots, and three peripheral devices—such as hard drives and CD-ROMs.

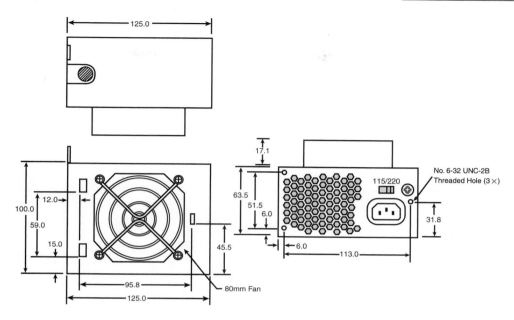

Figure 19.9 SFX/SFX12V rotated power supply with a recessed top-mounted 80mm fan.

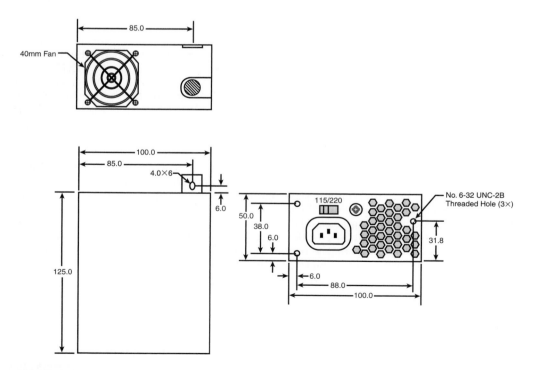

Figure 19.10 SFX/SFX12V low-profile power supply with internal 40mm fan.

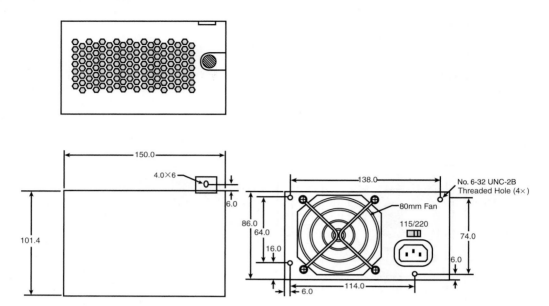

Figure 19.11   PS3 (SFX/SFX12V) power supply with internal 80mm fan.

Although Intel designed the SFX12V power supply specification with the microATX and FlexATX motherboard form factors in mind, SFX is a wholly separate standard that is compliant with other motherboards as well. For example, the PS3 variant of SFX12V can be used to replace standard ATX12V power supplies as long as the output capabilities and provided connectors match the system requirements. SFX power supplies use the same 20-pin or 24-pin connectors defined in the ATX/ATX12V standards and include both the Power_On and 5V_Standby outputs. SFX12V power supplies add the 4-pin +12V connector for CPU power, just as ATX12V supplies do. Whether you will use an ATX- or SFX-based power supply in a given system depends more on the case or chassis than the motherboard. Each has the same basic electrical connectors; the main difference is which type of power supply the case is physically designed to accept.

EPS/EPS12V

In 1998, a group of companies including Intel, Hewlett-Packard, NEC, Dell, Data General, Micron, and Compaq created the Server System Infrastructure (SSI), an industry initiative to promote industry-standard form factors covering common server hardware elements such as chassis, power supplies, motherboards, and other components. The idea was to be able to design network servers that could use industry-standard interchangeable parts. You can find out more about SSI at www.ssiforum.org. Although this book does not cover network servers, in many ways a low-end server is a high-end PC, and many high-end components that were once found only on servers have trickled down to standard PCs. This trickle-down theory is especially true when it comes to power supplies.

In 1998, the SSI created the entry-level power supply (EPS) specification, which defines an industry-standard power supply form factor for entry-level pedestal (standalone tower chassis) servers. The initial EPS standard was based on ATX, but with several enhancements. The first major enhancement was the use of a 24-pin main power connector, which eventually trickled down to the ATX12V as well as other power supply form factor specifications in 2003. EPS also originally called for the use of HCS terminals in the Molex Mini-Fit Jr.–based power supply connectors, which became standard in ATX12V in March 2005 as well. In addition, both the (now-obsolete) auxiliary 6-pin power connector, the 4-pin +12V power connector, and a variation of the 6-pin graphics power connector all appeared in the EPS specifications before ending up in ATX.

The EPS specification originally used a mechanical form factor identical to ATX, but the EPS form factor was later extended to support higher power outputs by allowing the body of the supply to be deeper if necessary. The ATX and the original EPS standards call for a supply that is 86mm tall by 150mm wide by 140mm deep, the same dimensions as the LPX or PS/2 form factors. EPS later added optional extended depths of 180mm and 230mm total. You may think these would require a custom EPS chassis, but in fact many (if not most) full-sized ATX tower chassis can handle these greater depths without interference, especially when using one of the newer breed of shorter-length optical drives (because one or more of the optical drives are often inline with the power supply).

With the improvements in EPS/EPS12V power supplies trickling down to ATX/ATX12V, I have studied the SSI EPS specifications to see what potential improvements might come to ATX. The main difference today between ATX and EPS with respect to connectors is the use of an 8-pin dual +12V connector in EPS12V instead of a 4-pin +12V connector in ATX12V. The 8-pin dual +12V connector is essentially the equivalent of two 4-pin connectors mated together and is used by entry-level servers to power multiple processors. Because of the way the connectors are designed, an 8-pin +12V connector can plug into a 4-pin +12V connector on a motherboard, with the unused pins simply hanging unused, offset to one side or the other.

The only other major difference between EPS12V and ATX12V is that EPS power supplies can be up to 180mm or 230mm deep, whereas ATX supplies are technically limited to 140mm depth according to the specification. An example of an EPS12V type supply is the Turbo-Cool 1KW (1-kilowatt) model from PC Power and Cooling (see Figure 19.12).

Figure 19.12   Turbo-Cool 1KW EPS12V form factor power supply (www.pcpower.com).

This power supply is basically a 230mm-deep EPS12V supply that works in place of or as an upgrade to an ATX12V supply as long as the chassis can accommodate the additional depth. EPS12V supplies are sometimes called *extended ATX* power supplies because of their optional extended length. If you plan on using one of these EPS12V power supplies in a standard ATX chassis, it's important that you measure the available space in your chassis to ensure you have the room behind the supply for the additional depth.

Connector compatibility isn't generally a problem because, by virtue of the Molex Mini-Fit Jr. connector design, you can plug a 24-pin main power connector into a 20-pin socket, as well as an 8-pin dual +12V connector into a 4-pin +12V socket.

If you have the room, an EPS12V power supply can be used with most ATX chassis and motherboards for the ultimate in high-output capabilities.

TFX12V

The TFX12V (thin form factor) power supply was originally introduced by Intel in April 2002 and is designed for small form factor (SFF) systems of about 9–15 liters in volume, primarily those using low-profile SFF chassis and microATX, FlexATX, or Mini-ITX motherboards. The basic shape of TFX12V is longer and narrower than the ATX- or SFX-based form factors, allowing it to more easily fit into low-profile systems. The dimensions of the TFX12V form factor are shown in Figure 19.13.

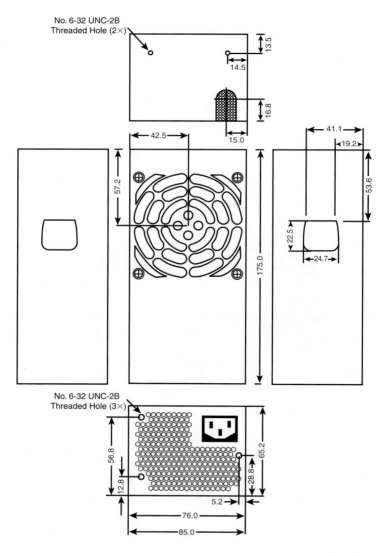

Figure 19.13 TFX12V power supply form factor dimensions.

TFX12V power supplies are designed to deliver nominal power output capabilities of 180–300 watts, which is more than adequate for the smaller systems for which they are designed. TFX12V supplies include a side-mounted internal 80mm fan that is usually thermostatically controlled, so as to run both coolly and quietly. A symmetrically designed mounting system allows the fan to be oriented facing either side inside the system for optimum cooling and flexibility in accommodating different chassis layouts (see Figure 19.14).

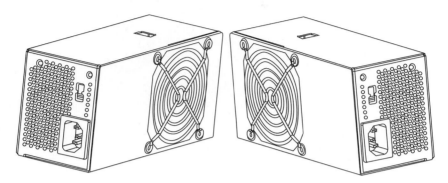

Figure 19.14   TFX12V power supplies are symmetrical and can be mounted with the fan facing either left or right.

Unlike SFX-based supplies, only one standard mechanical form factor exists for TFX12V supplies. TFX12V supplies have also always included the 4-pin +12V connector since the standard appeared in April 2002, well after the +12V connector had been included in other power supply form factors. TFX12V 1.2 (April 2003) added the Serial ATA power connector as an option, whereas the TFX12V 2.0 release (February 2004) made them mandatory and changed the main power connector from 20 pins to 24 pins. Revision 2.1 (July 2005) includes only minor updates and changes from the previous version.

CFX12V

The CFX12V (compact form factor) power supply was originally introduced by Intel in November 2003 and is designed for mid-sized BTX (balanced technology extended) systems of about 10–15 liters in volume, primarily using microBTX or picoBTX motherboards.

CFX12V power supplies are designed to deliver nominal power output capabilities of 220–300 watts, which is more than adequate for the mid-sized systems for which they are designed. CFX12V supplies include a rear-mounted internal 80mm fan that is typically thermostatically controlled, so as to run both coolly and quietly. The shape of the supply includes a ledge such that part of the supply can extend over the motherboard, reducing the overall size of the system (see Figure 19.15). The dimensions of the CFX12V form factor are shown in Figure 19.16.

CFX12V supplies have always included the 4-pin +12V connector since the standard first appeared in November 2003, well after the +12V connector had been included in other power supply form factors. TFX12V also included the 24-pin main power connector as well as Serial ATA power connectors as mandatory since its inception. The current CFX12V 1.2 release dates from 2005 and has only minor revisions over previous versions, including a change to HCS terminals in the connectors.

Figure 19.15 CFX12V power supply.

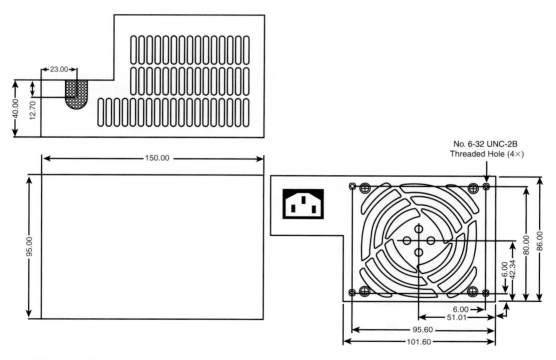

Figure 19.16 CFX12V power supply dimensions.

LFX12V

Intel originally introduced the LFX12V (low profile form factor) power supply in April 2004. It's designed for ultra-small BTX systems of about 6–9 liters in volume, primarily using picoBTX or nanoBTX motherboards.

LFX12V power supplies are designed to deliver nominal power output capabilities of 180–260 watts, which is ideal for the tiny systems for which they are designed. LFX12V supplies include an internal 60mm fan, which is 20mm smaller than that of the CFX12V design. Similar to the CFX12V fan, it is usually thermostatically controlled to ensure quiet operation while still providing adequate cooling. The shape of the supply includes a ledge such that part of the supply can extend over the motherboard, reducing the overall size of the system (see Figure 19.17). The dimensions of the LFX12V form factor are shown in Figure 19.18.

All LFX12V supplies include a 24-pin main motherboard power connector, a 4-pin +12V connector, and Serial ATA connectors. The current LFX12V 1.1 release dates from April 2005 and has only minor revisions over the previous version.

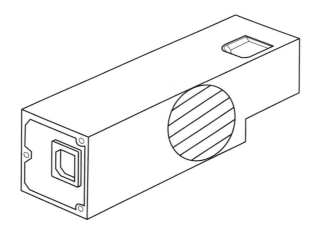

Figure 19.17   LFX12V power supply.

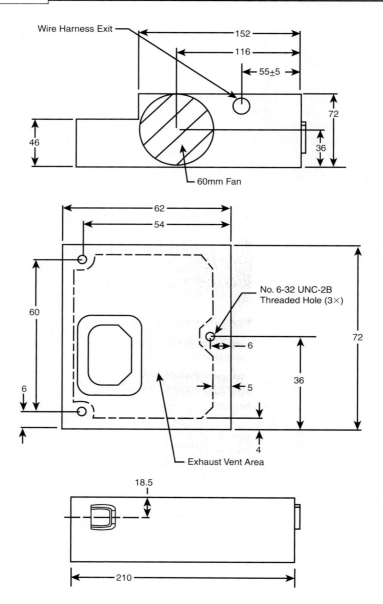

Figure 19.18   LFX12V power supply dimensions.

Power Switches

Three main types of power switches are used on PCs. They can be described as follows:

- Front panel motherboard-controlled switch (ATX and newer)
- Front panel power supply AC switch (AT/LPX; obsolete)
- Integral power supply AC switch (PC/XT/AT; obsolete)

ATX and Newer

All ATX and newer power supplies that employ the 20- or 24-pin motherboard connector use the PS_ON signal to power up the system. In this design, the power supply runs in standby mode when plugged in with the system off. The PS_ON signal is routed from the power supply through the motherboard to a low-voltage momentary contact DC switch on the front panel. As a result, the remote power switch does not physically control the power supply's access to the 120V AC power, as in older-style power supplies. Instead, the power supply's on or off status is toggled by the PS_ON signal received on the ATX Main power connector. This is sometimes called a *soft-off switch* because this is the name of the Advanced Configuration Power Interface (ACPI) state when the system is off but still receiving standby power.

The PS_ON signal can be manipulated physically by the computer's power switch or electronically by the motherboard under software control. PS_ON is an *active low signal*, meaning the power supply voltage outputs are disabled (the system is off) when the PS_ON is high (greater than or equal to 2.0V). This excludes the +5VSB (Standby) on pin 9 of the ATX main power connector, which is active whenever the power supply is connected to an AC power source. The power supply maintains the PS_ON signal at either 3.3V or +5V. This signal is then routed through the motherboard to the remote switch on the front of the case. When the switch is pressed, the PS_ON signal is grounded. When the power supply sees the PS_ON signal drop to 0.8V or less, the power supply (and system) is turned on. Thus, the remote switch in a system using an ATX or newer power supply carries up to only +5V of DC power, rather than the full 120V–240V AC current like that of the older AT/LPX form factors.

Caution

The continuous presence of the +5VSB power on pin 9 of the ATX main connector means the motherboard is always receiving standby power from the power supply when connected to an AC source, even when the computer is turned off. As a result, it is even more crucial to unplug an ATX system from the power source before working inside the case than it is on an earlier model system.

The remote switch on ATX and newer designs can only put the system in a soft-off state, in which the system appears off but is still receiving standby power. Some ATX and newer power supplies include a hard override AC power switch on the back, which essentially disconnects AC power from the system when turned off. With the AC switch off, the system no longer receives standby power and is essentially the same as being completely unplugged from an AC outlet.

Tip

The design of the ATX power switch is such that the motherboard actually controls the status of the power supply. On systems with full support for ACPI, when you press the power switch, the motherboard informs the OS to perform an orderly shutdown before the power is actually turned off. However, if the system is locked up or corrupted, it can remain running when you press the switch. In that situation, you can manually override the ACPI control by pressing the switch continuously for more than 4 seconds, which overrides the software control and forcibly turns off the system.

PC/XT/AT and LPX Power Switches

The earliest systems had power switches integrated or built directly into the power supply, which turned the main AC power to the system on and off. This was a simple design, but because the power supply was mounted in the rear right of the system, it required reaching around to the right side near the back of the system to actuate the switch. Also, switching the AC power directly meant the system couldn't be remotely started without special hardware.

Starting in the late 1980s, systems with LPX power supplies began using remote front panel switches. These were still AC switches; the only difference was that the AC switch was now mounted remotely (usually on the front panel of the chassis), rather than integrated in the power supply unit. The switch was connected to the power supply via a four-wire cable, and the ends of the cable were fitted with spade connector lugs, which plugged onto the spade connectors on the power switch. The cable from the power supply to the switch in the case contained four color-coded wires. In addition, a fifth wire supplying a ground connection to the case was sometimes included. The switch was usually included with the power supply and heavily shrink-wrapped or insulated where the connector lugs attached, to prevent electric shock.

This solved the ergonomic problem of reaching the switch, but it still didn't enable remote or automated system power-up without special hardware. Plus, you now had a 120V AC switch mounted in the chassis, with wires carrying dangerous voltage through the system. Some of these wires are hot anytime the system is plugged in (all are hot when the system's turned on), creating a dangerous environment for the average person when messing around inside the system.

Caution

At least two of the remote power switch leads to a remote-mounted AC power switch in an AT/LPX supply are energized with 120V AC at all times. You can be electrocuted if you touch the ends of these wires with the power supply plugged in, even if the unit is turned off! For this reason, always make sure the power supply is unplugged before connecting or disconnecting the remote power switch or touching any of the wires connected to it.

The four or five wires are usually color-coded as follows:

- **Brown and blue**—These wires are the live and neutral feed wires from the 120V power cord to the power supply. These are always hot when the power supply is plugged in.

- **Black and white**—These wires carry the AC feed from the switch back to the power supply. These leads should be hot only when the power supply is plugged in and the switch is turned on.

- **Green or green with a yellow stripe**—This is the ground lead. It should be connected to the PC case and should help ground the power supply to the case.

On the switch, the tabs for the leads are usually color-coded; if not, you'll find that most switches have two parallel tabs and two angled tabs. If no color-coding is on the switch, plug the blue and brown wires onto the tabs that are parallel to each other and the black and white wires to the tabs that are angled away from each other. If none of the tabs are angled, simply make sure the blue and brown wires are plugged into the most closely spaced tabs on one side of the switch and the black and white wires on the most closely spaced tabs on the other side (see Figure 19.19).

Caution

Although these wire color-codings and parallel/angled tabs are used on most power supplies, they are not necessarily 100% universal. I have encountered power supplies that do not use the same coloring or tab placement scheme described here. One thing is sure: Two of the wires will be hot with potentially fatal AC voltage anytime the power supply is plugged in. No matter what, always disconnect the power supply from the wall socket before handling any of these wires. Be sure to insulate the connections with electrical tape or heat-shrink tubing so you won't be able to touch the wires when working inside the case in the future.

As long as the blue and brown wires are on one set of tabs and the black and white leads are on the other, the switch and supply will work properly. If you incorrectly mix the leads, you will likely blow the circuit breaker for the wall socket because mixing them can create a direct short circuit.

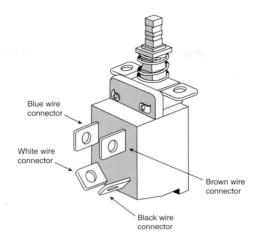

Figure 19.19 Power supply remote pushbutton switch connections.

Motherboard Power Connectors

Every PC power supply has connectors that attach to the motherboard, providing power to the motherboard; processor; memory; chipset; integrated components such as video, LAN, USB, and FireWire; and any cards plugged into bus slots. These connectors are very important—not only are these the main conduit through which power flows to your system, but attaching these connectors improperly can have a devastating effect on your PC, including burning up both your power supply and motherboard. Just as with the mechanical shape of the power supply, these connectors are usually designed to conform to one of several industry-standard specifications, which dictate the types of connectors used as well as the pinouts of the individual wires and terminals. Unfortunately, just as with the mechanical form factors, some PC manufacturers use power supplies with custom connectors or, worse yet, use standard connector types but with modified (incompatible) pinouts (meaning the signals and voltages are rearranged from standard specifications). Plugging a power supply with an incompatible pinout into a motherboard that uses a standard pinout (or vice versa) usually results in the destruction of either the board or the power supply—or both.

Just as I insist on industry-standard mechanical form factors in my systems, I also want to ensure that they use industry-standard connectors and pinouts. By only purchasing components that conform to industry standards, I can ensure the greatest flexibility and lowest cost for future upgrades and repairs.

Two main sets of motherboard power connectors have been used over the years: what I would call AT/LPX type and the ATX type. Each of these has minor variations; for example, the ATX type has evolved over the years, with new connectors coming (and some going) and modifications to existing connectors. The following sections detail the motherboard power connectors used by various types of industry-standard (and some not-so-standard) power supplies.

AT/LPX Power Supply Connectors

Industry-standard PC, XT, AT, Baby-AT, and LPX motherboards all use the same type of main power supply connectors. AT/LPX power supplies feature two main power connectors (P8 and P9), each with six pins that attach the power supply to the motherboard. The terminals used in these connectors are rated to handle up to 5 amps at up to 250V (even though the maximum used in a PC is +12V). These two connectors are shown in Figure 19.20.

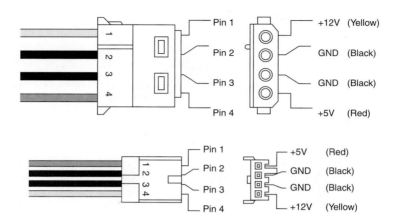

Figure 19.20 AT/LPX main P8/P9 (also called P1/P2) power connectors, side and terminal end view.

All AT/LPX power supplies that use the P8 and P9 connectors have them installed end to end so that the two black wires (ground connections) on both power connectors are next to each other when properly plugged in. Note the designations "P8" and "P9" are not fully standardized, although most use those designations because that is what IBM stamped on the originals. Some power supplies have them labeled as P1/P2 instead. Because these connectors usually have a clasp that prevents them from being inserted backward on the motherboard's pins, the major concern is getting the two connectors in the correct orientation side by side and also not offsetting by one or more pins side to side. Following the black-to-black rule and ensuring they are on-center keeps you safe. You must take care to ensure that no remaining unconnected motherboard pins exist between or on either side of the two connectors after you install them. A properly installed connector connects to and covers every motherboard power pin. If any power pins are showing on either side of or between the connectors, the entire connector assembly is installed incorrectly, which can result in catastrophic failure for the motherboard and everything plugged into it at the time of power-up. Figure 19.21 shows the P8 and P9 connectors (sometimes also called P1/P2) in their proper orientation when connecting them to a motherboard.

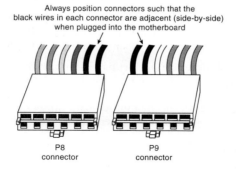

Figure 19.21 The P8/P9 power connectors (sometimes also called P1/P2) that connect an AT/LPX power supply to the motherboard.

Table 19.4 shows typical AT/LPX power supply connections.

Table 19.4   AT/LPX Power Supply Connectors (Wire End View)

Connector	Pin	Signal	Color[2]	Connector	Pin	Signal	Color[2]
P8 (or P1)	1	Power_Good (+5V)	Orange	P9 (or P2)	1	Ground	Black
	2	+5V[1]	Red		2	Ground	Black
	3	+12V	Yellow		3	−5V	White
	4	−12V	Blue		4	+5V	Red
	5	Ground	Black		5	+5V	Red
	6	Ground	Black		6	+5V	Red

1. *First-generation PC/XT motherboards and power supplies did not require this voltage, so the pin might be missing from the motherboard and terminal and the wire might be missing from the connector (P8 pin 2).*

2. *I have seen some supplies where the manufacturer did not follow industry-standard wire color-codes even though the signals were correct.*

Tip

Although older PC/XT power supplies do not have any connection at connector P8 pin 2, you still can use them on AT-type motherboards, or vice versa. The presence or absence of the +5V on that pin has little or no effect on system operation because the remaining +5V wires can usually carry the load.

Note that all the AT/LPX-type power supplies use the same connectors and pin configurations; there were never any nonstandard variations to my knowledge.

ATX and ATX12V Motherboard Power Connectors

Power supplies conforming to the original ATX and ATX12V 1.x form factor standards or variations thereof use the following three motherboard power connectors:

- 20-pin main power connector
- 6-pin auxiliary power connector
- 4-pin +12V power connector

The main power connector is always required, but the other two are optional depending on the application. Consequently, a given ATX or ATX12V power supply can have up to four different combinations of connectors, as listed here:

- Main power connector only
- Main and auxiliary
- Main and +12V
- Main, auxiliary, and +12V

The most common varieties are those including the main only and those with the main and +12V connectors. Most motherboards that use the +12V connector do not use the auxiliary connector, and vice versa.

The Reason for Multiple Motherboard Power Connectors

Only the 20-pin main power connector was included in the original ATX specification, and it was sufficient to power PC motherboards and processors in the mid-1990s, requiring 251 watts or less total power. However, by the late 1990s, motherboard and processor power requirements had increased, and in some systems the main power connector could no longer shoulder the load. Motherboards and processors that drew more than 251 total watts would potentially overheat the terminals and melt the connector housing—something I witnessed several times myself.

Rather than change the design of the main connector and cause incompatibilities with motherboards that didn't need the additional power, Intel added the auxiliary power connector as a fix to the ATX 2.02 specification in 1998. The auxiliary connector was designed to deliver up to 58 watts of additional +3.3V and +5V power to power-hungry motherboards, which often need the additional power for CPU, memory, and AGP slot voltage regulators. Even though incorporating the additional auxiliary connector was basically a good idea, most motherboards I saw continued to use only the single main power connector, even if it might be overloaded.

Although the auxiliary connector could provide extra +3.3V and +5V power, it did not provide any additional +12V power. The debut of the Pentium 4 processor in 2000 brought even greater power demands from the processor. CPUs run on very low voltages, which are normally provided via voltage regulators on the motherboard. These regulators take in the voltage provided by the power supply and convert it to that required by the processor. Power equals volts multiplied by amps. So, for the same power level, the more volts you provide the regulators, the fewer amps they require. Therefore, to reduce the overall current (amps) being delivered to the motherboard, a change was made to the CPU voltage regulators such that they would run on +12V power, instead of the +3.3V or +5V they had been previously using.

This unfortunately created another power problem: Even when both the main and auxiliary power connectors were combined, only a single +12V terminal was supplying up to 6 amps of current to the motherboard. So, to provide additional +12V power and preserve compatibility with the main and auxiliary connectors that had already been defined, in early 2000 Intel added the +12V power connector to the ATX 2.1 specification. This new connector was designed specifically to deliver up to 192 watts of power for the high-output voltage regulators required by the Pentium 4 and newer processors.

Power supplies with the +12V power connector were called *ATX12V supplies*, and a special ATX12V form factor specification was created just for the power supply. Because the +12V power connector was initially used on Pentium 4 motherboards, it became unofficially known as the *P4 connector*, even though AMD processor-based motherboards began using it also. By the end of 2001, most motherboards began requiring this connector and most power supplies being sold for PCs were the ATX12V type.

As a consequence of changing the CPU voltage regulators on the motherboard to use +12V power, the load on the +3.3V and +5V rails was reduced such that the auxiliary connector was no longer necessary; consequently, many ATX12V supplies came without it. The auxiliary connector was officially removed from the ATX12V 2.0 specification in 2000. Some ATX12V power supplies still continue to include the auxiliary power connector, and of course you should be sure it is present if required by your motherboard.

20-pin Main Power Connector

The 20-pin main power connector is standard for all power supplies conforming to the ATX and ATX12V 1.x power supply form factors and consists of a Molex Mini-Fit Jr. connector housing with female terminals. For reference, the connector is Molex part number 39-01-2200 (or equivalent) and the standard terminals are part number 5556 (see Figure 19.22). This is a 20-pin keyed connector with pins configured as shown in Table 19.5. The colors for the wires listed are those the ATX standard recommends; however, to enable them to vary from manufacturer to manufacturer, they are not required for compliance to the specification. I like to show these connector pinouts in a wire end view, which shows how the pins are arranged looking at the back of the connector (from the wire and not the terminal end). This is because it shows how they would be oriented if you were back-probing the connector with the connector plugged in.

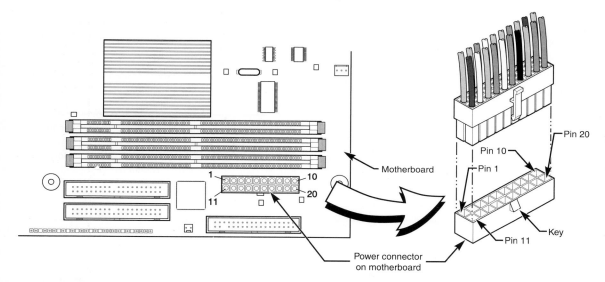

Figure 19.22   ATX 20-pin motherboard main power connector, perspective view.

Figure 19.23 shows a view of the connector as if you were looking at it facing the terminal end.

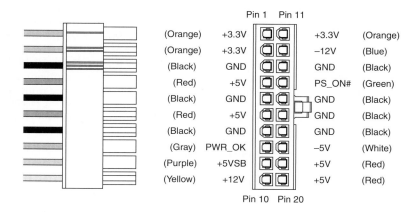

Figure 19.23   ATX 20-pin main power connector, side and terminal end view.

Table 19.5   ATX 20-pin Main Power Supply Connector Pinout (Wire End View)

Color	Signal	Pin	Pin	Signal	Color
Orange	+3.3V	11[1]	1	+3.3V	Orange
Blue	−12V	12	2	+3.3V	Orange
Black	GND	13	3	GND	Black
Green	PS_On	14	4	+5V	Red
Black	GND	15	5	GND	Black
Black	GND	16	6	+5V	Red
Black	GND	17	7	GND	Black
White	−5V	18[2]	8	Power_Good	Gray
Red	+5V	19	9	+5VSB (Standby)	Purple
Red	+5V	20	10	+12V	Yellow

1. Might have a second orange or brown wire, used for +3.3V sense feedback. The power supply uses this wire to monitor 3.3V regulation.

2. Pin 18 might be N/C (no connection) on some later model supplies or motherboards because −5V was removed from the ATX12V 1.3 and later specifications. Supplies with no connection at pin 18 should not be used with older motherboards that incorporate ISA Bus slots.

Note

The ATX supply features several voltages and signals not seen on earlier AT/LPX designs, such as the +3.3V, PS_On, and +5V_Standby. Therefore, adapting a standard LPX form factor supply to make it work properly in an ATX system is impossible, even though the shapes of the power supplies themselves are virtually identical.

However, because ATX is a superset of the older LPX power supply standard, you can use a connector adapter to allow an ATX power supply to connect to an older motherboard using AT/LPX connectors. PC Power and Cooling (www.pcpower.com) sells this type of adapter.

One of the most important issues with respect to power supply connectors is the capability to deliver sufficient power to the motherboard without overheating. It doesn't help to have a 500-watt power supply if the cables and connectors supplying power to the motherboard can handle only 250 watts before they start to melt. When talking about specific connectors, the current rating is stated in amperes per circuit, which is a measure of the amount of current that can be passed through a mated terminal that will allow no more than a 30° C (85° F) temperature rise over ambient 22° C (72° F). In other words, at a normal ambient temperature of 30° C (72° F), when operating under the maximum rated current load, the temperature of the mated terminals will not exceed 52° C (157° F). Because the ambient temperature inside a PC can run 40° C (104° F) or higher, running power connectors at maximum ratings can result in extremely high temperatures in the connectors.

The maximum current level is further de-rated or adjusted for the number of circuits in a given connector housing due to the heat of any adjacent terminals. For example, a power connector might be able to carry 8 amps per circuit in a 4-position connector, but the same connector and terminal design might be able to handle only 6 amps per circuit in a 20-position connector.

All the modern form factor power supplies since ATX have standardized on the use of Molex Mini-Fit Jr. connectors for the main and +12V connectors. A number of connector housings are used with anywhere from 4 to 24 positions or terminals. Molex makes three types of terminals for these connectors:

a standard version, an HCS version, and a Plus HCS version. The current ratings for these terminals are shown in Table 19.6.

Table 19.6   Current Ratings for Mini-Fit Jr. Connectors

Mini-Fit Jr. Terminal Type/No.	2–3 Pins (Amps/Pin)	4–6 Pins (Amps/Pin)	7–10 Pins (Amps/Pin)	12–24 Pins (Amps/Pin)
Standard/5556	9	8	7	6
HCS/44476	12	11	10	9
Plus HCS/45750	12	12	12	11

All ratings assume Mini-Fit Jr. connectors with 12–24 circuits using 18-gauge wire under standard temperature conditions.

The ATX main power connector is either a 20-pin or 24-pin connector, which, if standard terminals are used, is rated for up to 6 amps of current per terminal. If the connector were upgraded to HCS terminals, the rating would increase to 9 amps per terminal, and if upgraded to Plus HCS terminals, the rating would increase further to 11 amps per terminal. Prior to March 2005, all the power supply form factor specifications called for using standard terminals, but all the ratings from March 2005 to the present have changed to require HCS terminals instead. If your power supply connector has been overheating, you can easily install HCS or Plus HCS terminals to increase the power-handling capability of your connector by 50% or more.

By counting the number of terminals for each voltage level, you can calculate the power-handling capability of the connector as shown in Table 19.7.

Table 19.7   ATX 20-pin Main Power Connector Maximum Power Handling Capabilities

Volts	No. Pins	Using Std. Terminals (W)	Using HCS Terminals (W)	Using Plus HCS Terminals (W)
+3.3V	3	59.4	89.1	108.9
+5V	4	120	180	220
+12V	1	72	108	132
Total watts:		251.4	377.1	460.9

Standard terminals are rated 6 amps.

HCS terminals are rated 9 amps.

Plus HCS terminals are rated 11 amps.

All ratings assume Mini-Fit Jr. connectors with 12–24 circuits using 18-gauge wire under standard temperature conditions.

This means the total power-handling capacity of this connector is only 251 watts if standard terminals are being used, which is lower than many systems need today. Unfortunately, drawing more power than this maximum rating through the connector causes it to overheat. I'm sure you can appreciate how inadequate this has become today; for example, it certainly doesn't make sense to manufacture a 400- or 500-watt power supply if the main power connector can handle only 251 watts without melting! That would be like building a car that could go 200 mph and then equipping it with tires rated for only 100 mph. Everything would be fine until you exceeded the tires' rated speed, after which the results would not be pretty.

This is why the official power supply form factor specifications were updated in March 2005 to include HCS terminals, which have 50% greater power-handling capability than the standard terminals. Using HCS terminals, the power-handling capability of the 20-pin main connector alone increases to 377 watts, which is more than most systems need to run the entire system through all of the connectors combined.

6-pin Auxiliary Power Connector

As motherboards and processors have evolved, the need for power has become greater. Each of the terminals in the main power connector are rated for 6 amps (A) using standard terminals, which allows for a maximum supply of approximately 250 watts to the motherboard. Because motherboards with high-speed processors and multiple cards installed could draw more power than that and power supply manufacturers were building supplies with 300-watt and higher ratings, melted connectors were becoming more and more common. The terminals in the main connector overheated under such a load.

To allow for additional power from the supply to the motherboard, Intel modified the ATX specification to add a second auxiliary power connector for high power-drawing ATX motherboards and 250-watt or higher rated supplies. The criteria is such that, if the motherboard could draw more than 18A of +3.3V power and/or more than 24A of +5V power, the auxiliary connector is required to carry the additional load. These higher levels of power are needed in systems using 250- or 300-watt or greater supplies.

The 6-pin auxiliary power connector was added as a safety or stopgap measure in the ATX motherboard 2.02/2.03 and ATX12V 1.x power supply specifications for systems in which the +3.3V and +5V power draw could exceed the respective 18A and 24A maximums allowed using only the main connector with standard terminals. These conditions would normally be met in systems requiring 300W or higher output power supplies. The auxiliary power connector is a 6-pin Molex 90331-0010 connector, which is similar to the motherboard power connectors used on older AT/LPX power supplies for Baby-AT motherboards (see Figure 19.24).

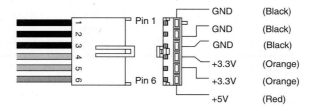

Figure 19.24 ATX 2.02/2.03 and ATX12V 1.x auxiliary power connector, side and terminal end view.

The pinouts of the auxiliary connector are shown in Table 19.8.

Table 19.8 ATX Auxiliary Power Connector Pinout

Pin	Signal	Color	Pin	Signal	Color
1	Gnd	Black	4	+3.3V	Orange
2	Gnd	Black	5	+3.3V	Orange
3	Gnd	Black	6	+5V	Red

Each terminal in the auxiliary power connector is rated to handle up to 5 amps of current, slightly less than the main power connector. By counting the number of terminals for each voltage level, you can calculate the power-handling capability of the connector as shown in Table 19.9.

Table 19.9   6-pin Auxiliary Power Connector Maximum Power-Handling Capabilities

Volts	No. Pins	Watts
+3.3V	2	33
+5V	1	25
Total watts:		58

Terminals are rated 5 amps.

Ratings assume 18-gauge wire under standard temperature conditions.

This means the total power-handling capacity of this connector is only 58 watts. Drawing more power than this maximum rating through the connector will cause it to overheat.

Combining the 20-pin main plus the auxiliary power connector would result in a maximum power-delivery capability to the motherboard of 309 watts.

Few motherboards actually used this connector, and few power supplies included it. Generally, if a motherboard includes this connector, you need a power supply that has it as well, but if the power supply includes the auxiliary connector but the motherboard does not, it can be left unconnected.

Starting in 2000, both motherboards and power supplies began including a different additional connector that was a better solution than the auxiliary connector. The most recent power supply form factor specifications have removed the auxiliary connector, rendering it an obsolete standard in modern systems.

ATX12V 2.x 24-pin Main Power Connector

Starting in June 2004, the new PCI Express bus first appeared on motherboards. PCI Express is a type of serial bus with standard slots having a single channel or lane of communications. These single-lane slots are called *x1 slots* and are designed for peripheral cards such as network cards, sound cards, and the like. PCI Express also includes a special higher-bandwidth slot with 16 lanes (called an *x16 slot*), which is especially designed for use by video cards. During development it was realized that PCI Express x16 video cards could draw more power than what was allowed by the existing 20-pin main and 6-pin auxiliary power supply connectors, especially when it came to +12V power.

The problem was that the 20-pin main connector had only a single +12V pin, but the new video cards required more +12V power than a single pin could safely deliver. The +12V connector that had already been added, as discussed in the next section, was specifically for the CPU and was unavailable to other devices. Rather than add another supplemental or auxiliary connector as it had done before, Intel eventually decided that it was finally time to upgrade the main power connector to supply more power.

The result was officially called ATX12V 2.0 and was released in February 2003. ATX12V 2.0 included two major changes from the previous ATX12V 1.x specifications: a new 24-pin main power connector and the elimination of the 6-pin auxiliary power connector. The new 24-pin main power connector included four more pins supplying additional +3.3V, +5V, and +12V power plus a ground. The inclusion of these extra pins delivered extra power to satisfy the power requirements for PCI Express video cards drawing up to 75 watts, but also made the older 6-pin auxiliary connector unnecessary.

The pinout of the new 24-pin main power connector started to be implemented in motherboards in mid-2004 (see Figure 19.25).

Note

Even though one of the design goals for increasing the main power connector to 24 pins was to provide extra power for PCI Express video cards, many if not most high-end video cards need more than the 75 watts available directly through the PCIe x16 slot. Video cards requiring more will have one or more additional power connectors on the card, which are used to draw power directly from the PSU.

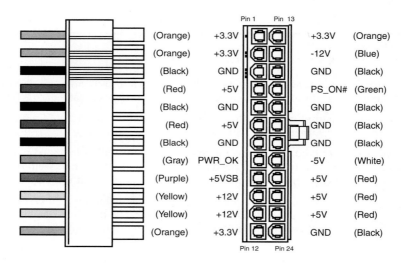

Figure 19.25   ATX12V 2.x 24-pin main power connector.

When looking at this image, it's important to keep in mind that pin 13 might have a second orange or brown wire for +3.3V sense feedback, used by the power supply to monitor 3.3V regulation. Also, pin 20 might be N/C (no connection) because –5V was removed from the ATX12V 2.01 and later specifications. Supplies with no connection at pin 20 should not be used with older motherboards that incorporate ISA Bus slots.

It is interesting to note that the 24-pin connector is not really that new; it first appeared in the Server System Infrastructure (SSI) Entry Power Supply (EPS) specification released in 1998. SSI (http://ssiforum.org/) is an initiative designed to create standard interfaces for server components, including power supplies. The 24-pin main power connector was first created for servers because, at the time, only servers needed the additional power. Today's PCs draw the same power levels as servers did years ago, so rather than reinvent an incompatible connector, the ATX12V 2.0 standard merely incorporated the 24-pin connector already specified in the SSI EPS standard.

Compared to the previous 20-pin design, the 24-pin main power connector includes additional +3.3V, +5V, and +12V terminals, allowing a substantially greater amount of power to be delivered to the motherboard. Each terminal in the main power connector is rated to handle up to 6 amps of current. By counting the number of terminals for each voltage level, you can calculate the power-handling capability of the connector as shown in Table 19.10.

Table 19.10   24-pin Main Power Connector Maximum Power-Handling Capabilities

Volts	No. Pins	Using Std. Terminals (W)	Using HCS Terminals (W)	Using Plus HCS Terminals (W)
+3.3V	4	79.2	118.8	145.2
+5V	5	150	225	275
+12V	2	144	216	264
Total watts:		373.2	559.8	684.2

Standard terminals are rated 6 amps.

HCS terminals are rated 9 amps.

Plus HCS terminals are rated 11 amps.

All ratings assume Mini-Fit Jr. connectors with 12–24 circuits using 18-gauge wire under standard temperature conditions.

This means the total power-handling capacity of this connector is 373 watts using standard terminals or 560 watts using HCS terminals, which is substantially higher than the 251 watts available in the previous 20-pin connector. Combining the 24-pin main and the 4-pin +12V power connector results in up to 565 watts (standard terminals) or 824 watts (using HCS terminals) total power available to the motherboard and processor! This is more than enough to support the highest-output power supplies on the market today, despite the fact that the power supply also has to supply power to the various disk drives in the system.

CPU Power Connectors

Power for the processor comes from a device called the *voltage regulator module (VRM)*, which is built into most modern motherboards. This device senses the CPU voltage requirements (usually via sense pins on the processor) and calibrates itself to provide the proper voltage to run the CPU. The design of a VRM enables it to run on either +5V or +12V for input power. Many have used +5V over the years, but starting in 2000 most converted to +12V because of the lower current requirements at that voltage. In addition, other devices might have already loaded the +5V, whereas only drive motors typically used the +12V prior to 2000. Whether the VRM on your board uses +5V or +12V depends on the particular motherboard or regulator design. Many modern voltage regulator ICs are designed to run on anything from a +4V to a +36V input, so it is up to the motherboard designer as to how they will be configured.

For example, I studied a system using a First International Computer (FIC) SD-11 motherboard, which used a Semtech SC1144ABCSW voltage regulator. This board design uses the +5V to convert to the lower voltage the CPU needs. Most motherboards use voltage regulator circuits controlled by chips from Semtech (http://www.semtech.com) or Linear Technology (http://www.linear.com). You can visit their sites for more data on these chips.

That motherboard accepted an Athlon 1GHz Cartridge version (Model 2), which according to AMD has a maximum power draw of 65W and a nominal voltage requirement of 1.8V. 65W at 1.8V would equate to 36.1A of current at that voltage (volts × amps = watts). If the voltage regulator used +5V as a feed, 65W would equate to only 13A at +5V. That would assume 100% efficiency in the regulator, which is impossible. Therefore, assuming 80% efficiency (which is typical), there would be about 16.25A actual draw on the +5V due to the regulator and processor combined.

When you consider that other circuits on the motherboard also use +5V power—remember that ISA or PCI cards are drawing that power as well—you can see how easy it is to overload the +5V lines from the supply to the motherboard.

Although most motherboard VRM designs up through the Pentium III and Athlon/Duron use +5V-based regulators, most systems since then use +12V-powered regulators. This is because the higher voltage significantly reduces the current draw. Using the same 65W AMD Athlon 1GHz CPU as an example, you would end up with the current draw at the various voltages shown in Table 19.11.

Table 19.11   Current Draw at Various Voltages

Watts	Volts	Amps	Amps at 80% Regulator Efficiency
65	1.8	36.1	—
65	3.3	19.7	24.6
65	5.0	13.0	16.3
65	12.0	5.4	6.8

As you can see, using +12V to power the chip results in only 5.4A of draw, or 6.8A assuming 80% efficiency on the part of the regulator.

So, modifying the motherboard VRM circuit to use the +12V power feed would seem simple. But as you'll recall from the preceding text, the ATX 2.03 specification has only a single +12V lead in the main power connector. Even the short-lived auxiliary connector had no +12V leads at all, so that was no help. Pulling up to 8A more through a single 18-gauge wire supplying +12V power to the motherboard is a recipe for a melted connector because the contacts in the main ATX connector are rated for only 6A using standard terminals. So, another solution was necessary.

Platform Compatibility Guide (PCG)

The amount of current drawn through the +12V connector is directly controlled by the processor. Modern motherboards are designed to support a wide range of different processors; however, because processor power consumption has increased, especially for high-end chips, the voltage regulator circuitry on a given motherboard may not have been designed to supply sufficient power to support all processors that might otherwise fit. To help eliminate the potential power problems that could result (including intermittent lockups or even damage such as damaged components or burned circuits), Intel created a power standard called the "Platform Compatibility Guide" (PCG). The PCG is marked on Intel boxed (retail) processors and motherboards. It is designed for system builders to use it as an easy way to know the power requirements of a processor and to ensure that the motherboard can meet those requirements.

The PCG is designated as a two- or three-digit alphanumeric value (for example, 05A), where the first two digits represent the year the particular specification was introduced and the optional third character stands for the market segment. PCG designations where the third character is A apply to processors and motherboards that fall in the low-end market (requiring less power), whereas designations where the third character is B apply to processors and motherboards that fall in the high-end market (requiring more power). Motherboards that support high-end processors by default also support low-end processors, but not the other way around. For example, you can install a processor with a PCG specification of 05A in a motherboard with a PCG specification of 05B, but if you install a 05B processor in a motherboard rated 05A, power problems will result. In other words, you can always install a processor with lower power requirements in a higher power capable motherboard, but not the other way around.

Although the PCG figures were specifically intended to apply to the processor and motherboard, they also can be used to specify minimum power supply requirements. Table 19.12 shows the PCG numbers and the power recommendations they prescribe.

Table 19.12   Intel Platform Compatibility Guide (PCG) +12V Connector Power Recommendations

PCG Number	Year Introduced	Market Segment	CPU Power Specification	Continuous +12V Rating	Peak +12V Rating
06	2006	All	65W	8 A	13 A
04A	2004	Low-end	84W	13 A	16.5 A
05A	2005	Low-end	95W	13 A	16.5 A
04B	2004	High-end	115W	13 A	16.5 A
05B	2005	High-end	130W	16 A	19 A

The power supply should be able to supply peak current for at least 10 ms.

Choosing a power supply with the required minimum output on the +12V connector helps to ensure proper operation of the system.

4-pin +12V CPU Power Connector

To augment the supply of +12V power to the motherboard, Intel created a new ATX12V power supply specification. This added a third power connector, called the *+12V connector*, specifically to supply additional +12V power to the board. The 4-pin +12V power connector is specified for all power supplies conforming to the ATX12V form factor and consists of a Molex Mini-Fit Jr. connector housing with female terminals. For reference, the connector is Molex part number 39-01-2040 and the terminals are part number 5556. This is the same style of connector as the ATX Main power connector, except with fewer pins.

This connector has two +12V power pins, each rated for 8A total using standard terminals (or up to 11A each using HCS terminals), allowing for up to 16A or more of additional +12V current to the motherboard, for a total of 22A of +12V when combined with the 20-pin main connector. The 4-pin +12V connector is shown in Figure 19.26.

Figure 19.26   +12V 4-pin CPU power connector, side and terminal end view.

The pinout of the +12V power connector is shown in Table 19.13.

Table 19.13   +12V 4-pin CPU Power Connector Pinout (Wire End View)

Color	Signal	Pin	Pin	Signal	Color
Yellow	+12V	3	1	Gnd	Black
Yellow	+12V	4	2	Gnd	Black

Using standard terminals, each pin in the +12V connector is rated to handle up to 8 amps of current, 11 amps with HCS terminals, or up to 12 amps with Plus HCS terminals. Even though it uses the same design and same terminals as the main power connector, the current rating per terminal is higher on this 4-pin connector than on the 20-pin main because there are fewer terminals overall. By counting the number of terminals for each voltage level, you can calculate the power-handling capability of the connector as shown in Table 19.14.

Table 19.14   4-pin +12V Power Connector Maximum Power-Handling Capabilities

Volts	No. Pins	Using Std. Terminals (W)	Using HCS Terminals (W)	Using Plus HCS Terminals (W)
+12V	2	192	264	288

Standard terminals are rated 8 amps.

HCS terminals are rated 11 amps.

Plus HCS terminals are rated 12 amps.

All ratings assume Mini-Fit Jr. connectors with 4–6 circuits using 18-gauge wire under standard temperature conditions.

This means the total power-handling capacity of this connector is 192 watts using standard terminals, which is available to and used only by the processor. Drawing more power than this maximum rating through the connector causes it to overheat, unless the HCS or Plus HCS terminals are used.

Combining the 20-pin main plus the 4-pin +12V power connector results in a maximum power-delivery capability to the motherboard of 443 watts (using standard terminals). The important thing to note is that adding the +12V connector provides the capability to support power supplies of up to 500 watts or more without overloading and melting the connectors.

Peripheral to 4-pin +12V CPU Power Adapters

If you are installing a new motherboard in a system that currently doesn't have the +12V connection for the CPU voltage regulator, an easy solution *may* be available; however, there are some caveats. Power adapters are available that convert one of the extra Peripheral power connectors found in most systems to a +12V 4-pin type. The drawback to this is that there are two +12V terminals in a +12V 4-pin connector, and only one +12V terminal in a Peripheral connector. If the adapter uses only a single Peripheral connector to power both +12V pins of the +12V connector, a serious power mismatch can result. Since the terminals in the Peripheral connector are only rated for 11A, and the two terminals in the +12V connector are also rated for up to 11A each, drawing more than 11A total can result in melted connectors at the Peripheral connector end. This is below the peak power requirements as recommended by the *Design Guide for Desktop Platform Form Factors* (www.formfactors.org), meaning these adapters do not conform to the latest standards. I did some calculations: Assuming a motherboard VRM (voltage regulator module) efficiency of 80%, a CPU power draw of 105W would just about equal 11A, the absolute limit of the connector. Since most CPUs can intermittently draw more than their nominal rating, I would hesitate to use one of these adapters on any processor drawing more than 75 watts, precluding their use with most mid- to high-end or multicore processors. An example of a Peripheral to +12V adapter is shown in Figure 19.27.

8-pin +12V CPU Power Connector

High-end motherboards often use multiple voltage regulators to supply power to the processor. To distribute the load among the additional voltage regulators, these boards may use two 4-pin +12V connectors; however, they are physically combined into a single 8-pin connector shell (see Figure 19.28). This type of CPU power connector was first defined in the EPS12V power supply specification version

1.6 released in the year 2000. Although this specification is intended for file servers, the increased power requirements of PC processors has caused this connector to appear on desktop PC motherboards as well.

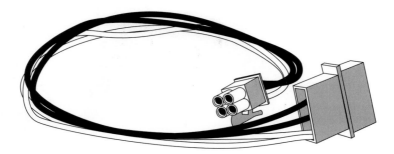

Figure 19.27   Peripheral to +12V power adapter.

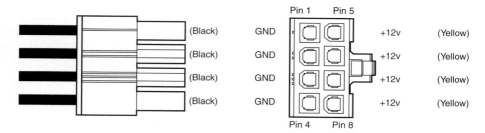

Figure 19.28   8-pin +12V CPU power connector, side and terminal end view.

The pinout of the 8-pin +12V CPU power connector is shown in Table 19.15.

Table 19.15   8-pin +12V CPU Power Connector Pinout (Wire End View)

Color	Signal	Pin	Pin	Signal	Color
Yellow	+12V	5	1	Gnd	Black
Yellow	+12V	6	2	Gnd	Black
Yellow	+12V	7	3	Gnd	Black
Yellow	+12V	8	4	Gnd	Black

Motherboards that utilize an 8-pin +12V CPU power connector must have signals connected to all 8-pins for the voltage regulators to function properly. Although a single 4-pin +12V power connector can fit (offset to one side or the other), doing so may result in only half of the voltage regulators functioning, possibly causing damage to the motherboard and/or processor. If your motherboard has an 8-pin +12V (CPU power) connector, you should either install a power supply with a matching 8-pin connector or use an adapter to convert the existing 4-pin connector on the power supply to an 8-pin connector to match the motherboard.

4-pin to 8-pin +12V CPU Power Adapters

If your power supply does not have a matching 8-pin +12V connector, you can use an adapter to convert an existing 4-pin connector to an 8-pin connector. An example of this is shown in Figure 19.29.

Figure 19.29 4-pin +12V to 8-pin +12V power adapter.

Adapters are available that also go the other way—that is, they convert an 8-pin CPU power connector to a 4-pin version. However, these are not always required because one can plug an 8-pin connector from a power supply into a 4-pin connector on a motherboard by simply offsetting the connector to one side when plugging it in. The only time the adapter would be needed is if there is a component on the board that is physically interfering with the portion of the connector that is offset.

Backward and Forward Compatibility

If you have reached this point, I'm sure you have some questions. For example, what happens if you purchase a new power supply that has a 24-pin main power connector but your motherboard has only a 20-pin main power socket? Likewise, what if you purchase a new motherboard that has a 24-pin main power socket but your power supply has only a 20-pin main power connector? The answers to these questions are surprising to say the least.

First, let me say that there are adapters that can convert a 24-pin connector to a 20-pin type, and the other way around, but surprisingly these adapters are *not* usually necessary, or even desirable. The plain truth is that compatibility has been engineered into the connectors, power supplies, and motherboards from the start.

If you look at the 24-pin main power connector diagram and compare it to the previous 20-pin design, you'll see that the extra 4 pins are all placed on one end of the connector and all the other pins are defined the same as they were previously. The design of these connectors is such that it allows an interesting bit of backward compatibility. The result is that you can plug a 24-pin main connector directly into a motherboard that has a 20-pin socket (and vice versa), without using an adapter! The trick is to position the connector such that the four extra pins are empty. Depending on the latch design, the latch on the side might not engage, but the connector will otherwise plug in and operate properly.

Figure 19.30 shows how you would connect a new power supply with a 24-pin connector to a motherboard that has only a 20-pin socket. The terminals on the 24-pin connector that are highlighted in gray would plug directly into the 20-pin socket, whereas the white highlighted terminals would remain free and unconnected.

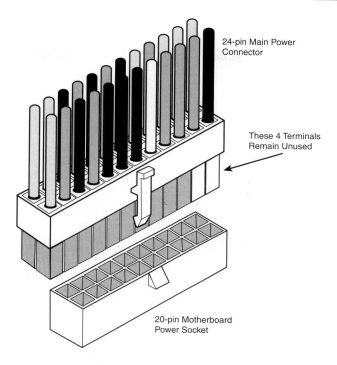

24-pin Main Power
Connector

These 4 Terminals
Remain Unused

20-pin Motherboard
Power Socket

Figure 19.30   Connecting a 24-pin main power connector to a 20-pin motherboard socket.

Logically this works because the first 20 pins of the 24-pin connector that match the 20-pin mother-board socket contain the correct signals in the correct positions. The only problem that might arise is if there are some components on the motherboard directly adjacent to the end of the 20-pin power socket that physically interfere with the four extra unused terminals on the 24-pin connector.

What about the opposite condition, in which you have a new motherboard with a 24-pin socket but your power supply has only a 20-pin connector? In this case, four terminals at the end of the mother-board socket are not connected. This also works because the 20-pin portion of both the connector and socket are the same. But this example raises another question: Will the motherboard operate properly without the extra power pins? Because the extra signals are merely additional voltage pins that are already present in the remaining part of the connector, the answer should be yes, but if the motherboard draws a lot of power, it can overload the remaining pins. After all, preventing overloads is the reason the extra pins were added in the first place.

Fortunately, even that problem has been solved. All the motherboards I've seen that use a 24-pin main power connector also have an additional peripheral (that is, disk drive) power connector onboard designed to provide the extra power that would be missing if you connected a 20-pin main power connector from your power supply. The documentation for the motherboard refers to this as an *alternate power connector*. Figure 19.31 shows an Intel D925XBC motherboard, which features 24-pin main, 4-pin +12V, and 4-pin alternate power connectors.

Regardless of whether you connect a 20- or 24-pin connector, the +12V power connector is always required because it provides power to the CPU. If you also plug a 24-pin main power connector into the 24-pin socket on the motherboard, the alternate power connection is unnecessary. However, you can plug a 20-pin main power connector into the 24-pin main power socket on the motherboard and then simply select a spare peripheral (disk drive) power connector from the power supply and plug it into the alternate power connector. Most power supplies have several extra peripheral power connectors for supporting additional drives. Using a 20-pin main and the alternate power connector satisfies the power requirements for the motherboard and any PCI Express x16 video cards, which can then draw up to 75 watts.

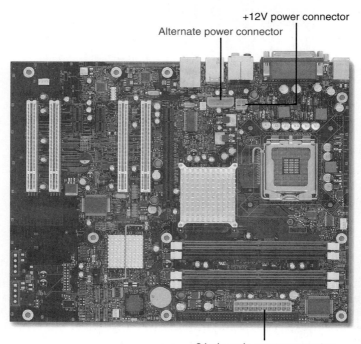

Figure 19.31   Intel D925XBC motherboard power connectors.

As a side note, you should be careful when plugging in the mismatched connectors so that they are offset properly. The main, +12V, and PCI Express graphics connectors are Molex Mini-Fit Jr.–type connectors that are keyed by virtue of a series of differently shaped plastic protrusions used around the terminals, which fit similarly shaped holes in the mating connectors. This keying is designed to prevent backward or improper off-center insertion, but I have found two problems with the keying that should be noted. One is that some alternate low-quality connector brands are built to looser tolerances than the original high-quality Molex versions, and the sloppier fit of the low-quality versions sometimes allows improper insertion. The other problem is that, with sufficient force, the keying on even the high-quality versions can be overcome. Because plugging a 20-pin connector into a 24-pin socket—or a 24-pin connector into a 20-pin socket—is designed to work even though they don't fully match up, you need to make sure you have the offsets correct or you risk damaging the board when you power it up.

Dell Proprietary (Nonstandard) ATX Design

If you currently own a desktop system made between 1996 and 2000 from Dell, you will definitely want to pay attention to this section. A potential booby trap is waiting to nail the unsuspecting owners of these systems who decide to upgrade either the motherboard or power supply. This hidden trap can cause the destruction of the motherboard, power supply, or both! Okay, now that I have your attention, read on....

As those of you who have attended my seminars or read previous editions of this book will know, I have long been a promoter of industry-standard components and wouldn't think of purchasing a desktop PC that didn't have what I consider an industry-standard form factor motherboard, power supply, and chassis (ATX, for example). I've been down the proprietary road before with systems from Packard Bell, Compaq, IBM, and other companies that used custom, unique, or proprietary components. For example, during a momentary lapse of reason in the early '90s, I purchased a Packard Bell system. I quickly outgrew the capabilities of the system, so I thought I'd upgrade it with a new motherboard and a faster processor. It was then that I discovered, to my horror, that LPX systems were not an interchangeable standard. Because of riser card differences, virtually no interchangeability of motherboards, riser cards, chassis, and power supplies existed. I had what I now refer to as a "disposable PC"—the kind you can't upgrade and have to throw away instead. Suddenly, the money I thought I had saved when initially purchasing the system paled in comparison to what I'd now have to spend to completely replace it. Lesson learned.

After several upgrade and repair experiences like that, I decided never again would I be trapped by systems using proprietary or nonstandard components. By purchasing only systems built with industry-standard parts, I could easily and inexpensively upgrade, maintain, or repair the systems for many years into the future. I have been preaching the gospel of industry-standard components in my seminars and in this book ever since.

Of course, building your own system from scratch is one way to avoid proprietary components, but often that route is more costly in both time and money than purchasing a prebuilt system. And what systems should I recommend for people who want an inexpensive prebuilt system but one that uses industry-standard parts so it can be inexpensively upgraded and repaired later? Although many system vendors and assemblers exist, I've settled on companies such as Gateway, MPC Computers (formerly MicronPC), and Dell. In fact, those are really the three largest system vendors that deal direct, and they mostly sell systems that use industry-standard ATX form factor components in all their main desktop system product lines. Or so I thought.

It seems that when Dell converted to the ATX motherboard form factor in mid-1996, it unfortunately defected from the newly released standard and began using specially modified Intel-supplied ATX motherboards with custom-wired power connectors. Inevitably, it also had custom power supplies made that duplicated the nonstandard pinout of the motherboard power connectors.

An even bigger crime than simply using nonstandard power connectors is that only the pinout is nonstandard; the connectors look like and are keyed the same as is dictated by true ATX. Therefore, nothing prevents you from plugging the Dell nonstandard power supply into a new industry-standard ATX motherboard you installed in your Dell case as an upgrade, or even plugging a new upgraded industry-standard ATX power supply into your existing Dell motherboard. But mixing either a new ATX board with the Dell supply or a new ATX supply with the existing Dell board is a recipe for silicon toast. How do you like your fried chips: medium or well-done?

Frankly, I'm amazed I haven't heard more about this because Dell has climbed to the lead in worldwide PC sales. In any case, I figure by getting this information out I can save thousands of innocent motherboards and power supplies from instant death upon installation.

If you've already fallen victim to this nasty circumstance, believe me, I feel your pain. I discovered this the hard way as well—by frying parts. At first, I thought the upgraded power supply I installed in one of my Dell systems was bad, especially considering the dramatic way it smoked when I turned on the system: I actually saw fire through the vents! Good thing I decided to check the color codes on the connectors and verify the pinout on another Dell system by using a voltmeter before I installed and fried a second supply. I was lucky in that the smoked supply didn't take the motherboard with it; I can only surmise that the supply fried so quickly it sacrificed itself and saved the motherboard. You might not be so lucky, and in most cases I'd expect you'd fry the board and supply together.

Call me a fool, but I didn't think I'd have to check the color-coding or get out my voltmeter to verify the Dell "pseudo-ATX" power connector pinouts before I installed a new ATX supply or motherboard. You'll also find that motherboard and power supply manufacturers don't like to replace these items under warranty when they are fried in this manner due to nonstandard connector wiring.

Dell's official explanation for its lack of conformance to the ATX standard was, "In the mid-90s the industry moved to a higher use of 3.3V motherboard components. Dell engineers designed a connector that supported the increased use of 3.3V current which differed from the industry proposed designs that we deemed less than robust." Unfortunately, this explanation doesn't hold much water because the standard ATX connector incorporated three 3.3V pins, allowing for up to 18A of current and the addition of the Auxiliary Connector added two more pins with 10A of additional current. Dell's pseudo-ATX design had only three 3.3V pins in the Auxiliary Connector, which could supply only up to 15A to the board. You can see that even the main ATX Connector alone had more 3.3V current than Dell's design using two connectors!

Because its technical explanation fails to address the issue, the only other reason I can imagine it did this is to lock people into purchasing replacement motherboards or power supplies from Dell. What makes this worse is that Dell uses virtually all Intel-manufactured boards in its systems. One system I have uses an Intel D815EEA motherboard, which is the same board used by many of the other major system builders, including Gateway and Micron. It's the same, except for the power connectors, that is. The difference is that Dell has Intel custom make the boards for with the nonstandard connectors. Everybody else gets virtually the same Intel boards, but with industry-standard connectors.

Tables 19.16 and 19.17 show the nonstandard Dell main and auxiliary power supply connections. This nonstandard wiring is used on Dell's pseudo-ATX systems.

Table 19.16   Dell Proprietary (Nonstandard) 20-pin ATX Main Power Connector Pinout (Wire End View)

Color	Signal	Pin	Pin	Signal	Color
Gray	PS_On	11	1	+5V	Red
Black	Gnd	12	2	Gnd	Black
Black	Gnd	13	3	+5V	Red
Black	Gnd	14	4	Gnd	Black
White	−5V	15	5	Power_Good	Orange
Red	+5V	16	6	+5VSB (Standby)	Purple
Red	+5V	17	7	+12V	Yellow
Red	+5V	18	8	−12V	Blue
KEY (blank)	—	19	9	Gnd	Black
Red	+5V	20	10	Gnd	Black

Table 19.17   Dell Proprietary (Nonstandard) ATX Auxiliary Power Connector Pinout

Pin	Signal	Color	Pin	Signal	Color
1	Gnd	Black	4	+3.3	Blue/White
2	Gnd	Black	5	+3.3	Blue/White
3	Gnd	Black	6	+3.3	Blue/White

At first I thought that if all Dell did was switch some of the terminals around, I could use a terminal pick to remove the terminals from the connectors (with the wires attached) and merely reinsert them into the proper connector positions, enabling me to use the Dell power supply with an upgraded ATX motherboard in the future. Unfortunately, if you study the Dell main and auxiliary connector pinouts I've listed here and compare them to the industry-standard ATX pinouts listed earlier, you'll see that not only are the voltage and signal positions changed, but the number of terminals carrying specific voltages and grounds has changed as well. You could modify a Dell supply to work with a standard ATX board or modify a standard ATX supply to work with a Dell board, but you'd have to do some cutting and splicing in addition to swapping some terminals around. Usually, it isn't worth the time and effort.

Systems known to have this nonstandard connector wiring include the following Dell models:

Dimension 2100	Dimension XPS Mxxx	OptiPlex GX115
Dimension 4100	Dimension XPS P133c MT	OptiPlex GX300
Dimension B1000R	Dimension XPS Pro 180n	OptiPlex GXa
Dimension L Series	Dimension XPS Rxxx	OptiPlex GXi
Dimension V350	Dimension XPS Txxx	Power Edge 2100
Dimension V400	OptiPlex G1	Power Edge 2200
Dimension XPS B Series	OptiPlex GX1	Precision Workstation 210
Dimension XPS Dxxx	OptiPlex GX110	Precision Workstation 400

If you do decide to upgrade the motherboard in any of these nonstandard Dell systems, a simple solution is available—just be sure you replace both the motherboard *and* power supply with industry-standard ATX components at the same time. That way nothing gets fried, and you'll be back to having a true industry-standard ATX system. If you want to replace just the Dell motherboard, you're out of luck unless you get your replacement board from Dell. On the other hand, if you want to replace just the power supply, you do have one alternative. PC Power and Cooling (www.pcpower.com) now makes several high-performance replacement power supplies with the modified Dell wiring. The internals are identical to its industry-standard, high-performance ATX supplies—only the number and arrangement of wires have changed.

Fortunately, starting in 2000, Dell switched to using industry-standard ATX power connections in its Dimension 4300, 4400, 8200, and most newer systems. That means barring any other unforeseen glitches, these systems should be more easily upgradeable by just replacing either the power supply or the motherboard alone.

Unfortunately, some of the newer Dell XPS systems use power supplies with proprietary form factors, which prevents you from installing an industry-standard replacement supply in the future. The bottom line is that, no matter which system you purchase, I recommend you check that it uses a power supply with an industry-standard form factor, both in regards to the electrical connectors and the physical shape.

Additional Power Connectors

Besides the motherboard power connectors, all power supplies include a variety of additional power connectors, mainly used for internally mounted drives but usable by other components as well. Most of these connectors are industry-standard types required by the various power supply form factor specifications. The following sections discuss the various types of additional device power connectors you're likely to find in your PC.

Peripheral Power Connectors

Perhaps the most common additional power connector seen on virtually all power supplies is the *peripheral power connector*, also called the *disk drive power connector*. What we know as the peripheral power connector was originally created by AMP as part of the commercial MATE-N-LOK series.

To determine the location of pin 1, carefully look at the connector. It is usually embossed in the plastic connector body; however, it is often tiny and difficult to read. Fortunately, these connectors are keyed and therefore difficult to insert incorrectly. Figure 19.32 shows the keying with respect to pin numbers on the larger drive power connector.

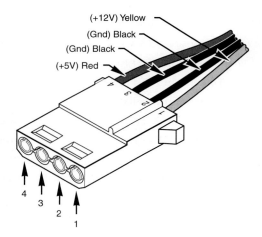

Figure 19.32   A peripheral power connector.

This is the one connector type that has been on all PC power supplies from the original IBM PC to the latest systems built today. It is most commonly known as a *disk drive connector*, but it is also used in some systems to provide additional power to the motherboard, video card, cooling fans, or just about anything that can use +5V or +12V power.

A peripheral power connector is a 4-pin connector with round terminals spaced 0.200" apart, rated to carry up to 11 amps per pin. Because there is one +12V pin and one +5V pin (the other two are grounds), the maximum power-handling capability of the peripheral connector is 187 watts. The plug is 0.830" wide, making it suitable for larger drives and devices.

Table 19.18 shows the peripheral power connector pinout and wire colors.

Table 19.18   Peripheral Power Connector Pinout (Large Drive Power Connector)

Pin	Signal	Color	Pin	Signal	Color
1	+12V	Yellow	3	Gnd	Black
2	Gnd	Black	4	+5V	Red

Floppy Power Connectors

When 3 1/2" floppy drives were first being integrated into PCs in the mid-1980s, it was clear that a smaller power connector was necessary. The answer came in what is now known as the *floppy power connector*, which was created by AMP as part of the EI (economy interconnection) series. These connectors are now used on all types of smaller drives and devices and feature the same +12V, +5V, and ground pins as the larger peripheral power connector. The floppy power connector has four pins spaced 2.5mm (0.098") apart, which makes the entire connector about half the overall width as the larger peripheral power connector. The pins are rated for only 2 amps each, giving a maximum power-handling capability of 34 watts.

Table 19.19 shows the pinouts for the smaller floppy drive power connector.

Table 19.19   3 1/2" Floppy Power Connector Pinout (Small Drive Power Connector)

Pin	Signal	Color	Pin	Signal	Color
1	+5V	Red	3	Gnd	Black
2	Gnd	Black	4	+12V	Yellow

The peripheral and floppy power connectors are universal with regard to pin configuration and even wire color. Figure 19.33 shows the peripheral and floppy power connectors.

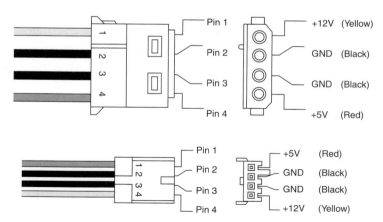

Figure 19.33   Peripheral and floppy power connectors.

The pin numbering and voltage designations are reversed on the floppy power connector. Be careful if you are making or using an adapter cable from one type of connector to another. Reversing the red and yellow wires will fry the drive or device you plug into.

Early power supplies featured only two peripheral power connectors, whereas later power supplies featured four or more of the larger peripheral (disk drive) connectors and one or two of the smaller floppy power connectors. Depending on their power ratings and intended uses, some supplies have as many as eight or more peripheral and/or floppy power connectors.

If you are adding drives and need additional power connectors, Y splitter cables (see Figure 19.34) as well as peripheral-to-floppy power connector adapters (see Figure 19.35) are available from many electronics supply houses (including RadioShack). These cables can adapt a single power connector to service two drives or enable you to convert the large peripheral power connector to a smaller floppy drive power connector. If you are using several Y-adapters, be sure that your total power supply output is capable of supplying the additional power and that you don't draw more power than a single connector can handle.

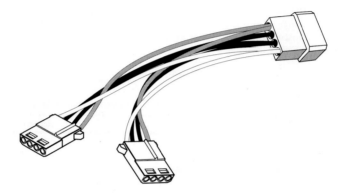

Figure 19.34   A common Y-adapter power cable.

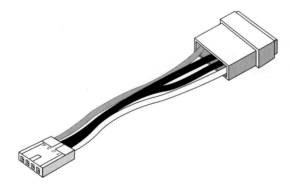

Figure 19.35   A peripheral-to-floppy power adapter cable.

Serial ATA Power Connectors

If you want to add Serial ATA drives to an existing system, you will need a newer power supply that includes a Serial ATA (SATA) power connector. The SATA power connector is a special 15-pin connector fed by only five wires, meaning three pins are connected directly to each wire. The overall width is about the same as the peripheral power connector, but the SATA connector is significantly thinner.

All the most recent power supply form factor specifications include SATA power connectors as mandatory for systems supporting SATA drives. Figure 19.36 shows a Serial ATA power connector.

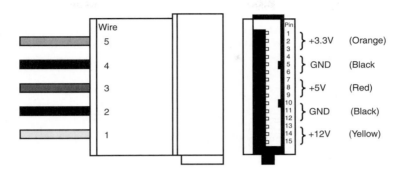

Figure 19.36 A Serial ATA power connector.

In the SATA power connector, each wire is connected to three terminal pins and the wire numbering is not in sync with the terminal numbering, which can be confusing.

If your power supply does not feature SATA power connectors, you can use an adapter to convert a standard peripheral power connector to a SATA power connector. However, such adapters do not include the +3.3V power. Fortunately, though, this is not a problem for most uses because most drives do not require +3.3V and use only +12V and +5V instead.

Figure 19.37 shows a peripheral-to-SATA power connector adapter.

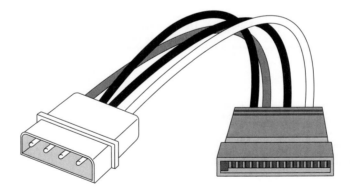

Figure 19.37 A peripheral-to-SATA power adapter.

PCI Express x16 Graphics Power Connectors

Althoughthe the ATX12V 2.x specification includes a new 24-pin main power connector with more power for devices such as video cards, the design was intended to power a video card drawing up to 75 watts maximum. Some video cards on the market are already drawing more power than that; for example, NVIDIA's GeForce 8800 Ultra draws 175 watts, and future cards might draw even more power. Greater than 75 watts cannot be provided via the motherboard directly, so the PCI-SIG (Special Interest Group) developed a standard for supplying at least 150 watts of power to the video card from the power supply via an additional graphics power connector. This will likely be included in future ATX12V power supply standards as well.

The PCI Express x16 Graphics Power specification consists of either a 6-pin or an 8-pin Molex Mini-Fit Jr. connector housing with female terminals that is used to provide power directly to the video card. For reference, the connector is similar to Molex part number 39-01-2060 (6-pin) or 39-01-2080 (8-pin), but with different keying to prevent interchanging them with +12V motherboard power connectors. The pinout of the connector is shown in Figure 19.38.

Figure 19.38   PCI Express x16 Graphics 6-pin power connector.

Pin 2 is technically listed as "not connected" in the official specification. Most graphics cards don't use it, but most power supplies do seem to include +12V there. The 8-pin version of the connector is the same as the 6-pin, with an additional pair of the +12V and ground pins added.

Each pin in the PCI Express graphics power connector is rated to handle up to 8 amps of current using standard terminals or 11 amps using HCS terminals. By counting the number of terminals for each voltage level, you can calculate the power-handling capability of the connector (see Table 19.20).

Table 19.20   PCI Express x16 Graphics Power Connector Maximum Power-Handling Capabilities

Connector Style	Volts	No. +12V Pins	Using Std. Terminals (W)	Using HCS Terminals (W)	Using Plus HCS Terminals (W)
6-pin	+12V	2	192	264	288
6-pin	+12V	3	288	396	432
8-pin	+12V	4	384	528	576

Only two +12V pins are required in the original 6-pin connector standard, even though most power supplies include three.

Standard terminals are rated 8 amps.

HCS terminals are rated 11 amps.

Plus HCS terminals are rated 12 amps.

All ratings assume Mini-Fit Jr. connectors using 18-gauge wire under standard temperature conditions.

Even though the specification calls for a delivery capability of only 150 watts, the total power-handling capacity of this connector is at least 192 watts using standard terminals, or 264 watts using HCS terminals. With additional terminals in the 6-pin and 8-pin versions, the power delivery capability increases to 528 watts using HCS terminals. This should be more than enough for even the most power-hungry video cards in the futurethe.

These connectors are often called *SLI* or *CrossFire* connectors because they are used by high-end PCI Express x16 boards with SLI or CrossFire capabilities. SLI and CrossFire are NVIDIA's and ATI's methods of using two video cards in unison, with each one drawing half of the screen for twice the performance. Each card can draw 150 watts or more, with many of the high-end cards using two on-board power connectors. This means that most power supplies that are rated as SLI- or CrossFire-ready include two or four of the 6/8-pin PCI Express x16 graphics power connectors. Using two video cards drawing 175 watts each means that if you have a 500-watt power supply, you will have only 150 watts of power left to run the motherboard, processor, and all the disk drives. With high-powered processors drawing 130 watts or more, this may not be enough. Systems using two or more high-end video cards require the highest-output supplies available, and some of the current ones are capable of putting out up to 1,000 watts (1 kilowatt) or more.

Note

NVIDIA has trademarked the term *SLI* as meaning *scalable link interface*, but its primary competitor—ATI—also uses similar dual-graphics card technology called CrossFire to achieve similar performance improvements.

If your existing power supply doesn't feature PCI Express x16 Graphics power connectors, you can use Y-adapters to convert two peripheral power connectors into a single 6-pin or 8-pin PCI Express x16 power connector. Note, however that these adapters will not help if the power supply is not capable of supplying sufficient total power.

Power Supply Specifications

Power supplies have several specifications that define their input and output capabilities as well as their operational characteristics. The following sections define and examine most of the common specifications related to power supplies.

Power Supply Loading

PC power supplies are of a *switching* rather than a *linear* design. The switching type of design uses a high-speed oscillator circuit to convert the higher wall-socket AC voltage to the much lower DC voltage used to power the PC and PC components. Switching-type power supplies are noted for being very efficient in size, weight, and energy in comparison to the linear design, which uses a large internal transformer to generate various outputs. This type of transformer-based design is inefficient in at least three ways. First, the output voltage of the transformer linearly follows the input voltage (hence the name *linear*), so any fluctuations in the AC power going into the system can cause problems with the output. Second, the high current-level (power) requirements of a PC system require the use of heavy wiring in the transformer. Third, the 60Hz frequency of the AC power supplied from your building is difficult to filter out inside the power supply, requiring large and expensive filter capacitors and rectifiers.

The switching supply, on the other hand, uses a switching circuit that chops up the incoming power at a relatively high frequency. This enables the use of high-frequency transformers that are much smaller and lighter. Also, the higher frequency is much easier and cheaper to filter out at the output, and the input voltage can vary widely. Input ranging from 90V to 135V still produces the proper output levels, and many switching supplies can automatically adjust to 240V input.

One characteristic of all switching-type power supplies is that they do not run without a *load*. Therefore, you must have something such as a motherboard and hard drive plugged in and drawing power for the supply to work. If you simply have the power supply on a bench with nothing plugged in to it, either the supply burns up or its protection circuitry shuts it down. Most power supplies are protected from no-load operation and shut down automatically. Some of the cheapest supplies, however, lack the protection circuit and relay and can be destroyed after a few seconds of no-load operation. A few power supplies have their own built-in load resistors, so they can run even though there isn't a normal load (such as a motherboard or hard disk) plugged in.

Some power supplies have minimum load requirements for both the +5V and +12V sides. According to IBM specifications for the 192-watt power supply used in the original AT, a minimum load of 7.0 amps was required at +5V and a minimum of 2.5 amps was required at +12V for the supply to work properly. As long as a motherboard was plugged into the power supply, the motherboard would draw sufficient +5V at all times to keep those circuits in the supply happy. However, +12V is typically used only by motors (and not motherboards), and the floppy or CD/DVD drive motors are off most of the time. Because floppy or optical (CD/DVD) drives don't present any +12V load unless they are spinning, systems without a hard disk drive could have problems because there wouldn't be enough load on the +12V circuit in the supply.

To alleviate problems, when IBM used to ship the original AT systems without a hard disk, it plugged the hard disk drive power cable into a large 5-ohm, 50-watt sandbar resistor that was mounted in a small, metal cage assembly where the drive would have been. The AT case had screw holes on top of where the hard disk would go, specifically designed to mount this resistor cage.

Note

Several computer stores I knew of in the mid-1980s ordered the diskless AT and installed their own 20MB or 30MB drives, which they could get more cheaply from sources other than IBM. They were throwing away the load resistors by the hundreds! I managed to grab a couple at the time, which is how I know the type of resistor they used.

This resistor would be connected between pin 1 (+12V) and pin 2 (Ground) on the hard disk power connector. This placed a 2.4-amp load on the supply's +12V output, drawing 28.8 watts of power (it would get hot!) and thus enabling the supply to operate normally. Note that the cooling fan in most power supplies draws approximately 0.1–0.25 amps, bringing the total load to 2.5 amps or more. If the load resistor were missing, the system would intermittently fail to start up.

Most of the power supplies in use today do not require as much of a load as the original IBM AT power supply. In most cases, a minimum load of 0–0.3 amps at +3.3V, 2.0–4.0 amps at +5V, and 0.5–1.0 amps at +12V is considered acceptable. Most motherboards easily draw the minimum +5V current by themselves. The standard power supply cooling fan draws only 0.1–0.25 amps, so the +12V minimum load might still be a problem for a diskless workstation. Generally, the higher the rating on the supply, the more minimum load required. However, exceptions do exist, so this is a specification you should check when evaluating power supplies.

Some switching power supplies have built-in load resistors and can run in a no-load situation. Most power supplies don't have internal load resistors but might require only a small load on the +5V line to operate properly. Some supplies, however, might require +3.3V, +5V, and +12V loads to work—the only way to know is by checking the documentation for the particular supply in question.

No matter what, if you want to properly and accurately bench test a power supply, be sure you place a load on at least one (or preferably all) of the positive voltage outputs. This is one reason it is best to test a supply while it is installed in the system, instead of testing it separately on the bench. For impromptu bench testing, you can use a spare motherboard and one or more hard disk drives to load the outputs.

Power Supply Ratings

A system manufacturer should be able to provide you the technical specifications of the power supplies it uses in its systems. This type of information can be found in the system's technical reference manual, as well as on stickers attached directly to the power supply. Power supply manufacturers can also supply this data, which is preferable if you can identify the manufacturer and contact them directly or via the Web.

The input specifications are listed as voltages, and the output specifications are listed as amps at several voltage levels. IBM reports output wattage level as "specified output wattage." If your manufacturer does not list the total wattage, you can convert amperage to wattage by using the following simple formula:

$$\text{watts} = \text{volts} \times \text{amps}$$

For example, if a motherboard is listed as drawing 6 amps of +5V current, that equals 30 watts of power according to the formula.

By multiplying the voltage by the amperage available at each main output and then adding the results, you can calculate the total capable output wattage of the supply. Note that only positive voltage outputs are normally used in calculating outputs; the negative outputs, Standby, Power_Good, or other signals that are not used to power components are exempt.

Table 19.21 shows the standard power supply output levels available in industry-standard form factors. Most manufacturers offer supplies with ratings from 100 watts to 450 watts or more. Table 19.21 and 19.22 show the rated outputs at each of the voltage levels for supplies with different manufacturer-specified output ratings.

Table 19.21 Typical Non-ATX Power Supply Output Ratings

Rated Output (Watts)	100W	150W	200W	250W	300W	375W	450W
Output current (amps):							
+5V	10.0	15.0	20.0	25.0	32.0	35.0	45.0
+12V	3.5	5.5	8.0	10.0	10.0	13.0	15.0
−5V	0.3	0.3	0.3	0.5	0.5	0.5	1.0
−12V	0.3	0.3	0.3	0.5	0.5	0.5	1.0
Calc. output (watts)	92	141	196	245	280	331	405

Adding a +3.3V output to the power supply modifies the equation significantly. Table 19.22 contains data for various ATX/ATX12V power supplies from PC Power and Cooling.

Table 19.22 PC Power and Cooling ATX/ATX12V Power Supply Output Ratings

Model (Rated Output)	235W	250W	275W	300W	350W	400W	425W	510W
+3.3V	13	13	14	14	28	40	40	30
+5V	22	25	30	30	32	40	40	40
+12V	8	10	10	12	15	15	15	34
−5V	0.3	0.3	0.3	0.3	0.3	0.3	0.3	0.3
−12V	0.5	0.5	1.0	1.0	0.8	1.0	1.0	2.0
+5VSB	2.0	2.0	2.0	2.0	2.0	2.0	2.0	3.0
Total watts (3.3+5+12)*	249	288	316	340	432	512	512	707
+3.3V and +5V Max.	125	150	150	150	215	300	300	300

Note the calculated maximum output is theoretical, assuming the maximum draw from the +3.3V, +5V, and +12V simultaneously. Virtually all power supplies place limits on the maximum combined draw for the +3.3V and +5V. This would make the true maximum rating somewhat less than the calculated maximum.

The 400W and 425W supplies listed here seem to have the same specs; however, the 400W version uses a special low-speed quiet fan that has slightly less cooling ability, hence the lower maximum rating figure.

If you compute the total output using the formula described earlier, these power supplies seem to produce an output that is much higher than their ratings. The 300W model, for example, comes out at 340 watts. However, notice that the supply also has a maximum combined output for the +3.3V and +5V of 150 watts. This means you can't draw the maximum rating on both the +5V and +3.3V circuits simultaneously but must keep the total combined draw between them at 150W or less. This brings the total output to a more logical 294 watts.

Most PC power supplies have ratings between 150 and 300 watts. Although lesser ratings are not usually desirable, you can purchase heavy-duty power supplies for most systems that have outputs as high as 600 watts or more.

The 300-watt and larger units are recommended for fully optioned desktops or tower systems. These supplies run any combination of motherboard and expansion card, as well as a large number of disk drives and other peripherals. In most cases, you can't exceed the ratings on these power supplies—the system will run out of room for additional items first!

Most power supplies are considered to be universal, or worldwide. That is, they also can run on the 240V, 50-cycle current used in Europe and many other parts of the world. Many power supplies that can switch from 120V to 240V input do so automatically, but a few require you to set a switch on the back of the power supply to indicate which type of power you will access.

Note

In North America, power companies are required to supply split-phase 240V (plus or minus 5%) AC, which equals two 120V legs. Resistive voltage drops in the building wiring can cause the 240V to drop to 220V or the 120V to drop to 110V by the time the power reaches an outlet at the end of a long circuit run. For this reason, the input voltage for an AC-powered device might be listed as anything between 220V and 240V, or 110V and 120V. I use the 240/120V numbers throughout this chapter because that is the intended standard figure.

Caution

If your supply does not switch input voltages automatically, make sure the voltage setting is correct. If you plug the power supply into a 120V outlet while it's set in the 240V setting, no damage will result, but the supply won't operate properly until you correct the setting. On the other hand, if you plug in to a 240V outlet and have the switch set for 120V, you can cause damage.

Other Power Supply Specifications

In addition to power output, many other specifications and features go into making a high-quality power supply. I have had many systems over the years. My experience has been that if a brownout occurs in a room with several systems running, the systems with higher-quality power supplies and higher output ratings are far more likely to make it through the power disturbances unscathed, whereas others choke.

High-quality power supplies also help protect your systems. A high-quality power supply from a vendor such as PC Power and Cooling will not be damaged if any of the following conditions occur:

- A 100% power outage of any duration
- A brownout of any kind

- A spike of up to 2,500V applied directly to the AC input (for example, a lightning strike or a lightning simulation test)

Decent power supplies have an extremely low current leakage to ground of less than 500 microamps. This safety feature is important if your outlet has a missing or an improperly wired ground line.

As you can see, these specifications are fairly tough and are certainly representative of a high-quality power supply. Make sure that your supply can meet these specifications.

You can also use many other criteria to evaluate a power supply. The power supply is a component many users ignore when shopping for a PC, and it is therefore one that some system vendors choose to skimp on. After all, a dealer is far more likely to be able to increase the price of a computer by spending money on additional memory or a larger hard drive than by installing a better power supply.

When buying a computer (or a replacement power supply), you always should learn as much as possible about the power supply. However, many consumers are intimidated by the vocabulary and statistics found in a typical power supply specification. Here are some of the most common parameters found on power supply specification sheets, along with their meanings:

- **Mean Time Between Failures (MTBF) or Mean Time To Failure (MTTF)**—The (calculated) average interval, in hours, that the power supply is expected to operate before failing. Power supplies typically have MTBF ratings (such as 100,000 hours or more) that are clearly not the result of real-time empirical testing. In fact, manufacturers use published standards to calculate the results based on the failure rates of the power supply's individual components. MTBF figures for power supplies often include the load to which the power supply was subjected (in the form of a percentage) and the temperature of the environment in which the tests were performed.

- **Input Range (or Operating Range)**—The range of voltages that the power supply is prepared to accept from the AC power source. For 120V AC power, an input range of 90V–135V is common; for 240V power, a 180V–270V range is typical.

- **Peak Inrush Current**—The greatest amount of current drawn by the power supply at a given moment immediately after it is turned on, expressed in terms of amps at a particular voltage. The lower the current, the less thermal shock the system experiences.

- **Hold-up Time**—The amount of time (in milliseconds) that a power supply can maintain output within the specified voltage ranges after a loss of input power. This enables your PC to continue running without resetting or rebooting if a brief interruption in AC power occurs. Values of 15–30 milliseconds are common for today's power supplies, and the higher (longer), the better. The ATX12V specification calls for a minimum of 17ms hold-up time.

- **Transient Response**—The amount of time (in microseconds) a power supply takes to bring its output back to the specified voltage ranges after a steep change in the output current. In other words, the amount of time it takes for the output power levels to stabilize after a device in the system starts or stops drawing power. Power supplies sample the current being used by the computer at regular intervals. When a device stops drawing power during one of these intervals (such as when a floppy drive stops spinning), the power supply might supply too high a voltage to the output for a brief time. This excess voltage is called *overshoot*, and the transient response is the time that it takes for the voltage to return to the specified level. This is seen as a spike in voltage by the system and can cause glitches and lockups. Once a major problem that came with switching power supplies, overshoot has been greatly reduced in recent years. Transient response values are sometimes expressed in time intervals, and at other times they are expressed in terms of a particular output change, such as "power output levels stay within regulation during output changes of up to 20%."

- **Overvoltage Protection**—Defines the trip points for each output at which the power supply shuts down or squelches that output. Values can be expressed as a percentage (for example, 120% for +3.3 and +5V) or as raw voltages (for example, +4.6V for the +3.3V output and +7.0V for the +5V output).

- **Maximum Load Current**—The largest amount of current (in amps) that safely can be delivered through a particular output. Values are expressed as individual amperages for each output voltage. With these figures, you can calculate not only the total amount of power the power supply can supply, but also how many devices using those various voltages it can support.

- **Minimum Load Current**—The smallest amount of current (in amps) that must be drawn from a particular output for that output to function. If the current drawn from an output falls below the minimum, the power supply could be damaged or automatically shut down.

- **Load Regulation (or Voltage Load Regulation)**—When the current drawn from a particular output increases or decreases, the voltage changes slightly as well—usually increasing as the current rises. Load regulation is the change in the voltage for a particular output as it transitions from its minimum load to its maximum load (or vice versa). Values, expressed in terms of a +/– percentage, typically range from +/–1% to +/–5% for the +3.3V, +5V, and +12V outputs.

- **Line Regulation**—The change in output voltage as the AC input voltage transitions from the lowest to the highest value of the input range. A power supply should be capable of handling any AC voltage in its input range with a change in its output of 1% or less.

- **Efficiency**—The ratio of power input to power output, expressed in terms of a percentage. Values of 65%–85% are common for power supplies today. The remaining 15%–35% of the power input is converted to heat during the AC/DC conversion process. Although greater efficiency means less heat inside the computer (always a good thing) and lower electric bills, it should not be emphasized at the expense of precision, stability, and durability, as evidenced in the supply's load regulation and other parameters.

- **Ripple (or Ripple and Noise, or AC Ripple, or PARD [Periodic and Random Deviation])**—The average voltage of all AC effects on the power supply outputs, usually measured in millivolts peak-to-peak or as a percentage of the nominal output voltage. The lower this figure, the better. Higher-quality units are typically rated at 1% ripple (or less), which if expressed in volts would be 1% of the output. Consequently, for +5V that would be 0.05V or 50mV (millivolts). Ripple can be caused by internal switching transients, feed through of the rectified line frequency, and other random noise.

Power Factor Correction

Recently, the power line efficiency and harmonic distortion generation of PC power supplies has come under examination. This generally falls under the topic of the power factor of the supply. Interest in power factor is not only due to an improvement in power efficiency, but also because of a reduction in the generation of harmonics back on the power line. In particular, new standards are now mandatory in many European Union (EU) countries that require harmonics be reduced below a specific amount. The circuitry required to do this is called *power factor correction (PFC)*.

The *power factor* measures how effectively electrical power is being used and is expressed as a number between 0 and 1. A high power factor means that electrical power is being used effectively, whereas a low power factor indicates poor utilization of electrical power. To understand the power factor, you must understand how power is used.

Generally, two types of loads are placed on AC power lines:

- **Resistive**—Power converted into heat, light, motion, or work

- **Inductive**—Sustains an electromagnetic field, such as in a transformer or motor

A resistive load is often called *working power* and is measured in kilowatts (KW). An inductive load, on the other hand, is often called *reactive power* and is measured in kilovolt-amperes-reactive (KVAR). Working power and reactive power together make up *apparent power*, which is measured in kilovolt-amperes (KVA). The power factor is measured as the ratio of working power to apparent power, or working power/apparent power (KW/KVA). The ideal power factor is 1, where the working power and apparent power are the same.

The concept of a resistive load or working power is fairly easy to understand. For example, a light bulb that consumes 100W of power generates 100W worth of heat and light. This is a pure resistive load. An inductive load, on the other hand, is a little harder to understand. Think about a transformer, which has coil windings to generate an electromagnetic field and then induce current in another set of windings. A certain amount of power is required to saturate the windings and generate the magnetic field, even though no work is being done. A power transformer that is not connected to anything is a perfect example of a pure inductive load. An apparent power draw exists to generate the fields, but no working power exists because no actual work is being done.

When the transformer is connected to a load, it uses both working power and reactive power. In other words, power is consumed to do work (for example, if the transformer is powering a light bulb), and apparent power is used to maintain the electromagnetic field in the transformer windings. In an AC circuit, these loads can become out of sync or phase, meaning they don't peak at the same time, which can generate harmonic distortions back down the power line. I've seen examples where electric motors have caused distortions in television sets plugged in to the same power circuit.

PFC usually involves adding capacitance to the circuit to maintain the inductive load without drawing additional power from the line. This makes the working power and apparent power the same, which results in a power factor of 1. It usually isn't just as simple as adding some capacitors to a circuit, although that can be done and is called *passive* power factor correction. *Active* power factor correction involves a more intelligent circuit designed to match the resistive and inductive loads so they are seen as the same by the electrical outlet.

A power supply with active power factor correction draws low distortion current from the AC source and has a power factor rating of 0.9 or greater. A nonpower factor corrected supply draws highly distorted current and is sometimes referred to as a *nonlinear* load. The power factor of a noncorrected supply is typically 0.6–0.8. Therefore, only 60% of the apparent power consumed is actually doing real work!

Having a power supply with active PFC might or might not lower your electric bill (it depends on how your power is measured), but it will definitely reduce the load on the building wiring. With PFC, all the power going into the supply is converted into actual work and the wiring is less overworked. For example, if you ran a number of computers on a single breaker-controlled circuit and found that you were blowing the breaker periodically, you could switch to systems with active PFC power supplies and reduce the load on the wiring by up to 40%, meaning you would be less likely to blow the breaker.

The International Electrical Committee (IEC) has released standards dealing with the low-frequency public supply system. The initial standards were 555.2 (Harmonics) and 555.3 (Flicker), but they have since been refined and are now available as IEC 1000-3-2 and IEC 1000-3-3, respectively. As governed by the EMC directive, most electrical devices sold within the member countries of the EU must meet the IEC standards. The IEC1000-3-2/3 standards became mandatory in 1997 and 1998.

Even if you don't live in a country where PFC is required, I highly recommend specifying PC power supplies with active PFC. The main benefits of PFC supplies is that they do not overheat building wiring or distort the AC source waveform, which causes less interference on the line for other devices.

Power Supply Safety Certifications

Many agencies around the world certify electric and electronic components for safety and quality. The most commonly known agency in the United States is Underwriters Laboratories, Inc. (UL). UL standard #60950—*Safety of Information Technology Equipment, Third Edition*—covers power supplies and other PC components. You should always purchase power supplies and other devices that are UL-certified. It has often been said that, although not every good product is UL-certified, no bad products are.

In Canada, electric and electronic products are certified by the Canadian Standards Agency (CSA). The German equivalents are TÜV Rheinland and VDE, and NEMKO operates in Norway. These agencies are responsible for certification of products throughout Europe. Power supply manufacturers that sell to an international market should have products that are certified at least by UL, the CSA, and TÜV— if not by all the agencies listed, and more.

Apart from UL-type certifications, many power supply manufacturers, even the most reputable ones, claim that their products have a Class B certification from the Federal Communications Commission, meaning that they meet FCC standards for electromagnetic and radio frequency interference (EMI/RFI). This is a contentious point, however, because the FCC does not certify power supplies as individual components. Title 47 of the Code of Federal Regulations, Part 15, Section 15.101(c) states the following:

> The FCC does NOT currently authorize motherboards, cases, and internal power supplies. Vendor claims that they are selling 'FCC-certified cases,' 'FCC-certified motherboards,' or 'FCC-certified internal power supplies' are false.

In fact, an FCC certification can be issued collectively only to a base unit consisting of a computer case, motherboard, and power supply. Thus, a power supply purported to be FCC-certified was actually certified along with a particular case and motherboard—not necessarily the same case and motherboard you are using in your system. This does not mean, however, that the manufacturer is being deceitful or that the power supply is inferior. If anything, this means that when evaluating power supplies, you should place less weight on the FCC certification than on other factors, such as UL certification.

Power-use Calculations

When expanding or upgrading your PC, you should ensure that your power supply is capable of providing sufficient current to power all the system's internal devices. One way to see whether your system is capable of expansion is to calculate the levels of power consumption by the various system components in your system, and then compare that to the rating on the power supply to see if it is up to the job. This calculation can also help you decide whether you must upgrade the power supply to a more capable unit. Unfortunately, these calculations can be difficult to make accurately because many manufacturers do not publish detailed power consumption data for their products. In some cases you can find the specs from a similar component and go by that data instead. Usually components of the same basic design, capability and vintage will have relatively the same power consumption characteristics. Table 19.23 shows the range of power usage for typical PC components I've observed over the last few years.

Table 19.23   Power Consumption Calculation

Component	Power Usage	Comments
Motherboard	50W-75W	Depends on the number of integrated components
Processor	25W-150W	For each physical processor (not cores), most are 50W to 100W
RAM	5W-15W	For each module (DIMM)

Table 19.23   Continued

Component	Power Usage	Comments
Integrated Video	5W-15W	Integrated into the north bridge chip
Discrete Video Card	25W-200W	For each video card
PCI Card	5W-15W	For each non-video card
PCIe Card	10W-25W	For each non-video card
Hard Disk Drive	15W-30W	For each drive, power use increased during startup
Optical Drive	15W-35W	For each drive
Cooling Fan	3W-5W	For each fan
USB/FireWire	2W-5W	For each used port

Of course power consumption can vary greatly for different devices such as processors and video cards, so if you want to be more informed, consult the data sheets or technical manuals for your specific components. Also these overall wattage figures do not give the breakdown covering which of the rails (+3.3V, +5V, or +12V) will be used by each device. In some cases, the combination of components used can exceed the available power on a single rail while still being under budget for the total wattage available from all of the rails combined. That is in fact one reason that people end up purchasing a power supply with a much higher watt rating than might seem necessary.

Once you've added everything up I recommend you multiply the total power consumed by all of your components by 1.5 in order to estimate the size of power supply required. This will allow some headroom for future expansion and also account for the fact that at certain times some devices can draw much more than their nominal power.

If you want an easier way to calculate your estimated power requirements, Asus has a fairly good power supply wattage calculator that you can use online at the following URL: http://support.asus.com/PowerSupplyCalculator/PSCalculator.aspx

By filling in all of the fields with the components in the intended system, the calculator will give you an estimate of the minimum power supply rating you should choose to power the system.

Different types of bus slots can provide different levels of power for cards. Fortunately, it is rare for any cards other than video cards to use the maximum allowable power. Table 19.24 shows the maximum power available per slot for different bus types.

Table 19.24   Maximum Available Power Per Bus Slot

Bus Type	+3.3V Current (amps)	+5V Current (amps)	+12V Current (amps)	Total Power (watts)
ISA	n/a	2.0	0.175	12.1
EISA	n/a	4.5	1.5	40.5
VL-bus	n/a	2.0	n/a	10
16-bit MCA	n/a	1.6	0.175	10.1
32-bit MCA	n/a	2.0	0.175	12.1
PCI	7.6	5	0.5	56
AGP	6	2	1	42
PCI Express	4.8	n/a	4.8	75

The biggest cause of power supply overload problems has historically been filling up the expansion slots (especially with multiple video cards), using high-powered processors, and adding more drives. Multiple hard drives, optical drives, and floppy drives can create quite a drain on the system power supply. Be sure you have enough +12V power to run all the drives you plan to install. Tower systems can be especially problematic because they have so many drive bays. Just because the case has room for the devices doesn't mean the power supply can support them. Be sure you have enough power to run all your expansion cards, especially video cards, but remember that most cards draw less than the maximum allowed. Today's newest processors can have very high current requirements for the +5V or +3.3V supplies. When selecting a power supply for your system, it pays to be conservative, so be sure to take into account any future upgrades or additions to the system.

Many people wait until an existing component fails to replace it with an upgraded version. If you are on a tight budget, this "if it ain't broke, don't fix it" attitude might be necessary. Power supplies, however, often do not fail completely all at once; they can fail in an intermittent fashion or allow fluctuating power levels to reach the system, which results in unstable operation. You might be blaming system lockups on software bugs when the culprit is an overloaded power supply. In addition, an inadequate or failing supply causing lockups can result in file system corruption, which causes even further system instabilities (that could remain present even after replacing the power supply). If you use bus-powered USB devices, a failing power supply can also cause these devices to fail or malfunction. If you have been running your original power supply for a long time and have upgraded your system in other ways, you should expect some problems, and you might want to consider reloading the operating system and applications from scratch.

Although there is certainly an appropriate place for the exacting power-consumption calculations you've read about in this section, a great many experienced PC users prefer the "don't worry about it" power calculation method. This technique consists of buying or building a system with a good-quality 500-watt or higher power supply (or upgrading to such a supply in an existing system) and then upgrading the system freely, without concern for power consumption.

Power Cycling

Should you turn off a system when it is not in use? To answer this frequent question, you should understand some facts about electrical components and what makes them fail. Combine this knowledge with information on power consumption, cost, and safety to come to your own conclusion. Because circumstances can vary, the best answer for your own situation might be different from the answer for others, depending on your particular needs and applications.

Frequently powering a system on and off does cause deterioration and damage to the components. This seems logical, but the simple reason is not obvious to most people. Many believe that flipping system power on and off frequently is harmful because it electrically "shocks" the system. The real problem, however, is temperature or thermal shock. As the system warms up, the components expand; as it cools off, the components contract. In addition, various materials in the system have different thermal expansion coefficients, so they expand and contract at different rates. Over time, thermal shock causes deterioration in many areas of a system.

From a pure system-reliability viewpoint, you should insulate the system from thermal shock as much as possible. When a system is turned on, the components go from ambient (room) temperature to as high as 185°F (85°C) within 30 minutes or less. When you turn off the system, the same thing happens in reverse, and the components cool back to ambient temperature in a short period of time.

Thermal expansion and contraction remains the single largest cause of component failure. Chip cases can split, allowing moisture to enter and contaminate them. Delicate internal wires and contacts can break, and circuit boards can develop stress cracks. Surface-mounted components expand and contract at rates different from the circuit boards on which they are mounted, causing enormous stress at the solder joints. Solder joints can fail due to the metal hardening from the repeated stress, resulting in cracks in the joint. Components that use heatsinks, such as processors, transistors, or voltage regulators, can overheat and fail because the thermal cycling causes heatsink adhesives to deteriorate and break the thermally conductive bond between the device and the heatsink. Thermal cycling also causes socketed devices and connections to loosen, or *creep*, which can cause a variety of intermittent contact failures.

◀◀ See "SIMMs, DIMMs, and RIMMs," p. 533.

Thermal expansion and contraction affect not only chips and circuit boards, but also things such as hard disk drives. Most hard drives today have sophisticated thermal compensation routines that make adjustments in head position relative to the expanding and contracting platters. Most drives perform this thermal compensation routine once every 5 minutes for the first 30 minutes the drive is running and then every 30 minutes thereafter. In older drives, this procedure can be heard as a rapid "tick-tick-tick-tick" sound.

In essence, anything you can do to keep the system at a constant temperature prolongs the life of the system, and the best way to accomplish this is to leave the system either permanently on or permanently off. Of course, if the system is never turned on in the first place, it should last a long time indeed!

Now, I am not saying that you should leave all systems on 24 hours a day. A system powered on and left unattended can be a fire hazard (I have witnessed at least two monitors spontaneously catch fire—luckily, I was there at the time), is a data security risk (from cleaning crews and other nocturnal visitors), can be easily damaged if moved while running, and wastes electrical energy.

Typical rates are 10 cents for a kilowatt-hour of electricity. Using this figure, combined with information about what a typical PC might consume, we can determine how much it will cost to run the system annually and what effect we can have on the operating cost by judiciously powering off or taking advantage of the various ACPI sleep, suspend, or Stand By modes that are available. ACPI stands for Advanced Power and Configuration Interface, and is described in more detail later in this chapter.

A typical desktop-style PC consumes anywhere from 75W to 300W when idling and from 150W to 600W under a load, depending on the configuration, age, and design of the system. This does not include monitors, which for LCDs range from 25W to 50W while active, while CRTs range from 75W to 150W or more. One PC and LCD display combination I tested consumed an average of 250W (0.25 kilowatts) of electricity during normal operation. The same system drew 200W when in ACPI S1 Stand By mode, only 8W while in ACPI S3 Stand By mode, and 7W of power while either turned off or hibernating (ACPI S4 mode).

Using those figures here are some calculations for annual power costs:

```
        Electricity Cost:   $0.10 Dollars per KWh
        PC/Display Power:   0.250 KW avg. while running
        PC/Display Power:   0.200 KW avg. while in ACPI S1 Stand By
        PC/Display Power:   0.008 KW avg. while in ACPI S3 Stand By
        PC/Display Power:   0.007 KW avg. while in ACPI S4 Stand By
        PC/Display Power:   0.007 KW avg. while OFF
              Work Hours:    2080 Per year
          Non-Work Hours:    6656 Per year
             Total Hours:    8736 Per year
-------------------------------------------------------------------
Annual Operating Cost:  $218.40 Left ON continuously
Annual Operating Cost:  $185.12 In S1 Stand By during non-work hours
```

```
Annual Operating Cost:     $57.32 In S3 Stand By during non-work hours
Annual Operating Cost:     $56.66 In S4 Stand By during non-work hours
Annual Operating Cost:     $56.66 Turned OFF during non-work hours
------------------------------------------------------------------
         Annual Savings:     $0.00 Left ON continuously
         Annual Savings:    $33.28 In S1 Stand By during non-work hours
         Annual Savings:   $161.08 In S3 Stand By during non-work hours
         Annual Savings:   $161.74 In S4 Stand By during non-work hours
         Annual Savings:   $161.74 Turned OFF during non-work hours
```

This means it would cost over $218 annually to run the system if it were left on continuously. However, if it were turned off during non-work hours, the annual operating cost would be reduced to $56, for an annual savings of over $161! As you can see, turning systems off when they are not in use can amount to a huge savings over time.

But even more interesting is that you don't have to turn a system all the way off to achieve this type of savings. When properly configured, most PCs will enter ACPI S3 Stand By mode either manually or after a pre-set period of inactivity, dropping to a power consumption level of 8W or less. In other words, if you configure the PC to enter S3 Stand By mode when not active, you can achieve nearly the same savings as if you were to turn it off completely. In the preceding example, it would only cost an additional $0.66 to keep the system in Stand By mode during non-work hours versus turned completely off, still resulting in an annual savings of over $161.

With the improved power management capabilities of modern hardware, combined with the stability and control features built in to modern operating systems such as Windows XP and Vista, you can set your systems to Stand By and Resume almost instantly, without having to go through the lengthy shutdown and cold boot startup procedures over and over again. I'm frankly surprised at how few people I see taking advantage of this, as it offers both cost savings and convenience.

The problem is that most desktop PCs have been configured to perform a full shutdown procedure when you press the power button, closing all open applications and shutting down the OS and system completely. Then when you turn the power back on, they do a cold boot, reload the OS, drivers and startup applications from scratch, after which you still have to open any other applications you normally use.

There is an alternative that is much better: that is, instead of shutting down normally, have the system save the full system context (state of the system, contents of RAM, and so on) in RAM before powering off, and then subsequently restore this context when powering on. Unfortunately, many systems don't come configured to take advantage of this type of suspend mode, especially older ones.

The key is in the system configuration, starting with one very important setting in the BIOS Setup. The setting is called ACPI suspend mode, and ideally you want it set so that the system will enter what is called the S3 state. S3 is sometimes called STR for Suspend to RAM. That has traditionally been the default setting for laptops; however, many if not most desktops unfortunately have ACPI suspend mode set to the S1 state by default. ACPI S1 is sometimes called POS for Power on Suspend, a state in which the screen blanks and CPU throttles down; however, almost everything else remains fully powered on. As an example, a system and LCD display that consumes 250W will generally drop to about 200W while in S1 Stand By, however the same system will drop to only 8W of power consumption in the S3 (Suspend To RAM) state.

When set to suspend in the S3 state, upon entering Stand By (either automatically or manually), the current system context is be saved in RAM and all of the system hardware (CPU, motherboard, fans, display, etc.) *except* RAM is be powered off. In this mode the system looks as if it is off and consumes virtually the same amount of power as if it were truly off. To resume, you merely press the power button just as if you were turning the system on normally. You can configure most systems to resume on a key press or mouse click as well. Then instead of performing a normal cold boot and full restart, the system almost instantly powers on and resumes from Stand By, restoring the previously saved context. Your OS, drivers, all open applications, and so on appear fully loaded just as they were when you "powered off."

As mentioned, many people have been using this capability on laptops, but few seem to be aware that you can use it on desktop systems also. To enable this deeper sleep capability, there are only two main steps:

1. Enter the BIOS Setup, select the Power menu, locate the ACPI suspend setting, and set it to enter the S3 state (sometimes called STR for Suspend to RAM). Save, exit, and restart. Table 5.29 in *Upgrading and Repairing PCs, 17th Edition*, shows how this setting appears on most Intel motherboards.

2. After Windows loads, open the Power Options tool in the Control Panel, then select the Advanced tab and set "When I press the power button on my computer" to Stand By.

I also recommend selecting the Hibernate tab and then checking the box to Enable Hibernation. This allows you to use the ACPI S4 (STD = Suspend to Disk) state in addition to S3. ACPI S4 is a lot like S3, except the system context is saved to disk (hiberfil.sys) instead of RAM, after which the system enters the G2/S5 state. The G2/S5 state is also known as Soft-Off, which is exactly the same as if the system were powered off normally. When you power on from Hibernation (S4), the system still cold boots; however, rather than reloading from scratch, Windows restores the system context from disk (hiberfil.sys) instead of rebooting normally. While hibernating isn't nearly as fast as S3 (Suspend to RAM), it is still much faster than a full shutdown and restart and works even if the system loses power completely while suspended.

Finally, to make the system enter Stand By mode automatically, select the Power Schemes tab, and under Settings for Custom Power Scheme, When Computer Is Plugged In, set System Standby to the duration of your choice. (I usually set it for 30 minutes.) This allows the system to automatically enter Stand By after the preset period of inactivity has elapsed.

Based on these facts, my recommendations are that you power on the systems at the beginning of the workday and then at the end of the workday, set the system to Stand By in either S3 (Suspend to RAM) or S4 (Hibernate) mode, rather than powering it off completely. By using S3 Stand By mode, you can effectively leave the system running all the time and yet still achieve nearly the same savings as if you turned it off completely. In any case, I don't recommend powering systems off for lunch, breaks, or any other short periods of time. If you are a home user, leave your computer on (possibly suspended) if you are going to be using it later in the day or if instant access is important. I'd normally recommend home users put their systems in S3 or S4 modes or turn off the system when leaving the house or when sleeping. Servers, of course, should be left on continuously; however, if you set the system to Wake on Lan (WOL) in both the BIOS Setup and in Windows, the system will effectively power off, and then automatically wake up anytime it is being accessed. The bottom line is that taking advantage of S3 mode can save a significant amount of energy (and money) over time. No matter what, these are just guidelines; if you can afford to leave your system on 24 hours a day, seven days a week, then make it so.

Power Management

As the standard PC configuration has grown to include capabilities formerly considered options, the power requirements of the system have increased steadily. Larger displays, DVD-ROM drives, and more powerful graphics cards all need more power to run, and the result is that the cost of operating a PC has risen steadily. To address these concerns, several programs and standards have been developed with the aim of reducing the power needed to run a PC as much as possible.

For standard desktop systems, power management is a matter of economy and convenience. By turning off specific components of the PC when they are not in use, you can reduce the electric bill and avoid having to power the computer up and down manually.

For portable systems, power management is far more important. Adding DVD-ROMs, speakers, and other components to a laptop or notebook computer reduces even further what is in many cases a short battery life. By adding new power management technology, a portable system can supply power only to the components it actually needs to run, thus extending the life of the battery charge.

Energy Star Systems

The EPA has started a certification program for energy-efficient PCs and peripherals. To be a member of this program, the PC or display must drop to a power draw at the outlet of 30 watts or less during periods of inactivity. Systems that conform to this specification get to wear the Energy Star logo. This is a voluntary program; however, many PC manufacturers are finding that it helps them sell their systems if they can advertise these systems as energy efficient.

One problem with this type of system is that the motherboard and disk drives can go to sleep, which means they can enter a standby mode in which they draw very little power. This causes havoc with some of the older power supplies because the low power draw does not provide enough of a load for them to function properly. Most of the newer supplies on the market, which are designed to work with these systems, have a very low minimum-load specification. I suggest you ensure that the minimum load will be provided by the equipment in your system if you buy a power supply upgrade. Otherwise, when the PC goes to sleep, it might take a power switch cycle to wake it up again. This problem would be most noticeable if you invested in a very high-output supply and used it in a system that draws very little power to begin with.

Advanced Power Management

Advanced Power Management (APM) is a specification jointly developed by Intel and Microsoft that defines a series of interfaces between power management–capable hardware and a computer's operating system. When it is fully activated, APM can automatically switch a computer between five states, depending on the system's current activity. Each state represents a further reduction in power use, accomplished by placing unused components into a low-power mode. The five system states are as follows:

- **Full On**—The system is completely operational, with no power management occurring.
- **APM Enabled**—The system is operational, with some devices being power managed. Unused devices can be powered down and the CPU clock slowed or stopped.
- **APM Standby**—The system is not operational, with most devices in a low-power state. The CPU clock can be slowed or stopped, but operational parameters are retained in memory. When triggered by a specific user or system activity, the system can return to the APM Enabled state almost instantaneously.
- **APM Suspend**—The system is not operational, with most devices unpowered. The CPU clock is stopped, and operational parameters are saved to disk for later restoration. When triggered by a wake-up event, the system returns to the APM Enabled state relatively slowly.
- **Off**—The system is not operational. The power supply is off.

APM requires support from both hardware and software to function. In this chapter, you've already seen how ATX-style power supplies can be controlled by software commands using the Power_On signal and the 6-pin optional power connector. Manufacturers are also integrating the same type of control features into other system components, such as motherboards, monitors, and disk drives.

Operating systems that support APM trigger power management events by monitoring the activities performed by the computer user and the applications running on the system. However, the OS does not directly address the power management capabilities of the hardware. All versions of Windows from 3.1 up include APM support.

A system can have many hardware devices and many software functions participating in APM functions, which makes communication difficult. To address this problem, both the operating system and the hardware have an abstraction layer that facilitates communication between the various elements of the APM architecture.

The operating system runs an APM driver that communicates with the various applications and software functions that trigger power management activities, while the system's APM-capable hardware devices all communicate with the system BIOS. The APM driver and the BIOS communicate directly, completing the link between the OS and the hardware.

Thus, for APM to function, support for the standard must be built into the system's individual hardware devices, the system BIOS, and the operating system (which includes the APM driver). Without all these components, APM activities can't occur.

Advanced Configuration and Power Interface

As power-management techniques continued to develop, maintaining the complex information states necessary to implement more advanced functions became increasingly difficult for the BIOS. Therefore, another standard was developed by Intel, Microsoft, and Toshiba. Called *Advanced Configuration and Power Interface (ACPI)*, this standard was designed to implement power-management functions in the operating system. Microsoft Windows 98 and later automatically use ACPI if ACPI functions are found in the system BIOS. The need to update system BIOSs for ACPI support is one reason many computer vendors have recommended performing a BIOS update before installing Windows 98 or later on older systems.

ACPI 1.0 was initially released in 1996 and first appeared in the Phoenix BIOS around that time. ACPI became a requirement for the Intel/Microsoft "PC'97" logo certification in 1996, which caused developers to work on integrating ACPI into system designs around that time. Intel included ACPI support in chipsets starting with the PIIX4E Southbridge in April 1998, and ACPI support was included in Windows starting with the release of Windows 98 (Jun. 25, 1998) as part of what Microsoft called its "OnNow" initiative. By the time Windows 2000 came out (Feb. 17, 2000), ACPI had universally replaced APM on new systems. The official ACPI specifications can be downloaded from www.acpi. info. Placing power management under the control of the OS enables a greater interaction with applications. For example, a program can indicate to the operating system which of its activities are crucial, forcing an immediate activation of the hard drive, and which can be delayed until the next time the drive is activated for some other reason. For example, a word processor may be set to automatically save files in the background, which an OS using ACPI can then delay until the drive is activated for some other reason, resulting in fewer random spin-ups of the drive.

ACPI goes far beyond the previous standard, Advanced Power Management (APM), which consisted mainly of processor, hard disk, and display control. ACPI controls not only power but also all the Plug and Play hardware configuration throughout the system. With ACPI, system configuration (Plug and Play) and power-management configuration are no longer controlled via the BIOS setup; they are instead controlled entirely within the operating system.

ACPI enables the system to automatically turn internal peripherals on and off (such as CD-ROM drives, network cards, hard disk drives, and modems) as well as external devices such as printers, monitors, or any devices connected to serial, parallel, USB, video, or other ports in the system. ACPI technology also enables peripherals to turn on or wake up the system. For example, a telephone answering machine application can request that it be able to respond to answer the telephone within 1 second. Not only is this possible, but if the user subsequently presses the power or sleep button, the system only goes into the deepest sleep state that is consistent with the ability to meet the telephone answering application's request.

ACPI enables system designers to implement a range of power-management features that are compatible with various hardware designs while using the same operating system driver. ACPI also uses the Plug and Play BIOS data structures and takes control over the Plug and Play interface, providing an operating system–independent interface for configuration and control.

ACPI defines several system states and substates. There are four Global System states labeled from G0 through G3, with G0 being the fully operational state and G3 being mechanically turned off. Global System states are immediately obvious to the user of the system and apply to the entire system as a whole. Within the G0 state, there are four CPU Power states (C0–C3) and four Device Power states (D0–D3) for each device. Within the C0 CPU Power state there are up to 16 CPU Performance states (P0–P15).

Device power states are states for individual devices when the system is in the G0 (Working) state. The device states may or may not be visible to the user. For example, it may be obvious when a hard disk has stopped or when the monitor is off; however, it may not be obvious that a modem or other device has been shut down. The device power states are somewhat generic; many devices do not have all four power states defined.

Within the G1 Global Sleep state, there are four Sleep states (S1–S4). The G2 Global Soft Off state is also known as the *S5 Sleep state*, in which case the system is powered off but still has standby power. Finally, G3 is the Mechanical Off state, where all power is disconnected from the system.

The following list shows the definitions and nested relationship of the various Global, CPU/Device Power, and Sleep states:

- **G0 Working**—This is the normal working state in which the system is running and fully operational. Within this state, the Processor and Device Power states apply. The Device Power states are defined as follows:

  - **G0/D0 Fully-On**—The device is fully active.

  - **G0/D1**—Depends on the device; uses less power than D0.

  - **G0/D2**—Depends on the device; uses less power than D1.

  - **G0/D3 Off**—The device is powered off (except for wake-up logic).

- The Processor Power states are defined as follows:

  - **G0/C0 CPU On**—Normal processor operation.

  - **G0/C1 CPU Halted**—The processor is halted.

  - **G0/C2 CPU Stopped**—The clock has been stopped.

  - **G0/C3 CPU/Cache Stopped**—The clock has been stopped and cache snoops are ignored.

- **G1 Sleeping**—The system appears to be off but is actually in one of four Sleep states—up to full hibernation. How quickly the system can return to G0 depends on which of the Sleep states the system has selected. In any of these Sleep states, system context, and status are saved such that they can be fully restored. The Sleep states available in the Global G1 state are defined as follows:

- **G1/S1 Halt**—A low-latency idle state. The CPU is halted; however, system context and status are fully retained.

- **G1/S2 Halt-Reset**—Similar to the S1 sleeping state except that the CPU and cache context is lost, and the CPU is reset upon wakeup.

- **G1/S3 Suspend to RAM**—All system context is lost except memory. The hardware maintains memory context. The CPU is reset and restores some CPU and L2 context upon wakeup.

- **G1/S4 Suspend to Disk (Hibernation)**—The system context and status (RAM contents) have been saved to nonvolatile storage—usually the hard disk. This is also known as *Hibernation*. To return to G0 (working) state, you must press the power button, and the system will restart, loading the saved context and status from where they were previously saved (normally the hard disk). Returning from G2/S5 to G0 requires a considerable amount of latency (time).

- **G2/S5 Soft Off**—This is the normal power-off state that occurs after you select Shutdown or press the power button to turn the system off. The system and all devices are essentially powered off; however, the system is still plugged in and standby power is coming from the power supply to the motherboard, allowing the system to wake up (power on) if commanded by an external device. No hardware context or status is saved. The system must be fully rebooted to return to the G0 (working) state.

- **G3 Mechanical Off**—Power is completely removed from the system. In most cases this means the system must be unplugged or the power turned off via a power strip. This is the only state in which it is save to disassemble the system. Except for the CMOS/clock circuitry, power consumption is completely zero.

In normal use, a system alternates between the G0 (Working) and G1 (Sleeping) states. In the G1 (Working) state, individual devices and processors can be power-managed via the Device Power (D1–D3) and Processor Power (C1–C3) states. Any device that is selectively turned off can be quickly powered on in a short amount of time, from virtually instantaneous to only a few seconds (such as a hard disk spinning up).

When the system is idle (no keyboard or mouse input) for a preset period of time, the system enters the Global G1 (Sleeping) state, which means also selecting one of the S1–S4 sleep states. In these states the system appears to be off, but all system context and status are saved, enabling the system to return to exactly where it left off, with varying amounts of latency. For example, returning to the G0 (Working) state from the G1/S4 (Hibernation) state requires more time than when returning from the G1/S3 (Suspend) state.

When the user presses the power button to turn the system off, or if she selects Shutdown via the operating system, the system enters the G2/S5 (Soft Off) state. In this state no context is saved, and the system is completely off except for standby power. Fully disconnecting AC or battery power causes the system to be in the Global G3 (Mechanical Off) state, which is the only state in which the system should be disassembled.

During the system setup and boot process, ACPI performs a series of checks and tests to see whether the system hardware and BIOS support ACPI. If support is not detected or is found to be faulty, the system typically reverts to standard Advanced Power Management control, which is referred to as *legacy power management* under ACPI. Virtually all ACPI problems are the result of partial or incomplete ACPI implementations or incompatibilities in either the BIOS or device drivers. If you encounter any of these errors, contact your motherboard manufacturer for an updated BIOS or the device manufacturers for updated drivers.

Power Supply Troubleshooting

Troubleshooting the power supply basically means isolating the supply as the cause of problems within a system and, if necessary, replacing it.

Caution

It is rarely recommended that an inexperienced user open a power supply to make repairs because of the dangerous high voltages present. Even when unplugged, power supplies can retain dangerous voltage and must be discharged (like a monitor) before service. Such internal repairs are beyond the scope of this book and are specifically not recommended unless the technician knows what she is doing.

Many symptoms lead me to suspect that the power supply in a system is failing. This can sometimes be difficult for an inexperienced technician to see because at times little connection seems to exist between the symptom and the cause—the power supply.

For example, in many cases a parity check error message can indicate a problem with the power supply. This might seem strange because the parity check message specifically refers to memory that has failed. The connection is that the power supply powers the memory, and memory with inadequate power fails.

It takes some experience to know when this type of failure is power related and not caused by the memory. One clue is the repeatability of the problem. If the parity check message (or other problem) appears frequently and identifies the same memory location each time, I would suspect that defective memory is the problem. However, if the problem seems random, or if the memory location the error message cites as having failed seems random, I would suspect improper power as the culprit. The following is a list of PC problems that often are related to the power supply:

- Any power-on or system startup failures or lockups
- Spontaneous rebooting or intermittent lockups during normal operation
- Intermittent parity check or other memory-type errors
- Hard disk and fan simultaneously failing to spin (no +12V)
- Overheating due to fan failure
- Small brownouts that cause the system to reset
- Electric shocks felt on the system case or connectors
- Slight static discharges that disrupt system operation
- Erratic recognition of bus-powered USB peripherals

In fact, just about any intermittent system problem can be caused by the power supply. I always suspect the supply when flaky system operation is a symptom. Of course, the following fairly obvious symptoms point right to the power supply as a possible cause:

- System that is completely dead (no fan, no cursor)
- Smoke
- Blown circuit breakers

If you suspect a power supply problem, some of the simple measurements and the more sophisticated tests outlined in this section can help you determine whether the power supply is at fault. Because these measurements might not detect some intermittent failures, you might have to use a spare power supply for a long-term evaluation. If the symptoms and problems disappear when a known good spare unit is installed, you have found the source of your problem.

Following is a simple flowchart to help you zero in on common power supply–related problems:

1. Check the AC power input. Make sure the cord is firmly seated in the wall socket and in the power supply socket. Try a different cord.

2. Check the DC power connections. Make sure the motherboard and disk drive power connectors are firmly seated and making good contact. Check for loose screws.

3. Check the DC power output. Use a digital multimeter to check for proper voltages. If it's below spec, replace the power supply.

4. Check the installed peripherals. Remove all boards and drives and retest the system. If it works, add items back in one at a time until the system fails again. The last item added before the failure returns is likely defective.

Many types of symptoms can indicate problems with the power supply. Because the power supply literally powers everything else in the system, everything from disk drive problems to memory problems to motherboard problems can often be traced back to the power supply as the root cause.

Overloaded Power Supplies

A weak or inadequate power supply can put a damper on your ideas for system expansion. Some systems are designed with beefy power supplies, as if to anticipate a great deal of system add-ons and expansion components. Most desktop or tower systems are built in this manner. Some systems have inadequate power supplies from the start, however, and can't adequately service the power-hungry options you might want to add.

The wattage rating can sometimes be very misleading. Not all 500-watt supplies are created the same. People familiar with high-end audio systems know that some watts are better than others. This is true for power supplies, too. Cheap power supplies might in fact put out the rated power, but at what temperature? Many cheap power supplies are rated at ridiculously low temperatures that will never be encountered in actual use. As the temperature goes up, the power output capability goes down, meaning that in some cases these supplies will only be capable of 50% less than their rating under normal use. Also, what about noise and distortion? Some of the supplies are under-engineered to just barely meet their specifications, whereas others might greatly exceed their specifications. Many of the cheaper supplies provide noisy or unstable power, which can cause numerous problems with the system. Another problem with under-engineered power supplies is that they can run hot and force the system to do so as well. The repeated heating and cooling of solid-state components eventually causes a computer system to fail, and engineering principles dictate that the hotter a PC's temperature, the shorter its life. Many people recommend replacing the original supply in a system with a heavier-duty model, which solves the problem. Because power supplies come in common form factors, finding a heavy-duty replacement for most systems is easy, as is the installation process.

Inadequate Cooling

Some of the available replacement power supplies have higher-capacity cooling fans than the originals, which can greatly prolong system life and minimize overheating problems—especially for the newer, hotter-running processors. If system noise is a problem, models with special fans can run more quietly than the standard models. These power supplies often use larger-diameter fans that spin more slowly, so they run more quietly but move the same amount of air as the smaller fans. PC Power and Cooling specializes in heavy-duty and quiet supplies.

Ventilation in a system is also important. You must ensure adequate airflow to cool the hotter items in the system. In most prebuilt systems, this is not much of a concern because most reputable manufacturers ensure that their systems have adequate ventilation to avoid overheating. If, however, you're building or upgrading a system, it's critical that your processor is cooled by an active heatsink and that the case include one or more cooling fans for additional ventilation. If you have free expansion slots, you should space out the boards in your system to permit airflow between them. Place the hottest-running boards nearest the fan or the ventilation holes in the system. Make sure that adequate airflow exists around the hard disk drive, especially for those that spin at high rates of speed. Some hard disks can generate quite a bit of heat during operation. If the hard disks overheat, data can be lost.

Always be sure you run your computer with the case cover on, especially if you have an older, loaded system using passive heatsinks. Removing the cover in that situation can actually cause the system to overheat. With the cover off, the power supply and chassis fans no longer draw air through the system. Instead, the fans end up cooling only the supply, and the rest of the system must be cooled by simple convection. Systems that use an active heatsink on the processor aren't as prone to this type of problem; in fact, the cooler air from outside the normally closed chassis can help them to run cooler.

In addition, be sure that any empty slot positions have the filler brackets installed. If you leave these brackets off after removing a card, the resultant hole in the case disrupts the internal airflow and can cause higher internal temperatures.

If you experience intermittent problems that you suspect are related to overheating, a higher-capacity replacement power supply is usually the best cure. Specially designed supplies with additional cooling fan capacity also can help. At least one company sells a device called a fan card, but I am not convinced these are a good idea. Unless the fan is positioned to draw air to or from outside the case, all it does is blow hot air around inside the system and provide a spot cooling effect for anything it is blowing on. In fact, adding fans in this manner can contribute to the overall heat inside the system because the fan consumes power and generates heat.

CPU and graphics card–mounted fans are an exception because they are designed only for spot cooling of the CPU or GPU. These two chips run so much hotter than the other components in the system that a conventional, passive heatsink can't do the job. In this case, a dedicated active heatsink placed directly over the chip draws heat away from it and provides a spot-cooling effect that keeps chip temperatures down. One drawback to these active processor cooling fans is that the processor could overheat instantly and be damaged if the heatsink's fan should fail. Most Intel processors since the Pentium III and current AMD processors have built-in safeguards that prevent damage by automatically shutting down the system or by throttling back the chip's clock speed if it overheats. Still, it is best not to depend on these safeguards because not all processors have them.

Using Digital Multimeters

One simple test you can perform on a power supply is to check the output voltages. This shows whether a power supply is operating correctly and whether the output voltages are within the correct tolerance range. Note that you must measure all voltages with the power supply connected to a proper load, which usually means testing while the power supply is still installed in the system and connected to the motherboard and peripheral devices.

Selecting a Meter

You need a simple digital multimeter (DMM) or digital volt-ohm meter (DVOM) to perform voltage and resistance checks on electronic circuits (see Figure 19.39). You should use only a DMM instead of the older needle-type multimeters because the older meters work by injecting 9V into the circuit when measuring resistance, which damages most computer circuits.

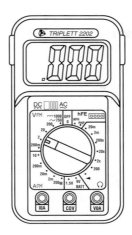

Figure 19.39   A typical DMM.

A DMM uses a much smaller voltage (usually 1.5V) when making resistance measurements, which is safe for electronic equipment. You can get a good DMM with many features from several sources. I prefer the small, pocket-size meters for computer work because they are easy to carry around.

Some features to look for in a good DMM are as follows:

- **Pocket size**—This is self-explanatory, but small meters that have many, if not all, of the features of larger ones are available. The elaborate features found on some of the larger meters are not really necessary for computer work.

- **Overload protection**—If you plug the meter into a voltage or current beyond the meter's capability to measure, the meter protects itself from damage. Cheaper meters lack this protection and can be easily damaged by reading current or voltage values that are too high.

- **Autoranging**—The meter automatically selects the proper voltage or resistance range when making measurements. This is preferable to the manual range selection; however, really good meters offer both autoranging capability and a manual range override.

- **Detachable probe leads**—The leads easily can be damaged, and sometimes a variety of differently shaped probes are required for different tests. Cheaper meters have the leads permanently attached, which means you can't easily replace them. Look for a meter with detachable leads that plug in to the meter.

- **Audible continuity test**—Although you can use the ohm scale for testing continuity (0 ohms indicates continuity), a continuity test function causes the meter to produce a beep noise when continuity exists between the meter test leads. By using the sound, you quickly can test cable assemblies and other items for continuity. After you use this feature, you will never want to use the ohms display for this purpose again.

- **Automatic power off**—These meters run on batteries, and the batteries can easily be worn down if the meter is accidentally left on. Good meters have an automatic shutoff that turns off the unit when it senses no readings for a predetermined period of time.

- **Automatic display hold**—This feature enables you to hold the last stable reading on the display even after the reading is taken. This is especially useful if you are trying to work in a difficult-to-reach area single-handedly.

- **Minimum and maximum trap**—This feature enables the meter to trap the lowest and highest readings in memory and hold them for later display, which is especially useful if you have readings that are fluctuating too quickly to see on the display.

Although you can get a basic pocket DMM for as little as $20, one with all these features is priced closer to $100, and some can be much higher. RadioShack carries some nice inexpensive units, and you can purchase the high-end models from electronics supply houses, such as Newark or Digi-Key.

Measuring Voltage

To measure voltages on a system that is operating, you must use a technique called *back probing* on the connectors (see Figure 19.40). You can't disconnect any of the connectors while the system is running, so you must measure with everything connected. Nearly all the connectors you need to probe have openings in the back where the wires enter the connector. The meter probes are narrow enough to fit into the connector alongside the wire and make contact with the metal terminal inside. The technique is called back probing because you are probing the connector from the back. You must use this back-probing technique to perform virtually all the following measurements.

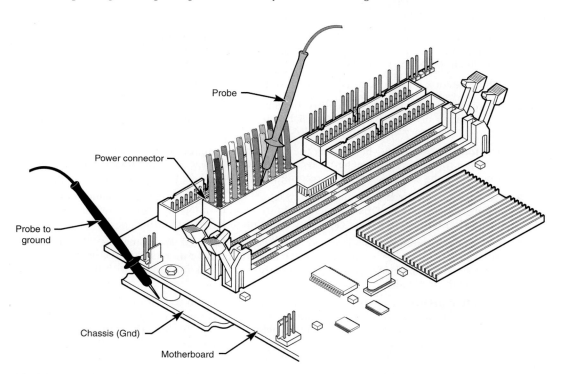

Probe

Power connector

Probe to ground

Chassis (Gnd)

Motherboard

Figure 19.40 Back probing the power supply connectors.

To test a power supply for proper output, check the voltage at the Power_Good pin (P8-1 on AT, Baby-AT, and LPX supplies; pin 8 on the ATX-type connector) for +3V to +6V of power. If the measurement is not within this range, the system never sees the Power_Good signal and therefore does not start or run properly. In most cases, the power supply is bad and must be replaced.

Continue by measuring the voltage ranges of the pins on the motherboard and drive power connectors. If you are measuring voltages for testing purposes, any reading within 10% of the specified voltage is considered acceptable, although most manufacturers of high-quality power supplies specify a tighter 5% tolerance. For ATX power supplies, the specification requires that voltages must be within 5% of the rating, except for the 3.3V current, which must be within 4%. The following table shows the voltage ranges within these tolerances.

Desired Voltage	Loose Tolerance		Tight Tolerance	
	Min. (–10%)	Max. (+8%)	Min. (–5%)	Max. (+5%)
+3.3V	2.97V	3.63V	3.135V	3.465V
+/–5.0V	4.5V	5.4V	4.75V	5.25V
+/–12.0V	10.8V	12.9V	11.4V	12.6V

The Power_Good signal has tolerances that are different from the other voltages, although it is nominally +5V in most systems. The trigger point for Power_Good is about +2.4V, but most systems require the signal voltage to be within the tolerances listed here:

Signal	Minimum	Maximum
Power_Good (+5V)	3.0V	6.0V

Replace the power supply if the voltages you measure are out of these ranges. Again, it is worth noting that any and all power supply tests and measurements must be made with the power supply properly loaded, which usually means it must be installed in a system and the system must be running.

Specialized Test Equipment

You can use several types of specialized test gear to test power supplies more effectively. Because the power supply is one of the most failure-prone items in PCs today, you should have these specialized items if you service many PC systems.

Digital Infrared Thermometer

One of the greatest additions to my toolbox is a digital infrared thermometer (illustrated in Chapter 22, "PC Diagnostics, Testing, and Maintenance"). They also are called noncontact thermometers because they measure by sensing infrared energy without having to touch the item they are reading. This enables me to make instant spot checks of the temperature of a chip, a board, or the system chassis. They are available from companies such as Raytek (http://www.raytek.com) for less than $100. To use these handheld items, you point at an object and then pull the trigger. Within seconds, the display shows a temperature readout accurate to +/–3°F (2°C). These devices are invaluable in checking to ensure the components in your system are adequately cooled.

Variable Voltage Transformer

When testing power supplies, it is sometimes desirable to simulate different AC voltage conditions at the wall socket to observe how the supply reacts. A variable voltage transformer is a useful test device for checking power supplies because it enables you to exercise control over the AC line voltage used as input for the power supply (see Figure 19.41). This device consists of a large transformer mounted in a housing with a dial indicator that controls the output voltage. You plug the line cord from the transformer into the wall socket and plug the PC power cord into the socket provided on the transformer. The knob on the transformer can be used to adjust the AC line voltage the PC receives.

Most variable transformers can adjust their AC outputs from 0V to 140V no matter what the AC input (wall socket) voltage is. Some can cover a range from 0V to 280V, as well. You can use the transformer to simulate brownout conditions, enabling you to observe the PC's response. Thus, you can check a power supply for proper Power_Good signal operation, among other things.

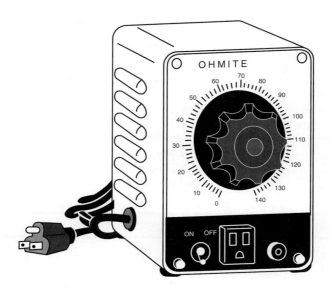

Figure 19.41   A variable voltage transformer.

By running the PC and dropping the voltage until the PC shuts down, you can see how much reserve is in the power supply for handling a brownout or other voltage fluctuations. If your transformer can output voltages in the 200V range, you can test the capability of the power supply to run on foreign voltage levels. A properly functioning supply should operate between 90V and 135V but should shut down cleanly if the voltage is outside that range.

One indication of a problem is seeing parity check-type error messages when you drop the voltage to 80V. This indicates that the Power_Good signal is not being withdrawn before the power supply output to the PC fails. The PC should simply stop operating as the Power_Good signal is withdrawn, causing the system to enter a continuous reset loop.

Variable voltage transformers are sold by a number of electronic parts supply houses, such as Newark InOne and Digi-Key. You should expect to pay anywhere from $100 to $300 for this device.

Repairing the Power Supply

Hardly anyone actually repairs power supplies anymore, primarily because simply replacing the supply with a new one is usually cheaper. Even high-quality power supplies are not that expensive when compared to the labor required to repair them.

A defective power supply is typically discarded unless it happens to be one of the higher-quality or more expensive units. In that case, it is usually wise to send the supply to a company that specializes in repairing power supplies and other components. These companies normally provide what is called *depot repair*, which means you send the supply to them and they repair it and return it to you. If time is of the essence, most of the depot repair companies immediately send you a functional equivalent to your defective supply and take yours in as a core charge. Depot repair is the recommended way to service many PC components, such as power supplies, monitors, and printers. If you take your PC to a conventional service outlet, they often determine which component has the problem and send it to be depot repaired. You can do that yourself and save the markup the repair shop usually charges in such cases.

For those with experience around high voltages, you might be able to repair a failing supply with two relatively simple operations (replacing the internal fuse or the fan); however, these require opening the supply—something I do not normally recommend. I mention it only as an alternative to replacement in some cases. Besides, in all cases where I've seen the internal fuse blown, there were more serious problems and just replacing the fuse only caused it to immediately blow again. On the other hand, if the only problem with the supply is that the fan has failed (motor or bearing failure), you might be able to save the supply from the trash by simply replacing the internal fan.

Most manufacturers try to prevent you from entering the supply by sealing it with special tamper-proof Torx screws. These screws use the familiar Torx star driver but also have a tamper-prevention pin in the center that prevents a standard driver from working. Most tool companies, such as Jensen or Specialized, sell sets of TT (tamperproof Torx) bits that remove the tamper-resistant screws. Other manufacturers rivet the power supply case shut, which means you must drill out the rivets to gain access.

Caution

The manufacturers place these obstacles there for a reason—to prevent entry by those who are inexperienced with high voltage. Consider yourself warned!

Obtaining Replacement Units

Most of the time, it is simply easier, safer, or less expensive (considering the time and materials involved) to replace the power supply than to repair it. As mentioned earlier, replacement power supplies are available from many manufacturers. Before you can shop for a supplier, however, you should consider other purchasing factors.

Deciding on a Power Supply

When you are shopping for a new power supply, you should take several factors into account. First, consider the power supply's shape, or form factor. Power supply form factors can differ in their physical sizes, shapes, screw-hole positions, connector types, and fan locations. When ordering a replacement supply, you need to know which form factor your system requires.

Some systems use proprietary power supply designs, which makes replacement more difficult. If a system uses one of the industry-standard form factor power supplies, replacement units with a variety of output levels and performance are available from hundreds of vendors. An unfortunate user of a system with a nonstandard form factor supply does not have this kind of choice and must get a replacement from the original manufacturer of the system—and usually must pay a much higher price for the unit. Although you can find high-quality, industry-standard form factor supplies for less than $50, the proprietary units from some manufacturers cost as much as $400 or more. PC buyers often overlook this and discover too late the consequences of having nonstandard components in a system.

◀◀ See "Power Supply Form Factors," p. 1212.

Name-brand systems on both the low and high end of the price scale are notorious for using proprietary form factor power supplies. For example, Dell has been using proprietary supplies in many of its systems. Be sure you consider this if you intend to own or use these types of systems out of warranty or plan significant upgrades during the life of the system. Personally, I always insist on systems that use industry-standard power supplies, such as the ATX12V form factor supply found in most systems today.

Sources for Replacement Power Supplies

Because one of the most failure-prone items in PC systems is the power supply, I am often asked to recommend a replacement. Literally hundreds of companies manufacture PC power supplies, and I certainly have not tested them all. I can, however, recommend some companies whose products I have come to know and trust.

Although other high-quality manufacturers exist, at this time I recommend power supplies from PC Power and Cooling and Antec, Inc.

Tip

My preferences for power supplies when building or upgrading systems include the Silencer models from PC Power and Cooling, due to their high output yet low-noise designs. For systems with up to a single high-performance video card I recommend the Silencer 470, which is a standard ATX-depth (140mm) 470W power supply. For larger systems with a bit more room in the chassis, possibly running multiple video cards and drives, I like the Silencer 610 and 750 models, which are extended-depth (180mm) 610W and 750W units. For building ultimate systems featuring dual quad-core processors, multiple video cards, and six or more hard drives, I recommend the Turbo-Cool 1KW, which is an extended-depth (230mm) unit featuring an incredible 1000W output rating (1100W peak). The 610 and up are probably overkill for most systems, but for those building high-performance systems, or for those who keep a system for a long time and put it through several upgrades, they can be an excellent choice.

PC Power and Cooling also has units available that fit some of Dell's proprietary designs. These units cost less than Dell's, are available with significantly higher output ratings, and bolt in as direct replacements.

Antec also offers high-quality power supplies, particularly its TruePower series. It also offers power supplies that can operate with no internal fan, resulting in the quietest design possible. It even has some power supplies with internal lighting for interesting visual effects when installed in windowed cases.

A high-quality power supply from one of these vendors can be one of the best cures for intermittent system problems and can go a long way toward ensuring trouble-free operation in the future.

Power Supply Tips and Recommendations

With backward compatibility ensuring that the new 24-pin ATX power connector will plug in to older 20-pin motherboard sockets, when purchasing a new power supply I now recommend only those units that include 24-pin main power connectors, which are usually sold as ATX12V 2.x or PCI Express models. For the most flexible and future-proof supply, also ensure that the power supply includes a 6-pin PCI Express graphics connector as well as integrated SATA drive power connectors. An example of a highly rated power supply incorporating all these features is the Turbo-Cool 510 Express/SLI from PC Power and Cooling (www.pcpower.com). Choosing a power supply with these features provides flexibility that allows it to work not only in newer systems, but also in virtually all older ATX systems—and with no adapters required.

◄◄   See "ATX12V 2.x 24-pin Main Power Connector," p. 1241.

Power-protection Systems

Power-protection systems do just what the name implies: They protect your equipment from the effects of power surges and power failures. In particular, power surges and spikes can damage computer equipment, and a loss of power can result in lost data. In this section, you learn about the four primary types of power-protection devices available and when you should use them.

Before considering any further levels of power protection, you should know that a quality power supply already affords you a substantial amount of protection. High-end power supplies from the vendors I recommend are designed to provide protection from higher-than-normal voltages and currents, and they provide a limited amount of power-line noise filtering. Some of the inexpensive aftermarket power supplies probably do not have this sort of protection. If you have an inexpensive computer, further protecting your system might be wise.

Caution

All the power-protection features in this chapter and the protection features in the power supply inside your computer require that the computer's AC power cable be connected to a ground.

Many older homes do not have three-prong (grounded) outlets to accommodate grounded devices.

Do not use a three-pronged adapter (that bypasses the three-prong requirement and enables you to connect to a two-prong socket) to plug a surge suppressor, computer, or UPS into a two-pronged outlet. They often don't provide a good ground and can inhibit the capabilities of your power-protection devices.

You also should test your power sockets to ensure they are grounded. Sometimes outlets, despite having three-prong sockets, are not connected to a ground wire; an inexpensive socket tester (available at most hardware stores) can detect this condition.

Of course, the easiest form of protection is to turn off and unplug your computer equipment (including your modem) when a thunderstorm is imminent. However, when this is not possible, other alternatives are available.

Power supplies should stay within operating specifications and continue to run a system even if any of these power line disturbances occur:

- Voltage drop to 80V for up to 2 seconds
- Voltage drop to 70V for up to .5 seconds
- Voltage surge of up to 143V for up to 1 second

Most high-quality power supplies (or the attached systems) will not be damaged by the following occurrences:

- Full power outage
- Any voltage drop (brownout)
- A spike of up to 2,500V

Because of their internal protection, many computer manufacturers that use high-quality power supplies state in their documentation that external surge suppressors are not necessary with their systems.

To verify the levels of protection built in to the existing power supply in a computer system, an independent laboratory subjected several unprotected PC systems to various spikes and surges of up to 6,000V—considered the maximum level of surge that can be transmitted to a system through an electrical outlet. Any higher voltage would cause the power to arc to the ground within the outlet. None of the systems sustained permanent damage in these tests. The worst thing that happened was that some of the systems rebooted or shut down when the surge was more than 2,000V. Each system restarted when the power switch was toggled after a shutdown.

I do not use any real form of power protection on my systems, and they have survived near-direct lightning strikes and powerful surges. The most recent incident, only 50 feet from my office, was a direct lightning strike to a brick chimney that blew the top of the chimney apart. None of my systems (which were running at the time) were damaged in any way from this incident; they just shut themselves down. I was able to restart each system by toggling the power switches. An alarm system located in the same office, however, was destroyed by this strike. I am not saying that lightning strikes or even much milder spikes and surges can't damage computer systems—another nearby lightning strike did destroy a modem and serial adapter installed in one of my systems. I was just lucky that the destruction did not include the motherboard.

This discussion points out an important oversight in some power-protection strategies: Do not forget to provide protection from spikes and surges on the phone line.

The automatic shutdown of a computer during power disturbances is a built-in function of most high-quality power supplies. You can reset the power supply by flipping the power switch from on to off and back on again. Some power supplies even have an auto-restart function. This type of power supply acts the same as others in a massive surge or spike situation: It shuts down the system. The difference is that after normal power resumes, the power supply waits for a specified delay of 3–6 seconds and then resets itself and powers the system back up. Because no manual switch resetting is required, this feature might be desirable in systems functioning as network servers or in those found in other unattended locations.

The first time I witnessed a large surge that caused an immediate shutdown of all my systems, I was extremely surprised. All the systems were silent, but the monitor and modem lights were still on. My first thought was that everything was blown, but a simple toggle of each system-unit power switch caused the power supplies to reset, and the units powered up with no problem. Since that first time, this type of shutdown has happened to me several times, always without further problems.

The following types of power-protection devices are explained in the sections that follow:

- Surge suppressors
- Phone-line surge protectors
- Line conditioners
- Standby power supplies (SPS)
- Uninterruptible power supplies (UPS)

Surge Suppressors (Protectors)

The simplest form of power protection is any one of the commercially available surge protectors—that is, devices inserted between the system and the power line. These devices, which cost between $20 and $200, can absorb the high-voltage transients produced by nearby lightning strikes and power equipment. Some surge protectors can be effective for certain types of power problems, but they offer only very limited protection.

Surge protectors use several devices, usually metal-oxide varistors (MOVs), that can clamp and shunt away all voltages above a certain level. MOVs are designed to accept voltages as high as 6,000V and divert any power above 200V to ground. MOVs can handle normal surges, but powerful surges such as direct lightning strikes can blow right through them. MOVs are not designed to handle a very high level of power and self-destruct while shunting a large surge. These devices therefore cease to function after either a single large surge or a series of smaller ones. The real problem is that you can't easily tell when they no longer are functional. The only way to test them is to subject the MOVs to a surge, which destroys them. Therefore, you never really know whether your so-called surge protector is protecting your system.

Some surge protectors have status lights that let you know when a surge large enough to blow the MOVs has occurred. A surge suppressor without this status indicator light is useless because you never know when it has stopped protecting.

Underwriters Laboratories has produced an excellent standard that governs surge suppressors, called UL 1449. Any surge suppressor that meets this standard is a very good one and definitely offers a line of protection beyond what the power supply in your PC already offers. The only types of surge suppressors worth buying, therefore, should have two features:

- Conformance to the UL 1449 standard
- A status light indicating when the MOVs are blown

Units that meet the UL 1449 specification say so on the packaging or directly on the unit. If this standard is not mentioned, it does not conform. Therefore, you should avoid it.

Another good feature to have in a surge suppressor is a built-in circuit breaker that can be manually reset rather than a fuse. The breaker protects your system if it or a peripheral develops a short. These better surge suppressors usually cost about $40.

Phone Line Surge Protectors

In addition to protecting the power lines, it is critical to provide protection to your systems from any connected phone lines. If you are using a modem or fax board that is plugged in to the phone system, any surges or spikes that travel through the phone line can damage your system. In many areas, the phone lines are especially susceptible to lightning strikes, which are the leading cause of fried modems and damage to the computer equipment attached to them.

Several companies manufacture or sell simple surge protectors that plug in between your modem and the phone line. These inexpensive devices can be purchased from most electronics supply houses. Some of the standard power line surge protectors include connectors for phone line protection as well.

Line Conditioners

In addition to high-voltage and current conditions, other problems can occur with incoming power. The voltage might dip below the level needed to run the system, resulting in a brownout. Forms of electrical noise other than simple voltage surges or spikes might travel through the power line, such as radio-frequency interference or electrical noise caused by motors or other inductive loads.

Remember two things when you wire together digital devices (such as computers and their peripherals):

- Any wire can act as an antenna and have voltage induced in it by nearby electromagnetic fields, which can come from other wires, telephones, CRTs, motors, fluorescent fixtures, static discharge, and, of course, radio transmitters.

- Digital circuitry responds with surprising efficiency to noise of even a volt or two, making those induced voltages particularly troublesome. The electrical wiring in your building can act as an antenna, picking up all kinds of noise and disturbances.

A line conditioner can handle many of these types of problems. A line conditioner is designed to remedy a variety of problems. It filters the power, bridges brownouts, suppresses high-voltage and current conditions, and generally acts as a buffer between the power line and the system. A line conditioner does the job of a surge suppressor, and much more. It is more of an active device, functioning continuously, rather than a passive device that activates only when a surge is present. A line conditioner provides true power conditioning and can handle myriad problems. It contains transformers, capacitors, and other circuitry that can temporarily bridge a brownout or low-voltage situation. These units usually cost $100–$300, depending on the power-handling capacity of the unit.

Backup Power

The next level of power protection includes backup power-protection devices. These units can provide power in case of a complete blackout, thereby providing the time necessary for an orderly system shutdown. Two types are available: the standby power supply (SPS) and the uninterruptible power supply (UPS). The UPS is a special device because it does much more than just provide backup power—it is also the best kind of line conditioner you can buy.

Standby Power Supplies

A standby power supply is known as an offline device: It functions only when normal power is disrupted. An SPS system uses a special circuit that can sense the AC line current. If the sensor detects a loss of power on the line, the system quickly switches over to a standby battery and power inverter. The power inverter converts the battery power to 120V AC power, which is then supplied to the system.

SPS systems do work, but sometimes a problem occurs during the switch to battery power. If the switch is not fast enough, the computer system shuts down or reboots anyway, which defeats the purpose of having the backup power supply. A truly outstanding SPS adds to the circuit a ferroresonant transformer, which is a large transformer with the capability to store a small amount of power and deliver it during the switch time. This device functions as a buffer on the power line, giving the SPS almost uninterruptible capability.

Tip

Look for SPS systems with a switch-over time of less than 10 milliseconds (ms). This is shorter than the hold-over time of typical power supplies.

SPS units also might have internal line conditioning of their own. Under normal circumstances, most cheaper units place your system directly on the regular power line and offer no conditioning. The addition of a ferroresonant transformer to an SPS gives it extra regulation and protection capabilities because of the buffer effect of the transformer. SPS devices without the ferroresonant transformer still require the use of a line conditioner for full protection. SPS systems usually cost between a hundred and several thousand dollars, depending on the quality and power-output capacity.

Uninterruptible Power Supplies

Perhaps the best overall solution to any power problem is to provide a power source that is conditioned and that can't be interrupted—which is the definition of an uninterruptible power supply. UPSs are known as online systems because they continuously function and supply power to your computer systems. Because some companies advertise ferroresonant SPS devices as though they were UPS devices, many now use the term *true UPS* to describe a truly online system. A true UPS system is constructed in much the same way as an SPS system; however, because the computer is always operating from the battery, there is no switching circuit.

In a true UPS, your system always operates from the battery. A voltage inverter converts from +12V DC to 120V AC. You essentially have your own private power system that generates power independently of the AC line. A battery charger connected to the line or wall current keeps the battery charged at a rate equal to or greater than the rate at which power is consumed.

When the AC current supplying the battery charger fails, a true UPS continues functioning undisturbed because the battery-charging function is all that is lost. Because the computer was already running off the battery, no switch takes place and no power disruption is possible. The battery begins discharging at a rate dictated by the amount of load your system places on the unit, which (based on the size of the battery) gives you plenty of time to execute an orderly system shutdown. Based on an appropriately scaled storage battery, the UPS functions continuously, generating power and preventing unpleasant surprises. When the line power returns, the battery charger begins recharging the battery, again with no interruption.

Note

Occasionally, a UPS can accumulate too much storage and not enough discharge. When this occurs, the UPS emits a loud alarm, alerting you that it's full. Simply unplugging the unit from the AC power source for a while can discharge the excess storage (as it powers your computer) and drain the UPS of the excess.

Many SPS systems are advertised as though they are true UPS systems. The giveaway is the unit's switch time. If a specification for switch time exists, the unit can't be a true UPS because UPS units never switch. However, a good SPS with a ferroresonant transformer can virtually equal the performance of a true UPS at a lower cost.

Note

Many UPSs and SPSs today come equipped with a cable and software that enables the protected computer to shut down in an orderly manner on receipt of a signal from the UPS. This way, the system can shut down properly even if the computer is unattended. Some operating systems designed for server environments contain their own UPS software components.

UPS cost is a direct function of both the length of time it can continue to provide power after a line current failure and how much power it can provide. You therefore should purchase a UPS that provides enough power to run your system and peripherals and enough time to close files and provide an orderly shutdown. Remember, however, to manually perform a system shutdown procedure during a power outage. You will probably need your monitor plugged into the UPS and the computer. Be sure the UPS you purchase can provide sufficient power for all the devices you must connect to it.

Because of a true UPS's almost total isolation from the line current, it is unmatched as a line conditioner and surge suppressor. The best UPS systems add a ferroresonant transformer for even greater power conditioning and protection capability. This type of UPS is the best form of power protection available. The price, however, can be high. To find out just how much power your computer system requires, look at the UL sticker on the back of the unit. This sticker lists the maximum power draw in watts, or sometimes in just volts and amperes. If only voltage and amperage are listed, multiply the two figures to calculate the wattage.

As an example, if the documentation for a system indicates that the computer can require as much as 120V at a maximum current draw of 5 amps, the maximum power the system can draw is about 550 watts. This wattage is for a system with every slot full, two hard disks, and one floppy—in other words, a system at the maximum possible level of expansion. The system should never draw any more power than that; if it does, a 5-amp fuse in the power supply will blow. This type of system usually draws an average of 300 watts. However, to be safe when you make calculations for UPS capacity, be conservative; use the 550-watt figure. Adding a monitor that draws 100 watts brings the total to 650 watts or more. Therefore, to run two fully loaded systems, you'd need a 1,100-watt UPS. And don't forget two monitors, each drawing 100 watts. Therefore, the total is 1,300 watts. A UPS of that capacity or greater costs approximately $500–$700. Unfortunately, that is what the best level of protection costs. Most companies can justify this type of expense only for critical-use PCs, such as network servers.

Note

The highest-capacity UPS sold for use with a conventional 15-amp outlet is about 1,400 watts. If it's any higher, you risk tripping a 15-amp circuit when the battery is charging heavily and the inverter is drawing maximum current.

In addition to the total available output power (wattage), several other factors can distinguish one UPS from another. The addition of a ferroresonant transformer improves a unit's power conditioning and buffering capabilities. Good units also have an inverter that produces a true sine wave output; the cheaper ones might generate a square wave. A square wave is an approximation of a sine wave with abrupt up-and-down voltage transitions. The abrupt transitions of a square wave are not compatible with some computer equipment power supplies. Be sure that the UPS you purchase produces power that is compatible with your computer equipment. Every unit has a specification for how long it can sustain output at the rated level. If your systems draw less than the rated level, you have some additional time.

Caution

Be careful! Most UPS systems are not designed for you to sit and compute for hours through an electrical blackout. They are designed to provide power only to essential components and to remain operating long enough to allow for an orderly shutdown. You pay a large amount for units that provide power for more than 15 minutes or so. At some point, it becomes more cost-effective to buy a generator than to keep investing in extended life for a UPS.

Some of the many sources of power protection equipment include American Power Conversion (APC) and Tripp Lite. These companies sell a variety of UPS, SPS, line, and surge protector products.

Caution

Don't connect a laser printer to a backed-up socket in any SPS or UPS unit. Such printers are electrically noisy and have widely varying current draws. This can be hard on the inverter in an SPS or a UPS and frequently cause the inverter to fail or detect an overload and shut down. Either case means that your system will lose power, too.

Printers are normally noncritical because whatever is being printed can be reprinted. Don't connect them to a UPS unless there's a good business need to do so.

Some UPSs and SPSs have sockets that are conditioned but not backed up—that is, they do not draw power from the battery. In cases such as this, you can safely plug printers and other peripherals into these sockets.

RTC/NVRAM (CMOS RAM) Batteries

Most PCs have a special type of chip in them that combines a real-time clock (RTC) with at least 64 bytes (including 14 bytes of clock data) of nonvolatile RAM (NVRAM) memory. This chip is officially called the RTC/NVRAM chip, but it is often referred to as the CMOS or CMOS RAM chip because the type of chip used is produced using a CMOS (complementary metal-oxide semiconductor) process. CMOS design chips are known for very low power consumption. This special RTC/NVRAM chip is designed to run off a battery for several years.

The original chip of this type was the Motorola MC146818, which was used in the IBM AT dating from August 1984. Although the chips used today have different manufacturers and part numbers, they all are designed to be compatible with this original Motorola part. Most modern motherboards have the RTC/NVRAM integrated in the motherboard chipset South Bridge or I/O Controller Hub (ICH) component, meaning no separate chip is required.

The function of the real-time clock should be obvious: The clock enables software to read the date and time and preserves the date and time data even when the system is powered off or unplugged. The NVRAM portion of the chip has another function: It is designed to store the basic system configuration, including the amount of memory installed, types of disk drives installed, Plug and Play device configuration, power-on passwords, and other information. Although some chips have been used that store up to 4KB or more of NVRAM, most motherboard chipsets with integrated RTC/NVRAM incorporate 256 bytes of NVRAM, of which the clock uses 14 bytes. The system reads this information every time you power it on.

Modern CMOS Batteries

Motherboard NVRAM (CMOS RAM) batteries come in many forms. Most are of a lithium design because they last 2–5 years or more. I have seen systems with conventional alkaline batteries mounted in a holder; these are much less desirable because they fail more frequently and do not last as long. Also, they are prone to leak, and if a battery leaks on the motherboard, the motherboard can be severely damaged. By far, the most commonly used battery for motherboards today is the coin cell, mounted in a holder that is part of the motherboard. Two main types of coin cells are used, differing in their chemistry. Most use a manganese dioxide (Mn02) cathode, designated by a *CR* prefix in the part number; others use a carbon monoflouride (CF) cathode, designated by a *BR* prefix in the part number. The CR types are more plentiful (and thus easier to get) and offer slightly higher capacity. The BR types are useful for higher-temperature operation (above 60°C or 140°F).

Because the CR series is cheaper and easier to obtain, it is generally what you will find in a PC. The other digits in the battery part number indicate the physical size of the battery. For example, the most common type of lithium coin cell used in PCs is the CR2032, which is 20mm in diameter (about the size of a quarter) and 3.2mm thick and uses a manganese dioxide cathode. These are readily available at electronics supply stores, camera shops, and even drugstores. Figure 19.42 shows a cutaway view of a CR2032 lithium coin cell battery.

Table 19.25 lists the specifications of the common 20mm diameter lithium coin cell batteries you might find in a PC.

Table 19.25   Common 20mm Lithium Coin Cell Specifications

Type	Voltage (V)	Capacity (mAh)	Diameter (mm)	Height (mm)
BR2016	3.00	75	20.00	1.60
BR2020	3.00	100	20.00	2.00
BR2032	3.00	190	20.00	3.20
CR2012	3.00	55	20.00	1.20
CR2016	3.00	90	20.00	1.60
CR2025	3.00	165	20.00	2.50
CR2032	3.00	220	20.00	3.20

BR = Carbon monoflouride (CF) cathode
CR = Manganese dioxide (MnO2) cathode

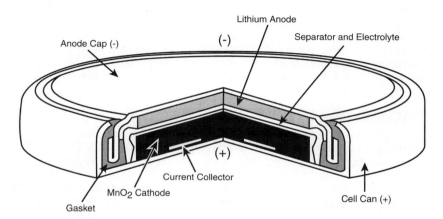

Figure 19.42   Cutaway view of a CR2032 lithium coin cell.

Estimated battery life can be calculated by dividing the battery capacity by the average current required. For example, a typical CR2032 battery is rated 220 mAh (milliamp hours), and the RTC/NVRAM circuit in most current motherboard chipsets draws 5 μA (microamps) with the power off. Battery life can therefore be calculated as follows:

220,000 μAh ÷ 5 μA = 44,000 hours = 5 years

If a thinner (and lower-capacity) battery such as the CR2025 is used, battery life will be shorter:

165,000 μAh ÷ 5 μA = 33,000 hours = 3.7 years

Battery life starts when the system is first assembled, which can be several months or more before you purchase the system, even if it is new. Also, the battery might be partially discharged before it is installed in the system; higher temperatures both in storage and in the system can contribute to shorter battery life. All these reasons and more can cause battery life to be less than what might be indicated by calculation.

As the battery drains, output voltage drops somewhat. Lower battery voltage can impair the accuracy of the RTC. Most lithium coin cell batteries are rated at 3V; however, actual readings on a new battery are usually higher. If your system clock seems inaccurate (it runs slow, for example), check the voltage on the CMOS battery. The highest accuracy is obtained if the battery voltage is maintained at 3.0V or higher. Lithium batteries normally maintain a fairly steady voltage until they are nearly fully discharged, whereupon the voltage quickly drops. If you check the battery voltage and find it is below 3.0V, consider replacing the battery, even if it is before the intended replacement time.

Obsolete or Unique CMOS Batteries

Although most modern systems use 3.0V coin cells, older systems have used a variety of battery types and voltages over the years. For example, some older systems have used 3.6V, 4.5V, and 6V types as well. If you are replacing the battery in an older machine, be sure your replacement is the same voltage as the one you removed from the system. Some motherboards can use batteries of several voltages, and you use a jumper or switch to select the various settings. If you suspect your motherboard has this capability, consult the documentation for instructions on changing the settings. Of course, the easiest thing to do is to replace the existing battery with another of the same type.

Some systems over the years have used a special type of chip that actually has the battery embedded within it. These are made by several companies, including Dallas Semiconductor and Benchmarq. These chips are notable for their long lives. Under normal conditions, the integral battery lasts for 10 years—which is, of course, longer than the useful life of the system. If your system uses one of the Dallas or Benchmarq modules, the battery and chip must be replaced as a unit because they are integrated. Most of the time, these chip/battery combinations are installed in a socket on the motherboard just in case a problem requires an early replacement. You can get new modules directly from the manufacturers for $18 or less, which is much more expensive than the coin-type lithium battery found in most modern systems. In fact, due to their expense and the fact that most motherboard chipset manufacturers have integrated the RTC/NVRAM functionality into the motherboard chipset, few if any modern PCs use these chip/battery modules.

Some systems do not use a battery at all. Hewlett-Packard, for example, includes a special capacitor in some of its systems that is automatically recharged anytime the system is plugged in. The system does not have to be running for the capacitor to charge; it only has to be plugged in. If the system is unplugged, the capacitor powers the RTC/NVRAM chip for up to a week or more. If the system remains unplugged for a duration longer than that, the NVRAM information is lost. In that case, these systems can reload the NVRAM from a backup kept in a special flash ROM chip contained on the motherboard. The only pieces of information that are actually missing when you repower the system are the date and time, which have to be reentered. By using the capacitor combined with an NVRAM backup in flash ROM, these systems have a very reliable solution that lasts indefinitely.

Many older systems use a separate battery that plugs in via a cable or that can even be directly soldered into the motherboard (mostly older, obsolete systems). For those older systems with the battery soldered in, a spare battery connector usually exists on the motherboard where you can insert a conventional plug-in battery if the original ever fails.

CMOS Battery Troubleshooting

Symptoms that indicate that the battery is about to fail include having to reset the clock on your PC every time you shut down the system (especially after moving it) and problems during the system's POST, such as drive-detection difficulties. If you experience problems such as these, you should make note of your system's CMOS settings and replace the battery as soon as possible.

Caution

When you replace a PC battery, be sure you get the polarity correct; otherwise, you will damage the RTC/NVRAM (CMOS) chip. Because the chip is soldered onto most motherboards, this can be an expensive mistake! The battery connector on the motherboard and the battery are usually keyed to prevent a backward connection. The pinout of this connector should be listed in your system documentation.

When you replace a battery, in most cases the existing data stored in the NVRAM is lost. Sometimes, however, the data remains intact for several minutes (I have observed NVRAM retain information with no power for an hour or more), so if you make the battery swap quickly, the information in the NVRAM might be retained. Just to be sure, I recommend that you record all the system configuration settings stored in the NVRAM by your system Setup program. In most cases, you should run the BIOS Setup program and copy or print out all the screens showing the various settings. Some Setup programs offer the capability to save the NVRAM data to a file for later restoration if necessary.

Tip

If your system BIOS is password-protected and you forget the password, one possible way to bypass the block is to remove the battery for a few minutes and then replace it. This resets the BIOS to its default settings, removing the password protection.

After replacing a battery, power up the system and use the Setup program to check the date and time setting and any other data that was stored in the NVRAM.

Building or Upgrading Systems

System Components

In these days of commodity parts and component pricing, building your own system from scratch is no longer the daunting process it once was. Every component necessary to build a PC system is available off the shelf at competitive pricing, and the system you build can use the same or even better components than the top name-brand systems.

There are, however, some cautions to heed. The main thing to note is that you rarely save money when building your own system; purchasing a complete system from a mail-order vendor or mass merchandiser is almost always less expensive. The reason for this is simple: Most system vendors who build systems to order use many, if not all, of the same components you can use when building your own system. The difference is that they buy these components in quantity and receive a much larger discount than you can by purchasing only one of a particular item.

In addition, you pay only one shipping and handling charge when you purchase a complete system instead of the multiple shipping charges you pay when you purchase separate components. In fact, the shipping and handling charges from ordering all the separate parts needed to build a PC through the mail often add up to $100 or more, and this doesn't count the additional time spent as well as additional telephone or Internet access charges accrued in the process. The cost rises further if you encounter problems with any of the components and have to make additional calls or pay for shipping charges to send improper or malfunctioning parts back for replacement. Also, many companies charge restocking fees if you purchase something and then determine you don't need it or can't use it.

If you purchase parts locally to avoid shipping charges, then you typically must pay the additional state sales tax, as well as the higher prices usually associated with retail store sales.

Then there is the included software. Although I can sometimes come close in price to a commercial system when building my own from scratch, the bundled software really adds value to the commercial system. For example, a copy of Windows costs $100 or more, an expense you'll have to include when building a new system from scratch. Besides the savings from the included OS, another contributing factor in the low cost of commercial systems is all the other programs they install. Most of the other software added to commercial systems contributes further to the system's low price. What I'm talking about is all the time- or feature-limited trial software, as well as pure advertisements and marketing gimmicks, often called *junkware*. Although it is unwelcome by most users and can be a chore to clean off, the truth of the matter is that the developers of these programs pay a significant amount of money to the larger OEMs to preload it on their systems. The revenue generated by installing junkware can shave many dollars off the price of a system, another reason it is hard to compete on price when building your own.

It is clear that the reasons for building a system from scratch often have less to do with saving money and more to do with the experience you gain and the results you achieve. In the end, by building your own you have a custom system that contains the exact components and features you have selected, without any of the extra junkware added. Most of the time when you buy a preconfigured system, you have to compromise in some way. For example, you might get the video adapter you want, but you would prefer a different make or model of motherboard. By building your own system, you can select the exact components you want and build the ultimate system for your needs. The experience is also very rewarding. You know exactly how your system is constructed and configured because you have done it yourself. This makes future support and installation of additional accessories much easier.

Another benefit of building your own system is that you are guaranteed an industry-standard system that will be easily upgradeable in the future. Many of the larger system vendors use proprietary components that can make future upgrades difficult or impossible. Of course, if you have been reading the book up to this point, you already know everything you need to ensure any preassembled systems you purchase would use industry-standard components and thus be upgradeable and repairable in the future.

You might be able to save some money using components from your current system when building your new system. The monitor, keyboard, mouse, storage devices, most PCI adapter cards, and even the case and power supply from your old system will likely work in a new system as well. Things you won't probably be able to reuse include motherboards, processors, memory, and video cards. For example, you might have recently upgraded the hard drive and optical drive in an attempt to extend the life of your current computer. In most cases, you can reinstall those components in any new system you build. One thing in particular I like to do is to take old systems that are being discarded and rebuild them using new components. Essentially, this means that I gut the system and reuse the case, fans, possibly the power supply, and as many other internal components as I can. Many of the cases used in older retail systems are attractive, well built, and accept industry standard components. By recycling the case and other parts in my new system builds, I can save both some money and a little bit of the environment at the same time.

So, if you are interested in a very rewarding and educational experience, want a customized and fully upgradeable system that is free from junkware, then building your own PC is the way to go.

Other candidates for building include those who use their PCs for specialized or high-end applications, such as extreme gaming, video or music editing, file or print serving, and so on. That way you can design and build a system that meets any and all of your custom specifications, including every individual component. Some even build as a matter of pride and bragging rights.

This chapter details the components necessary to assemble your own system, explains the assembly procedures, and lists some recommendations for components and their sources.

The components used in building a typical PC are as follows:

- Case and power supply
- Motherboard
- Processor with heatsink and fan
- Memory
- Floppy drive (optional)
- Hard disk drive
- Optical drive(s) (CD/DVD)
- Keyboard and pointing device (mouse)
- Video card and display
- Sound card and speakers
- Network card
- Modem (optional)
- Cables
- Hardware (nuts, bolts, screws, and brackets)
- Operating system software

Some of these components don't have to be purchased separately. For example, most motherboards have integrated sound and network cards, and some have integrated video as well. Each of these components is discussed in the following sections.

Case and Power Supply

The case and power supply unit (PSU) are typically sold as a unit, although some vendors do sell them separately. The power supplies included with lower-cost cases are often of lower quality or inadequate, so you might want to replace the existing PSU with one of your choosing. There are a multitude of chassis designs from which to choose, usually dependent on the motherboard form factor you want to use, the number of drive bays available, and whether the system is to be placed on a desktop, on the floor under the desk, on a shelf, or in some other location. There are cases with extra fans for cooling, front panel I/O and audio ports, removable side panels, and motherboard trays to make installing a motherboard easier, as well as cases that require no tools for assembly, rack-mounted versions, and more. For most custom-built systems, a mid-tower case supporting an ATX or microATX form factor motherboard, along with an ATX12V 2.x form factor PSU is the best choice. The ATX12V 2.x PSUs will have the 24-pin main power connector used on the latest boards, and the 24-pin connector is backward compatible, meaning it can be used with motherboards having only 20-pin main connectors as well (a 24-pin connector can plug directly into a 20-pin socket with 4 pins overhanging, or the overhanging 4-pin portion can be detached in some designs). The size and shape of a component is called the *form factor*. The most popular case form factors are as follows:

- Full-tower
- Mid- or mini-tower
- Desktop
- Low-profile (also called slimline)

These are not official form factors like those for motherboards and power supplies; however, each specific case is designed to accept a specific motherboard and power supply form factor. You have to ensure that the particular case you choose will accept the type of motherboard and power supply you want to use.

When deciding which type of case to purchase, you should consider where you will place your computer. Will it be on a desk? Or is it more feasible to put the system on the floor and just have the monitor, keyboard, and mouse on the desk? The amount of space you have available for the computer can affect other purchasing decisions, such as the length of the monitor, keyboard, and mouse cables.

After you have settled on a case form factor, you need to choose one that supports the motherboard and power supply form factors you want to use. The smaller mini-tower or slimline cases often accept only microATX, FlexATX, microBTX, or picoBTX motherboards, which somewhat limit your choices.

Within the ATX and BTX families, a larger case always accepts the smaller motherboards. For example, if a case accepts a full-size ATX motherboard, it also accepts microATX and FlexATX motherboards.

The same is true for BTX: A chassis that can handle BTX also accepts microBTX and picoBTX. FlexATX (and variations such as MiniITX), picoBTX, and nanoBTX motherboards are used in some of the latest small form factor systems.

◄◄   See "Motherboard Form Factors," p. 235.

Most mid-tower and larger cases accept full-size ATX boards, which have become the standard for most full-function systems. If you are interested in the most flexible type of case and power supply that will support the widest variety of future upgrades, I recommend getting a chassis that supports full-size ATX boards and ATX12V 2.x power supplies.

Important Considerations

Generally, any ATX case, motherboard, and power supply of sufficient wattage for your equipment can be put together to form the basis of a new system. I often recycle cases and power supplies from discarded systems when I build new systems. However, if you do this, there are some problems you should know about:

■ Many Dell systems built from 1996 through 2000 use nonstandard motherboards and power supplies with what appears to be a standard ATX power supply connectors; however, the pinout and voltage levels are changed. If you install a new motherboard in one of these systems, the power supply will plug into the new board, but the nonstandard wiring will likely destroy the power supply and possibly the new motherboard as well! Refer to Chapter 19, "Power Supplies," for more details.

This issue only affects the motherboard and power supply; the cases for those systems are standard ATX, and in fact they are built quite well. I have recycled many Dell chassis from that time period with all new internal components.

Many of Dell's newer systems also use nonstandard power supplies and motherboards, but these are more obvious in that they do not use standard form factors or connectors either, which means a standard ATX motherboard or power supply will not physically plug in. This makes an upgrade difficult or impossible, but at least you won't blow up any hardware in the process.

■ Newer processors require larger and more powerful heatsinks and fans for cooling. Be sure to use a heatsink designed for your particular processor, and make sure it is properly installed. These high-powered systems also require an ATX12V 2.x power supply, which has a 24-pin main connector plus an additional 4-pin 12V connector for the motherboard-based CPU voltage regulators.

The case you choose is really a matter of personal preference and system location. Most people feel that the tower systems are roomier and easier to work on, and the full-sized tower cases have a lot of bays for various storage devices. Tower cases typically have enough bays to hold floppy drives, multiple hard disk drives, optical drives, tape drives, and anything else you might want to install. However, some of the desktop cases can have as much room as the towers, particularly the mini- and mid-tower models. In fact, a tower case is sometimes considered a desktop case turned sideways, or vice versa. Some cases are convertible—that is, they can be used in either a desktop or tower orientation.

Tip

Mini-tower systems are an exception to the roomy tower case rule. These systems normally use the microATX, FlexATX, microBTX, or picoBTX motherboards and might have only two or three drive bays. These systems are compact and somewhat difficult to work on. These systems are, however, easily picked up and moved from one location to another.

When it comes to the power supply, the most important consideration is how many devices you plan to install in the system and how much power they require. Chapter 19 describes the process for calculating the power your system hardware requires and selecting an appropriate power supply for your needs.

◄◄ See "Power-use Calculations," p. 1266.

When you build your own system, you should always keep upgradeability and repairability in mind. A properly designed custom PC should last you far longer than an off-the-shelf model because you can more easily add or replace components. When choosing a case and power supply, leave yourself some room for expansion, on the assumption that you will eventually want to install additional drives or other new devices that appear on the market that you can't live without. To be specific, be sure you have at least a few empty internal drive bays and choose a higher output power supply than you initially need for your current equipment, so it won't be overtaxed when additional components are added later.

Processor

Both Intel and AMD sell processors through two primary channels or methods. They are referred to as *boxed* (or retail) and *OEM*.

- A boxed processor and an OEM processor might have the same specifications, but they are packaged differently, include different supplemental components, and have different warranties. Even though the boxed processors are sometimes also called *retail* processors, they are technically not intended to be sold in the normal retail channel. Both boxed and OEM processors are technically wholesale items and, as such, can be purchased from Intel or AMD only by signing up as a dealer with them and meeting their requirements to achieve and maintain dealer status. After you are registered as an Intel or AMD dealer, you can purchase boxed processors directly from them.

- OEM processors are sold only to major accounts that purchase hundreds of chips at a time. Although neither the boxed nor OEM processors are intended to be sold in the retail channel, after Intel or AMD sells them to one of their dealers, that dealer is free to resell the chips as he chooses. Therefore, an individual can purchase either boxed or OEM processors from many sources.

The most obvious difference between the boxed and OEM processors is the physical packaging. It could be argued that both technically come in boxes, but the Intel or AMD *boxed* processors come individually packaged in a colorful shrink-wrapped box that includes the processor, the heatsink and fan, installation instructions, a certificate of authenticity, warranty paperwork, and so on (see Figure 20.1).

On the other hand, OEM processors come in a much larger box with multiple trays containing up to 10 processors each, or up to 100 total. No heatsinks, fans, installation instructions, warranties, or other paperwork are included. These are purchased in large quantities by the major system manufacturers.

A boxed processor generally includes a three-year warranty direct with the processor manufacturer. So, if the CPU fails within 3 years of purchase, the end user can contact Intel or AMD directly and they will replace the chip. OEM processors have *no* warranty with the manufacturer (Intel or AMD); however, the company from which you purchased it will likely offer a 30- or 90-day warranty. The warranty length and the way in which it is administered are entirely up to the dealer from which you purchased the chip, which could be a problem if, for example, that dealer has gone out of business.

Figure 20.1   Boxed Intel Core 2 Duo processor. *Photo courtesy of Intel.*

Boxed processors also include a high-quality, manufacturer-supplied heatsink and cooling fan. Typically, the cooling system provided with a boxed processor is designed to work under worst-case thermal environments and is a very high-quality and heavy-duty unit. When you think about it, it wouldn't serve Intel or AMD to provide cheap heatsinks and fans on a processor they are warranting for three years!

OEM processors, on the other hand, include no heatsink or fan, but the dealer from which you purchase the processor will likely provide one. Unfortunately, these are often of very uneven quality and performance, up to the whims of the particular dealer you are using. With only a 30- or 90-day warranty, it doesn't matter as much if the manufacturer skimps on the heatsink because, if the chip fails beyond the short warranty period, the company isn't obligated to replace it. If you purchase an OEM processor with a motherboard, most dealers install the processor into the motherboard and provide a single warranty covering both items.

The motherboards you consider for new systems should most likely have one of the following processor sockets or slots:

- **Socket 775**—Supports the Core 2 Quad, Core 2 Duo, Pentium D, Celeron D, Pentium 4, and Celeron processors

- **Socket AM2**—Supports versions of the Athlon 64 X2, Athlon 64, and Sempron processors
- **Socket 939**—Supports versions of the Athlon 64 X2, Athlon 64 FX, and Athlon 64 processors

For very high-end or specialized systems, some might choose motherboards designed for server processors, such as the Intel Xeon and AMD Opteron. There are even motherboards designed to accept mobile (that is, laptop) processors, which are excellent for specialized low-power or low-heat systems. These motherboards might include sockets such as Socket F (AMD Opteron server), Socket S1 (AMD Turion mobile), Socket M (Core 2 Duo mobile), Socket 771 (Xeon server), and others.

The following socket types also can be purchased but are not compatible with the latest CPU models and will limit your future processor upgrade options:

- **Socket 478**—Supports the second- and third-generation Intel Pentium 4 and compatible Celeron processors
- **Socket 754**—Supports the Athlon 64 processors
- **Socket A (462)**—Supports the AMD Athlon, Athlon XP, and Duron processors
- **Socket 370 (also called PGA370)**—Supports the PGA versions of the Intel Pentium III and compatible Celeron processors

Because the motherboard you choose dictates or limits your choice in processor, you should choose your processor first, which will then dictate the type of CPU socket (or slot) that must be present on the motherboard. For more information on processors, refer to Chapter 3, "Microprocessor Types and Specifications."

◀◀ See "Processor Socket and Slot Types," p. 97.

Tip

Check the NewEgg.com site for information on motherboards and processors that are for sale. The site serves as a useful research tool for checking to see what components are currently available, what they cost, as well as specifications and compatibility requirements.

Motherboard

Several compatible form factors are used for motherboards. The form factor refers to the physical dimensions and size of the board and dictates into which type of case the board will fit. The types of compatible industry-standard motherboard form factors generally available for system builders are as follows:

- ATX and variants
- BTX and variants
- MiniITX (semiproprietary)

In general, you are safest sticking with the ATX form factor, or variants of ATX such as microATX. ATX is simply the most popular form factor family around, and with that you will have the widest choices in cases, motherboards, and power supplies.

BTX is the latest form factor, designed as an improved replacement for ATX; however, BTX is not physically compatible with and requires a different chassis from ATX. Although BTX is currently used by most of the major OEMs, BTX and variants have not taken off in the system builder market. Only a few BTX motherboards are available for Intel processors, and none for AMD processors. Because BTX was designed in part to help reduce the effects of hotter and hotter-running processors by better controlling airflow through the chassis, the recent trend in CPU design of increasing performance through design efficiency rather than ramp-ups in pure clock speed has diminished the need for it. Consequently, ATX has remained the dominant form factor for PCs and is likely to remain so for some time.

Note

For more information on all the motherboard form factors, refer to Chapter 4, "Motherboards and Buses." You can also find the reference standard documents detailing the modern form factors at the Desktop Form Factors website (www. formfactors.org).

In addition to processor support and form factor, you should consider several other features when selecting a motherboard. The following sections examine each feature.

Chipsets

Aside from the processor, the main component on a motherboard is called the *chipset*. This usually is a set of two chips that contains the main motherboard circuits. The two chips are often called the north bridge or MCH (Memory Controller Hub) and south bridge or ICH (I/O Controller Hub). The chips in the chipset replace the 150 or more distinct components that were used in the original IBM AT systems and enable a motherboard designer to easily create a functional system from just a few parts. The chipset contains most of the motherboard circuitry except the processor and memory in most systems.

Because the chipset really *is* the motherboard, the chipset used in a given motherboard has a profound effect on the performance of the board. It dictates all the performance parameters and limitations of the board, such as memory size and speed, processor types and speeds, supported buses and their speeds, and more.

Because chipsets are constantly being introduced and improved over time, I can't list all of them and their functions here; however, you will find a detailed description of many of them in Chapter 4. Several popular high-performance chipsets are on the market today.

◄◄   See "Chipsets," p. 273.
◄◄   See "Motherboard Selection Criteria (Knowing What to Look For)," p. 435.

Clearly, the selection of a chipset must be based largely on the processor you choose and the additional components you intend to install in the computer.

If you are intent on building the ultimate PC (at least by this week's standards), you also should consider the faster processors available. Be sure not to waste your investment on the most capable processor by using a chipset that doesn't fully exploit its capabilities.

When you are designing your system, carefully consider the number and type of expansion cards you intend to install. Then, ensure that the motherboard you select has the correct number of slots and that they are of the correct bus type for your peripherals (PCI, AGP, and PCI Express). Because most boards lack ISA slots, if you have any ISA peripherals, it is long past time that you replace them with more capable PCI or PCI Express versions.

The chipset dictates what types of bus slots can be included on the motherboard. Most recent chipsets include PCI and PCIe (PCI Express) slots only; if you have older ISA or AGP cards, most likely they won't be usable in any new system you build or buy.

When you buy a motherboard, I highly recommend you contact the chipset manufacturer and obtain the documentation (often called the *data book*) for your particular chipset. This explains how the memory and cache controllers, as well as many other devices in the system, operate. This documentation should also help describe the Advanced Chipset Setup functions in your system's Setup program. With this information, you might be able to fine-tune the motherboard configuration by altering the chipset features. Because chipsets are frequently discontinued and replaced with newer models, don't wait too long to get the chipset documentation because most manufacturers make it available only for chips currently in production.

Note

One interesting fact about chipsets is that in the volume the motherboard manufacturers purchase them, the chipsets usually cost about $40 each. If you have an older motherboard that needs repair, you usually can't purchase the chipsets because they aren't stocked by the manufacturer after they are discontinued. Not to mention that most chipsets feature surface mounting with ball grid array (BGA) packages that are extremely difficult to manually remove and replace. The low-cost chipset is one of the reasons motherboards have become disposable items that are rarely, if ever, repaired.

BIOS

Another important feature on the motherboard is the basic input/output system (BIOS). This is also called the ROM BIOS because the code is stored in a read-only memory (ROM) chip. There are several things to look for here. Most BIOS are supplied by one of the major BIOS manufacturers, such as AMI (American Megatrends International), Phoenix, or Award (owned by Phoenix). The BIOS is normally contained in a special type of reprogrammable chip called a flash ROM or EEPROM (electrically erasable programmable read-only memory). This enables you to download BIOS updates from the manufacturer and, using a program it supplies, easily update the code in your BIOS. Before purchasing a motherboard, check to see whether the motherboard is well supported and whether the manufacturer offers downloadable BIOS updates. If you can't easily find BIOS updates, drivers, and documentation for the board on the manufacturer's website, then you might want to choose a board from a different manufacturer that provides better support.

◄◄ See "Upgrading the BIOS," p. 459.

You also need to verify that the motherboard and BIOS support both the processor you plan to install initially and the processor you might upgrade to in the future. If the motherboard and chipset can handle a new processor but the BIOS cannot, a BIOS upgrade may be available to provide proper support.

Memory

Main memory typically is installed in the form of dual inline memory modules (DIMMs). Three physical types of main memory modules are commonly used in PC systems today, with several variations of each. The main types are as follows:

- 184-pin DDR DIMMs
- 240-pin DDR2 DIMMs
- 240-pin DDR3 DIMMs

Double data rate (DDR) SDRAM memory is an updated variation on SDRAM in which data is transferred twice as quickly, and it is the most common type of memory used in systems since 2004. DDR3 is the latest type of main memory on the market, and will be the eventual successor to DDR2.

◄◄ See "DDR SDRAM," p. 525.

Current motherboards use memory in either single-channel or dual-channel mode. In single-channel mode, each 64-bit wide DIMM is accessed individually, whereas in dual-channel mode the modules are accessed in pairs for higher performance. If you want to take advantage of the faster dual-channel mode, then make sure you purchase and install memory modules in matched pairs.

Memory modules are available with an extra error check bit for each 8 bits. These are called ECC (Error Correcting Code) modules. ECC support is normally found only in server-type motherboards and is rarely found in motherboards used in standard PCs. If you want to install the more expensive ECC modules in your system, make sure that your motherboard provides the necessary support.

◀◀ See "Parity and ECC," p. 557.

For more information on PC memory of all types, refer to Chapter 6, "Memory."

I/O Ports

Virtually all motherboards today have built-in I/O ports. In rare cases where these ports are not built in, they must be supplied via a plug-in expansion board that, unfortunately, wastes an expansion slot. The following ports might be included in any new system you assemble:

- PS/2 Keyboard connector (mini-DIN type)
- PS/2 Mouse port (mini-DIN type)
- Serial port
- Parallel port
- Four or more USB ports
- Two or more FireWire ports
- One or two analog VGA or DVI video connectors (integrated video)
- RJ-45 port for 10/100 or 10/100/1000 Ethernet
- Audio connectors (speakers, microphone, and so on)
- One or more parallel ATA ports
- Two or more serial ATA ports

Some motherboards lack the serial, parallel, keyboard, and mouse ports (referred to as *legacy ports*), instead relying on USB for those connections. You might want to avoid "legacy-free" motherboards if you still use peripherals with those types of connections. Most motherboards feature integrated sound, and many have optional integrated video as well.

All the integrated ports are supported either directly by the motherboard chipset or by an additional Super I/O chip and additional interface components. Adding the optional video and sound interfaces directly to the motherboard saves both money and the use of an expansion slot, especially important in the less expensive systems sold today. In the case of integrated video, however, you're likely to incur a performance hit as compared to having a separate AGP or PCI Express video card.

If these devices are not present on the motherboard, various Super I/O or multi-I/O boards that implement all these ports are available. Again, most of the newer versions of these boards use a single-chip implementation because it is cheaper and more reliable.

◀◀ See "Super I/O Chips," p. 367.

The primary drawback of having functions such as video and networking built into the motherboard, of course, is that you have little or no choice about the features or quality of the integrated adapters. Integrated components such as these are nearly always of serviceable quality, but they certainly do not push the performance envelope of higher-end expansion cards. Most people who decide to build a system themselves do so because they want optimum performance from every component, which you typically do not get from integrated video and sound.

Buying a motherboard with integrated adapters, however, does not preclude you from adding expansion devices of the same type. You usually can install a video or sound card into a system with an integrated sound or video adapter without major problems, except that the additional cost of the integrated component is wasted. You also might encounter difficulties with the automated hardware detection routines in operating systems such as Windows detecting the wrong adapter in your system, but you can remedy this by manually identifying the expansion card to the OS. If you want the convenience of integrated video but want to maintain the option of installing a faster PCI Express video card later, look for systems that provide both integrated video and the required PCIe x16 slot you'll need for your video card.

◄◄ See "Integrated Video/Motherboard Chipsets," p. 928.

If four or more USB ports exist, they often are split among two or more buses, with one set of connections on the back of the board and another set as a pin-header connector on the motherboard. A cable then plugs into this connector, enabling you to route the second USB bus port to the front of the PC case. Most newer cases have provisions for front-mounted USB ports in this manner, which makes temporarily connecting devices such as digital cameras or MP3 players for transferring files easier.

Note that if your motherboard has integrated devices such as video and sound, you must go into the BIOS Setup to disable these devices if you want to add a card-based replacement device. Check your BIOS Setup menus for an Enable/Disable setting for any integrated devices.

Hard Disk Drives

Your system also needs at least one hard disk drive. In most cases, a drive with a minimum capacity of 80GB is recommended, although in some cases you can get away with less for a low-end configuration. High-end systems should have drives of 400GB or higher. One of the cardinal rules of computer shopping is that you can never have too much storage. Buy as much as you can afford, and you'll almost certainly end up filling it anyway.

Tip

If you are an Internet user, one informal method of estimating how much disk space you will need is to go by the speed of your Internet connection. If you have a high-speed link, such as that provided by a DSL connection, a cable modem, or a LAN, you will find that the ease of downloading large amounts of data fills up disk space quickly. Similarly, if you have a large collection of CDs you want to store on your computer, I would recommend at least a 250GB hard drive. In addition, a removable storage system with a large capacity, such as a dual-layer DVD burner, is also a good idea.

Serial ATA has become the most popular hard disk interface, with many motherboards featuring six or more SATA connectors. Most still have a Parallel ATA port for optical drives; however, even those are now coming in SATA versions.

Many motherboards now feature RAID-compatible SATA interfaces. These enable you to install multiple drives in a number of array configurations, including RAID 0 (striped), RAID 1 (mirrored), and RAID 5 (striped with distributed parity). Using the RAID 1 or RAID 5 configurations are particularly useful for increased protection against data loss. RAID 1 requires matched pairs of drives, whereas RAID 5 requires three or more drives.

Most motherboards have built-in USB 2.0 ports, and many include IEEE 1394 (FireWire) ports as well. External USB and FireWire drives are very useful for backup purposes as well as for moving large amounts of data from system to system.

◄◄ See "PATA/SATA RAID," p. 634, and "Serial ATA," p. 605.

Several brands of high-quality hard disk drives are available from which to choose, and most offer similar performance within their price and capacity categories.

Removable Storage

Many of today's systems are no longer equipped with a 1.44MB 3 1/2" floppy drive because all systems today are capable of booting from CD, DVD, or even USB drives, thus making optical discs a useful high-capacity replacement for floppy or Zip drives.

However, for additional removable storage, I recommend a dual-layer DVD+/-RW (DVD-rewriteable) drive over floppy, Zip, or even CD-RW, regardless of your budget. These are now relatively inexpensive—often well under $50—and they allow you to use your choice of optical media, be it CD or DVD. Rewritable DVD media prices have also dropped considerably in recent years, making the cost per megabyte of storage superior to using rewritable CD media. Rewritable CDs store just 700MB of data compared to 4.7GB for a single-layer DVD and 8.4GB for a dual-layer DVD.

◀◀   See "DVD," p. 763.

Regardless of format, some form of optical drive is considered a mandatory item in any PC you construct if for no other reason than because almost all software is now distributed on CD-ROM or DVD. That said, while a rewritable DVD drive should be considered a required component in any new PC, an external hard drive is also worth considering if you need extra removable storage either for portability or for data backups. Even a dual-layer DVD cannot match the storage capacity of today's external hard drives, which can hold upward of 1TB of data. External enclosures that include USB 2.0 or FireWire ports (sometimes both) can now be had for around $30, and many of them include software that allows you to configure so-called "one-button backups" that let you simply press a button on the external drive and automatically back up your essential data.

On a smaller scale, USB-driven flash memory drives provide a much more compact storage solution that can be carried with you wherever you go. The first generation of flash drives often stored as little as 16MB of data, but today's larger devices can hold in excess of 8GB of data.

Input Devices

Obviously, your system needs a keyboard and some type of pointing device, such as a mouse. Different people prefer different types of keyboards, and the "feel" of one type can vary considerably from other types. If possible, I suggest you try a variety of keyboards until you find the type that suits you best. I prefer a stiff action with tactile feedback myself, but others prefer a lighter, quieter touch.

Keyboards and mice typically include connectors that can accommodate either PS/2 or USB ports. Even though PS/2 versions that plug into a 6-pin mini-DIN (PS/2) connector have traditionally been the most popular, USB has all but supplanted them at this point on newer systems. Wireless keyboards and mice often have no support at all for the venerable PS/2 port.

Though rarely an issue in new systems, it's important to keep in mind that, with any USB device, you must have support in the operating system for USB, and in the case of USB keyboards and mice, your system BIOS must support a function called *Legacy USB* or *USB Keyboard and Mouse* if you want to use the USB keyboard or mouse outside the Windows graphical user interface. Virtually all recent BIOSs have this feature. However, to enable you to use your USB keyboard or mouse on both new and older systems, I recommend you look for models that also support the traditional PS/2 ports. This type usually ships with a USB-to-PS/2 adapter. These adapters can also be purchased separately if necessary.

If you prefer a wireless keyboard or mouse, it used to be important that you chose one that uses RF (radio) instead of IR (infrared) signaling and one that could use a single transceiver for both the keyboard and mouse. In current products, that choice is largely made for you. However, you should keep in mind that RF signaling might use either short-range proprietary frequencies or the industry-standard

Bluetooth wireless network architecture. Bluetooth devices are preferable if you want to use the keyboard or mouse with a wide variety of devices or at distances greater than 6 feet or so from the system.

◀◀ See "Keyboards," p. 1059.

◀◀ See "Keyboard Technology," p. 1063.

Tip

You might be tempted to skimp on your keyboard and mouse to save a few dollars. Don't! You do all your interacting with your new PC through these devices, and cheap ones make their presence known every time you use your system. I insist on high-quality mechanical switch–type keyboards on all my systems.

The success of USB has changed the market so that there are virtually no limits to the types of devices available that can make use of the connection. Modems, keyboards, mice, optical drives, speakers, joysticks, hard drives, tape drives, floppy drives, scanners, cameras, MP3 players, and printers are just some of the devices available.

◀◀ See "USB Keyboards," p. 1075.

Video Card and Display

You need a video adapter and a monitor or display to complete your system. Numerous choices are available in this area, but the most important piece of advice I have to give is to choose a good monitor. The display is your main interface to the system and can be the cause of many hours of either pain or pleasure, depending on which monitor you choose. At this point the market for CRTs has died off, and I only recommend LCDs for new systems.

I usually recommend a minimum of a 17" LCD display running 1280×1024 SXGA (standard aspect ratio) or 1400×900 WSXGA+ (widescreen) resolution. If you go to a 19" or larger display, even higher resolutions are possible.

Most LCDs can be attached to a VGA analog port, but the most current models are designed to work with the DVI connector, which is rapidly becoming the default connector type on modern video cards. Another feature to look for is a low response time: Under 8ms (milliseconds) is considered good, and even lower numbers are better for fast gaming response.

In the past few years, video adapters had become standardized on the accelerated graphics port (AGP) interface. Today, however, video cards have made the leap to PCI Express. In some cases you will find graphics cards based on PCI as well. The only instance in which a PCI graphics card should be used in a desktop system is if you are adding a secondary video adapter for use with a second video display. Windows 98 and later supports multiple monitors on a single system, and it's a feature that can be very useful for a variety of applications. If performance is your ultimate goal and you can tolerate the added expense, look for a system that supports dual PCI Express x16 graphics cards. Both NVIDIA and ATI (now part of AMD) offer high-performance video chipsets that can be used to run dual video cards together to increase video display performance.

◀◀ See "Accelerated Graphics Port," p. 405.

◀◀ See "3D Graphics Accelerators," p. 951.

If you are installing a newer video card as a replacement upgrade to your current system, you can remove the existing video card and replace it with any video card that supports the motherboard's standard (be it AGP or PCI Express). In the case of older systems using AGP, you should ensure that the AGP slot and card are compatible because AGP has been implemented in multiple versions based on speed (4x, 8x, and so on). You can also replace an existing PCI video card with another PCI video card if there is no AGP slot, but you should consider a system upgrade instead to provide an AGP or a PCI Express slot for faster video.

Many motherboards with onboard video also have an AGP or a PCI Express video card slot; if your motherboard has one, you can insert the applicable card into this slot. The onboard video should be automatically disabled in most cases, although you might have to disable it in the BIOS setup in some cases.

Audio Hardware

All systems today should be capable of playing audio to some degree, which means you need at least a passable set of external speakers and either a motherboard with integrated audio or a separate sound card. Most systems today, even those without integrated video, now feature integrated audio, but it can be disabled if you prefer to add a dedicated high-quality sound card. Dedicated cards, such as Creative's X-Fi product line, are ideal if you want the best possible sound quality for DVD playback, audio capture and editing, or surround sound for gaming. Almost any motherboard-integrated audio system and sound card on the market today are compatible with the baseline Creative Sound Blaster series, Windows DirectSound, and other sound APIs.

Speakers designed for use with PCs range from tiny, underpowered devices to large audiophile class systems. Many of the top manufacturers of stereo speakers now produce speaker systems for PCs. Some include subwoofers or even a full Dolby 5.1, 6.1, or 7.1 surround sound implementation.

Accessories

Apart from the major components, you need several other accessories to complete your system. These are the small parts that can make the assembly process a pleasure or a chore. If you are purchasing your system components from mail-order sources, you should make a complete list of all the parts you need, right down to the last cable and screw, and be sure you have everything before you begin the assembly process. It is excruciating to have to wait several days with a half-assembled system for the delivery of a forgotten part.

Heatsinks/Cooling Fans

Most of today's faster processors produce a lot of heat, and this heat has to be dissipated so your system doesn't operate intermittently or even fail completely. Heatsinks are available in two main types: passive and active.

Passive heatsinks are simply finned chunks of metal (usually aluminum or copper) that are clipped or glued to the top of the processor. They act as a radiator and, in effect, give the processor more surface area to dissipate the heat. *Active* heatsinks, which include the heatsink itself and an attached fan, are required by most processors today because of their higher capacity and smaller space requirements. Often you have no control over which heatsink you use because it comes already attached to the processor. If you have to attach it yourself, you should use a thermal transfer grease or sticky tape to fill any air gaps between the heatsink and the processor. This allows for maximum heat transfer and the best efficiency.

Obviously, active heatsinks offer greater cooling capacity than the passive types. Boxed processors from Intel and AMD are sold with the heatsink and fan included. And although OEM processors don't include a heatsink from the processor manufacturer, most vendors who sell them add an aftermarket heatsink and fan to the package; often, aftermarket heatsinks and fans provide significantly better cooling than those shipped with boxed processors, making them more suitable for overclocking.

Caution

All modern heatsinks require that a thermal interface material (usually tape, grease, or paste) be applied to the base of the heatsink before installation. A small amount may be supplied with a new heatsink, but you may want to purchase some separately because the grease has to be cleaned off and reapplied every time you remove and reinstall the processor or heatsink.

Another consideration for cooling is with the case. The fan in the power supply and the one on the CPU heatsink are not enough for a modern high-performance system. I recommend you get a case that includes at least one additional cooling fan. This is typically mounted in the rear of the chassis, directing additional air out the back. Some cases include an extra fan in the front or side cover as well.

If you are upgrading an existing system, several companies make fan assemblies that insert into a drive bay for additional cooling. They take the place of a 5 1/4" drive and take air in through the front bezel, directing it back into the case. Bay-mounted fans are an especially good idea if you are using a 10,000 rpm or faster hard drive because they run extremely hot (most hard drives still spin at 7,200 rpm). There are even fan assemblies mounted on cards that blow air out the rear of the case. Keep in mind that it is best to keep the interior of the PC below 100°F; anything over 110° dramatically reduces component life and leads to stability problems.

Cables

PC systems need many different cables to hook up everything. These can include power cables or adapters, floppy drive cables, Parallel and Serial ATA drive cables, and many others. Frequently, the motherboard includes the cables for any of the internal ports, such as floppy or hard drives. Other external devices you purchase come with included cables, but in some cases, they aren't supplied.

If you build your system using all OEM (what the industry calls *white box*) components, be aware that these sometimes don't include the accessories, such as cables, software, and additional documentation, that you would get with a boxed-retail version of the same component.

Hardware

You might need screws, standoffs, mounting rails (if your case requires them), and other miscellaneous hardware to assemble your system. Most of these parts are included with the case or your other system components. This is especially true of any card or disk drive brackets or screws. When you purchase a component such as a hard drive, some vendors offer you the option of purchasing the bare drive or a kit containing the required cables and mounting hardware for the device. Most of the time bare drives don't include any additional hardware, but you might not need it anyway if the mounting hardware comes with your case. Even so, spending the few additional dollars for the complete drive kit is rarely a waste of money. Even if you're left with some extra bits and pieces after assembling your system, they will probably come in handy someday.

Hardware and Software Resources

When you are planning to build a system, it is important to consider how all your selected components will work together and how the software you run must support them. It is not enough to be sure that you have sufficient slots on the motherboard for all your expansion cards and enough bays in the case for all your drives. You must also consider the resources required for all the components.

For example, if you are planning to use FireWire devices, you need to know whether your new motherboard has FireWire ports built in or whether you will need to add a separate adapter card to achieve compatibility. With the many changes in processor speed and voltage, you also need to verify that the processor, memory, and motherboard combination you prefer will work correctly together.

Essentially, you should completely configure the system before you begin ordering any parts. Planning a system to this level of detail can be a lot of work, which is one reason—besides cost—that the vast majority of PCs are prebuilt.

Tip

In most cases, you can download or view online the manuals for the motherboard, processor, and other major components before you purchase them. Check the component vendors' websites for these manuals and technical notes and read
them carefully. You will need Adobe Acrobat Reader, available free from www.adobe.com, to view most online manuals.

Another consideration is the operating system and other software you need. Prebuilt systems nearly
always arrive with the operating system installed, but when you build your own, you must be prepared with a copy of your selected operating system.

The operating system you select for your new computer is another important decision. You must be
certain that the OS supports all the hardware you've selected, which can occasionally be a difficult
task. Today the main choices are Windows XP, Vista, or one of the Linux variants such as Ubuntu.
This is one area where building your own has real advantages; for example, after Vista was launched
in early 2007, many retail systems were only available with Vista, even though many people preferred
XP. In any case, when you build your own system, the choice of OS is entirely up to you.

About OEM Operating Systems

Because Microsoft doesn't allow OEM versions of its operating systems to be sold separately, if you intend to purchase
one, be sure you order an OEM edition of whatever operating system you will be running at the same time you buy your
hardware. The terms of the Microsoft dealer (or system builder) agreement allow dealers to sell the OS only with hardware. At one time you needed to buy a complete PC, a motherboard, or a hard disk to get an OEM version of the operating system, but you can now buy any hardware—even a device as inexpensive as a case fan or mouse—and qualify to
buy the OEM version. No matter what, be sure you get the original OEM version on CD-ROM or DVD-ROM.

Drivers for specific hardware components, such as your motherboard chipset, might also be a problem. It is a good idea to gather all the latest driver revisions for your hardware and intended OS, as
well as BIOS flashes, firmware updates, and other software components, and have them available
when you begin the assembly process. Placing them on a DVD or CD is a good idea; that way they
can be easily accessed and installed when necessary.

System Assembly and Disassembly

Actually assembling the system is easy after you have lined up all the components. In fact, you will
find the parts procurement phase the most lengthy and trying of the entire experience. Completing
the system is basically a matter of screwing everything together, plugging in all the cables and connectors, and configuring everything to operate properly together.

In short order, you will find out whether your system operates as you had planned or whether some
incompatibilities exist between some of the components. Be careful and pay attention to how you
install all your components. It is rare that a newly assembled system operates perfectly the first time,
even for experienced system builders. It is very easy to forget a jumper, switch, or cable connection
that later causes problems in system operation. Most people's first reaction when problems occur is to
blame defective hardware, but that is usually not the source. The problem can typically be traced to
some missed step or error made in the assembly process.

Above all, the most crucial rule of assembling your own system is to save every piece of documentation and software that comes with every component in your system. This material can be indispens-
able in troubleshooting problems you encounter during the assembly process or later. You should also
retain all the packing materials used to ship mail-order components to you until you are certain they
will not have to be returned.

Assembly Preparation

The process of physically assembling a PC requires only a few basic tools: a 1/4" nut driver or Phillips-head screwdriver for the external screws that hold the cover in place and a 3/16" nut driver or Phillips-head screwdriver for all the other screws. Needle-nose pliers can also help in removing motherboard standoffs, jumpers, and stubborn cable connectors. Because of marketplace standardization, only a couple types and sizes of screws (with a few exceptions) are used to hold a system together. Also, the physical arrangement of the major components is similar even among different manufacturers. Figure 20.2 shows the components that go into a typical system, and Figure 20.3 shows the system with those components assembled. Note that the components shown here are for a standard PC. Your final component list might vary.

You'll find more information on tools used to work on PCs in Chapter 22, "PC Diagnostics, Testing, and Maintenance."

Other tools you'll need are software related. You'll need an operating system install disc, and it is a good idea to have discs handy with any service packs, drivers, or other software you will want to install.

The following sections cover the assembly and disassembly procedure:

- Case or cover assembly
- Power supply
- Adapter boards
- Motherboard
- Disk drives

Later, you learn how to install and remove these components for several types of systems. With regard to assembly and disassembly, it is best to consider each system by the type of case it uses. All systems that have ATX-type cases, for example, are assembled and disassembled in much the same manner.

The following section lists assembly and disassembly instructions for several case types.

ESD Protection

One issue you must be aware of is electrostatic discharge (ESD) protection. Another is recording the configuration of the system with regard to the physical aspects of the system (such as jumper or switch settings and cable orientations) and the logical configuration of the system (especially in terms of elements such as CMOS settings).

When you are working on the internal components of a computer, you must take the necessary precautions to prevent accidental static discharges to the components. At any time, your body can hold a large static voltage charge that can easily damage components of your system. Before I ever put my hands into an open system, I first touch a grounded portion of the chassis, such as the power supply case. This action serves to equalize the electrical charges the device and my body might be carrying. Be sure the power supply is unplugged during all phases of the assembly process. Some will claim that you should leave the system plugged into provide an earth ground through the power cord and outlet, but that is unnecessary. If you leave the system plugged in, you open yourself up to other problems, such as accidentally turning it on or leaving it on when installing a board or device, which can damage the motherboard or other devices.

Caution

Also note that power supplies used in many systems today deliver a +5V current to the motherboard continuously—that is, whenever they are plugged in. Bottom line: Be sure any system you are working on is completely unplugged from the wall outlet.

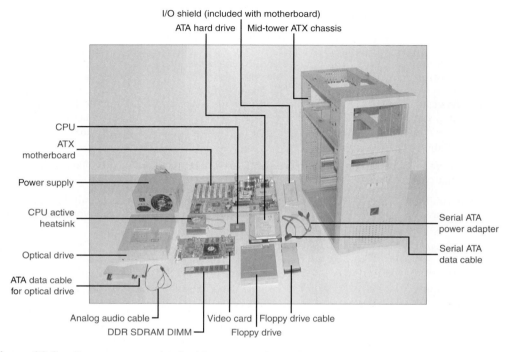

I/O shield (included with motherboard)
ATA hard drive | Mid-tower ATX chassis

CPU

ATX
motherboard

Power supply

CPU active
heatsink

Serial ATA
power adapter

Serial ATA
data cable

Optical drive

ATA data cable
for optical drive

Analog audio cable
DDR SDRAM DIMM

Video card | Floppy drive cable
Floppy drive

Figure 20.2 Components used in building a typical PC. The case and drive screws and the standoffs are not shown but are usually provided with the case and drives.

Figure 20.3 The completed system using all components shown in Figure 20.2.

High-end workbenches at repair facilities have the entire bench grounded, so it's not as big of a problem; however, you need something to be a good ground source to prevent a current from building up in you.

A more sophisticated way to equalize the charges between you and any of the system components is to use an ESD protection kit. These kits consist of a wrist strap and mat, with ground wires for attachment to the system chassis. When you are going to work on a system, you place the mat next to or partially below the system unit. Next, you clip the ground wire to both the mat and the system's chassis, tying the grounds together. You then put on the wrist strap and attach that wire to a ground. Because the mat and system chassis are already wired together, you can attach the wrist-strap wire to the system chassis or to the mat. If you are using a wrist strap without a mat, clip the wrist-strap wire to the system chassis. When clipping these wires to the chassis, be sure to use an area that is free of paint so a good ground contact can be achieved. This setup ensures that any electrical charges are carried equally by you and any of the components in the system, preventing the sudden flow of static electricity that can damage the circuits.

As you install or remove disk drives, adapter cards, and especially delicate items such as the entire motherboard, memory modules, or processors, you should place these components on the static mat. Sometimes people put the system unit on top of the mat, but the unit should be alongside the mat so you have room to lay out all the components as you work with them. If you are going to remove the motherboard from a system, be sure you leave enough room for it on the mat.

If you do not have such a mat, place the removed circuits and devices on a clean desk or table. Always pick up a loose adapter card by the metal bracket used to secure the card to the system. This bracket is tied into the ground circuitry of the card, so by touching the bracket first, you prevent a discharge from damaging the components of the card. If the circuit board has no metal bracket (a motherboard, for example), handle the board carefully by the edges, and try not to touch any of the connectors or components. If you don't have proper ESD equipment such as a wrist strap or mat, be sure to periodically touch the chassis while working inside the system to equalize any charge you might have built up.

Caution

Some people recommend placing loose circuit boards and chips on sheets of aluminum foil. I absolutely *do not recommend* this procedure because it can actually result in an explosion! Many motherboards, adapter cards, and other circuit boards today have built-in lithium or NiCad batteries. These batteries react violently when they are shorted out, which is exactly what you would be doing by placing such a board on a piece of aluminum foil. The batteries will quickly overheat and possibly explode like a large firecracker (with dangerous shrapnel). Because you will not always be able to tell whether a board has a battery built into it somewhere, the safest practice is to never place any board on any conductive metal surface.

Recording Physical Configuration

While you are assembling a system, you should record all the physical settings and configurations of each component, including jumper and switch settings, cable orientations and placement, ground wire locations, and even adapter board placement. Keep a notebook handy for recording these items, and write down all the settings. See Chapter 4 for more information on motherboard connector, jumper, and other component locations. Figure 20.4 shows a typical motherboard jumper.

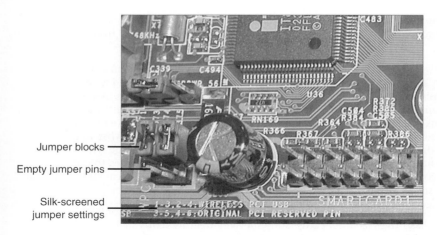

Jumper blocks

Empty jumper pins

Silk-screened jumper settings

Figure 20.4   The jumper position shown here is used to configure the motherboard's PCI and USB interface.

It is especially important to record all the jumper and switch settings on the motherboard, as well as those on any card you install in the system (cards seldom use jumpers or switches today, but some motherboards still do). If you accidentally disturb these jumpers or switches, you will know how they were originally set. This knowledge is very important if you do not have all the documentation for the system handy. Even if you do, undocumented jumpers and switches often do not appear in the manuals but must be set a certain way for the item to function. Also, record all cable orientations. Most name-brand systems use cables and connectors that are keyed so that they can't be plugged in backward, but some generic PCs do not have this added feature. You should mark or record what each cable was plugged into and its proper orientation. Ribbon cables usually have an odd-colored (red, green, blue, or black) wire at one end that indicates pin 1. There might also be a mark on the connector, such as a triangle or even the number 1. The devices the cables are plugged into are also marked in some way to indicate the orientation of pin 1. Often, a dot appears next to the pin 1 side of the connector, or a 1 or other mark might appear.

Although cable orientation and placement seem to be very simple, we rarely get through the entire course of my PC troubleshooting seminars without at least one group of people having cable-connection problems. Fortunately, in most cases (except power cables), plugging any of the ribbon cables inside the system backward doesn't cause any permanent damage.

Power and battery connections on pre-ATX systems are exceptions; plugging them in backward in most cases causes damage. In fact, plugging the motherboard power connectors in backward or in the wrong plug location on these older systems puts 12V where only 5V should be—a situation that can cause components of the board to violently explode. I know of several people who have facial scars caused by shrapnel from components that exploded because of improper power supply connections! As a precaution, I always turn my face away from the system when I power it on for the first time. If you are using an ATX board and power supply, there is little chance of this happening because of the keyed type of power connector used.

Plugging in the CMOS battery backward can damage the CMOS chip, which usually is soldered into the motherboard; in such a case, the motherboard must be replaced.

Finally, you should record miscellaneous items such as the placement of any ground wires, adapter cards, and anything else that you might have difficulty remembering later. Some configurations and setups might be particular about the slots in which the adapter cards are located, so you should put everything back exactly the way it was originally.

Motherboard Installation

When you are installing your system's motherboard, unpack the motherboard and check to ensure you have everything that should be included. If you purchase a new board, you typically get at least the motherboard, some I/O cables, and a manual. If you order the motherboard with a processor or memory, it is usually installed on the board for you but might also be included separately. Some board kits include an antistatic wrist strap to help prevent damage due to static electricity when installing the board.

Installing the CPU and Heatsink

Before your new motherboard is installed, you should install the processor and memory. This usually is much easier to do before the board is installed in the chassis. Some motherboards have jumpers that control both the CPU speed and the voltage supplied to it. If these are set incorrectly, the system might not operate at all, might operate erratically, or might possibly even damage the CPU. Modern boards control voltages either automatically or via the BIOS setup program. If you have any questions about the proper settings, contact the vendor who sold you the board before making any jumper changes.

◄◄ See "CPU Operating Voltages," p. 114.

All processors today run hot enough to require some form of heatsink to dissipate heat from the processor. To install the processor and heatsink, use the following procedure:

1. Prep the motherboard. Take the new motherboard out of the antistatic bag it was supplied in and set it on the bag or the antistatic mat, if you have one.

2. Install the processor. First, find pin 1 on the processor; it usually is denoted by a corner of the chip that is marked by a dot or bevel. Next, find the corresponding pin 1 of the socket for the CPU on the motherboard; it also is usually marked on the board or with a bevel in one corner of the socket. Be sure the pins on the processor are straight and not bent; if they are bent, the chip won't insert properly into the socket. If necessary, use small needle-nose pliers or a hemostat to carefully straighten any pins. Don't bend them too much—they might break off, ruining the chip. Insert the CPU into the socket by lifting the release lever until it is vertical. Then, align the pins on the processor with the holes in the socket and drop it down into place. If the processor does not seem to want to drop in all the way, remove it to check for proper alignment and any possibly bent pins. When the processor is fully seated in the socket, push the locking lever on the socket down until it latches to secure the processor (see Figure 20.5).

Note

If you require instructions for installing slot-based processors, refer to the section "Installing the CPU and Heatsink," in Chapter 22 of the 16th edition of this book.

3. Attach the heatsink. Most heatsinks clip to the socket with one or more retainer clips (see Figure 20.6). Be careful when attaching the clip to the socket; you don't want it to scrape against the motherboard, which can damage circuit traces or components. You also need to keep the heatsink steady on the chip while attaching the clips, so do not move, tilt, or slide the heatsink while you attach it. Most heatsinks have a preapplied thermal pad; otherwise, you will need to put a dab of heatsink thermal transfer compound (normally a white- or silver-colored grease) on the CPU before installing the heatsink. The exact amount required can vary, but you want just

enough to provide a very thin layer between the CPU and heatsink. Spread out the material with a plastic card (old credit cards work well) such that a very thin layer covers the heat spreader or CPU die, then remove or wipe off any excess. You can spread the material with your finger, however in that case I recommend you wear a rubber glove as you don't want oils and skin cells mixing with the thermal grease. The thermal grease fills any air gaps and enables the heatsink to work more efficiently. If the CPU has an active heatsink (with a fan), plug the fan power connector into one of the fan connectors supplied on the motherboard (see Figure 20.7). Optionally, some heatsinks use a disk drive power connector for fan power.

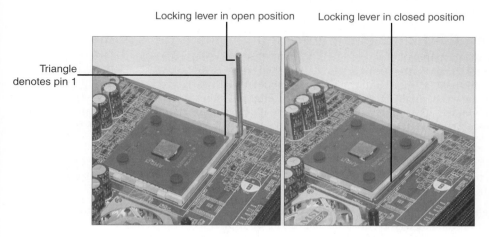

Figure 20.5 The lever on the socket locks the processor into the socket when lowered. Note the triangle on the corner of the processor, denoting pin 1.

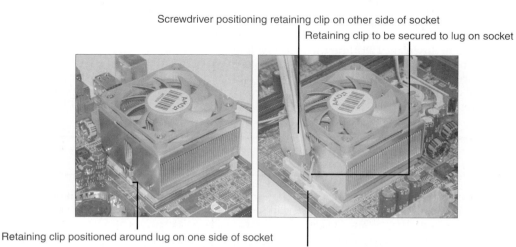

Figure 20.6 Attaching the heatsink to a socketed processor. The retaining clip is spring-loaded, so it must be positioned with a screwdriver or similar tool that can push the clip down and swing it into place.

Heatsink fan
power connector

Figure 20.7   Attaching the heatsink fan power connector to the motherboard.

4. Configure the motherboard jumpers (if necessary). Refer to the motherboard manufacturer's manual to set the jumpers, if any, to match the CPU you are going to install. Most of the time the motherboard BIOS handles this process, but if manual configuration is necessary, look for the diagram of the motherboard in the manual to find the jumper location, and look for the tables for the correct settings for your CPU. If the CPU supplied was already installed on the motherboard, the jumpers should already be correctly set for you, but it is still a good idea to check them.

Installing Memory Modules

To function, the motherboard must have memory installed on it. Modern motherboards use either DDR, DDR2, or DDR3 DIMMs. Depending on the module type, it will have a specific method of sliding into and clipping to the sockets. Usually, you install modules in the lowest-numbered sockets or banks first. Note that dual-channel boards perform best if modules are installed in matched pairs. Consult the motherboard documentation for more information on which sockets to use first and in what order and how to install the specific modules the board uses.

◄◄   See "Memory Banks," p. 555.

Because memory modules are keyed to the sockets by a notch on the side or bottom, they can go in only one way. Figure 20.8 shows how to install a DIMM; more detailed instructions for installing memory modules can be found in Chapter 6. Installing the modules might require some force, but you must ensure that you are installing the correct modules in the correct orientation or you might damage the modules and/or sockets.

Locking clips in open position

Locking clips in locked position; module is installed

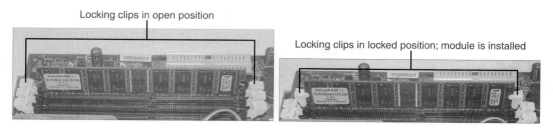

Figure 20.8   Installing the memory modules. Make sure the locking clips are open on both sides of the module before the module is inserted into the memory socket (left). Press down on the module until the module locking clips swing up into the locked position (right).

Caution

One of the more common failures I see are burnt pins on memory modules and sockets due to improper (backward) installation of the modules. Even though the modules and sockets are keyed, many people try to install them backward, and although they won't go in all the way due to the keying, they can be partially inserted that way. If you power on the system with the module partially inserted backward, in most cases you will damage both the module and motherboard. You may be able to use the remaining memory sockets, or the board may not work at all. Also, be careful not to damage the connector or the retaining latches on either side. If you damage the motherboard memory connector, you will probably have to replace the board.

Mounting the New Motherboard in the Case

The motherboard attaches to the case with one or more screws and standoffs (spacers). If you are using a new case, you might have to attach one or more standoffs in the proper holes before you can install the motherboard. Use the following procedure to install the new motherboard in the case:

1. Find the holes in the new motherboard for the standoffs. You should install standoffs in the chassis wherever there is a matching screw hole in the motherboard. Note that screw holes typically have a ring of solder around them, which acts as a grounding point. Sometimes boards will have other holes that are not designed for screws; these will not have the ground pad and should not use a standoff or screw (see Figure 20.9).

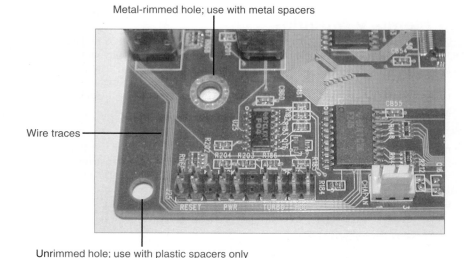

Metal-rimmed hole; use with metal spacers

Wire traces

Unrimmed hole; use with plastic spacers only

Figure 20.9 The corner of a typical motherboard. Be sure not to damage the wire traces when attaching the motherboard to the case.

2. Screw any standoffs into the new case in the proper positions to align with the screw holes in the motherboard (see Figure 20.10).

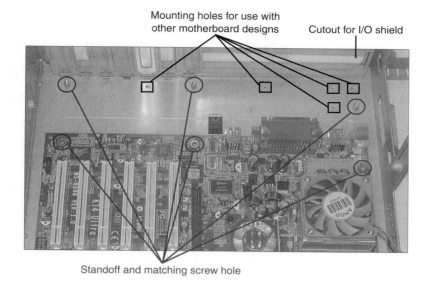

Mounting holes for use with other motherboard designs

Cutout for I/O shield

Standoff and matching screw hole

Figure 20.10   Make sure the standoffs align with the holes in the motherboard. Note that this chassis has a variety of mounting holes so you can adjust the position of the standoffs to match various motherboard designs.

3. Most motherboards today attach either directly to the chassis or to a removable motherboard tray. Figure 20.11 shows three types of standoffs, including two brass types and one plastic. One screws directly to the chassis or tray, whereas the others attach to the motherboard and then slide into notches in the case or tray. Most chassis use the metal screw-in standoffs; the other types are rarely used anymore.

Figure 20.11   Various types of motherboard standoffs, used to support the board when installed in the chassis or motherboard tray.

If the board uses the type of standoff that fits into slots in the chassis or tray, rather than screwing directly in, insert the standoffs directly into the new motherboard from underneath until they snap into place (see Figure 20.12). Or attach them to the board with a screw if necessary. Figure 20.13 shows a typical ATX-style motherboard with arrows indicating the typical location of the screw holes for mounting the motherboard to the case (see your motherboard manual for the exact location of these screw holes).

After you have inserted the standoffs and lined them up with the screw holes on the motherboard, carefully attach the screws to secure the motherboard to the motherboard tray or case, depending on your chassis design. Figure 20.14 shows a motherboard attached to a tray. Note the use of the thumb and forefinger to stabilize the screwdriver tip. This prevents accidental slippage of the screwdriver tip off of the screw, which is one of the biggest causes of new board failures.

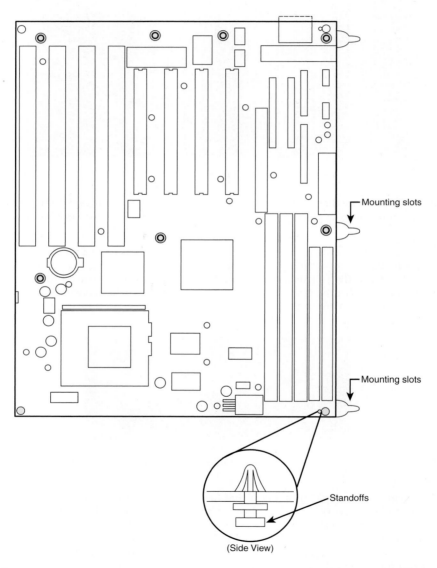

Figure 20.12 For Baby-AT boards, install the standoffs into the board, then set the board such that the standoffs are placed into the open part of the chassis mounting slots, and finally slide the board sideways to lock the standoffs in place.

Note

Refer to Chapter 19 for detailed coverage of the various types of power supply connectors, including the newer 24-pin ATX12V 2.x types.

Connecting I/O and Other Cables to the Motherboard

Several connections must be made between a motherboard and the case. These include LEDs for the hard disk and power, an internal speaker connection, a reset button, and a power button. Most modern motherboards also have several built-in I/O ports that have to be connected. This includes ATA/SATA host adapters, a floppy controller, and front-mounted USB or IEEE 1394 ports. Some boards also include additional items such as built-in video, sound, or SCSI adapters.

If the board is an ATX type, the connectors for all the external I/O ports are already built into the rear of the board. If you are using a legacy Baby AT–type board, you might have to install cables and brackets to run the serial, parallel, and other external I/O ports to the rear of the case.

If your motherboard has onboard I/O (nearly all PCs today use onboard I/O), use the following procedure to connect the cables:

1. Connect the floppy cable between the floppy drives and the 34-pin floppy controller connector on the motherboard.

2. Connect the Serial ATA and Parallel ATA cables to the drives and host adapter ports on the motherboard (see Figure 20.21). Typically, older systems will use the primary ATA channel connector for hard disks and the secondary channel for optical drives. Most newer systems will use Serial ATA connections for the hard drive and Parallel ATA for the optical drives, or possibly even SATA connections for all drives.

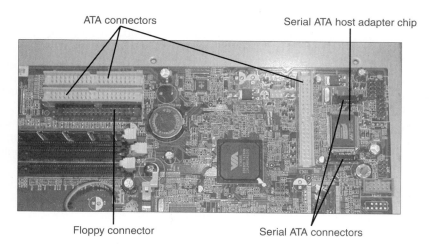

ATA connectors   Serial ATA host adapter chip

Floppy connector   Serial ATA connectors

Figure 20.21   Floppy, ATA, and Serial ATA hard drive connectors.

3. Attach the front-panel switch, LED, internal speaker wires, and front-mounted ports such as USB and IEEE 1394 from the case front panel to the motherboard. If they are not marked on the board, check where each one is on the diagram in the motherboard manual. Figure 20.22 shows the front-panel connectors. Unfortunately, even though there are standards for these types of

connections, many motherboard and chassis manufacturers don't follow the industry standards, and you might find some frustration in getting these connections right. Chapter 4 has detailed pinouts and connection diagrams for most motherboards and chassis.

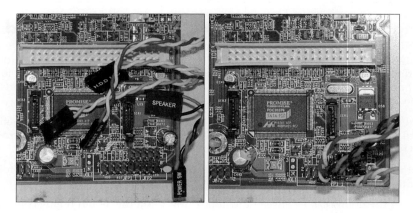

Figure 20.22   The motherboard front-panel connectors (speaker, power switch, LEDs, and so on) must be connected to the appropriate pins on the motherboard (bottom center).

Installing the Drives

At this point you should install your hard drive, floppy drive, and optical drive. This is covered in detail in Chapter 12, "Physical Drive Installation and Configuration."

The basic process for mounting optical drives, hard drives, and floppy drives is as follows:

1. Remove the drive bay plates (if needed). Simply bend or knock the plate out of the way.

2. To install an optical drive, simply slide the drive into the chassis. Note that it is easier to connect the ATA or SATA cable to the rear of the drive and make jumper selections before mounting the drive. Refer to Chapters 7 and 12 for more about ATA jumpers and drive installation. Note that some cases come with rails that must be added to 5 1/4"-wide drives, such as an optical drive. In such cases, use the screws from step 3 for the drive rails.

3. After the drive is in the bay, line up the drive-mounting screw holes on the drive with the holes in the case chassis. Secure the drive with four screws, using the ones that came with your case or the drive you are installing (see Figure 20.23). If the drive uses rails, the rails hold the drive in place.

4. If your system has a removable drive cage, for floppy and hard disk drives, you should remove the cage.

5. To install floppy and hard drives, slide your drives into the drive cage and secure them with the screws that came with your case or with the drive you are installing (see Figure 20.24). Many cases now feature sliding locks that allow you to install the drives without screws. As with an optical drive, it's easier to connect the floppy and ATA/SATA cables to the rear of the drives and make any jumper selections prior to placing the drives or the drive cage into the chassis.

Note

If your chassis does not include a removable drive cage, as shown in Figure 20.25, you'll simply have to mount the drives directly in the chassis.

Figure 20.23   Secure the drive to the chassis using four screws.

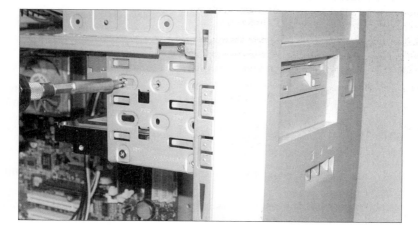

Figure 20.24   Use four screws to secure each drive to the drive bay. If your computer uses a removable drive cage, mount the drives to the drive cage in the same way.

   6. If your system has a removable drive cage, slide the drive cage back into the PC and secure it to the chassis using the screws provided with your case (see Figure 20.25).

3 1/2-inch drive cage

Figure 20.25 The drive cage inserts into the chassis and is usually held in place by two or four screws.

7. Connect the drive cables to the appropriate locations on your motherboard. Refer to Chapters 7 and 12 for more about jumper settings and cable connections for hard drives and floppy drives.

Installing the New Video Card and Driver Software

Follow these steps to install a new video card into a system:

1. If necessary, remove the screw and slot cover behind the expansion slot you want to use for the new video card.

2. Slide the video card straight down into the slot where it will be installed (typically an AGP or a PCI Express slot).

3. Push the card down into the slot, using a front-to-back rocking motion if necessary to get the edge connector to slide into the slot. Note many AGP and PCI Express cards feature a retaining tab at the end of the connector, which helps to secure the card in the slot. There are several different types of retainer designs used, and you will need to disengage this retainer when removing the card.

4. Use either the screw you removed during removal of the old card or the screw used in step 1 to fasten the card into place.

5. Attach the video cable from the monitor to the proper connector at the rear of the monitor. If the new card uses a DVI-I connector and the monitor uses the standard 15-pin VGA connector, use a DVI-to-VGA adapter (usually provided with the video card or available separately from stores that stock computer parts). If you're building a dual-display system, be sure to plug in your primary and secondary displays to the appropriate connectors.

Note

If you are replacing an existing video card (or switching from onboard video to an add-in video card), you should remove the existing installed video driver before powering down to install the new card. This helps prevent the system from improperly identifying the new video card and makes for a smoother upgrade. To do this, open the Windows Device Manager, select the existing display adapter, and select Remove or Uninstall. Do not reboot the system if asked; instead, you can power down and remove the existing video card.

After the entire system is assembled, when the system boots up, Windows should detect the new video card and automatically begin the driver installation process. At that point, follow the manufacturer's instructions for installing the latest video drivers for the new video card. After the video card drivers are installed, you can use the Windows Display properties to fine-tune its settings for resolution, color depth, or refresh rate if desired.

Installing Additional Expansion Cards

Many systems use additional expansion cards for wireless Ethernet, Internet connection (modem), sound, and SCSI adapters. These cards are plugged in to the bus slots present on the motherboard. To install these cards, follow these steps:

1. Insert each card by holding it carefully by the edges, being sure not to touch the chips and circuitry. Put the bottom-edge finger connector into the appropriate open slot (usually PCI or PCI Express). Firmly press down on the top of the card, exerting even pressure, until it snaps into place (see Figure 20.26).

2. Secure each card bracket with a screw (see Figure 20.27).

3. Attach any internal cables you might have removed earlier from the cards.

If there are multiple slots to choose from, try to consider airflow when choosing the slot to install a particular card. In some cases you might want to leave blank slots in between cards, or group all of the cards away from any video cards that might be installed, as video cards generally create more heat than all of the other cards combined.

Replacing the Cover and Connecting External Cables

Now the system should be nearly assembled. All that remains is installing the cover assembly and connecting any external devices that are cabled to the system. This normally includes a keyboard, mouse, monitor, speakers, and network cables. I usually don't like to install the case cover screws until I have tested the system and am sure everything is working properly.

Figure 20.26 This photo shows a video adapter being inserted into the slot.

Figure 20.27 Installing the screw to retain the card.

Running the Motherboard BIOS Setup Program (CMOS Setup)

Now that everything is connected, you can power up the system and run the BIOS Setup program. This enables you to configure the motherboard to access the installed devices and set the system date and time. The system POST (power-on self test) also runs to determine whether any major problems exist. To run the BIOS setup and configure the system, do the following:

1. Power on the monitor first and then the system unit. Observe the operation via the screen and listen for any beeps from the system speaker.

2. The system should automatically go through a power-on self test (POST) consisting of video BIOS checking, a RAM test, and usually an installed component report. If a fatal error occurs during the POST, you might not see anything onscreen and the system might beep several times, indicating a specific problem. Check the motherboard or BIOS documentation to determine what the beep codes mean. A list of POST codes is included in Chapter 22.

3. If there are no fatal errors, you should see the POST display onscreen. Depending on the type of motherboard BIOS, such as Phoenix, AMI, Award, or others, you have to press a key or series of keys to interrupt the normal boot sequence and get to the Setup program screens that enable you to enter important system information. Normally, the system indicates via the onscreen display which key to press to activate the BIOS Setup program during the POST, but if not, check the motherboard manual for the key(s) to press to enter the BIOS Setup. Common keys used to enter BIOS Setup are F1, F2, Del, F10, Esc, and Ins. Because the POST in modern motherboards is so fast, it is easy to miss the time you are supposed to hit the key, so I usually start tapping the key repeatedly just a second or two after powering on. In some cases this may generate a keyboard error message, which you can ignore as the BIOS setup screen appears.

4. After the Setup program is running, use the Setup program menus to enter the current date and time and any other changes from default settings you require. Note that the autodetect capabilities of most modern motherboards means that you may not need to make any changes at all—the default settings work for most normal setups. If you do make any changes, it is a good idea to note them, so you can quickly reset them again later if necessary.

5. Entering the hard drive information is most critical when building a new system. Most modern BIOSs feature an autodetect or auto-type setting for the drive; I recommend you choose that if it is available. This causes the BIOS to read the parameters directly from the drive, which eliminates a chance for errors—especially if the builder is less experienced.

6. After you have checked all the settings in the BIOS Setup, follow the instructions onscreen or in the motherboard manual to save the settings and exit the Setup menu.

◄◄ See "Running or Accessing the CMOS Setup Program," p. 476.

Troubleshooting New Installations

At this point, the system should reset and attempt to boot normally from either a floppy drive, optical drive, or a hard disk. Most modern OS come on a bootable CD or DVD, which should be inserted in the first optical drive. Upon starting, the system should boot and either reach an installation menu or a command prompt. If any problems exist, here are some basic items to check:

■ If the system won't power up at all, check the power cord. If the cord is plugged into a power strip, make sure the strip is switched on. Usually, a power switch can be found on the front of the case, but some power supplies have a switch on the back as well.

■ Check to see whether the power switch is connected properly inside the case. There is a cable connection from the switch to the motherboard; check both ends to ensure that they are connected properly.

- Check the main power connector from the supply to the board. Make sure the connectors are seated fully, and ensure that they are plugged in with the correct orientation.

- If the system appears to be running but you don't see anything on the display, check the monitor to ensure that it is plugged in, turned on, and properly and securely connected to the video card.

- Check the video card to ensure it is fully seated in the motherboard slot. Remove and reseat the video card, and possibly try a different slot if it is a PCI card.

- If the system beeps more than once, the BIOS is reporting a fatal error of some type. See the BIOS Error code listings in Chapter 22 for more information on what these codes mean. Also, consult your motherboard documentation—look in the BIOS section for a table of error codes.

- If the LED on your floppy drive, hard drive, or optical drive stays on continuously, the data cable is probably installed backward or is off by some pins. Check that the stripe on the cable is properly oriented toward pin 1 on both the drive and board connector ends. Also, check the drive jumpers for proper master/slave relationships.

When you are sure the system is up and running successfully, power it off and screw the chassis cover securely to the case. Now your new system should be ready for the operating system installation.

Installing the Operating System

If you are starting with a new drive, you must install the operating system. If you are using a non-Windows operating system, follow the documentation for the installation procedures.

On a newer system in which you are installing Windows XP or Vista, there isn't really anything you need to do, other than simply booting from the disc (you might have to enable the optical drive as a boot device in your BIOS Setup) and following the prompts to install the OS. Windows XP and Vista automatically recognize whether the hard drive needs to be partitioned and formatted and allow you to do that at the beginning part of the installation.

If you are installing Windows XP on a system with a SATA hard drive set in RAID or AHCI mode, you might need to press the F6 key at the beginning of the install, which will cause the installation to ask for a floppy disk with the appropriate drivers. You should have received a copy of this disk with your motherboard; if not, you can download a copy from the motherboard manufacturer. Obviously you will need a floppy drive installed for this to work; if you don't have a floppy, you can integrate most mass storage drivers into the XP installation disc using the driver packs found at www.driverpacks.net.

If you are installing Windows Vista, you won't need a floppy with storage drivers because Vista has them built in.

During the initial part of the installation you can delete any existing partitions and create new ones if desired. On a drive with no partitions, if you simply tell the installer to install Windows into "unpartitioned space," the installer automatically creates and formats a partition using all of the available space. If you want to do the partitioning and formatting manually (prior to installing the OS), you can follow the guidelines in the next few sections.

Partitioning the Drive with DOS and Windows 9x and Me

From the A:> prompt, with the startup disk inserted in the floppy drive, type the following command:

```
FDISK
```

This command is used to partition your drive. Follow the menus to create either a single partition for the entire drive or multiple partitions. Usually, the first partition must also be made active, which means it will be bootable. I recommend you answer Yes to the prompt `Do you wish to enable large disk support (Y/N)?`. This enables the partition to be created using the FAT32 or NTFS file system. Then, you can continue accepting default entries for all the prompts to partition the drive as a single bootable partition that covers the entire drive.

Next, exit FDISK; this restarts the system.

Note

Using FDISK was covered extensively in Chapter 12.

Formatting the Drive with DOS and Windows 9x and Me

After rebooting on the startup floppy, you need to format each partition you've created. The first partition is formatted using the FORMAT command as follows:

```
FORMAT C:
```

All other partitions are formatted in the same manner: Merely run the command, changing the drive letter for each partition that needs to be formatted.

After the FORMAT command completes on all the drives, you should reboot again from the startup floppy. Now you are ready to install Windows.

Note

Drive formatting was covered extensively in Chapter 9, "Hard Disk Storage." Refer to Chapter 12 for more details on installing and setting up a hard drive.

Preparing the Hard Drive with Windows 2000/XP/Vista

If you are using Windows 2000, XP, or Vista, the operating system prepares the drive for you during installation if you install the operating system to an empty drive. If unpartitioned space is available on an existing boot drive, you can direct Windows Setup to use that space and install as a "dual-boot" configuration. This configuration enables you to select your old version or new version of Windows each time you start your computer. You can also replace your existing version of Windows.

Installing Important Drivers

After installing the operating system, the first thing you need to do is install drivers for devices where drivers were not found on the Windows installation disc. This often includes things such as chipset drivers for your motherboard, drivers for newer video cards, USB 2.0 drivers, and more. Of these, the motherboard chipset drivers are the most critical and should be installed first. A disc containing these drivers should have been included with your motherboard; insert this disc and follow the prompts to install the chipset drivers. Then install other drivers, such as video, network, modem, and so on.

Disassembly/Upgrading Preparation

After you've built your system, you probably will have to open it again sometime to perform a repair or an upgrade. Before you power off the system for the last time and begin to open the case, you should learn and record several things about your computer. Often, when working on a system, you intentionally or accidentally wipe out the CMOS Setup information. Most systems use a special battery-powered CMOS clock and a data chip that is used to store the system's configuration information. If the battery is disconnected, or if certain pins are accidentally shorted, you can discharge the

CMOS memory and lose the setup. The CMOS memory in most systems is used to store simple things such as how many and what type of floppy drives are connected, how much memory is in the system, and the date and time.

A critical piece of information is the hard disk–type settings. Most modern BIOSs have an autodetect feature that reads the type information directly from the drive. I recommend you set the drive type to Auto, which automatically sets all the necessary parameters for you. With older BIOSs you must explicitly tell the system the parameters of the attached hard disk. Therefore, you need to know the current settings for cylinders, heads, and sectors per track.

If you do not enter the correct hard disk–type information in the CMOS Setup program, you will not be able to access the data on the hard disk. I know of several people who lost some or all of their data because they did not enter the correct type information when they reconfigured their systems. If this information is incorrect, the usual results are a missing operating system error message when the system starts and the inability to access the C: drive.

Most systems have the setup program built right into the ROM BIOS software. These built-in setup programs are activated by a key sequence usually entered during the POST. Most systems show a prompt on the screen during the POST indicating which key to press to enter the BIOS Setup.

The major vendors have standardized on these following keystrokes to enter the BIOS Setup—normally F1, F2, or the Del (Delete) key are used. If those don't work, others are listed in Chapter 5.

◀◀ See "Running or Accessing the CMOS Setup Program," p. 476.

After you're in the BIOS Setup main screen, you'll usually find a main menu allowing access to other menus and submenus offering various sections or screens.

Many setup programs allow for specialized control of the particular chipset used in the motherboard. These complicated settings can take up to several screens of information—I recommend you record any changes you make. Most systems return these settings to a BIOS default if the CMOS battery is removed, causing you to lose any customized settings you might have changed. See Chapter 5 for more information on the BIOS settings.

PC Mods: Overclocking and Cooling

Modifying, or *modding*, computer systems has been going on since even before the advent of the PC. In fact, because most of the early personal computers were either made from kits or entirely home built, custom modifications were the norm. And because of that, few systems were exactly alike. Even when fully functional personal computers and, more specifically, PCs came rolling off assembly lines in mass-produced fashion, people still found ways to make their own system different from all the others.

Computer modifications are usually designed to increase or improve performance or functionality in some way, but they can also be purely cosmetic in nature, or some combination of both. Because I am more into function than form, I will emphasize performance- or functionality-enhancing modifications over cosmetics in this chapter.

One of the primary modifications you can perform on a system is to make it run faster, which is usually called *overclocking*. When chips run faster, they run hotter, so cooling upgrades and modifications usually go hand-in-hand with overclocking. Systems that run cool tend to be more stable and more reliable, so even if you don't overclock your system, ensuring that it runs cool is essential for trouble-free operation. Many systems are not properly designed or configured for optimal cooling even at their standard speeds, much less when overclocked.

New interfaces bring new connectors to the PC, and many of these are more useful on the front of the system rather than in the back. Bringing modern interfaces to the front panel, adapting newer drives for different form factors, and adding windows, vents, and fans are all modifications that can be made to a chassis or case to improve or update it to handle the latest hardware.

Finally, you can perform purely cosmetic modifications, such as custom painting or internal lighting, which can make your system stand out from the rest. I cover the functional modifications in this chapter, with sound engineering principles applied such that you can either modify an existing system correctly or purchase new components with the desired features already integrated.

Note

If you are interested in the more cosmetic aspects of PC modding, such as adding interior lights, custom-dressed cables, clear windows on the side of your case, or even a custom paint job, a number of books on the market cover these topics. Check out *Maximum PC Guide to Extreme PC Mods*, by Paul Capello, published by Que.

Overclocking

One of the most popular performance-enhancing modifications of all time is overclocking, which can be defined as running all or part of the system faster than it was originally rated or intended to run. Overclocking is usually applied to the processor, but it can also be applied to other components in the system, including memory, video cards, bus speeds, and more.

Overclocking PCs dates all the way back to the original 4.77MHz IBM PC and 6MHz AT systems of the early 1980s. In fact, IBM made overclocking the AT easy because the quartz crystal that controlled the speed of the processor was socketed. You could obtain a faster replacement crystal for about a dollar and easily plug it in. The first several editions of this book covered how to perform this modification in detail, resulting in a system that was up to 1.5 times faster than it started out. Modern systems allow overclocking without replacing any parts by virtue of programmable timer chips and simple and easy-to-change BIOS Setup options.

Quartz Crystals

To understand overclocking, you need to know how computer system speeds are controlled. The main component controlling speed in a computer is a quartz crystal. Quartz is silicon dioxide (SiO_2) in crystalline form. Oxygen and silicon are the most common elements on earth (sand and rock are mostly silicon dioxide), and computer chips are made mainly from silicon. Quartz is a hard, transparent material with a density of 2649 kg/m^3 (1.531 oz/in^3) and a melting point of 1750° C (3182° F). Quartz is brittle but with a little bit of elasticity, which is perhaps its most useful attribute.

In crystalline form, quartz can be used to generate regular and consistent signal pulses to regulate electronic circuits, similar to the way a metronome can be used to regulate music. Quartz crystals are used because they are *piezoelectric*, which is defined as having a property that generates voltage when subjected to mechanical stress. The opposite is also true—that is, quartz generates mechanical stress when subjected to a voltage. Piezoelectricity was first discovered by Pierre and Jacques Curie in 1880, and it is the essential feature of quartz that makes it useful in electronic circuits.

The key to piezoelectricity is that when you twist, bend, deform, or simply apply pressure or stress to a quartz crystal, a small voltage is generated. This property is commonly used in sensors or transducers to detect pressure or sound waves. For example, the knock sensors used in virtually all modern automobile engines are based on quartz crystals that are sensitive to the vibrations produced in the engine block when detonation (uncontrolled burning of fuel) occurs. Because detonation can rapidly damage an engine, the engine management computer uses input from one or more knock sensors to retard the ignition timing upon sensing detonation, thus preventing engine damage. Some microphones and phonograph pickup devices also use quartz crystals for converting sound waves or the motion of the needle in the groove into a voltage.

Piezoelectricity works two ways, meaning that if a voltage is generated when you bend a crystal, likewise if you apply voltage to a crystal, it bends (contracts, expands, or twists) in a similar fashion. Although the crystal is mostly brittle in nature, it is still somewhat elastic, such that any deformation tends to snap back and then occur again, resonating or vibrating at a natural frequency as long as the voltage is present. Much like a tuning fork or the pipes in an organ, the natural resonant frequency depends on the size and shape of the crystal. In general, the smaller and thinner it is, the faster it vibrates.

The actual movement is exceedingly small, on the order of 68 nanometers (billionths of a meter) per centimeter, which in a normal crystal is only a few atoms in length. Although the movement is very small, it is also quite rapid, which means tremendous forces can be generated. For example, the surface acceleration of a 50MHz crystal can exceed five million times the force of gravity.

Crystal resonators are made from slabs of quartz sawed from raw quartz crystal stock. Although the stock can come from natural quartz, most crystals are made from synthetically grown quartz. The raw stock slabs are cut into squares, rounded, and ground into flat discs called *blanks*. The thinner the disc, the higher the resonant frequency; however, there are limits as to how thin the discs can be made before they break. The upper limit for fundamental mode resonators is approximately 50MHz. At that frequency, the discs are paper thin and are generally too fragile to withstand further grinding. Still, higher-frequency crystals can be achieved by using harmonics of the fundamental frequency, resulting in crystals of up to 200MHz or more. Even higher frequencies can be achieved by using frequency synthesizer circuits, which use a base crystal-generated frequency fed to a circuit that then generates multiples of frequency that can extend well into the gigahertz or terahertz range. In fact, crystal-based frequency synthesizer circuits are used to generate the high operating speeds of modern PCs.

The crystal packages, as well as the shape of the actual quartz crystals inside the packages, can vary. The packages are usually a metal can that is either cylindrical or oblong in shape, but they can also have other shapes or be constructed of plastic or other materials (see Figure 21.1).

The sliver of quartz inside the package is normally disc shaped, but it is shaped like a tuning fork in some examples. Figure 21.2 shows a cylindrical crystal package with the cover removed, exposing the tuning fork–shaped sliver of quartz inside.

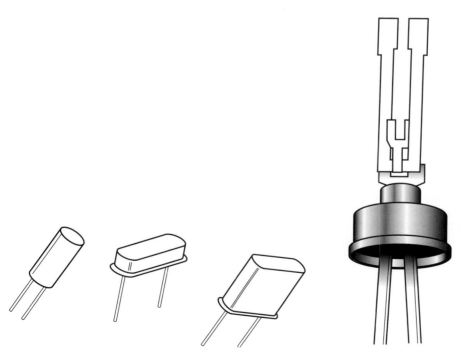

Figure 21.1   Crystal packages of varying shapes.

Figure 21.2   Crystal interior showing the quartz tuning fork.

Most crystals use a disc-shaped sliver of quartz as a resonator. The disc is contained in a hermetically sealed evacuated enclosure.

Figure 21.3 shows the interior view of a typical crystal with a disc-shaped resonator inside.

The quartz disc inside has electrodes on each side, allowing a voltage to be applied to the disc. The details are shown in Figure 21.4.

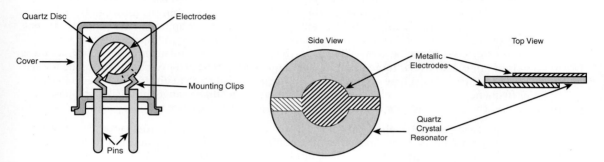

Figure 21.3   Crystal interior showing disc-shaped quartz resonator.

Figure 21.4   Disc-shaped quartz resonator details.

Walter G. Cady was the first to use a quartz crystal to control an electronic oscillator circuit in 1921. He published his results in 1922, which led to the development of the first crystal-controlled clock by Warren A. Marrison in 1927. Today, all modern computers have multiple internal oscillators and clocks, some for controlling bus and processor speeds and at least one for a standard time-of-day clock.

Overclocking History

Overclocking has been around since the beginning of computing. As long as there have been computers, there have been people trying to make them run faster. I began overclocking PCs back in the early 1980s, using a variety of devices on the market. The easiest system to overclock back then was the original IBM AT, which used a socketed crystal to run the processor. Two versions of the AT were available—one that used a 12MHz crystal and one that used a 16MHz crystal. The timer chip divided the crystal speed by 2, resulting in processor speeds of 6MHz and 8MHz.

A popular trick at the time was to remove the 12MHz or 16MHz crystals from their sockets and replace them with 18MHz or 20MHz crystals, which sped up the systems to 9MHz or 10MHz. Back in 1984, I was able to purchase crystals for as little as $1 each from RadioShack, and they could be changed in seconds. In my 6MHz system, I was able to use an 18MHz crystal to get the system to run at 9MHz. That was a 50% increase in speed for about $1! I also tried a 20MHz crystal (10MHz speed), but the system would not boot up at that speed, so I had to drop back to the 18MHz (9MHz speed) crystal instead.

Taking this further, some companies released variable frequency oscillators, which basically amounted to a variable-speed crystal you could use to replace the fixed stock crystal. A control panel was then mounted on the back of the system, which had an adjustment knob you could use to change the system speed. The most sophisticated of these was a product called the XCELX, which allowed you to adjust the original IBM AT from 6.5MHz to 12.7MHz. Figure 21.5 shows an XCELX, which dated from 1985.

The instructions told you to turn up the throttle until the system crashed and then back down a notch or two. How fast a given system would run depended on all the specific components contained within.

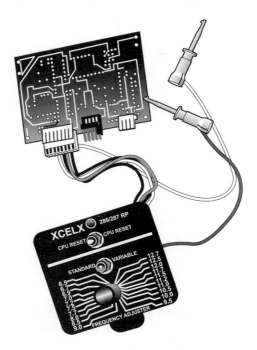

Figure 21.5 The XCELX frequency adjuster, a "throttle" that could be used to speed up the IBM AT.

I'm sure that few people are interested in overclocking systems that are more than 20 years old, but it is interesting to see that hotrodding PCs has been around for as long as PCs themselves have existed!

Modern PC Clocks

A modern PC has at least two crystals on the motherboard; the main crystal is used to control the speed of the motherboard and motherboard circuitry, and the other is used to control the real-time clock (RTC). The main crystal is always 14.31818MHz (it might be abbreviated as 14.318 or just 14.3), and the RTC crystal is always 32.768KHz.

Why 14.31818MHz?

The original 1981 vintage IBM PC ran at 4.77MHz, a speed derived by taking a 14.31818MHz crystal and using a divider circuit to divide the frequency by 3 to get 4.77MHz. Many people were confused as to why IBM chose to run the processor at 4.77MHz; after all, the 8088 processor they used was rated for 5MHz, and all they would have had to do to run it at that speed was change the main crystal from 14.318MHz to 15MHz instead. Well, the truth is that if they did that, they would have had to add more crystals to the design. You see, the same 14.318MHz crystal that was divided by 3 to run the processor was also divided by 4 to get 3.58MHz, which is the *exact* frequency needed for the NTSC color video modulation signal required to be compatible with color TV.

But that's not all: Another circuit divided the crystal frequency by 12 to get 1.193182MHz, which was used by an 8253 programmable three-channel 16-bit interval timer/counter chip. Each channel could be used to take an input clock signal and produce an output signal by dividing by an arbitrary 16-bit number. Channel 0 was used to make the time-of-day clock ticks. It was programmed by the BIOS to call INT 08h every 65,536 ticks, which was about 18.2 times per second (or about every 55 milliseconds). The software routines linked to INT 08h caused the time-of-day clock to be updated and could also chain to any other activities that needed to be done periodically. Channel 1 was used to tell the DMA to refresh the dynamic RAM every 72 cycles (about 15 microseconds), and channel 2 was used to make an audio signal for the speaker (beeps)—different tones could be made by changing the divisor.

So by carefully choosing a 14.318MHz crystal instead of 15MHz or some other speed, the IBM engineers were able to design a motherboard where a single crystal could be used to run the processor, video card, time-of-day clock, memory refresh, and even beep tones. The single-crystal design allowed the motherboard to be manufactured with fewer parts and at a lower cost.

As a testament to their foresight, all modern PCs are still controlled by a 14.318MHz crystal! This crystal, in conjunction with a frequency timing generator chip, is used to derive virtually all the frequencies used on a modern motherboard by the CPU, buses, memory, and more.

PCs don't run at 14.318MHz, so how can a crystal of that speed be used? And what happens when you install a different processor? How does the system adjust the bus and other speeds to accommodate the new chip? The answer is that a special chip called a *frequency timing generator (FTG)* or *frequency synthesizer* is used in conjunction with the crystal to derive the actual speeds of the system. Figure 21.6 shows a portion of a motherboard with an FTG chip with a 14.318MHz crystal below it.

Figure 21.6   An ICS 9250 frequency timing generator chip with a 14.318MHz crystal.

The real-time clock (RTC) in the original PC was notoriously inaccurate, so starting with the IBM AT in 1984, IBM added a separate 32.768KHz crystal to count time independent from the speed of the system. This crystal is used on all modern motherboards as well. Figure 21.7 shows a 32.768KHz crystal next to a chipset South Bridge or I/O controller hub, which contains the RTC circuitry and CMOS RAM.

Figure 21.7 Chipset South Bridge (I/O controller hub) incorporating an RTC, along with the 32.768KHz clock crystal.

Most frequency synthesizer chips used on PC motherboards are made by a handful of companies, including Integrated Device Technology (www.idt.com; formerly Integrated Circuit Systems) and Cypress Semiconductor (www.cypress.com; formerly International Microcircuits Inc [IMI]). These chips use phased locked loop (PLL) circuitry to generate synchronized processor, PCI, AGP, and other bus timing signals that are all derived from a single 14.318MHz crystal. The crystal and frequency synthesizer chip are usually situated near the processor and main chipset component of the motherboard.

The amazing thing about these chips is that most of them are programmable and adjustable, so they can change their frequency outputs via software, which results in the system running at different speeds. Because all CPUs are based on the speed of the CPU bus, when you change the CPU bus speed generated by the frequency synthesizer chip, you can change the speed of your processor. Because the PCI, AGP, and memory buses are often synchronized with the speed of the processor bus, when you change the processor bus speed by a given percentage, you also change the speed of those other buses by the same percentage. The software to accomplish this is built into the BIOS Setup menus of most modern motherboards.

Overclocking Tips

Most modern motherboards automatically read the CPU and memory components to determine their proper speed, timing, and voltage settings. Originally, these settings were controlled by jumpers and switches on 486 and Pentium boards, but in most modern boards you can enter the BIOS Setup to change these settings to manual and then use the menu options in the BIOS Setup to alter the speed of the system. Because such alterations can make the system unstable, most systems are designed to boot into the BIOS Setup at a default low speed so you are not locked out from making changes in the future. This makes overclocking as simple as changing a few menu options and then rebooting to test the selections you've made.

The concept for overclocking is simple: You change the settings to increase the speed of the processor, memory, buses, and so on until the system becomes unstable. Then you can go back in and reduce the settings until it is stable again. In this manner, you find the maximum sustainable speed for a system. Because each processor is different, even ones with the same ratings can end up allowing different maximum stable speeds.

Why can some chips be clocked faster than others? The reason is in how they are manufactured and marked. As an example, the first Pentium 4 chips based on the Prescott core used dies that were 112 square mm and made on 300mm wafers, resulting in a maximum of 631 dies per wafer. Typically, many of those dies wouldn't pass testing, but let's say that 80% (or 504 dies) did pass. Intel initially sold the Prescott core processors at speeds from 2.4GHz through 3.4GHz. This means that all the 500+ dies coming off the wafer were designed to potentially run as 3.4GHz (or faster) chips. They were tested after manufacture to see how fast they could actually run. Out of the 80% or so of the dies that worked, many ran at the highest tested speeds, while others only worked reliably at lower speeds. They were then sorted into bins and marked accordingly.

Early in manufacturing a given processor design, the sorted bins of chips at the end of the line would contain more that passed only the lower speed tests, and fewer that ran at the highest speeds. This is why the fastest chips are the most expensive—generally fewer of the chips produced on a given day will pass the testing at that speed. Eventually, however, as the manufacturing processes and chip design are tweaked, more and more of the finished chips end up passing the higher-speed tests. But because lower-speed chips are priced less and sell more, the manufacturer might have to dip into the faster bins and mark those chips at the lower speeds to fill the larger number of orders.

Essentially what I'm saying is that chipmakers such as Intel and AMD make all the chips on a wafer identically and try to make them so they will all run at the highest speeds. If you purchase one of the lesser-rated chips, you really have the same chip (die) as the higher-rated versions; the difference is the higher-rated ones are guaranteed to run at the higher speeds, whereas the lower-rated ones are not. That is where overclockers come in.

Users who overclock their systems purchase chips rated at lower speeds and essentially do their own testing to see if they will run at higher speeds. They can also start with the highest-rated chips and see whether they can run them even faster, but success there is much more limited. The most successful overclocking is almost always with the lowest-rated speed of a given design, and those chips are also sold for the lowest price. In other words, statistically you might be able to find many of the lowest-speed grade chips that are capable of running at the highest-speed grade (because they are essentially identical during manufacture); however, if you start with the highest-speed grade, you might be able to increase the speed only a very small percentage.

The key to remember is that a difference exists between the rated speed of a chip and the actual maximum speed at which it runs. Manufacturers such as Intel and AMD have to be conservative when they rate chips, so a chip of a given rating is almost always capable of running at least some margin of speed faster than the rating—the question is how much faster? Unfortunately the only way to know that is by trying it out—that is, by testing chips individually.

Bus Speeds and Multipliers

Modern processors run at a multiple of the motherboard speed, and the selected multiple is usually locked within the processor; therefore, all you can do to change speeds is to change the processor bus speed settings. The processor bus is also called the *CPU bus, front side bus (FSB)*, or *processor side bus (PSB)*, all of which are interchangeable terms.

For example, I built a system that uses an Intel Pentium 4 3.2E processor, which typically runs at 3200MHz on an 800MHz CPU bus. Thus, the processor is locked to run at four times the speed of the CPU bus. I was able to increase the CPU bus speed from 800MHz to 832MHz, which meant the processor speed increased from 3200MHz to 3328MHz, which is 128MHz faster than the rating. This took all of about 60 seconds to reboot, enter the BIOS Setup, make the changes in the menu, save, and reboot again. This was only a 4% increase in overall speed, but it didn't cost a penny and the system seemed to be just as stable as it was before.

Many motherboards allow changes in speed of up to 50% or more, but a processor rarely sustains speeds that far above its rating without locking up or crashing. Also note that, by increasing the speed of the processor bus, you may also be increasing the speed of the memory bus, PCI bus, PCI Express (or AGP) bus by the same percentage. Therefore, if your memory is unstable at the higher speed, the system will still crash, even though the processor might have been capable of sustaining it. The lowest common denominator prevails, which means your system will run faster only if all the components are up to the challenge.

Many motherboards allow voltage changes to be made for components such as processors, memory, and video cards. Be careful when making these changes because you can damage a component with improper voltage. Still, many overclockers have found that by tweaking the voltage up or down a tenth or so at a time, they can get a system to run more stable than had otherwise been possible.

Cooling

Heat can be a problem in any high-performance system. The higher-speed processors consume more power and therefore generate more heat. The processor is usually the single most power-hungry chip in a system, and in most situations, the fan inside your computer case is incapable of handling the load without some help.

Heatsinks

At one time, a *heatsink* (a special attachment for a chip that draws heat away from the chip) was needed only in systems in which processor heat was a problem. However, starting with the faster Pentium processors in the early 1990s, heatsinks have been a necessity for every processor since.

A heatsink works like the radiator in your car, pulling heat away from the engine. In a similar fashion, the heatsink conducts heat away from the processor so it can be vented out of the system. It does this by using a thermal conductor (usually metal) to carry heat away from the processor into fins that expose a high amount of surface area to moving air. This enables the air to be heated, thus cooling the heatsink and the processor as well. Just like the radiator in your car, the heatsink depends on airflow. With no moving air, a heatsink is incapable of radiating the heat away. To keep the engine in your car from overheating when the car is not moving, auto engineers incorporate a fan. Likewise, a fan is incorporated somewhere inside your PC to help move air across the heatsink and vent it out of the system. In some systems, the fan included in the power supply is enough when combined with a special heatsink design; in most cases, though, an additional fan must be attached directly over the processor heatsink to provide the necessary levels of cooling. Case fans are also typical in recent systems to assist in moving the hot air out of the system and replacing it with cooler air from the outside.

The heatsink is normally attached with clips or snap-in retainers. A variety of heatsinks and attachment methods exist. Figure 21.8 shows various passive heatsinks and attachment methods.

Tip

According to data from Intel, heatsink clips are the number-two destroyer of motherboards (screwdrivers are number one), which is one reason the company moved away from metal clips to plastic fasteners for its latest designs. When installing or removing a heatsink that is clipped on, be sure you don't scrape the surface of the motherboard. In most cases, the clips hook over protrusions in the socket. When you are installing or removing the clips, scratching or scraping the surface of the board right below where the clip ends attach is very easy. I like to place a thin sheet of plastic underneath the edge of the clip while I work, especially if board traces that can be scratched are in the vicinity.

Heatsinks are rated for their cooling performances. Typically, the ratings are expressed as a resistance to heat transfer in degrees centigrade per watt (°C/W), where lower is better. Note that the resistance varies according to the airflow across the heatsink.

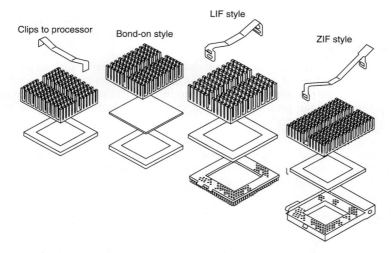

Figure 21.8   Passive heatsinks for socketed processors showing various attachment methods.

Active Heatsinks

To ensure a constant flow of air and more consistent performance, many heatsinks incorporate fans so they don't have to rely on the airflow within the system. Heatsinks with fans are referred to as *active* heatsinks (see Figure 21.9). Active heatsinks have a power connection. Older ones often used a spare disk drive power connector, but most recent heatsinks plug into dedicated heatsink power connections found on the newer motherboards.

The Socket 478 design uses two cams to engage the heatsink clips and place the system under tension. The force generated is 75 lbs., which produces a noticeable bow in the motherboard underneath the processor. This bow is normal, and the motherboard is designed to accommodate it. The high amount of force is necessary to prevent the heavier heatsinks from pulling up on the processor during movement or shipment of the system, and it ensures a good bond for the thermal interface material (thermal grease).

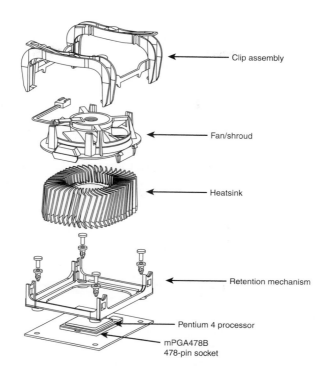

Clip assembly

Fan/shroud

Heatsink

Retention mechanism

Pentium 4 processor

mPGA478B
478-pin socket

Figure 21.9   Active heatsink suitable for a Pentium 4 processor using Socket 478.

Figure 21.10 shows the design used on most Socket AM2, 940, 939, and 754 processors, featuring a cam and clip assembly on one side. Similar to the Socket 478 double-cam assembly shown earlier, this design puts 75 lbs. of force between the heatsink and the processor. Bowing of the motherboard is prevented in this design by the use of a special stiffening plate (also called a *backing plate*) underneath the motherboard. The heatsink retention frame actually attaches to this plate through the board. The stiffening plate and retention frame normally come with the motherboard, but the heatsink with fan and the clip and cam assembly all come with the processor.

Tip

One of the best reasons to use the motherboard-based power connectors for the fan is that most recent system BIOS setup programs can display the fan performance and report it to a system monitoring program. Because some processors—particularly older Athlon processors—can be destroyed in a few moments by a malfunctioning processor heatsink fan, this feature can help prevent a disaster inside your system.

Active heatsinks use a fan or other electric cooling device that requires power to run. Active heatsinks also require power and usually plug into the motherboard CPU fan connector (or, in older systems, a disk drive power connector). If you do get a fan-type heatsink, be aware that some on the market are of very poor quality. The bad ones have motors that use sleeve bearings, which freeze up after a very short life. I recommend only fans with ball-bearing motors, which last about 10 times longer than the sleeve-bearing types. Of course, they cost more—but only about twice as much, so you'll save money in the long run.

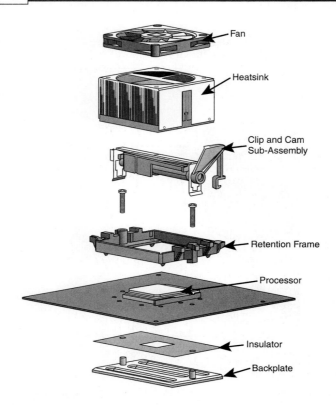

Figure 21.10   Active heatsink and cam retention mechanism used on Socket AM2, 940, 939, and 754 processors.

Newer fans include four-wire power connectors, which feature the standard power, ground, and tach wires found in three-wire fans, but also add a fourth wire for fan-speed control. These are known as PWM (Pulse Width Modulation) fans because they use pulse width modulation signals from the motherboard to control the fan speed more precisely and with more variations in speed. Standard three-wire fans have internal thermal resistors (thermistors) that control fan speed, and these normally offer only two-speed operation. With the PWM setup, the motherboard can monitor system and processor temperatures, and variably control the fan speed to maintain the desired temperatures.

Heatsinks designed for LGA775 sockets usually include plastic retainer clips that snap into holes in the motherboard. To install this type of heatsink, you merely align the tops of the clips such that the arrows are rotated all the way to the left (opposite the direction of the arrow) and then press the tops down until the bottom parts click and lock into the holes in the motherboard. To remove the heatsink, you insert a flat blade screwdriver into the slot under the arrows and then rotate the tops in the direction of the arrows. As you rotate each clip, it will pop out of the motherboard. Figure 21.11 shows an active heatsink for Socket LGA775 processors, featuring these snap-in retainers.

With the wide variety of processor designs on the market today, you also need to match the thermal output of the processor to the thermal-handling capability of the heatsink you plan to use. The heatsink performance required by a given processor depends on two main figures: the maximum allowable case temperature as well as the maximum power output. See the upcoming section

"Heatsink Ratings and Calculations" to see how you can calculate the maximum thermal resistance you will need. You can always install a heatsink with a lower thermal resistance, which will only improve the cooling, but you should never install a heatsink that has a higher thermal resistance than required by your processor.

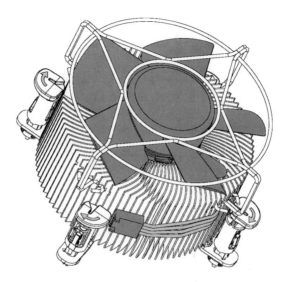

Figure 21.11   LGA775 boxed processor heatsink showing snap-in retainers and a four-wire PWM fan.

Processors sold as boxed or retail versions from Intel and AMD include high-quality active heatsinks designed to work under the worst possible ambient conditions. One of the main reasons I recommend purchasing boxed processors is that you are guaranteed to get a high-quality heatsink with the processor, one that is designed to cool the processor under the worst conditions and that should last the life of the system.

If you purchase an OEM processor that comes without a heatsink, you can expect to pay anywhere from $25 to $60 for a high-quality active fan heatsink, with some of the boutique models costing even more. You'll invariably pay more for the most efficient, best-cooling active heatsinks, and those overclockers who swear by these devices usually also believe that the extra expense is worthwhile.

Passive heatsinks are basically aluminum-finned radiators that rely on airflow from an external source. Passive heatsinks don't work well unless there is some airflow across the fins, usually provided by a chassis-mounted fan that sometimes features a duct to direct airflow directly through the fins on the heatsink. Integrating a passive heatsink is more difficult because you must ensure that the airflow comes from some other source; however, this can be more reliable and very cost effective if done correctly. This is why many of the larger name systems, such as those from Dell and Gateway, often use passive heatsinks with a ducted chassis fan. Systems built by individuals or smaller companies that don't have the ability to engineer a custom passive cooling solution should instead rely on an active heatsink with a built-in fan. An active heatsink provides a more certain cooling solution regardless of other airflow characteristics in the system.

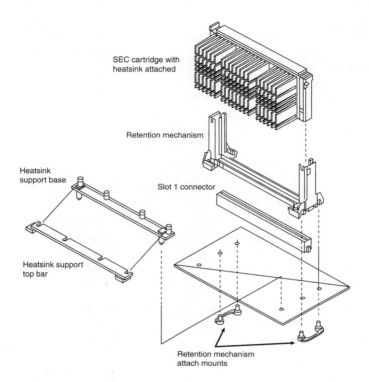

SEC cartridge with
heatsink attached

Retention mechanism

Heatsink
support base

Slot 1 connector

Heatsink support
top bar

Retention mechanism
attach mounts

Figure 21.12   A passive heatsink and supports used with Pentium II/III–SECC processors.

"Boutique" Heatsinks

A large market exists for high-end "boutique" heatsink products, many of which have shapes and designs that would qualify them more as industrial art than an internal computer component. These fancy heatsinks are very popular with overclockers as well as those who like to modify their systems in general.

Although I certainly appreciate a good-looking piece of hardware as much as anybody, as an engineer I am more concerned about performance than appearance. While most of the boutique designs do in fact have outstanding thermal performance, the actual level of performance is rarely documented (making comparisons difficult) and may come with other costs besides a high price. Some of the drawbacks I've seen in fancy aftermarket heatsinks include the following:

- **Size**—They are often very large, with a variety of shapes that may not fit all motherboards or chassis.
- **Weight**—They often exceed recommended maximum weights, potentially damaging the motherboard and/or processor socket if the system is shipped or moved.
- **Attachment**—They often have difficult-to-manage clips and brackets, and many installations require that the motherboard be removed.
- **Airflow**—They often don't provide the recommended omnidirectional airflow at the base needed to cool the CPU voltage regulators and North Bridge chip.

- **Documentation**—They often have no measured and tested information about their actual thermal performance.

- **Cost**—They generally cost many times more than standard units.

Perhaps my main beef is the lack of technical documentation. The primary specification for the thermal performance of a heatsink is the thermal resistance, specified in degrees Celsius per watt. The lower this figure, the better the performance. Unfortunately, most of the boutique heatsinks on the market don't include this figure in their specifications. Without knowing the thermal resistance, you have no easy way to compare the performance of one heatsink against another.

Heatsink Clamping Force

Heatsink clamping force is a potential threat to processors, especially if you are installing older processors such as the Athlon XP which use FC-PGA packaging. FC-PGA is so named because the raw processor die is placed upside down on top of the chip. This enables the heatsink to come in direct or near-direct contact with the die, resulting in the maximum heat transfer to the sink. Unfortunately, some problems have occurred that have forced chipmakers to modify their designs.

The main problem is one of force—too much and unevenly applied. Intel specifies a moderate 20-pound static load force for the heatsink on an FC-PGA die, whereas AMD specified a higher 30-pound static loading force for the spring clip to attach the heatsink on the Athlon, Duron, and Athlon XP processors. This has unfortunately resulted in many processors being damaged during heatsink installation. The reason for the higher static load on the AMD chips is to maximize the thermal transfer. Because the die rises up from the surface of the chip, the heatsink contacts only the die itself and overhangs in all directions. If, while installing the heatsink, you apply too much force to one corner or edge of the heatsink, you place an uneven force on the die and it will crack with a loud snap. This, of course, destroys the chip, and such damage is normally not covered under warranty by the chip manufacturer because it is considered improper handling and not a manufacturer defect. Although this cracking problem affected both AMD and Intel processors, it was much more of a problem with the AMD chips due to the higher force from the heatsink clip specified by AMD. These problems caused many vendors to provide a warranty for the processor only if it was sold with a motherboard and preinstalled by the vendor.

AMD added rubber pads near each of the four corners of the chip to help support the overhanging parts of the heatsink and prevent uneven forces that result in cracking. Unfortunately, even with these pads, you can still crack the die if you install the heatsink in a tilted or cockeyed position.

Today's Intel and AMD processors all include a metal cap called an *integrated heat spreader (IHS)* over the processor die. This protects the die from direct force and helps spread out the thermal contact point between the processor and heatsink. Most of the IHS-equipped chips allow up to a 100-pound static force from the heatsink and are virtually immune to the cracking problems related to improper heatsink installation. Intel's current heatsink designs for processors with integrated heat spreaders use a clamping force of 75 lbs. nominal on the processor. All Intel processors starting with the Pentium III/Celeron Tualatin (0.13-micron) include an IHS, as do all processors in the Athlon 64 family. In general, FC-PGA with the integrated heat spreader is called FC-PGA2 (see Figure 21.13) .

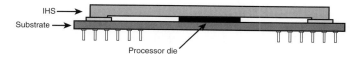

Figure 21.13   Side view of an FC-PGA2 processor showing the integrated heat spreader mounted on top of the die.

If you are installing an AMD or Intel processor that does not use an IHS metal cap, be extra careful to keep the heatsink flat and level with the surface of the die while attaching or removing the heatsink clip.

Heatsink Ratings and Calculations

When cooling a processor, the heatsink transfers heat from the processor to the air. This capability is expressed in a figure known as *thermal resistance*, which is measured in degrees Celsius per watt (C/W). The lower the figure, the lower the thermal resistance and the more heat the heatsink can remove from the CPU.

To calculate the heatsink required for your processor, you can use the following formula:

$$R_{total} = T_{case} - T_{inlet}/P_{power}$$

T_{case} is the maximum allowable CPU case temperature, T_{inlet} is the maximum allowable inlet temperature to the CPU heatsink, and P_{power} is the maximum power dissipation of the processor. For example, the Pentium 4 3.4E (Prescott) processor is rated for a maximum case temperature of 73°C and has a maximum TDP (Thermal Design Power) output of 103 watts. Intel recommends a maximum heatsink inlet temperature of 38° C, which means the heatsink required to properly cool this chip needs to be rated 0.34°C/W, or (73°C – 38°C) / 103 W.

A more extreme example is the Core 2 Extreme QX6800 quad-core processor, which is rated for a maximum 54.8°C at 130W TDP (Thermal Design Power). This would require an exceptionally high performance heatsink rated 0.13°C/W, or (54.8°C–38°C) / 130. A resistance rating this low usually requires some form of liquid cooling.

Another useful formula can be used to describe processor power:

$$P_{power} = C \times V^2 \times F$$

P_{power} is the maximum power output of the processor, C is the capacitance, V^2 is the voltage squared, and F is the frequency. From this you can see that if you double the frequency of a processor, it will consume twice as much power, and if you double the voltage, it will consume four times as much power. Consequently, if you lower the voltage by half, it will consume only one-fourth the power. These relationships are important to consider if you are overclocking your processor because a small increase in voltage will have a much more dramatic effect than a similar increase in speed.

In general, increasing the speed of a processor by 5% increases the power consumption by only the same amount. Using the previous heatsink calculation, if the processor speed was increased by 5%, the 103W processor would now draw 108.15W and the required heatsink rating would go from 0.34°C/W to 0.32°C/W, a proportional change. In most cases, unless you are overclocking to the extreme, the existing heatsink should work. As a compromise, you can try setting the voltage on manual and dropping it a small amount to compensate, thereby reducing the power consumption. Of course, when you drop the voltage, the CPU might become unstable, so this is something that needs to be tested. As you can see, changing all these settings in the interest of overclocking can take a lot of time when you consider all the testing required to ensure everything is working properly. You have to decide whether the rewards are worth the time and energy spent on setting it up and verifying the functionality.

Note that most professional heatsink manufacturers publish their °C/W ratings, whereas many of what I call the "boutique" heatsink vendors do not. In many cases the manufacturers of many of the more extreme heatsinks don't do the testing that the professional manufacturers do and are more interested in the looks than the actual performance.

Installing a Heatsink

To have the best possible transfer of heat from the processor to the heatsink, most heatsink manufacturers specify some type of thermal interface material to be placed between the processor and heatsink. This typically consists of a ceramic, alumina, or silver-based grease but can also be in the form of a special pad or even a type of double-stick tape. Some are called *phase-change* material because they change viscosity (become thinner) above certain temperatures, enabling them to better flow into minute gaps between the chip and heatsink. In general, thermal greases offer higher performance than phase-change materials, but because they always have a lower viscosity, they flow more easily, can be messy to apply, and (if too much is used) can spill from the sides onto the socket and motherboard.

No matter what type you use, a thermal interface aid such as thermal grease or phase-change material can improve heatsink performance dramatically compared to installing the heatsink dry. Thermal interface materials are rated by thermal conductance (in which case higher is better) or thermal resistance (in which case lower is better). Unfortunately, several industry-standard rating scales are used to measure performance, often making product comparisons difficult. Some measure the thermal conductivity; others measure the thermal resistance; and the scales used can vary greatly. The most commonly reported specification is thermal resistance in degrees centigrade per watt (°C/W) for an interface layer 0.001" thick and 1 square inch in size. For a given material, the thinner the interface layer or the larger the area, the lower the resistance. In addition, due to other variables such as surface roughness and pressure, it is often impossible to directly compare different materials even if they appear to use the same ratings scale.

As a means of offering some sort of comparison, let's look at the effect on processor temperatures by using thermal interface materials of different specifications. The Pentium 4 3.4E processor has one of the highest thermal outputs. It is rated at 103W thermal output with a surface area on the heat spreader of 1.5 square inches. Using thermal interface materials of different C/W specifications, Table 21.1 shows the rise in temperature that will result.

Table 21.1   Thermal Interface Material Resistance Versus CPU Temperature Rise for a 103W Pentium 4 Processor

Thermal Rating (°C/W)	Temperature Rise (°C)
0.000	0.00
0.005	0.34
0.010	0.69
0.020	1.37
0.030	2.06
0.040	2.75

Thermal Rating (°C/W)	Temperature Rise (°C)
0.050	3.43
0.060	4.12
0.070	4.81
0.080	5.49
0.090	6.18
0.100	6.87

Most of the better thermal greases are rated from 0.005 to 0.02 C/W per square inch, which would result in a rise of between 0.34° and 1.37°C. Even if there was a "perfect" thermal grease available, you would reduce the CPU temperature by only less than 2° over most of the products currently on the market. I've seen actual tests of multiple brands of thermal greases, and in most cases the differences in temperature readings between different brands are insignificant. For that reason, I generally don't get too excited about different brands of thermal grease; most of the premium products on the market have surprisingly similar performance.

You can purchase thermal grease in small single-use tubes or larger versions that can service multiple processor installations. Most of the recommended thermal greases include alumina or silver, which offer the lowest thermal resistances. Silver is generally the best but is significantly more expensive with real-world differences that are very slight. One brand (Arctic Silver) has even developed a following sufficient to cause others to counterfeit the product and name. The important thing to note is that, based on calculations as well as in tests I've seen, there has been only a couple of degrees difference in CPU temperature under full load when substituting one brand of thermal grease for another. If you want the best, choose a compound with embedded silver. The next best option is alumina and then the less expensive (and somewhat less effective) ceramic-based greases.

Figure 21.14 shows the thermal interface pad or grease positioned between the processor and heatsink.

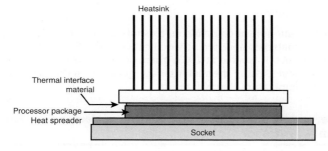

Figure 21.14   Thermal interface material helps transfer heat from the processor die to the heatsink.

The ATX and BTX motherboard families and matching cases used in virtually all desktop systems provide support for better processor cooling than the old Baby-AT form factor. Systems made from these types of motherboards and cases allow for improved cooling of the processor because the processor is repositioned in the case and room is provided for a chassis fan or even a duct to direct airflow over the processor. Most of these cases also feature one or more secondary fans to further assist in cooling. The larger case-mounted fans, especially those with ducts mounted directly over the processor, add to the cooling capability of the system.

◄◄   See "ATX" p. 249.

◄◄   See "BTX" p. 263.

Liquid Cooling

One of the more extreme methods for cooling a PC is to use some form of liquid cooling. Liquids have a much greater thermal carrying capacity than air, and as processors run hotter and hotter, it can be advantageous or even necessary in some situations to use a form of liquid cooling to dissipate the extreme levels of heat generated, especially in smaller or more confined spaces.

Several forms of liquid cooling are available, including the following:

- Heat pipes
- Water cooling
- Refrigeration

Each of these uses a liquid or vapor to absorb the heat of the processor or other components and take that heat to a heat exchanger where it must eventually be dispersed to the air. So, all liquid cooling involves air cooling as well; it just removes the exchange of heat to the air to a remote place. Also, the heat exchanger (radiator) used can be much larger than what would fit directly on the processor or other chips, which is another reason liquid cooling offers much greater cooling capacity.

Of all the types of liquid cooling available, heat pipes are the only type that is practical and cost-effective in production-level PCs. Water cooling and especially refrigeration are limited to those who are pursuing extreme overclocking and are willing to pay the high prices and put up with all the drawbacks and disadvantages that come with these two options.

Heat Pipes

Heat pipes were invented by George Grover at the Los Alamos National Laboratory in 1963. In simplest terms, a *heat pipe* is a thermal conductor designed to efficiently move heat from one place to another.

A typical heat pipe consists of a hermetically sealed tube incorporating a fine wick structure lining the inner walls, with a hollow core in the center. When constructed, the tube is first completely evacuated of air, then partially filled with a special fluid, and then sealed. The type of fluid and remaining vacuum inside allow the fluid to boil at relatively low temperatures. When the pipe is heated at one end, the fluid changes phase from liquid to vapor, absorbing a tremendous amount of heat in the process. The vapor then travels through the hollow core to the other end of the heat pipe where it condenses, changing phase again back into a liquid and releasing a tremendous amount of heat in the process. The liquid then travels back to the original end through the wick structure via capillary action (see Figure 21.15).

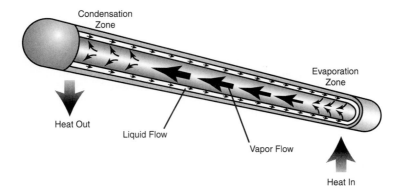

Figure 21.15 Heat pipe interior structure and function.

Heat pipes work by causing a liquid to change phase into a gas to absorb heat and then by causing the gas to change phase back into a liquid to release heat. The energy required to change phase is called the *latent heat of evaporation*. For example, the latent heat of evaporation for water is about

540 cal/g. Most heat pipes use water, ammonia, and methanol. The specific liquid is selected based on the temperature range at which the pipe will work. Water normally boils at 100°C (212°F); however, inside a heat pipe, the pressure is reduced by a partial vacuum such that the boiling point is at room temperature. Because of the heat of evaporation, a heat pipe is generally 10–10,000 times more thermally conductive than a solid copper rod of the same diameter and length.

Heat pipes cannot work alone. They need to be attached to the processor or other heat producing device at one end, and they must have some way of getting rid of the heat at the other end. Usually the condensing end is attached to a conventional heatsink, often with a fan. Figure 21.16 shows one of the heat pipe–based heatsinks used in the Shuttle line of small form factor systems.

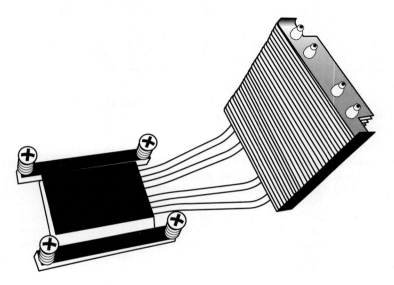

Figure 21.16   Heat pipe system with four pipes for cooling a processor.

In this example, a fan would be mounted on the back panel blowing through the fins attached to the ends of the heat pipes.

Heat pipes have many advantages. Because they are sealed and have no moving parts, they don't require any maintenance and don't wear out. If properly designed, they can even withstand freezing, although they won't work properly until the liquid inside is thawed. Heat pipes are also very compact and are ideal for small form factor system designs. This is one reason almost all laptop computers have been cooled by heat pipes since the early 1990s. Heat pipes are also widely used as integrated cooling systems for system chipsets and voltage regulators on high-performance systems to provide better cooling than passive or active heatsinks without the risk of fan failure. Some motherboard manufacturers are now providing heatpipes in some designs, while conversion kits are available for other motherboards. Figure 21.17 shows a typical high-performance desktop motherboard that uses heatpipes for chipset cooling.

Heat pipes are not only useful as a specific cooling solution, but can also be used to enhance conventional heatsinks. Embedded heat pipes inside a conventional heatsink can dramatically improve the thermal distribution within the heatsink. Figure 21.18 shows a heatsink with two heat pipes, allowing for greater transfer of heat from the bottom to the top of the sink.

Figure 21.17   Motherboard using heatpipe cooling for chipset and voltage regulator.

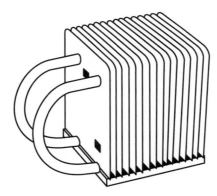

Figure 21.18   Heatsink with heat pipes for improved thermal distribution and performance.

Of all of the liquid cooling mechanisms, heat pipes have the most promise for future use in desktop computers.

Water Cooling

Water cooling is simple in concept but more complicated in reality. The idea is to circulate water over the processor or other components, thereby keeping them cool. The reality is a bit more difficult, making water cooling expensive, difficult to implement, and suitable only for extreme situations.

Water cooling involves several main components:

- **Water blocks**—Mounted on the processor and sometimes on the video card or chipset North Bridge, these are mostly blocks of metal with internal water passages and fittings to connect hoses.

- **Hoses and fittings**—These are used to interconnect all the components in the system.

- **Reservoir**—These are used to provide a sufficient amount of water to cool the components, as well as to cool the water for recirculation.

- **Pump**—A device used to move the water through the system.

- **Coolant**—The fluid, usually water, which is pumped through the system. Some systems use TEC devices (also known as Peltiers) to cool the water, in essence creating a refrigerated cooling system (albeit only for the processor and other components connected to the cooling system).

A diagram of a water cooling system using an external reservoir and pump is shown in Figure 21.19.

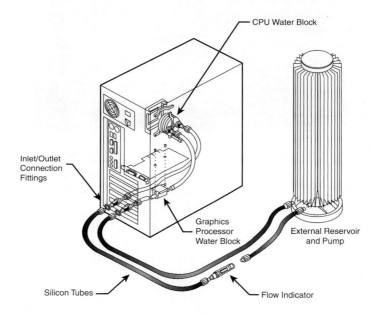

Figure 21.19 Zalman water cooling system with external reservoir and pump.

Some systems use pumps and reservoirs that are internal to the PC or that are mounted on the top, sides, or back. Placing the pump and reservoir inside can be difficult because these components require additional room.

Although water cooling systems can provide a tremendous amount of cooling capacity, they can be troublesome to use and maintain. Their primary disadvantages are that they require a pump to move the water and, if the pump fails, the system overheats. In addition, the water tends to cause corrosion in the pump, water blocks, and reservoirs and can even be subject to problems such as algae growth or other contamination. Finally, every fitting is the source of a potential leak and, if water leaks inside the system, it can cause the entire system to short out and fail. Water cooling systems also have a maintenance drawback: Periodic maintenance is necessary to prevent problems.

Contamination and corrosion have been major problems for water-cooled systems. Many people used plain water in their early designs, which as anybody familiar with automobiles knows allows corrosion and contamination to occur in short order. Using an automotive-style coolant is the best solution for most water cooling systems because the ethylene glycol–based coolants have additives that prevent corrosion and allow for long life. Still, the coolant should be periodically changed, and the water blocks, pump, and reservoir should be inspected for contamination and corrosion. Fittings should also be inspected for leaks periodically.

A good water cooling system can cost $200 or more, much more expensive than air cooling solutions or even heat pipes. They add a lot of visual appeal to a system; many systems use clear hoses and dyes to color the coolant for visual effect.

Due to the expense, maintenance required, potential for failure, and physical size of all the components, water cooling is best used in systems in which extreme overclocking or experimentation is the order. It will probably be a long time before water cooling reaches the point where it is used in commercially produced business or home PCs.

Intel Advanced Liquid Cooling Technology (ALCT)

The hottest processors can generate up to 130W in thermal output, called the TDP (Thermal Design Power), and require heatsinks with 0.13°C/W or lower thermal resistance. Most of the high-end heatsinks that have this level of performance use some form of liquid cooling to achieve very low thermal resistance figures. This includes heat pipes as well as more conventional liquid cooling. However, because conventional liquid cooling brings with it a host of other reliability and maintenance problems, several heatsink manufacturers have been looking to develop simple sealed liquid-cooled designs that will last several years with little or no maintenance. One such design has been proposed by Intel, variations of which are being offered by several of the larger heatsink manufacturers.

Intel refers to this new design as *ALCT*, for *Advanced Liquid Cooling Technology*. ALCT is basically a complete self-contained liquid-cooled heatsink that is both maintenance free and sealed for life. The ALCT includes two main components; an integrated pump and coldplate, along with a heat exchanger (radiator) with an attached 120mm fan. The radiator and pump are connected with flexible rubber hoses that are permanently attached. The pump and coldplate are fully integrated and completely sealed. The internal impeller is driven by a motor through a magnetic coupling, requiring no gaskets or seals. The entire unit is filled with coolant at the factory and permanently sealed so as to remain maintenance free. The reference design allows for a 0.13°C/W thermal resistance, which is enough for even the hottest-running processors. See Figure 21.20 for an example of the ALCT design.

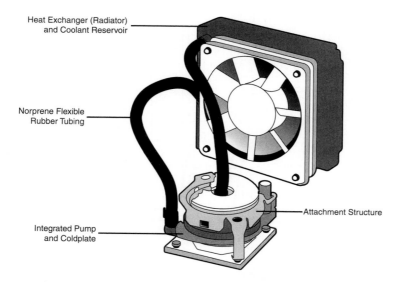

Figure 21.20 A liquid-cooled heatsink based on the ALCT (Advanced Liquid Cooling Technology) design. Heatsinks based on the sealed maintenance-free ALCT design may allow high-performance liquid cooling to appear even in future mainstream systems.

Refrigeration

On the extreme side of cooling, refrigeration enables the processor or other components to be reduced to below room temperature, allowing the extreme limits of overclocking and performance to be tested. When cooled to –40°C (also –40°F), a processor can be run at 33%–100% faster than rated. Unfortunately, this speed comes at a price—the refrigeration equipment is very expensive.

Because of the cost and expense, only a few companies have ever offered refrigerated chassis, mainly KryoTech, nVENTIV, and Asetek. In 1996, KryoTech introduced the first commercially available refrigerated PC. Unfortunately, due to costs and business concerns, it discontinued its chassis in 2002. nVENTIV, founded in 2000 as Chip-con, also introduced a refrigerated chassis, but went out of business in 2004. Kit Tronics (www.kit-tronics.com) sells cases with nVENTIV integrated cooling systems and other components. The survivor of the group, Asetek (www.asetek.com), produces the R134a-based VapoChill case and cooling system, and also offers the low-cost VapoChill Micro active heatsink, which cools only the processor, and also uses R134a coolant.

The key to refrigerated cooling at –40° is the CPU block, which not only has to cool the chip, but also has to prevent condensation from forming. Special insulation and sealing are key to making this work. You can purchase an entire chassis or just the lower cooling unit (see Figure 21.21), which can be used to adapt any system to refrigerated cooling. These cooling solutions sell from about $800 to $1,200, so this is not an inexpensive proposition. Still, if you must have the absolute fastest system on the block and you live for the ultimate in overclocking, the only way to go is refrigerated cooling.

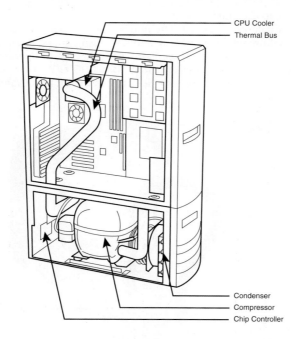

Figure 21.21   Asetek Lightspeed cooling unit.

Thermally Advantaged Chassis

With processors generating more and more heat these days, some recent breakthroughs in chassis engineering and design have allowed for even the fastest processors to be properly cooled, without a fortune needing to be spent on an excessive amount of fans or an expensive cooling solution.

PC power supplies have always contained a fan. For many years, that single fan in the power supply bore the responsibility of cooling not only the supply, but also the entire system and even the processor. In fact, PCs prior to the 486 didn't even use heatsinks on the processor because they generated only a couple of watts of heat. Passive heatsinks first became a standard fixture on processors with the 486DX2 in 1992, which used up to 5.7W of power. Active heatsinks first appeared on the retail Pentium processors from Intel (called Overdrive processors) and became a standard fixture on boxed or retail Pentium II and III and AMD Athlon models in 1997 and later. Most chassis up until that time did not incorporate a cooling fan, except for what was in the power supply.

Chassis fans first became popular in OEM systems in the mid-1990s because they usually used less expensive passive heatsinks on the processor. It was more efficient to use a single chassis fan to cool both the chassis and the processor and save money by using a passive heatsink (without a fan) on the processor. By 2000, with the Pentium 4, many systems began using both an active processor heatsink (with a fan) and a chassis fan. Most modern systems include three fans—one in the power supply, one in the active heatsink on the processor, and one for the rear of the chassis. Some systems have additional fans (a second rear fan and a front-mounted fan for cooling hard disk drives are popular add-ons), but three is the most common and most cost-effective design.

Unfortunately, with high-performance processors reaching and even exceeding the 100W power level, it has become impossible for a standard chassis design to cool the system without resorting to adding more fans or using more exotic (and expensive) liquid cooling setups. A minor breakthrough in chassis design has occurred that can allow even processors consuming more than 100W to be adequately cooled in a three-fan system, without employing exotic solutions or even adding any fans.

As you know from the formula earlier in this chapter, processor power consumption is proportional to speed and is proportional to the square of the voltage it consumes. Even though processor voltages have been decreasing, speeds have been increasing at a much more rapid pace, such that power consumption is reaching all-time high levels beyond 120W. To combat this heat, heatsink manufacturers have increased the efficiency of processor heatsinks significantly over the past 10–15 years. Heatsinks are available today with thermal resistances on the order of 0.33°C/W or less. Unfortunately, conventional air-cooled heatsinks are fast approaching the limits of the technology.

One cost-effective method of improving heatsink performance is to reduce the ambient temperature around the processor, which means lowering the temperature of air entering the heatsink. To ensure proper cooling for their boxed (retail) processors, Intel and AMD specify maximum temperature limits for the air that enters the heatsink fan assembly. If the air temperature entering the heatsink goes over that amount, the heatsink will not be able to adequately cool the processor. Because they must account for extreme circumstances, all modern systems and heatsinks are designed to operate properly if the external environmental ambient temperature in the room is 35°C (95°F). This means that, in general, PCs are designed to work in environments of up to that temperature. To operate in environments with higher temperatures than that, more specialized designs are required. Table 21.2 shows the maximum heatsink air inlet temperatures allowed for various processors with factory-installed heatsinks.

Table 21.2   Maximum Heatsink Inlet Temperatures for Various Processors

Environmental Temp.	Max. Heatsink Inlet Temp.	Processor Type
35°C (95°F)	45°C (113°F)	AMD K6, Pentium I, II, III
35°C (95°F)	42°C (107.6°F)	AMD Athlon, XP, 64, 64 FX
35°C (95°F)	40°C (104°F)	Pentium 4 Willamette, Northwood
35°C (95°F)	38°C (100.4°F)	Pentium 4 Northwood 3GHz+, Prescott 2.4GHz+, Core 2 Duo, Core 2 Extreme Quad Core

As you can see, for a long time new processors continually made more demands on system cooling. With the recent trend on the part of Intel and AMD to increase speed through chip design rather than pure clock speed increases, this trend has plateaued to an extent. The most demanding processors today require that the internal chassis temperature remain at or below 38°C (100.4°F), even if the system is running in a room temperature of 35°C (95°F). The internal temperature rise, or preheating of air inside the system, is typically caused by heat from components such as motherboard chipsets, graphics cards, memory, voltage regulators, disk drives, and other heat-generating components (including the processor itself). Even with all these devices producing heat, the specifications for many newer processors require that the air temperature inside the chassis at the heatsink can rise only to 3°C (5.4°F) over ambient. This places extreme demands on the chassis cooling.

Conventional chassis are incapable of maintaining that low of a differential between the chassis interior and ambient temperatures. The only way to achieve that has been by adding an excessive amount of fans to the system, which unfortunately adds cost and significantly adds to the noise level. Many systems with multiple fans on the front, rear, and sides are still incapable of maintaining only 3°C (5.4°F) over ambient at the processor heatsink. Fortunately, a simple solution was derived that not only solves the problem, but also adds no fans and very little cost to a system. The best part is that this new design can be added to most existing chassis for under $10 in parts and has an easy installation.

Both Intel and AMD have been releasing documents describing the thermal attributes of their processors and guides showing ideas for cooling systems and chassis designs that can adequately cool the system. Chassis that have been specifically designed to improve cooling for the processor by maintaining a temperature of 38°C or less at the processor heatsink inlet are often referred to as *thermally advantaged chassis*. Using a thermally advantaged chassis allows the processor to remain cool, even under extreme environmental conditions, and helps reduce noise. Most modern processors and chassis incorporate cooling systems that can adjust the speeds of the fans. If the temperatures remain below specific limits, the fans run at lower speeds, thus reducing the noise level. If temperatures rise, so do fan speeds and noise. In general, thermally advantaged chassis enable fan speeds to remain lower, resulting in quieter operation.

To meet the thermally advantaged chassis requirements, the following specifications are recommended:

- Accepts an industry-standard ATX, MicroATX, or FlexATX motherboard
- Accepts an industry-standard ATX, SFX, or TFX power supply with integral exhaust fan
- Uses a removable side cover with an adjustable processor duct and adapter card vent (see Figures 21.22–24, next section)
- Provides a primary chassis rear exhaust fan of 92mm or larger and an optional front-mounted 80mm fan (excluding any fans in the power supply)

Because a thermally advantaged chassis is much better at cooling for very little extra cost, I highly recommend you look for these features on the next system you buy or build.

Processor Duct

The latest advancement in chassis design, and a major feature of the thermally advantaged chassis discussed in the previous section, is the addition of a duct or air guide directly over the processor. This is called a *processor duct* or *chassis air guide*, and it essentially enables the processor heatsink to draw air directly from outside the chassis, greatly improving the thermal performance of the processor heatsink and easily meeting the requirement for a 38°C-or-lower heatsink inlet temperature. The specifications for this duct, and for an additional vent in the side cover for adapter cards such as graphics boards, can be found in an official standard called the Chassis Air Guide design guide, which was initially published in May 2002 and revised in September 2003. This guide details the dimensions and locations of the processor duct, as well as other attributes of the design, and is available from the Intel website.

Figure 21.22 shows a typical tower chassis with the processor duct installed in the side cover.

The processor duct is essentially a tube positioned directly over the processor heatsink, allowing it to pull cool air from outside the chassis. When viewed from the side, the duct is usually covered by a grille or vent cover. Figure 21.23 shows the processor duct and adapter card vents as viewed from the side.

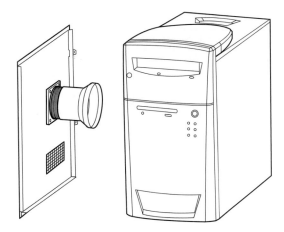

Figure 21.22 Thermally advantaged chassis featuring a processor air duct and adapter card vent in the side cover.

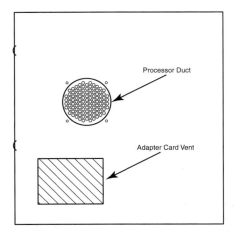

Figure 21.23 Thermally advantaged chassis processor duct and adapter card vent as viewed from the side.

The processor duct is the most important part of the thermally advantaged chassis design, and the placement of the duct is critical to its performance. The duct must be centered over the processor heatsink, and it must be positioned such that the end of the duct is spaced 12mm–20mm from the top of the heatsink. This ensures that the processor heatsink ingests only cool air from outside the chassis and enables some air to spill over to cool other parts of the system. Figure 21.23 shows the duct placement in relation to the top of the processor heatsink.

Because chassis can vary in size, shape, and dimension, the Chassis Air Guide standard details the placement of the processor duct and adapter card vent in relation to an industry-standard ATX motherboard.

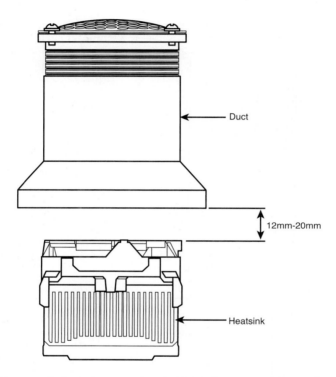

Figure 21.24   Processor air duct placement in relation to the processor heatsink.

The effect of the processor duct is quite noticeable in system operation. In a study done by Intel, it tested a system running Windows XP with a 3GHz Pentium 4 processor, a D865PERL motherboard, a GeForce4 video card, DDR400 memory, a hard drive, a CD-ROM drive, a sound card, and both rear- and front-mounted 80mm fans. The system was running in a 25°C (77°F) room, and the test results were as follows:

	Without CPU Duct	**With CPU Duct**
CPU inlet temp.	35°C (95°F)	28°C (82.4°F)
CPU fan speed	4050 rpm	2810 rpm
Sound level	39.8 Dba	29.9 Dba

As you can see, adding the duct dropped the temperature of the processor by 7°C (12.6°F), even while allowing the heatsink fan speed to drop to the lowest setting. The result is a processor that runs cooler, a fan that lasts longer, and less noise. As you can see, even with dual-chassis fans already in the system, the processor duct makes a huge difference.

By selecting a thermally advantaged chassis, you ensure that your processor remains cool under the most extreme environmental conditions, not to mention that you extend the life of the heatsink fan and cause your system to be much quieter overall.

Functional Chassis Mod: Adding a Processor Duct

Now that you know to look for a thermally advantaged chassis with a processor duct for your next system, what about the systems you already have? Fortunately, this is one modification that is extremely easy to perform to an existing system. Unlike purely cosmetic modifications, this mod benefits your system tremendously and is much more about function and performance than it is about looks.

After studying the Chassis Air Guide specifications, I thought this would be a perfect mod to perform to one of my existing systems. The benefits are obvious: A cooler processor is a happier processor, and the rest of the system is happier as well. If you had thoughts about overclocking, this modification will improve the cooling capability of your existing heatsink such that you won't need to replace it even in an overclocking situation.

After searching the local home improvement and hardware stores, I found the perfect solution for adding a processor duct to an existing system in the plumbing section! As I was looking over various fittings and parts to see what I could make work in the most efficient and least costly manner, I heard the inevitable "Can I help you?" from one of the store attendants. I thought to myself, "How am I going to answer? I mean, I can't really tell him I'm looking for parts to modify my computer! Ahh, what the heck," I thought. So, I said, "Okay, maybe you can help. I'm looking for parts that I can use to add a processor duct to my computer, which conforms to the official Chassis Air Guide 1.1 standard, thus making it a thermally advantaged chassis." "Um, never mind," was all he could say in response, as he walked away shaking his head.

After checking everything out, I found that I could design and install the modification using only two parts, as follows:

Item	P/N	Price
2" no-caulk shower drain (PVC)	30171	$5.97
4" flexible downspout connector (rubber)	PDSC 43	$2.99
	Total:	**$8.96**

I purchased these parts at Menards; however, any decent home improvement or hardware store should have them. The parts are shown in Figure 21.25.

The duct is exceedingly simple; it merely consists of the two pieces mated. The rubber downspout connector slips over the threaded end of the PVC shower drain and can be adjusted or even trimmed to get the precise distance from the top of the CPU heatsink.

Figure 21.25 2" no-caulk shower drain (for processor duct) and a 4" rubber flexible downspout connector (for processor duct).

To install the duct, follow these directions:

1. Remove the chassis side cover. Place a layer of masking tape completely covering the outer skin of the side cover to protect the paint from scratches when you are cutting the hole.

2. Looking at the cover as it would be positioned on the chassis, make a mark directly over the center position of the processor heatsink.

3. Using a hole saw, jigsaw, or other tools, cut a 3.25" (82.5mm) hole in the side cover, using the mark you made as the center point. The hole does not have to be cosmetically perfect or precise because the flange on the PVC shower drain will cover about a quarter of an inch of material beyond the hole.

4. Take the PVC shower drain and pull off the stainless steel strainer (it snaps off); then remove and discard the internal locknut, locknut spinner, and no-caulk gasket.

5. Unscrew the outer locknut, remove the paper and rubber gaskets, and discard the paper gasket.

6. Slide the PVC drain into the hole in the side cover, with the flange on the outside and the threaded portion on the inside.

7. Slip the rubber gasket over the threaded portion, and then screw on the outer locknut and tighten it down.

8. Take the rubber flexible downspout connector and slide the narrow portion over the threads on the PVC shower drain.

9. Place the cover and duct assembly back on the system for a trial fitting, look through the open duct, and measure the distance between the end of the rubber downspout connector and the top of the processor (see Figure 21.26).

10. Remove the side cover and duct assembly; then trim the rubber downspout connector with a knife or razor blade as necessary, so the distance from the end of the connector and the top of the CPU heatsink is between 12mm and 20mm (approx. 0.47"–0.79"). You might need to refit the cover several times when measuring and trimming.

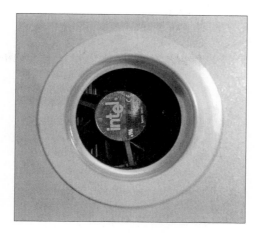

Figure 21.26   Peering through the duct to measure the clearance between the duct and processor heatsink.

11. Finally, snap the stainless steel strainer into place on the duct, and reinstall the side cover and duct assembly on the system (see Figure 21.27).

As you can see, the instructions are simple. The most difficult part is cutting the hole in the side cover. But even that isn't terribly hard, mainly because the flange of the drain covers an additional quarter of an inch of the cover, hiding the fact that the hole might be out of round or have rough edges.

Figure 21.28 shows the finished product, complete with stainless steel strainer.

Figure 21.27   Side cover with the duct being reinstalled on the chassis.

Figure 21.28   Processor duct and adapter card vent locations on the author's system.

The system I used already had a vent for the adapter card area. Plus, it uses a 92mm rear fan, so with the addition of the processor duct, it now fully meets the thermally advantaged chassis with Chassis Air Guide standards. Not only is it functional, but it actually looks pretty good, too. The stainless steel strainer adds an "industrial" look to the mod, adding a little form to the function.

Upon powering up the system with the duct in place, I immediately noticed that the processor was pulling air through the duct, allowing it to run noticeably cooler. Not bad for under $9 and about 15 minutes to cut the hole!

PC Diagnostics, Testing, and Maintenance

PC Diagnostics

No matter how well built your PC is and how well written its software, something is eventually going to go wrong, and you might not always have a support system available to resolve the problem. Diagnostic software can be vitally important to you anytime your computer malfunctions or you are in the process of upgrading a system component or especially building an entirely new system from scratch. This chapter examines the types of diagnostics software available, and particularly those utilities you might already own because they are included with common operating systems and hardware products.

You also might find that your system problems are caused by a hardware malfunction and that you must open the computer case to perform repairs. This chapter also examines the tools and testers used to upgrade and repair PCs—both the basic items every user should own and some of the more advanced devices.

Of course, the best way to deal with a problem is to prevent it from occurring in the first place. The preventive maintenance sections of this chapter describe the procedures you should perform on a regular basis to keep your system in good working order. This chapter describes several levels of diagnostic software that are either included with your system or available from your system manufacturer and third parties. This chapter describes how you can get the most from this software. It also details the various ROM BIOS audio codes and error codes and examines aftermarket diagnostics and public-domain diagnostic software.

Diagnostics Software

Several types of diagnostic software are available for PCs. Some diagnostic functions are integrated into the PC hardware or into peripheral devices, such as expansion cards, whereas others take the form of operating system utilities or separate software products. This software, some of which is included with the system when purchased, assists users in identifying many problems that can occur with a computer's components. In many cases, these programs can do most of the work in determining which PC component is defective or malfunctioning. The types of diagnostic software are as follows:

- **POST**—The power-on self test operates whenever any PC is powered up (switched on). These routines are contained within the motherboard ROM as well as ROMs on expansion cards.

- **Manufacturer-supplied diagnostics software**—Many of the larger manufacturers—especially high-end, name-brand manufacturers such as IBM, Hewlett-Packard, Dell, and others—make special diagnostics software expressly designed for their systems. This manufacturer-specific software normally consists of a suite of tests that thoroughly examines the system. In some cases, these utilities are included with the system, or you can download these diagnostics from the manufacturer's online services at no charge; otherwise, you might have to purchase them. Many vendors include a limited version of one of the aftermarket packages that has been customized for use with their systems. In some older IBM and Compaq systems, the diagnostic software is installed on a special partition on the hard drive and can be accessed during startup. This was a convenient way for those system manufacturers to ensure that users always had diagnostics available.

- **Peripheral diagnostics software**—Many hardware devices ship with specialized diagnostics software designed to test their particular functions. Adaptec SCSI host adapters, for example, include diagnostic functions in the card's ROM BIOS that you can access with a keystroke (Ctrl+A) at boot time. Sound cards normally include a diagnostic program on a disk along with the drivers, which test and verify all the card's functions. Network adapters usually include a diagnostic specific to that adapter on a disk, also normally with the drivers. Other devices or adapters also might provide a diagnostic program or disk, usually included with the drivers for the device.

- **Operating system diagnostics software**—Operating systems such as Windows, Linux, and so on, often include a variety of diagnostic software utilities designed to identify and monitor the performance of various components in the computer.

- **Aftermarket diagnostics software**—A number of manufacturers make general-purpose diagnostics software for PCs, both user-supported and commercial. This type of software is often bundled with other system maintenance and repair utilities to form a general PC software toolkit.

The Power-on Self Test

When IBM first began shipping the original PC in 1981, it included safety features that had never been seen in a personal computer. These features were the power-on self test (POST) and parity-checked memory. Although parity-checked or even error-correcting code (ECC) memory is no longer available in most low-end chipsets, every PC still executes a POST when you turn it on. The following sections provide more detail on the POST, a series of program routines buried in the motherboard ROM-BIOS chip that tests all the main system components at power-on time. This series of routines is partially responsible for the delay when you turn on your PC; the computer executes the POST before loading the operating system.

What Is Tested?

Whenever you start up your computer, it automatically performs a series of tests that checks the primary components in your system, such as the CPU, ROM, motherboard support circuitry, memory, and major peripherals such as the expansion chassis. These tests are brief and are designed to catch hard (not intermittent) errors. The POST procedures are not very thorough compared with available disk-based diagnostics. The POST process provides error or warning messages whenever it encounters a faulty component.

Although the diagnostics performed by the system POST are not very thorough, they are the first line of defense, especially when it comes to detecting severe motherboard problems. If the POST encounters a problem severe enough to keep the system from operating properly, it halts the system boot process and generates an error message that often identifies the cause of the problem. These POST-detected problems are sometimes called *fatal errors* because they prevent the system from booting.

How Errors Are Displayed

The POST tests normally provide three types of output messages: audio codes, onscreen text messages, and hexadecimal numeric codes that are sent to an I/O port address.

POST errors can be displayed in the following three ways:

- **Beep codes**—Heard through the speaker attached to the motherboard.
- **POST checkpoint codes**—Hexadecimal checkpoint codes sent to an I/O port address. A special card plugged into either an ISA or a PCI card slot is required to view these codes.
- **Onscreen messages**—Error messages displayed onscreen after the video adapter is initialized.

BIOS POST Beep Codes

Beep codes are used for fatal errors only, which are errors that occur so early in the process that the video card and other devices are not yet functional. Because no display is available, these codes take the form of a series of beeps that identify the faulty component. When your computer is functioning normally, you should hear one short beep when the system starts up at the completion of the POST, although some systems (such as Compaq's) beep twice at the end of a normal POST. If a problem is detected, a different number of beeps sounds, sometimes in a combination of short and long tones.

BIOS POST Checkpoint Codes

POST checkpoint codes are hexadecimal numeric codes written by POST routines to I/O port address 80h as each major step is begun. These are often simply called *POST codes*. These POST codes can only be read by a special adapter card plugged into one of the system slots. These cards originally were designed for system manufacturers to use for burn-in testing of the motherboard. Several companies make these cards available to technicians. Micro 2000, JDR Microdevices, eSupport, Ultra-X, and Trinitech (search for Omni Analyzer) are just a few manufacturers that market these POST cards. See the vendor list on the accompanying disc for more information about these manufacturers.

POST checkpoint codes can be used to track the system's progress through the boot process from power-on right up to the point at which the bootstrap loader runs (when the operating system load begins). When you plug a POST code reader card into a slot, during the POST you will see two-digit hexadecimal numbers flash on the card's display. If the system stops unexpectedly or hangs, you can identify the test that was in progress during the hang from the two-digit code. This step usually helps to identify the malfunctioning component.

Originally, most POST reader cards plugged into the 8-bit connector that is a part of the ISA or EISA bus. Some older PCI-based systems do still have ISA connectors that can use these cards. However, the motherboards found in newer PCs have no ISA slots at all, so obviously an ISA POST card won't work. Fortunately, the companies that make POST cards more often than not make PCI versions. Micro 2000 has a card called the Post-Probe, which has both ISA and PCI connectors on the same board. PC Certify has a similar card called the PCISA FlipPOST (see Figure 22.1).

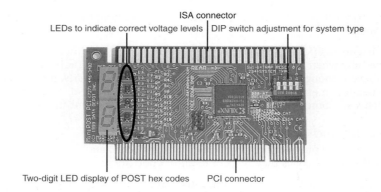

ISA connector

LEDs to indicate correct voltage levels | DIP switch adjustment for system type

Two-digit LED display of POST hex codes   PCI connector

Figure 22.1   The PC Certify PCISA FlipPOST diagnostics card works with both PCI- and ISA-based systems, and it also tests motherboard voltage levels.

Although rare at this point, if you maintain older Compaq or EISA-based systems from any vendor, these systems might use an I/O port address other than port 80. Simpler POST cards monitor only port 80, but some cards have DIP switches or jumper blocks to configure the card to monitor the different I/O port addresses these systems used.

Note

Listings for additional POST checkpoint codes can be found in the Technical Reference section of the accompanying DVD. Also, see Chapter 5, "BIOS," to learn more about working with your BIOS. Remember to consult your motherboard documentation for codes specific to your BIOS version. Also, the documentation included with the various POST cards covers most older as well as newer BIOS versions.

BIOS POST Onscreen Messages

Onscreen messages are brief messages that attempt to indicate a specific failure. These messages can be displayed only after the point at which the video adapter card and display have been initialized.

These different types of error messages are BIOS dependent and vary among BIOS manufacturers, and even in some cases among different BIOSs from the same manufacturer. The following sections list the codes used by the most popular ROM BIOS versions (AMI, Award, Phoenix, and IBM BIOS), but you should consult your motherboard or ROM BIOS manufacturer for the codes specific to your board and BIOS.

Most POST code cards come with documentation listing the POST checkpoint codes for various BIOS versions. If your BIOS is different from what I have listed here, consult the documentation for your BIOS or the information that came with your particular POST card.

AMI BIOS POST Error Codes

Table 22.1 lists the beep codes used by the AMI BIOS from American Megatrends.

Table 22.1   AMI BIOS POST Beep Codes

Beeps	Error Description	Action
1	Memory Refresh Error	Clean the memory contacts and reseat the modules. Remove all modules except the first bank. Replace the memory, power supply, and motherboard.
2	Memory Parity Error	Clean the memory contacts and reseat the modules. Remove all modules except the first bank. Replace the memory, power supply, and motherboard.
3	Base 64KB Memory Error	Clean the memory contacts and reseat the modules. Remove all modules except the first bank. Replace the memory, power supply, and motherboard.
4	Timer Error	Check for proper motherboard installation, loose screws, foreign objects causing shorts, and over-tightened screws. Replace the motherboard.
5	Processor Error	Check for proper motherboard installation, loose screws, foreign objects causing shorts, and over-tightened screws. Make sure the processor and heatsink are installed properly; remove and reseat them. Replace the processor. Replace the motherboard.
6	8042 – Gate A20 Error	Check for proper motherboard installation, loose screws, foreign objects causing shorts, and over-tightened screws. Replace the keyboard, motherboard, and processor.
7	Processor Exception Interrupt Error	Make sure the processor and heatsink are installed properly; remove and reseat them. Replace the processor. Replace the motherboard.
8	Display Memory Read/Write Error	Check the video card for proper installation. Try replacing the video card memory, and replace the video card. Replace the motherboard.
9	ROM Checksum Error	Try reseating the motherboard ROM chip. Try reflashing the motherboard ROM. Replace the motherboard.
10	CMOS Shutdown Register Read/Write Error	Replace the CMOS battery. Replace the motherboard.
11	Cache Memory Bad	Make sure cache settings in BIOS Setup are properly configured. Replace the processor. Replace the motherboard.
1 long, 3 short	Conventional/Extended Memory Error	Clean the memory contacts and reseat the modules. Remove all modules except the first bank. Replace the memory, power supply, and motherboard.
1 long, 8 short	Display/Retrace Error	Check the video card for proper installation. Try replacing the video card memory. Replace the video card. Replace the motherboard.

AMI BIOS codes used by permission of American Megatrends, Inc.

Phoenix Award BIOS, Award BIOS, Phoenix FirstBIOS

Phoenix Technologies has owned the former Award Software for a number of years but continues to market the Award BIOS, currently as Phoenix Award BIOS. This BIOS has also been referred to as the Phoenix FirstBIOS. Table 22.2 lists beep codes and Table 22.3 lists POST error messages for these BIOS versions.

Table 22.2   AwardBIOS/Phoenix FirstBIOS POST Beep Codes

Beeps	Error Description	Action
1 long, 2 short	Video Card Error	Check the video card for proper installation. Try removing and reinserting the video card. Replace the video card. Replace the motherboard.
1 long, 3 short	Video Card Error	Check the video card for proper installation. Try removing and reinserting the video card. Replace the video card. Replace the motherboard.
Continuous beeps	Memory Error	Clean the memory contacts and reseat the modules. Remove all modules except the first bank. Replace the memory, power supply, and motherboard.
High-frequency beeps while system operating	Overheating CPU	Check CPU active heatsink and case fan(s) for proper operation. Replace fans that are not working or are spinning too slowly. Use PC Health or hardware monitor in BIOS to check active heatsink (CPU fan) speed. Check airflow through case. Clean dirty or blocked air intakes or exhaust ports.
Repeating high/low	CPU	Incorrect CPU installation, CPU may be damaged or overheating. Check CPU active heatsink for proper operation. Use PC Health or hardware monitor in BIOS to check active heatsink (CPU fan) speed.

Table 22.3   AwardBIOS POST Onscreen Error Messages

Message	Description
BIOS ROM checksum error – System halted	The checksum of the BIOS code in the BIOS chip is incorrect, indicating the BIOS code might have become corrupt. Contact your system dealer to replace the BIOS.
CMOS battery failed	The CMOS battery is no longer functional. Contact your system dealer for a replacement battery.
CMOS checksum error Defaults loaded	Checksum of CMOS is incorrect, so the system loads the default equipment configuration. A checksum error can indicate that CMOS has become corrupt. This error might have been caused by a weak battery. Check the battery and replace if necessary.
CPU at nnnn	Displays the running speed of the CPU.
Display switch is set incorrectly	The display switch on the motherboard can be set to either monochrome or color. This message indicates the switch is set to a different setting than indicated in Setup. Determine which setting is correct, and then either turn off the system and change the jumper or enter Setup and change the VIDEO selection.
Press ESC to skip memory test=	The user can press Esc to skip the full memory test.
Floppy disk(s) fail	Can't find or initialize the floppy drive controller or the drive. Make sure the controller is installed correctly. If no floppy drives are installed, be sure the Diskette Drive selection in Setup is set to NONE or AUTO.

Table 22.3   Continued

Message	Description
HARD DISK initializing. Please wait a moment	Some hard drives require extra time to initialize.
HARD DISK INSTALLFAILURE	Can't find or initialize the hard drive controller or the drive. Make sure the controller is installed correctly. If no hard drives are installed, be sure the Hard Drive selection in Setup is set to NONE.
Hard disk(s) diagnosis fail	The system might run specific disk diagnostic routines. This message appears if one or more hard disks return an error when the diagnostics run.
Keyboard error or nokeyboard present	Can't initialize the keyboard. Make sure the keyboard is attached correctly and no keys are pressed during POST. To purposely configure the system without a keyboard, set the error halt condition in Setup to HALT ON ALL, BUT KEYBOARD. The BIOS then ignores the missing keyboard during POST.
Keyboard is locked out - Unlock the key	This message usually indicates that one or more keys have been pressed during the keyboard tests. Be sure no objects are resting on the keyboard.
Memory Test:	This message displays during a full memory test, counting down the memory areas being tested.
Memory test fail	If POST detects an error during memory testing, additional information appears giving specifics about the type and location of the memory error.
Override enabled - Defaults loaded	If the system can't boot using the current CMOS configuration, the BIOS can override the current configuration with a set of BIOS defaults designed for the most stable, minimal-performance system operations.
Press TAB to show POST screen	System OEMs might replace Phoenix Technologies' AwardBIOS POST display with their own proprietary displays. Including this message in the OEM display permits the operator to switch between the OEM display and the default POST display.
Primary master hard disk fail	POST detects an error in the primary master IDE hard drive.
Primary slave hard disk fail	POST detects an error in the secondary master IDE hard drive.
Resuming from disk, Press TAB to show POST screen	Phoenix Technologies offers a save-to-disk feature for notebook computers. This message might appear when the operator restarts the system after a save-to-disk shutdown.
Secondary master hard disk fail	POST detects an error in the primary slave IDE hard drive.
Secondary slave hard disk fail	POST detects an error in the secondary slave IDE hard drive.

PhoenixBIOS POST Error Codes

There have been several versions of the Phoenix BIOS over the years. Phoenix BIOS versions manufactured before 1994 supported 286 through 486 processors and used the beep codes shown in Table 22.4.

Table 22.4   PhoenixBIOS for 486 and Earlier Processors (pre-1994)

Beeps	Error Description	Action
1-2	Video Card Error	Check the video card for proper installation. Try replacing the video card memory, and replace the video card. Replace the motherboard.
1-3	CMOS RAM Read/Write Error	Replace the CMOS battery. Replace the motherboard.
1-1-4	ROM Checksum Error	Try reseating the motherboard ROM chip. Try reflashing the motherboard ROM. Replace the motherboard.
1-2-1	Timer Error	Check for proper motherboard installation, loose screws, foreign objects causing shorts, and over-tightened screws. Replace the motherboard.
1-2-2	DMA Initialization Error	Check for proper motherboard installation, loose screws, foreign objects causing shorts, and over-tightened screws. Replace the motherboard.
1-2-3	DMA Page Register Read/Write Error	Check for proper motherboard installation, loose screws, foreign objects causing shorts, and over-tightened screws. Replace the motherboard.
1-3-1	RAM Refresh Verification Error	Clean the memory contacts and reseat the modules. Remove all modules except the first bank. Replace the memory. Replace the power supply. Replace the motherboard.
1-3-3	First 64KB RAM Multibit Data Line Error	Clean the memory contacts and reseat the modules. Remove all modules except the first bank. Replace the memory, power supply, and motherboard.
1-3-4	First 64KB RAM Odd/Even Logic Error	Clean the memory contacts and reseat the modules. Remove all modules except the first bank. Replace the memory, power supply, and motherboard.
1-4-1	First 64KB RAM Address Line Error	Clean the memory contacts and reseat the modules. Remove all modules except the first bank. Replace the memory, power supply, and motherboard.
1-4-2	First 64KB RAM Parity Error	Clean the memory contacts and reseat the modules. Remove all modules except the first bank. Replace the memory. Replace the power supply. Replace the motherboard.
2-x-x*	First 64KB RAM Error	Clean the memory contacts and reseat the modules. Remove all modules except the first bank. Replace the memory. Replace the power supply. Replace the motherboard.
3-1-1	Slave DMA Register Error	Check for proper motherboard installation, loose screws, foreign objects causing shorts, and over-tightened screws. Replace the motherboard.
3-1-2	Master DMA Register Error	Check for proper motherboard installation, loose screws, foreign objects causing shorts, and over-tightened screws. Replace the motherboard.
3-1-3	Master Interrupt Mask Register Error	Check for proper motherboard installation, loose screws, foreign objects causing shorts, and over-tightened screws. Replace the motherboard.
3-1-4	Slave Interrupt Mask Register Error	Check for proper motherboard installation, loose screws, foreign objects causing shorts, and over-tightened screws. Replace the motherboard.
3-2-4	Keyboard Controller Error	Check for proper motherboard installation, loose screws, foreign objects causing shorts, and over-tightened screws. Replace the keyboard. Replace the motherboard. Replace the processor.

Table 22.4   Continued

Beeps	Error Description	Action
3-3-4	Screen Initialization Error	Check the video card for proper installation. Try replacing the video card memory, and replace the video card. Replace the motherboard.
3-4-1	Screen Retrace Error	Check the video card for proper installation. Try replacing the video card memory, and replace the video card. Replace the motherboard.
3-4-2	Video ROM Error	Check the video card for proper installation. Try replacing the video card memory, and replace the video card. Replace the motherboard.
4-2-1	Timer Interrupt Error	Check for proper motherboard installation, loose screws, foreign objects causing shorts, and over-tightened screws. Replace the motherboard.
4-2-2	Shutdown Error	Check for proper motherboard installation, loose screws, foreign objects causing shorts, and over-tightened screws. Replace the keyboard. Replace the motherboard. Replace the processor.
4-2-3	Gate A20 Error	Check for proper motherboard installation, loose screws, foreign objects causing shorts, and over-tightened screws. Replace the keyboard. Replace the motherboard. Replace the processor.
4-2-4	Unexpected Interrupt In Protected Mode	Check for a bad expansion card. Check for proper motherboard installation, loose screws, foreign objects causing shorts, and over-tightened screws. Replace the motherboard.
4-3-1	RAM Address Error >FFFh	Clean the memory contacts and reseat the modules. Remove all modules except the first bank. Replace the memory. Replace the power supply. Replace the motherboard.
4-3-3	Interval Timer Channel 2 Error	Check for proper motherboard installation, loose screws, foreign objects causing shorts, and over-tightened screws. Replace the motherboard.
4-3-4	Real Time Clock Error	Replace the CMOS battery. Replace the motherboard.
4-4-1	Serial Port Error	Reset the port configuration in BIOS Setup. Disable the port.
4-4-2	Parallel Port Error	Reset the port configuration in BIOS Setup. Disable the port.
4-4-3	Math Coprocessor Error	Check for proper motherboard installation, loose screws, foreign objects causing shorts, and over-tightened screws. Make sure the processor and heatsink are installed properly; remove and reseat them. Replace the processor. Replace the motherboard.
Low 1-1-2	System Board Select Error	Check for proper motherboard installation, loose screws, foreign objects causing shorts, and over- tightened screws. Make sure the processor and heatsink are installed properly; remove and reseat them. Replace the processor. Replace the motherboard.
Low 1-1-3	Extended CMOS RAM Error	Replace the CMOS battery. Replace the motherboard.

Second and third codes can be 1–4 beeps each, indicating different failed bits within the first 64KB of RAM.

PhoenixBIOS version 4 (the most recent edition is Version 4, Revision 6.0) supports Pentium and newer processors. The beep codes for this version are shown in Table 22.5.

Table 22.5   PhoenixBIOS Version 4 and Later POST Beep Codes

Beeps	Error Description	Description/Action
1-2-2-3	BIOS ROM Checksum Error	Try reseating the motherboard ROM chip. Try reflashing the motherboard ROM. Replace the motherboard.
1-3-1-1	DRAM Refresh Error	Clean the memory contacts and reseat the modules. Remove all modules except the first bank. Replace the memory. Replace the power supply. Replace the motherboard.
1-3-1-3	8742 Keyboard Controller Error	Check for proper motherboard installation, loose screws, foreign objects causing shorts, and over-tightened screws. Replace the keyboard. Replace the motherboard. Replace the processor.
1-3-4-1	Memory Address Line Error	Clean the memory contacts and reseat the modules. Remove all modules except the first bank. Replace the memory. Replace the power supply. Replace the motherboard.
1-3-4-3	Memory Low Byte Data Error	Clean the memory contacts and reseat the modules. Remove all modules except the first bank. Replace the memory. Replace the power supply. Replace the motherboard.
1-4-1-1	Memory High Byte Data Error	Clean the memory contacts and reseat the modules. Remove all modules except the first bank. Replace the memory. Replace the power supply. Replace the motherboard.
2-1-2-3	ROM Copyright Error	Try reseating the motherboard ROM chip. Try reflashing the motherboard ROM. Replace the motherboard.
2-2-3-1	Unexpected Interrupts	Check for a bad expansion card. Check for proper motherboard installation, loose screws, foreign objects causing shorts, and over-tightened screws. Replace the motherboard.
1-2	Video Card Error	Check the video card for proper installation. Try replacing the video card memory, and replace the video card. Replace the motherboard.

IBM BIOS POST Error Codes

The original IBM PC and AT systems used BIOSs developed by IBM. However, more recent IBM systems use BIOS products licensed from other vendors. Table 22.6 lists the beep codes for the IBM BIOS.

Table 22.6   IBM BIOS Beep Codes

Audio Code	Description
1 short beep	Normal POST—system okay
2 short beeps	POST error—view code onscreen
No beep	Power supply, motherboard
Continuous beep	Power supply, motherboard
Repeating short beeps	Power supply, motherboard
1 long, 1 short beep	Motherboard
1 long, 2 short beeps	Video card (MDA/CGA)
1 long, 3 short beeps	Video card (EGA/VGA)
3 long beeps	3270 keyboard card

IBM BIOS beep and alphanumeric error codes used by permission of IBM.

Table 22.7 lists the numeric error codes displayed by the IBM BIOS.

Table 22.7   IBM BIOS POST/Diagnostics Display Error Codes

Code	Description
1xx	System board errors
2xx	Memory (RAM) errors
3xx	Keyboard errors
4xx	Monochrome Display Adapter (MDA) errors
4xx	PS/2 system board parallel port errors (PS/2 systems only)
5xx	Color Graphics Adapter (CGA) errors
6xx	Floppy drive/controller errors
7xx	Math Coprocessor errors
9xx	Parallel printer adapter errors
10xx	Alternate parallel printer adapter errors
11xx	Primary Async Communications (Serial COM1:) errors
12xx	Alternate Async Communications (Serial COM2:, COM3:, and COM4:) errors
13xx	Game control adapter errors
14xx	Matrix printer errors
15xx	Synchronous Data Link Control (SDLC) Communications adapter errors
16xx	Display Station Emulation Adapter (DSEA) errors (5520, 525x)
17xx	ST-506/412 fixed disk and controller errors
18xx	I/O expansion unit errors
19xx	3270 PC attachment card errors
20xx	Binary Synchronous Communications (BSC) adapter errors
21xx	Alternate Binary Synchronous Communications (BSC) adapter errors
22xx	Cluster adapter errors
23xx	Plasma monitor adapter errors
24xx	Enhanced graphics adapter (EGA) or video graphics array (VGA) errors
25xx	Alternate Enhanced Graphics Adapter (EGA) errors
26xx	XT or AT/370 370-M (memory) and 370-P (processor) adapter errors
27xx	XT or AT/370 3277-EM (emulation) adapter errors
28xx	3278/79 emulation adapter or 3270 connection adapter errors
29xx	Color/graphics printer errors
30xx	Primary PC network adapter errors
31xx	Secondary PC network adapter errors
32xx	3270 PC or AT display and programmed symbols adapter errors
33xx	Compact printer errors
35xx	Enhanced display station emulation adapter (EDSEA) errors
36xx	General-purpose interface bus (GPIB) adapter errors
37xx	System board SCSI controller errors
38xx	Data acquisition adapter errors

Table 22.7   Continued

Code	Description
39xx	Professional graphics adapter (PGA) errors
44xx	5278 display attachment unit and 5279 display errors
45xx	IEEE interface adapter (IEEE 488) errors
46xx	A real-time interface coprocessor (ARTIC) multiport/2 adapter errors
48xx	Internal modem errors
49xx	Alternate internal modem errors
50xx	PC-convertible LCD errors
51xx	PC-convertible portable printer errors
56xx	Financial communication system errors
70xx	PhoenixBIOS/chipset unique error codes
71xx	Voice communications adapter (VCA) errors
73xx	3 1/2" external disk drive errors
74xx	IBM PS/2 display adapter (VGA Card) errors
74xx	8514/A display adapter errors
76xx	4216 PagePrinter adapter errors
84xx	PS/2 speech adapter errors
85xx	2MB XMA memory adapter or XMA adapter/A errors
86xx	PS/2 pointing device (mouse) errors
89xx	Musical Instrument Digital Interface (MIDI) adapter errors
91xx	IBM 3363 write-once read multiple (WORM) optical drive/adapter errors
96xx	SCSI adapter with cache (32-bit) errors
100xx	Multiprotocol adapter/A errors
101xx	300/1200bps internal modem/A errors
104xx	ESDI or MCA IDE fixed disk or adapter errors
107xx	5 1/4" external disk drive or adapter errors
112xx	SCSI adapter (16-bit without cache) errors
113xx	System board SCSI adapter (16-bit) errors
129xx	Processor complex (CPU board) errors
149xx	P70/P75 plasma display and adapter errors
152xx	XGA display adapter/A errors
164xx	120MB internal tape drive errors
165xx	6157 streaming tape drive or tape attachment adapter errors
166xx	Primary Token-Ring network adapter errors
167xx	Alternate Token-Ring network adapter errors
180xx	PS/2 wizard adapter errors
185xx	DBCS Japanese display adapter/A errors
194xx	80286 memory-expansion option memory-module errors
200xx	Image adapter/A errors

Table 22.7   Continued

Code	Description
208xx	Unknown SCSI device errors
209xx	SCSI removable disk errors
210xx	SCSI fixed disk errors
211xx	SCSI tape drive errors
212xx	SCSI printer errors
213xx	SCSI processor errors
214xx	SCSI write-once read multiple (WORM) drive errors
215xx	SCSI CD-ROM drive errors
216xx	SCSI scanner errors
217xx	SCSI magneto optical drive errors
218xx	SCSI jukebox changer errors
219xx	SCSI communications errors
243xxxx	XGA-2 adapter/A errors
1998xxxx	Dynamic configuration select (DCS) information codes
199900xx	Initial microcode load (IML) error
199903xx	No bootable device, initial program load (IPL) errors
199904xx	IML-to-system mismatch
199906xx	IML (boot) errors

IBM BIOS beep and alphanumeric error codes used by permission of IBM.

IBM/Lenovo Beep and Error Codes

IBM sold its Personal Computing Division to Lenovo in May 2005. Recent IBM and Lenovo systems use different beep codes than the original IBM PC and AT. Table 22.8 lists these beep codes.

Table 22.8   IBM/Lenovo BIOS POST/Diagnostics Display Error Codes

Audio Code	Description	Recommended Action/ Subsystem to Check
1-1-3	CMOS read/write error	1. Run Setup 2. System Board
1-1-4	ROM BIOS check error	1. System Board
1-2-X	DMA error	1. System Board
1-3-X	Memory module error	1. Memory Module 2. System Board
1-4-4	Keyboard error	1. Keyboard 2. System Board
1-4-X	Error detected in first 64KB of RAM	1. Memory Module 2. System Board
2-1-1, 2-1-2	Setup information may not be valid	1. Run Setup 2. System Board

Table 22.8 Continued

Audio Code	Description	Recommended Action/ Subsystem to Check
2-1-X	First 64KB of RAM failed	1. Memory Module 2. System Board
2-2-2		1. Video Adapter (if installed) 2. System Board
2-2-X	First 64KB of RAM failed	1. Memory Module 2. System Board
2-3-X	Memory failure	1. Memory Module 2. System Board
2-4-X	Setup or memory failure	1. Run Setup 2. Memory Module 3. System Board
3-1-X	DMA register failed	1. System Board
3-2-4	Keyboard controller failed	1. System Board 2. Keyboard
3-3-4	Screen initialization failed	1. Video Adapter (if installed) 2. System Board 3. Display
3-4-1	Screen retrace test detected an error	1. Video Adapter (if installed) 2. System Board 3. Display
3-4-2	POST is searching for video ROM	1. Video Adapter (if installed) 2. System Board
4	Video adapter failed	1. Video Adapter (if installed) 2. System Board
All other beep code sequences.	System board problem	1. System Board
One long and one short beep during POST.	Base 640 KB memory error or shadow RAM error	1. Memory Module 2. System Board
One long beep and two or three short beeps during POST.	Video error	1. Video Adapter (if installed) 2. System Board
Three short beeps during POST.	System board or memory problem	1. Memory 2. System Board
Continuous beep.	System board problem	1. System Board
Repeating short beeps.	Keyboard stuck key or cable problem	1. Keyboard stuck key? 2. Keyboard Cable 3. System Board

IBM BIOS beep and alphanumeric error codes used by permission of IBM.

POST Memory Count

On some PCs, the POST also displays the results of its system memory test on the monitor. The last number displayed is the amount of memory that tested successfully. For example, a system might display the following message:

```
32768 KB OK
```

The number displayed by the memory test should agree with the total amount of memory installed on the system motherboard. Some older systems display a slightly lower total because they deduct part or all of the 384KB of UMA (upper memory area) from the count. On old systems that use expanded memory cards, the memory on the card is not tested by the POST and does not count in the numbers reported. Also, this memory test is performed before any system software loads, so many memory managers or device drivers you might have installed do not affect the results of the test. If the POST memory test stops short of the expected total, the number displayed can indicate how far into the system memory array a memory error lies. This number can help you identify the exact module that is at fault and can be a valuable troubleshooting aid in itself.

Note

Many systems today are configured not to display memory or other information during boot. This default is sometimes referred to as "quiet boot." Some systems are configured not to beep during boot, even if there are problems.

To change how your system reports its configuration or startup problems, see Chapter 5, "BIOS."

Peripheral Diagnostics

Many types of diagnostic software are used with specific hardware products. This software can be integrated into the hardware, included with the hardware purchase, or sold as a separate product. The following sections examine several types of hardware-specific diagnostics.

Network Interface Diagnostics

Many network interface adapters are equipped with their own diagnostics, designed to test their own specialized functions. Depending on the network adapter, these tests might require you to boot with a DOS disk, or they might function within Windows.

The DIAG program included with all Linksys network interface cards, for example, performs the following internal tests on the Linksys EtherFast 10/100 Ethernet adapter:

- Configuration test
- I/O test
- ID test
- Internal Loopback test
- Link Status test
- Interrupt test
- Network Function test

The Network Function test sequence requires that you have another node installed on the same network with a Linksys adapter. By running the Diag software on both computers, you can configure one adapter to send data and the other to be the receiver. The sender transmits test messages to the receiver, which echoes the same messages back again. If the adapters and network are functioning properly, the messages should return to the sending system in exactly the same form as they were transmitted.

Other network adapters have similar testing capabilities, although the names of the tests might not be exactly the same.

If you do not have the driver or diagnostics files for your network adapter, you can normally download them free of charge from the manufacturers' respective websites.

Note

To create an MS-DOS boot disk in Windows XP or Vista that you can use to start the system before running DOS-based network diagnostics or other tests, insert a blank floppy disk into the A: drive, open My Computer, right-click the A: drive and select Format. Click the Create an MS-DOS Startup Disk checkbox, and then click OK.

General-purpose Diagnostics Programs

A large number of professional third-party diagnostics programs are available for PC systems. These are commercial programs used by technicians to perform testing of new systems (often called *burn-in testing*) or testing of existing systems either in the shop or in the field.

Most of the commercial PC diagnostics can test all your PC's key components. In addition, specific programs are available to test memory, floppy drives, hard disks, video adapters, and most other areas of the system. Here are some of the programs I recommend most highly:

- **AMIDiag Suite**—See www.ami.com for more information.
- **MicroScope**—See www.micro2000.com for more information.

Tip

Before trying a commercial diagnostic program to solve your problem, look in your operating system. Most operating systems today provide at least some of the diagnostic functions that diagnostic programs do. You might be able to save some time and money.

Unfortunately, no clear leader exists in the area of diagnostic software. Each program has unique advantages, and as a result, no program is universally better than another. When deciding which diagnostic programs to include in your arsenal, look for the features you need.

One of the most popular is AMIDiag Suite from AMI. This program runs on virtually any PC and tests most of the hardware in the system. AMIDiag Suite includes a native Windows version that also supports third-party diagnostics modules and a DOS version that can be used to test hardware, regardless of the operating system, by using a DOS boot disk to start the system. OEM and system integrators can also buy these and other AMIDiag components separately.

Operating System Diagnostics

In many cases, it might not be necessary to purchase third-party diagnostic software because your operating system has all the diagnostic tools you need. Windows includes a large selection of programs that enable you to view, monitor, and troubleshoot the hardware in your system.

Windows XP and Vista have numerous tools, utilities, and error-reporting features that can be useful in helping you determine the cause of problems. The most serious problems can be caused by corrupt files or buggy software on the system, as well as defective or incorrectly configured hardware, and will often result in a STOP or "blue-screen" error, causing Windows to enter a special debugging mode. When this happens, Windows XP and Vista are normally configured to save a dump of the error in a memory dump file, which can be useful if it is a software bug you are going to report to Microsoft. Still, it is always a good idea to write down the error for future reference.

Windows Vista also has the following new diagnostic and troubleshooting features:

- Integrated memory diagnostics that is run before the Windows desktop starts
- Problem Reports and Solutions for tracking problems reported to Microsoft and implementing suggested solutions
- System Diagnostics (system health) report on all subsystems, a part of the new Reliability and Performance Monitor

The Hardware Boot Process

The term *boot* comes from the word *bootstrap* and describes the method by which the PC becomes operational. Just as you pull on a large boot by the small strap attached to the back, a PC loads a large operating system by first loading a small program that can then pull the operating system into memory. The chain of events begins with the application of power and finally results in a fully functional computer system with software loaded and running. Each event is triggered by the event before it and initiates the event after it.

Tracing the system boot process might help you find the location of a problem if you examine the error messages the system displays when the problem occurs. If you see an error message that is displayed by only a particular program, you can be sure the program in question was at least loaded and partially running. Combine this information with the knowledge of the boot sequence, and you can at least tell how far the system's startup procedure had progressed before the problem occurred. You usually should look at whichever files or disk areas were being accessed during the failure in the boot process. Error messages displayed during the boot process and those displayed during normal system operation can be hard to decipher. However, the first step in decoding an error message is knowing where the message came from—which program actually generated or displayed it. The following programs are capable of displaying error messages during the boot process:

OS Independent

- Motherboard ROM BIOS
- Adapter card ROM BIOS extensions
- Master (partition) boot record (MBR)
- Volume boot record (VBR)

OS Dependent

- System files
- Device drivers (loaded through `CONFIG.SYS` or the Win Registry `SYSTEM.DAT`)
- Programs run by `AUTOEXEC.BAT`, the Windows Startup group, and the Registry

The first portion of the startup sequence is *operating system independent*, which means these steps are the same for all PCs no matter which operating system is installed. The latter portion of the boot sequence is *operating system dependent*, which means those steps can vary depending on which operating system is installed or being loaded. The following sections examine both the operating system–independent startup sequence and the operating system–dependent startup process for various operating systems. These sections provide a detailed account of many of the error messages that might occur during the boot process.

The Boot Process: Operating System Independent

If you have a problem with your system during startup and can determine where in this sequence of events your system has stalled, you know which events have occurred and probably can eliminate each of them as a cause of the problem. The following steps occur in a typical system startup regardless of which operating system you are loading:

1. You switch on electrical power to the system.

2. The power supply performs a self-test (known as the POST). When all voltages and current levels are acceptable, the supply indicates that the power is stable and sends the Power_Good signal to the motherboard. The time from switch-on to Power_Good is normally between 0.1 and 0.5 seconds.

3. The microprocessor timer chip receives the Power_Good signal, which causes it to stop generating a reset signal to the microprocessor.

◀◀ See "The Power Good Signal," p. 1210.

4. The microprocessor begins executing the ROM BIOS code, starting at memory address FFFF:0000. Because this location is only 16 bytes from the very end of the available ROM space, it contains a JMP (jump) instruction to the actual ROM BIOS starting address.

◀◀ See "Motherboard ROM BIOS," p. 446.

5. The ROM BIOS performs a test of the central hardware to verify basic system functionality. Any errors that occur are indicated by audio "beep" codes because the video system has not yet been initialized. If the BIOS is Plug and Play (PnP), the following steps are executed; if not, skip to step 10.

6. The Plug and Play BIOS checks nonvolatile random access memory (NVRAM) for input/output (I/O) port addresses, interrupt request lines (IRQs), direct memory access (DMA) channels, and other settings necessary to configure PnP devices on the computer.

7. All Plug and Play devices found by the Plug and Play BIOS are disabled to eliminate potential conflicts.

8. A map of used and unused resources is created.

9. The Plug and Play devices are configured and reenabled, one at a time. If your computer does not have a Plug and Play BIOS, PnP devices are initialized using their default settings. These devices can be reconfigured dynamically when Windows starts. At that point, Windows queries the Plug and Play BIOS for device information and then queries each Plug and Play device for its configuration.

10. The BIOS performs a video ROM scan of memory locations C000:0000–C780:0000 looking for video adapter ROM BIOS programs contained on a video adapter found either on a card plugged into a slot or integrated into the motherboard. If the scan locates a video ROM BIOS, it is tested by a checksum procedure. If the video BIOS passes the checksum test, the ROM is executed;

then the video ROM code initializes the video adapter and a cursor appears onscreen. If the checksum test fails, the following message appears:

```
C000 ROM Error
```

11. If the BIOS finds no video adapter ROM, it uses the motherboard ROM video drivers to initialize the video display hardware, and a cursor appears onscreen.

12. The motherboard ROM BIOS scans memory locations C800:0000–DF80:0000 in 2KB increments for any other ROMs located on any other adapter cards (such as SCSI adapters). If any ROMs are found, they are checksum-tested and executed. These adapter ROMs can alter existing BIOS routines and establish new ones.

13. Failure of a checksum test for any of these ROM modules causes the message

```
XXXX ROM Error
```

to appear, where the address XXXX indicates the segment address of the failed ROM module.

14. The ROM BIOS checks the word value at memory location 0000:0472 to see whether this start is a cold start or a warm start. A word value of 1234h in this location is a flag that indicates a warm start, which causes the BIOS to skip the memory test portion of the POST. Any other word value in this location indicates a cold start, and the BIOS performs the full POST procedure. Some system BIOSs let you control various aspects of the POST procedure, making it possible to skip the memory test, for example, which can be lengthy on a system with a lot of RAM.

15. If this is a cold start, the full POST executes; if this is a warm start, a mini-POST executes, minus the RAM test. Any errors found during the POST are reported by a combination of audio and displayed error messages. Successful completion of the POST is indicated by a single beep (with the exception of some Compaq computers, which beep twice).

16. The ROM BIOS searches for a boot record at cylinder 0, head 0, sector 1 (the very first sector) on the default boot drive. At one time, the default boot drive was always the first floppy disk, or A: drive. However, the BIOSs on today's systems often enable you to select the default boot device and the order in which the BIOS will look for other devices to boot from if necessary, using a floppy disk, hard disk, or even a CD-ROM drive in any order you choose. This sector is loaded into memory at 0000:7C00 and tested.

If a disk is in the drive but the sector can't be read, or if no disk is present, the BIOS continues with step 19.

Booting from CD, DVD, or Floppy

If you do want to boot from a CD-ROM or DVD-ROM, be sure the CD or DVD drive is listed before the hard disk in the boot devices menu in your BIOS setup. To ensure that you can boot from an emergency CD or floppy disk, I recommend setting the CD or DVD drive as the first and the floppy drive as the second boot device. A hard disk containing your operating system should be the third device in the boot device list. This enables you to always be ready for an emergency. So long as you do not start up the system with a floppy or bootable CD or DVD loaded, the BIOS bypasses both the CD/DVD and floppy disk drives and boots from the hard drive.

Note that not all operating system CDs are bootable. Windows 95 CDs are not bootable; however, with Windows 98/Me, Microsoft made the operating system CD-bootable, but only for OEM (original equipment manufacturer) versions. The retail versions of these Windows CDs are not bootable. On the other hand, Windows NT 4.0, Windows 2000, and Windows XP are shipped on bootable CDs, including all OEM, retail, and upgrade versions. Windows Vista is shipped on bootable DVDs, but bootable CDs are available upon special request.

Refer to Chapter 11, "Optical Storage," for information on how to make a bootable CD.

17. If you are booting from a floppy disk and the first byte of the volume boot record is less than 06h, or if the first byte is greater than or equal to 06h and the first nine words contain the same data pattern, this error message appears and the system stops:

```
602-Diskette Boot Record Error
```

18. If the volume boot record can't find or load the system files, or if a problem was encountered loading them, one of the following messages appears:

```
Non-System disk or disk error
Replace and strike any key when ready
Non-System disk or disk error
Replace and press any key when ready
Invalid system disk_
Replace the disk, and then press any key
Disk Boot failure
Disk I/O Error
```

All these messages originate in the volume boot record (VBR) and relate to VBR or system file problems.

19. If no boot record can be read from drive A: (such as when no disk is in the drive), the BIOS then looks for a master boot record (MBR) at cylinder 0, head 0, sector 1 (the very first sector) of the first hard disk. If this sector is found, it is loaded into memory address 0000:7C00 and tested for a signature.

20. If the last two (signature) bytes of the MBR are not equal to 55AAh, software interrupt 18h (Int 18h) is invoked on most systems. This causes the BIOS to display an error message that can vary for different BIOS manufacturers, but which is often similar to one of the following messages, depending on which BIOS you have.

IBM BIOS:

```
The IBM Personal Computer Basic_
Version C1.10 Copyright IBM Corp 1981
62940 Bytes free_
Ok_
```

Most IBM computers since 1987 display a strange character graphic depicting the front of a floppy drive, a 3 1/2" disk, and arrows prompting you to insert a disk in the drive and press the F1 key to proceed.

AMI BIOS:

```
NO ROM BASIC - SYSTEM HALTED
```

Compaq BIOS:

```
Non-System disk or disk error
replace and strike any key when ready
```

AwardBIOS:

```
DISK BOOT FAILURE, INSERT SYSTEM DISK AND PRESS ENTER
```

PhoenixBIOS:

```
No boot device available -
strike F1 to retry boot, F2 for setup utility
```

or

```
No boot sector on fixed disk -
strike F1 to retry boot, F2 for setup utility
```

Although the messages vary from BIOS to BIOS, the cause for each relates to specific bytes in the MBR, which is the first sector of a hard disk at the physical location cylinder 0, head 0, sector 1.

The problem involves a disk that either has never been partitioned or has had the Master Boot Sector corrupted. During the boot process, the BIOS checks the last two bytes in the MBR (first sector of the drive) for a signature value of 55AAh. If the last two bytes are not 55AAh, an Interrupt 18h is invoked, which calls the subroutine that displays one of the error messages just shown, which basically instructs the user to insert a bootable floppy to proceed.

The MBR (including the signature bytes) is written to the hard disk by the FDISK, Disk Management, or DISKPART programs. Immediately after a hard disk is low-level formatted, all the sectors are initialized with a pattern of bytes, and the first sector does not contain the 55AAh signature. In other words, these ROM error messages are exactly what you see if you attempt to boot from a hard disk that has been freshly low-level formatted but has not yet been partitioned or if the MBR has been corrupted such that the signature bytes were overwritten.

21. The MBR searches its built-in partition table entries for a boot indicator byte marking an active partition entry.

22. If none of the partitions are marked active (bootable), the BIOS invokes software interrupt 18h, which displays an error message (refer to step 20).

23. If any boot indicator byte in the MBR partition table is invalid, or if more than one indicates an active partition, the following message is displayed and the system stops:

```
Invalid partition table
```

24. If an active partition is found in the MBR, the partition boot record from the active partition is loaded and tested.

25. If the partition boot record can't be read successfully from the active partition within five retries because of read errors, the following message is displayed and the system stops:

```
Error loading operating system
```

26. The hard disk's partition boot record is tested for a signature. If it does not contain a valid signature of 55AAh as the last two bytes in the sector, the following message is displayed and the system stops:

```
Missing operating system
```

27. The volume boot record is executed as a program. This program looks for and loads the operating system kernel or system files. If the volume boot record can't find or load the system files, or if a problem was encountered loading them, one of the following messages appears:

```
Non-System disk or disk error
Replace and strike any key when ready
Non-System disk or disk error
Replace and press any key when ready
Invalid system disk_
Replace the disk, and then press any key
Disk Boot failure
Disk I/O Error
```

All these messages originate in the volume boot record (VBR) and relate to VBR or system file problems.

From this point forward, what happens depends on which operating system you have. The operating system–dependent boot procedures are discussed in the next several sections.

The DOS Boot Process

MS-DOS and similar operating systems (PC-DOS, DR-DOS, and Freedos) use the following boot process:

1. The initial system file (called IO.SYS or IBMBIO.COM) is executed.

2. The initialization code IO.SYS/IBMBIO.COM copies itself into the highest region of contiguoin IO.SYS/IBMBIO.COM copies itself into the highest region of contiguous DOS memory and transfers control to the copy. The initialization code copy then relocates MSDOS.SYS over the portion of IO.SYS in low memory that contains the initialization code because the initialization code no longer needs to be in that location.

3. The initialization code executes MSDOS.SYS (or IBMDOS.COM), which initializes the base device drivers, determines equipment status, resets the disk system, resets and initializes attached devices, and sets the system default parameters.

4. The full DOS file system is active, and control is returned to the IO.SYS initialization code.

5. The IO.SYS initialization code reads the CONFIG.SYS file multiple times.

6. When loading CONFIG.SYS, the DEVICE statements are first processed in the order in which they appear. Any device driver files named in those DEVICE statements are loaded and executed. Then, any INSTALL statements are processed in the order in which they appear; the programs named are loaded and executed. The SHELL statement is processed and loads the specified command processor with the specified parameters. If the CONFIG.SYS file contains no SHELL statement, the default \COMMAND.COM processor is loaded with default parameters. Loading the command processor overwrites the initialization code in memory (because the job of the initialization code is finished).

During the final reads of CONFIG.SYS, all the remaining statements are read and processed in a predetermined order. Therefore, the order of appearance for statements other than DEVICE, INSTALL, and SHELL in CONFIG.SYS is of no significance.

7. If AUTOEXEC.BAT is present, COMMAND.COM loads and runs AUTOEXEC.BAT. After the commands in AUTOEXEC.BAT have been executed, the DOS prompt appears (unless AUTOEXEC.BAT calls an application program or shell of some kind, in which case the user might operate the system without ever seeing a DOS prompt).

8. If no AUTOEXEC.BAT file is present, COMMAND.COM executes the internal DATE and TIME commands, displays a copyright message, and displays the DOS prompt.

Some minor variations from this scenario are possible, such as those introduced by other ROM programs in the various adapters that might be plugged into an expansion slot. Also, depending on the exact ROM BIOS programs involved, some of the error messages and sequences can vary. Generally, however, a computer follows this chain of events while "coming to life."

You can modify the system startup procedures by altering the CONFIG.SYS and AUTOEXEC.BAT files. These files control the configuration of DOS and allow special startup programs to be executed every time the system starts.

The Windows 9x/Me Boot Process

Knowing exactly how Windows 9x and Millennium Edition (Me) load and start can be helpful when troubleshooting startup problems. The Windows 9x boot process can be broken into three phases:

- The IO.SYS file is loaded and run. (Windows 9x's IO.SYS combines the functions of DOS's IO.SYS and MSDOS.SYS.)

- Real-mode configuration takes place.
- The WIN.COM file is loaded and run.

Windows Me's boot process is similar but does not perform the real-mode configuration step.

Phase 1—Loading and Running the IO.SYS File

IO.SYS is loaded first, and performs the following operations:

1. The initialization code initializes the base device drivers, determines equipment status, resets the disk system, resets and initializes attached devices, and sets the system default parameters.

2. The file system is activated, and control is returned to the IO.SYS initialization code.

3. The Starting Windows message is displayed for <n> seconds, or until you press a Windows function key. The amount of time the message is displayed is determined by the BootDelay=<n> line in the MSDOS.SYS file; the default is 2 seconds.

4. The IO.SYS initialization code reads the MSDOS.SYS configuration file. If you have multiple hardware profiles, you receive the following message and must choose a hardware configuration to use:

   Windows cannot determine what configuration your computer is in.

5. The LOGO.SYS file is loaded and displays a startup image onscreen.

6. If the DRVSPACE.INI or DBLSPACE.INI file exists, it is loaded into memory. IO.SYS also automatically loads HIMEM.SYS, IFSHLP.SYS, and SETVER.EXE.

7. The IO.SYS file checks the system Registry files (SYSTEM.DAT and USER.DAT) for valid data.

8. IO.SYS opens the SYSTEM.DAT file. If the SYSTEM.DAT file is not found, the SYSTEM.DA0 file is used for startup. If Windows 9x/Me starts successfully, the SYSTEM.DA0 file is copied to the SYSTEM.DAT file.

9. The DBLBUFF.SYS file is loaded if DoubleBuffer=1 is in the MSDOS.SYS file or if double buffering is enabled under the following Registry key:

   HKLM\System\CurrentControlSet\Control\WinBoot\DoubleBuffer

Note

Windows 9x Setup automatically enables double buffering if it detects that it is required.

10. If you have multiple hardware profiles, the hardware profile you chose is loaded from the Registry.

11. In Windows 9x/Me, the system looks in the Registry's Hkey_Local_Machine\System\CurrentControlSet key to load the device drivers and other parameters specified there before executing the CONFIG.SYS file.

Phase 2—Real-Mode Configuration

Some older hardware devices and programs require that drivers or files be loaded in real mode (16-bit mode) for them to work properly. To ensure backward compatibility, Windows 9x processes the _CONFIG.SYS and AUTOEXEC.BAT files if they exist. (Windows Me does not use real-mode drivers and skips this step.)

1. The `CONFIG.SYS` file is read if it exists, and the statements within are processed, including the loading of drivers into memory. If the `CONFIG.SYS` file does not exist, the `IO.SYS` file loads the following required drivers:

   - `IFSHLP.SYS`
   - `HIMEM.SYS`
   - `SETVER.EXE`

   `IO.SYS` obtains the location of these files from the `WinBootDir=` line of the `MSDOS.SYS` file and must be on the hard disk.

2. Windows reserves all global upper memory blocks (UMBs) for Windows 9x operating system use or for expanded memory support using the Expanded Memory Specification (EMS).

3. The `AUTOEXEC.BAT` file is processed if present, and any terminate-and-stay resident (TSR) programs listed within are loaded into memory.

Phase 3—Loading and Running the `WIN.COM` File

Windows 9x and Windows Me both perform the following steps:

1. The `WIN.COM` file is loaded and run.

2. The `WIN.COM` file accesses the `VMM32.VXD` file. If enough RAM is available, the `VMM32.VXD` file loads into memory; otherwise, it is accessed from the hard disk (resulting in a slower startup time).

3. The real-mode virtual device driver loader checks for duplicate virtual device drivers (VxDs) in the `WINDOWS\SYSTEM\VMM32` folder and the `VMM32.VXD` file. If a VxD exists in both the `WINDOWS\SYSTEM\VMM32` folder and the `VMM32.VXD` file, the duplicate VxD is "marked" in the `VMM32.VXD` file so that it is not loaded.

4. VxDs not already loaded by the `VMM32.VXD` file are loaded from the `[386 Enh]` section of the `WINDOWS\SYSTEM.INI` file.

Required VxDs

Some VxDs are required for Windows to run properly. These required VxDs are loaded automatically and do not require a Registry entry. Windows 9x requires the following VxDs:

BIOSXLAT	CONFIGMG	DYNAPAGE	DOSMGR
EBIOS	IFSMGR	INT13	IOS
PAGESWAP	SHELL	V86MMGR	VCD
VCACHE	VCOMM	VCOND	VDD
VDMAD	VFAT*VKD	VMCPD	VPICD
VTD	VTDAPI	VWIN32	VXDLDR

5. The real-mode virtual device driver loader checks that all required VxDs loaded successfully. If not, it attempts to load the drivers again.

6. After the real-mode virtual device driver loading is logged, driver initialization occurs. If any VxDs require real-mode initialization, they begin their processes in real mode.

7. VMM32 switches the computer's processor from real mode to protected mode.

8. A three-phase VxD initialization process occurs in which the drivers are loaded according to their InitDevice instead of the order in which they are loaded into memory.

9. After all the VxDs are loaded, the KRNL32.DLL, GDI.EXE, USER.EXE, and EXPLORER.EXE (the default Windows 9x GUI shell) files are loaded.

10. If a network is specified, the network environment and multiuser profiles are loaded. The user is prompted to log onto the installed network. Windows 9x/Me enables multiple users to save their custom desktop settings. When a user logs onto Windows, her desktop settings are loaded from the Registry. If the user does not log on, the desktop configuration uses a default desktop.

11. Programs in the StartUp group and the RunOnce Registry key are run during the last phase of the startup process. After each program in the RunOnce Registry key is started, the program is removed from the key.

Windows NT/2000/XP Startup

When you start a Windows NT, 2000, or XP system (which are all based on the same set of integral code), the boot process is different from that of a DOS or Windows 9x/Me system. Instead of the IO.SYS and MSDOS.SYS files used by 9x/Me, Windows NT/2000/XP use an OS loader program called Ntldr.

The basic Windows NT/2000/XP startup process is described in the following step-by-step procedures:

1. **The partition boot sector loads Ntldr (NT Loader)**. It then switches the processor to protected mode, starts the file system, and reads the contents of Boot.ini. The information in Boot.ini determines the startup options and initial boot menu selections (dual-booting, for example). If dual-booting is enabled and a non-NT/2000/XP OS is chosen, Bootsec.dos is loaded. If SCSI drives are present, Ntbootdd.sys is loaded, which contains the SCSI boot drivers.

2. **Ntdetect.com gathers hardware configuration data and passes this information to Ntldr**. If more than one hardware profile exists, Windows uses the correct one for the current configuration. If the ROM BIOS is ACPI compliant, Windows uses ACPI to enumerate and initialize devices.

3. **The kernel loads**. Ntldr passes information collected by Ntdetect.com to Ntoskrnl.exe. Ntoskrnl then loads the kernel, Hardware Abstraction Layer (Hal.dll), and Registry information. An indicator near the bottom of the screen details progress.

4. **Drivers load and the user logs on**. Networking-related components (for example, TCP/IP) load simultaneously with other services and the Begin Logon prompt appears onscreen. After a user logs on successfully, Windows updates the Last Known Good Configuration information to reflect the current configuration state.

5. **Plug and Play detects and configures new devices**. If new devices are detected, they are assigned resources. Windows extracts the necessary driver files from Driver.cab. If the driver files are not found, the user is prompted to provide them. Device detection occurs simultaneously with the operating system logon process.

The following files are processed during Windows NT/2000/XP startup:

- Ntldr
- Boot.ini
- Bootsect.dos (multiple-boot systems only)
- Ntbootdd.sys (loaded only for SCSI drives)
- Ntdetect.com

- Ntoskrnl.exe
- Hal.dll
- Files in systemroot\System32\Config (Registry)
- Files in systemroot\System32\Drivers (drivers)

Note

If you see error messages during startup or your system doesn't start properly, restart the system, press the F8 key (Windows 2000/XP only) to open the startup menu, and select Enable Boot Logging to create a file called `Ntbtlog.txt`. This file records events during startup and can help you determine which files or processes are not loading correctly.

Windows Vista Startup Differences

Although Microsoft Windows Vista, like Windows 2000 and Windows XP, has its roots in Windows NT 4.0, the boot process is different in some significant ways. Windows Vista uses three different components to replace `ntldr`:

- `bootmgr.exe`—Windows Boot Manager
- `winload.exe`—Windows operating system loader
- `winresume.exe`—Windows resume loader

Likewise, the traditional `boot.ini` boot configuration text file used in earlier NT-based versions of Windows is now replaced by the boot configuration data (BCD) store. The use of BCD enables a common interface for systems that use either traditional BIOS or the more recent extensible firmware interface (EFI) configuration methods. The configuration options in the BCD store are changed with the BCDEdit tool, a UAC-protected program.

`Bootmgr.exe` starts `winload.exe`, which loads Windows Vista, if no other operating system is present, using the settings in the BCD store. However, if a dual-boot configuration has been created by installing Windows Vista alongside a previous version of Windows, the Windows Boot Manager displays a selection menu listing Windows Vista and the previous version of Windows. For example, if Windows Vista is dual-booted with Windows XP, selecting the option to run the previous version of Windows causes the Windows Boot Manager to load Windows XP's `ntldr` as noted in the previous section. However, if Windows Vista is selected, `winload.exe` boots the system using the settings in the BCD store.

When a system running Windows Vista is hibernated, the BCD stores information about the state of the computer when it was hibernated. When the system resumes from hibernation, the `winresume.exe` program is used to restart Windows, using the hibernation information stored in the BCD as well as the contents of `hiberfil.sys`.

PC Maintenance Tools

To troubleshoot and repair PC systems properly, you need a few basic tools. If you intend to troubleshoot and repair PCs professionally, there are many more specialized tools you will want to purchase. These advanced tools enable you to more accurately diagnose problems and make jobs easier and faster. The basic tools that should be in every troubleshooter's toolbox are as follows:

- Simple hand tools for basic disassembly and reassembly procedures, including a flat blade and Phillips screwdrivers (both medium and small sizes), tweezers, an IC extraction tool, and a parts grabber or hemostat. Most of these items are included in $10–$20 starter toolkits found at most computer stores.

- Diagnostics software and hardware for testing components in a system.

- A multimeter that provides accurate measurements of voltage and resistance, as well as a continuity checker for testing cables and switches.
- Chemicals (such as contact cleaners), component freeze sprays, and compressed air for cleaning the system.
- Foam swabs, or lint-free cotton swabs if foam isn't available.
- Small nylon wire ties for "dressing" or organizing wires.

Some environments also might have the resources to purchase the following devices, although they're not required for most work:

- Memory-testing machines, used to evaluate the operation of single inline memory modules (SIMMs), dual inline memory modules (DIMMs), Rambus inline memory modules (RIMMs), or double data rate (DDR) DIMMs
- Serial and parallel loopback (or wrap) plugs to test serial and parallel ports
- A network cable scanner (if you work with networked PCs)
- A serial breakout box (if you use systems that operate over serial cables, such as Unix dumb terminals)
- A POST card (if you work with computers running DOS or other non-Windows operating systems, you might prefer to get a POST card that can also display IRQs and DMAs in use)

In addition, an experienced troubleshooter will probably want to have soldering and desoldering tools to fix bad serial cables. These tools are discussed in more detail in the following sections.

Hand Tools

When you work with PC systems, the tools required for nearly all service operations are simple and inexpensive. You can carry most of the required tools in a small pouch. Even a top-of-the-line "master mechanics" set fits inside a briefcase-sized container. The cost of these toolkits ranges from about $20 for a small service kit to $500 for one of the briefcase-sized deluxe kits. Compare these costs with what might be necessary for an automotive technician. An automotive service technician would have to spend $5,000–$10,000 or more for a complete set of tools. Not only are PC tools much less expensive, but I can tell you from experience that you don't get nearly as dirty working on computers as you do working on cars.

In this section, you learn about the tools required to assemble a kit that is capable of performing basic, board-level service on PC systems. One of the best ways to start such a set of tools is to purchase a small kit sold especially for servicing PCs.

Figure 22.2 shows some of the basic tools you can use to work on PCs. Many of these tools can be found in one of the small PC toolkits that sell for about $20.

Note

Some tools aren't recommended because they are of limited use. However, they normally come with these types of kits.

You use nut drivers to remove the hexagonal-headed screws that secure the system-unit covers, adapter boards, disk drives, and power supplies in most systems. The nut drivers work much better than conventional screwdrivers.

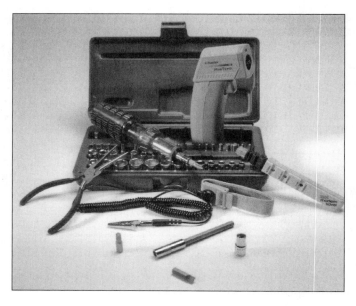

Figure 22.2   The basic tools you need to work on your PC are shown here.

Because some manufacturers have substituted Phillips-head screws for the more standard hexagonal-head screws, standard screwdrivers can be used for those systems. If slotted screws are used, they should be removed and replaced with Torx (preferred), hex, or Phillips-head screws that capture the driver tool and prevent it from slipping off the head of the screw. It is especially important never to allow slotted screws to be used on or near a motherboard because a flat-bladed screwdriver can very easily slip and damage the board.

Caution

When you are working in a cramped environment such as the inside of a computer case, screwdrivers with magnetic tips can be a real convenience, especially for retrieving that screw you dropped into the case. However, although I have used these types of screwdrivers many times with no problems, you should be aware of the damage a magnetic field can cause to magnetic storage devices such as floppy disks. Laying the screwdriver down on or near a floppy can damage the data on the disk. Fortunately, floppy disks aren't used that much anymore. Hard drives are shielded by a metal case; CD/DVD drives are not affected because they work optically; and memory and other chips are not affected by magnetic fields (unless they are magnitudes stronger than what you'll see in a hand tool).

Chip-extraction and insertion and -insertion tools are rarely needed these days because memory chips are mounted on SIMMs, RIMMs, or DIMMs and processors use zero insertion force (ZIF) sockets or other user-friendly connectors; however, in some cases they can be used as general-purpose prying or grabbing tools. The ZIF socket has a lever that, when raised, releases the grip on the pins of the processor, enabling you to easily lift it out with your fingers.

◀◀   See "Zero Insertion Force (ZIF)," p. 99.

However, if you work with older systems, you can use a chip extractor to install or remove memory chips (or other smaller chips) without bending any pins on the chip (see Figure 22.3). Usually, you pry out larger chips, such as microprocessors or ROMs, with the small screwdriver. Larger processors up through the 486 might require a chip extractor if they are mounted in the older low insertion force (LIF) socket. These chips have so many pins on them that a large amount of force is required to remove them, despite the fact that they call the socket "low insertion force." If you use a screwdriver on a large physical-size chip such as a 486, you risk cracking the case of the chip and permanently damaging it. The chip extractor tool for removing these chips has a very wide end with tines that fit between the pins on the chip to distribute the force evenly along the chip's underside. This minimizes the likelihood of breakage. Most of these types of extraction tools must be purchased specially for the chip you're trying to remove.

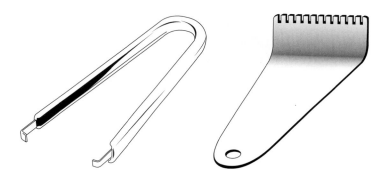

Figure 22.3   The chip extractor (left) is used to remove an individual RAM or ROM chip from a socket, but it would not be useful for a larger processor chip. Use an extractor such as the one on the right for extracting socketed processors—if the processor does not use a ZIF socket.

Tip

The older-style chip extractor shown on the left in Figure 22.3 does have another use as a keycap extractor. In fact, for this role it works quite well. By placing the tool over a keycap on a keyboard and squeezing the tool so the hooks grab under the keycap on opposite sides, you can cleanly and effectively remove the keycap from the keyboard without damage. This works much better than trying to pry off the caps with a screwdriver, which often results in damaging them or sending them flying across the room.

The tweezers and parts grabber can be used to hold any small screws or jumper blocks that are difficult to hold in your hand. The parts grabber is especially useful when you drop a small part into the interior of a system; usually, you can remove the part without completely disassembling the system (see Figure 22.4).

Finally, the Torx driver is a star-shaped driver that matches the special screws found in most systems (see Figure 22.5). Torx screws are vastly superior to other types of screws for computers because they offer greater grip and the tool is much less likely to slip. The most common cause of new motherboard failures is the use of slotted screwdrivers that slip off the screw head, scratching (and damaging) the motherboard. I never allow slotted screws or a standard flat-bladed screwdriver anywhere near the interior of my systems. You also can purchase tamperproof Torx drivers that can remove Torx screws with the tamper-resistant pin in the center of the screw. A tamperproof Torx driver has a hole drilled in it to allow clearance for the pin. Torx drivers come in a number of sizes, the most common being the T-10 and T-15.

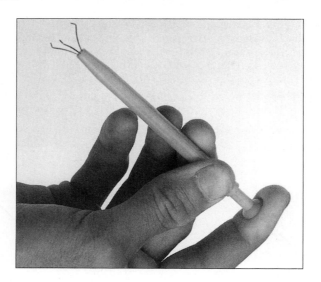

Figure 22.4 The parts grabber has three small metal prongs that can be extended to grab a part.

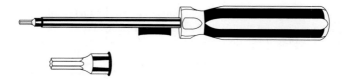

Figure 22.5 A Torx driver and bit.

Although this basic set is useful, you should supplement it with some other basic tools, such as the following:

- **Electrostatic discharge (ESD) protection kit**—This includes a wrist strap and mat (such as those from RadioShack or Stanley Supply & Services [formerly Jensen Tools and Contact East]) and prevents static damage to the components on which you are working. These kits consist of a wrist strap with a ground wire and a specially conductive mat with its own ground wire. You also can get just the wrist strap or the antistatic mat separately. In areas or times of the season when there is low humidity, static charges are much more likely to build up as you move, increasing the need for ESD protection. A wrist strap is shown in Figure 22.6.

- **Needle-nose pliers and hemostats (curved and straight)**—These are great for gripping small items and jumpers, straightening bent pins, and so on.

- **Electric screwdriver**—Combined with hex, Phillips, standard, and Torx bit sets, this tool really speeds up repetitive disassembly/assembly. Black and Decker offers the VersaPak VP750 (www.blackanddecker.com).

- **Flashlight**—You should preferably use a high-tech LED unit such as one from Lightwave (www.longlight.com), which enables you to see inside dark systems and are easy on batteries.

- **Wire cutter or stripper**—This is useful for making or repairing cables or wiring. For example, you'd need this (along with a crimping tool) to make 10BASE-T Ethernet cables using UTP cable and RJ-45 connectors (refer to Chapter 18, "Local Area Networking").

- **Vise or clamp**—This is used to install connectors on cables, crimp cables to the shape you want, and hold parts during delicate operations. In addition to the vise, RadioShack sells a nifty "extra hands" device that has two movable arms with alligator clips on the end. This type of device is very useful for making cables or for other delicate operations during which an extra set of hands to hold something might be useful.

- **Metal file**—This is used to smooth rough metal edges on cases and chassis and to trim the faceplates on disk drives for a perfect fit.

- **Markers, pens, and notepads**—Use these for taking notes, marking cables, and so on.

- **Windows 98/98SE or Me startup floppy**—These disks have DOS 7.1 or 8.0 and real-mode CD-ROM/DVD drivers, which can be used to boot test the system and possibly load other software.

- **Windows 2000/XP original (bootable) CD**—This can be used to boot test the system from a CD-ROM/DVD drive, to attempt system recovery, to install the OS, or to run other software. Microsoft also has a downloadable set of floppy disks (six disks for Windows XP) available at http://support.microsoft.com/. However, most systems capable of running Windows 2000 or XP should be able to boot from the CD.

- **Windows Vista original (bootable) DVD**—This can be used to boot test the system, install (or reinstall) the OS, or to run other programs. In the event of a system failure, you can run the new Recovery Environment, which provides access to System Restore, Complete PC Restore (Business and Ultimate editions only), a full-featured command prompt, memory diagnostics, and other options.

- **Diagnostics software**—This commercial, shareware, or freeware software can be used for PC hardware verification and testing.

- **Power-on self test (POST) card such as the Post Probe from www.micro2000.com**—This is used for displaying POST diagnostics codes on systems with fatal errors.

- **Nylon cable-ties**—These are used to help in routing and securing cables; neatly routed cables help to improve airflow in the system.

- **Digital pocket multimeter (such as those from RadioShack)**—This is used for checking power supply voltages, connectors, and cables for continuity.

- **Cleaning swabs, canned air (dust blower), and contact cleaner chemicals**—These are used for cleaning, lubricating, and enhancing contacts on circuit boards and cable connections. Products include those from www.chemtronics.com, as well as contact enhancer chemicals such as Stabilant 22a (www.stabilant.com).

- **Data transfer cables and adapters**—These are used for quickly connecting two systems and transferring data from one system to another. This includes serial and parallel cables (often called Laplink, Interlink, or Direct Cable Connect cables); Ethernet crossover cables; as well as more specialized USB-to-Ethernet, USB-to-USB, or USB-to-parallel adapters. I recommend using USB-to-USB or Ethernet for the fastest performance; I use serial and parallel cables only on systems that lack support for other interface types.

- **2 1/2" ATA drive cables and adapters**—These are used for connecting 2 1/2" ATA drives to laptop or desktop systems for transferring or recovering data. This includes 44-pin (2 1/2") ATA-to-40-pin (3 1/2") ATA ribbon cable/power adapters, 44-pin ATA-to-USB/FireWire adapters, and 2 1/2" USB/FireWire external drive enclosures.

- **3 1/2" drive enclosure**—A hard disk drive enclosure equipped with a USB 2.0 port enables you to recover data from a hard disk if the original host system is no longer functioning. Some enclosures support only ATA drives, but some recent models also support SATA hard disk drives.

- **External mouse, keyboard, and keyboard/mouse PS/2 Y adapter**—These are useful for operating a system in which the existing keyboard or pointing device is defective or difficult to use. The Y adapter is required on most laptops to use an external PS/2 keyboard alone or a PS/2 keyboard and mouse together.

- **USB powered hub, USB/FireWire cable adapter**—This is useful for connecting external USB devices, especially USB keyboards, mice, and external drives. The cable adapters and gender changers are recommended for connecting different types of USB and FireWire devices.

- **Spare screws, jumpers, standoffs, and so on**—These are used in case some go missing or are lost from the system you are working on.

- **Spare CR-2032 lithium coin cell batteries**—These are used as the CMOS RAM batteries in most systems, so it is a good idea to have a replacement or two on hand. Although a number of CR20xx battery types are available, most systems use the CR2032.

Safety

Before working on a system, you need to follow certain safety procedures. Some are to protect you, whereas others are to protect the system on which you are working.

From a personal safety point of view, there really isn't that much danger in working on a PC. Even if it is open with the power on, PCs run on only 3.3, 5, and 12 volts, meaning no dangerous, life-threatening voltages are present. However, dangerous voltages do exist inside the power supply and monitor. Most power supplies have 400 volts present at some points internally, and color displays have between 50,000 and 100,000 volts on the CRT! Normally, I treat the power supply and monitor as components that are replaced and not repaired, and I do not recommend you open either of them unless you really know what you are doing around high voltages.

Before working on a PC, you should unplug it from the wall. This is not really to protect you so much as it is to protect the system. A modern ATX form factor system is always partially running—that is, as long as the system is plugged in. So, even if it is off, standby voltages are present. To prevent damage to the motherboard, video card, and other cards, the system should be completely unplugged. If you accidentally turn the system all the way on, and plug in or remove a card, you can fry the card or motherboard.

Electrostatic discharge protection is another issue. While working on a PC, you should wear an ESD wrist strap that is clipped to the chassis of the machine (see Figure 22.6). This ensures that you and the system remain at the same electrical potential and prevents static electricity from damaging the system as you touch it. Some people feel that the system should be plugged in to provide an earth ground. That is not a good idea at all, as I previously mentioned. No "earth" ground is necessary; all that is important is that you and the system remain at the same electrical potential, which is accomplished via the strap. Another issue for personal safety is the use of a commercially available wrist strap, rather than making your own. Commercially made wrist straps feature an internal 1-meg ohm resistor designed to protect you. The resistor ensures that you are not the best path to ground should you touch any "hot" wire.

When you remove components from the system, they should be placed on a special conductive antistatic mat, which is also a part of any good ESD protection kit. The mat is also connected via a wire and clip to the system chassis. Any components removed from the system, especially items such as the processor, the motherboard, adapter cards, disk drives, and so on, should be placed on the mat. The connection between you, the mat, and the chassis will prevent any static discharges from damaging the components.

Note

It is possible (but not recommended) to work without an ESD protection kit if you're disciplined and careful about working on systems. If you don't have an ESD kit available, you can discharge yourself by touching any exposed metal on the chassis or case.

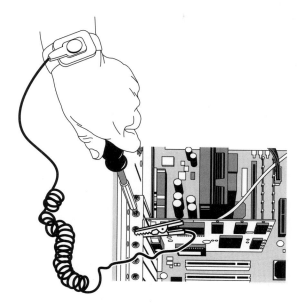

Figure 22.6   A typical ESD wrist strap clipped to a nonpainted surface in the case chassis.

The ESD kits, as well as all the other tools and much more, are available from a variety of tool vendors. Specialized Products Company and Stanley Supply & Services (formerly Jensen Tools and Contact East) are two of the most popular vendors of computer and electronic tools and service equipment. Their catalogs show an extensive selection of very high-quality tools. (These companies and several others are listed in the Vendor List on the accompanying disc.) With a simple set of hand tools, you will be equipped for nearly every PC repair or installation situation. The total cost of these tools should be less than $150, which is not much considering the capabilities they provide.

A Word About Hardware

This section discusses some problems you might encounter with the hardware (screws, nuts, bolts, and so on) used in assembling a system.

Types of Hardware

One of the biggest aggravations you encounter in dealing with various systems is the different hardware types and designs that hold the units together.

For example, most systems use screws that fit 1/4" or 3/16" hexagonal nut drivers. IBM used these screws in all its original PC, XT, and AT systems, and most other system manufacturers use this standard hardware as well. Some manufacturers use different hardware, however. Compaq, for example, uses Torx screws extensively in many of its systems. A Torx screw has a star-shaped hole driven by the correct-size Torx driver. These drivers carry size designations such as T-8, T-9, T-10, T-15, T-20, T-25, T-30, and T-40.

A variation on the Torx screw is the tamperproof Torx screw found in power supplies, monitors, hard drives, and other assemblies. These screws are identical to the regular Torx screws, except that a pin sticks up from the middle of the star-shape hole in the screw. This pin prevents the standard Torx driver from entering the hole to grip the screw; a special tamperproof driver with a corresponding hole for the pin is required. An alternative is to use a small chisel to knock out the pin in the screw. Usually, a device sealed with these types of screws is considered to be a replaceable unit that rarely, if ever, needs to be opened.

Caution

Note that devices sealed with tamperproof Torx screws generally have high voltages or other dangers waiting inside, so being able to bypass these screws doesn't mean it's always a good idea. Be sure you know what you are doing before disassembling devices such as monitors and power supplies.

Many manufacturers also use the more standard slotted-head and Phillips-head screws. Slotted-head screws should *never* be used in a computer because the screwdriver can very easily slip and damage a board. Using tools on these screws is relatively easy, but tools do not grip these fasteners as well as hexagonal head or Torx screws do. In addition, the heads can be stripped more easily than the other types. Extremely cheap versions tend to lose bits of metal as they're turned with a driver, and the metal bits can fall onto the motherboard. Stay away from cheap fasteners whenever possible; the headaches of dealing with stripped screws aren't worth it.

Some system manufacturers now use cases that snap together or use thumb screws. These are usually advertised as "no-tool" cases because you literally do not need any tools to remove the cover and access the major assemblies.

To make an existing case tool-free, you can replace the normal case screws with metal or plastic thumbscrews. However, you still should always use metal screws to install internal components, such as adapter cards, disk drives, power supplies, and the motherboard, because the metal screws provide a ground point for these devices.

English Versus Metric

Another area of aggravation with hardware is the fact that two types of thread systems exist: English and metric. IBM used mostly English-threaded fasteners in its original line of systems, but many other manufacturers used metric-threaded fasteners.

The difference between the two becomes especially apparent with disk drives. American-manufactured drives typically use English fasteners, whereas drives made in Japan, Taiwan, and other Pacific Rim countries (where most disk drives are now made) typically use metric. Whenever you replace a floppy drive in an older PC, you encounter this problem. Try to buy the correct screws and any other hardware, such as brackets, with the drive because they might be difficult to find as separate items. Many drive manufacturers offer retail drive kits that include all the required mounting components. The OEM's drive manual lists the correct data about a specific drive's hole locations and thread size.

Tip

Before you discard an obsolete computer, remove the screws and other reusable parts, such as drive bay and expansion slot cover plates, jumper blocks, drive rails, and so on. Label the bag or container with the name and model of the computer to help you more easily determine where else you can use the parts later.

Hard disks can use either English or metric fasteners; check your particular drive to see which type it uses. Most drives today use metric hardware.

Caution

Some screws in a system can be length-critical, especially screws used to retain hard disk drives. You can destroy some hard disks by using a mounting screw that's too long; the screw can puncture or dent the sealed disk chamber when you install the drive and fully tighten the screw. When you install a new drive in a system, always make a trial fit of the hardware to see how far the screws can be inserted into the drive before they interfere with its internal components. When in doubt, the drive manufacturer's OEM documentation will tell you precisely which screws are required and how long they should be. Most drives sold at retail include correct-length mounting screws, but OEM drives usually don't include screws or other hardware.

Test Equipment

In some cases, you must use specialized devices to test a system board or component. This test equipment is not expensive or difficult to use, but it can add much to your troubleshooting abilities.

Electrical Testing Equipment

I consider a voltmeter to be required gear for proper system testing. A multimeter can serve many purposes, including checking for voltage signals at various points in a system, testing the output of the power supply, and checking for continuity in a circuit or cable. An outlet tester is an invaluable accessory that can check the electrical outlet for proper wiring. This capability is useful if you believe the problem lies outside the computer system.

Loopback Connectors (Wrap Plugs)

For diagnosing serial- and parallel-port problems, you need loopback connectors (also called *wrap plugs*), which are used to circulate, or wrap, signals (see Figure 22.7). The plugs enable the serial, parallel or USB port to send data to itself for diagnostic purposes.

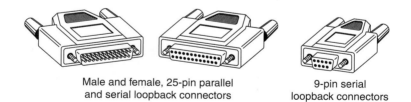

Male and female, 25-pin parallel
and serial loopback connectors

9-pin serial
loopback connectors

Figure 22.7 Typical wrap plugs, including 25-pin and 9-pin serial and 25-pin parallel versions.

Various types of loopback connectors are available. To accommodate all the ports you might encounter, you need one for the 25-pin serial port, one for the 9-pin serial port, one for the 25-pin parallel port, and one for USB 2.0/1.1 ports. Many companies, including IBM, sell the plugs separately, but be aware that you also need diagnostic software that can use them. Some diagnostic software products, such as Micro 2000's Micro-Scope, include loopback connectors with the product, or you can purchase serial and parallel loopback connectors as an option for about $30 a set. Note that there are some variations on how loopback connectors can be made, and not all versions work properly with all diagnostics software. You should therefore use the loopback connectors recommended by the diagnostics software you will be using.

IBM sells a special combination plug that includes all three legacy connector types in one compact unit. The device costs about the same as a normal set of wrap plugs. If you're handy, you can even make your own wrap plugs for testing. I include wiring diagrams for the three types of wrap plugs in Chapter 15, "I/O Interfaces from Serial and Parallel to IEEE 1394 and USB." In that chapter, you also will find a detailed discussion of serial and parallel ports.

Besides simple loopback connectors, you also might want to have a breakout box for your toolkit. A breakout box is a DB25 connector device that enables you to make custom temporary cables or even to monitor signals on a cable. For most PC troubleshooting uses, a "mini" breakout box works well and is inexpensive.

Note

USB loopback plugs and testing software are available from PassMark Software (www.passmark.com).

Meters

Some troubleshooting procedures require that you measure voltage and resistance. You take these measurements by using a handheld digital multimeter (DMM). The meter can be an analog device (using an actual meter) or a digital-readout device. The DMM has a pair of wires called test leads or probes. The test leads make the connections so that you can take readings. Depending on the meter's setting, the probes measure electrical resistance, direct-current (DC) voltage, or alternating-current (AC) voltage. Figure 22.8 shows a typical DMM being used to test the +12V circuit on an ATX motherboard.

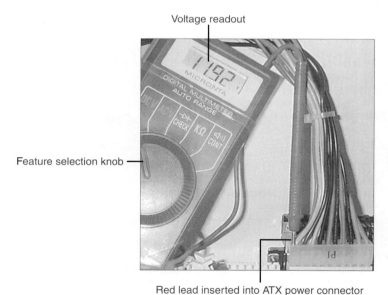

Voltage readout

Feature selection knob

Red lead inserted into ATX power connector

Figure 22.8   A typical digital multimeter tests a motherboard's +12V circuit.

Usually, each system-unit measurement setting has several ranges of operation. DC voltage, for example, usually can be read in several scales, to a maximum of 200 millivolts (mV), 2V, 20V, 200V, and

1,000V. Because computers use both +5V and +12V for various operations, you should use the 20V maximum scale for making your measurements. Making these measurements on the 200mV or 2V scale could "peg the meter" and possibly damage it because the voltage would be much higher than expected. Using the 200V or 1,000V scale works, but the readings at 5V and 12V are so small in proportion to the maximum that accuracy is low.

If you are taking a measurement and are unsure of the actual voltage, start at the highest scale and work your way down. Most of the better meters have autoranging capability—the meter automatically selects the best range for any measurement. This type of meter is much easier to operate. You simply set the meter to the type of reading you want, such as DC volts, and attach the probes to the signal source. The meter selects the correct voltage range and displays the value. Because of their design, these types of meters always have a digital display rather than a meter needle.

Caution

Whenever you are using a multimeter to test any voltage that could potentially be 50V or above (such as AC wall socket voltage), always use one hand to do the testing, not two. Either clip one lead to one of the sources and probe with the other or hold both leads in one hand.

If you hold a lead in each hand and accidentally slip, you can very easily become a circuit, allowing power to conduct or flow through you. When power flows from arm to arm, the path of the current is directly across the heart. The heart muscle tends to quit working when subjected to high voltages. It's funny that way.

I prefer the small digital meters; you can buy them for only slightly more than the analog style, and they're extremely accurate and much safer for digital circuits. Some of these meters are not much bigger than a cassette tape; they fit in a shirt pocket. RadioShack sells a good unit in the $25 price range; the meter (refer to Figure 22.8) is a half-inch thick, weighs 3 1/2 ounces, and is digital and autoranging, as well. This type of meter works well for most, if not all, PC troubleshooting and test uses.

Caution

You should be aware that many analog meters can be dangerous to digital circuits. These meters use a 9V battery to power the meter for resistance measurements. If you use this type of meter to measure resistance on some digital circuits, you can damage the electronics because you essentially are injecting 9V into the circuit. The digital meters universally run on 3V–5V or less.

Logic Probes and Logic Pulsers

A logic probe can be useful for diagnosing problems in digital circuits (see Figure 22.9). In a digital circuit, a signal is represented as either high (+5V) or low (0V). Because these signals are present for only a short time (measured in millionths of a second) or oscillate (switch on and off) rapidly, a simple voltmeter is useless. A logic probe is designed to display these signal conditions easily.

Logic probes are especially useful for troubleshooting a dead system. By using the probe, you can determine whether the basic clock circuitry is operating and whether other signals necessary for system operation are present. In some cases, a probe can help you cross-check the signals at each pin on an integrated circuit chip. You can compare the signals present at each pin with the signals a known-good chip of the same type would show—a comparison that is helpful in isolating a failed component. Logic probes also can be useful for troubleshooting some disk drive problems by enabling you to test the signals present on the interface cable or drive-logic board.

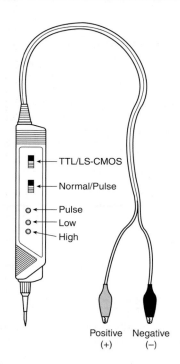

Figure 22.9   A typical logic probe.

A companion tool to the probe is the logic pulser. A *pulser* is designed to test circuit reaction by delivering a logical high (+5V) pulse into a circuit, usually lasting from 1 1/2 to 10 millionths of a second. Compare the reaction with that of a known-functional circuit. This type of device normally is used much less frequently than a logic probe, but in some cases it can be helpful for testing a circuit. Be careful however, because injecting 5V into a circuit designed for 3.3V or less can possibly cause damage.

Outlet (Receptacle) Testers

Outlet testers (also called *receptacle testers*) are very useful test tools. These simple, inexpensive devices, sold in hardware stores, test electrical outlets. You simply plug in the device, and three LEDs light up in various combinations, indicating whether the outlet is wired correctly (see Figure 22.10).

Although you might think that badly wired outlets would be a rare problem, I have seen a large number of installations in which the outlets were wired incorrectly. Most of the time, the problem is in the ground wire. An improperly wired outlet can result in unstable system operation, such as random parity checks and lockups. With an improper ground circuit, currents can begin flowing on the electrical ground circuits in the system. Because the system uses the voltage on the ground circuits as a comparative signal to determine whether bits are 0 or 1, a floating ground can cause data errors in the system.

Caution

Even if you use a surge protector, it will not protect your system from an improperly wired outlet. Therefore, you still should use an outlet tester to ensure your outlet is computer friendly.

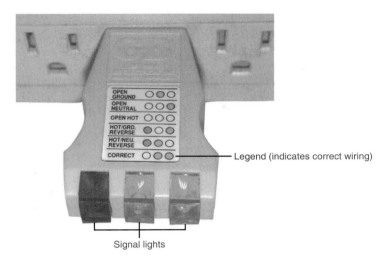

Figure 22.10 A typical outlet/receptacle tester.

Once, while running one of my PC troubleshooting seminars, I used a system that I literally could not approach without locking it up. Whenever I walked past the system, the electrostatic field generated by my body interfered with the system and the PC locked up, displaying a parity-check error message. The problem was that the hotel at which I was giving the seminar was very old and had no grounded outlets in the room. The only way I could prevent the system from locking up was to run the class in my stocking feet because my leather-soled shoes were generating the static charge.

Other symptoms of bad ground wiring in electrical outlets are continual electrical shocks when you touch the case or chassis of the system. These shocks indicate that voltages are flowing where they should not be. This problem also can be caused by bad or improper grounds within the system. By using the simple outlet tester, you can quickly determine whether the outlet is at fault.

If you just walk up to a system and receive an initial shock, it's probably only static electricity. Touch the chassis again without moving your feet. If you receive another shock, something is very wrong. In this case, the ground wire actually has voltage applied to it. You should check the outlet with an outlet/receptacle tester and, if it fails, have a professional electrician check the outlet immediately. If the outlet checks out, the power supply inside the PC is probably failing (even though the system might seem to be otherwise running normally). In such a case, it should be replaced.

Although I recommend using an outlet/receptacle tester, if you don't have one handy, you can test an outlet using a multimeter. First, remember to hold both leads in one hand. Test from one blade hole to another. This should read between 110V and 125V, depending on the electrical service in the area. Then, check from each blade to the ground (the round hole). One blade hole, the smaller one, should show a voltage almost identical to the one you got from the blade hole–to–blade hole test. The larger blade hole when measured to ground should show less than 0.5V.

Because ground and neutral are supposed to be tied together at the electrical panel, a large difference in these readings indicates that they are not tied together. However, small differences can be accounted for by current from other outlets down the line flowing on the neutral, when there isn't any on the ground.

If you don't get the results you expect, call an electrician to test the outlets for you. More weird computer problems are caused by improper grounding and other power problems than people like to believe.

Memory Testers

For high-volume service shops or large corporate environments servicing many systems, a dedicated memory tester can offer efficiency, performance, and accuracy far beyond running memory test software on a PC. These testers are table-top devices designed to evaluate all types of memory modules and even individual chips. The main drawback is that these testers can be somewhat expensive, costing upward of $2,500 or more, but the cost can be justified for those who need to test a lot of memory quickly and accurately.

Without one of these testers, you are reduced to testing memory by running diagnostic programs on the PC and testing the memory as it is installed. This can be very problematic because memory diagnostic programs can do only two things to the memory: write and read. A dedicated memory tester can do many things a memory diagnostic running in a PC can't do, such as

- Identify the type of memory
- Identify the memory speed
- Identify whether the memory has parity or is using bogus parity emulation
- Vary the refresh timing and access speed timing

- Locate single bit failures
- Detect power- and noise-related failures
- Detect solder opens and shorts
- Isolate timing-related failures
- Detect data retention errors

No conventional memory diagnostic software can do these things because it must rely on the fixed access parameters set up by the memory controller hardware in the motherboard chipset. This prevents the software from being capable of altering the timing and methods used to access the memory. You might have memory that fails in one system and works (mostly) in another when the chips are actually bad. This type of intermittent problem is almost impossible to detect with diagnostic software.

The bottom line is that there is no way you can test memory with true accuracy while it is installed in a PC; a memory tester is required for comprehensive and accurate testing. The price of a memory tester can be justified very easily in a shop environment where a lot of PCs are tested because many software and hardware upgrades today require the addition of new memory. With the large increases in the amount of memory in today's systems and the stricter timing requirements of newer motherboard designs, it has become even more important to be able to identify or rule out memory as a cause of system failure. Two companies making testers include CST (www.simmtester.com) and Tanisys (www.tanisys.com).

For smaller companies, repair shops, or individuals, a dedicated memory tester is far too expensive to justify, so for those applications you will be using a PC to test the memory instead. For PC-based memory testing, I recommend two programs:

- **Microsoft Windows Memory Diagnostic**—http://oca.microsoft.com/en/windiag.asp—Also included as part of Windows Vista
- **Memtest86**—http://www.memtest86.com

Both of these programs are available for downloading at no charge. They both offer a comprehensive set of memory tests in a bootable CD-ROM format. (The Windows Vista version of Microsoft Windows Memory Diagnostic can be run from the bootable Windows Vista DVD or configured to run the next time the system is started.) This means that no software needs to be installed on the PC being tested; you merely boot from the test CD and run the diagnostics. The bootable arrangement also means that testing can be done without interference from Windows or other protected-mode operating systems, thus improving the capability and accuracy of the test programs.

◄◄   See Chapter 6, "Memory," for more information on memory in general.

Special Tools for the Enthusiast

All the tools described so far are commonly used by most technicians. However, a few additional tools do exist that a true PC enthusiast might want to have.

Electric Screwdriver

Perhaps the most useful tool I use is an electric screwdriver. It enables me to disassemble and reassemble a PC in record time and makes the job not only faster but easier as well. I like the type with a clutch you can use to set how tight it will make the screws before slipping; such a clutch makes it even faster to use. If you use the driver frequently, it makes sense to use the type with replaceable, rechargeable batteries, so when one battery dies you can quickly replace it with a fresh one.

Caution

Note that using an electric screwdriver when installing a motherboard can be dangerous because the bit can easily slip off the screw and damage the board. A telltale series of swirling scratches near the screw holes on the board can be the result, for which most manufacturers rightfully deny a warranty claim. Be especially careful if your motherboard is retained with Phillips-head screws because they are extremely easy for the bit to slip out of. Normally, I recommend using only Torx-head or hex-head screws to retain the motherboard because they are far more resistant to having the bit slip out and cause damage.

With the electric screwdriver, I recommend getting a complete set of English and metric nut driver tips as well as various sizes of Torx, flat-head, and Phillips-head screwdriver tips.

Tamperproof Torx Bits

Devices such as power supplies and monitors are held together with tamperproof Torx screws. Tamperproof Torx driver sets are available from any good electronics tool supplier.

Temperature Probe

Determining the interior temperature of a PC is often useful when diagnosing whether heat-related issues are causing problems. This requires some way of measuring the temperature inside the PC, as well as the ambient temperature outside the system. The simplest and best tool I've found for the job is the digital thermometers sold at most auto parts stores for automobile use. They are designed to read the temperature inside and outside the car and normally come with an internal sensor, as well as one at the end of a length of wire.

With this type of probe, you can run the wired sensor inside the case (if it is metal, make sure it does not directly touch the motherboard or other exposed circuits where it might cause a short) with the wires slipped through a crack in the case or out one of the drive bays. Then, with the system running you can take the internal temperature as well as read the room's ambient temperature. Normally, the maximum limit for internal temperature should be 110°F (43°C) or less. If your system is running near or above that temperature, problems can be expected. You also can position the probe in the system to be near any heat producing devices, such as the processor, video card, and so on, to see the effect of the device. Probing the temperature with a device such as this enables you to determine whether additional cooling is necessary (that is, adding more cooling fans to the case) and enables you to check to see whether the added fans are helping.

Infrared Thermometer

Another useful temperature tool is a noncontact infrared (IR) thermometer, which is a special type of sensor that can measure the temperature of an object without physically touching it (see

Figure 22.11). You can take the temperature reading of an object in seconds by merely pointing the handheld device at the object you want to measure and pulling a trigger.

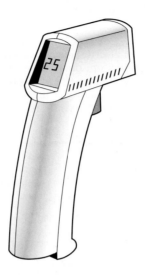

Figure 22.11   A noncontact infrared thermometer.

An IR thermometer works by capturing the infrared energy naturally emitted from all objects warmer than absolute zero (0° Kelvin). Infrared energy is a part of the electromagnetic spectrum with a frequency below that of visible light, which means it is invisible to the human eye. Infrared wavelengths are between 0.7 microns and 1,000 microns (millionths of a meter), although infrared thermometers typically measure radiation in the range 0.7–14 microns.

Because IR thermometers can measure the temperature of objects without touching them, they are ideal for measuring chip temperatures in a running system—especially the temperature of the CPU heatsink. By merely pointing the device at the top of the CPU and pulling the trigger, you can get a very accurate measurement in about 1 second. To enable more accuracy in positioning, many IR thermometers incorporate a laser pointer, which is used to aim the device.

IR thermometers are designed to measure IR radiation from a device; they can't be used to measure air temperature. The sensors are specifically designed so that the air between the sensor and target does not affect the temperature measurement.

Although several IR thermometers are available on the market, I use and recommend the Raytek (www.raytek.com) MiniTemp series, which consists of the MT2, MT4, and MT6. Look for these thermometers in the automotive section of the Raytek website. These units are all but identical; however, the MT4 includes a laser pointer for aiming and the MT6 includes a protective boot, improved distance to spot ratings (10:1 instead of 8:1), and a range of up to 6 feet (instead of 4 feet). The MT2 is capable of measuring temperatures between 0° and 525°F (–18°–270°C) in one-half of a second with an accuracy of about plus or minus 3°F (2°C). The MT4 tops out at 750°F (400°C), and the MT6 can measure temperatures between –20° and 932°F (–30°–500°C). They cost $80–$100 and are available from NAPA auto parts stores (these devices have many uses in automotive testing as well) and other tool outlets.

Large Claw-type Parts Grabber

One of the more useful tools in my toolbox is a large claw-type parts grabber, normally sold in stores that carry automotive tools. Having one of these around has saved many hours of frustration digging back into a system or behind a desk for a loose or dropped screw.

These grabbers are very similar to the small claw-type grabber included with most PC toolkits, except they are much larger—normally two feet or so in length. They can be useful if you drop a screw down inside a tower case, or even on the floor under or behind a desk or cabinet. Although magnetic parts grabbers are also available, I normally recommend the claw-type because using a powerful magnet near a computer can cause problems with any disk storage media you have about, or even the hard disk or CRT-type display.

Preventive Maintenance

Preventive maintenance is the key to obtaining years of trouble-free service from your computer system. A properly administered preventive maintenance program pays for itself by reducing problem behavior, data loss, and component failure and by ensuring a long life for your system. In several cases, I have "repaired" an ailing system with nothing more than a preventive maintenance session. Preventive maintenance also can increase your system's resale value because it will look and run better.

Developing a preventive maintenance program is important to everyone who uses or manages personal computer systems. The two types of preventive maintenance procedures are active and passive.

Passive preventive maintenance includes precautionary steps you can take to protect a system from the environment, such as using power-protection devices; ensuring a clean, temperature-controlled environment; and preventing excessive vibration. In other words, passive preventive maintenance means treating your system well and with care.

An *active* preventive maintenance program includes procedures that promote a longer, trouble-free life for your PC. This type of preventive maintenance primarily involves the periodic cleaning of the system and its components, as well as performing backups, antivirus and antispyware scans, and other software-related procedures. The following sections describe several active preventive maintenance procedures.

Active Preventive Maintenance Procedures

How often you should perform active preventive maintenance procedures depends on the system's environment and the quality of the system's components. If your system is in a dirty environment, such as a machine shop floor or a gas station service area, you might need to clean your system every three months or less. For normal office environments, cleaning a system every few months to a year is usually fine. However, if you open your system after one year and find dust bunnies inside, you should probably shorten the cleaning interval.

Other hard disk preventive maintenance procedures include making periodic backups of your data. Also, depending on which OS and file system you use, you should defragment hard disks at least once a month to maintain disk efficiency and speed.

The following is a sample weekly disk maintenance checklist:

- Back up any data or important files. The Windows Vista File and Folder Backup utility, the Windows XP NTBackup utility, and many third-party programs can be scheduled to run automatically to perform this step.
- Run a full system antivirus and antispyware scan. Before starting the scans, be sure to check for and install antivirus and antispyware software updates. Most of these programs have integrated

update routines that automatically check for updates on a weekly or monthly basis, or at some other interval you choose.

■ Run the Windows Disk Cleanup tool, which searches the system for files you can safely delete, such as

- Files in the Recycle Bin
- Temporary Internet files
- Windows temporary files
- Install programs for previously downloaded and installed programs
- System restore points except the most recent restore point
- Optional Windows components you are not using
- Installed programs you no longer use

■ Finally, run a disk-defragmenting program. Windows Vista's defragment programs runs automatically, but for a more thorough defragmentation, you may prefer a third-party program such as VOPT.

About System Restore

System Restore is an automatic service in Windows Me, XP, and Windows Vista that periodically creates restore points, which are snapshots of the Registry and certain other dynamic system files. These restore points do not include any user or application data and should therefore not be confused with, or used in place of, normal file or data backup procedures. The System Restore application (found in the Program menu under Accessories, System Tools) can be used to manually return a system to a previously created restore point, as well as to manually create a new restore point. You don't typically need to manually create restore points because they are automatically created at the following times:

■ Every time you install an application

■ Every time an update is installed with Automatic Updates

■ Every time an update is installed with Windows Update

■ Every time you install an unsigned driver

■ Every 24 hours if the system is turned on, or if it has been more than 24 hours since the last restore point was created

Even though you don't usually need to create restore points manually, I do recommend creating a manual restore point before editing the Registry directly because that essentially creates a backup of the Registry you can restore if your edit causes problems.

The Windows Vista System Restore program, unlike its predecessors, can be run without booting to the Windows Desktop. You can run it from the Windows Vista DVD's Recovery Environment to restore your system to an earlier condition.

The following are some monthly maintenance procedures you should perform:

■ Create an operating system startup disk, or ensure that you have access to a bootable OS installation CD for recovery purposes. The Complete PC Backup feature in Windows Vista Business and Ultimate editions creates a full operating system image that can be restored to an empty hard disk. Similar "bare metal" disaster recovery backups are available from third-party backup vendors.

- Check for and install any updated drivers for video cards, sound cards, modems, and other devices.

- Check for and install any operating system updates. If you have Automatic Updates turned on (recommended), this is done automatically for you.

- Clean the system, including the monitor screen, keyboard, CD/DVD drives, floppy drive, mouse, and so on.

- Check that all system fans are operating properly, including the CPU heatsink, power supply, and any chassis fans. You can use the system BIOS readout of fan speeds (located in the hardware monitor or PC health screens) to perform a quick check. Some motherboards and systems include utility programs that display this information within Windows. Open the system to examine any fans that aren't working or are running more slowly than normal.

System Backups

One of the most important preventive maintenance procedures is the performance of regular system backups. A sad reality in the computer repair and servicing world is that hardware can always be repaired or replaced, but data cannot. Many hard disk troubleshooting and service procedures, for example, require that you repartition or reformat the disk, which overwrites all existing data.

The hard disk drive capacity in a typical PC has grown far beyond the point at which floppy disks are a viable backup solution. Backup solutions that employ floppy disk drives, such as DOS backup software, are insufficient and too costly for hard disk backups in today's systems. Table 22.8 shows the number of units of various types of media required to back up an 80GB drive.

Table 22.8   Amounts and Costs of Various Media Required to Back Up a Full 80GB Drive

Media Type	Number Required	Unit Cost	Net Cost
1.44M floppy disks	54,883	$0.15	$8,232
80-minute/700MB CD-R discs	109	$0.25	$27
DVD+/-R discs	18	$0.50	$9
DVD+/-R DL discs	11	$2	$22
DAT DDS-4 tapes (native)	4	$9	$60
DAT DDS-4 tapes (compressed)	2	$9	$30
DAT72 tapes (native)	3	$15	$45
DAT72 tapes (compressed)	2	$15	$30

Assuming the drive were full, it would take 54,883 1.44MB floppy disks, for example, to back up an 80GB hard disk! That would cost more than $8,232 in disks, not to mention the time involved. As you can see, even using CDs would be miserable, requiring 109 discs to back up the entire drive. Using recordable DVDs, on the other hand, would require only 18 discs, or a bit over half that for dual-layer discs, which still wouldn't be much fun but might be adequate in a pinch. Tape, however, really shines here because it would require only two DAT DDS-4 or DAT72 tapes to back up the entire drive, meaning I would have to switch tapes in the drive only once.

The two main tape standards used for PC backups are Travan and DAT (digital audio tape). Travan drives are generally slower and hold less than the newest DAT drives, but both are available in relatively competitive versions. The latest Travan tape drives store 20GB/40GB (raw/compressed) on a single tape, whereas DAT72 drives store 36/72GB per tape. These tapes typically cost $15 or less. If you use larger drives, new versions of DAT and other technologies can be used to back up your drive.

Although the media for a CD-RW drive are quite inexpensive, it would take several discs to back up a multigigabyte hard drive, adding a measure of inconvenience to the backup process that makes it far less likely to be performed on a regular basis. Rewritable DVD drives can store 4.7GB (uncompressed) on a single DVD, and media costs drop to around $1 per disc in quantities. A rewritable DVD drive has about the same overall media costs for a backup as compared to a CD-RW drive, but reduces the amount of media required considerably. However, it still requires the operator to swap backup media periodically when more than 4.7GB of data must be backed up, and it requires you to use multiple sets of media.

Although tape or optical discs seem like a good alternative at a glance, the truth is that hard drives have increased in size well beyond what these backup media can handle. Even 80GB hard drives are considered quite small by today's standards, now that drives of 1TB or more are available. I just don't know anything that can adequately backup a large hard disk other than another large hard disk. With the relatively low cost of drives these days, this is an economical, fast, and efficient method; however, if a disaster occurs, such as theft or fire, you can still easily lose everything. Also, with only one backup, if your backup goes bad when you depend on it, you'll be without any other alternatives. I recommend making at least two or three backups of any important data, which usually requires many additional drives for backup.

A RAID 1 array automatically mirrors the contents of one drive to another (refer to Chapter 7, "The ATA/IDE Interface," for details); many motherboards now have built-in SATA RAID adapters. But RAID is not backup. RAID gives you redundancy, but backups are still important. I was reminded about this after building a server for a business that included six 320GB drives in a RAID 5 array. RAID 5 uses the capacity of one drive for parity storage, so the total capacity of the resulting volume was 1,600MB (1.6TB). All was fine until one of the drives failed. Due to the use of RAID 5, all of the data was still available; however, the array was now in a perilous state, because if another drive failed, all data would be lost. None of the data was backed up, so the business went out and purchased several USB external drives in order to back up the data as quickly as possible. There was a heart-stopping moment during the backup procedure when it seemed as if another one of the drives in the array had failed, resulting in a total loss of data! However, a reboot seemed to put things back in order, and the backup was completed successfully. After the backup was finished, the defective drive in the array was replaced (hot swapped) and the array began rebuilding itself automatically. After all of this sweat and downtime, the business owners realized that having a single 1.6TB server was dangerous; they realized that they needed another just to act as a backup of the first, plus at least one more set of 1.6TB worth of external drives for additional backups as well.

Because drive capacities have grown significantly in recent years, the best form of backup is often one or more external hard drives. You can perform hard disk–based backups for more than one system with an external hard drive. External hard disks are available in capacities up to 1TB or more and don't require media swapping. Some models even offer one-button backups. Small servers can easily be assembled with many terabytes worth of storage as well. However, you might eventually want to move the data on the external drive over to CD, DVD, or tape media for permanent storage. Hard drive prices have fallen such that backup from drive to drive is often the most economical alternative, given the relative capacity and speed available. In most cases, you should consider using two external drives of equal or larger capacity than your main drive. That way, you can alternate backups to the external drives and move one of them offsite between backups. This provides an extra level of protection and insurance from disaster.

Tip

No matter which backup solution you use, the entire exercise is pointless if you cannot restore your data from the storage medium. You should test your backup system by performing random file restores at regular intervals to ensure the viability of your data.

If your backup supports disaster recovery, be sure to test this feature as well by installing an empty drive and using the disaster recovery feature to rebuild the operating system and restore the data.

Cleaning a System

One of the most important operations in a good preventive maintenance program is regular and thorough cleaning of the system. Dust buildup on the internal components can lead to several problems. One is that the dust acts as a thermal insulator, which prevents proper system cooling. Excessive heat shortens the life of system components and adds to the thermal stress problem caused by greater temperature changes between the system's power-on and power-off states. Additionally, the dust can contain conductive elements that can cause partial short circuits in a system. Other elements in dust and dirt can accelerate corrosion of electrical contacts, resulting in improper connections. In all, the regular removal of any layer of dust and debris from within a computer system benefits that system in the long run.

Tip

Cigarette smoke contains chemicals that can conduct electricity and cause corrosion of computer parts. The smoke residue can infiltrate the entire system, causing corrosion and contamination of electrical contacts and sensitive components, such as floppy drive read/write heads and optical drive lens assemblies. You should avoid smoking near computer equipment and encourage your company to develop and enforce a similar policy.

Floppy disk drives are particularly vulnerable to the effects of dirt and dust. A floppy drive is essentially a large "hole" in the system case through which air continuously flows. Therefore, these drives accumulate a large amount of dust and chemical buildup within a short time. Hard disk drives, on the other hand, do not present quite the same problem. Because the head disk assembly (HDA) in a hard disk is a sealed unit with a single barometric vent, no dust or dirt can enter without passing through the barometric vent filter. This filter ensures that contaminating dust and particles cannot enter the interior of the HDA. Thus, cleaning a hard disk requires blowing off the dust and dirt from outside the drive. No internal cleaning is required.

Disassembly and Cleaning Tools

Properly cleaning the system and all the boards inside requires certain supplies and tools. In addition to the tools required to disassemble the unit, you should have these items:

- Contact cleaning solution
- Canned air
- A small brush
- Lint-free foam cleaning swabs
- Antistatic wrist-grounding strap

You also might want to acquire these optional items:

- Foam tape
- Low-volatile room-temperature vulcanizing (RTV) sealer
- Silicone-type lubricant
- Computer vacuum cleaner

These simple cleaning tools and chemical solutions enable you to perform most common preventive maintenance tasks.

Chemicals

Chemicals can be used to help clean, troubleshoot, and even repair a system. You can use several types of cleaning solutions with computers and electronic assemblies. Most fall into the following categories:

- Standard cleaners
- Contact cleaner/lubricants
- Dusters

Tip

The makeup of many of the chemicals used for cleaning electronic components has been changing because many of the chemicals originally used are now considered environmentally unsafe. They have been attributed to damaging the earth's ozone layer. Chlorine atoms from chlorofluorocarbons (CFCs) and chlorinated solvents attach themselves to ozone molecules and destroy them. Many of these chemicals are now strictly regulated by federal and international agencies in an effort to preserve the ozone layer. Most of the companies that produce chemicals used for system cleaning and maintenance have had to introduce environmentally safe replacements. The only drawback is that many of these safer chemicals cost more and usually do not work as well as those they've replaced.

Standard Cleaners

For the most basic function—cleaning components, electrical connectors, and contacts—one of the most useful chemicals is 1,1,1-trichloroethane. This substance is an effective cleaner that was at one time used to clean electrical contacts and components because it does not damage most plastics and board materials. In fact, trichloroethane is very useful for cleaning stains on the system case and keyboard as well. Unfortunately, trichloroethane is now being regulated as a chlorinated solvent, along with CFCs (chlorofluorocarbons) such as Freon, but electronic chemical-supply companies are offering several replacements.

Alternative cleaning solutions are available in a variety of types and configurations. You can use pure isopropyl alcohol, acetone, trichloroethane, or a variety of other chemicals. Most board manufacturers and service shops are now leaning toward alcohol, acetone, or other chemicals that do not cause ozone depletion and comply with government regulations and environmental safety.

Recently, new biodegradable cleaners described as "citrus-based cleaners" have become popular in the industry, and in many cases are more effective and more economical for circuit board and contact cleaning. These cleaners are commonly known as d-limonene or citrus terpenes and are derived from orange peels, which gives them a strong (but pleasant) citric odor. Another type of terpene is called a-pinene, and is derived from pine trees. You must exercise care when using these cleaners, however, because they can cause swelling of some plastics, especially silicone rubber and PVC.

You should make sure your cleaning solution is designed to clean computers or electronic assemblies. In most cases, this means that the solution should be chemically pure and free from contaminants or other unwanted substances. You should not, for example, use drugstore rubbing alcohol for cleaning electronic parts or contacts because it is not pure and could contain water or perfumes. The material must be moisture-free and residue-free. The solutions should be in liquid form, not a spray. Sprays can be wasteful, and you almost never spray the solution directly on components. Instead, wet a foam or chamois swab used for wiping the component. These electronic-component cleaning solutions are available at any good electronics parts store.

Contact Cleaner/Lubricants

These chemicals are similar to the standard cleaners but include a lubricating component. The lubricant eases the force required when plugging and unplugging cables and connectors, reducing strain on the devices. The lubricant coating also acts as a conductive protectant that insulates the contacts from corrosion. These chemicals can greatly prolong the life of a system by preventing intermittent contacts in the future.

A unique type of contact enhancer and lubricant called Stabilant 22 is currently on the market. This chemical, which you apply to electrical contacts, greatly enhances the connection and lubricates the contact point; it is much more effective than conventional contact cleaners or lubricants.

Stabilant 22 is a liquid-polymer semiconductor; it behaves like liquid metal and conducts electricity in the presence of an electric current. The substance also fills the air gaps between the mating surfaces of two items that are in contact, making the surface area of the contact larger and also keeping out oxygen and other contaminants that can corrode the contact point.

This chemical is available in several forms. Stabilant 22 is the concentrated version, whereas Stabilant 22a is a version diluted with isopropanol in a 4:1 ratio. An even more diluted 8:1-ratio version is sold in many high-end stereo and audio shops under the name Tweek. Just 15ml of Stabilant 22a sells for about $40; a liter of the concentrate costs about $4,000!

As you can plainly see, Stabilant 22 is fairly expensive, but little is required in an application, and nothing else has been found to be as effective in preserving electrical contacts. (NASA uses the chemical on spacecraft electronics.) An application of Stabilant can provide protection for up to 16 years, according to its manufacturer, D.W. Electrochemicals. You will find the company's address and phone number in the Vendor List on the accompanying disc.

Stabilant is especially effective on I/O slot connectors, adapter-card edge and pin connectors, disk drive connectors, power-supply connectors, and virtually any connector in the PC. In addition to enhancing the contact and preventing corrosion, an application of Stabilant lubricates the contacts, making insertion and removal of the connector easier.

Dusters

Compressed gas often is used as an aid in system cleaning. You use the compressed gas as a blower to remove dust and debris from a system or component. Originally, these dusters used CFCs (chlorofluorocarbons) such as Freon, whereas modern dusters use either HFCs (hydrofluorocarbons such as difluoroethane) or carbon dioxide, neither of which is known to damage the ozone layer. Be careful when you use these devices because some of them can generate a static charge when the compressed gas leaves the nozzle of the can. Be sure you are using the type approved for cleaning or dusting off computer equipment, and consider wearing a static grounding strap as a precaution. The type of compressed-air cans used for cleaning camera equipment can sometimes differ from the type used for cleaning static-sensitive computer components.

When using these compressed air products, be sure you hold the can upright so that only gas is ejected from the nozzle. If you tip the can, the raw propellant will come out as a cold liquid, which not only is wasteful but can damage or discolor plastics. You should use compressed gas only on equipment that is powered off, to minimize any chance of damage through short circuits.

Closely related to compressed-air products are chemical-freeze sprays. These sprays are used to quickly cool down a suspected failing component, which often temporarily restores it to normal operation. These substances are not used to repair a device, but to confirm that you have found a failed device. Often, a component's failure is heat-related, and cooling it temporarily restores it to normal operation. If the circuit begins operating normally, the device you are cooling is the suspect device.

Vacuum Cleaners

Some people prefer to use a vacuum cleaner instead of canned gas dusters for cleaning a system. Canned gas is usually better for cleaning in small areas. A vacuum cleaner is more useful when you are cleaning a system loaded with dust and dirt. You can use the vacuum cleaner to suck out the dust and debris instead of simply blowing it around on the other components, which sometimes happens with canned air. For onsite servicing (when you are going to the location of the equipment instead of the equipment coming to you), canned air is easier to carry in a toolkit than a small vacuum cleaner. Tiny vacuum cleaners also are available for system cleaning. These small units are easy to carry and can serve as an alternative to compressed air cans.

Some special vacuum cleaners are specifically designed for use on and around electronic components; they are designed to minimize electrostatic discharge (ESD) while in use. If you are using a regular vacuum cleaner and not one specifically designed with ESD protection, you should take precautions, such as wearing a grounding wrist strap. Also, if the cleaner has a metal nozzle, be careful not to touch it to the circuit boards or components you are cleaning.

Brushes and Swabs

You can use a small makeup, photographic, or paint brush to carefully loosen the accumulated dirt and dust inside a PC before spraying it with canned air or using the vacuum cleaner. Be careful about generating static electricity, however. In most cases, you should not use a brush directly on circuit boards, but only on the case interior and other parts, such as fan blades, air vents, and keyboards. Wear a grounded wrist strap if you are brushing on or near any circuit boards, and brush slowly and lightly to prevent static discharges from occurring.

Use cleaning swabs to wipe off electrical contacts and connectors, floppy or tape drive heads, and other sensitive areas. The swabs should be made of foam or synthetic chamois material that does not leave lint or dust residue. Unfortunately, proper foam or chamois cleaning swabs are more expensive than typical cotton swabs. Do not use cotton swabs because they leave cotton fibers on everything they touch. Cotton fibers are conductive in some situations and can remain on drive heads, which can scratch disks. Foam or chamois swabs can be purchased at most electronics supply stores.

Caution

One item to avoid is an eraser for cleaning contacts. Many people (including me) have recommended using a soft pencil-type eraser for cleaning circuit-board contacts. Testing has proven this to be bad advice for several reasons. One reason is that any such abrasive wiping on electrical contacts generates friction and an ESD. This ESD can be damaging to boards and components, especially the newer low-voltage devices. These devices are especially static sensitive, and cleaning the contacts without a proper liquid solution is not recommended. Also, the eraser will wear off the gold coating on many contacts, exposing the tin contact underneath, which rapidly corrodes when exposed to air.

Some companies sell premoistened contact cleaning pads soaked in a proper contact cleaner and lubricant. These pads are safe to wipe on conductors and contacts with no likelihood of ESD damage or abrasion of the gold plating.

Silicone Lubricants

You can use a silicone lubricant such as WD-40 to lubricate the door mechanisms on floppy disk drives and any other part of the system that might require clean, non-oily lubrication. Other items you can lubricate are the disk drive–head slider rails and even printer-head slider rails, to provide smoother operation.

Using silicone instead of conventional oils is important because silicone does not gum up and collect dust and other debris. Always use the silicone sparingly. Do not spray it anywhere near the equipment because it tends to migrate and will end up where it doesn't belong (such as on drive heads). Instead, apply a small amount to a toothpick or foam swab and dab the silicone lubricant on the components where needed. You can use a lint-free cleaning stick soaked in silicone to lubricate the metal print-head rails in a printer.

Obtaining the Required Tools and Accessories

You can obtain most of the cleaning chemicals and tools discussed in this chapter from an electronics supply house, or even your local RadioShack. A company called Chemtronics specializes in chemicals for the computer and electronics industry. These and other companies that supply tools, chemicals, and other computer and electronic cleaning supplies are listed in the Vendor List on the accompanying disc. With all these items on hand, you should be equipped for most preventive maintenance operations.

Disassembling and Cleaning Procedures

To properly clean your system, you must at least partially disassemble it. Some people go as far as to remove the motherboard. Removing the motherboard results in the best possible access to other areas of the system; but in the interest of saving time, you probably need to disassemble the system only to the point at which the motherboard is completely visible.

To do this, remove all the system's plug-in adapter cards and the disk drives. Complete system disassembly and reassembly procedures are listed in Chapter 20, "Building or Upgrading Systems." Although you can clean the heads of a floppy drive with a cleaning disk without opening the system unit's cover, you probably will want to do more thorough cleaning. In addition to the drive heads, you should clean and lubricate the door mechanism and clean any logic boards and connectors on the drive. This procedure usually requires removing the drive. If you use tape backup drives, you should use the cleaning cartridge recommended by the drive vendor and allow the system to dry thoroughly (if a wet-type cleaner is used) before performing a backup.

Next, do the same thing with the hard disk drives: Clean the logic boards and connectors, and lubricate the grounding strap. To do this, you must remove the hard disk assembly. As a precaution, be sure your data is backed up first.

Cleaning Boards

After reseating any socketed devices that might have crept out of their sockets (see the Technical Reference on the disc for details), the next step is to clean the boards and all connectors in the system. For this step, use the cleaning solutions and the lint-free swabs mentioned earlier.

First, clean the dust and debris off the board and then clean any connectors on the board. To clean the boards, using a vacuum cleaner designed for electronic assemblies and circuit boards or a duster can of compressed gas is usually best. The dusters are especially effective at blasting any dust and dirt off the boards.

Also, blow any dust out of the power supply, especially around the fan intake and exhaust areas. You do not need to disassemble the power supply to do this; simply use a duster can and blast the compressed air into the supply through the fan exhaust port. This will blow the dust out of the supply and clean off the fan blades and grill, which will help with system airflow.

Caution

Be careful with ESD, which can cause damage when you are cleaning electronic components. Take extra precautions in the dead of winter or in extremely dry, high-static environments. You can apply antistatic sprays and treatments to the work area to reduce the likelihood of ESD damage.

An antistatic wrist-grounding strap is recommended (refer to Figure 22.6 earlier in this chapter). This should be connected to a ground on the card or board you are wiping. This strap ensures that no electrical discharge occurs between you and the board. An alternative method is to keep a finger or thumb on the ground of the motherboard or card as you wipe it off.

Cleaning Connectors and Contacts

Cleaning the connectors and contacts in a system promotes reliable connections between devices. On a motherboard, you should clean the slot connectors, power supply connectors, keyboard and mouse connectors, and speaker connector. For most plug-in cards, you should clean the edge connectors that plug into slots on the motherboard and any other connectors, such as external ones mounted on the card bracket.

Submerge the lint-free swabs in the liquid cleaning solution. If you are using the spray, hold the swab away from the system and spray a small amount on the foam end until the solution starts to drip. Then, use the soaked foam swab to wipe the connectors on the boards. Presoaked wipes are the easiest to use—simply wipe them along the contacts to remove any accumulated dirt and leave a protective coating behind.

On the motherboard, pay special attention to the slot connectors. Be liberal with the liquid; resoak the foam swab repeatedly, and vigorously clean the connectors. Don't worry if some of the liquid drips on the surface of the motherboard. These solutions are entirely safe for the whole board and will not damage the components.

Use the solution to wash the dirt off the gold contacts in the slot connectors, and then clean any other connectors on the board. Clean the keyboard and mouse connectors, the grounding positions where screws ground the board to the system chassis, the power-supply connectors, the speaker connectors, and the battery connectors.

If you are cleaning a plug-in board, pay special attention to the edge connector that mates with the slot connector on the motherboard. When people handle plug-in cards, they often touch the gold contacts on these connectors. Touching the gold contacts coats them with oils and debris, which prevents proper contact with the slot connector when the board is installed. Make sure these gold contacts are free of all finger oils and residue. It is a good idea to use one of the contact cleaners that has a conductive lubricant, which makes it easier to push the adapter into the slot and also protects the contacts from corrosion.

You also should use the swab and solution to clean the ends of ribbon cables or other types of cables or connectors in a system. Clean the floppy drive cables and connectors, the hard disk cables and connectors, and any others you find. Don't forget to clean the edge connectors that are on the disk drive logic boards, as well as the power connectors to the drives.

Cleaning the Keyboard and Mouse

Keyboards and ball-type mice are notorious for picking up dirt and garbage. If you ever open up an older keyboard, you will be amazed at the junk you find in there.

To prevent problems, you should periodically clean the keyboard with a vacuum cleaner. An alternative method is to turn the keyboard upside down and shoot it with a can of compressed air. This blows out the dirt and debris that has accumulated inside the keyboard and possibly prevents future problems with sticking keys or dirty keyswitches.

If a particular key is stuck or making intermittent contact, you can soak or spray that switch with contact cleaner. The best way to do this is to first remove the keycap and then spray the cleaner into the switch. This usually does not require complete disassembly of the keyboard. Periodic vacuuming or compressed gas cleaning prevents more serious problems with sticking keys and keyswitches.

Most ball-type mice are easy to clean. In most cases, a twist-off locking retainer keeps the mouse ball retained in the body of the mouse. By removing the retainer, you cause the ball to drop out. After removing the ball, you should clean it with one of the electronic cleaners. I recommend a pure cleaner instead of a contact cleaner with lubricant because you do not want any lubricant on the mouse ball. Then, wipe off the rollers in the body of the mouse with the cleaner and some swabs.

To keep optical or laser mice clean, just check the bottom of the mouse for any dust or debris that might block the light or detector. Use compressed air to remove dust or other extraneous material.

Monthly cleaning of a mouse in this manner eliminates or prevents skipping or erratic movement. I also recommend a mouse pad for most ball-type mice because the pad prevents the mouse ball from picking up debris from your desk.

Other pointing devices requiring little or no maintenance are the IBM-designed TrackPoint and similar systems introduced by other manufacturers, such as the Glidepoint by Alps. These devices are totally sealed and use pressure transducers to control pointer movement. Optical mice that don't use a ball or roller mechanism also require little or no maintenance. Because they are sealed, cleaning need only be performed externally and is as simple as wiping off the device with a mild cleaning solution to remove oils and other deposits that have accumulated from handling them.

Hard Disk Maintenance

Certain preventive maintenance procedures protect your data and ensure that your hard disk works efficiently. Some of these procedures actually minimize wear and tear on your drive, which prolongs its life. Additionally, a high level of data protection can be implemented by performing some simple commands periodically. These commands provide methods for backing up (and possibly later restoring) critical areas of the hard disk that, if damaged, would disable access to all your files.

Defragmenting Files

Over time, as you delete and save files to a hard disk, the files become fragmented. This means they are split into many noncontiguous areas on the disk. One of the best ways to protect both your hard disk and the data on it is to periodically defragment the files on the disk. This serves two purposes. One is that by ensuring that all the files are stored in contiguous sectors on the disk, head movement and drive wear and tear is minimized. This has the added benefit of improving the speed at which the drive retrieves files by reducing the head thrashing that occurs every time it accesses a fragmented file.

The second major benefit, and in my estimation the more important of the two, is that in the case of a disaster in which the file system is severely damaged, the data on the drive can usually be recovered if the files are contiguous. On the other hand, if the files are split up in many pieces across the drive, figuring out which pieces belong to which files is virtually impossible without an intact file system. For the purposes of data integrity and protection, I recommend defragmenting your hard disk drives on a monthly basis.

The three main functions in most defragmentation programs are as follows:

- File defragmentation
- File packing (free space consolidation)
- File sorting

Defragmentation is the basic function, but most other programs also add file packing. Packing the files is optional on some programs because it usually takes additional time to perform. This function packs the files at the beginning of the disk so all free space is consolidated at the end of the disk. This feature minimizes future file fragmentation by eliminating any empty holes on the disk. Because all free space is consolidated into one large area, any new files written to the disk are capable of being written in a contiguous manner with no fragmentationr.

The last function, file sorting (sometimes called *optimizing*), is not usually necessary and is performed as an option by many defragmenting programs. This function adds a tremendous amount of time to the operation because it moves files based on how frequently they are used, even if they are not fragmented. This can have some benefit to performance because files stored near the beginning of a disk read faster than those stored near the middle or end. It can also be somewhat beneficial for disaster recovery purposes because you will have an idea of which files came before or after other files if a disaster occurs. Not all defragmenting programs offer file sorting, and the significant amount of extra time it takes may not be worth the benefits you will receive. Other programs can sort the order that files are listed in directories, which is a quick-and-easy operation compared to sorting the file ordering the disk.

Windows 9x/Me/2000/XP/Vista include a disk defragmentation program with the operating system, which you can use on any file system the OS supports. (Vista's defragmentation utility runs automatically.) For older DOS, Windows 3.x, and some versions of NT, you must purchase a third-party defragmentation program. Norton Utilities includes a disk defragmenter, as do many other utility packages.

If you elect to use a third-party product on a Windows 9x/Me/2000/XP/Vista system, be certain that it supports the file system you use on your drives. Running a FAT16 defragmentation program on a FAT32 drive can cause severe problems. An excellent third-party defrag program that works on all systems is VOPT by Golden Bow. See the Vendor List on the accompanying disc for more information on these programs.

Before you defragment your disks, you should run a disk repair program, such as ScanDisk or Norton Disk Doctor, even if you are not experiencing any problems. This ensures that your drives are in good working order before you begin the defragmentation process.

Windows Maintenance Wizard

Windows 98 and above include a Task Scheduler program that enables you to schedule programs for automatic execution at specified times. The Maintenance Wizard walks you through the steps of scheduling regular disk defragmentations, disk error scans, and deletions of unnecessary files. You can schedule these processes to execute during nonworking hours, so regular system activities are not disturbed.

Virus and Spyware Checking

Viruses and spyware are dangers to any system, and making scans with antivirus and antispyware utilities a regular part of your preventive maintenance program is a good idea. Many aftermarket utility packages are available that scan for and remove viruses and spyware. No matter which of these programs you use, you should perform a scan periodically, especially before making hard disk backups. This helps ensure that you catch any potential problem before it becomes a major catastrophe. In addition, selecting antivirus and antispyware products from vendors that provide regular updates is important. The updates include signatures that determine which virus or spyware programs the software can detect and cure, and because new virus and spyware programs are constantly being introduced, these updates are essential.

Tip

Because viruses and especially spyware are more dangerous and numerous than ever, turn on the firewall feature in your operating system and enable the automatic update feature found in most recent programs to keep your protection up to date. Even with a dialup connection, it takes only a few minutes a day to get downloads. If you have a broadband connection, the latest protection is downloaded in just a few moments. Using the firewall will help prevent many types of virus and other software exploits from attacking your system.

Passive Preventive Maintenance Procedures

Passive preventive maintenance involves taking care of the system by providing the best possible environment—both physical and electrical—for the system. Physical concerns are conditions such as ambient temperature, thermal stress from power cycling, dust and smoke contamination, and disturbances such as shock and vibration. Electrical concerns are items such as ESD, power-line noise, and radio-frequency interference. Each of these environmental concerns is discussed in the following sections.

Examining the Operating Environment

Oddly enough, one of the most overlooked aspects of microcomputer preventive maintenance is protecting the hardware—and the sizable financial investment it represents—from environmental abuse. Computers are relatively forgiving, and they are generally safe in an environment that is comfortable for people. Computers, however, are often treated with no more respect than desktop calculators. The result of this type of abuse is many system failures.

Before you set up a new PC, prepare a proper location for it that is free of airborne contaminants such as smoke or other pollution. Do not place your system in front of a window; the computer should not be exposed to direct sunlight or temperature variations. The environmental temperature should be as constant as possible. Power should be provided through properly grounded outlets and should be stable and free from electrical noise and interference. Keep your system away from radio transmitters or other sources of radio frequency energy.

Note

I also don't recommend using computer desks that place the system unit in a sealed cabinet; this is a good way to promote overheating.

Heating and Cooling

Thermal expansion and contraction from ambient temperature changes place stress on a computer system. Therefore, keeping the temperature in your office or room relatively constant is important to the successful operation of your computer system.

Temperature variations can lead to serious problems. You might encounter excessive chip creep, for example. If extreme variations occur over a short period, signal traces on circuit boards can crack and separate, solder joints can break, and contacts in the system can undergo accelerated corrosion. Solid-state components such as chips can be damaged also, and a host of other problems can develop.

Temperature variations can wreak havoc with hard disk drives, too. On some drives, writing to a disk at different ambient temperatures can cause data to be written at different locations relative to the track centers. This can cause read and write problems at a later time.

To ensure that your system operates in the correct ambient temperature, you must first determine your system's specified functional range. Most manufacturers provide data about the correct operating temperature range for their systems. Two temperature specifications might be available, one indicating allowable temperatures during operation and another indicating allowable temperatures under nonoperating conditions. IBM, for example, has indicate the following temperature ranges as acceptable for most of its systems. (Its personal computer products are now owned and sold by Lenovo.)

> System on: 60°–90° Fahrenheit
>
> System off: 50°–110° Fahrenheit

For the safety of the disk and the data it contains, avoid rapid changes in ambient temperatures. If rapid temperature changes occur—for example, when a new drive is shipped to a location during the winter and then brought indoors—let the drive acclimate to room temperature before turning it on. In extreme cases, condensation can form on the platters inside the drive head-disk assembly (HDA), which is disastrous for the drive if you turn it on before the condensation has a chance to evaporate. Most drive manufacturers specify a timetable to use as a guide in acclimating a drive to room temperature before operating it. You usually must wait several hours to a day before a drive is ready to use after it has been shipped or stored in a cold environment. Manufacturers normally advise that you leave the drive in its packing until it is acclimated. Removing the drive from a shipping carton when extremely cold increases the likelihood of condensation forming as the drive warms up.

Most office environments provide a stable temperature in which to operate a computer system, but some do not. Be sure to give some consideration to the placement of your equipment.

Power Cycling (On/Off)

As you have just learned, the temperature variations a system encounters greatly stress the system's physical components. The largest temperature variations a system encounters, however, are those that occur during the warm-up period right after you turn on the computer. Powering on a cold system subjects it to the greatest possible internal temperature variations. If you want a system to have the longest and most trouble-free life possible, you should limit the temperature variations in its environment. You can limit the extreme temperature cycling in two simple ways during a cold startup: Leave the system off all the time or leave it on all the time. Of these two possibilities, of course, you probably will want to choose the latter option. Leaving the power on is the best way I know to promote system reliability. If your only concern is system longevity, the simple recommendation is to keep the system unit powered on (or off!) continuously. In the real world, however, there are more variables to consider, such as the cost of electricity, the potential fire hazard of unattended running equipment, and other concerns, as well.

If you think about the way light bulbs typically fail, you can begin to understand how thermal cycling can be dangerous. Light bulbs burn out most often when you first turn them on because the filament must endure incredible thermal stress as it changes temperature, in less than one second, from ambient to several thousands of degrees. A bulb that remains on continuously lasts longer than one that is turned on and off repeatedly.

transmitter that suppresses spurious emissions. Unfortunately, problems sometimes persist until the transmitter is either switched off or moved some distance away from the affected computer.

Note

If you depend upon wireless Ethernet (Wi-Fi) networks, keep in mind that the popular 2.4GHz band used by 802.11b, 802.11g, and 802.11n networks is in the same general frequency band as Bluetooth and 2.4GHz wireless phones, so there's plenty of potential for interference.

To avoid interference from other 802.11-based networks, use a program such as Network Stumbler (www.netstumbler.com) to view the frequencies used by other nearby 802.11-based networks, and choose the least-crowded channel from 1, 6, or 11. (The other channels overlap substantially with each other.) To avoid conflicts with wireless phones, upgrade to 5.8GHz or 6GHz phones. To learn more about avoid conflicts with Bluetooth devices, see "Bluetooth," Chapter 18.

Dust and Pollutants

Dirt, smoke, dust, and other pollutants are bad for your system. The power-supply fan carries airborne particles through your system, and they collect inside. If your system is used in an extremely harsh environment, you might want to investigate some of the industrial systems on the market designed for harsh conditions.

Many companies make special hardened versions of their systems for harsh environments. Industrial systems typically use a different cooling system from the one used in regular PCs. A large cooling fan is used to pressurize the case rather than depressurize it. The air pumped into the case passes through a filter unit that must be cleaned and changed periodically. The system is pressurized so that no contaminated air can flow into it; air flows only outward. The only way air can enter is through the fan and filter system.

These systems also might have special keyboards impervious to liquids and dirt. Some flat-membrane keyboards are difficult to type on, but are extremely rugged; others resemble the standard types of keyboards but have a thin, plastic membrane that covers all the keys. You can add this membrane to normal types of keyboards to seal them from the environment.

A relatively new breed of humidifier can cause problems with computer equipment. This type of humidifier uses ultrasonics to generate a mist of water sprayed into the air. The extra humidity helps cure problems with static electricity resulting from a dry climate, but the airborne water contaminants can cause many problems. If you use one of these systems, you might notice a white, ash-like deposit forming on components. The deposit is the result of abrasive and corrosive minerals suspended in the vaporized water. If these deposits collect on the system components, they can cause all kinds of problems. The only safe way to run one of these ultrasonic humidifiers is to use distilled water. If you use a humidifier, be sure it does not generate these deposits.

If you do your best to keep the environment for your computer equipment clean, your system will run better and last longer. Also, you will not have to open up your unit as often for complete preventive maintenance cleaning.

Troubleshooting Tips and Techniques

Troubleshooting PC hardware problems can seem daunting to the uninitiated, but in reality it is much simpler than it seems. Most problems can be diagnosed and corrected using few, if any, special tools and can be accomplished by anybody who can apply simple deductive reasoning and logical thinking. PCs have become more complicated and yet simpler all at the same time. More and more complex internal circuits mean that there are potentially more things that can go wrong—more ways the system can fail. On the other hand, today's complex circuits are embedded into fewer boards, with fewer chips on each board and more serial interconnections using fewer pins (fewer wires). The internal consolidation means that isolating which replaceable component has failed is in many ways simpler than ever before. An understanding of the basics of how PCs work, combined with some very simple tools, some basic troubleshooting tips, and logical thinking and common sense, will enable you to effectively diagnose and repair your own systems, saving a tremendous amount of money over taking it to a shop. In some cases, you can save enough money to practically pay for an entire new system. The bottom line with troubleshooting PC problems is that a solution exists for every problem, and through simple practices combined with deductive reasoning, that solution can easily be found.

Modern PCs—More Complicated and More Reliable

Consider this: The modern PC is an incredible collection of hardware and software. Focusing specifically on the hardware, between 50 and more than 400 million transistors exist in modern processors. In addition, nearly 8.6 billion transistors are in 1GB of RAM; hundreds of millions of transistors exist in the motherboard chipset, video processor, and video RAM; and millions more are in the other adapter cards or logic boards in the system. Each of these billions of interconnected transistors must not only function properly, but also operate in an orderly fashion within strictly enforced timing windows, some of which are measured in picoseconds (trillionths of a second). When you realize that your PC will lock up or crash if any one of these transistors fails to operate properly and on time—and/or any one of the billions of circuit paths and interconnections between the transistors or devices containing them fails in any way—it is a wonder that PCs work at all!

Every time I turn on one of my systems and watch it boot up, I think about the billions upon billions of components and trillions upon trillions of machine/program steps and sequences that have to function properly to get there. As you can now see, many opportunities exist for problems to arise.

Although modern PCs are exponentially more complicated than their predecessors, from another point of view they have become simpler and more reliable. When you consider the complexity of the modern PC, it is not surprising that problems occasionally do arise. However, modern design and manufacturing techniques have made PCs more reliable and easier to service despite their ever-increasing internal complexity. Today's systems have fewer and fewer replaceable components and individual parts, which is a bit of a paradox. The truth is that, as PCs have become more complex, they have also become simpler and easier to service in many ways.

Industry-standard Replaceable Components

The use of industry-standard components is one of the key features of a PC. This means that virtually all the parts that make up a system are interchangeable with other systems in some manner. This also means that the parts are plentiful, inexpensive, and generally very easy to install. A typical PC contains the following replaceable components, most of which are made to industry standards for design and form factor:

- Motherboard
- Processor
- CPU heatsink/fan
- RAM
- CMOS battery
- Chassis with optional fan
- Power supply
- Video card*
- Monitor
- Sound card*
- Speakers
- Network card*
- Hard drive
- CD-ROM/RW drive
- DVD-ROM/+RW drive
- Floppy drive
- Drive cables
- Keyboard
- Mouse

May be integrated into the motherboard in some systems.

Although some of the more well-optioned systems might have even more components than listed here, you can see that most PCs have fewer than 20 replaceable "parts." Some can have as few as 10–15, depending on how many options are present and how they are integrated. From a hardware troubleshooting or repair perspective, one of these components is either improperly installed (configured) or defective. If it's improperly installed or configured, the component can be repaired by merely reinstalling it or configuring it properly. If it's truly defective, the component must simply be replaced. When a PC is broken down to the basic replaceable parts, you can see that it really isn't that complicated, which is why I've spent my career helping people to easily perform their own repairs or upgrades and even build entire systems from scratch.

Reinstall or Replace?

When dealing with hardware problems, the first simple truth to understand is that you do not usually *repair* anything—you *reinstall* or *replace* it instead. You reinstall because the majority of PC hardware problems are caused by a particular component being improperly installed or configured. I remember hearing from IBM many years ago that it had found that 60% or more of the problems handled by its service technicians were due to improper installation or configuration, meaning the hardware was not actually defective. This was, in fact, the major impetus behind the plug-and-play revolution, which has eliminated the need to manually configure jumpers and switches on most hardware devices. This has thus minimized the expertise necessary to install hardware properly and has also minimized installation, configuration, and resource conflict problems. Still, plug and play has sometimes been called *plug and pray* because it does not always work perfectly, sometimes requiring manual intervention to make it work properly.

You replace because of the economics of the situation with computer hardware. The bottom line is that it financially is much cheaper to replace a failed circuit board with a new one than to repair it. For example, you can purchase a new, state-of-the-art motherboard for around $100, but repairing an existing board normally costs much more than that. Modern boards use surface-mounted chips that have pin spacing measured in hundredths of an inch, requiring sophisticated and expensive equipment to attach and solder the chip. Even if you could figure out which chip had failed and had the equipment to replace it, the chips themselves are usually sold in quantities of thousands and obsolete chips are usually not available. The net effect of all of this is that the replaceable components in your PC have become disposable technology. Even a component as large and comprehensive as the motherboard is replaced rather than repaired.

Troubleshooting by Replacing Parts

You can troubleshoot a PC in several ways, but in the end it often comes down to simply reinstalling or replacing parts. That is why I normally use a simple "known-good spare" technique that requires very little in the way of special tools or sophisticated diagnostics. In its simplest form, say you have two identical PCs sitting side by side. One of them has a hardware problem; in this example let's say the memory module (DIMM) is defective. Depending on how and where the defect lies, this could manifest itself in symptoms ranging from a completely dead system to one that boots up normally but crashes when running Windows or software applications. You observe that the system on the left has the problem but the system on the right works perfectly—they are otherwise identical. The simplest technique for finding the problem would be to swap parts from one system to another, one at a time, retesting after each swap. At the point when the DIMMs were swapped, upon powering up and testing (in this case testing is nothing more than allowing the system to boot up and run some of the installed applications), the problem has now moved from one system to the other. Knowing that the last item swapped over was the DIMM, you have just identified the source of the problem! This did not require an expensive ($2,000 or more) DIMM test machine or any diagnostics software. Because components such as DIMMs are not economical to repair, replacing the defective DIMM would be the final solution.

Although this is very simplistic, it is often the quickest and easiest way to identify a problem component as opposed to specifically testing each item with diagnostics. Instead of having an identical system standing by to borrow parts from, most technicians have an inventory of what they call "known-good spare" parts. These are parts that have been previously used, are known to be functional, and can be used to replace a suspicious part in a problem machine. However, this is different from new replacement parts because, when you open a box containing a new component, you really can't be 100% sure that it works. I've been in situations in which I've had a defective component and replaced it with another (unknown to me) defective *new* component and the problem remained. Not knowing that the new part I just installed was also defective, I wasted a lot of time checking other parts that were not the problem. This technique is also effective because so few parts are needed to make up a PC and the known-good parts don't always have to be the same (for example, a lower-end video card can be substituted in a system to verify that the original card had failed).

Troubleshooting by the Bootstrap Approach

Another variation on this theme is the "bootstrap approach," which is especially good for what seems to be a dead system. In this approach, you take the system apart to strip it down to the bare-minimum necessary, functional components and then test it to see whether it works. For example, you might strip down a system to the chassis/power supply, bare motherboard, CPU (with heatsink), one bank of RAM, and a video card with display and then power it up to see whether it works. In that stripped configuration, you should see the POST or splash (logo) screen on the display, verifying that the motherboard, CPU, RAM, video card, and display are functional. If a keyboard is connected, you should see the three LEDs (capslock, scrlock, and numlock) flash within a few seconds after powering on. This indicates that the CPU and motherboard are functioning because the POST routines are testing the keyboard. After you get the system to a minimum of components that are functional, you should reinstall or add one part at a time, testing the system each time you make a change to verify it still works and that the part you added or changed is not the cause of a problem. Essentially, you are rebuilding the system from scratch using the existing parts, but doing it one step at a time.

Many times problems are caused by corrosion on contacts or connectors, so the mere act of disassembling and reassembling a PC will "magically" repair it. Over the years, I've disassembled, tested, and reassembled many systems only to find no problems after the reassembly. How can merely taking it apart and reassembling repair a problem? Although it might seem that nothing was changed and everything is installed exactly like it was before, in reality simply unplugging and replugging renews all the slot and cable connections between devices, which is often all the system needs. Some useful troubleshooting tips include the following:

- Eliminate unnecessary variables or components that are not pertinent to the problem.

- Reinstall, reconfigure, or replace only one component at a time.

- Test after each change you make.

- Keep a detailed record (write it down) of each step you take.

- Don't give up! Every problem has a solution.

- If you hit a roadblock, take a break or work on another problem. A fresh approach the next day often reveals things you overlooked.

- Don't overlook the simple or obvious. Double- and triple-check the installation and configuration of each component.

- Keep in mind that the power supply is one of the most failure-prone parts in a PC, as well as one of the most overlooked components. A high-output "known-good" spare power supply is highly recommended to use for testing suspect systems.

- Cables and connections are also a major cause of problems, so keep replacements of all types on hand.

Before starting any system troubleshooting, you should perform a few basic steps to ensure a consistent starting point and to enable isolating the failed component:

1. Turn off the system and any peripheral devices. Disconnect all external peripherals from the system, except for the keyboard and video display.

2. Make sure the system is plugged into a properly grounded power outlet.

3. Make sure the keyboard and video displays are connected to the system. Turn on the video display, and turn up the brightness and contrast controls to at least two-thirds of the maximum. Some displays have onscreen controls that might not be intuitive. Consult the display documentation for more information on how to adjust these settings. If you can't get any video display but the system seems to be working, try moving the card to a different slot (not possible with AGP video adapters) or try a different video card or monitor.

4. To enable the system to boot from a hard disk, make sure no floppy disk is in the floppy drive. Alternatively, put a known-good bootable floppy with DOS or diagnostics on it in the floppy drive for testing. On systems without floppy drives, use a bootable CD or DVD.

5. Turn on the system. Observe the power supply, chassis fans (if any), and lights on either the system front panel or power supply. If the fans don't spin and the lights don't light, the power supply or motherboard might be defective.

6. Observe the power-on self test (POST). If no errors are detected, the system beeps once and boots up. Errors that display onscreen (*nonfatal* errors) and that do not lock up the system display a text message that varies according to BIOS type and version. Record any errors that occur and refer to the disc accompanying this book for a list of BIOS error codes for more information on any specific codes you see. Errors that lock up the system (*fatal* errors) are indicated by a series of audible beeps. Refer to the disc for a list of beep error codes.

7. Confirm that the operating system loads successfully.

Problems During the POST

Problems that occur during the POST are usually caused by incorrect hardware configuration or installation. Actual hardware failure is a far less-frequent cause. If you have a POST error, check the following:

- Are all cables correctly connected and secured?
- Are the configuration settings correct in Setup for the devices you have installed? In particular, ensure the processor, memory, and hard drive settings are correct.
- Are all drivers properly installed?
- Are switches and jumpers on the baseboard correct, if changed from the default settings?
- Are all resource settings on add-in boards and peripheral devices set so that no conflicts exist—for example, two add-in boards sharing the same interrupt?
- Is the power supply set to the proper input voltage (110V–120V or 220V–240V)?
- Are adapter boards and disk drives installed correctly?
- Is a keyboard attached?
- Is a bootable hard disk (properly partitioned and formatted) installed?

- Does the BIOS support the drive you have installed, and if so, are the parameters entered correctly?
- Is a bootable floppy disk installed in drive A:?
- Are all memory SIMMs or DIMMs installed correctly? Try reseating them.
- Is the operating system properly installed?

Hardware Problems After Booting

If problems occur after the system has been running, and without you having made any hardware or software changes, a hardware fault possibly has occurred. Here is a list of items to check in that case:

- Try reinstalling the software that has crashed or refuses to run.
- Try clearing CMOS RAM and running Setup.
- Check for loose cables, a marginal power supply, or other random component failures.
- A transient voltage spike, power outage, or brownout might have occurred. Symptoms of voltage spikes include a flickering video display, unexpected system reboots, and the system not responding to user commands. Reload the software and try again.
- Try reseating the memory modules (SIMMs, DIMMs, or RIMMs).

Problems Running Software

Problems running application software (especially new software) are usually caused by or related to the software itself, or are due to the fact that the software is incompatible with the system. Here is a list of items to check in that case:

- Does the system meet the minimum hardware requirements for the software? Check the software documentation to be sure.
- Check to see that the software is correctly installed. Reinstall if necessary.
- Check to see that the latest drivers are installed.
- Scan the system for viruses using the latest antivirus software.

Problems with Adapter Cards

Problems related to add-in boards are usually related to improper board installation or resource (interrupt, DMA, or I/O address) conflicts. Chapter 4, "Motherboards and Buses," has a detailed discussion of these system resources, what they are, how to configure them, and how to troubleshoot them. Also be sure to check drivers for the latest versions and ensure that the card is compatible with your system and the operating system version you are using.

Sometimes adapter cards can be picky about which slot they are running in. Despite the fact that, technically, a PCI adapter should be able to run in any PCI slot (just as an ISA adapter should be able to run in any ISA slot), minor timing or signal variations sometimes occur from slot to slot. I have found on numerous occasions that simply moving a card from one slot to another can make a failing card begin to work properly. Sometimes moving a card works just by the inadvertent cleaning (wiping) of the contacts that takes place when removing and reinstalling the card, but in other cases I can duplicate the problem by inserting the card back into its original slot. When all else fails, try moving the cards around! Because some motherboards share a single IRQ between two PCI slots, between a PCI and an AGP slot, a PCI and a PCI-Express slot, or a PCI slot and an onboard device, changing one of the PCI cards to another slot can resolve conflicts.

Caution

Note that PCI cards become slot specific after their drivers are installed. By this I mean that if you move the card to another slot, the plug-and-play resource manager sees it as if you have removed one card and installed a new one. You therefore must install the drivers all over again for that card. Don't move a PCI card to a different slot unless you are prepared with all the drivers at hand to perform the driver installation. ISA cards don't share this quirk because the system is not aware of which slot an ISA card is in.

Top Troubleshooting Problems

These are some of the most frequently asked troubleshooting questions I receive.

When I power the system on, I see the power LED light and hear the fans spin, but nothing else ever happens.

The fact that the LEDs illuminate and fans spin indicates that the power supply is partially working, but that does not exclude it from being defective. This is a classic "dead" system, which can be caused by almost any defective hardware component. In my experiences I've had more problems with power supplies than most other components, so I recommend immediately using a multimeter to measure the outputs at the power supply connectors and ensure they are within the proper 5% tolerances of their rated voltages. Even if the voltage measurements checked out, you should swap in a high-quality, high-power, known-good spare supply and retest. If that doesn't solve the problem, you should revert to the bootstrap approach I mentioned earlier, which is to strip the system down to just the chassis/power supply, motherboard, CPU (with heatsink), one bank of RAM (one DIMM), and a video card and display. If the motherboard now starts, begin adding the components you removed one at a time, retesting after each change. If the symptoms remain, use a POST card (if you have one) to see whether the board is partially functional and where it stops. Also, try replacing the video card, RAM, CPU, and then finally the motherboard, and verify the CPU and (especially) the heatsink installation.

The system beeps when I turn it on, but there is nothing on the screen.

The beep indicates a failure detected by the ROM POST routines. Look up the beep code in the table corresponding to the ROM version in your motherboard. This can typically be found in the motherboard manual; however, you can also find the beep codes for the most popular AMI, Award, and PhoenixBIOS earlier in this chapter.

I see a STOP or STOP ERROR in Windows NT/2000/XP or Vista.

Many things, including corrupted files, viruses, incorrectly configured hardware, and failing hardware, can cause Windows STOP errors. The most valuable resource for handling any error message displayed by Windows is the Microsoft Knowledgebase (MSKB), an online compendium of more than 250,000 articles covering all Microsoft products. You can visit the MSKB at http://support.microsoft.com/, and from there you can use the search tool to retrieve information specific to your problem. For example, say you are receiving Stop 0x0000007B errors in Windows XP. In this case, you should visit the MSKB and enter the error message in the search box. In this case, I typed **stop 7B error Windows XP** in the box, and it returned two articles, one of which was Microsoft Knowledgebase Article number 324103, titled "HOW TO: Troubleshoot "Stop 0x0000007B" Errors in Windows XP." Upon this link, I was taken to the article at http://support.microsoft.com/default.aspx?scid=kb;en-us;324103, which has a complete description of the problem and solutions. The article states that this error could be caused by the following:

- Boot-sector viruses
- Device driver issues
- Hardware issues
- Other issues

The article explains each issue and solution in detail. All things considered, the MSKB is a valuable resource when dealing with any problems related to or reported by any version of Windows or any other Microsoft software.

I see Fatal Exception errors in Windows 95/98/Me.

This is the equivalent of the STOP error in Windows NT/2000/XP or Vista. As indicated in the previous answer, this can be caused by both hardware and software problems, and the best place to check for specific solutions is in the Microsoft Knowledgebase (MSKB) at http://support.microsoft.com/.

The system won't shut down in Windows.

This is another example where the MSKB comes to the rescue. For example, by searching for **shutdown problems Windows XP** (substitute the version of Windows you are using), you will quickly find several articles that can help you troubleshoot this type of problem. This problem has been caused by bugs in motherboard ROM (try upgrading your motherboard ROM to the latest version), bugs in the various Windows versions (visit www.windowsupdate.com and install the latest fixes, patches, and service packs), or in some cases configuration or hardware problems. I'll defer to the MSKB articles for more complete explanations of the Windows issues.

The power button won't turn off the system.

Desktop PCs built since 1996 mostly use the ATX or BTX form factors, which incorporate a special power supply design such that the power switch is connected to the motherboard and not the power supply directly. This enables the motherboard and operating system to control system shutdown, preventing an unexpected loss of power that can cause data loss or file system corruption. However, if the system experiences a problem and becomes frozen or locked up in some way, the motherboard might not respond to the power button, meaning it will not send a shutdown signal to the power supply. It might seem that you will have to pull the plug to power off the system, but fortunately a forced shutdown override is provided. Merely press and hold down the system power button (usually on the front of the chassis) for a minimum of 4 seconds, and the system should power off. The only drawback is that, because this type of shutdown is forced and under the control of the motherboard or operating system, unsaved data can be lost and some file system corruption can result. You should therefore run ScanDisk (found in the Windows Accessories, System Tools folder) in Windows 95/98/Me/NT/2000 or Chkdsk in Windows XP and Vista to check and correct any file-system issues after a forced shutdown.

The modem doesn't work.

First verify that the phone line is good and that you have a dial tone. Then check and, if necessary, replace the phone cable from the modem to the wall outlet. If the modem is integrated into the motherboard, check the BIOS Setup to ensure that the modem is enabled. Try clearing the Enhanced System Configuration Data (ESCD) option in the BIOS Setup. This forces the plug-and-play routines to reconfigure the system, which can resolve any conflicts. If the modem is internal and you aren't using the COM1/COM2 serial ports integrated into the motherboard (as for an external modem), try disabling the serial ports to free up additional system resources. Also, try removing and reinstalling the modem drivers, ensuring that you are using the most recent drivers from the modem manufacturer. If that doesn't help, try physically removing and reinstalling the modem. If the modem is internal, install it in a different slot. Or, if the modem is external, make sure it has power and is properly connected to the serial or USB port on the PC. Try replacing the external modem power brick and the serial/USB cable. Finally, if you get this far and it still doesn't work, try replacing the modem and finally the motherboard.

Note that modems are very susceptible to damage from nearby lightning strikes. Consider adding lighting arrestors or surge suppressors on the phone line running to the modem, and unplug the modem during storms. If the modem has failed after a storm, you can be almost certain that it has been damaged by lightning. The strike might have damaged the serial port or motherboard, in addition to the modem. Any items damaged by lightning will most likely need to be replaced.

The keyboard doesn't work.

The two primary ways to connect a keyboard to a PC are via the standard keyboard port (usually called a PS/2 port) and via USB. One problem is that some older systems that have USB ports cannot use a USB keyboard because USB support is provided by the operating system—for instance, if the motherboard has a USB port but does not include what is called USB Legacy Support in the BIOS. This support is specifically for USB keyboards (and mice) and was not common in systems until 1998 or later. Many systems that had such support in the BIOS still had problems with the implementation; in other words, they had bugs in the code that prevented the USB keyboard from working properly. If you are having problems with a USB keyboard, check to ensure that USB Legacy Support is enabled in the BIOS. If you are still having problems, make sure you have installed the latest BIOS for your motherboard and any Windows updates from Microsoft. Some older systems never could properly use a USB keyboard, in which case you should change to a PS/2 keyboard instead. Some keyboards feature both USB and PS/2 interfaces, which offer the flexibility to connect to almost any system.

If the keyboard is having problems, the quickest way to verify whether it is the keyboard or the motherboard is to simply replace the keyboard with a known-good spare. In other words, borrow a working keyboard from another system and try it. If it still doesn't work, the interface on the motherboard is most likely defective, which unfortunately means that the entire board must be replaced. If the spare keyboard works, then obviously the original keyboard was the problem. My favorite replacement keyboards come from the PC Keyboard Co. (www.pckeyboard.com), which makes the legendary buckling spring design originally developed by IBM. The company even offers versions with the TrackPoint pointing device built in, and you can select from PS/2 or USB port versions on many models.

I can't hear any sound from the speakers.

This can often be as simple as the speakers being unplugged, plugged into the wrong jacks, or powered off, so don't overlook the obvious and check to be sure! Also check the volume controls in Windows or your application to see that they are turned up and not muted. When you are sure the volume is turned up,the speakers have power and are plugged in, and the speaker configuration is correctly identified in Windows (some audio hardware uses a proprietary mixer control for this job) you need to verify whether the problem is with the speakers or the sound card. To do this most efficiently, you merely connect different known-good speakers and see whether they work. If they don't, clearly the issue is in the sound card—possibly the configuration of the card is incorrect or the card itself is defective. The first thing to try is clearing the ESCD in the BIOS Setup. This essentially forces the plug-and-play routines to reconfigure the system, which can resolve any conflicts. If this doesn't help, try removing and reinstalling the sound card drivers. Finally, if that doesn't help, physically remove and replace the card from the system. You might try replacing it first in the same slot and then in a different slot because timing issues can sometimes exist from one slot to the next. If that doesn't work, you must try replacing the card. If the sound "card" really isn't a card but is integrated into the motherboard, first try the ESCD reset and driver reinstallation. Then, if that doesn't work, you have to try disabling the integrated sound and perhaps installing a replacement card or replacement motherboard.

If your problem is only with playing audio CDs, check for a cable between the sound card and the drive. If there is no cable, check the properties for the drive in the Device Manager in Windows to see whether the Digital CD Audio option is checked (enabled). If it's not, enable it. If your system will not allow digital CD audio to be enabled, it is not supported and you must install an analog cable connected between the sound card and the drive.

The monitor appears completely garbled or unreadable.

A completely garbled screen is most often due to improper, incorrect, or unsupported settings for the refresh rate, resolution, or color depth. Using incorrect drivers can also cause this. To check the configuration of the card, the first step is to power on the system and verify whether you can see the POST or the system splash screen and enter the BIOS Setup. If the screen looks fine during the POST but goes crazy after Windows starts to load, the problem is almost certainly due to an incorrect setting or configuration of the card. To resolve this, open the special boot menu and select Windows Safe mode (hold down the F8 function key as Windows starts to load to display this menu).

This bypasses the current video driver and settings and places the system in the default VGA mode supported by the BIOS on the video card. When the Windows desktop appears, you can right-click the desktop, select Properties, and then either reconfigure the video settings or change drivers as necessary.

Note

Some motherboards (such as some ASUS models) use the F8 key to display a boot menu. On these and similar system, wait until the boot menu option is gone before pressing F8 to bring up the boot menu.

If the problem occurs from the moment you turn on the system—and even if you boot to a DOS floppy (such as a Windows 98 startup floppy)—a hardware problem definitely exists with the video card, cable, or monitor. First, replace the monitor with another one; if the cable is detachable, replace that, too. If replacing the monitor and cable does not solve the problem, the video card is probably defective. Either replace the card or, if it is a PCI-based card, move it to a different slot. If the video is integrated into the motherboard, you must add a separate card instead or replace the motherboard.

The image on the display is distorted (bent), shaking, or wavering.

This can often be caused by problems with the power line, such as an electric motor, an air conditioner, a refrigerator, a microwave oven, and so on, causing interference. Try replacing the power cord, plugging the monitor and/or the system into a different outlet, or moving it to a different location entirely. I've also seen this problem caused by local radio transmitters such as a nearby radio or television station or two-way radios being operated in the vicinity of the system. If the monitor is a CRT and the image is bent and discolored, it could be due to the shadow mask being magnetized. To demagnetize the mask you can turn the monitor on and off repeatedly; this causes the built-in degaussing coil around the perimeter of the tube to activate in an attempt to demagnetize the shadow mask. Some CRTs include a degauss feature in their onscreen menus, which if available would be preferred over turning the unit on and off. If degaussing seems to work partially but not completely, you might need to obtain a professional degaussing coil from an electronics or TV service shop to demagnetize the mask. Finally, if the problems persist, replace the monitor cable, try a different (known-good) monitor, and finally replace the video card.

I purchased a video card, and it won't fit in the slot.

Most video cards are designed to conform to the AGP 4X, AGP 8X, or PCI Express x16 specification. It is all but impossible to install a PCI Express x16 card into a non–PCI Express x16 slot, but problems can arise with AGP cards when they're used with older AGP systems.

Both AGP 4X and AGP8X are designed to run on only 1.5V.

Most older motherboards with AGP 2X slots are designed to accept only 3.3V cards. If you were to plug a 1.5V card into a 3.3V slot, both the card and motherboard could be damaged. Special keys have therefore been incorporated into the AGP specification to prevent such disasters. Typically, the slots and cards are keyed such that 1.5V cards fit only in 1.5V sockets and 3.3V cards fit only in 3.3V sockets. Additionally, universal sockets are available that accept either 1.5V or 3.3V cards. The keying for the AGP cards and connectors is dictated by the AGP standard as shown in Figure 22.12.

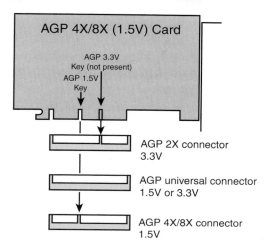

Figure 22.12 AGP 4X/8X (1.5V) card and how it relates to 3.3V, universal, and 1.5V AGP slots.

As you can see from Figure 22.12, AGP 4X or 8X (1.5V) cards fit only in 1.5V or universal (3.3V or 1.5V) slots. Due to the design of the connector and card keys, a 1.5V card cannot be inserted into a 3.3V slot. So, if your new AGP card won't fit in the AGP slot in your existing motherboard, consider that a good thing because, if you were able to plug it in, you would have fried both the card and the board! In a case such as this, you have to either return the 4X/8X card or get a new motherboard that supports 4X/8X (1.5V) cards.

I installed an upgraded processor, but it won't work.

First, make sure the motherboard supports the processor that is installed. Also make sure you are using the latest BIOS for your motherboard; check with the motherboard manufacturer to see whether any updates are available for download, and install them if any are available. Check the jumper settings (older boards) or BIOS Setup screens to verify that the processor is properly identified and set properly with respect to the FSB (or CPU bus) speed, clock multiplier, and voltage settings. On some systems, you may need to press Ctrl-F1 or some other special key combination in the system BIOS to display the setup screens used to configure processor and memory timings.

Make sure the processor is set to run at its rated speed and is not overclocked. If any of the CPU settings in the BIOS Setup are on manual override, set them to automatic instead. Then reseat the processor in the socket. Next, make sure the heatsink is properly installed and you are using thermal interface material (that is, thermal grease) at the mating junction between the CPU and heatsink.

Just because a processor fits in the socket (or slot) on your motherboard does not mean it will work. For a processor to work in a system, the following things are required:

■ **The CPU must fit in the socket**. Refer to Chapter 3, "Microprocessor Types and Specifications," for a complete guide to the various CPU socket types and which processors are compatible with them.

- **The motherboard must support the voltage required by the CPU.** Modern motherboards set voltages by reading voltage ID (VID) pins on the processor and then setting the onboard voltage regulator module (VRM) to the appropriate settings. Older boards might not support the generally lower voltage requirements of newer processors.

- **The motherboard ROM BIOS must support the CPU.** Modern boards also read the CPU to determine the proper FSB (or CPU bus) speed settings as well as the clock multiplier settings for the CPU. Many CPUs have different requirements for cache settings and initialization, as well as for bug fixes and workarounds.

- **The motherboard chipset must support the CPU.** In some cases, specific chipset models or revisions might be required to support certain processors.

Before purchasing an upgraded processor for your system, you should first check with the motherboard manufacturer to see whether your board supports the processor. If so, it will meet all the requirements listed previously. Often, BIOS updates are available that enable newer processors to be supported in older boards, beyond what was originally listed in the manual when you purchased the board. The only way to know for sure is to check with the motherboard manufacturer for updated information regarding supported processors for a particular board.

As a specific example, there are versions of the Pentium 4 that are single core, others that support hyper threading (HT) technology (one processor acts as if it were two processors), and some that actually have dual-cores, all of which physically fit into the same socket. If you have a system that uses the original single-core Pentium 4, it would be great to be able to simply purchase a replacement chip with either HT or true dual-cores. Unfortunately, many existing motherboards do not accept the HT or dual-core versions, even though they would physically plug in.

In another example, I had purchased a new motherboard and processor for a new system build, and upon initial power-on, the system didn't work at all. Upon investigation, I found that the new motherboard I had purchased did indeed support the processor I had installed, but only if the BIOS was upgraded to the latest version. Unfortunately the board I had must have been sitting on the shelf awhile because it came with an older BIOS version. All I had to do to solve the problem was to upgrade the BIOS, but how was I to do that since the board wouldn't even run with the processor until after the BIOS had been upgraded. I was in a classic chicken-before-the-egg situation. In the end I found a friend who had an older processor, one that would work with the older BIOS in my motherboard. I borrowed the chip and installed it just long enough to perform the BIOS upgrade, then I removed the borrowed chip, reinstalled the new one I had originally purchased, and the system now worked perfectly.

The important thing to learn from these examples is that before purchasing a processor for an existing board, make sure that the board will accept and work with the new chip and perform BIOS upgrades before beginning the processor upgrade process.

Some older motherboards might be capable of supporting a newer CPU with only a BIOS upgrade, but many boards do not meet the chipset, voltage, and front side bus speed requirements. In that case, you need a new processor, a new motherboard, and in all likelihood new memory to perform such an upgrade. In such cases, be sure to compare the cost of new components with the cost of a new system. It might make more sense to buy a new system.

The system runs fine for a few minutes but then freezes or locks up.

This is the classic symptom of a system that is overheating. Most likely the CPU is overheating, but other components such as the video card or motherboard chipset can also be overheating. If the system is new or custom built, the design might be insufficient for proper cooling, and bigger heatsinks, more fans, or other solutions might be required. If the system was working fine but now is exhibiting this problem, check to see whether the problem started after any recent changes were made. If so, then whatever change was made could be the cause of the problem. If no changes were made, most likely something such as a cooling fan is either failed or starting to fail.

Modern systems should have several fans, one inside the power supply, one on the CPU (or positioned to blow on the CPU), and optionally others for the chassis. Verify that any and all fans are properly installed and spinning. They should not be making grinding or growling noises, which usually indicates bearing failure. Many newer systems have thermostatically controlled fans; in these systems it is normal for the fan speeds to change with the temperature. Make sure that the chassis is several inches from walls and that the fan ports are unobstructed. Try removing and reseating the processor; then reinstall the CPU heatsink with new thermal interface material. Check the power supply and verify that it is rated sufficiently to power the system (most should be 300 watts or more). Use a digital multimeter to verify the voltage outputs of the power supply, which should be within +/–5% of the rated voltage at each pin. Try replacing the power supply with a high-quality replacement or known-good spare.

I am experiencing intermittent problems with the hard drive(s).

Many systems use ATA (AT-Attachment, commonly called IDE) interface drives, which consist of a drive and integrated controller, a ribbon cable, and a host adapter circuit in the motherboard. Typically, intermittent problems are found with the cable and the drive—it is far more rare that the host adapter fails or exhibits problems. Many problems occur with the cables. ATA drives use either 40-conductor or 80-conductor cables, with one 40-pin connector at either end and optionally one in the middle. Drives supporting transfer rates higher than ATA-33 (33MBps or Ultra DMA Mode 2) must use 80-conductor cables. Check the cable to ensure that it is not cut or damaged; then try unplugging and replugging it into the drive and motherboard. Check to see that the cable is not more than 18" (46cm) in length because that is the maximum allowed by the ATA specification. This is especially important when you are using the faster ATA-100 or ATA-133 transfer rates. Try replacing the cable with a new 80-conductor 18" version.

If replacing the cable does not help, replace the drive with a spare, install an OS, and test it to see whether the problem remains. If the problem does remain, the problem is with the motherboard, which will most likely need to be replaced. Alternatively, you could try adding a separate ATA 133 PCI card and attaching the drives to that, but in many cases a newer motherboard will give you more bang for your buck.

If the problem does not remain, the problem is most likely with your original drive. You can simply replace it or try testing, formatting, and reinstalling to see whether the drive can be repaired. To do this, you need the low-level format or test software provided by the drive manufacturer. You can find out more about where to get this for various makes of drives in Chapter 12, "Physical Drive Installation and Configuration."

If your system uses Serial ATA (SATA) hard disks, keep in mind that the cable and connector design used by some motherboards and SATA hard disks does not include a locking mechanism. The cable might have become disconnected from the motherboard or hard disk. SATA cables can also fail if they are bent or cut. Replace damaged cables and make sure the cable is connected to the drive and motherboard or host adapter card.

The system won't boot up; it says Missing operating system on the screen.

When your system boots, it reads the first sector from the hard disk—called the master boot record (MBR)—and runs the code contained in that sector. The MBR code then reads the partition table (also contained in the MBR) to determine which partition is bootable and where it starts. Then it loads the first sector of the bootable partition—called the volume boot record (VBR)—which contains the operating system–specific boot code. However, before executing the VBR, the MBR checks to ensure that the VBR ends with the signature bytes 55AAh. The Missing operating system message is displayed by the MBR if it finds that the first sector of the bootable partition (the VBR) does not end in 55AAh.

Several things can cause this to occur, including these:

- **The drive parameters entered in the BIOS Setup are incorrect or corrupted**. These are the parameters defining your drive that you entered in the BIOS Setup, and they're stored in a CMOS RAM chip powered by a battery on your motherboard. Incorrect parameters cause the MBR program to translate differently and read the wrong VBR sector, thus displaying the Missing operating system message. A dead CMOS battery can also cause this because it loses or corrupts the stored drive translation and transfer mode parameters. In fact, in my experience, a dead battery is one of the more likely causes. To repair, check and replace the CMOS battery, run the BIOS Setup, go to the hard drive parameter screen, and enter the correct drive parameters. Note that most drive parameters should be set to auto or autodetect.

- **The drive is not yet partitioned and formatted on this system**. This is a normal error if you try to boot the system from the hard disk before the OS installation is complete. Boot to an OS startup disk (floppy or CD) and run the SETUP program, which will prompt you through the partitioning and formatting process during the OS installation.

- **The MBR and/or partition tables are corrupt**. This can be caused by boot sector viruses, among other things. To repair this, *cold* boot (power off, then on) from a known, noninfected, write-protected floppy or bootable CD containing the FDISK program (preferably Win98 or later). Enter **FDISK/MBR** at the command prompt, which recopies the MBR code but doesn't alter the partition table. Then reboot. If the message persists, and you need to recover the data on the drive, you then must either rebuild the partition tables from scratch using a third-party utility such as the DISKEDIT program included with the Symantec Norton Utilities or hire a data recovery specialist who can do this for you. If you don't need to recover the data on the drive, simply reinstall the OS from scratch, which will prompt you through partitioning and formatting the drive.

- **The VBR is corrupt**. To repair with Windows 95/98/Me, secure a bootable floppy that was created by the same OS version as is on the hard disk and that contains the SYS command from that OS. Run SYS C:, which recopies a good VBR and system files to the volume. For Windows NT/2000/XP, you can use the Recovery Console or DiskProbe utilities (found on the bootable operating system CD). For Vista you can use the Windows RE (Recovery Environment), which is equivalent to the Recovery Console in XP and earlier.

The system is experiencing intermittent memory errors.

If the memory was recently added or some other change was made to the system, you should undo that addition/change to see whether it is the cause. If it's not, remove and reseat all memory modules. If the contacts look corroded, clean them with contact cleaner and then apply contact enhancer for protection. Check the memory settings in the BIOS Setup; generally, all settings should be on automatic. Next, upgrade to the latest BIOS for your motherboard, and remove all memory except one bank. Then run only one bank of memory, but in the second or third bank position. A socket can develop a problem, and most motherboards do not require that the sockets be filled in numerical order. Also, replace the remaining module with one of the others that was removed, a new module, or a known-good spare.

If you get this far, the problem is most likely either the motherboard or the power supply—or possibly some other component in the system. Remove other components from the system to see whether they are causing problems. Reseat the CPU, and replace the power supply with a high-quality new unit or a known-good spare. Finally, try replacing the motherboard.

The system locks up frequently and sometimes reboots on its own.

This is one of the classic symptoms of a power supply problem. The power supply is designed to send a special Power_Good signal to the motherboard when it has passed its own internal tests and outputs are stable. If this signal is dropped, even for an instant, the system resets. Problems with the power good circuit cause lockups and spontaneous rebooting. This can also be caused if the power at the wall outlet is not correct. Verify the power supply output with a digital multimeter—all outputs should be within +/–5% of the rated voltages. Use a tester for the wall outlet to ensure that it is properly wired, and verify that the voltage is near 120V. Replace the power cord or power strip between the power supply and wall outlet.

Unfortunately, the intermittent nature makes this problem hard to solve. If the problem is not with the wall outlet power, the best recourse is to replace the power supply with a high-quality new unit or a known-good spare of sufficient rating to handle the system (300 watts or higher recommended). If this doesn't help, reseat the CPU and reinstall the heatsink with new thermal interface material. Then reseat the memory modules, run only one bank of memory, and finally replace the motherboard.

I installed a 60GB drive in my system, but it is recognizing only 8.4GB.

Motherboard ROM BIOSs have been updated throughout the years to support larger and larger drives. BIOSs older than August 1994 are typically limited to drives of up to 528MB, whereas BIOSs older than January 1998 are limited to 8.4GB. Most BIOSs dated 1998 or newer support drives up to 137GB, and those dated September 2002 or newer should support drives larger than 137GB. These are only general guidelines; to accurately determine this for a specific system, you should check with your motherboard manufacturer. You can also use the BIOS Wizard utility from http://www.unicore.com/bioswiz/index2.html. It tells you the BIOS date from your system and specifically whether your system supports the Enhanced Hard Disk Drive specification, which means drives larger than 8.4GB.

If your BIOS does not support EDD (drives larger than 8.4GB), the three possible solutions are as follows:

- Upgrade your motherboard BIOS upgrade to a 1998 or newer version that supports >8.4GB.
- Install a BIOS upgrade card, such as the UltraATA cards from www.siig.com.
- Install a software patch to add >8.4GB support.

Of these, the first one is the most desirable because it is usually free. Visit your motherboard manufacturer's website to see whether it has any newer BIOSs available for your motherboard that will support large drives. If it doesn't, the next best thing is to use a card such as the UltraATA cards from SIIG. I almost never recommend the software patch solution because it merely installs a special driver in the boot sector area of the hard drive, which can result in numerous problems when booting from different drives, installing new drives, or recovering data.

The 137GB barrier is a bit more complicated because, in addition to BIOS issues, operating system and chipset-based ATA host adapter driver issues are involved. Drives larger than 137GB are accessed using 48-bit logical block address (LBA) numbers, which require BIOS support, chipset driver support, and operating system support. Generally, you need a BIOS with 48-bit LBA support (normally dated September 2002 or newer), the latest chipset driver such as the Intel Application Accelerator (for motherboards using Intel chipsets, at http://www.intel.com/support/chipsets/iaa/), and Windows XP with Service Pack 1 (or later) installed. If your motherboard BIOS does not provide the necessary support, one of the SIIG UltraATA cards listed earlier adds this support to your system. The original version of XP, as well as Windows 2000/NT or Windows 95/98/Me, does not currently provide native support for hard drives larger than 137GB.

If you have a system without BIOS support, check with your motherboard manufacturer for an update (or you can use a card with onboard BIOS). If your motherboard uses a non-Intel chipset, check with the motherboard or chipset manufacturer for driver updates to enable 48-bit LBA support.

My CD-ROM/DVD drive doesn't work.

CD and DVD drives are some of the more failure-prone components in a PC. It is not uncommon for one to suddenly fail after a year or so of use.

If you are having problems with a drive that was newly installed, check the installation and configuration of the drive. Check the jumper settings on the drive. If you're using an 80-conductor cable, the drive should be jumpered to Cable Select; if you're using a 40-conductor cable, the drive should be set to either master or slave (depending on whether it is the only drive on the cable). Check the cable to ensure that it is not nicked or cut and is a maximum of 18" long (the maximum allowed by the ATA specification). Replace the cable with a new one or a known-good spare, preferably using an 80-conductor cable. Make sure the drive power is connected, and verify that power is available at the connector using a digital multimeter. Also make sure the BIOS Setup is set properly for the drive, and verify that the drive is detected during the boot process. Finally, try replacing the drive and, if necessary, the motherboard.

If the drive had already been installed and was working before, first read different discs, preferably commercial-stamped discs rather than writeable or rewriteable ones. Then try the steps listed previously.

If you are using an SATA DVD drive in Windows Vista, you might need to configure the SATA host adapter the drive uses in PATA emulation mode rather than the native AHCI mode or install a hotfix (see Microsoft Knowledge Base article 928253).

My USB port or device doesn't work.

Make sure you have enabled the USB ports in the BIOS Setup. Make sure your operating system supports USB—for example Windows 95 and NT do not have USB support. Technically there were later versions of Windows 95 (called 95B and 95C) that did include USB support, but that support was unfortunately very limited and problematic. Windows 98 and later have proper support for USB. Try removing any hubs and plug the device having problems directly into the root hub connections on your system. Try replacing the cable. Many USB devices require additional power, so ensure that your device has an eternal power supply connected if one is required.

If the device requires USB 2.0 support, make sure your ports are configured to run in USB 2.0 (Hi-Speed USB) mode. Many systems also offer a USB 1.1-only mode. If the device is bus-powered, try replacing the system power supply; an overloaded or marginal power supply might not provide reliable power to USB ports.

I installed an additional memory module, but the system doesn't recognize it.

Verify that the memory is compatible with your motherboard. Many subtle variations exist on memory types that can appear to be identical on the surface. Just because it fits in the slot does not mean the memory will work properly with your system. Check your motherboard manual for the specific type of memory your system requires, and possibly for a list of supported modules. You can visit www.crucial.com and use its Memory Advisor Tool to determine the exact type of memory for a specific system or motherboard. Also note that all motherboards have limits to the amount of memory they support, and many boards today support only up to 512MB or 1GB. Again, consult the motherboard manual or manufacturer for information on the limits for your board.

If you are sure you have the correct type of memory, follow the memory troubleshooting steps listed previously for intermittent memory problems.

I installed a new drive, but it doesn't work and the drive LED remains lit.

This is the classic symptom for a cable plugged in backward. Both ATA and floppy drives are designed to use cables with keyed connectors; however, some cables are available that lack this keying, which means they can easily be installed backward. When the cable is installed backward into either the motherboard or the drive, the LED on the drive remains lit and the drive does not function. In some cases, this can also cause the entire system to freeze. Check the cables to ensure that they are plugged in properly at both ends; the stripe on the cable indicates pin-1 orientation. On the drive, pin-1 typically is oriented toward the power connector. On the motherboard, look for orientation marks silkscreened on the board or observe the orientation of the other cables plugged in (all cables follow the same orientation).

While I was updating my BIOS, the system froze and now the system is dead!

This can occur when a flash ROM upgrade goes awry. Fortunately, most motherboards have a recovery routine that can be enabled via a jumper on the board. When enabled, the recovery routine causes the system to look for a floppy with the BIOS update program on it. If you haven't done so already, you need to download an updated BIOS from the motherboard manufacturer and follow its directions for placing the BIOS update program on a bootable floppy. Then set BIOS recovery mode via the jumper on the motherboard, power on the system, and wait until the procedure completes. It usually take up to 5 minutes, and you might hear beeping to indicate the start and end of the procedure. When the recovery is complete, turn off the system and restore the recovery jumper to the original (normal) settings.

If your motherboard does not feature BIOS recovery capability, you might have to send the board to the manufacturer for repair.

I installed a new motherboard in an older Dell system, and nothing works.

Many older Dell Dimension systems built before 2001 (Dimension 4100, 8100, or older systems) do not fully conform to the ATX specification with respect to their power supplies and the power connectors on their motherboards. If you replace one of these nonstandard Dell power supplies with a standard ATX type, or replace the nonstandard Dell motherboard with a standard ATX type, you risk frying both the power supply and the motherboard. The older Dell systems can be upgraded only by replacing both the motherboard and the power supply at the same time.

Starting in 2001, Dell converted to using industry-standard ATX power supplies and motherboard power connectors for most (but not all) of its systems. Even though most Dell systems after 2001 use standard supplies, there are still some (like the XPS Gen 2, for example) built after that time that have used completely nonstandard power supplies.

I installed a PCI video card in an older system with PCI slots, and it doesn't work.

The PCI bus has gone through several revisions; most older slots are "2.0" type, and most newer cards need "2.1" or later PCI slots. The version of PCI your system has is dictated by the motherboard chipset. If you install a newer video or other PCI card that requires 2.1 slots in a system with 2.0 slots, often the system won't boot up or operate at all.

If you check the chipset reference information in Chapter 4, you might be able to determine which revision of PCI slots your motherboard has by knowing which chipset it has. If this is your problem, the only solution is to change either the card or motherboard so that they are both compatible.

Index

Numbers

THIS BOOK IS SAFARI ENABLED

INCLUDES FREE 45-DAY ACCESS TO THE ONLINE EDITION

The Safari® Enabled icon on the cover of your favorite technology book means the book is available through Safari Bookshelf. When you buy this book, you get free access to the online edition for 45 days.

Safari Bookshelf is an electronic reference library that lets you easily search thousands of technical books, find code samples, download chapters, and access technical information whenever and wherever you need it.

TO GAIN 45-DAY SAFARI ENABLED ACCESS TO THIS BOOK:

- Go to **http://www.quepublishing.com/safarienabled**
- Complete the brief registration form
- Enter the coupon code found in the front of this book on the "Copyright" page

If you have difficulty registering on Safari Bookshelf or accessing the online edition, please e-mail customer-service@safaribooksonline.com.

Get behind the Scenes to Stay Ahead of the Curve with Rough Cuts

When you need to gain early access to information on cutting edge technologies, turn to the Rough Cuts service from Safari Books Online. With Rough Cuts you'll access the book's content as it is being written.

You can choose to purchase online access to the book with unlimited viewing and PDF downloads of each revision, pre-purchase the print book, or get the best of both worlds—online access immediately and the print book later. Any way you cut it, you will receive the finished product as soon as it is published, whether as a pdf or as a printed book.

View Titles Available and Purchase **Rough Cuts** at

http://safari.informit.com/roughcuts

livelessons ▶

video instruction from technology experts

Trying to keep your skills up to date with the latest technology and advance your career?

Tired of expensive off-site training programs?

Wish you could learn from the best technologists in the industry?

LiveLessons: self-paced, personal video instruction from the world's leading technology experts

- INSTRUCTORS YOU TRUST
- CUTTING EDGE TOPICS
- CUSTOMIZED, SELF-PACED LEARNING
- LEARN BY DOING

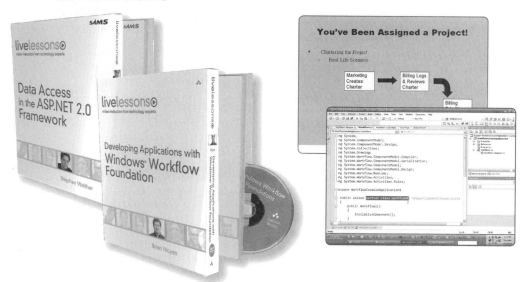

The power of the world's leading experts at your fingertips!

To learn more about **LiveLessons** visit
www.mylivelessons.com

 Addison Wesley PRENTICE HALL SAMS

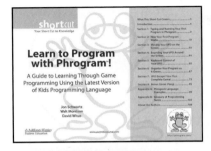

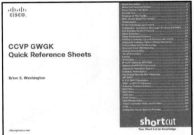

More knowledge from the PC hardware master!

For years, Scott Mueller has brought you the most complete, up-to-date information on PC hardware. Now, he has taken that formula for success and written more books, covering today's hottest topics in the manner you've grown to know and trust. Don't miss the newest books in the *Upgrading and Repairing* line!

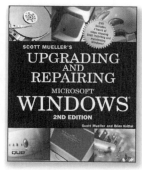

**Upgrading and Repairing
Microsoft Windows, Second Edition**
ISBN: 0-7897-3695-0
800 pp.

**Upgrading and Repairing
Laptops, Second Edition**
ISBN: 0-7897-3376-5
912 pp.

**Upgrading and Repairing
Servers**
ISBN: 0-7897-2815-X
1128 pp.

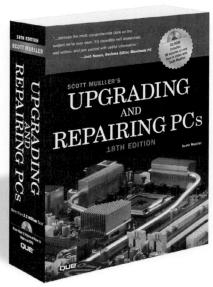

License Agreement

By opening this package, you are agreeing to be bound by the following agreement:

You may not copy or redistribute the entire media as a whole. Copying and redistribution of individual software programs on the media is governed by terms set by individual copyright holders.

The installer and code from the author(s) are copyrighted by the publisher and author(s). Individual programs and other items on the media are copyrighted by their various authors or other copyright holders. Some of the programs included with this product may be governed by an Open Source license, which allows redistribution; see the license information for each product for more information.

Other programs are included on the media by special permission from their authors.

This software is provided as is without warranty of any kind, either expressed or implied, including but not limited to the implied warranties of merchantability and fitness for a particular purpose. Neither the publisher nor its dealers or distributors assume any liability for any alleged or actual damages arising from the use of this program. (Some states do not allow for the exclusion of implied warranties, so the exclusion may not apply to you.)

Installing the DVD

The DVD accompanying this book is playable on both a standalone DVD player (DVD player attached to your television/home theater system) and a DVD drive installed in or connected to your PC.

Standalone DVD Video Players

To play the videos on this DVD, insert the DVD into your standalone DVD video player and navigate the menus using your DVD player's remote, just as you would do with any DVD.

Note

The DVD is coded for all regions. The extra features using Internet (Web) links are not active links; you must enter the specified URLs into your Web browser directly. Extra features and Windows Media Player–formatted videos are also available on Scott's Web site at www.upgradingandrepairing-pcs.com.

PC-Based DVD Drives

To play the DVD video content, do the following:

1. Insert the DVD into your PC's DVD drive.
2. Run your previously installed DVD player application and select Play.
3. Navigate the DVD menus as you would any standard DVD video.

Most DVD drives include a decoder/player application. If you do not currently have a DVD decoder/player installed on your system, you can do one of the following:

- Play the disc in a standard set-top DVD player.
- Use an existing DVD decoder with Windows Media Player 9 or later (visit www.microsoft.com/windows/windowsmedia).
- Purchase a DVD decoder to use with Windows Media Player.
- Purchase a complete decoder/player combination, such as PowerDVD by CyberLink (www.gocyberlink.com), or WinDVD by Intervideo (www.intervideo.com).

Here's how to access the Technical Reference files, previous editions of the book, and any other files on the DVD-ROM:

1. Insert the DVD into your PC's DVD drive.
2. Open My Computer.
3. Right-click the icon for the DVD drive containing the disc.
4. Select Explore.
5. Navigate through the folders and files just as if you were viewing files stored on your computer's hard drive.

Note

Many of the documents included in the Extras section of the DVD are in PDF format, which requires Adobe Acrobat to view. Acrobat is freely available at www.adobe.com.

System Requirements for DVD-ROM Video

The minimum system configuration is as follows:

- Intel or AMD processor, 400MHz or faster
- Windows 98SE/Me, 2000, XP, or Vista
- 64MB of RAM (Windows 2000/XP require 128MB; Vista requires 512MB)
- 4MB graphics card, 800 × 600 resolution, 16-bit color
- Direct Sound–compatible sound card
- 4X DVD-ROM drive (UDMA enabled)
- Direct Show–compliant DVD decoder/player software installed
- Direct X 7.0
- Internet Explorer 5.0

Access to DVD Content Without a DVD Player or DVD Drive

If you do not have a set-top DVD player or DVD drive, you can still access all the files included on the DVD-ROM by visiting www.upgradingandrepairingpcs.com. To access these materials on the Web, follow these steps:

1. Remove the DVD from the package insert and note the password on the DVD label.
2. Visit www.upgradingandrepairingpcs.com and follow the DVD link from the home page.
3. Enter your password as included on the DVD label.
4. You can then download any of the files provided there, including Windows Media Player versions of the videos, previous editions in PDF format, a vendor database, and more.